GREATER LONDON STREET ATLAS

KT-369-669

CONTENTS

HarperCollins*Publishers*

M25 LONDON ORBITAL MOTORWAY

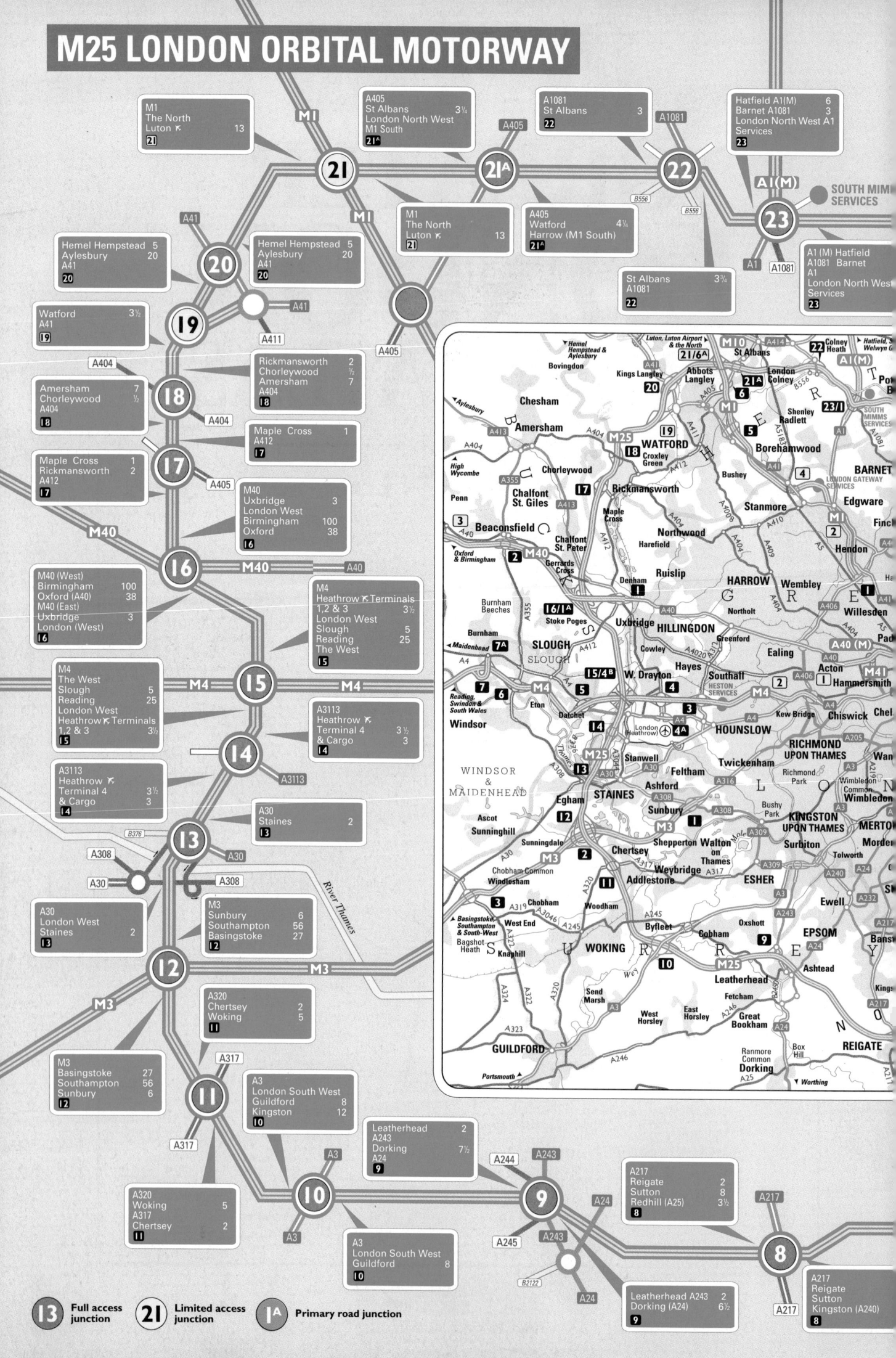

M1
The North
Luton ✈   13
21

A405
St Albans   3¼
London North West
M1 South
21A

A1081
St Albans   3
22

Hatfield A1(M)   6
Barnet A1081   3
London North West A1
Services
23

M1
The North
Luton ✈   13
21

A405
Watford   4¼
Harrow (M1 South)
21A

A1 (M) Hatfield
A1081 Barnet
A1
London North West
Services
23

St Albans   3¾
A1081
22

Hemel Hempstead 5
Aylesbury   20
A41
20

Hemel Hempstead 5
Aylesbury   20
A41
20

Watford   3½
A41
19

Rickmansworth   2
Chorleywood   2½
Amersham   7
A404
18

Amersham   7
Chorleywood   2½
A404
18

Maple Cross   1
A412
17

Maple Cross   1
Rickmansworth   2
A412
17

M40
Uxbridge   3
London West
Birmingham   100
Oxford   38
16

M40 (West)
Birmingham   100
Oxford (A40)   38
M40 (East)
Uxbridge   3
London (West)
16

M4
Heathrow ✈ Terminals
1,2 & 3   3½
London West
Slough   5
Reading   25
The West
15

M4
The West
Slough   5
Reading   25
London West
Heathrow ✈ Terminals
1,2 & 3   3½
15

A3113
Heathrow ✈
Terminal 4   3½
& Cargo   3
14

A3113
Heathrow ✈
Terminal 4   3½
& Cargo   3
14

A30
Staines   2
13

A30
London West
Staines   2
13

M3
Sunbury   6
Southampton   56
Basingstoke   27
12

M3
Basingstoke   27
Southampton   56
Sunbury   6
12

A320
Chertsey   2
Woking   5
11

A320
Woking   5
A317
Chertsey   2
11

A3
London South West
Guildford   8
Kingston   12
10

Leatherhead   2
A243
Dorking   7½
A24
9

A3
London South West
Guildford   8
10

A217
Reigate   2
Sutton   8
Redhill (A25)   3½
8

A217
Reigate
Sutton
Kingston (A240)
8

Leatherhead A243   2
Dorking (A24)   6½
9

13 Full access junction   **21** Limited access junction   **1A** Primary road junction

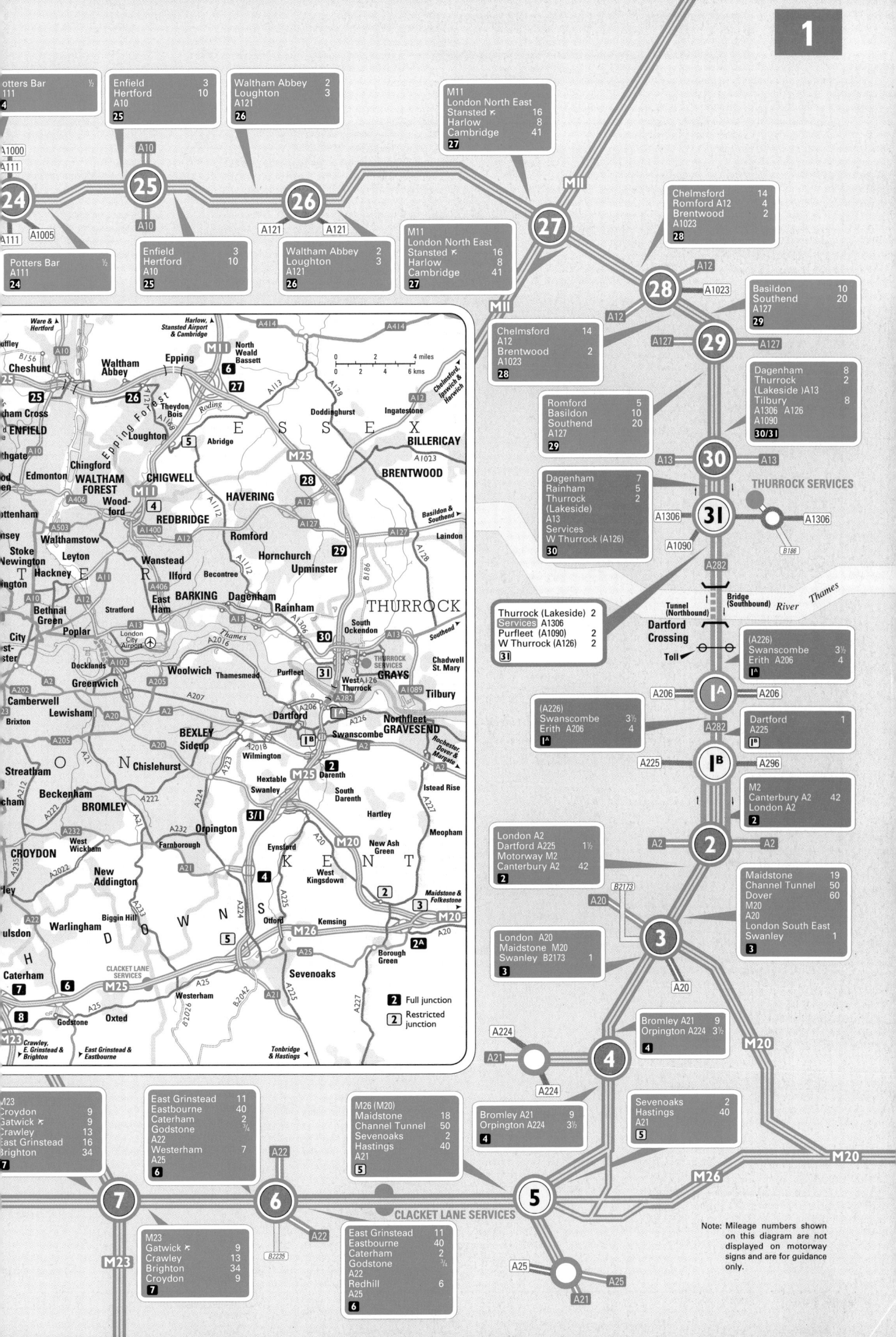

Potters Bar ½
A111
24

Enfield 3
Hertford 10
A10
25

Waltham Abbey 2
Loughton 3
A121
26

M11
London North East
Stansted ↗ 16
Harlow 8
Cambridge 41
27

A1000
A111

A10
A111
A1005

Chelmsford 14
Romford A12 4
Brentwood 2
A1023
28

24 **25** **26** **27**

A10
A121 A121

Potters Bar ½
A111
24

Enfield 3
Hertford 10
A10
25

Waltham Abbey 2
Loughton 3
A121
26

M11
London North East
Stansted ↗ 16
Harlow 8
Cambridge 41
27

A12
A1023
28

A12 A1023 **29** A127

Basildon 10
Southend 20
A127
29

Chelmsford 14
A12
Brentwood 2
A1023
28

A127 A127

Dagenham 8
Thurrock 2
(Lakeside)A13
Tilbury 8
A1306 A126
A1090
30/31

Romford 5
Basildon 10
Southend 20
A127
29

A13 **30** A13

THURROCK SERVICES

Dagenham 7
Rainham 5
Thurrock 2
(Lakeside)
A13
Services
W Thurrock (A126)
30

A1306 **31** A1306

B186

Thurrock (Lakeside) 2
Services A1306
Purfleet (A1090) 2
W Thurrock (A126) 2
31

A1090

A282

Tunnel Bridge River Thames
(Northbound) (Southbound)
Dartford
Crossing
Toll ◄

(A226)
Swanscombe 3½
Erith A206 4
1A

(A226)
Swanscombe 3½
Erith A206 4
1A

A206 **1A** A206

A282

Dartford 1
A225
1B

A225 **1B** A296

M2
Canterbury A2 42
London A2
2

London A2
Dartford A225 1½
Motorway M2
Canterbury A2 42
2

A2 **2** A2

Maidstone 19
Channel Tunnel 50
Dover 60
M20
A20
London South East
Swanley 1
3

B2173

A20

London A20
Maidstone M20
Swanley B2173 1
3

3

Bromley A21 9
Orpington A224 3½
4

A224

A21 **4** M20

A224

Sevenoaks 2
Hastings 40
A21
5

M23
Croydon 9
Gatwick ↗ 9
Crawley 13
East Grinstead 16
Brighton 34
7

East Grinstead 11
Eastbourne 40
Caterham 2
Godstone ¾
A22
Westerham 7
A25
6

A22

M26 (M20)
Maidstone 18
Channel Tunnel 50
Sevenoaks 2
Hastings 40
A21
5

Bromley A21 9
Orpington A224 3½
4

Sevenoaks 2
Hastings 40
A21
5

M26

M20

7 **6** A22 **5**

CLACKET LANE SERVICES

M23
Gatwick ↗ 9
Crawley 13
Brighton 34
Croydon 9
7

B2235

East Grinstead 11
Eastbourne 40
Caterham 2
Godstone ¾
A22
Redhill 6
A25
6

A25

A25 A25

A21

Note: Mileage numbers shown
on this diagram are not
displayed on motorway
signs and are for guidance
only.

2 M25 MILEAGE CHART

JUNCTION OF EXIT

Jct	Name	1	2	3	4	5	6	7	8	9	10	11	12	13	14	15	16	17	18	19	20	21	22	23	24	25	26	27	28	29	30	31
1	DARTFORD		1	4	8	12	22	25	28	35	41	46	48	51	53	55	59	53	52	49	48	45	40	37	34	28	25	21	13	10	5	4
2	A2	1		3	7	11	21	24	27	34	40	45	47	50	52	54	59	54	53	50	49	46	41	38	35	29	26	22	14	11	6	5
3	M20	4	3		4	8	18	21	24	31	37	42	44	47	49	51	56	57	56	53	52	49	44	41	38	32	29	25	17	14	9	8
4	A21	8	7	4		4	14	17	20	27	33	38	40	43	45	47	52	58	59	57	56	53	48	45	42	36	33	29	21	18	13	12
5	A26	12	11	8	4		10	13	16	23	29	34	36	39	41	43	48	54	55	58	59	52	52	49	46	40	37	33	25	22	17	16
6	A22	22	21	18	14	10		3	6	13	19	24	26	29	31	33	38	44	45	48	49	52	57	59	56	50	47	43	35	32	27	26
7	M23	25	24	21	17	13	3		3	10	16	21	23	26	28	30	35	41	42	45	46	49	54	57	59	53	50	46	38	35	30	29
8	REIGATE	28	27	24	20	16	6	3		7	13	18	20	23	25	27	32	38	39	42	43	46	51	54	57	56	53	49	41	38	33	32
9	LEATHERHEAD	35	34	31	27	23	13	10	7		6	11	13	16	18	20	25	31	32	35	36	39	44	47	50	56	56	54	48	45	40	39
10	A3	41	40	37	33	29	19	16	13	6		5	7	10	12	14	19	25	26	29	30	33	38	41	44	50	56	59	54	51	46	45
11	CHERTSEY	46	45	42	38	34	24	21	18	11	5		2	5	7	9	14	20	21	24	25	28	33	36	39	45	52	59	56	53	52	50
12	M3	48	47	44	40	36	26	23	20	13	7	2		3	5	7	12	18	19	22	23	26	31	34	37	43	50	58	58	53	53	52
13	A30	51	50	47	43	39	29	26	23	16	10	5	3		2	4	9	15	16	19	20	23	28	31	34	40	47	55	58	56	56	55
14	HEATHROW 4	53	52	49	45	41	31	28	25	18	12	7	5	2		2	7	13	14	17	18	21	26	29	32	38	45	53	56	58	58	57
15	M4, HEATHROW 1-3	55	54	51	47	43	33	30	27	20	14	9	7	4	2		5	11	12	15	16	19	24	27	30	36	43	51	54	59	59	59
16	M40	59	59	56	52	48	38	35	32	25	19	14	12	9	7	5		6	7	10	11	14	19	22	25	31	38	46	49	54	55	55
17	RICKMANSWORTH	53	54	57	58	54	44	41	38	31	25	20	18	15	13	11	6		1	4	5	8	13	16	19	25	32	40	43	48	48	49
18	A404	52	53	56	59	55	45	42	39	32	26	21	19	16	14	12	7	1		3	4	7	12	15	18	24	31	39	42	47	47	48
19	WATFORD	49	50	53	57	58	48	45	42	35	29	24	22	19	17	15	10	4	3		1	4	9	12	15	21	28	36	39	44	44	45
20	A41	48	49	52	56	59	49	46	43	36	30	25	23	20	18	16	11	5	4	1		3	8	11	14	20	27	35	38	43	43	44
21	M1	45	46	49	53	52	52	49	46	39	33	28	26	23	21	19	14	8	7	4	3		5	8	11	17	24	32	35	40	40	41
22	ST. ALBANS	40	41	44	48	52	57	54	51	44	38	33	31	28	26	24	19	13	12	9	8	5		3	6	12	19	27	30	35	35	36
23	A1 (M)	37	38	41	45	49	59	57	54	47	41	36	34	31	29	27	22	16	15	12	11	8	3		3	9	16	24	27	32	32	33
24	A111	34	35	38	42	46	56	59	57	50	44	39	37	34	32	30	25	19	18	15	14	11	6	3		6	13	21	24	29	29	30
25	A10	28	29	32	36	40	50	53	56	56	50	45	43	40	38	36	31	25	24	21	20	17	12	9	6		7	15	18	23	23	24
26	EPPING	25	26	29	33	37	47	50	53	56	56	52	50	47	45	43	38	32	31	28	27	24	19	16	13	7		4	12	15	20	21
27	M11	21	22	25	29	33	43	46	49	54	59	59	58	55	53	51	46	40	39	36	35	32	27	24	21	15	4		8	11	16	17
28	A12	13	14	17	21	25	35	38	41	48	54	56	58	58	56	54	49	43	42	39	38	35	30	27	24	18	12	8		3	8	9
29	A127	10	11	14	18	22	32	35	38	45	51	53	53	56	58	59	54	48	47	44	43	40	35	32	29	23	15	11	3		5	6
30	A13	5	6	9	13	17	27	30	33	40	46	52	53	56	58	59	55	48	47	44	43	40	35	32	29	23	20	16	8	5		1
31	A13	4	5	8	12	16	26	29	32	39	45	50	52	55	57	59	55	49	48	45	44	41	36	33	30	24	21	17	9	6	1	

JUNCTION OF ENTRY

Legend:
- Mileage Clockwise
- Mileage AntiClockwise

Note: This chart shows the shortest distance between junctions. The colours indicate whether the distance is clockwise or anticlockwise. The total distance around the M25 is approximately 117 miles.

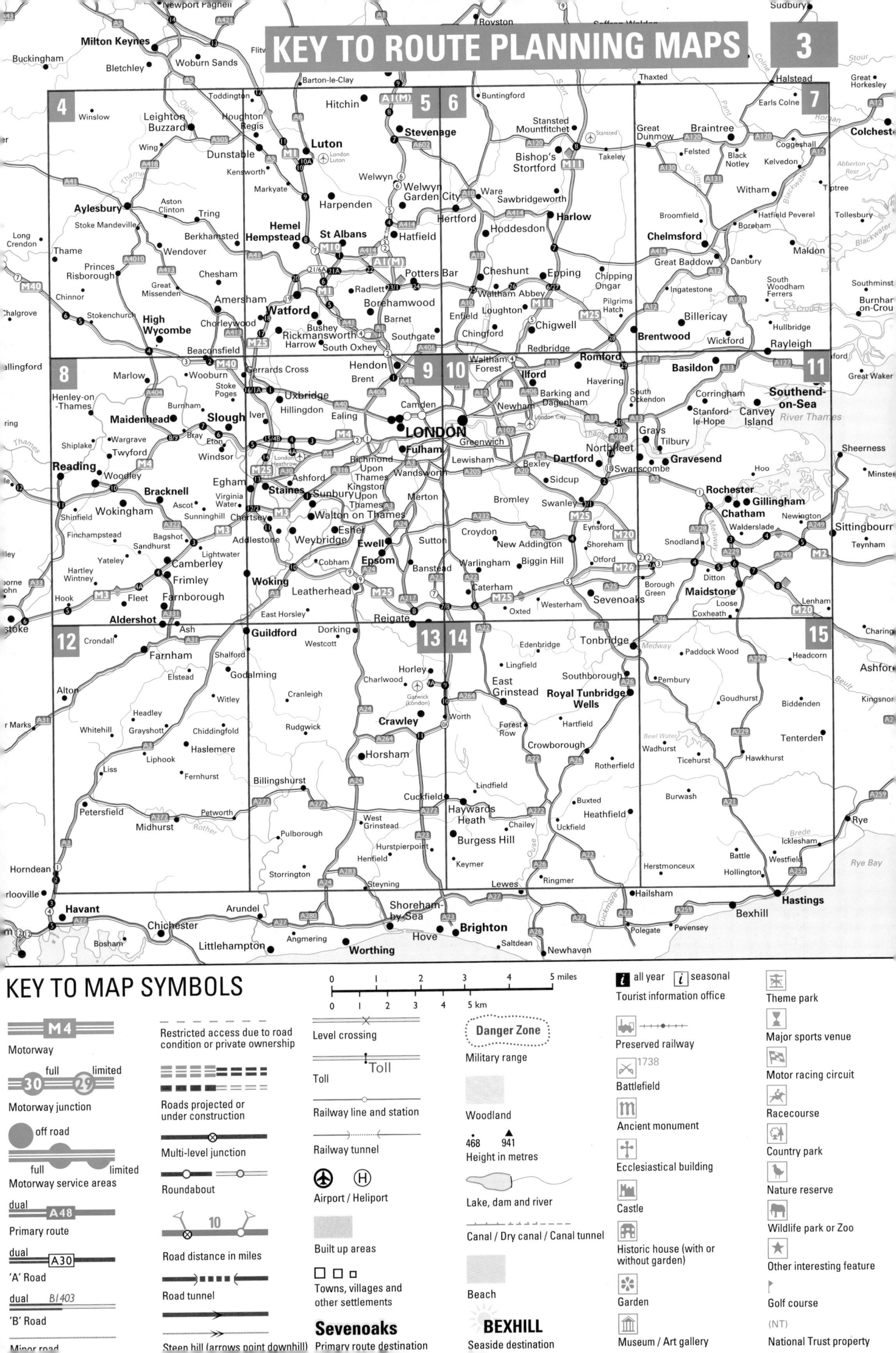

KEY TO ROUTE PLANNING MAPS
3
KEY TO MAP SYMBOLS
Motorway
Motorway junction
full
limited
off road
Motorway service areas
Primary route
dual
'A' Road
'B' Road
Minor road
Restricted access due to road condition or private ownership
Roads projected or under construction
Multi-level junction
Roundabout
Road distance in miles
Road tunnel
Steep hill (arrows point downhill)
Level crossing
Toll
Railway line and station
Railway tunnel
Airport / Heliport
Built up areas
Towns, villages and other settlements
Sevenoaks
Primary route destination
Danger Zone
Military range
Woodland
Height in metres
Lake, dam and river
Canal / Dry canal / Canal tunnel
Beach
BEXHILL
Seaside destination
all year
seasonal
Tourist information office
Preserved railway
Battlefield
Ancient monument
Ecclesiastical building
Castle
Historic house (with or without garden)
Garden
Museum / Art gallery
Theme park
Major sports venue
Motor racing circuit
Racecourse
Country park
Nature reserve
Wildlife park or Zoo
Other interesting feature
Golf course
(NT)
National Trust property
0 1 2 3 4 5 miles
0 1 2 3 4 5 km

Buckingham
Chantry Chapel
4
A421
A
12
Chase
A421
B4034
B
6
Woburn
Little Brickhill
C
Woburn Abbey
Padbury
Great Horwood
Little Horwood
Newton Longville
Ouzel
Great Brickhill
Milton
Adstock
B4033
Drayton Parslow
Stoke Hammond
Stockgrove
Potsgrove
A4012
Hillesden
Addington
Winslow Hall
Mursley
Heath and Reach
Battlesden
Steeple Claydon
Winslow
Swanbourne
A4146
Soulbury
Middle Claydon
A413
North End
B4032
Stewkley
Hockliffe
A4012
1
East Claydon
Claydon (NT)
Hoggeston
Calvert
Botolph Claydon
Granborough
South End
Linslade
Leighton Buzzard
Eggington
Leighton Buzzard Lt.Rly.
Stanbridge
Tilsworth
Gibbon
North Marston
Dunton
Burcott
Wing
A505
Cublington
Ascott (NT)
Billington
Eaton Green
Totternhoe
Grendon Underwood
A413
Oving
Whitchurch
Ledburn
Slapton
Eaton Bray
Pitchcott
A418
Quainton
10
Aston Abbotts
Mentmore
Mentmore
Horton
Kingswood
Hardwick
Nup End
Wingrave
Edlesborough
10
B488
Ivinghoe Aston
16
Weedon
Rowsham
Waddesdon
Cheddington
B489
Westcott
A41
Hulcott
Thame
Ivinghoe
15
Wotton Underwood
Waddesdon Manor (NT)
Akeman Street
Long Marston
Pitstone Green
2
Bierton
Dorton
Ashendon
Upper(Over) Winchendon
AYLESBURY
Puttenham
Marsworth
B489
Pitstone
Dorton
A4157
Wilstone
Hartwell
5
Wilstone Resr
New Mill
B488
Aldbury
Stone
Walton
A41
Buckland
Drayton Beauchamp
Lower(Nether) Winchendon
9
A413
Chilton
Upton
Hartwell
5
Aston Clinton
Tring
B4443
B4544
Dinton
Cuddington
Bishopstone
Easington
Westlington
Weston Turville
Halton
Zoological Museum
Wigginton
A4251
Long Crendon
Chearsley
Stoke Mandeville
A418
Ford
B4009
3
261
S
Hastoe
7
Notley Abbey (ruins)
North Lee
Haddenham
Kimble Wick
The
Three
Hundreds
Northchurch
Nash
Little Kimble
Coombe Hill
Wendover
Cholesbury
A41
Shabbington
Aston Sandford
Lee
8
Ellesborough
Butler's Cross
St Leonards
Buckland Common
A4129
Kingsey
Meadle
of
Aylesbury
A418
Owlswick
B4009
Great Kimble
Ashley Green
3
Ilmer
Thame
Rycote Chapel
Towersey
Longwick
Askett
Dunsmore
The Lee
Bellingdon
A416
Moreton
Thame
Monks Risborough
Lee Clump
A329
B4444
A413
Chartridge
Lye Green
Pitch Green
Little Hampden
9
A40
Chinnor & Princes Risborough Rly
Princes Risborough
Ballinger Common
Newtown
Emmington
B4445
CHESHAM
Henton
Saunderton
South Heath
B4012
Tetsworth
B4009
Bledlow
Loosley Row
B485
Sydenham
Great Missenden
Chesham Bois
Chinnor
Water
Speen
Little Missenden
Talmage
A40
Lacey Green
Prestwood
Hyde Heath
Postcombe
Adwell
South Weston
Aston Rowant
Kingston Blount
Upper North Dean
A4128
Little Kingshill
Saunderton Sta.
8
Hughenden Valley
Great Kingshill
Lewknor
Bradenham
AMERSHAM
Bledlow Ridge
Holmer Green
Chalfont
6
Easington
B4009
The City
A4010
Naphill
Cryers Hill
Penn Street
A404
A355
2
Stokenchurch
5
West Wycombe
Downley
Hughenden Manor (NT)
Hazlemere
Coleshill
Pyrton
Shirburn
255
Beacon's Bottom
A40
4
Watlington
8
Tylers Green
Winchmore Hill
West Wycombe Park (NT)
Christmas Common
B474
Chalfont St Giles
Penn
Milton's Cottage
Ibstone
M40
HIGH WYCOMBE
Bekonscot Model Village
B480
Northend
A40
Knotty Green
Seer Green
Cadmore End
Bolter End
8
1
Wycombe Marsh
Turville Heath
Booker
Lane End
Jordans
Forty Green
Greenfield
4
Turville
Fingest
Handy Cross
Loudwater
Holtspur
Beaconsfield
Cookley Green
Pishill
3
2
Russell's Water
Stonor Park
Frieth
8
Skirmett
B482
Flackwell Heath
A4094
B481
Park Corner
Maidensgrove
Stonor
Rockwell End
Little Marlow
Well End
Wooburn
Wooburn Green
Odds Farm Park
B480
A
B
C
Huntercombe End
Fawley
Middle Assendon
Lower Woodend
Marlow
A404
Bourne End
Hedsor
Hedgerley
Farnham
Nettlebed
Hambleden
11

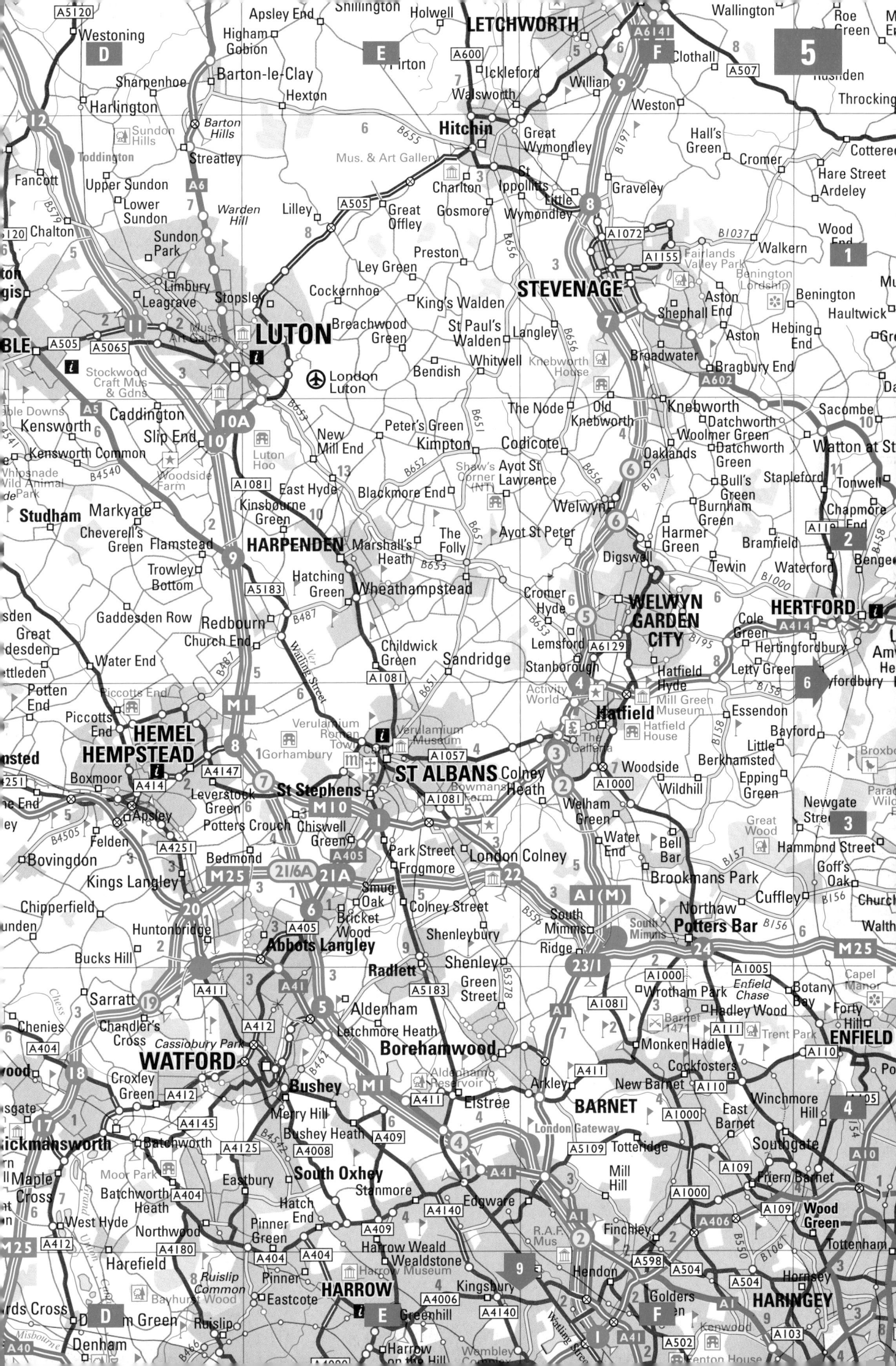

5
D
E
F
A5120
Westoning
Apsley End
Shillington
Holwell
LETCHWORTH
Wallington
Roe Green
Higham Gobion
Barton-le-Clay
Pirton
A600
Ickleford
A6141
Clothall
A507
Rushden
Sharpenhoe
Hexton
Walsworth
Willian
Weston
Throcking
Harlington
Barton Hills
Hitchin
Great Wymondley
Hall's Green
Cromer
Cottered
Sundon Hills
Toddington
Streatley
B655
Mus. & Art Gallery
Hare Street
Ardeley
Fancott
Upper Sundon
A6
Charlton
St Ippollitts
Graveley
Lower Sundon
Warden Hill
Lilley
A505
Great Offley
Gosmore
Little Wymondley
B579
Chalton
Sundon Park
Preston
A1072
B1037
Wood End
Walkern
A1155
Fairlands Valley Park
Benington Lordship
Ley Green
B656
STEVENAGE
Limbury
Leagrave
Stopsley
Cockernhoe
King's Walden
Aston
Benington
Aston End
Shephall
Haultwick
Breachwood Green
St Paul's Walden
Langley
Hebing End
LUTON
Mus. & Art Gallery
A505
A5065
Stockwood Craft Mus & Gdns
London Luton
Bendish
Whitwell
Knebworth House
Broadwater
Bragbury End
A602
A5
Caddington
10A
B653
The Node
Old Knebworth
Knebworth
Datchworth
Sacombe
Kensworth
Slip End
New Mill End
Peter's Green
Kimpton
B651
Codicote
Woolmer Green
Datchworth Green
Watton at Stone
Kensworth Common
Luton Hoo
Shaw's Corner (NT)
Ayot St Lawrence
Oaklands
Whipsnade Wild Animal Park
B4540
Woodside Farm
B652
B197
Stapleford
Tonwell
A1081
East Hyde
Blackmore End
Bull's Green
Burnham Green
Studham
Markyate
Kinsbourne Green
Welwyn
Chapmore End
Cheverell's Green
Flamstead
HARPENDEN
The Folly
Marshall's Heath
Ayot St Peter
Harmer Green
Bramfield
Digswell
Tewin
Waterford
Bengeo
Trowley Bottom
B653
Hatching Green
Wheathampstead
Cromer Hyde
B1000
A5183
Gaddesden Row
Redbourn
B487
WELWYN GARDEN CITY
HERTFORD
Great Gaddesden
Church End
Lemsford
Cole Green
A414
Hertingfordbury
Childwick Green
Sandridge
A6129
B195
Water End
Stanborough
Hatfield Hyde
Letty Green
Watling Street
Ver
A1081
B651
Activity World
Hatfield
Mill Green Museum
B158
Essendon
Potten End
Piccotts End
Piccotts End
Verulamium Roman Town
Verulamium Museum
The Galleria
Hatfield House
Bayford
HEMEL HEMPSTEAD
Gorhambury
A1057
ST ALBANS
Colney Heath
Little Berkhamsted
Woodside
M1
A4147
Boxmoor
A414
Leverstock Green
St Stephens
M10
A1081
Bowmans Farm
Wildhill
A1000
Epping Green
Newgate Street
Apsley
Welham Green
Potters Crouch
Chiswell Green
Park Street
B4505
Felden
A4251
Bedmond
A405
Frogmore
London Colney
Water End
Bell Bar
Great Wood
Hammond Street
Bovingdon
B157
Goff's Oak
M25
21/6A
21A
22
Brookmans Park
Kings Langley
Smug Oak
A1(M)
Cuffley
B156
Chipperfield
Bricket Wood
Colney Street
South Mimms
Northaw
Potters Bar
Huntonbridge
A405
B556
Abbots Langley
Shenleybury
Ridge
23/1
24
M25
Bucks Hill
Radlett
Shenley
B5378
A1000
A1005
Enfield Chase
Capel Manor
Botany Bay
Sarratt
A411
A41
A5183
Green Street
Wrotham Park
A1081
Hadley Wood
Forty Hill
Aldenham
Barnet 1471
A111
Trent Park
Chess
Chenies
Chandler's Cross
A412
Letchmore Heath
Monken Hadley
ENFIELD
A110
A404
Cassiobury Park
WATFORD
Borehamwood
Cockfosters
Croxley Green
Bushey
B462
M1
Aldenham Reservoir
A411
Arkley
New Barnet
A110
A4145
Merry Hill
Elstree
BARNET
Winchmore Hill
A412
A1000
East Barnet
Rickmansworth
Batchworth
B4542
Bushey Heath
A409
A4125
A4008
London Gateway
A5109
Totteridge
Southgate
A10
Moor Park
South Oxhey
Mill Hill
A109
Maple Cross
Batchworth Heath
A404
Eastbury
Stanmore
A41
Friern Barnet
A1000
West Hyde
Grand Union Canal
Northwood
Hatch End
Edgware
A4140
A406
A109
Wood Green
Pinner Green
A409
R.A.F. Mus
Finchley
B550
B106
M25
A412
A4180
A404
A404
Harrow Weald
Wealdstone
Harrow Museum
Tottenham
Harefield
A598
A504
Hornsey
Ruislip Common
Pinner
Hendon
A504
Bayhurst Wood
Eastcote
HARROW
A4006
Kingsbury
Golders Green
HARINGEY
Denham Green
Greenhill
A4140
Watling Street
A1
Ruislip
Kenwood
A103
Misbourne
A40
Denham
B466
Harrow on the Hill
Wembley
A41
A502
Kenton House

6
A
B
C
Roe Green
Mill End
Chipping
Anstey
Meesden
Wicken Bonhunt
Debden
Rushden
Wyddial
Brent Pelham
Clavering
Rickling
Prior's Hall Barn
Mole Hall
Throcking
Starling's Green
Quendon
Buntingford
Great Hormead
Stocking Pelham
Berden
Rickling Green
Hall's Green
Cromer
Cottered
Hare Street
Little Hormead
Hare Street
Barleycroft End
Henham
Ardeley
Aspenden
Furneux Pelham
East End
Ugley
Chickney
Westmill
Hay Street
Ugley Green
Manuden
Broxted
Walkern
Wood End
Patmore Heath
Elsenham
1
Benington Lordship
Great Munden
Nasty
Braughing
Farnham Green
Farnham
Stansted Mountfitchet
Aston
Benington
Albury
Hazel End
Molehill Green
Aston End
Haultwick
Puckeridge
Stansted
Aston
Hebing End
Green End
Standon
Little Hadham
Birchanger
Takeley Street
Takeley
Bragbury End
Collier's End
Hadham Ford
BISHOP'S STORTFORD
Birchanger Green
Dane End
Bury Green
Smith's Green
Datchworth
Sacombe
Much Hadham
Thorley Street
Hope End
Bulmer Green
Datchworth Green
Watton at Stone
High Cross
Hadham Cross
Thorley
Great Hallingbury
Hatfield Forest (NT)
Bacon End
Bull's Green
Stapleford
Tonwell
Wadesmill
Perry Green
Green Tye
Spellbrook
Little Hallingbury
Great Canfield
Burnham Green
Chapmore End
Thundridge
Baker's End
Allen's Green
Adventure Island Playbarn
Hatfield Broad Oak
Paynes Hall
Widford
Hatfield Heath
2
Tewin
Waterford
Bengeo
Ware
Wareside
Hunsdon
Sawbridgeworth
Aythorpe Roding
Sheering
HERTFORD
Great Amwell
Gilston Park
High Wych
Pye Corner
White Roding
Leaden Roding
Cole Green
Hertingfordbury
Little Amwell
St Margarets
Stanstead Abbotts
Eastwick
Churchgate Street
Matching
Matching Green
Letty Green
5
Bayfordbury
Hertford Heath
Hailey
Roydon
HARLOW
Matching Tye
Abbess Roding
Essendon
Rye Park
Little Parndon
Church Langley
Bayford
Hoddesdon
Great Parndon
Foster Street
Threshers Bush
Little Laver
Little Berkhamsted
Broxbourne
Spitalbrook
Roydon Hamlet
Broadley Common
Potter Street
Magdalen Laver
High Laver
Pickerells
Epping Green
Broxbourne
Paradise Wildlife Park
Nazeing
Hastingwood
North Weald Airfield
Moreton
Fyfield
Newgate Street
Wormley
Lower Nazeing
Epping Green
Bovinger
Bobbingworth
Clatterford
3
Great Wood
Thornwood Common
Tyler's Green
Shelley
Norton Mandeville
Hammond Street
Turnford
Bumble's Green
Epping Upland
North Weald Bassett
Chipping Ongar
Norton
Goff's Oak
Flamstead End
Coopersale Common
High Ongar
Cuffley
Churchgate
Cheshunt
Lee Valley
Cobbin's Brook
Hobbs Cross Open Farm
Epping
Toot Hill
Greensted
Potters Bar
Waltham Cross
Waltham Abbey
Upshire
Fiddlers Hamlet
Stanford Rivers
Stondon Massey
Capel Manor
Enfield Chase
Botany Bay
Theydon Bois
Stapleford Tawney
Little End
Kelvedon
Hadley Wood
Forty Hill
Sewardstone
Epping Forest
Navestock
Doddinghurst
Trent Park
ENFIELD
High Beach
Loughton
Passingford Bridge
Abridge
Navestock Side
Pilgrims Hatch
Ponders End
Stapleford Abbotts
Coxtie Green
Winchmore Hill
4
Chingford
Buckhurst Hill
Lambourne End
Bournebridge
Weald Park
South Weald
Southgate
Hainault Forest
Chigwell
Noak Hill
Havering-atte-Bower
Friern Barnet
Edmonton
Chigwell Row
Havering
Harold Hill
Woodford Green
Grange Hill
Hainault
Collier Row
Wood Green
WALTHAM FOREST
Woodford
Woodford Bridge
Fairlop Waters
Gidea Park
Roman Road
Harold Wood
Tottenham
Barkingside
Marks Gate
Hornsey
10
HARINGEY
Walthamstow
Wanstead
REDBRIDGE
Seven Kings
ROMFORD
Kenwood
Rush Green
Cranham
Kenwood House (NT)
Leyton
ILFORD
Hornchurch
M11
M25
A10
A120
A602
A414
A1170
A119
A1184
A1169
A1025
A1060
A128
A113
A1005
A1010
A1055
A112
A111
A110
A105
A104
A121
A1168
A1112
A1069
A1037
A1009
A109
A406
A503
A11
A1400
A118
A124
A123
A1083
A12
A127
A1023
A504
A103
A107
A114
A125
B1038
B1368
B1383
B1051
B1037
B1004
B1000
B158
B1197
B180
B181
B194
B1393
B1256
B156
B157
B184
B172
B175
B173
B170
B154
B137
B160
B179
B550
B106
Quin
Rib
Ash
Stort
Roding
Lea or Lee

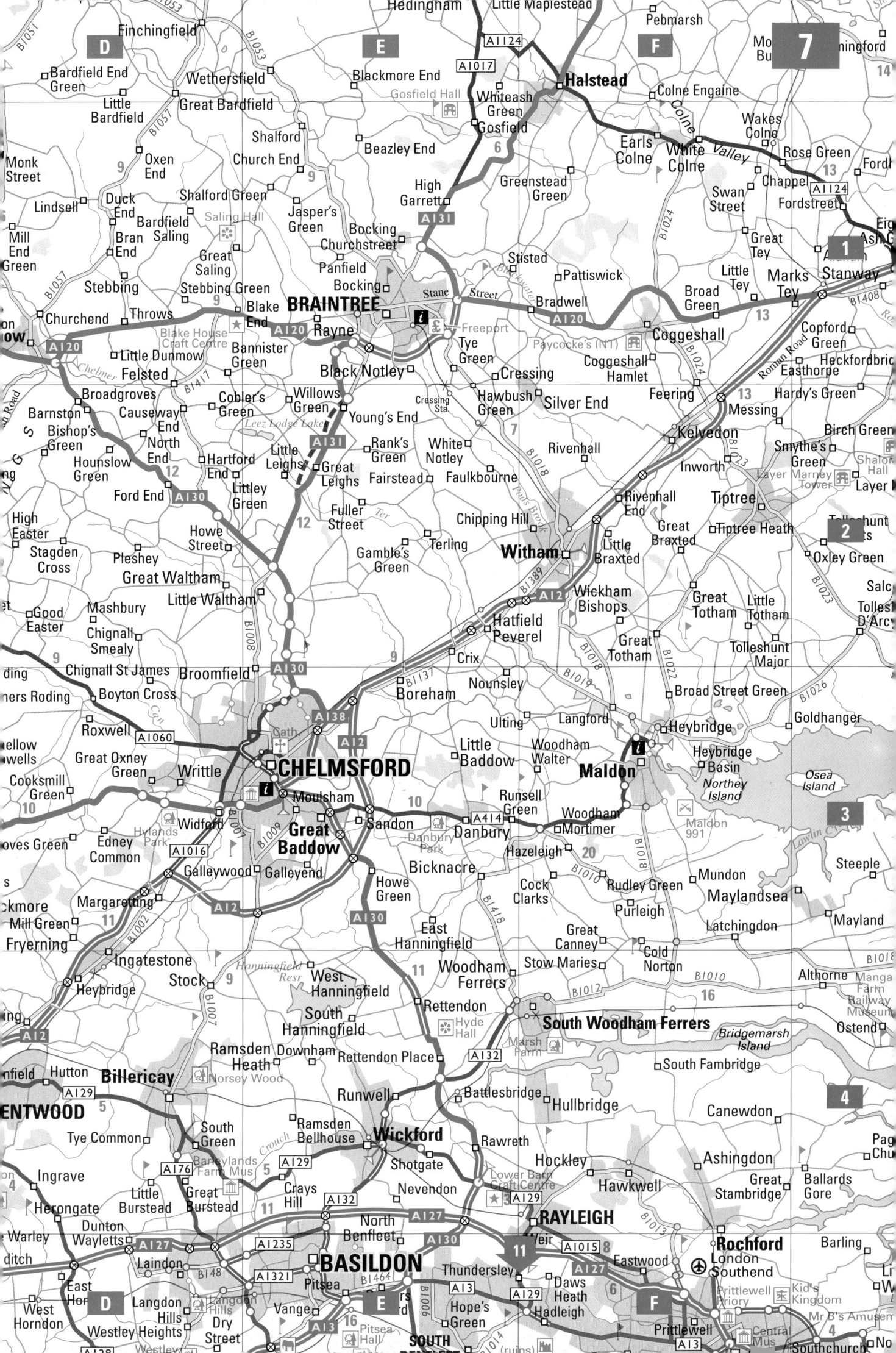

7
D
E
F
Hedingham
Little Maplestead
Pebmarsh
Finchingfield
Wethersfield
Bardfield End Green
Little Bardfield
Great Bardfield
Blackmore End
Gosfield Hall
Whiteash Green
Gosfield
Halstead
Colne Engaine
Colne Valley
Wakes Colne
Earls Colne
White Colne
Rose Green
Chappel
Fordstreet
Swan Street
Shalford
Church End
Beazley End
Oxen End
Monk Street
Lindsell
Duck End
Bran End
Bardfield Saling
Saling Hall
Shalford Green
Jasper's Green
High Garrett
Greenstead Green
Mill End Green
Great Saling
Bocking Churchstreet
Panfield
Bocking
Stisted
Pattiswick
Great Tey
Little Tey
Marks Tey
Stanway
Stebbing
Stebbing Green
BRAINTREE
Stane Street
Bradwell
Broad Green
Coggeshall
Churchend
Throws
Blake End
Rayne
Blake House Craft Centre
Freeport
Tye Green
Paycocke's (NT)
Copford Green
Little Dunmow
Felsted
Bannister Green
Black Notley
Cressing
Coggeshall Hamlet
Easthorpe
Heckfordbridge
Broadgroves
Cobler's Green
Willows Green
Hawbush Green
Silver End
Feering
Messing
Hardy's Green
Barnston
Causeway End
Leez Lodge Lakes
Young's End
Cressing Sta.
Kelvedon
Birch Green
Bishop's Green
North End
Little Leighs
Rank's Green
White Notley
Rivenhall
Smythe's Green
Hounslow Green
Hartford End
Great Leighs
Fairstead
Faulkbourne
Inworth
Layer Marney Tower
Layer
Ford End
Littley Green
Rivenhall End
Tiptree
High Easter
Howe Street
Fuller Street
Chipping Hill
Great Braxted
Tiptree Heath
Stagden Cross
Pleshey
Gamble's Green
Terling
Witham
Little Braxted
Oxley Green
Great Waltham
Little Waltham
Wickham Bishops
Great Totham
Little Totham
Good Easter
Mashbury
Chignall Smealy
Hatfield Peverel
Tolleshunt D'Arcy
Great Totham
Tolleshunt Major
Chignall St James
Broomfield
Crix
Boyton Cross
Boreham
Nounsley
Broad Street Green
Roxwell
Ulting
Langford
Heybridge
Goldhanger
Great Oxney Green
Writtle
CHELMSFORD
Little Baddow
Woodham Walter
Maldon
Heybridge Basin
Northey Island
Osea Island
Cooksmill Green
Moulsham
Runsell Green
Widford
Hylands Park
Sandon
Great Baddow
Danbury Park
Danbury
Woodham Mortimer
Maldon 991
Edney Common
Hazeleigh
Galleywood
Galleyend
Bicknacre
Howe Green
Cock Clarks
Rudley Green
Mundon
Steeple
Margaretting
Purleigh
Maylandsea
Mill Green
East Hanningfield
Great Canney
Latchingdon
Mayland
Fryerning
Ingatestone
Stow Maries
Cold Norton
Heybridge
Stock
Hanningfield Resr
West Hanningfield
Woodham Ferrers
Althorne
Mangapps Farm Railway Museum
Rettendon
South Hanningfield
Hyde Hall
South Woodham Ferrers
Ostend
Marsh Farm
Bridgemarsh Island
Ramsden Heath
Downham
Rettendon Place
South Fambridge
Hutton
Billericay
Norsey Wood
BRENTWOOD
Battlesbridge
Hullbridge
Runwell
Canewdon
Tye Common
South Green
Ramsden Bellhouse
Wickford
Rawreth
Ingrave
Barleylands Farm Mus
Shotgate
Hockley
Ashingdon
Lower Barn Craft Centre
Hawkwell
Great Stambridge
Ballards Gore
Herongate
Little Burstead
Great Burstead
Crays Hill
Nevendon
RAYLEIGH
Dunton Wayletts
North Benfleet
Rochford
Barling
Laindon
BASILDON
Weir
Eastwood
London Southend
Thundersley
Daws Heath
Prittlewell Priory
Kid's Kingdom
East Horndon
West Horndon
Langdon Hills
Pitsea
Vange
Hope's Green
Hadleigh
Mr B's Amusement
Westley Heights
Dry Street
Prittlewell
Central Mus
Southchurch
SOUTH
A1124
A1017
A131
A120
A130
A138
A12
A1060
A414
A1016
A132
A129
A176
A127
A1235
A1321
A13
A1015
B1053
B1051
B1057
B1417
B1024
B1408
B1023
B1018
B1389
B1019
B1022
B1026
B1137
B1008
B1007
B1009
B1002
B1010
B1418
B1012
B1013
B1148
B1464
B1006
B1014

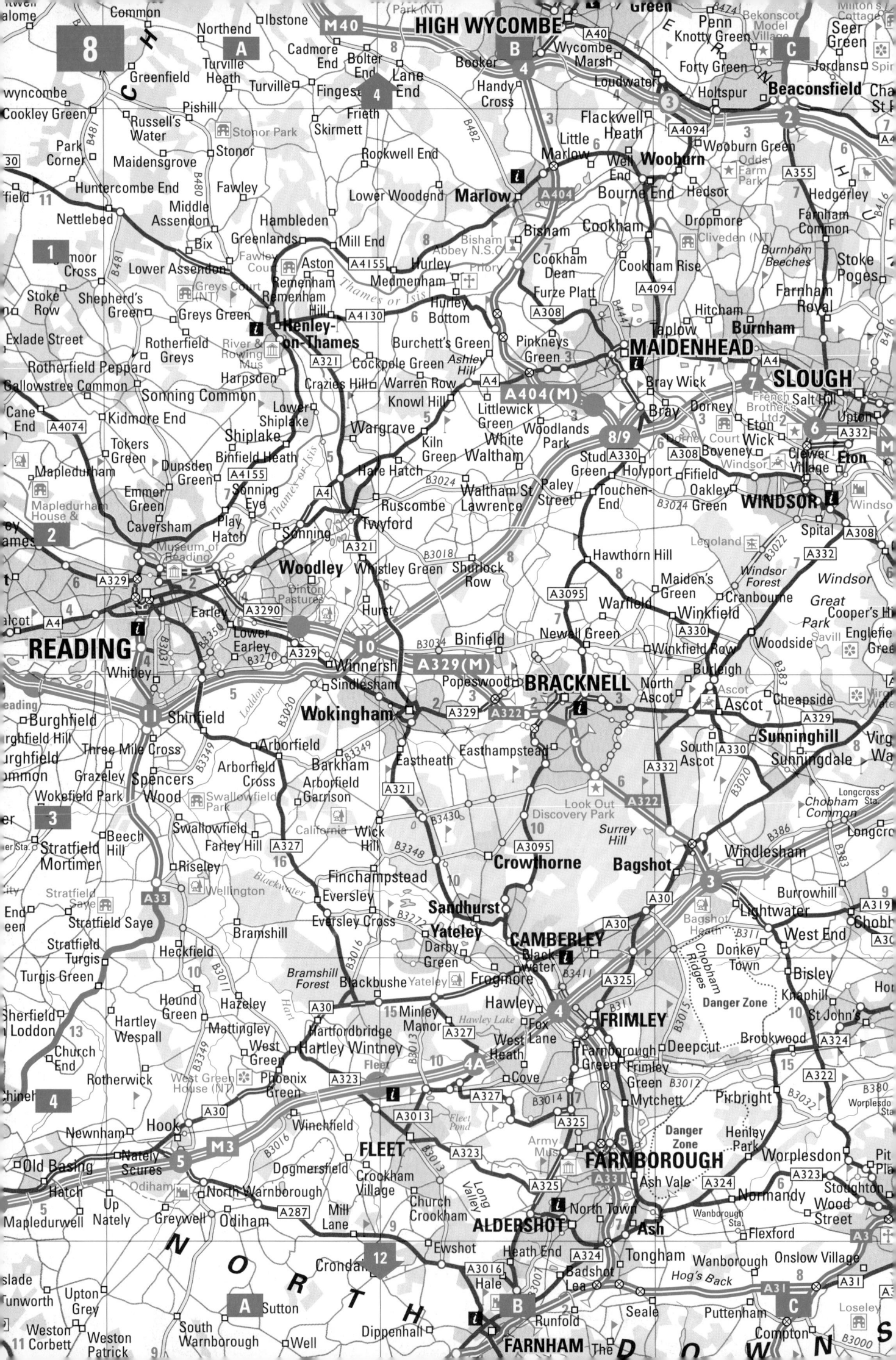

8
A
B
C
Common
Northend
Ibstone
M40
HIGH WYCOMBE
Penn
Knotty Green
Bekonscot Model Village
Seer Green
Jordans
Turville Heath
Cadmore End
Bolter End
Lane End
Booker
A40
Wycombe Marsh
Forty Green
Greenfield
Turville
Fingest
Frieth
Handy Cross
Loudwater
Holtspur
Beaconsfield
Cookley Green
Pishill
Skirmett
B482
Flackwell Heath
A4094
Russell's Water
Stonor Park
Little Marlow
Park Corner
B481
Stonor
Rockwell End
Well End
Wooburn
Wooburn Green
Odds Farm Park
A355
Maidensgrove
B480
Huntercombe End
Fawley
Lower Woodend
Marlow
A404
Bourne End
Hedsor
Hedgerley
Middle Assendon
Nettlebed
Hambleden
Dropmore
Farnham Common
Cookham
Bisham
Bisham Abbey N.S.C.
Greenlands
Mill End
Cliveden (NT)
Burnham Beeches
1
Bix
Fawley Court
Aston
A4155
Hurley
Priory
Cookham Dean
Cookham Rise
Stoke Poges
Lower Assendon
Remenham
Medmenham
Thames or Isis
Greys Court (NT)
Remenham Hill
Hurley Bottom
Furze Platt
A4094
Farnham Royal
Stoke Row
Shepherd's Green
Greys Green
A4130
A308
Hitcham
Henley-on-Thames
Taplow
Burnham
Exlade Street
Rotherfield Greys
River & Rowing Mus
Burchett's Green
Pinkneys Green
MAIDENHEAD
A321
Cockpole Green
Ashley Hill
A4
Rotherfield Peppard
Harpsden
Crazies Hill
Warren Row
Bray Wick
SLOUGH
Gallowstree Common
Sonning Common
A404(M)
Salt Hill
Cane End
Kidmore End
Lower Shiplake
Knowl Hill
Littlewick Green
Bray
Dorney
French Brothers Ltd
Upton
A4074
Shiplake
Wargrave
Woodlands Park
8/9
Eton
Tokers Green
Kiln Green
White Waltham
Dorney Court
Eton Wick
A332
Mapledurham
Binfield Heath
Hare Hatch
Stud Green
A330
Holyport
A308
Boveney
Windsor
Clewer Village
Eton
Dunsden Green
A4155
Mapledurham House
Emmer Green
Sonning Eye
A4
B3024
Waltham St Lawrence
Paley Street
Touchen-End
Fifield
Oakley Green
WINDSOR
Caversham
Play Hatch
Ruscombe
Twyford
B3024
Spital
A308
2
Sonning
Legoland
B3022
Museum of Reading
A321
B3018
Hawthorn Hill
A332
Woodley
Whistley Green
Shurlock Row
A329
Dinton Pastures
A3095
Maiden's Green
Windsor Forest
Windsor
Cranbourne
Earley
A3290
Hurst
Warfield
Great Park
Winkfield
Cooper's Hill
A4
Lower Earley
B3350
Newell Green
A330
Savill
Englefield Green
READING
B3031
B3270
A329
10
B3034
Binfield
Winkfield Row
Woodside
Whitley
Winnersh
A329(M)
Burleigh
B383
Sindlesham
Popeswood
BRACKNELL
North Ascot
Ascot
Cheapside
Burghfield
Shinfield
Loddon
B3030
Wokingham
A329
A322
Ascot
A329
Burghfield Hill
Sunninghill
Arborfield
B3349
Eastheath
Easthampstead
South Ascot
A330
Sunningdale
Burghfield Common
Three Mile Cross
Barkham
A332
Grazeley
Spencers Wood
Arborfield Cross
Arborfield Garrison
A321
B3020
Longcross Sta.
Wokefield Park
Swallowfield Park
Look Out Discovery Park
A322
Chobham Common
3
B3430
Surrey Hill
Longcross
Beech Hill
Swallowfield
California
Wick Hill
B386
Stratfield Mortimer
Farley Hill
A327
A3095
Windlesham
B3348
Crowthorne
Bagshot
B383
Riseley
16
Blackwater
Finchampstead
Stratfield Saye
Wellington
Eversley
Sandhurst
A30
Burrowhill
A33
Eversley Cross
B3272
Lightwater
A319
Stratfield Saye
Yateley
Bagshot Heath
A30
West End
Chobham
Bramshill
B3016
Darby Green
CAMBERLEY
Donkey Town
Stratfield Turgis
Heckfield
Blackwater
B3411
Chobham Ridges
Bisley
B3011
Bramshill Forest
Blackbushe
Yateley
Frogmore
A325
Turgis Green
Knaphill
Hound Green
Hazeley
Hart
A30
Minley Manor
Hawley
Hawley Lake
Fox Lane
4
B311
FRIMLEY
Danger Zone
St John's
Sherfield on Loddon
Hartley Wespall
Mattingley
Hartfordbridge
A327
West Heath
B3015
Brookwood
A324
West Green
Hartley Wintney
B3349
B3013
Fleet
4A
Farnborough Green
Deepcut
Church End
Rotherwick
West Green House (NT)
Phoenix Green
A323
Cove
Frimley Green
B3012
A322
B380
4
A327
Mytchett
Pirbright
B3032
Worplesdon Sta
B3014
Hook
A30
Winchfield
A3013
Fleet Pond
A325
Danger Zone
Henley Park
Newnham
Army Mus
M3
B3016
FLEET
A323
FARNBOROUGH
Worplesdon
Old Basing
Nately Scures
5
Dogmersfield
Crookham Village
B3013
A331
Ash Vale
A324
A323
Stoughton
Hatch
Odiham
North Warnborough
Long Valley
A325
Normandy
Wood Street
Up Nately
Mapledurwell
Greywell
Odiham
A287
Mill Lane
Church Crookham
North Town
Wanborough Sta
ALDERSHOT
Ash
Flexford
A3
Ewshot
Heath End
A324
Tongham
Wanborough
Onslow Village
12
Crondall
NORTH
A3016
Badshot Lea
Hog's Back
A31
A31
Hale
Upton Grey
Seale
Puttenham
Loseley
A
Sutton
B
C
Tunworth
Runfold
Weston Corbett
Weston Patrick
South Warnborough
Well
Dippenhall
FARNHAM
Compton
B3000

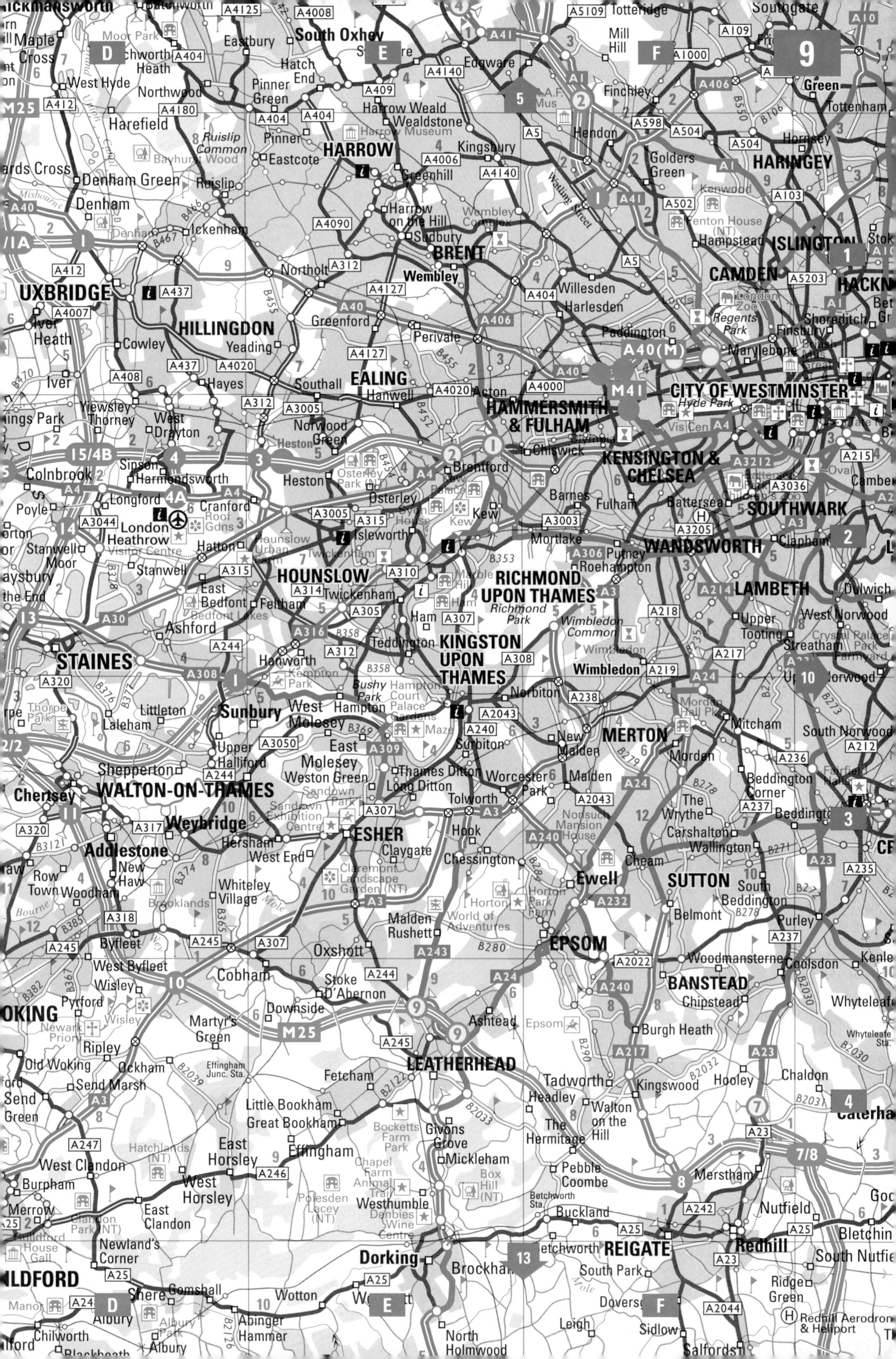

D
E
F
9
South Oxhey
Eastbury
Moor Park
Maple Cross
West Hyde
Northwood
Harefield
Hatch End
Pinner Green
Pinner
Eastcote
Ruislip Common
Bayhurst Wood
Harrow Weald
Wealdstone
Harrow Museum
HARROW
Greenhill
Harrow on the Hill
Sudbury
Edgware
Mill Hill
Totteridge
Southgate
Finchley
Hendon
Golders Green
Kingsbury
Wembley Complex
Wembley
BRENT
Watling Street
Hornsey
HARINGEY
Tottenham
Kenwood
Fenton House (NT)
Hampstead
ISLINGTON
CAMDEN
HACKNEY
London Zoo
Regents Park
Shoreditch
Finsbury
Marylebone
Denham Green
Denham
Ruislip
Ickenham
UXBRIDGE
HILLINGDON
Yeading
Cowley
Iver Heath
Iver
Northolt
Greenford
Perivale
Willesden
Harlesden
Paddington
CITY OF WESTMINSTER
Hyde Park
Vis Cen
Hayes
Southall
EALING
Hanwell
Acton
HAMMERSMITH & FULHAM
Olympia
Chiswick
KENSINGTON & CHELSEA
Yiewsley
West Drayton
Norwood Green
Heston
Brentford
Osterley Park (NT)
Osterley
Syon House
Kew
Barnes
Fulham
Battersea
Battersea Park Children's Zoo
SOUTHWARK
Oval
Camberwell
Sipson
Harmondsworth
Colnbrook
Longford
Cranford
Poyle
London Heathrow
Visitor Centre
Roof Gdns
Hatton
Hounslow Urban Farm
Isleworth
Twickenham
Mortlake
Putney
Roehampton
WANDSWORTH
Clapham
Stanwell Moor
Stanwell
HOUNSLOW
Marble Hill
RICHMOND UPON THAMES
Richmond Park
LAMBETH
Dulwich
East Bedfont
Feltham
Bedfont Lakes
Ham
Wimbledon Common
Wimbledon
Upper Tooting
West Norwood
Streatham
Crystal Palace Park
Farmyard
Ashford
STAINES
Hanworth
Kempton Park
Teddington
KINGSTON UPON THAMES
Norbiton
Upper Norwood
Thorpe Park
Laleham
Littleton
Sunbury
West Molesey
Hampton
Bushy Park
Hampton Court Palace Gardens
Maze
Surbiton
New Malden
MERTON
Morden Hall Pk
Mitcham
South Norwood
Upper Halliford
East Molesey
Morden
Shepperton
WALTON-ON-THAMES
Weston Green
Thames Ditton
Long Ditton
Worcester Park
Malden
Beddington Corner
Chertsey
Sandown Park
Sandown Exhibition Centre
Tolworth
Nonsuch Mansion House
The Wrythe
Carshalton
Beddington
Weybridge
Addlestone
Hersham
ESHER
Claygate
Hook
Chessington
Ewell
Cheam
Wallington
West End
New Haw
Row Town
Woodham
Brooklands
Whiteley Village
Claremont Landscape Garden (NT)
Horton Park Farm
World of Adventures
SUTTON
South Beddington
Belmont
Purley
Byfleet
West Byfleet
Wisley
Cobham
Oxshott
Malden Rushett
EPSOM
Woodmansterne
Coulsdon
Kenley
WOKING
Pyrford
Newark Priory
Ripley
Martyr's Green
Downside
Stoke D'Abernon
Ashtead
Epsom
BANSTEAD
Chipstead
Whyteleafe
Whyteleafe Sta.
Burgh Heath
Old Woking
Ockham
Effingham Junc. Sta.
Send Marsh
Send Green
Fetcham
LEATHERHEAD
Tadworth
Headley
Kingswood
Hooley
Chaldon
Caterham
Little Bookham
Great Bookham
Bocketts Farm Park
Givons Grove
Mickleham
Walton on the Hill
The Hermitage
Hatchlands (NT)
West Clandon
Burpham
East Horsley
Effingham
Chapel Farm Animal Trail
Box Hill (NT)
Pebble Coombe
Merstham
West Horsley
Polesden Lacey (NT)
Westhumble
Denbies Wine Centre
Betchworth Sta.
Buckland
Nutfield
Merrow
Clandon Park (NT)
East Clandon
Newland's Corner
Guildford House Gall
Bletchingley
GUILDFORD
Dorking
Brockham
Betchworth
REIGATE
Redhill
South Nutfield
South Park
Ridge Green
Shere
Gomshall
Wotton
Westcott
Dover's Green
Leigh
Sidlow
Redhill Aerodrome & Heliport
Manor
Albury
Albury Park
Abinger Hammer
Chilworth
Blackheath
North Holmwood
Salfords
M25
M4
M41
A40(M)
A1
A41
A406
A4
A3
A30
A308
A316
A309
A24
A23
A217
A243
A240
A232
A25
M1
13
10

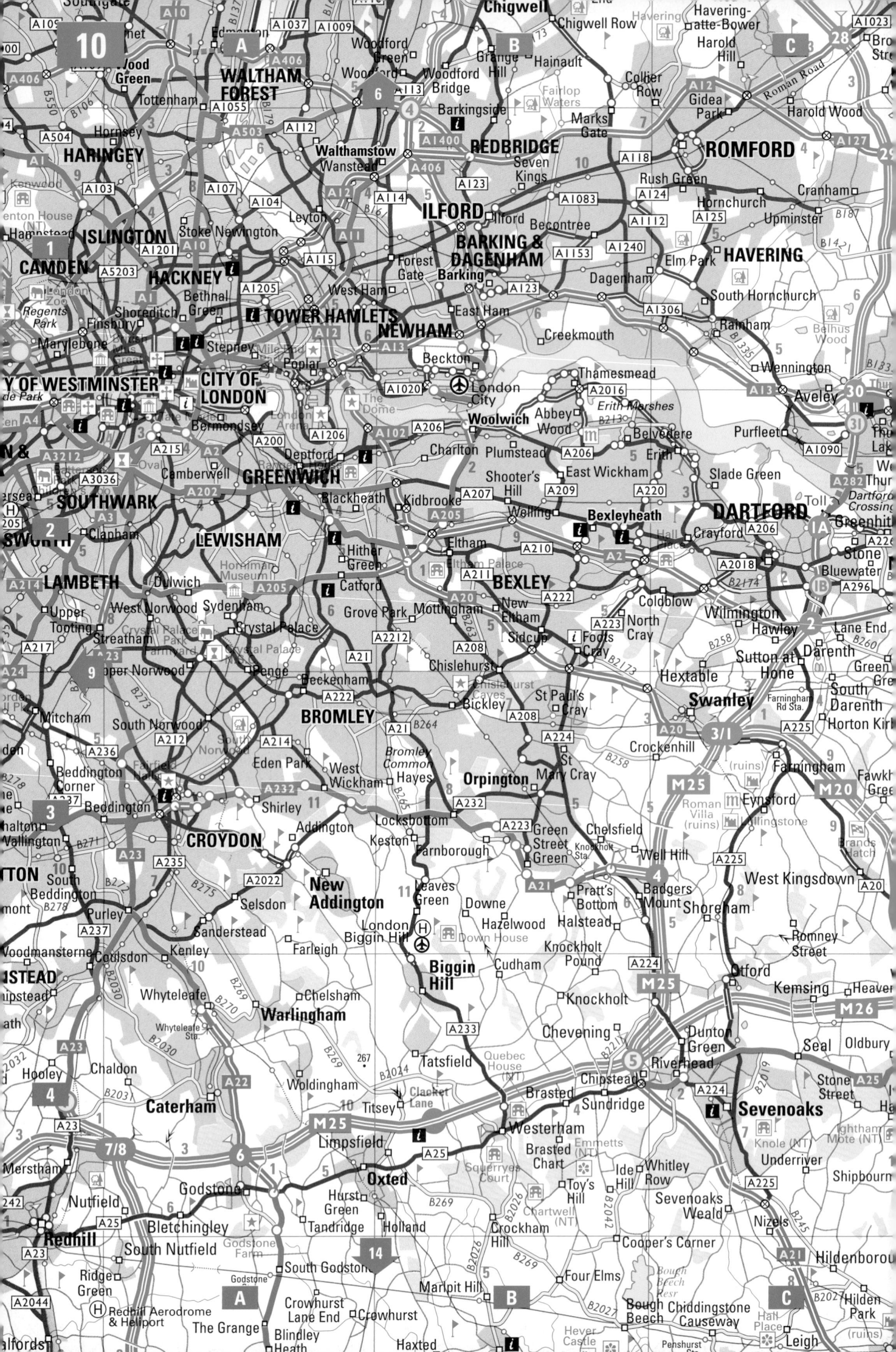

10
A
B
C
6
14
Chigwell
Chigwell Row
Havering-atte-Bower
Harold Hill
Edmonton
Wood Green
Tottenham
Woodford Green
Woodford Bridge
Grange Hill
Hainault
Collier Row
Fairlop Waters
Gidea Park
Roman Road
Harold Wood
WALTHAM FOREST
Barkingside
Marks Gate
Hornsey
HARINGEY
Walthamstow
Wanstead
REDBRIDGE
Seven Kings
ROMFORD
Rush Green
Cranham
Hornchurch
Upminster
ILFORD
Ilford
Becontree
Leyton
Stoke Newington
Hampstead
ISLINGTON
CAMDEN
HACKNEY
BARKING & DAGENHAM
Forest Gate
Barking
Elm Park
HAVERING
Dagenham
West Ham
Bethnal Green
Shoreditch
Finsbury
Regents Park
TOWER HAMLETS
NEWHAM
East Ham
South Hornchurch
Rainham
Belhus Wood
Marylebone
Stepney
Creekmouth
Wennington
Poplar
Beckton
Thamesmead
Y OF WESTMINSTER
CITY OF LONDON
London City
Aveley
The Dome
Abbey Wood
Erith Marshes
Bermondsey
Woolwich
Belvedere
Purfleet
Deptford
Charlton
Plumstead
Erith
Camberwell
GREENWICH
Shooter's Hill
East Wickham
Slade Green
SOUTHWARK
Blackheath
Kidbrooke
Welling
Bexleyheath
DARTFORD
Dartford Crossing
Greenhithe
Clapham
LEWISHAM
Hither Green
Eltham
Crayford
Stone
Bluewater
Horniman Museum
Eltham Palace
BEXLEY
LAMBETH
Dulwich
Catford
New Eltham
Coldblow
Wilmington
Lane End
Upper Tooting
West Norwood
Sydenham
Grove Park
Mottingham
North Cray
Hawley
Darenth
Streatham
Crystal Palace
Sidcup
Foots Cray
Sutton at Hone
Upper Norwood
Penge
Chislehurst
Hextable
Beckenham
Chislehurst Caves
St Paul's Cray
Swanley
South Darenth
Mitcham
South Norwood
BROMLEY
Bickley
Horton Kirby
Crockenhill
Eden Park
Bromley Common
West Wickham
Hayes
Orpington
St Mary Cray
Farningham
Beddington Corner
Beddington
Shirley
Eynsford
Roman Villa (ruins)
Addington
Locksbottom
Green Street Green
Chelsfield
Lullingstone
CROYDON
Keston
Farnborough
Knockholt Sta.
Well Hill
Brands Hatch
South Beddington
New Addington
Leaves Green
Pratt's Bottom
Badgers Mount
West Kingsdown
Selsdon
Downe
Shoreham
Purley
Sanderstead
London Biggin Hill
Hazelwood
Halstead
Down House
Romney Street
Farleigh
Knockholt Pound
Coulsdon
Kenley
Biggin Hill
Cudham
Otford
Kemsing
Heaverham
Whyteleafe
Chelsham
Knockholt
Warlingham
Whyteleafe Sta.
Chevening
Dunton Green
Seal
Oldbury
Tatsfield
Quebec House (NT)
Riverhead
Chaldon
Woldingham
Chipstead
Stone Street
Hooley
Caterham
Clacket Lane
Titsey
Brasted
Sundridge
Sevenoaks
Merstham
Limpsfield
Westerham
Emmetts (NT)
Knole (NT)
Ightham Mote (NT)
Brasted Chart
Underriver
Squerryes Court
Ide Hill
Whitley Row
Shipbourne
Godstone
Oxted
Toy's Hill
Nutfield
Hurst Green
Chartwell (NT)
Sevenoaks Weald
Bletchingley
Tandridge
Holland
Crockham Hill
Nizels
Redhill
South Nutfield
Godstone Farm
Cooper's Corner
Hildenborough
Ridge Green
South Godstone
Four Elms
Bough Beech Resr
Godstone
Marlpit Hill
Hilden Park
Redhill Aerodrome & Heliport
Crowhurst Lane End
Crowhurst
Bough Beech
Chiddingstone Causeway
The Grange
Blindley Heath
Haxted
Hever Castle
Penshurst
Leigh
M25
M20
M26
A2
A20
A21
A22
A23
A25

11
D
E
F
1
2
3
4
Tye Common
Green
Bellhouse
Crouch
Wickford
Rawreth
Hockley
Ashingdon
Ingrave
Barleylands Farm Mus
Crays Hill
Shotgate
Nevendon
Lower Barn Craft Centre
Hawkwell
Stambridge
Little Burstead
Great Burstead
Herongate
Dunton Wayletts
North Benfleet
RAYLEIGH
Rochford
Barling
Warley
Laindon
BASILDON
Weir
Eastwood
London Southend
Thundersley
Daws Heath
East Horndon
Pitsea
Bowers Gifford
Hope's Green
Hadleigh
Prittlewell Priory
Kid's Kingdom
West Horndon
Langdon Hills
Vange
Dry Street
Pitsea Hall
Wat Tyler
SOUTH BENFLEET
(ruins)
Prittlewell
Central Mus
Southchurch
Westley Heights
Zoo
Leigh-on-Sea
Westcliff-on-Sea
Peter Pan's Playground
Southend Pier
Sea Life Centre
Bulphan
One Tree Hill
Chapman Sands
Horndon on the Hill
Corringham
Fobbing
Leigh Beck
SOUTHEND-ON-SEA
Ockendon
Orsett
Coryton
Stanford-le-Hope
CANVEY ISLAND
Thames Haven
Mucking
THAMES
Blythe Sands
Linford
Chadwell St Mary
West Tilbury
East Tilbury
Tilbury
GRAYS
Fort
Halstow Marshes
St Mary's Marshes
Allhallows-on-Sea
Allhallows
Isle of Grain
St Mary's Hoo
Cliffe
Cooling
Northward Hill
Lower Stoke
Grain
Church Street
Danger Zone
High Halstow
Stoke
Stoke Saltings
Wallend
M.V. Princess Pocahontas
GRAVESEND
Milton Chantry
Lower Higham
Cliffe Woods
Chalk
Kingsnorth Power Station
Perry Street
Singlewell or Ifield
Shorne
Chattenden
Hoo
Queenborough
Higham
Upnor
Medway
Chetney Marshes
Southfleet
Thong
Shorne Ridgeway
Wainscott
Upper Upnor
Long Reach
Frindsbury
Chatham Historic Dockyard & Lifeboat Collection
Owletts (NT)
Guildhall Mus
Istead Rise
Cobham
Manor
Rochester Cath
Grange
Swale Sta.
Longfield
Cobham Hall
Strood
ROCHESTER
Brompton
GILLINGHAM
Upchurch
Iwade
New College
Longfield Hill
Camer
Sole Street
CHATHAM
Hook Green
Lower Halstow
Cuxton
Borstal
Luton
Kemsley
Luddesdown
Meopham
Rainham
Bobbing
Capstone
Wigmore
Newington
Milton Regis
Meopham Green
Halling
Wouldham
Hartlip
Walderslade
Ridley
Upper Halling
South Street
Harvel
SITTINGBOURNE
Lidsing
Borden
Holborough
Blue Bell Hill
Snodland
Burham
Oad Street
Bapchild
Bredhurst
Stockbury
Tunstall
Trosley
Kit's Coty House
Coldrum Long Barrow (NT)
Fairseat
Vigo Village
Birling
Ham Hill
Eccles
Little Kit's Coty House
Bredgar
Highsted
Ryarsh
Trottiscliffe
New Hythe
The Friars
Addington
Aylesford
Boxley
Abbey
Leybourne
Bicknor
West Malling
East Malling
Ditton
Sandling
Detling
Hucking
Milstead
Allington
Royal British Legion Village
Thurnham
Wormshill
Offham
Barming Sta
Broad Street
Frinstead
Platt
Leonard's Tower
St Leonard's Street
Maidstone
Wichling
MAIDSTONE
Mus & Art Gal
Bearsted
Eyhorne Manor
Hollingbourne
Great Comp
Crouch
East Barming
Eyhorne Street
West Street
Kent Street
Tovil
Stoneacre (NT)
Old Soar Manor (NT)
Wateringbury
Teston
Shepway
Leeds
Mereworth
Otham
Harrietsham
Warren Street
Dunk's Green
West Farleigh
East Farleigh
Dean Street
Leeds Castle & Gdns
West Peckham
Nettlestead Green
Nettlestead
Langley
Langley Heath
Broomfield
Lenham
Kingswood
Loose
Goose Green
Boughton Green
Sandway
Coxheath
Chart Corner
Five Wents
Lenham Heath
Hadlow
Yalding
Linton
Parkmlake
Liverton Street
Hale Street
Hunton
Boughton Monchelsea Place
Chart Sutton
Sutton Valence
Ulcombe
Grafty Green
Boughton Malherbe
East Peckham
Benover
Beult
Higham Wood
Gold Green
Beltring
Laddingford
Cross-at-Hand
Egerton
TONBRIDGE
Whetsted
Mockbeggar
Queen
Medway
A13
A127
A129
A130
A176
A132
A1235
A1321
A1015
A128
A1014
A1013
A1089
A126
A2260
A226
A227
A289
A228
A231
A230
A229
A2
A278
A249
A2045
A20
A26
A274
A250
M2
M20
B1013
B148
B1464
B1006
B1014
B1420
B1007
B188
B1016
B2001
B2000
B261
B260
B2004
B2097
B2016
B2015
B2010
B2163
B2160
15
187

NORTH DOWNS

Newnham · M3 · B3016 · FLEET · A323 · Army Mus · FARNBOROUGH · Worplesdon · Pitch Plac

Old Ba · 5 · Dogmersfield · Crookham Village · Long Valley · B · A325 · Ash Vale · A324 · Normandy · Stoughton

Odiham · North Warnborough · Church Crookham · A331 · North Town · Wanborough Sta · Wood Street · C

Up Nately · A287 · Mill Lane · 8 · ALDERSHOT · Ash · Flexford · A3

Mapledurwell · Greywell · Odiham · Ewshot · Heath End · A324 · Tongham · Wanborough · Onslow Village

Weston Corbett · South Warnborough · Crondall · A3016 · Hale · Badshot Lea · Hog's Back · A31 · A31

Upton Grey · Well · Dippenhall · B3001 · Seale · Puttenham · Compton · Loseley · B3000

Weston Patrick · Long Sutton · FARNHAM · The Sands · Charleshill · Peper Harow · Eashing

Thorpe · Wrecclesham · The Bourne · Lower Bourne · Waverley Abbey · Shackleford · Hurtmore · Godal

B3349 · Golden Pot · 225 · Bentley · Rowledge · Spreakley · Millbridge · Milford · Milford Sta · Winkworth Arboretum (NT) · Bus

Lasham · Coldrey · Upper Froyle · Bucks Horn Oak · Frensham · Frensham Lit. Pond · Witley Common (NT) · Wheelerstreet · Witley · Hydestile

Shalden · Holybourne · Blacknest · Batt's Corner · Dockenfield · Frensham (NT) · Rushmoor · Thursley · Bowlhead Green · Wormley · Witley Sta · Sandhills · Hambledon

Thedden Grange · Neatham · Binsted · Wheatley · Kingsley · Churt · Beacon Hill · Brook · A286 · A283

Beech · Alton · Wyck · Sleaford · Lindford · Arford · Headley Down · Hindhead · Gibbet Hill · Grayswood · Chiddingfo

Chawton · East Worldham · Headley · A287 · Grayshott · Educational Museum

Jane Austen's House · West Worldham · Bordon · Standford · Passfield · Bramshott · Haslemere · Lythe Hill · Ramsnest Commo

Lower Farringdon · Oakhanger · Whitehill · Conford · Shottermill · Hammer · Kingsley Green · Fisherstreet

Newton Valence · Selborne · Blackmoor · Danger Zone · Greatham · B3004 · Liphook · Camelsdale · Linchmere · Black Down

East Tisted · Oates Memorial & Gilbert White Museum · Empshott · Longmoor Camp · Langley · Northchapel · Fernhurst

Monkwood · Colemore · Hawkley · Liss Forest · Liss · East Liss · Rake · Milland · Lurgashall · Lickfold · Balls Cross

Privett · High Cross · Steep Marsh · Steep · Hill Brow · Redford · Henley · A283

Froxfield Green · Stoner Hill · Sheet · Petersfield · Rogate · Chithurst · Robins · Woolbeding · Lodsworth · Upperton · Gunters Bridge

Langrish · Stroud · Weston · Ramsdean · A272 · West Harting · Iping · Easebourne · River · Petw

Meon · Butser Hill · War Down · Nursted · Buriton · Nyewood · Trotton · Stedham · Midhurst · Cowdray House (Ruins) · Tillington · Bywo

Queen Elizabeth · South Harting · East Harting · Elsted · West Lavington · South Ambersham · Selham · Coultershaw Bridge

Clanfield · Uppark (NT) · Treyford · Didling · Bepton · Heyshott · Graffham · A285

Chalton · North Marden · Compton · East Marden · Chilgrove · Linch Down · Cocking · Duncton · East Lavington · Barlavington

Horndean · West Marden · Up Marden · Forestside · Bow Hill · Singleton · Charlton · East Dean · Upwaltham · Sutton · Bignor

Lovedean · Blendworth · Finchdean · Stansted Park · West Dean · Weald & Downland Open Air Museum · Goodwood · Slindon Estate (NT)

Cowplain · Rowland's Castle · Walderton · Stoughton · Kingley Vale · Goodwood House · Halnaker Hill · Madehurst

HAVANT · Red Hill · Woodend · Mid Lavant · Halnaker · Priory · Eartham · Dale Park · St. Nic

Bedhampton · Denvilles · Westbourne · West Stok · East Lavant · Strettington · Boxgrove · Denmans · Fontwell

Emsworth · Woodmancote · East Ashling · Tangmere

13
D
E
F
West Clandon
Burpham
Merrow
Hatchlands (NT)
East Horsley
West Horsley
Effingham
East Clandon
Clandon Park (NT)
Guildford House Gall
Newland's Corner
GUILDFORD
Manor
Chilworth
Blackheath
Albury
Albury Park
Albury Heath
Shere
Gomshall
Abinger Hammer
Wotton
Westcott
Dorking
Brockham
Grove
Mickleham
Box Hill (NT)
Westhumble
Denbies Wine Centre
Polesden Lacey (NT)
Chapel
Farley Green
Shamley Green
Bramley
Sutton Abinger
Peaslake
Holmbury St Mary
Friday Street
Abinger Common
Hurtwood Common
Stroud Common
Rowly
Grafham
Leith Hill
294
Tower (NT)
Coldharbour
Holmwood Sta.
North Holmwood
South Holmwood
Beare Green
Newdigate
Capel
Forest Green
Jayes Park
Ockley
Ewhurst
Ewhurst Green
Cranleigh
Vachery Pond
Walliswood
Oakwoodhill
Kingsfold
Ellen's Green
Alfold Crossways
Alfold
Bucks Green
Rudgwick
Rowhook
Warnham
Broadbridge Heath
Loxwood
Ifold
Slinfold
The Haven
HORSHAM
Buckman Corner
Christ's Hosp. Sta.
Denne Park
Roundstreet Common
Five Oaks
Itchingfield
Newpound Common
Barns Green
Kirdford
Fishers Farm Park
Billingshurst
Stane Street
Southwater
Brooks Green
Coneyhurst
Adversane
Burdocks
Coolham
Shipley
North Heath
Broadford Bridge
Gay Street
Broomer's Corner
Codmore Hill
Stopham
Nutbourne
West Chiltington
Dial Post
Pulborough
Pulborough Brooks R.S.P.B. Nature Reserve
Hardham
Wiggonholt
Thakeham
Warminghurst
Abingworth
Ashington
Greatham
Rackham
Parham
Cootham
Storrington
Sullington
Kithurst Hill
Hole Street
Washington
238
Amberley Museum
Amberley Sta.
North Stoke
South Stoke
Burpham
Harrow Hill
North End
Findon
Arundel
Warningcamp
Crossbush
Patching
Clapham
High Salvington
North Lancing
Pebble Coombe
Betchworth Sta.
Buckland
Betchworth
REIGATE
South Park
Merstham
Nutfield
Redhill
Bletchingley
South Nutfield
Ridge Green
Redhill Aerodrome & Heliport
Doversgreen
Sidlow
Salfords
Leigh
Norwood Hill
Parkgate
Horley
Hookwood
Povey Cross
Gatwick (London)
Tinsley Green
Burstow
Shipley Bridge
Charlwood
Gatwick Zoo
Gatwick Skyview
Lowfield Heath
County Oak
Copthorne
Ifieldwood
Rusper
Ifield
Three Bridges
Pound Hill
Crabbet Park
Lambs Green
Gossops Green
CRAWLEY
Worth
Tilgate Forest
Faygate
Buchan
Pease Pottage
Holmbush
Colgate
Roffey
St Leonard's Forest
High Beeches
Balcombe
Wakehurst Place (NT)
Selsfield
Ashfold Crossways
Handcross
Nymans (NT)
Mannings Heath
Monk's Gate
Lower Beeding
Slaugham
Staplefield
Brook Street
Borde Hill
Warninglid
Leonardslee
Nuthurst
Copsale
Maplehurst
The Bar
Crabtree
Whitemans Green
Cuckfield
Bolney
Ansty
Cowfold
West Grinstead
Partridge Green
Wineham
Hickstead
Twineham
Wivelsfield Sta.
Burgess Hill
Bines Green
Sayers Common
Albourne
Hurstpierpoint
Keymer
Hassocks
Danny
Henfield
Blackstone
Ashurst
Woodmancote
Muddleswood
Clayton
Ditchling
Ditchling Beacon
248
New Hall
Oreham Common
Pyecombe
Small Dole
Poynings
Fulking
Edburton
Steyning
Bramber
Upper Beeding
St Mary's
Botolphs
Coombes
Patcham
Coldean
Hollingbury
British Engineerium
Preston
Hangleton
Kingston by Sea
Portslade
West
A247 A246 A25 A248 A24 A29 A281 A264 A272 A283 A280 A23 A2044 A217 A242 A2011 A2220 A273 A2300 A2037 A1
M23
B2126 B2127 B2128 B2130 B2133 B2139 B2135 B2195 B2237 B2110 B2114 B2115 B2036 B2116 B2118 B2117 B2112 B2113
Mole
Arun
Adur
Rother

Merstham · Nutfield · Redhill · Bletchingley · South Nutfield · Godstone · Ridge Green · Outwood · Horne · Smallfield · Horley · Rovey Cross · Tinsley Green · Burstow · Shipley Bridge · Copthorne · Felbridge · Three Bridges · CRAWLEY · Worth · Pound Hill · Crabbet Park · Pease Pottage · High Beeches · Handcross · Nymans (NT) · Staplefield · Balcombe · Brook Street · Borde Hill · Ardingly · Lindfield · Cuckfield · Haywards Heath · Ansty · Sandrocks · Scayne's Hill · Wivelsfield · Wivelsfield Green · Burgess Hill · Hurstpierpoint · Keymer · Hassocks · Clayton · Pyecombe · Moulsecoomb · Preston · Patcham · Coldean · Hollingbury · Bevendean · Westdean

Godstone · Tandridge · Oxted · Limpsfield · Hurst Green · Holland · South Godstone · Godstone Farm · Crowhurst Lane End · Crowhurst · Blindley Heath · Haxted · Lingfield · Newchapel · Felcourt · Dormansland · Dormans Park · East Grinstead · Sackville College · Brockhurst · Crawley Down · Sunnyside · Saint Hill · Brambletye · Standen (NT) · Turners Hill · Selsfield Common · West Hoathly · Sharpthorne · Highbrook · Horsted Keynes · Paxhill Park · Chelwood Gate · Danehill · Sheffield Green · Sheffield Park (NT) · Fletching · North Chailey · Newick · Chailey · South Street · South Common · Spithurst · Barcombe Cross · Barcombe · Plumpton Green · Plumpton · East Chiltington · Westmeston · Cooksbridge · Ditchling · Streat · Offham · Hamsey · South Malling · Lewes · Mount Harry · Ditchling Beacon · Mount Caburn · Kingston near Lewes · Iford · Rodmell · Beddingham

Westerham · Brasted · Brasted Chart · Ide Hill · Whitley Row · Sevenoaks Weald · Nizels · Knole (NT) · Underriver · Shipbourn · Toy's Hill · Chartwell (NT) · Crockham Hill · Cooper's Corner · Four Elms · Marlpit Hill · Bough Beech · Chiddingstone Causeway · Hever Castle · Hever · Edenbridge · Marsh Green · Markbeech · Cowden Pound · Claydene · Cowden · Chiddingstone · Chiddingstone Hoath · Penshurst · Poundsbridge · Bidborough · Southborough · Speldhurst · Fordcombe · Blackham · Rusthall · Ashurst · Stone Cross · Langton Green · Groombridge · Eridge Green · Frant · Hammerwood · Holtye Common · Hartfield · Withyham · Upper Hartfield · Coleman's Hatch · Friar's Gate · Boarshead · Crowborough · Steel Cross · Mark Cross · Town Row · Rotherfield · Jarvis Brook · Poundgate · Duddleswell · Nutley · Heron's Ghyll · Fairwarp · High Hurstwood · Five Ashes · Butcher's Cross · Maresfield · Five Ash Down · Hadlow Down · Pound Green · Cross in Hand · Buxted · Ringles Cross · Piltdown · Uckfield · Blackboys · Stonebridge · Possingworth Park · Little London · New Town · Framfield · Ridgewood · Waldron · Foxhunt Green · Vine Cross · Halland · Shortgate · East Hoathly · Whitesmith · Laughton · Holme's Hill · Chiddingly · Muddles Green · Golden Cross · Hellingly · Lower Dicker · Upper Dicker · The Dicker · Ripe · Chalvington · Glynde · Glyndebourne · Ringmer · Glynde Place · West Firle · Selmeston · Berwick · Arlington · Michelham Priory

Ashdown Forest · Forest Row · Forest Way · Ashurstwood · Hartwell · Ashurst · Hartfield · Kidbrooke Park · Spring Hill · Wych Cross · Weir Wood Resr · Millennium Seed Bank · Wakehurst Place (NT) · Priest House

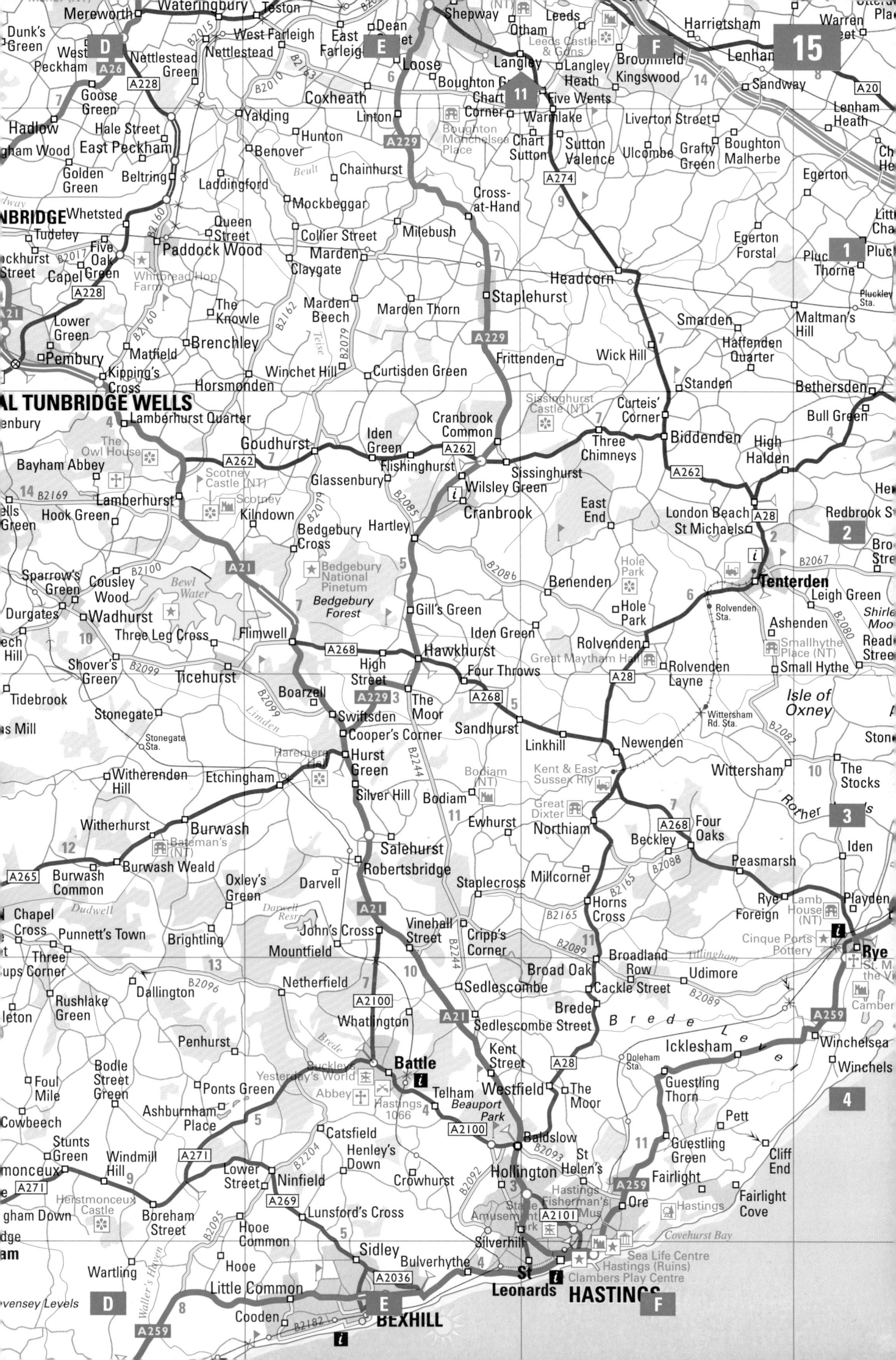

15
D
E
F
1
2
3
4
D
E
F
Mereworth
Wateringbury
Teston
Shepway
Otham
Leeds
Leeds Castle & Gdns
Harrietsham
Warren Street
Dunk's Green
West Peckham
Nettlestead Green
Nettlestead
West Farleigh
East Farleigh
Dean Street
Loose
Langley
Langley Heath
Broomfield
Kingswood
Lenham
Sandway
A20
Lenham Heath
Goose Green
Hadlow
Hale Street
East Peckham
Yalding
Hunton
Benover
Coxheath
Linton
Boughton Green
Chart Corner
Boughton Monchelsea Place
Chart Sutton
Five Wents
Warmlake
Sutton Valence
Liverton Street
Ulcombe
Grafty Green
Boughton Malherbe
Egerton
Golden Green
Beltring
Laddingford
Beult
Chainhurst
Mockbeggar
Cross-at-Hand
A274
A229
A228
A26
B2015
B2010
B2163
Whetsted
Tudeley
Five Oak Green
Capel
Queen Street
Paddock Wood
Whitbread Hop Farm
Collier Street
Marden
Claygate
Milebush
Egerton Forstal
Pluckley Thorne
Headcorn
Staplehurst
Pluckley Sta.
The Knowle
Marden Beech
Marden Thorn
Smarden
Maltman's Hill
Lower Green
Pembury
Matfield
Brenchley
Kipping's Cross
Horsmonden
Winchet Hill
Curtisden Green
Frittenden
Wick Hill
Haffenden Quarter
Standen
Bethersden
B2160
B2162
B2079
B2017
Teise
ROYAL TUNBRIDGE WELLS
Lamberhurst Quarter
The Owl House
Bayham Abbey
Goudhurst
Iden Green
Flishinghurst
Cranbrook Common
Sissinghurst Castle (NT)
Curteis' Corner
Biddenden
Three Chimneys
High Halden
Bull Green
A262
Scotney Castle (NT)
Lamberhurst
Hook Green
Kilndown
Glassenbury
Wilsley Green
Cranbrook
Sissinghurst
East End
London Beach
St Michaels
A28
Redbrook Street
B2169
B2085
Hartley
Bedgebury Cross
Bedgebury National Pinetum
Bedgebury Forest
B2086
Hole Park
Benenden
Tenterden
B2067
Leigh Green
Sparrow's Green
Cousley Wood
B2100
Bewl Water
Durgates
Wadhurst
A21
Gill's Green
Rolvenden Sta.
Ashenden
Three Leg Cross
Flimwell
Iden Green
Hole Park
Rolvenden
Smallhythe Place (NT)
Great Maytham Hall
Rolvenden Layne
Small Hythe
B2080
Shover's Green
B2099
Ticehurst
A268
High Street
Hawkhurst
Four Throws
Isle of Oxney
Tidebrook
Boarzell
The Moor
Stonegate
Stonegate Sta.
Limden
Swiftsden
Cooper's Corner
Sandhurst
Linkhill
Newenden
Wittersham Rd. Sta.
B2082
Haremere Hall
Hurst Green
B2244
Bodiam (NT)
Kent & East Sussex Rly
Wittersham
The Stocks
Witherenden Hill
Etchingham
Silver Hill
Bodiam
Great Dixter
Rother
Levels
Witherhurst
Burwash
Ewhurst
Northiam
Four Oaks
Beckley
Iden
Bateman's (NT)
Salehurst
Robertsbridge
Peasmarsh
Burwash Weald
Burwash Common
A265
Oxley's Green
Darvell
Staplecross
Millcorner
B2088
B2165
Horns Cross
Rye Foreign
Lamb House (NT)
Playden
Chapel Cross
Dudwell
Darwell Resr
John's Cross
Vinehall Street
Cripp's Corner
Punnett's Town
Brightling
Cinque Ports Pottery
Rye
Three Cups Corner
Mountfield
B2089
Broadland Row
Tillingham
Udimore
Broad Oak
Dallington
B2096
Netherfield
Sedlescombe
Cackle Street
Rushlake Green
A2100
Whatlington
Brede
Sedlescombe Street
Camber
A259
Winchelsea
Penhurst
Brede
Kent Street
Icklesham
Brede Level
Doleham Sta.
Bodle Street Green
Foul Mile
Battle
Yesterday's World
Abbey
Hastings 1066
Telham
Beauport Park
Westfield
The Moor
Guestling Thorn
Winchelsea Beach
Ponts Green
Ashburnham Place
Cowbeech
Catsfield
Pett
Baldslow
B2093
B2204
Henley's Down
Guestling Green
Stunts Green
Windmill Hill
Cliff End
Herstmonceux
A271
Lower Street
Ninfield
Crowhurst
Hollington
St Helen's
Fairlight
Hastings Fisherman's Mus
Ore
Fairlight Cove
B2092
Herstmonceux Castle
Boreham Street
A269
Lunsford's Cross
Stables Amusement Park
A2101
Hastings
Hooe Common
B2095
Covehurst Bay
Silverhill
Sea Life Centre
Hastings (Ruins)
Sidley
Bulverhythe
Hooe
Wartling
Waller's Haven
St Leonards
Clambers Play Centre
A2036
Little Common
HASTINGS
Pevensey Levels
Cooden
BEXHILL
B2182

KEY TO MAP SYMBOLS

i	Tourist information centre	⊖	Railway station
P	Short stay car park	⊖	London underground station
P	Long stay car park	⊖	Bus station

LUTON

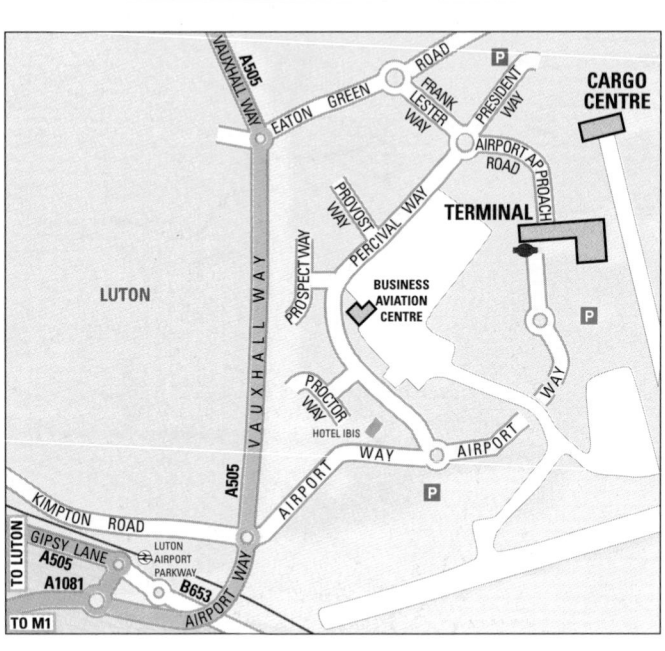

Tel. 01582 405100

STANSTED

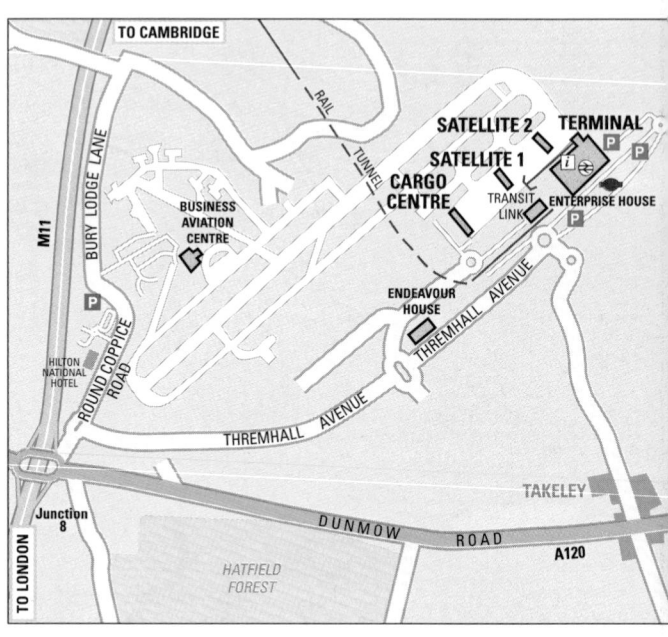

Tel. 01279 680500

HEATHROW

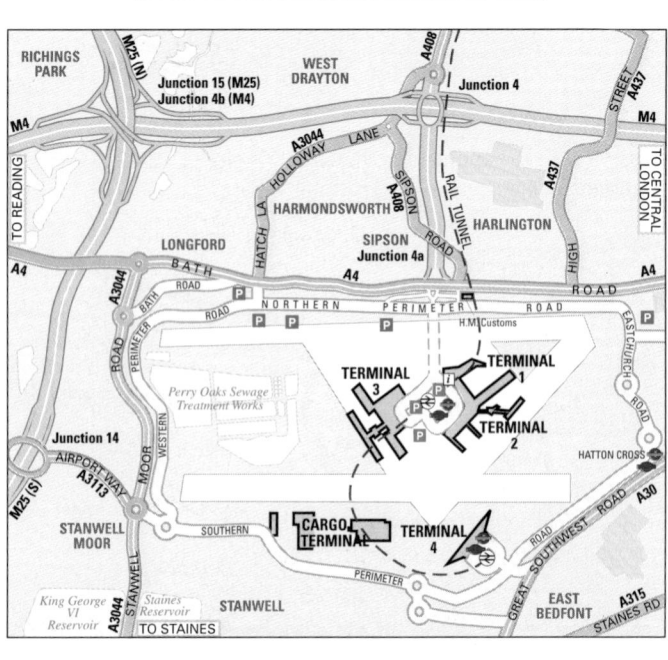

Tel. 0870 000123

GATWICK

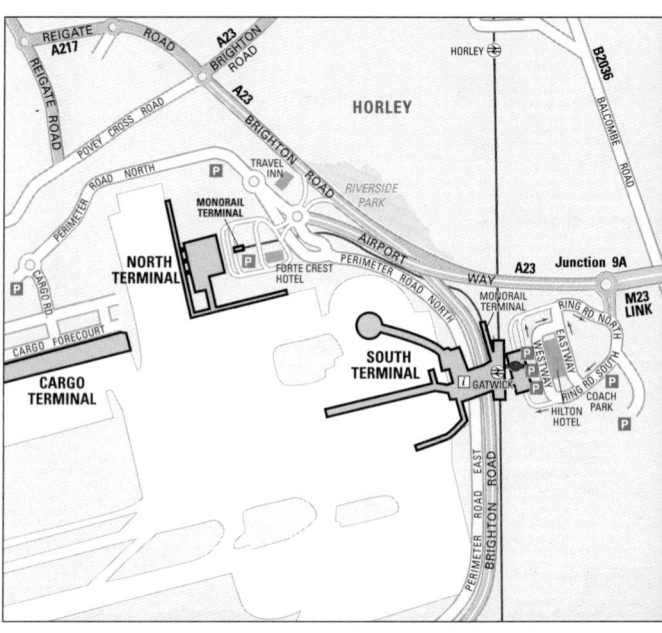

Tel. 01293 535353

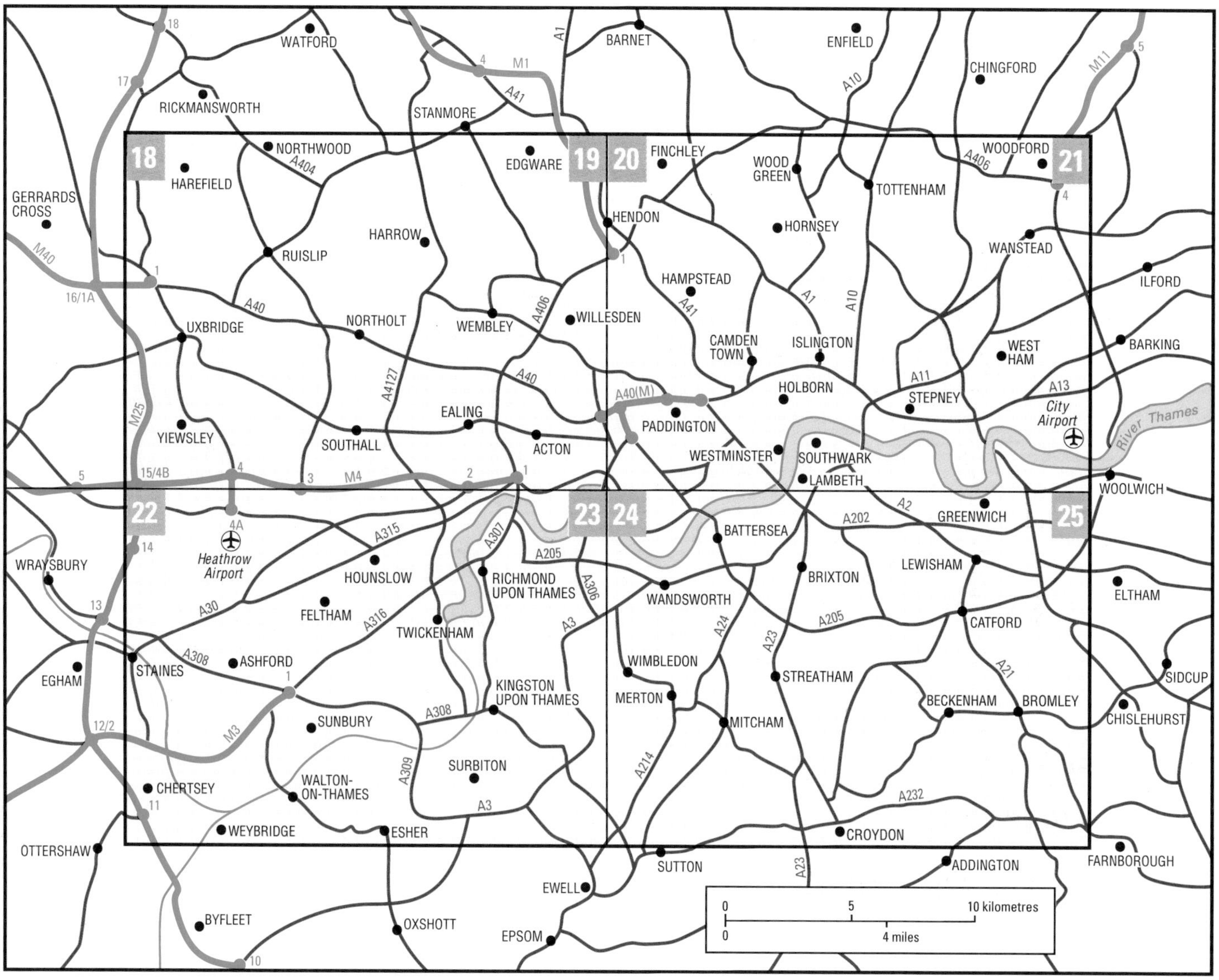

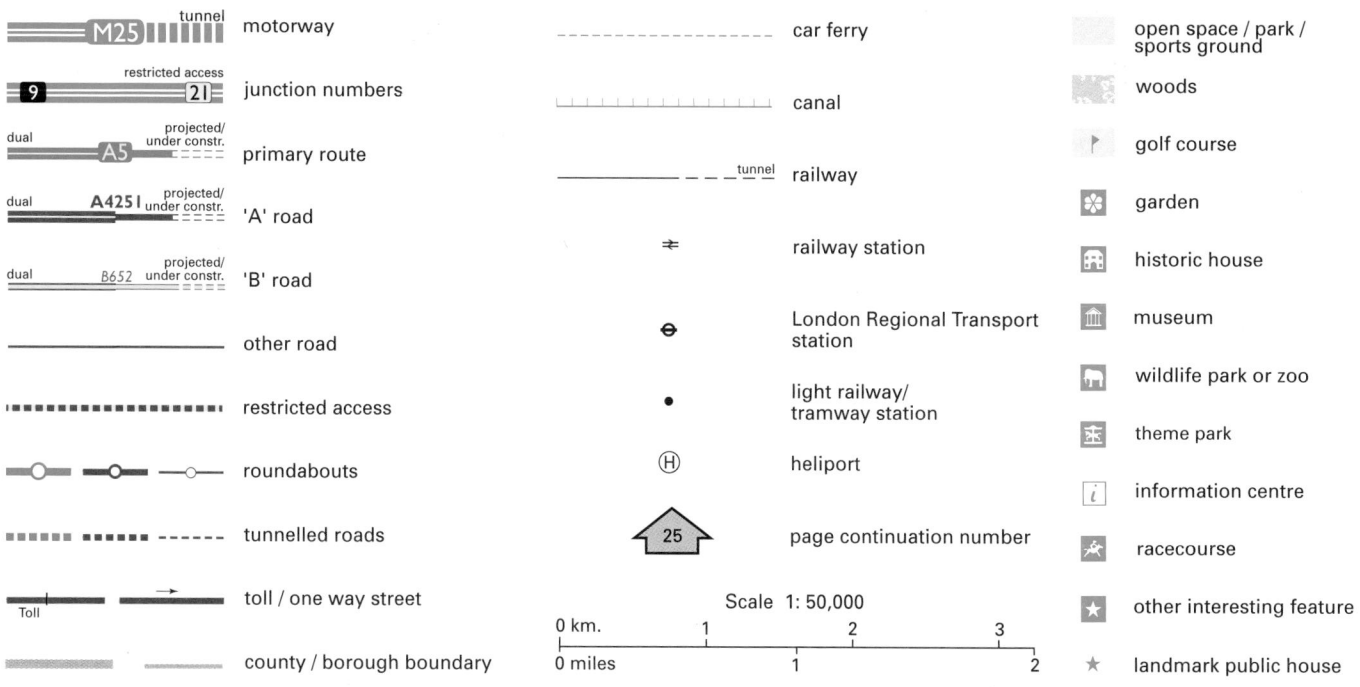

KEY TO MAP SYMBOLS

M25 tunnel	motorway
9 restricted access **21**	junction numbers
dual **A5** projected/under constr.	primary route
dual **A4251** projected/under constr.	'A' road
dual **B652** projected/under constr.	'B' road
———————	other road
■■■■■■■■	restricted access
roundabouts	roundabouts
■■■ ■■■ ----	tunnelled roads
Toll →	toll / one way street
county / borough boundary	county / borough boundary

– – – – – – – –	car ferry
┴┴┴┴┴┴┴┴	canal
——————— tunnel	railway
⇌	railway station
⊖	London Regional Transport station
•	light railway/tramway station
Ⓗ	heliport
25	page continuation number

Scale 1: 50,000

0 km.   1   2   3
0 miles   1   2

	open space / park / sports ground
	woods
►	golf course
✿	garden
🏠	historic house
🏛	museum
	wildlife park or zoo
	theme park
i	information centre
	racecourse
★	other interesting feature
★	landmark public house

18
NORTHWOOD
Hill End
Bishop's Wood
Pearson's Wood
Bishopswood Private Hospital
Mount Vernon Hospital
Wild Woods
Hatch End
Pinner Hill Golf Course
Northwood
Pinnerwood Park
Pinner Green
Harefield Hospital
Harefield
The Swan
Grand Union Canal
Northwood Golf Course
Northwood & Pinner Cottage Hospital
Northwood Hills
Haste Hill Golf Course
Copse Wood
St. Vincents Hospital (Orthopaedic)
Mad Bess Wood
Pinner
South Harefield
Bayhurst Wood Country Park
Ruislip Lido
Park Wood
RUISLIP
Eastcote Village
H I L L I N G D O N
Denham Green
The Nightingale
Denham
Government Offices
Eastcote
The Breakspear Arms
Ruislip Common
Rayners Lane
Ruislip Public Golf Course
Ruislip Manor
Buckinghamshire Golf Course
Uxbridge Golf Course
West Ruislip
DENHAM
Ruislip Gardens
Ickenham
South Ruislip
Northolt Aerodrome
Hillingdon
North Hillingdon
Northolt
Uxbridge
Civic Centre
London Golf Centre
Uxbridge Moor
Hillingdon Golf Course
Vine Inn
Rectory Park
The Red Lion
Prince of Wales
Yeading
Brunel University
Cowley
Hillingdon Hospital
Hayes End
Hayes Stadium
Hayes Cottage Hospital
HAYES
Iver
YIEWSLEY
Stockley Park Golf Course
SOUTHALL
Hayes Town
West Drayton
Thorney
Tower Arms
Hayes & Harlington
Holiday Inn Golf Course
Government Buildings
Southall
North Hyde
WEST DRAYTON
Prospect Park
Plough
Airlinks Golf Course
Heston Services
Cranford
22
WESTERN AVENUE
A40
M25
M4
A4020
A437
A312
A4180
A408
A404
A412

Canons Park
Edgware
Burnt Oak
Mill Hill Broadway
DEANSBROOK ROAD
WATLING AVENUE
Edgware Community Hospital
Burnt Oak
Copthall Stadium
GREAT NORTH
RAF Museums
Colindale Hospital
Colindale
AERODROME RD.
COLINDEEP LANE
Sunny Hill Park
Church Farm House Museum
Middx Uni.
Town Hall
Hendon Central
Hendon Park
HENDON
Hendon
Queensbury
Kingsbury Hospital
Prince of Wales
KINGSBURY ROAD
Kingsbury
Fryent Country Park
Barn Hill Open Space
Brent Town Hall
Brent Reservoir
NORTH CIRCULAR ROAD
Dollis Hill
DOLLIS HILL LANE
Gladstone Park
KENDAL RD.
ANSON RD.
Neasden
Willesden Green
20
HIGH ROAD
Willesden
Willesden Community Hospital
Kensal Rise
Willesden Junction
Harlesden
Stonebridge
Park Royal
Central Middlesex Hospital
Wormwood Scrubs
Linford Christie Stadium
Hammersmith Hospital
Q. Char. & Chelsea Hosp.
East Acton
B.B.C. T.V. Centre
Queens Park Rangers F.C.
WESTWAY
UXBRIDGE ROAD
Shepherd's Bush
GOLDHAWK ROAD
HAMMERSMITH
Ravenscourt Park
Town Hall
KING STREET
GREAT WEST ROAD
Castelnau
Stamford Brook
Turnham Green
CHISWICK HIGH ROAD
Bedford Park
Gunnersbury
Gunnersbury Park Museum
Gunnersbury Park
23
M4
Kew Bridge
ACTON
Acton Central
South Acton
Acton Main Line
West Acton
North Acton
North Ealing
EALING
Ealing Broadway
Ealing Town Hall
Ealing Civic Centre
Pitshanger Manor Museum
B.B.C. T.V. Studios
EALING GRN.
Uni.
South Ealing
Northfields
Little Ealing
Elevated Motorway
Boston Manor
BOSTON MANOR RD.
Brentford
Osterley Park
Osterley Park House
Wyke Green Golf Course
Hanwell
West Ealing
Drayton Green
Castle Bar Park
Brent Valley Golf Course
St. Bernard's Hospital
Ealing Hospital
BOSTON ROAD
UXBRIDGE ROAD
Greenford
Red Lion
RUISLIP ROAD
Perivale Park Golf Course
Athletics Stadium
South Greenford
Perivale
Ealing Golf Course
WESTERN AVENUE
Hanger Lane
HANGER LANE
Alperton
Perivale
Sudbury Golf Course
Horsenden Hill Golf Course
Sudbury Town
Sudbury
Sudbury Hill
South Harrow
Northolt Park
WHITTON AVE. W.
WHITTON AVE. E.
Sudbury and Harrow Road
WEMBLEY
North Wembley
Wembley Central
Wembley Arena
Wembley Stadium (under redevelopment)
GREAT CENTRAL WAY
Tokyngton
Wembley Park
The Mitre
EAST LANE
FORTY AVENUE
Preston Road
South Kenton
Kenton
Northwick Park
Uni. of Westminster (Harrow Campus)
Northwick Park and St. Mark's Hospital
Harrow on the Hill
HARROW
West Harrow
Headstone
Harrow Museum
Harrow & Wealdstone
Civic Centre
Belmont
HARROW WEALD
Harrow Weald Lake
Stanmore Park
Stanmore Golf Course
Canons Park
Government Buildings
The Masons Arms
The Green Man
Kenton
KENTON ROAD
St. Andrew's at Harrow
Clementine Churchill Hospital
BRENT
EALING
Grand Union Canal
River Brent

Finchley
Finchley Golf Course
West Finchley
Finchley Memorial Hospital
Coppetts Wood
Coppets Wood Hospital
Coldfall Wood
Bowes Park
Middx. Uni.
Bounds Green
Muswell Hill Golf Course
WOOD GREEN
Wood Green
Noel Park
Civic Centre
Alexandra Palace
Alexandra Palace Exhibition Centre
Alexandra Park
Muswell Hill
Middx. Uni.
Turnpike Lane
West Green
Black Boy
Hendon Golf Course
Church End
FINCHLEY
Finchley Central
The Queens Head
The London Museum of Jewish Life
Manor Cottage Tavern
East Finchley
St. Lukes Woodside Hospital
Highgate Wood
HORNSEY
Hornsey Central Hospital
Queen's Wood
Hornsey
HARINGEY
HARRINGAY
Harringay
St. Ann's Hospital
Harringay Green Lanes
Big Wood
Hampstead Garden Suburb
Highgate Golf Course
Highgate
Crouch End
Stroud Green
Crouch Hill
Manor House
Finsbury Park
STOKE NEWINGTON
Hendon Park
Brent Cross
Golders Green
Hampstead Golf Club
Athlone House
The Iveagh Bequest Kenwood House
HAMPSTEAD
Hampstead Heath
Parliament Hill
Highgate
The Flask
Whittington Hospital
Archway
Dartmouth Park
Upper Holloway
Child's Hill
Manor House Hospital
The Hill
Jack Straw's Castle
Queen Mary's Hospital
Burgh House
Keats House
Hampstead Heath
Gospel Oak
Tufnell Park
Clissold Park
Arsenal
Arsenal FC
Highbury
Cricklewood
King's College
Open University (Regional Centre)
Hampstead
The Flask
Royal Free Hospital
Belsize Park
Kentish Town
Holloway Road
Drayton Park
Uni.
ISLINGTON
Canonbury
Highbury & Islington
Brondesbury
West Hampstead (Thames Link)
Finchley Road and Frognal
Freud Man
Finchley Rd. & Frognal
Belsize Park
Chalk Farm
Caledonian Road
Barnsbury
Caledonian Rd. & Barnsbury
Business Design Cen.
Town Hall
Essex Road
Brondesbury Park
West Hampstead
South Hampstead
Swiss Cottage
CAMDEN
Primrose Hill
Camden Road
Camden Town
ST. PANCRAS
King's Cross
Kensal Rise
Kilburn
Queens Park
Kilburn High Road
Kilburn Park
St. John's Wood
London Zoo Conservation Education Cen.
Regents Park
Lord's Cricket Ground
Mornington Crescent
St. Pancras
British Library
Euston
King's Cross Thameslink
Angel
Kensal Green
Maida Vale
Regent's Park
Euston Sq.
Bloomsbury
Uni.
FINSBURY
St. Luke's
St. Charles Hospital
PADDINGTON
Warwick Avenue
Marylebone
Baker St.
Planetarium
Portland St.
Telecom Tower
Russell Square
Hosps.
Faringdon
Barbican
Mus. of London
Moorgate
Westbourne Park
MARYLEBONE
Edgware Road
Goodge St.
British Museum
HOLBORN
Holborn
Chancery Lane
CITY
Notting Hill
Royal Oak
Paddington
Oxford Circus
Soho
Tottenham Ct. Rd.
Guild Hall
St. Paul's
Mansion House
Bank
Ladbroke Grove
Latimer Road
Bayswater
Lancaster Gate
Marble Arch
Bond Street
Mayfair
Covent Garden
Leicester Sq.
National Gallery
Blackfriars
Millennium Bridge
Cannon Street
White City
Holland Park
Queensway
Hyde Park
WESTMINSTER
Piccadilly Circus
Temple
R. Nat. Theatre
Tate Modern
Southwark Cathedral
Shepherds Bush
Notting Hill Gate
Kensington Gardens
Albert Memorial Visitor's Cen.
Serpentine Gallery
Hyde Park Corner
Green Pk
Charing Cross
Embankment
Government Offices
London Eye
Waterloo East
Southwark
Waterloo
KENSINGTON
Kensington Palace
King's College
High Street Kensington
Royal Albert Hall
Imp. Coll
Knightsbridge
WESTMINSTER
Buckingham Palace
Q.E.II Conf. Cen.
St. James's Park
Waterloo Int.
Westminster
SOUTHWARK
Borough
Commonwealth Institute
KENSINGTON & CHELSEA
Kensington (Olympia)
Olympia
Science & Nat. Hist. Mus.
V. & A. Mus.
Cromwell Hosp.
Gloucester Road
D.E.T.R.
Victoria
St. City Hall
Westminster Cath.
Houses of Parliament
Lambeth North
Cathedral
Imperial War Mus.
Elephant & Castle
Hammersmith
Brompton
South Kensington
LAMBETH
Barons Court
West Kensington
Earls Court
CHELSEA
Pimlico
Nat. Army Mus.
Ranelagh Gardens
Vauxhall
The Oval
Kennington
Walworth
The Queens Club
Charing Cross Hospital
West Brompton
19
24

Banbury Reservoir
Lea Valley Park
Highams Park
Highams Park
Royal Oak
Walthamstow Greyhound Stadium
Tottenham Hotspur FC
White Hart Lane
Northumberland Park
Epping Forest
WOODFORD
Uni. of London
Woodford
Woodford Bridge
Higham Hill
WALTHAM FOREST
Tottenham Hale
Lockwood Reservoir
High Maynard Reservoir
South Woodford
South Woodford
The Cocked Hat
Roding Hospital
Clayhall
Wood Street
Epping Forest
Eagle Hotel
Blackhorse Road
Walthamstow Central
Vestry House Museum
Snaresbrook
Snares Brook
Hollow Pond
The George
South Tottenham
South Tottenham
Reservoir
Warwick Reservoirs
St. James Street
Walthamstow Queens Road
Whipps Cross Hospital
Redbridge
REDBRIDGE
Wanstead
WALTHAMSTOW
St. James's Park
Leytonstone
The Basin
Wanstead Golf Course
Wanstead Park
Springfield Park
Leyton Midland Road
Leytonstone
Stamford Hill
Walthamstow Marshes
Leytonstone High Road
REDBRIDGE
Aldersbrook
Cranbrook
Clapton
LEYTON
Ilford Golf Course
Rectory Road
Leyton Orient FC
Council Off.
Wanstead Flats
Lea Bridge
HACKNEY
Hackney Marsh
Leyton
Shacklewell
Lower Clapton
Clapton Park
Wanstead Park
Manor Park
Three Rabbits
Homerton Hospital
Wick Field
MAJOR ROAD
Hackney Downs
Hackney Central
Homerton
Hackney Wick
Hackney Wick
Maryland
Forest Gate
Woodgrange Park
Hackney
Town Hall
Hackney Museum
Stratford
Stratford
Victoria Park
WEST HAM
Upton
London Fields
Cultural Heritage Resources Museum
Old Ford
Pudding Mill La.
NEW PLAISTOW RD.
NEWHAM
East Ham
Upton Park
West Ham United. F.C.
Upton Park
Town Hall
EAST HAM
Haggerston
Royal Cricketer's
Bow
Plaistow
Plaistow
West Ham
TOWER HAMLETS
Bethnal Green
Museum of Childhood
Mile End
Mile End Park
Bow Church
Bromley By Bow
The London Gas Museum
Bethnal Green
Bow Road
Mile End
Devons Road
SHOREDITCH
Shoreditch
Stepney Green
Newham General Hospital
Terence McMillan Stadium
Bromley
Beckton
Whitechapel
Stepney
Custom House
Canning Town
Canning Town
Art Gall.
Whitechapel
Shadwell
Limehouse
Limehouse
All Saints
East India
Royal Victoria
Custom House
Prince Regent
Royal Albert
Beckton Park
Royal Albert Dock
Tower Gateway
Westferry
Poplar
Blackwall
Shadwell
Wapping
River Thames
Royal Victoria Dock
Wapping
West India Quay
Poplar
Canary Wharf
The Dome
London City Airport
Royal George V Dock
Tower Bridge
Rotherhithe Heritage Museum
Heron Quays
Brunel Engine House
Design Museum
Rotherhithe
North Greenwich
Thames Barrier Park
Silvertown & London City Airport
Silvertown
North Woolwich
Canada Water
South Quay
London Arena
Crossharbour
Thames Barrier
Thames Barrier Visitors Centre
Cubitt Town
Bermondsey
BERMONDSEY
Millwall
New Charlton
Surrey Quays
South Bermondsey
Mudchute
Woolwich Dockyard
Island Gardens
Deptford
Charlton
Charlton Athletic F.C.
Millwall F.C.
Greenwich District Hospital
Westcombe Park
Museum of Artillery
Livesey Museum
Charlton
Maze Hill

25

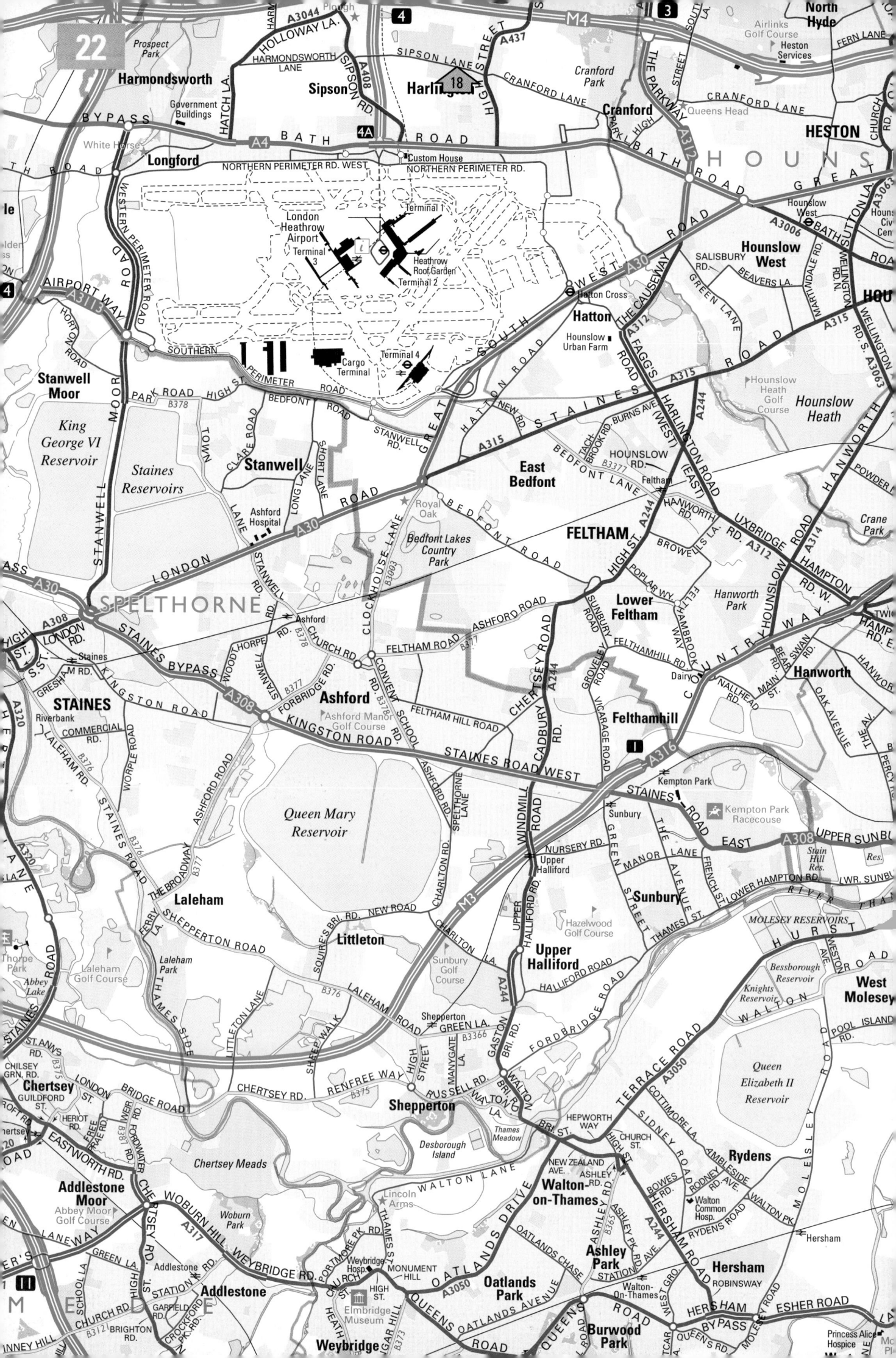
Harmondsworth
Prospect Park
HOLLOWAY LA.
A3044
Plough
HARMONDSWORTH LANE
Sipson
SIPSON RD.
A408
SIPSON LANE
Harlington
18
HIGH STREET
A437
M4
3
4
4A
Government Buildings
HATCH LA.
BYPASS
BATH ROAD
A4
White Horse
Longford
Custom House
NORTHERN PERIMETER RD. WEST
NORTHERN PERIMETER RD.
WESTERN PERIMETER ROAD
London Heathrow Airport
Terminal 1
Terminal 2
Terminal 3
Terminal 4
Heathrow Roof Garden
Cargo Terminal
SOUTHERN PERIMETER ROAD
AIRPORT WAY
A3113
HORTON ROAD
Stanwell Moor
STANWELL MOOR ROAD
King George VI Reservoir
Staines Reservoirs
PARK ROAD
HIGH ST.
B378
TOWN LANE
CLARE ROAD
BEDFONT ROAD
Stanwell
SHORT LANE
LONG LANE
STANWELL RD.
Ashford Hospital
LONDON ROAD
A30
SPELTHORNE
Cranford Park
CRANFORD LANE
Cranford
HIGH ST.
THE PARKWAY
A312
Queens Head
Airlinks Golf Course
Heston Services
North Hyde
FERN LANE
HESTON
CHURCH RD.
HOUNS
GREAT WEST ROAD
Hounslow West
A3006
BATH ROAD
SUTTON LA.
A3063
SALISBURY RD.
BEAVERS LA.
MARTINDALE RD.
WELLINGTON RD. N.
Hounslow West
GREEN LANE
Hatton Cross
Hatton
THE CAUSEWAY
Hounslow Urban Farm
FAGG'S ROAD
HATTON ROAD
STAINES ROAD
A315
Hounslow Heath Golf Course
Hounslow Heath
WELLINGTON RD. S.
NEW RD.
TACHBROOK RD.
BURNS AVE.
HARLINGTON ROAD (WEST)
HARLINGTON ROAD (EAST)
A244
East Bedfont
HOUNSLOW RD.
B3377
BEDFONT LANE
Feltham
HANWORTH RD.
HANWORTH ROAD
POWDER MILL
Crane Park
Royal Oak
BEDFONT ROAD
Bedfont Lakes Country Park
FELTHAM
HIGH ST.
BROWELLS LA.
UXBRIDGE RD.
A314
HAMPTON RD. W.
POPLAR WY.
Lower Feltham
Hanworth Park
CLOCKHOUSE LANE
B3003
ASHFORD ROAD
FELTHAM ROAD
B377
SUNBURY ROAD
FELTHAMBROOK WAY
FELTHAMHILL RD.
HOUNSLOW ROAD
COUNTRY WAY
Hanworth
BEAR RD.
SWAN RD.
MAIN ST.
NALLHEAD RD.
OAK AVENUE
THE AV.
Dairy
Ashford
CHURCH RD.
B378
STANWELL RD.
WOODTHORPE RD.
A308
LONDON RD.
HIGH ST.
Staines
STAINES BYPASS
KINGSTON ROAD
GRESHAM RD.
STAINES
Riverbank
COMMERCIAL RD.
LALEHAM RD.
B376
WORPLE ROAD
A320
Ashford
FORBRIDGE RD.
B377
CONVENT RD.
B3378
SCHOOL RD.
Ashford Manor Golf Course
FELTHAM HILL ROAD
CHERTSEY ROAD
CADBURY RD.
GROVELEY ROAD
VICARAGE ROAD
Felthamhill
1
A316
STAINES ROAD WEST
Kempton Park
STAINES ROAD EAST
Kempton Park Racecourse
Sunbury
ASHFORD ROAD
ASHFORD RD.
SPELTHORNE LANE
Queen Mary Reservoir
WINDMILL ROAD
NURSERY RD.
Upper Halliford
GREEN STREET
THE AVENUE
MANOR LANE
FRENCH ST.
A308
UPPER SUNBURY
Stain Hill Res.
Res.
LOWER HAMPTON RD.
LWR. SUNBURY
RIVER THAMES
STAINES ROAD
THE BROADWAY
B377
Laleham
CHARLTON RD.
M3
NEW ROAD
SQUIRE'S BRI. RD.
Littleton
SHEPPERTON ROAD
FERRY LA.
Laleham Park
Laleham Golf Course
Thorpe Park
Abbey Lake
CHARLTON LA.
Sunbury Golf Course
UPPER HALLIFORD RD.
Upper Halliford
A244
HALLIFORD ROAD
Hazelwood Golf Course
Sunbury
THAMES ST.
MOLESEY RESERVOIRS
HURST ROAD
WESTON AVE.
Bessborough Reservoir
Knights Reservoir
West Molesey
WALTON ROAD
POOL RD.
ISLAND
THAMES SIDE
B376
LALEHAM ROAD
LITTLETON LANE
SHEEP WALK
Shepperton
GREEN LA.
B3366
HIGH STREET
MANYGATE LA.
GASTON BRI. RD.
FORDBRIDGE ROAD
TERRACE ROAD
A3050
Queen Elizabeth II Reservoir
MOLESEY ROAD
STAINES ROAD
ST. ANN'S RD.
CHILSEY GRN. RD.
B375
Chertsey
GUILDFORD ST.
LONDON ST.
BRIDGE ROAD
HERIOT RD.
FREEMAN RD.
B387
WEIR RD.
FORDWATER RD.
CHERTSEY RD.
RENFREE WAY
B375
RUSSELL RD.
Shepperton
WALTON BRI. RD.
WALTON LA.
Thames Meadow
HEPWORTH WAY
CHURCH ST.
COTTIMORE LA.
SIDNEY ROAD
Rydens
EASTWORTH RD.
Chertsey Meads
Desborough Island
WALTON LANE
NEW ZEALAND AVE.
ASHLEY RD.
Walton-on-Thames
HIGH ST.
BOWES RD.
RODNEY RD.
AMBLESIDE AVE.
Walton Common Hosp.
WALTON PK.
Addlestone Moor
Abbey Moor Golf Course
CHERTSEY RD.
WOBURN HILL
A317
Woburn Park
Lincoln Arms
OATLANDS DRIVE
ASHLEY RD.
B365
ASHLEY PK. RD.
A244
HERSHAM ROAD
RYDENS ROAD
Hersham
GREEN LA.
Addlestone
STATION RD.
WEYBRIDGE RD.
PORTMORE PK. RD.
Weybridge Hosp.
THAMES ST.
MONUMENT HILL
OATLANDS CHASE
Ashley Park
STATION AVE.
Walton-On-Thames
WEST GRO.
Hersham
ROBINSWAY
11
SCHOOL LA.
HIGH ST.
Addlestone
GARFIELD RD.
CROCKFORD PK. RD.
CHURCH RD.
B3121
BRIGHTON RD.
CHURCH ST.
HIGH ST.
Elmbridge Museum
A3050
Oatlands Park
OATLANDS AVENUE
QUEENS ROAD
Burwood Park
HERSHAM BYPASS
ESHER ROAD
MOLESEY ROAD
QUEENS RD.
HEATH RD.
GAR HILL
B373
Weybridge
Princess Alice Hospice

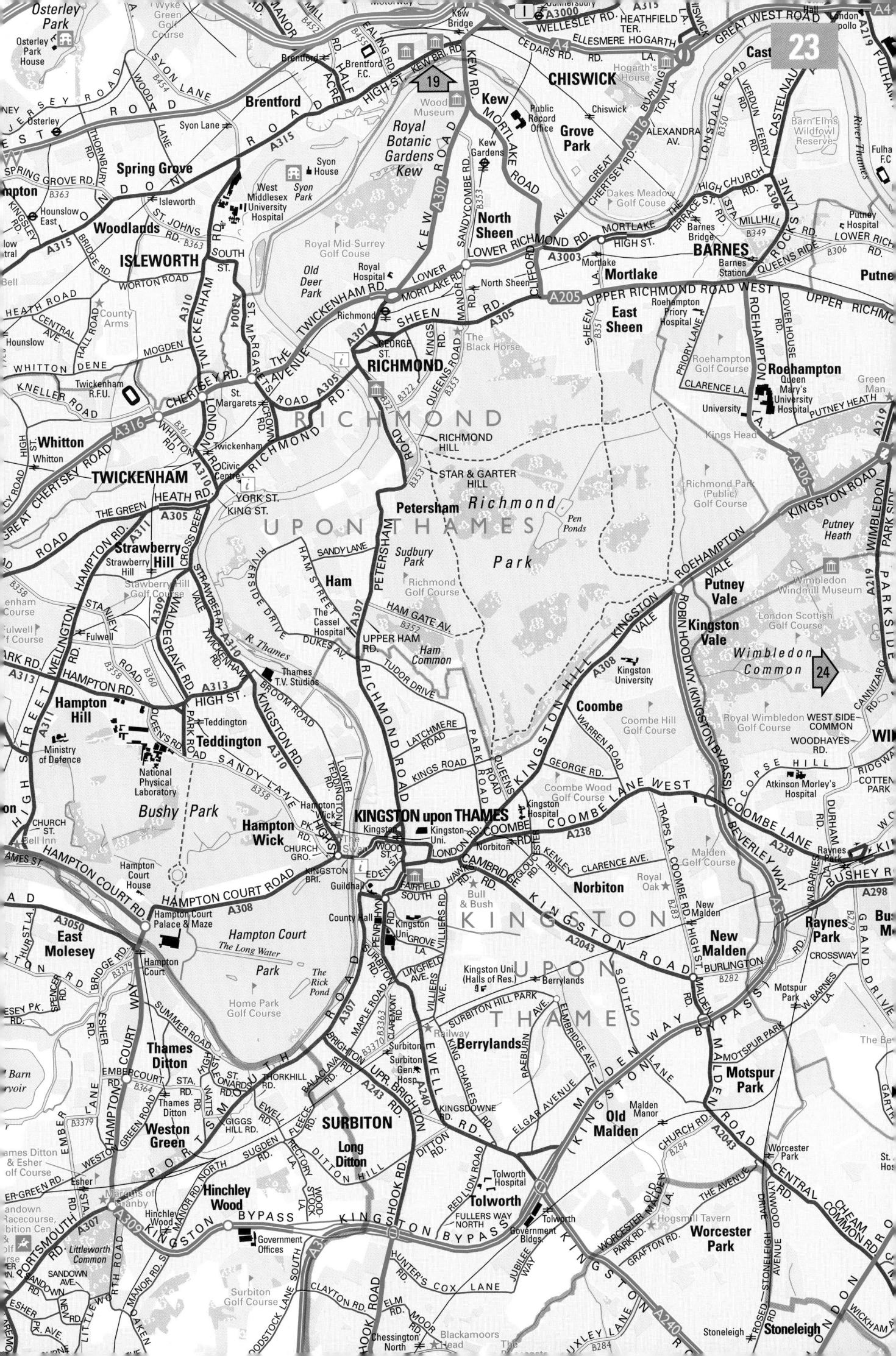
Osterley Park
Osterley Park House
Brentford
Brentford F.C.
Kew Bridge
19
Wood Museum
Kew
CHISWICK
Public Record Office
Grove Park
Chiswick
Hogarth's House
Royal Botanic Gardens Kew
Syon House
Syon Park
Spring Grove
West Middlesex University Hospital
Isleworth
Hounslow East
Woodlands
ISLEWORTH
North Sheen
Royal Mid-Surrey Golf Couse
Old Deer Park
Royal Hospital
Mortlake
BARNES
Barnes Bridge
Barnes Station
Dakes Meadow Golf Couse
Barn Elms Wildfowl Reserve
River Thames
East Sheen
Roehampton Priory Hospital
Richmond
RICHMOND
The Black Horse
Roehampton Golf Course
Roehampton
Queen Mary's University Hospital
University
Kings Head
Putney Hospital
County Arms
Hounslow
Twickenham R.F.U.
St. Margarets
Twickenham
Whitton
TWICKENHAM
RICHMOND UPON THAMES
RICHMOND HILL
STAR & GARTER HILL
Petersham
Richmond Park
Pen Ponds
Richmond Park (Public) Golf Course
Putney Heath
Strawberry Hill
Strawberry Hill Golf Course
Fulwell
Ham
Sudbury Park
Richmond Golf Course
The Cassel Hospital
Ham Common
Putney Vale
Kingston Vale
Wimbledon Windmill Museum
London Scottish Golf Course
Wimbledon Common
24
R. Thames
Thames T.V. Studios
Kingston University
Hampton Hill
Teddington
Ministry of Defence
National Physical Laboratory
Coombe
Coombe Hill Golf Course
Royal Wimbledon Golf Course
WEST SIDE COMMON
Atkinson Morley's Hospital
Bushy Park
Hampton Wick
Coombe Wood Golf Course
Kingston Hospital
KINGSTON upon THAMES
Kingston
Kingston Uni.
The Swan
Bell Inn
Hampton Court House
Guildhall
Norbiton
Bull & Bush
Royal Oak
Malden Golf Course
Raynes Park
County Hall
Hampton Court Palace & Maze
East Molesey
Hampton Court
The Long Water
Park
The Rick Pond
Home Park Golf Course
KINGSTON UPON THAMES
New Malden
Kingston Uni. (Halls of Res.)
Berrylands
Motspur Park
Railway
Thames Ditton
Surbiton
Surbiton Gen. Hosp.
Weston Green
Old Malden
Malden Manor
Worcester Park
SURBITON
Long Ditton
Hinchley Wood
Tolworth Hospital
Tolworth
Hogsmill Tavern
Esher
Marquis of Granby
Littleworth Common
Government Offices
Government Bldgs.
Surbiton Golf Course
Chessington North
Blackamoors Head
Stoneleigh
KINGSTON BYPASS
A3
A4
A205
A238
A240
A243
A298
A305
A306
A307
A308
A309
A310
A311
A313
A315
A316
A2043
A3003
A3050
HAMPTON COURT ROAD
UPPER RICHMOND ROAD WEST
KINGSTON ROAD
COOMBE LANE WEST
MALDEN WAY
PORTSMOUTH ROAD

24
20
23
CHELSEA
Pimlico
LAMBETH
Walworth
Kennington
Vauxhall
FULHAM
Walham Green
Sands End
Parsons Green
BATTERSEA
HAMMERSMITH & FULHAM
Putney
WANDSWORTH
Clapham
Stockwell
South Lambeth
Brixton
Clapham Park
LAMBETH
Herne Hill
Southfields
Earlsfield
Balham
Streatham Hill
Tulse Hill
West Dulwich
Wimbledon Park
Summerstown
Upper Tooting
West Norwood
Streatham
Streatham Park
Furzedown
Tooting Graveney
Collier's Wood
Norwood New Town
WIMBLEDON
Streatham Vale
MERTON
Norbury
MITCHAM
Bushey Mead
MORDEN
MERTON
Thornton Heath
St. Helier
Morden Park
Hackbridge
BEDDINGTON
North Cheam
SUTTON
CARSHALTON
WALLINGTON
River Thames
Battersea Park
Clapham Common
Wandsworth Common
Tooting Bec Common
Streatham Common
Mitcham Common
Brockwell Park
FULHAM PALACE ROAD
LILLIE ROAD
DAWES RD.
FULHAM RD.
NEW KINGS RD.
KING'S RD.
CHEYNE WK.
GROSVENOR RD.
NINE ELMS LA.
KENNINGTON LA.
BATTERSEA PARK RD.
WANDSWORTH ROAD
CLAPHAM ROAD
STOCKWELL RD.
BRIXTON ROAD
CAMBERWELL NEW RD.
COLDHARBOUR LA.
ACRE LA.
BATTERSEA RISE
NORTHCOTE ROAD
TRINITY ROAD
BALHAM HIGH RD.
TOOTING BEC RD.
STREATHAM HIGH RD.
LONDON RD.
CROYDON RD.
MITCHAM RD.
WIMBLEDON PARK SIDE
KINGSTON ROAD
WORPLE ROAD
DURNSFORD RD.
GARRATT LANE
MERTON RD.
PUTNEY HILL
WESTERN ROAD
MORDEN RD.
CROYDON ROAD
LONDON ROAD
PURLEY WAY
STONECOT HILL
ST. HELIER AVE.
BISHOPSFORD ROAD

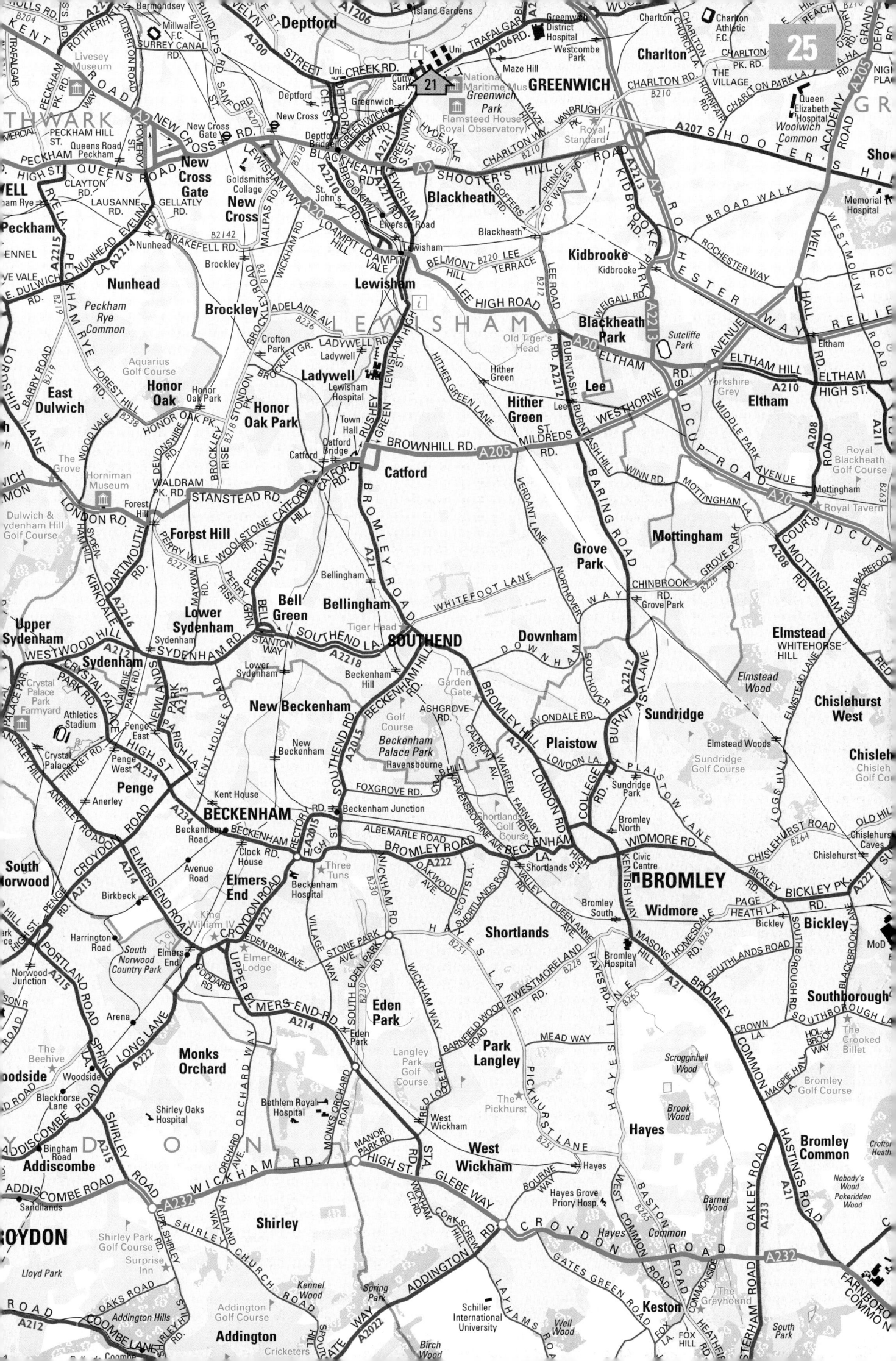
Deptford
Island Gardens
Greenwich District Hospital
Westcombe Park
Charlton
Charlton Athletic F.C.
Charlton
Maze Hill
Cutty Sark
National Maritime Mus
Greenwich Park
Flamsteed House (Royal Observatory)
GREENWICH
Royal Standard
Queen Elizabeth Hospital
Woolwich Common
Millwall F.C.
Bermondsey
Livesey Museum
Deptford
New Cross
New Cross Gate
Goldsmiths College
St. John's
Elverson Road
Blackheath
Blackheath
Lewisham
Kidbrooke
Kidbrooke
Memorial Hospital
Peckham
Peckham Rye
Nunhead
Nunhead
Brockley
Brockley
Lewisham
LEWISHAM
Blackheath Park
Sutcliffe Park
Old Tiger's Head
Lee
Eltham
Eltham
Yorkshire Grey
Peckham Rye Common
Aquarius Golf Course
Crofton Park
Ladywell
Ladywell
Lewisham Hospital
Hither Green
Hither Green
East Dulwich
Honor Oak
Honor Oak Park
Honor Oak Park
Town Hall
Catford Bridge
Catford
Catford
Lee
Royal Blackheath Golf Course
Mottingham
Royal Tavern
The Grove
Horniman Museum
Dulwich & Sydenham Hill Golf Course
Forest Hill
Forest Hill
Mottingham
Grove Park
Grove Park
Bellingham
Bellingham
Bell Green
Lower Sydenham
Upper Sydenham
Sydenham
Sydenham
Tiger Head
SOUTHEND
Downham
Elmstead
Elmstead Wood
Chislehurst West
Lower Sydenham
Beckenham Hill
The Garden Gate
Crystal Palace Park
Farmyard
Athletics Stadium
Crystal Palace
Penge East
Penge West
Penge
Anerley
New Beckenham
New Beckenham
Golf Course
Beckenham Palace Park
Ravensbourne
Plaistow
Sundridge
Elmstead Woods
Sundridge Golf Course
Sundridge Park
Kent House
BECKENHAM
Beckenham Road
Beckenham Junction
Clock House
Shortlands Golf Course
Bromley North
Civic Centre
Chislehurst
Chislehurst Caves
South Norwood
Avenue Road
Elmers End
Three Tuns
Beckenham Hospital
Birkbeck
Shortlands
BROMLEY
Widmore
Bromley South
Bickley
Bickley
MoD
King William IV
Harrington Road
South Norwood Country Park
Elmers End
Elmer Lodge
Shortlands
Bromley Hospital
Norwood Junction
Eden Park
Eden Park
Southborough
The Crooked Billet
Arena
The Beehive
Monks Orchard
Langley Park Golf Course
Park Langley
Scrogginhall Wood
Bromley Golf Course
Woodside
Woodside
Blackhorse Lane
Bethlem Royal Hospital
The Pickhurst
Brook Wood
Shirley Oaks Hospital
West Wickham
Hayes
Bromley Common
Croftor Heath
Bingham Road
Addiscombe
West Wickham
Hayes
Nobody's Wood
Pokeridden Wood
Sandilands
Hayes Grove Priory Hosp.
Barnet Wood
Shirley
Hayes Common
ROYDON
Shirley Park Golf Course
Surprise Inn
Lloyd Park
Kennel Wood
Spring Park
The Greyhound
Keston
Schiller International University
Well Wood
Addington Hills
Addington Golf Course
Addington
Cricketers
Birch Wood
South Park
FOX HILL
A2
A20
A21
A200
A202
A205
A206
A207
A208
A210
A212
A213
A214
A215
A222
A232
A233
A234
A1206
A2015
A2022
A2212
A2213
A2216
A2218
B207
B209
B210
B218
B219
B220
B226
B227
B228
B230
B236
B238
B251
B263
B264
B265
B2142
EVELYN STREET
CREEK RD.
TRAFALGAR RD.
CHARLTON RD.
SHOOTERS HILL
SHOOTER'S HILL ROAD
BROAD WALK
ROCHESTER WAY
ROCHESTER WAY RELIEF ROAD
KIDBROOKE PARK RD.
LEE HIGH ROAD
LEE TERRACE
BELMONT HILL
LOAMPIT VALE
LOAMPIT HILL
LEWISHAM WY.
BLACKHEATH RD.
GREENWICH HIGH RD.
NEW CROSS RD.
QUEENS ROAD
PECKHAM HIGH ST.
PECKHAM RYE
PECKHAM HILL ST.
RYE LA.
NUNHEAD LA.
EVELINA RD.
DRAKEFELL RD.
BROCKLEY ROAD
ADELAIDE AV.
LADYWELL RD.
LEWISHAM HIGH ST.
RUSHEY GREEN
BROWNHILL RD.
HITHER GREEN LANE
ST. MILDREDS RD.
WESTHORNE AVENUE
ELTHAM HILL
ELTHAM HIGH ST.
ELTHAM RD.
BURNT ASH HILL
BURNT ASH LANE
BARING ROAD
SIDCUP ROAD
SIDCUP BY-PASS
MOTTINGHAM LA.
MOTTINGHAM RD.
COURT RD.
GROVE PARK RD.
CHINBROOK RD.
WHITEFOOT LANE
VERDANT LANE
NORTHOVER
DOWNHAM WAY
SOUTHOVER
BROMLEY ROAD
BROMLEY HILL
LONDON RD.
STANSTEAD RD.
CATFORD HILL
PERRY HILL
PERRY VALE
WOOLSTONE RD.
DARTMOUTH RD.
KIRKDALE
SYDENHAM RD.
SYDENHAM HILL
WESTWOOD HILL
CRYSTAL PALACE PARK RD.
SOUTHEND LA.
BECKENHAM HILL RD.
SOUTHEND RD.
NEWLANDS PARK
PARISH LA.
KENT HOUSE RD.
HIGH ST.
CROYDON ROAD
ELMERS END ROAD
ANERLEY ROAD
PORTLAND ROAD
SPRING LA.
LONG LANE
SHIRLEY ROAD
ADDISCOMBE ROAD
WICKHAM RD.
BECKENHAM RD.
ALBEMARLE ROAD
BROMLEY ROAD
WIDMORE RD.
BICKLEY PK. RD.
PAGE HEATH LA.
SOUTHBOROUGH RD.
SOUTHLANDS ROAD
HOMESDALE RD.
MASONS HILL
KENTISH WAY
PLAISTOW LANE
LONDON LA.
COLLEGE RD.
HAYES LA.
HAYES RD.
WESTMORELAND RD.
BARNFIELD WOOD ROAD
MEAD WAY
PICKHURST LANE
WICKHAM WAY
SOUTH EDEN PARK RD.
STONE PARK AVE.
EDEN PARK AVE.
UPPER ELMERS END RD.
GODDARD RD.
ORCHARD WAY
MONKS ORCHARD ROAD
MANOR PARK RD.
HIGH ST.
GLEBE WAY
CROYDON ROAD
ADDINGTON RD.
CORKSCREW HILL
WEST COMMON ROAD
BASTON ROAD
GATES GREEN ROAD
LAYHAMS ROAD
OAKLEY ROAD
HASTINGS ROAD
COMMONSIDE
HEATHFIELD
SHIRLEY CHURCH ROAD
COOMBE LANE
OAKS ROAD
SHIRLEY HILLS RD.
FARNBOROUGH COMMON
CHISLEHURST ROAD
LOGS HILL
ELMSTEAD LANE
WHITEHORSE HILL
WELL HALL RD.
WESTMOUNT ROAD
OLD HILL
CRAB HILL
FOXGROVE RD.
RECTORY RD.
VILLAGE WAY
HAYES LANE
CROWN LA.
MAGPIE HALL LA.
BLACKBROOK LANE

KIMPTON

10   10A

STAPLEFORD   THUNDRIDGE

6

WELWYN

FLAMSTEAD   HARPENDEN   WHEATHAMPSTEAD   WELWYN   WARE
                                              GARDEN CITY
LITTLE   28   29   30   31   32   33
GADDESDEN   REDBOURN   HERTFORD
ASTON   STANST
CLINTON   ABBOT
TRING   4

NORTHCHURCH   BERKHAMSTED   ST. ALBANS   HATFIELD   HODDESDON
                        40   41   42   43   44   45   46   47   48   49
WENDOVER   38   39   HEMEL   BROXBOURNE
              BOURNE   HEMPSTEAD   POTTERS
              END   3

                                    21/6A   21A   22   BROOKMANS
                            BOVINGDON   PARK
              54   56   57   58   59   60   61   LONDON 62   63   64   65   66   67
GREAT   CHESHAM   CHIPPERFIELD   ABBOTS   COLNEY   POTTERS   CUFFLEY   CHESHUNT   W.
MISSENDEN   LANGLEY   20   BARS   23/1   24   A

                                              19   RADLETT
HAZLEMERE   AMERSHAM   LITTLE   EAST
                      CHALFONT   74   75   76   77   78   79   80   BARNET   82   83
              55   72   73   WATFORD   BOREHAMWOOD   BARNET   81   ENFIELD
                        CHORLEYWOOD   18   BUSHEY

HIGH   TYLERS   CHALFONT   RICKMANSWORTH   TOTTERIDGE   SOUTHGATE   CHINGF
WYCOMBE   GREEN   ST. GILES   17   97
              88   89   90   91   92   93   94   95   96   98   99   100   101
LOUDWATER   CHALFONT   HAREFIELD   NORTHWOOD   STANMORE   EDGWARE   FINCHLEY   WOOD   TOTTENHAM
              COMMON   GREEN
FLACKWELL   BEACONSFIELD   PINNER   HENDON   HORNSEY
HEATH   WOOBURN   GERRARDS   HARROW   KENTON   WALTHAMSTOW
MARLOW   CROSS   113   114   115   116   117   118   119   120   121   122   123
BOURNE   110   111   112   DENHAM   RUISLIP   STOKE   LEYTON
END   EGYPT   HAMPSTEAD   NEWINGTON
              16/1A   1   SUDBURY   WEMBLEY

FARNHAM   STOKE   UXBRIDGE   NORTHOLT   WILLESDEN   HACKNEY
COMMON   POGES   CAMDEN   ISLINGTON
130   131   132   133   134   135   136   137   138   139   TOWN   141   142   143
MAIDENHEAD   BURNHAM   IVER   YIEWSLEY   HAYES   SOUTHALL   EALING   ACTON   140   STEPNEY
A404(M)   SLOUGH   PADDINGTON   HOLBORN
ODLANDS   8/9   LANGLEY   WEST   HAMMERSMITH   WESTMINSTER   SOUTHWARK
K   ETON WICK   6   DRAYTON   154   155   156   157   158   159   160   161   162   163
150   151   152   153   4A   4   KEW   BARNES   LAMBETH   GREENWICH
HOLYPORT   WINDSOR   HEATHROW   BATTERSEA
              OLD   AIRPORT   BRIXTON   LEWISHAM
              WINDSOR   WRAYSBURY   LONDON   HOUNSLOW   WANDSWORTH   CATFORD
WINKFIELD   172   173   174   175   176   177   178   179   180   181   182   183
NFIELD   FELTHAM   TWICKENHAM   RICHMOND
              EGHAM   STAINES   ASHFORD   WIMBLEDON   STREATHAM
                              TEDDINGTON
BRACKNELL   ASCOT   VIRGINIA   SUNBURY   KINGSTON   MERTON   MITCHAM   BECKENHAM
              WATER   UPON THAMES
192   193   194   195   196   197   198   199   200   201   202   203
              CHERTSEY   WALTON-   SURBITON   CROYDON
BROOMHALL   ON-THAMES

BAGSHOT   LIGHTWATER   OTTERSHAW   WEYBRIDGE   ESHER   SUTTON   ADDING
              210   211   212   213   214   215   216   217   218   219   220   221
CAMBERLEY   CHOBHAM   BYFLEET   EWELL   PURLEY   SANDERSTEAD
BISLEY   OXSHOTT   EPSOM
FRIMLEY   WOKING   STOKE   ASHTEAD   BANSTEAD   WARLINGHAM
                              D'ABERNON   COULSDON
              226   227   228   229   230   231   232   233   234   235   236   237
MYTCHETT   PIRBRIGHT   RIPLEY   OCKHAM   FETCHAM   LEATHERHEAD   TADWORTH   HOOLEY   CATERHAM
              MAYFORD   WALTON
              JACOBS   EAST   GREAT   ON THE HILL
              WELL   HORSLEY   BOOKHAM
RNBOROUGH   242   243   244   245   246   247   248   249   250   251   252   253
ALDERSHOT   NORMANDY   STOUGHTON   EAST   REIGATE   REDHILL   GODSTONE
                              CLANDON
ALE   TONGHAM   GUILDFORD   GOMSHALL   WESTCOTT   DORKING   BROCKHAM   EARLSWOOD   SOUTH
                                                                   GODSTONE
              258   259   260   261   262   263   264   265   266   267
ILLBRIDGE   SHACKLEFORD   COMPTON   SHALFORD   ABINGER   NORTH   LEIGH   SALFORDS   BLINDLEY
                              HAMMER   HOLMWOOD   HEATH

ELSTEAD   GODALMING   SHAMLEY   HOLMBURY   BEARE   HORLEY   LIN
              GREEN   ST. MARY   GREEN   268   269
MILFORD   GRAFHAM   CHARLWOOD   GATWICK   NEWCHA
                        JAYES   AIRPORT   9A   9
WITLEY   PARK   LONDON

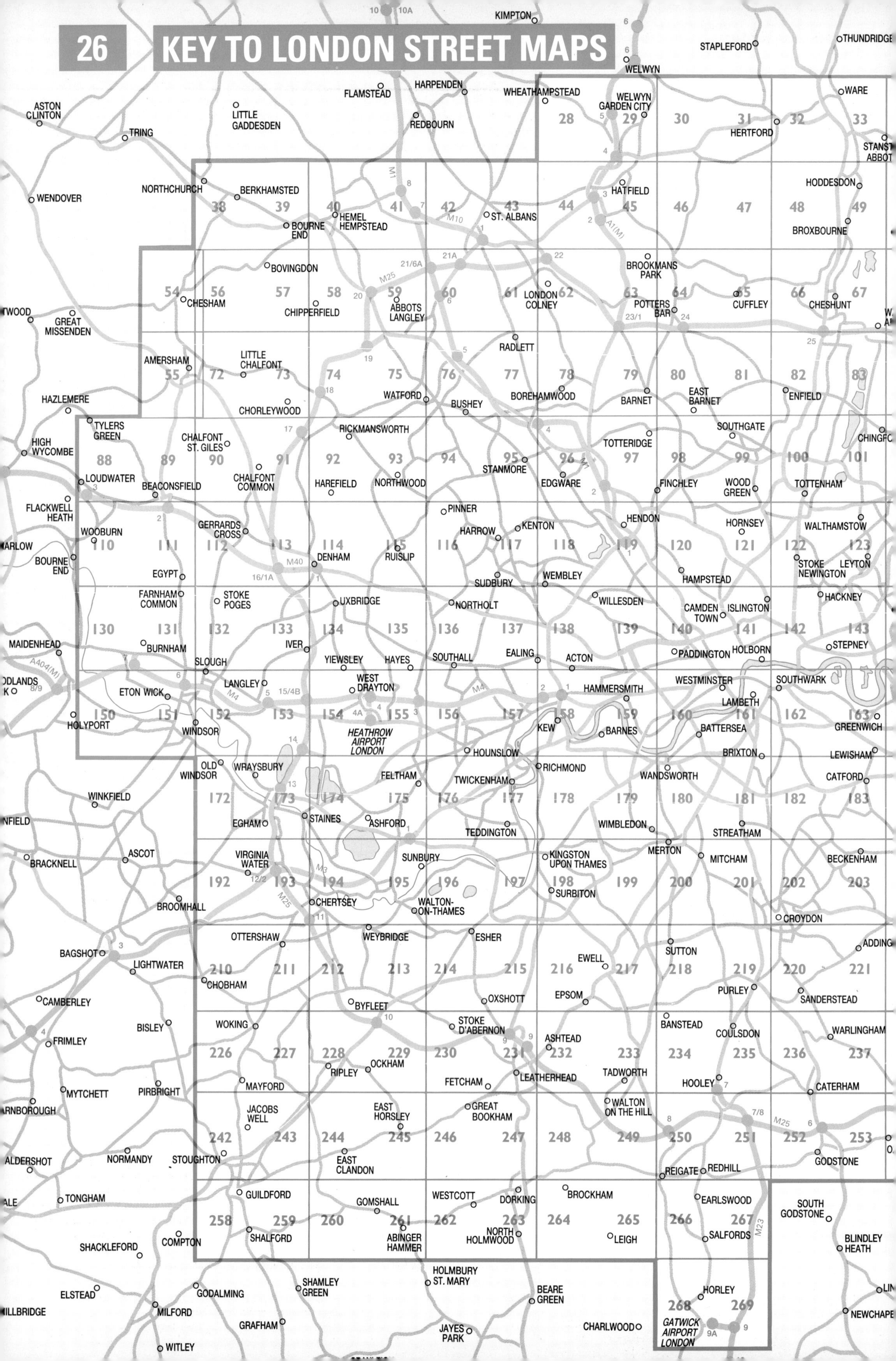

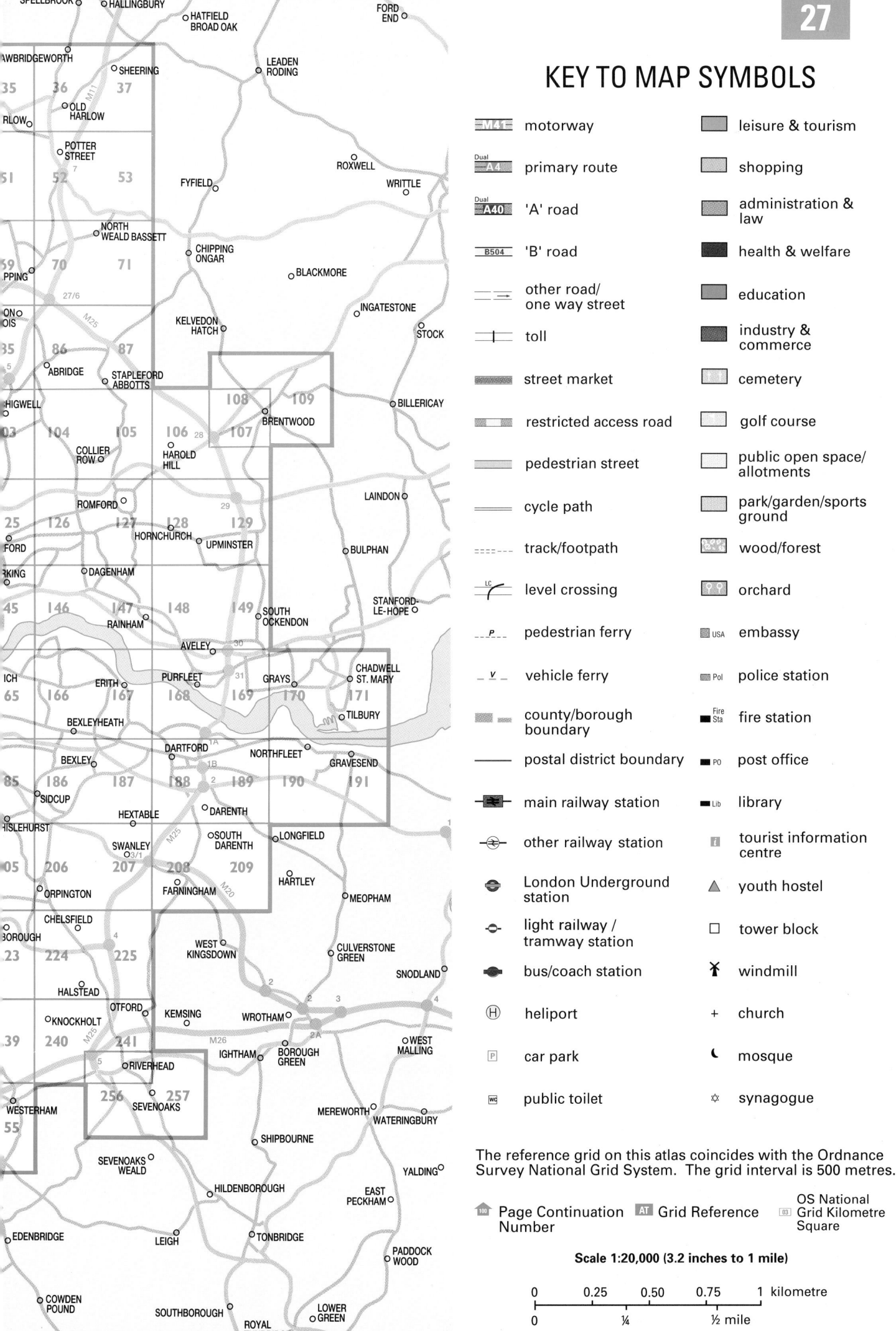

KEY TO MAP SYMBOLS

M41	motorway		leisure & tourism
Dual A4	primary route		shopping
Dual A40	'A' road		administration & law
B504	'B' road		health & welfare
	other road/ one way street		education
	toll		industry & commerce
	street market		cemetery
	restricted access road		golf course
	pedestrian street		public open space/ allotments
	cycle path		park/garden/sports ground
	track/footpath		wood/forest
LC	level crossing		orchard
P	pedestrian ferry	USA	embassy
V	vehicle ferry	Pol	police station
	county/borough boundary	Fire Sta	fire station
	postal district boundary	PO	post office
	main railway station	Lib	library
	other railway station	i	tourist information centre
	London Underground station	▲	youth hostel
	light railway / tramway station	□	tower block
	bus/coach station	✶	windmill
H	heliport	+	church
P	car park	☾	mosque
WC	public toilet	✡	synagogue

The reference grid on this atlas coincides with the Ordnance Survey National Grid System. The grid interval is 500 metres.

🏠 Page Continuation Number   AT Grid Reference   OS National Grid Kilometre Square

Scale 1:20,000 (3.2 inches to 1 mile)

0   0.25   0.50   0.75   1 kilometre

0   ¼   ½ mile

28
CL
CM
CN
CP
CQ
CR
CS
19
20
21
05
06
07
08
09
10
11
12
13
14
WHEATHAMPSTEAD
AL4
AL10
Lamer Farm
LAMER PARK
SCRATCHING GROVE
THREEGROVES WOOD
CHERRYTREE SPRING
CONEYDELL SPRING
DOWDELL'S WOOD
FISH WOOD
WARREN WOOD
BLADDER WOOD
Ayot Place
ROBINSON'S WOOD
AYOT GREENWAY
RIVER LEE OR LEA
GRAYS WOOD
Sparrowhall Farm
BOWLE'S WOOD
COWPER'S SPRING
PARK MEAD SPRING
CHARLIES CROFT
FLINT BRIDGE
BLUEBELL HILL WOOD
Glasshouse
FLINT BRIDGE PLANTATION
Clubhouse
Warren Farm
BROCKET PARK
Crooked Chimney PH
LAMB'S GROVE
Upper Cromer Hyde Farm
FLETCHER'S WICK
BENSTEAD'S WOOD
WET GROVE
LONG GROVE SPRING
LONG GROVE PLANTATION
Cromerhyde Farm
TITNOL'S WOOD
DOGSHEART SPRING
Symondshyde Farm
CHALKDELL WOOD
SYMONDSHYDE GREAT WOOD
HAMMOND'S WOOD
FURZE FIELD
HILL WOOD
HARLOWDELL SPRING
Wheathampstead House
Marford Farm
ALLOT
Devil's Dyke Earthworks
DAVID'S DINGLE
Chausdell Farm
The Slad Earthworks
Samuels Farm
Beech Hyde Farm
John Bunyan PH
MOAT
KENT'S DELL
SPRITE FIELD SPRING
PEARMANS SPRING
FURZEFIELD WOOD
COLEMAN GREEN
WELWYN HATFIELD
ST. ALBANS
Normansland Farm
Hammond's Farm
Cricket Ground
Pav
PLAYING FIELD
University of Hertfordshire Hall of Residence
PET CEM
HOME OFFICE
Fairfolds Farm
Sutton's Farm
Jersey Farm
Nashe's Farm
44
SAND AND GRAVEL PIT
Coll
Field Cen
Astwick Manor Farm
HATFIELD BUSINESS PARK
HOOK'S WOOD
SLEEVE HALL WOOD
CODICOTE ROAD B653
LOWER LUTON ROAD
CORY WRIGHT WAY
MARFORD ROAD B653
BEECH HYDE LANE
COLEMAN GREEN LANE
HAMMOND'S LANE
WOODCOCK HILL
COOPERS GREEN LANE
WATEREND LANE
CROMER HYDE LANE
HATFIELD ROAD
HAVILLAND WAY
MANOR RD
FROBISHER WAY
TOWER HILL LANE
SHEEPCOTE LANE
DROVERS LANE
WHEATHAMPSTEAD ROAD B651
LAMER LANE B651
Youth Cen
Hall
Lib
Sch
Fire Sta
Ten Cts
Memi
GRANARY CLO
CHURCH ST
HIGH ST
NECTON ROAD
GARRARD WAY
OFFAS WAY
TUDOR ROAD
CAESARS ROAD
NURSERIES ROAD
SAXON CLO
CONQUERORS HILL
BARTON RD
MALTINGS DRIVE
CANONS FIELD
GRD
ASH GROVE
BURY GREEN
HIGH MEADS
ROSE LANE
LANGLEY GROVE
SHOTFIELD
WOODCOCK HILL
HOUSE LANE
Home Farm
GOLF COURSE

Digswell
CT
CU
CV
CW
CX
CY
CZ
22
23
24
RIVER MIMRAM
PLAYING FIELD
HORSESHOE PLANTATION
RECTORY WOOD
White Hill Farm
Water Tower
The Frythe
HOMER'S WOOD
LONG SPRING
MITCHELL'S WOOD
Manor Farm
Saw Mill
Ayot Green
CAT'S GALLOWS
BROOK'S WOOD
TEMPLE WOOD
CONDUIT FIELD
SHERRARDSPARK WOOD
Sherrardspark
REDDINGS PLANTATION
Digswell House
Digswell Place
Digswell Place Stables
RESERVOIRS
WELWYN GARDEN CITY GOLF COURSE
Glasshouses
Brickwall House
Clubhouses
AL8
Junction 5
Lemsford
Sun Inn
Watercress Beds
THE COPPINS
SPORTS GRD
Handside
Welwyn Rugby Ground
Campus West
Superstore
BUS STA
The Howard Centre
WELWYN GARDEN CITY
Hunters Bridge
Works
Gas Works
SHIRE PARK
Lyles Bridge
MUNDELLS
Peartree
Fire sta
Superstore
YMCA
Twentieth Mile Bridge
Sports Centre
GOSLING SPORTS PARK
Ski slope
GOLF DRIVING RANGE
BURROWFIELD INDUSTIAL ESTATE
Elec Sta
HERTFORDSHIRE COUNTY POLICE HEADQUARTERS
BOATING LAKE
Lido
Pumping Station
Stanborough
Stanborough Bury Farm
SAILING LAKE
Woodhall
HATFIELD HYDE CEMETERY
KING GEORGE V PLAYING FIELD
Hatfield Hyde
Health Centre
Crest Hotel
QUEEN ELIZABETH II HOSPITAL
THE COMMONS
CRESWICK PLANTATION
LEA VALLEY WALK
Woodhall Farm
Junction 4
AL9
MILL GREEN GOLF COURSE
Sewage Works
Clubhouse
Cricket Ground
Hatfield Garden Village
PLAYING FIELD
Sports Centre
COUNCIL DEPOT
THE WARREN
Saw Mill
AL7
Holden
BESSEMER ROAD
BROADWATER ROAD
STANBOROUGH ROAD
CHEQUERS
HOWLANDS
DIGSWELL PARK ROAD
BRIDGE ROAD
A1(M)
A6129
A1000
B197
B195
B1000
B653
05
06
07
08
09
10
11
12
13
14
30
45

30
DA
DB
DC
DD
DE
DF
DG
26
27
28
05
06
07
08
09
10
11
12
13
14
Digswell
Tewin
Holdens
HOLDENS PLAYING FIELDS
PANSHANGER GOLF COMPLEX
Fairway Tavern PH
Clubhouse
DAWLEY PLANTATION
HOME WOOD
Weirs
AL6
WESTLEY WOOD
RECTORY WOOD
Tewin Bury Farm
Tewin Lodge
Tewin Mill Farm
Tewin Mill House
Muspatts Farm
FLEXLEYS WOOD
HOME WOOD
LAMB DELL WOOD
Marden Hill
RIVER MIMRAM
Warrengate Farm
PANSHANGER AERODROME
POPLARS GREEN
BROCKET HILL
Hangar
Flying School
HENRY WOOD
MONEYHOLE LANE PARK
HIGH GROVE
BIRCHALL WOOD
ROLLS WOOD
Panshanger
Peartree
Hall Grove
Hatfield Hyde
AL7
MUNDELLS
Works
SHIRE PARK
Superstore
Fire sta
29
KING GEORGE V PLAYING FIELD
QUEEN ELIZABETH II HOSPITAL
THE COMMONS
MILL GREEN GOLF COURSE
Sewage Works
Saw Mill
THE WARREN
AL9
GREAT CAPTAIN'S WOOD
Birchall
Cole Green
Munn's Farm
Holwell Hyde Farm
Holwell Court Farm
Holwell Court
Burnside Farm
HOLWELL CARAVAN SITE
Holwell Manor
Holwell Bridge
Essendon Mill
Essendonbury Farm
RIVER LEE
LEA VALLEY WALK
46
LONDON
HERTFORD ROAD
BIRCHALL LANE
B195
B1000
B1455
B158
A1000
A414
EAST HERTS
WELWYN HATFIELD

Bramfield
Waterford
Bengeo
HERTFORD
Hertingfordbury
Birch Green
Letty Green
SG14
SG13
HERTFORD COUNTY HOSPITAL
HERTFORD NORTH
HERTFORD CEMETERY
WATERFORD PLANTATION
WATERFORD MARSH
GREAT MOLE WOOD
LITTLE MOLE WOOD
ICEHOUSE WOOD
ELEVEN ACRE WOOD
LONG WOOD
BARNSLEYS WOOD
CHARTERSFIELD PLANTATION
SELEBROOM WOOD
HANGING GROVE
OAKFIELD PLANTATION
ARCHER'S SPRING
EVERGREEN WOOD
GARDEN WOOD
BLAKEMORE WOOD
LADY HUGHES'S WOOD
CHESHER'S PLANTATION
OSIER BEDS
CHISEL SHELF
RIVER MIMRAM
HERTINGFORDBURY ROAD
WELWYN ROAD
BYPASS
HIGH ROAD NORTH
A119
B1000
B158
A414
GASCOYNE WAY
TERRACE WOOD
SOUTHFIELD WOOD
CHALK DELL
GROTTO WOOD
GRAVEL PIT
THE PIGHTLE
SPRING WOOD
GRAVEFIELD GROVE
LARCH PLANTATION
HOOK'S GROVE
SAILOR'S GROVE
THE PINETUM
BAYFORD BROOK
RIVER LEE OR LEA
PONTERS GROVE
ST. JOHN'S WOOD
PRIEST WOOD
BARLEYCROFT GROVE
DEPOT
Kingfisher Garden Centre
Bayfordbury Park Farm
Field Station
Glasshouse
Home Farm
BROADGREEN
LOWER ROAD
HATFIELD ROAD
32
47
05
06
07
08
09
10
11
12
13
14
DH
DJ
DK
DL
DM
DN
DP
29
30
31

32
DQ
DR
DS
DT
DU
DV
DW
33
34
35
ST. JOHN'S WOOD
OAK WOOD
Pumping Station
Elec Sta
Depot
DEPOT
Works
05
06
07
08
09
10
11
12
13
14
RIVER BEANE
WATERFORD MARSH
NORTH ROAD
SG14
EIGHT ACRE PLANTATION
Ware Park Farm
COWSHED CORNER
Ware Park Manor
Nursery
MONASTERY
Bardon Farm
BENGEO MEADOWS
GREAT MOLE WOOD
Kennel Corner
Bengeo
LITTLE MOLE WOOD
THE WARREN
HARTHAM REC GRD
Swim Pool
Gas Works
MEAD BUS PARK
HERTFORD EAST
Superstore
HERTFORD NORTH
SPORTS GROUND
HERTFORD COUNTY HOSP
31
HERTFORD
COUNTY COURT
COUNTY HALL
PLAYING FIELD
BURIAL GRD
Fire Sta
FOXHOLES BUS PARK
University of Hertfordshire
BALLS PARK
THE CANAL
Tennis Courts
Cricket Ground
KING'S MEADS
RIVER LEE OR LEA
NEW RIVER
MANIFOLD DITCH
CHADWELL SPRINGS GOLF COURSE
Chadwell Spring
Clubhouse
WARE CEM
PLAYING FIELD
SPORTS GROUND
HOSP (closed)
Rush Green Farm
Foxholes Farm
Jenningsbury Court
MOAT
COVERED RESERVOIR
Amwell Place Farm
GREAT STOCK WOOD
LITTLE STOCK WOOD
Swallow Grove Farm
SG13
BALLS WOOD
HERTFORD HEATH NATURE RESERVE
HOBBYHORSE WOOD
BRICKENDON BROOK
Offices
48
Blackfields Farm
Clements Farm
Clements Cottages
Elbowlane Farm
SAILOR'S GROVE
TERRACE WOOD
Terrace Wood Nursery
Kingfisher Garden Centre
Station
Glasshouse
HOOK'S GROVE
A119
A414
B158
B1502
B1197
A1010
WARE ROAD
LONDON ROAD
HERTFORD ROAD

DX
DY
DZ
EA
EB
EC
ED
36
37
38
05
06
07
08
09
10
11
12
13
14
34
49
SG12
EN11
WARE
WESTERN HOUSE HOSP
KING GEORGE'S FLD
Arts Cen
JACKSON'S GROVE
PRIOR'S WOOD
DOGHOUSE WOOD
Mardocks Farm
LADY GROVE
YOUNG WOOD
Swades Farm
Newhole Farm
Ford
Watersplace Farm
Brokengall Hill
Widburyhill Farm
WIDBURY WOOD
MEAD WOOD
The Dairy Farm
EASNEYE WOOD
Coll
PLAYING FLD
Hardmead Lock
PETER'S WOOD
PLAYING FIELDS
POST WOOD
PRESDALES RECREATION GROUND
Amwellbury Farm
AMWELL QUARRY NATURE RESERVE
LEE NAVIGATION
LEE VALLEY CYCLE ROUTE
RIVER LEE
NEW RIVER
War Memorial
Van Hage Garden Centre
Great Amwell
Glasshouses
St. Margarets
Stanstead Lock
Stanstead Abbotts
Little Briggens Farm
LEAFYOAK WOOD
MUCH WOOD
GOLDING'S WOOD
HAILEY WOOD
PLAYING FIELDS
Haileybury College
Hailey House
Hailey Farm
The Galley Hall PH
Support Unit
St. Margarets Farm
Nursery
Coldharbour Farm
Ryegate Farm
RYE HOUSE MARSH NATURE RESERVE
Sludge Lagoons
Sewage Works
Filter Beds
Tanks
Rye House Gatehouse
RYE HOUSE
DELLS WOOD
CEM
SPORTS GRD
ALLOT
Youth Club
A1170
A10(T)
A414
B1004
B181
B1502
B180
HODDESDON BY-PASS
AMWELL ROAD
LONDON ROAD
STATION ROAD
HERTFORD ROAD
WARE ROAD
HARCAMLOW WAY
CAPPELL ROAD
ST MARGARET'S ROAD
CRANBOURNE DRIVE
ROYDON ROAD
HUNSDON ROAD
TOLL HOUSE STREAM
STANSTEAD MILL STREAM

EE
EF
EG
EH
EJ
EK
EL
40
41
42
05
06
07
08
09
10
11
12
13
14
13
12
11
14
33
50
SG12
EN11
CM19
Hunsdon
Hunsdonbury
Stanstead Abbotts
ROYDON
MOAT
New House Farm
HOGHAM'S WOOD
HOGHAM'S PLANTATION
TOWNLANDS
HULL WOOD
THISTLY WOOD
WARE ROAD
B1004
Little Samuels Farm
WIDFORD ROAD
B180
HUNSDON ROAD
Mardocks Farm
DOGHOUSE WOOD
LADY
YOUNG WOOD
HARCAMLOW
BIRCH PLANTATION
Fillets Farm
The Dairy Farm
MOAT WOOD
NEWGATE WOOD
BALLARD'S WOOD
THIRSTY SPRING
BLACK BUSHES
Halfway House Farm
THE WILDERNESS
SLOE GROVE
Waterfall
BURY PLANTATION
Nine Ashes Farm
Depot
Weir
EASTWICK ROAD
Hunsdon House
Little Briggens Farm
Olives Farm
SQUARE SPRING
HARCAMLOW WAY
LORD'S WOOD
LONG SPRING
POGDEN'S WOOD
HOUNDSON BROOK
Works
CAPPELL LA
ALLOT
PO
Sch
Brickhouse Farm
Briggens Home Farm
BRIGGENS HOUSE HOTEL GOLF COURSE
Briggens House Hotel
HUNSDON MEAD
ROYDON MEAD
A414
ROAD
EASTWICK
COLDHARBOUR WOOD
Coldharbour Farm
THE GROVE
Stanstead Bury
Stanstead Bury Farm
Ryegate Farm
Nursery
MAPLE CT
MARSH LANE
NETHERFIELD LANE
ROYDON ROAD
B181
KITTEN LANE
TROTTERS GAP
HIGH ST
SOUTH ST
MILL STREAM
STANSTEAD
LEE VALLEY
RYE ROAD
TOLL HOUSE STREET
Filter Beds
Tanks
Sludge Lagoons
Sewage Works
RYE HOUSE MARSH NATURE RESERVE
Rye House Gatehouse
RYE HOUSE SPEEDWAY
RYE HOUSE
RIVER STORT
ROYDON PARK LEISURE PARK
MILL STREAM
THREE FORESTS WAY
Lock
HARCAMLOW
RIVER STORT
EAST HERTS
EPPING FOREST
HERTFORDSHIRE
ESSEX
ROYDON LODGE CHALET ESTATE
Pumping Station
The New Inn
Temple Farm
Hall
HARLOW ROAD
ROYDON ROAD
East End Farm
HARLOW
EPPING FOREST
ROYDON PARK
HANSELLS MEAD
Tennis Cts
Pav
Pol
FB
LC
Lock

EM
EN
EP
EQ
ER
ES
ET
43
44
45
THE MANOR OF GROVES
GOLF COURSE
Clubhouse
The Manor of Groves Hotel
THE GROVE
LAWNS WOOD
EASTWICK WOOD
QUEEN'S WOOD
BATTLES WOOD
MAPLECROFT WOOD
BLACK HUT WOOD
GOLDEN GROVE
SAYES COPPICE
NEW PLANTATION
CM21
Great Pennys Farm
Overhall Farm
Dairy Cottages
Golden Hill
Channocks Farm
RECTORY PLANTATION
GIBSON'S SHAW
ROUNDSELL SHAW
TUCK'S SPRING
Eastwick Hall Farm
Offices
FOX EARTHS
Sayes Park Farm
High Wych Grange
Pole Hole Farm
Pole Hill
Redericks Farm
SAND AND GRAVEL PIT
HOLLINGSON MEADS
36
THE CHASE
The Mount
The Plume of Feathers PH
Hall
Fiddlers' Bridge
Eastwick
The Lion PH
Eastwick Manor
Eastwick Lodge Farm
The Dusty Miller PH
Research Laboratories
MEAD PARK ESTATE
Latton Lock
LATTON ISLAND
Warehouse
Works
Depot
Cinema
Queensgate Centre
Superstore
MARSHGATE SPRING
RIVER STORT (NAVIGATION)
PARNDON MEAD
Parndock Lock
Outdoor Pursuits Centre
HARLOW TOWN
EDINBURGH WAY
A414
A1169
FIFTH / ALLENDE AVENUE
RAM GORSE
SPORTS GROUND
ASH TREE FIELD
PLAYING FLD
Princes Gate
PETS CORNER
TOWN PARK
CM20
Mark Hall North
Mark Hall South
Little Parndon
PRINCESS ALEXANDRA HOSPITAL
Netteswell
Harlow College
HARLOW
HELIPAD
51
05
06
07
08
09
10
11
12
13
14
CANONS BROOK GOLF COURSE
GRAVEPIT SPRINGS
THE MOORS

EU
EV
EW
EX
EY
EZ
FA
47
48
49
SAWBRIDGEWORTH
THE MANOR OF GROVES
Clubhouse
GOLF COURSE
Manor of Groves Hotel
THE GROVE
CM21
BAKERS LANE
WYCH LANE
HIGH WYCH ROAD
Claylane Farm
05
06
07
08
09
10
11
12
13
14
Bakers Farm
PO
ALLOT
Sch
High Wych Grange
Sayes Park Farm
RIVERS HOSPITAL
ROWNEY WOOD
Rodney Bois Riding Stables
Rowney Farm
CHASEWAYS
A1184
PISHIOBURY DRIVE
UNION WOOD
Rowneybury
Lawrence House
Feakes Lock
THE OSIER BED
Nursery
Pumping Station
COV RES
Pump House
FOX EARTHS
REDERICKS LANE
Redericks Farm
Pole Hole Farm
CM20
35
POLLINGSON MEADS
SAND AND GRAVEL PIT
LATTON ISLAND
Latton Lock
HERTFORDSHIRE
ESSEX
EAST HERTS
RIVER STORT NAVIGATION
ASHPLANT
Works
CAMBRIDGE ROAD
HARLOW ROAD
Depot
Harlow Mill P.H.
MAPLE RIVER IND EST
Warehouses
TIP
Warehouse
HARLOW MILL
THE CRESCENT
HART ROAD
THE HOO
GUILFORDS
PINCEY BROOK
Ealing Bridge
MARSH LANE
Durrington Hall
Aylmers Farm
SHEERING ROAD
LOWER SHEERING ROAD
New House Farm
Harlowbury
Harlowbury Chapel
Mayfield Farm
EDINBURGH WAY
A414
Gas Works
Health Cen
MEAD PARK ESTATE
ATHENA EST
Superstores
Cinema
Queensgate Centre
Superstore
Princes Gate
Old Harlow
PLAYING FLD
THE OXLEYS
WATLINGTON ROAD
MULBERRY GREEN
Day Centre
Jocelyns Arts Cen
Health Cen
Clubhs
Fire Sta
Cricket Ground
Bowl Grn
SPORTS GRD
Rec Cen
CHIPPINGFIELD
ALLOT
PLAYING FIELD
B183
EPPING FOREST
HARLOW
BURIAL GROUND
Churchgate Manor Hotel
Tennis Court
Bowl Grn
Feltimores
Mark Hall North
Schs
Tennis Cts
MARK HALL MOORS
MARK HALL CYCLE MUS
MARK HALL PARK
FIRST AVE
GILDEN WAY
EAST PARK
THE CHANTRY
MOWBRAY ROAD
MANDELA AVENUE
FELMONGERS
Tennis Courts
PLAYING FIELDS
MARK HALL SPORTS GRD Clubhouse
Clubhouse
SPORTS GROUND
NORTEL
GRAVELPIT SPRING
Mulberry Green Factory
The Kennels
Essex Hunt Cottages
NEWSPOND SPRING
New Hall Farm
Hubbard's Hall
Hubbard's Hall Farm
Franklins Farm
VICARAGE WOOD
Mark Hall South
LADYSHOT SPORTS GROUND
MARKHALL WOOD
BRENTHALL WOOD
BARNSLEY WOOD
CHURCH LANGLEY
52
Church Langley Water Tower
Netteswell
SPORTS GRD
Clinic
PARSONAGE LEYS
HOME CLO
THE MOORS
GRAVEPIT SPRINGS
Potters Arms PH
Superstore

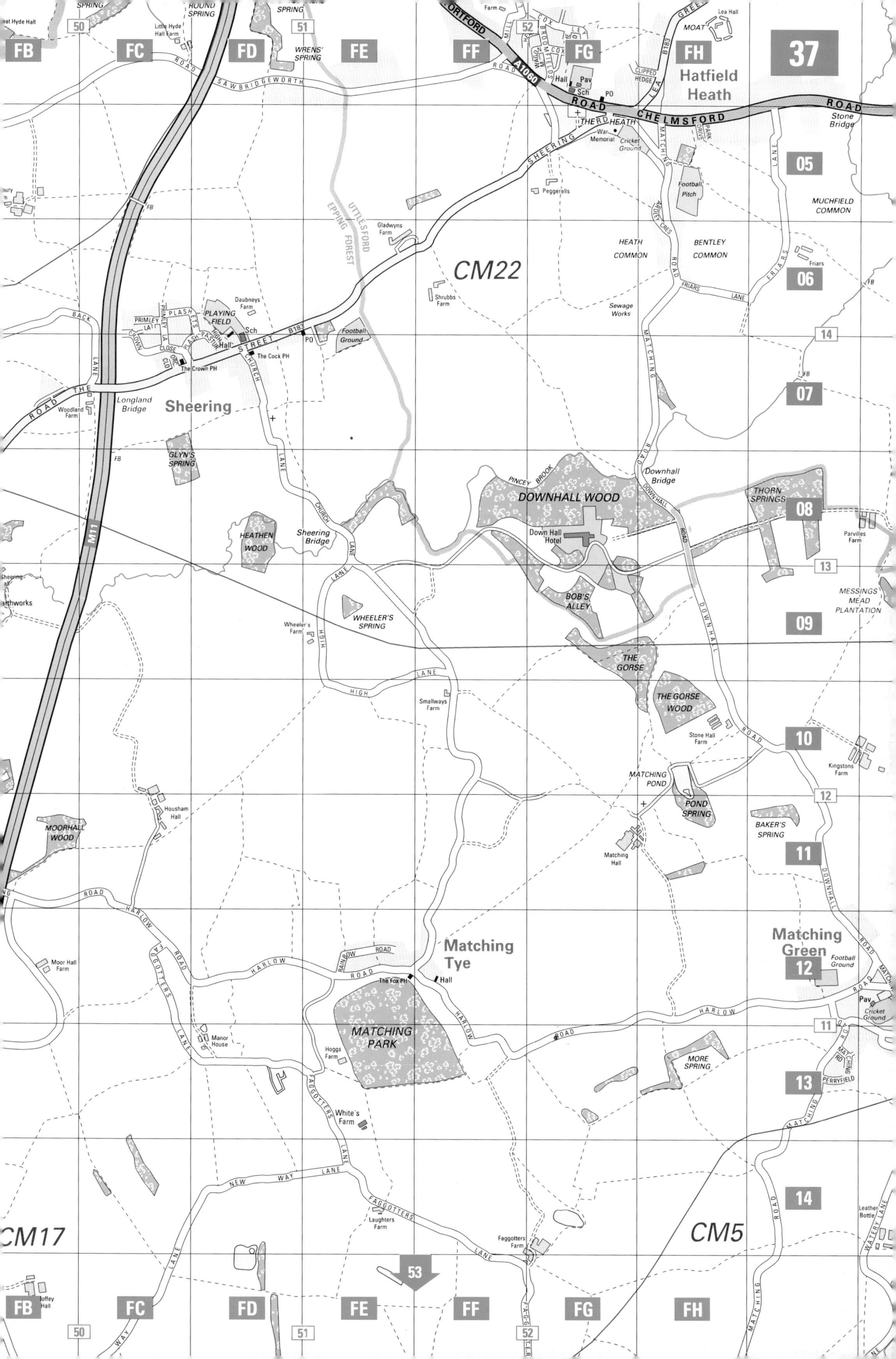
FB
FC
FD
FE
FF
FG
FH
50
51
52
Hatfield Heath
Sheering
Matching Tye
Matching Green
CM22
CM17
CM5
DOWNHALL WOOD
Down Hall Hotel
MATCHING PARK
HEATHEN WOOD
WHEELER'S SPRING
THE GORSE
THE GORSE WOOD
BOB'S ALLEY
THORN SPRINGS
POND SPRING
MORE SPRING
BAKER'S SPRING
MOORHALL WOOD
GLYN'S SPRING
WRENS' SPRING
MESSINGS MEAD PLANTATION
HEATH COMMON
BENTLEY COMMON
MUCHFIELD COMMON
MATCHING POND
Matching Hall
Housham Hall
Moor Hall Farm
Manor House
Hoggs Farm
White's Farm
Laughters Farm
Faggotters Farm
Smallways Farm
Stone Hall Farm
Kingstons Farm
Parvilles Farm
Wheeler's Farm
Shrubbs Farm
Gladwyns Farm
Daubneys Farm
Woodland Farm
Peggerells
Friars
Longland Bridge
Sheering Bridge
Downhall Bridge
Stone Bridge
Sewage Works
The Fox PH
The Cock PH
The Crown PH
Football Ground
Football Pitch
Cricket Ground
War Memorial
PLAYING FIELD
CHELMSFORD ROAD
SAWBRIDGEWORTH ROAD
HARLOW ROAD
DOWNHALL ROAD
MATCHING ROAD
FAGGOTTERS LANE
NEW WAY LANE
HIGH LANE
CHURCH LANE
FRIARS LANE
THE STREET
M11
A1060
B183
UTTLESFORD
EPPING FOREST
05
06
07
08
09
10
11
12
13
14
53

AS
AT
AU
AV
AW
AX
AY
98
99
00
NORTHCHURCH COMMON NT
NATIONA UST
BEECHES
Hill Farm
Northchurch Farm
Gorseside Farm
Pumping Sta
15
16
17
18
19
20
21
22
23
24
09
08
07
06
Dudswell
GRAND UNION CANAL
ALLOT
Rothschild Court
HIGH STREET
REC GRD
HP4
Well Farm
BERKHAMS
GOL
COU
Northchurch
BERKHAMSTED
Castle Hill Farm
Cricket Ground
Pav
SPORTS GRD
Tenn Cts
Bowl Grn
BERKHAMSTED CASTLE
BERKHAMSTED PLACE
PLAYING FIELD
New Farm
Sch
Tenn Ct
Clubhouse
Works
SHOOTERS DRIVING RANGE
Works
Comm Cen
GOSSOMS END HIGH STREET
Sports Cen
Health Cen
THE ROOKERY
Woodcock Hill
COX DELL
PLAYING FLD
THE PLANTATION
SHOOTERSWAY
BERKHAMSTED BYPASS
A4251
A416
A41
CORNER
LONDON ROAD
CIVIC CEN
REC GRD
ALLOT
CEM
THE MOOR
Fire & Amb Sta
ALLOT
KINGSHILL WAY
REC GRD
PLAYING FIELD
National Film and Television Archive
CEM
Ashlyns Farm
Ashlyns Hall
Marlin Chapel Farm
PANCAKE WOOD
HOCKERIDGE WOOD
WILLOW WOOD
The Old Farm
Hog Lane Farm
SANDPIT GREEN
DROPPING'S WOOD
COKER'S SPRING
Haresfoot Farm
William Hill Farm
Hockeridge Farm
CHESHAM ROAD
Brickies Farm
HP5
Harriotts End Farm
THE LARCHES
HEATHEN GROVE
DACORUM HERTFORDSHIRE
CHILTERN BUCKINGHAMSHIRE
Snowhill Farm
Old Oak Farm
Sewage Works
Brickies Farm
Ashley Green
Flamstead Farm
Whelpley Hill Farm
Kenmore Farm
GREAT WOOD
R'S GROVE
SHORT WOOD
56
Thorne Farm
PLAYING FLD
Sale's Farm
Spencer's Farm

39
AZ
BA
BB
BC
BD
BE
BF
01
02
03
09
08
07
06
GREAT FRITHSDEN COPSE
NATIONAL TRUST
LITTLE FRITHSDEN COPSE
Hollybush Farm
FRITHSDEN VINES
Alford Arms PH
NETTLEDEN ROAD
Nettleden Farm
Crossways Farm
HEIZDIN'S WOOD
Strathgade Farm
Red Lion PH
Watercress Beds
Gristy House Farm
15
Binghams Park Farm
Gaddesden Hall
Fish Farm
FISH PONDS
16
BROWN'S SPRING WOOD
Poultry Farm
HOLLYBUSH WOOD
Rumblers Farm
POTTEN END ROAD
Woodcroft Farm
Potten End Farm
CATSTAIL WOOD
New Farm
SPORTS GRD
ALLOT
VICARAGE ROAD
Potten End
THE SQ.
THE FRONT
Sch
P.O.
Hall
COMMON GRN
WATER END ROAD
The Red Lion PH
HEMPSTEAD LANE
RAMBLING WAY
DELL WOOD
Boxted Farm
17
WARNERS END WOOD
COV RES
Bowl Grn
Sch
PLAYING FIELD
Tenn Ct
Gutteridge Farm
Little Heath Park
Little Heath Small Farm
BERKHAMSTED LANE
GUTTERIDGE WOOD
LITTLE HEATH NT
BULLBEGGARS LANE
Boxted Pig Farm
FIELDS END LANE
POUCHEN END LANE
Little Heath Great Farm
Lower Little Heath Farm
Fields End Farm
ALLOT
SPORTS GROUND
Gadebridge
18
Pav
SPORTS GROUND
WARNERS END
Tennis Cts
PLAYING FIELD
Warners End
Sch
19
VALLEY
BULBEGGAR'S WOOD
HEATH LANE
HP1
40
Clinic
Comm Cen
William Crook House
Hammer
SHRUB HILL COMMON
NORTHRIDGE PARK
20
ALLOT
Berkhamsted Sewage Works
RIVER
Lock
GRAND
Lock
Chaulden
Sch
Comm Cen
Tudor Rose PH
21
Pouchen End Hall
Pouchen End Farm
A4251
LONDON ROAD
Broadway Farm
Pix Farm
PIX FARM LANE
UNION
ALLOT
CONVENT
Sch
CANAL
Lock
Lock
Watercress Beds
War Meml
Cress Farm
SUGAR LANE
CHAULDEN LANE PLAYING FIELD
Rugby Ground
Pav
22
Bourne End Farm
Bourne End
KINGS LANGLEY BYPASS
LONDON ROAD
BOXMOOR
COMMON
HEATH PARK
BOURNE END MILLS
Moorend Farm
HEMEL HEMPSTEAD
Swan PH
23
ROUGHDOWN COMMON
Travel Inn
A41
BERKHAMSTED BYPASS
Vale Farm
GREEN CROFT
HAY WOOD
Sch
Felden
HANGING WOOD
Clubhouse
HAY WOOD
BOXMOOR GOLF COURSE
24
Three Fields
COLESHILL WOOD
LITTLE HAY GOLF COMPLEX
Clubhouse
SHEETHANGER COMMON
Howe's Retreat
57
GORSEFIELD WOOD
BOX LANE
BURY WOOD
Felden Lodge
Tower Farm
Felden Grange
Felden Manor
HP3
COVERED RESERVOIR
DISUSED AIRFIELD
Longcroft Farm

BG
BH
BJ
BK
BL
BM
BN
05
06
07
09
08
15
16
17
18
19
20
21
22
23
24
39
58
VARNEY'S WOOD
Wood Farm
DODDS LANE
LEIGHTON BUZZARD ROAD
Red Lion PH
Strathgade Farm
POTTEN END HILL
Watercress Beds
Gristy House Farm
THRIFT WOOD
Noake Mill
Fish Farm
Piccotts End Garden Centre
Gaddesden Hall
FISH PONDS
Glasshouses
RIVER GADE
Electricity Sub Station
CATSTAIL WOOD
Piccotts End
New Farm House
DELL WOOD
Piccotts End Farm
Boars Head PH
Marchmont Farm
PICCOTTS END LANE
CYCLE TRACK
A4146
A4147
LINK ROAD
GROVEHILL PLAYING FIELDS
Grovehill
MARGARET LLOYD PARK
Health Cens
Youth Cen
PENNINE WAY SPORTS GRD
Clubhouse
PENNINE WAY SPORTS GROUND
HOWE GROVE
YEWTREE WOOD
REDBOURN ROAD
Superstore
WARNERS END WOOD
HOME WOOD
GADEBRIDGE
GADEBRIDGE PARK
SPORTS GROUND
Gadebridge
SPORTS GROUND
Highfield
RANDALL PARK
CYCLE TRACK
QUEENSWAY
HP1
WARNERS END
VALLEY
Varners End
Bowling Greens
OLD TOWN HALL ARTS CEN
West Herts Coll
Fire Sta
Amb Sta
TA Centre
KEEN FIELDS
Hammerfield
SHRUB HILL COMMON
NORTHRIDGE PARK
CONVENT
HEATH LANE CEMETERY
DACORUM CIVIC CENTRE
DACORUM PAVILION
Superstore
BUS STA
HEMEL HEMPSTEAD GENERAL HOSPITAL
HEMEL HEMPSTEAD
Adeyfield
ALLOT
ST ALBANS ROAD
A414
Superstore
Leisure World
JARMAN FIELDS
Hemel Ski Slope
Ashley Close
PLAYING FIELD
HP3
LIME WALK
Chaulden
Tudor Rose PH
CHAULDEN LANE PLAYING FIELD
Boxmoor
Cricket Ground
Sports Cen
Youth Cen
STATION ROAD
HEATH PARK
Cricket Ground
Clubho
Superstore
BOXMOOR
KINGS
LONDON ROAD
A4251
The Mallard PH
HEMEL HEMPSTEAD
ROUGHDOWN COMMON
Gas Works
Works
TWO WATERS ROAD
A41
Glasshouses
ORAM PLACE
Bennetts End
BELSWAINS PLAYING FIELDS
Felden
Three Fields Farm
A41 BY-PASS
Clubhouse
HOME WOOD
BOXMOOR GOLF CO
SHEETHANGER COMMON
Howe's Retreat
Felden Lodge
Tower Farm
Felden Manor
Apsley Mills Retail Park
APSLEY
GRAND UNION CANAL
SHENDISH GOLF COURSE
SPORTS GRD
HEN'S HEAD WOOD
LONGCROFT LANE
FLAUNDEN LANE
FEATHERBED LANE
HIGHCROFT ROAD

HP2
AL3
WD5
Wood End Farm
Cherry Tree Farm
Cherry Tree House
Eaton Lodge
High Grange
OIL DEPOT
Woodwells Farm
WOODWELLS FARM CEMETERY
LUCAS AEROSPACE SPORTS GROUND
MARCHMONT HOUSE POND
Forte Posthouse Hotel
BP Oil Offices
Depot
Junction 8
Junction 7
Leverstock Green
Westwick Farm
Westwick Row Farm
Westwick Hall
Westwick House
Corner Farm
Bunkers Farm
Well Farm
BLACKWATER WOOD
Highwood Hall Farm
High Herts Farm
The Swan PH
Rose Acre
Radio Station
GREAT FURZEFIELD WOOD
POTTERS CROUCH PLANTATION
LONGFIELD SPRING
Maidenscroft
Hill End Farm
Maynes Farm
Gorhambury (Ruins)
GORHAMBURY
CHALK DELL
Cricket Ground
THE WILDERNESS
KENTISH WOOD
THE VISTAS
WINDMILLHILL WOOD
BRUCE'S PLANTATION
BRICKKILN WOOD
CYPRESS WOOD
Kettlewell's Farm
Old Jeromes
Southend Farm
Butler's Farm
Hogg End
Bohemia House
Hill Farm
Potters Crouch
HEMEL HEMPSTEAD ROAD
PUNCH BOWL LANE
HOGG END LANE
BREAKSPEAR WAY
LEVERSTOCK GREEN ROAD
A4147
A414
M1
M10
59
42

42
BW
BX
BY
BZ
CA
CB
CC
12
13
14
09
08
07
06
15
16
17
18
19
20
21
22
23
24
41
60
Punch Bowl PH
Sewage Works
MILL STREAM
BUSH WOOD
Childwick Bury
SPRING WOOD
Bohemia House
Hill Farm
HILL
FARM LANE
PUNCH BOWL LANE
RIVER VER
WATLING STREET (ROMAN ROAD)
A5183
REDBOURN ROAD
New Jerome Cottage
MILL RACE
THE PLANTATION
TOULMIN DRIVE PLAYING FIELD
Pav
Woodlands
Ladygrove
LADIES GROVE WOOD
BATCH WOOD
Stafford Farm
Stafford Stud
Hogg End
HOGG END LANE
WHITEHEDGE SPRING
Tennis Cts
Sports Centre
Bowling Green
Clubhouse
BATCHWOOD GOLF COURSE
Bow Bridge
Old Jeromes
Butler's Farm
AL3
Maynes Farm
Nash's Lodge
DRIVE
WINDMILLHILL WOOD
CHURCHYARD MEADOW
THE WILDERNESS
ONE ACRE
CHALK DELL
GORHAMBURY
Cricket Ground
GILPINS
HUGO'S SPINNEY
Shepherds Cottages
Course of Roman Wall
Gorhambury (Ruins)
BRICKKILN WOOD
CYPRESS WOOD
The Fosse
LORD BACON'S MOUNT
Open Air Theatre
KINGSBURY WATER MILL MUSEUM
St. Michael's Bridge
VERULAMIUM MUSEUM
BELL MEADOW
TEMPLE WOOD
SITE OF ROMAN VERULAMIUM
BLUE HOUSE HILL
Prae Wood House
Praewood Farm
PRAE WOOD
Maynes Farm
SQUARE WOOD
VERULAMIUM PARK
Hypocaust
Tennis Courts
THE LAKE
RIVER VER
HEMEL HEMPSTEAD ROAD
A4147
Hill End Farm
Junction 7
RUNNING TRACK
ABBEY VIEW GOLF COURSE
Sports Centre
Superstore
Sch
ST. ALBAN'S SCHOOL PLAYING FIELD
PLAYING FIELD
St. Stephens
WATLING STREET
M10
LONGFIELD SPRING
Maidenscrouch Farm
MADAM'S WOOD
Windridge Farm
BIRCH WOOD
WINDRIDGE LANE
PARK WOOD
Westfield's Farm
LONG SPRING
Hollybush PH
Potters Crouch East Farm
Potters Crouch Farm
SQUARE WOOD
SCRUBBS WOOD
RAGGED HALL LANE
Cuckman's Farm
ALLOT
REC GRD
ST. JULIAN'S WOOD
M1
WD5
Potters Crouch
AL2
BEDMOND LANE
FURZEBUSHES
CHISWELL GREEN LANE
Plaistowes Farm

CD
CE
CF
CG
CH
CJ
CK
15
16
17
TOMPKINS SPRING
HOME OFFICE
PET CEM
Jersey Farm
JERSEY FARM OPEN SPACE
Sirdane House and Kennels
Nashe's Farm
Glasshouse
Carpenters Nursery
SANDRIDGEBURY
LONG SPRING
THE GLEN
BEECH BOTTOM DYKE
OLD ALBANIAN SPORTS GROUND
HARPENDEN ROAD
A1081
ST. ALBANS ROAD
Marshalswick
Oak Farm
09
08
07
06
18
19
20
21
22
23
24
Townsend
Youth Cen
Fire Sta
Amb Sta
BERNARDS HEATH
REC GRD
ALLOTMENTS
THE WICK
AL4
AL1
PLAYING FIELD
College Farm Buildings
Glasshouses
HOME WOOD
44
ST. ALBANS
Oaklands Coll
CIVIC OFFICES
CLARENCE PARK
HATFIELD ROAD
A1057
ST. ALBANS CEMETERY
War Memorial
Fleetville
Superstore
LONGACRES PLAYING FIELD
BRICK KNOLL PARK
Depot
ST. ALBANS CITY
The Maltings
SPHERE INDUSTRIAL ESTATE
RECREATION GROUND
The Camp
SPORTS GROUND
PLAYING FIELD
Home Farm
VERULAM GOLF COURSE
Tyttenhanger
PLAYING FIELDS
Highfield Farm
Highfield Hall
KNIGHT'S WOOD
NORTH ORBITAL TRADING ESTATE
BIRKLANDS PARK
CEM
Sopwell House Hotel
Sopwell Home Farm
Aylett Nursery
CHALKDELL WOOD
NORTH ORBITAL ROAD
A414
61
COPPICE WOOD
Hedges Farm
SPORTS GRD
PLAYING FIELD
RIVER VER
LONDON ROAD
A1081

44
CL
CM
CN
CP
CQ
CR
CS
19
20
21
28
62
15
16
17
18
19
20
21
22
23
24
09
08
07
06
Jersey Farm
HOME OFFICE
Fairfolds Farm
Sutton's Farm
WOODCOCK HILL
COOPERS GREEN
Coll
Field Cen
Astwick Manor Farm
MANOR RD
HATFIELD BUSINESS PARK
DE HAVILLAND WAY
FROBISHER WAY
AL10
SAND AND GRAVEL PIT
Nashe's Farm
HOOK'S WOOD
SLEEVE HALL WOOD
BALL'S COVERT
OAK WOOD
Beech Farm
Oak Farm
ASH GREEN
WELWYN HATFIELD
ST. ALBANS
ROUND WOOD
HOME COVERT
HATFIELD AERODROME (Disused)
Works
Comet Hotel
OAKLANDS LANE
COOPERS LANE
SANDPIT
Ninefields Nursery
Popefield Farm
College Farm Buildings
BAGGYMEAD SPRING
DRIVE
Coll
Glasshouses
Tenn Cts
PLAYING FIELD
HOME WOOD
43
ST. ALBANS ROAD
HATFIELD ROAD
A1057
Smallford
Wilkin's Green Farm
Nast Hyde Farm
Ellenbrook
Tennis Courts
COMET WAY
Junction 3
RYDER AVE
Sorting Office
ALBAN WAY
Smallford Nurseries
ALBAN INDUSTRIAL PARK
Superstore
Warehouse
Works
Depot
AL4
Sleapshyde Farm
SLEAPSHYDE
SMALLFORD LANE
A414
NORTH ORBITAL ROAD
JOHNSON'S SPRING
Smallford Farm
BUTTERWICK LANE
Coll
Hostel
Tennis Courts
Sch
PLAYING FIELD
Pav
SPORTS GROUND
HOSPITAL (closed)
HIXBERRY LANE
HEATH
Bullen's Green
Barley Mow Caravan Site
Barley Mow Stables
Barley Mow PH
SPORTS GROUND
Clubhouse
Roundhouse Farm
BUR GRD
Hall
Colney Heath
Pumping Station
ROESTOCK PARK
Queens Head PH
Colney Heath Farm
Roestock
PLAYING FIELD
Tyttenhanger
GREEN BARLEY
RIVER COLNE
PARK CORNER
HERTSMERE
SAND AND GRAVEL PIT
Highfield Farm
Highfield Hall
KNIGHT'S WOOD
Clinic
BLOUNT SPRING
Warren Farm
THE WARREN
FREDERICK'S WOOD
COURSERS ROAD
Tyttenhanger Farm
COPPICE WOOD
GARDEN WOOD
THE NEW PLANTATION
Tyttenhanger House
Coursers Farm
A1081
LONDON

CT
CU
CV
CW
CX
CY
CZ
22
23
24
Hatfield Garden Village
MILL GREEN GOLF COURSE
Sewage Works
Clubhouse
MT PLEASANT LA
COUNCIL DEPOT
29
Superstore
PLAYING FIELD
Sports Centre
COMET WAY
A1(M)
HERTFORD ROAD
A414
A1000
THE WARREN
THE BROADWATER
THE VINEYARD
15
16
17
18
19
20
21
22
23
24
09
08
07
06
The Ryde
Birchwood
HOME PARK
HATFIELD
Old Hatfield
THE OLD PALACE
HATFIELD HOUSE
NEW POND
HATFIELD PARK
THE FURZEFIELD
POLLARD WOOD
BRICKKILN WOOD
CONDUIT WOOD
WELLINGTON WOOD
THE ROUGHS
Parks Dairy
46
Roe Green
Oxlease
HOWE DELL
Home Farm
RESERVOIR
COOMBE WOOD
Hertfordshire University
South Hatfield
OXLEYS
SPORTS FIELD
HALFWAYOAK POND
MILLWARD'S PARK
GREAT NORTH ROAD
SOUTHWAY
A1001
Woodside Place Farm
WILDHILL
AL9
HATFIELD DISTRICT CEMETERY
Junction 2
SPORTS GROUND
WELHAM GREEN
Warehouses
Marshmoor Nurseries
Lower Woodside
Marshmoor Bridge
BUSH WOOD
Bell Bar Nursery
Rockwater Nursery
Nursery
The Cock O' the North PH
Skimpans Bridge
Youth & Comm Cen
REC GRD
Potterells Farm
THE LEGG
PELPIN'S WOOD
ROUND WOOD
63
BROOKMANS PARK GOLF COURSE
PLAYING FIELDS
NORTH MYMMS

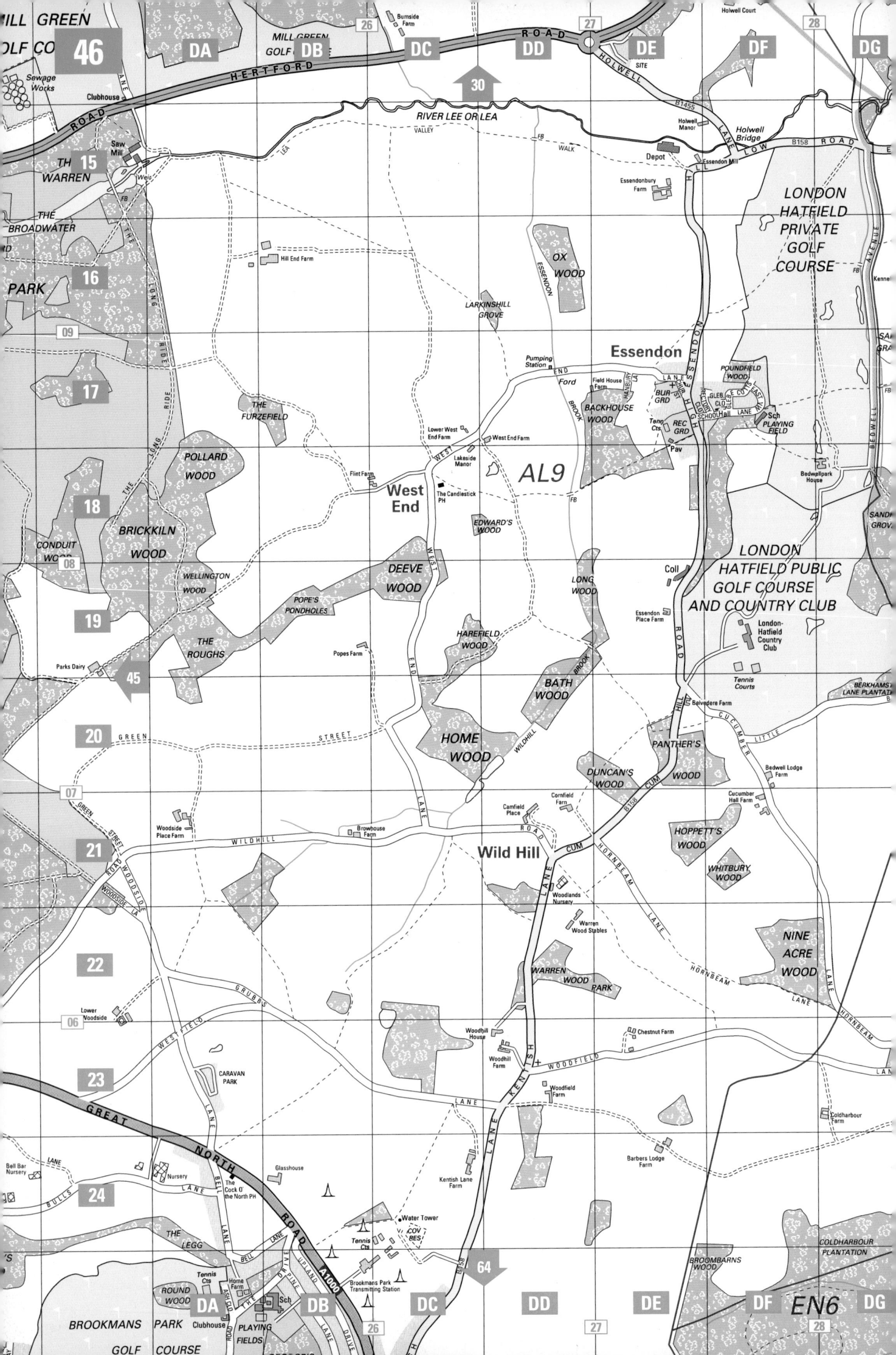

46
30
45
64
DA
DB
DC
DD
DE
DF
DG
MILL GREEN GOLF COURSE
HERTFORD ROAD
HOLWELL
Holwell Court
Burnside Farm
Sewage Works
Clubhouse
Saw Mill
THE WARREN
THE BROADWATER
PARK
RIVER LEE OR LEA
LEA VALLEY WALK
Holwell Manor
Holwell Bridge
Depot
Essendon Mill
Essendonbury Farm
LOW ROAD
B158
B1455
LONDON HATFIELD PRIVATE GOLF COURSE
Hill End Farm
OX WOOD
ESSENDON
LARKINSHILL GROVE
Essendon
Pumping Station
Ford
Field House Farm
BACKHOUSE WOOD
POUNDFIELD WOOD
THE FURZEFIELD
Lower West End Farm
West End Farm
Lakeside Manor
West End
The Candlestick PH
Flint Farm
AL9
POLLARD WOOD
BRICKKILN WOOD
CONDUIT WOOD
WELLINGTON WOOD
EDWARD'S WOOD
DEEVE WOOD
POPE'S PONDHOLES
LONG WOOD
Coll
LONDON HATFIELD PUBLIC GOLF COURSE AND COUNTRY CLUB
London-Hatfield Country Club
Essendon Place Farm
THE ROUGHS
Parks Dairy
Popes Farm
HAREFIELD WOOD
BATH WOOD
Tennis Courts
Belvedere Farm
BERKHAMSTEAD LANE PLANTATION
GREEN STREET
HOME WOOD
WILDHILL
PANTHER'S WOOD
DUNCAN'S WOOD
CUCUMBER LANE
Bedwell Lodge Farm
Cucumber Hall Farm
Woodside Place Farm
Browhouse Farm
Camfield Place
Cornfield Farm
Wild Hill
WILDHILL ROAD
CUM CUM
HOPPETT'S WOOD
WHITBURY WOOD
Woodlands Nursery
Warren Wood Stables
HORNBEAM LANE
NINE ACRE WOOD
WARREN WOOD PARK
Lower Woodside
GRUBBS LANE
WESTFIELD
Woodhill House
Woodhill Farm
Chestnut Farm
WOODFIELD
CARAVAN PARK
Woodfield Farm
KENTISH LANE
Coldharbour Farm
GREAT NORTH ROAD
Bell Bar Nursery
Nursery
The Cock O' the North PH
Glasshouse
Kentish Lane Farm
Barbers Lodge Farm
BULLS LANE
Water Tower
COV RES
THE LEGG
BELL LANE
Tennis Cts
Brookmans Park Transmitting Station
BROOMBARNS WOOD
COLDHARBOUR PLANTATION
ROUND WOOD
Home Farm
Sch
PLAYING FIELDS
BROOKMANS PARK GOLF COURSE
Clubhouse
A1000
EN6
BEDWELL AVENUE
Bedwellpark House
PLAYING FIELD

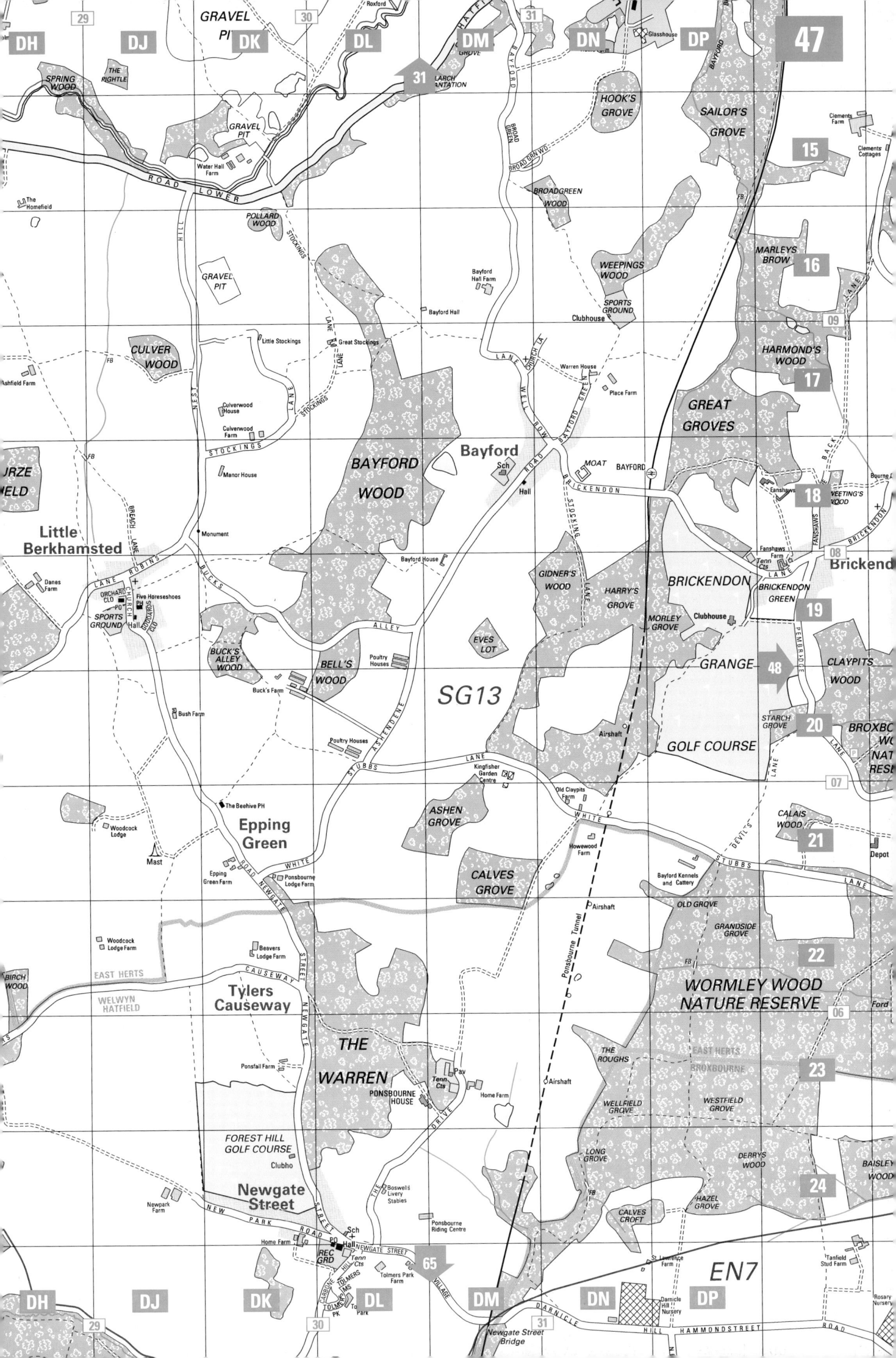
47
DH
DJ
DK
DL
DM
DN
DP
29
30
31
GRAVEL PIT
Roxford
Glasshouse
SPRING WOOD
THE PIGHTLE
31
LARCH PLANTATION
BAYFORD
BROAD GREEN
HOOK'S GROVE
SAILOR'S GROVE
BAYFORD
Clements Farm
Clements Cottages
15
GRAVEL PIT
Water Hall Farm
LOWER ROAD
BROAD GRN WD
BROADGREEN WOOD
The Homefield
POLLARD WOOD
HILL
STOCKINGS
GRAVEL PIT
Bayford Hall Farm
WEEPINGS WOOD
MARLEYS BROW
16
Bayford Hall
SPORTS GROUND
Clubhouse
09
LANE
Little Stockings
Great Stockings
HARMOND'S WOOD
17
CULVER WOOD
FB
Ashfield Farm
CHURCH LA
Warren House
Place Farm
WELL ROW
LANE
BAYFORD GREEN
STOCKINGS LANE
Culverwood House
Culverwood Farm
GREAT GROVES
NEST
STOCKINGS
Bayford
BAYFORD WOOD
Sch
MOAT
BAYFORD
BACK
Manor House
FB
ROAD
Hall
BRICKENDON
Fanshaws
Bourne
18
WEETING'S WOOD
BAYFORD WOOD
STOCKING
BREACH LANE
Little Berkhamsted
Monument
FANSHAWS
BRICKENDON
ROBINS
Bayford House
Fanshaws Farm
Tenn Cts
08
Brickend
LANE
Danes Farm
ORCHARD CLO
CHURCH
Five Horseshoes PH
PO
BUCKS
GIDNER'S WOOD
HARRY'S GROVE
BRICKENDON
BRICKENDON GREEN
19
SPORTS GROUND
GODDARDS CLO
Hall
ALLEY
EVES LOT
MORLEY GROVE
Clubhouse
PEMBRIDGE
BUCK'S ALLEY WOOD
BELL'S WOOD
Poultry Houses
GRANGE
48
CLAYPITS WOOD
Buck's Farm
SG13
Bush Farm
ASHENDENE
Airshaft
STARCH GROVE
20
BROXBO
Poultry Houses
GOLF COURSE
LANE
LANE
STUBBS
Kingfisher Garden Centre
07
Old Claypits Farm
The Beehive PH
ASHEN GROVE
CALAIS WOOD
Woodcock Lodge
Epping Green
WHITE
DEVIL'S
21
Mast
Howewood Farm
Depot
WHITE
STUBBS
Epping Green Farm
ROAD
Ponsbourne Lodge Farm
CALVES GROVE
Bayford Kennels and Cattery
LANE
NEWGATE
Airshaft
OLD GROVE
GRANDSIDE GROVE
Woodcock Lodge Farm
Beavers Lodge Farm
Ponsbourne Tunnel
22
FB
EAST HERTS
CAUSEWAY
BIRCH WOOD
STREET
WORMLEY WOOD NATURE RESERVE
WELWYN HATFIELD
Tylers Causeway
Ford
06
NEWGATE
THE WARREN
THE ROUGHS
EAST HERTS
BROXBOURNE
23
Ponsfall Farm
Tenn Cts
Pav
PONSBOURNE HOUSE
Home Farm
Airshaft
WELLFIELD GROVE
WESTFIELD GROVE
DRIVE
FOREST HILL GOLF COURSE
Clubho
LONG GROVE
DERRYS WOOD
BAISLEY WOOD
Newgate Street
FB
THE
Boswells Livery Stables
24
Newpark Farm
NEW PARK ROAD
STREET
HAZEL GROVE
CALVES CROFT
Ponsbourne Riding Centre
Sch
Home Farm
PO
Hall
NEWGATE STREET
REC GRD
Tenn Cts
65
St Lawrence Farm
EN7
Tanfield Stud Farm
CARBONE HILL
TOLMERS MS
Tolmers Park Farm
VILLAGE
Rosary Nursery
DH
DJ
DK
DL
DM
DN
DP
29
30
31
TOLMERS
PK
Park
Darnicle Hill Nursery
DARNICLE HILL
HAMMONDSTREET ROAD
Newgate Street Bridge

DQ
DR
DS
DT
DU
DV
DW
33
34
35
32
66
47
09
08
07
06
15
16
17
18
19
20
21
22
23
24
SAILOR'S GROVE
MARLEYS BROW
HARMOND'S WOOD
GREAT GROVES
BRICKENDON
MORLEY GROVE
GOLF COURSE
Brickendon
BRICKENDON GREEN
Fanshaws
Fanshaws Farm
SWEETING'S WOOD
Bourne Orchard
Well
Clements Farm
Clements Cottages
LIGHTS WOOD
Edwards Green Farm
Sewards Farm
Monks Green
Poultry Houses
THE GROVE
MONK'S WOOD
Blackfields Farm
MANGROVE LANE
SG13
JEPP'S WOOD
Jepps Farm
DALMOND'S WOOD
Highfield Farm
HIGHFIELD WOOD
HOBBYHORSE WOOD
Elbowlane Farm
ERMINE STREET (ROMAN)
Water Tower
The Huntsman PH
HODDESDON WOOD NATURE RESERVE
BRAMBLE'S WOOD
BOURNE WOOD
COWHEATH WOOD
CLAYPITS WOOD
STARCH GROVE
BROXBOURNE WOOD NATURE RESERVE
HEDGEROWS WOOD
Hedgegrove Farm
DANEMEAD WOOD
BROXBOURNE COMMON
BROAD RIDING WOOD
ROUND GROVE
HAYSTACK GROVE
MARTIN'S GREEN
NURSERY GROVE
CHESTNUT GROVE
GREAT GROVE
LITTLE GROVE
Broxbournebury Mansion Clubho
HERTFORDS GOLF COURS COUNT CLUB
SPITAL BROOK
CALAIS WOOD
Etridge Farm
Depot
Pembridge Lane Farm
STOCKING WOOD
PEMBRIDGE LANE
UPPER WHITE STUBBS
PARADISE WILDLIFE PARK
LOWER WHITE STUBBS
Edgewood Farm
Home Farm
Bayford Kennels and Cattery
WHITE STUBBS LANE
OLD GROVE
GRANDSIDE GROVE
BENCROFT WOOD NATURE RESERVE
MORTALS WOOD
BUSHY PIGHTLE
FIR GROVE
Birch Farm
COV RES
COLDHALL GREEN
White Stubbs Farm
Three Farm Stables
EAST HERTS
BROXBOURNE
WORMLEY WOOD NATURE RESERVE
Wormley West End
Ford
Manor Farm
Barleycroft Farm
The Woodman PH
Holborn Stud Farm
Tudor Farm
Manor House
Bury Farm
WORMLEY BROOK
FIRS WOOD
Brookfields Farm
Brookfields Nursery
BIGS GROVE
WESTFIELD GROVE
BEECH GROVE
NEW PLANTATION
BEAUMONT ROAD
DERRYS WOOD
BAISLEY'S WOOD
Beaumont Manor
Beaumont Manor Farm
BRAMBLE GROVE
THUNDERFIELD GROVE
HAZEL GROVE
Bread and Cheese Bridge
Cheshunt Park Farm
TURNFORD BROOK
PRIESTS OSIERS
SPRING WOOD
St Lawrence Farm
Tanfield Stud Farm
EN7
Danetree Nursery
Darnicle Hill Nursery
Rosary Nursery
Paradise Nursery
Dogge Hill
CROMWELL WOOD
Paradise House
Mast
HAMMONDSTREET ROAD
Francis Farm
APPLEBY STREET

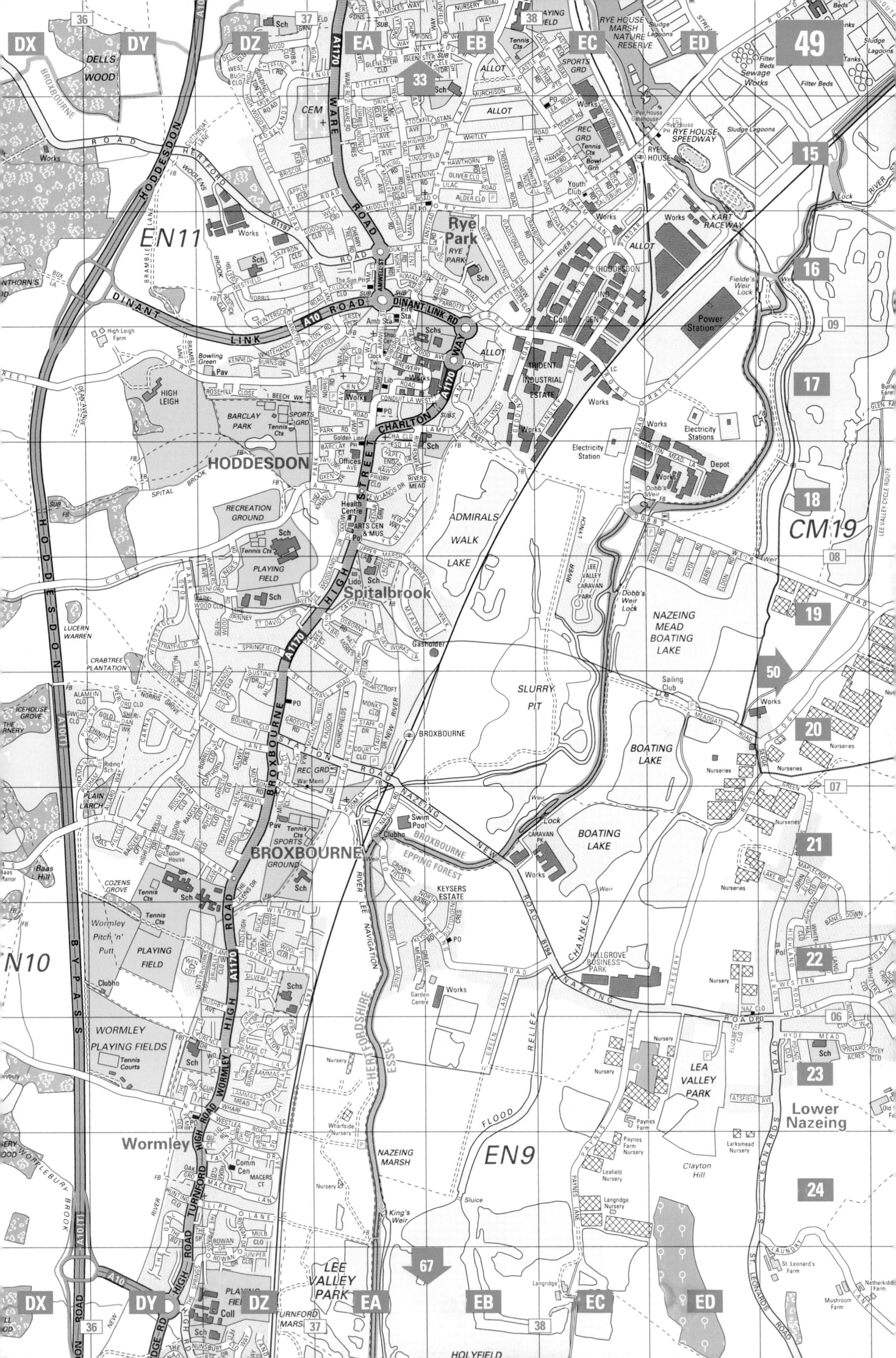
49
DX
DY
DZ
EA
EB
EC
ED
33
50
67
36
37
38
15
16
17
18
19
20
21
22
23
24
09
08
07
06
EN11
EN9
N10
CM19
HODDESDON
BROXBOURNE
Rye Park
Spitalbrook
Wormley
Lower Nazeing
DELLS WOOD
HODDESDON BY PASS
A10
A1170
DINANT LINK ROAD
BRAMBLE LANE
HIGH LEIGH
BARCLAY PARK
RECREATION GROUND
PLAYING FIELD
LUCERN WARREN
CRABTREE PLANTATION
ICEHOUSE GROVE
PLAIN LARCH
Baas Hill
COZENS GROVE
Wormley Pitch 'n' Putt
WORMLEY PLAYING FIELDS
HIGH STREET
CHARLTON WAY
STATION ROAD
SPORTS GROUND
ADMIRALS WALK LAKE
SLURRY PIT
NAZEING MEAD BOATING LAKE
BOATING LAKE
LEA VALLEY PARK
LEE VALLEY PARK
LEE VALLEY CARAVAN PARK
Dobb's Weir Lock
HILLGROVE BUSINESS PARK
KEYSERS ESTATE
NAZEING MARSH
King's Weir
RIVER LEE NAVIGATION
HERTFORDSHIRE
ESSEX
EPPING FOREST
NAZEING NEW ROAD
NAZEING ROAD
FLOOD RELIEF CHANNEL
PAYNES LANE
ST. LEONARDS ROAD
Clayton Hill
St. Leonard's Farm
Power Station
RYE HOUSE MARSH NATURE RESERVE
RYE HOUSE SPEEDWAY
KART RACEWAY
Sewage Works
Filter Beds
Sludge Lagoons
Fielde's Weir Lock
TRIDENT INDUSTRIAL ESTATE
HODDESDON IND CEN
Electricity Stations
Electricity Station
Sailing Club
Nurseries
HOLYFIELD
TURNFORD MARSH

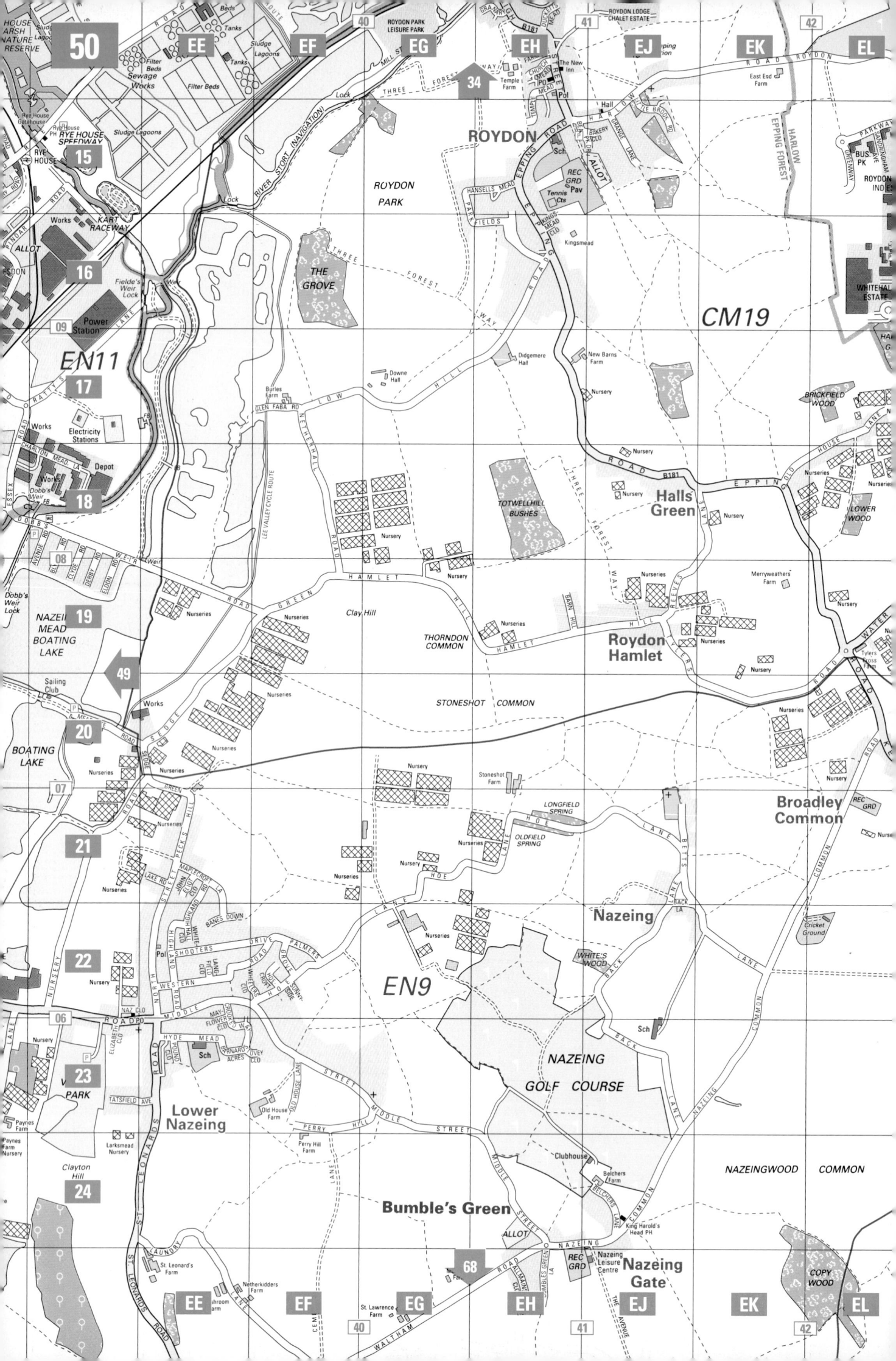
50
EE
EF
EG
EH
EJ
EK
EL
40
41
42
34
ROYDON PARK LEISURE PARK
ROYDON LODGE CHALET ESTATE
Sewage Works
Filter Beds
Sludge Lagoons
Tanks
Sludge Lagoons
Sludge Lagoons
RYE HOUSE SPEEDWAY
Rye House Gatehouse
RYE HOUSE
15
KART RACEWAY
Works
ALLOT
16
Fielde's Weir Lock
Power Station
09
EN11
17
RATTY'S LA
Works
Electricity Stations
CHARLTON MEAD LA
Works
Depot
Dobb's Weir
18
DOBBS WEIR RD
08
AVENUE RD
CLYDE RD
DERBY RD
ELDON RD
Dobb's Weir Lock
NAZEING MEAD BOATING LAKE
19
49
Sailing Club
20
BOATING LAKE
07
21
22
06
23
PARK
Paynes Farm
Paynes Farm Nursery
Clayton Hill
24
RIVER STORT (NAVIGATION)
Lock
THREE FOREST WAY
ROYDON PARK
THE GROVE
Temple Farm
The New Inn
ROYDON
EPPING ROAD
HARLOW RD
HANSELLS MEAD
PARK FIELDS
KINGSMEAD CLO
Sch
REC GRD
Pav
Tennis Cts
ALLOT
Kingsmead
East End Farm
ROYDON ROAD
HARLOW EPPING FOREST
BUS. PK
ROYDON IND ES
WHITEHALL ESTATE
CM19
Didgemere Hall
New Barns Farm
Downe Hall
Burles Farm
GLEN FABA RD
LOW HILL
NETHERHALL ROAD
Nursery
BRICKFIELD WOOD
Nursery
ROAD B181
TOTWELLHILL BUSHES
Halls Green
EPPING ROAD
OLD HOUSE LANE
Nurseries
LOWER WOOD
LEE VALLEY CYCLE ROUTE
HAMLET HILL
Clay Hill
Nurseries
Merryweathers Farm
THORNDON COMMON
Roydon Hamlet
TYLERS
Tylers Cross Farm
WATER LANE
STONESHOT COMMON
Works
SEDGE GREEN
Nurseries
Stoneshot Farm
LONGFIELD SPRING
HOE LANE
OLDFIELD SPRING
BETTS LANE
Broadley Common
REC GRD
PECKS HILL
NORTH STREET
LAKE RD
MAPLECROFT LA
BANES DOWN
SHOOTERS DRIVE
PALMERS GROVE
Nazeing
BACK LA
WHITE'S WOOD
Cricket Ground
EN9
WESTERN ROAD
MIDDLE ROAD
NAZ CLO
HYDE MEAD
Sch
ELIZABETH CLO
TATSFIELD AVE
Lower Nazeing
Old House Farm
OLD HOUSE LANE
PERRY HILL
Perry Hill Farm
MIDDLE STREET
NAZEING GOLF COURSE
BACK LANE
COMMON
NAZEING
Larksmead Nursery
Clubhouse
Belchers Farm
NAZEINGWOOD COMMON
Bumble's Green
King Harold's Head PH
ALLOT
68
REC GRD
Nazeing Leisure Centre
Nazeing Gate
COPY WOOD
St. Leonard's Farm
Netherkidders Farm
ST. LEONARDS ROAD
St. Lawrence Farm
WALTHAM ROAD
BUMBLES GREEN LA
THE AVENUE

51
EM
EN
EP
EQ
ER
ES
ET
43
44
45
35
52
69
15
16
17
18
19
20
21
22
23
24
09
08
07
06
Little Parndon
PRINCESS ALEXANDRA HOSPITAL
Netteswell
South
HARLOW
Harlow College
TOWN HALL
CM20
CM18
CM16
Pinnacles
Hare Street
Great Parndon
Katherines
Passmores
Tye Green
Brays Grove
Latton Bush
Stewards
Sumners
Kingsmoor
Epping Green
NEW FRONTIERS SCIENCE PARK
SMITHKLINE BEECHAM
HASELMERE PINNACLES ESTATE
Works
GYPSY SITE
HARLOW MUS
NETTLESWELL PLANTATION
PLAYING FIELD
SPORTS GROUND
Leisure Centre
Harlow Study & Visitors Centre
PARNDON WOOD NATURE RESERVE
PARNDON WOOD CEM
Crem
RISDEN'S WOOD
HOSPITAL WOOD
MAUND'S WOOD
BURNETT'S WOOD
MARK BUSHES
LATTON COMMON
GRAVEPIT SPRINGS
HARLOW
EPPING FOREST
COBBIN'S BROOK
A1025
A1169
B181
ELIZABETH WAY
THIRD AVENUE
SECOND AVENUE
FOURTH AVENUE
SOUTHERN WAY
KATHERINES WAY
VELIZY AVENUE
TENDRING ROAD
PARINGDON ROAD
COMMONSIDE ROAD
RYE HILL ROAD
EPPING ROAD
UPLAND ROAD
EPPING LANE
PARSLOE ROAD
WOOD LANE
Richmonds Farm
Blake's Farm
Lodge Farm
Summers Farm
The Travellers Friend PH
Epping Green House
Dorrington Farm
Water Tower
COV RES
Rivetts Farm
Marles Farm
Rose Farm
Hayleys Manor Farm
Pinch Timber Farm
Epping Bury Farm Centre
Goldings Farm
Stewards Farm Riding Centre

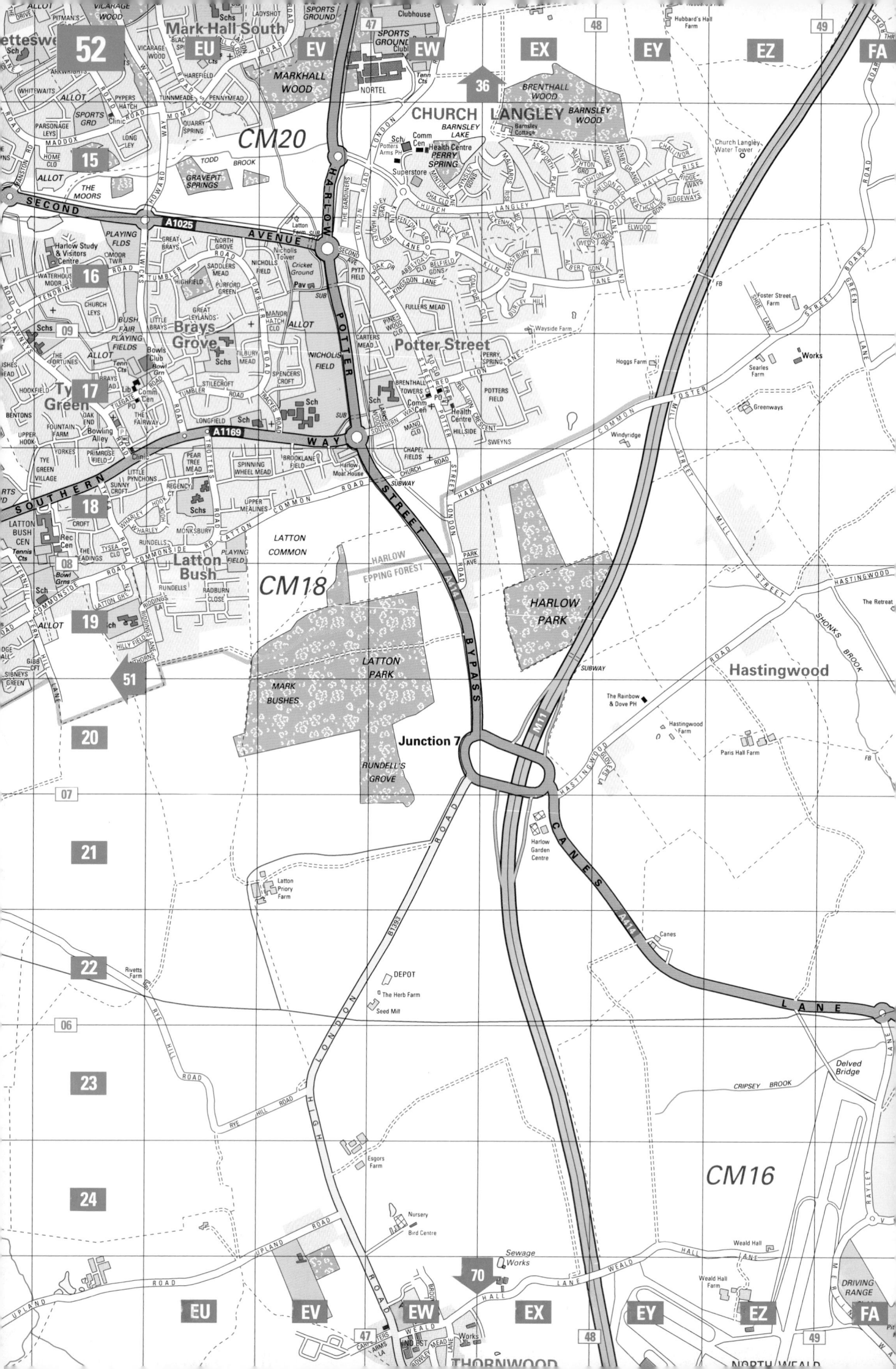

52
Mark Hall South
EU
EV
EW
EX
EY
EZ
FA
47
48
49
36
MARKHALL WOOD
NORTEL
BRENTHALL WOOD
CHURCH LANGLEY
BARNSLEY WOOD
BARNSLEY LAKE
PERRY SPRING
Church Langley Water Tower
CM20
TODD BROOK
GRAVEPIT SPRINGS
THE MOORS
SECOND AVENUE
A1025
HARLOW
POTTER
Harlow Study & Visitors Centre
Brays Grove
Potter Street
Tye Green
A1169
SOUTHERN WAY
LATTON COMMON
CM18
Latton Bush
HARLOW EPPING FOREST
HARLOW PARK
LATTON PARK
MARK BUSHES
RUNDELL'S GROVE
Junction 7
BYPASS
A414
M11
CANES
LANE
Hastingwood
The Rainbow & Dove PH
Hastingwood Farm
Paris Hall Farm
SHONKS BROOK
The Retreat
Foster Street Farm
Searles Farm
Greenways
Windyridge
Hoggs Farm
Wayside Farm
Harlow Garden Centre
Latton Priory Farm
Canes
DEPOT
The Herb Farm
Seed Mill
Rivetts Farm
RYE HILL ROAD
LONDON ROAD
HIGH ROAD
B1393
Delved Bridge
CRIPSEY BROOK
Esgors Farm
Nursery
Bird Centre
CM16
Sewage Works
70
UPLAND ROAD
Weald Hall
Weald Hall Farm
WEALD HALL LANE
DRIVING RANGE
THORNWOOD
NORTH WEALD
51
15
16
17
18
19
20
21
22
23
24
09
08
07
06

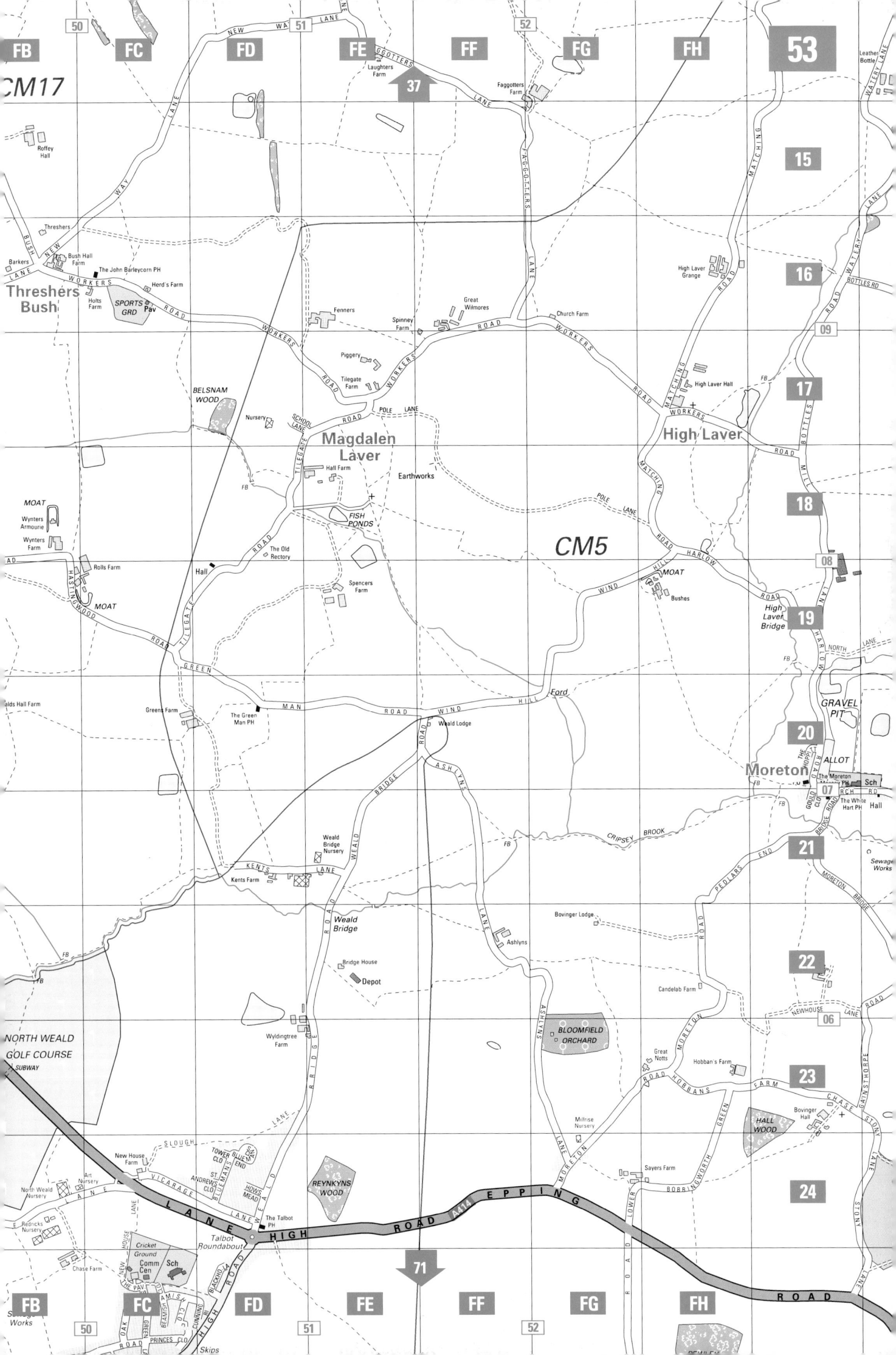
53
CM17
CM5
Threshers Bush
Magdalen Laver
High Laver
Moreton
Weald Bridge
NORTH WEALD GOLF COURSE
Talbot Roundabout
37
71
EPPING ROAD
HIGH ROAD
WORKERS ROAD
NEW WAY LANE
FAGGOTTERS LANE
MATCHING ROAD
HARLOW ROAD
WIND HILL
GREEN MAN ROAD
WEALD BRIDGE ROAD
ASHLYNS LANE
MORETON ROAD
HOBBANS FARM CHASE
BOBBINGWORTH
PEDLARS END
STONY LANE
VICARAGE LANE
KENTS LANE
POLE LANE
TILEGATE ROAD
HASTINGWOOD ROAD
BELSNAM WOOD
FISH PONDS
BLOOMFIELD ORCHARD
REYNKYNS WOOD
HALL WOOD
CRIPSEY BROOK
Sewage Works

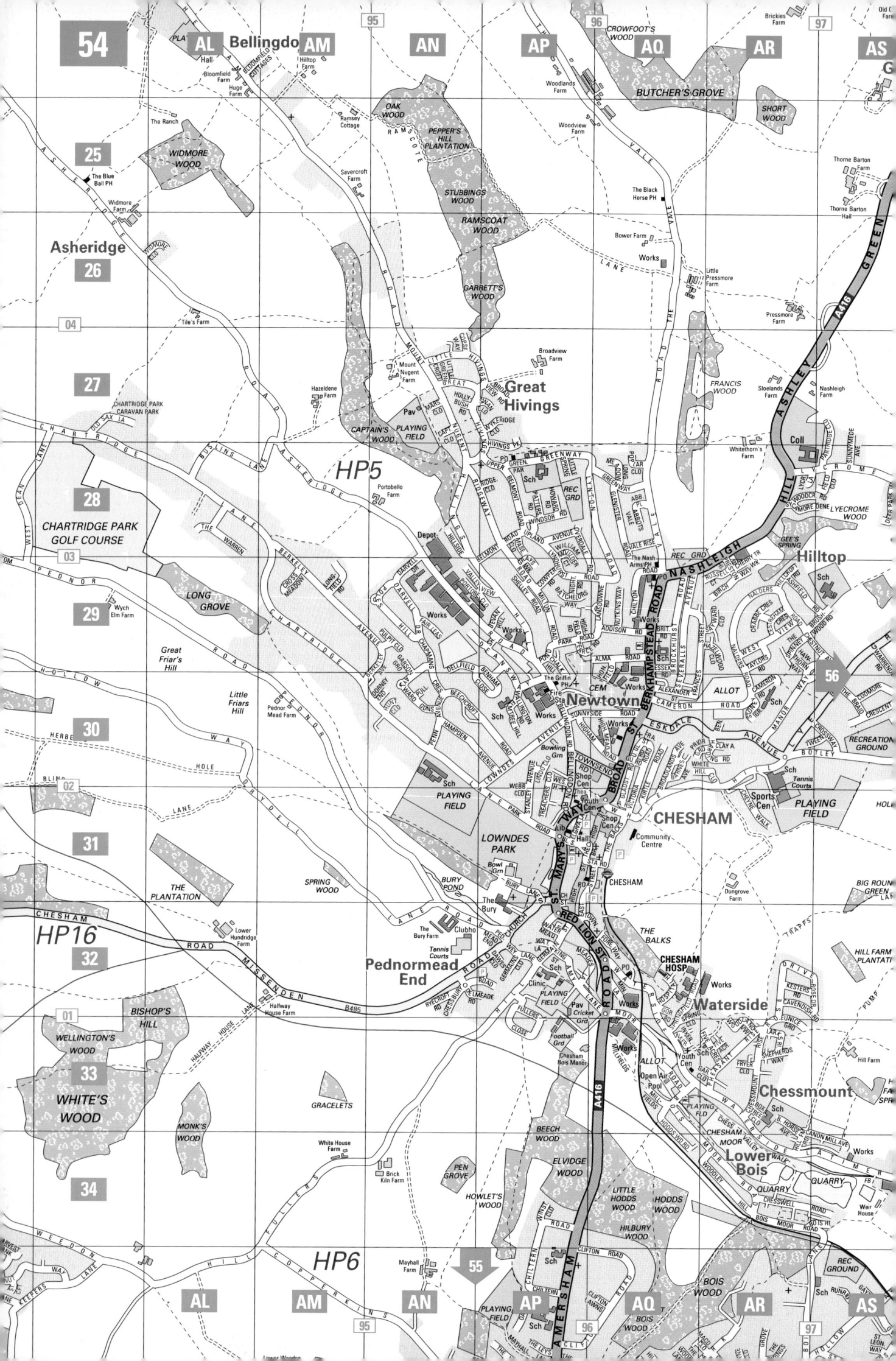

95   96   97

CROWFOOT'S
WOOD

BUTCHER'S GROVE

SHORT
WOOD

25

The Blue
Ball PH

WIDMORE
WOOD

The Black
Horse PH

26

Asheridge

Thorne Barton
Hall

Little
Pressmore
Farm

Pressmore
Farm

04

27

CHARTRIDGE PARK
CARAVAN PARK

HP5

FRANCIS
WOOD

Sloelands
Farm

Nashleigh
Farm

Whitethorn's
Farm

Great
Hivings

Coll

LYECROME
WOOD

28

CHARTRIDGE PARK
GOLF COURSE

Hilltop

03

29

Wych
Elm Farm

LONG
GROVE

Great Friar's
Hill

56

30

Little
Friars Hill

Pednor
Mead Farm

Newtown

CHESHAM

RECREATION
GROUND

02

31

THE
PLANTATION

SPRING
WOOD

LOWNDES
PARK

BIG ROUND
GREEN
FARM

HP16

32

CHESHAM   ROAD

Lower
Hundridge
Farm

Halfway
House Farm

Pednormead
End

CHESHAM
HOSP

Waterside

HILL FARM
PLANTATI

01

BISHOP'S
HILL

WELLINGTON'S
WOOD

Chessmount

33

WHITE'S
WOOD

GRACELETS

MONK'S
WOOD

White House
Farm

Brick
Kiln Farm

PEN
GROVE

BEECH
WOOD

ELVIDGE
WOOD

Lower
Bois

QUARRY

34

HOWLET'S
WOOD

LITTLE
HODDS
WOOD

HODDS
WOOD

HP6

HILBURY
WOOD

BOIS
WOOD

REC
GROUND

55

Mayhall
Farm

PLAYING
FIELD

95   96   97

AL
AM
AN
AP
AQ
AR
AS
54
HP6
HP5
HP7
HP8
Lower Bois
ELVIDGE WOOD
PEN GROVE
HOWLET'S WOOD
Brick Kiln Farm
Mayhall Farm
HILBURY WOOD
BOIS WOOD
GREAT BOIS WOOD
PLAYING FIELD
REC GROUND
Sewage Works
Blackwell Hall
Ivy House Farm
BLACKWELL STUBBS
Chesham Bois
CHESHAM BOIS COMMON
Lower Weedon Hill Farm
WEEDONHILL WOOD
HIGH SPRING
SPORTS GROUND
WINDMILL PLANTATION
OSTLER'S WOOD
SECOND CHARLSEYS WOOD
FIRST CHARLSEYS WOOD
HERVINES PARK
SPORTS GROUND
Quill Hall Farm
AMERSHAM
Allen's Barn Farm
ENGINE HOUSE WOOD
Cricket Ground
PARSONAGE WOOD
HIGH COPPICE
Amersham Old Town
BELLOUSE WOOD
WHEATLEY WOOD
ROUND DELL WOOD
FIRST WOOD
AMERSHAM HOSPITAL
Superstore
The Chequers PH
STANLEY WOOD
Shardeloes Farm
SECOND WOOD
HUNDRED ACRES
Crem
WILLOW WOOD
HOVEL WOOD
Gore Hill
RODGER'S WOOD
BRICKWELL'S WOOD
Depot
Cherry Tree Farm
Coleshill House
Coldharbour Farm
Cricket Ground
Water Twr
DAVID'S WOOD
Quarrendon Farm
Coleshill
Rushymead
BRENTFORD WOOD
DAY'S WOOD
Rushymead Farm
HIGH WOOD
Lower Bottom House Farm
The Red Lion PH
HERTS WOOD
COLESHILL COMMON
BOW WOOD
Upper Bottom House Farm
THE LARCHES
Grange Farm
89
72
A413
A404
A416
A355
AMERSHAM BYPASS
LONDON ROAD WEST
LONDON ROAD EAST
CHESHAM ROAD
AMERSHAM ROAD
WOODSIDE ROAD
STATION ROAD
GORE HILL
WHIELDEN LANE
WHITE LION ROAD
STANLEY HILL
35
36
37
38
39
40
41
42
43
44
95
96
97
98
99

56
AS
AT
AU
AV
AW
AX
AY
HP4
98
99
00
38
Ashley Green
Old Oak Farm
Brickies Farm
Sewage Works
Hall
PO
SNOW HILL
WHITE HILL
Whelpley Hill Farm
Kenmore Farm
GREAT WOOD
SHORT WOOD
Flamstead Farm
25
Thorne Barton Farm
Thorne Barton Hall
PLAYING FLD
The Warren
Sale's Farm
Spencer's Farm
Hemming's Farm
Berry Farm
Whelpley Hill
DELLS LANE
DEAN'S WOOD
Woodside
Grove Farm
GROVE LANE
26
Little Pressmore Farm
Pressmore Farm
04
ASHLEY GREEN ROAD
A416
LITTLE GROVE WOOD
FELMOOR WOOD
BUSH WOOD
Little Grove
Earthworks
FRANCIS WOOD
27
Nashleigh Farm
Torrington Farm
Moors Farm
Lye Green
Electricity Station
Depot
The Black Cat PH
Sch
Coll
Whitethorn's Farm
CROME ROAD
ORCHARD LEIGH
RUSHMERE
Orchard Leigh
B4505
BUCKINGHAMSHIRE
HERTFORDSHIRE
CHESHAM LANE
28
LYECROME WOOD
Lyegreen Farm
DEER PARK WK
GEE'S SPRING
NASHLEIGH HILL
Hilltop
03
New House Farm
POCKETSDELL LANE
Brockhurst Farm
Jasonhill Farm
29
HP5
Codmore
54
ALLOT
Manchant's Farm
CHILTERN LANE
DACORUM
Hall
Crab Tree Farm
30
RECREATION GROUND
BOTLEY ROAD
BOTLEY LA
PO
Sch
Botley
Comm Cen
SHANTOCK
CHESHAM AND LEY HILL GOLF COURSE
Cricket Grd
Game Farm
02
Sports Cen
Tennis Courts
PLAYING FIELD
CHESHAM
HOLLYBUSH WOOD
MAPLE TREE WOOD
KILN LANE
LITTLE WOOD
31
Clubhouse
Flaunden End Farm
SIMON DEAN'S WOOD
Cowcroft Farm
Dungrove Farm
BIG ROUND GREEN
ASHRIDGE RD
Ashridge Farm
COWCROFT WOOD
Barns
LONG KNOTTS
HORSE HILL
32
HILL FARM PLANTATION
CHESHAM HOSP
Works
Waterside
Brickworks
HORSEHILL SPRING
01
FURZEFIELD WOOD
PINNER GREEN
KNOTTS SPRING
Hill Farm
Youth Cen
Hockley Farm
33
Chessmount
HILL FARM SPRING
Cattle Shed
White End Park Farm
BLACKWELL HALL LANE
CODMORE WOOD ROAD
CODMORE WOOD
CHALK DELL
BUNN'S LANE
Lower Bois
QUARRY
Works
34
WYCHFIELD SPRING
Weir House
Works
FRITH WOOD
HP6
BOIS WOOD
REC GROUND
Sch
72
Sewage Works
CHESS VALLEY WALK
Blackwell Hall
Blackwell Farm
NETHER DITCH
FOUR ACRES
STOCKINGS
WEST JACK OF WADLEY'S

57
AZ
BA
BB
BC
BD
BE
BF
01
02
03
04
HP1
HP3
WD3
WD4
39
58
73
25
26
27
28
29
30
31
32
33
34
COLESHILL WOOD
HANGING WOOD
LITTLE HAY GOLF COMPLEX
Clubhouse
HAY WOOD
BOXMOOR GOLF CLUB
SHEETHANGER COMMON
Howe's Retreat
Felden Lodge
BURY WOOD
RAMACRE WOOD
GORSEFIELD WOOD
BOX LANE
FEATHERBED LANE
HIGHCROFT ROAD
Tower Farm
Felden Grange
Felden Manor
FELDEN LANE
UPPER BOURNE END LANE
COVERED RESERVOIR
BURY RISE
Longcroft Farm
B4505
BUSHFIELD ROAD
SHOTHANGER WAY
RAINHILL SPRING
HEMPSTEAD ROAD
DISUSED AIRFIELD
The Bobsleigh Inn
RAINHILL DELL
KINGSHILL DELL
SHORTRIDGE WOOD
OLD DEAN
YOUNG OFFENDERS INSTITUTION
Duckhall Farm
Honours Farm
Random Farm
HOMEFIELD SPRING
BULSTRODE LANE
STONEY LANE
Bury Farm
Sch
Lib
PO
Hall
Fire Sta
CHURCH STREET
MOLYNEAUX AVENUE
Dormers
Lane Farm
Nuffield Farm
BUCKLERS LANE
CHESHAM ROAD
CHIPPERFIELD ROAD
LONGCROFT LANE
FLAUNDEN LANE
BOVINGDON
Rent Street Farm
Street Farm
Darley Ash
Greinan Farm
Bulstrode Farm
Bovingdon Grange
Grange Farm
Pav
Football Grd
SPORTS GRD
Cross Farm
TOWER HILL
Green Farm
GREEN LANE
Bryant's Nursery
HUNTERS CLO
THE HOLLIES
MIDDLE LANE
Tenements Farm
Long Lane Farm
Stoney Lane Nurseries
NEW ROAD
The Boot PH
Tuffs Farm
Frenches Farm
SCATTERDELLS LANE
Riding School
Cottingham Farm
Bell Farm
Mast
Shantock Nursery
Meadow Way Farm
HOLLY HEDGES LANE
Chipperfield House
Chipperfield Garden Centre
Works
Depot
Crumlin Farm
Shantock Farm
Chiltern Farm
LONG LANE
VENUS HILL
Venus Hill Dairy Farm
New Maulden Farm
CHIPPERFIELD
WOODMAN'S WOOD
Two Brewers PH
War Memorial
ALLOT
Cricket Grd
Hogpits Bottom
FLAUNDEN PARK
Woodman's Farm
Rose Farm
HOGPITS BOTTOM
The Bricklayer's Arms PH
LOWER PLANTATION
OLLEBERRIE LANE
WINDMILL HILL
LITTLE WINDMILL HILL
CHIPPERFIELD COMMON
DUNNY LANE
Cherry Trees Farm
Stables
BIRCH LANE
HOG PITS
Dale Farm
Sharlowe's Farm
Olleberrie Farm
Flaunden
Hall
FLAUNDEN LANE
FLAUNDEN SPRING
FLAUNDEN HILL
Springview Farm
Whitedell Farm
BRAGMANS LANE
POLES HILL
PLOUGH LANE
LIMEDELL SPRING
Newhouse Farm
Rose Hall Farm
DEBARDINE WOOD
ROSEHALL WOOD
PLOUGH WOOD
HILLMEADS SPRING
PENMANS GREEN
Dellfield
Great Sarratt Hall Farm
HANGING CROFT
Moonshine Farm
CHENIES HILL
Mast
R.A.F. Chenies
DACORUM
THREE RIVERS
TOP SPRING
OLDCROFT WOOD
DAFFODIL SPRING
THE LANE
RED LION LANE
SARRATT
Martin Top Farm
HANGINGLANE WOOD
BRAMBLE CROFT

Felden
Apsley
HP3
SHEETHANGER COMMON
Felden Lodge
Howe's Retreat
Tower Farm
Felden Grange
Felden Manor
Longcroft Farm
APSLEY RETAIL PARK
Works
SHENDISH HOUSE GOLF COURSE
SPORTS GROUND
COCK'S HEAD WOOD
HEN'S HEAD WOOD
Cricket Ground
Manor Farm
Tennis Courts
Bowl Grn
SHENDISH HOUSE CONFERENCE & LEISURE CENTRE
GRAND UNION CANAL
GREAT WOOD
PHASELS WOOD
Phasels Wood Activity Centre
OLD DEAN
The Eagle Tavern PH
Barnes Lodge
RUCKLERS WOOD
MERCEYS WOOD
DARK WOOD
THE HANGINGS
THE NUCKET
Badgerdell
Barnes Farm
Bulstrode Farm
SCATTERDELLS WOOD
THE GROVE
THE WINGS
Sec Sch
Prim Sch
KING LANGLEY COMMON
Cricket Club
Hill Farm
Fire Sta
Priory (Remains of)
Kings Langley
Tenements Farm
The Boot PH
Tuffs Farm
Chipperfield House
Meggacres Farm
Whippendell Farm
Whippendell Bottom
Whippendell Hill
Kings Langley Riding School
Ballspond Farm
Garden Centre
Depot
Chipperfield
WD4
ROOKERY WOOD
Two Brewers PH
Rose Farm
CHIPPERFIELD COMMON
Manor House
Berrybush Farm
Sunbury Hill Farm
Langley Lodge
Langley Lodge Farm
Burlew Farm
Middle Farm
PENMAN'S GREEN
Belsize
The Plough PH
DACORUM
THREE RIVERS
Hillmeads Farm
Callipers Hall
Callipers Hall Farm
BERRYBUSHES WOOD
DEBARDINE WOOD
PLOUGH WOOD
Cart & Horses PH
Baytree Farm
Model Farm
SHEEPCOTE SPRING
HILLMEADS SPRING
Commonwood
Dellfield
Great Sarratt Hall Farm
Great Sarratt Hall
COMMONWOOD COMMON
Bucks Hill Farm
Bucks Hill
HAWK SPRING
BEECHEN BOTTOM
Little Westwood Farm
Sarratt
The Boot PH
HIGH SPRING
JUNIPER
Wayside Farm
Rectory Farm
A41 KINGS LANGLEY BYPASS
A4251 LONDON ROAD
HEMPSTEAD ROAD
HIGH STREET
RUCKLERS LANE
BARNES LANE
CHIPPERFIELD ROAD
BUCKS HILL
QUICKMOOR LANE
LANGLEY LODGE LANE
25 26 27 28 29 30 31 32 33 34
BG BH BJ BK BL BM BN
01 02 03 04 05 06 07
40 57 74

59
BP
BQ
BR
BS
BT
BU
BV
08
09
10
41
25
26
27
28
29
30
31
32
33
34
04
03
02
01
60
75
HP3
WD5
WD2
POTTERS CROUCH PLANTATION
APPSPOND
LONG DEANS
Highwood Hall Farm
Herts Farm
Bedmond House
Rose Acre
Radio Station
Hyde Meadow Farm
HYDE LANE SPRING
Hyde Springs
Hyde Lane Farm
Hyde Farm
Pimlico House
NEW PLANTATION
Little Abbots
Hart Hall
Green End Farm
White House Farm
Hart Hall Farm
Verulam Farm
NEWLANDS
ST. ALBANS THREE RIVERS
WELLFIELD SPRING
DEADMAN WOOD
BEDMOND WOOD
Serge Hill
Whitehouse Farm
White Hart PH
PIECORNER WOOD
HANGING WOOD
FURZEFIELD WOOD
JOB'S WOOD
Bedmond
BEDMOND PLAYING FIELDS
Prim Sch
MOOR WOOD
Bell Inn PH
Ninnings Farm
Millhouse Farm
Searches Farm
Poultry Farm
Tenements Farm
Hilltop Farm
ASH VIEW MOBILE HOME PARK
LONG SPRING
Benmore Farm
Glasshouse
GREAT NOTLEY
Junction 21 M25
Junction 6A M1
M25
M1
STOWES WOOD
Numbers Farm
Ovaltine Dairy Farm
Mansion House Farm
LITTLE NOTLEY
COVERED RESERVOIR
LONG WOOD
ROUND WOOD
Works
KINGS LANGLEY
CEM
Lib
Hall
PO
Youth Cen
Manor Lo
ABBOTS LANGLEY
MANOR HOUSE GROUNDS
Pav
Sch
Clinic
TANNERS WOOD
LEAVESDEN COUNTRY PARK
Fortunes Farm
BLOOM WOOD
Garston Manor Rehab. Cen
Sports Centre
Sec Sch
Garston Manor Sch
Junction 20
GRAND UNION CANAL
WATFORD ROAD
Hunton Bridge
The Kings Head PH
Langleybury
THE ROOKERY
SPORTS GROUND
HILL FARM IND EST
SOUTH WAY PLAYING FLD
Tennis Courts
Bowl Grn
Leavesden Studios
Hazelwood
Woodside
WOODSIDE STADIUM
Leisure Cen
WOODSIDE PLAYING FIELDS
ALBAN WOOD
Cricket Ground
Cinema
Leisure Centre
Comm Cen
Medical Cen
Leavesden Green
Kingswood
Garston
NORTH WATFORD CEMETERY
STANBOROUGH PARK
Airshafts
NORTH WESTERN AVENUE
NORTH ORBITAL ROAD
KINGSWAY
A405
A41
A412
ST ALBANS ROAD
WATFORD
RIVER GADE

BW
BX
BY
BZ
CA
CB
CC
12
13
14
42
59
76
25
26
27
28
29
30
31
32
33
34
04
03
02
01
APPSPOND WOOD
PARK WOOD
Holly Bush PH
Potters Crouch Farm
Potters Crouch East Farm
SQUARE WOOD
SCRUBBS WOOD
Westfields Farm
Cuckman's Farm
RAGGED HALL LANE
BEDMOND LANE
BLUNTS LANE
Potters Crouch
WELLFIELD SPRING
CHISWELL GREEN LANE
FURZEBUSHES LANE
Plaistowes Farm
NOKE LANE
Bone Hill
THE GDNS OF THE ROSE
Chiswellgreen Farm
The Three Hammers PH
AL2
Chiswell Green
WHITEHOUSE LANE
Whitehouse Farm
HANGING WOOD
FURZEFIELD WOOD
JOB'S WOOD
Millhouse Farm
SEARCHES LANE
Searches Farm
HOLT WOOD
Holt Farm
Moat
Noke Farm
Noke Lane Business Centre
The Noke Thistle Hotel
Burston Manor Farm
Garden Cen
Burston Nursery
Birchwood Farm
HOW WOOD
How Wood
BIRCH WOOD
Lido
Tennis Courts
SUNFOLKS
Kettlewell Farm
Lye House
Clubhouse
Cricket Ground
BLACKGREEN WOOD
Junction 21A
NORTH ORBITAL ROAD
M25
M1
A405
WD5
Tene Farm
Junction 21 M25
Junction 6A M1
WINCH HILL WOOD
Bricket Wood
ST. ALBANS
THREE RIVERS
CEM
CHEQUERS LANE
Fortunes Farm
Junction 6
BLOOM WOOD
Pav
Sch
BLACK GREEN
SMUG OAK GREEN BUSINESS CENTRE
Social Club
SMUG OAK GREEN
The Gate PH
SPORTS GROUND
BRICKET WOOD
Sports Centre
Prim Sch
Garston Manor Rehab. Cen
Sec Sch
Sports Centre
BENSKINS SPORTS GRD
Depot
Crem
Brookdell Farm
ST. ALBANS ROAD
PENFOLD PARK GOLF COURSE
NOTTLERS WOOD
Nottlers House
BRICKET WOOD COMMON
BUILDING RESEARCH ESTABLISHMENT
SPORTS GRD
Pumping Sta
JACK WILLIAM'S WOOD
NEW PLANTATION
WD2
Garston Manor Sch
Health Cen
Comm Cen
Leisure Cen
WOODSIDE STADIUM
PITCH
WOODSIDE PLAYING FIELDS
MUTCHETTS WOOD
Little Munden Farm
River Colne
COMMONMEADOW LANE
Cricket Ground
Cinema
Leisure Centre
KINGSWAY
Three Horseshoes PH
KYTES ESTATE
COLDHARBOUR PLANTATION
FOUR ACRE PLANTATION
GARSTON PARK
BUS GAR
CRAB WOOD
PEARTREE WOOD
Ford
HERTSMERE
Kingswood
Medical Cen
Garston Park Parade
A412
MUNDEN SPRING
Munden House
WATFORD
GARSTON
Garston
NORTH WATFORD CEMETERY
STANBOROUGH PARK
Meriden
Tenn Cts
Bowl Grn
SPORTS GROUND

CD
CE
CF
CG
CH
CJ
CK
15
16
17
43
AL1
AL4
AL2
WD7
VERULAM GOLF COURSE
NORTH ORBITAL ROAD
A414
LONDON ROAD
A1081
NORTH ORBITAL ROAD
CHALKDELL WOOD
Hedges Farm
Sopwell House
Mill Stream
River Ver
Park Street
PARK STREET
Frogmore
FROGMORE
FROGMORE HOME PARK
PARK INDUSTRIAL ESTATE
Radlett Aerodrome (Disused)
GRAVEL PIT
NAPSBURY HOSPITAL
Napsbury Farm
SHENLEY LANE
B5378
VERULAM R.F.C.
COLUMBANS SPORTS GRD
SPORTS GROUND
SPORTS GRD
Aylett Nursery
LONDON COLNEY
COPPICE WOOD
BIG MAYFIELD WOOD
BROAD COLNEY LAKES NATURE RESERVE
Broad Colney Bridge
River Colne
Fir Tree Farm
Superstore
ALL SAINTS PASTORAL CENTRE
25
26
27
28
29
30
31
32
33
34
62
77
04
03
02
01
M25
B556
QUARRY
COLNEY PARK
VENTURA PARK
OLD PARKBURY LANE
Old Parkbury
Colney Street Farm
The George & Dragon PH
The Red Cow PH
Colney Street
Colney Street Bridge
A5183
RADLETT ROAD
WATLING STREET
Harper Lane Rail Depot
HARPER LANE
The Black Horse PH
RADLETT GOLF RANGE
Houndswood
Houndswood Farm
HOUND'S WOOD
Harper Lodge Farm and Stables
HARPERBURY HOSPITAL
SPORTS GRDS
NINE ACRES
HERTSMERE
ST. ALBANS
Wild Farm
Moat
SHENLEYBURY
COW BANKS
SHENLEY PARK
PORTERS PARK GOLF COURSE
SAND PLANTATION
Cricket Ground
Clubhouse
Netherwylde Farm
Pumping Sta
Hill Farm
Starveacres
RIVERSIDE WAY
DROP LANE
Sewage Works
RADLETT
RADLETT ROAD
Auriol Farm
Wood Hall

CL
CM
CN
CP
CQ
CR
CS
19
20
21
44
GRAVEL PIT
Highfield Hall
Warren Farm
THE WARREN
FREDERICK'S WOOD
WELWYN HATFIELD
HERTSMERE
ST. ALBANS
A414 NORTH
LONDON COLNEY BYPASS
A1081
COPPICE WOOD
(SITE OF SPECIAL SCIENTIFIC INTEREST)
WHITE HORSE LANE
Tyttenhanger House
GARDEN WOOD
Tyttenhanger Farm
THE NEW PLANTATION
Coursers Farm
COURSERS ROAD
River Colne
FB
BIG MAYFIELD WOOD
Bowmansgreen Farm
AL4
WALSINGHAM WOOD
25
26
27
28
29
30
31
32
33
34
03
02
01
04
ALEXANDER RD
FIVE ACRES
HIGH STREET
Prim Sch
Rec Cen
Tenn Cts
PERHAM WAY
MORRIS WAY
Works
PO
MORRIS PLAYING FLD
Pav
LONDON COLNEY
ALLOT
Lib
Comm Cen
Prim Sch
COLLYER ROAD
ST ANNE'S ROAD
WALSINGHAM WAY
BROAD COLNEY LAKES NATURE RESERVE
LOWBELL LANE
COLNE GDNS
RIVERSIDE
WATERSIDE
WILLOWSIDE
BARNET ROAD
HAMSDALE
WYEDALE
ESKDALE
RIDGEVIEW LODGE
Junction 22
The Bell PH
Superstore
AL2
Tree Farm
Broad Colney Bridge
B5378
B556
BELL LANE
ST. ALBANS ROAD
M25
Gordon Hall Building
Tennis Courts
UNIVERSITY COLLEGE LONDON SPORTS GROUNDS
Salisbury Hall
Salisbury Hall Farm
MOAT
DE HAVILLAND MOSQUITO AIRCRAFT MUSEUM
ROUND WOOD
Redwell Wood Farm
REDWELL WOOD
61
SHENLEYBURY
FARM CLOSE
DELL GROVE
SHENLEYBURY COTTS
Sch
Ridgehill
PACKHORSE LANE
Southridge Animal Centre R.S.P.C.A.
WD7
HERTSMERE
ST. ALBANS
RECTORY LANE
BLACK LION HILL
COMBE WOOD
NORTH AVENUE
COW BANKS
KING CHARLES RD
Rectory Farm
Shenley Hill Stud Farm
Shenley Hill
Rabley Park Farm
Rabley Park
Catherine Bourne
St. Catherine's Farm
MIMMS LANE
Ravenscroft Court
DEEVES HALL LANE
Wild Farm
Moat
PORTERS PARK DRIVE
SHENLEY MANOR
GRACE AVENUE
SHENLEY PARK
The Black Lion PH
LONDON ROAD
CAGE POND RD
SPORTS GRD
Hall
Shenley
WD6
LITTLERIDGE WOOD
BIGPURSLEY WOOD
Ridge Farm
Tenn Cts
WALLED GDN
Cricket Ground
SAND PLANTATION
SPORTS GRD
Prim Sch
NEWCOME RD
BIRCH WD
The Garden Nursery
Tokonoma Bonsai
Pursley Farm
ALLOT
SPORTS GRD
GREEN STREET
Cricket Ground
78
LITTLEPURSLEY WOOD
CROSSOAKS LANE
Crossoaks
CROSS OAKS WOOD
SUMMERHOUSE
RADLETT LANE
THE GORSE
Auriol Farm
WOODHALL LANE
Wood Hall

63
CT
CU
CV
CW
CX
CY
CZ
22
23
24
45
64
79
25
26
27
28
29
30
31
32
33
34
AL9
EN6
BROOKMANS PARK
Water End
South Mimms
POTTERS BAR
Bentley Heath
Dancers
TH MYMMS PARK
North Mymms Park Training Centre
BROOKMANS PARK GOLF COURSE
POTTERS BAR GOLF COURSE
PELPIN'S WOOD
ROUND WOOD
THE LEGG
BRICK KILN WOOD
CANGSLEY WOOD
HAWKSHEAD WOOD
MYMMSHALL WOOD
PILVAGE WOOD
FURZEFIELD WOOD
GOBIONS OPEN SPACE
GOBIONS GARDEN
GOBIONS POND
Deep Bottom
SWALLOW HOLE
Royal Veterinary College (Hawkshead House)
Royal Veterinary College (Boltons Park Farm)
SPORTS GROUND
KING GEORGE V PLAYING FLDS
CRANBORNE INDUSTRIAL ESTATE
WELWYN HATFIELD
HERTSMERE
Site of Motte & Baileys
Forte Posthouse South Mimms
South Mimms Services
Nat Inst. for Biological Standards & Control
Junction 1 A1(M)
A1(M)
M25
B556
DIXONS HILL ROAD
SWANLAND ROAD
WARRENGATE ROAD
HAWKSHEAD LANE
HAWKSHEAD ROAD
MUTTON LANE
CECIL ROAD
BLANCHE LANE
ST. ALBANS ROAD
BAKER STREET
BENTLEY HEATH LANE
BRIDGEFOOT LANE
BULLS LANE
BRADMORE LANE
WISE'S LANE
STATION ROAD
MOFFATS LANE
BROOKMANS AVENUE
BLUEBRIDGE ROAD
DARKES LANE
THE AVENUE
HEATH ROAD
SUNNYBANK ROAD
Mimmshall Brook
Catherine Bourne

DA
DB
DC
DD
DE
DF
DG
26
27
28
46
63
80
25
26
27
28
29
30
31
32
33
34
04
03
02
01
M.K.M. Nurseries
Nursery
Glasshouse
The Cock o' the North PH
Kentish Lane Farm
Water Tower
COV RES
Tenn Cts
Brookmans Park Transmitting Station
THE LEGG
BELL LANE
ROUND WOOD
Home Farm
Tennis Courts
BROOKMANS PARK
GOLF COURSE
Clubhouse
Sec Sch
GEORGE'S WOOD
GREAT NORTH ROAD
A1000
UPLAND DRIVE
PINE GROVE
KENTISH LANE
B158
BROOMBARNS WOOD
COLDHARBOUR PLANTATION
Rowbourne Hill
GREAT
FB
BROOKMANS PARK
AVENUE
GEORGE'S WOOD ROAD
MOFFATS CL
PARK CL
MYMMS
BROOKMANS LANE
CALDER AVENUE
THE CLOSE
MOFFATS LANE
THE GROVE
SHRUBLANDS
CALDER AV
WOODLANDS
BLUEBRIDGE AV
GOBIONS OPEN SPACE
GOBIONS GARDEN
GOBIONS POND
DRIVE
SHEPHERDS WAY
B157
LYSLEY PL
RAMSEY CL
THE RIDGEWAY
SPORTS GROUND
Tennis Courts
Tenn Cen
CHAPEL CL
Queenswood Sch
AL9
Blue Bridge
Deep Bottom
SWALLOW HOLE
GOBIONS WOOD
WELL WOOD
LEGGATTS WOOD
WELL ROAD
HAWKSHEAD ROAD
SWANLEY BAR LANE
ORCHARD WY
SWANLEY CRES
Royal Veterinary College (Boltons Park Farm)
Leggatts Park
NYN POND
THE VINEYARD
WELWYN HATFIELD
HERTSMERE
POTTERS BAR
GOLF COURSE
JUDGES HILL
B156
NORTHAW PLACE
Northaw House
The Sun PH
Stud Farm
War Meml
CHURCH LA
VINEYARDS
Schs
Tenn Cts
SPORTS GRD
Two Brewers PH
Northaw
PO
NORTHAW
Springfield
GRESLEY CT
Prim Sch
Cricket Ground
GRN MEADOW
WESTWOOD CL
HEATH
MANOR WAY
MOUNTWAY
Sch
NEWLANDS
GRANGEWOOD
CRANMER CL
HEATHFIELD
OSBORNE RD
THORNTON ROAD
FRAMPTON RD
COOPERS RD
SPORTS GRD
HATFIELD RD
HERONFIELD
CHURCH ROAD
QUAKERS LANE
SANDRINGHAM
CEDAR CL
DRIVE
AVENUE
Sec Sch
SPORTS GROUND
Pav
Tennis Courts
COOPERS LANE
EN6
Morven (NT)
NORTHLANDS
Chequers PH
CAUSEWAY
B156
MOUNT GRACE ROAD
BILLY LOWS LANE
Clubhouse
MANOR ROAD
Works
STATION CLOSE
RITZ COURT
PO
PARK DR
DARKES
THE SERVICE RD
STRAFFORD GATE
DRIVE
LADBROOKE DRIVE
WAY
HIGHFIELD
PARKFIELD OPEN SPACE
RICHMOND CT
Works
BUS GAR
Elec Sta
Clinic
Lib
COTTON ROAD
OAKMERE LANE
TREWENNA DR
THE SPINNEY
TAVIST CL
STAPLETON ROAD
TIVERTON ROAD
HATHERL GDNS
TORRINGTON DR
Pol
Sch
HIGH STREET
Little Heath Riding Stables
HOOK WOOD
FISH POND
HOOK LANE
Oshwal House
Oshwal Centre
FIVE ACRE WOOD
FIR WOOD
Prim Sch
Youth & Comm Cen
COOPERS LANE
Superstore
Sta
POTTERS BAR
METROPOLITAN HO
Prim Sch
Potters Bar FC
Med Cen
OAKMERE PARK
CHACE AVENUE
THE WALK
Cricket Club
Bowls Club
Superstore
Offices
Fire Sta
Amb Sta
BIRCH GROVE
STRAFFORD GATE
MUTTON LANE
B556
War Meml
CEM
THE CLOSE
Prim Sch
Comm Cen
LAUREL FIELDS
CLIVE CLOSE
LAUREL AVENUE
ALLANDALE
OAKLANDS GDNS
SHERWOOD AVENUE
EMSCROFT GDNS
HEATHER WAY
ALLOT
DALESIDE DR
FAIRACRES CL
SUNNYBANK
THE BYWAY
BRACKENDALE
ELMROYD CL
AVENUE
THE SHRUBLANDS
AKROYD
Rydal Mount
Prim Sch
FIELD VIEW RD
THE GREENWAY
Prim Schs
MEADOW WAY
SUNNYBANK RD
HUNTER
WILLOW WA
BEECHWOOD
ASHWOOD
FIRS LA
CHERRY TREE LANE
WHALEY RD
ST JOHN'S
SOUTHGATE ROAD
A111
ST VINCENTS
ST FRANCIS
MANDEVILLE RD
TEMPEST
FORBES
CARPENTER
ALLOT
OAKMERE AVENUE
PARK AVENUE
KEMBLE CL
HONEYWOOD CL
CONINGSBY DR
Foxhole Hill
HERTSMERE
ENFIELD
Hooke Hill
POND WOOD
Turkey Brook
HILL RISE
HILL CREST
POTTERS BAR COMMUNITY HOSP
BYERS
POWIS CT
BARNET ROAD
DOVE LA
M25
FB
BENTLEY HEATH LANE
Elm Farm
Bentley Heath Farm
Bentley Heath
Ganwick Corner
Duke of York PH
Chase Farm
Junc 24
THE STAGG
FIR WOOD
Fenny Shade Hill
New Cottage Farm
Nursery
THE RIDGEWAY
A1005
Prep Sch
Water Tower
Plumridge Hill

65
47
66
81
Newgate Street
SG13
Justice Hill
WOOD
Grimes Bottom
Cuffley Camp
HOME WOOD
Carbone Bottom
Tolmers Scout Camp
WORMLEY WOOD
CHESHUNT COMMON
Cuffley
Goffs Oak
EN7
EN2
Coles Hill
KING GEORGE'S FIELD
NURSERY PLANTATION
CATTLEGATE WOOD
Cattlegate
Barvin Hill
South Hill
TILEKILN OSIERS
CATTLINS
DYSONS OSIERS
CINDER ASH
HERTFORDSHIRE
M25
CREWS HILL GOLF COURSE
Crews Hill
WHITEWEBBS WOOD
LONG GROVE
CALVES CROFT
St. Lawrence Farm
Darnicle Hill Nursery
Newgate Street Bridge
Postern Bridge
Burleigh Farm
Ashfield Nurseries
Theobold Nursery
Tolmers Park Farm
Tolmers Park
Thornton's Farm
Cuffley Hills Farm
Hempshill Brook
Northaw Brook
Turkey Brook
Cuffley Brook
Rags Brook
Turnford Brook
Soper's Viaduct
Colesdale Farm
Wells Farm
Cattlegate Farm
Woodhurst Farm
Owls Hall Farm
Holly Hill Farm
Robin Hill
Burnt Farm
Brook Farm
Poyndon Farm
Elm Farm
Rosebury Farm
Springfield Nursery
Weald View Nursery
Westgate Nursery
Tanfield Stud Farm
Sloeman's Farm
Glasgow Stud
Kings Oak Riding Stables
Oak Hill Farm
The Paddocks
Glasshouse
Garden Centre
Culver Garden Centre
Country World
Browns of Crews Hill Nurseries
Woldens Nursery & Garden Centre
Clubhouse
BROXBOURNE
WELWYN HATFIELD
THE RIDGEWAY
NORTHAW ROAD
WEST ROAD
CUFFLEY HILL
CATTLEGATE ROAD
HAMMOND STREET
NEWGATESTREET ROAD
OLD PARK RIDE
WHITEWEBBS ROAD
COOPERS LANE ROAD
BURNT FARM RIDE
DH
DJ
DK
DL
DM
DN
DP
29
30
31
25
26
27
28
29
30
31
32
33
34
04
03
02
01

DQ
DR
DS
DT
DU
DV
DW
48
82
65
25
26
27
28
29
30
31
32
33
34
04
03
02
01
DERRYS WOOD
BAISLEY'S WOOD
Turnford Brook
Beaumont Manor
Beaumont Manor Farm
Bread and Cheese Bridge
PRIESTS OSIERS
SPRING WOOD
Tanfield Stud Farm
Paradise Nursery
GAMMONS LANE
Rosary Nursery
Doggett Hill
CROMWELL WOOD
Paradise House
Mast
HAMMOND STREET
Gammon Farm
Francis Farm
APPLEBY STREET OPEN SPACE
Appleby Street Farm
Cheshunt Park Farm
Burleigh Farm
Ashfield Nurseries
Lamas Nursery
Burnham Nursery
Hammond Street
ROUNDCROFT
WOOD
CHESHUNT PARK
CHESHUNT GOLF COURSE
Nursery
Theobald Nursery
Cooksons Nursery
Small-Acre Nursery
CROUCH LANE
Elm Farm
Rosebury Farm
Malaya Farm
Burton Grange
Springfield Nursery
Weald View Nursery
Triangle Nursery
Twelve Acres Farm
White House Farm
Rags Brook
Clubhouse
CHESHUNT RESERVOIR (NORTH)
Prim Sch
Medical Cen
Flamstead End
Westgate Nursery
Longmead Nursery
Pylon Farm
Prince of Wales PH
Whitehouse Farm
The Goff's Oak PH
SPORTS GRD
Brynfield Nursery & Garden Centre
ROSEDALE SPORTS GROUND
FLAMSTEAD END REC GRD
The Jolly Bricklayers PH
Comm Cen
The Wheelwrights PH
Tudor Nursery
EN7
Goffs Oak
ALLOT
Colesgrove Manor
Poyndon Farm
Theolbalds Brook
GOFFS LANE
B156
SPORTS GRDS
MOAT
Sec Sch
Kobe Nursery
SILVER STREET
Rentokil Tropical Plants
Hope Nursery
Halstead Hill Nursery
ADATH YISROEL CEMETERY
Woodgreen Farm
CIVIC OFFICES
Crocodile PH
CEM
SPORTS GROUND
Broadfield Farm
Burnt Farm
Bury Green
Bury Green Farm
Albury Farm
OLD PARK RIDE
CATTLINS
DYSONS OSIERS
BURYGREEN PLANTATION
BROOM HILLS
HOME WOOD
HANGING PLANTATION
LIEUTENANT ELLIS WAY
GREAT CAMBRIDGE ROAD
A10
Temple Bar
Tesco Country Club
Spring Farm
HOME PLANTATION
Environmental Centre Farm
HERTFORDSHIRE
M25
CINDER ASH
Gunsite Farm Stables
SQUARE PLANTING
SOUTH OSIERS
Theobalds Park House
THEOBALDS PARK
Capel Manor Environmental Centre
Theobalds Park Farm
PARK LANE
Bullscross Farm
BULLSCROSS RIDE CEMETERY (JEWISH)
Theobalds Park Camping and Caravan Site
South Villa Nursery
COUNTY BROOK PLANTATION
BROXBOURNE
Junction 25
Sloeman's Farm
Whitewebbs Farm
Nursery
Pumping Station
Bulls Cross
Capel Manor Horticultural & Environmental Centre
Water World Aquatic & Garden
CAPEL HOUSE
Crews Hill
WHITEWEBBS LANE
Cricket Ground
SPORTS GROUND
BULLSMOOR LANE
Kings Oak Riding Stables

DX
DY
DZ
EA
EB
EC
ED
36
37
38
49
68
83
25
26
27
28
29
30
31
32
33
34
04
03
02
01
EN10
EN9
Wormley
Nazeing Marsh
Kings Weir
Paynes Farm Nursery
Leafield
Langridge Nursery
Clayton Hill
St. Leonards Farm
Netherkidders Farm
Turnford
Turnford Marsh
Turnford Place
Cheshunt Marriott Hotel
College
Aquaduct Lock
Holyfield Lake
Lee Valley Park
Sailing Club
Weir
Coleman's Shaw
Coleman's Lane
St. Leonards Road
Coach & Horses PH
Denver Lodge Farm
Holyfield Marsh
Holyfield Hill Farm
Marsh
Peartree Farm
Galleyhill Wood
Elec Station
The Nightleys
North Metropolitan Pit
Seventy Acres
Hayes Hill Farm
Hayes Hill
Holyfield
North Lodge Farm
Stubbings Hall Lane
Nursery
Grubbs Hill
Puck Lane
Homefield Wood
Nightingales
Cheshunt Lake
Turnershill Marsh
Holyfield Fishery
Holyfield Farm
Monkhams Hall
Young Mariners Base
Kennel Wood
Hooks Marsh
Cheshunt
Thistly Marsh
Cornmill Stream
Horsemill Stream
Claygate
Poultry Farm
River Lee Navigation
Lea Valley Walk
Grundy Park
Elm Arches
Hosp
Cheshunt Junction
Waltham Common Lock
Sluice
Waltham Abbey Woods
Lee Valley Park
Hall Marsh
Hall Marsh Scrape
Bowyer's Water
Small River Lea or Lee
Old River Lea or Lee
Cornmill Meadows
Mile Nursery
Langley Nursery
Lea Valley Nursery
Abbey View Nursery
Paternoster Hill Nursery
Epping Forest
Broxbourne
Hertfordshire
Essex
Theobalds Grove
Wheatsheaf PH
Marsh Bridge
Waltham Marsh
Crooked Mile Roundabout
Crooked Mile
Holyfield Road
Waltham Cross
Cheshunt Marsh
Britannia Nursery
Waltham Abbey (Ruins)
Abbey Gardens
Larsens Rec Grd
Prim Schs.
Highbridge St
Station Road
Eleanor Cross Rd
Small Lee Bridge
Waltham Lock
Superstores
Abbey Vw Roundabout
Lwr Island
Town Mead
Holdbrook
Leaside Trading Est
Sports Grd
Cem
Waltham Abbey FC
Swim Pool
Sports Ground
Pitches
Freezy Water
Rammey Marsh
M25
A10
A1170
A121
A1055
B194
B176
Cobbin's Brook
Sewardstone Roundabout
Quinton Hill Farm
Mollison Avenue
Monarchs Way
Hunt

68
EE
EF
EG
EH
EJ
EK
EL
Bumble's Green
50
Clayton
NAZEINGWOOD
COMMON
Clubhouse
Belchers Farm
King Harold's Head PH
Nazeing Gate
Leisure Cen
SPORTS GRD
ALLOT
COPY WOOD
25
26
27
28
29
30
31
32
33
34
St. Leonards Farm
Netherkidders Farm
Mushroom Farm
Mamelons Farm
St. Lawrence Farm
LAUNDRY LANE
CEMETERY LANE
WALTHAM ROAD
NAZEING ROAD
THE AVENUE
Harold's Park Farm
LONGFIELD SHAW
COLEMAN'S LANE
COLEMAN'S SHAW
ST. LEONARDS ROAD
B194
Coach & Horses PH
Denver Lodge Farm
GALLEYHILL GREEN
THE SPRINGS
DEERPARK WOOD
Marsh Hill
Galley Hill
Kennels
Claverhambury Manor
Claverhambury Farm
Claverhambury Carp Farm
CLAVERHAMBURY ROAD
Reevesgate Farm
Three Gates
LONGCROFT GROVE
COBBINSEND ROAD
STOCKING GROVE
Peartree Farm
GALLEYHILL WOOD
BROADGATE SPRINGS
BRAYSHILL SPRING
Holyfield
HOLYFIELD ROAD
North Lodge Farm
Aimes Green
Aimesgreen Farm
Nightingales
PUCK LANE
Cobbinsend Farm
Maynards Farm
EN9
MAPLE SPRINGS
BREACH BARN MOBILE HOME PARK
Cobbin's Brook
Monkhams Hall
67
KENNEL WOOD
Poultry Farm
Dallance Farm
Oakwood Nursery
Fourways Nursery
Breach Barns Farm
Obelisk
CLAYGATE LANE
Fernhall Farm
FERNHALL WOOD
The Cottage
BROOKMEADOW WOOD
Willows
Scatterbushes Cottage
Newhouse Farm
Home Farm
Nicholls Farm
FERNHALL LANE
LONG STREET
COBBIN POND
Mushroom Farm
Monkswood Nursery
Springfield Nursery
Upshire Nursery
ALLOT
Obelisk Farm
Glyn Gates
Temple Park Cottage
GDNS
The Temple
Abbey View Nursery
Knollys Nursery
Lea Valley Nursery
Warlies Park House
WARLIES PARK
Burgess Farm
Paternoster House
Paternoster Hill Nursery
Pickhill Farm
PICK HILL
GALLEY HILL
Upshire
Hall
Cricket Ground
Warlies Lodge
The Horseshoes PH
HORSESHOE HILL
CROWN HILL
PARKLANDS
Queens Head PH
Sec Sch
Sports Cen
Jubilee Ct
Prim Sch
Warlies Park Farm
SERGEANTS GREEN LA
RUGGED LANE
OXLEYS WOOD
WOODREDON FARM LANE
Copthall Green
Crown Hill Nursery
Comm Cen
Prim Schs.
SPORTS GROUND
Clubho.
Jessop
MONKSWOOD AVENUE
Prim Schs
Bowl Grn
LARSENS REC GRD
WOODGREEN ROAD
BLINDMANS LANE
BRAMBLY SHAW
Clinic
Works
The Sultan PH
Fire Sta
Woodgreen Farm
POTKILN WOOD
Green Lane Bungalows
SPORTS GRD
CEM
ALLOT
ROUNDHILLS
Waltham Abbey FC
Swim Pool
Prim Sch
Swallow Hotel
Southend Farm
Upshire Hall
SOUTHEND LANE
Works
Woodredon House
CLAY PIGEON RANGE
WOODBINE CLOSE
CONYBURY WOOD
SPORTS GROUND
WALTHAM ABBEY
84
The Lodge
Skillet Hill Farm
Sudbury Farm
Woodbine PH
Woodredon Farm
Woodredon Riding School
HONEY LANE
A121
M25
LODGE LANE
BEECHFIELD WALK
Sewardstone Roundabout
Quinton Hill Farm
SEWARDSTONE ROAD
Volunteer PH
40
41
42
04
03
02
01

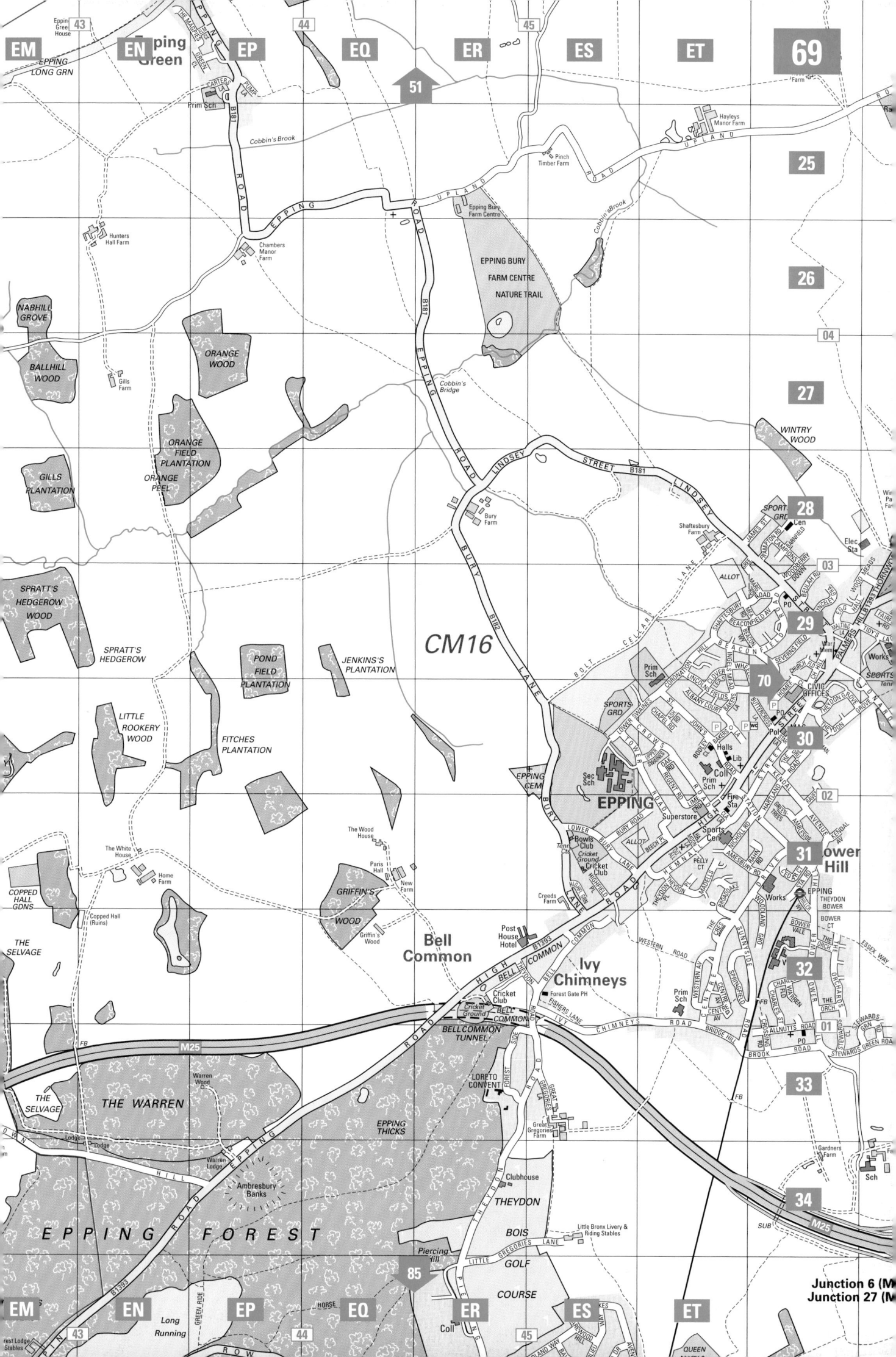

43 44 45

51

25

26

04

27

EPPING
LONG GRN

Eppin
Gree
House

ping
Green

Hayleys Manor Farm

Farm

Pinch Timber Farm

Cobbin's Brook

Hunters
Hall Farm

Chambers Manor
Farm

EPPING BURY
FARM CENTRE
NATURE TRAIL

Epping Bury
Farm Centre

Cobbins Brook

NABHILL
GROVE

ORANGE
WOOD

BALLHILL
WOOD

Gills
Farm

Cobbin's
Bridge

WINTRY
WOOD

GILLS
PLANTATION

ORANGE
FIELD
PLANTATION

ORANGE
PEEL

LINDSEY
STREET B181
LINDSEY

28

Shaftesbury
Farm

Elec
Sta

SPORTS
GRD
Cen

ALLOT

CM16

Bury
Farm

29

SPRATT'S
HEDGEROW
WOOD

Prim
Sch

War
Mem

Works
SPORTS

70

SPRATT'S
HEDGEROW

POND
FIELD
PLANTATION

JENKINS'S
PLANTATION

SPORTS
GRD

Halls

Lib

03

02

LITTLE
ROOKERY
WOOD

FITCHES
PLANTATION

EPPING
CEM

Prim
Sch

Col

Fire
Sta

30

EPPING

Superstore

Sports
Cen

ower
Hill

The Wood
House

Bowls
Club
Cricket
Ground
Cricket
Club

ALLOT

31

EPPING
THEYDON
BOWER

The White
House

Paris
Hall

Home
Farm

New
Farm

GRIFFIN'S
WOOD

Griffin's
Wood

Creeds
Farm

Works

BOWER
VALE

COPPED
HALL
GDNS

Copped Hall
(Ruins)

Bell
Common

Ivy
Chimneys

Prim
Sch

32

THE
SELVAGE

Post
House
Hotel

Forest Gate PH

FISHERS LANE

IVY CHIMNEYS

01

FB

FB

33

Cricket
Club

Cricket
Ground

BELL
COMMON

BELL COMMON
TUNNEL

WESTERN

ROAD

THE SELVAGE

M25

THE WARREN

Warren
Wood

LORETO
CONVENT

EPPING
THICKS

Gardners
Farm

34

Lodge

Warren
Lodge

Ambresbury
Banks

Clubhouse

THEYDON

SUB

M25

EPPING FOREST

BOIS

Little Bronx Livery &
Riding Stables

Piercing
Hill

85

GOLF

COURSE

43 44 45

Long
Running

Coll

52
THORNWOOD
NORTH WEALD
AIRFIELD
WINTRY WOOD
THE LOWER FOREST
EPPING PLAIN
ST. MARGARET'S HOSPITAL
SPENCER CLOSE HOSP
COOPERSALE
GERNON BUSHES
ROUGHTALLEY'S WOOD
NORTH WEALD GOLF COURSE
BIRCHING COPPICE
POSTERNIANE SPRING
HAWKSHILL WOOD
REDYN'S WOOD
FORTY ACRES
CM16
69
Bower Hill
EPPING
Fiddlers Hamlet
Mount End
Theydon Mount
HOBBS CROSS GOLF CENTRE
Junction 7
86
BARBER'S WOOD
M11
M25
Coopersale Farm
Coopersale House
Gaynes Park
Stonards Farm
Home Farm
The Merry Fiddlers PH
Masons Bridge Farm
Little Thorn Hall Farm
Gardners Farm
Farm Buildings
Sewage Works
Hornes Farm
Searles Hall
Sawkins Farm
North House
Mount Hill Farm
THE ROUGH PATCH
ICEHOUSE PLANTATION
LONG PLANTATION
Garnish Hall
Hayleys Manor Farm
Rose Farm
Bird Centre
Weald Hall
Weald Hall Farm
DRIVING RANGE
Wintry Park Farm
Shaftesbury Farm
WOODSIDE COMMERCIAL ESTATE
MOUNT QUARTER
ONGAR DOWN
GRAVELPIT WOOD
BEACHE WOOD

NORTH WEALD BASSETT
Greensted Green
Toot Hill
TOOT HILL GOLF COURSE
CM5
RM4
Talbot Roundabout
Skips Corner
Ongar Park Hall
Clunes House
Water Tower
Wealds Farm
Steers Farm
Does Farm
Freemans Farm
Clubhouse
Stewart's Farm
Cesslands Farm
Berwick Farm
Moat House
Mole Trap PH
Woodhatch Farm
Cold Hall Farm
Greensted House
Hardings Farm
Works
Willows Farm
Burrows Farm
Coleman's Farm
Newhouse
Clark's Farm
Stanford Rivers Hall Farm
The Drill House PH
Batt Livery Stable
White Bear PH
The Woodman PH
Murrells Farm
Traceys Farm
Houfields
Little Hall
Sayers Farm
New House Farm
The Talbot PH
Redricks Nursery
Chase Farm
Sewage Works
Bowling Green
Clubhouse
The Queens Head PH
Pol
PEWLEY WOOD
MILLER'S GROVE
DOLMAN'S SPRING
GREENSTED WOOD
ONGAR PARK WOOD
KNIGHTSLAND WOOD
NORTHLANDS WOOD
LONG SPRING
WELL EAVES
HANGING SPRING
ROUND SPRING
PARK SPRING
ICEHOUSE WOOD
TWENTYACRE WOOD
REYNKYNS WOOD
HIGH ROAD
EPPING ROAD
BLAKE HALL ROAD
PENSONS LANE
GREENSTED ROAD
TOOT HILL ROAD
MILL LANE
SCHOOL ROAD
SCHOOL LANE
COLEMANS LANE
BERWICK LANE
STAPLEFORD ROAD
TAWNEY COMMON
MUTTON ROW
OLD RECTORY ROAD
CHURCH ROAD
ESSEX WAY
53
87
25
26
27
28
29
30
31
32
33
34
FB
FC
FD
FE
FF
FG
FH
50
51
52
01
02
03
04

72
AS
AT
AU
AV
AW
AX
AY
98
99
00
56
55
90
35
36
37
38
39
40
41
42
43
44
Chesham Bois
BOIS WOOD
REC GROUND
BLACKWELL STUBBS
Sewage Works
Blackwell Hall
Blackwell Farm
Ivy House Farm
Works
Quarry
FRITH WOOD
NETHER DITCH
TOOLEY'S CROFT
STOCKINGS SPRING
FOUR ACRES
STAR CLUMP
JACK OF WADLEY'S SPRING
Latimer
PARKFIELD WOOD
Tennis Cts
PLAYING FIELD
RECTORY PLANTATION
Conf Cen
Training Centre
Latimer House
HP5
DUCK COVER
Weir
GREAT WATER
RIVER CHESS
MARKET READING WOOD
ROUND WOOD
LANE WOOD
HP6
Raans Farm
Quill Hall Farm
WEST WOOD
SPORTS GROUND
Tennis Courts
Pav
CHALFONT & LATIMER
LITTLE CHALFONT
LITTLE CHALFONT GOLF COURSE
STONYDEAN WOOD
LOUDHAM'S WOOD
Burton's Farm
Nightingales
BURTON'S WOOD
NIGHTINGALES WOOD
Rowood Farm
AMERSHAM
WOODSIDE ROAD
WHITE LION ROAD
A404
A416
A413
B4442
IND EST
Coll
Sch
Cricket Grd
Swim Pool
Amb Sta
Fire Sta
Youth Cen
Lib
Comm Cen
Health Cen
Pol
PO
PLAYING FIELD
Tenn Cts
SNELL'S WOOD
Snell's Farm
Little Kimblewick Farm
HP7
HOBB'S DELL
STANLEY WOOD
CEM
WILLOW WOOD
HOVEL WOOD
The Chequers PH
LONDON ROAD WEST
BYPASS
LONDON ROAD
EAST AMERSHAM ROAD
RIVER MISBOURNE
Depot
Clubhouse
HAREWOOD DOWNS GOLF COURSE
The Ivy House PH
Harewood Downs House
DOGGETT'S WOOD
Offices
Five Diamonds
The Gate House
The Shieling
POLLARDS WOOD
Pollards Park House
Elmswell House
SPORTS GROUND
Warren Farm
HP8
BAILEY WOOD
DAY'S WOOD
HIGH WOOD
BOW WOOD
STRATTON COPSE
Lower Bottom House Farm
Upper Bottom House Farm
BYCROFT PLANTATION
Misbourne Farm
BAILEY WOOD BELT
Vache Farm
RESERVOIR PLANTATION
KILNPOND WOOD
INFO CEN
THE LARCHES
Quarrendon Farm
WOOD
Coke's Farm
NIGHTINGALES LANE
96
97

73
57
74
91
HP3
WD3
Chenies
SARRATT
CHORLEYWOOD
Chorleywood Bottom
The Swillet
Heronsgate
MOUNT WOOD
BALDWIN'S WOOD
FLAUNDEN GROVE
CHORLEYWOOD COMMON
CHORLEYWOOD GOLF COURSE
AMERSHAM ROAD
RICKMANSWORTH ROAD
CHENIES ROAD
RIVER CHESS
Junction 18
M25
A404

74
BG
BH
BJ
BK
BL
BM
BN
05
06
07
Commonwood
Bucks Hill
58
Hillmeads Spring
Dellfield
Great Sarratt Hall
Commonwood Common
Bucks Hill Farm
Beechen Bottom
35
Daffodil Spring
Red Lion Lane
Bottom
Little Westwood Farm
Conference Centre
Great Westwood Farm
House
Sarratt
The Boot PH
High Spring
Old
Juniper Hill
Tennis Courts
Sports Ground
Pav
Wynyard Rd
Alexandra Rd
Downer Dr
Cricketers Inn PH
The Green
George St
Cardon Dr
Poultry Houses
Lane
Buckshill Bottom
36
PO
Prim Sch
Hall
Dimmocks Lane
Deadmans Ash Lane
Newhall Farm
Junction 19
Templepan Wood
Clutterbuck Lane
Ward's Nurseries
Sandfield Wood
Common
99
Adams Nurseries
Sarratt Road
Templepan Lane
Allot
White House
Yew Court Farm
37
Green End Farm
Chandlers Lane
Birch Spring
Dartpath Wood
Sarratt Bottom Cottages
Church Road
Mickleford Green Farm
Potten's Farm
White Shack Lane
The Grove Lodge
Great Wood
Stevens Nurseries
Sheepyard Spring
M25
Chandler's Farm
Valley
River Chess
Clarendon Arms PH
Fir Tree
38
New Model Farm
Sawpit Spring
Country Place
Coltspring Riding Stables
Coltyard Farm
Cottage Farm
Rousebarn
Blacketts Nurseries
Weir
98
Walk
Scrubbs Wood
Blunts Wood
Willow Wood
Harrocks Wood
New Hill
Chess Valley
Sarrattmill Bridge
Redhall Farm
Redhall
39
Water Works
Mead Spring
FB
Weirs
73
Welling Grove
Merlin's Wood
Micklefield Hall Farm
Micklefield Hall
Solesbridge
Cherry Walk
40
Beechen Hill
WD3
Merlin Spring
Beechengrove Wood
Millfield Plantation
Long Spring
Round Spring
Model Farm
York Ho Sch
Waterdell Spring
Dell Wood
97
Ladywood Cl
Upper Plantation
The Readings
Chess Way
Bridle Lane
Cem
Highlands Water Gardens
41
Millers Cl
The Gate PH
Warwick Ct
Solesbridge Mill Water Gardens
Trout Rise
Cherry Hill
Loudwater Hts
Whisperwood
Wagon Wy
Loudwater
Morning Rise
Waterdell House
Little Green Lane
Cricket Ground
Prim Sch
Rickmansworth Road
A404
Wyatts Cl
Little Lady's Wood
Troutstream Way
Loudwater House
Violet Way
Timber Ridge
Rooks Hill
Walden Lodge
Loudwater Lane
Thurlwood House
Croxley House
Killingdown Farm
Whitestocks Farm
Parrot's Dell
Croxley Green
White Horse PH
Junction 18
Chorleywood Road
Mont Au Source
Loudwater Drive
42
The Cedars
Home Wood
Chess Lane
Loudwater Farm
Baldwins Lane Recreation Ground
Copthorne Wood
Black Horse PH
96
Park Avenue
Chestnut Avenue
Clump Avenue
Glen Chess
Chess Valley Walk
River Chess
Watercress Beds
Sports Ground
Copthorne Road
Coach & Horses PH
Prim Sch
Bowl Grn
43
Allot
South Park Avenue
Round Spring
Lime Tree Wk
Lynwood Heights
Spencer Wk
Old Barn La
Pav
Sports Ground
Berry Lane
Berry Farm
The Screen
The Valley
Greenhills Cl
High Cl
Drive
Woodbank
Green La
Artichoke PH
New Road
Croxley Green
Solomon's Wood
The Climb
Sch
Rickmansworth Masonic Sch
West Herts Riding School
44
Pheasants Wood
Highfield Road
The Mount
Goosefields
Hockey Grd
Playing Field
Tenn Cts
Scotsbridge PH
Watford Road
Cricket Grd
Pav
Prim Sch
Upper Hill Rise
Arnett Way
Beacon Way
Shepherds Way
Clubhouse
Scots Hill
Sec Sch
Sports Ground
Queens Drive
Oakfield Avenue
Chorleywood Road Cemetery
92
Scots Br
Fortune Common
Chalmers Court
Croxley
M25
Rickmansworth Park
Park Road
PO
Tenn Club
Rickmansworth
The Cloisters
Caravan
Sec Sch
Sports Ground
Croxley

75
BP
BQ
BR
BS
BT
BU
BV
08
09
10
59
93
76
35
36
37
38
39
40
41
42
43
44
99
98
97
96
Langleybury
Leavesden Green
Kingswood
Garston
NORTH WATFORD
WATFORD
WEST WATFORD
Holywell
WD2
WD1
NORTH WESTERN AVENUE
NORTH WESTERN AV
HEMPSTEAD ROAD
A41
A411
A412
A4145
A4178
A4125
M25 LINK ROAD
Hunton Bridge Interchange
THREE RIVERS
WATFORD
HEATH WOOD
GROVE
PARK
WEST HERTFORDSHIRE GOLF COURSE
WHIPPENDELL WOOD
PLAYING FIELD
CASSIOBURY PARK
PADDLING POOLS
ROUGH WOOD
CHARLOTTE'S VALE
GRAND UNION CANAL
River Gade
River Colne
NORTH WATFORD CEMETERY
STANBOROUGH PARK
VICARAGE RD CEMETERY
CALLOWLAND REC GRD
GOODWOOD REC GRD
CHESLYN GDNS
West Herts College
Sports Complex
British Waterways
THE COLOSSEUM
TOWN HALL
WATFORD GENERAL HOSP
WATFORD FC
WATFORD STADIUM HALT (MATCH DAYS ONLY)
WATFORD NORTH
WATFORD JUNCTION
WATFORD WEST
WATFORD HIGH STREET
CROXLEY
CROXLEY GREEN
MOWAT INDUSTRIAL EST
EMPIRE CENTRE
Harlequin Centre
Charter Place
Electricity Transmission Station
KING GEORGE V PLAYING FIELDS
COMMON MOOR
LONG VALLEY WOOD
DURRANTS SPORTS GROUND
HOLYWELL IND EST
WOLSEY BUSINESS PARK
MOOR PARK INDUSTRIAL ESTATE
ST. ALBANS ROAD
RICKMANSWORTH ROAD
WIGGENHALL ROAD
VICARAGE ROAD
EXCHANGE RD
BEECHEN GROVE
TOLPITS LANE
EASTBURY ROAD
OXHEY PARK
CASSIOBURY PARK AVENUE
WATFORD FLDS
SPORTS GROUND

76
BW
BX
BY
BZ
CA
CB
CC
60
75
94
12
13
14
35
36
37
38
39
40
41
42
43
44
Garston
NORTH WATFORD CEMETERY
STANBOROUGH PARK
Meriden
WESTERN AVENUE
NORTH WESTERN AVENUE
NORTH WATFORD
WATFORD NORTH
MOWAT INDUSTRIAL EST
JACK NICKLAUS GOLF CENTRE
Junction 5
Berrygrove Interchange
ALDENHAM GOLF COURSE & COUNTRY CLUB
Aldenham
University of Hertfordshire
MUNDEN SPRING
River Colne
HERTSMERE
WATFORD
Bushey Hall Farm
Bushemill Bridge
EMPIRE CENTRE
COLONIAL WAY
Watford R.F.C.
WATFORD JUNCTION
British Telecom
WD1
WD2
RADLETT ROAD PLAYING FIELDS
STEPHENSON WAY
SCOTTS WOOD
BUSHEY HALL GOLF COURSE
West Herts Coll
ICEDALE WOODS
Hartspring Leisure Cen
The David Lloyd Club
The Purcell School
METROPOLITAN POLICE BUSHEY SPORTS GROUND
BUSHEY JEWISH CEMETERY
PLAYING FIELD
Watford Hilton National Hotel
WINFIELD MOBILE HOME PARK
Three Compasses PH
Patchetts Equestrian Centre
Delrow House
Holland Farm
The Lincolnsfields Centre
The U.S. International University-Europe
ELTON WAY (NORTH WESTERN AVENUE)
OTTERSPOOL WAY
BEECHEN GROVE
Harlequin Centre
Charter Place
WATFORD HIGH STREET
WATFORD FLDS
Colne Valley Water Company
Gas Works
WATFORD GENERAL HOSP
VICARAGE RD. CEMETERY
SPORTS GROUND
OXHEY
OXHEY PARK
Council Depot
Wiggenhall Bridge
BUSHEY
CHALK HILL
LONDON ROAD
HIGH STREET
MOAT FIELD REC GRD
KING GEORGE REC GROUND
BUSHEY GOLF COURSE & COUNTRY CLUB
Haydon Hill House
Open Air Pool
RUNNING TRACK
Watford Equestrian Centre
Watford Borough Council Nursery
Clubhouse
Superstore
Works

RADLETT
Letchmore Heath
ELSTREE
WD7
WD6
THE GORSE
GOLF COURSE
ELSTREE AERODROME
HILFIELD PARK RESERVOIR
ALDENHAM COUNTRY PARK
ALDENHAM RESERVOIR
ALDENHAM PARK WOODLAND
ALDENHAM PARK
ELSTREE GOLF COURSE
DRIVING RANGE
ELSTREE HILL OPEN SPACE
ELSTREE OPEN SPACE
CENTENNIAL PARK
KENDAL WOOD
LITTLE KENDALS WOOD
MOSES DELL
COBDENHILL DELL
WELLHOUSE DELL
SCRUBBITTS WOOD
FIR SPRING
PLAYING FIELD
SPORTS GROUND
Boydens Hill
MOATS
The Haberdasher's Aske's Sch for Boys
The Haberdasher's Aske's Sch for Girls
Lister Institute
Tabard R.F.C.
Radlett Cricket Club
Cricket Ground
Tenn & Squash Club
Clubhouse
Sewage Works
Flying Club
Hangars
Boathouse
Sailing Club
DAM
Pumping Sta
Gas Pumping Sta
CONVENT
Coll
Edgwarebury Hotel
Elstree Crematorium Cemetery
Watling Street
Cobden Hill
Watford Road
Elstree Road
Aldenham Road
Barnet Lane
Theobald Street
Tylers Way (North Western Av)
Elstree Hill North
Elstree Hill South
High Street
A5183
A411
A409
M1
Butterfly Lane
Hogg Lane
Wards Lane
Sawyers Lane
Hilfield Lane
Dagger Lane
Allum Lane
Common Lane
Radlett Lane
Watford Road
The Ridgeway
Loom Lane
Gills Hill Lane
Shenley Hill
Williams Way
Newberries Avenue
Craigweil Avenue
Letchmore Road
Christchurch Crescent
Aldenham Avenue
Tykes Water
Letchmore Lodge
Battle Axes PH
Cat & Fiddle PH
Waggon & Horses PH
Three Horseshoes PH
Medburn Bridge
North Medburn Farm
South Medburn Farm
Slades Farm
Little Kendals Farm
Kendal Hall Farm
Organ Hall Farm
Battlers Green Farm
Home Farm
Hilfield Farm
Hilfield Castle
Pages Farm
Caldecote Farm
Berkeley Cottage
Aldenham Cottage
Bhaktivedanta Manor
Aldenham Sch
Sports Cen
Prim Sch
Prep Sch
The Fruit Farm
Blackbirds Country Fare (Garden Centre)
Kemprow Farm
High Cross House
Starveacres
Medburn Cottages
Elli Dani Farm (Stables)
Auriol Farm
Wood Hall Farm
Wood Hall
Electricity Transfer Station
CD CE CF CG CH CJ CK
15 16 17
35 36 37 38 39 40 41 42 43 44
99 98 97 96
61
78
95

78
CL
CM
CN
CP
CQ
CR
CS
19
20
21
62
35
36
37
38
39
40
41
42
43
44
77
96
99
98
97
96
SAND PLANTATION
BIGPURSLEY WOOD
LITTLEPURSLEY WOOD
CROSS OAKS WOOD
Crossoaks Farm
CROSSOAKS LANE
The Garden Nursery
Tokonoma Bonsai
GREEN STREET
Cricket Ground
SPORTS GRD
ALLOT
Auriol Farm
WOODHALL
Wood Hall Farm
Wood Hall
Kitwells Farm
Villa Scalabrini
Lyndhurst
BIRCH WOOD
Catherine Bourne
WD7
Green Street
High Canons
High Canons Farm
Holmshill House
Buckettsland Farm
Wheatsheaf Farm
Maxwelton Nurseries
Well End Farm
Holly Cottage
Well End
Cowley Hill Farm
Strangeways Farm
Rowley Farm
Mops & Brooms PH
Gt Brookmead Sch
Health Cen
Prim Sch
Organ Hall Farm
AYCLIFFE ROAD PITCHES
Sec Sch
Sports Cen
ABERFORD LAKE
ABERFORD PARK
Comm Cen
SPORTS GROUND
MEADOW PARK
Borehamwood FC
Prim Schs
De Havilland College
THE VENUE
Swim Pool
CIVIC OFFS
ELSTREE WAY
A5135
BOREHAMWOOD IND PARK
G.E.C. SPORTS GROUND
Works
Elstree Moat House
Warehouses
B.B.C. Elstree Studios
Imperial Studios
Studios
BOREHAMWOOD
Superstore
MAXWELL PK
KING GEORGES PLAYING FLD
Depot
Boulevard 25 Retail Park
Metropolis Centre
Cinema
WD6
ELSTREE
DRIVING RANGE
GOLF
COURSE
Clubhouse
North Medburn Farm
North Medburn Stables
Waggon & Horses PH
Medburn Bridge
South Medburn Farm
ALDENHAM
PARK
ELSTREE & BOREHAMWOOD
Gas Works
ALLUM LANE
Elli Dani Farm (Stables)
HERTSMERE BOROUGH COUNCIL CEMETERY
ELSTREE HILL NORTH
ELSTREE HILL SOUTH
A5183
RIPON PARK
Furze Hill
TEMPSFORD GREEN
LAINGS PLAYING FIELD
A1 BARNET BYPASS
A411
BARNET LANE
ELSTREE TUNNEL
Woodcock Hill Farm
Deacons Hill
Airshafts
DEACONS HILL OPEN SPACE
SCRATCH WOOD
FROGHALL WOOD
BOYS HILL WOOD
THISTLE WOOD
Stirling Corner
ELSTREE PARK
ARKLEY PARK
Hyver Hall
GRAVEL PITWOOD
Elstree Manor
Penniwells Farm
The Leys
ELSTREE OPEN SPACE
Tennis Courts
Works

79
CT
CU
CV
CW
CX
CY
CZ
63
97
80
M25
Junction 23
(M25)
Junction 1
A1(M)
South Mimms
Depot
Works
Blanche Farm
BLANCHE LANE
ST. ALBANS ROAD
A1081
BARNET BYPASS
A1
Dancers Hill
Laurel Lodge
Laurel House
Dancershill House
DANCERS HILL ROAD
Norfolk Lodge
BAKER STREET
BENTLEY HEATH LANE
Elm Farm
Bentley Heath Farm
Bentley Heath
Mausoleum
Cricket Ground
Pav
Duke of York PH
WAGON ROAD
Tennis Courts
Open Air Pool
Wrotham Park
WROTHAM PARK
Deadman's Bottom
Home Farm
Lower Kitt's End Farm
Kitt's End
Kitt's End Farm
Dyrham Park Farm
DYRHAM LANE
Mimmshall Brook
BOTTOM
TROTTERS
Green Dragon Inn PH
DYRHAM PARK GOLF COURSE
Country Club
Tennis Courts
Open Air Pool
DYRHAM PARK
Knightsland Farm
Valentine's Farm
GALLEY LANE
BRIDGEDOWN GOLF COURSE
ALLOTMENTS
OLD FOLD MANOR GOLF COURSE
MOAT
Clubhouse
Old Fold Manor
Hadley High Stone
GREAT NORTH ROAD
A1000
HADLEY HIGHSTONE
Monken Hadley
Battle of Barnet 1471
Rectory Farm
Prim Sch
Jun Sch
St. Martha Convent
CAMLET
Bourne Hill
Fold Farm
WROTHAM PARK OPEN SPACE
EN5
Transformer Sta
High Barnet
BYNG ROAD PLAYING FIELDS
ALLOT
Barnet R.F.C.
Curriculum Centre
HADLEY GREEN
Hadley
KING GEORGE'S FIELD
BARNET
Homestead Farm
POOR CLARE MONASTERY
HERTFORDSHIRE
HERTSMERE
SPORTS GROUND
ARKLEY LANE OPEN SPACE
Woodlands Farm
ARKLEY LANE
TA Cen
Mkt
Lib
The Spires Shop Cen
Swim Pool
Sec Sch
Works
Tenn Cts
SPORTS GROUND
BARNET TRADING EST
Sports Cen
THE OLD BULL ARTS CEN
MUS
Barnet Coll
HIGH STREET
WOOD STREET
A411
Marie Foster Home
REC GRD
Pol
Sec Sch
HIGH BARNET
BARNET HILL
GREAT NORTH ROAD
WHALEBONE PARK
Water Tower
BARNET GENERAL HOSP
CEMETERY
CHIPPING BARNET
Nursery
Three Elms Farm
ARKLEY
ARKLEY RISE ESTATE OPEN SPACE
ARKLEY GOLF COURSE
Clubhouse
COV RES
ROWLEY GREEN ROAD
War Memorial
Arkley
Water Tower
PO
BARNET ROAD
Windmill
Barnet Gate
BELLS HILL ALLOT
ALLOT
Comm Cen
Prim Schs
Valley Cen
Cinema
Underhill
SPORTS GROUND
Clubhouse
BARNET FC
WHITINGS HILL OPEN SPACE
Youth & Comm Cen
SPORTS GROUND
Whitings Hill Farm
Cottage Farm
Ducks Island
Pav
GRANGE PLAYING FIELDS
PLAYING FIELD
Tennis Courts
DOLLIS VALLEY GREEN WK
BARNET PLAYING FIELDS
Pavs.
KING GEORGE V PLAYING FIELDS
OLD ELIZABETHANS (BARNET) MEMORIAL PLAYING FIELDS
Pav
MAYS LANE
Brent Lodge Farm
Dollis Brook
Sec Sch
OAKLANDS ROAD
SOUTH HERTS GOLF COURSE
N20
HENDON WOOD LANE

DA
DB
DC
DD
DE
DF
DG
M25
Junction 24
Bentley Heath
Ganwick Corner
WROTHAM PARK
HADLEY WOOD
ENFIELD
Monken Hadley
Battle of Barnet 1471
MONKEN HADLEY COMMON
HADLEYWOOD GOLF COURSE
EN4
EN5
Hadley
NEW BARNET
CHIPPING BARNET
Underhill
COCKFOSTERS
EAST BARNET
OAK HILL PARK
THE RIDGEWAY
STAGG HILL
COCKFOSTERS ROAD
GREAT NORTH ROAD
EAST BARNET ROAD
BARNET HILL
STATION ROAD
N20

81
M25
DH
DJ
DK
DL
DM
DN
DP
29
30
31
65
South Hill
Holly Hill Farm
Holyhill Brook
Oak Hill Farm
Glasgow Stud
Crews Hill
Culver Garden Centre
Country World
Nursery
Sloeman's Farm
Clubhouse
CREWS HILL GOLF COURSE
Woldens Nursery & Garden Centre
Browns of Crews Hill Nurseries
Woldens Nurseries
Pumping Station
Crews Hill
35
WHITEWEBBS PARK
Kings Oak Riding Stables
Tingeys Top Lane
Wildwoods Water Garden Centre
WILDWOOD
THE RIDGEWAY
Botany Bay
Pav
Cricket Ground
Botany Bay Farm
A1005
Kings Oak Plain
Glasshouses
Hill Side Nursery
36
SPORTS GROUND
Works
Prim Sch
99
Brayside Farm
Strayfield Road
Cricket Ground
Anglo Aquarium Plant
Queenswood Farm
37
Rectory Farm
Turkey Brook
Clay Hill
Clay Hill House
Kingswood
CHASE
Rendlesham Viaduct
Bandstand
EN2
HILLY FIELDS PARK
Cuckolds Hill
KING'S OAK PRIVATE HOSPITAL
CHASE FARM HOSPITAL
LAVENDER HILL CEMETERY
38
Park Farms
HADLEY ROAD
MOAT WOOD
Royal Chace Hotel
Parkside Farm
Pumping Station
Vicarage Farm
Camlet Hill
RIDE WOOD
Leeging Beech Gutter
Salmon's Brook
39
GORDON HILL
LAVENDER HILL
FISH POND
WILLIAMS WOOD
ICEHOUSE WOOD
Hog Hill
82
Middlesex University
Well
Monument
SHAWS WOOD
NUFFIELD HOSP
40
Merryhills Brook
SPORTS GROUND
TRENT PARK GOLF COURSE
TRIANGULAR WOOD
ALLOT
SLADES HILL
WINDMILL HILL
A110
41
World's End
ENFIELD CHASE
CHURCH
South Lodge Farm
Trent Park Equestrian Centre
ENFIELD ROAD
ENFIELD GOLF COURSE
Clubhouse
BOXER'S LAKE
SPORTS GROUND
Prim Sch
42
TOWN PARK
Clubhouse
CHEYNE WALK
96
BUSH HILL PARK GOLF COURSE
Oakwood
Sec Sch
GRANGE PARK
43
SPORTS GROUND
N21
Grange Park
PRIORY
OAKWOOD PARK
Pitch 'n' Putt
OAKWOOD
YACHTING POND
44
Hounsden Gutter
Hillel Sch
99
Chaseside Works
Salmon's Brook
DH
DJ
DK
DL
DM
DN
DP
WINCHMORE HILL
N14
29
30
31
Tenn & Squash Club
RIDGE AVENUE
GROVELANDS

82
DQ
DR
DS
DT
DU
DV
DW
33
34
35
66
M25
Junction 25
BULLSCROSS RIDE
CEMETERY (JEWISH)
COUNTY BROOK PLANTATION
Theobalds Park Camping and Caravan Site
Sloeman's Farm
Whitewebbs Farm
WHITEWEBBS
Bulls Cross
Capel Manor Horticultural & Environmental Centre
CAPEL HOUSE
Water World, Aquatic & Garden Centre
BULLSMOOR LANE
Crews Hill
WHITEWEBBS WOOD
WHITEWEBBS PARK
WHITEWEBBS GOLF COURSE
White Webbs House
Roman Villa
SPORTS GROUND
Myddelton Farm
BULLS CROSS FIELD
Myddelton House
Glasshouses
WILDWOOD
Kings Oak Riding Stables
Wiltwoods Water Garden Centre
Hill Side Nursery
Browns of Crews Hill Nurseries
Turkey Brook
New River (Old Course)
Cuffley Brook
EN2
Brayside Farm
Clubhouse
FORTY HALL COUNTRY PARK
Maiden's Bridge
Forty Hill
FORTY HALL & MUSEUM
Clock House
Clockhouse Nursery
GOUGH PARK
ALLOTMENTS
BRAMLEY HOUSE
Clay Hill
Clay Hill House
Bandstand
Kingswood
Rendlesham Viaduct
Anglo Aquarium Plant
Queenswood Farm
HILLY FIELDS PARK
CEDAR HILL CEMETERY
STRAYFIELD ROAD
CLAY HILL
TURKEY STREET
Bullsmoor
CEMETERY
Crematorium
War Memorial
THE DELL
GREAT CAMBRIDGE ROAD
HERTFORD ROAD
A10
A1010
HOE LANE
ENFIELD CEMETERY (JEWISH)
New River
QUEEN ELIZABETH STADIUM
David Lloyd Leisure Cen
EN1
ENFIELD PLAYING FIELDS
ENFIELD
SPORTS GROUND
BASEBALL GROUND
Pavilion
Enfield Town FC
ST. GEORGE'S FIELD
Boys Club
CARTERHATCH LANE
BRICK LANE
ENFIELD RETAIL PK
Superstores
Works
SOUTHBURY ROAD
SOUTHBURY Works
MARTINBRIDGE INDUSTRIAL ESTATE
Middlesex University
PROGRESS WAY
ALLOTMENTS
JUBILEE PARK
ENFIELD TOWN
CIVIC CENTRE
CHURCH ST
LONDON ROAD
SILVER STREET
BAKER STREET
A110
WINDMILL HILL
CECIL ROAD
ENFIELD CHASE
Holtwhites Hotel
TOWN PARK
Bowling Green
BUSH HILL PARK
BUSH HILL PARK GOLF COURSE
Salmon's Brook
A105
PARK AVENUE
VILLAGE ROAD
GRANGE PARK
THE RIDGEWAY
A1005
CHEYNE WALK
N21
GREEN DRAGON LANE
Hounsden Gutter
ENFIELD GOLF COURSE
GORDON HILL
SPORTS GROUND
LAVENDER HILL
CHASE SIDE
PARSONAGE LANE
CHASE GRN GDNS
Tenn & Squash Club
Bowls & Tenn Club
KING GEORGE'S FIELD
100
81

83
DX
DY
DZ
EA
EB
EC
ED
67
35
36
37
38
39
40
41
42
43
44
84
101
EN9
EN3
E4
Holdbrook
Freezy Water
RAMMEY MARSH
INNOVA BUSINESS PARK
Enfield Lock
ALBANY PARK
SOHAM LANE OPEN SPACE
PRINCE OF WALES OPEN SPACE
LEE VALLEY PARK
SEWARDSTONE MARSH
OSIERS
EPPING FOREST
ENFIELD
Sewardstone
Barn Hill
KING GEORGE'S RESERVOIR
BRIMSDOWN INDUSTRIAL ESTATE
BRIMSDOWN SPORTS GROUND
Brimsdown
DURANTS PARK
ALMA ROAD OPEN SPACE
CENTENARY ESTATE
PONDERS END IND EST
VALLEY LINK IND EST
RIVERSIDE IND EST
GILWELL PARK
BANCHET FIELD
THE QUICK
THE ROUGH
CARP LAKES
COVERED RESERVOIR
WEST ESSEX GOLF COURSE
FERNHILL WOOD
THOMPSON'S WOOD
Yardley Hill
THE HAWK WOOD
CHINGFORD GOLF COURSE
CHINGFORD PLAIN
POLE HILL
Sewardstone Roundabout
MOLLISON AVENUE
SEWARDSTONE ROAD
LEA VALLEY ROAD
MERIDIAN WAY
HERTFORD ROAD
M25
A1055
A112
A110
LEISURE

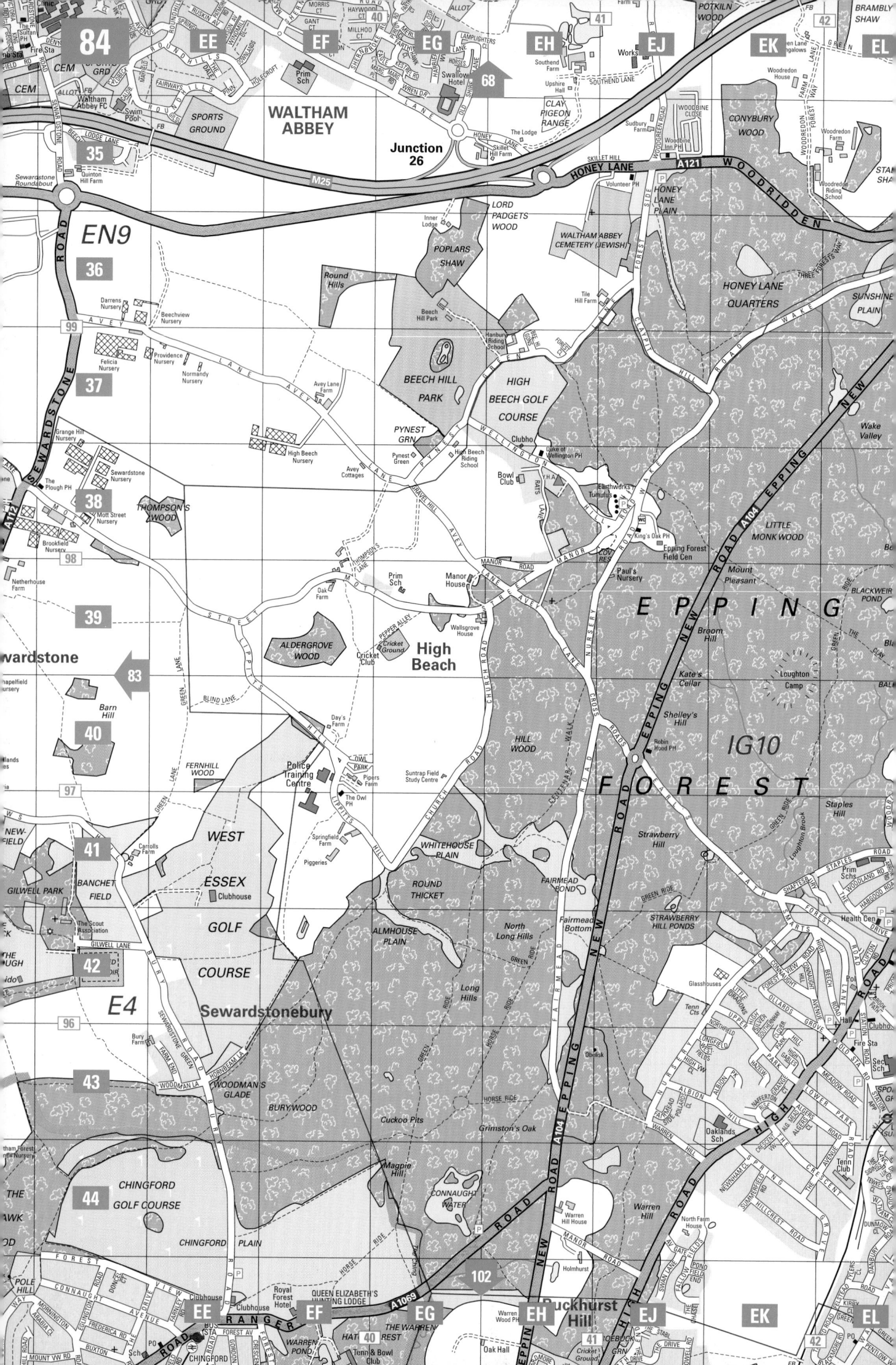

84
EE
EF
EG
EH
EJ
EK
EL
68
WALTHAM ABBEY
Junction 26
M25
HONEY LANE
A121
WOODRIDDEN
EN9
35
36
37
38
39
40
41
42
43
44
99
98
97
96
40
41
42
SEWARDSTONE ROAD
A112
AVEY LANE
MOTT STREET
LORD PADGETS WOOD
POPLARS SHAW
Round Hills
BEECH HILL PARK
HIGH BEECH GOLF COURSE
HONEY LANE PLAIN
HONEY LANE QUARTERS
CONYBURY WOOD
WALTHAM ABBEY CEMETERY (JEWISH)
SUNSHINE PLAIN
THOMPSON'S WOOD
ALDERGROVE WOOD
High Beach
83
Sewardstone
Barn Hill
FERNHILL WOOD
Police Training Centre
WEST ESSEX GOLF COURSE
Sewardstonebury
E4
BANCHET FIELD
GILWELL PARK
WHITEHOUSE PLAIN
ROUND THICKET
ALMHOUSE PLAIN
HILL WOOD
EPPING FOREST
A104
EPPING NEW ROAD
IG10
LITTLE MONK WOOD
Mount Pleasant
Broom Hill
Kate's Cellar
Loughton Camp
Shelley's Hill
Strawberry Hill
STRAWBERRY HILL PONDS
FAIRMEAD POND
Fairmead Bottom
North Long Hills
Long Hills
WOODMAN'S GLADE
BURY WOOD
Cuckoo Pits
Grimston's Oak
Magpie Hill
CONNAUGHT WATER
Warren Hill
CHINGFORD GOLF COURSE
CHINGFORD PLAIN
Royal Forest Hotel
QUEEN ELIZABETH'S HUNTING LODGE
A1069
RANGERS ROAD
102
Buckhurst Hill
CHINGFORD
Staples Hill
Wake Valley

85
EM
EN
EP
EQ
ER
ES
ET
43
44
45
69
86
103
35
36
37
38
39
40
41
42
43
44
99
98
97
96
EPPING FOREST
Ambresbury Banks
Warren Lodge
THEYDON BOIS GOLF COURSE
Little Bronx Livery & Riding Stables
Junction 6 (M
Junction 27 (M
LITTLE GREGORIES LANE
PIERCING HILL
Coll
Long Running
HORSE RIDE
GREEN RIDE
B1393
EPPING
Jacks Hill
B172
COPPICE ROW
Oak Hill
QUEEN MARY & WESTFIELD COLLEGE SPORTS GROUND
Pav
DUKES
HAREWOOD HILL
WOODLAND WAY
PURLIEU WAY
AVENUE
BALDOCKS RD
HEATH DR
THE WEIND
MORGAN CRESCENT
Prim Sch
ELIZABETH DR
ORCHARD DRIVE
BUXTON RD
BARN MEAD
Hall
PO
FOREST DRIVE
SLADE END
THEYDON BOIS
Sixteen Spring Jack PH
ROBINS LA
THEYDON PLAIN
THE COPPICE
Oak Hill Farm
Birch Hall
Birch Hall Farm
Dulsmead Hollow
COPLEY PLAIN
FURZE GROUND
RIDE
GREEN
THE DITCHES RIDE
GOLDINGS HILL
SIDNEY RD
Tenn Cts
Tenn Club
SPORTS GRD
Cricket Club
ALLOTS
Youth Cen
THEYDON GREEN
COPP ROW
ABRIDGE
Theydon Bois
Parsonage Farm
Blunts Farm
Depot
COOPERSALE
Thrifts Hall Farm
THE GREEN
POPLAR ROW
THRIFTS MEAD
Pol
WOBURN AV
HORNBEAM CL
PAKES WAY
GLADE
BLACKACRE ROAD
HILL ROAD
THEYDON PARK ROAD
CM16
BIRCH WOOD
RED OAK WOOD
GAUNT'S WOOD
LOUGHTON LANE
BROADSTROOD PLAIN
Ripley Grange
Debden Green
THEYDON BOIS CEMETERY
GREGSON'S RIDE
GOLDING'S HILL PONDS
DEBDEN ROAD
Coll
DEBDEN LANE
RIPLEY VW
LOUGHTON GOLF COURSE
Clubhouse
Sec Sch
Theydon Hall Farm
Theydon Hall
Nursery
BROADSTROOD
CAMPIONS
STANMORE WAY
A121
CLAY'S LANE
WILLINGALE ROAD
Prim Sch
JESSEL DR
M11
ALLOTS
Sch
AREWATER GRN
STONY PATH
HARWATER DR
MILLSMEAD WAY
SEDLEY RISE
ENGLANDS LANE
HILLCROFT
HILLYFIELDS
COLES GRN
PYRLES LANE
CHESTER RD
ROAD
LONG SHAW
B172
Plume of Feathers PH
MAPLE GATE
RECTORY
HILLYFIELDS OPEN SPACE
AVENUE DRIVE
Prim Sch
BURNEY DRIVE
ALLOTMENTS
FB
Debden
BROADFIELD SHAW
RM4
THEYDON MEAD
CEM
A1168
ROUNDMEAD AV
LAWTON RD
ROOKWOOD AV
WILLINGALE RD
Prim Sch
SPORTS GROUND
Pav
A113
LONDON ROAD
Abridge Park
Cricket Club
SPORTS GRD
Prim Sch
Printing Works
Tenn Cts
Clubhouse
River Roding
Bowl Grn
Tenn Cts
St. Lukes Sch
Coll
Sports Cen
Amb Sta
Clinic
Coll
Lib
Sir Winston Churchill PH
TORRINGTON
PROSPECT BUSINESS PARK
DEBDEN
SPORTS GROUND
BORDERS LANE
ALDERTON HILL
GHTON
OAKWOOD HILL INDUSTRIAL ESTATE
LANGSTON RD
CHIGWELL LANE
LORRY PK
IG7
DRIVING RANGE
Great Downs Farm
GRAVEL
Prim Schs
CHEQUERS
Clubhouse
SPORTS GROUND
Loughton Bridge
Junction 5
Clubhouse
Woolston Hall
Open Air Pool
Turnours Hall
Marchings
Marchings Farm
A1112
EPPING FOREST GOLF COURSE
OAKWOOD HILL
RIVER WAY
SOUTH VIEW RD
RIVERSIDE WALK
River Roding
SPORTS GROUND
Tenn Cts
PO
SPORTS GROUND
ABRIDGE ROAD
LANE
PUDDING LANE
Home Farm
Rolls Park
Rolls Park Farm
Pettits Hall
Taylor May's Farm
LOUGHTON
LANE

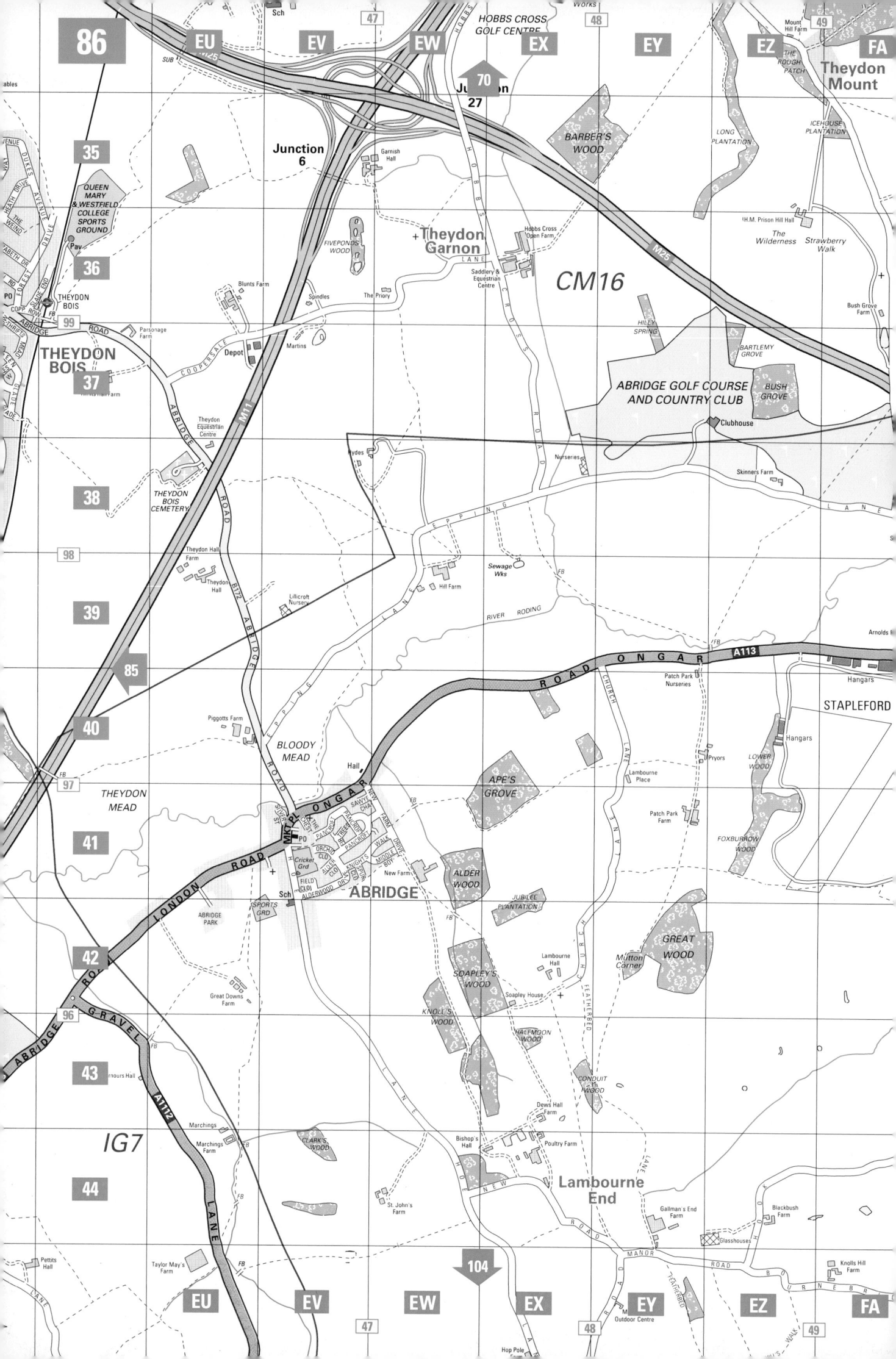

EU
EV
EW
EX
EY
EZ
FA
47
48
49
70
HOBBS CROSS GOLF CENTRE
Junction 27
Junction 6
M25
M11
Theydon Mount
THE ROUGH PATCH
LONG PLANTATION
ICEHOUSE PLANTATION
Mount Hill Farm
BARBER'S WOOD
Garnish Hall
QUEEN MARY & WESTFIELD COLLEGE SPORTS GROUND
Pav
H.M. Prison Hill Hall
The Wilderness
Strawberry Walk
FIVEPONDS WOOD
Theydon Garnon
Hobbs Cross Open Farm
Saddlery & Equestrian Centre
CM16
Blunts Farm
Spindles
The Priory
THEYDON BOIS
THEYDON BOIS
Parsonage Farm
Martins
Depot
COOPERSALE
HILLY SPRING
BARTLEMY GROVE
Bush Grove Farm
ABRIDGE GOLF COURSE AND COUNTRY CLUB
BUSH GROVE
Clubhouse
Theydon Equestrian Centre
Hydes
Nurseries
Skinners Farm
THEYDON BOIS CEMETERY
EPPING
LANE
Theydon Hall Farm
Theydon Hall
Sewage Wks
Hill Farm
Lillicroft Nursery
RIVER RODING
B172
ABRIDGE
ROAD
85
ONGAR ROAD
A113
Arnolds
Patch Park Nurseries
Hangars
STAPLEFORD
Piggotts Farm
BLOODY MEAD
Hall
CHURCH LANE
Pryors
LOWER WOOD
Lambourne Place
THEYDON MEAD
APE'S GROVE
Patch Park Farm
MKT PL
ONGAR
FOXBURROW WOOD
PO
Cricket Grd
New Farm
ALDER WOOD
ABRIDGE
LONDON ROAD
Sch
SPORTS GRD
ABRIDGE PARK
JUBILEE PLANTATION
GREAT WOOD
Mutton Corner
Lambourne Hall
SOAPLEY'S WOOD
Great Downs Farm
Soapley House
FEATHERBED
GRAVEL
KNOLL'S WOOD
HALFMOON WOOD
A1112
CONDUIT WOOD
Dews Hall Farm
Marchings
Marchings Farm
IG7
CLARK'S WOOD
Bishop's Hall
Poultry Farm
NEW
Lambourne End
St. John's Farm
Gallman's End Farm
Blackbush Farm
Glasshouses
MANOR ROAD
Knolls Hill Farm
Pettits Hall
Taylor May's Farm
104
Outdoor Centre
Hop Pole
35
36
37
38
39
40
41
42
43
44
96
97
98
99
FB

FB
FC
FD
FE
FF
FG
FH
50
51
52
SPRING
ROUND SPRING
WELL EAVES
ICEHO WOOD
Berwick Farm
70
Howfields
Little Tawney Hall
PARK SPRING
THE GROVE
TWENTYACRE WOOD
BERWICK HAM
Murrells Farm
Traceys Farm
White Bear PH
35
TENACRE WOOD
DOG KENNEL SPRING
36
STAPLEFORD ROAD
THE MOORS
BOB'S BARN WOOD
LANGFORD BOTTOM
STONYROCKS PLANTATION
BROOM WOOD
99
Stapleford Tawney
Great Tawney Hall
CM5
37
SHALES MORE
ROAD
A113
SHONKS
RAILMEAD PLANTATION
Mitchells Farm
Shonk's Mill Bridge
MILL ROAD
38
HOOK WOOD
Rose Hall Farm
RIVER RODING
EPPING FOREST
BRENTWOOD
98
LONDON ROAD
Clinic
Sutton's Farm
TAWNEY LANE
39
Howletts Hall
Dabbs Farm
Passingford Bridge
Waters Farm
ALBYNS LA
Yew Tree Farm
40
Navestock
97
B175
Green Farm
Grafton Farm
Hammonds Farm
Bons Farm
Albyns Farm
Albyns Hall
M25
MURTHERING LANE
41
The Rabbits PH
Forty Acre Farm
CURTISMILL GREEN
CURTIS MILL GRN
Lodge Farm
42
CHURCH LANE
Church Farm
Brook Farm
SUBWAY
Jenkins Farm
CURTIS MILL LANE
96
Battles Hall
Stapleford Abbotts
Sch
Hall
Belmont Farm
BOURNE BROOK
43
RM4
Tyseahill Farm
Spring Farm
CM14
Stapleford Hall Farm
GUTTERIDGE LA
High House Farm
Olives Farm
THE PADDOCKS
MOAT
Watton Farm
44
STAPLEFORD ABBOTTS GOLF COURSE
WATTON'S GREEN
PRIORS
Woodlands Farm
HORSEMAN SIDE
Nursery
Brook Farm
105
TYSEA HILL
Skips Corner Farm
Asheton Farm
Bournebridge Farm
Nuper's Hatch
EPPING
BRENTWOOD

HP15
HP10
HP13
AC
AD
AE
AF
AG
AH
AJ
91
92
93
94
45
46
47
48
49
50
51
52
53
54
TYLERS GREEN
COMMON WOOD
THE LARCHES
CHARCOLE GROVE
PENNHOUSE GROVE
PUGH'S WOOD
BROOK WOOD
ROUND WOOD
BRANCHES WOOD
Winchmore Hill Farm
GLORY BELT
Penn House
Pennstreet Farm
Pennhouse Farm
Puttenham Place Farm
Cricket Grd
Tennis Courts
Clubhouse
SPORTS GRD
The Old Queen's Head PH
The Red Lion PH
PLAYING FIELD
KING'S WOOD
Penn
VICARAGE WOOD
The Crown Inn PH
DOWNHAM GROVE
WESTFIELD PIECES
WITHERIDGE WOOD
GOMMS WOOD
PENBURY GROVE
Saucy Corner
CHURCH PATH WOOD
Stumpwell
LITTLE GOMMS WOOD
Fieldgrove Nurseries
POND WOOD
GATEMOOR WOOD
CORKERS WOOD
Town House Farm
Bottom Farm
STANDERS WOOD
Parsonage Farm
WYCOMBE HEIGHTS GOLF CENTRE
DRIVING RANGE
VINEYARD
COPPICE HOOP
Forty Green
The Royal Standard PH
LONGFIELD WOOD
Lude Farm
The Red Lion PH
REC GRD
THROSHERS WOOD
ROUNDHEADS WOOD
SNIGGS WOOD
Pitch 'n' Putt
MOBILE HOME PARK
CHILTERN WYCOMBE
HOGBACK WOOD
Electricity Station
Upper Derehams Farm
KING'S MEAD Cricket Grds
KINGSMEAD BUS PK
CEM
ALLOT
Holtspur Bottom Farm
Whitehouse Farm
LOUDWATER
KNAVES BEECH BUSINESS CENTRE
Superstore
Holtspur
CUT-THROAT WOOD
Youth Club
Bandstand
Clubhouse
Superstores
Junction 3
Highwayman's Farm
110
FLACKWELL HEATH
COURSE
REC GRD
The Three Horseshoes PH
Tenn Cts
Bowl Grn
Works
A40
M40
B474
LONDON ROAD
OXFORD ROAD
WYCOMBE ROAD
BOUNDARY ROAD
CHURCH ROAD
ELM ROAD
HAZLEMERE ROAD
COMMON WOOD
WITHERIDGE LANE
PENN STREET
CLAY LANE
PENN BOTTOM
BEACON HILL
HAMMERSLEY LANE
WHITEHOUSE LANE
RIDING LANE
GREGORIES ROAD
HOLTSPUR TOP LANE
HAMPDEN HILL
BURKES ROAD
WESTFIELD ROAD
FORTY GREEN ROAD
WOODSIDE ROAD

89
AK
AL
AM
AN
AP
AQ
AR
55
90
111
HP7
HP8
HP9
SL9
COLESHILL COMMON
HERTS WOOD
HERTFORDSHIRE WOOD
LITTLE LUCKINGS WOOD
ONGAR HILL DELLS
TALLY WOOD
GREAT LUCKINGS WOOD
GREAT BEARD'S WOOD
OWSLEARS WOOD
BROWN'S WOOD
NETHERLANDS WOOD
BIRCHEN SPRING
PEGGS WOOD
LEDBOROUGH WOOD
OLDFIELDS FURZE
YOUNG'S WOOD
HILL'S WOOD
HEATHFIELD GROVE
HODGEMOOR WOODS
HALES WOOD
WELPLEY'S WOOD
THE LARCHES
RAWLINGS DELL
BIG COPSE
LITTLE COPSE
STARVEACRE WOOD
BOTTOM WOOD
CLEARE CRAFT WOOD
BLUE CLOSE WOOD
BEACONSFIELD GOLF COURSE
THE MOUNT
WALK WOOD
LITTLE WALK WOOD
WHEATSHEAF WOOD
DEAN WOOD
PITLANDS WOOD
BIRCHLAND WOOD
THIRTY ACRE KNOLL
SEER GREEN
SPORTS GROUND
BON SECOURS HOSP
PLAYING FIELD
MODEL VILLAGE
AMERSHAM ROAD
LONDON END
LONDON ROAD
WYCOMBE END
OXFORD ROAD
LOWER PYEBUSHES
PYEBUSHES
BIRCH WOOD

90
AS
AT
AU
AV
AW
AX
AY
HP8
HP7
HP9
72
89
112
45
46
47
48
49
50
51
52
53
54
HODGEMOOR WOODS
CHALFONT ST. GILES
SEER GREEN
Jordans
Butlers Cross
CHALFONT PARK GOLF COURSE
GREYHOUND TRACK
Layter's Green
GOLDHILL COMMON
BAILEY WOOD
HALES WOOD
WELPLEY'S WOOD
PERRYFIELD PLANTATION
RUSHCROFT WOOD
BYCROFT PLANTATION
RESERVOIR PLANTATION
KILNPOND WOOD
OAK PLANTATION
DELLGARDEN PLANTATION
SHORTENILL WOOD
MILLFIELD PLANTATION
MILTON'S COTTAGE
Dibden Hill
TURNER'S WOOD
FOXDELL WOOD
PLAYING FIELD
OUTFIELD PLANTATION
BIRCH PLANTATION
MONAGUE'S DELL
FARM WOOD
ROUND WOOD
MIDDLE FARM
POND WARREN WOOD
LONG WOOD
GROVE WOOD
WELDERS WOOD
SPRING WOOD
WEEDONS DELL
MOUNTHILL WOOD
THE ASH BEDS
THIRTY ACRE KNOLL
GREAT LEGS WOOD
MALMS WOOD
HIGH WOOD
BEECH WOOD
BIRCH WOOD
BIRCHLAND WOOD
PITLANDS WOOD
WHEATSHEAF WOOD
DEAN WOOD
CRUTCHES WOOD
GREEN WOOD
BIG COPSE
LITTLE COPSE
RAWLINGS DELL
THE LARCHES
BOW WOOD
HIGH WOOD
Quakers Conference Centre
LONDON ROAD
AMERSHAM ROAD
GRAVEL HILL
A413

91
Chorleywood Bottom
The Swillet
Heronsgate
Mill End
Junction 17
Leisure centre
SPORTS GRD
PHILIPSHILL WOOD
NEWLAND PARK
Brunel University Buckinghamshire College
CHILTERN OPEN AIR MUSEUM
PLAYING FIELD
BOTTOM WOOD
LADYWALK WOOD
WD3
FIVE PLANTATIONS
HERTFORDSHIRE
BUCKINGHAMSHIRE
POLLARDSHILL WOOD
Maple Cross
MAPLE CROSS IND. ESTATE
BEECHEN WOOD
KILN WOOD
FRANKLIN'S SPRING
Maple Lodge Sewage Treatment Works
Sludge Drying Beds
SPRINGWELL LAKE
SPRINGWELL CHALK PIT
ROBERT'S WOOD
ROUND ROCKET PLANTATION
QUARRY & LANDFILL SITE
MIDDLE WOOD
BLOOM WOOD
LYNSTERS LAKE
PYNESFIELD LAKE
PARK WOO
GRAVEL PIT
CHALFONT ST.PETER
HOGTROUGH WOOD
GOLF COURSE
NOCKHILL WOOD
JUNIPER WOOD
DURDENT COURT CONFERENCE CENTRE
UB9
CHALFONT PARK
M25
A405
A412
ORBITAL ROAD
NORTH ORBITAL WAY
DENHAM WAY
73
113
45
46
47
48
49
50
51
52
53
54
92

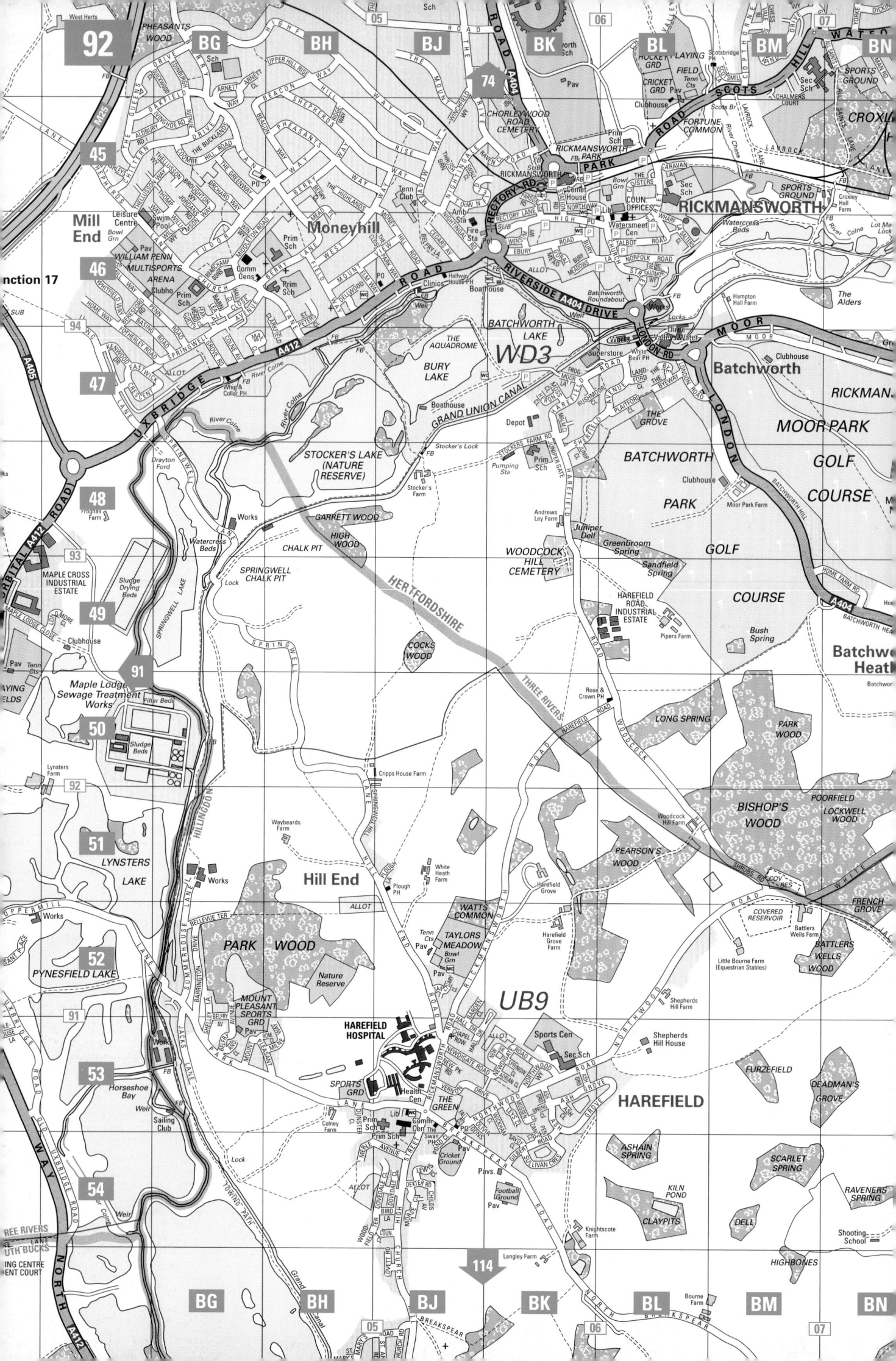
92
74
114
45
46
47
48
49
50
51
52
53
54
91
BG
BH
BJ
BK
BL
BM
BN
05
06
07
94
93
92
91
West Herts
PHEASANTS WOOD
Mill End
Moneyhill
Leisure Centre
Swim Pool
WILLIAM PENN MULTISPORTS ARENA
Junction 17
M25
A405
A412
UXBRIDGE ROAD
RICKMANSWORTH
Rickmansworth Park
CHORLEYWOOD ROAD CEMETERY
SCOTS HILL
CROXLEY
SPORTS GROUND
FORTUNE COMMON
RIVERSIDE DRIVE
A404
BATCHWORTH LAKE
THE AQUADROME
BURY LAKE
WD3
Batchworth
MOOR PARK
BATCHWORTH PARK GOLF COURSE
GRAND UNION CANAL
STOCKER'S LAKE (NATURE RESERVE)
GARRETT WOOD
HIGH WOOD
CHALK PIT
SPRINGWELL CHALK PIT
SPRINGWELL LAKE
HERTFORDSHIRE
THREE RIVERS
HILLINGDON
COCKS WOOD
WOODCOCK HILL CEMETERY
HAREFIELD ROAD INDUSTRIAL ESTATE
Batchworth Heath
MAPLE CROSS INDUSTRIAL ESTATE
Maple Lodge Sewage Treatment Works
LYNSTERS LAKE
PYNESFIELD LAKE
Horseshoe Bay
Hill End
PARK WOOD
LONG SPRING
BISHOP'S WOOD
POORFIELD
LOCKWELL WOOD
PEARSON'S WOOD
WATTS COMMON
TAYLORS MEADOW
MOUNT PLEASANT SPORTS GRD
HAREFIELD HOSPITAL
UB9
HAREFIELD
FRENCH GROVE
BATTLERS WELLS WOOD
FURZEFIELD
DEADMAN'S GROVE
ASHAIN SPRING
SCARLET SPRING
KILN POND
CLAYPITS
DELL
RAVENERS SPRING
HIGHBONES
Shooting School

BP
BQ
BR
BS
BT
BU
BV
08
09
10
Holywell
WATFORD STADIUM HALT (MATCH DAYS ONLY)
LONG VALLEY WOOD
COMMON MOOR
HOLYWELL IND EST
75
KING GEORGE V PLAYING FIELDS
Electricity Transmission Station
SPORTS GROUND
TOLPITS LANE
THE EBURY WAY CYCLE PATH
WOLSEY BUSINESS PARK
MOOR PARK INDUSTRIAL ESTATE
VALE INDUSTRIAL ESTATE
Moor Park Crossing
Brightwells Spring
HAMPERMILL LAKE
RUNNING TRACK
Tolpits Plantation
The Withey Bed Wood
Merchant Taylor's Sch
HAMPERMILL LANE
HAMPERMILL WOOD
BIG WOOD
Ox Pasture Spring
SOUTH OXHEY PLAYING FIELDS
OXHEY PARK GOLF COURSE
WD1
EASTBURY ROAD
BROOKDENE AVENUE
45
46
47
48
49
50
51
52
53
54
94
SANDY LODGE ROAD
GOLF COURSE
MOOR PARK
SANDY LODGE GOLF COURSE
Hampermill Spring
Round Spring
OLD FURZE FIELD
YOUNG HANGINGS
OLD HANGINGS
OXHEY
THE PLANTATION
BECK MASON'S WOOD
WOOD
SOUTH OXHEY
Moor Park
MOOR PARK ESTATE
Eastbury
BATHEND CLUMP
H.M.S. Warrior
PRESTWICK ROAD
BATCHWORTH LANE
THREE RIVERS
WILD WOODS
NANSOUND WOOD
NORTHWOOD
RICKMANSWORTH ROAD
MOUNT VERNON HOSPITAL
Frithwood Park
St. Helen's Sch
WATFORD ROAD
St. John's C of E Boys Sch
PINNER WOOD
PINNER HILL GOLF COURSE
PINNERWOOD PARK
HA6
HA5
GREEN LANE
HIGH STREET
HARROW STREET
HOGS BACK OPEN SPACE
THE GRAVEL PITS
Northwood Coll
NORTHWOOD GOLF COURSE
NORTHWOOD & PINNER COTTAGE HOSP
Northwood Hills
NORTHWOOD CEMETERY
HASTE HILL GOLF COURSE
RUISLIP NATURE RESERVE
COPSE WOOD
DUCKS HILL
PINNER GREEN
PLAYING FIELDS
115
ST. VINCENT'S ORTHOPAEDIC HOSPITAL
POOR'S FIELD
YOUNG WOOD
A4125
A4145
A4180
A404
B469

94
BW
BX
BY
BZ
CA
CB
CC
12
13
14
76
OXHEY PARK
BUSHEY
BUSHEY GOLF COURSE & COUNTRY CLUB
Open Air Pool
RUNNING TRACK
KING GEORGE V REC GROUND
Haydon Hill House
Watford Borough Council Nursery
Watford Equestrian Centre
Electricity Transmission Station
45
A4125
EASTBURY ROAD
BROOKDENE AVENUE
46
WD1
WATFORD HEATH
SPOILBANKS
SHERWOODS WOOD
GOLF DRIVING RANGE
MARGEHOLES WOOD
MERRY HILL
WD2
94
Ox Pasture Spring
47
PLAYING FIELDS
BIG WOOD
OXHEY PARK GOLF COURSE
Warren Dell
CARPENDERS PARK
Carpenders Park Farm
HARTSBOURNE GOLF COURSE & COUNTRY CLUB
CARPENDERS PARK
48
SOUTH OXHEY
POND WOOD
WOODWALKS
CARPENDERS PARK CEMETERY
HERTSMERE
MUTTON WOOD
LEVELS WOOD
93
OXHEY
49
WOOD
SANDPIT WOOD
GRIM'S DYKE GOLF COURSE
Grim's Dyke House Hotel
WEALD WOOD
93
B4542 OXHEY LANE
A4008
50
HERTFORDSHIRE
HARROW
STONY WOOD
Oxhey Lane Farm
Grimswood House
Highcroft
SPORTS GROUND
Elec Sta
THREE RIVERS
92
NANSCOT WOOD
SADDLERS MEAD REC GROUND
51
Pinnerwood Farm
SPORTS GROUND
HATCH END
SHAFTESBURY PLAYING FIELDS
52
PINNER WOOD
PINNER HILL GOLF COURSE
PINNERWOOD PARK
HILLINGDON
91
HATCH END
UXBRIDGE RD
A410
HARROW ARTS CENTRE
HATCH END PLAYING FIELD
RAGHUVANSHI CHARITABLE TRUST SPORTS GROUND
53
HA5
PINNER GREEN
PLAYING FIELDS
A404
54
PINNER PARK
Pinner Park Farm
HEADSTONE LANE
SPORTS GROUND
LITTLE COMMON
116
BLOOMSBURY COURT
CHISWICK COURT
RECREATION
ST. THOMAS' DRIVE
RICKMANSWORTH RD
UXBRIDGE ROAD

95
CD
CE
CF
CG
CH
CJ
CK
15
16
17
77
M1
A411
ELSTREE ROAD
WATFORD ROAD
BARNET
ELSTREE HILL OPEN SPACE
CENTENNIAL PARK
A41 BYPASS
ELSTREE OPEN SPACE
Edgwarebury Hotel
45
46
47
48
49
50
51
52
53
54
Junction 4
WD6
HERTSMERE
HARROW
B.U.P.A. HOSPITAL
BUSHEY HEATH
STANMORE COMMON
ROYAL NATIONAL ORTHOPAEDIC HOSP
Mike Heafey Sports & Rehabilitation Centre
Aspire Centre
Brockley Grange
Site of Sulloniacae Roman Settlement
PEAR WOOD
WOOD LANE
BROCKLEY HILL
EDGWARE WAY
A41 (WATFORD BYPASS)
WATLING STREET (ROMAN ROAD)
GROVE FIELDS
LITTLE COMMON
CLOISTERS WOOD
BROCKLEY HILL GOLF PARK
GOVT OFFICES
Canons Corner
SPUR ROAD
94
93
92
91
BENTLEY PRIORY
BENTLEY PRIORY OPEN SPACE
BENTLEY PRIORY NATURE RESERVE
DEER PARK
HA7
STANMORE HILL
A4140 COMMON
A409
A3
96
STANMORE
CHURCH RD
THE BDY
LONDON ROAD
A410
UXBRIDGE ROAD
HARROW WEALD CEMETERY
HARROW WEALD LAKE
Weald College
STANMORE PARK
Stanmore College
TEMPLE POND
STANMORE GOLF COURSE
ALLOTMENTS
STANMORE MARSH
PLAYING FIELD
HA8
N London Collegiate Sch
KING GEORGE V MEML GDNS
CANONS PARK
THE LAKE
SPORTS GROUND
PRINCE EDWARD PLAYING FIELD
HONEYPOT LANE
A4140
RECREATION GROUND
HARROW WEALD
BROOKSHILL
HIGH ROAD
BELMONT CIRCLE
BELMONT
CENTENARY PARK
QUEENSBURY
WEALDSTONE
117
BYRON REC GRD
GEORGE STREET

CL
CM
CN
CP
CQ
CR
CS
19
20
21
78
45
46
47
48
49
50
51
52
53
54
94
93
92
91
95
118
BARNET A411
DEACONS HILL OPEN SPACE
Deacons Hill
Woodcock Hill Farm
TUNNEL
Superstore
BARNET LANE
Stirling Corner
ELSTREE PARK
SCRATCH WOOD
FROGHALL WOOD
ARKLEY PARK
Hyver Hall
BOYS HILL WOOD
THISTLE WOOD
GRAVEL PITWOOD
CLUMP OF TREES WOOD
TARGET WOOD
MILL HILL GOLF COURSE
HEMMINGS WOOD
STONEY WOOD LAKE
STONEY WOOD
NUT WOOD
Elstree Manor
Penniwells Farm
Edgwarebury Hotel
ELSTREE OPEN SPACE
ELSTREE HILL SOUTH A5183
Junction 4
WD6
HERTSMERE
M1
BARNET
Depot
London Gateway Services
Travelodge Hotel
Brockley Grange
Site of Sulloniacae Roman Settlement
BROCKLEY HILL
EDGWARE WAY
WATLING STREET (ROMAN ROAD)
A41 (WATFORD BYPASS)
Bury Farm
EDGWAREBURY CEMETERY
CLAY LANE
REC GRD
SPORTS GRD
Clubhouse
EDGWAREBURY PARK
Pav
Tennis Courts
EDGWAREBURY GOLF COURSE
FISH POND
BROCKLEY GOLF
GOVT OFFICES
SPORTS GROUND
Canons Corner
SPUR ROAD
LONDON ROAD A410
STANMORE
SPUR RD ESTATE
STONEGROVE EST
STONEGROVE
THE LAKE
N London Collegiate Sch
KING GEORGE V MEML GDNS
CANONS PARK
THE SPINNEY
STONEGROVE PARK
HIGH STREET A5
STATION ROAD
EDGWARE
HA8
BUS STA
Broadwalk Shop Cen
BUS DEPOT
Deans Brook
ALLOTMENTS
CONVENT
EDGWARE WAY (WATFORD BYPASS)
HALE LANE A5100
Apex Corner
SELVAGE LANE
WATFORD WAY
LYNDHURST PARK
THE BASIN
SPORTS GROUND
CANONS PARK
WHITCHURCH LANE
GOVT BUILDINGS
Gas Works
PLAYING FIELD
HA7
CHANDOS RECREATION GROUND
PRINCE EDWARD PLAYING FIELD
BURNT OAK
EDGWARE COMMUNITY HOSPITAL
Hendon Coll
WATLING PARK
SPORTS GROUND
DEANSBROOK ROAD
BURNT OAK BROADWAY A5
SILKSTREAM PARK
ADASTRAL ESTATE
MONTROSE PLAYING FIELDS
COLINDALE HOSP
BLOOD TRANSFUSION CENTRE
NW9
BRIXTON EST
COLINDALE BUSINESS PK
CAPITOL IND PK
Yaohan Plaza
HONEYPOT LANE A4140
QUEENSBURY
CENTENARY PARK
Pitch 'n' Putt
The Flying Eagle Tavern PH
Green Man PH
ETON GROVE
COLINDALE
AEROVILLE

CT
CU
CV
CW
CX
CY
CZ
22
23
24
79
Barnet Gate
Ducks Island
Youth & Comm Cen
Whitings Hill Farm
Cottage Farm
GRANGE PLAYING FIELDS
PLAYING FIELD
Tennis Courts
KING GEORGE V PLAYING FIELDS
OLD ELIZABETHANS (BARNET) MEMORIAL PLAYING FIELDS
Brent Lodge Farm
Dollis Brook
Sec Sch
OAKLANDS ROAD
45
SOUTH HERTS GOLF COURSE
N20
OLD CHOLMELEIAN SPORTS GROUND
TOTTERIDGE FIELDS NATURE RESERVE
Mote End Farm
St. Edward's College
TOTTERIDGE PARK
TOTTERIDGE COMMON
A5109
TOTTERIDGE
War Memorial
46
Oak Lodge
Ellern Mede Farm
The Warren
Fairlawn
The Lynch House
VILLAGE
94
Orange Tree PH
Prim Sch
TOTTERIDGE GREEN
47
Cricket Grd Clubho.
HENDON PARK WOOD
HIGHWOOD HILL
Highwood House
Highwood Hill
Holcombe Dales
Consolata Missionary Coll
Folly Brook
DARLANDS LAKE NATURE RESERVE
48
THE REDDINGS
ABBEY
CONV
Jun Sch
Tenn Cts
Belmont Riding Centre
Belmont Farm
Folly Farm
SPORTS GROUND
Clubhouses
93
PLAYING FIELD
THE MILL FIELD
GROUNDS
NW7
St. Joseph's RC College
CHALET ESTATE
Three Hammers PH
Sports Cen
Prim Sch
Nursery
Pav
Burtonhole Farm
SPORTS GROUND
Clubhouse
SPORTS
49
RETREAT CENTRE
Nat Inst. for Medical Research
N12
Open Air Pool
Mill Hill Sch
COTTAGE HOMES
SPORTS
Elec Sta
98
SPORTS GRD
THE RIDGEWAY
B552
Prim Sch
Goodwyn Sch
GROUND
The Mount Sch
Oakfields
Frith Manor Equestrian Centre
Frith Manor Farm
Drivers Hill
Partingdale Manor
SPORTS GRD
50
Ridgeway House
Burton Bank
ARRANDENE OPEN SPACE
Milespit Hill
Watch Tower House
Wks
INGLIS BARRACKS
FINCHLEY
92
MILL HILL
Univ of London Observatory
Bowling Greens
Featherstone Hill
Cricket Club
MILL HILL PARK
MILL HILL CEM
BITTACY HILL PARK
Depot
GOLF
51
Nethercourt (Clubhouse)
Council Depot
Works
COURSE
MILL HILL EAST
Gas Works
WEST FINCHLEY
Superstore
Sec Sch
Prim Schs.
Comm Cen
Chase Lodge
CHASE LODGE PLAYING FIELD
52
PLAYING FIELD
METRO GOLF
Swim Pool
Clubhouse
HENDON
SPORTS GROUND
Crematorium
HENDON CEMETERY
Prim Sch
SPORTS GRD
91
Hendon Youth Cen
Swim Pool
COPTHALL
COPTHALL STADIUM
GOLF
Superstore
N3
53
FINCHLEY CENTRAL
Junction 2
Five Ways Corner
COPTHALL PLAYING FIELDS
Cricket Club
SPORTS GROUND
COURSE
Tennis Club
CHURCH END
Sec Sch
Comm Cen
A1
M1
GREAT NORTH WAY
Hendon R.F.C.
HOLDERS HILL
RAF MUSEUMS
NW4
Pav
Tennis Courts
SUNNY HILL PARK
WINDSOR OPEN SPACE
Coll
A504
54
The Queens Head PH
EAST END ROAD
Warehouses
119
GARDEN HO
College Farm
CT
CU
CV
CW
CX
CY
CZ
SPORTS GRD
22
CHURCH FARM HOUSE MUS
23
24
Prep Sch
Prim

DA
DB
DC
DD
DE
DF
DG
80
97
120
EAST BARNET
OAK HILL PARK
SOUTH HERTS GOLF COURSE
N20
WHETSTONE
OAKLEIGH PARK
EN4
BRUNSWICK PARK
NORTH MIDDLESEX GOLF COURSE
FRIARY PARK
FRIERN BARNET
BETHUNE GOLF COURSE
N12
NORTH FINCHLEY
TOTTERIDGE GREEN
FINCHLEY
N3
CHURCH END
COPPETTS WOOD
ST. PANCRAS & ISLINGTON CEMETERY
COLDFALL WOOD
N2
FINCHLEY MEMORIAL HOSP
COPPETTS WOOD HOSP
VICTORIA PARK
GLEBELANDS OPEN SPACE
AVENUE HOUSE GRDS
MUSWELL HILL SPORTS GROUND

99
DH
DJ
DK
DL
DM
DN
DP
29
30
31
81
121
45
46
47
48
49
50
51
52
53
54
91
92
93
94
100
OAKWOOD
OAKWOOD PARK
YACHTING POND
WINCHMORE HILL
GROVELANDS PARK
BOATING LAKE
N14
N21
N13
N22
OSIDGE
SOUTHGATE
Southgate Technical Coll
SOUTHGATE CEMETERY
HOSPITAL (CLOSED)
WOODCROFT SPORTS GROUND
THE PAULIN GROUND
CLOWES SPORTS GROUND
FIRS FARM PLAYING FIELD
PALMERS GREEN
HAZELWOOD SPORTS GRD
TATEM PARK REC GRD
HOLLYWOOD GDNS
ARNOS PARK
NEW SOUTHGATE
BROOMFIELD PARK
ARNOS GROVE
TOWN HALL
BOWES PARK
BOUNDS GREEN
TOTTENHALL SPORTS GROUND
BOUNDARY PLAYING FIELDS
NEW RIVER SPORTS CENTRE
MUSWELL HILL GOLF COURSE
SCOUT PARK
WOODSIDE PARK
CEM
PLAYING FIELD
Coll of N E London
Middlesex Uni
WOOD GREEN
TRAIN DEPOT
NOEL PARK
LORDSHIP RECREATION GROUND
ALEXANDRA PALACE
ALEXANDRA PARK
SPORTS GROUND
HORNSEY WATER TREATMENT WORKS
BELMONT REC GRD
DOWNHILLS PARK
MUSWELL HILL
HORNSEY
TURNPIKE LANE
CHASE SIDE
THE BOURNE
BOURNE HILL
HIGH STREET
CANNON HILL
ALDERMANS HILL
GREEN LANES
HEDGE LANE
BOWES ROAD
TELFORD ROAD
BOUNDS GREEN ROAD
NORTH CIRCULAR ROAD
HIGH ROAD
LORDSHIP LANE
WESTBURY AVENUE
THE BROADWAY
WATERFALL ROAD
A111
A1004
A1003
A1110
A109
A406
A105
B1452
B106
B151
A10
A1080

100
DQ
DR
DS
DT
DU
DV
DW
33
34
35
82
N21
N9
N13
N18
N17
N22
45
46
47
48
49
50
51
52
53
54
99
122
94
93
92
91
LOWER EDMONTON
EDMONTON
UPPER EDMONTON
TOTTENHAM
NOEL PARK
TOTTENHAM MARSHES
TOTTENHAM HALE
JUBILEE PARK
KING GEORGE'S FLD
EDMONTON CEMETERY
FIRS FARM PLAYING FIELDS
CLOWES SPORTS GROUND
THE PAULIN GROUND
CHURCH STREET REC GRD
CHURCHFIELD REC GRD
PYMMES PARK
TATEM PARK REC GRD
HOLLY-WOOD GDNS
TOTTENHALL SPORTS GROUND
BOUNDARY PLAYING FIELDS
NEW RIVER SPORTS CENTRE
TOTTENHAM CEMETERY
BRUCE CASTLE PARK
BRUCE CASTLE MUS
LORDSHIP RECREATION GROUND
BELMONT REC GRD
DOWNHILLS PARK
LEE VALLEY TECHNOPARK
DOWN LANE REC GRD
MILLMEAD INDUSTRIAL CENTRE
EDMONTON FEDERATION CEMETERY (JEWISH)
WESTERN SYNAGOGUE CEMETERY
CRAIG PARK
NORTH MIDDLESEX HOSPITAL
THE ROYAL LONDON ESTATE
TOTTENHAM HOTSPUR FC
WHITE HART LANE
GREAT CAMBRIDGE ROAD
HERTFORD ROAD
FORE STREET
HIGH ROAD
NORTH CIRCULAR ROAD
STERLING WAY
ANGEL ROAD
MERIDIAN WAY
WATERMEAD WAY
LORDSHIP LANE
THE ROUNDWAY
RIDGE AVENUE
GREEN LANES
WESTBURY AVENUE
BRUCE GROVE
CHURCH STREET
SILVER STREET
LEE VALLEY
LOCKWOOD RESERVOIR

101
DX
DY
DZ
EA
EB
EC
ED
36
37
38
83
45
46
47
48
49
50
51
52
53
54
91
92
93
94
102
123
CHINGFORD GOLF COURSE
CHINGFORD PLAIN
THE HAWK WOOD
POLE HILL
WILLIAM GIRLING RESERVOIR
LEISURE GOLF COURSE
LEA VALLEY PLAYING FIELDS
MANSFIELD PARK
CHINGFORD
E4
FRIDAY HILL
PIMP HALL PARK
RIDGEWAY PARK
CHINGFORD MOUNT CEMETERY
DEEPHAMS SEWAGE TREATMENT WORKS
LEE VALLEY PARK
CHINGFORD HATCH
LARKSWOOD PLAYING FIELDS
LARKS WOOD
JUBILEE SPORTS GRD
CHINGFORD HALL PARK
SOUTH CHINGFORD
HIGHAMS PARK
THE HIGHAMS PARK
BOATING LAKE
WOODFORD GOLF COURSE
LEA VALLEY VIADUCT
LEA VALLEY TRADING ESTATE
HASTINGWOOD TRADING ESTATE
BANBURY RESERVOIR
SALISBURY HALL BLADES PLAYING FIELDS
FAIRWAY GOLF RANGE
BRITANNIA SPORTS GROUND
WALTHAMSTOW GREYHOUND STADIUM
WADHAM LODGE SPORTS GROUND
HALE END
WOODFORD R.F.C.
EPPING FOREST
WALTHAMSTOW FOREST
SOUTHEND RD
NORTH CIRCULAR RD
E17
LLOYD PARK
HIGHAM HILL
HIGHAM HILL REC GRD
UPLANDS BUSINESS PARK
HIGHAMS LODGE BUSINESS CEN
WALTHAMSTOW
WALTHAM FOREST ATHLETICS GRD
CHESTNUTS SHOWGROUND
THORPE COOMBE HOSP
CHILDREN'S BOATING POND
A110
A112
A1009
A1037
A1055
A104
A406
A503
B160
B179

EE
EF
EG
EH
EJ
EK
EL
40
41
42
84
CHINGFORD GOLF COURSE
CHINGFORD PLAIN
Royal Forest Hotel
QUEEN ELIZABETH'S HUNTING LODGE
A1069
RANGERS ROAD
CHINGFORD
STATION ROAD
CONNAUGHT WATER
Magpie Hill
Buckhurst Hill
Warren Hill House
Holmhurst
Oak Hall
THE WARREN
HATCH FOREST
WARREN POND
BARN HOPPETT
CHINGFORD GREEN
WHITEHALL PLAIN
WHITEHALL ROAD
A110
FRIDAY HILL
E4
POLE HILL
45
46
47
48
49
50
51
52
53
54
91
92
93
94
PIMP HALL PARK
BLUEHOUSE GROVE
SPORTS GROUND
HATCH GROVE
REED'S FOREST
THE BIRBECK
OAKLEA CONF. CEN
HOLLY HOUSE HOSP
IG9
LORD'S BUSHES
Knighton Wood
Woodford Wells
BUCKHURST HILL
PALMERSTON ROAD
B170
EPPING NEW ROAD
A104
A121
HIGH ROAD
CHINGFORD FC
Hatch Plain
NEW ROAD
HATCH LA
CHINGFORD LANE
WOODFORD GOLF COURSE
The Lops
WOODFORD GREEN
JUBILEE SPORTS GR
101
HIGHAMS PARK
THE HIGHAMS PARK
BOATING LAKE
A1009
HALE END
WOODFORD R.F.C.
IG8
WOODFORD
BROADMEAD ROAD
SNAKES LANE
RODING VALLEY
Clubhouse
LUXBOROUGH LANE TREATMENT WORKS
RAY PARK
ASHTON PLAYING FIELD
SPORTS PITCH
RUNNING TRACK
Gas Works
LOUGHTON RUGBY Clubho. GROUND
BANCROFT RUGBY GROUND
SPORTS GRD
DARTNALLS PLAYING FLD
RODING VALLEY PARK
OLD MONOVIANS SPORTS GRD
WANSTEAD Clubhouse R.F.C.
PLAYING FLDS
BROADMEAD EST
A113
CHIGWELL ROAD
EPPING FOREST
WALTHAMSTOW FOREST
SOUTHEND ROAD
NORTH CIRCULAR RD
A406
Gates Corner
SOUTH WOODFORD
E18
124
UNI OF LONDON Halls of Residence
Snaresbrook Coll
REDBRIDGE
Hyland Ho Sch
A503
CHILDREN'S BOATING POND
SPORTS GROUND
Junction 4
WOODFORD TRADING ESTATE
Superstore
Elec Sta
PDSA Burial Grd
St. Swithan's Farm
B160
LARKSHALL ROAD
WINCHESTER ROAD
A11

103
EM
EN
EP
EQ
ER
ES
ET
85
104
125
43
44
45
45
46
47
48
49
50
51
52
53
54
91
92
93
94
FOREST GOLF
ABRIDGE
ROLLS PARK
Rolls Park Farm
Home Farm
Pettits Hall
Marchings Farm
Taylor May's Farm
Brownings Farm
Burnt House
Fulham's Farm
Old Farm
River Roding
RIVERSIDE
SPORTS GROUND
The David Lloyd Club
Pool
Tenn Cts
M11
RODING LANE
CHIGWELL
Bramstones
Rodings
Pav
Chigwell House
SPORTS GROUND
Sec Sch
Cricket Grd
Prim Sch
IG7
Chigwell Hall
Pavs.
CEM
METROPOLITAN POLICE SPORTS GRD
Olde King's Head PH
A113
HIGH ROAD
CHIGWELL ROW WATER WORKS
Filter Beds
RESERVOIR
Settling Tanks
RES
Chigwell Row
GRAVEL LANE
A1112
Girl Guide Camp Site
Chase Farm Riding Stables
The Maypole PH
Miller's Farm
ROMFORD
Ross Bridge
Oaks Farm
Hillside
White Ridge
COV RES
Chigwell Brook
Chigwell
Lib
Hall
PO
STATION RD
CHIGWELL
COOLGARDIE AVENUE
CHIGWELL PARK DRIVE
LYNDHURST RISE
Chigwell Brook
Nursery Farm
CHIGWELL CEMETERY
FROGHALL LANE
Forest House
LAMBOURNE ROAD
B173
Sch and Training Cen
PLAYING FIELD
Woodview
Fairview
Chig Well (Site of)
Gas Trans. Sta
Luxborough Nursery
SPORTS GROUND
Chigwell Nursery
Cedar Court Lodge
Clubhouse
CHIGWELL GOLF COURSE
HAINAULT ROAD
A123
MANOR ROAD
GRANGE HILL
Hall
Bald Hind PH
BROCKET WAY
Prim Sch
CONVENT OF THE SACRED HEART
Prim Sch
Grange Hill
L.R.T. DEPOT
Health Cen
Comm Cen
Lib
Fire Sta
TOMSWOOD ROAD
STRADBROKE DRIVE
FENCEPIECE ROAD
Kennels
Redbridge House (Guide Dogs for the Blind)
Orchard House
SPORTS GRD
Clubhouse
Claybury Hospital (Closed)
Redbridge
Claybury Hall
Forest House
HOSPITAL HILL WOOD
Claybury Woods
Hospital Hill
COCKED HAT PLANTATION
Tomswood Hill
Works
P. & U. Nedlloyd
HAINAULT
Bowl Grn
Bowl Club
HAINAULT RECREATION GROUND
FOREST ROAD PLAYING FIELD
ILFORD WANDERERS R.F.C.
FAIRLOP OAK PLAYING FIELD
SPORTS GROUND
BRACKEN INDUSTRIAL ESTATE
FOREST INDUSTRIAL PARK
Sailing Centre
FAIRLOP WATER
Forest Farm
FOREST ROAD
FAIRLOP
SPORTS GROUND
Sports Cen
Schs.
ALLOT
Fullwell Cross
Health Cen
Sch
IG6
FAIRLOP WATER GOLF COURSE
Hainault Farm
Cinema
Seven Kings Water
IG2
Riding School
PAINTERS ROAD
Aldborough Hall Farm
ALDBOROUGH HATCH
IG5
CLAYHALL
Clinic
Youth Cen
Sec Sch
Prim Sch
COCKED HAT PLANTATION
OWEN WATERS HO
RAVENSBOURNE GARDENS
FULLWELL AVENUE
Sec Sch
TIPTREE ESTATE
GARDEN OF REST
BARKINGSIDE CEM
BARKINGSIDE REC GRD
MAG CT
BARKINGSIDE
HIGH ST
Swim Pool
Barnardo Ho
VILLAGE GRN

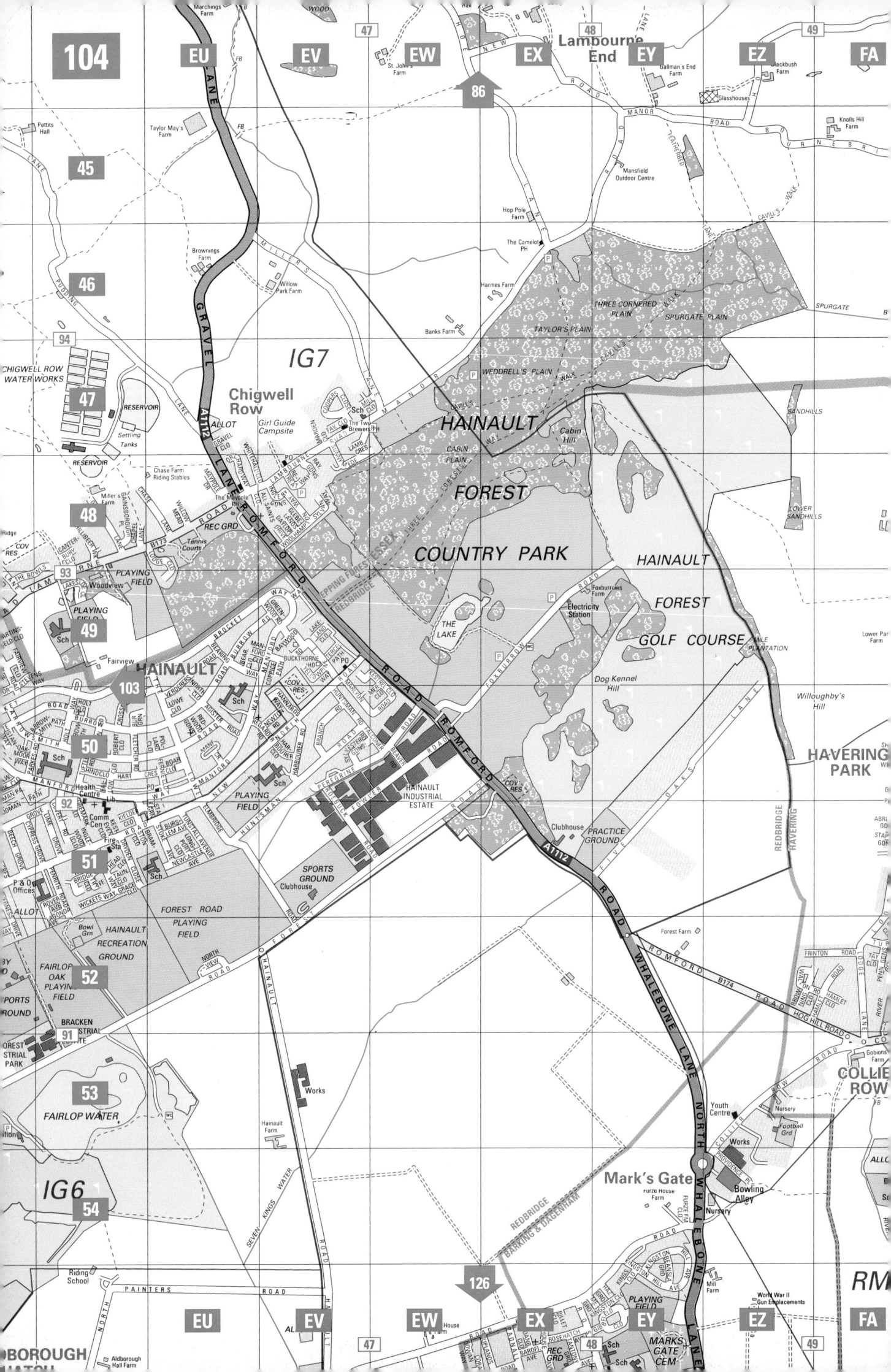

104
EU
EV
EW
EX
EY
EZ
FA
86
126
103
Lambourne End
Chigwell Row
IG7
IG6
HAINAULT
FOREST
COUNTRY PARK
HAINAULT FOREST GOLF COURSE
HAINAULT INDUSTRIAL ESTATE
HAVERING PARK
COLLIER ROW
Mark's Gate
FAIRLOP WATER
CHIGWELL ROW WATER WORKS
RESERVOIR
THE LAKE
Dog Kennel Hill
Cabin Hill
THREE CORNERED PLAIN
SPURGATE PLAIN
TAYLOR'S PLAIN
WEDDRELL'S PLAIN
CABIN PLAIN
FOREST ROAD PLAYING FIELD
HAINAULT RECREATION GROUND
FAIRLOP OAK PLAYING FIELD
SPORTS GROUND
PRACTICE GROUND
ROMFORD ROAD
WHALEBONE LANE NORTH
GRAVEL LANE
MANOR ROAD
FOREST ROAD
HAINAULT ROAD
PAINTERS ROAD
A1112
B174
B173
REDBRIDGE
HAVERING
ESSEX
BARKING & DAGENHAM
RM

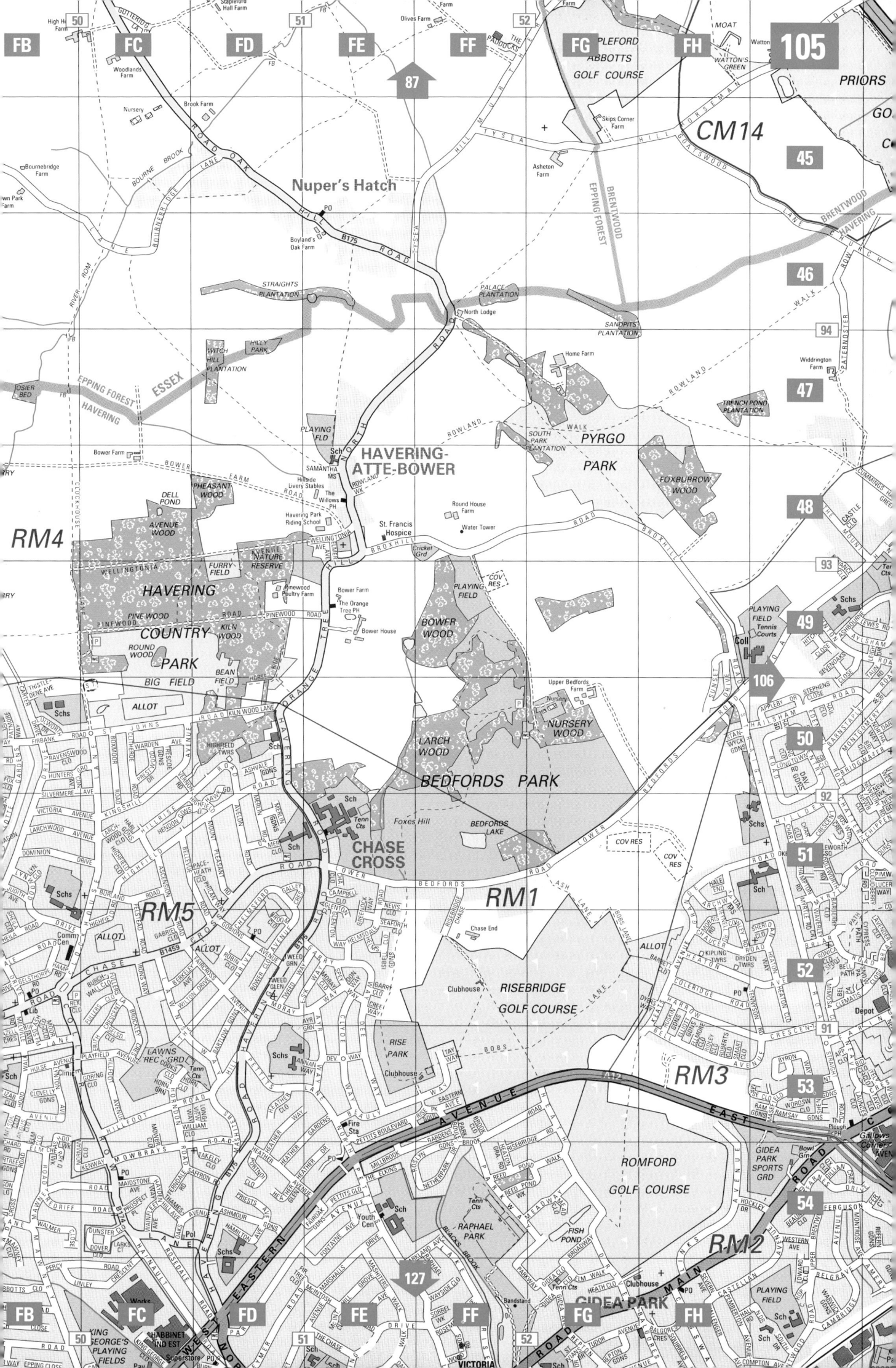

FB
FC
FD
FE
FF
FG
FH
50
51
52
87
Stapleford Abbotts Golf Course
Moat
Watton's Green
Priors
CM14
45
46
47
48
49
50
51
52
53
54
94
93
92
91
Nuper's Hatch
Tysea Hill
Horseman Hill
Goatswood Lane
Epping Forest
Brentwood
Havering
Essex
Straights Plantation
Palace Plantation
North Lodge
Sandpits Plantation
Witch Hill Plantation
Hilly Park
Osier Bed
Home Farm
Widdrington Farm
Trench Pond Plantation
Rowland Walk
South Park Plantation
Pyrgo Park
Foxburrow Wood
Playing Fld
Havering-atte-Bower
Bower Farm
Bower Earm Road
Pheasant Wood
Dell Pond
Avenue Wood
RM4
St. Francis Hospice
Round House Farm
Water Tower
Broxhill Road
Wellingtonia Ave
Nature Reserve
Furry Field
Havering
Country Park
Pinewood Road
Kiln Wood
Round Wood
Big Field
Bean Field
Bower Farm
The Orange Tree PH
Bower House
Bower Wood
Playing Field
Cov Res
Upper Bedfords Farm
Nursery Wood
Larch Wood
Bedfords Park
Foxes Hill
Bedfords Lake
Orange Tree Hill
Chase Cross
Lower Bedfords Road
Allot
Schs
St Johns Road
106
Coll
RM1
RM5
Chase End
Risebridge Golf Course
Clubhouse
Rise Park
RM3
A12
Eastern Avenue
Romford Golf Course
Raphael Park
Gidea Park Sports Grd
The Plough PH
Gallows Corner
RM2
Gidea Park
Main Road
127
Fish Pond
Lawns Rec Grd
King George's Playing Fields
Habbinet Ind Est
Superstore
Victoria
Havering Road
Mawney Road
Collier Row Road

FJ
FK
FL
FM
FN
FP
FQ
54
55
56
45
46
47
48
49
50
51
52
53
54
94
93
92
91
PRIORS
GOLF
COURSE
ESSEX
BRENTWOOD
HAVERING
Watton Farm
CURTIS PLANTATION
SEVENACRE PLANTATION
WABBING'S PLANTATION
Weald Bridge
The Chequers
WEALD BROOK
Frieze Hall
LOCKSMITH WOOD
GOLDSMITH WOOD
CM14
Hoo Hatch
Wright's Bridge
Old Macdonalds Farm Park
Wrightbridge Farm
Wealdside
Rochetts Farm
St. Vincent's Hamlet
M25
SUBWAY
Pentowan Farm
SPICE PITS WOOD
Spice Pits Farm
Hill Farm
NOAK HILL SPORTS GRD
Hall
Noak Hill
Widdrington Farm
TRENCH POND PLANTATION
RM4
THE OSIERS
BURNT WOOD
FOXBURROW WOOD
The Bear Inn
Manor Farm
DAGNAM PARK
FIR WOOD
COCK WOOD
ALDER WOOD
MAYLANDS
GOLF
COURSE
HATTER'S WOOD
Coll
Schs
PLAYING FIELD
Tennis Courts
MOAT
DUCK WOOD NATURE RESERVE
SPORTS GRD
Clubhouse
Maylands
CENTRAL
PARK
HAROLD
HILL
Swim Pool
Health Cen
Comm Cen
Youth Centre
Cricket Ground
SALE WOOD
SHOULDER OF MUTTON WOOD
RM3
The Saxon King PH
COV RES
HAROLD PARK
Sewage Works
Sludge Beds
INGREBOURNE RIVER
Paine's Bridge
ELMS INDUSTRIAL ESTATE
Works
Harold Court
HAROLD HILL INDUSTRIAL ESTATE
Depot
Superstore
COLCHESTER ROAD
A12
Nursery
King Harold PH
HAROLD WOOD
HAROLD WOOD HOSPITAL
Gallows Corner
The Plough PH
GIDEA PARK SPORTS GRD
ROMFORD GOLF COURSE
RM2
Ivy Lodge Farm
The Shepherd & Dog PH
Cockabourne Bridge
Pages Farm
Clinic
HAROLD WOOD PARK
SOUTHEND ARTERIAL ROAD
A127
128
105
Clubhouse
Tyes Farm
Ingrebourne Farm
RM

107
108
109
129
WEALD
COUNTRY
PARK
South Weald
BRENTWOOD
BROOK
STREET
WARLEY
Great
Warley
Junction
28
CM15
CM13
WARLEY HOSPITAL
HARTSWOOD HOSPITAL
MARILLAC HOSPITAL
LITTLE HIGHWOOD HOSP
HIGHWOOD HOSP
BRENTWOOD COMM HOSP
Anglia Polytechnic University
HIGH WOOD
CLEMENTS WOOD
HOLDEN'S WOOD
BARRACK WOOD
DONKEY LANE PLANTATION
HART'S WOOD
KENT'S WOOD
ELLEN'S WOOD
FOXBURROW WOOD
GOLF COURSE
WARLEY PLACE NATURE RESERVE
LITTLE WARLEY COMMON
BRENTWOOD
ESSEX
HAVERING

FS
FT
FU
FV
FW
FX
FY
58
59
60
41
42
43
44
45
46
47
48
49
50
96
95
94
93
106
107
Bentley
BENTLEY GOLF COURSE
PLAYING FIELD
Clubhouse
Ashwells Farm
Offices
MORES PLANTATION
Beads Hall Nursery
Straight Mile Nursery
Pilgrims Hall
Crow Green
Crow Green Farm
Wishfields Farm
Days Farm
BEARD'S HALL LAKE
RES
Bleak House Farm
Moat House
PILGRIM'S HATCH
CM15
Sumner's Farm
Howe's Farm
Brick House Farm
BRICK HOUSE WOOD
Graytoni Stud Farm
Canterbury Tye Farm
CANTERBURY TYE SPRING
White Horse PH
COXTIE GREEN ROAD
Coxtie Green Farm
Cricket Ground
Orchard Nursery
Black Horse PH
Brentwood Radio Station
SPORTS GRD
BISHOP'S HALL PARK
Comm Cen
SPORTS GROUND
Sports Centre
CIVIC AMENITY SITE
LARCH WOOD
TOWER PLANTATION
FOX WOOD
BROOM WOOD
LANGTONS WOOD
FOXDOWN WOOD
LODGE FIELD
THE FOREST
WEALD COUNTRY PARK
MARSH
LAKE FIELD
NURSERY FIELD
SOUTH WEALD LAKE
THE PARK
BELVEDERE FIELD
Langtons Farm
Cricket Ground
ALLOT
Nursery
HIGH WOOD
LARKINS PLAYING FIELDS
Calcott Hall Farm
THE SPINNEY
BRENTWOOD BYPASS
ONGAR ROAD
Sawyer's Hall Farm
PLAYING FIELDS
PLAYING FIELD
CONVENT OF MERCY
LITTLE HIGHWOOD HOSP
HIGHWOOD HOSP
Anglia Polytechnic University
Tennis Courts
BRENTWOOD SPORTS GRD
ESSEX NUFFIELD HOSP
HALL WOOD
Rochetts
Halfway House Farm
WEALD ROAD
Tower Arms PH
South Weald
CM14
FRONT PARK
Bennett's Farm
VICARAGE WOOD
Old Vicarage
THE OAKS
LOWER VICARAGE WOOD
Junction 28
Post House Hotel
Nags Head PH
BROOK STREET
Works
Grove Farm
THE GROVE
Putwell Bridge
Nursery
Mascalls
LOWER BELT
Leverton House
BRENTWOOD
LONDON ROAD CEMETERY
LA PLATA WOOD
Gas Works
HUBERT ROAD IND EST
IND EST
SPORTS GROUND
Sports Hall
SHENFIELD COMMON
COUNCIL OFF
PLAYING FLD
Superstore
Shop Cen
CATH
The Artichoke PH
Bowling Green
Tennis Courts
WARLEY
NAT RES
CEM
SPORTS GRD
WARLEY HOSPITAL
CEMETERY
DONKEY LANE PLANTATION
CLEMENTS WOOD
WARLEY PLAYING FIELDS
Coll
BARRACK WOOD
MARILLAC HOSPITAL
Depot
Great Ropers
Horse & Groom PH
A128
A12
A1023
B186

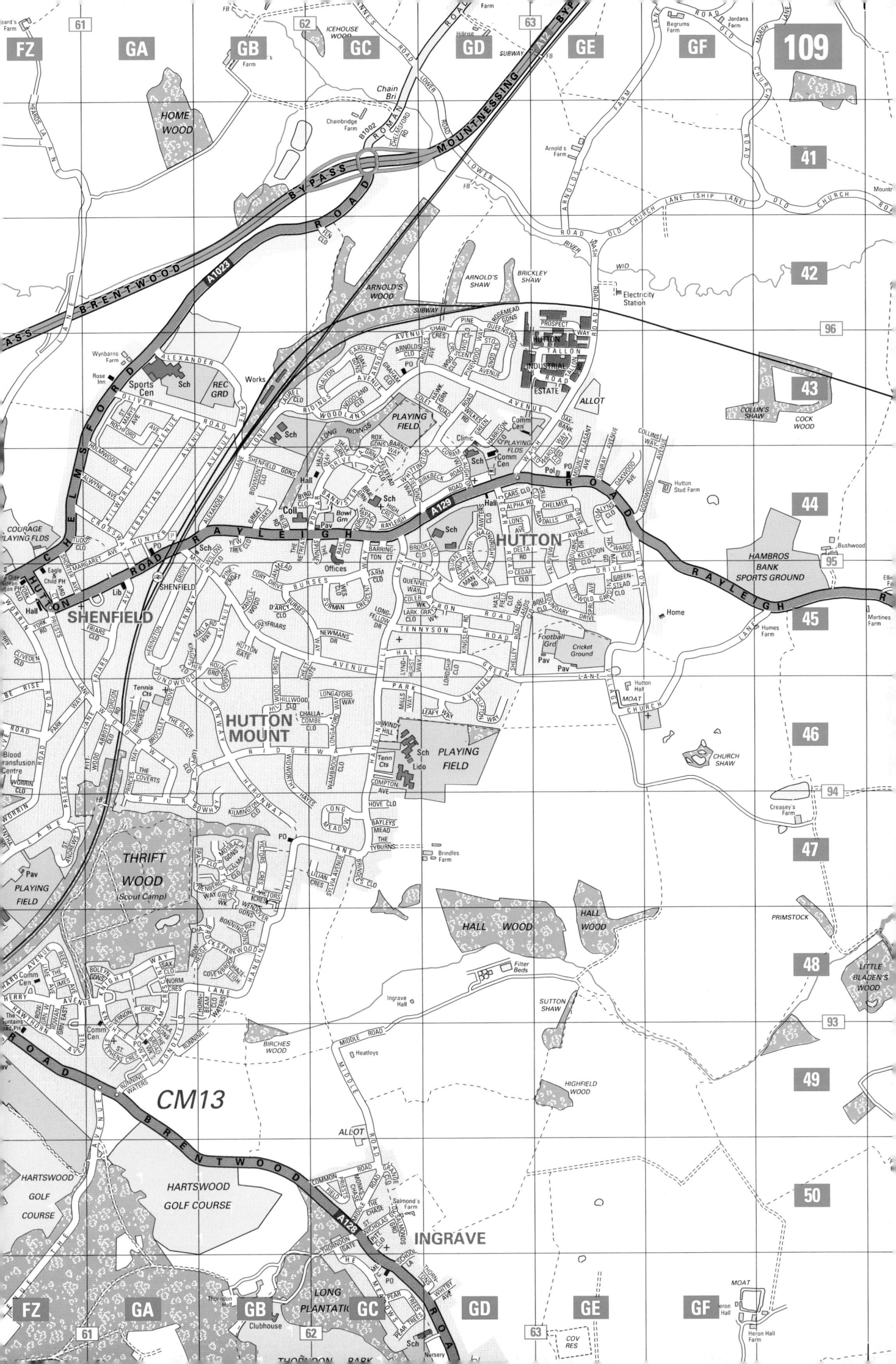

FZ
GA
GB
GC
GD
GE
GF
61
62
63
41
42
43
44
45
46
47
48
49
50
96
95
94
93
HOME WOOD
ICEHOUSE WOOD
Chain Bri
Chainbridge Farm
MOUNTNESSING BYPASS
A12
BRENTWOOD ROAD
A1023
CHELMSFORD ROAD
ARNOLD'S WOOD
ARNOLD'S SHAW
BRICKLEY SHAW
Electricity Station
RIVER WID
HUTTON INDUSTRIAL ESTATE
ALLOT
COLLIN'S SHAW
COCK WOOD
Hutton Stud Farm
HAMBROS BANK SPORTS GROUND
Bushwood
RAYLEIGH ROAD
A129
SHENFIELD
HUTTON
HUTTON MOUNT
PLAYING FIELD
Football Grd
Cricket Ground
Hutton Hall
CHURCH SHAW
Creasey's Farm
Humes Farm
Martines Farm
Brindles Farm
THRIFT WOOD (Scout Camp)
HALL WOOD
PRIMSTOCK
LITTLE BLADEN'S WOOD
Filter Beds
Ingrave Hall
SUTTON SHAW
BIRCHES WOOD
Heatleys
HIGHFIELD WOOD
CM13
ALLOT
HARTSWOOD GOLF COURSE
Salmond's Farm
INGRAVE
A128
LONG PLANTATION
Thorndon Hall
Clubhouse
MOAT
Heron Hall
Heron Hall Farm
COV RES
Nursery

FLACKWELL HEATH
FLACKWELL HEATH GOLF COURSE
Junction 3
WOOBURN GREEN
WOOBURN
WOOBURN PARK
WOOBURN COMMON
HP10
QUARRY
MILL WOOD
SHEEPCOTE WOODS
FARM WOOD
WASH HILL WOOD
THE SWILLEY
COVERED RESERVOIR
BOURNE END
SL8
WOOLMAN'S WOOD
THE DENE
PARK TOP
HEDSOR PARK
OAKEN GROVE
BURWOOD ESTATE
HOLLYBUSH WOOD
JOHNSON'S COPPICE
LAMBOURNE GOLF COURSE
ABBEY WOOD
ROOT MOUND
GULLEY WOOD
CADBROOK WOOD
LITTLE BARNS WOOD
LAMBOURNES WOOD
WYMERS WOOD
BRISTLES WOOD
ASHEN COPPICE
CLIVEDEN NT
Clivedon Hotel
COOKHAM
ODNEY COMMON
ODNEY CLUB SPORTS GRD
SL6
WINDSOR & MAIDENHEAD
WYCOMBE
SOUTH BUCKS
BUCKINGHAMSHIRE
RIVER THAMES
Cookham Bridge
Cookham Lock
OLD MEADOWS
NORTHERN WOODS
RONALD WOOD
Juniper Hill
Hawk's Hill
Tower Hill
White Hill
SOHO MILLS IND EST
CHALKPITS CARAVAN PARK
SPORTS GROUND
M40
A40 LONDON ROAD
OXFORD ROAD
WYCOMBE END
A4094
B440
AC AD AE AF AG AH AJ
88 89 86 87 91 92 93
55 56 57 58 59 60 61 62 63 64
130

HP9
SL9
SL2
Junction 2
Hedgerley
EGYPT
BURTLEY WOOD
BOWER WOOD
BURNHAM BEECHES
EGYPT WOODS
THE GROVE
HILL WOOD
BOVENEY WOOD
DORNEY WOOD
TWELVE ACRE WOOD
KILN WOOD
SCHOOL WOOD
TIMBER WOOD
STOKE WOOD
BLACK GROVE
HANGING WOOD
BIRCHLAND WOOD
PITLANDS WOOD
PYEBUSHES
GREEN BROOM
SAND AND GRAVEL PIT
RSBP NATURE RESERVE
CHURCH WOOD
BROCKHURST WOOD
INGRAM'S COPSE
Farnham Common
BURNHAM COMMON

AS
AT
AU
AV
AW
AX
AY
90
111
132
55
56
57
58
59
60
61
62
63
64
98
99
00
89
88
87
86
PITLANDS WOOD
BIRCHLAND WOOD
HIGH WOOD
Stampwell Farm
BIRCH WOOD
BEECH WOOD
MUMFORDS LANE
Mumfords Farm
SIBLET'S WOOD
Parkwood Farm
CARAVAN PARK
OXFORD ROAD
A40
Bellhouse Hotel
Wapsey's Wood Landfill Site
SAND AND GRAVEL PIT
BIRCHEN SPRING COPPICE
Jarretts Hill
WENT PLANTATION
CHILTERN
SOUTH BUCKS
SL9
BULSTRODE
PARK
Bulstrode
GROVE PLANTATION
MENAGERIE WOOD
Moat Farm
HEDGERLEY LANE
WAPSEYS LANE
Slade Farm
SUTTON'S WOOD
Mount Pleasant Farm
MOLL HAYES WOOD
Hedgerley
LEITH GROVE
RSBP NATURE RESERVE
CHURCH WOOD
SUBWAY
Ponders
Crab Hill
GERRARDS CROSS
GERRARDS CROSS COMMON
The Bull Hotel
CHANTRY WOOD
AUSTENWOOD COMMON
PLAYING FIELD
Raylands Farm
KILN WOOD
HANGING WOOD
HEDGERLEY PARK
MOUNTHILL WOOD
High Meadows
WINDSOR ROAD
Mount Hill Farm
DUKE'S ORCHARD
Riding Stables
M40
FOOTPATH WOOD
BLACK GROVE
Park House
Tara
Hedgerley Park Farm
PARKSIDE CEMETERY
PICKERIDGE WOOD
GRAVEL PIT
Pickeridge Farm
Kestrel Farm
Low Farm
SL3
HAY WOOD
FISH POND
Fulmer
Research Laboratories
Church Farm
Fulmer Farm
TIMBER WOOD
STOKE WOOD
SL2
TEMPLEWOOD LANE
STOKE COMMON ROAD
STOKE COMMON
BROCKHURST WOOD
INGRAM'S COPSE
FRAME WOOD
PENN WOOD
Fernacres Farm
Fernacres House
Black Firs
Framewood Manor
Wexham Place
Farnham Common
PARSON'S WOOD
B416

DENHAM AERODROME
DENHAM GOLF COURSE
DENHAM GREEN
Higher Denham
Tatling End
DENHAM
UB9
SL0
BUCKINGHAMS
NOCKHILL WOOD
JUNIPER WOOD
GREAT HALINGS WOOD
DENHAM MARSH WOOD
OAKEND WOOD
ROUND COPSE
SQUARE COPSE
QUARTERS WOOD
NORTHMOOR HILL WOOD
BATTLESFORD WOOD
RANSTON COVERT
WADLEY COVERT
NIGHTINGALE WOOD
HOLLY HILL WOOD
NEWSTEAD WOOD
COLLSELS WOOD
GALLOWS WOOD
LITTLE GALLOWS WOOD
MILL WOOD
THE RANCHO
TOM WILLIAM'S WOOD
CAPS WOOD
BAKER'S WOOD
GALDWINS WOOD
BROADSPRING WOOD
HAWKS WOOD
FURZENEY WOOD
GOSSAMS WOOD
BROWN'S WOOD
OLDHOUSE WOOD
PARKSPRING WOOD
MOUNT FIDGET WOOD
LONG COPPICE
LANGLEY COMMON
Junction 16 (M25)
Junction 1a (M40)
DURDENT COURT CONFERENCE CENTRE
MARTINSFIELD SPORTS GROUND
OXFORD ROAD
AMERSHAM ROAD
NORTH ORBITAL ROAD
DENHAM AVENUE
RIVER COLNE
RIVER MISBOURNE
M25
M40
A40
A412
A413

91
114
133

114
BG
BH
BJ
BK
BL
BM
BN
05
06
07
92
55
56
57
58
59
60
61
62
63
64
89
88
87
86
113
134
SOUTH HAREFIELD
UB9
UB10
Denham Green
Denham
Newyears Green
Junction 1
BAYHURST WOOD COUNTRY PARK
BUCKINGHAMSHIRE GOLF COURSE
DENHAM COUNTRY PARK
UXBRIDGE GOLF COURSE
HILLINGDON HOUSE FARM SPORTS GROUND
Grand Union Canal
NORTH ORBITAL ROAD
DENHAM ROAD
OXFORD ROAD
WESTERN AVENUE
HARVIL ROAD
BREAKSPEAR ROAD NORTH
NEW YEARS GREEN LANE
SWAKELEYS ROAD
PARK ROAD
MOORHALL ROAD
Broadwater Park
Rank Film Laboratories
PUBLIC TIP
Activities Centre
Glaxo Research Farm
Hillingdon Ski Centre
UXBRIDGE COMMON
RIVERSIDE WALK
Uxbridge

BP
BQ
BR
BS
BT
BU
BV
08
09
10
Northwood Hills
NORTHWOOD HILLS GOLF COURSE
NORTH CEMETERY
93
PINNER GREEN
COPSE WOOD
HA6
YOUNG WOOD
RUISLIP NATURE RESERVE
POOR'S FIELD
ST. VINCENT'S ORTHOPAEDIC HOSPITAL
RUISLIP LIDO
PARK WOOD
RUISLIP COMMON
Breakspear Crematorium
SPORTS GROUNDS
DUCKS HILL ROAD
BURY STREET
HIGH STREET
A4180
A404
PINNER ROAD
RICKMANSWORTH RD
UXBRIDGE
CUCKOO HILL
HA5
EASTCOTE VILLAGE
EASTCOTE HO GRD
Haydon Hall
EASTCOTE ROAD
FIELD END ROAD
GOVERNMENT OFFICES
KINGS COLLEGE PLAYING FIELDS
Eastcote Hockey & Badminton Club
BROADWOOD AVENUE
EASTCOTE
WARRENDER PARK
Swim Pool & Fitness Cen
RUISLIP
HA4
BURIAL GRD
WEST END RD
RUISLIP MANOR
RUISLIP GOLF COURSE
DRIVING RANGE
WEST RUISLIP
ICKENHAM
SPORTS GROUND
SPORTS GROUND
Ruislip R.F.C.
BESSINGBY FIELD
NEW POND FARM FIELDS
CAVENDISH REC GRD
PINE GDNS
VICTORIA ROAD
RUISLIP GARDENS
DEPOT
Compass Arts Thea
Ickenham Marsh
Yeading Brook
Canal Feeder
NORTHOLT AERODROME
135
HA4
Warehouse Hangar
Hangars
ODYSSEY BUSINESS PARK
SOUTH RUISLIP
SOUTH RUISLIP PLAYING FIELD
Works
Master Brewer Hotel
FREEZELAND COVERT
WESTERN AVENUE
116
55
56
57
58
59
60
61
62
63
64
86
87
88
89
REC GRD
REC GRD

116
BW
BX
BY
BZ
CA
CB
CC
94
115
136
12
13
14
55
56
57
58
59
60
61
62
63
64
86
87
88
89
PINNER GREEN
PINNER
LITTLE COMMON
PINNER MEMORIAL PARK
PINNER NEW CEMETERY
PINNER VILLAGE GARDENS
RECREATION GROUND
HEADSTONE MANOR
HEADST
NORTH HARROW
WEST HARROW
WEST HARROW REC GRD
SOUTH HARROW
RAYNERS LANE
EASTCOTE
EASTCOTE VILLAGE
CUCKOO HILL
HA5
HA2
HA4
THE CROFT PLAYING FIELD
ROXBOURNE PARK
Streamside Reservation
RECREATION GROUND
NEWTON PARK WEST
NEWTON FM ECOLOGY PK
CAVENDISH REC GRD
PINE GDNS
BESSINGBY FIELD
WARRENDER PARK
DEANE PARK
SOUTH RUISLIP
VICTORIA RETAIL PARK
FROGMORE ESTATE
SOLID WASTE TRANSFER STATION
ODYSSEY BUSINESS PARK
NORTHOLT RECREATION GRD
PLAYING FIELD
ALEXANDRA PARK
EARLSMEAD STADIUM
LORD HALSBURY MEMORIAL GRD
SPORTS GROUND
HILLINGDON
EALING
UXBRIDGE RD
A404 GEORGE V AVENUE
PINNER ROAD
STATION RD
A4090
ALEXANDRA AVENUE
IMPERIAL DRIVE
A312
NORTHOLT RD
A4180 WEST END ROAD
WHITTON AV W
YEADING BROOK

CD
CE
CF
CG
CH
CJ
CK
BELMONT
95
HA7
QUEENSBURY
WEALDSTONE
BYRON REC GRD
WEALDSTONE CEM
Leisure Centre
Sports Centre
DRIVING CENTRE
HARROW & WEALDSTONE
HA3
CIVIC AMENITY SITE
KENTON RECREATION GROUND
KENTON
KENTON ROAD
A4006
WOODCOCK PARK
CIVIC CENTRE
Superstore
Safari Cinema
St. Ann's Centre
COLLEGE BUS STA
HARROW ON THE HILL
University of Westminster
NORTHWICK PARK HOSPITAL
NORTHWICK PARK
Northwick Park Pavilion
THE TERRACE
HA1
MINIATURE RIFLE RANGE
HARROW SCHOOL PLAYING FIELDS
Harrow School Farm
JOHN BILLAM SPORTS GRD
PRESTON
118
PRESTON PARK
SOUTH KENTON
HARROW SCHOOL GOLF COURSE
PARK LAKE
HARROW ON THE HILL
ST. ANDREW'S AT HARROW HOSP
CLEMENTINE CHURCHILL HOSPITAL
CHASEWOOD PARK
NORTH WEMBLEY
WEMBLEY COMMERCIAL CENTRE
HA9
G.E.C. ESTATE
FORTY FARM SPORTS GROUND
VALE FARM SPORTS GROUND
WEMBLEY FC
KING EDWARD VII PARK
SPORTS GROUND
PLAYING FIELDS
EALING NORTHERN SPORTS GRD'
UB6
Sudbury Tower
SUDBURY
BARHAM PARK
HA0
WEMBLEY CENTRAL
137
SUDBURY TOWN
A404
A4005
A4088
A4140
A409
A312
A4089
55
56
57
58
59
60
61
62
63
64
86
87
88
89
15
16
17

118
CL
CM
CN
CP
CQ
CR
CS
HA7
HA8
HA3
HA9
NW9
NW10
QUEENSBURY
PRESTON
KINGSBURY
WEMBLEY PARK
WEMBLEY
KYNGTON
CHURCH END
KINGSBURY FRYENT COUNTRY PARK
FRYENT COUNTRY PARK
BARN HILL OPEN SPACE
ROE GREEN PARK
QUEENSBURY PARK
WOODCOCK PARK
PRESTON PARK
KING EDWARD VII PARK
SILVER JUBILEE PARK
WELSH HARP OPEN SPACE
ETON GROVE OPEN SPACE
SHERRINS FARM OPEN SPACE
CHURCH LANE REC GRD
KINGSBURY SPORTS GRD
BARDHILL SPORTS GRD
FORTY FARM SPORTS GROUND
JOHN BILLAM SPORTS GRD
COLINDALE HOSP
BLOOD TRANSFUSION CENTRE
KINGSBURY HOSPITAL
COLINDALE BUSINESS PK
CAPITOL IND PK
KINGSBURY TRADING EST
WEMBLEY COMMERCIAL CENTRE
G.E.C. ESTATE
Palace of Industry
WEMBLEY ARENA
OLYMPIC RETAIL PARK
WEMBLEY PARK BUSINESS CEN
CANNON TRADING EST
WEMBLEY STADIUM (Under Redevelopment)
Sunday Market
NEASDEN RAIL DEPOT
DRURY WAY IND EST
BRENT PARK
BRENT TOWN HALL
A4140
A4006
A4088
A4089
A404
A5
B4557
B4565
B454
KENTON ROAD
HONEYPOT LANE
FRYENT WAY
KINGSBURY ROAD
EDGWARE ROAD
SALMON STREET
FORTY LANE
FORTY AVENUE
BLACKBIRD HILL
NEASDEN LANE NORTH
WEMBLEY PARK DRIVE
BRIDGE RD
EMPIRE WAY
GREAT CENTRAL WAY
HARROW ROAD
HIGH ROAD
EALING ROAD
NORTH CIRCULAR ROAD
96
117
138

119
CT
CU
CV
CW
CX
CY
CZ
22
23
24
HILL
SUNNY HILL PARK
RAF MUSEUM
GARDEN HOSP
N3
HENDON
THE HYDE
NW4
HENDON PARK
HENDON CENTRAL
BRENT CROSS
Brent Cross Shopping Centre
Junction 1
BRENT RESERVOIR
NW11
GOLDERS GREEN
CLITTERHOUSE PLAYING FIELDS
CRICKLEWOOD
DOLLIS HILL
GLADSTONE PARK
NW2
CHILDS HILL
HAMPSTEAD CEMETERY
UNIVERSITY COLLEGE SCHOOL SPORTS GRD
WILLESDEN
97
120
139
55
56
57
58
59
60
61
62
63
64
NORTH CIRCULAR ROAD
FINCHLEY ROAD
HENDON WAY
EDGWARE ROAD
CRICKLEWOOD BROADWAY
GOLDERS GREEN ROAD
WATFORD WAY

DA
DB
DC
DD
DE
DF
DG
26
27
28
98
N3
55
56
57
58
59
119
60
87
61
62
86
63
64
89
88
140
N2
EAST FINCHLEY
NW11
N6
NW3
EAST FINCHLEY CEMETERY
Crematorium
HAMPSTEAD GARDEN SUBURB
BIG WOOD
LITTLE WOOD
FORTIS GREEN
CHERRY TREE WOOD
HIGHGATE WOOD
COLDFALL WOOD
NAT HOSP FOR NEUROLOGY & NEUROSURGERY
HIGHGATE GOLF COURSE
Clubhouse
HAMPSTEAD HEATH EXTENSION
HAMPSTEAD GOLF CLUB
Bunkers Hill
GOLDERS GREEN
HOOP LANE CEMETERY (JEWISH)
GARDEN OF REMEMBRANCE
GOLDERS GREEN DEPOT
Golders Green Hippodrome
TURNERS WOOD
NORTH WOOD
THE IVEAGH BEQUEST KENWOOD HOUSE
Kenwood House
ATHLONE HOUSE
SANDY HEATH
GOLDERS HILL PARK
CHILDS HILL
HILL GARDEN
WEST HEATH
LEG OF MUTTON POND
HEATHLANDS
VALE OF HEALTH
KENWOOD
HAMPSTEAD HEATH
LILY POND
CONCERT POND
KENWOOD LADIES POND
BIRD SANCTUARY POND
BOATING POND
HIGHGATE PONDS
HIGHGATE MEN'S POND
STOCK POND
VIADUCT POND
PARLIAMENT HILL
HAMPSTEAD PONDS
WHITESTONE POND
QUEEN MARY'S HOSP
FENTON HO
HAMPSTEAD
KEATS HOUSE
ROYAL FREE HOSP
LISMORE CIRCUS
GOSPEL OAK
ST. DOMINIC'S PRIORY
MAITLAND PARK EST
ATHLETICS TRACK
Lido
WEST HAMPSTEAD
Camden Arts Centre
TAVISTOCK CEN
MUSEUM
Uni of London King's Coll
Open Uni Regional Cen
HAMPSTEAD CEMETERY
BARNET
CAMDEN
HARINGEY
NORTH CIRCULAR ROAD
FALLODEN WAY
LYTTELTON ROAD
AYLMER ROAD
EAST END ROAD
GREAT NORTH ROAD
FORTIS GREEN
ARCHWAY ROAD
FINCHLEY ROAD
NORTH END ROAD
NORTH END WAY
SPANIARDS ROAD
HEATH STREET
HAMPSTEAD HIGH ST
ROSSLYN HILL
HAVERSTOCK HILL
HAMPSTEAD LANE
FORTUNE GREEN ROAD
WEST END LANE
HENDON WAY
A1
A5
A41
A406
A504
A502
A598
A1000
A407
B519
B510
B520

121
DH
DJ
DK
DL
DM
DN
DP
29
30
31
99
NOEL PARK
LORDSHIP RECREATION GROUND
ALEXANDRA PALACE
ALEXANDRA PARK
N22
MUSWELL HILL
HORNSEY
WEST GREEN
55
56
57
58
59
60
61
62
63
64
86
87
88
89
122
N8
HARRINGAY
CROUCH END
QUEEN'S WOOD
STROUD GREEN
FINSBURY PARK
N4
N19
UPPER HOLLOWAY
TUFNELL PARK
HOLLOWAY
N7
LOWER HOLLOWAY
KENTISH TOWN
HIGHBURY
N5
CANONBURY
141
PENTONVILLE PRISON
H.M. PRISON HOLLOWAY
WHITTINGTON HOSPITAL
HORNSEY CENTRAL HOSP
ST. ANN'S HOSPITAL
ARCHWAY
CLISSOLD PARK

122
DQ
DR
DS
DT
DU
DV
DW
100
121
142
33
34
35
55
56
57
58
59
60
61
62
63
64
86
87
88
89
N22
N17
N15
N4
N5
N16
E5
E8
NOEL PARK
LORDSHIP RECREATION GROUND
WEST GREEN
DOWNHILLS PARK
BELMONT REC GRD
TOTTENHAM HALE
TOTTENHAM MARSH
DOWN LANE REC GRD
LEE VALLEY TECHNOPARK
MILMEAD INDUSTRIAL CENTRE
LOCKWOOD INDUSTRIAL PARK
LOW MAYNARD RESERVOIR
CHESTNUTS REC GRD
ST. ANN'S HOSPITAL
SOUTH TOTTENHAM
SEVEN SISTERS
MARKFIELD REC GRD
RESERVOIR NUMBER ONE
RESERVOIR NUMBER THREE
WARWICK RESERVOIR EAST
WARWICK RESERVOIR WEST
COPPERMILL PLAYING FIELD
SPRINGHILL SPORTS GRD
SPRINGFIELD PARK
Walthamstow Marsh Nature Reserve
FINSBURY PARK
HARRINGAY
EAST RESERVOIR
WEST RESERVOIR
STAMFORD HILL
ABNEY PARK CEMETERY
STOKE NEWINGTON
CLISSOLD PARK
SPORTS GROUND
UPPER CLAPTON
SHACKLEWELL
HACKNEY DOWNS
HIGHBURY
CANONBURY
KINGSLAND
HACKNEY
WEST GREEN ROAD
SEVEN SISTERS ROAD
AMHURST PARK
STAMFORD HILL
HIGH ROAD
GREEN LANES
UPPER CLAPTON ROAD
LOWER CLAPTON ROAD
CLAPTON COMMON
STOKE NEWINGTON HIGH ST
BALLS POND RD
DALSTON LANE
GRAHAM ROAD
FERRY LANE
MONUMENT WAY
BROAD LANE
ST. ANN'S ROAD
REGTORY ROAD
PEMBURY ROAD
HIGHBURY PARK
ST. PAUL'S ROAD
A10
A503
A504
A105
A107
A104
A1199
A1201
A1207
A102
B152
B105
B104

DX
DY
DZ
EA
EB
EC
ED
36
37
38
101
124
143
55
56
57
58
59
60
61
62
63
64
86
87
88
89
HIGHAM HILL
LLOYD PARK
WALTHAMSTOW
UPPER WALTHAMSTOW
E17
EPPING FOREST
SNARESBROOK
WHIPPS CROSS HOSPITAL
LEYTONSTONE
E11
E10
LEYTON
E15
STRATFORD
HACKNEY MARSH
CLAPTON PARK
LOWER CLAPTON
HOMERTON
E9
HACKNEY WICK
LEA BRIDGE
LEYTON MARSHES
LEE VALLEY GOLF COURSE
WALTHAMSTOW CEM
ST. JAMES'S PARK
CIVIC AMENITY TIP
ALLOTMENTS
SEYMOUR ROAD PLAYING FIELD
MARSH LANE PLAYING FIELD
ST. PATRICK'S RC CEMETERY
RECREATION GROUND
ETON MANOR SPORTS GROUND
Lea Valley Sports Centre
LEE VALLEY PARK
WICK FIELD
EASTWAY CYCLE CIRCUIT
EASTWAY COMMERCIAL CENTRE
New Spitalfields Market
LEYTON ORIENT F.C.
SIDMOUTH PARK
DRAPERS FIELD REC GRD
JEWISH CEMETERY
LONDON INTERNATIONAL FREIGHT TERMINAL
FOREST BUSINESS PK
ROXWELL TRADING PK
CROMWELL IND EST
HIGHAMS LODGE BUSINESS CEN
Selbourne Walk Shop Cen
WALTHAMSTOW CENTRAL
WALTHAMSTOW QUEENS ROAD
LEYTON MIDLAND ROAD
LEYTONSTONE HIGH RD
LEYTONSTONE
LEYTON
BLACKHORSE ROAD
WOOD STREET
THORPE COOMBE HOSP
WALTHAM FOREST ATHLETICS GRD
CHESTNUTS SHOWGROUND
TOWN HALL
Waltham Forest Coll
ROUND POND
River Lee or Lea
River Lee Navigation
Flood Relief Channel
Dagenham Brook
FOREST ROAD
HOE STREET
LEA BRIDGE ROAD
CHURCH ROAD
HIGH ROAD LEYTON
LEYTONSTONE ROAD
WHIPPS CROSS ROAD
MARKHOUSE ROAD
BLACKHORSE ROAD
EASTWAY
RUCKHOLT ROAD
CHOBHAM ROAD
A503
A1006
A104
A112
A106
A114
A12
A11
B112
B113
B161

EE
EF
EG
EH
EJ
EK
EL
IG8
SOUTH WOODFORD
E18
EPPING FOREST
SPORTS GROUND
Junction 4
RODING HOSP
RECREATION GROUND
IG4
SNARESBROOK
SNARESBROOK CROWN COURT
EAGLE POND
HOLLOW POND
WHIPPS CROSS HOSPITAL
EPPING FOREST
RUGBY FOOTBALL GROUND
WANSTEAD GOLF COURSE
WANSTEAD
WANSTEAD FLATS
LEYTONSTONE
E11
THE BASIN
WANSTEAD GOLF COURSE
WANSTEAD PARK
BUSH WOOD
SHOULDER OF MUTTON POND
HERONRY POND
PERCH POND
ORNAMENTAL WATERS
ALDERSBROOK
CITY OF LONDON CEMETERY
WANSTEAD FLATS
MANOR PARK
MANOR PARK CEMETERY
WEST HAM CEMETERY
JEWISH CEMETERY
FOREST GATE
E7
WOODGRANGE PARK CEMETERY
PLASHET JEWISH CEMETERY
E15
STRATFORD
102
123
144
55
56
57
58
59
60
61
62
63
64
40
41
42
86
87
88
89

125
EM
EN
EP
EQ
ER
ES
ET
103
145
126
IG6
IG5
IG2
IG1
IG3
CLAYHALL
BARKINGSIDE
ALDBOROUGH HATCH
FAIRLOP WATER GOLF COURSE
GANTS HILL
NEWBURY PARK
VALENTINES PARK
SEVEN KINGS
SEVEN KINGS PARK
CRANBROOK
ILFORD
LOXFORD
SOUTH PARK
GOODMAYES PARK
MAYESBROOK PARK
BARKING PARK
KING GEORGE HOSP
KING GEORGE HOSPITAL
GOODMAYES HOSPITAL
EASTERN AVENUE
CRANBROOK ROAD
HIGH ROAD
GREEN LANE
LONGBRIDGE ROAD
WOODFORD AVENUE
ILFORD LANE
A123
A12
A118
A1083
A124
A406
55
56
57
58
59
60
61
62
63
64

126
EU
EV
EW
EX
EY
EZ
FA
47
48
49
104
125
146
Mark's Gate
Seven Kings Water
BARKING & DAGENHAM
REDBRIDGE
PAINTERS ROAD
Riding School
HAINAULT ROAD
ALDBOROUGH ROAD NORTH
IG2
Aldborough Hall Farm
Dick Turpin PH
Red House Farm
BILLET ROAD
Willow Farm
Little Heath Lodge
SPORTS GROUND
RM6
WHALEBONE LANE NORTH
A1112
Mill Farm
World War II Gun Emplacements
SPORTS GROUND
MARKS GATE CEM
Prim Sch
Clinic
Comm Cen & Lib
Pol
MOAT
Warren Farm
ARNEWAYS AVENUE
ROSEHATCH AV
SHEEPCOTES RD
PADNALL ROAD
EASTERN AVENUE
A12
Aldborough Hatch Farm
KING GEORGE HOSPITAL
GOODMAYES HOSPITAL
FORD'S SPORTS GROUND
Sports Cen
Tennis Courts
SPORTS GROUND
SPORTS GRD
PLAYING FIELD
KINGS PARK
Bandstand
Redbridge College
CHADWELL HEATH HOSPL
GRESHAM DRIVE
Works
Sec Sch
FRESHWELL AVENUE
ROCHFORD
HAVERING GDNS
Moby Dick PH
EASTERN AVENUE WEST
WARREN TER
GOLF DRIVING RANGE
ALLOT
Heath Club
Sec Sch
Prim Sch
Pitch 'n' Putt
ST. CHADS PARK
CHADWELL HEATH
Bowl Grns
Comm Cen
Superstore
Clinic
WESTLANDS PLAYING FIELDS
WEST HAM UNITED FC TRAINING GROUND
LONDON ROAD
HIGH ROAD
A118
SEVEN KINGS
Superstore
Superstores
Works
MIRRAVALE TRADING ESTATE
SELINAS LANE
FRESHWATER ROAD
CROW LANE
WHALEBONE LANE SOUTH
A112
GOODMAYES
The Kings PH
KINFAUNS ROAD
CASTLETON ROAD
The Lord Napier PH
GREEN LANE
IG3
GOODMAYES
RM8
SPORTS GROUND
Barking College
Royal Oak PH
A1083
The Matapan PH
Ship & Anchor PH
Three Travellers PH
Merry Fiddlers PH
Swim Pool
Superstore
GOODMAYES PARK
Bowling Club
Youth Cen
ALLOT
GOODMAYES PARK REC GRD
Mayes Brook
BECONTREE AVENUE
Day Hosp
VALENCE MOAT
VALENCE HO MUS
VALENCE PARK
BECONTREE
VALENCE CIRCUS
VALENCE WOOD ROAD
Comm Cen & Thea
Robin Hood PH
LONGBRIDGE ROAD
A124
WOOD LANE
Cherry Tree PH
RM9
Uni of East London
MAYESBROOK PARK
BARKING FC Clubhouse
SPORTS GRD
Youth Club
Schs
Lib
Hall
Clinic
Sec Sch
Leisure Centre
PARSLOES PARK
Bowling Green
Barking Coll
Comm Cen
HEATHWAY
A1240
A1153
PORTERS AVENUE
LODGE AVENUE
SPORTS GRD
BOATING LAKE
IVYHOUSE ROAD
DAGENHAM HEATHWAY
Shopping Centre
Church
Sports Cen
Prim Schs

127
FB
FC
FD
FE
FF
FG
FH
50
51
52
105
ROMFORD GOLF COURSE
RM2
GIDEA PARK
RM1
VICTORIA HOSP
KING GEORGE'S PLAYING FIELDS
HUBBINET IND EST
NORTH STREET
EASTERN
WEST
MAIN ROAD
A118
TOWN HALL
ROMFORD
COTTONS PARK
SPRING GARDENS IND EST
OLDCHURCH HOSPITAL
ROMFORD STADIUM
RM7
Romford Gas Works
JUTSUMS PARK
ROMFORD CEMETERY
RUSH GREEN
CROWLANDS SPORTS GROUND
OLDCHURCH PARK
HYLANDS PARK
RM11
Havering College
Ardleigh Green
55
56
57
58
59
60
61
62
63
64
88
89
86
87
128
HORNCHURCH ROAD
RUSH GREEN ROAD
A124
FORD SPORTS GROUND
BARKING & DAGENHAM
HAVERING
Barking College of Technology
CENTRAL PARK
FELS FIELD
WHITE HART LAKES
EASTBROOKEND CEMETERY
THE CHASE NATURE RESERVE
EASTBROOKEND COUNTRY PARK
RAINHAM ROAD
A125
HARROW LODGE PARK
BOATING LAKE
HORNCHURCH
RM12
ELM PARK
RM10
STERLING INDUSTRIAL ESTATE
DAGENHAM EAST
PONDFIELD PARK
Rhone-Poulenc Rorer
Beam River
147
SPORTS GROUND

128
FJ
FK
FL
FM
FN
FP
FQ
54
55
56
106
127
148
55
56
57
58
59
60
61
62
63
64
89
88
87
86
ROMFORD GOLF COURSE
RM2
RM3
RM11
RM12
HAROLD WOOD
HAROLD WOOD PARK
GIDEA PARK
Ardleigh Green
EMERSON PARK
HORNCHURCH
UPMINSTER
UPMINSTER GOLF COURSE
UPMINSTER PARK
Hacton
GAYNES PARKWAY
PARKLANDS OPEN SPACE
ST. GEORGES HOSPITAL
Havering College of Further Educ
Havering College
HORNCHURCH STADIUM
HORNCHURCH CEM
ELLIOT PLAYING FIELDS
FIELDERS SPORTS GRD
LANGTON GDNS
HYLANDS PARK
HAYNES PARK
ST. ANDREW'S PARK
ST. MARY'S CONVENT
SOUTHEND ARTERIAL ROAD
MAIN ROAD
HIGH STREET
UPMINSTER ROAD
ST. MARY'S LANE
A124
B187
Ingrebourne River
The Ravensbourne
INGREBOURNE VALLEY GREEN WAY
Palms Hotel
Tyes Farm
Ingrebourne Farm
Prospect Farm
Mount Pleasant Farm
Lillyputts Farm
Park Corner Farm
Lodge Farm
Rainham Lodge Farm
Gardners Cor Hall
Harwood Hall
Hacton House
Abattoir

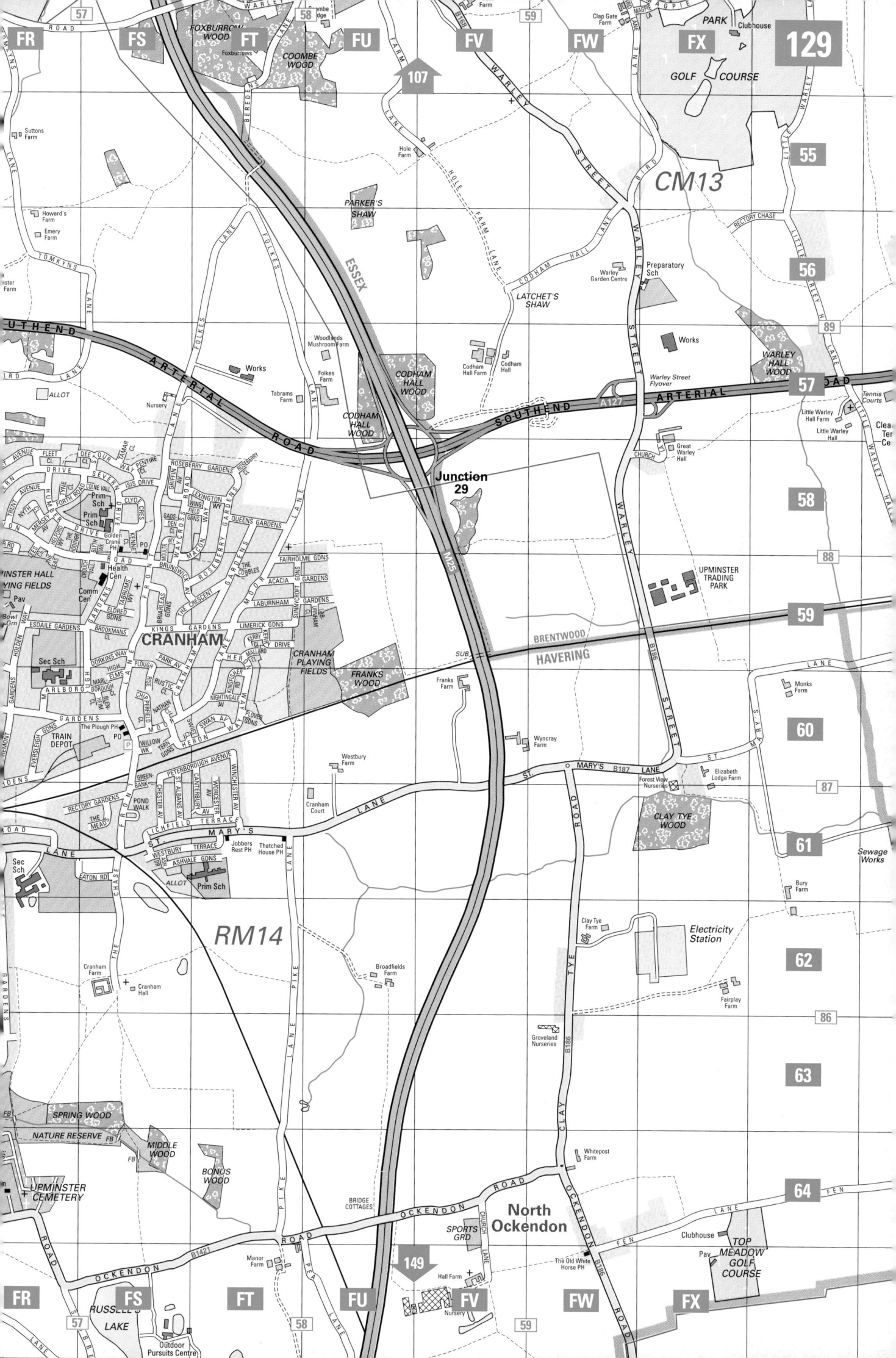
FR
FS
FT
FU
FV
FW
FX
107
149
55
56
57
58
59
60
61
62
63
64
86
87
88
89
CM13
RM14
CRANHAM
North Ockendon
Junction 29
M25
ESSEX
BRENTWOOD
HAVERING
SOUTHEND ARTERIAL ROAD
A127
B186
B187
B1421
B168
FOXBURROWS WOOD
Foxburrows
COOMBE WOOD
PARK GOLF COURSE
Clubhouse
Clap Gate Farm
Suttons Farm
Howard's Farm
Emery Farm
TOMKYNS LANE
Hole Farm
HOLE FARM LANE
PARKER'S SHAW
WARLEY STREET
BIRD LANE
LITTLE WARLEY HALL LANE
RECTORY CHASE
CODHAM HALL LANE
Warley Garden Centre
Preparatory Sch
LATCHET'S SHAW
Works
WARLEY HALL WOOD
Woodlands Mushroom Farm
Folkes Farm
Tabrams Farm
FOLKES LANE
Nursery
ALLOT
CODHAM HALL WOOD
Codham Hall Farm
Codham Hall
Warley Street Flyover
Little Warley Hall Farm
Little Warley Hall
Tennis Courts
Great Warley Hall
CHURCH
UPMINSTER TRADING PARK
UPMINSTER HALL PLAYING FIELDS
Pav
Health Cen
Comm Cen
Prim Sch
Sec Sch
CRANHAM PLAYING FIELDS
FRANKS WOOD
Franks Farm
Wyncray Farm
Monks Farm
TRAIN DEPOT
The Plough PH
Westbury Farm
ST. MARY'S LANE
Elizabeth Lodge Farm
Forest View Nurseries
CLAY TYE WOOD
Cranham Court
Jobbers Rest PH
Thatched House PH
Sewage Works
Bury Farm
Clay Tye Farm
Electricity Station
Broadfields Farm
Cranham Farm
Cranham Hall
Fairplay Farm
Groveland Nurseries
CLAY TYE ROAD
PIKE LANE
SPRING WOOD
NATURE RESERVE
MIDDLE WOOD
BONUS WOOD
UPMINSTER CEMETERY
Whitepost Farm
BRIDGE COTTAGES
OCKENDON ROAD
SPORTS GRD
FEN LANE
Clubhouse
TOP MEADOW GOLF COURSE
The Old White Horse PH
Manor Farm
Hall Farm
Nursery
RUSSELLS LAKE
Outdoor Pursuits Centre
PEA LANE

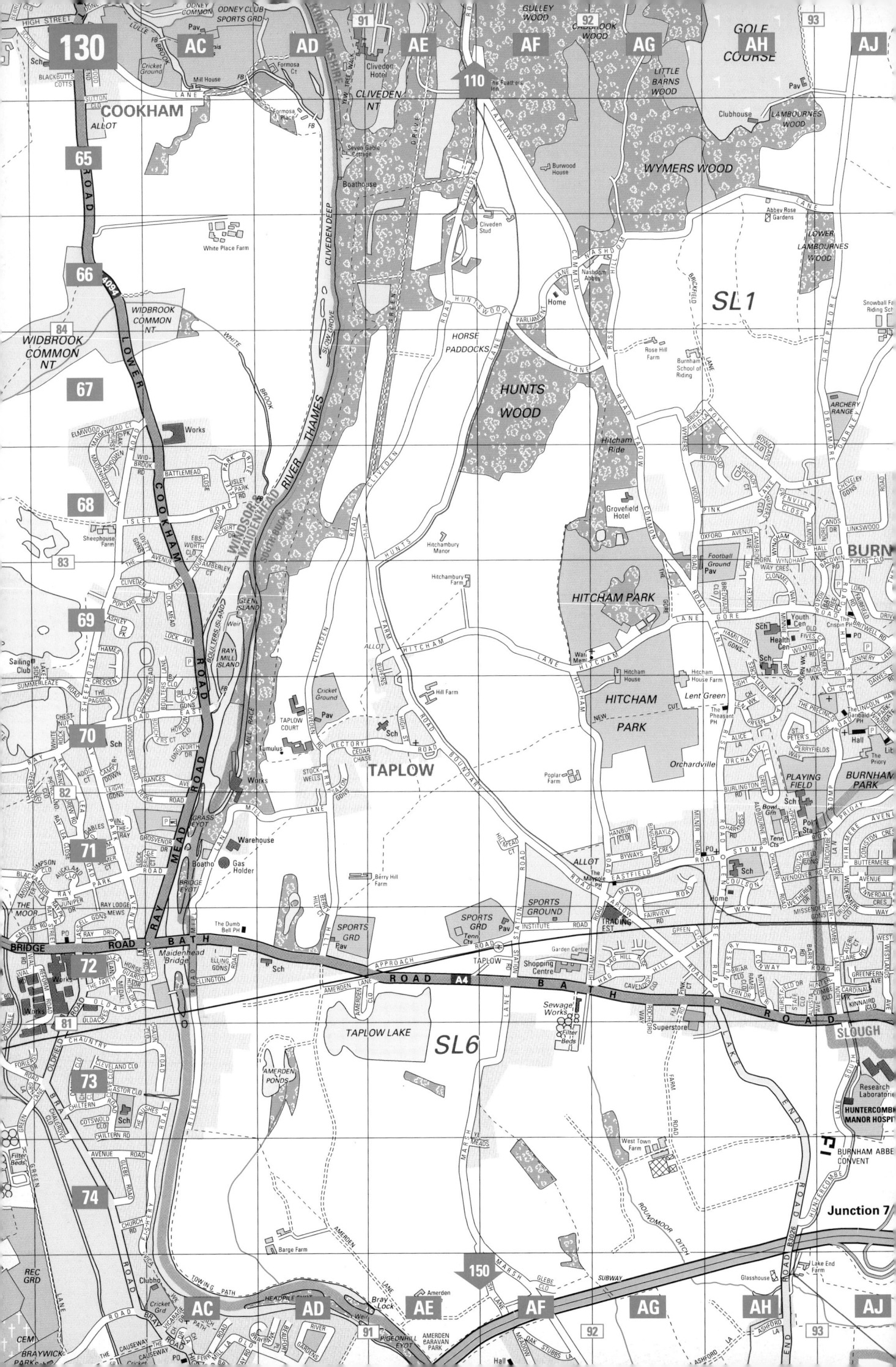

AC
AD
AE
AF
AG
AH
AJ
91
92
93
110
150
COOKHAM
ODNEY COMMON
ODNEY CLUB SPORTS GRD
HIGH STREET
Mill House
Formosa Ct
Formosa Place
Clivedon Hotel
CLIVEDEN NT
GULLEY WOOD
CADSHOOK WOOD
GOLF COURSE
LITTLE BARNS WOOD
Clubhouse
LAMBOURNES WOOD
WYMERS WOOD
Burwood House
Seven Gable Cottage
Boathouse
CLIVEDEN DEEP
Cliveden Stud
White Place Farm
Abbey Rose Gardens
LOWER LAMBOURNES WOOD
Nashdom Abbey
Home
SL1
Snowball Farm Riding Sch
WIDBROOK COMMON NT
84
HORSE PADDOCKS
Rose Hill Farm
Burnham School of Riding
HUNTS WOOD
ARCHERY RANGE
LOWER COOKHAM ROAD
A4094
65
66
67
68
69
70
71
72
73
74
Works
RIVER THAMES
WINDSOR & MAIDENHEAD
SOUTH BUCKS
Hitcham Ride
Grovefield Hotel
Sheephouse Farm
83
Hitchambury Manor
Hitchambury Farm
Football Ground
HITCHAM PARK
GLEN ISLAND
BOULTERS ISLAND
RAY MILL ISLAND
Weir
Sailing Club
ALLOT
Youth Cen
Health Cen
Sch
PO
HITCHAM LANE
Hitcham House
Hitcham House Farm
War Meml
Hill Farm
Cricket Ground
Lent Green
TAPLOW COURT
Tumulus
HITCHAM PARK
The Pheasant PH
TAPLOW
Orchardville
Poplar Farm
PLAYING FIELD
BURNHAM PARK
The Priory
82
Warehouse
Gas Holder
Boatho
GRASS EYOT
BRIDGE EYOT
Berry Hill Farm
SPORTS GROUND
SPORTS GRD
TRADING EST
The Maypole PH
The Dumb Bell PH
Maidenhead Bridge
BATH ROAD
A4
Garden Centre
Shopping Centre
Sewage Works
Filter Beds
Superstore
SLOUGH
81
TAPLOW LAKE
SL6
AMERDEN PONDS
Research Laboratories
HUNTERCOMBE MANOR HOSPITAL
BURNHAM ABBEY CONVENT
West Town Farm
Junction 7
ROUNDMOOR DITCH
B3026
Barge Farm
Lake End Farm
Glasshouse
Amerden
Bray Lock
PIGEONHILL EYOT
AMERDEN CARAVAN PARK
REC GRD
CEM
BRAYWICK
Cricket Grd
Clubho
TOWING PATH
HEADPILE EYOT
Hall

AK
AL
AM
AN
AP
AQ
AR
111
BURNHAM BEECHES
TOWER
DORNEYWOOD GARDENS
Dorneywood House
Pumpkin Hill
SEVEN WAYS PLAIN
UPPER POND
EAST BURNHAM COMMON
MIDDLE POND
JUNIPER GROVE
BURNHAM BEECHES GOLF COURSE
HAWTHORN DELL
EAST BURNHAM CONF CENTRE
SPORTS GROUND
INGRAM'S COPSE
Farnham Common
PARSON'S WOOD
OLD ORCHARD WOOD
65
66
67
68
69
70
71
72
73
74
SL2
FARNHAM PARK
GOLF COURSE
Clubhouses
SWILLY POND
THOMPKINS WOOD
Leys Farm
The Crown Inn
East Burnham
Kennedy's Garden Centre
Highfield Farm
Farnham Park Farm
Lock's Bottom
RUBBISH TIP
East Burnham Park
Allerds Farm
Farnham Common Nursery
FARNHAM PARK
Farnham Royal
Burnham Beeches Moat Hotel
GROVE WOOD
CHERRY ORCHARD NATURE PARK
Bottom Waltons
SOUTH BUCKS
GEORGE PITCHER MEMORIAL REC GRD
COCKSHERD WOOD
STOKE POGES GOLF COURSE
GARDENS OF REMEMBRANCE
132
BRITWELL EST
KENNEDY PARK
REC GRD
MANOR PARK
Electricity Station
SLOUGH TRADING ESTATE
Cockfield Br
Haymill Valley
BATH ROAD
A4
A355
B416
A332
GRANVILLE PLAYING FIELD
GODOLPHIN PLAYING FIELDS
SALT HILL PARK
SLOUGH
Thames Valley Univ
Ice Arena
Sports Cen
TOWN HALL
MERCIAN RECREATION GROUND
CIPPENHAM VILLAGE GREEN
CIPPENHAM
151
ALLOTMENTS
Copthorne Hotel
Courtyard Hotel
Switching Station
Filter Beds
Superstore
94
95
96

132
AS
AT
AU
AV
AW
AX
AY
98
99
00
STOKE COMMON
112
BROCKHURST WOOD
INGRAM'S COPSE
FRAME WOOD
PENN WOOD
Fernacres Farm
Fernacres House
Black Firs
Dar Alshams
Tenn Cts
Cricket Grd
FULMER
COMMON
Mill House Farm
Framewood Manor
Tennis Courts
Wexham Place
FULMER COMMON
Farnham Common
65
66
67
68
69
70
71
72
73
74
PARSON'S WOOD
OLD ORCHARD WOOD
SL2
84
FARNHAM PARK
GOLF COURSE
Clubhouses
STOKE POGES
Offices
Sch
Hall
PO
Lib
REC GRD
Pav
Tennis Cts
SPORTS GROUND
HOME WOOD
Eight Acres Farm
PLAYING FLD
Offices
UPTON WOOD
UPTON LAKE
Upton Farm
DOG KENNEL FIELD
Sefton Park
Home Farm
Hockley Hole
Clinic
The Stag PH
Wexham Street
Twin Trees Farm
THAMES VALLEY NUFFIELD HOSPITAL
The Plough PH
WEXHAM PARK GOLF COURSE
Clubhouse
ROWLEY WOOD
ROWLEYFIELD LARCHES
ROWLEY SLIP
Grange Farm
WEXHAM PARK GOLF COURSE
GROTES WOOD
GALLIONS WOOD
SPRING WOOD
HOLLYBUSH WOOD
Berry Farm
Snitterfield Farm
Glasshouses
Bell Farm
ROWLEY LAKE
Tithe Farm
B416
STOKE POGES GOLF COURSE
Monument
83
The Clock House
Stoke Park Farm
The Manor House
GRAY'S FIELD
Monument to Thomas Gray
Clubhouse
GARDENS OF REMEMBRANCE
131
Bowl Grn
SPORTS GROUND
Duffield House
Stoke Green
The Red Lion PH
WEXHAM PARK HOSPITAL
Amb Sta
Clubho
Cricket Ground
STOKE PARK PLAYING FIELD
Tumulus
STOKE PLACE CONFERENCE CENTRE
NOR PARK
82
THE LANES GOLF COURSE
Central Nursery
The Lodge
PLAYING FIELD
STONE'S WOOD
GRANVILLE PLAYING FIELD
Stokeplace Farm
Crematorium
SPORTS GRDS
ALLOT
All Souls Farm
The Green Man PH
CEMETERY
SLOUGH
SOUTH BUCKS
GEORGE GREEN
GODOLPHIN PLAYING FIELDS
81
Swim Pool
Youth & Comm Cen
UPTON LEA REC GRD
ROCHFORDS GARDENS
Slough Nursery
SL1
SALT HILL PARK
SLOUGH
Tennis Courts
Bowl Grn
GRAND UNION CANAL
Gas Works
A412
Lavender Farm
Ice Arena
Fire Sta
Thames Valley Univ
BRUNEL BUS STA
Superstore
Sports Cen
TOWN HALL
MONTEM PLEASURE GROUND
Shopping Cen
Shopping Centre
152
A4
WELLINGTON
A332
MAG CT
Works

133
AZ
BA
BB
BC
BD
BE
BF
01
02
03
113
153
134
SL0
UB9
SL3
BROWN'S WOOD
PARKSPRING WOOD
MOUNT FIDGET WOOD
BRIDGETTINE CONVENT
LANGLEY COMMON
STRAWBERRY WOOD
Pinewood Film Studios
Heatherden Hall
NATURE RESERVE
BLACK PARK COUNTRY PARK
Blackpark Lake
Centenary Lodge Visitors Centre
DIAMOND WOOD
CHESTNUT WOOD
FOXES GUTTER
COLUMN LARCHES
RHODODENDRON GARDENS
LANGLEY PARK WOOD
LANGLEY PARK COUNTRY PARK
ROUGHGROUND WOOD
ARBORETUM
Environmental Studies Centre
Langley Park House
OLDHOUSE WOOD
LONG COPPICE
Sevenhills Farm
PLAYING FIELD
THE CLUMP
Cherry Orchard Farm
Belle Farm
Dromenagh Farm
Copse Hill Farm
Southlands Manor
Round Coppice Farm
Kingcup Farm
Durham House
Cornerfields
Ivy House Farm
Brickfield Farm
BROOM WARREN
Stag & Hounds PH
Health Centre
Tennis Cts
REC GRD
Bowl Grn
Lib
Sch
PO
Home
Warren Lodge
Warren House
Warren House Farm
Crooked Billet PH
Five Points
Fernleigh
Park Lodge Farm
Brackenwood
Park Lodge
ALLOT
IVER HEATH
Home Cottage Farm
Perivale Livery Stables
Moorwards
Woodlands Park
CHANDLERS HILL
Mansfield Farm
Watergate Farm
Sub
UXBRIDGE
A4007
A412
M25
DENHAM ROAD
SLOUGH ROAD
CHURCH ROAD
PINEWOOD GREEN
PINEWOOD ROAD
SEVEN HILLS ROAD
BANGORS ROAD NORTH
BANGORS ROAD SOUTH
Bangors Park Farm
Norwood Grange
NORWOOD LANE
DELAFORD PARK
Delaford Manor
Coppins Farm
Coppins
Lower Delaford
Nursery
SPORTS GRD
Eureham Centre
Sports Centre
The Whip & Collar PH
Ashen Cross
BILLET LANE WOOD
Treal Farm
BELLSWOOD LANE
WOOD LANE
Shreding Green
Gurkha PH
Shredding Green Farm
LANGLEY PARK ROAD
Love Hill House Farm
Moat House
Clubhouse
IVER GOLF COURSE
Glasshouse
MOBILE HOMES PARK
GRAND UNION CANAL (SLOUGH ARM)
TOWING PATH
SOUTH BUCKS
BUCKINGHAMSHIRE
SLOUGH
CARAVAN PARK
Depot
Chequer Bridge
Works
LANGLEY BUSINESS CENTRE
IND EST
IVER
HIGH STREET
Iver Lodge
Delaford Park
BURIAL GRD
REC GRD
ALLOT
RIDGEWAY INDUSTRIAL ESTATE
Thorney Farm
Tower
COLN BROOK
FARLOWS LAKE
Sewage Works
Filter Beds
Huntsmoor Park Farm
65
66
67
68
69
70
71
72
73
74
81
82
83
84

134
BG
BH
BJ
BK
BL
BM
BN
05
06
07
114
133
154
65
66
67
68
69
70
71
72
73
74
84
83
82
81
UB9
UB10
UB8
UB7
SL0
UXBRIDGE
UXBRIDGE MOOR
COWLEY
IVER
YIEWSLEY
WEST DRAYTON
HILLINGDON
DENHAM ROAD
A412
A4020
A4007
A408
A408
B483
B470
M25
OXFORD ROAD
HIGH STREET
COWLEY ROAD
HILLINGDON ROAD
HILLINGDON HILL
HARLINGTON ROAD
FALLING LANE
DRAYTON PARK
ST. JOHNS ROAD
ROCKINGHAM RD
WINDSOR ST
NEW WINDSOR ST
PARK ROAD
FIELD HEATH ROAD
STATION ROAD
CHURCH ROAD
HORTON ROAD
KINGSTON LANE
ROYAL LANE
COLHAM AVENUE
FRAYS AVENUE
BUCKINGHAMSHIRE
SOUTH BUCKS
Grand Union Canal (Slough Arm)
Fray's River
Shire Ditch
River Pinn
Colne Brook
Alder Bourne
HILLINGDON HOUSE FARM SPORTS GROUNDS
UXBRIDGE COMMON
Uxbridge College
Ski Slopes
Hillingdon Ski Centre
UXBRIDGE STADIUM
Cricket Club
Cricket Ground
Open Air Pool
HIGHBRIDGE INDUSTRIAL ESTATE
The Pavilions
CIVIC OFFICES
Warehouses
Electricity Sub Station
MIDAS INDUSTRIAL ESTATE
SARUM COMPLEX
CHILTERN BUSINESS VILLAGE
Gas Works
COWLEY BUSINESS PARK
Brunel University
Halls of Residence
Sports Cen
HILLINGDON & UXBRIDGE CEMETERY
HILLINGDON GOLF COURSE
Clubhouse
R.A.F. Uxbridge
RIFLE RANGE
HILLINGDON COURT PARK
BIG CLUMP
ST. RAPHAELS CONVENT
R.A.F. SPORTS GRD
UNIVERSITY PLAYING FIELDS
Milton Hutchings Garden Centre
CONVENT
HILLINGDON HOSPITAL
COLHAM GREEN REC GRD
CONEY GREEN
Tudor Cottage
Stratford Bridge
COWLEY HALL REC GRD
HUNTSMOOR PARK
Huntsmoor Park Farm
Filter Beds
COWLEY LAKE
LITTLE BRITAIN LAKE
Packet Boat Nurseries
Little Britain Br
FARLOWS LAKE
Water Treatment Works
Sewage Works
Coal Depot
TOMO INDUSTRIAL EST
RAINBOW INDUSTRIAL ESTATE
HORTON IND PARK
LAWN FIELDS
SPORTS GROUND
Uxbridge FC
Apple Tree Roundabout
Colham Roundabout
THE RIDGEWAY ESTATE
THORNEY PARK GOLF COURSE
Thorney Farm
Thorney Wier House
Palmer's Moor Farm
Delaford Manor
Delaford Park
Coppins Farm
Coppins Cottages
Iver Lodge
Woodlands Park
Perivale Livery Stables
Moorwards
Park Farm
Mansfield Farm
Watergate Farm
Southlands Manor
Copse Hill Farm
Kingcup Farm
Brickfield Farm
Ivy House Farm
Oxford Road Nursery
Denham Lodge
Osborne Farm
Dog & Duck PH
Cornerfields
Round Coppice Farm
Old Mill Farm
Manor Farm
Paddington Packet Boat PH
Philpot's Bridge
Cowley Bri
Clisby's Br
Iver Bridge
Horton Bridge
Red Lion PH
Prince of Wales PH
Vine Inn PH
Common Plantation
PARK WOOD
Nature Reserve
PLAYING FIELD
SPORTS GRD

NORTHOLT AERODROME
HA4
NORTH HILLINGDON
WESTERN AVENUE
A40
UB5
WEST LONDON SHOOTING GROUNDS
YEADING BROOK MEADOWS NATURE RESERVE
YEADING
HAYES PARK
UB4
BELMORE PLAYING FIELDS
HAYES END
UXBRIDGE ROAD
A4020
HAYES
UB3
HAYES BYPASS
DAWLEY ROAD
STOCKLEY PARK
Grand Union Canal
HAYES TOWN
115
136
155
BP
BQ
BR
BS
BT
BU
BV
08
09
10
65
66
67
68
69
70
71
72
73
74

136
BW
BX
BY
BZ
CA
CB
CC
HA4
116
12
13
14
65
66
67
68
69
70
71
72
73
74
81
82
83
84
135
156
UB5
UB4
UB1
ODYSSEY BUSINESS PARK
FROGMORE ESTATE
SOLID WASTE TRANSFER STATION
NORTHOLT RECREATION GRD
LORD HALSBURY MEMORIAL REC GRD
SPORTS GROUND
NORTHOLT
ISLIP MANOR PARK
WESTERN AVENUE
CHURCH ROAD
MANDEVILLE ROAD
WEST END ROAD
LONDON GOLF CENTRE
BELVUE PARK
EALING GOLF RANGE
KELVIN INDUSTRIAL ESTATE
THE METROPOLITAN CENTRE
WEST LONDON SHOOTING GROUNDS
Down Barns Moated Site
LIME TREE PARK
PLAYING FIELDS
RECTORY PARK
SMITHS FARM EST
GREENFORD
RAVENOR PARK
RUISLIP ROAD
THE PARKWAY (HAYES BYPASS)
YEADING
SPORTS GROUND
KING GEORGE'S FIELD
GREENFORD PARK REC GRD
GREENFORD PARK CEMETERY
JUBILEE PARK
WARREN PARK
BROOKSIDE
UXBRIDGE ROAD
THE BROADWAY
HIGH STREET
SOUTHALL
SOUTHALL PARK
DORMER'S WELLS
WEST MIDDLESEX GOLF COURSE
GREENFORD ROAD
BELMORE PLAYING FIELDS
HAYES BYPASS
ELYSTAN BUSINESS CENTRE
HAYES METRO CENTRE
HEATHROW INTERCHANGE
BROOK INDUSTRIAL ESTATE
BARRATT INDUSTRIAL PARK
SOUTHALL RAILWAY CENTRE
SECURE PARKING
GRAND UNION CANAL (PADDINGTON BRANCH)
HILLINGDON
EALING
A312
A40
A4020
A3005
B455

137
CD
CE
CF
CG
CH
CJ
CK
15
16
17
117
138
157
65
66
67
68
69
70
71
72
73
74
81
82
83
84
SUDBURY
HA0
WEMBLEY
WHITTON AVENUE WEST
HARROW ROAD
SUDBURY & HARROW ROAD
SUDBURY TOWN
BRIDGEWATER ROAD
EALING ROAD
A4089
A4005
A4127
A40
A4020
B452
B455
B456
HORSENDEN WOOD
HORSENDEN HILL GOLF COURSE
HORSENDEN HILL
SUDBURY GOLF COURSE
SPORTS GROUND
BERKELEY FIELDS
GREAT BRAMSTONES
HOME MEAD
GRAND UNION CANAL (PADDINGTON BRANCH)
ALPERTON CEMETERY
ONE TREE HILL REC GRD
ALPERTON
UB6
PERIVALE WOOD
PERIVALE
PERIVALE INDUSTRIAL PARK
PERIVALE NEW BUSINESS CENTRE
WADSWORTH BUSINESS CENTRE
FLEETWAY BUSINESS PARK
SHERATON BUSINESS CEN
CAPITAL BUSINESS CEN
METROPOLITAN POLICE TRAFFIC UNIT
ALPERTON SPORTS GROUND
Westway Cross Shopping Park
GREENFORD
OLDFIELD REC GRD
EALING CENTRAL SPORTS GRD
SOUTH GREENFORD
WESTERN AVENUE
ATHLETICS STADIUM
PERIVALE PARK SPORTS GROUND
PERIVALE PARK GOLF COURSE
EALING GOLF COURSE
PITSHANGER PARK
River Brent
HANGER HILL PARK
HANGER LANE
BARCLAYS BANK SPORTS GROUND
CLEVELAND PARK
CUCKOO PARK
CASTLE BAR PARK
MONTPELIER PARK
W7
W5
W13
DRAYTON GREEN
WEST EALING
EALING
EALING BROADWAY
HAVEN GREEN
EALING COMMON
UXBRIDGE ROAD
NEW BROADWAY
THE BROADWAY
KENSINGTON & CHELSEA CEMETERY
HANWELL
HANWELL CEMETERY
CHURCHFIELDS RECREATION GROUND
BRENT VALLEY GOLF COURSE
Wharncliffe Viaduct
EALING HOSPITAL N.H.S. TRUST
WALPOLE PARK
PITSHANGER MANOR MUS
Thames Valley Uni
Ealing Studios
LAMMAS PARK

138
WEMBLEY
CL
CM
CN
CP
CQ
CR
CS
118
TOKYNGTON
CHURCH END
HA0
HA9
STONEBRIDGE PARK
STONEBRIDGE
ALPERTON
PARK ROYAL
HARLESDEN
NORTH ACTON
HANGER HILL PARK
WEST ACTON
W3
EALING
EALING COMMON
W5
ACTON
EAST ACTON
ACTON PARK
137
158
NORTH CIRCULAR ROAD
WESTERN AVENUE
HANGER LANE
EALING ROAD
UXBRIDGE ROAD
GUNNERSBURY AVENUE
HIGH STREET
THE MALL
HARROW ROAD
HILLSIDE
CRAVEN PARK
VICTORIA ROAD
HORN LANE
TOWNSEND INDUSTRIAL ESTATE
CENTRAL MIDDLESEX HOSPITAL
GIBBONS REC GRD
ONE TREE HILL REC GRD
BARCLAYS BANK SPORTS GROUND
NORTH THAMES GAS BOARD SPORTS GRD
NORTH ACTON PLAYING FIELDS
ACTON CEMETERY
PREMIER PARK
Princess Royal Distribution Centre
19
20
21

CT
CU
CV
CW
CX
CY
CZ
22
23
24
119
65
66
67
68
69
70
71
72
73
74
81
82
83
84
140
159
NW2
NW6
NW10
W9
W10
W11
W12
WILLESDEN
WILLESDEN GREEN
BRONDESBURY
BRONDESBURY PARK
KILBURN
KENSAL RISE
KENSAL GREEN
KENSAL TOWN
WEST KILBURN
MAIDA HILL
OLD OAK COMMON
WORMWOOD SCRUBS
NORTH KENSINGTON
NOTTING HILL
SHEPHERD'S BUSH
KENSINGTON
WESTBOURNE GREEN
WILLESDEN CEMETERY
ROUNDWOOD PARK
QUEEN'S PARK
PADDINGTON OLD CEMETERY
ST. MARY'S RC CEMETERY
KENSAL GREEN CEMETERY
GRAND UNION CANAL (Paddington Branch)
NORTH POLE INTERNATIONAL DEPOT
LITTLE WORMWOOD SCRUBS REC GRD
LINFORD CHRISTIE STADIUM
QUEEN CHARLOTTE & CHELSEA HOSP
HAMMERSMITH HOSPITAL
H.M. PRISON WORMWOOD SCRUBS
ST. CHARLES HOSP
PRINCESS LOUISE HOSP
WILLESDEN COMMUNITY HOSP
KING EDWARD VII SPORTS GRD
WILLESDEN STADIUM
RANGERS STADIUM QPR F.C.
HOLLAND PARK
WESTWAY
HARROW ROAD
WEST CROSS ROUTE M41
UXBRIDGE ROAD
HOLLAND PARK AVENUE
NOTTING HILL GATE
LADBROKE GROVE
WILLESDEN JUNCTION
WILLESDEN GREEN
KILBURN
BRONDESBURY
BRONDESBURY PARK
KENSAL RISE
QUEENS PARK
KENSAL GREEN
WESTBOURNE PARK
LATIMER ROAD
HOLLAND PARK
SHEPHERD'S BUSH
WHITE CITY

DA
DB
DC
DD
DE
DF
DG
26
27
28
120
WEST HAMPSTEAD
Camden Arts Centre
FINCHLEY ROAD & FROGNAL
WEST HAMPSTEAD (THAMESLINK)
WEST HAMPSTEAD
FINCHLEY ROAD
FREUD MUSEUM
TAVISTOCK CEN
ROYAL FREE HOSP
BELSIZE PARK
65
KILBURN
BRONDESBURY
SOUTH HAMPSTEAD
SWISS COTTAGE
CHALK FARM
66
NW6
PADDINGTON OLD CEMETERY
67
PRIMROSE HILL
PRIMROSE HILL
NW8
ABBEY ROAD EST
KILBURN
KILBURN PARK
KILBURN HIGH ROAD
68
LONDON ZOO
NW1
REGENT'S PARK
HOSPITAL OF ST. JOHN & ST. ELIZ
WELLINGTON HOSP
ST. JOHN'S WOOD
LORD'S CRICKET GROUND
LONDON CENTRAL MOSQUE
BOATING LAKE
QUEEN MARY'S GARDENS
83
WEST KILBURN
69
PADDINGTON RECREATION GROUND
MAIDA VALE
139
MAIDA HILL
W9
MAIDA VALE
LISSON GROVE
70
WARWICK AVENUE
Little Venice
MARYLEBONE
MADAME TUSSAUD'S
82
71
A40(M) WESTWAY
WESTBOURNE GREEN
PADDINGTON
ROYAL OAK
EDGWARE ROAD
ST. MARY'S HOSP
MARYLEBONE
72
W2
BAYSWATER
81
NOTTING HILL
73
QUEENSWAY
LANCASTER GATE
MARBLE ARCH
OXFORD STREET where marked is closed to through traffic (except buses & taxis) from 7a.m.-7p.m. Monday - Saturday
NOTTING HILL GATE
KENSINGTON GARDENS
HYDE PARK
74
HOLLAND PARK
ROUND POND
THE SERPENTINE
The Long Water
KENSINGTON
W8
KENSINGTON PALACE
SERPENTINE GALLERY
160
HOLLAND PARK
HOLLAND HOUSE
KENSINGTON ROAD
KENSINGTON GORE
KNIGHTSBRIDGE
BAYSWATER ROAD

141
DH
DJ
DK
DL
DM
DN
DP
N7
121
LOWER HOLLOWAY
KENTISH TOWN
CALEDONIAN PARK
SPORTS GRD
PENTONVILLE PRISON
BARNSBURY
CANONBURY
65
66
67
68
69
70
71
72
73
74
84
83
82
81
KING'S CROSS
CAMDEN TOWN
ISLINGTON
N1
ST. PANCRAS HOSP & HOSP FOR TROPICAL DISEASES
MORNINGTON CRESCENT
PENTONVILLE
SOMERS TOWN
BRITISH LIB
ST. GEORGE'S CATHEDRAL
EUSTON
ST. PANCRAS
FINSBURY
142
WC1
CORAM'S FIELDS
ST. LUKE'S
EC1
CLERKENWELL
RUSSELL SQUARE GDNS
GRAY'S INN GDNS
BLOOMSBURY
BRITISH MUSEUM
MIDDLESEX HOSP
HOLBORN
LINCOLN'S INN FIELDS
ST. BART'S HOSP
ST. PAUL'S CATH
SOHO
CAVENDISH SQUARE
OXFORD CIRCUS
COVENT GARDEN
STRAND
WC2
CHARING CROSS
EMBANKMENT
TRAFALGAR SQUARE
VICTORIA EMBANKMENT
RIVER THAMES
EC4
BLACKFRIARS
SOUTHWARK
SE1
SHAKESPEARE GLOBE THEATRE & EXHIBITION
TATE MODERN
ROYAL FESTIVAL HALL
QUEEN ELIZABETH HALL
HAYWARD GALLERY
WATERLOO
JUBILEE GARDENS
ST. JAMES'S
MARLBOROUGH HOUSE
GREEN PARK
ST. JAMES'S PARK
PICCADILLY
PALL MALL
161
WESTMINSTER BR
THE BOROUGH
29
30
31
BUCKINGHAM PALACE

DQ
DR
DS
DT
DU
DV
DW
33
34
35
122
162
141
65
66
67
68
69
70
71
72
73
74
84
83
82
81
CANONBURY
KINGSLAND
HACKNEY
DALSTON
E8
N1
DE BEAUVOIR TOWN
SOUTH HACKNEY
HOXTON
HAGGERSTON
E2
BETHNAL GREEN
SHOREDITCH
ST. LUKE'S
EC1
CLERKENWELL
BROADGATE
BARBICAN
EC2
E1
WHITECHAPEL
STEPNEY
EC4
EC3
WAPPING
SHADWELL
SE1
SOUTHWARK
THE BOROUGH
RIVER THAMES
TOWER OF LONDON
GUY'S HOSPITAL
LONDON FIELDS
REGENT'S CANAL
ST. PAUL'S CATH
TATE MODERN
LONDON BRIDGE

DX
DY
DZ
EA
EB
EC
ED
HOMERTON
MABLEY GREEN
E9
HACKNEY WICK
STADIUM (CLOSED)
VALLEY PARK
EASTWAY
123
LONDON INTERNATIONAL FREIGHT TERMINAL
STRATFORD
E15
65
66
67
68
69
70
71
72
73
74
VICTORIA PARK
WELL STREET COMMON
HERTFORD UNION CANAL
OLD FORD
BOW
MILE END
MILE END PARK
ROYAL LONDON HOSP (MILE END)
Queen Mary & Westfield Coll
ROYAL LON. HOSP (ST. CLEMENTS)
TOWER HAMLETS CEMETERY PARK
E3
BROMLEY
DEVONS EST
BOW BRIDGE EST
GROVE HALL PARK
THREE MILLS GREEN
LEE VALLEY PARK
Pumping Station
Stratford Mkt
WEST HAM
MEMORIAL RECREATION GROUND
144
LONDON GAS MUS
MEMORIAL GDNS
CODY ROAD BUSINESS CEN
MILE END STADIUM
LIMEHOUSE FIELDS EST
LOCKSLEY EST
BARTLETT PARK
LANSBURY EST
LANGDON PARK
E14
LIMEHOUSE
POPLAR
ALL SAINTS
EAST INDIA DOCK BASIN
BOW CREEK WATER PARK
CANNING TOWN
SILVERTOWN
RIVER THAMES
LIMEHOUSE REACH
CANARY WHARF
ISLE
WEST INDIA DOCKS
Billingsgate Fish Mkt
Blackwall Basin
BLACKWALL TUNNEL
THE DOME
MERIDIAN GARDENS
NORTH GREENWICH
SE10
SE16
RUSSIA DOCK WOODLAND
163
36
37
38
81
82
83
84
TOWER HAMLETS
NEWHAM
SOUTHWARK

144
EE
EF
EG
EH
EJ
EK
EL
E7
E15
E13
E16
SE10
40
41
42
124
143
164
65
66
67
68
69
70
71
72
73
74
84
83
82
81
FOREST GATE
STRATFORD
WEST HAM
WEST HAM PARK
UPTON
UPTON PARK
PLAISTOW
CANNING TOWN
CUSTOM HOUSE
SILVERTOWN
THE DOME
NORTH GREENWICH
ROYAL VICTORIA DOCK
WEST HAM UTD. F.C.
NEWHAM GENERAL HOSPITAL
PLAISTOW HOSP
EAST HAM MEM HOSP
EAST LONDON CEMETERY
Crematorium
MEMORIAL RECREATION GROUND
WOODGRANGE PARK CEMETERY
PLASHET JEWISH CEMETERY
PLASHET PARK
CHILDRENS ZOO
PRIORY PARK
BRAMPTON PARK
TERENCE McMILLAN STADIUM
BECKTON DISTRICT PARK NORTH
KING GEORGE V PARK
THREE MILLS GREEN
VALLEY PARK
BOW CREEK WATER PARK
EAST INDIA DOCK BASIN NATURE RESERVE
THAMES BARRIER PARK
THAMES FLOOD BARRIER
LOWER LEA CROSSING
SILVERTOWN WAY
NEWHAM WAY
ROMFORD ROAD
BARKING ROAD
PLAISTOW ROAD
WEST HAM LANE
MANOR ROAD
UPTON LANE
GREEN STREET
HIGH STREET
PRINCE REGENT LANE
NORTH WOOLWICH ROAD
CONNAUGHT BRIDGE
ROYAL ALBERT
Royal Albert Dock Regatta Centre
Grain Mills
Pontoon Dock
London City Airport Pier
Millennium Pier
Blackwall Tunnel
Blackwall Reach
Bow Creek
RIVER
WOOLWICH REACH
NEWHAM
GREENWICH
TOWER HAMLETS
A11
A12
A13
A112
A114
A118
A124
A1011
A1020
A102
B125
B164
B165
B167
Tate & Lyle Jetty

EM
EN
EP
EQ
ER
ES
ET
43
44
45
125
LOXFORD
LITTLE ILFORD PARK
BARKING PARK
THE LAKE
BARKING PARK REC GRD
Indoor Bowl Club
Bowling Greens
LONGBRIDGE ROAD
FANSHAWE AV
NORTHERN RELIEF ROAD
BARKING
TOWN HALL
SPORTS GRD
Sports Cen
RIPPLE ROAD
UPNEY
BOATING LAKE
Pitch 'n' Putt
65
66
67
68
69
70
71
72
73
74
83
84
82
81
146
165
RIPPLESIDE BURIAL GROUND
BARKING INDUSTRIAL PARK
ALFREDS WAY IND ESTATE
WAYSIDE COMMERCIAL EST
TRAIN DEPOT
IG11
GREAT FIELDS PARK
ALFREDS WAY
A13 (BARKING BYPASS)
ABBEY WHARF INDUSTRIAL ESTATE
KATELLA TRADING EST
LYON BUSINESS PARK
RIVERSIDE INDUSTRIAL ESTATE
City Farm & Ecology Park
RIVER ROAD BUSINESS PARK
TRAFALGAR BUSINESS CENTRE
BUZZARD CREEK INDUSTRIAL ESTATE
CREEKMOUTH
Gravel Works
BARKING FLOOD BARRIER
Barking or False Point
BARKING & DAGENHAM
LEWISHAM
River Roding
CUCKHOLD'S HAVEN
HAND TROUGH CREEK
Long Reach
Warpools Reach
Filter Beds
BECKTON REACH SEWAGE TREATMENT WORKS
Incinerator
Power Ho
Sludge Beds
Pump Sta
Pier
SPORTS GROUND
Refuse Transfer Sta
GOOSELEY'S PLAYING FIELDS
ALLOTMENTS
SPORTS GROUND
Gasholder
BARKING ROAD REC GRD
FLANDERS RD PLAYING FLDS
BARRINGTON PLAYING FLDS
Nature Reserve
NEWHAM WAY
Superstores
RETAIL PARK
Northern Outfall Sewer
Northern Outfall Sewage Works
ALPINE BUSINESS CEN
BECKTON
Gas Works
DLR DEPOT
NEW BECKTON PARK
GALLIONS REACH
Gallions Hotel
ALBERT WAY
BECKTON PARK
Uni of East London
ALBERT DOCK
ALBERT BASIN
AIRPORT
KING GEORGE V DOCK
Newham Coll of Further Ed
Motor Cross Track
BASIN SOUTH
WOOLWICH MANOR WAY
ROYAL DOCKS ROAD
A406
A117
A124
A123
A1153
GALLIONS REACH
MARGARET NESS OR TRIPCOCK POINT
THAMESMEAD
Thamesmere Lake
SE28
EASTERN WAY
CENTRAL WAY
BIRCHMERE
NORTH WOOLWICH
ROYAL VICTORIA GDNS
STANDARD INDUSTRIAL ESTATE
North Woolwich Pier
Woolwich Ferry Pier
WOOLWICH CROWN CT
H.M. PRISON BELMARSH
NEWHAM

146
EU
EV
EW
EX
EY
EZ
FA
47
48
49
126
BARKING FC
Clubhouse
SPORTS GRD
PARSLOES PARK
Barking Coll
Sports Cen
Sec Sch
Prim Schs
65
BOATING LAKE
BOATING LAKE
Pitch 'n' Putt
SPORTS GRD
SPORTS GRD
Health Centre
BECONTREE
DAGENHAM HEATHWAY
66
MAYBROOK MEADOW EST
84
A123
RIPPLESIDE BURIAL GROUND
67
CASTLE GREEN
GORESBROOK SPORTS GROUND
BARKING R.F.C.
Leisure Cen
DAGENHAM LEISURE PK
GORESBROOK PARK
BARKING INDUSTRIAL PARK
ALFREDS WAY IND ESTATE
WAYSIDE COMMERCIAL EST
RENWICK IND ESTATE
RIPPLESIDE COMMERCIAL ESTATE
MAYBELLS COMM EST
A13
RIPPLE ROAD
ALFREDS WAY
TRAIN DEPOT
68
LYON BUSINESS PARK
Freight Depot
FORD MOTOR
DAGENHAM DOCK
RM9
83
Youth & Comm Cen
SPORTS GRD
RIVERSIDE INDUSTRIAL ESTATE
69
City Farm & Ecology Park
RIVER ROAD BUSINESS PARK
IG11
COAL DEPOT
145
POWER STATION
Power Station
TRAFALGAR BUSINESS
70
CREEKMOUTH
Horse Shoe Corner
82
BUZZARD CREEK INDUSTRIAL ESTATE
Superstore
Oil Storage Depot
Depot
71
BARKING FLOOD BARRIER
Gravel Works
BARKING & DAGENHAM
Barking or False Point
Pier
Landing Stage
CROSSNESS LIGHTHOUSE
LEWISHAM
72
GREENWICH
BEXLEY
THAMESMEAD NORTH
Ecology Study Area
Crossway Lake
SE2
RIVERSIDE GOLF COURSE
81
Thamesmere Lake
Superstore
COVERED RESERVOIRS
MANORWAY GREEN
Crossness Sewage Treatment Works
Sludge Incinerator
73
Shop Cen
MOORINGS
Thamesmead Town FC
SPORTS GROUND
CROSSWAY PARK
THAMESMEAD
SPORTS GROUND
74
SPORTS GRD
SOUTHMERE PARK
ERITH MARSHES
A2016
LAKESIDE CENTRE
SOUTHMERE
BIRCHMERE PARK
EASTERN WAY
SE28
166
DA18
WOODLAND WAY
H.M. PRISON BELMARSH

FB
FC
FD
FE
FF
FG
FH
127
PARK
Dagenham East
Rhone Poulenc Rd
Pondfield Park
Western Avenue
South
Dagenham East
Sports Club
Bretons Equestrian Centre
Sports Ground
Brittons Playing Field
Manor Road Sports Grd
Rainham Road South
Dagenham Road
Rainham Road
A125
RM10
Old Dagenham Park
The Leys
Arena
Newtons Corner
South Hornchurch
Beam River
Barking & Dagenham
Havering
Rainham
Ingrebourne River
RM12
Hornchurch
Country Park
Airfield Wood
Flightway Wood
Farmfield Wood
Lowfield Wood
Albyns Farm
Superstore
65
66
67
68
69
70
71
72
73
74
84
83
82
81
148
Dovers Corner
The Albion PH
New Road
A1306
A1311
Link Road
Car Compound
Hornchurch Marshes
Riverside Sewage Works
Rainham Creek
Albright Industrial Estate
Denver Industrial Estate
Container Depot
Fairview Industrial Park
Rainham Sunday Market
Thames Avenue
Ferry Lane
Coldharbour Lane
A13
Thames Gateway
RM13
Wennington Road
B1335
Rainham Hall
Rainham Marshes
Silt Lagoons
Common Watercourse
Southall Bridge
South Hall Farm
Hornchurch Shoot
Old Man's Head
Jetty
DA17
Power Station (Closed)
Jenningtree Point Lighthouse
Jenningtree Point
Wharf
Pier
Erith
Wennington Marshes
167
50
51
52

FJ
FK
FL
FM
FN
FP
FQ
Hacton
128
RM12
HORNCHURCH
COUNTRY
PARK
AIRFIELD WOOD
PINEWOOD
FLIGHTWAY WOOD
FARMFIELD WOOD
LOWFIELD WOOD
ABBEY WOOD
BERWICK POND
SAND AND GRAVEL PIT
REFUSE TRANSFER STATION
PARKLANDS OPEN SPACE
Corbets Tey
WARWICK WOOD
RAINHAM CEMETERY (JEWISH)
SPRING FARM PARK
RM13
147
Wennington
RAINHAM MARSHES
Silt Lagoons
WENNINGTON MARSHES
SPORTS GROUND
168
65
66
67
68
69
70
71
72
73
74
54
55
56
84
83
82
81
White Post Corner
Southall Bridge
MOAT
Moor Hall
Sandy Lane Farm
SANDY LANE
A1306 NEW ROAD
A13
GATEWAY
WARWICK LANE
BERWICK POND ROAD
GERPINS LANE
PARK FARM ROAD
LAUNDERS LANE
WENNINGTON ROAD
UPMINSTER ROAD

North Ockendon
SOUTH OCKENDON
NORTH STIFFORD
RM15
BELHUS PARK
BELHUS WOODS COUNTRY PARK
BELHUS PARK GOLF COURSE
RUSSELL'S LAKE
COYS LAKE
SAND AND GRAVEL PIT
FREEMAN'S SHAW
WHITEHALL WOOD
LITTLE BRICKKILN WOOD
BRICKKILN WOOD
MIDDLE WOOD
BONUS WOOD
TOP MEADOW GOLF COURSE
THE WILDERNESS
CLAY PIT
Tumulus
MOAT
South Ockendon Hall
South Ockendon Hall Farm
LITTLE PALMER'S SHAW
GREAT PALMER'S SHAW
OAK WOOD
ASH PLANTATION
ROOKERY
LONG POND
The Ockendon Complex
BONNYGATE WOOD
DILKES PARK
South Ockendon Centre
SOUTH OCKENDON REC GRD
FORD AVELEY PLANT
South Ockendon Garden Centre
MILLARD'S GARDEN
BRANNETT'S WOOD
HANGMAN'S WOOD
LOW WELL WOOD
LOW WELL WOOD
BRICKBARN WOOD
COMBE WOOD
Mar Dyke
Junction 30
M25
HAVERING
THURROCK
OCKENDON ROAD
B1421
B186
B1335
STIFFORD ROAD
NORTH ROAD
SOUTH ROAD
FEN LANE
HALL LANE
WEST ROAD
DENNISES LANE
STUBBERS LANE
PEA LANE
PIKE LANE
DENNIS ROAD
SUNNINGS LANE
GREEN LANE
BUCKLES LANE
PILGRIMS LANE
ARTERIAL ROAD NORTH
THURROCK
A13
Manor Farm
Hall Farm
Nursery
Outdoor Pursuits Centre
Kemp's Farm
Groves Barns
Whitepost Farm
The Old White Horse PH
Royal Oak PH
Clubhouse
Bensons Farm
Little Mollands Farm
Hill Farm
Stifford Bridge
The Dog & Partridge PH
Police Dog Training
Pilgrims Caravan Park
Lakeside Coach Park
Thurrock Services
Arena Essex Raceway
Gas Works
Swimming Pool
Driving Range
SPORTS GROUND
THE SHRUBBERY
Depot
Works
FR FS FT FU FV FW FX
57 58 59
65 66 67 68 69 70 71 72 73 74
81 82 83 84
129
169

AC
AD
AE
AF
AG
AH
AJ
91
92
93
130
Junction
CONVENT
75
76
77
78
79
80
81
82
83
84
REC GRD
CEM
BRAYWICK PARK
Sch
Clubho
Cricket Grd
Cricket Ground
CAUSEWAY
THE CAUSEWAY
CHURCH PATH
CHURCH RD
GLEBE ROAD
FISHERY
ROAD
PO
HIGH ST
Bray
Home
Hall
ALLOT
Bray Bridge
THE CUT
HIBBERT
BRAYWICK RD
ASCOT A330 RD
WINDSOR
CANNON HILL ESTATE
CANNON HILL WAY
UPPER B3028 BRAY
PRIORS
IND EST
Works
Barge Farm
AMERDEN LANE
HEADPILE EYOT
TOWING PATH
Bray Lock
Weir
Amerden House
PIGEONHILL EYOT
AMERDEN CARAVAN PARK
RIVER GARDENS
OLD MILL LA
MILL LANE
M4
New Thames Bridge
OLD MARSH LANE
GLEBE CLO
SUBWAY
LUNDMOOR DITCH
MEADOW WAY
OAK STUBBS LA
Hall
Sch
HARCOURT
Dorney Reach
DORNEY REACH ROAD
Weir Bank
Weir Bank Stud Farm
MONKEY ISLAND
FB
ASHFORD LA
Glasshouse
Lake End Farm
B3026
LAKE END
Dorney
VILLAGE ROAD
COURT LANE
Dorney Court
Pigeonhouse Farm
Riding School
BRAY MARINA
GRAVEL PIT
Clubho
QUEEN'S EYOT
MONKEY ISLAND LANE
PO
A308
WINDSOR ROAD
TITHE BARN DR
BROAD PK
BUCKINGHAMSHIRE
RIVER THAMES
SOUTH BUCKS
WINDSOR & MAIDENHEAD
Bray Film Studios
Works
DOWN PLACE
Oakley Court Hotel
TOWING PATH
WINDSOR MARINA
MAIDENHEAD
The Guild House
Queen's Head PH
SL6
Stroud Farm
Wayside Stables Equestrian Centre
SPRINGFIELD
MOOR END
Works
HENDONS WAY
STOMPITS
BLIND LANE
Sch
77
76
The Retreat Farm
THE RETREAT
Bullock's Hatch Bridge
Fifield
Hare & Hounds PH
MANOR GROVE
MEADOW WAY
STEWART CLO
CONINGSBY LANE
Coningsby Farm
Grove House
GREEN LANE
FOREST GREEN ROAD
B3024
The Rising Sun PH
The White Hart PH
Ledger Farm
LEDGER LA
Fifield House
Cricket Ground
Pav
Sch
Banham Farm
Oakley Place Farm
Kimbers Farm
OAKLEY GREEN ROAD
Oakley Green
Bishops Farmhouse
BISHOPS FARM
B3383
DEDWORTH
Nags Head PH
Broom Farm
TARBAY LANE
PO
Ye Olde Red Lion PH
Windsor Garden Ce
CHARLTON WAY
Gale House Farm
Sch
Tarbay Farm
Braywood House
BRAY WOOD
Lakeside Racing Stables
FIFIELD LANE
DARKHOLE RIDE
Darkhole Bridge
Wakers Farm
Haws Far
ROAD DRIFT
New Lodge Farm
New Lodge
NOBBSCROOK
HOLLIDAY'S PLAIN
Nightingale Corner
St Leonard Farm
WINDSOR & MAIDENHEAD
BRACKNELL FOREST
Foliejon Park Farm
HOGOAK LANE
FISH POND
FOLIEJON PARK
Windsor Hill
NOBBSCROOK COPSE

151
AK
AL
AM
AN
AP
AQ
AR
94
95
96
131
152
75
76
77
78
79
80
81
82
83
84
CIPPENHAM
SL1
SL4
MERCIAN RECREATION GROUND
Sludge Beds
Filter Beds
Sludge Bed
WATER POLLUTION CONTROL WORKS
Pumping Station
M4
SLOUGH
WINDSOR & MAIDENHEAD
SOUTH BUCKS
Junction 6
ETON WICK
ETON WICK COMMON
Eton Common Farm
Saddocks Farm
Manor Farm
NORTH FIELD
Bell Farm
Tilson Bridge
NEY COMMON
ETON GREAT COMMON
Crown Farm
ETON WICK REC GRD
SOUTH FIELD
Boveney
Boveney Court Farm
Boveney Lock
RIVER THAMES
OLD TOWING PATH
ROYAL WINDSOR RACECOURSE
Parade Ring
Grandstand
Stands
Stables
WINDSOR RACECOURSE YACHT BASIN
WINDSOR RACECOURSE PARK HOMES
MILL STREAM
SUTHERLAND GRANGE
Cuckoo Weir
Long Bri
Bird Sanctuary
Elizabeth Bri
CLEWER VILLAGE
ALLOT
Works
Windsor Lad PH
MAIDENHEAD ROAD
A308
A332
A355
B3026
B3024
B3022
B3173
RELIEF ROAD
ETON RELIEF ROAD
WINDSOR & ETON RELIEF ROAD
CHALVEY
Ice Arena
Sports Cen
MONTEM PLEASURE GROUND
Courtyard Hotel
Copthorne Hotel
Switching Station
REC GRD
PLAYING FIELD
ALLOTMENTS
Schs
Superstore
SALT HILL PARK
Tennis Courts
Thames Valley Univ
WELLINGTON ST
MONTEM ROAD
AGARS PLOUGH PLAYING FIELDS
Agars Plough
Cricket Ground
Fifteen Arch Bri
THE PLAYING FIELDS
ETON GOLF COURSE
Open Air Pool
Folly Bri
Eton Coll
Eton College
Tennis Courts
RECREATION GROUND
SOUTH MEADOW
ETON
THE BROCAS
BATHS ISLAND
Eton Coll Boathouse
DEADWATER AIT
FIREWORK AIT
Windsor Bri
WINDSOR & ETON RIVERSIDE
Romney Lock
HOME PARK RECREATION GROUND
KING EDWARD VII AVE
WINDSOR CASTLE
EAST LAWN
South Slopes
Royal Mews Riding School
Cambridge Gate
GOLF COURSE
WINDSOR
LEISURE CENTRE
ALEXANDRA GDNS
COACH PARK
VANSITTART IND EST
WINDSOR & ETON CENTRAL
GUILDHALL
Theatre Royal
MUS
Hotel
Victoria Barracks
DEDWORTH
DEDWORTH MANOR
Dedworth Manor
OPEN SPACE
Comm Cen
CLEWER MEMORIAL REC GRD
Clubhouse
RUNNING TRACK
Youth & Comm Cen
MAG CT
Fire Sta
Pol Sta
HOSP
GOSLAR WAY
Clewer Green
Clewer New Town
CONV
PRINCESS MARGARET HOSPITAL
Combermere Barracks
KING EDWARD VII HOSP
HOUSEHOLD CAVALRY MUS
TA Centre
WINDSOR CEMETERY
Football Grd
QUEEN MARY'S PLANTATION
CAVALRY EXERCISE GROUNDS
Queen Anne's Gate
RIFLE RANGE
HOG COMMON
GARRISON SPORTS GROUND
Queens Cottages
Shaw Farm
Clayhall Farm
FROGMORE GDNS
Royal Mausoleum
Long Walk Gate
ASH PLANTATION
WITHY COVER
DININGROOM CLOSE
SPITAL MEADOW
PADDOCKHILL COPSE
NEW COVER
LEGO LAND
Palatine Gate
WINKFIELD ROAD
KINGS ROAD
ALBERT ROAD
CONSORT'S DRIVE
Superstore
Coll

152
SLOUGH
SALT HILL PARK
AS
AT
AU
AV
AW
AX
AY
98
99
00
132
75
76
77
78
79
80
81
82
83
84
151
172
Thames Valley Univ
BRUNEL BUS STA
WELLINGTON ST
WELLINGTON
Superstore
Shopping Cen
Shopping Centre
Royal Mail
Ice Arena
Town Hall
Sports Cen
MONTEM
CHALVEY
ALVEY
UPTON HOSPITAL
ALBERT ST
A412
MERE RD
YEW TREE ROAD
UPTON
LASCELLES PLAYING FIELDS
Upton Park
HERSCHEL PARK
UXBRIDGE RD
SUSSEX PLACE
LONDON ROAD
A4
A332
WINDSOR ROAD
PLAYING FIELD
SL1
SL4
UPTON COURT
PARK LANE
UPTON PARK
AGARS PLOUGH PLAYING FIELDS
Cricket Ground
RUNNING TRACK
ETON GOLF COURSE
Open Air Pool
Fifteen Arch Bri
PLAYING FIELDS
POCOCKS LANE
B3026
ETON
Pumping Station
Eton College
THE HOME PARK RECREATION GROUND
DATCHET GOLF COURSE
Victoria Bridge
KING EDWARD VII AVENUE
B470
RUGBY GROUNDS
Clubhouse
SLOUGH WINDSOR & MAIDENHEAD
DITTON PARK
KEDERMISTER PARK
M4
DEFENCE RESEARCH AGENCY
KING'S OAK
Offices
Riding Court Farm
FISH POND
DITTON PARK
ROMNEY
Romney Lock
WINDSOR & ETON RIVERSIDE
WINDSOR CASTLE
EAST LAWN
South Slopes
Royal Mews Riding School
Cambridge Gate
GOLF COURSE
WINDSOR
Victoria Barracks
THE HOME PARK
Adelaide Lodge
Long Walk Gate
FROGMORE GDNS
Frogmore House
Royal Mausoleum
Prince Consort's Home Farm
Windsor Hall
Glasshouses
ROYAL GARDENS
Shaw Farm
Clayhall Farm
ALBERT ROAD
A308
KING EDWARD VII HOSP
PRINCESS MARGARET HOSPITAL
GARRISON SPORTS GROUND
Queens Cottages
DATCHET
The Green
DATCHET RECREATION GROUND
DATCHET CEMETERY
MAJORS ROAD
RIVER THAMES
SOUTHLEA ROAD
B3021
Southlea
Southlea Farm
MILL PLACE CARAVAN SITE
The Rising Sun PH
Albert Bridge
NICKCROFT AIT
Sludge Lagoon
Sludge Lagoons
Filter Bed
Sludge Bed
Sewage Works
HAM ISLAND
Ham Bridge
HAM LANE
Manor Farm
The Lord Nelson PH
Old Windsor Lock
St George's Farm
SUNNYMEAD
Boathouse
Sunny

AZ
BA
BB
BC
BD
BE
BF
01
02
03
133
IVER GOLF COURSE
Clubhouse
Glasshouse
SOUTH BUCKS
BUCKINGHAMSHIRE
SLOUGH
GRAND UNION
(SLOUGH ARM)
TOWING PATH
CARAVAN
Works
Depot
CANAL
IND EST
LANGLEY
IVER
Chequer Bridge
Withy Bridge
Thorney Farm
75
76
77
78
79
80
81
82
83
84
RICHINGS PARK
SPORTS GRD
Tennis Cts
Bowl Grn
Lib
Tower Arms PH
THORNEY MILL RD
SL0
LANGLEY BUSINESS CENTRE
SPORTS GRD
Coll
Hall
PO
LANGLEY MEMORIAL GROUND
Comm Cen
Sch
Tenn Cts
Warehouse
Swimming Pool
HARVEY PARK
Youth & Comm Cen
Health Centre
Pol Sta
ALLOT
RICHINGS PARK GOLF COURSE
Clubho
HOME WOOD
Old Slade Farm
Sutton Court Farm
Garden Centre
OAK PLANTATION
M4
OLD WOOD
Sewage Works
Filter Beds
Heathrow Marriott Hotel
LONDON ROAD
Junction 5
BRANDS HILL
Heathrow Ambassador Hotel
COLNBROOK BYPASS
A4
COLNBROOK
REC GRD
Brook Farm
Tanhouse Farm
Greyhound PH
Warehouses
154
Depot
M25
Moor Roundabout
THE QUEEN MOTHER RESERVOIR
Clubhouse
SL3
Colnbrook Bridge
GRAVEL PIT
POYLE
Warehouses
DRIVING RANGE
Pav
Longford Roundabout
Mad Bridge
Moor Bridge
HILLINGDON
POYLE CHANNEL
Poyle Lodge
Manor Farm
POYLE IND EST
MCKAY TRD EST
TRIDENT IND EST
Poyle Farm
The Golden Cross PH
WRAYSBURY RIVER
BEDFORD COURT ESTATE
Pickins Piece
Works
Ashgood Farm
Berkyn Manor Farm
COLNE BROOK
ARTHUR JACOB NATURE RESERVE
Weir
The Crown PH
The Five Bells PH
Horton
Clubhouse
STANWELL ROAD
HORTON ROAD
Lintells Bridge
Junction 14
AIRPORT
A3113
SURREY
WINDSOR & MAIDENHEAD
COPPERMILL ROAD
Inlet Pier
WRAYSBURY
TW19
173
REC GRD
Hall
STANWELL MOOR
PO

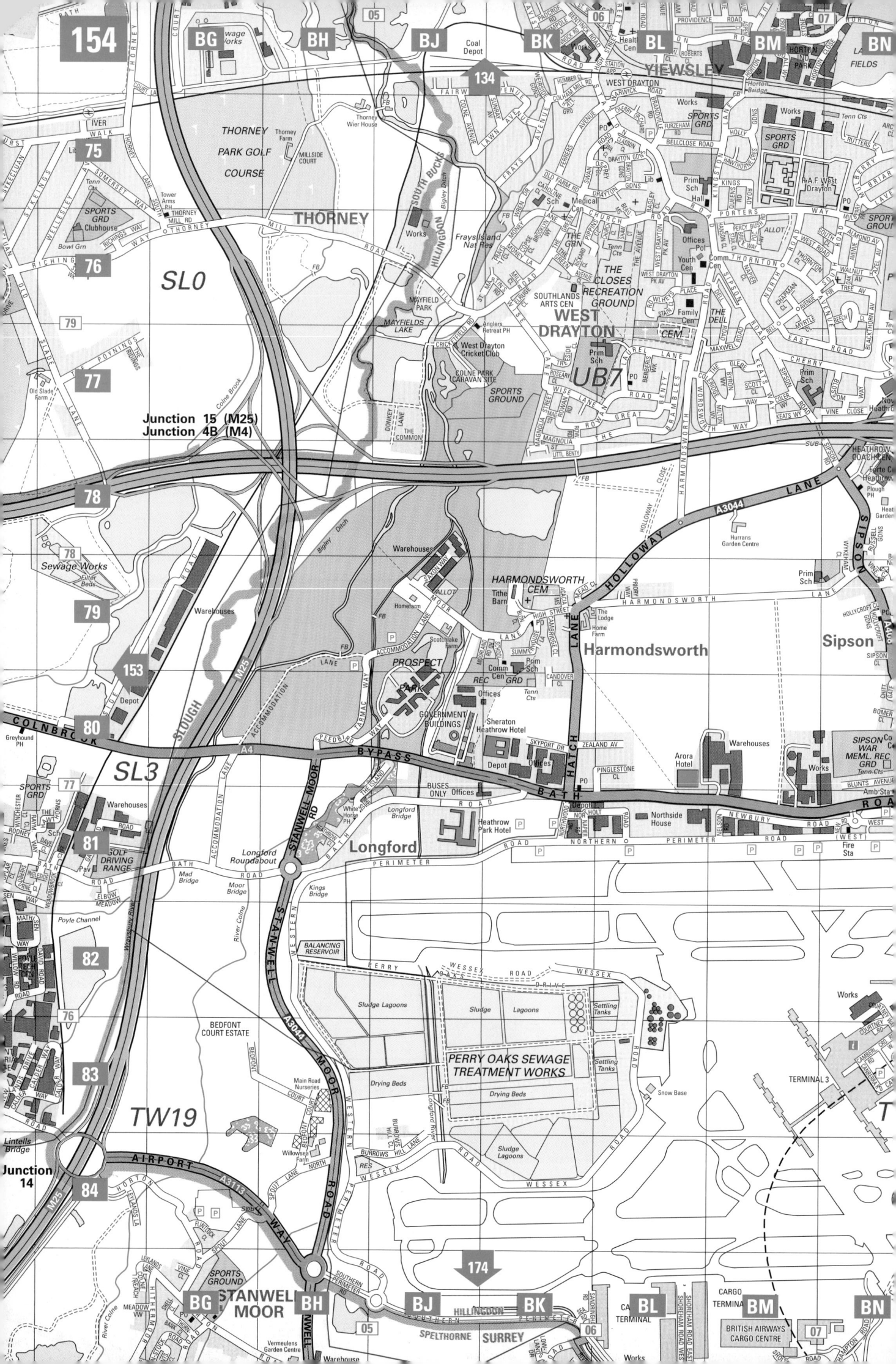

BP
BQ
BR
BS
BT
BU
BV
08
09
10
135
E.M.I. SPORTS GROUND
HAYES TOWN
Grand Union Canal
Stockley Bridge
Starveall Bridge
STOCKLEY PARK
ADLER IND EST
ABERGLEN INDUSTRIAL ESTATE
WARNFORD IND EST
PROVIDENT INDUSTRIAL ESTATE
PETER JAMES BUSINESS CENTRE
HAYES & HARLINGTON
Speedmarque Centre
THE SQUIRRELS TRADING ESTATE
INTERNATIONAL TRADING EST
GOVERNMENT BUILDINGS
BOURNE FARM FIELD
ALLOTMENTS
PINKWELL PARK
UB3
NORTH HYDE ROAD
STATION ROAD
CHERRY LANE CEMETERY
SAM PHILP REC GRD
M4
Junction 4
Junction 3
IMPERIAL COLLEGE SPORTS GROUND
LITTLE HARLINGTON FIELD
SIPSON MEADOW
SPORTS GROUND
HARLINGTON
HIGH STREET
CRANE MEADOW
CRANFORD
PARK
AVENUE PARK
CRANFORD
THE PARKWAY
HAYES BY PASS
HOUNSLOW
HILLINGDON
Superstore
Western International Market
HARLEQUIN CENTRE
David Lloyd Club
AIRLINK
AIR LINKS INDUSTRIAL ESTATE
SPITFIRE ESTATE
BRITISH AIRWAYS SPORTS GROUND
PARKWAY TRADING ESTATE
REDWOOD ESTATE
TW5
Junction 4A
Edwardian Int Hotel
Marriott Hotel
Sheraton Skyline Hotel
Heathrow Airport Visitors Cen
Renaissance Hotel
Cardinal Pt
BATH ROAD
NORTHERN PERIMETER ROAD
CUSTOM HOUSE
HEATHROW AIRPORT (LONDON)
Maintenance Area
Hangar
Perishable Handling Facility
Speedbird House
Boadicea House
Comet House
TERMINAL 1
HEATHROW TERMINALS 1, 2 & 3
TERMINAL 2
TW4
HATTON
HATTON CROSS
GREAT SOUTH WEST ROAD
A30
BALANCING RESERVOIR
RADIUS PARK
HASLEMERE HEATHROW ESTATE
HEATHROW INT TRADING ESTATE
RIFLE RANGE
GREEN LANE OPEN SPACE
HOUNSLOW HEATH GOLF COURSE
DONKEY WOOD
THE CAUSEWAY
MERCURY CENTRE
TW14
175
BEDFONT RECREATION GROUND
HEATHROW TERMINAL 4
Heathrow Hilton Hotel
156
75
76
77
78
79
80
81
82
83
84

SOUTHALL
UB1
136
BW
BX
BY
BZ
CA
CB
CC
12
13
14
HEATHROW INTERCHANGE
BROOK INDUSTRIAL ESTATE
BEACONSFIELD ROAD
SECURE PARKING
Gas Works
GRAND UNION CANAL (PADDINGTON BRANCH)
HILLINGDON
EALING
BARRATT INDUSTRIAL PARK
SOUTHALL RAILWAY CENTRE
MIDDLESEX BUSINESS CENTRE
FEATHERSTONE IND EST
Balfour Business Centre
THE PARKWAY
HAYES
75
76
77
78
79
80
81
82
83
84
Junction 3
Western International Market
HARLEQUIN CENTRE
SOUTHALL REC GRD
NORWOOD GREEN
UB2
TENTELOW LANE SPORTS GROUND
Grand Union Canal
NORTH HYDE
AIRLINKS
GOLF
COURSE
Heston Services
BRITISH AIRWAYS SPORTS GROUND
SPITFIRE ESTATE
AIR LINKS INDUSTRIAL ESTATE
Concorde Centre
PARKWAY TRADING ESTATE
Thorncliffe Hotel
HESTON PARK
HESTON
HESTON INDUSTRIAL MALL
155
TW5
SUTTON PLAYING FIELD
SPORTS GROUND
Osterley Park Farm
GREAT WEST ROAD
BATH ROAD
LAMPTON
LAMPTON PARK
HOUNSLOW CIVIC CENTRE
HOUNSLOW WEST
BEAVERSFORD PARK
HOUNSLOW WEST
Cavalry Barracks
TW4
HOUNSLOW
HOUNSLOW HEATH
GREEN LANE OPEN SPACE
RIFLE RANGE
DONKEY WOOD
HEATHROW INT. TRADING ESTATE
Cranebank
HASLEMERE HEATHROW
BALANCING RESERVOIR
MERCURY CENTRE
CENTRAL PARK EST
Garden Centre
Treaty Centre
Hounslow Centre
DERBY ESTATE
INWOOD
TW3
176
Metropolitan Police
STAINES ROAD
WELLINGTON ROAD N
A3006
A3005
A3063
A315
A312
A4127
A4

157
CD
CE
CF
CG
CH
CJ
CK
HANWELL
HANWELL CEMETERY
EALING HOSPITAL N.H.S. TRUST
THE BROADWAY
BROADWAY
W7
BRENT RIVER PARK
ELTHORNE PARK
ELTHORNE PARK EXTENSION
WATERSIDE TRADING CENTRE
RIVER BRENT BUS. PARK
W13
LAMMAS PARK
WALPOLE PARK
SOUTH EALING
NORTHFIELDS
LITTLE EALING
W5
SOUTH EALING CEMETERY
LONDON PLAYING FIELDS
BOSTON MANOR
BOSTON MANOR PARK
BOSTON MANOR ROAD
Junction 2
OSTERLEY PARK
WYKE GREEN GOLF COURSE
MACFARLANE SPORT FIELD
WEST CROSS CENTRE
GREAT WEST ROAD
TW7
TW8
BRENTFORD
BRENTFORD F.C.
LONDON RD
Brunel University (Osterley Campus)
SPRING GROVE
ISLEWORTH
WOODLANDS
WEST MIDDLESEX UNIVERSITY HOSP
MOGDEN WATER TREATMENT WORKS
SYON PARK
SYON HOUSE
Battles of Brentford 1016 & 1642
Duke of Northumberland Estate
RIVER THAMES
ROYAL BOTANIC GARDENS
KEW
KEW PALACE
QUEEN'S COTTAGE GARDENS
ROYAL MID-SURREY GOLF COURSE (OLD DEER PARK)
TW9
OBSERVATORY GARDENS
OLD DEER PARK RECREATION GROUND
RICHMOND ATHLETIC GROUND
RICHMOND GREEN
TW1
ST. MARGARETS
TWICKENHAM ROAD
ISLEWORTH AIT
137
158
177
75
76
77
78
79
80
81
82
83
84
15
16
17

158
CL
CM
CN
CP
CQ
CR
CS
W5
W3
W4
TW8
TW9
SW14
138
157
178
19
20
21
75
76
77
78
79
80
81
82
83
84
EALING COMMON
ACTON PARK
SOUTH ACTON
ACTON TOWN
BEDFORD PARK
SOUTH EALING
LITTLE EALING
SOUTH EALING CEMETERY
POPEFIELD PLAYING FIELDS
SPORTS GROUND
SOUTHFIELDS PLAYING FIELDS
GUNNERSBURY PARK
GUNNERSBURY PARK MUSEUM
BOATING LAKE
Miniature Golf
POTOMAC (FISH POND)
KENSINGTON CEMETERY
International Sch of London
GUNNERSBURY
GUNNERSBURY TRIANGLE NATURE RESERVE
CHISWICK PARK
ACTON GRN COMMON
CHISWICK COMMON
CLAYPONDS HOSP
CARVILLE HALL PARK NORTH
CARVILLE HALL PARK
Junction 2
Junction 1
PHOENIX PARK
Smithkline Beecham
Agfa Gevaert
Data General Twr
Leisure Cen
KEW BRIDGE STEAM MUS
THE MUSICAL MUS
BRENTFORD
BRENTFORD FC
BRENTFORD AIT
WATERMANS ARTS CEN
OLIVER'S ISLAND
KEW
KEW GREEN
KEW PALACE
ROYAL BOTANIC GARDENS
The Princess of Wales Conservatory
THE POND
Temple of Arethosa
Palm House
ARBORETUM
THE LAKE
WATER LILY POND
QUEEN'S COTTAGE GARDENS
MARIANNE NORTH GALLERY
Restaurant Pavilion
Pagoda
PUBLIC RECORD OFFICE
Sewage Works
RIVER THAMES
THAMES
GROVE PARK
CHISWICK
CHISWICK HOUSE GROUNDS
CHISWICK HOUSE
CHISWICK CEMETERY
CIVIL SERVICE SPORTS GROUND
DUKE'S MEADOW
DUKE'S MEADOW GOLF COURSE
Chiswick R.F.C.
UNI WEST. SPORTS GRD
STADIUM
CIVIC AMENITY SITE
Crematorium
HAMMERSMITH CEMETERY
NORTH SHEEN CEMETERY
NORTH SHEEN
MORTLAKE
Courage Brewery
RICHMOND UPON THAMES
HOUNSLOW
BARNES HOSP
EAST SHEEN
PESTHOUSE COMMON
EAST SHEEN COMMON (N T)
PALEWELL COMMON
ROYAL MID-SURREY GOLF COURSE (OLD DEER PARK)
RICHMOND ATHLETIC GROUND
ROYAL HOSP
London Welsh R.F.C.
RICHMOND
RICHMOND GREEN
Richmond Palace Remains
SYON HOUSE
Battles of Brentford 1016 & 1642
NORTH CIRCULAR ROAD
GUNNERSBURY AVENUE
CHISWICK HIGH ROAD
GREAT WEST RD
KEW BRIDGE ROAD
KEW ROAD
MORTLAKE ROAD
SOUTH CIRCULAR ROAD
LOWER RICHMOND RD
UPPER RICHMOND ROAD
UPPER RICHMOND ROAD WEST
LOWER MORTLAKE ROAD
SHEEN ROAD
MORTLAKE HIGH ST
CLIFFORD AVENUE
GREAT CHISWICK BR
CHERTSEY ROAD
BURLINGTON LANE
ELLESMERE ROAD
CEDARS RD
HIGH STREET
A4020
A4000
A406
A315
A3000
A4
A205
A316
A307
A305
A3003
B491
B409
B4491

CT
CU
CV
CW
CX
CY
CZ
22
23
24
139
SHEPHERD'S BUSH
W12
W8
W6
W14
SW5
SW13
SW6
SW15
SW18
KENSINGTON
HOLLAND PARK
HOLLAND HOUSE
KENSINGTON (OLYMPIA)
OLYMPIA
EARLS COURT
WEST KENSINGTON
WEST BROMPTON
HAMMERSMITH
HAMMERSMITH FLYOVER
HAMMERSMITH CEMETERY
CHARING CROSS HOSP
RIVERSIDE STUDIOS
RAVENSCOURT PARK
STAMFORD BROOK
CHISWICK EYOT
CHISWICK LODGE HOSP
CASTELNAU
BARN ELMS WILDFOWL RESERVE
BARN ELMS PLAYING FIELDS
BARN ELMS SCHOOL SPORTS CENTRE
HARROD'S SPORTS GRD
LEG OF MUTTON NATURE RESERVE
BARNES
BARNES COMMON
PUTNEY COMMON
PUTNEY HOSP
PUTNEY BRIDGE
PUTNEY
FULHAM
FULHAM CEMETERY
FULHAM PALACE
FULHAM PALACE GARDENS
BISHOP'S PARK
PARSONS GREEN
EEL BROOK COMMON
HURLINGHAM PARK
HURLINGHAM CLUB
THE QUEENS TENNIS CLUB
WANDSWORTH PARK
WANDSWORTH
RIVER THAMES
HAMMERSMITH & FULHAM
RICHMOND UPON THAMES
ROEHAMPTON
ROEHAMPTON HOSPITAL
75
76
77
78
79
80
81
82
83
84
160
179

160
DA
DB
DC
DD
DE
DF
DG
26
27
28
140
159
180
KENSINGTON GARDENS
HYDE PARK
ROUND POND
THE SERPENTINE
KENSINGTON
HOLLAND PARK
W8
SW7
SW5
SW10
SW3
SW6
SW11
SW15
SW18
SOUTH KENSINGTON
EARLS COURT
WEST BROMPTON
BROMPTON
CHELSEA
BELGRAVIA
WALHAM GREEN
PARSONS GREEN
SANDS END
BATTERSEA PARK
WANDSWORTH
CLAPHAM JUNCTION
KENSINGTON ROAD
KENSINGTON GORE
KNIGHTSBRIDGE
CROMWELL ROAD
BROMPTON ROAD
FULHAM ROAD
KINGS ROAD
CHEYNE WALK
CHELSEA EMBANKMENT
WANDSWORTH BRIDGE ROAD
LAVENDER HILL
ST. JOHN'S HILL
HAMMERSMITH & FULHAM
WANDSWORTH
75
76
77
78
79
80
81
82
83
84

DH
DJ
DK
DL
DM
DN
DP
29
30
31
141
ST. JAMES'S
GREEN PARK
ST. JAMES'S PARK
BUCKINGHAM PALACE
WESTMINSTER
VICTORIA
HOUSES OF PARLIAMENT
WATERLOO
SOUTHWARK
SE1
THE BOROUGH
75
76
NEWINGTON
LAMBETH
SW1
SE11
PIMLICO
77
78
VAUXHALL
RIVER THAMES
KENNINGTON
79
NINE ELMS
SW8
162
80
SOUTH LAMBETH
CAMBERWELL
SE5
81
SW9
82
STOCKWELL
83
CLAPHAM
BRIXTON
84
SE24
SW4
181
RUSKIN PARK
KENNINGTON PARK
MYATT'S FIELDS
KING'S COLLEGE HOSPITAL
WESTMINSTER BR
LAMBETH BR
VAUXHALL BR
GROSVENOR ROAD
WANDSWORTH ROAD
CLAPHAM ROAD
BRIXTON ROAD
COLDHARBOUR LANE
CAMBERWELL NEW ROAD
KENNINGTON PARK ROAD
ACRE LANE
CLAPHAM HIGH STREET
STOCKWELL ROAD
SOUTH LAMBETH ROAD
VAUXHALL BRIDGE ROAD
MILLBANK
ALBERT EMBANKMENT
NINE ELMS LANE
BATTERSEA PARK ROAD
DENMARK HILL

162
DQ
DR
DS
DT
DU
DV
DW
33
34
35
142
161
182
75
76
77
78
79
80
81
82
83
84
SE1
SOUTHWARK
THE BOROUGH
NEWINGTON
SE17
WALWORTH
BERMONDSEY
WAPPING
THE POOL
SE11
CAMBERWELL
PECKHAM
SE5
SE15
SE22
SE24
SW9
KENNINGTON PARK
BURGESS PARK
RUSKIN PARK
PECKHAM RYE COMMON
PECKHAM RYE PARK
GUY'S HOSPITAL
KING'S COLLEGE HOSPITAL
THE MAUDSLEY HOSPITAL
KING'S COLLEGE HOSP DULWICH
ST. MARY'S CATHEDRAL
TOWER BRIDGE EXPERIENCE
LOUGHBOROUGH JUNCTION
EAST DULWICH
PECKHAM RYE
NEW KENT ROAD
OLD KENT ROAD
WALWORTH ROAD
CAMBERWELL ROAD
DENMARK HILL
JAMAICA ROAD
SOUTHWARK PARK ROAD
ROTHERHITHE NEW ROAD
PECKHAM HIGH ST
QUEENS ROAD
CAMBERWELL CH ST
COLDHARBOUR LANE
DOG KENNEL HILL

163
DX
DY
DZ
EA
EB
EC
ED
36
37
38
143
164
183
75
76
77
78
79
80
81
82
83
84
THE DOME
NORTH GREENWICH
SE10
SE16
SE14
SE8
SE4
SE13
E14
ISLE
OF
DOGS
WEST INDIA DOCKS
CANARY WHARF
MILLWALL OUTER DOCK
MILLWALL INNER DOCK
MUDCHUTE PARK
MILLWALL PARK
ISLAND GARDENS
CUBITT TOWN
GREENLAND DOCK
SOUTH DOCK
SURREY DOCKS WATER SPORTS CEN
RUSSIA DOCK WOODLAND
DEPTFORD PARK
DEPTFORD
PEPYS PARK
GREENWICH
GREENWICH PARK
NATIONAL MARITIME MUSEUM
QUEEN'S HOUSE
FLAMSTEED HOUSE (Old Royal Observatory)
CUTTY SARK
GIPSY MOTH IV
GREENWICH REACH
LIMEHOUSE REACH
THE WILDERNESS (DEER PARK)
BLACKHEATH
NEW CROSS
NEW CROSS GATE
ST JOHN'S
LEWISHAM
HILLY FIELDS
BROCKLEY
BROCKLEY CEMETERY
LADYWELL CEMETERY
LADYWELL
TELEGRAPH HILL PARK
FORDHAM PARK
FOLKESTONE GDNS
Goldsmiths College (Univ of Lon)
Uni of Greenwich
Lewisham Centre
MANOR HOUSE GARDENS
MANOR PARK
EVELYN STREET
CREEK ROAD
ROMNEY RD
TRAFALGAR ROAD
SHOOTER'S HILL ROAD
BLACKHEATH ROAD
BLACKHEATH HILL
LOAMPIT VALE
LOAMPIT HILL
LEWISHAM WAY
LEWISHAM HIGH ST
LEE BRIDGE
WESTFERRY ROAD
MANCHESTER ROAD
PRESTONS ROAD
BLACKWALL TUNNEL APPROACH
TOWER HAMLETS
SOUTHWARK
GREENWICH

THE DOME
NORTH GREENWICH
SE10
E16
RIVER THAMES
WOOLWICH REACH
THAMES FLOOD BARRIER
SILVERTOWN
THAMES BARRIER PARK
LYLE PARK
NORTH WOOLWICH ROAD
RUSSIAN SUBMARINE
NEW CHARLTON
MARYON PARK
MARYON WILSON PARK
CHARLTON
SE7
CHARLTON PARK
HORNFAIR PARK
GREENWICH DISTRICT HOSP
EAST GREENWICH PLEASAUNCE
NATIONAL MARITIME MUSEUM
GREENWICH PARK
BLACKHEATH
SE3
KIDBROOKE
BLACKHEATH PARK
SE13
LEE
SE12
SUTCLIFFE PARK
SHOOTER'S HILL ROAD
ROCHESTER WAY RELIEF RD
EE
EF
EG
EH
EJ
EK
EL
75
76
77
78
79
80
81
82
83
84
144
163
184

165
AIRPORT
KING GEORGE V DOCK
THAMESMEAD
EM
EN
EP
EQ
ER
ES
ET
43
44
45
145
Newham Coll of Further Ed
Warehouses
ROYAL VICTORIA GDNS
NORTH WOOLWICH
STANDARD INDUSTRIAL ESTATE
North Woolwich Pier
Woolwich Ferry Pier
GALLIONS REACH
NEWHAM
GREENWICH
SE28
WOOLWICH CROWN CT
H.M. PRISON BELMARSH
EASTERN WAY
WESTERN WAY
BROADWATER
BROADWATER GRN
WOOLWICH FREE FERRY
WOOLWICH FOOT TUNNEL
SE. London Aquatic Cen
THAMESMEAD WEST
Works
75
76
77
78
79
80
81
82
83
84
BIRCHMERE
ABBEY WOOD PARK
SE2
PLUMSTEAD GARDENS
PLUMSTEAD ROAD
PLUMSTEAD HIGH STREET
PLUMSTEAD
WOOLWICH ARSENAL
Woolwich Coll of FE
ROLTHORNE EST
Royal Artillery Barracks
ARTILLERY PLACE
WOOLWICH
BARRACK FIELD
WOOLWICH COMMON
GRAND DEPOT ROAD
JOHN WILSON ST
PLUMSTEAD COMMON
SE18
WINN'S COMMON
BOSTALL WOODS
BOSTALL HEATH
WOOLWICH CEM
WOOLWICH CEMETERY
ROCK. GDNS
166
Royal Military Academy
SHREWSBURY PARK
SHOOTER'S HILL GOLF COURSE
SHOOTER'S HILL
CLOTHWORKERS WOOD
EAST WICKHAM
EAST WICKHAM OPEN SPACE
HILLVIEW CEMETERY
SHOOTER'S HILL
BELLEGROVE ROAD
A207
CASTLEWOOD THERAPY CENTRE
ELTHAM COMMON
MEMORIAL HOSPITAL
Severndroog Castle
Jackwood House
CASTLE WOOD
JACK WOOD
OXLEAS WOOD
OXLEAS MEADOW
ELTHAM COMMON
GREENWICH
BEXLEY
DA16
WELLING
WELLING WAY
FALCONWOOD
FALCONWOOD FIELD
SHEPHERDLEAS WOOD
ELTHAM PARK NORTH
ELTHAM PARK SOUTH
SE9
ROCHESTER WAY RELIEF ROAD
ELTHAM CEMETERY
Crematorium
ELTHAM WARREN GOLF COURSE
185
DA15
EAST ROCHESTER WAY
SPORTS GROUND
Environment Curriculum Service
A2
A205
A206
A209
A2016

166
THAMESMEAD
EU
EV
EW
EX
EY
EZ
FA
47
48
49
SOUTHMERE PARK
ERITH MARSHES
LAKESIDE CENTRE
SOUTHMERE
146
BIRCHMERE PARK
SE28
DA18
WOODLAND WAY
EASTERN WAY
75
H.M. PRISON BELMARSH
ABBEY WOOD PARK
THISTLEBROOK INDUSTRIAL EST
76
ABBEY WOOD
HARROW MANORWAY
79
REC GRD
PLUMSTEAD GARDENS
77
LESSNESS ABBEY WOOD
Lessness Abbey (Ruins)
78
HIGH STREET
SE2
BOSTALL HEATH
BOSTALL HILL
A206
A2041
KNEE HILL
WOOLWICH ROAD
HURST ESTATE
WEST HEATH
BELVEDERE SPORTS GRD
WINN'S COMMON
BOSTALL HEATH
CLAM FIELD RECREATION GROUND
BOSTALL WOODS
GOLDIE LEIGH HOSPITAL
SE18
165
WOOLWICH CEM
WOOLWICH CEMETERY
PLUMSTEAD CEMETERY
80
EAST WICKHAM
EAST WICKHAM OPEN SPACE
DA16
81
STEVENS PARK
82
BEXLEYHEATH
WELLING
83
A207
WELLING HIGH STREET
PARK VIEW ROAD
CROOK LOG
BROADWAY
BEXLEYHEATH CEMETERY
PLAYING FIELD
84
DANSON
PARK
186
A221
DANSON ROAD
DA6
BEXLEYHEATH
ROCHESTER WAY
BLACKFEN

FB
FC
FD
FE
FF
FG
FH
147
168
187
75
76
77
78
79
80
81
82
83
84
50
51
52
RAINHAM MARSHES
Silt Lagoons
WENNINGTON MARSHES
RM13
RIVER THAMES
ERITH REACH
ERITH RANDS
FREIGHTMASTER ESTATE
Coldharbour Point
HELIPAD
Warehouse
HAVERING
BEXLEY
THURROCK
BELVEDERE INDUSTRIAL ESTATE
Erith Oil Works
DA17
BELVEDERE
LESSNESS HEATH
ERITH
EUROPA TRADING ESTATE
ERITH & DISTRICT HOSP
ERITH STADIUM
ERITH REC GRD
NORTHUMBERLAND HEATH
DA8
MANFORD IND EST
ANCHOR BAY IND EST
THE CHURCH TRADING EST
DARENT INDUSTRIAL PARK
The Saltings
Sailing Club
SLADE GREEN
HOWBURY LANE REC GRDS
CRAYFORD MARSHES
RAIL DEPOT
BURSTED WOOD
BARNEHURST
BARNEHURST GOLF COURSE
MARTENS GROVE PARK
SHENSTONE PARK
BAKERS FIELD
DA1
BARNES CRAY
Depot & Civic Amenity Site
ACORN INDUSTRIAL PARK
CRAYFORD
THAMESMEAD SPINE RD
BRONZE AGE WAY
A2016
FRASER ROAD
A206
BEXLEY ROAD
NORTHEND ROAD
THAMES ROAD
PERRY STREET
A2000
WATLING STREET
LONDON ROAD
A207
A220
A223
UNIVERSITY WAY
BURNHAM ROAD

RAINHAM MARSHES
Silt Lagoons
FJ
FK
FL
FM
FN
FP
FQ
54
55
56
148
Works
PURFLEET IND PARK
Nursery
LONDON ROAD
A1306
Bowling Green
Clubhouse
SPORTS GROUND
PURFLEET
THAMES
A13
WENNINGTON MARSHES
AVELEY MARSHES
RIFLE RANGES
RM13
RM
COV RES
Fanns Farm
Depot
Mar Dyke
75
76
77
78
79
80
81
82
83
84
HELIPAD
Jetty
HAVERING
THURROCK
BEXLEY
TANK HILL ROAD
A1090
ARTERIAL
Prim Sch
PO
Oil Depot
Oil Storage Tanks
PURFLEET
CHALK PIT
Beacon Hill
RM19
Harrisons Wharf
Mill
Crayford Ness
DA8
Works
DARENT INDUSTRIAL PARK
FLOOD BARRIER
The Saltings
Sailing Club
Pier
MANFORD IND EST
167
DARTFORD SALT MARSHES
DARTFORD
THURROCK
KENT
Chimney
Longreach Sewage Treatment Works
DA1
CRAYFORD MARSHES
SPORTS
SPORTS GRD
Pav
Clubhouse
MOAT
Howbury Farm
RAIL DEPOT
JOYCE GREEN HOSPITAL
Littlebrook Power Station
Joyce Green Farm
River Darent
Chemical Works
Tenn Cts
UNIVERSITY WAY
A206
DARTFORD NORTHERN BYPASS
Depot & Civic Amenity Site
West Kent Main Sewer
CEM
DARTFORD FRESH MARSHES
MILLSIDE INDUSTRIAL ESTATE
BURNHAM ROAD
A2026
GLAXOWELLCOME
BARNES CRAY
CRAYFORD MARSHES
Prim Sch
Stanham Farm
Stanham River
Holiday Inn Express
Stakis County Court Hotel
TOLL
CROSSWAYS BUS PARK
B2228
VICTORIA INDUSTRIAL PARK
Gas Works
188
Youth Cen
Comm
Junction 1a
REC GRD
Pav
APPROACH ROAD

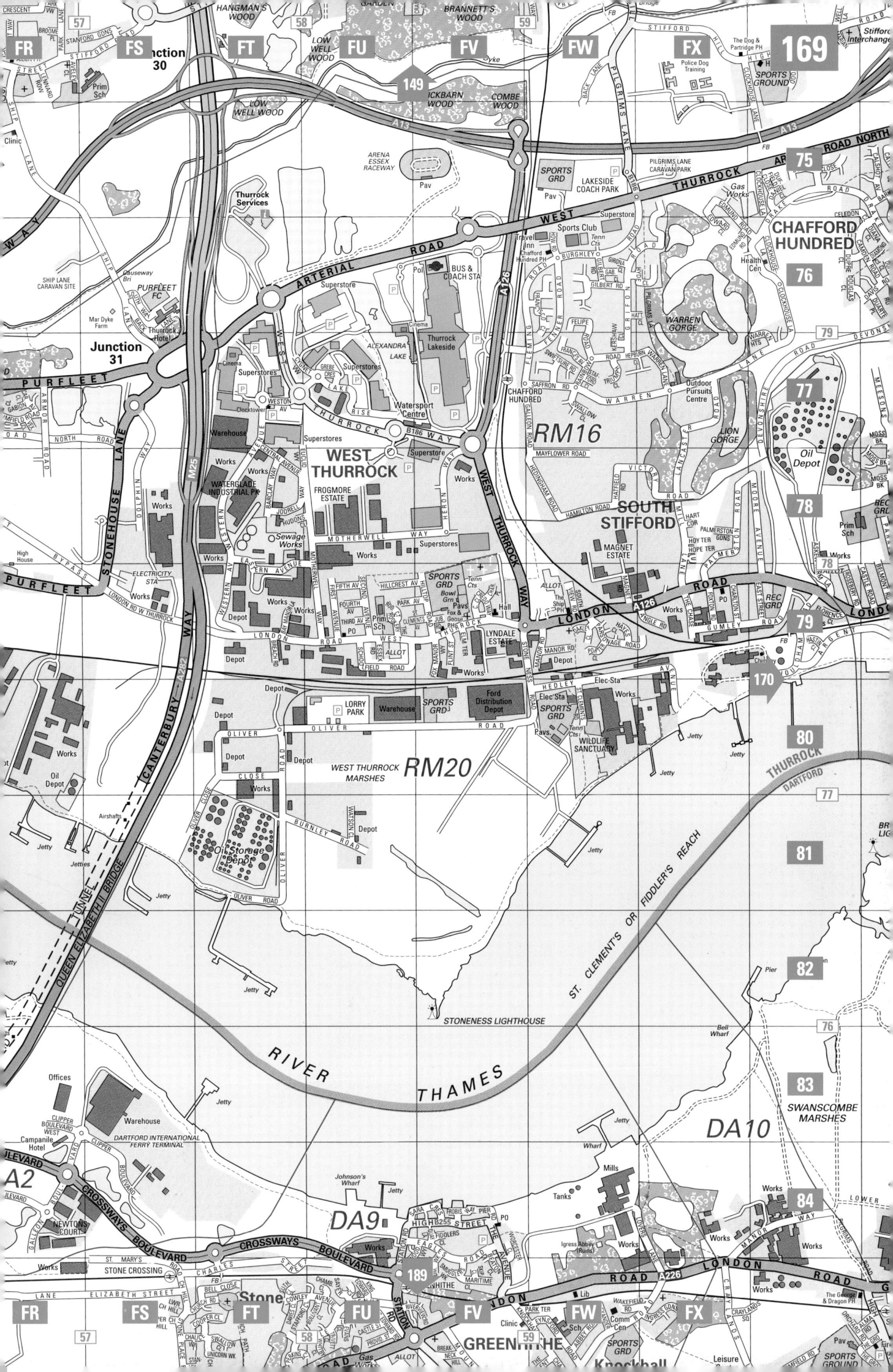

169
FR
FS
FT
FU
FV
FW
FX
57
58
59
149
170
189
Junction 30
Junction 31
HANGMAN'S WOOD
BRANNETT'S WOOD
LOW WELL WOOD
ICKBARN WOOD
COMBE WOOD
STIFFORD HILL
Stifford Interchange
The Dog & Partridge PH
Police Dog Training
SPORTS GROUND
CLOCKHOUSE LANE
PILGRIMS LANE
BACK LANE
A13
ARENA ESSEX RACEWAY
Pav
SPORTS GRD
LAKESIDE COACH PARK
PILGRIMS LANE CARAVAN PARK
ARTERIAL ROAD NORTH
ARTERIAL ROAD WEST
THURROCK
Thurrock Services
Superstore
Sports Club
Travel Inn
Chafford Hundred PH
BURGHLEY ROAD
GILBERT RD
Gas Works
CHAFFORD HUNDRED
Health Cen
WARREN GORGE
SHIP LANE CARAVAN SITE
Causeway Bri
PURFLEET FC
Mar Dyke Farm
Thurrock Hotel
PURFLEET BYPASS
BUS & COACH STA
Pol
Cinema
Thurrock Lakeside
ALEXANDRA LAKE
Superstores
Watersport Centre
THURROCK WAY
B186
A126
WEST THURROCK WAY
CHAFFORD HUNDRED
SAFFRON RD
WARREN LANE
Outdoor Pursuits Centre
LION GORGE
RM16
MAYFLOWER ROAD
VICTORY ROAD
HAMILTON ROAD
SOUTH STIFFORD
MAGNET ESTATE
Oil Depot
Prim Sch
WEST THURROCK
FROGMORE ESTATE
MOTHERWELL WAY
Sewage Works
WATERGLADE INDUSTRIAL PK
Works
Warehouse
Clocktower
STONEHOUSE LANE
ARMOR ROAD
NORTH ROAD
DOLPHIN WAY
M25
A282
CANTERBURY WAY
High House
ELECTRICITY STA
LONDON RD W THURROCK
Depot
LONDON ROAD
HILLCREST AV
LYNDALE ESTATE
STONE NESS ROAD
MANOR RD
HEDLEY AVENUE
Elec Sta
Ford Distribution Depot
LORRY PARK
Warehouse
WILDLIFE SANCTUARY
Jetty
OLIVER ROAD
OLIVER CLOSE
WEST THURROCK MARSHES
RM20
BURNLEY ROAD
Airshafts
Oil Storage Depot
Jetties
QUEEN ELIZABETH II BRIDGE
TUNNEL
THURROCK
DARTFORD
ST. CLEMENT'S OR FIDDLER'S REACH
STONENESS LIGHTHOUSE
RIVER THAMES
Pier
Bell Wharf
SWANSCOMBE MARSHES
DA10
Offices
CLIPPER BOULEVARD WEST
Campanile Hotel
Warehouse
DARTFORD INTERNATIONAL FERRY TERMINAL
A2
CROSSWAYS BOULEVARD
NEWTONS COURT
Johnson's Wharf
DA9
HIGH STREET
B255
Wharf
Mills
Tanks
Igress Abbey (Ruins)
LONDON ROAD
A226
ST. MARY'S ROAD
STONE CROSSING
CHARLES STREET
ELIZABETH STREET
Stone
STATION RD
Clinic
GREENHITHE
Knockhall
Comm Cen
Sch
SPORTS GRD
Lib
The George & Dragon PH
Leisure
MANOR WAY
Works
75
76
77
78
79
80
81
82
83
84

FY
FZ
GA
GB
GC
GD
GE
162
RM16
Stifford Interchange
Hogg Lane Roundabout
ARTERIAL ROAD NORTH STIFFORD
THURROCK
A13
A1012
CHAFFORD HUNDRED
ELIZABETH ROAD
HOGG LANE
THURROCK COMMUNITY HOSPITAL
THURROCK ATHLETICS STADIUM
KING GEORGE'S FIELD
Blackshots Leisure Centre
Sockett's Heath
STANFORD ROAD
A1013
Little Thurrock
HANGMAN'S WOOD
WARREN GORGE
LION GORGE
Oil Depot
GRAYS
RM17
SOUTHEND ROAD
PALMERS AV
GRAYS NEW CEMETERY
SOUTH STIFFORD
LONDON ROAD
A126
ORSETT ROAD
CIVIC OFFICES
EAST THURROCK RD
BROADWAY
DOCK ROAD
169
LITTLE THURROCK MARSHES
THURROCK PARK IND EST
Thurrock Yacht Club
RIVER THAMES
NORTHFLEET HOPE
BROADNESS LIGHTHOUSE
BROADNESS SALT MARSHES
Radar Mast
SWANSCOMBE MARSHES
DA10
DA11
BOTANY MARSHES
TILBURY DOCKS
NORTHFLEET INDUSTRIAL ESTATE
LONDON ROAD
A226
GALLEY HILL ROAD
STONEBRIDGE ROAD
190
EBBSFLEET INDUSTRIAL ESTATE
KENT
THURROCK
GRAVESHAM
DARTFORD
75
76
77
78
79
80
81
82
83
84
61
62
63

171
GF
GG
GH
GJ
GK
GL
GM
64
65
66
ORSETT GOLF COURSE
Orsett Heath
CHADWELL ST. MARY
Linford
SS17
Muckingford
West Tilbury
Low Street
TILBURY
TILBURY MARSHES
WEST TILBURY MARSHES
EAST TILBURY MARSHES
WALTHAM COMMON
RM18
PARSONAGE COMMON
HALLHILL COMMON
RAINBOW WOOD
ASHEN SHAW
GRAVEL PIT
OLD HOUSE WOOD
SHROVE HILL WOOD
TERRELS HEATH
Thurrock Technical College
ST. MARY'S CEM
KING GEORGE'S FIELD
SPORTS GROUND
KARTING TRACK
Tilbury Fort
MOAT
Tilbury Energy & Environmental Centre
Tilbury B Power Station
Electricity Station
Sewage Works
CUSTOM HOUSE
Warehouses
Cold Storage
Tidal Basin
DRY DOCK
RIVER THAMES
THURROCK
GRAVESHAM
GRAVESEND REACH
GRAVESEND
191
A126
A128
A1089
B149
BRENTWOOD ROAD
CHADWELL HILL
ST. CHAD'S ROAD
DOCK ROAD
FERRY ROAD
FORT ROAD
MUCKINGFORD ROAD
LINFORD ROAD
RECTORY ROAD
CHURCH ROAD
STATION ROAD
BUCKINGHAM HILL ROAD
HIGH HOUSE LANE
TURNPIKE LANE
GUN HILL
BLUE ANCHOR LANE
LOW STREET LANE
COAL ROAD
COOPERS SHAW ROAD
BIGGIN LANE
SANDY LANE
CHADWELL BYPASS
HEATH ROAD
RIVER VIEW
Hob Hill
Hutts Hill
Broom Hill
Biggin Farm
Tally Ho Riding School
Hobhill Farm
Gunhill Farm
West Tilbury Hall
The Kings Head PH
Manor Farm
Holford Farm
Blue Anchor Cottage
Mill House Farm
High House
Becksland
Ashlea Farm
Brook Farm
Whittakers Nursery
The Fox PH
Greyhound PH
Chadwell Place
Poultry Farm
Merie Loots Farm
George & Dragon PH
Sutton's Farm
Walton's Hall
Bowaters Farm
The Worlds End PH
Tilbury FC
Works
Jetty
Pier
75
76
77
78
79
80
81
82
83
84

AS
AT
AU
AV
AW
AX
AY
98
99
00
152
192
85
86
87
88
89
90
91
92
93
94
74
73
72
71
ALBERT ROAD
A308
STRAIGHT ROAD
OLD WINDSOR
SL4
SL5
TW20
HAM LANE
Manor Farm
St. George's Farm
Old Windsor Lock
REMENHA PARK
ALLOT
The Wheatsheaf PH
Hall
Lib
CHURCH ROAD
The Priory
The Manor
MOAT
Tileplace Farm
CLAYHALL LANE
MILLERS LANE
Peter's Hill
NEWMEADOW PLANTATION
PLAYING FLD
Sch
The Oxford Blue PH
Mount Place
CRIMP HILL
CEM
HOSPITAL (closed)
Woodside Farm
Bear's Rails
RUSH POND
BATTLE BOURNE
HOLLY DRIVE
LONG WALK
GALLOP
Health Cen
BURFIELD RD
B3021
Burfield Lodge
Priory Stables
FRIARY ISLAND
MANOR FARM ESTATE
RIVER THAMES
WHARF ROAD
OUSELEY ROAD
THE EMBANKMENT
The Bells of Ouseley PH
Old Ferry House
FERRY ROAD
WINDSOR ROAD
Manor Farm
ST. ANDREW'S CLO
PRINCE OF WALES POND
OLD WINDSOR WOOD
WITHY BED
LIDDELL PLANTATION
DUKE OF YORK PLANTATION
OLD COVERT
WILD BORE ENCLOSURE
Beaumont College Fm
War Meml
REC GRD
Tenn Cts
RECREATION GROUND
Pav
RUNNYMEDE
WINDSOR & MAIDENHEAD
SURREY
Runnymede House
Priest Hill House
South Lodge Farm
Home Farm
PLAYING FLD
MAGNA CARTA ISLAND
PATS CROFT EYOT
JFK Memorial
Magna Carta Monument
Priest Hill Farm
COOPER'S HILL SLOPES NT
MARCHIONESS OF HERTFORD PLANTATION
PRINCESS CHRISTIAN PLANTATION
PRINCE CONSORTS PLANTATION
SULTAN PLANTATION
Snow Hill
PRINCE OF WALES PLANTATION
QUEEN VICTORIA'S PLANTATION
Spring Hill
GORE PLANTATION
Cookes Hill
Beech Hill
Ridgemead House
Park Place
The Dell
Bishops Gate
BISHOPSGATE ROAD
Fox & Hounds PH
Main Gate Lodges
Chapel Lodge
Royal Lodge
PLAYING FLDS
Pumping Station
COVERED RESERVOIR
PRIEST HILL
ST. JUDE'S ROAD
A328
Brunel University Runnymede Campus
Cooper's Hill
COPPER'S HILL COPPICE
Air Forces Memorial
SPORTS GROUND
Brunel University Kingswood
RUNNYMEDE PARK
CONSERVATORY COVERT
OX POND
GREENBROOM COVERT
KING GEORGE VI CORONATION GROVE
COW POND
Chaplain's Lodge
Bishopsgate House
Dell Park Farm
Round Oak
Castle Hill
ANUGRAHA CONFERENCE CENTRE
Tennis Courts
Castlehill Farm
ENGLEFIELD GREEN
Englefield Green
The Vinery
CUMBERLAND LODGE
Park Close
The Sun PH
CHAPEL WOOD
Cumberland Gate
WILDERNESS
WINDSOR
GREAT
PARK
Glasshouses
Parkside House
Meadow Cottage Farm
THE SAVILL GARDENS
RHODODENDRON RIDE
Temple Hill
SMITH'S LAWN
SPORTS GRD
ST. JUDE'S CEMETERY
HOSP
Health Cen
Ripley Springs
Royal Holloway College
Athlone Hall
Cameron Hall
Theatre
Glasshouses
CORK CLUMP
Prince Consort's Statue
FUZZY CLUMP
ALDER COVER
Cumberland Obelisk
OBELISK POND
Parkwood
FRANK'S PLANTATION
SCARLETOAK PLANTATION
Egham Wick
Lubbock House
LONDON ROAD
A30
EGHAM
POLO GROUNDS
The Flying Barn
EGHAM WICK PLANTATION
Breakheart Hill
WEEDEN'S FIELD
JOHNSON'S POND
HEATHER GARDEN
DARKHOLE CLUMP
High Flyer's
OXHED
Eton Bridge
Royal Holloway
B388
BAKEHAM LANE
PRUNE HILL
ROBERTS WAY
HARVEST ROAD
MIDDLE HILL
BARLEY MOW ROAD
BISHOPSGATE ROAD
Barley Mow PH
NORTHCROFT ROAD
VICTORIA STREET
BOND STREET
MAGNA ROAD
ARCHWOOD
KINGS LANE
WICK LANE
WICK ROAD

173
AZ
BA
BB
BC
BD
BE
BF
01
02
03
153
193
174
Junction 14
Junction 13
WRAYSBURY
RESERVOIR
SL3
WINDSOR & MAIDENHEAD
SURREY
SPELTHORNE
TW19
TW18
TW20
KING GEORGE VI RESERVOIR
STANWELL MOOR
STAINES MOOR
RUBBISH DUMP
GRAVEL PIT
HERON LAKE
QUEENSMEAD LAKE
RUNNYMEDE NT
RUNNYMEDE PLEASURE GROUND
THE ISLAND
Hythe End
Pooley Green
Egham Hythe
EGHAM
Thorpe Lea
STAINES
M25
A30
A308
A320
A3044
B376
B3376
B388
STAINES BYPASS
LONDON ROAD
THE CAUSEWAY
THE GLANTY
CHERTSEY LANE
STAINES RESERVOIRS AQUEDUCT
RIVER COLNE
Egham Sports Centre
ELMSLEIGH CENTRE
TOWN HALL
Runnymede Hotel
Bellweir Lock
Penton Hook Lock
Crabtree Corner
THORPE INDUSTRIAL
71
72
73
74
85
86
87
88
89
90
91
92
93
94

Junction 14
BG
BH
BJ
BK
BL
BM
BN
05
06
07
154
STANWELL MOOR
CARGO TERMINAL
CARGO TERMINAL
HILLINGDON
SPELTHORNE
85
86
87
88
89
90
91
92
93
94
74
73
72
71
KING GEORGE VI RESERVOIR
STAINES RESERVOIRS
TW19
STANWELL
RECREATION GROUND
BLACKBURN TRADING ESTATE
CAMGATE ESTATE
SURREY
ASHFORD HOSPITAL
BURIAL GROUND
PLAYING FIELDS
173
A30
A3044
A308
A3113
STAINES
ELMSLEIGH CENTRE
SHORTWOOD COMMON
ASHFORD PARK
REC GROUND
ASHFORD
ASHFORD MANOR GOLF COURSE
STAINES PARK MINI RAILWAY
FORDBRIDGE PARK
GRAVEL PIT
SPORTS GROUND
TW18
TW17
194
QUEEN MARY
Penton Hook Lock

175
BP
BQ
BR
BS
BT
BU
BV
08
09
10
155
TW6
TERMINAL 4
HEATHROW TERMINAL 4
Heathrow Hilton Hotel
Hangars
BUS STA
SOUTHERN PERIMETER ROAD
GREAT SOUTH-WEST ROAD
A30
HATTON
RADIUS PARK
HATTON CROSS
THE CAUSEWAY
A312
FAGGS ROAD
BALANCING RESERVOIR
ALLOT
TIP
Works
Warehouse
MERCURY CENTRE
IND EST
Hounslow Urban Farm
Amb Sta
Fire Sta
CEM
Superstore
Mast
TW14
Football Ground
Bowl Grn
Lido
REC GRD
Sch
DUKES GREEN
Fagg's Bridge
THE GRIFFIN CENTRE
STAINES ROAD
HOUNSLOW HEATH GOLF COURSE
DONKEY WOOD
FAIRWAY ESTATE
85
86
87
88
89
90
91
92
93
94
74
73
72
71
Baber Bridge
HOUNSLOW HEATH
DUKE OF NORTHUMBERLAND'S RIVER
HILLINGDON
HOUNSLOW
The Two Bridges
Catering Centre
LONGFORD RIVER
STAINES ROAD
A315
BEDFONT GREEN
Clinic
Health Centre
PLAYING FIELD
SPORTS GRD
Grandstand
BEDFONT LANE REC GRD
FELTHAM ARENAS
FELTHAM PARK
HARLINGTON ROAD WEST
HOUNSLOW ROAD
A244
Clockhouse Roundabout
Royal Oak PH
NEW SQUARE
EAST BEDFONT
BEDFONT LAKES COUNTRY PARK
B3003
BEDFONT ROAD
GROSVENOR PARK
Superstore
Health Cen
FELTHAM
Depot
SPORTS GRD
176
Hanworth Park House
HANWORTH
TW13
PARK
H.M. YOUNG OFFENDER INSTITUTION AND REMAND CENTRE
LOWER FELTHAM
HIGH STREET
ASHFORD RD
SPELTHORNE
HOUNSLOW
ASHFORD INDUSTRIAL ESTATE
Cricket Grd
Scout Hall
Hanworth Garden Centre
RECTORY MEADOW
A316
B377
RIFLE RANGE
LAKESIDE SPORTS GRD
Staines R.F.C.
Clubho
SPORTS GRD
FELTHAMHILL
Running Horse PH
KING GEORGE'S FIELD
SURREY
BP International Ltd
Pumping Station
Filter Beds
RESERVOIR
TW15
TW16
CHERTSEY ROAD
REC GRD
STAINES RESERVOIRS AQUEDUCT
KEMPTON PARK (Only Open On Race Days)
A308
STAINES ROAD WEST
SPORTS GROUND
Water Works
M3
Junction 1
195
Superstore
Shopping Centre
Fire Sta
SUNBURY
Warehouses
TRADING ESTATE
ASHFORD COMMON WATER TREATMENT WORKS
COV RES
Grandstands
Grandstand
PARK
RACECOURSE
PLAYING FIELD
RUGBY GROUND
Sports Cen
Tennis Cts
DOLPHIN ESTATE

176
BW
BX
BY
BZ
CA
CB
CC
TW3
156
TW4
HOUNSLOW
HEATH
TW14
HOUNSLOW HEATH GOLF COURSE
HOUNSLOW HEATH GOLF COURSE
STAINES ROAD
A315
A312
A3063
A314
A244
A316
A313
A311
A308
HARLINGTON ROAD WEST
HARLINGTON ROAD EAST
HOUNSLOW ROAD
UXBRIDGE ROAD
HANWORTH ROAD
GREAT CHERTSEY RD
TWICKENHAM RD
STAINES ROAD
COUNTRY WAY
WHITTON
FELTHAM
FELTHAM ARENAS
TW13
HANWORTH PARK
HANWORTH
TW12
TW16
KEMPTON PARK
RACECOURSE
RESERVOIR
HAMPTON
FULWELL GOLF COURSE
FULWELL PARK
TWICKENHAM PARK GOLF COURSE
CRANE PARK
NATURE RESERVE
BOROUGH CEMETERY
HEATHFIELD REC GRD
TWICKENHAM CEMETERY
HANWORTH TRADING ESTATE
APEX RETAIL PARK
SPORTS GROUND
PLAYING FIELDS
Police Training Centre
Hanworth Park House
Twickenham R.F.C. Clubhouse
HALF MOON COVERT
CARLISLE PARK
KINGSWAY BUSINESS PARK
HYDES FIELD
RECTORY MEADOW
STAINES RESERVOIRS AQUEDUCT
RIVER CRANE
175
196
85
86
87
88
89
90
91
92
93
94
74
73
72
71
12
13
14

177
CD
CE
CF
CG
CH
CJ
CK
15
16
17
157
TW9
TW6
TW2
TW1
TW10
TW11
KT2
MOGDEN WATER TREATMENT WORKS
OLD DEER PARK
REC GRD
RICHMOND GREEN
ST MARGARETS
IVYBRIDGE ESTATE
TWICKENHAM TRADING ESTATE
THE RUGBY FOOTBALL UNION TWICKENHAM
RICHMOND UPON THAMES COLLEGE
HARLEQUINS FC (RUGBY)
HOUNSLOW
RICHMOND UPON THAMES
RICHMOND
MARBLE HILL
MARBLE HILL HOUSE
MARBLE HILL PARK
PETERSHAM MEADOWS
GLOVER'S ISLAND
EEL PIE ISLAND
TWICKENHAM
HAM HOUSE NT
HAM HOUSE GARDENS NT
KING GEORGE'S FIELD
POLO GROUND
THE COPSE
HAM PLAYING FIELD
SANDY LANE EST
HAM
ST. MICHAEL'S CONVENT
HAM COMMON
RICHMOND GOLF COURSE
SUDBROOK
The Wilderness
PETERSHAM
STRAWBERRY HILL
STRAWBERRY HILL GOLF COURSE
St. Mary's Training College
TEDDINGTON CEM
CASSEL HOSPITAL
Teddington Lock
Teddington Weir
Thames TV Studios
The Lensbury Club
SHELL SPORTS GRD
TROWLOCK ISLAND
TEDDINGTON
NORMANSFIELD HOSPITAL (closed)
BROOM ROAD REC GRD
STEVEN'S EYOT
HAMPTON HILL
NATIONAL PHYSICAL LABORATORY
CANAL PLANTATION
ROUND PLANTATION
BUSHY HOUSE
BUSHY PARK
WOODLAND GARDEN
BROOM CLUMPS
LEG OF MUTTON POND
HERON POND
OVAL PLANTATION
HAMPTON WICK
KINGSTON
Kingston College of F.E.
178
197
85
86
87
88
89
90
91
92
93
94
71
72
73
74
A316
A310
A305
A3004
A307
A309
A311
A313
B360

CL
CM
CN
CP
CQ
CR
CS
19
20
21
158
TW9
SW14
TW1
TW10
KT2
RICHMOND
RICHMOND PARK
PETERSHAM
PETERSHAM PARK
HAM COMMON
COOMBE
EAST SHEEN
UPPER RICHMOND ROAD WEST
SHEEN ROAD
QUEENS ROAD
PETERSHAM ROAD
RICHMOND ROAD
KINGSTON HILL
KINGSTON VALE
ROBIN HOOD WAY
COOMBE LANE WEST
RIVER THAMES
EAST SHEEN COMMON (N T)
EAST SHEEN CEMETERY
RICHMOND CEMETERY
PESTHOUSE COMMON
PALEWELL COMMON
PALEWELL PLAYING FIELDS
TECK PLANTATION
SHEEN WOOD
The Bog
ADAM'S POND
SHEEN CROSS WOOD
POLO FIELD
CONDUIT WOOD
BARN WOOD POND
SAW PIT PLANTATION
JUBILEE PLANTATION
DUCHESS WOOD
WHITE LODGE PLANTATIONS
White Lodge (The Royal Ballet Sch)
KIDNEY WOOD
SIDMOUTH WOOD
QUEEN ELIZABETH'S PLANTATION
LEG OF MUTTON POND
PEN PONDS
KING GEORGE V JUBILEE PLANTATION
DEER PARK
TREEBOX WOOD
SPANKER'S HILL WOOD
LAWN PLANTATION
POND PLANTATION
Tercentenary Plantation
Pond Slade
MARTIN'S POND
PRINCE CHARLES'S SPINNEY
GIBBET WOOD
HAM CROSS PLANTATION
ISABELLA PLANTATION
THOMSON'S POND
PEG'S POND
STILL POND
HIGH WOOD
Deer Fold
Broomfield Hill
BROOMFIELD HILL PLANTATION
Kingston Uni (Dorich House)
Kingston University (Kingston Hill)
Kingston University (Coombehurst)
CORONATION PLANTATION
DANN'S POND
Thatchedhouse Lodge
GALLOW'S POND
Kings Clump
Dark Hill
Ladderstile Gate
Kingston Gate
Robin Hood Gate
Roehampton Gate
Richmond Gate
Ham Gate
Ham Bottom
Ham Dip
Ham Cross
KING HENRY VIII MOUND
RICHMOND GOLF COURSE SUDBROOK PARK
The Wilderness
Ormeley Lodge
TERRACE GDNS
TERRACE FIELD
PETERSHAM MEADOWS
GLOVER'S ISLAND
MEADOWBANK
THE COPSE
Ham Polo Club
COOMBE HILL GOLF COURSE
COOMBE WOOD GOLF COURSE
THE WATERGARDENS
KINGSTON HOSPITAL
THE BANK OF ENGLAND SPORTS GROUND
BROOM ROAD REC GRD
TROWLOCK ISLAND
STEVEN'S EYOT
Open During Daylight Hours Only
SAWYER'S HILL
HORSE RIDE
CYCLE PATH
A305
A307
A308
A238
B351
B352

CT
CU
CV
CW
CX
CY
CZ
22
23
24
159
ROEHAMPTON
PUTNEY
SW15
WANDSWORTH
EAST PUTNEY
UPPER RICHMOND ROAD
WEST HILL
PUTNEY HILL
QUEEN MARY'S UNI HOSP
ROEHAMPTON PLAYING FIELDS
PUTNEY HEATH
ROYAL HOSPITAL
Whitelands Training Coll
SW18
SOUTHFIELDS
ROEHAMPTON LANE
KINGSTON ROAD
TIBBET'S RIDE
Tibbet's Corner
WIMBLEDON PARK SIDE
PUTNEY VALE CEMETERY
Crematorium
Superstore
PUTNEY VALE
WINDMILL MUSEUM
Clubhouse
Queen's Mere
LONDON SCOTTISH GOLF COURSE
WIMBLEDON
COMMON
PARKSIDE CLINIC
Roehampton Institute of Adult Ed
Southlands Coll
WIMBLEDON PARK
ATHLETICS TRACK
GOLF COURSE
ALL ENGLAND LAWN TENNIS & CROQUET CLUB
Indoor Tenn
MUS
ROYAL WIMBLEDON GOLF COURSE
CANNIZARO PARK
Cannizaro House (Hotel)
RUSHMERE POND
Caesar's Camp
LADY JANE'S WOOD
HIGH ST WIMBLEDON
WIMBLEDON HILL RD
MUS OF LOCAL HISTORY
King's Coll Sch
Southside Ho
WOLFSON MED. REHAB CENTRE
ATKINSON MORLEY'S HOSPITAL
COPSE HILL
OBERON PLAYING FIELD
SW20
DUNDONALD REC GRD
WIMBLEDON
Shop Cen
THE BROADWAY
SW19
SOUTH PARK GDNS
MERTON PARK
KINGSTON ROAD
COTTENHAM PARK
WEST BARNES
DURNSFORD ROAD
85
86
87
88
89
90
91
92
93
94
180
199
71
72
73
74

DA
DB
DC
DD
DE
DF
DG
26
27
28
160
200
179
71
72
73
74
85
86
87
88
89
90
91
92
93
94
WANDSWORTH
WANDSWORTH TOWN
SW11
SW17
SW18
SW19
SOUTHFIELDS
EARLSFIELD
SUMMERSTOWN
WIMBLEDON PARK
UPPER TOOTING
BALHAM
TOOTING GRAVENEY
COLLIER'S WOOD
SOUTH WIMBLEDON
MERTON
H.M. PRISON WANDSWORTH
WANDSWORTH CEMETERY
CENTRAL LONDON GOLF CENTRE
SPRINGFIELD HOSPITAL
STREATHAM CEMETERY
WIMBLEDON STADIUM
WIMBLEDON CEMETERY
LAMBETH CEMETERY
ST. GEORGE'S HOSPITAL
LONDON ROAD CEMETERY
FIGGE'S MARSH
KING GEORGE'S PARK
WANDSWORTH COMMON
BOLINGBROKE HOSP
SPENCER PARK
DUNDONALD REC GRD
GREENLEA PARK
WANDLE PARK
MERTON HIGH STREET
TRINITY ROAD
GARRATT LANE
MERTON ROAD
DURNSFORD ROAD
HAYDONS ROAD
TOOTING HIGH STREET
MITCHAM ROAD
BURNTWOOD LANE
WEST HILL
KINGSTON ROAD
THE BROADWAY
HIGH STREET COLLIERS WOOD

DH
DJ
DK
DL
DM
DN
DP
161
CLAPHAM PARK
SW4
SW2
BRIXTON
H.M. PRISON BRIXTON
SE24
BROCKWELL PARK
HERNE HILL
SE21
TULSE HILL
STREATHAM HILL
TOOTING BEC COMMON
182
WEST NORWOOD CEMETERY
WEST NORWOOD
SE27
STREATHAM PARK
STREATHAM
STREATHAM COMMON
SW16
THE ROOKERY
NORWOOD GROVE RECREATION GROUND
PLAYING FIELD
BIGGIN WOOD
SE19
NORWOOD NEW TOWN
STREATHAM VALE
NORBURY PARK
NORBURY
201
NATIONAL WESTMINSTER BANK SPORTS GROUND
85
86
87
88
89
90
91
92
93
94
29
30
31
71
72
73
74

182
DQ
DR
DS
DT
DU
DV
DW
33
34
35
162
181
202
85
86
87
88
89
90
91
92
93
94
74
73
72
71
SE24
SE15
SE22
SE21
SE27
SE26
SE19
SE20
HERNE HILL
BROCKWELL PARK
EAST DULWICH
DULWICH
DULWICH PARK
TULSE HILL
WEST DULWICH
WEST NORWOOD
WEST NORWOOD CEMETERY
UPPER SYDENHAM
NORWOOD
NORWOOD NEW TOWN
NORWOOD PARK
CRYSTAL PALACE PARK
CRYSTAL PALACE ATHLETICS STADIUM
National Sports Cen
UPPER NORWOOD
PECKHAM RYE COMMON
PECKHAM RYE PARK
CAMBERWELL OLD CEMETERY
HORNIMAN GDNS
HORNIMAN MUS
DULWICH & SYDENHAM HILL GOLF COURSE
SYDENHAM HILL WOOD (NATURE RESERVE)
DULWICH WOOD
SOUTH BANK UNIVERSITY SPORTS GROUND
DULWICH PICTURE GALL
HERNE HILL STADIUM
KING'S COLL HOSP DULWICH
WESTOW PARK
UPPER NORWOOD REC GRD
PENGE
SYDENHAM
HALF MOON LANE
VILLAGE WAY
DULWICH COMMON
LORDSHIP LANE
LONDON ROAD
THURLOW PARK ROAD
CROXTED ROAD
SOUTH CROXTED ROAD
NORWOOD ROAD
KNIGHTS HILL
BEULAH HILL
CENTRAL HILL
CROWN DALE
WESTWOOD HILL
CRYSTAL PALACE PARADE
CRYSTAL PALACE PARK ROAD
ANERLEY HILL
ANERLEY ROAD
CHURCH ROAD
WESTOW HILL
GIPSY HILL
DULWICH WOOD PK
COLLEGE RD
KIRKDALE
DARTMOUTH ROAD
HIGH ST
A205
A215
A2199
A2214
A2216
A212
A214
A234

183
DX
DY
DZ
EA
EB
EC
ED
36
37
38
163
SE13
SE4
SE6
SE23
BR3
BR2
BROCKLEY
LADYWELL
HONOR OAK PARK
HONOR OAK SPORTS GRD
BROCKLEY CEMETERY
LADYWELL CEMETERY
UNIVERSITY LEWISHAM HOSP
LADYWELL UNIT
LEWISHAM PARK
MANOR PARK
HITHER GREEN
MANOR HOUSE GARDENS
GUY'S U.M.D.S. ATHLETIC GRD
CATFORD GREYHOUND STADIUM
LADYWELL FIELDS
BLYTHE HILL FIELDS
BROCKLEY HILL PARK
MOUNTFIELD PARK PLAYING FIELDS
BROWNHILL ROAD
SOUTH CIRCULAR ROAD
A205
CATFORD
CATFORD ROAD
CATFORD HILL
A212
A21
BROMLEY ROAD
RUSHEY GRN
LEWISHAM HIGH STREET
PRIVATE BANKS SPORTS GRD
FOREST HILL
STANSTEAD ROAD
PERRY HILL
BELL GREEN
BELLINGHAM
FORSTER MEMORIAL PARK
SPORTS GROUND
LOWER SYDENHAM
MAYOW PARK
SOUTHEND
SOUTHEND LANE
A2218
SOUTHEND PARK
HOME PARK
NAT WEST BANK SPORTS GRD
LLOYDS BANK SPORTS GRD
NEW BECKENHAM
BECKENHAM HILL
BECKENHAM PLACE PARK
GOLF COURSE
SUMMERHOUSE HILL WOOD
ASH PLANTATION
LEWISHAM BOROUGH SPORTS GROUND
MIDLAND BANK SPORTS GROUND
WARREN AVE PLAYING FIELDS
DOWNHAM
DOWNHAM FIELDS
H.S.B.C. GROUP SPORTS GRD
CATOR PARK
C.G.U. CUACO SPORTS GRD
BECKENHAM
BECKENHAM JUNCTION
SOUTHEND ROAD
A2015
SHORTLANDS GOLF COURSE
BROMLEY PARK
THE SLOANE HOSPITAL
KENT HOUSE
LEWISHAM BROMLEY
BEXLEY PLANTATION
203
184
85
86
87
88
89
90
91
92
93
94
71
72
73
74

184
EE
EF
EG
EH
EJ
EK
EL
164
183
204
40
41
42
85
86
87
88
89
90
91
92
93
94
74
73
72
71
HITHER GREEN
SE12
SE6
BR1
BR2
LEE
ELTHAM
MOTTINGHAM
GROVE PARK
DOWNHAM
PLAISTOW
SUNDRIDGE
ELMSTEAD
BROMLEY PARK
MANOR PARK
SPORTS GROUNDS
FOOTBALL PITCHES
SUTCLIFFE PARK
OLD COLFEIANS SPORTS GROUND
CIVIL SERVICE SPORTS GROUNDS
MIDDLE PARK FIELD
QUEENSCROFT REC GRD
UNI OF GREENWICH ATHLETIC GRD
KING JOHN PLAYING FIELDS
NORTHBROOK PARK
HITHER GREEN CEMETERY
UNI OF WESTMINSTER SPORTS GROUND
MOTTINGHAM SPORTS GROUND
PLAYING FIELD
LOWER MARVELS WOOD
MARVELS WOOD
GROVE PARK CEMETERY
ELMSTEAD WOOD
CHINBROOK MEADOWS
DOWNHAM FIELDS
DOWNHAM PLAYING FIELDS
SHAFTESBURY PARK REC GRD
KING'S MEADOW PLAYING FIELDS
SUNDRIDGE PARK GOLF COURSE
Sundridge Park Management Cen
ROCKPIT WOOD
LOGSHILL WOOD
LEWISHAM BOROUGH SPORTS GROUND
MIDLAND BANK SPORTS GROUND
WARREN AVE PLAYING FIELDS
SHORTLANDS GOLF COURSE
THE SLOANE HOSPITAL
ASH PLANTATION
SOUTH CIRCULAR ROAD
A205
A20
A210
A2212
A21
A2213
B226
ELTHAM ROAD
SIDCUP ROAD
WESTHORNE AVENUE
BURNT ASH HILL
BARING ROAD
BROMLEY ROAD
LONDON ROAD
BURNT ASH LANE
ST. MILDREDS ROAD
KIDBROOKE PARK ROAD
ELTHAM HILL
MOTTINGHAM LANE
GROVE PARK ROAD
CHINBROOK ROAD
COLLEGE RD
SUNDRIDGE PARK
BROMLEY NORTH
GROVE PARK
RAVENSBOURNE
ELMSTEAD WOODS

185
EM
EN
EP
EQ
ER
ES
ET
43
44
45
165
186
205
A16
ELTHAM PARK SOUTH
ELTHAM WARREN GOLF COURSE
ELTHAM CEMETERY
Crematorium
ROCHESTER WAY RELIEF ROAD
EAST ROCHESTER WAY
BEXLEY ROAD
BLACKFEN ROAD
A210
AVERY HILL
AVERY HILL PARK
University of Greenwich Avery Hill Campus
CAMBRIDGE MISSION SPORTS GROUND
CHARLTON ATHLETIC FC TRAINING GRD
MILLWALL FC TRAINING GRD
FOOTSCRAY PLAYING FIELDS
FOOTSCRAY ROAD
A211
ROYAL BLACKHEATH GOLF COURSE
SE9
TARN BIRD SANCTUARY
THE TARN
FAIRY HILL REC GRD
NEW ELTHAM
SIDCUP ROAD
A20
BLACKFEN
HOLLY OAK WOOD PK
DA15
LAMORBEY
OLD FARM PARK
KING GEORGE'S REC GRD
GAELIC ATH. ASSOC. SPORTS GRD
LONGLANDS
JACK NICKLAUS GOLF CENTRE
FLAMINGO PK SPORTS GRD
LONGLANDS REC GRD
MAIN ROAD
SIDCUP
DA14
SIDCUP BY-PASS
STATION ROAD
A222
SIDCUP PLACE
BELMONT LANE OPEN SPACE
DOG RACING TRACK
CHISLEHURST CEMETERY
Hoblands Wood
OLD ELTHAMIANS SPORTS GRD
UNIVERSITY COLLEGE LONDON SPORTS GRD
BR7
CHISLEHURST WEST
WHYTES WOODLAND
CHISLEHURST
CAMDEN PARK
CHISLEHURST GOLF COURSE
CHISLEHURST COMMON
PERRY STREET
SCADBURY PARK NATURE RESERVE
Scadbury Moated Manor House Site
PARK WOOD
Frognal Corner
QUEEN MARY'S HOSP
A208
WHITE HORSE HILL
RED HILL
HIGH STREET
BROMLEY ROAD
BROMLEY LANE
A222

EU
EV
BEXLEY
EW
EX
EY
EZ
FA
47
48
49
166
DANSON
DA16
The Boathouse Function Suite
THE LAKE
PARK
BEXLEYHEATH
GOLF
COURSE
ROCHESTER WAY
ROCHESTER ROAD
BLACKFEN ROAD
A210
A2
A221
A207
A222
A223
A224
A211
A20
85
86
87
88
89
90
91
92
93
94
74
73
72
71
BLACKFEN
HOLLYOAK WOOD PARK
WILLERSLEY PARK
MARLBOROUGH PARK
DA15
MORBEY
SIDCUP GOLF COURSE
Rose Bruford College
LAMORBEY PARK
PENHILL PARK
PENHILL ROAD
RIVERSIDE WALK
BEXLEY PARK WOOD
HURST ROAD
SIDCUP CEM
RUTLAND SHAW
ALBANY PARK
ABBEYHILL PARK
KING GEORGE'S REC GROUND
185
LONGLANDS REC GRD
Sidcup Arts Cen
WARING PARK
NORTH CRAY WOOD
FOOTS CRAY MEADOWS
STABLE MEADOW
Five Arch Bridge
Foots Cray Place
DAVID LLOYD CLUB
SPORTS GROUND
THE ALDERS
NORTH CRAY
NORTH CRAY ROAD
GATTONS WOOD
DA14
SIDCUP
SIDCUP PLACE
SIDCUP HIGH ST
SIDCUP HILL
SIDCUP BYPASS
QUEEN MARY'S HOSP
Frognal House
GARDEN SHAW
FOOTS CRAY
MAIDSTONE ROAD
RUXLEY CORNER INDUSTRIAL ESTATE
Ruxley Corner
RUXLEY WOOD
EDGINGTON WAY
SCADBURY PARK NATURE RESERVE
LITTLE WOOD
Bank's Shaw
Spring Shaw
Square Clump
Bushy Clump
Irish Plantation
WOOD
BR5
206
SEVENOAKS WAY
Profiles Ski Centre
Sports Club
RUXLEY GOLF COURSE
DRIVING RANGE
BEXLEY
BROMLEY

FB
FC
FD
FE
FF
FG
FH
167
CRAYFORD MARSHES
DA1
ACORN INDUSTRIAL PARK
SHENSTONE PARK
WATLING STREET
LONDON ROAD
A207
A223
A220
CRAYFORD
CRAYFORD STADIUM
RECREATION GROUND
HALL PLACE GARDENS
HALL PLACE
RUGBY GRD
ST. MARY'S REC GRD
QUARRY
OLD BEXLEY
CHURCHFIELD WOOD
DA5
DARTFORD HEATH
ROCHESTER WAY
DARTFORD ROAD
A2018
A226
A2
COLDBLOW
SHEPHERDS LANE
PRINCES ROAD
OLD BEXLEY LANE
BEXLEY HOSPITAL
PLAYING FIELDS
DARTFORD GOLF COURSE
BRICKHILL WOOD
North West Kent College of Technology
University of Greenwich
188
85
86
87
88
89
90
91
92
93
94
73
74
72
71
JOYDEN'S WOOD
JOYDENS WOOD
Hook Green
ROWHILL WOOD
DA2
ROWHILL WOOD
BR8
BIRCHWOOD PARK GOLF COURSE
Stonehill Woods Caravan Park
HEXTABLE
RECREATION GROUND
HEXTABLE GDNS
TOURIST RAILWAY
Swanley Village
WILMIN
DARTFORD
SEVENOAKS
KENT
207
50
51
52

188
FJ
FK
FL
FM
FN
FP
FQ
54
55
56
168
208
187
85
86
87
88
89
90
91
92
93
94
74
73
72
71
DARTFORD FRESH MARSHES
CRAYFORD MARSHES
DA1
BR8
DA
DARTFORD
NEW TOWN
WILMINGTON
HAWLEY
DARENTH
SUTTON AT HONE
Swanley Village
Junction 1a
Junction 1b
Junction 2
DARTFORD GOLF COURSE
BROOKLANDS LAKE
North West Kent College of Technology
University of Greenwich
WEST HILL HOSP
LIVINGSTONE HOSP
STONE HOUSE HOSPITAL
ARCHERY HOUSE
GLAXOWELLCOME CHEMICAL WORKS
VICTORIA IND EST
MILLSIDE INDUSTRIAL ESTATE
DARTFORD TRADE PARK
CENTRAL PARK
WELLCOME SPORTS GROUND
OAKFIELD PARK
BOW ARROW LANE CEM
WATLING STREET CEM
Leigh City Tech Coll
ST. JOHN'S JERUSALEM
DEER PARK
BURNHAM ROAD
VICTORIA ROAD
HYTHE ST
WEST HILL
EAST HILL (WATLING ST)
HIGH ST
LOWFIELD STREET
HAWLEY ROAD
PRINCES ROAD
DARTFORD BYPASS
SHIREHALL ROAD
MAIN ROAD
SEVENOAKS ROAD
DARTFORD TUNNEL APPROACH
A206
A2026
A226
A2018
A225
A296
A2
A282
M25
B2174
B258
B260
B2200
B2228

189
FR
FS
FT
FU
FV
FW
FX
57
58
59
169
Johnson's Wharf
Jetty
CROSSWAYS BOULEVARD
STONE CROSSING
Stone
GREENHITHE
Knockhall
Ingress Abbey
LONDON ROAD
A226
Gas Works
DA9
Greenhithe Technical Centre
Stone Castle
Leisure Centre
HERITAGE PARK
NATURE RESERVE
Aikerden Farm
Western Cross Farm
STONE REC GRD
STONE CEM
War Memorial
The Bull PH
Bluewater Shopping Centre
THE VILLAGE
BLUEWATER PARKWAY
WATER CIRCUS
WATLING STREET
A296
B255
BEAN ROAD
DA10
85
86
87
88
89
90
91
92
93
94
CHALK PIT
Works
73
74
A2 BYPASS
WATLING STREET
DARENTH WOOD
THE THRIFT
Caravan Site
190
The Royal Oak PH
Knoxfield Caravan Park
Arrow Riding Centre
BURIAL GRD
DARTFORD ROAD
Badger's Mount
Bean Farm
BEAN
LADIES WOOD
LORDS WOOD
BEACON COUNTRY PARK
Youth Club
Cherwell Farm
Betsham
B262
72
71
North End Farm
Manor House Farm
DA13
Cricket Grd
Westwood Farm
The Wheatsheaf PH
HIGH CROSS ROAD
BETSHAM ROAD
HOOK GREEN
Manor Farm Garden Centre
SHELLBANK
PLAYING FLD
Green Street Green
The Ship PH
SANDBANKS
B260
DA4
St. Margaret's Farm
209
Walnut Tree Farm
Chalkcroft
Ryecroft Farm
RYECROFTS WOOD
DARTFORD SEVENOAKS
SOUTH DARENTH
Gill's Farm
CHALK PIT
REC GRD

FY
FZ
GA
GB
GC
GD
GE
61
62
63
170
85
86
87
88
89
90
91
92
93
94
189
74
73
72
71
SWANSCOMBE
NORTHFLEET
DA11
DA10
DA2
DA13
Betsham
Southfleet
Hook Green
Redstreet
Northfleet Green
Wombwell Park
Istead
GALLEY HILL ROAD
LONDON ROAD
STONEBRIDGE ROAD
HIGH STREET
WATLING STREET
SPRINGHEAD ROAD
THAMES WAY
STATION ROAD
PARK CORNER ROAD
SOUTHFLEET ROAD
NORTHFLEET INDUSTRIAL ESTATE
EBBSFLEET INDUSTRIAL ESTATE
SPORTS GROUND
BLUE CIRCLE SPORTS GRD
NORTHFLEET URBAN COUNTRY PARK
SPRINGHEAD ENTERPRISE PARK
SPRINGHEAD REC GROUND
NORTHFLEET CEMETERY
CHALK PIT
Electricity Station
Sewage Works
Filter Beds
Springhead Nurseries
Water Works
North End Farm
Highfield Farm
Mates Farm
Manor House Farm
Court Lodge Farm
Scadbury Manor
Northfleet Green Farm
Chapter Farm
Manor Farm
Hook Place Farm
Westwood Farm
Brakefield House
Cherwell Farm
Alkerden Farm
MADAM WOOD
COURT WOOD
COURTWOOD SHAW
Robins Creek
Northfleet Hope
RIVER
DARTFORD
GRAVESHAM

GF
GG
GH
GJ
GK
GL
GM
171
THAMES
REACH
GRAVESEND
THURROCK
GRAVESHAM
KENT
GRAVESEND
Milton
Denton
Chalk
Westcourt
Windmill Hill
Kings Farm
Parrock Farm
Riverview Park
Singlewell
MID KENT GOLF COURSE
WESTCOURT MARSHES
GREAT CLANE LANE MARSHES
CLAYLANE WOOD
DA12
OVERCLIFFE
ROCHESTER ROAD
WROTHAM ROAD
WATLING STREET
HUNTONDOWN WOOD
GREYHOUND RACING TRACK
TWENTY ACRE WOOD
GRAVEHILL WOOD
JENNY LEE SMITH GOLF COURSE
SPORTS GROUND
Leisure Centre
Tollgate Motel
Services
85
86
87
88
89
90
91
92
93
94
64
65
66
71
72
73
74

192
AS
AT
AU
AV
AW
AX
AY
98
99
00
172
210
CORK CLUMP
FUZZY CLUMP
ALDER COVER
OBELISK POND
SCARLETOAK PLANTATION
FRANK'S PLANTATION
POLO GROUNDS
Pav
The Flying Barn
Breakheart Hill
WEEDEN'S FIELD
JOHNSON'S POND
HEATHER GARDEN
High Flyer's Hill
DARKHOLE CLUMP
OXHED CLUMP
Eton Bridge
Larch Bri
Totem Pole
WICK POND
WINTER GARDEN
Boathouse
The Punch Bowl
THE VALLEY GARDENS
BROAD VIRGINIA WATER PLANTATIONS
EGHAM WICK PLANTATION
Lubbock House
LARKSFIELD
ROBERTS WAY
Royal Holloway College
Research Centre
Sch
Callow Hill
GREAT WOOD
VIRGINIA WATER
Botany Bay Point
FROSTFARM PLANTATION
BLACKNEST
A329
ROAD
LONDON ROAD
Wheatsheaf PH
Virginia Lodge
Cascade Bridge
CHRISTCHURCH ROAD
B389
BELVEDERE WOOD
Belvedere Fort
CEDAR DRIVE
SL5
GU25
GU24
A30
VIRGINIA BEECHES
HOLLOW LANE
THE DELL
Stroude Farm
Stroude Crossing
PIPERS END
HEATH RISE
HEATH CLO
GORSE HILL ROAD
PLAYING FLD
TROTSWORTH AVE
STATION APP
PO
Lib
VIRGINIA WATER
WAVERLEY COPSE
KING'S COPSE
GENERAL'S COPSE
DUKE'S COPSE
Broom Hill
WENTWORTH POND
Clubhouse
Tennis Courts
Wellington Bri
WENTWORTH
Wentworth
The Dormy House
Ingliston House
Podenhale
GOLF COURSE
GREAT WOOD
BEECH WOOD
Knowle Hill
KNOWLE GROVE
KING GEORGE V PLAYING FIELD
Comm Cen
TRUMPS GREEN
The Klondyke Piggeries
Waterloo Bridge
Fairview Farm
Trumps Farm
Longcross Bri
M3
LONGCROSS
Depots
CHOBHAM LANE
KITSMEAD
BOG WOOD
CHERTSEY COMMON
Hersham Farm
DICKEN'S WOOD
Barrowhills
Tenn Cts
MILITARY GOLF COURSE
Grangewood
B386
LONGCROSS ROAD
Longcross
Works
Hillside
Flutters Hill
Longcross House
Lily Pond Farm
Glasshouse
ACCOMMODATION ROAD
Little Arm
Long Arm
Ship Hill
Memorial Cross
B383
Oystershell Hill
Rushy Pond
CHERTSEY ROAD
WINDSOR ROAD
SUBWAY
CHOBHAM COMMON
RUNNYMEDE
SURREY HEATH
95
96
97
98
99
100
101
102
103
104
69
68
67
66

193
TW18
TW20
KT16
KT15
AZ
BA
BB
BC
BD
BE
BF
01
02
03
173
194
211
95
96
97
98
99
100
101
102
103
104
69
68
67
66
Stroude
Thorpe Green
THORPE
Thorpe Industrial Park
Crabtree Corner
Great Fosters Hotel
Luddington House
LONGSIDE LAKE
SPORTS GROUND
THORPE CEM
Manor Lake
Fleet Lake
THORPE PARK
St. Ann's Lake
Abbey Lake
Britannia Arena
Water Gardens
Mountbatten Pavilion
Penton Hook Marina
Penton Hook Island
Penton Hook Lock
Yacht Basin
Penton Park Caravan Park
Fishing Temple Mobile Home Park
Laleham Burway
Junction 2 (M3)
Junction 12 (M25)
ST. ANN'S HILL PARK
Anchor Copse
St. Ann's Chapel (remains of)
Sewage Works
Filter Beds
Sludge Lagoons
Redlands Farm
Lyne Farm
Lyne Court
The Brooks Riding Centre
THE ROUGH
Merrywood Farm
Walnut Tree Farm
Elm Farm Caravan Park
LYNE
Lyne Copse
Hersham Copse
Recreation Ground
FAN GROVE
Fangrove Caravan Park
Great Cockrow Railway
Cockcrow Hill
Hardwick Court Farm
Tara House
Druidswood
Grange Gardens Nursery
Lynefield Farm
Hillside Farm
Gogmore Fm Pk
Cricket Ground
Abbey Fields Rec Grd
Abbey Bridge
Earthworks
CHERTSEY
Chertsey Mus
ADDLESTONE MOOR
Addlestone Cemetery
Abbey Moor Golf Course
Woodside Farm
Simplemarsh Farm
Convent
Junction 11
St. Peter's Hosp
Runnymede Hosp
Abraham Cowley Unit
Bournewood Hospital
Home Wood
Fox Hills
Foxhills Country Club
FOXHILLS GOLF COURSE
Kitchenride Corner
Silverlands Park Nursery
Westbrook Farm
Trys Hill Farm
Fan Court
Fox Hill Farm
France Farm
Silverlands Farm
M25
M3
A320
A317
B388
B389
B386
B375
Chertsey Lane
Staines Road
Thorpe Bypass
Guildford Road
Pyrcroft Rd
Chilsey Green Rd
Mill House Lane
Lyne Crossing Road
Almners Road
Holloway Hill
St. Peter's Way
Eastworth Road

QUEEN MARY RESERVOIR
TW18
KT16
KT15
LALEHAM
CHERTSEY
ADDLESTONE MOOR
CHERTSEY MEADS
WOBURN PARK
LALEHAM GOLF COURSE
LALEHAM BURWAY
LALEHAM PARK
PENTON HOOK
PENTON HOOK ISLAND
PENTON HOOK MARINA
PENTON PARK
ABBEY LAKE
FLEET LAKE
SPORTS GROUND
GRAVEL PIT
ROUND COPSE
RECREATION GROUND
ABBEY MOOR GOLF COURSE
ADDLESTONE CEMETERY
St. George's College
Lee International Studios Shepperton
Chertsey Lock
Penton Hook Lock
Dumsey Eyot
Dockett Eddy
Dockett Point
PHARAOH'S ISLAND
HAMHAUGH ISLAND
Hamhaugh Point
The Bull Dogs
Weybridge Lock
Black Boy Bridge
WEYBRIDGE BUSINESS PARK
Charlton Quarry
Gas Pipeline Station
Pumping Station
Water Works
Laleham Abbey
Sweep's Bridge
Squires Bridge
Fordwater Bridge
Abbey Bridge
Abbey Chase House
Junction 11
RIVER THAMES
ABBEY RIVER
RIVER WEY
SPELTHORNE
RUNNYMEDE
M3
M25
A317
A320
B375
B376
B377
174
193
212
BG
BH
BJ
BK
BL
BM
BN
05
06
07
95
96
97
98
99
100
101
102
103
104
69
68
67
66

195
BP
BQ
BR
BS
BT
BU
BV
08
09
10
175
Junction 1
ASHFORD COMMON
WATER TREATMENT
WORKS
SPORTS GRD
PLAYING FIELD
RUGBY GROUND
LONDON IRISH RUFC
GAFLAC SPORTS GRD
CEDARS REC GRD
KEMPTON
PARK
RACECOURSE
95
96
97
98
99
100
101
102
103
104
68
69
67
66
TW16
SUNBURY
SUNBURY PARK
HAZELWOOD GOLF COURSE
SUNBURY CEMETERY
UPPER HALLIFORD
SUNBURY GOLF COURSE
M3
A244
A308
A3050
A317
B375
B376
B385
B3366
Refuse Transfer Station
WATER TREATMENT WORKS
Sunbury Locks
SUNBURY LOCK AIT
Gas Works
GRAVEL PIT
KT12
APPS COURT GREEN
196
SHEPPERTON
SHEPPERTON BUSINESS PARK
Shepperton Moat House
SHEPPERTON MARINA
BISHOP DUPPA'S REC GRD
GIBBS MARINA
LAS PALMAS ESTATE
DESBOROUGH ISLAND
THAMES MEADOW
Cowey Sale
RIVER ASH
Gaston Bridge
WHEATLEY'S AIT
Sports Centre
Jungle Garden Centre
Squires Garden Centre
Grange Farm
Vicarage Farm
Longmere Farm
Ash Farm Stables
Watersplash Farm
Riding School
KT13
REC GRD
ENGINE RIVER
BROAD WATER
Broadwater Farm
Oatlands Park Hotel
SPORTS GROUND
ASHLEY PARK SPORTS GRD
ELM GROVE REC GRD
WALTON-ON-THAMES
ASHLEY PARK
WALTON-ON-THAMES
BRIDGE STREET
HEPWORTH WAY
NEW ZEALAND AVENUE
HIGH ST
TERRACE ROAD
HERSHAM ROAD
WALTON BRIDGE RD
UPPER HALLIFORD BYPASS
OATLANDS DRIVE
QUEENS ROAD
STAINES ROAD WEST
WINDMILL ROAD
HALLIFORD ROAD
GASTON BRIDGE ROAD
WALTON LANE
213
OATLANDS PARK
RYDENS
HOSP
PLAYING FIELD

BW
BX
BY
BZ
CA
CB
CC
12
13
14
176
195
214
HAMPTON
PARK
RACECOURSE
Grandstands
Grandstand
PLAYING FIELD
HALF MOON COVERT
HYDES FIELD
Portlane Bridge
KINGSWAY BUSINESS PARK
UPPER SUNBURY ROAD
A308
RICHMOND UPON THAMES
STAIN HILL RESERVOIRS
GRAND JUNCTION RESERVOIR
WATER WORKS
Filter Beds
TW12
KENTON COURT MEADOW
SUNBURY COURT
SUNBURY COURT ISLAND
RIVER THAMES
SUNNYSIDE RESERVOIR
PLATT'S EYOT
HURST
GARRICK'S AIT
SURREY
ELMBRIDGE
TW16
SUNBURY
SWAN'S REST ISLAND
RIVERMEAD ISLAND
RIVERSIDE ARTS CENTRE
MOLESEY RESERVOIRS
HURST ROAD
A3050
WATER TREATMENT WORKS
Sunbury Locks
SUNBURY LOCK AIT
Gas Works
BESSBOROUGH RESERVOIR
KNIGHTS RESERVOIR
GRAVEL PIT
Apps Court Farm
APPS COURT GREEN
WALTON ROAD
B369
KT12
WEST MOLESEY
MOLESEY HOSP
REC GROUND
Swim Pool
FOOTBALL GRD
DEAD RIVER
QUEEN ELIZABETH II RESERVOIR
SAND & GRAVEL PIT
ISLAND BARN RESERVOIR
RIVER MOLE
RIVER EMBER
Pumping Station
Clubhouse
KT10
Filter Beds
Sewage Works
Fieldcommon Farm
RYDENS ROAD REC GRD
Esher R.F.C.
HERSHAM TRADING ESTATE
HERSHAM
SANDOWN INDUSTRIAL PARK
LOWER GREEN
Metropolitan Police Dog Training Centre
SANDOWN GOLF COURSE
DRIVING RANGE
RACECOURSE
Sandown Ski Slope
The Warren
Clubhouses
RYDENS
ELM GROVE REC GRD
HOSP
Fire Sta
Offices
WALTON-ON-THAMES
CORONATION PLAYING FIELDS
Weylands Equestrian Centre
South Weylands Farm
West Weylands Farm
ESHER
A244
A317
A311
95
96
97
98
99
100
101
102
103
104
69
68
67
66

197
CD
CE
CF
CG
CH
CJ
CK
15
16
17
177
215
198
TW11
KT1
KT6
KT7
KT9
BUSHY
PARK
HAMPTON COURT
HOME PARK
PARK
GOLF
COURSE
HAMPTON WICK
EAST MOLESEY
THAMES DITTON
WESTON GREEN
HINCHLEY WOOD
LONG DITTON
SURBITON
KINGSTON UPON THAMES
TLEWORTH COMMON
THAMES DITTON & ESHER GOLF COURSE
ESHER
ROUND PLANTATION
WATERHOUSE WOODLAND GARDEN
WATERHOUSE POND
BROOM CLUMPS
WARREN PLANTATION
HALF MOON PLANTATION
LEG OF MUTTON POND
HERON POND
OVAL PLANTATION
BOATING POOL
FISHER'S POND
Red Brick Bridge
Diana Fountain
Hampton Court House
Hampton Court Gate
THE ROYAL PADDOCKS
HAMPTON WICK POND
THE KINGSFIELD
ASH ISLAND
HAMPTON COURT GREEN
MAZE
HAMPTON COURT GDNS
HAMPTON COURT PALACE
THE NORTH CANAL
THE LONG WATER
THE SOUTH CANAL
PRIVY GDN
Stud House
The Wilderness
Parkfield
THE RICK POND
RAVENS AIT
Watersports Centre
THAMES DITTON ISLAND
BOYLE FARM ISLAND
THAMES MARINA
DITTON FIELD
SPORTS GROUND
PLAYING FIELDS
CEMETERY
Cockcrow Hill
KING EDWARD REC GRD
PLAYING FIELD
Kingston University
Kingston Coll
Hillcroft College
SURBITON HOSP
DSS OFFICES
The Waffrons
Telegraph Hill
Scilly Isles
HAMPTON COURT ROAD
HAMPTON COURT WAY
PORTSMOUTH ROAD
KINGSTON BYPASS
UPPER BRIGHTON ROAD
EWELL ROAD
HOOK ROAD
A307
A308
A309
A3
A240
A243
B364
B3364

198
CL
CM
CN
CP
CQ
CR
CS
19
20
21
178
197
216
95
96
97
98
99
100
101
102
103
104
69
68
67
66
COURSE
COOMBE
COOMBE WOOD GOLF COURSE
KT2
KINGSTON HOSPITAL
NORBITON
KINGSTON UPON THAMES
KINGSTON CEMETERY
KT1
NEW MALDEN
KT8
River Thames
HAMPTON WICK POND
SURBITON CEMETERY
BERRYLANDS
GREEN LANE REC GRD
KT3
HOGSMILL PUBLIC OPEN SPACE
KT5
SURBITON GENERAL HOSP
KT6
SURBITON
FISHPONDS OPEN SPACE
ALEXANDRA REC GRD
HOGSMILL OPEN SPACE
MALDEN MANOR
OLD MALDEN
MAORI SPORTS GROUND
LONG DITTON
Cockcrow Hill
TOLWORTH HOSPITAL
TOLWORTH
KINGSTON UNIVERSITY SPORTS GRD
RIVERHILL SPORTS GRD
WANDGAS ATHLETIC GROUND
KING GEORGES FIELD
KING EDWARD REC GRD
KING GEORGE'S TRADING EST
HOOK RISE SOUTH IND PK
KINGSTON BYPASS
MALDEN WAY
KINGSTON ROAD
COOMBE LANE WEST
PORTSMOUTH ROAD
EWELL ROAD
HOOK ROAD
BRIGHTON ROAD
SURBITON HILL ROAD
CAMBRIDGE ROAD
LONDON ROAD
SURREY
RAVENS AIT

199
CT
CU
CV
CW
CX
CY
CZ
179
217
COPSE HILL
WOLFSON MED. REHAB CENTRE
ATKINSON MORLEY'S HOSPITAL
SW20
OBERON PLAYING FIELD
COTTENHAM PARK
COTTENHAM PK REC GRD
COOMBE LANE
A238
KINGSTON ROAD
WORPLE ROAD
DUNDONALD REC GRD
NELSON HOSP
WIMBLEDON CHASE
MERTON
MERTON PARK
SW19
MORDEN
SOUTH MERTON
MOSTYN GARDENS
RAYNES PARK
RAYNES PARK SPORTS GRD
BUSHEY ROAD
A298
PRINCE GEORGE'S PLAYING FIELD
The David Lloyd Club
JOSEPH HOOD RECREATION GROUND
MESSINES PLAYING FLD
BUSHEY MEAD
CANNON HILL COMMON
RAYNES PARK PLAYING FIELDS
WEST BARNES
KINGSTON BYPASS
BEVERLEY WAY
KINGSTON UPON THAMES
MERTON
MOTSPUR PARK
UNIVERSITY OF LONDON ATHLETIC GROUND
THE SIR JOSEPH HOOD MEMORIAL PLAYING FIELDS
B.B.C. SPORTS GRD
OLD BLUES R.F.C.
MORDEN CEMETERY
Crematorium
MERTON & SUTTON JOINT CEMETERY
MORDEN PARK
MORDEN PARK SPORTS GROUND
MORDEN PLAYING FIELDS
SPORTS GROUND
SM4
KING GEORGE'S FIELD
MANOR PARK REC GRD
GARTH ROAD IND CEN
Sewage Treatment Works
ST. ANTHONY'S HOSP
SM3
SUTTON CEMETERY
KIMPTON TRADE BUSINESS CENTRE
REIGATE AVENUE REC GRD
EPSOM ROAD
A24
MALDEN GRN
WORCESTER PARK
A2043
CENTRAL ROAD
CHEAM COMMON ROAD
LONDON ROAD
NORTH CHEAM
KT4
CUDDINGTON REC GRD
SM1
COLLINGWOOD PARK
Sutton Utd. FC
ST. DUNSTAN'S HILL
OLDFIELDS ROAD
A217
95
96
97
98
99
100
101
102
103
104
200
22
23
24

200
DA
DB
DC
DD
DE
DF
DG
SOUTH WIMBLEDON
COLLIER'S WOOD
LONDON ROAD CEMETERY
FIGGE'S MARSH
MERTON
MERTON PARK
SW19
MORDEN
MORDEN HALL PARK
PHIPPS BRIDGE
MITCHAM
CR4
RAVENSBURY PARK
MORDEN SOUTH
MORDEN PARK SPORTS GROUND
SM4
ST. HELIER
MORDEN REC.GRD
POULTER PARK
WILLOW BUSINESS CENTRE
CARSHALTON SPORTS ARENA
ST. HELIER OPEN SPACE
SM5
ROSEHILL
ST. HELIER HOSP
QUEEN MARY'S HOSP FOR CHILDREN
SUTTON CEMETERY
SM3
BENHILTON
THE WRYTHE
DALE PARK
ROYSTON PARK
SM1
COLLINGWOOD PARK
180
199
218
26
27
28

201
SE19
DH
DJ
DK
DL
DM
DN
DP
29
30
31
STREATHAM VALE
NORBURY PARK
NORBURY
NATIONAL WESTMINSTER BANK SPORTS GROUND
181
95
96
97
98
99
100
101
102
103
104
STREATHAM PARK
CEMETERY
PLAYING FIELDS
SW16
POLLARDS HILL
MERTON
CROYDON
GREEN LANE SPORTS GROUND
CR7
THORNTON HEATH
TCHAM
PLAYING FIELD
SHERWOOD PK
COMMON
CROYDON CEMETERY
Croydon Boys FC
Croydon Athletic FC
Crematorium
MAYDAY HOSPITAL
202
QUEEN'S ROAD CEMETERY
BROAD GREEN
THORNTON ROAD RETAIL PK
MERTON
SUTTON
RIFLE RANGE
BEDDINGTON LANE
Sewage Works
Sludge Beds
Filter Beds
RESERVOIR
MILE ROAD
PIONEERS INDUSTRIAL PARK
CR0
WADDON MARSH
WADDON
WANDLE PARK
SM6
BEDDINGTON
ACKBRIDGE
SPORTS GRD
PLAYING FIELDS
BEDDINGTON PARK
THE GRANGE GARDENS
CROYDON SUB STATION
PROGRESS BUSINESS PK
MILL LANE TRADING ESTATE
WEST CROYDON
Whitgift Centre
FAIRFIELD HALLS
219
DUPPAS HILL
Tertiary Centre
Croydon Flyover
MITCHAM ROAD
CROYDON ROAD
LONDON ROAD
PURLEY WAY
ROMAN WAY
DUPPAS HILL RD
A23
A236
A232
A235
A212
A213
B272
B273
68
67
66
69

202
DQ
DR
DS
DT
DU
DV
DW
33
34
35
182
UPPER NORWOOD
WESTOW PARK
BEULAH HILL
THE LAWNS
BEAULIEU HEIGHTS
SYLVAN ESTATE
SOUTH NORWOOD GROUNDS
ORCHARD SCHOOL SPORTS CENTRE
SPORTS GROUND
SOUTH NORWOOD LAKE
SE20
ANERLEY
BETTS PARK
SOUTH PENGE PARK EST
95
96
97
98
99
100
101
102
103
104
69
68
67
66
GREEN LANE SPORTS GROUND
GRANGEWOOD PARK
SOUTH NORWOOD
BECKENHAM CEMETERY
CR7
SE25
SELHURST PARK
THORNTON HEATH
SOUTH NORWOOD REC GRD
NORWOOD JUNCTION
CROYDON SPORTS ARENA
Croydon FC
ARENA
SELHURST
RAIL DEPOT
WOOD SIDE
QUEEN'S ROAD CEMETERY
MAYDAY HOSPITAL
201
BROAD GREEN
ASHBURTON PARK
Davidson Centre
CR0
ADDISCOMBE
CROYDON
REC GRD
WANDLE PARK
WHITGIFT PLAYING FIELDS
SHIRLEY PARK
GOLF COURSE
HOCKEY PITCH
LLOYD PARK
SPORTS GROUND
PARK HILL
DUPPAS HILL
Croydon Flyover
COOMBE PARK
220
Whitgift Centre
EAST CROYDON
WEST CROYDON
FAIRFIELD HALLS

203
DX
DY
DZ
EA
EB
EC
ED
183
BECKENHAM
RAVENSBOURNE
WARREN AVE PLAYING FIELDS
SHORTLANDS GOLF COURSE
95
BROMLEY PARK
THE SLOANE HOSPITAL
96
97
SHORTLANDS
98
99
100
101
102
103
104
204
221
36
37
38
66
67
68
69
KENT HOUSE
BECKENHAM JUNCTION
BECKENHAM ROAD
BECKENHAM HOSPITAL
CROYDON RD REC GROUND
ELMERS END
BR3
KELSEY PARK
HIGH STREET
MANOR ROAD
BROMLEY ROAD
CROYDON ROAD
UPPER ELMERS END
HARVINGTON PLAYING FIELD
EDEN PARK
Langley Court (Research Laboratories)
PARK LANGLEY
LANGLEY PARK GOLF COURSE
LANGLEY PARK SPORTS GRD
MONKS ORCHARD
BETHLEM ROYAL HOSPITAL
HIGH BROOM WOOD
CROUCH OAK WOOD
BLAKE REC GRD
WEST WICKHAM
SPRING PARK WOOD
CR0
SHIRLEY
FOXES WOOD
KENNEL WOOD
SPRING PARK
SPARROWS DEN PLAYING FIELDS
BR4
CONEY HALL REC GRD
Schiller International University
EMMAUS CONF. CENTRE
Old Beccehamian R.F.C.
ADDINGTON GOLF COURSE
Shirley Wanderers
Pumping Station
PINEWOODS
SOUTH EDEN PARK RD
BECKENHAM ROAD
GLEBE WAY
ADDINGTON ROAD
WICKHAM WAY
HAYES LANE
PICKHURST LANE

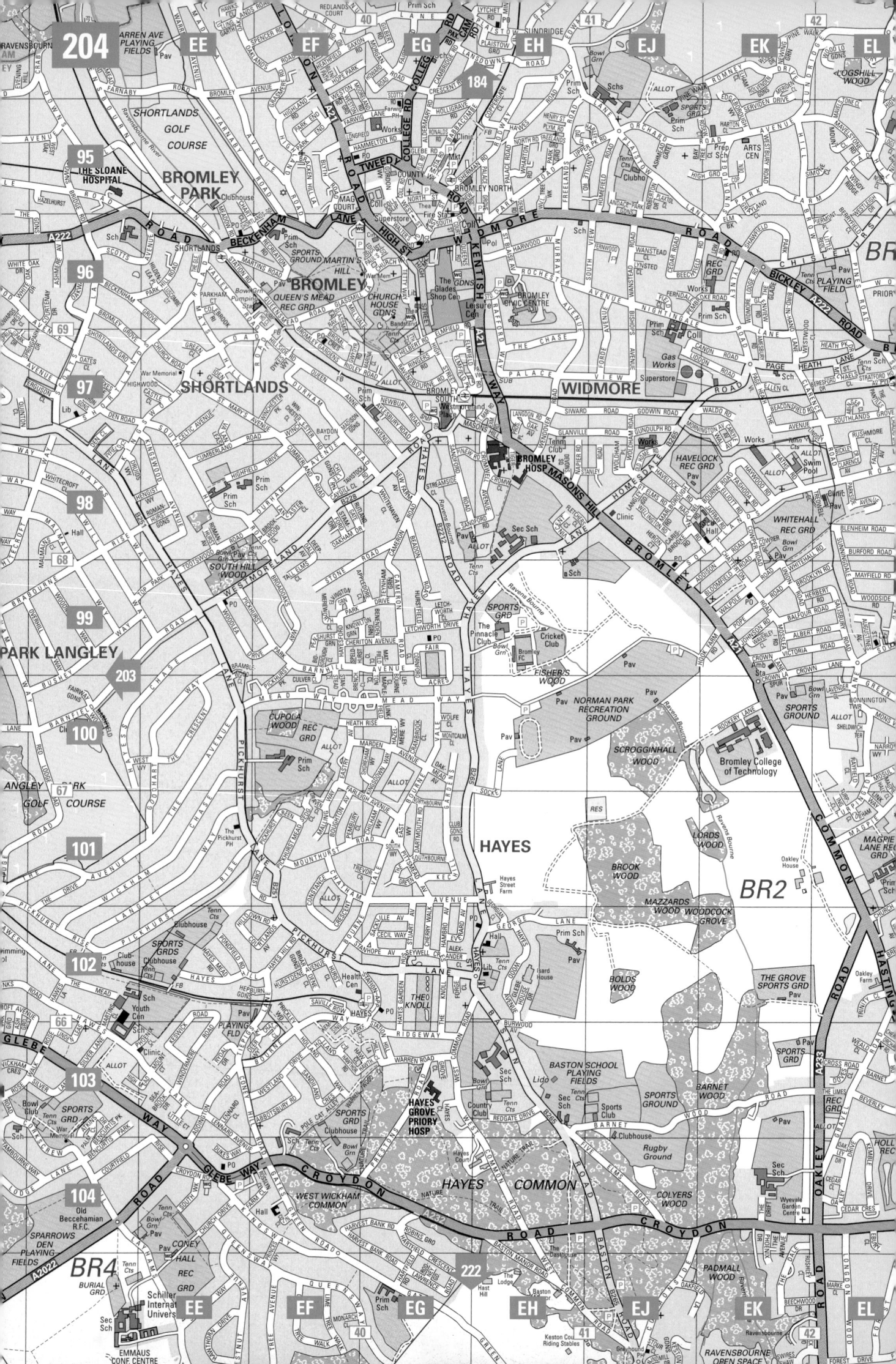
204
EE
EF
EG
EH
EJ
EK
EL
40
41
42
184
95
96
97
98
99
100
101
102
103
104
69
68
67
66
203
222
BROMLEY PARK
BROMLEY
SHORTLANDS
WIDMORE
PARK LANGLEY
HAYES
HAYES COMMON
BR2
BR4
SHORTLANDS GOLF COURSE
THE SLOANE HOSPITAL
BROMLEY HOSP
BROMLEY CIVIC CENTRE
The Glades Shop Cen
QUEEN'S MEAD REC GRD
MARTIN'S HILL
CHURCH HOUSE GDNS
SOUTH HILL WOOD
CUPOLA WOOD
NORMAN PARK RECREATION GROUND
SCROGGINHALL WOOD
Bromley College of Technology
LORDS WOOD
BROOK WOOD
MAZZARDS WOOD
WOODCOCK GROVE
BOLDS WOOD
HAVELOCK REC GRD
WHITEHALL REC GRD
FISHER'S WOOD
THE GROVE SPORTS GRD
BASTON SCHOOL PLAYING FIELDS
BARNET WOOD
COLYERS WOOD
PADMALL WOOD
HAYES GROVE PRIORY HOSP
WEST WICKHAM COMMON
CONEY HALL REC GRD
SPARROWS DEN PLAYING FIELDS
LOGSHILL WOOD
MAGPIE LANE REC GRD
RAVENSBOURNE OPEN SPACE
EMMAUS CONF. CENTRE
A21
A222
A232
A233
A2022
B265
B251
B228
B2212
WIDMORE ROAD
BICKLEY ROAD
MASONS HILL
BROMLEY COMMON
OAKLEY ROAD
HASTINGS ROAD
CROYDON ROAD
GLEBE WAY
BASTON ROAD
HAYES LANE
PICKHURST LANE
WICKHAM ROAD
LONDON ROAD
TWEEDY ROAD
HIGH ST
KENTISH WAY
BECKENHAM ROAD
WESTMORELAND ROAD
HAYES ROAD
HAYES STREET FARM
Gas Works
Superstore

205
EM
EN
EP
EQ
ER
ES
ET
43
44
45
185
223
206
CAMDEN PARK
CHISLEHURST GOLF COURSE
CHISLEHURST COMMON
NATURE RESERVE
PARK WOOD
Icehouse Wood
Holbrook Wood
The Larches
Scadbury Moated Manor House Site
Field Study Centre
CHALKPIT WOOD
BANSOME WOOD
CHISLEHURST
BIRCH WOOD
GOSHILL WOOD
POND WOOD
BR7
HAWKWOOD ESTATE NT
WALK WOOD
ST. PAUL'S CRAY COMMON
PETTS WOOD NT
Edlmann Memorial Wood
Willett Memorial Wood
Kyd Brook
Hawkwood Farm
Tongs Farm
Piggeries
Chislehurst Junction
GREAT THRIFT
HOBLINGWELL WOOD
HOBLINGWELL WOOD REC GRD
ST. PAUL'S CRAY
ST. MARY CRAY
BICKLEY
Bickley Junction
M.O.D.
Bickley Manor Hotel
BLACKBROOK WOOD
Bromley High Sch
THORNET WOOD
JUBILEE COUNTRY PARK
Petts Wood Junction
Southborough Lane Stables
PETTS WOOD
BR5
POVEREST
COVET WOOD
POVEREST REC GRD
SOUTHBOROUGH OPEN SPACE
SOUTHBOROUGH RECREATION GROUND
PARKFIELD
Bromley Common
PLAYING FIELD
Scrubs Farm
SPARROW WOOD
SPARROW COMMON
ROUNDABOUT WOOD
CROFTON HEATH
CLAY WOOD
GUMPING COMMON
PETTS WOOD REC GRD
NOBODY'S WOOD
POKERIDDEN WOOD
ORPINGTON
BR6
FARNBOROUGH REC GRD
FARNBOROUGH HOSPITAL
NEWSTEAD WOOD
DARRICK COMMON
DARRICK WOOD
PERRY HALL ROAD
CHISLEHURST ROAD
ORPINGTON ROAD
SPUR ROAD
CROFTON ROAD
FARNBOROUGH COMMON
SPORTS GROUND
95
96
97
98
99
100
101
102
103
104

206
EU
EV
EW
EX
EY
EZ
FA
47
48
49
186
205
224
95
96
97
98
99
100
101
102
103
104
69
68
67
66
NATURE RESERVE
WOOD
Bushy Clump
Plantation
PLAYING FIELD
Field Study Cen
Youth Centre
RUXLEY WOOD
DA14
BY PASS
A20
RUXLEY GOLF COURSE
DRIVING RANGE
Golf Centre
Sports Club
Profiles Ski Centre
CRAY VALLEY GOLF COURSE
Barnfield Bank
Pilgrim Hill
CHAPMANS LANE
Lower Hockenden Farm
Simon's Field Shaw
The Small House
PAULS CRAY HILL PARK
HIGHLANDS WOOD
HOCKENDEN WOOD
BR5
BR 7
ST. PAUL'S CRAY
HOBLINGWELL WOOD
Sports Cen
CRAYFIELD IND PARK
MURRAY BUS. CEN
SEVENOAKS WAY
A224
ST MARY CRAY
STAR LANE
SANDWAY PK
NUGENT IND PK
THE WARREN
Sheepcote Farm
Ringland Farm
CHILDS WOOD
POVEREST
ST. MARY CRAY
ST. MARY CRAY REC GRD
DERRY DOWNS
Grigg's Cross
CROCKENHILL ROAD
B258
Blueberry Farm
Kevington Farm
Waldens Farm
KYNASTON WOOD
Walden Manor
Depot
Heather's Holding
Bleak House Farm
COVET
POVEREST REC GRD
ALLOT
PERRY HALL ROAD
A208
PRIORY GDNS
BROMLEY MUS
GRASSMEADE RECREATION GROUND
ORPINGTON
RAMSDEN
PLAYING FIELD
COCKMANNINGS ROAD
HOLLINGBOURNE TOWER
BEKESBOURNE TOWER
GRIFF'S WOOD
Eastwood Farm
Piggery
Byways Nurseries
SAGE WENTS
BR6
Cookham Hill Farm
Cookham Farm
SPUR ROAD
A232
A223
A224 (ORPINGTON BYPASS)
GODDINGTON
GODDINGTON PARK
ROUNDS SMALLAMS
LILLY'S WOOD
BLACK BUSH WOOD
ORPINGTON HOSPITAL
SPORTS GRD
SEVENOAKS ROAD

207
HEXTABLE
RECREATION GROUND
PLAYING FIELDS
TOURIST RAILWAY
NEW BARN PARK
Swanley Village
SWANLEY BYPASS
SWANLEY
GOLDSEL RD IND EST
MORETON IND EST
PEDHAM PLACE ESTATE
TEARDROP IND EST
DRIVING RANGE
Broom Hill
BR8
Junction 3(M25)
Junction 1(M20)
M25
M20
A20
B2173
B258
BIRCH WOOD
Windmill Hill Wood
TILE KILNS WOOD
CROCKENHILL
CACKETSHILL WOOD
Westerd Farm
PEDHAM PLACE GOLF CENTRE
Capricorn Farm
HEATHFIELD SHAW
HORNCROSS SHAW
Hulberry
DA4
LULLINGSTONE ROMAN VILLA (REMAINS OF)
THE ROUGHET
ASHEN BANK
LULLINGSTONE PARK
Skeet Hill
KENT
BROMLEY
SEVENOAKS
DARTFORD
FB FC FD FE FF FG FH
50 51 52
187
208
225
95 96 97 98 99 100 101 102 103 104
69 68 67 66

FJ
FK
FL
FM
FN
FP
FQ
54
55
56
188
207
95
96
97
98
99
100
101
102
103
104
69
68
67
66
Swanley Village
SUTTON AT HONE
FARNINGHAM
EYNSFORD
FARNINGHAM WOOD NATURE RESERVE
PEDHAM PLACE GOLF CENTRE
Junction 3(M25)
Junction 1(M20)
BR8
DA4
RAM'S WOOD
THE FOLLY
FRANKS
WESTMINSTER FIELD
DRIVING RANGE
PLAYING FIELD
EYNSFORD CASTLE
FIRPOUND SHAW
OLIVERS SHAW
ALCHIN'S WOOD
POLLY SHAW
SANDHOLE SHAW
LULLINGSTONE ROMAN VILLA (REMAINS OF)
Farningham Road
Swanley Village Nursery
Creswick Nurseries
Homefield Farm
Pedham Place Farm
Capricorn Farm
Beesfield Farm
Charton Manor Farm
Pollyhaugh Farm
Newbarn Farm
Lullingston Park Farm
Gorse Hill Farm
Eglantine Farm
Greenacres Nursery
Beechenley Nursery
Highlands Poultry Farm
Coldharbour Farm
Gildenhill Farm
Hill Farm
Hill House
Franks Hall
The Farningham PH
Pied Bull PH
The Bull PH
The Fighting Cocks PH
Mill House
Clubhouse
Pumping Station
Home Farm
Eynsford Nursery
Furlongs Farm
Tweed House
Tweed Hill
MORETON IND EST
PEDHAM PLACE ESTATE
TEARDROP IND EST
COVERED RESERVOIRS
WADARD TERRACE
LONDON ROAD
GORSE HILL
DARTFORD ROAD
MAIN ROAD
HIGH STREET
STATION ROAD
CALFSTOCK LANE
FRANKS LANE
EGLANTINE LANE
DONKEY LANE
MAPLESCOMBE LANE
CROCKENHILL LANE
PAREPENNY LANE
SHIP LANE
SWANLEY VILLAGE ROAD
FARNINGHAM HILL ROAD
BUTTON STREET
M25
M20
A20
A225

209
189
FR
FS
FT
FU
FV
FW
FX
57
58
59
95
96
97
98
99
100
101
102
103
104
69
68
67
66
SOUTH DARENTH
DA2
DA3
TN15
CHALK PIT
REC GRD
Works
LONGFIELD
HART
Walnut Tree Farm
Ryecroft Farm
Chalkcroft
RYECROFTS WOOD
Orchard View
Gill's Farm
GILL'S ROAD
DARTFORD
SEVENOAKS
GREEN STREET
B260
B255
WHITEHILL ROAD
NORTHDOWN
MAIN ROAD
ESSEX
KENT
STATION ROAD
CAVENDISH SQ
BRAMBLEFIELD
LONGFIELD
Dean Bottom Farm
Pinden End Farm
Rabbits Farm
RABBITS ROAD
WILSON
Tuppence Farm
ALLOT
SOUTHDOWNS
PRINCE CHARLES AVE
AVENUE
CANADA FARM ROAD
CHURCHDOWN WOOD
Churchdown Farm
FAWKHAM
CASTLE HILL
Northdown Country Riding Club
Beeches Farm
Canada Farm
Hill Barn Farm
SCUDDERS ROAD
CORINTHIAN
SPORTS GRD
Tennis Cts
Football Grd
Sports Cen
GOLF COURSE
PENNIS LA
Gay Dawn Farm
Pennis Farm
VALLEY
Lone Oak Farm
Kentdown Mushroom Farm
Nursery
Electricity Station
SCHOOL LANE
HORTON WOOD
MUSSENDEN
GROVE WOOD
Grove Farm
Hall
Sch
HOPKINS SPRING WOOD
HATCHFIELD WOOD
MANOR ROAD
PENNIS WOOD
YEWFIELD SHAW
PARKFIELD WOOD
FAWKHAM MANOR HOSPITAL
Fawkham Manor Farm
Clubhouse
REDLIBBETS GOLF COURSE
NEW ASH GREEN
The Rookery Pig Farm
FB
M20
GABRIEL SPRING ROAD
GABRIELSPRING WOOD
Speedgate Farm
SPEEDGATE HILL
White House Farm
THREE GATES ROAD
CHOAKS WOOD
The Rising Sun PH
War Meml
PO
Fawkham Green
Westyoke Farm
WEST YOKE
BUTCHERS
Eaglesfield Equestrian Centre
Beechcroft Farm Industries
Greyhound Schooling Establishment
Woodhall Farm
SCRATCHERS
Works
BRANDS HATCH KARTING
BRANDS HATCH RD
Sports Centre
SAXTEN'S WOOD
CAGE'S WOOD
Brands Hatch Place Hotel
SHETLEY SHAWS
Brands Hatch Thistle Hotel
BRANDS HATCH
ROGERS WOOD
GALLOWS WOOD
Landway Farm
REDHILL ROAD
White Swan PH
Ash Place Farm
Sports Cen
RECREATION GROUND
Tennis Cts
The Royal Oak PH
Shopping Cen
Comm Cen
Bovis Offices
Lib
ASH ROAD
Black Lion PH
ALLOT
PLAYING FIELD
MERTON AVE
BANCKSIDE
OLD DOWNS
CHURCH
STACK LANE
CARMELITE WAY
ROUND ASH WAY
Clubho
Bowl Grn
CULVEY CLO
COLT STEAD
MILLFIELD
CHAPEL WOOD

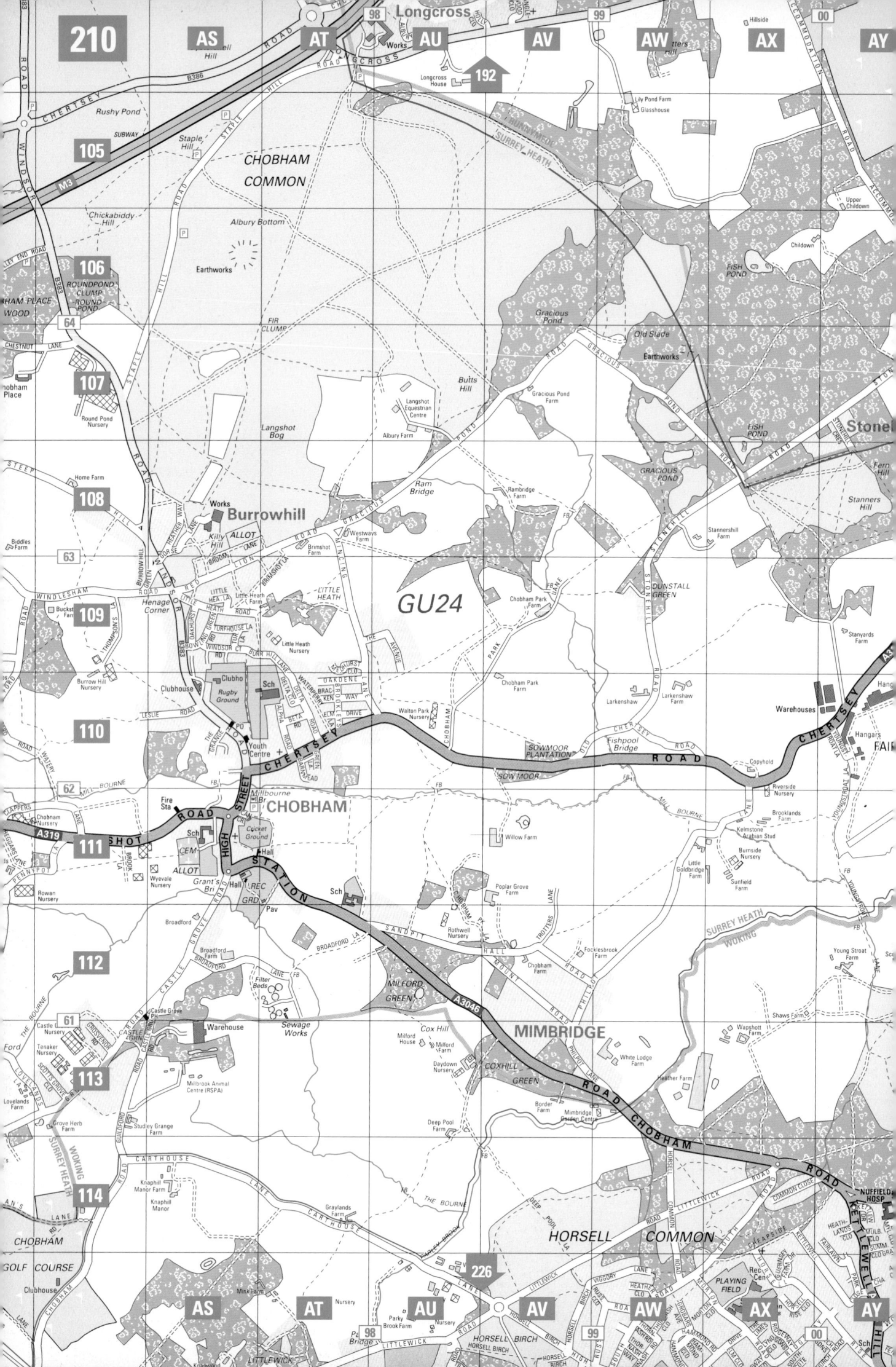

210
Longcross
192
CHOBHAM COMMON
Burrowhill
GU24
CHOBHAM
MIMBRIDGE
HORSELL COMMON
226
Chobham Place Wood
Chobham Golf Course
Rushy Pond
Staple Hill
Chickabiddy Hill
Albury Bottom
Earthworks
Roundpond Clump
Fir Clump
Langshot Bog
Gracious Pond
Old Slade
Butts Hill
Fish Pond
Stanners Hill
Fern Hill
Ram Bridge
Little Heath
Dunstall Green
Henage Corner
Sowmoor Plantation
Sow Moor
Fishpool Bridge
Milford Green
Coxhill Green
Cox Hill
Horsell Birch
Chertsey Road
Windsor Road
Staple Hill Road
Gracious Pond Road
Stonehill Road
Chobham Park Lane
High Street
Station Road
Bagshot Road
Guildford Road
Castle Grove Road
Carthouse Lane
Littlewick Road
Philpot Lane
Mill Bourne
The Bourne
Sewage Works
Filter Beds
Warehouse
Warehouses
Hangars
Nuffield Hosp
Playing Field
SURREY HEATH
RUNNYMEDE
WOKING
M3
A319
A3046
B383
B386

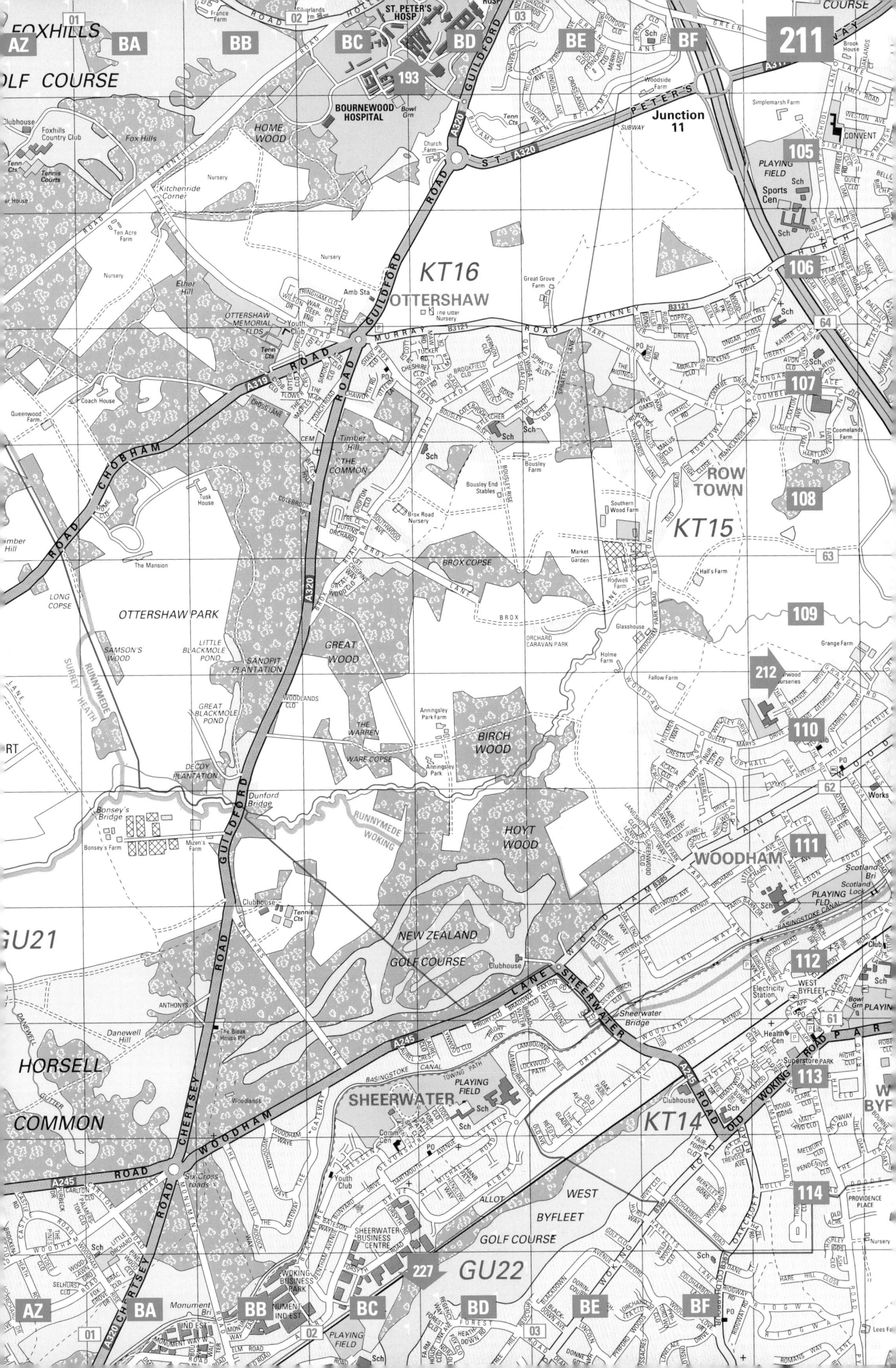
FOXHILLS
GOLF COURSE
Foxhills Country Club
Fox Hills
ST. PETER'S HOSP
BOURNEWOOD HOSPITAL
HOME WOOD
Kitchenride Corner
Ten Acre Farm
Nursery
Ether Hill
OTTERSHAW MEMORIAL FLDS
KT16
OTTERSHAW
Great Grove Farm
Junction 11
ST. PETER'S WAY
GUILDFORD ROAD
MURRAY ROAD
SPINNEY HILL
CHOBHAM ROAD
Queenwood Farm
Coach House
Tusk House
The Mansion
Timber Hill
THE COMMON
Bousley Farm
Bousley End Stables
Brox Road Nursery
BROX COPSE
Southern Wood Farm
Market Garden
Rodwell Farm
ROW TOWN
KT15
Hall's Farm
LONG COPSE
OTTERSHAW PARK
SAMSON'S WOOD
LITTLE BLACKMOLE POND
SANDPIT PLANTATION
GREAT WOOD
GREAT BLACKMOLE POND
THE WARREN
Anningsley Park Farm
BIRCH WOOD
WARE COPSE
Anningsley Park
ORCHARD CARAVAN PARK
Glasshouse
Holme Farm
Fallow Farm
Grange Farm
DECOY PLANTATION
Dunford Bridge
Bonsey's Bridge
Bonsey's Farm
Mizen's Farm
HOYT WOOD
RUNNYMEDE
WOKING
SURREY HEATH
WOODHAM
Scotland Bri
Scotland Lock
BASINGSTOKE CANAL
GU21
Clubhouse
NEW ZEALAND GOLF COURSE
SHEERWATER
Sheerwater Bridge
WEST BYFLEET
Electricity Station
HORSELL COMMON
Danewell Hill
The Bleak House PH
SHEERWATER
PLAYING FIELD
KT14
Six Cross roads
WEST BYFLEET GOLF COURSE
SHEERWATER BUSINESS CENTRE
WOKING BUSINESS PARK
MONUMENT IND EST
Monument Bri
GU22
105
106
107
108
109
110
111
112
113
114
193
212
227
AZ BA BB BC BD BE BF
01 02 03
61 62 63 64

212
BG
BH
BJ
BK
BL
BM
BN
05
06
07
194
211
228
Junction 11
105
106
107
108
109
110
111
112
113
114
64
63
62
61
ADDLESTONE
KT15
NEW HAW
ROW TOWN
WOODHAM
CENTRAL VETERINARY LABORATORY
BROOKLANDS
Airfield (Disused)
BROOKLANDS INDUSTRIAL ESTATE
BROOKLANDS MUSEUM
Brooklands Technical Coll
WEYBRIDGE BUSINESS PARK
TRADING ESTATE
St. George's College
MEADOWLANDS PARK
VICTORY PARK
SAYES COURT PUBLIC OPEN SPACE
Crockford Bridge
MILL POND
Coxes Lock
Addlestone Junction
Weybridge Junction
Nine Arches Bridge
Seven Arches Bridge
Byfleet Junction
BYFLEET & NEW HAW
Electricity Station
HEATHERVALE REC GRD
HEATHERVALE CARAVAN PARK
Botton Lock
Scotland Lock
CAMPHILL INDUSTRIAL ESTATE
BASINGSTOKE CANAL
RIVER WEY NAVIGATION
RIVER WEY
DARTNELL PARK
BYFLEET INDUSTRIAL ESTATE
WEST BYFLEET
BROADOAKS GOVT OFFICES
KT14
TINS WOOD
DODD'S WOOD
OLDWOOD POND
GU23
BYFLEET
Murray's Bridge
Dodd's Bridge
Sheerwater Bridge
Plough Bridge
Bluegates Hole
The Island
COMMON MEADOWS
BUXTON
A317
A318
A245
M25
B3121
B385
B367
B374
HIGH STREET
BRIGHTON RD
NEW HAW ROAD
BYFLEET ROAD
OYSTER LANE
PARVIS ROAD
WOODHAM LANE
OLD WOKING ROAD
WEYBRIDGE ROAD
CHURCH ROAD
STATION ROAD
WELLINGTON WAY
SHEERWATER ROAD
WOKING
RUNNYMEDE
ELMBRIDGE
GUILDFORD
Black Boy Bridge
Weybridge Lock
WEYBRI

BP
BQ
BR
BS
BT
BU
BV
08
09
10
195
OATLANDS PARK
Oatlands Park Hotel
ASHLEY PARK
WALTON-ON-THAMES
BURWOOD PARK
KT12
KT13
105
106
107
108
109
110
111
112
113
114
64
63
62
61
QUEENS ROAD
HERSHAM ROAD
BURWOOD ROAD
OATLANDS DRIVE
A3050
A317
B365
B372
B373
A244
WALTON COMMON
UPPER COMMON
ST. GEORGE'S HILL
ST. GEORGE'S HILL GOLF COURSE
WHITELEY VILLAGE
FLAGSTAFF HOUSE CONFERENCE CENTRE
BURHILL GOLF COURSE
NEW BURHILL GOLF COURSE
214
RIVER MOLE
SEVEN HILLS ROAD
NOTRE DAME CONVENT
Seven Hills Estate
Walton Firs Scout Camp
Beards Hill
Strawberry Hill
Dick Turpin's Cottage
Norwood Farm
Hook's Corner
OLD COMMON
BYFLEET ROAD
A245
ESHER ROAD
PORTSMOUTH ROAD
A307
A3
COBHAM HOSP
FOXHOLM COVERT
SILVER MERE
SILVERMERE GOLF COURSE
DRIVING RANGE
KT11
Hilton National Cobham
Heyswood Girl Guide Camp
THE BROOM
PAINSHILL PARK
229
THE LAKE
WHEEL ISLAND
Red Hill
Oak Pollard
COBHAM
STOKE ROAD
RIVER HILL
MILL RD
Cobham Court
HIGH ST
BETWEEN STREETS
Cricket Ground
Football Grd
Youth Cen
Running Mare PH

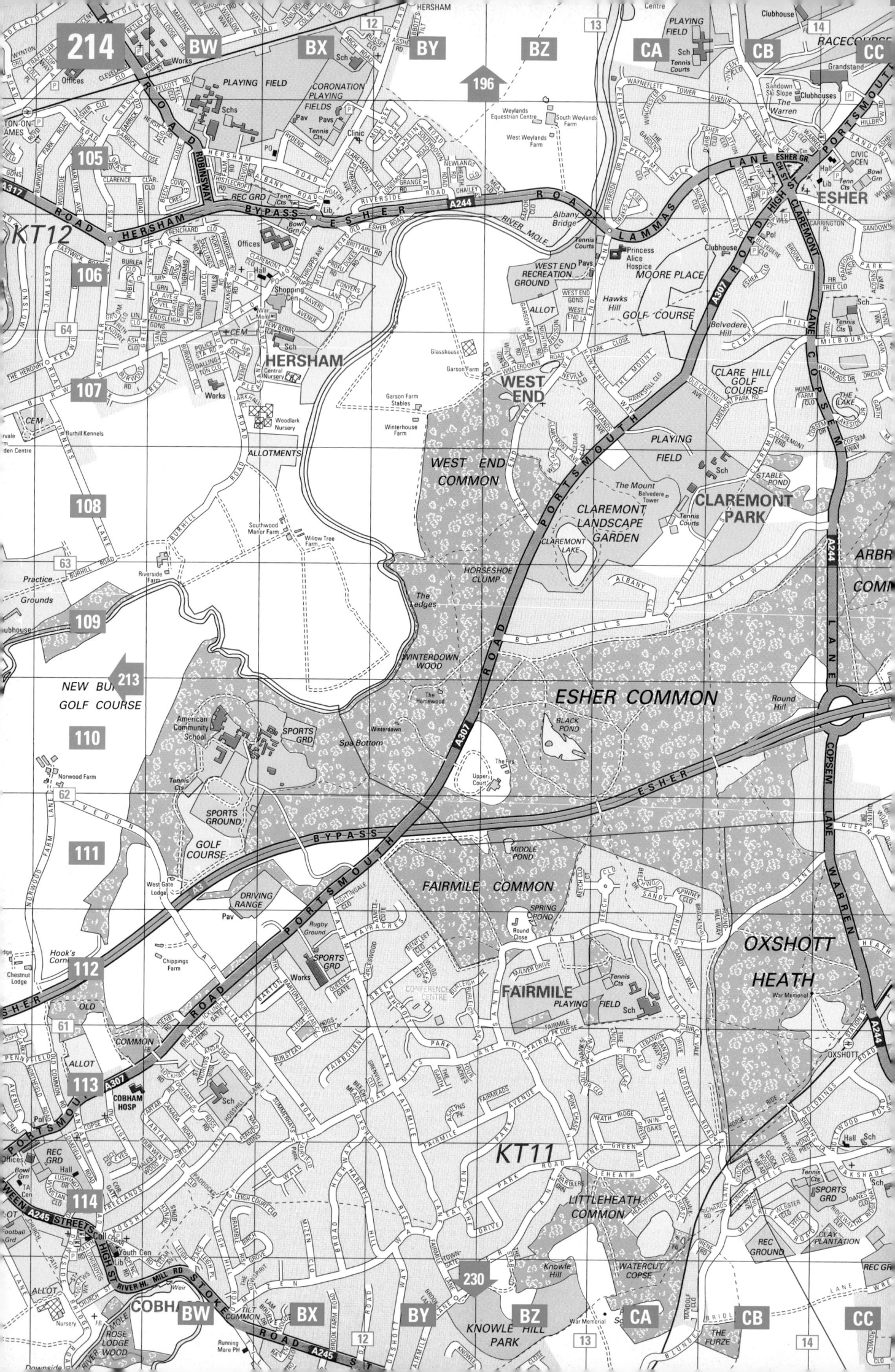
HERSHAM
ESHER
WEST END
CLAREMONT PARK
CLAREMONT LANDSCAPE GARDEN
ESHER COMMON
WEST END COMMON
FAIRMILE COMMON
FAIRMILE
OXSHOTT HEATH
LITTLEHEATH COMMON
KNOWLE HILL PARK
COBHAM
KT12
KT11
NEW BURHILL GOLF COURSE
AMERICAN COMMUNITY SCHOOL
PORTSMOUTH ROAD
ESHER BYPASS
HERSHAM ROAD
A307
A244
A245
A3
196
213
230

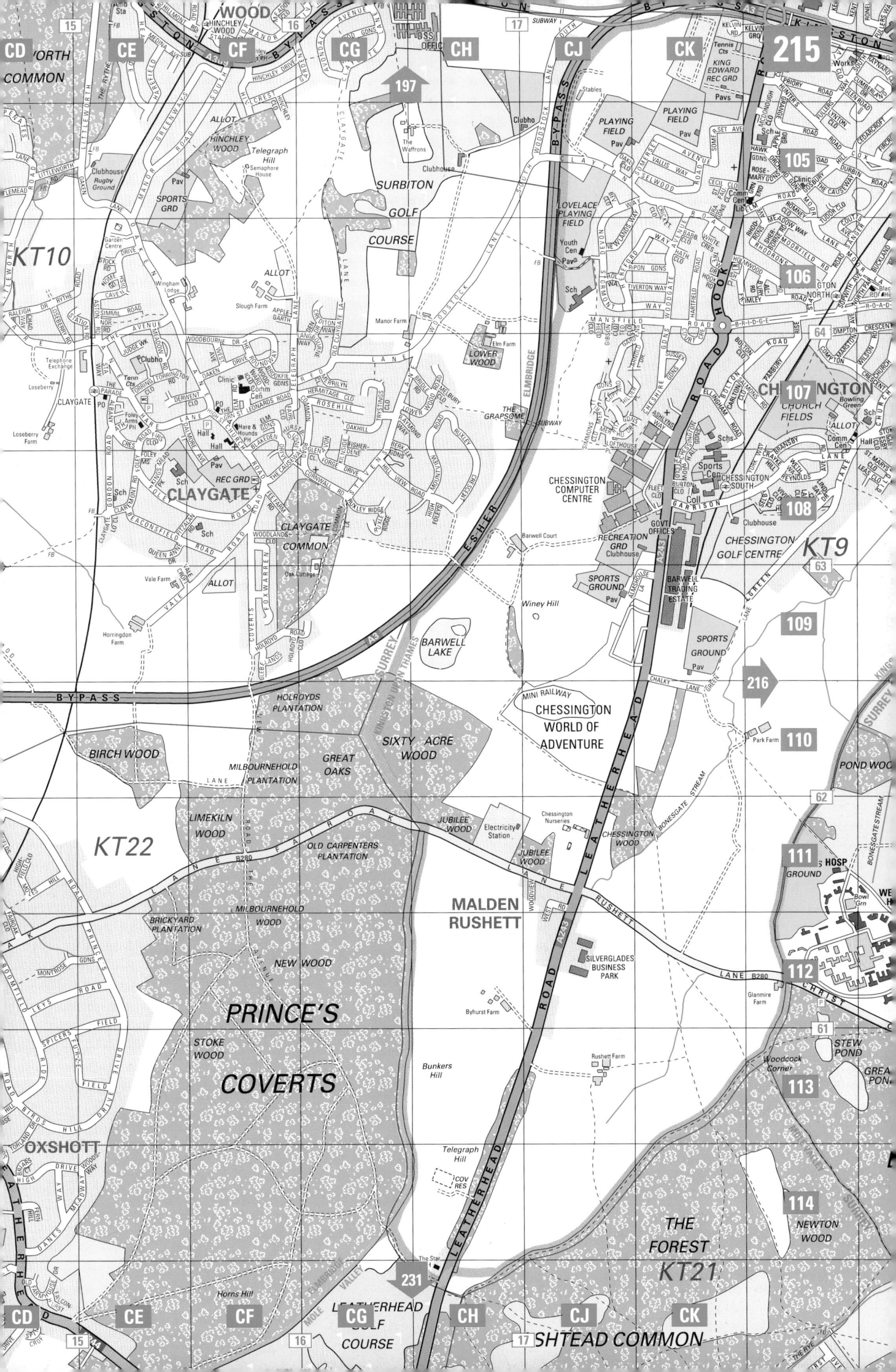
215
197
216
231
CD
CE
CF
CG
CH
CJ
CK
15
16
17
105
106
107
108
109
110
111
112
113
114
64
63
62
61
KT10
KT9
KT22
KT21
WOOD
HINCHLEY WOOD
KINGSTON BYPASS
COMMON
LITTLEWORTH
Clubhouse
Rugby Ground
ALLOT
HINCHLEY WOOD
Telegraph Hill
Semaphore House
SPORTS GRD
Pav
The Waffrons
Clubhouse
SURBITON GOLF COURSE
Clubho
PLAYING FIELD
KING EDWARD REC GRD
Tennis Cts
Pavs
LOVELACE PLAYING FIELD
Youth Cen
Sch
Garden Centre
Wingham Lodge
Slough Farm
Manor Farm
Elm Farm
LOWER WOOD
Telephone Exchange
Loseberry
CLAYGATE
Loseberry Farm
Clubho
Tenn Cts
Foley Arms PH
Clinic
Comm Cen
Hare & Hounds PH
Hall
REC GRD
Pav
Sch
CLAYGATE
CLAYGATE COMMON
Oak Cottage
Vale Farm
ALLOT
Horringdon Farm
THE GRAPSOME
ELMBRIDGE
SUBWAY
ESHER BYPASS
CHESSINGTON COMPUTER CENTRE
Barwell Court
RECREATION GRD
Clubhouse
GOVT OFFICES
SPORTS GROUND
Pav
BARWELL TRADING ESTATE
Coll
Sports Cen
CHESSINGTON SOUTH
Clubhouse
CHESSINGTON GOLF CENTRE
CHESSINGTON
CHURCH FIELDS
Bowling Green
Winey Hill
BARWELL LAKE
SPORTS GROUND
Pav
CHALKY LANE
HOLROYDS PLANTATION
SURREY
KINGSTON UPON THAMES
SIXTY ACRE WOOD
MINI RAILWAY
CHESSINGTON WORLD OF ADVENTURE
Park Farm
BIRCH WOOD
MILBOURNEHOLD PLANTATION
GREAT OAKS
LIMEKILN WOOD
OLD CARPENTERS PLANTATION
JUBILEE WOOD
Electricity Station
Chessington Nurseries
JUBILEE WOOD
CHESSINGTON WOOD
BONESGATE STREAM
POND WOOD
FAIROAK LANE
B280
MALDEN RUSHETT
RUSHETT LANE
BRICKYARD PLANTATION
MILBOURNEHOLD WOOD
SILVERGLADES BUSINESS PARK
NEW WOOD
Byhurst Farm
Glanmire Farm
PRINCE'S COVERTS
STOKE WOOD
Rushett Farm
Bunkers Hill
STEW POND
Woodcock Corner
LEATHERHEAD ROAD
A243
OXSHOTT
Telegraph Hill
COV RES
THE FOREST
NEWTON WOOD
The Star
Horns Hill
MOLE VALLEY
LEATHERHEAD GOLF COURSE
ASHTEAD COMMON

216
CL
CM
CN
CP
CQ
CR
CS
198
215
232
19
20
21
105
106
107
108
109
110
111
112
113
114
64
63
62
61
KINGSTON BYPASS
KING GEORGES FIELD
HOOK RISE SOUTH IND PK
KING GEORGE'S TRADING EST
KING EDWARD REC GRD
SPORTS GROUND
COX LANE
HOOK ROAD
A243
MANSFIELD ROAD
CHESSINGTON NORTH
CHESSINGTON
CHURCH FIELDS
KT9
CHESSINGTON SOUTH
CHESSINGTON GOLF CENTRE
BARWELL BUSINESS PARK
CHALKY LANE
LEATHERHEAD ROAD
CHESSINGTON WOOD
Park Farm
Castle Hill
Earthworks
BUTCHERS GROVE
HORTON PARK COUNTRY CLUB GOLF COURSE
GREAT WOOD
HOOK ARENA SPORTS GROUND
KINGSTON UPON THAMES
EPSOM & EWELL
SURREY
FOUR ACRE WOOD
HORTON COUNTRY PARK
POND WOOD
Bonesgate Stream
KT19
ST. EBBA'S HOSPITAL
HORTON
Horton Park Children's Farm
LONG GROVE
Hospital Closed
SPORTS GROUND
EPSOM & EWELL NEW COTTAGE HOSP
WEST PARK HOSPITAL
CHRIST CHURCH ROAD
Horton Lane
HOGSMILL RIVERSIDE OPEN SPACE
KING GEORGE V REC GRD
WEST EWELL
PLAYING FIELD
RUXLEY LANE
CHESSINGTON ROAD
B284
OLD HALEYBURIANS R.F.C.
WORCESTER PARK
NONSUCH INDUSTRIAL ESTATE
LONGMEAD BUSINESS PARK
COURT REC GRD
WEST STREET
HIGH STREET
UPPER HIGH STREET
TOWN HALL
SOUTH STREET
ASHLEY AVENUE
ASHLEY CENTRE
KT18
MOUNTHILL GDNS
ROSEBERY PARK
EPSOM
EPSOM COMMON
STEW POND
GREAT POND
Woodcock Corner
NEWTON WOOD
FOREST
KT21
DORKING ROAD
A24
ASHTEAD COMMON
THE GREENWAY
WOODCOTE GREEN
STAMFORD GRN

217
CT
CU
CV
CW
CX
CY
CZ
22
23
24
KT4
CUDDINGTON REC GRD
STONELEIGH
NORTH CHEAM
SM1
COLLINGWOOD PARK
WEST SUTTON
SM3
CHEAM REC GRD
NONSUCH PARK
Nonsuch Mansion House
OAK PLANTATION
THE WOOD
Diana's Dyke
CHEAM PARK
CHEAM
PERRETS FIELD
SEARS PARK
Sutton Water Services
EWELL BYPASS
LONDON ROAD
EWELL ROAD
CHEAM ROAD
BELMONT RISE
ST. DUNSTAN'S HILL
SM2
EAST EWELL
EWELL
KT17
CUDDINGTON GOLF COURSE
SM7
BANSTEAD DOWNS GOLF COURSE
NORTH LOOE
SURREY
EPSOM & EWELL
SUTTON
REIGATE ROAD
COLLEGE ROAD
FIR TREE ROAD
WINKWORTH ROAD
BRIGHTON ROAD
NORK
EPSOM DOWNS
Epsom College
ALEXANDRA REC GRD
RIFLE RANGE
BANSTEAD
199
218
233
105
106
107
108
109
110
111
112
113
114
64
63
62
61

218
DA
DB
DC
DD
DE
DF
DG
26
27
28
200
217
234
SM1
SM2
SM5
SM7
105
106
107
108
109
110
111
112
113
114
61
62
63
64
COLLINGWOOD PARK
Sutton Utd. FC
ROYSTON PARK
THE WRYTHE REC GRD
Carshalton Athletic FC
THE GROVE
WEST SUTTON
CARSHALTON
SUTTON
CARSHALTON PARK
CARSHALTON WAR MEMORIAL HOSP
CARSHALTON BEECHES
CHEAM
OVERTON PARK REC GRD
HOSP
SUTTON HOSPITAL
ROYAL MARSDEN HOSP
BELMONT
BANSTEAD DOWNS
BANSTEAD COMMON
GOLF COURSE
DOWNVIEW PRISON
HIGHDOWN PRISON
OAKS SPORTS CENTRE GOLF COURSE
Oaks Sports Cen
THE OAKS PARK
LITTLE WOODCOTE
WELLFIELD PLANTATION
PLAYING FIELD
RIFLE RANGE
BANSTEAD
WOODMANSTERNE PARK RECREATION GROUND
SPORTS GROUND
BIG WOOD
RIFFET WOOD
CLOCKHOUSE REC GRD
WOODMANSTERNE
ST. DUNSTAN'S HILL
BELMONT RISE
BRIGHTON ROAD
CARSHALTON ROAD
HIGH STREET
POUND STREET
GROSVENOR
CHEAM ROAD
WOODMANSTERNE ROAD
WOODMANSTERNE LANE
CROYDON LANE
WINKWORTH ROAD
CROYDON ROAD
SUTTON LANE
BANSTEAD ROAD
FREEDOWN LANE
SURREY
SUTTON
REIGATE & BANSTEAD

DH
DJ
DK
DL
DM
DN
DP
201
105
106
107
108
109
110
111
112
113
114
220
235
29
30
31
64
63
62
61
BEDDINGTON
THE GRANGE GARDENS
PARK
CROYDON ROAD
A232
WALLINGTON
SM6
SOUTH BEDDINGTON
BANDON HILL CEMETERY
MELLOWS PARK
SPORTS GROUNDS
ROUNDSHAW PLAYING FIELD
ROUNDSHAW OPEN SPACE
ROUNDSHAW PARK
PURLEY WAY PLAYING FIELDS
PURLEY WAY
CR0
CR2
CR5
CR8
DUPPAS HILL
DUPPAS HILL RD
Tertiary Centre
Croydon Flyover
HALING PARK
SOUTH CROYDON
SOUTH CROYDON REC GRD
STAFFORD CROSS IND EST
Hilton National Hotel
Leisure Cen
Country Club
WOODCOTE
WOODCOTE ROAD
A237
WOODCOTE LANE
FOXLEY LANE
A2022
SUTTON
CROYDON
PURLEY
PURLEY HOSP
ROTARY FIELD
Superstore
GODSTONE ROAD
DOWNS COURT ROAD
MITCHLEY
RIDDLESDOWN WOOD
COOMBE WOOD
FOXLEY WOOD
HIGHER DRIVE REC GRD
REEDHAM
REC GRD
KENLEY
BRIGHTON ROAD
A23
A235
A22
A2030
SMITHAM BOTTOM
SMITHAM
WOODCOTE GROVE REC GRD
WOODCOTE PARK GOLF COURSE
Woodcote Grove House
Orford House
New Lodge
Market Garden
GROVE WOOD HILL
COULSDON COURT
HARTLEY BUSHES

220
DQ
DR
DS
DT
DU
DV
DW
33
34
35
202
105
106
107
108
109
110
111
112
113
114
64
63
62
61
219
236
SHIRLEY PARK
GOLF COURSE
WHITGIFT PLAYING FIELDS
LLOYD PARK
COOMBE PARK
SPORTS GROUND
PLAYING FIELD
Coombe Farm
Oaks Farm
Geoffrey Harris Ho
Coombe Lodge
Central Nursery
COOMBE WOOD
ADDINGTON
BALLARDS PLANTATION
Cottage in the Woods
Sports Hall
Open Air Pool
SPORTS GROUND
Clubhouse
REC GRD
PARK HILL
The Water Tower
DUPPAS HILL
Croydon Flyover
HALING PARK
SOUTH CROYDON
CR0
Haling Cottage
War Memorial
Leisure Cen
Amb Sta
Comm Cen
PURLEY WAY PLAYING FIELDS
SPORTS GROUND
HALING GROVE
SOUTH CROYDON REC GRD
COV RES
SANDERSTEAD
PURLEY OAKS
Royal Oak Ho
Red Deer PH
Blue Anchor PH
Swan & Sugar Loaf PH
CROHAM HURST
CROHAM HURST GOLF COURSE
Breakneck Hill
Tumulus
THRIFT WOOD
LITTLEHEATH WOODS
Hook's Hill
DAYS ACRE
SANDERSTEAD
SANDERSTEAD PLANTATION
CR2
SELSDON PARK HOTEL GOLF COURSE
Selsdon Park Hotel
SPORTS GRD
NEWLANDS WOOD
PURLEY BEECHES
PURLEY DOWNS GOLF COURSE
ROTARY FIELD
PURLEY HOSP
PURLEY
RIDDLESDOWN
RIDDLESDOWN WOOD
COOMBES WOOD
Keepers Cottage
MITCHLEY WOOD
RAGGED WOOD
AINSLEY BERRY SHAW
KINGS WOOD
CR8
FOXLEY WOOD
HIGHER DRIVE REC GRD
KENLEY
SPORTS GROUND
SURREY
TANDRIDGE
COOMBE ROAD
A212
BRIGHTON ROAD
A235
SELSDON ROAD
B275
ADDINGTON ROAD
A2022
RECTORY PARK
MITCHLEY AVENUE
SANDERSTEAD ROAD
B269
GODSTONE ROAD
DOWNS COURT ROAD
PURLEY DOWNS ROAD
CROHAM ROAD
CROHAM VALLEY ROAD
UPPER SELSDON ROAD
LIMPSFIELD ROAD
PARK LANE
HIGH ST
SOUTH END
PARK HILL
A2039
A232
A23
PURLEY WAY

DX
DY
DZ
EA
EB
EC
ED
36
37
38
203
105
106
107
108
109
110
111
112
113
114
222
237
64
63
62
61
BR4
CR0
CR6
FOXES WOOD
PINEWOODS
ADDINGTON GOLF COURSE
Clubhouse
KENNEL WOOD
THREEHALFPENNY WOOD
SPRING PARK
PLAYING FIELD
SPARROWS DEN PLAYING FIELDS
Old Beccehamian R.F.C.
CONEY HALL REC GRD
BURIAL GRD
Schiller Internat Univers
EMMAUS CONF. CENTRE
Pumping Station
Shirley Wanderers R.F.C.
Rugby Grd
Fox Hill
FOXHILL SHAW
BIRCH WOOD
ADDINGTON
ADDINGTON PALACE GOLF COURSE
Addington Palace Sports Centre
Addington Palace (Royal Sch of Church Music)
ADDINGTON PARK
Pavilion
ADDINGTON VILLAGE
The Cricketers Inn
KENT GATE WAY
ADDINGTON ROAD
A2022
A212
GRAVEL HILL
ROWDOWN FIELDS
SPORTS GROUND
BROMLEY
CROYDON
CASTLE HILL RUFFS
BRADMANSHILL WOOD
Micklenam Way Electricity Sta
NEW ADDINGTON
ROWDOWN WOOD
ADDINGTON VALE
SELSDON PARK ROAD
FALCONWOOD MEADOW
Featherbed Lane Water Works
FORESTDALE
Clubhouse
REC GRD
KING HENRY'S DRIVE
NORTH DOWN REC GRD
PARKWAY
Health Cen
Resource Cen
Comm Cens
Swim Pool
Mkt
Lib
Sports Centre
SPORTS GROUND
SELSDON WOOD NT
STEVEN'S LARCH
ADDINGTON COURT (PUBLIC) GOLF COURSE
BEARS WOOD
(Scout Camp)
TANDRIDGE
SURREY
FRITH WOOD
BIRCHEN SHAW
MILNE PARK
Clubhouse
SPORTS GROUND
Croydon R.F.C.
THREECORNER GROVE
GREENHILL SHAW
HILLOCKS WOOD
BROOM WOOD
PUPLET WOOD
Haggler's Dean
Farleigh Dean
FRYLANDS WOOD
(Scout Camp)
FARLEIGH COURT GOLF COURSE
DUMPSEY DERRY
CRAB WOOD
CHAPEL HILL
LIMEKILN SHAW
COLDBLOW SHAW
BOGRAMS WOOD
BEECHES SHAW
WELLS SHAW
HODGE GROVE
HOGCROFT SHAW
Elm Farm
Farleigh House Farm
Farleigh Court
North Lodge
South Lodge
Fairchildes Farm
White Bear Inn PH
Fickleshole Farm
Cox's Cottage
MOSSYHILL SHAW
FARLEIGH
Farleigh Cottages
Farleigh Court Manor House
Little Farleigh Green Farm
LITTLE FARLEIGH GREEN
LITTLE GREAT HILL
OAKEN SHAW
MOSESHILL SHAW
GT FARLEIGH GRN
GREAT PARK WOOD
Scotshall Farm
FIVE ACRE SHAW
Harrow Inn PH
WARLINGHAM PARK HOSPITAL

EE
EF
EG
EH
EJ
EK
EL
40
41
42
HAYES
COMMON
GLEBE WAY
CROYDON ROAD
WICKHAM COMMON
COLYERS WOOD
204
BR4
SPARROWS DEN PLAYING FIELDS
A2022
R.F.C.
CONEY HALL REC GRD
Schiller International University
Sec Sch
EMMAUS CONF. CENTRE
BURIAL GRD
105
106
107
108
109
110
111
112
113
114
QUEENSWAY
KINGSWAY
CHURCH DRIVE
LAYHAMS ROAD
HARVEST BANK RD
ROBINS GRO
HARTFIELD CRESCENT
LAWRENCE RD
Prim Sch
MONARCH CL
HAWTHORN DRIVE
CHESTNUT AVE
BIRCH TREE AVENUE
CHERRY TREE WALK
LIME TREE WALK
SYLVAN WAY
WELL WOOD
GATES GREEN ROAD
Rouse Farm
Hast Hill
The Lodge
BASTON MANOR ROAD
Baston Manor
WEST COMMON ROAD
BASTON ROAD
COMMONSIDE
Keston Court Riding Stables
PADMALL WOOD
RAVENSBOURNE OPEN SPACE
KESTON COMMON
FOREST DRIVE
LAKES ROAD
HEATHFIELD
KESTON AV
FISHPONDS ROAD
Keston
The Fox PH
FOX LANE
LEAFY GROVE
WESTERHAM ROAD
A233
Earthworks
War Meml
Caesar's Camp
Holwood
Redwood
Seismograph Services Co H.
Cricket Ground
64
63
62
61
BROMLEY
CROYDON
LONG SHAW
COOPER'S WOOD
Elm Farm
Raithes Organic Worm Farm
ALLOT
JACKASS LANE
Foxhill Farm
JACKASS SHAW
Fortune Bank Farm
Nash Farm
Longfield Cottage
NASH LANE
North Pole Farm
NORTH POLE LANE
Layham's Cattery
FULLER'S WOOD
JAMES'S WOOD
Stables
BR2
War Bank
CASTLE HILL RUFFS
BRADMANSHILL WOOD
Five Oaks Equestrian Centre
RUSHFIELD SHAW
BROOMFIELDBANK SHAW
Mickleham Way Electricity Sta
Keston Court Farm
RECTORY ROAD
Scout Camp
Milchden
CHURCH ROAD
Glebe Farm
DOWNE ROAD
Keston Fruit Farm
BLACKNESS LANE
Leaves Green
Metropolitan Police Dog Training Centre
NEW ADDINGTON
ROWDOWN WOOD
Comm Cen
Prim Schs.
Pitch 'n' Putt
HENRY'S AVENUE
KESTREL WAY
Layham's Farm
Racing Circuit
Kimberley Farm
ADDINGTON VALE
221
VULCAN WAY
Works
Gas Works
The Vale Farm
Resource Cen
FURZE BOTTOM
Prim Schs.
Crown Inn PH
Clubhouse
SPORTS GROUND
Holmshaw Farm
HOPPERSNATCH SHAW
Greyhound Training Kennels
Bradmore
Greenacres Riding School
LEAVES GREEN ROAD
Colinette Farm
High House Farm
ASHMORE LANE
Milking Lane Farm
MILKING LANE
The Kings Arms PH
Clubhouse
ARNHEM DRIVE
UVEDALE
MILNE PARK
MILNE PARK EAST
MILNE PARK WEST
FAIRCHILDES AVENUE
Higham's Hill
Highams Hill Farm
Croydon R.F.C.
TERMINAL
HELIPAD
Prim Sch
Sec Sch
THREECORNER GROVE
SHEEPBARN LANE
MORTIMER ROAD
KEITH PARK
GRICE AV
HANBURY DR
CHAPEL HILL
JEWELS WOOD
JEWELS HILL
SALT BOX HILL
REC GRD
Barracks (Disused)
Hangars
LONDON BIGGIN HILL AIRPORT
BOGRAMS WOOD
North Lodge
South Lodge
Fairchildes Farm
White Bear Inn PH
FAIRCHILDES LANE
BLACKMANS LANE
Blackman's Cottages
Cox's Cottage
CR6
OAKLANDS LANE
MAIN ROAD
A233
TN16
Hangars
CUDHAM LODGE WOODS
SOW WOOD
CHURCH HILL
TANDRIDGE
SURREY
BROMLEY
SKID HILL LANE
238
Skid Hill House
Hill Farm
AIRPORT INDUSTRIAL ESTATE
BIGGIN HILL BUSINESS PARK
Hangar
VICTOR
CHRISTY ROAD
SUNNINGVALE
GREAT HILL SHAW
FIVE ACRE SHAW
MIDDLEY
LITTLE EAT HILL
Costains Farm

223
FARNBOROUGH
FARNBOROUGH HOSPITAL
ORPINGTON HOSPITAL
FARNBOROUGH COMMON
SEVENOAKS WAY
SEVENOAKS ROAD
HIGH STREET
Green Street Green
BR6
HIGH ELMS GOLF COURSE
Clubhouse
Downe
DARWIN MUSEUM
Hazelwood
TN14
NEW YEARS WOOD
Single Street
Cudham
CUCKOO WOOD
WHITELANDS WOOD
NINHAMS WOOD
BROOM BANK
DOWNE BANK (NATURE RESERVE)
205
224
239
A21
A223
B2158

ORPINGTON BYPASS
A224
A21
A223
COURT ROAD
SEVENOAKS ROAD
SEVENOAKS WAY
FARNBOROUGH WAY
HIGH STREET
CHELSFIELD
BR6
PRATT'S BOTTOM
CHELSFIELD DOWN GOLF COURSE
BROKE HILL GOLF COURSE
CHELSFIELD PARK HOSPITAL
Maypole
KNOCKHOLT
HALSTEAD
Knockholt Pound
Singles Cross
NEW YEARS WOOD
HIGH WOOD
PERRY WOOD
CHARM WOOD
RUSHMOOR HILL WOOD
DEERLEAP WOOD
PIECE WOOD
LITTLE MOLLOMS WOOD
FOXBERRY WOOD
HOMEFIELD SPRING
GLENTRAMMON REC GRD
SPORTS GRD
PLAYING FIELD
EU
EV
EW
EX
EY
EZ
FA
206
223
240

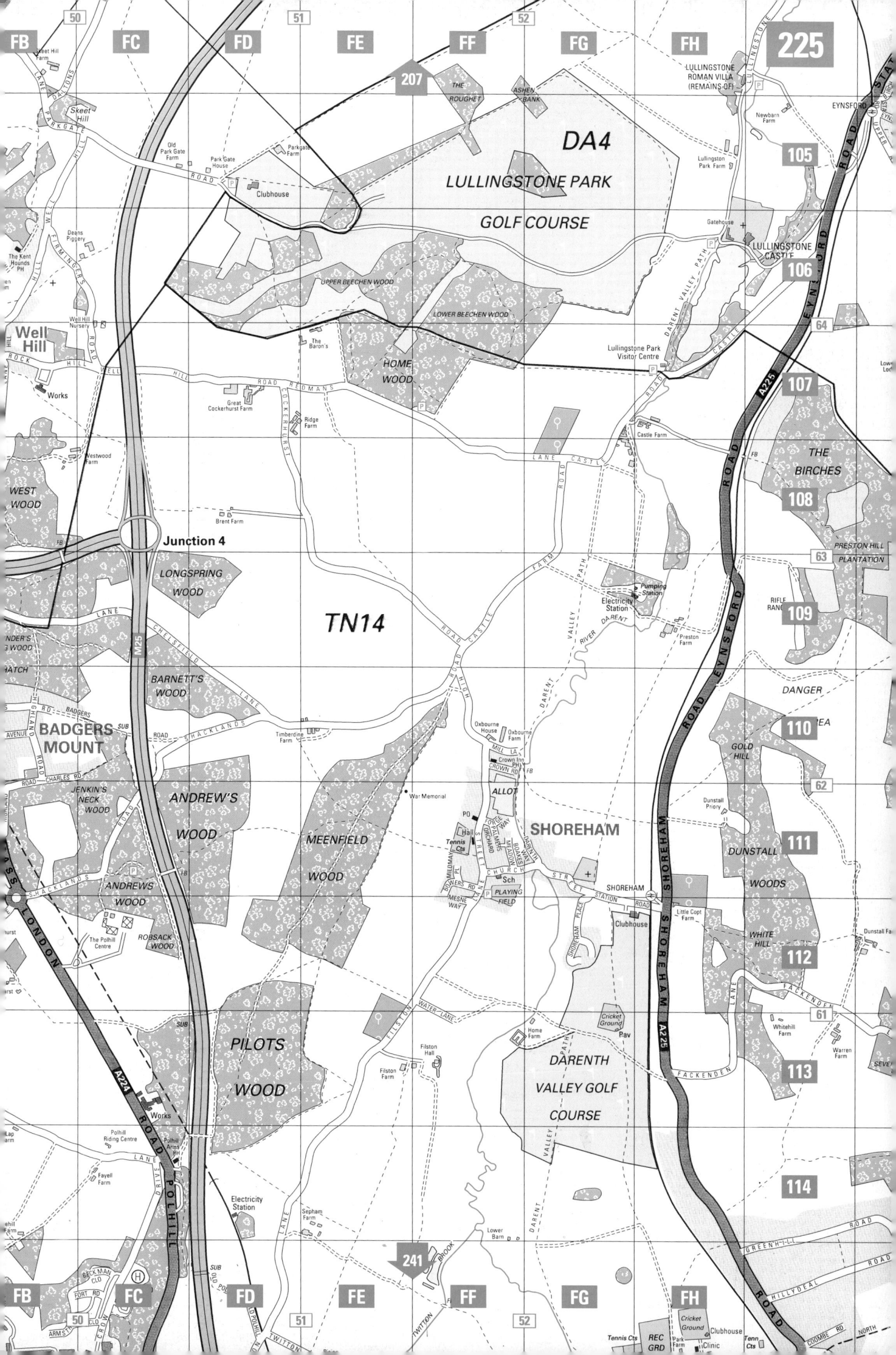

207
DA4
LULLINGSTONE PARK
GOLF COURSE
LULLINGSTONE ROMAN VILLA (REMAINS OF)
EYNSFORD
Newbarn Farm
Lullingston Park Farm
Gatehouse
LULLINGSTONE CASTLE
DARENT VALLEY PATH
Lullingstone Park Visitor Centre
THE ROUGHET
ASHEN BANK
Parkgate Farm
Old Park Gate Farm
Park Gate House
Clubhouse
UPPER BEECHEN WOOD
LOWER BEECHEN WOOD
HOME WOOD
Skeet Hill Farm
Skeet Hill
PARKGATE
Deans Piggery
The Kent Hounds PH
Well Hill Nursery
Well Hill
Works
The Baron's
REDMANS
Great Cockerhurst Farm
COCKERHURST
Ridge Farm
Castle Farm
CASTLE LANE
Westwood Farm
WEST WOOD
Brent Farm
Junction 4
LONGSPRING WOOD
M25
TN14
Pumping Station
Electricity Station
RIVER DARENT
Preston Farm
THE BIRCHES
PRESTON HILL PLANTATION
RIFLE RANGE
DANGER AREA
GOLD HILL
CHELSFIELD LANE
BARNETT'S WOOD
BADGERS MOUNT
SHACKLANDS ROAD
Timberdine Farm
Oxbourne House
Oxbourne Farm
MILL LA
Crown Inn PH
CROWN RD
ALLOT
War Memorial
JENKIN'S NECK WOOD
ANDREW'S WOOD
MEENFIELD WOOD
SHOREHAM
Dunstall Priory
DUNSTALL WOODS
PO
Hall
Tennis Cts
CHURCH STREET
Sch
PLAYING FIELD
MESNE WAY
STATION ROAD
Clubhouse
Little Copt Farm
WHITE HILL
Dunstall Farm
ANDREWS WOOD
The Polhill Centre
ROBSACK WOOD
LONDON ROAD
A224
PILOTS WOOD
FILSTON LANE
WATER LANE
Filston Hall
Filston Farm
Cricket Ground
Pav
Home Farm
DARENTH VALLEY GOLF COURSE
FACKENDEN LANE
Whitehill Farm
Warren Farm
SHOREHAM ROAD
EYNSFORD ROAD
A225
Works
Polhill Riding Centre
Polhill Arms PH
Fayell Farm
POLHILL
Electricity Station
Sepham Farm
Lower Barn
241
GREEN HILL ROAD
HILLYDEAL ROAD
COOMBE RD
BECKMAN CLO
FORT RD
Cricket Ground
Clubhouse
Tennis Cts
REC GRD
Clinic
TWITTON

AS
AT
AU
AV
AW
AX
AY
98
99
00
210
242
GU21
GU24
GU3
CHOBHAM
GOLF COURSE
Clubhouse
115
116
117
118
119
120
121
122
123
124
59
58
57
56
HORSELL COMMON
HORSELL BIRCH
LITTLEWICK COMMON
TRACIOUS COPSE
GOLDSWORTH PARK REC GROUND
GOLDSWORTH PARK TRADING ESTATE
Sports Centre
Goldsworth Park
WATERERS PARK
Knaphill
St. John's
Mount Hermon
Hook Heath
WOKING GOLF COURSE
WOKING CEMETERY
BROOKWOOD LYE
WEST HILL GOLF COURSE
WORPLESDON GOLF COURSE
FISHER'S HILL
SMART'S HEATH
PREY HEATH
Mayford
HOE VALLEY LINEAR PARK
SUTTON GREEN GOLF COURSE
BRIDLEY COPSE
WHITMOOR
WORPLESDON
Burdenshot Hill
Kemishford Bridge
MARLANDS IND EST
LOCKFIELD DRIVE
A324
A320
B380
BASINGSTOKE CANAL
HORSELL IND EST
BUTT'S ROAD IND EST
Pye Hill
Beech Hill
Mayford Centre
SPORTS GROUND
Jackman's Garden Centre
Crastock Manor
Bridley Manor
Bridley Manor Farm
Rickford Mill
Blanketmill
Rye Farm
Hockley Lands
Havering Farm
Suttongreen Nurseries
Briarwood Nursery
Blackhorse Nurseries
Brook Farm
Fishers Hill House
Knaphill Manor Farm
Knaphill Manor
Mink Farm
Westbury Farm
Parley Bridge
Parley Brook Farm
Lantana Nursery
Openwood
Bonnieshott Wood Farm
Loampits Farm

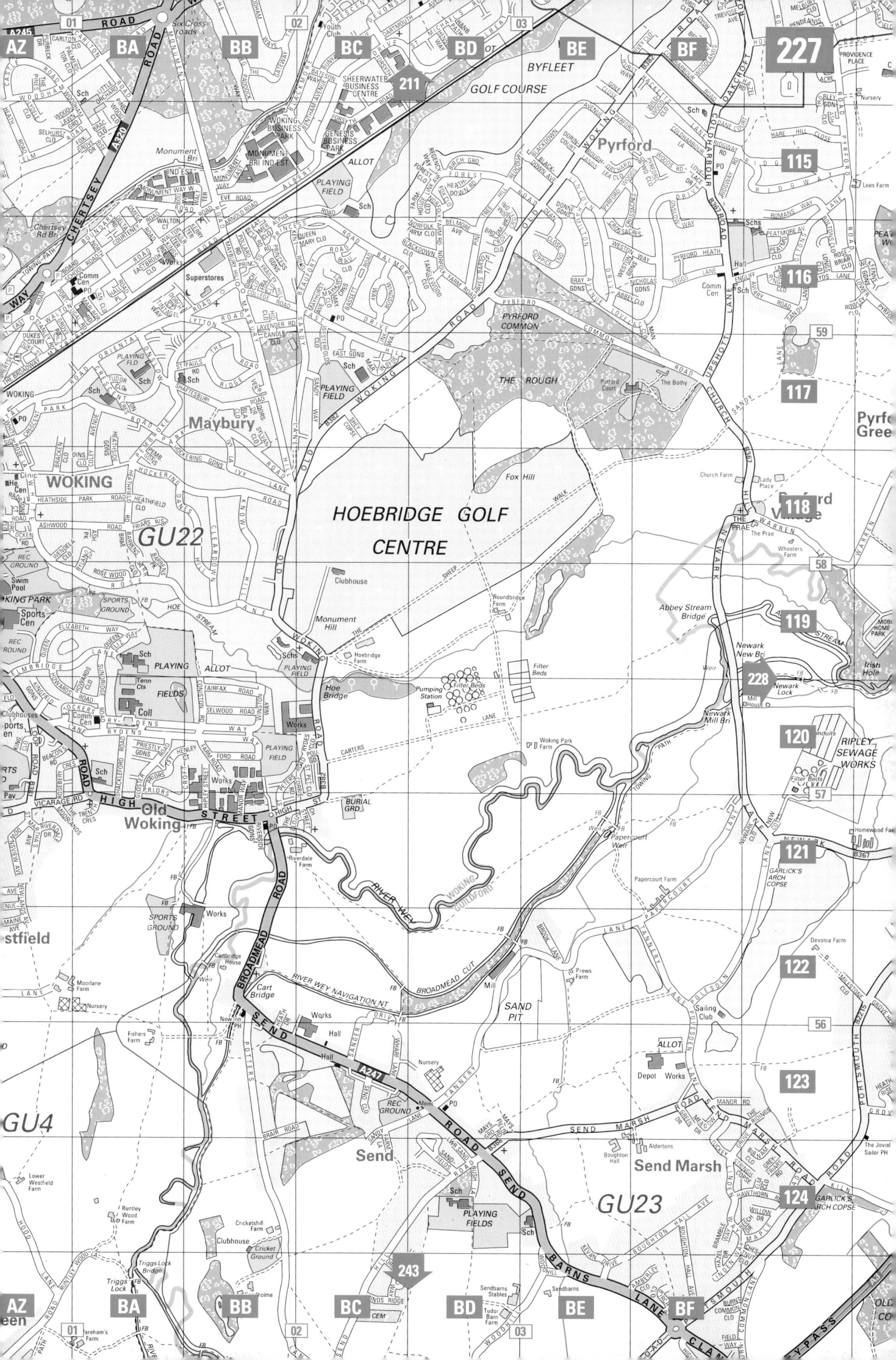

227
211
228
243
AZ
BA
BB
BC
BD
BE
BF
BYFLEET GOLF COURSE
Pyrford
Maybury
WOKING
GU22
HOEBRIDGE GOLF CENTRE
PYRFORD COMMON
THE ROUGH
Old Woking
HIGH STREET
BROADMEAD ROAD
SEND ROAD
SEND BARNS LANE
RIVER WEY NAVIGATION NT
BROADMEAD CUT
RIVER WEY
Send
Send Marsh
GU23
GU4
RIPLEY SEWAGE WORKS
Newark Lock
Papercourt Weir
Abbey Stream Bridge
Newark New Bri
Newark Mill Bri
SAND PIT
Pyrford Village
Woking Business Park
Sheerwater Business Centre
Genesis Business Park
Monument Bri Ind Est
Six Cross-roads
Chertsey Rd Bri
Superstores
Fox Hill
Clubhouse
Monument Hill
Hoe Bridge
Pumping Station
Filter Beds
Cart Bridge
Triggs Lock
Garlick's Arch Copse
PORTSMOUTH ROAD
A320
A245
A247
B367
B382
B368
B2215
115
116
117
118
119
120
121
122
123
124
01
02
03
56
57
58
59

228
BYFLEET
BG
BH
BJ
BK
BL
BM
BN
05
06
07
212
KT14
Murray's Bridge
Dodd's Bridge
PROVIDENCE PLACE
Clubhouse
Nursery
COMMON MEADOWS
RIVER WEY
BUXTON WOOD
M25
WOKING
GUILDFORD
115
116
117
118
119
120
121
122
123
124
59
58
57
56
Lees Farm
PEATMOOR WOOD
PYRFORD MARINA
LOCK COPSE
The Anchor PH
Pyrford Lock
Sewage Works
Filter Beds
Church Farm
Wisley Bridge
Wisley Bri
Wisley
SPORTS GRD
Tennis Cts
Deers Farm
COLDHARBOUR ROAD
RIDGWAY
Schs
Hall
Comm Cen
Sch
Hospital (Closed)
Pyrford Place Farm
PYRFORD
THE WISLEY
GOLF COURSE
Clubhouse
DRIVING RANGE
Wren's Nest Pinetum
WISLEY
COMMON
Pyrford Court
GU22
Pyrford Green
Green Farm
GOLF
Clubhouse
COURSE
Home Farm
Pyrford Place
Aberconway House
WISLEY GARDEN (RHS)
Glasshouse
Battleston Hill
Glasshouses
OCKHAM COMMON
Elm Corner
DISUSED AI
Church Farm
Lady Place
Pyrford Village
The Prae
Wheelers Farm
Ockham Mill Farm
Nursery
Ockham Mill
Walsham Lock
WALSHAM PLANTATION
Weir
MOBILE HOME PARK
Abbey Stream
ABBEY STREAM
Newark New Bri
Irish Hole
227
Newark Lock
Mill House
Newark Mill Bri
WALSHAM MEADOW
Stratford Bridge
Nutberry Fruit Farm
Dunsborough Farm
Dunsborough Park
RIPLEY GREEN
Conduits
RIPLEY SEWAGE WORKS
Filter Beds
SPORTS GRD
The Half Moon PH
PORTSMOUTH ROAD
BYPASS
Old Rectory Farm
Chestnut Farm
Papercourt Weir
Homewood Farm
NEWARK LANE
B367
HIGH STREET
GARLICK'S ARCH COPSE
Papercourt Farm
Sch
Hall
Pol
Chapel Farm
PLAYING FIELD
Ripley
OCKHAM PARK
Ockham Park House
ALLOT
RIPLEY
A3
PARK WOOD
GU23
Devonia Farm
B2215
B2039
Ockham Park Farm
Sailing Club
Services
Services
Guileshill Farm
ALLOT
Depot
Heath Rise
GROVE HEATH
Grove Heath Farm
The Jovial Sailor PH
LOVELAND'S COPSE
ROBOROW WOOD
BACHELOR'S COPSE
Ryde Farm
Aldertons
Boughton Hall
Send Marsh
SEND MARSH ROAD
GARLICK'S ARCH COPSE
GROVE HEATH CT
HUNGRY HILL
BRAMBLERIDE COPSE
244
Three Bridges
SHEPPARDSGROVE COPSE

229
BP
BQ
BR
BS
BT
BU
BV
08
09
10
213
230
245
115
116
117
118
119
120
121
122
123
124
59
58
57
56
GUILDFORD
Long Orchard Farm
Bramble Hedge Farm
Foxwarren Park
BELT WOOD
Heyswood Girl Guide Camp
THE BROOM
PAINSHILL PARK
Gothic Temple
Grotto
Chinese Bridge
THE LAKE
Wood Hill
WHEEL ISLAND
Red Hill
The Tower
Tower Hill
Oak Pollard
Red Hill
Junction 10
CHATLEY WOOD
Redhill Bottom
Cockrow Hill
Tumulus
Sandpit Hill
Chatley Farm
KT11
CURRIE'S CLUMP
CHATLEY HEATH
THE BOGS
BREACH HILL WOOD
Telegraph Hill
Chatley Semaphore
OCKHAM COMMON
LODGE COPSE
RIVER MOLE
HATCHFORD WOOD
HATCHFORD PARK
HUNT'S COPSE
BRAMBLE WOOD
Poynters Farm
Pointers Grn
LITTLE BRICKFIELD COPSE
BRICKFIELD COPSE
Halfpenny Cross
Cold Norton Farm
Hazeldene Farm
NORTON WOOD
Poultry Houses
The Black Swan PH
Martyr's Green
Pound Farm
ELMBRIDGE
GUILDFORD
Bridge End Farm
Upton Farm
TANNERS COPSE
TRULLIBER COPSE
School Farm
CHAFFERS COPSE
HOOK WOOD
STUMPS GROVE
Barnsthorns
Blackmoor Farm
Slade Farm
BARNSTHORNS WOOD
Blue Ride
THE DRIFT GOLF COURSE
Clubhouse
THE DRIFT
THE FOREST
Broom House
Football Grd
Pav
Tennis Cts
Sch
COBHAM
Cobham Court Farm
Downside Bridge
ROSE LODGE WOOD
Cobham Park Nursery
Works
Cobham Stud Farm
Cossins House
Cossins Farm
Downside
Pondtail Farm
DOWNSIDE COMMON
ALLOT
Hall
BEAUMONT PLANTATION
Highway Farm
New Barn Farm
Bull Riding Farm
OLD OAK COMMON
THE NEW PRESERVE
PEAKED ROUGH
ROUNDABOUT
Hurst Hill
Newmarsh Farm
Gun Club
NEW BARN WOOD
CLAMP ROUGH
BUSHY THICKET
THICKET COPSE
Banks Way House
LITTLE MORNSHILL WOOD
GREAT MORNSHILL WOOD
BANK'S COMMON
The Lord Howard PH
GALLOWS GROVE
KT24
EFFINGHAM JUNCTION
Depot
PO
EFFINGHAM COMMON
Slater's Oak
Norwood Farm
Cricket Grd
Lower Farm
PIKES POOL
Hook Farm
Indian Farm
Running Mare PH
Youth Cen
Football Grd
Cricket Ground
M25
A3
A245
B366
B2039
PORTSMOUTH ROAD
OCKHAM LANE
POINTERS ROAD
OLD LANE
PLOUGH LANE
CHILBROOK ROAD
DOWNSIDE ROAD
HORSLEY ROAD
GOOSE GRN
NORTON LANE
BOOKHAM ROAD
EFFINGHAM COMMON ROAD
LOWER FARM ROAD
DRIFT ROAD
OCKHAM ROAD NORTH
HIGH ST
BETWEEN STREETS
RIVER HILL
MILL RD
STOKE

BW
BX
BY
BZ
CA
CB
CC
12
13
14
214
229
246
115
116
117
118
119
120
121
122
123
124
59
58
57
56
COBHAM
Stoke D' Abernon
Downside
KT11
KT24
KT23
A245
M25
STOKE ROAD
WOODLANDS
HIGH ST
RIVER HI. MILL RD
TILT ROAD
LITTLEHEATH COMMON
KNOWLE HILL PARK
Knowle Hill
WATERCUT COPSE
Polyapes Scout Camp
War Memorial
THE FURZE
REC GROUND
CLAY PLANTATION
SPORTS GRD
THE COPSE
Mast
RECREATION GRD
COBHAM CEM
COBHAM & STOKE D'ABERNON
SPORTS GROUND
Tennis Courts
Pav
Lower Farm
Manor Farm
Garden Centre
Old Parks
Woodland Court Farm
OLD PARKS COPSE
HEATHFIELD COPSE
RIVER MOLE
Weir
Stoke D' Abernon Bridge
ELMBRIDGE
MOLE VALLEY
Slyfield House
Little Slyfield
Slyfield Farm
LITTLE WOOD
BUSHY COPSE
Bookham Lodge Stud
Bookham Lodge
Sheepbell Farm
LADY CHEWTONS WOOD
Barracks Farm
Mark Oak Nursery
ROSE LODGE WOOD
Downside Bridge
Running Mare PH
Elm Farm
Cobham Park Nursery
Works
PARK WOOD
BIG ROUNDABOUT
LITTLE ROUNDABOUT
Cobham Stud Farm
Cossins House
Cossins Farm
DOWNSIDE COMMON
Downside Farm
BEAUMONT PLANTATION
MUGGERIDGE WOOD
WRENS HILL WOOD
New Barn Farm
THORNETS WOOD
SPRING MEADOW WOOD
DOWN WOOD
CHASEMORE WOOD
Chasemore Farm
WITHY BED
Bull Riding Farm
PEAKED
NEW BARN WOOD
HUNDRED POND BRI WOOD
Hundred Pond Bri
Hill Farm
THE BIRCHES
GREAT BOOKHAM COMMON NT
LITTLE BOOKHAM COMMON
BANK'S COMMON NT
Bank's Farm
Isle of White
Manor Cottage
Newmarsh Farm
Gun Club
BUSHY THICKET
THICKET COPSE
Banks Way House
LITTLE MORNSHILL WOOD
GREAT MORNSHILL WOOD
EFFINGHAM JUNCTION
ALLOT
Bookham Tunnel
BOOKHAM
BOOKHAM IND EST
Long Maddox Farm
Slater's Oak
Norwood Farm
Cricket Grd
Lower Farm
PIKES POOL
HERONS REACH
MALLARDS MERE
OAKEN WOOD
Indian Farm
Hook Farm
THORNET WOOD
Little Bookham
GREAT BOOKHAM
Youth Centre
Sch
Hall
PO

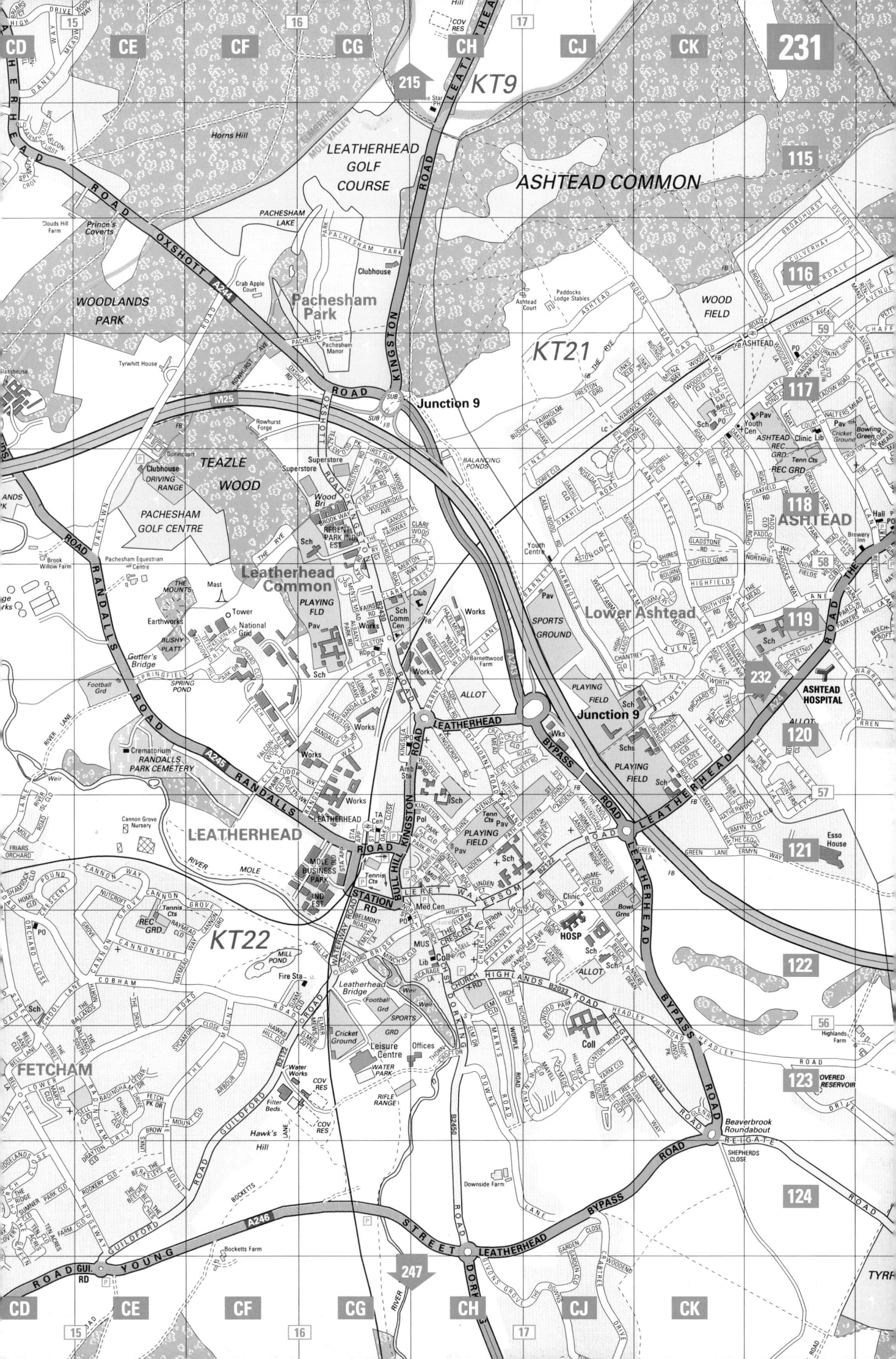

231
CD
CE
CF
CG
CH
CJ
CK
15
16
17
215
KT9
KT21
KT22
247
232
115
116
117
118
119
120
121
122
123
124
59
58
57
56
Horns Hill
LEATHERHEAD GOLF COURSE
ASHTEAD COMMON
PACHESHAM LAKE
Clouds Hill Farm
Prince's Coverts
Crab Apple Court
Clubhouse
Pachesham Park
Pachesham Manor
WOODLANDS PARK
Tyrwhitt House
Ashtead Court
Paddocks Lodge Stables
WOOD FIELD
ASHTEAD
Junction 9
Rowhurst Forge
Dorincourt
Clubhouse
DRIVING RANGE
TEAZLE WOOD
PACHESHAM GOLF CENTRE
Superstore
BALANCING PONDS
ASHTEAD REC GRD
Tenn Cts
Bowling Green
Cricket Ground
ASHTEAD
Brewery Inn
Brook Willow Farm
Pachesham Equestrian Centre
Leatherhead Common
PLAYING FLD
THE MOUNTS
Mast
Tower
National Grid
Earthworks
BUSHY PLATT
Gutter's Bridge
SPRING POND
Football Grd
Youth Centre
SPORTS GROUND
Lower Ashtead
ASHTEAD HOSPITAL
PLAYING FIELD
Barnettwood Farm
ALLOT
Crematorium
RANDALLS PARK CEMETERY
Weir
Cannon Grove Nursery
LEATHERHEAD
RIVER MOLE
MOLE BUSINESS PARK
IND EST
Esso House
FRIARS ORCHARD
REC GRD
Tennis Cts
MILL POND
Fire Sta
Leatherhead Bridge
Football Grd
SPORTS GRD
Cricket Ground
Leisure Centre
Offices
WATER PARK
RIFLE RANGE
Water Works
COV RES
Filter Beds
Hawk's Hill
FETCHAM
HOSP
Coll
Highlands Farm
COVERED RESERVOIR
Beaverbrook Roundabout
SHEPHERDS CLOSE
Downside Farm
Bocketts Farm
M25
A244
A245
A243
A24
A246
B2430
B2122
B2033
B2450
OXSHOTT ROAD
KINGSTON ROAD
RANDALLS ROAD
LEATHERHEAD BYPASS ROAD
LEATHERHEAD ROAD
GUILDFORD ROAD
YOUNG STREET
REIGATE ROAD
HEADLEY ROAD
DORKING ROAD
EPSOM ROAD
HIGHLANDS ROAD
STATION RD
BULL HILL
COBHAM ROAD
ASHTEAD WOODS ROAD

232
EPSOM COMMON
FOREST
NEWTON WOOD
EPSOM
216
EPSOM GENERAL HOSP
DORKING ROAD
A24
THE RYE
WOOD FIELD
ASHTEAD
Ashtead Park
PLAYING FIELDS
City of London Freemen's School
Woodcote
WOODCOTE PARK GOLF COURSE
Woodcote Park Hotel
Woodcote Stud Farm
THE GROVE
THE STREET
EPSOM ROAD
ASHTEAD HOSPITAL
LEATHERHEAD ROAD
Lower Ashtead
231
KT21
KT18
KT22
Langley Vale
LANGLEY BOTTOM WOOD
MOLE VALLEY
EPSOM & EWELL
Chance Farm Stud
Esso House
M25
ADDLESTEAD WOOD
LITTLE HURST WOOD
Tyrrell's Wood
TYRRELL'S WOOD
HEADLEY COURT
HAMBLETON WOOD
HOOK WOOD
GREAT HURST WOOD
COSTAL WOOD
OYSTER HILL NT
NOWER WOOD
248
TYRRELL'S WOOD GOLF COURSE
PIGNUT WOOD
COVERED RESERVOIR
Beaverbrook Roundabout
LEATHERHEAD BYPASS RD
REIGATE ROAD
B2033
Headley
CL CM CN CP CQ CR CS
115 116 117 118 119 120 121 122 123 124
19 20 21

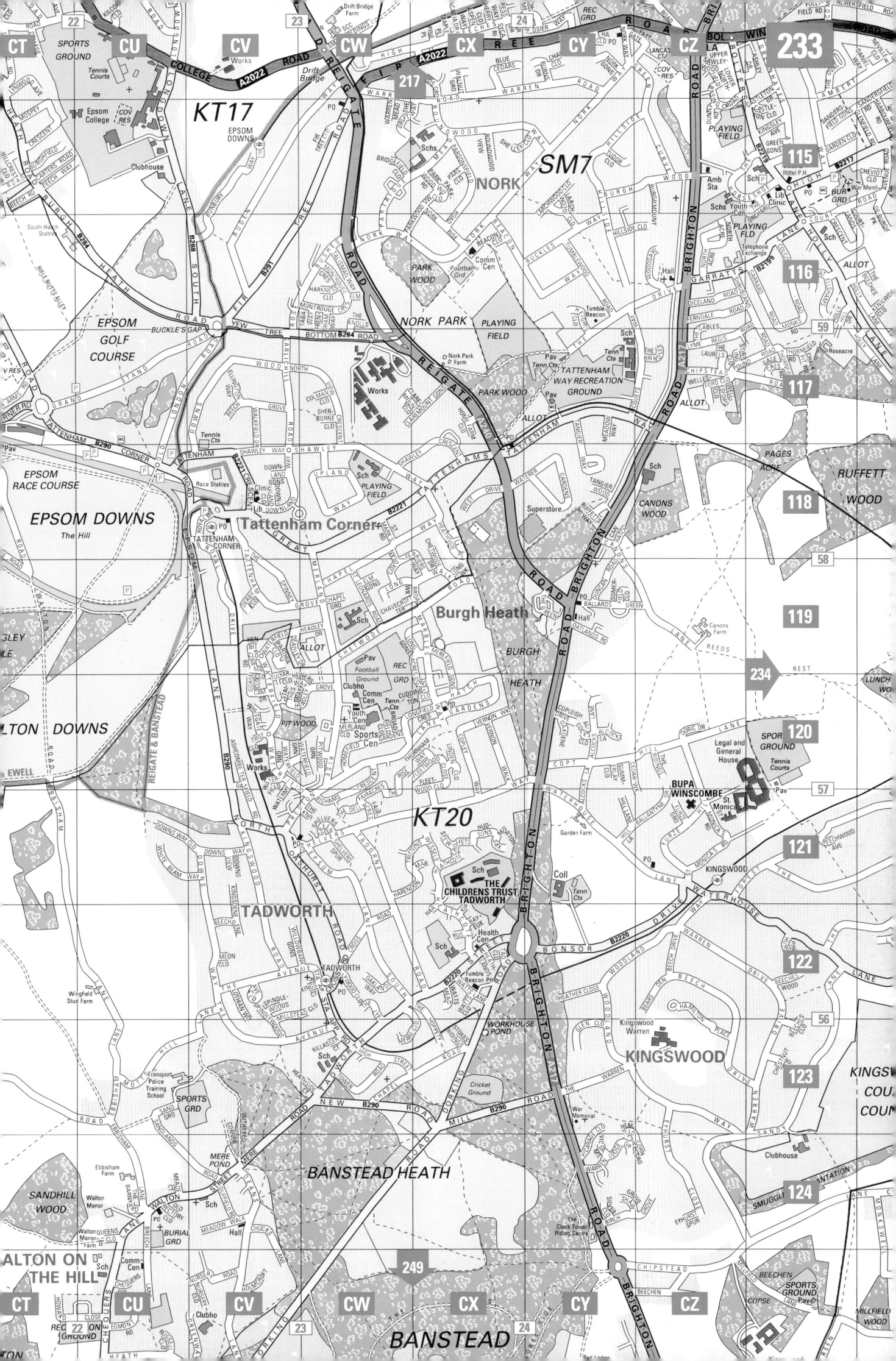
CT
CU
CV
CW
CX
CY
CZ
22
23
24
217
115
116
117
118
119
120
121
122
123
124
59
58
57
56
234
249
KT17
SM7
KT20
NORK
EPSOM DOWNS
The Hill
EPSOM RACE COURSE
EPSOM GOLF COURSE
Epsom College
SPORTS GROUND
BUCKLE'S GAP
NORK PARK
PARK WOOD
PLAYING FIELD
TATTENHAM WAY RECREATION GROUND
Tattenham Corner
TATTENHAM CORNER
Race Stables
Burgh Heath
BURGH HEATH
CANONS WOOD
Canons Farm
PAGES ACRE
RUFFETT WOOD
Superstore
PIT WOOD
Sports Cen
Works
Legal and General House
BUPA WINSCOMBE
St. Monica's
Garden Farm
THE CHILDRENS TRUST TADWORTH
TADWORTH
KINGSWOOD
Kingswood Warren
WORKHOUSE POND
Cricket Ground
BANSTEAD HEATH
BANSTEAD
SANDHILL WOOD
Ebbisham Farm
Walton Manor
Wingfield Stud Farm
Transport Police Training School
MERE POND
BURIAL GRD
The Clock Tower Riding Centre
BEECHEN
SPORTS GROUND
MILLFIELD WOOD
COPSE
Clubhouse
DOWNS
REIGATE ROAD
BRIGHTON ROAD
A217
A2022
A240
B290
B284
B2220
B2221
B291
B288
ALTON ON THE HILL

WINKWORTH ROAD
BANSTEAD
SM7
WOODMANSTERNE
THE SHRUBBERY
SCRATCH WOOD
GREAT SOLOM'S WOOD
PARK DOWNS
RUFFETT WOOD
PAGES ACRE
CANONS WOOD
NATURE RESERVE
BANSTEAD WOOD
FAMES ROUGH
CHIPSTEAD BOTTOM
CHIPHOUSE WOOD
WELL COPSE
LUNCH WOOD
SPORTS GROUND
Legal and General House
KT20
OUTWOOD
OUTWOOD SHAW
Chipstead Bottom
POORFIELD WOOD
CHIPSTEAD GOLF COURSE
CHIPSTEAD MEADS REC GRD
EMBERS SHAW
THE LONG PLANTATION
THE BELT
KINGSWOOD
KINGSWOOD GOLF COURSE AND COUNTRY CLUB
SMUGGLERS PIT PLANTATION
TOP SHAW
ROUND WOOD
THE RUFFETT
RUFFETTS WOOD
Mugswell
MILLFIELD WOOD
BEECHEN COPSE
Kingswood Warren
Eyhurst Park
Eyhurst Farm
Pigeonhouse Farm
Shabden Park
Manor Park
Noke Farm
Reeves Rest
Park Farm
Banstead Place
Courtlands Farm
Mint Farm
Perrotts Farm
Canons Farm
DA
DB
DC
DD
DE
DF
DG
26
27
28
218
233
250
115
116
117
118
119
120
121
122
123
124

235
219
236
251
DH
DJ
DK
DL
DM
DN
DP
29
30
31
115
116
117
118
119
120
121
122
123
124
59
58
57
56
CR8
CR5
CR3
RH1
WOODCOTE PARK GOLF COURSE
COULSDON
Coulsdon South
SMITHAM
KENLEY
COULSDON MANOR GOLF COURSE
HARTLEY BUSHES
Old Coulsdon
GRANGE PARK
FARTHING OR FAIRDEAN DOWNS
POSTERN WOOD
STONYFIELD SHAW
ULLSWATER CRESCENT TRADING ESTATE
MARLFIELD SHAW
STAR SHAW
THREE CORNERED SHAW
DEVILSDEN WOOD
DITCHES SHAW
BOXERS WOOD
HAPPY VALLEY PARK
SPARKLIE WOOD
THE DEVILS DEN
PETERSHOLE SHAW
Star Bridge
Forge Bridge
HOSPITAL (closed)
THE GULLET
NETHERNE WOOD
FIGGS WOOD
BROAD WOOD
PILES WOOD
GRASSCUTS SHAW
LORD'S WOOD
FURZEFIELD WOOD
ALDERSTEAD HEATH
SPARTICLES WOOD
Chaldon
Rook Hill
WILLEY BROOM WOOD
FRYERN BROOM WOOD
HAPPY VALLEY GOLF COURSE
COULSDON COMMON
BETTS MEAD RECREATION GROUND
HOME WOOD
LIFECARE TRUST
Caterham Barracks (closed)
RIFLE RANGES
CROYDON
TANDRIDGE
SURREY
REIGATE & BANSTEAD
BRIGHTON ROAD
WOODCOTE GROVE ROAD A237
Mersham Tunnel
Airshafts
Junction 7

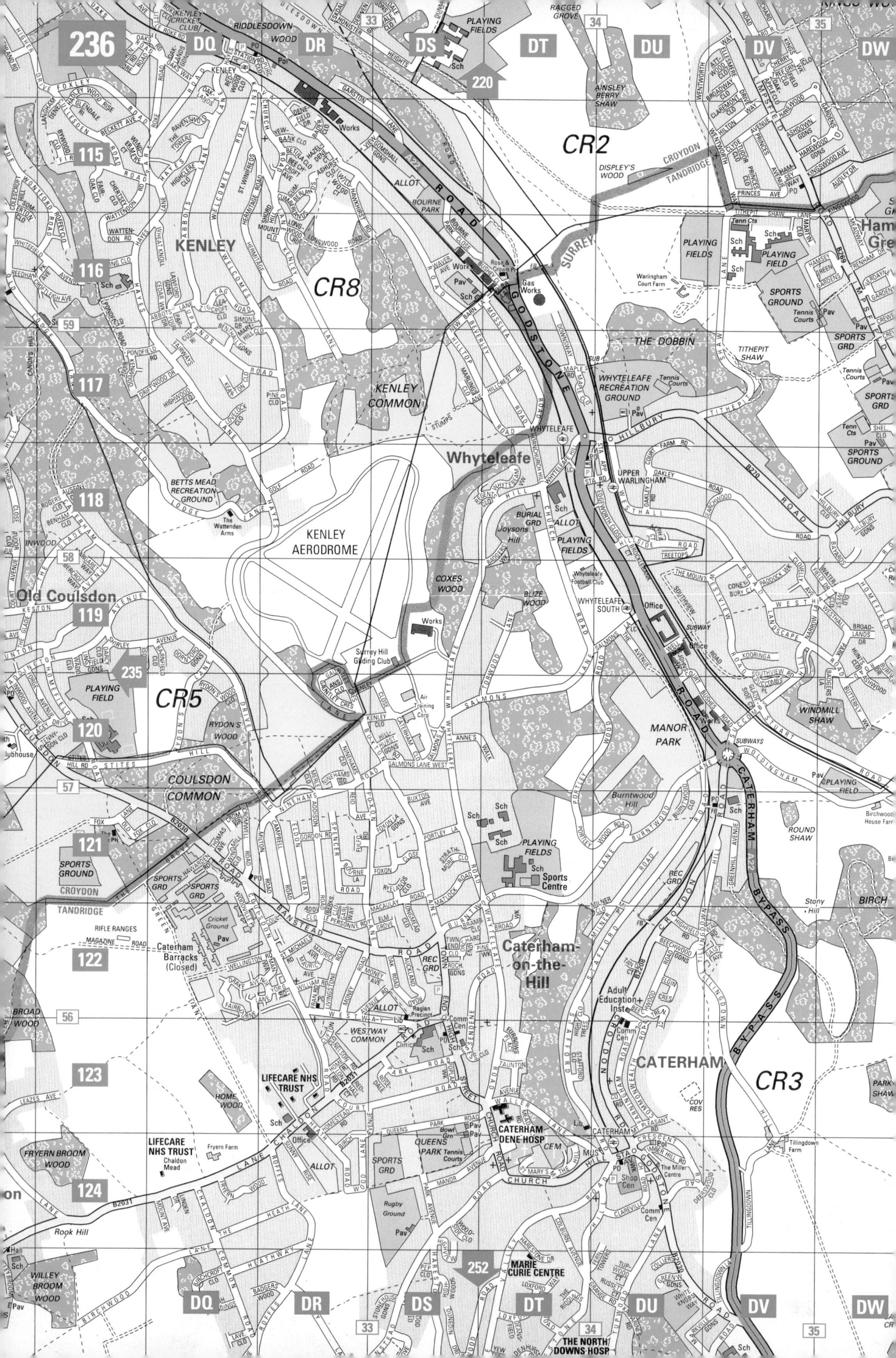

236
DQ
DR
DS
DT
DU
DV
DW
33
34
35
220
235
252
115
116
117
118
119
120
121
122
123
124
59
58
57
56
KENLEY
CR8
CR2
CR5
CR3
RIDDLESDOWN WOOD
PLAYING FIELDS
RAGGED GROVE
AINSLEY BERRY SHAW
DISPLEY'S WOOD
CROYDON
TANDRIDGE
SURREY
BOURNE PARK
KENLEY COMMON
Whyteleafe
WHYTELEAFE
WHYTELEAFE RECREATION GROUND
THE DOBBIN
TITHEPIT SHAW
UPPER WARLINGHAM
Warlingham Court Farm
SPORTS GROUND
BETTS MEAD RECREATION GROUND
The Wattenden Arms
KENLEY AERODROME
Old Coulsdon
COXES WOOD
BLIZE WOOD
Joysons Hill
WHYTELEAFE SOUTH
Whyteleafe Football Club
Surrey Hill Gliding Club
Air Training Corp
RYDON'S WOOD
COULSDON COMMON
MANOR PARK
Burntwood Hill
WINDMILL SHAW
ROUND SHAW
Birchwood House Farm
Stony Hill
BIRCH
RIFLE RANGES
Caterham Barracks (Closed)
Cricket Ground
Caterham-on-the-Hill
WESTWAY COMMON
Raglan Precinct
Sports Centre
Adult Education Inst
CATERHAM
LIFECARE NHS TRUST
HOME WOOD
CATERHAM DENE HOSP
QUEENS PARK
Rugby Ground
BROAD WOOD
FRYERN BROOM WOOD
Fryern Farm
Chaldon Mead
Rook Hill
WILLEY BROOM WOOD
MARIE CURIE CENTRE
THE NORTH DOWNS HOSP
Tillingdown Farm
PARK SHAW
GODSTONE ROAD
CATERHAM BYPASS
A22
B2030
B2031
B270
B269
B2208

FARLEIGH
Chelsham
Woldingham
Garden Village
WOLDINGHAM
CR6
FARLEIGH COURT
GOLF COURSE
GREATPARK WOOD
HOLT WOOD
LITTLEPARK
WOOD
HENLEY
WOOD
DUKE'S DENE
GOLF
COURSE
HALLILOO
PLANTATION
SLINES
OAK
WORMS
HEATH
GREENHILL
SHAW
WHISTLERS
WOOD
TITSEY
PLANTATIO
LUMBERDINE
WOOD
ASHEN
SHAW
HONEYOAK
WOOD
NORTH
DOWNS
GOLF
COURSE
CHALK PITS
221
238
253
115
116
117
118
119
120
121
122
123
124
DX
DY
DZ
EA
EB
EC
ED

238
EE
EF
EG
EH
EJ
EK
EL
222
237
254
AIRPORT
BIGGIN HILL
CR6
CR3
RH8
Titsey
SURREY
TANDRIDGE
BROMLEY
MOLLARDS WOOD
OWLS WOOD
HONEYOAK WOOD
LUMBERDINE WOOD
ASHEN SHAW
PITCHERS WOOD
TITSEY PLANTATION
LONG COPPICE
ROUND WOOD
PARK WOOD GOLF COURSE
LIMEHOUSE BOTTOM
WESTMORE GREEN
BEAVER WATER WORLD
SPORTS GRD
CLARKSLANE SHAW
COLDHARBOUR BEECHES
HIGH TREES
Botley Hill
BIGGIN HILL BUS. PK
AIRPORT IND EST
BIGGIN HILL CEM
REC GRD
A233
MAIN ROAD
CROYDON ROAD
B269
CLARKS LANE
TITSEY HILL
PILGRIMS LANE
BEDDLESTEAD LANE
HESIERS ROAD
NORHEADS LANE
LUSTED HALL LANE
SUNNINGVALE AVENUE
115
116
117
118
119
120
121
122
123
124
40
41
42
56
57
58
59

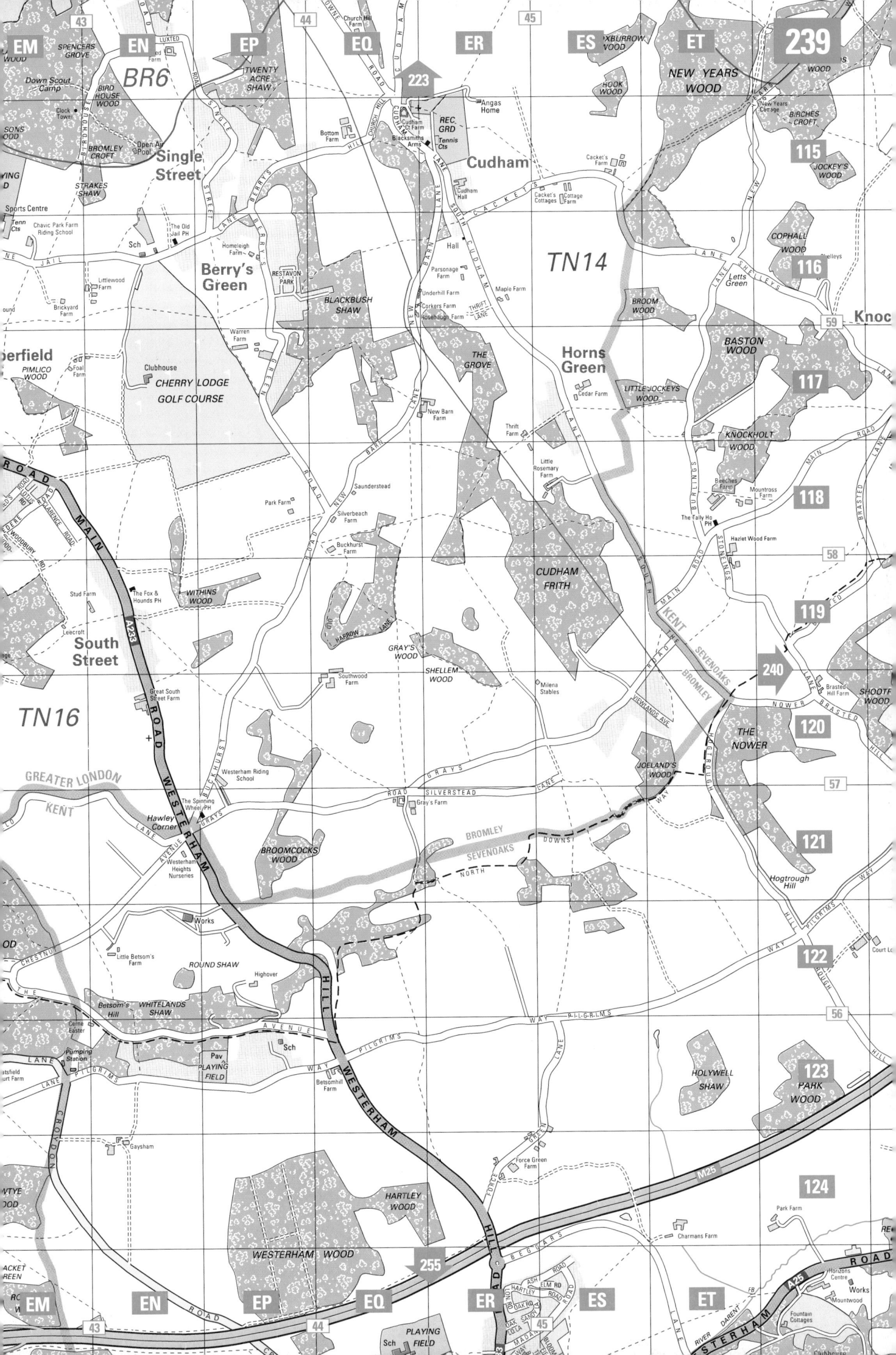

239
43
44
45
EM
EN
EP
EQ
ER
ES
ET
223
SPENCERS GROVE
LUXTED
BR6
TWENTY ACRE SHAW
Church Hill Farm
CUDHAM
Down Scout Camp
BIRD HOUSE WOOD
Clock Tower
BIRDHOUSE
Open Air Pool
BROMLEY CROFT
Single Street
SINGLE STREET
STRAKES SHAW
Sports Centre
Tenn Cts
Chavic Park Farm Riding School
JAIL LANE
Sch
The Old Jail PH
BERRY'S LANE
BERRY'S GREEN
Homeleigh Farm
Berry's Green
RESTAVON PARK
BLACKBUSH SHAW
Littlewood Farm
Brickyard Farm
Warren Farm
Bottom Farm
CHURCH HILL
Cudham Ct Farm
Blacksmiths Arms
REC GRD
Tennis Cts
Angas Home
Cudham
Cudham Hall
Hall
CUDHAM LANE
SOUTH CUDHAM
CACKETS LANE
Cacket's Farm
Cacket's Cottages
Cottage Farm
Parsonage Farm
Underhill Farm
Corkers Farm
Rosehaugh Farm
THRIFT LANE
Maple Farm
NEW BARN LANE
THE GROVE
TN14
OXBURROW WOOD
HOOK WOOD
NEW YEARS WOOD
New Years Cottage
BIRCHES CROFT
115
JOCKEY'S WOOD
COPHALL WOOD
116
Shelleys
Letts Green
SHELLEYS LANE
BROOM WOOD
59
Knoc
BASTON WOOD
117
Horns Green
Cedar Farm
LITTLE JOCKEYS WOOD
Thrift Farm
Little Rosemary Farm
KNOCKHOLT WOOD
BURLINGS LANE
MAIN ROAD
Beeches Farm
Mountross Farm
118
The Tally Ho PH
Hazlet Wood Farm
STONINGS
58
BRASTED
119
240
Brasted Hill Farm
SHOOTF WOOD
NOWER
THE NOWER
120
HOGTROUGH
57
121
Hogtrough Hill
PILGRIMS WAY
122
Court Lo
56
123
PARK WOOD
124
Park Farm
erfield
PIMLICO WOOD
Foal Farm
Clubhouse
CHERRY LODGE GOLF COURSE
MAIN ROAD
A233
Park Farm
Saunderstead
Silverbeach Farm
Buckhurst Farm
WITHINS WOOD
Stud Farm
The Fox & Hounds PH
Leecroft
South Street
HARROW LANE
GRAY'S WOOD
SHELLEM WOOD
CUDHAM FRITH
KENT
SEVENOAKS
BROMLEY
MAIN ROAD
VIEWLANDS AVE
Milena Stables
Southwood Farm
Great South Street Farm
TN16
WESTERHAM ROAD
BUCKHURST
Westerham Riding School
GRAYS ROAD
SILVERSTEAD LANE
Gray's Farm
JOELAND'S WOOD
GREATER LONDON
KENT
Hawley Corner
The Spinning Wheel PH
BROMLEY
SEVENOAKS
DOWNS
NORTH
WAY
BROOMCOCKS WOOD
Westerham Heights Nurseries
Works
CHESTNUT
Little Betsom's Farm
ROUND SHAW
Highover
Betsom's Hill
WHITELANDS SHAW
AVENUE
Cerne Easter
Pumping Station
Sch
Pav
PLAYING FIELD
PILGRIMS WAY
HILL
Betsomhill Farm
WESTERHAM
LANE
HOLYWELL SHAW
Gaysham
CROYDON
Force Green Farm
FORCE GREEN
M25
HARTLEY WOOD
WESTERHAM WOOD
255
BEGGARS
Charmans Farm
ROAD
A25
Horizons Centre
Works
Mountwood
Fountain Cottages
RIVER DARENT
FB
STERHAM
ASH
ELM RD
HARTLEY ROAD
OAK RD
SANDY LA
OAK LO LA
MADAN
BLOOM
LONDON RD
PLAYING FIELD
Sch
EM
EN
EP
EQ
ER
ES
ET
43
44
45

NEW YEARS WOOD
NEWLANDS WOOD
HAYMAN'S WOOD
BIRCHES CROFT
LONG BOTTOM SHAW
JOCKEY'S WOOD
HAWFIELD WOOD
224
Singles Cross
Knockholt Pound
Warehouses
CHAPEL CROFT
Works
Curry Farm
Blueberry Farm
The Spinney Nurseries
Whitelegg's Garden Centre
Clinic
Comm Cen
Ivy Farm
Bowl Grn
Football Ground
The Grange
Harrow PH
Meadow Fm
Aldwyn House
Warren Farm
Rose Cottage Farm
The Mill House
COPHALL WOOD
Sheileys
Letts Green
BROOM WOOD
LEES WOOD
DUTCHMORE WOOD
Homefield
Court Lodge
Knockholt
COOPER'S WOOD
BASTON WOOD
War Meml
Sch
The Crown PH
ASHFIELD WOOD
STAR HILL WOOD
LITTLE JOCKEYS WOOD
ASH PLATT
KNOCKHOLT BEECHES
Masts
SAND BANKS
MINNY WOOD
KNOCKHOLT WOOD
COV RES
Keepers Cottage
Beeches Farm
Mountross Farm
The Tally Ho PH
Hazlet Wood Farm
CHEVENING PARK
SUMMERHOUSE WOOD
PARK WOOD
Sundridge Hill
THE SPINNEY
ROUGHFIELDS WOOD
HAGBUSH WOOD
Chevening
Chevening House
Well
BURIAL GROUND
Shootfield
TN14
Home Farm
Brasted Hill Farm
SHOOTFIELD WOOD
THE NOWER
JOELAND'S WOOD
HOME WOOD
Chevening Cross
Grove House
CLAYPIT SHAW
Oveny Green Farm
Farm
Combe Bank Farm
Ovenden Lodge
Junction
Hogtrough Hill
Court Lodge Farm
COMBEBANK WOOD
Combe Bank Wood
M25
Willow
TN16
COMBE WOOD
B2211
PLAYING FLD
Sch
PARK WOOD
Pumping Station
ST. MARTINS MEADOW
Tanners
Pav
SPORTS GROUND
Little Coombe Bank
Council Yard
Offices
Glass
Warren Farm
Mill Farm
The Stanhope Arms PH
The Old Rectory
PYM ORCHARD
Bowl Grn
The Lamb PH
Brasted
Sundridge
Depots
The White Horse PH
Hall
The Old Rectory
Park Farm
Charmans Farm
REC GRD
Bull Inn
White Hart Inn
Orchard Farm
Brasted Place
THE ROOKERIES
Sch
THE WARREN
Horizons Centre
Works
Mountwood
Fountain Cottages
Brasted Place Farm
Long Barn
A25
EU EV EW EX EY EZ FA
47 48 49
115 116 117 118 119 120 121 122 123 124
56 57 58 59
239
KENT
SEVENOAKS
BROMLEY

241
FB
FC
FD
FE
FF
FG
FH
225
115
116
117
118
119
120
121
122
123
124
257
256
50
51
52
56
57
58
59
Twitton
OTFORD
OTFORD CEMETERY
Otford Junction
DEFENCE RESEARCH AGENCY
CHALK PIT
OLD GROVE
HELIPAD
Electricity Station
Sepham Farm
Lower Barn
RIVER DARENT
Frog Farm
Homestead Farm
Hopgarden Farm
BLUEBELL WOOD
Broughton House
Donnington Manor Hotel
Great Dunton Farm
Morants Court
Morants Court Cross
Morants Court Farm
The Rose & Crown PH
Dunton Green
ALDER SHAW
EDWARD SHAW
HOME WOOD
DUNTON GREEN
Rye House Farm
WICKENS CARAVAN SITE
GRAVEL PIT
Bartram Farm
RIVERSIDE RETAIL PARK
Superstore
THE MOORS
RAKEFIELD WOOD
Longford
RYE WOOD
Depots
EAST LAKE
SEVENOAKS WILDFOWL RESERVE
WEST LAKE
Visitors Cen
Bradbourne Farm & Riding Centre
SEVENOAKS BUSINESS CEN
SEVENOAKS HOSP
CHIPSTEAD LAKE
Windmill Farm
Froghole
Chipstead
Riverhead
ALLOTMENTS
RIVERHEAD PARKLAND
FISH PONDS
ANT WOOD
MONTREAL PARK
ASH PLAT WOOD
Obelisk
OBELISK WOOD
TN13
Bessels Green
COLD ARBOR WOOD
Salters Heath Farm
Brittains Farm
SEVENOAKS
SPORTS GRD
PLAYING FIELD
KNOLE PADDOCK
PLAYING FLD
KNOLE ENVIRONMENTAL PARK
LITTLE BRITAIN'S WOOD
MIDDLINGS WOOD
OXEN SHA
M25
M26
A224
A225
A25
A21
B2042
B2020
POLHILL
LONDON ROAD
MORANTS COURT ROAD
PILGRIMS WAY
NORTH DOWNS WAY
STATION RD
HIGH STREET
SEVENOAKS ROAD
OTFORD ROAD
VESTRY ROAD
BRADBOURNE VALE ROAD
SEAL ROAD
ST JOHN'S HILL
DARTFORD ROAD
WESTERHAM ROAD
WORSHIPS HILL
AMHERST HILL
LONDON ROAD
BOTOLPH'S ROAD
COLD ARBOR ROAD
SEVENOAKS

AS
AT
AU
AV
AW
AX
AY
226
258
GU3
GU2
GU22
Worplesdon
WHITMOOR COMMON
WHITMOOR POND
POOR JACK'S WOOD
WHITMOOR WOOD
BRIDLEY COPSE
RICKFORD COMMON
ROKER PARK GOLF COURSE
Fairlands
Rydeshill
BROADSTREET COMMON
Park Barn
Pitch Place
Stoughton
Bellfields
Jacobs Well
Woodbridge Hill
STRINGER'S COMMON
BRITTEN'S POND
STOKE NEW CEMETERY
ROYAL SURREY COUNTY HOSPITAL
University of Surrey
CATHEDRAL
Guildford Park
CATHEDRAL HILL IND EST
GUILDFORD BUSINESS PARK
RESEARCH PARK
HENMAN SPORTS GROUND
PERRY HILL
WORPLESDON ROAD
ALDERSHOT ROAD
SALT BOX ROAD
WOKING ROAD
GUILDFORD BYPASS
A322
A323
A320
A25
A246
A3100
125
126
127
128
129
130
131
132
133
134
54
53
52
51
98
99
00

243
Send Marsh
GU23
GU4
227
244
259
PLAYING FIELDS
Sendgrove
SUTTON PARK
Sutton Place
BURPHAM COURT FARM PARK
Bower's Lock
Broadoak Bridge
RIVER WEY
RIVER WEY NAVIGATION NT
WOKING
GUILDFORD
FRITHYS WOOD
COTTS WOOD
HIGHCOTTS WOOD
Burpham
SUTHERLAND MEMORIAL PARK
Superstore
COPSE EDGE
MERROW COMMON
CLANDON PARK
Bushy Hill
Merrow
SURREY CRICKET CENTRE
GUILDFORD GOLF COURSE
THE WILD WOOD
THE WILDERNESS
CHALK PIT
Clandon House
The Manor Hotel
LONDON ROAD
RIPLEY BYPASS
GUILDFORD BYPASS
EPSOM ROAD
BOXGROVE ROAD
A3
A3100
A247
A25
A246
B2215
B2234
THE STREET
125
126
127
128
129
130
131
132
133
134
54
53
52
51
01
02
03
AZ
BA
BB
BC
BD
BE
BF

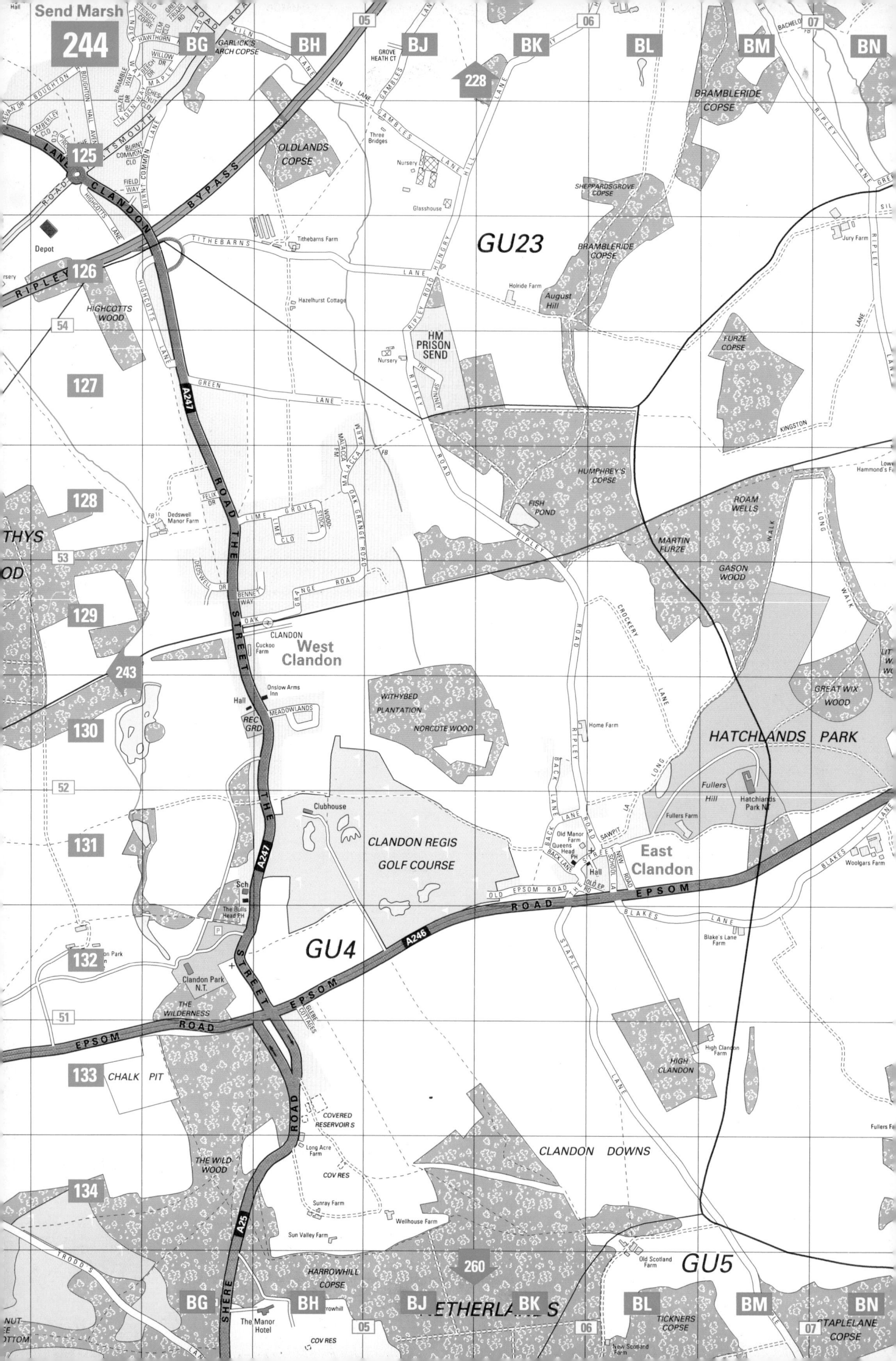

Send Marsh
244
BG
BH
BJ
BK
BL
BM
BN
05
06
07
228
GARLICK'S ARCH COPSE
GROVE HEATH CT
KILN LANE
GAMBLES LANE
HILL
Three Bridges
Nursery
Glasshouse
OLDLANDS COPSE
BRAMBLERIDE COPSE
SHEPPARDSGROVE COPSE
BRAMBLERIDE COPSE
Jury Farm
RIPLEY LANE
125
126
127
128
129
130
131
132
133
134
54
53
52
51
CLANDON
BYPASS
A3
Depot
HIGHCOTTS WOOD
HIGHCOTTS LANE
TITHEBARNS LANE
Tithebarns Farm
Hazelhurst Cottage
HUNGRY HILL LANE
GU23
Holride Farm
August Hill
FURZE COPSE
HM PRISON SEND
Nursery
THE SPINNEY
RIPLEY ROAD
GREEN LANE
A247
KINGSTON
HUMPHREY'S COPSE
FISH POND
Lower Hammond's Fa
ROAM WELLS
MARTIN FURZE
GASON WOOD
LONG WALK
MALACCA FM
FB
Dedswell Manor Farm
FELIX DR
LIME GROVE
LIME CLO
WOODSTOCK
OAK GRANGE ROAD
GRANGE ROAD
DEDSWELL DR
BENNET WAY
CROCKERY LANE
THE STREET
OAK
CLANDON
Cuckoo Farm
West Clandon
243
Onslow Arms Inn
Hall
REC GRD
MEADOWLANDS
WITHYBED PLANTATION
NORCOTE WOOD
Home Farm
GREAT WIX WOOD
HATCHLANDS PARK
Fullers Hill
Hatchlands Park NT
Fullers Farm
Clubhouse
CLANDON REGIS GOLF COURSE
BACK LANE
Old Manor Farm
Queens Head PH
SAWPIT LA
East Clandon
SCHOOL LA
NEW ROAD
Hall
OLD EPSOM ROAD
OLD EP RD
EPSOM ROAD
BLAKES LANE
Woolgars Farm
Sch
The Bulls Head PH
P
A246
GU4
Blake's Lane Farm
Clandon Park N.T.
THE WILDERNESS
GLEBE COTTAGES
STAPLE LANE
High Clandon Farm
HIGH CLANDON
CHALK PIT
COVERED RESERVOIRS
Fullers Fa
Long Acre Farm
CLANDON DOWNS
THE WILD WOOD
COV RES
Sunray Farm
Wellhouse Farm
Sun Valley Farm
A25
TRODDS LANE
260
Old Scotland Farm
GU5
HARROWHILL COPSE
SHERE ROAD
NETHERLANDS
The Manor Hotel
COV RES
TICKNERS COPSE
STAPLELANE COPSE
New Scotland Farm

245
BP
BQ
BR
BS
BT
BU
BV
229
246
261
East Horsley
West Horsley
KT24
RH5
GREATLEE WOOD
LOLLESWORTH WOOD
FRENCHLANDS COPSE
Management Centre
GUILDFORD ROAD
EPSOM
A246
B2039
OCKHAM ROAD SOUTH
OCKHAM ROAD NORTH
WESTON WOOD
SHEEP LEAS
GREEN DENE PLANTATION
MOUNTAIN WOOD
EFFINGHAM FOREST
HANGERS WOOD
OLDLANDS WOOD
BUCKLES PLANTATION
PARK WOOD
LITTLELEE WOOD
EFFINGHAM GOLF COURSE
UPPER COMMON
UPPER WESTON WOOD
HOOK WOOD
TYRRELSWOOD
DAWS DENE
King's Hills
Troy Bridge
Crocknorth Farm
Hookwood Farm
Woodcote Farm
Warren Farm
Orestan Farm
Place Farm
Manor Farm

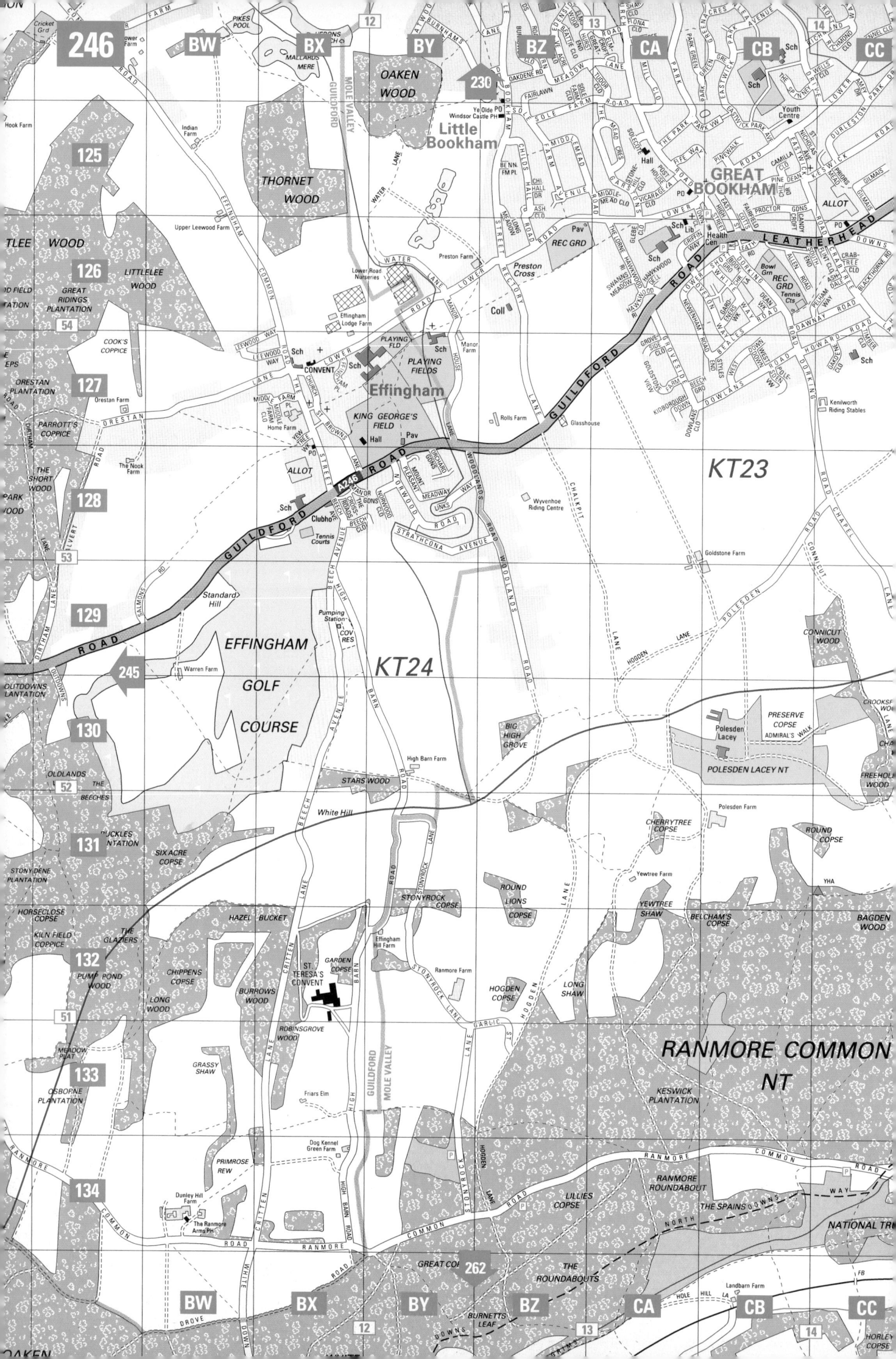

246
BW
BX
BY
BZ
CA
CB
CC
12
13
14
230
245
262
125
126
127
128
129
130
131
132
133
134
54
53
52
51
Cricket Grd
Pikes Pool
Herons
Mallards Mere
Oaken Wood
Mole Valley
Guildford
Little Bookham
Great Bookham
Ye Olde PO
Windsor Castle PH
Hook Farm
Indian Farm
Thornet Wood
Upper Leewood Farm
Effingham Common
Water Lane
Lower Road Nurseries
Effingham Lodge Farm
Preston Farm
Preston Cross
Rectory Lane
Manor House Lane
Manor Farm
Coll
Playing Fld
Playing Fields
Sch
Convent
Effingham
King George's Field
Hall
Pav
Allot
Clubho
Tennis Courts
Orestan Lane
Orestan Farm
Home Farm
The Nook Farm
Cook's Coppice
Orestan Plantation
Parrott's Coppice
The Short Wood
Tlee Wood
Littlelee Wood
Great Ridings Plantation
Guildford Road
A246
Leatherhead Road
Rolls Farm
Glasshouse
Wyvenhoe Riding Centre
Strathcona Avenue
Woodlands Road
Chalkpit Lane
KT23
KT24
Goldstone Farm
Kenilworth Riding Stables
Dorking Road
Chapel Road
Connicut Lane
Polesden Lane
Hogden Lane
Connicut Wood
Standard Hill
Salmons Rd
Pumping Station
Cov Res
Effingham Golf Course
Warren Farm
Dirtham Lane
Calvert Lane
Outdowns Plantation
Big High Grove
High Barn Farm
Stars Wood
Barn Road
Beech Avenue
High Barn Road
White Hill
Preserve Copse
Admiral's Walk
Polesden Lacey
Polesden Lacey NT
Polesden Farm
Cherrytree Copse
Round Copse
Freehold Wood
Crooksfield Wood
Oldlands
The Beeches
Puckles Plantation
Six Acre Copse
Stony Dene Plantation
Horseclose Copse
Kiln Field Coppice
The Glaziers
Pump Pond Wood
Hazel Bucket
Chippens Copse
Long Wood
Burrows Wood
Stonyrock Copse
Stonyrock Lane
Round Lions Copse
Yewtree Farm
Yewtree Shaw
Belcham's Copse
YHA
Bagden Wood
Effingham Hill Farm
Garden Copse
St. Teresa's Convent
Ranmore Farm
Hogden Copse
Long Shaw
Garlic St
Critten Lane
Robinsgrove Wood
Grassy Shaw
Meadow Plat
Osborne Plantation
Friars Elm
Ranmore Common NT
Keswick Plantation
Dog Kennel Green Farm
Primrose Rew
Ranmore Common Road
Ranmore Roundabout
Lillies Copse
The Spains
North Downs Way
National Trust
Dunley Hill Farm
The Ranmore Arms PH
Ranmore Road
Great Copse
The Roundabouts
Burnetts Leaf
White Down
Drove Road
Hole Hill La
Landbarn Farm
FB
Horley Copse
Sole Farm Road
Fairlawn
Oakdene Rd
Eastwick Park Ave
Youth Centre
Lower Road
Post House La
Vicarage Cl
Health Cen
Lib
PO
Rec Grd
Bowl Grn
Tennis Cts
Dawnay Road
Howard Road
Dowlans Rd
Kidborough Down
Allot
Gilmais
Middlemead

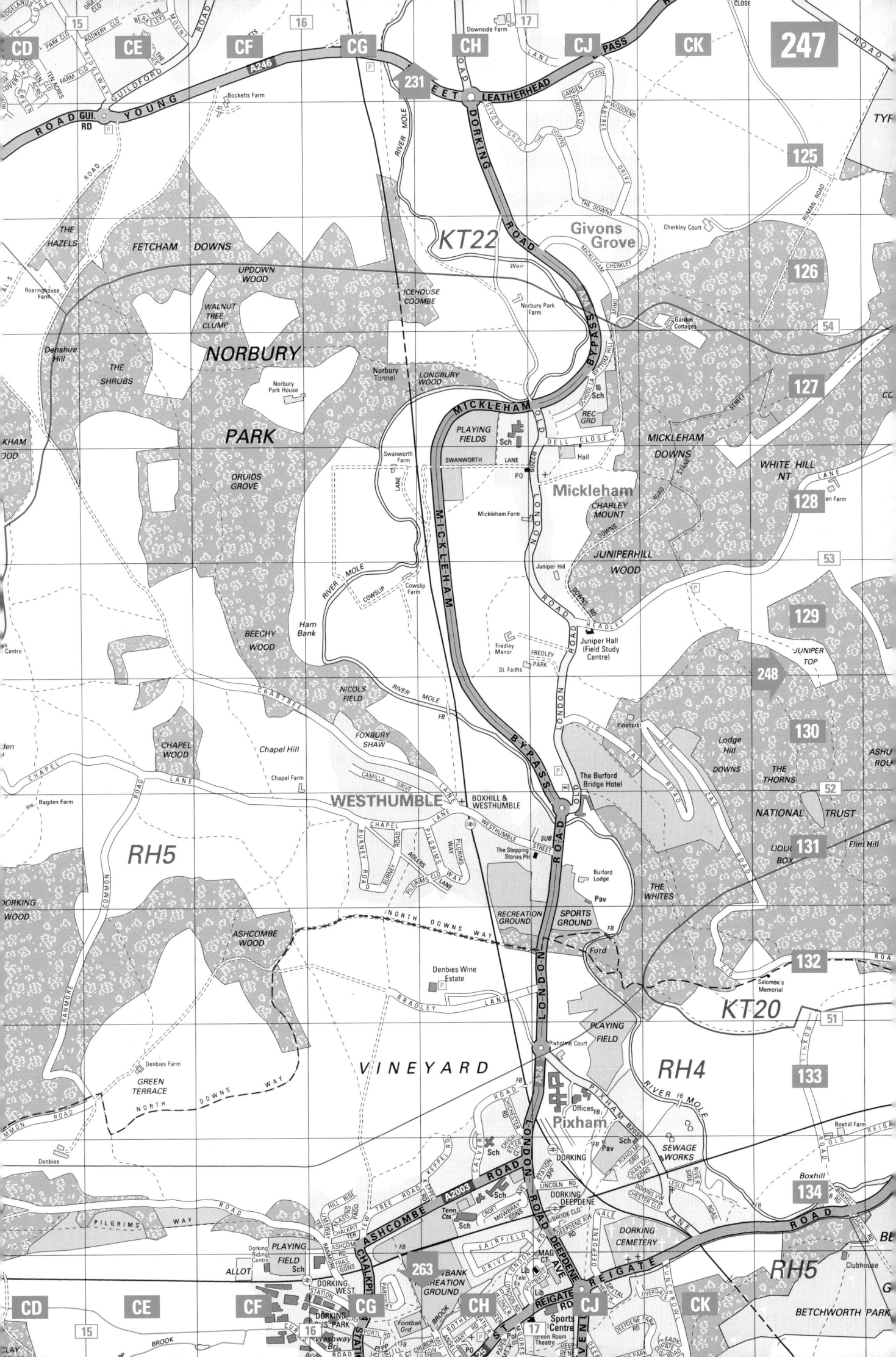
CD
CE
CF
CG
CH
CJ
CK
15
16
17
231
A246
GUILDFORD ROAD
YOUNG STREET
LEATHERHEAD BYPASS
Bocketts Farm
Downside Farm
DORKING ROAD
RIVER MOLE
GIVONS GROVE
THE DOWNS
GARDEN CLO
WOODEND
CRABTREE DRIVE
125
THE HAZELS
FETCHAM DOWNS
UPDOWN WOOD
KT22
Givons Grove
Cherkley Court
ROMAN ROAD
Roaringhouse Farm
WALNUT TREE CLUMP
ICEHOUSE COOMBE
Weir
Norbury Park Farm
MICKLEHAM DRIVE
CHERKLEY HILL
126
Garden Cottages
54
Denshire Hill
THE SHRUBS
NORBURY
Norbury Park House
Norbury Tunnel
LONGBURY WOOD
A24 BYPASS
SCHOOL LA
BYTTOM HILL
Sch
REC GRD
127
PARK
MICKLEHAM
PLAYING FIELDS
DELL CLOSE
Hall
MICKLEHAM DOWNS
WHITE HILL NT
Swanworth Farm
SWANWORTH LANE
B2209
PO
Mickleham
DRUIDS GROVE
CHARLEY MOUNT
128
Mickleham Farm
OLD LONDON ROAD
JUNIPERHILL WOOD
53
Juniper Hill
DOWNS RD
RIVER MOLE
COWSLIP
Cowslip Farm
MICKLEHAM BYPASS
129
HEADLEY ROAD
Ham Bank
BEECHY WOOD
Juniper Hall (Field Study Centre)
Fredley Manor
FREDLEY PARK
St. Faiths
JUNIPER TOP
248
NICOLS FIELD
RIVER MOLE
FB
CRABTREE
Pinehurst
ZIG ZAG ROAD
130
FOXBURY SHAW
CHAPEL WOOD
Chapel Hill
Lodge Hill
DOWNS
THE THORNS
CHAPEL LANE
CAMILLA DRIVE
Chapel Farm
The Burford Bridge Hotel
52
WESTHUMBLE
BOXHILL & WESTHUMBLE
NATIONAL TRUST
Bagden Farm
CHAPEL LANE
WESTHUMBLE STREET
BURNEY ROAD
PILGRIMS WAY
ADLERS LANE
PILGRIMS CLO
RH5
The Stepping Stones PH
131
Flint Hill
Burford Lodge
Pav
THE WHITES
DORKING WOOD
COMMON
RECREATION GROUND
SPORTS GROUND
NORTH DOWNS WAY
ASHCOMBE WOOD
FB
Ford
132
Denbies Wine Estate
Salomons Memorial
BRADLEY LANE
LONDON ROAD
KT20
51
RANMORE
PLAYING FIELD
Pixholme Court
VINEYARD
RH4
A24
133
Denbies Farm
GREEN TERRACE
NORTH DOWNS WAY
Offices
PIXHAM LANE
B2038
RIVER MOLE
Pixham
Boxhill Farm
OLD REIGATE RD
CHICHESTER RD
Sch
SEWAGE WORKS
Denbies
DORKING
STATION APP
LINCOLN RD
A2003
ASHCOMBE ROAD
Boxhill
134
DORKING DEEPDENE
PILGRIMS WAY
HILL RISE
KEPPEL RD
Tenn Cts
Sch
CROFT
MOWBRAY GDNS
DEEPDENE AVE
DORKING CEMETERY
REIGATE ROAD
Dorking Riding Centre
PLAYING FIELD
FAIRFIELD DRIVE
Sch
263
MAG CT
Lib
Clubhouse
ALLOT
DORKING WEST
RECREATION GROUND
REIGATE RD
RH5
CHALKPIT
DORKING DEEPDENE
PUNCHBOWL LANE
BETCHWORTH PARK
CD
CE
CF
CG
CH
CJ
CK
DORKING BUS PARK
Washway Bri
Football Grd
BROOK
Sports Centre
Green Room Theatre
DEEPDENE PARK RD
15
16
17
BROOK

248
CL
CM
CN
CP
CQ
CR
CS
19
20
21
232
KT22
NOWER WOOD
PIGNUT WOOD
Court Farm
Clubhouse
TYRRELL'S WOOD GOLF COURSE
OYSTER HILL NT
GREAT HURST WOOD
COSTAL WOOD
Headley
Tumber Farm
Glasshouses
Nursery
PO
125
Cherkley Court
126
CHERKLEY WOOD
HEADLEY WARREN NATURE RESERVE
Heath Farm
54
Garden Cottages
127
GOODMAN'S FURZE
Cricket Grd
Clubhouse
COCKSHOT WOOD
DEAN WOOD
MOLE VALLEY
REIGATE & BANSTEAD
KT18
MICKLEHAM DOWNS
WHITE HILL NT
HERRING GROVE
128
Warren Farm
HEADLEY HEATH NT
Headley Grove Farm
HEADLEY GROVE
Pebble Coombe
RH5
53
Pebble Coombe
PEBBLE COOMBE
HEADLEY RESERVOIR
129
HEADLEY PLANTATION
JUNIPER TOP
247
Bellasis
HEATH PLANTATION
BATCHELOR'S ROUGH
Pinehurst
130
Lodge Hill
DOWNS
THE THORNS
ASHURST ROUGH
BRAMBLE HALL WOOD
MERRYWOOD PARK
Prestige Farm
SURREY HILLS
Hand in Hand PH
Maybury Farm
BETCHWORTH HILLS WOOD
52
NATIONAL TRUST
WILTON BANK
Birchingrove Farm
BOX HILL
CHALK PIT
131
LIQUOR BOX
Flint Hill
THE BIRCHES
KT20
CARAVAN PARK
THE WHITES
MOBILE HOMES PARK
BETCHWORTH CLUMP
CHALK PIT
MOBILE HOMES PARK
Chestnut Lodge Farm
BETCHWORTH
132
Salomon's Memorial
Brockham Warren
OAK WOOD
BROCKHAM HILLS
Sunny Banks Farm
Depot
51
DUKES PLANTATION
REIGATE ROAD
The Michael Seymour Nursery
133
RH4
RH3
RIVER MOLE
Boxhill Farm
Cottage Farm
A25
Broome Park
SEWAGE WORKS
Deepdene Bridge
Boxhill Bridge
134
DORKING CEMETERY
BETCHWORTH PARK
Betchworth Castle Remains
BROCKHAM BIG FIELD
Clubhouse
BETCHWORTH
Midland Bank College
Sch
Clubhouse
GOLF COURSE
264
Borough Bridge
Brockham Court Farm
Betchworth House

249
233
250
265
BANSTEAD HEATH
BANSTEAD KT20 HEATH
WALTON ON THE HILL
WALTON HEATH GOLF COURSE
WALTON HEATH
LOWER KINGSWOOD
Mogador
Margery
Buckland
RH2
REIGATE
REIGATE HEATH GOLF COURSE
REIGATE HEATH
REIGATE PRIORY PLAYING FIELDS
REIGATE PARK
LITTLE HEATH
Walton Oaks Offices
ROUND WOOD
DEWRIDING PLANTATION
Lady Hill
Thistle Hill
Buckland Hills
NORTH DOWNS WAY
PILGRIMS' WAY
Mount Hill
Conibury Hill
Juniper Hill
Colley Hill
THE HORSESHOE
THE SADDLE KNOB
QUEEN'S PARK
MARGERY WOOD NT
FOUR ACRE UPPER WOODS
COLLEYLAND SHAW
BUSHY SHAW
BUSHFIELD COPPICE
COLLEY COPSE
COLLEY WOOD
SAND AND GRAVEL PIT
TAP WOOD
ROUND ALDERS
THE ALDERS
MOLE VALLEY
REIGATE & BANSTEAD
M25
A217
A25
B2032
B2220
BRIGHTON ROAD
REIGATE ROAD
BUCKLAND ROAD
WEST STREET
HIGH STREET
DORKING ROAD
GAS STATION
CHUSSEX PLAIN
Kingswood Fields
GRUB WOOD
MILLFIELD WOOD
Clock Tower Riding Centre
Red Lodge
Wayside Farm
Dent's Farm
Underhill Farm
Kemp's Farm
Dowde's Farm
Glebe House
Petty's Farm
Dungate's Farm
Wonham Hill
Wonham Mill
MILL POND
Dungate Manor
Heathfield Farm
Jolly Farmers PH
High Trees Garden Centre
Buckland Nurseries
The Black Horse PH
Mint Arms PH
Kingswood Hall
Kingswood Grange
Kingswood Manor
Orchard Cottage Riding Stables
Broadleas
Fairhall
Margery Hall
COVERED RESERVOIR
Water Tower

250
DA
DB
DC
DD
DE
DF
DG
26
27
28
234
249
266
Mugswell
CR5
KT20
RH2
LOWER KINGSWOOD
Margery
Junction 8
Gatton
Coles Meads
REIGATE
REDHILL
Kingswood Fields
Kingswood Grange
Kingswood Manor
MILLFIELD WOOD
GRUB WOOD
FURZEFIELD COPSE
GATWICK WOOD
LONG WOOD
LITTLE WOOD
COLTS BUSHES
UPPER GATTON WOOD
DELL WOOD
UPPER GATTON PARK
FURZEFIELD SHAW
BOARS GREEN SHAW
Boars Green Farm
Park Farm
Reeves Rest
Southerns Farm
Home Field Farm
Highways Livery Stables
Ashtead Hill
JUBILEE PLANTATIONS
PARK SHAW
MANSHIPS SHAW
Kingswood Hill
GATTON FIELD SHAW
CATSBRAIN EAST
GLEBE SHAW
GROVE SHAW
MAJORITY PLANTATION
THE CROSSWAYS
Crossways Farm
GATLANDS SHAW
CATSBRAIN SHAW
TOWER WOOD
PLAYING FIELD
HIGH BEECHES
Whitehall Farm
GATTON BOTTOM
GOLF
HALFMOON CLUMP
THE BURPIT
HOP GARDEN POND
ENGINE POND
THE LAKE
SERPENTINE WOOD
GREENCLUMP HILL
TEMPLE WOOD
GREAT BUCK WOOD
WINGATE HILL
NUT WOOD NT
TWO ACRE WOOD
BLACKHORSE WOOD
FOUR ACRE UPPER WOODS
THE BEECHES
Reigate Hill
Rock Farm
Margery Hall
Margery Farm
Nursery
COVERED RESERVOIR
MARGERY WOOD NT
Water Tower
Colley Hill
QUEEN'S PARK
Kingswood Hall
COLLEY COPSE
COLLEY WOOD
Broadleas
Orchard Cottage Riding Stables
BEECHEN
SPORTS GROUND
COPSE
REC GRD
Bowling Green
Mint Arms PH
The Fox PH
Well House PH
Yew Tree PH
A217
A25
A23
A242
M25
B2034
BRIGHTON ROAD
REIGATE HILL
GATTON PARK ROAD
CROYDON ROAD
REIGATE ROAD
LONDON ROAD
HIGH STREET
CHURCH STREET
STATION RD
QUEENSWAY
HATCHLANDS RD
WRAY COMMON
Sports Cen
ALLOT
TA Centre
Johnston House
Site of Reigate Castle
Superstore
Clinic
Offices
Fire Sta
Comm Cen
Cricket Ground
Fire Brigade Headquarters
REIGATE CEMETERY
REIGATE POL STA
East Surrey Coll
Health Cen
BUS DEPOT
PLAYING FIELDS
REIGATE PRIORY
PRIORY POND
REIGATE PARK
COMMON
Works
Tennis Courts
Clubhouse
Belfry Shop Cen
Harlequin Thea
REDSTONE MANOR
Stables

251
252
235
267
DH
DJ
DK
DL
DM
DN
DP
29
30
31
CR3
RH1
125
126
127
128
129
130
131
132
133
134
54
53
52
51
SPARTICLES WOOD
ALDERSTEAD HEATH
WOOD
Chaldon Mead
DEAN LANE
ROOK LANE
B2031
Rook Hill
Hall
Sch
WILLEY BROOM WOOD
Clubhouse
Pav
SIX BROTHERS FIELD
BIRCHWOOD
BIRCHCROFT CLO
BADGERS WOOD
HEATHWAY
COMMON ROAD
LAVE CLO
FARM LANE
ROFFES LANE
Mersham Tunnel
Airshafts
Junction 7
COVERED RESERVOIR
Alderstead Farm
ALDERSTEAD HILL
THE SHRUBBERY
BEECH ROAD
SHEPHERDS HILL
LONDON ROAD
CHURCH HILL
Uplands Farm
Tollsworth Manor
Earthworks
PILGRIMS' WAY
PILGRIMS LANE
HILLTOP LANE
Hilltop Farm
Hilltop House
Masts
RIDGEBUSHES WOOD
Willey Park Farm
GRUBS WOOD
White Hill
LIME WORKS ROAD
JOLIFFE RD
M23
M25
A23
NORTH DOWNS WAY
SUB
Ockley Hill
Junction 8 (M23)
Junction 7(M25)
ROCKSHAW ROAD
SPRING BOTTOM ROAD
Rockshaw Cottage
SPRING BOTTOM
QUARRY WOOD
Quarry Hall Farm
ROCKY SHAW
PENDELL WOOD
BLACK BUSH
HERONSWOOD MERE
ASHCOMBE RD
NORTH ROAD
SOUTH ROAD
HIGH ST
Hall
Cricket Ground
Home Farm
MERSTHAM
STATION RD
QUALITY ST
FURZEFIELD WOOD
LAXTON GDNS
RADSTOCK WAY
MALMSTONE AVENUE
HUDDLESTONE CRES
MANSFIELD
CHESTERTON DRIVE
Comm Cen
PORTLAND HOUSE
PORTLAND DRIVE
NAILSWORTH CRES
DUNDREY
DELABOLE
CHILMARK GDNS
RADSTOCK
BOLSOVER GRO
BLETCHINGLEY ROAD
WORSTED GREEN
Health Cen
Lib
Clubhouse
SUTTON GDNS
TAYNTON DRIVE
Darby House
PLAYING FIELDS
Tennis Courts
SPORTS GROUND
ALLOT
South Merstham
Warwick Wold
WARWICK WOLD RD
OAKWOOD
FURZEFIELD WOOD
MERSTHAM ROAD
REDHILL BROOK
FB
SAND PIT
THE GROVE
THE CROSSWAYS
MANOR RD
ALBERT RD
ENDSLEIGH RD
SOUTHCOTE RD
DEVON ROAD
DEANS RD
MELTON RD
BOURNE RD
WYCLIFFE GDNS
CHILBERTON DR
SEWAGE WORKS
REIGATE & BANSTEAD
TANDRIDGE
Works
QUARRYSIDE BUSINESS PARK
ALLOT
BATTLEBRIDGE LANE
SAND PIT
HOLMETHORPE INDUSTRIAL ESTATE
HOLMETHORPE AVENUE
Ford Bridge
MILL LANE
MERCERS PARK COUNTRY PARK
Clubhouse
Mercers Farm
Pendell Farm
WATER LANE
PLAYING FIELD
PENDELL COURT
Pendell House
Brewer Street Farm
Lake Farm
Holmethorpe
REDHILL BROOK
NUTFIELD MARSH ROAD
Cricket Ground
Pav
Inn on the Pond
CHILMEAD LANE
Chilmead Farm
SAND PIT
Glebe House
COCKLEY PLANTATION
SANDY LANE
LITTLE COMMON LANE
Nursery
Dormers Farm
BLETCHINGLEY
ALLOT
STYCHENS LANE
CLARE COTTS
BOTERY'S CROSS
OVERDALE
BIG COMMON LANE
CASTLE SQ
Sports Hall
Coll
HIGH ST
Castle Hill
STANLEY'S WOOD
COOMBES COPPICE
Robert Denholm House
Capenor Nursery
SAND AND GRAVEL PIT
LAND FILL SITE
PARK WOOD
Nutfield Court
CHURCH HILL
Nutfield
SPORTS GRD
Hall
BLETCHINGLEY ROAD
NUTFIELD CEMETERY
A25
ROAD HIGH STREET
Sch
PO
FOX HOLE
Holmesdale
COPPERS HILL
DEANS LA
Works
NORTH PARK
PLAYING FIELD
Nutfield Priory Hotel
Nutfield Lodge
Stockers Hill
Furze Hill
Priory Farm Plant Centre
Priory Farm
STENERS HILL
Sandhills
FULLERS WOOD LANE
NUTFIELD PRIORY LAKE
HOGTROUGH LANE
SANDY LANE
BOWER HILL
BRAES MEAD
KENTWYNS RISE
Kentwyns
Lyttel Hall
GREENSAND WAY
Sandhills Farm
REDSTONE CEMETERY
CORMONGERS LANE
MID STREET
WHITEHILL
PLACE FARM

252
DQ
DR
DS
DT
DU
DV
DW
236
251
125
126
127
128
129
130
131
132
133
134
33
34
35
54
53
52
51
CR3
RH1
Rook Hill
WILLEY BROOM WOOD
RIDGEBUSHES WOOD
Hilltop House
Willey Park Farm
White Hill
QUARRY HANGERS
SPRING BOTTOM
QUARRY WOOD
Quarry Hall Farm
ROCKY SHAW
BLACK BUSHES
PENDELL WOOD
GRUBS WOOD
The Harrow PH
Arthur's Seat
CONDUIT SHAW
KITCHEN COPSE
Place Farm
Brewer Street Farm
Pendell Farm
Pendell House
PENDELL COURT
Lake Farm
COCKLEY PLANTATION
Nursery
Dormers Farm
BLETCHINGLEY
Castle Hill
COOMBES COPPICE
STANLEY'S WOOD
Castlehill Farm
Sandhills
Sandhills Farm
BLETCHINGLEY GOLF COURSE
Clubhouse
The Plough Inn
SPORTS GRD
Bowling Green
PLAYING FIELDS
CROOKEDFIELD SHAW
MARIE CURIE CENTRE
THE NORTH DOWNS HOSP
Sports Centre
PLAYING FIELD
Rugby Ground
EIGHT ACRE WOOD
The Chalet Farm
The Chalet
Paddock Barn
OLDPARK SHAW
TEN ACRE SHAW
TUPWOOD SCRUBS
The Moyle House
FOSTERDOWN WOOD
Kennels & Cattery
Gravelly Hill
Water Twr
The Mound
Roughets House
DIALBANK WOOD
THE DEVIL'S HOLE
KENNEL SHAW
Tyler's Green
Fire Sta
North Park Farm
SAND PIT
ELM PLATT
Godstone
GODSTONE GREEN
White Hart PH
Youth Cen
Knights Garden Centre Ivy Mill
Stangrave Hall Stables
Waterhouse Farm
SUNNYBANK VILLAS
Nettletons Nursery
Garston Park
HARLINGS SHAW
TILBURSTOWHILL PLANTATION
Tilburstow Hill
GRAVELHILL WOOD
Coldharbour Farm
Coldharbour House
ELEVEN ACRE SHAW
LONG SHAW
Tilburstowhill Farm
M25
M23
A25
A22
B2235
B2030
GODSTONE ROAD
CATERHAM
BLETCHINGLEY ROAD
HIGH STREET
CASTLE STREET
OXTED ROAD
NORTH DOWNS WAY
HARESTONE VALLEY ROAD
WHITEHILL LANE
ROUGHETTS LANE
NORTH PARK LANE
RABIES HEATH ROAD
TILBURSTOW HILL
GREENSAND WAY

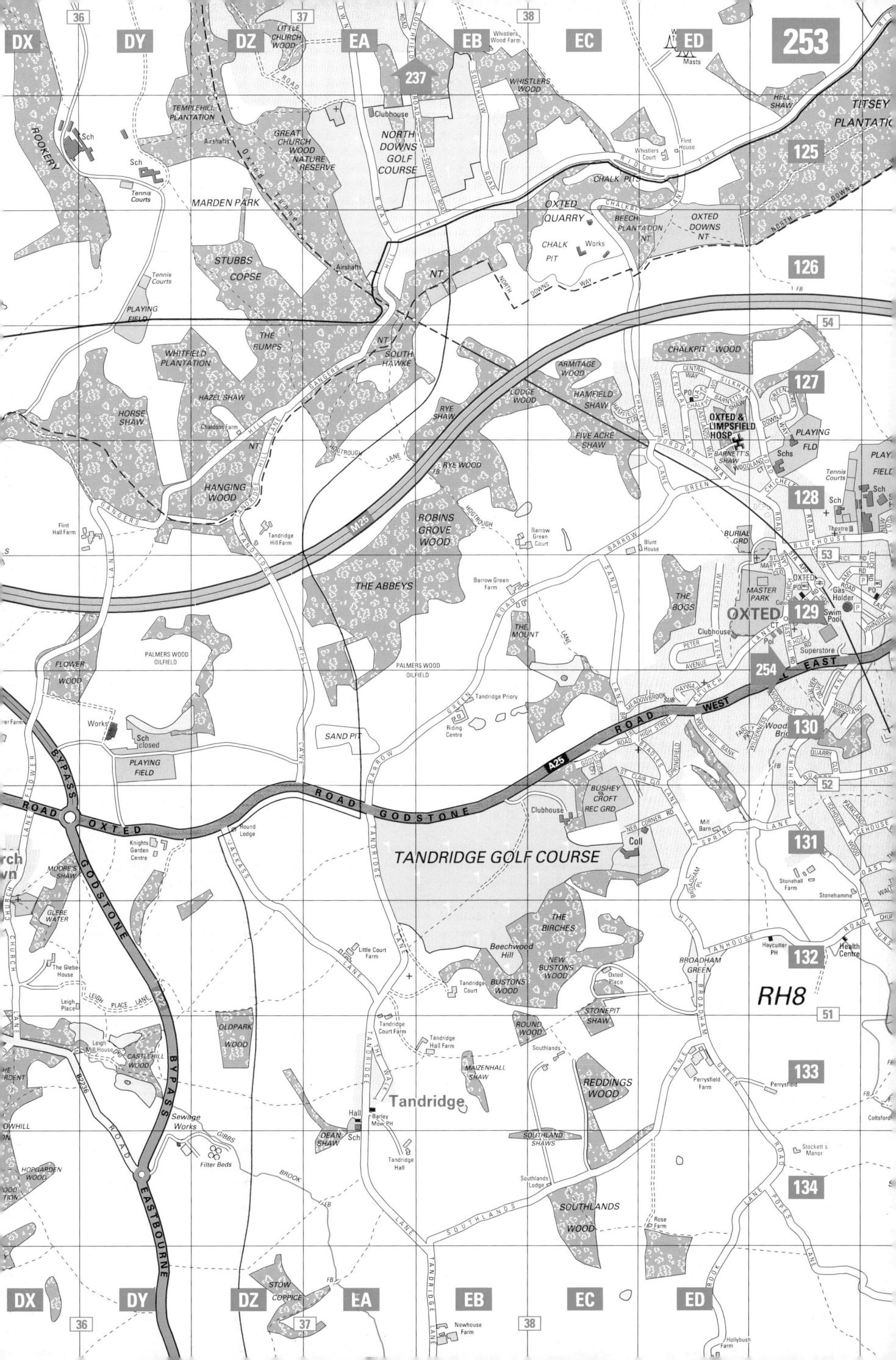

DX
DY
DZ
EA
EB
EC
ED
36
37
38
237
254
125
126
127
128
129
130
131
132
133
134
54
53
52
51
OXTED
Tandridge
RH8
TANDRIDGE GOLF COURSE
NORTH DOWNS GOLF COURSE
MARDEN PARK
STUBBS COPSE
THE RUMPS
WHITFIELD PLANTATION
HAZEL SHAW
HORSE SHAW
HANGING WOOD
TEMPLEHILL PLANTATION
GREAT CHURCH WOOD NATURE RESERVE
LITTLE CHURCH WOOD
ROOKERY
WHISTLERS WOOD
OXTED QUARRY
CHALK PIT
BEECH PLANTATION NT
OXTED DOWNS NT
TITSEY PLANTATION
HELL SHAW
CHALKPIT WOOD
ARMITAGE WOOD
HAMFIELD SHAW
LODGE WOOD
FIVE ACRE SHAW
RYE SHAW
RYE WOOD
ROBINS GROVE WOOD
THE ABBEYS
SOUTH HAWKE
OXTED & LIMPSFIELD HOSP
PLAYING FLD
BURIAL GRD
MASTER PARK
THE BOGS
THE MOUNT
PALMERS WOOD OILFIELD
FLOWER WOOD
SAND PIT
PLAYING FIELD
BUSHEY CROFT REC GRD
THE BIRCHES
Beechwood Hill
NEW BUSTONS WOOD
BUSTONS WOOD
STONEPIT SHAW
ROUND WOOD
OLDPARK WOOD
MAIZENHALL SHAW
REDDINGS WOOD
SOUTHLAND SHAWS
SOUTHLANDS WOOD
DEAN SHAW
STOW COPPICE
CASTLEHILL WOOD
MOORE'S SHAW
GLEBE WATER
HOPGARDEN WOOD
BROADHAM GREEN
M25
A25
A22
B2236
GODSTONE ROAD
OXTED ROAD
GODSTONE BYPASS
EASTBOURNE ROAD
THE RIDGE
NORTH DOWNS WAY
GANGERS HILL
HOGTROUGH LANE
BARROW GREEN ROAD
TANDRIDGE LANE
TANDRIDGE HILL LANE
SOUTHLANDS LANE
TANHOUSE ROAD
SPRING LANE
BROADHAM GREEN
ROOK LANE
POPES LANE
GIBBS BROOK
JACKASS LANE
Whistlers Wood Farm
Whistlers Court
Flint House
Masts
Clubhouse
Sch
Tennis Courts
Airshafts
Chaldons Farm
Flint Hall Farm
Tandridge Hill Farm
Barrow Green Court
Blunt House
Barrow Green Farm
Tandridge Priory
Riding Centre
Works
Round Lodge
Knights Garden Centre
The Glebe House
Leigh Place
Leigh Mill House
Sewage Works
Filter Beds
Little Court Farm
Tandridge Court
Tandridge Court Farm
Tandridge Hall Farm
Tandridge Hall
Barley Mow PH
Hall
Southlands
Southlands Lodge
Rose Farm
Newhouse Farm
Hollybush Farm
Perrysfield Farm
Perrysfield
Stockett's Manor
Coltsford
Oxted Place
Coll
Mill Barn
Stonehall Farm
Stonehamme
Haycutter PH
Health Centre
Superstore
Swim Pool
Gas Holder
Theatre
Schs
Clubhouse
Pol

EE
EF
EG
EH
EJ
EK
EL
40
41
42
238
CR3
HELL SHAW
TITSEY PLANTATION
TITSEY PLACE GARDENS
Titsey Place
Titsey
CHURCH WOOD
ROUGHFIELD SHAW
SQUARE WOOD
Whistlers Court
125
RIDGE
PILGRIMS WAY
NORTH DOWNS WAY
BARTON SHAW
Pitchfont Farm
Limpsfield Lodge Farm
TITSEY PARK
BEECH PLANTATION NT
OXTED DOWNS NT
126
Park Farm
Clacket Lane Services
TITSEY WOOD
M25
54
CHALKPIT WOOD
127
ASHEN COPPICE
Broomlands Farm
OXTED & LIMPSFIELD HOSP
PLAYING FLD
Schs
SAND PIT
PLAYING FIELDS
PLAYING FIELD
Tennis Courts
Sports Hall
GRUBSTREET SHAW
GRUBSTREET COPSE
128
BURIAL GRD
Theatre
REC GRD
Tennis Club
Blunt House
53
LIMPSFIELD
THE
129
MASTER PARK
OXTED
Gas Holder
Swim Pool
Health Cen
Lib
PO
Pebble Hill
Cricket Ground
Clubhouse
Pebble Hill House
Court Langley
ALLOT
A25
WESTERHAM ROAD
WESTERHAM HILL
EAST HILL
WEST HILL
Fire Sta
Superstore
Pol
253
LIMPSFIELD COMMON
NT
ANDREWS WOOD
130
Woodhurst Bridge
Wildshaw
Swallowfield
Limpsfield Tunnel
WEST HEATH
STONESWOOD ROAD
CHAPEL ROAD
52
B269
HATCH
Sch
PLAYING FIELD
Mill Barn
131
Coll
CROCKED
LITTLE HEATH NT
Chartfield House
Tenchley's Park
THE ALDERS
TENCHLEY'S WOOD
Stonehall Farm
Stonehamme
Boulthurst Farm
HURST GREEN
Abbeyfield
Comm Cen
Haycutter PH
Health Centre
132
LOAMPIT WOOD
RH8
Hurst Green
Whitegates Farm
Crabbett Wood
51
CRABBETT WOOD
Crabbett Wood Farm
Tenchleys Manor
Pav
RUNNING TRACK
Doghurst
ITCHINGWOOD COMMON
133
Perrysfield
Coltsford Mill
FAIRVIEW IND EST
Red Lane Farm
Holland
Stockett's Manor
PARISHCROFT WOOD
Parishcroft Wood Farm
134
Sewage Works
Depot
Filter Beds
PONDERDICK SHAW
The Diamond
Connerton Stables
Stockenden Farm
Rose Farm
Clubhouse
Rugby Ground
HONESLAND WOOD
COLLESTERS WOOD
Upper Gr Farm
MOLLSTONES WOOD
Hollybush Farm

255
EM
EN
EP
EQ
ER
ES
ET
43
44
45
239
M25
HARTLEY WOOD
WESTERHAM WOOD
WESTERHAM
PLAYING FIELD
Sch
ALLOT
Offices
Pav
Depot
KINGS GEORGES FIELD
Tenn Cts
Lib
Fire Sta
PO
BURIAL GRD
Statues
QUEBEC HOUSE
MKT SQ
VIC. HILL SQ
LONDON ROAD
HIGH STREET
A25
A233
B2024
BRASTED ROAD
WESTERHAM ROAD
CROYDON ROAD
BEGGARS LANE
RIVER DARENT
Charmans Farm
Horizons Centre
Works
Mountwood
Fountain Cottages
Clubhouse
Cricket Grd
PONDS
WESTERHAM GOLF COURSE
125
126
127
128
129
130
131
132
133
134
54
53
52
51
TN16
TN8
Hosey Hill
DUNSDALE WOOD
Dunsdale House
Dunsdale Wood Farm
Dunsdale Farm House
The Granary
Glebe House
Gillhams Farm
Piper's Farm
Foxwold
MANNING'S WOOD
PIPERS GREEN
STANHO WOOD
SQUERRYES PARK
SQUERRYES COURT
Cenotaph
Squerryes Home Farm
SPRING SHAW
LODGES WOOD
SAND PIT
Green Croft Farm
WET WOOD
DEVIL OF KENT
SURREY
KENT
FARLEY COMMON
Farley Grange
Covers Farm
Westwood Farm
Cross Dyke
Grasshopper PH
Moorhouse Farm
Moor House
MOORHOUSE BANK
MOORHOUSE BANK COMMON NT
Clubhouse
CRONKLANDS
THE HIGH CHART
Goodley Stock
GOODLEY STOCK ROAD
TOWER WOOD
Tower
HOSEY COMMON
Valance End
BURIAL GRD
FRENCH STREET
French Street Farm
French Street House
Outridge
Cobb Cottage
MAPLETON ROAD
Moorcroft Place
HOSEY COMMON ROAD
B2026
Crockham House
Kent Hatch
THE CHART
NT
SCEARN BANK
Curie Centre
COV RES
Kent Hatch House
B269
CROCKHAMHILL COMMON
Chartwell NT
Chartwell House
Chartwell Farm
BUDDLES WOOD
BROWNS'S OVEN WOOD
CASTLE GR
The Warren
Hopland
The Red House
Crockham Hill Farm
Froghole Farm
Manners
ROUNDMEAD SHAW
Trevereux
Froghole
Little Court
GUDGE WOOD
PUDDLEDOCK LANE
DERBY WOOD
CHANDLER WOOD
TIES WOOD
Sch
PO
Hall
OAKDALE LANE
SMITHS LANE
Crockham Hill
Coachmans
KENT BROOK
FB
TANDRIDGE
SEVENOAKS
Swaynesland
Hurst Farm
DAIRY LANE
Old Dairy Farm
Clubhouse
PLAYING FIELD
DENNETTSLAND ROAD
Dennett Lodge Farm
POOTINGS LANE
SPOUT LANE
MAIN ROAD
B2026
Obriss Farm
LONGCROFT WOOD
HATCROFT WOOD
GUILDABLES WOOD
Redland Farm
Coakham

FA
FB
FC
FD
FE
FF
FG
241
240
121
122
123
124
125
126
127
128
129
130
Longford
SEVENOAKS WILDFOWL
TN14
WEST LAKE
CHIPSTEAD LAKE
Junction 5
Chipstead
Riverhead
Sundridge
Bessels Green
MONTREAL PARK
TN13
SEVENOAKS
Kippington
RED GROVE
GREAT BRITAIN'S WOOD
MILL BANK WOOD
WHITLEY FOREST
HYDE'S FOREST
DUST WOOD
Goathurst Common
SHEEPHILL WOOD
PITFIELD WOOD
Douglas Hill
Bayley's Hill
STUBBS WOOD
RAKEFIELD WOOD
CLAYPIT SHAW
COLD ARBOR WOOD
THE WARREN
LITTLE BRITAIN'S WOOD
GREENLANE WOOD
FURZEFIELD WOOD
MILL WATER BOTTOM WOOD
MILDRIDGE WOOD
ROUNDABOUT WOOD
KEATING WOOD
BROCKHILL WOODS
SEVENOAKS BYPASS
WESTERHAM ROAD
BRADBOURNE
LONDON ROAD
Seven Wents
Chevening Cross

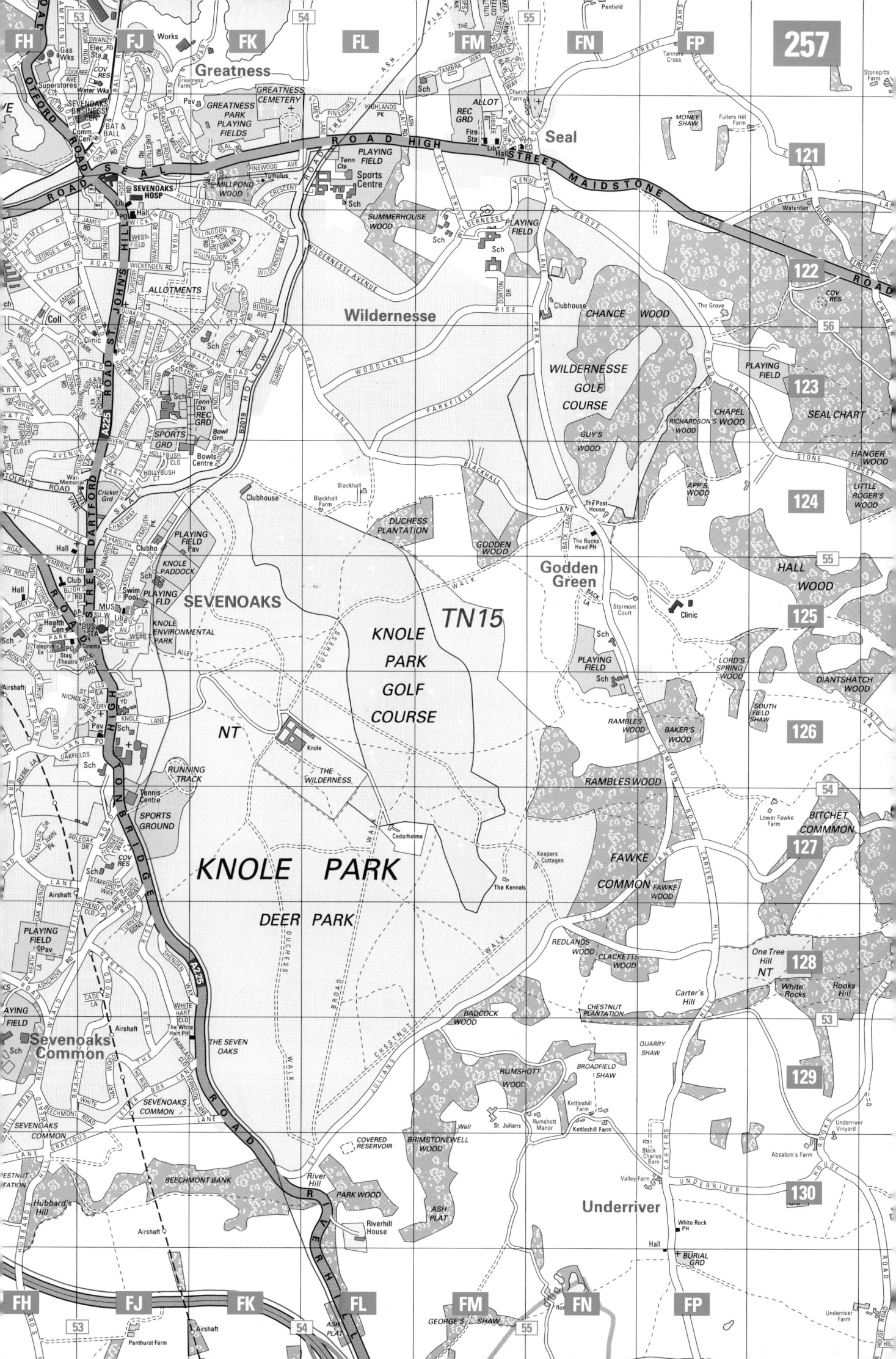

FH
FJ
FK
FL
FM
FN
FP
53
54
55
56
Greatness
Works
Greatness Farm
GREATNESS CEMETERY
GREATNESS PARK PLAYING FIELDS
SEVENOAKS BUSINESS CEN
Superstores
Water Wks
Gas Wks
Elec Sta
COV RES
BAT & BALL
Comm Cen
OTFORD ROAD
SEAL ROAD
SEVENOAKS HOSP
MILLPOND WOOD
Tumulus
PINEWOOD AVE
THE CRESCENT
HILLINGDON
HIGHLANDS PK
PLAYING FIELD
Tenn Cts
Sports Centre
Sch
SUMMERHOUSE WOOD
WILDERNESSE AVENUE
WILDERNESSE
PLAYING FIELD
ALLOT
REC GRD
Fire Sta
Lib
Hall
PO
Seal
HIGH STREET
MAIDSTONE ROAD
A25
Church Farm
Penfield
Tanners Cross
NOAH'S
MONEY SHAW
Fullers Hill Farm
Stonepitts Farm
121
122
123
124
125
126
127
128
129
130
FOUNTAIN
Waterden
COV RES
The Grove
PLAYING FIELD
SEAL CHART
CHAPEL WOOD
RICHARDSON'S WOOD
HANGER WOOD
LITTLE ROGER'S WOOD
STONE STREET
APP'S WOOD
HALL WOOD
Clubhouse
CHANCE WOOD
WILDERNESSE GOLF COURSE
GUY'S WOOD
Wildernesse
WOODLAND
PARKFIELD
BLACKHALL
Blackhall
Blackhall Farm
DUCHESS PLANTATION
GODDEN WOOD
The Post House
The Bucks Head PH
Godden Green
Stormont Court
Clinic
LORD'S SPRING WOOD
DIANTSHATCH WOOD
SOUTH FIELD SHAW
PLAYING FIELD
RAMBLES WOOD
BAKER'S WOOD
FAWKE COMMON ROAD
Lower Fawke Farm
BITCHET COMMON
FAWKE COMMON
FAWKE WOOD
REDLANDS WOOD
CLACKETTS WOOD
One Tree Hill NT
White Rocks
Rooks Hill
Carter's Hill
CHESTNUT PLANTATION
BADCOCK WOOD
QUARRY SHAW
RUMSHOTT WOOD
BROADFIELD SHAW
Kettleshill Farm
St. Julians
Rumshott Manor
Well
BRIMSTONEWELL WOOD
Black Charles Barn
Underriver Vinyard
Absalom's Farm
Valley Farm
UNDERRIVER
Underriver
White Rock PH
Hall
BURIAL GRD
ASH PLAT
Riverhill House
River Hill
PARK WOOD
COVERED RESERVOIR
GEORGE'S SHAW
Underriver Farm
KNOLE PARK
DEER PARK
KNOLE PARK GOLF COURSE
TN15
NT
Knole
THE WILDERNESS
Cedarholme
Keepers Cottages
The Kennels
Clubhouse
DUCHESS WALK
BROAD WALK
CHESTNUT WALK
JULIANS
SEVENOAKS
KNOLE PADDOCK
PLAYING FIELD
PLAYING FLD
Swim Pool
KNOLE ENVIRONMENTAL PARK
RUNNING TRACK
Tennis Centre
SPORTS GROUND
THE SEVEN OAKS
The White Hart PH
SEVENOAKS COMMON
Sevenoaks Common
BEECHMONT BANK
Hubbard's Hill
Airshaft
Panthurst Farm
DARTFORD ROAD
A225
ST. JOHN'S HILL
HIGH STREET
TONBRIDGE ROAD
RIVERHILL
ALLOTMENTS
SPORTS GRD
REC GRD
Bowls Centre
Cricket Grd
War Memorial
Coll
Clinic
Club
Health Cen
BUS STA
Stag Theatre
Cinema
KNOLE LANE
Pav
PLAYING FIELD

242
ROYAL SURREY COUNTY HOSPITAL
GU2
Stag Hill
CATHEDRAL
Guildford Park
THE PHILIP HENMAN SPORTS GROUND
STRAWBERRY GROVE
DEAN BOTTOM
MANOR COPSE
Onslow Village
GUILDFORD
GUILDFORD CEMETERY
GU1
Charlotte
HOG'S BACK
SUNNYDOWN PLANTATION
PICCARD'S ROUGH
Artington
SURREY POLICE HQ
EAST WARREN
GU3
LOSELEY PARK
Littleton
RUSH CROFT
ASHEN COPSE
PIPKIN COPSE
PUDDOCK COPSE
BURL'S REW
OLD CLAYPITS WOOD
SHALFORD PARK
SHALFORD
Peasmarsh
RIVERWAY ESTATE
TRUNLEY HEATH
Binscombe
GU7
BROADWATER PARK
FARNCOMBE GOLF COURSE
FARNCOMBE
BRAMLEY GOLF COURSE
RIVER WEY GODALMING NAVIGATION NT
AS
AT
AU
AV
AW
AX
AY
135
136
137
138
139
140
141
142
143
144
98
99
00
49
48
47
46

GUILDFORD
GOLF
COURSE
MERROW
DOWNS
WALNUT
TREE
BOTTOM
HAREWARREN
THE
ROUGHS
URN
FIELD
PLAYING
FIELD
ST. LUKE'S
HOSPITAL
M.A.F.F.
ALBURY
DOWNS
PEWLEY DOWN
GU4
GU5
CHANTRIES
FARTHING
COPSE
HALFPENNY
COPSE
St. Martha's
Hill
LIDWELL
COPSE
POSTFORD
POND
Chilworth
Manor
MUD
WOOD
Chilworth
CHILWORTH
FISH
POND
BRADSTONE
BROOK SPORTS
GROUND
SHALFORD
COMMON
WONERSH
COMMON
LOCKNER
HOLT
NATIONAL
TRUST
Tangley
Hill
ROSEMARY
HILL
FRIARY
Blackheath
BLACKHEATH
CUCKOO
COPSE
BELMONT
COPSE
Tower
Chinthurst
Hill
BRITISH
RED CROSS
MUSEUM
DERRY'S
WOOD
Derry's
Hill
ST. MARY'S
INSTITUTE
NORTHBROOK
HILL
ST. JOHN'S
SEMINARY
Wonersh
HEATHFIELDS
JUGS
COPSE
The Hallams
Hallams
Court
Hallam's Farm
Watercress
Beds
Holmcroft
Nursery
Southlands
Equestrian
Centre
Lower
Chinthurst
Farm
Great Tangley
Manor
House
Great Tangley
Manor Farm
Hornhatch
Farm
Bradstone
Brook
Lockner Farm
Lockner Holt
Newbarn
White
Lane
Farm
Newlands
The Manor
Hotel
Tyting Farm
St. Martha's
Priory Lodge
Great
Halfpenny Farm
Great
Halfpenny
Little
Halfpenny
Farm
Manor
Farm
South
Warren
Farm
Whinney
Hill
Warren
Farm
Burwood
Farm
A246
A248
A25
A281
B2128
243
260
135
136
137
138
139
140
141
142
143
144
49
48
47
46
AZ
BA
BB
BC
BD
BE
BF
01
02
03

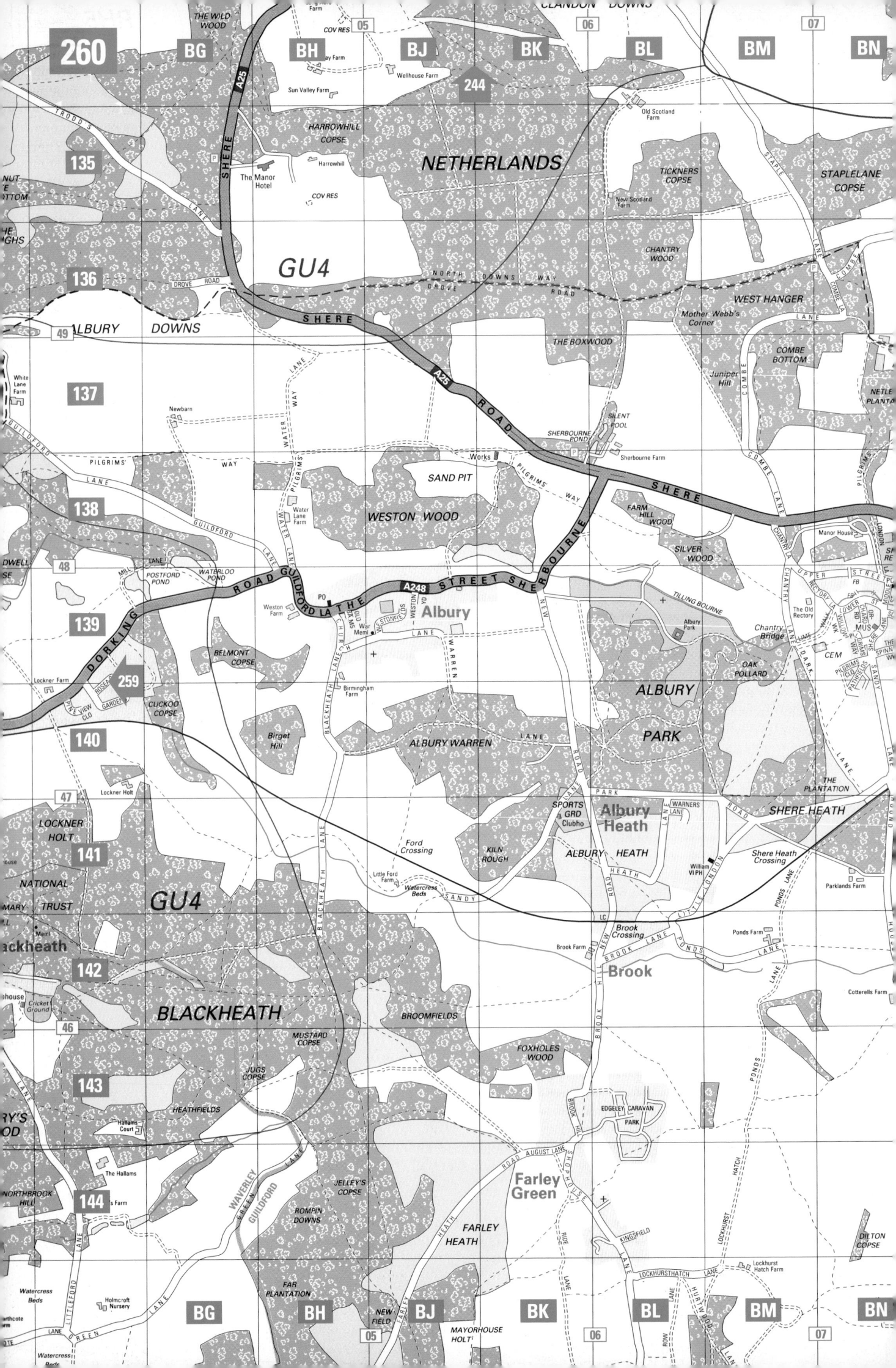
BG
BH
BJ
BK
BL
BM
BN
244
259
GU4
NETHERLANDS
HARROWHILL COPSE
The Manor Hotel
TICKNERS COPSE
STAPLELANE COPSE
CHANTRY WOOD
WEST HANGER
ALBURY DOWNS
THE BOXWOOD
COMBE BOTTOM
Juniper Hill
SILENT POOL
SHERBOURNE POND
Sherbourne Farm
SAND PIT
WESTON WOOD
FARM HILL WOOD
SILVER WOOD
Albury
BELMONT COPSE
CUCKOO COPSE
Birget Hill
ALBURY WARREN
ALBURY PARK
OAK POLLARD
Chantry Bridge
THE PLANTATION
SHERE HEATH
Albury Heath
ALBURY HEATH
KILN ROUGH
Ford Crossing
Shere Heath Crossing
LOCKNER HOLT
NATIONAL TRUST
Blackheath
BLACKHEATH
Brook
Brook Crossing
BROOMFIELDS
MUSTARD COPSE
FOXHOLES WOOD
JUGS COPSE
HEATHFIELDS
EDGELEY CARAVAN PARK
Farley Green
JELLEY'S COPSE
ROMPIN DOWNS
FARLEY HEATH
FAR PLANTATION
MAYORHOUSE HOLT
DILTON COPSE
The Hallams
Hallams Court
Holmcroft Nursery
Lockhurst Hatch Farm
Cotterells Farm
Ponds Farm
Parklands Farm
Brook Farm
Little Ford Farm
Lockner Farm
Lockner Holt
Birmingham Farm
Weston Farm
Water Lane Farm
Newbarn
White Lane Farm
Old Scotland Farm
New Scotland Farm
Wellhouse Farm
Sun Valley Farm
Harrowhill
COV RES
NORTH DOWNS WAY
SHERE ROAD
DORKING ROAD
GUILDFORD ROAD
THE STREET
A25
A248
135
136
137
138
139
140
141
142
143
144
05
06
07
49
48
47
46

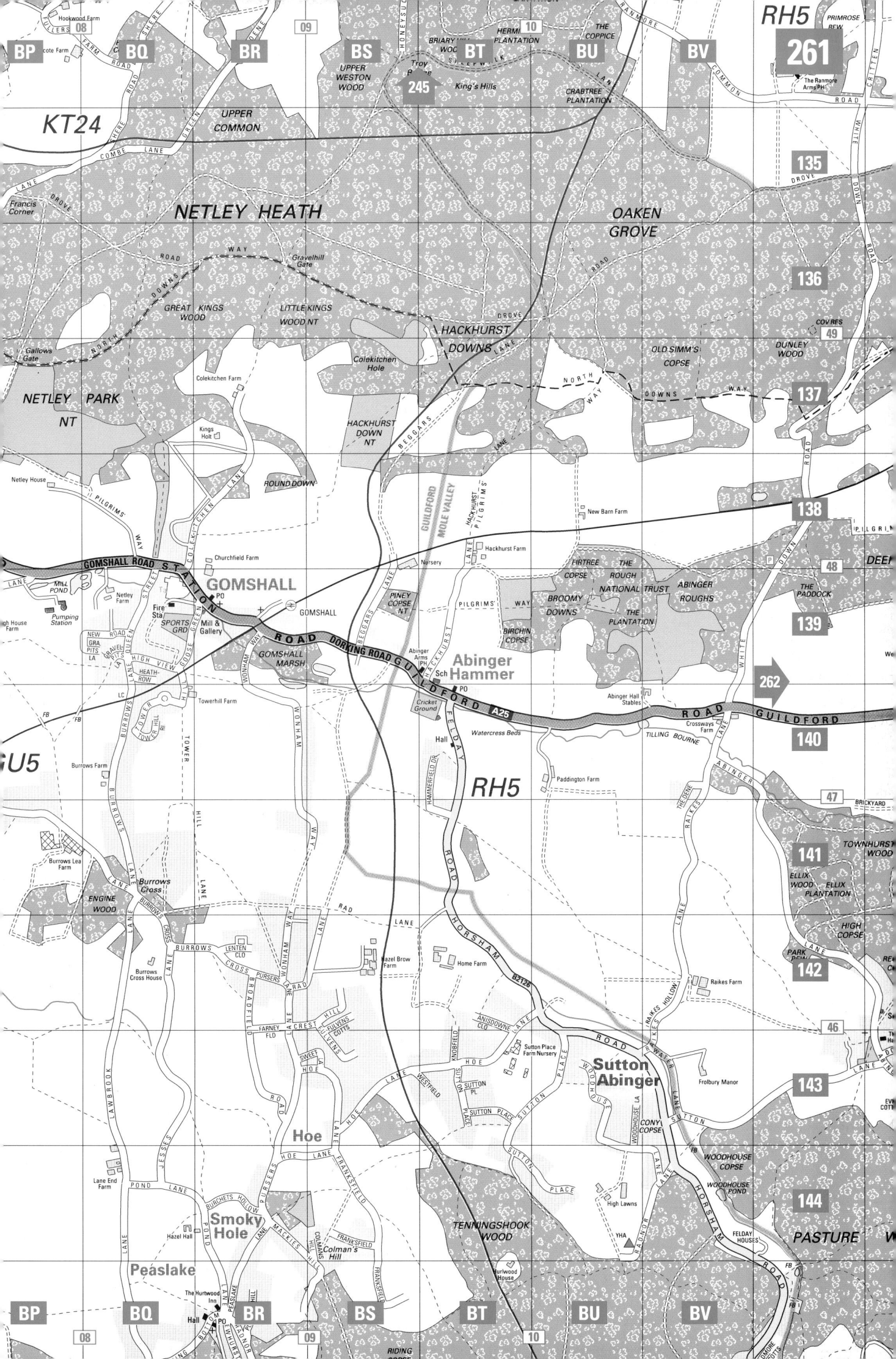
RH5
261
245
262
KT24
GU5
RH5
BP
BQ
BR
BS
BT
BU
BV
08
09
10
135
136
137
138
139
140
141
142
143
144
49
48
47
46
NETLEY HEATH
OAKEN GROVE
NETLEY PARK NT
UPPER COMMON
UPPER WESTON WOOD
King's Hills
CRABTREE PLANTATION
THE COPPICE
HACKHURST DOWNS
GREAT KINGS WOOD
LITTLE KINGS WOOD NT
Gravelhill Gate
Gallows Gate
Francis Corner
Colekitchen Hole
Colekitchen Farm
HACKHURST DOWN NT
OLD SIMM'S COPSE
DUNLEY WOOD
Kings Holt
Netley House
ROUND DOWN
New Barn Farm
Hackhurst Farm
Churchfield Farm
Nursery
GOMSHALL
Netley Farm
Mill Pond
Pumping Station
Fire Sta
SPORTS GRD
Mill & Gallery
GOMSHALL MARSH
PINEY COPSE NT
FIRTREE COPSE
THE ROUGH
NATIONAL TRUST
ABINGER ROUGHS
BROOMY DOWNS
THE PLANTATION
BIRCHIN COPSE
THE PADDOCK
Abinger Hammer
Abinger Arms PH
Sch
PO
Cricket Ground
Towerhill Farm
Abinger Hall Stables
Crossways Farm
Watercress Beds
TILLING BOURNE
Hall
Paddington Farm
Burrows Farm
Burrows Lea Farm
Burrows Cross
ENGINE WOOD
TOWNHURST WOOD
ELLIX WOOD
ELLIX PLANTATION
HIGH COPSE
Hazel Brow Farm
Home Farm
Raikes Farm
Burrows Cross House
Sutton Place Farm Nursery
Sutton Abinger
Frolbury Manor
CONY COPSE
Hoe
WOODHOUSE COPSE
WOODHOUSE POND
Lane End Farm
Smoky Hole
Hazel Hall
High Lawns
YHA
TENNINGSHOOK WOOD
Colman's Hill
PASTURE
FELDAY HOUSES
Hurtwood House
Peaslake
The Hurtwood Inn
Hall
The Ranmore Arms PH
GOMSHALL ROAD
STATION ROAD
DORKING ROAD
GUILDFORD ROAD
A25
B2126
HORSHAM ROAD
FELDAY ROAD
GUILDFORD MOLE VALLEY
PILGRIMS' WAY
NORTH DOWNS WAY
COMBE LANE
BEGGARS LANE
WONHAM WAY
HACKHURST LANE
WHITE DOWN LANE
ABINGER LANE
RAIKES LANE
RAIKES HOLLOW
SUTTON LANE
SUTTON PLACE
HOE LANE
PURSERS LANE
BURROWS LANE
LAWBROOK LANE
JESSES LANE
POND LANE
FRANKSFIELD
MACKIES HILL
COLMANS HILL
BROADFIELD ROAD
ANISDOWNE CLO
KNOBFIELD
WESTFIELD
SWEET LA
CREST HILL
FULVENS
FULVENS COTTS
FARNEY FLD
LENTEN CLO
TOWER HILL
TOWER HILL RI
HIGH VIEW
HEATH ROW
QUEEN STREET
GRAVEL PITS LA
NEW ROAD
COLEKITCHEN LANE
HAMMERFIELD DR
THE DENE
WOODHOUSE LA
BURCHETS HOLLOW
RADNOR ROAD
RANMORE COMMON ROAD
BRICKYARD
COV RES
FB

BW
BX
BY
BZ
CA
CB
CC
12
13
14
135
136
137
138
139
140
141
142
143
144
49
48
47
46
246
261
RANMORE COMMON ROAD
PRIMROSE REW
The Ranmore Arms PH
HIGH BARN ROAD
CRITTEN
STONYROCK
LILLIES COPSE
RANMORE ROUNDABOUT
THE SPAIL
NATIONAL TRUST
NORTH DOWNS WAY
GREAT COPSE
THE ROUNDABOUTS
Landbarn Farm
HOLE HILL LA
BURNETTS LEAF
PILGRIMS WAY
DROVE ROAD
WHITE DOWN ROAD
OAKEN GROVE
WHITE DOWNS
Picketts Hole
HOLEHILL COPSE
BUSHY PLAT
Bushy Plat Farm
HORLEY COPSE
HURST COPSE
Dene Farm
Hole Hill
Rokefield
Coomb Farm
COV RES
OLD SIMM'S COPSE
DUNLEY WOOD
FB
WESTCOTT
SPRINGFIELD
ST JOHN'S ROAD
REC GRD
COOMBE COPSE
MILL POND
Rookery Farm
DEERLEAP RD
SAND RD
The Cricketers PH
PO
THE PADDOCK
PARSONAGE LA
STONES LA
COAST HILL LA
Park Farm
HILL GUILDFORD
WESTCOTT HEATH
LOGMORE LANE
HEATH RISE
THE HILDENS
A25
Rookery Hill Farm
HOLCOMBE COPSE
THE ROOKERY
ROOKERY DRIVE
DEERLEAP WOOD
THE PADDOCK
LAISURE COPSE
ABINGER ROUGHS
NATIONAL TRUST
THE PLANTATION
ROOKERY WOOD
FIR PLANTATION
Wotton
RH5
Westlane Farm
WEST LANE
Wotton Hatch PH
ICEHOUSE WOOD
PIPP BROOK
HANGER WOOD
LONGMOOR WOOD
FURZEFIELD COPSE
FURZEFIELD PLANTATION
THE TOLT
Coast Hill Farm
SHEEPHOUSE
FURZE FIELD
SHEEPHOUSE GRN
WILLIAM EVELYN
COAST ROAD
GUILDFORD ROAD
Crossways
TILLING BOURNE
Manor Farm
THE ROUNDABOUT
GREEN BROOM
HORSLEY COPSE
WOTTON DRIVE
SYLVANUS WOOD
BRITT'S WOOD
HOLLOW LANE
FIRTREE PLAT
BRICKYARD LANE
WOTTON
Wotton House
DAMPHURST WOOD
Oldpark Hill
Weirs
Weir
WOLVENS LANE
Logmore Green Farm
ALDER COPSE
RAIKES LANE
TOWNHURST WOOD
CHANDLERS WOOD
ELLIX WOOD
ELLIX PLANTATION
WHITINGS WOOD
STONEPIT COPSE
BRIDLEGATE COPSE
HIGH COPSE
PARK REW
RECTORY COPSE
MUNDIES PLANTATION
BUSHY WOOD
THE WILDERNESS
STABLE COPSE
Squire's Farm
Raikes Farm
RAIKES HOLLOW
WATERFALL COPSE
SQUIRE'S
Sch
The Abinger Hatch PH
DONKEY LANE
Abinger Common
SIMONS COPSE
NOONS CORNER ROAD
NOONS COPSE
Noons Corner
WESTCOTT GORE
MILL POND
FRIDAY STREET
Home Farm
Stephan Langton PH
TILLING BOURNE
TANKARDS POND
EVELYN COTTAGES
GLEBE LA
WOODHOUSE COPSE
WOODHOUSE POND
SUTTON LANE
CONY COPSE
WOODHOUSE LA
ABINGER COMMON
NATIONAL TRUST
SEVERELLS COPSE
TOWER COPSE
Goddard's
WHITEBERRY ROAD
BROOKWICK COPSE
PASTURE WOOD
FELDAY HOUSES
HAM ROAD
ABINGER COMMON ROAD
LEITH HILL LANE
PARKHURST WOOD
Park House Farm
King George's Hill
LEMON'S FARM RD
Lemon's Farm
LEYLANDS LANE
Shootlands
YHA
RADNOR ROAD
FELDAY COTTS
Leylands Farm
THE DUKE'S WARREN

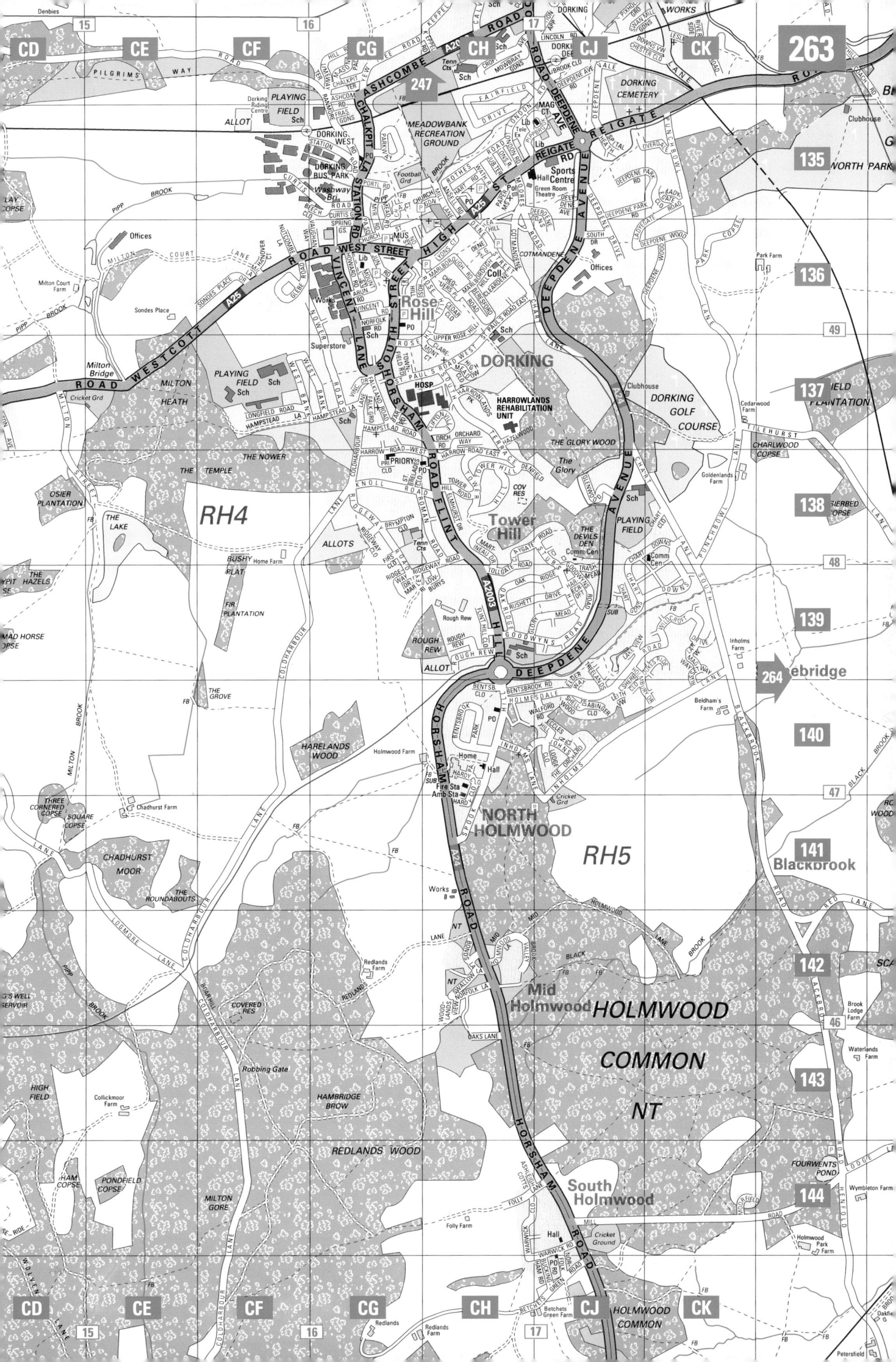

263
247
264
Denbies
CD
CE
CF
CG
CH
CJ
CK
15
16
17
PILGRIMS' WAY
ASHCOMBE ROAD
A25
DORKING
WORKS
DORKING CEMETERY
PLAYING FIELD
Sch
ALLOT
Dorking Riding Centre
DORKING WEST
MEADOWBANK RECREATION GROUND
DORKING BUS PARK
Washway Bri
Football Grd
Sports Centre
Green Room Theatre
REIGATE RD
REIGATE ROAD
HIGH ST
WEST STREET
DEEPDENE AVENUE
Clubhouse
NORTH PARK
135
136
137
138
139
140
141
142
143
144
49
48
47
46
Offices
Milton Court Farm
Sondes Place
Works
Rose Hill
Superstore
WESTCOTT ROAD
Milton Bridge
Cricket Grd
MILTON HEATH
DORKING
HOSP
HARROWLANDS REHABILITATION UNIT
DORKING GOLF COURSE
Park Farm
Cedarwood Farm
FIELD PLANTATION
CHARLWOOD COPSE
Goldenlands Farm
THE GLORY WOOD
The Glory
THE NOWER
THE TEMPLE
OSIER PLANTATION
THE LAKE
RH4
ALLOTS
Tower Hill
THE DEVILS DEN
PLAYING FIELD
Comm Cen
BUSHY PLAT
Home Farm
FIR PLANTATION
THE HAZELS
MAD HORSE COPSE
Rough Rew
ROUGH REW
ALLOT
A2003
A24
DEEPDENE
Inholms Farm
ebridge
Beldham's Farm
THE GROVE
HARELANDS WOOD
Holmwood Farm
Fire Sta
Amb Sta
Hall
Cricket Grd
NORTH HOLMWOOD
RH5
Blackbrook
THREE CORNERED COPSE
SQUARE COPSE
Chadhurst Farm
CHADHURST MOOR
THE ROUNDABOUTS
Works
HORSHAM ROAD
Redlands Farm
Mid Holmwood
HOLMWOOD COMMON NT
Brook Lodge Farm
Waterlands Farm
COVERED RES
Robbing Gate
HIGH FIELD
Collickmoor Farm
HAMBRIDGE BROW
REDLANDS WOOD
FOURWENTS POND
Wymbleton Farm
HAM COPSE
PONDFIELD COPSE
MILTON GORE
South Holmwood
Folly Farm
Cricket Ground
Holmwood Park Farm
COLDHARBOUR LANE
WOLVEN LANE
Betchets Green Farm
HOLMWOOD COMMON
Redlands
Redlands Farm
Petersfield

CL
CM
CN
CP
CQ
CR
CS
19
20
21
248
263
135
136
137
138
139
140
141
142
143
144
49
48
47
46
BETCHWORTH PARK GOLF COURSE
BETCHWORTH PARK
BROCKHAM BIG FIELD
BETCHWORTH
Midland Bank College
RH3
RH5
BROCKHAM
DORKING CEMETERY
DORKING GOLF COURSE
FIELD PLANTATION
CHARLWOOD COPSE
OSIERBED COPSE
Strood Green
Stonebridge
Blackbrook
HOLMWOOD COMMON NT
ROOTHILL WOOD
HIGHRIDGE WOOD
Root Hill
Brockham Park
Bunce Common
HOOK COPSE
SCAMMELLS GROVE
HITHER HAWESREW
SNELLING PLANTED FIELD
NEW BARN SHAW
BIRCH PLATT'S
SIX ACRE COPSE
FURZEFIELD COPSE
OLDPARK WOOD
DENDY'S WOOD
GADBROOK COPSE
THE ROUGH
TWEED WOOD
TWENTY ACRE SHAW
JESSIES ROUGH
KILN COPSE
ORCHARD COPSE
BROOKFIELD COPSE
SEWAGE WORKS
FOURWENTS POND
HOLMWOOD COMMON
Tanner's Bridge
Borough Bridge
Betchworth Bridge
Boxhill Bridge
Deepdene Bridge
Betchworth Castle Remains
Brockham Court Farm
Pondtail Farm
Park Farm
Cedarwood Farm
Goldenlands Farm
Feltons Farm
Bushbury Farm
Stroodgreen Farm
Gadbrook Farm
Gadbrook House
Hall Farm
Ashcroft Farm
Hook Farm
Root Hill Farm
Great Brockhamhurst
Great Brockhamhurst Farm
Blunts Place Farm
Oakleigh Grange
Westwood Farm
Shellwood Manor
Shellwood Farm
Inholms Farm
Beldham's Farm
Brook Lodge Farm
Waterlands Farm
Hawesrew Farm
Lodge Farm
Wymbleton Farm
Holmwood Park Farm
Oakfield F
Swires Farm
Petersfield Farm
Ewood Farm
Hammond's Farm
Betchworth House
The Dolphin PH
Bowling Green

265
266
249
REIGATE
REIGATE HEATH
REIGATE PARK
REIGATE PRIORY
PRIORY POND
PLAYING FIELDS
Park Hill
South Park
RH2
Leigh
Nalderswood
Ironsbottom
Dawesgreen
SAND AND GRAVEL PIT
Dungate's Farm
THE ALDERS
Wonham Hill
Wonham Manor
Wonham Mill
MILL POND
Clubhouse
Heathfield Nursery
Skimmington Castle PH
Dungate Manor
Heathfield Farm
Heathfield
Trumpet Hill
Little Santon Farm
AGLAND COPSE
ALDERNESS WOOD
GUZZLE COPSE
Snowerhill Farm
Ricebridge Farm
Rice Bridge
JOHN'S COPSE
RIDING'S COPSE
KNIGHT'S GORSE
GAD BROOK
WALLACE BROOK
Flanchford Farm
Little Flanchford Farm
Flanchford Bridge
MILL POND
SLIPSHATCH WOOD
WITHY WOOD
HILLY FURZE FIELD
Hartswood Farm
REIGATE GRAMMAR SCHOOL PLAYING FIELDS
Tapner's Bridge
MARK MEAD PLANTATION
PLAYING FIELD
MOAT
Leigh Place
Seven Stars PH
The Plough PH
BUTLER'S SHAW
BIRCHETT COPSE
MOLE VALLEY
REIGATE & BANSTEAD
RIVER MOLE
Bures Manor
ALDER COPSE
Leigh Bridge
BELL COPSE
Dabdon Bridge
DEANOAK BROOK
BROWN'S COPSE
Clayhill Farm
Lowbridge Farm
Oak Farm
Old Swains Farmhouse
Dene Farm
Stumblehole Farm
MAGPIE WOOD
DULANDS COPSE
RIGDEN ROUGH
Ashurst Farm
SWAINS COPSE
Dean Oak Farm
Wolvers Home Farm
HILLY COPSE
Mynthurst
Fortune Farm
BUSH HOUSE COPSE
Ridgewood
ORCHARD FOUR ACRE PLANTATION
PARKHOUSE COPSE
Glasshouses
Nutley Dean Farm
Duxhurst Farm
CRUTCHFIELD LANE
SANDEAN COPSE
FLANCHFORD ROAD
SLIPSHATCH ROAD
CLAYHALL LANE
LITTLETON LANE
TRUMPETS HILL ROAD
SANDY LANE
RICEBRIDGE LANE
TAPNERS ROAD
LEIGH PLACE ROAD
SMALLS HILL ROAD
CLAYHILL ROAD
DEAN OAK LANE
IRONSBOTTOM
WHITEHALL LANE
PARK LANE
PRICES LANE
SANDCROSS LANE
NORTH ROAD
CHURCH ROAD
ALEXANDER ROAD
STUART ROAD
EDES FIELDS
CT
CU
CV
CW
CX
CY
CZ
22
23
24
135
136
137
138
139
140
141
142
143
144
46
47
48
49

DA
DB
DC
DD
DE
DF
DG
REIGATE
REDHILL
250
REIGATE PRIORY PLAYING FIELDS
REIGATE PARK
Park Hill
REDHILL COMMON
Mead Vale
Earlswood
Woodhatch
South Park
SPORTS GROUND
EARLSWOOD COMMON
REDHILL AND REIGATE GOLF COURSE
EARLSWOOD LAKES
SEWAGE WORKS
REDWOOD HOSPITAL
Doversgreen
REIGATE GRAMMAR SCHOOL PLAYING FIELDS
RH2
265
FELLAND COPSE
HOME GROVE
BENTING WOOD
HOLLOW SHAW
Sidlow
Sidlow Bridge
RIVER MOLE
Irons Bottom
SALFORDS
Salford's Bridge
MAGPIE WOOD
SAXLEY HILL
SAXONS HILL
RH6
BUSH HOUSE COPSE
COLLENDEAN COPSE
268
REIGATE ROAD
A217
A2044
A23
BRIGHTON ROAD
135
136
137
138
139
140
141
142
143
144
49
48
47
46
26
27
28

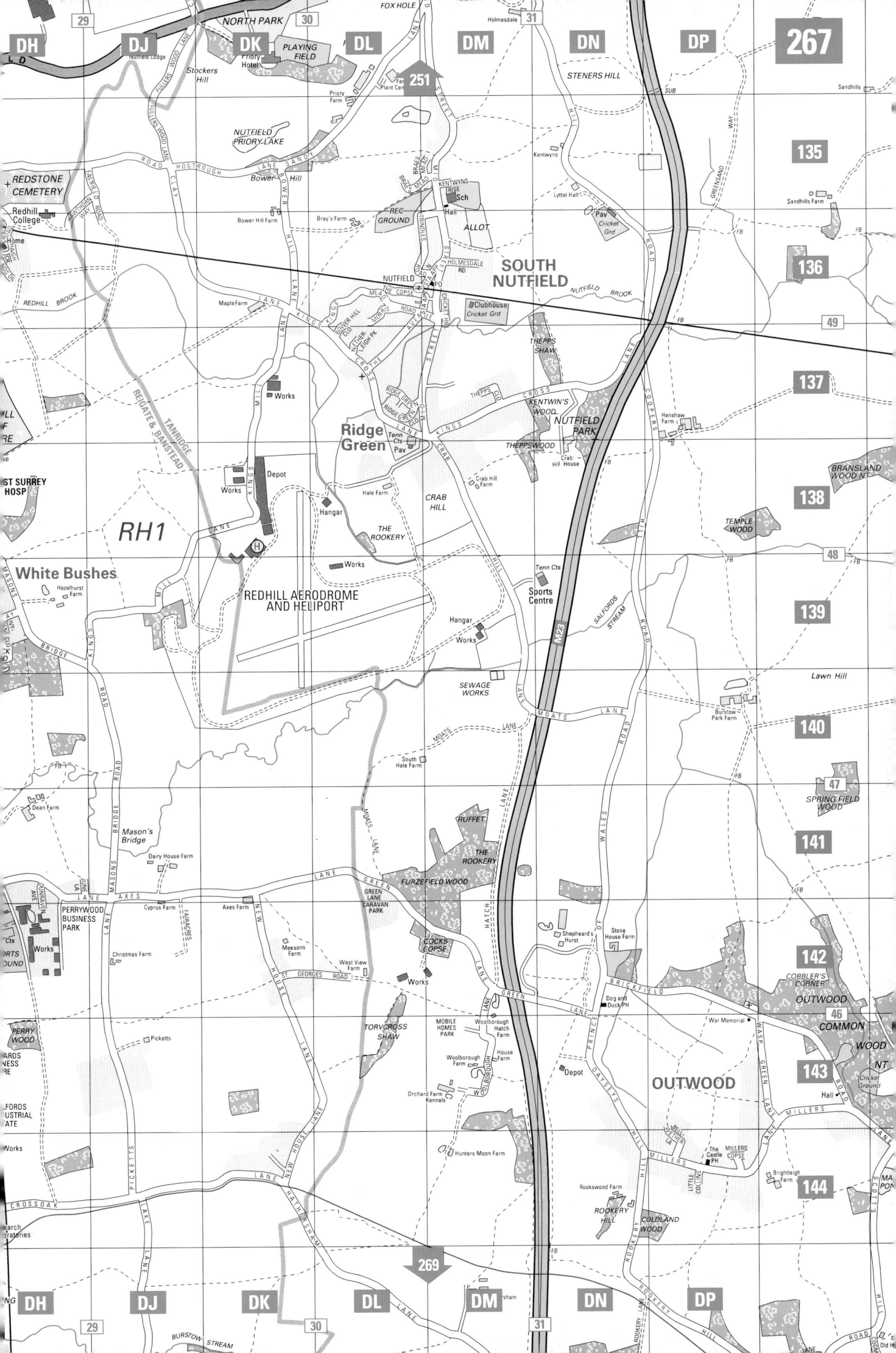
NORTH PARK
PLAYING FIELD
Nutfield Lodge
Priory Hotel
Stockers Hill
FOX HOLE
Holmesdale
STENERS HILL
Sandhills
Priory Farm
Plant Cen
NUTFIELD PRIORY LAKE
HOGTROUGH
SANDY LANE
Bower Hill
REDSTONE CEMETERY
Redhill College
Home
Bower Hill Farm
Bray's Farm
REC GROUND
Sch
Hall
ALLOT
KENTWYNS RISE
Kentwyns
Lyttel Hall
Pav
Cricket Grd
GREENSAND WAY
Sandhills Farm
FB
SOUTH NUTFIELD
HOLMESDALE RD
NUTFIELD
PO
NUTFIELD BROOK
REDHILL BROOK
Maple Farm
Clubhouse
Cricket Grd
THE COPSE
MORRIS ROAD
KINGS CROSS LANE
BOWER HILL CLO
NETHERLEIGH PK
THEPPS SHAW
THEPPS CLO
KENTWIN'S WOOD
NUTFIELD PARK
COOPERS HILL ROAD
Henshaw Farm
Works
REIGATE & BANSTEAD
TANRIDGE
RIDGE GREEN
Ridge Green
Tenn Cts
Pav
THEPPSWOOD
Crab Hill House
CRAB HILL
BRANSLAND WOOD NT
ST SURREY HOSP
Depot
Works
KINGS MILL LANE
Hale Farm
Crab Hill Farm
Hangar
THE ROOKERY
TEMPLE WOOD
RH1
White Bushes
Hazelhurst Farm
REDHILL AERODROME AND HELIPORT
Tenn Cts
Sports Centre
M23
SALFORDS STREAM
Hangar
Works
KINGS ROAD
BRIDGE
Lawn Hill
SEWAGE WORKS
Burstow Park Farm
MOATS LANE
South Hale Farm
SPRING FIELD WOOD
Dean Farm
Mason's Bridge
MASONS BRIDGE ROAD
RUFFET
THE ROOKERY
HATCH LANE
WALES ROAD
Dairy House Farm
AXES LANE
GREEN LANE
FURZEFIELD WOOD
GREEN LANE CARAVAN PARK
PERRYWOOD BUSINESS PARK
DUNRAVEN AVE
Cyprus Farm
Axes Farm
FAIRACRES
Shepheard's Hurst
Stone House Farm
COCKS COPSE
Meesons Farm
Christmas Farm
West View Farm
ST GEORGES ROAD
Works
BRICKFIELD
Dog and Duck PH
COBBLER'S CORNER
OUTWOOD COMMON
PERRY WOOD
TORVCROSS SHAW
MOBILE HOMES PARK
Woolborough Hatch Farm
War Memorial
WOOD NT
Picketts
House Farm
Woolborough Farm
Depot
PRINCE OF WALES ROAD
DAYSEYS HILL
OUTWOOD
Cricket Ground
Hall
WASP GREEN LANE
MILLERS LANE
Orchard Farm Kennels
WOOLBOROUGH LANE
BELLWETHER LA
The Castle PH
MILLERS COPSE
Works
Hunters Moon Farm
PICKETTS LANE
NEW HOUSE LANE
CROSSOAK LANE
HATHERSHAM LANE
LITTLE COLLINS
Brightleigh Farm
Rooksword Farm
ROOKERY HILL
COLDLAND WOOD
ROOKERY LANE
SCOTTS HILL
FB
BURSTOW STREAM
ROOKERY HILL
ROAD

251
269

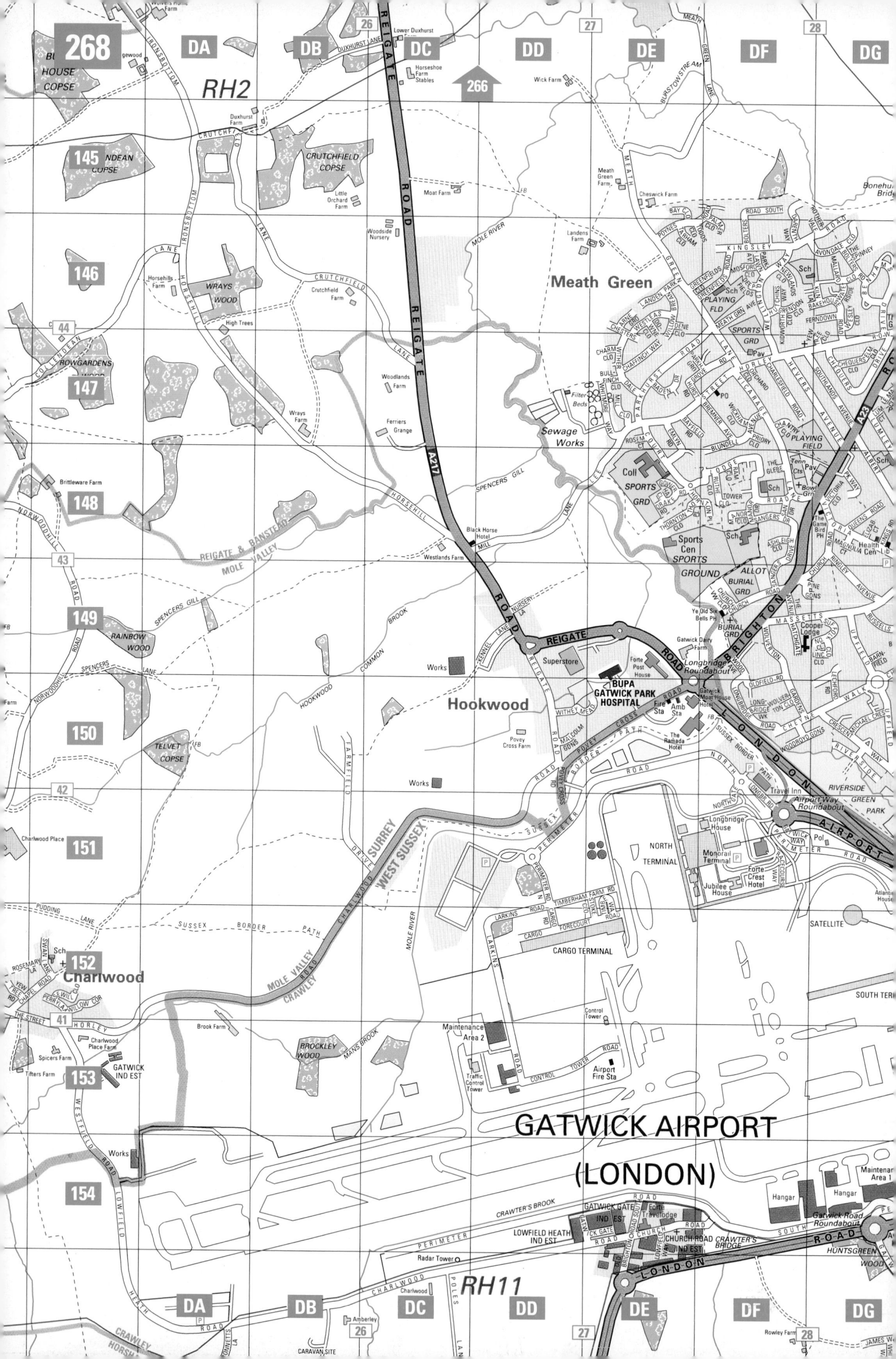

DA
DB
DC
DD
DE
DF
DG
26
27
28
266
RH2
Duxhurst Lane
Lower Duxhurst
Horseshoe Farm Stables
Wick Farm
Meath Green Lane
Burstow Stream
Ironsbottom
Duxhurst Farm
Crutchfield Lane
Crutchfield Copse
145
146
147
148
149
150
151
152
153
154
44
43
42
41
Moat Farm
Little Orchard Farm
Woodside Nursery
Meath Green Farm
Cheswick Farm
Landens Farm
Mole River
Meath Green
Horsehills Farm
Wrays Wood
Crutchfield Farm
High Trees
Rowgardens
Woodlands Farm
Ferriers Grange
Wrays Farm
Filter Beds
Sewage Works
Brittleware Farm
Norwoodhill Road
Reigate & Banstead
Mole Valley
Spencers Gill
Horsehill
Black Horse Hotel
Mill Lane
Westlands Farm
Reigate Road
A217
Rainbow Wood
Spencers Lane
Common Brook
Hookwood
Works
Hookwood
Superstore
Forte Post House
BUPA GATWICK PARK HOSPITAL
Longbridge Roundabout
Gatwick Dairy Farm
Ye Old Six Bells PH
Brighton Road
A23
Povey Cross Farm
Povey Cross Road
Telvet Copse
Farmfield Drive
Surrey
West Sussex
Sussex Border Path
The Ramada Hotel
Travel Inn
Airport Way Roundabout
London Road
Riverside Green Park
Longbridge House
North Terminal
Monorail Terminal
Forte Crest Hotel
Jubilee House
Perimeter Road
Satellite
Charlwood Place
Pudding Lane
Charlwood
The Street
Horley Road
Charlwood Road
Mole River
Larkins Road
Timberham Farm Rd
Cargo Forecourt Road
Cargo Terminal
South Terminal
Brook Farm
Charlwood Place Farm
Spicers Farm
Tilters Farm
Gatwick Ind Est
Brockley Wood
Mans Brook
Maintenance Area 2
Control Tower
Airport Fire Sta
Traffic Control Tower
Control Tower Road
GATWICK AIRPORT
(LONDON)
Westfield Road
Lowfield Road
Hangar
Maintenance Area 1
Gatwick Road Roundabout
Crawter's Brook
Gatwick Gate Ind Est
Forte Travelodge
Lowfield Heath Ind Est
Church Road Ind Est
Crawter's Bridge
Huntsgreen Wood
Radar Tower
Perimeter Road South
Charlwood Road
Poles Lane
RH11
Amberley
Caravan Site
Rowley Farm
Crawley
Horsham

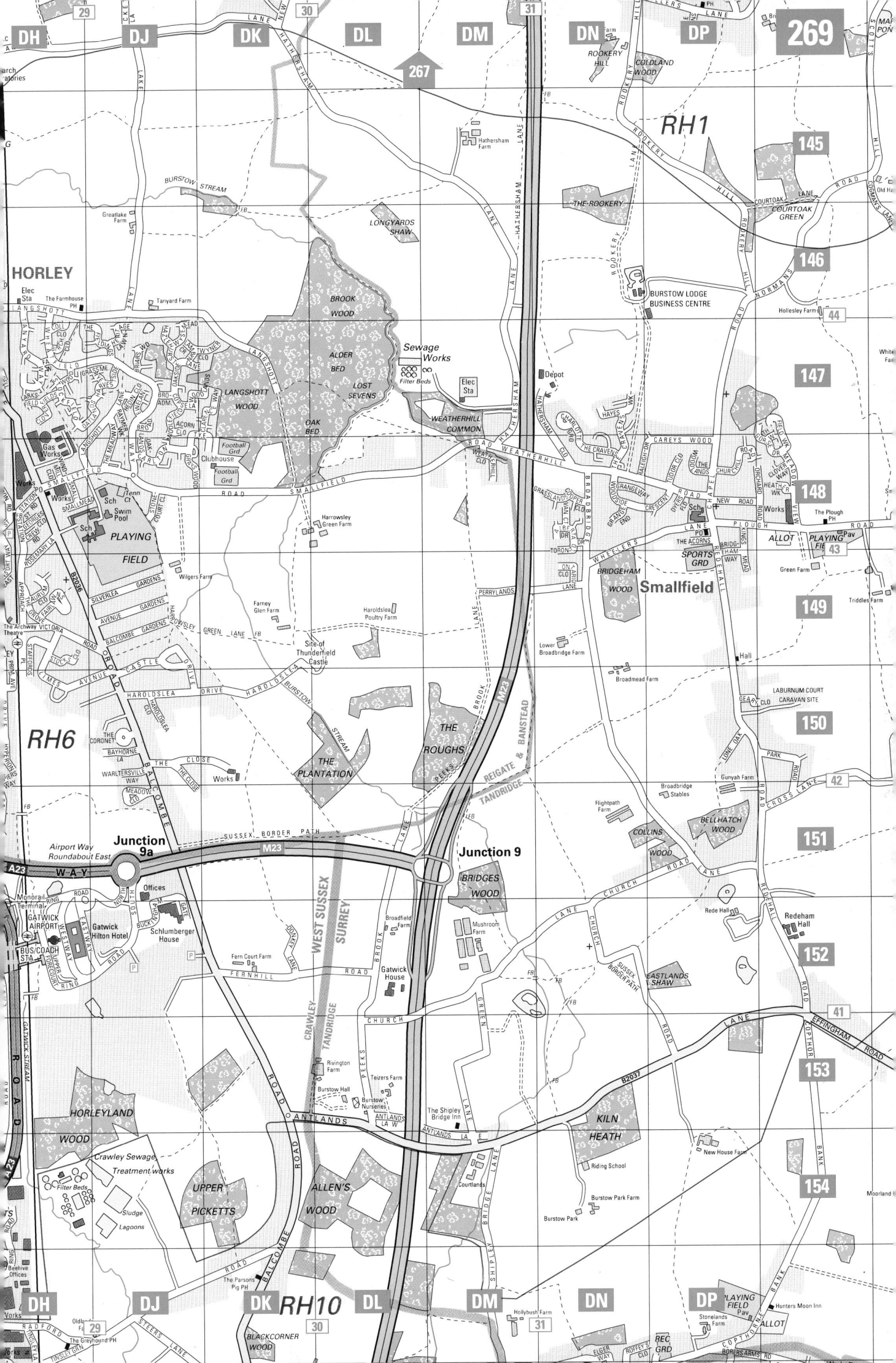
269
267
DH
DJ
DK
DL
DM
DN
DP
29
30
31
44
43
42
41
145
146
147
148
149
150
151
152
153
154
RH1
RH6
RH10
HORLEY
Smallfield
Junction 9a
Junction 9
Airport Way Roundabout East
GATWICK AIRPORT
Gatwick Hilton Hotel
Schlumberger House
Offices
Monorail Terminal
BUS/COACH STA
Sewage Works
Filter Beds
Elec Sta
Gas Works
ROOKERY HILL
COLDLAND WOOD
THE ROOKERY
COURTOAK GREEN
BURSTOW LODGE BUSINESS CENTRE
Hollesley Farm
Hathersham Farm
BURSTOW STREAM
Greatlake Farm
LONGYARDS SHAW
BROOK WOOD
ALDER BED
LOST SEVENS
OAK BED
LANGSHOTT WOOD
WEATHERHILL COMMON
Depot
The Farmhouse PH
Tanyard Farm
Football Grd
Clubhouse
Swim Pool
PLAYING FIELD
Harrowsley Green Farm
Wilgers Farm
Farney Glen Farm
Haroldslea Poultry Farm
Site of Thunderfield Castle
THE ROUGHS
THE PLANTATION
BRIDGEHAM WOOD
Lower Broadbridge Farm
Broadmead Farm
LABURNUM COURT CARAVAN SITE
Gunyah Farm
Broadbridge Stables
Flightpath Farm
COLLINS WOOD
BELLHATCH WOOD
Rede Hall
Redeham Hall
EASTLANDS SHAW
BRIDGES WOOD
Mushroom Farm
Broadfield Farm
Gatwick House
Fern Court Farm
Rivington Farm
Burstow Hall
Burstow Nurseries
Teizers Farm
The Shipley Bridge Inn
KILN HEATH
Riding School
New House Farm
Burstow Park Farm
Burstow Park
Courtlands
HORLEYLAND WOOD
Crawley Sewage Treatment works
Sludge Lagoons
UPPER PICKETTS
ALLEN'S WOOD
The Parsons Pig PH
BLACKCORNER WOOD
Hollybush Farm
Stonelands Farm
Hunters Moon Inn
PLAYING FIELD
ALLOT
Moorland
The Plough PH
Green Farm
Triddles Farm
White Farm
SPORTS GRD
The Archway Theatre
The Greyhound PH
Works
Sch
PO
Hall
Pav
FB
SUSSEX BORDER PATH
WEST SUSSEX
SURREY
REIGATE & BANSTEAD
TANDRIDGE
CRAWLEY
M23
A23
B2036
B2037
BALCOMBE ROAD
SMALLFIELD ROAD
WEATHERHILL ROAD
HATHERSHAM LANE
ROOKERY HILL
NORMANS ROAD
PLOUGH LANE
REDEHALL ROAD
CHURCH LANE
CHURCH ROAD
FERNHILL ROAD
ANTLANDS LANE
SHIPLEY BRIDGE LANE
PEEKS BROOK LANE
EFFINGHAM ROAD
COPTHORNE BANK
CROSS LANE
HAROLDSLEA DRIVE
LANGSHOTT
RADFORD ROAD
STEERS LANE
TINSLEY GRN
BORERS ARMS RD
ELGER WAY
REC GRD

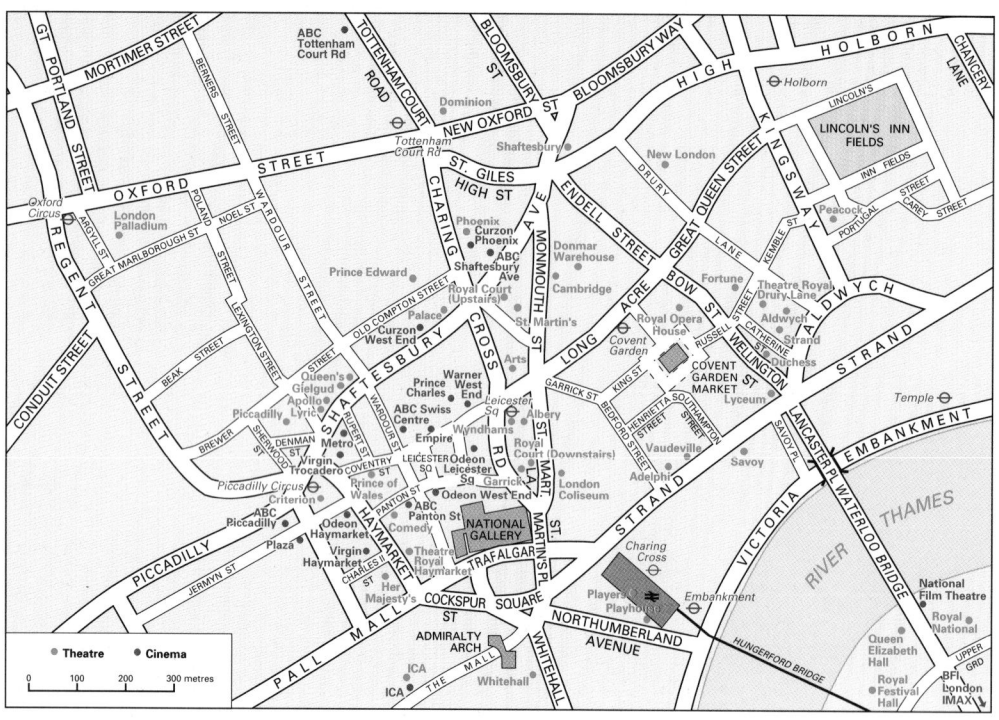

THEATRES

Adelphi 020 7344 0055
Albery 020 7369 1730
Aldwych 020 7416 6003
Apollo 020 7416 6022
Arts 020 7836 2132
Cambridge 020 7494 5054
Comedy 020 7369 1731
Criterion 020 7369 1747
Dominion 020 7656 1888
Donmar Warehouse 020 7369 1732
Duchess 020 7494 5075
Fortune 020 7836 2238
Garrick 020 7494 5085
Gielgud 020 7494 5065
Her Majesty's 020 7494 5400
ICA 020 7930 3647
London Coliseum 020 7632 8300
London Palladium 020 7494 5020
Lyceum 020 7420 8191
Lyric 020 7494 5045
New London 020 7405 0072
Palace 020 7434 0909
Peacock 020 7314 8800
Phoenix 020 7369 1733
Piccadilly 020 7369 1734
Players 020 7839 1134
Playhouse 020 7839 4401
Prince Edward 020 7734 8951
Prince of Wales 020 7839 5987
Queen Elizabeth Hall
  020 7960 4242
Queen's 020 7494 5041
Royal Court Theatre Downstairs
  020 7565 5000
Royal Court Theatre Upstairs
  020 7565 5000
Royal Festival Hall
  020 7960 4242
Royal National 020 7452 3000
Royal Opera House
  020 7304 4000
St. Martin's 020 7836 1443
Savoy 020 7836 8888
Shaftesbury 020 7379 5399
Strand 020 7930 8800
Theatre Royal, Drury Lane
  020 7494 5550
Theatre Royal, Haymarket
  020 7930 8800
Vaudeville 020 7836 9987
Whitehall 020 7369 1735
Wyndhams 020 7369 1736

CINEMAS

ABC Panton St 020 7930 0631
ABC Piccadilly 020 7437 3561
ABC Shaftesbury Avenue
  020 7836 6279
ABC Swiss Centre
  020 7439 4470
ABC Tottenham Court Rd
  020 7636 6148
BFI London IMAX 020 7902 1200

Curzon Phoenix 020 7369 1721
Curzon West End 020 7369 1722
Empire 020 7437 1234
ICA 020 7930 3647
Metro 020 7437 0757
National Film Theatre
  020 7928 3232
Odeon Haymarket
  0426 915353
Odeon Leicester Sq
  020 8315 4215

Odeon Mezzanine
(Odeon Leicester Sq)
  020 8315 4215
Odeon West End
  020 8315 4221
Plaza 020 7437 1234
Prince Charles 020 7437 8181
Virgin Haymarket 0870 907 0712
Virgin Trocadero 0870 907 0716
Warner West End 020 7437 4347

WEST END SHOPPING

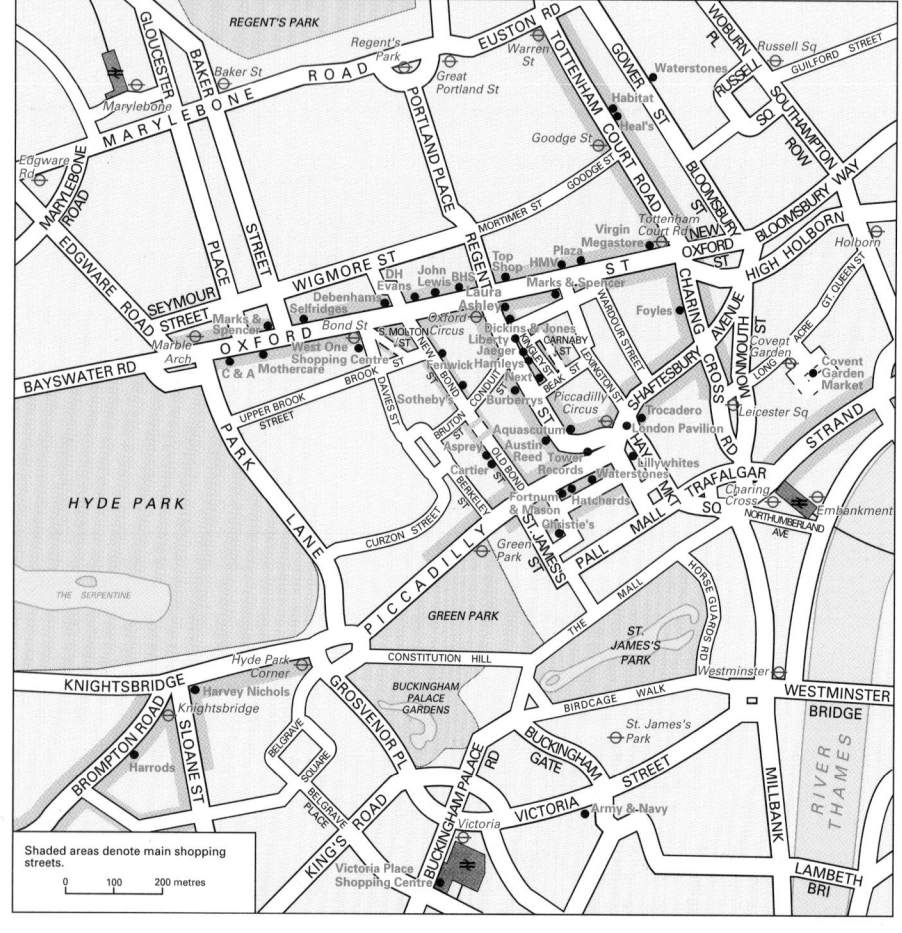

SHOPS

Aquascutum 020 7734 6090
Army & Navy 020 7834 1234
Asprey 020 7493 6767
Austin Reed 020 7734 6789
BHS (Oxford St) 020 7629 2011
C & A 020 7629 7272
Cartier 020 7493 6962
Christie's 020 7839 9060
Covent Garden Market 020 7836 9137
DH Evans 020 7629 8800
Debenhams 020 7580 3000
Dickins & Jones 020 7734 7070
Fenwick 020 7629 9161
Fortnum & Mason 020 7734 8040
Foyles 020 7437 5660
Habitat (Tottenham Court Rd)
  020 7631 3880
Hamleys 020 7734 3161
Harrods 020 7730 1234
Harvey Nichols 020 7235 5000
Hatchards 020 7439 9921
Heal's 020 7636 1666
HMV 020 7631 3423
Jaeger 020 7200 4000
John Lewis 020 7629 7711
Laura Ashley (Regent St) 020 7355 1363
Liberty 020 7734 1234
Lillywhites 020 7930 3181
London Pavilion 020 7437 1838
Marks & Spencer
  (Marble Arch) 020 7935 7954
Marks & Spencer (Oxford St)
  020 7437 7722
Mothercare 020 7580 1688
Next (Regent St) 020 7434 2515
Plaza on Oxford St 020 7637 8811
Selfridges 020 7629 1234
Sotheby's 020 7493 8080
Top Shop & Top Man 020 7636 7700
Tower Records 020 7439 2500
Trocadero 020 7439 1791
Victoria Place Shopping Centre
  020 7931 8811
Virgin Megastore 020 7580 5822
Waterstones 020 7636 1577
Waterstones 020 7851 2400

SHOOT UP HILL
Kilburn
St. John's Wood
MAIDA VALE
FINCHLEY ROAD
HAVERSTOCK HILL
CHALK FARM ROAD
Primrose Hill
PRINCE ALBERT ROAD
272
St. John's Wood
A41
Regent's Park
ALBANY ST
EDGWARE ROAD
MARYLEBONE STA.
MARYLEBONE
WESTWAY A404
A5
PADDINGTON STA.
Bayswater
BAYSWATER
SUSSEX GARDENS ROAD
Marble Arch
OXFORD
REGENT STREET
TOTTENHAM COURT ROAD
Soho
Covent Garden
KENTISH TOWN RD
CAMDEN ROAD
A503
YORK WAY
A5200
CALEDONIAN ROAD
Camden Town
ST. PANCRAS STA.
273 **274**
EUSTON ROAD
EUSTON STA.
KINGS CROSS STA.
PENTONVILLE RD
GRAY'S INN ROAD
Islington
A1
A1200 A104
ST. PAUL'S ROAD
ESSEX ROAD
NEW NORTH ROAD
CITY ROAD
GOSWELL ROAD
CLERKENWELL ROAD
A201
A1
FLEET ST
EMBANKMENT
A44
St. Paul's
OLD STREET
LONDON WALL
IA1211
City
DALSTON LA A104
Hackney
A10
WELL STREET A106
MAIRE STREET
VICTORIA PARK RD
KINGSLAND ROAD
HACKNEY RD
BETHNAL GREEN ROAD
275
Bethnal Green
MILE END ROAD A11
Stepney
COMMERCIAL ROAD A13
LIVERPOOL STREET STA.
Mayfair
PICCADILLY
PARK LANE
276
Kensington Gardens
Hyde Park
Kensington
Holland Park
KENSINGTON HIGH STREET
KENSINGTON ROAD A315
Knightsbridge
A4
CROMWELL ROAD
Earls Court
WARWICK ROAD
BROMPTON ROAD
A308
Chelsea
KING'S A3217
OLD ROAD
FULHAM
A304 A308
A3331
A3220
Battersea Park
A3216
BATTERSEA PARK RD
NINE ELMS LANE
A3025
Green Park
THE MALL
St. James's Park
WHITEHALL
VICTORIA STREET
Belgravia
VICTORIA STA.
VAUXHALL BRIDGE
A202 ROAD
A3213
Westminster
ALBERT EMBANKMENT
277 **278**
CHARING CROSS STA.
WATERLOO INT. STA.
WATERLOO STA.
Lambeth
LAMBETH ROAD
KENNINGTON RD
BLACKFRIARS ROAD
Southwark
LONDON BRIDGE STA.
TOOLEY ST
BLACKFRIARS
A2
A3
A201
CAMBERWELL
Bermondsey
OLD KENT ROAD
Kennington
CAMBERWELL NEW ROAD
WANDSWORTH ROAD
A203
CLAPHAM ROAD
A3
BRIXTON ROAD
A23
A202
The Tower
279
Wapping
THE HIGHWAY A1203
ROTHERHITHE TUNNEL
RIVER THAMES
JAMAICA ROAD
ROTHERHITHE NEW ROAD
Southwark Park
LOWER ROAD A200
Peckham
PECKHAM ROAD
A202
QUEENS ROAD
A2
RIVER THAMES

0 ___ 1 mile

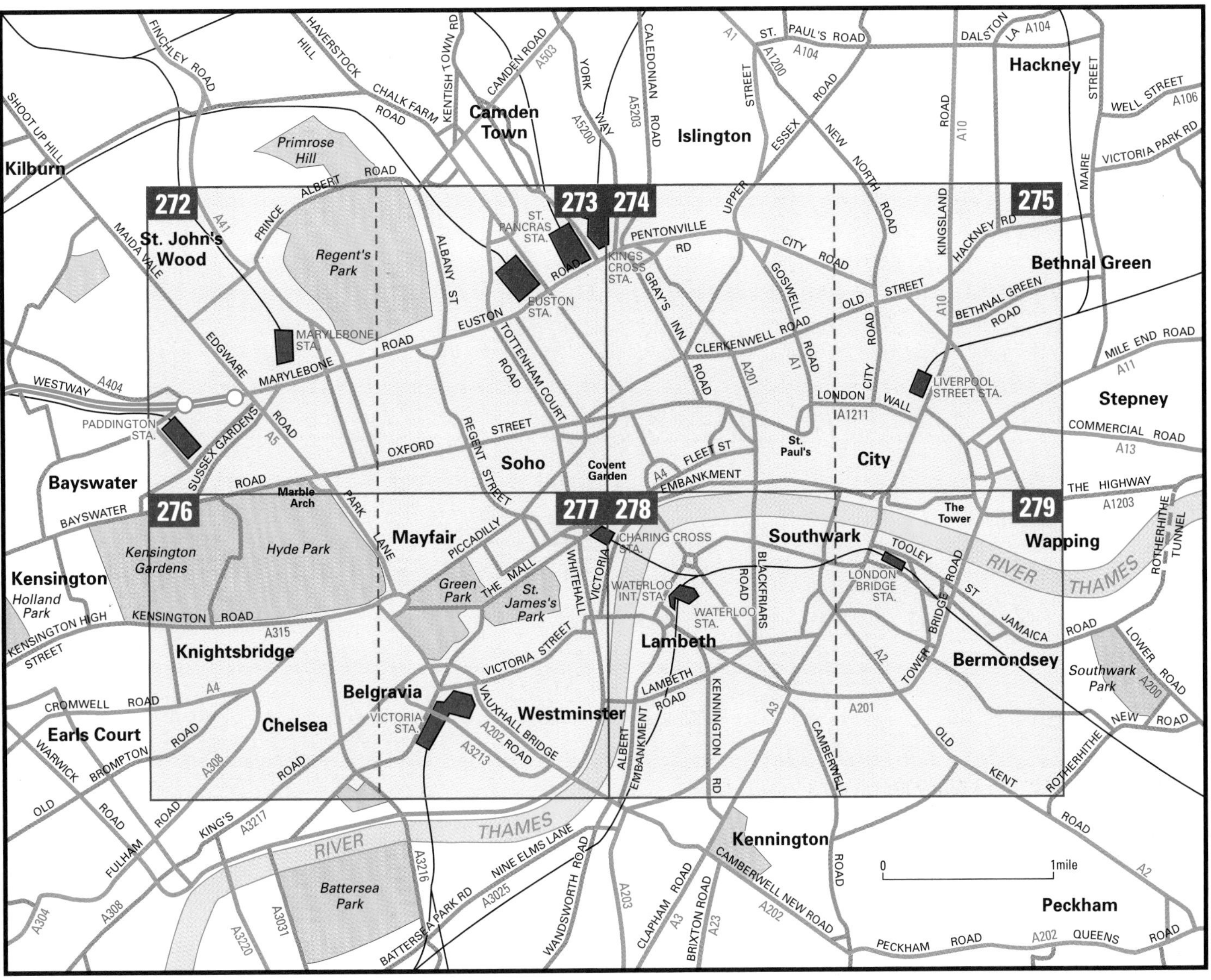

KEY TO MAP SYMBOLS

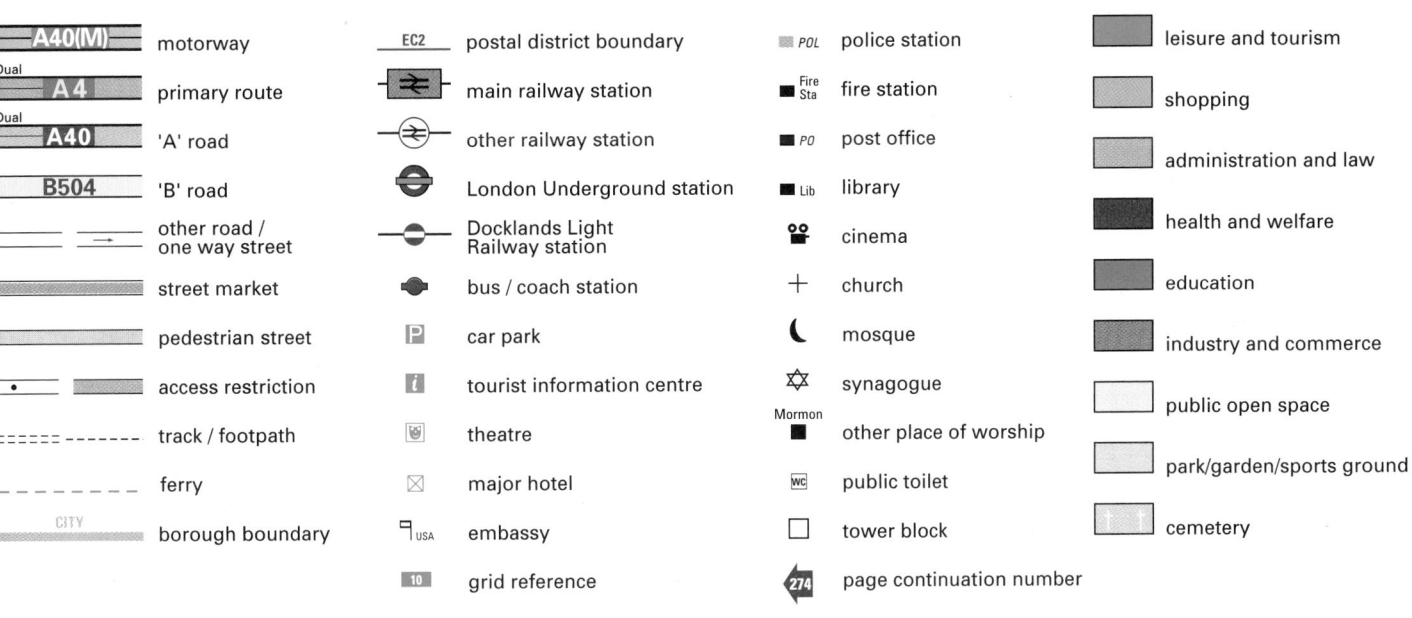

A40(M)	motorway
Dual A4	primary route
Dual A40	'A' road
B504	'B' road
	other road / one way street
	street market
	pedestrian street
	access restriction
------	track / footpath
	ferry
CITY	borough boundary

EC2	postal district boundary
	main railway station
	other railway station
	London Underground station
	Docklands Light Railway station
	bus / coach station
P	car park
i	tourist information centre
	theatre
⊠	major hotel
USA	embassy
10	grid reference

POL	police station
Fire Sta	fire station
PO	post office
Lib	library
	cinema
+	church
☽	mosque
✡	synagogue
Mormon	other place of worship
WC	public toilet
□	tower block
274	page continuation number

	leisure and tourism
	shopping
	administration and law
	health and welfare
	education
	industry and commerce
	public open space
	park/garden/sports ground
	cemetery

Scale 1: 10,000 (6.3 inches to 1 mile)

0 ___ 0.25 ___ 0.50 ___ 0.75 ___ 1 kilometre
0 ___ 1/4 ___ 1/2 mile

272
A
B
C
D
E
F
G
1
2
3
4
5
6
7
8
9
10
140
276
REGENT'S PARK
NW1
NW8
W1
W2
ST. JOHN'S WOOD
LISSON GROVE
MARYLEBONE
LORD'S CRICKET GROUND
M.C.C. MUSEUM
LORD'S TAVERN
HOSP OF ST. JOHN & ST. ELIZABETH
CONVENT OF MERCY
WELLINGTON HOSP N
WELLINGTON HOSP S
WELLINGTON ROAD
PRINCE ALBERT ROAD
PARK ROAD
ST. JOHN'S WOOD ROAD
GROVE END ROAD
LISSON GROVE
EDGWARE ROAD
MARYLEBONE ROAD
BAKER STREET
GLOUCESTER PLACE
OXFORD STREET
BAYSWATER ROAD
SUSSEX GARDENS
PRAED ST
WIGMORE ST
PORTMAN SQUARE
SEYMOUR PL
PARK LANE
A41
A5205
A5
A501
A40(M)
A40
A4205
A4209
B507
WINFIELD HOUSE
London Central Mosque
BOATING LAKE
QUEEN MARY'S GARDENS
OPEN AIR THEATRE
THE HOLME
REGENT'S COLLEGE
Clarence Gate
LONDON BUSINESS SCH
ROYAL COLL OF OBSTETRICIANS & GYNAECOLOGISTS
SHERLOCK HOLMES MUS
MADAME TUSSAUD'S
PLANETARIUM
BAKER STREET
MARYLEBONE
EDGWARE ROAD
MARBLE ARCH
PADDINGTON
LANCASTER GATE
ST. MARY'S HOSP
Paddington Basin
PADDINGTON GREEN
CITY OF WESTMINSTER COLL
WALLACE COLLECTION
SELFRIDGES
Speaker's Corner
Marlborough Gate
Victoria Gate
BROOK GATE
OXFORD S[T] where marked is closed to through traffic (except buses & taxis) from 7a.m. - 7p.m. Monday - Saturday

273
H
J
K
L
M
N
P
SOMERS TOWN
ST. PANCRAS
BLOOMSBURY
SOHO
STRAND
WC1
WC2
KING'S CROSS
EUSTON
ST. PANCRAS
BRITISH LIBRARY
THE BRITISH MUSEUM
RUSSELL SQUARE GARDENS
MORNINGTON CRESCENT
REGENT'S PARK
EUSTON ROAD
OXFORD STREET
NEW OXFORD ST
TOTTENHAM COURT RD
OXFORD CIRCUS
COVENT GARDEN
LEICESTER SQ.
HOLBORN
WHARFDALE RD
CALEDONIAN
A5202
A4200
A400
A4201
A501
A40
A401
B506
B502
B504
B406
B401
141
274
277
1
2
3
4
5
6
7
8
9
10

274
A
B
C
D
E
F
G
1
2
3
4
5
6
7
8
9
10
141
273
278
KING'S CROSS
ST. PANCRAS
BRITISH LIBRARY
KING'S CROSS & ST. PANCRAS
KING'S CROSS THAMESLINK
PENTONVILLE
PENTONVILLE ROAD
A501
ANGEL
FINSBURY
ST. PANCRAS
WC1
CLERKENWELL
BLOOMSBURY
THE BRITISH MUSEUM
HOLBORN
LINCOLN'S INN FIELDS
WC2
STRAND
EC4
COVENT GARDEN
RUSSELL SQUARE GARDENS
CORAM'S FIELDS
GRAY'S INN GARDENS
MOUNT PLEASANT SORTING OFFICE
ROYAL COURTS OF JUSTICE
SOMERSET HOUSE
ROYAL OPERA HOUSE
FARRINGDON
CHANCERY LANE
TEMPLE
BLACKFRIARS
CITY THAMESLINK
EMBANKMENT
VICTORIA
RIVER THAMES
H.M.S. PRESIDENT
H.Q.S. WELLINGTON
KING'S REACH
CALEDONIAN ROAD
YORK WAY
EUSTON ROAD
GRAY'S INN ROAD
KING'S CROSS ROAD
FARRINGDON ROAD
ROSEBERY AV
CLERKENWELL ROAD
THEOBALD'S ROAD
GUILFORD STREET
SOUTHAMPTON ROW
KINGSWAY
HIGH HOLBORN
NEW OXFORD ST
SHAFTESBURY AV
CHARING CROSS RD
ALDWYCH
FLEET STREET
STRAND
CHARTERHOUSE ST
HOLBORN VIADUCT
NEW BRIDGE ST
ST. JOHN ST
GOSWELL ROAD
CITY ROAD
A1
A4
A40
A201
A401
A5200
A5201
B502
B500
B504
B521
B400
B401
B402
NATIONAL GALLERY
CLEOPATRA'S NEEDLE

275
HOXTON
ST. LUKE'S
SHOREDITCH
BROADGATE
BARBICAN
CITY
EC2
EC3
HAGGERSTON PARK
SPORTS GROUND
SHOREDITCH PARK
HACKNEY ROAD
KINGSLAND ROAD
NEW NORTH RD
CITY ROAD
OLD STREET
GREAT EASTERN STREET
SHOREDITCH HIGH STREET
BETHNAL GREEN ROAD
COMMERCIAL STREET
BISHOPSGATE
LONDON WALL
HOUNDSDITCH
MIDDLESEX STREET
WHITECHAPEL HIGH ST
MANSELL ST
LEMAN STREET
MINORIES
FENCHURCH ST
LEADENHALL ST
CORNHILL
CHEAPSIDE
QUEEN VICTORIA ST
CANNON ST
THREADNEEDLE ST
GRACECHURCH ST
KING WILLIAM ST
EASTCHEAP
LOWER THAMES ST
UPPER THAMES ST
ROYAL MINT ST
COLUMBIA RD
OLD NICHOL ST
BRICK LANE
CHISWELL STREET
FINSBURY SQ
BUNHILL ROW
BUNHILL FIELDS
BUNHILL FIELDS BURIAL GRD
MOORFIELDS EYE HOSP
GEFFRYE MUSEUM
HACKNEY COMM COLL
OLD SPITALFIELDS MARKET
LIVERPOOL STREET
MOORGATE
BANK
Bank of England
Stock Exch
ST. PAUL'S CATHEDRAL
MANSION HOUSE
MONUMENT
ALDGATE
ALDGATE EAST
TOWER GATEWAY
TOWER HILL
TOWER OF LONDON
CANNON ST
FENCHURCH ST
OLD STREET
SHOREDITCH
The Guildhall
Lloyds of London
Site of Billingsgate
Old Mkt
London Commodity Ex
SHAKESPEARE'S GLOBE THEATRE & EXHIBITION
Southwark Bridge
142
279

276
272
140
160
OXFORD STREET where marked is closed to through traffic (except buses & taxis) from 7a.m. - 7p.m. Monday - Saturday
HYDE PARK
W2
SW7
SW3
KENSINGTON GARDENS
BELGRAVIA
BROMPTON
THE SERPENTINE
The Lido
Pier
THE LONG WATER
The Fountains
Bird Sanctuary
Speke's Monument
Peter Pan
Serpentine Gallery
Clubhouse
Bandstand
War Memorial
Achilles Statue
Speakers Corner
Centre Fountain
Putting Green
Albert Memorial
BAYSWATER ROAD
THE (NORTH CARRIAGE DRIVE) RING
THE (WEST CARRIAGE DRIVE) RING
SERPENTINE ROAD
ROTTEN ROW
SOUTH CARRIAGE DRIVE
KENSINGTON GORE
KENSINGTON RD
KNIGHTSBRIDGE
A315
A4
A40
A4202
A3216
A3217
A3214
A308
B304
B310
B319
B302
Marble Arch
Cumberland Gate
Lancaster Gate
Victoria Gate
Marlborough Gate
Brook Gate
Grosvenor Gate
Stanhope Gate
Curzon Gate
Queen Elizabeth Gate
Hyde Park Corner
Albert Gate
Edinburgh Gate
Rutland Gate
Prince of Wales Gate
Coalbrookdale Gate
Alexandra Gate
Apsley House Wellington Mus
Hyde Park Barracks
Royal Albert Hall
Royal Coll of Art
Royal Coll of Music
Imperial Coll
Science Museum
Natural History Museum
Earth Galleries
Victoria & Albert Museum
Brompton Oratory
Holy Trinity
Harrods
Harvey Nichols
Sloane Street
Sloane Square
Cadogan Square
Pont Street
Cromwell Road
South Kensington
Fulham Road
King's Road
Sydney Street
Royal Marsden Hosp
Royal Brompton Hosp
Chelsea Coll of Art & Design
Duke of York's Headquarters
Burton's Court
Chelsea Barracks
Peter Jones
Lower Sloane St
Pimlico Road
Samuel Lewis Trust Dwellings
Sutton Est
Park Lane
Belgrave Square
Eaton Square
A B C D E F G
1 2 3 4 5 6 7 8 9 10

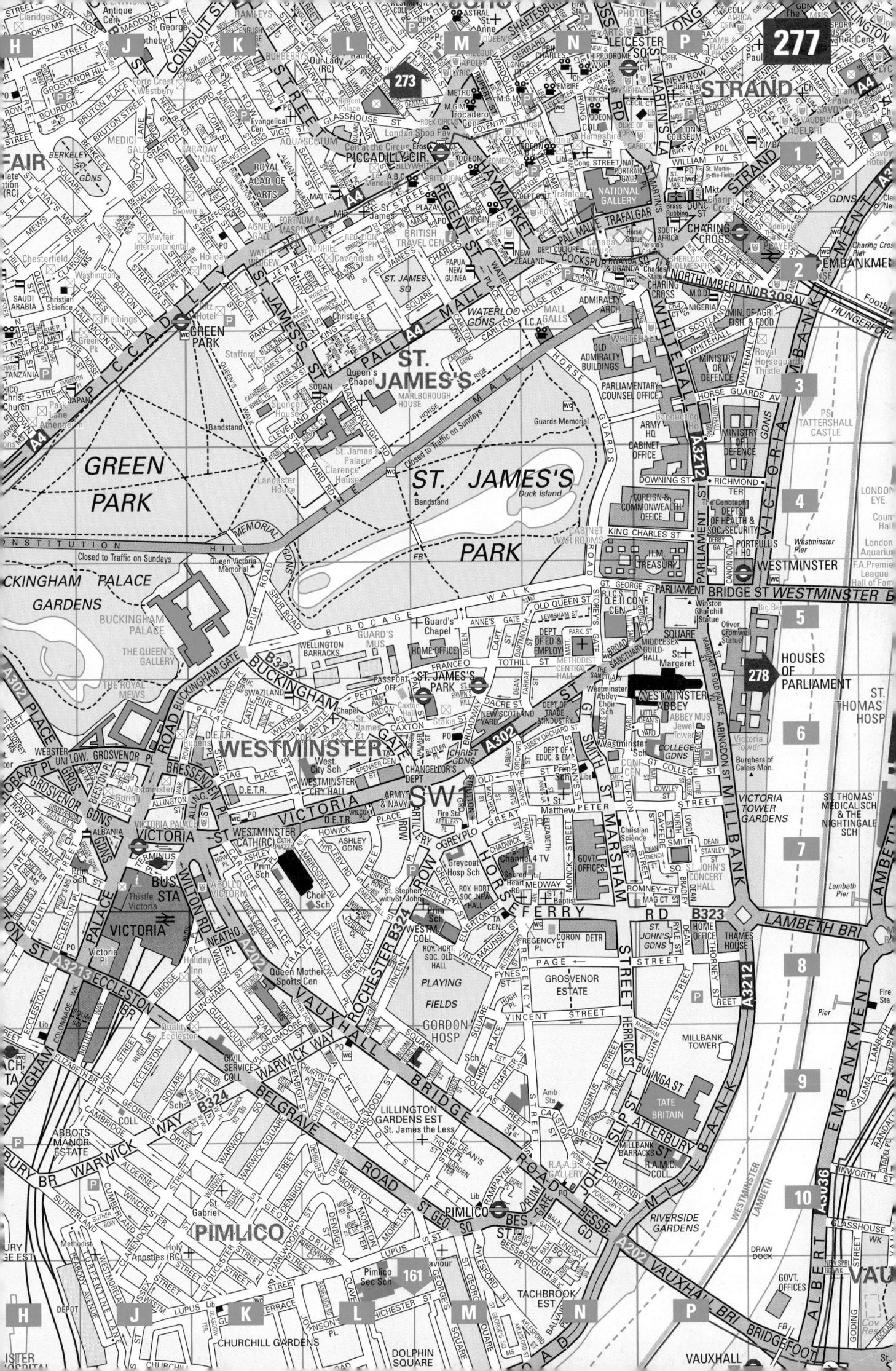

277
273
278
161
H
J
K
L
M
N
P
1
2
3
4
5
6
7
8
9
10
STRAND
PICCADILLY CIR.
LEICESTER SQ
TRAFALGAR
NATIONAL GALLERY
CHARING CROSS
EMBANKMENT
ROYAL ACAD. OF ARTS
HAYMARKET
REGENT ST
PALL MALL
PICCADILLY
GREEN PARK
ST. JAMES'S
ST. JAMES'S PARK
THE MALL
CONSTITUTION HILL
BUCKINGHAM PALACE GARDENS
BUCKINGHAM PALACE
THE QUEEN'S GALLERY
THE ROYAL MEWS
BIRDCAGE WALK
WHITEHALL
HORSE GUARDS
MINISTRY OF DEFENCE
DOWNING ST
FOREIGN & COMMONWEALTH OFFICE
H.M. TREASURY
WESTMINSTER
WESTMINSTER ABBEY
HOUSES OF PARLIAMENT
WESTMINSTER BRIDGE
VICTORIA
VICTORIA ST
SW1
VICTORIA TOWER GARDENS
LAMBETH BRI
MILLBANK
MILLBANK TOWER
TATE BRITAIN
PLAYING FIELDS
GORDON HOSP
VAUXHALL BRIDGE ROAD
BELGRAVE ROAD
WARWICK WAY
PIMLICO
RIVERSIDE GARDENS
VAUXHALL
ALBERT EMBANKMENT
VICTORIA EMBANKMENT
LONDON EYE
ST. THOMAS' HOSP
CHURCHILL GARDENS
DOLPHIN SQUARE
TACHBROOK EST

278
A
B
C
D
E
F
G
1
2
3
4
5
6
7
8
9
10
274
277
161
STRAND
EC4
RIVER THAMES
KING'S REACH
VICTORIA EMBANKMENT
WATERLOO BRI
BLACKFRIARS BRI
BLACKFRIARS
WESTMINSTER BRI
LAMBETH BRI
VAUXHALL BRI
CHARING CROSS
EMBANKMENT
WESTMINSTER
WATERLOO
WATERLOO INTERNATIONAL
WATERLOO EAST
LAMBETH NORTH
SOUTHWARK
KENNINGTON
VAUXHALL
LAMBETH
SE11
SE1
TRAFALGAR
NATIONAL GALLERY
WHITEHALL
HOUSES OF PARLIAMENT
WESTMINSTER ABBEY
MINISTRY OF DEFENCE
H.M. TREASURY
VICTORIA TOWER GARDENS
MILLBANK
MILLBANK TOWER
TATE BRITAIN
THAMES HOUSE
LAMBETH PALACE GDNS
ARCHBISHOP'S PARK
ST. THOMAS' HOSP
LONDON EYE
County Hall
London Aquarium
JUBILEE GDNS
ROYAL FESTIVAL HALL
QUEEN ELIZABETH HALL & PURCELL ROOM
HAYWARD GALLERY
ROYAL NATIONAL
NAT FILM THEA
The London Television Centre
IMAX
SOMERSET HOUSE
KING'S COLL UNI OF LON
H.M.S. PRESIDENT
GERALDINE MARY HARMSWORTH PARK
IMPERIAL WAR MUS
FLORENCE NIGHTINGALE MUS
PS TATTERSHALL CASTLE
STAMFORD STREET
YORK ROAD
THE CUT
WESTMINSTER BR ROAD
ST. GEORGE'S ROAD
LAMBETH ROAD
KENNINGTON ROAD
KENNINGTON LANE
LAMBETH WK
BOROUGH
SOUTHWARK UNION
A3200
A301
A302
A3036
A3203
A23
A201
A3204
A3211
A3212
A202
A3
A4
B308
B323

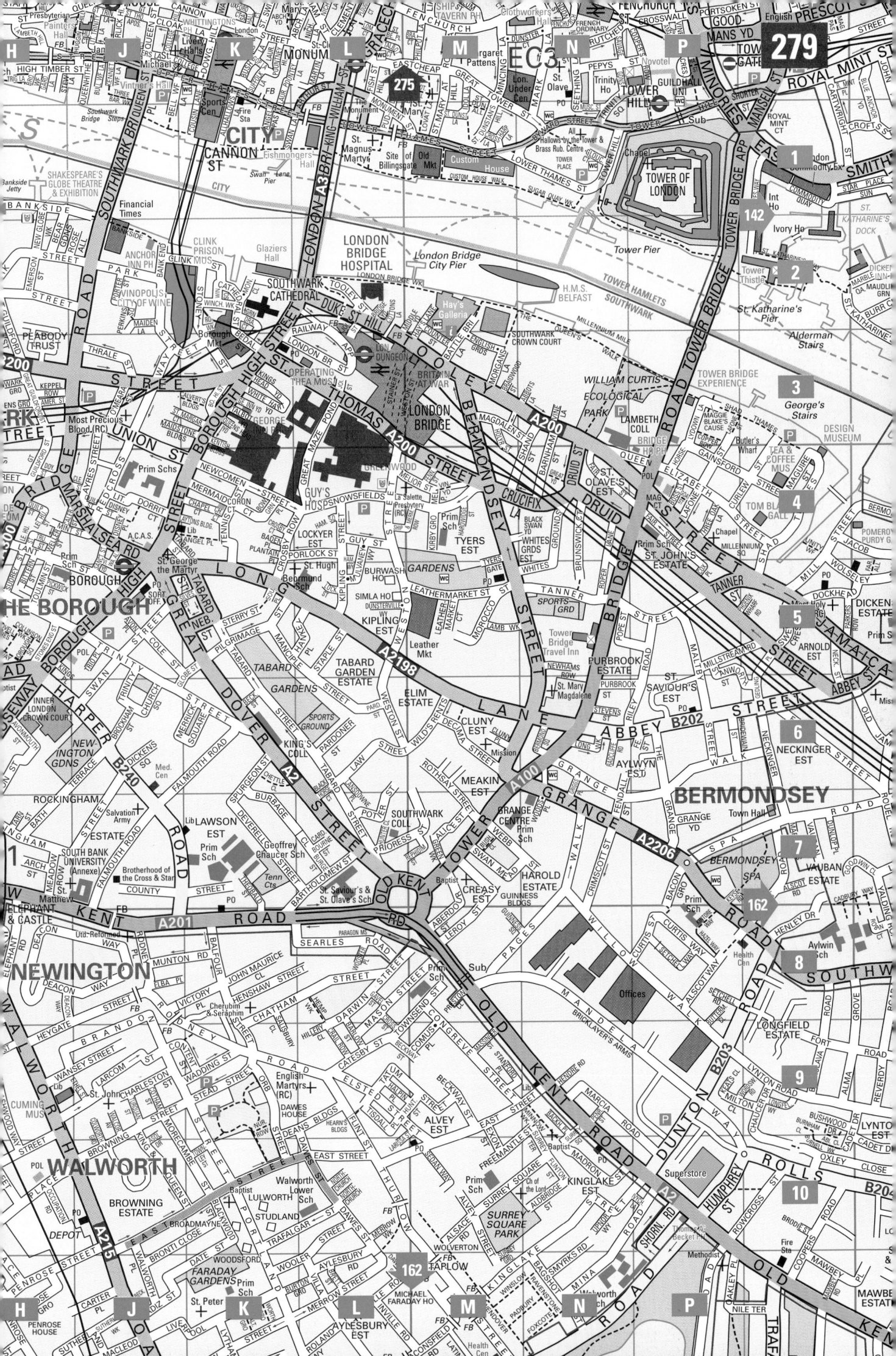

279
H
J
K
L
M
N
P
275
EC3
CITY
CANNON ST
MONUMENT
TOWER HILL
TOWER OF LONDON
Tower Pier
St. Katharine's Pier
ST. KATHARINE'S DOCK
1
2
3
4
5
6
7
8
9
10
142
162
SHAKESPEARE'S GLOBE THEATRE & EXHIBITION
Financial Times
CLINK PRISON MUS
Glaziers Hall
LONDON BRIDGE HOSPITAL
London Bridge City Pier
H.M.S. BELFAST
SOUTHWARK CATHEDRAL
Borough Mkt
Hay's Galleria
SOUTHWARK CROWN COURT
LON DUNGEON
BRITAIN AT WAR
LONDON BRIDGE
TOWER BRIDGE EXPERIENCE
WILLIAM CURTIS ECOLOGICAL PARK
DESIGN MUSEUM
George's Stairs
Alderman Stairs
GUY'S HOSP
TYERS EST
Leather Mkt
TABARD GARDEN ESTATE
ELIM ESTATE
PURBROOK ESTATE
ST. SAVIOUR'S EST
NECKINGER EST
BERMONDSEY
Town Hall
BERMONDSEY SPA
VAUBAN ESTATE
THE BOROUGH
BOROUGH
INNER LONDON CROWN COURT
NEW-INGTON GDNS
ROCKINGHAM ESTATE
SOUTH BANK UNIVERSITY (Annexe)
ELEPHANT & CASTLE
LAWSON EST
Geoffrey Chaucer Sch
KING'S COLL
SOUTHWARK COLL
MEAKIN EST
GRANGE CENTRE
HAROLD ESTATE
CREASY EST
OLD KENT RD
NEWINGTON
WALWORTH
CUMING MUS
BROWNING ESTATE
FARADAY GARDENS
AYLESBURY EST
ALVEY EST
SURREY SQUARE PARK
KINGLAKE EST
Superstore
LONGFIELD ESTATE
Offices
BRICKLAYER'S ARMS
A200
A2198
A2
A100
A201
A215
A2206
B202
B203
B240

The following is a comprehensive listing of the places of interest which appear in this atlas. Bold references can be found within the Central London enlarged scale section (pages 272-279).

The following is a comprehensive listing of all named places which appear in this atlas. Bold references can be found within the Central London enlarged scale section (pages 272-276). Postal information is in either London postal district or non-London post town form. For an explanation of post town abbreviations please consult page 287.

Downside, Cob. 229 BV118
Ducks Island, Barn. 79 CX44
Dulwich SE21 182 DS87
Dunton Grn., Sev. 241 FC119
Ealing W5 137 CJ73
Earls Ct. SW5 159 CZ78
Earlsfield SW18 180 DC88
Earlswood, Red. 266 DF136
East Acton W3 138 CR74
East Barnet, Barn. 80 DE44
East Bedfont, Felt. 175 BS88
East Burnham, Slou. 131 AN67
East Clandon, Guil. 244 BL131
East Dulwich SE22 182 DU86
East Ewell, Sutt. 217 CX110
East Finchley N2 120 DD56
East Ham E6 144 EL68
East Horsley, Lthd. 245 BS128
East Molesey, E.Mol. 197 CD97
East Sheen SW14 158 CR84
East Wickham, Well. 166 EU80
Eastbury, Nthwd. 93 BS49
Eastcote, Pnr. 116 BW58
Eastcote Village, Pnr. 115 BV57
Eastwick, Harl. 35 EP11
Eden Pk., Beck. 203 EA99
Edgware, Edg. 96 CP50
Edmonton N9 100 DU49
Effingham, Lthd. 246 BY127
Egham, Egh. 173 BA93
Egham Hythe, Stai. 173 BE93
Egham Wick, Egh. 172 AU94
Egypt, Slou. 111 AQ63
Ellenbrook, Hat. 44 CR19
Elm Cor., Wok. 228 BN119
Elm Pk., Horn. 127 FH64
Elmers End, Beck. 203 DY97
Elmstead, Chis. 184 EK92
Elstree, Borwd. 77 CJ44
Eltham SE9 184 EK86
Emerson Pk., Horn. 128 FL58
Enfield, Enf. 82 DT41
Enfield Highway, Enf. 82 DW41
Enfield Lock, Enf. 83 DZ37
Enfield Town, Enf. 82 DR40
Enfield Wash, Enf. 83 DX38
Englefield Grn., Egh. 172 AV92
Epping, Epp. 69 ES31
Epping Grn., Epp. 51 EN24
Epping Grn., Hert. 47 DK21
Epsom, Epsom 216 CQ114
Erith, Erith 167 FD79
Esher, Esher 214 CC105
Essendon, Hat. 46 DE17
Eton, Wind. 151 AQ80
Eton Wick, Wind. 151 AL77
Ewell, Epsom 217 CU110
Eynsford, Dart. 208 FL103
Fairmile, Cob. 214 BZ112
Falconwood, Well. 165 ER83
Farleigh, Warl. 221 DZ114
Farley Grn., Guil. 260 BK144
Farnborough, Orp. 223 EP106
Farncombe, Gdmg. 258 AT144
Farnham Common, Slou. 131 AQ65
Farnham Royal, Slou. 131 AQ68
Farningham, Dart. 208 FM100
Fawkham Grn., Long. 209 FV103
Felden, Hem.H. 40 BG24
Feltham, Felt. 175 BU89
Felthamhill, Felt. 175 BT92
Fetcham, Lthd. 231 CD123
Fiddlers Hamlet, Epp. 70 EW32
Fifield, Maid. 150 AD81
Finchley N3 98 DB53
Finsbury EC1 274 E2
Finsbury Pk. N4 121 DN60
Flamstead End, Wal.Cr. 66 DU28
Flaunden, Hem.H. 57 BB33
Fleetville, St.Alb. 43 CG20
Foots Cray, Sid. 186 EV93
Forest Gate E7 124 EG64
Forest Hill SE23 183 DX88
Forestdale, Croy. 221 EA109
Fortis Grn. N2 120 DF56
Forty Grn., Beac. 88 AH50
Forty Hill, Enf. 82 DS37
Freezy Water, Wal.Cr. 83 DY35
Friday Hill E4 101 ED47
Friern Barnet N11 98 DE49
Froghole, Eden. 255 ER133
Frogmore, St.Alb. 61 CE28
Fulham SW6 159 CY82
Fullwell Cross, Ilf. 103 ER53
Fulmer, Slou. 112 AX63
Furzedown SW17 180 DG92
Gadebridge, Hem.H. 39 BF18
Gants Hill, Ilf. 125 EN57
Ganwick Cor., Barn. 80 DB35
Garston, Wat. 76 BW35
Gatton, Reig. 250 DF128
George Grn., Slou. 132 AX72
Gerrards Cross, Ger.Cr. 112 AX58
Gidea Pk., Rom. 127 FG55
Givons Gro., Lthd. 247 CJ126
Goathurst Common, Sev. 256 FB130
Godden Grn., Sev. 257 FN125
Goddington, Orp. 206 EW104
Godstone, Gdse. 252 DV131
Goffs Oak, Wal.Cr. 66 DQ29
Golders Grn. NW11 120 DA59
Goldsworth Pk., Wok. 226 AU117
Gomshall, Guil. 261 BR139
Goodley Stock, West. 255 EP130
Goodmayes, Ilf. 126 EV61
Gospel Oak NW5 120 DG63
Grange Hill, Chig. 103 ER51
Grange Pk. N21 81 DP43
Gravesend, Grav. 191 GJ85
Grays, Grays 170 GA78
Great Amwell, Ware 33 DZ10
Great Bookham, Lthd. 246 CB125
Great Hivings, Chesh. 54 AP27
Great Parndon, Harl. 51 EP17
Great Warley, Brwd. 107 FU53
Green St., Borwd. 78 CP37
Green St. Grn., Dart. 189 FU93
Green St. Grn., Orp. 223 ES107
Greenford, Grnf. 136 CB69
Greenhithe, Green. 189 FV85
Greensted Grn., Ong. 71 FH28
Greenwich SE10 163 ED79
Grove Pk. SE12 184 EG89
Grove Pk. W4 158 CQ80
Grovehill, Hem.H. 40 BL16
Guildford, Guil. 258 AV137
Guildford Pk., Guil. 258 AV135
Gunnersbury W4 158 CP77
Hackbridge, Wall. 201 DH103
Hackney E8 142 DV65
Hackney Wick E9 123 DZ64
Hacton, Rain. 128 FM64
Hadley, Barn. 79 CZ40
Hadley Wd., Barn. 80 DD38
Haggerston E2 142 DT68
Hainault, Ilf. 103 ES52
Hale End E4 101 ED51
Hall Gro., Welw.G.C. 30 DB11
Halls Grn., Harl. 50 EJ18
Halstead, Sev. 224 EZ113
Ham, Rich. 177 CJ90
Hammerfield, Hem.H. 40 BH20
Hammersmith W6 159 CW78
Hammond St., Wal.Cr. 66 DR26
Hampstead NW3 120 DD63
Hampstead Gdn. Suburb N2 120 DC57
Hampton, Hmptn. 196 CB95
Hampton Hill, Hmptn. 177 CD93
Hampton Wick, Kings.T. 197 CH95
Hamsey Grn., Warl. 236 DW116
Handside, Welw.G.C. 29 CV10
Hanwell W7 137 CF74
Hanworth, Felt. 176 BX91
Hare St., Harl. 51 EP16
Harefield, Uxb. 92 BL53
Harlesden NW10 138 CS68
Harlington, Hayes 155 BQ79
Harlow, Harl. 51 ER15
Harmondsworth, West Dr. 154 BK79
Harold Hill, Rom. 106 FM50
Harold Pk., Rom. 106 FN52
Harold Wd., Rom. 106 FL54
Harringay N8 121 DN57
Harrow, Har. 117 CD59
Harrow on the Hill, Har. 117 CE61
Harrow Weald, Har. 95 CD53
Hastingwood, Harl. 52 EZ19
Hatch End, Pnr. 94 BY51
Hatfield, Hat. 45 CV17
Hatfield Gdn. Village, Hat. 29 CU14
Hatfield Hyde, Welw.G.C. 29 CZ12
Hatton, Felt. 155 BT84
Havering Pk., Rom. 104 FA50
Havering-atte-Bower, Rom. 105 FE48
Hawley, Dart. 188 FM92
Hayes, Brom. 204 EH101
Hayes, Hayes 135 BS72
Hayes End, Hayes 135 BQ71
Hayes Town, Hayes 155 BS75
Hazelwood, Sev. 223 ER111
Headley, Epsom 248 CQ125
Headstone, Har. 116 CC56
Hedgerley, Slou. 111 AR60
Hemel Hempstead, Hem.H. 40 BK21
Hendon NW4 119 CV56
Herne Hill SE24 182 DQ85
Heronsgate, Rick. 91 BD45
Hersham, Walt. 214 BX107
Hertford, Hert. 31 DP10
Hertford Heath, Hert. 32 DW12
Hertingfordbury, Hert. 31 DL10
Heston, Houns. 156 BZ80
Hextable, Swan. 187 FG94
High Barnet, Barn. 79 CX40
High Beach, Loug. 84 EG39
High Laver, Ong. 53 FH17
Higham Hill E17 101 DY54
Highams Pk. E4 101 ED50
Highbury N5 121 DP64
Higher Denham, Uxb. 113 BC59
Highfield, Hem.H. 40 BL18
Highgate N6 120 DG61
Highwood Hill NW7 97 CU47
Hill End, Uxb. 92 BH51
Hillingdon, Uxb. 134 BN69
Hilltop, Chesh. 54 AR28
Hinchley Wd., Esher 197 CF104
Hither Grn. SE13 184 EE86
Hoddesdon, Hodd. 49 DZ18
Hoe, Guil. 261 BR143
Hogpits Bottom, Hem.H. 57 BA31
Holborn WC2 274 B8
Holdbrook, Wal.Cr. 67 EA34
Holdens, Welw.G.C. 30 DA06
Holders Hill NW4 97 CX54
Holland, Oxt. 254 EG134
Holloway N7 121 DL63
Holmethorpe, Red. 251 DH132
Holtspur, Beac. 88 AF54
Holyfield, Wal.Abb. 67 ED28
Holywell, Wat. 75 BS44
Homerton E9 123 DY64
Honor Oak SE23 182 DW86
Honor Oak Pk. SE4 183 DY86
Hook Grn., Dart. 187 FG91
Hook Grn., Grav. 190 FZ93
Hook Heath, Wok. 226 AV120
Hookwood, Horl. 268 DC150
Hooley, Couls. 234 DG122
Horley, Horl. 269 DH146
Hornchurch, Horn. 128 FJ61
Horns Grn., Sev. 239 ES117
Hornsey N8 121 DM55
Horsell, Wok. 226 AY116
Horton, Epsom 216 CP110
Horton, Slou. 153 BA83
Horton Kirby, Dart. 209 FR98
Hosey Hill, West. 255 ES127
Hounslow, Houns. 156 BZ84
Hounslow W., Houns. 156 BX83
How Wd., St.Alb. 60 CC27
Hoxton N1 275 M1
Hulberry, Swan. 207 FG103
Hunsdon, Ware 34 EJ06
Hunsdonbury, Ware 34 EJ08
Hunton Bri., Kings L. 59 BP33
Hurst Grn., Oxt. 254 EG132
Hutton, Brwd. 109 GD44
Hutton Mt., Brwd. 109 GB46
Hyde, The NW9 119 CT56
Hythe End, Stai. 173 BB90
Ickenham, Uxb. 115 BQ62
Ilford, Ilf. 125 EQ62
Ingrave, Brwd. 109 GC50
Irons Bottom, Reig. 266 DA142
Isleworth, Islw. 157 CF83
Islington N1 141 DN67
Istead Ri., Grav. 190 GE94
Iver, Iver 133 BF72
Iver Heath, Iver 133 BD69
Ivy Chimneys, Epp. 69 ES32
Jacobs Well, Guil. 242 AY129
Jersey Fm., St.Alb. 43 CK15
Jordans, Beac. 90 AT52
Joydens Wd., Bex. 187 FC92
Katherines, Harl. 51 EM18
Kenley, Ken. 236 DQ116
Kennington SE11 161 DN79
Kensal Grn. NW10 139 CW69
Kensal Ri. NW6 139 CX68
Kensal Town W10 139 CX70
Kensington W8 159 CZ75
Kent Hatch, Eden. 255 EP131
Kentish Town NW5 141 DJ65
Kenton, Har. 117 CH57
Keston, Brom. 222 EJ106
Kew, Rich. 158 CN79
Kidbrooke SE3 164 EH83
Kilburn NW6 139 CZ68
King's Cross N1 141 DK67
Kings Fm., Grav. 191 GJ90
Kings Langley, Kings L. 58 BM30
Kingsbury NW9 118 CP58
Kingsland N1 142 DS65
Kingsmoor, Harl. 51 EQ20
Kingston upon Thames, Kings.T. 198 CL96
Kingston Vale SW15 178 CS91
Kingswood, Tad. 233 CZ123
Kingswood, Wat. 59 BV34
Kippington, Sev. 256 FG126
Kitt's End, Barn. 79 CY37
Knockhall, Green. 189 FW85
Knockholt, Sev. 240 EU116
Knockholt Pound, Sev. 240 EY116
Knotty Grn., Beac. 88 AJ48
Ladywell SE13 183 EA85
Laleham, Stai. 194 BJ97
Lambeth SE1 278 B6
Lambourne End, Rom. 86 EX44
Lamorbey, Sid. 185 ET88
Lampton, Houns. 156 CB81
Lane End, Dart. 189 FR92
Langley, Slou. 153 BA76
Langley Vale, Epsom 232 CR119
Langleybury, Kings L. 59 BP34
Latimer, Chesh. 72 AY36
Latton Bush, Harl. 52 EU18
Layter's Grn., Ger.Cr. 90 AV54
Lea Bri. E5 123 DX62
Leatherhead, Lthd. 231 CF121

285

Sendgrove, Wok.	243	BC126
Seven Kings, Ilf.	125	ES59
Sevenoaks, Sev.	257	FJ125
Sevenoaks Common, Sev.	257	FH129
Sewardstone E4	83	EC39
Sewardstonebury E4	84	EE42
Shacklewell N16	122	DT63
Shadwell E1	142	DW73
Shalford, Guil.	258	AX141
Sheering, B.Stort.	37	FC07
Sheerwater, Wok.	211	BC113
Shenfield, Brwd.	109	FZ45
Shenley, Rad.	62	CN33
Shepherd's Bush W12	139	CW74
Shepperton, Shep.	195	BP101
Shere, Guil.	260	BN139
Sherrardspark, Welw.G.C.	29	CV07
Shirley, Croy.	203	DX104
Shooter's Hill SE18	165	EQ81
Shoreditch E1	**275**	**P5**
Shoreham, Sev.	225	FG111
Shortlands, Brom.	204	EE93
Shreding Grn., Iver	133	BC72
Sidcup, Sid.	185	ET91
Sidlow, Reig.	266	DB141
Silvertown E16	164	EJ75
Single St., West.	239	EN115
Singlewell, Grav.	191	GK93
Sipson, West Dr.	154	BN79
Slough, Slou.	132	AS74
Smallfield, Horl.	269	DP149
Smallford, St.Alb.	44	CP19
Smoky Hole, Guil.	261	BR144
Snaresbrook E11	124	EE57
Sockett's Heath, Grays	170	GD76
Soho W1	**273**	**M10**
Somers Town NW1	**273**	**N2**
South Acton W3	158	CN76
South Beddington, Wall.	219	DK107
South Chingford E4	101	DZ50
South Croydon, S.Croy.	220	DQ107
South Darenth, Dart.	209	FR95
South Hackney E9	142	DW66
South Hampstead NW6	140	DB66
South Harefield, Uxb.	114	BJ56
South Harrow, Har.	116	CB62
South Hatfield, Hat.	45	CU20
South Holmwood, Dor.	263	CJ144
South Hornchurch, Rain.	147	FE67
South Kensington SW7	160	DB76
South Lambeth SW8	161	DL81
South Merstham, Red.	251	DJ130
South Mimms, Pot.B.	63	CT32
South Norwood SE25	202	DT97
South Nutfield, Red.	267	DM136
South Ockendon, S.Ock.	149	FW70
South Oxhey, Wat.	94	BW48
South Pk., Reig.	266	DA138
South Ruislip, Ruis.	116	BW64
South Stifford, Grays	169	FW78
South St., West.	239	EM119
South Tottenham N15	122	DS57
South Weald, Brwd.	108	FS47
South Wimbledon SW19	180	DB94
South Woodford E18	102	EF54
Southall, Sthl.	136	BX74
Southborough, Brom.	205	EM100
Southend SE6	183	EB91
Southfields SW18	180	DA88
Southfleet, Grav.	190	GB93
Southgate N14	99	DJ47
Southlea, Slou.	152	AV82
Southwark SE1	**278**	**G3**
Spitalbrook, Hodd.	49	EA19
Spring Gro., Islw.	157	CF81
Staines, Stai.	174	BG91
Stamford Hill N16	122	DS60
Stanborough, Welw.G.C.	29	CT12
Stanmore, Stan.	95	CG50
Stanstead Abbotts, Ware	33	ED11
Stanwell, Stai.	174	BL87
Stanwell Moor, Stai.	174	BG85
Stapleford Abbotts, Rom.	87	FC43
Stapleford Tawney, Rom.	87	FC37
Stepney E1	142	DW71
Stewards, Harl.	51	ER19
Stockwell SW9	161	DK83
Stoke D'Abernon, Cob.	230	BZ116
Stoke Grn., Slou.	132	AU70
Stoke Newington N16	122	DS61
Stoke Poges, Slou.	132	AT66
Stone, Green.	189	FT85
Stonebridge NW10	138	CP67
Stonebridge, Dor.	264	CL139
Stonehill, Cher.	210	AY107
Stoneleigh, Epsom	217	CU106
Stoughton, Guil.	242	AV131
Strand WC2	**273**	**P10**
Stratford E15	143	EC65
Strawberry Hill, Twick.	177	CE90
Streatham SW16	181	DL91
Streatham Hill SW2	181	DM87
Streatham Pk. SW16	181	DJ91
Streatham Vale SW16	181	DK94
Strood Grn., Bet.	264	CP138
Stroud Grn. N4	121	DM58
Stroude, Vir.W.	193	AZ96

Sudbury, Wem.	117	CG64
Summerstown SW17	180	DB90
Sumners, Harl.	51	EN19
Sunbury, Sun.	195	BV97
Sundridge, Brom.	184	EJ93
Sundridge, Sev.	240	EZ124
Sunnymeads, Stai.	152	AY84
Surbiton, Surb.	198	CM101
Sutton, Sutt.	218	DB107
Sutton Abinger, Dor.	261	BU143
Sutton at Hone, Dart.	188	FN94
Sutton Grn., Guil.	243	AZ125
Swanley, Swan.	207	FE98
Swanley Village, Swan.	207	FH95
Swanscombe, Swans.	190	FZ86
Swillet, The, Rick.	73	BB44
Sydenham SE26	182	DW92
Tadworth, Tad.	233	CV122
Tandridge, Oxt.	253	EA133
Taplow, Maid.	130	AE70
Tatling End, Ger.Cr.	113	BB61
Tatsfield, West.	238	EL120
Tattenham Cor., Epsom	233	CV118
Teddington, Tedd.	177	CG93
Tewin, Welw.	30	DE05
Thames Ditton, T.Ditt.	197	CF100
Thamesmead SE28	145	ET74
Thamesmead N. SE28	146	EX72
Thamesmead W. SE18	165	EQ76
Theydon Bois, Epp.	85	ET37
Theydon Garnon, Epp.	86	EW36
Theydon Mt., Epp.	70	FA34
Thorney, Iver	154	BH76
Thornton Heath, Th.Hth.	201	DP98
Thornwood, Epp.	70	EW25
Thorpe, Egh.	193	BC97
Thorpe Grn., Egh.	193	BA98
Thorpe Lea, Egh.	173	BB93
Threshers Bush, Harl.	53	FB16
Tilbury, Til.	171	GG81
Titsey, Oxt.	254	EH125
Tokyngton, Wem.	138	CP65
Tolworth, Surb.	198	CN103
Toot Hill, Ong.	71	FF30
Tooting Graveney SW17	180	DE93
Tottenham N17	100	DS53
Tottenham Hale N17	122	DV55
Totteridge N20	97	CY46
Tower Hill, Dor.	263	CH138
Townsend, St.Alb.	43	CD17
Tufnell Pk. N7	121	DK63
Tulse Hill SE21	182	DQ88
Turnford, Brox.	67	DZ26
Twickenham, Twick.	177	CG89
Twitton, Sev.	241	FE116
Tye Grn., Harl.	51	ET17
Tylers Causeway, Hert.	47	DK22
Tyler's Grn., Gdse.	252	DV129
Tyrrell's Wd., Lthd.	232	CM123
Tyttenhanger, St.Alb.	44	CL23
Underhill, Barn.	80	DA43
Underriver, Sev.	257	FN130
Upminster, Upmin.	128	FQ62
Upper Clapton E5	122	DV60
Upper Edmonton N18	100	DU51
Upper Elmers End, Beck.	203	DZ99
Upper Halliford, Shep.	195	BS97
Upper Holloway N19	121	DJ62
Upper Norwood SE19	182	DR94
Upper Sydenham SE26	182	DU91
Upper Tooting SW17	180	DE90
Upper Walthamstow E17	123	EB56
Upshire, Wal.Abb.	68	EJ32
Upton E7	144	EH66
Upton, Slou.	152	AU76
Upton Pk. E6	144	EJ67
Upton Pk., Slou.	152	AT76
Uxbridge, Uxb.	134	BK66
Uxbridge Moor, Iver	134	BG67
Uxbridge Moor, Uxb.	134	BG67
Vauxhall SE11	161	DL78
Virginia Water, Vir.W.	192	AW97
Waddon, Croy.	201	DN103
Walham Grn. SW6	160	DB80
Wallington, Wall.	219	DJ106
Waltham Abbey, Wal.Abb.	84	EF35
Waltham Cross, Wal.Cr.	67	DZ33
Walthamstow E17	101	EB54
Walton on the Hill, Tad.	249	CT125
Walton-on-Thames, Walt.	195	BT103
Walworth SE17	**279**	**H10**
Wandsworth SW18	179	CZ85
Wanstead E11	124	EH59
Wapping E1	142	DU74
Ware, Ware	33	DZ06
Warley, Brwd.	108	FV50
Warlingham, Warl.	237	DX118
Warners End, Hem.H.	39	BE19
Warwick Wold, Red.	251	DN129
Water End, Hat.	63	CV26
Waterford, Hert.	31	DM05
Waterside, Chesh.	54	AR32
Watford, Wat.	75	BT41
Watford Heath, Wat.	94	BY46
Wealdstone, Har.	117	CF55
Welham Grn., Hat.	45	CV23
Well End, Borwd.	78	CR38

Well Hill, Orp.	225	FB107
Welling, Well.	166	EU83
Welwyn Gdn. City, Welw.G.C.	29	CX10
Wembley, Wem.	118	CL63
Wembley Pk., Wem.	118	CM61
Wennington, Rain.	148	FK73
Wentworth, Vir.W.	192	AS100
West Acton W3	138	CN72
West Barnes, N.Mal.	199	CU99
West Brompton SW10	160	DB79
West Byfleet, W.Byf.	212	BH113
West Clandon, Guil.	244	BH129
West Drayton, West Dr.	154	BK76
West Dulwich SE21	182	DR90
West End, Esher	214	BZ107
West End, Hat.	46	DC18
West Ewell, Epsom	216	CS108
West Grn. N15	122	DQ56
West Ham E15	144	EF66
West Hampstead NW6	120	DB64
West Harrow, Har.	116	CC59
West Heath SE2	166	EX79
West Hendon NW9	118	CS59
West Horsley, Lthd.	245	BP127
West Kilburn W9	139	CZ69
West Molesey, W.Mol.	196	BZ98
West Norwood SE27	182	DQ90
West Thurrock, Grays	169	FU78
West Tilbury, Til.	171	GL79
West Watford, Wat.	75	BU42
West Wickham, W.Wick.	203	EC103
Westbourne Grn. W2	140	DA71
Westcott, Dor.	262	CC138
Westcourt, Grav.	191	GL89
Westerham, West.	255	EQ126
Westfield, Wok.	227	AZ122
Westhumble, Dor.	247	CG131
Westminster SW1	**277**	**K6**
Weston Grn., T.Ditt.	197	CF102
Wexham St., Slou.	132	AW67
Weybridge, Wey.	212	BN105
Wheathampstead, St.Alb.	28	CL06
Whelpley Hill, Chesh.	56	AX26
Whetstone N20	98	DB47
White Bushes, Red.	267	DH139
Whitechapel E1	142	DU72
Whiteley Village, Walt.	213	BS110
Whitton, Twick.	176	CB87
Whyteleafe, Cat.	236	DS118
Widmore, Brom.	204	EH97
Wild Hill, Hat.	46	DD21
Wildernesse, Sev.	257	FL122
Willesden NW10	139	CT65
Willesden Grn. NW10	139	CV66
Wilmington, Dart.	188	FJ91
Wimbledon SW19	179	CY93
Wimbledon Pk. SW19	179	CZ90
Winchmore Hill N21	99	DM45
Winchmore Hill, Amer.	88	AJ45
Windmill Hill, Grav.	191	GG88
Windsor, Wind.	152	AS81
Wisley, Wok.	228	BL116
Woking, Wok.	227	AZ118
Woldingham, Cat.	237	EB122
Woldingham Gdn. Village, Cat.	237	DY121
Wombwell Pk., Grav.	190	GD89
Wonersh, Guil.	259	BB144
Wooburn, H.Wyc.	110	AD58
Wooburn Grn., H.Wyc.	110	AF56
Wood Grn. N22	99	DL53
Woodbridge Hill, Guil.	242	AU132
Woodcote, Epsom	232	CQ116
Woodcote, Pur.	219	DK111
Woodford, Wdf.Grn.	102	EH51
Woodford Bri., Wdf.Grn.	103	EM52
Woodford Grn., Wdf.Grn.	102	EF49
Woodford Wells, Wdf.Grn.	102	EH49
Woodhall, Welw.G.C.	29	CY11
Woodham, Add.	211	BF111
Woodhatch, Reig.	266	DC137
Woodlands, Islw.	157	CE82
Woodmansterne, Bans.	234	DE115
Woodside, Croy.	202	DU99
Woodside, Wat.	59	BU33
Woolwich SE18	165	EN78
Worcester Pk., Wor.Pk.	199	CT103
World's End, Enf.	81	DN41
Wormley, Brox.	49	DY24
Wormley W. End, Brox.	48	DS22
Wotton, Dor.	262	BZ139
Wraysbury, Stai.	173	AZ86
Wrythe, The, Cars.	200	DE103
Yeading, Hayes	135	BV69
Yiewsley, West Dr.	134	BL74

General Abbreviations

All.	Alley	Coron.	Coroners	Gdns.	Gardens	Mt.	Mount	Sq.	Square
Allot.	Allotments	Cors.	Corners	Govt.	Government	Mus.	Museum	St.	Saint
Amb.	Ambulance	Cotts.	Cottages	Gra.	Grange	N.	North	St.	Street
App.	Approach	Cov.	Covered	Grd.	Ground	N.T.	National Trust	Sta.	Station
Arc.	Arcade	Crem.	Crematorium	Grds.	Grounds	Nat.	National	Sts.	Streets
Av./Ave.	Avenue	Cres.	Crescent	Grn.	Green	P.H.	Public House	Sub.	Subway
Bdy.	Broadway	Ct.	Court	Grns.	Greens	P.O.	Post Office	Swim.	Swimming
Bk.	Bank	Cts.	Courts	Gro.	Grove	Par.	Parade	T.A.	Territorial Army
Bldgs.	Buildings	Ctyd.	Courtyard	Gros.	Groves	Pas.	Passage	T.H.	Town Hall
Boul.	Boulevard	Dep.	Depot	Gt.	Great	Pav.	Pavilion	Tenn.	Tennis
Bowl.	Bowling	Dev.	Development	Ho.	House	Pk.	Park	Ter.	Terrace
Br./Bri.	Bridge	Dr.	Drive	Hos.	Houses	Pl.	Place	Thea.	Theatre
C. of E.	Church of England	Dws.	Dwellings	Hosp.	Hospital	Pol.	Police	Trd.	Trading
Cath.	Cathedral	E.	East	Hts.	Heights	Prec.	Precinct	Twr.	Tower
Cem.	Cemetery	Ed.	Education	Ind.	Industrial	Prim.	Primary	Twrs.	Towers
Cen.	Central, Centre	Elec.	Electricity	Int.	International	Prom.	Promenade	Uni.	University
Cft.	Croft	Embk.	Embankment	Junct.	Junction	Pt.	Point	Vil.	Villa, Villas
Cfts.	Crofts	Est.	Estate	La.	Lane	Quad.	Quadrant	Vw.	View
Ch.	Church	Ex.	Exchange	Las.	Lanes	R.C.	Roman Catholic	W.	West
Chyd.	Churchyard	Exhib.	Exhibition	Lib.	Library	Rd.	Road	Wd.	Wood
Cin.	Cinema	F.B.	Footbridge	Lo.	Lodge	Rds.	Roads	Wds.	Woods
Circ.	Circus	F.C.	Football Club	Lwr.	Lower	Rec.	Recreation	Wf.	Wharf
Cl./Clo.	Close	Fld.	Field	Mag.	Magistrates	Res.	Reservoir	Wk.	Walk
Co.	County	Flds.	Fields	Mans.	Mansions	Ri.	Rise	Wks.	Works
Coll.	College	Fm.	Farm	Mem.	Memorial	S.	South	Yd.	Yard
Comm.	Community	Gall.	Gallery	Mkt.	Market	Sch.	School		
Conv.	Convent	Gar.	Garage	Mkts.	Markets	Sec.	Secondary		
Cor.	Corner	Gdn.	Garden	Ms.	Mews	Shop.	Shopping		

Post Town Abbreviations

Abb.L.	Abbots Langley	Chig.	Chigwell	Hert.	Hertford	Rain.	Rainham	Twick.	Twickenham
Add.	Addlestone	Chis.	Chislehurst	Hmptn.	Hampton	Red.	Redhill	Upmin.	Upminster
Amer.	Amersham	Cob.	Cobham	Hodd.	Hoddesdon	Reig.	Reigate	Uxb.	Uxbridge
Ash.	Ashtead	Couls.	Coulsdon	Horl.	Horley	Rich.	Richmond	Vir.W.	Virginia Water
Ashf.	Ashford	Craw.	Crawley	Horn.	Hornchurch	Rick.	Rickmansworth	W.Byf.	West Byfleet
B.End	Bourne End	Croy.	Croydon	Houns.	Hounslow	Rom.	Romford	W.Mol.	West Molesey
B.Stort.	Bishop's Stortford	Dag.	Dagenham	Ilf.	Ilford	Ruis.	Ruislip	W.Wick.	West Wickham
Bans.	Banstead	Dart.	Dartford	Islw.	Isleworth	S.Croy.	South Croydon	Wal.Abb.	Waltham Abbey
Bark.	Barking	Dor.	Dorking	Ken.	Kenley	S.le H.	Stanford le Hope	Wal.Cr.	Waltham Cross
Barn.	Barnet	E.Mol.	East Molesey	Kes.	Keston	S.Ock.	South Ockendon	Wall.	Wallington
Beac.	Beaconsfield	Eden.	Edenbridge	Kings L.	Kings Langley	Saw.	Sawbridgeworth	Walt.	Walton-on-Thames
Beck.	Beckenham	Edg.	Edgware	Kings.T.	Kingston upon Thames	Sev.	Sevenoaks	Warl.	Warlingham
Belv.	Belvedere	Egh.	Egham	Long.	Longfield	Shep.	Shepperton	Wat.	Watford
Berk.	Berkhamsted	Enf.	Enfield	Loug.	Loughton	Sid.	Sidcup	Wdf.Grn.	Woodford Green
Bet.	Betchworth	Epp.	Epping	Lthd.	Leatherhead	Slou.	Slough	Well.	Welling
Bex.	Bexley	Felt.	Feltham	Maid.	Maidenhead	St.Alb.	St. Albans	Welw.	Welwyn
Bexh.	Bexleyheath	Gat.	Gatwick	Mitch.	Mitcham	Stai.	Staines	Welw.G.C.	Welwyn Garden City
Borwd.	Borehamwood	Gdmg.	Godalming	Mord.	Morden	Stan.	Stanmore	Wem.	Wembley
Brent.	Brentford	Gdse.	Godstone	N.Mal.	New Malden	Sthl.	Southall	West Dr.	West Drayton
Brom.	Bromley	Ger.Cr.	Gerrards Cross	Nthlt.	Northolt	Sun.	Sunbury-on-Thames	West.	Westerham
Brox.	Broxbourne	Grav.	Gravesend	Nthwd.	Northwood	Surb.	Surbiton	Wey.	Weybridge
Brwd.	Brentwood	Green.	Greenhithe	Ong.	Ongar	Sutt.	Sutton	Whyt.	Whyteleafe
Buck.H.	Buckhurst Hill	Grnf.	Greenford	Orp.	Orpington	Swan.	Swanley	Wind.	Windsor
Cars.	Carshalton	Guil.	Guildford	Oxt.	Oxted	Swans.	Swanscombe	Wok.	Woking
Cat.	Caterham	H.Wyc.	High Wycombe	Pnr.	Pinner	T.Ditt.	Thames Ditton	Wor.Pk.	Worcester Park
Ch.St.G.	Chalfont St. Giles	Har.	Harrow	Pot.B.	Potters Bar	Tad.	Tadworth		
Cher.	Chertsey	Harl.	Harlow	Pur.	Purley	Tedd.	Teddington		
Chesh.	Chesham	Hat.	Hatfield	Purf.	Purfleet	Th.Hth.	Thornton Heath		
Chess.	Chessington	Hem.H.	Hemel Hempstead	Rad.	Radlett	Til.	Tilbury		

Notes

A strict word-by-word alphabetical order is followed in the index whereby generic terms such as Avenue, Close, Gardens etc., although abbreviated, are ordered in their expanded form. So, for example, Abbot St. comes before Abbots Ave., and Abbots Ri. comes before Abbots Rd.

Street names preceded by a definite article (i.e. The) are indexed from their second word onwards with the article being placed at the end of the name,
e.g. Avenue, The, or Long Walk, The

The alphabetical order extends to include postal information so that where two or more streets have exactly the same name, London post town references are given first in alpha-numeric order and are followed by non-London post town references in alphabetic order,
e.g. Abbey Gdns. NW8 is followed by Abbey Gdns. W6 and then Abbey Gdns., Chertsey.

In some cases there are two or more streets of the same name in the same postal area. In order to aid correct location, extra information will be given in brackets,
e.g. High St., Epsom and High St. (Ewell), Epsom.

The street name and postal district or post town of an entry is followed by the page number and grid reference on which the name will be found, e.g. Abbey Road SW19 will be found on page 180 and in square DC94. Likewise, Norfolk Crescent, Sidcup will be found on page 185 and in square ES87 (within postal district DA15).

All streets within the Central London enlarged-scale section (pages 272-279) are shown in **bold type** when named in the index, e.g. **Abbey St. SE1** will be found on page **279** and in square **N6**. Certain streets may also be duplicated on parts of pages 140-142 and 160-162. In these cases the Central London section reference is always given first in bold type, followed by the same name in standard type, e.g.

    Abbey Orchard St. SW1 277 N6
    Abbey Orchard St. SW1 161 DK76

The index also contains some roads for which there is insufficient space to name on the map. The adjoining, or nearest named thoroughfare to such roads is shown in *italics*, and the reference indicates where the unnamed road is located off the named thoroughfare,
e.g. Oyster Catchers Close E16 is off *Freemasons Road* and is located off this road on page 144 in square EH72.

A.C. Ct., T.Ditt. 197 CG100
Harvest La.
A1(M) Business Pk., Hat. 45 CW23
Aaron Hill Rd. E6 145 EN71
Abberley Ms. SW4 161 DH83
Cedars Rd.
Abberton Wk., Rain. 147 FE66
Ongar Way
Abbess Clo. E6 144 EL71
Oliver Gdns.
Abbess Clo. SW2 181 DP88
Abbeville Rd. N8 121 DK56
Barrington Rd.
Abbeville Rd. SW4 181 DJ86
Abbey Ave., St.Alb. 42 CA23
Abbey Ave., Wem. 138 CL68
Abbey Clo., Hayes 135 BV74
Abbey Clo., Nthlt. 136 BZ69
Invicta Gro.
Abbey Clo., Pnr. 115 BV55
Abbey Clo., Rom. 127 FG58
Abbey Clo., Slou. 131 AL73
Abbey Clo., Wok. 227 BE116
Abbey Ct., Wal.Abb. 67 EB34
Abbey Cres., Belv. 166 FA77
Abbey Dr. SW17 180 DG92
Church La.
Abbey Dr., Abb.L. 59 BU32
Abbey Dr., Stai. 194 BJ97
Abbey Gdns. NW8 140 DC68
Abbey Gdns. SE16 162 DU77
Monnow Rd.
Abbey Gdns. W6 159 CY79
Abbey Gdns., Cher. 194 BG100
Abbey Gdns., Wal.Abb. 67 EC33
Abbey Grn., Cher. 194 BG100
Abbey Gro. SE2 166 EV77
Abbey Ind. Est., Wem. 138 CM67
Abbey La. E15 143 EC68
Abbey La., Beck. 183 EA94
Abbey Mead Ind. Pk., Wal.Abb. 67 EC34
Abbey Ms. E17 123 EA57
Leamington Ave.
Abbey Mill End, St.Alb. 42 CC21
Abbey Mill La., St.Alb. 42 CC21
Abbey Mills, St.Alb. 42 CC21
Abbey Orchard St. SW1 277 N6
Abbey Orchard St. SW1 161 DK76
Abbey Par. SW19 180 DC94
Merton High St.
Abbey Par. W5 138 CM69
Hanger La.
Abbey Pk., Beck. 183 EA94
Abbey Pk. La., Slou. 111 AL61
Abbey Pl., Dart. 188 FK85
Priory Rd.
Abbey Retail Pk., Bark. 145 EP67
Abbey Rd. E15 144 EE68
Abbey Rd. NW6 140 DB66
Abbey Rd. NW8 140 DC68
Abbey Rd. NW10 138 CP68
Abbey Rd. SE2 166 EX77
Abbey Rd. SW19 180 DC94
Abbey Rd., Bark. 145 EQ67
Abbey Rd., Belv. 166 EX77
Abbey Rd., Bexh. 166 EY84
Abbey Rd., Cher. 194 BH101
Abbey Rd., Croy. 201 DP104
Abbey Rd., Enf. 82 DS43
Abbey Rd., Grav. 191 GL88
Abbey Rd., Green. 189 FW85
Abbey Rd., Ilf. 125 ER57
Abbey Rd., Shep. 194 BN102
Abbey Rd., S.Croy. 221 DX110
Abbey Rd., Vir.W. 192 AX99
Abbey Rd., Wal.Cr. 67 DY34
Abbey Rd., Wok. 226 AW117
Abbey Rd. Est. NW8 140 DB67
Abbey St. E13 144 EG70
Abbey St. SE1 279 N6
Abbey St. SE1 162 DS76
Abbey Ter. SE2 166 EW77
Abbey Vw. NW7 97 CT48
Abbey Vw., Wal.Abb. 67 EB33
Abbey Vw., Wat. 76 BX36
Abbey Vw. Rd., St.Alb. 42 CC20
Abbey Vw. Roundabout, Wal.Abb. 67 EB33
Abbey Wk., W.Mol. 196 CB97
Abbey Way SE2 166 EX76
Abbey Wf. Ind. Est., Bark. 145 ER68
Abbey Wd. La., Rain. 148 FK68
Abbey Wd. Rd. SE2 166 EV77
Abbeydale Clo., Harl. 52 EW16
Abbeydale Rd., Wem. 138 CN67
Abbeyfield Est. SE16 162 DW77
Abbeyfield Rd. SE16 162 DW77
Abbeyfields Clo. NW10 138 CN68
Abbeyhill Rd., Sid. 186 EW89
Abbot Clo., Stai. 174 BK94
Abbot Clo., W.Byf. 212 BK110
Abbot Rd., Guil. 258 AX136
Abbot St. E8 142 DT65
Abbots Ave., Epsom 216 CN111
Abbots Ave., St.Alb. 43 CE23
Abbots Ave. W., St.Alb. 43 CD23
Abbots Clo. N1 142 DQ65
Alwyne Rd.
Abbots Clo., Brwd. 109 GA46
Abbots Clo., Guil. 258 AS137
Abbots Clo., Orp. 205 EQ102
Abbots Clo., Rain. 148 FJ68
Abbots Clo., Ruis. 116 BX62
Abbots Dr., Har. 116 CA61
Abbots Dr., Vir.W. 192 AW98
Abbots Fld., Grav. 191 GJ93
Ruffets Wd.
Abbots Gdns. N2 120 DD56
Abbots Gdns. W8 160 DB76
St. Mary's Pl.
Abbots Grn., Croy. 221 DX107
Abbots La. SE1 279 N3
Abbots La., Ken. 236 DQ116
Abbots Manor Est. SW1 277 H10
Abbots Manor Est. SW1 161 DH77
Abbots Pk. SW2 181 DN88
Abbots Pk., St.Alb. 43 CF22
Abbot's Pl. NW6 140 DB67
Abbots Ri., Kings L. 58 BM26
Abbots Ri., Red. 250 DG132
Abbots Ri., Ware 33 ED11
Abbot's Rd. E6 144 EK67
Abbots Rd., Abb.L. 59 BS30
Abbots Rd., Edg. 96 CQ52
Abbots Ter. N8 121 DL58
Abbots Vw., Kings L. 58 BM27
Abbots Wk. W8 160 DB76
St. Mary's Pl.
Abbots Wk., Cat. 236 DU122
Tillingdown Hill
Abbots Way, Beck. 203 DY99
Abbots Way, Guil. 243 BD133
Abbotsbury Clo. E15 143 EC68
Abbotsbury Clo. W14 159 CZ75
Abbotsbury Rd.
Abbotsbury Gdns., Pnr. 116 BW58
Abbotsbury Ms. SE15 162 DW83
Abbotsbury Rd. W14 159 CY75
Abbotsbury Rd., Brom. 204 EF103
Abbotsbury Rd., Mord. 200 DB99
Abbotsford Ave. N15 122 DQ56
Abbotsford Clo., Wok. 227 BA117
Onslow Cres.
Abbotsford Gdns., Wdf.Grn. 102 EG52
Abbotsford Lo., Nthwd. 93 BS50
Abbotsford Rd., Ilf. 126 EU61
Abbotshade Rd. SE16 143 DX74
Abbotshall Ave. N14 99 DJ48
Abbotshall Rd. SE6 183 ED88
Abbotsleigh Clo., Sutt. 218 DB108
Abbotsleigh Rd. SW16 181 DJ91
Abbotsmede Clo., Twick. 177 CF89
Abbotstone Rd. SW15 159 CW83
Abbotsweld, Harl. 51 ER18
Abbotswell Rd. SE4 183 DZ85
Abbotswood, Guil. 243 AZ132
Abbotswood Clo., Belv. 166 EY76
Coptefield Dr.
Abbotswood Clo., Guil. 243 AZ131
Abbotswood Dr., Wey. 213 BR110
Abbotswood Gdns., Ilf. 125 EM55
Abbotswood Rd. SE22 162 DS84
Abbotswood Rd. SW16 181 DK90
Abbotswood Way, Hayes 135 BV74
Abbott Ave. SW20 199 CX96
Abbott Clo., Hmptn. 176 BY93
Abbott Clo., Nthlt. 136 BZ65
Abbott Rd. E14 143 EC71
Abbotts Clo. SE28 146 EW73
Abbotts Clo., Rom. 127 FB55
Abbotts Clo., Swan. 207 FG98
Abbotts Clo., Uxb. 134 BK71
Abbotts Cres. E4 101 ED49
Abbotts Cres., Enf. 81 DP40
Abbotts Dr., Wal.Abb. 68 EG34
Abbotts Dr., Wem. 117 CH61
Abbotts Pk. Rd. E10 123 EC59
Abbotts Pl., Chesh. 54 AQ28
Abbotts Rd., Barn. 80 DB42
Abbotts Rd., Mitch. 201 DJ98
Abbotts Rd., Sthl. 136 BY74
Abbotts Rd., Sutt. 199 CZ104
Abbott's Tilt, Walt. 196 BY104
Abbotts Vale, Chesh. 54 AQ28
Abbotts Wk., Bexh. 166 EX80
Abbotts Wk., Wind. 151 AL82
Abbotts Way, Slou. 131 AK74
Abbotts Way, Ware 33 ED11
Abbs Cross Gdns., Horn. 128 FJ60
Abbs Cross La., Horn. 128 FJ62
Abchurch La. EC4 275 L10
Abchurch La. EC4 142 DR73
Abchurch Yd. EC4 275 K10
Abdale Rd. W12 139 CV74
Abel Clo., Hem.H. 40 BN20
Abenberg Way, Brwd. 109 GB47
Aberavon Rd. E3 143 DY69
Abercairn Rd. SW16 181 DJ94
Aberconway Rd., Mord. 200 DB97
Abercorn Clo. NW7 97 CY52
Abercorn Clo. NW8 140 DC69
Abercorn Clo., S.Croy. 221 DX112
Abercorn Cres., Har. 116 CB60
Abercorn Gdns., Har. 117 CK59
Abercorn Gdns., Rom. 126 EV58
Abercorn Gro., Ruis. 115 BR56
Abercorn Pl. NW8 140 DC69
Abercorn Rd. NW7 97 CY52
Abercorn Rd., Stan. 95 CJ52
Abercorn Way SE1 162 DU78
Abercorn Way, Wok. 226 AU118
Abercrombie Dr., Enf. 82 DU39
Abercrombie St. SW11 160 DE82
Abercrombie Way, Harl. 51 EQ17
Aberdale Gdns., Pot.B. 63 CZ33
Aberdare Clo., W.Wick. 203 EC103
Aberdare Gdns. NW6 140 DB66
Aberdare Gdns. NW7 97 CX52
Aberdare Rd., Enf. 82 DW42
Aberdeen Ave., Slou. 131 AN73
Aberdeen La. N5 121 DP64
Aberdeen Par. N18 100 DV50
Angel Rd.
Aberdeen Pk. N5 122 DQ64
Aberdeen Pk. Ms. N5 122 DQ63
Aberdeen Pl. NW8 140 DD70
Aberdeen Rd. N5 122 DQ63
Aberdeen Rd. N18 100 DV50
Aberdeen Rd. NW10 119 CT64
Aberdeen Rd., Croy. 220 DQ105
Aberdeen Rd., Har. 95 CF54
Aberdeen Sq. E14 143 DZ74
Westferry Circ.
Aberdeen Ter. SE3 163 ED82
Aberdour Rd., Ilf. 126 EV62
Aberdour St. SE1 279 M8
Aberdour St. SE1 162 DS77
Aberfeldy St. E14 143 EC72
Aberford Gdns. SE18 164 EL81
Aberford Rd., Borwd. 78 CN40
Aberfoyle Rd. SW16 181 DK93
Abergeldie Rd. SE12 184 EH86
Aberglen Ind. Est., Hayes 155 BR75
Abernethy Rd. SE13 164 EE84
Abersham Rd. E8 122 DT64
Abery St. SE18 165 ES77
Abingdon Clo. NW1 141 DK65
Camden Sq.
Abingdon Clo. SE1 162 DT77
Bushwood Dr.
Abingdon Clo. SW19 180 DC93
Abingdon Clo., Uxb. 134 BM67
Abingdon Clo., Wok. 226 AV118
Abingdon Pl., Pot.B. 64 DB32
Abingdon Rd. N3 98 DC54
Abingdon Rd. SW16 201 DL96
Abingdon Rd. W8 160 DA76
Abingdon St. SW1 277 P6
Abingdon St. SW1 161 DL76
Abingdon Vil. W8 160 DA76
Abingdon Way, Orp. 224 EV105
Abinger Ave., Sutt. 217 CW109
Abinger Clo., Bark. 126 EU63
Abinger Clo., Brom. 204 EL97
Abinger Clo., Dor. 263 CJ140
Abinger Clo., Wall. 219 DL106
Garden Clo.
Abinger Common Rd., Dor. 262 BY144
Abinger Dr., Red. 266 DE136
Abinger Gdns., Islw. 157 CE83
Abinger Gro. SE8 163 DZ79
Abinger La., Dor. 261 BV140
Abinger Ms. W9 140 DA70
Warlock Rd.
Abinger Rd. W4 158 CS76
Abinger Way, Guil. 243 BB129
Ablett St. SE16 162 DW78
Abney Gdns. N16 122 DT61
Stoke Newington High St.
Aboyne Dr. SW20 199 CU96
Aboyne Est. SW17 180 DD90
Aboyne Rd. NW10 118 CS62
Aboyne Rd. SW17 180 DD90
Abridge Clo., Wal.Cr. 83 DX35
Abridge Gdns., Rom. 104 FA51
Abridge Pk. (Abridge), Rom. 86 EU42
Abridge Rd., Chig. 85 ER44
Abridge Rd., Epp. 85 ES36
Abridge Rd. (Abridge), Rom. 86 EU39
Abridge Way, Bark. 146 EV69
Abyssinia Clo. SW11 160 DE84
Cairns Rd.
Acacia Ave. N17 100 DR52
Acacia Ave., Brent. 157 CH80
Acacia Ave., Hayes 135 BT72
Acacia Ave., Horn. 127 FF61
Acacia Ave., Mitch. 201 DH96
Acacia Rd.
Acacia Ave., Ruis. 115 BU60
Acacia Ave., Shep. 194 BN99
Acacia Ave., Stai. 152 AY84
Acacia Ave., Wem. 118 CL64
Acacia Ave., West Dr. 134 BM73
Acacia Ave., Wok. 226 AX120
Acacia Clo. SE8 163 DY77
Acacia Clo. SE20 202 DU96
Selby Rd.
Acacia Clo., Add. 211 BF110
Acacia Clo., Orp. 205 ER99
Acacia Clo., Stan. 95 CE51
Acacia Clo., Wal.Cr. 66 DS27
Acacia Dr., Add. 211 BF110
Acacia Dr., Bans. 217 CX114
Acacia Dr., Sutt. 199 CZ102
Acacia Dr., Upmin. 128 FN63
Acacia Gdns. NW8 140 DD68
Acacia Rd.
Acacia Gdns., Upmin. 129 FT59
Acacia Gdns., W.Wick. 203 EC103
Acacia Gro. SE21 182 DR89
Acacia Gro., Berk. 38 AV20
Acacia Gro., N.Mal. 198 CR97
Acacia Ms., West Dr. 154 BK79
Acacia Pl. NW8 140 DD68
Acacia Rd. E11 124 EE61
Acacia Rd. E17 123 DY58
Acacia Rd. N22 99 DN53
Acacia Rd. NW8 140 DD68
Acacia Rd. SW16 201 DL95
Acacia Rd. W3 138 CQ73
Acacia Rd., Beck. 203 DZ97
Acacia Rd., Dart. 188 FK88
Acacia Rd., Enf. 82 DR39
Acacia Rd., Green. 189 FS86
Acacia Rd., Guil. 242 AX134
Acacia Rd., Hmptn. 176 CA93
Acacia Rd., Mitch. 201 DH96
Acacia Rd., Stai. 174 BH92
Acacia St., Hat. 45 CU21
Acacia Wk., Swan. 207 FD96
Walnut Way
Acacia Way, Sid. 185 ET88
Academy Gdns., Croy. 202 DT102
Academy Gdns., Nthlt. 136 BX68
Academy Pl. SE18 165 EM81
Academy Rd. SE18 165 EM81
Acanthus Dr. SE1 162 DU78
Acanthus Rd. SW11 160 DG83
Accommodation La., West Dr. 154 BJ79
Accommodation Rd. NW11 119 CZ59
Accommodation Rd., Cher. 192 AX104
Acer Ave., Hayes 136 BY71
Acer Ave., Rain. 148 FK69
Acer Rd., West. 238 EK116
Acers, St.Alb. 60 CC28
Acfold Rd. SW6 160 DB81
Achilles Clo. SE1 162 DU78
Achilles Clo., Hem.H. 40 BM18
Achilles Pl., Wok. 226 AW117
Achilles Rd. NW6 120 DA64
Achilles St. SE14 163 DY80
Achilles Way W1 276 G3
Acklam Rd. W10 139 CZ71
Acklington Dr. NW9 96 CS53
Ackmar Rd. SW6 160 DA81
Ackroyd Dr. E3 143 DZ71
Ackroyd Rd. SE23 183 DX87
Ackworth Clo. N9 100 DW45
Turin Rd.
Acland Clo. SE18 165 ER80
Clothworkers Rd.
Acland Cres. SE5 162 DR84
Acland Rd. NW2 139 CV65
Acme Rd., Wat. 75 BU38
Acock Gro., Nthlt. 116 CB64
Dorchester Rd.
Acol Cres., Ruis. 115 BV64
Acol Rd. NW6 140 DA66
Aconbury Rd., Dag. 146 EV67
Acorn Clo. E4 101 EB50
The Lawns
Acorn Clo., Chis. 185 EQ92
Acorn Clo., Enf. 81 DP39
Acorn Clo., Horl. 269 DJ147
Acorn Clo., Stan. 95 CH52
Acorn Ct., Ilf. 125 ES58
Acorn Gdns. SE19 202 DT95
Acorn Gdns. W3 138 CR71
Acorn Gro., Hayes 155 BT80
Acorn Gro., Ruis. 115 BT63
Acorn Gro., Tad. 233 CY124
Warren Lo. Dr.
Acorn Gro., Wok. 226 AY121
Old Sch. Pl.
Acorn Ind. Pk., Dart. 187 FG85
Acorn La. (Cuffley), Pot.B. 65 DL29
Acorn Par. SE15 162 DV80
Carlton Gro.
Acorn Pl., Wat. 75 BU37
Acorn Rd., Dart. 187 FF85
Acorn Rd., Hem.H. 40 BN21
Acorn St., Ware 34 EK08
Acorn Wk. SE16 143 DY74
Acorn Way SE23 183 DX90
Acorn Way, Orp. 223 EP105
Acorns, The, Chig. 103 ES49
Acorns, The, Horl. 269 DP148
Acorns Clo., Hmptn. 176 CB93
Acorns Way, Esher 214 CC106
Acre Dr. SE22 162 DU84
Acre La. SW2 161 DL84
Acre La., Cars. 218 DG105
Acre La., Wall. 218 DG105
Acre Pas., Wind. 151 AR81
Madeira Wk.
Acre Path, Nthlt. 136 BY65
Arnold Rd.
Acre Rd. SW19 180 DD93
Acre Rd., Dag. 147 FB66
Acre Rd., Kings.T. 198 CL95
Acre Vw., Horn. 128 FL56
Acre Way, Nthwd. 93 BT53
Acrefield Rd., Ger.Cr. 112 AX55
Acres End, Amer. 55 AS39
Acres Gdns., Tad. 233 CX119
Acrewood, Hem.H. 40 BL20
Acrewood Way, St.Alb. 44 CM20
Acris St. SW18 180 DC85
Acton Clo. N9 100 DU47
Acton Clo. (Cheshunt), Wal.Cr. 67 DY31
Acton Hill Ms. W3 138 CP74
Uxbridge Rd.
Acton La. NW10 138 CS68
Acton La. W3 158 CQ75
Acton La. W4 158 CR76
Acton Ms. E8 142 DT67
Acton Pk. Ind. Est. W3 158 CR75
Acton St. WC1 274 B3
Acton St. WC1 141 DM69
Acuba Rd. SW18 180 DB89
Acworth Clo. N9 100 DW45
Turin Rd.
Ada Gdns. E14 143 ED72
Ada Gdns. E15 144 EF67
Ada Pl. E2 142 DU67
Ada Rd. SE5 162 DS80
Ada Rd., Wem. 117 CK62
Ada St. E8 142 DV67
Adair Clo. SE25 202 DV97
Adair Rd. W10 139 CY70
Adair Twr. W10 139 CY70
Appleford Rd.
Adam & Eve Ct. W1 273 L8
Adam & Eve Ms. W8 160 DA76
Adam Clo., Slou. 131 AN74
Telford Dr.
Adam Ct. SW7 160 DC77
Gloucester Rd.
Adam Pl. N16 122 DT61
Stoke Newington High St.
Adam Rd. E4 101 DZ51
Adam St. WC2 278 A1
Adam St. WC2 141 DL73
Adam Wk. SW6 159 CW80
Adams Clo. N3 98 DA52
Falkland Ave.
Adams Clo. NW9 118 CP61
Adams Clo., Surb. 198 CM100
Adams Ct. EC2 275 L8
Adams Gdns. Est. SE16 162 DW75
St. Marychurch St.
Adams Pl. E14 143 EB74
North Colonnade
Adams Pl. N7 121 DM64
George's Rd.
Adams Rd. N17 100 DS54
Adams Rd., Beck. 203 DY99
Adams Row W1 276 G1
Adams Row W1 140 DG73
Adams Sq., Bexh. 166 EY83
Regency Way
Adams Wk., Kings.T. 198 CL96
Adams Way, Croy. 202 DT100
Adamsfield, Wal.Cr. 66 DU27
Adamson Rd. E16 144 EG72
Adamson Rd. NW3 140 DD66
Adamsrill Clo., Enf. 82 DR44
Adamsrill Rd. SE26 183 DY91
Adare Wk. SW16 181 DM90
Adastral Est. NW9 96 CS53
Adcock Wk., Orp. 223 ET105
Borkwood Pk.
Adderley Gdns. SE9 185 EN91
Adderley Gro. SW11 180 DG85
Culmstock Rd.
Adderley Rd., Har. 95 CF53
Adderley St. E14 143 EC72
Addington Border, Croy. 221 DY110
Addington Clo., Wind. 151 AN83
Addington Ct. SW14 158 CR83
Addington Dr. N12 98 DC51
Addington Gro. SE26 183 DY91
Addington Rd. E3 143 EA69
Addington Rd. E16 144 EE70
Addington Rd. N4 121 DN58
Addington Rd., Croy. 201 DN102
Addington Rd., S.Croy. 220 DU111
Addington Rd., W.Wick. 204 EE103
Addington Sq. SE5 162 DQ79
Addington St. SE1 278 C5
Addington Village Rd., Croy. 221 EA106
Addis Clo., Enf. 83 DX39
Addiscombe Ave., Croy. 202 DU101
Addiscombe Clo., Har. 117 CJ57
Addiscombe Ct. Rd., Croy. 202 DS102
Addiscombe Gro., Croy. 202 DR103
Addiscombe Rd., Croy. 202 DS103
Addiscombe Rd., Wat. 75 BV42
Addison Ave. N14 81 DH44
Addison Ave. W11 139 CY74
Addison Ave., Houns. 156 CC81
Addison Bri. Pl. W14 159 CZ77
Addison Clo., Cat. 236 DR122
Addison Clo., Nthwd. 93 BU53
Addison Clo., Orp. 205 EQ100
Addison Cres. W14 159 CY76
Addison Dr. SE12 184 EH85
Eltham Rd.
Addison Gdns. W14 159 CX76
Addison Gdns., Grays 170 GC77
Palmers Dr.
Addison Gdns., Surb. 198 CM98
Addison Gro. W4 158 CS76
Addison Pl. W11 139 CY74
Addison Pl., Sthl. 136 CA73
Longford Ave.
Addison Rd. E11 124 EG58
Addison Rd. E17 123 EB57
Addison Rd. SE25 202 DU98
Addison Rd. W14 159 CZ76
Addison Rd., Brom. 204 EJ99
Addison Rd., Cat. 236 DR121
Addison Rd., Chesh. 54 AQ29
Addison Rd., Enf. 82 DW39
Addison Rd., Guil. 258 AY135
Addison Rd., Ilf. 103 EQ53
Addison Rd., Tedd. 177 CH93
Addison Rd., Wok. 227 AZ117
Chertsey Rd.
Addison Way NW11 119 CZ56
Addison Way, Hayes 135 BU72
Addison Way, Nthwd. 93 BT53
Addison's Clo., Croy. 203 DZ103
Addle Hill EC4 274 G10
Addle St. EC2 275 J7
Addlestone Moor, Add. 194 BJ103
Addlestone Pk., Add. 212 BH106
Addlestone Rd., Add. 212 BL105
Adecroft Way, W.Mol. 196 CC97
Adela Ave., N.Mal. 199 CV99
Adela St. W10 139 CY70
Kensal Rd.
Adelaide Ave. SE4 163 DZ84
Adelaide Clo., Enf. 82 DT38
Adelaide Clo., Slou. 151 AN75
Amerden Way
Adelaide Clo., Stan. 95 CG49
Adelaide Cotts. W7 157 CF75
Adelaide Gdns., Rom. 126 EY57
Adelaide Gro. W12 139 CU74
Adelaide Pl., Wey. 213 BR105
Adelaide Rd. E10 123 EC62
Adelaide Rd. NW3 140 DD66
Adelaide Rd. SW18 180 DA85
Putney Bri. Rd.
Adelaide Rd. W13 137 CG74
Adelaide Rd., Ashf. 174 BK92
Adelaide Rd., Chis. 185 EP92
Adelaide Rd., Houns. 156 BY81
Adelaide Rd., Ilf. 125 EP61
Adelaide Rd., Rich. 158 CM84
Adelaide Rd., Sthl. 156 BY77
Adelaide Rd., Surb. 198 CL99
Adelaide Rd., Tedd. 177 CF93
Adelaide Rd., Til. 171 GF81
Adelaide Rd., Walt. 195 BU104
Adelaide Sq., Wind. 151 AR82
Adelaide St. WC2 277 P1
Adelaide St., St.Alb. 43 CD19
Adelaide Ter., Brent. 157 CK78
Adelaide Wk. SW9 161 DN84
Sussex Wk.
Adelina Gro. E1 142 DW71
Adelina Ms. SW12 181 DK88
King's Ave.
Adeline Pl. WC1 273 N7
Adeline Pl. WC1 141 DK71
Adeliza Clo., Bark. 145 EP66
North St.
Adelphi Cres., Hayes 135 BT69
Adelphi Cres., Horn. 127 FG61
Adelphi Gdns., Slou. 152 AS75
Adelphi Rd., Epsom 216 CR113
Adelphi Ter. WC2 278 A1
Adelphi Way, Hayes 135 BT69
Aden Gro. N16 122 DR63
Aden Rd., Enf. 83 DY42
Aden Rd., Ilf. 125 EP59
Aden Ter. N16 122 DR63
Adeney Clo. W6 159 CX79
Adenmore Rd. SE6 183 EA87
Adeyfield Gdns., Hem.H. 40 BM19
Adeyfield Rd., Hem.H. 40 BK19
Adhern Ct., St.Alb. 43 CJ22
Adie Rd. W6 159 CW76
Adine Rd. E13 144 EH70
Adler Ind. Est., Hayes 155 BR75
Adler St. E1 142 DU72
Adlers La., Dor. 247 CG131
Adley St. E5 123 DY64
Adlington Clo. N18 100 DS50
Admaston Rd. SE18 165 EQ80
Admiral Clo., Orp. 206 EX98
Admiral Ct. NW4 119 CU57
Barton Clo.
Admiral Pl. SE16 143 DY74
Admiral Seymour Rd. SE9 165 EM84
Admiral Sq. SW10 160 DD81
Admiral St. SE8 163 EA81
Admiral St., Hert. 32 DU09
Admiral Wk. W9 140 DA71
Admiral Way, Berk. 38 AT17
Tortoiseshell Way
Admirals Clo. E18 124 EH56
Admirals Clo., St.Alb. 44 CS23
Admirals Ct., Guil. 243 BB133
Admiral's Rd., Lthd. 247 CD126
Admirals Wk. NW3 120 DC62
Admiral's Wk., Dor. 246 CB130
Admirals Wk., Green. 189 FV85
Admirals Wk., Hodd. 49 EA19
Admirals Wk., St.Alb. 43 CG23
Admiral's Wk., The, Couls. 235 DM120
Goodenough Way
Admirals Way E14 163 EA75
Admiralty Clo. SE8 163 EA80
Reginald Sq.
Admiralty Rd., Tedd. 177 CF93
Adnams Wk., Rain. 147 FF65
Lovell Wk.
Adolf St. SE6 183 EB91
Adolphus Rd. N4 121 DP61
Adolphus St. SE8 163 DZ80
Adomar Rd., Dag. 126 EX62
Adpar St. W2 140 DD70
Adrian Ave. NW2 119 CV60
North Circular Rd.
Adrian Clo. (Harefield), Uxb. 92 BK53
Adrian Ms. SW10 160 DB79
Adrian Rd., Abb.L. 59 BS31
Adrienne Ave., Sthl. 136 BZ70
Adstock Ms., Ger.Cr. 90 AX53
Church La.
Adstock Way, Grays 170 FZ77
Advance Rd. SE27 182 DQ91
Advent Way N18 101 DX50
Advice Ave., Grays 170 GA75
Adys Rd. SE15 162 DT83
Aerodrome Rd. NW4 119 CT55
Aerodrome Rd. NW9 97 CT54
Aerodrome Way, Houns. 156 BW79
Aeroville NW9 96 CS54
Affleck St. N1 274 C1
Afghan Rd. SW11 160 DE82
Afton Dr., S.Ock. 149 FV72

Agamemnon Rd. NW6 119 CZ64
Agar Clo., Surb. 198 CM103
Agar Gro. NW1 141 DJ66
Agar Gro. Est. NW1 141 DK66
Agar Pl. NW1 141 DJ66
Agar St. WC2 277 P1
Agar St. WC2 141 DL73
Agars Plough, Slou. 152 AU79
Agate Clo. E16 144 EK72
Agate Rd. W6 159 CW76
Agates La., Ash. 231 CK118
Agatha Clo. E1 142 DV74
Prusom St.
Agaton Rd. SE9 185 EQ89
Agave Rd. NW2 119 CW63
Agdon St. EC1 274 F4
Agdon St. EC1 141 DP70
Agincourt Rd. NW3 120 DF63
Agister Rd., Chig. 104 EU50
Agnes Ave., Ilf. 125 EP63
Agnes Clo. E6 145 EN73
Agnes Gdns., Dag. 126 EX63
Agnes Rd. W3 139 CT74
Agnes Scott Ct., Wey. 195 BP104
Palace Dr.
Agnes St. E14 143 DZ72
Agnesfield Clo. N12 98 DE51
Agnew Rd. SE23 183 DX87
Agraria Rd., Guil. 258 AV135
Agricola Ct. E3 143 DZ67
Parnell Rd.
Agricola Pl., Enf. 82 DT43
Aidan Clo., Dag. 126 EY63
Aileen Wk. E15 144 EF66
Ailsa Ave., Twick. 177 CG85
Ailsa Rd., Twick. 177 CH85
Ailsa St. E14 143 EC71
Ainger Ms. NW3 140 DF66
Ainger Rd.
Ainger Rd. NW3 140 DF66
Ainsdale Clo., Orp. 205 ER102
Ainsdale Cres., Pnr. 116 CA55
Ainsdale Dr. SE1 162 DU78
Ainsdale Rd. W5 137 CK70
Ainsdale Rd., Wat. 94 BW48
Ainsdale Way, Wok. 226 AU118
Ainsley Ave., Rom. 127 FB58
Ainsley Clo. N9 100 DS46
Ainsley St. E2 142 DV69
Ainslie Wk. SW12 181 DH87
Ainslie Wd. Cres. E4 101 EB50
Ainslie Wd. Gdns. E4 101 EB49
Ainslie Wd. Rd. E4 101 EA50
Ainsty Est. SE16 163 DX75
Ainsworth Clo. NW2 119 CU62
Ainsworth Clo. SE15 162 DS82
Lyndhurst Gro.
Ainsworth Rd. E9 142 DW66
Ainsworth Rd., Croy. 201 DP103
Ainsworth Way NW8 140 DC67
Aintree Ave. E6 144 EL67
Aintree Clo., Grav. 191 GH90
Aintree Clo., Slou. 153 BE81
Aintree Clo., Uxb. 135 BP72
Craig Dr.
Aintree Cres., Ilf. 103 EQ54
Aintree Est. SW6 159 CY80
Dawes Rd.
Aintree Gro., Upmin. 128 FM62
Aintree Rd., Grnf. 137 CH68
Aintree St. SW6 159 CY80
Air Links Ind. Est., Houns. 156 BW78
Air St. W1 277 L1
Air St. W1 141 DJ73
Airdrie Clo. N1 141 DM66
Airdrie Clo., Hayes 136 BY71
Glencoe Rd.
Aire Dr., S.Ock. 149 FV70
Airedale, Hem.H. 40 BL17
Airedale Ave. W4 159 CT77
Airedale Ave. S. W4 159 CT78
Netheravon Rd. S.
Airedale Clo., Dart. 188 FQ88
Airedale Rd. SW12 180 DF87
Airedale Rd. W5 157 CJ76
Airey Neave Ct., Grays 170 GA75
Airfield Way, Horn. 147 FH65
Airlie Gdns. W8 140 DA74
Campden Hill Rd.
Airlie Gdns., Ilf. 125 EP60
Airport Ind. Est., West. 222 EK114
Airport Roundabout E16 144 EK74
Connaught Bri.
Airport Way, Gat. 268 DG151
Airport Way, Stai. 153 BF84
Airthrie Rd., Ilf. 126 EV61
Aisgill Ave. W14 159 CZ78
Aisher Rd. SE28 146 EW73
Aisher Way, Sev. 241 FD119
London Rd.
Aislibie Rd. SE12 164 EE84
Aitken Clo. E8 142 DU67
Pownall Rd.
Aitken Clo., Mitch. 200 DF101
Aitken Rd. SE6 183 EB89
Aitken Rd., Barn. 79 CW43
Ajax Ave. NW9 118 CS55
Ajax Ave., Slou. 131 AP73
Ajax Rd. NW6 120 DA64
Akabusi Clo., Croy. 202 DU100
Akehurst La., Sev. 257 FJ125
Akehurst St. SW15 179 CU86
Akeman Clo., St.Alb. 42 BZ22
Meautys
Akenside Rd. NW3 120 DD64
Akerman Rd. SW9 161 DP82
Akerman Rd., Surb. 197 CJ100
Akers Way, Rick. 73 BD44
Alabama St. SE18 165 ER80
Alacross Rd. W5 157 CJ75
Alamein Clo., Brox. 49 DX20
Alamein Gdns., Dart. 189 FR87
Alamein Rd., Swans. 189 FX86
Alan Clo., Dart. 168 FJ84
Alan Dr., Barn. 79 CY44
Alan Gdns., Rom. 126 FA59
Alan Hocken Way E15 144 EE68
Alan Rd. SW19 179 CY92
Alan Way, Slou. 132 AY72
Alanbrooke, Grav. 191 GJ87
Alandale Dr., Pnr. 93 BV54
Alander Ms. E17 123 EC56
Alanthus Clo. SE12 184 EF86
Alaska St. SE1 278 D3
Alba Clo., Hayes 136 BX70
Ramulis Dr.
Alba Gdns. NW11 119 CY58
Alba Pl. W11 139 CZ72
Portobello Rd.
Albacore Cres. SE13 183 EB86
Albain Cres., Ashf. 174 BL89
Alban Ave., St.Alb. 43 CD18
Alban Cres., Borwd. 78 CP39
Alban Cres. (Farningham), Dart. 208 FN102
Alban Highwalk EC2 142 DQ71
London Wall
Alban Ind. Pk., St.Alb. 44 CN20
Alban Pk., St.Alb. 44 CM20
Alban Way, Hat. 44 CR19
Alban Way, St.Alb. 43 CE22
Albans Vw., Wat. 59 BV33
Albany W1 277 K1
Albany, The, Wdf.Grn. 102 EF49
Albany Clo. N15 121 DP56
Albany Clo. SW14 158 CP84
Albany Clo., Bex. 186 EW87
Albany Clo., Esher 214 CA109
Albany Clo., Reig. 250 DA131
Albany Clo., Uxb. 114 BN64
Albany Clo. (Bushey), Wat. 77 CD44
Albany Ct. E4 83 EB44
Chelwood Clo.
Albany Ct., Epp. 69 ET30
Albany Ctyd. W1 277 L1
Albany Cres., Edg. 96 CN52
Albany Cres., Esher 215 CE107
Albany Gate, Chesh. 54 AP30
Bellingdon Rd.
Albany Mans. SW11 160 DE80
Albany Ms. N1 141 DN66
Barnsbury Pk.
Albany Ms. SE5 162 DQ79
Albany Rd.
Albany Ms., Brom. 184 EG93
Avondale Rd.
Albany Ms., Kings.T. 177 CK93
Albany Ms., St.Alb. 60 CA27
North Orbital Rd.
Albany Ms., Sutt. 218 DB106
Camden Rd.
Albany Pk., Slou. 153 BD80
Albany Pk. Ave., Enf. 82 DW39
Albany Pk. Rd., Kings.T. 178 CL93
Albany Pk. Rd., Lthd. 231 CG119
Albany Pas., Rich. 178 CM85
Albany Pl. N7 121 DN63
Benwell Rd.
Albany Pl., Brent. 158 CL79
Albany Rd.
Albany Pl., Egh. 173 BB91
Albany Quay, Ware 33 DY06
Albany Rd. E10 123 EA59
Albany Rd. E12 124 EK63
Albany Rd. E17 123 DZ58
Albany Rd. N4 121 DM58
Albany Rd. N18 100 DV50
Albany Rd. SE5 162 DR79
Albany Rd. SW19 180 DB92
Albany Rd. W13 137 CH73
Albany Rd., Belv. 166 EZ79
Albany Rd., Bex. 186 EW87
Albany Rd., Brent. 157 CK79
Albany Rd., Brwd. 108 FV44
Albany Rd., Chis. 185 EP92
Albany Rd., Enf. 83 DX37
Albany Rd., Horn. 127 FG60
Albany Rd., N.Mal. 198 CS98
Albany Rd., Rich. 178 CM85
Albert Rd.
Albany Rd., Rom. 126 EZ58
Albany Rd., Walt. 214 BW105
Albany Rd., Wind. 151 AQ82
Albany Rd. (Old Windsor), Wind. 172 AU85
Albany St. NW1 141 DH68
Albany Ter. NW1 141 DH70
Marylebone Rd.
Albany Vw., Buck.H. 102 EG46
Albanys, The, Reig. 250 DA132
Albatross Gdns., S.Croy. 221 DX111
Albatross St. SE18 165 ES80
Albatross Way SE16 163 DX75
Albemarle SW19 179 CX89
Albemarle App., Ilf. 125 EP58
Albemarle Ave., Pot.B. 64 DB33
Albemarle Ave., Twick. 176 BZ88
Albemarle Ave. (Cheshunt), Wal.Cr. 66 DW28
Albemarle Clo., Grays 170 GA75
Albemarle Gdns., Ilf. 125 EP58
Albemarle Gdns., N.Mal. 198 CR98
Albemarle Pk., Stan. 95 CJ50
Marsh La.
Albemarle Rd., Barn. 98 DE45
Albemarle Rd., Beck. 203 EB95
Albemarle St. W1 277 J1
Albemarle St. W1 141 DH73
Albemarle Way EC1 274 F5
Albeny Gate, St.Alb. 43 CD21
Alberon Gdns. NW11 119 CZ56
Albert Ave. E4 101 EA49
Albert Ave. SW8 161 DM80
Albert Ave., Cher. 194 BG97
Albert Bri. SW3 160 DE79
Albert Bri. SW11 160 DE79
Albert Bri. Rd. SW11 160 DE80
Albert Carr Gdns. SW16 181 DL92
Albert Clo. E9 142 DV67
Northiam St.
Albert Clo. N22 99 DK53
Albert Clo., Grays 170 GC76
Albert Clo., Slou. 152 AT76
Albert St.
Albert Ct. SW7 160 DD75
Albert Cres. E4 101 EA49
Albert Dr. SW19 179 CY89
Albert Dr., Wok. 211 BD114
Albert Embk. SE1 161 DL78
Albert Gdns. E1 143 DX72
Albert Gdns., Harl. 52 EX16
Albert Gate SW1 276 E4
Albert Gate SW1 160 DF75
Albert Gro. SW20 199 CX95
Albert Hall Mans. SW7 160 DD75
Kensington Gore
Albert Mans. SW11 160 DF81
Albert Bri. Rd.
Albert Ms. E14 143 DY73
Narrow St.
Albert Ms. W8 160 DC76
Victoria Gro.
Albert Murray Clo., Grav. 191 GJ87
Albert Pl. N3 98 DA53
Albert Pl. N17 122 DT55
High Rd.
Albert Pl. W8 160 DB75
Albert Pl. (Eton Wick), Wind. 151 AN78
Common Rd.
Albert Rd. E10 123 EC61
Albert Rd. E16 144 EL74
Albert Rd. E17 123 EA57
Albert Rd. E18 124 EH55
Albert Rd. N4 121 DM60
Albert Rd. N15 122 DS58
Albert Rd. N22 99 DJ53
Albert Rd. NW4 119 CX56
Albert Rd. NW6 139 CZ68
Albert Rd. NW7 97 CT50
Albert Rd. SE9 184 EL90
Albert Rd. SE20 183 DX94
Albert Rd. SE25 202 DU98
Albert Rd. W5 137 CH70
Albert Rd., Add. 194 BK104
Albert Rd., Ashf. 174 BM92
Albert Rd., Ash. 232 CM118
Albert Rd., Barn. 80 DC42
Albert Rd., Belv. 166 EZ78
Albert Rd., Bex. 186 FA86
Albert Rd., Brom. 204 EK99
Albert Rd., Buck.H. 102 EK47
Albert Rd., Chesh. 54 AQ31
Albert Rd., Dag. 126 FA60
Albert Rd., Dart. 188 FJ90
Albert Rd., Egh. 172 AX93
Albert Rd., Epsom 217 CT113
Albert Rd., Hmptn. 176 CC92
Albert Rd., Har. 116 CC55
Albert Rd., Hayes 155 BS76
Albert Rd., Horl. 268 DG148
Albert Rd., Houns. 156 CA84
Albert Rd., Ilf. 125 EP62
Albert Rd., Kings.T. 198 CM96
Albert Rd., Mitch. 200 DF97
Albert Rd., N.Mal. 199 CT98
Albert Rd., Orp. 224 EU106
Albert Rd. (St. Mary Cray), Orp. 206 EV100
Albert Rd., Red. 251 DJ129
Albert Rd., Rich. 178 CL85
Albert Rd., Rom. 127 FF57
Albert Rd., Sthl. 156 BX76
Albert Rd., Sutt. 218 DD106
Albert Rd., Swans. 190 FZ86
Albert Rd., Tedd. 177 CF93
Albert Rd., Twick. 177 CF88
Albert Rd., Warl. 237 DZ117
Albert Rd., West Dr. 134 BL74
Albert Rd., Wind. 151 AR83
Albert Rd. Est., Belv. 166 EZ78
Albert Rd. N., Reig. 249 CZ133
Albert Rd. N., Wat. 75 BV41
Albert Rd. S., Wat. 75 BV41
Albert Sq. E15 124 EE64
Albert Sq. SW8 161 DM80
Albert St. N12 98 DC50
Albert St. NW1 141 DH67
Albert St., Brwd. 108 FW50
Albert St., St.Alb. 43 CD21
Albert St., Slou. 152 AT76
Albert St., Wind. 151 AP81
Albert Ter. NW1 140 DG67
Albert Ter. NW10 138 CR67
Albert Ter., Buck.H. 102 EK47
Albert Ter. Ms. NW1 140 DG67
Regents Pk. Rd.
Albert Way SE15 162 DV80
Alberta Ave., Sutt. 217 CY105
Alberta Dr., Horl. 269 DN148
Alberta Est. SE17 278 G10
Alberta Est. SE17 161 DP78
Alberta Rd., Enf. 82 DT44
Alberta Rd., Erith 167 FC81
Alberta St. SE17 278 F10
Alberta St. SE17 161 DP78
Albertine Clo., Epsom 233 CV116
Rose Bushes
Albion Ave. N10 98 DG53
Albion Ave. SW8 161 DK82
Albion Bldgs. EC1 142 DQ71
Bartholomew Clo.
Albion Clo. W2 272 C10
Albion Clo., Hert. 32 DS08
Albion Clo., Rom. 127 FD58
Albion Clo., Slou. 132 AU74
Albion Cres., Ch.St.G. 90 AV48
Albion Dr. E8 142 DT66
Albion Est. SE16 163 DX75
Albion Gdns. W6 159 CV77
Albion Gro. N16 122 DS63
Albion Hill SE13 163 EB82
Albion Hill, Loug. 84 EJ43
Albion Ho., Slou. 153 BB78
Albion Ms. N1 141 DN67
Albion Ms. NW6 139 CZ66
Kilburn High Rd.
Albion Ms. W2 272 C9
Albion Ms. W2 140 DE72
Albion Ms. W6 159 CV77
Galena Rd.
Albion Par. N16 122 DR63
Albion Rd.
Albion Par., Grav. 191 GK86
Albion Pk., Loug. 84 EK43
Albion Pl. EC1 274 F6
Albion Pl. EC1 141 DP71
Albion Pl. SE25 202 DU97
High St.
Albion Pl. W6 159 CV77
Albion Rd. E17 123 EC55
Albion Rd. N16 122 DR63
Albion Rd. N17 100 DT54
Albion Rd., Bexh. 166 EZ84
Albion Rd., Ch.St.G. 90 AV47
Albion Rd., Grav. 191 GJ87
Albion Rd., Hayes 135 BS72
Albion Rd., Houns. 156 CA84
Albion Rd., Kings.T. 198 CQ95
Albion Rd., Reig. 266 DC135
Albion Rd., St.Alb. 43 CF20
Albion Rd., Sutt. 218 DD107
Albion Rd., Twick. 177 CE88
Albion Sq. E8 142 DT66
Albion St. SE16 162 DW75
Albion St. W2 272 C9
Albion St. W2 140 DE72
Albion St., Croy. 201 DP102
Albion Ter. E8 142 DT66
Albion Ter., Grav. 191 GJ86
Albion Vil. Rd. SE26 182 DW90
Albion Way EC1 275 H7
Albion Way SE13 163 EC84
Albion Way, Wem. 118 CP62
North End Rd.
Albion Yd. E1 142 DV71
Albright Ind. Est., Rain. 147 FF71
Albrighton Rd. SE22 162 DS83
Albuhera Clo., Enf. 81 DN39
Albury Ave., Bexh. 166 EY82
Albury Ave., Islw. 157 CF80
Albury Ave., Sutt. 217 CW109
Albury Clo., Cher. 192 AU104
Albury Clo., Hmptn. 176 CA93
Albury Dr., Pnr. 94 BX52
Albury Gro. Rd. (Cheshunt), Wal.Cr. 67 DX30
Albury Heath, Guil. 260 BK141
Albury Ms. E12 124 EJ60
Albury Pk., Guil. 260 BL140
Albury Ride (Cheshunt), Wal.Cr. 67 DX31
Albury Rd., Chess. 216 CL106
Albury Rd., Guil. 259 AZ135
Albury Rd., Red. 251 DJ129
Albury Rd., Walt. 213 BS107
Albury St. SE8 163 EA79
Albury Wk. (Cheshunt), Wal.Cr. 67 DX32
Albyfield, Brom. 205 EM97
Albyn Rd. SE8 163 EA81
Albyns Clo., Rain. 147 FG66
Albyns La., Rom. 87 FC40
Alcester Cres. E5 122 DV61
Alcester Rd., Wall. 219 DH105
Alcock Clo., Wall. 219 DK108
Alcock Rd., Houns. 156 BX80
Alcocks Clo., Tad. 233 CY120
Alcocks La., Tad. 233 CY121
Alconbury, Welw.G.C. 30 DE09
Alconbury Rd. E5 122 DU61
Alcorn Clo., Sutt. 200 DA103
Alcott Clo. W7 137 CF71
Westcott Cres.
Alcuin Ct., Stan. 95 CJ52
Old Ch. La.
Aldborough Rd., Dag. 147 FC65
Aldborough Rd., Upmin. 128 FM61
Aldborough Rd. N., Ilf. 125 ET57
Aldborough Rd. S., Ilf. 125 ES60
Aldborough Spur, Slou. 132 AS72
Aldbourne Rd. W12 139 CT74
Aldbourne Rd., Slou. 130 AH71
Aldbridge St. SE17 279 N10
Aldbridge St. SE17 162 DS78
Aldburgh Ms. W1 272 G8
Aldbury Ave., Wem. 138 CP66
Aldbury Clo., St.Alb. 43 CJ15
Sandringham Cres.
Aldbury Clo., Wat. 76 BX36
Aldbury Gro., Welw.G.C. 30 DB09
Aldbury Ms. N9 100 DR45
Aldbury Rd., Rick. 91 BF45
Aldebert Ter. SW8 161 DL80
Aldeburgh Clo. E5 122 DV61
Southwold Rd.
Aldeburgh Pl., Wdf.Grn. 102 EG49
Aldeburgh St. SE10 164 EG78
Alden Ave. E15 144 EF69
Alden Vw., Wind. 151 AK81
Aldenham Ave., Rad. 77 CG36
Aldenham Dr., Uxb. 135 BP70
Aldenham Gro., Rad. 61 CH34
Aldenham Rd., Borwd. 77 CH42
Aldenham Rd., Rad. 77 CG35
Aldenham Rd., Wat. 76 BX44
Aldenham Rd. (Bushey), Wat. 76 BZ41
Aldenham Rd. (Letchmore Heath), Wat. 77 CE39
Aldenham St. NW1 273 L1
Aldenham St. NW1 141 DK68
Aldenholme, Wey. 213 BS107
Aldensley Rd. W6 159 CV76
Alder Ave., Upmin. 128 FM63
Alder Clo. SE15 162 DT79
Alder Clo., Egh. 172 AY92
Alder Clo., Hodd. 49 EB15
Alder Clo., St.Alb. 60 CB28
Alder Clo., Slou. 131 AM74
Alder Cft., Couls. 235 DM116
Alder Dr., S.Ock. 149 FW70
Laburnum Gro.
Alder Gro. NW2 119 CV61
Alder Ms. N19 121 DJ61
Bredgar Rd.
Alder Rd. SW14 158 CR83
Alder Rd., Iver 133 BC68
Alder Rd., Sid. 185 ET90
Alder Rd. (Denham), Uxb. 134 BJ65
Alder Wk., Ilf. 125 EQ64
Alder Wk., Wat. 75 BV35
Aspen Pk. Dr.
Alder Way, Swan. 207 FD96
Alderbourne La., Iver 113 AZ64
Alderbourne La., Slou. 112 AX63
Alderbrook Rd. SW12 181 DH86
Alderbury Rd. SW13 159 CU79
Alderbury Rd., Slou. 153 AZ75
Alderbury Rd. W., Slou. 153 AZ75
Aldercombe La., Cat. 252 DS127
Aldercroft, Couls. 235 DM116
Aldergrove Gdns., Houns. 156 BY82
Bath Rd.
Aldergrove Wk., Horn. 148 FJ65
Airfield Way
Alderholt Way SE15 162 DT80
Daniel Gdns.
Alderley Ct., Berk. 38 AV20
Alderman Ave., Bark. 146 EU69
Alderman Clo., Hat. 45 CW24
Alderman Judge Mall, Kings.T. 198 CL96
Eden St.
Aldermanbury EC2 275 J8
Aldermanbury EC2 142 DQ72
Aldermanbury Sq. EC2 275 J7
Aldermans Hill N13 99 DL49
Alderman's Wk. EC2 275 M7
Aldermary Rd., Brom. 204 EG95
Aldermoor Rd. SE6 183 DZ90
Alderney Ave., Houns. 156 CB80
Alderney Gdns., Nthlt. 136 BZ66
Alderney Rd. E1 143 DX70
Alderney Rd., Erith 167 FG80
Alderney St. SW1 277 J10
Alderney St. SW1 161 DH77
Alders, The N21 81 DN44
Alders, The, Felt. 176 BY91
Alders, The, Houns. 156 BZ79
Alders, The, W.Byf. 212 BJ112
Alders, The, W.Wick. 203 EB102
Alders Ave., Wdf.Grn. 102 EE51
Alders Clo. E11 124 EH61
Aldersbrook Rd.
Alders Clo. W5 157 CK76
Alders Clo., Edg. 96 CQ50
Alders Ct., Welw.G.C. 30 DA09
Alders Gro., E.Mol. 197 CD99
Esher Rd.
Alders Rd., Edg. 96 CQ50
Alders Rd., Reig. 250 DB132
Aldersbrook Ave., Enf. 82 DS40
Aldersbrook Dr., Kings.T. 178 CM93
Aldersbrook La. E12 125 EM62
Aldersbrook Rd. E11 124 EH61
Aldersbrook Rd. E12 124 EK62
Aldersey Gdns., Bark. 145 ER65
Aldersey Rd., Guil. 243 AZ134
Aldersford Clo. SE4 183 DX85
Aldersgate St. EC1 275 H8
Aldersgate St. EC1 142 DQ71
Aldersgrove, Wal.Abb. 68 EE34
Roundhills
Aldersgrove Ave. SE9 184 EJ90
Aldershot Rd. NW6 139 CZ67
Aldershot Rd., Guil. 242 AT132
Alderside Wk., Egh. 172 AY92
Aldersmead Ave., Croy. 203 DX100
Aldersmead Rd., Beck. 183 DY94
Alderson Pl., Sthl. 136 CC74
Alderson St. W10 139 CY70
Kensal Rd.
Alderstead Heath, Red. 235 DK124
Alderstead La., Red. 251 DK125
Alderton Clo. NW10 118 CR62
Alderton Clo., Brwd. 108 FV43
Alderton Clo., Loug. 85 EN42
Alderton Cres. NW4 119 CV57
Alderton Hall La., Loug. 85 EN42
Alderton Hill, Loug. 84 EL43
Alderton Ms., Loug. 85 EN42
Alderton Hall La.
Alderton Ri., Loug. 85 EN42
Alderton Rd. SE24 162 DQ83
Alderton Rd., Croy. 202 DT101
Alderton Way NW4 119 CV57
Alderton Way, Loug. 85 EM43
Alderville Rd. SW6 159 CZ82
Alderwick Dr., Houns. 157 CD83
Alderwood Clo., Cat. 252 DS125
Alderwood Clo., Rom. 86 EV41
Alderwood Dr., Rom. 86 EV41
Alderwood Rd. SE9 185 ER86
Aldford St. W1 276 F2
Aldford St. W1 140 DG74
Aldgate EC3 275 P9
Aldgate EC3 142 DT72
Aldgate Ave. E1 275 P8
Aldgate High St. EC3 275 P9
Aldgate High St. EC3 142 DT72
Aldham Dr., S.Ock. 149 FW71
Aldin Ave. N., Slou. 152 AU75
Aldin Ave. S., Slou. 152 AU75
Aldine Ct. W12 139 CW74
Aldine St.
Aldine Pl. W12 139 CW74
Uxbridge Rd.
Aldine St. W12 159 CW75
Aldingham Ct., Horn. 127 FG64
Easedale Dr.
Aldingham Gdns., Horn. 127 FG64
Aldington Clo., Dag. 126 EW59
Aldington Rd. SE18 164 EK76
Aldis Ms. SW17 180 DE92
Aldis St.
Aldis St. SW17 180 DE92
Aldock, Welw.G.C. 30 DA12
Aldred Rd. NW6 120 DA64
Aldren Rd. SW17 180 DC90
Aldrich Cres., Croy. 221 EC109
Aldrich Gdns., Sutt. 199 CZ104
Aldrich Ter. SW18 180 DC89
Lidiard Rd.
Aldriche Way E4 101 EC51
Aldridge Ave., Edg. 96 CP48
Aldridge Ave., Enf. 83 EA38
Aldridge Ave., Ruis. 116 BX61
Aldridge Ave., Stan. 96 CL53
Aldridge Ri., N.Mal. 198 CS101
Aldridge Rd., Slou. 131 AN70
Aldridge Rd. Vil. W11 139 CZ71
Aldridge Wk. N14 99 DL45
Aldrington Rd. SW16 181 DJ92
Aldsworth Clo. W9 140 DB70
Aldwick, St.Alb. 43 CH22
Aldwick Clo. SE9 185 ER90
Aldwick Rd., Croy. 201 DM104
Aldworth Gro. SE13 183 EC86
Aldworth Rd. E15 144 EE66
Aldwych WC2 274 B10
Aldwych WC2 141 DM73
Aldwych Ave., Ilf. 125 EQ56
Aldwych Clo., Horn. 127 FG61
Aldwych Underpass WC2 141 DM72
Kingsway
Aldykes, Hat. 45 CT18
Alers Rd., Bexh. 186 EX85
Alesia Clo. N22 99 DL52
Nightingale Rd.
Alestan Beck Rd. E16 144 EK72
Fulmer Rd.
Alexa Ct. W8 160 DA77
Lexham Gdns.
Alexander Ave. NW10 139 CV66
Alexander Clo., Barn. 80 DD42
Alexander Clo., Brom. 204 EG102
Alexander Clo., Sid. 185 ES85
Alexander Clo., Sthl. 136 CC74
Alexander Clo., Twick. 177 CF89
Alexander Ct., Wal.Cr. 67 DX30
Alexander Evans Ms. SE23 183 DX88
Sunderland Rd.
Alexander Godley Clo., Ash. 232 CM119
Alexander La., Brwd. 109 GB44
Alexander Ms. W2 140 DB72
Alexander St.
Alexander Pl. SW7 276 B8
Alexander Pl. SW7 160 DE77
Alexander Rd. N19 121 DL62
Alexander Rd., Bexh. 166 EX82
Alexander Rd., Chis. 185 EP92
Alexander Rd., Couls. 235 DH115
Alexander Rd., Egh. 173 BC92
Alexander Rd., Green. 189 FW85
Alexander Rd., Hert. 31 DN09
Alexander Rd., Reig. 266 DA137
Alexander Rd., St.Alb. 61 CK25

Alexander Sq. SW3 276 B8
Alexander Sq. SW3 160 DE77
Alexander St. W2 140 DA72
Alexander St., Chesh. 54 AQ30
Alexanders Wk., Cat. 252 DT126
Alexandra Ave. N22 99 DK53
Alexandra Ave. SW11 160 DG81
Alexandra Ave. W4 158 CR80
Alexandra Ave., Har. 116 BZ60
Alexandra Ave., Sthl. 136 BZ73
Alexandra Ave., Sutt. 200 DA104
Alexandra Ave., Warl. 237 DZ117
Alexandra Clo., Ashf. 175 BR94
Alexandra Rd.
Alexandra Clo., Grays 171 GH75
Alexandra Clo., Har. 116 CA62
Alexandra Ave.
Alexandra Clo., Stai. 174 BK93
Alexandra Clo., Swan. 207 FE96
Alexandra Clo., Walt. 195 BU103
Alexandra Cotts. SE14 163 DZ81
Alexandra Ct. N14 81 DJ43
Alexandra Ct., Ashf. 175 BR93
Alexandra Rd.
Alexandra Ct., Wem. 118 CM63
Alexandra Cres., Brom. 184 EF93
Alexandra Dr. SE19 182 DS92
Alexandra Dr., Surb. 198 CN101
Alexandra Gdns. N10 121 DH56
Alexandra Gdns. W4 158 CR80
Alexandra Gdns., Cars. 218 DG109
Alexandra Gdns., Houns. 156 CB82
Alexandra Gro. N4 121 DP60
Alexandra Gro. N12 98 DB50
Alexandra Ms. N2 120 DF55
Fortis Grn.
Alexandra Ms. SW19 180 DA93
Alexandra Rd.
Alexandra Palace N22 99 DK54
Alexandra Palace Way N22 121 DJ55
Alexandra Pk. Rd. N10 99 DH54
Alexandra Pk. Rd. N22 99 DK54
Alexandra Pl. NW8 140 DC67
Alexandra Pl. SE25 202 DR99
Alexandra Pl., Croy. 202 DS102
Alexandra Rd.
Alexandra Pl., Guil. 259 AZ136
Alexandra Rd. E6 145 EN69
Alexandra Rd. E10 123 EC62
Alexandra Rd. E17 123 DZ58
Alexandra Rd. E18 124 EH55
Alexandra Rd. N8 121 DN55
Alexandra Rd. N9 100 DV45
Alexandra Rd. N10 99 DH52
Alexandra Rd. N15 122 DR57
Alexandra Rd. NW4 119 CX56
Alexandra Rd. NW8 140 DC66
Alexandra Rd. SE26 183 DX93
Alexandra Rd. SW14 158 CR83
Alexandra Rd. SW19 179 CZ93
Alexandra Rd. W4 158 CR75
Alexandra Rd., Add. 212 BK105
Alexandra Rd., Ashf. 175 BR94
Alexandra Rd., Borwd. 78 CR38
Alexandra Rd., Brent. 157 CK79
Alexandra Rd., Brwd. 108 FW48
Alexandra Rd., Croy. 202 DS102
Alexandra Rd., Egh. 172 AW93
Alexandra Rd., Enf. 83 DX42
Alexandra Rd., Epsom 217 CT113
Alexandra Rd., Erith 167 FF79
Alexandra Rd., Grav. 191 GL87
Alexandra Rd., Hem.H. 40 BK19
Alexandra Rd., Houns. 156 CB82
Alexandra Rd., Kings L. 58 BN29
Alexandra Rd. (Chipperfield), Kings L. 58 BG30
Alexandra Rd., Kings.T. 178 CN94
Alexandra Rd., Mitch. 180 DE94
Alexandra Rd., Rain. 147 FF67
Alexandra Rd., Rich. 158 CM82
Alexandra Rd., Rick. 74 BG36
Alexandra Rd., Rom. 127 FF58
Alexandra Rd. (Chadwell Heath), Rom. 126 EX58
Alexandra Rd., St.Alb. 43 CE20
Alexandra Rd., Slou. 151 AR76
Alexandra Rd., T.Ditt. 197 CF99
Alexandra Rd., Til. 171 GF82
Alexandra Rd., Twick. 177 CJ86
Alexandra Rd., Uxb. 134 BK68
Alexandra Rd., Warl. 237 DY117
Alexandra Rd., Wat. 75 BU40
Alexandra Rd., West. 238 EH119
Alexandra Rd., Wind. 151 AR82
Alexandra Sq., Mord. 200 DA99
Alexandra St. E16 144 EG71
Alexandra St. SE14 163 DY80
Alexandra Ter., Guil. 258 AY135
Alexandra Wk. SE19 182 DS92
Alexandra Way, Epsom 216 CN111
Alexandra Way, Wal.Cr. 67 DZ34
Alexandria Rd. W13 137 CG73
Alexis St. SE16 162 DU77
Alfan La., Dart. 187 FD92
Alfearn Rd. E5 122 DW63
Alford Clo., Guil. 243 BB131
Alford Grn., Croy. 221 ED107
Alford Pl. N1 275 J1
Alford Rd. SW8 161 DK81
Alford Rd., Erith 167 FD78
Alfoxton Ave. N15 121 DP56
Alfred Clo. W4 158 CR77
Belmont Rd.
Alfred Gdns., Sthl. 136 BY73
Alfred Ms. W1 273 M6
Alfred Ms. W1 141 DK71
Alfred Pl. WC1 273 M6
Alfred Pl. WC1 141 DK71
Alfred Pl., Grav. 191 GF88
Alfred Prior Ho. E12 125 EN63
Alfred Rd. E15 124 EF64
Alfred Rd. SE25 202 DU99
Alfred Rd. W2 140 DA71
Alfred Rd. W3 138 CQ74
Alfred Rd., Belv. 166 EZ78
Alfred Rd., Brwd. 108 FX47
Alfred Rd., Buck.H. 102 EK47
Alfred Rd., Dart. 188 FL91
Alfred Rd., Felt. 176 BW89
Alfred Rd., Grav. 191 GH89
Alfred Rd., Kings.T. 198 CL97
Alfred Rd., S.Ock. 148 FQ74
Alfred Rd., Sutt. 218 DC106
Alfred St. E3 143 DZ69
Alfred St., Grays 170 GC79
Alfreda St. SW11 161 DH81
Alfred's Gdns., Bark. 145 ES68
Alfreds Way, Bark. 145 EQ69
Alfreds Way Ind. Est., Bark. 146 EU67
Alfreton Clo. SW19 179 CX90
Alfriston Ave., Croy. 201 DL101
Alfriston Ave., Har. 116 CA58
Alfriston Clo., Surb. 198 CM99
Alfriston Rd. SW11 180 DF85
Algar Clo., Islw. 157 CG83
Algar Rd.
Algar Clo., Stan. 95 CF50
Algar Rd., Islw. 157 CG83
Algarve Rd. SW18 180 DB88
Algernon Rd. NW4 119 CU58
Algernon Rd. NW6 140 DA67
Algernon Rd. SE13 163 EB84
Algers Clo., Loug. 84 EK43
Algers Mead, Loug. 84 EK43
Algers Rd., Loug. 84 EK43
Algiers Rd. SE13 163 EA84
Alibon Gdns., Dag. 126 FA64
Alibon Rd., Dag. 126 FA64
Alice Ct. SW15 159 CZ84
Deodar Rd.
Alice Gilliatt Ct. W14 159 CZ79
Alice La. E3 143 DZ67
Alice La., Slou. 130 AH70
Alice Ms., Tedd. 177 CF92
Luther Rd.
Alice Ruston Pl., Wok. 226 AW119
Alice St. SE1 279 M7
Alice St. SE1 162 DS76
Alice Thompson Clo. SE12 184 EJ89
Alice Walker Clo. SE24 161 DP84
Shakespeare Rd.
Alice Way, Houns. 156 CB84
Alicia Ave., Har. 117 CH56
Alicia Clo., Har. 117 CJ56
Alicia Gdns., Har. 117 CJ56
Alie St. E1 142 DT72
Alington Cres. NW9 118 CQ60
Alington Gro., Wall. 219 DJ109
Alison Clo. E6 145 EN72
Alison Clo., Croy. 203 DX102
Shirley Oaks Rd.
Alison Clo., Wok. 226 AY115
Aliwal Rd. SW11 160 DE84
Alkerden La., Green. 189 FW86
Alkerden La., Swans. 189 FX86
Alkerden Rd. W4 158 CS78
Alkham Rd. N16 122 DT61
All Hallows Rd. N17 100 DS53
All Saints Clo. N9 100 DT47
All Saints Clo., Chig. 104 EV48
All Saints Clo., Swans. 190 FZ85
High St.
All Saints Cres., Wat. 60 BX33
All Saints Dr. SE3 164 EE82
All Saints Dr., S.Croy. 220 DT112
All Saints La., Rick. 74 BN44
All Saints Ms., Har. 95 CE51
All Saints Pas. SW18 180 DB85
Wandsworth High St.
All Saints Rd. SW19 180 DC94
All Saints Rd. W3 158 CQ76
All Saints Rd. W11 139 CZ71
All Saints Rd., Grav. 191 GF88
All Saints Rd., Sutt. 200 DB104
All Saints St. N1 141 DM68
All Saints Twr. E10 123 EB59
All Souls Ave. NW10 139 CV68
All Souls Pl. W1 273 J7
Allan Barclay Clo. N15 122 DT58
High Rd.
Allan Clo., N.Mal. 198 CR99
Allan Way W3 138 CQ71
Allandale, Hem.H. 40 BK19
Allandale, St.Alb. 42 CB23
Allandale Ave. N3 119 CY55
Allandale Cres., Pot.B. 63 CY32
Allandale Pl., Orp. 206 EX104
Allandale Rd., Enf. 83 DX36
Allandale Rd., Horn. 127 FF59
Allard Clo., Orp. 206 EW101
Allard Clo. (Cheshunt), Wal.Cr. 66 DT27
Allard Cres. (Bushey), Wat. 94 CC46
Allard Gdns. SW4 181 DK85
Allard Way, Brox. 49 DY21
Allardyce St. SW4 161 DM84
Allbrook Clo., Tedd. 177 CE92
Allcot Clo., Felt. 175 BT88
Allcroft Rd. NW5 120 DG64
Alldicks Rd., Hem.H. 40 BM22
Allen Clo., Mitch. 201 DH95
Allen Clo., Rad. 62 CL32
Russet Dr.
Allen Clo., Sun. 195 BV95
Allen Ct., Dor. 263 CH136
High St.
Allen Ct., Grnf. 117 CF64
Allen Ct., Hat. 45 CV20
Drakes Way
Allen Edwards Dr. SW8 161 DL81
Allen Ho. Pk., Wok. 226 AW120
Allen Pl., Twick. 177 CG88
Church St.
Allen Rd. E3 143 DZ68
Allen Rd. N16 122 DS63
Allen Rd., Beck. 203 DX96
Allen Rd., Croy. 201 DM101
Allen Rd., Lthd. 246 CB126
Allen Rd., Rain. 148 FJ69
Allen Rd., Sun. 195 BV95
Allen St. W8 160 DA76
Allenby Ave., S.Croy. 220 DQ109
Allenby Clo., Grnf. 136 CA69
Allenby Cres., Grays 170 GB78
Allenby Dr., Horn. 128 FL60
Allenby Rd. SE23 183 DY90
Allenby Rd., Sthl. 136 CA72
Allenby Rd., West. 238 EL117
Allendale Ave., Sthl. 136 CA72
Allendale Clo. SE5 162 DR81
Daneville Rd.
Allendale Clo. SE26 183 DX92
Allendale Clo., Dart. 189 FR88
Princes Rd.
Allendale Rd., Grnf. 137 CH65
Allende Ave., Harl. 35 EQ12
Allens Rd., Enf. 82 DW43
Allensbury Pl. NW1 141 DK66
Allenswood Rd. SE9 164 EL83
Allerds Rd., Slou. 131 AM67
Allerford Ct., Har. 116 CB57
Allerford Rd. SE6 183 EB91
Allerton Clo., Borwd. 78 CM38
Allerton Ct. NW4 97 CX54
Holders Hill Rd.
Allerton Rd. N16 122 DQ61
Allerton Rd., Borwd. 78 CL38
Allerton Wk. N7 121 DM61
Durham Rd.
Allestree Rd. SW6 159 CY80
Alleyn Cres. SE21 182 DR89
Alleyn Pk. SE21 182 DR89
Alleyn Pk., Sthl. 156 BZ77
Alleyn Rd. SE21 182 DR90
Alleyndale Rd., Dag. 126 EW61
Allfarthing La. SW18 180 DB86
Allgood Clo., Mord. 199 CX100
Allgood St. E2 142 DT68
Hackney Rd.
Allhallows La. EC4 279 K1
Allhallows Rd. E6 144 EL71
Allhusen Gdns., Slou. 112 AY63
Alderbourne La.
Alliance Clo., Wem. 117 CK63
Alliance Rd. E13 144 EJ70
Alliance Rd. SE18 166 EU79
Alliance Rd. W3 138 CP70
Allied Way W3 158 CS75
Larden Rd.
Allingham Clo. W7 137 CF73
Allingham Ct., Gdmg. 258 AT144
Summers Rd.
Allingham Ms. N1 142 DQ68
Allingham St.
Allingham Rd., Reig. 266 DA137
Allingham St. N1 142 DQ68
Allington Ave. N17 100 DS51
Allington Clo. SW19 179 CX92
High St. Wimbledon
Allington Clo., Grav. 191 GM88
Farley Rd.
Allington Clo., Grnf. 136 CC66
Allington Ct. SW19 179 CX92
High St. Wimbledon
Allington Ct., Enf. 83 DX43
Allington Ct., Slou. 132 AT73
Myrtle Cres.
Allington Rd. NW4 119 CV57
Allington Rd. W10 139 CY68
Allington Rd., Har. 116 CC57
Allington Rd., Orp. 205 ER103
Allington St. SW1 277 K7
Allington St. SW1 161 DH76
Allison Clo. SE10 163 EC81
Dartmouth Hill
Allison Clo., Wal.Abb. 68 EG32
Allison Gro. SE21 182 DS88
Allison Rd. N8 121 DN57
Allison Rd. W3 138 CQ72
Allitsen Rd. NW8 272 B1
Allitsen Rd. NW8 140 DE68
Allmains Clo., Wal.Abb. 68 EH25
Allnutt Way SW4 181 DK85
Allnutts Rd., Epp. 70 EU33
Alloa Rd. SE8 163 DX78
Alloa Rd., Ilf. 126 EU61
Allonby Dr., Ruis. 115 BP59
Allonby Gdns., Wem. 117 CJ60
Allotment La., Sev. 257 FJ122
Alloway Clo., Wok. 226 AV118
Inglewood
Alloway Rd. E3 143 DY69
Allsop Pl. NW1 272 E5
Allsop Pl. NW1 140 DF70
Allum Clo., Borwd. 78 CL42
Allum Gro., Tad. 233 CV121
Preston La.
Allum La., Borwd. 78 CM42
Allum Way N20 98 DC46
Allwood Clo. SE26 183 DX91
Allwood Rd., Wal.Cr. 66 DT27
Allyn Clo., Stai. 173 BF93
Penton Rd.
Alma Ave. E4 101 EC52
Alma Ave., Horn. 128 FL63
Alma Clo., Wok. 226 AS118
Alma Cres., Sutt. 217 CY106
Alma Cut, St.Alb. 43 CE21
Alma Gro. SE1 162 DT77
Alma Pl. NW10 139 CV69
Harrow Rd.
Alma Pl. SE19 182 DT94
Alma Pl., Th.Hth. 201 DN99
Alma Rd. N10 98 DG52
Alma Rd. SW18 180 DC85
Alma Rd., Berk. 38 AS17
Alma Rd., Cars. 218 DE106
Alma Rd., Chesh. 54 AQ29
Alma Rd., Enf. 83 DY43
Alma Rd., Esher 197 CE102
Alma Rd., Orp. 206 EX103
Alma Rd., Reig. 250 DB133
Alma Rd., St.Alb. 43 CE21
Alma Rd., Sid. 186 EU90
Alma Rd., Sthl. 136 BY73
Alma Rd., Swans. 190 FZ85
Alma Rd., Wind. 151 AQ82
Alma Rd. (Eton Wick), Wind. 151 AM77
Alma Row, Har. 95 CD53
Alma Sq. NW8 140 DC69
Alma St. E15 123 ED65
Alma St. NW5 141 DH65
Alma Ter. SW18 180 DD87
Alma Ter. W8 160 DA76
Allen St.
Almack Rd. E5 122 DW63
Almeida St. N1 141 DP66
Almer Rd. SW20 179 CU94
Almeric Rd. SW11 160 DF84
Almington St. N4 121 DM60
Almners Rd., Cher. 193 BA102
Almond Ave. W5 158 CL76
Almond Ave., Cars. 200 DF103
Almond Ave., Uxb. 115 BP62
Almond Ave., West Dr. 154 BN76
Almond Ave., Wok. 226 AX121
Almond Clo. SE15 162 DU82
Almond Clo., Brom. 205 EN101
Almond Clo., Egh. 172 AV93
Almond Clo., Grays 171 GG76
Almond Clo., Guil. 242 AX130
Almond Clo., Hayes 135 BS73
Almond Clo., Ruis. 115 BT62
Roundways
Almond Clo., Shep. 195 BQ96
Almond Clo., Wind. 151 AP82
Almond Dr., Swan. 207 FD96
Almond Gro., Brent. 157 CH80
Almond Rd. N17 100 DU52
Almond Rd. SE16 162 DV77
Almond Rd., Dart. 188 FQ87
Almond Rd., Epsom 216 CR111
Almond Rd., Slou. 130 AH68
Almond Wk., Hat. 45 CU21
Southdown Rd.
Almond Way, Borwd. 78 CP42
Almond Way, Brom. 205 EN101
Almond Way, Har. 94 CB54
Almond Way, Mitch. 201 DK99
Almonds, The, St.Alb. 43 CH24
Almonds Ave., Buck.H. 102 EG47
Almons Way, Slou. 132 AV71
Almorah Rd. N1 142 DR66
Almorah Rd., Houns. 156 BX81
Alms Heath, Wok. 229 BP121
Almshouse La., Chess. 215 CJ109
Almshouse La., Enf. 82 DV37
Almshouses, The, Dor. 263 CH135
Cotmandene
Alnwick Gro., Mord. 200 DB98
Bordesley Rd.
Alnwick Rd. E16 144 EJ72
Alnwick Rd. SE12 184 EH87
Alperton La., Grnf. 137 CK69
Alperton La., Wem. 137 CK69
Alperton St. W10 139 CY70
Alpha Clo. NW1 272 C3
Alpha Ct., Whyt. 236 DU118
Alpha Gro. E14 163 EA75
Alpha Pl. NW6 140 DA68
Alpha Pl. SW3 160 DE79
Alpha Rd. E4 101 EB48
Alpha Rd. N18 100 DU51
Alpha Rd. SE14 163 DZ81
Alpha Rd., Brwd. 109 GD44
Alpha Rd., Croy. 202 DS102
Alpha Rd., Enf. 83 DY42
Alpha Rd., Surb. 198 CM100
Alpha Rd., Tedd. 177 CD92
Alpha Rd., Uxb. 135 BP70
Alpha Rd., Wok. 227 BB116
Alpha Rd. (Chobham), Wok. 210 AT110
Alpha St. SE15 162 DU82
Alpha St. N., Slou. 152 AU75
Alpha St. S., Slou. 152 AT76
Alpha Way, Egh. 193 BC95
Alphabet Gdns., Cars. 200 DD100
Alphabet Sq. E3 143 EA71
Hawgood St.
Alphea Clo. SW19 180 DE94
Courtney Rd.
Alpine Ave., Surb. 198 CQ103
Alpine Clo., Croy. 202 DS104
Alpine Copse, Brom. 205 EN96
Alpine Gro. E9 142 DW66
Alpine Rd. SE16 162 DW77
Alpine Rd., Red. 250 DG131
Alpine Rd., Walt. 195 BU101
Alpine Vw., Cars. 218 DE106
Alpine Wk., Stan. 95 CE47
Alpine Way E6 145 EN71
Alresford Rd., Guil. 258 AU135
Alric Ave. NW10 138 CR66
Alric Ave., N.Mal. 198 CS97
Alroy Rd. N4 121 DN59
Alsace Rd. SE17 279 M10
Alsace Rd. SE17 162 DS78
Alscot Rd. SE1 162 DT77
Alscot Way SE1 279 P8
Alscot Way SE1 162 DT77
Alsford Wf., Berk. 38 AW18
Alsike Rd. SE2 166 EX76
Alsike Rd., Erith 166 EY76
Alsom Ave., Wor.Pk. 217 CU105
Alsop Clo., St.Alb. 62 CM27
Halsey Pk.
Alston Clo., Surb. 197 CH101
Alston Rd. N18 100 DV50
Alston Rd. SW17 180 DD91
Alston Rd., Barn. 79 CY41
Alston Rd., Hem.H. 40 BG21
Alt Gro. SW19 179 CZ94
St. George's Rd.
Altair Clo. N17 100 DT51
Altair Way, Nthwd. 93 BT49
Altash Way SE9 185 EM89
Altenburg Ave. W13 157 CH76
Altenburg Gdns. SW11 160 DF84
Alterton Clo., Wok. 226 AU117
Altham Gro., Harl. 35 ET12
Altham Rd., Pnr. 94 BY52
Althea St. SW6 160 DB83
Althorne Gdns. E18 124 EF56
Althorne Rd., Red. 266 DG136
Althorne Way, Dag. 126 FA61
Althorp Clo., Barn. 97 CU45
Althorp Rd. SW17 180 DF88
Althorp Rd., St.Alb. 43 CE19
Althorpe Gro. SW11 160 DD81
Westbridge Rd.
Althorpe Ms. SW11 160 DD81
Westbridge Rd.
Althorpe Rd., Har. 116 CC57
Altmore Ave. E6 145 EM66
Alton Ave., Stan. 95 CF52
Alton Clo., Bex. 186 EY88
Alton Clo., Islw. 157 CF82
Alton Ct., Stai. 193 BE95
Alton Gdns., Beck. 183 EA94
Alton Gdns., Twick. 177 CD86
Alton Rd. N17 122 DR55
Alton Rd. SW15 179 CU88
Alton Rd., Croy. 201 DN104
Alton Rd., Rich. 158 CL84
Alton St. E14 143 EB71
Altona Rd., H.Wyc. 88 AD52
Altona Way, Slou. 131 AP72
Altwood Clo., Slou. 131 AL71
Burnham La.
Altyre Clo., Beck. 203 DZ99
Altyre Rd., Croy. 202 DR103
Altyre Way, Beck. 203 DZ99
Aluric Clo., Grays 171 GH77
Alva Way, Wat. 94 BX47
Alvanley Gdns. NW6 120 DB64
Alverstoke Rd., Rom. 106 FL52
Alverston Gdns. SE25 202 DS99
Alverstone Ave. SW19 180 DA89
Alverstone Ave., Barn. 98 DE45
Alverstone Gdns. SE9 185 EQ88
Alverstone Rd. E12 125 EN63
Alverstone Rd. NW2 139 CW66
Alverstone Rd., N.Mal. 199 CT98
Alverstone Rd., Wem. 118 CM60
Alverton, St.Alb. 42 CC17
Green La.
Alverton St. SE8 163 DZ78
Alveston Ave., Har. 117 CH55
Alvey Est. SE17 279 M9
Alvey Est. SE17 162 DS77
Alvey St. SE17 279 M10
Alvey St. SE17 162 DS78
Alvia Gdns., Sutt. 218 DC105
Alvington Cres. E8 122 DT64
Alvista Ave., Maid. 130 AH72
Alway Ave., Epsom 216 CQ106
Alwen Gro., S.Ock. 149 FV71
Alwold Cres. SE12 184 EH86
Alwyn Ave. W4 158 CR78
Alwyn Clo., Borwd. 78 CM44
Alwyn Clo., Croy. 221 EB108
Alwyn Gdns. NW4 119 CU56
Alwyn Gdns. W3 138 CP72
Alwyne Ave., Brwd. 109 GA44
Alwyne Ct., Wok. 226 AY116
Alwyne La. N1 141 DP66
Alwyne Vil.
Alwyne Pl. N1 142 DQ65
Alwyne Rd. N1 142 DQ66
Alwyne Rd. SW19 179 CZ93
Alwyne Rd. W7 137 CE73
Alwyne Sq. N1 142 DQ65
Alwyne Vil. N1 141 DP66
Alwyns Clo., Cher. 194 BG100
Alwyns La.
Alwyns La., Cher. 193 BF100
Alyngton, Berk. 38 AS16
Alyth Gdns. NW11 120 DA58
Alzette Ho. E2 143 DX69
Amalgamated Dr., Brent. 157 CG79
Amanda Clo., Chig. 103 ER51
Amanda Ct., Slou. 152 AX76
Amanda Ms., Rom. 127 FC57
Amazon St. E1 142 DV72
Hessel St.
Ambassador Clo., Houns. 156 BY82
Ambassador Gdns. E6 145 EM71
Ambassador Sq. E14 163 EB77
Ambassador's Ct. SW1 277 L3
Amber Ave. E17 101 DY53
Amber Ct. SW17 180 DG91
Brudenell Rd.
Amber Gro. NW2 119 CX60
Prayle Gro.
Amber St. E15 143 ED65
Salway Rd.
Ambercroft Way, Couls. 235 DP119
Amberden Ave. N3 120 DA55
Ambergate St. SE17 278 G10
Ambergate St. SE17 161 DP78
Amberley Clo., Orp. 223 ET106
Warnford Rd.
Amberley Clo., Pnr. 116 BZ55
Amberley Clo., Wok. 243 BF125
Amberley Ct., Maid. 130 AC69
Amberley Ct., Sid. 186 EW92
Amberley Dr., Add. 211 BF110
Amberley Gdns., Enf. 100 DS45
Amberley Gdns., Epsom 217 CT105
Amberley Gro. SE26 182 DV91
Amberley Gro., Croy. 202 DT101
Amberley Rd. E10 123 EB59
Amberley Rd. N13 99 DM47
Amberley Rd. SE2 166 EX79
Amberley Rd. W9 140 DA71
Amberley Rd., Buck.H. 102 EJ46
Amberley Rd., Enf. 100 DT45
Amberley Rd., Slou. 131 AL71
Amberley Way, Houns. 176 BW85
Amberley Way, Mord. 199 CZ101
Amberley Way, Rom. 127 FB56
Amberley Way, Uxb. 134 BL69
Amberry Ct., Harl. 35 ER14
Amberside Clo., Islw. 177 CD86
Amberwood Ri., N.Mal. 198 CS100
Amblecote, Cob. 214 BY112
Amblecote Clo. SE12 184 EH90
Amblecote Meadows SE12 184 EH90
Amblecote Rd. SE12 184 EH90
Ambler Rd. N4 121 DP62
Ambleside, Brom. 183 ED93
Ambleside, Epp. 70 EU31
Ambleside Ave. SW16 181 DK91
Ambleside Ave., Beck. 203 DY99
Ambleside Ave., Horn. 127 FH64
Ambleside Ave., Walt. 196 BW102
Ambleside Clo. E9 122 DW64
Churchill Wk.
Ambleside Clo. E10 123 EB59
Ambleside Clo., Red. 267 DH139
Ambleside Cres., Enf. 83 DX41
Ambleside Dr., Felt. 175 BT88
Ambleside Gdns. SW16 181 DK92
Ambleside Gdns., Ilf. 124 EL56
Ambleside Gdns., S.Croy. 221 DX109
Ambleside Gdns., Sutt. 218 DC107
Ambleside Gdns., Wem. 117 CK60
Ambleside Rd. NW10 139 CT66
Ambleside Rd., Bexh. 166 FA82
Ambleside Wk., Uxb. 134 BK67
High St.
Ambleside Way, Egh. 173 BB94
Ambrey Way, Wall. 219 DK109
Ambrook Rd., Belv. 166 FA76
Ambrosden Ave. SW1 277 L7
Ambrosden Ave. SW1 161 DJ76
Ambrose Ave. NW11 119 CY59
Ambrose Clo. E6 144 EL71
Lovage App.
Ambrose Clo., Dart. 167 FF84
Ambrose Clo., Orp. 205 ET104
Stapleton Rd.
Ambrose Ms. SW11 160 DE82
Ambrose St. SE16 162 DV77
Ambrose Wk. E3 143 EA68
Malmesbury Rd.
Amelia St. SE17 278 G10
Amelia St. SE17 161 DP78
Amen Cor. EC4 274 G9
Amen Cor. SW17 180 DF93
Amen Ct. EC4 274 G8
Amenity Way, Mord. 199 CW101
Amerden Clo., Maid. 130 AD72
Amerden La., Maid. 130 AD74
Amerden Way, Slou. 151 AN75
America Sq. EC3 275 P10
America St. SE1 279 H3
Amerland Rd. SW18 179 CZ86
Amersham, Rick. 73 BA39
Amersham Ave. N18 100 DR51
Amersham Bypass, Amer. 55 AL38
Amersham Clo., Rom. 106 FM51
Amersham Dr., Rom. 106 FL51
Amersham Gro. SE14 163 DZ80
Amersham Pl., Amer. 72 AW39
Amersham Rd. SE14 163 DZ81
Amersham Rd., Amer. 89 AP46

Amersham Rd. (Chesham Bois), Amer. 55 AP35
Amersham Rd. (Little Chalfont), Amer. 72 AX39
Amersham Rd., Beac. 89 AM53
Amersham Rd., Ch.St.G. 72 AU43
Amersham Rd., Chesh. 54 AQ32
Amersham Rd., Croy. 202 DQ100
Amersham Rd., Ger.Cr. 90 AX49
Amersham Rd., Rick. 73 BB39
Amersham Rd., Rom. 106 FL51
Amersham Vale SE14 163 DZ80
Amersham Wk., Rom. 106 FM51
Amersham Rd.
Amersham Way, Amer. 72 AX39
Amery Gdns. NW10 139 CV67
Amery Gdns., Rom. 128 FK55
Amery Rd., Har. 117 CG61
Ames Rd., Swans. 190 FY86
Amesbury, Wal.Abb. 68 EG32
Amesbury Ave. SW2 181 DL89
Amesbury Clo., Epp. 69 ET31
Amesbury Rd.
Amesbury Clo., Wor.Pk. 199 CW102
Amesbury Dr. E4 83 EB44
Amesbury Rd., Brom. 204 EK97
Amesbury Rd., Dag. 146 EX66
Amesbury Rd., Epp. 69 ET31
Amesbury Rd., Felt. 176 BX89
Amethyst Rd. E15 123 ED63
Amey Dr., Lthd. 230 CC124
Amherst Ave. W13 137 CJ72
Amherst Clo., Orp. 206 EU98
Amherst Dr., Orp. 205 ET98
Amherst Hill, Sev. 256 FE122
Amherst Rd. W13 137 CJ72
Amherst Rd., Sev. 257 FH122
Amhurst Gdns., Islw. 157 CF81
Amhurst Par. N16 122 DT59
Amhurst Pk.
Amhurst Pk. N16 122 DR59
Amhurst Pas. E8 122 DU64
Amhurst Rd. E8 122 DV64
Amhurst Rd. N16 122 DU63
Amhurst Ter. E8 122 DU63
Amhurst Wk. SE28 146 EU74
Pitfield Cres.
Amidas Gdns., Dag. 126 EV63
Amiel St. E1 142 DW70
Amies St. SW11 160 DF83
Amina Way SE16 162 DU76
Yalding Rd.
Amis Ave., Add. 212 BG110
Amis Ave., Epsom 216 CP107
Amis Rd., Wok. 226 AS119
Amity Gro. SW20 199 CW95
Amity Rd. E15 144 EF67
Ammanford Gdn. NW9 118 CS58
Ruthin Clo.
Amner Rd. SW11 180 DG86
Amor Rd. W6 159 CW76
Amott Rd. SE15 162 DU83
Amoy Pl. E14 143 EA72
Ampere Way, Croy. 201 DL101
Ampleforth Rd. SE2 166 EV75
Ampthill Sq. Est. NW1 273 L1
Ampton Pl. WC1 274 B3
Ampton St. WC1 274 B3
Ampton St. WC1 141 DM69
Amroth Clo. SE23 182 DV88
Amstel Way, Wok. 226 AT118
Amsterdam Rd. E14 163 EC76
Amundsen Ct. E14 163 EA78
Napier Ave.
Amwell Clo., Enf. 82 DR43
Amwell Clo., Wat. 76 BY35
Phillipers
Amwell Common, Welw.G.C. 30 DB10
Amwell Ct., Hodd. 49 EA16
Amwell Ct., Wal.Abb. 68 EF33
Amwell Ct. Est. N4 122 DQ60
Amwell End, Ware 33 DX06
Amwell Hill, Ware 33 DZ08
Amwell La., Ware 33 EA09
Amwell St. EC1 274 D2
Amwell St. EC1 141 DN69
Amwell St., Hodd. 49 EA16
Amy Clo., Wall. 219 DL108
Mollison Dr.
Amy La., Chesh. 54 AP32
Amy Rd., Oxt. 254 EE129
Amy Warne Clo. E6 144 EL70
Evelyn Denington Rd.
Amyand Cotts., Twick. 177 CH86
Amyand Pk. Rd.
Amyand La., Twick. 177 CH87
Marble Hill Gdns.
Amyand Pk. Gdns., Twick. 177 CH87
Amyand Pk. Rd.
Amyand Pk. Rd., Twick. 177 CG87
Amyruth Rd. SE4 183 EA85
Anatola Rd. N19 121 DH61
Dartmouth Pk. Hill
Ancaster Cres., N.Mal. 199 CU100
Ancaster Ms., Beck. 203 DX97
Ancaster Rd., Beck. 203 DX97
Ancaster St. SE18 165 ES80
Anchor & Hope La. SE7 164 EH76
Anchor Bay Ind. Est., Erith 167 FG79
Anchor Boul., Dart. 168 FQ84
Anchor Clo. (Cheshunt), Wal.Cr. 67 DX28
Anchor Dr., Rain. 147 FH69
Anchor La., Hem.H. 40 BH22
Anchor Ms. SW12 181 DH86
Hazelbourne Rd.
Anchor St. SE16 162 DV77
Anchor Wf. E3 143 EB71
Watts Gro.
Anchor Yd. EC1 275 J4
Anchorage Clo. SW19 180 DA92
Anchorage Pt. Ind. Est. SE7 164 EJ76
Ancill Clo. W6 159 CY79
Ancona Rd. NW10 139 CU68
Ancona Rd. SE18 165 ER78
Andace Pk. Gdns., Brom. 204 EJ95
Andalus Rd. SW9 161 DL83
Ander Clo., Wem. 117 CK63
Andermans, Wind. 151 AK81
Anderson Clo. N21 81 DM43
Anderson Clo. W3 138 CR72
Anderson Clo., Epsom 216 CP112
Anderson Clo., Sutt. 200 DA102
Anderson Clo. (Harefield), Uxb. 92 BG53
Anderson Dr., Ashf. 175 BQ91
Anderson Ho., Bark. 145 ER68
The Coverdales
Anderson Pl., Houns. 156 CB84
Anderson Rd. E9 143 DX65
Anderson Rd., Rad. 62 CN33
Anderson Rd., Wey. 195 BR104
Anderson Rd., Wdf.Grn. 124 EK55
Anderson St. SW3 276 D10
Anderson St. SW3 160 DF78
Anderson Way, Belv. 167 FB75
Anderton Clo. SE5 162 DR83
Andmark Ct., Sthl. 136 BZ74
Herbert Rd.
Andover Ave. E16 144 EK72
King George Ave.
Andover Clo., Epsom 216 CR111
Andover Clo., Felt. 175 BT88
Andover Clo., Grnf. 136 CB70
Ruislip Rd.
Andover Clo., Uxb. 134 BH68
Andover Pl. NW6 140 DB68
Andover Rd. N7 121 DM61
Andover Rd., Orp. 205 ER102
Andover Rd., Twick. 177 CD88
Andre St. E8 122 DU64
Andrea Ave., Grays 170 GA75
Andrew Borde St. WC2 273 N8
Andrew Clo., Bex. 187 FD85
Andrew Clo., Dart. 187 FD85
Andrew Clo., Ilf. 103 ER51
Andrew Clo. (Shenley), Rad. 62 CM33
Andrew Hill La., Slou. 111 AQ60
Andrew Pl. SW8 161 DK81
Cowthorpe Rd.
Andrew St. E14 143 EC72
Andrewes Gdns. E6 144 EL72
Andrewes Ho. EC2 142 DQ71
Fore St.
Andrews Clo. E6 144 EL72
Linton Gdns.
Andrews Clo., Buck.H. 102 EJ47
Andrews Clo., Epsom 217 CT114
Andrews Clo., Har. 117 CD59
Bessborough Rd.
Andrews Clo., Hem.H. 40 BK18
Church St.
Andrews Clo., Orp. 206 EX97
Andrews Clo., Wor.Pk. 199 CX103
Andrews Crosse WC2 274 D9
Andrews La. (Cheshunt), Wal.Cr. 66 DU28
Andrews Pl. SE9 185 EP86
Andrew's Rd. E8 142 DV67
Andrews Wk. SE17 161 DP79
Dale Rd.
Andrews Way, Slou. 131 AK73
Andrewsfield, Welw.G.C. 30 DC09
Andwell Clo. SE2 166 EV75
Anelle Ri., Hem.H. 40 BM24
Anerley Gro. SE19 182 DT94
Anerley Hill SE19 182 DT93
Anerley Pk. SE20 182 DU94
Anerley Pk. Rd. SE20 182 DV94
Anerley Rd. SE19 182 DU94
Anerley Rd. SE20 182 DU94
Anerley Sta. Rd. SE20 202 DV95
Anerley St. SW11 160 DF82
Anerley Vale SE19 182 DT94
Anfield Clo. SW12 181 DJ87
Belthorn Cres.
Angas Ct., Wey. 213 BQ106
Angel All. E1 142 DU72
Whitechapel Rd.
Angel Clo. N18 100 DT49
Angel Cor. Par. N18 100 DU50
Fore St.
Angel Ct. EC2 275 L8
Angel Ct. EC2 142 DR72
Angel Ct. SW1 277 L3
Angel Ct. SW17 180 DF91
Angel Gate EC1 274 G2
Angel Gate, Guil. 258 AX135
High St.
Angel Hill, Sutt. 200 DB104
Sutton Common Rd.
Angel Hill Dr., Sutt. 200 DB104
Angel La. E15 143 ED65
Angel La., Hayes 135 BR71
Angel Ms. N1 274 E1
Angel Ms. N1 141 DN68
Angel Ms. SW15 179 CU87
Roehampton High St.
Angel Pas. EC4 279 K1
Angel Pl. N18 100 DU50
Angel Pl. SE1 279 K4
Angel Rd. N18 100 DV50
Angel Rd., Har. 117 CE58
Angel Rd., T.Ditt. 197 CG101
Angel Rd. Wks. N18 100 DW50
Angel Sq. EC1 274 E1
Angel St. EC1 275 H8
Angel St. EC1 142 DQ72
Angel Wk. W6 159 CW77
Angel Way, Rom. 127 FE57
Angelfield, Houns. 156 CB84
Angelica Clo., West Dr. 134 BL72
Lovibonds Ave.
Angelica Dr. E6 145 EN71
Angelica Gdns., Croy. 203 DX102
Angelica Rd., Guil. 242 AU130
Angell Pk. Gdns. SW9 161 DN83
Angell Rd. SW9 161 DN83
Angerstein La. SE3 164 EF80
Angle Clo., Uxb. 134 BN67
Angle Grn., Dag. 126 EW60
Angle Pl., Berk. 38 AU19
Angle Rd., Grays 169 FX79
Anglefield Rd., Berk. 38 AU19
Anglers Clo., Rich. 177 CJ91
Locksmeade Rd.
Angler's La. NW5 141 DH65
Angles Rd. SW16 181 DL91
Anglesea Ave. SE18 165 EP77
Anglesea Cen., Grav. 191 GH86
New Rd.
Anglesea Pl., Grav. 191 GH86
Clive Rd.
Anglesea Rd. SE18 165 EP77
Anglesea Rd., Kings.T. 197 CK98
Anglesea Rd., Orp. 206 EW100
Anglesea Ter. W6 159 CV76
Wellesley Ave.
Anglesey Clo., Ashf. 174 BN91
Anglesey Ct. Rd., Cars. 218 DG107
Anglesey Dr., Rain. 147 FG71
Anglesey Gdns., Cars. 218 DG107
Anglesey Rd., Enf. 82 DV42
Anglesey Rd., Wat. 94 BW50
Anglesmede Cres., Pnr. 116 CA55
Anglesmede Way, Pnr. 116 BZ55
Anglia Clo. N17 100 DV52
Park La.
Anglia Ho. E14 143 DY72
Anglia Wk. E6 145 EM67
Anglian Clo., Wat. 76 BW40
Anglian Rd. E11 123 ED62
Anglo Rd. E3 143 DZ68
Angrave Ct. E8 142 DT67
Angrave Pas. E8 142 DT67
Haggerston Rd.
Angus Clo., Chess. 216 CN106
Angus Dr., Ruis. 116 BW63
Angus Gdns. NW9 96 CR53
Angus Rd. E13 144 EJ69
Angus St. SE14 163 DY80
Anhalt Rd. SW11 160 DE80
Anisdowne Clo., Dor. 261 BT142
Ankerdine Cres. SE18 165 EN80
Ankerwycke Priory, Stai. 172 AY88
Anlaby Rd., Tedd. 177 CE92
Anley Rd. W14 159 CX75
Anmersh Gro., Stan. 95 CK53
Ann La. SW10 160 DD80
Ann Moss Way SE16 162 DW76
Ann St. SE18 165 ER77
Anna Clo. E8 142 DT67
Anna Neagle Clo. E7 124 EG63
Dames Rd.
Annabel Clo. E14 143 EB72
Annalee Gdns., S.Ock. 149 FV71
Annalee Rd., S.Ock. 149 FV71
Annan Way, Rom. 105 FD53
Annandale Gro., Uxb. 115 BQ62
Thorpland Ave.
Annandale Rd. SE10 164 EF79
Annandale Rd. W4 158 CS77
Annandale Rd., Croy. 202 DU103
Annandale Rd., Guil. 258 AV136
Annandale Rd., Sid. 185 ES87
Anne Boleyn's Wk., Kings.T. 178 CL92
Anne Boleyn's Wk., Sutt. 217 CX108
Anne Case Ms., N.Mal. 198 CR97
Sycamore Gro.
Anne of Cleves Rd., Dart. 188 FK85
Anne St. E13 144 EG70
Anne Way, Ilf. 103 EQ51
Anne Way, W.Mol. 196 CB98
Anners Clo., Egh. 193 BC97
Anne's Wk., Cat. 236 DS120
Annesley Ave. NW9 118 CR55
Annesley Clo. NW10 118 CS62
Annesley Dr., Croy. 203 DZ104
Annesley Rd. SE3 164 EH81
Annesley Wk. N19 121 DJ61
Annett Clo., Shep. 195 BS98
Annett Rd., Walt. 195 BU101
Annette Clo., Har. 95 CE54
Spencer Rd.
Annette Cres. N1 142 DQ66
Essex Rd.
Annette Rd. N7 121 DM63
Annie Besant Clo. E3 143 DZ67
Annifer Way, S.Ock. 149 FV71
Anning St. EC2 275 N4
Annington Rd. N2 120 DF55
Annis Rd. E9 143 DY65
Ann's Clo. SW1 276 E5
Ann's Pl. E1 275 P7
Annsworthy Ave., Th.Hth. 202 DR97
Grange Pk. Rd.
Annsworthy Cres. SE25 202 DR96
Grange Rd.
Ansculf Rd., Slou. 131 AN69
Ansdell Rd. SE15 162 DW82
Ansdell St. W8 160 DB76
Ansdell Ter. W8 160 DB76
Ansdell St.
Ansell Gro., Cars. 200 DG102
Ansell Rd. SW17 180 DE90
Ansell Rd., Dor. 263 CH135
Anselm Clo., Croy. 202 DT104
Park Hill Ri.
Anselm Rd. SW6 160 DA79
Anselm Rd., Pnr. 94 BZ52
Ansford Rd., Brom. 183 EC92
Ansleigh Pl. W11 139 CX73
Ansley Clo., S.Croy. 220 DV114
Anslow Gdns., Iver 133 BD68
Anslow Pl., Slou. 130 AJ71
Anson Clo., Hem.H. 57 AZ27
Anson Clo., Ken. 236 DR120
Anson Clo., Rom. 105 FB54
Anson Clo., St.Alb. 43 CJ22
Anson Rd. N7 121 DK63
Anson Rd. NW2 119 CX64
Anson Ter., Nthlt. 136 CB65
Anson Wk., Nthwd. 93 BQ49
Anstead Dr., Rain. 147 FG68
Anstey Rd. SE15 162 DU83
Anstey Wk. N15 121 DP56
Anstice Clo. W4 158 CS80
Anston Ct., Guil. 242 AS134
Southway
Anstridge Path SE9 185 ER86
Anstridge Rd. SE9 185 ER86
Antelope Ave., Grays 170 GA76
Hogg La.
Antelope Rd. SE18 165 EM76
Anthony Clo. NW7 96 CS49
Anthony Clo., Sev. 256 FE121
Anthony Clo., Wat. 94 BW46
Anthony La., Swan. 207 FG95
Anthony Rd. SE25 202 DU100
Anthony Rd., Borwd. 78 CM40
Anthony Rd., Grnf. 137 CE68
Anthony Rd., Well. 166 EU81
Anthony St. E1 142 DV72
Commercial Rd.
Anthony Way, Slou. 131 AK73
Anthonys, Wok. 211 BA112
Anthorne Clo., Pot.B. 64 DB31
Anthus Ms., Nthwd. 93 BS52
Antigua Clo. SE19 182 DR92
Salters Hill
Antigua Wk. SE19 182 DR92
Antill Rd. E3 143 DY69
Antill Rd. N15 122 DT56
Antill Ter. E1 143 DX72
Antlands La., Horl. 269 DK153
Antlands La. E., Horl. 269 DM153
Antlands La. W., Horl. 269 DL153
Antlers Hill E4 83 EB43
Antoinette Ct., Abb.L. 59 BT29
Anton Cres., Sutt. 200 DA104
Anton Rd., S.Ock. 149 FV70
Anton St. E8 122 DU64
Antoneys Clo., Pnr. 94 BX54
Briarswood Way
Antonine Gate, St.Alb. 42 CA21
Antrim Gro. NW3 140 DF65
Antrim Mans. NW3 140 DE65
Antrim Rd. NW3 140 DF65
Antrobus Clo., Sutt. 217 CZ106
Antrobus Rd. W4 158 CQ77
Anugraha Conference Cen., Egh. 172 AU91
Anvil Clo. SW16 181 DJ94
Anvil Ct., Slou. 153 BA77
Blacksmith Row
Anvil La., Cob. 213 BU114
Anvil Pl., St.Alb. 60 CA26
Anvil Rd., Sun. 195 BU98
Anworth Clo., Wdf.Grn. 102 EH51
Anyards Rd., Cob. 213 BV113
Apeldoorn Dr., Wall. 219 DL109
Aperdele Rd., Lthd. 231 CG118
Aperfield Rd., Erith 167 FF79
Aperfield Rd., West. 238 EL117
Apers Ave., Wok. 227 AZ121
Apex Clo., Beck. 203 EB95
Apex Clo., Wey. 195 BR104
Apex Cor. NW7 96 CR49
Apex Twr., N.Mal. 198 CS97
Apley Rd., Reig. 266 DA137
Aplin Way, Islw. 157 CE81
Apollo Ave., Brom. 204 EH95
Rodway Rd.
Apollo Ave., Nthwd. 93 BU50
Apollo Clo., Horn. 127 FH61
Apollo Pl. E11 124 EE62
Apollo Pl. SW10 160 DD80
Apollo Way SE28 165 ER76
Broadwater Rd.
Apollo Way, Hem.H. 40 BM18
Apostle Way, Th.Hth. 201 DP96
Apothecary St. EC4 274 F9
Appach Rd. SW2 181 DN86
Apple Cotts., Hem.H. 57 BA27
Apple Garth, Brent. 157 CK77
Apple Gro., Chess. 216 CL105
Apple Gro., Enf. 82 DS41
Apple Mkt., Kings.T. 197 CK96
Eden St.
Apple Orchard, Swan. 207 FD98
Apple Orchard, The, Hem.H. 40 BM18
Highfield La.
Apple Rd. E11 124 EE62
Apple Tree Ave., Uxb. 134 BM71
Apple Tree Ave., West Dr. 134 BM71
Apple Tree Roundabout, West Dr. 134 BM73
Apple Tree Yd. SW1 277 L2
Appleby Clo. E4 101 EC51
Appleby Clo. N15 122 DR57
Appleby Clo., Twick. 177 CD89
Appleby Dr., Rom. 106 FJ50
Appleby Gdns., Felt. 175 BT88
Appleby Grn., Rom. 106 FJ50
Appleby Dr.
Appleby Rd. E8 142 DU66
Appleby Rd. E16 144 EF72
Appleby St. E2 142 DT68
Appleby St. (Cheshunt), Wal.Cr. 66 DT26
Applecroft, Berk. 38 AS17
Applecroft, St.Alb. 60 CB28
Applecroft Rd., Welw.G.C. 29 CV09
Appledore Ave., Bexh. 167 FC81
Appledore Ave., Ruis. 115 BV62
Appledore Clo. SW17 180 DF89
Appledore Clo., Brom. 204 EF99
Appledore Clo., Edg. 96 CN53
Appledore Clo., Rom. 106 FJ53
Appledore Cres., Sid. 185 ES90
Appledown Ri., Couls. 235 DJ115
Applefield, Amer. 72 AW39
Appleford Clo., Hodd. 49 DZ15
Appleford Rd. W10 139 CY70
Applegarth, Croy. 221 EB108
Applegarth, Esher 215 CF106
Applegarth Dr., Dart. 188 FL89
Applegarth Dr., Ilf. 125 ET56
Applegarth Rd. SE28 146 EV74
Applegarth Rd. W14 159 CX76
Applegate, Brwd. 108 FT43
Appleshaw Clo., Grav. 191 GG92
Appleton Clo., Amer. 72 AV40
Appleton Gdns., N.Mal. 199 CU100
Appleton Rd. SE9 164 EL83
Appleton Rd., Loug. 85 EP41
Appleton Sq., Mitch. 200 DE95
Appleton Way, Horn. 128 FK60
Appletree Clo. SE20 202 DV95
Jasmine Gro.
Appletree Clo., Lthd. 230 CC122
Kennel La.
Appletree Ct., Guil. 243 BD131
Old Merrow St.
Appletree Gdns., Barn. 80 DE42
Appletree La., Slou. 152 AW76
Appletree Wk., Chesh. 54 AR34
Cresswell Rd.
Appletree Wk., Wat. 59 BV34
Applewood Clo. N20 98 DE46
Applewood Clo. NW2 119 CV62
Appold St. EC2 275 M6
Appold St. EC2 142 DS71
Appold St., Erith 167 FF79
Apprentice Way E5 122 DV63
Clarence Rd.
Approach, The NW4 119 CX57
Approach, The W3 138 CR72
Approach, The, Enf. 82 DV40
Approach, The, Lthd. 230 BY123
Maddox La.
Approach, The, Orp. 205 ET103
Approach, The, Pot.B. 63 CZ32
Approach, The, Upmin. 128 FP62
Approach Clo. N16 122 DS64
Cowper Rd.
Approach Rd. E2 142 DW68
Approach Rd. SW20 199 CW96
Approach Rd., Ashf. 175 BQ93
Approach Rd., Barn. 80 DD42
Approach Rd., Maid. 130 AC72
Approach Rd., Pur. 219 DP112
Approach Rd., St.Alb. 43 CE21
Approach Rd., W.Mol. 196 CA99
Appspond La., St.Alb. 41 BV23
Aprey Gdns. NW4 119 CW56
April Clo. W7 137 CE73
April Clo., Ash. 232 CM117
April Clo., Felt. 175 BU90
April Clo., Orp. 223 ET106
Briarswood Way
April Glen SE23 183 DX90
April St. E8 122 DT63
Aprilwood Clo., Add. 211 BF111
Apsledene, Grav. 191 GK93
Miskin Way
Apsley Clo., Har. 116 CC57
Apsley Gra., Hem.H. 58 BL25
London Rd.
Apsley Mills Retail Pk., Hem.H. 40 BL24
Apsley Rd. SE25 202 DV98
Apsley Rd., N.Mal. 198 CQ97
Apsley Way NW2 119 CU61
Apsley Way W1 276 G4
Aquarius Business Pk. NW2 119 CU60
Aquarius Way, Nthwd. 93 BU50
Aquila Clo., Lthd. 232 CL121
Aquila St. NW8 140 DD68
Aquinas St. SE1 278 E3
Aquis Ct., St.Alb. 42 CC20
Arabella Dr. SW15 158 CS84
Arabia Clo. E4 101 ED45
Arabin Rd. SE4 163 DY84
Araglen Ave., S.Ock. 149 FV71
Aragon Ave., Epsom 217 CV109
Aragon Ave., T.Ditt. 197 CF99
Aragon Clo., Brom. 205 EM102
Aragon Clo., Croy. 222 EE110
Aragon Clo., Enf. 81 DM38
Aragon Clo., Hem.H. 41 BQ15
Aragon Clo., Loug. 84 EL44
Aragon Clo., Rom. 105 FB51
Aragon Clo., Sun. 175 BT94
Aragon Dr., Ilf. 103 EQ52
Aragon Dr., Ruis. 116 BX60
Aragon Ms. E1 142 DU74
Thomas More St.
Aragon Rd., Kings.T. 178 CL92
Aragon Rd., Mord. 199 CX100
Aragon Wk., W.Byf. 212 BM113
Aran Ct., Wey. 195 BR103
Mallards Reach
Aran Dr., Stan. 95 CJ49
Aran Hts., Ch.St.G. 90 AV49
Arandora Cres., Rom. 126 EV59
Arbery Rd. E3 143 DY69
Arbor Clo., Beck. 203 EB96
Arbor Ct. N16 122 DR61
Lordship Rd.
Arbor Rd. E4 101 ED48
Arborfield Clo. SW2 181 DM88
Arborfield Clo., Slou. 152 AS76
Arbour, The, Hert. 32 DR11
Arbour Clo., Brwd. 108 FW50
Arbour Clo., Lthd. 231 CF123
Arbour Rd., Enf. 83 DX42
Arbour Sq. E1 143 DX72
Arbour Vw., Amer. 72 AV39
Arbour Way, Horn. 127 FH64
Arbroath Grn., Wat. 93 BU48
Arbroath Rd. SE9 164 EL83
Arbrook Clo., Orp. 206 EU97
Arbrook La., Esher 214 CC107
Arbury Ter. SE26 182 DV90
Oaksford Ave.
Arbuthnot La., Bex. 186 EY86
Arbuthnot Rd. SE14 163 DX82
Arbutus Clo., Red. 266 DC137
Arbutus Rd., Red. 266 DC136
Arbutus St. E8 142 DS67
Arcade, The EC2 275 M7
Arcade, The, Croy. 202 DQ104
High St.
Arcade, The, Hat. 45 CV17
Kennelwood La.
Arcade Pl., Rom. 127 FE57
Arcadia Ave. N3 98 DA53
Arcadia Clo., Cars. 218 DG105
Arcadia St. E14 143 EA72
Arcadian Ave., Bex. 186 EY86
Arcadian Clo., Bex. 186 EY86
Arcadian Gdns. N22 99 DM52
Arcadian Rd., Bex. 186 EY86
Arcany Rd., S.Ock. 149 FV70
Arch Rd., Walt. 196 BX104
Arch St. SE1 279 H7
Arch St. SE1 162 DQ76
Archangel St. SE16 163 DX75
Archates Ave., Grays 170 GA76
Archbishops Pl. SW2 181 DM86
Archdale Pl., N.Mal. 198 CP97
Archdale Rd. SE22 182 DT85
Archel Rd. W14 159 CZ79
Archer Clo., Kings L. 58 BM29
Archer Clo., Kings.T. 178 CL94
Archer Ho. SW11 160 DD81
Vicarage Cres.
Archer Ms., Hmptn. 176 CC93
Windmill Rd.
Archer Rd. SE25 202 DV98
Archer Rd., Orp. 206 EU99
Archer St. W1 273 M10
Archer Ter., West Dr. 134 BL73
Yew Ave.
Archer Way, Swan. 207 FF96
Archers, Harl. 51 EP20
Archers Clo., Hert. 32 DQ08
Archers Ct., S.Ock. 149 FV71
Archers Dr., Enf. 82 DW40
Archers Fld., St.Alb. 43 CF18
Archers Ride, Welw.G.C. 30 DB11
Archers Wk. SE15 162 DT81
Wodehouse Ave.
Archery Clo. W2 272 C9
Archery Clo. W2 140 DE72
Archery Clo., Har. 117 CF55
Archery Rd. SE9 185 EM85
Arches, The SW6 159 CZ82
Munster Rd.
Arches, The WC2 278 A2
Arches, The, Har. 116 CB61
Archfield, Welw.G.C. 29 CY06
Archibald Ms. W1 276 G2
Archibald Ms. W1 140 DG74
Archibald Rd. N7 121 DK63
Archibald Rd., Rom. 106 FN53
Archibald St. E3 143 EA69
Archie Clo., West Dr. 154 BN75
Archway, Rom. 105 FH51
Archway Clo. N19 121 DJ61
St. Johns Way
Archway Clo. SW19 180 DB91
Archway Clo. W10 139 CX71
Archway Clo., Wall. 201 DK104

Archway Mall N19 121 DJ61
Magdala Ave.
Archway Ms., Dor. 263 CG135
Chapel Ct.
Archway Pl., Dor. 263 CG135
Chapel Ct.
Archway Rd. N6 120 DG58
Archway Rd. N19 121 DJ60
Archway St. SW13 158 CS83
Arcola St. E8 122 DT64
Arctic St. NW5 120 DG64
Gillies St.
Arcus Rd., Brom. 184 EE93
Ardbeg Rd. SE24 182 DR86
Arden Clo., Har. 117 CD62
Arden Clo., Hem.H. 57 BA28
Arden Clo., Reig. 266 DB138
Arden Clo. (Bushey), Wat. 95 CF45
Arden Ct. Gdns. N2 120 DD58
Arden Cres. E14 163 EA77
Arden Cres., Dag. 146 EW66
Arden Est. N1 275 M1
Arden Est. N1 142 DS68
Arden Gro., Orp. 223 EP105
Arden Ms. E17 123 EB57
Arden Mhor, Pnr. 115 BV56
Arden Rd. N3 119 CY55
Arden Rd. W13 137 CJ73
Ardens Way, St.Alb. 43 CK17
Ardent Clo. SE25 202 DS97
Ardesley Wd., Wey. 213 BS105
Ardfern Ave. SW16 201 DN97
Ardfillan Rd. SE6 183 ED88
Ardgowan Rd. SE6 184 EE87
Ardilaun Rd. N5 122 DQ63
Ardingly Clo., Croy. 203 DX104
Ardleigh Clo., Horn. 128 FK55
Ardleigh Ct., Brwd. 109 FZ45
Ardleigh Gdns., Brwd. 109 GE44
Fairview Ave.
Ardleigh Gdns., Sutt. 200 DA101
Ardleigh Grn. Rd., Horn. 128 FK57
Ardleigh Ho., Bark. 145 EQ67
St. Ann's
Ardleigh Ms., Ilf. 125 EP62
Bengal Rd.
Ardleigh Rd. E17 101 DZ53
Ardleigh Rd. N1 142 DR65
Ardleigh Ter. E17 101 DZ53
Ardley Clo. NW10 118 CS62
Ardley Clo. SE6 183 DY90
Ardley Clo., Ruis. 115 BQ59
Ardley Cres., B.Stort. 37 FH05
Ardlui Rd. SE27 182 DQ89
Ardmay Gdns., Surb. 198 CL99
Ardmere Rd. SE13 183 ED86
Ardmore Ave., Guil. 242 AV132
Ardmore La., Buck.H. 102 EH45
Ardmore Pl., Buck.H. 102 EH45
Ardmore Rd., S.Ock. 149 FV70
Ardmore Way, Guil. 242 AV132
Ardoch Rd. SE6 183 ED89
Ardra Rd. N9 101 DX48
Ardross Ave., Nthwd. 93 BS50
Ardrossan Clo., Slou. 131 AQ75
Ardrossan Gdns., Wor.Pk. 199 CU104
Ardshiel Clo. SW15 159 CX83
Bemish Rd.
Ardshiel Dr., Red. 266 DE136
Ardwell Ave., Ilf. 125 EQ57
Ardwell Rd. SW2 181 DL89
Ardwick Rd. NW2 120 DA63
Arena, The, Enf. 83 DZ38
Arewater Grn., Loug. 85 EM39
Argali Ho., Erith 166 EY76
Kale Rd.
Argall Ave. E10 123 DX59
Argall Way E10 123 DX60
Argent Clo., Egh. 173 BC93
Holbrook Meadow
Argent St. SE1 278 G4
Argent St., Grays 170 FY79
Argenta Way NW10 138 CP66
Argles Clo., Green. 189 FU85
Cowley Ave.
Argon Ms. SW6 160 DA80
Argon Rd. N18 100 DW50
Argosy Gdns., Stai. 173 BF93
Argosy La., Stai. 174 BK87
Argus Clo., Rom. 105 FB53
Argus Way W3 158 CP76
Argus Way, Nthlt. 136 BY69
Argyle Ave., Houns. 176 CA86
Argyle Clo. W13 137 CG70
Argyle Gdns., Upmin. 129 FR61
Argyle Pas. N17 100 DT53
Argyle Pl. W6 159 CV77
Argyle Rd. E1 143 DX70
Argyle Rd. E15 124 EE63
Argyle Rd. E16 144 EJ72
Argyle Rd. N12 98 DA50
Argyle Rd. N17 100 DU53
Argyle Rd. N18 100 DU49
Argyle Rd. W13 137 CG71
Argyle Rd., Barn. 79 CW42
Argyle Rd., Grnf. 137 CF69
Argyle Rd., Har. 116 CB57
Argyle Rd., Houns. 176 CB85
Argyle Rd., Ilf. 125 EN61
Argyle Rd., Sev. 257 FH125
Argyle Rd., Tedd. 177 CE92
Argyle Sq. WC1 274 A2
Argyle Sq. WC1 141 DL69
Argyle St. WC1 273 P2
Argyle St. WC1 141 DL69
Argyle Wk. WC1 274 A3
Argyle Way SE16 162 DU78
Argyll Ave., Slou. 131 AN73
Argyll Ave., Sthl. 136 CB74
Argyll Clo. SW9 161 DM83
Dalyell Rd.
Argyll Gdns., Edg. 96 CP54
Argyll Rd. W8 160 DA75
Argyll Rd., Grays 170 GA78
Argyll Rd., Hem.H. 40 BL15
Argyll St. W1 273 K9
Argyll St. W1 141 DJ72
Arica Rd. SE4 163 DY84
Ariel Clo., Grav. 191 GM91
Ariel Rd. NW6 140 DA65
Ariel Way W12 139 CW74
Ariel Way, Houns. 155 BV83
Arisdale Ave., S.Ock. 149 FV71
Aristotle Rd. SW4 161 DK83
Ark Ave., Grays 170 GA76
Arkell Gro. SE19 181 DP94
Arkindale Rd. SE6 183 EC90
Arkley Ct., Hem.H. 41 BP15
Arkley Rd.
Arkley Cres. E17 123 DZ57
Arkley Dr., Barn. 79 CU42
Arkley La., Barn. 79 CU41
Arkley Pk., Barn. 78 CR44
Arkley Rd. E17 123 DZ57
Arkley Rd., Hem.H. 41 BP15
Arkley Vw., Barn. 79 CV42
Arklow Ms., Surb. 198 CL103
Vale Rd. S.
Arklow Rd. SE14 163 DZ79
Arkwright Rd. NW3 120 DC64
Arkwright Rd., Slou. 153 BE82
Arkwright Rd., S.Croy. 220 DT110
Arkwright Rd., Til. 171 GG82
Arkwrights, Harl. 35 ET14
Arlesey Clo. SW15 179 CY86
Lytton Gro.
Arlesford Rd. SW9 161 DL83
Arlingford Rd. SW2 181 DN85
Arlington N12 98 DA48
Arlington Ave. N1 142 DQ68
Arlington Clo., Sid. 185 ES87
Arlington Clo., Sutt. 200 DA103
Arlington Clo., Twick. 177 CJ86
Arlington Ct., Hayes 155 BR78
Shepiston La.
Arlington Ct., Reig. 250 DB132
Oakfield Dr.
Arlington Cres., Wal.Cr. 67 DY34
Arlington Dr., Cars. 200 DF103
Arlington Dr., Ruis. 115 BR58
Arlington Gdns. W4 158 CQ78
Arlington Gdns., Ilf. 125 EN60
Arlington Gdns., Rom. 106 FL53
Arlington Lo. SW2 161 DM84
Arlington Lo., Wey. 213 BP105
Arlington Ms., Twick. 177 CH86
Arlington Rd.
Arlington Pl. SE10 163 EC80
Greenwich S. St.
Arlington Rd. N14 99 DH47
Arlington Rd. NW1 141 DH67
Arlington Rd. W13 137 CH72
Arlington Rd., Ashf. 174 BM92
Arlington Rd., Rich. 177 CK89
Arlington Rd., Surb. 197 CK100
Arlington Rd., Tedd. 177 CF91
Arlington Rd., Twick. 177 CJ86
Arlington Rd., Wdf.Grn. 102 EG53
Arlington Sq. N1 142 DQ67
Arlington St. SW1 277 K2
Arlington St. SW1 141 DJ74
Arlington Way EC1 274 E2
Arlington Way EC1 141 DN69
Arliss Way, Nthlt. 136 BW67
Arlow Rd. N21 99 DN46
Armada Ct. SE8 163 EA79
Watergate St.
Armada Ct., Grays 170 GA76
Hogg La.
Armada St. SE8 163 EA79
Armada Way E6 145 EQ73
Armadale Clo. N17 122 DV56
Armadale Rd. SW6 160 DA80
Armadale Rd., Felt. 175 BU85
Armadale Rd., Wok. 226 AU117
Armagh Rd. E3 143 DZ67
Armand Clo., Wat. 75 BT38
Armfield Clo., W.Mol. 196 BZ99
Armfield Cres., Mitch. 200 DF96
Armfield Rd., Enf. 82 DR39
Arminger Rd. W12 139 CV74
Armistice Gdns. SE25 202 DU97
Penge Rd.
Armitage Clo., Rick. 74 BK42
Armitage Rd. NW11 119 CZ60
Armitage Rd. SE10 164 EF78
Armor Rd., Purf. 169 FR77
Armour Clo. N7 141 DM65
Roman Way
Armoury Dr., Grav. 191 GJ87
Armoury Rd. SE8 163 EB82
Armoury Way SW18 180 DA85
Armstead Wk., Dag. 146 FA66
Armstrong Ave., Wdf.Grn. 102 EE51
Armstrong Clo. E6 145 EM72
Porter Rd.
Armstrong Clo., Dag. 126 EX60
Palmer Rd.
Armstrong Clo., Pnr. 115 BU58
Armstrong Clo., Sev. 241 FB115
Armstrong Clo., Walt. 195 BU100
Sunbury La.
Armstrong Cres., Barn. 80 DD41
Armstrong Gdns., Rad. 62 CL32
Armstrong Pl., Hem.H. 40 BK19
High St.
Armstrong Rd. SW7 160 DD76
Armstrong Rd. W3 139 CT74
Armstrong Rd., Egh. 172 AW93
Armstrong Rd., Felt. 176 BY92
Armstrong Way, Sthl. 156 CB75
Armytage Rd., Houns. 156 BX80
Arnal Cres. SW18 179 CY87
Arncliffe Clo. N11 98 DG51
Kettlewell Clo.
Arncroft Ct., Bark. 146 EV69
Renwick Rd.
Arndale Cen. SW18 180 DB86
Arndale Wk. SW18 180 DB85
Garratt La.
Arndale Way, Egh. 173 BA92
Church Rd.
Arne Gro., Horl. 268 DE146
Arne Gro., Orp. 205 ET104
Arne St. WC2 274 A9
Arne St. WC2 141 DL72
Arne Wk. SE3 164 EF84
Arnett Clo., Rick. 74 BG44
Arnett Sq. E4 101 DZ51
Silver Birch Ave.
Arnett Way, Rick. 74 BG44
Arneway St. SW1 277 N7
Arneways Ave., Rom. 126 EX55
Arnewood Clo. SW15 179 CU88
Arnewood Clo., Lthd. 214 CB113
Arney's La., Mitch. 200 DG100
Arngask Rd. SE6 183 ED87
Arnhem Ave., S.Ock. 148 FQ74
Arnhem Dr., Croy. 221 ED111
Arnhem Pl. E14 163 EA76
Arnhem Way SE22 182 DS85
East Dulwich Gro.
Arnhem Wf. E14 163 EA76
Arnhem Pl.
Arnison Rd., E.Mol. 197 CD98
Arnold Ave. E., Enf. 83 EA38
Arnold Ave. W., Enf. 83 DZ38
Arnold Circ. E2 275 P3
Arnold Circ. E2 142 DT69
Arnold Clo., Har. 118 CM59
Arnold Cres., Islw. 177 CD85
Arnold Dr., Chess. 215 CK107
Arnold Est. SE1 162 DT75
Arnold Gdns. N13 99 DP50
Arnold Pl., Til. 171 GJ81
Kipling Ave.
Arnold Rd. E3 143 EA69
Arnold Rd. N15 122 DT55
Arnold Rd. SW17 180 DF94
Arnold Rd., Dag. 146 EZ66
Arnold Rd., Grav. 191 GK89
Arnold Rd., Nthlt. 136 BX65
Arnold Rd., Stai. 174 BJ94
Arnold Rd., Wok. 227 BB115
Arnolds Ave., Brwd. 109 GC43
Arnolds Clo., Brwd. 109 GC43
Arnolds Fm. La., Brwd. 109 GE41
Arnolds La. (Sutton at Hone), Dart. 188 FM93
Arnos Gro. N14 99 DK49
Arnos Rd. N11 99 DJ50
Arnott Clo. SE28 146 EW73
Applegarth Rd.
Arnott Clo. W4 158 CR77
Fishers La.
Arnould Ave. SE5 162 DR84
Arnsberg Way, Bexh. 166 FA84
Arnside Gdns., Wem. 117 CK60
Arnside Rd., Bexh. 166 FA81
Arnside St. SE17 162 DQ79
Arnulf St. SE6 183 EB91
Arnulls Rd. SW16 181 DN93
Arodene Rd. SW2 181 DM86
Arosa Rd., Twick. 177 CK86
Arragon Gdns. SW16 181 DL94
Arragon Gdns., W.Wick. 203 EB104
Arragon Rd. E6 144 EK67
Arragon Rd. SW18 180 DB88
Arragon Rd., Twick. 177 CG87
Arran Clo., Erith 167 FD79
Arran Clo., Hem.H. 41 BQ22
Arran Clo., Wall. 219 DH105
Arran Dr. E12 124 EK60
Arran Ms. W5 138 CM74
Arran Rd. SE6 183 EB89
Arran Wk. N1 142 DQ66
Arran Way, Esher 196 CB103
Arranmore Ct. (Bushey), Wat. 76 BY42
Bushey Hall Rd.
Arras Ave., Mord. 200 DC99
Arretine Clo., St.Alb. 42 BZ22
Arrol Rd., Beck. 202 DW97
Arrow Rd. E3 143 EB69
Arrowscout Wk., Nthlt. 136 BY69
Argus Way
Arrowsmith Clo., Chig. 103 ET50
Arrowsmith Path, Chig. 103 ET50
Arrowsmith Rd., Chig. 103 ES50
Arrowsmith Rd., Loug. 84 EL41
Arsenal Rd. SE9 165 EM82
Artemis Clo., Grav. 191 GL87
Arterberry Rd. SW20 179 CW94
Arterial Ave., Rain. 147 FH70
Arterial Rd. N. Stifford, Grays 170 FY75
Arterial Rd. Purfleet, Purf. 168 FN76
Arterial Rd. W. Thurrock, Grays 169 FU76
Artesian Clo. NW10 138 CR66
Artesian Clo., Horn. 127 FF58
Artesian Gro., Barn. 80 DC42
Artesian Rd. W2 140 DA72
Artesian Wk. E11 124 EE62
Arthingworth St. E15 144 EE67
Arthur Ct. W2 140 DB72
Queensway
Arthur Gro. SE18 165 EQ77
Arthur Henderson Ho. SW6 159 CZ82
Arthur Horsley Wk. E7 124 EF64
Magpie Clo.
Arthur Rd. E6 145 EM68
Arthur Rd. N7 121 DM63
Arthur Rd. N9 100 DT47
Arthur Rd. SW19 180 DA90
Arthur Rd., Kings.T. 178 CN94
Arthur Rd., N.Mal. 199 CV99
Arthur Rd., Rom. 126 EW59
Arthur Rd., St.Alb. 43 CH20
Arthur Rd., Slou. 151 AR75
Arthur Rd., West. 238 EJ115
Arthur Rd., Wind. 151 AP81
Arthur St. EC4 279 L1
Arthur St., Erith 167 FF80
Arthur St., Grav. 191 GG87
Arthur St., Grays 170 GC79
Arthur St. (Bushey), Wat. 76 BX42
Arthur St. W., Grav. 191 GG87
Arthur Toft Ho., Grays 170 GB79
New Rd.
Arthurdon Rd. SE4 183 EA85
Arthur's Bri. Rd., Wok. 226 AX117
Artichoke Dell, Rick. 73 BE43
Artichoke Hill E1 142 DV73
Pennington St.
Artichoke Pl. SE5 162 DR81
Camberwell Ch. St.
Artillery Clo., Ilf. 125 EQ58
Horns Rd.
Artillery La. E1 275 N7
Artillery La. E1 142 DS71
Artillery La. W12 139 CU72
Artillery Pas. E1 275 N7
Artillery Pl. SE18 165 EM77
Artillery Pl. SW1 277 M7
Artillery Pl., Har. 94 CC52
Chicheley Rd.
Artillery Rd., Guil. 242 AX134
Artillery Row SW1 277 M7
Artillery Row SW1 161 DK76
Artillery Row, Grav. 191 GJ87
Artillery Ter., Guil. 242 AX134
Artington Clo., Orp. 223 EQ105
Artington Wk., Guil. 258 AW137
Artisan Clo. E6 145 EP72
Ferndale St.
Artisan Cres., St.Alb. 42 CC19
Artizan St. E1 275 N8
Arundel Ave., Epsom 217 CV110
Arundel Ave., Mord. 199 CZ98
Arundel Ave., S.Croy. 220 DU110
Arundel Clo. E15 124 EE63
Arundel Clo. SW11 180 DE85
Chivalry Rd.
Arundel Clo., Bex. 186 EZ86
Arundel Clo., Croy. 201 DP104
Arundel Clo., Hmptn. 176 CB92
Arundel Clo., Hem.H. 41 BP19
Arundel Clo. (Cheshunt), Wal.Cr. 66 DW29
Arundel Ct. N12 98 DE51
Arundel Ct., Har. 116 CA63
Arundel Ct., Slou. 152 AX77
Arundel Dr., Borwd. 78 CQ43
Arundel Dr., Har. 116 BZ63
Arundel Dr., Orp. 224 EV106
Arundel Dr., Wdf.Grn. 102 EG52
Arundel Gdns. N21 99 DN46
Arundel Gdns. W11 139 CZ73
Arundel Gdns., Edg. 96 CR52
Arundel Gdns., Ilf. 126 EU61
Arundel Great Ct. WC2 274 C10
Arundel Gro. N16 122 DS64
Arundel Pl. N1 141 DN65
Arundel Rd., Abb.L. 59 BU32
Arundel Rd., Barn. 80 DE41
Arundel Rd., Croy. 202 DR100
Arundel Rd., Dart. 168 FJ84
Arundel Rd., Dor. 263 CG136
Arundel Rd., Houns. 156 BW83
Arundel Rd., Kings.T. 198 CP96
Arundel Rd., Rom. 106 FM52
Arundel Rd., Sutt. 217 CZ108
Arundel Rd., Uxb. 134 BH68
Arundel Sq. N7 141 DN65
Arundel St. WC2 274 C10
Arundel St. WC2 141 DM73
Arundel Ter. SW13 159 CV79
Arundell Gro., St.Alb. 43 CD16
Arvon Rd. N5 121 DN64
Asbaston Ter., Ilf. 125 EQ64
Buttsbury Rd.
Ascalon St. SW8 161 DJ80
Ascension Rd., Rom. 105 FC51
Ascham Dr. E4 101 EB52
Rushcroft Rd.
Ascham End E17 101 DY53
Ascham St. NW5 121 DJ64
Aschurch Rd., Croy. 202 DT101
Ascot Clo., Borwd. 78 CN43
Ascot Clo., Ilf. 103 ES51
Ascot Clo., Nthlt. 116 CA64
Ascot Gdns., Enf. 82 DW37
Ascot Gdns., Horn. 128 FL63
Ascot Gdns., Sthl. 136 BZ71
Ascot Ms., Wall. 219 DJ109
Ascot Rd. E6 145 EM69
Ascot Rd. N15 122 DR57
Ascot Rd. N18 100 DU49
Ascot Rd. SW17 180 DG93
Ascot Rd., Felt. 174 BN89
Ascot Rd., Grav. 191 GH90
Ascot Rd., Orp. 205 ET98
Ascot Rd., Wat. 75 BS43
Ascots La., Hat. 29 CY14
Ascots La., Welw.G.C. 29 CY14
Ascott Ave. W5 158 CL75
Ash Clo. SE20 202 DW96
Ash Clo., Abb.L. 59 BR32
Ash Clo., Brwd. 108 FT43
Ash Clo., Cars. 200 DF103
Ash Clo., Edg. 96 CQ49
Ash Clo., Hat. 64 DA25
Ash Clo., N.Mal. 198 CR96
Ash Clo., Orp. 205 ER99
Ash Clo., Red. 251 DJ130
Ash Clo., Rom. 105 FB52
Ash Clo., Sid. 186 EV90
Ash Clo., Slou. 153 BB76
Ash Clo., Stan. 95 CG51
Ash Clo., Swan. 207 FC96
Ash Clo. (Harefield), Uxb. 92 BK53
Ash Clo., Wat. 75 BV35
Ash Clo., Wok. 226 AY120
Ash Clo. (Pyrford), Wok. 228 BG115
Ash Copse, St.Alb. 60 BZ31
Ash Ct., Epsom 216 CQ105
Ash Dr., Hat. 45 CU21
Ash Dr., Red. 267 DH136
Ash Grn. (Denham), Uxb. 134 BH65
Ash Gro. E8 142 DV67
Ash Gro. N13 100 DQ48
Ash Gro. NW2 119 CX63
Ash Gro. SE20 202 DW96
Ash Gro. W5 158 CL75
Ash Gro., Amer. 55 AN36
Ash Gro., Enf. 100 DS45
Ash Gro., Felt. 175 BS88
Ash Gro., Guil. 242 AU134
Ash Gro., Hayes 135 BR73
Ash Gro., Hem.H. 40 BM24
Ash Gro., Houns. 156 BX81
Ash Gro., Slou. 132 AT66
Ash Gro., Sthl. 136 CA71
Ash Gro., Stai. 174 BJ93
Ash Gro. (Harefield), Uxb. 92 BK53
Ash Gro., Wem. 117 CG63
Ash Gro., West Dr. 134 BM73
Ash Gro., W.Wick. 203 EC103
Ash Gros., Saw. 36 FA05
Ash Hill Clo. (Bushey), Wat. 94 CB46
Ash Hill Dr., Pnr. 116 BW55
Ash Ind. Est., Harl. 51 EM16
Flex Meadow
Ash Island, E.Mol. 197 CD97
Ash La., Horn. 128 FN56
Southend Arterial Rd.
Ash La., Rom. 105 FG51
Ash La., Wind. 151 AK82
Ash Ms., Epsom 216 CS113
Ash Platt, The, Sev. 257 FL121
Ash Platt Rd., Sev. 257 FL121
Ash Ride, Enf. 81 DN35
Ash Rd. E15 124 EE64
Ash Rd., Croy. 203 EA103
Ash Rd., Dart. 188 FK88
Ash Rd. (Hawley), Dart. 188 FM91
Ash Rd., Grav. 191 GJ91
Ash Rd., Orp. 223 ET108
Ash Rd., Shep. 194 BN98
Ash Rd., Sutt. 199 CY101
Ash Rd., West. 255 ER125
Ash Rd., Wok. 226 AX120
Ash Row, Brom. 205 EN101
Ash Tree Clo., Croy. 203 DY100
Ash Tree Clo., Surb. 198 CL102
Ash Tree Dell NW9 118 CQ57
Ash Tree Fld., Harl. 35 EN13
Ash Tree Rd., Wat. 75 BV36
Ash Tree Way, Croy. 203 DY99
Ash Vale, Rick. 91 BD50
Ash Wk. SW2 181 DM88
Ash Wk., S.Ock. 149 FX69
Ash Wk., Wem. 117 CJ63
Ashan Ct., Ashf. 175 BS94
Ashbeam Clo., Brwd. 107 FW51
Canterbury Way
Ashbourne Ave. E18 124 EH56
Ashbourne Ave. N20 98 DF47
Ashbourne Ave. NW11 119 CZ57
Ashbourne Ave., Bexh. 166 EY80
Ashbourne Ave., Har. 117 CD61
Ashbourne Clo. N12 98 DB49
Ashbourne Clo. W5 138 CN71
Ashbourne Clo., Couls. 235 DJ118
Ashbourne Ct. E5 123 DY63
Daubeney Rd.
Ashbourne Gro. NW7 96 CR50
Ashbourne Gro. SE22 182 DT85
Ashbourne Gro. W4 158 CS78
Ashbourne Par. W5 138 CM70
Ashbourne Rd.
Ashbourne Ri., Orp. 223 ER105
Ashbourne Rd. W5 138 CM71
Ashbourne Rd., Brox. 49 DZ21
Ashbourne Rd., Mitch. 180 DG93
Ashbourne Rd., Rom. 106 FJ49
Ashbourne Sq., Nthwd. 93 BS51
Ashbourne Ter. SW19 180 DA94
Ashbourne Way NW11 119 CZ57
Ashbourne Ave.
Ashbridge Rd. E11 124 EF59
Ashbridge St. NW8 272 B5
Ashbridge St. NW8 140 DE70
Ashbrook Rd. N19 121 DK60
Ashbrook Rd., Dag. 127 FB62
Ashbrook Rd., Wind. 172 AV87
Ashburn Gdns. SW7 160 DC77
Ashburn Pl. SW7 160 DC77
Ashburnham Ave., Har. 117 CF58
Ashburnham Clo. N2 120 DD55
Ashburnham Clo., Sev. 257 FJ127
Fiennes Way
Ashburnham Clo., Wat. 93 BU48
Ashburnham Dr.
Ashburnham Dr., Wat. 93 BU48
Ashburnham Gdns., Har. 117 CF58
Ashburnham Gdns., Upmin. 128 FP60
Ashburnham Gro. SE10 163 EB80
Ashburnham Pk., Esher 214 CC105
Ashburnham Pl. SE10 163 EB80
Ashburnham Retreat SE10 163 EB80
Ashburnham Rd. NW10 139 CW69
Ashburnham Rd. SW10 160 DC80
Ashburnham Rd., Belv. 167 FC77
Ashburnham Rd., Rich. 177 CH89
Ashburton Ave., Croy. 202 DV102
Ashburton Ave., Ilf. 125 ES63
Ashburton Clo., Croy. 202 DU102
Ashburton Ct., Pnr. 116 BX55
Ashburton Gdns., Croy. 202 DU103
Ashburton Gro. N7 121 DN63
Ashburton Rd. E16 144 EG72
Ashburton Rd., Croy. 202 DU102
Ashburton Rd., Ruis. 115 BU61
Ashburton Ter. E13 144 EG68
Grasmere Rd.
Ashbury Clo., Hat. 44 CS18
Ashbury Cres., Guil. 243 BC132
Ashbury Dr., Uxb. 115 BP61
Ashbury Gdns., Rom. 126 EX57
Ashbury Pl. SW19 180 DC93
Ashbury Rd. SW11 160 DF83
Ashby Ave., Chess. 216 CN107
Ashby Clo., Horn. 128 FN60
Holme Rd.
Ashby Gdns., St.Alb. 43 CD24
Ashby Gro. N1 142 DQ66
Ashby Ms. SE4 163 DZ82
Ashby Rd. N15 122 DU57
Ashby Rd. SE4 163 DZ82
Ashby Rd., Wat. 75 BU38
Ashby St. EC1 274 G3
Ashby Wk., Croy. 202 DQ100
Ashby Way, West Dr. 154 BN80
Ashchurch Gro. W12 159 CU75
Ashchurch Pk. Vil. W12 159 CU76
Ashchurch Ter. W12 159 CU76
Ashcombe, Welw.G.C. 29 CY05
Ashcombe Ave., Surb. 197 CK101
Ashcombe Gdns., Edg. 96 CN49
Ashcombe Pk. NW2 118 CS62
Ashcombe Rd. SW19 180 DA92
Ashcombe Rd., Cars. 218 DG107
Ashcombe Rd., Dor. 247 CG134
Ashcombe Rd., Red. 251 DJ127
Ashcombe Sq., N.Mal. 198 CQ97
Ashcombe St. SW6 160 DB82
Ashcombe Ter., Tad. 233 CV120
Ashcroft, Guil. 258 AY141
Ashcroft, Pnr. 94 CA51
Ashcroft Ave., Sid. 186 EU86
Ashcroft Ct., Brox. 49 DZ22
Winford Dr.
Ashcroft Ct., Slou. 130 AH68
Ashcroft Cres., Sid. 186 EU86
Ashcroft Dr., Uxb. 113 BF58
Ashcroft Pk., Cob. 214 BY112
Ashcroft Ri., Couls. 235 DL116
Ashcroft Rd. E3 143 DY69
Ashcroft Rd., Chess. 198 CM104
Ashcroft Sq. W6 159 CW77
King St.
Ashdale, Lthd. 246 CC126
Ashdale Clo., Stai. 174 BL89
Ashdale Clo., Twick. 176 CC87
Ashdale Gro., Stan. 95 CF51
Ashdale Rd. SE12 184 EH88
Ashdale Way, Twick. 176 CC87
Ashdale Clo.
Ashdales, St.Alb. 43 CD24
Ashdene SE15 162 DV81
Ashdene, Pnr. 116 BW55
Ashdene Clo., Ashf. 175 BQ94
Ashdon Clo., Brwd. 109 GC44
Poplar Dr.
Ashdon Clo., S.Ock. 149 FV72
Afton Dr.
Ashdon Clo., Wdf.Grn. 102 EH51
Ashdon Rd. NW10 138 CS67
Ashdon Rd. (Bushey), Wat. 76 BX41
Ashdown Clo., Beck. 203 EB96
Ashdown Clo., Bex. 187 FC87
Ashdown Clo., Reig. 266 DB138
Ashdown Cres. NW5 120 DG64
Queens Cres.

Ashdown Cres. (Cheshunt), Wal.Cr. 67 DY28
Ashdown Dr., Borwd. 78 CL40
Ashdown Est. E11 124 EE63
High Rd. Leytonstone
Ashdown Gdns., S.Croy. 236 DV115
Ashdown Rd., Enf. 82 DW41
Ashdown Rd., Epsom 217 CT113
Ashdown Rd., Kings.T. 198 CL96
Ashdown Rd., Reig. 266 DB138
Ashdown Rd., Uxb. 134 BN68
Ashdown Wk. E14 163 EA77
Ashdown Wk., Rom. 105 FB54
Ashdown Way SW17 180 DG89
Ashdown Way, Amer. 55 AR36
Chestnut La.
Ashen E6 145 EN72
Downings
Ashen Dr., Dart. 187 FG86
Ashen Gro. SW19 180 DA90
Ashen Vale, S.Croy. 221 DX109
Ashenden Rd. E5 123 DX64
Ashenden Rd., Guil. 242 AT134
Ashenden Wk., Slou. 111 AR63
Ashendene Rd., Hert. 47 DL20
Ashentree Ct. EC4 274 E9
Asher Loftus Way N11 98 DF51
Asher Way E1 142 DU73
Asheridge Rd., Chesh. 54 AM28
Ashfield Ave., Felt. 175 BV88
Ashfield Ave. (Bushey), Wat. 76 CB44
Ashfield Clo., Beck. 183 EA94
Ashfield Clo., Rich. 178 CL88
Ashfield La., Chis. 185 EQ93
Ashfield Par. N14 99 DK46
Ashfield Rd. N4 122 DQ58
Ashfield Rd. N14 99 DJ48
Ashfield Rd. W3 139 CT74
Ashfield Rd., Chesh. 54 AR29
Ashfield St. E1 142 DV71
Ashfield Yd. E1 142 DV71
Ashfield St.
Ashfields, Loug. 85 EM40
Ashfields, Wat. 75 BT35
Ashford Ave. N8 121 DL56
Ashford Ave., Ashf. 175 BP93
Ashford Ave., Brwd. 108 FV48
Ashford Ave., Hayes 136 BX72
Ashford Clo. E17 123 DZ58
Ashford Clo., Ashf. 174 BL91
Ashford Cres., Ashf. 174 BL90
Ashford Cres., Enf. 82 DW40
Ashford Gdns., Cob. 230 BX116
Ashford Grn., Wat. 94 BX50
Ashford Ind. Est., Ashf. 175 BQ91
Ashford La., Maid. 150 AG75
Ashford La., Wind. 150 AH75
Ashford Rd. E6 145 EN65
Ashford Rd. E18 102 EH54
Ashford Rd. NW2 119 CX63
Ashford Rd., Ashf. 175 BP94
Ashford Rd., Felt. 175 BR91
Ashford Rd., Iver 133 BC67
Ashford Rd., Stai. 194 BK95
Ashford St. N1 275 M2
Ashgrove Rd., Ashf. 175 BQ92
Ashgrove Rd., Brom. 183 ED93
Ashgrove Rd., Ilf. 125 ET60
Ashgrove Rd., Sev. 256 FG127
Ashingdon Clo. E4 101 EC48
Ashington Rd. SW6 159 CZ82
Ashlake Rd. SW16 181 DL91
Ashland Pl. W1 272 F6
Ashland Pl. W1 140 DG71
Ashlar Pl. SE18 165 EP77
Masons Hill
Ashlea Rd., Ger.Cr. 90 AY54
Ashleigh Ave., Egh. 173 BC94
Ashleigh Clo., Amer. 55 AS39
Ashleigh Clo., Horl. 268 DF148
Ashleigh Cotts., Dor. 263 CH144
Ashleigh Gdns., Sutt. 200 DB103
Ashleigh Gdns., Upmin. 129 FR62
Ashleigh Rd. SE20 202 DV97
Ashleigh Rd. SW14 158 CS83
Ashley Ave., Epsom 216 CR113
Ashley Ave., Ilf. 103 EP54
Ashley Ave., Mord. 200 DA99
Chalgrove Ave.
Ashley Cen., Epsom 216 CR113
Ashley Clo. NW4 97 CW54
Ashley Clo., Lthd. 246 BZ125
Ashley Clo., Pnr. 93 BV54
Ashley Clo., Sev. 257 FH124
Ashley Clo., Walt. 195 BS102
Ashley Clo., Welw.G.C. 29 CW07
Ashley Ct., Epsom 216 CR113
Ashley Ct., Hat. 45 CV17
Ashley Ct., Wok. 226 AT118
Ashley Cres. N22 99 DN54
Ashley Cres. SW11 160 DG83
Ashley Dr., Bans. 218 DA114
Ashley Dr., Borwd. 78 CQ43
Ashley Dr., H.Wyc. 88 AC45
Ashley Dr., Islw. 157 CE79
Ashley Dr., Twick. 176 CB88
Ashley Dr., Walt. 195 BU104
Ashley Gdns. N13 100 DQ49
Ashley Gdns. SW1 277 L7
Ashley Gdns. SW1 161 DJ76
Ashley Gdns., Guil. 259 AZ141
Ashley Gdns., Orp. 223 ES106
Ashley Gdns., Rich. 177 CK89
Ashley Gdns., Wem. 118 CL61
Ashley Grn. La., Chesh. 54 AR27
Ashley Grn. Rd., Chesh. 54 AR27
Ashley Gro., Loug. 84 EL41
Staples Rd.
Ashley La. NW4 97 CW54
Ashley La., Croy. 219 DP105
Ashley Pk. Ave., Walt. 195 BT103
Ashley Pk. Cres., Walt. 195 BT102
Ashley Pk. Rd., Walt. 195 BU103
Ashley Pl. SW1 277 K7
Ashley Pl. SW1 161 DJ76
Ashley Ri., Walt. 213 BT105
Ashley Rd. E4 101 EA50
Ashley Rd. E7 144 EJ66
Ashley Rd. N17 122 DU55
Ashley Rd. N19 121 DL60
Ashley Rd. SW19 180 DB93
Ashley Rd., Dor. 262 CC137
Ashley Rd., Enf. 82 DW40
Ashley Rd., Epsom 216 CR114
Ashley Rd., Hmptn. 196 CA95
Ashley Rd., Hert. 31 DN10
Ashley Rd., Rich. 158 CL83
Jocelyn Rd.
Ashley Rd., St.Alb. 43 CJ20
Ashley Rd., Sev. 257 FH124
Ashley Rd., T.Ditt. 197 CF100
Ashley Rd., Th.Hth. 201 DM98
Ashley Rd., Uxb. 134 BH68
Ashley Rd., Walt. 195 BU102
Ashley Rd., Wok. 226 AT118
Ashley Sq., Epsom 216 CR113
Ashley Wk. NW7 97 CW52
Ashleys, Rick. 91 BF45
Ashlin Rd. E15 123 ED63
Ashling Rd., Croy. 202 DU102
Ashlone Rd. SW15 159 CW83
Ashlyn Clo. (Bushey), Wat. 76 BY42
Ashlyn Gro., Horn. 128 FK55
Ashlyns Ct., Berk. 38 AV20
Ashlyns La., Ong. 53 FF20
Ashlyns Pk., Cob. 214 BY113
Ashlyns Rd., Berk. 38 AV20
Ashlyns Rd., Epp. 69 ET30
Ashlyns Way, Chess. 215 CK107
Ashmead N14 81 DJ44
Ashmead Dr. (Denham), Uxb. 114 BG61
Ashmead Gate, Brom. 204 EJ95
Ashmead La. (Denham), Uxb. 114 BG61
Ashmead Rd. SE8 163 EA82
Ashmead Rd., Felt. 175 BU88
Ashmeads Ct. (Shenley), Rad. 61 CK33
Porters Pk. Dr.
Ashmere Ave., Beck. 203 ED96
Ashmere Clo., Sutt. 217 CW106
Ashmere Gro. SW2 161 DL84
Ashmill St. NW1 272 B6
Ashmill St. NW1 140 DE71
Ashmole Pl. SW8 161 DM79
Ashmole St. SW8 161 DM79
Ashmore Ct., Houns. 156 CA79
Wheatlands
Ashmore Gdns., Hem.H. 41 BP21
Ashmore Gro., Well. 165 ER83
Ashmore La., Kes. 222 EH111
Ashmore Rd. W9 139 CZ70
Ashmount Est. N19 121 DK59
Ashmount Rd.
Ashmount Rd. N15 122 DT57
Ashmount Rd. N19 121 DJ59
Ashmount Ter. W5 157 CK77
Murray Rd.
Ashmour Gdns., Rom. 105 FD54
Ashneal Gdns., Har. 117 CD62
Ashness Gdns., Grnf. 137 CH65
Ashness Rd. SW11 180 DF85
Ashridge Clo., Har. 117 CJ58
Ashridge Clo., Hem.H. 57 BA28
Ashridge Cres. SE18 165 EQ80
Ashridge Dr., St.Alb. 60 BY30
Ashridge Dr., Wat. 94 BW50
Ashridge Gdns. N13 99 DK50
Ashridge Gdns., Pnr. 116 BY56
Ashridge Ri., Berk. 38 AT18
Ashridge Rd., Chesh. 56 AW31
Ashridge Way, Mord. 199 CZ97
Ashridge Way, Sun. 175 BU93
Ashtead Gap, Lthd. 231 CG116
Kingston Rd.
Ashtead Rd. E5 122 DU59
Ashtead Wds. Rd., Ash. 231 CJ116
Ashton Clo., Sutt. 218 DA105
Ashton Clo., Walt. 213 BV107
Ashton Gdns., Houns. 156 BZ84
Ashton Gdns., Rom. 126 EY58
Ashton Rd. E15 123 ED64
Ashton Rd., Enf. 83 DY36
Ashton Rd., Rom. 106 FK52
Ashton Rd., Wok. 226 AT117
Ashton St. E14 143 EC73
Ashtree Ave., Mitch. 200 DE96
Ashtree Clo., Orp. 223 EP105
Broadwater Gdns.
Ashtree Ct., St.Alb. 43 CF20
Granville Rd.
Ashtree Way, Hem.H. 40 BG21
Ashurst Clo. SE20 202 DV95
Ashurst Clo., Dart. 167 FF83
Ashurst Clo., Ken. 236 DR115
Ashurst Clo., Nthwd. 93 BS52
Ashurst Dr., Ilf. 125 EP58
Ashurst Dr., Shep. 194 BL99
Ashurst Dr., Tad. 248 CP130
Ashurst Rd. N12 98 DE50
Ashurst Rd., Barn. 80 DF43
Ashurst Rd., Tad. 233 CV121
Ashurst Wk., Croy. 202 DV103
Ashvale Dr., Upmin. 129 FS61
Ashvale Gdns., Rom. 105 FD50
Ashvale Gdns., Upmin. 129 FS61
Ashvale Rd. SW17 180 DF92
Ashview Clo., Ashf. 174 BL93
Ashview Gdns., Ashf. 174 BL92
Ashville Rd. E11 123 ED61
Ashwater Rd. SE12 184 EG88
Ashwell Clo. E6 144 EL72
Northumberland Rd.
Ashwell St., St.Alb. 43 CD19
Ashwells Way, Ch.St.G. 90 AW47
Ashwin St. E8 142 DT65
Ashwindham Ct., Wok. 226 AT118
Raglan Rd.
Ashwood, Warl. 236 DW120
Ashwood Ave., Rain. 147 FH70
Ashwood Ave., Uxb. 134 BN72
Ashwood Gdns., Croy. 221 EB107
Ashwood Gdns., Hayes 155 BT77
Cranford Dr.
Ashwood Pk., Lthd. 230 CC123
Ashwood Pk., Wok. 227 BA118
Ashwood Rd. E4 101 ED48
Ashwood Rd., Egh. 172 AV93
Ashwood Rd., Pot.B. 64 DD33
Ashwood Rd., Wok. 227 AZ118
Ashworth Clo. SE5 162 DR82
Hascombe Ter.
Ashworth Pl., Guil. 242 AT134
Ashworth Pl., Harl. 52 EX15
Ashworth Rd. W9 140 DB69
Aske St. N1 275 M2
Askern Clo., Bexh. 166 EX84
Askew Cres. W12 159 CT75
Askew Fm. La., Grays 170 FY78
Askew Rd. W12 139 CT74
Askew Rd., Nthwd. 93 BR47
Askham Ct. W12 139 CU74
Askham Rd. W12 139 CU74
Askill Dr. SW15 179 CY85
Keswick Rd.
Askwith Rd., Rain. 147 FD69
Asland Rd. E15 144 EE67
Aslett St. SW18 180 DB87
Asmar Clo., Couls. 235 DL115
Asmara Rd. NW2 119 CY64
Asmuns Hill NW11 120 DA57
Asmuns Pl. NW11 119 CZ57
Asolando Dr. SE17 279 J9
Aspasia Clo., St.Alb. 43 CF21
Aspdin Rd., Grav. 190 GD90
Aspen Clo. N19 121 DJ61
Hargrave Pk.
Aspen Clo. W5 158 CM75
Aspen Clo., Cob. 230 BY116
Aspen Clo., Guil. 243 BD131
Aspen Clo., Orp. 224 EU106
Aspen Clo., St.Alb. 60 BY30
Aspen Clo., Slou. 131 AP71
Birch Gro.
Aspen Clo., Stai. 173 BF90
Aspen Clo., Swan. 207 FD95
Aspen Clo., West Dr. 134 BM74
Aspen Copse, Brom. 205 EM96
Aspen Ct., Hayes 155 BS77
Aspen Dr., Wem. 117 CG63
Aspen Gdns. W6 159 CV78
Aspen Gdns., Mitch. 200 DG99
Aspen Grn., Erith 166 EZ76
Aspen Gro., Upmin. 128 FN63
Aspen La., Nthlt. 136 BY69
Aspen Pk. Dr., Wat. 75 BV35
Aspen Sq., Wey. 195 BR104
Oatlands Dr.
Aspen Way E14 143 EB73
Aspen Way, Bans. 217 CX114
Aspen Way, Enf. 83 DX35
Aspen Way, Felt. 175 BV90
Aspen Way, S.Ock. 149 FX69
Aspen Way, Welw.G.C. 30 DC10
Aspenlea Rd. W6 159 CX79
Aspern Gro. NW3 120 DE64
Aspfield Row, Hem.H. 40 BH18
Aspinall Rd. SE4 163 DX83
Aspinden Rd. SE16 162 DV77
Aspley Rd. SW18 180 DB85
Asplins Rd. N17 100 DU53
Asquith Clo., Dag. 126 EW60
Crystal Way
Ass Ho. La., Har. 94 CB49
Assam St. E1 142 DU72
White Ch. La.
Assata Ms. N1 141 DP65
St. Paul's Rd.
Assembly Pas. E1 142 DW71
Assembly Wk., Cars. 200 DE101
Assher Rd., Walt. 196 BY104
Assheton Rd., Beac. 89 AK51
Assurance Cotts., Belv. 166 EZ78
Heron Hill
Astall Clo., Har. 95 CE53
Astbury Rd. SE15 162 DW81
Aste St. E14 163 EC75
Astell St. SW3 276 C10
Astell St. SW3 160 DE78
Asters, The, Wal.Cr. 66 DR28
Asteys Row N1 141 DP66
River Pl.
Asthall Gdns., Ilf. 125 EQ56
Astle St. SW11 160 DG82
Astleham Rd., Shep. 194 BL97
Astley, Grays 170 FZ79
Astley Ave. NW2 119 CW64
Astley Rd., Hem.H. 40 BJ20
Aston Ave., Har. 117 CJ59
Aston Clo., Ash. 231 CJ118
Aston Clo., Sid. 186 EU90
Aston Clo., Wat. 76 BW40
Aston Clo. (Bushey), Wat. 76 CC44
Aston Grn., Houns. 156 BW82
Aston Mead, Wind. 151 AL81
Aston Ms., Rom. 126 EW59
Reynolds Ave.
Aston Rd. SW20 199 CW96
Aston Rd. W5 137 CK72
Aston Rd., Esher 215 CE106
Aston St. E14 143 DY72
Aston Ter. SW12 181 DH86
Cathles Rd.
Aston Way, Epsom 233 CT116
Aston Way, Pot.B. 64 DD32
Astons Rd., Nthwd. 93 BQ48
Astonville St. SW18 180 DA88
Astor Ave., Rom. 127 FC58
Astor Clo., Add. 212 BK105
Astor Clo., Kings.T. 178 CP93
Astoria Wk. SW9 161 DN83
Astra Clo., Horn. 147 FH65
Astra Dr., Grav. 191 GL92
Astrop Ms. W6 159 CW76
Astrop Ter. W6 159 CW76
Astwick Ave., Hat. 45 CT15
Astwood Ms. SW7 160 DB77
Asylum Arch Rd., Red. 266 DF137
Asylum Rd. SE15 162 DV80
Atalanta Clo., Pur. 219 DN110
Atalanta St. SW6 159 CX81
Atbara Ct., Tedd. 177 CH93
Atbara Rd., Tedd. 177 CH93
Atcham Rd., Houns. 156 CC84
Atcost Rd., Bark. 146 EU71
Atheldene Rd. SW18 180 DB88
Athelney St. SE6 183 EA90
Athelstan Clo., Rom. 106 FM54
Athelstan Rd.
Athelstan Rd., Kings.T. 198 CM98
Athelstan Rd., Rom. 106 FM53
Athelstan Wk. N., Welw.G.C. 29 CY10
Athelstan Wk. S., Welw.G.C. 29 CX10
Athelstan Way, Orp. 206 EU95
Athelstane Gro. E3 143 DZ68
Athelstane Ms. N4 121 DN60
Stroud Grn. Rd.
Athelstone Rd., Har. 95 CD54
Athelstone Rd., Hem.H. 40 BM23
Athena Clo., Har. 117 CE61
Byron Hill Rd.
Athena Clo., Kings.T. 198 CM97
Athena Pl., Nthwd. 93 BT53
The Dr.
Athenaeum Pl. N10 121 DH55
Fortis Grn. Rd.
Athenaeum Rd. N20 98 DC46
Athenlay Rd. SE15 183 DX85
Athens Gdns. W9 140 DA70
Elgin Ave.
Atherden Rd. E5 122 DW63
Atherfield Rd., Reig. 266 DC137
Atherfold Rd. SW9 161 DL83
Atherley Way, Houns. 176 BZ87
Atherstone Ct. W2 140 DB71
Delamere Ter.
Atherstone Ms. SW7 160 DC77
Atherton Clo., Guil. 258 AY140
Atherton Clo., Stai. 174 BK86
Atherton Ct. (Eton), Wind. 151 AR80
Meadow La.
Atherton Dr. SW19 179 CX91
Atherton Gdns., Grays 171 GJ77
Atherton Hts., Wem. 137 CJ65
Atherton Ms. E7 144 EF65
Atherton Pl., Har. 117 CD55
Atherton Pl., Sthl. 136 CB73
Longford Ave.
Atherton Rd. E7 124 EF64
Atherton Rd. SW13 159 CU80
Atherton Rd., Ilf. 102 EL54
Atherton St. SW11 160 DE82
Athlon Rd., Wem. 137 CK68
Athlone, Esher 215 CE107
Athlone Clo. E5 122 DV63
Goulton Rd.
Athlone Clo., Rad. 77 CH36
Athlone Rd. SW2 181 DM87
Athlone Sq., Wind. 151 AQ81
Alma Rd.
Athlone St. NW5 140 DG65
Athol Clo., Pnr. 93 BV53
Athol Gdns., Pnr. 93 BV53
Athol Rd., Erith 167 FC78
Athol Sq. E14 143 EC72
Athol Way, Uxb. 134 BN69
Athole Gdns., Enf. 82 DS43
Atholl Rd., Ilf. 126 EU59
Atkins Clo., Wok. 226 AU118
Greythorne Rd.
Atkins Dr., W.Wick. 203 ED103
Atkins Rd. E10 123 EB58
Atkins Rd. SW12 181 DK87
Atkinson Clo., Orp. 224 EU106
Martindale Ave.
Atkinson Rd. E16 144 EJ71
Atlanta Boul., Rom. 127 FE58
Atlantic Rd. SW9 161 DN84
Atlas Gdns. SE7 164 EJ77
Atlas Ms. E8 142 DT65
Tyssen St.
Atlas Ms. N7 141 DM65
Atlas Rd. E13 144 EG68
Atlas Rd. N11 99 DH51
Atlas Rd. NW10 138 CS69
Atlas Rd., Dart. 168 FM83
Cornwall Rd.
Atlas Rd., Wem. 118 CQ63
Atley Rd. E3 143 EA67
Atlip Rd., Wem. 138 CL67
Atney Rd. SW15 159 CY84
Atria Rd., Nthwd. 93 BU50
Attenborough Clo., Wat. 94 BY48
Harrow Way
Atterbury Clo., West. 255 ER126
Atterbury Rd. N4 121 DN58
Atterbury St. SW1 277 N9
Atterbury St. SW1 161 DL77
Attewood Ave. NW10 118 CS62
Attewood Rd., Nthlt. 136 BY65
Attfield Clo. N20 98 DD47
Attimore Clo., Welw.G.C. 29 CV10
Attimore Rd., Welw.G.C. 29 CV10
Attle Clo., Uxb. 134 BN68
Attlee Clo., Hayes 135 BV69
Attlee Clo., Th.Hth. 202 DQ100
Attlee Ct., Grays 170 GA76
Attlee Dr., Dart. 188 FN85
Attlee Rd. SE28 146 EV73
Attlee Rd., Hayes 135 BU69
Attlee Ter. E17 123 EB56
Attneave St. WC1 274 D3
Attwood Clo., S.Croy. 220 DV114
Atwater Clo. SW2 181 DN88
Atwell Clo. E10 123 EB58
Belmont Pk. Rd.
Atwell Rd. SE15 162 DU82
Rye La.
Atwood, Lthd. 230 BY124
Atwood Ave., Rich. 158 CN82
Atwood Rd. W6 159 CV77
Atwoods All., Rich. 158 CN81
Leyborne Pk.
Aubert Pk. N5 121 DP63
Aubert Rd. N5 121 DP63
Aubretia Clo., Rom. 106 FL53
Aubrey Ave., St.Alb. 61 CJ26
Aubrey Pl. NW8 140 DC68
Violet Hill
Aubrey Rd. E17 123 EA55
Aubrey Rd. N8 121 DL57
Aubrey Rd. W8 139 CZ74
Aubrey Wk. W8 139 CZ74
Aubreys Rd., Hem.H. 39 BE20
Aubyn Hill SE27 182 DQ91
Aubyn Sq. SW15 159 CU84
Auckland Ave., Rain. 147 FF69
Auckland Clo. SE19 202 DT95
Auckland Clo., Enf. 82 DV37
Auckland Clo., Til. 171 GG82
Auckland Gdns. SE19 202 DS95
Auckland Hill SE27 182 DQ91
Auckland Ri. SE19 202 DS95
Auckland Rd. E10 123 EB62
Auckland Rd. SE19 202 DT95
Auckland Rd. SW11 160 DE84
Auckland Rd., Cat. 236 DS122
Auckland Rd., Ilf. 125 EP60
Auckland Rd., Kings.T. 198 CM98
Auckland Rd., Pot.B. 63 CY32
Auckland St. SE11 161 DM78
Kennington La.
Auden Pl. NW1 140 DG67
Audleigh Pl., Chig. 103 EN51
Audley Clo. N10 99 DH52
Audley Clo. SW11 160 DG83
Audley Clo., Add. 212 BH106
Audley Clo., Borwd. 78 CN41
Audley Ct. E18 124 EF56
Audley Ct., Pnr. 94 BW54
Rickmansworth Rd.
Audley Dr. E16 144 EH74
Wesley Ave.
Audley Dr., Warl. 236 DW115
Audley Firs, Walt. 214 BW105
Audley Gdns., Ilf. 125 ET61
Audley Gdns., Loug. 85 EQ40
Audley Gdns., Wal.Abb. 67 EC34
Audley Pl., Sutt. 218 DA108
Audley Rd. NW4 119 CV58
Audley Rd. W5 138 CM71
Audley Rd., Enf. 81 DP40
Audley Rd., Rich. 178 CM85
Audley Sq. W1 276 G2
Audley Wk., Orp. 206 EW100
Audrey Clo., Beck. 203 EB100
Audrey Gdns., Wem. 117 CH61
Audrey Rd., Ilf. 125 EP62
Audrey St. E2 142 DU68
Audric Clo., Kings.T. 198 CN95
Audwick Clo. (Cheshunt), Wal.Cr. 67 DX28
Augur Clo., Stai. 173 BF92
Augurs La. E13 144 EH69
August End, Slou. 132 AY72
August La., Guil. 260 BK144
Augusta Clo., W.Mol. 196 BZ97
Freeman Dr.
Augusta Rd., Twick. 176 CC89
Augusta St. E14 143 EB72
Augustine Clo., Slou. 153 BE83
Augustine Ct., Wal.Abb. 67 EB33
Beaulieu Dr.
Augustine Rd. W14 159 CX76
Augustine Rd., Grav. 191 GJ87
Augustine Rd., Har. 94 CB53
Augustine Rd., Orp. 206 EX97
Augustus Clo., Brent. 157 CJ80
Augustus Clo., St.Alb. 42 CA22
Augustus La., Orp. 206 EU103
Augustus Rd. SW19 179 CY88
Augustus St. NW1 273 J1
Augustus St. NW1 141 DH68
Aulton Pl. SE11 161 DN78
Aultone Way, Cars. 200 DF104
Aultone Way, Sutt. 200 DB103
Aurelia Gdns., Croy. 201 DM99
Aurelia Rd., Croy. 201 DL100
Auriel Ave., Dag. 147 FD65
Auriga Ms. N16 122 DR64
Auriol Clo., Wor.Pk. 198 CS104
Auriol Pk. Rd.
Auriol Dr., Grnf. 137 CD66
Auriol Dr., Uxb. 134 BN65
Auriol Pk. Rd., Wor.Pk. 198 CS104
Auriol Rd. W14 159 CY77
Aurum Clo., Horl. 269 DH149
Austell Gdns. NW7 96 CS48
Austen Clo. SE28 146 EV74
Austen Clo., Green. 189 FW85
Austen Clo., Loug. 85 ER41
Austen Clo., Til. 171 GJ82
Coleridge Rd.
Austen Gdns., Dart. 168 FM84
Austen Ho. NW6 140 DA69
Austen Rd., Erith 167 FB80
Austen Rd., Guil. 259 AZ135
Austen Rd., Har. 116 CB61
Austenway, Ger.Cr. 112 AY55
Austenwood Clo., Ger.Cr. 90 AW54
Austenwood La., Ger.Cr. 90 AX54
Austin Ave., Brom. 204 EL99
Austin Clo. SE23 183 DZ87
Austin Clo., Couls. 235 DP118
Austin Clo., Twick. 177 CJ85
Austin Ct. E6 144 EJ67
Kings Rd.
Austin Friars EC2 275 L8
Austin Friars EC2 142 DR72
Austin Friars Pas. EC2 275 L8
Austin Friars Sq. EC2 275 L8
Austin Rd. SW11 160 DG81
Austin Rd., Grav. 191 GF88
Austin Rd., Hayes 155 BT75
Austin Rd., Orp. 206 EU100
Austin St. E2 275 P3
Austin St. E2 142 DT69
Austin Waye, Uxb. 134 BJ67
Austin's La., Uxb. 115 BR63
Austins Mead, Hem.H. 57 BB28
Austins Pl., Hem.H. 40 BK19
St. Mary's Rd.
Austral Clo., Sid. 185 ET90
Austral Dr., Horn. 128 FK59
Austral St. SE11 278 F8
Austral St. SE11 161 DP77
Australia Rd. W12 139 CV73
Australia Rd., Slou. 132 AV74
Austyn Gdns., Surb. 198 CP102
Autumn Clo. SW19 180 DC93
Autumn Clo., Enf. 82 DU39
Autumn Clo., Slou. 131 AM74
Autumn Dr., Sutt. 218 DB109
Autumn Glades, Hem.H. 41 BQ22
Autumn Gro., Welw.G.C. 30 DB11
Autumn St. E3 143 EA67
Auxiliaries Way, Uxb. 113 BF57
Avalon Clo. SW20 199 CY96
Avalon Clo. W13 137 CG71
Avalon Clo., Enf. 81 DN40
Avalon Clo., Orp. 206 EX104
Avalon Clo., Wat. 60 BY32
Avalon Rd. SW6 160 DB81
Avalon Rd. W13 137 CG70
Avalon Rd., Orp. 206 EV103
Avard Gdns., Orp. 223 EQ105
Avarn Rd. SW17 180 DF93
Ave Maria La. EC4 274 G9
Ave Maria La. EC4 141 DP72
Avebury, Slou. 131 AN74
Avebury Ct. N1 142 DR67
Poole St.
Avebury Ct., Hem.H. 40 BN18
Avebury Pk., Surb. 197 CK101
Avebury Rd. E11 123 ED60
Southwest Rd.
Avebury Rd. SW19 199 CZ95
Avebury Rd., Orp. 205 ER104
Avebury St. N1 142 DR67
Poole St.
Aveley Bypass, S.Ock. 148 FQ73
Aveley Clo., Erith 167 FF79
Aveley Clo., S.Ock. 149 FR74
Aveley Rd., Rom. 127 FD56
Aveley Rd., Upmin. 148 FP65
Aveline St. SE11 278 D10
Aveline St. SE11 161 DN78
Aveling Clo., Pur. 219 DM113
Aveling Pk. Rd. E17 101 EA54
Avelon Rd., Rain. 147 FG67
Avelon Rd., Rom. 105 FD51
Avenell Rd. N5 121 DP62
Avening Rd. SW18 180 DA87
Brathway Rd.

Avening Ter. SW18 180 DA86
Avenons Rd. E13 144 EG70
Avenue, The E4 101 ED51
Avenue, The (Leytonstone) E11 124 EF61
Avenue, The (Wanstead) E11 124 EF61
Avenue, The N3 98 DA54
Avenue, The N8 121 DN55
Avenue, The N10 99 DJ54
Avenue, The N11 99 DH49
Avenue, The N17 100 DS54
Avenue, The NW6 139 CX67
Avenue, The SE7 164 EJ80
Avenue, The SE10 163 ED80
Avenue, The SW4 180 DG85
Avenue, The SW11 180 DF87
Bellevue Rd.
Avenue, The SW18 180 DE87
Avenue, The W4 158 CS76
Avenue, The W13 137 CH73
Avenue, The, Add. 212 BG110
Avenue, The, Amer. 55 AQ38
Avenue, The, Barn. 79 CY41
Avenue, The, Beck. 203 EB95
Avenue, The, Bet. 248 CN134
Avenue, The, Bex. 186 EX86
Avenue, The, Brwd. 109 FZ50
Avenue, The, Brom. 204 EK97
Avenue, The, Cars. 218 DG108
Avenue, The, Couls. 235 DK115
Avenue, The, Croy. 202 DS104
Avenue, The, Egh. 173 BB91
Avenue, The, Epsom 217 CV108
Avenue, The, Esher 215 CE107
Avenue, The, Grav. 191 GG88
Avenue, The, Green. 169 FV84
Avenue, The, Guil. 242 AS127
Avenue, The, Hmptn. 176 BZ93
Avenue, The, Har. 95 CF53
Avenue, The, Hem.H. 39 BE19
Avenue, The, Hert. 31 DP07
Avenue, The, Hodd. 49 DZ19
Avenue, The, Horl. 268 DF149
Avenue, The, Horn. 128 FJ61
Avenue, The, Houns. 176 CB85
Avenue, The (Cranford), Houns. 155 BU81
Avenue, The, Islw. 157 CD79
Avenue, The, Kes. 204 EK104
Avenue, The, Lthd. 215 CF112
Avenue, The, Loug. 84 EK44
Avenue, The, Maid. 130 AC69
Avenue, The, Nthwd. 93 BQ51
Avenue, The, Orp. 205 ET103
Avenue, The (St. Paul's Cray), Orp. 186 EV94
Avenue, The, Pnr. 116 BZ58
Avenue, The (Hatch End), Pnr. 94 CA52
Avenue, The, Pot.B. 63 CZ30
Avenue, The, Rad. 61 CG33
Avenue, The, Red. 267 DL137
Avenue, The, Rich. 158 CM82
Avenue, The, Rom. 127 FD56
Avenue, The, Slou. 111 AP63
Avenue, The (Datchet), Slou. 152 AV81
Avenue, The, Stai. 194 BH95
Avenue, The (Sunnymeads), Stai. 152 AX83
Avenue, The, Sun. 195 BV95
Avenue, The, Surb. 198 CM100
Avenue, The, Sutt. 217 CZ109
Avenue, The (Cheam), Sutt. 217 CW108
Avenue, The, Tad. 233 CV122
Avenue, The, Twick. 177 CH85
Avenue, The (Cowley), Uxb. 134 BK70
Avenue, The (Ickenham), Uxb. 114 BN63
Avenue, The, Wal.Abb. 68 EJ25
Avenue, The, Wat. 75 BV40
Avenue, The (Bushey), Wat. 76 BZ42
Avenue, The, Wem. 118 CM61
Avenue, The, West Dr. 154 BL76
Avenue, The, W.Wick. 203 ED101
Avenue, The, West. 239 EM122
Avenue, The, Whyt. 236 DU119
Avenue, The, Wind. 172 AV85
Avenue, The, Wok. 210 AT109
Avenue, The, Wor.Pk. 199 CT103
Avenue App., Kings L. 58 BN30
Avenue Clo. N14 81 DJ44
Avenue Clo. NW8 140 DE67
Avenue Clo., Houns. 155 BU81
The Ave.
Avenue Clo., Rom. 106 FM52
Avenue Clo., Tad. 233 CV122
Avenue Clo., West Dr. 154 BK76
Avenue Cres. W3 158 CP75
Avenue Cres., Houns. 155 BV80
Avenue Dr., Slou. 133 AZ71
Avenue Elmers, Surb. 198 CL99
Avenue Gdns. SE25 202 DU97
Avenue Gdns. SW14 158 CS83
Avenue Gdns. W3 158 CP75
Avenue Gdns., Horl. 269 DJ149
Avenue Gdns., Houns. 155 BU80
The Ave.
Avenue Gdns., Tedd. 177 CF94
Avenue Gate, Loug. 84 EJ44
Avenue Ind. Est. E4 101 DZ51
Avenue Ms. N10 121 DH55
Avenue Pk. Rd. SE27 181 DP89
Avenue Ri. (Bushey), Wat. 76 CA43
Avenue Rd. E7 124 EH64
Avenue Rd. N6 121 DJ59
Avenue Rd. N12 98 DC49
Avenue Rd. N14 99 DJ45
Avenue Rd. N15 122 DR57
Avenue Rd. NW3 140 DD66
Avenue Rd. NW8 140 DD67
Avenue Rd. NW10 139 CT68
Avenue Rd. SE20 202 DW95
Avenue Rd. SE25 202 DU96
Avenue Rd. SW16 201 DK96
Avenue Rd. SW20 199 CV96
Avenue Rd. W3 158 CP75
Avenue Rd., Bans. 234 DB115
Avenue Rd., Beck. 202 DW95
Avenue Rd., Belv. 167 FC77
Avenue Rd., Bexh. 166 EY83
Avenue Rd., Brent. 157 CJ78
Avenue Rd., Brwd. 108 FW49
Avenue Rd., Cat. 236 DR122
Avenue Rd., Cob. 230 BX116
Avenue Rd., Epp. 85 ER36
Avenue Rd., Epsom 216 CR114
Avenue Rd., Erith 167 FC80
Avenue Rd., Felt. 175 BT90
Avenue Rd., Hmptn. 196 CB95
Avenue Rd., Hodd. 49 ED19
Avenue Rd., Islw. 157 CF81
Avenue Rd., Kings.T. 198 CL97
Avenue Rd., N.Mal. 198 CS98
Avenue Rd., Pnr. 116 BY55
Avenue Rd. (Chadwell Heath), Rom. 126 EV59
Avenue Rd. (Harold Wd.), Rom. 106 FM52
Avenue Rd., St.Alb. 43 CE19
Avenue Rd., Sev. 257 FJ124
Avenue Rd., Sthl. 156 BZ75
Avenue Rd., Stai. 173 BD92
Avenue Rd., Sutt. 218 DA110
Avenue Rd., Tedd. 177 CG94
Avenue Rd., Wall. 219 DJ108
Avenue Rd., West. 238 EL120
Avenue Rd., Wdf.Grn. 102 EJ51
Avenue S., Surb. 198 CM101
Avenue Ter., N.Mal. 198 CQ97
Kingston Rd.
Avenue Ter., Wat. 76 BY44
Averil Ct., Maid. 130 AJ72
Averil Gro. SW16 181 DP93
Averill St. W6 159 CX79
Avern Gdns., W.Mol. 196 CB98
Avern Rd., W.Mol. 196 CB98
Avery Fm. Row SW1 276 G9
Avery Gdns., Ilf. 125 EM57
Avery Hill Rd. SE9 185 ER86
Avery Row W1 273 H10
Avery Row W1 141 DH73
Avey La., Loug. 84 EH39
Avey La., Wal.Abb. 83 ED36
Avia Clo., Hem.H. 40 BK24
Aviary Clo. E16 144 EF71
Aviary Rd., Wok. 228 BG116
Aviemore Clo., Beck. 203 DZ99
Aviemore Way, Beck. 203 DY99
Avignon Rd. SE4 163 DX83
Avington Clo., Guil. 242 AY134
London Rd.
Avington Ct. SE1 162 DS77
Old Kent Rd.
Avington Gro. SE20 182 DW94
Avington Way SE15 162 DT80
Daniel Gdns.
Avion Cres. NW9 97 CU53
Avior Dr., Nthwd. 93 BT49
Avis Gro., Croy. 221 DY110
Avis Sq. E1 143 DX72
Avoca Rd. SW17 180 DG91
Avocet Ms. SE28 165 ER76
Avon Clo., Add. 212 BG107
Avon Clo., Grav. 191 GK89
Avon Clo., Hayes 136 BW70
Avon Clo., Slou. 131 AL73
Avon Clo., Sutt. 218 DC105
Avon Clo., Wat. 60 BW34
Avon Clo., Wor.Pk. 199 CU103
Avon Ct., Grnf. 136 CB70
Braund Ave.
Avon Grn., S.Ock. 149 FV72
Avon Ms., Pnr. 94 BZ53
Avon Path, S.Croy. 220 DQ107
Avon Pl. SE1 279 J5
Avon Rd. E17 123 ED55
Avon Rd. SE4 163 EA83
Avon Rd., Grnf. 136 CA70
Avon Rd., Sun. 175 BT94
Avon Rd., Upmin. 129 FR58
Avon Sq., Hem.H. 40 BM15
Avon Way E18 124 EG55
Avondale Ave. N12 98 DB50
Avondale Ave. NW2 118 CS62
Avondale Ave., Barn. 98 DF46
Avondale Ave., Esher 197 CG104
Avondale Ave., Stai. 173 BF94
Avondale Ave., Wor.Pk. 199 CT102
Avondale Clo., Horl. 268 DG146
Avondale Clo., Loug. 103 EM45
Avondale Clo., Walt. 214 BW106
Pleasant Pl.
Avondale Ct. E11 124 EE60
Avondale Ct. E16 144 EE71
Avondale Rd.
Avondale Ct. E18 102 EH53
Avondale Cres., Enf. 83 DY41
Avondale Cres., Ilf. 124 EK57
Avondale Dr., Hayes 135 BU74
Avondale Dr., Loug. 103 EM45
Avondale Gdns., Houns. 176 BZ85
Avondale Ms., Brom. 184 EG93
Avondale Rd.
Avondale Pk. Gdns. W11 139 CY73
Avondale Pk. Rd. W11 139 CY73
Avondale Pavement SE1 162 DU78
Avondale Sq.
Avondale Ri. SE15 162 DT83
Avondale Rd. E16 144 EE71
Avondale Rd. E17 123 EA59
Avondale Rd. N3 98 DC53
Avondale Rd. N13 99 DN47
Avondale Rd. N15 121 DP57
Avondale Rd. SE9 184 EL89
Avondale Rd. SW14 158 CR83
Avondale Rd. SW19 180 DB92
Avondale Rd., Ashf. 174 BK90
Avondale Rd., Brom. 184 EE93
Avondale Rd., Har. 117 CF55
Avondale Rd., S.Croy. 220 DQ107
Avondale Rd., Well. 166 EW82
Avondale Sq. SE1 162 DU78
Avonley Rd. SE14 162 DW80
Avonmead, Wok. 226 AW118
Silversmiths Way
Avonmore Ave., Guil. 243 AZ133
Avonmore Gdns. W14 159 CY77
Avonmore Rd.
Avonmore Pl. W14 159 CY77
Avonmore Rd.
Avonmore Rd. W14 159 CZ77
Avonmouth Rd., Dart. 188 FK85
Avonmouth St. SE1 279 H6
Avonmouth St. SE1 162 DQ76
Avontar Rd., S.Ock. 149 FV70
Avonwick Rd., Houns. 156 CB82
Avril Way E4 101 EC50
Avro Way, Wall. 219 DL108
Avro Way, Wey. 212 BL111
Awlfield Ave. N17 100 DR53
Awliscombe Rd., Well. 165 ET82
Axe St., Bark. 145 EQ67
Axes La., Red. 267 DJ141
Axholme Ave., Edg. 96 CN53
Axminster Cres., Well. 166 EW81
Axminster Rd. N7 121 DL62
Axtaine Rd., Orp. 206 EX101
Axtane, Grav. 190 FZ94
Axtane Clo. (Sutton at Hone), Dart. 208 FQ96
Axwood, Epsom 232 CQ115
Aybrook St. W1 272 F7
Aybrook St. W1 140 DG71
Aycliffe Clo., Brom. 205 EM98
Aycliffe Dr., Hem.H. 40 BL15
Aycliffe Rd. W12 139 CT74
Aycliffe Rd., Borwd. 78 CL39
Ayebridges Ave., Egh. 173 BC94
Aylands Clo., Wem. 118 CL61
Preston Rd.
Aylands Rd., Enf. 82 DW36
Ayles Rd., Hayes 135 BV69
Aylesbury Clo. E7 144 EF65
Atherton Rd.
Aylesbury Cres., Slou. 131 AR72
Aylesbury End, Beac. 89 AL54
Aylesbury Est. SE17 162 DR78
Villa St.
Aylesbury Rd. SE17 162 DR78
Aylesbury Rd., Brom. 204 EG97
Aylesbury St. EC1 274 F5
Aylesbury St. EC1 141 DP70
Aylesbury St. NW10 118 CR62
Aylesford Ave., Beck. 203 DY99
Aylesford St. SW1 277 M10
Aylesford St. SW1 161 DK78
Aylesham Clo. NW7 97 CU52
Aylesham Rd., Orp. 205 ET101
Aylestone Ave. NW6 139 CX67
Aylesworth Ave., Slou. 131 AN69
Doddsfield Rd.
Aylesworth Spur, Wind. 172 AV87
Aylets Fld., Harl. 51 ES18
Aylett Rd. SE25 202 DV98
Aylett Rd., Islw. 157 CE82
Aylett Rd., Upmin. 128 FQ61
Ayley Cft., Enf. 82 DU43
Ayliffe Clo., Kings.T. 198 CN96
Cambridge Gdns.
Aylmer Clo., Stan. 95 CG49
Aylmer Dr., Stan. 95 CG49
Aylmer Par. N2 120 DF57
Aylmer Rd.
Aylmer Rd. E11 124 EF60
Aylmer Rd. N2 120 DE57
Aylmer Rd. W12 159 CT75
Aylmer Rd., Dag. 126 EY62
Ayloffe Rd., Dag. 146 EZ65
Ayloffs Clo., Horn. 128 FL57
Ayloffs Wk., Horn. 128 FK57
Aylsham Dr., Uxb. 115 BR61
Aylsham La., Rom. 106 FJ49
Aylsham Rd., Hodd. 49 EC16
Aylton Est. SE16 162 DW75
Renforth St.
Aylward Gdns., Chesh. 54 AN30
Aylward Rd. SE23 183 DX89
Aylward Rd. SW20 199 CZ96
Aylward St. E1 142 DW72
Aylwards Ri., Stan. 95 CG49
Aylwyn Est. SE1 279 P6
Aylwyn Est. SE1 162 DS76
Aymer Clo., Stai. 193 BE95
Aymer Dr., Stai. 193 BE95
Aynho St., Wat. 75 BV43
Aynhoe Rd. W14 159 CX77
Aynscombe Angle, Orp. 206 EU101
Aynscombe La. SW14 158 CQ83
Aynscombe Path SW14 158 CQ82
Thames Bank
Aynsley Gdns., Harl. 52 EW15
Ayot Grn., Welw. 29 CU07
Ayot Greenway, St.Alb. 28 CN06
Ayot Little Grn., Welw. 29 CT06
Ayot Path, Borwd. 78 CN37
Ayr Ct. W3 138 CN71
Monks Dr.
Ayr Grn., Rom. 105 FE52
Ayr Way, Rom. 105 FE52
Ayres Clo. E13 144 EG69
Ayres Cres. NW10 138 CR66
Ayres St. SE1 279 J4
Ayres St. SE1 162 DQ75
Ayron Rd., S.Ock. 149 FV70
Ayrsome Rd. N16 122 DS62
Ayrton Rd. SW7 160 DD76
Wells Way
Aysgarth Rd. SE21 182 DS86
Aytoun Pl. SW9 161 DM82
Aytoun Rd. SW9 161 DM82
Azalea Clo. W7 137 CF74
Azalea Clo., Ilf. 125 EP64
Azalea Ct., Wok. 226 AX119
Azalea Ct., Wdf.Grn. 102 EE52
The Bridle Path
Azalea Dr., Swan. 207 FD98
Azalea Wk., Pnr. 115 BV57
Azalea Wk., Sthl. 156 CC75
Navigator Dr.
Azalea Way, Slou. 132 AY72
Blinco La.
Azenby Rd. SE15 162 DT82
Azile Everitt Ho. SE18 165 EQ78
Vicarage Pk.
Azof St. SE10 164 EE77

B

Baalbec Rd. N5 121 DP64
Baas Hill, Brox. 49 DX21
Baas Hill Clo., Brox. 49 DY21
Baas La., Brox. 49 DY21
Babbacombe Clo., Chess. 215 CK106
Babbacombe Gdns., Ilf. 124 EL56
Babbacombe Rd., Brom. 204 EG95
Baber Dr., Felt. 176 BW86
Babington Ri., Wem. 138 CN65
Babington Rd. NW4 119 CV56
Babington Rd. SW16 181 DK92
Babington Rd., Dag. 126 EW64
Babington Rd., Horn. 127 FH60
Babmaes St. SW1 277 L1
Babylon La., Tad. 250 DA127
Bacchus Wk. N1 275 M1
Bachelors Acre, Wind. 151 AR81
Bachelor's La., Wok. 228 BM124
Baches St. N1 275 L3
Baches St. N1 142 DR69
Back, The, Berk. 39 BB16
Back Ch. La. E1 142 DU73
Back Grn., Walt. 214 BW107
Back Hill EC1 274 D5
Back Hill EC1 141 DN70
Back La. N8 121 DL57
Back La. NW3 120 DC63
Heath St.
Back La., Bex. 186 FA87
Back La., B.Stort. 36 FA06
Back La., Brent. 157 CK79
Back La., Ch.St.G. 90 AU48
Back La., Edg. 96 CQ53
Back La., Grays 149 FW74
Back La., Guil. 244 BK131
Back La., Hert. 48 DQ18
Back La., Purf. 169 FS76
Back La., Rich. 177 CJ90
Back La., Rick. 73 BB38
Back La., Rom. 126 EY59
St. Chad's Rd.
Back La. (Godden Grn.), Sev. 257 FN124
Back La. (Ide Hill), Sev. 256 FB128
Back La., Wal.Abb. 50 EJ22
Back La., Wat. 77 CE39
Back La., Welw. 30 DE05
Back Path, Red. 252 DQ133
Back Rd., Sid. 186 EU91
Back St., Harl. 36 EW11
Broadway Ave.
Backhouse Pl. SE17 279 N9
Backley Gdns. SE25 202 DU100
Backs, The, Chesh. 54 AQ31
Bacon Gro. SE1 279 P7
Bacon Gro. SE1 162 DT76
Bacon La. NW9 118 CP56
Bacon La., Edg. 96 CN53
Bacon Link, Rom. 105 FB51
Bacon St. E1 142 DT70
Bacon St. E2 142 DT70
Bacon Ter., Dag. 126 EV64
Fitzstephen Rd.
Bacons Dr. (Cuffley), Pot.B. 65 DL29
Bacons La. N6 120 DG60
Bacons Mead (Denham), Uxb. 114 BG61
Bacton NW5 120 DG64
Bacton St. E2 142 DW69
Roman Rd.
Badburgham Ct., Wal.Abb. 68 EF33
Baddow Clo., Dag. 146 FA67
Baddow Clo., Wdf.Grn. 102 EK51
Baddow Wk. N1 142 DQ67
Baden Clo., Stai. 174 BG94
Baden Dr., Horl. 268 DE147
Baden Pl. SE1 279 K4
Baden Powell Clo., Dag. 146 EY67
Baden Powell Clo., Surb. 198 CM103
Baden Powell Rd., Sev. 256 FE122
Baden Rd. N8 121 DK56
Baden Rd., Guil. 242 AU132
Baden Rd., Ilf. 125 EP64
Bader Clo., Ken. 236 DR115
Bader Clo., Welw.G.C. 30 DC09
Bader Gdns., Slou. 151 AN75
Bader Wk., Grav. 190 GE90
Bader Way, Rain. 147 FG65
Badger Clo., Felt. 175 BU90
Sycamore Clo.
Badger Clo., Guil. 242 AV131
Badger Clo., Houns. 156 BW83
Badger Clo., Ilf. 125 EQ59
Badger Way, Hat. 45 CV20
Badgers Clo., Ashf. 174 BM92
Fordbridge Rd.
Badgers Clo., Borwd. 78 CM40
Kingsley Ave.
Badgers Clo., Enf. 81 DP41
Badgers Clo., Har. 117 CD58
Badgers Clo., Hayes 135 BS73
Badgers Clo., Hert. 32 DV09
Badgers Clo., Wok. 226 AW118
Badgers Copse, Orp. 205 ET103
Badgers Copse, Wor.Pk. 199 CT103
Badgers Cft. N20 97 CY46
Badgers Cft. SE9 185 EN90
Badgers Cft., Brox. 49 DY21
Badgers Cft., Hem.H. 41 BR21
Badgers Hill, Vir.W. 192 AW99
Badgers Hole, Croy. 221 DX105
Badgers La., Warl. 236 DW119
Badgers Mt., Grays 171 GF75
Badgers Ri., Sev. 224 FA110
Badgers Rd., Sev. 225 FB110
Badgers Wk., N.Mal. 198 CS96
Badgers Wk., Pur. 219 DK111
Badgers Wk., Rick. 73 BF42
Badgers Wk., Whyt. 236 DT119
Badgers Wd., Cat. 252 DQ125
Badgers Wd., Slou. 111 AQ64
Badingham Dr., Lthd. 231 CE123
Badlis Rd. E17 123 EA55
Badlow Clo., Erith 167 FE80
Badminton Clo., Borwd. 78 CN40
Badminton Clo., Har. 117 CE56
Badminton Clo., Nthlt. 136 CA65
Badminton Ms. E16 144 EG74
Hanameel St.
Badminton Pl., Brox. 49 DY20
Badminton Rd. SW12 180 DG86
Badsworth Rd. SE5 162 DQ80
Baffin Way E14 143 EC73
Prestons Rd.
Bagden Hill, Dor. 247 CD130
Bagley Clo., West Dr. 154 BL75
Bagley's La. SW6 160 DB81
Bagleys Spring, Rom. 126 EY56
Bagot Clo., Ash. 232 CM116
Bagshot Ct. SE18 165 EN81
Prince Imperial Rd.
Bagshot Rd., Egh. 172 AW94
Bagshot Rd., Enf. 100 DT45
Bagshot St. SE17 162 DS78
Bahram Rd., Epsom 216 CR110
Baildon St. SE8 163 EA80
Watson's St.
Bailey Clo. E4 101 EC49
Bailey Clo., Purf. 169 FR77
Gabion Ave.
Bailey Clo., Wind. 151 AN82
Bailey Pl. SE26 183 DX93
Bailey Rd., Dor. 262 CC137
Baillie Clo., Rain. 147 FH70
Baillie Rd., Guil. 259 AZ135
Baillies Wk. W5 157 CK75
Liverpool Rd.
Bainbridge Rd., Dag. 126 EZ63
Bainbridge St. WC1 273 N8
Bainbridge St. WC1 141 DK72
Baines Clo., S.Croy. 220 DQ106
Brighton Rd.
Bainton Mead, Wok. 226 AU117
Baird Ave., Sthl. 136 CB73
Baird Clo. NW9 118 CQ58
Baird Clo., Slou. 151 AP75
Haig Dr.
Baird Clo. (Bushey), Wat. 76 CB44
Ashfield Ave.
Baird Gdns. SE19 182 DS91
Baird Rd., Enf. 82 DV42
Baird St. EC1 275 J4
Bairstow Clo., Borwd. 78 CL39
Baizdon Rd. SE3 164 EE82
Bakeham La., Egh. 192 AX95
Bakehouse Rd., Horl. 268 DF146
Baker Boy La., Croy. 221 DZ112
Baker Hill Clo., Grav. 191 GF91
Baker La., Mitch. 200 DG96
Baker Pas. NW10 138 CS67
Acton La.
Baker Rd. NW10 138 CS67
Baker Rd. SE18 164 EL80
Baker St. NW1 272 E5
Baker St. NW1 140 DF70
Baker St. W1 272 E6
Baker St. W1 140 DF71
Baker St., Enf. 82 DR41
Baker St., Hert. 32 DS09
Baker St., Pot.B. 79 CY35
Baker St., Wey. 212 BN105
Bakers Ave. E17 123 EB58
Bakers Ct. SE25 202 DS97
Bakers End SW20 199 CY96
Bakers Fld. N7 121 DK63
Crayford Rd.
Bakers Gdns., Cars. 200 DE103
Bakers Gro., Welw.G.C. 30 DC08
Bakers Hill E5 122 DW60
Bakers Hill, Barn. 80 DB40
Bakers La. N6 120 DF57
Bakers La., Epp. 69 ET30
Bakers La., Saw. 35 ES05
Bakers Mead, Gdse. 252 DW130
Baker's Ms. W1 272 F8
Bakers Ms., Orp. 223 ET107
Bakers Orchard, H.Wyc. 110 AE58
Bakers Pas. NW3 120 DC63
Heath St.
Baker's Rents E2 275 P3
Bakers Rd., Uxb. 134 BK66
Bakers Rd. (Cheshunt), Wal.Cr. 66 DV30
Bakers Row E15 144 EE68
Baker's Row EC1 274 D5
Baker's Row EC1 141 DN70
Bakers Wd., Uxb. 113 BD60
Baker's Yd. EC1 141 DN70
Baker's Row
Baker's Yd., Uxb. 134 BK66
Bakers Rd.
Bakery Clo. SW9 161 DM81
Bakery Clo., Harl. 50 EJ15
Bakery Path, Edg. 96 CP51
Station Rd.
Bakery Pl. SW11 160 DF84
Altenburg Gdns.
Bakewell Way, N.Mal. 198 CS96
Bala Gdn. NW9 118 CS58
Snowdon Dr.
Balaam St. E13 144 EG69
Balaams La. N14 99 DK47
Balaclava Rd. SE1 162 DT77
Balaclava Rd., Surb. 197 CJ101
Balcaskie Rd. SE9 185 EM85
Balchen Rd. SE3 164 EK82
Balchier Rd. SE22 182 DV86
Balchins La., Dor. 262 CA138
Balcombe Clo., Bexh. 166 EX84
Balcombe Gdns., Horl. 269 DJ149
Balcombe Rd., Craw. 269 DK154
Balcombe Rd., Horl. 269 DH147
Balcombe St. NW1 272 D5
Balcombe St. NW1 140 DF70
Balcon Way, Borwd. 78 CQ39
Balcorne St. E9 142 DW66
Balder Ri. SE12 184 EH89
Balderton St. W1 272 G9
Balderton St. W1 140 DG72
Baldock St. E3 143 EB68
Baldock St., Ware 33 DX06
Baldock Way, Borwd. 78 CM39
Baldocks Rd., Epp. 85 ES35
Baldry Gdns. SW16 181 DL93
Baldwin Cres. SE5 162 DQ81
Baldwin Cres., Guil. 243 BC132
Baldwin Rd., Beac. 89 AP54
Baldwin Rd., Slou. 130 AJ69
Baldwin St. EC1 275 K3
Baldwin Ter. N1 142 DQ68
Baldwins, Welw.G.C. 30 DC09
Baldwin's Gdns. EC1 274 D6
Baldwin's Gdns. EC1 141 DN71
Baldwins Hill, Loug. 85 EM40
Baldwins La., Rick. 75 BP42
Baldwins Shore, Wind. 151 AR79
Baldwyn Gdns. W3 138 CR73
Baldwyns Pk., Bex. 187 FD89
Baldwyns Rd., Bex. 187 FD89
Balfe St. N1 274 A1
Balfe St. N1 141 DL68
Balfern Gro. W4 158 CS78
Balfern St. SW11 160 DE81
Balfont Clo., S.Croy. 220 DU113
Balfour Ave. W7 137 CF74
Balfour Ave., Wok. 226 AY122
Balfour Gro. N20 98 DF48
Balfour Ho. W10 139 CX71
St. Charles Sq.
Balfour Ms. N9 100 DU48
The Bdy.
Balfour Ms. W1 276 G2
Balfour Pl. SW15 159 CV84
Balfour Pl. W1 276 G1
Balfour Rd. N5 122 DQ63
Balfour Rd. SE25 202 DU98
Balfour Rd. SW19 180 DB94
Balfour Rd. W3 138 CQ71
Balfour Rd. W13 157 CG75
Balfour Rd., Brom. 204 EK99
Balfour Rd., Cars. 218 DF108
Balfour Rd., Grays 170 GC77
Balfour Rd., Har. 117 CD57
Balfour Rd., Houns. 156 CB83
Balfour Rd., Ilf. 125 EP61
Balfour Rd., Sthl. 156 BX76

Baron Wk. E16 144 EF71
Baron Wk., Mitch. 200 DE98
Baroness Rd. E2 142 DT69
Diss St.
Baronet Gro. N17 100 DU53
St. Paul's Rd.
Baronet Rd. N17 100 DU53
Barons, The, Twick. 177 CH86
Barons Ct., Wall. 201 DK104
Whelan Way
Barons Ct. Rd. W14 159 CY78
Barons Gate, Barn. 80 DE44
Barons Gate, Epsom 232 CQ116
Barons Keep W14 159 CY78
Barons Mead, Har. 117 CE56
Barons Pl. SE1 278 E5
Barons Pl. SE1 161 DN75
Barons Wk., Croy. 203 DY100
Barons Way, Egh. 173 BD93
Barons Way, Reig. 266 DA138
Baronsfield Rd., Twick. 177 CH86
Baronsmead Rd. SW13 159 CU81
Baronsmede W5 158 CM75
Baronsmere Rd. N2 120 DE56
Barque Ms. SE8 163 EA79
Watergate St.
Barr Rd., Grav. 191 GM89
Barr Rd., Pot.B. 64 DC33
Barra Clo., Hem.H. 41 BP23
Barra Hall Circ., Hayes 135 BS72
Barra Hall Rd., Hayes 135 BS73
Barrack La., Wind. 151 AR81
Barrack Path, Wok. 226 AT118
Barrack Rd., Guil. 242 AU132
Barrack Rd., Houns. 156 BX84
Barrack Row, Grav. 191 GH86
Barracks, The, Add. 194 BH104
Barracks Hill, Amer. 89 AM45
Barracks La., Barn. 79 CY41
High St.
Barrards Way, Beac. 89 AQ51
Barratt Ave. N22 99 DM54
Barratt Ind. Pk., Sthl. 156 CA75
Barratt Way, Har. 117 CD55
Tudor Rd.
Barrenger Rd. N10 98 DF53
Barrens Brae, Wok. 227 BA118
Barrens Clo., Wok. 227 BA119
Barrens Pk., Wok. 227 BA118
Barrett Clo., Rom. 105 FH52
Barrett Rd. E17 123 EC56
Barrett Rd., Lthd. 231 CD124
Barrett St. W1 272 G9
Barrett St. W1 140 DG72
Barretts Grn. Rd. NW10 138 CQ68
Barretts Gro. N16 122 DS64
Barretts Rd., Sev. 241 FD120
Barrhill Rd. SW2 181 DL89
Barricane, Wok. 226 AV119
Barrie Clo., Couls. 235 DJ115
Barrie Est. W2 140 DD73
Craven Ter.
Barrie Ho. W3 158 CP75
Barriedale SE14 163 DY82
Barrier App. SE7 164 EK76
Barringer Sq. SW17 180 DG91
Barrington Clo. NW5 120 DG64
Barrington Clo., Ilf. 103 EM53
Barrington Clo., Loug. 85 EQ42
Barrington Rd.
Barrington Ct., Brwd. 109 GC44
Barrington Ct., Dor. 263 CG137
Barrington Rd.
Barrington Dr. (Harefield), Uxb. 92 BG52
Barrington Grn., Loug. 85 EQ42
Barrington Lo., Wey. 213 BQ106
Barrington Pk. Gdns., Ch.St.G. 90 AX46
Barrington Rd. E12 145 EN65
Barrington Rd. N8 121 DK57
Barrington Rd. SW9 161 DP83
Barrington Rd., Bexh. 166 EX82
Barrington Rd., Dor. 263 CG137
Barrington Rd., Loug. 85 EQ41
Barrington Rd., Pur. 219 DJ112
Barrington Rd., Sutt. 200 DA102
Barrington Vil. SE18 165 EN81
Barrow Ave., Cars. 218 DF108
Barrow Clo. N21 99 DP48
Barrow Grn. Rd., Oxt. 253 EA130
Barrow Hedges Clo., Cars. 218 DE108
Barrow Hedges Way, Cars. 218 DE108
Barrow Hill, Wor.Pk. 198 CS103
Barrow Hill Clo., Wor.Pk. 198 CS103
Barrow Hill
Barrow Hill Est. NW8 140 DE68
Barrow Hill Rd.
Barrow Hill Rd. NW8 272 B1
Barrow Hill Rd. NW8 140 DE68
Barrow La. (Cheshunt), Wal.Cr. 66 DT30
Barrow Pt. Ave., Pnr. 94 BY54
Barrow Pt. La., Pnr. 94 BY54
Barrow Rd. SW16 181 DK93
Barrow Rd., Croy. 219 DN106
Barrow Wk., Brent. 157 CJ78
Glenhurst Rd.
Barrowdene Clo., Pnr. 94 BY54
Paines La.
Barrowell Grn. N21 99 DP47
Barrowfield Clo. N9 100 DV48
Barrowgate Rd. W4 158 CQ78
Barrows Rd., Harl. 51 EM15
Barrowsfield, S.Croy. 220 DT112
Barrs Rd. NW10 138 CR66
Barry Ave. N15 122 DT58
Craven Pk. Rd.
Barry Ave., Bexh. 166 EY80
Barry Ave., Wind. 151 AQ80
Barry Clo., Grays 171 GG75
Barry Clo., Orp. 205 ES104
Barry Clo., St.Alb. 60 CB25
Barry Rd. E6 144 EL72
Barry Rd. NW10 138 CQ66
Barry Rd. SE22 182 DU86
Bars, The, Guil. 258 AX135
Barset Rd. SE15 162 DW83
Barson Clo. SE20 182 DW94
Barston Rd. SE27 182 DQ90
Barstow Cres. SW2 181 DM88
Bartel Clo., Hem.H. 41 BR22
Bartelotts Rd., Slou. 131 AK70
Barter St. WC1 274 A7
Barter St. WC1 141 DL71
Barters Wk., Pnr. 116 BY55
High St.
Barth Rd. SE18 165 ES77
Bartholomew Clo. EC1 275 H7
Bartholomew Clo. EC1 142 DQ71
Bartholomew Clo. SW18 160 DC84
London Wall
Bartholomew Ct., Dor. 263 CG137
South St.
Bartholomew Dr., Rom. 106 FK54
Bartholomew La. EC2 275 L9
Bartholomew Pl. EC1 275 H7
Bartholomew Rd. NW5 141 DJ65
Bartholomew Sq. E1 142 DV70
Coventry Rd.
Bartholomew Sq. EC1 275 J4
Bartholomew Sq. EC1 142 DQ70
Bartholomew St. SE1 279 K7
Bartholomew St. SE1 162 DR76
Bartholomew Vil. NW5 141 DJ65
Bartholomew Way, Swan. 207 FE97
Bartle Ave. E6 144 EL68
Bartle Rd. W11 139 CY72
Bartlett Clo. E14 143 EA72
Bartlett Ct. EC4 274 E8
Bartlett Rd., Grav. 191 GG88
Bartlett Rd., West. 255 EQ126
Bartlett St., S.Croy. 220 DR106
Bartletts Mead, Hert. 32 DR06
Bartletts Pas. EC4 274 E8
Bartlow Gdns., Rom. 105 FD53
Barton, The, Cob. 214 BW112
Barton Ave., Rom. 127 FB60
Barton Clo. E6 145 EM72
Barton Clo. E9 122 DW64
Churchill Wk.
Barton Clo. NW4 119 CU56
Barton Clo. SE15 162 DV83
Kirkwood Rd.
Barton Clo., Add. 212 BG107
Barton Clo., Bexh. 186 EY85
Barton Clo., Chig. 103 EQ47
Barton Clo., Shep. 195 BP100
Barton Grn., N.Mal. 198 CR96
Barton Meadows, Ilf. 125 EQ56
Barton Rd. W14 159 CY78
Barton Rd. (Sutton at Hone), Dart. 188 FP94
Barton Rd., Guil. 259 BA144
Barton Rd., Horn. 127 FG60
Barton Rd., Sid. 186 EY93
Barton Rd., Slou. 153 AZ75
Barton St. SW1 277 P6
Barton Way, Borwd. 78 CN40
Barton Way, Rick. 75 BP43
Bartons, The, Borwd. 77 CK44
Bartonway NW8 140 DD68
Queen's Ter.
Bartram Clo., Uxb. 135 BP70
Lees Rd.
Bartram Rd. SE4 183 DY85
Bartrams La., Barn. 80 DC38
Bartrop Clo., Wal.Cr. 66 DR28
Poppy Wk.
Barville Clo. SE4 163 DY84
St. Norbert Rd.
Barwell Trd. Est., Chess. 215 CK109
Barwick Rd. E7 124 EH63
Barwood Ave., W.Wick. 203 EB102
Basden Gro., Felt. 176 CA89
Basedale Rd., Dag. 146 EV66
Baseing Clo. E6 145 EN73
Basford Way, Wind. 151 AK83
Bashley Rd. NW10 138 CR70
Basil Ave. E6 144 EL68
Basil Gdns. SE27 182 DQ92
Basil Gdns., Croy. 203 DX102
Primrose La.
Basil St. SW3 276 D6
Basil St. SW3 160 DF76
Basildene Rd., Houns. 156 BX82
Basildon Ave., Ilf. 103 EN53
Basildon Clo., Sutt. 218 DB109
Basildon Clo., Wat. 75 BQ44
Basildon Rd. SE2 166 EU78
Basildon Sq., Hem.H. 40 BM16
Basilon Rd., Bexh. 166 EY82
Basin S. E16 145 EP74
Basing Clo., T.Ditt. 197 CF101
Basing Ct. SE15 162 DT81
Basing Dr., Bex. 186 EZ86
Basing Hill NW11 119 CZ60
Basing Hill, Wem. 118 CM61
Basing Ho., Bark. 145 ER67
St. Margarets
Basing Ho. Yd. E2 275 N2
Basing Pl. E2 275 N2
Basing Rd., Bans. 217 CZ114
Basing Rd., Rick. 91 BF46
Basing St. W11 139 CZ72
Basing Way N3 120 DB55
Basing Way, T.Ditt. 197 CF101
Basingdon Way SE5 162 DR84
Basingfield Rd., T.Ditt. 197 CF101
Basinghall Ave. EC2 275 K7
Basinghall Ave. EC2 142 DR71
Basinghall Gdns., Sutt. 218 DB109
Basinghall St. EC2 275 K8
Basinghall St. EC2 142 DQ71
Basire St. N1 142 DQ67
Baskerville Rd. SW18 180 DE87
Basket Gdns. SE9 184 EL85
Baslow Clo., Har. 95 CD53
Baslow Wk. E5 123 DX63
Overbury St.
Basnett Rd. SW11 160 DG83
Basque Ct. SE16 163 DX75
Poolmans St.
Bassano St. SE22 182 DT85
Bassant Rd. SE18 165 ET79
Bassein Pk. Rd. W12 159 CT75
Basset Clo., Add. 212 BH110
Bassett Clo., Sutt. 218 DB109
Bassett Gdns., Epp. 71 FB26
Bassett Gdns., Islw. 156 CC80
Bassett Ho., Dag. 146 EV67
Bassett Rd. W10 139 CX72
Bassett Rd., Uxb. 134 BJ66
New Windsor St.
Bassett Rd., Wok. 227 BC116
Bassett St. NW5 140 DG65
Bassett Way, Grnf. 136 CB72
Bassett Way, Slou. 131 AL70
Pemberton Rd.
Bassetts Clo., Orp. 223 EP105
Bassetts Way, Orp. 223 EP105
Bassil Rd., Hem.H. 40 BK21
Bassingbourne Clo., Brox. 49 DZ20
Bassingburn Wk., Welw.G.C. 29 CZ10
Bassingham Rd. SW18 180 DC87
Bassingham Rd., Wem. 137 CK65
Bassishaw Highwalk EC2 142 DQ71
London Wall
Basswood Clo. SE15 162 DV83
Linden Gro.
Bastable Ave., Bark. 145 ES68
Bastion Highwalk EC2 142 DQ71
London Wall
Bastion Ho. EC2 142 DQ71
London Wall
Bastion Rd. SE2 166 EU78
Baston Manor Rd., Brom. 204 EH104
Baston Rd., Brom. 204 EH102
Bastwick St. EC1 275 H4
Bastwick St. EC1 142 DQ70
Basuto Rd. SW6 160 DA81
Bat & Ball Rd., Sev. 257 FJ121
Batavia Clo., Sun. 196 BW95
Batavia Ms. SE14 163 DY80
Goodwood Rd.
Batavia Rd. SE14 163 DY80
Batavia Rd., Sun. 195 BV95
Batchelor St. N1 141 DN68
Batchelors Way, Amer. 55 AR39
Batchelors Way, Chesh. 54 AP29
Batchwood Dr., St.Alb. 42 CB19
Batchwood Gdns., St.Alb. 43 CD17
Batchwood Grn., Orp. 206 EU97
Batchwood Vw., St.Alb. 42 CC18
Batchworth Heath Hill, Rick. 92 BN49
Batchworth Hill, Rick. 92 BM48
Batchworth La., Nthwd. 93 BS50
Batchworth Roundabout, Rick. 92 BK46
Bate St. E14 143 DZ73
Three Colt St.
Bateman Clo., Bark. 145 EQ65
Glenny Rd.
Bateman Ho. SE17 161 DP79
Otto St.
Bateman Rd. E4 101 EA51
Bateman Rd., Rick. 74 BN44
Bateman St. W1 273 M9
Bateman's Bldgs. W1 273 M9
Bateman's Row EC2 275 N4
Bateman's Row EC2 142 DS70
Bates Clo., Slou. 132 AY72
Bates Cres. SW16 181 DJ94
Bates Cres., Croy. 219 DN106
Bates Rd., Rom. 106 FN52
Bates Wk., Add. 212 BJ107
Bateson St. SE18 165 ES77
Bateson Way, Wok. 211 BC114
Batford Clo., Welw.G.C. 30 DB10
Waterford Grn.
Bath Clo. SE15 162 DV80
Asylum Rd.
Bath Ct. EC1 274 D5
Bath Ho. Rd., Croy. 201 DL102
Bath Pas., Kings.T. 197 CK96
St. James Rd.
Bath Pl. EC2 275 M3
Bath Pl., Barn. 79 CZ41
Bath Rd. E7 144 EK65
Bath Rd. N9 100 DV47
Bath Rd. W4 158 CS77
Bath Rd., Dart. 187 FH87
Bath Rd., Hayes 155 BQ81
Bath Rd., Houns. 156 BW81
Bath Rd., Maid. 130 AC72
Bath Rd., Mitch. 200 DD97
Bath Rd., Rom. 126 EY58
Bath Rd., Slou. 131 AK72
Bath Rd. (Colnbrook), Slou. 153 BB79
Bath Rd., West Dr. 154 BK81
Bath St. EC1 275 J3
Bath St. EC1 142 DR69
Bath St., Grav. 191 GH86
Bath Ter. SE1 279 H7
Bath Ter. SE1 162 DQ76
Bathgate Rd. SW19 179 CX90
Baths Rd., Brom. 204 EK98
Bathurst Ave. SW19 200 DB95
Brisbane Ave.
Bathurst Clo., Iver 153 BF75
Bathurst Gdns. NW10 139 CV68
Bathurst Rd., Hem.H. 40 BK17
Bathurst Rd., Ilf. 125 EP60
Bathurst St. W2 140 DD73
Bathurst Wk., Iver 153 BE75
Bathway SE18 165 EN77
Batley Clo., Mitch. 200 DF101
Batley Pl. N16 122 DT62
Batley Rd. N16 122 DT62
Stoke Newington High St.
Batley Rd., Enf. 82 DQ39
Batman Clo. W12 139 CV74
Baton Clo., Purf. 169 FR77
Brimfield Rd.
Batoum Gdns. W6 159 CW76
Batson St. W12 159 CU75
Batsworth Rd., Mitch. 200 DD97
Batten Ave., Wok. 226 AS119
Batten Clo. E6 145 EM72
Savage Gdns.
Batten St. SW11 160 DE83
Battenburg Wk. SE19 182 DS92
Brabourne Clo.
Batterdale, Hat. 45 CW17
Battersby Rd. SE6 183 ED89
Battersea Bri. SW3 160 DD80
Battersea Bri. SW11 160 DD80
Battersea Bri. Rd. SW11 160 DE80
Battersea Ch. Rd. SW11 160 DD81
Battersea High St. SW11 160 DD81
Battersea Pk. SW11 160 DF80
Battersea Pk. Rd. SW8 161 DH81
Battersea Pk. Rd. SW11 160 DE82
Battersea Ri. SW11 180 DE85
Battersea Sq. SW11 160 DD81
Battersea High St.
Battery Rd. SE28 165 ES75
Battis, The, Rom. 127 FE58
Waterloo Rd.
Battishill Gdns. N1 141 DP66
Waterloo Ter.
Battishill St. N1 141 DP66
Waterloo Ter.
Battle Bri. La. SE1 279 M3
Battle Bri. La. SE1 142 DS74
Battle Bri. Rd. NW1 273 P1
Battle Bri. Rd. NW1 141 DL68
Battle Clo. SW19 180 DC93
North Rd.
Battle Rd., Belv. 167 FC77
Battle Rd., Erith 167 FC77
Battlebridge La., Red. 251 DH130
Battledean Rd. N5 121 DP64
Battlefield Rd., St.Alb. 43 CF18
Battlemead Clo., Maid. 130 AC68
Battlers Grn. Dr., Rad. 77 CE37
Batts Hill, Red. 250 DE132
Batts Hill, Reig. 250 DD132
Batty St. E1 142 DU72
Baudwin Rd. SE6 184 EE89
Baugh Rd., Sid. 186 EW92
Baulk, The SW18 180 DA87
Bavant Rd. SW16 201 DL96
Bavaria Rd. N19 121 DL61
Bavdene Ms. NW4 119 CV56
The Burroughs
Bavent Rd. SE5 162 DQ82
Bawdale Rd. SE22 182 DT85
Bawdsey Ave., Ilf. 125 ET56
Bawtree Clo., Sutt. 218 DC110
Bawtree Rd. SE14 163 DY80
Bawtree Rd., Uxb. 134 BK65
Bawtry Rd. N20 98 DF48
Baxendale N20 98 DC47
Baxendale St. E2 142 DU69
Baxter Ave., Red. 250 DE134
Baxter Clo., Sthl. 156 CB75
Baxter Clo., Uxb. 135 BP69
Baxter Rd. E16 144 EJ72
Baxter Rd. N1 142 DR65
Baxter Rd. N18 100 DV49
Baxter Rd. NW10 138 CS70
Baxter Rd., Ilf. 125 EP64
Bay Clo., Horl. 268 DE145
Bay Ct. W5 158 CL76
Popes La.
Bay Manor La., Grays 169 FT79
Bay Tree Clo., Brom. 204 EJ95
Bay Tree Ct., Slou. 130 AJ69
Bayards, Warl. 236 DW118
Baycroft Clo., Pnr. 116 BW55
Baydon Ct., Brom. 204 EF97
Bayes Clo. SE26 182 DW92
Bayeux, Tad. 233 CX122
Bayfield Rd. SE9 164 EK84
Bayfield Rd., Horl. 268 DE147
Bayford Clo., Hem.H. 41 BQ15
Bayford Clo., Hert. 32 DQ11
Bayford Grn., Hert. 47 DN17
Bayford La., Hert. 31 DM14
Bayford Ms. E8 142 DV66
Bayford St.
Bayford Rd. NW10 139 CX69
Bayford St. E8 142 DV66
Bayham Pl. NW1 141 DJ67
Bayham Rd. W4 158 CR76
Bayham Rd. W13 137 CH73
Bayham Rd., Mord. 200 DB98
Bayham Rd., Sev. 257 FJ123
Bayham St. NW1 141 DJ67
Bayhorne La., Horl. 269 DJ150
Bayhurst Dr., Nthwd. 93 BT51
Bayley Cres., Slou. 130 AG71
Bayley St. WC1 273 M7
Bayley St. WC1 141 DK71
Bayley Wk. SE2 166 EY78
Woolwich Rd.
Bayleys Mead, Brwd. 109 GC47
Baylie Ct., Hem.H. 40 BL19
Baylie La.
Baylie La., Hem.H. 40 BL19
Baylin Rd. SW18 180 DB86
Garratt La.
Baylis Par., Slou. 132 AS72
Oatlands Dr.
Baylis Rd. SE1 278 D5
Baylis Rd. SE1 161 DN75
Baylis Rd., Slou. 131 AR73
Bayliss Ave. SE28 146 EX73
Bayliss Clo. N21 81 DL43
Macleod Rd.
Bayly Rd., Dart. 188 FN86
Baymans Wd., Brwd. 109 FZ47
Bayne Clo. E6 145 EM72
Savage Gdns.
Bayne Hill, Beac. 89 AR52
Bayne Hill Clo., Beac. 89 AR52
Baynes Clo., Enf. 82 DU40
Baynes Ms. NW3 140 DD65
Belsize La.
Baynes St. NW1 141 DJ66
Baynham Clo., Bex. 186 EZ86
Bayonne Rd. W6 159 CY79
Bayshill Ri., Nthlt. 136 CB65
Bayston Rd. N16 122 DT62
Bayswater Rd. W2 272 A10
Bayswater Rd. W2 140 DB73
Baythorne St. E3 143 DZ71
Baytree Clo., St.Alb. 60 CB27
Baytree Clo., Sid. 185 ET88
Baytree Clo., Wal.Cr. 66 DT27
Baytree Rd. SW2 161 DM84
Baytree Wk., Wat. 75 BT38
Baywood Sq., Chig. 104 EV49
Bazalgette Clo., N.Mal. 198 CR99
Bazalgette Gdns., N.Mal. 198 CR99
Bazely St. E14 143 EC73
Bazile Rd. N21 81 DN44
Beach Gro., Felt. 176 CA89
Beacham Clo. SE7 164 EK78
Beachborough Rd., Brom. 183 EC91
Beachcroft Rd. E11 124 EE62
Beachcroft Way N19 121 DK60
Beachy Rd. E3 143 EA66
Beacon Clo., Bans. 233 CX116
Beacon Clo., Ger.Cr. 90 AY52
Beacon Clo., Uxb. 114 BK64
Beacon Dr., Dart. 189 FV90
Beacon Gate SE14 163 DX83
Beacon Gro., Cars. 218 DG105
Beacon Hill N7 121 DL64
Beacon Hill, H.Wyc. 88 AD48
Beacon Hill, Purf. 168 FP78
Beacon Hill, Wok. 226 AV119
Beacon Ri., Sev. 256 FG126
Beacon Rd. SE13 183 ED86
Beacon Rd., Erith 167 FH80
Beacon Rd., Houns. 174 BN86
Beacon Rd., Ware 33 EA05
Beacon Rd. Roundabout, Houns. 174 BN86
Beacon Way, Bans. 233 CX116
Beacon Way, Beac. 88 AG54
Holtspur Way
Beacon Way, Rick. 92 BG45
Beaconfield Ave., Epp. 69 ET29
Beaconfield Rd., Epp. 69 ET29
Beaconfield Way, Epp. 69 ET29
Beaconfields, Sev. 256 FF126
Beacons, The, Loug. 85 EN38
Beacons Clo. E6 144 EL71
Oliver Gdns.
Beaconsfield Clo. N11 98 DG49
Beaconsfield Clo. SE3 164 EG79
Beaconsfield Clo. W4 158 CQ78
Beaconsfield Clo., Hat. 45 CW17
Beaconsfield Common La., Slou. 111 AQ58
Beaconsfield Par. SE9 184 EL91
Beaconsfield Rd.
Beaconsfield Pl., Epsom 216 CS112
Beaconsfield Rd. E10 123 EC61
Beaconsfield Rd. E16 144 EF70
Beaconsfield Rd. E17 123 DZ58
Beaconsfield Rd. N9 100 DU49
Beaconsfield Rd. N11 98 DG48
Beaconsfield Rd. N15 122 DS56
Beaconsfield Rd. NW10 139 CT65
Beaconsfield Rd. SE3 164 EF80
Beaconsfield Rd. SE9 184 EL89
Beaconsfield Rd. SE17 162 DR78
Beaconsfield Rd. W4 158 CR76
Beaconsfield Rd. W5 157 CJ75
Beaconsfield Rd., Bex. 187 FD89
Beaconsfield Rd., Brom. 204 EK97
Beaconsfield Rd., Croy. 202 DR100
Beaconsfield Rd., Enf. 83 DX37
Beaconsfield Rd., Epsom 232 CR119
Beaconsfield Rd., Esher 215 CE108
Beaconsfield Rd., Hat. 45 CW17
Beaconsfield Rd., Hayes 136 BW74
Beaconsfield Rd., N.Mal. 198 CR96
Beaconsfield Rd., St.Alb. 43 CE20
Beaconsfield Rd., Slou. 131 AQ68
Beaconsfield Rd., Sthl. 136 BX74
Beaconsfield Rd., Surb. 198 CM101
Beaconsfield Rd., Twick. 177 CH86
Beaconsfield Rd., Wok. 227 AZ120
Beaconsfield Ter., Rom. 126 EX58
Beaconsfield Ter. Rd. W14 159 CY76
Beaconsfield Wk. E6 145 EN72
East Ham Manor Way
Beaconsfield Wk. SW6 159 CZ81
Beacontree Ave. E17 101 ED53
Beacontree Rd. E11 124 EF59
Beadles La., Oxt. 253 ED130
Beadlow Clo., Cars. 200 DD100
Olveston Wk.
Beadman Pl. SE27 181 DP91
Norwood High St.
Beadman St. SE27 181 DP91
Beadnell Rd. SE23 183 DX88
Beadon Rd. W6 159 CW77
Beadon Rd., Brom. 204 EG98
Beads Hall La., Brwd. 108 FV42
Beaford Gro. SW20 199 CY97
Beagle Clo., Felt. 175 BV91
Beagle Clo., Rad. 77 CF37
Beagles Clo., Orp. 206 EX103
Beak St. W1 273 L10
Beak St. W1 141 DJ73
Beal Clo., Well. 166 EU81
Beal Rd., Ilf. 125 EN61
Beale Clo. N13 99 DP50
Beale Pl. E3 143 DZ68
Beale Rd. E3 143 DZ67
Beales La., Wey. 194 BN104
Beales Rd., Lthd. 246 CB127
Bealings Way, Beac. 89 AK50
Beam Ave., Dag. 147 FB67
Beam Way, Dag. 147 FD66
Beaminster Gdns., Ilf. 103 EP54
Beamish Clo., Epp. 71 FC25
Beamish Dr. (Bushey), Wat. 94 CC46
Beamish Rd. N9 100 DU46
Beamish Rd., Orp. 206 EW101
Bean La., Dart. 189 FV89
Bean Rd., Bexh. 166 EX84
Bean Rd., Green. 189 FV85
Beanacre Clo. E9 143 DZ65
Beane Rd., Hert. 31 DP09
Beanshaw SE9 185 EN91
Beansland Gro., Rom. 104 EY54
Bear All. EC4 274 F8
Bear Clo., Rom. 127 FB58
Bear Gdns. SE1 279 H2
Bear Gdns. SE1 142 DQ74
Bear La. SE1 278 G2
Bear La. SE1 141 DP74
Bear Rd., Felt. 176 BX92
Bear St. WC2 273 N10
Beard Rd., Kings.T. 178 CM92
Beardell St. SE19 182 DT93
Beardow Gro. N14 81 DJ44
Beard's Hill, Hmptn. 196 CA95
Beard's Hill Clo., Hmptn. 196 CA95
Beard's Hill
Beards Rd., Ashf. 175 BS93
Beardsfield E13 144 EG67
Valetta Gro.
Beardsley Ter., Dag. 126 EV64
Fitzstephen Rd.
Beardsley Way W3 158 CR75
Bearfield Rd., Kings.T. 178 CL94
Bearing Clo., Chig. 104 EU49
Bearing Way, Chig. 104 EU49
Bears Den, Tad. 233 CZ122
Bearstead Ri. SE4 183 DZ85
Bearstead Ter., Beck. 203 EA95
Copers Cope Rd.
Bearswood End, Beac. 89 AL51
Bearwood Clo., Add. 212 BG107
Ongar Pl.
Bearwood Clo., Pot.B. 64 DD31
Beasley's Ait La., Sun. 195 BT100
Beasleys Yd., Uxb. 134 BJ66
Warwick Pl.
Beaton Clo., Green. 169 FV84
Beatrice Ave. SW16 201 DM97
Beatrice Ave., Wem. 118 CL64
Beatrice Clo. E13 144 EG70
Chargeable La.
Beatrice Clo., Pnr. 115 BU56
Reid Clo.
Beatrice Ct., Buck.H. 102 EK47
Beatrice Gdns., Grav. 190 GE89
Beatrice Pl. W8 160 DB76
Beatrice Rd. E17 123 EA57
Beatrice Rd. N4 121 DN59
Beatrice Rd. N9 100 DW45
Beatrice Rd. SE1 162 DU77
Beatrice Rd., Oxt. 254 EE129
Beatrice Rd., Rich. 178 CM85
Albert Rd.
Beatrice Rd., Sthl. 136 BZ74
Beatson Wk. SE16 143 DY74
Beattie Clo., Lthd. 230 BZ124

Beattock Ri. N10 121 DH56
Beatty Ave., Guil. 243 BA133
Beatty Rd. N16 122 DS63
Beatty Rd., Stan. 95 CJ51
Beatty Rd., Wal.Cr. 67 DZ34
Beatty St. NW1 141 DJ68
Beattyville Gdns., Ilf. 125 EN55
Beauchamp Clo. W4 158 CQ76
Church Path
Beauchamp Ct., Stan. 95 CJ50
Hardwick Clo.
Beauchamp Gdns., Rick. 92 BG46
Beauchamp Pl. SW3 276 C6
Beauchamp Pl. SW3 160 DE76
Beauchamp Rd. E7 144 EH66
Beauchamp Rd. SE19 202 DR95
Beauchamp Rd. SW11 160 DE84
Beauchamp Rd., E.Mol. 196 CB99
Beauchamp Rd., Sutt. 218 DA106
Beauchamp Rd., Twick. 177 CG87
Beauchamp Rd., W.Mol. 196 CB99
Beauchamp St. EC1 274 D7
Beauchamp Ter. SW15 159 CV83
Dryburgh Rd.
Beauclare Clo., Lthd. 231 CK121
Hatherwood
Beauclerc Rd. W6 159 CV76
Beauclerk Clo., Felt. 175 BV88
Florence Rd.
Beaudesert Ms., West Dr. 154 BL75
Beaufort E6 145 EN71
Newark Knok
Beaufort Ave., Har. 117 CG56
Beaufort Clo. E4 101 EB51
Higham Sta. Ave.
Beaufort Clo. SW15 179 CV87
Beaufort Clo. W5 138 CM71
Beaufort Clo., Epp. 70 FA26
Beaufort Clo., Grays 170 FZ76
Clifford Rd.
Beaufort Clo., Reig. 249 CZ133
Beaufort Clo., Rom. 127 FC56
Beaufort Clo., Wok. 227 BC116
Beaufort Ct., Rich. 177 CJ91
Beaufort Rd.
Beaufort Dr. NW11 120 DA56
Beaufort Gdns. NW4 119 CW58
Beaufort Gdns. SW3 276 C6
Beaufort Gdns. SW3 160 DE76
Beaufort Gdns. SW16 181 DM94
Beaufort Gdns., Houns. 156 BY81
Beaufort Gdns., Ilf. 125 EN60
Beaufort Ms. SW6 159 CZ79
Lillie Rd.
Beaufort Pk. NW11 120 DA56
Beaufort Pl., Maid. 150 AD75
Beaufort Rd. W5 138 CM71
Beaufort Rd., Kings.T. 198 CL98
Beaufort Rd., Reig. 249 CZ133
Beaufort Rd., Rich. 177 CJ91
Beaufort Rd., Ruis. 115 BR61
Lysander Rd.
Beaufort Rd., Twick. 177 CJ87
Beaufort Rd., Wok. 227 BC116
Beaufort St. SW3 160 DD79
Beaufort Way, Epsom 217 CU108
Beauforts, Egh. 172 AW92
Beaufoy Rd. N17 100 DS52
Beaufoy Wk. SE11 278 C9
Beaufoy Wk. SE11 161 DM77
Beaulieu Ave. E16 144 EH74
Beaulieu Ave. SE26 182 DV91
Beaulieu Clo. NW9 118 CS56
Beaulieu Clo. SE5 162 DR83
Beaulieu Clo., Houns. 176 BZ85
Beaulieu Clo., Mitch. 200 DG95
Beaulieu Clo., Slou. 152 AV81
Beaulieu Clo., Twick. 177 CK86
Beaulieu Clo., Wat. 94 BW46
Beaulieu Dr., Pnr. 116 BX58
Beaulieu Dr., Wal.Abb. 67 EB32
Beaulieu Gdns. N21 100 DQ45
Beaulieu Pl. W4 158 CQ76
Rothschild Rd.
Beauly Way, Rom. 105 FE53
Beaumanor Gdns. SE9 185 EN91
Beaumaris Dr., Wdf.Grn. 102 EK52
Beaumayes Clo., Hem.H. 40 BH21
Beaumont Ave. W14 159 CZ78
Beaumont Ave., Har. 116 CB58
Beaumont Ave., Rich. 158 CM83
Beaumont Ave., St.Alb. 43 CH18
Beaumont Ave., Wem. 117 CJ64
Beaumont Clo., Kings.T. 178 CN94
Beaumont Clo., Rom. 106 FJ54
Beaumont Cres. W14 159 CZ78
Beaumont Cres., Rain. 147 FG65
Beaumont Dr., Ashf. 175 BR92
Beaumont Dr., Grav. 190 GE87
Beaumont Dr., St.Alb. 43 CE18
Beaumont Gdns. NW3 120 DA62
Beaumont Gdns., Brwd. 109 GC44
Bannister Dr.
Beaumont Gate, Rad. 77 CH35
Shenley Hill
Beaumont Gro. E1 143 DX70
Beaumont Ms. W1 272 G6
Beaumont Pk. Dr., Harl. 50 EH15
Beaumont Pl. W1 273 L4
Beaumont Pl. W1 141 DJ70
Beaumont Pl., Barn. 79 CZ39
Beaumont Pl., Islw. 177 CF85
Beaumont Ri. N19 121 DK60
Beaumont Rd. E10 123 EB59
Beaumont Rd. E13 144 EH69
Beaumont Rd. SE19 182 DQ93
Beaumont Rd. SW19 179 CY87
Beaumont Rd. W4 158 CQ76
Beaumont Rd., Brox. 48 DR24
Beaumont Rd., Orp. 205 ER100
Beaumont Rd., Pur. 219 DN113
Beaumont Rd., Slou. 131 AR70
Beaumont Rd., Wind. 151 AQ82
Beaumont Sq. E1 143 DX70
Beaumont St. W1 272 G6
Beaumont St. W1 140 DG71
Beaumont Vw. (Cheshunt), Wal.Cr. 66 DR26
Beaumont Wk. NW3 140 DF66
Beaumonts, Red. 266 DF142
Beauvais Ter., Nthlt. 136 BX69
Beauval Rd. SE22 182 DT86
Beaver Clo. SE20 182 DU94
Lullington Rd.
Beaver Clo., Hmptn. 196 CB95
Beaver Gro., Nthlt. 136 BY69
Jetstar Way
Beaver Rd., Ilf. 104 EW50
Beaverbank Rd. SE9 185 ER88
Beavers Clo., Guil. 242 AS133
Beavers Cres., Houns. 156 BW84
Beavers La., Houns. 156 BW83
Beavers La. Camp, Houns. 156 BW83
Beavers La.
Beaverwood Rd., Chis. 185 ES93
Beavor Gro. W6 159 CU77
Beavor La.
Beavor La. W6 159 CU77
Bebbington Rd. SE18 165 ES77
Bebletts Clo., Orp. 223 ET106
Bec Clo., Ruis. 116 BX62
Beccles Dr., Bark. 145 ES65
Beccles St. E14 143 DZ73
Beck Clo. SE13 163 EB81
Beck Ct., Beck. 203 DX97
Beck La., Beck. 203 DX97
Beck River Pk., Beck. 203 EA95
Rectory Rd.
Beck Rd. E8 142 DV67
Beck Way, Beck. 203 DZ97
Beckenham Business Cen., Beck. 183 DY93
Beckenham Gdns. N9 100 DS48
Beckenham Gro., Brom. 203 ED96
Beckenham Hill Rd. SE6 183 EB92
Beckenham Hill Rd., Beck. 183 EB92
Beckenham La., Brom. 204 EE96
Beckenham Pl. Pk., Beck. 183 EB94
Beckenham Rd., Beck. 203 DX95
Beckenham Rd., W.Wick. 203 EB101
Beckenshaw Gdns., Bans. 234 DD115
Beckers, The N16 122 DU62
Rectory Rd.
Becket Ave. E6 145 EN69
Becket Clo. SE25 202 DU100
Becket Clo., Brwd. 107 FW51
Becket Fold, Har. 117 CF57
Courtfield Cres.
Becket Rd. N18 100 DW49
Becket St. SE1 279 K6
Beckets Sq., Berk. 38 AU17
Bridle Way
Beckett Ave., Ken. 235 DP115
Beckett Clo. NW10 138 CR65
Beckett Clo. SW16 181 DK89
Beckett Clo., Belv. 166 EY76
Tunstock Way
Beckett Wk., Beck. 183 DY93
Becketts, Hert. 31 DN10
Becketts Ave., St.Alb. 42 CC17
Becketts Clo., Felt. 175 BV86
Becketts Clo., Orp. 205 ET104
Becketts Pl., Kings.T. 197 CK95
Beckford Dr., Orp. 205 ER101
Beckford Pl. SE17 162 DQ78
Walworth Rd.
Beckford Rd., Croy. 202 DT100
Beckingham Rd., Guil. 242 AU133
Beckings Way, H.Wyc. 110 AC56
Becklow Gdns. W12 159 CU75
Becklow Rd.
Becklow Ms. W12 159 CT75
Becklow Rd.
Becklow Rd. W12 159 CU75
Beckman Clo., Sev. 241 FC115
Becks Rd., Sid. 186 EU90
Beckton Pk. Roundabout E16 145 EM73
Royal Albert Way
Beckton Rd. E16 144 EF71
Beckway Rd. SW16 201 DK96
Beckway St. SE17 279 L9
Beckway St. SE17 162 DR77
Beckwith Rd. SE24 182 DR86
Beclands Rd. SW17 180 DG93
Becmead Ave. SW16 181 DK91
Becmead Ave., Har. 117 CH57
Becondale Rd. SE19 182 DS92
Becontree Ave., Dag. 126 EV63
Bective Pl. SW15 159 CZ84
Bective Rd.
Bective Rd. E7 124 EG63
Bective Rd. SW15 159 CZ84
Becton Pl., Erith 167 FB80
Bedale Rd., Enf. 82 DQ38
Bedale Rd., Rom. 106 FN50
Bedale St. SE1 279 K3
Bedale St. SE1 142 DR74
Bedale Wk., Dart. 188 FP88
Princes Ave.
Beddington Cross, Croy. 201 DL101
Beddington Fm. Rd.
Beddington Fm. Rd., Croy. 201 DL102
Beddington Gdns., Cars. 218 DG107
Beddington Gdns., Wall. 219 DH107
Beddington Grn., Orp. 205 ET95
Beddington Gro., Wall. 219 DK106
Beddington La., Croy. 201 DJ99
Beddington Path, Orp. 205 ET95
Beddington Rd., Ilf. 125 ET59
Beddington Rd., Orp. 205 ES96
Beddington Trd. Pk. W., Croy. 201 DL102
Beddlestead La., Warl. 238 EF117
Bede Clo., Pnr. 94 BX53
Bede Rd., Rom. 126 EW58
Bedenham Way SE15 162 DT80
Daniel Gdns.
Bedens Rd., Sid. 186 EY93
Bedfont Clo., Felt. 175 BQ86
Bedfont Clo., Mitch. 200 DG96
Bedfont Ct., Stai. 154 BH84
Bedfont Ct. Est., Stai. 154 BG83
Bedfont Grn. Clo., Felt. 175 BQ88
Bedfont La., Felt. 175 BS87
Bedfont Rd., Felt. 175 BQ88
Bedfont Rd., Stai. 174 BL86
Bedford Ave. WC1 273 N7
Bedford Ave. WC1 141 DK71
Bedford Ave., Amer. 72 AW39
Bedford Ave., Barn. 79 CZ43
Bedford Ave., Hayes 135 BV72
Bedford Ave., Slou. 131 AM72
Bedford Clo. N10 98 DG52
Bedford Clo. W4 158 CS79
Bedford Clo., Rick. 73 BB38
Bedford Clo., Wok. 226 AW115
Bedford Cor. W4 158 CS77
The Ave.
Bedford Ct. WC2 277 P1
Bedford Cres., Enf. 83 DY35
Bedford Dr., Slou. 111 AP64
Bedford Gdns. W8 140 DA74
Bedford Gdns., Horn. 128 FJ61
Bedford Hill SW12 181 DH88
Bedford Hill SW16 181 DH88
Bedford Ho. SW4 161 DK84
Bedford Ms. N2 120 DE55
Bedford Rd.
Bedford Pk., Croy. 202 DQ102
Bedford Pk. Cor. W4 158 CS77
Bath Rd.
Bedford Pk. Rd., St.Alb. 43 CE20
Bedford Pas. SW6 159 CY80
Dawes Rd.
Bedford Pl. W1 273 L6
Bedford Pl. WC1 273 P6
Bedford Pl. WC1 141 DL71
Bedford Pl., Croy. 202 DR102
Bedford Rd. E6 145 EN67
Bedford Rd. E17 101 EA54
Bedford Rd. E18 102 EG54
Bedford Rd. N2 120 DE55
Bedford Rd. N8 121 DK58
Bedford Rd. N9 100 DV45
Bedford Rd. N15 122 DS56
Bedford Rd. N22 99 DL53
Bedford Rd. NW7 96 CS48
Bedford Rd. SW4 161 DL83
Bedford Rd. W4 158 CR76
Bedford Rd. W13 137 CH73
Bedford Rd., Dart. 188 FN87
Bedford Rd., Grav. 191 GF89
Bedford Rd., Grays 170 GB78
Bedford Rd., Guil. 258 AW135
Bedford Rd., Har. 116 CC58
Bedford Rd., Ilf. 125 EP62
Bedford Rd., Nthwd. 93 BQ48
Bedford Rd., Orp. 206 EV103
Bedford Rd., Ruis. 115 BT63
Bedford Rd., St.Alb. 43 CE21
Bedford Rd., Sid. 185 ES90
Bedford Rd., Twick. 177 CD90
Bedford Rd., Wor.Pk. 199 CW103
Bedford Row WC1 274 C6
Bedford Row WC1 141 DM71
Bedford Sq. WC1 273 N7
Bedford Sq. WC1 141 DK71
Bedford St. WC2 273 P10
Bedford St. WC2 141 DL73
Bedford St., Berk. 38 AX19
Bedford St., Wat. 75 BV39
Bedford Ter. SW2 181 DL85
Lyham Rd.
Bedford Way WC1 273 N5
Bedford Way WC1 141 DK70
Bedfordbury WC2 273 P10
Bedgebury Gdns. SW19 179 CY89
Bedgebury Rd. SE9 164 EK84
Bedivere Rd., Brom. 184 EG90
Bedlow Way, Croy. 219 DM105
Bedmond La., Abb.L. 59 BV25
Bedmond La., St.Alb. 42 BZ22
Bedmond La. (Potters Crouch), St.Alb. 42 BW24
Bedmond Rd., Abb.L. 59 BT29
Bedmond Rd., Hem.H. 41 BQ21
Bedonwell Rd. SE2 166 EY79
Bedonwell Rd., Belv. 166 FA79
Bedonwell Rd., Bexh. 166 FA79
Bedser Clo. SE11 161 DM79
Harleyford Rd.
Bedser Clo., Th.Hth. 202 DQ97
Bedser Dr., Grnf. 117 CD64
Bedster Gdns., W.Mol. 196 CB96
Bedwardine Rd. SE19 182 DS94
Bedwell Ave., Hat. 46 DG18
Bedwell Ave., Hert. 46 DG17
Bedwell Clo., Welw.G.C. 29 CY10
Bedwell Gdns., Hayes 155 BS78
Bedwell Rd. N17 100 DS53
Bedwell Rd., Belv. 166 FA78
Bedwin Way SE16 162 DV78
Catlin St.
Beeby Rd. E16 144 EH71
Beech Ave. N20 98 DE46
Beech Ave. W3 138 CS74
Beech Ave., Brent. 157 CH80
Beech Ave., Brwd. 109 FZ48
Beech Ave., Buck.H. 102 EH47
Beech Ave., Enf. 81 DN35
Beech Ave., Lthd. 246 BX128
Beech Ave., Rad. 61 CG33
Beech Ave., Ruis. 115 BV60
Beech Ave., Sid. 186 EU87
Beech Ave., S.Croy. 220 DR111
Beech Ave., Swan. 207 FF98
Beech Ave., Upmin. 128 FP62
Beech Ave., West. 238 EK119
Westmore Rd.
Beech Bottom, St.Alb. 43 CD17
Beech Clo. N9 82 DU44
Beech Clo. SE8 163 DZ79
Clyde St.
Beech Clo. SW15 179 CU87
Beech Clo. SW19 179 CW93
Beech Clo., Ashf. 175 BR92
Beech Clo., Cars. 200 DF103
Beech Clo., Cob. 214 CA112
Beech Clo., Dor. 263 CG135
Beech Clo., Hat. 45 CU19
Beech Clo., Horn. 127 FH62
Beech Clo., Lthd. 246 BX128
Beech Clo., Loug. 85 EP40
Cedar Dr.
Beech Clo., Stai. 174 BK87
St. Marys Cres.
Beech Clo., Sun. 196 BX96
Harfield Rd.
Beech Clo., Walt. 214 BW105
Beech Clo., Ware 33 DX08
Beech Clo., W.Byf. 212 BL112
Beech Clo., West Dr. 154 BN76
Beech Clo. Ct., Cob. 214 BZ111
Beech Copse, Brom. 205 EM96
Beech Copse, S.Croy. 220 DS106
Beech Ct. E17 123 ED55
Beech Ct. SE9 184 EL86
Beech Ct., Ilf. 125 EN62
Riverdene Rd.
Beech Ct., Surb. 198 CL101
Beech Cres., Tad. 248 CQ130
Beech Dell, Kes. 223 EM105
Beech Dr. N2 120 DF55
Beech Dr., Berk. 38 AW20
Beech Dr., Borwd. 78 CM40
Beech Dr., Reig. 250 DD134
Beech Dr., Saw. 36 EW07
Beech Dr., Tad. 233 CZ122
Beech Dr., Wok. 228 BG124
Beech Fm. Rd., Warl. 237 EC120
Beech Gdns. EC2 142 DQ71
Aldersgate St.
Beech Gdns. W5 158 CL75
Beech Gdns., Dag. 147 FB66
Beech Gdns., Wok. 226 AY115
Beech Gro., Add. 212 BH105
Beech Gro., Amer. 55 AQ39
Beech Gro., Cat. 252 DS126
Beech Gro., Croy. 221 DY110
Beech Gro., Epsom 233 CV117
Beech Gro., Guil. 242 AT134
Beech Gro., Ilf. 103 ES51
Beech Gro., Lthd. 246 CA127
Beech Gro., Mitch. 201 DK98
Beech Gro., N.Mal. 198 CR97
Beech Gro., S.Ock. 148 FQ74
Beech Gro., Wok. 226 AX123
Beech Hall Cres. E4 101 ED52
Beech Hall Rd. E4 101 EC52
Beech Hill, Barn. 80 DD38
Beech Hill, Wok. 226 AX123
Beech Hill Ave., Barn. 80 DC39
Beech Hill Ct., Berk. 38 AX18
Beech Hill Gdns., Wal.Abb. 84 EH37
Beech Holt, Lthd. 231 CJ122
Beech Ho., Croy. 221 EB107
Beech Ho. Rd., Croy. 202 DR104
Beech Hyde La., St.Alb. 28 CM07
Beech La., Beac. 90 AS52
Beech La., Buck.H. 102 EH47
Beech La., Guil. 258 AW137
Beech Lawn, Guil. 259 AZ135
Beech Lawns N12 98 DD50
Beech Lo., Stai. 173 BE92
Beech Pk., Amer. 72 AV39
Beech Pl., Epp. 69 ET31
Beech Pl., St.Alb. 43 CD17
Beech Rd. N11 99 DL51
Beech Rd. SW16 201 DL96
Beech Rd., Dart. 188 FK88
Beech Rd., Epsom 233 CT115
Beech Rd., Felt. 175 BS87
Beech Rd., Orp. 224 EU108
Beech Rd., Red. 251 DJ126
Beech Rd., Reig. 250 DA131
Beech Rd., St.Alb. 43 CE17
Beech Rd., Sev. 257 FH125
Victoria Rd.
Beech Rd., Slou. 152 AY75
Beech Rd., Wat. 75 BU37
Beech Rd., West. 238 EH118
Beech Rd., Wey. 213 BR105
Beech Row, Rich. 178 CL91
Beech St. EC2 275 H6
Beech St. EC2 142 DQ71
Beech St., Rom. 127 FC56
Beech Tree Clo., Stan. 95 CJ50
Beech Tree Glade E4 102 EF46
Forest Side
Beech Tree Pl., Sutt. 218 DB106
St. Nicholas Way
Beech Wk. NW7 96 CS51
Beech Wk., Dart. 167 FG84
Beech Wk., Epsom 217 CU111
Beech Wk., Hodd. 49 DZ17
Beech Way NW10 138 CR66
Beech Way, Epsom 233 CT115
Beech Way, S.Croy. 221 DX113
Beech Way, Twick. 176 CA90
Beech Waye, Ger.Cr. 113 AZ59
Beechall, Cher. 211 BC108
Beechcroft, Ash. 232 CM119
Beechcroft, Chis. 185 EN94
Beechcroft Ave. NW11 119 CZ59
Beechcroft Ave., Bexh. 167 FD81
Beechcroft Ave., Har. 116 CA59
Beechcroft Ave., Ken. 236 DR115
Beechcroft Ave., N.Mal. 198 CQ95
Beechcroft Ave., Rick. 75 BQ44
Beechcroft Ave., Sthl. 136 BZ74
Beechcroft Clo., Houns. 156 BY80
Beechcroft Clo., Orp. 223 ER105
Beechcroft Gdns., Wem. 118 CM62
Beechcroft Manor, Wey. 195 BR104
Beechcroft Rd. E18 102 EH54
Beechcroft Rd. SW14 158 CQ83
Elm Rd.
Beechcroft Rd. SW17 180 DE89
Beechcroft Rd., Chesh. 54 AN30
Beechcroft Rd., Chess. 198 CM104
Beechcroft Rd., Orp. 223 ER105
Beechcroft Rd. (Bushey), Wat. 76 BY43
Beechdale N21 99 DM47
Beechdale Rd. SW2 181 DM86
Beechdene, Tad. 233 CV122
Beechen Cliff Way, Islw. 157 CF81
Henley Clo.
Beechen Gro., Pnr. 116 BZ55
Beechen Gro., Wat. 76 BW42
Beechen La., Tad. 249 CZ125
Beechenlea La., Swan. 207 FG98
Beeches, The, Amer. 55 AN36
Woodfield Pk.
Beeches, The, Bans. 234 DB116
Beeches, The, Beac. 88 AH54
Beeches, The, Brwd. 108 FV48
Beeches, The, Guil. 259 AZ134
Beeches, The, Houns. 156 CB81
Beeches, The, Lthd. 231 CE124
Beeches, The, Rick. 73 BF43
Beeches, The, St.Alb. 61 CE27
Beeches, The, Til. 171 GH82
Beeches Ave., Cars. 218 DE108
Beeches Clo. SE20 202 DW95
Genoa Rd.
Beeches Clo., Tad. 234 DA123
Beeches Ct., Brom. 184 EG93
Avondale Rd.
Beeches Dr., Slou. 111 AP63
Beeches Pk., Beac. 89 AK53
Beeches Rd. SW17 180 DE90
Beeches Rd., Slou. 111 AP64
Beeches Rd., Sutt. 199 CY102
Beeches Wk., Cars. 218 DD109
Beeches Way, B.End 110 AD61
Harvest Hill
Beeches Wd., Tad. 234 DA122
Beechfield, Bans. 218 DB113
Beechfield, Hodd. 33 EA13
Beechfield, Kings L. 58 BM30
Beechfield, Saw. 36 EZ05
Beechfield Cotts., Brom. 204 EJ96
Widmore Rd.
Beechfield Gdns., Rom. 127 FC59
Beechfield Rd. N4 122 DQ58
Beechfield Rd. SE6 183 DZ88
Beechfield Rd., Brom. 204 EJ96
Beechfield Rd., Erith 167 FE80
Beechfield Rd., Hem.H. 40 BH21
Beechfield Rd., Ware 33 DZ05
Beechfield Rd., Welw.G.C. 29 CY10
Beechfield Wk., Wal.Abb. 83 ED35
Beechhill Rd. SE9 185 EN85
Beechmeads, Cob. 214 BX113
Beechmont Ave., Vir.W. 192 AX99
Beechmont Clo., Brom. 184 EE92
Beechmont Rd., Sev. 257 FH129
Beechmore Gdns., Sutt. 199 CX103
Beechmore Rd. SW11 160 DF81
Beechmount Ave. W7 137 CD71
Beecholm Ms., Wal.Cr. 67 DX28
Beecholme, Bans. 217 CY114
Beecholme Ave., Mitch. 201 DH95
Beecholme Est. E5 122 DV62
Prout Rd.
Beechpark Way, Wat. 75 BS37
Beechtree Ave., Egh. 172 AV93
Beechvale Clo. N12 98 DE50
Beechway, Bex. 186 EX86
Beechway, Guil. 243 BB133
Beechwood Ave. N3 119 CZ55
Beechwood Ave., Amer. 72 AW38
Beechwood Ave., Couls. 235 DH115
Beechwood Ave., Grnf. 136 CB69
Beechwood Ave., Har. 116 CB62
Beechwood Ave., Hayes 135 BR73
Beechwood Ave., Orp. 223 ES106
Beechwood Ave., Pot.B. 64 DB33
Beechwood Ave., Rich. 158 CN81
Beechwood Ave., Rick. 73 BB42
Beechwood Ave., Ruis. 115 BT61
Beechwood Ave., St.Alb. 43 CH18
Beechwood Ave., Stai. 174 BH93
Beechwood Ave., Sun. 175 BU93
Beechwood Ave., Tad. 234 DA121
Beechwood Ave., Th.Hth. 201 DP98
Beechwood Ave., Uxb. 134 BN72
Beechwood Ave., Wey. 213 BS105
Beechwood Circle, Har. 116 CB62
Beechwood Gdns.
Beechwood Clo. NW7 96 CR50
Beechwood Clo., Amer. 72 AW39
Beechwood Clo., Hert. 32 DT09
Beechwood Clo., Surb. 197 CK101
Beechwood Clo. (Cheshunt), Wal.Cr. 66 DS26
Beechwood Clo., Wey. 213 BS105
Beechwood Clo., Wok. 226 AS117
Beechwood Ct., Cars. 218 DF105
Beechwood Ct., Sun. 175 BU93
Beechwood Cres., Bexh. 166 EX83
Beechwood Dr., Cob. 214 CA111
Beechwood Dr., Kes. 222 EK105
Beechwood Dr., Wdf.Grn. 102 EF50
Beechwood Gdns. NW10 138 CM69
St. Annes Gdns.
Beechwood Gdns., Cat. 236 DU122
Beechwood Gdns., Har. 116 CB62
Beechwood Gdns., Ilf. 125 EM57
Beechwood Gdns., Rain. 147 FH71
Beechwood Gdns., Slou. 152 AS75
Beechwood Gro. W3 138 CS73
East Acton La.
Beechwood Gro., Surb. 197 CJ101
Beechwood La., Warl. 237 DX119
Beechwood Manor, Wey. 213 BS105
Beechwood Ms. N9 100 DU47
Beechwood Pk. E18 124 EG55
Beechwood Pk., Hem.H. 39 BF24
Beechwood Pk., Lthd. 231 CJ123
Beechwood Ri., Chis. 185 EP91
Beechwood Ri., Wat. 75 BV36
Beechwood Rd. E8 142 DT65
Beechwood Rd. N8 121 DK56
Beechwood Rd., Beac. 88 AJ53
Beechwood Rd., Cat. 236 DU122
Beechwood Rd., Slou. 131 AR71
Beechwood Rd., S.Croy. 220 DS109
Beechwood Rd., Vir.W. 192 AU101
Beechwood Rd., Wok. 226 AS117
Beechwood Vil., Red. 266 DG144
Beechwoods Ct. SE19 182 DT92
Crystal Palace Par.
Beechworth Clo. NW3 120 DA61
Beecot La., Walt. 196 BW103
Beecroft Rd. SE4 183 DY85
Beehive Clo. E8 142 DT66
Beehive Clo., Borwd. 77 CK44
Beehive Clo., Uxb. 134 BM66
Honey Hill
Beehive Grn., Welw.G.C. 30 DA11
Beehive La., Ilf. 125 EM58
Beehive La., Welw.G.C. 30 DA12
Beehive Pas. EC3 275 M9
Beehive Pl. SW9 161 DN83
Beehive Rd., Stai. 173 BF92
Beehive Rd. (Cheshunt), Wal.Cr. 65 DP28
Beehive Way, Reig. 266 DB138
Beeken Dene, Orp. 223 EQ105
Isabella Dr.
Beel Clo., Amer. 72 AW39
Beeleigh Rd., Mord. 200 DB98
Beesfield La. (Farningham), Dart. 208 FN101
Beeston Clo. E8 122 DU64
Ferncliff Rd.
Beeston Clo., Wat. 94 BX49
Beeston Dr., Wal.Cr. 67 DX27
Beeston Pl. SW1 277 J7
Beeston Pl. SW1 161 DH76
Beeston Rd., Barn. 80 DD44
Beeston Way, Felt. 176 BW86
Beethoven Rd., Borwd. 77 CK44
Beethoven St. W10 139 CY69
Beeton Clo., Pnr. 94 CA52
Begbie Rd. SE3 164 EJ81
Beggars Bush La., Wat. 75 BR43
Beggars Hill, Epsom 217 CT108
Beggars Hollow, Enf. 82 DR37
Beggars La., Dor. 261 BS139
Beggars La., West. 255 ER125
Beggars Roost La., Sutt. 218 DA107
Begonia Clo. E6 144 EL71
Begonia Pl., Hmptn. 176 CA93
Gresham Rd.
Begonia Wk. W12 139 CT72
Du Cane Rd.
Beira St. SW12 181 DH87
Beken Ct., Wat. 76 BW35
Bekesbourne St. E14 143 DY72
Ratcliffe La.
Bekesbourne Twr., Orp. 206 EX102
Belcher Rd., Hodd. 49 EA16
Amwell St.
Belchers La., Wal.Abb. 50 EJ24
Belcroft Clo., Brom. 184 EF94
Hope Pk.

Beldam Haw, Sev. 224 FA112
Beldham Gdns., W.Mol. 196 CB97
Belfairs Dr., Rom. 126 EW59
Belfairs Grn., Wat. 94 BX50
Heysham Dr.
Belfast Ave., Slou. 131 AQ72
Belfast Rd. N16 122 DT61
Belfast Rd. SE25 202 DV98
Belfield Gdns., Harl. 52 EW16
Belfield Rd., Epsom 216 CR109
Belfont Wk. N7 121 DL63
Belford Gro. SE18 165 EN77
Belford Rd., Borwd. 78 CM38
Belfort Rd. SE15 162 DW82
Belfry Ave. (Harefield), Uxb. 92 BG53
Belfry Clo. SE16 162 DV78
Masters Dr.
Belfry La., Rick. 92 BJ46
Belgrade Rd. N16 122 DS63
Belgrade Rd., Hmptn. 196 CB95
Belgrave Ave., Rom. 128 FJ55
Belgrave Ave., Wat. 75 BT43
Belgrave Clo. N14 81 DJ43
Prince George Ave.
Belgrave Clo. NW7 96 CR50
Belgrave Clo. W3 158 CQ75
Avenue Rd.
Belgrave Clo., Orp. 206 EW98
Belgrave Clo., St.Alb. 43 CJ16
Belgrave Clo., Walt. 213 BV105
Belgrave Cres., Sun. 195 BV95
Belgrave Dr., Kings L. 59 BQ28
Belgrave Gdns. N14 81 DK43
Belgrave Gdns. NW8 140 DB67
Belgrave Gdns., Stan. 95 CJ50
Copley Rd.
Belgrave Manor, Wok. 226 AY119
Belgrave Ms., Uxb. 134 BK70
Belgrave Ms. N. SW1 276 F5
Belgrave Ms. N. SW1 160 DG76
Belgrave Ms. S. SW1 276 G6
Belgrave Ms. S. SW1 160 DG76
Belgrave Ms. W. SW1 276 F6
Belgrave Ms. W. SW1 160 DG76
Belgrave Pl. SW1 276 G6
Belgrave Pl. SW1 160 DG76
Belgrave Pl., Slou. 152 AV75
Clifton Rd.
Belgrave Rd. E10 123 EC60
Belgrave Rd. E11 124 EG61
Belgrave Rd. E13 144 EJ70
Belgrave Rd. E17 123 EA57
Belgrave Rd. SE25 202 DT98
Belgrave Rd. SW1 277 K9
Belgrave Rd. SW1 161 DH77
Belgrave Rd. SW13 159 CT80
Belgrave Rd., Houns. 156 BZ83
Belgrave Rd., Ilf. 125 EM60
Belgrave Rd., Mitch. 200 DD97
Belgrave Rd., Slou. 132 AS73
Belgrave Rd., Sun. 195 BV95
Belgrave Sq. SW1 276 F6
Belgrave Sq. SW1 160 DG76
Belgrave St. E1 143 DX72
Belgrave Ter., Wdf.Grn. 102 EG48
Belgrave Wk., Mitch. 200 DD97
Belgrave Yd. SW1 277 H7
Belgravia Clo., Barn. 79 CZ41
Belgravia Gdns., Brom. 184 EE93
Belgravia Ho. SW4 181 DL86
Belgravia Ms., Kings.T. 197 CK98
Belgrove St. WC1 273 P2
Belgrove St. WC1 141 DL69
Belham Rd., Kings L. 58 BM28
Belham Wk. SE5 162 DR81
D'Eynsford Rd.
Belhaven Ct., Borwd. 78 CM39
Belinda Rd. SW9 161 DP83
Belitha Vil. N1 141 DM66
Bell Ave., Rom. 105 FH53
Bell Ave., West Dr. 154 BM77
Bell Bri. Rd., Cher. 193 BF102
Bell Clo., Abb.L. 59 BT27
Bell Clo., Beac. 89 AM53
Bell Clo., Green. 189 FT85
Bell Clo., Pnr. 116 BW55
Bell Clo., Ruis. 115 BT62
Bell Clo., Slou. 132 AV71
Bell Common, Epp. 69 ES32
Bell Ct., Surb. 198 CP103
Barnsbury La.
Bell Cres., Couls. 235 DH121
Maple Way
Bell Dr. SW18 179 CY87
Bell Fm. Ave., Dag. 127 FC62
Bell Gdns. E17 123 DZ57
Markhouse Rd.
Bell Gdns., Orp. 206 EW99
Bell Grn. SE26 183 DZ90
Bell Grn., Hem.H. 57 BB27
Bell Grn. La. SE26 183 DY92
Bell Hill, Croy. 202 DQ104
Surrey St.
Bell Ho. Rd., Rom. 127 FC60
Bell Inn Yd. EC3 275 L9
Bell La. E1 275 P7
Bell La. E1 142 DT71
Bell La. E16 144 EG74
Bell La. NW4 119 CX56
Bell La., Abb.L. 59 BT27
Bell La., Amer. 72 AV39
Bell La., Berk. 38 AS18
Bell La., Brox. 49 DY21
Bell La., Enf. 83 DX38
Bell La., Hat. 64 DA25
Bell La., Hert. 32 DR09
Bell La., Hodd. 49 EA17
Bell La., Lthd. 231 CD123
Bell La., St.Alb. 62 CL29
Bell La., Twick. 177 CG88
The Embk.
Bell La., Wem. 117 CK61
Magnet Rd.
Bell La. (Eton Wick), Wind. 151 AM77
Bell La. Clo., Lthd. 231 CD123
Bell Mead, Saw. 36 EY05
Bell Meadow SE19 182 DS91
Dulwich Wd. Ave.
Bell Meadow, Gdse. 252 DV132
Hickmans Clo.
Bell Par., Wind. 151 AM82
St. Andrews Ave.
Bell Rd., E.Mol. 197 CD99
Bell Rd., Enf. 82 DR39
Bell Rd., Houns. 156 CB84
Bell St. NW1 272 B6
Bell St. NW1 140 DE71
Bell St., Reig. 250 DA134
Bell St., Saw. 36 EY05
Bell Vw., Wind. 151 AM83
Bell Vw. Clo., Wind. 151 AM82
Bell Wk., Saw. 36 EY05
London Rd.
Bell Water Gate SE18 165 EN76
Bell Weir Clo., Stai. 173 BB89
Bell Wf. La. EC4 275 J10
Bell Wf. La. EC4 142 DQ73
Bell Yd. WC2 274 D8
Bell Yd. WC2 141 DN72
Bellamy Clo. E14 163 EA75
Byng St.
Bellamy Clo. W14 159 CZ78
Aisgill Ave.
Bellamy Clo., Edg. 96 CQ48
Bellamy Clo., Uxb. 114 BN62
Bellamy Clo., Wat. 75 BU39
Bellamy Dr., Stan. 95 CH53
Bellamy Rd. E4 101 EB51
Bellamy Rd., Enf. 82 DR40
Bellamy Rd. (Cheshunt), Wal.Cr. 67 DY29
Bellamy St. SW12 181 DH87
Bellasis Ave. SW2 181 DL89
Bellclose Rd., West Dr. 154 BL75
Belle Vue, Grnf. 137 CD67
Belle Vue Clo., Stai. 194 BG95
Belle Vue Est. NW4 119 CW56
Bell La.
Belle Vue La. (Bushey), Wat. 95 CD46
Belle Vue Pk., Th.Hth. 202 DQ97
Belle Vue Rd. E17 101 ED54
Belle Vue Rd. NW4 119 CW56
Bell La.
Belle Vue Rd., Orp. 223 EN110
Standard Rd.
Belle Vue Rd., Ware 33 DZ06
Bellefield Rd., Orp. 206 EV99
Bellefields Rd. SW9 161 DM83
Bellegrove Clo., Well. 165 ET82
Bellegrove Par., Well. 165 ET83
Bellegrove Rd.
Bellegrove Rd., Well. 165 ER82
Bellenden Rd. SE15 162 DT82
Bellestaines Pleasaunce E4 101 EA47
Belleville Rd. SW11 180 DF85
Bellevue Ms. N11 98 DG50
Bellevue Rd.
Bellevue Par. SW17 180 DE88
Bellevue Rd.
Bellevue Pl. E1 142 DW70
Bellevue Pl., Slou. 152 AT76
Albert St.
Bellevue Rd. N11 98 DG49
Bellevue Rd. SW13 159 CU82
Bellevue Rd. SW17 180 DE88
Bellevue Rd. W13 137 CH70
Bellevue Rd., Bexh. 186 EZ85
Bellevue Rd., Horn. 128 FM60
Bellevue Rd., Kings.T. 198 CL97
Bellevue Rd., Rom. 105 FC51
Bellevue Ter. (Harefield), Uxb. 92 BG52
Bellew St. SW17 180 DC90
Bellfield, Croy. 221 DY109
Bellfield Ave., Har. 95 CD51
Bellfields Ct., Guil. 242 AW130
Oak Tree Dr.
Bellfields Rd., Guil. 242 AX132
Bellflower Clo. E6 144 EL71
Sorrel Gdns.
Bellflower Path, Rom. 106 FJ52
Bellgate, Hem.H. 40 BL17
Bellgate Ms. NW5 121 DH62
York Ri.
Bellhouse La., Brwd. 108 FS43
Bellingdon Rd., Chesh. 54 AP30
Bellingham Ct., Bark. 146 EV69
Renwick Rd.
Bellingham Grn. SE6 183 EA90
Bellingham Rd. SE6 183 EB90
Bellman Ave., Grav. 191 GL88
Bellmarsh Rd., Add. 212 BH105
Bellmount Wd. Ave., Wat. 75 BS39
Bello Clo. SE24 181 DP87
Bellot Gdns. SE10 164 EE78
Bellot St. SE10 164 EE78
Bellring Clo., Belv. 166 FA79
Bells All. SW6 160 DA82
Bells Gdn. Est. SE15 162 DU80
Buller Clo.
Bells Hill, Barn. 79 CX43
Bell's Hill, Slou. 132 AU67
Bells Hill Grn., Slou. 132 AU66
Bells La., Slou. 153 BB83
Bellswood La., Iver 133 BB71
Belltrees Gro. SW16 181 DM92
Bellwether La., Red. 267 DP143
Bellwood Rd. SE15 163 DX84
Belmarsh Rd. SE28 165 ES75
Western Way
Belmont, Slou. 131 AN71
Belmont Ave. N9 100 DU46
Belmont Ave. N13 99 DL50
Belmont Ave. N17 122 DQ55
Belmont Ave., Barn. 80 DF43
Belmont Ave., Guil. 242 AT131
Belmont Ave., N.Mal. 199 CU99
Belmont Ave., Sthl. 156 BY76
Belmont Ave., Upmin. 128 FM61
Belmont Ave., Well. 165 ES83
Belmont Ave., Wem. 138 CM67
Belmont Circle, Har. 95 CH53
Belmont Clo. E4 101 ED50
Belmont Clo. N20 98 DB46
Belmont Clo. SW4 161 DJ83
Belmont Clo., Barn. 80 DF42
Belmont Clo., Uxb. 134 BK65
Belmont Clo., Wdf.Grn. 102 EH49
Belmont Ct. NW11 119 CZ57
Belmont Gro. SE13 163 ED83
Belmont Gro. W4 158 CR77
Belmont Rd.
Belmont Hall Ct. SE13 163 ED83
Belmont Gro.
Belmont Hill SE13 163 ED83
Belmont Hill, St.Alb. 43 CD21
Belmont La., Chis. 185 EQ92
Belmont La., Stan. 95 CJ52
Belmont Ms. SW19 179 CX89
Chapman Sq.
Belmont Pk. SE13 163 ED84
Belmont Pk. Clo. SE13 163 ED84
Belmont Pk.
Belmont Pk. Rd. E10 123 EB58
Belmont Ri., Sutt. 217 CZ109
Belmont Rd. N15 122 DQ56
Belmont Rd. N17 122 DQ56
Belmont Rd. SE25 202 DV99
Belmont Rd. SW4 161 DJ83
Belmont Rd. W4 158 CR77
Belmont Rd., Beck. 203 DZ96
Belmont Rd., Chesh. 54 AP28
Belmont Rd., Chis. 185 EP92
Belmont Rd., Erith 166 FA80
Belmont Rd., Grays 170 FZ78
Belmont Rd., Har. 117 CF55
Belmont Rd., Hem.H. 40 BL24
Belmont Rd., Horn. 128 FK62
Belmont Rd., Ilf. 125 EQ62
Belmont Rd., Lthd. 231 CG122
Belmont Rd., Reig. 266 DC135
Belmont Rd., Sutt. 218 DA110
Belmont Rd., Twick. 177 CD89
Belmont Rd., Uxb. 134 BK66
Belmont Rd., Wall. 219 DH106
Belmont Rd. (Bushey), Wat. 76 BY43
Belmont St. NW1 140 DG66
Belmont Ter. W4 158 CR77
Belmont Rd.
Belmor, Borwd. 78 CN43
Belmore Ave., Hayes 135 BU72
Belmore Ave., Wok. 227 BD116
Belmore La. N7 121 DK64
Belmore St. SW8 161 DK81
Beloe Clo. SW15 159 CU83
Belper Ct. E5 123 DX63
Pedro St.
Belsham St. E9 142 DW65
Belsize Ave. N13 99 DM51
Belsize Ave. NW3 140 DE65
Belsize Ave. W13 157 CH76
Belsize Clo., Hem.H. 40 BN21
Belsize Clo., St.Alb. 43 CJ15
Belsize Ct. NW3 120 DE64
Belsize La.
Belsize Cres. NW3 120 DD64
Belsize Gdns., Sutt. 218 DB105
Belsize Gro. NW3 140 DE65
Belsize La. NW3 140 DD65
Belsize Ms. NW3 140 DD65
Belsize La.
Belsize Pk. NW3 140 DD65
Belsize Pk. Gdns. NW3 140 DE65
Belsize Pk. Ms. NW3 140 DD65
Belsize La.
Belsize Pl. NW3 140 DD65
Belsize La.
Belsize Rd. NW6 140 DC66
Belsize Rd., Har. 95 CD52
Belsize Rd., Hem.H. 40 BN21
Belsize Sq. NW3 140 DD65
Belsize Ter. NW3 140 DD65
Belson Rd. SE18 165 EM77
Belswains Grn., Hem.H. 40 BL23
Belswains La.
Belswains La., Hem.H. 58 BM25
Beltana Dr., Grav. 191 GL91
Beltane Dr. SW19 179 CX90
Belthorn Cres. SW12 181 DJ87
Beltinge Rd., Rom. 128 FM55
Belton Rd. E7 144 EH66
Belton Rd. E11 124 EE63
Belton Rd. N17 122 DS55
Belton Rd. NW2 139 CU65
Belton Rd., Berk. 38 AU18
Belton Rd., Sid. 186 EU91
Belton Way E3 143 EA71
Beltona Gdns. (Cheshunt), Wal.Cr. 67 DX27
Beltran Rd. SW6 160 DB82
Beltwood Rd., Belv. 167 FC77
Belvedere Ave. SW19 179 CY92
Belvedere Ave., Ilf. 103 EP54
Belvedere Bldgs. SE1 278 G5
Belvedere Clo., Esher 214 CB106
Belvedere Clo., Grav. 191 GJ88
Belvedere Clo., Guil. 242 AV132
Belvedere Clo., Tedd. 177 CE92
Belvedere Clo., Wey. 212 BN106
Belvedere Ct. N2 120 DD57
Belvedere Dr. SW19 179 CY92
Belvedere Gdns., St.Alb. 60 CA27
Belvedere Gdns., W.Mol. 196 BZ99
Belvedere Gro. SW19 179 CY92
Belvedere Ho., Felt. 175 BU88
Belvedere Ind. Est., Belv. 167 FC76
Belvedere Ms. SE15 162 DV83
Belvedere Pl. SE1 278 G5
Belvedere Pl. SE1 161 DP75
Belvedere Rd. E10 123 DY60
Belvedere Rd. SE1 278 C4
Belvedere Rd. SE1 141 DM74
Belvedere Rd. SE2 146 EX74
Belvedere Rd. SE19 182 DT94
Belvedere Rd. W7 157 CF76
Belvedere Rd., Bexh. 166 EZ83
Belvedere Rd., Brwd. 108 FT48
Belvedere Rd., West. 239 EM118
Belvedere Sq. SW19 179 CY92
Belvedere Strand NW9 97 CT54
Belvedere Way, Har. 118 CL58
Belvoir Clo. SE9 184 EL90
Belvoir Rd. SE22 182 DU87
Belvue Clo., Nthlt. 136 CA66
Belvue Rd., Nthlt. 136 CA66
Bembridge Clo. NW6 139 CY66
Bembridge Ct., Slou. 152 AT76
Park St.
Bembridge Gdns., Ruis. 115 BR61
Bemerton Est. N1 141 DM66
Bemerton St. N1 141 DM67
Bemish Rd. SW15 159 CX83
Bempton Dr., Ruis. 115 BV61
Bemsted Rd. E17 123 DZ55
Ben Hale Clo., Stan. 95 CH49
Ben Jonson Rd. E1 143 DY71
Ben Smith Way SE16 162 DU76
Jamaica Rd.
Ben Tillet Clo., Bark. 146 EU66
Ben Tillett Clo. E16 145 EM74
Newland St.
Benares Rd. SE18 165 ET77
Benbow Clo., St.Alb. 43 CH22
Benbow Rd. W6 159 CV76
Benbow St. SE8 163 EA79
Benbow Waye, Uxb. 134 BJ71
Benbrick Rd., Guil. 258 AU135
Benbury Clo., Brom. 183 EC92
Bence, The, Egh. 193 BB97
Bench Fld., S.Croy. 220 DT107
Bench Manor Cres., Ger.Cr. 90 AW54
Benchleys Rd., Hem.H. 39 BF21
Bencombe Rd., Pur. 219 DN114
Bencroft (Cheshunt), Wal.Cr. 66 DU26
Bencroft Rd. SW16 181 DJ94
Bencroft Rd., Hem.H. 40 BL20
Bencurtis Pk., W.Wick. 203 ED104
Bendall Ms. NW1 272 C6
Bendemeer Rd. SW15 159 CX83
Bendish Rd. E6 144 EL66
Bendmore Ave. SE2 166 EU78
Bendon Valley SW18 180 DB87
Bendysh Rd. (Bushey), Wat. 76 BY41
Benedict Clo., Belv. 166 EY76
Tunstock Way
Benedict Clo., Orp. 205 ES104
Benedict Dr., Felt. 175 BR87
Benedict Rd. SW9 161 DM83
Benedict Rd., Mitch. 200 DD97
Benedict Way N2 120 DC55
Benedictine Gate, Wal.Cr. 67 DY27
Benen-Stock Rd., Stai. 173 BF85
Benenden Grn., Brom. 204 EG99
Benets Rd., Horn. 128 FN60
Benett Gdns. SW16 201 DL96
Benfleet Clo., Cob. 214 BY112
Benfleet Clo., Sutt. 200 DC104
Benford Rd., Hodd. 49 DZ19
Bengal Ct. EC3 142 DR72
Birchin La.
Bengal Rd., Ilf. 125 EP63
Bengarth Dr., Har. 95 CD54
Bengarth Rd., Nthlt. 136 BX67
Bengeo Meadows, Hert. 32 DR06
Bengeo Ms., Hert. 32 DQ06
Bengeo St.
Bengeo St., Hert. 32 DQ06
Bengeworth Rd. SE5 162 DQ83
Bengeworth Rd., Har. 117 CG61
Benham Clo. SW11 160 DD83
Benham Clo., Chesh. 54 AP29
Benham Clo., Chess. 215 CJ107
Merritt Gdns.
Benham Clo., Couls. 235 DP118
Benham Gdns., Houns. 156 BZ84
Benham Rd. W7 137 CE71
Benhams Clo., Horl. 268 DG146
Benhams Dr., Horl. 268 DG146
Benhams Pl. NW3 120 DC63
Holly Wk.
Benhill Ave., Sutt. 218 DB105
Benhill Rd. SE5 162 DR80
Benhill Rd., Sutt. 200 DC104
Benhill Wd. Rd., Sutt. 200 DC104
Benhilton Gdns., Sutt. 200 DB104
Benhurst Ave., Horn. 127 FH62
Benhurst Clo., S.Croy. 221 DX110
Benhurst Ct. SW16 181 DN92
Benhurst Gdns., S.Croy. 220 DW110
Benhurst La. SW16 181 DN92
Benin St. SE13 183 ED87
Benison Ct., Slou. 152 AT76
Osborne St.
Benjafield Clo. N18 100 DV49
Brettenham Rd.
Benjamin Clo. E8 142 DU67
Benjamin Clo., Horn. 127 FG58
Benjamin St. EC1 274 F6
Benjamin St. EC1 141 DP71
Benledi St. E14 143 ED72
Benn St. E9 143 DY65
Bennerley Rd. SW11 180 DE85
Bennet's Hill EC4 274 G10
Bennetsfield Rd., Uxb. 135 BP74
Bennett Clo., Cob. 213 BU113
Bennett Clo., Kings.T. 197 CJ95
Bennett Clo., Nthwd. 93 BT52
Bennett Clo., Well. 166 EU82
Bennett Clo., Welw.G.C. 29 CZ13
Bennett Gro. SE13 163 EB81
Bennett Pk. SE3 164 EF83
Bennett Rd. E13 144 EJ70
Bennett Rd. N16 122 DS63
Bennett Rd., Rom. 126 EY58
Bennett St. SW1 277 K2
Bennett St. W4 158 CS79
Bennett Way, Dart. 189 FR91
Bennett Way, Guil. 244 BG129
Bennetts, Chesh. 54 AR30
Bennetts Ave., Croy. 203 DY103
Bennetts Ave., Grnf. 137 CE67
Bennetts Castle La., Dag. 126 EW63
Bennetts Clo. N17 100 DT51
Bennetts Clo., Mitch. 201 DH95
Bennetts Clo., St.Alb. 44 CR23
Meadway
Bennetts Clo., Slou. 131 AN74
Bennetts Copse, Chis. 184 EL93
Bennetts End Clo., Hem.H. 40 BM22
Bennetts End Rd., Hem.H. 40 BM21
Bennetts Fm. Pl., Lthd. 246 BZ125
Bennetts Gate, Hem.H. 40 BN23
Bennetts End Rd.
Bennetts Way, Croy. 203 DY103
Bennetts Yd. SW1 277 N7
Bennetts Yd., Uxb. 134 BJ66
High St.
Benning Clo., Wind. 151 AK83
Benningholme Rd., Edg. 96 CS51
Bennington Rd. N17 100 DS53
Bennington Rd., Wdf.Grn. 102 EE52
Bennions Clo., Horn. 148 FK65
Franklin Rd.
Bennison Dr., Rom. 106 FK54
Benn's Wk., Rich. 158 CL84
Rosedale Rd.
Benrek Clo., Ilf. 103 EQ53
Bensbury Clo. SW15 179 CV87
Bensham Clo., Th.Hth. 202 DQ98
Bensham Gro., Th.Hth. 202 DQ96
Bensham La., Croy. 201 DP101
Bensham La., Th.Hth. 201 DP98
Bensham Manor Rd., Th.Hth. 202 DQ98
Bensington Ct., Felt. 175 BR86
Benskin Rd., Wat. 75 BU43
Benskins La. (Havering-atte-Bower), Rom. 106 FK46
Bensley Clo. N11 98 DF50
Benson Ave. E6 144 EJ68
Benson Clo., Houns. 156 CA84
Benson Clo., Slou. 132 AU74
Benson Clo., Uxb. 134 BL71
Benson Quay E1 142 DW73
Garnet St.
Benson Rd. SE23 182 DW88
Benson Rd., Croy. 201 DN104
Benson Rd., Grays 170 GB79
Bentfield Gdns. SE9 184 EJ90
Aldersgrove Ave.
Benthal Rd. N16 122 DU61
Benthall Gdns., Ken. 236 DQ116
Bentham Ave., Wok. 227 BC115
Bentham Ct. N1 142 DQ66
Rotherfield St.
Bentham Rd. E9 143 DX65
Bentham Rd. SE28 146 EV73
Bentham Wk. NW10 118 CQ64
Bentinck Clo., Ger.Cr. 112 AX57
Bentinck Ms. W1 272 G8
Bentinck Pl. NW8 272 B1
Bentinck Rd., West Dr. 134 BK74
Bentinck St. W1 272 G8
Bentinck St. W1 140 DG72
Bentley Dr. NW2 119 CZ62
Bentley Dr., Harl. 52 EW16
Bentley Dr., Ilf. 125 EQ58
Bentley Dr., Wey. 212 BN109
Bentley Heath La., Barn. 63 CY34
Bentley Ms., Enf. 82 DR44
Bentley Pk., Slou. 131 AK68
Bentley Rd. N1 142 DS65
Tottenham Rd.
Bentley Rd., Hert. 31 DL08
Bentley Rd., Slou. 131 AN74
Bentley St., Grav. 191 GJ86
Bentley Way, Stan. 95 CG50
Bentley Way, Wdf.Grn. 102 EG47
Benton Rd., Ilf. 125 ER60
Benton Rd., Wat. 94 BX50
Bentons, Harl. 51 ES17
Bentons La. SE27 182 DQ91
Bentons Ri. SE27 182 DR92
Bentry Clo., Dag. 126 EY61
Bentry Rd., Dag. 126 EY61
Bentsbrook Clo., Dor. 263 CH140
Bentsbrook Pk., Dor. 263 CH140
Bentsbrook Rd., Dor. 263 CH140
Bentsley Clo., St.Alb. 43 CJ16
Bentworth Rd. W12 139 CV72
Benwell Ct., Sun. 195 BU95
Benwell Rd. N7 121 DN63
Benwick Clo. SE16 162 DV76
Benworth St. E3 143 DZ69
Benyon Path, S.Ock. 149 FW68
Tyssen Pl.
Benyon Rd. N1 142 DR67
Southgate Rd.
Beomonds Row, Cher. 194 BG101
Berber Rd. SW11 180 DF85
Berberis Clo., Guil. 242 AW132
Berberis Wk., West Dr. 154 BL77
Berberry Clo., Edg. 96 CQ49
Larkspur Gro.
Berceau Wk., Wat. 75 BS39
Bercta Rd. SE9 185 EQ89
Bere St. E1 143 DX73
Cranford St.
Berecroft, Harl. 51 ER20
Beredens La., Brwd. 129 FT55
Berefeld, Hem.H. 40 BK18
Berenger Wk. SW10 160 DD80
Blantyre St.
Berens Rd. NW10 139 CX69
Berens Rd., Orp. 206 EX99
Berens Way, Chis. 205 ET98
Beresford Ave. N20 98 DF47
Beresford Ave. W7 137 CD71
Beresford Ave., Slou. 132 AW73
Beresford Ave., Surb. 198 CP102
Beresford Ave., Twick. 177 CJ86
Beresford Ave., Wem. 138 CM67
Beresford Dr., Brom. 204 EK97
Beresford Dr., Wdf.Grn. 102 EJ49
Beresford Gdns., Enf. 82 DS42
Beresford Gdns., Houns. 176 BZ85
Beresford Gdns., Rom. 126 EY57
Beresford Rd. E4 102 EE46
Beresford Rd. E17 101 EB53
Beresford Rd. N2 120 DE55
Beresford Rd. N5 122 DQ64
Beresford Rd. N8 121 DN57
Beresford Rd., Dor. 263 CH136
Beresford Rd., Grav. 190 GE87
Beresford Rd., Har. 117 CD57
Beresford Rd., Kings.T. 198 CM95
Beresford Rd., N.Mal. 198 CQ98
Beresford Rd., Rick. 91 BF46
Beresford Rd., St.Alb. 43 CH21
Beresford Rd., Sthl. 136 BX74
Beresford Rd., Sutt. 217 CZ108
Beresford Sq. SE18 165 EP77
Beresford St. SE18 165 EP76
Beresford Ter. N5 122 DQ64
Berestede Rd. W6 159 CT78
Bergen Sq. SE16 163 DY76
Norway Gate
Berger Clo., Orp. 205 ER100
Berger Rd. E9 143 DX65
Berghem Ms. W14 159 CX76
Blythe Rd.
Berghers Hill, H.Wyc. 110 AF59
Bergholt Ave., Ilf. 124 EL57
Bergholt Cres. N16 122 DS59
Bergholt Ms. NW1 141 DJ66
Rossendale Way
Bericot Way, Welw.G.C. 30 DC09
Bering Sq. E14 163 EA78
Napier Ave.
Bering Wk. E16 144 EK72
Berisford Ms. SW18 180 DC86
Berkeley Ave., Bexh. 166 EX81
Berkeley Ave., Chesh. 54 AM28
Berkeley Ave., Grnf. 137 CE65
Berkeley Ave., Houns. 155 BU82
Berkeley Ave., Ilf. 103 EN54
Berkeley Ave., Rom. 105 FC52
Berkeley Clo., Abb.L. 59 BT32
Berkeley Clo., Borwd. 78 CN43
Berkeley Clo., Chesh. 54 AN30
Berkeley Ave.
Berkeley Clo., Horn. 128 FP61
Berkeley Clo., Kings.T. 178 CL94
Berkeley Clo., Orp. 205 ES101
Berkeley Clo., Pot.B. 63 CY32
Berkeley Clo., Ruis. 115 BU62
Berkeley Clo., Stai. 173 BD89
Berkeley Clo., Ware 32 DW05
Berkeley Ct. N14 81 DJ44
Berkeley Ct., Guil. 242 AY134
London Rd.
Berkeley Ct., Wall. 201 DJ104
Berkeley Ct., Wey. 195 BR103
Berkeley Cres., Barn. 80 DD43

Berkeley Cres., Dart. 188 FM88
Berkeley Dr., Horn. 128 FN60
Berkeley Gdns. N21 100 DR45
Berkeley Gdns. W8 140 DA74
Brunswick Gdns.
Berkeley Gdns., Esher 215 CG107
Berkeley Gdns., Walt. 195 BT101
Berkeley Gdns., W.Byf. 211 BF114
Berkeley Ho. E3 143 EA70
Berkeley Ms. W1 272 E8
Berkeley Pl. SW19 179 CX93
Berkeley Pl., Epsom 232 CR115
Berkeley Rd. E12 124 EL64
Berkeley Rd. N8 121 DK57
Berkeley Rd. N15 122 DR58
Berkeley Rd. NW9 118 CN56
Berkeley Rd. SW13 159 CU81
Berkeley Rd., H.Wyc. 88 AC53
Berkeley Rd., Uxb. 135 BQ66
Berkeley Sq. W1 277 J1
Berkeley Sq. W1 141 DH73
Berkeley St. W1 277 J1
Berkeley St. W1 141 DH73
Berkeley Wk. N7 121 DM61
Durham Rd.
Berkeley Waye, Houns. 156 BX80
Berkeleys, The, Lthd. 231 CE124
Berkhampstead Rd., Belv. 166 FA78
Berkhampstead Rd., Chesh. 54 AQ30
Berkhamsted Ave., Wem. 138 CM65
Berkhamsted Bypass, Berk. 38 AV21
Berkhamsted Bypass, Hem.H. 39 BB23
Berkhamsted Hill, Berk. 38 AY17
Berkhamsted Pl., Berk. 38 AW17
Berkhamsted Rd., Hem.H. 39 BD17
Berkley Ave., Wal.Cr. 67 DX34
Berkley Clo., St.Alb. 43 CJ16
Berkley Ct., Berk. 38 AW18
Mill St.
Berkley Ct., Guil. 242 AY134
London Rd.
Berkley Ct., Rick. 75 BR43
Mayfare
Berkley Dr., W.Mol. 196 BZ97
Berkley Gro. NW1 140 DF66
Berkley Rd.
Berkley Rd. NW1 140 DF66
Berkley Rd., Beac. 89 AK49
Berkley Rd., Grav. 191 GH86
Berks Hill, Rick. 73 BC43
Berkshire Ave., Slou. 131 AP72
Berkshire Clo., Cat. 236 DR122
Berkshire Gdns. N13 99 DN51
Berkshire Gdns. N18 100 DV50
Berkshire Rd. E9 143 DZ65
Berkshire Sq., Mitch. 201 DL98
Berkshire Way
Berkshire Way, Horn. 128 FN57
Berkshire Way, Mitch. 201 DL98
Bermans Clo., Brwd. 109 GB47
Hanging Hill La.
Bermans Way NW10 118 CS63
Bermondsey Sq. SE1 279 N6
Bermondsey St. SE1 279 M3
Bermondsey St. SE1 162 DS75
Bermondsey Wall E. SE16 162 DU75
Bermondsey Wall W. SE16 162 DU75
Bermuda Rd., Til. 171 GG82
Bernal Clo. SE28 146 EX73
Haldane Rd.
Bernard Ashley Dr. SE7 164 EH78
Bernard Ave. W13 157 CH76
Bernard Cassidy St. E16 144 EF71
Bernard Gdns. SW19 179 CZ92
Bernard Gro., Wal.Abb. 67 EB33
Beaulieu Dr.
Bernard Rd. N15 122 DT57
Bernard Rd., Rom. 127 FC59
Bernard Rd., Wall. 219 DH105
Bernard St. WC1 273 P5
Bernard St. WC1 141 DL70
Bernard St., Grav. 191 GH86
Bernard St., St.Alb. 43 CD19
Bernards Clo., Ilf. 103 EQ51
Bernato Clo., W.Byf. 212 BL112
Viscount Gdns.
Bernays Clo., Stan. 95 CJ51
Bernays Gro. SW9 161 DM84
Berne Rd., Th.Hth. 202 DQ99
Bernel Dr., Croy. 203 DZ104
Berners Clo., Slou. 131 AL73
Berners Dr. W13 137 CG72
Berners Dr., Brox. 49 DZ23
Berners Way
Berners Dr., St.Alb. 43 CE23
Berners Ms. W1 273 L7
Berners Ms. W1 141 DJ71
Berners Pl. W1 273 L8
Berners Pl. W1 141 DJ72
Berners Rd. N1 141 DN67
Berners Rd. N22 99 DN53
Berners St. W1 273 L7
Berners St. W1 141 DJ71
Berners Way, Brox. 49 DZ23
Bernersmede SE3 164 EG83
Blackheath Pk.
Berney Rd., Croy. 202 DR101
Bernice Clo., Rain. 148 FJ70
Bernville Way, Har. 118 CM57
Kenton Rd.
Bernwell Rd. E4 102 EE48
Berridge Grn., Edg. 96 CN52
Berridge Ms. NW6 120 DA64
Hillfield Rd.
Berridge Rd. SE19 182 DR92
Berries, The, St.Alb. 43 CG16
Berriman Rd. N7 121 DM62
Berrington Dr., Lthd. 229 BT124
Berriton Rd., Har. 116 BZ60
Berry Ave., Wat. 75 BV36
Berry Clo. N21 99 DP46
Berry Clo. NW10 138 CS66
Berry Clo., Horn. 128 FJ64
Airfield Way
Berry Clo., Rick. 92 BH45
Berry Ct., Houns. 176 BZ85
Berry Fld. Pk., Amer. 55 AP37
Berry Gro. La. (Bushey), Wat. 76 CA39
Berry Hill, Maid. 130 AD70
Berry Hill, Stan. 95 CK49
Berry La. SE21 182 DR91
Berry La., Rick. 92 BH46
Berry Meade, Ash. 232 CM117
Berry Pl. EC1 274 G3
Berry St. EC1 274 G4
Berry St. EC1 141 DP70
Berry Wk., Ash. 232 CM119
Berry Way W5 158 CL76
Berry Way, Rick. 92 BH45
Berrybank Clo. E4 101 EC47
Greenbank Clo.
Berrydale Rd., Hayes 136 BY70
Berryfield, Slou. 132 AW72
Berryfield Clo. E17 123 EB56
Berryfield Clo., Brom. 204 EL95
Berryfield Rd. SE17 278 G10
Berryfield Rd. SE17 161 DP78
Berryhill SE9 165 EP84
Berryhill Gdns. SE9 165 EP84
Berrylands SW20 199 CW97
Berrylands, Orp. 206 EW104
Berrylands, Surb. 198 CN99
Berrylands Rd., Surb. 198 CM100
Berryman Clo., Dag. 126 EW62
Bennetts Castle La.
Berrymans La. SE26 183 DX91
Berrymead, Hem.H. 40 BM18
Berrymead Gdns. W3 138 CQ74
Berrymede Rd. W4 158 CR76
Berrys Grn. Rd., West. 239 EP115
Berrys Hill, West. 239 EP115
Berrys La., W.Byf. 212 BK111
Berryscroft Ct., Stai. 174 BJ94
Berryscroft Rd.
Berryscroft Rd., Stai. 174 BJ94
Bersham La., Grays 170 FZ77
Bert Rd., Th.Hth. 202 DQ99
Bertal Rd. SW17 180 DD91
Berther Rd., Horn. 128 FK59
Berthold Ms., Wal.Abb. 67 EB33
Berthon St. SE8 163 EA80
Bertie Rd. NW10 139 CU65
Bertie Rd. SE26 183 DX93
Bertram Cotts. SW19 180 DA94
Hartfield Rd.
Bertram Rd. NW4 119 CU58
Bertram Rd., Enf. 82 DU42
Bertram Rd., Kings.T. 178 CN94
Bertram St. N19 121 DH61
Bertram Way, Enf. 82 DT42
Bertrand St. SE13 163 EB83
Bertrand Way SE28 146 EV73
Berwick Ave., Hayes 136 BX72
Berwick Ave., Slou. 131 AP72
Berwick Clo., Beac. 89 AP54
Berwick Clo., Stan. 95 CF52
Gordon Ave.
Berwick Clo., Wal.Cr. 67 EA34
Berwick Cres., Sid. 185 ES86
Berwick La., Ong. 71 FE33
Berwick Pond Clo., Rain. 148 FK68
Berwick Pond Rd., Rain. 148 FL68
Berwick Pond Rd., Upmin. 148 FM66
Berwick Rd. E16 144 EH72
Berwick Rd. N22 99 DP53
Berwick Rd., Borwd. 78 CM38
Berwick Rd., Rain. 148 FK68
Berwick Rd., Well. 166 EV81
Berwick St. W1 273 M9
Berwick St. W1 141 DK72
Berwick Way, Orp. 206 EU102
Berwick Way, Sev. 257 FH121
Berwyn Ave., Houns. 156 CB81
Berwyn Rd. SE24 181 DP88
Berwyn Rd., Rich. 158 CP84
Beryl Ave. E6 144 EL71
Beryl Ho. SE18 165 ET78
Spinel Clo.
Beryl Rd. W6 159 CX78
Berystede, Kings.T. 178 CP94
Besant Ct. N1 122 DR64
Newington Grn. Rd.
Besant Rd. NW2 119 CY63
Besant Wk. N7 121 DM61
Newington Barrow Way
Besant Way NW10 118 CQ64
Besley St. SW16 181 DJ93
Bessant Dr., Rich. 158 CP81
Bessborough Gdns. SW1 277 N10
Bessborough Gdns. SW1 161 DK78
Bessborough Pl. SW1 277 N10
Bessborough Pl. SW1 161 DK78
Bessborough Rd. SW15 179 CU88
Bessborough Rd., Har. 117 CD60
Bessborough St. SW1 277 M10
Bessborough St. SW1 161 DK78
Bessels Grn. Rd., Sev. 256 FD123
Bessels Meadow, Sev. 256 FD124
Bessels Way, Sev. 256 FC124
Bessemer Rd. SE5 162 DQ82
Bessemer Rd., Welw.G.C. 29 CY05
Bessie Lansbury Clo. E6 145 EN72
Bessingby Rd., Ruis. 115 BU61
Bessingham Wk. SE4 163 DX84
Frendsbury Rd.
Besson St. SE14 162 DW81
Bessy St. E2 142 DW69
Roman Rd.
Bestobell Rd., Slou. 131 AQ72
Bestwood St. SE8 163 DX77
Beswick Ms. NW6 140 DB65
Lymington Rd.
Beta Rd., Wok. 227 BB116
Beta Rd. (Chobham), Wok. 210 AT110
Beta Way, Egh. 193 BC95
Betam Rd., Hayes 155 BR75
Betchworth Clo., Sutt. 218 DD106
Turnpike La.
Betchworth Rd., Ilf. 125 ES61
Betchworth Way, Croy. 221 EC109
Betenson Ave., Sev. 256 FF122
Betham Rd., Grnf. 137 CD69
Bethany Waye, Felt. 175 BS87
Bethecar Rd., Har. 117 CE57
Bethel Rd., Sev. 257 FJ123
Bethel Rd., Well. 166 EW83
Bethell Ave. E16 144 EF70
Bethell Ave., Ilf. 125 EN59
Bethersden Clo., Beck. 183 DZ94
Bethnal Grn. Rd. E1 275 P4
Bethnal Grn. Rd. E1 142 DT70
Bethnal Grn. Rd. E2 275 P4
Bethnal Grn. Rd. E2 142 DT70
Bethune Ave. N11 98 DF49
Bethune Rd. N16 122 DR59
Bethune Rd. NW10 138 CR70
Bethwin Rd. SE5 161 DP80
Betjeman Clo., Couls. 235 DM117
Betjeman Clo., Pnr. 116 CA56
Betjeman Clo., Wal.Cr. 66 DU28
Rosedale Way
Betjeman Way, Hem.H. 40 BH18
Betley Ct., Walt. 195 BV104
Betony Clo., Croy. 203 DX102
Primrose La.
Betony Rd., Rom. 106 FK51
Cloudberry Rd.
Betoyne Ave. E4 102 EE49
Betsham Rd., Erith 167 FF80
Betsham Rd., Grav. 189 FX92
Betsham Rd., Swans. 190 FY87
Betstyle Rd. N11 99 DH49
Betterton Dr., Sid. 186 EY89
Betterton Rd., Rain. 147 FE69
Betterton St. WC2 273 P9
Betterton St. WC2 141 DL72
Bettles Clo., Uxb. 134 BJ68
Wescott Way
Bettons Pk. E15 144 EE67
Bettridge Rd. SW6 159 CZ82
Betts Clo., Beck. 203 DY96
Kendall Rd.
Betts La., Wal.Abb. 50 EJ21
Betts Ms. E17 123 DZ58
Queen's Rd.
Betts Rd. E16 144 EH73
Victoria Dock Rd.
Betts St. E1 142 DV73
The Highway
Betts Way SE20 202 DV95
Betts Way, Surb. 197 CH102
Betula Clo., Ken. 236 DR115
Betula Wk., Rain. 148 FK69
Between Sts., Cob. 213 BU114
Beulah Ave., Th.Hth. 201 DM98
Beulah Rd.
Beulah Clo., Edg. 96 CP48
Beulah Cres., Th.Hth. 202 DQ96
Beulah Gro., Croy. 202 DQ100
Beulah Hill SE19 181 DP93
Beulah Path E17 123 EB57
Addison Rd.
Beulah Rd. E17 123 EB57
Beulah Rd. SW19 179 CZ94
Beulah Rd., Epp. 70 EU29
Beulah Rd., Horn. 128 FJ62
Beulah Rd., Sutt. 218 DA105
Beulah Rd., Th.Hth. 202 DQ97
Beulah Wk., Cat. 237 DY120
Beult Rd., Dart. 167 FG83
Bev Callender Clo. SW8 161 DH83
Daley Thompson Way
Bevan Ave., Bark. 146 EU66
Bevan Clo., Hem.H. 40 BK22
Bevan Ct., Croy. 219 DN106
Bevan Hill, Chesh. 54 AP29
Bevan Ho., Grays 170 GD75
Laird Ave.
Bevan Pl., Swan. 207 FE98
Bevan Rd. SE2 166 EV78
Bevan Rd., Barn. 80 DF42
Bevan St. N1 142 DQ67
Bevan Way, Horn. 128 FM63
Bevans Clo., Green. 189 FW86
Johnsons Way
Bevenden St. N1 275 L2
Bevenden St. N1 142 DR69
Bevercote Wk., Belv. 166 EZ79
Osborne Rd.
Beveridge Rd. NW10 138 CS66
Curzon Cres.
Beverley Ave. SW20 199 CT95
Beverley Ave., Houns. 156 BZ84
Beverley Ave., Sid. 185 ET87
Beverley Clo. N21 100 DQ46
Beverley Clo. SW11 160 DD84
Maysoule Rd.
Beverley Clo. SW13 159 CT82
Beverley Clo., Add. 212 BK106
Beverley Clo., Brox. 49 DY21
Beverley Clo., Chess. 215 CJ105
Beverley Clo., Enf. 82 DS42
Beverley Clo., Epsom 217 CW111
Beverley Clo., Horn. 128 FM59
Beverley Clo., Wey. 195 BS103
Beverley Cotts. SW15 178 CR91
Kingston Vale
Beverley Ct. N14 99 DJ45
Beverley Ct. SE4 163 DZ83
Beverley Ct., Slou. 152 AV75
Dolphin Rd.
Beverley Cres., Wdf.Grn. 102 EH53
Beverley Dr., Edg. 118 CP55
Beverley Gdns. NW11 119 CY59
Beverley Gdns. SW13 159 CT83
Beverley Gdns., Horn. 128 FM59
Beverley Gdns., St.Alb. 43 CK16
Beverley Gdns., Stan. 95 CG53
Beverley Gdns. (Cheshunt), Wal.Cr. 66 DT30
Beverley Gdns., Welw.G.C. 30 DC09
Beverley Gdns., Wem. 118 CM60
Beverley Gdns., Wor.Pk. 199 CU102
Green La.
Beverley Hts., Reig. 250 DB132
Beverley Ho. NW8 272 B3
Beverley La. SW15 179 CT90
Beverley La., Kings.T. 178 CS94
Beverley Ms. E4 101 ED51
Beverley Rd.
Beverley Path SW13 159 CT82
Beverley Rd. E4 101 ED51
Beverley Rd. E6 144 EK69
Beverley Rd. SE20 202 DV96
Wadhurst Clo.
Beverley Rd. SW13 159 CT83
Beverley Rd. W4 159 CT78
Beverley Rd., Bexh. 167 FC82
Beverley Rd., Brom. 204 EL103
Beverley Rd., Dag. 126 EY63
Beverley Rd., Kings.T. 197 CJ95
Beverley Rd., Mitch. 201 DK98
Beverley Rd., N.Mal. 199 CU98
Beverley Rd., Ruis. 115 BU61
Beverley Rd., Sthl. 156 BY76
Beverley Rd., Sun. 195 BT95
Beverley Rd., Whyt. 236 DS116
Beverley Rd., Wor.Pk. 199 CW103
Beverley Way SW20 199 CT95
Beverley Way, N.Mal. 199 CT95
Beversbrook Rd. N19 121 DK62
Beverston Ms. W1 272 D7
Beverstone Rd. SW2 181 DM85
Beverstone Rd., Th.Hth. 201 DN98
Bevil Ct., Hodd. 33 EA14
Molesworth
Bevill Allen Clo. SW17 180 DF92
Bevill Clo. SE25 202 DU97
Bevin Clo. SE16 143 DY74
Stave Yd. Rd.
Bevin Ct. WC1 141 DN69
Holford St.
Bevin Rd., Hayes 135 BU69
Bevin Sq. SW17 180 DF90
Bevin Way WC1 274 D2
Bevington Rd. W10 139 CY71
Bevington Rd., Beck. 203 EB96
Bevington St. SE16 162 DU75
Bevis Clo., Dart. 188 FQ86
Bevis Marks EC3 275 N8
Bevis Marks EC3 142 DS72
Bewcastle Gdns., Enf. 81 DL42
Bewdley St. N1 141 DN66
Bewick St. SW8 161 DH82
Bewley Clo. (Cheshunt), Wal.Cr. 67 DX31
Bewley St. E1 142 DV73
Dellow St.
Bewlys Rd. SE27 181 DP92
Bexhill Clo., Felt. 176 BY89
Bexhill Rd. N11 99 DK50
Bexhill Rd. SE4 183 DZ86
Bexhill Rd. SW14 158 CQ83
Bexhill Wk. E15 144 EE68
Mitre Rd.
Bexley Clo., Dart. 187 FE85
Bexley Gdns. N9 100 DR48
Bexley Gdns., Rom. 126 EV57
Bexley High St., Bex. 186 FA87
Bexley La., Dart. 187 FE85
Bexley La., Sid. 186 EW91
Bexley Rd. SE9 185 EP85
Bexley Rd., Erith 167 FC80
Bexley St., Wind. 151 AQ81
Beyers Gdns., Hodd. 33 EA14
Beyers Prospect, Hodd. 33 EA14
Beyers Ride, Hodd. 33 EA13
Beynon Rd., Cars. 218 DF106
Bianca Ho. N1 142 DS68
Crondall St.
Bianca Rd. SE15 162 DT79
Bibsworth Rd. N3 97 CZ54
Bibury Clo. SE15 162 DS79
Bicester Rd., Rich. 158 CN83
Bickenhall St. W1 272 E6
Bickenhall St. W1 140 DF71
Bickersteth Rd. SW17 180 DF93
Bickerton Rd. N19 121 DJ61
Bickley Cres., Brom. 204 EL98
Bickley Pk. Rd., Brom. 204 EL97
Bickley Rd. E10 123 EB59
Bickley Rd., Brom. 204 EK96
Bickley St. SW17 180 DE92
Bicknell Rd. SE5 162 DQ83
Bickney Way, Lthd. 230 CC122
Bicknoller Clo., Sutt. 218 DB110
Bicknoller Rd., Enf. 82 DT39
Bicknor Rd., Orp. 205 ES101
Bidborough Clo., Brom. 204 EF99
Bidborough St. WC1 273 P3
Bidborough St. WC1 141 DK69
Biddenden Way SE9 185 EN91
Biddenden Way, Grav. 190 GE94
Biddenham Turn, Wat. 76 BW35
Bidder St. E16 144 EE71
Biddestone Rd. N7 121 DM63
Biddles Clo., Slou. 131 AL74
Biddulph Rd. W9 140 DB69
Biddulph Rd., S.Croy. 220 DQ109
Bideford Ave., Grnf. 137 CH68
Bideford Clo., Edg. 96 CN53
Bideford Clo., Felt. 176 BZ90
Bideford Clo., Rom. 106 FJ53
Bideford Gdns., Enf. 100 DS45
Bideford Rd., Brom. 184 EF90
Bideford Rd., Enf. 83 DZ38
Bideford Rd., Ruis. 115 BV62
Bideford Rd., Well. 166 EV80
Bideford Spur, Slou. 131 AP69
Bidhams Cres., Tad. 233 CW121
Bidwell Gdns. N11 99 DJ52
Bidwell St. SE15 162 DV81
Big Common La., Red. 251 DP133
Big Hill E5 122 DV60
Bigbury Clo. N17 100 DR52
Weir Hall Rd.
Bigbury Rd. N17 100 DS52
Barkham Rd.
Biggerstaff Rd. E15 143 EC67
Biggerstaff St. N4 121 DN61
Biggin Ave., Mitch. 200 DF95
Biggin Hill SE19 181 DP94
Biggin Hill Clo., Kings.T. 177 CJ92
Biggin La., Grays 171 GH79
Biggin Way SE19 181 DP94
Bigginwood Rd. SW16 181 DP94
Biggs Row SW15 159 CX83
Felsham Rd.
Bigland St. E1 142 DV72
Bignell Rd. SE18 165 EP78
Bignold Rd. E7 124 EG63
Bigwood Rd. NW11 120 DB57
Biko Clo., Uxb. 134 BJ72
Sefton Way
Bill Hamling Clo. SE9 185 EM89
Billet Clo., Rom. 126 EX55
Billet La., Berk. 38 AU18
Billet La., Horn. 128 FK60
Billet La., Iver 133 BB69
Billet La., Slou. 133 BB69
Billet Rd. E17 101 DX54
Billet Rd., Rom. 126 EV55
Billet Rd., Stai. 174 BG90
Farnell Rd.
Billets Hart Clo. W7 157 CE75
Billing Pl. SW10 160 DB80
Billing Rd. SW10 160 DB80
Billing St. SW10 160 DB80
Billingford Clo. SE4 163 DX84
Billings Clo., Dag. 146 EW66
Ellerton Rd.
Billington Rd. SE14 163 DX80
Billiter Sq. EC3 275 N10
Billiter St. EC3 275 N9
Billiter St. EC3 142 DS72
Billockby Clo., Chess. 216 CM107
Billson St. E14 163 EC77
Billy Lows La., Pot.B. 64 DA31
Bilsby Gro. SE9 184 EK91
Bilton Clo., Slou. 153 BE82
Bilton Rd., Erith 167 FG79
Bilton Rd., Grnf. 137 CJ67
Bilton Way, Enf. 83 DY39
Bilton Way, Hayes 155 BV75
Bina Gdns. SW5 160 DC77
Bincote Rd., Enf. 81 DM41
Binden Rd. W12 159 CT76
Bindon Grn., Mord. 200 DB98
Binfield Rd. SW4 161 DL81
Binfield Rd., S.Croy. 220 DT106
Binfield Rd., W.Byf. 212 BL112
Bingfield St. N1 141 DL67
Bingham Clo., S.Ock. 149 FV72
Bingham Ct. N1 141 DP66
Halton Rd.
Bingham Dr., Stai. 174 BK94
Bingham Dr., Wok. 226 AT118
Bingham Pl. W1 272 F6
Bingham Rd., Croy. 202 DU102
Bingham Rd., Slou. 130 AG71
Bingham St. N1 142 DR65
Bingley Rd. E16 144 EJ72
Bingley Rd., Grnf. 136 CC71
Bingley Rd., Hodd. 49 EC17
Bingley Rd., Sun. 175 BU94
Binney St. W1 272 G10
Binney St. W1 140 DG72
Binns Rd. W4 158 CS78
Binns Ter. W4 158 CS78
Binns Rd.
Binscombe Cres., Gdmg. 258 AS144
Binsey Wk. SE2 146 EW74
Binyon Cres., Stan. 95 CF50
Birbetts Rd. SE9 185 EM89
Birch Ave. N13 100 DQ48
Birch Ave., Cat. 236 DR124
Birch Ave., Lthd. 231 CF120
Birch Ave., West Dr. 134 BM72
Birch Circle, Gdmg. 258 AT143
Birch Clo. E16 144 EE71
Birch Clo. N19 121 DJ61
Hargrave Pk.
Birch Clo. SE15 162 DU82
Bournemouth Rd.
Birch Clo., Add. 212 BK109
Birch Clo., Amer. 55 AS37
Birch Clo., Brent. 157 CH80
Birch Clo., Buck.H. 102 EK48
Birch Clo., Dart. 208 FK104
Birch Clo., Houns. 157 CD83
Birch Clo., Rom. 127 FB55
Birch Clo., Sev. 257 FH123
Birch Clo., S.Ock. 149 FX69
Birch Clo., Tedd. 177 CG92
Birch Clo., Wok. 226 AW119
Birch Clo. (Send Marsh), Wok. 243 BF125
Birch Copse, St.Alb. 60 BY30
Birch Ct., Nthwd. 93 BQ51
Rickmansworth Rd.
Birch Cres., Horn. 128 FL56
Birch Cres., S.Ock. 149 FX69
Birch Cres., Uxb. 134 BM67
Birch Dr., Hat. 45 CU19
Birch Dr., Rick. 91 BD50
Birch Gdns., Dag. 127 FC62
Birch Grn. NW9 96 CS52
Clayton Fld.
Birch Grn., Hem.H. 39 BF19
Birch Grn., Hert. 31 DJ11
Birch Grn., Stai. 173 BF90
Birch Gro. E11 124 EE62
Birch Gro. SE12 184 EF87
Birch Gro. W3 138 CN74
Birch Gro., Cob. 214 BW114
Birch Gro., Pot.B. 64 DA32
Birch Gro., Shep. 195 BS96
Birch Gro., Slou. 131 AP71
Birch Gro., Tad. 233 CY124
Birch Gro., Well. 166 EU84
Birch Gro., Wind. 151 AK81
Birch Gro., Wok. 227 BD115
Birch Hill, Croy. 221 DX106
Birch La., Hem.H. 57 BB33
Birch La., Pur. 219 DL111
Birch Leys, Hem.H. 41 BQ15
Hunters Oak
Birch Mead, Orp. 205 EN103
Birch Pk., Har. 94 CC52
Birch Pl., Green. 189 FS86
Birch Rd., Felt. 176 BX92
Birch Rd., Gdmg. 258 AT143
Birch Rd., Rom. 127 FB55
Birch Row, Brom. 205 EN101
Birch Tree Ave., W.Wick. 222 EF106
Birch Tree Clo., Chesh. 56 AV30
Birch Tree Wk., Wat. 75 BT37
Birch Tree Way, Croy. 202 DV103
Birch Vale, Cob. 214 CA113
Birch Vw., Epp. 70 EV29
Birch Wk., Borwd. 78 CN39
Birch Wk., Erith 167 FC79
Birch Wk., Mitch. 201 DH95
Birch Wk., W.Byf. 212 BG112
Birch Way, Chesh. 54 AR29
Birch Way, Hat. 45 CV16
Crawford Rd.
Birch Way, St.Alb. 61 CK27
Birch Way, Warl. 237 DY118
Birch Wd., Rad. 62 CN34
Birchall La., Hert. 30 DD11
Birchall La., Welw.G.C. 30 DD11
Birchall Wd., Welw.G.C. 30 DC10
Bircham Path SE4 163 DX84
St. Norbert Rd.
Birchanger Rd. SE25 202 DU99
Birchcroft Clo., Cat. 252 DQ125
Birchdale, Ger.Cr. 112 AX60
Birchdale Clo., W.Byf. 212 BJ111
Birchdale Gdns., Rom. 126 EX59
Birchdale Rd. E7 124 EJ64
Birchdene Dr. SE28 166 EU75
Birchen Clo. NW9 118 CR61
Birchen Gro. NW9 118 CR61
Birchend Clo., S.Croy. 220 DR107
Bircherley Ct., Hert. 32 DR09
Priory St.
Bircherley St., Hert. 32 DR09
Railway St.
Birches, The N21 81 DM44
Birches, The SE7 164 EH79
Birches, The, Brwd. 108 FY48
Birches, The, Epp. 71 FB26
Birches, The, Hem.H. 39 BF23
Birches, The, Lthd. 245 BS126
Birches, The, Orp. 223 EN105
Birches, The, Swan. 207 FE96
Birches, The (Bushey), Wat. 76 CC43
Birches, The, Wok. 227 AZ118
Heathside Rd.
Birches Clo., Epsom 232 CS115
Birches Clo., Mitch. 200 DF97
Birches Clo., Pnr. 116 BY57

Birchfield Clo., Add. 212 BH105
Birchfield Clo., Couls. 235 DM116
Birchfield Gro., Epsom 217 CW110
Birchfield Rd. (Cheshunt), Wal.Cr. 66 DV29
Birchfield St. E14 143 EA73
Birchgate Ms., Tad. 233 CW121
Bidhams Cres.
Birchin La. EC3 275 L9
Birchin La. EC3 142 DR72
Birchington Clo., Bexh. 167 FB81
Birchington Clo., Orp. 206 EW102
Hart Dyke Rd.
Birchington Rd. N8 121 DK58
Birchington Rd. NW6 140 DA67
Birchington Rd., Surb. 198 CM101
Birchington Rd., Wind. 151 AN82
Birchlands Ave. SW12 180 DF87
Birchmead, Wat. 75 BT38
Birchmead Ave., Pnr. 116 BW56
Birchmead Clo., St.Alb. 43 CD17
Birchmere Row SE3 164 EF82
Birchmore Wk. N5 122 DQ62
Birchville Ct. (Bushey), Wat. 95 CE46
Heathbourne Rd.
Birchway, Hat. 45 CV16
Crawford Rd.
Birchway, Hayes 135 BU74
Birchway, Red. 267 DH136
Birchwood, Wal.Abb. 68 EE34
Roundhills
Birchwood Ave. N10 120 DG55
Birchwood Ave., Beck. 203 DZ98
Birchwood Ave., Hat. 45 CU16
Birchwood Ave., Sid. 186 EV89
Birchwood Ave., Wall. 200 DG104
Birchwood Clo., Brwd. 107 FW51
Canterbury Way
Birchwood Clo., Hat. 45 CU16
Birchwood Clo., Horl. 269 DH147
Birchwood Clo., Mord. 200 DB98
Birchwood Ct. N13 99 DP50
Birchwood Ct., Edg. 96 CQ54
Birchwood Dr. NW3 120 DB62
Birchwood Dr., Dart. 187 FE91
Birchwood Dr., W.Byf. 212 BG112
Birchwood Gro., Hmptn. 176 CA93
Birchwood La., Cat. 251 DP125
Birchwood La., Esher 215 CD109
Birchwood La., Lthd. 215 CF110
Birchwood La., Sev. 240 EZ115
Birchwood Pk. Ave., Swan. 207 FE97
Birchwood Rd. SW17 181 DH92
Birchwood Rd., Dart. 187 FD93
Birchwood Rd., Orp. 205 ER98
Birchwood Rd., Swan. 207 FC95
Birchwood Rd., W.Byf. 212 BG112
Birchwood Ter., Swan. 207 FC95
Birchwood Rd.
Birchwood Way, St.Alb. 60 CB28
Bird in Bush Rd. SE15 162 DU80
Bird La., Brwd. 129 FX55
Bird La., Upmin. 129 FR57
Bird La. (Harefield), Uxb. 92 BJ54
Bird St. W1 272 G9
Bird Wk., Twick. 176 BZ88
Bird-in-Hand La., Brom. 204 EK96
Bird-in-Hand Pas. SE23 182 DW89
Dartmouth Rd.
Birdbrook Clo., Brwd. 109 GB44
Birdbrook Clo., Dag. 147 FC66
Birdbrook Rd. SE3 164 EJ83
Birdcage Wk. SW1 277 L5
Birdcage Wk. SW1 161 DJ75
Birdcage Wk., Harl. 35 EQ14
Birdcroft Rd., Welw.G.C. 29 CX10
Birdham Clo., Brom. 204 EL99
Birdhouse La., Orp. 239 EN115
Birdhurst Ave., S.Croy. 220 DR105
Birdhurst Gdns., S.Croy. 220 DR105
Birdhurst Ri., S.Croy. 220 DS106
Birdhurst Rd. SW18 160 DC84
Birdhurst Rd. SW19 180 DE93
Birdhurst Rd., S.Croy. 220 DS106
Birdie Way, Hert. 32 DV08
Birdlip Clo. SE15 162 DS79
Birds Clo., Welw.G.C. 30 DB11
Birds Fm. Ave., Rom. 105 FB53
Birds Hill Dr., Lthd. 215 CD113
Birds Hill Ri., Lthd. 215 CD113
Birds Hill Rd., Lthd. 215 CD112
Birdsfield La. E3 143 DZ67
Birdswood Dr., Wok. 226 AS120
Birdwood Clo., S.Croy. 221 DX111
Birdwood Clo., Tedd. 177 CE91
Birfield Rd., H.Wyc. 88 AC53
Birkbeck Ave. W3 138 CQ73
Birkbeck Ave., Grnf. 136 CC67
Birkbeck Gdns., Wdf.Grn. 102 EF47
Birkbeck Gro. W3 158 CR75
Birkbeck Hill SE21 181 DP89
Birkbeck Ms. E8 122 DT64
Sandringham Rd.
Birkbeck Pl. SE21 182 DQ88
Birkbeck Rd. E8 122 DT64
Birkbeck Rd. N8 121 DL56
Birkbeck Rd. N12 98 DC50
Birkbeck Rd. N17 100 DT53
Birkbeck Rd. NW7 97 CT50
Birkbeck Rd. SW19 180 DB92
Birkbeck Rd. W3 138 CR74
Birkbeck Rd. W5 157 CJ77
Birkbeck Rd., Beck. 202 DW96
Birkbeck Rd., Brwd. 109 GD44
Birkbeck Rd., Enf. 82 DR39
Birkbeck Rd., Ilf. 125 ER57
Birkbeck Rd., Rom. 127 FD60
Birkbeck Rd., Sid. 186 EU90
Birkbeck St. E2 142 DV69
Birkbeck Way, Grnf. 136 CC67
Birkdale Ave., Pnr. 116 CA55
Birkdale Ave., Rom. 106 FM52
Birkdale Clo. SE16 162 DV78
Masters Dr.
Birkdale Clo., Orp. 205 ER101
Birkdale Gdns., Croy. 221 DX105
Birkdale Gdns., Wat. 94 BX48
Birkdale Rd. SE2 166 EU77
Birkdale Rd. W5 138 CL71
Birken Ms., Nthwd. 93 BP50
Birkenhead Ave., Kings.T. 198 CM96
Birkenhead St. WC1 274 A2
Birkenhead St. WC1 141 DL69
Birkett Way, Ch.St.G. 72 AX41
Birkhall Rd. SE6 183 ED88
Birkheads Rd., Reig. 250 DA133
Birklands La., St.Alb. 43 CH24
Birklands Pk., St.Alb. 43 CH24
Birkwood Clo. SW12 181 DK87
Birley Rd. N20 98 DC47
Birley Rd., Slou. 131 AR72
Birley St. SW11 160 DG82
Birling Rd., Erith 167 FD80
Birnam Rd. N4 121 DM61
Birnham Clo., Wok. 228 BG124
Birse Cres. NW10 118 CS63
Birstall Grn., Wat. 94 BX49
Birstall Rd. N15 122 DS57
Birtley Path, Borwd. 78 CL39
Biscay Rd. W6 159 CX78
Biscoe Clo., Houns. 156 CA79
Biscoe Way SE13 163 ED83
Bisenden Rd., Croy. 202 DS103
Bisham Clo., Cars. 200 DF102
Bisham Gdns. N6 120 DG60
Bishop Butt Clo., Orp. 205 ET104
Stapleton Rd.
Bishop Clo. W4 158 CQ78
Bishop Duppa's Pk., Shep. 195 BR101
Bishop Fox Way, W.Mol. 196 BZ98
Bishop Ken Rd., Har. 95 CF54
Bishop Kings Rd. W14 159 CY77
Bishop Rd. N14 99 DH45
Bishop Sq., Hat. 44 CS17
Bishop St. N1 142 DQ67
Bishop Way NW10 138 CS66
Bishop Wilfred Wd. Clo. SE15 162 DU82
Moncrieff St.
Bishop's Ave. E13 144 EH67
Bishop's Ave. SW6 159 CX82
Bishops Ave., Borwd. 78 CM43
Bishops Ave., Brom. 204 EJ96
Bishops Ave., Nthwd. 93 BS49
Bishops Ave., Rom. 126 EW58
Bishops Ave., The N2 120 DD59
Bishops Bri. W2 140 DC71
Bishops Bri. Rd. W2 140 DC72
Bishops Clo. E17 123 EB56
Bishops Clo. N19 121 DJ62
Wyndham Cres.
Bishops Clo. SE9 185 EQ89
Bishops Clo., Barn. 79 CX44
Bishop's Clo., Couls. 235 DN118
Bishops Clo., Enf. 82 DV40
Central Ave.
Bishops Clo., Hat. 45 CT18
Bishops Clo., Rich. 177 CK90
Bishops Clo., St.Alb. 43 CG16
Bishop's Clo., Sutt. 200 DA104
Bishops Clo., Uxb. 134 BN68
Bishop's Ct. EC4 274 F8
Bishop's Ct. WC2 274 D8
Bishops Ct., Green. 189 FS85
Chalice Way
Bishops Ct., Wal.Cr. 66 DV30
Churchgate
Bishops Dr., Felt. 175 BR86
Bishops Dr., Nthlt. 136 BY67
Bishops Fm. Clo., Wind. 150 AH82
Bishops Garth, St.Alb. 43 CG16
Bishops Clo.
Bishops Gro. N2 120 DD58
Bishops Gro., Hmptn. 176 BZ91
Bishop's Hall, Kings.T. 197 CK96
Bishops Hall Rd., Brwd. 108 FV44
Bishops Hill, Walt. 195 BU101
Bishops Mead, Hem.H. 40 BH22
Bishops Orchard, Slou. 131 AP69
Bishop's Pk. SW6 159 CX82
Bishop's Pk. Rd. SW6 159 CX82
Bishops Pk. Rd. SW16 201 DL95
Bishops Pl., Sutt. 218 DC106
Lind Rd.
Bishops Ri., Hat. 45 CT18
Bishops Rd. N6 120 DG58
Bishops Rd. SW6 159 CZ81
Bishops Rd. W7 157 CE75
Bishops Rd., Croy. 201 DP101
Bishops Rd., Hayes 135 BQ71
Bishops Rd., Slou. 152 AU75
Bishops Ter. SE11 278 E8
Bishops Ter. SE11 161 DN77
Bishops Wk., Chis. 205 EQ95
Bishops Wk., Croy. 221 DX106
Bishops Wk., H.Wyc. 110 AE58
Bishop's Wk., Pnr. 116 BY55
High St.
Bishops Way E2 142 DV68
Bishops Way, Egh. 173 BD93
Bishops Wd., Wok. 226 AT117
Bishopsfield, Harl. 51 ER18
Bishopsford Rd., Mord. 200 DC101
Bishopsgate EC2 275 N7
Bishopsgate EC2 142 DS72
Bishopsgate Arc. EC2 275 N7
Bishopsgate Chyd. EC2 275 M8
Bishopsgate Rd., Egh. 172 AT90
Bishopsmead Clo., Lthd. 245 BS128
Ockham Rd. S.
Bishopsmead Dr., Lthd. 245 BT129
Bishopsmead Par., Lthd. 245 BS129
Ockham Rd. S.
Bishopsthorpe Rd. SE26 183 DX91
Bishopswood Rd. N6 120 DF59
Biskra, Wat. 75 BU39
Bisley Clo., Wal.Cr. 67 DX33
Bisley Clo., Wor.Pk. 199 CW102
Bispham Rd. NW10 138 CM69
Bisson Rd. E15 143 EC68
Bisterne Ave. E17 123 ED55
Bitchet Rd., Sev. 257 FP127
Bittacy Clo. NW7 97 CX51
Bittacy Hill NW7 97 CX51
Bittacy Pk. Ave. NW7 97 CX51
Bittacy Ri. NW7 97 CW51
Bittacy Rd. NW7 97 CX51
Bittams La., Cher. 211 BD105
Bittern Clo., Hayes 136 BX71
Bittern Clo. (Cheshunt), Wal.Cr. 66 DQ25
Bittern St. SE1 279 H5
Bitterne Dr., Wok. 226 AT117
Bittoms, The, Kings.T. 197 CK97
Bixley Clo., Sthl. 156 BZ77
Black Acre Clo., Amer. 55 AS39
Black Boy La. N15 122 DQ57
Black Boy Wd., St.Alb. 60 CA30
Black Cut, St.Alb. 43 CE21
Black Eagle Clo., West. 255 EQ127
Black Fan Clo., Enf. 82 DQ39
Black Fan Rd., Welw.G.C. 30 DA08
Black Friars Ct. EC4 274 F10
Black Friars La. EC4 274 F10
Black Friars La. EC4 141 DP73
Black Gates, Pnr. 116 BZ55
Church La.
Black Horse Ave., Chesh. 54 AR33
Black Horse Clo., Wind. 151 AK82
Black Horse Ct. SE1 279 L6
Black Lake Clo., Egh. 193 BA95
Black Lion Ct., Harl. 36 EW11
Black Lion Hill, Rad. 62 CL32
Black Lion La. W6 159 CU77
Black Lion Ms. W6 159 CU77
Black Lion La.
Black Pk. Rd., Slou. 132 AY68
Black Path E10 123 DX59
Black Prince Clo., W.Byf. 212 BM114
Black Prince Rd. SE1 278 B9
Black Prince Rd. SE1 161 DM77
Black Prince Rd. SE11 278 C9
Black Prince Rd. SE11 161 DM77
Black Rod Clo., Hayes 155 BT76
Black Swan Ct., Ware 33 DX06
Baldock St.
Black Swan Yd. SE1 279 N4
Black Thorne Rd., West. 238 EK115
Blackacre Rd., Epp. 85 ES37
Blackall St. EC2 275 M4
Blackberry Clo., Guil. 242 AV131
Blackberry Clo., Shep. 195 BS98
Cherry Way
Blackberry Fm. Clo., Houns. 156 BY80
Blackberry Fld., Orp. 206 EU95
Blackbird Hill NW9 118 CQ61
Blackbird Yd. E2 142 DT69
Ravenscroft St.
Blackbirds La., Wat. 77 CD35
Blackborne Rd., Dag. 146 FA65
Blackborough Clo., Reig. 250 DC134
Blackborough Rd., Reig. 266 DB135
Blackbridge Rd., Wok. 226 AX119
Blackbrook La., Brom. 205 EN97
Blackbrook Rd., Dor. 263 CK140
Blackburn, The, Lthd. 230 BZ124
Little Bookham St.
Blackburn Rd. NW6 140 DB65
Blackburn Trd. Est., Stai. 174 BM86
Blackburne's Ms. W1 272 F10
Blackburne's Ms. W1 140 DG73
Blackbury Clo., Pot.B. 64 DC31
Blackbush Ave., Rom. 126 EX57
Blackbush Clo., Sutt. 218 DB108
Blackbush Spring, Harl. 36 EU14
Blackdale (Cheshunt), Wal.Cr. 66 DU27
Blackdown Ave., Wok. 227 BE115
Blackdown Clo. N2 98 DC54
Blackdown Clo., Wok. 227 BC116
Blackdown Ter. SE18 165 EN80
Prince Imperial Rd.
Blackett Clo., Stai. 193 BE96
Blackett St. SW15 159 CX83
Blacketts Wd. Dr., Rick. 73 BB43
Blackfen Rd., Sid. 185 ES85
Blackford Clo., S.Croy. 219 DP109
Blackford Rd., Wat. 94 BX50
Blackford's Path SW15 179 CU87
Roehampton High St.
Blackfriars Bri. EC4 274 F10
Blackfriars Bri. EC4 141 DP73
Blackfriars Bri. SE1 274 F10
Blackfriars Bri. SE1 141 DP73
Blackfriars Pas. EC4 274 F10
Blackfriars Rd. SE1 278 F5
Blackfriars Rd. SE1 141 DP74
Blackhall La., Sev. 257 FK123
Blackhall Pl., Sev. 257 FL124
Blackhall La.
Blackheath Ave. SE10 163 ED80
Blackheath Gro. SE3 164 EF82
Blackheath Gro., Guil. 259 BB143
Blackheath Hill SE10 163 EC81
Blackheath La., Guil. 259 BB143
Blackheath Pk. SE3 164 EF83
Blackheath Ri. SE13 163 EC82
Blackheath Rd. SE10 163 EB81
Blackheath Vale SE3 164 EE82
Blackheath Village SE3 164 EF82
Blackhills, Esher 214 BZ109
Blackhorse Clo., Amer. 72 AT38
Blackhorse Cres., Amer. 55 AS38
Blackhorse La. E17 123 DX56
Blackhorse La., Croy. 202 DU101
Blackhorse La., Epp. 71 FD25
Blackhorse La., Pot.B. 62 CS30
Blackhorse La., Reig. 250 DB129
Blackhorse Ms. E17 123 DX55
Blackhorse Rd.
Blackhorse Rd. E17 123 DX56
Blackhorse Rd. SE8 163 DY78
Blackhorse Rd., Sid. 186 EU91
Blackhorse Rd., Wok. 226 AS122
Blacklands Dr., Hayes 135 BQ70
Blacklands Meadow, Red. 251 DL133
Blacklands Rd. SE6 183 EC91
Blacklands Ter. SW3 276 D9
Blacklands Ter. SW3 160 DF77
Blackley Clo., Wat. 75 BT37
Blackmans Clo., Dart. 188 FJ88
Blackmans La., Warl. 222 EE114
Blackmead, Sev. 241 FD119
London Rd.
Blackmoor La., Wat. 75 BR43
Blackmore Ave., Sthl. 137 CD74
Blackmore Clo., Grays 170 GC78
Blackmore Ct., Wal.Abb. 68 EG33
Blackmore Cres., Wok. 211 BC114
Blackmore Rd., Buck.H. 102 EL45
Blackmore Way, Uxb. 134 BK65
Blackmores, Harl. 51 EP15
Blackmores Gro., Tedd. 177 CG93
Blackness La., Kes. 222 EK109
Blackness La., Wok. 226 AY119
Blacknest Rd., Vir.W. 192 AT97
Blackpond La., Slou. 131 AP65
Blackpool Gdns., Hayes 135 BS70
Blackpool Rd. SE15 162 DV82
Blacks Rd. W6 159 CW77
Queen Caroline St.
Blackshaw Pl. N1 142 DS66
Hertford Rd.
Blackshaw Rd. SW17 180 DC91
Blacksmith Clo., Ash. 232 CM119
Rectory La.
Blacksmith Clo., Ware 33 DZ08
Blacksmith La., Guil. 259 BC139
Blacksmith Row, Slou. 153 BA77
Blacksmiths Clo., Rom. 126 EW58
Blacksmiths Hill, S.Croy. 220 DU113
Blacksmiths La., Cher. 194 BG101
Blacksmiths La., Orp. 206 EW99
Blacksmiths La., Rain. 147 FF67
Blacksmiths La., St.Alb. 42 CB20
Blacksmiths La., Stai. 194 BH97
Blacksmiths La., Uxb. 113 BC61
Blackstock Ms. N4 121 DP61
Blackstock Rd.
Blackstock Rd. N4 121 DP61
Blackstock Rd. N5 121 DP61
Blackstone Clo., Red. 266 DE135
Blackstone Est. E8 142 DV66
Blackstone Hill, Red. 250 DE134
Blackstone Rd. NW2 119 CW64
Blackthorn Ave., West Dr. 154 BN77
Blackthorn Clo., Reig. 266 DC136
Blackthorn Clo., St.Alb. 43 CJ17
Blackthorn Clo., Wat. 59 BV32
Blackthorn Ct., Houns. 156 BY80
Blackthorn Dell, Slou. 152 AW76
Blackthorn Gro., Bexh. 166 EY83
Blackthorn Rd., Reig. 266 DB136
Blackthorn Rd., Welw.G.C. 30 DA10
Blackthorn St. E3 143 EA70
Blackthorn Way, Brwd. 108 FX50
Blackthorne Ave., Croy. 202 DW101
Blackthorne Clo., Hat. 45 CT21
Blackthorne Dr. E4 101 ED49
Blackthorne Rd., Lthd. 246 CC126
Blackthorne Rd., Slou. 153 BE83
Blacktree Ms. SW9 161 DN83
Blackwall La. SE10 164 EE78
Blackwall Pier E14 144 EE73
Blackwall Tunnel E14 143 ED74
Blackwall Tunnel App. SE10 164 EE75
Blackwall Tunnel Northern App. E3 143 EA68
Blackwall Tunnel Northern App. E14 143 EA68
Blackwall Way E14 143 EC73
Blackwater Clo. E7 124 EF63
Blackwater Clo., Rain. 147 FE71
Blackwater La., Hem.H. 41 BS23
Blackwater Rd., Sutt. 218 DB105
High St.
Blackwater St. SE22 182 DT85
Blackwell Clo. E5 123 DX63
Blackwell Clo., Har. 95 CD52
Blackwell Dr., Wat. 76 BW44
Blackwell Gdns., Edg. 96 CN48
Blackwell Hall La., Chesh. 72 AT35
Blackwell Rd., Kings L. 58 BN29
Blackwood Clo., W.Byf. 212 BJ112
Blackwood St. SE17 279 K10
Blackwood St. SE17 162 DR78
Blade Ms. SW15 159 CZ84
Deodar Rd.
Bladen Clo., Wey. 213 BR107
Blades Clo., Lthd. 231 CK120
Blades Ct. SW15 159 CZ84
Deodar Rd.
Bladindon Dr., Bex. 186 EW87
Bladon Clo., Guil. 243 BA133
Bladon Gdns., Har. 116 CB58
Blagdens Clo. N14 99 DJ47
Blagdens La. N14 99 DK47
Blagdon Rd. SE13 183 EB86
Blagdon Rd., N.Mal. 199 CT98
Blagdon Wk., Tedd. 177 CJ93
Blagrove Rd. W10 139 CY71
Blair Ave. NW9 118 CS59
Blair Ave., Esher 196 CC103
Blair Clo. N1 142 DQ65
Blair Clo., Hayes 155 BU77
Blair Clo., Sid. 185 ES85
Blair Dr., Sev. 257 FH123
Blair Rd., Slou. 132 AS74
Blair St. E14 143 EC72
Blairderry Rd. SW2 181 DL89
Blairhead Dr., Wat. 93 BV48
Blake Ave., Bark. 145 ES67
Blake Clo. W10 139 CW71
Blake Clo., Cars. 200 DE101
Blake Clo., Rain. 147 FF67
Blake Clo., St.Alb. 43 CG23
Blake Clo., Well. 165 ES81
Blake Gdns. SW6 160 DB81
Blake Gdns., Dart. 168 FM84
Blake Hall Cres. E11 124 EG60
Blake Hall Rd. E11 124 EG59
Blake Hall Rd., Ong. 71 FG27
Blake Ho., Beck. 183 EA93
Blake Rd. E16 144 EF70
Blake Rd. N11 99 DJ52
Blake Rd., Croy. 202 DS103
Blake Rd., Mitch. 200 DE97
Blake St. SE8 163 EA79
Watergate St.
Blakeborough Dr., Rom. 106 FL54
Blakeden Dr., Esher 215 CF107
Blakehall Rd., Cars. 218 DF107
Blakeley Cotts. SE10 163 ED75
Tunnel Ave.
Blakemere Rd., Welw.G.C. 29 CX07
Blakemore Rd. SW16 181 DL90
Blakemore Rd., Th.Hth. 201 DM99
Blakemore Way, Belv. 166 EY76
Blakeney Ave., Beck. 203 DZ95
Blakeney Clo. E8 122 DU64
Ferncliff Rd.
Blakeney Clo. N20 98 DC46
Blakeney Clo. NW1 141 DK66
Rossendale Way
Blakeney Clo., Epsom 216 CR111
Blakeney Rd., Beck. 183 DZ94
Blakenham Rd. SW17 180 DF91
Blaker Ct. SE7 164 EJ80
Fairlawn
Blaker Rd. E15 143 EC67
Blakes Ave., N.Mal. 199 CT99
Blakes Ct., Saw. 36 EY05
Church St.
Blake's Grn., W.Wick. 203 EC102
Blakes La., Guil. 244 BL132
Blakes La., Lthd. 244 BN131
Blakes La., N.Mal. 199 CT99
Blakes Rd. SE15 162 DS80
Blakes Ter., N.Mal. 199 CU99
Blakes Way, Til. 171 GJ82
Coleridge Rd.
Blakesley Ave. W5 137 CJ72
Blakesley Wk. SW20 199 CZ96
Kingston Rd.
Blakesware Gdns. N9 100 DR45
Blakewood Clo., Felt. 176 BW91
Blanch Clo. SE15 162 DW80
Culmore Rd.
Blanchard Clo. SE9 184 EL90
Blanchard Way E8 142 DU65
Blanchards Hill, Guil. 242 AY126
Blanche La., Pot.B. 63 CT34
Blanche St. E16 144 EF70
Blanchedowne SE5 162 DR84
Blanchland Rd., Mord. 200 DB99
Blanchmans Rd., Warl. 237 DY118
Bland St. SE9 164 EK84
Blandfield Rd. SW12 180 DG86
Blandford Ave., Beck. 203 DY96
Blandford Ave., Twick. 176 CB88
Blandford Clo. N2 120 DC56
Blandford Clo., Croy. 201 DL104
Blandford Clo., Rom. 127 FB56
Blandford Clo., Slou. 152 AX76
Blandford Clo., Wok. 227 BB117
Blandford Ct., Slou. 152 AX76
Blandford Rd. S.
Blandford Cres. E4 101 EC45
Blandford Rd. W4 158 CS76
Blandford Rd. W5 157 CK75
Blandford Rd., Beck. 202 DW96
Blandford Rd., St.Alb. 43 CG20
Blandford Rd., Sthl. 156 CA77
Blandford Rd., Tedd. 177 CD92
Blandford Rd. N., Slou. 152 AX76
Blandford Rd. S., Slou. 152 AX76
Blandford Sq. NW1 272 C5
Blandford Sq. NW1 140 DE70
Blandford St. W1 272 E8
Blandford St. W1 140 DG71
Blandford Waye, Hayes 136 BW72
Blaney Cres. E6 145 EP69
Blanford Rd., Reig. 266 DC135
Blanmerle Rd. SE9 185 EP88
Blann Clo. SE9 184 EK86
Blantyre St. SW10 160 DD80
Blantyre Wk. SW10 160 DD80
Blantyre St.
Blashford NW3 140 DF66
Blashford St. SE13 183 ED87
Blasker Wk. E14 163 EA78
Blattner Clo., Borwd. 78 CL42
Blawith Rd., Har. 117 CE56
Blaxland Ter. (Cheshunt), Wal.Cr. 67 DX28
Davison Dr.
Blaydon Clo. N17 100 DV52
Blaydon Clo., Ruis. 115 BS59
Blaydon Wk. N17 100 DV52
Blays Clo., Egh. 172 AW93
Blays La., Egh. 172 AV94
Bleak Hill La. SE18 165 ET79
Blean Gro. SE20 182 DW94
Bleasdale Ave., Grnf. 137 CG68
Blechynden St. W10 139 CX73
Bramley Rd.
Bleddyn Clo., Sid. 186 EW86
Bledlow Clo. SE28 146 EW73
Bledlow Ri., Grnf. 136 CC68
Bleeding Heart Yd. EC1 274 E7
Blegborough Rd. SW16 181 DJ93
Blencarn Clo., Wok. 226 AT116
Blendon Dr., Bex. 186 EX86
Blendon Path, Brom. 184 EF94
Blendon Rd., Bex. 186 EW86
Blendon Ter. SE18 165 EQ78
Blendworth Way SE15 162 DS80
Daniel Gdns.
Blenheim Ave., Ilf. 125 EN58
Blenheim Clo. N21 100 DQ46
Elm Pk. Rd.
Blenheim Clo. SW20 199 CW97
Blenheim Clo., Dart. 188 FJ86
Blenheim Clo., Grnf. 137 CD68
Leaver Gdns.
Blenheim Clo., Rom. 127 FC56
Blenheim Clo., Saw. 36 EW07
Blenheim Clo., Slou. 133 AZ74
Blenheim Clo., Upmin. 129 FS60
Blenheim Clo., Wall. 219 DJ108
Blenheim Clo., Wat. 94 BX45
Blenheim Clo., W.Byf. 211 BF113
Madeira Rd.
Blenheim Ct. N19 121 DL61
Marlborough Rd.
Blenheim Ct., Sid. 185 ER90
Blenheim Cres. W11 139 CY72
Blenheim Cres., Ruis. 115 BR61
Blenheim Cres., S.Croy. 220 DQ108
Blenheim Dr., Well. 165 ET81
Blenheim Gdns. NW2 119 CW64
Blenheim Gdns. SW2 181 DM86
Blenheim Gdns., Kings.T. 178 CP94
Blenheim Gdns., S.Croy. 220 DU112
Blenheim Gdns., S.Ock. 148 FP74
Blenheim Gdns., Wall. 219 DJ107
Blenheim Gdns., Wem. 118 CL62
Blenheim Gdns., Wok. 226 AV119
Blenheim Gro. SE15 162 DU82
Blenheim Pk. Rd., S.Croy. 220 DQ109
Blenheim Pas. NW8 140 DC68
Blenheim Ter.
Blenheim Ri. N15 122 DT56
Talbot Rd.
Blenheim Rd. E6 144 EK69
Blenheim Rd. E15 124 EE63
Blenheim Rd. E17 123 DX55
Blenheim Rd. NW8 140 DC68
Blenheim Rd. SE20 182 DW94
Maple Rd.
Blenheim Rd. SW20 199 CW97
Blenheim Rd. W4 158 CS76
Blenheim Rd., Abb.L. 59 BU33
Blenheim Rd., Barn. 79 CX41
Blenheim Rd., Brwd. 108 FU44
Blenheim Rd., Brom. 204 EL98
Blenheim Rd., Dart. 188 FJ86
Blenheim Rd., Epsom 216 CR111
Blenheim Rd., Har. 116 CB58
Blenheim Rd., Nthlt. 136 CB65
Blenheim Rd., Orp. 206 EW103
Blenheim Rd., St.Alb. 43 CF19
Blenheim Rd., Sid. 186 EW88
Blenheim Rd., Slou. 152 AX77
Blenheim Rd., Sutt. 200 DA104
Blenheim St. W1 273 H9
Blenheim Ter. NW8 140 DC68
Blenheim Way, Epp. 70 FA27
Blenheim Way, Islw. 157 CG81
Blenkarne Rd. SW11 180 DF86
Blenkin Clo., St.Alb. 42 CC16
Bleriot Rd., Houns. 156 BW80
Blessbury Rd., Edg. 96 CQ53
Blessing Way, Bark. 146 EW69
Blessington Clo. SE13 163 ED83
Blessington Rd. SE13 163 ED83
Bletchingley Clo., Red. 251 DJ129
Bletchingley Clo., Th.Hth. 201 DP98

Boundary Way, Wok. 227 BA115
Boundary Yd., Wok. 227 BA116
Boundary Rd.
Boundfield Rd. SE6 184 EE90
Bounds Grn. Rd. N11 99 DJ51
Bounds Grn. Rd. N22 99 DJ51
Bourchier Clo., Sev. 257 FH126
Bourchier St. W1 273 M10
Bourdon Pl. W1 273 J10
Bourdon Rd. SE20 202 DW96
Bourdon St. W1 277 H1
Bourdon St. W1 141 DH73
Bourke Clo. NW10 138 CS65
Mayo Rd.
Bourke Clo. SW4 181 DL86
Bourke Hill, Couls. 234 DF118
Bourlet Clo. W1 273 K7
Bourn Ave. N15 122 DR56
Bourn Ave., Barn. 80 DD43
Bourn Ave., Uxb. 134 BN70
Bournbrook Rd. SE3 164 EK83
Bourne, The N14 99 DK46
Bourne, The, Hem.H. 57 BA27
Bourne, The, Ware 33 DX05
Bourne Ave. N14 99 DL47
Bourne Ave., Cher. 194 BG97
Eastern Ave.
Bourne Ave., Hayes 155 BQ76
Bourne Ave., Ruis. 116 BW64
Bourne Ave., Wind. 151 AQ84
Bourne Clo., Brox. 49 DZ20
Bourne Clo., Guil. 259 BB140
Bourne Clo., Ware 33 DX05
Bourne Clo., W.Byf. 212 BH113
Bourne Ct., Ruis. 115 BV64
Bourne Dr., Mitch. 200 DD96
Bourne End, Horn. 128 FN59
Bourne End La., Hem.H. 39 BC22
Bourne End Rd., Maid. 110 AD63
Bourne End Rd., Nthwd. 93 BS49
Bourne Est. EC1 274 D6
Bourne Est. EC1 141 DN71
Bourne Gdns. E4 101 EB49
Bourne Gro., Ash. 231 CK119
Bourne Hill N13 99 DL46
Bourne Ind. Pk., Dart. 187 FE85
Bourne Rd.
Bourne La., Cat. 236 DR121
Bourne Mead, Bex. 187 FC85
Bourne Meadow, Egh. 193 BB98
Bourne Pk. Clo., Ken. 236 DS116
Bourne Pl. W4 158 CR78
Dukes Ave.
Bourne Rd. E7 124 EF62
Bourne Rd. N8 121 DL58
Bourne Rd., Berk. 38 AT18
Bourne Rd., Bex. 187 FB87
Bourne Rd., Brom. 204 EK98
Bourne Rd., Dart. 187 FD85
Bourne Rd., Gdmg. 258 AT144
Bourne Rd., Grav. 191 GM89
Bourne Rd., Red. 251 DJ130
Bourne Rd., Slou. 151 AQ75
Bourne Rd., Vir.W. 192 AX99
Bourne Rd. (Bushey), Wat. 76 CA43
Bourne St. SW1 276 F9
Bourne St. SW1 160 DG77
Bourne St., Croy. 201 DP103
Waddon New Rd.
Bourne Ter. W2 140 DB71
Bourne Vale, Brom. 204 EG101
Bourne Vw., Grnf. 137 CF65
Bourne Vw., Ken. 236 DR115
Bourne Way, Add. 212 BJ106
Bourne Way, Brom. 204 EF103
Bourne Way, Epsom 216 CQ105
Bourne Way, Sutt. 217 CZ106
Bourne Way, Swan. 207 FC97
Bourne Way, Wok. 227 BA115
Bourne Way (Mayford), Wok. 226 AX122
Bournebridge Clo., Brwd. 109 GE45
Bournebridge La., Rom. 104 EZ45
Bournefield Rd., Whyt. 236 DT118
Godstone Rd.
Bournehall Ave. (Bushey), Wat. 76 CA43
Bournehall La. (Bushey), Wat. 76 CA44
Bournehall Rd. (Bushey), Wat. 76 CA44
Bournemead Ave., Nthlt. 135 BU68
Bournemead Clo., Nthlt. 135 BU68
Bournemead Way, Nthlt. 135 BV68
Bournemouth Clo. SE15 162 DU82
Bournemouth Rd. SE15 162 DU82
Bournemouth Rd. SW19 200 DA95
Bourneside, Vir.W. 192 AU101
Bourneside Cres. N14 99 DK46
Bourneside Gdns. SE6 183 EC92
Bourneside Rd., Add. 212 BK105
Bournevale Rd. SW16 181 DL91
Bournewood Rd. SE18 166 EU80
Bournewood Rd., Orp. 206 EV101
Bournville Rd. SE6 183 EA87
Bournwell Clo., Barn. 80 DF41
Bourton Clo., Hayes 135 BU74
Avondale Dr.
Bousfield Rd. SE14 163 DX82
Bousley Ri., Cher. 211 BD107
Boutflower Rd. SW11 160 DE84
Bouverie Gdns., Har. 117 CK58
Bouverie Gdns., Pur. 219 DL114
Bouverie Ms. N16 122 DS61
Bouverie Rd.
Bouverie Pl. W2 272 A8
Bouverie Pl. W2 140 DD72
Bouverie Rd. N16 122 DS61
Bouverie Rd., Couls. 234 DG118
Bouverie Rd., Har. 116 CC58
Bouverie St. EC4 274 E9
Bouverie St. EC4 141 DN72
Bouverie Way, Slou. 152 AY78
Bouvier Rd., Enf. 82 DW38
Boveney Clo., Slou. 151 AN75
Amerden Way
Boveney New Rd. (Eton Wick), Wind. 151 AL77
Boveney Rd. SE23 183 DX87
Boveney Rd., Wind. 150 AJ77
Boveney Wd. La., Slou. 110 AJ62
Bovey Way, S.Ock. 149 FV71
Bovill Rd. SE23 183 DX87
Bovingdon Ave., Wem. 138 CN65
Bovingdon Clo. N19 121 DJ61
Junction Rd.
Bovingdon Cres., Wat. 60 BX34
Bovingdon La. NW9 96 CS53
Bovingdon Rd. SW6 160 DB81
Bovingdon Sq., Mitch. 201 DL98
Leicester Ave.
Bow Arrow La., Dart. 188 FN86
Bow Bri. Est. E3 143 EB69
Bow Chyd. EC4 275 J9
Bow Common La. E3 143 DY70
Bow Ind. Pk. E15 143 EA66
Bow La. EC4 275 J9
Bow La. EC4 142 DQ72
Bow La. N12 98 DC53
Bow La., Mord. 199 CY100
Bow Rd. E3 143 DZ69
Bow St. E15 124 EE64
Bow St. WC2 274 A9
Bow St. WC2 141 DL72
Bowater Clo. NW9 118 CR57
Bowater Clo. SW2 181 DL86
Bowater Pl. SE3 164 EH80
Bowater Ridge, Wey. 213 BR110
Bowater Rd. SE18 164 EK76
Bowden Clo., Felt. 175 BS88
Bowden Dr., Horn. 128 FL60
Bowden St. SE11 161 DN78
Bowditch SE8 163 DZ78
Bowdon Rd. E17 123 EA59
Bowen Dr. SE21 182 DS90
Bowen Rd., Har. 116 CC59
Bowen St. E14 143 EB72
Bowens Wd., Croy. 221 DZ109
Bower Ave. SE10 164 EE81
Bower Clo., Nthlt. 136 BW68
Bower Clo., Rom. 105 FD52
Bower Ct., Epp. 70 EU32
Bower Ct., Wok. 227 BB116
Princess Rd.
Bower Fm. Rd. (Havering-atte-Bower), Rom. 105 FC48
Bower Hill, Epp. 70 EU32
Bower Hill Clo., Red. 267 DL137
Bower Hill Ind. Est., Epp. 70 EU32
Bower Hill La., Red. 267 DK135
Bower La. (Eynsford), Dart. 208 FL103
Bower Rd., Swan. 187 FG94
Bower St. E1 143 DX72
Bower Ter., Epp. 70 EU32
Bower Hill
Bower Vale, Epp. 70 EU32
Bower Way, Slou. 131 AL73
Bowerdean St. SW6 160 DB81
Bowerman Ave. SE14 163 DY79
Bowerman Rd., Grays 171 GG77
Bowers Ave., Grav. 191 GF91
Bowers Clo., Guil. 243 BA130
Cotts Wd. Dr.
Bowers Fm. Dr., Guil. 243 BA130
Bowers La., Guil. 243 BA129
Bowers Rd., Sev. 225 FF111
Bowers Wk. E6 145 EM72
Bowes Clo., Sid. 186 EV86
Bowes Rd. N11 99 DH50
Bowes Rd. N13 99 DL50
Bowes Rd. W3 138 CS73
Bowes Rd., Dag. 126 EW63
Bowes Rd., Stai. 173 BE92
Bowes Rd., Walt. 195 BV103
Bowes-Lyon Clo., Wind. 151 AQ81
Alma Rd.
Bowes-Lyon Ms., St.Alb. 43 CD20
Lower Dagnall St.
Bowfell Rd. W6 159 CW79
Bowford Ave., Bexh. 166 EY81
Bowgate, St.Alb. 43 CE19
Bowhay, Brwd. 109 GA47
Bowhill Clo. SW9 161 DN80
Bowie Clo. SW4 181 DK87
Bowl Ct. EC2 275 N5
Bowl Ct. EC2 142 DS70
Bowland Rd. SW4 161 DK84
Bowland Rd., Wdf.Grn. 102 EJ51
Bowland Yd. SW1 276 E5
Bowlers Orchard, Ch.St.G. 90 AU48
Bowles Grn., Enf. 82 DV36
Bowles Rd. SE1 162 DU79
Old Kent Rd.
Bowley Clo. SE19 182 DT93
Bowley La. SE19 182 DT92
Bowling Clo., Uxb. 134 BM67
Birch Cres.
Bowling Ct., Wat. 75 BU42
Bowling Grn. Clo. SW15 179 CV87
Bowling Grn. La. EC1 274 E4
Bowling Grn. La. EC1 141 DN70
Bowling Grn. Pl. SE1 279 K4
Bowling Grn. Pl. SE1 162 DR75
Bowling Grn. Rd., Wok. 210 AS109
Bowling Grn. Row SE18 165 EM76
Samuel St.
Bowling Grn. St. SE11 161 DN79
Bowling Grn. Wk. N1 275 M2
Bowling Rd., Ware 33 DY06
Bowls, The, Chig. 103 ES49
Bowls Clo., Stan. 95 CH50
Bowman Ave. E16 144 EF73
Bowman Ms. SW18 179 CZ88
Bowmans Clo. W13 137 CH74
Bowmans Clo., Pot.B. 64 DD32
Bowmans Clo., Slou. 130 AH67
Bowmans Ct., Hem.H. 40 BK18
Bowmans Grn., Wat. 76 BX36
Bowmans Lea SE23 182 DW87
Bowmans Meadow, Wall. 201 DH104
Bowmans Ms. E1 142 DU72
Hooper St.
Bowmans Ms. N7 121 DL62
Seven Sisters Rd.
Bowmans Pl. N7 121 DL62
Holloway Rd.
Bowmans Rd., Dart. 187 FF87
Bowman's Trd. Est. NW9 118 CM55
Westmoreland Rd.
Bowmead SE9 185 EM89
Bowmont Clo., Brwd. 109 GB44
Bowmore Wk. NW1 141 DK66
St. Paul's Cres.
Bown Clo., Til. 171 GH82
Bowness Clo. E8 142 DT65
Beechwood Rd.
Bowness Cres. SW15 178 CS92
Bowness Dr., Houns. 156 BY84
Bowness Rd. SE6 183 EB87
Bowness Rd., Bexh. 167 FB82
Bowness Way, Horn. 127 FG64
Bowood Rd. SW11 160 DG84
Bowood Rd., Enf. 83 DX40
Bowring Grn., Wat. 94 BW50
Bowrons Ave., Wem. 137 CK66
Bowry Dr., Stai. 173 AZ86
Bowsprit, The, Cob. 230 BW115
Bowstridge La., Ch.St.G. 90 AW48
Bowyer Clo. E6 145 EM71
Bowyer Cres., Uxb. 113 BF58
Bowyer Dr., Slou. 131 AL74
Bowyer Pl. SE5 162 DR80
Bowyer St. SE5 162 DQ80
Bowyers, Hem.H. 40 BK18
Bowyers Clo., Ash. 232 CM118
Box La., Bark. 146 EV68
Box La., Hem.H. 39 BE24
Box La., Hodd. 49 DX16
Box Ridge Ave., Pur. 219 DM112
Box Tree Clo., Chesh. 54 AR33
Box Wk., Lthd. 245 BS132
Boxall Rd. SE21 182 DS86
Boxfield, Welw.G.C. 30 DB12
Boxford Clo., S.Croy. 221 DX112
Boxgrove Ave., Guil. 243 BA132
Boxgrove La., Guil. 243 BA133
Boxgrove Rd. SE2 166 EW76
Boxgrove Rd., Guil. 243 BA133
Boxhill, Hem.H. 40 BK18
Boxhill Rd., Dor. 248 CL133
Boxhill Rd., Tad. 248 CM132
Boxhill Way, Bet. 264 CP138
Boxley Rd., Mord. 200 DC98
Boxley St. E16 144 EH74
Boxmoor Rd., Har. 117 CH56
Boxmoor Rd., Rom. 105 FC50
Boxoll Rd., Dag. 126 EZ63
Boxted Clo., Buck.H. 102 EL46
Boxted Rd., Hem.H. 39 BE18
Boxtree La., Har. 94 CC53
Boxtree Rd., Har. 95 CD52
Boxtree Wk., Orp. 206 EX102
Eldred Dr.
Boxwell Rd., Berk. 38 AV19
Boxwood Clo., West Dr. 154 BM75
Hawthorne Cres.
Boxwood Way, Warl. 237 DX117
Boxworth Clo. N12 98 DD50
Boxworth Gro. N1 141 DM67
Richmond Ave.
Boyard Rd. SE18 165 EP78
Boyce Clo., Borwd. 78 CL39
Boyce St. SE1 278 C3
Boyce Way E13 144 EG70
Boycroft Ave. NW9 118 CQ58
Boyd Ave., Sthl. 136 BZ74
Boyd Clo., Kings.T. 178 CN94
Crescent Rd.
Boyd Rd. SW19 180 DD93
Boyd St. E1 142 DU72
Boydell Ct. NW8 140 DD66
St. John's Wd. Pk.
Boyfield St. SE1 278 G5
Boyfield St. SE1 161 DP75
Boyland Rd., Brom. 184 EF92
Boyle Ave., Stan. 95 CG51
Boyle Clo., Uxb. 134 BM68
Boyle Fm. Rd., T.Ditt. 197 CG100
Boyle St. W1 273 K10
Boyne Ave. NW4 119 CX56
Boyne Rd. SE13 163 EC83
Boyne Rd., Dag. 126 FA62
Boyne Ter. Ms. W11 139 CZ74
Boyseland Ct., Edg. 96 CQ47
Boyson Rd. SE17 162 DR79
Boythorn Way SE16 162 DV78
Credon Rd.
Boyton Clo. E1 143 DX70
Stayner's Rd.
Boyton Clo. N8 121 DL55
Boyton Rd. N8 121 DL55
Brabant Ct. EC3 275 M10
Brabant Rd. N22 99 DM54
Brabazon Ave., Wall. 219 DL108
Brabazon Rd., Houns. 156 BW80
Brabazon Rd., Nthlt. 136 CA68
Brabazon St. E14 143 EB72
Brabourn Gro. SE15 162 DW82
Brabourne Clo. SE19 182 DS92
Brabourne Cres., Bexh. 166 EZ79
Brabourne Hts. NW7 96 CS48
Brabourne Ri., Beck. 203 EC99
Brace Clo. (Cheshunt), Wal.Cr. 65 DP25
Bracewell Ave., Grnf. 117 CF64
Bracewell Rd. W10 139 CW71
Bracewood Gdns., Croy. 202 DT104
Bracey Ms. N4 121 DL61
Bracey St.
Bracey St. N4 121 DL61
Bracken, The E4 101 EC47
Hortus Rd.
Bracken Ave. SW12 180 DG86
Bracken Ave., Croy. 203 EB104
Bracken Clo. E6 145 EM71
Bracken Clo., Borwd. 78 CP39
Bracken Clo., Lthd. 230 BZ124
Bracken Clo., Slou. 111 AR63
Bracken Clo., Sun. 175 BT93
Cavendish Rd.
Bracken Clo., Twick. 176 CA87
Hedley Rd.
Bracken Clo., Wok. 227 AZ118
Bracken Dr., Chig. 103 EP51
Bracken End, Islw. 177 CD85
Bracken Gdns. SW13 159 CU82
Bracken Hill Clo., Brom. 204 EF95
Bracken Hill La.
Bracken Hill La., Brom. 204 EF95
Bracken Ind. Est., Ilf. 103 ET52
Bracken Ms. E4 101 EC47
Hortus Rd.
Bracken Ms., Rom. 126 FA58
Bracken Path, Epsom 216 CP113
Bracken Way, Guil. 242 AS132
Bracken Way, Wok. 210 AT110
Brackenbridge Dr., Ruis. 116 BX62
Brackenbury Gdns. W6 159 CV76
Brackenbury Rd. N2 120 DC55
Brackenbury Rd. W6 159 CV76
Brackendale N21 99 DM47
Brackendale, Pot.B. 64 DA33
Brackendale Clo., Houns. 156 CB81
Brackendale Gdns., Upmin. 128 FQ63
Brackendene, Dart. 187 FE91
Brackendene, St.Alb. 60 BZ30
Brackendene Clo., Wok. 227 BA115
Brackenfield Clo. E5 122 DV63
Tiger Way
Brackenforde, Slou. 152 AW75
Brackenhill, Cob. 214 CA111
Brackens, The, Enf. 100 DS45
Brackens, The, Hem.H. 40 BK19
Heather Way
Brackens, The, Orp. 224 EU106
Brackens Dr., Brwd. 108 FW50
Brackenside, Horl. 269 DH147
Stockfield
Brackenwood, Sun. 195 BU95
Brackley, Wey. 213 BR106
Brackley Clo., Wall. 219 DL108
Brackley Rd. W4 158 CS78
Brackley Rd., Beck. 183 DZ94
Brackley Sq., Wdf.Grn. 102 EK52
Brackley St. EC1 275 H6
Brackley Ter. W4 158 CS78
Bracklyn Clo. N1 142 DR68
Parr St.
Bracklyn Ct. N1 142 DR68
Wimbourne St.
Bracklyn St. N1 142 DR68
Bracknell Clo. N22 99 DN53
Bracknell Gdns. NW3 120 DB63
Bracknell Gate NW3 120 DB64
Bracknell Pl., Hem.H. 40 BM16
Bracknell Way NW3 120 DB63
Bracondale, Esher 214 CC107
Bracondale Rd. SE2 166 EU77
Brad St. SE1 278 E3
Bradbery, Rick. 91 BD50
Bradbourne Pk. Rd., Sev. 256 FG123
Bradbourne Rd., Bex. 186 FA87
Bradbourne Rd., Grays 170 GB79
Bradbourne Rd., Sev. 257 FH122
Bradbourne St. SW6 160 DA82
Bradbourne Vale Rd., Sev. 256 FF122
Bradbury Clo., Borwd. 78 CP39
Bradbury Clo., Sthl. 156 BZ77
Bradbury Gdns., Slou. 112 AX63
Bradbury Ms. N16 122 DS64
Bradbury St.
Bradbury St. N16 122 DS64
Braddock Clo., Islw. 157 CF83
Braddon Rd., Rich. 158 CM83
Braddyll St. SE10 164 EE78
Braden St. W9 140 DB70
Shirland Rd.
Bradenham Ave., Well. 166 EU84
Bradenham Clo. SE17 162 DR79
Bradenham Rd., Har. 117 CH56
Bradenham Rd., Hayes 135 BS69
Bradenhurst Clo., Cat. 252 DT125
Bradfield Clo., Guil. 243 BA131
Bradfield Clo., Wok. 226 AY118
Bradfield Dr., Bark. 126 EU64
Bradfield Rd. E16 164 EG75
Bradfield Rd., Ruis. 116 BY64
Bradford Clo. N17 100 DS51
Commercial Rd.
Bradford Clo. SE26 182 DV91
Coombe Rd.
Bradford Clo., Brom. 205 EM102
Bradford Dr., Epsom 217 CT107
Bradford Rd. W3 158 CS75
Warple Way
Bradford Rd., Ilf. 125 ER60
Bradford Rd., Rick. 91 BC45
Bradford Rd., Slou. 131 AN72
Bradgate (Cuffley), Pot.B. 65 DK27
Bradgate Clo. (Cuffley), Pot.B. 65 DK28
Bradgate Rd. SE6 183 EA86
Brading Cres. E11 124 EH61
Brading Rd. SW2 181 DM87
Brading Rd., Croy. 201 DM100
Bradiston Rd. W9 139 CZ69
Bradleigh Ave., Grays 170 GC77
Bradley Clo. N7 141 DM65
Sutterton St.
Bradley Clo., Sutt. 218 DA110
Station Rd.
Bradley Gdns. W13 137 CH72
Bradley La., Dor. 247 CG132
Bradley Ms. SW17 180 DF88
Bellevue Rd.
Bradley Rd. N22 99 DM54
Bradley Rd. SE19 182 DQ93
Bradley Rd., Enf. 83 DY38
Bradley Rd., Slou. 131 AR73
Bradley Stone Rd. E6 145 EM71
Bradley's Clo. N1 141 DN68
White Lion St.
Bradman Row, Edg. 96 CQ52
Pavilion Way
Bradmead SW8 161 DH80
Bradmore Grn., Couls. 235 DM118
Coulsdon Rd.
Bradmore Grn., Hat. 63 CY26
Bradmore Ho. E1 142 DW71
Bradmore La., Hat. 63 CW26
Bradmore Pk. Rd. W6 159 CV76
Bradmore Way, Couls. 235 DL117
Bradmore Way, Hat. 63 CY26
Bradshaw Clo. SW19 180 DA93
Bradshaw Clo., Wind. 151 AL81
Bradshaw Rd., Wat. 76 BW39
Bradshawe Waye, Uxb. 134 BL71
Bradshaws, Hat. 45 CT22
Bradshaws Clo. SE25 202 DU97
Bradstock Rd. E9 143 DX65
Bradstock Rd., Epsom 217 CU106
Bradwell Ave., Dag. 126 FA61
Bradwell Clo. E18 124 EF56
Bradwell Clo., Horn. 147 FH65
Bradwell Grn., Brwd. 109 GC44
Bradwell Ms. N18 100 DU49
Lyndhurst Rd.
Bradwell Rd., Buck.H. 102 EL46
Bradwell St. E1 143 DX69
Brady Ave., Loug. 85 EQ40
Brady St. E1 142 DV70
Bradymead E6 145 EP72
Warwall
Braemar Ave. N22 99 DL53
Braemar Ave. NW10 118 CR62
Braemar Ave. SW19 180 DA89
Braemar Ave., Bexh. 167 FC84
Braemar Ave., S.Croy. 220 DQ109
Braemar Ave., Th.Hth. 201 DN97
Braemar Ave., Wem. 137 CK66
Braemar Gdns. NW9 96 CR53
Braemar Gdns., Horn. 128 FN58
Braemar Gdns., Sid. 185 ER90
Braemar Gdns., Slou. 151 AN75
Braemar Gdns., W.Wick. 203 EC102
Braemar Rd. E13 144 EF70
Braemar Rd. N15 122 DS57
Braemar Rd., Brent. 158 CL79
Braemar Rd., Wor.Pk. 199 CV104
Braes Mead, Red. 267 DL135
Braes St. N1 141 DP66
Braeside, Add. 212 BH111
Braeside, Beck. 183 EA92
Braeside Ave. SW19 199 CY95
Braeside Ave., Sev. 256 FF124
Braeside Clo., Pnr. 94 CA52
The Ave.
Braeside Clo., Sev. 256 FF123
Braeside Cres., Bexh. 167 FC84
Braeside Rd. SW16 181 DJ94
Braesyde Clo., Belv. 166 EZ77
Brafferton Rd., Croy. 220 DQ105
Braganza St. SE17 278 F10
Braganza St. SE17 161 DP78
Bragg Clo., Dag. 146 EV65
Porters Ave.
Bragmans La., Hem.H. 57 BB34
Bragmans La., Rick. 57 BD33
Braham St. E1 142 DT72
Braid, The, Chesh. 54 AS30
Braid Ave. W3 138 CS72
Braid Clo., Felt. 176 BZ89
Braidwood Rd. SE6 183 ED88
Braidwood St. SE1 279 M3
Brailsford Clo., Mitch. 180 DE94
Brailsford Rd. SW2 181 DN85
Brain Clo., Hat. 45 CV17
Brainton Ave., Felt. 175 BV87
Braintree Ave., Ilf. 124 EL56
Braintree Rd., Dag. 126 FA62
Braintree Rd., Ruis. 115 BV63
Braintree St. E2 142 DW69
Braithwaite Ave., Rom. 126 FA59
Braithwaite Gdns., Stan. 95 CJ53
Braithwaite Rd., Enf. 83 DZ41
Brakefield Rd., Grav. 190 GB93
Brakey Hill, Red. 252 DS134
Brakynbery, Berk. 38 AS16
Bramah Grn. SW9 161 DN81
Bramalea Clo. N6 120 DG58
Bramall Clo. E15 124 EF64
Idmiston Rd.
Bramber Ct., Brent. 158 CL77
Sterling Pl.
Bramber Ct., Slou. 131 AN74
Bramber Rd. N12 98 DE50
Bramber Rd. W14 159 CZ79
Bramble Ave., Dart. 189 FW90
Bramble Banks, Cars. 218 DG109
Bramble Clo., Cat. 236 DS122
Burntwood La.
Bramble Clo., Croy. 221 EA105
Bramble Clo., Guil. 242 AS132
Bramble Clo., Red. 266 DG136
Bramble Clo., Shep. 195 BR98
Halliford Clo.
Bramble Clo., Stan. 95 CK52
Bramble Clo., Uxb. 134 BM71
Bramble Clo., Wat. 59 BU34
Bramble Cft., Erith 167 FC77
Bramble Gdns. W12 139 CT73
Wallflower St.
Bramble La., Amer. 55 AS41
Bramble La., Hmptn. 176 BZ93
Bramble La., Hodd. 49 DY16
Bramble La., Sev. 257 FH128
Bramble La., Upmin. 148 FQ67
Bramble Mead, Ch.St.G. 90 AU48
Bramble Ri., Cob. 214 BW114
Bramble Ri., Harl. 35 EQ14
Bramble Rd., Hat. 44 CR18
Bramble Wk., Epsom 216 CP114
Bramble Way, Wok. 227 BF124
Brambleacres Clo., Sutt. 218 DA108
Bramblebury Rd. SE18 165 EQ78
Brambledene Clo., Wok. 226 AW118
Brambledown, Stai. 194 BH95
Brambledown Clo., W.Wick. 204 EE99
Brambledown Rd., Cars. 218 DG108
Brambledown Rd., S.Croy. 220 DS108
Brambledown Rd., Wall. 219 DH108
Bramblefield Clo., Long. 209 FX97
Brambles, The, Chig. 103 EQ50
Clayside
Brambles, The, St.Alb. 43 CD22
Brambles, The, Wal.Cr. 67 DX31
Brambles, The, West Dr. 154 BL77
Brambles Clo., Cat. 236 DS122
Brambles Clo., Islw. 157 CH80
Brambles Fm. Dr., Uxb. 134 BN69
Brambletye Pk. Rd., Red. 266 DF136
Bramblewood, Red. 251 DH129
Bramblewood Clo., Cars. 200 DE102
Brambling Clo., Wat. 76 BY42
Brambling Ri., Hem.H. 40 BL17
Bramblings, The E4 101 ED49
Bramcote Ave., Mitch. 200 DF98
Bramcote Ct., Mitch. 200 DF98
Bramcote Ave.
Bramcote Gro. SE16 162 DW78
Bramcote Rd. SW15 159 CV84
Bramdean Cres. SE12 184 EG88
Bramdean Gdns. SE12 184 EG88
Bramerton Rd., Beck. 203 DZ97
Bramerton St. SW3 160 DE79
Bramfield, Wat. 60 BY34
Garston La.
Bramfield Ct. N4 122 DQ61
Queens Dr.
Bramfield Ct., Hert. 31 DN08
Windsor Dr.
Bramfield La., Hert. 31 DL05
Bramfield Rd. SW11 180 DE86
Bramfield Rd., Hert. 31 DL06
Bramford Ct. N14 99 DK47
Bramford Rd. SW18 160 DC84
Bramham Gdns. SW5 160 DB78
Bramham Gdns., Chess. 215 CK105
Bramhope La. SE7 164 EH79
Bramlands Clo. SW11 160 DE83
Bramleas, Wat. 75 BT42
Bramley Ave., Couls. 235 DJ115
Bramley Clo. E17 101 DY54
Bramley Clo. N14 81 DH43
Bramley Clo., Cher. 194 BH102
Bramley Clo., Grav. 191 GF94
Bramley Clo., Hayes 135 BU73
Orchard Rd.
Bramley Clo., Orp. 205 EP102
Bramley Clo., Red. 266 DE136
Abinger Dr.
Bramley Clo., S.Croy. 219 DP106
Bramley Clo., Stai. 174 BJ93
Bramley Clo., Swan. 207 FE98
Bramley Clo., Twick. 176 CC86
Bramley Ct., Wat. 59 BV31
Orchard Ave.

Bramley Ct., Well. 166 EV81
Bramley Cres. SW8 161 DK80
Pascal St.
Bramley Cres., Ilf. 125 EN58
Bramley Gdns., Wat. 94 BW50
Bramley Hill, S.Croy. 219 DP106
Bramley Pl., Dart. 167 FG84
Bramley Rd. N14 81 DH43
Bramley Rd. W5 157 CJ76
Bramley Rd. W10 139 CX73
Bramley Rd., Sutt. 218 DD106
Bramley Rd. (Cheam), Sutt. 217 CX109
Bramley Shaw, Wal.Abb. 68 EF33
Bramley Wk., Horl. 269 DJ148
Carlton Tye
Bramley Way, Ash. 232 CM117
Bramley Way, Houns. 176 BZ85
Bramley Way, St.Alb. 43 CJ21
Bramley Way, W.Wick. 203 EB103
Brammas Clo., Slou. 151 AQ76
Brampton Clo. E5 122 DV61
Brampton Clo. (Cheshunt), Wal.Cr. 66 DU28
Brampton Gdns. N15 122 DQ57
Brampton Rd.
Brampton Gdns., Walt. 214 BW106
Brampton Gro. NW4 119 CV56
Brampton Gro., Har. 117 CG56
Brampton Gro., Wem. 118 CN60
Brampton La. NW4 119 CW56
Brampton Pk. Rd. N22 121 DN55
Brampton Rd. E6 144 EK69
Brampton Rd. N15 122 DQ57
Brampton Rd. NW9 118 CN56
Brampton Rd. SE2 166 EW79
Brampton Rd., Bexh. 166 EX80
Brampton Rd., Croy. 202 DT101
Brampton Rd., St.Alb. 43 CG19
Brampton Rd., Uxb. 135 BP68
Brampton Rd., Wat. 93 BU48
Brampton Ter., Borwd. 78 CN38
Bramshaw Gdns., Wat. 94 BX50
Bramshaw Ri., N.Mal. 198 CS100
Bramshaw Rd. E9 143 DX65
Bramshill Clo., Chig. 103 ES50
Tine Rd.
Bramshill Gdns. NW5 121 DH62
Bramshill Rd. NW10 139 CT68
Bramshot Ave. SE7 164 EG79
Bramshot Way, Wat. 93 BU47
Bramston Clo., Ilf. 103 ET51
Bramston Rd. NW10 139 CU68
Bramston Rd. SW17 180 DC90
Bramwell Clo., Sun. 196 BX96
Bramwell Ms. N1 141 DM67
Brancaster Dr. NW7 97 CT52
Brancaster La., Pur. 220 DQ112
Brancaster Pl., Loug. 85 EM41
Brancaster Rd. E12 125 EM63
Brancaster Rd. SW16 181 DL90
Brancaster Rd., Ilf. 125 ER58
Brancepeth Gdns., Buck.H. 102 EG47
Branch Clo., Hat. 45 CW16
Branch Hill NW3 120 DC62
Branch Pl. N1 142 DR67
Branch Rd. E14 143 DY73
Branch Rd., Ilf. 104 EV50
Branch Rd., St.Alb. 42 CB19
Branch Rd. (Park St.), St.Alb. 61 CD27
Branch St. SE15 162 DS80
Brancker Clo., Wall. 219 DL108
Brown Clo.
Brancker Rd., Har. 117 CK55
Brancroft Way, Enf. 83 DY39
Brand St. SE10 163 EC80
Brandlehow Rd. SW15 159 CZ84
Brandon Clo., Grays 170 FZ75
Brandon Clo. (Cheshunt), Wal.Cr. 66 DS26
Brandon Est. SE17 161 DP79
Brandon Gros. Ave., S.Ock. 149 FW69
Brandon Ms. EC2 142 DR71
Moor La.
Brandon Rd. E17 123 EC55
Brandon Rd. N7 141 DL66
Brandon Rd., Dart. 188 FM87
Brandon Rd., Sthl. 156 BZ78
Brandon Rd., Sutt. 218 DB105
Brandon St. SE17 279 J9
Brandon St. SE17 162 DQ77
Brandon St., Grav. 191 GH87
Brandram Rd. SE13 164 EE83
Brandreth Rd. E6 145 EM72
Brandreth Rd. SW17 181 DH89
Brandries, The, Wall. 201 DK104
Brands Rd., Slou. 153 BB79
Brandsland, Reig. 266 DB138
Brandville Gdns., Ilf. 125 EP56
Brandville Rd., West Dr. 154 BL75
Brandy Way, Sutt. 218 DA108
Branfill Rd., Upmin. 128 FP61
Brangbourne Rd., Brom. 183 EC92
Brangton Rd. SE11 161 DM78
Brangwyn Cres. SW19 200 DD95
Branksea St. SW6 159 CY80
Branksome Ave. N18 100 DT50
Branksome Clo., Hem.H. 40 BN19
Branksome Clo., Walt. 196 BX103
Branksome Rd. SW2 181 DL85
Branksome Rd. SW19 200 DA95
Branksome Way, Har. 118 CL58
Branksome Way, N.Mal. 198 CQ95
Bransby Rd., Chess. 216 CL107
Branscombe Gdns. N21 99 DN45
Branscombe St. SE13 163 EB83
Bransdale Clo. NW6 140 DB67
West End La.
Bransell Clo., Swan. 207 FC100
Bransgrove Rd., Edg. 96 CM53
Branston Cres., Orp. 205 ER102
Branstone Rd., Rich. 158 CM81
Branton Rd., Green. 189 FT86
Brants Wk. W7 137 CE70
Brantwood Ave., Erith 167 FC80
Brantwood Ave., Islw. 157 CG84
Brantwood Clo. E17 123 EB55
Brantwood Clo., W.Byf. 212 BG113
Brantwood Gdns.
Brantwood Dr., W.Byf. 211 BF113
Brantwood Gdns., Enf. 81 DL42
Brantwood Gdns., Ilf. 124 EL56
Brantwood Gdns., W.Byf. 211 BF113
Brantwood Rd. N17 100 DU51
Brantwood Rd. SE24 182 DQ85
Brantwood Rd., Bexh. 167 FB82
Brantwood Rd., S.Croy. 220 DQ109
Brantwood Way, Orp. 206 EW97
Brasenose Dr. SW13 159 CW79
Brasher Clo., Grnf. 117 CD64
Brass Tally All. SE16 163 DX75
Middleton Dr.
Brassey Clo., Felt. 175 BT88
Brassey Hill, Oxt. 254 EG130
Brassey Rd. NW6 139 CZ65
Brassey Rd., Oxt. 254 EF130
Brassey Sq. SW11 160 DG83
Brassie Ave. W3 138 CS72
Brasted Clo. SE26 182 DW91
Brasted Clo., Bexh. 186 EX85
Brasted Clo., Orp. 206 EU103
Brasted Clo., Sutt. 218 DA110
Brasted Hill Rd., Sev. 240 EU120
Brasted Hill Rd., West. 240 EV121
Brasted La., Sev. 240 EU119
Brasted Rd., Erith 167 FE80
Brasted Rd., West. 255 ER126
Brathway Rd. SW18 180 DA87
Bratley St. E1 142 DU70
Weaver St.
Brattle Wd., Sev. 257 FH129
Braund Ave., Grnf. 136 CB70
Braundton Ave., Sid. 185 ET88
Braunston Dr., Hayes 136 BY70
Bravington Clo., Shep. 194 BM99
Bravington Pl. W9 139 CZ70
Bravington Rd.
Bravington Rd. W9 139 CZ68
Brawlings La., Ger.Cr. 91 BA49
Brawne Ho. SE17 161 DP79
Hillingdon St.
Braxfield Rd. SE4 163 DY84
Braxted Pk. SW16 181 DM93
Bray NW3 140 DE66
Bray Clo., Borwd. 78 CQ39
Bray Clo., Maid. 150 AC75
Bray Rd.
Bray Ct., Maid. 150 AC77
Bray Cres. SE16 163 DX75
Marlow Way
Bray Dr. E16 144 EF73
Bray Gdns., Wok. 227 BE116
Bray Pas. E16 144 EG73
Bray Pl. SW3 276 D9
Bray Pl. SW3 160 DF77
Bray Rd. NW7 97 CX51
Bray Rd., Cob. 230 BY116
Bray Rd., Guil. 258 AV135
Bray Rd., Maid. 150 AC75
Brayards Rd. SE15 162 DV82
Brayards Rd. Est. SE15 162 DV82
Braybank, Maid. 150 AC75
Braybourne Clo., Uxb. 134 BJ65
Braybourne Dr., Islw. 157 CF80
Braybrook St. W12 139 CT71
Braybrooke Gdns. SE19 182 DT94
Fox Hill
Brayburne Ave. SW4 161 DJ82
Braycourt Ave., Walt. 195 BV101
Braydon Rd. N16 122 DU60
Brayfield Rd., Maid. 150 AC75
Brayfield Ter. N1 141 DN66
Lofting Rd.
Brayford Sq. E1 142 DW72
Summercourt Rd.
Brays Mead, Harl. 51 ET17
Brayton Gdns., Enf. 81 DK42
Braywood Ave., Egh. 173 AZ93
Braywood Rd. SE9 165 ER84
Braziers Fld., Hert. 32 DT09
Brazil Clo., Croy. 201 DL101
Breach Barns La., Wal.Abb. 68 EF30
Galley Hill
Breach La., Dag. 146 FA69
Breach La., Hert. 47 DJ18
Breach Rd., Grays 169 FT79
Bread & Cheese La. (Cheshunt), Wal.Cr. 66 DR25
Bread St. EC4 275 J9
Bread St. EC4 142 DQ73
Breakfield, Couls. 235 DL116
Breakmead, Welw.G.C. 30 DB11
Breakneck Hill, Green. 189 FV85
Breaks Rd., Hat. 45 CV17
Breakspear Ave., St.Alb. 43 CF21
Breakspear Ct., Abb.L. 59 BT30
Breakspear Path (Harefield), Uxb. 114 BJ55
Breakspear Rd., Ruis. 115 BP58
Breakspear Rd. N. (Harefield), Uxb. 114 BN57
Breakspear Rd. S. (Ickenham), Uxb. 114 BM62
Breakspear Way, Hem.H. 41 BQ20
Breakspeare Clo., Wat. 75 BV38
Breakspeare Rd., Abb.L. 59 BS31
Breakspears Dr., Orp. 206 EU95
Breakspears Ms. SE4 163 EA82
Breakspears Rd.
Breakspears Rd. SE4 163 DZ84
Bream Clo. N17 122 DV56
Bream Gdns. E6 145 EN69
Bream St. E3 143 EA66
Breamore Clo. SW15 179 CU88
Breamore Rd., Ilf. 125 ET61
Bream's Bldgs. EC4 274 D8
Bream's Bldgs. EC4 141 DN72
Breamwater Gdns., Rich. 177 CH90
Brearley Clo., Edg. 96 CQ52
Pavilion Way
Brearley Clo., Uxb. 134 BL65
Breasley Clo. SW15 159 CV84
Brechin Pl. SW7 160 DC77
Rosary Gdns.
Brecken Clo., St.Alb. 43 CG16
Brecknock Rd. N7 121 DJ63
Brecknock Rd. N19 121 DJ63
Brecknock Rd. Est. N7 121 DJ63
Breckonmead, Brom. 204 EJ96
Wanstead Rd.
Brecon Clo., Mitch. 201 DL97
Brecon Clo., Wor.Pk. 199 CW103
Brecon Rd. W6 159 CY79
Brecon Rd., Enf. 82 DW42
Brede Clo. E6 145 EN69
Bredgar Rd. N19 121 DJ61
Bredhurst Clo. SE20 182 DW93
Bredon Rd. SE5 162 DQ83
Bredon Rd., Croy. 202 DT101
Bredune, Ken. 236 DR115
Church Rd.
Bredward Clo., Slou. 130 AH69
Breech La., Tad. 233 CU124
Breer St. SW6 160 DB83
Breeze Ter. (Cheshunt), Wal.Cr. 67 DX28
Collet Clo.
Breezers Hill E1 142 DU73
Pennington St.
Brember Rd., Har. 116 CC61
Bremer Ms. E17 123 EB56
Church La.
Bremer Rd., Stai. 174 BG90
Bremner Ave., Horl. 268 DF147
Bremner Clo., Swan. 207 FG98
Bremner Rd. SW7 160 DC75
Brenchley Ave., Grav. 191 GH92
Brenchley Clo., Brom. 204 EF100
Brenchley Clo., Chis. 205 EN95
Brenchley Gdns. SE23 182 DW86
Brenchley Rd., Orp. 205 ET95
Brenda Rd. SW17 180 DF89
Brendans Clo., Horn. 128 FL60
Brende Gdns., W.Mol. 196 CB98
Brendon Ave. NW10 118 CS63
Brendon Clo., Erith 167 FE81
Brendon Clo., Esher 214 CC107
Brendon Clo., Hayes 155 BQ80
Brendon Ct., Rad. 61 CH34
The Ave.
Brendon Dr., Esher 214 CC107
Brendon Gdns., Har. 116 CB63
Brendon Gdns., Ilf. 125 ES57
Brendon Gro. N2 98 DC54
Brendon Rd. SE9 185 ER89
Brendon Rd., Dag. 126 EZ60
Brendon St. W1 272 C8
Brendon St. W1 140 DE72
Brendon Way, Enf. 100 DS45
Brenley Clo., Mitch. 200 DG97
Brenley Gdns. SE9 164 EK84
Brennan Rd., Til. 171 GH82
Brent, The, Dart. 188 FN87
Brent Clo., Bex. 186 EY88
Brent Clo., Dart. 188 FP86
Brent Cres. NW10 138 CM68
Brent Cross Gdns. NW4 119 CX58
Haley Rd.
Brent Cross Shop. Cen. NW4 119 CW59
Brent Grn. NW4 119 CW57
Brent Grn. Wk., Wem. 118 CQ62
Brent La., Dart. 188 FM87
Brent Lea, Brent. 157 CJ80
Brent Pk. NW10 118 CR64
Brent Pk. Rd. NW4 119 CV59
Brent Pk. Rd. NW9 119 CU60
Brent Pl., Barn. 80 DA43
Brent Rd. E16 144 EG71
Brent Rd. SE18 165 EP80
Brent Rd., Brent. 157 CJ79
Brent Rd., S.Croy. 220 DV109
Brent Rd., Sthl. 156 BW76
Brent Side, Brent. 157 CJ79
Brent St. NW4 119 CW56
Brent Ter. NW2 119 CW61
Brent Vw. Rd. NW9 119 CU59
Brent Way N3 98 DA51
Brent Way, Brent. 157 CK80
Brent Way, Dart. 188 FP86
Brent Way, Wem. 138 CP65
Brentcot Clo. W13 137 CH70
Brentfield NW10 138 CP66
Brentfield Clo. NW10 138 CR65
Normans Mead
Brentfield Gdns. NW2 119 CX59
Hendon Way
Brentfield Rd. NW10 138 CR65
Brentfield Rd., Dart. 188 FN86
Brentford Business Cen., Brent. 157 CJ80
Brentford Clo., Hayes 136 BX70
Brenthall Twrs., Harl. 52 EW17
Brentham Way W5 137 CK70
Brenthouse Rd. E9 142 DV66
Brenthurst Rd. NW10 139 CT65
Brentlands Dr., Dart. 188 FN88
Brentmead Clo. W7 137 CE73
Brentmead Gdns. NW10 138 CM68
Brentmead Pl. NW11 119 CX58
North Circular Rd.
Brenton St. E14 143 DY72
Brentside Clo. W13 137 CG70
Brentside Executive Cen., Brent. 157 CH79
Brentvale Ave., Sthl. 137 CD74
Brentvale Ave., Wem. 138 CM67
Brentwick Gdns., Brent. 158 CL77
Brentwood Bypass, Brwd. 108 FS49
Brentwood Clo. SE9 185 EQ88
Brentwood Ct., Add. 212 BH105
Brentwood Ho. SE18 164 EK80
Shooter's Hill Rd.
Brentwood Pl., Brwd. 108 FX46
Brentwood Rd., Brwd. 109 GA49
Brentwood Rd., Grays 171 GH77
Brentwood Rd., Rom. 127 FF58
Brereton Ct., Hem.H. 40 BL22
Brereton Rd. N17 100 DT52
Bressenden Pl. SW1 277 J6
Bressenden Pl. SW1 161 DH76
Bressey Ave., Enf. 82 DU39
Bressey Gro. E18 102 EF54
Bretlands Rd., Cher. 193 BE103
Brett Clo. N16 122 DS61
Yoakley Rd.
Brett Clo., Nthlt. 136 BX69
Broomcroft Ave.
Brett Ct. N9 100 DW47
Brett Cres. NW10 138 CR66
Brett Gdns., Dag. 146 EY66
Brett Ho. Clo. SW15 179 CX86
Putney Heath La.
Brett Pas. E8 122 DV64
Kenmure Rd.
Brett Pl., Wat. 75 BU37
The Harebreaks
Brett Rd. E8 122 DV64
Brett Rd., Barn. 79 CW43
Brettell St. SE17 162 DR78
Merrow St.
Brettenham Ave. E17 101 EA53
Brettenham Rd. E17 101 EA54
Brettenham Rd. N18 100 DV49
Brettgrave, Epsom 216 CQ110
Brevet Clo., Purf. 169 FR77
Brew Ho. Rd., Bet. 264 CQ138
Tanners Meadow
Brewer St. W1 273 L10
Brewer St. W1 141 DJ73
Brewer St., Red. 252 DQ131
Brewer's Fld., Dart. 188 FJ91
Brewer's Grn. SW1 277 M6
Brewers Hall Gdns. EC2 275 J7
Brewers La., Rich. 177 CK85
George St.
Brewery Clo., Wem. 117 CG64
Brewery La., Sev. 257 FJ125
High St.
Brewery La., Twick. 177 CF87
Brewery La., W.Byf. 212 BL113
Brewery Rd. N7 141 DL66
Brewery Rd. SE18 165 ER78
Brewery Rd., Brom. 204 EL102
Brewery Rd., Hodd. 49 EA17
Brewery Rd., Wok. 226 AX117
Brewery Sq. SE1 142 DT74
Horselydown La.
Brewhouse La. E1 142 DV74
Brewhouse La., Hert. 32 DQ09
St. Andrew St.
Brewhouse Rd. SE18 165 EM77
Brewhouse St. SW15 159 CY83
Brewhouse Wk. SE16 143 DY74
Brewhouse Yd. EC1 274 F4
Brewhouse Yd., Grav. 191 GH86
Queen St.
Brewood Rd., Dag. 146 EV65
Brewster Gdns. W10 139 CW71
Brewster Ho. E14 143 DZ73
Brewster Rd. E10 123 EB60
Brian Ave., S.Croy. 220 DS112
Brian Clo., Horn. 127 FH63
Brian Rd., Rom. 126 EW57
Briane Rd., Epsom 216 CQ110
Briant St. SE14 163 DX81
Briants Clo., Pnr. 94 BZ54
Briar Ave. SW16 181 DM94
Briar Banks, Cars. 218 DG109
Briar Clo. N2 120 DB55
Briar Clo. N13 100 DQ48
Briar Clo., Berk. 39 BA16
Briar Clo., Buck.H. 102 EK47
Briar Clo., Hmptn. 176 BZ92
Briar Clo., Islw. 177 CF85
Briar Clo., Maid. 130 AH72
Briar Clo. (Cheshunt), Wal.Cr. 66 DW29
Briar Clo., W.Byf. 212 BH111
Briar Ct., Sutt. 217 CW105
Briar Cres., Nthlt. 136 CB65
Briar Gdns., Brom. 204 EF102
Briar Gro., S.Croy. 220 DU113
Briar Hill, Pur. 219 DL111
Briar La., Cars. 218 DG109
Briar La., Croy. 221 EB105
Briar Pas. SW16 201 DL97
Briar Pl. SW16 201 DM97
Briar Rd. NW2 119 CW63
Briar Rd. SW16 201 DL97
Briar Rd., Bex. 187 FD90
Briar Rd., Har. 117 CJ57
Briar Rd., Rom. 106 FJ52
Briar Rd., St.Alb. 43 CK17
Briar Rd., Shep. 194 BM99
Briar Rd., Twick. 177 CE88
Briar Rd., Wat. 59 BU34
Briar Rd., Wok. 227 BB123
Briar Wk. SW15 159 CV84
Briar Wk. W10 139 CY70
Droop St.
Briar Wk., Edg. 96 CQ52
Briar Wk., W.Byf. 212 BG112
Briar Way, Berk. 38 AW20
Briar Way, Guil. 243 BB130
Briar Way, Slou. 131 AQ71
Briar Way, West Dr. 154 BN75
Briarbank Rd. W13 137 CG72
Briarcliff, Hem.H. 39 BE19
Briardale Gdns. NW3 120 DA62
Briarfield Ave. N3 98 DB54
Briaris Clo. N17 100 DV52
Briarleas Gdns., Upmin. 129 FS59
Briarley Clo., Brox. 49 DZ22
Briars, The, Hert. 32 DU09
Briars, The, Rick. 74 BH36
Briars, The, Slou. 153 AZ78
Briars, The (Cheshunt), Wal.Cr. 67 DY31
Briars, The (Bushey), Wat. 95 CE45
Briars Clo., Hat. 45 CU18
Briars Ct., Lthd. 215 CD114
Briars La., Hat. 45 CU18
Briars Rd., Maid. 130 AH72
Briars Wk., Rom. 106 FM54
Briars Wd., Hat. 45 CT18
Briars Wd., Horl. 269 DJ147
Briarswood, Wal.Cr. 66 DR28
Briarswood Way, Orp. 223 ET106
Briarwood Clo. NW9 118 CQ58
Briarwood Clo., Felt. 175 BS90
Briarwood Dr., Nthwd. 93 BU54
Briarwood Rd. SW4 181 DK85
Briarwood Rd., Epsom 217 CU107
Briary Clo. NW3 140 DE66
Fellows Rd.
Briary Ct., Sid. 186 EV92
Briary Gdns., Brom. 184 EH92
Briary Gro., Edg. 96 CP54
Briary La. N9 100 DT48
Brick, The, Ware 32 DV05
Brick Ct. EC4 274 D9
Brick Fm. Clo., Rich. 158 CP81
Brick Kiln Clo., Wat. 76 BY44
Brick Kiln La., Oxt. 254 EJ131
Brick Knoll Pk., St.Alb. 43 CJ21
Brick La. E1 142 DT71
Brick La. E2 142 DT69
Brick La., Enf. 82 DV40
Brick La., Stan. 95 CK52
Honeypot La.
Brick St. W1 277 H3
Brick St. W1 141 DH74
Brickcroft, Brox. 67 DY26
Brickenden Ct., Wal.Abb. 68 EF33
Brickendon La., Hert. 32 DQ12
Bricket Rd., St.Alb. 43 CD20
Brickett Clo., Ruis. 115 BQ57
Brickfield, Hat. 45 CU21
Brickfield Ave., Hem.H. 41 BP21
Brickfield Clo., Brent. 157 CJ80
Brickfield Cotts. SE18 165 ET79
Brickfield Fm. Gdns., Orp. 223 EQ105
Brickfield La., Barn. 79 CT44
Brickfield La., Hayes 155 BR79
Brickfield La., Slou. 130 AG66
Brickfield Rd. SW19 180 DB91
Brickfield Rd., Epp. 70 EX29
Brickfield Rd., Red. 267 DN142
Brickfield Rd., Th.Hth. 201 DP95
Brickfields, Har. 117 CD61
Brickfields La., Epp. 70 EX29
Brickfield Rd.
Brickfields Way, West Dr. 154 BM76
Bricklayer's Arms SE1 279 N8
Bricklayer's Arms SE1 162 DS77
Brickmakers La., Hem.H. 41 BP21
Brickwall Clo., Welw. 29 CU07
Brickwall La., Ruis. 115 BS60
Brickwood Clo. SE26 182 DV90
Brickwood Rd., Croy. 202 DS103
Brickyard La., Dor. 262 BW141
Bride Ct. EC4 274 F9
Bride La. EC4 274 F9
Bride St. N7 141 DM65
Brideale Clo. SE15 162 DT80
Colegrove Rd.
Bridewain St. SE1 162 DT76
Bridewell Pl. E1 142 DV74
Brewhouse La.
Bridewell Pl. EC4 274 F9
Bridford Ms. W1 273 J6
Bridge, The, Har. 117 CE55
Bridge App. NW1 140 DG66
Bridge Ave. W6 159 CW78
Bridge Ave. W7 137 CD71
Bridge Ave., Upmin. 128 FN61
Bridge Barn La., Wok. 226 AW117
Bridge Clo. W10 139 CX72
Kingsdown Clo.
Bridge Clo., Brwd. 109 FZ49
Bridge Clo., Enf. 82 DV40
Bridge Clo., Rom. 127 FE58
Bridge Clo., Slou. 131 AM73
Bridge Clo., Walt. 195 BT101
Bridge Clo., W.Byf. 212 BM112
Bridge Clo., Wok. 226 AW117
Bridge Cotts., Upmin. 129 FU64
Bridge Dr. N13 99 DM49
Bridge End E17 101 EC53
Bridge Gdns., Ashf. 175 BQ94
Bridge Gdns., E.Mol. 197 CD98
Bridge Gate N21 100 DQ45
Ridge Ave.
Bridge Hill, Epp. 69 ET33
Bridge Ho. Quay E14 143 EC74
Prestons Rd.
Bridge La. NW11 119 CY57
Bridge La. SW11 160 DE81
Bridge La., Vir.W. 192 AY99
Bridge Meadows SE14 163 DX79
Bridge Pk. SW18 180 DA85
Bridge Pk. St., Slou. 153 BD80
Bridge Pl. SW1 277 J8
Bridge Pl. SW1 161 DH77
Bridge Pl., Amer. 55 AS38
Bridge Pl., Croy. 202 DR101
Bridge Pl., Wat. 76 BX43
Bridge Rd. E6 145 EM66
Bridge Rd. E15 143 ED66
Bridge Rd. E17 123 DZ59
Bridge Rd. N9 100 DU48
The Bdy.
Bridge Rd. N22 99 DL53
Bridge Rd. NW10 138 CS65
Bridge Rd., Beck. 183 DZ94
Bridge Rd., Bexh. 166 EY82
Bridge Rd., Cher. 194 BH101
Bridge Rd., Chess. 216 CL106
Bridge Rd., Croy. 202 DQ104
Duppas Hill Rd.
Bridge Rd., E.Mol. 197 CD99
Bridge Rd., Epsom 217 CT112
Bridge Rd., Erith 167 FF81
Bridge Rd., Grays 170 GB78
Bridge Rd., Houns. 157 CD83
Bridge Rd., Islw. 157 CD83
Bridge Rd., Kings L. 59 BQ33
Bridge Rd., Orp. 206 EV100
Bridge Rd., Rain. 147 FF70
Bridge Rd., Sthl. 156 BZ75
Bridge Rd., Sutt. 218 DB107
Bridge Rd., Twick. 177 CH86
Bridge Rd., Uxb. 134 BJ68
Bridge Rd., Wall. 219 DJ106
Bridge Rd., Welw.G.C. 29 CW08
Bridge Rd., Wem. 118 CN62
Bridge Rd., Wey. 212 BM105
Bridge Rd. E., Welw.G.C. 29 CY08
Bridge Row, Croy. 202 DR102
Cross Rd.
Bridge St. SW1 277 P5
Bridge St. SW1 161 DL75
Bridge St. W4 158 CR77
Bridge St., Berk. 38 AX19
Bridge St., Guil. 258 AW135
Bridge St., Hem.H. 40 BJ21
Bridge St., Lthd. 231 CG122
Bridge St., Pnr. 116 BX55
Bridge St., Rich. 177 CK85
Bridge St., Slou. 153 BD80
Bridge St., Stai. 173 BE91
Bridge St., Walt. 195 BS102
Bridge Ter. E15 143 ED66
Bridge Vw. W6 159 CW78
Bridge Way N11 99 DJ48
Pymmes Grn. Rd.
Bridge Way NW11 119 CZ57
Bridge Way, Cob. 213 BT113
Bridge Way, Couls. 234 DE119
Bridge Way, Twick. 176 CC87
Bridge Way, Uxb. 115 BP64
Bridge Wf., Cher. 194 BJ102
Bridge Wf. Rd., Islw. 157 CH83
Church St.
Bridge Wks., Uxb. 134 BJ70
Bridge Yd. SE1 279 L2
Bridgefield Clo., Bans. 233 CW115
Bridgefield Rd., Sutt. 218 DA107
Bridgefields, Welw.G.C. 29 CZ08
Bridgefoot SE1 161 DL78
Bridgefoot La., Pot.B. 63 CX33
Bridgeham Clo., Wey. 212 BN106
Mayfield Rd.
Bridgeham Way, Horl. 269 DP148
Bridgehill Clo., Guil. 242 AU132
Bridgeland Rd. E16 144 EG73
Bridgeman Dr., Wind. 151 AN82
Bridgeman Rd. N1 141 DM66
Bridgeman Rd., Tedd. 177 CG93
Bridgeman St. NW8 272 B1
Bridgeman St. NW8 140 DE68
Bridgen Rd., Bex. 186 EY86
Bridgend Rd. SW18 160 DC84
Bridgend Rd., Enf. 82 DW35
Bridgenhall Rd., Enf. 82 DT39

Brodie Rd., Guil. 258 AY135
Brodie St. SE1 162 DT78
Coopers Rd.
Brodlove La. E1 143 DX73
Brodrick Gro. SE2 166 EV77
Brodrick Rd. SW17 180 DE89
Brograve Gdns., Beck. 203 EB96
Broke Ct., Guil. 243 BC131
Speedwell Clo.
Broke Fm. Dr., Orp. 224 EX109
Broke Wk. E8 142 DU67
Broken Furlong (Eton), Wind. 151 AQ78
Broken Wf. EC4 275 H10
Brokengate La., Uxb. 113 BC60
Brokes Cres., Reig. 250 DA132
Brokes Rd., Reig. 250 DA130
Brokesley St. E3 143 DZ70
Bromar Rd. SE5 162 DS83
Bromborough Grn., Wat. 94 BW50
Brome Rd. SE9 165 EM83
Bromefield, Stan. 95 CJ53
Bromefield Ct., Wal.Abb. 68 EG33
Bromehead Rd. E1 142 DW72
Bromell's Rd. SW4 161 DJ84
Bromet Clo., Wat. 75 BT38
Hempstead Rd.
Bromfelde Rd. SW4 161 DK82
Bromfelde Wk. SW4 161 DK82
Bromfield St. N1 141 DN68
Bromford Clo., Oxt. 254 EG133
Bromhall Rd., Dag. 146 EV65
Bromhedge SE9 185 EM90
Bromholm Rd. SE2 166 EV76
Bromleigh Clo. (Cheshunt), Wal.Cr. 67 DY28
Martins Dr.
Bromleigh Ct. SE23 182 DV89
Lapse Wd. Wk.
Bromley, Grays 170 FZ79
Bromley Ave., Brom. 184 EE94
Bromley Common, Brom. 204 EJ98
Bromley Cres., Brom. 204 EF97
Bromley Cres., Ruis. 115 BT63
Bromley Gdns., Brom. 204 EF97
Bromley Gro., Brom. 203 ED96
Bromley Hall Rd. E14 143 EC71
Bromley High St. E3 143 EB69
Bromley Hill, Brom. 184 EE93
Bromley La., Chis. 185 EQ94
Bromley Pk., Brom. 204 EF95
London Rd.
Bromley Pl. W1 273 K6
Bromley Rd. E10 123 EB58
Bromley Rd. E17 123 EA55
Bromley Rd. N17 100 DR48
Bromley Rd. N18 100 DT53
Bromley Rd. SE6 183 EB88
Bromley Rd., Beck. 203 EB95
Bromley Rd., Brom. 203 EC96
Bromley Rd. (Downham), Brom. 183 EC91
Bromley Rd., Chis. 205 EP95
Bromley St. E1 143 DX71
Brompton Arc. SW3 276 D5
Brompton Clo. SE20 202 DU96
Selby Rd.
Brompton Clo., Houns. 176 BZ85
Brompton Dr., Erith 167 FH80
Brompton Gro. N2 120 DE56
Brompton Pk. Cres. SW6 160 DB79
Brompton Pl. SW3 276 C6
Brompton Pl. SW3 160 DE76
Brompton Rd. SW1 276 C6
Brompton Rd. SW1 160 DE76
Brompton Rd. SW3 276 C6
Brompton Rd. SW3 160 DE76
Brompton Rd. SW7 276 C6
Brompton Rd. SW7 160 DE76
Brompton Sq. SW3 276 B6
Brompton Sq. SW3 160 DE76
Brompton Ter. SE18 165 EN81
Prince Imperial Rd.
Bromwich Ave. N6 120 DG61
Bromyard Ave. W3 138 CS74
Bromyard Ho. SE15 162 DV80
Bromycroft, Slou. 131 AN69
Brondesbury Ct. NW2 139 CW65
Brondesbury Ms. NW6 140 DA66
Willesden La.
Brondesbury Pk. NW2 139 CV65
Brondesbury Pk. NW6 139 CX66
Brondesbury Rd. NW6 139 CZ68
Brondesbury Vil. NW6 139 CZ68
Bronsart Rd. SW6 159 CY80
Bronsdon Way, Uxb. 113 BF61
Bronson Rd. SW20 199 CX96
Bronte Clo. E7 124 EG63
Bective Rd.
Bronte Clo., Erith 167 FB80
Bronte Clo., Ilf. 125 EN57
Bronte Clo., Til. 171 GJ82
Bronte Gro., Dart. 168 FM84
Bronte Ho. NW6 140 DA69
Bronte Vw., Grav. 191 GJ88
Bronti Clo. SE17 162 DQ78
Bronze Age Way, Belv. 167 FC76
Bronze Age Way, Erith 167 FC76
Bronze St. SE8 163 EA80
Brook Ave., Dag. 147 FB66
Brook Ave., Edg. 96 CP51
Brook Ave., Wem. 118 CN62
Brook Clo. NW7 97 CY52
Frith Ct.
Brook Clo. SW17 180 DG89
Balham High Rd.
Brook Clo. SW20 199 CV97
Brook Clo. W3 138 CN74
West Lo. Ave.
Brook Clo., Borwd. 78 CP41
Brook Clo., Dor. 247 CJ134
Brook Clo., Epsom 216 CS109
Gibraltar Cres.
Brook Clo., Rom. 105 FF53
Brook Clo., Ruis. 115 BS59
Brook Clo., Stai. 174 BM87
Brook Cres. E4 101 EA49
Brook Cres. N9 100 DV49
Brook Cres., Slou. 131 AL72
Brook Dr. SE11 278 E7
Brook Dr. SE11 161 DN77
Brook Dr., Har. 116 CC56
Brook Dr., Rad. 61 CF33
Brook Dr., Ruis. 115 BS58
Brook Dr., Sun. 175 BS92
Chertsey Rd.
Brook End, Saw. 36 EX05
Brook Fm. Rd., Cob. 230 BX115
Brook Gdns. E4 101 EB49
Brook Gdns. SW13 159 CT83
Brook Gdns., Kings.T. 198 CQ95
Brook Gate W1 276 E1
Brook Gate W1 140 DF73
Brook Grn. W6 159 CX77
Brook Hill, Guil. 260 BK143
Brook Hill, Oxt. 253 EC130
Brook Ind. Est., Hayes 136 BX74
Brook La. SE3 164 EH82
Brook La., Berk. 38 AV18
Brook La., Bex. 186 EX86
Brook La., Brom. 184 EG93
Brook La., Guil. 260 BL142
Brook La., Saw. 36 EX05
Brook La., Wok. 227 BE122
Brook La. N., Brent. 157 CK78
Brook Mead, Epsom 216 CS107
Brook Meadow N12 98 DB49
Brook Meadow Clo., Wdf.Grn. 102 EE51
Brook Par., Chig. 103 EP48
High Rd.
Brook Pk. Clo. N21 81 DP44
Brook Path, Loug. 84 EL42
Brook Path, Slou. 131 AM73
Brook Pl., Barn. 80 DA43
Brook Ri., Chig. 103 EN48
Brook Rd. N8 121 DL56
Brook Rd. N22 121 DM55
Brook Rd. NW2 119 CU61
Brook Rd., Borwd. 78 CN40
Brook Rd., Brwd. 108 FT48
Brook Rd., Buck.H. 102 EG47
Brook Rd., Epp. 70 EU33
Brook Rd., Grav. 190 GE88
Brook Rd., Guil. 259 BC140
Brook Rd., Ilf. 125 ES58
Brook Rd., Loug. 84 EL43
Brook Rd., Red. 266 DF135
Brook Rd. (Merstham), Red. 251 DJ129
Brook Rd., Rom. 105 FF53
Brook Rd., Saw. 36 EX06
Brook Rd., Surb. 198 CL103
Brook Rd., Swan. 207 FD97
Brook Rd., Th.Hth. 202 DQ98
Brook Rd., Twick. 177 CG86
Brook Rd., Wal.Cr. 67 DZ34
Brook Rd. S., Brent. 157 CK79
Brook St. N17 100 DT54
High Rd.
Brook St. W1 272 G10
Brook St. W1 141 DH72
Brook St. W2 272 A10
Brook St. W2 140 DD73
Brook St., Belv. 167 FB78
Brook St., Brwd. 107 FR50
Brook St., Erith 167 FB79
Brook St., Kings.T. 198 CL96
Brook St., Wind. 151 AR82
Brook Vale, Erith 167 FB81
Brook Valley, Dor. 263 CH142
Brook Wk. N2 98 DD53
Brook Wk., Edg. 96 CR51
Brook Way, Chig. 103 EN48
Brook Way, Lthd. 231 CG118
Brook Way, Rain. 147 FH71
Brookbank, H.Wyc. 110 AC60
Brookbank Ave. W7 137 CD71
Brookbank Rd. SE13 163 EA83
Brookdale N11 99 DJ49
Brookdale Ave., Upmin. 128 FN62
Brookdale Clo., Upmin. 128 FP62
Brookdale Rd. E17 123 EA55
Brookdale Rd. SE6 183 EB86
Brookdale Rd., Bex. 186 EY86
Brookdene Ave., Wat. 93 BV45
Brookdene Dr., Nthwd. 93 BT52
Brookdene Rd. SE18 165 ET77
Brooke Ave., Har. 116 CC62
Brooke Clo. (Bushey), Wat. 94 CC45
Brooke Rd. E5 122 DU62
Brooke Rd. E17 123 EC56
Brooke Rd. N16 122 DT62
Brooke Rd., Grays 170 GA78
Brooke St. EC1 274 D7
Brooke St. EC1 141 DN71
Brooke Way (Bushey), Wat. 94 CC45
Richfield Rd.
Brookehowse Rd. SE6 183 EB90
Brookend Rd., Sid. 185 ES88
Brooker Rd., Wal.Abb. 67 EC34
Brookers Clo., Ash. 231 CJ117
Brooke's Ct. EC1 274 D6
Brookes Mkt. EC1 274 E6
Brookfield N6 120 DG62
Brookfield, Epp. 70 EW25
Brookfield, Gdmg. 258 AU143
Brookfield, Wok. 226 AV116
Brookfield Ave. E17 123 EC56
Brookfield Ave. NW7 97 CV51
Brookfield Ave. W5 137 CK70
Brookfield Ave., Sutt. 218 DD105
Brookfield Cen. (Cheshunt), Wal.Cr. 67 DX27
Brookfield Clo. NW7 97 CV51
Brookfield Clo., Brwd. 109 GC44
Brookfield Clo., Cher. 211 BD107
Brookfield Clo., Red. 266 DG140
Brookfield Ct., Grnf. 136 CC69
Brookfield Ct., Har. 117 CK57
Brookfield Cres. NW7 97 CV51
Brookfield Cres., Har. 118 CL57
Brookfield Gdns., Esher 215 CF107
Brookfield Gdns. (Cheshunt), Wal.Cr. 67 DX27
Brookfield La. (Cheshunt), Wal.Cr. 67 DX27
Brookfield La. W. (Cheshunt), Wal.Cr. 66 DV28
Brookfield Pk. NW5 121 DH62
Brookfield Path, Wdf.Grn. 102 EE51
Brookfield Retail Pk. (Cheshunt), Wal.Cr. 67 DX26
Brookfield Rd. E9 143 DY65
Brookfield Rd. N9 100 DU48
Brookfield Rd. W4 158 CR75
Brookfield Rd., H.Wyc. 110 AD60
Brookfields, Enf. 83 DX42
Brookfields, Saw. 36 EX05
Brookfields Ave., Mitch. 200 DE99
Brookhill Clo. SE18 165 EP78
Brookhill Clo., Barn. 80 DE43
Brookhill Rd. SE18 165 EP78
Brookhill Rd., Barn. 80 DE43
Brookhouse Dr., H.Wyc. 110 AC60
Brookhouse Gdns. E4 102 EE49
Brookhurst Rd., Add. 212 BH107
Brooking Rd. E7 124 EG64
Brookland Clo. NW11 120 DA56
Brookland Garth NW11 120 DB56
Brookland Hill NW11 120 DA56
Brookland Ri. NW11 120 DA56
Brooklands, Dart. 188 FL88
Brooklands App., Rom. 127 FD56
Brooklands Ave. SW19 180 DB89
Brooklands Ave., Sid. 185 ER89
Brooklands Clo., Cob. 230 BY115
Brooklands Clo., Rom. 127 FD56
Marshalls Rd.
Brooklands Clo., Sun. 195 BS95
Brooklands Ct., Add. 212 BK110
Brooklands Dr., Grnf. 137 CK67
Brooklands Gdns., Horn. 128 FJ57
Brooklands Gdns., Pot.B. 63 CY32
Brooklands Ind. Est., Wey. 212 BL110
Brooklands La., Rom. 127 FD56
Brooklands La., Wey. 212 BM107
Brooklands Pk. SE3 164 EG83
Brooklands Rd., Rom. 127 FD56
Brooklands Rd., T.Ditt. 197 CF102
Brooklands Rd., Wey. 213 BP107
Brooklands Way, Red. 250 DE132
Brooklane Fld., Harl. 52 EV18
Brooklea Clo. NW9 96 CS53
Brookleys, Wok. 210 AT110
Brooklyn Ave. SE25 202 DV98
Brooklyn Ave., Loug. 84 EL42
Brooklyn Clo., Cars. 200 DE103
Brooklyn Clo., Wok. 226 AY119
Brooklyn Ct., Wok. 226 AY119
Brooklyn Rd.
Brooklyn Gro. SE25 202 DV98
Brooklyn Rd. SE25 202 DV98
Brooklyn Rd., Brom. 204 EK99
Brooklyn Rd., Wok. 226 AY118
Brooklyn Way, West Dr. 154 BK76
Brookmans Ave., Hat. 63 CY26
Brookmans Clo., Upmin. 129 FS59
Brookmarsh Trd. Est. SE10 163 EB80
Norman Rd.
Brookmead Ave., Brom. 205 EM99
Brookmead Clo., Orp. 206 EV101
Brookmead Rd., Croy. 201 DJ100
Brookmead Way, Orp. 206 EV100
Brookmeads Est., Mitch. 200 DE99
Brookmill Clo., Wat. 93 BV45
Brookside Rd.
Brookmill Rd. SE8 163 EA81
Brooks Ave. E6 145 EM70
Brooks Clo. SE9 185 EN89
Brooks Clo., Wey. 212 BN110
Brooks Ct. E15 123 EB64
Clays La.
Brooks Ct., Hert. 31 DM08
Brooks La. W4 158 CN79
Brook's Ms. W1 273 H10
Brook's Ms. W1 141 DH73
Brooks Rd. E13 144 EG67
Brooks Rd. W4 158 CN78
Brooks Way, Orp. 206 EW96
Brooksbank St. E9 143 DX65
Brooksby Ms. N1 141 DN66
Brooksby St.
Brooksby St. N1 141 DN66
Brooksby's Wk. E9 123 DX64
Brookscroft, Croy. 221 DY110
Brookscroft Rd. E17 101 EB53
Brooksfield, Welw.G.C. 30 DB08
Brookshill, Har. 95 CD50
Brookshill Ave., Har. 95 CD50
Brookshill Dr., Har. 95 CD50
Brookside N21 81 DM44
Brookside, Barn. 80 DE44
Brookside, Cars. 218 DG106
Brookside, Cher. 193 BE101
Brookside, Guil. 242 AX129
Brookside, Harl. 51 EM18
Brookside, Hat. 44 CR18
Brookside, Hert. 32 DS09
Brookside, Hodd. 49 EA17
Brookside, Horn. 128 FL57
Brookside, Ilf. 103 EQ51
Brookside, Orp. 205 ET101
Brookside, Pot.B. 63 CU32
Brookside, Slou. 153 BC80
Brookside, Uxb. 134 BM66
Brookside, Wal.Abb. 68 EE33
Broomstick Hall Rd.
Brookside Ave., Ashf. 174 BJ92
Brookside Ave., Stai. 152 AY83
Brookside Clo., Barn. 79 CY44
Brookside Clo., Felt. 175 BU90
Sycamore Clo.
Brookside Clo., Har. 117 CK57
Brookside Clo. (Kenton), Har. 116 BY63
Brookside Cres. (Cuffley), Pot.B. 65 DL27
Brookside Cres., Wor.Pk. 199 CU102
Green La.
Brookside Gdns., Enf. 82 DV37
Brookside Rd. N9 100 DV49
Brookside Rd. N19 121 DJ61
Junction Rd.
Brookside Rd. NW11 119 CY58
Brookside Rd., Grav. 191 GF94
Brookside Rd., Hayes 136 BW73
Brookside Rd., Wat. 93 BV45
Brookside S., Barn. 98 DG45
Brookside Wk. N3 97 CY54
Brookside Wk. N12 98 DA51
Brookside Wk. NW4 119 CY56
Brookside Wk. NW11 119 CY56
Brookside Way, Croy. 203 DX100
Brooksville Ave. NW6 139 CY67
Brookview Rd. SW16 181 DJ92
Brookville Rd. SW6 159 CZ80
Brookway SE3 164 EG83
Brookwood, Horl. 269 DH147
Stockfield
Brookwood Ave. SW13 159 CT82
Brookwood Clo., Brom. 204 EF98
Brookwood Rd. SW18 179 CZ88
Brookwood Rd., Houns. 156 CB81
Broom Ave., Orp. 206 EV96
Broom Clo., Brom. 204 EL100
Broom Clo., Esher 214 CB106
Broom Clo., Hat. 45 CT21
Broom Clo., Tedd. 177 CK94
Broom Clo. (Cheshunt), Wal.Cr. 66 DU27
Broom Gdns., Croy. 203 EA104
Broom Gro., Wat. 75 BU38
Broom Hall, Lthd. 214 CC114
Broom Hill, Hem.H. 39 BE21
Broom Hill, Slou. 132 AU66
Broom La., Wok. 210 AS109
Broom Leys, St.Alb. 43 CK17
Broom Lock, Tedd. 177 CJ93
Broom Mead, Bexh. 186 FA85
Broom Pk., Tedd. 177 CK94
Broom Rd., Croy. 203 EA104
Broom Rd., Tedd. 177 CH92
Broom Water, Tedd. 177 CJ93
Broom Water W., Tedd. 177 CJ92
Broom Way, Wey. 213 BS105
Broomcroft Ave., Nthlt. 136 BW69
Broomcroft Clo., Wok. 227 BD116
Broomcroft Dr., Wok. 227 BD116
Broome Clo., Epsom 248 CQ126
Broome Pl., S.Ock. 149 FR74
Broome Rd., Hmptn. 176 BZ94
Broome Way SE5 162 DQ80
Broomer Pl., Wal.Cr. 66 DW29
Broomfield E17 123 DZ59
Broomfield, Guil. 242 AS133
Broomfield, Harl. 36 EV12
Broomfield, St.Alb. 60 CC27
Broomfield, Stai. 174 BG93
Broomfield, Sun. 195 BU95
Broomfield Ave. N13 99 DM50
Broomfield Ave., Brox. 67 DY26
Broomfield Ave., Loug. 85 EM44
Broomfield Clo., Guil. 242 AS132
Broomfield Clo., Rom. 105 FD52
Broomfield Ct., Wey. 213 BP107
Broomfield La. N13 99 DM49
Broomfield Pk., Dor. 262 CC137
Broomfield Pl. W13 137 CH74
Broomfield Rd.
Broomfield Ride, Lthd. 215 CD112
Broomfield Ri., Abb.L. 59 BR32
Broomfield Rd. N13 99 DL50
Broomfield Rd. W13 137 CH74
Broomfield Rd., Add. 212 BH111
Broomfield Rd., Beck. 203 DY97
Broomfield Rd., Bexh. 186 FA85
Broomfield Rd., Rich. 158 CM81
Broomfield Rd., Rom. 126 EX59
Broomfield Rd., Sev. 256 FF122
Broomfield Rd., Surb. 198 CM102
Broomfield Rd., Swans. 190 FY86
Broomfield Rd., Tedd. 177 CJ93
Melbourne Rd.
Broomfield St. E14 143 EA71
Broomfields, Esher 214 CC106
Broomgrove Gdns., Edg. 96 CN53
Broomgrove Rd. SW9 161 DM82
Broomhall End, Wok. 226 AY116
Broomhall La.
Broomhall La., Wok. 226 AY116
Broomhall Rd., S.Croy. 220 DR109
Broomhall Rd., Wok. 226 AY116
Broomhill Ri., Bexh. 186 FA85
Broomhill Rd. SW18 180 DA85
Broomhill Rd., Dart. 187 FH86
Broomhill Rd., Ilf. 126 EU61
Broomhill Rd., Orp. 206 EU101
Broomhill Rd., Wdf.Grn. 102 EG51
Broomhill Wk., Wdf.Grn. 102 EF52
Broomhills, Grav. 190 FY91
Betsham Rd.
Broomhills, Welw.G.C. 30 DA08
Broomhouse La. SW6 160 DA82
Broomhouse Rd. SW6 160 DA82
Broomlands La., Oxt. 254 EL127
Broomloan La., Sutt. 200 DA103
Brooms Clo., Welw.G.C. 29 CX06
Broomsleigh St. NW6 119 CZ64
Broomstick Hall Rd., Wal.Abb. 68 EE33
Broomstick La., Chesh. 56 AU30
Broomwood Clo., Croy. 203 DX99
Broomwood Gdns., Brwd. 108 FU44
Broomwood Rd. SW11 180 DF86
Broomwood Rd., Orp. 206 EV96
Broseley Gdns., Rom. 106 FL49
Broseley Gro. SE26 183 DY92
Broseley Rd., Rom. 106 FL49
Broster Gdns. SE25 202 DT97
Brough Clo. SW8 161 DL80
Kenchester Clo.
Brough Clo., Kings.T. 177 CK92
Brougham Rd. E8 142 DU67
Brougham Rd. W3 138 CQ72
Brougham St. SW11 160 DF82
Broughinge Rd., Borwd. 78 CP40
Broughton Ave. N3 119 CY55
Broughton Ave., Rich. 177 CH90
Broughton Dr. SW9 161 DN84
Broughton Gdns. N6 121 DJ58
Broughton Rd. SW6 160 DB82
Broughton Rd. W13 137 CH73
Broughton Rd., Orp. 205 ER103
Broughton Rd., Sev. 241 FG116
Broughton Rd., Th.Hth. 201 DN100
Broughton Rd. App. SW6 160 DB82
Wandsworth Bri. Rd.
Broughton St. SW8 160 DG82
Broughton Way, Rick. 92 BG45
Brouncker Rd. W3 158 CQ75
Brow, The, Ch.St.G. 90 AX48
Brow, The, Red. 266 DG139
Spencer Way
Brow, The, Wat. 59 BV33
Brow Clo., Orp. 206 EX101
Brow Cres.
Brow Cres., Orp. 206 EW102
Browells La., Felt. 175 BV89
Brown Clo., Wall. 219 DL108
Brown Hart Gdns. W1 272 G10
Brown Hart Gdns. W1 140 DG73
Brown Rd., Grav. 191 GL88
Brown St. W1 272 D8
Brown St. W1 140 DF72
Browne Clo., Brwd. 108 FV46
Browne Clo., Rom. 105 FB50
Bamford Way
Brownfield St. E14 143 EB72
Brownfields, Welw.G.C. 29 CZ08
Browngraves Rd., Hayes 155 BQ80
Brownhill Rd. SE6 183 EB87
Browning Ave. W7 137 CF72
Browning Ave., Sutt. 218 DE105
Browning Ave., Wor.Pk. 199 CV102
Browning Clo. E17 123 EC56
Browning Clo. W9 140 DC70
Randolph Ave.
Browning Clo., Hmptn. 176 BZ91
Browning Clo., Rom. 104 EZ52
Browning Clo., Well. 165 ES81
Browning Est. SE17 279 J10
Browning Est. SE17 162 DQ78
Browning Ho. W12 139 CW72
Wood La.
Browning Ms. W1 273 H7
Browning Rd. E11 124 EF59
Browning Rd. E12 145 EM65
Browning Rd., Dart. 168 FM84
Browning Rd., Enf. 82 DR38
Browning Rd., Lthd. 247 CD125
Browning St. SE17 279 J10
Browning St. SE17 162 DQ78
Browning Wk., Til. 171 GJ82
Coleridge Rd.
Browning Way, Houns. 156 BX81
Brownlea Gdns., Ilf. 126 EU61
Brownlow Ms. WC1 274 C5
Brownlow Ms. WC1 141 DM70
Brownlow Rd. E7 124 EH63
Woodford Rd.
Brownlow Rd. E8 142 DT67
Brownlow Rd. N3 98 DB52
Brownlow Rd. N11 99 DL51
Brownlow Rd. NW10 138 CS66
Brownlow Rd. W13 137 CG74
Brownlow Rd., Berk. 38 AW18
Brownlow Rd., Borwd. 78 CN42
Brownlow Rd., Croy. 220 DS105
Brownlow Rd., Red. 250 DE134
Brownlow St. WC1 274 C7
Brownrigg Rd., Ashf. 174 BN91
Brown's Bldgs. EC3 275 N9
Brown's Bldgs. EC3 142 DS72
Browns La. NW5 121 DH64
Browns La., Lthd. 246 BX127
Browns Rd. E17 123 EA55
Browns Rd., Surb. 198 CM101
Browns Spring, Berk. 39 BC16
Brownspring Dr. SE9 185 EP91
Brownswell Rd. N2 98 DD54
Brownswood Rd. N4 121 DP62
Brownswood Rd., Beac. 89 AK51
Brox La., Cher. 211 BC108
Brox Rd., Cher. 211 BC109
Broxash Rd. SW11 180 DG86
Broxbourne Ave. E18 124 EH56
Broxbourne High St., Hodd. 49 EA19
Broxbourne Rd. E7 124 EG62
Broxbourne Rd., Orp. 205 ET101
Broxbournebury Ms., Brox. 48 DW21
White Stubbs La.
Broxburn Dr., S.Ock. 149 FV73
Broxburn Par., S.Ock. 149 FV73
Broxburn Dr.
Broxhill Rd. (Havering-atte-Bower), Rom. 105 FE48
Broxholm Rd. SE27 181 DN90
Broxted Ms., Brwd. 109 GC44
Bannister Dr.
Broxted Rd. SE6 183 DZ89
Broxwood Way NW8 140 DE67
Bruce Ave., Horn. 128 FK61
Bruce Ave., Shep. 195 BQ100
Bruce Castle Rd. N17 100 DT53
Bruce Clo. W10 139 CY71
Ladbroke Gro.
Bruce Clo., Slou. 131 AN74
Bruce Clo., Well. 166 EV81
Bruce Clo., W.Byf. 212 BK113
Bruce Dr., S.Croy. 221 DX109
Bruce Gdns. N20 98 DF48
Balfour Gro.
Bruce Gro. N17 100 DS53
Bruce Gro., Orp. 206 EU101
Bruce Gro., Wat. 76 BW38
Bruce Hall Ms. SW17 180 DG91
Brudenell Rd.
Bruce Rd. E3 143 EB69
Bruce Rd. NW10 138 CR66
Bruce Rd. SE25 202 DR98
Bruce Rd., Barn. 79 CY41
St. Albans Rd.
Bruce Rd., Har. 95 CE54
Bruce Rd., Mitch. 180 DG94
Bruce Wk., Wind. 151 AK82
Tinkers La.
Bruce Way, Wal.Cr. 67 DX33
Bruces Wf. Rd., Grays 170 GA79
Bruckner St. W10 139 CZ69
Brudenell, Wind. 151 AM83
Brudenell Rd. SW17 180 DF90
Bruffs Meadow, Nthlt. 136 BY65
Bruges Pl. NW1 141 DJ66
Randolph St.
Brumana Clo., Wey. 213 BP106
Elgin Rd.
Brumfield Rd., Epsom 216 CQ106
Brummel Clo., Bexh. 167 FC83
Brune St. E1 275 P7
Brune St. E1 142 DT71
Brunel Clo. SE19 182 DT93
Brunel Clo., Houns. 155 BV80
Brunel Clo., Nthlt. 136 BZ69
Brunel Clo., Rom. 127 FE56
Brunel Clo., Til. 171 GH83
Brunel Est. W2 140 DA71
Brunel Pl., Sthl. 136 CB72
Brunel Rd. E17 123 DY58
Brunel Rd. SE16 162 DW75
Brunel Rd. W3 138 CS71
Brunel Rd., Wdf.Grn. 103 EM50
Brunel St. E16 144 EF72
Victoria Dock Rd.
Brunel Wk. N15 122 DS56
Brunel Wk., Twick. 176 CA87
Stephenson Rd.
Brunel Way, Slou. 132 AT74
Brunner Clo. NW11 120 DC57
Brunner Ct., Cher. 211 BC106
Brunner Rd. E17 123 DZ57
Brunner Rd. W5 137 CK70
Bruno Pl. NW9 118 CQ61
Brunswick Ave. N11 98 DG48
Brunswick Ave., Upmin. 129 FS59
Brunswick Cen. WC1 273 P4
Brunswick Clo., Bexh. 166 EX84
Brunswick Clo., Pnr. 116 BY58
Brunswick Clo., T.Ditt. 197 CF102
Brunswick Clo., Twick. 177 CD90
Brunswick Clo., Walt. 196 BW103
Brunswick Ct. EC1 141 DP69
Northampton Sq.
Brunswick Ct. SE1 279 N5
Brunswick Ct. SE1 162 DS75
Brunswick Ct., Barn. 80 DD43
Brunswick Ct., Upmin. 129 FS59
Waycross Rd.

Brunswick Cres. N11 98 DG48
Brunswick Gdns. W5 138 CL69
Brunswick Gdns. W8 140 DA74
Brunswick Gdns., Ilf. 103 EQ52
Brunswick Gro. N11 98 DG48
Brunswick Gro., Cob. 214 BW113
Brunswick Ind. Pk. N11 99 DH49
Brunswick Ms. SW16 181 DK93
Potters La.
Brunswick Ms. W1 272 E8
Brunswick Pk. SE5 162 DR81
Brunswick Pk. Gdns. N11 98 DG47
Brunswick Pk. Rd. N11 98 DG47
Brunswick Pl. N1 275 L3
Brunswick Pl. N1 142 DR69
Brunswick Pl. SE19 182 DU94
Brunswick Quay SE16 163 DX76
Brunswick Rd. E10 123 EC60
Brunswick Rd. E14 143 EC72
Blackwall Tunnel Northern App.
Brunswick Rd. N15 122 DS57
Brunswick Rd. W5 137 CK70
Brunswick Rd., Bexh. 166 EX84
Brunswick Rd., Enf. 83 EA38
Brunswick Rd., Kings.T. 198 CN95
Brunswick Rd., Sutt. 218 DB105
Brunswick Sq. N17 100 DT51
Brunswick Sq. WC1 274 A5
Brunswick Sq. WC1 141 DL70
Brunswick St. E17 123 EC57
Brunswick Vil. SE5 162 DS81
Brunswick Wk., Grav. 191 GK86
Brunswick Way N11 99 DH49
Brunton Pl. E14 143 DY72
Brushfield St. E1 275 N7
Brushfield St. E1 142 DS71
Brushrise, Wat. 75 BU36
Brushwood Dr., Rick. 73 BC42
Brushwood Rd., Chesh. 54 AR29
Brussels Rd. SW11 160 DD84
Bruton Clo., Chis. 185 EM94
Bruton La. W1 277 J1
Bruton La. W1 141 DH73
Bruton Pl. W1 277 J1
Bruton Pl. W1 141 DH73
Bruton Rd., Mord. 200 DC99
Bruton St. W1 277 J1
Bruton St. W1 141 DH73
Bruton Way W13 137 CG71
Bryan Ave. NW10 139 CV66
Bryan Clo., Sun. 175 BU94
Bryan Rd. SE16 163 DZ75
Bryan's All. SW6 160 DB82
Wandsworth Bri. Rd.
Bryanston Ave., Twick. 176 CB88
Bryanston Clo., Sthl. 156 BZ77
Bryanston Ms. E. W1 272 D7
Bryanston Ms. W. W1 272 D7
Bryanston Pl. W1 272 D7
Bryanston Pl. W1 140 DF71
Bryanston Rd., Til. 171 GJ82
Bryanston Sq. W1 272 D7
Bryanston Sq. W1 140 DF71
Bryanston St. W1 272 D9
Bryanston St. W1 140 DF72
Bryanstone Ave., Guil. 242 AT130
Bryanstone Clo., Guil. 242 AT130
Bryanstone Gro., Guil. 242 AT130
Bryanstone Rd. N8 121 DK57
Bryanstone Rd., Wal.Cr. 67 DZ34
Bryant Ave., Rom. 106 FK53
Bryant Ave., Slou. 131 AR71
Bryant Clo., Barn. 79 CZ43
Bryant Ct. E2 142 DT68
Bryant Ind. Est., Rom. 106 FK54
Bryant Rd., Nthlt. 136 BW69
Bryant St. E15 143 ED66
Bryantwood Rd. N7 121 DN64
Bryce Rd., Dag. 126 EW63
Brycedale Cres. N14 99 DK49
Bryden Clo. SE26 183 DY92
Brydges Pl. WC2 277 P1
Brydges Rd. E15 123 ED64
Brydon Wk. N1 141 DL67
Outram Pl.
Bryer Ct. EC2 142 DQ71
Aldersgate St.
Bryer Pl., Wind. 151 AK83
Bryett Rd. N7 121 DL62
Brymay Clo. E3 143 EA68
Brympton Clo., Dor. 263 CG138
Bryn-y-Mawr Rd., Enf. 82 DT42
Brynford Clo., Wok. 226 AY115
Brynmaer Rd. SW11 160 DF81
Bryony Clo., Loug. 85 EP42
Bryony Clo., Uxb. 134 BM71
Bryony Rd. W12 139 CU73
Bryony Rd., Guil. 243 BB131
Bryony Way, Sun. 175 BT93
Bubblestone Rd., Sev. 241 FH116
Buccleuch Rd., Slou. 152 AU80
Buchan Clo., Uxb. 134 BJ69
Buchan Rd. SE15 162 DW83
Buchanan Clo. N21 81 DM43
Buchanan Clo., S.Ock. 148 FQ74
Buchanan Ct., Borwd. 78 CQ40
Buchanan Gdns. NW10 139 CV68
Bucharest Rd. SW18 180 DC87
Buck Hill Wk. W2 276 A1
Buck La. NW9 118 CR57
Buck St. NW1 141 DH66
Buck Wk. E17 123 ED56
Foresters Dr.
Buckbean Path, Rom. 106 FJ52
Clematis Clo.
Buckden Clo. N2 120 DF56
Southern Rd.
Buckden Clo. SE12 184 EF86
Upwood Rd.
Buckettsland La., Borwd. 78 CR38
Buckfast Rd., Mord. 200 DB98
Buckfast St. E2 142 DU69
Buckham Thorns Rd., West. 255 EQ126
Buckhold Rd. SW18 180 DA86
Buckhurst Ave., Cars. 200 DE102
Buckhurst Ave., Sev. 257 FJ125
Buckhurst Clo., Red. 250 DE132
Buckhurst La., Sev. 257 FJ125
Buckhurst Rd., West. 239 EP121
Buckhurst St. E1 142 DV70
Buckhurst Way, Buck.H. 102 EK49
Buckingham Arc. WC2 278 A1
Buckingham Ave. N20 98 DC45
Buckingham Ave., Felt. 175 BV86
Buckingham Ave., Grnf. 137 CG67
Buckingham Ave., Slou. 131 AL72
Buckingham Ave., Th.Hth. 201 DN95
Buckingham Ave., Well. 165 ES84
Buckingham Ave., W.Mol. 196 CB97
Buckingham Ave. E., Slou. 131 AQ72
Buckingham Clo. W5 137 CJ71
Buckingham Clo., Enf. 82 DS40
Buckingham Clo., Guil. 243 AZ133
Buckingham Clo., Hmptn. 176 BZ92
Buckingham Clo., Horn. 128 FK58
Buckingham Clo., Orp. 205 ES101
Buckingham Ct. NW4 119 CU55
Buckingham Dr., Chis. 185 EP92
Buckingham Gdns., Edg. 96 CM52
Buckingham Gdns., Slou. 152 AT75
Buckingham Gdns., Th.Hth. 201 DN96
Buckingham Gdns., W.Mol. 196 CB96
Buckingham Ave.
Buckingham Gate SW1 277 K5
Buckingham Gate SW1 161 DJ76
Buckingham Gro., Uxb. 134 BN68
Buckingham La. SE23 183 DY87
Buckingham Ms. N1 142 DS65
Buckingham Rd.
Buckingham Ms. NW10 139 CT68
Buckingham Rd.
Buckingham Ms. SW1 277 K6
Buckingham Palace Rd. SW1 277 H9
Buckingham Palace Rd. SW1 161 DH77
Buckingham Pl. SW1 277 K6
Buckingham Rd. E10 123 EB62
Buckingham Rd. E11 124 EJ57
Buckingham Rd. E15 124 EF64
Buckingham Rd. E18 102 EF53
Buckingham Rd. N1 142 DS65
Buckingham Rd. N22 99 DL53
Buckingham Rd. NW10 139 CT68
Buckingham Rd., Borwd. 78 CR42
Buckingham Rd., Edg. 96 CM52
Buckingham Rd., Grav. 190 GD87
Dover Rd.
Buckingham Rd., Hmptn. 176 BZ91
Buckingham Rd., Har. 117 CD57
Buckingham Rd., Ilf. 125 ER61
Buckingham Rd., Kings.T. 198 CM98
Buckingham Rd., Mitch. 201 DL99
Buckingham Rd., Rich. 177 CK89
Buckingham Rd., Wat. 76 BW37
Buckingham St. WC2 278 A1
Buckingham Way, Wall. 219 DJ109
Buckland Ave., Slou. 152 AV77
Buckland Cres. NW3 140 DD66
Buckland Cres., Wind. 151 AM81
Buckland La., Bet. 249 CU130
Buckland La., Tad. 249 CU130
Buckland Ri., Pnr. 94 BW53
Buckland Rd. E10 123 EC61
Buckland Rd., Chess. 216 CM106
Buckland Rd., Orp. 223 ES105
Buckland Rd., Reig. 249 CX133
Buckland Rd., Sutt. 217 CW110
Buckland Rd., Tad. 249 CZ128
Buckland St. N1 275 L1
Buckland St. N1 142 DR68
Buckland Wk. W3 158 CQ75
Church Rd.
Buckland Wk., Mord. 200 DC98
Buckland Way, Wor.Pk. 199 CW102
Bucklands, The, Rick. 92 BG45
Bucklands Rd., Tedd. 177 CJ93
Buckle St. E1 142 DT72
Leman St.
Bucklebury Clo., Maid. 150 AC78
Buckleigh Ave. SW20 199 CY97
Buckleigh Rd. SW16 181 DK93
Buckleigh Way SE19 202 DT95
Buckler Gdns. SE9 185 EM90
Southold Ri.
Bucklers All. SW6 159 CZ79
Bucklers Clo., Brox. 49 DZ22
Bucklers Ct., Brwd. 108 FW50
Bucklers Way, Cars. 200 DF104
Bucklersbury EC4 275 K9
Bucklersbury EC4 142 DR72
Bucklersbury Pas. EC4 275 K9
Buckles Ct., Belv. 166 EX76
Fendyke Rd.
Buckles La., S.Ock. 149 FW71
Buckles Way, Bans. 233 CY116
Buckley Clo., Dart. 167 FF82
Buckley Rd. NW6 139 CZ66
Buckley St. SE1 278 D3
Buckmaster Clo. SW9 161 DM83
Stockwell Pk. Rd.
Buckmaster Rd. SW11 160 DE84
Bucknall St. WC2 273 N8
Bucknall St. WC2 141 DK72
Bucknalls Clo., Wat. 60 BY32
Bucknalls Dr., St.Alb. 60 BZ31
Bucknalls La., Wat. 60 BX32
Bucknell Clo. SW2 161 DM84
Buckner Rd. SW2 161 DM84
Bucknills Clo., Epsom 216 CP114
Buckrell Rd. E4 101 ED47
Bucks All., Hert. 47 DK19
Bucks Ave., Wat. 94 BY45
Bucks Clo., W.Byf. 212 BH114
Bucks Cross Rd., Grav. 191 GF90
Bucks Cross Rd., Orp. 224 EY106
Bucks Hill, Kings L. 58 BK34
Buckstone Clo. SE23 182 DW86
Buckstone Rd. N18 100 DU50
Buckters Rents SE16 143 DY74
Buckthorne Ho., Chig. 104 EV49
Buckthorne Rd. SE4 183 DY86
Buckton Rd., Borwd. 78 CM38
Budd Clo. N12 98 DB49
Buddcroft, Welw.G.C. 30 DB08
Buddings Circle, Wem. 118 CQ62
Budd's All., Twick. 177 CJ85
Arlington Clo.
Budebury Rd., Stai. 174 BG92
Budge La., Mitch. 200 DF101
Budge Row EC4 275 K10
Budgen Dr., Red. 250 DG131
Budge's Wk. W2 140 DC73
Budgin's Hill, Orp. 224 EV112
Budleigh Cres., Well. 166 EW81
Budoch Ct., Ilf. 126 EU61
Budoch Dr., Ilf. 126 EU61
Buer Rd. SW6 159 CY82
Buff Ave., Bans. 218 DB114
Buffins, Maid. 130 AE69
Bug Hill, Warl. 237 DX120
Bugsby's Way SE7 164 EH77
Bugsby's Way SE10 164 EF77
Bulbourne Clo., Berk. 38 AT17
Bulbourne Clo., Hem.H. 40 BG21
Bulganak Rd., Th.Hth. 202 DQ98
Bulinga St. SW1 277 P9
Bulinga St. SW1 161 DK77
Bulkeley Ave., Wind. 151 AP83
Bulkeley Clo., Egh. 172 AW92
Bull All., Well. 166 EV83
Welling High St.
Bull Clo., Grays 170 FZ75
Bull Hill, Dart. 208 FQ98
Bull Hill, Lthd. 231 CG121
Bull Inn Ct. WC2 278 A1
Bull La. N18 100 DS50
Bull La., Chis. 185 ER94
Bull La., Dag. 127 FB62
Bull La., Ger.Cr. 112 AX55
Bull Plain, Hert. 32 DR09
Bull Rd. E15 144 EF68
Bull Stag Grn., Hat. 45 CW16
Bull Wf. La. EC4 275 J10
Bull Yd., Grav. 191 GH86
High St.
Bullace Clo., Hem.H. 40 BG19
Bullace La., Dart. 188 FL86
High St.
Bullace Row SE5 162 DQ81
Camberwell Rd.
Bullards Pl. E2 143 DX69
Bullbanks Rd., Belv. 167 FC77
Bullbeggars La., Berk. 39 AZ20
Bullbeggars La., Wok. 226 AV116
Bullbeggars Rd., Gdse. 252 DW132
Bullen St. SW11 160 DE82
Bullens Grn. La., St.Alb. 44 CS23
Buller Clo. SE15 162 DU80
Buller Rd. N17 100 DU54
Buller Rd. N22 99 DN54
Buller Rd. NW10 139 CX69
Chamberlayne Rd.
Buller Rd., Bark. 145 ES66
Buller Rd., Th.Hth. 202 DR96
Bullers Clo., Sid. 186 EY92
Bullers Wd. Dr., Chis. 184 EL94
Bullescroft Rd., Edg. 96 CN48
Bullfinch Clo., Horl. 268 DE147
Bullfinch Clo., Sev. 256 FD122
Bullfinch Dene, Sev. 256 FD122
Bullfinch La., Sev. 256 FD122
Bullfinch Rd., S.Croy. 221 DX110
Bullhead Rd., Borwd. 78 CQ41
Bullied Way SW1 277 J9
Bullivant Clo., Green. 189 FU85
Bullivant St. E14 143 EC73
Bullocks La., Hert. 32 DQ11
Bullrush Clo., Croy. 202 DS100
Bullrush Clo., Hat. 45 CV19
Bullrush Gro., Uxb. 134 BJ70
Bull's All. SW14 158 CR82
Bulls Bri. Ind. Est., Sthl. 155 BV76
Hayes Rd.
Bulls Bri. Rd., Sthl. 155 BV76
Bulls Cross, Enf. 82 DU37
Bulls Cross Ride, Wal.Cr. 82 DU35
Bulls Gdns. SW3 276 C8
Bull's Head Pas. EC3 275 M9
Bulls La., Hat. 45 CX24
Bullsbrook Rd., Hayes 136 BW74
Bullsland Gdns., Rick. 73 BB44
Bullsland La., Ger.Cr. 91 BB45
Bullsland La., Rick. 73 BB44
Bullsmoor Clo., Wal.Cr. 82 DW35
Bullsmoor Gdns., Wal.Cr. 82 DV35
Bullsmoor La., Enf. 82 DW35
Bullsmoor La., Wal.Cr. 82 DU35
Bullsmoor Ride, Wal.Cr. 82 DW35
Bullsmoor Way, Wal.Cr. 82 DV35
Bullwell Cres. (Cheshunt), Wal.Cr. 67 DY29
Bulmer Gdns., Har. 117 CK59
Bulmer Ms. W11 140 DA73
Ladbroke Rd.
Bulmer Pl. W11 140 DA74
Bulmer Wk., Rain. 148 FJ68
Bulow Est. SW6 160 DB82
Broughton Rd.
Bulstrode Ave., Houns. 156 BZ82
Bulstrode Ct., Ger.Cr. 112 AX58
Heathfield Way
Bulstrode Gdns., Houns. 156 BZ83
Bulstrode La., Hem.H. 58 BG27
Bulstrode La., Kings L. 57 BE29
Bulstrode Pl. W1 272 G7
Bulstrode Rd., Houns. 156 CA83
Bulstrode St. W1 272 G8
Bulstrode St. W1 140 DG72
Bulstrode Way, Ger.Cr. 112 AX57
Bulwer Ct. Rd. E11 123 ED60
Bulwer Gdns., Barn. 80 DC42
Bulwer Rd.
Bulwer Rd. E11 123 ED59
Bulwer Rd. N18 100 DS49
Bulwer Rd., Barn. 80 DB42
Bulwer St. W12 139 CW74
Bumbles Grn. La., Wal.Abb. 68 EH25
Bunbury Way, Epsom 233 CV116
Bunby Rd., Slou. 132 AT66
Bunce Common Rd., Reig. 264 CR141
Bunce Dr., Cat. 236 DQ121
Coulsdon Rd.
Buncefield La., Hem.H. 41 BQ17
Bunces Clo. (Eton Wick), Wind. 151 AP78
Bunces La., Wdf.Grn. 102 EF52
Bundys Way, Stai. 173 BF93
Bungalow Rd. SE25 202 DS98
Bungalow Rd., Wok. 229 BQ124
Bungalows, The SW16 181 DH94
Bungalows, The, Wall. 219 DH106
Bunhill Row EC1 275 K4
Bunhill Row EC1 142 DR70
Bunhouse Pl. SW1 276 F10
Bunhouse Pl. SW1 160 DG78
Bunkers Hill NW11 120 DC59
Bunkers Hill, Belv. 166 FA77
Bunkers Hill, Sid. 186 EZ90
Bunkers La., Hem.H. 58 BN25
Bunning Way N7 141 DL66
Bunns La. NW7 97 CT51
Bunn's La., Chesh. 56 AT34
Bunnsfield, Welw.G.C. 30 DC08
Bunsen St. E3 143 DY68
Kenilworth Rd.
Bunten Meade, Slou. 131 AP74
Bunting Clo. N9 101 DX46
Dunnock Clo.
Bunting Clo., Mitch. 200 DF99
Buntingbridge Rd., Ilf. 125 ER57
Bunton St. SE18 165 EN76
Bunyan Ct. EC2 142 DQ71
Beech St.
Bunyan Rd. E17 123 DY55
Bunyard Dr., Wok. 211 BC114
Bunyons Clo., Brwd. 107 FW51
Essex Way
Buonaparte Ms. SW1 277 M10
Burbage Clo. SE1 279 K7
Burbage Clo. SE1 162 DR76
Burbage Clo. (Cheshunt), Wal.Cr. 67 DZ31
Burbage Rd. SE21 182 DR86
Burbage Rd. SE24 182 DQ86
Burberry Clo., N.Mal. 198 CS96
Burbidge Rd., Shep. 194 BN98
Burbridge Way N17 100 DT54
Burch Rd., Grav. 191 GF86
Burcham St. E14 143 EB72
Burcharbro Rd. SE2 166 EX79
Burchell Ct. (Bushey), Wat. 94 CC45
Catsey La.
Burchell Rd. E10 123 EB60
Burchell Rd. SE15 162 DV81
Burchets Hollow, Guil. 261 BR144
Burchett Way, Rom. 126 EZ58
Burchetts Way, Shep. 195 BP100
Burchwall Clo., Rom. 105 FC52
Burcote, Wey. 213 BR107
Burcote Rd. SW18 180 DD88
Burcott Gdns., Add. 212 BJ107
Burcott Rd., Pur. 219 DN114
Burden Clo., Brent. 157 CJ78
Burden Way E11 124 EH61
Brading Cres.
Burden Way, Guil. 242 AV129
Burdenshot Hill, Guil. 242 AU125
Burdenshott Ave., Rich. 158 CP84
Burdenshott Rd., Guil. 242 AU125
Burdenshott Rd., Wok. 226 AU124
Burder Clo. N1 142 DS65
Burder Rd. N1 142 DS65
Balls Pond Rd.
Burdett Ave. SW20 199 CU95
Burdett Clo. W7 157 CF75
Cherington Rd.
Burdett Clo., Sid. 186 EY92
Burdett Ms. NW3 140 DD65
Belsize Cres.
Burdett Ms. W2 140 DB72
Hatherley Gro.
Burdett Rd. E3 143 DZ70
Burdett Rd. E14 143 DZ70
Burdett Rd., Croy. 202 DR100
Burdett Rd., Rich. 158 CM83
Burdett St. SE1 278 D6
Burdetts Rd., Dag. 146 EZ67
Burdock Clo., Croy. 203 DX102
Burdock Rd. N17 122 DU55
Burdon La., Sutt. 217 CY108
Burdon Pk., Sutt. 217 CZ109
Burfield Clo. SW17 180 DD91
Burfield Clo., Hat. 45 CU16
Burfield Dr., Warl. 236 DW119
Burfield Rd., Rick. 73 BB43
Burfield Rd., Wind. 172 AU87
Burford Clo., Dag. 126 EW62
Burford Clo., Ilf. 125 EQ56
Burford Clo., Uxb. 114 BL63
Burford Gdns. N13 99 DM48
Burford Gdns., Hodd. 49 EB16
Burford La., Epsom 217 CW111
Burford Ms., Hodd. 49 EA16
Burford St.
Burford Pl., Hodd. 49 EA16
Burford St.
Burford Rd. E6 144 EL69
Burford Rd. E15 143 ED66
Burford Rd. SE6 183 DZ89
Burford Rd., Brent. 158 CL78
Burford Rd., Brom. 204 EL98
Burford Rd., Sutt. 200 DA103
Burford Rd., Wor.Pk. 199 CT101
Burford St., Hodd. 49 EA17
Burford Wk. SW6 160 DB80
Cambria St.
Burford Way, Croy. 221 EC107
Burgate Clo., Dart. 167 FF83
Burge St. SE1 279 L7
Burge St. SE1 162 DR76
Burges Clo., Horn. 128 FM58
Burges Ct. E6 145 EN66
Burges Gro. SW13 159 CV80
Burges Rd. E6 144 EL66
Burges Way, Stai. 174 BG92
Burgess Ave. NW9 118 CR58
Burgess Clo., Felt. 176 BY91
Burgess Clo. (Cheshunt), Wal.Cr. 66 DQ25
Burgess Ct., Borwd. 78 CM38
Belford Rd.
Burgess Hill NW2 120 DA63
Burgess Rd. E15 124 EE63
Burgess Rd., Sutt. 218 DB105
Burgess St. E14 143 EA71
Burgess Wd. Gro., Beac. 88 AH53
Burgess Wd. Rd., Beac. 88 AH53
Burgess Wd. Rd. S., Beac. 110 AH55
Burgett Rd., Slou. 151 AP76
Burgh Heath Rd., Epsom 217 CT114
Burgh Mt., Bans. 233 CZ115
Burgh St. N1 141 DP68
Burgh Wd., Bans. 233 CY115
Burghfield, Epsom 233 CT115
Burghfield Rd., Grav. 191 GF94
Burghill Rd. SE26 183 DY91
Burghley Ave., Borwd. 78 CQ43
Burghley Ave., N.Mal. 198 CR95
Burghley Hall Clo. SW19 179 CY88
Princes Way
Burghley Pl., Mitch. 200 DG99
Burghley Rd. E11 124 EE60
Burghley Rd. N8 121 DN55
Burghley Rd. NW5 121 DH64
Burghley Rd. SW19 179 CX91
Burghley Rd., Grays 169 FW76
Burghley Twr. W3 139 CT73
Burgon St. EC4 274 G9
Burgos Clo., Croy. 219 DN107
Burgos Gro. SE10 163 EB81
Burgoyne Hatch, Harl. 36 EU14
Momples Rd.
Burgoyne Rd. N4 121 DP58
Burgoyne Rd. SE25 202 DT98
Burgoyne Rd. SW9 161 DM83
Burgoyne Rd., Sun. 175 BS93
Burgundy Cft., Welw.G.C. 29 CZ11
Burgwood Gro., Beac. 88 AH53
Burham Clo. SE20 182 DW94
Maple Rd.
Burhill Gro., Pnr. 94 BY54
Burhill Rd., Walt. 213 BV109
Burke Clo. SW15 158 CS84
Burke St. E16 144 EF72
Burkes Clo., Beac. 110 AH55
Burkes Cres., Beac. 89 AK53
Burkes Rd., Beac. 110 AJ55
Burket Clo., Sthl. 156 BZ77
Kingsbridge Rd.
Burland Rd. SW11 180 DF85
Burland Rd., Brwd. 108 FX46
Burland Rd., Rom. 105 FC51
Burlea Clo., Walt. 213 BV106
Burleigh Ave., Sid. 185 ET85
Burleigh Ave., Wall. 200 DG104
Burleigh Clo., Add. 212 BH106
Burleigh Gdns. N14 99 DJ46
Burleigh Gdns., Ashf. 175 BQ92
Burleigh Ho. W10 139 CX71
St. Charles Sq.
Burleigh Mead, Hat. 45 CW16
Burleigh Pk., Cob. 214 BY112
Burleigh Pl. SW15 179 CX85
Burleigh Rd., Add. 212 BH106
Burleigh Rd., Enf. 82 DS42
Burleigh Rd., Hem.H. 41 BQ21
Burleigh Rd., Hert. 32 DU08
Burleigh Rd., St.Alb. 43 CH20
Burleigh Rd., Sutt. 199 CY102
Burleigh Rd., Uxb. 135 BP67
Burleigh Rd. (Cheshunt), Wal.Cr. 67 DY32
Burleigh St. WC2 274 B10
Burleigh Wk. SE6 183 EC88
Muirkirk Rd.
Burleigh Way, Enf. 82 DR41
Church St.
Burleigh Way (Cuffley), Pot.B. 65 DL30
Burley Clo. E4 101 EA50
Burley Clo. SW16 201 DK96
Burley Hill, Harl. 52 EX16
Burley Orchard, Cher. 194 BG100
Burley Rd. E16 144 EJ72
Burlingham Clo., Guil. 243 BD132
Gilliat Dr.
Burlings La., Sev. 239 ET118
Burlington Arc. W1 277 K1
Burlington Arc. W1 141 DJ73
Burlington Ave., Rich. 158 CN81
Burlington Ave., Rom. 127 FB58
Burlington Ave., Slou. 152 AS75
Burlington Clo. E6 144 EL72
Northumberland Rd.
Burlington Clo. W9 139 CZ70
Burlington Clo., Felt. 175 BR87
Burlington Clo., Orp. 205 EP103
Burlington Clo., Pnr. 115 BV55
Burlington Gdns. W1 277 K1
Burlington Gdns. W1 141 DJ73
Burlington Gdns. W3 138 CQ74
Burlington Gdns. W4 158 CQ78
Burlington Gdns., Rom. 126 EY59
Burlington La. W4 158 CS80
Burlington Ms. SW15 179 CZ85
Upper Richmond Rd.
Burlington Ms. W3 138 CQ74
Burlington Pl. SW6 159 CY82
Burlington Rd.
Burlington Pl., Wdf.Grn. 102 EG48
Burlington Ri., Barn. 98 DE46
Burlington Rd. N10 98 DG54
Tetherdown
Burlington Rd. N17 100 DU53
Burlington Rd. SW6 159 CY82
Burlington Rd. W4 158 CQ78
Burlington Rd., Enf. 82 DR39
Burlington Rd., Islw. 157 CD81
Burlington Rd., N.Mal. 199 CU98
Burlington Rd., Slou. 130 AH70
Burlington Rd., Th.Hth. 202 DQ96
Burma Rd. N16 122 DR63
Burma Rd., Wok. 192 AT103
Burman Clo., Dart. 188 FQ87
Burmester Rd. SW17 180 DC90
Burn Clo., Add. 212 BK105
Burn Side N9 100 DW48
Burn Wk., Slou. 130 AH69
Wilmot Rd.
Burnaby Cres. W4 158 CP79
Burnaby Gdns. W4 158 CQ79
Burnaby Rd., Grav. 190 GE87
Burnaby St. SW10 160 DC80
Burnbrae Clo. N12 98 DB51
Burnbury Rd. SW12 181 DJ88
Burncroft Ave., Enf. 82 DW40
Burne Jones Ho. W14 159 CZ77
Burne St. NW1 272 B6
Burne St. NW1 140 DE71
Burnell Ave., Rich. 177 CJ92
Burnell Ave., Well. 166 EU82
Burnell Gdns., Stan. 95 CK53
Burnell Rd., Sutt. 218 DB105
Burnell Wk. SE1 162 DT78
Cadet Dr.
Burnell Wk., Brwd. 107 FW51
Burnels Ave. E6 145 EN69
Burness Clo. N7 141 DM65
Roman Way
Burness Clo., Uxb. 134 BK68
Whitehall Rd.
Burnet Ave., Guil. 243 BB131
Woodruff Ave.
Burnet Clo., Hem.H. 40 BL21
Burnet Gro., Epsom 216 CQ113
Burnett Clo. E9 122 DW64
Burnett Pk., Harl. 51 EP20
Burnett Rd., Erith 168 FK79
Burnett Sq., Hert. 31 DM08
Burnetts Rd., Wind. 151 AL81
Burney Ave., Surb. 198 CM99
Burney Clo., Lthd. 246 CC125
Burney Dr., Loug. 85 EP40
Burney Rd., Dor. 247 CG131
Burney St. SE10 163 EC80
Burnfoot Ave. SW6 159 CY81
Burnfoot Ct. SE22 182 DV88
Burnham NW3 140 DE66
Burnham Ave., Beac. 111 AN55
Burnham Ave., Uxb. 115 BQ63
Burnham Clo. NW7 97 CU52
Burnham Clo. SE1 162 DT77
Cadet Dr.
Burnham Clo., Enf. 82 DS38

Burnham Clo., Har. 117 CG56
Burnham Clo., Wind. 151 AK82
Burnham Ct. NW4 119 CW56
Burnham Cres. E11 124 EJ56
Burnham Cres., Dart. 168 FJ84
Burnham Dr., Reig. 250 DA133
Burnham Dr., Wor.Pk. 199 CX103
Burnham Gdns., Croy. 202 DT101
Burnham Gdns., Hayes 155 BR76
Burnham Gdns., Houns. 155 BV81
Burnham La., Slou. 131 AL70
Burnham Rd. E4 101 DZ50
Burnham Rd., Dag. 146 EV66
Burnham Rd., Dart. 168 FJ84
Burnham Rd., Mord. 200 DB99
Burnham Rd., Rom. 127 FD55
Burnham Rd., St.Alb. 43 CG20
Burnham Rd., Sid. 186 EY89
Burnham St. E2 142 DW69
Burnham St., Kings.T. 198 CN95
Burnham Wk., Slou. 111 AN64
Burnham Way SE26 183 DZ92
Burnham Way W13 157 CH77
Burnhams Rd., Lthd. 230 BY124
Burnhill Rd., Beck. 203 EA96
Burnley Clo., Wat. 94 BW50
Burnley Rd. NW10 119 CU64
Burnley Rd. SW9 161 DM82
Burnley Rd., Grays 169 FT81
Burns Ave., Felt. 175 BU86
Burns Ave., Rom. 126 EW59
Burns Ave., Sid. 186 EU86
Burns Ave., Sthl. 136 CA73
Burns Clo. E17 123 EC56
Burns Clo. SW19 180 DD93
North Rd.
Burns Clo., Erith 167 FF81
Burns Clo., Hayes 135 BT71
Burns Clo., Well. 165 ET81
Burns Dr., Bans. 217 CY114
Burns Pl., Til. 171 GH81
Burns Rd. NW10 139 CT67
Burns Rd. SW11 160 DF82
Burns Rd. W13 157 CH75
Burns Rd., Wem. 137 CK68
Burns Way, Brwd. 109 GD45
Burns Way, Houns. 156 BX82
Burnsall St. SW3 276 C10
Burnsall St. SW3 160 DE78
Burnside, Ash. 232 CM118
Burnside, Hert. 31 DN10
Burnside, Hodd. 49 DZ17
Burnside, St.Alb. 43 CH22
Burnside, Saw. 36 EX05
Burnside Ave. E4 101 DZ51
Burnside Clo. SE16 143 DX74
Burnside Clo., Barn. 80 DA41
Burnside Clo., Hat. 45 CU15
Homestead Rd.
Burnside Clo., Twick. 177 CG86
Burnside Cres., Wem. 137 CK67
Burnside Rd., Dag. 126 EW61
Burnside Ter., Harl. 36 EZ12
Hobbs Cross Rd.
Burnt Ash Hill SE12 184 EF86
Burnt Ash La., Brom. 184 EG93
Burnt Ash Rd. SE12 184 EF85
Burnt Common Clo., Wok. 243 BF125
Burnt Common La., Wok. 244 BG125
Burnt Fm. Ride, Enf. 65 DP34
Burnt Fm. Ride, Wal.Cr. 65 DP31
Burnt Ho. La., Dart. 188 FL91
Burnt Mill, Harl. 35 EQ13
Burnt Mill Clo., Harl. 35 EQ12
Burnt Mill La.
Burnt Mill La., Harl. 35 EQ12
Burnt Oak Bdy., Edg. 96 CP52
Burnt Oak Flds., Edg. 96 CQ53
Burnt Oak La., Sid. 186 EU89
Burnthwaite Rd. SW6 160 DA80
Burntmill Cor., Harl. 35 EQ11
Eastwick Rd.
Burntwood, Brwd. 108 FW48
Gerrard Cres.
Burntwood Ave., Horn. 128 FK58
Burntwood Clo. SW18 180 DD88
Burntwood Clo., Cat. 236 DU121
Burntwood Gra. Rd. SW18 180 DD88
Burntwood Gro., Sev. 257 FH127
Burntwood La. SW17 180 DE89
Burntwood La., Cat. 236 DS122
Burntwood Rd., Sev. 257 FH128
Burntwood Vw. SE19 182 DT92
Bowley La.
Burnway, Horn. 128 FL59
Buross St. E1 142 DV72
Commercial Rd.
Burpham La., Guil. 243 BA130
Burr Clo. E1 142 DU74
Burr Clo., Bexh. 166 EZ83
Burr Clo., St.Alb. 62 CL27
Burr Hill La., Wok. 210 AS109
Burr Rd. SW18 180 DA87
Burrage Gro. SE18 165 EQ77
Burrage Pl. SE18 165 EP78
Burrage Rd. SE18 165 EQ78
Burrard Rd. E16 144 EH72
Burrard Rd. NW6 120 DA63
Burrell, The, Dor. 262 CC137
Burrell Clo., Croy. 203 DY100
Burrell Clo., Edg. 96 CP47
Burrell Row, Beck. 203 EA96
High St.
Burrell St. SE1 278 F2
Burrell St. SE1 141 DP74
Burrell Twr. E10 123 EA59
Burrells Wf. Sq. E14 163 EB78
Burrfield Dr., Orp. 206 EX99
Burritt Rd., Kings.T. 198 CN96
Burroughs, The NW4 119 CV57
Burroughs Gdns. NW4 119 CV56
Burroughs Par. NW4 119 CV56
The Burroughs
Burrow Clo., Chig. 103 ET50
Burrow Rd.
Burrow Grn., Chig. 103 ET50
Burrow Rd. SE22 162 DS84
Burrow Rd., Chig. 103 ET50
Burrow Wk. SE21 182 DQ87
Rosendale Rd.
Burroway Rd., Slou. 153 BB76
Burrowfield, Welw.G.C. 29 CX11
Burrowfield Ind. Est., Welw.G.C. 29 CX12
Burrows Clo., Guil. 242 AT133
Burrows Clo., H.Wyc. 88 AC45
Burrows Clo., Lthd. 230 BZ124
Burrows Cross, Guil. 261 BQ141
Burrows Hill Clo., Houns. 154 BJ84
Burrows Hill La., Houns. 154 BH84
Burrows La., Guil. 261 BQ140
Burrows Ms. SE1 278 F4
Burrows Rd. NW10 139 CW69
Bursdon Clo., Sid. 185 ET89
Burses Way, Brwd. 109 GB45
Bursland Rd., Enf. 83 DX42
Burslem Ave., Ilf. 104 EU51
Burslem St. E1 142 DU72
Burstead Clo., Cob. 214 BX112
Burstock Rd. SW15 159 CY84
Burston Dr., St.Alb. 60 CC28
Burston Rd. SW15 179 CX85
Burston Vil. SW15 179 CX85
St. John's Ave.
Burstow Rd. SW20 199 CY95
Burt Rd. E16 144 EJ74
Burtenshaw Rd., T.Ditt. 197 CG101
Burtley Clo. N4 122 DQ60
Burton Ave., Wat. 75 BU42
Burton Clo., Chess. 215 CK108
Burton Clo., Horl. 268 DG149
Burton Ct. SW3 160 DF78
Franklin's Row
Burton Gdns., Houns. 156 BZ81
Burton Gro. SE17 162 DR78
Portland St.
Burton La. SW9 161 DN82
Burton La. (Cheshunt), Wal.Cr. 66 DS29
Burton Ms. SW1 276 G9
Burton Pl. WC1 273 N3
Burton Rd. E18 124 EH55
Burton Rd. NW6 139 CZ66
Burton Rd. SW9 161 DP82
Burton Rd., Kings.T. 178 CL94
Burton Rd., Loug. 85 EQ42
Burton St. WC1 273 N3
Burton St. WC1 141 DK69
Burton Way, Wind. 151 AL82
Burtonhole Clo. NW7 97 CX49
Burtonhole La. NW7 97 CY49
Burtons La., Ch.St.G. 72 AW40
Burtons La., Rick. 73 BA43
Burtons Rd., Hmptn. 176 CB91
Burtons Way, Ch.St.G. 72 AW40
Burtwell La. SE27 182 DR91
Burwash Ct., Orp. 206 EW99
Rookery Gdns.
Burwash Ho. SE1 279 L5
Burwash Rd. SE18 165 ER78
Burway Cres., Cher. 194 BG97
Burwell Ave., Grnf. 137 CE65
Burwell Clo. E1 142 DV72
Bigland St.
Burwell Rd. E10 123 DY60
Burwell Wk. E3 143 EA70
Burwood Ave., Brom. 204 EH103
Burwood Ave., Ken. 219 DP114
Burwood Ave., Pnr. 116 BW57
Burwood Clo., Guil. 243 BD133
Burwood Clo., Reig. 250 DD134
Burwood Clo., Surb. 198 CN102
Burwood Clo., Walt. 214 BW107
Burwood Gdns., Rain. 147 FF69
Burwood Pk. Rd., Walt. 213 BV105
Burwood Pl. W2 272 C8
Burwood Pl. W2 140 DE72
Burwood Rd., Walt. 213 BS108
Bury Ave., Hayes 135 BS68
Bury Ave., Ruis. 115 BQ58
Bury Clo. SE16 143 DX74
Rotherhithe St.
Bury Clo., Wok. 226 AX116
Bury Ct. EC3 275 N8
Bury Flds., Guil. 258 AW136
Bury Grn., Hem.H. 40 BJ19
Bury Grn. Rd. (Cheshunt), Wal.Cr. 66 DU31
Bury Gro., Mord. 200 DB99
Bury Hill, Hem.H. 40 BH19
Bury Hill Clo., Hem.H. 40 BJ19
Bury La., Chesh. 54 AP31
Bury La., Epp. 69 ES31
Bury La., Rick. 92 BK46
Bury La., Wok. 226 AW116
Bury Meadows, Rick. 92 BK46
Bury Pl. WC1 273 P7
Bury Pl. WC1 141 DL71
Bury Ri., Hem.H. 57 BD25
Bury Rd. E4 84 EE43
Bury Rd. N22 121 DN55
Bury Rd., Dag. 127 FB64
Bury Rd., Epp. 69 ES31
Bury Rd., Harl. 36 EW11
Bury Rd., Hat. 45 CW17
Bury Rd., Hem.H. 40 BJ19
Bury St. EC3 275 N9
Bury St. EC3 142 DS72
Bury St. N9 100 DU46
Bury St. SW1 277 K2
Bury St. SW1 141 DJ74
Bury St., Guil. 258 AW136
Bury St., Ruis. 115 BR57
Bury St. W. N9 100 DR45
Bury Wk. SW3 276 B9
Bury Wk. SW3 160 DE78
Burycroft, Welw.G.C. 29 CY06
Burydell La., St.Alb. 61 CD27
Buryholme, Brox. 49 DZ23
Busbridge Ho. E14 143 EA71
Brabazon St.
Busby Ms. NW5 141 DK65
Torriano Ave.
Busby Pl. NW5 141 DK65
Busby St. E2 142 DT70
Chilton St.
Bush Clo., Add. 212 BJ106
Bush Clo., Ilf. 125 ER57
Bush Cotts. SW18 180 DA85
Putney Bri. Rd.
Bush Ct. W12 159 CX75
Bush Elms Rd., Horn. 127 FG59
Bush Fair, Harl. 52 EU17
Tilegate Rd.
Bush Gro. NW9 118 CQ59
Bush Gro., Stan. 95 CK53
Bush Hall La., Hat. 45 CX15
Bush Hill N21 100 DQ45
Bush Hill Rd. N21 82 DR44
Bush Hill Rd., Har. 118 CM58
Bush Ind. Est. NW10 138 CR70
Bush La. EC4 275 K10
Bush La., Wok. 227 BD124
Bush Rd. E8 142 DV67
Bush Rd. E11 124 EF59
Bush Rd. SE8 163 DX77
Bush Rd., Buck.H. 102 EK49
Bush Rd., Rich. 158 CM79
Bush Rd., Shep. 194 BM99
Bushbaby Clo. SE1 279 M7
Bushbarns (Cheshunt), Wal.Cr. 66 DU29
Bushberry Rd. E9 143 DY65
Bushbury La., Bet. 264 CN139
Bushby Ave., Brox. 49 DZ22
Bushell Clo. SW2 181 DM89
Bushell Grn. (Bushey), Wat. 95 CD47
Bushell St. E1 142 DU74
Hermitage Wall
Bushell Way, Chis. 185 EN92
Bushetts Gro., Red. 251 DH128
Bushey Ave. E18 124 EF55
Bushey Ave., Orp. 205 ER101
Bushey Clo. E4 101 EC48
Bushey Clo., Pur. 236 DS116
Bushey Clo., Uxb. 115 BP61
Bushey Clo., Welw.G.C. 30 DB10
Bushey Ct. SW20 199 CV96
Bushey Cft., Harl. 51 ES17
Bushey Cft., Oxt. 253 EC130
Bushey Down SW12 181 DH89
Bedford Hill
Bushey Grn., Welw.G.C. 30 DB10
Bushey Gro. Rd. (Bushey), Wat. 76 BX42
Bushey Hall Dr. (Bushey), Wat. 76 BY42
Bushey Hall Rd. (Bushey), Wat. 76 BX42
Bushey Hill Rd. SE5 162 DS81
Bushey La., Sutt. 218 DA105
Bushey Lees, Sid. 185 ET86
Fen Gro.
Bushey Ley, Welw.G.C. 30 DB10
Bushey Mill Cres., Wat. 76 BW37
Bushey Mill La., Wat. 76 BW37
Bushey Mill La. (Bushey), Wat. 76 BZ40
Bushey Rd. E13 144 EJ68
Bushey Rd. N15 122 DS58
Bushey Rd. SW20 199 CV97
Bushey Rd., Croy. 203 EA103
Bushey Rd., Hayes 155 BS77
Bushey Rd., Sutt. 218 DB105
Bushey Rd., Uxb. 114 BN61
Bushey Shaw, Ash. 231 CH117
Bushey Vw. Wk., Wat. 76 BX40
Bushey Way, Beck. 203 ED100
Bushfield Clo., Edg. 96 CP47
Bushfield Cres., Edg. 96 CP47
Bushfield Dr., Red. 266 DG139
Bushfield Rd., Hem.H. 57 BC25
Bushfield Wk., Swans. 190 FY86
Bushfields, Loug. 85 EN43
Bushgrove Rd., Dag. 126 EX63
Bushmead Clo. N15 122 DT56
Copperfield Dr.
Bushmoor Cres. SE18 165 EQ80
Bushnell Rd. SW17 181 DH89
Bushway, Dag. 126 EX63
Bushwood E11 124 EF60
Bushwood Clo., Hat. 45 CV23
Dellsome La.
Bushwood Dr. SE1 162 DT77
Bushwood Rd., Rich. 158 CN79
Bushy Hill Dr., Guil. 243 BB132
Bushy Pk., Hmptn. 197 CF95
Bushy Pk., Tedd. 197 CF95
Bushy Pk. Gdns., Tedd. 177 CD92
Bushy Pk. Rd., Tedd. 177 CH94
Bushy Rd., Lthd. 230 CB122
Bushy Rd., Tedd. 177 CF93
Buslins La., Chesh. 54 AL28
Butcher Row E1 143 DX73
Butcher Row E14 143 DX73
Butcher Wk., Swans. 190 FY87
Manor Rd.
Butchers La., Sev. 209 FX103
Butchers Rd. E16 144 EG72
Bute Ave., Rich. 178 CL89
Bute Ct., Wall. 219 DJ106
Bute Rd.
Bute Gdns. W6 159 CX77
Bute Gdns., Wall. 219 DJ106
Bute Gdns. W., Wall. 219 DJ106
Bute Rd., Croy. 201 DN102
Bute Rd., Ilf. 125 EP57
Bute Rd., Wall. 219 DJ105
Bute St. SW7 160 DD77
Bute Wk. N1 142 DR65
Marquess Rd.
Butler Ave., Har. 117 CD59
Butler Ho., Grays 170 GA79
Argent St.
Butler Pl. SW1 277 M6
Butler Rd. NW10 139 CT66
Curzon Cres.
Butler Rd., Dag. 126 EV63
Butler Rd., Har. 116 CC59
Butler St. E2 142 DW69
Knottisford St.
Butler St., Uxb. 135 BP70
Butler Wk., Grays 170 GD77
Palmers Dr.
Butlers Clo., Amer. 55 AN37
Butlers Clo., Wind. 151 AK82
Butlers Ct. Rd., Beac. 89 AK54
Butlers Dene Rd., Cat. 237 DZ119
Butlers Dr. E4 83 EC38
Butlers Hill, Lthd. 245 BP130
Butlers Wf. SE1 162 DT75
Lafone St.
Butt Fld. Vw., St.Alb. 42 CC24
Buttell Clo., Grays 170 GD78
Butter Hill, Cars. 200 DG104
Butter Hill, Dor. 263 CG136
South St.
Butter Hill, Wall. 200 DG104
Buttercross La., Epp. 70 EU30
Buttercup Clo., Rom. 106 FK53
Copperfields Way
Buttercup Sq., Stai. 174 BK88
Diamedes Ave.
Butterfield, H.Wyc. 110 AD59
Butterfield Clo. N17 100 DQ51
Devonshire Rd.
Butterfield Clo. SE16 162 DV75
Wilson Gro.
Butterfield Clo., Twick. 177 CF86
Rugby Rd.
Butterfield La., St.Alb. 43 CE24
Butterfield Sq. E6 145 EM72
Harper Rd.
Butterfields E17 123 EC57
Butterfly La. SE9 185 EP86
Butterfly La., Borwd. 77 CG41
Butterfly Wk. SE5 162 DR81
Denmark Hill
Butterfly Wk., Warl. 236 DW120
Butteridges Clo., Dag. 146 EZ67
Butterly Ave., Dart. 188 FM89
Buttermere Ave., Slou. 130 AJ71
Buttermere Clo. E15 123 ED63
Buttermere Clo. SE1 279 P8
Buttermere Clo., Felt. 175 BT88
Buttermere Clo., Mord. 199 CX100
Buttermere Clo., St.Alb. 43 CH21
Buttermere Dr. SW15 179 CY85
Buttermere Gdns., Pur. 220 DR113
Buttermere Rd., Orp. 206 EX98
Buttermere Wk. E8 142 DT65
Buttermere Way, Egh. 173 BB94
Keswick Rd.
Buttersweet Ri., Saw. 36 EY06
Brook Rd.
Butterwick W6 159 CW77
Butterwick, Wat. 76 BY36
Butterwick La., St.Alb. 44 CN22
Butterworth Gdns., Wdf.Grn. 102 EG51
Buttesland St. N1 275 L2
Buttesland St. N1 142 DR69
Buttfield Clo., Dag. 147 FB65
Buttlehide, Rick. 91 BD50
Buttmarsh Clo. SE18 165 EP78
Button St., Swan. 208 FJ96
Buttondene Cres., Brox. 49 EB22
Butts, The, Brent. 157 CK79
Butts, The, Brox. 49 DY24
Butts, The, Sev. 241 FH116
Butts, The, Sun. 196 BW97
Elizabeth Gdns.
Butts Cotts., Felt. 176 BZ90
Butts Cres., Felt. 176 CA90
Butts End, Hem.H. 40 BG18
Butts Grn. Rd., Horn. 128 FK58
Butts Piece, Nthlt. 135 BV68
Longhook Gdns.
Butts Rd., Brom. 184 EE92
Butts Rd., Wok. 226 AY117
Butts Rd. Ind. Est., Wok. 226 AY118
Buttsbury Rd., Ilf. 125 EQ64
Buttsmead, Nthwd. 93 BQ52
Buxted Rd. E8 142 DT66
Buxted Rd. N12 98 DE50
Buxted Rd. SE22 162 DS84
Buxton Ave., Cat. 236 DS121
Buxton Clo., St.Alb. 43 CK17
Buxton Clo., Wdf.Grn. 102 EK51
Buxton Ct. N1 275 J2
Buxton Cres., Sutt. 217 CY105
Buxton Dr. E11 124 EE56
Buxton Dr., N.Mal. 198 CR96
Buxton Gdns. W3 138 CP73
Buxton La., Cat. 236 DR120
Buxton Path, Wat. 94 BW48
Buxton Rd. E4 101 ED45
Buxton Rd. E6 144 EL69
Buxton Rd. E15 124 EE64
Buxton Rd. E17 123 DY56
Buxton Rd. N19 121 DK60
Buxton Rd. NW2 139 CV65
Buxton Rd. SW14 158 CS83
Buxton Rd., Ashf. 174 BK92
Buxton Rd., Epp. 85 ES36
Buxton Rd., Erith 167 FD80
Buxton Rd., Grays 170 GE75
Buxton Rd., Ilf. 125 ES58
Buxton Rd., Th.Hth. 201 DP99
Buxton Rd., Wal.Abb. 68 EG32
Buxton St. E1 142 DT70
Buzzard Creek Ind. Est., Bark. 145 ET71
By the Mt., Welw.G.C. 29 CX10
By the Wd., Wat. 94 BX47
By-Wood End, Ger.Cr. 91 AZ50
Byam St. SW6 160 DC82
Byards Cft. SW16 201 DK95
Byatt Wk., Hmptn. 176 BY93
Victors Dr.
Bybend Clo., Slou. 131 AP67
Bychurch End, Tedd. 177 CF92
Church Rd.
Bycliffe Ter., Grav. 191 GF87
Bycroft Rd., Sthl. 136 CA70
Bycroft St. SE20 183 DX94
Parish La.
Bycullah Ave., Enf. 81 DP41
Bycullah Rd., Enf. 81 DP41
Byde St., Hert. 32 DQ08
Bye, The W3 138 CS72
Bye Way, The, Har. 95 CE53
Byegrove Rd. SW19 180 DD93
Byers Clo., Pot.B. 64 DC34
Byewaters, Wat. 75 BQ44
Byeway, The SW14 158 CQ83
Byeway, The, Rick. 92 BL47
Byeways, Twick. 176 CB90
Byeways, The, Ash. 231 CK118
Skinners La.
Byeways, The, Surb. 198 CN99
Byfeld Gdns. SW13 159 CU81
Byfield, Welw.G.C. 29 CY06
Byfield Clo. SE16 163 DY75
Byfield Pas., Islw. 157 CG83
Byfield Rd., Islw. 157 CG83
Byfleet Ind. Est., W.Byf. 212 BK111
Byfleet Rd., Add. 212 BK109
Byfleet Rd., Cob. 212 BN112
Byford Clo. E15 144 EE66
Bygrove, Croy. 221 EB107
Bygrove St. E14 143 EB72
Byland Clo. N21 99 DM45
Bylands, Wok. 227 BA119
Bylands Clo. SE2 166 EV76
Finchale Rd.
Bylands Clo. SE16 143 DX74
Rotherhithe St.
Byne Rd. SE26 182 DW93
Byne Rd., Cars. 200 DE103
Bynes Rd., S.Croy. 220 DR108
Byng Dr., Pot.B. 64 DA31
Byng Pl. WC1 273 M5
Byng Pl. WC1 141 DK70
Byng Rd., Barn. 79 CX41
Byng St. E14 163 EA75
Bynghams, Harl. 51 EM17
Bynon Ave., Bexh. 166 EY83
Byre, The N14 81 DH44
Farm La.
Byre Rd. N14 80 DG44
Farm La.
Byrefield Rd., Guil. 242 AT131
Byrne Rd. SW12 181 DH88
Byron Ave. E12 144 EL65
Byron Ave. E18 124 EF55
Byron Ave. NW9 118 CP56
Byron Ave., Borwd. 78 CN43
Byron Ave., Couls. 235 DL115
Byron Ave., Houns. 155 BU82
Byron Ave., N.Mal. 199 CU99
Byron Ave., Sutt. 218 DD105
Byron Ave., Wat. 76 BX39
Byron Ave. E., Sutt. 218 DD105
Byron Clo. E8 142 DU67
Byron Clo. SE26 183 DY91
Porthcawe Rd.
Byron Clo. SE28 146 EW74
Byron Clo., Hmptn. 176 BZ91
Byron Clo., Wal.Cr. 66 DT27
Allard Clo.
Byron Clo., Walt. 196 BY102
Byron Clo., Wok. 226 AS117
Byron Ct. W9 140 DA70
Lanhill Rd.
Byron Ct., Enf. 81 DP40
Bycullah Rd.
Byron Ct., Har. 117 CE58
Byron Dr. N2 120 DD58
Byron Dr., Erith 167 FB80
Byron Gdns., Sutt. 218 DD105
Byron Gdns., Til. 171 GJ81
Byron Hill Rd., Har. 117 CD60
Byron Ho., Beck. 183 EA93
Byron Ho., Slou. 153 BB78
Byron Ms. NW3 120 DE64
Byron Ms. W9 140 DA70
Shirland Rd.
Byron Pl., Lthd. 231 CH122
Byron Rd. E10 123 EB60
Byron Rd. E17 123 EA55
Byron Rd. NW2 119 CV61
Byron Rd. NW7 97 CU50
Byron Rd. W5 138 CM74
Byron Rd., Add. 212 BK105
Byron Rd., Brwd. 109 GD45
Byron Rd., Dart. 168 FP84
Byron Rd., Har. 117 CE58
Byron Rd. (Wealdstone), Har. 95 CF54
Byron Rd., S.Croy. 220 DV110
Byron Rd., Wem. 117 CJ62
Byron St. E14 143 EC72
St. Leonards Rd.
Byron Ter. N9 100 DW45
Byron Way, Hayes 135 BT70
Byron Way, Nthlt. 136 BY69
Byron Way, Rom. 106 FJ53
Byron Way, West Dr. 154 BM77
Bysouth Clo. N15 122 DR56
Bysouth Clo., Ilf. 103 EP53
Bythorn St. SW9 161 DM83
Byton Rd. SW17 180 DF93
Byttom Hill, Dor. 247 CJ127
Byward Ave., Felt. 176 BW86
Byward St. EC3 279 N1
Byward St. EC3 142 DS73
Bywater Pl. SE16 143 DY74
Bywater St. SW3 276 D10
Bywater St. SW3 160 DF78
Byway, The, Epsom 217 CT105
Byway, The, Pot.B. 64 DA33
Byway, The, Sutt. 218 DD109
Byways, Berk. 38 AY18
Byways, Slou. 130 AG71
Bywell Pl. W1 273 K7
Bywood Ave., Croy. 202 DW100
Bywood Clo., Ken. 235 DP115
Byworth Wk. N19 121 DK60
Courtauld Rd.

C

C.I. Twr., N.Mal. 198 CS97
Cabbell Pl., Add. 212 BJ105
Cabbell St. NW1 272 B7
Cabbell St. NW1 140 DE71
Cabell Rd., Guil. 242 AS133
Cabinet Way E4 101 DZ51
Cable Pl. SE10 163 EC81
Diamond Ter.
Cable St. E1 142 DU73
Cable Trade Pk. SE7 164 EJ77
Cabot Sq. E14 143 EA74
Cabot Way E6 144 EK67
Parr Rd.
Cabrera Ave., Vir.W. 192 AW100
Cabrera Clo., Vir.W. 192 AX100
Cabul Rd. SW11 160 DE82
Cackets La., Sev. 239 ER115
Cactus Clo. SE15 162 DS82
Lyndhurst Gro.
Cactus Wk. W12 139 CT73
Du Cane Rd.
Cadbury Clo., Islw. 157 CG81
Cadbury Clo., Sun. 175 BS94
Cadbury Rd., Sun. 175 BS94
Cadbury Way SE16 162 DU76
Yalding Rd.
Caddington Clo., Barn. 80 DE43
Caddington Rd. NW2 119 CY62
Caddis Clo., Stan. 95 CF52
Daventer Dr.
Caddy Clo., Egh. 173 BA92
Cade La., Sev. 257 FJ128
Cade Rd. SE10 163 ED81
Cadell Clo. E2 142 DT69
Shipton St.
Cader Rd. SW18 180 DC86
Cadet Dr. SE1 162 DT77
Cadet Pl. SE10 164 EE78
Cadiz Ct., Dag. 147 FD66
Rainham Rd. S.
Cadiz Rd., Dag. 147 FC66
Cadiz St. SE17 162 DQ78
Cadley Ter. SE23 182 DW89
Cadlocks Hill, Sev. 224 EZ110
Cadman Clo. SW9 161 DP80
Langton Rd.
Cadmer Clo., N.Mal. 198 CS98
Cadmore Ct., Hert. 31 DM07
The Ridgeway
Cadmore La. (Cheshunt), Wal.Cr. 67 DX28
Cadmus Clo. SW4 161 DK83
Aristotle Rd.
Cadogan Ave., Dart. 189 FR87

Canford Rd. SW11 180 DG85
Cangels Clo., Hem.H. 39 BF22
Canham Rd. SE25 202 DS97
Canham Rd. W3 158 CS75
Canmore Gdns. SW16 181 DJ94
Cann Hall Rd. E11 124 EE63
Canning Cres. N22 99 DM53
Canning Cross SE5 162 DS82
Canning Pas. W8 160 DC76
Canning Pl. W8 160 DC76
Canning Pl. Ms. W8 160 DC76
Canning Pl.
Canning Rd. E15 144 EE68
Canning Rd. E17 123 DY56
Canning Rd. N5 121 DP62
Canning Rd., Croy. 202 DT103
Canning Rd., Har. 117 CF55
Cannington Rd., Dag. 146 EW65
Cannizaro Rd. SW19 179 CW93
Cannon Clo. SW20 199 CW97
Cannon Clo., Hmptn. 176 CB93
Hanworth Rd.
Cannon Cres., Wok. 210 AS111
Cannon Dr. E14 143 EA73
Cannon Gro., Lthd. 231 CE122
Cannon Hill N14 99 DK48
Cannon Hill NW6 120 DA64
Cannon Hill Clo., Maid. 150 AC77
Cannon Hill La. SW20 199 CY97
Cannon La. NW3 120 DD62
Cannon La., Pnr. 116 BY60
Cannon Ms., Wal.Abb. 67 EB33
Cannon Mill Ave., Chesh. 54 AR33
Cannon Pl. NW3 120 DD62
Cannon Pl. SE7 164 EL78
Cannon Rd. N14 99 DL48
Cannon Rd., Bexh. 166 EY81
Cannon Rd., Wat. 76 BW43
Cannon St. EC4 275 H9
Cannon St. EC4 142 DQ72
Cannon St., St.Alb. 43 CD19
Cannon St. Rd. E1 142 DV72
Cannon Trd. Est., Wem. 118 CP63
Cannon Wk., Grav. 191 GJ87
Cannon Way, Lthd. 231 CE121
Cannon Way, W.Mol. 196 CA98
Cannon Wf. Business Cen. SE8 163 DY77
Cannonbury Ave., Pnr. 116 BX58
Cannons Meadow, Welw. 30 DE05
Cannonside, Lthd. 231 CE122
Canon Ave., Rom. 126 EW57
Canon Beck Rd. SE16 162 DW75
Canon Hill, Couls. 235 DN118
Canon Mohan Clo. N14 81 DH44
Farm La.
Canon Rd., Brom. 204 EJ97
Canon Row SW1 277 P5
Canon Row SW1 161 DL75
Canon St. N1 142 DQ67
Canonbie Rd. SE23 182 DW87
Canonbury Cres. N1 142 DQ66
Canonbury Gro. N1 142 DQ66
Canonbury La. N1 141 DP66
Canonbury Pk. N. N1 142 DQ65
Canonbury Pk. S. N1 142 DQ65
Canonbury Pl. N1 141 DP65
Canonbury Rd. N1 141 DP65
Canonbury Rd., Enf. 82 DS39
Canonbury Sq. N1 141 DP66
Canonbury St. N1 142 DQ66
Canonbury Vil. N1 141 DP66
Canonbury Yd. N1 142 DQ67
New N. Rd.
Canons Brook, Harl. 51 EN15
Canons Clo. N2 120 DD59
Canons Clo., Edg. 96 CM51
Canons Clo., Rad. 77 CH35
Canons Clo., Reig. 249 CZ133
Canons Cor., Edg. 96 CL49
Canons Dr., Edg. 96 CL51
Canons Gate, Harl. 35 EN13
Canons Gate (Cheshunt), Wal.Cr. 67 DZ26
Canons Hatch, Tad. 233 CY118
Canon's Hill, Couls. 235 DN118
Canons La., Tad. 233 CY118
Canons Pk. Clo., Edg. 96 CL52
Donnefield Ave.
Canons Rd., Ware 32 DW05
Canons Wk., Croy. 203 DX104
Canonsleigh Rd., Dag. 146 EV66
Canopus Way, Nthwd. 93 BU49
Canopus Way, Stai. 174 BL87
Canrobert St. E2 142 DV69
Cantelowes Rd. NW1 141 DK65
Canterbury Ave., Ilf. 124 EL59
Canterbury Ave., Sid. 186 EW89
Canterbury Ave., Slou. 131 AQ70
Canterbury Ave., Upmin. 129 FT60
Canterbury Clo. E6 145 EM72
Harper Rd.
Canterbury Clo., Amer. 55 AS39
Canterbury Clo., Beck. 203 EB95
Canterbury Clo., Chig. 103 ET48
Canterbury Clo., Dart. 188 FN87
Canterbury Clo., Grnf. 136 CB72
Canterbury Clo., Nthwd. 93 BT51
Canterbury Cres. SW9 161 DN83
Canterbury Gro. SE27 181 DP90
Canterbury Par., S.Ock. 149 FW69
Canterbury Pl. SE17 278 G9
Canterbury Pl. SE17 161 DP77
Canterbury Rd. E10 123 EC59
Canterbury Rd. NW6 140 DA68
Canterbury Rd., Borwd. 78 CN40
Canterbury Rd., Croy. 201 DM101
Canterbury Rd., Felt. 176 BY90
Canterbury Rd., Grav. 191 GJ89
Canterbury Rd., Guil. 242 AT132
Canterbury Rd., Har. 116 CB57
Canterbury Rd., Mord. 200 DC99
Canterbury Rd., Wat. 75 BV40
Canterbury Ter. NW6 140 DA68
Canterbury Way, Brwd. 107 FW51
Canterbury Way, Grays 169 FS80
Canterbury Way, Rick. 75 BQ41
Cantley Gdns. SE19 202 DT95
Cantley Gdns., Ilf. 125 EQ58
Cantley Rd. W7 157 CG76
Canton St. E14 143 EA72
Cantrell Rd. E3 143 DZ70
Cantwell Rd. SE18 165 EP80
Canute Gdns. SE16 163 DX77
Canvey St. SE1 278 G2
Cape Clo., Bark. 145 EQ65
North St.
Cape Rd. N17 122 DU55
High Cross Rd.
Cape Rd., St.Alb. 43 CH20
Cape Yd. E1 142 DU74
Asher Way
Capel Ave., Wall. 219 DM106
Capel Clo. N20 98 DC48
Capel Clo., Brom. 204 EL102
Capel Ct. EC2 275 L9
Capel Ct. SE20 202 DW95
Melvin Rd.
Capel Gdns., Ilf. 125 ET63
Capel Gdns., Pnr. 116 BZ56
Capel Pl., Dart. 188 FJ91
Capel Pt. E7 124 EH63
Capel Rd. E7 124 EH63
Capel Rd. E12 124 EJ63
Capel Rd., Barn. 80 DE44
Capel Rd., Enf. 82 DV36
Capel Rd., Wat. 76 BY44
Capel Vere Wk., Wat. 75 BS39
Capell Ave., Rick. 73 BC43
Capell Rd., Rick. 73 BD43
Capell Way, Rick. 73 BD43
Capella Rd., Nthwd. 93 BT50
Capener's Clo. SW1 276 F5
Capern Rd. SW18 180 DC88
Cargill Rd.
Capital Business Cen., Wem. 137 CK68
Capital Interchange Way, Brent. 158 CN78
Capital Pl., Croy. 219 DM106
Stafford Rd.
Capitol Ind. Pk. NW9 118 CQ55
Capitol Way NW9 118 CQ55
Capland St. NW8 272 A4
Capland St. NW8 140 DD70
Caple Par. NW10 138 CS68
Harley Rd.
Caple Rd. NW10 139 CT68
Capon Clo., Brwd. 108 FV46
Caponfield, Welw.G.C. 30 DB11
Cappell La., Ware 33 EC09
Capper St. WC1 273 L5
Capper St. WC1 141 DJ70
Caprea Clo., Hayes 136 BX71
Triandra Way
Capri Rd., Croy. 202 DT102
Capstan Clo., Rom. 126 EV58
Capstan Ct., Dart. 168 FQ84
Capstan Ride, Enf. 81 DN40
Capstan Rd. SE8 163 DZ77
Capstan Sq. E14 163 EC75
Capstan Way SE16 143 DY74
Capstan's Wf., Wok. 226 AT118
Capstone Rd., Brom. 184 EF91
Captain Cook Clo., Ch.St.G. 90 AV49
Captains Clo., Chesh. 54 AN27
Captains Wk., Berk. 38 AX20
Capthorne Ave., Har. 116 BY60
Capuchin Clo., Stan. 95 CH51
Capulet Ms. E16 144 EG74
Hanover Ave.
Capworth St. E10 123 EA60
Caractacus Cottage Vw., Wat. 93 BU45
Caractacus Grn., Wat. 75 BT44
Caradoc Clo. W2 140 DA72
Caradoc St. SE10 164 EE78
Caradon Clo. E11 124 EE61
Brockway Clo.
Caradon Clo., Wok. 226 AV118
Caradon Way N15 122 DR56
Caravan La., Rick. 92 BL45
Caravel Clo. E14 163 EA76
Tiller Rd.
Caravel Clo., Grays 170 FZ76
Caravel Ms. SE8 163 EA79
Watergate St.
Caravelle Gdns., Nthlt. 136 BX69
Javelin Way
Caraway Clo. E13 144 EH71
Caraway Pl., Guil. 242 AU129
Caraway Pl., Wall. 201 DH104
Carberry Rd. SE19 182 DS93
Carbery Ave. W3 158 CM75
Carbis Clo. E4 101 ED46
Carbis Rd. E14 143 DZ72
Carbone Hill, Hert. 65 DK26
Carbone Hill (Cuffley), Pot.B. 65 DJ27
Carbuncle Pas. Way N17 100 DU54
Carburton St. W1 273 J6
Carburton St. W1 141 DH71
Carbury Clo., Horn. 148 FJ65
Cardale St. E14 163 EC76
Plevna St.
Cardamom Clo., Guil. 242 AU130
Carde Clo., Hert. 31 DM08
Carden Rd. SE15 162 DV83
Cardiff Rd. W7 157 CG76
Cardiff Rd., Enf. 82 DV42
Cardiff Rd., Wat. 75 BV44
Cardiff St. SE18 165 ES80
Cardiff Way, Abb.L. 59 BU32
Cardigan Clo., Slou. 131 AM73
Cardigan Clo., Wok. 226 AS118
Bingham Dr.
Cardigan Gdns., Ilf. 126 EU61
Cardigan Rd. E3 143 DZ68
Cardigan Rd. SW13 159 CU82
Cardigan Rd. SW19 180 DC93
Haydons Rd.
Cardigan Rd., Rich. 178 CL86
Cardigan St. SE11 278 D10
Cardigan St. SE11 161 DN78
Cardigan Wk. N1 142 DQ66
Ashby Gro.
Cardinal Ave., Borwd. 78 CP41
Cardinal Ave., Kings.T. 178 CL92
Cardinal Ave., Mord. 199 CY100
Cardinal Bourne St. SE1 279 L7
Cardinal Bourne St. SE1 162 DR76
Cardinal Clo., Chis. 205 ER95
Cardinal Clo., Edg. 96 CR52
Abbots Rd.
Cardinal Clo., Mord. 199 CY101
Cardinal Clo., S.Croy. 220 DU113
Cardinal Clo. (Cheshunt), Wal.Cr. 66 DT26
Adamsfield
Cardinal Clo., Wor.Pk. 217 CU105
Cardinal Cres., N.Mal. 198 CQ96
Cardinal Dr., Ilf. 103 EQ51
Cardinal Dr., Walt. 196 BX102
Cardinal Gro., St.Alb. 42 CB22
Cardinal Pl. SW15 159 CX84
Cardinal Rd., Felt. 175 BV88
Cardinal Rd., Ruis. 116 BX60
Cardinal Way, Har. 117 CE55
Wolseley Rd.
Cardinal Way, Rain. 148 FK68
Cardinals Wk., Hmptn. 176 CC94
Cardinals Wk., Maid. 130 AJ72
Cardinals Wk., Sun. 175 BS93
Cardinals Way N19 121 DK60
Cardine Ms. SE15 162 DV80
Cardingham, Wok. 226 AU117
Cardington Sq., Houns. 156 BX84
Cardington St. NW1 273 K2
Cardington St. NW1 141 DJ69
Cardozo Rd. N7 121 DL64
Cardrew Ave. N12 98 DD50
Cardrew Clo. N12 98 DE50
Cardross St. W6 159 CV76
Cardwell Rd. N7 121 DL63
Cardwell Rd. SE18 165 EM77
Cardwells Keep, Guil. 242 AU131
Cardy Rd., Hem.H. 40 BH20
Carew Clo. N7 121 DM61
Carew Clo., Couls. 235 DP119
Carew Rd. N17 100 DU54
Carew Rd. W13 157 CJ75
Carew Rd., Ashf. 175 BQ93
Carew Rd., Mitch. 200 DG96
Carew Rd., Nthwd. 93 BS51
Carew Rd., Th.Hth. 201 DP97
Carew Rd., Wall. 219 DJ107
Carew St. SE5 162 DQ82
Carew Way, Wat. 94 BZ48
Carey Clo., Wind. 151 AP83
Carey Ct., Bexh. 187 FB85
Carey Gdns. SW8 161 DJ81
Carey La. EC2 275 H8
Carey Pl. SW1 277 M9
Carey Rd., Dag. 126 EY63
Carey St. WC2 274 C9
Carey St. WC2 141 DM72
Carey Way, Wem. 118 CQ63
Careys Cft., Berk. 38 AU16
Careys Wd., Horl. 269 DP148
Carfax Pl. SW4 161 DK84
Holwood Pl.
Carfax Rd., Hayes 155 BT78
Carfax Rd., Horn. 127 FF63
Carfree Clo. N1 141 DN66
Bewdley St.
Cargill Rd. SW18 180 DB88
Cargo Forecourt Rd., Gat. 268 DD152
Cargo Rd., Gat. 268 DD152
Cargreen Pl. SE25 202 DT98
Cargreen Rd.
Cargreen Rd. SE25 202 DT98
Carholme Rd. SE23 183 DZ88
Carisbrook Rd., Brwd. 108 FV44
Carisbrooke Ave., Bex. 186 EX88
Carisbrooke Ave., Wat. 76 BX39
Carisbrooke Clo., Enf. 82 DT39
Carisbrooke Clo., Horn. 128 FN60
Carisbrooke Clo., Stan. 95 CK54
Carisbrooke Ct., Slou. 132 AT73
Carisbrooke Gdns. SE15 162 DT80
Commercial Way
Carisbrooke Rd. E17 123 DY56
Carisbrooke Rd., Brom. 204 EJ98
Carisbrooke Rd., Mitch. 201 DK98
Carisbrooke Rd., St.Alb. 60 CB26
Carker's La. NW5 121 DH64
Carl Ekman Ho., Grav. 190 GD87
Carlbury Clo., St.Alb. 43 CH21
Carleton Ave., Wall. 219 DK109
Carleton Clo., Esher 197 CD102
Carleton Pl. (Horton Kirby), Dart. 208 FQ98
Carleton Rd. N7 121 DK64
Carleton Rd., Dart. 188 FN87
Carleton Rd. (Cheshunt), Wal.Cr. 67 DX28
Carleton Vil. NW5 121 DJ64
Leighton Gro.
Carlile Clo. E3 143 DZ68
Carlina Gdns., Wdf.Grn. 102 EH50
Carlingford Gdns., Mitch. 180 DF94
Carlingford Rd. N15 121 DP55
Carlingford Rd. NW3 120 DD63
Carlingford Rd., Mord. 199 CX100
Carlisle Ave. EC3 275 N9
Carlisle Ave. W3 138 CS72
Carlisle Ave., St.Alb. 43 CD18
Carlisle Clo., Kings.T. 198 CN95
Carlisle Clo., Pnr. 116 BY59
Carlisle Gdns., Har. 117 CK59
Carlisle Gdns., Ilf. 124 EL58
Carlisle La. SE1 278 C7
Carlisle La. SE1 161 DM76
Carlisle Ms. NW8 272 A6
Carlisle Ms. NW8 140 DD71
Carlisle Pl. N11 99 DH49
Carlisle Pl. SW1 277 K7
Carlisle Pl. SW1 161 DJ76
Carlisle Rd. E10 123 EA60
Carlisle Rd. N4 121 DN59
Carlisle Rd. NW6 139 CY67
Carlisle Rd. NW9 118 CQ55
Carlisle Rd., Dart. 188 FN86
Carlisle Rd., Hmptn. 176 CB94
Carlisle Rd., Rom. 127 FG57
Carlisle Rd., Slou. 131 AR73
Carlisle Rd., Sutt. 217 CZ106
Carlisle St. W1 273 M9
Carlisle Wk. E8 142 DT65
Laurel St.
Carlisle Way SW17 180 DG92
Carlos Pl. W1 276 G1
Carlos Pl. W1 140 DG73
Carlow St. NW1 141 DJ68
Arlington Rd.
Carlton Ave. N14 81 DK43
Carlton Ave., Felt. 176 BW86
Carlton Ave., Green. 189 FS86
Carlton Ave., Har. 117 CH57
Carlton Ave., Hayes 155 BS77
Carlton Ave., S.Croy. 220 DS108
Carlton Ave. E., Wem. 118 CL60
Carlton Ave. W., Wem. 117 CH61
Carlton Clo. NW3 120 DA61
Carlton Clo., Borwd. 78 CR42
Carlton Clo., Chess. 215 CK107
Carlton Clo., Edg. 96 CN50
Carlton Clo., Nthlt. 116 CC64
Whitton Ave. W.
Carlton Clo., Upmin. 128 FP61
Carlton Clo., Wok. 211 AZ114
Carlton Ct. SW9 161 DP81
Carlton Ct., Ilf. 125 ER55
Carlton Ct., Uxb. 134 BK71
Carlton Cres., Sutt. 217 CY105
Carlton Dr. SW15 179 CY85
Carlton Dr., Ilf. 125 ER55
Carlton Gdns. SW1 277 M3
Carlton Gdns. SW1 141 DK74
Carlton Gdns. W5 137 CJ72
Carlton Grn., Red. 250 DE131
Carlton Gro. SE15 162 DV81
Carlton Hill NW8 140 DB68
Carlton Ho. Ter. SW1 277 M3
Carlton Ho. Ter. SW1 141 DK74
Carlton Par., Orp. 206 EV101
Carlton Par., Sev. 257 FJ122
St. John's Hill
Carlton Pk. Ave. SW20 199 CW96
Carlton Pl., Felt. 175 BT87
Carlton Pl., Nthwd. 93 BP50
Carlton Rd. E11 124 EF60
Carlton Rd. E12 124 EK63
Carlton Rd. E17 101 DY53
Carlton Rd. N4 121 DN59
Carlton Rd. N11 98 DG50
Carlton Rd. SW14 158 CQ83
Carlton Rd. W4 158 CR75
Carlton Rd. W5 137 CJ73
Carlton Rd., Erith 167 FB79
Carlton Rd., Grays 171 GF75
Carlton Rd., N.Mal. 198 CS96
Carlton Rd., Red. 250 DE131
Carlton Rd., Reig. 250 DD132
Carlton Rd., Rom. 127 FG57
Carlton Rd., Sid. 185 ET92
Carlton Rd., Slou. 132 AV73
Carlton Rd., S.Croy. 220 DR107
Carlton Rd., Sun. 175 BT94
Carlton Rd., Walt. 195 BV101
Carlton Rd., Well. 166 EV83
Carlton Rd., Wok. 211 BA114
Carlton Sq. E1 143 DX70
Argyle Rd.
Carlton St. SW1 277 M1
Carlton Ter. E11 124 EH57
Carlton Ter. N18 100 DR48
Carlton Ter. SE26 182 DW90
Carlton Twr. Pl. SW1 276 E6
Carlton Twr. Pl. SW1 160 DF76
Carlton Tye, Horl. 269 DJ147
Carlton Vale NW6 140 DB68
Carlton Vil. SW15 179 CW85
St. John's Ave.
Carlwell St. SW17 180 DE92
Carlyle Ave., Brom. 204 EK97
Carlyle Ave., Sthl. 136 BZ73
Carlyle Clo. N2 120 DC58
Carlyle Clo. NW10 138 CR67
Carlyle Clo., W.Mol. 196 CB96
Carlyle Gdns., Sthl. 136 BZ73
Carlyle Pl. SW15 159 CX84
Carlyle Rd. E12 124 EL63
Carlyle Rd. SE28 146 EV73
Carlyle Rd. W5 157 CJ78
Carlyle Rd., Croy. 202 DU103
Carlyle Rd., Stai. 173 BF94
Carlyle Sq. SW3 160 DD78
Carlyon Ave., Har. 116 BZ63
Carlyon Clo., Wem. 138 CL67
Carlyon Rd., Hayes 136 BW72
Carlyon Rd., Wem. 138 CL68
Carmalt Gdns. SW15 159 CW84
Carmalt Gdns., Walt. 214 BW106
Carmarthen Gdn. NW9 118 CS58
Snowdon Dr.
Carmarthen Rd., Slou. 132 AS73
Carmel Clo., Wok. 226 AY118
Carmel Ct. W8 160 DB75
Holland St.
Carmel Ct., Wem. 118 CP61
Carmelite Clo., Har. 94 CC53
Carmelite Rd., Har. 94 CC53
Carmelite St. EC4 274 E10
Carmelite St. EC4 141 DN73
Carmelite Wk., Har. 94 CC53
Carmelite Way, Har. 94 CC54
Carmen Ct., Borwd. 78 CM38
Belford Rd.
Carmen St. E14 143 EB72
Carmichael Clo. SW11 160 DD83
Darien Rd.
Carmichael Clo., Ruis. 115 BU63
Carmichael Ms. SW18 180 DD87
Carmichael Rd. SE25 202 DU99
Carminia Rd. SW17 181 DH89
Carnaby Rd., Brox. 49 DY20
Carnaby St. W1 273 K9
Carnaby St. W1 141 DJ72
Carnac St. SE27 182 DR91
Carnach Grn., S.Ock. 149 FV73
Carnanton Rd. E17 101 ED53
Carnarvon Ave., Enf. 82 DT41
Carnarvon Dr., Hayes 155 BQ76
Carnarvon Rd. E10 123 EC58
Carnarvon Rd. E15 144 EF65
Carnarvon Rd. E18 102 EF53
Carnarvon Rd., Barn. 79 CY41
Carnation Clo., Rom. 127 FE61
Carnation St. SE2 166 EV78
Carnbrook Rd. SE3 164 EK83
Carnecke Gdns. SE9 184 EL85
Carnegie Clo., Surb. 198 CM103
Fullers Ave.
Carnegie Pl. SW19 179 CX90
Carnegie Rd., St.Alb. 43 CD16
Carnegie St. N1 141 DM67
Carnforth Clo., Epsom 216 CP107
Carnforth Gdns., Horn. 127 FG64
Carnforth Rd. SW16 181 DK94
Carnie Lo. SW17 181 DH90
Manville Rd.
Carnoustie Dr. N1 141 DM66
Carnwath Rd. SW6 160 DA83
Caro La., Hem.H. 40 BN22
Carol St. NW1 141 DJ67
Carolina Clo. E15 124 EE64
Carolina Rd., Th.Hth. 201 DP96
Caroline Clo. N10 99 DH54
Alexandra Pk. Rd.
Caroline Clo. SW16 181 DM91
Caroline Clo. W2 140 DB73
Bayswater Rd.
Caroline Clo., Croy. 220 DS105
Brownlow Rd.
Caroline Clo., Islw. 157 CD80
Caroline Clo., West Dr. 154 BK75
Caroline Ct., Ashf. 175 BP93
Caroline Ct., Stan. 95 CG51
The Chase
Caroline Gdns. SE15 162 DV80
Caroline Pl. SW11 160 DG82
Caroline Pl. W2 140 DB73
Caroline Pl., Hayes 155 BS80
Caroline Pl., Wat. 76 BY44
Caroline Pl. Ms. W2 140 DB73
Orme La.
Caroline Rd. SW19 179 CZ94
Caroline St. E1 143 DX72
Caroline Ter. SW1 276 F9
Caroline Ter. SW1 160 DG77
Caroline Wk. W6 159 CY79
Carolyn Clo., Wok. 226 AT119
Carolyn Dr., Orp. 206 EU104
Caroon Dr., Rick. 74 BH36
Carpenders Ave., Wat. 94 BY48
Carpenter Clo., Epsom 217 CT109
West St.
Carpenter Gdns. N21 99 DP47
Carpenter St. W1 277 H1
Carpenter Way, Pot.B. 64 DC33
Carpenters Arms La., Epp. 70 EV25
Carpenters Ct., Twick. 177 CE89
Carpenters Path, Brwd. 109 GD43
Carpenters Pl. SW4 161 DK84
Carpenters Rd. E15 143 EB65
Carpenters Rd., Enf. 82 DW36
Carpenters Wd. Dr., Rick. 73 BB42
Carr Gro. SE18 164 EL77
Carr Rd. E17 101 DZ54
Carr Rd., Nthlt. 136 CB65
Carr St. E14 143 DY71
Carrara Wk. SW9 161 DN84
Somerleyton Rd.
Carriage Dr. E. SW11 160 DG80
Carriage Dr. N. SW11 160 DG79
Carriage Dr. S. SW11 160 DF81
Carriage Dr. W. SW11 160 DF80
Carriage Ms., Ilf. 125 EQ61
Carriage Pl. N16 122 DR62
Carriageway, The, Sev. 240 EW124
Carrick Clo., Islw. 157 CG83
Carrick Dr., Ilf. 103 EQ53
Carrick Dr., Sev. 257 FH123
Carrick Gdns. N17 100 DS52
Flexmere Rd.
Carrick Gate, Esher 196 CC104
Carrick Ms. SE8 163 EA79
Watergate St.
Carriden Ct., Hert. 31 DM07
The Ridgeway
Carrill Way, Belv. 166 EX77
Carrington Ave., Borwd. 78 CP43
Carrington Ave., Houns. 176 CB85
Carrington Clo., Barn. 79 CU43
Carrington Clo., Borwd. 78 CQ43
Carrington Clo., Croy. 203 DY101
Carrington Clo., Kings.T. 178 CQ92
Carrington Clo., Red. 250 DF133
Carrington Gdns. E7 124 EH63
Woodford Rd.
Carrington Pl., Esher 214 CB106
Carrington Rd., Dart. 188 FM86
Carrington Rd., Rich. 158 CN84
Carrington Rd., Slou. 132 AS73
Carrington Sq., Har. 94 CC52
Carrington St. W1 277 H3
Carrol Clo. NW5 121 DH63
Carroll Ave., Guil. 243 BB134
Carroll Clo. E15 124 EF64
Carroll Hill, Loug. 85 EM41
Carron Clo. E14 143 EB72
Carronade Pl. SE28 165 EQ76
Carroun Rd. SW8 161 DM80
Carrow Rd., Dag. 146 EV66
Carrow Rd., Walt. 196 BX104
Kenilworth Dr.
Carroway La., Grnf. 137 CD69
Cowgate Rd.
Carrs La. N21 82 DQ43
Carshalton Gro., Sutt. 218 DD105
Carshalton Pk. Rd., Cars. 218 DF106
Carshalton Pl., Cars. 218 DG105
Carshalton Rd., Bans. 218 DF114
Carshalton Rd., Cars. 218 DC106
Carshalton Rd., Mitch. 200 DG98
Carshalton Rd., Sutt. 218 DC106
Carsington Gdns., Dart. 188 FK89
Carslake Rd. SW15 179 CW86
Carson Rd. E16 144 EG70
Carson Rd. SE21 182 DR89
Carson Rd., Barn. 80 DF42
Carstairs Rd. SE6 183 EC90
Carston Clo. SE12 184 EG85
Carswell Clo., Brwd. 109 GD44
Carswell Clo., Ilf. 124 EK56
Roding La. S.
Carswell Rd. SE6 183 EC87
Cart La. E4 101 ED45
Cart Path, Wat. 60 BW33
Cartbridge Clo., Wok. 227 BB123
Send Rd.
Cartel Clo., Purf. 169 FR77
Carter Clo., Rom. 105 FB52
Carter Clo., Wall. 219 DK108
Carter Clo., Wind. 151 AN82
Carter Ct. EC4 141 DP72
Carter La.
Carter Dr., Rom. 105 FB52
Carter La. EC4 274 G9
Carter La. EC4 141 DP72
Carter Pl. SE17 162 DQ78
Carter Rd. E13 144 EH67
Carter Rd. SW19 180 DD93
Carter St. SE17 162 DQ79
Carter Wk., H.Wyc. 88 AC47
Carteret St. SW1 277 M5
Carteret St. SW1 161 DK75
Carteret Way SE8 163 DY77
Carterhatch La., Enf. 82 DU40
Carterhatch Rd., Enf. 82 DW40
Carters Clo., Wor.Pk. 199 CX103
Carters Cotts., Red. 266 DE136
Kings Ave.
Carters Hill, Sev. 257 FP127
Carters Hill Clo. SE9 184 EJ88
Carters La. SE23 183 DY89
Carters La., Epp. 51 EP24
Carters La., Wok. 227 BC120
Carters Mead, Harl. 52 EV17
Carters Rd., Epsom 233 CT115
Carters Row, Grav. 191 GF88
Carters Yd. SW18 180 DA85
Wandsworth High St.
Cartersfield Rd., Wal.Abb. 67 EC34
Cartersmeade Clo., Horl. 269 DH147
Wheatfield Way
Carthew Rd. W6 159 CV76
Carthew Vil. W6 159 CV76

Carthouse La., Wok. 210 AT114
Carthusian St. EC1 275 H6
Carthusian St. EC1 142 DQ71
Cartier Circle E14 143 EB74
Carting La. WC2 278 A1
Carting La. WC2 141 DL73
Cartmel Clo. N17 100 DV52
Heybourne Rd.
Cartmel Clo., Reig. 250 DE133
Cartmel Gdns., Mord. 200 DC99
Cartmel Rd., Bexh. 166 FA81
Carton St. W1 272 E8
Cartwright Gdns. WC1 273 P3
Cartwright Gdns. WC1 141 DL69
Cartwright Rd., Dag. 146 EZ66
Cartwright St. E1 142 DT73
Cartwright Way SW13 159 CV80
Carve Ley, Welw.G.C. 30 DB10
Carver Clo. W4 158 CQ76
Carver Rd. SE24 182 DQ86
Carville Cres., Brent. 158 CL78
Cary Rd. E11 124 EE63
Cary Wk., Rad. 61 CH34
Carysfort Rd. N8 121 DK57
Carysfort Rd. N16 122 DR62
Cascade Ave. N10 121 DJ56
Cascade Clo., Buck.H. 102 EK47
Cascade Rd.
Cascade Clo., Orp. 206 EW97
Cascade Rd., Buck.H. 102 EK47
Cascades, Croy. 221 DZ110
Caselden Clo., Add. 212 BJ106
Casella Rd. SE14 163 DX80
Casewick Rd. SE27 181 DP91
Casimir Rd. E5 122 DV62
Casino Ave. SE24 182 DQ85
Caspian St. SE5 162 DR80
Caspian Wk. E16 144 EK72
Caspian Wf. E3 143 EB71
Violet Rd.
Cassandra Clo., Nthlt. 117 CD63
Cassandra Gate, Wal.Cr. 67 DZ27
Casselden Rd. NW10 138 CR66
Cassidy Rd. SW6 160 DA80
Cassilda Rd. SE2 166 EU77
Cassilis Rd., Twick. 177 CH85
Cassio Rd., Wat. 75 BV41
Cassiobridge, Wat. 75 BR42
Cassiobridge Rd., Wat. 75 BS42
Cassiobury Ave., Felt. 175 BT86
Cassiobury Ct., Wat. 75 BT40
Cassiobury Dr., Wat. 75 BT40
Cassiobury Pk., Wat. 75 BS41
Cassiobury Pk. Ave., Wat. 75 BS41
Cassiobury Rd. E17 123 DX57
Cassis Ct., Loug. 85 EQ42
Cassland Rd. E9 142 DW66
Cassland Rd., Th.Hth. 202 DR98
Casslee Rd. SE6 183 DZ87
Cassocks Sq., Shep. 195 BR101
Casson St. E1 142 DU71
Casstine Clo., Swan. 187 FF94
Castalia Sq. E14 163 EC75
Roserton St.
Castalia St. E14 163 EC75
Plevna St.
Castano Ct., Abb.L. 59 BS31
Castell Rd., Loug. 85 EQ39
Castellain Rd. W9 140 DB70
Castellan Ave., Rom. 127 FH55
Castellane Clo., Stan. 95 CF52
Daventer Dr.
Castello Ave. SW15 179 CW85
Castelnau SW13 159 CV79
Castelnau Gdns. SW13 159 CV79
Arundel Ter.
Castelnau Pl. SW13 159 CV79
Castelnau
Castelnau Row SW13 159 CV79
Lonsdale Rd.
Casterbridge NW6 140 DB67
Casterbridge Rd. SE3 164 EG83
Casterton St. E8 142 DV65
Wilton Way
Castile Rd. SE18 165 EN77
Castillon Rd. SE6 184 EE89
Castlands Rd. SE6 183 DZ89
Castle Ave. E4 101 ED50
Castle Ave., Epsom 217 CU109
Castle Ave., Rain. 147 FE66
Castle Ave., Slou. 152 AU79
Castle Ave., West Dr. 134 BL73
Castle Baynard St. EC4 274 G10
Castle Clo. E9 123 DY64
Swinnerton St.
Castle Clo. SW19 179 CX90
Castle Clo. W3 158 CP75
Park Rd. E.
Castle Clo., Brom. 204 EE97
Castle Clo., Hodd. 33 EC14
Castle Clo., Red. 252 DQ133
Castle Clo., Reig. 266 DB138
Castle Clo., Rom. 106 FJ48
Castle Clo., Sun. 175 BS94
Mill Fm. Ave.
Castle Clo. (Bushey), Wat. 76 CB44
Castle Ct. EC3 275 L9
Castle Ct. SE26 183 DY91
Champion Rd.
Castle Dr., Horl. 269 DJ149
Castle Dr., Ilf. 124 EL58
Castle Dr., Reig. 266 DA138
Castle Fm. Rd., Sev. 225 FF109
Castle Gdns., Dor. 248 CM134
Castle Gateway, Berk. 38 AW17
Castle Grn., Wey. 195 BS104
Castle Gro. Rd., Wok. 210 AS112
Castle Hill, Berk. 38 AW17
Castle Hill, Guil. 258 AX136
Castle Hill, Long. 209 FX99
Castle Hill, Wind. 151 AR81
Castle Hill Ave., Berk. 38 AW18
Castle Hill Ave., Croy. 221 EB109
Castle Hill Clo., Berk. 38 AV18
Castle Hill Rd., Egh. 172 AV90
Castle La. SW1 277 L6
Castle La. SW1 161 DJ76
Castle Mead, Hem.H. 40 BH22
Castle Ms. N12 98 DC50
Castle Rd.
Castle Ms. NW1 141 DH65
Castle Rd.
Castle Par., Epsom 217 CU108
Ewell Bypass
Castle Pl. NW1 141 DH65
Castle Pl. W4 158 CS77
Windmill Rd.
Castle Pt. E13 144 EJ68
Castle Rd. N12 98 DC50
Castle Rd. NW1 141 DH65
Castle Rd., Couls. 234 DE120
Castle Rd., Dag. 146 EV67
Castle Rd., Dart. 225 FH107
Castle Rd., Enf. 83 DY39
Castle Rd., Grays 170 FZ79
Castle Rd., Hodd. 33 EC14
Castle Rd., Islw. 157 CF82
Castle Rd., Nthlt. 136 CB65
Castle Rd., St.Alb. 43 CH20
Castle Rd., Sev. 225 FG108
Castle Rd., Sthl. 156 BZ76
Castle Rd., Swans. 190 FZ86
Castle Rd., Wey. 195 BR104
Castle Rd., Wok. 211 AZ114
Castle Sq., Guil. 258 AX136
Castle Sq., Red. 252 DQ133
Castle St. E6 144 EJ68
Castle St., Berk. 38 AW19
Castle St., Green. 189 FU85
Castle St., Guil. 258 AX136
Castle St., Hert. 32 DQ10
Castle St., Kings.T. 198 CL96
Castle St., Red. 251 DP133
Castle St., Slou. 152 AT76
Castle St., Swans. 190 FZ86
Castle Vw., Epsom 216 CP114
Castle Vw. Rd., Wey. 213 BP105
Castle Wk., Reig. 250 DA134
High St.
Castle Wk., Sun. 196 BW97
Elizabeth Gdns.
Castle Way SW19 179 CX90
Castle Way, Epsom 217 CU109
Castle Ave.
Castle Way, Felt. 176 BW91
Castle Yd. N6 120 DG59
North Rd.
Castle Yd. SE1 278 G2
Castle Yd., Rich. 177 CK85
Hill St.
Castlebar Hill W5 137 CH71
Castlebar Ms. W5 137 CJ71
Castlebar Pk. W5 137 CH71
Castlebar Rd. W5 137 CJ71
Castlebrook Clo. SE11 278 F8
Castlebrook Clo. SE11 161 DP77
Castlecombe Dr. SW19 179 CX87
Castlecombe Rd. SE9 184 EL91
Castledine Rd. SE20 182 DV94
Castlefield Rd., Reig. 250 DA134
Castleford Ave. SE9 185 EP88
Castleford Clo. N17 100 DT51
Castlegate, Rich. 158 CM83
Castlehaven Rd. NW1 141 DH66
Castleleigh Ct., Enf. 82 DR43
Castlemaine Ave., Epsom 217 CV109
Castlemaine Ave., S.Croy. 220 DT106
Castlemaine Twr. SW11 160 DF81
Castlereagh St. W1 272 D8
Castleton Ave., Bexh. 167 FD81
Castleton Ave., Wem. 118 CL63
Castleton Clo., Bans. 234 DA115
Castleton Clo., Croy. 203 DY100
Castleton Dr., Bans. 234 DA115
Castleton Gdns., Wem. 118 CL62
Castleton Rd. E17 101 ED54
Castleton Rd. SE9 184 EK91
Castleton Rd., Ilf. 126 EU60
Castleton Rd., Mitch. 201 DK98
Castleton Rd., Ruis. 116 BX60
Castletown Rd. W14 159 CY78
Castleview Clo. N4 122 DQ60
Castleview Gdns., Ilf. 124 EL58
Castleview Rd., Slou. 152 AW77
Castlewood Dr. SE9 165 EM82
Castlewood Rd. N15 122 DU58
Castlewood Rd. N16 122 DU59
Castlewood Rd., Barn. 80 DD41
Castor La. E14 143 EB73
Cat Hill, Barn. 80 DE44
Catalina Ave. (Chafford Hundred), Grays 170 FZ75
Catalpa Clo., Guil. 242 AW132
Cedar Way
Cater Gdns., Guil. 242 AT132
Caterham Ave., Ilf. 103 EM54
Caterham Bypass, Cat. 236 DV120
Caterham Clo., Cat. 236 DS120
Caterham Ct., Wal.Abb. 68 EF34
Shernbroke Rd.
Caterham Dr., Couls. 235 DP118
Caterham Rd. SE13 163 EC83
Catesby St. SE17 279 L9
Catesby St. SE17 162 DR77
Catford Bdy. SE6 183 EB87
Catford Hill SE6 183 DZ89
Catford Ms. SE6 183 EB87
Holbeach Rd.
Catford Rd. SE6 183 EA87
Cathall Rd. E11 123 ED62
Catham Clo., St.Alb. 43 CH22
Cathay St. SE16 162 DV75
Cathay Wk., Nthlt. 136 CA68
Brabazon Rd.
Cathcart Dr., Orp. 205 ES103
Cathcart Hill N19 121 DJ62
Cathcart Rd. SW10 160 DC79
Cathcart St. NW5 141 DH65
Cathedral Clo., Guil. 258 AV135
Cathedral Ct., St.Alb. 42 CB22
Cathedral Hill Ind. Est., Guil. 242 AU133
Cathedral Piazza SW1 277 K7
Cathedral Pl. EC4 275 H8
Cathedral St. SE1 279 K2
Cathedral St. SE1 142 DR74
Cathedral Vw., Guil. 242 AT134
Catherall Rd. N5 122 DQ62
Catherine Clo., Brwd. 108 FU43
Catherine Clo., Grays 170 FZ75
Catherine Clo., Hem.H. 41 BP15
Parr Cres.
Catherine Clo., Loug. 85 EM44
Roding Gdns.
Catherine Clo., W.Byf. 212 BL114
Catherine Ct. N14 81 DJ43
Conisbee Ct.
Catherine Dr., Rich. 158 CL84
Catherine Dr., Sun. 175 BT93
Catherine Gdns., Houns. 157 CD84
Catherine Griffiths Ct. EC1 274 E4
Catherine Gro. SE10 163 EB81
Catherine Howard Ct., Wey. 195 BP104
Old Palace Rd.
Catherine Pl. SW1 277 K6
Catherine Pl. SW1 161 DJ76
Catherine Rd., Enf. 83 DY36
Catherine Rd., Rom. 127 FH57
Catherine Rd., Surb. 197 CK99
Catherine St. WC2 274 B10
Catherine St. WC2 141 DM73
Catherine St., St.Alb. 43 CD19
Catherine Wheel All. E1 275 N7
Catherine Wheel Rd., Brent. 157 CK80
Catherine Wheel Yd. SW1 277 K3
Catherine's Clo., West Dr. 154 BK76
Money La.
Cathles Rd. SW12 181 DH86
Cathnor Rd. W12 159 CV75
Catisfield Rd., Enf. 83 DY37
Catkin Clo., Hem.H. 40 BH19
Catlin Cres., Shep. 195 BR99
Catlin Gdns., Gdse. 252 DV130
Catlin St. SE16 162 DU78
Catlin St., Hem.H. 40 BH23
Catling Clo. SE23 182 DW90
Catlins La., Pnr. 115 BV55
Cato Rd. SW4 161 DK83
Cato St. W1 272 C7
Cato St. W1 140 DE71
Cator Clo., Croy. 222 EE111
Cator Cres., Croy. 221 ED111
Cator La., Beck. 203 DZ96
Cator Rd. SE26 183 DX93
Cator Rd., Cars. 218 DF106
Cator St. SE15 162 DT79
Catsey La. (Bushey), Wat. 94 CC45
Catsey Wds. (Bushey), Wat. 94 CC45
Catterick Clo. N11 98 DG51
Catterick Way, Borwd. 78 CM39
Cattistock Rd. SE9 184 EL92
Cattlegate Hill, Pot.B. 65 DK31
Cattlegate Rd., Enf. 65 DL34
Cattlegate Rd., Pot.B. 65 DK31
Cattley Clo., Barn. 79 CY42
Wood St.
Cattlins Clo., Wal.Cr. 66 DT29
Catton St. WC1 274 B7
Catton St. WC1 141 DM71
Cattsdell, Hem.H. 40 BL18
Caulfield Rd. E6 145 EM66
Caulfield Rd. SE15 162 DV82
Causeway, The N2 120 DE56
Causeway, The SW18 160 DB84
Causeway, The SW19 179 CX92
Causeway, The, Cars. 200 DG104
Causeway, The, Chess. 216 CL105
Causeway, The, Egh. 173 BC91
Causeway, The, Esher 215 CF108
Causeway, The, Felt. 155 BU84
Causeway, The, Maid. 150 AC75
Causeway, The, Pot.B. 64 DC31
Causeway, The, St.Alb. 42 CB22
King Harry La.
Causeway, The, Stai. 173 BC91
Causeway, The, Sutt. 218 DC109
Causeway, The, Tedd. 177 CF93
Broad St.
Causeway Clo., Pot.B. 64 DD31
Causeway Ct., Wok. 226 AT118
Bingham Dr.
Causeyware Rd. N9 100 DV45
Causton Rd. N6 121 DH59
Causton St. SW1 277 N9
Causton St. SW1 161 DK77
Cautherly La., Ware 33 DZ10
Cautley Ave. SW4 181 DJ85
Cavalier Clo., Rom. 126 EX56
Cavalier Gdns., Hayes 135 BR72
Hanover Circle
Cavalry Barracks, Houns. 156 BX83
Cavalry Cres., Houns. 156 BX84
Cavalry Cres., Wind. 151 AQ83
Cavalry Gdns. SW15 179 CZ85
Upper Richmond Rd.
Cavan Dr., St.Alb. 43 CD15
Cavaye Pl. SW10 160 DC78
Fulham Rd.
Cave Rd. E13 144 EH68
Cave Rd., Rich. 177 CJ91
Cave St. N1 141 DM68
Carnegie St.
Cavell Cres., Dart. 168 FN84
Cavell Cres., Rom. 106 FL54
Cavell Dr., Enf. 81 DN40
Cavell Rd. N17 100 DR52
Cavell Rd. (Cheshunt), Wal.Cr. 66 DT27
Cavell St. E1 142 DV71
Cavell Way, Epsom 216 CN111
Cavendish Ave. N3 98 DA54
Cavendish Ave. NW8 272 A1
Cavendish Ave. NW8 140 DD68
Cavendish Ave. W13 137 CG71
Cavendish Ave., Erith 167 FC79
Cavendish Ave., Har. 117 CD63
Cavendish Ave., Horn. 147 FH65
Cavendish Ave., N.Mal. 199 CV99
Cavendish Ave., Ruis. 115 BV64
Cavendish Ave., Sev. 256 FG122
Cavendish Ave., Sid. 186 EU87
Cavendish Ave., Well. 165 ET83
Cavendish Ave., Wdf.Grn. 102 EH53
Cavendish Clo. N18 100 DV50
Cavendish Rd.
Cavendish Clo. NW6 139 CZ66
Cavendish Rd.
Cavendish Clo. NW8 272 A2
Cavendish Clo. NW8 140 DD69
Cavendish Clo., Amer. 72 AV39
Cavendish Clo., Hayes 135 BS71
Westacott
Cavendish Clo., Maid. 130 AG72
Cavendish Clo., Sun. 175 BT93
Cavendish Ct. EC3 275 N8
Cavendish Ct., Rick. 75 BR43
Mayfare
Cavendish Ct., Sun. 175 BT93
Cavendish Cres., Borwd. 78 CN42
Cavendish Cres., Horn. 147 FH65
Cavendish Dr. E11 123 ED60
Cavendish Dr., Edg. 96 CM51
Cavendish Dr., Esher 215 CE106
Cavendish Gdns., Bark. 125 ES64
Cavendish Gdns., Ilf. 125 EN60
Cavendish Gdns., Red. 250 DG133
Cavendish Gdns., Rom. 126 EY57
Cavendish Ms. N. W1 273 J6
Cavendish Ms. S. W1 273 J7
Cavendish Par., Houns. 156 BY82
Bath Rd.
Cavendish Pl. W1 273 J8
Cavendish Pl. W1 141 DH72
Cavendish Rd. E4 101 EC51
Cavendish Rd. N4 121 DN58
Cavendish Rd. N18 100 DV50
Cavendish Rd. NW6 139 CY66
Cavendish Rd. SW12 181 DH86
Cavendish Rd. SW19 180 DD94
Cavendish Rd. W4 158 CQ81
Cavendish Rd., Barn. 79 CW41
Cavendish Rd., Chesh. 54 AR32
Cavendish Rd., Croy. 201 DP102
Cavendish Rd., N.Mal. 199 CT99
Cavendish Rd., Red. 250 DG134
Cavendish Rd., St.Alb. 43 CF20
Cavendish Rd., Sun. 175 BT93
Cavendish Rd., Sutt. 218 DC108
Cavendish Rd., Wey. 213 BP109
Cavendish Rd., Wok. 226 AX119
Cavendish Sq. W1 273 J8
Cavendish Sq. W1 141 DH72
Cavendish Sq., Long. 209 FX97
Cavendish St. N1 275 K1
Cavendish St. N1 142 DR68
Cavendish Ter., Felt. 175 BU89
High St.
Cavendish Way, Hat. 45 CT18
Cavendish Way, W.Wick. 203 EB102
Cavenham Clo., Wok. 226 AY119
Cavenham Gdns., Horn. 128 FJ57
Cavenham Gdns., Ilf. 125 ER62
Caverleigh Way, Wor.Pk. 199 CU102
Caversham Ave. N13 99 DN48
Caversham Ave., Sutt. 199 CY103
Caversham Flats SW3 160 DF79
Caversham St.
Caversham Rd. N15 122 DQ56
Caversham Rd. NW5 141 DJ65
Caversham Rd., Kings.T. 198 CM96
Caversham St. SW3 160 DF79
Caverswall St. W12 139 CW72
Caveside Clo., Chis. 205 EN95
Cavill's Wk., Rom. 104 EW47
Cawcott Dr., Wind. 151 AL81
Cawdor Ave., S.Ock. 149 FU73
Cawdor Cres. W7 157 CG77
Cawley Hatch, Harl. 51 EM15
Cawnpore St. SE19 182 DS92
Cawsey Way, Wok. 226 AY117
Caxton Ave., Add. 212 BG107
Caxton Dr., Uxb. 134 BK68
Chiltern Vw. Rd.
Caxton Gdns., Guil. 242 AV133
Caxton Gro. E3 143 EA69
Caxton Hill, Hert. 32 DS09
Caxton Hill Extension Rd., Hert. 32 DT09
Caxton La., Oxt. 254 EL131
Caxton Ms., Brent. 157 CK79
The Butts
Caxton Ri., Red. 250 DG133
Caxton Rd. N22 99 DM54
Caxton Rd. SW19 180 DC92
Caxton Rd. W12 159 CX75
Caxton Rd., Hodd. 33 EB13
Caxton Rd., Sthl. 156 BX76
Caxton St. SW1 277 L6
Caxton St. SW1 161 DJ76
Caxton St. N. E16 144 EF73
Victoria Dock Rd.
Caxton Way, Rom. 127 FE56
Caxton Way, Wat. 75 BR44
Caxtons Ct., Guil. 243 BA132
Caygill Clo., Brom. 204 EF98
Cayley Clo., Wall. 219 DL108
Cayley Rd., Sthl. 156 CB76
McNair Rd.
Cayton Pl. EC1 275 K3
Cayton Rd., Grnf. 137 CE68
Cayton St. EC1 275 K3
Cazenove Rd. E17 101 EA53
Cazenove Rd. N16 122 DT61
Cearn Way, Couls. 235 DM115
Cearns Ho. E6 144 EK67
Cecil Ave., Bark. 145 ER66
Cecil Ave., Enf. 82 DT42
Cecil Ave., Grays 170 FZ75
Cecil Ave., Horn. 128 FL55
Cecil Ave., Wem. 118 CM64
Cecil Clo. W5 137 CK71
Helena Rd.
Cecil Clo., Ashf. 175 BQ93
Cecil Clo., Chess. 215 CK105
Cecil Ct. WC2 277 N1
Cecil Ct., Barn. 79 CX41
Cecil Cres., Hat. 45 CV16
Cecil Pk., Pnr. 116 BY56
Cecil Pl., Mitch. 200 DF99
Cecil Rd. E11 124 EE62
Cecil Rd. E13 144 EG67
Cecil Rd. E17 101 EA53
Cecil Rd. N10 99 DH54
Cecil Rd. N14 99 DJ46
Cecil Rd. NW9 118 CS55
Cecil Rd. NW10 138 CS67
Cecil Rd. SW19 180 DB94
Cecil Rd. W3 138 CQ71
Cecil Rd., Ashf. 175 BQ94
Cecil Rd., Croy. 201 DM100
Cecil Rd., Enf. 82 DR42
Cecil Rd., Grav. 191 GF88
Cecil Rd., Har. 117 CE55
Cecil Rd., Hert. 32 DQ12
Cecil Rd., Hodd. 49 EC15
Cecil Rd., Houns. 156 CC82
Cecil Rd., Ilf. 125 EP63
Cecil Rd., Iver 133 BE72
Cecil Rd., Pot.B. 63 CU32
Cecil Rd., Rom. 126 EX59
Cecil Rd., St.Alb. 43 CF20
Cecil Rd., Sutt. 217 CZ107
Cecil Rd. (Cheshunt), Wal.Cr. 67 DX32
Cecil St., Wat. 75 BV38
Cecil Way, Brom. 204 EG102
Cecil Way, Slou. 131 AM70
Cecile Pk. N8 121 DL58
Cecilia Clo. N2 120 DC55
Cecilia Rd. E8 122 DU64
Cedar Ave., Barn. 98 DE45
Cedar Ave., Cob. 230 BW115
Cedar Ave., Enf. 82 DW40
Cedar Ave., Grav. 191 GJ91
Cedar Ave., Hayes 135 BU72
Cedar Ave., Rom. 126 EY57
Cedar Ave., Ruis. 136 BW65
Cedar Ave., Sid. 186 EU87
Cedar Ave., Twick. 176 CB86
Cedar Ave., Upmin. 128 FN63
Cedar Ave., Wal.Cr. 67 DX33
Cedar Ave., West Dr. 134 BM74
Cedar Chase, Maid. 130 AD70
Cedar Clo. SE21 182 DQ88
Cedar Clo. SW15 178 CR91
Cedar Clo., Borwd. 78 CP42
Cedar Clo., Brwd. 109 GD45
Cedar Clo., Brom. 204 EL104
Cedar Clo., Buck.H. 102 EK47
Cedar Clo., Cars. 218 DF107
Cedar Clo., Dor. 263 CH136
Cedar Clo., E.Mol. 197 CE98
Cedar Rd.
Cedar Clo., Epsom 217 CT114
Cedar Clo., Esher 214 BZ108
Cedar Clo., Hert. 31 DP09
Cedar Clo., Pot.B. 64 DA30
Cedar Clo., Reig. 266 DC136
Cedar Clo., Rom. 127 FC56
Cedar Clo., Saw. 36 EY06
Cedar Clo., Stai. 194 BJ96
Cedar Clo., Swan. 207 FC96
Cedar Clo., Ware 33 DX07
Cedar Clo., Warl. 237 DY118
Cedar Copse, Brom. 205 EM96
Cedar Ct. E8 142 DT66
Cedar Ct. N1 142 DQ66
Essex Rd.
Cedar Ct. SE9 184 EL86
Cedar Ct. SW19 179 CX90
Cedar Ct., Egh. 173 BA91
Cedar Ct., Epp. 70 EU31
Cedar Ct., St.Alb. 43 CK20
Cedar Cres., Brom. 204 EL104
Cedar Dr. N2 120 DE56
Cedar Dr. (Sutton at Hone), Dart. 208 FP96
Cedar Dr., Lthd. 231 CE122
Cedar Dr., Loug. 85 EP40
Cedar Dr., Pnr. 94 CA51
Cedar Gdns., Sutt. 218 DC107
Cedar Gdns., Upmin. 128 FQ62
Cedar Gdns., Wok. 226 AV118
St. John's Rd.
Cedar Grn., Hodd. 49 EA18
Cedar Gro. W5 158 CL76
Cedar Gro., Amer. 55 AR39
Cedar Gro., Bex. 186 EW86
Cedar Gro., Sthl. 136 CA71
Cedar Gro., Wey. 213 BQ105
Cedar Hts., Rich. 178 CL88
Cedar Hill, Epsom 232 CQ116
Cedar Ho., Croy. 221 EB107
Cedar Ho., Sun. 175 BT94
Cedar Lawn Ave., Barn. 79 CY43
Cedar Mt. SE9 184 EK88
Cedar Pk., Chig. 103 EP49
High Rd.
Cedar Pk. Gdns., Rom. 126 EX59
Cedar Pk. Rd., Enf. 82 DQ38
Cedar Pl. SE7 164 EJ78
Floyd Rd.
Cedar Pl., Nthwd. 93 BQ51
Cedar Ri. N14 98 DG45
Cedar Ri., S.Ock. 149 FX70
Sycamore Way
Cedar Rd. N17 100 DT53
Cedar Rd. NW2 119 CW63
Cedar Rd., Berk. 38 AX20
Cedar Rd., Brwd. 109 GD44
Cedar Rd., Brom. 204 EJ96
Cedar Rd., Cob. 213 BV114
Cedar Rd., Croy. 202 DS103
Cedar Rd., Dart. 188 FK88
Cedar Rd., E.Mol. 197 CE98
Cedar Rd., Enf. 81 DP38
Cedar Rd., Erith 167 FG81
Cedar Rd., Felt. 175 BR88
Cedar Rd., Grays 171 GG76
Cedar Rd., Hat. 45 CU19
Cedar Rd., Horn. 128 FJ62
Cedar Rd., Houns. 156 BW82
Cedar Rd., Rom. 127 FC56
Cedar Rd., Sutt. 218 DC107
Cedar Rd., Tedd. 177 CG92
Cedar Rd., Wat. 76 BW44
Cedar Rd., Wey. 212 BN105
Cedar Rd., Wok. 226 AV120
Cedar Ter., Rich. 158 CM84
Cedar Ter. Rd., Sev. 257 FJ123
Cedar Tree Gro. SE27 181 DP92
Cedar Vista, Rich. 158 CL81
Kew Rd.
Cedar Wk., Hem.H. 40 BK22
Cedar Wk., Ken. 236 DQ116
Cedar Wk., Tad. 233 CY120
Cedar Wk., Wal.Abb. 67 ED34
Cedar Wk., Welw.G.C. 30 DB10
Cedar Way NW1 141 DK66
Cedar Way, Berk. 38 AX20
Cedar Way, Guil. 242 AW132
Cedar Way, Slou. 152 AY78
Cedar Way, Sun. 175 BS94
Cedar Wd. Dr., Wat. 75 BV35
Cedarcroft Rd., Chess. 216 CM105
Cedarhurst, Brom. 184 EE94
Elstree Hill
Cedarhurst Dr. SE9 184 EJ85
Cedarne Rd. SW6 160 DB80
Cedars, Bans. 218 DF114
Cedars, The E15 144 EF67
Portway
Cedars, The W13 137 CJ72
Heronsforde
Cedars, The, Buck.H. 102 EG46
Cedars, The, Guil. 243 BA131
Cedars, The, Lthd. 231 CK121
Cedars, The, Reig. 250 DD134
Cedars, The, Tedd. 177 CF93
Adelaide Rd.
Cedars, The, W.Byf. 212 BM112
Cedars Ave. E17 123 EA57
Cedars Ave., Mitch. 200 DG98
Cedars Ave., Rick. 92 BJ46
Cedars Clo. NW4 119 CX55
Cedars Clo., Ger.Cr. 90 AY50
Cedars Ct. N9 100 DS47
Church St.
Cedars Dr., Uxb. 134 BM68
Cedars Ms. SW4 161 DH84
Cedars Rd.
Cedars Rd. E15 144 EE65
Cedars Rd. N9 100 DU47
Church St.
Cedars Rd. N21 99 DP47
Cedars Rd. SW4 161 DH83
Cedars Rd. SW13 159 CT82
Cedars Rd. W4 158 CQ78

Charles Clo., Sid. 186 EV91
Charles Cobb Gdns., Croy. 219 DN106
Charles Coveney Rd. SE15 162 DT81
Charles Cres., Har. 117 CD59
Charles Dickens Ho. E2 142 DV69
Charles Flemwell Ms. E16 144 EG74
Hanameel St.
Charles Gdns., Slou. 132 AV72
Borderside
Charles Grinling Wk. SE18 165 EN77
Charles Ho. N17 100 DT52
Love La.
Charles Ho., Wind. 151 AQ81
Alma Rd.
Charles La. NW8 272 A1
Charles Pl. NW1 273 L3
Charles Rd. E7 144 EJ66
Lens Rd.
Charles Rd. SW19 200 DA95
Charles Rd. W13 137 CG71
Charles Rd., Dag. 147 FD65
Charles Rd., Rom. 126 EX59
Charles Rd., Sev. 225 FB110
Charles Rd., Stai. 174 BK93
Charles II Pl. SW3 160 DF78
King's Rd.
Charles II St. SW1 277 M2
Charles II St. SW1 141 DK74
Charles Sevright Dr. NW7 97 CX50
Charles Sq. N1 275 L3
Charles Sq. N1 142 DR69
Charles Sq. Est. N1 142 DR69
Pitfield St.
Charles St. E16 144 EK74
Charles St. SW13 158 CS82
Charles St. W1 277 H2
Charles St. W1 141 DH74
Charles St., Berk. 38 AV19
Charles St., Cher. 193 BF102
Charles St., Croy. 202 DQ104
Charles St., Enf. 82 DT43
Charles St., Epp. 70 EU32
Charles St., Grays 170 GB79
Charles St., Green. 189 FS85
Charles St., Hem.H. 40 BJ21
Charles St., Houns. 156 BZ82
Charles St., Uxb. 135 BP70
Charles St., Wind. 151 AQ81
Charles Whincup Rd. E16 144 EH74
Charlesfield SE9 184 EJ90
Charlesfield Rd., Horl. 268 DF147
Charleston Clo., Felt. 175 BU90
Charleston St. SE17 279 J9
Charleston St. SE17 162 DQ77
Charlesworth Clo., Hem.H. 40 BK22
Charleville Circ. SE26 182 DU92
Charleville Rd. W14 159 CY78
Charlie Chaplin Wk. SE1 141 DN74
Waterloo Rd.
Charlieville Rd., Erith 167 FC80
Northumberland Pk.
Charlmont Rd. SW17 180 DF93
Charlock Way, Guil. 243 BB131
Charlock Way, Wat. 75 BT44
Charlotte Clo., Bexh. 186 EY85
Charlotte Despard Ave. SW11 160 DG81
Charlotte Gdns., Rom. 105 FB51
Charlotte Gro., Horl. 269 DN147
Charlotte Ms. W1 273 L6
Charlotte Ms. W10 139 CX72
Charlotte Ms. W14 159 CY77
Munden St.
Charlotte Pl. NW9 118 CQ57
Uphill Dr.
Charlotte Pl. SW1 277 K9
Charlotte Pl. W1 273 L7
Charlotte Pl., Grays 169 FV79
Charlotte Rd. EC2 275 M4
Charlotte Rd. EC2 142 DS70
Charlotte Rd. SW13 159 CT81
Charlotte Rd., Dag. 147 FB65
Charlotte Rd., Wall. 219 DJ107
Charlotte Row SW4 161 DJ83
North St.
Charlotte Sq., Rich. 178 CM86
Greville Rd.
Charlotte St. W1 273 L6
Charlotte St. W1 141 DJ71
Charlotte Ter. N1 141 DM67
Charlow Clo. SW6 160 DC82
Townmead Rd.
Charlton Ave., Walt. 213 BV105
Charlton Ch. La. SE7 164 EJ78
Charlton Clo., Hodd. 49 EA17
Charlton Clo., Slou. 151 AP75
Haig Dr.
Charlton Clo., Uxb. 115 BP61
Charlton Cres., Bark. 145 ET68
Charlton Dene SE7 164 EJ80
Charlton Dr., West. 238 EK117
Charlton Gdns., Couls. 235 DJ118
Charlton Kings, Wey. 195 BS104
Charlton Kings Rd. NW5 121 DK64
Charlton La. SE7 164 EK78
Charlton La., Shep. 195 BQ97
Charlton Mead La., Hodd. 49 ED18
Charlton Mead La. S., Hodd. 49 ED18
Charlton Mead La.
Charlton Pk. La. SE7 164 EK80
Charlton Pk. Rd. SE7 164 EK79
Charlton Pl. N1 141 DP68
Charlton Pl., Wind. 150 AJ82
Charlton Row
Charlton Rd. N9 101 DX46
Charlton Rd. NW10 138 CS67
Charlton Rd. SE3 164 EG80
Charlton Rd. SE7 164 EH79
Charlton Rd., Har. 117 CK56
Charlton Rd., Shep. 195 BQ97
Charlton Rd., Wem. 118 CM60
Charlton Row, Wind. 150 AJ82
Charlton Sq., Wind. 150 AJ82
Charlton Row
Charlton St., Grays 169 FX79
Charlton Wk., Wind. 150 AJ82
Charlton Row
Charlton Way SE3 164 EE81
Charlton Way, Hodd. 49 EA17
Charlton Way, Wind. 150 AJ82
Charlwood, Croy. 221 DZ109
Charlwood Clo., Har. 95 CE52
Kelvin Cres.
Charlwood Dr., Lthd. 231 CD115
Charlwood Pl. SW1 277 L9
Charlwood Pl. SW1 161 DJ77
Charlwood Rd. SW15 159 CX83
Charlwood Rd., Horl. 268 DB152
Charlwood Sq., Mitch. 200 DD97
Charlwood St. SW1 277 L9
Charlwood St. SW1 161 DJ78
Charlwood Ter. SW15 159 CX84
Cardinal Pl.
Charm Clo., Horl. 268 DE147
Charman Rd., Red. 250 DE134
Charmans La., Reig. 264 CS140
Charmian Ave., Stan. 117 CK55
Charminster Ave. SW19 200 DB96
Charminster Ct., Surb. 197 CK100
Charminster Rd. SE9 184 EK91
Charminster Rd., Wor.Pk. 199 CX102
Charmouth Ct., St.Alb. 43 CG17
Charmouth Rd., St.Alb. 43 CG18
Charmouth Rd., Well. 166 EW81
Charmwood La., Orp. 224 EV109
Charne, The, Sev. 241 FG117
Charnock, Swan. 207 FE98
Charnock Rd. E5 122 DV62
Charnwood Ave. SW19 200 DA96
Charnwood Clo., N.Mal. 198 CS98
Charnwood Dr. E18 124 EH55
Charnwood Gdns. E14 163 EA77
Charnwood Pl. N20 98 DC48
Charnwood Rd. SE25 202 DR99
Charnwood Rd., Enf. 82 DV36
Charnwood Rd., Uxb. 134 BN68
Charnwood St. E5 122 DU61
Charrington Rd., Croy. 201 DP103
Drayton Rd.
Charrington St. NW1 141 DK68
Charsley Clo., Amer. 72 AW39
Charsley Rd. SE6 183 EB89
Chart Clo., Brom. 204 EE96
Chart Clo., Croy. 202 DW100
Stockbury Rd.
Chart Clo., Dor. 263 CK140
Chart Downs, Dor. 263 CJ139
Chart Gdns., Dor. 263 CJ139
Chart La., Dor. 263 CH136
Chart La., Reig. 250 DB134
Chart La. S., Dor. 263 CJ138
Chart St. N1 275 L2
Chart St. N1 142 DR69
Charta Rd., Egh. 173 BC93
Charter Ave., Ilf. 125 ER60
Charter Clo., St.Alb. 43 CD20
Charter Clo., Slou. 152 AT76
Osborne St.
Charter Ct., N.Mal. 198 CS97
Charter Cres., Houns. 156 BY84
Charter Dr., Amer. 72 AT38
Charter Dr., Bex. 186 EY87
Charter Pl., Uxb. 134 BK66
Charter Pl., Wat. 76 BW41
Charter Rd., Kings.T. 198 CP97
Charter Rd., Slou. 131 AL73
Charter Rd., The, Wdf.Grn. 102 EE51
Charter Sq., Kings.T. 198 CP96
Charter Way N3 119 CZ56
Charter Way N14 81 DJ44
Charterhouse Ave., Wem. 117 CJ63
Charterhouse Bldgs. EC1 274 G5
Charterhouse Dr., Sev. 256 FG123
Charterhouse Ms. EC1 274 G6
Charterhouse Rd., Orp. 206 EU104
Charterhouse Sq. EC1 274 G6
Charterhouse Sq. EC1 141 DP71
Charterhouse St. EC1 274 E7
Charterhouse St. EC1 141 DP71
Charteris Rd. N4 121 DN60
Charteris Rd. NW6 139 CZ67
Charteris Rd., Wdf.Grn. 102 EH52
Charters Clo. SE19 182 DS92
Charters Cross, Harl. 51 ER18
Chartfield Ave. SW15 179 CV85
Chartfield Rd., Reig. 266 DC135
Chartfield Sq. SW15 179 CX85
Chartham Gro. SE27 181 DN90
Royal Circ.
Chartham Rd. SE25 202 DV97
Chartley Ave. NW2 118 CS62
Chartley Ave., Stan. 95 CF51
Charton Clo., Belv. 166 EZ79
Nuxley Rd.
Chartridge Clo., Barn. 79 CU43
Chartridge Clo. (Bushey), Wat. 76 CC44
Chartridge La., Chesh. 54 AM29
Chartridge Way, Hem.H. 41 BQ20
Chartway, Reig. 250 DB134
Chartway, Sev. 257 FJ124
Chartwell Clo. SE9 185 EQ89
Chartwell Clo., Croy. 202 DR102
Tavistock Rd.
Chartwell Clo., Grnf. 136 CB67
Chartwell Clo., Wal.Abb. 68 EE33
Chartwell Dr., Orp. 223 ER106
Chartwell Gdns., Sutt. 217 CY105
Chartwell Gate, Beac. 89 AK53
Chartwell Pl., Epsom 216 CS114
Chartwell Pl., Har. 117 CD61
Chartwell Pl., Sutt. 217 CZ105
Chartwell Rd., Nthwd. 93 BT51
Chartwell Way SE20 202 DV95
Charville La., Hayes 135 BS68
Charville La. W., Uxb. 135 BP69
Charwood SW16 181 DN91
Charwood Clo. (Shenley), Rad. 62 CL33
Chasden Rd., Hem.H. 39 BF17
Chase, The E12 124 EK63
Chase, The SW4 161 DH83
Chase, The SW16 181 DM94
Chase, The SW20 199 CY95
Chase, The, Ash. 231 CJ118
Chase, The, Bexh. 167 FB83
Chase, The (Cromwell Rd.), Brwd. 108 FV49
Chase, The (Ingrave), Brwd. 109 GC50
Chase, The (Seven Arches Rd.), Brwd. 108 FX48
Chase, The (Woodman Rd.), Brwd. 108 FX50
Chase, The, Brom. 204 EH97
Chase, The, Chesh. 54 AP29
Chalk Hill
Chase, The, Chig. 103 EQ49
Chase, The, Couls. 219 DJ114
Chase, The, Edg. 96 CP53
Chase, The, Grays 169 FX79
Chase, The, Guil. 258 AU135
Chase, The, Hem.H. 40 BL21
Turners Hill
Chase, The (Tylers Grn.), H.Wyc. 88 AC46
Chase, The (Wooburn), H.Wyc. 110 AF59
Chase, The, Horn. 127 FE62
Chase, The (East Horsley), Lthd. 245 BT126
Chase, The (Oxshott), Lthd. 230 CC115
Chase, The, Loug. 102 EJ45
Chase, The, Pnr. 116 BZ56
Chase, The (Eastcote), Pnr. 116 BW58
Chase, The, Rad. 77 CF35
Chase, The, Reig. 250 DD134
Chase, The, Rom. 127 FE55
Chase, The (Chadwell Heath), Rom. 126 EY58
Chase, The (Rush Grn.), Rom. 127 FD62
Chase, The, Stan. 95 CG50
Chase, The, Sun. 195 BV95
Chase, The, Tad. 234 DA122
Chase, The, Upmin. 129 FS62
Chase, The, Uxb. 114 BN64
Chase, The, Wall. 219 DL106
Chase, The (Cheshunt), Wal.Cr. 65 DP28
Chase, The, Ware 33 EA09
Chase, The, Wat. 75 BS42
Chase Clo., Amer. 55 AN43
Chase Clo., H.Wyc. 88 AC46
Chase Ct. Gdns., Enf. 82 DQ41
Chase Cross Rd., Rom. 105 FC52
Chase End, Epsom 216 CR112
Chase Gdns. E4 101 EA49
Chase Gdns., Twick. 177 CD86
Chase Grn., Enf. 82 DQ41
Chase Grn. Ave., Enf. 81 DP40
Chase Hill, Enf. 82 DQ41
Chase Ho. Gdns., Horn. 128 FM57
Great Nelmes Chase
Chase La., Ilf. 125 ER57
Chase Ridings, Enf. 81 DN40
Chase Rd. N14 81 DK44
Chase Rd. NW10 138 CR70
Chase Rd. W3 138 CR70
Chase Rd., Brwd. 108 FW48
Chase Rd., Epsom 216 CR112
Chase Side N14 80 DG44
Chase Side, Enf. 82 DQ41
Chase Side Ave. SW20 199 CY95
Chase Side Ave., Enf. 82 DQ40
Chase Side Cres., Enf. 82 DQ39
Chase Side Pl., Enf. 82 DQ40
Chase Side
Chase Sq., Grav. 191 GH86
Princes St.
Chase Way N14 99 DH47
Chasefield Clo., Guil. 243 BA131
Chasefield Rd. SW17 180 DF91
Chaseley Dr. W4 158 CP81
Wellesley Rd.
Chaseley Dr., S.Croy. 220 DR110
Chaseley St. E14 143 DY72
Chasemore Clo., Mitch. 200 DF101
Chasemore Gdns., Croy. 219 DP106
Thorneloe Gdns.
Chaseside Clo., Rom. 105 FE51
Chaseside Gdns., Cher. 194 BH101
Chaseville Pk. Rd. N21 81 DL43
Chaseways, Saw. 36 EW07
Chasewood Ave., Enf. 81 DP40
Chasewood Pk., Har. 117 CF62
Chastilian Rd., Dart. 187 FF87
Chatelet Clo., Horl. 269 DH147
Chatfield, Slou. 131 AN71
Chatfield Ct., Cat. 236 DR122
Yorke Gate Rd.
Chatfield Dr., Guil. 243 BC132
Kingfisher Dr.
Chatfield Rd. SW11 160 DC83
Chatfield Rd., Croy. 201 DP102
Chatham Ave., Brom. 204 EF101
Chatham Clo. NW11 120 DA57
Chatham Clo., Sutt. 199 CZ101
Chatham Hill Rd., Sev. 257 FJ121
Chatham Pl. E9 142 DW65
Chatham Rd. E17 123 DY55
Chatham Rd. E18 102 EF54
Grove Hill
Chatham Rd. SW11 180 DF86
Chatham Rd., Kings.T. 198 CN96
Chatham Rd., Orp. 223 EQ106
Chatham St. SE17 279 K8
Chatham St. SE17 162 DR77
Chatsfield, Epsom 217 CU110
Chatsfield Pl. W5 138 CL72
Chatsworth Ave. NW4 97 CW54
Chatsworth Ave. SW20 199 CY95
Chatsworth Ave., Brom. 184 EH91
Chatsworth Ave., Sid. 186 EU88
Chatsworth Ave., Wem. 118 CM64
Chatsworth Clo. NW4 97 CW54
Chatsworth Clo., Borwd. 78 CN41
Chatsworth Clo., W.Wick. 204 EF103
Chatsworth Ct. W8 160 DA77
Chatsworth Ct., Stan. 95 CJ50
Marsh La.
Chatsworth Cres., Houns. 157 CD84
Chatsworth Dr., Enf. 100 DU45
Chatsworth Est. E5 123 DX63
Elderfield Rd.
Chatsworth Gdns. W3 138 CP73
Chatsworth Gdns., Har. 116 CB60
Chatsworth Gdns., N.Mal. 199 CT99
Chatsworth Par., Orp. 205 EQ99
Queensway
Chatsworth Pl., Lthd. 215 CD113
Chatsworth Pl., Mitch. 200 DF97
Chatsworth Pl., Tedd. 177 CG91
Chatsworth Ri. W5 138 CM70
Chatsworth Rd. E5 122 DW62
Chatsworth Rd. E15 124 EF64
Chatsworth Rd. NW2 139 CX65
Chatsworth Rd. W4 158 CQ79
Chatsworth Rd. W5 138 CM70
Chatsworth Rd., Croy. 220 DR105
Chatsworth Rd., Dart. 188 FJ85
Chatsworth Rd., Hayes 135 BV70
Chatsworth Rd., Sutt. 217 CX106
Chatsworth Way SE27 181 DP90
Chatteris Ave., Rom. 106 FJ51
Chattern Hill, Ashf. 175 BP91
Chattern Rd., Ashf. 175 BQ91
Chatterton Rd. N4 121 DP62
Chatterton Rd., Brom. 204 EK98
Chatto Rd. SW11 180 DF85
Chaucer Ave., Hayes 135 BU71
Chaucer Ave., Houns. 155 BV82
Chaucer Ave., Rich. 158 CN82
Chaucer Ave., Wey. 212 BN108
Chaucer Clo. N11 99 DJ50
Chaucer Clo., Bans. 217 CY114
Chaucer Clo., Berk. 38 AT18
Chaucer Clo., Til. 171 GJ82
Chaucer Ct. N16 122 DS63
Chaucer Ct., Guil. 258 AW137
Lawn Rd.
Chaucer Dr. SE1 162 DT77
Chaucer Gdns., Sutt. 200 DA104
Chaucer Grn., Croy. 202 DV101
Chaucer Ho., Sutt. 200 DA104
Chaucer Pk., Dart. 188 FM87
Chaucer Rd. E7 144 EG65
Chaucer Rd. E11 124 EG58
Chaucer Rd. E17 101 EC54
Chaucer Rd. SE24 181 DN85
Chaucer Rd. W3 138 CQ74
Chaucer Rd., Ashf. 174 BL91
Chaucer Rd., Grav. 190 GD90
Chaucer Rd., Rom. 105 FH52
Chaucer Rd., Sid. 186 EW88
Chaucer Rd., Sutt. 218 DA105
Chaucer Rd., Well. 165 ES81
Chaucer Way SW19 180 DD93
Chaucer Way, Add. 212 BG107
Chaucer Way, Dart. 168 FN84
Chaucer Way, Hodd. 33 EA13
Chaulden Ho. Gdns., Hem.H. 39 BF21
Chaulden La., Hem.H. 39 BD22
Chaulden Ter., Hem.H. 39 BF21
Chauncey Clo. N9 100 DU48
Chauncy Ave., Pot.B. 64 DC33
Chaundrye Clo. SE9 184 EL86
Chauntler Clo. E16 144 EH72
Chauntry Clo., Maid. 130 AC73
Chave Rd., Dart. 188 FL90
Chavecroft Ter., Epsom 233 CW119
Chaworth Rd., Cher. 211 BC107
Cheam Clo., Tad. 233 CV121
Waterfield
Cheam Common Rd., Wor.Pk. 199 CV103
Cheam Mans., Sutt. 217 CY108
Cheam Pk. Way, Sutt. 217 CY107
Cheam Rd., Epsom 217 CU109
Cheam Rd., Sutt. 217 CZ107
Cheam Rd. (East Ewell), Sutt. 217 CX110
Cheam St. SE15 162 DV83
Evelina Rd.
Cheapside EC2 275 J9
Cheapside EC2 142 DQ72
Cheapside N13 100 DQ49
Taplow Rd.
Cheapside, Wok. 210 AX114
Cheapside La., Uxb. 113 BF62
Chedburgh, Welw.G.C. 30 DD08
Cheddar Rd., Houns. 154 BN82
Cromer Rd.
Cheddar Waye, Hayes 135 BV72
Cheddington Rd. N18 100 DS48
Chedworth Clo. E16 144 EF72
Hallsville Rd.
Cheelson Rd., S.Ock. 149 FW68
Cheeseman Clo., Hmptn. 176 BY93
Cheesemans Ter. W14 159 CZ78
Cheffins Rd., Hodd. 33 DZ14
Chelford Rd., Brom. 183 ED92
Chelmer Cres., Bark. 146 EV68
Chelmer Dr., Brwd. 109 GE44
Chelmer Dr., S.Ock. 149 FW73
Chelmer Rd. E9 123 DX64
Chelmer Rd., Grays 171 GG78
Chelmer Rd., Upmin. 129 FR58
Chelmsford Ave., Rom. 105 FD52
Chelmsford Clo. E6 145 EM72
Guildford Rd.
Chelmsford Clo. W6 159 CX79
Chelmsford Clo., Sutt. 218 DA109
Chelmsford Dr., Upmin. 128 FM62
Chelmsford Gdns., Ilf. 124 EL59
Chelmsford Rd. E11 123 ED60
Chelmsford Rd. E17 123 EA58
Chelmsford Rd. E18 102 EF53
Chelmsford Rd. N14 99 DJ45
Chelmsford Rd., B.Stort. 37 FH05
Chelmsford Rd., Brwd. 109 FZ44
Chelmsford Rd., Hert. 31 DN10
Chelmsford Sq. NW10 139 CW67
Chelsea Bri. SW1 161 DH79
Chelsea Bri. SW8 161 DH79
Chelsea Bri. Rd. SW1 276 F10
Chelsea Bri. Rd. SW1 160 DG78
Chelsea Cloisters SW3 160 DE77
Lucan Pl.
Chelsea Clo. NW10 138 CR67
Winchelsea Rd.
Chelsea Clo., Edg. 96 CN54
Chelsea Clo., Hmptn. 176 CC93
Chelsea Clo., Wor.Pk. 199 CU101
Chelsea Embk. SW3 160 DE79
Chelsea Flds., Hodd. 33 EB13
Chelsea Gdns., Sutt. 217 CY105
Chelsea Harbour SW10 160 DD81
Chelsea Harbour Dr. SW10 160 DC81
Chelsea Manor Gdns. SW3 160 DE79
Chelsea Manor St. SW3 160 DE78
Chelsea Ms., Horn. 127 FH60
St. Leonards Way
Chelsea Pk. Gdns. SW3 160 DD79
Chelsea Sq. SW3 276 A10
Chelsea Sq. SW3 160 DD78
Chelsea Wf. SW10 160 DD80
Chelsfield Ave. N9 101 DX45
Chelsfield Gdns. SE26 182 DW90
Chelsfield Grn. N9 101 DX45
Chelsfield Ave.
Chelsfield Hill, Orp. 224 EW109
Chelsfield La., Orp. 224 FA108
Chelsfield La. (Chelsfield), Orp. 206 EX101
Chelsfield La., Sev. 225 FC109
Chelsfield Rd., Orp. 206 EW100
Chelsham Clo., Warl. 237 DY118
Limpsfield Rd.
Chelsham Common Rd., Warl. 237 EA117
Chelsham Ct. Rd., Warl. 237 ED118
Chelsham Rd. SW4 161 DK83
Chelsham Rd., S.Croy. 220 DR107
Chelsham Rd., Warl. 237 DZ118
Chelsing Ri., Hem.H. 41 BQ21
Chelston App., Ruis. 115 BU61
Chelston Rd., Ruis. 115 BU60
Chelsworth Clo., Rom. 106 FM53
Chelsworth Dr.
Chelsworth Dr. SE18 165 ER79
Chelsworth Dr., Rom. 106 FL53
Cheltenham Ave., Twick. 177 CG87
Cheltenham Clo., Grav. 191 GJ92
Cheltenham Clo., N.Mal. 198 CQ97
Northcote Rd.
Cheltenham Clo., Nthlt. 136 CB65
Cheltenham Gdns. E6 144 EL68
Cheltenham Gdns., Loug. 84 EL44
Cheltenham Pl. W3 138 CP74
Cheltenham Pl., Har. 118 CL56
Cheltenham Rd. E10 123 EC58
Cheltenham Rd. SE15 162 DW84
Cheltenham Rd., Orp. 206 EU104
Cheltenham Ter. SW3 276 E10
Cheltenham Ter. SW3 160 DF78
Cheltenham Vil., Stai. 173 BF86
Chelverton Rd. SW15 159 CX84
Chelveston, Welw.G.C. 30 DD08
Chelwood Ave., Hat. 45 CU16
Chelwood Clo. E4 83 EB44
Chelwood Clo., Epsom 217 CT112
Chelwood Clo., Nthwd. 93 BQ52
Chelwood Gdns., Rich. 158 CN82
Chelwood Gdns. Pas., Rich. 158 CN82
Chelwood Gdns.
Chelwood Wk. SE4 163 DY84
Chenappa Clo. E13 144 EG69
Chenduit Way, Stan. 95 CF50
Chene Dr., St.Alb. 43 CD18
Cheney Rd. NW1 273 P1
Cheney Rd. NW1 141 DL68
Cheney Row E17 101 DZ53
Cheney St., Pnr. 116 BW57
Cheneys Rd. E11 124 EE62
Chenies, The, Dart. 187 FE91
Chenies, The, Orp. 205 ES100
Chenies Ave., Amer. 72 AW39
Chenies Ct., Hem.H. 41 BP15
Datchet Clo.
Chenies Hill, Hem.H. 57 BB34
Chenies Ms. WC1 273 M5
Chenies Par., Amer. 72 AW40
Chenies Pl. NW1 141 DK68
Chenies Rd., Rick. 73 BD40
Chenies St. WC1 273 M6
Chenies St. WC1 141 DK71
Chenies Way, Wat. 93 BS45
Cheniston Clo., W.Byf. 212 BG113
Madeira Rd.
Cheniston Gdns. W8 160 DB76
Chennells, Hat. 45 CT19
Chepstow Ave., Horn. 128 FL62
Chepstow Clo. SW15 179 CY86
Lytton Gro.
Chepstow Cres. W11 140 DA73
Chepstow Cres., Ilf. 125 ES58
Chepstow Gdns., Sthl. 136 BZ72
Chepstow Pl. W2 140 DA72
Chepstow Ri., Croy. 202 DS104
Chepstow Rd. W2 140 DA72
Chepstow Rd. W7 157 CG76
Chepstow Rd., Croy. 202 DS104
Chepstow Vil. W11 139 CZ73
Chepstow Way SE15 162 DT81
Chequer St. EC1 275 J5
Chequer St., St.Alb. 43 CD20
Chequer Tree Clo., Wok. 226 AS116
Chequers, Hat. 29 CX13
Chequers, Welw.G.C. 29 CX12
Chequers Clo. NW9 118 CS55
Chequers Clo., Horl. 268 DG147
Chequers Clo., Orp. 205 ET98
Chequers Clo., Tad. 249 CU125
Chequers Dr., Horl. 268 DG147
Chequers Fld., Welw.G.C. 29 CX12
Chequers Gdns. N13 99 DP50
Chequers Hill, Amer. 55 AR40
Chequers La., Dag. 146 EZ70
Chequers La., Tad. 249 CU125
Chequers La., Wat. 60 BW30
Chequers Orchard, Iver 133 BF72
Chequers Par. SE9 185 EM86
Eltham High St.
Chequers Pl., Dor. 263 CH136
Chequers Rd., Brwd. 106 FM46
Chequers Rd., Loug. 85 EN43
Chequers Rd., Rom. 106 FL47
Chequers Sq., Uxb. 134 BJ66
High St.
Chequers Wk., Wal.Abb. 68 EF33
Chequers Way N13 100 DQ50
Chequers Yd., Dor. 263 CH136
Chequers Pl.
Cherbury Clo. SE28 146 EX72
Cherbury Ct. N1 142 DR68
Cherbury St.
Cherbury St. N1 275 L1
Cherbury St. N1 142 DR68
Cherchefelle Ms., Stan. 95 CH50
Cherimoya Gdns., W.Mol. 196 CB97
Kelvinbrook
Cherington Rd. W7 137 CF74
Cheriton Ave., Brom. 204 EF99
Cheriton Ave., Ilf. 103 EM54
Cheriton Clo. W5 137 CJ71
Cheriton Clo., Barn. 80 DF41
Cheriton Clo., St.Alb. 43 CK16
Cheriton Ct., Walt. 196 BW102
St. Johns Dr.
Cheriton Dr. SE18 165 ER80
Cheriton Sq. SW17 180 DG89
Cherkley Hill, Lthd. 247 CJ126
Cherries, The, Slou. 132 AV72
Cherry Acre, Ger.Cr. 90 AX49
Cherry Ave., Brwd. 109 FZ48
Cherry Ave., Slou. 152 AX75
Cherry Ave., Sthl. 136 BX74
Cherry Ave., Swan. 207 FD97
Cherry Blossom Clo. N13 99 DP50
Cherry Bounce, Hem.H. 40 BK18
Cherry Clo. E17 123 EB57
Eden Rd.
Cherry Clo. SW2 181 DN87
Tulse Hill
Cherry Clo. W5 157 CK76
Cherry Clo., Bans. 217 CX114
Cherry Clo., Cars. 200 DF103
Cherry Clo., Mord. 199 CY98
Cherry Clo., Ruis. 115 BT62
Roundways
Cherry Cres., Brent. 157 CH80
Cherry Cft., Welw.G.C. 29 CX05
Cherry Dr., Beac. 88 AH51
Cherry Gdn. St. SE16 162 DV75
Cherry Gdns., Dag. 126 EZ64
Cherry Gdns., Nthlt. 136 CB66
Cherry Garth, Brent. 157 CK77
Cherry Grn. Clo., Red. 267 DH136

Cherry Gro., Hayes 135 BV74
Cherry Gro., Uxb. 135 BP71
Cherry Hill, Barn. 80 DB44
Cherry Hill, Har. 95 CE51
Cherry Hill, Rick. 74 BH41
Cherry Hill, St.Alb. 60 CA25
Cherry Hill Gdns., Croy. 219 DM105
Cherry Hills, Wat. 94 BY50
Cherry Hollow, Abb.L. 59 BT31
Cherry La., West Dr. 154 BM77
Cherry La. Roundabout, West Dr. 155 BP77
Cherry Laurel Wk. SW2 181 DM86
Beechdale Rd.
Cherry Orchard, Amer. 55 AS37
Cherry Orchard, Ash. 232 CP118
Cherry Orchard, Hem.H. 40 BG18
Cherry Orchard, Slou. 132 AV66
Cherry Orchard, Stai. 174 BG92
Cherry Orchard, West Dr. 154 BL75
Cherry Orchard Clo., Orp. 206 EW99
Cherry Orchard Gdns., Croy. 202 DR103
Oval Rd.
Cherry Orchard Gdns., W.Mol. 196 BZ97
Cherry Orchard Rd., Brom. 204 EL103
Cherry Orchard Rd., Croy. 202 DR103
Cherry Orchard Rd., W.Mol. 196 BZ97
Cherry Ri., Ch.St.G. 90 AX47
Cherry Rd., Enf. 82 DW38
Cherry St., Rom. 127 FD57
Cherry St., Wok. 226 AY118
Cherry Tree Ave., Guil. 242 AT134
Cherry Tree Ave., St.Alb. 61 CK26
Cherry Tree Ave., Stai. 174 BH93
Cherry Tree Ave., West Dr. 134 BM72
Cherry Tree Clo. E9 142 DW67
Moulins Rd.
Cherry Tree Clo., Grays 170 GC79
Cherry Tree Clo., Rain. 147 FG68
Cherry Tree Clo., Wem. 117 CF63
Cherry Tree Ct. NW9 118 CQ56
Cherry Tree Ct., Couls. 235 DM117
Cherry Tree Dr. SW16 181 DL90
Cherry Tree Dr., S.Ock. 149 FX70
Cherry Tree Grn., Hert. 31 DM07
Cherry Tree Grn., S.Croy. 220 DV114
Cherry Tree La., Dart. 187 FF90
Cherry Tree La., Epsom 216 CN112
Christ Ch. Rd.
Cherry Tree La., Hem.H. 41 BQ15
Cherry Tree La., Iver 134 BG67
Cherry Tree La., Pot.B. 64 DB34
Cherry Tree La., Rain. 147 FE69
Cherry Tree La., Rick. 91 BC46
Cherry Tree La., Slou. 133 AZ65
Cherry Tree Ri., Buck.H. 102 EJ49
Cherry Tree Rd. E15 124 EE63
Wingfield Rd.
Cherry Tree Rd. N2 120 DF56
Cherry Tree Rd., Beac. 110 AH55
Cherry Tree Rd., Hodd. 49 EA16
Cherry Tree Rd., Slou. 131 AQ66
Cherry Tree Rd., Wat. 75 BV36
Cherry Tree Wk. EC1 275 J5
Cherry Tree Wk., Beck. 203 DZ98
Cherry Tree Wk., Chesh. 54 AR29
Cherry Tree Wk., W.Wick. 222 EF105
Cherry Tree Way, H.Wyc. 88 AC46
Cherry Tree Way, Stan. 95 CH51
Cherry Wk., Brom. 204 EG102
Cherry Wk., Grays 171 GG76
Cherry Wk., Rain. 147 FF68
Cherry Wk., Rick. 74 BJ40
Cherry Way, Epsom 216 CR107
Cherry Way, Hat. 45 CU21
Cherry Way, Shep. 195 BR98
Cherry Way, Slou. 153 BC83
Cherry Wd. Clo., Beac. 89 AR50
Cherry Wd. Way W5 138 CN71
Hanger Vale La.
Cherrycot Hill, Orp. 223 ER105
Cherrycot Ri., Orp. 223 EQ105
Cherrycroft Gdns., Pnr. 94 BZ52
Westfield Pk.
Cherrydale, Wat. 75 BT42
Cherrydown Ave. E4 101 DZ48
Cherrydown Clo. E4 101 DZ48
Cherrydown Rd., Sid. 186 EX89
Cherrydown Wk., Rom. 105 FB54
Cherrytree La., Ger.Cr. 90 AX54
Cherrywood Ave., Egh. 172 AV94
Cherrywood Clo. E3 143 DY69
Cherrywood Clo., Kings.T. 178 CN94
Cherrywood Dr. SW15 179 CX85
Cherrywood Dr., Grav. 190 GE91
Cherrywood La., Mord. 199 CY98
Cherston Gdns., Loug. 85 EN42
Cherston Rd.
Cherston Rd., Loug. 85 EN42
Chertsey Bri. Rd., Cher. 194 BK101
Chertsey Clo., Ken. 235 DP115
Chertsey Cres., Croy. 221 EC110
Chertsey Dr., Sutt. 199 CY103
Chertsey La., Cher. 193 BF97
Chertsey La., Epsom 216 CN112
Chertsey La., Stai. 173 BE92
Chertsey Rd. E11 123 ED61
Chertsey Rd., Add. 194 BH103
Chertsey Rd., Ashf. 175 BR94
Chertsey Rd., Felt. 175 BS92
Chertsey Rd., Ilf. 125 ER63
Chertsey Rd., Shep. 194 BK101
Chertsey Rd., Sun. 175 BR94
Chertsey Rd., Twick. 177 CF86
Chertsey Rd., W.Byf. 212 BK111
Chertsey Rd., Wok. 227 AZ116
Chertsey Rd. (Chobham), Wok. 210 AT110
Chertsey St. SW17 180 DG92
Chertsey St., Guil. 258 AX135
Cherubs, The, Slou. 131 AQ65
Chervil Clo., Felt. 175 BU90
Chervil Ms. SE28 146 EV74
Cherwell Clo., Rick. 74 BN43
Cherwell Clo., Slou. 153 BB79
Tweed Rd.
Cherwell Ct., Epsom 216 CQ105
Cherwell Gro., S.Ock. 149 FV73
Cherwell Way, Ruis. 115 BQ58
Cheryls Clo. SW6 160 DB81
Cheselden Rd., Guil. 258 AY135
Cheseman St. SE26 182 DV90
Chesfield Rd., Kings.T. 178 CL94
Chesham Ave., Orp. 205 EP100
Chesham Clo. SW1 276 F7
Chesham Clo., Rom. 127 FD56
Chesham Clo., Sutt. 217 CY110
Chesham Ct., Nthwd. 93 BT51
Frithwood Ave.
Chesham Cres. SE20 202 DW96
Chesham La., Ch.St.G. 90 AY48
Chesham La., Ger.Cr. 90 AY49
Chesham Ms. SW1 276 F6
Chesham Ms. SW1 160 DG76
Chesham Ms., Guil. 259 AZ135
Chesham Rd.
Chesham Pl. SW1 276 F7
Chesham Pl. SW1 160 DG76
Chesham Rd. SE20 202 DW96
Chesham Rd. SW19 180 DD92
Chesham Rd., Amer. 55 AQ36
Chesham Rd., Berk. 38 AV21
Chesham Rd., Chesh. 54 AL32
Chesham Rd., Guil. 259 AZ135
Chesham Rd., Hem.H. 56 AY27
Chesham Rd., Kings.T. 198 CN95
Chesham St. NW10 118 CR62
Chesham St. SW1 276 F7
Chesham St. SW1 160 DG76
Chesham Ter. W13 157 CH75
Chesham Way, Wat. 75 BS44
Cheshire Clo. E17 101 EB53
Cheshire Clo. SE4 163 DZ82
Cheshire Clo., Cher. 211 BD107
Cheshire Clo., Horn. 128 FN57
Cheshire Clo., Mitch. 201 DL97
Cheshire Ct. EC4 274 E9
Cheshire Ct., Slou. 152 AV75
Clements Clo.
Cheshire Gdns., Chess. 215 CK107
Cheshire Rd. N22 99 DM52
Cheshire St. E2 142 DT70
Chesholm Rd. N16 122 DS62
Cheshunt Link Rd. (Cheshunt), Wal.Cr. 66 DW33
Cheshunt Pk. (Cheshunt), Wal.Cr. 66 DV26
Cheshunt Rd. E7 144 EH65
Cheshunt Rd., Belv. 166 FA78
Cheshunt Wash (Cheshunt), Wal.Cr. 67 DY27
Chesil Ct. E2 142 DV68
Chesil Way, Hayes 135 BT69
Chesilton Rd. SW6 159 CZ81
Chesley Gdns. E6 144 EK68
Cheslyn Gdns., Wat. 75 BT37
Chesney Cres., Croy. 221 EC108
Chesney St. SW11 160 DG81
Chesnut Est. N17 122 DT55
Chesnut Gro. N17 122 DT55
Chesnut Rd.
Chesnut Rd. N17 122 DT55
Chess Clo., Chesh. 72 AX36
Chess Clo., Rick. 74 BK42
Chess Hill, Rick. 74 BK42
Chess La., Rick. 74 BK42
Chess Vale Ri., Rick. 74 BM44
Chess Valley Wk., Chesh. 54 AR33
Chess Valley Wk., Rick. 74 BL44
Chess Way, Rick. 74 BG41
Chessbury Rd., Chesh. 54 AN32
Chessfield Pk., Amer. 72 AY39
Chessholme Ct., Sun. 175 BS94
Scotts Ave.
Chessholme Rd., Ashf. 175 BQ93
Chessington Ave. N3 119 CY55
Chessington Ave., Bexh. 166 EY80
Chessington Clo., Epsom 216 CQ107
Chessington Ct., Pnr. 116 BZ56
Chessington Hall Gdns., Chess. 215 CK108
Chessington Hill Pk., Chess. 216 CN106
Chessington Lo. N3 119 CZ55
Chessington Rd., Epsom 217 CT109
Chessington Way, W.Wick. 203 EB103
Chessmount Ri., Chesh. 54 AR33
Chesson Rd. W14 159 CZ79
Chesswood Way, Pnr. 94 BX54
Chester Ave., Rich. 178 CM85
Chester Ave., Twick. 176 BZ88
Chester Ave., Upmin. 129 FS61
Chester Clo. SW1 276 G5
Chester Clo. SW1 160 DG75
Chester Clo. SW13 159 CV83
Chester Clo., Ashf. 175 BR92
Chester Clo., Dor. 247 CJ134
Chester Clo., Guil. 242 AT132
Chester Clo., Loug. 85 EQ39
Chester Clo., Pot.B. 64 DB29
Chester Clo., Sutt. 200 DA103
Chester Clo., Uxb. 135 BP72
Dawley Ave.
Chester Clo. N. NW1 273 J2
Chester Clo. S. NW1 273 J3
Chester Cotts. SW1 276 F9
Chester Ct. NW1 273 J2
Chester Ct. SE5 162 DR80
Chester Cres. E8 142 DT65
Ridley Rd.
Chester Dr., Har. 116 BZ58
Chester Gdns. W13 137 CG72
Chester Gdns., Enf. 82 DV44
Chester Gdns., Mord. 200 DC100
Chester Gate NW1 273 H3
Chester Gate NW1 141 DH69
Chester Grn., Loug. 85 EQ39
Chester Ms. SW1 277 H6
Chester Ms. SW1 161 DH76
Chester Path, Loug. 85 EQ39
Chester Pl. NW1 273 J2
Chester Rd. E7 144 EK66
Chester Rd. E11 124 EH58
Chester Rd. E16 144 EE70
Chester Rd. E17 123 DX57
Chester Rd. N9 100 DV46
Chester Rd. N17 122 DR55
Chester Rd. N19 121 DH61
Chester Rd. NW1 272 G3
Chester Rd. NW1 140 DG69
Chester Rd. SW19 179 CW93
Chester Rd., Borwd. 78 CQ41
Chester Rd., Chig. 103 EN48
Chester Rd., Houns. 155 BV83
Chester Rd. (Heathrow Airport), Houns. 154 BN83
Chester Rd., Ilf. 125 ET60
Chester Rd., Lthd. 245 BV129
Dirtham La.
Chester Rd., Loug. 85 EP40
Chester Rd., Nthwd. 93 BS52
Chester Rd., Sid. 185 ES85
Chester Rd., Slou. 131 AR72
Chester Rd., Wat. 75 BU43
Chester Row SW1 276 F9
Chester Row SW1 160 DG77
Chester Sq. SW1 277 H8
Chester Sq. SW1 161 DH76
Chester Sq. Ms. SW1 277 H7
Chester St. E2 142 DU70
Chester St. SW1 276 G6
Chester St. SW1 160 DG76
Chester Ter. NW1 273 H2
Chester Way SE11 278 E9
Chester Way SE11 161 DN77
Chesterfield Clo., Orp. 206 EX98
Chesterfield Dr., Dart. 187 FH85
Chesterfield Dr., Esher 197 CG103
Chesterfield Dr., Sev. 256 FD122
Chesterfield Gdns. N4 121 DP57
Chesterfield Gdns. SE10 163 ED80
Crooms Hill
Chesterfield Gdns. W1 277 H2
Chesterfield Gdns. W1 141 DH74
Chesterfield Gro. SE22 182 DT85
Chesterfield Hill W1 277 H1
Chesterfield Hill W1 141 DH73
Chesterfield Ms. N4 121 DP57
Chesterfield Gdns.
Chesterfield Ms., Ashf. 174 BL91
Chesterfield Rd.
Chesterfield Rd. E10 123 EC58
Chesterfield Rd. N3 98 DA51
Chesterfield Rd. W4 158 CQ79
Chesterfield Rd., Ashf. 174 BL91
Chesterfield Rd., Barn. 79 CX43
Chesterfield Rd., Enf. 83 DY37
Chesterfield Rd., Epsom 216 CR108
Chesterfield St. W1 277 H2
Chesterfield St. W1 141 DH74
Chesterfield Wk. SE10 163 ED81
Chesterfield Way SE15 162 DW80
Chesterfield Way, Hayes 155 BU75
Chesterford Gdns. NW3 120 DB63
Chesterford Ho. SE18 164 EK80
Shooter's Hill Rd.
Chesterford Rd. E12 125 EM64
Chesters, Horl. 268 DE146
Chesters, The, N.Mal. 198 CS95
Chesterton Clo. SW18 180 DA85
Ericcson Clo.
Chesterton Clo., Chesh. 54 AP29
Milton Rd.
Chesterton Clo., Grnf. 136 CB68
Chesterton Dr., Red. 251 DL128
Chesterton Dr., Stai. 174 BM88
Chesterton Grn., Beac. 89 AL52
Chesterton Rd. E13 144 EG69
Chesterton Rd. W10 139 CX71
Chesterton Sq. W8 159 CZ77
Pembroke Rd.
Chesterton Ter. E13 144 EG69
Chesterton Ter., Kings.T. 198 CN96
Chesterton Way, Til. 171 GJ82
Chesthunte Rd. N17 100 DQ53
Chestnut All. SW6 159 CZ79
Lillie Rd.
Chestnut Ave. E7 124 EH63
Chestnut Ave. N8 121 DL57
Chestnut Ave. SW14 158 CR83
Thornton Rd.
Chestnut Ave., Brent. 157 CK77
Chestnut Ave., Brwd. 108 FS45
Chestnut Ave., Buck.H. 102 EK48
Chestnut Ave., Chesh. 54 AR29
Chestnut Ave., E.Mol. 197 CF97
Chestnut Ave., Edg. 96 CL51
Chestnut Ave., Epsom 216 CS105
Chestnut Ave., Esher 197 CD101
Chestnut Ave., Grays 170 GB75
Chestnut Ave. (Bluewater), Green. 189 FT87
Chestnut Ave., Guil. 258 AW137
Chestnut Ave., Hmptn. 176 CA94
Chestnut Ave., Horn. 127 FF61
Chestnut Ave., Nthwd. 93 BT54
Chestnut Ave., Rick. 74 BG43
Chestnut Ave., Slou. 152 AY75
Chestnut Ave., Tedd. 197 CF96
Chestnut Ave., Vir.W. 192 AT98
Chestnut Ave., Walt. 213 BS110
Chestnut Ave., Wem. 117 CH64
Chestnut Ave., West Dr. 134 BM73
Chestnut Ave., W.Wick. 222 EE106
Chestnut Ave., West. 238 EK123
Chestnut Ave., Wey. 213 BQ108
Chestnut Ave. N. E17 123 EC56
Chestnut Ave. S. E17 123 EC56
Chestnut Clo. N14 81 DJ43
Chestnut Clo. N16 122 DR61
Lordship Gro.
Chestnut Clo. SE6 183 EC92
Chestnut Clo. SE14 163 DZ83
Shardeloes Rd.
Chestnut Clo. SW16 181 DN91
Chestnut Clo., Add. 212 BK106
Chestnut Clo., Amer. 55 AR37
Chestnut Clo., Ashf. 175 BP91
Chestnut Clo., Berk. 39 BB17
Chestnut Clo., Buck.H. 102 EK47
Chestnut Clo., Cars. 200 DF102
Chestnut Clo., Egh. 172 AW93
Chestnut Clo., Ger.Cr. 91 AZ53
Chestnut Clo., Grav. 191 GF86
Burch Rd.
Chestnut Clo., Hayes 135 BS73
Chestnut Clo., Horn. 128 FJ63
Lancaster Dr.
Chestnut Clo., Orp. 224 EU106
Chestnut Clo., Red. 267 DH136
Haigh Cres.
Chestnut Clo., Sid. 186 EU88
Chestnut Clo., Sun. 175 BT93
Chestnut Clo., Tad. 234 DA123
Chestnut Clo., Ware 34 EK06
Chestnut Clo., West Dr. 155 BP80
Chestnut Clo., Wok. 228 BG124
Chestnut Copse, Oxt. 254 EH132
Chestnut Ct. SW6 159 CZ79
North End Rd.
Chestnut Ct., Amer. 55 AR37
Chestnut Ct., Surb. 198 CL101
Penners Gdns.
Chestnut Dr. E11 124 EG58
Chestnut Dr., Berk. 38 AX20
Chestnut Dr., Bexh. 166 EX83
Chestnut Dr., Egh. 172 AX93
Chestnut Dr., Har. 95 CF52
Chestnut Dr., Pnr. 116 BX58
Chestnut Dr., St.Alb. 43 CH18
Chestnut Dr., Wind. 151 AL84
Chestnut Glen, Horn. 127 FF61
Chestnut Gro. SE20 182 DW94
Chestnut Gro. SW12 180 DG87
Chestnut Gro. W5 157 CK76
Chestnut Gro., Barn. 80 DF43
Chestnut Gro., Brwd. 108 FW47
Chestnut Gro., Dart. 187 FD91
Chestnut Gro., Ilf. 103 ES51
Chestnut Gro., Islw. 157 CG84
Chestnut Gro., Mitch. 201 DK98
Chestnut Gro., N.Mal. 198 CR97
Chestnut Gro., S.Croy. 220 DV108
Chestnut Gro., Stai. 174 BJ93
Chestnut Gro., Wem. 117 CH64
Chestnut Gro., Wok. 226 AY120
Chestnut La. N20 97 CY46
Chestnut La., Amer. 55 AR36
Chestnut La., Sev. 257 FH124
Chestnut La., Wey. 213 BP106
Chestnut Manor Clo., Stai. 174 BH92
Chestnut Mead, Red. 250 DE133
Oxford Rd.
Chestnut Pl., Ash. 232 CL119
Chestnut Pl., Epsom 217 CU111
Chestnut Ri. SE18 165 ER79
Chestnut Ri. (Bushey), Wat. 94 CB45
Chestnut Rd. SE27 181 DP90
Chestnut Rd. SW20 199 CX96
Chestnut Rd., Ashf. 175 BP91
Chestnut Rd., Beac. 88 AH54
Chestnut Rd., Dart. 188 FK88
Chestnut Rd., Enf. 83 DY36
Chestnut Rd., Guil. 242 AX134
Chestnut Rd., Horl. 269 DH146
Chestnut Rd., Kings.T. 178 CL94
Chestnut Rd., Twick. 177 CE89
Chestnut Wk., Epp. 51 EP24
Epping Rd.
Chestnut Wk., Ger.Cr. 90 AY52
Chestnut Wk., Sev. 257 FL129
Chestnut Wk., Shep. 195 BS99
Chestnut Wk., Walt. 213 BS109
Octagon Rd.
Chestnut Wk., Wat. 75 BU37
Chestnut Wk., W.Byf. 212 BL112
Royston Rd.
Chestnut Wk., Wdf.Grn. 102 EG50
Chestnut Way, Felt. 175 BV90
Chestnuts, Brwd. 109 GB45
Chestnuts, The SE14 163 DZ81
Chestnuts, The, Hem.H. 39 BF24
Chestnuts, The, Hert. 32 DR09
Chestnuts, The, Horl. 269 DH146
Chestnuts, The, Rom. 86 EV41
Chestnuts, The, Walt. 195 BU103
Cheston Ave., Croy. 203 DY103
Chestwood Gro., Uxb. 134 BM66
Cheswick Clo., Dart. 167 FF84
Chesworth Clo., Erith 167 FE81
Chettle Clo. SE1 279 K6
Chettle Ct. N8 121 DN58
Chetwode Dr., Epsom 233 CX118
Chetwode Rd. SW17 180 DF90
Chetwode Rd., Tad. 233 CW119
Chetwood Wk. E6 144 EL72
Chetwynd Ave., Barn. 98 DF46
Chetwynd Dr., Uxb. 134 BM68
Chetwynd Rd. NW5 121 DH63
Cheval Pl. SW7 276 C6
Cheval Pl. SW7 160 DE76
Cheval St. E14 163 EA76
Chevalier Clo., Stan. 96 CL49
Cheveley Clo., Rom. 106 FM53
Chelsworth Dr.
Cheveley Gdns., Slou. 130 AJ68
Chevely Clo., Epp. 70 EX29
Cheveney Wk., Brom. 204 EG97
Marina Clo.
Chevening La., Sev. 240 EY116
Chevening Rd. NW6 139 CX68
Chevening Rd. SE10 164 EF78
Chevening Rd. SE19 182 DR93
Chevening Rd., Sev. 240 EZ119
Chevenings, The, Sid. 186 EW90
Cheverton Rd. N19 121 DK60
Chevet St. E9 123 DY64
Kenworthy Rd.
Chevington Way, Horn. 128 FK63
Cheviot Clo., Bans. 234 DB115
Cheviot Clo., Bexh. 167 FE82
Cheviot Clo., Enf. 82 DR40
Cheviot Clo., Hayes 155 BR80
Cheviot Clo., Sutt. 218 DD109
Cheviot Clo. (Bushey), Wat. 76 CC44
Cheviot Gdns. NW2 119 CX61
Cheviot Gdns. SE27 181 DP91
Cheviot Gate NW2 119 CY61
Cheviot Rd. SE27 181 DN92
Cheviot Rd., Horn. 127 FG60
Cheviot Rd., Slou. 153 BA78
Cheviot Way, Ilf. 125 ES56
Cheviots, Hat. 45 CU21
Cheviots, Hem.H. 40 BM17
Chevron Clo. E16 144 EG72
Chevy Rd., Sthl. 156 CC75
Chewton Rd. E17 123 DY56
Cheyham Gdns., Sutt. 217 CX110
Cheyham Way, Sutt. 217 CY110
Cheyne Ave. E18 124 EF55
Cheyne Ave., Twick. 176 BZ88
Cheyne Clo. NW4 119 CW57
Cheyne Clo., Amer. 55 AR36
Cheyne Clo., Brom. 204 EL104
Cedar Cres.
Cheyne Clo., Ger.Cr. 112 AY60
Cheyne Clo., Ware 33 DX05
Cheyne Ct. SW3 160 DF79
Flood St.
Cheyne Ct., Bans. 234 DB115
Park Rd.
Cheyne Gdns. SW3 160 DE79
Cheyne Hill, Surb. 198 CM98
Cheyne Ms. SW3 160 DE79
Cheyne Path W7 137 CF72
Copley Clo.
Cheyne Pl. SW3 160 DF79
Cheyne Rd., Ashf. 175 BR93
Cheyne Row SW3 160 DE79
Cheyne Wk. N21 81 DP43
Cheyne Wk. NW4 119 CW58
Cheyne Wk. SW3 160 DE79
Cheyne Wk. SW10 160 DD80
Cheyne Wk., Chesh. 54 AR31
Cheyne Wk., Croy. 202 DU103
Cheyne Wk., Horl. 268 DF150
Cheyne Wk., Long. 209 FX97
Cavendish Sq.
Cheyney Rd., Ashf. 175 BR93
Cheyneys Ave., Edg. 95 CK51
Chichele Gdns., Croy. 220 DT105
Brownlow Rd.
Chichele Rd. NW2 119 CX64
Chichele Rd., Oxt. 254 EE128
Chicheley Gdns., Har. 94 CC52
Chicheley Rd., Har. 94 CC52
Chicheley St. SE1 278 C4
Chicheley St. SE1 161 DM75
Chichester Ave., Ruis. 115 BR61
Chichester Clo. E6 144 EL72
Chichester Clo. SE3 164 EJ81
Chichester Clo., Dor. 247 CH134
Chichester Clo., Hmptn. 176 BZ93
Maple Clo.
Chichester Clo., S.Ock. 148 FQ74
Chichester Ct., Epsom 217 CT109
Chichester Ct., Slou. 152 AV75
Chichester Ct., Stan. 118 CL55
Chichester Dr., Pur. 219 DM112
Chichester Dr., Sev. 256 FF125
Chichester Gdns., Ilf. 124 EL59
Chichester Ms. SE27 181 DN91
Chichester Rents WC2 274 D8
Chichester Ri., Grav. 191 GK91
Chichester Rd. E11 124 EE62
Chichester Rd. N9 100 DU46
Chichester Rd. NW6 140 DA68
Chichester Rd. W2 140 DB71
Chichester Rd., Croy. 202 DS104
Chichester Rd., Dor. 247 CH133
Chichester Rd., Green. 189 FT85
Chichester Row, Amer. 55 AR38
Chichester St. SW1 161 DJ78
Chichester Way E14 163 ED77
Chichester Way, Felt. 176 BW87
Chichester Way, Wat. 60 BY33
Chicksand St. E1 142 DT71
Chiddingfold N12 98 DA48
Chiddingstone Ave., Bexh. 166 EZ80
Chiddingstone Clo., Sutt. 218 DA110
Chiddingstone St. SW6 160 DA82
Chieftan Dr., Purf. 168 FM77
Chieveley Rd., Bexh. 167 FB84
Chiffinch Gdns., Grav. 190 GE90
Chignell Pl. W13 137 CG74
Broadway
Chigwell Hill E1 142 DV73
Pennington St.
Chigwell Hurst Ct., Pnr. 116 BX55
Chigwell La., Loug. 85 EQ43
Chigwell Pk., Chig. 103 EP49
Chigwell Pk. Dr., Chig. 103 EN48
Chigwell Ri., Chig. 103 EN47
Chigwell Rd. E18 124 EH55
Chigwell Rd., Wdf.Grn. 102 EJ54
Chigwell Vw., Rom. 104 FA51
Lodge La.
Chilberton Dr., Red. 251 DJ130
Chilbrook Rd., Cob. 229 BU118
Chilcot Clo. E14 143 EB72
Grundy St.
Chilcote La., Amer. 72 AV39
Chilcott Rd., Wat. 75 BS36
Childebert Rd. SW17 181 DH89
Childeric Rd. SE14 163 DY80
Childerley St. SW6 159 CX81
Fulham Palace Rd.
Childers, The, Wdf.Grn. 103 EM50
Childers St. SE8 163 DY79
Childs Ave. (Harefield), Uxb. 92 BJ54
Childs Clo., Horn. 128 FJ58
Childs Cres., Swans. 189 FX86
Childs Hall Clo., Lthd. 246 BZ125
Childs Hall Rd.
Childs Hall Dr., Lthd. 246 BZ125
Childs Hall Rd., Lthd. 246 BZ125
Childs Hill Wk. NW2 119 CZ62
Childs La. SE19 182 DS93
Westow St.
Child's Pl. SW5 160 DA77
Child's St. SW5 160 DA77
Child's Wk. SW5 160 DA77
Child's Pl.
Childs Way NW11 119 CZ57
Childwick Ct., Hem.H. 40 BN23
Rumballs Rd.
Chilham Clo., Bex. 186 EZ87
Chilham Clo., Grnf. 137 CG68
Chilham Clo., Hem.H. 40 BL21
Chilham Rd. SE9 184 EL91
Chilham Way, Brom. 204 EG101
Chillerton Rd. SW17 180 DG92
Chillingworth Gdns., Twick. 177 CF90
Tower Rd.
Chillingworth Rd. N7 121 DN64
Liverpool Rd.
Chilmans Dr., Lthd. 246 CB125
Chilmark Gdns., N.Mal. 199 CT101
Chilmark Gdns., Red. 251 DL129
Chilmark Rd. SW16 201 DK96
Chilmead La., Red. 251 DK132
Chilsey Grn. Rd., Cher. 193 BE100
Chiltern Ave., Amer. 55 AR38
Chiltern Ave., Twick. 176 CA88
Chiltern Ave. (Bushey), Wat. 76 CC44
Chiltern Business Village, Uxb. 134 BH68
Chiltern Clo., Berk. 38 AT18
Chiltern Clo., Bexh. 167 FE81
Cumbrian Ave.
Chiltern Clo., Borwd. 78 CM40
Chiltern Clo., Croy. 202 DS104
Chiltern Clo. (Ickenham), Uxb. 115 BP61
Chiltern Clo. (Cheshunt), Wal.Cr. 65 DP27
Chiltern Clo. (Bushey), Wat. 76 CB44
Chiltern Clo., Wok. 226 AW122
Chiltern Clo., Wor.Pk. 199 CW103
Cotswold Way
Chiltern Dene, Enf. 81 DM42
Chiltern Dr., Rick. 91 BF45
Chiltern Dr., Surb. 198 CP99
Chiltern Gdns. NW2 119 CX62
Chiltern Gdns., Brom. 204 EF98
Chiltern Gdns., Horn. 128 FJ62
Chiltern Hill, Ger.Cr. 90 AY53
Chiltern Hills Rd., Beac. 88 AJ53
Chiltern Par., Amer. 55 AQ37
Chiltern Pk. Ave., Berk. 38 AU17
Chiltern Rd. E3 143 EA70

Chiltern Rd., Amer. 55 AP35
Chiltern Rd., Grav. 190 GE90
Chiltern Rd., Ilf. 125 ES56
Chiltern Rd., Pnr. 116 BW57
Chiltern Rd., St.Alb. 43 CJ15
Chiltern Rd., Slou. 130 AH71
Chiltern Rd., Sutt. 218 DB109
Chiltern St. W1 272 F6
Chiltern St. W1 140 DG71
Chiltern Vw. Rd., Uxb. 134 BJ68
Chiltern Way, Wdf.Grn. 102 EG48
Chilterns, Berk. 38 AT17
Chilterns, Hat. 45 CU21
Chilterns, Hem.H. 40 BL18
Chilterns, The, Sutt. 218 DB109
Gatton Clo.
Chilthorne Clo. SE6 183 DZ87
Ravensbourne Pk. Cres.
Chilton Ave. W5 157 CK77
Chilton Clo., H.Wyc. 88 AC45
Chilton Ct., Hert. 31 DM07
The Ridgeway
Chilton Ct., Walt. 213 BU105
Chilton Grn., Welw.G.C. 30 DC09
Chilton Gro. SE8 163 DX77
Chilton Rd., Chesh. 54 AQ29
Chilton Rd., Edg. 96 CN51
Manor Pk. Cres.
Chilton Rd., Grays 171 GG76
Chilton Rd., Rich. 158 CN83
Chilton St. E2 142 DT70
Chiltonian Ind. Est. SE12 184 EF86
Chiltons, The E18 102 EG54
Grove Hill
Chiltons Clo., Bans. 234 DB115
High St.
Chilver St. SE10 164 EF78
Chilwell Gdns., Wat. 94 BW49
Chilwick, Slou. 131 AM69
Chilworth Ct. SW19 179 CX88
Windlesham Gro.
Chilworth Gdns., Sutt. 200 DC104
Chilworth Ms. W2 140 DC72
Chilworth Rd., Guil. 260 BG139
Chilworth St. W2 140 DC72
Chimes Ave. N13 99 DN50
Chinbrook Cres. SE12 184 EH90
Chinbrook Rd.
Chinbrook Est. SE9 184 EK90
Chinbrook Rd. SE12 184 EH90
Chinchilla Dr., Houns. 156 BW82
Chindit Clo., Brox. 49 DY20
Chindits La., Brwd. 108 FW50
Chine, The N10 121 DJ56
Chine, The N21 81 DP44
Chine, The, Dor. 263 CH135
High St.
Chine, The, Wem. 117 CH64
Ching Ct. WC2 273 P9
Ching Way E4 101 DZ51
Chingdale Rd. E4 102 EE48
Chingford Ave. E4 101 EB48
Chingford Hall Est. E4 101 DZ51
Chingford Ind. Cen. E4 101 DY50
Chingford La., Wdf.Grn. 102 EE49
Chingford Mt. Rd. E4 101 EA49
Chingford Rd. E4 101 EA51
Chingford Rd. E17 101 EB53
Chingley Clo., Brom. 184 EE93
Chinnery Clo., Enf. 82 DT39
Garnault Rd.
Chinnor Cres., Grnf. 136 CB68
Chinthurst La., Guil. 258 AY141
Chinthurst Pk., Guil. 258 AY142
Chip St. SW4 161 DK84
Chipka St. E14 163 EC75
Chipley St. SE14 163 DY79
Chipmunk Gro., Nthlt. 136 BY69
Argus Way
Chippendale All., Uxb. 134 BK66
Chippendale Waye
Chippendale St. E5 123 DX62
Chippendale Waye, Uxb. 134 BK66
Chippenham Ave., Wem. 118 CP64
Chippenham Clo., Pnr. 115 BT56
Chippenham Clo., Rom. 106 FK50
Chippenham Rd.
Chippenham Gdns. NW6 140 DA69
Chippenham Gdns., Rom. 106 FK50
Chippenham Ms. W9 140 DA70
Chippenham Rd. W9 140 DA70
Chippenham Rd., Rom. 106 FK51
Chippenham Wk., Rom. 106 FK51
Chippenham Rd.
Chipperfield Clo., Upmin. 129 FS60
Chipperfield Rd., Hem.H. 40 BJ24
Chipperfield Rd. (Bovingdon), Hem.H. 57 BB27
Chipperfield Rd., Kings L. 58 BK29
Chipperfield Rd., Orp. 206 EU95
Chipping Clo., Barn. 79 CY41
St. Albans Rd.
Chippingfield, Harl. 36 EW12
Chipstead, Ger.Cr. 90 AW53
Chipstead Ave., Th.Hth. 201 DP98
Chipstead Clo. SE19 182 DT94
Chipstead Clo., Couls. 234 DG116
Chipstead Clo., Red. 266 DG136
Chipstead Clo., Sutt. 218 DB109
Chipstead Ct., Wok. 226 AS117
Creston Ave.
Chipstead Gdns. NW2 119 CV61
Chipstead Gate, Couls. 235 DJ119
Woodfield Clo.
Chipstead La., Couls. 234 DB124
Chipstead La., Sev. 256 FC122
Chipstead La., Tad. 249 CZ125
Chipstead Pk., Sev. 256 FD122
Chipstead Pk. Clo., Sev. 256 FC122
Chipstead Pl. Gdns., Sev. 256 FC122
Chipstead Rd., Bans. 233 CZ117
Chipstead Rd., Erith 167 FE80
Chipstead Sta. Par., Couls. 234 DF118
Station App.
Chipstead St. SW6 160 DA81
Chipstead Valley Rd., Couls. 234 DG116
Chipstead Way, Bans. 234 DF115
Chirk Clo., Hayes 136 BY70
Braunston Dr.
Chirton Wk., Wok. 226 AU118
Shilburn Way
Chisenhale Rd. E3 143 DY68
Chisholm Rd., Croy. 202 DS103
Chisholm Rd., Rich. 178 CM86
Chisledon Wk. E9 143 DZ65
Osborne Rd.
Chislehurst Ave. N12 98 DC52
Chislehurst Rd., Brom. 204 EK96
Chislehurst Rd., Chis. 204 EK96
Chislehurst Rd., Orp. 205 ES98
Chislehurst Rd., Rich. 178 CL86
Chislehurst Rd., Sid. 186 EU92
Chislet Clo., Beck. 183 EA94
Abbey La.
Chisley Rd. N15 122 DS58
Chiswell Ct., Wat. 76 BW38
Chiswell Grn. La., St.Alb. 60 BX25
Chiswell Sq. SE3 164 EH82
Brook La.
Chiswell St. EC1 275 J6
Chiswell St. EC1 142 DQ71
Chiswick Bri. SW14 158 CQ82
Chiswick Bri. W4 158 CQ82
Chiswick Clo., Croy. 201 DM104
Chiswick Common Rd. W4 158 CR77
Chiswick Ct., Pnr. 116 BZ55
Chiswick High Rd. W4 158 CR77
Chiswick High Rd., Brent. 158 CM78
Chiswick Ho. Grds. W4 158 CR79
Chiswick La. W4 158 CS78
Chiswick La. S. W4 159 CT78
Chiswick Mall W4 159 CT79
Chiswick Mall W6 159 CT79
Chiswick Quay W4 158 CQ81
Chiswick Rd. N9 100 DU47
Chiswick Rd. W4 158 CQ77
Chiswick Roundabout W4 158 CN78
Chiswick High Rd.
Chiswick Sq. W4 158 CS79
Hogarth Roundabout
Chiswick Staithe W4 158 CQ81
Chiswick Ter. W4 158 CQ77
Acton La.
Chiswick Village W4 158 CP78
Chiswick Wf. W4 159 CT79
Chittenden Cotts., Wok. 228 BL116
Chitterfield Gate, West Dr. 154 BN80
Chitty St. W1 273 L6
Chitty St. W1 141 DJ71
Chittys Common, Guil. 242 AT130
Chitty's La., Dag. 126 EX61
Chittys Wk., Guil. 242 AT130
Chivalry Rd. SW11 180 DE85
Chivenor Gro., Kings.T. 177 CK92
Chivers Rd. E4 101 EB48
Choats Manor Way, Bark. 146 EW70
Choats Rd., Bark. 146 EW68
Choats Rd., Dag. 146 EY69
Chobham Clo., Cher. 211 BB107
Chobham Gdns. SW19 179 CX89
Chobham La., Wok. 192 AT104
Chobham Pk. La., Wok. 210 AU110
Chobham Rd. E15 123 ED64
Chobham Rd., Cher. 211 BA108
Chobham Rd., Wok. 226 AY116
Chobham Rd. (Horsell), Wok. 210 AW113
Choir Grn., Wok. 226 AS117
Semper Clo.
Cholmeley Cres. N6 121 DH59
Cholmeley Pk. N6 121 DH60
Cholmley Gdns. NW6 120 DA64
Fortune Grn. Rd.
Cholmley Rd., T.Ditt. 197 CH100
Cholmondeley Ave. NW10 139 CU68
Cholmondeley Wk., Rich. 177 CJ85
Choppins Ct. E1 142 DV74
Wapping La.
Chopwell Clo. E15 143 ED66
Bryant St.
Chorleywood Bottom, Rick. 73 BD43
Chorleywood Clo., Rick. 92 BK45
Nightingale Rd.
Chorleywood Cres., Orp. 205 ET96
Chorleywood Lo. La., Rick. 73 BF41
Rickmansworth Rd.
Chorleywood Rd., Rick. 74 BK44
Choumert Gro. SE15 162 DU82
Choumert Rd. SE15 162 DT83
Choumert Sq. SE15 162 DU82
Chow Sq. E8 122 DT64
Arcola St.
Chrislaine Clo. (Stanwell), Stai. 174 BK86
High St.
Chrisp St. E14 143 EB71
Christ Ch. Mt., Epsom 216 CP112
Christ Ch. Pas. EC1 274 G8
Christ Ch. Path, Hayes 155 BQ76
Christ Ch. Rd., Beck. 203 EA96
Fairfield Rd.
Christ Ch. Rd., Epsom 216 CL112
Christ Ch. Rd., Surb. 198 CM100
Christchurch Ave. N12 98 DC51
Christchurch Ave. NW6 139 CY66
Christchurch Ave., Erith 167 FD79
Christchurch Ave., Har. 117 CH56
Christchurch Ave., Rain. 147 FF68
Christchurch Ave., Tedd. 177 CG92
Christchurch Ave., Wem. 138 CL65
Christchurch Clo. SW19 180 DD94
Christchurch Clo., Enf. 82 DQ40
Christchurch Clo., St.Alb. 42 CC19
Christchurch Cres., Grav. 191 GJ87
Christchurch Rd.
Christchurch Cres., Rad. 77 CG36
Christchurch Gdns., Epsom 216 CP111
Christchurch Gdns., Har. 117 CG56
Christchurch Grn., Wem. 138 CL65
Christchurch Hill NW3 120 DD62
Christchurch La., Barn. 79 CY40
Christchurch Pk., Sutt. 218 DC108
Christchurch Pas. NW3 120 DC62
Christchurch Pas., Barn. 79 CY41
Christchurch Pl., Epsom 216 CP111
Christchurch Rd. N8 121 DL58
Christchurch Rd. SW2 181 DM88
Christchurch Rd. SW14 178 CP85
Christchurch Rd. SW19 180 DD94
Christchurch Rd., Dart. 188 FJ86
Christchurch Rd., Grav. 191 GJ88
Christchurch Rd., Hem.H. 40 BK19
Christchurch Rd., Houns. 154 BN83
Courtney Rd.
Christchurch Rd., Ilf. 125 EP60
Christchurch Rd., Pur. 219 DP110
Christchurch Rd., Sid. 185 ET91
Christchurch Rd., Til. 171 GG81
Christchurch Rd., Vir.W. 192 AU97
Christchurch Sq. E9 142 DW67
Victoria Pk. Rd.
Christchurch St. SW3 160 DF79
Christchurch Ter. SW3 160 DF79
Christchurch St.
Christchurch Way SE10 164 EE77
Christchurch Way, Wok. 227 AZ117
Church St. E.
Christian Ct. SE16 143 DZ74
Christian Flds. SW16 181 DN94
Christian Flds. Ave., Grav. 191 GJ91
Christian Sq., Wind. 151 AQ81
Alma Rd.
Christian St. E1 142 DU72
Christie Clo., Brox. 49 DZ21
Christie Dr., Croy. 202 DU99
Christie Gdns., Rom. 126 EV58
Christie Rd. E9 143 DY65
Christie Wk., Cat. 236 DQ121
Coulsdon Rd.
Christies Ave., Sev. 224 FA110
Christina Sq. N4 121 DP60
Adolphus Rd.
Christina St. EC2 275 M4
Christine Worsley Clo. N21 99 DP47
Highfield Rd.
Christmas La., Slou. 111 AQ62
Christopher Ave. W7 157 CG76
Christopher Clo. SE16 163 DX75
Christopher Clo., Horn. 128 FK63
Chevington Way
Christopher Clo., Sid. 185 ET85
Christopher Clo., Tad. 233 CW123
High St.
Christopher Ct., Hem.H. 40 BK23
Seaton Rd.
Christopher Ct., Tad. 233 CW123
Christopher Gdns., Dag. 126 EX64
Wren Rd.
Christopher Pl. NW1 273 N3
Christopher Pl., St.Alb. 43 CD20
Market Pl.
Christopher Rd., Sthl. 155 BV77
Christopher St. EC2 275 L5
Christopher St. EC2 142 DR70
Christopher's Ms. W11 139 CY74
Penzance St.
Christy Rd., West. 238 EJ115
Chryssell Rd. SW9 161 DN80
Chrystie La., Lthd. 246 CB126
Chubworthy St. SE14 163 DY79
Chucks La., Tad. 233 CV124
Chudleigh Cres., Ilf. 125 ES63
Chudleigh Gdns., Sutt. 200 DC104
Chudleigh Rd. NW6 139 CX66
Chudleigh Rd. SE4 183 DZ85
Chudleigh Rd., Rom. 106 FL49
Chudleigh Rd., Twick. 177 CE86
Chudleigh St. E1 143 DX72
Chudleigh Way, Ruis. 115 BU60
Chulsa Rd. SE26 182 DV92
Chumleigh St. SE5 162 DS79
Chumleigh Wk., Surb. 198 CM98
Church All., Croy. 201 DN102
Church All., Wat. 76 CC38
Church App. SE21 182 DR90
Church App., Egh. 193 BC97
Church App., Sev. 239 EQ115
Cudham La. S.
Church App., Stai. 174 BK86
Church Ave. E4 101 ED51
Church Ave. NW1 141 DH65
Kentish Town Rd.
Church Ave. SW14 158 CR83
Church Ave., Beck. 203 EA95
Church Ave., Nthlt. 136 BZ66
Church Ave., Pnr. 116 BY58
Church Ave., Ruis. 115 BR60
Church Ave., Sid. 186 EU92
Church Ave., Sthl. 156 BY76
Church Clo. N20 98 DE48
Church Clo. W8 160 DB75
Kensington Ch. St.
Church Clo., Add. 212 BH105
Church Clo., Edg. 96 CQ50
Church Clo., Hayes 135 BR71
Church Clo., Hert. 47 DJ19
Goddards Clo.
Church Clo., Lthd. 231 CD124
Church Clo., Loug. 85 EM40
Church Clo., Nthwd. 93 BT52
Church Clo. (Cuffley), Pot.B. 65 DL29
Church Clo., Rad. 77 CG36
Church Clo., Stai. 194 BJ97
The Bdy.
Church Clo., Tad. 249 CZ127
Buckland Rd.
Church Clo., Uxb. 134 BH68
Church Clo., West Dr. 154 BL76
Church Clo., Wind. 151 AR79
Church Clo., Wok. 226 AX116
Church Ct., Reig. 250 DB134
Church Ct., Rich. 177 CK85
George St.
Church Cres. E9 143 DX66
Church Cres. N3 97 CZ53
Church Cres. N10 121 DH56
Church Cres. N20 98 DE48
Church Cres., St.Alb. 42 CC19
Church Cres., Saw. 36 EZ05
Forebury Ave.
Church Cres., S.Ock. 149 FW69
Church Cft., St.Alb. 43 CJ23
Church Dr. NW9 118 CR60
Church Dr., Har. 116 BZ58
Church Dr., Maid. 150 AC75
Church Dr., W.Wick. 204 EE104
Church Elm La., Dag. 146 FA65
Church End E17 123 EB56
Church End NW4 119 CV55
Church End, Harl. 51 EN17
Church Entry EC4 274 G9
Church Fm. Clo., Swan. 207 FC100
Church Fm. La., Sutt. 217 CY107
Church Fm. Way, Wat. 76 CB38
Church Fld., Dart. 188 FK89
Church Fld., Epp. 70 EU29
Church Fld., Rad. 77 CG36
Church Fld., Sev. 256 FE122
Church Gdns. W5 157 CK75
Church Gdns., Dor. 263 CG135
Church Gdns., Wem. 117 CG63
Church Gate SW6 159 CY83
Church Grn., Hayes 135 BT72
Church Grn., St.Alb. 43 CD19
Hatfield Rd.
Church Grn., Walt. 214 BW107
Church Gro. SE13 163 EB84
Church Gro., Amer. 72 AY39
Church Gro., Kings.T. 197 CJ95
Church Gro., Slou. 132 AW71
Church Hill E17 123 EA56
Church Hill N21 99 DM45
Church Hill SE18 165 EM76
Church Hill SW19 179 CZ92
Church Hill, Abb.L. 59 BT26
Church Hill, Cars. 218 DF106
Church Hill, Cat. 236 DT124
Church Hill, Dart. 188 FK90
Church Hill (Crayford), Dart. 167 FE84
Church Hill, Epp. 70 EU30
Church Hill, Green. 189 FS85
Church Hill, Guil. 260 BN139
Church Hill, Har. 117 CE60
Church Hill, Hert. 32 DV11
Church Hill, Loug. 84 EL41
Church Hill, Orp. 206 EU101
Church Hill, Pur. 219 DL110
Church Hill (Merstham), Red. 251 DH126
Church Hill (Nutfield), Red. 251 DM133
Church Hill, Sev. 239 EQ115
Church Hill (Harefield), Uxb. 114 BJ55
Church Hill, Welw.G.C. 29 CU10
Church Hill, West. 238 EK122
Church Hill (Horsell), Wok. 226 AX116
Church Hill (Pyrford), Wok. 227 BF117
Church Hill Rd. E17 123 EB56
Church Hill Rd., Barn. 98 DF45
Church Hill Rd., Surb. 198 CL99
Church Hill Rd., Sutt. 217 CX105
Church Hill Wd., Orp. 205 ET99
Church Hollow, Purf. 168 FN78
Church Hyde SE18 165 ES79
Old Mill Rd.
Church Island, Stai. 173 BD91
Church La. E11 124 EE60
Church La. E17 123 EB56
Church La. N2 120 DD55
Church La. N8 121 DM56
Church La. N9 100 DU47
Church La. N17 100 DS53
Church La. NW9 118 CQ61
Church La. SW17 181 DH91
Church La. SW19 199 CZ95
Church La. W5 157 CJ75
Church La. (Nork), Bans. 233 CX117
Reigate Rd.
Church La., Berk. 38 AW19
Church La., B.Stort. 37 FD07
Church La. (Doddinghurst), Brwd. 129 FW58
Church La. (Hutton), Brwd. 109 GE46
Church La., Brom. 204 EL102
Church La., Brox. 48 DV21
Church La., Cat. 235 DN123
Church La., Chess. 216 CM107
Church La., Chis. 205 EQ95
Church La., Couls. 234 DG122
Church La., Dag. 147 FB65
Church La., Enf. 82 DR41
Church La., Epp. 71 FB27
Church La., Epsom 233 CX117
Reigate Rd.
Church La. (Headley), Epsom 232 CQ124
Church La., Ger.Cr. 90 AX53
Church La., Gdse. 253 DX132
Church La., Guil. 260 BH139
Church La. (Worplesdon), Guil. 242 AS127
Church La., Har. 95 CF53
Church La., Hat. 45 CW18
Church La., Hem.H. 57 BB27
Church La., Hert. 47 DM17
Church La., Horl. 269 DL153
Church La., Kings L. 58 BN29
Church La., Loug. 85 EM41
Church La., Maid. 150 AC75
Church La., Oxt. 253 ED130
Church La., Pnr. 116 BY55
Church La., Pot.B. 64 DG30
Church La., Purf. 168 FN78
London Rd. Purfleet
Church La. (Wennington), Rain. 148 FK72
Church La., Red. 252 DR133
Church La., Rich. 178 CL88
Church La. (Mill End), Rick. 92 BG46
Church La. (Sarratt), Rick. 73 BF38
Church La., Rom. 127 FE56
Church La. (Abridge), Rom. 86 EY40
Church La. (Stapleford Abbotts), Rom. 87 FC42
Church La., St.Alb. 44 CP22
Church La. (Stoke Poges), Slou. 132 AT70
Church La. (Wexham), Slou. 132 AV70
Church La., Tedd. 177 CF92
Church La., T.Ditt. 197 CF100
Church La., Twick. 177 CG88
Church La., Upmin. 129 FV64
Church La., Uxb. 134 BH68
Church La., Wall. 201 DK104
Church La. (Cheshunt), Wal.Cr. 66 DW29
Church La., Warl. 237 DX117
Church La. (Chelsham), Warl. 237 EB117
Church La., Wat. 76 CB38
Church La., West. 238 EK122
Church La., Wind. 151 AR81
Church La. (Send), Wok. 243 BB126
Church La. Ave., Couls. 235 DH122
Church La. Dr., Couls. 235 DH122
Church Langley Way, Harl. 52 EW15
Church Leys, Harl. 51 ET16
Church Manor Est. SW9 161 DN80
Vassall Rd.
Church Manorway SE2 165 ET77
Church Manorway, Erith 167 FD76
Church Mead, Harl. 34 EH14
Church Meadow, Surb. 197 CJ103
Church Ms., Ware 33 DX06
Church St.
Church Mill Gra., Harl. 36 EY11
Church Mt. N2 120 DD57
Church Paddock Ct., Wall. 201 DK104
Church Pas. EC2 142 DQ72
Gresham St.
Church Pas., Barn. 79 CZ42
Wood St.
Church Pas., Surb. 198 CL99
Church Path E11 124 EG57
Church Path E17 123 EB56
St. Mary Rd.
Church Path N12 98 DC50
Church Path N17 100 DS52
White Hart La.
Church Path N20 98 DC49
Church Path NW10 138 CS66
Church Path SW14 158 CR83
Church Path SW19 200 DA96
Church Path W4 158 CQ76
Church Path W7 136 CA74
Church Path, Cob. 213 BU114
Church Path, Couls. 235 DN118
Canon's Hill
Church Path, Croy. 202 DQ103
Church Path, Grav. 190 GC86
Church Path, Grays 170 GA79
Church Path, Green. 189 FT86
London Rd.
Church Path, Maid. 150 AC75
Church Path, Mitch. 200 DE97
Church Path, Sthl. 156 BZ76
Church Path, Ware 33 DZ09
Church Path, Wok. 227 AZ117
High St.
Church Pl. SW1 277 L1
Church Pl. W5 157 CK75
Church Gdns.
Church Pl., Mitch. 200 DE97
Church Pl., Twick. 177 CH88
Church St.
Church Pl. (Ickenham), Uxb. 115 BQ62
Church Ri. SE23 183 DX88
Church Ri., Chess. 216 CM107
Church Rd. E10 123 EB61
Church Rd. E12 124 EL64
Church Rd. E17 101 DY54
Church Rd. N6 120 DG58
Church Rd. N17 100 DS53
Church Rd. NW4 119 CV56
Church Rd. NW10 138 CS65
Church Rd. SE19 202 DS95
Church Rd. SW13 159 CT82
Church Rd. (Wimbledon) SW19 179 CY91
Church Rd. W3 138 CQ74
Church Rd. W7 137 CF74
Church Rd., Add. 212 BG106
Church Rd., Ashf. 174 BM90
Church Rd., Ash. 231 CK117
Church Rd., Bark. 145 EQ65
Church Rd., Beac. 89 AR51
Church Rd., Berk. 39 BB16
Church Rd., Bexh. 166 EZ82
Church Rd., B.End 110 AD62
Church Rd., Brom. 204 EG96
Church Rd. (Shortlands), Brom. 204 EE97
Church Rd., Buck.H. 102 EH46
Church Rd., Cat. 236 DT123
Church Rd. (Woldingham), Cat. 237 DX122
Church Rd., Craw. 268 DE154
Church Rd., Croy. 201 DP104
Church Rd. (Sutton at Hone), Dart. 188 FL94
Church Rd., E.Mol. 197 CD98
Church Rd., Egh. 173 AZ92
Church Rd., Enf. 82 DW44
Church Rd., Epsom 216 CS112
Church Rd. (West Ewell), Epsom 216 CR108
Church Rd., Erith 167 FD78
Church Rd., Esher 215 CF107
Church Rd., Felt. 176 BX92
Church Rd., Grav. 191 GJ94
Church Rd., Green. 189 FS85
Church Rd., Guil. 258 AX135
Church Rd., Harl. 52 EW18
Church Rd., Hayes 135 BT72
Church Rd., Hem.H. 41 BQ21
Church Rd., Hert. 32 DQ08
Church Rd. (Little Berkhamsted), Hert. 47 DJ19
Church Rd. (Penn), H.Wyc. 88 AD47
Church Rd., Horl. 268 DF149
Church Rd. (Smallfield), Horl. 269 DN152
Church Rd. (Cranford), Houns. 155 BV78
Church Rd. (Heston), Houns. 156 CA80
Church Rd., Ilf. 125 ES58
Church Rd., Islw. 157 CD81
Church Rd., Iver 133 BC69
Church Rd., Ken. 236 DR115
Church Rd., Kes. 222 EK108
Church Rd., Kings.T. 198 CM96
Church Rd., Lthd. 231 CH122
Church Rd. (Great Bookham), Lthd. 230 BZ123
Church Rd., Loug. 84 EH40
Church Rd., Mitch. 200 DD96
Church Rd., Nthlt. 136 BZ66
Church Rd., Nthwd. 93 BT52
Church Rd. (Chelsfield), Orp. 224 EW108
Church Rd. (Farnborough), Orp. 223 EQ106
Church Rd., Pot.B. 64 DB30
Church Rd., Pur. 219 DL110
Church Rd., Red. 266 DE136
Church Rd., Reig. 266 DA136
Church Rd., Rich. 178 CL85
Church Rd. (Ham), Rich. 178 CM92
Church Rd. (Harold Wd.), Rom. 106 FN53
Church Rd. (Havering-atte-Bower), Rom. 106 FJ46
Church Rd. (Halstead), Sev. 224 EY111
Church Rd. (Seal), Sev. 257 FM121
Church Rd., Shep. 195 BP101
Church Rd., Sid. 186 EU91
Church Rd., Slou. 131 AQ69
Church Rd., Sthl. 156 BZ76
Church Rd., Stan. 95 CH50
Church Rd., Surb. 197 CJ102
Church Rd., Sutt. 217 CY107
Church Rd., Swan. 208 FK95
Church Rd. (Crockenhill), Swan. 207 FD101
Church Rd., Swans. 190 FZ86
Church Rd., Tedd. 177 CE91
Church Rd., Til. 171 GF81
Church Rd. (West Tilbury), Til. 171 GL79
Church Rd. (Cowley), Uxb. 134 BK70

Col - Coo This index reads in the sequence: Street Name / Postal District or Post Town / Map Page Number / Grid Reference

Columbia Ctyd. E14 143 EA74
West India Ave.
Columbia Rd. E2 275 P2
Columbia Rd. E2 142 DT69
Columbia Rd. E13 144 EF70
Columbia Sq. SW14 158 CQ84
Upper Richmond Rd. W.
Columbia Wf. Rd., Grays 170 GA79
Columbine Ave. E6 144 EL71
Columbine Ave., S.Croy. 219 DP108
Columbine Way SE13 163 EC82
Columbine Way, Rom. 106 FL53
Columbus Ct. SE16 142 DW74
Rotherhithe St.
Columbus Gdns., Nthwd. 93 BU53
Columbus Sq., Erith 167 FF79
Colva Wk. N19 121 DH61
Chester Rd.
Colvestone Cres. E8 122 DT64
Colview Ct. SE9 184 EK88
Mottingham La.
Colville Est. N1 142 DS67
Colville Gdns. W11 139 CZ72
Colville Hos. W11 139 CZ72
Colville Ms. W11 139 CZ72
Lonsdale Rd.
Colville Pl. W1 273 L7
Colville Rd. E11 123 EC62
Colville Rd. E17 101 DY54
Colville Rd. N9 100 DV46
Colville Rd. W3 158 CP76
Colville Rd. W11 139 CZ72
Colville Sq. W11 139 CZ72
Colville Sq. Ms. W11 139 CZ72
Portobello Rd.
Colville Ter. W11 139 CZ72
Colvin Clo. SE26 182 DW92
Colvin Gdns. E4 101 EC48
Colvin Gdns. E11 124 EH56
Colvin Gdns., Ilf. 103 EQ53
Colvin Gdns., Wal.Cr. 83 DX35
Colvin Rd. E6 144 EL66
Colvin Rd., Th.Hth. 201 DN99
Colwall Gdns., Wdf.Grn. 102 EG50
Colwell Rd. SE22 182 DT85
Colwick Clo. N6 121 DK59
Colwith Rd. W6 159 CW79
Colwood Gdns. SW19 180 DD94
Colworth Gro. SE17 279 J9
Colworth Rd. E11 124 EE58
Colworth Rd., Croy. 202 DU102
Colwyn Ave., Grnf. 137 CF68
Colwyn Clo. SW16 181 DJ92
Colwyn Cres., Houns. 156 CC81
Colwyn Grn. NW9 118 CS58
Snowdon Dr.
Colwyn Rd. NW2 119 CV62
Colyer Clo. N1 141 DM68
Colyer Clo. SE9 185 EP89
Colyer Rd., Grav. 190 GC89
Colyers Clo., Erith 167 FD81
Colyers La., Erith 167 FC81
Colyers Wk., Erith 167 FE81
Colyers La.
Colyton Clo., Well. 166 EX81
Colyton Clo., Wem. 137 CJ65
Bridgewater Rd.
Colyton Clo., Wok. 226 AW118
Colyton Rd. SE22 182 DV85
Colyton Way N18 100 DU50
Combe Ave. SE3 164 EF80
Combe Bank Dr., Sev. 240 EY122
Combe La., Guil. 260 BM138
Combe La., Walt. 213 BT109
Combe Lo. SE7 164 EJ79
Elliscombe Rd.
Combe Martin, Kings.T. 178 CQ92
Combe Ms. SE3 164 EF80
Combe Rd., Gdmg. 258 AT143
Combe Rd., Wat. 75 BT44
Combe St., Hem.H. 40 BJ20
Combedale Rd. SE10 164 EG78
Combemartin Rd. SW18 179 CY87
Comber Clo. NW2 119 CV62
Comber Gro. SE5 162 DQ81
Combermere Rd. SW9 161 DM83
Combermere Rd., Mord. 200 DB100
Comberton Rd. E5 122 DV61
Combeside SE18 165 ET80
Combwell Cres. SE2 166 EU76
Comely Bank Rd. E17 123 EC57
Comer Cres., Sthl. 156 CC75
Windmill Ave.
Comeragh Clo., Wok. 226 AU119
Comeragh Ms. W14 159 CY78
Comeragh Rd. W14 159 CY78
Comerford Rd. SE4 163 DY84
Comet Clo. E12 124 EK63
Comet Clo., Purf. 168 FN77
Comet Clo., Wat. 59 BT34
Comet Pl. SE8 163 EA80
Comet Rd., Hat. 45 CT17
Comet Rd., Stai. 174 BK87
Comet St. SE8 163 EA80
Comet Way, Hat. 44 CS19
Comforts Fm. Ave., Oxt. 254 EF133
Comfrey Ct., Grays 170 GD79
Commerce Rd. N22 99 DM53
Commerce Rd., Brent. 157 CJ80
Commerce Way, Croy. 201 DM103
Commercial Pl., Grav. 191 GJ86
Commercial Rd. E1 142 DU72
Commercial Rd. E14 142 DW72
Commercial Rd. N17 100 DS51
Commercial Rd. N18 100 DS50
Commercial Rd., Guil. 258 AX135
Commercial Rd., Stai. 174 BG93
Commercial St. E1 275 P5
Commercial St. E1 142 DT70
Commercial Way NW10 138 CP68
Commercial Way SE15 162 DT80
Commercial Way, Wok. 226 AY117
Commerell St. SE10 164 EE78
Commodity Quay E1 142 DT73
East Smithfield
Commodore Sq. SW10 160 DD81
Commodore St. E1 143 DY70
Common, The W5 138 CL73
Common, The, Berk. 39 AZ17
Common, The, Guil. 258 AY141
Common, The (Wonersh), Guil. 259 BB143
Common, The, Hat. 45 CU17
Common, The, Kings L. 58 BG32
Common, The, Rich. 177 CK90
Common, The, Sthl. 156 BW77
Common, The, Stan. 95 CE47
Common, The, West Dr. 154 BJ77
Common Clo., Wok. 210 AX114
Common Gate Rd., Rick. 73 BD43
Common Grn., Berk. 39 BB17
Common La., Add. 212 BJ109
Common La., Dart. 187 FG89
Common La., Esher 215 CG108
Common La., Kings L. 58 BM28
Common La., Rad. 77 CE39
Common La., Slou. 111 AK62
Common La., Wat. 77 CE39
Common La. (Eton), Wind. 151 AR78
Common Rd. SW13 159 CU83
Common Rd., Brwd. 109 GC50
Common Rd., Esher 215 CG107
Common Rd., Lthd. 230 BY121
Common Rd., Red. 266 DF136
Common Rd., Rick. 73 BD42
Common Rd., Slou. 110 AH61
Common Rd. (Langley), Slou. 153 BA77
Common Rd., Stan. 95 CD49
Common Rd., Wal.Abb. 50 EL21
Common Rd., Wind. 150 AJ77
Common Rd. (Eton Wick), Wind. 151 AN77
Common Wd., Slou. 111 AQ63
Common Wd. La., H.Wyc. 88 AD46
Commondale SW15 159 CW83
Commonfield La. SW17 180 DE92
Tooting Gro.
Commonfield Rd., Bans. 218 DA114
Commonfields, Harl. 35 ES14
Commonmeadow La., Wat. 60 CB33
Commons, The, Welw.G.C. 30 DA12
Commons La., Hem.H. 40 BL19
Commonside, Epsom 232 CN115
Commonside, Harl. 51 ES19
Fern Hill La.
Commonside, Kes. 222 EJ105
Commonside, Lthd. 230 CA122
Commonside Clo., Couls. 235 DP120
Coulsdon Rd.
Commonside Clo., Sutt. 218 DB111
Downs Rd.
Commonside E., Mitch. 200 DF97
Commonside Rd., Harl. 51 ES19
Commonside W., Mitch. 200 DF97
Commonwealth Ave. W12 139 CV73
Commonwealth Ave., Hayes 135 BR72
Commonwealth Rd. N17 100 DU52
Commonwealth Rd., Cat. 236 DU123
Commonwealth Way SE2 166 EV78
Commonwood La., Kings L. 74 BH35
Community Clo., Houns. 155 BV81
Community Clo., Uxb. 115 BQ62
Community La. N7 121 DK64
Community Rd. E15 123 ED64
Community Rd., Grnf. 136 CC67
Community Way, Rick. 75 BP43
Barton Way
Como Rd. SE23 183 DY89
Como St., Rom. 127 FD57
Compass Hill, Rich. 177 CK86
Compayne Gdns. NW6 140 DB66
Comport Grn., Croy. 222 EE112
Compton Ave. E6 144 EK68
Compton Ave. N1 141 DP65
Compton Ave. N6 120 DE59
Compton Ave., Brwd. 109 GC46
Compton Ave., Rom. 127 FH55
Compton Clo. E3 143 EA71
Compton Clo. NW1 273 J3
Compton Clo. NW11 119 CX62
The Vale
Compton Clo. W13 137 CG72
Compton Clo., Edg. 96 CQ52
Pavilion Way
Compton Clo., Esher 214 CC106
Compton Ct. SE19 182 DS92
Victoria Cres.
Compton Ct., Slou. 131 AL72
Brook Cres.
Compton Cres. N17 100 DQ52
Compton Cres. W4 158 CQ79
Compton Cres., Chess. 216 CL107
Compton Cres., Nthlt. 136 BX67
Compton Gdns., Add. 212 BH106
Monks Cres.
Compton Gdns., St.Alb. 60 CB26
Compton Pas. EC1 274 G4
Compton Pl. WC1 273 P4
Compton Pl., Erith 167 FF79
Compton Pl., Wat. 94 BY48
Compton Ri., Pnr. 116 BY57
Compton Rd. N1 141 DP65
Compton Rd. N21 99 DN46
Compton Rd. NW10 139 CX69
Compton Rd. SW19 179 CZ93
Compton Rd., Croy. 202 DV102
Compton Rd., Hayes 135 BS73
Compton St. EC1 274 F4
Compton St. EC1 141 DP70
Compton Ter. N1 141 DP65
Comreddy Clo., Enf. 81 DP39
Comus Pl. SE17 279 M9
Comus Pl. SE17 162 DS77
Comyn Rd. SW11 160 DE84
Comyne Rd., Wat. 75 BT36
Comyns, The (Bushey), Wat. 94 CC46
Comyns Clo. E16 144 EF71
Comyns Rd., Dag. 146 FA66
Conant Ms. E1 142 DU73
Back Ch. La.
Conaways Clo., Epsom 217 CU110
Concanon Rd. SW2 161 DM84
Concert Hall App. SE1 278 C3
Concert Hall App. SE1 141 DM74
Concord Clo., Nthlt. 136 BX69
Britannia Clo.
Concord Rd. W3 138 CP70
Concord Rd., Enf. 82 DW43
Concorde Clo., Houns. 156 CB82
Lampton Rd.
Concorde Clo., Uxb. 134 BL68
Concorde Dr. E6 145 EM71
Concorde Dr., Hem.H. 40 BK20
Concorde Way, Slou. 151 AQ75
Concourse, The N9 100 DU47
New Rd.
Concourse, The NW9 97 CT53
Condell Rd. SW8 161 DJ81
Conder St. E14 143 DY72
Salmon La.
Conderton Rd. SE5 162 DQ83
Condor Ct., Guil. 258 AW136
Millmead Ter.
Condor Path, Nthlt. 136 CA68
Brabazon Rd.
Condor Rd., Stai. 194 BH97
Condor Wk., Horn. 147 FH66
Heron Flight Ave.
Condover Cres. SE18 165 EP80
Condray Pl. SW11 160 DE80
Conduit, The, Red. 252 DR129
Conduit Ave. SE10 163 ED81
Crooms Hill
Conduit Ct. WC2 273 P10
Conduit La. N18 100 DW50
Conduit La., Croy. 220 DU106
Conduit La., Enf. 83 DY44
Morson Rd.
Conduit La., Slou. 152 AY78
Conduit La., S.Croy. 220 DU106
Conduit La. E., Hodd. 49 EB17
Conduit La. W., Hodd. 49 EA17
Conduit Ms. W2 140 DD72
Conduit Pas. W2 140 DD72
Conduit Pl.
Conduit Pl. W2 140 DD72
Conduit Rd. SE18 165 EP78
Conduit Rd., Slou. 152 AY78
Conduit St. W1 273 J10
Conduit St. W1 141 DH73
Conduit Way NW10 138 CQ66
Conegar Ct., Slou. 132 AS74
Conewood St. N5 121 DP62
Coney Acre SE21 182 DQ88
Coney Burrows E4 102 EE47
Wyemead Cres.
Coney Clo., Hat. 45 CV19
Coney Gro., Uxb. 134 BN69
Coney Hill Rd., W.Wick. 204 EE103
Coney Way SW8 161 DM79
Coneyberry, Reig. 266 DD138
Coneybury, Red. 252 DS134
Coneybury Clo., Warl. 236 DV119
Coneydale, Welw.G.C. 29 CX07
Coneygrove Path, Nthlt. 136 BY65
Arnold Rd.
Conference Clo. E4 101 EC47
Greenbank Clo.
Conference Rd. SE2 166 EW77
Conford Dr., Guil. 258 AY141
Congleton Gro. SE18 165 EQ78
Congo Rd. SE18 165 ER78
Congress Rd. SE2 166 EW77
Congreve Rd. SE9 165 EM83
Congreve Rd., Wal.Abb. 68 EE33
Congreve St. SE17 279 M8
Congreve St. SE17 162 DS77
Congreve Wk. E16 144 EK71
Conical Cor., Enf. 82 DQ40
Coniers Way, Guil. 243 BB131
Conifer Ave., Rom. 105 FB50
Conifer Clo., Orp. 223 ER105
Conifer Clo., Reig. 250 DA132
Conifer Clo., Wal.Cr. 66 DT29
Conifer Dr., Brwd. 108 FX50
Conifer Gdns. SW16 181 DL90
Conifer Gdns., Enf. 82 DS44
Conifer Gdns., Sutt. 200 DB103
Conifer La., Egh. 173 BC92
Conifer Way, Hayes 135 BU73
Longmead Rd.
Conifer Way, Swan. 207 FC95
Conifer Way, Wem. 117 CJ62
Conifers, Wey. 195 BS104
Conifers, The, Hem.H. 39 BF23
Conifers, The, Wat. 76 BW35
Conifers Clo., Tedd. 177 CJ94
Coniger Rd. SW6 160 DA82
Coningesby Dr., Wat. 75 BS39
Coningham Ms. W12 139 CU74
Percy Rd.
Coningham Rd. W12 139 CV74
Coningsby Bank, St.Alb. 42 CC24
Coningsby Clo., Hat. 45 CX24
Coningsby Cotts. W5 157 CK75
Coningsby Rd.
Coningsby Dr., Pot.B. 64 DD33
Coningsby Gdns. E4 101 EB51
Coningsby La., Maid. 150 AC81
Coningsby Rd. N4 121 DP59
Coningsby Rd. W5 157 CJ75
Coningsby Rd., S.Croy. 220 DQ109
Conington Rd. SE13 163 EB82
Conisbee Ct. N14 81 DJ43
Conisborough Cres. SE6 183 EC90
Coniscliffe Clo., Chis. 205 EN95
Coniscliffe Rd. N13 100 DQ48
Conista Ct., Wok. 226 AT116
Roundthorn Way
Coniston Ave., Bark. 145 ES66
Coniston Ave., Grnf. 137 CH69
Coniston Ave., Upmin. 128 FQ63
Coniston Ave., Well. 165 ES83
Coniston Clo. N20 98 DC48
Coniston Clo. SW13 159 CT80
Lonsdale Rd.
Coniston Clo. SW20 199 CX100
Coniston Clo. W4 158 CQ81
Coniston Clo., Bark. 145 ES66
Coniston Ave.
Coniston Clo., Bexh. 167 FC81
Coniston Clo., Dart. 187 FH88
Coniston Clo., Erith 167 FE80
Coniston Clo., Hem.H. 41 BQ21
Coniston Gdns. N9 100 DW46
Coniston Gdns. NW9 118 CR57
Coniston Gdns., Ilf. 124 EL56
Coniston Gdns., Pnr. 115 BU56
Coniston Gdns., Sutt. 218 DD107
Coniston Gdns., Wem. 117 CJ60
Coniston Ho. SE5 162 DQ80
Coniston Rd. N10 99 DH54
Coniston Rd. N17 100 DU51
Coniston Rd., Bexh. 167 FC81
Coniston Rd., Brom. 184 EE93
Coniston Rd., Couls. 235 DJ116
Coniston Rd., Croy. 202 DU101
Coniston Rd., Kings L. 58 BM28
Coniston Rd., Twick. 176 CB86
Coniston Rd., Wok. 227 BB120
Coniston Wk. E9 122 DW64
Clifden Rd.
Coniston Way, Chess. 198 CL104
Coniston Way, Egh. 173 BB94
Coniston Way, Horn. 127 FG64
Coniston Way, Reig. 250 DE133
Conistone Way N7 141 DL66
Conlan St. W10 139 CY70
Conley Rd. NW10 138 CS65
Conley St. SE10 164 EE78
Pelton Rd.
Connaught Ave. E4 101 ED45
Connaught Ave. SW14 158 CQ83
Connaught Ave., Ashf. 174 BL91
Connaught Ave., Barn. 98 DF46
Connaught Ave., Enf. 82 DS40
Connaught Ave., Grays 170 GB75
Connaught Ave., Houns. 176 BY85
Connaught Ave., Loug. 84 EK42
Connaught Bri. E16 144 EK73
Connaught Clo. E10 123 DY61
Connaught Clo. W2 272 B9
Connaught Clo., Enf. 82 DS40
Connaught Clo., Hem.H. 40 BN18
Connaught Clo., Sutt. 200 DD103
Connaught Clo., Uxb. 135 BQ70
New Rd.
Connaught Dr. NW11 120 DA56
Connaught Dr., Wey. 212 BN111
Connaught Gdns. N10 121 DH57
Connaught Gdns. N13 99 DP49
Connaught Gdns., Berk. 38 AT16
Connaught Gdns., Mord. 200 DC98
Connaught Hill, Loug. 84 EK42
Connaught La., Ilf. 125 ER61
Connaught Rd.
Connaught Ms. SE18 165 EN78
Connaught Ms. W2 272 D9
Connaught Ms., Ilf. 125 ER61
Connaught Rd.
Connaught Pl. W2 272 D10
Connaught Pl. W2 140 DF73
Connaught Rd. E4 102 EE45
Connaught Rd. E11 123 ED60
Connaught Rd. E16 144 EK74
Connaught Rd. E17 123 EA57
Connaught Rd. N4 121 DN59
Connaught Rd. NW10 138 CS67
Connaught Rd. SE18 165 EN78
Connaught Rd. W13 137 CH73
Connaught Rd., Barn. 79 CX44
Connaught Rd., Har. 95 CF53
Connaught Rd., Horn. 128 FK62
Connaught Rd., Ilf. 125 ER61
Connaught Rd., N.Mal. 198 CS98
Connaught Rd., Rich. 178 CM85
Albert Rd.
Connaught Rd., St.Alb. 42 CC18
Connaught Rd., Slou. 152 AV75
Connaught Rd., Sutt. 200 DD103
Connaught Rd., Tedd. 177 CD92
Connaught Roundabout E16 144 EK73
Connaught Bri.
Connaught Sq. W2 272 D9
Connaught Sq. W2 140 DF72
Connaught St. W2 272 B9
Connaught St. W2 140 DE72
Connaught Way N13 99 DP49
Connell Cres. W5 138 CM70
Connemara Clo., Borwd. 78 CR44
Percheron Rd.
Connicut La., Lthd. 246 CB128
Connington Cres. E4 101 ED48
Conniston Cres., Slou. 130 AJ71
Connop Rd., Enf. 83 DX38
Connor Rd., Dag. 126 EZ63
Connor St. E9 143 DX67
Lauriston Rd.
Conolly Rd. W7 137 CE74
Conquerors Hill, St.Alb. 28 CL07
Conquest Rd., Add. 212 BG106
Conrad Clo., Grays 170 GB75
Conrad Dr., Wor.Pk. 199 CW102
Conrad Gdns., Grays 170 GA75
Conrad Ho. N16 122 DS64
Cons St. SE1 278 E4
Consfield Ave., N.Mal. 199 CU98
Consort Clo., Brwd. 108 FW50
Consort Ms., Islw. 177 CD85
Consort Rd. SE15 162 DV81
Consort Way, Horl. 268 DG148
Consort Way, Uxb. 113 BF58
Consort Way E., Horl. 269 DH149
Constable Ave. E16 144 EH74
Wesley Ave.
Constable Clo. NW11 120 DB58
Constable Clo., Hayes 135 BQ69
Charville La.
Constable Cres. N15 122 DU57
Constable Gdns., Edg. 96 CN53
Constable Gdns., Islw. 177 CD85
Constable Ms., Dag. 126 EV63
Stonard Rd.
Constable Rd., Grav. 190 GE90
Constable Wk. SE21 182 DT90
Constance Cres., Brom. 204 EF101
Constance Rd., Croy. 201 DP101
Constance Rd., Enf. 82 DS44
Constance Rd., Sutt. 218 DC105
Constance Rd., Twick. 176 CB87
Constance St. E16 144 EL74
Albert Rd.
Constantine Pl., Uxb. 134 BM67
Vine La.
Constantine Rd. NW3 120 DE63
Constitution Hill SW1 277 H4
Constitution Hill SW1 161 DH75
Constitution Hill, Grav. 191 GJ88
Constitution Hill, Wok. 226 AY119
Constitution Ri. SE18 165 EN81
Consul Ave., Dag. 147 FC69
Consul Gdns., Swan. 187 FG93
Princes Rd.
Content St. SE17 279 J9
Content St. SE17 162 DR77
Contessa Clo., Orp. 223 ES106
Control Twr. Rd., Gat. 268 DD153
Control Twr. Rd., Houns. 154 BN83
Convair Wk., Nthlt. 136 BX69
Kittiwake Rd.
Convent Clo., Beck. 183 EC94
Convent Gdns. W5 157 CJ77
Convent Gdns. W11 139 CZ72
Kensington Pk. Rd.
Convent Hill SE19 182 DQ93
Convent La., Cob. 213 BS111
Seven Hills Rd.
Convent Rd., Ashf. 174 BN92
Convent Rd., Wind. 151 AN82
Convent Way, Sthl. 156 BW77
Conway Clo., H.Wyc. 88 AC53
Conway Clo., Rain. 147 FG66
Conway Clo., Stan. 95 CG51
Conway Cres., Grnf. 137 CE68
Conway Cres., Rom. 126 EW59
Conway Dr., Ashf. 175 BQ93
Conway Dr., Hayes 155 BQ76
Conway Dr., Sutt. 218 DB107
Conway Gdns., Enf. 82 DS38
Conway Gdns., Grays 170 GB80
Conway Gdns., Mitch. 201 DK98
Conway Gdns., Wem. 117 CJ59
Conway Gro. W3 138 CR71
Conway Ms. W1 273 K5
Conway Rd. N14 99 DL48
Conway Rd. N15 121 DP57
Conway Rd. NW2 119 CW61
Conway Rd. SE18 165 ER77
Conway Rd. SW20 199 CW95
Conway Rd., Felt. 176 BX92
Conway Rd., Houns. 176 BZ87
Conway Rd. (Heathrow Airport), Houns. 155 BP83
Inner Ring E.
Conway Rd., Maid. 130 AH72
Conway St. E13 144 EG70
Conway St. W1 273 K5
Conway St. W1 141 DJ71
Conway Wk., Hmptn. 176 BZ93
Fearnley Cres.
Conybeare NW3 140 DE66
King Henry's Rd.
Conybury Clo., Wal.Abb. 68 EG32
Conyer St. E3 143 DY68
Conyers, Harl. 35 EQ13
Conyers Clo., Walt. 214 BX106
Conyers Clo., Wdf.Grn. 102 EE51
Conyers Rd. SW16 181 DK92
Conyers Way, Loug. 85 EP41
Cooden Clo., Brom. 184 EH94
Plaistow La.
Cooderidge Clo. N17 100 DT51
Brantwood Rd.
Cook Ct. SE16 142 DW74
Rotherhithe St.
Cook Rd., Dag. 146 EY67
Cook Sq., Erith 167 FF80
Cooke Clo. E14 143 EA74
Cabot Sq.
Cookes Clo. E11 124 EF61
Cookes La., Sutt. 217 CY107
Cookham Clo., Sthl. 156 CB75
Cookham Cres. SE16 163 DX75
Marlow Way
Cookham Dene Clo., Chis. 205 ER95
Cookham Hill, Orp. 206 FA104
Cookham Rd., Sid. 206 FA95
Cookham Rd., Swan. 206 FA95
Cookhill Rd. SE2 166 EV75
Cooks Clo., Rom. 105 FC53
Cook's Hole Rd., Enf. 81 DP38
Cooks Mead (Bushey), Wat. 76 CB44
Cook's Rd. E15 143 EB68
Cooks Rd. SE17 161 DP79
Cooks Spinney, Harl. 36 EU13
Cooks Vennel, Hem.H. 40 BG18
Cooks Way, Hat. 45 CV20
Cookson Gro., Erith 167 FB80
Cool Oak La. NW9 118 CS59
Coolfin Rd. E16 144 EG72
Coolgardie Ave. E4 101 EC50
Coolgardie Ave., Chig. 103 EN48
Coolgardie Rd., Ashf. 175 BQ92
Coolhurst Rd. N8 121 DK58
Coomassie Rd. W9 139 CZ70
Bravington Rd.
Coombe, The, Bet. 248 CR131
Coombe Ave., Croy. 220 DS105
Coombe Ave., Sev. 241 FH120
Coombe Bank, Kings.T. 198 CS95
Coombe Clo., Edg. 96 CM54
Coombe Clo., Houns. 156 CA84
Coombe Cor. N21 99 DP46
Coombe Cres., Hmptn. 176 BY94
Coombe Dr., Add. 211 BF107
Coombe Dr., Kings.T. 178 CR94
Coombe Dr., Ruis. 115 BV60
Coombe End, Kings.T. 178 CR94
Coombe Gdns. SW20 199 CU96
Coombe Gdns., Berk. 38 AT18
Coombe Gdns., N.Mal. 199 CT98
Coombe Hts., Kings.T. 178 CS94
Coombe Hill Ct., Wind. 151 AL83
Coombe Hill Glade, Kings.T. 178 CS94
Coombe Hill Rd., Kings.T. 178 CS94
Coombe Hill Rd., Rick. 92 BG45
Coombe Ho. Chase, N.Mal. 198 CR95
Coombe La. SW20 199 CV96
Coombe La., Croy. 220 DV106
Coombe La. W., Kings.T. 199 CU95
Coombe Lea, Brom. 204 EL97
Coombe Neville, Kings.T. 178 CR94
Coombe Pk., Kings.T. 178 CR92
Coombe Ridings, Kings.T. 178 CQ92
Coombe Ri., Brwd. 109 FZ46
Coombe Ri., Kings.T. 198 CQ95
Coombe Rd. N22 99 DN53
Coombe Rd. NW10 118 CR62
Coombe Rd. SE26 182 DV91
Coombe Rd. W4 158 CS78
Coombe Rd. W13 157 CH76
Northcroft Rd.
Coombe Rd., Croy. 220 DR105
Coombe Rd., Grav. 191 GJ89
Coombe Rd., Hmptn. 176 BZ93
Coombe Rd., Kings.T. 198 CN95
Coombe Rd., N.Mal. 198 CS96
Coombe Rd., Rom. 128 FM55
Coombe Rd. (Bushey), Wat. 94 CC45
Coombe Vale, Ger.Cr. 112 AY60
Coombe Wk., Sutt. 200 DB104
Coombe Way, W.Byf. 212 BM112
Coombe Wd. Hill, Pur. 220 DQ112
Coombe Wd. Rd., Kings.T. 178 CQ92
Coombefield Clo., N.Mal. 198 CS99
Coombehurst Clo., Barn. 80 DF40
Coombelands La., Add. 212 BG107
Coomber Way, Croy. 201 DK101
Coombermere Clo., Wind. 151 AP82
Coombes Rd., Dag. 146 EZ67
Coombes Rd., St.Alb. 61 CJ26
Coombewood Dr., Rom. 126 EZ58
Coombfield Dr., Dart. 189 FR91
Coombs St. N1 274 G1
Coombs St. N1 141 DP68
Coomer Ms. SW6 159 CZ79
Coomer Pl.

Coomer Pl. SW6 159 CZ79
Coomer Rd. SW6 159 CZ79
Coomer Pl.
Cooms Wk., Edg. 96 CQ53
East Rd.
Cooper Ave. E17 101 DX53
Cooper Clo. SE1 278 E5
Cooper Clo., Green. 189 FS85
Cooper Clo., Horl. 269 DN148
Cooper Ct. E15 123 EB64
Clays La.
Cooper Cres., Cars. 200 DF104
Cooper Rd. NW4 119 CX58
Cooper Rd. NW10 119 CU64
Cooper Rd., Croy. 219 DN105
Cooper Rd., Guil. 258 AY136
Cooper St. E16 144 EF71
Lawrence St.
Cooper Way, Slou. 151 AP76
Cooperage Clo. N17 100 DT51
Brantwood Rd.
Coopers Clo. E1 142 DW70
Coopers Clo., Chig. 104 EV47
Coopers Clo., Dag. 147 FB65
Coopers Clo. 209 FR95
(South Darenth), Dart.
Coopers Clo., Stai. 173 BE92
Coopers Cres., Borwd. 78 CQ39
Coopers Grn. La., Hat. 28 CR14
Coopers Grn. La., St.Alb. 44 CL17
Coopers Grn. La., 29 CU12
Welw.G.C.
Coopers Hill La., Egh. 172 AW90
Coopers Hill Rd., Red. 251 DM133
Coopers La. E10 123 EB60
Coopers La. NW1 141 DK68
Cooper's La. SE12 184 EH89
Coopers La., Pot.B. 64 DD31
Coopers La. Rd., Pot.B. 64 DE31
Coopers Rd. SE1 162 DT78
Coopers Rd., Grav. 190 GE88
Coopers Rd., Pot.B. 64 DC30
Cooper's Row EC3 275 P10
Coopers Row, Iver 133 BD70
Coopers Shaw Rd., Til. 171 GK80
Coopers Wk. E15 123 ED64
Maryland St.
Coopers Wk. (Cheshunt), 67 DX28
Wal.Cr.
Cooper's Yd. SE19 182 DS93
Westow Hill
Coopersale Clo., Wdf.Grn. 102 EJ52
Navestock Cres.
Coopersale Common, Epp. 70 EX28
Coopersale La., Epp. 86 EU37
Coopersale Rd. E9 123 DX64
Coopersale St., Epp. 70 EW32
Coote Gdns., Dag. 126 EZ62
Coote Rd., Bexh. 166 EZ81
Coote Rd., Dag. 126 EZ62
Cope Pl. W8 160 DA76
Cope St. SE16 163 DX77
Copeland Dr. E14 163 EA77
Copeland Rd. E17 123 EB57
Copeland Rd. SE15 162 DU82
Copeman Clo. SE26 182 DW92
Copeman Rd., Brwd. 109 GD45
Copenhagen Gdns. W4 158 CQ75
Copenhagen Pl. E14 143 DZ72
Copenhagen St. N1 141 DL67
Copenhagen Way, Walt. 195 BV104
Copers Cope Rd., Beck. 183 DZ93
Copford Clo., Wdf.Grn. 102 EL51
Copford Wk. N1 142 DQ67
Popham St.
Copgate Path SW16 181 DM93
Copinger Wk., Edg. 96 CP53
North Rd.
Copland Ave., Wem. 117 CK64
Copland Clo., Wem. 117 CJ64
Copland Ms., Wem. 138 CL65
Copland Rd.
Copland Rd., Wem. 138 CL65
Copleigh Dr., Tad. 233 CY120
Copleston Ms. SE15 162 DT82
Copleston Rd.
Copleston Pas. SE15 162 DT83
Copleston Rd. SE15 162 DT83
Copley Clo. SE17 161 DP79
Hillingdon St.
Copley Clo. W7 137 CF71
Copley Clo., Red. 250 DE132
Copley Clo., Wok. 226 AS119
Copley Dene, Brom. 204 EK95
Copley Pk. SW16 181 DM93
Copley Rd., Stan. 95 CJ50
Copley St. E1 143 DX71
Stepney Grn.
Copley Way, Tad. 233 CX120
Copmans Wick, Rick. 73 BD43
Copnor Way SE15 162 DS80
Diamond St.
Coppard Gdns., Chess. 215 CJ107
Copped Hall SE21 182 DR89
Glazebrook Clo.
Coppelia Rd. SE3 164 EF84
Coppen Rd., Dag. 126 EZ59
Copper Beech Clo. NW3 140 DD65
Daleham Ms.
Copper Beech Clo., Grav. 191 GK87
Copper Beech Clo., Hem.H. 39 BF23
Copper Beech Clo., Ilf. 103 EN53
Copper Beech Clo., Orp. 206 EW99
Rookery Gdns.
Copper Beech Clo., Wind. 151 AK81
Copper Beech Clo., Wok. 226 AV121
Copper Beech Ct., Loug. 85 EN39
Copper Beech Rd., S.Ock. 149 FW69
Copper Beeches, Islw. 157 CD81
Eversley Cres.
Copper Clo. SE19 182 DT94
Auckland Rd.
Copper Mead Clo. NW2 119 CW62
Copper Mill Dr., Islw. 157 CF82
Copper Mill La. SW17 180 DC91
Copper Ridge, Ger.Cr. 91 AZ50
Copper Row SE1 279 P3
Copper Row SE1 142 DT74
Copperas St. SE8 163 EB79
Copperbeech Clo. NW3 120 DD64
Akenside Rd.
Copperdale Rd., Hayes 155 BU75
Copperfield, Chig. 103 ER51
Copperfield App., Chig. 103 ER51
Copperfield Ave., Uxb. 134 BN71
Copperfield Clo., S.Croy. 220 DQ111
Copperfield Ct., Lthd. 231 CG121
Kingston Rd.
Copperfield Ct., Pnr. 116 BZ56
Copperfield Way
Copperfield Dr. N15 122 DT56
Copperfield Gdns., Brwd. 108 FV46
Copperfield Ms. N18 100 DS50
Copperfield Ri., Add. 211 BF106
Copperfield Rd. E3 143 DY70
Copperfield Rd. SE28 146 EW72
Copperfield St. SE1 278 G4
Copperfield St. SE1 161 DP75
Copperfield Way, Chis. 185 EQ93
Copperfield Way, Pnr. 116 BZ56
Copperfields, Beac. 89 AL50
Copperfields, Lthd. 230 CC122
Copperfields, Welw.G.C. 30 DC10
Forresters Dr.
Copperfields Way, Rom. 106 FK53
Coppergate Clo., Brom. 204 EH95
Copperkins Gro., Amer. 55 AP36
Copperkins La., Amer. 55 AM35
Coppermill La. E17 122 DW58
Coppermill La., Rick. 91 BE52
Coppermill La., Uxb. 91 BE52
Coppermill Rd., Stai. 173 BB86
Copperwood, Hert. 32 DT09
Coppetts Clo. N12 98 DE52
Coppetts Rd. N10 98 DG54
Coppice, The, Ashf. 175 BP93
School Rd.
Coppice, The, Beac. 89 AR51
School La.
Coppice, The, Enf. 81 DP42
Thornton Rd.
Coppice, The, Hem.H. 41 BP19
Coppice, The, Wat. 76 BW44
Coppice, The, West Dr. 134 BL72
Coppice Clo. SW20 199 CW97
Coppice Clo., Hat. 45 CT22
Coppice Clo., Ruis. 115 BR58
Coppice Clo., Stan. 95 CF51
Coppice Dr. SW15 179 CV86
Coppice Dr., Stai. 172 AX87
Coppice End, Wok. 227 BE116
Coppice Fm. Rd., H.Wyc. 88 AC45
Coppice La., Reig. 249 CZ132
Coppice Path, Chig. 104 EV49
Coppice Row, Epp. 85 EM36
Coppice Wk. N20 98 DA48
Coppice Way E18 124 EF56
Coppice Way, Slou. 111 AR61
Coppies Gro. N11 98 DG49
Copping Clo., Croy. 220 DS105
Tipton Dr.
Coppings, The, Hodd. 33 EA14
Danemead
Coppins, The, Croy. 221 EB107
Coppins, The, Har. 95 CE51
Coppins Clo., Berk. 38 AS19
Coppins La., Iver 133 BF71
Coppock Clo. SW11 160 DE82
Coppsfield, W.Mol. 196 CA97
Hurst Rd.
Copse, The E4 102 EF46
Copse, The, Amer. 55 AQ38
Copse, The, Beac. 88 AJ51
Copse, The, Cat. 252 DU126
Tupwood La.
Copse, The, Hem.H. 39 BE18
Copse, The, Hert. 32 DU09
Copse, The, Lthd. 230 CB123
Copse, The, Red. 267 DL136
Copse Ave., W.Wick. 203 EB104
Copse Clo. SE7 164 EH79
Copse Clo., Guil. 259 BC140
Copse Clo., Nthwd. 93 BQ54
Copse Clo., Slou. 131 AM74
Copse Clo., West Dr. 154 BK76
Copse Edge Ave., 217 CT113
Epsom
Copse Glade, Surb. 197 CK102
Copse Hill SW20 179 CV94
Copse Hill, Harl. 51 EP18
Copse Hill, Pur. 219 DL113
Copse Hill, Sutt. 218 DB108
Copse La., Beac. 90 AS52
Copse La., Horl. 269 DJ147
Copse Rd., Cob. 213 BV113
Copse Rd., Red. 266 DC136
Copse Rd., Wok. 226 AT118
Copse Vw., S.Croy. 221 DX109
Copse Way, Chesh. 54 AN27
Copse Wd., Iver 133 BD67
Copse Wd. Ct., Reig. 250 DE132
Green La.
Copse Wd. Way, Nthwd. 93 BQ52
Copsem Dr., Esher 214 CB107
Copsem La., Esher 214 CB107
Copsem La., Lthd. 214 CC111
Copsem Way, Esher 214 CC107
Copsen Wd., Lthd. 214 CC111
Copsewood Clo., Sid. 185 ES86
Copsewood Rd., Wat. 75 BV39
Copshall Clo., Harl. 51 ES19
Copsleigh Ave., Red. 266 DG141
Copsleigh Clo., Red. 266 DG140
Copsleigh Way, Red. 266 DG140
Copt Hill La., Tad. 233 CY120
Coptefield Dr., Belv. 166 EX76
Coptfold Rd., Brwd. 108 FW47
Copthall Ave. EC2 275 L8
Copthall Ave. EC2 142 DR72
Copthall Bldgs. EC2 275 K8
Copthall Clo. EC2 275 K8
Copthall Clo., Ger.Cr. 91 AZ52
Copthall Cor., Ger.Cr. 90 AY52
Copthall Dr. NW7 97 CU52
Copthall Gdns. NW7 97 CU52
Copthall Gdns., Twick. 177 CF88
Copthall La., Ger.Cr. 90 AY52
Copthall Rd. E., Uxb. 114 BN61
Copthall Rd. W., Uxb. 114 BN61
Copthall Way, Add. 211 BF110
Copthorn Ave., Brox. 49 DZ20
Copthorne Ave. SW12 181 DK87
Copthorne Ave., Brom. 205 EM103
Copthorne Ave., Ilf. 103 EP51
Copthorne Chase, Ashf. 174 BM91
Ford Rd.
Copthorne Clo., Rick. 74 BM43
Copthorne Clo., Shep. 195 BQ100
Copthorne Gdns., Horn. 128 FN57
Copthorne Ms., Hayes 155 BS77
Copthorne Ri., S.Croy. 220 DR113
Copthorne Rd., Lthd. 231 CH120
Copthorne Rd., Rick. 74 BM44
Coptic St. WC1 273 P7
Coptic St. WC1 141 DL71
Copwood Clo. N12 98 DD49
Coral Clo., Rom. 126 EW55
Coral Row SW11 160 DC83
Gartons Way
Coral St. SE1 278 E5
Coral St. SE1 161 DN75
Coraline Clo., Sthl. 136 BZ69
Coralline Wk. SE2 166 EW75
Corals Mead, Welw.G.C. 29 CX10
Coram Clo., Berk. 38 AW20
Coram Grn., Brwd. 109 GD44
Coram St. WC1 273 P5
Coram St. WC1 141 DL70
Coran Clo. N9 101 DX45
Corban Rd., Houns. 156 CA83
Corbar Clo., Barn. 80 DD38
Corbet Clo., Wall. 200 DG102
Corbet Ct. EC3 275 L9
Corbet Pl. E1 275 P6
Corbet Rd., Epsom 216 CS110
Corbets Ave., Upmin. 128 FP64
Corbets Tey Rd., Upmin. 128 FP63
Corbett Clo., Croy. 221 ED112
Corbett Gro. N22 99 DL52
Corbett Ho., Wat. 94 BW48
Corbett Rd. E11 124 EJ58
Corbett Rd. E17 123 EC55
Corbetts La. SE16 162 DW77
Rotherhithe New Rd.
Corbetts Pas. SE16 162 DW77
Rotherhithe New Rd.
Corbicum E11 124 EE59
Corbiere Ct. SW19 179 CX93
Thornton Rd.
Corbiere Ho. N1 142 DS67
Corbins La., Har. 116 CB62
Corbridge Cres. E2 142 DV68
Corby Clo., Egh. 172 AW93
Corby Clo., St.Alb. 60 CA25
Corby Cres., Enf. 81 DL42
Corby Dr., Egh. 172 AV93
Corby Rd. NW10 138 CR68
Corby Way E3 143 EA70
Knapp Rd.
Corbylands Rd., Sid. 185 ES87
Corbyn St. N4 121 DL60
Corcorans, Brwd. 108 FV44
Cord Way E14 163 EA76
Mellish St.
Corde Way, Slou. 151 AQ75
Cordelia Clo. SE24 161 DP84
Cordelia Gdns., Stai. 174 BL87
Cordelia Rd., Stai. 174 BL87
Cordelia St. E14 143 EB72
Cordell Clo. (Cheshunt), 67 DY28
Wal.Cr.
Corder Clo., St.Alb. 42 CA23
Corderoy Pl., Cher. 193 BE100
Cording St. E14 143 EB71
Chrisp St.
Cordingley Rd., Ruis. 115 BR61
Cordons Clo., Ger.Cr. 90 AX53
Cordova Rd. E3 143 DY69
Cordrey Gdns., Couls. 235 DL115
Cordwainers Wk. E13 144 EG68
Clegg St.
Cordwell Rd. SE13 184 EE85
Corelli Rd. SE3 164 EL82
Corfe Ave., Har. 116 CA63
Corfe Clo., Ash. 231 CJ118
Corfe Clo., Hayes 136 BW72
Corfe Clo., Hem.H. 40 BL21
Corfe Gdns., Slou. 131 AN73
Avebury
Corfe Twr. W3 158 CP75
Corfield Rd. N21 81 DM43
Corfield St. E2 142 DV69
Corfton Rd. W5 138 CL72
Coriander Ave. E14 143 ED72
Coriander Cres., Guil. 242 AU129
Cories Clo., Dag. 126 EX61
Corinium Clo., Wem. 118 CM63
Corinium Gate, St.Alb. 42 CA22
Corinne Rd. N19 121 DJ63
Corinthian Manorway, Erith 167 FD77
Corinthian Rd., Erith 167 FD77
Cork Sq. E1 142 DV74
Smeaton St.
Cork St. W1 277 K1
Cork St. W1 141 DJ73
Cork St. Ms. W1 277 K1
Cork Tree Way E4 101 DY50
Corker Wk. N7 121 DM61
Corkran Rd., Surb. 197 CK101
Corkscrew Hill, W.Wick. 203 ED103
Corlett St. NW1 272 B6
Corlett St. NW1 140 DE71
Cormongers La., Red. 251 DJ134
Cormont Rd. SE5 161 DP81
Cormorant Clo. E17 101 DX53
Banbury Rd.
Cormorant Rd. E7 124 EF64
Cormorant Wk., Horn. 147 FH65
Heron Flight Ave.
Corn Cft., Hat. 45 CV16
Corn Mead, Welw.G.C. 29 CW06
Corn Mill Dr., Orp. 205 ET101
Corn Way E11 123 ED62
Cornbury Rd., Edg. 95 CK52
Cornelia Pl., Erith 167 FE79
Queen St.
Cornelia St. N7 141 DM65
Cornell Clo., Sid. 186 EY93
Cornell Way, Rom. 104 FA50
Corner, The, W.Byf. 212 BG113
Old Woking Rd.
Corner Grn. SE3 164 EG82
Corner Hall, Hem.H. 40 BJ22
Corner Hall Ave., Hem.H. 40 BK22
Corner Ho. St. WC2 277 P2
Corner Mead NW9 97 CT52
Corner Vw., Hat. 45 CW24
Cornerfield, Hat. 45 CV15
Corners, Welw.G.C. 30 DA07
Cornerside, Ashf. 175 BQ94
Corney Reach Way W4 158 CS80
Corney Rd. W4 158 CS79
Cornfield Clo., Uxb. 134 BK68
The Greenway
Cornfield Rd., Reig. 266 DC135
Cornfield Rd. (Bushey), 76 CB42
Wat.
Cornfields, Gdmg. 258 AU143
Cornfields, Hem.H. 40 BH21
Cornflower La., Croy. 203 DX102
Cornflower Ter. SE22 182 DV86
Cornflower Way, Rom. 106 FL53
Cornford Clo., Brom. 204 EG99
Cornford Gro. SW12 181 DH89
Cornhill EC3 275 L9
Cornhill EC3 142 DR72
Cornhill Clo., Add. 194 BH103
Cornhill Dr., Enf. 83 DY37
Ordnance Rd.
Cornish Ct. N9 100 DV45
Cornish Gro. SE20 182 DV94
Cornish Ho. SE17 161 DP79
Otto St.
Cornish Ho., Brent. 158 CM78
Green Dragon La.
Cornmill, Wal.Abb. 67 EB33
Cornmill La. SE13 163 EB83
Cornmill Ms., Wal.Abb. 67 EB33
Highbridge St.
Cornmow Dr. NW10 119 CT64
Cornshaw Rd., Dag. 126 EX60
Cornsland, Brwd. 108 FX48
Cornsland Ct., Brwd. 108 FW48
Cornthwaite Rd. E5 122 DW62
Cornwall Ave. E2 142 DW69
Cornwall Ave. N3 98 DA52
Cornwall Ave. N22 99 DL53
Cornwall Ave., Esher 215 CF108
The Causeway
Cornwall Ave., Slou. 131 AQ70
Cornwall Ave., Sthl. 136 BZ71
Cornwall Ave., Well. 165 ES83
Cornwall Ave., W.Byf. 212 BM114
Cornwall Clo., Bark. 145 ET65
Cornwall Clo., Horn. 128 FN56
Cornwall Clo., Wal.Cr. 67 DY33
Cornwall Clo. (Eton Wick), 151 AL78
Wind.
Cornwall Cres. W11 139 CY73
Cornwall Dr., Orp. 186 EW94
Cornwall Gdns. NW10 139 CV65
Cornwall Gdns. SW7 160 DC76
Cornwall Gdns. Wk. SW7 160 DB76
Cornwall Gdns.
Cornwall Gate, Purf. 168 FN77
Fanns Ri.
Cornwall Gro. W4 158 CS78
Cornwall Ms. S. SW7 160 DC76
Cornwall Ms. W. SW7 160 DB76
Cornwall Gdns.
Cornwall Rd. N4 121 DN59
Cornwall Rd. N15 122 DR57
Cornwall Rd. N18 100 DU50
Fairfield Rd.
Cornwall Rd. SE1 278 D2
Cornwall Rd. SE1 141 DN74
Cornwall Rd., Brwd. 108 FV43
Cornwall Rd., Croy. 201 DP103
Cornwall Rd., Dart. 168 FM83
Cornwall Rd., Esher 215 CG108
Cornwall Rd., Har. 116 CC58
Cornwall Rd., Pnr. 94 BZ52
Cornwall Rd., Ruis. 115 BT62
Cornwall Rd., St.Alb. 43 CE22
Cornwall Rd., Sutt. 217 CZ108
Cornwall Rd., Twick. 177 CG87
Cornwall Rd., Uxb. 134 BK65
Cornwall Rd., Wind. 172 AU86
Cornwall St. E1 142 DV73
Watney St.
Cornwall Ter. NW1 272 E5
Cornwall Ter. Ms. NW1 272 E5
Cornwall Way, Stai. 173 BE93
Cornwallis Ave. N9 100 DV47
Cornwallis Ave. SE9 185 ER89
Cornwallis Clo., Erith 167 FF79
Cornwallis Gro. N9 100 DV47
Cornwallis Rd. E17 123 DX56
Cornwallis Rd. N9 100 DV47
Cornwallis Rd. N19 121 DL61
Cornwallis Rd., Dag. 126 EX63
Cornwallis Sq. N19 121 DL61
Cornwallis Wk. SE9 165 EM83
Cornwell Ave., Grav. 191 GJ90
Cornwood Clo. N2 120 DD57
Cornwood Dr. E1 142 DW72
Cornworthy Rd., Dag. 126 EW64
Corona Rd. SE12 184 EG87
Coronation Ave. N16 122 DT62
Victorian Rd.
Coronation Ave., Slou. 132 AY71
Coronation Ave., Wind. 152 AT82
Coronation Clo., Bex. 186 EX86
Coronation Clo., Ilf. 125 EQ56
Coronation Dr., Horn. 127 FH63
Coronation Hill, Epp. 69 ET30
Coronation Rd. E13 144 EJ69
Coronation Rd. NW10 138 CM69
Coronation Rd., Hayes 155 BT77
Coronation Rd., Ware 33 DX05
Coronation Wk., Twick. 176 CA88
Coronet, The, Horl. 269 DJ150
Coronet St. N1 275 M3
Coronet St. N1 142 DS69
Corporation Ave., Houns. 156 BY84
Corporation Row EC1 274 E4
Corporation Row EC1 141 DN70
Corporation St. E15 144 EE68
Corporation St. N7 121 DL64
Corral Gdns., Hem.H. 40 BM19
Corran Way, S.Ock. 149 FV73
Corrance Rd. SW2 161 DL84
Corri Ave. N14 99 DK49
Corrib Dr., Sutt. 218 DE106
Corrie Gdns., Vir.W. 192 AW101
Corrie Rd., Add. 212 BK105
Corrie Rd., Wok. 227 BC120
Corrigan Ave., Couls. 218 DG114
Corringham Ct. NW11 120 DB59
Corringham Rd.
Corringham Ct., St.Alb. 43 CF19
Lemsford Rd.
Corringham Rd. NW11 120 DA59
Corringham Rd., Wem. 118 CN61
Corringway NW11 120 DB59
Corringway W5 138 CN70
Corsair Clo., Stai. 174 BK87
Corsair Rd., Stai. 174 BL87
Corscombe Clo., Kings.T. 178 CQ92
Corsehill St. SW16 181 DJ93
Corsham St. N1 275 L3
Corsham St. N1 142 DR69
Corsica St. N5 141 DP65
Corsley Way E9 143 DZ65
Osborne Rd.
Cortayne Rd. SW6 159 CZ82
Cortis Rd. SW15 179 CV86
Cortis Ter. SW15 179 CV86
Corunna Rd. SW8 161 DJ81
Corunna Ter. SW8 161 DJ81
Corve La., S.Ock. 149 FV73
Corvette Sq. SE10 163 ED79
Feathers Pl.
Corwell Gdns., Uxb. 135 BQ72
Corwell La., Uxb. 135 BQ72
Cory Dr., Brwd. 109 GB45
Cory Wright Way, St.Alb. 28 CL06
Coryton Path W9 139 CZ70
Ashmore Rd.
Cosbycote Ave. SE24 182 DQ85
Cosdach Ave., Wall. 219 DK108
Cosedge Cres., Croy. 219 DN106
Cosgrove Clo. N21 100 DQ47
Cosgrove Clo., Hayes 136 BY70
Kingsash Dr.
Cosmo Pl. WC1 274 A6
Cosmur Clo. W12 159 CT76
Cossall Wk. SE15 162 DV81
Cosser St. SE1 278 D6
Cosser St. SE1 161 DN76
Costa St. SE15 162 DU82
Costead Manor Rd., 108 FV46
Brwd.
Costell's Meadow, West. 255 ER126
Coston Wk. SE4 163 DX84
Frendsbury Rd.
Costons Ave., Grnf. 137 CD69
Costons La., Grnf. 137 CD69
Cosway St. NW1 272 C6
Cosway St. NW1 140 DE71
Cotall St. E14 143 EA72
Coteford Clo., Loug. 85 EP40
Coteford Clo., Pnr. 115 BU57
Coteford St. SW17 180 DF91
Cotelands, Croy. 202 DS104
Cotesbach Rd. E5 122 DW62
Cotesmore Gdns., Dag. 126 EW63
Cotesmore Rd., Hem.H. 39 BE21
Cotford Rd., Th.Hth. 202 DQ98
Cotham St. SE17 279 J9
Cotherstone, Epsom 216 CR110
Cotherstone Rd. SW2 181 DM88
Cotland Acres, Red. 266 DD136
Cotlandswick, St.Alb. 61 CJ26
Cotleigh Ave., Bex. 186 EX89
Cotleigh Rd. NW6 140 DA66
Cotleigh Rd., Rom. 127 FD58
Cotman Clo. NW11 120 DC58
Cotman Clo. SW15 179 CW86
Westleigh Ave.
Cotman Gdns., Edg. 96 CN54
Cotman Ms., Dag. 126 EW64
Highgrove Rd.
Cotmandene, Dor. 263 CH136
Cotmandene Cres., Orp. 206 EU96
Cotmans Clo., Hayes 135 BU74
Coton Rd., Well. 166 EU83
Cotsford Ave., N.Mal. 198 CQ99
Cotswold, Hem.H. 40 BL17
Mendip Way
Cotswold Ave. (Bushey), 76 CC44
Wat.
Cotswold Clo., Bexh. 167 FE82
Cotswold Clo., Kings.T. 178 CP93
Cotswold Clo., St.Alb. 43 CJ15
Chiltern Rd.
Cotswold Clo., Slou. 151 AQ76
Cotswold Clo., Stai. 174 BG92
Cotswold Clo., Uxb. 134 BJ67
Cotswold Ct. N11 98 DG49
Cotswold Gdns. E6 144 EK69
Cotswold Gdns. NW2 119 CX61
Cotswold Gdns., Brwd. 109 GE45
Cotswold Gdns., Ilf. 125 ER59
Cotswold Gate NW2 119 CY60
Cotswold Gdns.
Cotswold Grn., Enf. 81 DM42
Cotswold Way
Cotswold Ms. SW11 160 DD81
Battersea High St.
Cotswold Ri., Orp. 205 ET100
Cotswold Rd., Grav. 190 GE90
Cotswold Rd., Hmptn. 176 CA93
Cotswold Rd., Rom. 106 FM54
Cotswold Rd., Sutt. 218 DB110
Cotswold St. SE27 181 DP91
Norwood High St.
Cotswold Way, Enf. 81 DM42
Cotswold Way, Wor.Pk. 199 CW103
Cotswolds, Hat. 45 CU20
Cottage Ave., Brom. 204 EL102
Cottage Clo., Cher. 211 BC107
Cottage Clo., Rick. 74 BM44
Scots Hill
Cottage Clo., Ruis. 115 BR60
Cottage Clo., Wat. 75 BT40
Cottage Fm. Way, Egh. 193 BC97
Green Rd.
Cottage Fld. Clo., Sid. 186 EW88
Cottage Gdns., Wal.Cr. 66 DW29
Cottage Grn. SE5 162 DR80
Cottage Gro. SW9 161 DL83
Cottage Gro., Surb. 197 CK100
Cottage Homes NW7 97 CU49
Cottage Pk. Rd., Slou. 111 AR61
Cottage Pl. SW3 276 B6
Cottage Pl. SW3 160 DE76
Cottage Rd., Epsom 216 CR108
Cottage St. E14 143 EB73
Cottage Wk. N16 122 DT62
Smalley Clo.
Cottage Wk. SE15 162 DT80
Sumner Est.
Cottenham Dr. NW9 119 CT55
Cottenham Dr. SW20 179 CV94
Cottenham Par. SW20 199 CV96
Durham Rd.
Cottenham Pk. Rd. SW20 179 CV94
Cottenham Pl. SW20 179 CV94
Cottenham Rd. E17 123 DZ56
Cotterells, Hem.H. 40 BJ21
Cotterells Hill, Hem.H. 40 BJ20
Cotterill Rd., Surb. 198 CL103
Cottesbrook St. SE14 163 DY80
Nynehead St.
Cottesbrooke Clo., Slou. 153 BD81
Cottesloe Ms. SE1 278 E6
Cottesmore Ave., Ilf. 103 EN54
Cottesmore Gdns. W8 160 DB76
Cottimore Ave., Walt. 195 BV102
Cottimore Cres., Walt. 195 BV101
Cottimore La., Walt. 195 BV101
Cottimore Ter., Walt. 195 BV101
Cottingham Chase, Ruis. 115 BU62
Cottingham Rd. SE20 183 DX94
Cottingham Rd. SW8 161 DM80
Cottington Rd., Felt. 176 BX91
Cottington St. SE11 278 E10
Cottle St. SE16 162 DW75
St. Marychurch St.
Cotton Ave. W3 138 CR72

Cotton Clo., Dag. 146 EW66
Ellerton Rd.
Cotton Dr., Hert. 32 DV08
Cotton Fld., Hat. 45 CV16
Cotton Hill, Brom. 183 ED91
Cotton La., Dart. 188 FQ86
Cotton La., Green. 188 FQ85
Cotton Rd., Pot.B. 64 DC31
Cotton Row SW11 160 DC83
Cotton St. E14 143 EC73
Cottongrass Clo., Croy. 203 DX102
Cornflower La.
Cottonmill Cres., St.Alb. 43 CD21
Cottonmill La., St.Alb. 43 CD22
Cottons App., Rom. 127 FD57
Cottons Ct., Rom. 127 FD57
Cottons Gdns. E2 275 N2
Cottons La. SE1 279 L2
Cotts Clo. W7 137 CF71
Westcott Cres.
Cotts Wd. Dr., Guil. 243 BA129
Couchmore Ave., Esher 197 CE103
Couchmore Ave., Ilf. 103 EM54
Coulgate St. SE4 163 DY83
Coulsdon Ct. Rd., Couls. 235 DM116
Coulsdon La., Couls. 234 DF119
Coulsdon Pl., Cat. 236 DR122
Coulsdon Ri., Couls. 235 DL117
Coulsdon Rd., Cat. 236 DQ121
Coulsdon Rd., Couls. 235 DM115
Coulser Clo., Hem.H. 40 BG17
Coulson Clo., Dag. 126 EW59
Coulson St. SW3 276 D10
Coulson St. SW3 160 DF77
Coulson Way, Slou. 130 AH71
Coulter Clo., Hayes 136 BY70
Coulter Clo. (Cuffley), Pot.B. 65 DK27
Coulter Rd. W6 159 CV76
Coulton Ave., Grav. 190 GE87
Council Ave., Grav. 190 GC86
Councillor St. SE5 162 DQ80
Counter Ct. SE1 142 DR74
Southwark St.
Counter St. SE1 279 M3
Counters Clo., Hem.H. 40 BG20
Countess Clo. (Harefield), Uxb. 92 BJ54
Countess Rd. NW5 121 DJ64
Countisbury Ave., Enf. 100 DT45
Countisbury Gdns., Add. 212 BH106
Addlestone Pk.
Country Way, Felt. 175 BV93
Country Way, Sun. 175 BU94
County Gdns., Bark. 145 ES68
River Rd.
County Gate SE9 185 EQ90
County Gate, Barn. 80 DB44
County Gro. SE5 162 DQ81
County Rd. E6 145 EP71
County Rd., Th.Hth. 201 DP96
County St. SE1 279 J7
County St. SE1 162 DR76
Coupland Pl. SE18 165 EQ78
Courage Clo., Horn. 128 FJ58
Courage Wk., Brwd. 109 GD44
Wainwright Ave.
Courcy Rd. N8 121 DN55
Courier Rd., Dag. 147 FC70
Courland Gro. SW8 161 DK81
Courland Rd., Add. 194 BH104
Courland St. SW8 161 DK81
Course, The SE9 185 EN90
Coursers Rd., St.Alb. 62 CN27
Court, The, Ruis. 116 BY63
Court, The, Warl. 237 DY118
Court Ave., Belv. 166 EZ78
Court Ave., Couls. 235 DN118
Court Ave., Rom. 106 FN52
Court Bushes Rd., Whyt. 236 DU119
Court Clo., Har. 118 CL55
Court Clo., Maid. 150 AC77
Court Clo., Twick. 176 CB90
Court Clo., Wall. 219 DK108
Court Clo. Ave., Twick. 176 CB90
Court Cres., Chess. 215 CK106
Court Cres., Slou. 131 AR72
Court Cres., Swan. 207 FE98
Court Downs Rd., Beck. 203 EB96
Court Dr., Croy. 219 DM105
Court Dr., Maid. 130 AC68
Court Dr., Stan. 96 CL49
Court Dr., Sutt. 218 DE105
Court Dr., Uxb. 134 BM67
Court Fm. Ave., Epsom 216 CR106
Court Fm. Ind. Est., Stai. 174 BM86
Court Fm. Rd. SE9 184 EK89
Court Fm. Rd., Nthlt. 136 CA66
Court Fm. Rd., Warl. 236 DU118
Court Gdns. N7 141 DN65
Court Grn. Hts., Wok. 226 AW120
Court Haw, Bans. 234 DE115
Court Hill, Couls. 234 DE118
Court Hill, S.Croy. 220 DS112
Court Ho. Gdns. N3 98 DA51
Court La. SE21 182 DS86
Court La., Epsom 216 CQ113
Court La., Iver 134 BG74
Court La., Slou. 131 AK69
Court La., Wind. 150 AG76
Court La. Gdns. SE21 182 DS87
Court Lawns, H.Wyc. 88 AC46
Court Lo. Rd., Horl. 268 DE147
Court Mead, Nthlt. 136 BZ69
Court Par., Wem. 117 CH62
Court Rd. SE9 184 EL89
Court Rd. SE25 202 DT96
Court Rd., Bans. 234 DA116
Court Rd., Cat. 236 DR123
Court Rd., Dart. 189 FS92
Court Rd., Gdse. 252 DW131
Court Rd., Maid. 130 AC69
Court Rd., Orp. 206 EV101
Court Rd., Sthl. 156 BZ77
Court Rd., Uxb. 115 BP64
Court St. E1 142 DV71
Durward St.
Court St., Brom. 204 EG96
Court Way NW9 118 CS56
Court Way W3 138 CQ71
Court Way, Ilf. 125 EQ55
Court Way, Rom. 106 FL54
Court Way, Twick. 177 CF87
Court Wd. Dr., Sev. 256 FG124
Court Wd. Gro., Croy. 221 DZ111
Court Wd. La., Croy. 221 DZ111
Court Yd. SE9 184 EL86
Courtauld Clo. SE28 146 EU74
Pitfield Cres.
Courtauld Rd. N19 121 DK60
Courtaulds, Kings L. 58 BH30
Courtenay Ave. N6 120 DE59
Courtenay Ave., Har. 94 CC53
Courtenay Ave., Sutt. 218 DA109
Courtenay Dr., Beck. 203 ED96
Courtenay Dr., Grays 170 FZ76
Clifford Rd.
Courtenay Gdns., Har. 94 CC54
Courtenay Gdns., Upmin. 128 FQ60
Courtenay Ms. E17 123 DY57
Cranbrook Ms.
Courtenay Pl. E17 123 DY57
Courtenay Rd. E11 124 EF62
Courtenay Rd. E17 123 DX56
Courtenay Rd. SE20 183 DX94
Courtenay Rd., Wem. 117 CK62
Courtenay Rd., Wok. 227 BA116
Courtenay Rd., Wor.Pk. 199 CW104
Courtenay Sq. SE11 161 DN78
Courtenay St.
Courtenay St. SE11 278 D10
Courtenay St. SE11 161 DN78
Courtens Ms., Stan. 95 CJ52
Courtfield W5 137 CJ71
Castlebar Hill
Courtfield Ave., Har. 117 CF57
Courtfield Clo., Brox. 49 EA20
Stafford Dr.
Courtfield Cres., Har. 117 CF57
Courtfield Gdns. SW5 160 DB77
Courtfield Gdns. W13 137 CG72
Courtfield Gdns., Ruis. 115 BT61
Courtfield Gdns. (Denham), Uxb. 114 BG62
Courtfield Ms. SW5 160 DB77
Courtfield Gdns.
Courtfield Ri., W.Wick. 203 ED104
Courtfield Rd. SW7 160 DB77
Courtfield Rd., Ashf. 175 BP93
Courthill Rd. SE13 163 EC84
Courthope Rd. NW3 120 DF63
Courthope Rd. SW19 179 CY92
Courthope Rd., Grnf. 137 CD68
Courthope Vil. SW19 179 CY94
Courthouse Rd. N12 98 DB51
Courtland Ave. E4 102 EF47
Courtland Ave. NW7 96 CR48
Courtland Ave. SW16 181 DM94
Courtland Ave., Ilf. 125 EM61
Courtland Dr., Chig. 103 EP48
Courtland Gro. SE28 146 EX73
Courtland Rd. E6 144 EL67
Harrow Rd.
Courtlands, Rich. 158 CN84
Courtlands Ave. SE12 184 EH85
Courtlands Ave., Brom. 204 EF102
Courtlands Ave., Esher 214 BZ107
Courtlands Ave., Hmptn. 176 BZ93
Courtlands Ave., Rich. 158 CP82
Courtlands Ave., Slou. 152 AX77
Courtlands Clo., Ruis. 115 BT59
Courtlands Clo., S.Croy. 220 DT110
Courtlands Clo., Wat. 75 BS35
Courtlands Cres., Bans. 234 DA115
Courtlands Dr., Epsom 216 CS107
Courtlands Dr., Wat. 75 BS37
Courtlands Rd., Surb. 198 CN101
Courtleas, Cob. 214 CA113
Courtleet Dr., Erith 167 FB81
Courtleigh Ave., Barn. 80 DD38
Courtleigh Gdns. NW11 119 CY56
Courtman Rd. N17 100 DQ52
Courtmead Clo. SE24 182 DQ86
Courtnell St. W2 140 DA72
Courtney Clo. SE19 182 DS93
Courtney Cres., Cars. 218 DF108
Courtney Pl., Croy. 201 DN104
Courtney Rd. N7 121 DN64
Bryantwood Rd.
Courtney Rd. SW19 180 DE94
Courtney Rd., Croy. 201 DN104
Courtney Rd., Grays 171 GJ75
Courtney Rd., Houns. 154 BN83
Courtney Way, Houns. 154 BN82
Courtrai Rd. SE23 183 DY86
Courtside N8 121 DK58
Courtway, Wdf.Grn. 102 EJ50
Courtway, The, Wat. 94 BY47
Courtyard, The N1 141 DM66
Courtyards, The, Slou. 153 BA75
Waterside Dr.
Cousin La. EC4 279 K1
Cousins Clo., West Dr. 134 BL73
Couthurst Rd. SE3 164 EH79
Coutts Ave., Chess. 216 CL106
Coutts Cres. NW5 120 DG62
Coval Gdns. SW14 158 CP84
Coval La. SW14 158 CP84
Coval Rd. SW14 158 CP84
Coveham Cres., Cob. 213 BU113
Covelees Wall E6 145 EN72
Covell Ct. SE8 163 EA80
Reginald Sq.
Covenbrook, Brwd. 109 GB48
Covent Gdn. WC2 274 A10
Covent Gdn. WC2 141 DL73
Coventry Clo. E6 145 EM72
Harper Rd.
Coventry Clo. NW6 140 DA67
Kilburn High Rd.
Coventry Cross E3 143 EC70
Gillender St.
Coventry Rd. E1 142 DV70
Coventry Rd. E2 142 DV70
Coventry Rd. SE25 202 DU98
Coventry Rd., Ilf. 125 EP60
Coventry St. W1 277 M1
Coventry St. W1 141 DK73
Coverack Clo. N14 81 DJ44
Coverack Clo., Croy. 203 DY101
Coverdale, Hem.H. 40 BL17
Coverdale Clo., Stan. 95 CH50
Coverdale Ct., Enf. 83 DY37
Raynton Rd.
Coverdale Gdns., Croy. 202 DT104
Park Hill Ri.
Coverdale Rd. N11 98 DG51
Coverdale Rd. NW2 139 CX66
Coverdale Rd. W12 139 CV74
Coverdale Way, Slou. 131 AL70
Coverdales, The, Bark. 145 ER68
Coverley Clo. E1 142 DU71
Coverley Clo., Brwd. 107 FW51
Wilmot Grn.
Covert, The, Nthwd. 93 BQ53
Covert, The, Orp. 205 ES100
Covert Rd., Ilf. 103 ET51
Covert Way, Barn. 80 DC40
Coverton Rd. SW17 180 DE92
Coverts, The, Brwd. 109 GA46
Coverts Rd., Esher 215 CF109
Covet Wd. Clo., Orp. 205 ET100
Lockesley Dr.
Covey Clo. SW19 200 DB96
Covington Gdns. SW16 181 DP94
Covington Way SW16 181 DM93
Cow La., Grnf. 137 CD68
Cow La., Wat. 76 BW36
Cow Leaze E6 145 EN72
Cowan Clo. E6 144 EL71
Oliver Gdns.
Cowbridge, Hert. 32 DQ09
Cowbridge La., Bark. 145 EP66
Cowbridge Rd., Har. 118 CM56
Cowcross St. EC1 274 F6
Cowcross St. EC1 141 DP71
Cowden Rd., Orp. 205 ET101
Cowden St. SE6 183 EA91
Cowdenbeath Path N1 141 DM67
Cowdray Rd., Uxb. 135 BQ67
Cowdray Way, Horn. 127 FF63
Cowdrey Clo., Enf. 82 DS40
Cowdrey Ct., Dart. 187 FH87
Cowdrey Rd. SW19 180 DB92
Cowdry Rd. E9 143 DY65
Wick Rd.
Cowen Ave., Har. 116 CC61
Cowgate Rd., Grnf. 137 CD68
Cowick Rd. SW17 180 DF91
Cowings Mead, Nthlt. 136 BY66
Cowland Ave., Enf. 82 DW42
Cowleaze Rd., Kings.T. 198 CL95
Cowles (Cheshunt), Wal.Cr. 66 DT27
Cowley Ave., Cher. 193 BF101
Cowley Ave., Green. 189 FU85
Cowley Business Pk., Uxb. 134 BJ69
Cowley Clo., S.Croy. 220 DW109
Cowley Cres., Uxb. 134 BJ71
Cowley Cres., Walt. 214 BW105
Cowley Hill, Borwd. 78 CP37
Cowley La. E11 124 EE62
Cathall Rd.
Cowley La., Cher. 193 BF101
Cowley Mill Rd., Uxb. 134 BH68
Cowley Pl. NW4 119 CW57
Cowley Rd. E11 124 EH57
Cowley Rd. SW9 161 DN81
Cowley Rd. SW14 158 CS83
Cowley Rd. W3 139 CT74
Cowley Rd., Ilf. 125 EM59
Cowley Rd., Rom. 105 FH52
Cowley Rd., Uxb. 134 BJ68
Cowley St. SW1 277 P6
Cowling Clo. W11 139 CY74
Wilsham St.
Cowlins, Harl. 36 EX11
New Rd.
Cowper Ave. E6 144 EL66
Cowper Ave., Sutt. 218 DD105
Cowper Ave., Til. 171 GH81
Cowper Clo., Brom. 204 EK98
Cowper Clo., Cher. 193 BF100
Cowper Clo., Well. 186 EU85
Cowper Ct., Wat. 75 BU37
Cowper Cres., Hert. 31 DP07
Cowper Gdns. N14 81 DJ44
Cowper Gdns., Wall. 219 DJ107
Cowper Rd. N14 99 DH46
Cowper Rd. N16 122 DS64
Cowper Rd. N18 100 DU50
Cowper Rd. SW19 180 DC93
Cowper Rd. W3 138 CR74
Cowper Rd. W7 137 CF73
Cowper Rd., Belv. 166 FA77
Cowper Rd., Berk. 38 AV19
Cowper Rd., Brom. 204 EK98
Cowper Rd., Chesh. 54 AP29
Cowper Rd., Hem.H. 40 BH22
Cowper Rd., Kings.T. 178 CM92
Cowper Rd., Rain. 147 FG70
Cowper Rd., Slou. 131 AN70
Cowper Rd., Welw.G.C. 29 CZ11
Cowper St. EC2 275 L4
Cowper St. EC2 142 DR70
Cowper Ter. W10 139 CX71
St. Marks Rd.
Cowslip Clo., Uxb. 134 BL66
Cowslip La., Dor. 247 CG129
Cowslip La., Wok. 226 AU115
Carthouse La.
Cowslip Rd. E18 102 EH54
Cowslips, Welw.G.C. 30 DC10
Cowthorpe Rd. SW8 161 DK81
Cox Clo., Rad. 62 CM32
Cox La., Chess. 216 CM105
Cox La., Epsom 216 CP106
Coxdean, Epsom 233 CW119
Coxe Pl., Har. 117 CG56
Coxfield Clo., Hem.H. 40 BL21
Toms Cft.
Coxley Ri., Pur. 220 DQ113
Coxmount Rd. SE7 164 EK78
Cox's Wk. SE21 182 DU88
Coxson Pl. SE1 279 P5
Coxwell Rd. SE18 165 ER78
Coxwell Rd. SE19 182 DS94
Coxwold Path, Chess. 216 CL108
Garrison La.
Cozens La. E., Brox. 49 DZ22
Cozens La. W., Brox. 49 DY22
Cozens Rd., Ware 33 DZ06
Crab Hill, Beck. 183 ED94
Crab Hill La., Red. 267 DM138
Crab La., Wat. 76 CB35
Crabbe Cres., Chesh. 54 AR29
Crabbs Cft. Clo., Orp. 223 EQ106
Ladycroft Way
Crabtree Ave., Rom. 126 EX56
Crabtree Ave., Wem. 138 CL68
Crabtree Clo. E2 275 P1
Crabtree Clo. E2 142 DT68
Crabtree Clo., Beac. 88 AH54
Crabtree Clo., Hem.H. 40 BK22
Crabtree Clo., Lthd. 246 CC126
Crabtree Clo. (Bushey), Wat. 76 CB43
Crabtree Ct. E15 123 EB64
Clays La.
Crabtree Dr., Lthd. 247 CJ125
Crabtree La. SW6 159 CX80
Crabtree La., Dor. 247 CF130
Crabtree La., Hem.H. 40 BK22
Crabtree La., Lthd. 246 CC126
Crabtree Manorway N., Belv. 167 FC75
Crabtree Manorway S., Belv. 167 FC76
Crabtree Rd., Egh. 193 BC96
Crabtree Wk. SE15 162 DT81
Lisford St.
Crace St. NW1 273 M2
Crackley Meadow, Hem.H. 41 BP15
Craddock Rd., Enf. 82 DT41
Craddock St. NW5 140 DG65
Prince of Wales Rd.
Craddocks Ave., Ash. 232 CL117
Craddocks Par., Ash. 232 CL117
Cradhurst Clo., Dor. 262 CC137
Cradley Rd. SE9 185 ER88
Cragg Ave., Rad. 77 CF36
Craig Dr., Uxb. 135 BP72
Craig Gdns. E18 102 EF54
Craig Mt., Rad. 77 CH35
Craig Pk. Rd. N18 100 DV50
Craig Rd., Rich. 177 CJ91
Craigavon Rd., Hem.H. 40 BM16
Craigdale Rd., Horn. 127 FF58
Craigen Ave., Croy. 202 DV102
Craigerne Rd. SE3 164 EH80
Craigholm SE18 165 EN82
Craiglands, St.Alb. 43 CK16
Craigmore Twr., Wok. 226 AY119
Guildford Rd.
Craigmuir Pk., Wem. 138 CM67
Craignair Rd. SW2 181 DN87
Craignish Ave. SW16 201 DM96
Craigs Ct. SW1 277 P2
Craigs Wk. (Cheshunt), Wal.Cr. 67 DX28
Davison Dr.
Craigton Rd. SE9 165 EM84
Craigweil Ave., Rad. 77 CH35
Craigweil Clo., Stan. 95 CK50
Craigweil Dr., Stan. 95 CK50
Craigwell Ave., Felt. 175 BU90
Craigwell Clo., Stai. 193 BE95
Craik Ct. NW6 139 CZ68
Carlton Vale
Crail Row SE17 279 L9
Crakell Rd., Reig. 266 DC135
Cramer St. W1 272 G7
Crammerville Wk., Rain. 147 FH70
Cramond Clo. W6 159 CY79
Cramond Ct., Felt. 175 BR88
Kilross Rd.
Crampshaw La., Ash. 232 CM119
Crampton Rd. SE20 182 DW93
Crampton St. SE17 279 H9
Crampton St. SE17 162 DQ77
Cramptons Rd., Sev. 241 FH120
Cranberry Clo., Nthlt. 136 BX68
Parkfield Ave.
Cranberry La. E16 144 EE70
Cranborne Ave., Sthl. 156 CA77
Cranborne Ave., Surb. 198 CN104
Cranborne Clo., Pot.B. 63 CY31
Cranborne Cres., Pot.B. 63 CY31
Cranborne Gdns., Upmin. 128 FP61
Cranborne Ind. Est., Pot.B. 63 CY30
Cranborne Rd., Bark. 145 ER67
Cranborne Rd., Hat. 45 CV17
Cranborne Rd., Hodd. 49 EB16
Cranborne Rd., Pot.B. 63 CY30
Cranborne Rd. (Cheshunt), Wal.Cr. 67 DX32
Cranborne Waye, Hayes 136 BW73
Cranbourn All. WC2 273 N10
Cranbourn Pas. SE16 162 DV75
Marigold St.
Cranbourn St. WC2 273 N10
Cranbourn St. WC2 141 DK73
Cranbourne Ave. E11 124 EH56
Cranbourne Ave., Wind. 151 AM82
Cranbourne Clo. SW16 201 DL97
Cranbourne Clo., Hert. 32 DQ12
Cranbourne Clo., Horl. 269 DH146
Cranbourne Clo., Slou. 131 AQ74
Cranbourne Dr., Hodd. 33 EB13
Cranbourne Dr., Pnr. 116 BX57
Cranbourne Gdns. NW11 119 CY57
Cranbourne Gdns., Ilf. 125 EQ55
Cranbourne Gdns., Welw.G.C. 29 CZ10
Cranbourne Rd. E12 124 EL64
High St. N.
Cranbourne Rd. E15 123 EC63
Cranbourne Rd. N10 99 DH54
Cranbourne Rd., Nthwd. 115 BT55
Cranbourne Rd., Slou. 131 AQ74
Cranbrook Clo., Brom. 204 EG100
Cranbrook Dr., Esher 196 CC102
Cranbrook Dr., Rom. 127 FH56
Cranbrook Dr., St.Alb. 44 CL20
Cranbrook Dr., Twick. 176 CB88
Cranbrook Ms. E17 123 DZ57
Cranbrook Pk. N22 99 DM53
Cranbrook Ri., Ilf. 125 EM59
Cranbrook Rd. SE8 163 EA81
Cranbrook Rd. SW19 179 CY94
Cranbrook Rd. W4 158 CS78
Cranbrook Rd., Barn. 80 DD44
Cranbrook Rd., Bexh. 166 EZ81
Cranbrook Rd., Houns. 156 BZ84
Cranbrook Rd., Ilf. 125 EN60
Cranbrook Rd., Th.Hth. 202 DQ96
Cranbrook St. E2 143 DX68
Mace St.
Cranbury Rd. SW6 160 DB82
Crane Ave. W3 138 CQ73
Crane Ave., Islw. 177 CG85
Crane Clo., Dag. 146 FA65
Crane Clo., Har. 116 CC62
Crane Ct. EC4 274 E9
Crane Ct., Epsom 216 CQ105
Crane Gdns., Hayes 155 BT77
Crane Gro. N7 141 DN65
Crane Lo. Rd., Houns. 155 BV79
Crane Mead SE16 163 DX77
Crane Mead, Ware 33 DY07
Crane Pk. Rd., Twick. 176 CB89
Crane Rd., Twick. 177 CE88
Crane St. SE10 163 ED78
Crane St. SE15 162 DT81
Crane Way, Twick. 176 CC87
Cranebrook, Twick. 176 CC89
Manor Rd.
Cranefield Dr., Wat. 60 BY32
Craneford Clo., Twick. 177 CF87
Craneford Way, Twick. 177 CE87
Cranell Grn., S.Ock. 149 FV74
Cranes Dr., Surb. 198 CL98
Cranes Pk., Surb. 198 CL98
Cranes Pk. Ave., Surb. 198 CL98
Cranes Pk. Cres., Surb. 198 CM98
Cranes Way, Borwd. 78 CQ43
Cranesbill Clo. NW9 118 CR55
Colindale Ave.
Craneswater, Hayes 155 BT80
Craneswater Pk., Sthl. 156 BZ78
Cranfield Clo. SE27 182 DQ90
Dunelm Gro.
Cranfield Ct., Wok. 226 AU118
Martindale Rd.
Cranfield Cres. (Cuffley), Pot.B. 65 DL29
Cranfield Dr. NW9 96 CS52
Cranfield Rd. SE4 163 DZ83
Cranfield Rd. E., Cars. 218 DG109
Cranfield Rd. W., Cars. 218 DF109
Cranfield Row SE1 278 E6
Cranford Ave. N13 99 DL50
Cranford Ave., Stai. 174 BL87
Cranford Clo. SW20 199 CV95
Cranford Clo., Pur. 220 DQ113
Cranford Clo., Stai. 174 BL87
Canopus Way
Cranford Cotts. E1 143 DX73
Cranford St.
Cranford Ct., Hert. 31 DM07
The Ridgeway
Cranford Dr., Hayes 155 BT77
Cranford La., Hayes 155 BR79
Cranford La. (Cranford), Houns. 155 BT81
Cranford La. (Hatton Cross), Houns. 155 BT83
Cranford La. (Heston), Houns. 156 BX80
Cranford Pk. Rd., Hayes 155 BT77
Cranford Ri., Esher 214 CC106
Cranford Rd., Dart. 188 FL88
Cranford St. E1 143 DX73
Cranford Way N8 121 DM57
Cranham Gdns., Upmin. 129 FS60
Cranham Rd., Horn. 127 FH58
Cranhurst Rd. NW2 119 CW64
Cranleigh Clo. SE20 202 DV96
Cranleigh Clo., Bex. 187 FB86
Cranleigh Clo., Orp. 206 EU104
Cranleigh Clo., S.Croy. 220 DU112
Cranleigh Clo. (Cheshunt), Wal.Cr. 66 DU28
Cranleigh Dr., Swan. 207 FE99
Cranleigh Gdns. N21 81 DN43
Cranleigh Gdns. SE25 202 DS97
Cranleigh Gdns., Bark. 145 ER66
Cranleigh Gdns., Har. 118 CL57
Cranleigh Gdns., Kings.T. 178 CM93
Cranleigh Gdns., Loug. 85 EM44
Cranleigh Gdns., S.Croy. 220 DU112
Cranleigh Gdns., Sthl. 136 BZ72
Cranleigh Gdns., Sutt. 200 DB103
Cranleigh Gdns. Ind. Est., Sthl. 136 BZ72
Cranleigh Ms. SW11 160 DE82
Cranleigh Rd. N15 122 DQ57
Cranleigh Rd. SW19 200 DA97
Cranleigh Rd., Esher 196 CC102
Cranleigh Rd., Felt. 175 BT91
Cranleigh Rd., Guil. 259 BB144
Cranleigh St. NW1 273 L1
Cranleigh St. NW1 141 DJ68
Cranley Clo., Guil. 243 BA134
Cranley Dene Ct. N10 121 DH56
Cranley Dr., Ilf. 125 EQ59
Cranley Dr., Ruis. 115 BT61
Cranley Gdns. N10 121 DJ56
Cranley Gdns. N13 99 DM48
Cranley Gdns. SW7 160 DC78
Cranley Gdns., Wall. 219 DJ108
Cranley Ms. SW7 160 DC78
Cranley Par. SE9 184 EL91
Beaconsfield Rd.
Cranley Pl. SW7 160 DD77
Cranley Rd. E13 144 EH71
Cranley Rd., Guil. 243 AZ134
Cranley Rd., Ilf. 125 EQ58
Cranley Rd., Walt. 213 BS106
Cranmer Ave. W13 157 CH76
Cranmer Clo., Mord. 199 CX100
Cranmer Clo., Pot.B. 64 DB30
Cranmer Clo., Ruis. 116 BX60
Cranmer Clo., Stan. 95 CJ52
Cranmer Clo., Warl. 237 DY117
Cranmer Clo., Wey. 213 BR108
Cranmer Ct. SW3 276 C9
Cranmer Ct. SW4 161 DK83
Cranmer Ct., Hmptn. 176 CB92
Cranmer Rd.
Cranmer Fm. Clo., Mitch. 200 DF98
Cranmer Gdns., Dag. 127 FC63
Cranmer Gdns., Warl. 237 DY117
Cranmer Rd. E7 124 EH63
Cranmer Rd. SW9 161 DN80
Cranmer Rd., Croy. 201 DP104
Cranmer Rd., Edg. 96 CP48
Cranmer Rd., Hmptn. 176 CB92
Cranmer Rd., Hayes 135 BR72
Cranmer Rd., Kings.T. 178 CL92
Cranmer Rd., Mitch. 200 DF98
Cranmer Rd., Sev. 256 FE123
Cranmer Ter. SW17 180 DD92
Cranmore Ave., Islw. 156 CC80
Cranmore Cotts., Lthd. 245 BP129
Cranmore Ct., St.Alb. 43 CF19
Cranmore La., Lthd. 245 BP129
Cranmore Rd., Brom. 184 EE90
Cranmore Rd., Chis. 185 EM92
Cranmore Way N10 121 DJ56
Cranston Clo., Houns. 156 BY82
Cranston Clo., Reig. 266 DB135
Cranston Clo., Uxb. 115 BR61
Cranston Est. N1 275 L1
Cranston Est. N1 142 DR68
Cranston Gdns. E4 101 EB50
Cranston Pk. Ave., Upmin. 128 FQ63
Cranston Rd. SE23 183 DY88
Cranstoun Clo., Guil. 242 AT130
Cranswick Rd. SE16 162 DV78
Crantock Rd. SE6 183 EB89
Cranwell Clo. E3 143 EB70
Cranwell Gro., Shep. 194 BM98
Cranwell Rd., Houns. 155 BP82
Cranwich Ave. N21 100 DR45
Cranwich Rd. N16 122 DR59
Cranwood St. EC1 275 K3
Cranwood St. EC1 142 DR69
Cranworth Cres. E4 101 ED46
Cranworth Gdns. SW9 161 DN81

Craster Rd. SW2 181 DM87
Crathie Rd. SE12 184 EH86
Cravan Ave., Felt. 175 BU89
Craven Ave. W5 137 CJ73
Craven Ave., Sthl. 136 BZ71
Craven Clo., Hayes 135 BU72
Craven Gdns. SW19 180 DA92
Craven Gdns., Bark. 145 ES68
Craven Gdns., Ilf. 103 ER54
Craven Gdns. (Collier Row), Rom. 104 FA50
Craven Gdns. (Harold Wd.), Rom. 106 FQ51
Craven Hill W2 140 DC73
Craven Hill Gdns. W2 140 DC73
Craven Hill Ms. W2 140 DC73
Craven Ms. SW11 160 DG83
Taybridge Rd.
Craven Pk. NW10 138 CS67
Craven Pk. Ms. NW10 138 CS67
Craven Pk. Rd. N15 122 DT58
Craven Pk. Rd. NW10 138 CS67
Craven Pas. WC2 277 P2
Craven Pas. WC2 141 DL74
Craven Rd. NW10 138 CR67
Craven Rd. W2 140 DC73
Craven Rd. W5 137 CJ73
Craven Rd., Croy. 202 DV102
Craven Rd., Kings.T. 198 CM95
Craven Rd., Orp. 206 EX104
Craven St. WC2 277 P2
Craven St. WC2 141 DL74
Craven Ter. W2 140 DC73
Craven Wk. N16 122 DU59
Cravens, The, Horl. 269 DN148
Crawford Ave., Wem. 117 CK64
Crawford Clo., Islw. 157 CE82
Crawford Compton Clo., Horn. 148 FJ65
Crawford Est. SE5 162 DQ82
Crawford Gdns. N13 99 DP48
Crawford Gdns., Nthlt. 136 BZ69
Crawford Ms. W1 272 D7
Crawford Pas. EC1 274 D5
Crawford Pl. W1 272 C8
Crawford Pl. W1 140 DE72
Crawford Rd. SE5 162 DQ81
Crawford Rd., Hat. 45 CU16
Crawford St. W1 272 D7
Crawford St. W1 140 DF71
Crawfords, Swan. 187 FE94
Crawley Dr., Hem.H. 40 BM16
Crawley Rd. E10 123 EB60
Crawley Rd. N22 100 DQ54
Crawley Rd., Enf. 100 DS45
Crawshaw Rd., Cher. 211 BD107
Crawshay Clo., Sev. 256 FG123
Crawshay Ct. SW9 161 DN81
Eythorne Rd.
Crawthew Gro. SE22 162 DT84
Cray Ave., Ash. 232 CL116
Cray Ave., Orp. 206 EV100
Cray Clo., Dart. 167 FG84
Cray Riverway, Dart. 187 FF85
Cray Rd., Belv. 166 FA79
Cray Rd., Sid. 186 EW94
Cray Rd., Swan. 207 FB100
Cray Valley Rd., Orp. 206 EU99
Craybrooke Rd., Sid. 186 EV91
Crayburne, Grav. 190 FZ92
Craybury End SE9 185 EQ89
Craydene Rd., Erith 167 FF81
Crayford Clo. E6 144 EL71
Neatscourt Rd.
Crayford High St., Dart. 167 FE84
Crayford Rd. N7 121 DK63
Crayford Rd., Dart. 187 FF85
Crayford Way, Dart. 187 FF85
Crayke Hill, Chess. 216 CL108
Craylands, Orp. 206 EW97
Craylands La., Swans. 189 FX85
Craylands Sq., Swans. 189 FX85
Crayle St., Slou. 131 AN69
Craymill Sq., Dart. 167 FF82
Crayonne Clo., Sun. 195 BS95
Crayside Ind. Est., Dart. 167 FH84
Thames Rd.
Crealock Gro., Wdf.Grn. 102 EF50
Crealock St. SW18 180 DB86
Creasey Clo., Horn. 127 FH61
St. Leonards Way
Creasy Clo., Abb.L. 59 BT31
Creasy Est. SE1 279 M7
Creasy Est. SE1 162 DS76
Crebor St. SE22 182 DU86
Credenhall Dr., Brom. 205 EM102
Credenhill St. SW16 181 DJ93
Crediton Hill NW6 120 DB64
Crediton Rd. E16 144 EG72
Pacific Rd.
Crediton Rd. NW10 139 CX67
Crediton Way, Esher 215 CG106
Credo Way, Grays 169 FV79
Credon Rd. E13 144 EJ68
Credon Rd. SE16 162 DV78
Cree Way, Rom. 105 FE52
Creechurch La. EC3 275 N9
Creechurch La. EC3 142 DS72
Creechurch Pl. EC3 275 N9
Creed Ct. EC4 141 DP72
Ludgate Hill
Creed La. EC4 274 G9
Creek, The, Grav. 190 GB85
Creek, The, Sun. 195 BU99
Creek Rd. SE8 163 EA79
Creek Rd. SE10 163 EA79
Creek Rd., Bark. 145 ET69
Creek Rd., E.Mol. 197 CE98
Creekside SE8 163 EB80
Creekside, Rain. 147 FE70
Creeland Gro. SE6 183 DZ88
Catford Hill
Crefeld Clo. W6 159 CX79
Creffield Rd. W3 138 CM73
Creffield Rd. W5 138 CM73
Creighton Ave. E6 144 EK68
Creighton Ave. N2 120 DE55
Creighton Ave. N10 120 DE55
Creighton Ave., St.Alb. 43 CD24
Creighton Clo. W12 139 CV73
Bloemfontein Rd.
Creighton Rd. N17 100 DS52
Creighton Rd. NW6 139 CX68
Creighton Rd. W5 157 CK76
Cremer St. E2 275 P1
Cremer St. E2 142 DT68
Cremorne Est. SW10 160 DD79
Milman's St.
Cremorne Gdns., Epsom 216 CR109
Cremorne Rd. SW10 160 DC80
Cremorne Rd., Grav. 191 GF87
Crescent EC3 275 P10
Crescent, The E17 123 DY57
Crescent, The N11 98 DF49
Crescent, The NW2 119 CV62
Crescent, The SW13 159 CT82
Crescent, The SW19 180 DA90
Crescent, The W3 138 CS72
Crescent, The, Abb.L. 59 BT30
Crescent, The, Ashf. 174 BM92
Crescent, The, Barn. 80 DB41
Crescent, The, Beck. 203 EA95
Crescent, The, Bex. 186 EW87
Crescent, The, Cat. 237 EA123
Crescent, The, Cher. 194 BG97
Western Ave.
Crescent, The, Croy. 202 DR99
Crescent, The, Egh. 172 AY93
Crescent, The, Epp. 69 ET32
Crescent, The, Epsom 216 CN114
Crescent, The, Grav. 191 GF89
Crescent, The, Green. 189 FW85
Crescent, The, Guil. 242 AU133
Crescent, The, Harl. 36 EW09
Crescent, The, Har. 117 CD60
Crescent, The, Hayes 155 BQ80
Crescent, The, Horl. 268 DG150
Crescent, The, Ilf. 125 EN58
Crescent, The, Lthd. 231 CH122
Crescent, The, Loug. 84 EK43
Crescent, The, N.Mal. 198 CQ96
Crescent, The, Reig. 250 DB134
Chartway
Crescent, The, Rick. 75 BP44
Crescent, The, St.Alb. 60 CA30
Crescent, The, Sev. 257 FK121
Crescent, The, Shep. 195 BT101
Crescent, The, Sid. 185 ET91
Crescent, The, Slou. 152 AS75
Crescent, The, Sthl. 156 BZ75
Crescent, The, Surb. 198 CL99
Crescent, The, Sutt. 218 DD105
Crescent, The (Belmont), Sutt. 218 DA111
Crescent, The, Upmin. 129 FS59
Crescent, The, Wat. 76 BW42
Crescent, The (Aldenham), Wat. 76 CB37
Crescent, The, Wem. 117 CH61
Crescent, The, W.Mol. 196 CA98
Crescent, The, W.Wick. 204 EE100
Crescent, The, Wey. 194 BN104
Crescent Ave., Grays 170 GD78
Crescent Ave., Horn. 127 FF61
Crescent Cotts., Sev. 241 FE120
Crescent Dr., Brwd. 108 FY46
Crescent Dr., Orp. 205 EP100
Crescent E., Barn. 80 DC38
Crescent Gdns. SW19 180 DA90
Crescent Gdns., Ruis. 115 BV58
Crescent Gdns., Swan. 207 FC96
Crescent Gro. SW4 161 DJ84
Crescent Gro., Mitch. 200 DE98
Crescent La. SW4 181 DK85
Crescent Ms. N22 99 DL53
Palace Gates Rd.
Crescent Pl. SW3 276 B8
Crescent Pl. SW3 160 DE77
Crescent Ri. N22 99 DK53
Crescent Ri., Barn. 80 DE43
Crescent Rd. E4 102 EE45
Crescent Rd. E6 144 EJ67
Crescent Rd. E10 123 EB61
Crescent Rd. E13 144 EG67
Crescent Rd. E18 102 EJ54
Crescent Rd. N3 97 CZ53
Crescent Rd. N8 121 DK59
Crescent Rd. N9 100 DU46
Crescent Rd. N11 98 DF49
Crescent Rd. N15 121 DP55
Carlingford Rd.
Crescent Rd. N22 99 DK53
Crescent Rd. SE18 165 EP78
Crescent Rd. SW20 199 CX95
Crescent Rd., Barn. 80 DE43
Crescent Rd., Beck. 203 EB96
Crescent Rd., Brwd. 108 FV49
Crescent Rd., Brom. 184 EG94
Crescent Rd., Cat. 236 DU124
Crescent Rd., Dag. 127 FB63
Crescent Rd., Enf. 81 DP41
Crescent Rd., Erith 167 FF79
Crescent Rd., Hem.H. 40 BK20
Crescent Rd., Kings.T. 178 CN94
Crescent Rd., Red. 252 DQ133
Crescent Rd., Reig. 266 DA136
Crescent Rd., Shep. 195 BQ99
Crescent Rd., Sid. 185 ET90
Crescent Rd., S.Ock. 168 FQ75
Crescent Row EC1 275 H5
Crescent Stables SW15 159 CY84
Upper Richmond Rd.
Crescent St. N1 141 DM66
Crescent Vw., Loug. 84 EK44
Crescent Wk., S.Ock. 168 FQ75
Crescent Way N12 98 DE51
Crescent Way SE4 163 EA83
Crescent Way SW16 181 DM94
Crescent Way, Horl. 268 DG150
Crescent Way, Orp. 223 ES106
Crescent Way, S.Ock. 149 FR74
Crescent W., Barn. 80 DC38
Crescent Wd. Rd. SE26 182 DU90
Cresford Rd. SW6 160 DB81
Crespigny Rd. NW4 119 CV58
Cress End, Rick. 92 BG46
Springwell Ave.
Cress Rd., Slou. 151 AP75
Cressage Clo., Sthl. 136 CA70
Cressall Clo., Lthd. 231 CH120
Cresset Clo., Ware 33 EC12
Cresset Rd. E9 142 DW65
Cresset St. SW4 161 DK83
Cressfield Clo. NW5 120 DG64
Cressida Rd. N19 121 DJ60
Cressingham Gro., Sutt. 218 DC105
Cressingham Rd. SE13 163 EC83
Cressingham Rd., Edg. 96 CR51
Cressington Clo. N16 122 DS64
Wordsworth Rd.
Cresswell Gdns. SW5 160 DC78
Cresswell Pk. SE3 164 EF83
Cresswell Pl. SW10 160 DC78
Cresswell Rd. SE25 202 DU98
Cresswell Rd., Chesh. 54 AR34
Cresswell Rd., Felt. 176 BY91
Cresswell Rd., Twick. 177 CK86
Cresswell Way N21 99 DN45
Cressy Ct. E1 142 DW71
Cressy Pl.
Cressy Ct. W6 159 CV76
Cressy Pl. E1 142 DW71
Cressy Rd. NW3 120 DF63
Crest, The N13 99 DN49
Crest, The NW4 119 CW57
Crest, The, Saw. 36 EX05
Crest, The, Surb. 198 CN99
Crest, The (Cheshunt), Wal.Cr. 65 DP27
Orchard Way
Crest Ave., Grays 170 GB80
Crest Clo., Sev. 225 FB111
Crest Dr., Enf. 82 DW38
Crest Gdns., Ruis. 116 BW62
Crest Hill, Guil. 261 BR142
Crest Pk., Hem.H. 41 BQ19
Crest Rd. NW2 119 CT62
Crest Rd., Brom. 204 EF101
Crest Rd., S.Croy. 220 DV108
Crest Vw., Green. 169 FU84
Woodland Way
Crest Vw., Pnr. 116 BX56
Crest Vw. Dr., Orp. 205 EP99
Cresta Dr., Add. 211 BF110
Crestbrook Ave. N13 99 DP48
Crestbrook Pl. N13 99 DP48
Crestfield St. WC1 274 A2
Crestfield St. WC1 141 DL69
Cresthill Ave., Grays 170 GC77
Creston Ave., Wok. 226 AS116
Creston Way, Wor.Pk. 199 CX102
Crestway SW15 179 CV86
Crestwood Way, Houns. 176 BZ85
Creswick Ct., Welw.G.C. 29 CX10
Creswick Rd. W3 138 CP73
Creswick Wk. E3 143 EA69
Malmesbury Rd.
Creswick Wk. NW11 119 CZ56
Crete Hall Rd., Grav. 190 GD86
Creton St. SE18 165 EN76
Crewdson Rd. SW9 161 DN80
Crewdson Rd., Horl. 269 DH148
Crewe Curve, Berk. 38 AT16
Crewe Pl. NW10 139 CT69
Crewe's Ave., Warl. 236 DW116
Crewe's Clo., Warl. 236 DW117
Crewe's Fm. La., Warl. 237 DY117
Crewe's La., Warl. 236 DW117
Crews St. E14 163 EA77
Crewys Rd. NW2 119 CZ61
Crewys Rd. SE15 162 DV82
Crib St., Ware 33 DX05
Crichton Ave., Wall. 219 DK106
Crichton Rd., Cars. 218 DF107
Cricket Fld. Rd., Uxb. 134 BK67
Cricket Grn., Mitch. 200 DF97
Cricket Grd. Rd., Chis. 205 EP95
Cricket Hill, Red. 267 DM136
Cricket La., Beck. 183 DY93
Cricket Way, Wey. 195 BS103
Cricketers Arms Rd., Enf. 82 DQ40
Cricketers Clo. N14 99 DJ45
Cricketers Clo., Chess. 215 CK105
Cricketers Clo., Erith 167 FE78
Cricketers Clo., St.Alb. 43 CE19
Stonecross
Cricketers Ct. SE11 278 F9
Cricketers Ct. SE11 161 DP77
Cricketers Ms. SW18 180 DB85
East Hill
Cricketers Ter., Cars. 200 DE104
Wrythe La.
Cricketfield Rd. E5 122 DV63
Cricketfield Rd., West Dr. 154 BJ77
Cricklade Ave. SW2 181 DL89
Cricklade Ave., Rom. 106 FK51
Cricklewood Bdy. NW2 119 CX62
Cricklewood La. NW2 119 CX63
Cricklewood Trd. Est. NW2 119 CY62
Cridland St. E15 144 EF67
Church St.
Crieff Ct., Tedd. 177 CJ94
Crieff Rd. SW18 180 DC86
Criffel Ave. SW2 181 DK89
Crimp Hill Rd., Egh. 172 AU90
Crimp Hill Rd., Wind. 172 AT87
Crimscott St. SE1 279 N7
Crimscott St. SE1 162 DS76
Crimsworth Rd. SW8 161 DK81
Crinan St. N1 141 DL68
Cringle St. SW8 161 DJ80
Cripplegate St. EC2 275 H6
Cripps Grn., Hayes 135 BV70
Stratford Rd.
Crisp Rd. W6 159 CW78
Crispe Ho., Bark. 145 ER68
Dovehouse Mead
Crispen Rd., Felt. 176 BY91
Crispian Clo. NW10 118 CS63
Crispin Clo., Ash. 232 CM118
Crispin Clo., Croy. 201 DL103
Harrington Clo.
Crispin Cres., Croy. 201 DK104
Crispin Rd., Edg. 96 CQ51
Crispin St. E1 275 P7
Crispin St. E1 142 DT71
Crispin Way, Slou. 111 AR63
Criss Cres., Ger.Cr. 90 AW54
Criss Gro., Ger.Cr. 90 AW54
Cristowe Rd. SW6 159 CZ82
Criterion Ms. N19 121 DK61
Critten La., Dor. 246 BX134
Crockenhall Way, Grav. 190 GE94
Crockenhill La., Dart. 208 FJ102
Crockenhill La., Swan. 207 FG101
Crockenhill Rd., Orp. 206 EX99
Crockenhill Rd., Swan. 206 EZ100
Crockerton Rd. SW17 180 DF89
Crockery La., Guil. 244 BL129
Crockford Clo., Add. 212 BJ105
Crockford Pk. Rd., Add. 212 BJ106
Crockham Way SE9 185 EN91
Crocknorth Rd., Lthd. 245 BT132
Crocus Clo., Croy. 203 DX102
Cornflower La.
Crocus Fld., Barn. 79 CZ44
Croffets, Tad. 233 CX121
Croft, The E4 102 EE47
Croft, The NW10 139 CT68
Croft, The W5 138 CL71
Croft, The, Barn. 79 CX42
Croft, The, Brox. 49 DY23
Croft, The, Houns. 156 BY79
Croft, The, Loug. 85 EN40
Croft, The, Pnr. 116 BZ59
Rayners La.
Croft, The, Ruis. 116 BW63
Croft, The, St.Alb. 60 CA25
Croft, The, Swan. 207 FC97
Croft, The, Welw.G.C. 29 CZ12
Croft, The, Wem. 117 CJ64
Croft Ave., Dor. 247 CH134
Croft Ave., W.Wick. 203 EC102
Croft Clo. NW7 96 CS48
Croft Clo., Belv. 166 EZ78
Croft Clo., Chis. 185 EM91
Croft Clo., Hayes 155 BQ80
Croft Clo., Kings L. 58 BG30
Croft Clo., Uxb. 134 BN66
Croft End Clo., Chess. 198 CM104
Ashcroft Rd.
Croft End Rd., Kings L. 58 BG30
Croft Fld., Hat. 45 CU18
Croft Fld., Kings L. 58 BG30
Croft Gdns. W7 157 CG75
Croft Gdns., Ruis. 115 BT60
Croft La., Kings L. 58 BG30
Croft Lo. Clo., Wdf.Grn. 102 EH51
Croft Meadow, Kings L. 58 BG30
Croft Ms. N12 98 DC48
Croft Rd. SW16 201 DN95
Croft Rd. SW19 180 DC94
Croft Rd., Brom. 184 EG93
Croft Rd., Cat. 237 DZ122
Croft Rd., Enf. 83 DY39
Croft Rd., Ger.Cr. 90 AY54
Croft Rd., Sutt. 218 DE106
Croft Rd., Ware 32 DW05
Croft Rd., West. 255 EP126
Croft St. SE8 163 DY77
Croft Wk., Brox. 49 DZ23
The Cft.
Croft Way NW3 120 DA63
Ferncroft Ave.
Croft Way, Sev. 256 FF125
Croft Way, Sid. 185 ES90
Croftdown Rd. NW5 120 DG62
Crofters, The, Wind. 172 AU86
Crofters Clo., Islw. 177 CD85
Ploughmans End
Crofters Ct. SE8 163 DY77
Croft St.
Crofters Mead, Croy. 221 DZ109
Crofters Rd., Nthwd. 93 BS49
Crofters Way NW1 141 DK67
Crofthill Rd., Slou. 131 AP70
Croftleigh Ave., Pur. 235 DP116
Crofton, Ash. 232 CL118
Crofton Ave. W4 158 CR80
Crofton Ave., Bex. 186 EX87
Crofton Ave., Orp. 205 EQ103
Crofton Ave., Walt. 196 BW104
Crofton Clo., Cher. 211 BC108
Crofton Gro. E4 101 ED49
Crofton La., Orp. 205 ES101
Crofton Pk. Rd. SE4 183 DZ86
Crofton Rd. E13 144 EH70
Crofton Rd. SE5 162 DS81
Crofton Rd., Grays 170 GE76
Crofton Rd., Orp. 205 EN104
Crofton Ter. E5 123 DY64
Studley Clo.
Crofton Ter., Rich. 158 CM84
Crofton Way, Barn. 80 DB44
Wycherley Cres.
Crofton Way, Enf. 81 DN40
Croftongate Way SE4 183 DY85
Crofts, The, Hem.H. 41 BP21
Crofts, The, Shep. 195 BS98
Crofts La. N22 99 DN52
Glendale Ave.
Crofts Path, Hem.H. 40 BN22
Crofts Rd., Har. 117 CG58
Crofts St. E1 142 DU73
Croftside SE25 202 DU97
Sunny Bank
Croftway NW3 120 DA63
Croftway, Rich. 177 CH90
Crogsland Rd. NW1 140 DG66
Croham Clo., S.Croy. 220 DS107
Croham Manor Rd., S.Croy. 220 DS108
Croham Mt., S.Croy. 220 DS108
Croham Pk. Ave., S.Croy. 220 DT106
Croham Rd., S.Croy. 220 DS106
Croham Valley Rd., S.Croy. 220 DT107
Croindene Rd. SW16 201 DL95
Cromartie Rd. N19 121 DK59
Cromarty Rd., Edg. 96 CP47
Crombie Clo., Ilf. 125 EM57
Crombie Rd., Sid. 185 ER88
Cromer Clo., Uxb. 135 BQ72
Dawley Ave.
Cromer Hyde La., Welw.G.C. 28 CR10
Cromer Pl., Orp. 205 ER102
Andover Rd.
Cromer Rd. E10 123 ED58
James La.
Cromer Rd. N17 100 DU54
Cromer Rd. SE25 202 DV97
Cromer Rd. SW17 180 DG93
Cromer Rd., Barn. 80 DC42
Cromer Rd., Horn. 128 FK59
Cromer Rd., Houns. 154 BN83
Cromer Rd., Rom. 127 FC58
Cromer Rd. (Chadwell Heath), Rom. 126 EY58
Cromer Rd., Wat. 76 BW38
Cromer Rd., Wdf.Grn. 102 EG49
Cromer Rd. W., Houns. 154 BN83
Cromer St. WC1 274 A3
Cromer St. WC1 141 DL69
Cromer Ter. E8 122 DU64
Ferncliff Rd.
Cromer Vil. Rd. SW18 179 CZ86
Cromford Clo., Orp. 205 ES104
Cromford Path E5 123 DX63
Overbury St.
Cromford Rd. SW18 180 DA85
Cromford Way, N.Mal. 198 CR95
Cromlix Clo., Chis. 205 EP96
Crompton St. W2 140 DD70
Cromwell Ave. N6 121 DH60
Cromwell Ave. W6 159 CV78
Cromwell Ave., Brom. 204 EH98
Cromwell Ave., N.Mal. 199 CT99
Cromwell Ave. (Cheshunt), Wal.Cr. 66 DU30
Cromwell Clo. E1 142 DU74
Vaughan Way
Cromwell Clo. N2 120 DD56
Cromwell Clo. W3 138 CQ74
High St.
Cromwell Clo., Brom. 204 EH98
Cromwell Clo., Ch.St.G. 90 AW48
Cromwell Clo., St.Alb. 43 CK15
Cromwell Clo., Walt. 195 BV102
Cromwell Cres. SW5 160 DA77
Cromwell Dr., Slou. 132 AS72
Cromwell Gdns. SW7 276 A7
Cromwell Gdns. SW7 160 DD76
Cromwell Gro. W6 159 CW76
Cromwell Gro., Cat. 236 DQ121
Cromwell Ind. Est. E10 123 DY60
Cromwell Ms. SW7 276 A8
Cromwell Ms. SW7 160 DD77
Cromwell Pl. N6 121 DH60
Cromwell Pl. SW7 276 A8
Cromwell Pl. SW7 160 DD77
Cromwell Pl. SW14 158 CQ83
Cromwell Pl. W3 138 CQ74
Grove Pl.
Cromwell Rd. E7 144 EJ66
Cromwell Rd. E17 123 EC57
Cromwell Rd. N3 98 DC53
Cromwell Rd. N10 98 DG52
Cromwell Rd. SW5 160 DB77
Cromwell Rd. SW7 160 DB77
Cromwell Rd. SW9 161 DP81
Cromwell Rd. SW19 180 DA92
Cromwell Rd., Beck. 203 DY96
Cromwell Rd., Borwd. 78 CL39
Cromwell Rd., Brwd. 108 FV49
Cromwell Rd., Cat. 236 DQ121
Cromwell Rd., Croy. 202 DR101
Cromwell Rd., Felt. 175 BV88
Cromwell Rd., Grays 170 GA77
Cromwell Rd., Hayes 135 BR72
Cromwell Rd., Hert. 32 DT08
Cromwell Rd., Houns. 156 CA84
Cromwell Rd., Kings.T. 198 CL95
Cromwell Rd., Red. 250 DF133
Cromwell Rd., Tedd. 177 CG93
Cromwell Rd. (Cheshunt), Wal.Cr. 66 DV28
Cromwell Rd., Walt. 196 BW102
Cromwell Rd., Ware 33 DZ05
Cromwell Rd., Wem. 138 CL68
Cromwell Rd., Wor.Pk. 198 CR104
Cromwell St., Houns. 156 CA84
Cromwell Twr. EC2 142 DQ71
Whitecross St.
Cromwell Wk., Red. 250 DF134
Cromwells Mere, Rom. 105 FD51
Havering Rd.
Crondace Rd. SW6 160 DA81
Crondall St. N1 275 L1
Crondall St. N1 142 DR68
Cronin St. SE15 162 DT80
Cronks Hill, Red. 266 DC136
Cronks Hill, Reig. 266 DC136
Cronks Hill Clo., Red. 266 DD136
Cronks Hill Rd., Red. 266 DD136
Crook Log, Bexh. 166 EX83
Crooke Rd. SE8 163 DY78
Crooked Billet SW19 179 CW93
Woodhayes Rd.
Crooked Billet Roundabout E17 101 EA52
Crooked Billet Yd. E2 142 DS69
Kingsland Rd.
Crooked La., Grav. 191 GH86
Crooked Mile, Wal.Abb. 67 EC33
Crooked Mile Roundabout, Wal.Abb. 67 EC33
Crooked Usage N3 119 CY55
Crooked Way, Wal.Abb. 50 EE22
Crookham Rd. SW6 159 CZ81
Crookhams, Welw.G.C. 30 DA07
Crookston Rd. SE9 165 EN83
Croombs Rd. E16 144 EJ71
Crooms Hill SE10 163 ED80
Crooms Hill Gro. SE10 163 EC80
Crop Common, Hat. 45 CV16
Cropley Ct. N1 142 DR68
Cropley St.
Cropley St. N1 142 DR68
Croppath Rd., Dag. 126 FA63
Cropthorne Ct. W9 140 DC69
Maida Vale
Crosby Clo., Beac. 111 AM55
Crosby Clo., Felt. 176 BY91
Crosby Clo., St.Alb. 43 CJ23
Crosby Ct. SE1 279 K4
Crosby Rd. E7 144 EG65
Crosby Rd., Dag. 147 FB68
Crosby Row SE1 279 K5
Crosby Row SE1 162 DR75
Crosby Sq. EC3 275 M9
Crosby Wk. E8 142 DT65
Laurel St.
Crosby Wk. SW2 181 DN87
Crosier Rd. (Ickenham), Uxb. 115 BQ63
Crosier Way, Ruis. 115 BS62
Crosland Pl. SW11 160 DG83
Taybridge Rd.
Cross Ave. SE10 163 ED79
Cross Clo. SE15 162 DV81
Gordon Rd.
Cross Deep, Twick. 177 CF90
Cross Deep Gdns., Twick. 177 CF89
Cross Keys Clo. N9 100 DU47
Balham Rd.
Cross Keys Clo. W1 272 G7
Cross Keys Clo., Sev. 256 FG127
Brittains La.
Cross Keys Sq. EC1 275 H7
Cross Lances Rd., Houns. 156 CB84
Cross La. EC3 279 M1
Cross La. N8 121 DM56
Cross La., Beac. 111 AM55
Cross La., Bex. 186 EZ87
Cross La., Cher. 211 BB107
Chobham Rd.
Cross La., Hert. 31 DP09
Cross La. E., Grav. 191 GH89
Cross La. Footpath, Cher. 211 BB107
Cross La. W., Grav. 191 GH89
Cross Las., Ger.Cr. 91 AZ50
Cross Las., Guil. 243 AZ134
Cross Las. Clo., Ger.Cr. 91 AZ50
Cross Las.
Cross Meadow, Chesh. 54 AM29
Cross Oak, Wind. 151 AN82
Cross Oak Rd., Berk. 38 AU20
Cross Rd. E4 102 EE46
Cross Rd. N11 99 DH50
Cross Rd. N22 99 DN52

Cro - Cut This index reads in the sequence: Street Name / Postal District or Post Town / Map Page Number / Grid Reference

Cross Rd. SE5 162 DS82
Cross Rd. SW19 180 DA94
Cross Rd., Brom. 204 EL103
Cross Rd., Croy. 202 DR102
Cross Rd., Dart. 188 FJ86
Cross Rd. (Hawley), Dart. 188 FM91
Cross Rd., Enf. 82 DS42
Cross Rd., Felt. 176 BY91
Cross Rd., Grav. 191 GF86
Cross Rd., Har. 117 CD56
Cross Rd. (South Harrow), Har. 116 CB62
Cross Rd. (Wealdstone), Har. 95 CG54
Cross Rd., Hert. 32 DQ08
Cross Rd., Kings.T. 178 CM94
Cross Rd., Orp. 206 EV99
Cross Rd., Pur. 219 DP113
Cross Rd., Rom. 126 FA55
Cross Rd. (Chadwell Heath), Rom. 126 EW59
Cross Rd., Sid. 186 EV91
Sidcup Hill
Cross Rd., Sutt. 218 DD106
Cross Rd. (Belmont), Sutt. 218 DA110
Cross Rd., Tad. 233 CW122
Cross Rd., Uxb. 134 BJ66
New Windsor St.
Cross Rd., Wal.Cr. 67 DY33
Cross Rd., Wat. 76 BY44
Cross Rd., Wey. 195 BR104
Cross Rd., Wdf.Grn. 103 EM51
Cross Rds., Loug. 84 EH40
Cross St. N1 141 DP67
Cross St. SW13 158 CS82
Cross St., Erith 167 FE78
Bexley Rd.
Cross St., Hmptn. 176 CC92
Cross St., Harl. 51 ER15
Cross St., St.Alb. 43 CD20
Spencer St.
Cross St., Uxb. 134 BJ66
Cross St., Ware 33 DY06
Cross St., Wat. 76 BW41
Cross Way, The, Har. 95 CE54
Cross Ways, Hem.H. 41 BP20
Crossacres, Wok. 227 BE116
Crossbow Rd., Chig. 103 ET50
Crossbrook, Hat. 44 CS19
Crossbrook Rd. SE3 164 EL82
Crossbrook St. (Cheshunt), Wal.Cr. 67 DX31
Crossett Grn., Hem.H. 41 BQ22
Crossfell Rd., Hem.H. 41 BQ22
Crossfield Clo., Berk. 38 AT19
Crossfield Pl., Wey. 213 BP108
Crossfield Rd. N17 122 DQ55
Crossfield Rd. NW3 140 DD66
Crossfield Rd., Hodd. 49 EB15
Crossfield St. SE8 163 EA80
Crossfields, Loug. 85 EP43
Crossfields, St.Alb. 42 CB23
Crossford St. SW9 161 DM82
Crossgate, Edg. 96 CN48
Crossgate, Grnf. 137 CH65
Crossing Rd., Epp. 70 EU32
Crossland Rd., Red. 250 DG134
Crossland Rd., Th.Hth. 201 DP100
Crosslands, Cher. 211 BE105
Crosslands Ave. W5 138 CM74
Crosslands Ave., Sthl. 156 BZ78
Crosslands Rd., Epsom 216 CR107
Crosslet St. SE17 279 L8
Crosslet Vale SE10 163 EB81
Blackheath Rd.
Crossley Clo., West. 238 EK115
Crossley St. N7 141 DN65
Crossleys, Ch.St.G. 90 AW49
Crossmead SE9 185 EM88
Crossmead, Wat. 75 BV44
Crossmead Ave., Grnf. 136 CA69
Crossmount Ho. SE5 162 DQ80
Crossness La. SE28 146 EX73
Crossness Rd., Bark. 145 ET69
Crossoak La., Red. 266 DG144
Crossoaks La., Borwd. 78 CR35
Crossoaks La. (South Mimms), Pot.B. 62 CS34
Crosspath, The, Rad. 77 CG35
Crossroads, The, Lthd. 246 BX128
Crossthwaite Ave. SE5 162 DR84
Crosswall EC3 275 P10
Crosswall EC3 142 DT73
Crossway N12 98 DD51
Crossway N16 122 DS64
Crossway NW9 119 CT56
Crossway SE28 146 EW72
Crossway SW20 199 CW98
Crossway W13 137 CG70
Crossway, Chesh. 54 AS30
Crossway, Dag. 126 EW62
Crossway, Enf. 100 DS45
Crossway, Hayes 135 BU74
Crossway, Orp. 205 ER98
Crossway, Pnr. 93 BV54
Crossway, Ruis. 116 BW63
Crossway, Walt. 195 BV103
Crossway, Welw.G.C. 29 CW05
Crossway, Wdf.Grn. 102 EJ49
Crossway, The N22 99 DP52
Crossway, The SE9 184 EK89
Crossway, The, Uxb. 134 BM68
Crossways N21 82 DQ44
Crossways, Beac. 89 AM54
Crossways, Berk. 38 AT20
Crossways, Brwd. 109 GA44
Crossways, Egh. 173 BD93
Crossways, Lthd. 246 BX127
The St.
Crossways, Rom. 127 FH55
Crossways, S.Croy. 221 DY108
Crossways, Sun. 175 BT94
Crossways, Sutt. 218 DD109
Crossways, West. 238 EJ120
Crossways, The, Couls. 235 DM119
Crossways, The, Guil. 258 AT136
Crossways, The, Houns. 156 BZ80
Crossways, The, Red. 251 DJ130
Crossways, The, Wem. 118 CN61
Crossways Boul., Dart. 168 FQ84
Crossways Boul., Green. 169 FT84
Crossways Business Pk., Dart. 168 FQ84
Crossways La., Reig. 250 DC128
Crossways Rd., Beck. 203 EA98
Crossways Rd., Mitch. 201 DH97
Crosswell Clo., Shep. 195 BQ96
Crosthwaite Way, Slou. 131 AK71
Croston St. E8 142 DU67
Crothall Clo. N13 99 DM48
Crouch Ave., Bark. 146 EV68
Crouch Clo., Beck. 183 EA93
Abbey La.
Crouch Cft. SE9 185 EN90
Crouch End Hill N8 121 DK59
Crouch Hall Rd. N8 121 DK58
Crouch Hill N4 121 DL58
Crouch Hill N8 121 DL58
Crouch La. (Cheshunt), Wal.Cr. 66 DQ28
Crouch Oak La., Add. 212 BJ105
Crouch Rd. NW10 138 CR66
Crouch Rd., Grays 171 GG78
Crouch Valley, Upmin. 129 FS59
Crouchfield, Hem.H. 40 BH21
Crouchfield, Hert. 32 DQ06
Crouchman's Clo. SE26 182 DT90
Crow Clo., Warl. 237 DY118
Crow Dr., Sev. 241 FC115
Crow Grn. La., Brwd. 108 FU43
Crow Grn. Rd., Brwd. 108 FT43
Crow La., Rom. 126 EZ59
Crow Piece La., Slou. 131 AM66
Crowborough Clo., Warl. 237 DY118
Crowborough Dr., Warl. 237 DY118
Crowborough Path, Wat. 94 BX49
Prestwick Rd.
Crowborough Rd. SW17 180 DG93
Crowden Way SE28 146 EW73
Crowder St. E1 142 DV73
Crowfoot Clo. E9 123 DZ64
Lee Conservancy Rd.
Crowhurst Clo. SW9 161 DN82
Crowhurst Mead, Gdse. 252 DW130
Crowhurst Way, Orp. 206 EW99
Crowland Ave., Hayes 155 BS77
Crowland Gdns. N14 99 DL45
Crowland Rd. N15 122 DT57
Crowland Rd., Th.Hth. 202 DR98
Crowland Ter. N1 142 DR66
Crowland Wk., Mord. 200 DB100
Crowlands Ave., Rom. 127 FB58
Crowley Cres., Croy. 219 DN106
Crowline Wk. N1 142 DR65
Clephane Rd.
Crowmarsh Gdns. SE23 182 DW87
Tyson Rd.
Crown Arc., Kings.T. 197 CK96
Union St.
Crown Ash Hill, West. 222 EH114
Crown Ash La., West. 238 EG116
Crown Clo. E3 143 EA67
Crown Clo. NW6 140 DB65
Crown Clo. NW7 97 CT47
Crown Clo., B.Stort. 37 FC07
Crown Clo., Hayes 155 BT75
Station Rd.
Crown Clo., Orp. 224 EU105
Crown Clo., Walt. 196 BW101
Crown Ct. EC2 275 J9
Crown Ct. SE12 184 EH86
Crown Ct. WC2 274 A9
Crown Ct., Brom. 204 EK99
Victoria Rd.
Crown Dale SE19 181 DP93
Crown Gate, Harl. 51 ER15
Crown Hts., Guil. 258 AY137
Crown Hill, Croy. 202 DQ103
Church St.
Crown Hill, Epp. 69 EM33
Crown Hill, Wal.Abb. 69 EM33
Crown La. N14 99 DJ46
Crown La. SW16 181 DN92
Crown La., Brom. 204 EK99
Crown La., Chis. 205 EQ95
Crown La., H.Wyc. 88 AF48
Crown La., Mord. 200 DB97
Crown La., Slou. 131 AN67
Crown La., Vir.W. 192 AX100
Crown La. Gdns. SW16 181 DN92
Crown La.
Crown La. Spur, Brom. 204 EK100
Crown Meadow, Slou. 153 BB80
Crown Ms. E13 144 EJ67
Waghorn Rd.
Crown Ms. W6 159 CU77
Crown Office Row EC4 274 D10
Crown Pas. SW1 277 L3
Crown Pas. SW1 141 DJ74
Crown Pas., Wat. 76 BW42
The Cres.
Crown Pl. EC2 275 M6
Crown Pl. EC2 142 DS71
Crown Pl. NW5 141 DH65
Kentish Town Rd.
Crown Pt. Par. SE19 181 DP93
Beulah Hill
Crown Ri., Cher. 193 BF102
Crown Ri., Wat. 60 BW34
Crown Rd. N10 98 DG52
Crown Rd., Borwd. 78 CN39
Crown Rd., Enf. 82 DV42
Crown Rd., Grays 170 GA79
Crown Rd., Ilf. 125 ER56
Crown Rd., Mord. 200 DB98
Crown Rd., N.Mal. 198 CQ95
Crown Rd., Orp. 224 EU106
Crown Rd., Ruis. 116 BX64
Crown Rd., Sev. 225 FF110
Crown Rd., Slou. 153 BB80
Crown Rd., Sutt. 218 DB105
Crown Rd., Twick. 177 CH86
Crown Rd., Vir.W. 192 AW100
Crown Sq., Wok. 227 AZ117
Commercial Way
Crown St. SE5 162 DQ80
Crown St. W3 138 CP74
Crown St., Brwd. 108 FW47
Crown St., Dag. 147 FC65
Crown St., Egh. 173 BA91
Crown St., Har. 117 CD60
Crown Ter., Rich. 158 CM84
Crown Wk., Uxb. 134 BJ66
Oxford Rd.
Crown Wk., Wem. 118 CM62
Crown Way, West Dr. 134 BM74
Crown Wds. La. SE9 165 EP82
Crown Wds. La. SE18 165 EP82
Crown Wds. Way SE9 185 ER85
Crown Wks. E2 142 DV68
Temple St.
Crown Yd., Houns. 156 CC83
High St.
Crowndale Rd. NW1 141 DJ68
Crownfield, Brox. 49 EA21
Crownfield Ave., Ilf. 125 ES57
Crownfield Rd. E15 123 ED64
Crownfields, Sev. 257 FH125
Crownhill Rd. NW10 139 CT67
Crownhill Rd., Wdf.Grn. 102 EL52
Crownmead Way, Rom. 127 FB56
Crownstone Rd. SW2 181 DN85
Crowntree Clo., Islw. 157 CF79
Crows Rd. E15 143 ED69
Crows Rd., Epp. 69 ET30
Crowshott Ave., Stan. 95 CJ53
Crowstone Rd., Grays 170 GC75
Crowther Ave., Brent. 158 CL77
Crowther Rd. SE25 202 DU98
Crowthorne Clo. SW18 179 CZ88
Crowthorne Rd. W10 139 CX72
Croxdale Rd., Borwd. 78 CM40
Croxden Clo., Edg. 118 CM55
Croxden Wk., Mord. 200 DC100
Croxford Gdns. N22 99 DP52
Croxford Way, Rom. 127 FD60
Horace Ave.
Croxley Clo., Orp. 206 EV96
Croxley Grn., Orp. 206 EV95
Croxley Rd. W9 139 CZ69
Croxley Vw., Wat. 75 BS44
Croxted Clo. SE21 182 DQ87
Croxted Rd. SE21 182 DQ87
Croxted Rd. SE24 182 DQ87
Croyde Ave., Grnf. 136 CC69
Croyde Ave., Hayes 155 BS77
Croyde Clo., Sid. 185 ER87
Croydon Flyover, Croy. 219 DP105
Croydon Gro., Croy. 201 DP102
Croydon La., Bans. 218 DC114
Croydon La. S., Bans. 218 DB114
Croydon Rd. E13 144 EF70
Croydon Rd. SE20 202 DV96
Croydon Rd., Beck. 203 DY98
Croydon Rd., Brom. 204 EF104
Croydon Rd., Cat. 236 DU122
Croydon Rd., Croy. 219 DH105
Croydon Rd., Houns. 155 BP82
Croydon Rd., Kes. 204 EJ104
Croydon Rd., Mitch. 200 DG98
Croydon Rd., Reig. 250 DB134
Croydon Rd., Wall. 219 DH105
Croydon Rd., Warl. 237 EC119
Croydon Rd., W.Wick. 204 EE104
Croydon Rd., West. 239 EM123
Croyland Rd. N9 100 DU46
Croylands Dr., Surb. 198 CL101
Croysdale Ave., Sun. 195 BU97
Crozier Dr., S.Croy. 220 DV110
Crozier Ter. E9 123 DX64
Crucible Clo., Rom. 126 EV58
Crucifix La. SE1 279 M4
Crucifix La. SE1 162 DS75
Cruden Ho. SE17 161 DP79
Hillingdon St.
Cruden Rd., Grav. 191 GM90
Cruden St. N1 141 DP67
Cruick Ave., S.Ock. 149 FW73
Cruikshank Rd. E15 124 EE63
Cruikshank St. WC1 274 D2
Cruikshank St. WC1 141 DN69
Crum Clo., Slou. 130 AJ72
Crummock Gdns. NW9 118 CS57
Crumpsall St. SE2 166 EW77
Crundale Ave. NW9 118 CN57
Crundale Twr., Orp. 206 EW102
Crunden Rd., S.Croy. 220 DR108
Crusader Clo., Purf. 168 FN77
Centurion Way
Crusader Gdns., Croy. 202 DS104
Cotelands
Crusader Way, Wat. 75 BT44
Crushes Clo., Brwd. 109 GE44
Crusoe Ms. N16 122 DR61
Crusoe Rd., Erith 167 FD78
Crusoe Rd., Mitch. 180 DF94
Crutched Friars EC3 275 N10
Crutched Friars EC3 142 DS73
Crutches La., Beac. 90 AS51
Crutchfield La., Horl. 268 DA145
Crutchfield La., Walt. 195 BV103
Crutchley Rd. SE6 184 EE89
Crystal Ave., Horn. 128 FL63
Crystal Ct. SE19 182 DT92
College Rd.
Crystal Ho. SE18 165 ET78
Spinel Clo.
Crystal Palace Par. SE19 182 DT93
Crystal Palace Pk. Rd. SE26 182 DU92
Crystal Palace Rd. SE22 162 DU84
Crystal Palace Sta. Rd. SE19 182 DU93
Anerley Hill
Crystal Ter. SE19 182 DR93
Crystal Vw. Ct., Brom. 183 ED91
Winlaton Rd.
Crystal Way, Dag. 126 EW60
Crystal Way, Har. 117 CF57
Cuba Dr., Enf. 82 DW40
Cuba St. E14 163 EA75
Cubitt Sq., Sthl. 136 CC74
Windmill Ave.
Cubitt Steps E14 143 EA74
Cabot Sq.
Cubitt St. WC1 274 B3
Cubitt St. WC1 141 DM69
Cubitt St., Croy. 219 DM106
Cubitt Ter. SW4 161 DJ83
Cubitts Yd. WC2 274 A10
Cublands, Hert. 32 DV09
Cuckmans Dr., St.Alb. 60 CA25
Cuckoo Ave. W7 137 CE70
Cuckoo Dene W7 137 CD71
Cuckoo Hall La. N9 100 DW45
Cuckoo Hill, Pnr. 116 BW55
Cuckoo Hill Dr., Pnr. 116 BW55
Cuckoo Hill Rd., Pnr. 116 BW56
Cuckoo La. W7 137 CE73
Cuckoo Pound, Shep. 195 BS99
Cucumber La., Hat. 46 DF20
Cucumber La., Hert. 46 DG23
Cudas Clo., Epsom 217 CT105
Cuddington Ave., Wor.Pk. 199 CT104
Cuddington Clo., Tad. 233 CW120
Cuddington Pk. Clo., Bans. 217 CZ113
Cuddington Way, Sutt. 217 CX112
Cudham Clo., Sutt. 218 DA110
Cudham Dr., Croy. 221 EC110
Cudham La. N., Orp. 223 ES110
Cudham La. N., Sev. 223 ER112
Cudham La. S., Sev. 239 ER116
Cudham Pk. Rd., Sev. 223 ES110
Cudham Rd., Orp. 223 EN111
Cudham Rd., West. 238 EL120
Cudham St. SE6 183 EC87
Cudworth St. E1 142 DV70
Cuff Cres. SE9 184 EK86
Cuff Pt. E2 275 P2
Cuff Pt. E2 142 DT69
Cuffley Ave., Wat. 60 BX34
Cuffley Ct., Hem.H. 41 BQ15
Cuffley Hill (Cheshunt), Wal.Cr. 65 DN29
Cugley Rd., Dart. 188 FQ87
Culford Gdns. SW3 276 E9
Culford Gdns. SW3 160 DF77
Culford Gro. N1 142 DS65
Culford Ms. N1 142 DS65
Culford Rd.
Culford Rd. N1 142 DS66
Culford Rd., Grays 170 GC75
Culgaith Gdns., Enf. 81 DL42
Cullen Sq., S.Ock. 149 FW73
Cullen Way NW10 138 CQ70
Cullera Clo., Nthwd. 93 BT51
Cullerne Clo., Epsom 217 CT110
Cullesden Rd., Ken. 235 DP115
Culling Rd. SE16 162 DW76
Lower Rd.
Cullings Ct., Wal.Abb. 68 EF33
Cullington Clo., Har. 117 CG56
Cullingworth Rd. NW10 119 CU64
Culloden Clo. SE16 162 DU78
Culloden Rd., Enf. 81 DP40
Culloden St. E14 143 EC72
Cullum St. EC3 275 M10
Culmington Rd. W13 157 CJ75
Culmington Rd., S.Croy. 220 DQ109
Culmore Cross SW12 181 DH88
Culmore Rd. SE15 162 DV80
Culmstock Rd. SW11 180 DG85
Culpeper Clo., Ilf. 103 EP51
Culross Clo. N15 122 DQ56
Culross St. W1 276 F1
Culross St. W1 140 DG73
Culsac Rd., Surb. 198 CL103
Culver Dr., Oxt. 254 EE130
Culver Gro., Stan. 95 CJ54
Culver Rd., St.Alb. 43 CE19
Culverden Rd. SW12 181 DJ89
Culverden Rd., Wat. 93 BV48
Culverhay, Ash. 232 CL116
Culverhouse Gdns. SW16 181 DM90
Culverlands Clo., Stan. 95 CH49
Culverley Rd. SE6 183 EB88
Culvers Ave., Cars. 200 DF103
Culvers Cft., Beac. 89 AQ51
Culvers Retreat, Cars. 200 DF102
Culvers Way, Cars. 200 DF103
Culverstone Clo., Brom. 204 EF100
Culvert La., Uxb. 134 BH68
Culvert Pl. SW11 160 DG82
Culvert Rd. N15 122 DS57
Culvert Rd. SW11 160 DF82
Culworth St. NW8 272 B1
Cum Cum Hill, Hat. 46 DD21
Cumberland Ave. NW10 138 CP69
Cumberland Ave., Grav. 191 GJ87
Cumberland Ave., Guil. 242 AU129
Cumberland Ave., Horn. 128 FL62
Cumberland Ave., Slou. 131 AQ70
Cumberland Ave., Well. 165 ES83
Cumberland Clo. E8 142 DT65
Cumberland Clo. SW20 179 CX94
Lansdowne Rd.
Cumberland Clo., Amer. 72 AV39
Cumberland Clo., Epsom 216 CS110
Cumberland Clo., Hem.H. 41 BS24
Cumberland Clo., Hert. 31 DP06
Cumberland Clo., Horn. 128 FL62
Cumberland Clo., Ilf. 103 EQ53
Carrick Dr.
Cumberland Clo., Twick. 177 CH86
Westmorland Clo.
Cumberland Cres. W14 159 CY77
Cumberland Dr., Bexh. 166 EY80
Cumberland Dr., Chess. 198 CM104
Cumberland Dr., Dart. 188 FM87
Cumberland Dr., Esher 197 CG103
Cumberland Gdns. NW4 97 CY54
Cumberland Gdns. WC1 274 C2
Cumberland Gate W1 272 D10
Cumberland Gate W1 140 DF73
Cumberland Mkt. NW1 273 J2
Cumberland Mkt. NW1 141 DH69
Cumberland Mkt. Est. NW1 273 J2
Cumberland Mills Sq. E14 163 ED78
Saunders Ness Rd.
Cumberland Pk. W3 139 CU69
Cumberland Pl. NW1 273 H2
Cumberland Pl. SE6 184 EF88
Cumberland Pl., Sun. 195 BU98
Cumberland Rd. E12 124 EK63
Cumberland Rd. E13 144 EH71
Cumberland Rd. E17 101 DY54
Cumberland Rd. N9 100 DW46
Cumberland Rd. N22 99 DM54
Cumberland Rd. SE25 202 DV100
Cumberland Rd. SW13 159 CT81
Cumberland Rd. W3 138 CQ73
Cumberland Rd. W7 157 CF75
Cumberland Rd., Ashf. 174 BK90
Cumberland Rd., Brom. 204 EE98
Cumberland Rd., Har. 116 CB57
Cumberland Rd., Rich. 158 CN80
Cumberland Rd., Stan. 118 CM55
Cumberland St. SW1 277 J10
Cumberland St. SW1 161 DH78
Cumberland St., Stai. 173 BD92
Cumberland Ter. NW1 273 H2
Cumberland Ter. Ms. NW1 273 H1
Cumberland Vil. W3 138 CQ73
Cumberland Rd.
Cumberlands, Ken. 236 DR115
Cumberlow Ave. SE25 202 DT97
Cumberlow Pl., Hem.H. 41 BQ21
Cumbernauld Gdns., Sun. 175 BT92
Cumberton Rd. N17 100 DR53
Cumbrae Gdns., Surb. 197 CJ102
Cumbrian Ave., Bexh. 167 FE81
Cumbrian Gdns. NW2 119 CX61
Cumbrian Way, Uxb. 134 BK66
Chippendale Waye
Cumley Rd., Ong. 71 FE30
Cumming St. N1 274 B1
Cumming St. N1 141 DM68
Cummings Hall La., Rom. 106 FJ48
Cumnor Gdns., Epsom 217 CU107
Cumnor Ri., Ken. 236 DQ117
Cumnor Rd., Sutt. 218 DC107
Cunard Cres. N21 82 DR44
Cunard Pl. EC3 275 N9
Cunard Rd. NW10 138 CR69
Cunard St. SE5 162 DS79
Albany Rd.
Cunard Wk. SE16 163 DY77
Cundalls Rd., Ware 33 DY05
Cundy Rd. E16 144 EJ72
Cundy St. SW1 276 G9
Cundy St. SW1 160 DG77
Cundy St. Est. SW1 276 G9
Cunliffe Clo., Epsom 232 CP124
Cunliffe Rd., Epsom 217 CT105
Cunliffe St. SW16 181 DJ93
Cunningham Ave., Enf. 83 DY36
Cunningham Ave., Guil. 243 BA133
Cunningham Ave., St.Alb. 43 CF22
Cunningham Clo., Rom. 126 EW57
Cunningham Clo., W.Wick. 203 EB103
Cunningham Hill Rd., St.Alb. 43 CF22
Cunningham Pk., Har. 116 CC57
Cunningham Pl. NW8 140 DD70
Cunningham Ri., Epp. 71 FC25
Cunningham Rd. N15 122 DU56
Cunningham Rd., Bans. 234 DD115
Cunningham Rd. (Cheshunt), Wal.Cr. 67 DY27
Cunnington St. W4 158 CQ76
Cupar Rd. SW11 160 DG81
Cupola Clo., Brom. 184 EH92
Cureton St. SW1 277 N9
Cureton St. SW1 161 DK77
Curfew Bell Rd., Cher. 193 BF101
Curfew Ho., Bark. 145 EQ67
St. Ann's
Curfew Yd., Wind. 151 AR80
Thames St.
Curlew Clo. SE28 146 EX73
Curlew Clo., Berk. 38 AW20
Curlew Clo., S.Croy. 221 DX111
Curlew Ct., Brox. 49 DZ23
Curlew Ct., Surb. 198 CM104
Curlew Gdns., Guil. 243 BD132
Curlew St. SE1 279 P4
Curlew St. SE1 162 DT75
Curlew Way, Hayes 136 BX71
Curlews, The, Grav. 191 GK89
Curling Clo., Couls. 235 DM120
Curling La., Grays 170 FZ78
Curling Vale, Guil. 258 AU136
Curnick's La. SE27 182 DQ91
Chapel Rd.
Curnock Est. NW1 141 DJ67
Plender St.
Curran Ave., Sid. 185 ET85
Curran Ave., Wall. 200 DG104
Curran Clo., Uxb. 134 BJ70
Currey Rd., Grnf. 137 CD65
Curricle St. W3 138 CS74
Currie Hill Clo. SW19 179 CZ91
Currie St., Hert. 32 DS09
Curries La., Slou. 111 AK64
Curry Ri. NW7 97 CX51
Cursitor St. EC4 274 D8
Cursitor St. EC4 141 DN72
Curtain Pl. EC2 142 DS69
Curtain Rd.
Curtain Rd. EC2 275 M5
Curtain Rd. EC2 142 DS70
Curteys, Harl. 36 EX10
Curthwaite Gdns., Enf. 81 DK42
Curtis Clo., Rick. 92 BG46
Curtis Dr. W3 138 CR72
Curtis Fld. Rd. SW16 181 DM91
Curtis Gdns., Dor. 263 CG135
Curtis La., Wem. 138 CL65
Montrose Cres.
Curtis Mill Grn., Rom. 87 FE42
Curtis Mill La., Rom. 87 FE42
Curtis Rd., Dor. 263 CF135
Curtis Rd., Epsom 216 CQ105
Curtis Rd., Hem.H. 41 BR21
Curtis Rd., Horn. 128 FM60
Curtis Rd., Houns. 176 BY87
Curtis St. SE1 279 P8
Curtis St. SE1 162 DT77
Curtis Way SE1 279 P8
Curtis Way SE1 162 DT77
Curtis Way SE28 146 EV73
Tawney Rd.
Curtis Way, Berk. 38 AX20
Curtismill Clo., Orp. 206 EV97
Curtismill Way, Orp. 206 EV97
Curvan Clo., Epsom 217 CT110
Curve, The W12 139 CU73
Curwen Ave. E7 124 EH63
Woodford Rd.
Curwen Rd. W12 159 CU75
Curzon Ave., Beac. 89 AK51
Curzon Ave., Enf. 83 DX43
Curzon Ave., H.Wyc. 88 AC45
Curzon Ave., Stan. 95 CG53
Curzon Clo., H.Wyc. 88 AC45
Curzon Clo., Orp. 223 ER105
Curzon Clo., Wey. 212 BN105
Curzon Rd.
Curzon Cres. NW10 139 CT66
Curzon Cres., Bark. 145 ET68
Curzon Dr., Grays 170 GC80
Curzon Gate W1 276 G3
Curzon Gate W1 140 DG74
Curzon Mall, Slou. 152 AT75
High St.
Curzon Pl. W1 276 G3
Curzon Pl., Pnr. 116 BW57
Curzon Rd. N10 99 DH54
Curzon Rd. W5 137 CH70
Curzon Rd., Th.Hth. 201 DN100
Curzon Rd., Wey. 212 BN105
Curzon St. W1 276 G3
Curzon St. W1 140 DG74
Cusack Clo., Twick. 177 CF91
Waldegrave Rd.
Cussons Clo. (Cheshunt), Wal.Cr. 66 DU29
Custom Ho. Reach SE16 163 DZ75
Custom Ho. Wk. EC3 279 M1
Custom Ho. Wk. EC3 142 DS73
Cut, The SE1 278 E4
Cut, The SE1 161 DN75
Cut, The, Slou. 131 AN70
Long Furlong Dr.
Cut Hills, Egh. 192 AU97
Cutcombe Rd. SE5 162 DQ82
Cuthberga Clo., Bark. 145 EQ66
George St.
Cuthbert Gdns. SE25 202 DS97

323

Dat - Den This index reads in the sequence: Street Name / Postal District or Post Town / Map Page Number / Grid Reference

Datchet Rd. SE6 183 DZ90
Datchet Rd., Slou. 152 AT77
Datchet Rd. (Horton), Slou. 153 AZ83
Datchet Rd., Wind. 151 AR80
Datchet Rd. (Old Windsor), Wind. 152 AU84
Datchworth Ct. N4 122 DQ62
Queens Dr.
Datchworth Turn, Hem.H. 41 BQ20
Date St. SE17 162 DQ78
Daubeney Gdns. N17 100 DQ52
Daubeney Rd. E5 123 DY63
Daubeney Rd. N17 100 DQ52
Daubeney Twr. SE8 163 DZ77
Dault Rd. SW18 180 DC86
Davall Ho., Grays 170 GA79
Argent St.
Davema Clo., Chis. 205 EN95
Brenchley Clo.
Davenant Rd. N19 121 DK61
Davenant Rd., Croy. 219 DP105
Duppas Hill Rd.
Davenant St. E1 142 DU71
Davenham Ave., Nthwd. 93 BT50
Davenport Clo., Tedd. 177 CG93
Davenport Rd. SE6 183 EB86
Davenport Rd., Sid. 186 EX89
Daventer Dr., Stan. 95 CF52
Daventry Ave. E17 123 EA57
Daventry Clo., Slou. 153 BF81
Daventry Gdns., Rom. 106 FJ50
Daventry Grn., Rom. 106 FJ50
Hailsham Rd.
Daventry Rd., Rom. 106 FJ50
Daventry St. NW1 272 B6
Daventry St. NW1 140 DE71
Davern Clo. SE10 164 EF77
Davey Clo. N7 141 DM65
Davey Rd. E9 143 EA66
Davey St. SE15 162 DT79
David Ave., Grnf. 137 CE69
David Clo., Hayes 155 BR80
David Dr., Rom. 106 FN51
David Ms. W1 272 E6
David Rd., Dag. 126 EY61
David Rd., Slou. 153 BF82
David St. E15 143 ED65
Davidge St. SE1 278 F5
Davidge St. SE1 161 DP75
Davids Rd. SE23 182 DW88
David's Way, Ilf. 103 ES52
Davidson Gdns. SW8 161 DL80
Davidson La., Har. 117 CF59
Grove Hill
Davidson Rd., Croy. 202 DT100
Davidson Way, Rom. 127 FE58
Davies Clo., Croy. 202 DU100
Davies Clo., Rain. 148 FJ69
Davies La. E11 124 EE61
Davies Ms. W1 273 H10
Davies St. W1 273 H10
Davies St. W1 141 DH73
Davies St., Hert. 32 DS09
Davies Way, H.Wyc. 88 AC54
Davington Gdns., Dag. 126 EV64
Davington Rd., Dag. 146 EV65
Davinia Clo., Wdf.Grn. 103 EM51
Deacon Way
Davis Ave., Grav. 190 GE88
Davis Clo., Sev. 257 FJ122
Davis Rd. W3 139 CT74
Davis Rd., Chess. 216 CN105
Davis Rd., Grays 170 FZ76
Davis Rd., S.Ock. 149 FR74
Davis Rd., Wey. 212 BM110
Davis St. E13 144 EH68
Davison Clo., Wal.Cr. 67 DX28
Davison Dr. (Cheshunt), Wal.Cr. 67 DX28
Davisville Rd. W12 159 CU75
Davos Clo., Wok. 226 AY119
Davys Clo., St.Alb. 28 CL08
Davys Pl., Grav. 191 GL93
Dawell Dr., West. 238 EJ117
Dawes Ave., Horn. 128 FK62
Dawes Ave., Islw. 177 CG85
Dawes Clo., Chesh. 54 AP32
Dawes Clo., Green. 189 FT85
Dawes Ct., Esher 214 CB105
Dawes E. Rd., Slou. 130 AJ70
Dawes Ho. SE17 279 L9
Dawes La., Rick. 73 BE37
Dawes Moor Clo., Slou. 132 AW72
Dawes Rd. SW6 159 CY80
Dawes Rd., Uxb. 134 BL68
Dawes St. SE17 279 L10
Dawes St. SE17 162 DR78
Dawley, Welw.G.C. 29 CZ06
Dawley Ave., Uxb. 135 BQ71
Dawley Ct., Hem.H. 40 BN16
Dawley Grn., S.Ock. 149 FU72
Dawley Par., Hayes 135 BQ73
Dawley Rd.
Dawley Ride, Slou. 153 BE81
Dawley Rd., Hayes 155 BS76
Dawlish Ave. N13 99 DL49
Dawlish Ave. SW18 180 DB89
Dawlish Ave., Grnf. 137 CG68
Dawlish Dr., Ilf. 125 ES63
Dawlish Dr., Pnr. 116 BY57
Dawlish Dr., Ruis. 115 BU61
Dawlish Rd. E10 123 EC61
Dawlish Rd. N17 122 DU55
Dawlish Rd. NW2 139 CX65
Dawlish Wk., Rom. 106 FJ53
Neave Cres.
Dawn Clo., Houns. 156 BY83
Dawn Cres. E15 143 ED67
Bridge Rd.
Dawn Redwood Clo., Slou. 153 BA83
Dawnay Gdns. SW18 180 DD89
Dawnay Rd. SW18 180 DC89
Dawnay Rd., Lthd. 246 CB126
Dawpool Rd. NW2 119 CT61
Daws Hill E4 83 EC41
Daws La. NW7 97 CT50
Dawson Ave., Bark. 145 ET66
Dawson Ave., Orp. 206 EV96
Dawson Clo. SE18 165 EQ77
Dawson Clo., Hayes 135 BR71
Dawson Clo., Wind. 151 AN82
Dawson Dr., Rain. 147 FH66
Dawson Dr., Swan. 187 FE93
Dawson Gdns., Bark. 145 ET66
Dawson Ave.
Dawson Hts. Est. SE22 182 DU87
Dawson Pl. W2 140 DA73
Dawson Rd. NW2 119 CW64
Dawson Rd., Kings.T. 198 CM97
Dawson Rd., W.Byf. 212 BK111
Dawson St. E2 142 DT68
Dax Ct., Sun. 196 BW97
Thames St.
Day Spring, Guil. 242 AV130
Daybrook Rd. SW19 200 DB96
Daye Mead, Welw.G.C. 30 DB12
Daylesford Ave. SW15 159 CU84
Daylop Dr., Chig. 104 EV48
Daymer Gdns., Pnr. 115 BV56
Daymerslea Ridge, Lthd. 231 CJ121
Days Acre, S.Croy. 220 DT110
Days Clo., Hat. 45 CT18
Days La., Brwd. 108 FU42
Days La., Sid. 185 ES87
Days Mead, Hat. 45 CT18
Daysbrook Rd. SW2 181 DM88
Dayseys Hill, Red. 267 DN143
Dayton Dr., Erith 168 FK78
Dayton Gro. SE15 162 DW81
De Barowe Ms. N5 121 DP63
Leigh Rd.
De Beauvoir Cres. N1 142 DS67
De Beauvoir Est. N1 142 DR67
De Beauvoir Rd. N1 142 DS67
De Beauvoir Sq. N1 142 DS66
De Bohun Ave. N14 81 DH44
De Brome Rd., Felt. 176 BW88
De Burgh Pk., Bans. 234 DB115
De Crespigny Pk. SE5 162 DR82
De Frene Rd. SE26 183 DX91
De Havilland Ave., Hat. 44 CS17
De Havilland Clo., Hat. 45 CT17
De Havilland Ct., Rad. 62 CL32
Armstrong Gdns.
De Havilland Dr., Wey. 212 BL111
De Havilland Rd., Edg. 96 CP54
De Havilland Rd., Houns. 156 BW80
De Havilland Rd., Wall. 219 DL108
De Havilland Way, Abb.L. 59 BT32
De Havilland Way, Stai. 174 BK86
De Lapre Clo., Orp. 206 EX101
De Lara Way, Wok. 226 AX118
De Laune St. SE17 161 DP78
De Luci Rd., Erith 167 FC78
De Lucy St. SE2 166 EV77
De Mandeville Gate, Enf. 82 DU42
Southbury Rd.
De Mel Clo., Epsom 216 CN112
Trotter Way
De Montfort Par. SW16 181 DL90
Streatham High Rd.
De Montfort Rd. SW16 181 DL90
De Morgan Rd. SW6 160 DB83
De Quincey Ms. E16 144 EG74
Wesley Ave.
De Quincey Rd. N17 100 DR53
De Ros Pl., Egh. 173 BA93
De Salis Rd., Uxb. 135 BQ70
De Tany Ct., St.Alb. 43 CD21
De Vere Cotts. W8 160 DC76
Canning Pl.
De Vere Gdns. W8 160 DC75
De Vere Gdns., Ilf. 125 EM61
De Vere Ms. W8 160 DC76
Canning Pl.
De Vere Wk., Wat. 75 BS40
De Walden St. W1 272 G7
Deacon Clo., Cob. 229 BV119
Deacon Clo., Pur. 219 DL109
Deacon Clo., St.Alb. 43 CD24
Creighton Ave.
Deacon Fld., Guil. 242 AV133
Midleton Rd.
Deacon Ms. N1 142 DR66
Deacon Pl., Cat. 236 DQ121
Coulsdon Rd.
Deacon Rd. NW2 119 CU64
Deacon Rd., Kings.T. 198 CM95
Deacon Way SE17 279 H8
Deacon Way SE17 162 DQ77
Deacon Way, Wdf.Grn. 103 EM52
Deacons Clo., Borwd. 78 CN42
Deacons Clo., Pnr. 93 BV54
Deacons Hill, Wat. 76 BW44
Deacon's Hill Rd., Borwd. 78 CM42
Deacons Leas, Orp. 223 ER105
Deacons Ri. N2 120 DD57
Deacons Wk., Hmptn. 176 BZ91
Bishops Gro.
Deaconsfield Rd., Hem.H. 40 BK23
Deadfield La., Hert. 30 DF13
Deadhearn La., Ch.St.G. 90 AY46
Deadman's Ash La., Rick. 74 BH36
Deakin Clo., Wat. 93 BS45
Chenies Way
Deal Ave., Slou. 131 AM72
Deal Ms. W5 157 CK77
Darwin Rd.
Deal Porters Way SE16 162 DW76
Deal Rd. SW17 180 DG93
Deal St. E1 142 DU71
Deal Wk. SW9 161 DN80
Mandela St.
Deal's Gateway SE10 163 EB81
Blackheath Rd.
Dealtry Rd. SW15 159 CW84
Dean Ave., Hodd. 49 DX17
Dean Bradley St. SW1 277 P7
Dean Bradley St. SW1 161 DL76
Dean Clo. E9 122 DW64
Churchill Wk.
Dean Clo. SE16 143 DX74
Surrey Water Rd.
Dean Clo., Uxb. 134 BM66
Dean Clo., Wind. 151 AK83
Dean Clo., Wok. 227 BE115
Dean Ct., Wem. 117 CH62
Dean Dr., Stan. 96 CL54
Dean Farrar St. SW1 277 M6
Dean Farrar St. SW1 161 DK76
Dean Fld., Hem.H. 57 BA27
Dean Gdns. E17 123 ED56
Dean Gdns. W13 137 CH74
Northfield Ave.
Dean La., Red. 235 DH123
Dean Oak La., Reig. 265 CW144
Dean Rd. NW2 139 CW65
Dean Rd. SE28 146 EU73
Dean Rd., Croy. 220 DR105
Dean Rd., Hmptn. 176 BZ92
Dean Rd., Houns. 176 CB85
Dean Ryle St. SW1 277 P8
Dean Ryle St. SW1 161 DL77
Dean Stanley St. SW1 277 P7
Dean Stanley St. SW1 161 DL76
Dean St. E7 124 EG64
Dean St. W1 273 M8
Dean St. W1 141 DK72
Dean Trench St. SW1 277 P7
Dean Trench St. SW1 161 DL76
Dean Wk., Edg. 96 CQ51
Deansbrook Rd.
Dean Wk., Lthd. 246 CB126
Dean Way, Sthl. 156 CB75
Dean Wd. Rd., Beac. 89 AR52
Deanacre Clo., Ger.Cr. 90 AY51
Deancroft Rd., Ger.Cr. 90 AY51
Deancross St. E1 142 DW72
Deane Ave., Ruis. 116 BW64
Deane Cft. Rd., Pnr. 116 BW58
Deane Way, Ruis. 115 BV58
Deanery Clo. N2 120 DE56
Deanery Ms. W1 276 G2
Deanery Rd. E15 144 EE65
Deanery Rd., Eden. 255 EQ134
Deanery St. W1 276 G2
Deanery St. W1 140 DG74
Deanhill Rd. SW14 158 CP84
Deans Bldgs. SE17 279 K9
Deans Bldgs. SE17 162 DR77
Deans Clo. W4 158 CP79
Deans Clo., Abb.L. 59 BR32
Deans Clo., Amer. 72 AT37
Park Rd.
Dean's Clo., Croy. 202 DT104
Deans Clo., Edg. 96 CQ51
Deans Clo., Slou. 132 AV67
Deans Clo., Tad. 233 CV124
Deans La.
Deans Ct. EC4 274 G9
Deans Dr. N13 99 DP51
Deans Dr., Edg. 96 CR50
Deans Gdns., St.Alb. 43 CG16
Dean's Gate Clo. SE23 183 DX90
Deans La. W4 158 CP79
Deans La., Edg. 96 CQ51
Deans La., Red. 251 DN133
Deans La., Tad. 233 CV124
Deans Ms. W1 273 J8
Dean's Pl. SW1 277 M10
Dean's Pl. SW1 161 DK78
Deans Rd. W7 137 CF74
Deans Rd., Brwd. 108 FV48
Deans Rd., Red. 251 DJ130
Deans Rd., Sutt. 200 DB104
Deans Wk., Couls. 235 DN118
Deans Way, Edg. 96 CQ50
Dean's Yd. SW1 277 N6
Deansbrook Clo., Edg. 96 CQ52
Deansbrook Rd., Edg. 96 CQ51
Deanscroft Ave. NW9 118 CQ61
Deansfield, Cat. 252 DT125
Deansway N2 120 DD56
Deansway N9 100 DS48
Deansway, Chesh. 54 AP29
Deansway, Hem.H. 40 BM23
Deanway, Ch.St.G. 90 AU48
De'Arn Gdns., Mitch. 200 DE97
Dearne Clo., Stan. 95 CG50
Dearsley Ho., Rain. 147 FD68
Dearsley Rd., Enf. 82 DU41
Deason St. E15 143 EC67
High St.
Debden Clo., Kings.T. 177 CK92
Debden Clo., Wdf.Grn. 102 EJ52
Debden La., Loug. 85 EP38
Debden Rd., Loug. 85 EP38
Debden Wk., Horn. 147 FH65
Debenham Rd. (Cheshunt), Wal.Cr. 66 DV27
Debnams Rd. SE16 162 DW77
Rotherhithe New Rd.
Deborah Clo., Islw. 157 CE81
Deborah Cres., Ruis. 115 BR59
Debrabant Clo., Erith 167 FD79
Deburgh Rd. SW19 180 DC94
Decies Way, Slou. 132 AU67
Decima St. SE1 279 M6
Decima St. SE1 162 DS76
Deck Clo. SE16 163 DX75
Thame Rd.
Decoy Ave. NW11 119 CY57
Dedswell Dr., Guil. 244 BG129
Dedworth Dr., Wind. 151 AM81
Dedworth Rd., Wind. 150 AJ82
Dee, The, Hem.H. 40 BM15
Dee Clo., Upmin. 129 FS58
Dee Rd., Rich. 158 CM84
Dee St. E14 143 EC72
Dee Way, Epsom 216 CS110
Dee Way, Rom. 105 FE52
Deeley Rd. SW8 161 DK81
Deena Clo. W3 138 CM72
Deena Clo., Slou. 131 AL73
Deep Acres, Amer. 55 AN36
Deep Fld., Slou. 152 AV80
Deep Pool La., Wok. 210 AV114
Deepdale SW19 179 CX91
Deepdale Ave., Brom. 204 EF98
Deepdale Clo. N11 98 DG51
Ribblesdale Ave.
Deepdene W5 138 CM70
Deepdene, Pot.B. 63 CX31
Deepdene Ave., Croy. 202 DT104
Deepdene Ave., Dor. 263 CH139
Deepdene Ave. Rd., Dor. 247 CJ134
Deepdene Clo. E11 124 EG56
Deepdene Ct. N21 81 DP44
Deepdene Dr., Dor. 263 CJ135
Deepdene Gdns. SW2 181 DM87
Deepdene Gdns., Dor. 263 CH135
Deepdene Pk. Rd., Dor. 263 CJ135
Deepdene Path, Loug. 85 EN42
Deepdene Rd. SE5 162 DR84
Deepdene Rd., Loug. 85 EN42
Deepdene Rd., Well. 166 EU83
Deepdene Vale, Dor. 263 CJ135
Deepdene Wd., Dor. 263 CJ136
Deepfield Way, Couls. 235 DL116
Deepfields, Horl. 268 DF146
Deepwell Clo., Islw. 157 CG81
Deepwood La., Grnf. 137 CD69
Cowgate Rd.
Deer Pk., Harl. 51 EN18
Deer Pk. Clo., Kings.T. 178 CP94
Deer Pk. Gdns., Mitch. 200 DD97
Deer Pk. Rd. SW19 200 DB96
Deer Pk. Wk., Chesh. 54 AS28
Deer Pk. Way, W.Wick. 204 EF103
Deerbarn Rd., Guil. 242 AV133
Deerbrook Rd. SE24 181 DP88
Deerdale Rd. SE24 162 DQ84
Deere Ave., Rain. 147 FG65
Deerfield Clo., Ware 33 DX05
Deerhurst Clo., Felt. 175 BU91
Deerhurst Cres., Hmptn. 176 CC92
Deerhurst Rd. NW2 139 CX65
Deerhurst Rd. SW16 181 DM92
Deerings Dr., Pnr. 115 BU57
Deerings Rd., Reig. 250 DB134
Deerleap Gro. E4 83 EB43
Deerleap La., Sev. 224 EX113
Deerleap Rd., Dor. 262 CB137
Deers Fm. Clo., Wok. 228 BL116
Deerswood Ave., Hat. 45 CV20
Deerswood Clo., Cat. 236 DU124
Deeside Rd. SW17 180 DD90
Deeves Hall La., Pot.B. 62 CS33
Defiance Wk. SE18 165 EM76
Defiant Way, Wall. 219 DL108
Defoe Ave., Rich. 158 CN80
Defoe Clo. SE16 163 DZ75
Vaughan St.
Defoe Clo. SW17 180 DE93
Defoe Clo., Erith 167 FE81
Selkirk Dr.
Defoe Ho. EC2 142 DQ71
Beech St.
Defoe Par., Grays 171 GH76
Defoe Rd. N16 122 DS61
Defoe Way, Rom. 104 FA51
Degema Rd., Chis. 185 EP92
Dehar Cres. NW9 119 CT59
Dehavilland Clo., Nthlt. 136 BX69
Deimos Dr., Hem.H. 40 BN17
Dekker Rd. SE21 182 DS86
Delabole Rd., Red. 251 DL129
Delacourt Rd. SE3 164 EH80
Old Dover Rd.
Delafield Rd. SE7 164 EH78
Delafield Rd., Grays 170 GD78
Delaford Rd. SE16 162 DV78
Delaford St. SW6 159 CY80
Delagarde Rd., West. 255 EQ126
Delahay Ri., Berk. 38 AV17
Delamare Cres., Croy. 202 DW100
Delamare Rd. (Cheshunt), Wal.Cr. 67 DZ30
Delamere Gdns. NW7 96 CR51
Delamere Rd. SW20 199 CX95
Delamere Rd. W5 138 CL74
Delamere Rd., Borwd. 78 CP39
Delamere Rd., Hayes 136 BX73
Delamere Rd., Reig. 266 DB138
Delamere Ter. W2 140 DB71
Delancey Pas. NW1 141 DH67
Delancey St.
Delancey St. NW1 141 DH67
Delaporte Clo., Epsom 216 CS112
Delargy Clo., Grays 171 GH76
Delaware Rd. W9 140 DB70
Delawyk Cres. SE24 182 DQ86
Delcombe Ave., Wor.Pk. 199 CW102
Delderfield, Lthd. 231 CK120
Delfcroft, Ware 32 DW05
Delft Way SE22 182 DS85
East Dulwich Gro.
Delhi Rd., Enf. 100 DT45
Delhi St. N1 141 DL67
Delia St. SW18 180 DB87
Delius Clo., Borwd. 77 CJ44
Delius Gro. E15 143 ED68
Dell, The SE2 166 EU78
Dell, The SE19 202 DT95
Dell, The, Bex. 187 FE88
Dell, The, Brent. 157 CJ79
Dell, The, Brwd. 107 FV51
Dell, The, Felt. 175 BV87
Harlington Rd. W.
Dell, The, Ger.Cr. 90 AY51
Dell, The, Hert. 32 DQ12
Dell, The, H.Wyc. 88 AC46
Dell, The, Horl. 269 DH147
Dell, The, Nthwd. 93 BS47
Dell, The, Pnr. 94 BX54
Dell, The, Rad. 77 CG36
Dell, The, Reig. 250 DA133
Dell, The, St.Alb. 43 CG18
Dell, The, Tad. 233 CW121
Dell, The, Wem. 117 CH64
Dell, The, Wok. 226 AW118
Dell, The, Wdf.Grn. 102 EH48
Dell Clo. E15 143 ED67
Dell Clo., Dor. 247 CJ127
Dell Clo., Lthd. 231 CE123
Dell Clo., Slou. 111 AQ64
Dell Clo., Wall. 219 DK105
Dell Clo., Wdf.Grn. 102 EH48
Dell Fm. Rd., Ruis. 115 BR57
Dell La., Epsom 217 CU106
Dell Lees, Beac. 89 AQ51
Dell Meadow, Hem.H. 40 BL24
Belswains La.
Dell Ri., St.Alb. 60 CB26
Dell Rd., Enf. 82 DW38
Dell Rd., Epsom 217 CU107
Dell Rd., Grays 170 GB77
Dell Rd., Wat. 75 BU37
Dell Rd., West Dr. 154 BM76
Dell Side, Wat. 75 BU37
The Harebreaks
Dell Wk., N.Mal. 198 CS96
Dell Way W13 137 CJ72
Della Path E5 122 DV62
Napoleon Rd.
Dellbow Rd., Felt. 175 BV85
Central Way
Dellcott Clo., Welw.G.C. 29 CW08
Dellcut Rd., Hem.H. 40 BN18
Dellfield, Chesh. 54 AN29
Dellfield, St.Alb. 43 CG21
Dellfield Ave., Berk. 38 AV17
Dellfield Clo., Beck. 183 EC94
Foxgrove Rd.
Dellfield Clo., Berk. 38 AU17
Dellfield Clo., Rad. 77 CE35
Dellfield Clo., Wat. 75 BU40
Dellfield Cres., Uxb. 134 BJ70
Dellfield Par. (Cowley), Uxb. 134 BJ70
High St.
Dellfield Rd., Hat. 45 CU18
Dellmeadow, Abb.L. 59 BS30
Dellors Clo., Barn. 79 CX43
Dellow Clo., Ilf. 125 ER59
Dellow St. E1 142 DV73
Dells, The, Hem.H. 41 BP21
Dells Clo. E4 101 EB45
Dell's Ms. SW1 277 L9
Dells Wd. Clo., Hodd. 33 DZ14
Dellside (Harefield), Uxb. 114 BJ57
Dellsome La., Hat. 45 CV23
Dellsome La., St.Alb. 44 CS23
Dellwood, Rick. 92 BH46
Dellwood Gdns., Ilf. 125 EN55
Delmar Ave., Hem.H. 41 BR21
Delmare Clo. SW9 161 DM84
Brighton Ter.
Delme Cres. SE3 164 EH82
Delmeade Rd., Chesh. 54 AN32
Delmey Clo., Croy. 202 DT104
Radcliffe Rd.
Deloraine St. SE8 163 EA81
Delorme St. W6 159 CX79
Delta Bungalows, Horl. 268 DG150
Michael Cres.
Delta Clo., Wok. 210 AT110
Delta Clo., Wor.Pk. 199 CT104
Delta Ct. NW2 119 CU61
Delta Dr., Horl. 268 DG150
Cheyne Wk.
Delta Gain, Wat. 94 BX47
Delta Gro., Nthlt. 136 BX69
Delta Rd., Brwd. 109 GD44
Delta Rd., Wok. 227 BA116
Delta Rd. (Chobham), Wok. 210 AT110
Delta Rd., Wor.Pk. 198 CS104
Delta St. E2 142 DU69
Wellington Row
Delta Way, Egh. 193 BC95
Delvan Clo. SE18 165 EN80
Ordnance Rd.
Delvers Mead, Dag. 127 FC63
Delverton Rd. SE17 161 DP78
Delves, Tad. 233 CX121
Heathcote
Delvino Rd. SW6 160 DA81
Demesne Rd., Wall. 219 DK106
Demeta Clo., Wem. 118 CQ62
Dempster Clo., Surb. 197 CJ101
Dempster Rd. SW18 180 DC85
Den Clo., Beck. 203 ED97
Den Rd., Brom. 203 ED97
Denbar Par., Rom. 127 FC56
Mawney Rd.
Denberry Dr., Sid. 186 EV90
Denbigh Clo. NW10 138 CS66
Denbigh Clo. W11 139 CZ73
Denbigh Clo., Chis. 185 EM93
Denbigh Clo., Hem.H. 40 BL21
Denbigh Clo., Horn. 128 FN56
Denbigh Clo., Ruis. 115 BT61
Denbigh Clo., Sthl. 136 BZ72
Denbigh Clo., Sutt. 217 CZ106
Denbigh Dr., Hayes 155 BQ75
Denbigh Gdns., Rich. 178 CM85
Denbigh Ms. SW1 277 K9
Denbigh Pl. SW1 277 K10
Denbigh Pl. SW1 161 DJ78
Denbigh Rd. E6 144 EK69
Denbigh Rd. W11 139 CZ73
Denbigh Rd. W13 137 CH73
Denbigh Rd., Houns. 156 CB82
Denbigh Rd., Sthl. 136 BZ72
Denbigh St. SW1 277 K9
Denbigh St. SW1 161 DJ77
Denbigh Ter. W11 139 CZ73
Denbridge Rd., Brom. 205 EM96
Denby Gra., Harl. 52 EY15
Denby Rd., Cob. 214 BW112
Dendridge Clo., Enf. 82 DV37
Dene, The W13 137 CH71
Dene, The, Croy. 221 DX105
Dene, The, Dor. 261 BV141
Dene, The, Sev. 257 FH126
Dene, The, Sutt. 217 CZ111
Dene, The, Wem. 118 CL63
Dene, The, W.Mol. 196 BZ99
Dene Ave., Houns. 156 BZ83
Dene Ave., Sid. 186 EV87
Dene Clo. SE4 163 DY83
Dene Clo., Brom. 204 EF102
Dene Clo., Couls. 234 DE119
Dene Clo., Dart. 187 FE91
Dene Clo., Guil. 243 BB132
Dene Clo., Horl. 268 DE146
Dene Clo., Wor.Pk. 199 CT103
Dene Ct., Stan. 95 CJ50
Marsh La.
Dene Dr., Orp. 206 EV104
Dene Gdns., Stan. 95 CJ50
Dene Gdns., T.Ditt. 197 CG103
Dene Holm Rd., Grav. 190 GD90
Dene Path, S.Ock. 149 FU72
Dene Pl., Wok. 226 AV118
Dene Rd. N11 98 DF46
Dene Rd., Ash. 232 CM119
Dene Rd., Buck.H. 102 EK46
Dene Rd., Dart. 188 FM87
Dene Rd., Guil. 258 AY135
Dene Rd., Nthwd. 93 BS51
Dene St., Dor. 263 CH136
Dene St. Gdns., Dor. 263 CH136
Denecroft Cres., Uxb. 135 BP67
Denecroft Gdns., Grays 170 GD76
Denefield Dr., Ken. 236 DR115
Denehurst Gdns. NW4 119 CW58
Denehurst Gdns. W3 138 CP74
Denehurst Gdns., Rich. 158 CN84
Denehurst Gdns., Twick. 177 CD87
Denehurst Gdns., Wdf.Grn. 102 EH49
Denewood, Barn. 80 DC43
Denewood Clo., Wat. 75 BT37
Denewood Rd. N6 120 DF58
Denfield, Dor. 263 CH138
Dengie Wk. N1 142 DQ67
Basire St.
Denham Ave., Uxb. 113 BF61
Denham Clo., Hem.H. 40 BN15
Denham Clo. (Denham), Uxb. 114 BG62
Denham Clo., Well. 166 EW83
Park Vw. Rd.
Denham Ct. Dr. (Denham), Uxb. 114 BH63
Denham Cres., Mitch. 200 DF98
Denham Dr., Esher 215 CG106
Denham Dr., Ilf. 125 EQ58
Denham Grn. Clo. (Denham), Uxb. 114 BG59
Denham Grn. La., Uxb. 113 BE57
Denham La., Ger.Cr. 90 AY50
Denham Rd. N20 98 DF48
Denham Rd., Egh. 173 BA91
Denham Rd., Epsom 217 CT112
Denham Rd., Felt. 176 BW86
Denham Rd., Iver 133 BD67
Denham St. SE10 164 EG78

Dunoon Rd. SE23 182 DW87
Dunottar Clo., Red. 266 DD136
Dunraven Ave., Red. 267 DH141
Dunraven Dr., Enf. 81 DN40
Dunraven Rd. W12 139 CU74
Dunraven St. W1 272 E10
Dunsany Rd. W14 159 CX76
Dunsborough Pk., Wok. 228 BJ120
Dunsbury Clo., Sutt. 218 DB109
Nettlecombe Clo.
Dunsdon Ave., Guil. 258 AX135
Dunsfold Ri., Couls. 219 DK113
Dunsfold Way, Croy. 221 EB108
Dunsford Way SW15 179 CV86
Dover Pk. Dr.
Dunsmore Clo., Hayes 136 BY70
Kingsash Dr.
Dunsmore Clo. (Bushey), Wat. 77 CD44
Dunsmore Rd., Walt. 195 BV100
Dunsmore Way (Bushey), Wat. 77 CD44
Dunsmure Rd. N16 122 DS60
Dunspring La., Ilf. 103 EP54
Dunstable Clo., Rom. 106 FK51
Dunstable Rd.
Dunstable Ms. W1 272 G6
Dunstable Rd., Rich. 158 CL84
Dunstable Rd., Rom. 106 FK51
Dunstable Rd., W.Mol. 196 BZ98
Dunstall Grn., Wok. 210 AW109
Dunstall Rd. SW20 179 CV93
Dunstall Way, W.Mol. 196 CB97
Dunstalls, Harl. 51 EN19
Dunstan Clo. N2 120 DC55
Thomas More Way
Dunstan Rd. NW11 119 CZ60
Dunstan Rd., Couls. 235 DK117
Dunstans Gro. SE22 182 DV86
Dunstans Rd. SE22 182 DU87
Dunster Ave., Mord. 199 CX102
Dunster Clo., Barn. 79 CX42
Dunster Clo., Rom. 105 FC54
Dunster Clo. (Harefield), Uxb. 92 BH53
Dunster Ct. EC3 275 N10
Dunster Cres., Horn. 128 FN61
Dunster Dr. NW9 118 CQ60
Dunster Gdns. NW6 139 CZ66
Dunster Gdns., Slou. 131 AN73
Avebury
Dunster Way, Har. 116 BY62
Dunsters Mead, Welw.G.C. 30 DA11
Dunsterville Way SE1 279 L5
Dunston Rd. E8 142 DT67
Dunston Rd. SW11 160 DG82
Dunston St. E8 142 DT67
Dunton Clo., Surb. 198 CL102
Dunton Rd. E10 123 EB59
Dunton Rd. SE1 279 P10
Dunton Rd. SE1 162 DT78
Dunton Rd., Rom. 127 FE56
Duntshill Rd. SW18 180 DB88
Dunvegan Clo., W.Mol. 196 CB98
Dunvegan Rd. SE9 165 EM84
Dunwich Rd., Bexh. 166 EZ81
Dunworth Ms. W11 139 CZ72
Portobello Rd.
Duplex Ride SW1 276 E5
Dupont Rd. SW20 199 CX96
Dupont St. E14 143 DY71
Maroon St.
Duppas Ave., Croy. 219 DP105
Violet La.
Duppas Clo., Shep. 195 BR99
Green La.
Duppas Hill La., Croy. 219 DP105
Duppas Hill Rd.
Duppas Hill Rd., Croy. 219 DP105
Duppas Hill Ter., Croy. 201 DP104
Duppas Rd., Croy. 201 DN104
Dupre Clo., Grays 170 FY76
Dupre Cres., Beac. 89 AP54
Dupre Wk., H.Wyc. 110 AD59
Stratford Dr.
Dupree Rd. SE7 164 EH78
Dura Den Clo., Beck. 183 EB94
Durand Clo., Cars. 200 DF102
Durand Gdns. SW9 161 DM81
Durand Way NW10 138 CQ66
Durands Wk. SE16 163 DZ75
Durant Rd., Swan. 187 FG93
Durant St. E2 142 DU69
Durants Pk. Ave., Enf. 83 DX42
Durants Rd., Enf. 82 DW42
Durban Gdns., Dag. 147 FC66
Durban Rd. E15 144 EE69
Durban Rd. E17 101 DZ53
Durban Rd. N17 100 DS51
Durban Rd. SE27 182 DQ91
Durban Rd., Beck. 203 DZ96
Durban Rd., Ilf. 125 ES60
Durban Rd. E., Wat. 75 BU42
Durban Rd. W., Wat. 75 BU42
Durbin Rd., Chess. 216 CL105
Durdans Rd., Sthl. 136 BZ72
Durell Gdns., Dag. 126 EX64
Durell Rd., Dag. 126 EX64
Durfold Dr., Reig. 250 DC134
Durford Cres. SW15 179 CV88
Durham Ave., Brom. 204 EF98
Durham Ave., Houns. 156 BZ78
Durham Ave., Rom. 128 FJ56
Durham Ave., Slou. 131 AN72
Durham Ave., Wdf.Grn. 102 EK50
Durham Clo. SW20 199 CV96
Durham Rd.
Durham Clo., Guil. 242 AT132
Durham Clo., Saw. 36 EW06
Durham Clo., Ware 33 EB10
Durham Ct., Brom. 184 EF91
Durham Ho. St. WC2 278 A1
Durham Pl. SW3 160 DF78
Smith St.
Durham Pl., Ilf. 125 EQ63
Eton Rd.
Durham Ri. SE18 165 EQ78
Durham Rd. E12 124 EK63
Durham Rd. E16 144 EE70
Durham Rd. N2 120 DE55
Durham Rd. N7 121 DM61
Durham Rd. N9 100 DU47
Durham Rd. SW20 199 CV95
Durham Rd. W5 157 CK76
Durham Rd., Borwd. 78 CQ41
Durham Rd., Brom. 204 EF97
Durham Rd., Dag. 127 FC64
Durham Rd., Felt. 176 BW87
Durham Rd., Har. 116 CB57
Durham Rd., Sid. 186 EV92
Durham Row E1 143 DY71
Durham St. SE11 161 DM78
Durham Ter. W2 140 DB72
Durham Wf., Brent. 157 CJ80
High St.
Durham Yd. E2 142 DV69
Teesdale St.
Duriun Way, Erith 167 FH80
Durleston Pk. Dr., Lthd. 246 CC125
Durley Ave., Pnr. 116 BY59
Durley Gdns., Orp. 224 EV105
Durley Rd. N16 122 DS59
Durlston Rd. E5 122 DU61
Durlston Rd., Kings.T. 178 CL93
Durndale La., Grav. 190 GE91
Durnell Way, Loug. 85 EN41
Durnford St. N15 122 DS57
Durnford St. SE10 163 EC79
Greenwich Ch. St.
Durning Rd. SE19 182 DR92
Durnsford Ave. SW19 180 DA89
Durnsford Rd. N11 99 DK53
Durnsford Rd. SW19 180 DA89
Durrant Pl., Chesh. 54 AN27
Great Hivings
Durrant Way, Orp. 223 ER106
Durrant Way, Swans. 190 FY87
Durrants Clo., Rain. 148 FJ68
Durrants Dr., Rick. 75 BQ42
Durrants Hill Rd., Hem.H. 40 BK23
Durrants La., Berk. 38 AS19
Durrants Rd., Berk. 38 AT18
Durrell Rd. SW6 159 CZ81
Durrell Way, Shep. 195 BR100
Durrington Ave. SW20 199 CW95
Durrington Pk. Rd. SW20 179 CW94
Durrington Rd. E5 123 DY63
Dursley Clo. SE3 164 EJ82
Dursley Gdns. SE3 164 EK81
Dursley Rd. SE3 164 EJ82
Durward St. E1 142 DV71
Durweston Ms. W1 272 E6
Durweston St. W1 272 E6
Durweston St. W1 140 DF71
Dury Falls Clo., Horn. 128 FM60
Dury Rd., Barn. 79 CZ39
Dutch Barn Clo., Stai. 174 BK86
Dutch Elm Ave., Wind. 152 AT80
Dutch Gdns., Kings.T. 178 CP93
Windmill Ri.
Dutch Yd. SW18 180 DA85
Wandsworth High St.
Duthie St. E14 143 EC73
Prestons Rd.
Dutton St. SE10 163 EC81
Dutton Way, Iver 133 BE72
Duxberry Clo., Brom. 204 EL99
Southborough La.
Duxford Clo., Horn. 147 FH65
Duxford Ho. SE2 166 EX75
Wolvercote Rd.
Duxhurst La., Reig. 266 DB144
Duxons Turn, Hem.H. 41 BP19
Maylands Ave.
Dwight Ct. SW6 159 CY82
Burlington Rd.
Dwight Rd., Wat. 93 BR45
Dye Ho. La. E3 143 EA67
Dyer's Bldgs. EC1 274 D7
Dyers Fld., Horl. 269 DP148
Dyers Hall Rd. E11 124 EE60
Dyers La. SW15 159 CV84
Dyers Way, Rom. 105 FH52
Dyke Dr., Orp. 206 EW102
Dykes Path, Wok. 227 BC115
Bentham Ave.
Dykes Way, Brom. 204 EF97
Dykewood Clo., Bex. 187 FE90
Dylan Clo., Borwd. 95 CK45
Coates Rd.
Dylan Rd. SE24 161 DP84
Dylan Rd., Belv. 166 FA76
Dylan Thomas Ho. N8 121 DM56
Dylways SE5 162 DR84
Dymchurch Clo., Ilf. 103 EN54
Dymchurch Clo., Orp. 223 ES105
Dymes Path SW19 179 CX89
Queensmere Rd.
Dymock St. SW6 160 DB83
Dymoke Grn., St.Alb. 43 CG16
Dymoke Rd., Horn. 127 FF59
Dymokes Way, Hodd. 33 EA14
Dymond Est. SW17 180 DE90
Glenburnie Rd.
Dyne Rd. NW6 139 CZ66
Dyneley Rd. SE12 184 EJ91
Dynevor Rd. N16 122 DS62
Dynevor Rd., Rich. 178 CL85
Dynham Rd. NW6 140 DA66
Dyott St. WC1 273 P8
Dyott St. WC1 141 DK72
Dyrham La., Barn. 79 CU36
Dysart Ave., Kings.T. 177 CJ92
Dysart St. EC2 275 M5
Dyson Clo., Wind. 151 AP83
Dyson Rd. E11 124 EE58
Dyson Rd. E15 144 EF65
Dysons Clo., Wal.Cr. 67 DX33
Dysons Rd. N18 100 DV50

E

Eade Rd. N4 122 DQ59
Eagans Clo. N2 120 DE55
Market Pl.
Eagle Ave., Rom. 126 EY58
Eagle Clo. SE16 162 DW78
Varcoe Rd.
Eagle Clo., Enf. 82 DW42
Eagle Clo., Horn. 147 FH65
Eagle Clo., Wall. 219 DL107
Eagle Clo., Wal.Abb. 68 EG34
Eagle Ct. EC1 274 F6
Eagle Ct. EC1 141 DP71
Eagle Ct., Hert. 32 DV08
Eagle Dr. NW9 96 CS54
Eagle Hill SE19 182 DR93
Eagle La. E11 124 EG56
Eagle Ms. N1 142 DS65
Tottenham Rd.
Eagle Pl. SW1 277 L1
Eagle Pl. SW7 160 DC78
Old Brompton Rd.
Eagle Rd., Guil. 242 AX134
Eagle Rd., Wem. 137 CK66
Eagle St. WC1 274 B7
Eagle St. WC1 141 DM71
Eagle Ter., Wdf.Grn. 102 EH52
Eagle Way, Brwd. 107 FV51
Eagle Way, Grav. 190 GA85
Eagle Way, Hat. 45 CU20
Eagle Wf. E14 143 EB71
Broomfield St.
Eagle Wf. Rd. N1 142 DQ68
Eagles Dr., West. 238 EK118
Eagles Rd., Green. 169 FV84
Eaglesfield Rd. SE18 165 EP80
Ealdham Sq. SE9 164 EJ84
Ealing Clo., Borwd. 78 CR39
Ealing Downs Ct., Grnf. 137 CG69
Perivale La.
Ealing Grn. W5 137 CK74
Ealing Pk. Gdns. W5 157 CJ77
Ealing Rd., Brent. 157 CK78
Ealing Rd., Nthlt. 136 CA66
Ealing Rd., Wem. 138 CL67
Ealing Village W5 138 CL72
Eamont Clo., Ruis. 115 BP59
Allonby Dr.
Eamont St. NW8 140 DE68
Eardemont Clo., Dart. 167 FF84
Eardley Cres. SW5 160 DA78
Eardley Pt. SE18 165 EP77
Wilmount St.
Eardley Rd. SW16 181 DJ92
Eardley Rd., Belv. 166 FA78
Eardley Rd., Sev. 257 FH124
Earl Clo. N11 99 DH50
Earl Ri. SE18 165 ER77
Earl Rd. SW14 158 CQ84
Elm Rd.
Earl Rd., Grav. 190 GE89
Earl St. EC2 275 M6
Earl St. EC2 142 DR71
Earl St., Wat. 76 BW41
Earldom Rd. SW15 159 CW84
Earle Gdns., Kings.T. 178 CL93
Earleswood, Cob. 214 BX112
Earlham Gro. E7 124 EF64
Earlham Gro. N22 99 DM52
Earlham St. WC2 273 N9
Earlham St. WC2 141 DK72
Earls Ct. Gdns. SW5 160 DB77
Earls Ct. Rd. SW5 160 DA77
Earls Ct. Rd. W8 160 DA76
Earls Ct. Sq. SW5 160 DB78
Earls Cres., Har. 117 CE56
Earls La., Pot.B. 62 CS32
Earls La., Slou. 131 AL74
Earl's Path, Loug. 84 EJ40
Earls Ter. W8 159 CZ76
Earls Wk. W8 160 DA76
Earls Wk., Dag. 126 EV63
Earls Way, Orp. 205 ET103
Station Rd.
Earlsbrook Rd., Red. 266 DF136
Earlsdown Ho., Bark. 145 ER68
Wheelers Cross
Earlsferry Way N1 141 DM67
Earlsfield, Maid. 150 AC77
Earlsfield Rd. SW18 180 DC88
Earlshall Rd. SE9 165 EM84
Earlsmead, Har. 116 BZ63
Earlsmead Rd. N15 122 DT57
Earlsmead Rd. NW10 139 CW68
Earlsthorpe Ms. SW12 180 DG86
Earlsthorpe Rd. SE26 183 DX91
Earlstoke St. EC1 274 F2
Earlston Gro. E9 142 DV67
Earlswood Ave., Th.Hth. 201 DN99
Earlswood Clo. SE10 164 EE78
Earlswood St.
Earlswood Gdns., Ilf. 125 EN55
Earlswood Rd., Red. 266 DF136
Earlswood St. SE10 164 EE78
Early Ms. NW1 141 DH67
Arlington Rd.
Earnshaw St. WC2 273 N8
Earnshaw St. WC2 141 DK72
Earsby St. W14 159 CY77
Easby Cres., Mord. 200 DB100
Easebourne Rd., Dag. 126 EW64
Easedale Dr., Horn. 127 FG64
Easedale Ho., Islw. 177 CF85
Easington Pl., Guil. 259 AZ135
Maori Rd.
Easington Way, S.Ock. 149 FU71
Easley's Ms. W1 272 G8
East Acton La. W3 138 CS74
East Arbour St. E1 143 DX72
East Ave. E12 144 EL66
East Ave. E17 123 EB56
East Ave., Hayes 155 BT75
East Ave., Sthl. 136 BZ73
East Ave., Wall. 219 DM106
East Ave., Walt. 213 BT110
Octagon Rd.
East Bank N16 122 DS59
East Barnet Rd., Barn. 80 DE44
East Burnham La., Slou. 131 AN67
East Burrow Fld., Welw.G.C. 29 CX11
East Churchfield Rd. W3 138 CR74
East Clo. W5 138 CN70
East Clo., Barn. 80 DG42
East Clo., Grnf. 136 CC68
East Clo., Rain. 147 FH70
East Clo., St.Alb. 60 CB25
East Common, Ger.Cr. 112 AY58
East Ct., Wem. 117 CJ61
East Cres. N11 98 DF49
East Cres., Enf. 82 DT43
East Cres., Wind. 151 AM81
East Cres. Rd., Grav. 191 GJ86
East Cross Route E3 143 EA67
East Dene Dr., Rom. 106 FK50
East Dr., Cars. 218 DE109
East Dr., Nthwd. 93 BS47
East Dr., Orp. 206 EV100
East Dr., St.Alb. 44 CL19
East Dr., Saw. 36 EY06
East Dr., Slou. 132 AS69
East Dr., Vir.W. 192 AV100
East Dr., Wat. 75 BV35
East Duck Lees La., Enf. 83 DY42
East Dulwich Gro. SE22 182 DS86
East Dulwich Rd. SE15 162 DT84
East Dulwich Rd. SE22 162 DT84
East End Rd. N2 120 DC55
East End Rd. N3 98 DA54
East End Way, Pnr. 116 BY55
East Entrance, Dag. 147 FB68
East Ferry Rd. E14 163 EB76
East Flint, Hem.H. 39 BF19
East Gdns. SW17 180 DE93
East Gdns., Wok. 227 BC117
East Gate, Harl. 35 ER14
East Gorse, Croy. 221 DY112
East Grn., Hem.H. 58 BM25
East Hall La., Rain. 148 FK72
East Hall Rd., Orp. 206 EY101
East Ham Ind. Est. E6 144 EL70
East Ham Manor Way E6 145 EN72
East Harding St. EC4 274 E8
East Heath Rd. NW3 120 DD62
East Hill SW18 180 DB85
East Hill, Dart. 188 FM87
East Hill (South Darenth), Dart. 208 FQ95
East Hill, Oxt. 254 EE129
East Hill, S.Croy. 220 DS110
East Hill, Wem. 118 CN61
East Hill, West. 238 EH118
East Hill, Wok. 227 BC116
East Hill Dr., Dart. 188 FM87
East Hill Rd., Oxt. 254 EE129
East Holme, Erith 167 FD81
East India Dock Rd. E14 143 ED72
East Kent Ave., Grav. 190 GC86
East La. SE16 162 DU75
East La., Abb.L. 59 BU29
East La., Dart. 209 FR96
East Hill
East La., Kings.T. 197 CK97
East La., Lthd. 245 BQ126
East La., Wat. 59 BU29
East La., Wem. 117 CK62
East Lo. La., Enf. 81 DK36
East Mascalls SE7 164 EJ79
Mascalls Rd.
East Mead, Ruis. 116 BX62
East Mead, Welw.G.C. 30 DB12
East Meads, Guil. 258 AT135
East Mill, Grav. 191 GF86
East Milton Rd., Grav. 191 GK87
East Mimms, Hem.H. 40 BL19
East Mt. St. E1 142 DV71
East Pk., Harl. 36 EW12
East Pk., Saw. 36 EY06
East Pk. Clo., Rom. 126 EX57
East Parkside SE10 164 EE75
East Pas. EC1 274 G6
East Pier E1 142 DV74
Wapping High St.
East Pl. SE27 182 DQ91
Pilgrim Hill
East Poultry Ave. EC1 274 F7
East Ramp, Houns. 155 BP81
East Ridgeway (Cuffley), Pot.B. 65 DL29
East Rd. E15 144 EG67
East Rd. N1 275 K3
East Rd. N1 142 DR69
East Rd. SW19 180 DC93
East Rd., Barn. 98 DG46
East Rd., Edg. 96 CP53
East Rd., Enf. 82 DW38
East Rd., Felt. 175 BR87
East Rd., Harl. 36 EV11
East Rd., Kings.T. 198 CL95
East Rd., Reig. 249 CZ133
East Rd. (Chadwell Heath), Rom. 126 EY57
East Rd. (Rush Grn.), Rom. 127 FD59
East Rd., Well. 166 EV82
East Rd., West Dr. 154 BM77
East Rd., Wey. 213 BR108
East Rochester Way SE9 165 ES84
East Rochester Way, Bex. 186 EX86
East Rochester Way, Sid. 165 ES84
East Row E11 124 EG58
East Row W10 139 CY70
East Shalford La., Guil. 258 AY139
East Sheen Ave. SW14 158 CR84
East Smithfield E1 142 DT73
East St. SE17 279 J10
East St. SE17 162 DQ78
East St., Bark. 145 EQ66
East St., Bexh. 166 FA84
East St., Brent. 157 CJ80
East St., Brom. 204 EG96
East St., Cher. 194 BG101
East St., Chesh. 54 AP32
East St., Epsom 216 CS112
East St., Grays 170 GC79
East St. (South Stifford), Grays 170 FY79
East St., Hem.H. 40 BK20
East St., Lthd. 246 CB125
East St., Ware 33 DX06
East Surrey Gro. SE15 162 DT80
East Tenter St. E1 142 DT72
East Ter., Grav. 191 GJ86
East Thurrock Rd., Grays 170 GB79
East Twrs., Pnr. 116 BX57
East Vw. E4 101 EC50
East Vw., Barn. 79 CZ41
East Vw., Hat. 46 DF17
East Wk., Barn. 98 DG45
East Wk., Harl. 35 ER14
East Wk., Hayes 135 BU74
East Wk., Reig. 250 DB134
East Way E11 124 EH57
East Way, Beac. 88 AG54
East Way, Brom. 204 EG101
East Way, Croy. 203 DY103
East Way, Guil. 242 AT134
East Way, Hayes 135 BU74
East Way, Ruis. 115 BU60
East Woodside, Bex. 186 EY88
Maiden Erlegh Ave.
Eastbank Rd., Hmptn. 176 CC92
Eastbourne Ave. W3 138 CR72
Eastbourne Gdns. SW14 158 CQ83
Eastbourne Ms. W2 140 DC72
Eastbourne Rd. E6 145 EN69
Eastbourne Rd. E15 144 EE67
Eastbourne Rd. N15 122 DS58
Eastbourne Rd. SW17 180 DG93
Eastbourne Rd. W4 158 CQ79
Eastbourne Rd., Brent. 157 CJ78
Eastbourne Rd., Felt. 176 BX89
Eastbourne Rd., Gdse. 253 DY134
Eastbourne Rd., Slou. 131 AM72
Eastbourne Ter. W2 140 DC72
Eastbournia Ave. N9 100 DV48
Eastbridge, Slou. 132 AV74
Victoria Rd.
Eastbrook Ave. N9 100 DW45
Eastbrook Ave., Dag. 127 FC63
Eastbrook Clo., Wok. 227 BA116
Eastbrook Dr., Rom. 127 FE62
Eastbrook Rd. SE3 164 EH80
Eastbrook Rd., Wal.Abb. 68 EE33
Eastbrook Way, Hem.H. 40 BL20
Eastbury Ave., Bark. 145 ES67
Eastbury Ave., Enf. 82 DS39
Eastbury Ave., Nthwd. 93 BS50
Eastbury Clo., Nthwd. 93 BT50
Eastbury Ave.
Eastbury Ct., Bark. 145 ES67
Eastbury Ct., St.Alb. 43 CF19
Eastbury Gro. W4 158 CS78
Eastbury Ho., Bark. 145 ET67
Eastbury Pl., Nthwd. 93 BT50
Eastbury Ave.
Eastbury Rd. E6 145 EN70
Eastbury Rd., Kings.T. 178 CL94
Eastbury Rd., Nthwd. 93 BS51
Eastbury Rd., Orp. 205 ER100
Eastbury Rd., Rom. 127 FD58
Eastbury Rd., Wat. 93 BV45
Eastbury Sq., Bark. 145 ET67
Eastbury Ter. E1 143 DX70
Eastcastle St. W1 273 K8
Eastcastle St. W1 141 DJ72
Eastcheap EC3 275 L10
Eastcheap EC3 142 DR73
Eastchurch Rd., Houns. 155 BS82
Eastcombe Ave. SE7 164 EH79
Eastcote, Orp. 205 ET102
Eastcote Ave., Grnf. 117 CG64
Eastcote Ave., Har. 116 CB61
Eastcote Ave., W.Mol. 196 BZ99
Eastcote La., Har. 116 CA62
Eastcote La., Nthlt. 136 CA66
Eastcote La. N., Nthlt. 136 BZ65
Eastcote Pl., Pnr. 115 BV58
Eastcote Rd., Har. 116 CC62
Eastcote Rd., Pnr. 116 BX57
Eastcote Rd. (Eastcote Village), Pnr. 115 BU58
Eastcote Rd., Ruis. 115 BS59
Eastcote Rd., Well. 165 ER82
Eastcote St. SW9 161 DM82
Eastcote Vw., Pnr. 116 BW56
Eastcroft, Slou. 131 AP70
Eastcroft Rd., Epsom 216 CS108
Eastdean Ave., Epsom 216 CP113
Eastdown Pk. SE13 163 ED84
Eastergate, Beac. 88 AJ51
Eastern Ave. E11 124 EJ58
Eastern Ave., Cher. 194 BG97
Eastern Ave., Grays 169 FT78
Eastern Ave., Ilf. 124 EL58
Eastern Ave., Pnr. 116 BX59
Eastern Ave., Rom. 126 EW56
Eastern Ave., S.Ock. 148 FQ74
Eastern Ave., Wal.Cr. 67 DY33
Eastern Ave. E., Rom. 127 FD55
Eastern Ave. W., Rom. 126 EY56
Eastern Dr., B.End 110 AC59
Eastern Ind. Est., Erith 166 FA75
Eastern Pathway, Horn. 148 FJ67
Eastern Perimeter Rd., Houns. 155 BT83
Eastern Rd. E13 144 EH68
Eastern Rd. E17 123 EC57
Eastern Rd. N2 120 DF55
Eastern Rd. N22 99 DL53
Eastern Rd. SE4 163 EA84
Eastern Rd., Grays 170 GD77
Eastern Rd., Rom. 127 FE57
Eastern Vw., West. 238 EJ117
Eastern Way SE2 146 EX74
Eastern Way SE28 166 EU75
Eastern Way, Belv. 167 FB75
Eastern Way, Erith 146 EX74
Eastern Way, Grays 170 GA79
Easternville Gdns., Ilf. 125 EQ58
Eastfield Ave., Wat. 76 BX39
Eastfield Clo., Slou. 152 AU76
St. Laurence Way
Eastfield Cotts., Hayes 155 BS78
Eastfield Ct., St.Alb. 43 CK17
Southfield Way
Eastfield Gdns., Dag. 126 FA63
Eastfield Par., Pot.B. 64 DD32
Eastfield Rd. E17 123 EA56
Eastfield Rd. N8 121 DL55
Eastfield Rd., Brwd. 108 FX47
Eastfield Rd., Dag. 126 FA63
Eastfield Rd., Enf. 83 DX38
Eastfield Rd., Red. 267 DJ135
Eastfield Rd., Slou. 130 AG71
Eastfield Rd., Wal.Cr. 67 DY32
Eastfields, Pnr. 116 BW57
Eastfields Rd. W3 138 CQ71
Eastfields Rd., Mitch. 200 DG96
Eastgate, Bans. 217 CY114
Eastgate Clo. SE28 146 EX72
Eastgate Gdns., Guil. 258 AY135
Eastglade, Nthwd. 93 BS50
Eastglade, Pnr. 116 BY55
Eastham Clo., Barn. 79 CY43
Eastham Cres., Brwd. 109 GA49
Eastholm NW11 120 DB56
Eastholme, Hayes 135 BU74
Eastlake Rd. SE5 161 DP82
Eastlands Clo., Oxt. 253 ED127
Eastlands Way
Eastlands Cres. SE21 182 DT86
Eastlands Way, Oxt. 253 ED127
Eastlea Ave., Wat. 76 BY37
Eastlea Ms. E16 144 EE70
Desford Rd.
Eastleigh Ave., Har. 116 CB61
Eastleigh Clo. NW2 118 CS62
Eastleigh Clo., Sutt. 218 DB108
Eastleigh Rd. E17 101 DZ54
Eastleigh Rd., Bexh. 167 FC82
Eastleigh Rd., Houns. 155 BT83
Cranford La.
Eastleigh Wk. SW15 179 CU87
Eastleigh Way, Felt. 175 BU88
Eastman Rd. W3 138 CR74
Eastman Way, Hem.H. 40 BN17
Eastmead, Wok. 227 BA116
Eastmead Ave., Grnf. 136 CB69
Eastmead Clo., Brom. 204 EL96
Eastmearn Rd. SE21 182 DQ89
Eastmont Rd., Esher 197 CF103

Eastmoor Pl. SE7 164 EK76
Eastmoor St.
Eastmoor St. SE7 164 EK76
Eastney Rd., Croy. 201 DP102
Eastney St. SE10 163 ED78
Eastnor, Hem.H. 57 BA28
Eastnor Clo., Reig. 265 CZ137
Eastnor Rd. SE9 185 EQ88
Eastnor Rd., Reig. 266 DA136
Easton Gdns., Borwd. 78 CR42
Easton St. WC1 274 D3
Eastor, Welw.G.C. 30 DA06
Eastry Ave., Brom. 204 EF100
Eastry Rd., Erith 166 FA80
Eastside Rd. NW11 119 CZ56
Eastview Ave. SE18 165 ES80
Eastville Ave. NW11 119 CZ58
Eastway E9 143 DZ65
Eastway E10 123 EC63
Eastway E15 123 EA64
Eastway, Epsom 216 CQ112
Eastway, Gat. 269 DH152
Eastway, Mord. 199 CX99
Eastway, Wall. 219 DJ105
Eastway Commercial Cen. E9 123 EA64
Eastwell Clo., Beck. 203 DY95
Eastwick Cres., Rick. 91 BF47
Eastwick Dr., Lthd. 230 CB122
Eastwick Hall La., Harl. 35 EN09
Eastwick Pk. Ave., Lthd. 230 CB124
Eastwick Rd., Harl. 35 EP11
Eastwick Rd., Lthd. 246 CB125
Eastwick Rd., Walt. 213 BV106
Eastwick Rd. (Hunsdonbury), Ware 34 EK08
Eastwick Rd. (Stanstead Abbotts), Ware 34 EF12
Eastwick Row, Hem.H. 40 BN21
Eastwood Clo. E18 102 EG54
George La.
Eastwood Clo. N17 100 DV52
Northumberland Gro.
Eastwood Ct., Hem.H. 40 BN19
Eastwood Dr., Rain. 147 FH72
Eastwood Rd. E18 102 EG54
Eastwood Rd. N10 98 DG54
Eastwood Rd., Guil. 259 AZ144
Eastwood Rd., Ilf. 126 EU59
Eastwood Rd., West Dr. 154 BN75
Eastwood St. SW16 181 DJ93
Eastworth Rd., Cher. 193 BF102
Eatington Rd. E10 123 ED57
Eaton Clo. SW1 276 F9
Eaton Clo. SW1 160 DG77
Eaton Clo., Stan. 95 CH49
Eaton Ct., Guil. 243 BA132
Eaton Dr. SW9 161 DP84
Eaton Dr., Kings.T. 178 CN94
Eaton Dr., Rom. 105 FB52
Eaton Gdns., Dag. 146 EY66
Eaton Gate SW1 276 F8
Eaton Gate SW1 160 DG77
Eaton Gate, Nthwd. 93 BQ51
Eaton La. SW1 277 J7
Eaton La. SW1 161 DH76
Eaton Ms. N. SW1 276 F8
Eaton Ms. N. SW1 160 DG76
Eaton Ms. S. SW1 276 G8
Eaton Ms. S. SW1 161 DH76
Eaton Ms. W. SW1 276 G8
Eaton Ms. W. SW1 160 DG77
Eaton Pk., Cob. 214 BY114
Eaton Pk. Rd. N13 99 DN47
Eaton Pk. Rd., Cob. 214 BY114
Eaton Pl. SW1 276 F7
Eaton Pl. SW1 160 DG76
Eaton Ri. E11 124 EJ57
Eaton Ri. W5 137 CK72
Eaton Rd. NW4 119 CW57
Eaton Rd., Enf. 82 DS41
Eaton Rd., Hem.H. 41 BP17
Eaton Rd., Houns. 157 CD84
Eaton Rd., St.Alb. 43 CH20
Eaton Rd., Sid. 186 EX89
Eaton Rd., Sutt. 218 DD107
Eaton Rd., Upmin. 129 FS61
Eaton Row SW1 277 H7
Eaton Row SW1 161 DH76
Eaton Sq. SW1 277 H6
Eaton Sq. SW1 160 DG77
Eaton Sq., Long. 209 FX97
Bramblefield Clo.
Eaton Ter. SW1 276 F8
Eaton Ter. SW1 160 DG77
Eaton Ter. Ms. SW1 276 F8
Eaton Wk. SE15 162 DT80
Sumner Est.
Eatons Mead E4 101 EA47
Eatonville Rd. SW17 180 DF89
Eatonville Vil. SW17 180 DF89
Eatonville Rd.
Ebbas Way, Epsom 232 CP115
Ebberns Rd., Hem.H. 40 BL23
Ebbisham Clo., Dor. 263 CG136
Nower Rd.
Ebbisham Dr. SW8 161 DM79
Ebbisham La., Tad. 233 CU123
Ebbisham Rd., Epsom 216 CP114
Ebbisham Rd., Wor.Pk. 199 CW103
Ebbsfleet Ind. Est., Grav. 190 GA85
Ebbsfleet Rd. NW2 119 CY63
Ebbsfleet Wk., Grav. 190 GB86
Ebdon Way SE3 164 EH83
Ebenezer St. N1 275 K2
Ebenezer St. N1 142 DR69
Ebenezer Wk. SW16 201 DJ95
Ebley Clo. SE15 162 DT79
Ebner St. SW18 180 DB85
Ebor St. E1 275 P4
Ebor St. E1 142 DT70
Ebrington Rd., Har. 117 CK58
Ebsworth Clo., Maid. 130 AC68
Ebsworth St. SE23 183 DX87
Eburne Rd. N7 121 DL62
Ebury Bri. SW1 277 H10
Ebury Bri. SW1 161 DH78
Ebury Bri. Est. SW1 277 H10
Ebury Bri. Est. SW1 161 DH78
Ebury Bri. Rd. SW1 160 DG78
Ebury Clo., Kes. 204 EL104
Ebury Clo., Nthwd. 93 BQ50
Ebury Ms. SE27 181 DP90
Ebury Ms. SW1 277 H8
Ebury Ms. SW1 161 DH77
Ebury Ms. E. SW1 277 H8
Ebury Rd., Rick. 92 BK46
Ebury Rd., Wat. 76 BW41
Ebury Sq. SW1 276 G9
Ebury Sq. SW1 160 DG77
Ebury St. SW1 277 H8
Ebury St. SW1 160 DG77
Ebury Way, The, Rick. 93 BP45
Ebury Way, The, Wat. 93 BP45
Eccles Hill, Dor. 263 CJ140
Eccles Rd. SW11 160 DF84
Ecclesbourne Clo. N13 99 DN50
Ecclesbourne Gdns. N13 99 DN50
Ecclesbourne Rd. N1 142 DQ66
Ecclesbourne Rd., Th.Hth. 202 DQ99
Eccleston Bri. SW1 277 J8
Eccleston Bri. SW1 161 DH77
Eccleston Clo., Barn. 80 DF42
Eccleston Clo., Orp. 205 ER102
Eccleston Cres., Rom. 126 EU59
Eccleston Ms. SW1 276 G7
Eccleston Ms. SW1 160 DG76
Eccleston Pl. SW1 277 H8
Eccleston Pl. SW1 161 DH77
Eccleston Rd. W13 137 CG73
Eccleston Sq. SW1 277 J9
Eccleston Sq. SW1 161 DH77
Eccleston Sq. Ms. SW1 277 K9
Eccleston St. SW1 277 H7
Eccleston St. SW1 160 DG76
Ecclestone Ct., Wem. 118 CL64
St. John's Rd.
Ecclestone Pl., Wem. 118 CM64
Echelforde Dr., Ashf. 174 BN91
Echo Hts. E4 101 EB46
Mount Echo Dr.
Echo Pit Rd., Guil. 258 AY138
Echo Sq., Grav. 191 GJ89
Old Rd. E.
Eckersley St. E1 142 DU70
Buxton St.
Eckford St. N1 141 DN68
Eckstein Rd. SW11 160 DE84
Eclipse Rd. E13 144 EH71
Ecob Clo., Guil. 242 AT130
Ecton Rd., Add. 212 BH105
Ector Rd. SE6 184 EE89
Edbrooke Rd. W9 140 DA70
Eddiscombe Rd. SW6 159 CZ82
Eddy Clo., Rom. 127 FB58
Eddy St., Berk. 38 AU18
Eddystone Rd. SE4 183 DY85
Eddystone Wk., Stai. 174 BL87
Clare Rd.
Ede Clo., Houns. 156 BZ83
Eden Clo. NW3 120 DA61
Eden Clo. W8 160 DA76
Adam & Eve Ms.
Eden Clo., Add. 212 BH110
Eden Clo., Bex. 187 FD91
Eden Clo., Slou. 153 BA78
Eden Clo., Wem. 137 CK67
Eden Grn., S.Ock. 149 FV71
Bovey Way
Eden Gro. E17 123 EB57
Eden Gro. N7 121 DM64
Eden Gro. Rd., W.Byf. 212 BL113
Eden Ms. SW17 180 DC90
Huntspill St.
Eden Pk. Ave., Beck. 203 DY98
Eden Pl., Grav. 191 GH87
Lord St.
Eden Rd. E17 123 EB57
Eden Rd. SE27 181 DP92
Eden Rd., Beck. 203 DY98
Eden Rd., Bex. 187 FC91
Eden Rd., Croy. 220 DR105
Eden St., Kings.T. 197 CK96
Eden Wk., Kings.T. 198 CL96
Eden St.
Eden Way, Beck. 203 DZ99
Eden Way, Warl. 237 DY118
Edenbridge Clo. SE16 162 DV78
Masters Dr.
Edenbridge Clo., Orp. 206 EX98
Edenbridge Rd. E9 143 DX66
Edenbridge Rd., Enf. 82 DS44
Edencourt Rd. SW16 181 DH93
Edencroft, Guil. 259 AZ144
Edendale Rd., Bexh. 167 FD81
Edenfield Gdns., Wor.Pk. 199 CT104
Edenhall Clo., Hem.H. 41 BR21
Edenhall Clo., Rom. 106 FJ50
Edenhall Glen, Rom. 106 FJ50
Edenhall Rd., Rom. 106 FJ50
Edenham Way W10 139 CZ71
Elkstone Rd.
Edenhurst Ave. SW6 159 CZ83
Edenside Rd., Lthd. 230 BZ124
Edensor Gdns. W4 158 CS80
Edensor Rd. W4 158 CS80
Edenvale Clo., Mitch. 180 DG94
Edenvale Rd.
Edenvale Rd., Mitch. 180 DG94
Edenvale St. SW6 160 DB82
Ederline Ave. SW16 201 DM97
Edes Flds., Reig. 265 CY136
Edgar Clo., Swan. 207 FF97
Edgar Kail Way SE22 162 DS84
Edgar Rd. E3 143 EB69
Edgar Rd., Houns. 176 BZ87
Edgar Rd., Rom. 126 EX59
Edgar Rd., S.Croy. 220 DR109
Edgar Rd., West Dr. 134 BL73
Edgar Rd., West. 238 EK121
Edgarley Ter. SW6 159 CY81
Edgars Ct., Welw.G.C. 29 CY10
Edgbaston Dr., Rad. 62 CL32
Edgbaston Rd., Wat. 93 BV48
Edge Clo., Wey. 212 BN108
Edge Hill SE18 165 EP79
Edge Hill SW19 179 CX94
Edge Hill Ave. N3 120 DA55
Edge Hill Ct. SW19 179 CX94
Edge St. W8 140 DA74
Kensington Ch. St.
Edgeborough Way, Brom. 184 EK94
Edgebury, Chis. 185 EP91
Edgebury Wk., Chis. 185 EQ91
Edgecombe Ho. SW19 179 CY88
Edgecoombe, S.Croy. 220 DW108
Edgecoombe Clo., Kings.T. 178 CR94
Edgecot Gro. N15 122 DR57
Oulton Rd.
Edgecote Clo. W3 138 CQ74
Cheltenham Pl.
Edgefield Ave., Bark. 145 ET66
Edgefield Clo., Dart. 188 FP89
Edgefield Clo., Red. 266 DG139
Edgehill Ct., Walt. 196 BW102
St. Johns Dr.
Edgehill Gdns., Dag. 126 FA63
Edgehill Rd. W13 137 CJ71
Edgehill Rd., Chis. 185 EQ90
Edgehill Rd., Mitch. 201 DH95
Edgehill Rd., Pur. 219 DN110
Edgel St. SW18 160 DB84
Ferrier St.
Edgeley, Lthd. 230 BY124
Edgeley La. SW4 161 DK83
Edgeley Rd.
Edgeley Rd. SW4 161 DK83
Edgell Clo., Vir.W. 193 AZ97
Edgell Rd., Stai. 173 BF92
Edgepoint Clo. SE27 181 DP92
Knights Hill
Edgewood Dr., Orp. 223 ET106
Edgewood Grn., Croy. 203 DX102
Edgeworth Ave. NW4 119 CU57
Edgeworth Clo. NW4 119 CU57
Edgeworth Clo., Whyt. 236 DU118
Edgeworth Cres. NW4 119 CU57
Edgeworth Rd. SE9 164 EJ84
Edgeworth Rd., Barn. 80 DE42
Edgington Rd. SW16 181 DK93
Edgington Way, Sid. 186 EW94
Edgware Ct., Edg. 96 CN51
Cavendish Dr.
Edgware Rd. NW2 119 CV60
Edgware Rd. NW9 118 CR55
Edgware Rd. W2 272 C8
Edgware Rd. W2 140 DE72
Edgware Rd. Subway W2 140 DE71
Edgware Rd.
Edgware Way, Edg. 96 CM49
Edgwarebury Gdns., Edg. 96 CN50
Edgwarebury La., Borwd. 96 CL45
Edgwarebury La., Edg. 96 CN49
Edinburgh Ave., Rick. 74 BG44
Edinburgh Ave., Slou. 131 AN71
Edinburgh Clo. E2 142 DW68
Russia La.
Edinburgh Clo., Pnr. 116 BX59
Edinburgh Clo., Uxb. 115 BP63
Edinburgh Ct. SW20 199 CX99
Edinburgh Cres., Wal.Cr. 67 DY33
Edinburgh Dr., Abb.L. 59 BU32
Edinburgh Dr., Rom. 127 FC56
Eastern Ave. W.
Edinburgh Dr., Stai. 174 BK93
Edinburgh Dr. (Denham), Uxb. 113 BF58
Edinburgh Dr. (Ickenham), Uxb. 115 BP63
Edinburgh Gdns., Wind. 151 AR82
Edinburgh Gate SW1 276 D4
Edinburgh Gate SW1 160 DF75
Edinburgh Ho. W9 140 DC69
Edinburgh Ms., Til. 171 GH82
Edinburgh Pl., Harl. 36 EU11
Edinburgh Rd. E13 144 EH68
Edinburgh Rd. E17 123 EA57
Edinburgh Rd. N18 100 DU50
Edinburgh Rd. W7 157 CF75
Edinburgh Rd., Sutt. 200 DC103
Edinburgh Way, Harl. 35 ER12
Edington Rd. SE2 166 EV76
Edington Rd., Enf. 82 DW40
Edis St. NW1 140 DG67
Edison Ave., Horn. 127 FF61
Edison Clo. E17 123 EA57
Exeter Rd.
Edison Clo., Horn. 127 FF60
Edison Ave.
Edison Clo., St.Alb. 43 CJ21
Edison Dr., Sthl. 136 CB72
Edison Gro. SE18 165 ET80
Edison Rd. N8 121 DK58
Edison Rd., Brom. 204 EG96
Edison Rd., Enf. 83 DZ40
Edison Rd., Well. 165 ET81
Edith Cavell Clo. N19 121 DK59
Hornsey Ri. Gdns.
Edith Gdns., Surb. 198 CP101
Edith Gro. SW10 160 DC79
Edith Rd. E6 144 EK66
Edith Rd. E15 123 ED64
Chandos Rd.
Edith Rd. N11 99 DK52
Edith Rd. SE25 202 DR99
Edith Rd. SW19 180 DB93
Edith Rd. W14 159 CY77
Edith Rd., Orp. 224 EU106
Edith Rd., Rom. 126 EX58
Edith Row SW6 160 DB81
Edith St. E2 142 DU68
Edith Ter. SW10 160 DC80
Edith Turbeville Ct. N19 121 DL59
Hillrise Rd.
Edith Vil. W14 159 CZ77
Edith Yd. SW10 160 DC80
World's End Est.
Edithna St. SW9 161 DL83
Edlyn Clo., Berk. 38 AT18
Edmansons Clo. N17 100 DS53
Bruce Gro.
Edmeston Clo. E9 143 DY65
Edmond Beaufort Dr., St.Alb. 43 CD18
Edmond Halley Way SE10 164 EE75
Edmonds Ct., W.Mol. 196 CB98
Avern Rd.
Edmonton Grn. N9 100 DV47
Hertford Rd.
Edmund Rd. (Chafford Hundred), Grays 169 FX75
Edmund Rd., Mitch. 200 DE97
Edmund Rd., Orp. 206 EW100
Edmund Rd., Rain. 147 FE68
Edmund Rd., Well. 166 EU83
Edmund St. SE5 162 DR80
Edmund Way, Slou. 132 AV71
Edmunds Ave., Orp. 206 EX97
Edmunds Clo., Hayes 136 BW71
Edmunds Clo., Hert. 31 DM08
Edmunds Twr., Harl. 51 EQ15
Edmunds Wk. N2 120 DD56
Edna Rd. SW20 199 CX96
Edna St. SW11 160 DE81
Edric Rd. SE14 163 DX80
Edrich Ho. SW4 161 DL81
Edrick Rd., Edg. 96 CQ51
Edrick Wk., Edg. 96 CQ51
Edridge Clo., Horn. 128 FK64
Edridge Clo. (Bushey), Wat. 76 CC43
Edridge Rd., Croy. 202 DQ104
Edulf Rd., Borwd. 78 CP39
Edward Amey Clo., Wat. 76 BW36
Edward Ave. E4 101 EB51
Edward Ave., Mord. 200 DD99
Edward Clo. N9 100 DT45
Edward Clo., Abb.L. 59 BT32
Edward Clo. (Chafford Hundred), Grays 169 FX76
Edward Clo., Hmptn. 176 CC92
Edward Rd.
Edward Clo., Nthlt. 136 BW68
Edward Clo., Rom. 128 FJ55
Edward Clo., St.Alb. 43 CF21
Edward Ct. E16 144 EG71
Alexandra St.
Edward Ct., Hem.H. 40 BK24
King Edward St.
Edward Ct., Stai. 174 BJ93
Elizabeth Ave.
Edward Ct., Wal.Abb. 68 EF33
Edward Gro., Barn. 80 DD43
Edward Ms. NW1 273 J1
Edward Pauling Ho., Felt. 175 BT87
Edward Pl. SE8 163 DZ79
Edward Rd. E17 123 DX56
Edward Rd. SE20 183 DX94
Edward Rd., Barn. 80 DD43
Edward Rd., Brom. 184 EH94
Edward Rd., Chis. 185 EP92
Edward Rd., Couls. 235 DK115
Edward Rd., Croy. 202 DS101
Edward Rd., Felt. 175 BR85
Edward Rd., Hmptn. 176 CC92
Edward Rd., Har. 116 CC55
Edward Rd., Nthlt. 136 BW68
Edward Rd., Rom. 126 EY58
Edward Rd., West. 238 EL118
Edward II Ave., W.Byf. 212 BM114
Edward Sq. N1 141 DM67
Caledonian Rd.
Edward Sq. SE16 143 DY74
Rotherhithe St.
Edward St. E16 144 EG70
Edward St. SE8 163 DZ79
Edward St. SE14 163 DY80
Edward Temme Ave. E15 144 EF66
Edward Tyler Rd. SE12 184 EH89
Edward Way, Ashf. 174 BM89
Edwardes Pl. W8 159 CZ76
Edwardes Sq.
Edwardes Sq. W8 160 DA76
Edward's Ave., Ruis. 135 BV65
Edwards Clo., Brwd. 109 GE44
Edwards Clo., Wor.Pk. 199 CX103
Edwards Cotts. N1 141 DP65
Compton Ave.
Edwards Ct., Slou. 152 AS75
Edwards Dr. N11 99 DK52
Gordon Rd.
Edwards Gdns., Swan. 207 FD98
Ladds Way
Edwards La. N16 122 DR61
Edwards Ms. N1 141 DN66
Edwards Ms. W1 272 F9
Edwards Ms. W1 140 DG72
Edwards Rd., Belv. 166 FA77
Edwards Way, Brwd. 109 GE44
Edwards Yd., Wem. 138 CL67
Mount Pleasant
Edwin Ave. E6 145 EN68
Edwin Clo., Bexh. 166 EZ79
Edwin Clo., Rain. 147 FF69
Edwin Pl., Croy. 202 DR102
Cross Rd.
Edwin Rd., Dart. 187 FH90
Edwin Rd., Edg. 96 CR51
Edwin Rd., Lthd. 245 BQ125
Edwin Rd., Twick. 177 CE88
Edwin St. E1 142 DW70
Edwin St. E16 144 EG71
Edwin St., Grav. 191 GH87
Edwina Gdns., Ilf. 124 EL57
Edwin's Mead E9 123 DY63
Lindisfarne Way
Edwyn Clo., Barn. 79 CW44
Eel Brook Studios SW6 160 DA80
Moore Pk. Rd.
Eel Pie Island, Twick. 177 CG88
Effie Pl. SW6 160 DA80
Effie Rd. SW6 160 DA80
Effingham Clo., Sutt. 218 DB108
Effingham Common Rd., Lthd. 229 BU123
Effingham Ct., Wok. 226 AY118
Constitution Hill
Effingham Pl., Lthd. 246 BX127
Effingham Rd. N8 121 DN57
Effingham Rd. SE12 184 EE85
Effingham Rd., Croy. 201 DM101
Effingham Rd., Reig. 266 DB135
Effingham Rd., Surb. 197 CH101
Effort St. SW17 180 DE92
Effra Par. SW2 181 DN85
Effra Rd. SW2 161 DN84
Effra Rd. SW19 180 DB93
Egan Way, Hayes 135 BS73
Egbert St. NW1 140 DG67
Egdean Wk., Sev. 257 FJ123
Egerton Ave., Swan. 187 FF94
Egerton Clo., Dart. 187 FH88
Egerton Clo., Pnr. 115 BU56
Egerton Ct., Guil. 242 AS134
Egerton Rd.
Egerton Cres. SW3 276 C8
Egerton Cres. SW3 160 DE77
Egerton Dr. SE10 163 EB81
Egerton Gdns. NW4 119 CV56
Egerton Gdns. NW10 139 CW67
Egerton Gdns. SW3 276 B7
Egerton Gdns. SW3 160 DE76
Egerton Gdns. W13 137 CH72
Egerton Gdns., Ilf. 125 ET62
Egerton Gdns. Ms. SW3 276 C7
Egerton Gdns. Ms. SW3 160 DE76
Egerton Pl. SW3 276 C7
Egerton Pl. SW3 160 DE76
Egerton Pl., Wey. 213 BQ107
Egerton Rd. N16 122 DT59
Egerton Rd. SE25 202 DS97
Egerton Rd., Berk. 38 AU17
Egerton Rd., Guil. 242 AS134
Egerton Rd., N.Mal. 199 CT98
Egerton Rd., Slou. 131 AL70
Egerton Rd., Twick. 177 CE87
Egerton Rd., Wem. 138 CM66
Egerton Rd., Wey. 213 BQ107
Egerton Ter. SW3 276 C7
Egerton Ter. SW3 160 DE76
Egerton Way, Hayes 155 BP80
Egg Hall, Epp. 70 EU29
Egham Bypass, Egh. 172 AY92
Egham Clo. SW19 179 CY89
Winterfold Clo.
Egham Clo., Sutt. 199 CY103
Egham Cres., Sutt. 199 CX104
Egham Hill, Egh. 172 AX93
Egham Rd. E13 144 EH71
Eghams Clo., Beac. 88 AJ51
Eghams Wd. Rd., Beac. 88 AH51
Eglantine La. (Horton Kirby), Dart. 208 FN101
Eglantine Rd. SW18 180 DC85
Egleston Rd., Mord. 200 DB100
Egley Dr., Wok. 226 AX120
Egley Rd., Wok. 226 AX122
Eglington Ct. SE17 162 DQ79
Carter St.
Eglington Rd. E4 101 ED45
Eglinton Hill SE18 165 EP79
Eglinton Rd. SE18 165 EN79
Eglinton Rd., Swans. 190 FZ86
Eglise Rd., Warl. 237 DY117
Egliston Ms. SW15 159 CW83
Egliston Rd. SW15 159 CW83
Eglon Ms. NW1 140 DF66
Berkley Rd.
Egmont Ave., Surb. 198 CM102
Egmont Pk. Rd., Tad. 249 CU125
Egmont Rd., N.Mal. 199 CT98
Egmont Rd., Surb. 198 CM102
Egmont Rd., Sutt. 218 DC108
Egmont Rd., Walt. 195 BV101
Egmont St. SE14 163 DX80
Egmont Way, Tad. 233 CY119
Oatlands Rd.
Egremont Gdns., Slou. 131 AN74
Egremont Rd. SE27 181 DN90
Egret Way, Hayes 136 BX71
Egypt La., Slou. 111 AP61
Eider Clo. E7 124 EF64
Eider Clo., Hayes 136 BX71
Cygnet Way
Eight Acres, Slou. 130 AH70
Eighteenth Rd., Mitch. 201 DL98
Eighth Ave. E12 125 EM63
Eighth Ave., Hayes 135 BU74
Eileen Rd. SE25 202 DR99
Eindhoven Clo., Cars. 200 DG102
Eisenhower Dr. E6 144 EL71
Elaine Gro. NW5 120 DG64
Elam Clo. SE5 161 DP82
Elam St. SE5 161 DP82
Elan Rd., S.Ock. 149 FU71
Eland Pl., Croy. 201 DP104
Eland Rd.
Eland Rd. SW11 160 DF83
Eland Rd., Croy. 201 DP104
Elba Pl. SE17 279 J8
Elbe St. SW6 160 DC82
Elberon Ave., Croy. 201 DJ100
Elborough Rd. SE25 202 DU99
Elborough St. SW18 180 DA88
Elbow La., Hert. 48 DV17
Elbow Meadow, Slou. 153 BF81
Elbury Dr. E16 144 EG72
Elcho St. SW11 160 DE80
Elcot Ave. SE15 162 DV80
Elder Ave. N8 121 DL57
Elder Clo., Guil. 243 BA131
Elder Clo., Sid. 185 ET88
Elder Clo., West Dr. 134 BL73
Yew Ave.
Elder Ct. (Bushey), Wat. 95 CE47
Elder Gdns. SE27 182 DQ91
Gladstone Ter.
Elder Oak Clo. SE20 202 DV95
Elder Rd. SE27 182 DQ92
Elder St. E1 275 P5
Elder St. E1 142 DT71
Elder Wk. N1 141 DP67
Essex Rd.
Elder Way, Dor. 263 CJ140
Elder Way, Rain. 148 FK69
Elder Way, Slou. 153 AZ75
Elderbek Clo., Wal.Cr. 66 DU28
Elderberry Gro. SE27 182 DQ92
Linton Gro.
Elderberry Rd. W5 158 CL75
Elderberry Way, Wat. 75 BV35
Elderfield, Harl. 36 EX11
Elderfield Pl. SW17 181 DH91
Elderfield Rd. E5 122 DW63
Elderfield Rd., Slou. 132 AT65
Elderfield Wk. E11 124 EH57
Elderflower Way E15 144 EE66
Eldersley Clo., Red. 250 DF132
Elderslie Clo., Beck. 203 EB99
Elderslie Rd. SE9 185 EN85
Elderton Rd. SE26 183 DY91
Eldertree Pl., Mitch. 201 DJ95
Eldertree Way
Eldertree Way, Mitch. 201 DH95
Elderwood Pl. SE27 182 DQ92
Elder Rd.
Eldon Ave., Borwd. 78 CN40
Eldon Ave., Croy. 202 DW103
Eldon Ave., Houns. 156 CA80
Eldon Gro. NW3 120 DD64
Eldon Pk. SE25 202 DV98
Eldon Rd. E17 123 DZ56
Eldon Rd. N9 100 DW47
Eldon Rd. N22 99 DP53
Eldon Rd. W8 160 DB76
Eldon Rd., Cat. 236 DR121
Eldon Rd., Hodd. 49 ED19
Eldon St. EC2 275 L7
Eldon St. EC2 142 DR71
Eldon Way NW10 138 CP68
Eldred Dr., Orp. 206 EW102
Eldred Gdns., Upmin. 129 FS59
Eldred Rd., Bark. 145 ES67
Eldrick Ct., Felt. 175 BR88
Kilross Rd.
Eldridge Clo., Felt. 175 BU88
Eleanor Ave., Epsom 216 CR110
Eleanor Ave., St.Alb. 43 CD18
Eleanor Clo. N15 122 DT55
Arnold Rd.
Eleanor Clo. SE16 163 DX75
Eleanor Cres. NW7 97 CX49
Eleanor Cross Rd., Wal.Cr. 67 DY34
Eleanor Gdns., Barn. 79 CX43

Eleanor Gdns., Dag. 126 EZ62
Eleanor Gro. SW13 158 CS83
Eleanor Gro. (Ickenham), Uxb. 115 BP62
Eleanor Rd. E8 142 DV66
Eleanor Rd. E15 144 EF65
Eleanor Rd. N11 99 DL51
Eleanor Rd., Ger.Cr. 90 AW53
Eleanor Rd., Hert. 32 DQ08
Eleanor Rd., Wal.Cr. 67 DY33
Eleanor St. E3 143 EA69
Eleanor Wk. SE18 165 EM77
Samuel St.
Eleanor Way, Brwd. 108 FX50
Eleanor Way, Wal.Cr. 67 DZ33
Electric Ave. SW9 161 DN84
Electric Ave., Enf. 83 DZ36
Electric La. SW9 161 DN84
Electric Par., Surb. 197 CK100
Elephant & Castle SE1 278 G7
Elephant & Castle SE1 161 DP77
Elephant La. SE16 162 DW75
Elephant Rd. SE17 279 H8
Elephant Rd. SE17 162 DQ77
Elers Rd. W13 157 CJ75
Elers Rd., Hayes 155 BR77
Eleven Acre Ri., Loug. 85 EM41
Eley Est. N18 100 DW50
Eley Rd. N18 101 DX50
Elf Row E1 142 DW73
Elfin Gro., Tedd. 177 CF92
Broad St.
Elfindale Rd. SE24 182 DQ85
Elford Clo. SE3 164 EH84
Elfort Rd. N5 121 DN63
Elfrida Cres. SE6 183 EA91
Elfrida Rd., Wat. 76 BW43
Elfwine Rd. W7 137 CE71
Elgal Clo., Orp. 223 EP106
Orchard Rd.
Elgar Ave. NW10 138 CR65
Mitchellbrook Way
Elgar Ave. SW16 201 DL97
Elgar Ave. W5 158 CL75
Elgar Ave., Surb. 198 CP101
Elgar Clo. E13 144 EJ68
Bushey Rd.
Elgar Clo. SE8 163 EA80
Comet St.
Elgar Clo., Borwd. 95 CK45
Elgar Clo., Buck.H. 102 EK47
Elgar Clo., Uxb. 114 BN61
Elgar Gdns., Til. 171 GH81
Elgar St. SE16 163 DY76
Elgin Ave. W9 140 DB69
Elgin Ave., Ashf. 175 BQ93
Elgin Ave., Har. 95 CH54
Elgin Ave., Rom. 106 FP52
Elgin Cres. W11 139 CZ72
Elgin Cres., Cat. 236 DU122
Elgin Cres., Houns. 155 BS82
Eastern Perimeter Rd.
Elgin Dr., Nthwd. 93 BS52
Elgin Gdns., Guil. 243 BA133
Elgin Ms. W11 139 CY72
Ladbroke Gro.
Elgin Ms. N. W9 140 DB69
Randolph Ave.
Elgin Ms. S. W9 140 DB69
Randolph Ave.
Elgin Rd. N22 99 DJ54
Elgin Rd., Brox. 49 DZ23
Elgin Rd., Croy. 202 DT102
Elgin Rd., Ilf. 125 ES60
Elgin Rd., Sutt. 200 DC104
Elgin Rd., Wall. 219 DJ107
Elgin Rd. (Cheshunt), Wal.Cr. 66 DW30
Elgin Rd., Wey. 212 BN106
Elgiva La., Chesh. 54 AP31
Elgood Ave., Nthwd. 93 BU51
Elgood Clo. W11 139 CY73
Avondale Pk. Rd.
Elham Clo., Brom. 184 EK94
Elia Ms. N1 274 F1
Elia Ms. N1 141 DP68
Elia St. N1 274 F1
Elia St. N1 141 DP68
Elias Pl. SW8 161 DN79
Elibank Rd. SE9 165 EN84
Elim Est. SE1 279 M6
Elim Est. SE1 162 DS76
Elim Way E13 144 EF69
Eliot Bank SE23 182 DV89
Eliot Cotts. SE3 164 EE82
Eliot Pl.
Eliot Dr., Har. 116 CB61
Eliot Gdns. SW15 159 CU84
Eliot Hill SE13 163 EC82
Eliot Ms. NW8 140 DC68
Eliot Pk. SE13 163 EC83
Eliot Pl. SE3 164 EE82
Eliot Rd., Dag. 126 EX63
Eliot Rd., Dart. 188 FP85
Eliot Vale SE3 163 ED82
Elizabeth Ave. N1 142 DQ66
Elizabeth Ave., Amer. 72 AV39
Elizabeth Ave., Enf. 81 DP41
Elizabeth Ave., Ilf. 125 ER61
Elizabeth Ave., Stai. 174 BJ93
Elizabeth Blackwell Ho. N22 99 DN53
Progress Way
Elizabeth Bri. SW1 277 H9
Elizabeth Bri. SW1 161 DH77
Elizabeth Clo. E14 143 EB72
Grundy St.
Elizabeth Clo. W9 140 DC70
Randolph Ave.
Elizabeth Clo., Barn. 79 CX41
Elizabeth Clo., Rom. 105 FB53
Elizabeth Clo., Sutt. 217 CZ105
Elizabeth Clo., Til. 171 GH82
Elizabeth Clo., Wal.Abb. 49 ED23
Elizabeth Clo., Welw.G.C. 30 DC09
Elizabeth Clyde Clo. N15 122 DS56
Elizabeth Cotts., Rich. 158 CM81
Elizabeth Ct. SW1 277 N7
Elizabeth Ct., Gdmg. 258 AS144
Elizabeth Ct., Grav. 191 GG86
St. James's Rd.
Elizabeth Ct., Horl. 268 DG148
Elizabeth Ct., St.Alb. 43 CK17
Villiers Cres.
Elizabeth Ct., Wat. 75 BT38
Elizabeth Dr., Epp. 85 ES36
Elizabeth Est. SE17 162 DR79
Elizabeth Fry Rd. E8 142 DV66
Lamb La.
Elizabeth Gdns. W3 139 CT74
Elizabeth Gdns., Stan. 95 CJ51
Elizabeth Gdns., Sun. 196 BW97
Elizabeth Huggins Cotts., Grav. 191 GH89
Elizabeth Ms. NW3 140 DE65
Elizabeth Pl. N15 122 DR56
Elizabeth Ride N9 100 DV45
Elizabeth Rd. E6 144 EK67
Elizabeth Rd. N15 122 DS57
Elizabeth Rd., Brwd. 108 FV44
Elizabeth Rd., Gdmg. 258 AS144
Elizabeth Rd., Grays 170 FZ76
Elizabeth Rd., Rain. 147 FH71
Elizabeth Sq. SE16 143 DY73
Rotherhithe St.
Elizabeth St. SW1 276 G8
Elizabeth St. SW1 160 DG77
Elizabeth St., Green. 189 FS85
Elizabeth Ter. SE9 185 EM86
Elizabeth Way SE19 182 DR94
Elizabeth Way, Felt. 176 BW91
Elizabeth Way, Harl. 51 EM16
Elizabeth Way, Orp. 206 EW99
Elizabeth Way, Slou. 132 AT67
Elizabethan Clo., Stai. 174 BK87
Elizabethan Way
Elizabethan Way, Stai. 174 BK87
Elkanette Ms. N20 98 DC47
Ridgeview Rd.
Elkington Rd. E13 144 EH70
Elkins, The, Rom. 105 FE54
Elkins Gdns., Guil. 243 BA131
Elkins Rd., Slou. 112 AS61
Elkstone Rd. W10 139 CZ71
Ella Rd. N8 121 DL59
Ellaline Rd. W6 159 CX79
Ellanby Cres. N18 100 DV50
Elland Rd. SE15 162 DW84
Elland Rd., Walt. 196 BX103
Ellement Clo., Pnr. 116 BX57
Ellen Clo., Brom. 204 EK97
Ellen Clo., Hem.H. 40 BM19
Ellen Ct. N9 100 DW47
Densworth Gro.
Ellen St. E1 142 DU72
Ellen Webb Dr., Har. 117 CE55
Ellenborough Pl. SW15 159 CU84
Ellenborough Rd. N22 100 DQ53
Ellenborough Rd., Sid. 186 EX92
Ellenbridge Way, S.Croy. 220 DS109
Ellenbrook Clo., Wat. 75 BV39
Hatfield Rd.
Ellenbrook Cres., Hat. 44 CR18
Ellenbrook La.
Ellenbrook La., Hat. 44 CR18
Elleray Rd., Tedd. 177 CF93
Ellerby St. SW6 159 CX81
Ellerdale Clo. NW3 120 DC63
Ellerdale Rd.
Ellerdale Rd. NW3 120 DC64
Ellerdale St. SE13 163 EB84
Ellerdine Rd., Houns. 156 CC84
Ellerker Gdns., Rich. 178 CL86
Ellerman Ave., Twick. 176 BZ88
Ellerman Rd., Til. 171 GF82
Ellerslie, Grav. 191 GK87
Ellerslie Gdns. NW10 139 CU67
Ellerslie Rd. W12 139 CV74
Ellerslie Sq. Ind. Est. SW2 181 DL85
Ellerton Gdns., Dag. 146 EW66
Ellerton Rd. SW13 159 CU81
Ellerton Rd. SW18 180 DD88
Ellerton Rd. SW20 179 CU94
Ellerton Rd., Dag. 146 EW66
Ellerton Rd., Surb. 198 CM103
Ellery Rd. SE19 182 DR94
Ellery St. SE15 162 DV82
Elles Ave., Guil. 243 BB134
Ellesborough Clo., Wat. 94 BW50
Ellesmere Ave. NW7 96 CR48
Ellesmere Ave., Beck. 203 EB96
Ellesmere Clo. E11 124 EF57
Ellesmere Clo., Ruis. 115 BQ59
Ellesmere Dr., S.Croy. 220 DV114
Ellesmere Gdns., Ilf. 124 EL57
Ellesmere Gro., Barn. 79 CZ43
Ellesmere Rd. E3 143 DY68
Ellesmere Rd. NW10 119 CU64
Ellesmere Rd. W4 158 CR79
Ellesmere Rd., Berk. 38 AX19
Ellesmere Rd., Grnf. 136 CC70
Ellesmere Rd., Twick. 177 CJ86
Ellesmere Rd., Wey. 213 BS108
Ellesmere St. E14 143 EB72
Ellice Rd., Oxt. 254 EF128
Elliman Ave., Slou. 132 AS73
Ellingfort Rd. E8 142 DV66
Ellingham Clo., Hem.H. 40 BN18
Ellingham Rd. E15 123 ED63
Ellingham Rd. W12 159 CU75
Ellingham Rd., Chess. 215 CK107
Ellingham Rd., Hem.H. 40 BM19
Ellington Ct., Maid. 130 AC72
Ellington Rd.
Ellington Gdns., Maid. 130 AC72
Ellington Rd. N10 121 DH56
Ellington Rd., Felt. 175 BT91
Ellington Rd., Houns. 156 CB82
Ellington Rd., Maid. 130 AC72
Ellington St. N7 141 DN65
Ellington Way, Epsom 233 CV117
Elliot Clo. E15 144 EE66
Elliot Clo., Welw.G.C. 29 CX12
Elliot Rd. NW4 119 CV58
Elliot Rd., Stan. 95 CG51
Elliott Ave., Ruis. 115 BV61
Elliott Clo., Wem. 118 CM62
Elliott Gdns., Rom. 105 FH53
Elliott Gdns., Shep. 194 BN98
Elliott Rd. SW9 161 DP80
Elliott Rd. W4 158 CS77
Elliott Rd., Brom. 204 EK98
Elliott Rd., Th.Hth. 201 DP98
Elliott Sq. NW3 140 DE66
Elliott St., Grav. 191 GK87
Elliotts Clo. (Cowley), Uxb. 134 BJ71
Elliotts La., Sev. 240 EW124
Elliott's Pl. N1 141 DP67
St. Peters St.
Elliotts Row SE11 278 F8
Elliotts Row SE11 161 DP77
Ellis Ave., Ger.Cr. 91 AZ53
Ellis Ave., Guil. 258 AT136
Ellis Ave., Rain. 147 FG71
Ellis Ave., Slou. 152 AS75
Ellis Clo. NW10 139 CW65
High Rd.
Ellis Clo. SE9 185 EQ89
Ellis Clo., Couls. 235 DM120
Ellis Ct. W7 137 CF71
Ellis Fm. Clo., Wok. 226 AX122
Ellis Ms. SE7 164 EJ79
Ellis Rd., Couls. 235 DM120
Ellis Rd., Mitch. 200 DF100
Ellis Rd., Sthl. 136 CC74
Ellis St. SW1 276 E8
Ellis St. SW1 160 DF77
Ellis Way, Dart. 188 FM89
Elliscombe Rd. SE7 164 EJ78
Ellisfield Dr. SW15 179 CT87
Ellison Clo., Wind. 151 AM83
Ellison Gdns., Sthl. 156 BZ77
Ellison Rd. SW13 159 CT82
Ellison Rd. SW16 181 DK94
Ellison Rd., Sid. 185 ER88
Elliston Ho. SE18 165 EN77
Ellmore Clo., Rom. 105 FH53
Ellora Rd. SW16 181 DK92
Ellsworth St. E2 142 DV69
Ellwood Ct. W9 140 DB70
Clearwell Dr.
Ellwood Gdns., Wat. 59 BV34
Ellwood Ri., Ch.St.G. 90 AW47
Elm Ave. W5 138 CL74
Elm Ave., Cars. 218 DF110
Elm Ave., Ruis. 115 BU60
Elm Ave., Upmin. 128 FP62
Elm Ave., Wat. 94 BY45
Elm Bank, Brom. 204 EK96
Elm Bank Gdns. SW13 158 CS82
Elm Clo. E11 124 EH58
Elm Clo. N19 121 DJ61
Hargrave Pk.
Elm Clo. NW4 119 CX57
Elm Clo. SW20 199 CW98
Grand Dr.
Elm Clo., Amer. 55 AQ38
Elm Clo., Buck.H. 102 EK47
Elm Clo., Cars. 200 DF102
Elm Clo., Dart. 188 FJ88
Elm Clo., Epp. 51 EP24
Elm Clo., Har. 116 CB58
Elm Clo., Hayes 135 BU72
Elm Clo., Lthd. 231 CH122
Elm Clo., Rom. 105 FB53
Elm Clo., Slou. 131 AQ65
Elm Clo., S.Croy. 220 DS107
Elm Clo., Stai. 174 BK88
Elm Clo., Surb. 198 CQ101
Elm Clo., Tad. 248 CQ130
Elm Clo., Twick. 176 CB89
Elm Clo., Wal.Abb. 67 ED34
Elm Clo., Warl. 237 DX117
Elm Clo., Wok. 226 AX115
Elm Clo. (Send Marsh), Wok. 228 BG124
Elm Ct. EC4 274 D10
Elm Ct., Mitch. 200 DF96
Armfield Cres.
Elm Ct., Sun. 175 BT94
Elm Cres. W5 138 CL74
Elm Cres., Kings.T. 198 CL95
Elm Cft., Slou. 152 AW81
Elm Dr., Har. 116 CB58
Elm Dr., Hat. 45 CU19
Elm Dr., Lthd. 231 CH123
Elm Dr., St.Alb. 43 CJ20
Elm Dr., Sun. 196 BW96
Elm Dr., Swan. 207 FD96
Elm Dr. (Cheshunt), Wal.Cr. 67 DY28
Elm Dr., Wok. 210 AT110
Elm Friars Wk. NW1 141 DK66
Elm Gdns. N2 120 DC55
Elm Gdns., Enf. 82 DR38
Elm Gdns., Epp. 71 FB26
Elm Gdns., Epsom 233 CW119
Elm Gdns., Esher 215 CF107
Elm Gdns., Mitch. 201 DK98
Elm Gdns., Welw.G.C. 29 CV09
Elm Grn. W3 138 CS72
Elm Grn., Hem.H. 39 BE18
Elm Gro. N8 121 DL58
Elm Gro. NW2 119 CX63
Elm Gro. SE15 162 DT82
Elm Gro. SW19 179 CY94
Elm Gro., Berk. 38 AV19
Elm Gro., Cat. 236 DS122
Elm Gro., Epsom 216 CQ114
Elm Gro., Erith 167 FD80
Elm Gro., Har. 116 CA59
Elm Gro., Horn. 128 FL58
Elm Gro., Kings.T. 198 CL95
Elm Gro., Orp. 205 ET102
Elm Gro., Sutt. 218 DB105
Elm Gro., Wat. 75 BU37
Elm Gro., West Dr. 134 BM73
Willow Ave.
Elm Gro., Wdf.Grn. 102 EF50
Elm Gro. Par., Wall. 200 DG104
Butter Hill
Elm Gro. Rd. SW13 159 CU82
Elm Gro. Rd. W5 158 CL75
Elm Gro. Rd., Cob. 230 BX116
Elm Hall Gdns. E11 124 EH57
Elm La. SE6 183 DZ89
Elm La., Wok. 228 BM118
Elm Lawn Clo., Uxb. 134 BL66
Park Rd.
Elm Ms., Rich. 178 CM86
Grove Rd.
Elm Par., Horn. 127 FH63
St. Nicholas Ave.
Elm Pk. SW2 181 DM86
Elm Pk., Stan. 95 CH50
Elm Pk. Ave. N15 122 DT57
Elm Pk. Ave., Horn. 127 FG63
Elm Pk. Ct., Pnr. 116 BW55
Elm Pk. Gdns. NW4 119 CX57
Elm Pk. Gdns. SW10 160 DD78
Elm Pk. La. SW3 160 DD78
Elm Pk. Mans. SW10 160 DC79
Park Wk.
Elm Pk. Rd. E10 123 DY60
Elm Pk. Rd. N3 97 CZ52
Elm Pk. Rd. N21 100 DQ45
Elm Pk. Rd. SE25 202 DT97
Elm Pk. Rd. SW3 160 DD79
Elm Pk. Rd., Pnr. 94 BW54
Elm Pl. SW7 160 DD78
Elm Quay Ct. SW8 161 DK79
Elm Rd. E7 144 EF65
Elm Rd. E11 123 ED61
Elm Rd. E17 123 EC57
Elm Rd. N22 99 DP53
Granville Rd.
Elm Rd. SW14 158 CQ83
Elm Rd., Barn. 79 CZ42
Elm Rd., Beck. 203 DZ96
Elm Rd., Chess. 216 CL105
Elm Rd., Dart. 188 FK88
Elm Rd., Epsom 217 CT107
Elm Rd., Erith 167 FG81
Elm Rd., Esher 215 CF107
Elm Rd., Felt. 175 BR88
Elm Rd., Gdmg. 258 AT143
Elm Rd., Grav. 191 GJ90
Elm Rd., Grays 170 GC79
Elm Rd., Green. 189 FS86
Elm Rd., H.Wyc. 88 AD46
Elm Rd., Hodd. 49 EA17
Taverners Way
Elm Rd., Kings.T. 198 CM95
Elm Rd., Lthd. 231 CH122
Elm Rd., N.Mal. 198 CR98
Elm Rd., Orp. 224 EU108
Elm Rd., Pur. 219 DP113
Elm Rd., Red. 250 DE134
Elm Rd., Rom. 105 FB54
Elm Rd., Sid. 186 EU91
Elm Rd., S.Ock. 148 FQ74
Elm Rd., Th.Hth. 202 DR98
Elm Rd., Wall. 200 DG102
Elm Rd., Warl. 237 DX117
Elm Rd., Wem. 118 CL64
Elm Rd., West. 255 ES125
Elm Rd., Wind. 151 AP83
Elm Rd., Wok. 226 AX118
Elm Rd. (Horsell), Wok. 227 AZ115
Elm Rd. W., Sutt. 199 CZ101
Elm Row NW3 120 DC62
Elm St. WC1 274 C5
Elm St. WC1 141 DM70
Elm Ter. NW2 120 DA62
Elm Ter. NW3 120 DE63
Constantine Rd.
Elm Ter. SE9 185 EN86
Elm Ter., Grays 169 FV79
Elm Ter., Har. 95 CD52
Elm Tree Ave., Esher 197 CD101
Elm Tree Clo. NW8 140 DD69
Elm Tree Clo., Ashf. 175 BP92
Convent Rd.
Elm Tree Clo., Cher. 193 BE103
Green La.
Elm Tree Clo., Horl. 268 DG147
Elm Tree Clo., Nthlt. 136 BZ68
Elm Tree Rd. NW8 140 DD69
Elm Wk. NW3 120 DA61
Elm Wk. SW20 199 CW99
Elm Wk., Orp. 205 EM104
Elm Wk., Rad. 77 CF36
Elm Wk., Rom. 127 FG55
Elm Way N11 98 DG51
Elm Way NW10 118 CS63
Elm Way, Brwd. 108 FU49
Elm Way, Epsom 216 CR106
Elm Way, Rick. 92 BH46
Elm Way, Wor.Pk. 199 CW104
Elmar Grn., Slou. 131 AN69
Elmar Rd. N15 122 DR56
Elmbank N14 99 DL45
Elmbank Ave., Barn. 79 CW42
Elmbank Ave., Egh. 172 AV93
Elmbank Ave., Guil. 258 AU135
Elmbank Way W7 137 CD71
Elmbourne Dr., Belv. 167 FB77
Elmbourne Rd. SW17 180 DG90
Elmbridge, Harl. 36 EZ12
Elmbridge Ave., Surb. 198 CP99
Elmbridge Clo., Ruis. 115 BU58
Elmbridge Dr., Ruis. 115 BT57
Elmbridge La., Wok. 227 AZ119
Elmbridge Rd., Ilf. 104 EU51
Elmbridge Wk. E8 142 DU66
Wilman Gro.
Elmbrook Clo., Sun. 195 BV95
Elmbrook Gdns. SE9 164 EL84
Elmbrook Rd., Sutt. 217 CZ105
Elmcote Way, Rick. 74 BM44
Elmcourt Rd. SE27 181 DP89
Elmcroft N8 121 DM57
Elmcroft, Lthd. 230 CA124
Elmcroft Ave. E11 124 EH57
Elmcroft Ave. N9 82 DV44
Elmcroft Ave. NW11 119 CZ59
Elmcroft Ave., Sid. 185 ET86
Elmcroft Clo. E11 124 EH56
Elmcroft Clo. W5 137 CK72
Elmcroft Clo., Chess. 198 CL104
Elmcroft Clo., Felt. 175 BT86
Elmcroft Cres. NW11 119 CY59
Elmcroft Cres., Har. 116 CA55
Elmcroft Dr., Ashf. 174 BN92
Elmcroft Dr., Chess. 198 CL104
Elmcroft Gdns. NW9 118 CN57
Elmcroft Rd., Orp. 206 EU101
Elmcroft St. E5 122 DW63
Elmdale Rd. N13 99 DM50
Elmdene, Surb. 198 CQ102
Elmdene Ave., Horn. 128 FM57
Elmdene Clo., Beck. 203 DZ99
Elmdene Rd. SE18 165 EP78
Elmdon Rd., Houns. 156 BX82
Elmdon Rd. (Hatton Cross), Houns. 155 BT83
Elmer Ave. (Havering-atte-Bower), Rom. 105 FE48
Elmer Clo., Enf. 81 DM41
Elmer Clo., Rain. 147 FG66
Elmer Cotts., Lthd. 231 CG123
Elmer Gdns., Edg. 96 CP52
Elmer Gdns., Islw. 157 CD83
Elmer Gdns., Rain. 147 FG66
Elmer Ms., Lthd. 231 CG122
Elmer Rd. SE6 183 EC87
Elmers Dr., Tedd. 177 CH93
Kingston Rd.
Elmers End Rd. SE20 202 DW96
Elmers End Rd., Beck. 202 DW96
Elmers Rd. SE25 202 DU101
Elmerside Rd., Beck. 203 DY98
Elmfield, Lthd. 230 CA123
Elmfield Ave. N8 121 DL57
Elmfield Ave., Mitch. 200 DG95
Elmfield Ave., Tedd. 177 CF92
Elmfield Clo., Grav. 191 GH88
Elmfield Clo., Har. 117 CE61
Elmfield Clo., Pot.B. 63 CY33
Elmfield Pk., Brom. 204 EG97
Elmfield Rd. E4 101 EC47
Elmfield Rd. E17 123 DX58
Elmfield Rd. N2 120 DD55
Elmfield Rd. SW17 180 DG89
Elmfield Rd., Brom. 204 EG97
Elmfield Rd., Pot.B. 63 CY33
Elmfield Rd., Sthl. 156 BY76
Elmfield Way W9 140 DA71
Elmfield Way, S.Croy. 220 DT109
Elmgate Ave., Felt. 175 BV90
Elmgate Gdns., Edg. 96 CR50
Elmgreen Clo. E15 144 EE67
Church St. N.
Elmgrove Cres., Har. 117 CF57
Elmgrove Gdns., Har. 117 CG57
Elmgrove Rd., Croy. 202 DV101
Elmgrove Rd., Har. 117 CF57
Elmgrove Rd., Wey. 212 BN105
Elmhurst, Belv. 166 EY79
Elmhurst Ave. N2 120 DD55
Elmhurst Ave., Mitch. 181 DH94
Elmhurst Ct., Guil. 259 AZ135
Lower Edgeborough Rd.
Elmhurst Dr. E18 102 EG54
Elmhurst Dr., Dor. 263 CH138
Elmhurst Dr., Horn. 128 FJ60
Elmhurst Gdns. E18 102 EH53
Elmhurst Dr.
Elmhurst Rd. E7 144 EH66
Elmhurst Rd. N17 100 DT54
Elmhurst Rd. SE9 184 EL89
Elmhurst Rd., Enf. 82 DW37
Elmhurst Rd., Slou. 153 BA76
Elmhurst St. SW4 161 DK83
Elmhurst Vil. SE15 162 DW84
Cheltenham Rd.
Elmhurst Way, Loug. 103 EM45
Elmington Clo., Bex. 187 FB86
Elmington Est. SE5 162 DR80
Elmington Rd. SE5 162 DR81
Elmira St. SE13 163 EB83
Elmlea Dr., Hayes 135 BS71
Grange Rd.
Elmlee Clo., Chis. 185 EM93
Elmley Clo. E6 144 EL71
Northumberland Rd.
Elmley St. SE18 165 ER77
Elmore Clo., Wem. 138 CL68
Elmore Rd. E11 123 EC62
Elmore Rd., Couls. 234 DF121
Elmore Rd., Enf. 83 DX39
Elmore St. N1 142 DQ66
Elmores, Loug. 85 EN41
Elmpark Gdns., S.Croy. 220 DW110
Elmroyd Ave., Pot.B. 63 CZ33
Elmroyd Clo., Pot.B. 63 CZ33
Elms, The SW13 159 CT83
Elms, The, Hert. 32 DU09
Elms Ave. N10 121 DH55
Elms Ave. NW4 119 CX57
Elms Ct., Wem. 117 CF63
Elms Cres. SW4 181 DJ86
Elms Fm. Rd., Horn. 128 FJ64
Elms Gdns., Dag. 126 EZ63
Elms Gdns., Wem. 117 CG63
Elms Ind. Est., Rom. 106 FP52
Elms La., Wem. 117 CG63
Elms Ms. W2 140 DD73
Elms Pk. Ave., Wem. 117 CG63
Elms Rd. SW4 181 DJ85
Elms Rd., Ger.Cr. 90 AY52
Elms Rd., Har. 95 CE52
Elms Rd., Ware 33 EA05
Elmscott Gdns. N21 82 DQ44
Elmscott Rd., Brom. 184 EF92
Elmscroft N8 121 DM57
Tottenham La.
Elmscroft Gdns., Pot.B. 63 CY32
Elmsdale Rd. E17 123 DZ56
Elmshaw Rd. SW15 179 CU85
Elmshorn, Epsom 233 CW116
Elmshott La., Slou. 131 AL73
Elmshurst Cres. N2 120 DD56
Elmside, Croy. 221 EB107
Elmside, Guil. 258 AU135
Elmside Rd., Wem. 118 CN62
Elmsleigh Ave., Har. 117 CH56
Elmsleigh Cen., The, Stai. 173 BF91
Elmsleigh Ct., Sutt. 200 DB104
Elmsleigh Rd., Stai. 173 BF92
Thames St.
Elmsleigh Rd., Twick. 177 CD89
Elmslie Clo., Epsom 216 CQ114
Elmslie Clo., Wdf.Grn. 103 EM51
Elmslie Pt. E3 143 DZ71
Elmstead Ave., Chis. 185 EM92
Elmstead Ave., Wem. 118 CL60
Elmstead Clo. N20 98 DA47
Elmstead Clo., Epsom 216 CS106
Elmstead Clo., Sev. 256 FE122
Elmstead Cres., Well. 166 EW79
Elmstead Gdns., Wor.Pk. 199 CU104
Elmstead Glade, Chis. 185 EM93
Elmstead La., Chis. 185 EM92
Elmstead Rd., Erith 167 FE81
Elmstead Rd., Ilf. 125 ES61
Elmstead Rd., W.Byf. 212 BG113
Elmstone Rd. SW6 160 DA81
Elmsway, Ashf. 174 BM92
Elmswood, Lthd. 230 BZ124
Elmsworth Ave., Houns. 156 CB82
Elmton Way E5 122 DU62
Rendlesham Rd.
Elmtree Clo., W.Byf. 212 BL113
Elmtree Hill, Chesh. 54 AP30
Elmtree Rd., Tedd. 177 CE91
Elmwood, Saw. 36 EZ06
Elmwood, Welw.G.C. 29 CV10
Elmwood Ave. N13 99 DL50
Elmwood Ave., Borwd. 78 CP42
Elmwood Ave., Felt. 175 BU89
Elmwood Ave., Har. 117 CG57
Elmwood Clo., Ash. 231 CK117
Elmwood Clo., Epsom 217 CU108
Elmwood Clo., Wall. 200 DG103
Elmwood Ct., Ash. 231 CK117
Elmwood Clo.
Elmwood Ct., Wem. 117 CG62
Elmwood Cres. NW9 118 CQ56
Elmwood Dr., Bex. 186 EY87

Etchingham Rd. E15 123 EC63
Eternit Wk. SW6 159 CW81
Etfield Gro., Sid. 186 EV92
Ethel Bailey Clo., Epsom 216 CN112 *Christ Ch. Rd.*
Ethel Rd. E16 144 EH72
Ethel Rd., Ashf. 174 BL92
Ethel St. SE17 279 H9
Ethel Ter., Orp. 224 EW109
Ethelbert Clo., Brom. 204 EG97
Ethelbert Gdns., Ilf. 125 EM57
Ethelbert Rd. SW20 199 CX95
Ethelbert Rd., Brom. 204 EG97
Ethelbert Rd., Dart. 188 FL91
Ethelbert Rd., Erith 167 FC80
Ethelbert Rd., Orp. 206 EX97
Ethelbert St. SW12 181 DH88 *Fernlea Rd.*
Ethelburga Rd., Rom. 106 FM53
Ethelburga St. SW11 160 DE81
Ethelden Rd. W12 139 CV74
Etheldene Ave. N10 121 DJ56
Ethelred Clo., Welw.G.C. 29 CZ10
Ethelwine Pl., Abb.L. 59 BT30 *The Cres.*
Etheridge Grn., Loug. 85 EQ41 *Etheridge Rd.*
Etheridge Rd. NW2 119 CW59
Etheridge Rd., Loug. 85 EP40
Etherley Rd. N15 122 DQ57
Etherow St. SE22 182 DU86
Etherstone Grn. SW16 181 DN91 *Etherstone Rd.*
Etherstone Rd. SW16 181 DN91
Ethnard Rd. SE15 162 DV79
Ethorpe Clo., Ger.Cr. 112 AY57
Ethorpe Cres., Ger.Cr. 112 AY57
Ethronvi Rd., Bexh. 166 EY83
Etloe Rd. E10 123 EA61
Etna Rd., St.Alb. 43 CD19
Eton Ave. N12 98 DC52
Eton Ave. NW3 140 DD66
Eton Ave., Barn. 80 DE44
Eton Ave., Houns. 156 BZ79
Eton Ave., N.Mal. 198 CR99
Eton Ave., Wem. 117 CH63
Eton Clo. SW18 180 DB87
Eton Clo., Slou. 152 AU79
Eton College Rd. NW3 140 DF65
Eton Ct. NW3 140 DD66 *Eton Ave.*
Eton Ct., Stai. 173 BF92 *Richmond Rd.*
Eton Ct., Wem. 117 CJ63 *Eton Ave.*
Eton Ct. (Eton), Wind. 151 AR80
Eton Garages NW3 140 DE65 *Lambolle Pl.*
Eton Gro. NW9 118 CN55
Eton Gro. SE13 164 EE83
Eton Hall NW3 140 DF65 *Eton College Rd.*
Eton Pl. NW3 140 DG66 *Haverstock Hill*
Eton Ri. NW3 140 DF65 *Eton College Rd.*
Eton Rd. NW3 140 DF66
Eton Rd., Hayes 155 BT80
Eton Rd., Ilf. 125 EQ64
Eton Rd., Orp. 224 EV105
Eton Rd., Slou. 152 AT78
Eton Sq. (Eton), Wind. 151 AR80
Eton St., Rich. 178 CL85
Eton Vil. NW3 140 DF65
Eton Way, Dart. 168 FJ84
Eton Wick Rd. (Eton Wick), Wind. 151 AL77
Etta St. SE8 163 DY79
Etton Clo., Horn. 128 FL61
Ettrick St. E14 143 EC72
Etwell Pl., Surb. 198 CM100
Euclid Way, Grays 169 FU77
Eugene Clo., Rom. 128 FJ56
Eugenia Rd. SE16 162 DW77
Eunice Gro., Chesh. 54 AR33
Eureka Rd., Kings.T. 198 CN96 *Washington Rd.*
Europa Pk. Rd., Guil. 242 AW133
Europa Pl. EC1 275 H3
Europa Rd., Hem.H. 40 BM17 *Jupiter Dr.*
Europa Trd. Est., Erith 167 FD78
Europe Rd. SE18 165 EM76
Eustace Rd. E6 144 EL69
Eustace Rd. SW6 160 DA80
Eustace Rd., Guil. 243 BD132
Eustace Rd., Rom. 126 EX59
Euston Ave., Wat. 75 BT43
Euston Cen. NW1 141 DJ70 *Triton Sq.*
Euston Gro. NW1 273 M3
Euston Gro. NW1 141 DK69
Euston Rd. N1 273 P2
Euston Rd. N1 141 DK70
Euston Rd. NW1 273 J5
Euston Rd. NW1 141 DH70
Euston Rd., Croy. 201 DN102
Euston Sq. NW1 273 M3
Euston Sq. NW1 141 DK69
Euston Sta. Colonnade NW1 273 M3
Euston St. NW1 273 L4
Euston St. NW1 141 DJ69
Eva Rd., Rom. 126 EW59
Evandale Rd. SW9 161 DN82
Evangelist Rd. NW5 121 DH63
Evans Ave., Wat. 75 BT35
Evans Clo. E8 142 DT65 *Buttermere Wk.*
Evans Clo., Green. 189 FU85
Evans Clo., Rick. 74 BN43 *New Rd.*
Evans Gro., Felt. 176 CA89
Evans Gro., St.Alb. 43 CJ16
Evans Rd. SE6 184 EE89
Evansdale, Rain. 147 FF69 *New Zealand Way*
Evanston Ave. E4 101 EC52
Evanston Gdns., Ilf. 124 EL58
Eve Rd. E11 124 EE63
Eve Rd. E15 144 EE68
Eve Rd. N17 122 DS55
Eve Rd., Islw. 157 CG84
Eve Rd., Wok. 227 BB115
Evelina Rd. SE15 162 DW83
Evelina Rd. SE20 183 DX94
Eveline Lowe Est. SE16 162 DU76
Eveline Rd., Mitch. 200 DF95
Evelyn Ave. NW9 118 CR56
Evelyn Ave., Ruis. 115 BT58
Evelyn Clo., Twick. 176 CB87
Evelyn Clo., Wok. 226 AX120
Evelyn Ct. N1 275 K1
Evelyn Cres., Sun. 195 BT95
Evelyn Denington Rd. E6 144 EL70
Evelyn Dr., Pnr. 94 BX52
Evelyn Fox Ct. W10 139 CW71
Evelyn Gdns. SW7 160 DD78
Evelyn Gdns., Gdse. 252 DW130
Evelyn Gdns., Rich. 158 CL84 *Kew Rd.*
Evelyn Gro. W5 138 CM74
Evelyn Gro., Sthl. 136 BZ72
Evelyn Rd. E16 144 EH74
Evelyn Rd. E17 123 EC56
Evelyn Rd. SW19 180 DB92
Evelyn Rd. W4 158 CR76
Evelyn Rd., Barn. 80 DF42
Evelyn Rd., Rich. 158 CL83
Evelyn Rd. (Ham), Rich. 177 CJ90
Evelyn Sharp Clo., Rom. 128 FK55 *Amery Gdns.*
Evelyn St. SE8 163 DY78
Evelyn Ter., Rich. 158 CL83
Evelyn Wk. N1 275 K1
Evelyn Wk. N1 142 DR68
Evelyn Wk., Brwd. 107 FW51 *Wilmot Grn.*
Evelyn Way, Cob. 230 BZ116
Evelyn Way, Epsom 216 CN111
Evelyn Way, Sun. 195 BT95
Evelyn Way, Wall. 219 DK105
Evelyn Yd. W1 273 M8
Evelyns Clo., Uxb. 134 BN72
Evening Hill, Beck. 183 EC94
Evensyde, Wat. 75 BR44
Evenwood Clo. SW15 179 CY85
Everard Ave., Brom. 204 EG102
Everard Ave., Slou. 152 AS75
Everard Clo., St.Alb. 43 CD22
Everard La., Cat. 236 DU122 *Tillingdown Hill*
Everard Way, Wem. 118 CL62
Everatt Clo. SW18 179 CZ86 *Amerland Rd.*
Everdon Rd. SW13 159 CU79
Everest Clo., Grav. 190 GE90
Everest Ct., Wok. 226 AS116 *Langmans Way*
Everest Pl. E14 143 EC71
Everest Pl., Swan. 207 FD98
Everest Rd. SE9 185 EM85
Everest Rd., Stai. 174 BK87
Everest Way, Hem.H. 40 BN19
Everett Clo., Pnr. 115 BT55
Everett Clo. (Cheshunt), Wal.Cr. 66 DQ26
Everett Clo., Wat. 95 CE46
Everett Wk., Belv. 166 EZ78 *Osborne Rd.*
Everglade, West. 238 EK118
Everglade Strand NW9 97 CT53
Evergreen Ct., Stai. 174 BK87
Evergreen Oak Ave., Wind. 152 AU83
Evergreen Wk., Hem.H. 40 BL22 *Redwood Dr.*
Evergreen Way, Hayes 135 BT73
Evergreen Way, Stai. 174 BK87
Everilda St. N1 141 DM67
Evering Rd. E5 122 DT62
Evering Rd. N16 122 DT62
Everington Rd. N10 98 DF54
Everington St. W6 159 CX79
Everitt Rd. NW10 138 CR69
Everlands Clo., Wok. 226 AY118
Everlasting La., St.Alb. 42 CC18
Everleigh St. N4 121 DM60
Eversfield Gdns. NW7 96 CS52
Eversfield Rd., Reig. 250 DB134
Eversfield Rd., Rich. 158 CM82
Evershed Wk. W4 158 CR77
Eversholt St. NW1 273 L1
Eversholt St. NW1 141 DJ68
Evershot Rd. N4 121 DM60
Eversleigh Gdns., Upmin. 129 FR60
Eversleigh Rd. E6 144 EK67
Eversleigh Rd. N3 97 CZ52
Eversleigh Rd. SW11 160 DG82
Eversleigh Rd., Barn. 80 DC43
Eversley Ave., Bexh. 167 FD82
Eversley Ave., Wem. 118 CN61
Eversley Clo. N21 81 DM44
Eversley Cres. N21 81 DM44
Eversley Cres., Islw. 157 CD81
Eversley Cres., Ruis. 115 BS61
Eversley Cross, Bexh. 167 FE82
Eversley Mt. N21 81 DM44
Eversley Pk. SW19 179 CV92
Eversley Pk. Rd. N21 81 DM44
Eversley Rd. SE7 164 EH79
Eversley Rd. SE19 182 DR94
Eversley Rd., Surb. 198 CM98
Eversley Way, Croy. 221 EA105
Eversley Way, Egh. 193 BC96
Everthorpe Rd. SE15 162 DT83
Everton Bldgs. NW1 273 K3
Everton Dr., Stan. 118 CM55
Everton Rd., Croy. 202 DU102
Evesham Ave. E17 101 EA54
Evesham Clo., Grnf. 136 CB68
Evesham Clo., Reig. 249 CZ133
Evesham Clo., Sutt. 218 DA108
Evesham Grn., Mord. 200 DB100
Evesham Rd. E15 144 EF67
Evesham Rd. N11 99 DJ50
Evesham Rd., Felt. 176 BW87 *Sparrow Fm. Dr.*
Evesham Rd., Grav. 191 GK89
Evesham Rd., Mord. 200 DB100
Evesham Rd., Reig. 249 CZ134
Evesham Rd. N., Reig. 249 CZ133
Evesham St. W11 139 CX73
Evesham Wk. SE5 162 DR82 *Love Wk.*
Evesham Wk. SW9 161 DN82
Evesham Way SW11 160 DG83
Evesham Way, Ilf. 125 EN55
Evreham Rd., Iver 133 BE72
Evry Rd., Sid. 186 EW93
Ewald Rd. SW6 159 CZ82
Ewan Rd., Rom. 106 FK54
Ewanrigg Ter., Wdf.Grn. 102 EJ50
Ewart Gro. N22 99 DN53
Ewart Pl. E3 143 DZ68
Ewart Rd. SE23 183 DX87
Ewe Clo. N7 141 DL65
Ewelands, Horl. 269 DJ147
Ewell Bypass, Epsom 217 CU108
Ewell Ct. Ave., Epsom 216 CS106
Ewell Downs Rd., Epsom 217 CU111
Ewell Ho. Gro., Epsom 217 CT110
Ewell Pk. Gdns., Epsom 217 CU108
Ewell Pk. Way, Epsom 217 CU107
Ewell Rd., Surb. 198 CL100
Ewell Rd. (Long Ditton), Surb. 197 CH101
Ewell Rd., Sutt. 217 CY107
Ewellhurst Rd., Ilf. 102 EL54
Ewelme Rd. SE23 182 DW88
Ewen Cres. SW2 181 DN88
Ewer St. SE1 279 H3
Ewer St. SE1 142 DQ74
Ewhurst Ave., S.Croy. 220 DT109
Ewhurst Clo., Sutt. 217 CW109
Ewhurst Ho. E1 142 DW71
Ewhurst Rd. SE4 183 DZ86
Exbury Rd. SE6 183 EA89
Excel Ct. WC2 277 N1
Excelsior Clo., Kings.T. 198 CN96 *Washington Rd.*
Excelsior Gdns. SE13 163 EC82
Exchange Arc. EC2 275 N6
Exchange Bldgs. E1 142 DS72 *Cutler St.*
Exchange Ct. WC2 278 A1
Exchange Pl. EC2 275 M6
Exchange Rd., Wat. 75 BV42
Exchange Sq. EC2 275 M6
Exchange Sq. EC2 142 DS71
Exchange St., Rom. 127 FE57
Exeforde Ave., Ashf. 174 BN91
Exeter Clo. E6 145 EM72 *Harper Rd.*
Exeter Clo., Wat. 76 BW40
Exeter Gdns., Ilf. 124 EL60
Exeter Ho. SW15 179 CW86 *Putney Heath*
Exeter Ms. NW6 140 DB65 *West Hampstead Ms.*
Exeter Pl., Guil. 242 AT132
Exeter Rd. E16 144 EG71
Exeter Rd. E17 123 EA57
Exeter Rd. N9 100 DW47
Exeter Rd. N14 99 DH46
Exeter Rd. NW2 119 CY64
Exeter Rd., Croy. 202 DS101
Exeter Rd., Dag. 147 FB65
Exeter Rd., Enf. 83 DX41
Exeter Rd., Felt. 176 BZ90
Exeter Rd., Grav. 191 GK90
Exeter Rd., Har. 116 BY61
Exeter Rd., Houns. 155 BS82
Exeter Rd., Well. 165 ET82
Exeter St. WC2 274 A10
Exeter St. WC2 141 DL73
Exeter Way SE14 163 DZ80
Exeter Way, Houns. 155 BS83
Exford Gdns. SE12 184 EH88
Exford Rd. SE12 184 EH89
Exhibition Clo. W12 139 CW73
Exhibition Rd. SW7 276 A5
Exhibition Rd. SW7 160 DD75
Exmoor Clo., Ilf. 103 EQ53
Exmoor St. W10 139 CX70
Exmouth Mkt. EC1 274 D4
Exmouth Mkt. EC1 141 DN70
Exmouth Ms. NW1 273 L3
Exmouth Pl. E8 142 DV66
Exmouth Rd. E17 123 DZ57
Exmouth Rd., Brom. 204 EH97
Exmouth Rd., Grays 170 GB79
Exmouth Rd., Hayes 135 BS69
Exmouth Rd., Ruis. 116 BW62
Exmouth Rd., Well. 166 EW81
Exmouth St. E1 142 DW72 *Commercial Rd.*
Exning Rd. E16 144 EF70
Exon St. SE17 279 M10
Exon St. SE17 162 DS78
Explorer Ave., Stai. 174 BL87
Explorer Dr., Wat. 75 BT44
Express Dr., Ilf. 126 EV60
Exton Cres. NW10 138 CQ66
Exton Gdns., Dag. 126 EW64
Exton St. SE1 278 D3
Exton St. SE1 141 DN74
Eyebright Clo., Croy. 203 DX102 *Primrose La.*
Eyhurst Ave., Horn. 127 FG62
Eyhurst Clo. NW2 119 CU61
Eyhurst Clo., Tad. 233 CZ123
Eyhurst Pk., Tad. 234 DC123
Eyhurst Spur, Tad. 233 CZ124
Eylewood Rd. SE27 182 DQ92
Eynella Rd. SE22 182 DT87
Eynham Rd. W12 139 CW72
Eynsford Clo., Orp. 205 EQ101
Eynsford Cres., Bex. 186 EW88
Eynsford Rd., Green. 189 FW85
Eynsford Rd., Ilf. 125 ES61
Eynsford Rd., Sev. 225 FH110
Eynsford Rd., Swan. 207 FD100
Eynsham Dr. SE2 166 EU77
Eynswood Dr., Sid. 186 EV92
Eyot Gdns. W6 159 CT78
Eyot Grn. W4 159 CT79 *Chiswick Mall*
Eyre Clo., Rom. 127 FH56
Eyre Ct. NW8 140 DD68 *Finchley Rd.*
Eyre St. Hill EC1 274 D5
Eyston Dr., Wey. 212 BN110
Eythorne Rd. SW9 161 DN81
Eywood Rd., St.Alb. 42 CC22
Ezra St. E2 142 DT69

F

Faber Gdns. NW4 119 CU57
Fabian Rd. SW6 159 CZ80
Fabian St. E6 145 EM70
Fackenden La., Sev. 225 FH113
Factory La. N17 100 DT54
Factory La., Croy. 201 DN102
Factory Path, Stai. 173 BE91 *Mustard Mill Rd.*
Factory Rd. E16 144 EL74
Factory Rd., Grav. 190 GC86
Factory Sq. SW16 181 DL93
Factory Yd. W7 137 CE74 *Uxbridge Rd.*
Faesten Way, Bex. 187 FE90
Faggotters La., Harl. 37 FC12
Faggotters La., Ong. 53 FG16
Faggotts Clo., Rad. 77 CJ35
Faggs Rd., Felt. 175 BU85
Fagnall La., Amer. 88 AJ45
Fagus Ave., Rain. 148 FK69
Faints Clo., Wal.Cr. 66 DT29
Fair Acres, Brom. 204 EG99
Fair Clo. (Bushey), Wat. 94 CB45 *Claybury*
Fair Grn., Saw. 36 EY05 *The Sq.*
Fair La., Couls. 250 DC125
Fair Leas, Chesh. 54 AN29
Fair St. SE1 279 N4
Fair St., Houns. 156 CC83 *High St.*
Fairacre, Hem.H. 40 BM24
Fairacre, N.Mal. 198 CS97
Fairacres SW15 159 CU84
Fairacres, Cob. 214 BX112
Fairacres, Croy. 221 DZ109
Fairacres, Ruis. 115 BT59
Fairacres, Tad. 233 CW121
Fairacres, Wind. 151 AK82
Fairacres Clo., Pot.B. 63 CZ33
Fairbairn Clo., Pur. 219 DN113
Fairbairn Grn. SW9 161 DN81
Fairbank Ave., Orp. 205 EP103
Fairbank Est. N1 142 DR68 *East Rd.*
Fairbanks Rd. N17 122 DT55
Fairborne Way, Guil. 242 AU131
Fairbourne, Cob. 214 BX113
Fairbourne Clo., Wok. 226 AU118 *Abercorn Way*
Fairbourne La., Cat. 236 DQ122
Fairbourne Rd. N17 122 DS55
Fairbridge Rd. N19 121 DK61
Fairbrook Clo. N13 99 DN50
Fairbrook Rd. N13 99 DN51
Fairburn Clo., Borwd. 78 CN39
Fairburn Ct. SW15 179 CY85 *Mercier Rd.*
Fairby Rd. SE12 184 EH85
Faircharm Trd. Est. SE8 163 EB80
Fairchild Clo. SW11 160 DD82 *Wye St.*
Fairchild Pl. EC2 275 N5
Fairchild St. EC2 275 N5
Fairchildes Ave., Croy. 221 ED112
Fairchildes La., Warl. 221 ED114
Fairclough St. E1 142 DU72
Faircroft, Slou. 131 AP70
Faircross Ave., Bark. 145 EQ65
Faircross Ave., Rom. 105 FD52
Faircross Way, St.Alb. 43 CG19
Fairdale Gdns. SW15 159 CV84
Fairdale Gdns., Hayes 135 BU74
Fairdene Rd., Couls. 235 DK118
Fairey Ave., Hayes 155 BT77
Fairfax Ave., Epsom 217 CV109
Fairfax Ave., Red. 250 DE133
Fairfax Clo., Walt. 195 BV102
Fairfax Gdns. SE3 164 EK81
Fairfax Ms. E16 144 EH74 *Wesley Ave.*
Fairfax Ms. SW15 159 CW84 *Upper Richmond Rd.*
Fairfax Ms., Amer. 55 AN40
Fairfax Pl. NW6 140 DC66
Fairfax Rd. N8 121 DN56
Fairfax Rd. NW6 140 DC66
Fairfax Rd. W4 158 CS76
Fairfax Rd., Grays 170 GB78
Fairfax Rd., Hert. 32 DT08
Fairfax Rd., Tedd. 177 CG93
Fairfax Rd., Til. 171 GF81
Fairfax Rd., Wok. 227 BB120
Fairfax Way N10 98 DG52 *Cromwell Rd.*
Fairfield App., Stai. 172 AX86
Fairfield Ave. NW4 119 CV58
Fairfield Ave., Edg. 96 CP51
Fairfield Ave., Horl. 268 DG149
Fairfield Ave., Ruis. 115 BQ59
Fairfield Ave., Slou. 152 AW80
Fairfield Ave., Stai. 173 BF91
Fairfield Ave., Twick. 176 CB88
Fairfield Ave., Upmin. 128 FQ62
Fairfield Ave., Wat. 94 BW48
Fairfield Clo. N12 98 DC49
Fairfield Clo., Dor. 247 CH134 *Fairfield Dr.*
Fairfield Clo., Enf. 83 DY42 *Scotland Grn. Rd. N.*
Fairfield Clo., Epsom 216 CS106
Fairfield Clo., Hat. 45 CW15
Fairfield Clo., Horn. 127 FG60
Fairfield Clo., Mitch. 180 DE94
Fairfield Clo., Nthwd. 93 BP50 *Thirlmere Gdns.*
Fairfield Clo., Rad. 77 CE37
Fairfield Clo., Sid. 185 ET86
Fairfield Clo., Slou. 152 AX80
Fairfield Cotts., Lthd. 246 CB125
Fairfield Ct. NW10 139 CU67
Fairfield Cres., Edg. 96 CP51
Fairfield Dr. SW18 180 DB85
Fairfield Dr., Brox. 49 DZ24
Fairfield Dr., Dor. 247 CH134
Fairfield Dr., Grnf. 137 CJ67
Fairfield Dr., Har. 116 CC55
Fairfield Dr., Slou. 130 AJ69
Fairfield E., Kings.T. 198 CL96
Fairfield Gdns. N8 121 DL57 *Elder Ave.*
Fairfield Gro. SE7 164 EK78
Fairfield Ind. Est., Kings.T. 198 CM97
Fairfield La., Slou. 131 AP68
Fairfield N., Kings.T. 198 CL96
Fairfield Pk., Cob. 214 BX114
Fairfield Path, Croy. 202 DR104
Fairfield Pathway, Horn. 148 FJ66
Fairfield Pl., Kings.T. 198 CL97
Fairfield Ri., Guil. 242 AT133
Fairfield Rd. E3 143 EA68
Fairfield Rd. E17 101 DY54
Fairfield Rd. N8 121 DL57
Fairfield Rd. N18 100 DU49
Fairfield Rd. W7 157 CG76
Fairfield Rd., Beck. 203 EA96
Fairfield Rd., Bexh. 166 EZ82
Fairfield Rd., Brwd. 108 FW48
Fairfield Rd., Brom. 184 EG94
Fairfield Rd., Croy. 202 DS104
Fairfield Rd., Epp. 70 EV29
Fairfield Rd., Hodd. 49 EA15
Fairfield Rd., Ilf. 145 EP65
Fairfield Rd., Kings.T. 198 CL96
Fairfield Rd., Lthd. 231 CH121
Fairfield Rd., Orp. 205 ER100
Fairfield Rd., Sthl. 136 BZ72
Fairfield Rd., Stai. 172 AX86
Fairfield Rd., Uxb. 134 BK65
Fairfield Rd., West Dr. 134 BL74
Fairfield Rd., Wdf.Grn. 102 EG51
Fairfield S., Kings.T. 198 CL96
Fairfield St. SW18 180 DB85
Fairfield Wk., Lthd. 231 CH121 *Fairfield Rd.*
Fairfield Wk. (Cheshunt), Wal.Cr. 67 DY28
Fairfield Way, Barn. 80 DA43
Fairfield Way, Couls. 219 DK114
Fairfield Way, Epsom 216 CS106
Fairfield W., Kings.T. 198 CL96
Fairfields, Cher. 194 BG102
Fairfields, Grav. 191 GL92
Fairfields Clo. NW9 118 CQ57
Fairfields Cres. NW9 118 CQ56
Fairfields Rd., Houns. 156 CC83
Fairfolds, Wat. 76 BY36
Fairfoot Rd. E3 143 EA70
Fairford Ave., Bexh. 167 FD81
Fairford Ave., Croy. 203 DX99
Fairford Clo., Croy. 203 DY99
Fairford Clo., Reig. 250 DC132
Fairford Clo., Rom. 106 FP51 *Fairford Way*
Fairford Clo., W.Byf. 211 BF114
Fairford Gdns., Wor.Pk. 199 CT103
Fairford Way, Rom. 106 FP51
Fairgreen, Barn. 80 DF41
Fairgreen E., Barn. 80 DF41
Fairgreen Rd., Th.Hth. 201 DP99
Fairham Ave., S.Ock. 149 FU73
Fairhaven, Egh. 173 AZ92
Fairhaven Ave., Croy. 203 DX100
Fairhaven Cres., Wat. 93 BU48
Fairhaven Rd., Red. 250 DG130
Fairhazel Gdns. NW6 140 DB65
Fairhill, Hem.H. 40 BM24
Fairholme, Felt. 175 BR87
Fairholme Ave., Rom. 127 FG57
Fairholme Clo. N3 119 CY56
Fairholme Cres., Ash. 231 CJ117
Fairholme Cres., Hayes 135 BT70
Fairholme Gdns. N3 119 CY55
Fairholme Gdns., Upmin. 129 FT59
Fairholme Rd. W14 159 CY78
Fairholme Rd., Ashf. 174 BL92
Fairholme Rd., Croy. 201 DN101
Fairholme Rd., Har. 117 CF57
Fairholme Rd., Ilf. 125 EM59
Fairholme Rd., Sutt. 217 CZ107
Fairholt Clo. N16 122 DS60
Fairholt Rd. N16 122 DR60
Fairholt St. SW7 276 C6
Fairkytes Ave., Horn. 128 FK60
Fairland Rd. E15 144 EF65
Fairlands Ave., Buck.H. 102 EG47
Fairlands Ave., Sutt. 200 DA103
Fairlands Ave., Th.Hth. 201 DM98
Fairlands Ct. SE9 185 EN86 *North Pk.*
Fairlawn SE7 164 EJ79
Fairlawn, Lthd. 230 BZ124
Fairlawn Ave. N2 120 DE56
Fairlawn Ave. W4 158 CQ77
Fairlawn Ave., Bexh. 166 EX82
Fairlawn Clo. N14 81 DJ44
Fairlawn Clo., Esher 215 CF107
Fairlawn Clo., Felt. 176 BZ91
Fairlawn Clo., Kings.T. 178 CQ93
Fairlawn Dr., Red. 266 DE136
Fairlawn Dr., Wdf.Grn. 102 EG52
Fairlawn Gdns., Sthl. 136 BZ73
Fairlawn Gro. W4 158 CQ77
Fairlawn Gro., Bans. 218 DD113
Fairlawn Pk. SE26 183 DY92
Fairlawn Pk., Wind. 151 AL84
Fairlawn Pk., Wok. 210 AY114
Fairlawn Rd. SW19 179 CZ94
Fairlawn Rd., Bans. 218 DD112
Fairlawn Rd., Cars. 218 DC111
Fairlawns, Add. 211 BF111
Fairlawns, Brwd. 108 FU48
Fairlawns, Horl. 269 DH149
Fairlawns, Pnr. 94 BW54
Fairlawns, Sun. 195 BU97
Fairlawns, Twick. 177 CJ86
Fairlawns, Wat. 75 BT38 *Langley Rd.*
Fairlawns, Wey. 213 BS106
Fairlawns Clo., Horn. 128 FM59
Fairlawns Clo., Stai. 174 BH93
Fairlea Pl. W5 137 CK70
Fairley Way (Cheshunt), Wal.Cr. 66 DV28
Fairlie Gdns. SE23 182 DW87
Fairlie Rd., Slou. 131 AN72
Fairlight Ave. E4 101 ED47
Fairlight Ave. NW10 138 CS68
Fairlight Ave., Wind. 151 AR82
Fairlight Ave., Wdf.Grn. 102 EG51
Fairlight Clo. E4 101 ED47
Fairlight Clo., Wor.Pk. 217 CW105
Fairlight Dr., Uxb. 134 BK65
Fairlight Rd. SW17 180 DD91
Fairlop Clo., Horn. 147 FH65
Fairlop Gdns., Ilf. 103 EQ52
Fairlop Rd. E11 123 ED59
Fairlop Rd., Ilf. 103 EQ54
Fairmark Dr., Uxb. 134 BN65
Fairmead, Brom. 205 EM98
Fairmead, Surb. 198 CP102
Fairmead, Wok. 226 AW118
Fairmead Clo., Brom. 205 EM98
Fairmead Clo., Houns. 156 BX80
Fairmead Clo., N.Mal. 198 CR97
Fairmead Cres., Edg. 96 CQ48
Fairmead Gdns., Ilf. 124 EL57
Fairmead Rd. N19 121 DK62
Fairmead Rd., Croy. 201 DM102
Fairmead Rd., Loug. 84 EH42
Fairmead Side, Loug. 84 EJ43
Fairmeads, Cob. 214 BZ113
Fairmeads, Loug. 85 EP40

Fairmile Ave. SW16 181 DK92
Fairmile Ave., Cob. 214 BY114
Fairmile La., Cob. 214 BX112
Fairmile Pk. Copse, Cob. 214 BZ112
Fairmile Pk. Rd., Cob. 214 BZ113
Fairmont Clo., Belv. 166 EZ78
Lullingstone Rd.
Fairmount Rd. SW2 181 DM86
Fairoak Clo., Ken. 235 DP115
Fairoak Clo., Lthd. 215 CD112
Fairoak Clo., Orp. 205 EP101
Fairoak Dr. SE9 185 ER85
Fairoak Gdns., Rom. 105 FE54
Fairoak La., Chess. 215 CH111
Fairoak La., Lthd. 214 CC113
Fairs Rd., Lthd. 231 CG119
Fairseat Clo. (Bushey), Wat. 95 CE47
Hive Rd.
Fairstead Wk. N1 142 DQ67
Popham Rd.
Fairstone Ct., Horl. 269 DH147
Tanyard Way
Fairthorn Rd. SE7 164 EG78
Fairtrough Rd., Orp. 224 EV113
Fairview, Epsom 217 CW111
Fairview, Erith 167 FF80
Guild Rd.
Fairview, Pot.B. 64 DB29
Hawkshead Rd.
Fairview Ave., Brwd. 109 GE45
Fairview Ave., Rain. 148 FK68
Fairview Ave., Wem. 137 CK65
Fairview Ave., Wok. 227 AZ118
Fairview Clo. E17 101 DY53
Fairview Clo., Chig. 103 ES49
Fairview Clo., Wok. 227 AZ118
Fairview Ave.
Fairview Ct., Ashf. 174 BN92
Fairview Cres., Har. 116 CA60
Fairview Dr., Chig. 103 ES49
Fairview Dr., Orp. 223 ER105
Fairview Dr., Shep. 194 BM99
Fairview Dr., Wat. 75 BS36
Fairview Gdns., Wdf.Grn. 102 EH53
Fairview Ind. Pk., Rain. 147 FE71
Fairview Pl. SW2 181 DM87
Fairview Rd. N15 122 DT57
Fairview Rd. SW16 201 DM95
Fairview Rd., Chig. 103 ES49
Fairview Rd., Enf. 81 DN39
Fairview Rd., Epsom 217 CT111
Fairview Rd., Grav. 190 GD94
Fairview Rd., Maid. 130 AG72
Fairview Rd., Slou. 131 AM70
Fairview Rd., Sutt. 218 DD106
Fairview Way, Edg. 96 CN49
Fairwater Ave., Well. 166 EU84
Fairwater Dr., Add. 212 BK109
Fairway SW20 199 CW97
Fairway, Bexh. 186 EY85
Fairway, Cars. 218 DC111
Fairway, Cher. 194 BH102
Fairway, Guil. 243 BD134
Fairway, Hem.H. 40 BM24
Fairway, Orp. 205 ER99
Fairway, Saw. 36 EY05
Fairway, Vir.W. 192 AW100
Fairway, Ware 32 DW07
Fairway, Wdf.Grn. 102 EJ50
Fairway, The N13 100 DQ48
Fairway, The N14 81 DH44
Fairway, The NW7 96 CR48
Fairway, The W3 138 CS72
Fairway, The, Abb.L. 59 BR32
Fairway, The, Barn. 80 DB44
Fairway, The, Brom. 205 EM99
Fairway, The, Grav. 191 GG89
Fairway, The, Harl. 51 ET17
Fairway, The, H.Wyc. 110 AC56
Fairway, The, Lthd. 231 CG118
Fairway, The, N.Mal. 198 CR95
Fairway, The, Nthlt. 136 CC65
Fairway, The, Nthwd. 93 BS49
Fairway, The, Ruis. 116 BX62
Fairway, The, Slou. 130 AJ69
Fairway, The, Upmin. 128 FQ59
Fairway, The, Uxb. 134 BM68
Fairway, The, Wem. 117 CH62
Fairway, The, W.Mol. 196 CB97
Fairway, The, Wey. 212 BN111
Fairway Ave. NW9 118 CP55
Fairway Ave., Borwd. 78 CP40
Fairway Ave., West Dr. 134 BJ74
Fairway Clo. NW11 120 DC59
Fairway Clo., Croy. 203 DY99
Fairway Clo., Epsom 216 CQ105
Fairway Clo., Houns. 176 BW85
Fairway Clo., St.Alb. 60 CC27
Fairway Clo., West Dr. 134 BK74
Fairway Ave.
Fairway Clo., Wok. 226 AV119
Fairway Ct. NW7 96 CR48
The Fairway
Fairway Ct., Hem.H. 40 BM24
Fairway
Fairway Dr. SE28 146 EX72
Fairway Dr., Dart. 188 FP87
Fairway Dr., Grnf. 136 CB66
Fairway Gdns., Beck. 203 ED100
Fairway Gdns., Ilf. 125 EQ64
Fairways, Ashf. 175 BP93
Fairways, Ken. 236 DQ117
Fairways, Stan. 96 CL54
Fairways, Tedd. 177 CK94
Fairways, Wal.Abb. 68 EE34
Fairways, Wal.Cr. 67 DX26
Fairweather Clo. N15 122 DS56
Fairweather Rd. N16 122 DU58
Fairwell La., Lthd. 245 BP128
Fairwyn Rd. SE26 183 DY91
Fakenham Clo. NW7 97 CU52
Fakenham Clo., Nthlt. 136 CA65
Goodwood Dr.
Fakruddin St. E1 142 DU70
Falaise, Egh. 172 AY92
Falcon Ave., Brom. 204 EL98
Falcon Ave., Grays 170 GB79
Falcon Clo. SE1 278 G2
Falcon Clo. W4 158 CQ79
Sutton La. S.
Falcon Clo., Dart. 188 FM85
Falcon Clo., Hat. 45 CU20
Falcon Clo., Nthwd. 93 BS52
Falcon Clo., Saw. 36 EW06
Falcon Clo., Wal.Abb. 68 EG34
Kestrel Rd.
Falcon Ct. EC4 274 D9
Falcon Ct. EC4 141 DN72
Falcon Ct., Wok. 211 BC114
Blackmore Cres.
Falcon Cres., Enf. 83 DX43
Falcon Dr., Stai. 174 BK86
Falcon Gro. SW11 160 DE83
Falcon Ho. W13 137 CF70
Falcon La. SW11 160 DE83
Falcon Ms., Grav. 190 GE88
Falcon Pk. Ind. Est. NW10 119 CT64
Falcon Ridge, Berk. 38 AW20
Falcon Rd. SW11 160 DE82
Falcon Rd., Enf. 83 DX43
Falcon Rd., Guil. 258 AX135
Falcon Rd., Hmptn. 176 BZ94
Falcon St. E13 144 EG70
Falcon Ter. SW11 160 DE83
Falcon Way E11 124 EG56
Falcon Way E14 163 EB77
Falcon Way NW9 96 CS54
Falcon Way, Felt. 175 BV85
Falcon Way, Har. 118 CL57
Falcon Way, Horn. 147 FG66
Falcon Way, Sun. 195 BS96
Falcon Way, Wat. 60 BY34
Falcon Way, Welw.G.C. 29 CY07
Falconberg Ct. W1 273 N8
Falconberg Ms. W1 273 M8
Falconer Rd., Ilf. 104 EV50
Falconer Rd. (Bushey), Wat. 76 BZ44
Falconer Wk. N7 121 DM61
Newington Barrow Way
Falconers Pk., Saw. 36 EX06
Falconhurst, Lthd. 231 CD115
Falcons Cft., H.Wyc. 110 AE55
Falconwood, Egh. 172 AY92
Falconwood, Lthd. 229 BT124
Falconwood Ave., Well. 165 ER82
Falconwood Par., Well. 165 ES84
Falconwood Rd., Croy. 221 EA108
Falcourt Clo., Sutt. 218 DB106
Falkirk Clo., Horn. 128 FN60
Falkirk Gdns., Wat. 94 BX50
Blackford Rd.
Falkirk Ho. W9 140 DB69
Falkirk St. N1 275 N1
Falkirk St. N1 142 DS68
Falkland Ave. N3 98 DA52
Falkland Ave. N11 98 DG49
Falkland Gdns., Dor. 263 CG137
Harrow Rd. W.
Falkland Gro., Dor. 263 CG137
Falkland Pk. Ave. SE25 202 DS97
Falkland Pl. NW5 121 DJ64
Falkland Rd.
Falkland Rd. N8 121 DN56
Falkland Rd. NW5 121 DJ64
Falkland Rd., Barn. 79 CY40
Falkland Rd., Dor. 263 CG137
Fallaize Ave., Ilf. 125 EP63
Riverdene Rd.
Falling La., West Dr. 134 BL73
Falloden Way NW11 120 DA56
Fallow Clo., Chig. 103 ET50
Fallow Ct. SE16 162 DU78
Argyle Way
Fallow Ct. Ave. N12 98 DC52
Fallow Flds., Loug. 102 EJ45
Fallowfield, Stan. 95 CG48
Fallowfield, Welw.G.C. 29 CZ06
Fallowfield Clo. (Harefield), Uxb. 92 BJ53
Fallowfield Ct., Stan. 95 CG48
Fallowfield Wk., Hem.H. 40 BG17
Tollpit End
Fallowfield Way, Horl. 269 DH147
Fallowfields Dr. N12 98 DE51
Fallows Clo. N2 98 DC54
Fallsbrook Rd. SW16 181 DJ94
Falman Clo. N9 100 DU46
Croyland Rd.
Falmer Rd. E17 123 EB55
Falmer Rd. N15 122 DQ57
Falmer Rd., Enf. 82 DS42
Falmouth Ave. E4 101 ED50
Falmouth Clo. N22 99 DM52
Truro Rd.
Falmouth Clo. SE12 184 EF85
Falmouth Gdns., Ilf. 124 EL57
Falmouth Rd. SE1 279 J6
Falmouth Rd. SE1 162 DQ76
Falmouth Rd., Slou. 131 AN72
Falmouth Rd., Walt. 214 BW105
Falmouth St. E15 123 ED64
Falstaff Gdns., St.Alb. 42 CC23
Falstaff Ms., Hmptn. 177 CD92
Hampton Rd.
Falstone, Wok. 226 AV118
Fambridge Clo. SE26 183 DZ91
Fambridge Rd., Dag. 126 FA60
Famet Ave., Pur. 220 DQ113
Famet Clo., Pur. 220 DQ113
Famet Wk., Pur. 220 DQ113
Fane St. W14 159 CZ79
North End Rd.
Fanhams Rd., Ware 33 DY05
Fann St. EC1 275 H5
Fann St. EC1 142 DQ70
Fann St. EC2 275 H5
Fann St. EC2 142 DQ70
Fanns Ri., Purf. 168 FN77
Fanshaw St. N1 275 M2
Fanshaw St. N1 142 DS69
Fanshawe Ave., Bark. 145 EQ65
Fanshawe Cres., Dag. 126 EY64
Fanshawe Cres., Horn. 128 FK58
Fanshawe Cres., Ware 32 DW05
Fanshawe Rd., Grays 171 GG76
Fanshawe Rd., Rich. 177 CJ91
Fanshawe St., Hert. 31 DP08
Fanshaws La., Hert. 48 DQ18
Fanthorpe St. SW15 159 CW83
Far End, Hat. 45 CV21
Faraday Ave., Sid. 186 EU89
Faraday Clo. N7 141 DM65
Bride St.
Faraday Clo., Slou. 131 AP71
Faraday Clo., Wat. 75 BR44
Faraday Rd. E15 144 EF65
Faraday Rd. SW19 180 DA93
Faraday Rd. W3 138 CQ73
Faraday Rd. W10 139 CY71
Faraday Rd., Slou. 131 AP71
Faraday Rd., Sthl. 136 CB73
Faraday Rd., Well. 166 EU83
Faraday Rd., W.Mol. 196 CA98
Faraday Way SE18 164 EK76
Faraday Way, Croy. 201 DM102
Ampere Way
Faraday Way, Orp. 206 EV98
Fareham Rd., Felt. 176 BW87
Fareham St. W1 273 M8
Farewell Pl., Mitch. 200 DE95
Faringdon Ave., Brom. 205 EP100
Faringdon Ave., Rom. 106 FJ53
Faringford Clo., Pot.B. 64 DD31
Faringford Rd. E15 144 EE66
Farington Acres, Wey. 195 BR104
Faris Barn Dr., Add. 211 BF112
Faris La., Add. 211 BF111
Farjeon Rd. SE3 164 EK81
Farland Rd., Hem.H. 41 BP20
Farleigh Ave., Brom. 204 EF100
Farleigh Border, Croy. 221 DY112
Farleigh Ct., Guil. 242 AS134
Park Barn Dr.
Farleigh Ct. Rd., Warl. 221 DZ114
Farleigh Dean Cres., Croy. 221 EB111
Farleigh Pl. N16 122 DT63
Farleigh Rd.
Farleigh Rd. N16 122 DT63
Farleigh Rd., Add. 212 BG111
Farleigh Rd., Warl. 237 DX118
Farleton Clo., Wey. 213 BR107
Farley Dr., Ilf. 125 ES60
Farley Heath, Guil. 260 BJ144
Farley La., West. 255 EP127
Farley Nursery, West. 255 EQ127
Farley Pk., Oxt. 253 ED130
Farley Pl. SE25 202 DU98
Farley Rd. SE6 183 EB87
Farley Rd., Grav. 191 GM88
Farley Rd., S.Croy. 220 DV108
Farleycroft, West. 255 EQ126
Farleys Clo., Lthd. 245 BQ126
Farlington Pl. SW15 179 CV87
Roehampton La.
Farlow Clo., Grav. 191 GF90
Farlow Rd. SW15 159 CX83
Farlton Rd. SW18 180 DB87
Farm Ave. NW2 119 CY62
Farm Ave. SW16 181 DL91
Farm Ave., Har. 116 BZ59
Farm Ave., Swan. 207 FC97
Farm Ave., Wem. 137 CJ65
Farm Clo., Amer. 72 AX39
Farm Clo., Barn. 79 CW43
Farm Clo., Borwd. 77 CK38
Farm Clo., Brwd. 109 GC45
Farm Clo., Buck.H. 102 EJ48
Farm Clo., Cher. 193 BA100
Farm Clo., Couls. 234 DF120
Farm Clo., Dag. 147 FC66
Farm Clo., Guil. 242 AX131
Waterside Rd.
Farm Clo., Harl. 34 EH14
Farm Clo., Hert. 31 DN09
Farm Clo. (East Horsley), Lthd. 245 BT128
Farm Clo. (Fetcham), Lthd. 231 CD124
Farm Clo., Maid. 150 AC78
Farm Clo. (Cuffley), Pot.B. 65 DK27
Farm Clo., Rad. 62 CL30
Farm Clo., Shep. 194 BN101
Farm Clo., Sthl. 136 CB73
Farm Clo., Stai. 173 BE92
Farm Clo., Sutt. 218 DD108
Farm Clo., Uxb. 115 BP61
Farm Clo., Wall. 219 DJ110
Farm Clo. (Cheshunt), Wal.Cr. 66 DW30
Farm Clo., Welw.G.C. 29 CW09
Farm Clo., W.Byf. 212 BM112
Farm Clo., W.Wick. 204 EE104
Farm Ct. NW4 119 CU55
Farm Cres., Slou. 132 AV71
Farm Dr., Croy. 203 DZ103
Farm Dr., Pur. 219 DK112
Farm End E4 84 EE43
Farm End, Nthwd. 93 BP53
Drakes Dr.
Farm Fld., Wat. 75 BS38
Farm Flds., S.Croy. 220 DS111
Farm Gro., Beac. 88 AJ50
Farm Hill Rd., Wal.Abb. 67 EC34
Farm Ho. Clo., Brox. 67 DZ25
Farm La. N14 80 DG44
Farm La. SW6 160 DA79
Farm La., Add. 212 BG107
Farm La., Ash. 232 CN116
Farm La., Beac. 89 AR52
Farm La., Cars. 218 DF110
Farm La., Croy. 203 DZ103
Farm La., Epsom 232 CP120
Farm La., Hodd. 49 EC15
Farm La., Lthd. 245 BT128
Farm La., Pur. 219 DJ110
Farm La., Rick. 74 BH41
Farm La., Slou. 131 AR73
Whitby Rd.
Farm La., Wok. 227 BC123
Farm Lea, H.Wyc. 110 AF56
Farm Pl. W8 140 DA74
Uxbridge St.
Farm Pl., Berk. 38 AT18
Farm Pl., Dart. 167 FG84
Farm Rd. N21 100 DQ46
Farm Rd., Edg. 96 CP51
Farm Rd., Esher 196 CB102
Farm Rd., Grays 171 GF75
Farm Rd., Houns. 176 BY88
Farm Rd., Maid. 130 AG72
Farm Rd., Mord. 200 DB99
Farm Rd., Nthwd. 93 BQ50
Farm Rd., Rain. 148 FJ69
Farm Rd., Rick. 73 BA42
Farm Rd., St.Alb. 43 CH19
Farm Rd., Sev. 257 FJ121
Farm Rd., Stai. 174 BH93
Farm Rd., Sutt. 218 DD108
Farm Rd., Warl. 237 DY119
Farm Rd., Wok. 227 BB120
Farm St. W1 277 H1
Farm St. W1 141 DH73
Farm Vale, Bex. 187 FB86
Farm Vw., Tad. 249 CZ127
Farm Wk. NW11 119 CZ57
Farm Wk., Guil. 258 AT136
Wilderness Rd.
Farm Wk., Horl. 268 DF148
Court Lo. Rd.
Farm Way, Buck.H. 102 EJ49
Farm Way, Horn. 127 FH63
Farm Way, Nthwd. 93 BS49
Farm Way, Stai. 173 BF86
Farm Way (Bushey), Wat. 76 CB42
Farm Way, Wor.Pk. 199 CW104
Farm Yd., Wind. 151 AR80
Farman Gro., Nthlt. 136 BX69
Wayfarer Rd.
Farmborough Clo., Har. 117 CD59
Pool Rd.
Farmcote Rd. SE12 184 EG88
Farmcroft, Grav. 191 GG89
Farmdale Rd. SE10 164 EG78
Farmdale Rd., Cars. 218 DE108
Farmer Rd. E10 123 EB60
Farmer St. W8 140 DA74
Uxbridge St.
Farmers Clo., Wat. 59 BV33
Farmers Ct., Wal.Abb. 68 EG33
Winters Way
Farmers Rd. SE5 161 DP80
Farmers Rd., Stai. 173 BE92
Farmers Way, Beac. 89 AQ51
Farmfield Dr., Horl. 268 DB150
Farmfield Rd., Brom. 184 EE92
Farmhouse Clo., Wok. 227 BD115
Farmhouse La., Hem.H. 40 BN18
Farmhouse Rd. SW16 181 DJ94
Farmilo Rd. E17 123 DZ59
Farmington Ave., Sutt. 200 DD104
Farmland Wk., Chis. 185 EP92
Farmlands, Enf. 81 DN39
Farmlands, Pnr. 115 BU56
Farmlands, The, Nthlt. 136 BZ65
Farmleigh N14 99 DJ45
Farmleigh Gro., Walt. 213 BS106
Farmstead Rd. SE6 183 EB91
Farmstead Rd., Har. 95 CD53
Farmview, Cob. 230 BX116
Farmway, Dag. 126 EW63
Farnaby Dr., Sev. 256 FF126
Farnaby Rd. SE9 164 EJ84
Farnaby Rd., Brom. 183 ED94
Farnan Ave. E17 101 EA54
Farnan Rd. SW16 181 DL92
Farnborough Ave. E17 123 DY55
Farnborough Ave., S.Croy. 221 DX108
Farnborough Clo., Wem. 118 CP61
Chalkhill Rd.
Farnborough Common, Orp. 205 EM104
Farnborough Cres., Brom. 204 EF102
Saville Row
Farnborough Cres., S.Croy. 221 DY109
Farnborough Hill, Orp. 223 ER106
Farnborough Way SE15 162 DT80
Chandler Way
Farnborough Way, Orp. 223 EQ105
Farnburn Ave., Slou. 131 AP71
Farncombe St. SE16 162 DU75
Farncombe St., Gdmg. 258 AS144
Farndale Ave. N13 99 DP48
Farndale Cres., Grnf. 136 CC69
Farnell Ms. SW5 160 DB78
Earls Ct. Sq.
Farnell Rd., Islw. 157 CD83
Farnell Rd., Stai. 174 BG90
Farnes Dr., Rom. 106 FJ54
Farney Fld., Guil. 261 BR142
Farnham Clo. N20 98 DC45
Farnham Clo., Hem.H. 57 BA28
Farnham Clo., Saw. 36 EW06
Farnham Gdns. SW20 199 CV96
Farnham La., Slou. 131 AL69
Farnham Pk. La., Slou. 131 AQ66
Farnham Pl. SE1 278 G3
Farnham Rd., Guil. 258 AS137
Farnham Rd., Ilf. 125 ET59
Farnham Rd., Rom. 106 FK50
Farnham Rd., Slou. 131 AQ71
Farnham Rd., Well. 166 EW82
Farnham Royal SE11 161 DM78
Farningham Cres., Cat. 236 DU123
Commonwealth Rd.
Farningham Hill Rd. (Farningham), Dart. 208 FJ99
Farningham Rd. N17 100 DU52
Farningham Rd., Cat. 236 DU123
Farnley, Wok. 226 AT117
Farnley Rd. E4 102 EE45
Farnley Rd. SE25 202 DR98
Farnol Rd., Dart. 168 FN84
Faro Clo., Brom. 205 EN96
Faroe Rd. W14 159 CX76
Farorna Wk., Enf. 81 DN39
Farquhar Rd. SE19 182 DT92
Farquhar Rd. SW19 180 DA90
Farquhar St., Hert. 32 DQ08
Farquharson Rd., Croy. 202 DQ102
Farr Ave., Bark. 146 EU68
Farr Rd., Enf. 82 DR39
Farraline Rd., Wat. 75 BV42
Farrance Rd., Rom. 126 EY58
Farrance St. E14 143 DZ72
Farrans Ct., Har. 117 CH59
Farrant Ave. N22 99 DN54
Farrant Clo., Orp. 224 EU108
Farrant Way, Borwd. 78 CL39
Farrell Ho. E1 142 DW72
Farren Rd. SE23 183 DY89
Farrer Ms. N8 121 DJ56
Farrer Rd.
Farrer Rd. N8 121 DJ56
Farrer Rd., Har. 118 CL57
Farrer's Pl., Croy. 221 DX105
Farriday Clo., St.Alb. 43 CE16
Farrier Clo., Sun. 195 BU98
Farrier Clo., Uxb. 134 BN72
Horseshoe Dr.
Farrier Rd., Nthlt. 136 CA68
Farrier St. NW1 141 DH66
Farrier Wk. SW10 160 DC79
Farriers, Ware 33 EA09
Farriers Clo., Epsom 216 CS112
Portland Pl.
Farriers Clo., Grav. 191 GM88
Farriers Ct., Wat. 59 BV32
Farriers End, Brox. 67 DZ26
Farriers Rd., Epsom 216 CS112
Farriers Way, Borwd. 78 CQ44
Farringdon La. EC1 274 E5
Farringdon La. EC1 141 DN70
Farringdon Rd. EC1 274 D4
Farringdon Rd. EC1 141 DN70
Farringdon St. EC4 274 F8
Farringdon St. EC4 141 DP71
Farringford Clo., St.Alb. 60 CA26
Farrington Ave., Orp. 206 EV97
Farrington Pl., Chis. 185 ER94
Farrington Pl., Nthwd. 93 BT49
Farrins Rents SE16 143 DY74
Farrow La. SE14 162 DW80
Farrow Pl. SE16 163 DY76
Ropemaker Rd.
Farthing All. SE1 162 DU75
Wolseley St.
Farthing Clo., Dart. 168 FM84
Farthing Flds. E1 142 DV74
Raine St.
Farthing Grn. La., Slou. 132 AU68
Farthing St., Orp. 223 EM108
Farthingale Ct., Wal.Abb. 68 EG34
Farthingale La., Wal.Abb. 68 EG34
Farthingale Wk. E15 143 ED66
Farthings, Wok. 226 AS116
Farthings, The, Hem.H. 40 BH20
Farthings, The, Kings.T. 198 CN95
Brunswick Rd.
Farthings Clo. E4 102 EE48
Farthings Clo., Pnr. 115 BV58
Farwell Rd., Sid. 186 EV90
Farwig La., Brom. 204 EF95
Fashion St. E1 275 P7
Fashion St. E1 142 DT71
Fashoda Rd., Brom. 204 EK98
Fassett Rd. E8 142 DU65
Fassett Rd., Kings.T. 198 CL98
Fassett Sq. E8 142 DU65
Fassnidge Way, Uxb. 134 BJ66
Oxford Rd.
Fauconberg Rd. W4 158 CQ79
Faulkner Clo., Dag. 126 EX59
Faulkner St. SE14 162 DW81
Faulkner's All. EC1 274 F6
Faulkners Rd., Walt. 214 BW106
Fauna Clo., Rom. 126 EW59
Faunce St. SE17 161 DP78
Harmsworth St.
Favart Rd. SW6 160 DA81
Faverolle Grn., Wal.Cr. 67 DX28
Faversham Ave. E4 102 EE46
Faversham Ave., Enf. 82 DR44
Faversham Clo., Chig. 104 EV47
Faversham Rd. SE6 183 DZ87
Faversham Rd., Beck. 203 DZ96
Faversham Rd., Mord. 200 DB100
Fawcett Clo. SW11 160 DD82
Fawcett Clo. SW16 181 DN91
Fawcett Est. E5 122 DU60
Fawcett Rd. NW10 139 CT67
Fawcett Rd., Croy. 201 DP104
Fawcett Rd., Wind. 151 AP81
Fawcett St. SW10 160 DC79
Fawcus Clo., Esher 215 CF107
Dalmore Ave.
Fawe Pk. Rd. SW15 159 CZ84
Fawe St. E14 143 EB71
Fawke Common Rd., Sev. 257 FN126
Fawkes Ave., Dart. 188 FM89
Fawkham Grn. Rd. (Fawkham Grn.), Long. 209 FV104
Fawkham Rd., Long. 209 FX98
Fawkon Wk., Hodd. 49 EA18
Taverners Way
Fawley Rd. NW6 120 DB64
Fawn Ct., Hat. 45 CW16
Fawn Rd. E13 144 EJ68
Fawn Rd., Chig. 103 ET50
Fawnbrake Ave. SE24 181 DP85
Fawns Manor Clo., Felt. 175 BQ88
Fawns Manor Rd., Felt. 175 BR88
Fawood Ave. NW10 138 CR66
Fawsley Clo., Slou. 153 BE80
Fawters Clo., Brwd. 109 GD44
Fay Grn., Abb.L. 59 BR33
Fayerfield, Pot.B. 64 DD31
Faygate Cres., Bexh. 186 FA85
Faygate Rd. SW2 181 DM89
Fayland Ave. SW16 181 DJ92
Faymore Gdns., S.Ock. 149 FU72
Feacey Down, Hem.H. 40 BH18
Fearn Clo., Lthd. 245 BS129
Fearney Mead, Rick. 92 BG46
Fearnley Cres., Hmptn. 176 BY92
Fearnley Rd., Welw.G.C. 29 CW10
Fearnley St., Wat. 75 BV42
Fearns Mead, Brwd. 108 FW50
Bucklers Ct.
Fearon St. SE10 164 EG78
Feather Dell, Hat. 45 CT18
Featherbed La., Abb.L. 59 BV26
Sergehill La.
Featherbed La., Croy. 221 DZ108
Featherbed La., Rom. 86 EX42
Featherbed La., Warl. 221 ED113
Feathers La., Stai. 173 BA89
Feathers Pl. SE10 163 ED79
Featherstone Ave. SE23 182 DV89
Featherstone Gdns., Borwd. 78 CQ42
Featherstone Ind. Est., Sthl. 156 BY75
Featherstone Rd. NW7 97 CV51
Featherstone Rd., Sthl. 156 BY76
Featherstone St. EC1 275 K4
Featherstone St. EC1 142 DR70
Featherstone Ter., Sthl. 156 BY76
Featley Rd. SW9 161 DP83
Federal Rd., Grnf. 137 CJ68
Federal Way, Wat. 76 BW38
Federation Rd. SE2 166 EV77
Fee Fm. Rd., Esher 215 CF108
Feenan Highway, Til. 171 GH80
Felbridge Ave., Stan. 95 CG53
Felbridge Clo. SW16 181 DN91
Felbridge Clo., Sutt. 218 DC109
Felbrigge Rd., Ilf. 125 ET61
Felcott Clo., Walt. 196 BW104
Felcott Rd., Walt. 196 BW104
Felday Hos., Dor. 261 BV144
Felday Rd. SE13 183 EB86
Felday Rd., Dor. 261 BT140
Felden Clo., Pnr. 94 BY52
Felden Clo., Wat. 60 BX34
Felden Dr., Hem.H. 40 BG24
Felden La., Hem.H. 40 BG24
Felden Rd., Hem.H. 39 BF23
Felden St. SW6 159 CZ81
Feldman Clo. N16 122 DU60
Felgate Ms. W6 159 CV77
Felhampton Rd. SE9 185 EP89
Felhurst Cres., Dag. 127 FB63

Felicia Way, Grays 171 GH77
Felipe Rd., Grays 169 FW76
Felix Ave. N8 121 DL58
Felix Dr., Guil. 244 BG128
Felix La., Shep. 195 BS100
Felix Rd. W13 137 CG73
Felix Rd., Walt. 195 BU100
Felix St. E2 142 DV68
Hackney Rd.
Felixstowe Rd. N9 100 DU49
Felixstowe Rd. N17 122 DT55
Felixstowe Rd. NW10 139 CV69
Felixstowe Rd. SE2 166 EV76
Fell Rd., Croy. 202 DQ104
Fell Wk., Edg. 96 CP53
East Rd.
Felland Way, Reig. 266 DD138
Fellbrigg Rd. SE22 182 DT85
Fellbrigg St. E1 142 DV70
Headlam St.
Fellbrook, Rich. 177 CH90
Fellmongers Yd., Croy. 202 DQ103
Surrey St.
Fellowes Clo., Hayes 136 BX70
Paddington Clo.
Fellowes La., St.Alb. 44 CR23
Fellowes Rd., Cars. 200 DE104
Fellows Ct. E2 275 P1
Fellows Ct. E2 142 DT68
Fellows Rd. NW3 140 DD66
Felltram Way SE7 164 EG78
Woolwich Rd.
Felmersham Clo. SW4 161 DK84
Haselrigge Rd.
Felmingham Rd. SE20 202 DW96
Felmongers, Harl. 36 EV13
Felnex Trd. Est., Wall. 200 DG103
Fels Clo., Dag. 127 FB62
Fels Fm. Ave., Dag. 127 FC62
Felsberg Rd. SW2 181 DL86
Felsham Rd. SW15 159 CX83
Felspar Clo. SE18 165 ET78
Felstead Ave., Ilf. 103 EN53
Felstead Clo., Brwd. 109 GC44
Felstead Gdns. E14 163 EC78
Ferry St.
Felstead Rd. E11 124 EG59
Felstead Rd., Epsom 216 CR111
Felstead Rd., Loug. 102 EL45
Felstead Rd., Orp. 206 EU103
Felstead Rd., Rom. 105 FC51
Felstead Rd., Wal.Cr. 67 DY32
Felstead St. E9 143 DZ65
Felsted Rd. E16 144 EK72
Feltham Ave., E.Mol. 197 CE98
Feltham Hill Rd., Ashf. 175 BP92
Feltham Hill Rd., Felt. 175 BU91
Feltham Rd., Ashf. 175 BP91
Feltham Rd., Mitch. 200 DF96
Feltham Rd., Red. 266 DF139
Feltham Wk., Red. 266 DF139
Felthambrook Way, Felt. 175 BV90
Felton Clo., Borwd. 78 CL38
Felton Clo., Brox. 67 DZ25
Felton Clo., Orp. 205 EP100
Felton Gdns., Bark. 145 ES67
Sutton Rd.
Felton Lea, Sid. 185 ET92
Felton Rd. W13 157 CJ75
Camborne Ave.
Felton Rd., Bark. 145 ES68
Sutton Rd.
Felton St. N1 142 DR67
Fen Clo., Brwd. 109 GC42
Fen Ct. EC3 275 M10
Fen Gro., Sid. 185 ET86
Fen La., Upmin. 129 FW64
Fen St. E16 144 EF73
Victoria Dock Rd.
Fencepiece Rd., Chig. 103 EQ50
Fencepiece Rd., Ilf. 103 EQ50
Fenchurch Ave. EC3 275 M9
Fenchurch Ave. EC3 142 DS72
Fenchurch Bldgs. EC3 275 N9
Fenchurch Pl. EC3 275 N10
Fenchurch St. EC3 275 M10
Fenchurch St. EC3 142 DS73
Fendall Rd., Epsom 216 CQ106
Fendall St. SE1 279 N7
Fendall St. SE1 162 DS76
Fendt Clo. E16 144 EF73
Bowman Ave.
Fendyke Rd., Belv. 166 EX76
Fenelon Pl. W14 159 CZ77
Fengates Rd., Red. 250 DE134
Fenham Rd. SE15 162 DU80
Fenman Ct. N17 100 DV53
Shelbourne Rd.
Fenman Gdns., Ilf. 126 EV60
Fenn Clo., Brom. 184 EG93
Fenn St. E9 122 DW64
Fennel Clo. E16 144 EE70
Cranberry La.
Fennel Clo., Croy. 203 DX102
Primrose La.
Fennel Clo., Guil. 243 BB131
Fennel St. SE18 165 EN79
Fennells, Harl. 51 EQ20
Fennells Mead, Epsom 217 CT109
Fenner Clo. SE16 162 DV77
Layard Rd.
Fenner Ho., Walt. 213 BU105
Fenner Rd., Grays 169 FW77
Fenner Sq. SW11 160 DD83
Thomas Baines Rd.
Fenning St. SE1 279 M4
Fennings, The, Amer. 55 AR36
Fenns Way, Wok. 226 AY115
Fennycroft Rd., Hem.H. 39 BF17
Fens Way, Swan. 187 FG93
Fensomes All., Hem.H. 40 BK19
Queensway
Fenstanton Ave. N12 98 DD50
Fenswood Clo., Bex. 186 FA86
Fentiman Rd. SW8 161 DL79
Fentiman Way, Horn. 128 FL60
Fenton Ave., Stai. 174 BJ93
Fenton Clo. E8 142 DT65
Laurel St.
Fenton Clo. SW9 161 DM82
Fenton Clo., Chis. 185 EM92
Fenton Clo., Red. 250 DG134
Fenton Gra., Harl. 52 EW16
Fenton Rd. N17 100 DQ52
Fenton Rd., Red. 250 DG134
Fentons Ave. E13 144 EH68
Fentum Rd., Guil. 242 AU132
Fenwick Clo. SE18 165 EN79
Ritter St.
Fenwick Clo., Wok. 226 AV118
Fenwick Gro. SE15 162 DU83
Fenwick Path, Borwd. 78 CM38
Fenwick Pl. SW9 161 DL83
Fenwick Rd. SE15 162 DU83
Ferdinand Pl. NW1 140 DG66
Ferdinand St.
Ferdinand St. NW1 140 DG65
Fergus Rd. N5 121 DP64
Calabria Rd.
Ferguson Ave., Grav. 191 GJ91
Ferguson Ave., Rom. 106 FJ54
Ferguson Ave., Surb. 198 CM99
Ferguson Clo. E14 163 EA77
Ferguson Clo., Brom. 203 EC97
Ferguson Ct., Rom. 106 FK54
Ferguson Dr. W3 138 CR72
Ferme Pk. Rd. N4 121 DL57
Ferme Pk. Rd. N8 121 DL57
Fermor Rd. SE23 183 DY88
Fermoy Rd. W9 139 CZ70
Fermoy Rd., Grnf. 136 CB70
Fern Ave., Mitch. 201 DK98
Fern Clo., Brox. 49 DZ23
Fern Clo., Erith 167 FH81
Hollywood Way
Fern Clo., Warl. 237 DY118
Fern Dells, Hat. 45 CT19
Fern Dene W13 137 CH71
Templewood
Fern Dr., Hem.H. 40 BL21
Fern Gro., Felt. 175 BV87
Fern Gro., Welw.G.C. 29 CX05
Fern Hill La., Harl. 51 ES19
Fern La., Houns. 156 BZ78
Fern Leys, St.Alb. 43 CJ17
Fern Rd., Maid. 130 AH72
Fern St. E3 143 EA70
Fern Twrs., Cat. 252 DU125
Fern Wk. SE16 162 DU78
Argyle Way
Fern Wk., Ashf. 174 BK92
Ferndale Rd.
Fern Way, Wat. 75 BU35
Fernbank, Buck.H. 102 EH46
Fernbank Ave., Horn. 128 FJ63
Fernbank Ave., Walt. 196 BY101
Fernbank Ave., Wem. 117 CF63
Fernbank Ms. SW12 181 DJ86
Fernbank Rd., Add. 212 BG106
Fernbrook Ave., Sid. 185 ES85
Blackfen Rd.
Fernbrook Cres. SE13 184 EE86
Fernbrook Dr., Har. 116 CB59
Fernbrook Rd. SE13 184 EE86
Ferncliff Rd. E8 122 DU64
Ferncroft Ave. N12 98 DE51
Ferncroft Ave. NW3 120 DA62
Ferncroft Ave., Ruis. 116 BW61
Ferndale, Brom. 204 EJ96
Ferndale, Guil. 242 AS132
Ferndale Ave. E17 123 ED57
Ferndale Ave., Cher. 193 BE104
Ferndale Ave., Houns. 156 BY83
Ferndale Clo., Bexh. 166 EY81
Ferndale Ct. SE3 164 EF80
Ferndale Cres., Uxb. 134 BJ69
Ferndale Rd. E7 144 EH66
Ferndale Rd. E11 124 EE61
Ferndale Rd. N15 122 DT58
Ferndale Rd. SE25 202 DV99
Ferndale Rd. SW4 161 DL84
Ferndale Rd. SW9 161 DM83
Ferndale Rd., Ashf. 174 BK92
Ferndale Rd., Bans. 233 CZ116
Ferndale Rd., Enf. 83 DY37
Ferndale Rd., Grav. 191 GH89
Ferndale Rd., Rom. 105 FC54
Ferndale Rd., Wok. 227 AZ116
Ferndale St. E6 145 EP73
Ferndale Ter., Har. 117 CF56
Ferndale Way, Orp. 223 ER106
Ferndell Ave., Bex. 187 FD90
Ferndene Ri., Gdmg. 258 AS144
Fernden Way, Rom. 127 FB58
Ferndene, St.Alb. 60 BZ31
Ferndene Rd. SE24 162 DQ84
Ferndown, Horl. 268 DF146
Ferndown, Horn. 128 FM58
Ferndown, Nthwd. 93 BU54
Ferndown Ave., Orp. 205 ER102
Ferndown Clo., Guil. 259 BA135
Ferndown Clo., Pnr. 94 BY52
Ferndown Clo., Sutt. 218 DD107
Ferndown Ct., Guil. 242 AW133
Ferndown Gdns., Cob. 214 BW113
Ferndown Rd. SE9 184 EK87
Ferndown Rd., Wat. 94 BW48
Fernecroft, St.Alb. 42 CC23
Fernery, The, Stai. 173 BE92
Fernes Clo., Uxb. 134 BJ72
Ferney Ct., W.Byf. 212 BK112
Ferney Rd.
Ferney Meade Way, Islw. 157 CG82
Ferney Rd., Barn. 98 DG45
Ferney Rd., W.Byf. 212 BK112
Fernhall Dr., Ilf. 124 EK57
Fernhall La., Wal.Abb. 68 EK31
Fernham Rd., Th.Hth. 202 DQ97
Fernhead Rd. W9 139 CZ70
Fernheath Way, Dart. 187 FD92
Fernhill, Harl. 51 ES19
Fernhill, Lthd. 215 CD114
Fernhill Clo., Wok. 226 AW120
Fernhill Ct. E17 101 ED54
Fernhill Gdns., Kings.T. 177 CK92
Fernhill La., Wok. 226 AW120
Fernhill Pk., Wok. 226 AW120
Fernhill Rd., Horl. 269 DK152
Fernhill St. E16 145 EM74
Fernhills, Kings L. 59 BR33
Fernholme Rd. SE15 183 DX85
Fernhurst Clo., Beac. 89 AM53
Fernhurst Gdns., Edg. 96 CN51
Fernhurst Rd. SW6 159 CY81
Fernhurst Rd., Ashf. 175 BQ91
Fernhurst Rd., Croy. 202 DU101
Fernie Clo., Chig. 104 EU50
Fernihough Clo., Wey. 212 BN111
Fernlands Clo., Cher. 193 BE104
Fernlea, Lthd. 230 CB124
Fernlea Rd. SW12 181 DH88
Fernlea Rd., Mitch. 200 DG96
Fernleigh Clo., Croy. 219 DN105
Stafford Rd.
Fernleigh Ct., Har. 94 CB54
Fernleigh Ct., Wem. 118 CL61
Fernleigh Rd. N21 99 DN47
Ferns, The, Beac. 89 AM54
Ferns Clo., Enf. 83 DY36
Ferns Clo., S.Croy. 220 DV110
Ferns Rd. E15 144 EF65
Fernsbury St. WC1 274 D3
Fernsham Wk., Slou. 111 AQ64
Fernshaw Rd. SW10 160 DC79
Fernside NW11 120 DA61
Finchley Rd.
Fernside, Buck.H. 102 EH46
Fernside Ave. NW7 96 CR48
Fernside Ave., Felt. 175 BV91
Fernside La., Sev. 257 FJ129
Fernside Rd. SW12 180 DF88
Fernsleigh Clo., Ger.Cr. 90 AY51
Fernthorpe Rd. SW16 181 DJ93
Ferntower Rd. N5 122 DR64
Fernville La., Hem.H. 40 BK20
Midland Rd.
Fernways, Ilf. 125 EP63
Cecil Rd.
Fernwood Ave. SW16 181 DK91
Fernwood Ave., Wem. 117 CJ64
Bridgewater Rd.
Fernwood Clo., Brom. 204 EJ96
Fernwood Cres. N20 98 DF48
Ferny Hill, Barn. 80 DF38
Ferranti Clo. SE18 164 EK76
Ferraro Clo., Houns. 156 CA79
Ferrers Ave., Wall. 219 DK105
Ferrers Ave., West Dr. 154 BK75
Ferrers Rd. SW16 181 DK92
Ferrestone Rd. N8 121 DM56
Ferriby Clo. N1 141 DN66
Bewdley St.
Ferrier Pt. E16 144 EH71
Forty Acre La.
Ferrier St. SW18 160 DB84
Ferriers Way, Epsom 233 CW118
Ferring Clo., Har. 116 CC60
Ferrings SE21 182 DS89
Ferris Ave., Croy. 203 DZ104
Ferris Rd. SE22 162 DU84
Ferro Rd., Rain. 147 FG70
Ferron Rd. E5 122 DV62
Ferrour Ct. N2 120 DD55
Ferry Ave., Stai. 173 BE94
Ferry La. N17 122 DV56
Ferry La. SW13 159 CT79
Ferry La., Brent. 158 CL79
Ferry La., Cher. 194 BG100
Ferry La., Guil. 258 AW138
Portsmouth Rd.
Ferry La., Rain. 147 FE72
Ferry La., Rich. 158 CM79
Ferry La., Shep. 194 BN102
Ferry La. (Hythe End), Stai. 173 BB89
Ferry La. (Laleham), Stai. 194 BJ97
Ferry Pl. SE18 165 EN76
Woolwich High St.
Ferry Rd. SW13 159 CU80
Ferry Rd., Maid. 150 AC75
Ferry Rd., Tedd. 177 CH92
Ferry Rd., T.Ditt. 197 CH100
Ferry Rd., Til. 171 GG83
Ferry Rd., Twick. 177 CH88
Ferry Rd., W.Mol. 196 CA97
Ferry Sq., Brent. 157 CK79
Ferry Sq., Shep. 195 BP101
Ferry St. E14 163 EC78
Ferryhills Clo., Wat. 94 BW48
Ferrymead Ave., Grnf. 136 CA69
Ferrymead Dr., Grnf. 136 CA68
Ferrymead Gdns., Grnf. 136 CC68
Ferrymoor, Rich. 177 CH90
Ferryby Rd., Grays 171 GH76
Feryngs Clo., Harl. 36 EX11
Watlington Rd.
Fesants Cft., Harl. 36 EV12
Festing Rd. SW15 159 CX83
Festival Clo., Bex. 186 EX88
Festival Clo., Erith 167 FF80
Betsham Rd.
Festival Clo., Uxb. 135 BP67
Festival Path, Wok. 226 AT119
Festival Wk., Cars. 218 DF106
Fetcham Common La., Lthd. 230 CB121
Fetcham Pk. Dr., Lthd. 231 CE123
Fetherstone Clo., Pot.B. 64 DD32
Fetter La. EC4 274 E9
Fetter La. EC4 141 DN72
Ffinch St. SE8 163 EA80
Fiddicroft Ave., Bans. 218 DB114
Fiddlebridge La., Hat. 45 CT17
Fiddlers Clo., Green. 169 FV84
Fidler Pl. (Bushey), Wat. 76 CB44
Ashfield Ave.
Field Clo. E4 101 EB51
Field Clo., Brom. 204 EJ96
Field Clo., Buck.H. 102 EJ48
Field Clo., Chesh. 54 AS28
Field Clo., Chess. 215 CJ106
Field Clo., Guil. 243 BD132
Field Clo., Hayes 155 BQ80
Field Clo., Houns. 155 BV81
Field Clo., Rom. 86 EV41
Field Clo., Ruis. 115 BQ60
Field Way
Field Clo., St.Alb. 43 CG16
Field Clo., S.Croy. 220 DV114
Field Clo., W.Mol. 196 CB99
Field Ct. WC1 274 C7
Field Ct., Oxt. 254 EE127
Field End, Barn. 79 CV42
Field End, Couls. 219 DK114
Field End, Nthlt. 136 BX65
Field End, Ruis. 136 BW65
Field End, Twick. 177 CF91
Field End Clo., Wat. 94 BY45
Field End Rd., Pnr. 115 BV58
Field End Rd., Ruis. 116 BY63
Field La., Brent. 157 CJ80
Field La., Gdmg. 258 AT144
The Oval
Field La., Tedd. 177 CG92
Field Mead NW7 96 CS52
Field Mead NW9 96 CS52
Field Pl., Gdmg. 258 AS144
George Rd.
Field Pl., N.Mal. 199 CT100
Field Rd. E7 124 EG63
Field Rd. N17 122 DR55
Field Rd. W6 159 CY78
Field Rd., Felt. 175 BV86
Field Rd., Hem.H. 40 BN21
Field Rd., S.Ock. 148 FQ74
Field Rd., Uxb. 113 BD63
Field Rd., Wat. 76 BY44
Field St. WC1 274 B2
Field St. WC1 141 DM69
Field Vw., Egh. 173 BC92
Field Vw., Felt. 175 BR91
Field Vw. Ri., St.Alb. 60 BY29
Field Vw. Rd., Pot.B. 64 DA33
Field Way NW10 138 CQ66
Twybridge Way
Field Way, Berk. 38 AY21
Field Way, Croy. 221 EB107
Field Way, Ger.Cr. 90 AX52
Field Way, Grnf. 136 CB67
Field Way, Hem.H. 57 BA27
Field Way, Hodd. 33 EC13
Field Way, Rick. 92 BH46
Field Way, Ruis. 115 BQ60
Field Way, Uxb. 134 BK70
Field Way, Wok. 243 BF125
Fieldcommon La., Walt. 196 BY102
Fieldend Rd. SW16 201 DJ95
Fielders Clo., Enf. 82 DS42
Woodfield Clo.
Fielders Clo., Har. 116 CC60
Fielders Grn., Guil. 243 BA134
Fielders Way (Shenley), Rad. 62 CL33
Fieldfare Rd. SE28 146 EW73
Fieldgate La., Mitch. 200 DE97
Fieldgate St. E1 142 DU71
Fieldhouse Clo. E18 102 EG53
Fieldhouse Rd. SW12 181 DJ88
Fieldhurst, Slou. 153 AZ78
Fieldhurst Clo., Add. 212 BH106
Fielding Ave., Til. 171 GH81
Fielding Ave., Twick. 176 CC90
Fielding Ho. NW6 140 DA69
Fielding Ms. SW13 159 CV79
Castelnau
Fielding Rd. W4 158 CR76
Fielding Rd. W14 159 CX76
Fielding St. SE17 162 DQ79
Fielding Wk. W13 157 CH76
Fielding Way, Brwd. 109 GC44
Fieldings, The SE23 182 DW88
Fieldings, The, Horl. 269 DJ147
Fieldings, The, Wok. 226 AT116
Fieldings Rd. (Cheshunt), Wal.Cr. 67 DZ29
Fields Ct., Pot.B. 64 DD33
Fields End La., Hem.H. 39 BD18
Fields Est. E8 142 DU66
Fields Pk. Cres., Rom. 126 EX57
Fieldsend Rd., Sutt. 217 CY106
Fieldside Clo., Orp. 223 EQ105
State Fm. Ave.
Fieldside Rd., Brom. 183 ED92
Fieldview SW18 180 DD88
Fieldview, Horl. 269 DH147
Stockfield
Fieldway, Amer. 55 AP41
Fieldway, Dag. 126 EV63
Fieldway, Orp. 205 ER100
Fieldway, Ware 33 EB11
Fieldway Cres. N5 121 DN64
Fiennes Clo., Dag. 126 EW60
Fiennes Way, Sev. 257 FJ127
Fiesta Dr., Dag. 147 FC70
Fife Rd. E16 144 EG71
Fife Rd. N22 99 DP52
Fife Rd. SW14 178 CQ85
Fife Rd., Kings.T. 198 CL96
Fife Ter. N1 141 DM68
Fifehead Clo., Ashf. 174 BL93
Fifeway, Lthd. 246 CA125
Fifield La., Wind. 150 AD84
Fifield Path SE23 183 DX90
Bampton Rd.
Fifield Rd., Maid. 150 AD80
Fifth Ave. E12 125 EM63
Fifth Ave. W10 139 CY69
Fifth Ave., Grays 169 FU79
Fifth Ave., Harl. 35 EQ12
Fifth Ave., Hayes 135 BT74
Fifth Ave., Wat. 76 BX35
Fifth Cross Rd., Twick. 177 CD89
Fifth Way, Wem. 118 CP63
Fig St., Sev. 256 FF129
Fig Tree Clo. NW10 138 CS67
Craven Pk.
Fig Tree Hill, Hem.H. 40 BK19
Figges Rd., Mitch. 180 DG94
Filby Rd., Chess. 216 CM107
Filey Ave. N16 122 DU60
Filey Clo., Sutt. 218 DC108
Filey Clo., West. 238 EH119
Filey Spur, Slou. 151 AP75
Filey Waye, Ruis. 115 BU61
Filigree Ct. SE16 143 DZ74
Silver Wk.
Fillebrook Ave., Enf. 82 DS40
Fillebrook Rd. E11 123 ED60
Filmer La., Sev. 257 FL121
Filmer Rd. SW6 159 CY81
Filmer Rd., Wind. 151 AK82
Filston La., Sev. 241 FD116
Filston Rd., Erith 167 FB78
Riverdale Rd.
Finborough Rd. SW10 160 DB78
Finborough Rd. SW17 180 DF93
Finch Ave. SE27 182 DR91
Finch Clo. NW10 118 CR64
Finch Clo., Barn. 80 DA43
Finch Clo., Hat. 45 CU20
Eagle Way
Finch Dr., Felt. 176 BX87
Finch End, H.Wyc. 88 AC47
Finch Grn., Rick. 73 BF42
Finch La. EC3 275 L9
Finch La., Amer. 72 AT42
Finch La., Beac. 88 AJ50
Finch La. (Bushey), Wat. 76 CA43
Finch Ms. SE15 162 DT80
Finch Rd., Berk. 38 AU19
Finch Rd., Guil. 242 AX134
Finchale Rd. SE2 166 EU76
Fincham Clo., Uxb. 115 BQ61
Aylsham Dr.
Finchdale, Hem.H. 40 BG20
Finchdean Way SE15 162 DT80
Daniel Gdns.
Finches, The, Hert. 32 DV09
Finches Ri., Guil. 243 BC132
Finchingfield Ave., Wdf.Grn. 102 EJ52
Finchley Clo., Dart. 188 FN86
Finchley Ct. N3 98 DB51
Finchley La. NW4 119 CW56
Finchley Pk. N12 98 DC49
Finchley Pl. NW8 140 DD68
Finchley Rd. NW2 120 DA62
Finchley Rd. NW3 140 DC65
Finchley Rd. NW8 140 DD67
Finchley Rd. NW11 119 CZ58
Finchley Rd., Grays 170 GB79
Finchley Way N3 98 DA52
Finchmoor, Harl. 51 ER18
Finck St. SE1 278 C5
Finden Rd. E7 124 EH64
Findhorn Ave., Hayes 135 BV71
Findhorn St. E14 143 EC72
Findlay Dr., Guil. 242 AT130
Findon Clo. SW18 180 DA86
Wimbledon Pk. Rd.
Findon Clo., Har. 116 CB62
Findon Gdns., Rain. 147 FG71
Findon Rd. N9 100 DV46
Findon Rd. W12 159 CU75
Fine Bush La. (Harefield), Uxb. 115 BP58
Fingal St. SE10 164 EF78
Finglesham Clo., Orp. 206 EX102
Westwell Clo.
Finians Clo., Uxb. 134 BM66
Finland Quay SE16 163 DY76
Finland Rd. SE4 163 DY83
Finland St. SE16 163 DY76
Finlay Gdns., Add. 212 BJ105
Finlay St. SW6 159 CX81
Finlays Clo., Chess. 216 CN106
Finnart Clo., Wey. 213 BQ105
Finnart Ho. Dr., Wey. 213 BQ105
Vaillant Rd.
Finnis St. E2 142 DV69
Finnymore Rd., Dag. 146 EY66
Finsbury Ave. EC2 275 L7
Finsbury Circ. EC2 275 L7
Finsbury Circ. EC2 142 DR71
Finsbury Cotts. N22 99 DL52
Clarence Rd.
Finsbury Est. EC1 274 F3
Finsbury Est. EC1 141 DN69
Finsbury Ho. N22 99 DL53
Finsbury Mkt. EC2 275 M5
Finsbury Mkt. EC2 142 DS70
Finsbury Pk. Ave. N4 122 DQ58
Finsbury Pk. Rd. N4 121 DP62
Finsbury Pavement EC2 275 L6
Finsbury Pavement EC2 142 DR71
Finsbury Rd. N22 99 DM53
Finsbury Sq. EC2 275 L6
Finsbury Sq. EC2 142 DR71
Finsbury St. EC2 275 K6
Finsbury St. EC2 142 DR71
Finsbury Way, Bex. 186 EZ86
Finsen Rd. SE5 162 DQ83
Finstock Rd. W10 139 CX72
Finucane Dr., Orp. 206 EW101
Finucane Gdns., Rain. 147 FG65
Finucane Ri. (Bushey), Wat. 94 CC47
Finway Ct., Wat. 75 BT43
Whippendell Rd.
Finway Rd., Hem.H. 41 BP16
Fiona Clo., Lthd. 230 CA124
Fir Clo., Walt. 195 BU101
Fir Dene, Orp. 205 EM104
Fir Gra. Ave., Wey. 213 BP106
Fir Gro., N.Mal. 199 CT100
Fir Gro., Wok. 226 AU119
Fir Pk., Harl. 51 EP18
Fir Rd., Felt. 176 BX92
Fir Rd., Sutt. 199 CZ102
Fir Tree Ave., Mitch. 200 DG96
Fir Tree Ave., Slou. 132 AT70
Fir Tree Ave., West Dr. 154 BN76
Fir Tree Clo. SW16 181 DJ92
Fir Tree Clo. W5 138 CL72
Fir Tree Clo., Epsom 217 CT105
Fir Tree Clo., Esher 214 CC106
Fir Tree Clo., Grays 170 GD79
Fir Tree Clo., Hem.H. 40 BN21
Fir Tree Clo., Lthd. 231 CJ123
Fir Tree Clo., Orp. 223 ET106
Highfield Ave.
Fir Tree Clo., Rom. 127 FD55
Fir Tree Gdns., Croy. 221 EA105
Fir Tree Gro., Cars. 218 DF108
Fir Tree Hill, Rick. 74 BM38
Fir Tree Pl., Ashf. 174 BN92
Percy Ave.
Fir Tree Rd., Bans. 217 CW114
Fir Tree Rd., Epsom 233 CV116
Fir Tree Rd., Guil. 242 AX131
Fir Tree Rd., Houns. 156 BY84
Fir Tree Rd., Lthd. 231 CJ123
Fir Tree Wk., Dag. 127 FC62
Wheel Fm. Dr.
Fir Tree Wk., Enf. 82 DR41
Fir Tree Wk., Reig. 250 DD134
Fir Trees, Rom. 86 EV41
Fir Trees Clo. SE16 143 DY74
Firbank Clo. E16 144 EK71
Firbank Clo., Enf. 82 DQ42
Gladbeck Way
Firbank Dr., Wat. 94 BY45
Firbank Dr., Wok. 226 AV119
Firbank La., Wok. 226 AV119
Firbank Pl., Egh. 172 AV93
Firbank Rd. SE15 162 DV82
Firbank Rd., Rom. 105 FB50
Firbank Rd., St.Alb. 43 CF16
Fircroft Clo., Slou. 132 AU65
Fircroft Clo., Wok. 227 AZ118
Fircroft Ct., Wok. 227 AZ118
Fircroft Clo.
Fircroft Gdns., Har. 117 CE62
Fircroft Rd. SW17 180 DF89
Fircroft Rd., Chess. 216 CM105
Firdene, Surb. 198 CQ102
Fire Bell All., Surb. 198 CL100
Fire Sta. All., Barn. 79 CZ40
Christchurch La.
Firecrest Dr. NW3 120 DB62
Firefly Clo., Wall. 219 DL108
Firefly Gdns. E6 144 EL70
Jack Dash Way

Firethorn Clo., Edg. 96 CQ49
Larkspur Gro.
Firfield Rd., Add. 212 BG105
Firfields, Wey. 213 BP107
Firham Pk. Ave., Rom. 106 FN52
Firhill Rd. SE6 183 EA91
Firlands, Horl. 269 DH147
Stockfield
Firlands, Wey. 213 BS107
Firmin Rd., Dart. 188 FJ85
Firmingers Rd., Orp. 225 FB106
Firs, The E17 123 DY57
Leucha Rd.
Firs, The N20 98 DD46
Firs, The W5 137 CK71
Firs, The, Bex. 187 FD88
Dartford Rd.
Firs, The, Brwd. 108 FU44
Firs, The, Cat. 236 DR122
Yorke Gate Rd.
Firs, The, Guil. 258 AV138
Firs, The, St.Alb. 43 CH24
Firs, The, Tad. 249 CZ126
Brighton Rd.
Firs, The, Wal.Cr. 66 DS27
Firs, The, Welw.G.C. 29 CW05
Firs Ave. N10 120 DG55
Firs Ave. N11 98 DG51
Firs Ave. SW14 158 CQ84
Firs Ave., Wind. 151 AM83
Firs Clo. N10 120 DG55
Firs Ave.
Firs Clo. SE23 183 DX87
Firs Clo., Dor. 263 CG138
Firs Clo., Esher 215 CE107
Firs Clo., Hat. 45 CV19
Firs Clo., Mitch. 201 DH96
Firs Dr., Houns. 155 BV80
Firs Dr., Loug. 85 EN39
Firs Dr., Slou. 133 AZ74
Firs End, Ger.Cr. 112 AY55
Southside
Firs La. N13 100 DQ48
Firs La. N21 100 DQ47
Firs La., Pot.B. 64 DB33
Firs Pk. Ave. N21 100 DR46
Firs Pk. Gdns. N21 100 DQ46
Firs Rd., Ken. 235 DP115
Firs Wk., Nthwd. 93 BR51
Firs Wk., Wdf.Grn. 102 EG50
Firs Wd. Clo., Pot.B. 64 DF32
Firsby Ave., Croy. 203 DX102
Firsby Rd. N16 122 DT60
Firscroft N13 100 DQ48
Firsdene Clo., Cher. 211 BD107
Slade Rd.
Firsgrove Cres., Brwd. 108 FV49
Firsgrove Rd., Brwd. 108 FV49
Firside Gro., Sid. 185 ET88
First Ave. E12 124 EL63
First Ave. E13 144 EG69
First Ave. E17 123 EA57
First Ave. N18 100 DW49
First Ave. NW4 119 CW56
First Ave. SW14 158 CS83
First Ave. W3 139 CT74
First Ave. W10 139 CZ70
First Ave., Amer. 55 AQ40
First Ave., Bexh. 166 EW80
First Ave., Dag. 147 FB68
First Ave., Enf. 82 DT44
First Ave., Epsom 216 CS109
First Ave., Grav. 190 GE88
First Ave., Grays 169 FU79
First Ave., Hayes 135 BT74
First Ave., Rom. 126 EW57
First Ave., Walt. 195 BV100
First Ave., Wat. 76 BW35
First Ave., Wem. 117 CK61
First Ave., W.Mol. 196 BZ98
First Avenue-Mandela Ave., Harl. 35 ET13
First Clo., W.Mol. 196 CC97
First Cres., Slou. 131 AQ71
First Cross Rd., Twick. 177 CE89
First Dr. NW10 138 CQ66
First Slip, Lthd. 231 CG118
First St. SW3 276 C8
First St. SW3 160 DE77
First Way, Wem. 118 CP63
Firstway SW20 199 CW96
Firsway, Guil. 242 AT133
Firswood Ave., Epsom 217 CT106
Firth Gdns. SW6 159 CY81
Firtree Clo. (Stoneleigh), Epsom 233 CV116
Firtree Ct., Borwd. 78 CM42
Firwood Ave., St.Alb. 44 CL20
Firwood Clo., Wok. 226 AS119
Firwood Rd., Vir.W. 192 AS100
Fish St. Hill EC3 275 L10
Fish St. Hill EC3 142 DR73
Fisher Clo., Croy. 202 DT102
Grant Rd.
Fisher Clo., Grnf. 136 CA69
Gosling Clo.
Fisher Clo., Kings L. 58 BN29
Fisher Clo., Walt. 213 BV105
Fisher Rd., Har. 95 CF54
Fisher St. E16 144 EG71
Fisher St. WC1 274 B7
Fisher St. WC1 141 DM71
Fisherman Clo., Rich. 177 CJ91
Locksmeade Rd.
Fishermans Dr. SE16 163 DX75
Fishermans Hill, Grav. 190 GB85
Fisherman's Wk. E14 143 EA74
Fishermans Wk. SE28 165 ES75
Tugboat St.
Fishers, Horl. 269 DJ147
Ewelands
Fishers Clo., Wal.Cr. 67 EA34
Fishers Clo. (Bushey), Wat. 76 BY41
Fishers Ct. SE14 163 DX81
Besson St.
Fishers Hatch, Harl. 35 ES14
School La.
Fishers La. W4 158 CR77
Fishers La., Epp. 69 ES32
Fishers Way, Belv. 147 FC74
Fishersdene, Esher 215 CG107
Fisherton St. NW8 140 DD70
Fishery Pas., Hem.H. 40 BG22
Fishery Rd.
Fishery Rd., Hem.H. 40 BG22
Fishery Rd., Maid. 130 AC74
Fishponds Rd. SW17 180 DE91
Fishponds Rd., Kes. 222 EK106
Fishpool St., St.Alb. 42 CB20
Fisons Rd. E16 144 EG74
Fitzalan Rd. N3 119 CY55
Fitzalan Rd., Esher 215 CE108
Fitzalan St. SE11 278 C8
Fitzalan St. SE11 161 DM77
Fitzgeorge Ave. W14 159 CY77
Fitzgeorge Ave., N.Mal. 198 CR95
Fitzgerald Ave. SW14 158 CS83
Fitzgerald Clo. E11 124 EG57
Fitzgerald Rd.
Fitzgerald Ho. E14 143 EB72
Fitzgerald Ho., Hayes 135 BV74
Fitzgerald Rd. E11 124 EG57
Fitzgerald Rd. SW14 158 CR83
Fitzgerald Rd., T.Ditt. 197 CG100
Fitzhardinge St. W1 272 F8
Fitzhardinge St. W1 140 DG72
Fitzhugh Gro. SW18 180 DD86
Fitzhugh Gro. Est. SW18 180 DD86
Fitzilian Ave., Rom. 106 FM53
Fitzjames Ave. W14 159 CY77
Fitzjames Ave., Croy. 202 DU103
Fitzjohn Ave., Barn. 79 CY43
Fitzjohn Clo., Guil. 243 BC131
Fitzjohn's Ave. NW3 120 DD64
Fitzmaurice Pl. W1 277 J2
Fitzmaurice Pl. W1 141 DH73
Fitzneal St. W12 139 CT72
Fitzrobert Pl., Egh. 173 BA93
Fitzroy Clo. N6 120 DF60
Fitzroy Ct. W1 273 L5
Fitzroy Cres. W4 158 CR80
Fitzroy Gdns. SE19 182 DS94
Fitzroy Ms. W1 273 K5
Fitzroy Pk. N6 120 DF60
Fitzroy Rd. NW1 140 DG67
Fitzroy Sq. W1 273 K5
Fitzroy Sq. W1 141 DJ70
Fitzroy St. W1 273 K5
Fitzroy St. W1 141 DJ70
Fitzroy Yd. NW1 140 DG67
Fitzroy Rd.
Fitzstephen Rd., Dag. 126 EV64
Fitzwarren Gdns. N19 121 DJ60
Fitzwilliam Ave., Rich. 158 CM82
Fitzwilliam Ct., Harl. 36 EY11
Fitzwilliam Ms. E16 144 EG74
Hanover Ave.
Fitzwilliam Rd. SW4 161 DJ83
Fitzwygram Clo., Hmptn. 176 CC92
Five Acre NW9 97 CT53
Five Acres, Chesh. 54 AR33
Five Acres, Harl. 51 ES18
Five Acres, H.Wyc. 110 AE56
Five Acres, Kings L. 58 BM29
Five Acres, St.Alb. 61 CK25
Five Acres Ave., St.Alb. 60 BZ29
Five Bell All. E14 143 DZ73
Three Colt St.
Five Elms Rd., Brom. 204 EH104
Five Elms Rd., Dag. 126 EZ62
Five Flds. Clo., Wat. 94 BZ48
Five Oaks, Add. 211 BF107
Five Oaks La., Chig. 104 EY51
Five Wents, Swan. 207 FG96
Fiveacre Clo., Th.Hth. 201 DN100
Fiveash Rd., Grav. 191 GF87
Fives Ct. SE11 278 F8
Fiveways Rd. SW9 161 DP82
Fladbury Rd. N15 122 DR58
Fladgate Rd. E11 124 EE58
Flag Clo., Croy. 203 DX102
Flag Wk., Pnr. 115 BU58
Eastcote Rd.
Flags, The, Hem.H. 41 BP20
Flagstaff Clo., Wal.Abb. 67 EB33
Flagstaff Rd., Wal.Abb. 67 EB33
Flambard Rd., Har. 117 CG58
Flamborough Clo., West. 238 EH119
Flamborough Rd., Ruis. 115 BU62
Flamborough Spur, Slou. 151 AN75
Flamborough St. E14 143 DY72
Flamingo Gdns., Nthlt. 136 BY69
Jetstar Way
Flamingo Wk., Horn. 147 FG65
Flamstead End Rd. (Cheshunt), Wal.Cr. 66 DV28
Flamstead Gdns., Dag. 146 EW66
Flamstead Rd.
Flamstead Rd., Dag. 146 EW66
Flamsted Ave., Wem. 138 CN65
Flamsteed Rd. SE7 164 EL78
Flanchford Rd. W12 159 CT76
Flanchford Rd., Reig. 265 CT140
Flanders Ct., Egh. 173 BC92
Flanders Cres. SW17 180 DF94
Flanders Rd. E6 145 EM68
Flanders Rd. W4 158 CS77
Flanders Way E9 143 DX65
Flank St. E1 142 DU73
Dock St.
Flash La., Enf. 81 DP37
Flask Cotts. NW3 120 DD63
New End Sq.
Flask Wk. NW3 120 DD63
Flat Iron Sq. SE1 142 DQ74
Union St.
Flatfield Rd., Hem.H. 40 BN22
Flaunden Bottom, Chesh. 72 AY36
Flaunden Bottom, Hem.H. 57 AZ34
Flaunden Hill, Hem.H. 57 AZ33
Flaunden La., Hem.H. 57 BB32
Flaunden La., Rick. 57 BD33
Flaunden Pk., Hem.H. 57 BA32
Flavell Ms. SE10 164 EE78
Flavian Clo., St.Alb. 42 BZ22
Flaxen Clo. E4 101 EB48
Flaxen Rd.
Flaxen Rd. E4 101 EB48
Flaxley Rd., Mord. 200 DB100
Flaxman Ct. W1 273 M9
Flaxman Rd. SE5 161 DP82
Flaxman Ter. WC1 273 N3
Flaxman Ter. WC1 141 DK69
Flaxton Rd. SE18 165 ER81
Flecker Clo., Stan. 95 CF50
Fleece Dr. N9 100 DU49
Fleece Rd., Surb. 197 CJ102
Fleece Wk. N7 141 DL65
Manger Rd.
Fleeming Clo. E17 101 DZ54
Pennant Ter.
Fleeming Rd. E17 101 DZ54
Fleet Ave., Dart. 188 FQ88
Fleet Ave., Upmin. 129 FR58
Fleet Clo., Ruis. 115 BQ58
Fleet Clo., Upmin. 129 FR58
Fleet Clo., W.Mol. 196 CA99
Fleet La., W.Mol. 196 BZ100
Fleet Pl. EC4 141 DN72
Farringdon St.
Fleet Rd. NW3 120 DE64
Fleet Rd., Dart. 188 FP88
Fleet Rd., Grav. 190 GC90
Fleet Sq. WC1 274 B3
Fleet St. EC4 274 D9
Fleet St. EC4 141 DN72
Fleet St. Hill E1 142 DU70
Weaver St.
Fleetdale Par., Dart. 188 FQ88
Fleet Ave.
Fleetside, W.Mol. 196 BZ99
Fleetway, Egh. 193 BC97
Fleetway Business Pk., Grnf. 137 CH68
Fleetwood Clo. E16 144 EK71
Fleetwood Clo., Ch.St.G. 90 AU49
Fleetwood Clo., Chess. 215 CK108
Fleetwood Clo., Croy. 202 DS104
Chepstow Ri.
Fleetwood Clo., Tad. 233 CX120
Fleetwood Ct. E6 145 EM71
Evelyn Denington Rd.
Fleetwood Ct., W.Byf. 212 BG113
Fleetwood Gro. W3 138 CS73
East Acton La.
Fleetwood Rd. NW10 119 CU64
Fleetwood Rd., Kings.T. 198 CP97
Fleetwood Rd., Slou. 132 AT74
Fleetwood Sq., Kings.T. 198 CP97
Fleetwood St. N16 122 DS61
Stoke Newington Ch. St.
Fleetwood Way, Wat. 94 BW49
Fleming Clo. (Cheshunt), Wal.Cr. 66 DU26
Fleming Ct. W2 140 DD71
St. Marys Ter.
Fleming Ct., Croy. 219 DN106
Fleming Cres., Hert. 31 DN09
Windsor Dr.
Fleming Dr. N21 81 DM43
Sydenham Ave.
Fleming Gdns., Rom. 106 FK54
Bartholomew Dr.
Fleming Gdns., Til. 171 GJ81
Fielding Ave.
Fleming Mead, Mitch. 180 DE94
Fleming Rd. SE17 161 DP79
Fleming Rd., Grays 169 FW77
Fleming Rd., Sthl. 136 CB72
Fleming Way SE28 146 EX73
Fleming Way, Islw. 157 CF83
Flemings, Brwd. 107 FW51
Flemish Flds., Cher. 194 BG101
Flemming Ave., Ruis. 115 BV60
Flempton Rd. E10 123 DY60
Fletcher Clo. E6 145 EP72
Trader Rd.
Fletcher Clo., Cher. 211 BE107
Fletcher La. E10 123 EC59
Fletcher Path SE8 163 EA80
New Butt La.
Fletcher Rd. W4 158 CQ76
Fletcher Rd., Cher. 211 BD107
Fletcher Rd., Chig. 103 ET50
Fletcher St. E1 142 DU73
Fletcher Way, Hem.H. 40 BJ18
Fletchers Clo., Brom. 204 EH98
Fletching Rd. E5 122 DW62
Fletching Rd. SE7 164 EJ79
Fletton Rd. N11 99 DL52
Fleur de Lis St. E1 275 N5
Fleur de Lis St. E1 142 DS70
Fleur Gates SW19 179 CX87
Princes Way
Flex Meadow, Harl. 50 EL16
Flexley Wd., Welw.G.C. 29 CZ06
Flexmere Gdns. N17 100 DR53
Flexmere Rd.
Flexmere Rd. N17 100 DR53
Flight App. NW9 97 CT54
Flimwell Clo., Brom. 184 EE92
Flinders Clo., St.Alb. 43 CG22
Flint Clo., Bans. 218 DB114
Flint Clo., Lthd. 246 CC126
Flint Clo., Red. 250 DF133
Flint Down Clo., Orp. 206 EU95
Flint Hill, Dor. 263 CH138
Flint Hill Clo., Dor. 263 CH139
Flint St. SE17 279 L9
Flint St. SE17 162 DR77
Flint St., Grays 169 FV79
Flint Way, St.Alb. 42 CC16
Flintlock Clo., Stai. 154 BG84
Flintmill Cres. SE3 164 EL82
Flinton St. SE17 279 N10
Flinton St. SE17 162 DS78
Flitcroft St. WC2 273 N8
Flock Mill Pl. SW18 180 DB88
Flockton St. SE16 162 DU75
George Row
Flodden Rd. SE5 162 DQ81
Flood La., Twick. 177 CG88
Church La.
Flood Pas. SE18 165 EM77
Samuel St.
Flood St. SW3 160 DE78
Flood Wk. SW3 160 DE79
Flora Clo. E14 143 EB72
Flora Gdns. W6 159 CV77
Ravenscourt Rd.
Flora Gdns., Croy. 221 EC111
Flora Gdns., Rom. 126 EW58
Flora Gro., St.Alb. 43 CF21
Flora St., Belv. 166 EZ78
Victoria St.
Floral Ct., Ash. 231 CJ118
Rosedale
Floral Dr., St.Alb. 61 CK26
Floral St. WC2 273 P10
Floral St. WC2 141 DL73
Florence Ave., Add. 212 BG111
Florence Ave., Enf. 82 DQ41
Florence Ave., Mord. 200 DC99
Florence Cantwell Wk. N19 121 DL59
Hillrise Rd.
Florence Clo., Grays 170 FY79
Florence Clo., Harl. 52 EW17
Florence Clo., Horn. 128 FL61
Florence Clo., Walt. 195 BV101
Florence Rd.
Florence Clo., Wat. 75 BU35
Florence Dr., Enf. 82 DQ41
Florence Gdns. W4 158 CQ79
Florence Gdns., Rom. 126 EW59
Roxy Ave.
Florence Gdns., Stai. 174 BH94
Florence Nightingale Ho. N1 142 DR65
Clephane Rd.
Florence Rd. E6 144 EJ67
Florence Rd. E13 144 EF68
Florence Rd. N4 121 DN60
Florence Rd. SE2 166 EW76
Florence Rd. SE14 163 DZ81
Florence Rd. SW19 180 DB93
Florence Rd. W4 158 CR76
Florence Rd. W5 138 CL73
Florence Rd., Beck. 203 DX96
Florence Rd., Brom. 204 EG95
Florence Rd., Felt. 175 BV88
Florence Rd., Kings.T. 178 CM94
Florence Rd., S.Croy. 220 DR109
Florence Rd., Sthl. 156 BX77
Florence Rd., Walt. 195 BV101
Florence St. E16 144 EF70
Florence St. N1 141 DP66
Florence St. NW4 119 CW56
Florence Ter. SE14 163 DZ81
Florence Way SW12 180 DF88
Florfield Pas. E8 142 DV65
Reading La.
Florfield Rd. E8 142 DV65
Reading La.
Florian Ave., Sutt. 218 DD105
Florian Rd. SW15 159 CY84
Florida Clo. (Bushey), Wat. 95 CD47
Florida Rd., Guil. 258 AY140
Florida Rd., Th.Hth. 201 DP95
Florida St. E2 142 DU69
Floriston Ave., Uxb. 135 BQ66
Floriston Clo., Stan. 95 CH53
Floriston Gdns., Stan. 95 CH53
Floss St. SW15 159 CW82
Flower & Dean Wk. E1 142 DT71
Thrawl St.
Flower Cres., Cher. 211 BB107
Flower La. NW7 97 CT50
Flower La., Gdse. 253 DX131
Flower Pot Clo. N15 122 DT58
St. Ann's Rd.
Flower Wk., Guil. 258 AW137
Flower Wk., The SW7 160 DC75
Flowerfield, Sev. 241 FF117
Flowerhill Way, Grav. 190 GE94
Flowers Ms. N19 121 DJ61
Tollhouse Way
Flowersmead SW17 180 DG89
Floyd Rd. SE7 164 EJ78
Floyds La., Wok. 228 BG116
Fludyer St. SE13 164 EE84
Flyer's Way, The, West. 255 ER126
Folair Way SE16 162 DV78
Catlin St.
Fold Cft., Harl. 35 EN14
Foley Clo., Beac. 88 AJ51
Foley Ms., Esher 215 CE107
Foley Rd., Esher 215 CE108
Foley Rd., West. 238 EK118
Foley St. W1 273 K7
Foley St. W1 141 DJ71
Folgate St. E1 275 N6
Folgate St. E1 142 DS71
Foliot St. W12 139 CT72
Folkes La., Upmin. 129 FT57
Folkestone Ct., Slou. 153 BA78
Folkestone Rd. E6 145 EN68
Folkestone Rd. E17 123 EB56
Folkestone Rd. N18 100 DU49
Folkingham La. NW9 96 CR53
Folkington Cor. N12 97 CZ50
Follet Dr., Abb.L. 59 BT31
Follett Clo., Wind. 172 AV86
Follett St. E14 143 EC72
Folly, The, Hert. 32 DR09
Folly Ave., St.Alb. 42 CC19
Folly Clo., Rad. 77 CF36
Folly La. E4 101 DZ52
Folly La. E17 101 DY53
Folly La., Dor. 263 CH144
Folly La., St.Alb. 42 CC19
Folly Ms. W11 139 CZ72
Portobello Rd.
Folly Pathway, Rad. 77 CF35
Folly Vw., Ware 33 EB10
Folly Wall E14 163 EC75
Follyfield Rd., Bans. 218 DA114
Font Hills N2 98 DC54
Fontaine Rd. SW16 181 DM94
Fontarabia Rd. SW11 160 DG84
Fontayne Ave., Chig. 103 EQ49
Fontayne Ave., Rain. 147 FE66
Fontenoy Rd. SW12 181 DH89
Fonteyne Gdns., Wdf.Grn. 102 EK54
Lechmere Ave.
Fonthill Clo. SE20 202 DU96
Selby Rd.
Fonthill Ms. N4 121 DN61
Lennox Rd.
Fonthill Rd. N4 121 DM60
Fontley Way SW15 179 CU87
Fontmell Clo., Ashf. 174 BN92
Fontmell Clo., St.Alb. 43 CE18
Fontmell Pk., Ashf. 174 BM92
Fontwell Clo., Har. 95 CE52
Fontwell Clo., Nthlt. 136 CA65
Fontwell Dr., Brom. 205 EN99
Fontwell Pk. Gdns., Horn. 128 FL63
Football La., Har. 117 CE60
Footbury Hill Rd., Orp. 206 EU101
Footpath, The SW15 179 CU85
Foots Cray High St., Sid. 186 EW93
Foots Cray La., Sid. 186 EW88
Footscray Rd. SE9 185 EN86
Footway, The SE9 185 EQ87
Forbench Clo., Wok. 228 BH122
Forbes Ave., Pot.B. 64 DD33
Forbes Clo. NW2 119 CU62
Forbes Clo., Horn. 127 FH60
St. Leonards Way
Forbes Ct. SE19 182 DS92
Forbes St. E1 142 DU72
Ellen St.
Forbes Way, Ruis. 115 BV61
Forburg Rd. N16 122 DU60
Force Grn. La., West. 239 ER124
Ford Clo. E3 143 DY68
Roman Rd.
Ford Clo., Ashf. 174 BL93
Ford Clo., Har. 117 CD59
Ford Clo., Rain. 147 FF66
Ford Clo., Shep. 194 BN98
Ford Clo., Th.Hth. 201 DP100
Ford Clo. (Bushey), Wat. 76 CC42
Ford End, Uxb. 113 BF61
Ford End, Wdf.Grn. 102 EH51
Ford La., Iver 134 BG72
Ford La., Rain. 147 FF66
Ford Rd. E3 143 DY67
Ford Rd., Ashf. 174 BM91
Ford Rd., Cher. 194 BH102
Ford Rd., Dag. 146 EZ66
Ford Rd., Grav. 190 GB85
Ford Rd. (Old Woking), Wok. 227 BB120
Ford Sq. E1 142 DV71
Ford St. E3 143 DY67
Ford St. E16 144 EF72
Fordbridge Clo., Cher. 194 BH102
Fordbridge Rd., Ashf. 174 BL93
Fordbridge Rd., Shep. 195 BS100
Fordbridge Rd., Sun. 195 BS100
Fordcroft Rd., Orp. 206 EV99
Forde Ave., Brom. 204 EJ97
Fordel Rd. SE6 183 ED88
Fordham Clo., Barn. 80 DE41
Fordham Clo., Horn. 128 FN59
Fordham Rd., Barn. 80 DD41
Fordham St. E1 142 DU72
Fordhook Ave. W5 138 CM73
Fordingley Rd. W9 139 CZ69
Fordington Rd. N6 120 DF57
Fordmill Rd. SE6 183 EA89
Fords Gro. N21 100 DQ46
Fords Pk. Rd. E16 144 EG72
Fordwater Rd., Cher. 194 BH102
Fordwater Trd. Est., Cher. 194 BH102
Fordwich Clo., Hert. 31 DN09
Fordwich Clo., Orp. 205 ET101
Fordwich Hill, Hert. 31 DN09
Fordwich Ri., Hert. 31 DN09
Fordwich Rd., Welw.G.C. 29 CW10
Fordwych Rd. NW2 119 CY64
Fordyce Clo., Horn. 128 FM59
Fordyce Rd. SE13 183 EC86
Fordyke Rd., Dag. 126 EZ61
Fore St. EC2 275 J7
Fore St. EC2 142 DQ71
Fore St. N9 100 DU50
Fore St. N18 100 DT51
Fore St., Harl. 36 EW11
Fore St., Hat. 45 CW17
Fore St., Hert. 32 DR09
Fore St., Pnr. 115 BU57
Fore St. Ave. EC2 275 K7
Forebury, The, Saw. 36 EY05
Forebury Ave., Saw. 36 EZ05
Forebury Cres., Saw. 36 EZ05
Forefield, St.Alb. 60 CA27
Foreland Ct. NW4 97 CY53
Foreland St. SE18 165 ER77
Plumstead Rd.
Forelands Way, Chesh. 54 AQ32
Foreman Ct. W6 159 CW77
Hammersmith Bdy.
Foremark Clo., Ilf. 103 ET50
Foreshore SE8 163 DZ77
Forest, The E11 124 EE56
Forest App. E4 102 EE45
Forest App., Wdf.Grn. 102 EF52
Forest Ave. E4 102 EE45
Forest Ave., Chig. 103 EN50
Forest Ave., Hem.H. 40 BK22
Forest Business Pk. E17 123 DX59
Forest Clo. E11 124 EF57
Forest Clo., Chis. 205 EN95
Forest Clo., Lthd. 245 BT125
Forest Clo., Wal.Abb. 84 EH37
Forest Clo., Wok. 227 BD115
Forest Clo., Wdf.Grn. 102 EH48
Forest Ct. E4 102 EF46
Forest Ct. E11 124 EE56
Forest Cres., Ash. 232 CN116
Forest Cft. SE23 182 DV89
Forest Dr. E12 124 EK62
Forest Dr., Epp. 85 ES36
Forest Dr., Kes. 222 EL105
Forest Dr., Sun. 175 BT94
Forest Dr., Tad. 233 CY121
Forest Dr., Wdf.Grn. 101 ED52
Forest Dr. E. E11 123 ED59
Forest Dr. W. E11 123 EC59
Forest Edge, Buck.H. 102 EJ49
Forest Gdns. N17 100 DT54
Forest Gate NW9 118 CS57
Forest Glade E4 102 EE49
Forest Glade E11 124 EE58
Forest Glade, Epp. 70 EY28
Forest Grn. Rd., Maid. 150 AD82
Forest Grn. Rd., Wind. 150 AD82
Forest Gro. E8 142 DT66
Forest Hts., Buck.H. 102 EG47
Forest Hill Business Cen. SE23 182 DW89
Forest Hill Ind. Est. SE23 182 DW89
Perry Vale
Forest Hill Rd. SE22 182 DV85
Forest Hill Rd. SE23 182 DV85
Forest Ind. Pk., Ilf. 103 ES53
Forest La. E7 124 EE64
Forest La. E15 124 EE64
Forest La., Chig. 103 EN50
Forest La., Lthd. 229 BT124
Forest Mt. Rd., Wdf.Grn. 101 ED52
Forest Ridge, Beck. 203 EA97
Forest Ridge, Kes. 222 EL105
Forest Ri. E17 123 ED57
Forest Rd. E7 124 EG63
Forest Rd. E8 142 DT65
Forest Rd. E11 123 ED59
Forest Rd. E17 122 DW56
Forest Rd. N9 100 DV46
Forest Rd. N17 122 DW56
Forest Rd., Enf. 83 DY36
Forest Rd., Erith 167 FG81
Forest Rd., Felt. 176 BW89
Forest Rd., Ilf. 103 ES53
Forest Rd., Lthd. 229 BU123
Forest Rd., Loug. 84 EK41
Forest Rd., Rich. 158 CN80
Forest Rd., Rom. 127 FB55

Freightmaster Est., Rain. 167 FG76
Freke Rd. SW11 160 DG83
Fremantle Ho., Til. 171 GF81
Leicester Rd.
Fremantle Rd., Belv. 166 FA77
Fremantle Rd., Ilf. 103 EQ54
Fremont St. E9 142 DW67
French Gdns., Cob. 214 BW114
French Horn La., Hat. 45 CV17
French Ordinary Ct. EC3 275 N10
French Pl. E1 275 N3
French Row, St.Alb. 43 CD20
Market Pl.
French St., Sun. 196 BW96
French St., West. 255 ES128
Frenchaye, Add. 212 BJ106
Frenches, The, Red. 250 DG132
Frenches Ct., Red. 250 DG132
Frenches Rd.
Frenches Dr., Red. 250 DG132
The Frenches
Frenches Rd., Red. 250 DG132
Frenchlands Hatch, Lthd. 245 BS127
French's Clo., Ware 33 EB11
French's Wells, Wok. 226 AV117
Frenchum Gdns., Slou. 131 AL73
Frendsbury Rd. SE4 163 DY84
Frensham (Cheshunt), Wal.Cr. 66 DT27
Frensham Clo., Sthl. 136 BZ70
Frensham Ct., Mitch. 200 DD97
Phipps Bri. Rd.
Frensham Dr. SW15 179 CU89
Frensham Dr., Croy. 221 EC108
Frensham Rd. SE9 185 ER89
Frensham Rd., Ken. 219 DP114
Frensham St. SE15 162 DU79
Frensham Way, Epsom 233 CW116
Frere St. SW11 160 DE82
Fresh Wf. Rd., Bark. 145 EP67
Freshborough Ct., Guil. 259 AZ135
Lower Edgeborough Rd.
Freshfield Ave. E8 142 DT66
Freshfield Clo. SE13 163 ED84
Marischal Rd.
Freshfield Dr. N14 99 DH45
Freshfields, Croy. 203 DZ101
Freshfields Ave., Upmin. 128 FP64
Freshford St. SW18 180 DC90
Freshmount Gdns., Epsom 216 CP111
Freshwater Clo. SW17 180 DG93
Freshwater Rd. SW17 180 DG93
Freshwater Rd., Dag. 126 EX60
Freshwaters, Harl. 35 ES14
School La.
Freshwell Ave., Rom. 126 EW56
Freshwood Clo., Beck. 203 EB95
Freshwood Way, Wall. 219 DH109
Freston Gdns., Barn. 80 DG43
Freston Pk. N3 97 CZ54
Freston Rd. W10 139 CX73
Freston Rd. W11 139 CX73
Freta Rd., Bexh. 186 EZ85
Fretherne Rd., Welw.G.C. 29 CX09
Frewin Rd. SW18 180 DD88
Friar Ms. SE27 181 DP90
Prioress Rd.
Friar Rd., Hayes 136 BX70
Friar Rd., Orp. 206 EU99
Friar St. EC4 274 G9
Friars, The, Chig. 103 ES49
Friars, The, Harl. 51 EN17
Friars Ave. N20 98 DE48
Friars Ave. SW15 179 CT90
Friars Ave., Brwd. 109 GA46
Friars Clo. E4 101 EC48
Friars Clo. N2 120 DD56
Friars Clo., Brwd. 109 GA45
Friars Clo., Nthlt. 136 BX69
Broomcroft Ave.
Friars Fld., Berk. 38 AS16
Herons Elm
Friars Gdns. W3 138 CR72
St. Dunstans Ave.
Friars Gate, Guil. 258 AU136
Friars Gate Clo., Wdf.Grn. 102 EG49
Friars La., B.Stort. 37 FH06
Friars La., Rich. 177 CK85
Friars Mead E14 163 EC76
Friars Ms. SE9 185 EN85
Friars Orchard, Lthd. 231 CD121
Friars Pl. La. W3 138 CR73
Friars Ri., Wok. 227 BA118
Friars Rd. E6 144 EK67
Friars Rd., Vir.W. 192 AX98
Friars Stile Pl., Rich. 178 CL86
Friars Stile Rd.
Friars Stile Rd., Rich. 178 CL86
Friars Wk. N14 99 DH46
Friars Wk. SE2 166 EX78
Friars Way W3 138 CR72
Friars Way, Cher. 194 BG99
Friars Way, Kings L. 58 BN30
Friars Way (Bushey), Wat. 76 BZ39
Friars Wd., Croy. 221 DY109
Friarscroft, Brox. 49 EA20
Friary, The, Wind. 172 AW86
Friary Bri., Guil. 258 AW136
Friary Clo. N12 98 DE50
Friary Ct. SW1 277 L3
Friary Ct., Wok. 226 AT118
Friary Est. SE15 162 DU79
Friary Island, Stai. 172 AW86
Friary La., Wdf.Grn. 102 EG49
Friary Pas., Guil. 258 AW136
Friary St.
Friary Rd. N12 98 DD49
Friary Rd. SE15 162 DU80
Friary Rd. W3 138 CQ72
Friary Rd., Stai. 172 AW87
Friary St., Guil. 258 AW136
Friary Way N12 98 DE49
Friday Hill E4 102 EE47
Friday Hill E. E4 102 EE48
Friday Hill W. E4 102 EE47
Friday Rd., Erith 167 FD78
Friday Rd., Mitch. 180 DF94
Friday St. EC4 275 H9
Friday St. EC4 142 DQ72
Friday St., Dor. 262 BY143
Frideswide Pl. NW5 121 DJ64
Islip St.
Friend St. EC1 274 F2
Friend St. EC1 141 DP69
Friendly Pl. SE13 163 EB81
Lewisham Rd.
Friendly St. SE8 163 EA81
Friendly St. Ms. SE8 163 EA82
Friendly St.
Friends Ave., Wal.Cr. 67 DX31
Friends Rd., Croy. 202 DR104
Friends Rd., Pur. 219 DP112
Friends Wk., Stai. 173 BF92
South St.
Friends Wk., Uxb. 134 BK66
Bakers Rd.
Friendship Wk., Nthlt. 136 BX69
Wayfarer Rd.
Friern Barnet La. N11 98 DE49
Friern Barnet La. N20 98 DE49
Friern Barnet Rd. N11 98 DF50
Friern Bri. Retail Pk. N11 99 DH51
Friern Ct. N20 98 DD48
Friern Mt. Dr. N20 98 DC45
Friern Pk. N12 98 DC50
Friern Rd. SE22 182 DU86
Friern Watch Ave. N12 98 DC49
Frigate Ms. SE8 163 EA79
Watergate St.
Frimley Ave., Horn. 128 FN60
Frimley Ave., Wall. 219 DL106
Frimley Clo. SW19 179 CY89
Frimley Clo., Croy. 221 EC108
Frimley Ct., Sid. 186 EW92
Frimley Cres., Croy. 221 EC108
Frimley Gdns., Mitch. 200 DE97
Frimley Rd., Chess. 216 CL106
Frimley Rd., Hem.H. 39 BE19
Frimley Rd., Ilf. 125 ES62
Frimley Vw., Wind. 151 AK81
Frimley Way E1 143 DX70
Fringewood Clo., Nthwd. 93 BP53
Frinsted Clo., Orp. 206 EX98
Frinsted Rd., Erith 167 FD80
Frinton Clo., Wat. 93 BV47
Frinton Dr., Wdf.Grn. 101 ED52
Frinton Ms., Ilf. 125 EN58
Bramley Cres.
Frinton Rd. E6 144 EK69
Frinton Rd. N15 122 DS58
Frinton Rd. SW17 180 DG93
Frinton Rd., Rom. 104 EZ52
Frinton Rd., Sid. 186 EY89
Friston Path, Chig. 103 ES50
Friston St. SW6 160 DB82
Friswell Pl., Bexh. 166 FA84
Frith Ct. NW7 97 CY52
Frith Knowle, Walt. 213 BV106
Frith La. NW7 97 CY52
Frith Rd. E11 123 EC63
Frith Rd., Croy. 202 DQ103
Frith St. W1 273 M9
Frith St. W1 141 DK72
Fritham Clo., N.Mal. 198 CS100
Frithe, The, Slou. 132 AV72
Friths Dr., Reig. 250 DB131
Frithsden Copse, Berk. 39 AZ15
Frithsden Rd., Berk. 38 AY17
Frithville Gdns. W12 139 CW74
Frithwald Rd., Cher. 193 BF101
Frithwood Ave., Nthwd. 93 BS51
Frizlands La., Dag. 127 FB63
Frobisher Clo., Ken. 236 DR117
Hayes La.
Frobisher Clo., Pnr. 116 BX59
Frobisher Cres., Stai. 174 BL87
Frobisher Gdns., Guil. 243 BA133
Frobisher Gdns., Stai. 174 BL87
Frobisher Cres.
Frobisher Pas. E14 143 EA74
North Colonnade
Frobisher Rd. E6 145 EM72
Frobisher Rd. N8 121 DN56
Frobisher Rd., Erith 167 FF80
Frobisher Rd., St.Alb. 43 CJ22
Frobisher St. SE10 164 EE79
Frobisher Way, Grav. 191 GL92
Frobisher Way, Green. 169 FV84
Frobisher Way, Hat. 44 CR15
Frog La., Guil. 242 AY125
Frog La., Rain. 147 FD71
Froggy La., Uxb. 113 BD61
Froghall La., Chig. 103 ER49
Froghole La., Eden. 255 ER132
Frogley Rd. SE22 162 DT84
Frogmoor La., Rick. 92 BK47
Frogmore SW18 180 DA85
Frogmore, St.Alb. 61 CD27
Frogmore Ave., Hayes 135 BS70
Frogmore Clo., Slou. 151 AN75
Frogmore Clo., Sutt. 199 CX104
Frogmore Dr., Wind. 152 AS81
Frogmore Est., Ruis. 116 BX64
Frogmore Gdns., Hayes 135 BS70
Frogmore Gdns., Sutt. 217 CY105
Frogmore Home Pk., St.Alb. 61 CD28
Frogmore Ind. Est. NW10 138 CQ69
Frogmore Rd., Hem.H. 40 BK23
Frognal NW3 120 DC64
Frognal Ave., Har. 117 CF56
Frognal Ave., Sid. 186 EU92
Frognal Clo. NW3 120 DC64
Frognal Ct. NW3 140 DC65
Frognal Gdns. NW3 120 DC63
Frognal La. NW3 120 DB64
Frognal Par. NW3 140 DC65
Frognal Ct.
Frognal Pl., Sid. 186 EU93
Frognal Ri. NW3 120 DC63
Frognal Way NW3 120 DC63
Froissart Rd. SE9 184 EK85
Frome Rd. N22 121 DP55
Westbury Ave.
Frome Sq., Hem.H. 40 BN15
Waveney
Frome St. N1 142 DQ68
Fromer Rd., H.Wyc. 110 AD59
Fromondes Rd., Sutt. 217 CY106
Front, The, Berk. 39 BB16
Front La., Upmin. 129 FS59
Frostic Wk. E1 142 DT71
Froude St. SW8 161 DH82
Frowick Clo., Hat. 45 CV23
Frowyke Cres., Pot.B. 63 CU32
Fruen Rd., Felt. 175 BT87
Fry Clo., Rom. 104 FA50
Fry Rd. E6 144 EK66
Fry Rd. NW10 139 CT67
Fryatt Rd. N17 100 DR52
Fryatt St. E14 144 EE72
Orchard Pl.
Fryent Clo. NW9 118 CN58
Fryent Cres. NW9 118 CS58
Fryent Flds. NW9 118 CS58
Fryent Gro. NW9 118 CS58
Fryent Way NW9 118 CN58
Fryer Clo., Chesh. 54 AR33
Fryern Wd., Cat. 236 DQ124
Frye's Bldgs. N1 141 DN68
Upper St.
Frying Pan All. E1 275 P7
Fryston Ave., Couls. 219 DH114
Fryston Ave., Croy. 202 DU103
Fryth Mead, St.Alb. 42 CB19
Fuchsia Clo., Rom. 127 FE61
Fuchsia St. SE2 166 EV78
Fulbeck Dr. NW9 96 CS53
Fulbeck Wk., Edg. 96 CP47
Bushfield Cres.
Fulbeck Way, Har. 94 CC54
Fulbourne Clo., Red. 250 DE132
Dennis Clo.
Fulbourne Rd. E17 101 EC53
Fulbourne St. E1 142 DV71
Durward St.
Fulbrook Ave., Add. 212 BG111
Fulbrook La., S.Ock. 149 FT73
Fulbrook Ms. N19 121 DJ63
Junction Rd.
Fulbrook Rd. N19 121 DJ63
Junction Rd.
Fulford Gro., Wat. 93 BV47
Fulford Rd., Cat. 236 DR121
Fulford Rd., Epsom 216 CR108
Fulford St. SE16 162 DV75
Fulham Bdy. SW6 160 DA80
Fulham Clo., Uxb. 135 BQ70
Uxbridge Rd.
Fulham Ct. SW6 160 DA80
Fulham Rd.
Fulham High St. SW6 159 CY82
Fulham Palace Rd. SW6 159 CX80
Fulham Palace Rd. W6 159 CW78
Fulham Pk. Gdns. SW6 159 CZ82
Fulham Pk. Rd. SW6 159 CZ82
Fulham Rd. SW3 160 DC79
Fulham Rd. SW6 159 CY82
Fulham Rd. SW10 160 DB80
Fulkes Cotts., Lthd. 245 BP128
Fullarton Cres., S.Ock. 149 FT72
Fullbrooks Ave., Wor.Pk. 199 CT102
Fuller Clo. E2 142 DU70
St. Matthew's Row
Fuller Clo., Orp. 223 ET106
Fuller Gdns., Wat. 75 BV37
Fuller Rd.
Fuller Rd., Dag. 126 EV62
Fuller Rd., Wat. 75 BV37
Fuller St. NW4 119 CW56
Fuller Ter., Ilf. 125 EQ64
Oaktree Gro.
Fuller Way, Hayes 155 BT78
Fuller Way, Rick. 74 BN43
Fullers Ave., Surb. 198 CM103
Fullers Ave., Wdf.Grn. 102 EF52
Fullers Clo., Chesh. 54 AP32
Fullers Clo., Rom. 105 FC52
Fullers Clo., Wal.Abb. 68 EG33
Fullers Fm. Rd., Lthd. 245 BP134
Fullers Hill, Amer. 54 AM34
Fullers Hill, Chesh. 54 AM34
Fullers Hill, West. 255 ER126
High St.
Fullers La., Rom. 105 FC52
Fullers Mead, Harl. 52 EW16
Fullers Rd. E18 102 EF53
Fullers Way N., Surb. 198 CM104
Fullers Way S., Chess. 216 CL105
Fullers Wd., Croy. 221 EA106
Fullers Wd. La., Red. 251 DJ134
Fullerton Clo., W.Byf. 212 BM114
Fullerton Dr., W.Byf. 212 BL114
Fullerton Rd. SW18 180 DC85
Fullerton Rd., Cars. 218 DE109
Fullerton Rd., Croy. 202 DT101
Fullerton Rd., W.Byf. 212 BL114
Fullerton Way, W.Byf. 212 BL114
Fullmer Way, Add. 211 BF110
Fullwell Ave., Ilf. 103 EM53
Fullwell Cross Roundabout, Ilf. 103 ER54
Fencepiece Rd.
Fullwoods Ms. N1 275 L2
Fulmar Ct., Surb. 198 CM100
Fulmar Cres., Hem.H. 40 BG21
Fulmar Rd., Horn. 147 FG66
Fulmead St. SW6 160 DB81
Fulmer Clo., Hmptn. 176 BY92
Fulmer Common Rd., Iver 133 BA65
Fulmer Common Rd., Slou. 112 AX64
Fulmer Dr., Ger.Cr. 112 AX61
Fulmer La., Ger.Cr. 113 BA62
Fulmer La., Slou. 112 AY62
Fulmer Ri. Est., Slou. 133 AZ65
Fulmer Rd. E16 144 EK71
Fulmer Rd., Ger.Cr. 112 AY59
Fulmer Rd., Slou. 112 AX63
Fulmer Way W13 157 CH76
Fulmer Way, Ger.Cr. 112 AY58
Fulready Rd. E10 123 ED57
Fulstone Clo., Houns. 156 BZ84
Fulthorp Rd. SE3 164 EF82
Fulton Ms. W2 140 DC73
Porchester Ter.
Fulton Rd., Wem. 118 CN62
Fulvens, Guil. 261 BS142
Fulvens Cotts., Guil. 261 BS142
Fulwell Pk. Ave., Twick. 176 CB89
Fulwell Rd., Tedd. 177 CD91
Fulwich Rd., Dart. 188 FM86
Fulwood Ave., Wem. 138 CM67
Fulwood Clo., Hayes 135 BT72
Fulwood Gdns., Twick. 177 CF86
Fulwood Pl. WC1 274 C7
Fulwood Pl. WC1 141 DM71
Fulwood Wk. SW19 179 CY88
Furber St. W6 159 CV76
Furham Feild, Pnr. 94 CA52
Furley Rd. SE15 162 DU80
Furlong Clo., Wall. 200 DG102
Furlong Rd. N7 141 DN65
Furlong Rd., Dor. 262 CC137
Furlong Way, Ware 33 DZ09
Furlongs, Hem.H. 40 BG19
Furlough, The, Wok. 227 BA117
Pembroke Rd.
Furmage St. SW18 180 DB87
Furmingers Rd., Orp. 225 FB106
Furneaux Ave. SE27 181 DP92
Furner Clo., Dart. 167 FF83
Furness Clo., Grays 171 GH78
Furness Pl., Wind. 150 AJ82
Furness Row
Furness Rd. NW10 139 CU68
Furness Rd. SW6 160 DB82
Furness Rd., Har. 116 CB59
Furness Rd., Mord. 200 DB101
Furness Row, Wind. 150 AJ82
Furness Sq., Wind. 150 AJ82
Furness Row
Furness Wk., Wind. 150 AJ82
Furness Row
Furness Way, Horn. 127 FG64
Furness Way, Wind. 150 AJ82
Furnival Ave., Slou. 131 AP71
Furnival Clo., Vir.W. 192 AX100
Furnival St. EC4 274 D8
Furnival St. EC4 141 DN72
Furrow La. E9 122 DW64
Furrowfield, Hat. 45 CV16
Cob Mead
Furrows, The (Harefield), Uxb. 114 BJ57
Furrows, The, Walt. 196 BW103
Furrows Pl., Cat. 236 DT123
Fursby Ave. N3 98 DA51
Furse Ave., St.Alb. 43 CG17
Further Acre NW9 97 CT54
Further Grn. Rd. SE6 184 EE87
Furtherfield, Abb.L. 59 BS32
Furtherfield Clo., Croy. 201 DN100
Furtherground, Hem.H. 40 BL21
Furze Clo., Red. 250 DF133
Furze Clo., Wat. 94 BW50
Furze Fm. Clo., Rom. 104 EY54
Furze Fld., Lthd. 215 CD113
Furze Gro., Tad. 233 CZ121
Furze Hill, Pur. 219 DL111
Furze Hill, Red. 250 DE133
Linkfield La.
Furze Hill, Tad. 233 CZ120
Furze La., Gdmg. 258 AT143
Furze La., Pur. 219 DL111
Furze Rd., Add. 211 BF107
Furze Rd., Hem.H. 39 BE21
Furze Rd., Th.Hth. 202 DQ97
Furze St. E3 143 EA71
Furze Vw., Rick. 73 BC44
Furzebushes La., St.Alb. 60 BY25
Furzedown Dr. SW17 181 DH92
Furzedown Rd. SW17 181 DH92
Furzedown Rd., Sutt. 218 DC111
Furzefield (Cheshunt), Wal.Cr. 66 DV28
Furzefield Clo., Chis. 185 EP93
Furzefield Cres., Reig. 266 DC136
Furzefield Rd. SE3 164 EH79
Furzefield Rd., Beac. 88 AJ52
Furzefield Rd., Reig. 266 DC136
Furzefield Rd., Welw.G.C. 29 CY10
Furzeground Way, Uxb. 135 BQ74
Furzeham Rd., West Dr. 154 BL75
Furzehill Rd., Borwd. 78 CN42
Furzen Clo., Slou. 131 AN69
Furzen Cres., Hat. 45 CT21
Furzewood, Sun. 195 BU95
Fuschia Ct., Wdf.Grn. 102 EE52
The Bridle Path
Fusedale Way, S.Ock. 149 FT73
Fuzzens Wk., Wind. 151 AL82
Fyfe Way, Brom. 204 EG96
Widmore Rd.
Fyfield Clo., Brom. 203 ED98
Fyfield Ct. E7 144 EG65
Fyfield Rd. E17 123 ED55
Fyfield Rd. SW9 161 DN83
Fyfield Rd., Enf. 82 DS41
Fyfield Rd., Rain. 147 FF67
Fyfield Rd., Wdf.Grn. 102 EJ52
Fynes St. SW1 277 M8
Fynes St. SW1 161 DK77

G

G.E.C. Est., Wem. 117 CK62
Gabion Ave., Purf. 169 FR77
Gable Clo. SE26 182 DV91
Lawrie Pk. Ave.
Gable Clo., Abb.L. 59 BS32
Gable Clo., Dart. 187 FG85
Gable Clo., Pnr. 94 CA52
Gable Ct. SE26 182 DV92
Lawrie Pk. Ave.
Gables, The, Bans. 233 CZ117
Gables, The, Hem.H. 40 BK19
Chapel St.
Gables, The, Lthd. 214 CC112
Gables, The, Wem. 118 CM63
Gables Ave., Ashf. 174 BM92
Gables Ave., Borwd. 78 CM41
Gables Clo. SE5 162 DS81
Gables Clo. SE12 184 EG88
Gables Clo., Ger.Cr. 90 AY49
Gables Clo., Slou. 152 AU79
Gables Clo., Wok. 227 AZ120
Kingfield Rd.
Gabriel Clo., Felt. 176 BX91
Gabriel Clo. (Chafford Hundred), Grays 169 FW76
Gabriel Clo., Rom. 105 FC52
Gabriel Spring Rd. (Fawkham Grn.), Long. 209 FR103
Gabriel Spring Rd. (East), Long. 209 FS103
Gabriel St. SE23 183 DX87
Gabrielle Clo., Wem. 118 CM62
Gabrielle Ct. NW3 140 DD65
Gabriels Gdns., Grav. 191 GL92
Gad Clo. E13 144 EH69
Gadbrook Rd., Bet. 264 CQ140
Gaddesden Ave., Wem. 138 CM65
Gaddesden Cres., Wat. 60 BX34
Gaddesdon Gro., Welw.G.C. 30 DC09
Widford Rd.
Gade Ave., Wat. 75 BS42
Gade Bank, Rick. 75 BR42
Gade Clo., Hayes 135 BV74
Gade Clo., Hem.H. 40 BH17
Gade Clo., Wat. 75 BS42
Gade Twr., Hem.H. 58 BN25
Gade Valley Clo., Kings L. 58 BN28
Gade Vw. Gdns., Kings L. 59 BQ32
Gadebridge La., Hem.H. 40 BH18
Gadebridge Rd., Hem.H. 40 BG18
Gadesden Rd., Epsom 216 CQ107
Gadeview Rd., Hem.H. 40 BK24
Gadsbury Clo. NW9 119 CT58
Gadsden Clo., Upmin. 129 FS58
Gadswell Clo., Wat. 76 BX36
Gadwall Clo. E16 144 EH72
Freemasons Rd.
Gadwall Way SE28 165 ER75
Gage Rd. E16 144 EE71
Malmesbury Rd.
Gage St. WC1 274 A6
Gainford St. N1 141 DN67
Richmond Ave.
Gainsboro Gdns., Grnf. 117 CE64
Gainsborough Ave. E12 125 EN64
Gainsborough Ave., Dart. 188 FJ85
Gainsborough Ave., St.Alb. 43 CF19
Gainsborough Ave., Til. 171 GG81
Gainsborough Clo., Beck. 183 EA94
Gainsborough Clo., Esher 197 CE102
Lime Tree Ave.
Gainsborough Ct. N12 98 DB50
Gainsborough Ct. W12 159 CW75
Lime Gro.
Gainsborough Ct., Walt. 213 BU105
Gainsborough Dr., Grav. 190 GD90
Gainsborough Dr., S.Croy. 220 DU113
Gainsborough Gdns. NW3 120 DD62
Gainsborough Gdns. NW11 119 CZ59
Gainsborough Gdns., Edg. 96 CM54
Gainsborough Gdns., Islw. 177 CD85
Gainsborough Ms. SE26 182 DV90
Panmure Rd.
Gainsborough Pl., Chig. 103 ET48
Gainsborough Rd. E11 124 EE59
Gainsborough Rd. E15 144 EE69
Gainsborough Rd. N12 98 DB50
Gainsborough Rd. W4 159 CT77
Gainsborough Rd., Dag. 126 EV63
Gainsborough Rd., Epsom 216 CQ110
Gainsborough Rd., Hayes 135 BQ68
Gainsborough Rd., N.Mal. 198 CR101
Gainsborough Rd., Rain. 147 FG67
Gainsborough Rd., Rich. 158 CM83
Gainsborough Rd., Wdf.Grn. 102 EL51
Gainsborough Sq., Bexh. 166 EX83
Regency Way
Gainsford Rd. E17 123 DZ56
Gainsford St. SE1 279 P4
Gainsford St. SE1 162 DT75
Gainswood, Welw.G.C. 29 CY10
Mill Grn. Rd.
Gairloch Rd. SE5 162 DS82
Gaisford St. NW5 141 DJ65
Gaist Ave., Cat. 236 DV122
Gaitskell Rd. SE9 185 EQ88
Galahad Clo., Slou. 151 AN75
Mitchell Clo.
Galahad Rd., Brom. 184 EG90
Galata Rd. SW13 159 CU80
Galatea Sq. SE15 162 DV83
Scylla Rd.
Galbraith St. E14 163 EC76
Galdana Ave., Barn. 80 DC41
Gale Clo., Hmptn. 176 BY93
Stewart Clo.
Gale Clo., Mitch. 200 DD97
Gale Cres., Bans. 234 DA117
Gale St. E3 143 EA71
Gale St., Dag. 146 EX67
Galeborough Ave., Wdf.Grn. 101 ED52
Galen Clo., Epsom 216 CN111
Williams Evans Rd.
Galen Pl. WC1 274 A7
Galena Ho. SE18 165 ET78
Grosmont Rd.
Galena Rd. W6 159 CV77
Gales Clo., Guil. 243 BD132
Gilliat Dr.
Gales Gdns. E2 142 DV69
Gales Way, Wdf.Grn. 102 EL52
Galesbury Rd. SW18 180 DC86
Galey Grn., S.Ock. 149 FV71
Bovey Way
Galgate Clo. SW19 179 CY88
Gallants Fm. Rd., Barn. 98 DE45
Galleon Boul., Dart. 169 FR84
Galleon Clo. SE16 163 DX75
Kinburn St.
Galleon Clo., Erith 167 FD77
Galleon Rd., Grays 169 FW77
Galleons La., Slou. 132 AW70
Gallery Gdns., Nthlt. 136 BX68
Gallery Rd. SE21 182 DR88
Galley Grn., Hert. 33 EA13
Galley Hill, Hem.H. 39 BF18
Galley Hill, Wal.Abb. 68 EF30
Galley Hill Rd., Grav. 190 FZ85
Galley La., Barn. 79 CV41
Galleymead Rd., Slou. 153 BF81
Galleywall Rd. SE16 162 DV77
Galleywood Cres., Rom. 105 FD51
Gallia Rd. N5 121 DP64
Galliard Clo. N9 82 DW44
Galliard Rd. N9 100 DU46
Gallions Clo., Bark. 146 EU69
Gallions Rd. E16 145 EP73
Gallions Rd. SE7 164 EH77
Gallions Roundabout E16 145 EP73
Gallions Vw. Rd. SE28 165 ER75
Goldfinch Rd.
Gallon Clo. SE7 164 EJ77
Gallop, The, S.Croy. 220 DV108
Gallop, The, Sutt. 218 DC108
Gallosson Rd. SE18 165 ES77
Galloway Clo., Brox. 67 DZ26
Galloway Path, Croy. 220 DR105
Galloway Rd. W12 139 CU74
Gallows Cor., Rom. 106 FJ53
Gallows Hill, Kings L. 59 BQ31

Gallows Hill La., Abb.L. 59 BQ32
Gallus Clo. N21 81 DM44
Gallus Sq. SE3 164 EH83
Gallys Rd., Wind. 151 AK82
Galpins Rd., Th.Hth. 201 DM98
Galsworthy Ave., Rom. 126 EV59
Galsworthy Clo. SE28 146 EV74
Galsworthy Cres. SE3 164 EJ81
Merriman Rd.
Galsworthy Rd. NW2 119 CY63
Galsworthy Rd., Cher. 194 BG101
Galsworthy Rd., Kings.T. 178 CP94
Galsworthy Rd., Til. 171 GJ81
Galsworthy Ter. N16 122 DS62
Hawksley Rd.
Galton St. W10 139 CY70
Galva Clo., Barn. 80 DG42
Galvani Way, Croy. 201 DM102
Ampere Way
Galveston Rd. SW15 179 CZ85
Galvin Rd., Slou. 131 AQ74
Galvins Clo., Guil. 242 AU131
Galway Clo. SE16 162 DV78
Masters Dr.
Galway St. EC1 275 J3
Galway St. EC1 142 DQ69
Gambetta St. SW8 161 DH82
Gambia St. SE1 278 G3
Gambles La., Wok. 228 BJ124
Gambole Rd. SW17 180 DE91
Games Rd., Barn. 80 DF41
Gamlen Rd. SW15 159 CX84
Gammon Clo., Hem.H. 40 BN21
Gammons Fm. Clo., Wat. 75 BT36
Gammons La., Brox. 66 DT25
Gammons La., Wat. 75 BV38
Gamuel Clo. E17 123 EA58
Gander Grn. La., Sutt. 199 CY103
Ganders Ash, Wat. 59 BU33
Gandhi Clo. E17 123 EA58
Gandolfi St. SE15 162 DS79
St. Georges Way
Gane Clo., Wall. 219 DL108
Kingsford Ave.
Gangers Hill, Gdse. 253 DY128
Ganghill, Guil. 243 BA132
Gant Ct., Wal.Abb. 68 EF34
Ganton St. W1 273 K10
Ganton Wk., Wat. 94 BY49
Woodhall La.
Gantshill Cres., Ilf. 125 EN57
Gantshill Cross, Ilf. 125 EN58
Eastern Ave.
Ganymede Pl., Hem.H. 40 BM18
Jupiter Dr.
Gap Rd. SW19 180 DA92
Garage Rd. W3 138 CN72
Garbrand Wk., Epsom 217 CT109
Garbutt Pl. W1 272 G6
Garbutt Rd., Upmin. 128 FQ61
Gard St. EC1 274 G2
Garden Ave., Bexh. 166 FA83
Garden Ave., Hat. 45 CU22
Garden Ave., Mitch. 181 DH94
Garden City, Edg. 96 CN51
Garden Clo. E4 101 EA50
Garden Clo. SE12 184 EH90
Garden Clo. SW15 179 CV87
Garden Clo., Add. 212 BK105
Garden Clo., Ashf. 175 BQ93
Garden Clo., Bans. 234 DA115
Garden Clo., Barn. 79 CW42
Garden Clo., Hmptn. 176 BZ92
Garden Clo., Lthd. 231 CJ124
Garden Clo., Nthlt. 136 BY67
Garden Clo., Ruis. 115 BS61
Garden Clo., St.Alb. 43 CH19
Garden Clo., Wall. 219 DL106
Garden Clo., Wat. 75 BT40
Garden Cotts., Orp. 206 EW96
Main Rd.
Garden Ct. EC4 274 D10
Garden Ct. SE15 162 DT81
Sumner Est.
Garden Ct., Rich. 158 CM81
Lichfield Rd.
Garden Ct., Stan. 95 CJ50
Marsh La.
Garden Ct., Welw.G.C. 29 CZ08
Tewin Rd.
Garden Ct., W.Mol. 196 CB98
Avern Rd.
Garden End, Amer. 55 AS37
Garden Fld. La., Berk. 39 AZ21
Garden La. SW2 181 DM88
Christchurch Rd.
Garden La., Brom. 184 EH93
Garden Ms. W2 140 DA73
Linden Gdns.
Garden Ms., Slou. 132 AT74
Littledown Rd.
Garden Pl., Dart. 188 FK90
Garden Reach, Ch.St.G. 72 AX41
Garden Rd. NW8 140 DC69
Garden Rd. SE20 202 DW95
Garden Rd., Abb.L. 59 BS31
Garden Rd., Brom. 184 EH94
Garden Rd., Rich. 158 CN83
Garden Rd., Sev. 257 FK122
Garden Rd., Walt. 195 BV100
Garden Row SE1 278 F7
Garden Row SE1 161 DP76
Garden Row, Grav. 191 GF90
Garden St. E1 143 DX71
Garden Ter. SW1 277 M10
Garden Ter. Rd., Harl. 36 EW11
Garden Wk. EC2 275 M3
Garden Wk., Beck. 203 DZ95
Hayne Rd.
Garden Wk., Couls. 235 DH123
Garden Way NW10 138 CQ65
Garden Way, Loug. 85 EN38
Gardeners Clo. N11 98 DG47
Gardeners Rd., Croy. 201 DP102
Gardeners Wk., Lthd. 246 CB126
Gardenia Rd., Enf. 82 DS44
Gardenia Way, Wdf.Grn. 102 EG50
Gardens, The SE22 162 DU84
Gardens, The, Beck. 203 EC96
Gardens, The, Esher 214 CA105
Gardens, The, Felt. 175 BR86
Gardens, The, Har. 116 CC58
Gardens, The, Hat. 63 CY27
Gardens, The, Pnr. 116 BZ58
Gardens, The, Wat. 75 BT40
Gardiner Ave. NW2 119 CW64
Gardiner Clo., Dag. 126 EX63
Gardiner Clo., Enf. 83 DX44
Gardiner Clo., Orp. 206 EW96
Gardiners, The, Harl. 52 EV16
Gardner Clo. E11 124 EH58
Gardner Gro., Felt. 176 BZ89
Gardner Rd. E13 144 EH70
Gardner Rd., Guil. 242 AX134
Gardners La. EC4 275 H10
Gardnor Rd. NW3 120 DD63
Flask Wk.
Garendon Gdns., Mord. 200 DB101
Garendon Rd., Mord. 200 DB101
Gareth Clo., Wor.Pk. 199 CX103
Burnham Dr.
Gareth Gro., Brom. 184 EG91
Garfield Ms. SW11 160 DG83
Garfield Rd.
Garfield Pl., Wind. 151 AR82
Albany Rd.
Garfield Rd. E4 101 ED46
Garfield Rd. E13 144 EF70
Garfield Rd. SW11 160 DG83
Garfield Rd. SW19 180 DC92
Garfield Rd., Add. 212 BJ106
Garfield Rd., Enf. 82 DW42
Garfield Rd., Twick. 177 CG88
York St.
Garfield St., Wat. 75 BV38
Garford St. E14 143 EA73
Garganey Wk. SE28 146 EX73
Gargles Clo., Green. 189 FU85
Cowley Ave.
Garibaldi Rd., Red. 266 DF135
Garibaldi St. SE18 165 ES77
Garland Clo., Hem.H. 40 BK19
Garland Clo., Wal.Cr. 67 DY31
Garland Rd. SE18 165 ER80
Garland Rd., Stan. 96 CL53
Garland Rd., Ware 33 DY06
Garland Way, Cat. 236 DR122
Garland Way, Horn. 128 FL56
Garlands Ct., Croy. 220 DR105
Chatsworth Rd.
Garlands Rd., Lthd. 231 CH121
Garlands Rd., Red. 266 DF135
Garlic St., Dor. 246 BZ132
Garlichill Rd., Epsom 233 CV117
Garlick Hill EC4 275 J10
Garlick Hill EC4 142 DQ73
Garlies Rd. SE23 183 DY90
Garlinge Rd. NW2 139 CZ65
Garman Clo. N18 100 DR50
Garman Rd. N17 100 DW52
Garnault Ms. EC1 274 E3
Garnault Pl. EC1 274 E3
Garnault Rd., Enf. 82 DT38
Garner Dr., Brox. 67 DY26
Garner Rd. E17 101 EC53
Garner St. E2 142 DU68
Coate St.
Garners Clo., Ger.Cr. 91 AZ51
Garners End, Ger.Cr. 90 AY51
Garners Rd., Ger.Cr. 90 AY51
Garnet Clo., Slou. 151 AN75
Mitchell Clo.
Garnet Rd. NW10 138 CS65
Garnet Rd., Th.Hth. 202 DR98
Garnet St. E1 142 DW73
Garnet Wk. E6 144 EL71
Kingfisher St.
Garnett Clo. SE9 165 EM83
Garnett Clo., Wat. 76 BX37
Garnett Dr., St.Alb. 60 BZ29
Garnett Rd. NW3 120 DF64
Garnett Way E17 101 DY53
McEntee Ave.
Garnham Clo. N16 122 DT61
Garnham St.
Garnham St. N16 122 DT61
Garnies Clo. SE15 162 DT80
Garnon Mead, Epp. 70 EX28
Garrad's Rd. SW16 181 DK90
Garrard Clo., Bexh. 166 FA83
Garrard Clo., Chis. 185 EP92
Garrard Rd., Bans. 234 DA116
Garrard Rd., Slou. 131 AL70
Garrard Wk. NW10 138 CS65
Garnet Rd.
Garratt Clo., Croy. 219 DL105
Garratt La. SW17 180 DD91
Garratt La. SW18 180 DB85
Garratt Rd., Edg. 96 CN52
Garratt Ter. SW17 180 DE91
Garratts La., Bans. 233 CZ116
Garratts Rd. 94 CC45
(Bushey), Wat.
Garrett Clo. W3 138 CR71
Jenner Ave.
Garrett Clo., Chesh. 54 AR33
Garrett St. EC1 275 J4
Garrick Ave. NW11 119 CY58
Garrick Clo. SW18 160 DC84
Garrick Clo. W5 138 CL70
Garrick Clo., Rich. 177 CK85
The Grn.
Garrick Clo., Stai. 174 BG94
Garrick Clo., Walt. 213 BV105
Garrick Cres., Croy. 202 DS103
Garrick Dr. NW4 97 CW54
Garrick Dr. SE28 165 ER76
Broadwater Rd.
Garrick Gdns., W.Mol. 196 CA97
Garrick Pk. NW4 97 CX54
Garrick Rd. NW9 119 CT58
Garrick Rd., Grnf. 136 CB70
Garrick Rd., Rich. 158 CN82
Garrick St. WC2 273 P10
Garrick St. WC2 141 DL73
Garrick St., Grav. 191 GH86
Barrack Row
Garrick Way NW4 119 CX56
Garrison Clo. SE18 165 EN80
Red Lion La.
Garrison La., Chess. 215 CK108
Garrison Par., Purf. 168 FN77
Comet Clo.
Garrolds Clo., Swan. 207 FD96
Garron La., S.Ock. 149 FT72
Garry Clo., Rom. 105 FE52
Garry Way, Rom. 105 FE52
Garsdale Clo. N11 98 DG51
Garside Clo. SE28 165 ER76
Goosander Way
Garside Clo., Hmptn. 176 CB93
Garsington Ms. SE4 163 DZ83
Garsmouth Way, Wat. 76 BX36
Garson Gro., Chesh. 54 AN29
Garson La., Stai. 172 AX87
Garson Mead, Esher 214 BZ106
Garson Rd., Esher 214 BZ107
Garston Cres., Wat. 60 BW34
Garston Dr., Wat. 60 BW34
Garston La., Ken. 220 DR114
Garston La., Wat. 60 BX34
Garston Pk. Par., Wat. 60 BX34
Garstons, The, Lthd. 246 CA125
Garter Way SE16 163 DX75
Poolmans St.
Garth, The, Abb.L. 59 BR33
Garth, The, Cob. 214 BY113
Garth, The, Hmptn. 176 CB93
Uxbridge Rd.
Garth, The, Har. 118 CM58
Garth Clo. W4 158 CR78
Garth Clo., Kings.T. 178 CM92
Garth Clo., Mord. 199 CX101
Garth Clo., Ruis. 116 BX60
Garth Ct. W4 158 CR78
Garth Rd.
Garth Ms. W5 138 CL70
Greystoke Gdns.
Garth Rd. NW2 119 CZ61
Garth Rd. W4 158 CR79
Garth Rd., Kings.T. 178 CM92
Garth Rd., Mord. 199 CW100
Garth Rd., Sev. 257 FJ128
Garth Rd., S.Ock. 149 FW70
Garth Rd. Ind. Cen., 199 CX101
Mord.
Garthland Dr., Barn. 79 CV43
Garthorne Rd. SE23 183 DX87
Garthside, Rich. 178 CL92
Garthway N12 98 DE51
Gartlett Rd., Wat. 76 BW41
Gartmoor Gdns. SW19 179 CZ88
Gartmore Rd., Ilf. 125 ET60
Garton Pl. SW18 180 DC86
Gartons Clo., Enf. 82 DW43
Gartons Way SW11 160 DC83
Garvary Rd. E16 144 EH72
Garvin Ave., Beac. 89 AL53
Garvock Dr., Sev. 256 FG126
Garway Rd. W2 140 DB72
Gas Wks. La., Brox. 49 EA19
Gascoigne Gdns., 102 EE52
Wdf.Grn.
Gascoigne Pl. E2 275 P3
Gascoigne Pl. E2 142 DT69
Gascoigne Rd., Bark. 145 EQ67
Gascoigne Rd., Croy. 221 EC110
Gascoigne Rd., Wey. 195 BP104
Gascons Gro., Slou. 131 AN70
Gascony Ave. NW6 140 DA66
Gascoyne Clo., Pot.B. 63 CU32
Gascoyne Clo., Rom. 106 FK52
Gascoyne Dr., Dart. 167 FF82
Gascoyne Rd. E9 143 DX66
Gascoyne Way, Hert. 32 DQ09
Gaselee St. E14 143 EC73
Gasholder Pl. SE11 161 DM78
Kennington La.
Gaskarth Rd. SW12 181 DH86
Gaskarth Rd., Edg. 96 CQ53
Gaskell Rd. N6 120 DF58
Gaskell St. SW4 161 DL82
Gaskin St. N1 141 DP67
Gaspar Clo. SW5 160 DB77
Courtfield Gdns.
Gaspar Ms. SW5 160 DB77
Courtfield Gdns.
Gassiot Rd. SW17 180 DF91
Gassiot Way, Sutt. 200 DD104
Gasson Rd., Swans. 190 FY86
Gastein Rd. W6 159 CX79
Gaston Bell Clo., Rich. 158 CM83
Gaston Bri. Rd., Shep. 195 BR100
Gaston Rd., Mitch. 200 DG97
Gaston Way, Shep. 195 BQ99
Gataker St. SE16 162 DV76
Gatcombe Rd. E16 144 EG74
Gatcombe Rd. N19 121 DK62
Gatcombe Way, Barn. 80 DF41
Gate Clo., Borwd. 78 CQ39
Gate End, Nthwd. 93 BU52
Gate Ms. SW7 276 C5
Gate Ms. SW7 160 DE75
Gate St. WC2 274 B8
Gatecroft, Hem.H. 40 BM22
Gateforth St. NW8 272 B5
Gateforth St. NW8 140 DE70
Gatehill Rd., Nthwd. 93 BT52
Gatehope Dr., S.Ock. 149 FT72
Gatehouse Clo., 178 CQ94
Kings.T.
Gatehouse Sq. SE1 142 DQ74
Southwark Bri. Rd.
Gateley Rd. SW9 161 DM83
Gater Dr., Enf. 82 DR39
Gates Grn. Rd., Kes. 222 EG105
Gates Grn. Rd., W.Wick. 204 EF104
Gatesborough St. EC2 275 M4
Gatesden Rd., Lthd. 230 CC123
Gateshead Rd., Borwd. 78 CM39
Gateside Rd. SW17 180 DF90
Gatestone Rd. SE19 182 DS93
Gateway SE17 162 DQ79
Gateway, Wey. 195 BP104
Palace Dr.
Gateway, The, Wok. 211 BB114
Gateway Arc. N1 141 DP68
Islington High St.
Gateway Clo., Nthwd. 93 BQ51
Gateway Ind. Est. NW10 139 CT69
Gateway Ms. E8 122 DT64
Shacklewell La.
Gateway Rd. E10 123 EB62
Gateways, Guil. 243 BA134
Gateways, The SW3 276 C9
Gateways, The SW3 160 DF77
Gateways, The, Wal.Cr. 66 DR28
Gatewick Clo., Slou. 132 AW74
Gatfield Gro., Felt. 176 CA89
Gathorne Rd. N22 99 DN54
Gathorne St. E2 143 DX68
Mace St.
Gatley Ave., Epsom 216 CP106
Gatley Dr., Guil. 243 AZ131
Gatliff Rd. SW1 161 DH78
Gatling Rd. SE2 166 EU78
Gatting Clo., Edg. 96 CQ52
Pavilion Way
Gatting Way, Uxb. 134 BL65
Gatton Bottom, Red. 250 DG127
Gatton Bottom, Reig. 250 DC130
Gatton Clo., Reig. 250 DC131
Gatton Clo., Sutt. 218 DB109
Gatton Pk., Reig. 250 DG128
Gatton Pk. Rd., Red. 250 DD132
Gatton Pk. Rd., Reig. 250 DD132
Gatton Rd. SW17 180 DE91
Gatton Rd., Reig. 250 DC132
Gattons Way, Sid. 186 EZ91
Gatward Clo. N21 81 DP44
Gatward Grn. N9 100 DS47
Gatwick Gate, Craw. 268 DE154
Gatwick Gate Ind. Est., 268 DE154
Craw.
Gatwick Rd. SW18 179 CZ87
Gatwick Rd., Gat. 268 DG154
Gatwick Rd., Grav. 191 GH90
Gatwick Way, Gat. 268 DF151
Gatwick Way, Horn. 128 FM63
Haydock Clo.
Gauden Clo. SW4 161 DK83
Gauden Rd. SW4 161 DK82
Gaumont App., Wat. 75 BV41
Gaumont Ter. W12 159 CW75
Lime Gro.
Gaunt St. SE1 279 H6
Gauntlet Clo., Nthlt. 136 BY66
Gauntlet Cres., Ken. 236 DR120
Gauntlett Ct., Wem. 117 CH64
Gauntlett Rd., Sutt. 218 DD106
Gautrey Rd. SE15 162 DW82
Gautrey Sq. E6 145 EM72
Gavel St. SE17 279 L8
Gavell Rd., Cob. 213 BU113
Gavenny Path, S.Ock. 149 FT72
Gaverick St. E14 163 EA77
Gaveston Clo., W.Byf. 212 BM113
Gaveston Dr., Berk. 38 AV17
Gaveston Rd., Lthd. 231 CG120
Gaveston Rd., Slou. 131 AM69
Gavestone Cres. SE12 184 EH87
Gavestone Rd. SE12 184 EH87
Gaviller Pl. E5 122 DV63
Clarence Rd.
Gavin St. SE18 165 ES77
Gavina Clo., Mord. 200 DE99
Gaviots Clo., Ger.Cr. 113 AZ60
Gaviots Grn., Ger.Cr. 112 AY60
Gaviots Way, Ger.Cr. 112 AY59
Gawber St. E2 142 DW69
Gawsworth Clo. E15 124 EE64
Ash Rd.
Gawthorne Ave. NW7 97 CY50
Lane App.
Gawthorne Ct. E3 143 EA68
Mostyn Gro.
Gay Clo. NW2 119 CV64
Gay Gdns., Dag. 127 FC63
Gay Rd. E15 143 ED68
Gay St. SW15 159 CX83
Gaydon Ho. W2 140 DB71
Gaydon La. NW9 96 CS53
Gayfere Rd., Epsom 217 CU106
Gayfere Rd., Ilf. 125 EM55
Gayfere St. SW1 277 P7
Gayfere St. SW1 161 DL76
Gayford Rd. W12 159 CT75
Gayhurst SE17 162 DR79
Hopwood Rd.
Gayhurst Rd. E8 142 DU66
Gayler Clo., Red. 252 DT133
Gaylor Rd., Nthlt. 116 BZ64
Gaylor Rd., Til. 170 GE81
Gaynes Ct., Upmin. 128 FP63
Gaynes Hill Rd., Wdf.Grn. 102 EL51
Gaynes Pk. Rd., Upmin. 128 FN63
Gaynes Rd., Upmin. 128 FP61
Gaynesford Rd. SE23 183 DX89
Gaynesford Rd., Cars. 218 DF108
Gaysham Ave., Ilf. 125 EN57
Gaysham Hall, Ilf. 125 EP55
Gayton Clo., Amer. 55 AS35
Gayton Clo., Ash. 232 CL118
Gayton Ct., Har. 117 CF58
Gayton Cres. NW3 120 DD63
Gayton Rd. NW3 120 DD63
Gayton Rd. SE2 166 EW76
Florence Rd.
Gayton Rd., Har. 117 CF58
Gayville Rd. SW11 180 DF86
Gaywood Ave. 67 DX30
(Cheshunt), Wal.Cr.
Gaywood Clo. SW2 181 DM88
Gaywood Est. SE1 278 G7
Gaywood Est. SE1 161 DP76
Gaywood Rd. E17 123 EA55
Gaywood Rd., Ash. 232 CM118
Gaywood St. SE1 278 G7
Gaza St. SE17 161 DP78
Braganza St.
Gazelda Vil., Wat. 76 BX43
Lower High St.
Gazelle Glade, Grav. 191 GM92
Gean Wk., Hat. 45 CU21
Southdown Rd.
Geariesville Gdns., Ilf. 125 EP56
Geary Clo., Horl. 269 DP150
Geary Dr., Brwd. 108 FW46
Geary Rd. NW10 119 CU64
Geary St. N7 121 DM64
Geddes Pl., Bexh. 166 FA84
Market Pl.
Geddes Rd. 76 CC42
(Bushey), Wat.
Geddings Rd., Hodd. 49 EB17
Gedeney Rd. N17 100 DQ53
Gedling Pl. SE1 162 DT75
Gee St. EC1 275 H4
Gee St. EC1 142 DQ70
Geere Rd. E15 144 EF67
Gees Ct. W1 272 G9
Geffrye Ct. N1 275 N1
Geffrye Est. N1 142 DS68
Stanway St.
Geffrye St. E2 142 DT68
Geisthorp Ct., Wal.Abb. 68 EG33
Winters Way
Geldart Rd. SE15 162 DV80
Geldeston Rd. E5 122 DU61
Gell Clo., Uxb. 114 BM62
Gellatly Rd. SE14 162 DW82
Gelsthorpe Rd., Rom. 105 FB52
Gemini Gro., Nthlt. 136 BY69
Javelin Way
General Gordon Pl. 165 EP77
SE18
General Wolfe Rd. SE10 163 ED81
Generals Wk., The, Enf. 83 DY37
Genesis Business Pk., 227 BC115
Wok.
Genesta Rd. SE18 165 EP79
Geneva Clo., Shep. 195 BS96
Geneva Dr. SW9 161 DN84
Geneva Gdns., Rom. 126 EY57
Geneva Rd., Kings.T. 198 CL98
Geneva Rd., Th.Hth. 202 DQ99
Genever Clo. E4 101 EA50
Genista Rd. N18 100 DV50
Genoa Ave. SW15 179 CW85
Genoa Rd. SE20 202 DW95
Genotin Rd., Enf. 82 DR41
Genotin Ter., Enf. 82 DR41
Genotin Rd.
Gentian Row SE13 163 EC81
Sparta St.
Gentlemans Row, Enf. 82 DQ41
Gentry Gdns. E13 144 EG70
Whitwell Rd.
Genyn Rd., Guil. 258 AV135
Geoffrey Ave., Rom. 106 FN51
Geoffrey Clo. SE5 162 DQ82
Geoffrey Gdns. E6 144 EL68
Geoffrey Rd. SE4 163 DZ83
George Avey Cft., Epp. 71 FB26
George Beard Rd. SE8 163 DZ77
George Comberton Wk. 125 EN64
E12
Gainsborough Ave.
George Ct. WC2 278 A1
George Cres. N10 98 DG52
George Crook's Ho., 170 GB79
Grays
New Rd.
George Downing Est. 122 DT61
N16
Cazenove Rd.
George V Ave., Pnr. 116 CA55
George V Clo., Pnr. 116 CA55
George V Ave.
George V Way, Grnf. 137 CH67
George V Way, Rick. 74 BG36
George Gange Way, Har. 117 CE55
George Grn. Dr., Slou. 133 AZ72
George Grn. Rd., Slou. 132 AX72
George Gro. Rd. SE20 202 DU95
George Inn Yd. SE1 279 K3
George La. E18 102 EG54
George La. SE13 183 EC86
George La., Brom. 204 EH102
George Lansbury Ho. 99 DN53
N22
Progress Way
George Loveless Ho. E2 142 DT69
Diss St.
George Lowe Ct. W2 140 DB71
Bourne Ter.
George Mathers Rd. 278 F8
SE11
George Mathers Rd. 161 DP77
SE11
George Ms. NW1 273 K3
George Ms., Enf. 82 DR41
Sydney Rd.
George Pl. N17 122 DS55
Dongola Rd.
George Rd. E4 101 EA51
George Rd., Gdmg. 258 AS144
George Rd., Guil. 242 AX134
George Rd., Kings.T. 178 CP94
George Rd., N.Mal. 199 CT98
George Row SE16 162 DU75
George Sq. SW19 199 CZ97
Mostyn Rd.
George St. E16 144 EF72
George St. W1 272 E8
George St. W1 140 DG72
George St. W7 137 CE74
The Bdy.
George St., Bark. 145 EQ66
George St., Berk. 38 AX19
George St., Chesh. 54 AQ30
Berkhampstead Rd.
George St., Croy. 202 DR103
George St., Grays 170 GA79
George St., Hem.H. 40 BK19
George St., Hert. 32 DQ09
George St., Houns. 156 BZ82
George St., Rich. 177 CK85
George St., Rom. 127 FF58
George St., St.Alb. 43 CD20
George St., Sthl. 156 BY77
George St., Stai. 173 BF91
George St., Sutt. 218 DB106
George St., Uxb. 134 BK66
George St., Wat. 76 BW42
George Tilbury Ho., 171 GH75
Grays
George Wyver Clo. SW19 179 CY87
Beaumont Rd.
George Yd. EC3 275 L9
George Yd. W1 272 G10
George Yd. W1 140 DG73
Georgelands (Ripley), 228 BH121
Wok.
Georges Clo., Orp. 206 EW97
Georges Dr., Brwd. 108 FT43
Georges Dr., H.Wyc. 110 AC56
Georges Mead, Borwd. 77 CK44
George's Rd. N7 121 DM64
Georges Rd., West. 238 EK120
Georges Sq. SW6 159 CZ79
North End Rd.
Georges Ter., Cat. 236 DQ122
Coulsdon Rd.
George's Wd. Rd., Hat. 64 DA26
Georgetown Clo. SE19 182 DR92
St. Kitts Ter.
Georgette Pl. SE10 163 EC80
King George St.
Georgeville Gdns., Ilf. 125 EP56
Georgewood Rd., 58 BM25
Hem.H.
Georgia Rd., N.Mal. 198 CQ98
Georgia Rd., Th.Hth. 201 DP95
Georgian Clo., Brom. 204 EH101
Georgian Clo., Stai. 174 BH91
Georgian Clo., Stan. 95 CG52
Georgian Clo., Uxb. 114 BL63
Georgian Ct. SW16 181 DL91
Gleneldon Rd.
Georgian Ct., Wem. 138 CN65
Georgian Way, Har. 117 CD61
Georgiana St. NW1 141 DJ67
Georgina Gdns. E2 142 DT69
Columbia Rd.
Geraint Rd., Brom. 184 EG91
Gerald Ms. SW1 276 G8
Gerald Rd. E16 144 EF70
Gerald Rd. SW1 276 G8
Gerald Rd. SW1 160 DG77

Gerald Rd., Dag. 126 EZ61
Gerald Rd., Grav. 191 GL87
Geraldine Rd. SW18 180 DC85
Geraldine Rd. W4 158 CN79
Geraldine St. SE11 278 F7
Geraldine St. SE11 161 DP76
Geralds Gro., Bans. 217 CX114
Gerard Ave., Houns. 176 CA87
Redfern Ave.
Gerard Gdns., Rain. 147 FE68
Gerard Rd. SW13 159 CT81
Gerard Rd., Har. 117 CG58
Gerards Clo. SE16 162 DW78
Gerda Rd. SE9 185 EQ89
Gerdview Dr., Dart. 188 FJ91
Germain St., Chesh. 54 AP32
Germains Clo., Chesh. 54 AP32
Germander Way E15 144 EE69
Gernon Clo., Rain. 148 FK68
Jordans Way
Gernon Rd. E3 143 DY68
Geron Way NW2 119 CV60
Gerpins La., Upmin. 148 FM68
Gerrard Cres., Brwd. 108 FW48
Gerrard Gdns., Pnr. 115 BU57
Gerrard Pl. W1 273 N10
Gerrard Rd. N1 141 DP68
Gerrard St. W1 273 M10
Gerrard St. W1 141 DK73
Gerrards Clo. N14 81 DJ43
Gerrards Cross Rd., Slou. 132 AU66
Gerrards Mead, Bans. 233 CZ117
Garratts La.
Gerridge St. SE1 278 E5
Gerridge St. SE1 161 DN76
Gerry Raffles Sq. E15 143 ED65
Salway Rd.
Gertrude Rd., Belv. 166 FA77
Gertrude St. SW10 160 DC79
Gervaise Clo., Slou. 131 AM74
Gervase Clo., Wem. 118 CQ62
Gervase Rd., Edg. 96 CQ53
Gervase St. SE15 162 DV80
Gews Cor. (Cheshunt), Wal.Cr. 67 DX29
Ghent St. SE6 183 EA89
Ghent Way E8 142 DT65
Tyssen St.
Giant Arches Rd. SE24 182 DQ87
Giant Tree Hill (Bushey), Wat. 95 CD46
Gibb Cft., Harl. 51 ES19
Gibbard Ms. SW19 179 CX92
Gibbfield Clo., Rom. 126 EY55
Gibbins Rd. E15 143 EC66
Gibbon Rd. SE15 162 DW82
Gibbon Rd. W3 138 CS73
Gibbon Rd., Kings.T. 198 CL95
Gibbon Wk. SW15 159 CU84
Swinburne Rd.
Gibbons Clo., Borwd. 78 CL39
Gibbons Rd. NW10 138 CR65
Gibbs Ave. SE19 182 DR92
Gibbs Clo. SE19 182 DR92
Gibbs Clo. (Cheshunt), Wal.Cr. 67 DX29
Gibbs Couch, Wat. 94 BX48
Gibbs Grn. W14 159 CZ78
Gibbs Grn., Edg. 96 CQ50
Gibbs Rd. N18 100 DW49
Gibbs Sq. SE19 182 DR92
Gibraltar Clo., Brwd. 107 FW51
Essex Way
Gibraltar Cres., Epsom 216 CS110
Gibraltar Ho., Brwd. 107 FW51
Gibraltar Wk. E2 142 DT69
Gibson Clo. E1 142 DW70
Colebert Ave.
Gibson Clo. N21 81 DN44
Gibson Clo., Chess. 215 CJ107
Gibson Clo., Epp. 71 FC25
Beamish Clo.
Gibson Clo., Grav. 191 GF90
Gibson Clo., Islw. 157 CD83
Gibson Clo., Slou. 153 AZ78
Gibson Gdns. N16 122 DT61
Northwold Rd.
Gibson Pl., Stai. 174 BJ86
Gibson Rd. SE11 278 C9
Gibson Rd. SE11 161 DM77
Gibson Rd., Dag. 126 EW60
Gibson Rd., Sutt. 218 DB106
Gibson Rd., Uxb. 114 BM63
Gibson Sq. N1 141 DN67
Gibson St. SE10 164 EE78
Gibson's Hill SW16 181 DN93
Gidd Hill, Couls. 234 DG116
Gidea Ave., Rom. 127 FG55
Gidea Clo., Rom. 127 FG55
Gidea Clo., S.Ock. 149 FW69
Tyssen Pl.
Gideon Clo., Belv. 167 FB77
Gideon Ms. W5 157 CK75
Gideon Rd. SW11 160 DG83
Gidian Ct., St.Alb. 61 CD27
Giesbach Rd. N19 121 DJ61
Giffard Rd. N18 100 DS50
Giffard Way, Guil. 242 AU131
Giffin St. SE8 163 EA80
Gifford Gdns. W7 137 CD71
Gifford Pl., Brwd. 108 FX50
Blackthorn Way
Gifford St. N1 141 DL66
Giffordside, Grays 171 GH78
Gift La. E15 144 EE67
Giggs Hill, Orp. 206 EU96
Giggs Hill Gdns., T.Ditt. 197 CG102
Giggs Hill Rd., T.Ditt. 197 CG101
Gilbert Clo. SE18 165 EM81
Gilbert Clo., Swans. 189 FX86
Gilbert Gro., Edg. 96 CR53
Gilbert Ho. EC2 142 DQ71
Fore St.
Gilbert Ho. SE8 163 EA79
McMillan St.
Gilbert Pl. WC1 273 P7
Gilbert Rd. SE11 278 E9
Gilbert Rd. SE11 161 DN77
Gilbert Rd. SW19 180 DC94
Gilbert Rd., Belv. 166 FA76
Gilbert Rd., Brom. 184 EG94
Gilbert Rd., Grays 169 FW76
Gilbert Rd., Pnr. 116 BX56
Gilbert Rd., Rom. 127 FF56
Gilbert Rd. (Harefield), Uxb. 92 BK54
Gilbert St. E15 124 EE63
Gilbert St. W1 272 G10
Gilbert St. W1 140 DG72
Gilbert St., Enf. 82 DW37
Gilbert St., Houns. 156 CC83
High St.
Gilbert Way, Berk. 38 AU19
Gilbert Way, Croy. 201 DL102
Beddington Fm. Rd.
Gilbey Clo., Uxb. 115 BP63
Gilbey Rd. SW17 180 DE91
Gilbey Wk., H.Wyc. 110 AD59
Stratford Dr.
Gilbeys Yd. NW1 141 DH67
Oval Rd.
Gilbourne Rd. SE18 165 ET79
Gilda Ave., Enf. 83 DY43
Gilda Cres. N16 122 DU60
Gildea Clo., Pnr. 94 CA52
Gildea St. W1 273 J7
Gilden Clo., Harl. 36 EY11
Gilden Cres. NW5 120 DG64
Gilden Way, Harl. 36 EW12
Gildenhill Rd., Swan. 188 FJ93
Gilders, Saw. 36 EX05
Gilders Rd., Chess. 216 CM107
Gildersome St. SE18 165 EN79
Nightingale Vale
Giles Clo., Rain. 148 FK68
Giles Coppice SE19 182 DT91
Giles Travers Clo., Egh. 193 BC97
Gilfrid Clo., Uxb. 135 BP72
Craig Dr.
Gilhams Ave., Bans. 217 CY112
Gilkes Cres. SE21 182 DS86
Gilkes Pl. SE21 182 DS86
Gill Ave. E16 144 EG72
Gill Clo., Wat. 75 BQ44
Gill Cres., Grav. 191 GF90
Gill St. E14 143 DZ72
Gillam Way, Rain. 147 FG65
Gillan Grn. (Bushey), Wat. 94 CC47
Gillards Ms. E17 123 EA56
Gillards Way
Gillards Way E17 123 EA56
Gillender St. E3 143 EC70
Gillender St. E14 143 EC70
Gillespie Rd. N5 121 DN62
Gillett Ave. E6 144 EL68
Gillett Pl. N16 122 DS64
Gillett St.
Gillett Rd., Th.Hth. 202 DR98
Gillett St. N16 122 DS64
Gillette Cor., Islw. 157 CG80
Gillfoot NW1 273 L1
Gillfoot NW1 141 DJ68
Gillham Ter. N17 100 DU51
Gilliam Gro., Pur. 219 DN110
Gillian Ave., St.Alb. 42 CC24
Gillian Cres., Rom. 106 FJ54
Gillian Pk. Rd., Sutt. 199 CZ102
Gillian St. SE13 183 EB85
Gilliat Clo., Iver 133 BE72
Dutton Way
Gilliat Dr., Guil. 243 BD132
Gilliat Rd., Slou. 132 AS73
Gilliat's Grn., Rick. 73 BD42
Gillies St. NW5 120 DG64
Gilling Ct. NW3 140 DE65
Gillingham Ms. SW1 277 K8
Gillingham Rd. NW2 119 CY62
Gillingham Row SW1 277 K8
Gillingham St. SW1 277 K8
Gillingham St. SW1 161 DH77
Gillison Wk. SE16 162 DU76
Tranton Rd.
Gillman Dr. E15 144 EF67
Gillmans Rd., Orp. 206 EV102
Gills Hill, Rad. 77 CF35
Gills Hill La., Rad. 77 CF36
Gills Hollow, Rad. 77 CF36
Gill's Rd., Dart. 209 FS95
Gillum Clo., Barn. 98 DF46
Gilmais, Lthd. 246 CC125
Gilman Cres., Wind. 151 AK83
Gilmore Clo., Slou. 152 AW75
Gilmore Clo., Uxb. 114 BN62
Gilmore Cres., Ashf. 174 BN92
Gilmore Rd. SE13 163 ED84
Gilmour Clo., Wal.Cr. 82 DU35
Gilpin Ave. SW14 158 CR84
Gilpin Clo. W2 140 DC71
Porteus Rd.
Gilpin Clo., Mitch. 200 DE96
Gilpin Cres. N18 100 DT50
Gilpin Cres., Twick. 176 CB87
Gilpin Rd. E5 123 DY63
Gilpin Rd., Ware 33 DY07
Gilpin Way, Hayes 155 BR80
Gilpin's Gallop, Ware 33 EB11
Gilpins Ride, Berk. 38 AX18
Gilroy Clo., Rain. 147 FF65
Gilroy Way, Orp. 206 EV101
Gilsland, Wal.Abb. 84 EE35
Gilsland Rd., Th.Hth. 202 DR98
Gilstead Ho., Bark. 146 EV68
Gilstead Rd. SW6 160 DB82
Gilston Rd. SW10 160 DC78
Gilton Rd. SE6 184 EE90
Giltspur St. EC1 274 G8
Giltspur St. EC1 141 DP72
Gilwell Clo. E4 83 EB42
Antlers Hill
Gilwell La. E4 83 EC42
Gilwell Pk. E4 83 EC41
Gimcrack Hill, Lthd. 231 CH123
Dorking Rd.
Gippeswyck Clo., Pnr. 94 BX53
Uxbridge Rd.
Gipsy Hill SE19 182 DS92
Gipsy La. SW15 159 CU83
Gipsy La., Grays 170 GC79
Gipsy Rd. SE27 182 DQ91
Gipsy Rd., Well. 166 EX81
Gipsy Rd. Gdns. SE27 182 DQ91
Giralda Clo. E16 144 EK71
Fulmer Rd.
Giraud St. E14 143 EB72
Girdlers Rd. W14 159 CX77
Girdlestone Wk. N19 121 DJ61
Girdwood Rd. SW18 179 CY87
Girling Way, Felt. 155 BU83
Girona Clo. (Chafford Hundred), Grays 169 FW76
Gironde Rd. SW6 159 CZ80
Girtin Rd. (Bushey), Wat. 76 CB43
Girton Ave. NW9 118 CN55
Girton Clo., Nthlt. 136 CC65
Girton Ct., Wal.Cr. 67 DY30
Girton Gdns., Croy. 203 EA104
Girton Rd. SE26 183 DX92
Girton Rd., Nthlt. 136 CC65
Girton Vil. W10 139 CX72
Girton Way, Rick. 75 BQ43
Gisborne Gdns., Rain. 147 FF69
Gisbourne Clo., Wall. 201 DK104
Gisburn Rd. N8 121 DM56
Gisburne Way, Wat. 75 BU37
Gissing Wk. N1 141 DN66
Lofting Rd.
Gittens Clo., Brom. 184 EF91
Given Wilson Wk. E13 144 EF68
Givons Gro., Lthd. 247 CH125
Glacier Way, Wem. 137 CK68
Gladbeck Way, Enf. 81 DP42
Gladding Rd. E12 124 EK63
Gladding Rd. (Cheshunt), Wal.Cr. 65 DP25
Glade, The N21 81 DM44
Glade, The SE7 164 EJ80
Glade, The, Brwd. 109 GA46
Glade, The, Brom. 204 EK96
Glade, The, Couls. 235 DN119
Glade, The, Croy. 203 DX99
Glade, The, Enf. 81 DN41
Glade, The, Epsom 217 CU106
Glade, The, Ger.Cr. 112 AX60
Glade, The, H.Wyc. 88 AC46
Glade, The, Ilf. 103 EM53
Glade, The, Lthd. 230 CA122
Glade, The, Sev. 257 FH123
Glade, The, Stai. 174 BH94
Glade, The, Sutt. 217 CY109
Glade, The, Tad. 234 DA121
Glade, The, Upmin. 128 FQ64
Glade, The, Welw.G.C. 29 CW07
Glade, The, W.Byf. 211 BE113
Glade, The, W.Wick. 203 EB104
Glade, The, Wdf.Grn. 102 EH48
Glade Clo., Hem.H. 40 BH17
Glade Clo., Surb. 197 CK103
Glade Ct., Ilf. 103 EM53
The Glade
Glade Gdns., Croy. 203 DY101
Glade La., Sthl. 156 CB75
Glade Spur, Tad. 234 DB121
Glades, The, Grav. 191 GK93
Glades, The, Hem.H. 39 BE19
Glades Pl., Brom. 204 EG96
Widmore Rd.
Glades Shop. Cen., The, Brom. 204 EG96
Gladeside N21 81 DM44
Gladeside, Croy. 203 DX100
Gladeside, St.Alb. 43 CK17
Gladeside Clo., Chess. 215 CK108
Leatherhead Rd.
Gladeside Ct., Warl. 236 DV120
Gladesmore Rd. N15 122 DT58
Gladeswood Rd., Belv. 167 FB77
Gladeway, The, Wal.Abb. 67 ED33
Gladiator St. SE23 183 DY86
Glading Ter. N16 122 DT62
Gladioli Clo., Hmptn. 176 CA93
Gresham Rd.
Gladsdale Dr., Pnr. 115 BU56
Gladsmuir Clo., Walt. 196 BW103
Gladsmuir Rd. N19 121 DJ60
Gladsmuir Rd., Barn. 79 CY40
Gladstone Ave. E12 144 EL66
Gladstone Ave. N22 99 DN54
Gladstone Ave., Felt. 175 BU86
Gladstone Ave., Twick. 177 CD87
Gladstone Clo., Ware 33 DX05
High Oak Rd.
Gladstone Ms. NW6 139 CZ66
Cavendish Rd.
Gladstone Ms. SE20 182 DW94
Gladstone Par. NW2 119 CV60
Edgware Rd.
Gladstone Pk. Gdns. NW2 119 CV62
Gladstone Pl. E3 143 DZ68
Roman Rd.
Gladstone Pl., Barn. 79 CX42
Gladstone Rd. SW19 180 DA94
Gladstone Rd. W4 158 CR76
Acton La.
Gladstone Rd., Ash. 231 CK118
Gladstone Rd., Buck.H. 102 EH46
Gladstone Rd., Chesh. 54 AQ31
Gladstone Rd., Croy. 202 DR101
Gladstone Rd., Dart. 188 FM86
Gladstone Rd., Hodd. 49 EB16
Gladstone Rd., Kings.T. 198 CN97
Gladstone Rd., Orp. 223 EQ106
Gladstone Rd., Sthl. 156 BY76
Gladstone Rd., Surb. 197 CK103
Gladstone Rd., Ware 33 DX05
Gladstone Rd., Wat. 76 BW41
Gladstone St. SE1 278 F6
Gladstone St. SE1 161 DP76
Gladstone Ter. SE27 182 DQ91
Gladstone Ter. SW8 161 DH81
Gladstone Way, Har. 117 CE55
Gladstone Way, Slou. 131 AN74
Gladwell Rd. N8 121 DM58
Gladwell Rd., Brom. 184 EG93
Gladwyn Rd. SW15 159 CX83
Gladys Rd. NW6 140 DA66
Glaisyer Way, Iver 133 BC68
Glamis Clo. (Cheshunt), Wal.Cr. 66 DU29
Glamis Cres., Hayes 155 BQ76
Glamis Dr., Horn. 128 FL60
Glamis Pl. E1 142 DW73
Glamis Rd. E1 142 DW73
Glamis Way, Nthlt. 136 CC65
Glamorgan Clo., Mitch. 201 DL97
Glamorgan Rd., Kings.T. 177 CJ94
Glanfield, Hem.H. 40 BL17
Bathurst Rd.
Glanfield Rd., Beck. 203 DZ98
Glanleam Rd., Stan. 95 CK49
Glanmead, Brwd. 108 FY46
Glanmor Rd., Slou. 132 AV73
Glanthams Clo., Brwd. 109 FZ47
Glanthams Rd., Brwd. 109 FZ47
Glanty, The, Egh. 173 BB91
Glanville Dr., Horn. 128 FM60
Glanville Rd. SW2 181 DL85
Glanville Rd., Brom. 204 EH97
Glasbrook Ave., Twick. 176 BZ88
Glasbrook Rd. SE9 184 EK87
Glaserton Rd. N16 122 DS59
Glasford St. SW17 180 DF93
Glasgow Ho. W9 140 DB68
Glasgow Rd. E13 144 EH68
Glasgow Rd. N18 100 DV50
Aberdeen Rd.
Glasgow Rd., Slou. 131 AN72
Glasgow Ter. SW1 161 DJ78
Glass St. E2 142 DV70
Coventry Rd.
Glass Yd. SE18 165 EN76
Woolwich High St.
Glasse Clo. W13 137 CG73
Glasshill St. SE1 278 G4
Glasshill St. SE1 161 DP75
Glasshouse All. EC4 274 E9
Glasshouse Flds. E1 143 DX73
Glasshouse St. W1 277 L1
Glasshouse St. W1 141 DJ73
Glasshouse Wk. SE11 278 A10
Glasshouse Wk. SE11 161 DL78
Glasshouse Yd. EC1 275 H5
Glasslyn Rd. N8 121 DK57
Glassmill La., Brom. 204 EF96
Glastonbury Ave., Wdf.Grn. 102 EK52
Glastonbury Clo., Orp. 206 EW102
Glastonbury Rd. N9 100 DT46
Glastonbury Rd., Mord. 200 DA101
Glastonbury St. NW6 119 CZ64
Glaucus St. E3 143 EB71
Glazbury Rd. W14 159 CY77
Glazebrook Clo. SE21 182 DR89
Glazebrook Rd., Tedd. 177 CF94
Glean Wk., Hat. 45 CU21
Southdown Rd.
Gleave Clo., St.Alb. 43 CH19
Glebe, The SE3 164 EE83
Glebe, The SW16 181 DK91
Glebe, The, Chis. 205 EQ95
Glebe, The, Horl. 268 DF148
Glebe, The, Kings L. 58 BN29
Glebe, The, Reig. 265 CU141
Glebe, The, Wat. 60 BW33
Glebe, The, West Dr. 154 BM77
Glebe, The, Wor.Pk. 199 CT102
Glebe Ave., Enf. 81 DP41
Glebe Ave., Har. 118 CL55
Glebe Ave., Mitch. 200 DE96
Glebe Ave., Ruis. 135 BV65
Glebe Ave., Uxb. 115 BQ63
Glebe Ave., Wdf.Grn. 102 EG51
Glebe Clo. W4 158 CS78
Glebe St.
Glebe Clo., Ger.Cr. 90 AX52
Glebe Clo., Hat. 46 DF17
Glebe Clo., Hem.H. 40 BL23
Glebe Clo., Lthd. 246 CA126
Glebe Clo., S.Croy. 220 DT111
Glebe Clo., Uxb. 115 BQ63
Glebe Cotts., Guil. 244 BH132
Glebe Cotts., Hat. 46 DF17
Glebe Cotts., Sutt. 218 DB105
Vale Rd.
Glebe Cotts., West. 240 EV123
Glebe Ct. W7 137 CD73
Glebe Ct., Guil. 243 AZ134
Glebe Ct., Mitch. 200 DF97
Glebe Ct., Stan. 95 CJ50
Glebe Rd.
Glebe Cres. NW4 119 CW56
Glebe Cres., Har. 118 CL55
Glebe Gdns., N.Mal. 198 CS101
Glebe Gdns., W.Byf. 212 BK114
Glebe Ho. Dr., Brom. 204 EH102
Glebe Hyrst SE19 182 DT91
Giles Coppice
Glebe Hyrst, S.Croy. 220 DT112
Glebe La., Barn. 79 CU43
Glebe La., Dor. 262 BX143
Glebe La., Har. 118 CL56
Glebe La., Sev. 257 FH126
Glebe Path, Mitch. 200 DE97
Glebe Pl. SW3 160 DE79
Glebe Pl. (Horton Kirby), Dart. 208 FQ98
Glebe Rd. E8 142 DT66
Middleton Rd.
Glebe Rd. N3 98 DC53
Glebe Rd. N8 121 DM56
Glebe Rd. NW10 139 CT65
Glebe Rd. SW13 159 CU82
Glebe Rd., Ash. 231 CK118
Glebe Rd., Brom. 204 EG95
Glebe Rd., Cars. 218 DF107
Glebe Rd., Dag. 147 FB65
Glebe Rd., Dor. 263 CF136
Glebe Rd., Egh. 173 BC93
Glebe Rd., Ger.Cr. 90 AW53
Glebe Rd., Grav. 191 GF88
Glebe Rd., Hayes 135 BT74
Glebe Rd., Hert. 32 DR07
Glebe Rd., Rain. 148 FJ69
Glebe Rd., Red. 235 DH124
Glebe Rd., Stai. 174 BH92
Glebe Rd., Stan. 95 CJ50
Glebe Rd., Sutt. 217 CY109
Glebe Rd., Uxb. 134 BJ68
Glebe Rd., Warl. 237 DX117
Glebe Rd., Wind. 172 AV85
Glebe Side, Twick. 177 CF87
Glebe St. W4 158 CS78
Glebe Ter. E3 143 EA69
Bow Rd.
Glebe Way, Amer. 55 AR36
Glebe Way, Erith 167 FE79
Glebe Way, Felt. 176 CA90
Glebe Way, Horn. 128 FL59
Glebe Way, S.Croy. 220 DT111
Glebe Way, W.Wick. 203 EC103
Glebefield, The, Sev. 256 FF123
Glebeland, Hat. 45 CW18
St. Etheldredas Dr.
Glebeland Gdns., Shep. 195 BQ100
Glebelands, Chig. 104 EV48
Glebelands, Dart. 167 FF84
Glebelands, Esher 215 CF109
Glebelands, Harl. 35 ET12
Glebelands, H.Wyc. 88 AC47
Glebelands, W.Mol. 196 CB99
Glebelands Ave. E18 102 EG54
Glebelands Ave., Ilf. 125 ER59
Glebelands Clo. SE5 162 DS83
Grove Hill Rd.
Glebelands Rd., Felt. 175 BU87
Glebeway, Wdf.Grn. 102 EJ50
Gledhow Gdns. SW5 160 DC77
Gledhow Wd., Tad. 234 DB121
Gledstanes Rd. W14 159 CY78
Gledwood Ave., Hayes 135 BT71
Gledwood Cres., Hayes 135 BT71
Gledwood Dr., Hayes 135 BT71
Gledwood Gdns., Hayes 135 BT71
Gleed Ave. (Bushey), Wat. 95 CD47
Gleeson Dr., Orp. 223 ET106
Glegg Pl. SW15 159 CX84
Glen, The, Add. 211 BF106
Glen, The, Brom. 204 EE96
Glen, The, Croy. 203 DX103
Glen, The, Enf. 81 DP42
Glen, The, Hem.H. 40 BM15
Glen, The, Nthwd. 93 BR52
Glen, The, Orp. 205 EM104
Glen, The, Pnr. 116 BY59
Glen, The (Eastcote), Pnr. 115 BV57
Glen, The, Rain. 148 FJ70
Glen, The, Slou. 152 AW77
Glen, The, Sthl. 156 BZ78
Glen, The, Wem. 117 CK63
Glen Albyn Rd. SW19 179 CX89
Glen Ave., Ashf. 174 BN91
Glen Clo., Shep. 194 BN98
Glen Clo., Tad. 233 CY123
Glen Cres., Wdf.Grn. 102 EH51
Glen Faba Rd., Harl. 50 EF17
Glen Gdns., Croy. 201 DN104
Glen Ri., Wdf.Grn. 102 EH51
Glen Rd. E13 144 EJ70
Glen Rd. E17 123 DZ57
Glen Rd., Chess. 198 CL104
Glen Rd. End, Wall. 219 DH109
Glen Ter. E14 163 EC75
Manchester Rd.
Glen Vw., Grav. 191 GJ88
Glen Wk., Islw. 177 CD85
Glen Way, Wat. 75 BS38
Glena Mt., Sutt. 218 DC105
Glenaffric Ave. E14 163 ED77
Glenalla Rd., Ruis. 115 BT59
Glenalmond Rd., Har. 118 CL56
Glenalvon Way SE18 164 EL77
Glenarm Rd. E5 122 DW64
Glenavon Clo., Esher 215 CG107
Glenavon Gdns., Slou. 152 AW77
Glenavon Rd. E15 144 EE66
Glenbarr Clo. SE9 165 EP83
Dumbreck Rd.
Glenbow Rd., Brom. 184 EE93
Glenbrook N., Enf. 81 DM42
Glenbrook Rd. NW6 120 DA64
Glenbrook S., Enf. 81 DM42
Glenbuck Ct., Surb. 197 CK100
Glenbuck Rd.
Glenbuck Rd., Surb. 197 CK100
Glenburnie Rd. SW17 180 DF90
Glencairn Dr. W5 137 CJ70
Glencairn Rd. SW16 181 DL94
Glencairne Clo. E16 144 EK71
Glencoe Ave., Ilf. 125 ER59
Glencoe Dr., Dag. 126 FA63
Glencoe Rd., Hayes 136 BX71
Glencoe Rd. (Bushey), Wat. 76 CA44
Glencoe Rd., Wey. 194 BN104
Glencorse Grn., Wat. 94 BX49
Caldwell Rd.
Glendale, Hem.H. 40 BH20
Glendale, Swan. 207 FF99
Glendale Ave. N22 99 DN52
Glendale Ave., Edg. 96 CM49
Glendale Ave., Rom. 126 EW59
Glendale Clo. SE9 165 EN83
Dumbreck Rd.
Glendale Clo., Brwd. 108 FY46
Glendale Clo., Wok. 226 AW118
Glendale Dr. SW19 179 CZ92
Glendale Dr., Guil. 243 BC131
Glendale Gdns., Wem. 117 CK60
Glendale Ms., Beck. 203 EB95
Glendale Ri., Ken. 235 DP115
Glendale Rd., Erith 167 FC77
Glendale Rd., Grav. 190 GE91
Glendale Wk. (Cheshunt), Wal.Cr. 67 DY30
Glendale Way SE28 146 EW73
Glendall St. SW9 161 DM84
Glendarvon St. SW15 159 CX83
Glendene Ave., Lthd. 245 BS126
Glendevon Clo., Edg. 96 CP48
Tayside Dr.
Glendish Rd. N17 100 DV53
Glendor Gdns. NW7 96 CR49
Glendower Cres., Orp. 206 EU100
Glendower Gdns. SW14 158 CR83
Glendower Rd.
Glendower Pl. SW7 160 DD77
Glendower Rd. E4 101 ED46
Glendower Rd. SW14 158 CR83
Glendown Rd. SE2 166 EU78
Glendun Rd. W3 138 CS73
Gleneagle Ms. SW16 181 DK92
Ambleside Ave.
Gleneagle Rd. SW16 181 DK92
Gleneagles, Stan. 95 CH51
Gleneagles Clo. SE16 162 DV78
Ryder Dr.
Gleneagles Clo., Orp. 205 ER102
Gleneagles Clo., Rom. 106 FM52
Gleneagles Clo., Stai. 174 BK86
Gleneagles Clo., Wat. 94 BX49
Gleneagles Grn., Orp. 205 ER102
Tandridge Dr.
Gleneagles Twr., Sthl. 136 CC72
Gleneldon Ms. SW16 181 DL91
Gleneldon Rd. SW16 181 DL91
Glenelg Rd. SW2 181 DL85
Glenesk Rd. SE9 165 EN83
Glenester Clo., Hodd. 33 EA14
Glenfarg Rd. SE6 183 ED88
Glenferrie Rd., St.Alb. 43 CG20
Glenfield Clo., Bet. 264 CP138
Glenfield Cres., Ruis. 115 BR59
Glenfield Rd. SW12 181 DJ88
Glenfield Rd. W13 157 CH75
Glenfield Rd., Ashf. 175 BP93
Glenfield Rd., Bans. 234 DB115
Glenfield Rd., Bet. 264 CP138
Glenfield Ter. W13 157 CH75
Glenfinlas Way SE5 161 DP80
Glenforth St. SE10 164 EF78
Glengall Causeway E14 163 EA76
Glengall Gro. E14 163 EC76
Glengall Rd. NW6 139 CZ67
Glengall Rd. SE15 162 DT79
Glengall Rd., Bexh. 166 EY83
Glengall Rd., Edg. 96 CP48
Glengall Rd., Wdf.Grn. 102 EG51

Glengall Ter. SE15 162 DT79
Glengarnock Ave. E14 163 EC77
Glengarry Rd. SE22 182 DS85
Glenham Dr., Ilf. 125 EP57
Glenhaven Ave., Borwd. 78 CN41
Glenhead Clo. SE9 165 EP83
Dumbreck Rd.
Glenheadon Clo., Lthd. 231 CK123
Glenheadon Ri.
Glenheadon Ri., Lthd. 231 CK123
Glenhill Clo. N3 98 DA54
Glenhouse Rd. SE9 185 EN85
Glenhurst Ave. NW5 120 DG63
Glenhurst Ave., Bex. 186 EZ88
Glenhurst Ave., Ruis. 115 BQ59
Glenhurst Ct. SE19 182 DT92
Glenhurst Ri. SE19 182 DQ94
Glenhurst Rd. N12 98 DD50
Glenhurst Rd., Brent. 157 CJ79
Glenilla Rd. NW3 140 DE65
Glenister Ho., Hayes 135 BV74
Glenister Pk. Rd. SW16 181 DK94
Glenister Rd. SE10 164 EF78
Glenister Rd., Chesh. 54 AQ28
Glenister St. E16 145 EN74
Glenlea Rd. SE9 185 EM85
Glenlion Ct., Wey. 195 BR104
Glenloch Rd. NW3 140 DE65
Glenloch Rd., Enf. 82 DW40
Glenluce Rd. SE3 164 EG79
Glenlyn Ave., St.Alb. 43 CH21
Glenlyon Rd. SE9 185 EN85
Glenmere Ave. NW7 97 CU52
Glenmill, Hmptn. 176 BZ92
Glenmire Ter., Ware 33 ED11
Glenmore Clo., Add. 194 BH104
Glenmore Gdns., Abb.L. 59 BU32
Stewart Clo.
Glenmore Rd. NW3 140 DE65
Glenmore Rd., Well. 165 ET81
Glenmore Way, Bark. 146 EU68
Glenmount Path SE18 165 EQ78
Raglan Rd.
Glenn Ave., Pur. 219 DP111
Glennie Rd. SE27 181 DN90
Glenny Rd., Bark. 145 EQ65
Glenorchy Clo., Hayes 136 BY71
Glenparke Rd. E7 144 EH65
Glenrosa Gdns., Grav. 191 GM92
Glenrosa St. SW6 160 DC82
Glenrose Ct., Sid. 186 EV92
Glenroy St. W12 139 CW72
Glensdale Rd. SE4 163 DZ83
Glenshee Clo., Nthwd. 93 BQ51
Rickmansworth Rd.
Glenshiel Rd. SE9 185 EN85
Glenside, Chig. 103 EP51
Glenside Cotts., Slou. 152 AT76
Upton Pk.
Glentanner Way SW17 180 DD90
Aboyne Rd.
Glentham Gdns. SW13 159 CV79
Glentham Rd.
Glentham Rd. SW13 159 CU79
Glenthorne Ave., Croy. 202 DV102
Glenthorne Clo., Sutt. 200 DA102
Glenthorne Clo., Uxb. 134 BN69
Uxbridge Rd.
Glenthorne Gdns., Ilf. 125 EN55
Glenthorne Gdns., Sutt. 200 DA102
Glenthorne Ms. W6 159 CV77
Glenthorne Rd.
Glenthorne Rd. E17 123 DY57
Glenthorne Rd. N11 98 DF50
Glenthorne Rd. W6 159 CW77
Glenthorne Rd., Kings.T. 198 CM98
Glenthorpe Rd., Mord. 199 CX99
Glenton Clo., Rom. 105 FE51
Glenton Rd. SE13 164 EE84
Glenton Way, Rom. 105 FE52
Glentrammon Ave., Orp. 223 ET107
Glentrammon Clo., Orp. 223 ET107
Glentrammon Gdns., Orp. 223 ET107
Glentrammon Rd., Orp. 223 ET107
Glentworth Pl., Slou. 131 AQ74
Glentworth St. NW1 272 E5
Glentworth St. NW1 140 DF70
Glenure Rd. SE9 185 EN85
Glenview SE2 166 EX79
Glenview Gdns., Hem.H. 40 BH20
Glenview Rd.
Glenview Rd., Brom. 204 EK96
Glenview Rd., Hem.H. 40 BH20
Glenville Ave., Enf. 82 DQ38
Glenville Gro. SE8 163 DZ80
Glenville Ms. SW18 180 DB87
Glenville Rd., Kings.T. 198 CN95
Glenwood, Brox. 49 DZ19
Glenwood, Dor. 263 CJ138
Glenwood, Welw.G.C. 30 DD10
Glenwood Ave. NW9 118 CS60
Glenwood Ave., Rain. 147 FH70
Glenwood Clo., Har. 117 CF57
Glenwood Dr., Rom. 127 FG56
Glenwood Gdns., Ilf. 125 EN57
Glenwood Gro. NW9 118 CQ60
Glenwood Rd. N15 121 DP57
Glenwood Rd. NW7 96 CS48
Glenwood Rd. SE6 183 DZ88
Glenwood Rd., Epsom 217 CU107
Glenwood Rd., Houns. 157 CD83
Glenwood Way, Croy. 203 DX100
Glenworth Ave. E14 163 ED77
Glevum Clo., St.Alb. 42 BZ22
Gliddon Rd. W14 159 CY77
Glimpsing Grn., Erith 166 EY76
Glisson Rd., Uxb. 134 BN68
Gload Cres., Orp. 206 EX103
Global App. E3 143 EB68
Hancock Rd.
Globe Ct., Hert. 32 DQ07
Grove Wk.
Globe Ind. Estates, Grays 170 GC78
Globe Pond Rd. SE16 143 DY74
Globe Rd. E1 142 DW69
Globe Rd. E2 142 DW69
Globe Rd. E15 124 EF64
Globe Rd., Horn. 127 FG58
Globe Rd., Wdf.Grn. 102 EJ51
Globe Rope Wk. E14 163 EC77
Globe St. SE1 279 J6
Globe St. SE1 162 DR76
Globe Ter. E2 142 DW69
Globe Rd.
Globe Yd. W1 273 H9
Glory Clo., H.Wyc. 110 AF56
Glory Hill La., Beac. 110 AF55
Glory Mead, Dor. 263 CH139
Glory Mill La., H.Wyc. 110 AE56
Glossop Rd., S.Croy. 220 DR109
Gloster Rd., N.Mal. 198 CS98
Gloster Rd., Wok. 227 BA121
Gloucester Arc. SW7 160 DC77
Gloucester Rd.
Gloucester Ave. NW1 140 DG66
Gloucester Ave., Grays 170 GC75
Gloucester Ave., Horn. 128 FN56
Gloucester Ave., Sid. 185 ES89
Gloucester Ave., Slou. 131 AQ71
Gloucester Ave., Wal.Cr. 67 DY33
Gloucester Ave., Well. 165 ET84
Gloucester Circ. SE10 163 EC80
Gloucester Clo. NW10 138 CR66
Gloucester Clo., S.Ock. 149 FW69
South Rd.
Gloucester Clo., T.Ditt. 197 CG102
Gloucester Ct. EC3 279 N1
Gloucester Ct., Rich. 158 CN80
Gloucester Ct., Til. 171 GF82
Dock Rd.
Gloucester Ct. (Denham), Uxb. 114 BG58
Moorfield Rd.
Gloucester Cres. NW1 141 DH67
Gloucester Cres., Stai. 174 BK93
Gloucester Dr. N4 121 DP61
Gloucester Dr. NW11 120 DA56
Gloucester Dr., Stai. 173 BC90
Gloucester Gdns. NW11 119 CZ59
Gloucester Gdns. W2 140 DC72
Bishops Bri. Rd.
Gloucester Gdns., Barn. 80 DG42
Gloucester Gdns., Ilf. 124 EL59
Gloucester Gdns., Sutt. 200 DB103
Gloucester Gate NW1 141 DH68
Gloucester Gate Ms. NW1 141 DH68
Gloucester Gate
Gloucester Gro., Edg. 96 CR53
Gloucester Gro. Est. SE15 162 DS79
Gloucester Ho. N7 121 DL62
Gloucester Ho. NW6 140 DA68
Gloucester Ms. E10 123 EA59
Gloucester Rd.
Gloucester Ms. W2 140 DC72
Gloucester Ms. W. W2 140 DC72
Cleveland Ter.
Gloucester Par., Sid. 186 EU85
Gloucester Pl. NW1 272 D4
Gloucester Pl. NW1 140 DF70
Gloucester Pl. W1 272 E6
Gloucester Pl. W1 140 DF71
Gloucester Pl., Wind. 151 AR82
Gloucester Pl. Ms. W1 272 E7
Gloucester Rd. E10 123 EA59
Gloucester Rd. E11 124 EH57
Gloucester Rd. E12 125 EM62
Gloucester Rd. E17 101 DX54
Gloucester Rd. N17 100 DR54
Gloucester Rd. N18 100 DT50
Gloucester Rd. SW7 160 DC77
Gloucester Rd. W3 158 CQ75
Gloucester Rd. W5 157 CJ75
Gloucester Rd., Barn. 80 DC43
Gloucester Rd., Belv. 166 EZ78
Gloucester Rd., Brwd. 108 FV43
Gloucester Rd., Croy. 202 DR100
Gloucester Rd., Dart. 187 FH87
Gloucester Rd., Enf. 82 DQ38
Gloucester Rd., Felt. 176 BW88
Gloucester Rd., Grav. 191 GJ91
Gloucester Rd., Guil. 242 AT132
Gloucester Rd., Hmptn. 176 CB94
Gloucester Rd., Har. 116 CB57
Gloucester Rd., Houns. 156 BY84
Gloucester Rd., Kings.T. 198 CP96
Gloucester Rd., Red. 250 DF133
Gloucester Rd., Rich. 158 CN80
Gloucester Rd., Rom. 127 FE58
Gloucester Rd., Tedd. 177 CE92
Gloucester Rd., Twick. 176 CC88
Gloucester Sq. E2 142 DU67
Whiston Rd.
Gloucester Sq. W2 272 A9
Gloucester Sq. W2 140 DD72
Gloucester Sq., Wok. 226 AY117
Church St. E.
Gloucester St. SW1 161 DJ78
Gloucester Ter. W2 140 DD73
Gloucester Wk. W8 160 DA75
Gloucester Wk., Wok. 227 AZ117
Church St. E.
Gloucester Way EC1 274 E3
Gloucester Way EC1 141 DN69
Glover Clo. SE2 166 EW77
Glover Clo., Wal.Cr. 66 DT27
Allwood Rd.
Glover Dr. N18 100 DW51
Glover Rd., Pnr. 116 BX58
Glovers Clo., Hert. 32 DQ11
Glovers Gro., Ruis. 115 BP59
Glovers La., Harl. 52 EY20
Glovers Rd., Reig. 266 DB135
Gloxinia Rd., Grav. 190 GB93
Gloxinia Wk., Hmptn. 176 CA93
The Ave.
Glycena Rd. SW11 160 DF83
Glyn Ave., Barn. 80 DD42
Glyn Clo. SE25 202 DS96
Glyn Clo., Epsom 217 CU109
Glyn Ct. SW16 181 DN90
Glyn Davies Clo., Sev. 241 FE120
Glyn Dr., Sid. 186 EV91
Glyn Rd. E5 123 DX63
Glyn Rd., Enf. 82 DW42
Glyn Rd., Wor.Pk. 199 CX103
Glyn St. SE11 161 DM78
Kennington La.
Glynde Ms. SW3 276 C7
Glynde Rd., Bexh. 166 EX83
Glynde St. SE4 183 DZ86
Glyndebourne Pk., Orp. 205 EP103
Glyndon Rd. SE18 165 EQ77
Glynfield Rd. NW10 138 CS66
Glynne Rd. N22 99 DN54
Glynswood, Ger.Cr. 91 AZ52
Glynwood Ct. SE23 182 DW89
Goat La., Enf. 82 DT38
Goat La., Surb. 197 CH103
Goat Rd., Mitch. 200 DG101
Goat St. SE1 279 P4
Goat Wf., Brent. 158 CL79
Goaters All. SW6 159 CZ80
Goatsfield Rd., West. 238 EJ120
Goatswood La., Rom. 105 FH45
Gobions Ave., Rom. 105 FD52
Gobions Way, Pot.B. 64 DB28
Swanley Bar La.
Goblins Grn., Welw.G.C. 29 CX10
Godalming Ave., Wall. 219 DL106
Godalming Rd. E14 143 EB71
Godbold Rd. E15 144 EE69
Goddard Clo., Shep. 194 BM97
Magdalene Rd.
Goddard Rd., Beck. 203 DX98
Goddards Clo., Hert. 47 DJ19
Goddards Way, Ilf. 125 ER60
Goddington Chase, Orp. 224 EV105
Goddington La., Orp. 206 EU104
Godfrey Ave., Nthlt. 136 BY67
Godfrey Ave., Twick. 177 CD87
Godfrey Hill SE18 164 EL77
Godfrey Rd. SE18 165 EM77
Godfrey St. E15 143 EC68
Godfrey St. SW3 276 C10
Godfrey St. SW3 160 DE78
Godfrey Way, Houns. 176 BZ87
Goding St. SE11 161 DL78
Godley Rd. SW18 180 DD88
Godley Rd., W.Byf. 212 BM114
Godliman St. EC4 275 H9
Godliman St. EC4 142 DQ72
Godman Rd. SE15 162 DV82
Godman Rd., Grays 171 GG76
Godolphin Clo. N13 99 DP51
Godolphin Clo., Sutt. 217 CZ111
Godolphin Pl. W3 138 CR73
Vyner Rd.
Godolphin Rd. W12 159 CV75
Godolphin Rd., Beac. 89 AQ51
Godolphin Rd., Slou. 131 AR73
Godolphin Rd., Wey. 213 BR107
Godric Cres., Croy. 221 ED110
Godson Rd., Croy. 201 DN104
Godson St. N1 141 DN68
Godstone Bypass, Gdse. 252 DW129
Godstone Grn., Gdse. 252 DV131
Godstone Grn. Rd., Gdse. 252 DV131
Godstone Hill, Gdse. 252 DV127
Godstone Rd., Cat. 236 DU124
Godstone Rd., Ken. 219 DN112
Godstone Rd., Oxt. 253 EA131
Godstone Rd., Pur. 219 DN112
Godstone Rd., Red. 252 DR133
Godstone Rd., Sutt. 218 DC105
Godstone Rd., Twick. 177 CG86
Godstone Rd., Whyt. 236 DT116
Godstow Rd. SE2 166 EW75
Godwin Clo. E4 83 EC38
Godwin Clo. N1 142 DQ68
Napier Gro.
Godwin Clo., Epsom 216 CQ107
Godwin Ct. NW1 141 DJ68
Crowndale Rd.
Godwin Rd. E7 124 EH63
Godwin Rd., Brom. 204 EJ97
Goffers Rd. SE3 163 ED81
Goffs Cres. (Cheshunt), Wal.Cr. 65 DP29
Goffs La. (Cheshunt), Wal.Cr. 66 DR29
Goffs Oak Ave. (Cheshunt), Wal.Cr. 65 DP28
Goffs Rd., Ashf. 175 BR93
Gogmore Fm. Clo., Cher. 193 BF101
Gogmore La., Cher. 193 BF101
Goidel Clo., Wall. 219 DK105
Golborne Gdns. W10 139 CZ70
Golborne Rd.
Golborne Ms. W10 139 CY71
Portobello Rd.
Golborne Rd. W10 139 CY71
Gold Clo., Brox. 49 DY20
Gold Hill, Edg. 96 CR51
Gold Hill E., Ger.Cr. 90 AX54
Gold Hill N., Ger.Cr. 90 AW53
Gold Hill W., Ger.Cr. 90 AW54
Gold La., Edg. 96 CR51
Golda Clo., Barn. 79 CX44
Goldace, Grays 170 FZ79
Goldbeaters Gro., Edg. 96 CS51
Goldcliff Clo., Mord. 200 DA100
Goldcrest Clo. E16 144 EK71
Sheerwater Rd.
Goldcrest Clo. SE28 146 EW73
Goldcrest Clo., Horl. 268 DE147
Wither Dale
Goldcrest Ms. W5 137 CK71
Montpelier Ave.
Goldcrest Way, Croy. 221 ED109
Goldcrest Way, Pur. 219 DK110
Goldcrest Way (Bushey), Wat. 94 CC46
Goldcroft, Hem.H. 40 BN22
Golden Ct., Rich. 177 CK85
George St.
Golden Cres., Hayes 135 BT74
Golden Cross Ms. W11 139 CZ72
Basing St.
Golden Dell, Welw.G.C. 29 CZ13
Golden La. EC1 275 H5
Golden La. EC1 142 DQ70
Golden La. Est. EC1 275 H5
Golden Manor W7 137 CE73
Golden Oak Clo., Slou. 131 AQ65
Golden Plover Clo. E16 144 EH72
Maplin Rd.
Golden Sq. W1 273 L10
Golden Sq. W1 141 DJ73
Golden Yd. NW3 120 DC63
Heath St.
Golders Clo., Edg. 96 CP50
Golders Gdns. NW11 119 CY59
Golders Grn. Cres. NW11 119 CZ59
Golders Grn. Rd. NW11 119 CY58
Golders Manor Dr. NW11 119 CX58
Golders Pk. Clo. NW11 120 DB60
Golders Ri. NW4 119 CX57
Golders Way NW11 119 CZ59
Goldfinch Clo., Orp. 224 EU106
Goldfinch Gdns., Guil. 243 BD133
Goldfinch Rd. SE28 165 ER76
Goldfinch Rd., S.Croy. 221 DY110
Goldfinch Way, Borwd. 78 CN42
Goldfort Wk., Wok. 226 AS116
Langmans Way
Goldhawk Ms. W12 159 CV75
Devonport Rd.
Goldhawk Rd. W6 159 CT77
Goldhawk Rd. W12 159 CU76
Goldhaze Clo., Wdf.Grn. 102 EK52
Goldhurst Ter. NW6 140 DB66
Golding Clo., Chess. 215 CJ107
Coppard Gdns.
Golding Rd., Sev. 257 FJ122
Golding St. E1 142 DU72
Golding Ter. SW11 160 DG82
Longhedge St.
Goldingham Ave., Loug. 85 EQ40
Goldings, The, Wok. 226 AT116
Goldings Cres., Hat. 45 CV17
Goldings Hill, Loug. 85 EN39
Goldings La., Hert. 31 DN06
Goldings Ri., Loug. 85 EN39
Goldings Rd., Loug. 85 EN39
Goldington Clo., Hodd. 33 DZ14
Goldington Cres. NW1 141 DK68
Goldington St. NW1 141 DK68
Goldman Clo. E2 142 DU70
Goldney Rd. W9 140 DA70
Goldrill Dr. N11 98 DG47
Goldrings Rd., Lthd. 214 CB113
Goldsboro Rd. SW8 161 DK81
Goldsborough Cres. E4 101 EB47
Goldsdown Clo., Enf. 83 DY40
Goldsdown Rd., Enf. 83 DX40
Goldsel Rd., Swan. 207 FD99
Goldsel Rd. Ind. Est., Swan. 207 FE98
Goldsmid St. SE18 165 ES78
Sladedale Rd.
Goldsmith, Grays 170 FZ79
Goldsmith Ave. E12 144 EL65
Goldsmith Ave. NW9 119 CT58
Goldsmith Ave. W3 138 CR73
Goldsmith Ave., Rom. 126 FA59
Goldsmith Clo. W3 138 CS74
East Acton La.
Goldsmith Clo., Har. 116 CB60
Goldsmith La. NW9 118 CP56
Goldsmith Rd. E10 123 EA60
Goldsmith Rd. E17 101 DX54
Goldsmith Rd. N11 98 DF50
Goldsmith Rd. SE15 162 DU81
Goldsmith Rd. W3 138 CR74
Goldsmith St. EC2 275 J8
Goldsmiths Clo., Wok. 226 AW118
Goldsmith's Row E2 142 DU68
Goldsmith's Sq. E2 142 DU68
Goldstone Clo., Ware 33 DX05
High Oak Rd.
Goldstone Fm. Vw., Lthd. 246 CA127
Goldsworth Orchard, Wok. 226 AU118
St. John's Rd.
Goldsworth Pk. Trd. Est., Wok. 226 AU116
Goldsworth Rd., Wok. 226 AW118
Goldsworthy Gdns. SE16 162 DW77
Goldsworthy Way, Slou. 130 AJ72
Goldwell Rd., Th.Hth. 201 DM98
Goldwin Clo. SE14 162 DW81
Goldwing Clo. E16 144 EG72
Golf Clo., Stan. 95 CJ52
Golf Clo., Th.Hth. 201 DN95
Kensington Ave.
Golf Clo. (Bushey), Wat. 76 BX41
Golf Clo., Wok. 211 BE114
Golf Club Dr., Kings.T. 178 CR94
Golf Club Rd., Hat. 64 DA26
Golf Club Rd., Wey. 213 BP109
Golf Club Rd., Wok. 226 AU120
Golf Ho. Rd., Oxt. 254 EJ129
Golf Links Ave., Grav. 191 GH92
Golf Ride, Enf. 81 DN35
Golf Rd. W5 138 CM72
Boileau Rd.
Golf Rd., Brom. 205 EN97
Golf Rd., Ken. 236 DR118
Golf Side, Sutt. 217 CY111
Golf Side, Twick. 177 CD90
Golfe Rd., Ilf. 125 ER62
Golfside Clo. N20 98 DE48
Golfside Clo., N.Mal. 198 CS96
Goliath Clo., Wall. 219 DL108
Gollogly Ter. SE7 164 EJ78
Gombards, St.Alb. 43 CD19
Gombards All., St.Alb. 43 CD20
Worley Rd.
Gomer Gdns., Tedd. 177 CG93
Gomer Pl., Tedd. 177 CG93
Gomm Rd. SE16 162 DW76
Gomms Wd. Clo., Beac. 88 AH51
Gomshall Ave., Wall. 219 DL106
Gomshall Gdns., Ken. 236 DS115
Gomshall La., Guil. 260 BN139
Gomshall Rd., Guil. 261 BQ138
Gomshall Rd., Sutt. 217 CW110
Gondar Gdns. NW6 119 CZ64
Gonnerston, St.Alb. 42 CC19
Kings Rd.
Gonson Pl. SE8 163 EA79
Gonson St. SE8 163 EB79
Gonston Clo. SW19 179 CY89
Boddicott Clo.
Gonville Ave., Rick. 75 BP44
Gonville Cres., Nthlt. 136 CB65
Gonville Rd., Th.Hth. 201 DM99
Gonville St. SW6 159 CY83
Putney Bri. App.
Goodall Rd. E11 123 EC62
Gooden Ct., Har. 117 CE62
Goodenough Clo., Couls. 235 DN120
Goodenough Rd. SW19 179 CZ94
Goodenough Way, Couls. 235 DM120
Gooderham Ho., Grays 171 GH75
Goodge Pl. W1 273 L7
Goodge St. W1 273 L7
Goodge St. W1 141 DJ71
Goodhall St. NW10 138 CS69
Goodhart Pl. E14 143 DY73
Goodhart Way, W.Wick. 204 EE101
Goodhew Rd., Croy. 202 DU100
Gooding Clo., N.Mal. 198 CQ98
Goodinge Clo. N7 141 DL65
Goodlake Ct., Uxb. 113 BF59
Goodley Stock Rd., Eden. 255 EP131
Goodley Stock Rd., West. 255 EP128
Goodman Cres. SW2 181 DK89
Goodman Pk., Slou. 132 AW74
Goodman Pl., Stai. 173 BF91
High St.
Goodman Rd. E10 123 EC59
Goodmans Ct., Wem. 117 CK63
Goodman's Stile E1 142 DU72
Goodmans Yd. E1 275 P10
Goodmans Yd. E1 142 DT73
Goodmayes Ave., Ilf. 126 EU60
Goodmayes La., Ilf. 126 EU63
Goodmayes Rd., Ilf. 126 EU60
Goodmead Rd., Orp. 206 EU101
Goodrich Clo., Wat. 75 BU35
Goodrich Rd. SE22 182 DT86
Goods Way NW1 141 DL68
Goodson Rd. NW10 138 CS66
Goodway Gdns. E14 143 ED72
Goodwin Ave., Brwd. 109 GE44
Goodwin Clo. SE16 162 DU76
Goodwin Clo., Mitch. 200 DD97
Goodwin Ct., Wal.Cr. 67 DY28
Goodwin Dr., Sid. 186 EX90
Goodwin Gdns., Croy. 219 DP107
Goodwin Meadows, H.Wyc. 110 AE57
Goodwin Rd. N9 100 DW46
Goodwin Rd. W12 159 CU75
Goodwin Rd., Croy. 219 DP106
Goodwin Rd., Slou. 131 AM69
Goodwin St. N4 121 DN61
Fonthill Rd.
Goodwins Ct. WC2 273 P10
Goodwood Ave., Enf. 82 DW37
Goodwood Ave., Horn. 128 FL63
Goodwood Ave., Wat. 75 BS35
Goodwood Clo., Hodd. 49 EA16
Goodwood Clo., Mord. 200 DA98
Goodwood Clo., Stan. 95 CJ50
Goodwood Cres., Grav. 191 GJ92
Goodwood Dr., Nthlt. 136 CA65
Goodwood Path, Borwd. 78 CN41
Stratfield Rd.
Goodwood Rd. SE14 163 DY80
Goodwood Rd., Red. 250 DF132
Goodwyn Ave. NW7 96 CS50
Goodwyns Pl., Dor. 263 CH139
Goodwyns Vale N10 98 DG53
Goodyers Ave., Rad. 61 CF33
Goodyers Gdns. NW4 119 CX57
Goosander Way SE28 165 ER76
Goose Acre, Chesh. 56 AT30
Goose Grn., Cob. 229 BU119
Goose Grn., Guil. 261 BQ139
Goose Grn., Hodd. 49 DY17
Lord St.
Goose Grn., Slou. 131 AP68
Goose Grn. Clo., Orp. 206 EU96
Goose La., Wok. 226 AV122
Goose Rye Rd., Guil. 242 AT125
Goose Sq. E6 145 EM72
Harper Rd.
Gooseacre, Welw.G.C. 29 CZ11
Gooseacre La., Har. 117 CK57
Goosecroft, Hem.H. 39 BF19
Goosefields, Rick. 74 BJ44
Gooseley La. E6 145 EN69
Goosens Clo., Sutt. 218 DC106
Turnpike La.
Gooshays Dr., Rom. 106 FL50
Gooshays Gdns., Rom. 106 FL51
Gophir La. EC4 275 K10
Gopsall St. N1 142 DR67
Goral Mead, Rick. 92 BK46
Gordon Ave. E4 102 EE51
Gordon Ave. SW14 158 CS84
Gordon Ave., Horn. 127 FF61
Gordon Ave., S.Croy. 220 DQ110
Gordon Ave., Stan. 95 CH51
Gordon Ave., Twick. 177 CG85
Gordon Clo. E17 123 EA58
Gordon Clo. N19 121 DJ60
Highgate Hill
Gordon Clo., Cher. 193 BE104
Gordon Clo., St.Alb. 43 CH21
Kitchener Clo.
Gordon Clo., Stai. 174 BH93
Gordon Ct. W12 139 CW72
Gordon Cres., Croy. 202 DS102
Gordon Cres., Hayes 155 BU76
Gordon Dr., Cher. 193 BE104
Gordon Dr., Shep. 195 BR100
Gordon Gdns., Edg. 96 CP54
Gordon Gro. SE5 161 DP82
Gordon Hill, Enf. 82 DQ39
Gordon Ho. Rd. NW5 120 DG63
Gordon Pl. W8 160 DA75
Gordon Pl., Grav. 191 GJ86
East Ter.
Gordon Prom., Grav. 191 GJ86
Gordon Prom. E., Grav. 191 GJ86
Gordon Rd. E4 102 EE45
Gordon Rd. E11 124 EG58
Gordon Rd. E15 123 EC63
Gordon Rd. E18 102 EH53
Gordon Rd. N3 97 CZ52
Gordon Rd. N9 100 DV47
Gordon Rd. N11 99 DK52
Gordon Rd. SE15 162 DV82
Gordon Rd. W4 158 CP79
Gordon Rd. W5 137 CJ73
Gordon Rd. W13 137 CH73
Gordon Rd., Ashf. 174 BL90
Gordon Rd., Bark. 145 ES67
Gordon Rd., Beck. 203 DZ97
Gordon Rd., Belv. 167 FC77
Gordon Rd., Brwd. 109 GA46
Gordon Rd., Cars. 218 DF107
Gordon Rd., Cat. 236 DR121
Gordon Rd., Chesh. 54 AQ32
Gordon Rd., Dart. 188 FK87
Gordon Rd., Enf. 82 DQ39
Gordon Rd., Esher 215 CE108
Gordon Rd., Grav. 190 GE87
Gordon Rd., Grays 171 GF75
Gordon Rd., Har. 117 CE55
Gordon Rd., Houns. 156 CC84
Gordon Rd., Ilf. 125 ER62
Gordon Rd., Kings.T. 198 CM95
Gordon Rd., Red. 250 DG131
Gordon Rd., Rich. 158 CM82
Gordon Rd., Rom. 126 EZ58
Gordon Rd., Sev. 257 FH125
Gordon Rd., Shep. 195 BR100
Gordon Rd., Sid. 185 ES85
Gordon Rd., Sthl. 156 BY77
Gordon Rd., Stai. 173 BC91
Gordon Rd., Surb. 198 CM101
Gordon Rd., Wal.Abb. 67 EA34
Gordon Rd., West Dr. 134 BL73
Gordon Rd., Wind. 151 AM82
Gordon Sq. WC1 273 N5
Gordon Sq. WC1 141 DK70
Gordon St. E13 144 EG69
Grange Rd.
Gordon St. WC1 273 M4
Gordon St. WC1 141 DK70

Gordon Way, Barn. 79 CZ42
Gordon Way, Brom. 204 EG95
Gordon Way, Ch.St.G. 90 AV48
Gordonbrock Rd. SE4 183 EA85
Gordondale Rd. SW19 180 DA89
Gordons Way, Oxt. 253 ED128
Gore Clo. (Harefield), Uxb. 114 BH56
Gore Ct. NW9 118 CN57
Gore Hill, Amer. 55 AP43
Gore Rd. E9 142 DW67
Gore Rd. SW20 199 CW96
Gore Rd., Dart. 188 FQ90
Gore Rd., Slou. 130 AH69
Gore St. SW7 160 DC76
Gorefield Pl. NW6 140 DA68
Gorelands La., Ch.St.G. 90 AX46
Gorell Rd., Beac. 89 AP54
Goresbrook Rd., Dag. 146 EV67
Goresbrook Village, Dag. 146 EV67
Goresbrook Rd.
Gorham Dr., St.Alb. 43 CE23
Gorham Pl. W11 139 CY73
Mary Pl.
Gorhambury Dr., St.Alb. 42 BZ19
Goring Clo., Rom. 105 FC53
Goring Gdns., Dag. 126 EW63
Goring Rd. N11 99 DL51
Goring Rd., Dag. 147 FD65
Goring Rd., Stai. 173 BD92
Goring St. EC3 275 N8
Goring St. EC3 142 DS72
Goring Way, Grnf. 136 CC68
Gorings Sq., Stai. 173 BE91
Gorle Clo., Wat. 59 BU34
Gorleston Rd. N15 122 DR57
Gorleston St. W14 159 CY77
Gorman Rd. SE18 165 EM77
Gorringe Ave. (South Darenth), Dart. 209 FR96
Gorringe Pk. Ave., Mitch. 180 DF94
Gorse Clo. E16 144 EG72
Gorse Clo., Hat. 45 CT21
Gorse Clo., Tad. 233 CV120
Gorse Ct., Guil. 243 BC132
Kingfisher Dr.
Gorse Hill (Farningham), Dart. 208 FN101
Gorse Hill La., Vir.W. 192 AX98
Gorse Hill Rd., Vir.W. 192 AX98
Gorse La., Wok. 210 AS108
Gorse Meade, Slou. 131 AP74
Gorse Ri. SW17 180 DG92
Gorse Rd., Croy. 221 EA105
Gorse Rd., Orp. 206 EZ102
Gorse Wk., West Dr. 134 BL72
Gorselands Clo., W.Byf. 212 BJ111
Gorseway, Rom. 127 FE61
Gorsewood Rd., Wok. 226 AS119
Gorst Rd. NW10 138 CQ70
Gorst Rd. SW11 180 DF86
Gorsuch Pl. E2 275 P2
Gorsuch St. E2 275 P2
Gorsuch St. E2 142 DT69
Gosberton Rd. SW12 180 DG88
Gosbury Hill, Chess. 216 CL105
Gosden Common, Guil. 258 AY143
Gosden Hill Rd., Guil. 243 BC130
Gosfield Rd., Dag. 126 FA61
Gosfield Rd., Epsom 216 CR112
Gosfield St. W1 273 K6
Gosfield St. W1 141 DJ71
Gosford Gdns., Ilf. 125 EM57
Gosforth La., Wat. 94 BW48
Gosforth Path, Wat. 93 BU48
Goshawk Gdns., Hayes 135 BS69
Goslar Way, Wind. 151 AP82
Goslett Yd. WC2 273 N9
Gosling Clo., Grnf. 136 CA69
Gosling Grn., Slou. 152 AY76
Gosling Rd., Slou. 152 AY76
Gosling Way SW9 161 DN81
Gospatrick Rd. N17 100 DQ53
Gospel Oak Est. NW5 120 DF64
Gosport Dr., Horn. 148 FJ65
Gosport Rd. E17 123 DZ57
Gosport Wk. N17 122 DV57
Yarmouth Cres.
Gosport Way SE15 162 DT80
Pentridge St.
Goss Hill, Dart. 188 FJ93
Goss Hill, Swan. 188 FJ93
Gossage Rd. SE18 165 ER78
Ancona Rd.
Gossage Rd., Uxb. 134 BM66
Gossamers, The, Wat. 76 BY36
Gosselin Rd., Hert. 32 DQ07
Gosset St. E2 142 DT69
Gosshill Rd., Chis. 205 EN96
Gossington Clo., Chis. 185 EP91
Beechwood Ri.
Gossoms End, Berk. 38 AU18
Gossoms Ryde, Berk. 38 AU18
Gosterwood St. SE8 163 DY79
Gostling Rd., Twick. 176 CA88
Goston Gdns., Th.Hth. 201 DN97
Goswell Hill, Wind. 151 AR81
Goswell Rd. EC1 275 H5
Goswell Rd. EC1 141 DP69
Goswell Rd., Wind. 151 AR80
Gothic Clo., Dart. 188 FK90
Gothic Ct., Hayes 155 BR79
Sipson La.
Gothic Rd., Twick. 177 CD89
Gottfried Ms. NW5 121 DJ63
Fortess Rd.
Goudhurst Rd., Brom. 184 EE92
Gouge Ave., Grav. 190 GE88
Gough Rd. E15 124 EF63
Gough Rd., Enf. 82 DV40
Gough Sq. EC4 274 E8
Gough Sq. EC4 141 DN72
Gough St. WC1 274 C4
Gough St. WC1 141 DM70
Gough Wk. E14 143 EA72
Saracen St.
Gould Clo., Hat. 45 CV24
Gould Ct. SE19 182 DT92
Gould Ct., Guil. 243 BD132
Eustace Rd.
Gould Rd., Felt. 175 BS87
Gould Rd., Twick. 177 CE88
Gould Ter. E8 122 DV64
Kenmure Rd.
Goulding Gdns., Th.Hth. 201 DP96
Goulds Grn., Uxb. 135 BP72
Goulston St. E1 275 P8
Goulston St. E1 142 DT72
Goulton Rd. E5 122 DV63
Gourley Pl. N15 122 DS57
Gourley St.
Gourley St. N15 122 DS57
Gourock Rd. SE9 185 EN85
Govan St. E2 142 DU67
Whiston Rd.
Government Row, Enf. 83 EA38
Governors Ave., Uxb. 113 BF57
Governors Clo., Amer. 72 AT37
Govett Ave., Shep. 195 BQ99
Govier Clo. E15 144 EE66
Gowan Ave. SW6 159 CY81
Gowan Rd. NW10 139 CV65
Gowar Fld., Pot.B. 63 CU32
Gower, The, Egh. 193 BB97
Gower Clo. SW4 181 DJ86
Gower Ct. WC1 273 M4
Gower Ms. WC1 273 M7
Gower Ms. WC1 141 DK71
Gower Pl. WC1 273 L4
Gower Pl. WC1 141 DJ70
Gower Rd. E7 144 EG65
Gower Rd., Horl. 268 DE148
Gower Rd., Islw. 157 CF79
Gower Rd., Wey. 213 BR107
Gower St. WC1 273 M5
Gower St. WC1 141 DJ70
Gowers, The, Amer. 55 AS36
Gowers, The, Harl. 36 EU13
Gowers La., Grays 171 GF75
Gower's Wk. E1 142 DU72
Gowland Pl., Beck. 203 DZ96
Gowlett Rd. SE15 162 DU83
Gowrie Rd. SW11 160 DG83
Graburn Way, E.Mol. 197 CD97
Grace Ave., Bexh. 166 EZ82
Grace Ave. (Shenley), Rad. 61 CK33
Grace Clo. SE9 184 EK90
Grace Clo., Borwd. 78 CR39
Grace Clo., Edg. 96 CQ52
Pavilion Way
Grace Clo., Ilf. 103 ET51
Grace Ct., Slou. 131 AQ74
Grace Jones Clo. E8 142 DU65
Parkholme Rd.
Grace Path SE26 182 DW91
Silverdale
Grace Pl. E3 143 EB69
St. Leonards St.
Grace Rd., Croy. 202 DQ100
Grace St. E3 143 EB69
Gracechurch St. EC3 275 L10
Gracechurch St. EC3 142 DR73
Gracedale Rd. SW16 181 DH92
Gracefield Gdns. SW16 181 DL90
Grace's All. E1 142 DU73
Graces Ms. SE5 162 DS82
Graces Rd. SE5 162 DS82
Gracious La., Sev. 256 FG130
Gracious La. End, Sev. 256 FF130
Gracious Pond Rd., Wok. 210 AT108
Gradient, The SE26 182 DU91
Graeme Rd., Enf. 82 DR40
Graemesdyke Ave. SW14 158 CP84
Graemesdyke Rd., Berk. 38 AU20
Grafton Clo. W13 137 CG72
Grafton Clo., Houns. 176 BY88
Grafton Clo., Slou. 132 AY72
Grafton Clo., W.Byf. 211 BF113
Madeira Rd.
Grafton Clo., Wor.Pk. 198 CS104
Grafton Ct., Felt. 175 BR88
Loxwood Clo.
Grafton Cres. NW1 141 DH65
Grafton Gdns. N4 122 DQ58
Grafton Gdns., Dag. 126 EY61
Grafton Ho. E3 143 EA69
Grafton Ms. W1 273 K5
Grafton Pk. Rd., Wor.Pk. 198 CS103
Grafton Pl. NW1 273 M3
Grafton Pl. NW1 141 DK69
Grafton Rd. NW5 120 DG64
Grafton Rd. W3 138 CQ73
Grafton Rd., Croy. 201 DN102
Grafton Rd., Dag. 126 EY61
Grafton Rd., Enf. 81 DM41
Grafton Rd., Har. 116 CC57
Grafton Rd., N.Mal. 198 CS97
Grafton Rd., Wor.Pk. 198 CR104
Grafton Sq. SW4 161 DJ83
Grafton St. W1 277 J1
Grafton St. W1 141 DH73
Grafton Ter. NW5 120 DF64
Grafton Way W1 273 K5
Grafton Way W1 141 DJ70
Grafton Way WC1 273 K5
Grafton Way WC1 141 DJ70
Grafton Way, W.Mol. 196 BZ98
Grafton Yd. NW5 141 DH65
Prince of Wales Rd.
Graftons, The NW2 120 DA62
Hermitage La.
Graham Ave. W13 157 CH75
Graham Ave., Brox. 49 DY20
Graham Ave., Mitch. 200 DG95
Graham Clo., Brwd. 109 GC43
Graham Clo., Croy. 203 EA103
Graham Clo., St.Alb. 43 CD22
Graham Gdns., Surb. 198 CL102
Graham Rd. E8 142 DU65
Graham Rd. E13 144 EG70
Graham Rd. N15 121 DP55
Graham Rd. NW4 119 CV58
Graham Rd. SW19 179 CZ94
Graham Rd. W4 158 CR76
Graham Rd., Bexh. 166 FA84
Graham Rd., Hmptn. 176 CA91
Graham Rd., Har. 117 CE55
Graham Rd., Mitch. 200 DG95
Graham Rd., Pur. 219 DN113
Graham St. N1 274 G1
Graham St. N1 141 DP68
Graham Ter. SW1 276 F9
Graham Ter. SW1 160 DG77
Grahame Pk. Est. NW9 97 CT53
Grahame Pk. Way NW7 97 CT52
Grahame Pk. Way NW9 97 CT54
Grainger Clo., Nthlt. 116 CC64
Lancaster Rd.
Grainger Rd. N22 100 DQ53
Grainger Rd., Islw. 157 CF82
Grainge's Yd., Uxb. 134 BJ66
Cross St.
Gramer Clo. E11 123 ED61
Norman Rd.
Grampian Clo., Hayes 155 BR80
Grampian Clo., Orp. 205 ET100
Cotswold Ri.
Grampian Gdns. NW2 119 CY60
Grampian Way, Slou. 153 BA78
Granard Ave. SW15 179 CV85
Granard Rd. SW12 180 DF87
Granaries, The, Wal.Abb. 68 EE34
Granary, The, Harl. 34 EH14
Granary Clo. N9 100 DW45
Turin Rd.
Granary Clo., Horl. 268 DG146
Waterside
Granary Rd. E1 142 DV70
Granary St. NW1 141 DK67
Granby Bldgs. SE11 278 B9
Granby Pk. Rd. (Cheshunt), Wal.Cr. 66 DT28
Granby Rd. SE9 165 EM82
Granby Rd., Grav. 190 GC86
Granby St. E2 142 DT70
Granby Ter. NW1 273 K1
Granby Ter. NW1 141 DJ68
Grand Arc. N12 98 DC50
Ballards La.
Grand Ave. EC1 274 G6
Grand Ave. N10 120 DG56
Grand Ave., Surb. 198 CP99
Grand Ave., Wem. 118 CN64
Grand Ave. E., Wem. 118 CP64
Grand Depot Rd. SE18 165 EN78
Grand Dr. SW20 199 CW96
Grand Dr., Sthl. 156 CC75
Grand Junct. Wf. N1 275 H1
Grand Junct. Wf. N1 142 DQ68
Grand Par. Ms. SW15 179 CY85
Upper Richmond Rd.
Grand Stand Rd., Epsom 233 CT117
Grand Union Canal Wk. W7 157 CE76
Grand Union Clo. W9 139 CZ71
Woodfield Rd.
Grand Union Cres. E8 142 DU66
Grand Union Ind. Est. NW10 138 CP68
Grand Union Wk. NW1 141 DH66
Grand Vw. Ave., West. 238 EJ117
Grand Wk. E1 143 DY70
Solebay St.
Granden Rd. SW16 201 DL96
Grandfield Ave., Wat. 75 BT39
Grandis Cotts., Wok. 228 BH122
Grandison Rd. SW11 180 DF85
Grandison Rd., Wor.Pk. 199 CW103
Granfield St. SW11 160 DD81
Grange, The N2 98 DD54
Central Ave.
Grange, The N20 98 DC46
Grange, The SE1 279 P6
Grange, The SE1 162 DT76
Grange, The SW19 179 CX93
Grange, The, Croy. 203 DZ103
Grange, The, Dart. 209 FR95
Grange, The, Walt. 195 BV103
Grange, The, Wem. 138 CN66
Grange, The, Wind. 172 AV85
Grange, The, Wok. 210 AS110
Grange, The, Wor.Pk. 198 CR104
Grange Ave. N12 98 DC50
Grange Ave. N20 97 CY45
Grange Ave. SE25 202 DS96
Grange Ave., Barn. 98 DE46
Grange Ave., Stan. 95 CH54
Grange Ave., Twick. 177 CE89
Grange Ave., Wdf.Grn. 102 EG51
Grange Clo., Brwd. 109 GC50
Grange Clo., Edg. 96 CQ50
Grange Clo., Ger.Cr. 90 AY53
Grange Clo., Grav. 191 GF91
Grange Clo., Guil. 242 AV130
Grange Clo., Hayes 135 BS71
Grange Clo., Hem.H. 40 BN21
Grange Clo., Hert. 31 DP09
Grange Clo., Houns. 156 BZ79
Grange Clo., Lthd. 231 CK120
Grange Clo. (Bletchingley), Red. 252 DR133
Grange Clo. (Merstham), Red. 251 DH128
Grange Clo., Sid. 186 EU90
Grange Clo., Stai. 172 AY86
Grange Clo., Wat. 75 BU39
Grange Clo., W.Mol. 196 CB98
Grange Clo., West. 255 EQ126
Grange Clo., Wdf.Grn. 102 EG52
Grange Ct. E8 142 DT66
Grange Ct. WC2 274 C9
Grange Ct., Chig. 103 EQ47
Grange Ct., Loug. 84 EK43
Grange Ct., Nthlt. 136 BW68
Grange Ct., Stai. 174 BG92
Grange Ct., Wal.Abb. 67 EC34
Grange Ct., Walt. 195 BU103
Grange Cres. SE28 146 EW72
Grange Cres., Chig. 103 ER50
Grange Cres., Dart. 188 FP86
Grange Dr., Chis. 184 EL93
Grange Dr., H.Wyc. 110 AD60
Grange Dr., Orp. 224 EW109
Rushmore Hill
Grange Dr., Red. 251 DH128
London Rd. S.
Grange Dr., Wok. 210 AY114
Grange End, Horl. 269 DN148
Grange Fm. Clo., Har. 116 CC61
Grange Flds., Ger.Cr. 90 AY53
Lower Rd.
Grange Gdns. N14 99 DK46
Grange Gdns. NW3 120 DB62
Grange Gdns. SE25 202 DS96
Grange Gdns., Bans. 218 DB113
Grange Gdns., Pnr. 116 BZ56
Grange Gdns., Slou. 111 AR64
Grange Gdns., Ware 33 DY07
Grange Gro. N1 142 DQ65
Grange Hill SE25 202 DS96
Grange Hill, Edg. 96 CQ50
Grange Ho., Bark. 145 ER67
St. Margarets
Grange La. SE21 182 DT89
Grange La., Harl. 50 EJ15
Grange La., Wat. 77 CD39
Grange Mans., Epsom 217 CT108
Grange Meadow, Bans. 218 DB113
Grange Ms. SE10 163 ED80
Crooms Hill
Grange Pk. W5 138 CL74
Grange Pk., Wok. 210 AY114
Grange Pk. Ave. N21 81 DP44
Grange Pk. Pl. SW20 179 CV94
Grange Pk. Rd. E10 123 EB60
Grange Pk. Rd., Th.Hth. 202 DR98
Grange Pl. NW6 140 DA66
Grange Pl., Stai. 194 BJ96
Grange Rd. E10 123 EA60
Grange Rd. E13 144 EF69
Grange Rd. E17 123 DY57
Grange Rd. N6 120 DG58
Grange Rd. N17 100 DU51
Grange Rd. N18 100 DU51
Grange Rd. NW10 139 CV65
Grange Rd. SE1 279 N7
Grange Rd. SE1 162 DS76
Grange Rd. SE19 202 DR98
Grange Rd. SE25 202 DR98
Grange Rd. SW13 159 CU81
Grange Rd. W4 158 CP78
Grange Rd. W5 137 CK74
Grange Rd., Add. 212 BG110
Grange Rd., Borwd. 78 CM43
Grange Rd., Cat. 252 DU125
Grange Rd., Chess. 216 CL105
Grange Rd., Edg. 96 CR51
Grange Rd., Egh. 173 AZ92
Grange Rd., Ger.Cr. 90 AY53
Grange Rd., Grav. 191 GG87
Grange Rd., Grays 170 GB79
Grange Rd., Guil. 242 AV129
Grange Rd., Har. 117 CG58
Grange Rd. (South Harrow), Har. 117 CD61
Grange Rd., Hayes 135 BS72
Grange Rd., Ilf. 125 EP63
Grange Rd., Kings.T. 198 CL97
Grange Rd., Lthd. 231 CK120
Grange Rd., Orp. 205 EQ103
Grange Rd., Rom. 105 FH52
Grange Rd., Sev. 256 FG127
Grange Rd., S.Croy. 220 DQ110
Grange Rd., S.Ock. 148 FQ74
Grange Rd., Sthl. 156 BY75
Grange Rd., Sutt. 218 DA108
Grange Rd., Th.Hth. 202 DR98
Grange Rd., Walt. 214 BY105
Grange Rd. (Bushey), Wat. 76 BY43
Grange Rd., W.Mol. 196 CB98
Grange Rd., Wok. 210 AY114
Grange St. N1 142 DR67
Grange St., St.Alb. 43 CD19
Grange Vale, Sutt. 218 DB108
Grange Vw. Rd. N20 98 DC46
Grange Wk. SE1 279 N6
Grange Wk. SE1 162 DS76
Grange Way, Erith 167 FH80
Grange Way, Iver 133 BF72
Grange Yd. SE1 279 P7
Grange Yd. SE1 162 DT76
Grangecliffe Gdns. SE25 202 DS96
Grangecourt Rd. N16 122 DS60
Grangedale Clo., Nthwd. 93 BS53
Grangefields Rd., Guil. 242 AX128
Grangehill Pl. SE9 165 EM83
Westmount Rd.
Grangehill Rd. SE9 165 EM83
Grangemill Rd. SE6 183 EA90
Grangemill Way SE6 183 EA89
Grangemount, Lthd. 231 CK120
Granger Way, Rom. 127 FG58
Grangeway N12 98 DB49
Grangeway NW6 140 DA66
Messina Ave.
Grangeway, Horl. 269 DN148
Grangeway, Wdf.Grn. 102 EJ49
Grangeway, The N21 81 DP44
Grangeway Gdns., Ilf. 124 EL57
Grangeways Clo., Grav. 191 GF91
Grangewood, Bex. 186 EZ88
Hurst Rd.
Grangewood, Pot.B. 64 DB30
Grangewood, Slou. 132 AW71
Grangewood Ave., Grays 170 GE76
Grangewood Ave., Rain. 148 FJ70
Grangewood Clo., Brwd. 109 GA48
Knight's Way
Grangewood Clo., Pnr. 115 BU57
Grangewood Dr., Sun. 175 BT94
Forest Dr.
Grangewood La., Beck. 183 DZ93
Grangewood St. E6 144 EJ67
Grangewood Ter. SE25 202 DR97
Grange Rd.
Granham Gdns. N9 100 DT47
Granite St. SE18 165 ET78
Granleigh Rd. E11 124 EE61
Gransden Ave. E8 142 DV66
Gransden Rd. W12 159 CT75
Wendell Rd.
Grant Ave., Slou. 132 AS72
Grant Clo. N14 99 DJ45
Grant Clo., Shep. 195 BP100
Grant Pl., Croy. 202 DT102
Grant Rd. SW11 160 DD84
Grant Rd., Croy. 202 DT102
Grant Rd., Har. 117 CF55
Grant St. E13 144 EG69
Grant St. N1 141 DN68
Chapel Mkt.
Grant Way, Islw. 157 CG79
Grantbridge St. N1 141 DP68
Grantchester Clo., Har. 117 CF62
Grantham Clo., Edg. 96 CL48
Grantham Gdns., Rom. 126 EZ58
Grantham Gdns., Ware 33 DY05
Grantham Grn., Borwd. 78 CQ43
Grantham Pl. W1 277 H3
Grantham Rd. E12 125 EN63
Grantham Rd. SW9 161 DL82
Grantham Rd. W4 158 CS80
Grantley Clo., Guil. 258 AY141
Grantley Gdns., Guil. 242 AU133
Grantley Rd., Guil. 242 AU133
Grantley Rd., Houns. 156 BW82
Grantley St. E1 143 DX69
Grantock Rd. E17 101 ED53
Granton Ave., Upmin. 128 FM61
Granton Rd. SW16 201 DJ95
Granton Rd., Ilf. 126 EU60
Granton Rd., Sid. 186 EW93
Grants Clo. NW7 97 CW52
Grants La., Oxt. 254 EJ133
Grantully Rd. W9 140 DB69
Grantwood Clo., Red. 267 DH139
Bushfield Dr.
Granville Ave. N9 100 DW48
Granville Ave., Felt. 175 BU89
Granville Ave., Houns. 176 CA85
Granville Ave., Slou. 131 AR71
Granville Clo., Croy. 202 DS103
Granville Clo., W.Byf. 212 BM113
Church Rd.
Granville Clo., Wey. 213 BQ107
Granville Ct. N1 142 DR67
Granville Dene, Hem.H. 57 BA27
Granville Gdns. SW16 201 DM95
Granville Gdns. W5 138 CM74
Granville Gdns., Hodd. 33 EA13
Granville Gro. SE13 163 EC83
Granville Ms., Sid. 186 EU91
Granville Pk. SE13 163 EC83
Granville Pl. (North Finchley) N12 98 DC52
High Rd.
Granville Pl. W1 272 F9
Granville Pl. W1 140 DG72
Granville Pl., Pnr. 94 BX54
Elm Pk. Rd.
Granville Rd. E17 123 EB58
Granville Rd. E18 102 EH54
Granville Rd. N4 121 DM58
Granville Rd. N12 98 DB52
Granville Rd. N13 99 DM51
Russell Rd.
Granville Rd. N22 99 DP53
Granville Rd. NW2 119 CZ61
Granville Rd. NW6 140 DA68
Granville Rd. SW18 180 DA87
Granville Rd. SW19 180 DA94
Russell Rd.
Granville Rd., Barn. 79 CW42
Granville Rd., Berk. 38 AS17
Granville Rd., Epp. 70 EV29
Granville Rd., Grav. 191 GF88
Granville Rd., Hayes 155 BT77
Granville Rd., Ilf. 125 EP60
Granville Rd., Oxt. 254 EF129
Granville Rd., St.Alb. 43 CF20
Granville Rd., Sev. 256 FG124
Granville Rd., Sid. 186 EU91
Granville Rd., Uxb. 135 BP65
Granville Rd., Wat. 76 BW42
Granville Rd., Well. 166 EW83
Granville Rd., West. 255 EQ126
Granville Rd., Wey. 213 BQ108
Granville Rd., Wok. 227 AZ120
Granville Sq. SE15 162 DS80
Granville Sq. WC1 274 C3
Granville Sq. WC1 141 DM69
Granville St. WC1 274 C3
Grape St. WC2 273 P8
Graphite Sq. SE11 278 B10
Grasdene Rd. SE18 166 EU80
Grasmere Ave. SW15 178 CR91
Grasmere Ave. SW19 200 DA97
Grasmere Ave. W3 138 CQ73
Grasmere Ave., Houns. 176 CB86
Grasmere Ave., Orp. 205 EP104
Grasmere Ave., Ruis. 115 BQ59
Grasmere Ave., Slou. 132 AU73
Grasmere Ave., Wem. 117 CK59
Grasmere Clo., Felt. 175 BT88
Grasmere Clo., Guil. 243 BB133
Grasmere Clo., Hem.H. 41 BP22
Grasmere Clo., Loug. 85 EM40
Grasmere Clo., Wat. 59 BV32
Grasmere Ct. N22 99 DM51
Palmerston Rd.
Grasmere Gdns., Har. 95 CG54
Grasmere Gdns., Ilf. 125 EM57
Grasmere Gdns., Orp. 205 EP104
Grasmere Rd. E13 144 EG68
Grasmere Rd. N10 99 DH53
Grasmere Rd. N17 100 DU51
Grasmere Rd. SE25 202 DV100
Grasmere Rd. SW16 181 DM92
Grasmere Rd., Bexh. 167 FC81
Grasmere Rd., Brom. 204 EF95
Grasmere Rd., Orp. 205 EP104
Grasmere Rd., Pur. 219 DP111
Grasmere Rd., St.Alb. 43 CH22
Grasmere Way, W.Byf. 212 BM112
Grass Pk. N3 97 CZ53
Grass Warren, Welw. 30 DE06
Grassfield Clo., Couls. 235 DJ119
Grassingham End, Ger.Cr. 90 AY52
Grassingham Rd., Ger.Cr. 90 AY52
Grassington Clo. N11 98 DG51
Ribblesdale Ave.
Grassington Clo., St.Alb. 60 CA30
Grassington Rd., Sid. 186 EU91
Grasslands, Horl. 269 DN148
Grassmere, Horl. 269 DJ147
Grassmere Clo., Egh. 173 BB94
Keswick Rd.
Grassmere Rd., Horn. 128 FM56
Grassmount SE23 182 DV89
Grassmount, Pur. 219 DJ110
Grassway, Wall. 219 DJ105
Grassy Clo., Hem.H. 40 BG19
Grassy La., Sev. 257 FH126
Grasvenor Ave., Barn. 80 DA44
Grately Way SE15 162 DT80
Daniel Gdns.
Gratton Dr., Wind. 151 AL84
Gratton Rd. W14 159 CY76
Gratton Ter. NW2 119 CX62
Gravel Clo., Chig. 104 EU47
Gravel Hill N3 97 CZ54
Gravel Hill, Bexh. 187 FB85
Gravel Hill, Croy. 221 DX107
Gravel Hill, Ger.Cr. 90 AY51
Gravel Hill, Hem.H. 40 BH20
Gravel Hill, Lthd. 231 CH121
North St.
Gravel Hill, Loug. 84 EG38
Gravel Hill, Uxb. 114 BK64
Gravel Hill Clo., Bexh. 187 FB85
Gravel Hill Ter., Hem.H. 40 BG21
Gravel La. E1 275 P8
Gravel La., Hem.H. 40 BG21
Gravel Path, Berk. 38 AX19
Gravel Path, Hem.H. 40 BG20
Gravel La.
Gravel Pit La. SE9 185 EQ85
Gravel Pit Way, Orp. 206 EU103
Gravel Rd., Brom. 204 EL103
Gravel Rd., Dart. 188 FP94
Gravel Rd., Twick. 177 CE88
Graveley Ave., Borwd. 78 CQ42
Graveley Ct., Hem.H. 41 BQ21

Graveley Dell, Welw.G.C. 30 DB10
Waterford Grn.
Gravelly Hill, Cat. 252 DS128
Gravelly Ride SW19 179 CV91
Gravelpits La., Guil. 261 BQ139
Gravelwood Clo., Chis. 185 EQ90
Gravely Way, H.Wyc. 88 AF45
Graveney Gro. SE20 182 DW94
Graveney Rd. SW17 180 DE91
Gravesend Rd. W12 139 CU73
Gravetts La., Guil. 242 AS131
Gray Ave., Dag. 126 EZ60
Gray Gdns., Rain. 147 FG65
Gray Pl., Cher. 211 BC107
Murray Rd.
Gray St. SE1 278 E5
Grayburn Clo., Ch.St.G. 90 AU47
Grayham Cres., N.Mal. 198 CR98
Grayham Rd., N.Mal. 198 CR98
Grayland Clo., Brom. 204 EK95
Graylands, Epp. 85 ER37
Graylands, Wok. 226 AY116
Graylands Clo., Wok. 226 AY116
Grayling Clo. E16 144 EE70
Cranberry La.
Grayling Ct., Berk. 38 AT17
Tortoiseshell Way
Grayling Rd. N16 122 DR61
Grayling Sq. E2 142 DU69
Graylings, The, Abb.L. 59 BR33
Grays End Clo., Grays 170 GA76
Grays Fm. Rd., Orp. 206 EV95
Gray's Inn WC1 274 C6
Gray's Inn WC1 141 DN71
Gray's Inn Pl. WC1 274 C7
Gray's Inn Rd. WC1 274 B3
Gray's Inn Rd. WC1 141 DM70
Gray's Inn Sq. WC1 274 C6
Grays La., Ashf. 175 BP91
Gray's La., Ash. 232 CM119
Gray's La., Epsom 232 CP121
Shepherds' Wk.
Grays Pk. Rd., Slou. 132 AU68
Grays Pl., Slou. 132 AT74
Grays Rd., Gdmg. 258 AT144
Grays Rd., Slou. 132 AT74
Grays Rd., Uxb. 134 BL67
Grays Rd., West. 239 EP121
Grays Wk., Brwd. 109 GD45
Grays Wk., Chesh. 54 AP29
Grays Wd., Horl. 269 DJ148
Gray's Yd. W1 272 G9
Grayscroft Rd. SW16 181 DK94
Graysfield, Welw.G.C. 30 DA12
Grayshott Rd. SW11 160 DG82
Grayswood Gdns. SW20 199 CV96
Farnham Gdns.
Graywood Ct. N12 98 DC52
Grazebrook Rd. N16 122 DR61
Grazeley Clo., Bexh. 187 FC85
Grazeley Ct. SE19 182 DS91
Gipsy Hill
Grazings, The, Hem.H. 40 BM18
Great Acre Ct. SW4 161 DK84
St. Alphonsus Rd.
Great Bell All. EC2 275 K8
Great Benty, West Dr. 154 BL77
Great Bois Wd., Amer. 55 AP36
Bois Ave.
Great Braitch La., Hat. 28 CS13
Great Brays, Harl. 52 EU16
Great Break, Welw.G.C. 30 DB10
Great Brownings SE21 182 DT91
Great Bushey Dr. N20 98 DB46
Great Cambridge Rd. N9 100 DT46
Great Cambridge Rd. N17 100 DR50
Great Cambridge Rd. N18 100 DR50
Great Cambridge Rd., Brox. 67 DY26
Great Cambridge Rd., Enf. 82 DU42
Great Cambridge Rd. (Cheshunt), Wal.Cr. 66 DW34
Great Castle St. W1 273 J8
Great Castle St. W1 141 DJ72
Great Cen. Ave., Ruis. 116 BW64
Great Cen. St. NW1 272 D6
Great Cen. St. NW1 140 DF71
Great Cen. Way NW10 118 CS64
Great Cen. Way, Wem. 118 CQ63
Great Chapel St. W1 273 M8
Great Chapel St. W1 141 DK72
Great Chertsey Rd. W4 158 CQ82
Great Chertsey Rd., Felt. 176 CA90
Great Ch. La. W6 159 CX78
Great College St. SW1 277 P6
Great College St. SW1 161 DL76
Great Conduit, Welw.G.C. 30 DC08
Great Cross Ave. SE10 164 EE80
Great Cullings, Rom. 127 FE61
Great Cumberland Ms. W1 272 D9
Great Cumberland Pl. W1 272 D8
Great Cumberland Pl. W1 140 DF72
Great Dell, Welw.G.C. 29 CX07
Great Dover St. SE1 279 J5
Great Dover St. SE1 162 DR75
Great Eastern Rd. E15 143 ED66
Great Eastern Rd., Brwd. 108 FW49
Great Eastern St. EC2 275 M3
Great Eastern St. EC2 142 DS69
Great Eastern Wk. EC2 275 N7
Great Ellshams, Bans. 234 DA116
Great Elms Rd., Brom. 204 EJ98
Great Elms Rd., Hem.H. 40 BM24
Great Fld. NW9 96 CS53
Great Fleete Way, Bark. 146 EW68
Great Galley Clo., Bark. 146 EV69
Great Ganett, Welw.G.C. 30 DB11
Great Gdns. Rd., Horn. 127 FH58
Great George St. SW1 277 N5
Great George St. SW1 161 DK75
Great Goodwin Dr., Guil. 243 BB132
Great Gregories La., Epp. 69 ES33
Great Gro. (Bushey), Wat. 76 CB42
Great Gros., Wal.Cr. 66 DS28
Great Guildford St. SE1 279 H3
Great Guildford St. SE1 142 DQ74
Great Harry Dr. SE9 185 EN90
Great Heart, Hem.H. 40 BL18
Great Heath, Hat. 45 CV15
Great Hivings, Chesh. 54 AN27
Great James St. WC1 274 B5
Great James St. WC1 141 DM71
Great Julians, Rick. 74 BN42
Grove Cres.
Great Lake Ct., Horl. 269 DH147
Tanyard Way
Great Ley, Welw.G.C. 29 CY11
Great Leylands, Harl. 52 EU16
Great Marlborough St. W1 273 K9
Great Marlborough St. W1 141 DJ72
Great Maze Pond SE1 279 L4
Great Maze Pond SE1 162 DR75
Great Meadow, Brox. 49 EA22
Great Molewood, Hert. 31 DP06
Great Nelmes Chase, Horn. 128 FM57
Great New St. EC4 274 E8
Great Newport St. WC2 141 DK73
Cranbourn St.
Great N. Rd. N2 120 DE56
Great N. Rd. N6 120 DE56
Great N. Rd., Barn. 79 CZ38
Great N. Rd. (New Barnet), Barn. 80 DA43
Great N. Rd., Hat. 64 DB27
Great N. Rd., Pot.B. 64 DB27
Great N. Rd., Welw. 29 CV05
Great N. Rd., Welw.G.C. 29 CU08
Great N. Way NW4 97 CW54
Great Oaks, Brwd. 109 GB44
Great Oaks, Chig. 103 EQ49
Great Oaks Pk., Guil. 243 BB129
Great Ormond St. WC1 274 A6
Great Ormond St. WC1 141 DL71
Great Owl Rd., Chig. 103 EN48
Great Palmers, Hem.H. 40 BM15
Great Pk., Kings L. 58 BM30
Great Percy St. WC1 274 C2
Great Percy St. WC1 141 DM69
Great Peter St. SW1 277 M7
Great Peter St. SW1 161 DK76
Great Plumtree, Harl. 35 ET13
Great Portland St. W1 273 J6
Great Portland St. W1 141 DH71
Great Pulteney St. W1 273 L10
Great Pulteney St. W1 141 DJ73
Great Quarry, Guil. 258 AX137
Great Queen St. WC2 274 A9
Great Queen St. WC2 141 DL72
Great Queen St., Dart. 188 FM87
Great Rd., Hem.H. 40 BM19
Great Ropers La., Brwd. 107 FU51
Great Russell St. WC1 273 N8
Great Russell St. WC1 141 DL71
Great St. Helens EC3 275 M8
Great St. Helens EC3 142 DS72
Great St. Thomas Apostle EC4 275 J10
Great Scotland Yd. SW1 277 P3
Great Scotland Yd. SW1 141 DL74
Great Slades, Pot.B. 63 CZ33
Great Smith St. SW1 277 N6
Great Smith St. SW1 161 DK76
Great South-West Rd., Felt. 175 BQ87
Great South-West Rd., Houns. 155 BT84
Great Spilmans SE22 182 DS85
Great Strand NW9 97 CT53
Great Sturgess Rd., Hem.H. 39 BF20
Great Suffolk St. SE1 278 G3
Great Suffolk St. SE1 161 DP75
Great Sutton St. EC1 274 G5
Great Sutton St. EC1 141 DP70
Great Swan All. EC2 275 K8
Great Tattenhams, Epsom 233 CV118
Great Thrift, Orp. 205 EQ98
Great Till Clo., Sev. 241 FE116
Great Titchfield St. W1 273 K8
Great Titchfield St. W1 141 DJ72
Great Twr. St. EC3 275 M10
Great Twr. St. EC3 142 DS73
Great Trinity La. EC4 275 J10
Great Turnstile WC1 274 C7
Great Warley St., Brwd. 107 FU53
Great W. Rd. W4 158 CP78
Great W. Rd. W6 159 CT78
Great W. Rd., Brent. 158 CP78
Great W. Rd., Houns. 156 BX82
Great W. Rd., Islw. 157 CF80
Great Western Rd. W2 139 CZ71
Great Western Rd. W9 139 CZ71
Great Western Rd. W11 139 CZ71
Great Wf. Rd. E14 143 EB74
Churchill Pl.
Great Whites Rd., Hem.H. 40 BM22
Great Winchester St. EC2 275 L8
Great Winchester St. EC2 142 DR72
Great Windmill St. W1 273 M10
Great Windmill St. W1 141 DK73
Great Woodcote Dr., Pur. 219 DK110
Great Woodcote Pk., Pur. 219 DK110
Great Yd. SE1 279 N4
Greatdown Rd. W7 137 CF70
Greatfield Ave. E6 145 EM70
Greatfield Clo. N19 121 DJ63
Warrender Rd.
Greatfield Clo. SE4 163 EA84
Greatfields Dr., Uxb. 134 BN71
Greatfields Rd., Bark. 145 ER67
Greatford Dr., Guil. 243 BD134
Greatham Rd. (Bushey), Wat. 76 BX41
Greatham Wk. SW15 179 CU88
Greathurst End, Lthd. 230 BZ124
Greatness La., Sev. 257 FJ121
Greatness Rd., Sev. 257 FJ121
Greatorex St. E1 142 DU71
Greatwood, Chis. 185 EN94
Greatwood Clo., Cher. 211 BC109
Greaves Clo., Bark. 145 ES66
Norfolk Rd.
Greaves Pl. SW17 180 DE91
Grebe Ave., Hayes 136 BX72
Cygnet Way
Grebe Clo. E7 124 EF64
Cormorant Rd.
Grebe Clo. E17 101 DY52
Grebe Crest, Grays 169 FU77
Grecian Cres. SE19 181 DP93
Greding Wk., Brwd. 109 GB47
Gredo Ho., Bark. 146 EV69
Greek Ct. W1 273 N9
Greek St. W1 273 N9
Greek St. W1 141 DK72
Greek Yd. WC2 273 P10
Green, The E4 101 EC46
Green, The E11 124 EH58
Green, The E15 144 EE65
Green, The N9 100 DU47
Green, The N14 99 DK48
Green, The N21 99 DN45
Green, The SW14 158 CQ83
Green, The SW19 179 CX92
Green, The W3 138 CS72
Green, The W5 137 CK74
High St.
Green, The, Amer. 55 AR38
Batchelors Way
Green, The, Berk. 39 BB17
Green, The, Bexh. 166 FA81
Green, The, Brom. 204 EG101
Green, The, Cars. 218 DG105
Green, The, Cat. 237 EA123
Green, The, Ch.St.G. 90 AW47
High St.
Green, The, Croy. 221 DZ109
Green, The, Epp. 85 ES37
Green, The, Epsom 217 CU111
Green, The, Esher 215 CF107
Green, The, Felt. 175 BV89
Green, The, Hayes 135 BS72
Wood End
Green, The, Hem.H. 57 BA27
Green, The, H.Wyc. 110 AE57
Green, The, Houns. 156 CA79
Heston Rd.
Green, The, Lthd. 231 CD124
Green, The, Mord. 199 CY98
Green, The, N.Mal. 198 CQ97
Green, The (Pratt's Bottom), Orp. 224 EW110
Rushmore Hill
Green, The (St. Paul's Cray), Orp. 186 EV94
The Ave.
Green, The, Rain. 148 FL73
Green, The, Rich. 177 CK85
Green, The (Croxley Grn.), Rick. 74 BN44
Green, The (Sarratt), Rick. 74 BG35
Green, The, Sev. 257 FK122
Green, The, Shep. 195 BS98
Green, The, Sid. 186 EU91
Green, The, Slou. 130 AH70
Green, The (Chalvey), Slou. 151 AR75
Green, The (Datchet), Slou. 152 AV80
Green, The, S.Ock. 149 FW69
Green, The, Sthl. 156 BY76
Green, The, Stai. 172 AY86
Green, The, Sutt. 200 DB104
Green, The, Tad. 233 CY119
Green, The, Til. 171 GL79
Green, The, Twick. 177 CE89
Green, The (Harefield), Uxb. 92 BJ53
Green, The (Ickenham), Uxb. 115 BQ61
Green, The, Wal.Abb. 67 EC34
Sewardstone Rd.
Green, The (Cheshunt), Wal.Cr. 66 DW28
Green, The, Walt. 213 BS110
Octagon Rd.
Green, The, Warl. 237 DX117
Green, The, Wat. 77 CE39
Green, The, Well. 165 ES84
Green, The, Wem. 117 CG61
Green, The, West Dr. 154 BK76
Green, The, West. 255 ER126
Green, The, Wdf.Grn. 102 EG50
Green Acres, Croy. 202 DT104
Green Acres, Hem.H. 41 BR21
Green Acres, Welw.G.C. 29 CZ12
Green Arbour Ct. EC1 274 F8
Green Ave. NW7 96 CR49
Green Ave. W13 157 CH76
Green Bank E1 142 DV74
Green Bank N12 98 DB49
Green Clo. NW9 118 CQ58
Green Clo. NW11 120 DC59
Green Clo., Brom. 204 EE97
Green Clo., Cars. 200 DF103
Green Clo., Epp. 51 EP24
Green Clo., Felt. 176 BY92
Green Clo., Hat. 63 CY26
Station Rd.
Green Clo., Maid. 130 AH72
Green Clo. (Cheshunt), Wal.Cr. 67 DY32
Green Common La., H.Wyc. 110 AG59
Green Ct. Rd., Swan. 207 FD100
Green Cres., H.Wyc. 110 AC56
Green Cft., Edg. 96 CQ50
Deans La.
Green Cft., Hat. 45 CU15
Talbot Rd.
Green Curve, Bans. 217 CZ114
Green Dale SE5 162 DR84
Green Dale SE22 182 DS85
Green Dale Clo. SE22 182 DS85
Green Dale
Green Dell Way, Hem.H. 41 BQ21
Green Dene, Lthd. 245 BT131
Green Dragon Ct. SE1 279 K2
Green Dragon La. N21 81 DP44
Green Dragon La., Brent. 158 CL78
Green Dragon Yd. E1 142 DU71
Old Montague St.
Green Dr., Slou. 152 AY77
London Rd.
Green Dr., Sthl. 136 CA74
Green Dr., Wok. 227 BF123
Green E. Rd., Beac. 90 AS52
Green Edge, Wat. 75 BU35
Clarke Grn.
Green End N21 99 DP47
Green End, Chess. 216 CL105
Green End Gdns., Hem.H. 40 BG21
Green End La., Hem.H. 39 BF20
Green End Rd., Hem.H. 40 BG20
Green Gdns., Orp. 223 EQ106
Green Glade, Epp. 85 ES37
Green Glades, Horn. 128 FM58
Green Hill, Buck.H. 102 EJ46
Green Hill, Orp. 222 EL112
Green Hill La., Warl. 237 DY117
Sunny Bank
Green Hundred Rd. SE15 162 DU79
Green La. E4 84 EE41
Green La. NW4 119 CX57
Green La. SE9 185 EN89
Green La. SE20 183 DX94
Green La. SW16 181 DM94
Green La. W7 157 CE75
Green La., Add. 194 BG104
Green La., Amer. 55 AS38
Green La. (Chesham Bois), Amer. 55 AR35
Green La., Ash. 231 CJ117
Green La., Brwd. 108 FU46
Greenshaw
Green La. (Pilgrims Hatch), Brwd. 108 FV43
Green La. (Warley), Brwd. 107 FU52
Green La., Brox. 49 EB23
Green La., Cher. 193 BE103
Green La., Chesh. 56 AV34
Green La., Chess. 216 CL109
Green La., Chig. 103 ER47
Green La., Chis. 185 EP91
Green La., Cob. 214 BY112
Green La., Couls. 250 DA125
Green La., Dag. 126 EX61
Green La., Edg. 96 CN50
Green La., Egh. 173 BB92
Green La. (Thorpe), Egh. 193 BD95
Green La., Felt. 176 BY92
Green La., Guil. 243 BB134
Green La. (Shamley Grn.), Guil. 260 BG144
Green La. (West Clandon), Guil. 244 BG127
Green La., Harl. 52 FA16
Green La., Har. 117 CE62
Green La., Hem.H. 41 BQ21
Green La. (Bovingdon), Hem.H. 57 BA28
Green La., Horl. 269 DM152
Green La., Houns. 155 BV83
Green La., Ilf. 125 EQ61
Green La., Lthd. 231 CK121
Green La. (Fifield), Maid. 150 AC81
Green La., Mord. 200 DB100
Green La., N.Mal. 198 CQ99
Green La., Nthwd. 93 BT52
Green La., Pur. 219 DJ111
Green La., Red. 250 DE132
Green La. (Bletchingley), Red. 252 DS131
Green La. (Outwood), Red. 267 DL141
Green La. (White Bushes), Red. 266 DG139
Green La., Reig. 249 CZ134
Green La., Rick. 74 BM43
Green La., St.Alb. 42 CC17
Green La., Shep. 195 BQ100
Green La., Slou. 130 AJ69
Green La. (Datchet), Slou. 152 AV81
Green La. (Farnham Common), Slou. 111 AP64
Green La., S.Ock. 149 FR69
Green La., Stai. 193 BE95
Green La., Stan. 95 CH49
Green La., Sun. 175 BT94
Green La., Tad. 249 CZ126
Green La., Th.Hth. 201 DN95
Green La., Upmin. 149 FR68
Green La., Uxb. 135 BQ71
Green La., Wal.Abb. 68 EJ34
Green La., Walt. 213 BV107
Green La., Warl. 237 DY116
Green La., Wat. 94 BW46
Green La. (Panshanger), Welw.G.C. 30 DD10
Green La., W.Byf. 212 BM112
Green La., W.Mol. 196 CB99
Green La., Wind. 151 AN82
Green La. (Chobham), Wok. 210 AT110
Green La. (Mayford), Wok. 226 AV121
Copper Beech Clo.
Green La. (Ockham), Wok. 229 BP124
Green La., Wor.Pk. 199 CU102
Green La. Ave., Walt. 214 BW106
Green La. Caravan Pk., Red. 267 DL141
Green La. Clo., Amer. 55 AR36
Green La. Clo., Cher. 193 BE103
Green La. Clo., W.Byf. 212 BM112
Green La. Gdns., Th.Hth. 202 DQ96
Green La. W., Wok. 244 BN125
Green Las. N4 122 DQ60
Green Las. N8 121 DP55
Green Las. N13 99 DM51
Green Las. N15 121 DP55
Green Las. N16 122 DQ62
Green Las. N21 99 DP46
Green Las., Epsom 216 CS109
Green Las., Hat. 29 CT13
Green Las., Welw.G.C. 29 CT11
Green Lawns, Ruis. 116 BW60
Green Leaf Ave., Wall. 219 DK105
Green Leas, Sun. 175 BT94
Green Leas, Wal.Abb. 67 ED34
Roundhills
Green Leas Clo., Sun. 175 BT93
Green Leas
Green Man Gdns. W13 137 CG73
Green Man La. W13 137 CG74
Green Man La., Felt. 155 BU84
Green Man Pas. W13 137 CG73
Green Man Rd., Ong. 53 FC19
Green Man Roundabout E11 124 EF59
Green Manor Way, Grav. 170 FZ84
Green Mead, Esher 214 BZ107
Winterdown Gdns.
Green Meadow, Pot.B. 64 DA30
Green Moor Link N21 99 DP45
Green N. Rd., Beac. 90 AS51
Green Pk., Stai. 173 BE90
Green Pk. Way, Grnf. 137 CE67
Green Pl., Dart. 187 FE85
Green Pt. E15 144 EE65
Green Pond Clo. E17 123 DZ55
Green Pond Rd. E17 123 DY55
Green Ride, Epp. 85 EP35
Green Ride, Loug. 84 EG43
Green Rd. N14 81 DH44
Green Rd. N20 98 DC48
Green Rd., Egh. 193 BA99
Green Sand Rd., Red. 250 DG133
Noke Dr.
Green Shield Ind. Est. E16 144 EG74
Bradfield Rd.
Green St. E7 144 EH65
Green St. E13 144 EJ67
Green St. W1 272 E10
Green St. W1 140 DG73
Green St., Borwd. 78 CN36
Green St., Enf. 82 DW40
Green St., Hat. 45 CZ20
Green St., Hert. 32 DR09
Green St., Rad. 78 CN36
Green St., Rick. 73 BC41
Green St., Sun. 195 BU95
Green St. Grn. Rd., Dart. 188 FP88
Green Tiles La., Uxb. 113 BF58
Green Vale W5 138 CM72
Green Vale, Bexh. 186 EX85
Green Verges, Stan. 95 CK52
Green Vw., Chess. 216 CM108
Green Vw. Clo., Hem.H. 57 BA29
Green Wk. NW4 119 CX57
Green Wk. SE1 279 M7
Green Wk., Dart. 167 FF84
Green Wk., Hmptn. 176 BZ93
Orpwood Clo.
Green Wk., Ruis. 115 BT60
Green Wk., Sthl. 156 CA78
Green Wk., Wdf.Grn. 102 EL45
Green Wk., The E4 101 EC46
Green Way SE9 184 EK85
Green Way, Brom. 204 EL100
Green Way, Red. 250 DE132
Green Way, Slou. 130 AH69
Green Way, Sun. 195 BU98
Green W. Rd., Beac. 90 AS52
Green Wrythe Cres., Cars. 200 DE102
Green Wrythe La., Cars. 200 DD100
Greenacre, Dart. 188 FL89
Oakfield La.
Greenacre, Wind. 151 AL82
Greenacre, Wok. 226 AS116
Mead Ct.
Greenacre Clo., Barn. 79 CZ38
Greenacre Clo., Nthlt. 116 BZ64
Eastcote La.
Greenacre Clo., Swan. 207 FE98
Greenacre Ct., Egh. 172 AW93
Greenacre Gdns. E17 123 EC56
Greenacre Pl., Wall. 201 DH103
Park Rd.
Greenacre Sq. SE16 163 DX75
Fishermans Dr.
Greenacre Wk. N14 99 DL48
Greenacres SE9 185 EN86
Greenacres, Epp. 69 ET29
Greenacres, Lthd. 230 CB124
Greenacres, Oxt. 254 EE127
Greenacres (Bushey), Wat. 95 CD47
Greenacres Ave., Uxb. 114 BM62
Greenacres Clo., Orp. 223 EQ105
Greenacres Clo., Rain. 148 FL69
Greenacres Dr., Stan. 95 CH52
Greenall Clo. (Cheshunt), Wal.Cr. 67 DY30
Greenaway Gdns. NW3 120 DB63
Greenbank (Cheshunt), Wal.Cr. 66 DV28
Greenbank Ave., Wem. 117 CG64
Greenbank Clo. E4 101 EC47
Greenbank Clo., Rom. 106 FK48
Greenbank Cres. NW4 119 CY56
Greenbank Rd., Wat. 75 BR36
Greenbanks, Dart. 188 FL89
Greenbanks, St.Alb. 43 CF22
Colindale Ave.
Greenbanks, Upmin. 129 FS60
Greenbay Rd. SE7 164 EK80
Greenberry St. NW8 272 B1
Greenberry St. NW8 140 DE68
Greenbrook Ave., Barn. 80 DC39
Greenbury Clo., Rick. 73 BC41
Green St.
Greencoat Pl. SW1 277 L8
Greencoat Pl. SW1 161 DJ77
Greencoat Row SW1 277 L7
Greencoates, Hert. 32 DS10
Greencourt Ave., Croy. 202 DV103
Greencourt Ave., Edg. 96 CP53
Greencourt Gdns., Croy. 202 DV102
Greencourt Rd., Orp. 205 ER99
Greencrest Pl. NW2 119 CV62
Dollis Hill La.
Greencroft, Guil. 243 BB134
Greencroft Ave., Ruis. 116 BW61
Greencroft Clo. E6 144 EL71
Neatscourt Rd.
Greencroft Gdns. NW6 140 DB66
Greencroft Gdns., Enf. 82 DS41
Greencroft Rd., Houns. 156 BZ81
Greendale Ms., Slou. 132 AU73
Greendale Wk., Grav. 190 GE90
Greene Fld. Rd., Berk. 38 AW19
Greene Fielde End, Stai. 174 BK94
Berryscroft Rd.
Greene Wk., Berk. 38 AX20
Greenend Rd. W4 158 CS75
Greenfarm Clo., Orp. 223 ET106
Greenfern Ave., Slou. 130 AJ72
Greenfield, Hat. 45 CX15
Greenfield, Welw.G.C. 29 CX06
Greenfield Ave., Surb. 198 CP101
Greenfield Ave., Wat. 94 BX47
Greenfield End, Ger.Cr. 91 AZ52
Greenfield Gdns. NW2 119 CY61
Greenfield Gdns., Dag. 146 EX67
Greenfield Gdns., Orp. 205 ER101
Greenfield Link, Couls. 235 DL115
Greenfield Rd. E1 142 DU71
Greenfield Rd. N15 122 DS57
Greenfield Rd., Dag. 146 EW67
Greenfield Rd., Dart. 187 FD92
Greenfield St., Wal.Abb. 67 EC34
Greenfield Way, Har. 116 CB55
Greenfields, Loug. 85 EN42
Greenfields (Cuffley), Pot.B. 65 DL30
South Dr.
Greenfields Clo., Brwd. 107 FW51
Essex Way
Greenfields Clo., Horl. 268 DE146
Greenfields Clo., Loug. 85 EN42
Greenfields Rd., Horl. 268 DF146
Greenford Ave. W7 137 CE70
Greenford Ave., Sthl. 136 BZ73

Greenford Gdns., Grnf. 136 CB69
Greenford Rd., Grnf. 136 CC71
Greenford Rd., Har. 137 CD68
Greenford Rd., Sthl. 136 CC74
Greenford Rd., Sutt. 218 DB105
Greengate, Grnf. 137 CH65
Greengate St. E13 144 EH68
Greenhalgh Wk. N2 120 DC56
Greenham Clo. SE1 278 D5
Greenham Clo. SE1 161 DN75
Greenham Cres. E4 101 DZ51
Greenham Rd. N10 98 DG54
Greenham Wk., Wok. 226 AW118
Greenhayes Ave., Bans. 218 DA114
Greenhayes Clo., Reig. 250 DC134
Greenhayes Gdns., Bans. 234 DA115
Greenheys Clo., Nthwd. 93 BS53
Greenheys Dr. E18 124 EF55
Greenheys Pl., Wok. 227 AZ118
White Rose La.
Greenhill NW3 120 DD63
Hampstead High St.
Greenhill SE18 165 EM78
Greenhill, Sutt. 200 DC103
Greenhill, Wem. 118 CP61
Greenhill Ave., Cat. 236 DV121
Greenhill Cres., Wat. 75 BS44
Greenhill Gdns., Guil. 243 BC131
Greenhill Gdns., Nthlt. 136 BZ68
Greenhill Gro. E12 124 EL63
Greenhill Pk. NW10 138 CS67
Greenhill Pk., Barn. 80 DB43
Greenhill Rd. NW10 138 CS67
Greenhill Rd., Grav. 191 GF89
Greenhill Rd., Har. 117 CE58
Greenhill Ter. SE18 165 EM78
Greenhill Ter., Nthlt. 136 BZ68
Greenhill Way, Croy. 221 DX111
Greenhill Way, Har. 117 CE58
Greenhill Way, Wem. 118 CP61
Greenhills, Harl. 51 ES15
Greenhills Clo., Rick. 74 BH43
Greenhill's Rents EC1 274 G6
Greenhills Ter. N1 142 DR65
Baxter Rd.
Greenhithe Clo., Sid. 185 ES87
Greenholm Rd. SE9 185 EP85
Greenhurst La., Oxt. 254 EF132
Greenhurst Rd. SE27 181 DN92
Greening St. SE2 166 EW77
Greenland Cres., Sthl. 156 BW76
Greenland Ms. SE8 163 DX78
Trundleys Rd.
Greenland Pl. NW1 141 DH67
Greenland Rd.
Greenland Quay SE16 163 DX77
Greenland Rd. NW1 141 DJ67
Greenland Rd., Barn. 79 CW44
Greenland St. NW1 141 DH67
Camden High St.
Greenlands Rd., Stai. 174 BG91
Greenlands Rd., Wey. 195 BP104
Greenlaw Gdns., N.Mal. 199 CT101
Greenlaw St. SE18 165 EN76
Greenlea Pk. SW19 200 DD95
Greenleaf Clo. SW2 181 DN87
Tulse Hill
Greenleaf Rd. E6 144 EJ67
Redclyffe Rd.
Greenleaf Rd. E17 123 DZ55
Greenleafe Dr., Ilf. 125 EP56
Greenleaves Ct., Ashf. 175 BP93
Redleaves Ave.
Greenleigh Ave., Orp. 206 EV98
Greenman St. N1 142 DQ66
Greenmead Clo. SE25 202 DU99
Greenmeads, Wok. 226 AY122
Greenmoor Rd., Enf. 82 DW40
Greeno Cres., Shep. 194 BN99
Greenoak Pl., Barn. 80 DF41
Cockfosters Rd.
Greenoak Ri., West. 238 EJ118
Greenoak Way SW19 179 CX91
Greenock Rd. SW16 201 DK95
Greenock Rd. W3 158 CP76
Greenock Rd., Slou. 131 AN72
Greenock Way, Rom. 105 FE52
Greenpark Ct., Wem. 137 CJ66
Greens Clo., The, Loug. 85 EN40
Green's Ct. W1 273 M10
Green's End SE18 165 EP77
Greensand Clo. (South Merstham), Red. 251 DK128
Greensand Rd., Red. 250 DG133
Greensand Way, Bet. 264 CM136
Old Sch. La.
Greensand Way, Dor. 263 CK136
Punchbowl La.
Greenshank Clo. E17 101 DY52
Banbury Rd.
Greenshaw, Brwd. 108 FV46
Greenside, Bex. 186 EY88
Greenside, Borwd. 78 CN38
Greenside, Dag. 126 EW60
Greenside, Slou. 131 AN71
Greenside, Swan. 207 FD96
Greenside Clo. N20 98 DD47
Greenside Clo. SE6 183 ED89
Greenside Clo., Guil. 243 BC132
Foxglove Gdns.
Greenside Rd. W12 159 CU76
Greenside Rd., Croy. 201 DN101
Greenside Rd., Wey. 195 BP104
Greenside Wk., West. 238 EH118
Kings Rd.
Greenslade Ave., Ash. 232 CP119
Greenslade Rd., Bark. 145 ER66
Greensleeves Clo., St.Alb. 43 CJ21
Greenstead, Saw. 36 EY06
Greenstead Ave., Wdf.Grn. 102 EJ52
Greenstead Clo., Brwd. 109 GE45
Greenstead Clo., Wdf.Grn. 102 EJ51
Greenstead Gdns.
Greenstead Gdns. SW15 179 CU85
Greenstead Gdns., Wdf.Grn. 102 EJ51
Greensted Rd., Loug. 102 EL45
Greensted Rd., Ong. 71 FG28
Greenstone Ms. E11 124 EG58
Greensward (Bushey), Wat. 76 CB44
Greenvale, Welw.G.C. 30 DA10
Greenvale Rd. SE9 165 EM84
Greenview Ave., Beck. 203 DY100
Greenview Ave., Croy. 203 DY100
Greenview Ct., Ashf. 174 BM91
Village Way
Greenway N14 99 DL47
Greenway N20 98 DA47
Greenway SW20 199 CW98
Greenway, Berk. 38 AT19
Greenway, Brwd. 109 GA45
Greenway, Chesh. 54 AP28
Greenway, Chis. 185 EN92
Greenway, Dag. 126 EW61
Greenway, Harl. 50 EL15
Greenway, Har. 118 CL57
Greenway, Hayes 135 BV70
Greenway, Hem.H. 41 BP20
Greenway, Lthd. 230 CB123
Greenway, Pnr. 93 BV54
Greenway, Rom. 106 FP51
Greenway, Wall. 219 DJ105
Greenway, West. 238 EJ120
Greenway, Wdf.Grn. 102 EJ50
Greenway, The NW9 96 CR54
Greenway, The, Enf. 83 DX35
Greenway, The, Ger.Cr. 112 AX55
Greenway, The, Har. 95 CE53
Greenway, The, Houns. 156 BZ84
Greenway, The, Orp. 206 EV100
Greenway, The, Oxt. 254 EH133
Greenway, The, Pnr. 116 BZ58
Greenway, The, Pot.B. 64 DA33
Greenway, The, Rick. 92 BG45
Greenway, The, Slou. 131 AK74
Greenway, The, Uxb. 134 BJ68
Greenway, The (Ickenham), Uxb. 115 BQ61
Greenway Ave. E17 123 ED56
Greenway Clo. N4 122 DQ61
Greenway Clo. N11 98 DG51
Greenway Clo. N15 122 DT56
Copperfield Dr.
Greenway Clo. N20 98 DA47
Greenway Clo. NW9 96 CR54
Greenway Clo., W.Byf. 212 BG113
Greenway Dr., Stai. 194 BK95
Greenway Gdns. NW9 96 CR54
Greenway Gdns., Croy. 203 DZ104
Greenway Gdns., Grnf. 136 CA69
Greenway Gdns., Har. 95 CE53
Greenway Par., Chesh. 54 AP28
Greenways, Abb.L. 59 BS32
Greenways, Beck. 203 EA96
Greenways, Egh. 172 AY92
Greenways, Esher 215 CE105
Greenways, Hert. 31 DN09
Greenways, Tad. 249 CV125
Greenways (Cheshunt), Wal.Cr. 65 DP29
Greenways, Wok. 227 BA117
Pembroke Rd.
Greenways, The, Twick. 177 CG86
Greenwell Clo., Gdse. 252 DV130
Greenwell St. W1 273 J5
Greenwell St. W1 141 DH70
Greenwich Ch. St. SE10 163 EC79
Greenwich Cres. E6 144 EL71
Swan App.
Greenwich Foot Tunnel E14 163 EC78
Greenwich Foot Tunnel SE10 163 EC78
Greenwich High Rd. SE10 163 EB81
Greenwich Ind. Est. SE7 164 EH77
Greenwich Mkt. SE10 163 EC79
Greenwich Pk. SE10 164 EE80
Greenwich Pk. St. SE10 163 ED78
Greenwich S. St. SE10 163 EB81
Greenwich Vw. Pl. E14 163 EB76
Greenwood, The, Guil. 243 BA134
Greenwood Ave., Dag. 127 FB63
Greenwood Ave., Enf. 83 DY40
Greenwood Ave. (Cheshunt), Wal.Cr. 66 DV31
Greenwood Clo., Add. 211 BF111
Greenwood Clo., Amer. 55 AS38
Greenwood Clo., Beac. 89 AQ51
Farmers Way
Greenwood Clo., Mord. 199 CY98
Greenwood Clo., Orp. 205 ES100
Greenwood Clo., Sid. 186 EU89
Hurst Rd.
Greenwood Clo., T.Ditt. 197 CG102
Greenwood Clo. (Cheshunt), Wal.Cr. 66 DV31
Greenwood Ave.
Greenwood Clo. (Bushey), Wat. 95 CE45
Langmead Dr.
Greenwood Ct. SW1 277 K10
Greenwood Ct. SW1 161 DJ78
Greenwood Dr. E4 101 EC50
Avril Way
Greenwood Dr., Red. 266 DG139
Greenwood Dr., Wat. 59 BV34
Greenwood Gdns. N13 99 DP48
Greenwood Gdns., Cat. 252 DU125
Greenwood Gdns., Ilf. 103 EQ52
Greenwood Gdns. (Shenley), Rad. 62 CL33
Greenwood Ho., Grays 170 GA79
Argent St.
Greenwood La., Hmptn. 176 CB92
Greenwood Pk., Kings.T. 178 CS94
Greenwood Pl. NW5 121 DH64
Highgate Rd.
Greenwood Rd. E8 142 DU65
Greenwood Rd. E13 144 EF68
Maud Rd.
Greenwood Rd., Bex. 187 FD91
Greenwood Rd., Chig. 104 EV48
Greenwood Rd., Croy. 201 DP101
Greenwood Rd., Islw. 157 CE83
Greenwood Rd., Mitch. 201 DK97
Greenwood Rd., T.Ditt. 197 CG102
Greenwood Rd., Wok. 226 AS120
Greenwood Ter. NW10 138 CR67
Greenwood Way, Sev. 256 FF125
Greenwoods, The, Har. 116 CC61
Sherwood Rd.
Greenyard, Wal.Abb. 67 EC33
Greer Rd., Har. 94 CC53
Greet St. SE1 278 E3
Greet St. SE1 141 DN74
Greg Clo. E10 123 EC58
Gregor Ms. SE3 164 EG80
Gregories Fm. La., Beac. 89 AK53
Gregories Rd., Beac. 88 AH53
Gregory Ave., Pot.B. 64 DC33
Gregory Cres. SE9 184 EK87
Gregory Dr., Wind. 172 AV86
Gregory Ms., Wal.Abb. 67 EB33
Beaulieu Dr.
Gregory Pl. W8 160 DB75
Gregory Rd., Rom. 126 EX56
Gregory Rd., Slou. 111 AR61
Gregory Rd., Sthl. 156 CA76
Gregson Clo., Borwd. 78 CQ39
Gregson's Ride, Loug. 85 EN38
Greig Clo. N8 121 DL57
Greig Ter. SE17 161 DP79
Lorrimore Sq.
Grena Gdns., Rich. 158 CM84
Grena Rd., Rich. 158 CM84
Grenaby Ave., Croy. 202 DR101
Grenaby Rd., Croy. 202 DR101
Grenada Rd. SE7 164 EJ80
Grenade St. E14 143 DZ73
Grenadier Clo., St.Alb. 43 CJ21
Grenadier St. E16 145 EN74
Grenadine Clo., Wal.Cr. 66 DT27
Allwood Rd.
Grendon Clo., Horl. 268 DF146
Grendon Gdns., Wem. 118 CN61
Grendon St. NW8 272 B4
Grendon St. NW8 140 DE70
Grenfell Ave., Horn. 127 FF60
Grenfell Clo., Borwd. 78 CQ39
Grenfell Gdns., Har. 118 CL59
Grenfell Rd. W11 139 CX73
Grenfell Rd., Beac. 89 AL52
Grenfell Rd., Mitch. 180 DF93
Grenfell Twr. W11 139 CX73
Grenfell Wk. W11 139 CX73
Grennell Clo., Sutt. 200 DD103
Grennell Rd., Sutt. 200 DC103
Grenoble Gdns. N13 99 DN51
Grenville Ave., Brox. 49 DZ21
Grenville Clo. N3 97 CZ53
Grenville Clo., Cob. 214 BY113
Grenville Clo., Slou. 130 AH68
Grenville Clo., Surb. 198 CQ102
Grenville Clo., Wal.Cr. 67 DX32
Grenville Gdns., Wdf.Grn. 102 EJ53
Grenville Ms. SW7 160 DC77
Grenville Ms., Hmptn. 176 CB92
Grenville Pl. NW7 96 CR50
Grenville Pl. SW7 160 DC76
Grenville Rd. N19 121 DL60
Grenville Rd., Croy. 221 EC109
Grenville St. WC1 274 A5
Grenville St. WC1 141 DL70
Gresford Clo., St.Alb. 43 CK20
Gresham Ave. N20 98 DF49
Gresham Ave., Warl. 237 DY118
Gresham Clo., Bex. 186 EY86
Gresham Clo., Brwd. 108 FW48
Gresham Clo., Enf. 82 DQ41
Gresham Clo., Oxt. 254 EF128
Gresham Ct., Berk. 38 AV20
Gresham Dr., Rom. 126 EV57
Gresham Gdns. NW11 119 CY60
Gresham Rd. E6 145 EM68
Gresham Rd. E16 144 EH72
Gresham Rd. NW10 118 CR64
Gresham Rd. SE25 202 DU98
Gresham Rd. SW9 161 DN83
Gresham Rd., Beck. 203 DY96
Gresham Rd., Brwd. 108 FW48
Gresham Rd., Edg. 96 CM51
Gresham Rd., Hmptn. 176 CA93
Gresham Rd., Houns. 156 CC81
Gresham Rd., Oxt. 254 EF128
Gresham Rd., Slou. 131 AN72
Gresham Rd., Stai. 173 BF92
Gresham Rd., Uxb. 134 BN68
Gresham St. EC2 275 H8
Gresham St. EC2 142 DQ72
Gresham Way SW19 180 DA90
Gresley Clo. E17 123 DY58
Gresley Clo. N15 122 DR56
Clinton Rd.
Gresley Clo., Welw.G.C. 29 CY08
Gresley Ct., Pot.B. 64 DC29
Gresley Rd. N19 121 DJ60
Gresse St. W1 273 M7
Gresse St. W1 141 DK71
Gressenhall Rd. SW18 179 CZ86
Gresswell Clo., Sid. 186 EU90
Greswell St. SW6 159 CX81
Greta Bank, Lthd. 245 BQ126
Gretton Rd. N17 100 DS52
Greville Ave., S.Croy. 221 DX110
Greville Clo., Ash. 232 CL119
Greville Clo., Guil. 242 AS134
Greville Clo., Hat. 45 CV24
Greville Clo., Twick. 177 CH87
Greville Ct., Lthd. 246 CC125
Keswick Rd.
Greville Hall NW6 140 DB68
Greville Ms. NW6 140 DB68
Greville Rd.
Greville Pk. Ave., Ash. 232 CL118
Greville Pk. Rd., Ash. 232 CL118
Greville Pl. NW6 140 DB68
Greville Rd. E17 123 EC56
Greville Rd. NW6 140 DB67
Greville Rd., Rich. 178 CM86
Greville St. EC1 274 E7
Greville St. EC1 141 DN71
Grey Alders, Bans. 217 CW114
High Beeches
Grey Clo. NW11 120 DC58
Grey Eagle St. E1 275 P6
Grey Eagle St. E1 142 DT71
Grey Twrs. Ave., Horn. 128 FK60
Grey Twrs. Gdns., Horn. 128 FK60
Grey Twrs. Ave.
Greycaine Rd., Wat. 76 BX37
Greycoat Pl. SW1 277 M7
Greycoat Pl. SW1 161 DK76
Greycoat St. SW1 277 M7
Greycoat St. SW1 161 DK76
Greycot Rd., Beck. 183 EA92
Greyfell Clo., Stan. 95 CH50
Coverdale Clo.
Greyfields Clo., Pur. 219 DP113
Greyfriars, Brwd. 109 GB45
Greyfriars Pas. EC1 274 G8
Greyfriars Rd., Wok. 228 BG124
Greygoose Pk., Harl. 51 EN18
Greyhound Hill NW4 119 CU55
Greyhound La. SW16 181 DK93
Greyhound La., Grays 171 GG75
Greyhound La., Pot.B. 63 CU33
Greyhound Rd. N17 122 DS55
Greyhound Rd. NW10 139 CV69
Greyhound Rd. W6 159 CX79
Greyhound Rd. W14 159 CX79
Greyhound Rd., Sutt. 218 DC106
Greyhound Ter. SW16 201 DJ95
Greyhound Way, Dart. 187 FE86
Greys Pk. Clo., Kes. 222 EJ106
Greystead Rd. SE23 182 DW87
Greystoke Ave., Pnr. 116 CA55
Greystoke Clo., Berk. 38 AU20
Greystoke Dr., Ruis. 115 BP58
Greystoke Gdns. W5 138 CL70
Greystoke Gdns., Enf. 81 DK42
Greystoke Pk. Ter. W5 137 CK69
Greystoke Pl. EC4 274 D8
Greystoke Rd., Slou. 131 AM71
Greystone Clo., S.Croy. 220 DW111
Greystone Gdns., Har. 117 CJ58
Greystone Gdns., Ilf. 103 EQ54
Greystone Path E11 124 EF59
Grove Rd.
Greystones Clo., Red. 266 DD136
Hardwick Rd.
Greystones Dr., Reig. 250 DC132
Greyswood St. SW16 181 DH93
Greythorne Rd., Wok. 226 AU118
Grice Ave., West. 222 EH113
Gridiron Pl., Upmin. 128 FP62
Grierson Rd. SE23 183 DX87
Grieves Rd., Grav. 191 GF90
Griffetts Yd., Chesh. 54 AP30
Bellingdon Rd.
Griffin Ave., Upmin. 129 FS58
Griffin Clo. NW10 119 CV64
Griffin Clo., Slou. 151 AQ75
Griffin Manor Way SE28 165 ER76
Griffin Rd. N17 100 DS54
Griffin Rd. SE18 165 ER78
Griffin Wk., Green. 189 FT85
Church Rd.
Griffin Way, Lthd. 246 CA126
Griffin Way, Sun. 195 BU96
Griffins, The, Grays 170 GB75
Griffith Clo., Dag. 126 EW60
Gibson Rd.
Griffiths Clo., Wor.Pk. 199 CV103
Griffiths Rd. SW19 180 DA94
Griffiths Way, St.Alb. 42 CC22
Grifon Rd., Grays 169 FW76
Griggs App., Ilf. 125 EQ61
Griggs Gdns., Horn. 128 FJ64
Tylers Cres.
Griggs Pl. SE1 279 N7
Griggs Rd. E10 123 EC58
Grilse Clo. N9 100 DV49
Grimsby St. E2 142 DU70
Cheshire St.
Grimsdells La., Amer. 55 AR37
Grimsdyke Cres., Barn. 79 CW41
Grimsdyke Rd., Pnr. 94 BY52
Grimsel Path SE5 161 DP80
Laxley Clo.
Grimshaw Clo. N6 120 DG59
Grimshaw Way, Rom. 127 FF57
Grimston Rd. SW6 159 CZ82
Grimston Rd., St.Alb. 43 CF21
Grimstone Clo., Rom. 105 FB51
Grimthorpe Clo., St.Alb. 43 CD17
Grimwade Ave., Croy. 202 DU104
Grimwade Clo. SE15 162 DW83
Grimwade Cres. SE15 162 DW83
Evelina Rd.
Grimwood Rd., Twick. 177 CF87
Grindal St. SE1 278 D5
Grindall Clo., Croy. 219 DP105
Hillside Rd.
Grindcobbe, St.Alb. 43 CD23
Grindleford Ave. N11 98 DG47
Grindley Gdns., Croy. 202 DT100
Grinling Pl. SE8 163 EA79
Grinstead Rd. SE8 163 DY78
Grisedale Clo., Pur. 220 DS114
Grisedale Gdns., Pur. 220 DS114
Grittleton Ave., Wem. 138 CP65
Grittleton Rd. W9 140 DA70
Grizedale Ter. SE23 182 DV89
Grobars Ave., Wok. 226 AW115
Grocer's Hall Ct. EC2 275 K9
Grogan Clo., Hmptn. 176 BZ93
Groom Cres. SW18 180 DD87
Groom Pl. SW1 276 G6
Groom Pl. SW1 160 DG76
Groom Rd., Brox. 67 DZ26
Groom Wk., Guil. 242 AY130
Slyfield Grn.
Groombridge Clo., Walt. 213 BV106
Groombridge Clo., Well. 186 EU85
Groombridge Rd. E9 143 DX66
Groomfield Clo. SW17 180 DG91
Grooms Cotts., Chesh. 56 AV30
Grooms Dr., Pnr. 115 BU57
Grosmont Rd. SE18 165 ET78
Grosse Way SW15 179 CV86
Grosvenor Ave. N5 122 DQ64
Grosvenor Ave. SW14 158 CS83
Grosvenor Ave., Cars. 218 DF107
Grosvenor Ave., Har. 116 CB58
Grosvenor Ave., Hayes 135 BS68
Grosvenor Ave., Kings L. 59 BQ28
Grosvenor Ave., Rich. 178 CL85
Grosvenor Rd.
Grosvenor Clo., Iver 133 BD69
Grosvenor Clo., Loug. 85 EP39
Grosvenor Cotts. SW1 276 F8
Grosvenor Ct. N14 99 DJ45
Grosvenor Ct. NW6 139 CX67
Christchurch Ave.
Grosvenor Ct., Guil. 243 BA132
London Rd.
Grosvenor Ct., Rick. 75 BR43
Mayfare
Grosvenor Ct., Slou. 132 AS72
Stoke Poges La.
Grosvenor Cres. NW9 118 CN56
Grosvenor Cres. SW1 276 G5
Grosvenor Cres. SW1 160 DG75
Grosvenor Cres., Dart. 188 FK85
Grosvenor Cres., Uxb. 135 BP66
Grosvenor Cres. Ms. SW1 276 F5
Grosvenor Cres. Ms. SW1 160 DG75
Grosvenor Dr., Horn. 128 FJ60
Grosvenor Dr., Loug. 85 EP39
Grosvenor Dr., Maid. 130 AC71
Grosvenor Est. SW1 277 N8
Grosvenor Est. SW1 161 DK77
Grosvenor Gdns. E6 144 EK69
Grosvenor Gdns. N10 121 DJ55
Grosvenor Gdns. N14 81 DK43
Grosvenor Gdns. NW2 119 CW64
Grosvenor Gdns. NW11 119 CZ58
Grosvenor Gdns. SW1 277 H6
Grosvenor Gdns. SW1 161 DH76
Grosvenor Gdns. SW14 158 CS83
Grosvenor Gdns., Kings.T. 177 CK93
Grosvenor Gdns., Upmin. 129 FR60
Grosvenor Gdns., Wall. 219 DJ108
Grosvenor Gdns., Wdf.Grn. 102 EG51
Grosvenor Gdns. Ms. E. SW1 277 J6
Grosvenor Gdns. Ms. N. SW1 277 H7
Grosvenor Gdns. Ms. S. SW1 277 J7
Grosvenor Gate W1 276 E1
Grosvenor Gate W1 140 DF73
Grosvenor Hill SW19 179 CY93
Grosvenor Hill W1 273 H10
Grosvenor Hill W1 141 DH73
Grosvenor Pk. SE5 162 DQ79
Grosvenor Pk. Rd. E17 123 EA57
Grosvenor Path, Loug. 85 EP39
Grosvenor Pl. SW1 276 G5
Grosvenor Pl. SW1 160 DG75
Grosvenor Pl., Wey. 195 BR104
Vale Rd.
Grosvenor Ri. E. E17 123 EB57
Grosvenor Rd. E6 144 EK67
Grosvenor Rd. E7 144 EH65
Grosvenor Rd. E10 123 EC60
Grosvenor Rd. E11 124 EG57
Grosvenor Rd. N3 97 CZ52
Grosvenor Rd. N9 100 DV46
Grosvenor Rd. N10 99 DH53
Grosvenor Rd. SE25 202 DU98
Grosvenor Rd. SW1 161 DH79
Grosvenor Rd. W4 158 CP78
Grosvenor Rd. W7 137 CG74
Grosvenor Rd., Belv. 166 FA79
Grosvenor Rd., Bexh. 186 EX85
Grosvenor Rd., Borwd. 78 CN41
Grosvenor Rd., Brent. 157 CK79
Grosvenor Rd., Brox. 49 DZ20
Grosvenor Rd., Dag. 126 EZ60
Grosvenor Rd., Epsom 232 CR119
Grosvenor Rd., Houns. 156 BZ83
Grosvenor Rd., Ilf. 125 EQ62
Grosvenor Rd., Nthwd. 93 BT50
Grosvenor Rd., Orp. 205 ES100
Grosvenor Rd., Rich. 178 CL85
Grosvenor Rd., Rom. 127 FD59
Grosvenor Rd., St.Alb. 43 CE21
Grosvenor Rd., Sthl. 156 BZ76
Grosvenor Rd., Stai. 174 BG94
Grosvenor Rd., Twick. 177 CG87
Grosvenor Rd., Wall. 219 DH107
Grosvenor Rd., Wat. 76 BW42
Grosvenor Rd., W.Wick. 203 EB102
Grosvenor Sq. W1 272 G10
Grosvenor Sq. W1 140 DG73
Grosvenor Sq., Kings L. 59 BQ28
Grosvenor Ave.
Grosvenor St. W1 273 H10
Grosvenor St. W1 141 DH73
Grosvenor Ter. SE5 161 DP80
Grosvenor Ter., Hem.H. 40 BG21
Grosvenor Vale, Ruis. 115 BT61
Grosvenor Way E5 122 DW61
Grosvenor Wf. Rd. E14 163 ED77
Grote's Bldgs. SE3 164 EE82
Grote's Pl. SE3 164 EE82
Groton Rd. SW18 180 DB89
Grotto, The, Ware 33 DX07
Grotto Pas. W1 272 G6
Grotto Rd., Twick. 177 CF89
Grotto Rd., Wey. 195 BP104
Ground La., Hat. 45 CV16
Grove, The E15 144 EE65
Grove, The N3 98 DA53
Grove, The N4 121 DM59
Grove, The N6 120 DG60
Grove, The N8 121 DK57
Grove, The N13 99 DN49
Grove, The N14 81 DJ43
Grove, The NW9 118 CR57
Grove, The NW11 119 CY59
Grove, The W5 137 CK74
Grove, The, Add. 212 BH106
Grove, The, Amer. 55 AR36
Grove, The, Bexh. 166 EX84
Grove, The, Brwd. 108 FT49
Grove, The, Cat. 235 DP121
Grove, The, Chesh. 72 AX36
Grove, The, Couls. 235 DK115
Grove, The, Edg. 96 CP49
Grove, The, Egh. 173 BA92
Grove, The, Enf. 81 DN40
Grove, The, Epsom 216 CS113
Grove, The (Ewell), Epsom 217 CT110
Grove, The, Esher 196 CB102
Grove, The, Grav. 191 GH87
Grove, The, Grnf. 136 CC72
Grove, The, Hat. 64 DA27
Grove, The, Horl. 269 DH149
Grove, The, Islw. 157 CE81
Grove, The, Pot.B. 64 DC32
Grove, The, Rad. 61 CG34
Grove, The, Sid. 186 EY92
Grove, The, Slou. 152 AU75
Grove, The, Stan. 95 CG47
Grove, The, Swan. 207 FF97
Grove, The, Swans. 190 FZ85
Grove, The, Tedd. 177 CG91
Grove, The, Twick. 177 CH86
Bridge Rd.
Grove, The, Upmin. 128 FP63
Grove, The, Uxb. 114 BN64
Grove, The, Walt. 195 BV101
Grove, The, Wat. 75 BQ37
Grove, The, W.Wick. 203 EB104
Grove, The, West. 238 EK118
Grove, The, Wok. 227 AZ116
Grove Ave. N3 98 DA52
Grove Ave. N10 99 DJ54
Grove Ave. W7 137 CE72
Grove Ave., Epsom 216 CS113
Grove Ave., Pnr. 116 BY56
Grove Ave., Sutt. 218 DA107
Grove Ave., Twick. 177 CF88
Grove Bank, Wat. 94 BX46
Grove Clo. N14 99 DH45
Avenue Rd.
Grove Clo. SE23 183 DX88
Grove Clo., Brom. 204 EG103
Grove Clo., Felt. 176 BY91
Grove Clo., Ger.Cr. 90 AW53
Grove La.

Grove Clo., Kings.T. 198 CM98
Grove Clo., Slou. 152 AU76
Alpha St. S.
Grove Clo., Uxb. 114 BN64
Grove Clo., Wind. 172 AV87
Grove Cor., Lthd. 246 CA126
Lower Shott
Grove Cotts. SW3 160 DE79
Grove Ct. SE3 164 EG81
Grove Ct., E.Mol. 197 CD99
Walton Rd.
Grove Ct., Wal.Abb. 67 EB33
Highbridge St.
Grove Cres. E18 102 EF54
Grove Cres. NW9 118 CQ56
Grove Cres. SE5 162 DS82
Grove Cres., Felt. 176 BY91
Grove Cres., Kings.T. 198 CL97
Grove Cres., Rick. 74 BN42
Grove Cres., Walt. 195 BV101
Grove Cres. Rd. E15 143 ED65
Grove End E18 102 EF54
Grove Hill
Grove End NW5 121 DH63
Chetwynd Rd.
Grove End, Ger.Cr. 90 AW53
Grove End Gdns. NW8 140 DD68
Grove End Rd.
Grove End La., Esher 197 CD102
Grove End Rd. NW8 140 DD69
Grove Fm. Ct., Mitch. 200 DF98
Brookfields Ave.
Grove Fm. Pk., Nthwd. 93 BR50
Grove Footpath, Surb. 198 CL98
Grove Gdns. E15 144 EE65
Grove Gdns. NW4 119 CU56
Grove Gdns. NW8 272 C3
Grove Gdns., Dag. 127 FC62
Grove Gdns., Enf. 83 DX39
Grove Gdns., Tedd. 177 CG91
Grove Grn. Rd. E11 123 EC62
Grove Hall Ct. NW8 140 DC69
Hall Rd.
Grove Hall Rd., Wat. 76 BY42
Grove Heath Ct., Wok. 228 BJ124
Grove Heath N., Wok. 228 BH122
Grove Heath Rd. (Ripley), Wok. 228 BH123
Grove Hill E18 102 EF54
Grove Hill, Ger.Cr. 90 AW52
Grove Hill, Har. 117 CE59
Grove Hill Rd. SE5 162 DS83
Grove Hill Rd., Har. 117 CE59
Grove Ho. Rd. N8 121 DL56
Grove La. SE5 162 DR81
Grove La., Beac. 89 AL53
Grove La., Chesh. 56 AU27
Grove La., Chig. 103 ET48
Grove La., Couls. 218 DG113
Grove La., Epp. 70 EU30
High St.
Grove La., Ger.Cr. 90 AV53
Grove La., Kings.T. 198 CL98
Grove La., Uxb. 134 BM70
Grove La. Ter. SE5 162 DS83
Grove La.
Grove Lea, Hat. 45 CU21
Grove Mkt. Pl. SE9 185 EM86
Grove Mead, Hat. 45 CT18
Grove Meadow, Welw.G.C. 30 DC09
Grove Ms. W6 159 CW76
Grove Ms. W11 139 CZ72
Portobello Rd.
Grove Mill La., Wat. 75 BP37
Grove Mill Pl., Cars. 200 DG104
Grove Pk. E11 124 EH58
Grove Pk. NW9 118 CQ56
Grove Pk. SE5 162 DS82
Grove Pk. Ave. E4 101 EB52
Grove Pk. Bri. W4 158 CQ80
Grove Pk. Gdns. W4 158 CP79
Grove Pk. Ms. W4 158 CQ80
Grove Pk. Rd. N15 122 DS56
Grove Pk. Rd. SE9 184 EJ90
Grove Pk. Rd. W4 158 CP80
Grove Pk. Rd., Rain. 147 FG67
Grove Pk. Ter. W4 158 CP79
Grove Pas. E2 142 DV68
Grove Pas., Tedd. 177 CG92
Grove Path (Cheshunt), Wal.Cr. 66 DU31
Grove Pl. NW3 120 DD63
Christchurch Hill
Grove Pl. SW12 181 DH86
Cathles Rd.
Grove Pl. W3 138 CQ74
Grove Pl. W5 137 CK74
The Gro.
Grove Pl., Bark. 145 EQ67
Clockhouse Ave.
Grove Pl., Hat. 45 CW24
Dixons Hill Rd.
Grove Pl., Wat. 76 CB39
Hartspring La.
Grove Pl., Wey. 213 BQ106
Princes Rd.
Grove Rd. E3 143 DX67
Grove Rd. E4 101 EB49
Grove Rd. E11 124 EF59
Grove Rd. E17 123 EB57
Grove Rd. E18 102 EF54
Grove Rd. N11 99 DH50
Grove Rd. N12 98 DD50
Grove Rd. N15 122 DS57
Grove Rd. NW2 139 CW65
Grove Rd. SW13 159 CT82
Grove Rd. SW19 180 DC94
Grove Rd. W3 138 CQ74
Grove Rd. W5 137 CK73
Grove Rd., Amer. 72 AT37
Grove Rd., Ash. 232 CM118
Grove Rd., Barn. 80 DE41
Grove Rd., Beac. 89 AK53
Grove Rd., Belv. 166 EZ79
Grove Rd., Bexh. 167 FC84
Grove Rd., Borwd. 78 CN39
Grove Rd., Brent. 157 CJ78
Grove Rd., Cher. 193 BF100
Grove Rd., E.Mol. 197 CD98
Grove Rd., Edg. 96 CN51
Grove Rd., Epsom 216 CS113
Grove Rd., Grav. 190 GB85
Grove Rd., Grays 170 GC79
Grove Rd., Guil. 243 BC134
Grove Rd., Hem.H. 40 BG22
Grove Rd., Horl. 268 DE147
Grove Rd., Houns. 156 CA84
Grove Rd., Islw. 157 CE81
Grove Rd., Mitch. 201 DH96
Grove Rd., Nthwd. 93 BR50
Grove Rd., Oxt. 253 EC134
Southlands La.
Grove Rd., Pnr. 116 BZ57
Grove Rd., Rich. 178 CM86
Grove Rd., Rick. 92 BG47
Grove Rd., Rom. 126 EV59
Grove Rd., St.Alb. 43 CD21
Grove Rd., Sev. 257 FJ121
Grove Rd. (Seal), Sev. 257 FN122
Grove Rd., Shep. 195 BQ100
Grove Rd., Slou. 131 AK68
Grove Rd., Surb. 197 CK99
Grove Rd., Sutt. 218 DB107
Grove Rd., Th.Hth. 201 DN98
Grove Rd., Twick. 177 CD90
Grove Rd., Uxb. 134 BK66
Grove Rd., Ware 33 DZ05
Grove Rd., West. 238 EJ120
Grove Rd., Wind. 151 AQ82
Grove Rd., Wok. 227 AZ116
Grove Rd. W., Enf. 82 DW37
Grove Shaw, Tad. 233 CY124
Grove St. N18 100 DT51
Grove St. SE8 163 DZ77
Grove Ter. NW5 121 DH62
Grove Ter., Tedd. 177 CG91
Grove Ter. Ms. NW5 121 DH62
Grove Ter.
Grove Vale SE22 162 DT84
Grove Vale, Chis. 185 EN93
Grove Vil. E14 143 EB73
Grove Wk., Hert. 32 DQ07
Grove Way, Esher 196 CC101
Grove Way, Rick. 73 BB43
Grove Way, Uxb. 134 BK66
Grove Way, Wem. 118 CP64
Grove Wd. Hill, Couls. 219 DK114
Grovebarns, Stai. 174 BG93
Grovebury Clo., Erith 167 FD79
Grovebury Gdns., St.Alb. 60 CC27
Grovebury Rd. SE2 166 EV75
Grovedale Clo. (Cheshunt), Wal.Cr. 66 DT30
Grovedale Rd. N19 121 DK61
Groveherst Rd., Dart. 168 FM83
Grovehill Rd., Red. 250 DE134
Groveland Ave. SW16 181 DM94
Groveland Ct. EC4 275 J9
Groveland Rd., Beck. 203 DZ97
Groveland Way, N.Mal. 198 CQ99
Grovelands, Hem.H. 41 BQ18
Grovelands, St.Alb. 60 CB27
Grovelands, W.Mol. 196 CA98
Grovelands Clo. SE5 162 DS82
Grovelands Clo., Har. 116 CB62
Grovelands Ct. N14 99 DK45
Grovelands Rd. N13 99 DM49
Grovelands Rd. N15 122 DU58
Grovelands Rd., Orp. 186 EU94
Grovelands Rd., Pur. 219 DL112
Grovelands Way, Grays 170 FZ78
Groveley Rd., Sun. 175 BS92
Grover Clo., Hem.H. 40 BK18
Grover Rd., Wat. 94 BX45
Groves Clo., B.End 110 AC60
Groveside, Lthd. 246 CA127
Groveside Clo. W3 138 CN72
Groveside Clo., Cars. 200 DE103
Groveside Clo., Lthd. 246 CA127
Groveside Rd. E4 102 EE47
Grovestile Waye, Felt. 175 BR87
Groveway SW9 161 DM81
Groveway, Dag. 126 EX63
Grovewood, Rich. 158 CN81
Sandycombe Rd.
Grovewood Clo., Rick. 73 BB43
Grovewood Pl., Wdf.Grn. 103 EM51
Grubb St., Oxt. 254 EJ128
Grubbs La., Hat. 46 DA22
Grummant Rd. SE15 162 DT81
Grundy St. E14 143 EB72
Gruneisen Rd. N3 98 DB52
Guardian Clo., Horn. 127 FH60
Guards Club Rd., Maid. 130 AC72
Guards Rd., Wind. 150 AJ82
Guards Wk., Wind. 150 AJ82
Guards Rd.
Guardsman Clo., Brwd. 108 FX50
Gubbins La., Rom. 106 FM52
Gubyon Ave. SE24 181 DP85
Guerin Sq. E3 143 DZ69
Malmesbury Rd.
Guernsey Clo., Guil. 243 BA129
Cotts Wd. Dr.
Guernsey Clo., Houns. 156 CA81
Guernsey Fm. Dr., Wok. 226 AX115
Guernsey Gro. SE24 182 DQ87
Guernsey Rd. E11 123 ED60
Guessens Ct., Welw.G.C. 29 CW09
Guessens Gro., Welw.G.C. 29 CW09
Guessens Rd., Welw.G.C. 29 CW09
Guessens Wk., Welw.G.C. 29 CW08
Guibal Rd. SE12 184 EH87
Guild Rd. SE7 164 EK78
Guild Rd., Erith 167 FF80
Guildcroft, Guil. 243 BA134
Guildersfield Rd. SW16 181 DL94
Guildford & Godalming Bypass, Guil. 258 AS137
Guildford Ave., Felt. 175 BT89
Guildford Business Pk., Guil. 242 AV133
Guildford Bypass, Guil. 243 AZ131
Guildford Gdns., Rom. 106 FL51
Guildford Gro. SE10 163 EB81
Guildford La., Guil. 260 BH139
Guildford La., Wok. 226 AX120
Guildford Lo. Dr., Lthd. 245 BT129
Guildford Pk. Ave., Guil. 258 AV135
Guildford Pk. Rd., Guil. 258 AV135
Guildford Rd. E6 144 EL72
Guildford Rd. E17 101 EC53
Guildford Rd. SW8 161 DL81
Guildford Rd., Cher. 193 BE102
Guildford Rd., Croy. 202 DR100
Guildford Rd. (Abinger Hammer), Dor. 261 BS139
Guildford Rd. (Westcott), Dor. 262 CA138
Guildford Rd., Gdmg. 258 AU144
Guildford Rd., Guil. 242 AX127
Guildford Rd., Ilf. 125 ES61
Guildford Rd., Lthd. 247 CE125
Guildford Rd. (East Horsley), Lthd. 245 BT130
Guildford Rd. (Great Bookham), Lthd. 246 BZ127
Guildford Rd., Rom. 106 FL51
Guildford Rd., St.Alb. 43 CH21
Guildford Rd., Wok. 226 AY119
Guildford Rd. (Mayford), Wok. 226 AX122
Guildford St., Cher. 193 BF102
Guildford St., Stai. 174 BG93
Guildford Way, Wall. 219 DL106
Guildhall Bldgs. EC2 142 DR72
Basinghall St.
Guildhall Yd. EC2 275 K8
Guildhouse St. SW1 277 K8
Guildhouse St. SW1 161 DJ77
Guildown Ave. N12 98 DB49
Guildown Ave., Guil. 258 AV137
Guildown Rd., Guil. 258 AV137
Guildsway E17 101 DZ53
Guileshill La., Wok. 228 BL123
Guilford Ave., Surb. 198 CM99
Guilford Pl. WC1 274 B5
Guilford Pl. WC1 141 DM70
Guilford St. WC1 273 P5
Guilford St. WC1 141 DL70
Guilford Vil., Surb. 198 CM100
Alpha Rd.
Guilfords, Harl. 36 EX10
Guilsborough Clo. NW10 138 CS66
Guinevere Gdns., Wal.Cr. 67 DY31
Guinness Bldgs. SE1 279 M7
Guinness Bldgs. SE1 162 DS77
Guinness Clo. E9 143 DY66
Guinness Clo., Hayes 155 BR76
Guinness Ct., Wok. 226 AT118
Iveagh Rd.
Guinness Sq. SE1 279 M8
Guinness Trust Bldgs. SE11 278 G10
Guinness Trust Bldgs. SE11 161 DP78
Guinness Trust Bldgs. SW3 276 D9
Guinness Trust Bldgs. SW9 161 DP84
Guinness Trust Est. N16 122 DS60
Holmleigh Rd.
Guion Rd. SW6 159 CZ82
Gull Clo., Wall. 219 DL108
Gull Wk., Horn. 147 FH66
Heron Flight Ave.
Gulland Clo. (Bushey), Wat. 76 CC43
Gulland Wk. N1 142 DQ65
Clephane Rd.
Gullbrook, Hem.H. 40 BG20
Gullet Wd. Rd., Wat. 75 BU35
Gulliver Clo., Nthlt. 136 BZ67
Gulliver Rd., Sid. 185 ES89
Gulliver St. SE16 163 DZ76
Gulphs, The, Hert. 32 DR09
Gulston Wk. SW3 276 E9
Gulston Wk. W11 139 CZ72
Basing St.
Gumleigh Rd. W5 157 CJ77
Gumley Gdns., Islw. 157 CG83
Gumley Rd., Grays 169 FX79
Gumping Rd., Orp. 205 EQ103
Gun Hill, Til. 171 GK79
Gun St. E1 275 P7
Gun St. E1 142 DT71
Gundulph Rd., Brom. 204 EJ97
Gunfleet Clo., Grav. 191 GL87
Gunmakers La. E3 143 DY67
Gunn Rd., Swans. 190 FY86
Gunnell Clo. SE26 182 DU92
Gunnell Clo., Croy. 202 DU100
Gunner La. SE18 165 EN78
Gunners Gro. E4 101 EC48
Gunners Rd. SW18 180 DD89
Gunnersbury Ave. W3 158 CN76
Gunnersbury Ave. W4 158 CN76
Gunnersbury Ave. W5 138 CM74
Gunnersbury Clo. W4 158 CP78
Grange Rd.
Gunnersbury Ct. W3 158 CP75
Bollo La.
Gunnersbury Cres. W3 158 CN75
Gunnersbury Dr. W5 158 CM75
Gunnersbury Gdns. W3 158 CN75
Gunnersbury La. W3 158 CN76
Gunnersbury Ms. W4 158 CP78
Chiswick High Rd.
Gunnersbury Pk. W3 158 CM77
Gunnersbury Pk. W5 158 CM77
Gunning Rd., Grays 170 GD78
Gunning St. SE18 165 ES77
Gunpowder Sq. EC4 274 E8
Gunstor Rd. N16 122 DS63
Gunter Gro. SW10 160 DC79
Gunter Gro., Edg. 96 CR53
Gunterstone Rd. W14 159 CY77
Gunthorpe St. E1 142 DT72
Gunton Rd. E5 122 DV62
Gunton Rd. SW17 180 DG93
Gunwhale Clo. SE16 143 DX74
Gurdon Rd. SE7 164 EG78
Gurnard Clo., West Dr. 134 BK73
Trout Rd.
Gurnell Gro. W13 137 CF70
Gurnells Rd., Beac. 89 AQ50
Gurney Clo. E15 124 EE64
Gurney Rd.
Gurney Clo. E17 101 DX53
Gurney Clo., Bark. 145 EP65
Gurney Ct. Rd., St.Alb. 43 CF18
Gurney Cres., Croy. 201 DM102
Gurney Dr. N2 120 DC57
Gurney Rd. E15 124 EE64
Gurney Rd., Cars. 218 DG105
Gurney Rd., Nthlt. 135 BV69
Gurney's Clo., Red. 266 DF135
Guthrie St. SW3 276 B10
Gutter La. EC2 275 J8
Gutter La. EC2 142 DQ72
Gutteridge La., Rom. 87 FC44
Guy Barnett Gro. SE3 164 EG83
Casterbridge Rd.
Guy Rd., Wall. 201 DK104
Guy St. SE1 279 L4
Guy St. SE1 162 DR75
Guyatt Gdns., Mitch. 200 DG96
Ormerod Gdns.
Guyscliff Rd. SE13 183 EC85
Guysfield Clo., Rain. 147 FG67
Guysfield Dr., Rain. 147 FG67
Gwalior Rd. SW15 159 CX83
Felsham Rd.
Gwendolen Ave. SW15 179 CX85
Gwendolen Clo. SW15 179 CX85
Gwendoline Ave. E13 144 EH67
Gwendwr Rd. W14 159 CY78
Gwent Clo., Wat. 60 BX34
Gwillim Clo., Sid. 186 EU85
Gwydor Rd., Beck. 203 DX98
Gwydyr Rd., Brom. 204 EF97
Gwyn Clo. SW6 160 DC80
Gwynn Rd., Grav. 190 GC89
Gwynne Ave., Croy. 203 DX101
Gwynne Clo. W4 159 CT79
Gwynne Clo., Wind. 151 AL81
Gwynne Pk. Ave., Wdf.Grn. 103 EM51
Gwynne Pl. WC1 274 C3
Gwynne Rd. SW11 160 DD82
Gwynne Rd., Cat. 236 DQ121
Coulsdon Rd.
Gwynne Vaughan Ave., Guil. 242 AU130
Gwynns Wk., Hert. 32 DS09
Gyfford Wk., Wal.Cr. 66 DV31
Gylcote Clo. SE5 162 DR84
Gyles Pk., Stan. 95 CJ53
Gyllyngdune Gdns., Ilf. 125 ET61
Gypsy Clo., Ware 33 DZ11
Gypsy La., Hat. 29 CZ13
Gypsy La., Kings L. 75 BR35
Gypsy La., Slou. 112 AS62
Gypsy La., Ware 33 DZ11

H

Ha-Ha Rd. SE18 165 EM79
Haarlem Rd. W14 159 CX76
Haberdasher Est. N1 142 DR69
Haberdasher St.
Haberdasher Pl. N1 275 L2
Haberdasher St. N1 275 L2
Haberdasher St. N1 142 DR69
Habgood Rd., Loug. 84 EL41
Haccombe Rd. SW19 180 DC93
Haydons Rd.
Hackbridge Grn., Wall. 200 DG103
Hackbridge Pk. Gdns., Cars. 200 DG103
Hackbridge Rd., Wall. 200 DG103
Hackett La., Saw. 35 ET05
Hacketts La., Wok. 211 BF114
Hackford Rd. SW9 161 DM81
Hackforth Clo., Barn. 79 CV43
Hackhurst La., Dor. 261 BT139
Hackington Cres., Beck. 183 EA93
Hackney Clo., Borwd. 78 CR43
Hackney Gro. E8 142 DV65
Reading La.
Hackney Rd. E2 275 P3
Hackney Rd. E2 142 DT69
Hacton Dr., Horn. 128 FK63
Hacton La., Horn. 128 FM64
Hacton La., Upmin. 128 FM64
Hadden Rd. SE28 165 ES76
Hadden Way, Grnf. 137 CD65
Haddestoke Gate (Cheshunt), Wal.Cr. 67 DZ26
Haddington Rd., Brom. 183 ED90
Haddo St. SE10 163 EB79
Haddon Clo., Borwd. 78 CN41
Haddon Clo., Enf. 82 DU44
Haddon Clo., Hem.H. 40 BN21
Haddon Clo., N.Mal. 199 CT99
Haddon Clo., Wey. 195 BR104
Haddon Rd., Orp. 206 EW99
Haddon Rd., Rick. 73 BC43
Haddon Rd., Sutt. 218 DB105
Haddonfield SE8 163 DX77
Hadfield Clo., Sthl. 136 BZ69
Adrienne Ave.
Hadfield Rd., Stai. 174 BK86
Hadleigh Clo. E1 142 DW70
Mantus Rd.
Hadleigh Clo. SW20 199 CZ96
Hadleigh Ct., Brox. 49 DZ22
Hadleigh Dr., Sutt. 218 DA109
Hadleigh Rd. N9 100 DV45
Hadleigh St. E2 142 DW70
Hadleigh Wk. E6 144 EL72
Hadley Clo. N21 81 DN44
Hadley Clo., Borwd. 78 CM44
Hadley Common, Barn. 80 DA40
Hadley Gdns. W4 158 CR78
Hadley Gdns., Sthl. 156 BZ78
Hadley Gra., Harl. 52 EW15
Hadley Grn., Barn. 79 CZ40
Hadley Grn. Rd., Barn. 79 CZ40
Hadley Grn. W., Barn. 79 CZ40
Hadley Gro., Barn. 79 CY40
Hadley Highstone, Barn. 79 CZ39
Hadley Pl., Wey. 212 BN108
Hadley Ridge, Barn. 79 CZ41
Hadley Rd. (Hadley Wd.), Barn. 81 DH38
Hadley Rd. (New Barnet), Barn. 80 DB42
Hadley Rd., Belv. 166 EZ77
Hadley Rd., Enf. 81 DL38
Hadley Rd., Mitch. 201 DK98
Hadley St. NW1 141 DH65
Hadley Way N21 81 DN44
Hadley Wd. Ri., Ken. 235 DP115
Hadlow Ct., Slou. 131 AQ73
Hadlow Pl. SE19 182 DU94
Hadlow Rd., Sid. 186 EU91
Hadlow Rd., Well. 166 EW80
Hadlow Way, Grav. 190 GE94
Hadrian Clo., St.Alb. 42 CA22
Hadrian Clo., Stai. 174 BL88
Hadrian Way
Hadrian Clo., Wall. 219 DL108
Hadrian Est. E2 142 DU68
Hadrian St. SE10 164 EE78
Hadrian Way, Stai. 174 BK87
Hadrians Ride, Enf. 82 DT43
Hadyn Pk. Rd. W12 159 CU75
Hafer Rd. SW11 160 DF84
Hafton Rd. SE6 184 EE88
Hag Hill La., Maid. 130 AG72
Hag Hill Ri., Maid. 130 AG72
Hagden La., Wat. 75 BT43
Haggard Rd., Twick. 177 CG87
Haggerston Rd. E8 142 DT66
Haggerston Rd., Borwd. 78 CL38
Hagsdell La., Hert. 32 DR09
Hagsdell Rd., Hert. 32 DR09
Hague St. E2 142 DU69
Derbyshire St.
Haig Clo., St.Alb. 43 CH21
Kitchener Clo.
Haig Dr., Slou. 151 AP75
Haig Gdns., Grav. 191 GJ87
Haig Pl., Mord. 200 DA100
Green La.
Haig Rd., Grays 171 GG76
Haig Rd., Stan. 95 CJ50
Haig Rd., Uxb. 135 BP71
Haig Rd., West. 238 EL117
Haig Rd. E. E13 144 EJ69
Haig Rd. W. E13 144 EJ69
Haigh Cres., Red. 267 DH136
Haigville Gdns., Ilf. 125 EP56
Hailes Clo. SW19 180 DC93
North Rd.
Hailey Ave., Hodd. 33 EA13
Hailey La., Hert. 33 DX13
Hailey Rd., Erith 166 FA75
Haileybury Ave., Enf. 82 DT44
Haileybury Rd., Orp. 224 EU105
Hailsham Ave. SW2 181 DM89
Hailsham Clo., Rom. 106 FJ50
Hailsham Clo., Surb. 197 CK101
Hailsham Dr., Har. 117 CD55
Hailsham Gdns., Rom. 106 FJ50
Hailsham Rd. SW17 180 DG93
Hailsham Rd., Rom. 106 FJ50
Hailsham Ter. N18 100 DQ50
Haimo Rd. SE9 184 EK85
Hainault Ct. E17 123 ED56
Hainault Gore, Rom. 126 EY57
Hainault Gro., Chig. 103 EQ49
Hainault Rd. E11 123 EC60
Hainault Rd., Chig. 103 EP48
Hainault Rd., Rom. 105 FC54
Hainault Rd. (Chadwell Heath), Rom. 126 EZ58
Hainault Rd. (Hainault), Rom. 126 EV55
Hainault St. SE9 185 EP88
Hainault St., Ilf. 125 EP61
Haines Ct., Wey. 213 BR106
St. George's Lo.
Haines Wk., Mord. 200 DB101
Dorchester Rd.
Haines Way, Wat. 59 BU34
Hainford Clo. SE4 163 DX84
Haining Clo. W4 158 CN78
Wellesley Rd.
Hainthorpe Rd. SE27 181 DP90
Hainton Clo. E1 142 DV72
Halberd Ms. E5 122 DV61
Knightland Rd.
Halbutt Gdns., Dag. 126 EZ62
Halbutt St., Dag. 126 EZ63
Halcomb St. N1 142 DS67
Halcot Ave., Bexh. 187 FB85
Halcrow St. E1 142 DV71
Newark St.
Halcyon Ct., Wem. 118 CP62
Coffers Circle
Halcyon Way, Horn. 128 FM60
Haldan Rd. E4 101 EC51
Haldane Clo. N10 99 DH52
Haldane Gdns., Grav. 190 GC88
Haldane Pl. SW18 180 DB88
Haldane Rd. E6 144 EK69
Haldane Rd. SE28 146 EX73
Haldane Rd. SW6 159 CZ80
Haldane Rd., Sthl. 136 CC72
Haldens, Welw.G.C. 29 CZ06
Haldon Clo., Chig. 103 ES50
Arrowsmith Rd.
Haldon Rd. SW18 179 CZ85
Hale, The E4 101 ED52
Hale, The N17 122 DU56
Hale Clo. E4 101 EC48
Hale Clo., Edg. 96 CQ50
Hale Clo., Orp. 223 EQ105
Hale Dr. NW7 96 CQ51
Hale End, Rom. 105 FH51
Hale End, Wok. 226 AV121
Hale End Clo., Ruis. 115 BU58
Hale End Rd. E4 101 ED51
Hale End Rd. E17 101 ED53
Hale End Rd., Wdf.Grn. 101 ED52
Hale Gdns. N17 122 DU55
Hale Gdns. W3 138 CN74
Hale Gro. Gdns. NW7 96 CR50
Hale La. NW7 96 CR50
Hale La., Edg. 96 CP50
Hale La., Sev. 241 FE117
Hale Path SE27 181 DP91
Hale Pit Rd., Lthd. 246 CC126
Hale Rd. E6 144 EL70
Hale Rd. N17 122 DU55
Hale Rd., Hert. 32 DR10
Hale St. E14 143 EB73
Hale St., Stai. 173 BE91
Hale Wk. W7 137 CE71
Halefield Rd. N17 100 DU53
Hales Oak, Lthd. 246 CC126
Hales Pk., Hem.H. 41 BQ19
Hales Pk. Clo., Hem.H. 41 BQ19
Hales St. SE8 163 EA80
Deptford High St.
Halesowen Rd., Mord. 200 DB101
Haleswood, Cob. 213 BV114
Haleswood Rd., Hem.H. 41 BP19
Halesworth Clo. E5 122 DW61
Theydon Rd.
Halesworth Clo., Rom. 106 FL52
Halesworth Rd. SE13 163 EB83
Halesworth Rd., Rom. 106 FL51
Haley Rd. NW4 119 CW58
Half Acre, Brent. 157 CK79
Half Acre Rd. W7 137 CE74
Half Moon Ct. EC1 275 H7
Half Moon Cres. N1 141 DM68
Half Moon La. SE24 182 DQ86
Half Moon La., Epp. 69 ET31
Half Moon Meadow, Hem.H. 41 BP15
Half Moon Pas. E1 142 DT72
Braham St.
Half Moon St. W1 277 J2
Half Moon St. W1 141 DH74
Half Moon Yd., St.Alb. 43 CD20
Chequer St.
Halfacre Hill, Ger.Cr. 91 AZ53
Halfhide La. (Cheshunt), Wal.Cr. 67 DX27

Halfhides, Wal.Abb. 67 ED33
Halford Clo., Edg. 96 CP54
Halford Rd. E10 123 ED57
Halford Rd. SW6 160 DA79
Halford Rd., Rich. 178 CL85
Halford Rd., Uxb. 114 BN64
Halfpenny Clo., Guil. 259 BD140
Halfpenny La., Guil. 259 BC136
Halfway Ct., Purf. 168 FN77
Thamley
Halfway Grn., Walt. 195 BV104
Halfway Ho. La., Amer. 54 AL33
Halfway St., Sid. 185 ER87
Haliburton Rd., Twick. 177 CG85
Haliday Wk. N1 142 DR65
Balls Pond Rd.
Halidon Clo. E9 122 DW64
Urswick Rd.
Halidon Ri., Rom. 106 FP51
Halifax Rd., Enf. 82 DQ40
Halifax Rd., Grnf. 136 CB67
Halifax Rd., Rick. 91 BC45
Halifax St. SE26 182 DV91
Halifax Way, Welw.G.C. 30 DE09
Halifield Dr., Belv. 166 EY76
Haling Down Pas., S.Croy. 220 DQ109
Haling Gro., S.Croy. 220 DQ108
Haling Pk., S.Croy. 220 DQ107
Haling Pk. Gdns., S.Croy. 219 DP107
Haling Pk. Rd., S.Croy. 219 DP106
Haling Rd., S.Croy. 220 DR107
Halings La., Uxb. 113 BD56
Halkin Arc. SW1 276 F6
Halkin Arc. SW1 160 DG76
Halkin Ms. SW1 276 F6
Halkin Pl. SW1 276 F6
Halkin Pl. SW1 160 DG76
Halkin St. SW1 276 G5
Halkin St. SW1 160 DG75
Halkingcroft, Slou. 152 AW75
Hall, The SE3 164 EG83
Hall Ave. N18 100 DR51
Weir Hall Ave.
Hall Ave., S.Ock. 148 FQ74
Hall Clo. W5 138 CL71
Hall Clo., Gdmg. 258 AS144
Hall Clo., Rick. 92 BG46
Hall Ct., Slou. 152 AV80
Hall Ct., Tedd. 177 CF92
Teddington Pk.
Hall Cres., S.Ock. 168 FQ75
Hall Dene Clo., Guil. 243 BC133
Hall Dr. SE26 182 DW92
Hall Dr. W7 137 CE72
Hall Dr. (Harefield), Uxb. 92 BJ53
Hall Fm. Clo., Stan. 95 CH49
Hall Fm. Dr., Twick. 177 CD87
Hall Gdns. E4 101 DZ49
Hall Gdns., St.Alb. 44 CR23
Hall Gate NW8 140 DC69
Hall Rd.
Hall Grn. La., Brwd. 109 GC45
Hall Gro., Welw.G.C. 30 DB11
Hall Heath Clo., St.Alb. 43 CH18
Hall Hill, Oxt. 253 ED131
Hall Hill, Sev. 257 FP123
Hall La. E4 101 DY50
Hall La. NW4 97 CU53
Hall La., Brwd. 109 FZ44
Hall La., Hayes 155 BR80
Hall La., S.Ock. 149 FX68
Hall La., Upmin. 128 FQ55
Hall Meadow, Slou. 130 AJ68
Hall Oak Wk. NW6 139 CZ65
Maygrove Rd.
Hall Pk., Berk. 38 AY20
Hall Pk. Gate, Berk. 38 AY21
Hall Pk. Hill, Berk. 38 AY21
Hall Pk. Rd., Upmin. 128 FQ64
Hall Pl. W2 140 DD70
Hall Pl., Wok. 227 BA116
Hall Pl. Clo., St.Alb. 43 CE19
Hall Pl. Cres., Bex. 187 FC85
Hall Pl. Dr., Wey. 213 BS106
Hall Pl. Gdns., St.Alb. 43 CE19
Hall Rd. E6 145 EM67
Hall Rd. E15 123 ED63
Hall Rd. NW8 140 DC69
Hall Rd., Dart. 168 FM84
Hall Rd., Grav. 190 GC90
Hall Rd., Hem.H. 41 BP18
Hall Rd., Islw. 177 CD85
Hall Rd., Rom. 126 EW58
Hall Rd. (Gidea Pk.), Rom. 127 FH55
Hall Rd., S.Ock. 168 FQ75
Hall Rd., Wall. 219 DH109
Hall St. EC1 274 G2
Hall St. EC1 141 DP69
Hall St. N12 98 DC50
Hall Ter., Rom. 106 FN52
Hall Ter., S.Ock. 169 FR75
Hall Vw. SE9 184 EK89
Hall Way, Pur. 219 DP113
Hallam Clo., Chis. 185 EM92
Hallam Clo., Wat. 76 BW40
Hallam Gdns., Pnr. 94 BY52
Hallam Ms. W1 273 J6
Hallam Rd. N15 121 DP56
Hallam Rd. SW13 159 CV83
Hallam St. W1 273 J5
Hallam St. W1 141 DH71
Halland Way, Nthwd. 93 BR51
Halley Gdns. SE13 163 ED84
Halley Rd. E7 144 EJ65
Halley Rd. E12 144 EK65
Halley St. E14 143 DY71
Halleys App., Wok. 226 AU118
Halleys Ct., Wok. 226 AU118
Halleys App.
Halleys Ridge, Hert. 31 DN10
Halleys Wk., Add. 212 BJ108
Hallfield Est. W2 140 DC72
Hallford Way, Dart. 188 FJ85
Halliards, The, Walt. 195 BU100
Felix Rd.
Halliday Clo. (Shenley), Rad. 62 CL32
Halliday Sq., Sthl. 137 CD74
Halliford Clo., Shep. 195 BR98
Halliford Rd., Shep. 195 BS99
Halliford Rd., Sun. 195 BT99
Halliford St. N1 142 DQ66
Halling Hill, Harl. 35 ET13
Hallingbury Ct. E17 123 EB55
Hallington Clo., Wok. 226 AV117
Halliwell Rd. SW2 181 DM86
Halliwick Rd. N10 98 DG53
Hallmark Trd. Est. NW10 118 CQ63
Great Cen. Way
Hallmead Rd., Sutt. 200 DB104
Hallmores, Brox. 49 EA19
Hallowell Ave., Croy. 219 DL105
Hallowell Clo., Mitch. 200 DG97
Hallowell Rd., Nthwd. 93 BS52
Hallowes Cres., Wat. 93 BU48
Hayling Rd.
Hallowfield Way, Mitch. 200 DE97
Hallside Rd., Enf. 82 DT38
Hallsland Way, Oxt. 254 EF132
Hallsville Rd. E16 144 EF72
Hallswelle Rd. NW11 119 CZ57
Hallwood Cres., Brwd. 108 FY45
Hallywell Cres. E6 145 EM71
Halons Rd. SE9 185 EN87
Halpin Pl. SE17 279 L9
Halsbrook Rd. SE3 164 EK83
Halsbury Clo., Stan. 95 CH49
Halsbury Rd. W12 139 CV74
Halsbury Rd. E., Nthlt. 116 CC63
Halsbury Rd. W., Nthlt. 116 CB64
Halse Dr., Slou. 111 AM63
Halsend, Hayes 135 BV74
Halsey Ms. SW3 276 D8
Halsey Pk., St.Alb. 62 CM27
Halsey Pl., Wat. 75 BV38
Halsey Rd., Wat. 75 BV41
Halsey St. SW3 276 D8
Halsey St. SW3 160 DF77
Halsford Bri. Ind. Est., Brwd. 108 FW47
Halsham Cres., Bark. 145 ET65
Halsmere Rd. SE5 161 DP81
Halstead Clo., Croy. 202 DQ104
Charles St.
Halstead Ct. N1 275 L1
Halstead Gdns. N21 100 DR46
Halstead Hill (Cheshunt), Wal.Cr. 66 DS29
Halstead La., Sev. 224 EZ114
Halstead Rd. E11 124 EG57
Halstead Rd. N21 100 DQ46
Halstead Rd., Enf. 82 DS42
Halstead Rd., Erith 167 FE81
Halstead Way, Brwd. 109 GC44
Halston Clo. SW11 180 DF86
Halstow Rd. NW10 139 CX69
Halstow Rd. SE10 164 EG78
Halsway, Hayes 135 BU74
Halt Robin La., Belv. 167 FB77
Halt Robin Rd.
Halt Robin Rd., Belv. 166 FA77
Halter Clo., Borwd. 78 CR43
Clydesdale Clo.
Halton Cross St. N1 141 DP67
Halton Pl. N1 142 DQ67
Dibden St.
Halton Rd. N1 141 DP66
Halton Rd., Grays 171 GJ76
Haltside, Hat. 44 CS19
Halwick Clo., Hem.H. 40 BH21
Ham, The, Brent. 157 CJ80
Ham Clo., Rich. 177 CJ90
Ham Common, Rich. 178 CM91
Ham Fm. Rd., Rich. 177 CK91
Ham La., Egh. 172 AV91
Ham La., Wind. 152 AW84
Ham Pk. Rd. E7 144 EF66
Ham Pk. Rd. E15 144 EF66
Ham Ridings, Rich. 178 CM92
Ham St., Rich. 177 CH88
Ham Vw., Croy. 203 DY100
Ham Yd. W1 273 M10
Hambalt Rd. SW4 181 DJ85
Hamble Clo., Ruis. 115 BS61
Chichester Ave.
Hamble Clo., Wok. 226 AU117
Hamble Ct., Kings.T. 177 CK94
Hamble La., S.Ock. 149 FT71
Hamble St. SW6 160 DB83
Hamble Wk., Nthlt. 136 CA68
Brabazon Rd.
Hamble Wk., Wok. 226 AU118
Denton Way
Hambledon Clo., Uxb. 135 BP71
Aldenham Dr.
Hambledon Gdns. SE25 202 DT97
Hambledon Hill, Epsom 232 CQ116
Hambledon Pl. SE21 182 DS88
Hambledon Rd. SW18 179 CZ87
Hambledon Rd., Cat. 236 DQ121
Coulsdon Rd.
Hambledon Vale, Epsom 232 CQ116
Hambledown Rd., Sid. 185 ER87
Hambleton Clo., Wor.Pk. 199 CW103
Cotswold Way
Hamblings Clo., Rad. 61 CK33
Hambridge Way SW2 181 DN87
Hambro Ave., Brom. 204 EG102
Hambro Rd. SW16 181 DK93
Hambro Rd., Brwd. 108 FX47
Hambrook Rd. SE25 202 DV97
Hambrough Rd., Sthl. 136 BY74
Hamburgh Ct., Wal.Cr. 67 DX28
Hamden Cres., Dag. 127 FB62
Hamel Clo., Har. 117 CK55
Hamelin St. E14 143 EC72
St. Leonards Rd.
Hamels Dr., Hert. 32 DV08
Hamer Clo., Hem.H. 57 BA28
Hamerton Rd., Grav. 190 GB85
Hameway E6 145 EN70
Hamfield Clo., Oxt. 253 EC127
Hamfrith Rd. E15 144 EF65
Hamhaugh Island, Shep. 194 BN103
Hamilton Ave. N9 100 DU45
Hamilton Ave., Cob. 213 BU113
Hamilton Ave., Hodd. 49 EA15
Hamilton Ave., Ilf. 125 EP56
Hamilton Ave., Rom. 105 FD54
Hamilton Ave., Surb. 198 CP102
Hamilton Ave., Sutt. 199 CY103
Hamilton Ave., Wok. 227 BE115
Hamilton Clo. N17 122 DT55
Hamilton Clo. NW8 140 DD69
Hamilton Clo. SE16 163 DY75
Somerford Way
Hamilton Clo., Barn. 80 DE42
Hamilton Clo., Cher. 193 BF102
Hamilton Clo., Epsom 216 CQ112
Hamilton Clo., Felt. 175 BT92
Hamilton Clo., Guil. 242 AU129
Hamilton Clo., Pot.B. 63 CU33
Hamilton Clo., Pur. 219 DP112
Hamilton Clo., St.Alb. 60 CA30
Hamilton Clo., Stan. 95 CF47
Hamilton Ct. W5 138 CM73
Hamilton Ct. W9 140 DC69
Maida Vale
Hamilton Ct., Hat. 45 CV20
Cooks Way
Hamilton Ct., Lthd. 246 CB125
Eastwick Pk. Ave.
Hamilton Cres. N13 99 DN49
Hamilton Cres., Brwd. 108 FW49
Hamilton Cres., Har. 116 BZ62
Hamilton Cres., Houns. 176 CB85
Hamilton Dr., Guil. 242 AU129
Hamilton Dr., Rom. 106 FL54
Hamilton Gdns. NW8 140 DC69
Hamilton Gdns., Slou. 130 AH69
Hamilton Gordon Ct., Guil. 242 AW133
Langley Clo.
Hamilton La. N5 121 DP63
Hamilton Pk.
Hamilton Mead, Hem.H. 57 BA27
Hamilton Ms. W1 277 H4
Hamilton Pk. N5 121 DP63
Hamilton Pk. W. N5 121 DP63
Hamilton Pl. W1 276 G3
Hamilton Pl. W1 140 DG74
Hamilton Pl., Guil. 242 AU129
Hamilton Pl., Sun. 175 BV94
Hamilton Pl., Tad. 233 CZ122
Hamilton Rd. E15 144 EE69
Hamilton Rd. E17 101 DY54
Hamilton Rd. N2 120 DC55
Hamilton Rd. N9 100 DU45
Hamilton Rd. NW10 119 CU64
Hamilton Rd. NW11 119 CX59
Hamilton Rd. SE27 182 DR91
Hamilton Rd. SW19 180 DB94
Hamilton Rd. W4 158 CS75
Hamilton Rd. W5 138 CL73
Hamilton Rd., Barn. 80 DE42
Hamilton Rd., Berk. 38 AV19
Hamilton Rd., Bexh. 166 EY82
Hamilton Rd., Brent. 157 CK79
Hamilton Rd., Felt. 175 BT91
Hamilton Rd., Grays 169 FW78
Hamilton Rd., Har. 117 CE57
Hamilton Rd., Hayes 135 BV73
Hamilton Rd., Ilf. 125 EP63
Hamilton Rd., Kings L. 59 BQ33
Hamilton Rd., Rom. 127 FH57
Hamilton Rd., St.Alb. 43 CG19
Hamilton Rd., Sid. 186 EU91
Hamilton Rd., Slou. 131 AN72
Hamilton Rd., Sthl. 136 BZ74
Hamilton Rd., Th.Hth. 202 DR97
Hamilton Rd., Twick. 177 CE88
Hamilton Rd., Uxb. 134 BK71
Hamilton Rd., Wat. 93 BV48
Hamilton Sq. SE1 279 L4
Hamilton St. SE8 163 EA79
Deptford High St.
Hamilton St., Wat. 76 BW43
Hamilton Ter. NW8 140 DB68
Hamilton Wk., Erith 167 FF80
Hamilton Way N3 98 DA51
Hamilton Way N13 99 DP49
Hamilton Way, Wall. 219 DK109
Hamlea Clo. SE12 184 EF85
Hamlet, The SE5 162 DR83
Hamlet, The, Berk. 39 BA16
Hamlet Clo. SE13 164 EE84
Old Rd.
Hamlet Clo., Rom. 104 FA52
Hamlet Gdns. W6 159 CU77
Hamlet Hill, Harl. 50 EF19
Hamlet Rd. SE19 182 DT94
Hamlet Rd., Rom. 104 FA52
Hamlet Sq. NW2 119 CY62
Cricklewood Trd. Est.
Hamlet Sq. NW11 119 CY62
The Vale
Hamlet Way SE1 279 L4
Hamlets Way E3 143 DZ70
Hamlin Cres., Pnr. 116 BW57
Hamlin Rd., Sev. 256 FE121
Hamlyn Clo., Edg. 96 CL48
Hamlyn Gdns. SE19 182 DS94
Hamm Ct., Wey. 194 BM104
Hamm Moor La., Add. 212 BL106
Hammarskjold Rd., Harl. 35 ER13
Hammelton Grn. SW9 161 DP81
Cromwell Rd.
Hammelton Rd., Brom. 204 EF95
Hammer La., Hem.H. 40 BM19
Hammer Par., Wat. 59 BU33
Hammerfield Dr., Dor. 261 BT141
Hammers Gate, St.Alb. 60 CA25
Hammers La. NW7 97 CU50
Hammersley La., H.Wyc. 88 AC49
Hammersmith Bri. SW13 159 CV78
Hammersmith Bri. Rd. W6 159 CW78
Hammersmith Bdy. W6 159 CW77
Hammersmith Flyover W6 159 CW78
Hammersmith Gro. W6 159 CW76
Hammersmith Rd. W6 159 CX77
Hammersmith Rd. W14 159 CX77
Hammersmith Ter. W6 159 CU78
Hammet Clo., Hayes 136 BX71
Willow Tree La.
Hammett St. EC3 275 P10
Hammond Ave., Mitch. 201 DH96
Hammond Clo., Barn. 79 CY43
Hammond Clo., Grnf. 117 CD64
Lilian Board Way
Hammond Clo., Hmptn. 196 CA95
Hammond Clo. (Cheshunt), Wal.Cr. 66 DS26
Hammond Clo., Wok. 226 AW115
Hammond End, Slou. 111 AP63
Hammond Rd., Enf. 82 DV40
Hammond Rd., Sthl. 156 BY76
Hammond Rd., Wok. 226 AW115
Hammond St. NW5 141 DJ65
Hammond Way SE28 146 EV73
Oriole Way
Hammonds Clo., Dag. 126 EW62
Hammonds La., Brwd. 107 FV51
Hammond's La., Hat. 28 CN12
Hammond's La., St.Alb. 28 CN12
Hammondstreet Rd. (Cheshunt), Wal.Cr. 66 DR26
Hamond Clo., S.Croy. 219 DP109
Hamonde Clo., Edg. 96 CP47
Hampden Ave., Beck. 203 DY96
Hampden Ave., Chesh. 54 AN30
Hampden Clo. NW1 273 N1
Hampden Clo., Epp. 70 FA27
Hampden Clo., Slou. 132 AU69
Hampden Cres., Brwd. 108 FW49
Hampden Cres. (Cheshunt), Wal.Cr. 66 DV31
Hampden Gurney St. W1 272 D9
Hampden Hill, Beac. 88 AH53
Hampden Hill, Ware 33 DZ05
Hampden Hill Clo., Ware 33 DZ05
Hampden Hill
Hampden La. N17 100 DT53
Hampden Pl., St.Alb. 61 CE29
Hampden Rd. N8 121 DN56
Hampden Rd. N10 98 DG52
Hampden Rd. N17 100 DU53
Hampden Rd. N19 121 DK61
Holloway Rd.
Hampden Rd., Beck. 203 DY96
Hampden Rd., Ger.Cr. 90 AX53
Hampden Rd., Grays 170 GB78
Hampden Rd., Har. 94 CC53
Hampden Rd., Kings.T. 198 CN97
Hampden Rd., Rom. 105 FB52
Hampden Rd., Slou. 153 AZ76
Hampden Sq. N14 99 DH46
Osidge La.
Hampden Way N14 99 DH47
Hampden Way, Wat. 75 BS36
Hampermill La., Wat. 93 BT47
Hampshire Ave., Slou. 131 AQ71
Hampshire Clo. N18 100 DV50
Berkshire Gdns.
Hampshire Hog La. W6 159 CV77
King St.
Hampshire Rd. N22 99 DM52
Hampshire Rd., Horn. 128 FN56
Hampshire St. NW5 141 DK65
Torriano Ave.
Hampson Way SW8 161 DM81
Hampstead Clo. SE28 146 EV74
Hampstead Gdns. NW11 120 DA58
Hampstead Gdns., Rom. 126 EV57
Hampstead Grn. NW3 120 DE64
Hampstead Gro. NW3 120 DC62
Hampstead Hts. N2 120 DC56
Hampstead High St. NW3 120 DC63
Hampstead Hill Gdns. NW3 120 DD63
Hampstead La. N6 120 DD59
Hampstead La. NW3 120 DD59
Hampstead La., Dor. 263 CG137
Hampstead Rd. NW1 273 K1
Hampstead Rd. NW1 141 DJ68
Hampstead Rd., Dor. 263 CG137
Hampstead Sq. NW3 120 DC62
Hampstead Wk. E3 143 DZ67
Parnell Rd.
Hampstead Way NW11 120 DC60
Hampton Clo. N11 99 DH50
Balmoral Ave.
Hampton Clo. NW6 140 DA69
Hampton Clo. SW20 179 CW94
Hampton Ct. N1 141 DP65
Upper St.
Hampton Ct. Ave., E.Mol. 197 CD99
Hampton Ct. Cres., E.Mol. 197 CD97
Hampton Ct. Palace, E.Mol. 197 CE97
Hampton Ct. Par., E.Mol. 197 CE98
Creek Rd.
Hampton Ct. Rd., E.Mol. 197 CF97
Hampton Ct. Rd., Hmptn. 196 CC96
Hampton Ct. Rd., Kings.T. 197 CJ96
Hampton Ct. Way, E.Mol. 197 CE100
Hampton Ct. Way, T.Ditt. 197 CE103
Hampton Cres., Grav. 191 GF89
Hampton Fm. Ind. Est., Felt. 176 BY90
Hampton Gdns., Saw. 36 EV08
Hampton Gro., Epsom 217 CT111
Hampton La., Felt. 176 BY91
Hampton Mead, Loug. 85 EP41
Hampton Ms. NW10 138 CR69
Minerva Rd.
Hampton Ri., Har. 118 CL58
Hampton Rd. E4 101 DZ50
Hampton Rd. E7 124 EH64
Hampton Rd. E11 123 ED60
Hampton Rd., Croy. 202 DQ100
Hampton Rd., Hmptn. 177 CD92
Hampton Rd., Ilf. 125 EP63
Hampton Rd., Red. 266 DF139
Hampton Rd., Tedd. 177 CD92
Hampton Rd., Twick. 177 CD90
Hampton Rd., Wor.Pk. 199 CU103
Hampton Rd. E., Felt. 176 BZ90
Hampton Rd. W., Felt. 176 BY89
Hampton St. SE1 278 G9
Hampton St. SE1 161 DP77
Hampton St. SE17 278 G9
Hampton St. SE17 161 DP77
Hamsey Grn. Gdns., Warl. 236 DV116
Hamsey Way, S.Croy. 236 DV115
Hamshades Clo., Sid. 185 ET90
Hamstel Rd., Harl. 35 EP13
Hanah Ct. SW19 179 CX94
Hanameel St. E16 144 EH74
Hanbury Clo. NW4 119 CW55
Parson St.
Hanbury Clo., Slou. 130 AG71
Hanbury Clo. (Cheshunt), Wal.Cr. 67 DX29
Hanbury Clo., Ware 33 DY06
Hanbury Dr. N21 81 DM43
Hanbury Dr., West. 222 EH113
Hanbury La., Hat. 46 DE17
Hanbury Ms. N1 142 DQ67
Mary St.
Hanbury Path, Wok. 211 BD114
Hanbury Rd. N17 100 DV54
Hanbury Rd. W3 158 CP75
Hanbury St. E1 275 P6
Hanbury St. E1 142 DT71
Hanbury Wk., Bex. 187 FE90
Hancock Ct., Borwd. 78 CQ39
Hancock Rd. E3 143 EC69
Hancock Rd. SE19 182 DR93
Hancroft Rd., Hem.H. 40 BM22
Hand Ct. WC1 274 C7
Hand Ct. WC1 141 DM71
Hand La., Saw. 36 EW06
Handa Clo., Hem.H. 41 BP23
Handa Wk. N1 142 DR65
Clephane Rd.
Handcroft Rd., Croy. 201 DP101
Handel Clo., Edg. 96 CM51
Handel Cres., Til. 171 GG80
Handel Pl. NW10 138 CR65
Mitchellbrook Way
Handel St. WC1 273 P4
Handel St. WC1 141 DL70
Handel Way, Edg. 96 CN52
Handen Rd. SE12 184 EE85
Handforth Rd. SW9 161 DN80
Handforth Rd., Ilf. 125 EP62
Winston Way
Handley Rd. E9 142 DW66
Handowe Clo. NW4 119 CU56
Handpost Hill, Pot.B. 65 DH28
Hands Wk. E16 144 EG72
Handside Clo., Welw.G.C. 29 CW09
Handside Clo., Wor.Pk. 199 CX102
Carters Clo.
Handside Grn., Welw.G.C. 29 CW08
Handside La., Welw.G.C. 29 CV11
Handsworth Ave. E4 101 ED51
Handsworth Rd. N17 122 DR55
Handsworth Way, Wat. 93 BU48
Hayling Rd.
Handtrough Way, Bark. 145 EP68
Fresh Wf. Rd.
Hanford Clo. SW18 180 DA88
Hanford Rd., S.Ock. 148 FQ74
Hanford Row SW19 179 CW93
Hangar Ruding, Wat. 94 BZ48
Hanger Clo., Hem.H. 40 BH21
Hanger Grn. W5 138 CN70
Hanger Hill, Wey. 213 BP107
Hanger La. W5 138 CM70
Hanger Vale La. W5 138 CM72
Hanger Vw. Way W3 138 CN72
Hanging Hill La., Brwd. 109 GB48
Hangrove Hill, Orp. 223 EP113
Hankey Pl. SE1 279 L5
Hankey Pl. SE1 162 DR75
Hankins La. NW7 96 CS48
Hanley Clo., Wind. 151 AK81
Hanley Pl., Beck. 183 EA94
Hanley Rd. N4 121 DL60
Hanmer Wk. N7 121 DM62
Newington Barrow Way
Hannah Clo. NW10 118 CQ63
Hannah Clo., Beck. 203 EC97
Hannah Mary Way SE1 162 DU77
Simms Rd.
Hannah Ms., Wall. 219 DJ108
Hannards Way, Chig. 104 EV50
Hannay La. N8 121 DK59
Hannay Wk. SW16 181 DK89
Hannell Rd. SW6 159 CY80
Hannen Rd. SE27 181 DP90
Norwood High St.
Hannibal Rd. E1 142 DW71
Hannibal Rd., Stai. 174 BK87
Hannibal Way, Croy. 219 DM106
Hannington Rd. SW4 161 DH83
Hanover Ave. E16 144 EG74
Hanover Ave., Felt. 175 BU88
Hanover Circle, Hayes 135 BQ72
Hanover Clo., Egh. 172 AV93
Hanover Clo., Red. 251 DJ128
Hanover Clo., Rich. 158 CN80
Hanover Clo., Slou. 152 AU76
Hanover Clo., Sutt. 217 CZ105
Hanover Ct. W12 139 CU74
Uxbridge Rd.
Hanover Ct., Dor. 263 CF136
Hanover Ct., Guil. 242 AX132
Riverside
Hanover Ct., Hodd. 49 EA16
Jersey Clo.
Hanover Ct., Wok. 226 AY119
Midhope Rd.
Hanover Dr., Chis. 185 EQ91
Hanover Gdns. SE11 161 DN79
Hanover Gdns., Ilf. 103 EQ52
Hanover Gate NW1 272 C3
Hanover Gate NW1 140 DE69
Hanover Grn., Hem.H. 40 BG22
Hanover Mead, Maid. 150 AC76
Hanover Pk. SE15 162 DU81
Hanover Pl. E3 143 DZ69
Brokesley St.
Hanover Pl. WC2 274 A9
Hanover Rd. N15 122 DT56
Hanover Rd. NW10 139 CW66
Hanover Rd. SW19 180 DC94
Hanover Sq. W1 273 J9
Hanover Sq. W1 141 DH72
Hanover St. W1 273 J9
Hanover St. W1 141 DH72
Hanover St., Croy. 201 DP104
Abbey Rd.
Hanover Ter. NW1 272 D3
Hanover Ter. NW1 140 DE69
Hanover Ter., Islw. 157 CG81
Hanover Ter. Ms. NW1 272 C3
Hanover Wk., Hat. 45 CT21
Hanover Wk., Wey. 195 BS104
Hanover Way, Bexh. 166 EX83
Hanover Way, Wind. 151 AM82
Hanover W. Ind. Est. NW10 138 CR68
Hanover Yd. N1 141 DP68
Noel Rd.
Hans Cres. SW1 276 D6
Hans Cres. SW1 160 DF76
Hans Pl. SW1 276 E6
Hans Pl. SW1 160 DF76
Hans Rd. SW3 276 D6
Hans Rd. SW3 160 DF76
Hans St. SW1 276 E7
Hansard Ms. W14 159 CX75
Holland Rd.
Hansart Way, Enf. 81 DN39
The Ridgeway
Hanselin Clo., Stan. 95 CF50
Chenduit Way
Hansells Mead, Harl. 50 EG15
Hansen Dr. N21 81 DM43
Hansha Dr., Edg. 96 CR53
Hansler Gro., E.Mol. 197 CD99
Hansler Rd. SE22 182 DT85
Hansol Rd., Bexh. 186 EY85
Hanson Clo. SW12 181 DH87
Hanson Clo. SW14 158 CQ83
Hanson Clo., Beck. 183 EB93
Hanson Clo., Guil. 243 AZ131
Hanson Clo., Loug. 85 EQ40
Hanson Dr.
Hanson Clo., West Dr. 154 BM76
Hanson Dr., Loug. 85 EQ40
Hanson Gdns., Sthl. 156 BY75
Hanson Grn., Loug. 85 EQ40
Hanson Dr.

Hanson St. W1 273 K6
Hanson St. W1 141 DJ71
Hanway Pl. W1 273 M8
Hanway Rd. W7 137 CD72
Hanway St. W1 273 M8
Hanway St. W1 141 DK72
Hanworth La., Cher. 193 BF102
Hanworth Rd., Felt. 175 BV88
Hanworth Rd., Hmptn. 176 BZ91
Hanworth Rd., Houns. 156 CB83
Hanworth Rd., Red. 266 DF139
Hanworth Rd., Sun. 175 BU94
Hanworth Ter., Houns. 156 CB84
Hanworth Trd. Est., Felt. 176 BY90
Hanyards End (Cuffley), Pot.B. 65 DL28
Hanyards La. (Cuffley), Pot.B. 65 DK28
Hapgood Clo., Grnf. 117 CD64
Harads Pl. E1 142 DU73
Ensign St.
Harben Rd. NW6 140 DC66
Harberson Rd. E15 144 EF67
Harberson Rd. SW12 181 DH88
Harberton Rd. N19 121 DJ60
Harberts Rd., Harl. 51 EP16
Harbet Rd. E4 101 DX50
Harbet Rd. N18 101 DX50
Harbet Rd. W2 272 A7
Harbet Rd. W2 140 DD71
Harbex Clo., Bex. 187 FB87
Harbinger Rd. E14 163 EB77
Harbledown Pl., Orp. 206 EW98
Okemore Gdns.
Harbledown Rd. SW6 160 DA81
Harbledown Rd., S.Croy. 220 DU111
Harbord Clo. SE5 162 DR82
De Crespigny Pk.
Harbord St. SW6 159 CX81
Harborne Clo., Wat. 94 BW50
Harborough Ave., Sid. 185 ES87
Harborough Clo., Slou. 131 AK74
West Pt.
Harborough Rd. SW16 181 DM91
Harbour Ave. SW10 160 DC81
Harbour Ex. Sq. E14 163 EB75
Harbour Rd. SE5 162 DQ83
Harbourer Clo., Ilf. 104 EV50
Harbourer Rd., Ilf. 104 EV50
Harbourfield Rd., Bans. 234 DB115
Harbridge Ave. SW15 179 CT87
Harbury Rd., Cars. 218 DE109
Harbut Rd. SW11 160 DD84
Harcamlow Way, Harl. 36 EU10
Harcamlow Way, Ware 33 EC05
Harcombe Rd. N16 122 DS62
Harcourt Ave. E12 125 EM63
Harcourt Ave., Edg. 96 CQ48
Harcourt Ave., Sid. 186 EW86
Harcourt Ave., Wall. 219 DH105
Harcourt Clo., Egh. 173 BC93
Harcourt Clo., Islw. 157 CG83
Harcourt Clo., Maid. 150 AF76
Harcourt Fld., Wall. 219 DH105
Harcourt La., Maid. 150 AF76
Harcourt Rd.
Harcourt Ms., Rom. 127 FF57
Harcourt Rd. E15 144 EF68
Harcourt Rd. N22 99 DK53
Harcourt Rd. SE4 163 DY84
Harcourt Rd. SW19 180 DA94
Russell Rd.
Harcourt Rd., Bexh. 166 EY84
Harcourt Rd., Maid. 150 AF76
Harcourt Rd., Th.Hth. 201 DM100
Harcourt Rd., Wall. 219 DH105
Harcourt Rd. (Bushey), Wat. 76 CC43
Harcourt Rd., Wind. 151 AL81
Harcourt St. W1 272 C7
Harcourt St. W1 140 DE71
Harcourt Ter. SW10 160 DB78
Hardcastle Clo., Croy. 202 DU100
Hardcourts Clo., W.Wick. 203 EB104
Hardel Ri. SW2 181 DP89
Hardel Wk. SW2 181 DN87
Papworth Way
Hardell Clo., Egh. 173 BA92
Harden Rd., Grav. 191 GF90
Hardens Manorway SE7 164 EK76
Harders Rd. SE15 162 DV82
Hardess St. SE24 162 DQ83
Herne Hill Rd.
Hardie Clo. NW10 118 CR64
Hardie Rd., Dag. 127 FC62
Harding Clo. SE17 162 DQ79
Hillingdon St.
Harding Clo., Croy. 202 DT104
Harding Clo., Wat. 60 BW33
Harding Ho., Hayes 135 BV72
Harding Rd., Bexh. 166 EZ82
Harding Rd., Chesh. 54 AR30
Harding Rd., Epsom 232 CS119
Harding Rd., Grays 171 GG76
Hardinge Clo., Uxb. 135 BP72
Dawley Ave.
Hardinge La. E1 142 DW72
Hardinge St.
Hardinge Rd. N18 100 DS50
Hardinge Rd. NW10 139 CV67
Hardinge St. E1 142 DW72
Hardings, Welw.G.C. 30 DC08
Hardings Clo., Iver 133 BD69
Harding's Clo., Kings.T. 198 CM95
Hardings La. SE20 183 DX93
Hardings Row, Iver 133 BC69
Hardley Cres., Horn. 128 FK56
Hardman Rd. SE7 164 EH78
Hardman Rd., Kings.T. 198 CL96
Hardwick Clo., Lthd. 230 CC115
Hardwick Clo., Stan. 95 CJ50
Hardwick Cres., Dart. 188 FP86
Hardwick Grn. W13 137 CH71
Hardwick La., Cher. 193 BC101
Hardwick Rd., Red. 266 DD136
Hardwick St. EC1 274 E3
Hardwick St. EC1 141 DN69
Hardwicke Ave., Houns. 156 CA81
Hardwicke Gdns., Amer. 55 AS38
Hardwicke Pl., St.Alb. 61 CK27
Hardwicke Rd. N13 99 DL51
Hardwicke Rd. W4 158 CR77
Hardwicke Rd., Reig. 250 DA133
Hardwicke Rd., Rich. 177 CJ91
Hardwicke St., Bark. 145 EQ67
Hardwicks Way SW18 180 DA85
Buckhold Rd.
Hardwidge St. SE1 279 M4
Hardy Ave. E16 144 EG74
Wesley Ave.
Hardy Ave., Grav. 190 GE89
Hardy Ave., Ruis. 115 BV64
Hardy Clo. SE16 163 DX75
Middleton Dr.
Hardy Clo., Barn. 79 CY44
Hardy Clo., Dor. 263 CH141
Hardy Clo., Horl. 268 DE148
Hardy Clo., Pnr. 116 BX59
Hardy Clo., Slou. 131 AN74
Hardy Gro., Dart. 168 FN84
Hardy Rd. E4 101 DZ51
Hardy Rd. SE3 164 EF80
Hardy Rd. SW19 180 DB94
Hardy Rd., Hem.H. 40 BM19
Hardy Way, Enf. 81 DN39
Hare & Billet Rd. SE3 163 ED81
Hare Ct. EC4 274 D9
Hare Cres., Wat. 59 BU32
Hare Hall La., Rom. 127 FH56
Hare Hill, Add. 211 BE107
Hare Hill Clo., Wok. 228 BG115
Hare La., Esher 215 CD106
Hare La., Hat. 45 CV20
Hare Marsh E2 142 DU70
Cheshire St.
Hare Pl. EC4 274 E9
Hare Row E2 142 DV68
Hare St. SE18 165 EN76
Hare St., Harl. 51 EP15
Hare St. Springs, Harl. 51 EP15
Hare Ter., Grays 169 FX78
Mill La.
Hare Wk. N1 275 N1
Hare Wk. N1 142 DS68
Harebell, Welw.G.C. 29 CY12
Harebell Clo., Hert. 32 DV09
Harebell Dr. E6 145 EN71
Harebell Hill, Cob. 214 BX114
Harebell Way, Rom. 106 FK52
Harebreaks, The, Wat. 75 BV38
Harecastle Clo., Hayes 136 BY70
Braunston Dr.
Harecourt Rd. N1 142 DQ65
Harecroft, Dor. 263 CJ139
Harecroft, Lthd. 230 CB123
Haredale Rd. SE24 162 DQ84
Haredon Clo. SE23 182 DW87
Harefield, Esher 197 CE104
Harefield, Harl. 36 EU14
Harefield Ave., Sutt. 217 CY109
Harefield Clo., Enf. 81 DN39
Harefield Ms. SE4 163 DZ83
Harefield Pl., St.Alb. 43 CK17
Harefield Rd. N8 121 DK57
Harefield Rd. SE4 163 DZ83
Harefield Rd. SW16 181 DM94
Harefield Rd., Rick. 92 BK50
Harefield Rd., Sid. 186 EX89
Harefield Rd., Uxb. 134 BK65
Harefield Rd. Ind. Est., Rick. 92 BL49
Harehatch La., Slou. 111 AL60
Harelands Clo., Wok. 226 AW117
Harendon, Tad. 233 CW121
Harepark Clo., Hem.H. 39 BF19
Hares Bank, Croy. 221 ED110
Haresfield Rd., Dag. 146 FA65
Harestone Dr., Cat. 236 DT124
Harestone Hill, Cat. 252 DT126
Harestone La., Cat. 252 DS125
Harestone Valley Rd., Cat. 252 DS126
Hareward Rd., Guil. 243 BC132
Harewood, Rick. 74 BH43
Harewood Ave. NW1 272 C5
Harewood Ave. NW1 140 DE70
Harewood Ave., Nthlt. 136 BY66
Harewood Clo., Nthlt. 136 BZ66
Harewood Clo., Reig. 250 DC132
Harewood Dr., Ilf. 103 EM54
Harewood Gdns., S.Croy. 236 DV115
Harewood Hill, Epp. 85 ES35
Harewood Pl. W1 273 J9
Harewood Pl., Slou. 152 AU76
Harewood Rd. SW19 180 DE93
Harewood Rd., Brwd. 108 FV44
Harewood Rd., Ch.St.G. 72 AW41
Harewood Rd., Islw. 157 CF80
Harewood Rd., S.Croy. 220 DS107
Harewood Rd., Wat. 93 BV48
Harewood Row NW1 272 C6
Harewood Ter., Sthl. 156 BZ77
Harfield Gdns. SE5 162 DS83
Harfield Rd., Sun. 196 BX96
Harford Clo. E4 101 EB45
Harford Dr., Wat. 75 BS38
Harford Rd. E4 101 EB45
Harford St. E1 143 DY70
Harford Wk. N2 120 DD57
Harfst Way, Swan. 207 FC95
Hargood Clo., Har. 118 CL58
Hargood Rd. SE3 164 EJ81
Hargrave Pk. N19 121 DJ61
Hargrave Pl. N7 121 DK64
Brecknock Rd.
Hargrave Rd. N19 121 DJ61
Hargreaves Ave. (Cheshunt), Wal.Cr. 66 DV30
Hargreaves Clo. (Cheshunt), Wal.Cr. 66 DV31
Hargwyne St. SW9 161 DM83
Haringey Pk. N8 121 DL58
Haringey Pas. N4 121 DP57
Warham Rd.
Haringey Pas. N8 121 DP58
Haringey Rd. N8 121 DL56
Harington Ter. N9 100 DR48
Harington Ter. N18 100 DR48
Harkett Clo., Har. 95 CF54
Byron Rd.
Harkett Ct., Har. 95 CF54
Harkness (Cheshunt), Wal.Cr. 66 DU29
Harkness Clo., Epsom 233 CW116
Harkness Clo., Rom. 106 FM50
Harkness Rd., Slou. 130 AH71
Harland Ave., Croy. 202 DT104
Harland Ave., Sid. 185 ER90
Harland Clo. SW19 200 DB97
Harland Rd. SE12 184 EG88
Harlands Gro., Orp. 223 EP105
Pinecrest Gdns.
Harlech Gdns., Houns. 156 BW79
Harlech Gdns., Pnr. 116 BX59
Harlech Rd. N14 99 DL48
Harlech Rd., Abb.L. 59 BU31
Harlech Twr. W3 158 CP75
Harlequin Ave., Brent. 157 CG79
Harlequin Cen., Wat. 76 BW42
Harlequin Clo., Hayes 136 BX71
Cygnet Way
Harlequin Clo., Islw. 177 CE85
Harlequin Ho., Erith 166 EY76
Kale Rd.
Harlequin Rd., Tedd. 177 CH94
Harlescott Rd. SE15 163 DX84
Harlesden Clo., Rom. 106 FM52
Harlesden Gdns. NW10 139 CT67
Harlesden La. NW10 139 CU67
Harlesden Rd. NW10 139 CU67
Harlesden Rd., Rom. 106 FM51
Harlesden Rd., St.Alb. 43 CG20
Harlesden Wk., Rom. 106 FM52
Harlesden Rd.
Harleston Clo. E5 122 DW61
Theydon Rd.
Harley Clo., Wem. 137 CK65
Harley Ct. E11 124 EG59
Blake Hall Rd.
Harley Ct., St.Alb. 43 CK16
Villiers Cres.
Harley Cres., Har. 117 CD56
Harley Gdns. SW10 160 DC78
Harley Gdns., Orp. 223 ES105
Harley Gro. E3 143 DZ69
Harley Pl. W1 273 H7
Harley Pl. W1 141 DH71
Harley Rd. NW3 140 DD66
Harley Rd. NW10 138 CS68
Harley Rd., Har. 117 CD56
Harley St. W1 273 H7
Harley St. W1 141 DH70
Harleyford, Brom. 204 EH95
Harleyford Rd. SE11 161 DM79
Harleyford St. SE11 161 DN79
Harlinger St. SE18 164 EL76
Harlings, Hert. 32 DW13
Harlington Clo., Hayes 155 BQ80
New Rd.
Harlington Rd., Bexh. 166 EY83
Harlington Rd., Houns. 155 BT84
Harlington Rd., Uxb. 135 BP71
Harlington Rd. E., Felt. 175 BV87
Harlington Rd. W., Felt. 175 BV86
Harlow Common, Harl. 52 EW18
Harlow Ct., Hem.H. 40 BN16
Harlow Gdns., Rom. 105 FC51
Harlow Potter St. Bypass, Harl. 52 EV15
Harlow Rd. N13 100 DR48
Harlow Rd., B.Stort. 37 FB07
Harlow Rd., Harl. 50 EJ15
Harlow Rd. (Matching Tye), Harl. 37 FC12
Harlow Rd. (Old Harlow), Harl. 36 FA09
Harlow Rd., Ong. 53 FH18
Harlow Rd., Rain. 147 FF67
Harlow Rd., Saw. 36 EW08
Harlton Ct., Wal.Abb. 68 EF34
Harlyn Dr., Pnr. 115 BV55
Harman Ave., Grav. 191 GH92
Harman Ave., Wdf.Grn. 102 EF52
Harman Clo. E4 101 ED49
Harman Clo. NW2 119 CY62
Harman Dr. NW2 119 CY62
Harman Dr., Sid. 185 ET86
Harman Pl., Pur. 219 DP111
Harman Rd., Enf. 82 DT43
Harmer Rd., Swans. 190 FZ86
Harmer St., Grav. 191 GJ86
Harmondsworth La., West Dr. 154 BL79
Harmondsworth Rd., West Dr. 154 BL78
Harmony Clo. NW11 119 CY57
Harmony Clo., Hat. 45 CU16
Harmony Clo., Wall. 219 DL109
Harmony Way NW4 119 CW56
Victoria Rd.
Harmood Gro. NW1 141 DH66
Clarence Way
Harmood Pl. NW1 141 DH66
Harmood St.
Harmood St. NW1 141 DH66
Harms Gro., Guil. 243 BC131
Harmsworth Ms. SE11 278 F7
Harmsworth St. SE17 161 DP78
Harmsworth Way N20 97 CZ46
Harness Rd. SE28 166 EU75
Harness Way, St.Alb. 43 CK17
Harnetts Clo., Swan. 207 FD100
Harold Ave., Belv. 166 EZ78
Harold Ave., Hayes 155 BT76
Harold Ct. Rd., Rom. 106 FP51
Harold Cres., Wal.Abb. 67 EC32
Harold Est. SE1 279 N7
Harold Est. SE1 162 DS76
Harold Gibbons Ct. SE7 164 EJ79
Victoria Way
Harold Pl. SE11 161 DN78
Harold Rd. E4 101 EC49
Harold Rd. E11 124 EE60
Harold Rd. E13 144 EH67
Harold Rd. N8 121 DM57
Harold Rd. N15 122 DT57
Harold Rd. NW10 138 CR69
Harold Rd. SE19 182 DR94
Harold Rd., Dart. 188 FM91
Harold Rd., Sutt. 218 DD105
Harold Rd., Wdf.Grn. 102 EG53
Harold Vw., Rom. 106 FM54
Harolds Clo., Harl. 51 EM16
Harolds Rd., Harl. 50 EL16
Haroldslea, Horl. 269 DK150
Haroldslea Clo., Horl. 269 DJ150
Haroldslea Dr., Horl. 269 DJ150
Haroldstone Rd. E17 123 DX57
Harp All. EC4 274 F8
Harp Island Clo. NW10 118 CR61
Harp La. EC3 279 M1
Harp Rd. W7 137 CF70
Harpenden Rd. E12 124 EJ61
Harpenden Rd. SE27 181 DP90
Harpenden Rd., St.Alb. 43 CD18
Harper Clo. N14 81 DJ43
Alexandra Ct.
Harper La., Rad. 61 CG32
Harper Rd. E6 145 EM72
Harper Rd. SE1 279 H6
Harper Rd. SE1 162 DQ76
Harpers Yd. N17 100 DT53
Ruskin Rd.
Harpesford Ave., Vir.W. 192 AV99
Harpley Sq. E1 142 DW69
Harpour Rd., Bark. 145 EQ65
Harps Oak La., Red. 250 DF125
Harpsden St. SW11 160 DG81
Harpsfield Bdy., Hat. 45 CT17
Harptree Way, St.Alb. 43 CG18
Harpur Ms. WC1 274 B6
Harpur St. WC1 274 B6
Harpur St. WC1 141 DM71
Harpurs, Tad. 233 CX122
Harraden Rd. SE3 164 EJ81
Harrap Chase, Grays 170 FZ78
Harrap St. E14 143 EC73
Harrier Ave. E11 124 EH58
Eastern Ave.
Harrier Clo., Horn. 147 FH65
Harrier Ms. SE28 165 ER76
Harrier Rd. NW9 96 CS54
Harrier Way E6 145 EM71
Harrier Way, Wal.Abb. 68 EG34
Harriers Clo. W5 138 CL73
Harries Clo., Chesh. 54 AP30
Deansway
Harries Rd., Hayes 136 BW70
Harriescourt, Wal.Abb. 68 EG32
Harriet Clo. E8 142 DU67
Harriet Gdns., Croy. 202 DU103
Harriet St. SW1 276 E5
Harriet Tubman Clo. SW2 181 DN87
Harriet Wk. SW1 276 E5
Harriet Wk. SW1 160 DF75
Harriet Way (Bushey), Wat. 95 CD45
Harringay Gdns. N8 121 DP56
Harringay Rd. N15 121 DP57
Harrington Clo. NW10 118 CR62
Harrington Clo., Croy. 201 DL103
Harrington Clo., Reig. 265 CU141
Harrington Clo., Wind. 151 AM84
Harrington Ct. W10 139 CZ69
Dart St.
Harrington Gdns. SW7 160 DB77
Harrington Hill E5 122 DV60
Harrington Rd. E11 124 EE60
Harrington Rd. SE25 202 DV98
Harrington Rd. SW7 160 DD77
Harrington Sq. NW1 273 K1
Harrington Sq. NW1 141 DJ68
Harrington St. NW1 273 K2
Harrington St. NW1 141 DJ69
Harrington Way SE18 164 EK76
Harriott Clo. SE10 164 EF77
Harriotts Clo., Ash. 231 CJ120
Harriotts La.
Harriotts La., Ash. 231 CJ119
Harris Clo., Enf. 81 DP39
Harris Clo., Grav. 190 GE90
Harris Clo., Houns. 156 CA81
Harris La., Rad. 62 CN34
Harris Rd., Bexh. 166 EY81
Harris Rd., Dag. 126 EZ64
Harris Rd., Wat. 75 BU35
Harris St. E17 123 DZ59
Harris St. SE5 162 DR80
Harris Way, Sun. 195 BS95
Harrison Clo. N20 98 DE46
Harrison Clo., Brwd. 109 GD43
Harrison Clo., Nthwd. 93 BQ51
Harrison Clo., Reig. 266 DB135
Harrison Ct., Shep. 195 BP99
Greeno Cres.
Harrison Dr., Epp. 71 FB26
Harrison Rd., Dag. 147 FB65
Harrison St. WC1 274 A3
Harrison St. WC1 141 DL69
Harrison Wk. (Cheshunt), Wal.Cr. 67 DX30
Harrison Way, Sev. 256 FG122
Harrison Way, Slou. 131 AK74
Harrisons Ri., Croy. 201 DP104
Harrisons Wf., Purf. 168 FN78
Harris's La., Ware 32 DW05
Harrogate Ct., Slou. 153 BA78
Harrogate Rd., Wat. 94 BW48
Harrold Rd., Dag. 126 EV64
Harrow Ave., Enf. 82 DT44
Harrow Bottom Rd., Vir.W. 193 AZ100
Harrow Clo., Add. 194 BH103
Harrow Clo., Chess. 215 CK108
Harrow Clo., Dor. 263 CG137
Harrow Rd. W.
Harrow Cres., Rom. 105 FH52
Harrow Dr. N9 100 DT46
Harrow Dr., Horn. 127 FH59
Harrow Flds. Gdns., Har. 117 CE62
Harrow Gdns., Orp. 224 EV105
Harrow Gdns., Warl. 237 DZ116
Harrow Gate Gdns., Dor. 263 CH138
Horsham Rd.
Harrow Grn. E11 124 EE62
Harrow Rd.
Harrow La. E14 143 EC73
Harrow La., Gdmg. 258 AS144
Farncombe St.
Harrow Manorway SE2 146 EW74
Harrow Pk., Har. 117 CE61
Harrow Pas., Kings.T. 197 CK96
Market Pl.
Harrow Pl. E1 275 N8
Harrow Pl. E1 142 DS72
Harrow Rd. E6 144 EL67
Harrow Rd. E11 124 EE62
Harrow Rd. NW10 139 CV69
Harrow Rd. W2 139 CZ70
Harrow Rd. W9 139 CZ70
Harrow Rd. W10 139 CX70
Harrow Rd., Bark. 145 ES67
Harrow Rd., Cars. 218 DE106
Harrow Rd., Felt. 174 BN88
Harrow Rd., Ilf. 125 EQ63
Harrow Rd., Sev. 240 EY115
Harrow Rd., Slou. 153 AZ76
Harrow Rd., Warl. 237 DZ115
Harrow Rd., Wem. 117 CJ64
Harrow Rd. (Tokyngton), Wem. 138 CP65
Harrow Rd. E., Dor. 263 CH138
Harrow Rd. W., Dor. 263 CG138
Harrow Vw., Har. 117 CD56
Harrow Vw., Hayes 135 BU72
Harrow Vw., Uxb. 135 BQ69
Harrow Vw. Rd. W5 137 CH70
Harrow Way, Shep. 195 BQ96
Harrow Way, Wat. 94 BY48
Harrow Weald Pk., Har. 95 CD51
Harroway Rd. SW11 160 DD82
Harrowby Gdns., Grav. 190 GE89
Harrowby St. W1 272 C8
Harrowby St. W1 140 DE72
Harrowdene Clo., Wem. 117 CK63
Harrowdene Gdns., Tedd. 177 CG93
Harrowdene Rd., Wem. 117 CK62
Harrowes Meade, Edg. 96 CN48
Harrowgate Rd. E9 143 DY65
Harrowlands Pk., Dor. 263 CH137
Harrowsley Ct., Horl. 269 DH147
Tanyard Way
Harrowsley Grn. La., Horl. 269 DJ149
Harston Dr., Enf. 83 EA38
Hart Clo., Red. 252 DT134
Hart Cor., Grays 169 FX78
Hart Cres., Chig. 103 ET50
Hart Dyke Cres., Swan. 207 FD97
Hart Dyke Rd.
Hart Dyke Rd., Orp. 206 EW102
Hart Dyke Rd., Swan. 207 FD96
Hart Gdns., Dor. 263 CH135
Hart Rd.
Hart Gro. W5 138 CN74
Hart Gro., Sthl. 136 CA71
Hart Rd., Dor. 263 CH135
Hart Rd., Harl. 36 EW10
Hart Rd., St.Alb. 43 CD21
Hart Rd., W.Byf. 212 BL113
Hart St. EC3 275 N10
Hart St., Brwd. 108 FW47
Harte Rd., Houns. 156 BZ82
Hartfield Ave., Borwd. 78 CN43
Hartfield Ave., Nthlt. 135 BV68
Hartfield Clo., Borwd. 78 CN43
Hartfield Ct., Ware 33 DX05
Hartfield Cres. SW19 179 CZ94
Hartfield Cres., W.Wick. 204 EG104
Hartfield Gro. SE20 202 DV95
Hartfield Pl., Grav. 190 GD87
Hartfield Rd. SW19 179 CZ94
Hartfield Rd., Chess. 215 CK106
Hartfield Rd., W.Wick. 222 EG105
Hartfield Ter. E3 143 EA68
Hartford Ave., Har. 117 CG55
Hartford Rd., Bex. 186 FA86
Hartford Rd., Epsom 216 CN107
Hartforde Rd., Borwd. 78 CN40
Harthall La., Hem.H. 59 BS26
Harthall La., Kings L. 59 BP28
Hartham Clo. N7 121 DL64
Hartham Clo., Islw. 157 CG81
Hartham La., Hert. 32 DQ09
Hartham Rd. N7 121 DL64
Hartham Rd. N17 100 DT54
Hartham Rd., Islw. 157 CF81
Harting Rd. SE9 184 EL91
Hartington Clo., Har. 117 CE63
Hartington Ct. W4 158 CP80
Hartington Pl., Reig. 250 DA132
Reigate Hill
Hartington Rd. E16 144 EH72
Hartington Rd. E17 123 DY58
Hartington Rd. SW8 161 DL81
Hartington Rd. W4 158 CP80
Hartington Rd. W13 137 CH73
Hartington Rd., Sthl. 156 BY75
Hartington Rd., Twick. 177 CH87
Hartismere Rd. SW6 159 CZ80
Hartlake Rd. E9 143 DX65
Hartland Clo. N21 82 DQ44
Elmscott Gdns.
Hartland Clo., Add. 212 BJ109
Hartland Clo., Edg. 96 CN47
Hartland Clo., Slou. 131 AR74
Hartland Dr., Edg. 96 CN47
Hartland Dr., Ruis. 115 BV62
Hartland Rd. E15 144 EF66
Hartland Rd. N11 98 DF50
Hartland Rd. NW1 141 DH66
Hartland Rd. NW6 139 CZ68
Hartland Rd., Add. 212 BG108
Hartland Rd., Epp. 70 EU31
Hartland Rd., Hmptn. 176 CB91
Hartland Rd., Horn. 127 FG61
Hartland Rd., Islw. 157 CG83
Hartland Rd., Mord. 200 DA101
Hartland Rd. (Cheshunt), Wal.Cr. 67 DX30
Hartland Way, Croy. 203 DY103
Hartland Way, Mord. 199 CZ101
Hartlands Clo., Bex. 186 EZ86
Hartley Ave. E6 144 EL67
Hartley Ave. NW7 97 CT50
Hartley Clo. NW7 97 CT50
Hartley Clo., Brom. 205 EM96
Hartley Clo., Slou. 132 AW67
Hartley Copse, Wind. 172 AU86
Hartley Down, Pur. 219 DM113
Hartley Fm. Est., Pur. 235 DM115
Hartley Hill, Pur. 235 DM115
Hartley Old Rd., Pur. 219 DM114
Hartley Rd. E11 124 EF60
Hartley Rd., Croy. 201 DP101
Hartley Rd., Well. 166 EW80
Hartley Rd., West. 255 ER125
Hartley St. E2 142 DW69
Hartley Way, Pur. 235 DM115
Hartmann Rd. E16 144 EK74
Hartmoor Ms., Enf. 83 DX37
Ordnance Rd.
Hartnoll St. N7 121 DM64
Eden Gro.
Harton Clo., Brom. 204 EK95
Harton Rd. N9 100 DV47
Harton St. SE8 163 EA81
Harts Clo. (Bushey), Wat. 76 CA40
Harts Gdns., Guil. 242 AV131
Harts Gro., Wdf.Grn. 102 EG50
Harts La. SE14 163 DY80
Harts La., Bark. 145 EP65
Hartsbourne Ave. (Bushey), Wat. 94 CC47
Hartsbourne Clo. (Bushey), Wat. 95 CD47
Hartsbourne Rd. (Bushey), Wat. 95 CD47
Hartsbourne Way, Hem.H. 41 BQ21
Hartscroft, Croy. 221 DY109
Hartshill Clo., Uxb. 134 BN65
Hartshill Rd., Grav. 191 GF89
Hartshill Wk., Wok. 226 AV116
Sythwood

Hartshorn All. EC3 275 N9
Hartshorn Gdns. E6 145 EN70
Hartslands Rd., Sev. 257 FJ123
Hartslock Dr. SE2 166 EX75
Hartsmead Rd. SE9 185 EM89
Hartsmoor Ms., Enf. 83 DX37
Hartspiece Rd., Red. 266 DG136
Hartspring La. (Bushey), Wat. 76 CA39
Hartsway, Enf. 82 DW42
Hartswood, Dor. 263 CK139
Wildcroft Dr.
Hartswood Ave., Reig. 266 DA138
Hartswood Clo., Brwd. 108 FY49
Hartswood Gdns. W12 159 CT76
Hartswood Grn. (Bushey), Wat. 95 CD47
Hartswood Rd. W12 159 CT75
Hartswood Rd., Brwd. 108 FY49
Hartsworth Clo. E13 144 EF68
Hartville Rd. SE18 165 ES77
Hartwell Clo., H.Wyc. 88 AC45
Hartwell Dr. E4 101 EC51
Hartwell Dr., Beac. 89 AK52
Hartwell St. E8 142 DT65
Dalston La.
Harvard Hill W4 158 CP79
Harvard La. W4 158 CP78
Harvard Rd. SE13 183 EC85
Harvard Rd. W4 158 CP78
Harvard Rd., Islw. 157 CE81
Harvard Wk., Horn. 127 FG63
Harvel Clo., Orp. 206 EU97
Harvel Cres. SE2 166 EX78
Harvest Bank Rd., W.Wick. 204 EF104
Harvest Ct., Shep. 194 BN98
Harvest End, Wat. 76 BX36
Harvest Hill, B.End 110 AC61
Harvest La., Loug. 84 EL43
High Rd.
Harvest La., T.Ditt. 197 CG100
Harvest Mead, Hat. 45 CV17
Harvest Rd., Egh. 172 AX92
Harvest Rd., Felt. 175 BU91
Harvest Rd. (Bushey), Wat. 76 CB42
Harvest Way, Swan. 207 FD101
Harvester Rd., Epsom 216 CR110
Harvesters, St.Alb. 43 CK16
Harvesters Clo., Islw. 177 CD85
Harvestside, Horl. 269 DJ147
Harvey, Grays 170 GB75
Harvey Cen., Harl. 51 EQ15
Harvey Gdns. E11 124 EF60
Harvey Rd.
Harvey Gdns. SE7 164 EK77
Harvey Gdns., Loug. 85 EP41
Harvey Ho., Brent. 158 CL78
Green Dragon La.
Harvey Orchard, Beac. 88 AJ52
Harvey Pt. E16 144 EH71
Fife Rd.
Harvey Rd. E11 124 EF60
Harvey Rd. N8 121 DM57
Harvey Rd. SE5 162 DR81
Harvey Rd., Guil. 258 AY136
Harvey Rd., Houns. 176 BZ87
Harvey Rd., Ilf. 125 EP64
Harvey Rd., Nthlt. 136 BW66
Harvey Rd., Rick. 74 BN44
Harvey Rd., St.Alb. 61 CJ26
Harvey Rd., Slou. 153 BB76
Harvey Rd., Uxb. 134 BN68
Harvey Rd., Walt. 195 BU101
Harvey St. N1 142 DR67
Harveyfields, Wal.Abb. 67 EC34
Harveys La., Rom. 127 FD61
Harvil Rd. (Harefield), Uxb. 114 BK58
Harvil Rd. (Ickenham), Uxb. 114 BL60
Harvill Rd., Sid. 186 EX92
Harvington Wk. E8 142 DU66
Wilman Gro.
Harvist Est. N7 121 DN63
Harvist Rd. NW6 139 CX68
Harwater Dr., Loug. 85 EM40
Harwell Clo., Ruis. 115 BR60
Harwell Pas. N2 120 DF56
Harwich La. EC2 275 N6
Harwich La. EC2 142 DS71
Harwich Rd., Slou. 131 AN72
Harwood Ave., Brom. 204 EH96
Harwood Ave., Horn. 128 FL55
Harwood Ave., Mitch. 200 DE97
Harwood Clo. N12 98 DE51
Summerfields Ave.
Harwood Clo., Welw. 30 DE05
Harwood Clo., Welw.G.C. 29 CY05
Harwood Clo., Wem. 117 CK63
Harrowdene Rd.
Harwood Dr., Uxb. 134 BM67
Harwood Gdns., Wind. 172 AV87
Harwood Hall La., Upmin. 148 FP65
Harwood Hill, Welw.G.C. 29 CY06
Harwood Pk., Red. 266 DG143
Harwood Rd. SW6 160 DA80
Harwood Ter. SW6 160 DB81
Harwoods Rd., Wat. 75 BU42
Harwoods Yd. N21 99 DN45
Wades Hill
Hascombe Ter. SE5 162 DR82
Hasedines Rd., Hem.H. 40 BG19
Haselbury Rd. N9 100 DS49
Haselbury Rd. N18 100 DS49
Haseldine Meadows, Hat. 45 CT19
Haseldine Rd., St.Alb. 61 CK26
Haseley End SE23 182 DW87
Tyson Rd.
Haselrigge Rd. SW4 161 DK84
Haseltine Rd. SE26 183 DZ91
Haselwood Dr., Enf. 81 DP42
Haskard Rd., Dag. 126 EX63
Haskell Ho. NW10 138 CR67
Hasker St. SW3 276 C8
Hasker St. SW3 160 DE77
Haslam Ave., Sutt. 199 CY102
Haslam Clo. N1 141 DN66
Haslam Clo., Uxb. 115 BQ61
Haslam St. SE15 162 DT80
Haslemere Ave. NW4 119 CX58
Haslemere Ave. SW18 180 DB89
Haslemere Ave. W7 157 CG76
Haslemere Ave. W13 157 CG76
Haslemere Ave., Barn. 98 DF46
Haslemere Ave., Houns. 156 BW82
Haslemere Ave., Mitch. 200 DD96
Haslemere Clo., Hmptn. 176 BZ92
Haslemere Clo., Wall. 219 DL106
Stafford Rd.
Haslemere Est., Harl. 51 EM15
Haslemere Gdns. N3 119 CZ55
Haslemere Heathrow Est., Houns. 155 BV82
Haslemere Pinnacles Est., Harl. 51 EN16
Haslemere Rd. N8 121 DK59
Haslemere Rd. N21 99 DP47
Haslemere Rd., Bexh. 166 EZ82
Haslemere Rd., Ilf. 125 ET61
Haslemere Rd., Th.Hth. 201 DP99
Haslemere Rd., Wind. 151 AN81
Hasler Clo. SE28 146 EV73
Haslett Rd., Shep. 195 BS96
Haslewood Ave., Hodd. 49 EA17
Hasluck Gdns., Barn. 80 DC44
Hassard St. E2 142 DT68
Hackney Rd.
Hassendean Rd. SE3 164 EH79
Hassett Rd. E9 143 DX65
Hassock Wd., Kes. 222 EK105
Hassocks Clo. SE26 182 DV90
Hassocks Rd. SW16 201 DK95
Hassop Rd. NW2 119 CX63
Hassop Wk. SE9 184 EL91
Hasted Clo., Green. 189 FW86
Hasted Rd. SE7 164 EK78
Hastings Ave., Ilf. 125 EQ56
Hastings Clo. SE15 162 DU80
Hastings Clo., Barn. 80 DC42
Leicester Rd.
Hastings Clo., Grays 170 FY79
Hastings Clo., Maid. 150 AC77
Hastings Dr., Surb. 197 CJ100
Hastings Ho. SE18 165 EM77
Hastings Rd. N11 99 DJ50
Hastings Rd. N17 122 DR55
Hastings Rd. W13 137 CH73
Hastings Rd., Brom. 204 EL102
Hastings Rd., Croy. 202 DT102
Hastings Rd., Rom. 127 FH57
Hastings St. WC1 273 P3
Hastings St. WC1 141 DL69
Hastings Way, Rick. 75 BP42
Hastings Way (Bushey), Wat. 76 BY42
Hastingwood Rd., Harl. 52 EX20
Hastingwood Trd. Est. N18 101 DX51
Hastoe Clo., Hayes 136 BY70
Kingsash Dr.
Hat and Mitre Ct. EC1 274 G5
Hatch, The, Enf. 83 DX39
Hatch, The, Wind. 150 AJ80
Hatch Clo., Add. 194 BH104
Hatch Gdns., Tad. 233 CX120
Hatch Gro., Rom. 126 EY56
Hatch La. E4 101 ED49
Hatch La., Bans. 234 DF115
Rectory La.
Hatch La., Couls. 234 DG115
Hatch La., West Dr. 154 BK80
Hatch La., Wind. 151 AN83
Hatch La., Wok. 229 BP120
Hatch Pl., Kings.T. 178 CM92
Hatch Rd. SW16 201 DL96
Hatch Rd., Brwd. 108 FU43
Hatch Side, Chig. 103 EN50
Hatcham Pk. Ms. SE14 163 DX81
Hatcham Pk. Rd.
Hatcham Pk. Rd. SE14 163 DX81
Hatcham Rd. SE15 162 DW79
Hatchard Rd. N19 121 DK61
Hatchcroft NW4 119 CV55
Hatchett Rd., Felt. 175 BQ88
Hatchgate, Horl. 268 DF149
Hatchgate Gdns., Slou. 131 AK69
Hatchlands Rd., Red. 250 DE134
Hatchwood Clo., Wdf.Grn. 102 EF49
Sunset Ave.
Hatcliffe Clo. SE3 164 EF83
Hatcliffe St. SE10 164 EF78
Woolwich Rd.
Hatfield Ave., Hat. 44 CS15
Hatfield Clo. SE14 163 DX80
Reaston St.
Hatfield Clo., Brwd. 109 GD45
Hatfield Clo., Horn. 128 FK64
Hatfield Clo., Ilf. 125 EP55
Hatfield Clo., Mitch. 200 DD98
Hatfield Clo., Sutt. 218 DA109
Hatfield Clo., W.Byf. 212 BH112
Hatfield Cres., Hem.H. 40 BM16
Hatfield Ho., Hat. 45 CX18
Hatfield Mead, Mord. 200 DA99
Central Rd.
Hatfield Pk., Hat. 45 CV18
Hatfield Rd. E15 124 EE64
Hatfield Rd. W4 158 CR75
Hatfield Rd. W13 137 CG74
Hatfield Rd., Ash. 232 CM119
Hatfield Rd., Dag. 146 EY66
Hatfield Rd., Grays 169 FW78
Hatfield Rd., Hert. 30 DF12
Hatfield Rd., Pot.B. 64 DC30
Hatfield Rd., St.Alb. 43 CE20
Hatfield Rd., Slou. 152 AU75
Hatfield Rd., Wat. 75 BV39
Hatfields SE1 278 E2
Hatfields SE1 141 DP74
Hatfields, Loug. 85 EP41
Hathaway Clo., Brom. 205 EM102
Hathaway Clo., Ruis. 115 BT63
Stafford Rd.
Hathaway Clo., Stan. 95 CG50
Hathaway Ct., St.Alb. 44 CL20
Hathaway Cres. E12 145 EM65
Hathaway Gdns. W13 137 CF71
Hathaway Gdns., Grays 170 GB76
Hathaway Rd.
Hathaway Gdns., Rom. 126 EX57
Hathaway Rd., Croy. 201 DP101
Hathaway Rd., Grays 170 GB77
Hatherleigh Clo., Chess. 215 CK106
Hatherleigh Clo., Mord. 200 DA98
Hatherleigh Gdns., Pot.B. 64 DD32
Hatherleigh Rd., Ruis. 115 BU61
Hatherleigh Way, Rom. 106 FK53
Hatherley Cres., Sid. 186 EU89
Hatherley Gdns. E6 144 EK69
Hatherley Gdns. N8 121 DL58
Hatherley Gro. W2 140 DB72
Hatherley Ms. E17 123 EA56
Hatherley Rd. E17 123 DZ56
Hatherley Rd., Rich. 158 CM82
Hatherley Rd., Sid. 186 EU91
Hatherley St. SW1 277 L8
Hathern Gdns. SE9 185 EN91
Hatherop Rd., Hmptn. 176 BZ94
Hathersham Clo., Horl. 269 DN147
Hathersham La., Horl. 267 DL144
Hatherwood, Lthd. 231 CK121
Hathorne Clo. SE15 162 DV82
Hathway St. SE15 162 DW82
Gibbon Rd.
Hathway Ter. SE14 162 DW82
Gibbon Rd.
Hatley Ave., Ilf. 125 EQ56
Hatley Clo. N11 98 DF50
Hatley Rd. N4 121 DM61
Hatteraick St. SE16 162 DW75
Brunel Rd.
Hatters La., Wat. 75 BR44
Hattersfield Clo., Belv. 166 EZ77
Hatton Ave., Slou. 131 AR70
Hatton Clo. SE18 165 ER80
Hatton Clo., Grav. 190 GE90
Hatton Clo. (Chafford Hundred), Grays 169 FX76
Hatton Ct. E5 123 DY63
Gilpin Rd.
Hatton Gdn. EC1 274 E6
Hatton Gdn. EC1 141 DN71
Hatton Gdns., Mitch. 200 DF99
Hatton Grn., Felt. 155 BU84
Hatton Gro., West Dr. 154 BK75
Hatton Ho. E1 142 DU73
Wellclose Sq.
Hatton Pl. EC1 274 E5
Hatton Pl. EC1 141 DN70
Hatton Rd., Croy. 201 DN102
Hatton Rd., Felt. 175 BQ87
Hatton Rd. (Cheshunt), Wal.Cr. 67 DX29
Hatton Row NW8 272 A5
Hatton St. NW8 272 A5
Hatton Wall EC1 274 D6
Hatton Wall EC1 141 DN71
Haunch of Venison Yd. W1 273 H9
Havana Clo., Rom. 127 FE57
Havana Rd. SW19 180 DA89
Havannah St. E14 163 EA75
Havant Rd. E17 123 EC55
Havant Way SE15 162 DT80
Daniel Gdns.
Havelock Pl., Har. 117 CE58
Havelock Rd. N17 100 DU54
Havelock Rd. SW19 180 DC92
Havelock Rd., Belv. 166 EZ77
Havelock Rd., Brom. 204 EJ98
Havelock Rd., Croy. 202 DT102
Havelock Rd., Dart. 187 FH87
Havelock Rd., Grav. 191 GF88
Havelock Rd., Har. 117 CE55
Havelock Rd., Kings L. 58 BN28
Havelock Rd., Sthl. 156 BZ76
Havelock St. N1 141 DL67
Havelock St., Ilf. 125 EP61
Havelock Ter. SW8 161 DH80
Havelock Wk. SE23 182 DW88
Haven, The SE26 182 DV92
Springfield Rd.
Haven, The, Grays 171 GF78
Haven, The, Rich. 158 CN83
Haven Clo. SE9 185 EM90
Haven Clo. SW19 179 CX90
Haven Clo., Grav. 191 GF94
Haven Clo., Hat. 45 CT17
Haven Clo., Hayes 135 BS71
Haven Clo., Sid. 186 EW93
Haven Clo., Swan. 207 FF96
Haven Grn. W5 137 CK72
Haven Grn. Ct. W5 137 CK72
Haven Grn.
Haven La. W5 138 CL72
Haven Pl. W5 137 CK73
The Bdy.
Haven Pl., Grays 170 GC75
Haven Rd., Ashf. 175 BP91
Haven St. NW1 141 DH66
Castlehaven Rd.
Haven Ter. W5 137 CK73
The Bdy.
Havengore Ave., Grav. 191 GL87
Havenhurst Ri., Enf. 81 DN40
Havensfield, Kings L. 58 BH31
Nunfield
Havenwood, Wem. 118 CP62
Havenwood Clo., Brwd. 107 FW51
Wilmot Grn.
Havercroft Clo., St.Alb. 42 CB22
King Harry La.
Haverfield Gdns., Rich. 158 CN80
Haverfield Rd. E3 143 DY69
Haverford Way, Edg. 96 CM53
Haverhill Rd. E4 101 EC46
Haverhill Rd. SW12 181 DJ88
Havering Dr., Rom. 127 FE56
Havering Gdns., Rom. 126 EW57
Havering Rd., Rom. 127 FD55
Havering St. E1 143 DX72
Devonport St.
Havering Way, Bark. 146 EV69
Havers Ave., Walt. 214 BX106
Haversfield Est., Brent. 158 CL78
Haversham Clo., Twick. 177 CK86
Haversham Pl. N6 120 DF61
Haverstock Hill NW3 120 DE64
Haverstock Rd. NW5 120 DG64
Haverstock St. N1 274 G1
Haverstock St. N1 141 DP68
Haverthwaite Rd., Orp. 205 ER103
Havil St. SE5 162 DS80
Havisham Pl. SE19 181 DP93
Haward Rd., Hodd. 49 EC15
Hawarden Gro. SE24 182 DQ87
Hawarden Hill NW2 119 CU62
Hawarden Rd. E17 123 DX56
Hawarden Rd., Cat. 236 DQ121
Hawbridge Rd. E11 123 ED60
Hawes Clo., Nthwd. 93 BT52
Hawes La. E4 83 EC38
Hawes La., W.Wick. 203 ED102
Hawes Rd. N18 100 DV51
Hawes Rd., Brom. 204 EH95
Hawes Rd., Tad. 233 CX120
Hatch Gdns.
Hawes St. N1 141 DP66
Haweswater Dr., Wat. 60 BW33
Haweswater Ho., Islw. 177 CF85
Hawfield Bank, Orp. 206 EX104
Hawfield Gdns., St.Alb. 61 CD26
Hawgood St. E3 143 EA71
Hawk Clo., Wal.Abb. 68 EG34
Hawkdene E4 83 EB44
Hawke Pk. Rd. N22 121 DP55
Hawke Pl. SE16 163 DX75
Middleton Dr.
Hawke Rd. SE19 182 DS93
Hawkenbury, Harl. 51 EN17
Hawker Clo., Wall. 219 DL108
Hawkes Clo., Grays 170 GB79
New Rd.
Hawke's Pl., Sev. 256 FG127
Hawkes Rd., Mitch. 200 DE95
Hawkesbury Rd. SW15 179 CV85
Hawkesfield Rd. SE23 183 DY89
Hawkesley Clo., Twick. 177 CG91
Hawkesworth Clo., Nthwd. 93 BS52
Hawkewood Rd., Sun. 195 BU97
Hawkhirst Rd., Ken. 236 DR115
Hawkhurst, Cob. 214 CA114
Hawkhurst Gdns., Chess. 216 CL105
Hawkhurst Gdns., Rom. 105 FD51
Hawkhurst Rd. SW16 201 DK95
Hawkhurst Way, N.Mal. 198 CR99
Hawkhurst Way, W.Wick. 203 EB103
Hawkinge Wk., Orp. 206 EV97
Farrington Ave.
Hawkinge Way, Horn. 148 FJ65
Hawkins Ave., Grav. 191 GJ91
Hawkins Clo. NW7 96 CR50
Hale La.
Hawkins Clo., Borwd. 78 CQ40
Banks Rd.
Hawkins Clo., Har. 117 CD59
Hawkins Rd., Tedd. 177 CH93
Hawkins Way SE6 183 EA91
Hawkley Gdns. SE27 181 DP89
Hawkridge Clo., Rom. 126 EW59
Hawkridge Dr., Grays 170 GD78
Hawks Hill, B.End 110 AC61
Hawks Hill, Lthd. 231 CF123
Guildford Rd.
Hawks Hill Clo., Lthd. 231 CF123
Hawks Ms. SE10 163 EC80
Luton Pl.
Hawks Rd., Kings.T. 198 CM96
Hawksbrook La., Beck. 203 EB100
Hawkshaw Clo. SW2 181 DL87
Tierney Rd.
Hawkshead Clo., Brom. 184 EE94
Hawkshead La., Hat. 63 CW28
Hawkshead Rd. NW10 139 CT66
Hawkshead Rd. W4 158 CS75
Hawkshead Rd., Pot.B. 64 DB29
Hawkshill, St.Alb. 43 CG21
Hawkshill Clo., Esher 214 CA107
Hawkshill Dr., Hem.H. 39 BE23
Hawkshill Rd., Slou. 131 AN69
Hawkshill Way, Esher 214 BZ107
Hawkslade Rd. SE15 183 DX85
Hawksley Rd. N16 122 DS62
Hawksmead Clo., Enf. 83 DX35
Hawksmoor, Rad. 62 CN33
Hawksmoor Clo. E6 144 EL72
Allhallows Rd.
Hawksmoor Clo. SE18 165 ES78
Hawksmoor Grn., Brwd. 109 GD43
Hawksmoor Ms. E1 142 DV73
Cable St.
Hawksmoor St. W6 159 CX79
Hawksmouth E4 101 EB45
Hawkstone Rd. SE16 162 DW77
Hawksview, Cob. 214 BZ113
Hawksway, Stai. 173 BF90
Hawkswell Clo., Wok. 226 AT117
Hawkswell Wk., Wok. 226 AS117
Lockfield Dr.
Hawkswood Gro., Slou. 133 AZ65
Hawkswood La., Ger.Cr. 113 AZ64
Hawkwell Ct. E4 101 EC48
Colvin Gdns.
Hawkwell Ho., Dag. 126 FA60
Hawkwell Wk. N1 142 DQ67
Basire St.
Hawkwood Cres. E4 83 EB44
Hawkwood Dell, Lthd. 246 CA126
Hawkwood La., Chis. 205 EQ95
Hawkwood Mt. E5 122 DV60
Hawkwood Ri., Lthd. 246 CA126
Hawlands Dr., Pnr. 116 BY59
Hawley Clo., Hmptn. 176 BZ93
Hawley Cres. NW1 141 DH66
Hawley Ms. NW1 141 DH66
Hawley St.
Hawley Rd. N18 101 DX50
Hawley Rd. NW1 141 DH66
Hawley Rd., Dart. 188 FL89
Hawley St. NW1 141 DH66
Hawley Way, Ashf. 174 BN92
Haws La., Stai. 174 BG86
Hawstead La., Orp. 224 EZ106
Hawstead Rd. SE6 183 EB86
Hawsted, Buck.H. 102 EH45
Hawthorn Ave. N13 99 DL50
Hawthorn Ave., Brwd. 109 FZ48
Hawthorn Ave., Cars. 218 DG108
Hawthorn Ave., Rain. 147 FH70
Hawthorn Ave., Rich. 158 CL82
Kew Rd.
Hawthorn Ave., Th.Hth. 201 DP95
Hawthorn Cen., Har. 117 CF56
Hawthorn Clo., Abb.L. 59 BU32
Magnolia Ave.
Hawthorn Clo., Bans. 217 CY114
Hawthorn Clo., Grav. 191 GH91
Hawthorn Clo., Hmptn. 176 CA92
Hawthorn Clo., Hert. 31 DN08
Hawthorn Clo., Houns. 155 BV80
Hawthorn Clo., Orp. 205 ER100
Hawthorn Clo., Red. 266 DG139
Bushfield Dr.
Hawthorn Clo., Wat. 75 BT38
Hawthorn Clo., Wok. 226 AY120
Hawthorn Cotts., Well. 166 EU83
Hook La.
Hawthorn Ct., Rich. 158 CP81
West Hall Rd.
Hawthorn Cres. SW17 180 DG92
Hawthorn Cres., S.Croy. 220 DW111
Hawthorn Dr., Har. 116 BZ58
Hawthorn Dr. (Denham), Uxb. 134 BJ65
Hawthorn Dr., W.Wick. 222 EE105
Hawthorn Gdns. W5 157 CK76
Hawthorn Gro. SE20 182 DV94
Hawthorn Gro., Barn. 79 CT44
Hawthorn Gro., Enf. 82 DR38
Hawthorn Hatch, Brent. 157 CH80
Hawthorn La., Sev. 256 FF122
Hawthorn La., Slou. 131 AL66
Hawthorn Ms. NW7 97 CY53
Holders Hill Rd.
Hawthorn Pl., Erith 167 FC78
Hawthorn Pl., H.Wyc. 88 AC47
Hawthorn Rd. N8 121 DK55
Hawthorn Rd. N18 100 DT50
Hawthorn Rd. NW10 139 CU66
Hawthorn Rd., Bexh. 166 EZ84
Hawthorn Rd., Brent. 157 CH80
Hawthorn Rd., Buck.H. 102 EK49
Hawthorn Rd., Dart. 188 FK88
Hawthorn Rd., Hodd. 49 EB15
Hawthorn Rd., Stai. 173 BC91
Hawthorn Rd., Sutt. 218 DE107
Hawthorn Rd., Wall. 219 DH108
Hawthorn Rd., Wok. 226 AX120
Hawthorn Rd. (Send Marsh), Wok. 227 BF124
Hawthorn Wk. W10 139 CY70
Droop St.
Hawthorn Way, Add. 212 BJ110
Hawthorn Way, Chesh. 54 AR29
Hawthorn Way, Red. 267 DH136
Hawthorn Way, St.Alb. 42 CA24
Hawthorn Way, Shep. 195 BR98
Hawthorn Way, Stai. 174 BK87
Hawthornden Clo. N12 98 DE51
Fallowfields Dr.
Hawthorndene Clo., Brom. 204 EG103
Hawthorndene Rd., Brom. 204 EF103
Hawthorne Ave., Har. 117 CG58
Hawthorne Ave., Mitch. 200 DD96
Hawthorne Ave., Ruis. 115 BV58
Hawthorne Ave. (Cheshunt), Wal.Cr. 66 DV31
Hawthorne Ave., West. 238 EK115
Hawthorne Clo. N1 142 DS65
Hawthorne Clo., Brom. 205 EM97
Hawthorne Clo., Sutt. 200 DB103
Aultone Way
Hawthorne Clo. (Cheshunt), Wal.Cr. 66 DV31
Hawthorne Ct., Nthwd. 93 BU54
Ryefield Cres.
Hawthorne Ct., Walt. 196 BX103
Ambleside Ave.
Hawthorne Cres., Slou. 132 AS72
Hawthorne Cres., West Dr. 154 BM75
Hawthorne Fm. Ave., Nthlt. 136 BY67
Hawthorne Gro. NW9 118 CQ59
Hawthorne La., Hem.H. 39 BF19
Hawthorne Ms., Grnf. 136 CC72
Greenford Rd.
Hawthorne Pl., Epsom 216 CS112
Hawthorne Pl., Hayes 135 BT73
Hawthorne Rd. E17 123 EA55
Hawthorne Rd., Brom. 205 EM97
Hawthorne Rd., Rad. 61 CG34
Hawthorne Way N9 100 DS47
Hawthorne Way, Guil. 243 BB130
Hawthornes, Hat. 45 CT20
Hazel Gro.
Hawthorns, Harl. 51 ET19
Hawthorns, Welw.G.C. 29 CX07
Hawthorns, Wdf.Grn. 102 EG48
Hawthorns, The, Berk. 38 AU18
Hawthorns, The, Epsom 217 CT107
Ewell Bypass
Hawthorns, The, Hem.H. 39 BF24
Hawthorns, The, Loug. 85 EN42
Hawthorns, The, Oxt. 254 EG132
Hawthorns, The, Rick. 91 BD50
Hawthorns, The, Slou. 153 BF81
Hawtrees, Rad. 77 CF35
Hawtrey Ave., Nthlt. 136 BX68
Hawtrey Clo., Slou. 152 AV75
Hawtrey Dr., Ruis. 115 BU59
Hawtrey Rd. NW3 140 DE66
Hawtrey Rd., Wind. 151 AQ82
Haxted Rd., Brom. 204 EH95
North Rd.
Hay Clo. E15 144 EE66
Hay Clo., Borwd. 78 CQ40
Hay Currie St. E14 143 EB72
Hay Hill W1 277 J1
Hay Hill W1 141 DH73
Hay La. NW9 118 CR56
Hay La., Slou. 112 AX63
Hay St. E2 142 DU67
Haybourn Mead, Hem.H. 40 BH21
Hayburn Way, Horn. 127 FF60
Haycroft Clo., Couls. 235 DP118
Caterham Dr.
Haycroft Gdns. NW10 139 CU67
Haycroft Rd. SW2 181 DL85
Haycroft Rd., Surb. 198 CL104
Hayday Rd. E16 144 EG71
Hayden Ct., Add. 212 BH111
Hayden Way, Rom. 105 FC54
Haydens Clo., Orp. 206 EW100
Haydens Pl. W11 139 CZ72
Portobello Rd.
Haydens Rd., Harl. 51 EQ15
Haydn Ave., Pur. 219 DN114
Haydns Ms. W3 138 CQ72
Emanuel Ave.
Haydock Ave., Nthlt. 136 CA65
Haydock Clo., Horn. 128 FM63
Haydock Grn., Nthlt. 136 CA65
Haydock Ave.
Haydon Clo. NW9 118 CQ56
Haydon Clo., Enf. 82 DS44
Mortimer Dr.
Haydon Dr., Pnr. 115 BU56
Haydon Pk. Rd. SW19 180 DB92
Haydon Pl., Guil. 258 AX135
Haydon Rd., Dag. 126 EW61
Haydon Rd., Wat. 76 BY44
Haydon St. EC3 275 P10
Haydon Wk. E1 142 DT73
Mansell St.
Haydon Way SW11 160 DD84
St. John's Hill
Haydons Rd. SW19 180 DB92
Hayes, The, Epsom 232 CR119
Hayes Barton, Wok. 227 BD116

Hector St. SE18 165 ES77
Heddington Gro. N7 121 DM64
Heddon Clo., Islw. 157 CG84
Heddon Ct. Ave., Barn. 80 DF43
Heddon Rd., Barn. 80 DF43
Heddon St. W1 273 K10
Heddon St. W1 141 DJ73
Hedge Hill, Enf. 81 DP39
Hedge La. N13 99 DP48
Hedge Lea, H.Wyc. 110 AD55
Hedge Pl. Rd., Green. 189 FT86
Hedge Row, Hem.H. 40 BG18
Hedge Wk. SE6 183 EB91
Hedgebrooms, Welw.G.C. 30 DC08
Hedgeley, Ilf. 125 EM56
Hedgemans Rd., Dag. 146 EX66
Hedgemans Way, Dag. 146 EY65
Hedger St. SE11 278 F8
Hedgerley Ct., Wok. 226 AW117
Hedgerley Gdns., Grnf. 136 CC68
Hedgerley Hill, Slou. 111 AR62
Hedgerley La., Beac. 111 AN56
Hedgerley La., Ger.Cr. 112 AV59
Hedgerley La., Slou. 112 AS58
Hedgerow, Ger.Cr. 90 AY54
Hedgerow Wk., Wal.Cr. 67 DX30
Hedgerows, Saw. 36 EZ05
Hedgerows, The, Grav. 190 GE89
Hedgers Gro. E9 143 DY65
Hedges, The, St.Alb. 42 CC16
Hedges Clo., Hat. 45 CV17
Hedgeside, Berk. 39 BA16
Hedgeside Rd., Nthwd. 93 BQ50
Hedgeway, Guil. 258 AU136
Hedgewood Gdns., Ilf. 125 EN57
Hedgley St. SE12 184 EF85
Hedingham Clo. N1 142 DQ66
Popham Rd.
Hedingham Clo., Horl. 269 DJ147
Hedingham Rd., Dag. 126 EV64
Hedingham Rd., Grays 169 FW78
Hedingham Rd., Horn. 128 FN60
Hedley Ave., Grays 169 FW80
Hedley Clo., Rom. 127 FE57
High St.
Hedley Rd., St.Alb. 43 CH20
Hedley Rd., Twick. 176 CA87
Hedley Row N5 122 DR64
Poets Rd.
Hedley Vw., H.Wyc. 88 AD54
Hedsor Hill, B.End 110 AC61
Hedsor La., H.Wyc. 110 AF60
Hedworth Ave., Wal.Cr. 67 DX33
Heenan Clo., Bark. 145 EQ65
Glenny Rd.
Heene Rd., Enf. 82 DR39
Heideck Gdns., Brwd. 109 GB47
Victors Cres.
Heidegger Cres. SW13 159 CV79
Trinity Ch. Rd.
Heigham Rd. E6 144 EK66
Heighams, Harl. 51 EM18
Heighton Gdns., Croy. 219 DP106
Heights, The SE7 164 EJ78
Heights, The, Beck. 183 EC94
Heights, The, Hem.H. 40 BH18
Saturn Way
Heights, The, Loug. 85 EM40
Heights, The, Nthlt. 116 BZ64
Heights, The, Wal.Abb. 68 EH25
Heights, The, Wey. 212 BN110
Heights Clo. SW20 179 CV94
Heights Clo., Bans. 233 CY116
Heiron St. SE17 161 DP79
Helby Rd. SW4 181 DK86
Helder Gro. SE12 184 EF87
Helder St., S.Croy. 220 DR107
Heldmann Clo., Houns. 157 CD84
Helen Ave., Felt. 175 BV87
Helen Clo. N2 120 DC55
Thomas More Way
Helen Clo., Dart. 187 FH87
Helen Clo., W.Mol. 196 CB98
Helen Rd., Horn. 128 FK55
Helen St. SE18 165 EP77
Wilmount St.
Helena Clo., Barn. 80 DD38
Helena Clo., Wall. 219 DL108
Helena Pl. E9 142 DW67
Fremont St.
Helena Rd. E13 144 EF68
Helena Rd. E17 123 EA57
Helena Rd. NW10 119 CV64
Helena Rd. W5 137 CK71
Helena Rd., Wind. 151 AR82
Helena Sq. SE16 143 DY73
Rotherhithe St.
Helens Gate, Wal.Cr. 67 DZ26
Helen's Pl. E2 142 DW69
Roman Rd.
Helenslea Ave. NW11 119 CZ60
Helford Clo., Ruis. 115 BS61
Chichester Ave.
Helford Wk., Wok. 226 AU118
Helford Way, Upmin. 129 FR58
Helgiford Gdns., Sun. 175 BS94
Helions Rd., Harl. 51 EP15
Helix Gdns. SW2 181 DM86
Helix Rd.
Helix Rd. SW2 181 DM86
Helleborine, Grays 170 FZ78
Hellings St. E1 142 DU74
Wapping High St.
Helm Clo., Epsom 216 CN112
Helme Clo. SW19 179 CZ92
Helmet Row EC1 275 J4
Helmet Row EC1 142 DQ70
Helmsdale, Wok. 226 AV118
Winnington Way
Helmsdale Clo., Hayes 136 BY70
Berrydale Rd.
Helmsdale Clo., Rom. 105 FE52
Helmsdale Rd. SW16 201 DJ95
Helmsdale Rd., Rom. 105 FE52
Helmsley Pl. E8 142 DV66
Helsinki Sq. SE16 163 DY76
Finland St.
Helston Clo., Pnr. 94 BZ52
Helston Gro., Hem.H. 40 BK15
Helston La., Wind. 151 AP81
Helston Pl., Abb.L. 59 BT32
Shirley Rd.
Helvellyn Clo., Egh. 173 BB94
Helvetia St. SE6 183 DZ89
Hemans St. SW8 161 DK80
Hemberton Rd. SW9 161 DL83
Hemel Hempstead Rd., Hem.H. 41 BR22
Hemel Hempstead Rd., St.Alb. 42 BW22
Hemel Hempstead Rd. (Redbourn), St.Alb. 41 BQ15
Hemery Rd., Grnf. 117 CD64
Heming Rd., Edg. 96 CP52
Hemingford Clo. N12 98 DD50
Hemingford Rd. N1 141 DM67
Hemingford Rd., Sutt. 217 CW105
Hemingford Rd., Wat. 75 BS36
Hemington Ave. N11 98 DF50
Hemlock Clo., Tad. 233 CY124
Warren Lo. Dr.
Hemlock Rd. W12 139 CT73
Hemmen La., Hayes 135 BT72
Hemming Clo., Hmptn. 196 CA95
Chandler Clo.
Hemming St. E1 142 DU70
Hemming Way, Wat. 75 BU35
Hemmings, The, Berk. 38 AT20
Hemmings Clo., Sid. 186 EV89
Hemnall St., Epp. 69 ET31
Hemp Wk. SE17 279 L8
Hemp Wk. SE17 162 DR77
Hempshaw Ave., Bans. 234 DF116
Hempson Ave., Slou. 152 AW76
Hempstall, Welw.G.C. 30 DB11
Linces Way
Hempstead Clo., Buck.H. 102 EG47
Hempstead La., Berk. 39 BB17
Hempstead Rd. E17 101 ED54
Hempstead Rd., Hem.H. 57 BA27
Hempstead Rd., Kings L. 58 BM26
Hempstead Rd., Wat. 75 BT39
Hemsby Rd., Chess. 216 CM107
Hemstal Rd. NW6 140 DA66
Hemsted Rd., Erith 167 FE80
Hemswell Dr. NW9 96 CS53
Hemsworth Ct. N1 142 DS68
Hemsworth St.
Hemsworth St. N1 142 DS68
Hemus Pl. SW3 160 DE78
Chelsea Manor St.
Hemwood Rd., Wind. 151 AK83
Hen & Chicken Ct. EC4 141 DN72
Fleet St.
Henbane Path, Rom. 106 FK52
Clematis Clo.
Henbit Clo., Tad. 233 CV119
Henbury Way, Wat. 94 BX48
Henchley Dene, Guil. 243 BD131
Henchman St. W12 139 CT72
Hencroft St. N., Slou. 152 AT75
Hencroft St. S., Slou. 152 AT76
Osborne St.
Hendale Ave. NW4 119 CU55
Henderson Ave., Guil. 242 AV129
Henderson Clo. NW10 138 CQ65
Henderson Clo., Horn. 127 FH61
St. Leonards Way
Henderson Clo., St.Alb. 42 CC16
Henderson Dr. NW8 140 DD70
Cunningham Pl.
Henderson Dr., Dart. 168 FM84
Henderson Pl., Abb.L. 59 BT27
Henderson Rd. E7 144 EJ65
Henderson Rd. N9 100 DV46
Henderson Rd. SW18 180 DE87
Henderson Rd., Croy. 202 DR100
Henderson Rd., Hayes 135 BU69
Henderson Rd., West. 222 EJ112
Hendham Rd. SW17 180 DE89
Hendon Ave. N3 97 CZ54
Hendon Gdns., Rom. 105 FC51
Hendon Hall Ct. NW4 119 CX55
Hendon La. N3 119 CY55
Hendon Pk. Row NW11 119 CZ58
Hendon Rd. N9 100 DU47
Hendon Way NW2 119 CZ62
Hendon Way NW4 119 CV58
Hendon Way, Stai. 174 BK86
Hendon Wd. La. NW7 79 CT44
Hendre Rd. SE1 279 N9
Hendren Clo., Grnf. 117 CD64
Dimmock Dr.
Hendrick Ave. SW12 180 DF87
Heneage Cres., Croy. 221 EC110
Heneage La. EC3 275 N9
Heneage St. E1 142 DT71
Henfield Clo. N19 121 DJ60
Henfield Clo., Bex. 186 FA86
Henfield Rd. SW19 199 CZ95
Henfold La., Dor. 264 CL144
Hengelo Gdns., Mitch. 200 DD98
Hengist Rd. SE12 184 EH87
Hengist Rd., Erith 167 FB80
Hengist Way, Brom. 204 EE98
Hengrave Rd. SE23 183 DX87
Hengrove Ct., Bex. 186 EY88
Hurst Rd.
Hengrove Cres., Ashf. 174 BK90
Henhurst Rd., Grav. 191 GL94
Henley Ave., Sutt. 199 CY104
Henley Bank, Guil. 258 AU136
Henley Clo., Grnf. 136 CC68
Henley Clo., Islw. 157 CF81
Henley Ct. N14 99 DJ45
Henley Ct., Wok. 227 BA120
Henley Cross SE3 164 EH83
Henley Deane, Grav. 190 GE91
Henley Dr. SE1 162 DT77
Henley Dr., Kings.T. 179 CT94
Henley Gdns., Pnr. 115 BV55
Henley Gdns., Rom. 126 EY57
Henley Rd. E16 165 EM75
Henley Rd. N18 100 DS49
Henley Rd. NW10 139 CW67
Henley Rd., Ilf. 125 EQ63
Henley Rd., Slou. 131 AL72
Henley St. SW11 160 DG82
Henley Way, Felt. 176 BX92
Henlow Pl., Rich. 177 CK89
Sandpits Rd.
Hennel Clo. SE23 182 DW90
Hennessy Ct., Wok. 211 BC113
Henniker Gdns. E6 144 EK69
Henniker Ms. SW3 160 DD79
Callow St.
Henniker Pt. E15 124 EE64
Henniker Rd. E15 123 ED64
Henning St. SW11 160 DE81
Henningham Rd. N17 100 DR53
Henrietta Clo. SE8 163 EA79
Henrietta Ms. WC1 274 A4
Henrietta Pl. W1 273 H9
Henrietta Pl. W1 141 DH72
Henrietta St. E15 123 EC64
Henrietta St. WC2 274 A10
Henrietta St. WC2 141 DL73
Henriques St. E1 142 DU72
Henry Clo., Enf. 82 DS38
Henry Cooper Way SE9 184 EK90
Henry Darlot Dr. NW7 97 CX50
Henry Dickens Ct. W11 139 CX74
Henry Doulton Dr. SW17 181 DH91
Henry Jackson Rd. SW15 159 CX83
Henry Rd. E6 144 EL68
Henry Rd. N4 122 DQ60
Henry Rd., Barn. 80 DD43
Henry Rd., Slou. 151 AR75
Henry St., Brom. 204 EH95
Henry St., Grays 170 GC79
East Thurrock Rd.
Henry St., Hem.H. 40 BK24
Henry Wells Sq., Hem.H. 40 BL16
Aycliffe Dr.
Henry's Ave., Wdf.Grn. 102 EF50
Henry's Wk., Ilf. 103 ER52
Henryson Rd. SE4 183 EA85
Hensford Gdns. SE26 182 DV91
Wells Pk. Rd.
Henshall St. N1 142 DR65
Henshaw St. SE17 279 K8
Henshaw St. SE17 162 DR77
Henshawe Rd., Dag. 126 EX62
Henshill Pt. E3 143 EB69
Bromley High St.
Henslow Way, Wok. 211 BD114
Henslowe Rd. SE22 182 DU85
Henson Ave. NW2 119 CW64
Henson Clo., Orp. 205 EP103
Henson Path, Har. 117 CK55
Henson Pl., Nthlt. 136 BW67
Henstridge Pl. NW8 140 DE68
Henty Clo. SW11 160 DE80
Henty Wk. SW15 179 CV85
Henville Rd., Brom. 204 EH95
Henwick Rd. SE9 164 EK83
Henwood Side, Wdf.Grn. 103 EM51
Love La.
Hepburn Clo. (Chafford Hundred), Grays 169 FW77
Hepburn Gdns., Brom. 204 EE102
Hepburn Ms. SW11 180 DF85
Webbs Rd.
Hepple Clo., Islw. 157 CH82
Hepplestone Clo. SW15 179 CV86
Dover Pk. Dr.
Hepscott Rd. E9 143 EA66
Hepworth Ct., Bark. 126 EU64
Hepworth Gdns., Bark. 126 EU64
Hepworth Rd. SW16 181 DL94
Hepworth Wk. NW3 120 DE64
Haverstock Hill
Hepworth Way, Walt. 195 BT102
Heracles Clo., Wall. 219 DL108
Herald Gdns., Wall. 201 DH104
Herald St. E2 142 DV70
Three Colts La.
Herald Wk., Dart. 188 FM85
Temple Hill Sq.
Herald's Ct. SE11 278 F9
Herald's Pl. SE11 278 E8
Herbal Hill EC1 274 E5
Herbal Hill EC1 141 DN70
Herbert Cres. SW1 276 E6
Herbert Cres., Wok. 226 AS118
Herbert Gdns. NW10 139 CV68
Herbert Gdns. W4 158 CP79
Magnolia Rd.
Herbert Gdns., Rom. 126 EX59
Herbert Pl. SE18 165 EP79
Plumstead Common Rd.
Herbert Rd. E12 124 EL63
Herbert Rd. E17 123 DZ59
Herbert Rd. N11 99 DL52
Herbert Rd. N15 122 DT57
Herbert Rd. NW9 119 CU58
Herbert Rd. SE18 165 EN80
Herbert Rd. SW19 179 CZ94
Herbert Rd., Bexh. 166 EY82
Herbert Rd., Brom. 204 EK99
Herbert Rd., Horn. 128 FL59
Herbert Rd., Ilf. 125 ES61
Herbert Rd., Kings.T. 198 CM97
Herbert Rd., Sthl. 136 BZ74
Herbert Rd., Swan. 187 FH93
Herbert Rd., Swans. 190 FZ86
Herbert St. E13 144 EG68
Herbert St. NW5 140 DG65
Herbert St., Hem.H. 40 BK19
St. Mary's Rd.
Herbert Ter. SE18 165 EP79
Herbert Rd.
Herbrand St. WC1 273 P4
Herbrand St. WC1 141 DL70
Hercies Rd., Uxb. 134 BM66
Hercules Pl. N7 121 DL62
Hercules St.
Hercules Rd. SE1 278 C7
Hercules Rd. SE1 161 DM76
Hercules St. N7 121 DL62
Hercules Twr. SE14 163 DY79
Milton Ct. Rd.
Hereford Ave., Barn. 98 DF46
Hereford Clo., Epsom 216 CR113
Hereford Clo., Guil. 242 AT132
Hereford Clo., Stai. 194 BH95
Hereford Copse, Wok. 226 AV119
Hereford Gdns. SE13 184 EE85
Longhurst Rd.
Hereford Gdns., Ilf. 124 EL59
Hereford Gdns., Pnr. 116 BY57
Hereford Gdns., Twick. 176 CC88
Hereford Ho. NW6 140 DA68
Hereford Ms. W2 140 DA72
Hereford Rd.
Hereford Pl. SE14 163 DZ80
Hereford Retreat SE15 162 DU80
Bird in Bush Rd.
Hereford Rd. E11 124 EH57
Hereford Rd. W2 140 DA72
Hereford Rd. W3 138 CP73
Hereford Rd. W5 157 CJ76
Hereford Rd., Felt. 176 BW88
Hereford Sq. SW7 160 DC77
Hereford St. E2 142 DU70
Hereford Way, Chess. 215 CJ106
Herent Dr., Ilf. 125 EM55
Hereward Ave., Pur. 219 DN111
Hereward Clo., Wal.Abb. 67 ED32
Hereward Gdns. N13 99 DN50
Hereward Grn., Loug. 85 EQ39
Hereward Rd. SW17 180 DF91
Herga Ct., Har. 117 CE62
Herga Ct., Wat. 75 BU40
Herga Rd., Har. 117 CF56
Herington Gro., Brwd. 109 GA45
Heriot Ave. E4 101 EA47
Heriot Rd. NW4 119 CW57
Heriot Rd., Cher. 194 BG101
Heriots Clo., Stan. 95 CG49
Heritage Clo. SW9 161 DP83
Heritage Clo., Uxb. 134 BJ70
Heritage Hill, Kes. 222 EJ106
Heritage Lawn, Horl. 269 DJ147
Heritage Vw., Har. 117 CF62
Heritage Wk., Rick. 73 BE41
Chenies Rd.
Herkomer Clo. (Bushey), Wat. 76 CB44
Herkomer Rd. (Bushey), Wat. 76 CA43
Herlwyn Ave., Ruis. 115 BS62
Herlwyn Gdns. SW17 180 DF91
Hermes Pt. W9 140 DA70
Hermes St. N1 274 D1
Hermes Wk., Nthlt. 136 CA68
Hotspur Rd.
Hermes Way, Wall. 219 DK108
Hermiston Ave. N8 121 DL57
Hermit Pl. NW6 140 DB67
Belsize Rd.
Hermit Rd. E16 144 EF71
Hermit St. EC1 274 F2
Hermit St. EC1 141 DP69
Hermitage, The SE23 182 DW88
Hermitage, The SW13 159 CT81
Hermitage, The, Felt. 175 BT90
Hermitage, The, Rich. 178 CL85
Hermitage, The, Uxb. 134 BL65
Hermitage Clo. E18 124 EF56
Hermitage Clo., Enf. 81 DP40
Hermitage Clo., Esher 215 CG107
Hermitage Clo., Shep. 194 BN98
Hermitage Clo., Slou. 152 AW76
Hermitage Ct. E18 124 EG56
Hermitage Ct. NW2 120 DA62
Hermitage La.
Hermitage Ct., Pot.B. 64 DC33
Southgate Rd.
Hermitage Gdns. NW2 120 DA62
Hermitage Gdns. SE19 182 DQ93
Hermitage La. N18 100 DR50
Hermitage La. NW2 120 DA62
Hermitage La. SE25 202 DU100
Hermitage La. SW16 181 DM94
Hermitage La., Croy. 202 DU100
Hermitage La., Wind. 151 AN83
Hermitage Path SW16 201 DL95
Hermitage Rd. N4 121 DP59
Hermitage Rd. N15 121 DP59
Hermitage Rd. SE19 182 DQ94
Hermitage Rd., Ken. 236 DQ116
Hermitage Row E8 122 DU64
Hermitage St. W2 140 DD71
Hermitage Wk. E18 124 EF56
Hermitage Wall E1 142 DU74
Hermitage Way, Stan. 95 CG53
Hermitage Wds. Cres., Wok. 226 AS119
Hermon Gro., Hayes 135 BU74
Hermon Hill E11 124 EG57
Hermon Hill E18 124 EG57
Herndon Clo., Egh. 173 BA91
Herndon Rd. SW18 180 DC85
Herne Clo. NW10 118 CR64
North Circular Rd.
Herne Ct., Ch.St.G. 90 AV48
Herne Hill SE24 182 DQ86
Herne Hill Rd. SE24 162 DQ83
Herne Ms. N18 100 DU49
Lyndhurst Rd.
Herne Pl. SE24 181 DP85
Herne Rd., Surb. 197 CK103
Herne Rd. (Bushey), Wat. 76 CB44
Herneshaw, Hat. 45 CT20
Hazel Gro.
Herns La., Welw.G.C. 30 DB08
Herns Way, Welw.G.C. 30 DA07
Heron Clo. E17 101 DZ54
Heron Clo. NW10 138 CS65
Heron Clo., Buck.H. 102 EG46
Heron Clo., Guil. 242 AV131
Heron Clo., Rick. 92 BK47
Heron Clo., Saw. 36 EX06
Heron Clo., Uxb. 134 BK65
Heron Ct., Brom. 204 EJ98
Heron Cres., Sid. 185 ES90
Heron Dale, Add. 212 BK106
Heron Dr. N4 122 DQ61
Heron Dr., Slou. 153 BB77
Heron Dr., Ware 33 EC12
Heron Flight Ave., Horn. 147 FG66
Heron Hill, Belv. 166 EZ77
Heron Ms., Ilf. 125 EP61
Balfour Rd.
Heron Pl. SE16 143 DY74
Heron Quay E14 143 EA74
Heron Rd. SE24 162 DQ84
Heron Rd., Croy. 202 DS103
Tunstall Rd.
Heron Rd., Twick. 157 CG84
Heron Sq., Rich. 177 CK85
Bridge St.
Heron Wk., Nthwd. 93 BS49
Heron Wk., Wok. 211 BC114
Blackmore Cres.
Heron Way, Grays 169 FV78
Heron Way, Hat. 45 CU19
Heron Way, Upmin. 129 FS60
Herondale, S.Croy. 221 DX109
Herondale Ave. SW18 180 DD88
Heronfield, Egh. 172 AV93
Heronfield, Pot.B. 64 DC30
Herongate Rd. E12 124 EJ61
Herongate Rd., Swan. 187 FE93
Herongate Rd. (Cheshunt), Wal.Cr. 67 DY27
Heronry, The, Walt. 213 BU107
Herons, The E11 124 EF58
Herons Cft., Wey. 213 BR107
Herons Elm, Berk. 38 AS16
Heron's Pl., Islw. 157 CH83
Herons Ri., Barn. 80 DE42
Herons Way, St.Alb. 43 CG24
Herons Wd., Harl. 35 EP13
Herons Wd. Ct., Horl. 269 DH147
Tanyard Way
Heronsforde W13 137 CJ72
Heronsgate, Edg. 96 CN50
Heronsgate Rd., Rick. 73 BB44
Heronslea, Wat. 76 BW36
Heronslea Dr., Stan. 96 CL50
Heronswood, Wal.Abb. 68 EE34
Roundhills
Heronswood Pl., Welw.G.C. 30 DA10
Heronswood Rd., Welw.G.C. 30 DA09
Heronway, Brwd. 109 GB46
Heronway, Wdf.Grn. 102 EJ49
Herrick Rd. N5 122 DQ62
Herrick St. SW1 277 N8
Herrick St. SW1 161 DK77
Herries St. W10 139 CY68
Herringham Rd. SE7 164 EJ76
Herrings La., Cher. 194 BG100
Herrongate Clo., Enf. 82 DT40
Hersant Clo. NW10 139 CU67
Herschel Pk. Dr., Slou. 152 AT75
Herschel St., Slou. 152 AT75
Herschell Rd. SE23 183 DY87
Hersham Bypass, Walt. 213 BV106
Hersham Clo. SW15 179 CU87
Hersham Gdns., Walt. 214 BW105
Hersham Rd., Walt. 195 BU102
Hersham Trd. Est., Walt. 196 BY103
Hertford Ave. SW14 178 CS85
Hertford Clo., Barn. 80 DD41
Hertford Pl. W1 273 K5
Hertford Rd. N1 142 DS67
Hertford Rd. N2 120 DE55
Hertford Rd. N9 100 DV47
Hertford Rd., Bark. 145 EP66
Hertford Rd., Barn. 80 DC41
Hertford Rd., Enf. 82 DW41
Hertford Rd., Hat. 30 DA14
Hertford Rd., Hert. 30 DF08
Hertford Rd. (Hertford Heath), Hert. 32 DW13
Hertford Rd. (Marden Hill), Hert. 30 DG06
Hertford Rd., Hodd. 49 DY15
Hertford Rd., Ilf. 125 ES58
Hertford Rd., Wal.Cr. 83 DX36
Hertford Rd., Ware 32 DW07
Hertford Rd. (Great Amwell), Ware 33 DZ11
Hertford Rd., Welw. 30 DA05
Hertford Rd. (Tewin), Welw. 30 DE05
Hertford Sq., Mitch. 201 DL98
Hertford Way
Hertford St. W1 277 H2
Hertford St. W1 141 DH74
Hertford Wk., Belv. 166 FA78
Hoddesdon Rd.
Hertford Way, Mitch. 201 DL98
Hertingfordbury Rd., Hert. 31 DM10
Hertslet Rd. N7 121 DM62
Hertsmere Rd. E14 143 EA73
Hervey Clo. N3 98 DA53
Hervey Pk. Rd. E17 123 DY56
Hervey Rd. SE3 164 EH81
Hervines Ct., Amer. 55 AQ37
Hervines Rd., Amer. 55 AP37
Hesa Rd., Hayes 135 BU72
Hesewall Clo. SW4 161 DJ82
Brayburne Ave.
Hesiers Hill, Warl. 238 EE117
Hesiers Rd., Warl. 238 EE117
Hesketh Ave., Dart. 188 FP88
Hesketh Pl. W11 139 CY73
Hesketh Rd. E7 124 EG62
Heslop Rd. SW12 180 DF88
Hesper Ms. SW5 160 DB78
Hesperus Cres. E14 163 EB77
Hessel Rd. W13 157 CG75
Hessel St. E1 142 DV72
Hesselyn Dr., Rain. 147 FH66
Hessle Gro., Epsom 217 CT111
Hester Rd. N18 100 DU50
Hester Rd. SW11 160 DE80
Hester Ter., Rich. 158 CN83
Chilton Rd.
Hestercombe Ave. SW6 159 CY82
Hesterman Way, Croy. 201 DM102
Heston Ave., Houns. 156 BY80
Heston Gra. La., Houns. 156 BZ79
Heston Ind. Mall, Houns. 156 BZ80
Heston Rd., Houns. 156 CA80
Heston Rd., Red. 266 DF138
Heston St. SE14 163 DZ81
Heston Wk., Red. 266 DF138
Heswell Grn., Wat. 93 BU48
Fairhaven Cres.
Hetchleys, Hem.H. 40 BG17
Hetherington Clo., Slou. 131 AM69
Hetherington Rd. SW4 161 DL84
Hetherington Rd., Shep. 195 BQ96
Hetherington Way, Uxb. 114 BL63
Hethersett Clo., Reig. 250 DC131
Hetley Gdns. SE19 182 DT94
Fox Hill
Hetley Rd. W12 139 CV74
Heton Gdns. NW4 119 CU56
Heusden Way, Ger.Cr. 113 AZ60
Hevelius Clo. SE10 164 EF78
Hever Ct. Rd., Grav. 191 GJ93
Hever Cft. SE9 185 EN91
Hever Gdns., Brom. 205 EN97
Heverham Rd. SE18 165 ES77
Hevers Ave., Horl. 268 DF147
Heversham Rd., Bexh. 166 FA82
Hewens Rd., Hayes 135 BQ70
Hewens Rd., Uxb. 135 BQ70
Hewer St. W10 139 CX71
Hewers Way, Tad. 233 CV120
Hewett Clo., Stan. 95 CH49
Hewett Pl., Swan. 207 FD98
Hewett Rd., Dag. 126 EX63
Hewett St. EC2 275 N5
Hewins Clo., Wal.Abb. 68 EE33
Broomstick Hall Rd.
Hewish Rd. N18 100 DS49
Hewison St. E3 143 DZ68
Hewitt Ave. N22 99 DP54
Hewitt Clo., Croy. 203 EA104
Hewitt Rd. N8 121 DN57
Hewitts Rd., Orp. 224 EZ108
Hewlett Rd. E3 143 DY68
Hexagon, The N6 120 DF60
Hexal Rd. SE6 184 EE90
Hexham Gdns., Islw. 157 CG80

Hexham Rd. SE27 182 DQ89
Hexham Rd., Barn. 80 DB42
Hexham Rd., Mord. 200 DB102
Hextalls La., Red. 252 DR128
Heybourne Rd. N17 100 DV52
Heybridge Ave. SW16 181 DL94
Heybridge Dr., Ilf. 125 ER55
Heybridge Way E10 123 DY59
Heydons Clo., St.Alb. 43 CD18
Heyford Ave. SW8 161 DL80
Heyford Ave. SW20 199 CZ97
Heyford Rd., Mitch. 200 DE96
Heyford Rd., Rad. 77 CF37
Heyford Ter. SW8 161 DL80
Heyford Ave.
Heyford Way, Hat. 45 CW16
Heygate St. SE17 279 H9
Heygate St. SE17 162 DQ77
Heylyn Sq. E3 143 DZ69
Malmesbury Rd.
Heymede, Lthd. 231 CJ123
Heynes Rd., Dag. 126 EW63
Heysham Dr., Wat. 94 BW50
Heysham La. NW3 120 DB62
Heysham Rd. N15 122 DR58
Heythorp St. SW18 179 CZ88
Heythorpe Clo., Wok. 226 AT117
Kenton Way
Heythrop Dr. (Ickenham), Uxb. 114 BM63
Heywood Ave. NW9 96 CS53
Heyworth Rd. E5 122 DV63
Heyworth Rd. E15 124 EF64
Hibbert Ave., Wat. 76 BX38
Hibbert Lo., Ger.Cr. 90 AX54
Gold Hill E.
Hibbert Rd. E17 123 DZ59
Hibbert Rd., Har. 95 CF54
Hibbert St. SW11 160 DD83
Hibberts All., Wind. 151 AR81
Peascod St.
Hibberts Way, Ger.Cr. 112 AY56
North Pk.
Hibbs Clo., Swan. 207 FD96
Hibernia Dr., Grav. 191 GM90
Hibernia Gdns., Houns. 156 CA84
Hibernia Pt. SE2 166 EX75
Wolvercote Rd.
Hibernia Rd., Houns. 156 CA84
Hibiscus Clo., Edg. 96 CQ49
Campion Way
Hichisson Rd. SE15 182 DW85
Hickin Clo. SE7 164 EK77
Hickin St. E14 163 EC76
Plevna St.
Hickling Rd., Ilf. 125 EP64
Hickman Ave. E4 101 EC51
Hickman Clo. E16 144 EK71
Hickman Clo., Brox. 49 DX20
Hickman Rd., Rom. 126 EW59
Hickmans Clo., Gdse. 252 DW132
Hickmore Wk. SW4 161 DJ83
Hickory Clo. N9 100 DU45
Hicks Ave., Grnf. 137 CD69
Hicks Clo. SW11 160 DE83
Hicks St. SE8 163 DY78
Hidalgo Ct., Hem.H. 40 BM18
Hidcote Clo., Wok. 227 BB116
Hidcote Gdns. SW20 199 CV97
Hide E6 145 EN72
Downings
Hide Pl. SW1 277 M9
Hide Pl. SW1 161 DK77
Hide Rd., Har. 117 CD56
Hideaway, The, Abb.L. 59 BU31
Hides, The, Harl. 35 ER14
Hides St. N7 141 DM65
Sheringham Rd.
Higgins Wk., Hmptn. 176 BY93
Abbott Clo.
High, The, Harl. 51 ER15
High Acres, Abb.L. 59 BR32
High Barn La., Dor. 246 BX134
High Barn Rd., Lthd. 246 BX129
High Beech, S.Croy. 220 DS108
High Beech Rd., Loug. 84 EK42
High Beeches, Bans. 217 CX114
High Beeches, Ger.Cr. 112 AX60
High Beeches, Orp. 224 EU107
High Beeches, Sid. 186 EY92
High Beeches Clo., Pur. 219 DK110
High Bois La., Amer. 55 AR35
Bois La.
High Bri. SE10 163 ED78
High Bri. Wf. SE10 163 ED78
High Broom Cres., W.Wick. 203 EB101
High Canons, Borwd. 78 CQ37
High Cedar Dr. SW20 179 CV94
High Clandon, Guil. 244 BL133
High Clo., Rick. 74 BJ43
High Coombe Pl., Kings.T. 178 CR93
High Coppice, Amer. 55 AQ39
High Cross, Wat. 77 CD37
High Cross Cen. N15 122 DU56
High Cross Rd. N17 122 DU55
High Dells, Hat. 45 CT19
High Dr., Cat. 237 EA122
High Dr., Lthd. 215 CD114
High Dr., N.Mal. 198 CQ95
High Elms, Chig. 103 ES49
High Elms, Upmin. 129 FS60
High Elms, Wdf.Grn. 102 EG50
High Elms Clo., Nthwd. 93 BR51
High Elms La., Wat. 59 BV31
High Elms Rd., Orp. 223 EP110
High Firs, Rad. 77 CF35
High Firs, Swan. 207 FE98
High Foleys, Esher 215 CH108
High Gables, Loug. 84 EK43
High Garth, Esher 214 CC107
High Gro. SE18 165 ER80
High Gro., Brom. 204 EJ95
High Gro., St.Alb. 43 CD18
High Gro., Welw.G.C. 29 CW08
High Hill Est. E5 122 DV60
Mount Pleasant La.
High Hill Ferry E5 122 DV60
High Hill Rd., Warl. 237 EC115
High Holborn WC1 274 A8
High Holborn WC1 141 DL72
High Ho. La., Til. 171 GJ75
High La. W7 137 CD72
High La., B.Stort. 37 FE09
High La., Cat. 237 DZ119
High La., Warl. 237 DZ118
High Lawns, Har. 117 CE62
High Level Dr. SE26 182 DU91
High Mead, Chig. 103 EQ47
High Mead, Har. 117 CE57
High Mead, W.Wick. 203 ED103
High Meadow Clo., Dor. 263 CH137
High Meadow Clo., Pnr. 115 BV56
Daymer Gdns.
High Meadow Cres. NW9 118 CR57
High Meadow Pl., Cher. 193 BF100
High Meadows, Chig. 103 ER50
High Meads Rd. E16 144 EK72
Fulmer Rd.
High Mt. NW4 119 CU58
High Oak Rd., Ware 33 DX05
High Oaks, Enf. 81 DM38
High Oaks, St.Alb. 42 CC15
High Oaks Rd., Welw.G.C. 29 CV08
High Pk. Ave., Lthd. 245 BT126
High Pk. Ave., Rich. 158 CN81
High Pk. Rd., Rich. 158 CN81
High Pastures, B.Stort. 37 FD07
High Path SW19 200 DB95
High Path Rd., Guil. 243 BC134
High Pewley, Guil. 258 AY136
High Pine Clo., Wey. 213 BQ106
High Pines, Warl. 236 DW119
High Pt. N6 120 DG59
High Pt. SE9 185 EP90
High Pt., Wey. 212 BN106
High Ridge (Cuffley), Pot.B. 65 DL27
High Ridge Clo., Hem.H. 58 BK25
High Ridge Rd., Hem.H. 58 BK25
High Rd. N2 98 DD54
High Rd. N11 99 DH50
High Rd. N12 98 DC51
High Rd. N15 122 DT58
High Rd. N17 100 DT53
High Rd. N20 98 DC45
High Rd. N22 121 DN55
High Rd. (Willesden) NW10 139 CT65
High Rd., Brox. 49 DZ23
High Rd., Buck.H. 102 EH47
High Rd., Chig. 103 EM50
High Rd., Couls. 234 DE124
High Rd. (Wilmington), Dart. 188 FJ90
High Rd., Epp. 69 ER32
High Rd. (North Weald Bassett), Epp. 71 FB27
High Rd. (Thornwood), Epp. 70 EV28
High Rd. (Harrow Weald), Har. 95 CE52
High Rd., Hat. 46 DD17
High Rd., Ilf. 125 EP62
High Rd. (Seven Kings), Ilf. 125 ET60
High Rd., Loug. 102 EJ45
High Rd., Pnr. 115 BV56
High Rd., Reig. 250 DC127
High Rd. (Chadwell Heath), Rom. 126 EV60
High Rd., Uxb. 134 BJ71
High Rd. (Bushey), Wat. 95 CD46
High Rd. (Leavesden Grn.), Wat. 75 BT35
High Rd., Wem. 117 CK64
High Rd., W.Byf. 212 BK112
High Rd. Ickenham, Uxb. 115 BP62
High Rd. Leyton E10 123 EB60
High Rd. Leyton E15 123 EC62
High Rd. Leytonstone E11 124 EE63
High Rd. Leytonstone E15 124 EE63
High Rd. Turnford, Brox. 67 DY25
High Rd. Woodford Grn. E18 102 EG54
High Rd. Woodford Grn., Wdf.Grn. 102 EF52
High Rd. Wormley (Turnford), Brox. 49 DY24
High Silver, Loug. 84 EK42
High Standing, Cat. 252 DQ125
High St. E11 124 EG57
High St. E13 144 EG68
High St. E15 143 EC68
High St. E17 123 DZ57
High St. N8 121 DL56
High St. N14 99 DK46
High St. NW7 97 CV49
High St. (Harlesden) NW10 139 CT68
High St. SE20 182 DV93
High St. (South Norwood) SE25 202 DT98
High St. W3 138 CP74
High St. W5 137 CK73
High St., Abb.L. 58 BN29
High St. (Bedmond), Abb.L. 59 BS31
High St., Add. 212 BH105
High St., Amer. 55 AM38
High St., Bans. 234 DA115
High St., Barn. 79 CY41
High St., Beck. 203 EA95
High St., Berk. 38 AW19
High St. (Elstree), Borwd. 77 CK44
High St., Brent. 157 CK79
High St., Brwd. 108 FW47
High St., Brom. 204 EG96
High St., Brox. 49 DZ21
High St., Cars. 218 DG105
High St., Cat. 236 DS123
High St., Ch.St.G. 90 AW48
High St., Chesh. 54 AP31
High St., Chis. 185 EP93
High St., Cob. 213 BV114
High St., Croy. 202 DQ103
High St., Dart. 188 FL87
High St. (Bean), Dart. 189 FV90
High St. (Eynsford), Dart. 208 FL103
High St. (Farningham), Dart. 208 FL100
High St., Dor. 263 CH136
High St., Edg. 96 CN51
High St., Egh. 173 BA92
High St. (Ponders End), Enf. 82 DW42
High St., Epp. 69 ET31
High St., Epsom 216 CR113
High St. (Ewell), Epsom 217 CT110
High St., Esher 214 CB105
High St. (Claygate), Esher 215 CF107
High St., Felt. 175 BT90
High St., Ger.Cr. 90 AY53
High St., Gdse. 252 DV131
High St., Grav. 191 GH86
High St. (Northfleet), Grav. 190 GB86
High St., Grays 170 GA79
High St., Green. 169 FV84
High St., Guil. 258 AX135
High St., Hmptn. 196 CB95
High St., Harl. 36 EW11
High St. (Roydon), Harl. 34 EH14
High St., Har. 117 CE60
High St. (Wealdstone), Har. 117 CE55
High St., Hayes 155 BS78
High St., Hem.H. 40 BK19
High St. (Bovingdon), Hem.H. 57 BA27
High St., Hodd. 49 EA17
High St., Horl. 269 DH148
High St., Horn. 128 FK60
High St., Houns. 156 CC83
High St. (Cranford), Houns. 155 BU81
High St., Ilf. 103 EQ54
High St., Iver 133 BE72
High St., Kings L. 59 BT27
High St., Kings.T. 197 CK97
High St. (Hampton Wick), Kings.T. 197 CJ95
High St., Lthd. 231 CH122
High St. (Great Bookham), Lthd. 246 CB125
High St. (Oxshott), Lthd. 215 CD113
High St. (Bray), Maid. 150 AC75
High St. (Taplow), Maid. 130 AE70
High St., N.Mal. 198 CS97
High St., Nthwd. 93 BT53
High St., Orp. 206 EU103
High St. (Downe), Orp. 223 EN111
High St. (Farnborough), Orp. 223 EP106
High St. (Green St. Grn.), Orp. 223 ET108
High St. (St. Mary Cray), Orp. 206 EW100
High St., Oxt. 253 ED130
High St. (Limpsfield), Oxt. 254 EG128
High St., Pnr. 116 BY55
High St., Pot.B. 64 DC33
High St., Purf. 168 FN78
London Rd. Purfleet
High St., Pur. 219 DN111
High St., Red. 250 DF134
High St. (Bletchingley), Red. 252 DQ133
High St. (Merstham), Red. 251 DH128
High St. (Nutfield), Red. 251 DM133
High St., Reig. 250 DA134
High St., Rick. 92 BK46
High St., Rom. 127 FE57
High St., Ruis. 115 BS59
High St., St.Alb. 43 CD20
High St. (Colney Heath), St.Alb. 44 CP22
High St. (London Colney), St.Alb. 61 CJ25
High St., Sev. 257 FJ126
High St. (Chipstead), Sev. 256 FC122
High St. (Otford), Sev. 241 FF116
High St. (Seal), Sev. 257 FL121
High St. (Shoreham), Sev. 225 FF110
High St., Shep. 195 BP101
High St., Slou. 152 AT75
High St. (Burnham), Slou. 130 AJ69
High St. (Chalvey), Slou. 151 AQ76
High St. (Colnbrook), Slou. 153 BC80
High St. (Datchet), Slou. 152 AV81
High St. (Langley), Slou. 153 AZ78
High St., S.Ock. 149 FR74
High St., Sthl. 136 BZ74
High St., Stai. 173 BF91
High St. (Stanwell), Stai. 174 BK86
High St. (Wraysbury), Stai. 172 AY86
High St., Sutt. 218 DB105
High St. (Cheam), Sutt. 217 CY107
High St., Swan. 207 FF97
High St., Swans. 190 FZ85
High St., Tad. 233 CW123
High St., Tedd. 177 CF92
High St., T.Ditt. 197 CG101
High St., Th.Hth. 202 DQ98
High St. (Whitton), Twick. 176 CC87
High St., Uxb. 134 BK67
High St. (Cowley), Uxb. 134 BJ70
High St. (Harefield), Uxb. 92 BJ54
High St., Wal.Cr. 67 DY34
High St. (Cheshunt), Wal.Cr. 67 DX29
High St., Walt. 195 BU102
High St., Ware 33 DX06
High St. (Hunsdon), Ware 34 EK06
High St. (Stanstead Abbotts), Ware 33 EC11
High St., Wat. 75 BV42
High St. (Bushey), Wat. 76 CA44
High St., Wem. 118 CM63
High St., West Dr. 154 BK79
High St. (Yiewsley), West Dr. 134 BK74
High St., W.Mol. 196 CA98
High St., W.Wick. 203 EB102
High St., West. 255 EQ127
High St. (Brasted), West. 240 EV124
High St., Wey. 212 BN105
High St., Wind. 151 AR81
High St. (Eton), Wind. 151 AR79
High St., Wok. 227 AZ117
High St. (Chobham), Wok. 210 AS111
High St. (Horsell), Wok. 226 AV115
High St. (Old Woking), Wok. 227 BA121
High St. (Ripley), Wok. 228 BH122
High St. Colliers Wd. SW19 180 DD94
High St. Grn., Hem.H. 40 BN18
High St. Ms. SW19 179 CY92
High St. N. E6 144 EL67
High St. N. E12 124 EL64
High St. S. E6 145 EM68
High St. Wimbledon SW19 179 CX92
High Timber St. EC4 275 H10
High Timber St. EC4 142 DQ73
High Tor Clo., Brom. 184 EH94
Babbacombe Rd.
High Tree Clo., Add. 211 BF106
High Tree Clo., Saw. 36 EX06
High Tree Ct. W7 137 CE73
High Trees SW2 181 DN88
High Trees, Barn. 80 DE43
High Trees, Croy. 203 DY102
High Trees Clo., Cat. 236 DT123
High Trees Ct., Brwd. 108 FW49
Warley Mt.
High Trees Rd., Reig. 266 DC135
High Vw., Guil. 261 BQ139
High Vw., Hat. 45 CT20
High Vw., Pnr. 116 BW56
High Vw., Rick. 74 BG42
High Vw., Sutt. 217 CZ111
High Vw., Wat. 75 BT44
High Vw. Ave., Grays 170 GC78
High Vw. Clo. SE19 202 DT96
High Vw. Clo., Loug. 84 EJ43
High Vw. Rd. E18 124 EF55
High Vw. Rd., Guil. 258 AS137
High Wickfield, Welw.G.C. 30 DC10
Amwell Common
High Wd. Rd., Hodd. 33 DZ14
High Worple, Har. 116 BZ59
High Wych La., Saw. 36 EU05
High Wych Rd., Saw. 35 ES09
Higham Hill Rd. E17 101 DY54
Higham Mead, Chesh. 54 AQ30
Higham Pl. E17 123 DY55
Higham Rd. N17 122 DR55
Higham Rd., Chesh. 54 AP30
Higham Rd., Wdf.Grn. 102 EG51
Higham Sta. Ave. E4 101 EB51
Higham St. E17 123 DY55
Higham Vw., Epp. 71 FB26
Highams Lo. Business Cen. E17 123 DY55
Highams Pk. Ind. Est. E4 101 EC51
Highbank Way N8 121 DN58
Highbanks Clo., Well. 166 EV80
Highbanks Rd., Pnr. 94 CB50
Highbarns, Hem.H. 58 BN25
Highbarrow Rd., Croy. 202 DU101
Highbridge Ind. Est., Uxb. 134 BJ66
Highbridge Rd., Bark. 145 EP67
Highbridge St., Wal.Abb. 67 EA33
Highbrook Rd. SE3 164 EK83
Highbury Ave., Hodd. 49 EA15
Highbury Ave., Th.Hth. 201 DN96
Highbury Clo., N.Mal. 198 CQ98
Highbury Clo., W.Wick. 203 EB103
Highbury Cor. N5 141 DN65
Highbury Cres. N5 121 DN64
Highbury Est. N5 122 DQ64
Highbury Gdns., Ilf. 125 ES61
Highbury Gra. N5 121 DP63
Highbury Gro. N5 141 DP65
Highbury Hill N5 121 DN62
Highbury Ms. N7 141 DN65
Holloway Rd.
Highbury New Pk. N5 122 DQ64
Highbury Pk. N5 121 DP62
Highbury Pk. Ms. N5 122 DQ63
Highbury Gra.
Highbury Pl. N5 141 DP65
Highbury Quad. N5 122 DQ62
Highbury Rd. SW19 179 CY92
Highbury Sta. Rd. N1 141 DN65
Highbury Ter. N5 121 DP64
Highbury Ter. Ms. N5 121 DP64
Highclere, Guil. 243 BA132
Highclere Clo., Ken. 236 DQ115
Highclere Ct., St.Alb. 43 CE19
Avenue Rd.
Highclere Dr., Hem.H. 40 BN24
Highclere Rd., N.Mal. 198 CR97
Highclere St. SE26 183 DY91
Highcliffe Dr. SW15 179 CT86
Highcliffe Gdns., Ilf. 124 EL57
Highcombe SE7 164 EH79
Highcombe Clo. SE9 184 EK88
Highcotts La., Guil. 243 BF126
Highcotts La., Wok. 243 BF125
Highcroft NW9 118 CR57
Highcroft Ave., Wem. 138 CN67
Highcroft Ct., Lthd. 230 CA123
Highcroft Gdns. NW11 119 CZ58
Highcroft Rd. N19 121 DL59
Highcroft Rd., Hem.H. 58 BG25
Highcross Rd., Grav. 189 FX92
Highcross Way SW15 179 CU88
Highdaun Dr. SW16 201 DM98
Highdown, Wor.Pk. 199 CT103
Highdown La., Sutt. 218 DB111
Highdown Rd. SW15 179 CV86
Higher Dr., Bans. 217 CX112
Higher Dr., Lthd. 245 BS127
Higher Dr., Pur. 219 DN113
Higher Grn., Epsom 217 CU113
Highfield, Bans. 234 DE117
Highfield, Ch.St.G. 90 AX47
Highfield, Felt. 175 BU88
Highfield, Guil. 258 AY142
Highfield, Harl. 52 EU16
Highfield, Kings L. 58 BL28
Highfield, Wat. 94 BZ48
Highfield Ave. NW9 118 CQ57
Highfield Ave. NW11 119 CX59
Highfield Ave., Erith 167 FB79
Highfield Ave., Grnf. 117 CE64
Highfield Ave., Orp. 223 ET106
Highfield Ave., Pnr. 116 BZ57
Highfield Ave., Wem. 118 CM62
Highfield Clo. N22 99 DN53
Highfield Clo. NW9 118 CQ57
Highfield Clo. SE13 183 ED87
Highfield Clo., Amer. 55 AR37
Highfield Clo., Egh. 172 AW93
Highfield Clo., Lthd. 215 CD111
Highfield Clo., Nthwd. 93 BS53
Highfield Clo., Rom. 105 FC51
Highfield Clo., Surb. 197 CJ102
Highfield Clo., W.Byf. 212 BG113
Highfield Ct. N14 81 DJ44
Highfield Cres., Horn. 128 FM61
Highfield Cres., Nthwd. 93 BS53
Highfield Dr., Brom. 204 EE98
Highfield Dr., Brox. 49 DY21
Highfield Dr., Epsom 217 CT108
Highfield Dr. (Ickenham), Uxb. 114 BL63
Highfield Dr., W.Wick. 203 EB103
Highfield Gdns. NW11 119 CY58
Highfield Gdns., Grays 170 GD75
Highfield Grn., Epp. 69 ES31
Highfield Hill SE19 182 DR94
Highfield La., Hem.H. 40 BM18
Highfield La., St.Alb. 43 CJ22
Highfield Link, Rom. 105 FD51
Highfield Pk. Dr., St.Alb. 43 CH23
Highfield Pl., Epp. 69 ES31
Highfield Rd. N21 99 DP47
Highfield Rd. NW11 119 CY58
Highfield Rd. W3 138 CP71
Highfield Rd., Berk. 38 AX20
Highfield Rd., Bexh. 186 EZ85
Highfield Rd., Brom. 205 EM98
Highfield Rd., Cat. 236 DU122
Highfield Rd., Cher. 194 BG102
Highfield Rd., Chesh. 54 AP29
Highfield Rd., Chis. 205 ET97
Highfield Rd., Dart. 188 FK87
Highfield Rd., Felt. 175 BU88
Highfield Rd., Hert. 32 DR11
Highfield Rd., Horn. 128 FM61
Highfield Rd., Islw. 157 CF81
Highfield Rd., Nthwd. 93 BS53
Highfield Rd., Pur. 219 DM110
Highfield Rd., Rom. 105 FC52
Highfield Rd., Sun. 195 BT98
Highfield Rd., Surb. 198 CQ101
Highfield Rd., Sutt. 218 DE106
Highfield Rd. (Cheshunt), Wal.Cr. 66 DS26
Highfield Rd., Walt. 195 BU102
Highfield Rd. (Bushey), Wat. 76 BY43
Highfield Rd., W.Byf. 212 BG113
Highfield Rd., West. 238 EJ117
Highfield Rd., Wind. 151 AM83
Highfield Rd., Wdf.Grn. 102 EL52
Highfield Rd. S., Dart. 188 FK87
Highfield Twrs., Rom. 105 FD50
Highfield Way, Horn. 128 FM61
Highfield Way, Pot.B. 64 DB32
Highfield Way, Rick. 74 BH44
Highfields, Ash. 231 CK119
Highfields, Lthd. 231 CD124
Highfields (East Horsley), Lthd. 245 BS128
Highfields (Cuffley), Pot.B. 65 DL28
Highfields, Rad. 77 CF35
Highfields Gro. N6 120 DF60
Highgate Ave. N6 121 DH58
Highgate Clo. N6 120 DG59
Highgate Gro., Saw. 36 EX05
Highgate High St. N6 120 DG60
Highgate Hill N6 121 DH60
Highgate Hill N19 121 DH60
Highgate Rd. NW5 121 DH63
Highgate Wk. SE23 182 DW89
Highgate W. Hill N6 120 DG61
Highgrove, Brwd. 108 FV44
Highgrove Clo. N11 98 DG50
Balmoral Ave.
Highgrove Clo., Chis. 204 EL95
Highgrove Ct., Beck. 183 EA94
Park Rd.
Highgrove Ms., Cars. 200 DF104
Highgrove Ms., Grays 170 GC78
Highgrove Rd., Dag. 126 EW64
Highgrove Way, Ruis. 115 BU58
Highland Ave. W7 137 CE72
Highland Ave., Brwd. 108 FW46
Highland Ave., Dag. 127 FC62
Highland Ave., Loug. 84 EL44
Highland Cotts., Wall. 219 DH105
Highland Ct. E18 102 EH53
Highland Cft., Beck. 183 EB92
Highland Dr., Hem.H. 41 BP20
Highland Dr. (Bushey), Wat. 94 CC45
Highland Pk., Felt. 175 BT91
Highland Rd. SE19 182 DS93
Highland Rd., Amer. 55 AR39
Highland Rd., Bexh. 166 FA84
Highland Rd., Brom. 204 EF95
Highland Rd., Nthwd. 93 BT54
Highland Rd., Pur. 219 DN114
Highland Rd., Sev. 225 FB110
Highland Rd., Wal.Abb. 50 EE22
Highlands, Ash. 231 CJ119
Highlands, Hat. 45 CW15
Highlands, Wat. 94 BW46
Highlands, The, Edg. 96 CP54
Highlands, The, Lthd. 245 BS125
Highlands, The, Pot.B. 80 DB43
Highlands, The, Rick. 92 BH45
Highlands Ave. N21 81 DM43
Highlands Ave. W3 138 CQ73
Highlands Ave., Lthd. 231 CJ122
Highlands Clo. N4 121 DL59
Mount Vw. Rd.
Highlands Clo., Ger.Cr. 90 AY52
Highlands Clo., Houns. 156 CB81
Highlands Clo., Lthd. 231 CH122
Highlands End, Ger.Cr. 91 AZ52
Highlands Gdns., Ilf. 125 EM60
Highlands Heath SW15 179 CW87
Highlands Hill, Swan. 207 FG96
Highlands La., Ger.Cr. 91 AZ51
Highlands La., Wok. 226 AY122
Highlands Pk., Lthd. 231 CK123
Highlands Pk., Sev. 257 FL121
Highlands Rd., Barn. 80 DA43
Highlands Rd., Beac. 89 AQ50
Highlands Rd., Lthd. 231 CH122
Highlands Rd., Orp. 206 EV101
Highlands Rd., Reig. 250 DD133
Highlea Clo. NW9 96 CS53
Highlever Rd. W10 139 CW71
Highmead SE18 165 ET80
Highmead Cres., Wem. 138 CM66
Highmoor, Amer. 55 AR39
Highmore Rd. SE3 164 EE79
Highover Pk., Amer. 55 AQ40
Highridge Clo., Epsom 232 CS115
Highridge La., Bet. 264 CP140
Highshore Rd. SE15 162 DT82
Highstead Cres., Erith 167 FE81
Highstone Ave. E11 124 EG58
Highview, Cat. 236 DS124
Highview, Nthlt. 136 BY69
Highview Ave., Edg. 96 CQ49
Highview Ave., Wall. 219 DM106
Highview Clo., Pot.B. 64 DC33
Highview Cres., Brwd. 109 GC44
Highview Gdns. N3 119 CY55
Highview Gdns. N11 99 DJ50
Highview Gdns., Edg. 96 CQ49
Highview Gdns., Pot.B. 64 DC33
Highview Gdns., St.Alb. 43 CJ15
Highview Gdns., Upmin. 128 FP61
Highview Ho., Rom. 126 EY56
Highview Rd. SE19 182 DR93
Highview Rd. W13 137 CG71
Highview Rd., Sid. 186 EV91
Highway, The E1 142 DV73
Highway, The E14 142 DV73

Highway, The, Orp. 224 EV106
Highway, The, Stan. 95 CF53
Highway, The, Sutt. 218 DC109
Highwold, Couls. 234 DG118
Highwood, Brom. 204 EE97
Highwood Ave. N12 98 DC49
Highwood Ave. (Bushey), Wat. 76 BZ39
Highwood Clo., Brwd. 108 FV45
Highwood Clo., Ken. 236 DQ117
Highwood Clo., Orp. 205 EQ103
Highwood Dr., Orp. 205 EQ103
Highwood Gdns., Ilf. 125 EM57
Highwood Gro. NW7 96 CR50
Highwood Hall La., Hem.H. 59 BQ25
Highwood Hill NW7 97 CT48
Highwood La., Loug. 85 EN43
Highwood Rd. N19 121 DL62
Highwoods, Cat. 252 DS125
Highwoods, Lthd. 231 CJ121
Highworth Rd. N11 99 DK51
Hilary Ave., Mitch. 200 DG97
Hilary Clo. SW6 160 DB80
Hilary Clo., Erith 167 FC81
Hilary Clo., Horn. 128 FK64
Hilary Rd. W12 139 CT72
Hilary Rd., Slou. 152 AY75
Hilbert Rd., Sutt. 199 CX104
Hilborough Way, Orp. 223 ER106
Hilbury Clo., Amer. 55 AQ35
Hilda May Ave., Swan. 207 FD97
Hilda Rd. E6 144 EK66
Hilda Rd. E16 144 EE70
Hilda Ter. SW9 161 DN82
Hilda Vale Clo., Orp. 223 EP105
Hilda Vale Rd., Orp. 223 EN105
Hilden Dr., Erith 167 FH80
Hildenborough Gdns., Brom. 184 EE93
Hildenlea Pl., Brom. 204 EE96
Hildenley Clo., Red. 251 DK128
Malmstone Ave.
Hildens, The, Dor. 262 CB138
Hilders, The, Ash. 232 CP117
Hildreth St. SW12 181 DH88
Hildyard Rd. SW6 160 DA79
Hiley Rd. NW10 139 CW69
Hilfield La., Wat. 77 CD41
Hilfield La. S. (Bushey), Wat. 77 CF44
Hilgay, Guil. 243 AZ134
Hilgay Clo., Guil. 243 AZ134
Hilgrove Rd. NW6 140 DC66
Hiliary Gdns., Stan. 95 CJ54
Hilljon Cres., Ger.Cr. 90 AY53
Hill, The, Cat. 236 DT124
Hill, The, Grav. 190 GC86
Hill, The, Harl. 36 EW11
Hill Ave., Amer. 55 AQ38
Hill Barn, S.Croy. 220 DS111
Hill Brow, Brom. 204 EK95
Hill Brow, Dart. 187 FF86
Hill Clo. NW2 119 CV62
Hill Clo. NW11 120 DA58
Hill Clo., Barn. 79 CW43
Hill Clo., Chis. 185 EP92
Hill Clo., Grav. 190 GE94
Hill Clo., Har. 117 CE62
Hill Clo., H.Wyc. 110 AF56
Hill Clo., Pur. 220 DQ113
Hill Clo., Stan. 95 CH49
Hill Clo., Wok. 226 AX115
Hill Common, Hem.H. 40 BN24
Hill Ct., Gdmg. 258 AS144
Hill Ct., Nthlt. 116 CA64
Hill Cres. N20 98 DB47
Hill Cres., Bex. 187 FC88
Hill Cres., Har. 117 CG57
Hill Cres., Horn. 128 FJ58
Hill Cres., Surb. 198 CM99
Hill Cres., Wor.Pk. 199 CW103
Hill Crest, Pot.B. 64 DC34
Hill Crest, Sev. 256 FG122
Hill Crest, Sid. 186 EU87
Hill Dr. NW9 118 CQ60
Hill Dr. SW16 201 DM97
Hill End, Orp. 205 ET103
The App.
Hill End La., St.Alb. 43 CJ23
Hill End Rd. (Harefield), Uxb. 92 BH51
Hill Fm. App., H.Wyc. 110 AE55
Hill Fm. Ave., Wat. 59 BU33
Hill Fm. Clo., Wat. 59 BU33
Hill Fm. Ind. Est., Wat. 59 BT33
Hill Fm. La., Ch.St.G. 90 AT46
Hill Fm. Rd. W10 139 CW71
Hill Fm. Rd., Chesh. 54 AR34
Hill Fm. Rd., Ger.Cr. 90 AY52
Hill Fm. Rd., Maid. 130 AD68
Hill Fm. Rd., Uxb. 115 BR63
Austin's La.
Hill Gro., Rom. 127 FE55
Hill Ho. Ave., Stan. 95 CF52
Hill Ho. Clo. N21 99 DN45
Hill Ho. Clo., Ger.Cr. 90 AY52
Rickmansworth La.
Hill Ho. Dr., Reig. 266 DB136
Hill Ho. Dr., Wey. 212 BN111
Hill Ho. Rd. SW16 181 DM92
Hill La., Orp. 207 FB104
Hill La., Ruis. 115 BQ60
Hill La., Tad. 233 CY121
Hill Ley, Hat. 45 CT18
Hill Leys (Cuffley), Pot.B. 65 DL28
Hill Meadow, Amer. 55 AM36
Hill Pk. Dr., Lthd. 231 CF119
Hill Path SW16 181 DM92
Valley Rd.
Hill Pl., Slou. 131 AP66
Hill Ri. N9 82 DV44
Hill Ri. NW11 120 DB56
Hill Ri. SE23 182 DV88
London Rd.
Hill Ri., Dart. 189 FR92
Hill Ri., Dor. 247 CG134
Hill Ri., Esher 197 CH103
Hill Ri., Ger.Cr. 90 AX54
Hill Ri., Grnf. 136 CC66
Hill Ri., Pot.B. 64 DC34
Hill Ri. (Cuffley), Pot.B. 65 DK27
Hill Ri., Rich. 177 CK85
Hill Ri., Rick. 74 BH44
Hill Ri., Ruis. 115 BQ60
Hill Ri., Slou. 153 BA79
Hill Ri., Upmin. 128 FN61
Hill Ri. Cres., Ger.Cr. 90 AX54
Hill Rd. N10 98 DF53
Hill Rd. NW8 140 DC68
Hill Rd., Brwd. 108 FU48
Hill Rd., Cars. 218 DE107
Hill Rd., Dart. 188 FL89
Hill Rd., Epp. 85 ES37
Hill Rd., Har. 117 CG57
Hill Rd., Hem.H. 39 BE21
Hill Rd., Lthd. 230 CB122
Hill Rd., Mitch. 201 DH95
Hill Rd., Nthwd. 93 BR51
Hill Rd., Pnr. 116 BY57
Hill Rd., Pur. 219 DM112
Hill Rd., Sutt. 218 DB106
Hill Rd., Wem. 117 CH62
Hill St. W1 276 G2
Hill St. W1 141 DH74
Hill St., Rich. 177 CK85
Hill St., St.Alb. 42 CC20
Hill Top NW11 120 DB56
Hill Top, Loug. 85 EN40
Hill Top, Mord. 200 DA100
Hill Top, Sutt. 199 CZ101
Hill Top Clo., Loug. 85 EN41
Hill Top Pl., Loug. 85 EN41
Hill Top Vw., Wdf.Grn. 103 EM51
Hill Vw., Berk. 38 AU17
Hill Vw. Clo., Tad. 233 CW121
Shelvers Way
Hill Vw. Cres., Orp. 205 ET102
Hill Vw. Dr., Well. 165 ES82
Hill Vw. Gdns. NW9 118 CR57
Hill Vw. Rd., Esher 215 CG108
Hill Vw. Rd., Orp. 205 ET102
Hill Vw. Rd., Stai. 172 AX86
Hill Vw. Rd., Twick. 177 CG86
Hill Vw. Rd., Wok. 227 AZ118
Hill Waye, Ger.Cr. 113 AZ58
Hillars Heath Rd., Couls. 235 DL115
Hillary Ave., Grav. 190 GE90
Hillary Cres., Walt. 196 BW102
Hillary Ri., Barn. 80 DA42
Hillary Rd., Hem.H. 40 BN20
Hillary Rd., Sthl. 156 CA76
Hillbeck Clo. SE15 162 DW80
Hillbeck Way, Grnf. 137 CD67
Hillborne Clo., Hayes 155 BU78
Hillborough Ave., Sev. 257 FK122
Hillborough Clo. SW19 180 DC94
Hillbrook Gdns., Wey. 212 BN108
Hillbrook Rd. SW17 180 DF90
Hillbrow, N.Mal. 199 CT97
Hillbrow Clo., Bex. 187 FD91
Hillbrow Cotts., Gdse. 252 DW132
Hillbrow Ct., Gdse. 252 DW132
Hillbrow Rd., Brom. 184 EE94
Hillbrow Rd., Esher 214 CC105
Hillbury, Hat. 45 CT19
Hillbury Ave., Har. 117 CH57
Hillbury Clo., Warl. 236 DW118
Hillbury Gdns., Warl. 236 DW118
Hillbury Rd. SW17 181 DH90
Hillbury Rd., Warl. 236 DU117
Hillbury Rd., Whyt. 236 DU117
Hillcote Ave. SW16 181 DN94
Hillcourt Ave. N12 98 DB51
Hillcourt Est. N16 122 DR60
Hillcourt Rd. SE22 182 DV86
Hillcrest N6 120 DG59
Hillcrest N21 99 DP45
Hillcrest, Hat. 45 CU18
Hillcrest, St.Alb. 42 CB22
Hillcrest, Wey. 213 BP105
Hillcrest Ave. NW11 119 CY57
Hillcrest Ave., Cher. 211 BE105
Hillcrest Ave., Edg. 96 CP49
Hillcrest Ave., Grays 169 FU79
Hillcrest Ave., Pnr. 116 BX56
Hillcrest Clo. SE26 182 DU91
Hillcrest Clo., Beck. 203 DZ99
Hillcrest Clo., Epsom 233 CT115
Hillcrest Dr., Green. 189 FV85
Riverview Rd.
Hillcrest Gdns. N3 119 CY56
Hillcrest Gdns. NW2 119 CU62
Hillcrest Gdns., Esher 197 CF104
Hillcrest Par., Couls. 219 DH114
Hillcrest Rd. E17 101 ED54
Hillcrest Rd. E18 102 EF54
Hillcrest Rd. W3 138 CN74
Hillcrest Rd. W5 138 CL71
Hillcrest Rd., Brom. 184 EG92
Hillcrest Rd., Dart. 187 FF87
Hillcrest Rd., Guil. 242 AT133
Hillcrest Rd., Horn. 127 FG59
Hillcrest Rd., Loug. 84 EK44
Hillcrest Rd., Ong. 71 FE30
Hillcrest Rd., Orp. 206 EU103
Hillcrest Rd., Pur. 219 DM110
Hillcrest Rd., Rad. 62 CN33
Hillcrest Rd., West. 238 EK116
Hillcrest Rd., Whyt. 236 DT117
Hillcrest Vw., Beck. 203 DZ100
Hillcrest Way, Epp. 70 EU31
Hillcrest Waye, Ger.Cr. 113 AZ58
Hillcroft, Loug. 85 EN40
Hillcroft Ave., Pnr. 116 BZ58
Hillcroft Ave., Pur. 219 DJ113
Hillcroft Cres. W5 138 CL72
Hillcroft Cres., Ruis. 116 BX62
Hillcroft Cres., Wat. 93 BV46
Hillcroft Cres., Wem. 118 CM63
Hillcroft Rd. E6 145 EP71
Hillcroft Rd., Chesh. 54 AR29
Hillcroft Rd., H.Wyc. 88 AC46
Hillcroome Rd., Sutt. 218 DD107
Hillcross Ave., Mord. 199 CZ99
Hilldale Rd., Sutt. 217 CZ105
Hilldeane Rd., Pur. 219 DN109
Hilldene Ave., Rom. 106 FJ51
Hilldene Clo., Rom. 106 FK50
Hilldown Rd. SW16 181 DL94
Hilldown Rd., Brom. 204 EE102
Hilldown Rd., Hem.H. 40 BG18
Hilldrop Cres. N7 121 DK64
Hilldrop Est. N7 121 DK64
Hilldrop La. N7 121 DK64
Hilldrop Rd. N7 121 DK64
Hilldrop Rd., Brom. 184 EG93
Hillend SE18 165 EN81
Hillersdon, Slou. 132 AV71
Hillersdon Ave. SW13 159 CU82
Hillersdon Ave., Edg. 96 CM50
Hillery Clo. SE17 279 L9
Hilley Fld. La., Lthd. 230 CC122
Hillfield, Hat. 45 CV15
Hillfield Ave. N8 121 DL57
Hillfield Ave. NW9 118 CS57
Hillfield Ave., Wem. 138 CL66
Hillfield Clo., Guil. 243 BC132
Hillfield Clo., Har. 116 CC56
Hillfield Clo., Red. 250 DG134
Hillfield Ct. NW3 120 DE64
Hillfield Ct., Hem.H. 40 BL20
Hillfield Par., Mord. 200 DE100
Hillfield Pk. N10 121 DH56
Hillfield Pk. N21 99 DN47
Hillfield Pk. Ms. N10 121 DH56
Hillfield Rd. NW6 119 CZ64
Hillfield Rd., Ger.Cr. 90 AY52
Hillfield Rd., Hmptn. 176 BZ94
Hillfield Rd., Hem.H. 40 BK20
Hillfield Rd., Red. 250 DG134
Hillfield Rd., Sev. 241 FE120
Hillfield Sq., Ger.Cr. 90 AY52
Hillfoot Ave., Rom. 105 FC53
Hillfoot Rd., Rom. 105 FC53
Hillford Pl., Red. 266 DG140
Hillgate Pl. SW12 181 DH87
Hillgate Pl. W8 140 DA74
Hillgate St. W8 140 DA74
Hillgrove, Ger.Cr. 90 AY53
Hillgrove Business Pk., Wal.Abb. 49 EC22
Hillhouse, Wal.Abb. 68 EF33
Hillhouse Rd., Dart. 188 FQ87
Hillhurst Gdns., Cat. 236 DS120
Hilliard Rd., Nthwd. 93 BT53
Hilliards Ct. E1 142 DV74
Wapping High St.
Hilliards Rd., Uxb. 134 BK72
Hillier Clo., Barn. 80 DB44
Hillier Gdns., Croy. 219 DN106
Crowley Cres.
Hillier Pl., Chess. 215 CJ107
Hillier Rd. SW11 180 DF86
Hillier Rd., Guil. 243 BA134
Hilliers Ave., Uxb. 134 BN69
Harlington Rd.
Hilliers La., Croy. 201 DL104
Hillingdale, West. 238 EH118
Hillingdon Ave., Sev. 257 FJ121
Hillingdon Ave., Stai. 174 BL88
Hillingdon Hill, Uxb. 134 BL69
Hillingdon Ri., Sev. 257 FK122
Hillingdon Rd., Bexh. 167 FC82
Hillingdon Rd., Grav. 191 GG89
Hillingdon Rd., Uxb. 134 BL67
Hillingdon Rd., Wat. 59 BU34
Hillingdon St. SE5 161 DP79
Hillingdon St. SE17 161 DP79
Hillington Gdns., Wdf.Grn. 102 EK54
Hillman Clo., Horn. 128 FK55
Hillman Clo., Uxb. 114 BL64
Hillman Dr. W10 139 CW70
Hillman St. E8 142 DV65
Hillmarton Rd. N7 121 DL64
Hillmay Dr., Hem.H. 40 BJ21
Hillmead, Berk. 38 AU20
Hillmead Ct., Maid. 130 AF71
Hillmead Dr. SW9 161 DP84
Hillmont Rd., Esher 197 CE104
Hillmore Gro. SE26 183 DX92
Hillreach SE18 165 EM78
Hillrise, Walt. 195 BT101
Hillrise Ave., Wat. 76 BX38
Hillrise Rd. N19 121 DL59
Hillrise Rd., Rom. 105 FC51
Hills Chase, Brwd. 108 FW49
Hills La., Nthwd. 93 BS53
Hills Ms. W5 138 CL73
Hills Pl. W1 273 K9
Hills Rd., Buck.H. 102 EH46
Hillsborough Grn., Wat. 93 BU48
Ashburnham Dr.
Hillsborough Rd. SE22 182 DS85
Hillsgrove, Well. 166 EW80
Hillside NW9 118 CR56
Hillside NW10 138 CQ67
Hillside SW19 179 CX93
Hillside, Bans. 233 CY115
Hillside, Barn. 80 DC43
Hillside, Chesh. 54 AN28
Hillside, Dart. 189 FS92
Hillside (Farningham), Dart. 208 FM101
Hillside, Erith 167 FD77
Hillside, Grays 170 GD77
Hillside, Harl. 52 EW17
Hillside, Hat. 45 CU18
Hillside, Hodd. 49 DZ16
Hillside, Slou. 152 AS75
Hillside (Harefield), Uxb. 114 BJ57
Hillside, Vir.W. 192 AW100
Hillside, Ware 32 DW07
Hillside, Welw.G.C. 30 DB12
Hillside, Wok. 226 AX120
Hillside, The, Orp. 224 EV109
Hillside Ave. N11 98 DF51
Hillside Ave., Borwd. 78 CP42
Hillside Ave., Grav. 191 GK89
Hillside Ave., Pur. 219 DP113
Hillside Ave. (Cheshunt), Wal.Cr. 67 DX31
Hillside Ave., Wem. 118 CM63
Hillside Ave., Wdf.Grn. 102 EJ50
Hillside Clo. NW8 140 DB68
Hillside Clo., Abb.L. 59 BS32
Hillside Clo., Bans. 233 CY116
Hillside Clo., Bet. 264 CN135
Hillside Clo., Ch.St.G. 90 AV48
Hillside Clo., Ger.Cr. 90 AY51
Hillside Clo., Mord. 199 CY98
Hillside Clo., Wdf.Grn. 102 EJ50
Hillside Ct., St.Alb. 43 CE19
Hillside Rd.
Hillside Ct., Swan. 207 FG98
Hillside Cres., Enf. 82 DR38
Hillside Cres., Har. 116 CC60
Hillside Cres., Nthwd. 93 BU53
Hillside Cres. (Cheshunt), Wal.Cr. 67 DX31
Hillside Cres., Ware 33 EB11
Hillside Cres., Wat. 76 BY44
Hillside Dr., Edg. 96 CN51
Hillside Dr., Grav. 191 GK89
Hillside Est. N15 122 DT58
Hillside Gdns. E17 123 ED55
Hillside Gdns. N6 120 DG58
Hillside Gdns. SW2 181 DN89
Hillside Gdns., Add. 211 BF106
Hillside Gdns., Barn. 79 CY42
Hillside Gdns., Berk. 38 AX20
Hillside Gdns., Bet. 248 CN134
Hillside Gdns., Edg. 96 CM49
Hillside Gdns., Har. 118 CL59
Hillside Gdns., Nthwd. 93 BU52
Hillside Gdns., Wall. 219 DJ108
Hillside Gate, St.Alb. 43 CE19
Hillside Gro. N14 99 DK45
Hillside Gro. NW7 97 CU52
Hillside La., Brom. 204 EG103
Hillside La., Ware 33 EA10
Hillside Pas. SW2 181 DM89
Hillside Ri., Nthwd. 93 BU52
Hillside Rd. N15 122 DS59
Hillside Rd. SW2 181 DN89
Hillside Rd. W5 138 CL71
Hillside Rd., Ash. 232 CM117
Hillside Rd., Brom. 204 EF97
Hillside Rd., Couls. 235 DL118
Hillside Rd., Croy. 219 DP106
Hillside Rd., Dart. 187 FG86
Hillside Rd., Epsom 217 CW110
Hillside Rd., Nthwd. 93 BU52
Hillside Rd., Pnr. 93 BV52
Hillside Rd., Rad. 77 CH35
Hillside Rd., Rick. 73 BC43
Hillside Rd., St.Alb. 43 CE19
Hillside Rd., Sev. 257 FK123
Hillside Rd., Sthl. 136 CA70
Hillside Rd., Surb. 198 CM99
Hillside Rd., Sutt. 217 CZ108
Hillside Rd. (Bushey), Wat. 76 BY43
Hillside Rd., West. 238 EL119
Hillside Rd., Whyt. 236 DU118
Hillside Ter., Hert. 32 DQ11
Hillside Wk., Brwd. 108 FU48
Hillsleigh Rd. W8 139 CZ74
Hillsmead Way, S.Croy. 220 DU113
Hillspur Clo., Guil. 242 AT133
Hillspur Rd., Guil. 242 AT133
Hillstowe St. E5 122 DW61
Hilltop Clo., Guil. 242 AT130
Hilltop Clo., Lthd. 231 CJ123
Hilltop Clo. (Cheshunt), Wal.Cr. 66 DT26
Hilltop Gdns. NW4 97 CV53
Great N. Way
Hilltop Gdns., Dart. 188 FM85
Hilltop Gdns., Orp. 205 ES103
Hilltop La., Cat. 251 DN126
Hilltop La., Red. 251 DN126
Hilltop Ri., Lthd. 246 CC126
Hilltop Rd. NW6 140 DA66
Hilltop Rd., Berk. 38 AW20
Hilltop Rd., Grays 169 FV79
Hilltop Rd., Kings L. 59 BR27
Hilltop Rd., Reig. 266 DB136
Hilltop Rd., Whyt. 236 DS117
Hilltop Wk., Cat. 237 DY120
Hilltop Way, Stan. 95 CG48
Hillview SW20 179 CV94
Hillview, Mitch. 201 DL98
Hillview Ave., Har. 118 CL57
Hillview Ave., Horn. 128 FJ58
Hillview Clo., Pnr. 94 BZ51
Hillview Clo., Pur. 219 DP111
Hillview Ct., Wok. 227 AZ118
Hillview Cres., Guil. 242 AT132
Hillview Cres., Ilf. 125 EM58
Hillview Dr., Red. 266 DG135
Philanthropic Rd.
Hillview Gdns. NW4 119 CX56
Hillview Gdns., Har. 116 CA55
Hillview Gdns. (Cheshunt), Wal.Cr. 67 DX27
Hillview Rd. NW7 97 CX49
Hillview Rd., Chis. 185 EN92
Hillview Rd., Pnr. 94 BZ52
Hillview Rd., Sutt. 200 DC104
Hillway N6 120 DG61
Hillway NW9 118 CS60
Hillway, Amer. 55 AP41
Hillwood Clo., Brwd. 109 GB46
Hillwood Gro., Brwd. 109 GB46
Hillworth Rd. SW2 181 DN87
Hilly Fld., Harl. 51 ET19
Hilly Flds. Cres. SE4 163 EA83
Hillyard Rd. W7 137 CE71
Hillyard St. SW9 161 DN81
Hillyfield E17 123 DY55
Hillyfields, Loug. 85 EN40
Hillyfields, Welw.G.C. 30 DC08
Hilperton Rd., Slou. 152 AS75
Hilsea St. E5 122 DW63
Hilton Ave. N12 98 DD50
Hilton Clo., Uxb. 134 BH68
Hilton Ct., Horl. 269 DK147
Clarence Way
Hilton Way, S.Croy. 236 DV115
Hilversum Cres. SE22 182 DS85
East Dulwich Gro.
Himalayan Way, Wat. 75 BT44
Himley Rd. SW17 180 DE92
Hinchcliffe Clo., Wall. 219 DM108
Hinchley Clo., Esher 197 CF104
Hinchley Dr., Esher 197 CF104
Hinchley Way, Esher 197 CG104
Hinckley Rd. SE15 162 DU84
Hind Clo., Chig. 103 ET50
Hind Ct. EC4 274 E9
Hind Cres., Erith 167 FD79
Hind Gro. E14 143 EA72
Hind Ter., Grays 169 FX78
Mill La.
Hinde Ms. W1 140 DG72
Marylebone La.
Hinde St. W1 272 G8
Hinde St. W1 140 DG72
Hindes Rd., Har. 117 CD57
Hindhead Clo. N16 122 DS60
Hindhead Clo., Uxb. 135 BP71
Aldenham Dr.
Hindhead Gdns., Nthlt. 136 BY67
Hindhead Grn., Wat. 94 BW50
Hindhead Way, Wall. 219 DL106
Hindmans Rd. SE22 182 DU85
Hindmans Way, Dag. 146 EZ70
Hindmarsh Clo. E1 142 DU73
Cable St.
Hindrey Rd. E5 122 DV64
Hindsley's Pl. SE23 182 DW89
Hinkler Clo., Wall. 219 DL108
Hinkler Rd., Har. 117 CK55
Hinkley Clo. (Harefield), Uxb. 114 BJ56
Hinksey Clo., Slou. 153 BB76
Hinksey Path SE2 166 EX76
Hinstock Rd. SE18 165 EQ79
Hinton Ave., Houns. 156 BX84
Hinton Clo. SE9 184 EL88
Hinton Rd. N18 100 DS49
Hinton Rd. SE24 161 DP83
Hinton Rd., Slou. 131 AL73
Hinton Rd., Uxb. 134 BJ67
Hinton Rd., Wall. 219 DJ107
Hintons, Harl. 51 EM19
Hipley Ct., Guil. 259 BA135
Warren Rd.
Hipley St., Wok. 227 BB121
Hippodrome Ms. W11 139 CY73
Portland Rd.
Hippodrome Pl. W11 139 CY73
Hiscocks Ho. NW10 138 CQ66
Hitcham La., Slou. 130 AE69
Hitcham Rd. E17 123 DZ59
Hitcham Rd., Maid. 130 AF72
Hitcham Rd., Slou. 130 AF70
Hitchcock Clo., Shep. 194 BM97
Hitchen Hatch La., Sev. 256 FG124
Hitchens Clo., Hem.H. 39 BF19
Hitchin Clo., Rom. 106 FJ49
Hitchin Sq. E3 143 DY68
Hitchings Way, Reig. 266 DA138
Hither Fm. Rd. SE3 164 EJ83
Hither Grn. La. SE13 183 EC85
Hither Meadow, Ger.Cr. 90 AY53
Lower Rd.
Hitherbaulk, Welw.G.C. 29 CY11
Hitherbroom Rd., Hayes 135 BU74
Hitherbury Clo., Guil. 258 AW137
Hitherfield Rd. SW16 181 DM89
Hitherfield Rd., Dag. 126 EY61
Hitherlands SW12 181 DH89
Hithermoor Rd., Stai. 174 BG86
Hitherway, Welw.G.C. 29 CX05
Hitherwell Dr., Har. 95 CD53
Hitherwood Clo., Horn. 128 FK63
Swanbourne Dr.
Hitherwood Clo., Reig. 250 DE132
Hitherwood Dr. SE19 182 DT91
Hive Clo. (Bushey), Wat. 95 CD47
Hive La., Grav. 190 GB86
Hive Rd. (Bushey), Wat. 95 CD47
Hivings Hill, Chesh. 54 AN28
Hivings Pk., Chesh. 54 AP28
Hixberry La., St.Alb. 43 CK21
Hoadly Rd. SW16 181 DK90
Hobart Clo. N20 98 DE47
Oakleigh Rd. N.
Hobart Clo., Hayes 136 BX70
Hobart Dr., Hayes 136 BX70
Hobart Gdns., Th.Hth. 202 DR97
Hobart La., Hayes 136 BX70
Hobart Pl. SW1 277 H6
Hobart Pl. SW1 161 DH76
Hobart Pl., Rich. 178 CM86
Chisholm Rd.
Hobart Rd., Dag. 126 EX63
Hobart Rd., Hayes 136 BX70
Hobart Rd., Ilf. 103 EQ54
Hobart Rd., Til. 171 GG81
Hobart Rd., Wor.Pk. 199 CV104
Hobart Wk., St.Alb. 43 CF16
Valley Rd.
Hobarts Dr., Uxb. 113 BF58
Hobbans Fm. Chase, Ong. 53 FH23
Hobbayne Rd. W7 137 CD72
Hobbes Wk. SW15 179 CV85
Hobbs Clo., St.Alb. 44 CL21
Hobbs Clo. (Cheshunt), Wal.Cr. 67 DX29
Hobbs Clo., W.Byf. 212 BH113
Hobbs Cross Rd., Epp. 86 EW35
Hobbs Cross Rd., Harl. 36 EY12
Hobbs Grn. N2 120 DC55
Hobbs Hill, Hem.H. 40 BM23
Hobbs Hill Rd., Hem.H. 40 BL24
Hobbs Ms., Ilf. 125 ET61
Ripley Rd.
Hobbs Pl. Est. N1 142 DS67
Pitfield St.
Hobbs Rd. SE27 182 DQ91
Hobbs Way, Welw.G.C. 29 CW10
Hobday St. E14 143 EB71
Hobill Wk., Surb. 198 CM100
Hoblands End, Chis. 185 ES93
Hobletts Rd., Hem.H. 40 BM19
Hobsons Clo., Hodd. 33 DZ14
Hobsons Pl. E1 142 DU71
Hanbury St.
Hobtoe Rd., Harl. 35 EN14
Hobury St. SW10 160 DC79
Hockenden La., Swan. 206 FA97
Hocker St. E2 275 P3
Hockeridge Bottom, Berk. 38 AT21
Hockering Gdns., Wok. 227 BA118
Hockering Rd., Wok. 227 BA118
Hockett Clo. SE8 163 DY77
Hocklands, Welw.G.C. 30 DC08
Hockley Ave. E6 144 EL68
Hockley Dr., Rom. 105 FH54
Hockley La., Slou. 132 AV67
Hockley Ms., Bark. 145 ES68
Hocroft Ave. NW2 119 CZ62
Hocroft Rd. NW2 119 CZ63
Hocroft Wk. NW2 119 CZ62
Hodder Dr., Grnf. 137 CF68
Hoddesdon Bypass, Brox. 49 DX24
Hoddesdon Bypass, Hert. 33 DZ13
Hoddesdon Ind. Cen., Hodd. 49 EC16
Hoddesdon Rd., Belv. 166 FA78
Hoddesdon Rd., Brox. 67 DX27
Hoddesdon Rd., Hodd. 49 DY15
Hoddesdon Rd., Ware 33 EC11
Hodds Wd. Rd., Chesh. 54 AQ33
Hodford Rd. NW11 119 CZ61
Hodges Way, Wat. 75 BU44
Hodgkin Clo. SE28 146 EX73
Fleming Way
Hodgson Gdns., Guil. 243 AZ131
Sutherland Dr.
Hodings Rd., Harl. 35 EP14
Hodister Clo. SE5 162 DQ80
Badsworth Rd.
Hodnet Gro. SE16 163 DX77
Hodsoll Ct., Orp. 206 EX99
Hodson Clo., Har. 116 BZ62
Hodson Cres., Orp. 206 EX99
Hoe, The, Wat. 94 BX47
Hoe La., Dor. 261 BT143
Hoe La., Enf. 82 DU38
Hoe La., Guil. 261 BR144
Hoe La., Rom. 86 EV41

Hoe - Hom This index reads in the sequence: Street Name / Postal District or Post Town / Map Page Number / Grid Reference

Hoe La., Wal.Abb. 50 EF22
Hoe La., Ware 33 DX09
Hoe Meadow, Beac. 88 AJ51
Hoe St. E17 123 EA56
Hoebrook Clo., Wok. 226 AX121
Hoecroft, Wal.Abb. 50 EF22
Hoestock Rd., Saw. 36 EX05
Hofland Rd. W14 159 CX76
Hog Hill Rd., Rom. 104 EZ52
Hog Pits, Hem.H. 57 BB32
Hogan Ms. W2 140 DD71
Porteus Rd.
Hogan Way E5 122 DU61
Geldeston Rd.
Hogarth Ave., Ashf. 175 BQ93
Hogarth Ave., Brwd. 108 FY48
Hogarth Clo. E16 144 EK71
Hogarth Clo. W5 138 CL71
Hogarth Clo., Slou. 131 AL73
Hogarth Ct. EC3 275 N10
Hogarth Ct. SE19 182 DT91
Fountain Dr.
Hogarth Ct. (Bushey), Wat. 94 CB45
Steeplands
Hogarth Cres. SW19 200 DD95
Hogarth Cres., Croy. 202 DQ101
Hogarth Gdns., Houns. 156 CA80
Hogarth Hill NW11 119 CZ56
Hogarth La. W4 158 CS79
Hogarth Pl. SW5 160 DB77
Hogarth Rd.
Hogarth Reach, Loug. 85 EM43
Hogarth Rd. SW5 160 DB77
Hogarth Rd., Dag. 126 EV64
Hogarth Rd., Edg. 96 CN54
Hogarth Roundabout W4 158 CS79
Hogarth Roundabout Flyover W4 158 CS79
Burlington La.
Hogarth Way, Hmptn. 196 CC95
Hogback Wd. Rd., Beac. 88 AH51
Hogden La., Dor. 246 BZ134
Hogden La., Lthd. 246 CA129
Hogfair La., Slou. 130 AJ69
Hogg End La., Hem.H. 41 BR17
Hogg End La., St.Alb. 41 BT17
Hogg La., Borwd. 77 CG42
Hogg La., Grays 170 GA76
Hogg La. Roundabout, Grays 170 FZ75
Hogpits Bottom, Hem.H. 57 BA32
Hogs Back, Guil. 258 AS137
Hogs La., Grav. 190 GD90
Hogs Orchard, Swan. 207 FH95
School La.
Hogscross La., Couls. 234 DF123
Hogsdell La., Hert. 32 DV11
Hogshead Pas. E1 142 DV73
Pennington St.
Hogshill La., Cob. 213 BV114
Hogsmill Way, Epsom 216 CQ106
Hogtrough Hill, West. 239 ET120
Hogtrough La., Oxt. 253 EA128
Hogtrough La., Red. 267 DJ135
Holbeach Gdns., Sid. 185 ES86
Holbeach Ms. SW12 181 DH88
Harberson Rd.
Holbeach Rd. SE6 183 EA87
Holbeck La. (Cheshunt), Wal.Cr. 66 DT26
Holbeck Row SE15 162 DU80
Holbein Gate, Nthwd. 93 BS50
Holbein Ms. SW1 276 F10
Holbein Ms. SW1 160 DG78
Holbein Pl. SW1 276 F9
Holbein Pl. SW1 160 DG77
Holbein Ter., Dag. 126 EV63
Marlborough Rd.
Holberton Gdns. NW10 139 CV69
Holborn EC1 274 D7
Holborn EC1 141 DN71
Holborn Circ. EC1 274 E7
Holborn Clo., St.Alb. 43 CK15
Holborn Pl. WC1 274 B7
Holborn Rd. E13 144 EH70
Holborn Viaduct EC1 274 E7
Holborn Viaduct EC1 141 DN71
Holborn Way, Mitch. 200 DF96
Holbreck Pl., Wok. 227 AZ118
Heathside Rd.
Holbrook Clo. N19 121 DH60
Dartmouth Pk. Hill
Holbrook Clo., Enf. 82 DT39
Holbrook La., Chis. 185 ER94
Holbrook Meadow, Egh. 173 BC93
Holbrook Rd. E15 144 EF68
Holbrook Way, Brom. 205 EM100
Holbrooke Ct. N7 121 DL63
Holbrooke Pl., Rich. 177 CK85
Hill Ri.
Holburne Clo. SE3 164 EJ81
Holburne Gdns. SE3 164 EK81
Holburne Rd. SE3 164 EJ81
Holcombe Hill NW7 97 CU48
Highwood Hill
Holcombe Rd. N17 122 DT55
Holcombe Rd., Ilf. 125 EN59
Holcombe St. W6 159 CV77
Holcon Ct., Red. 250 DG131
Holcote Clo., Belv. 166 EY76
Blakemore Way
Holcroft Rd. E9 142 DW66
Holdbrook N., Wal.Cr. 67 DZ34
Eleanor Way
Holdbrook S., Wal.Cr. 67 DZ34
Queens Way
Holdbrook Way, Rom. 106 FM54
Holden Ave. N12 98 DB50
Holden Ave. NW9 118 CQ60
Holden Clo., Dag. 126 EV62
Holden Clo., Hert. 32 DS08
Holden Gdns., Brwd. 108 FX50
Holden Pt. E15 143 ED65
Waddington Rd.
Holden Rd. N12 98 DB50
Holden St. SW11 160 DG82
Holden Way, Upmin. 129 FR59
Holdenby Rd. SE4 183 DY85
Holdenhurst Ave. N12 98 DB52
Holder Clo. N3 98 DB52
Holderness Way SE27 181 DP92
Holdernesse Clo., Islw. 157 CG81
Holdernesse Rd. SW17 180 DF90
Holders Hill Ave. NW4 97 CX54
Holders Hill Circ. NW7 97 CY52
Dollis Rd.
Holders Hill Cres. NW4 97 CX54
Holders Hill Dr. NW4 119 CX55
Holders Hill Gdns. NW4 97 CY54
Holders Hill Rd. NW4 97 CX54
Holders Hill Rd. NW7 97 CY53
Holdgate St. SE7 164 EK76
Westmoor St.
Holdings, The, Hat. 45 CX16
Hole Fm. La., Brwd. 107 FU53
Hole Hill La., Dor. 262 CB136
Holecroft, Wal.Abb. 68 EE34
Holford Pl. WC1 274 C2
Holford Rd. NW3 120 DC62
Holford Rd., Grays 171 GK76
Holford Rd., Guil. 243 BC134
Holford Rd., S.le H. 171 GL75
Holford St. WC1 274 D2
Holford St. WC1 141 DN69
Holgate Ave. SW11 160 DD83
Holgate Gdns., Dag. 126 FA64
Holgate Rd., Dag. 126 FA64
Holland Ave. SW20 199 CT95
Holland Ave., Sutt. 218 DA109
Holland Clo., Barn. 98 DD45
Holland Clo., Brom. 204 EF103
Holland Clo., Red. 250 DF134
Holland Clo., Rom. 127 FC57
Holland Clo., Stan. 95 CH50
Holland Cres., Oxt. 254 EG133
Holland Dr. SE23 183 DY90
Holland Gdns. W14 159 CY76
Holland Gdns., Egh. 193 BF96
Holland Gdns., Wat. 76 BW35
Holland Gro. SW9 161 DN80
Holland La., Oxt. 254 EG133
Holland Pk. W8 159 CZ75
Holland Pk. W11 159 CZ75
Holland Pk. Ave. W11 159 CY75
Holland Pk. Ave., Ilf. 125 ES58
Holland Pk. Gdns. W14 139 CY74
Holland Pk. Ms. W11 139 CY74
Holland Pk. Rd. W14 159 CZ76
Holland Pas. N1 142 DQ67
Basire St.
Holland Pl. W8 160 DB75
Kensington Ch. St.
Holland Rd. E6 145 EM67
Holland Rd. E15 144 EE69
Holland Rd. NW10 139 CU67
Holland Rd. SE25 202 DU99
Holland Rd. W14 159 CX75
Holland Rd., Oxt. 254 EG133
Holland Rd., Wem. 137 CK65
Holland St. SE1 278 G2
Holland St. SE1 141 DP74
Holland St. W8 160 DA75
Holland Vil. Rd. W14 159 CY75
Holland Wk. N19 121 DK60
Duncombe Rd.
Holland Wk. W8 159 CZ75
Holland Wk., Stan. 95 CG50
Holland Way, Brom. 204 EF103
Hollands, The, Felt. 176 BX91
Hollands, The, Wor.Pk. 199 CT102
Hollands Cft., Ware 34 EK06
Hollar Rd. N16 122 DT62
Stoke Newington High St.
Hollen St. W1 273 M8
Hollen St. W1 141 DJ72
Holles Clo., Hmptn. 176 CA93
Holles St. W1 273 J8
Holles St. W1 141 DH72
Holley Rd. W3 158 CS75
Hollickwood Ave. N12 98 DF51
Holliday Sq. SW11 160 DD83
Fowler Clo.
Holliday St., Berk. 38 AX19
Hollidge Way, Dag. 147 FB65
Hollier Ct., Hat. 45 CV17
Holliers Way, Hat. 45 CU18
Hollies, The E11 124 EG57
Hollies, The N20 98 DD46
Oakleigh Pk. N.
Hollies, The, Grav. 191 GK93
Hollies, The, Har. 117 CG56
Hollies, The, Hem.H. 57 BA29
Hollies, The, Welw.G.C. 29 CV13
Hollies Ave., Sid. 185 ET89
Hollies Ave., W.Byf. 211 BF113
Hollies Clo. SW16 181 DN93
Hollies Clo., Twick. 177 CF89
Hollies Ct., Add. 212 BJ106
Hollies End NW7 97 CV50
Hollies Rd. W5 157 CJ77
Hollies Way SW12 180 DG87
Bracken Ave.
Hollies Way, Pot.B. 64 DC31
Holligrave Rd., Brom. 204 EG95
Hollingbourne Ave., W13 166 EZ80
Hollingbourne Gdns. W13 137 CH71
Hollingbourne Rd. SE24 182 DQ85
Hollingbourne Twr., Orp. 206 EX102
Hollingsworth Rd., Croy. 220 DV107
Hollington Cres., N.Mal. 199 CT100
Hollington Rd. E6 145 EM69
Hollington Rd. N17 100 DU54
Hollingworth Clo., W.Mol. 196 BZ98
Hollingworth Rd., Orp. 205 EP100
Hollingworth Way, West. 255 ER126
Hollis Pl., Grays 170 GA77
Ward Ave.
Hollman Gdns. SW16 181 DP93
Hollow, The, Wdf.Grn. 102 EF49
Hollow Clo., Guil. 258 AV135
Lynwood
Hollow Cotts., Purf. 168 FN78
Hollow Hill La., Iver 133 BB73
Hollow La., Dor. 262 BX140
Hollow La., Vir.W. 192 AW97
Hollow Wk., Rich. 158 CL80
Kew Rd.
Hollow Way La., Amer. 55 AS35
Hollow Way La., Chesh. 72 AT35
Holloway Clo., West Dr. 154 BL78
Holloway Dr., Vir.W. 192 AY98
Holloway Hill, Cher. 193 BC104
Holloway La., Rick. 73 BB38
Holloway La., West Dr. 154 BL79
Holloway Rd. E6 145 EM69
Holloway Rd. E11 124 EE62
Holloway Rd. N7 141 DN65
Holloway Rd. N19 121 DK61
Holloway St., Houns. 156 CB83
Holloways La., Hat. 45 CX23
Hollowfield Ave., Grays 170 GD77
Hollowfield Wk., Nthlt. 136 BY65
Hollows, The, Brent. 158 CM79
Kew Bri. Rd.
Holly Ave., Add. 212 BG110
Holly Ave., Stan. 96 CL54
Holly Ave., Walt. 196 BX102
Holly Bank Rd., Wok. 226 AV119
Holly Bush Hill NW3 120 DC63
Holly Bush La., Hmptn. 176 BZ94
Holly Bush La., Sev. 257 FJ124
Holly Bush Steps NW3 120 DC63
Heath St.
Holly Bush Vale NW3 120 DC63
Heath St.
Holly Clo. NW10 138 CS66
Holly Clo., Buck.H. 102 EK48
Holly Clo., Cher. 192 AU104
Holly Clo., Egh. 172 AV93
Holly Clo., Felt. 176 BY92
Holly Clo., Hat. 45 CT19
Holly Clo., Slou. 111 AQ63
Holly Clo., Wall. 219 DH108
Holly Clo., Wok. 226 AV119
Holly Cottage Ms., Uxb. 134 BN71
Pield Heath Rd.
Holly Cres., Beck. 203 DZ99
Holly Cres., Wind. 151 AK82
Holly Cres., Wdf.Grn. 101 ED52
Holly Cft., Hert. 31 DN08
Holly Cross Rd., Ware 33 DZ07
Holly Dr. E4 101 EB45
Holly Dr., Berk. 38 AX20
Holly Dr., Brent. 157 CG79
Holly Dr., Pot.B. 64 DB33
Holly Dr., S.Ock. 149 FX70
Holly Dr., Wind. 172 AS85
Holly Fm. Rd., Sthl. 156 BY78
Holly Fld., Harl. 51 EQ18
Holly Gdns., West Dr. 154 BM75
Holly Grn., Wey. 213 BR105
Holly Gro. NW9 118 CQ59
Holly Gro. SE15 162 DT82
Holly Gro., Pnr. 94 BY53
Holly Gro. (Bushey), Wat. 95 CD45
Holly Gro. Rd., Hert. 31 DH07
Holly Hedge Ter. SE13 183 ED85
Holly Hedges La., Hem.H. 57 BC30
Holly Hedges La., Rick. 57 BD32
Holly Hill N21 81 DM44
Holly Hill NW3 120 DC63
Holly Hill Dr., Bans. 234 DA116
Holly Hill Rd., Belv. 167 FB78
Holly Hill Rd., Erith 167 FB78
Holly Ho., Brwd. 108 FX46
Sawyers Hall La.
Holly La., Bans. 234 DA116
Holly La. E., Bans. 234 DB116
Holly La. W., Bans. 234 DB117
Holly Lea, Guil. 242 AX128
Holly Lo. Gdns. N6 120 DG61
Holly Ms. SW10 160 DC78
Drayton Gdns.
Holly Mt. NW3 120 DC63
Holly Bush Hill
Holly Pk. N3 119 CZ55
Holly Pk. N4 121 DM59
Holly Pk. Est. N4 121 DM59
Blythwood Rd.
Holly Pk. Gdns. N3 120 DA55
Holly Pk. Rd. N11 98 DG50
Holly Pk. Rd. W7 137 CF74
Holly Pl. NW3 120 DC63
Holly Wk.
Holly Rd. E11 124 EF59
Holly Rd. W4 158 CR77
Dolman Rd.
Holly Rd., Dart. 188 FK88
Holly Rd., Enf. 83 DX36
Holly Rd., Hmptn. 176 CC93
Holly Rd., Houns. 156 CB84
Holly Rd., Orp. 224 EU108
Holly Rd., Reig. 266 DB136
Holly Rd., Twick. 177 CG88
Holly St. E8 142 DT65
Holly St. Est. E8 142 DT66
Holly Ter. N6 120 DG60
Highgate W. Hill
Holly Ter. N20 98 DC47
Swan La.
Holly Tree Ave., Swan. 207 FE96
Holly Tree Clo., Chesh. 56 AV31
Holly Tree Rd., Cat. 236 DS122
Elm Gro.
Holly Vw. Clo. NW4 119 CU58
Holly Village N6 121 DH61
Swains La.
Holly Wk. NW3 120 DC63
Holly Wk., Enf. 82 DR41
Holly Wk., Rich. 158 CL82
Holly Wk., Welw.G.C. 29 CW05
Holly Way, Mitch. 201 DK98
Hollybank Clo., Hmptn. 176 CA92
Hollybank Rd., W.Byf. 212 BG114
Hollyberry La. NW3 120 DC63
Holly Wk.
Hollybrake Clo., Chis. 185 ER94
Hollybush Ave., St.Alb. 42 CA24
Hollybush Clo. E11 124 EG57
Hollybush Clo., Berk. 39 BD16
Hollybush Clo., Har. 95 CE53
Hollybush Clo., Sev. 257 FJ124
Hollybush Clo., Wat. 94 BW45
Hollybush Ct., Sev. 257 FJ124
Hollybush Gdns. E2 142 DV69
Hollybush Hill E11 124 EF58
Hollybush Hill, Slou. 132 AU66
Hollybush La., Amer. 55 AR36
Hollybush La., Hem.H. 39 BF19
Hollybush La., Iver 133 BB72
Hollybush La., Orp. 224 FA107
Hollybush La., Uxb. 113 BC61
Hollybush La., Welw.G.C. 29 CZ12
Hollybush La., Wok. 228 BK119
Hollybush Pl. E2 142 DV69
Bethnal Grn. Rd.
Hollybush Rd., Chesh. 54 AN27
Hollybush Rd., Grav. 191 GJ89
Hollybush Rd., Kings.T. 178 CL92
Hollybush St. E13 144 EH69
Hollybush Wk. SW9 161 DP84
Hollybush Way, Wal.Cr. 66 DU28
Hollycombe, Egh. 172 AW91
Hollycroft Ave. NW3 120 DA62
Hollycroft Ave., Wem. 118 CM61
Hollycroft Clo., S.Croy. 220 DS106
Hollycroft Clo., West Dr. 154 BN79
Hollycroft Gdns., West Dr. 154 BN79
Hollydale Clo., Nthlt. 116 CB63
Dorchester Rd.
Hollydale Dr., Brom. 205 EM104
Hollydale Rd. SE15 162 DW81
Hollydell, Hert. 32 DQ11
Hollydene SE15 162 DV81
Hollydown Way E11 123 ED62
Hollyfield, Hat. 45 CU21
Hollyfield Ave. N11 98 DF50
Hollyfield Rd., Surb. 198 CM101
Hollyfields, Brox. 67 DY26
Hollyhedge Rd., Cob. 213 BV114
Hollyhock Clo., Hem.H. 39 BE19
Hollymead, Cars. 200 DF104
Hollymead Rd., Couls. 234 DG118
Hollymeoak Rd., Couls. 235 DH119
Hollymoor La., Epsom 216 CR110
Hollymount Clo. SE10 163 EC81
Hollytree Clo. SW19 179 CX88
Hollytree Clo., Ger.Cr. 90 AY50
Hollywood Ct., Borwd. 78 CM42
Deacon's Hill Rd.
Hollywood Gdns., Hayes 135 BV72
Hollywood Ms. SW10 160 DC79
Hollywood Rd.
Hollywood Rd. E4 101 DY50
Hollywood Rd. SW10 160 DC79
Hollywood Way, Erith 167 FH81
Hollywood Way, Wdf.Grn. 101 ED52
Hollywoods, Croy. 221 DZ109
Holm Clo., Add. 211 BE112
Holm Gro., Uxb. 134 BN66
Holm Oak Clo. SW15 179 CZ86
West Hill
Holm Oak Ms. SW4 181 DL85
King's Ave.
Holm Wk. SE3 164 EG82
Blackheath Pk.
Holman Rd. SW11 160 DD82
Holman Rd., Epsom 216 CQ106
Holmbank Dr., Shep. 195 BS98
Holmbridge Gdns., Enf. 83 DX42
Holmbrook Dr. NW4 119 CX57
Holmbury Ct. SW17 180 DF90
Holmbury Ct. SW19 180 DE94
Cavendish Rd.
Holmbury Dr., Dor. 263 CJ139
Holmbury Gdns., Hayes 135 BT74
Church Rd.
Holmbury Gro., Croy. 221 DZ108
Holmbury Pk., Brom. 184 EL94
Holmbury Vw. E5 122 DV60
Holmbush Rd. SW15 179 CY86
Holmcote Gdns. N5 122 DQ64
Holmcroft, Tad. 249 CV125
Holmcroft Way, Brom. 205 EM99
Holmdale Clo., Borwd. 78 CM40
Holmdale Gdns. NW4 119 CX57
Holmdale Rd. NW6 120 DA64
Holmdale Rd., Chis. 185 EQ92
Holmdale Ter. N15 122 DS59
Holmdene Ave. NW7 97 CU51
Holmdene Ave. SE24 182 DQ85
Holmdene Ave., Har. 116 CB55
Holmdene Clo., Beck. 203 EC96
Holme Chase, Wey. 213 BQ107
Holme Clo., Hat. 45 CT15
Holme Clo. (Cheshunt), Wal.Cr. 67 DY31
Holme Lacey Rd. SE12 184 EF86
Holme Lea, Wat. 60 BW34
Kingsway
Holme Pk., Borwd. 78 CM40
Holme Rd. E6 144 EL67
Holme Rd., Hat. 45 CT15
Holme Rd., Horn. 128 FN60
Holme Way, Stan. 95 CF51
Holmead Rd. SW6 160 DB80
Holmebury Clo. (Bushey), Wat. 95 CE47
Holmedale, Slou. 132 AW73
Holmefield Ct. NW3 140 DE65
Holmes Ave. E17 123 DZ55
Holmes Ave. NW7 97 CY50
Holmes Meadow, Harl. 51 EP21
Holmes Pl. SW10 160 DC79
Fulham Rd.
Holmes Rd. NW5 121 DH64
Holmes Rd. SW19 180 DC94
Holmes Rd., Twick. 177 CF89
Holmes Ter. SE1 278 D4
Holmes Ter. SE1 161 DN75
Holmesdale, Wal.Cr. 83 DX35
Holmesdale Ave. SW14 158 CP83
Holmesdale Clo. SE25 202 DT97
Holmesdale Clo., Guil. 243 BB133
Holmesdale Hill (South Darenth), Dart. 208 FQ95
Holmesdale Rd. N6 121 DH59
Holmesdale Rd. SE25 202 DR99
Holmesdale Rd., Bexh. 166 EX82
Holmesdale Rd., Croy. 202 DR99
Holmesdale Rd. (South Darenth), Dart. 208 FQ95
Holmesdale Rd., Dor. 263 CH140
Holmesdale Rd., Red. 267 DM136
Holmesdale Rd., Reig. 250 DA133
Holmesdale Rd., Rich. 158 CM81
Holmesdale Rd., Tedd. 177 CJ94
Holmesdale Ter., Dor. 263 CH140
Holmesdale Rd.
Holmesley Rd. SE23 183 DY86
Holmethorpe Ave., Red. 251 DH131
Holmethorpe Ind. Est., Red. 251 DH131
Holmewood Gdns. SW2 181 DM87
Holmewood Rd. SE25 202 DS97
Holmewood Rd. SW2 181 DL87
Holmfield Ave. NW4 119 CX57
Holmhurst Rd., Belv. 167 FB78
Holmlea Rd., Slou. 152 AX81
Holmlea Wk., Slou. 152 AW81
Holmleigh Ave., Dart. 168 FJ84
Holmleigh Rd. N16 122 DS60
Holmleigh Rd. Est. N16 122 DT60
Holmleigh Rd.
Holms St. E2 142 DU68
Holmsdale Clo., Iver 133 BF72
Holmsdale Gro., Bexh. 167 FE82
Holmsdale Rd., Sev. 257 FJ123
Holmshaw Clo. SE26 183 DY91
Holmshill La., Borwd. 78 CS36
Holmside Ri., Wat. 93 BV48
Holmside Rd. SW12 180 DG86
Holmsley Clo., N.Mal. 199 CT100
Holmstall Ave., Edg. 118 CQ55
Holmwood Ave., Brwd. 109 GA43
Holmwood Ave., S.Croy. 220 DT113
Holmwood Clo., Add. 212 BG106
Holmwood Clo., Har. 116 CC55
Holmwood Clo., Lthd. 245 BS128
Holmwood Clo., Nthlt. 136 CB65
Holmwood Clo., Sutt. 217 CX109
Holmwood Gdns. N3 98 DA54
Holmwood Gdns., Wall. 219 DH107
Holmwood Gro. NW7 96 CR50
Holmwood Rd., Chess. 215 CK106
Holmwood Rd., Enf. 83 DX36
Holmwood Rd., Ilf. 125 ES61
Holmwood Rd., Sutt. 217 CW110
Holmwood Vw. Rd., Dor. 263 CH142
Horsham Rd.
Holmwood Vil. SE7 164 EG78
Woolwich Rd.
Holne Chase N2 120 DC58
Holne Chase, Mord. 199 CZ100
Holness Rd. E15 144 EF65
Holroyd Clo., Esher 215 CF109
Holroyd Rd. SW15 159 CW84
Holroyd Rd., Esher 215 CF109
Holstein Ave., Wey. 212 BN105
Holstein Way, Erith 166 EY76
Holstock Rd., Ilf. 125 EQ62
Holsworth Clo., Har. 116 CC57
Holsworthy Sq. WC1 274 C5
Holsworthy Way, Chess. 215 CJ106
Holt, The, Hem.H. 40 BL21
Turners Hill
Holt, The, Ilf. 103 EQ51
Holt, The, Wall. 219 DJ105
Holt, The, Welw.G.C. 30 DD10
Holt Clo. N10 120 DG56
Holt Clo. SE28 146 EV73
Holt Clo., Borwd. 78 CM42
Holt Clo., Chig. 103 ET50
Holt Ct. E15 123 EC64
Clays La.
Holt Rd. E16 144 EL74
Holt Rd., Wem. 117 CH62
Holt Way, Chig. 103 ET50
Holton St. E1 143 DX70
Holtsmere Clo., Wat. 76 BW35
Holtspur Ave., H.Wyc. 110 AE56
Holtspur Clo., Beac. 88 AG54
Holtspur La., H.Wyc. 110 AE57
Holtspur Top La., Beac. 88 AG54
Holtspur Way, Beac. 88 AG54
Holtwhite Ave., Enf. 82 DQ40
Holtwhites Hill, Enf. 81 DP39
Holtwood Rd., Lthd. 214 CC114
Holwell Caravan Site, Hat. 30 DE14
Holwell Hyde, Welw.G.C. 30 DC11
Holwell Hyde La., Welw.G.C. 30 DC12
Holwell La., Hat. 30 DE14
Holwell Pl., Pnr. 116 BY56
Holwell Rd., Welw.G.C. 29 CY10
Holwood Clo., Walt. 196 BW103
Holwood Pk. Ave., Orp. 223 EM105
Holwood Pl. SW4 161 DK84
Holy Cross Hill, Brox. 48 DU24
Holy Wk., Brox. 49 EA19
St. Catherines Rd.
Holybourne Ave. SW15 179 CU87
Holyfield Rd., Wal.Abb. 67 EC29
Holyhead Clo. E3 143 EA69
Holyhead Clo. E6 145 EM71
Valiant Way
Holyoak Rd. SE11 278 F8
Holyoake Ave., Wok. 226 AW117
Holyoake Ct. SE16 163 DZ75
Bryan Rd.
Holyoake Cres., Wok. 226 AW117
Holyoake Ter., Sev. 256 FG124
Holyoake Wk. N2 120 DC55
Holyoake Wk. W5 137 CJ70
Holyport Rd. SW6 159 CW80
Holyrood Ave., Har. 116 BY63
Holyrood Cres., St.Alb. 43 CD24
Holyrood Gdns., Edg. 118 CP55
Holyrood Gdns., Grays 171 GJ77
Holyrood Ms. E16 144 EG74
Wesley Ave.
Holyrood Rd., Barn. 80 DC44
Holyrood St. SE1 279 M3
Holywell Clo. SE3 164 EG79
Holywell Clo. SE16 162 DV78
Masters Dr.
Holywell Clo., Stai. 174 BL88
Holywell Hill, St.Alb. 43 CD21
Holywell Ind. Est., Wat. 75 BR44
Holywell La. EC2 275 N4
Holywell La. EC2 142 DS70
Holywell Rd., Wat. 75 BU43
Holywell Row EC2 275 M5
Holywell Row EC2 142 DS70
Holywell Way, Stai. 174 BL88
Home Barn Ct., Lthd. 246 BX127
The St.
Home Clo., Brox. 49 DZ24
Home Clo., Cars. 200 DF103
Home Clo., Harl. 35 ET14
Home Clo., Lthd. 231 CD121
Home Clo., Nthlt. 136 BZ69
Home Ct., Felt. 175 BU88
Home Fm. Clo., Bet. 264 CS135
Home Fm. Clo., Epsom 233 CX117
Home Fm. Clo., Esher 214 CB107
Home Fm. Clo., Shep. 195 BS98
Home Fm. Clo., T.Ditt. 197 CF101
Home Fm. Gdns., Walt. 196 BW103
Home Fm. Rd., Rick. 92 BN49
Home Fm. Way, Slou. 132 AW67
Home Fld., Berk. 39 BB16
Home Gdns., Dag. 127 FC62
Home Gdns., Dart. 188 FL86
Home Hill, Swan. 187 FF94
Home Lea, Orp. 223 ET106
Home Ley, Welw.G.C. 29 CY09
Home Mead, Stan. 95 CJ53
Home Mead Clo., Grav. 191 GH87
Home Meadow, Bans. 234 DA116
Holly La.
Home Meadow, Slou. 131 AQ68
Home Meadow, Welw.G.C. 29 CZ09
Home Orchard, Dart. 188 FL86
Home Pk., Oxt. 254 EG131
Home Pk. Mill Link Rd., Kings L. 59 BP31
Home Pk. Rd. SW19 180 DA90
Home Pk. Wk., Kings.T. 197 CK98
Home Rd. SW11 160 DE82
Home Way, Rick. 91 BF46

Homecroft Gdns., Loug. 85 EP42
Homecroft Rd. N22 100 DQ53
Homecroft Rd. SE26 182 DW92
Homedean Rd., Sev. 256 FC122
Homefarm Clo., Cher. 211 BA108
Homefarm Rd. W7 137 CE72
Homefield, Hem.H. 57 BB28
Homefield, Wal.Abb. 68 EG32
Homefield, Walt. 214 BX105
Homefield Ave., Ilf. 125 ES57
Homefield Clo. NW10 138 CQ65
Homefield Clo., Add. 211 BE112
Homefield Clo., Epp. 70 EU30
Homefield Clo., Hayes 136 BW70
Homefield Clo., Horl. 269 DH147
Tanyard Way
Homefield Clo., Lthd. 231 CJ121
Homefield Clo., Orp. 206 EV98
Homefield Clo., Swan. 207 FF97
Homefield Fm. Rd., Dart. 208 FM96
Homefield Gdns. N2 120 DD55
Homefield Gdns., Mitch. 200 DC96
Homefield Gdns., Tad. 233 CW120
Homefield Ms., Beck. 203 EA95
Homefield Pk., Sutt. 218 DB107
Homefield Ri., Orp. 206 EU102
Homefield Rd. SW19 179 CX93
Homefield Rd. W4 159 CT77
Homefield Rd., Brom. 204 EJ95
Homefield Rd., Couls. 235 DP119
Homefield Rd., Edg. 96 CR51
Homefield Rd., Hem.H. 40 BN20
Homefield Rd., Rad. 77 CF37
Homefield Rd., Rick. 73 BC42
Green St.
Homefield Rd., Sev. 256 FE122
Homefield Rd., Walt. 196 BY101
Homefield Rd., Ware 33 DY05
Homefield Rd., Warl. 236 DW119
Homefield Rd. (Bushey), Wat. 76 CA43
Homefield Rd., Wem. 117 CG63
Homefield St. N1 275 M1
Homefield St. N1 142 DS68
Homeland Dr., Sutt. 218 DB109
Homelands, Lthd. 231 CJ121
Homelands Dr. SE19 182 DS94
Homeleigh Ct., Wal.Cr. 66 DV29
Homeleigh Rd. SE15 183 DX85
Homemead SW12 181 DJ89
Homemead Rd., Brom. 205 EM99
Homemead Rd., Croy. 201 DJ100
Homer Clo., Bexh. 167 FC81
Homer Dr. E14 163 EA77
Homer Rd. E9 143 DY65
Homer Rd., Croy. 203 DX100
Homer Row W1 272 C7
Homer Row W1 140 DE71
Homer St. W1 272 C7
Homer St. W1 140 DE71
Homerfield, Welw.G.C. 29 CW08
Homers Rd., Wind. 151 AK81
Homersham Rd., Kings.T. 198 CN96
Homerswood La., Welw. 29 CU05
Homerton Gro. E9 123 DX64
Homerton High St. E9 122 DW64
Homerton Rd. E9 123 DY64
Homerton Row E9 122 DW64
Homerton Ter. E9 142 DW65
Morning La.
Homesdale Clo. E11 124 EG57
Homesdale Rd., Brom. 204 EJ98
Homesdale Rd., Cat. 236 DR123
Homesdale Rd., Orp. 205 ES101
Homesfield NW11 120 DA57
Homestall Rd. SE22 182 DW85
Homestead, The N11 99 DH49
Homestead, The, Dart. 188 FJ86
Homestead Clo., St.Alb. 60 CC27
Homestead Ct., Welw.G.C. 29 CZ11
Homestead Gdns., Esher 215 CE106
Homestead La., Welw.G.C. 29 CZ12
Homestead Paddock N14 81 DH43
Homestead Pk. NW2 119 CT62
Homestead Rd. SW6 159 CZ80
Homestead Rd., Cat. 236 DR123
Homestead Rd., Dag. 126 EZ61
Homestead Rd., Hat. 45 CU15
Homestead Rd., Orp. 224 EV108
Homestead Rd., Rick. 92 BK45
Park Rd.
Homestead Rd., Stai. 174 BH93
Homestead Way, Croy. 221 EC111
Homesteads, The, Ware 34 EK07
Hunsdon Rd.
Homewaters Ave., Sun. 195 BT95
Homeway, Rom. 106 FP51
Homewillow Clo. N21 81 DP44
Homewood, Slou. 132 AX72
Homewood Ave. (Cuffley), Pot.B. 65 DL27
Old Cote Dr.
Homewood Clo., Hmptn. 176 BZ93
Fearnley Cres.
Homewood Cres., Chis. 185 ES93
Homewood La., Pot.B. 65 DJ27
Homewood Rd., St.Alb. 43 CH17
Honduras St. EC1 275 H4
Honey Brook, Wal.Abb. 68 EE33
Honey Clo., Dag. 147 FB65
Honey Hill, Uxb. 134 BM66
Honey La. EC2 275 J9
Honey La., Wal.Abb. 84 EG35
Honeybourne Rd. NW6 120 DB64
Honeybourne Way, Orp. 205 ER102
Honeybrook Rd. SW12 181 DJ87
Honeycrock La., Red. 266 DG141
Honeycroft, Loug. 85 EN42
Honeycroft, Welw.G.C. 29 CW10
Honeycroft Dr., St.Alb. 43 CJ22
Honeycroft Hill, Uxb. 134 BL66
Honeycross Rd., Hem.H. 39 BE21
Honeyden Rd., Sid. 186 EY93
Honeyman Clo. NW6 139 CX66
Honeymeade, Saw. 36 EW08
Honeypot Clo. NW9 118 CM56
Honeypot La. NW9 118 CM55
Honeypot La., Brwd. 108 FU48
Honeypot La., Stan. 118 CM55
Honeypots Rd., Wok. 226 AX122
Honeysett Rd. N17 100 DT54
Reform Row
Honeysuckle Bottom, Lthd. 245 BS134
Honeysuckle Clo., Brwd. 108 FV43
Honeysuckle Clo., Hert. 32 DU09
Honeysuckle Clo., Horl. 269 DJ147
Briars Wd.
Honeysuckle Clo., Iver 133 BC72
Honeysuckle Clo., Rom. 106 FK51
Cloudberry Rd.
Honeysuckle Clo., Sthl. 136 BY73
Honeysuckle Fld., Chesh. 54 AQ30
Honeysuckle Gdns., Croy. 203 DX102
Primrose La.
Honeysuckle Gdns., Hat. 45 CV19
Honeysuckle La., Dor. 263 CJ139
Treelands
Honeywell Rd. SW11 180 DF86
Honeywood Clo., Pot.B. 64 DE33
Honeywood Rd. NW10 139 CT68
Honeywood Rd., Islw. 157 CG84
Honeywood Wk., Cars. 218 DF105
Honister Clo., Stan. 95 CH53
Honister Gdns., Stan. 95 CH52
Honister Hts., Pur. 220 DR114
Honister Pl., Stan. 95 CH53
Honiton Rd. NW6 139 CZ68
Honiton Rd., Rom. 127 FD58
Honiton Rd., Well. 165 ET82
Honley Rd. SE6 183 EB87
Honnor Rd., Stai. 174 BK94
Honor Oak Pk. SE23 182 DW86
Honor Oak Ri. SE23 182 DW86
Honor Oak Rd. SE23 182 DW88
Hoo, The, Harl. 36 EW10
Hood Ave. N14 81 DH44
Hood Ave. SW14 178 CQ85
Hood Ave., Orp. 206 EV99
Hood Clo., Croy. 201 DP102
Parson's Mead
Hood Ct. EC4 274 E9
Hood Rd. SW20 179 CT94
Hood Rd., Rain. 147 FE67
Hood Wk., Rom. 105 FB53
Hoodcote Gdns. N21 99 DP45
Hook, The, Barn. 80 DD44
Hook Fm. Rd., Brom. 204 EK99
Hook Gate, Enf. 82 DV36
Hook Grn. La., Dart. 187 FF90
Hook Grn. Rd., Grav. 190 FY94
Hook Heath Ave., Wok. 226 AV119
Hook Heath Gdns., Wok. 226 AT121
Hook Heath Rd., Wok. 226 AT121
Hook Hill, S.Croy. 220 DS110
Hook Hill La., Wok. 226 AV121
Hook Hill Pk., Wok. 226 AV121
Hook La., Guil. 260 BN140
Hook La., Pot.B. 64 DF32
Hook La., Rom. 86 EZ44
Hook La., Well. 185 ET85
Hook Ri. N., Surb. 198 CN104
Hook Ri. S., Surb. 198 CN104
Hook Ri. S. Ind. Pk., Surb. 198 CN104
Hook Rd., Chess. 215 CK106
Hook Rd., Epsom 216 CR111
Hook Rd., Surb. 198 CL104
Hook Wk., Edg. 96 CQ51
Hooke Rd., Lthd. 245 BT125
Hookers Rd. E17 123 DX55
Hookfield, Epsom 216 CQ113
Hookfield, Harl. 51 ES17
Hookfields, Grav. 190 GE90
Hooking Grn., Har. 116 CB57
Hooks Clo. SE15 162 DV81
Woods Rd.
Hooks Hall Dr., Dag. 127 FC62
Hooks Way SE22 182 DU88
Dulwich Common
Hookstone Way, Wdf.Grn. 102 EK52
Hookwood Cor., Oxt. 254 EH128
Hookwood La.
Hookwood La., Oxt. 254 EH128
Hookwood Rd., Orp. 224 EW111
Hooley La., Red. 266 DF135
Hoop La. NW11 119 CZ59
Hooper Rd. E16 144 EG72
Hooper St. E1 142 DU72
Hooper's Ct. SW3 276 D5
Hoopers Yd., Sev. 257 FJ126
Hop Gdns. WC2 277 P1
Hope Clo. N1 142 DQ65
Wallace Rd.
Hope Clo. SE12 184 EH90
Hope Clo., Sutt. 218 DC106
Hope Clo., Wdf.Grn. 102 EJ51
West Gro.
Hope Grn., Wat. 59 BU33
Hope Pk., Brom. 184 EF94
Hope Rd., Swans. 190 FZ86
High St.
Hope St. SW11 160 DD83
Hope Ter., Grays 169 FX78
Hope Wf. SE16 162 DW75
St. Marychurch St.
Hopedale Rd. SE7 164 EH79
Hopefield Ave. NW6 139 CY68
Hopes Clo., Houns. 156 CA79
Old Cote Dr.
Hopetown St. E1 142 DT71
Brick La.
Hopewell Dr., Grav. 191 GM92
Hopewell St. SE5 162 DR80
Hopewell Yd. SE5 162 DR80
Hopewell St.
Hopfield, Wok. 226 AY116
Hopfield Ave., W.Byf. 212 BL112
Hopgarden La., Sev. 256 FG128
Hopgood St. W12 139 CW74
Macfarlane Rd.
Hopground Clo., St.Alb. 43 CG22
Hopkins Clo. N10 98 DG52
Cromwell Rd.
Hopkins Clo., Rom. 128 FJ55
Hopkins Ms. E15 144 EF67
West Rd.
Hopkins St. W1 273 L9
Hopkinsons Pl. NW1 140 DG67
Fitzroy Rd.
Hoppers Rd. N13 99 DN47
Hoppers Rd. N21 99 DN47
Hoppett Rd. E4 102 EE48
Hoppety, The, Tad. 233 CX122
Hopping La. N1 141 DP65
St. Mary's Gro.
Hoppingwood Ave., N.Mal. 198 CS97
Hoppit Rd., Wal.Abb. 67 EB32
Hoppner Rd., Hayes 135 BQ68
Hopton Ct., Guil. 242 AS134
Park Barn Dr.
Hopton Gdns. SE1 278 G2
Hopton Gdns. SE1 141 DP74
Hopton Gdns., N.Mal. 199 CU100
Hopton Rd. SW16 181 DL92
Hopton St. SE1 278 G2
Hopton St. SE1 141 DP74
Hopwood Clo. SW17 180 DC90
Hopwood Clo., Wat. 75 BR36
Hopwood Rd. SE17 162 DR79
Hopwood Wk. E8 142 DU66
Wilman Gro.
Horace Ave., Rom. 127 FC60
Horace Rd. E7 124 EH63
Horace Rd., Ilf. 125 EQ55
Horace Rd., Kings.T. 198 CM97
Horatio Ct. SE16 142 DW74
Rotherhithe St.
Horatio Pl. E14 163 EC75
Cold Harbour
Horatio Pl. SW19 180 DA94
Kingston Rd.
Horatio St. E2 142 DT68
Horatius Way, Croy. 219 DM106
Horbury Cres. W11 140 DA73
Horbury Ms. W11 139 CZ73
Ladbroke Rd.
Horder Rd. SW6 159 CY81
Hordle Gdns., St.Alb. 43 CF21
Hordle Prom. E. SE15 162 DT80
Daniel Gdns.
Hordle Prom. N. SE15 162 DT80
Daniel Gdns.
Hordle Prom. S. SE15 162 DT80
Pentridge St.
Hordle Prom. W. SE15 162 DS80
Diamond St.
Horizon Way SE7 164 EH77
Horksley Gdns., Brwd. 109 GC44
Bannister Dr.
Horle Wk. SE5 161 DP82
Lilford Rd.
Horley Clo., Bexh. 186 FA85
Horley Lo. La., Red. 266 DF143
Horley Rd. SE9 184 EL91
Horley Rd., Red. 266 DF136
Horley Row, Horl. 268 DF147
Hormead Rd. W9 139 CZ70
Horn Clo., Hert. 32 DQ11
Horn La. SE10 164 EG77
Horn La. W3 138 CQ73
Horn La., Bexh. 167 FC82
Windermere Rd.
Horn La., Wdf.Grn. 102 EG51
Horn Link Way SE10 164 EG77
Horn Pk. Clo. SE12 184 EH85
Horn Pk. La. SE12 184 EH85
Hornbeam Ave., Upmin. 128 FN63
Hornbeam Chase, S.Ock. 149 FX69
Hornbeam Clo. NW7 97 CT48
Marsh La.
Hornbeam Clo. SE11 278 D8
Hornbeam Clo., Borwd. 78 CN39
Hornbeam Clo., Brwd. 109 GB48
Hornbeam Clo., Buck.H. 102 EK48
Hornbeam Rd.
Hornbeam Clo., Epp. 85 ES37
Hornbeam Clo., Hert. 31 DP08
Hornbeam Clo., Ilf. 125 ER64
Hornbeam Clo., Nthlt. 116 BZ64
Hornbeam Cres., Brent. 157 CH80
Hornbeam Gdns., Slou. 152 AU76
Upton Rd.
Hornbeam Gro. E4 102 EE48
Hornbeam La. E4 84 EE43
Hornbeam La., Bexh. 167 FC82
Hornbeam La., Hat. 46 DE21
Hornbeam Rd., Buck.H. 102 EK48
Hornbeam Rd., Epp. 85 ER37
Hornbeam Rd., Guil. 242 AW131
Hornbeam Rd., Hayes 136 BW71
Hornbeam Rd., Reig. 266 DB137
Hornbeam Ter., Cars. 200 DE102
Hornbeam Twr. E11 123 ED62
Hollydown Way
Hornbeam Wk., Rich. 178 CM90
Hornbeam Wk., Walt. 213 BT109
Octagon Rd.
Hornbeam Way, Brom. 205 EN100
Hornbeam Way, Wal.Cr. 66 DT29
Hornbeams, St.Alb. 60 BZ30
Hornbeams, The, Harl. 35 EQ13
Hornbeams Ave., Enf. 82 DW35
Hornbeams Ri. N11 98 DG51
Hornbill Clo., Uxb. 134 BK72
Hornblower Clo. SE16 163 DY77
Greenland Quay
Hornbuckle Clo., Har. 117 CD61
Hornby Clo. NW3 140 DD66
Horncastle Clo. SE12 184 EG87
Horncastle Rd. SE12 184 EG87
Hornchurch Clo., Kings.T. 177 CK91
Hornchurch Hill, Whyt. 236 DT117
Hornchurch Rd., Horn. 127 FG60
Horndean Clo. SW15 179 CU88
Bessborough Rd.
Horndon Clo., Rom. 105 FC53
Horndon Grn., Rom. 105 FC53
Horndon Rd., Rom. 105 FC53
Horne Rd., Shep. 194 BM98
Horne Way SW15 159 CW82
Horner La., Mitch. 200 DD96
Hornets, The, Wat. 75 BV42
Hornfair Rd. SE7 164 EJ79
Hornford Way, Rom. 127 FE59
Hornhatch, Guil. 259 BB140
Hornhatch Clo., Guil. 259 BB140
Hornhatch La., Guil. 259 BA140
Hornhill Rd., Ger.Cr. 91 BB50
Hornhill Rd., Rick. 91 BD50
Horniman Dr. SE23 182 DV88
Horning Clo. SE9 184 EL91
Hornminster Glen, Horn. 128 FN61
Horns End Pl., Pnr. 116 BW56
Horns Mill Rd., Hert. 32 DQ12
Horns Rd., Hert. 32 DQ10
Horns Rd., Ilf. 125 EQ58
Hornsby La., Grays 171 GG75
Hornsey La. N6 121 DH60
Hornsey La. N19 121 DJ59
Hornsey La. Est. N19 121 DK59
Hornsey La.
Hornsey La. Gdns. N6 121 DJ59
Hornsey Pk. Rd. N8 121 DM55
Hornsey Ri. N19 121 DK59
Hornsey Ri. Gdns. N19 121 DK59
Hornsey Rd. N7 121 DL61
Hornsey Rd. N19 121 DL61
Hornsey St. N7 121 DM64
Hornsfield, Welw.G.C. 30 DC08
Hornshay St. SE15 162 DW79
Hornton Pl. W8 160 DA75
Hornton St. W8 160 DA75
Horsa Clo., Wall. 219 DL108
Horsa Rd. SE12 184 EJ87
Horsa Rd., Erith 167 FC80
Horse and Dolphin Yd. W1 273 N10
Horse Fair, Kings.T. 197 CK96
Horse Guards Ave. SW1 277 P3
Horse Guards Ave. SW1 141 DL74
Horse Guards Rd. SW1 277 N3
Horse Guards Rd. SW1 141 DK74
Horse Hill, Chesh. 56 AX32
Horse Leaze E6 145 EN72
Horse Ride SW1 277 M3
Horse Ride SW1 141 DJ74
Horse Ride, Dor. 263 CD144
Wolvens La.
Horse Ride, Lthd. 245 BQ132
Epsom Rd.
Horse Rd. E7 124 EH62
Centre Rd.
Horse Shoe Cres., Nthlt. 136 CA68
Horse Shoe Grn., Sutt. 200 DB103
Aultone Way
Horse Yd. N1 141 DP67
Essex Rd.
Horsebridge Clo., Dag. 146 EY67
Horsecroft, Bans. 233 CZ117
Lyme Regis Rd.
Horsecroft Clo., Orp. 206 EV102
Horsecroft Pl., Harl. 50 EL16
Horsecroft Rd., Edg. 96 CR52
Horsecroft Rd., Harl. 50 EL16
Horsecroft Rd., Hem.H. 40 BG22
Horseferry Pl. SE10 163 EC79
Horseferry Rd. E14 143 DY73
Horseferry Rd. SW1 277 M7
Horseferry Rd. SW1 161 DK77
Horsehill, Horl. 268 DA146
Horselers, Hem.H. 40 BN23
Horsell Birch, Wok. 226 AV115
Horsell Common, Wok. 210 AV114
Horsell Common Rd., Wok. 210 AW114
Horsell Ct., Cher. 194 BH101
Stepgates
Horsell Moor, Wok. 226 AX117
Horsell Pk., Wok. 226 AX116
Horsell Pk. Clo., Wok. 226 AX116
Horsell Ri., Wok. 226 AX115
Horsell Ri. Clo., Wok. 226 AX115
Horsell Rd. N5 121 DN64
Horsell Rd., Orp. 206 EV95
Horsell Vale, Wok. 226 AY115
Horsell Way, Wok. 226 AW116
Horselydown La. SE1 279 P4
Horselydown La. SE1 162 DT75
Horseman Side, Brwd. 105 FH46
Horsemans Ride, St.Alb. 60 CA26
Horsemoor Clo., Slou. 153 BA77
Parlaunt Rd.
Horsenden Ave., Grnf. 117 CE64
Horsenden Cres., Grnf. 117 CF64
Horsenden La. N., Grnf. 137 CF65
Horsenden La. S., Grnf. 137 CG68
Horseshoe, The, Bans. 233 CZ115
Horseshoe, The, Couls. 219 DK113
Horseshoe, The, Hem.H. 41 BQ22
Horseshoe Clo. E14 163 EC78
Ferry St.
Horseshoe Clo. NW2 119 CV61
Horseshoe Clo., Wal.Abb. 68 EG34
Horseshoe Cres., Beac. 89 AL54
Horseshoe Dr., Uxb. 134 BN72
Horseshoe Hill, Slou. 110 AJ63
Horseshoe Hill, Wal.Abb. 68 EJ33
Horseshoe La. N20 97 CX46
Horseshoe La., Enf. 82 DQ41
Chase Side
Horseshoe La., Wat. 59 BV32
Horseshoe La. E., Guil. 243 BB133
Horseshoe La. W., Guil. 243 BB133
Horseshoe Ridge, Wey. 213 BQ111
Horsfeld Gdns. SE9 184 EL85
Horsfeld Rd. SE9 184 EK85
Horsfield Clo., Dart. 188 FQ87
Horsford Rd. SW2 181 DM85
Horsham Ave. N12 98 DE50
Horsham Rd., Bexh. 186 FA86
Horsham Rd., Dor. 263 CG137
Horsham Rd. (North Holmwood), Dor. 263 CH140
Horsham Rd. (Sutton Abinger), Dor. 261 BT142
Horsham Rd., Felt. 175 BQ86
Horsham Rd., Guil. 258 AX142
Horsley Clo., Epsom 216 CR113
Horsley Dr., Croy. 221 EC108
Horsley Dr., Kings.T. 177 CK92
Horsley Rd. E4 101 EC47
Horsley Rd., Brom. 204 EH95
Palace Rd.
Horsley Rd., Cob. 229 BU122
Horsley St. SE17 162 DR79
Horsleys, Rick. 91 BD50
Horsmonden Clo., Orp. 205 ES101
Horsmonden Rd. SE4 183 DZ85
Hortensia Rd. SW10 160 DC80
Horticultural Pl. W4 158 CR78
Heathfield Ter.
Horton Ave. NW2 119 CY63
Horton Bri. Rd., West Dr. 134 BM74
Horton Clo., Maid. 130 AC70
Horton Clo., West Dr. 134 BM74
Horton Footpath, Epsom 216 CQ111
Horton Gdns., Epsom 216 CQ111
Horton Hill
Horton Hill, Epsom 216 CQ111
Horton Ind. Pk., West Dr. 134 BM74
Horton La., Epsom 216 CP110
Horton Rd. E8 142 DV65
Horton Rd. (Horton Kirby), Dart. 208 FQ98
Horton Rd., Slou. 153 BA82
Horton Rd. (Datchet), Slou. 152 AV80
Horton Rd. (Poyle), Slou. 153 BE83
Horton Rd., Stai. 174 BG85
Horton Rd., West Dr. 134 BN74
Horton St. SE13 163 EB83
Horton Way, Croy. 203 DX99
Horton Way (Farningham), Dart. 208 FM101
Hortons Way, West. 255 ER126
Hortus Rd. E4 101 EC47
Hortus Rd., Sthl. 156 BZ75
Horvath Clo., Wey. 213 BR105
Horwood Clo., Rick. 92 BG45
Thellusson Way
Horwood Ct., Wat. 76 BX37
Hosack Rd. SW17 180 DF89
Hoser Ave. SE12 184 EG89
Hosey Common Rd., Eden. 255 EQ133
Hosey Common Rd., West. 255 ER130
Hosey Hill, West. 255 ER127
Hosier La. EC1 274 F7
Hosier La. EC1 141 DP71
Hoskins Clo. E16 144 EJ72
Hoskins Clo., Hayes 155 BT78
Cranford Dr.
Hoskins Rd., Oxt. 254 EE129
Hoskins St. SE10 163 ED78
Hoskins Wk., Oxt. 254 EE129
Hospital Bri. Rd., Twick. 176 CB87
Hospital Hill, Chesh. 54 AQ32
Hospital La., Islw. 177 CF85
Hospital Rd. E9 123 DX64
Homerton Row
Hospital Rd., Houns. 156 CA83
Hospital Rd., Sev. 257 FJ121
Hotham Clo. (Sutton at Hone), Dart. 188 FN94
Hotham Clo., Swan. 207 FH95
Hotham Clo., W.Mol. 196 CA97
Garrick Gdns.
Hotham Rd. SW15 159 CW83
Hotham Rd. SW19 180 DC94
Hotham Rd. Ms. SW19 180 DC94
Haydons Rd.
Hotham St. E15 144 EE67
Hothfield Pl. SE16 162 DW76
Lower Rd.
Hotspur Rd., Nthlt. 136 CA68
Hotspur St. SE11 278 D10
Hotspur St. SE11 161 DN78
Houblon Rd., Rich. 178 CL85
Houblons Hill, Epp. 70 EW31
Houghton Clo. E8 142 DT65
Buttermere Wk.
Houghton Clo., Hmptn. 176 BY93
Houghton Rd. N15 122 DT57
West Grn. Rd.
Houghton St. WC2 274 C9
Houlder Cres., Croy. 219 DP107
Hound Ho. Rd., Guil. 260 BN141
Houndsden Rd. N21 81 DM44
Houndsditch EC3 275 N8
Houndsditch EC3 142 DS72
Houndsfield Rd. N9 100 DV45
Hounslow Ave., Houns. 176 CB85
Hounslow Gdns., Houns. 176 CB85
Hounslow Rd. (Feltham), Felt. 175 BV88
Hounslow Rd. (Hanworth), Felt. 176 BX91
Hounslow Rd., Twick. 176 CB86
House La., St.Alb. 43 CK16
Housefield Way, St.Alb. 43 CJ23
Houseman Way SE5 162 DR80
Hopewell St.
Housewood End, Hem.H. 40 BH17
Houston Pl., Esher 197 CE102
Lime Tree Ave.
Houston Rd. SE23 183 DY89
Hove Ave. E17 123 DZ57
Hove Clo., Brwd. 109 GC47
Hove Gdns., Sutt. 200 DB102
Hoveden Rd. NW2 119 CY64
Hoveton Rd. SE28 146 EW72
How La., Couls. 234 DF119
How Wd., St.Alb. 60 CB28
Howard Agne Clo., Hem.H. 57 BA27
Howard Ave., Bex. 186 EW88
Howard Ave., Epsom 217 CU110
Howard Ave., Slou. 131 AR71
Howard Business Pk., Wal.Abb. 67 ED33
Howard Clo.
Howard Clo. N11 98 DG47
Howard Clo. NW2 119 CY63
Howard Clo. W3 138 CP72
Howard Clo., Ash. 232 CM118
Howard Clo., Hmptn. 176 CC93
Howard Clo., Lthd. 231 CJ123
Windmill Dr.
Howard Clo. (West Horsley), Lthd. 245 BR125
Howard Clo., Loug. 84 EL44
Howard Clo., St.Alb. 43 CH22
Howard Clo., Sun. 175 BT93
Catherine Dr.
Howard Clo., Tad. 249 CT125
Howard Clo., Wal.Abb. 67 ED34
Howard Clo., Wat. 75 BU37
Howard Clo. (Bushey), Wat. 95 CE45
Howard Cres., Beac. 89 AQ50
Howard Dr., Borwd. 78 CR42
Howard Gdns., Guil. 243 BA133
Howard Ms. N5 121 DP63
Hamilton Pk.
Howard Pl. SW1 277 K7
Howard Ridge, Guil. 243 BA130
Howard Rd. E6 145 EM68
Howard Rd. E11 124 EE62
Howard Rd. E17 123 EA55
Howard Rd. N15 122 DS58
Howard Rd. N16 122 DR63
Howard Rd. NW2 119 CX63
Howard Rd. SE20 202 DW95
Howard Rd. SE25 202 DU99
Howard Rd., Bark. 145 ER67
Howard Rd., Beac. 89 AQ50
Howard Rd., Brom. 184 EG94
Howard Rd., Chesh. 54 AP28
Howard Rd., Couls. 235 DJ115
Howard Rd., Dart. 188 FN86
Howard Rd., Dor. 263 CG136
Howard Rd. (North Holmwood), Dor. 263 CJ140
Holmesdale Rd.
Howard Rd., Grays 169 FW76
Howard Rd., Ilf. 125 EP63
Howard Rd., Islw. 157 CF83
Howard Rd., Lthd. 229 BU122
Howard Rd. (Great Bookham), Lthd. 246 CB127
Howard Rd., N.Mal. 198 CS97
Howard Rd., Reig. 266 DB135

Howard Rd., Sthl. 136 CB72
Howard Rd., Surb. 198 CM100
Howard Rd., Upmin. 128 FQ61
Howard St., T.Ditt. 197 CH101
Howard Wk. N2 120 DC56
Howard Way, Barn. 79 CX43
Howard Way, Harl. 35 ET12
Howards Clo., Pnr. 93 BV54
Howards Clo., Wok. 227 BA120
Howards Crest Clo., Beck. 203 CE96
Howards Dr., Hem.H. 39 BF17
Howards La. SW15 159 CV84
Howards La., Add. 211 BE107
Howards Rd. E13 144 EG69
Howards Rd., Wok. 227 AZ120
Howards Thicket, Ger.Cr. 112 AW61
Howards Wd. Dr., Ger.Cr. 112 AX61
Howardsgate, Welw.G.C. 29 CX08
Howarth Ct. E15 123 EC64
Clays La.
Howarth Rd. SE2 166 EU78
Howberry Clo., Edg. 95 CK51
Howberry Rd., Edg. 95 CK51
Howberry Rd., Stan. 95 CK51
Howberry Rd., Th.Hth. 202 DR95
Howbury La., Erith 167 FG82
Howbury Rd. SE15 162 DW83
Howcroft Cres. N3 98 DA52
Howcroft La., Grnf. 137 CD69
Cowgate Rd.
Howden Clo. SE28 146 EX73
Howden Rd. SE25 202 DT96
Howden St. SE15 162 DU83
Howe Clo., Rad. 62 CL32
Howe Clo., Rom. 104 FA53
Howe Dell, Hat. 45 CV18
Howe Dr., Beac. 89 AK50
Howe Dr., Cat. 236 DR122
Yorke Gate Rd.
Howe Rd., Hem.H. 40 BN22
Howell Clo., Rom. 126 EX57
Howell Hill Clo., Epsom 217 CW111
Howell Hill Gro., Epsom 217 CW110
Howell Wk. SE1 278 G9
Howes Clo. N3 120 DA55
Howfield Grn., Hodd. 33 DZ14
Howfield Pl. N17 122 DT55
Howgate Rd. SW14 158 CR83
Howick Pl. SW1 277 L7
Howick Pl. SW1 161 DJ76
Howicks Grn., Welw.G.C. 30 DA12
Howie St. SW11 160 DE80
Howitt Clo. NW3 140 DE65
Howitt Rd.
Howitt Rd. NW3 140 DE65
Howland Est. SE16 162 DW76
Howland Garth, St.Alb. 42 CC24
Howland Ms. E. W1 273 L6
Howland St. W1 273 K6
Howland St. W1 141 DJ71
Howland Way SE16 163 DY75
Howlands, Welw.G.C. 29 CX12
Howletts La., Ruis. 115 BQ57
Howletts Rd. SE24 182 DQ86
Howley Pl. W2 140 DC71
Howley Rd., Croy. 201 DP104
Hows Clo., Uxb. 134 BJ67
Hows Rd.
Hows Mead, Epp. 53 FD24
Hows Rd., Uxb. 134 BJ67
Hows St. E2 142 DT68
Howsman Rd. SW13 159 CU79
Howson Rd. SE4 163 DY84
Howson Ter., Rich. 178 CL86
Howton Pl. (Bushey), Wat. 95 CD46
Hoxton Mkt. N1 275 M3
Hoxton Sq. N1 275 M3
Hoxton Sq. N1 142 DS69
Hoxton St. N1 275 N3
Hoxton St. N1 142 DS67
Hoy St. E16 144 EF72
Hoy Ter., Grays 169 FX78
Hoylake Cres. (Ickenham), Uxb. 115 BP61
Hoylake Gdns., Mitch. 201 DJ97
Hoylake Gdns., Rom. 106 FN52
Hoylake Gdns., Ruis. 115 BV60
Hoylake Gdns., Wat. 94 BX49
Hoylake Rd. W3 138 CS72
Hoyland Clo. SE15 162 DV80
Commercial Way
Hoyle Rd. SW17 180 DE92
Hubbard Dr., Chess. 215 CJ107
Hubbard Rd. SE27 182 DQ91
Hubbard St. E15 144 EE67
Hubbards Chase, Horn. 128 FN57
Hubbards Clo., Horn. 128 FN57
Hubbard's Hill, Sev. 257 FH130
Hubbards Rd., Rick. 73 BD43
Hubbinet Ind. Est., Rom. 127 FC55
Hubert Day Clo., Beac. 89 AK52
Seeleys Rd.
Hubert Gro. SW9 161 DL83
Hubert Rd. E6 144 EK69
Hubert Rd., Brwd. 108 FV48
Hubert Rd., Rain. 147 FF69
Hubert Rd., Slou. 152 AX76
Hubert Rd. Ind. Est., Brwd. 108 FV48
Hucknall Clo., Rom. 106 FM51
Huddart St. E3 143 EA71
Huddleston Clo. E2 142 DW68
Huddleston Rd. N7 121 DK63
Huddlestone Cres., Red. 251 DK128
Huddlestone Rd. E7 124 EF63
Huddlestone Rd. NW2 139 CV65
Hudons Clo., Grays 169 FT78
Hudson Ave., Uxb. 113 BF58
Hudson Clo., St.Alb. 43 CD22
Hudson Clo., Wat. 75 BT36
Hudson Ct. E14 163 EA78
Napier Ave.
Hudson Ct. SW19 180 DB94
Hudson Ct., Guil. 242 AT133
Cobbett Rd.
Hudson Gdns., Orp. 223 ET107
Superior Dr.
Hudson Pl. SE18 165 EQ78
Hudson Rd., Bexh. 166 EZ82
Hudson Rd., Hayes 155 BR79
Hudsons, Tad. 233 CX121
Hudson's Pl. SW1 277 J8
Huggin Ct. EC4 275 J10
Huggin Hill EC4 275 J10
Huggins La., Hat. 45 CW23
Huggins Pl. SW2 181 DM88
Roupell Rd.
Hugh Dalton Ave. SW6 159 CZ79
Hugh Gaitskell Clo. SW6 159 CZ79
Hugh Ms. SW1 277 J9
Hugh Pl. SW1 277 M8
Hugh St. SW1 277 J9
Hugh St. SW1 161 DH77
Hughan Rd. E15 123 ED64
Hughenden Ave., Har. 117 CH57
Hughenden Gdns., Nthlt. 136 BW69
Hughenden Rd., St.Alb. 43 CH17
Hughenden Rd., Slou. 131 AR72
Hughenden Rd., Wor.Pk. 199 CU101
Hughendon Ter. E15 123 EC63
Westdown Rd.
Hughes Rd., Ashf. 175 BQ94
Hughes Rd., Grays 171 GG76
Hughes Rd., Hayes 135 BV73
Hughes Wk., Croy. 202 DQ101
St. Saviours Rd.
Hugh's Twr., Harl. 35 ER14
Hugo Gdns., Rain. 147 FG65
Hugo Gryn Way, Rad. 62 CL31
Farm Clo.
Hugo Rd. N19 121 DJ63
Hugon Rd. SW6 160 DB83
Huguenot Pl. E1 142 DT71
Huguenot Pl. SW18 180 DC85
Huguenot Sq. SE15 162 DV83
Scylla Rd.
Hull Clo. SE16 163 DX75
Hull Clo., Slou. 151 AQ75
Hull Clo., Sutt. 218 DB110
Yarbridge Clo.
Hull Gro., Harl. 51 EN20
Hull St. EC1 275 H3
Hullbridge Ms. N1 142 DR67
Sherborne St.
Hulletts La., Brwd. 108 FT43
Hulse Ave., Bark. 145 ER65
Hulse Ave., Rom. 105 FB53
Hulse Ter., Ilf. 125 EQ64
Buttsbury Rd.
Hulsewood Clo., Dart. 187 FH90
Hulton Clo., Lthd. 231 CJ123
Windmill Dr.
Hulverston Clo., Sutt. 218 DB110
Humber Ave., S.Ock. 149 FT72
Humber Clo., West Dr. 134 BK74
Humber Dr. W10 139 CX70
Humber Dr., Upmin. 129 FR58
Humber Rd. NW2 119 CV61
Humber Rd. SE3 164 EF79
Humber Rd., Dart. 188 FK85
Humber Way, Slou. 153 BA77
Humberstone Rd. E13 144 EJ69
Humberton Clo. E9 123 DY64
Marsh Hill
Humbolt Clo., Guil. 242 AS134
Humbolt Rd. W6 159 CY79
Hume Ave., Til. 171 GG83
Hume Ter. E16 144 EJ72
Prince Regent La.
Hume Way, Ruis. 115 BU58
Humes Ave. W7 157 CE76
Hummer Rd., Egh. 173 BA91
Humphrey Clo., Ilf. 103 EM53
Humphrey Clo., Lthd. 230 CC122
Humphrey St. SE1 279 P10
Humphrey St. SE1 162 DT78
Humphries Clo., Dag. 126 EZ63
Hundred Acre NW9 97 CT54
Hundred Acres La., Amer. 55 AR40
Hungerdown E4 101 EC46
Hungerford Ave., Slou. 132 AS71
Hungerford Bri. SE1 278 A2
Hungerford Bri. SE1 141 DL74
Hungerford Bri. WC2 278 A2
Hungerford Bri. WC2 141 DL74
Hungerford La. WC2 277 P2
Hungerford Rd. N7 121 DL64
Hungerford Sq., Wey. 213 BR105
Rosslyn Pk.
Hungerford St. E1 142 DV72
Commercial Rd.
Hungry Hill, Wok. 228 BK124
Hungry Hill La.
Hungry Hill La., Wok. 228 BK124
Hunsdon, Welw.G.C. 30 DD09
Hunsdon Clo., Dag. 146 EY65
Hunsdon Dr., Sev. 257 FH123
Hunsdon Rd. SE14 163 DX79
Hunsdon Rd. (Stanstead Abbotts), Ware 34 EE11
Hunslett St. E2 142 DW68
Royston St.
Hunston Rd., Mord. 200 DB102
Hunt Clo., St.Alb. 43 CK17
Villiers Cres.
Hunt Rd., Grav. 190 GE90
Hunt Rd., Sthl. 156 CA76
Hunt St. W11 139 CX74
Hunt Way SE22 182 DU88
Dulwich Common
Hunter Ave., Brwd. 109 GA44
Hunter Clo. SE1 279 L7
Hunter Clo. SW12 180 DG88
Balham Pk. Rd.
Hunter Clo., Borwd. 78 CQ43
Hunter Clo., Pot.B. 64 DB33
Hunter Dr., Horn. 128 FJ63
Hunter Ho., Felt. 175 BU88
Hunter Rd. SW20 199 CW95
Hunter Rd., Guil. 258 AY135
Hunter Rd., Ilf. 125 EP64
Hunter Rd., Th.Hth. 202 DR97
Hunter St. WC1 274 A4
Hunter St. WC1 141 DL70
Hunter Wk. E13 144 EG68
Hunter Wk., Borwd. 78 CQ43
Ashley Dr.
Huntercombe Clo., Maid. 130 AH72
Huntercombe La. N., Maid. 130 AJ72
Huntercombe La. N., Slou 130 AJ71
Huntercombe La. S., Maid. 130 AH74
Huntercombe Spur, Slou. 130 AJ73
Huntercrombe Gdns., Wat. 94 BW49
Hunters, The, Beck. 203 EC95
Hunters Clo., Bex. 187 FE90
Hunters Clo., Chesh. 54 AN30
Hunters Clo., Epsom 216 CQ113
Marshalls Clo.
Hunters Clo., Hem.H. 57 BA29
Hunters Ct., Rich. 177 CK85
Friars La.
Hunters Gro., Har. 117 CJ56
Hunters Gro., Hayes 135 BU74
Hunters Gro., Orp. 223 EP105
Hunters Gro., Rom. 105 FB50
Hunters Hall Rd., Dag. 126 FA63
Hunters Hill, Ruis. 116 BW62
Hunters La., Wat. 59 BT33
Hunters Meadow SE19 182 DS91
Dulwich Wd. Ave.
Hunters Oak, Hem.H. 41 BP15
Hunters Pk., Berk. 38 AY18
Hunters Reach, Wal.Cr. 66 DT29
Hunters Ride, St.Alb. 60 CA31
Hunters Rd., Chess. 198 CL104
Hunters Sq., Dag. 126 FA63
Hunters Wk., Sev. 224 EY114
Hunters Way, Croy. 220 DS105
Brownlow Rd.
Hunters Way, Enf. 81 DN39
Hunters Way, Welw.G.C. 29 CZ12
Huntersfield Clo., Reig. 250 DB131
Hunting Clo., Esher 214 CA105
Hunting Gate, Hem.H. 40 BL16
Hunting Gate Clo., Enf. 81 DN41
Hunting Gate Dr., Chess. 216 CL108
Hunting Gate Ms., Sutt. 200 DB104
Hunting Gate Ms., Twick. 177 CE88
Colne Rd.
Huntingdon Clo., Brox. 49 DY24
Huntingdon Clo., Mitch. 201 DL97
Huntingdon Gdns. W4 158 CQ80
Huntingdon Gdns., Wor.Pk. 199 CW104
Huntingdon Rd. N2 120 DE55
Huntingdon Rd. N9 100 DW46
Huntingdon Rd., Red. 250 DF134
Huntingdon Rd., Wok. 226 AT117
Huntingdon St. E16 144 EF72
Huntingdon St. N1 141 DM66
Huntingfield, Croy. 221 DZ108
Huntingfield Rd. SW15 179 CU85
Huntingfield Way, Egh. 173 BD93
Huntings Rd., Dag. 146 FA65
Huntland Clo., Rain. 147 FH71
Huntley Ave., Grav. 190 GB86
Huntley Dr. N3 98 DA51
Huntley St. WC1 273 L5
Huntley St. WC1 141 DJ70
Huntley Way SW20 199 CU96
Huntly Rd. SE25 202 DS98
Hunton Bri. Hill, Kings L. 59 BQ33
Hunton St. E1 142 DU70
Hunt's Clo. SE3 164 EG82
Hunt's Ct. WC2 277 N1
Hunts La. E15 143 EC68
Hunts La., Maid. 130 AE68
Hunts Mead, Enf. 83 DX41
Hunts Mead Clo., Chis. 185 EM94
Hunts Slip Rd. SE21 182 DS90
Huntsman Clo., Warl. 236 DW119
Huntsman Rd., Ilf. 104 EU51
Huntsman St. SE17 279 L9
Huntsman St. SE17 162 DR77
Huntsmans Clo., Felt. 175 BV91
Huntsmans Clo., Lthd. 231 CD124
The Grn.
Huntsmans Dr., Upmin. 128 FQ64
Huntsmill Rd., Hem.H. 39 BE21
Huntsmoor Rd., Epsom 216 CR106
Huntspill St. SW17 180 DC90
Huntswood La., Maid. 130 AE66
Huntsworth La., Slou. 130 AF67
Huntsworth Ms. NW1 272 D5
Hurdwick Pl. NW1 141 DJ68
Harrington Sq.
Hurley Clo., Walt. 195 BV103
Hurley Cres. SE16 163 DX75
Marlow Way
Hurley Gdns., Guil. 243 BA130
Hurley Rd. SE11 278 E9
Hurley Rd. SE11 161 DN77
Hurley Rd., Grnf. 136 CB72
Hurlfield, Dart. 188 FJ90
Hurlford, Wok. 226 AU117
Hurlingham Ct. SW6 159 CZ83
Hurlingham Gdns. SW6 159 CZ83
Hurlingham Rd. SW6 159 CZ82
Hurlingham Rd., Bexh. 166 EZ80
Hurlingham Sq. SW6 160 DB83
Peterborough Rd.
Hurlock St. N5 121 DP62
Hurlstone Rd. SE25 202 DR99
Hurn Ct. Rd., Houns. 156 BX82
Renfrew Rd.
Hurnford Clo., S.Croy. 220 DS110
Huron Clo., Orp. 223 ET107
Winnipeg Dr.
Huron Rd. SW17 180 DG89
Hurren Clo. SE3 164 EE83
Hurricane Way, Abb.L. 59 BU32
Abbey Dr.
Hurricane Way, Epp. 70 FA27
Hurry Clo. E15 144 EE66
Hursley Rd., Chig. 103 ET50
Tufter Rd.
Hurst Ave. E4 101 EA49
Hurst Ave. N6 121 DJ58
Hurst Clo. E4 101 EA48
Hurst Clo. NW11 120 DB58
Hurst Clo., Brom. 204 EF102
Hurst Clo., Chess. 216 CN106
Hurst Clo., Nthlt. 116 BZ64
Hurst Clo., Welw.G.C. 30 DC10
Hurst Clo., Wok. 226 AW120
Hurst Cft., Guil. 258 AY137
Hurst Dr., Tad. 249 CU126
Hurst Dr., Wal.Cr. 67 DX34
Hurst Est. SE2 166 EX78
Hurst Grn. Clo., Oxt. 254 EG132
Hurst Grn. Rd., Oxt. 254 EF132
Hurst Gro., Walt. 195 BT102
Hurst La. SE2 166 EX78
Hurst La., E.Mol. 196 CC98
Hurst La., Egh. 193 BA96
Hurst La., Epsom 232 CQ124
Hurst Pk. Ave., Horn. 128 FL63
Newmarket Way
Hurst Pl., Nthwd. 93 BP53
Hurst Ri., Barn. 80 DA41
Hurst Rd. E17 123 EB55
Hurst Rd. N21 99 DN46
Hurst Rd., Bex. 186 EW88
Hurst Rd., Buck.H. 102 EK46
Hurst Rd., Croy. 220 DR106
Hurst Rd., E.Mol. 196 CA97
Hurst Rd., Epsom 216 CR111
Hurst Rd. (Headley), Epsom 232 CR123
Hurst Rd., Erith 167 FC80
Hurst Rd., Horl. 268 DE147
Hurst Rd., Sid. 186 EU89
Hurst Rd., Slou. 131 AK71
Hurst Rd., Tad. 233 CU123
Hurst Rd., Walt. 196 BW99
Hurst Rd., W.Mol. 196 CA97
Hurst Springs, Bex. 186 EY88
Hurst St. SE24 181 DP86
Hurst Vw. Rd., S.Croy. 220 DS108
Hurst Way, Sev. 257 FJ127
Hurst Way, S.Croy. 220 DS107
Hurst Way, Wok. 211 BE114
Hurstbourne, Esher 215 CF107
Hurstbourne Gdns., Bark. 145 ES65
Hurstbourne Rd. SE23 183 DY88
Hurstcourt Rd., Sutt. 200 DB103
Hurstdene Ave., Brom. 204 EF102
Hurstdene Ave., Stai. 174 BH93
Hurstdene Gdns. N15 122 DS59
Hurstfield, Brom. 204 EG99
Hurstfield Cres., Hayes 135 BS70
Hurstfield Dr., Maid. 130 AH72
Hurstfield Rd., W.Mol. 196 CA97
Hurstlands, Oxt. 254 EG132
Hurstlands Clo., Horn. 128 FJ59
Hurstleigh Clo., Red. 250 DF132
Hurstleigh Dr., Red. 250 DF132
Hurstleigh Gdns., Ilf. 103 EM53
Hurstlings, Welw.G.C. 30 DB10
Hurstmead Ct., Edg. 96 CP49
Hurstway Wk. W11 139 CX73
Hurstwood Ave. E18 124 EH56
Hurstwood Ave., Bex. 186 EY88
Hurstwood Ave., Bexh. 167 FE81
Hurstwood Ave., Brwd. 108 FV45
Ongar Rd.
Hurstwood Ave., Erith 167 FE81
Hurstwood Ct., Upmin. 128 FQ60
Hurstwood Dr., Brom. 205 EM97
Hurstwood Rd. NW11 119 CY56
Hurtwood Rd., Walt. 196 BZ101
Hurworth Rd., Slou. 152 AW76
Huson Clo. NW3 140 DE66
Hussars Clo., Houns. 156 BY83
Husseywell Cres., Brom. 204 EG102
Hutchings Rd., Beac. 89 AK50
Hutchings St. E14 163 EA75
Hutchings Wk. NW11 120 DB56
Hutchingsons Rd., Croy. 221 EC111
Hutchins Clo. E15 143 EC66
Gibbins Rd.
Hutchins Clo., Horn. 128 FL62
Hutchins Rd. SE28 146 EU73
Hutchins Way, Horl. 268 DF146
Hutchinson Ter., Wem. 117 CK62
Hutton Clo., Grnf. 117 CD64
Mary Peters Dr.
Hutton Clo., Hert. 31 DN09
Hutton Clo., Wdf.Grn. 102 EH51
Hutton Dr., Brwd. 109 GC45
Hutton Gdns., Har. 94 CC52
Hutton Gate, Brwd. 109 GB45
Hutton Gro. N12 98 DB50
Hutton Ind. Est., Brwd. 109 GE43
Hutton La., Har. 94 CC52
Hutton Rd., Brwd. 109 FZ45
Hutton Row, Edg. 96 CQ52
Pavilion Way
Hutton St. EC4 274 E9
Hutton Village, Brwd. 109 GE44
Hutton Wk., Har. 94 CC52
Huxbear St. SE4 183 DZ85
Huxley Clo., Nthlt. 136 BY67
Huxley Clo., Uxb. 134 BK70
Huxley Dr., Rom. 126 EV59
Huxley Gdns. NW10 138 CM69
Huxley Par. N18 100 DR50
Huxley Pl. N13 99 DP49
Huxley Rd. E10 123 EC61
Huxley Rd. N18 100 DR49
Huxley Rd., Well. 165 ET83
Huxley Sayze N18 100 DR50
Huxley St. W10 139 CY69
Hyacinth Clo., Hmptn. 176 CA93
Gresham Rd.
Hyacinth Clo., Ilf. 145 EP65
Hyacinth Ct., Pnr. 116 BW55
Tulip Ct.
Hyacinth Dr., Uxb. 134 BL66
Hyacinth Rd. SW15 179 CU88
Hyburn Clo., Hem.H. 41 BP21
Hyburn Clo., St.Alb. 60 BZ30
Hycliffe Gdns., Chig. 103 EQ49
Hyde, The NW9 118 CS57
Hyde, The, Ware 32 DV05
Hyde Ave., Pot.B. 64 DB33
Hyde Clo. E13 144 EG68
Hyde Clo., Ashf. 175 BS93
Hyde Ter.
Hyde Clo., Barn. 79 CZ41
Hyde Clo. (Chafford Hundred), Grays 169 FX76
Hyde Ct. N20 98 DD48
Hyde Cres. NW9 118 CS57
Hyde Dr., Orp. 206 EV98
Hyde Est. Rd. NW9 119 CT57
Hyde Grn., Beac. 89 AM52
Hyde Ho. NW9 118 CS57
Hyde La. SW11 160 DE81
Battersea Bri. Rd.
Hyde La., Hem.H. 59 BR26
Hyde La. (Bovingdon), Hem.H. 57 AZ27
Hyde La., St.Alb. 61 CE28
Hyde La., Wok. 228 BN120
Hyde Mead, Wal.Abb. 50 EE23
Hyde Meadows, Hem.H. 57 BA28
Hyde Pk. SW7 276 C2
Hyde Pk. SW7 140 DF74
Hyde Pk. W1 276 C2
Hyde Pk. W1 140 DF74
Hyde Pk. W2 276 C2
Hyde Pk. W2 140 DF74
Hyde Pk. Ave. N21 100 DQ47
Hyde Pk. Cor. W1 276 G4
Hyde Pk. Cor. W1 160 DG75
Hyde Pk. Cres. W2 272 B9
Hyde Pk. Cres. W2 140 DE72
Hyde Pk. Gdns. N21 100 DQ46
Hyde Pk. Gdns. W2 272 A10
Hyde Pk. Gdns. W2 140 DD73
Hyde Pk. Gdns. Ms. W2 272 A10
Hyde Pk. Gate SW7 160 DC75
Hyde Pk. Gate Ms. SW7 160 DC75
Hyde Pk. Gate
Hyde Pk. Pl. W2 272 C10
Hyde Pk. Pl. W2 140 DE73
Hyde Pk. Sq. W2 272 B9
Hyde Pk. Sq. W2 140 DE72
Hyde Pk. Sq. Ms. W2 272 B9
Hyde Pk. St. W2 272 B9
Hyde Pk. St. W2 140 DE72
Hyde Rd. N1 142 DR67
Hyde Rd., Bexh. 166 EZ82
Hyde Rd., Rich. 178 CM85
Albert Rd.
Hyde Rd., S.Croy. 220 DS113
Hyde Rd., Wat. 75 BU40
Hyde St. SE8 163 EA79
Deptford High St.
Hyde Ter., Ashf. 175 BS93
Hyde Vale SE10 163 EC80
Hyde Valley, Welw.G.C. 29 CZ11
Hyde Wk., Mord. 200 DA101
Hyde Way N9 100 DT47
Hyde Way, Hayes 155 BT77
Hyde Way, Welw.G.C. 29 CY09
Hydefield Clo. N21 100 DR46
Hydefield Ct. N9 100 DS47
Hyder Rd., Grays 171 GJ76
Hyderabad Way E15 144 EE66
Hydes Pl. N1 141 DP66
Compton Ave.
Hydeside Gdns. N9 100 DT47
Hydethorpe Ave. N9 100 DT47
Hydethorpe Rd. SW12 181 DJ88
Hyland Clo., Horn. 127 FH59
Hyland Way, Horn. 127 FH59
Hylands Clo., Epsom 232 CQ115
Hylands Ms., Epsom 232 CQ115
Hylands Rd. E17 101 ED54
Hylands Rd., Epsom 232 CQ115
Hylle Clo., Wind. 151 AL81
Hylton St. SE18 165 ET77
Hyndewood SE23 183 DX90
Hyndman St. SE15 162 DV79
Hynton Rd., Dag. 126 EW61
Hyperion Ct., Hem.H. 40 BM17
Saturn Way
Hyperion Pl., Epsom 216 CR109
Hyperion Wk., Horl. 269 DH150
Hyrons Clo., Amer. 55 AS38
Hyrons La., Amer. 55 AR38
Hyrstdene, S.Croy. 219 DP105
Hyson Rd. SE16 162 DV77
Galleywall Rd.
Hythe, The, Stai. 173 BE92
Hythe Ave., Bexh. 166 EZ80
Hythe Clo. N18 100 DU49
Hythe Clo., Orp. 206 EW98
Sandway Rd.
Hythe End Rd., Stai. 173 AZ89
Hythe Fld. Ave., Egh. 173 BD93
Hythe Pk. Rd., Egh. 173 BC92
Hythe Path, Th.Hth. 202 DR97
Hythe Rd. NW10 139 CU70
Hythe Rd., Stai. 173 BD92
Hythe Rd., Th.Hth. 202 DR96
Hythe St., Dart. 188 FL86
Hythe St. Lwr., Dart. 188 FL85
Hyver Hill NW7 78 CR44

I

Ian Sq., Enf. 83 DX39
Lansbury Rd.
Ibbetson Path, Loug. 85 EP41
Ibbotson Ave. E16 144 EF72
Ibbott St. E1 142 DW70
Mantus Rd.
Iberian Ave., Wall. 219 DK105
Ibis La. W4 158 CQ81
Ibis Way, Hayes 136 BX72
Cygnet Way
Ibscott Clo., Dag. 147 FC65
Ibsley Gdns. SW15 179 CU88
Ibsley Way, Barn. 80 DE43
Ice Wf. Marina N1 141 DL68
New Wf. Rd.
Icehouse Wd., Oxt. 254 EE131
Iceland Rd. E3 143 EA67
Iceni Ct. E3 143 DZ67
Roman Rd.
Ickburgh Est. E5 122 DV62
Ickburgh Rd.
Ickburgh Rd. E5 122 DV62
Ickenham Clo., Ruis. 115 BR61
Ickenham Rd., Ruis. 115 BR60
Ickenham Rd. (Ickenham), Uxb. 115 BQ61
Ickleton Rd. SE9 184 EL91
Icklingham Gate, Cob. 214 BW112
Icklingham Rd.
Icklingham Rd., Cob. 214 BW112
Icknield Clo., St.Alb. 42 BZ22
Icknield Dr., Ilf. 125 EP57
Ickworth Pk. Rd. E17 123 DY56
Ida Rd. N15 122 DR57
Ida St. E14 143 EC72
Iden Clo., Brom. 204 EE97
Idlecombe Rd. SW17 180 DG93
Idmiston Rd. E15 124 EF64
Idmiston Rd. SE27 182 DQ90
Idmiston Rd., Wor.Pk. 199 CT101
Idmiston Sq., Wor.Pk. 199 CT101
Idol La. EC3 279 M1
Idonia St. SE8 163 DZ80
Iffley Clo., Uxb. 134 BK66
Iffley Rd. W6 159 CV76
Ifield Clo., Red. 266 DE137
Ifield Rd. SW10 160 DB79
Ifield Way, Grav. 191 GK93
Ifold Rd., Red. 266 DG136
Ifor Evans Pl. E1 143 DX70
Mile End Rd.
Ightham Rd., Erith 166 FA80
Ikea Twr. NW10 118 CR64
Ikona Ct., Wey. 213 BQ106
Ilbert St. W10 139 CX69
Ilchester Gdns. W2 140 DB73
Ilchester Pl. W14 159 CZ76
Ilchester Rd., Dag. 126 EV64
Ildersly Gro. SE21 182 DR89
Ilderton Rd. SE15 162 DW80

Ilderton Rd. SE16 162 DV78
Ilex Clo., Egh. 172 AV94
Ilex Clo., Sun. 196 BW96
Oakington Dr.
Ilex Ct., Berk. 38 AV19
Ilex Ho. N4 121 DM59
Ilex Rd. NW10 139 CT65
Ilex Way SW16 181 DN92
Ilford Hill, Ilf. 125 EN62
Ilford La., Ilf. 125 EP62
Ilfracombe Cres., Horn. 128 FJ63
Ilfracombe Gdns., Rom. 126 EV59
Ilfracombe Rd., Brom. 184 EF90
Iliffe St. SE17 278 G10
Iliffe St. SE17 161 DP78
Iliffe Yd. SE17 278 G10
Ilkeston Ct. E5 123 DX63
Overbury St.
Ilkley Clo. SE19 182 DR93
Ilkley Rd. E16 144 EJ71
Ilkley Rd., Wat. 94 BX50
Illingworth, Wind. 151 AL83
Illingworth Clo., Mitch. 200 DD97
Illingworth Way, Enf. 82 DS42
Ilmington Rd., Har. 117 CK58
Ilminster Gdns. SW11 160 DE84
Imber Clo. N14 99 DJ45
Imber Clo., Esher 197 CD102
Ember La.
Imber Ct. Ind. Est., E.Mol. 197 CD100
Imber Gro., Esher 197 CD101
Imber Pk. Rd., Esher 197 CD102
Imber St. N1 142 DR67
Imer Pl., T.Ditt. 197 CF101
Imperial Ave. N16 122 DT62
Victorian Rd.
Imperial Business & Retail Pk., Grav. 191 GF86
Imperial Clo., Har. 116 CA58
Imperial College Rd. SW7 160 DD76
Imperial Cres., Wey. 195 BQ104
Churchill Dr.
Imperial Dr., Grav. 191 GM92
Imperial Dr., Har. 116 CA59
Imperial Gdns., Mitch. 201 DH97
Imperial Ms. E6 144 EJ68
Central Pk. Rd.
Imperial Rd. N22 99 DL53
Imperial Rd. SW6 160 DC81
Imperial Rd., Felt. 175 BS87
Imperial Rd., Wind. 151 AN83
Imperial Sq. SW6 160 DB81
Imperial St. E3 143 EC69
Imperial Way, Chis. 185 EQ90
Imperial Way, Croy. 219 DM107
Imperial Way, Har. 118 CL58
Imperial Way, Wat. 76 BW39
Inca Dr. SE9 185 EP87
Ince Rd., Walt. 213 BS108
Inchmery Rd. SE6 183 EB89
Inchwood, Croy. 221 EB105
Indells, Hat. 45 CT19
Independent Pl. E8 122 DT64
Downs Pk. Rd.
Independents Rd. SE3 164 EF83
Blackheath Village
Inderwick Rd. N8 121 DM57
Indescon Ct. E14 163 EB75
India Pl. WC2 274 B10
India Rd., Slou. 152 AV75
India St. EC3 275 P9
India Way W12 139 CV73
Indigo Ms. E14 143 EC73
Ashton St.
Indigo Ms. N16 122 DR62
Indus Rd. SE7 164 EJ80
Industry Ter. SW9 161 DN83
Canterbury Cres.
Ingal Rd. E13 144 EG70
Ingate Pl. SW8 161 DH81
Ingatestone Rd. E12 124 EJ60
Ingatestone Rd. SE25 202 DV98
Ingatestone Rd., Wdf.Grn. 102 EG52
Ingelow Rd. SW8 161 DH82
Ingels Mead, Epp. 69 ET29
Ingersoll Rd. W12 139 CV74
Ingersoll Rd., Enf. 82 DW38
Ingestre Pl. W1 273 L9
Ingestre Rd. E7 124 EG63
Ingestre Rd. NW5 121 DH63
Ingham Clo., S.Croy. 221 DX109
Ingham Rd. NW6 120 DA63
Ingham Rd., S.Croy. 220 DW109
Ingle Clo., Pnr. 116 BY55
Inglebert St. EC1 274 D2
Ingleboro Dr., Pur. 220 DR113
Ingleborough St. SW9 161 DN82
Ingleby Dr., Har. 117 CD62
Ingleby Gdns., Chig. 104 EV48
Ingleby Rd., Dag. 147 FB65
Ingleby Rd., Grays 171 GH76
Ingleby Rd., Ilf. 125 EP60
Ingleby Way, Chis. 185 EN92
Ingleby Way, Wall. 219 DK109
Ingledew Rd. SE18 165 ER78
Inglefield, Pot.B. 64 DA30
Ingleglen, Horn. 128 FN59
Ingleglen, Slou. 111 AP64
Inglehurst, Add. 212 BH110
Inglehurst Gdns., Ilf. 125 EM57
Inglemere Rd. SE23 183 DX90
Inglemere Rd., Mitch. 180 DF94
Ingles, Welw.G.C. 29 CX06
Inglesham Wk. E9 143 DZ65
Ingleside, Slou. 153 BE81
Ingleside Clo., Beck. 183 EA94
Ingleside Gro. SE3 164 EF79
Inglethorpe St. SW6 159 CX81
Ingleton Ave., Well. 186 EU85
Ingleton Rd. N18 100 DU51
Ingleton Rd., Cars. 218 DE109
Ingleton St. SW9 161 DN82
Ingleway N12 98 DD51
Inglewood, Cher. 193 BF104
Inglewood, Croy. 221 DY109
Inglewood, Wok. 226 AV118
Inglewood Clo. E14 163 EA77
Inglewood Clo., Horn. 128 FK63
Inglewood Clo., Ilf. 103 ET51
Inglewood Copse, Brom. 204 EL96
Inglewood Rd. NW6 120 DA64
Inglewood Rd., Bexh. 167 FD84
Inglis Barracks NW7 97 CY51
Inglis Rd. W5 138 CM73
Inglis Rd., Croy. 202 DT102
Inglis St. SE5 161 DP81
Ingoldsby Rd., Grav. 191 GL88
Ingram Ave. NW11 120 DC59
Ingram Clo. SE11 278 C8
Ingram Clo., Stan. 95 CJ50
Ingram Rd. N2 120 DE56
Ingram Rd., Dart. 188 FL88
Ingram Rd., Grays 170 GD77
Ingram Rd., Th.Hth. 202 DQ95
Ingram Way, Grnf. 137 CD67
Ingrams Clo., Walt. 214 BW106
Ingrave Ho., Dag. 146 EV67
Ingrave Rd., Brwd. 108 FX47
Ingrave Rd., Rom. 127 FD56
Ingrave St. SW11 160 DD83
Ingrebourne Gdns., Upmin. 128 FQ60
Ingrebourne Rd., Rain. 147 FH70
Ingrebourne Valley Grn. Way, Horn. 128 FK64
Ingress Gdns., Green. 189 FX85
Ingress St. W4 158 CS78
Devonshire Rd.
Ingreway, Rom. 106 FP51
Inholms La., Dor. 263 CH140
Inigo Jones Rd. SE7 164 EL80
Inigo Pl. WC2 273 P10
Inkerman Rd. NW5 141 DH65
Inkerman Rd., St.Alb. 43 CE21
Inkerman Rd. (Eton Wick), Wind. 151 AM77
Inkerman Rd., Wok. 226 AS118
Inkerman Ter. W8 160 DA76
Allen St.
Inkerman Ter., Chesh. 54 AQ33
Inkerman Way, Wok. 226 AS118
Inks Grn. E4 101 EC50
Inman Rd. NW10 138 CS67
Inman Rd. SW18 180 DC87
Inmans Row, Wdf.Grn. 102 EG49
Inner Circle NW1 272 F2
Inner Circle NW1 140 DG69
Inner Pk. Rd. SW19 179 CX88
Inner Ring E., Houns. 155 BP83
Inner Ring W., Houns. 154 BN83
Inner Temple La. EC4 274 D9
Innes Clo. SW20 199 CY96
Innes Ct., Hem.H. 40 BK22
Innes Gdns. SW15 179 CV86
Innes Yd., Croy. 202 DQ104
Whitgift St.
Inniskilling Rd. E13 144 EJ68
Innova Business Pk., Enf. 83 DZ36
Innova Way, Enf. 83 DZ36
Innovation Clo., Wem. 138 CL67
Inskip Clo. E10 123 EB61
Inskip Dr., Horn. 128 FL60
Inskip Rd., Dag. 126 EX60
Institute Pl. E8 122 DV64
Amhurst Rd.
Institute Rd., Dor. 262 CC137
Guildford Rd.
Institute Rd., Epp. 70 EX29
Institute Rd., Maid. 130 AF72
Instone Clo., Wall. 219 DL108
Instone Rd., Dart. 188 FK87
Integer Gdns. E11 123 ED59
Forest Rd.
Interchange E. Ind. Est. E5 122 DW60
Theydon Rd.
International Ave., Houns. 156 BW78
International Trd. Est., Sthl. 155 BV76
Inver Clo. E5 122 DW61
Theydon Rd.
Inver Ct. W2 140 DB72
Inverness Ter.
Inveraray Pl. SE18 165 ER79
Old Mill Rd.
Inverclyde Gdns., Rom. 126 EX56
Inveresk Gdns., Wor.Pk. 199 CT104
Inverforth Clo. NW3 120 DC61
North End Way
Inverforth Rd. N11 99 DH50
Inverine Rd. SE7 164 EH78
Invermore Pl. SE18 165 EQ77
Inverness Ave., Enf. 82 DS39
Inverness Dr., Ilf. 103 ES51
Inverness Gdns. W8 140 DB74
Vicarage Gate
Inverness Ms. W2 140 DB73
Inverness Ter.
Inverness Pl. W2 140 DB73
Inverness Rd. N18 100 DV50
Aberdeen Rd.
Inverness Rd., Houns. 156 BZ84
Inverness Rd., Sthl. 156 BY77
Inverness Rd., Wor.Pk. 199 CX102
Inverness St. NW1 141 DH67
Inverness Ter. W2 140 DB73
Inverton Rd. SE15 163 DX84
Invicta Clo., Chis. 185 EN92
Invicta Gro., Nthlt. 136 BZ69
Invicta Plaza SE1 278 F2
Invicta Rd. SE3 164 EG80
Invicta Rd., Dart. 188 FP86
Inville Rd. SE17 162 DR78
Inwen Ct. SE8 163 DY78
Inwood Ave., Couls. 235 DN120
Inwood Ave., Houns. 156 CC83
Inwood Clo., Croy. 203 DY103
Inwood Ct., Walt. 196 BW103
Inwood Rd., Houns. 156 CB84
Inworth St. SW11 160 DE82
Inworth Wk. N1 142 DQ67
Popham St.
Ion Sq. E2 142 DU68
Hackney Rd.
Iona Clo. SE6 183 EA87
Iona Clo., Mord. 200 DB101
Iona Cres., Slou. 131 AL72
Ionian Way, Hem.H. 40 BM18
Jupiter Dr.
Ipswich Rd. SW17 180 DG93
Ipswich Rd., Slou. 131 AN73
Ireland Clo. E6 145 EM71
Bradley Stone Rd.
Ireland Pl. N22 99 DL52
Whittington Rd.
Ireland Yd. EC4 274 G9
Ireland Yd. EC4 141 DP72
Irene Rd. SW6 160 DA81
Irene Rd., Cob. 214 CB114
Irene Rd., Orp. 205 ET101
Ireton Ave., Walt. 195 BS103
Ireton Clo. N10 98 DG52
Cromwell Rd.
Ireton Pl., Grays 170 GA77
Russell Rd.
Ireton St. E3 143 EA70
Tidworth Rd.
Iris Ave., Bex. 186 EY86
Iris Clo. E6 144 EL70
Iris Clo., Brwd. 108 FV43
Iris Clo., Croy. 203 DX102
Iris Clo., Surb. 198 CM101
Iris Ct., Pnr. 116 BW55
Iris Cres., Bexh. 166 EZ79
Iris Path, Rom. 106 FJ52
Clematis Clo.
Iris Rd., Epsom 216 CP106
Iris Way E4 101 DZ51
Irkdale Ave., Enf. 82 DT39
Iron Bri. Clo. NW10 118 CS64
Iron Bri. Clo., Sthl. 136 CC74
Iron Bri. Rd., Uxb. 154 BN75
Iron Bri. Rd., West Dr. 154 BN75
Iron Dr., Hert. 32 DV08
Iron Mill La., Dart. 167 FE84
Iron Mill Pl. SW18 180 DB86
Garratt La.
Iron Mill Pl., Dart. 167 FF84
Iron Mill Rd. SW18 180 DB86
Ironmonger La. EC2 275 K9
Ironmonger Pas. EC1 275 J4
Ironmonger Row EC1 275 J4
Ironmonger Row EC1 142 DQ69
Ironmongers Pl. E14 163 EA77
Spindrift Ave.
Irons Bottom, Horl. 268 DA146
Irons Way, Rom. 105 FC52
Ironsbottom, Reig. 265 CZ143
Ironside Clo. SE16 163 DX75
Kinburn St.
Irvine Ave., Har. 117 CG55
Irvine Clo. N20 98 DE47
Irvine Gdns., S.Ock. 149 FT72
Irvine Pl., Vir.W. 192 AY99
Irvine Way, Orp. 205 ET101
Irving Ave., Nthlt. 136 BX67
Irving Gro. SW9 161 DM82
Irving Rd. W14 159 CX76
Irving St. WC2 277 N1
Irving St. WC2 141 DK73
Irving Wk., Swans. 190 FY87
Durrant Way
Irving Way NW9 119 CT57
Irving Way, Swan. 207 FD96
Irwin Ave. SE18 165 ES80
Irwin Clo., Uxb. 114 BN62
Irwin Gdns. NW10 139 CV67
Irwin Rd., Guil. 258 AU136
Isabel Gate (Cheshunt), Wal.Cr. 67 DZ26
Isabel St. SW9 161 DM81
Isabella Clo. N14 99 DJ45
Isabella Dr., Orp. 223 EQ105
Isabella Rd. E9 122 DW64
Isabella St. SE1 278 F3
Isabella St. SE1 141 DP74
Isabelle Clo., Wal.Cr. 66 DQ29
Isambard Clo., Uxb. 134 BK69
Isambard Ms. E14 163 EC76
Isambard Pl. SE16 142 DW74
Rotherhithe St.
Isbell Gdns., Rom. 105 FE52
Isbells Dr., Reig. 266 DB136
Isel Way SE22 182 DS85
East Dulwich Gro.
Isenburg Way, Hem.H. 40 BK15
Isham Rd. SW16 201 DL96
Isis Clo. SW15 159 CW84
Isis Clo., Ruis. 115 BQ58
Isis Dr., Upmin. 129 FS58
Isis St. SW18 180 DC89
Isla Rd. SE18 165 EQ79
Island, The, Stai. 173 BA90
Island, The, West Dr. 154 BH81
Island Clo., Stai. 173 BE91
Island Fm. Ave., W.Mol. 196 BZ99
Island Fm. Rd., W.Mol. 196 BZ99
Island Rd., Mitch. 180 DF94
Island Row E14 143 DZ72
Commercial Rd.
Islay Gdns., Houns. 176 BX85
Islay Wk. N1 142 DQ66
Douglas Rd.
Isledon Rd. N7 121 DN62
Islehurst Clo., Chis. 205 EN95
Islet Pk. Dr., Maid. 130 AC68
Islet Pk. Rd., Maid. 130 AC68
Isleworth Business Complex, Islw. 157 CF82
St. John's Rd.
Isleworth Prom., Twick. 157 CH84
Islington Grn. N1 141 DP67
Islington High St. N1 274 E1
Islington High St. N1 141 DP68
Islington Pk. Ms. N1 141 DN66
Islington Pk. St.
Islington Pk. St. N1 141 DN66
Islip Gdns., Edg. 96 CR52
Islip Gdns., Nthlt. 136 BY66
Islip Manor Rd., Nthlt. 136 BY66
Islip St. NW5 121 DJ64
Ismailia Rd. E7 144 EH66
Ismay Ct., Slou. 132 AS73
Elliman Ave.
Isom Clo. E13 144 EJ70
Belgrave Rd.
Istead Ri., Grav. 191 GF94
Itchingwood Common Rd., Oxt. 254 EJ133
Ivanhoe Clo., Uxb. 134 BK71
Ivanhoe Dr., Har. 117 CG55
Ivanhoe Rd. SE5 162 DT83
Ivanhoe Rd., Houns. 156 BX83
Ivatt Pl. W14 159 CZ78
Ivatt Way N17 121 DP55
Ive Fm. Clo. E10 123 EA61
Ive Fm. La. E10 123 EA61
Iveagh Ave. NW10 138 CN68
Iveagh Clo. E9 143 DX67
Iveagh Clo. NW10 138 CN68
Iveagh Clo., Nthwd. 93 BP53
Iveagh Rd., Guil. 258 AV135
Iveagh Rd., Wok. 226 AT118
Iveagh Ter. NW10 138 CN68
Iveagh Ave.
Ivedon Rd., Well. 166 EW82
Iveley Rd. SW4 161 DJ82
Iver La., Uxb. 134 BH71
Iver Rd., Brwd. 108 FV44
Iver Rd., Iver 134 BG72
Iverdale Clo., Iver 133 BC73
Ivere Dr., Barn. 80 DB44
Iverhurst Clo., Bexh. 186 EX85
Iverna Ct. W8 160 DA76
Iverna Gdns. W8 160 DA76
Iverna Gdns., Felt. 175 BR85
Ivers Way, Croy. 221 EB108
Iverson Rd. NW6 139 CZ65
Ives Gdns., Rom. 127 FF56
Sims Clo.
Ives Rd. E16 144 EE71
Ives Rd., Hert. 31 DP08
Ives Rd., Slou. 153 AZ76
Ives St. SW3 276 C8
Ives St. SW3 160 DE77
Ivestor Ter. SE23 182 DW87
Ivimey St. E2 142 DU69
Ivinghoe Clo., Enf. 82 DS40
Ivinghoe Clo., St.Alb. 43 CJ15
Highview Gdns.
Ivinghoe Clo., Wat. 76 BX35
Ivinghoe Rd., Dag. 126 EV64
Ivinghoe Rd., Rick. 92 BG45
Ivinghoe Rd. (Bushey), Wat. 95 CD45
Ivins Rd., Beac. 88 AG54
Ivor Clo., Guil. 259 AZ135
Ivor Gro. SE9 185 EP88
Ivor Pl. NW1 272 D5
Ivor Pl. NW1 140 DF70
Ivor St. NW1 141 DJ66
Ivory Ct., Hem.H. 40 BL23
Ivory Sq. SW11 160 DC83
Gartons Way
Ivorydown, Brom. 184 EG91
Ivy Bower Clo., Green. 189 FV85
Riverview Rd.
Ivy Chimneys Rd., Epp. 69 ES32
Ivy Clo., Dart. 188 FN87
Ivy Clo., Grav. 191 GJ90
Ivy Clo., Har. 116 BZ63
Ivy Clo., Pnr. 116 BW59
Ivy Clo., Sun. 196 BW96
Ivy Cotts. E14 143 EB73
Grove Vil.
Ivy Ct. SE16 162 DU78
Argyle Way
Ivy Cres. W4 158 CQ77
Ivy Cres., Slou. 131 AM73
Ivy Gdns. N8 121 DL58
Ivy Gdns., Mitch. 201 DK97
Ivy Ho. La., Berk. 38 AY19
Ivy Ho. La., Sev. 241 FD118
Ivy Ho. Rd., Uxb. 115 BP62
Ivy La., Houns. 156 BZ84
Ivy La., Sev. 240 EY116
Ivy La., Wok. 227 BB117
Ivy Lea, Rick. 92 BG46
Springwell Ave.
Ivy Lo. La., Rom. 106 FP53
Ivy Mill Clo., Gdse. 252 DV132
Ivy Mill La., Gdse. 252 DU132
Ivy Pl., Surb. 198 CM100
Alpha Rd.
Ivy Rd. E16 144 EG72
Pacific Rd.
Ivy Rd. E17 123 EA58
Ivy Rd. N14 99 DJ45
Ivy Rd. NW2 119 CW63
Ivy Rd. SE4 163 DZ84
Ivy Rd. SW17 180 DE92
Tooting High St.
Ivy Rd., Houns. 156 CB84
Ivy Rd., Surb. 198 CN102
Ivy St. N1 142 DS68
Ivy Ter., Hodd. 49 EC15
Ivy Wk., Dag. 146 EY65
Ivybridge, Brox. 49 EA19
Ivybridge Clo., Twick. 177 CG87
Ivybridge Clo., Uxb. 134 BL69
Ivybridge Est., Islw. 177 CF85
Ivybridge La. WC2 278 A1
Ivychurch Clo. SE20 182 DW94
Ivychurch La. SE17 279 P10
Ivydale Rd. SE15 163 DX83
Ivydale Rd., Cars. 200 DF103
Ivyday Gro. SW16 181 DM90
Ivydene, W.Mol. 196 BZ99
Ivydene Clo., Red. 267 DH139
Ivydene Clo., Sutt. 218 DC105
Ivyhouse Rd., Dag. 146 EX65
Ivymount Rd. SE27 181 DN90
Ixworth Pl. SW3 276 B10
Ixworth Pl. SW3 160 DE78
Izane Rd., Bexh. 166 EZ84

J

Jacaranda Clo., N.Mal. 198 CS97
Jack Barnett Way N22 99 DM54
Jack Clow Rd. E15 144 EE68
Jack Cornwell St. E12 125 EN63
Jack Dash Way E6 144 EL70
Jack Stevens Clo., Harl. 52 EW17
Hillside
Jack Walker Ct. N5 121 DP63
Jackass La., Kes. 222 EH107
Jackass La., Oxt. 253 DZ131
Jackdaws, Welw.G.C. 30 DC09
Jackets La., Nthwd. 93 BP53
Jackets La. (Harefield), Uxb. 92 BN52
Jacketts Fld., Abb.L. 59 BT31
Jacklin Grn., Wdf.Grn. 102 EG49
Jackman Ms. NW10 118 CS62
Jackman St. E8 142 DV67
Jackmans La., Wok. 226 AU119
Jacks La. (Harefield), Uxb. 92 BG53
Jackson Clo. E9 142 DW66
Jackson Clo., Epsom 216 CR114
Jackson Clo., Green. 189 FU85
Cowley Ave.
Jackson Clo., Horn. 128 FM56
Jackson Clo., Uxb. 134 BL66
Jackson Rd.
Jackson Rd. N7 121 DM63
Jackson Rd., Bark. 145 ER67
Jackson Rd., Barn. 80 DE44
Jackson Rd., Brom. 204 EL103
Jackson Rd., Uxb. 134 BL66
Jackson St. SE18 165 EN79
Jackson Way, Sthl. 156 CB75
Jacksons Dr., Wal.Cr. 66 DU28
Jacksons La. N6 120 DG59
Jacksons Pl., Croy. 202 DR102
Cross Rd.
Jacksons Way, Croy. 203 EA104
Jacob Ho., Erith 166 EX75
Kale Rd.
Jacob St. SE1 162 DU75
Jacobs Ave., Rom. 106 FL54
Jacobs Clo., Dag. 127 FB63
Jacobs Clo., Wind. 151 AL81
Jacobs Ho. E13 144 EJ69
Jacobs Ladder, Hat. 45 CW18
The Bdy.
Jacobs La., Dart. 208 FQ97
Jacob's Well Ms. W1 272 G8
Jacob's Well Rd., Guil. 242 AX129
Jacqueline Clo., Nthlt. 136 BZ67
Canford Ave.
Jade Clo. E16 144 EK72
Jade Clo. NW2 119 CX59
Marble Dr.
Jade Clo., Dag. 126 EW60
Jaffe Rd., Ilf. 125 EQ60
Jaffray Pl. SE27 181 DP91
Chapel Rd.
Jaffray Rd., Brom. 204 EK98
Jaggard Way SW12 180 DF87
Jagger Clo., Dart. 188 FQ87
Jago Clo. SE18 165 EQ79
Jago Wk. SE5 162 DR80
Jail La. (Biggin Hill), West. 238 EK115
Jamaica Rd. SE1 162 DU75
Jamaica Rd. SE16 162 DV75
Jamaica Rd., Th.Hth. 201 DP100
Jamaica St. E1 142 DW72
James Ave. NW2 119 CW64
James Ave., Dag. 126 EZ60
James Bedford Clo., Pnr. 94 BW54
James Boswell Clo. SW16 181 DN91
Curtis Fld. Rd.
James Clo. E13 144 EG68
Richmond St.
James Clo. NW11 119 CY58
Woodlands
James Clo., Rom. 127 FG57
James Clo. (Bushey), Wat. 76 BY43
Aldenham Rd.
James Collins Clo. W9 139 CZ70
Fermoy Rd.
James Ct. N1 142 DQ66
Morton Rd.
James Dudson Ct. NW10 138 CQ66
James Gdns. N22 99 DP52
James Hammett Ho. E2 142 DT69
Ravenscroft St.
James Joyce Wk. SE24 161 DP84
Shakespeare Rd.
James La. E10 123 ED59
James La. E11 123 ED58
James Martin Clo. (Denham), Uxb. 114 BG58
James Newman Ct. SE9 185 EN90
Great Harry Dr.
James Pl. N17 100 DT53
James Rd., Dart. 187 FF87
James Rd., Guil. 258 AW142
James Sinclair Pt. E13 144 EJ67
James St. W1 272 G8
James St. W1 140 DG72
James St. WC2 274 A10
James St., Bark. 145 EQ66
James St., Enf. 82 DT43
James St., Epp. 69 ET28
James St., Houns. 157 CD83
James St., Wind. 151 AR81
James Ter. SW14 158 CR83
Addington Ct.
James Yd. E4 101 ED51
Larkshall Rd.
Jameson Clo. W3 158 CQ75
Acton La.
Jameson Ct., St.Alb. 43 CF19
Avenue Rd.
Jameson St. W8 140 DA74
James's Cotts., Rich. 158 CN80
Kew Rd.
Jamestown Rd. NW1 141 DH67
Jamestown Way E14 143 ED73
Jamieson Ho., Houns. 176 BZ86
Jamnagar Clo., Stai. 173 BF93
Jane St. E1 142 DV72
Commercial Rd.
Janet St. E14 163 EA76
Janeway Pl. SE16 162 DV75
Janeway St.
Janeway St. SE16 162 DU75
Janice Ms., Ilf. 125 EP62
Oakfield Rd.
Janmead, Brwd. 109 GB45
Janoway Hill La., Wok. 226 AW119
Firbank La.
Jansen Wk. SW11 160 DD84
Hope St.
Janson Clo. E15 124 EE64
Janson Rd.
Janson Clo. NW10 118 CR62
Janson Rd. E15 124 EE64
Jansons Rd. N15 122 DS55
Japan Cres. N4 121 DM59
Japan Rd., Rom. 126 EX58
Japonica Clo., Wok. 226 AW118
Jardine Rd. E1 143 DX73
Jarman Clo., Hem.H. 40 BL22
Jarmans Way, Hem.H. 40 BM21
Jarrah Cotts., Purf. 169 FR79
London Rd. Purfleet
Jarrett Clo. SW2 181 DP88
Jarrow Clo., Mord. 200 DB99
Jarrow Rd. N17 122 DV56
Jarrow Rd. SE16 162 DW77
Jarrow Rd., Rom. 126 EW58
Jarrow Way E9 123 DY63
Jarvis Cleys (Cheshunt), Wal.Cr. 66 DT26
Jarvis Clo., Bark. 145 ER67
Westbury Rd.
Jarvis Clo., Barn. 79 CX43
Jarvis Rd. SE22 162 DS84
Melbourne Gro.
Jarvis Rd., S.Croy. 220 DR107
Jarvis Way, Rom. 106 FL54
Jasmin Clo., Nthwd. 93 BT53
Jasmin Rd., Epsom 216 CP106
Jasmin Way, Hem.H. 39 BE19
Jasmine Clo., Ilf. 125 EP64
Jasmine Clo., Orp. 205 EP103
Jasmine Clo., Red. 266 DG139
Spencer Way
Jasmine Clo., Sthl. 136 BY73
Jasmine Clo., Wok. 226 AT116
Jasmine Dr., Hert. 32 DU09

Jas - Kei This index reads in the sequence: Street Name / Postal District or Post Town / Map Page Number / Grid Reference

Jasmine Gdns., Croy. 203 EB104
Jasmine Gdns., Har. 116 CA61
Jasmine Gdns., Hat. 45 CU16
Jasmine Gro. SE20 202 DV95
Jasmine Rd., Rom. 127 FE61
Jasmine Ter., West Dr. 154 BN75
Jasmine Way, E.Mol. 197 CE98
Hampton Ct. Way
Jason Clo., Brwd. 108 FT49
Jason Clo., Red. 266 DE139
Jason Clo., Wey. 213 BQ106
Jason Ct. W1 140 DG72
Marylebone La.
Jason Wk. SE9 185 EN91
Jasons Dr., Guil. 243 BC131
Jasons Hill, Chesh. 56 AV30
Jasper Clo., Enf. 82 DW38
Jasper Pas. SE19 182 DT93
Jasper Rd. E16 144 EK72
Jasper Rd. SE19 182 DT92
Jasper Wk. N1 275 K2
Javelin Way, Nthlt. 136 BX69
Jay Gdns., Chis. 185 EM91
Jay Ms. SW7 160 DC75
Jaycroft, Enf. 81 DN39
The Ridgeway
Jays Covert, Couls. 234 DG120
Jebb Ave. SW2 181 DL86
Jebb St. E3 143 EA68
Jedburgh Rd. E13 144 EJ69
Jedburgh St. SW11 160 DG84
Jeddo Rd. W12 159 CT75
Jefferson Clo. W13 157 CH76
Jefferson Clo., Ilf. 125 EP57
Jefferson Clo., Slou. 153 BA77
Jefferson Wk. SE18 165 EN79
Kempt St.
Jeffreys Pl. NW1 141 DJ66
Jeffreys St.
Jeffreys Rd. SW4 161 DL82
Jeffreys Rd., Enf. 83 DZ41
Jeffreys St. NW1 141 DH66
Jeffreys Wk. SW4 161 DL82
Jeffries Ho. NW10 138 CR67
Jeffries Pas., Guil. 258 AX135
High St.
Jeffries Rd., Lthd. 245 BP131
Jeffries Rd., Ware 33 DY06
Jeffs Clo., Hmptn. 176 CB93
Uxbridge Rd.
Jeffs Rd., Sutt. 217 CZ105
Jeger Ave. E2 142 DT67
Jeken Rd. SE9 164 EJ84
Jelf Rd. SW2 181 DN85
Jellicoe Ave., Grav. 191 GJ90
Jellicoe Ave. W., Grav. 191 GJ90
Kitchener Ave.
Jellicoe Clo., Slou. 151 AP75
Jellicoe Gdns., Stan. 95 CF51
Jellicoe Rd. E13 144 EG70
Jutland Rd.
Jellicoe Rd. N17 100 DR52
Jellicoe Rd., Wat. 75 BU44
Jemmett Clo., Kings.T. 198 CP95
Jengar Clo., Sutt. 218 DB105
Jenkins Ave., St.Alb. 60 BY30
Jenkins La. E6 145 EN68
Jenkins La., Bark. 145 EP68
Jenkins Rd. E13 144 EH70
Jenner Ave. W3 138 CR71
Jenner Ho. SE3 164 EE79
Jenner Pl. SW13 159 CV79
Jenner Rd. N16 122 DT61
Jenner Rd., Guil. 258 AY135
Jennery La., Slou. 130 AJ69
Jennett Rd., Croy. 201 DN104
Jennifer Rd., Brom. 184 EF90
Jennings Clo., Add. 212 BJ109
Woodham La.
Jennings Fld., H.Wyc. 110 AC56
Jennings Rd. SE22 182 DT86
Jennings Rd., St.Alb. 43 CF19
Jennings Way, Barn. 79 CW41
Jennings Way, Hem.H. 40 BL22
Jenningtree Rd., Erith 167 FH80
Jenningtree Way, Belv. 167 FC75
Jenny Hammond Clo. E11 124 EF62
Newcomen Rd.
Jenny Path, Rom. 106 FK52
Jenson Way SE19 182 DT94
Jenton Ave., Bexh. 166 EY81
Jephson Rd. E7 144 EJ66
Jephson St. SE5 162 DR81
Grove La.
Jephtha Rd. SW18 180 DA86
Jeppos La., Mitch. 200 DF98
Jerdan Pl. SW6 160 DA80
Jeremiah St. E14 143 EB72
Jeremys Grn. N18 100 DV49
Jermyn St. SW1 277 K2
Jermyn St. SW1 141 DK73
Jerningham Ave., Ilf. 103 EP54
Jerningham Rd. SE14 163 DY82
Jerome Cres. NW8 272 B4
Jerome Cres. NW8 140 DE70
Jerome Dr., St.Alb. 42 CA22
Jerome St. E1 275 P6
Jerounds, Harl. 51 EP17
Jerrard St. N1 275 N1
Jerrard St. SE13 163 EB83
Jersey Ave., Stan. 95 CH54
Jersey Clo., Cher. 193 BF104
Jersey Clo., Guil. 243 BB129
Weybrook Dr.
Jersey Clo., Hodd. 49 EA16
Jersey Dr., Orp. 205 ER100
Jersey La., St.Alb. 43 CH18
Jersey Par., Houns. 156 CB81
Jersey Rd. E11 123 ED60
Jersey Rd. E16 144 EJ72
Prince Regent La.
Jersey Rd. SW17 181 DH93
Jersey Rd. W7 157 CG75
Jersey Rd., Houns. 156 CB81
Jersey Rd., Ilf. 125 EP63
Jersey Rd., Islw. 157 CE79
Jersey Rd., Rain. 147 FG66
Jersey St. E2 142 DV69
Bethnal Grn. Rd.
Jerusalem Pas. EC1 274 F5
Jervis Ave., Enf. 83 DY35
Jervis Ct. W1 273 J9
Jerviston Gdns. SW16 181 DN93
Jesmond Ave., Wem. 138 CM65
Jesmond Clo., Mitch. 201 DH97
Jesmond Rd., Croy. 202 DT101
Jesmond Way, Stan. 96 CL50
Jessam Ave. E5 122 DV60
Jessamine Pl., Dart. 188 FQ87
Jessamine Rd. W7 137 CE74
Jessamine Ter., Swan. 207 FC95
Birchwood Rd.
Jessamy Rd., Wey. 195 BP103
Jesse Rd. E10 123 EC60
Jessel Dr., Loug. 85 EQ39
Jesses La., Guil. 261 BQ144
Jessett Clo., Erith 167 FD77
West St.
Jessica Rd. SW18 180 DC86
Jessie Blythe La. N19 121 DL59
Jessiman Ter., Shep. 194 BN99
Jessop Ave., Sthl. 156 BZ77
Jessop Rd. SE24 161 DP84
Milkwood Rd.
Jessop Sq. E14 143 EA74
Heron Quay
Jessops Way, Croy. 201 DJ100
Jessup Clo. SE18 165 EQ77
Jetstar Way, Nthlt. 136 BY69
Jetty Wk., Grays 170 GA79
Jevington Way SE12 184 EH88
Jewel Rd. E17 123 EA55
Jewels Hill, West. 222 EG112
Jewry St. EC3 275 P9
Jewry St. EC3 142 DT72
Jew's Row SW18 160 DC84
Jews Wk. SE26 182 DV91
Jeymer Ave. NW2 119 CV64
Jeymer Dr., Grnf. 136 CC67
Jeypore Pas. SW18 180 DC86
Jeypore Rd.
Jeypore Rd. SW18 180 DC87
Jillian Clo., Hmptn. 176 CA94
Jim Bradley Clo. SE18 165 EN77
John Wilson St.
Jim Desormeaux Bungalows, Harl. 35 ES13
School La.
Jinnings, The, Welw.G.C. 30 DA12
Joan Cres. SE9 184 EK87
Joan Gdns., Dag. 126 EY61
Joan Rd., Dag. 126 EY61
Joan St. SE1 278 F3
Joan St. SE1 141 DP74
Jocelyn Rd., Rich. 158 CL83
Jocelyn St. SE15 162 DU81
Jocelyns, Harl. 36 EW11
Jocketts Hill, Hem.H. 39 BF20
Jocketts Rd., Hem.H. 39 BF21
Jockey's Flds. WC1 274 C6
Jockey's Flds. WC1 141 DM71
Jodane St. SE8 163 DZ77
Jodrell Clo., Islw. 157 CG81
Jodrell Rd. E3 143 DZ67
Jodrell Way, Grays 169 FT78
Joel St., Nthwd. 115 BU55
Joel St., Pnr. 115 BU55
Johanna St. SE1 278 D5
John Adam St. WC2 278 A1
John Adam St. WC2 141 DL73
John Aird Ct. W2 140 DC71
John Archer Way SW18 180 DD86
John Ashby Clo. SW2 181 DL86
John Austin Clo., Kings.T. 198 CM95
Queen Elizabeth Rd.
John Barnes Wk. E15 144 EF65
John Bradshaw Rd. N14 99 DK46
High St.
John Burns Dr., Bark. 145 ES66
John Campbell Rd. N16 122 DS64
John Carpenter St. EC4 274 F10
John Carpenter St. EC4 141 DP73
John Cobb Rd., Wey. 212 BN108
John Cornwell VC Ho. E12 125 EN63
John Ct., Hodd. 33 EA14
Molesworth
John Eliot Clo., Wal.Abb. 50 EE21
John Felton Rd. SE16 162 DU75
John Fisher St. E1 142 DU73
John Gooch Dr., Enf. 81 DP39
John Harrison Way SE10 164 EF76
John Horner Ms. N1 142 DQ68
Frome St.
John Islip St. SW1 277 P9
John Islip St. SW1 161 DL77
John Keats Ho. N22 99 DM52
John Maurice Clo. SE17 279 K8
John Maurice Clo. SE17 162 DR77
John McKenna Wk. SE16 162 DU76
Tranton Rd.
John Newton Ct., Well. 166 EV83
Danson La.
John Parker Clo., Dag. 147 FB66
John Parker Sq. SW11 160 DD83
Thomas Baines Rd.
John Penn St. SE13 163 EB81
John Perrin Pl., Har. 118 CL59
John Princes St. W1 273 J8
John Princes St. W1 141 DH72
John Rennie Wk. E1 142 DV74
Wine Clo.
John Roll Way SE16 162 DU76
John Ruskin St. SE5 161 DP80
John Russell Clo., Guil. 242 AU131
John Silkin La. SE8 163 DX77
John Smith Ave. SW6 159 CZ80
John Spencer Sq. N1 141 DP65
John St. E15 144 EF67
John St. SE25 202 DU98
John St. WC1 274 C5
John St. WC1 141 DM70
John St., Enf. 82 DT43
John St., Grays 170 GC79
John St., Houns. 156 BY82
John Tate Rd., Hert. 32 DT10
John Taylor Ct., Slou. 131 AQ74
John Trundle Ct. EC2 142 DQ71
Beech St.
John Walsh Twr. E11 124 EF61
John Williams Clo. SE14 163 DX79
John Wilson St. SE18 165 EN76
John Woolley Clo. SE13 164 EE84
Johnby Clo., Enf. 83 DY37
Manly Dixon Dr.
Johns Ave. NW4 119 CW56
Johns Clo., Ashf. 175 BQ91
John's La., Berk. 38 AT21
Johns La., Mord. 200 DC99
John's Ms. WC1 274 C5
John's Ms. WC1 141 DM70
John's Pl. E1 142 DV72
Damien St.
Johns Rd., West. 238 EK120
John's Ter., Croy. 202 DR102
John's Ter., Rom. 106 FP51
Johns Wk., Whyt. 236 DU119
Johnsdale, Oxt. 254 EF129
Johnson Clo. E8 142 DU67
Johnson Clo., Grav. 190 GD90
Johnson Ct., Hem.H. 40 BL22
Johnson Rd., Brom. 204 EK99
Johnson Rd., Croy. 202 DR101
Johnson Rd., Houns. 156 BW80
Johnson St. E1 142 DW73
Cable St.
Johnson St., Sthl. 156 BW76
Johnsons Ave., Sev. 225 FB110
Johnsons Clo., Cars. 200 DF104
Johnson's Ct. EC4 141 DN72
Fleet St.
Johnsons Ct., Sev. 257 FM121
School La.
Johnsons Dr., Hmptn. 196 CC95
Johnson's Pl. SW1 161 DJ78
Johnsons Way NW10 138 CP70
Johnsons Way, Green. 189 FW86
Johnsons Yd., Uxb. 134 BJ66
Redford Way
Johnston Clo. SW9 161 DM81
Hackford Rd.
Johnston Grn., Guil. 242 AU130
Johnston Rd., Wdf.Grn. 102 EG50
Johnston Ter. NW2 119 CX62
Campion Ter.
Johnston Wk., Guil. 242 AU130
Johnstone Rd. E6 145 EM69
Joiner St. SE1 279 L3
Joiner's Arms Yd. SE5 162 DR81
Denmark Hill
Joiners Clo., Chesh. 56 AV30
Joiners Clo., Ger.Cr. 91 AZ52
Joiners La., Ger.Cr. 90 AY53
Joiners Way, Ger.Cr. 90 AY52
Joinville Pl., Add. 212 BK105
Jolliffe Rd., Red. 251 DJ126
Jollys La., Har. 117 CD60
Jollys La., Hayes 136 BX71
Jonathan Ct. W4 158 CS77
Windmill Rd.
Jonathan St. SE11 278 B10
Jonathan St. SE11 161 DM78
Jones Rd. E13 144 EH70
Holborn Rd.
Jones Rd. (Cheshunt), Wal.Cr. 65 DP30
Jones St. W1 277 H1
Jones Wk., Rich. 178 CM86
Pyrland Rd.
Jones Way, Slou. 111 AR61
Jonquil Clo., Welw.G.C. 30 DB11
Jonquil Gdns., Hmptn. 176 BZ93
Partridge Rd.
Jonson Clo., Hayes 135 BU71
Jonson Clo., Mitch. 201 DH98
Jordan Clo., Dag. 127 FB63
Muggeridge Rd.
Jordan Clo., Har. 116 BZ62
Hamilton Cres.
Jordan Clo., S.Croy. 220 DT111
Jordan Clo., Wat. 75 BT35
Jordan Rd., Grnf. 137 CH67
Jordans Clo., Guil. 243 BA133
Beatty Ave.
Jordans Clo., Islw. 157 CE81
Jordans Clo., Red. 266 DG139
Spencer Way
Jordans Clo., Stai. 174 BJ87
Jordans La., Beac. 90 AS53
Jordans Rd., Rick. 92 BG45
Jordans Way, Beac. 90 AT51
Jordans Way, Rain. 148 FK68
Jordans Way, St.Alb. 60 BZ30
Joseph Ave. W3 138 CR72
Joseph Locke Way, Esher 196 CA103
Mill Rd.
Joseph Powell Clo. SW12 181 DH86
Hazelbourne Rd.
Joseph Ray Rd. E11 124 EE61
Joseph St. E3 143 DZ70
Josephine Ave. SW2 181 DM85
Josephine Ave., Tad. 249 CZ126
Josephine Clo., Tad. 249 CZ127
Joseph's Rd., Guil. 242 AW133
Joshua St. E14 143 EC72
St. Leonards Rd.
Joslin Rd., Purf. 168 FQ78
Joslyn Clo., Enf. 83 EA38
Joubert St. SW11 160 DF82
Journeys End, Slou. 132 AS71
Jowett St. SE15 162 DT80
Joy Rd., Grav. 191 GJ88
Joyce Ave. N18 100 DT50
Joyce Ct., Wal.Abb. 67 ED34
Joyce Dawson Way SE28 146 EU73
Thamesmere Dr.
Joyce Grn. La., Dart. 168 FL81
Joyce Grn. Wk., Dart. 168 FM84
Joyce Page Clo. SE7 164 EK79
Lansdowne La.
Joyce Wk. SW2 181 DN86
Joydens Wd. Rd., Bex. 187 FD91
Joydon Dr., Rom. 126 EV58
Joyes Clo., Rom. 106 FK49
Joyners Clo., Dag. 126 EZ63
Joyners Fld., Harl. 51 EQ19
Jubb Powell Ho. N15 122 DS58
Jubilee Ave. E4 101 EC51
Jubilee Ave., Rom. 127 FB57
Jubilee Ave., St.Alb. 61 CK26
Jubilee Ave., Twick. 176 CC87
Jubilee Ave., Ware 33 DZ05
Jubilee Clo. NW9 118 CR58
Jubilee Clo., Green. 189 FW86
Jubilee Clo., Pnr. 94 BW54
Jubilee Clo., Rom. 127 FB57
Jubilee Clo., Stai. 174 BJ87
Jubilee Ct., Hat. 45 CV15
Jubilee Ct., Stai. 174 BG92
Leacroft
Jubilee Ct., Wal.Abb. 68 EF33
Jubilee Cres. E14 163 EC76
Jubilee Cres. N9 100 DU46
Jubilee Cres., Add. 212 BK106
Jubilee Cres., Grav. 191 GL89
Jubilee Dr., Ruis. 116 BX63
Jubilee Gdns., Sthl. 136 CA72
Jubilee Pl. SW3 276 C10
Jubilee Pl. SW3 160 DE78
Jubilee Ri., Sev. 257 FM121
Jubilee Rd., Grays 169 FV79
Jubilee Rd., Grnf. 137 CH67
Jubilee Rd., Orp. 224 FA107
Jubilee Rd., Sutt. 217 CX108
Jubilee Rd., Wat. 75 BU38
Jubilee St. E1 142 DW72
Jubilee Ter., Bet. 264 CP138
Jubilee Ter., Dor. 263 CH135
Jubilee Wk., Wat. 93 BV49
Jubilee Way SW19 200 DB95
Jubilee Way, Chess. 216 CN105
Jubilee Way, Felt. 175 BT88
Jubilee Way, Sid. 186 EU89
Judd St. WC1 273 P3
Judd St. WC1 141 DL69
Jude St. E16 144 EF72
Judeth Gdns., Grav. 191 GL92
Judge Heath La., Hayes 135 BQ72
Judge Heath La., Uxb. 135 BQ72
Judge St., Wat. 75 BV38
Judge Wk., Esher 215 CE107
Judges Hill, Pot.B. 64 DE29
Judith Ave., Rom. 105 FB51
Juer St. SW11 160 DE80
Juglans Rd., Orp. 206 EU102
Julia Gdns., Bark. 146 EX68
Julia Garfield Ms. E16 144 EH74
Wesley Ave.
Julia St. NW5 120 DG63
Oak Village
Julian Ave. W3 138 CP73
Julian Clo., Barn. 80 DB41
Julian Clo., Wok. 226 AW118
Julian Hill, Har. 117 CE61
Julian Hill, Wey. 212 BN108
Julian Pl. E14 163 EB78
Julian Rd., Orp. 224 EU107
Juliana Clo. N2 120 DB55
East End Rd.
Julians Clo., Sev. 256 FG127
Julians Way, Sev. 256 FG127
Julien Rd. W5 157 CJ76
Julien Rd., Couls. 235 DK115
Juliette Rd. E13 144 EF68
Juliette Way, S.Ock. 168 FM75
Junction App. SE13 163 EC83
Junction App. SW11 160 DE83
Junction Ave. W10 139 CW69
Harrow Rd.
Junction Ms. W2 272 B8
Junction Pl. W2 272 B8
Junction Rd. E13 144 EH68
Junction Rd. N9 100 DU46
Junction Rd. N17 122 DU55
Junction Rd. N19 121 DJ63
Junction Rd. W5 157 CK77
Junction Rd., Ashf. 175 BQ92
Junction Rd., Brent. 157 CK77
Junction Rd., Brwd. 108 FW49
Junction Rd., Dart. 188 FK86
Junction Rd., Dor. 263 CG136
Junction Rd., Har. 117 CE58
Junction Rd., Rom. 127 FF56
Junction Rd., S.Croy. 220 DR106
Junction Rd. E., Rom. 126 EY61
Kenneth Rd.
Junction Rd. W., Rom. 126 EY59
June Clo., Couls. 219 DH114
June La., Red. 267 DH141
Junewood Clo., Add. 211 BF111
Juniper Ave., St.Alb. 60 CA31
Juniper Clo., Barn. 79 CX43
Juniper Clo., Brox. 67 DZ25
Juniper Clo., Chess. 216 CM107
Juniper Clo., Guil. 242 AV129
Juniper Clo., Reig. 266 DC136
Juniper Clo., Rick. 92 BK48
Juniper Clo., Wem. 118 CM64
Juniper Clo., West. 238 EL117
Juniper Ct., Slou. 152 AU75
Nixey Clo.
Juniper Cres. NW1 140 DG66
Juniper Gdns. SW16 201 DJ95
Leonard Rd.
Juniper Gdns. (Shenley), Rad. 62 CL33
Juniper Gdns., Sun. 175 BT93
Juniper Gate, Rick. 92 BK47
Juniper Grn., Hem.H. 39 BE20
Juniper Gro., Wat. 75 BU38
Juniper La. E6 144 EL71
Juniper La., H.Wyc. 110 AD56
Juniper Rd., Ilf. 125 EN63
Juniper Rd., Reig. 266 DC136
Juniper St. E1 142 DW73
Juniper Wk., Bet. 264 CQ136
Warrenne Rd.
Juniper Wk., Swan. 207 FD96
Pear Tree Clo.
Juniper Way, Hayes 135 BR73
Juniper Way, Rom. 106 FL53
Juno Rd., Hem.H. 40 BM17
Saturn Way
Juno Way SE14 163 DX79
Jupiter Dr., Hem.H. 40 BM18
Jupiter Way N7 141 DM65
Jupp Rd. E15 143 ED66
Jupp Rd. W. E15 143 EC67
Jurgens Rd., Purf. 169 FR79
London Rd. Purfleet
Justice Wk. SW3 160 DE79
Lawrence St.
Justin Clo., Brent. 157 CK80
Justin Rd. E4 101 DZ51
Jute La., Enf. 83 DY40
Jutland Clo. N19 121 DL60
Sussex Way
Jutland Gdns., Couls. 235 DL120
Goodenough Way
Jutland Pl., Egh. 173 BC92
Mullens Rd.
Jutland Rd. E13 144 EG70
Jutland Rd. SE6 183 EC87
Jutsums Ave., Rom. 127 FB58
Jutsums La., Rom. 127 FB58
Juxon Clo., Har. 94 CB53
Augustine Rd.
Juxon St. SE11 278 C8
Juxon St. SE11 161 DM77

K

Kaduna Clo., Pnr. 115 BU57
Kale Rd., Erith 166 EY75
Kambala Rd. SW11 160 DD83
Kandlewood, Brwd. 109 GB45
Kangley Bri. Rd. SE26 183 DZ92
Kaplan Dr. N21 81 DM43
Kara Way NW2 119 CX63
Karen Clo., Brwd. 108 FW45
Karen Clo., Rain. 147 FE68
Karen Ct. SE4 163 DZ82
Wickham Rd.
Karen Ct., Brom. 204 EF95
Blyth Rd.
Karen Ter. E11 124 EF61
Montague Rd.
Karenza Ct., Wem. 117 CJ59
Lulworth Ave.
Karina Clo., Chig. 103 ES50
Karoline Gdns., Grnf. 137 CD68
Oldfield La. N.
Kashgar Rd. SE18 165 ET77
Kashmir Clo., Add. 212 BK109
Kashmir Rd. SE7 164 EK80
Kassala Rd. SW11 160 DF81
Katella Trd. Est., Bark. 145 ES69
Kates Clo., Barn. 79 CU43
Kates Cft., Welw.G.C. 29 CY13
Katharine St., Croy. 202 DQ104
Katherine Clo. SE16 143 DX74
Rotherhithe St.
Katherine Clo., Add. 212 BG107
Katherine Clo., Hem.H. 40 BL23
Katherine Clo., H.Wyc. 88 AC47
Katherine Gdns. SE9 164 EK84
Katherine Gdns., Ilf. 103 EQ52
Katherine Rd. E6 144 EK66
Katherine Rd. E7 124 EJ64
Katherine Rd., Twick. 177 CG88
London Rd.
Katherine Sq. W11 139 CY74
Wilsham St.
Katherines Way, Harl. 51 EN18
Kathleen Ave. W3 138 CQ71
Kathleen Ave., Wem. 138 CL66
Kathleen Rd. SW11 160 DF83
Katrine Sq., Hem.H. 40 BK16
Kavanaghs Rd., Brwd. 108 FU48
Kavanaghs Ter., Brwd. 108 FV48
Kavanaghs Rd.
Kay Rd. SW9 161 DL82
Kay St. E2 142 DU68
Kay St. E15 143 ED66
Kay St., Well. 166 EV81
Kaye Ct., Guil. 242 AW131
Kaye Don Way, Wey. 212 BN111
Kayemoor Rd., Sutt. 218 DE108
Kaywood Clo., Slou. 152 AW76
Kean St. WC2 274 B9
Kean St. WC2 141 DM72
Kearton Clo., Ken. 236 DQ117
Keary Rd., Swans. 190 FY87
Keatley Grn. E4 101 DZ51
Keats Ave. E16 144 EH74
Wesley Ave.
Keats Ave., Red. 250 DG132
Keats Ave., Rom. 105 FH52
Keats Clo. E11 124 EH57
Nightingale La.
Keats Clo. NW3 120 DE63
Keats Gro.
Keats Clo. SE1 279 P9
Keats Clo. SW19 180 DD93
North Rd.
Keats Clo., Chig. 103 EQ51
Keats Clo., Enf. 83 DX43
Keats Clo., Hayes 135 BU71
Keats Gdns., Til. 171 GH82
Keats Gro. NW3 120 DD63
Keats Ho., Beck. 183 EA93
Keats La., Wind. 151 AR79
Keats Pl. EC2 275 K7
Keats Rd., Belv. 167 FC76
Keats Rd., Well. 165 ES81
Keats Wk., Brwd. 109 GD45
Byron Rd.
Keats Way, Croy. 202 DW100
Keats Way, Grnf. 136 CB71
Keats Way, West Dr. 154 BM77
Keble Clo., Nthlt. 116 CC64
Keble Clo., Wor.Pk. 199 CT102
Keble Pl. SW13 159 CV79
Somerville Ave.
Keble St. SW17 180 DC91
Keble Ter., Abb.L. 59 BT32
Kechill Gdns., Brom. 204 EG101
Kedelston Ct. E5 123 DX63
Redwald Rd.
Kedleston Dr., Orp. 205 ET99
Kedleston Wk. E2 142 DV69
Middleton St.
Keedonwood Rd., Brom. 184 EE92
Keefield, Harl. 51 EP20
Keel Clo. SE16 143 DX74
Keel Clo., Bark. 146 EY69
Choats Rd.
Keel Dr., Slou. 151 AP75
Keele Clo., Wat. 76 BW40
Keeler Clo., Wind. 151 AL83
Keeley Rd., Croy. 202 DQ103
Keeley St. WC2 274 B9
Keeley St. WC2 141 DM72
Keeling Rd. SE9 184 EK85
Keely Clo., Barn. 80 DE43
Keemor Clo. SE18 165 EN80
Llanover Rd.
Keens Clo. SW16 181 DK92
Keens La., Guil. 242 AT130
Keens Pk. Rd., Guil. 242 AT130
Keens Rd., Croy. 220 DQ105
Keens Yd. N1 141 DP65
St. Paul's Rd.
Keensacre, Iver 133 BD68
Keep, The SE3 164 EG82
Keep, The, Kings.T. 178 CM93
Keep La. N11 98 DG49
Gardeners Clo.
Keepers Clo., Guil. 243 BD131
Keepers Fm. Clo., Wind. 151 AL82
Keepers Ms., Tedd. 177 CJ93
Keepers Wk., Vir.W. 192 AX99
Keesey St. SE17 162 DR79
Keetons Rd. SE16 162 DV76
Keevil Dr. SW19 179 CX87
Keighley Clo. N7 121 DL64
Penn Rd.
Keighley Rd., Rom. 106 FL52
Keightley Dr. SE9 185 EQ88
Keilder Clo., Uxb. 134 BN68
Charnwood Rd.

Kew Foot Rd., Rich. 158 CL84
Kew Gdns. Rd., Rich. 158 CM80
Kew Grn., Rich. 158 CN79
Kew Meadow Path, Rich. 158 CN81
Kew Palace, Rich. 158 CL80
Kew Rd., Rich. 158 CL83
Kewferry Dr., Nthwd. 93 BP50
Kewferry Rd., Nthwd. 93 BQ51
Key Clo. E1 142 DV70
Keybridge Ho. SW8 161 DL79
Keyes Rd. NW2 119 CX64
Keyes Rd., Dart. 168 FM84
Keyfield Ter., St.Alb. 43 CD21
Keymer Clo., West. 238 EJ116
Keymer Rd. SW2 181 DM89
Keynes Clo. N2 120 DF55
Keynsham Ave., Wdf.Grn. 102 EE49
Keynsham Gdns. SE9 184 EL85
Keynsham Rd. SE9 184 EK85
Keynsham Rd., Mord. 200 DB102
Keynsham Wk., Mord. 200 DB102
Keynton Clo., Hert. 31 DM08
Keys, The, Brwd. 107 FW51
Eagle Way
Keyse Rd. SE1 279 P7
Keysers Est., Brox. 49 EB21
Keysers Rd., Brox. 49 EA22
Keysham Ave., Houns. 155 BU81
The Ave.
Keystone Cres. N1 274 A1
Keywood Dr., Sun. 175 BU93
Keyworth Clo. E5 123 DY63
Keyworth St. SE1 278 G6
Keyworth St. SE1 161 DP76
Kezia St. SE8 163 DY78
Trundleys Rd.
Khalsa Ave., Grav. 191 GJ87
Khama Rd. SW17 180 DE91
Khartoum Pl., Grav. 191 GJ86
Khartoum Rd. E13 144 EH69
Khartoum Rd. SW17 180 DD91
Khartoum Rd., Ilf. 125 EP64
Khyber Rd. SW11 160 DE82
Kibes La., Ware 33 DX06
Kibworth St. SW8 161 DM80
Kidborough Down, Lthd. 246 CA127
Kidbrooke Gdns. SE3 164 EG82
Kidbrooke Gro. SE3 164 EG81
Kidbrooke La. SE9 164 EL84
Kidbrooke Pk. Clo. SE3 164 EH81
Kidbrooke Pk. Rd. SE3 164 EH81
Kidbrooke Way SE3 164 EH82
Kidd Pl. SE7 164 EL78
Kidderminster Pl., Croy. 201 DP102
Kidderminster Rd.
Kidderminster Rd., Croy. 201 DP102
Kidderminster Rd., Slou. 131 AN69
Kidderpore Ave. NW3 120 DA63
Kidderpore Gdns. NW3 120 DA63
Kidlington Way NW9 96 CS54
Kidworth Clo., Horl. 268 DF147
Kielder Clo., Ilf. 103 ET51
Kiffen St. EC2 275 L4
Kilberry Clo., Islw. 157 CD81
Kilbride Ct., Hem.H. 40 BL16
Aycliffe Dr.
Kilburn Bri. NW6 139 CZ66
Kilburn High Rd.
Kilburn Bldgs. NW6 140 DB67
Kilburn High Rd.
Kilburn Gate NW6 140 DB68
Kilburn Priory
Kilburn High Rd. NW6 139 CZ66
Kilburn La. W9 139 CX69
Kilburn La. W10 139 CX69
Kilburn Pk. Rd. NW6 140 DA69
Kilburn Pl. NW6 140 DA67
Kilburn Priory NW6 140 DB67
Kilburn Sq. NW6 140 DA67
Kilburn High Rd.
Kilburn Vale NW6 140 DB67
Belsize Rd.
Kilby Clo., Wat. 76 BX35
Kilcorral Clo., Epsom 217 CU114
Kildare Clo., Ruis. 116 BW60
Kildare Gdns. W2 140 DA72
Kildare Rd. E16 144 EG71
Kildare Ter. W2 140 DA72
Kildare Wk. E14 143 EA72
Farrance St.
Kildonan Clo., Wat. 75 BT39
Kildoran Rd. SW2 181 DL85
Kildowan Rd., Ilf. 126 EU60
Kilfillan Gdns., Berk. 38 AU20
Kilgour Rd. SE23 183 DY86
Kilkie St. SW6 160 DC82
Killarney Rd. SW18 180 DC86
Killasser Ct., Tad. 233 CW123
Killburns Mill Clo., Wall. 219 DH105
London Rd.
Killearn Rd. SE6 183 ED88
Killester Gdns., Wor.Pk. 217 CV105
Killewarren Way, Orp. 206 EW100
Killick Clo., Sev. 256 FE121
Killick St. N1 141 DM68
Killieser Ave. SW2 181 DL89
Killip Clo. E16 144 EF72
Killowen Ave., Nthlt. 116 CC64
Killowen Rd. E9 143 DX65
Killy Hill, Wok. 210 AS108
Killyon Rd. SW8 161 DJ82
Killyon Ter. SW8 161 DJ82
Kilmaine Rd. SW6 159 CY80
Kilmarnock Gdns., Dag. 126 EW62
Lindsey Rd.
Kilmarnock Pk., Reig. 250 DB132
Kilmarnock Rd., Wat. 94 BX49
Kilmarsh Rd. W6 159 CW77
Kilmartin Ave. SW16 201 DM97
Kilmartin Rd., Ilf. 126 EU61
Kilmartin Way, Horn. 127 FH64
Kilmeston Way SE15 162 DT80
Daniel Gdns.
Kilmington Clo., Brwd. 109 GB47
Kilmington Rd. SW13 159 CU79
Kilmiston Ave., Shep. 195 BQ100
Kilmorey Rd., Twick. 157 CH84
Kilmorie Rd. SE23 183 DY88
Kiln Ave., Amer. 72 AW38
Kiln Clo., Hayes 155 BR79
Brickfield La.
Kiln Ct., Beac. 110 AH55
Kiln Flds., B.End 110 AE61
Kiln Grd., Hem.H. 40 BN22
Kiln Ho. Clo., Ware 33 DY05
Kiln La., Bet. 264 CP135
Kiln La., Chesh. 56 AV31
Kiln La., Epsom 216 CS111
Kiln La., Harl. 52 EW15
Kiln La., H.Wyc. 110 AC60
Kiln La., Horl. 268 DG146
Kiln La., Slou. 111 AQ60
Kiln La., Wok. 228 BG124
Kiln Ms. SW17 180 DD92
Kiln Pl. NW5 120 DG64
Kiln Rd., Epp. 70 FA27
Kiln Wk., Red. 267 DH139
Bushfield Dr.
Kiln Way, Grays 170 FZ78
Kiln Way, Nthwd. 93 BS51
Kiln Wd. La., Rom. 105 FD50
Kilncroft, Hem.H. 41 BP22
Kilndown, Grav. 191 GJ93
Kilner St. E14 143 EA71
Kilnfield, Welw.G.C. 29 CZ06
Kilnside, Esher 215 CG108
Kilnwood, Sev. 224 EZ113
Kilpatrick Way, Hayes 136 BY71
Kilravock St. W10 139 CY69
Kilross Rd., Felt. 175 BR88
Kilrue La., Walt. 213 BT105
Kilrush Ter., Wok. 227 BA116
Kilsby Wk., Dag. 146 EV65
Rugby Rd.
Kilsha Rd., Walt. 195 BV100
Kilsmore La., Wal.Cr. 67 DX28
Kilvinton Dr., Enf. 82 DR38
Kilworth Ave., Brwd. 109 GA44
Kilworth Clo., Welw.G.C. 30 DB11
Kimbell Gdns. SW6 159 CY81
Kimbell Pl. SE3 164 EJ84
Tudway Rd.
Kimber Clo., Wind. 151 AM83
Kimber Ct., Guil. 243 BD132
Gilliat Dr.
Kimber Rd. SW18 180 DA87
Kimberley Ave. E6 144 EL68
Kimberley Ave. SE15 162 DV82
Kimberley Ave., Ilf. 125 ER59
Kimberley Ave., Rom. 127 FC58
Kimberley Clo., Horl. 268 DF148
Court Lo. Rd.
Kimberley Clo., Slou. 153 AZ77
Kimberley Dr., Sid. 186 EX89
Kimberley Gdns. N4 121 DP57
Kimberley Gdns., Enf. 82 DT41
Kimberley Gate, Brom. 184 EF94
Oaklands Rd.
Kimberley Pl., Pur. 219 DN111
Brighton Rd.
Kimberley Ride, Cob. 214 CB113
Littleheath La.
Kimberley Rd. E4 102 EE46
Kimberley Rd. E11 123 ED61
Kimberley Rd. E16 144 EF70
Kimberley Rd. E17 101 DZ53
Kimberley Rd. N17 100 DU54
Kimberley Rd. N18 100 DV51
Kimberley Rd. NW6 139 CY67
Kimberley Rd. SW9 161 DL82
Kimberley Rd., Beck. 203 DX96
Kimberley Rd., Croy. 201 DP100
Kimberley Rd., St.Alb. 42 CC19
Kimberley Way E4 102 EE46
Kimbers Dr., Slou. 131 AK69
Kimble Clo., Wat. 75 BS44
Kimble Cres. 94 CC45
(Bushey), Wat.
Kimble Rd. SW19 180 DD93
Kimbolton Clo. SE12 184 EF86
Kimbolton Grn., Borwd. 78 CQ42
Kimbolton Row SW3 276 B9
Kimmeridge Gdns. 184 EL91
SE9
Kimmeridge Rd. SE9 184 EL91
Kimps Way, Hem.H. 40 BN23
Kimpton Ave., Brwd. 108 FV45
Kimpton Clo., Hem.H. 41 BP15
Kimpton Pl., Wat. 60 BX34
Kimpton Rd. SE5 162 DR81
Kimpton Rd., Sutt. 199 CZ103
Kimpton Trade Business 199 CZ103
Cen., Sutt.
Kimptons Clo., Pot.B. 63 CX33
Kimptons Mead, Pot.B. 63 CX32
Kinburn Dr., Egh. 172 AY92
Kinburn St. SE16 163 DX75
Kincaid Rd. SE15 162 DV80
Kincardine Gdns. W9 139 CZ70
Harrow Rd.
Kinch Gro., Wem. 118 CM59
Kincraig Dr., Sev. 256 FG124
Kinder Clo. SE28 146 EX73
Kinder St. E1 142 DV72
Cannon St. Rd.
Kinderscout, Hem.H. 40 BN22
Kindersley Way, Abb.L. 59 BQ31
Kinetic Cres., Enf. 83 DZ36
Kinfauns Ave., Horn. 128 FJ58
Kinfauns Rd. SW2 181 DN89
Kinfauns Rd., Ilf. 126 EU60
King Acre Ct., Stai. 173 BE90
Victoria Rd.
King Alfred Ave. SE6 183 EA90
King Alfred Rd., Rom. 106 FM54
King & Queen Clo. SE9 184 EL91
St. Keverne Rd.
King & Queen St. SE17 279 J9
King & Queen St. SE17 162 DQ78
King Arthur Clo. SE15 162 DW80
King Arthur Ct., Wal.Cr. 67 DX31
King Charles Cres., 198 CM101
Surb.
King Charles Rd., Rad. 62 CL32
King Charles Rd., Surb. 198 CM99
King Charles St. SW1 277 N4
King Charles St. SW1 161 DK75
King Charles Ter. E1 142 DV73
Sovereign Clo.
King Charles Wk. SW19 179 CY88
Princes Way
King David La. E1 142 DW73
King Edward Ave., Dart. 188 FK86
King Edward Ave., Rain. 148 FK68
King Edward Ct., Wind. 151 AR81
King Edward Dr., Chess. 198 CL104
Kelvin Gro.
King Edward Dr., Grays 170 GE75
King Edward Ms. SW13 159 CU81
King Edward Rd. E10 123 EC60
King Edward Rd. E17 123 DY55
King Edward Rd., Barn. 80 DA42
King Edward Rd., Brwd. 108 FW48
King Edward Rd., Rad. 62 CM33
King Edward Rd., Rom. 127 FF58
King Edward Rd., Wal.Cr. 67 DY33
King Edward Rd., Wat. 76 BY44
King Edward VII Ave., 152 AS80
Wind.
King Edward St. EC1 275 H8
King Edward St. EC1 142 DQ72
King Edward St., Hem.H. 40 BJ24
King Edward St., Slou. 151 AR75
King Edward III Ms. SE16 162 DV75
Paradise St.
King Edward Wk. SE1 278 E6
King Edward Wk. SE1 161 DN76
King Edward's Gdns. W3 138 CN74
King Edwards Gro., Tedd. 177 CH93
King Edward's Pl. W3 138 CN74
King Edward's Gdns.
King Edwards Rd. E9 142 DV67
King Edwards Rd. N9 100 DV45
King Edwards Rd., Bark. 145 ER67
King Edward's Rd., Enf. 83 DX42
King Edwards Rd., Ruis. 115 BR60
King Edwards Rd., Ware 33 DY05
King Frederik IX Twr. 163 DZ76
SE16
Finland St.
King Gdns., Croy. 219 DP106
King George Ave. E16 144 EK72
King George Ave., Ilf. 125 ER57
King George Ave., Walt. 196 BX102
King George Ave. 76 CB44
(Bushey), Wat.
King George Clo., Rom. 127 FC55
King George Clo., Sun. 175 BT92
King George V Rd., Amer. 55 AR38
King George Rd., 67 EC34
Wal.Abb.
King George Rd., Ware 33 DY05
King George VI Ave., 200 DF98
Mitch.
King George VI Ave., 238 EK116
West.
King George Sq., Rich. 178 CM86
King George St. SE10 163 EC80
King Georges Ave., Wat. 75 BS43
King Georges Dr., Add. 212 BG110
King Georges Dr., Sthl. 136 BZ71
King Georges Rd., Brwd. 108 FV44
King George's Trd. Est., 216 CN105
Chess.
King Harolds Way, Bexh. 166 EX80
King Harry La., St.Alb. 42 CA21
King Harry St., Hem.H. 40 BK21
King Henry Ms., Orp. 223 ET106
Osgood Ave.
King Henry St. N16 122 DS64
King Henry Ter. E1 142 DV73
Sovereign Clo.
King Henry's Dr., Croy. 221 EC109
King Henry's Ms., Enf. 83 EA37
King Henry's Rd. NW3 140 DE66
King Henry's Rd., Kings.T. 198 CP97
King Henry's Wk. N1 142 DS65
King James Ave. (Cuffley), 65 DL29
Pot.B.
King James Ct. SE1 161 DP75
Borough Rd.
King James St. SE1 278 G5
King James St. SE1 161 DP75
King John Ct. EC2 275 N4
King John St. E1 143 DX71
King John's Clo., Stai. 172 AW86
King Johns Wk. SE9 184 EK88
King Sq. EC1 275 H3
King Stable Ct., Wind. 151 AR80
King Stable St.
King Stable St., Wind. 151 AR80
King Stairs Clo. SE16 162 DV75
Elephant La.
King St. E13 144 EG70
King St. EC2 275 J9
King St. EC2 142 DQ72
King St. N2 120 DD55
King St. N17 100 DT53
King St. SW1 277 L3
King St. SW1 141 DJ74
King St. W3 138 CP74
King St. W6 159 CU77
King St. WC2 273 P10
King St. WC2 141 DL73
King St., Cher. 194 BG102
King St., Chesh. 54 AP32
King St., Grav. 191 GH86
King St., Rich. 177 CK85
King St., Sthl. 156 BY76
King St., Twick. 177 CG88
King St., Wat. 76 BW42
King William IV Gdns. 182 DW93
SE20
St. John's Rd.
King William La. SE10 164 EE78
Orlop St.
King William St. EC4 279 L1
King William St. EC4 142 DR73
King William Wk. SE10 163 EC79
Kingaby Gdns., Rain. 147 FG66
Kingcup Clo., Croy. 203 DX102
Primrose La.
Kingdon Rd. NW6 140 DA65
Kingfield Clo., Wok. 227 AZ120
Kingfield Dr., Wok. 227 AZ120
Kingfield Gdns., Wok. 227 AZ119
Kingfield Rd. W5 137 CK70
Kingfield Rd., Wok. 226 AY120
Kingfield St. E14 163 EC77
Kingfisher Ave. E11 124 EH58
Eastern Ave.
Kingfisher Clo. SE28 146 EW73
Kingfisher Clo., Brwd. 109 GA45
Kingfisher Clo., Har. 95 CF52
Kingfisher Clo., Nthwd. 93 BP53
Kingfisher Clo., Orp. 206 EX98
Kingfisher Clo., Walt. 214 BY106
Old Esher Rd.
Kingfisher Clo., Ware 33 EC12
Lawrence Ave.
Kingfisher Ct. SW19 179 CY89
Queensmere Rd.
Kingfisher Ct., Wok. 211 BC114
Blackmore Cres.
Kingfisher Dr., Guil. 243 BC132
Kingfisher Dr., Red. 250 DG131
Kingfisher Dr., Rich. 177 CH91
Kingfisher Dr., Stai. 173 BF91
Kingfisher Gdns., S.Croy. 221 DX111
Kingfisher Lure, Kings L. 59 BP29
Kingfisher Lure, Rick. 74 BH42
Kingfisher Rd., Upmin. 129 FT60
Kingfisher Sq. SE8 163 DZ79
Kingfisher St. E6 144 EL71
Kingfisher Wk. NW9 96 CS54
Eagle Dr.
Kingfisher Way NW10 138 CR65
Kingfisher Way, Beck. 203 DX99
Kingham Clo. SW18 180 DC87
Kingham Clo. W11 159 CY75
Kinghorn St. EC1 275 H7
Kinglake Ct., Wok. 226 AS118
Raglan Rd.
Kinglake Est. SE17 279 N10
Kinglake St. SE17 162 DS78
Kingly Ct. W1 273 K10
Kingly St. W1 273 K9
Kingly St. W1 141 DJ72
Kings Arbour, Sthl. 156 BY78
Kings Arms Ct. E1 142 DU71
Old Montague St.
Kings Arms Yd. EC2 275 K8
Kings Ave. N10 120 DG55
Kings Ave. N21 99 DP46
King's Ave. SW4 181 DK87
King's Ave. SW12 181 DK88
Kings Ave. W5 137 CK72
Kings Ave., Brom. 184 EF93
Kings Ave., Buck.H. 102 EK47
Kings Ave., Cars. 218 DE108
Kings Ave., Grnf. 136 CB72
Kings Ave., Hem.H. 40 BM24
Kings Ave., Houns. 156 CB81
Kings Ave., N.Mal. 198 CS98
Kings Ave., Red. 266 DE136
Kings Ave., Rom. 126 EZ58
Kings Ave., Sun. 175 BT92
Kings Ave., Wat. 75 BT42
Kings Ave., W.Byf. 212 BK112
Kings Ave., Wdf.Grn. 102 EH50
Kings Bench St. SE1 278 G4
Kings Bench Wk. EC4 274 E9
Kings Chace Vw., Enf. 81 DN40
Crofton Way
Kings Chase, Brwd. 108 FW48
Kings Chase, E.Mol. 196 CC97
Kings Clo. E10 123 EB59
Kings Clo. NW4 119 CX56
Kings Clo., Beac. 110 AG55
Kings Clo., Ch.St.G. 90 AX47
Kings Clo., Dart. 167 FE84
Kings Clo., Kings L. 58 BH31
Kings Clo., Nthwd. 93 BT51
Kings Clo., Stai. 174 BK94
Kings Clo., T.Ditt. 197 CG100
Kings Clo., Walt. 195 BV102
King's Clo., Wat. 75 BV42
Lady's Clo.
Kings College Rd. NW3 140 DE66
Kings College Rd., Ruis. 115 BT58
Kings Ct. E13 144 EH67
Kings Ct. W6 159 CU77
King St.
Kings Ct., Berk. 38 AW18
Lower Kings Rd.
Kings Ct., Tad. 233 CW122
Kings Ct., Wem. 118 CP61
Kings Ct. S. SW3 160 DE78
Chelsea Manor Gdns.
Kings Cres. N4 122 DQ62
Kings Cres. Est. N4 122 DQ61
King's Cross Bri. N1 274 A2
Kings Cross La., Red. 267 DK136
King's Cross Rd. WC1 274 C2
King's Cross Rd. WC1 141 DM69
Kings Dr., Edg. 96 CM49
Kings Dr., Grav. 191 GH90
Kings Dr., Surb. 198 CN101
Kings Dr., Tedd. 177 CD92
Kings Dr., T.Ditt. 197 CH100
Kings Dr., Wem. 118 CP61
Kings Dr., The, Walt. 213 BT109
Kings Fm. Ave., Rich. 158 CN84
Kings Fm. Rd., Rick. 73 BD44
Kings Gdns. NW6 140 DA66
West End La.
Kings Gdns., Ilf. 125 ER60
Kings Gdns., Upmin. 129 FS59
King's Garth Ms. SE23 182 DW89
London Rd.
Kings Grn., Loug. 84 EL41
Kings Gro. SE15 162 DV80
Kings Gro., Rom. 127 FG57
Kings Hall Rd., Beck. 183 DY94
Kings Head Hill E4 101 EB45
Kings Head La., W.Byf. 212 BK111
Kings Head Yd. SE1 279 K3
Kings Highway SE18 165 ES79
Kings Hill, Loug. 84 EL40
Kings Keep, Kings.T. 198 CL98
Beaufort Rd.
Kings La., Egh. 172 AU92
Kings La., Kings L. 58 BG31
Kings La., Sutt. 218 DD107
Kings Langley Bypass, 39 BD22
Hem.H.
Kings Langley Bypass, 58 BK28
Kings L.
Kings Lynn Clo., Rom. 106 FK51
Kings Lynn Dr.
Kings Lynn Dr., Rom. 106 FK51
Kings Lynn Path, Rom. 106 FK51
Kings Lynn Dr.
Kings Mead, Horl. 269 DP148
Kings Mead, Red. 267 DL136
Kings Mead Pk., Esher 215 CE108
Kings Meadow, Kings L. 58 BN28
Kings Ms. SW4 181 DL85
King's Ave.
King's Ms. WC1 274 C5
King's Ms. WC1 141 DM71
Kings Ms., Chig. 103 EQ47
Kings Mill La., Red. 267 DJ139
Kings Oak, Rom. 126 FA55
King's Orchard SE9 184 EL86
Kings Paddock, Hmptn. 196 CC95
Kings Par., Cars. 200 DE104
Wrythe La.
King's Pas. E11 124 EE59
Kings Pas., Kings.T. 197 CK96
Kings Pl. SE1 279 H5
Kings Pl. W4 158 CQ78
Kings Pl., Buck.H. 102 EJ47
King's Reach Twr. SE1 278 E2
King's Reach Twr. SE1 141 DN74
King's Ride Gate, Rich. 158 CN84
Kings Rd. E4 101 ED46
Kings Rd. E6 144 EJ67
Kings Rd. E11 124 EE59
King's Rd. N17 100 DT53
Kings Rd. N18 100 DU50
Kings Rd. N22 99 DM53
Kings Rd. NW10 139 CV66
Kings Rd. SE25 202 DU97
King's Rd. SW1 160 DF78
King's Rd. SW3 276 C10
King's Rd. SW3 160 DF78
King's Rd. SW6 160 DB81
King's Rd. SW10 160 DB81
Kings Rd. SW14 158 CR83
Kings Rd. SW19 180 DA93
Kings Rd. W5 137 CK71
Kings Rd., Add. 212 BH110
Kings Rd., Bark. 145 EQ66
North St.
Kings Rd., Barn. 79 CW41
Kings Rd., Berk. 38 AU20
Kings Rd., Brwd. 108 FW47
Kings Rd., Ch.St.G. 90 AW47
Kings Rd., Egh. 173 BA91
Kings Rd., Felt. 176 BW88
Kings Rd., Guil. 242 AX134
Kings Rd. (Shalford), 258 AY141
Guil.
Kings Rd., Har. 116 BZ61
Kings Rd., Hert. 32 DU08
Kings Rd., Horl. 268 DG148
Kings Rd., Kings.T. 178 CL94
Kings Rd., Mitch. 200 DG97
Kings Rd., Orp. 223 ET105
Kings Rd., Rich. 178 CM85
Kings Rd., Rom. 127 FG57
Kings Rd., St.Alb. 42 CC20
Kings Rd. 61 CJ26
(London Colney), St.Alb.
Kings Rd., Slou. 152 AS76
Kings Rd., Surb. 197 CJ102
Kings Rd., Sutt. 218 DA110
Kings Rd., Tedd. 177 CD92
Kings Rd., Twick. 177 CH86
King's Rd., Uxb. 134 BK68
Kings Rd., Wal.Cr. 67 DY34
Kings Rd., Walt. 195 BV103
Kings Rd., West Dr. 154 BM75
Kings Rd., West. 238 EH118
Kings Rd., Wind. 151 AR84
Kings Rd., Wok. 227 BA116
Kings Rd. Bungalows, 116 BZ62
Har.
Kings Rd.
King's Scholars' Pas. 277 K8
SW1
King's Ter. NW1 141 DJ67
Plender St.
Kings Ter., Islw. 157 CG83
Worple Rd.
Kings Wk., Grays 170 GA79
King's Wk., Kings.T. 197 CK95
Kings Wk., S.Croy. 220 DV114
Kings Way, Har. 117 CE56
Kingsand Rd. SE12 184 EG89
Kingsash Dr., Hayes 136 BY70
Kingsbridge Ave. W3 158 CM75
Kingsbridge Circ., Rom. 106 FL52
Kingsbridge Clo., Rom. 106 FL51
Kingsbridge Cres., Sthl. 136 BZ71
Kingsbridge Rd. W10 139 CW72
Kingsbridge Rd., Bark. 145 ER68
Kingsbridge Rd., Mord. 199 CX101
Kingsbridge Rd., Rom. 106 FL51
Kingsbridge Rd., Sthl. 156 BZ77
Kingsbridge Rd., Walt. 195 BV101
Kingsbridge Way, 135 BS69
Hayes
Kingsbrook, Lthd. 231 CG118
Ryebrook Rd.
Kingsbury Ave., St.Alb. 42 CC19
Kingsbury Circle NW9 118 CN57
Kingsbury Cres., Stai. 173 BD91
Kingsbury Dr., Wind. 172 AU87
Kingsbury Rd. N1 142 DS65
Kingsbury Rd. NW9 118 CP57
Kingsbury Ter. N1 142 DS65
Kingsbury Trd. Est. NW9 118 CR58
Kingsclere Clo. SW15 179 CU87
Kingsclere Pl., Enf. 82 DQ40
Chase Side
Kingscliffe Gdns. SW19 179 CZ88
Kingscote Rd. W4 158 CR76
Kingscote Rd., Croy. 202 DV101
Kingscote Rd., N.Mal. 198 CR97
Kingscote St. EC4 274 F10
Kingscourt Rd. SW16 181 DK90
Kingscroft, Welw.G.C. 30 DB08
Kingscroft Rd. NW2 139 CZ65
Kingscroft Rd., Bans. 234 DD115
Kingscroft Rd., Lthd. 231 CH120
Kingsdale Gdns. W11 139 CX74
Kingsdale Rd. SE18 165 ET80
Kingsdale Rd. SE20 183 DX94
Kingsdale Rd., Berk. 38 AU20
Kingsdene, Tad. 233 CV121
Kingsdon La., Harl. 52 EW16
Kingsdown Ave. W3 138 CS73
Kingsdown Ave. W13 157 CH75
Kingsdown Ave., S.Croy. 219 DP109
Kingsdown Clo. SE16 162 DV78
Masters Dr.
Kingsdown Clo. W10 139 CX72
Kingsdown Clo., Grav. 191 GM88
Farley Rd.
Kingsdown Rd. E11 124 EE62
Kingsdown Rd. N19 121 DL61
Kingsdown Rd., Epsom 217 CU113
Kingsdown Rd., Sutt. 217 CY106
Kingsdown Way, Brom. 204 EG101
Kingsdowne Rd., Surb. 198 CL101
Kingsend, Ruis. 115 BR60
Kingsfield, Guil. 260 BL144
Kingsfield, Hodd. 49 EA15
Kingsfield, Wind. 151 AK81
Kingsfield Ave., Har. 116 CB56
Kingsfield Ct., Wat. 94 BX45
Kingsfield Dr., Enf. 83 DX35
Kingsfield Ho. SE9 184 EK90
Kingsfield Rd., Har. 117 CD59
Kingsfield Rd., Wat. 94 BX45
Kingsfield Ter., Dart. 188 FK86
Priory Rd.
Kingsfield Way, Enf. 83 DX35
Kingsford Ave., Wall. 219 DL108
Kingsford St. NW5 120 DF64
Kingsford Way E6 145 EM71
Kingsgate, Wem. 118 CQ62
Kingsgate Ave. N3 120 DA55
Kingsgate Clo., Bexh. 166 EY81
Kingsgate Clo., Orp. 206 EW97
Main Rd.
Kingsgate Pl. NW6 140 DA66
Kingsgate Rd. NW6 140 DA66

Laburnum Gro., Ruis. 115 BR58
Laburnum Gro., St.Alb. 60 CB25
Laburnum Gro., Slou. 153 BB79
Laburnum Gro., S.Ock. 149 FW69
Laburnum Gro., Sthl. 136 BZ70
Laburnum Ho., Dag. 126 FA61
Bradwell Ave.
Laburnum Pl., Egh. 172 AV93
Laburnum Rd. SW19 180 DC94
Laburnum Rd., Cher. 194 BG102
Laburnum Rd., Epp. 70 EW29
Laburnum Rd., Epsom 216 CS113
Laburnum Rd., Hayes 155 BT77
Laburnum Rd., Hodd. 49 EB15
Laburnum Rd., Mitch. 200 DG96
Laburnum Rd., Wok. 226 AX119
Laburnum St. E2 142 DT67
Laburnum Wk., Horn. 128 FJ64
Laburnum Way, Brom. 205 EN101
Laburnum Way, Stai. 174 BM88
Laburnum Way (Cheshunt), Wal.Cr. 65 DP28
Millcrest Rd.
Lacebark Clo., Sid. 185 ET87
Lacey Ave., Couls. 235 DN120
Lacey Clo. N9 100 DU47
Lacey Clo., Egh. 173 BD94
Lacey Dr., Couls. 235 DN120
Lacey Dr., Dag. 126 EV63
Lacey Dr., Edg. 96 CL49
Lacey Dr., Hmptn. 196 BZ95
Lacey Grn., Couls. 235 DN120
Lacey Wk. E3 143 EA68
Lackford Rd., Couls. 234 DF118
Lackington St. EC2 275 L6
Lackington St. EC2 142 DR71
Lackmore Rd., Enf. 82 DW35
Lacock Clo. SW19 180 DC93
Lacon Rd. SE22 162 DU84
Lacy Rd. SW15 159 CX84
Ladas Rd. SE27 182 DQ91
Ladbroke Cres. W11 139 CY72
Ladbroke Gro.
Ladbroke Gdns. W11 139 CZ73
Ladbroke Gro. W10 139 CX70
Ladbroke Gro. W11 139 CY72
Ladbroke Gro., Red. 250 DG133
Ladbroke Ms. W11 139 CY74
Ladbroke Rd.
Ladbroke Rd. W11 139 CZ74
Ladbroke Rd., Enf. 82 DT44
Ladbroke Rd., Epsom 216 CR114
Ladbroke Rd., Horl. 269 DH146
Ladbroke Rd., Red. 250 DG133
Ladbroke Sq. W11 139 CZ73
Ladbroke Ter. W11 139 CZ73
Ladbroke Wk. W11 139 CZ74
Ladbrook Clo., Pnr. 116 BZ57
Ladbrook Rd. SE25 202 DR97
Ladbrooke Clo., Pot.B. 64 DA32
Strafford Gate
Ladbrooke Cres., Sid. 186 EX90
Ladbrooke Dr., Pot.B. 64 DA32
Ladbrooke Rd., Slou. 151 AQ76
Ladderstile Ride, Kings.T. 178 CP92
Ladderswood Way N11 99 DJ50
Ladds Way, Swan. 207 FD98
Ladies Gro., St.Alb. 42 CB19
Lady Booth Rd., Kings.T. 198 CL96
Lady Dock Path SE16 163 DY75
Salter Rd.
Lady Gro., Welw.G.C. 29 CY13
Lady Hay, Wor.Pk. 199 CT103
Lady Margaret Rd. N19 121 DJ63
Lady Margaret Rd. NW5 121 DJ64
Lady Margaret Rd., Sthl. 136 BZ71
Lady Somerset Rd. NW5 121 DH63
Ladybower Ct. E5 123 DY63
Gilpin Rd.
Ladycroft Gdns., Orp. 223 EQ106
Ladycroft Rd. SE13 163 EB83
Ladycroft Wk., Stan. 95 CK53
Ladycroft Way, Orp. 223 EQ106
Ladyday Pl., Slou. 131 AQ74
Glentworth Pl.
Ladyegate Clo., Dor. 263 CK135
Ladyegate Rd., Dor. 263 CJ136
Ladyfield Clo., Loug. 85 EP42
Ladyfields, Grav. 191 GF91
Ladyfields, Loug. 85 EP42
Ladygate La., Ruis. 115 BP58
Ladygrove, Croy. 221 DY109
Ladygrove Dr., Guil. 243 BA129
Ladymead, Guil. 242 AW133
Ladymeadow, Kings L. 58 BK27
Lady's Clo., Wat. 75 BV42
Ladyshot, Harl. 36 EU14
Ladysmith Ave. E6 144 EL68
Ladysmith Ave., Ilf. 125 ER59
Ladysmith Rd. E16 144 EF69
Ladysmith Rd. N17 100 DU54
Ladysmith Rd. N18 100 DV50
Ladysmith Rd. SE9 185 EN86
Ladysmith Rd., Enf. 82 DS41
Ladysmith Rd., Har. 95 CE54
Ladysmith Rd., St.Alb. 43 CD19
Ladythorpe Clo., Add. 212 BH105
Church Rd.
Ladywalk, Rick. 91 BE50
Ladywell Clo. SE4 163 DZ84
Adelaide Ave.
Ladywell Hts. SE4 183 DZ86
Ladywell Prospect, Saw. 36 FA06
Ladywell Rd. SE13 183 EA85
Ladywell St. E15 144 EF67
Plaistow Gro.
Ladywood Ave., Orp. 205 ES99
Ladywood Clo., Rick. 74 BH41
Ladywood Rd., Dart. 189 FS92
Ladywood Rd., Hert. 31 DM09
Ladywood Rd., Surb. 198 CN103
Lafone Ave., Felt. 176 BW88
Alfred Rd.
Lafone St. SE1 279 P4
Lafone St. SE1 162 DT75
Lagado Ms. SE16 143 DX74
Lagger, The, Ch.St.G. 90 AV48
Lagger Clo., Ch.St.G. 90 AV48
Laglands Clo., Reig. 250 DC132
Lagonda Ave., Ilf. 103 ET51
Lagonda Way, Dart. 168 FJ84
Arundel Rd.
Lagoon Rd., Orp. 206 EV99
Laidlaw Dr. N21 81 DM43
Chadwick Ave.
Laidon Sq., Hem.H. 40 BK16
Laing Clo., Ilf. 103 ER51
Laing Dean, Nthlt. 136 BW67
Laings Ave., Mitch. 200 DF96
Lainlock Pl., Houns. 156 CB81
Spring Gro. Rd.
Lainson St. SW18 180 DA87
Laird Ave., Grays 170 GD75
Laird Ho. SE5 142 DQ80
Lairdale Clo. SE21 182 DQ88
Lairs Clo. N7 141 DL65
Manger Rd.
Laitwood Rd. SW12 181 DH88
Lake, The (Bushey), Wat. 94 CC46
Lake Ave., Brom. 184 EG93
Lake Ave., Rain. 148 FK68
Lake Ave., Slou. 131 AR73
Lake Clo. SW19 179 CZ92
Lake Rd.
Lake Clo., W.Byf. 212 BK112
Lake Dr. (Bushey), Wat. 94 CC47
Lake End Ct., Maid. 130 AH72
Taplow Rd.
Lake End Rd., Maid. 130 AH73
Lake End Rd., Wind. 150 AH75
Lake Gdns., Dag. 126 FA64
Lake Gdns., Rich. 177 CH89
Lake Gdns., Wall. 201 DH104
Lake Ho. Rd. E11 124 EG62
Lake La., Horl. 267 DJ144
Lake Ri., Grays 169 FU77
Lake Ri., Rom. 127 FF55
Lake Rd. SW19 179 CZ92
Lake Rd., Croy. 203 DZ103
Lake Rd., Rom. 126 EX56
Lake Rd., Vir.W. 192 AV98
Lake Rd., Wal.Abb. 50 EE21
Lake Vw., Dor. 263 CJ139
Lake Vw., Edg. 96 CM50
Lake Vw., Pot.B. 64 DC33
Lake Vw. Rd., Sev. 256 FG123
Lakedale Rd. SE18 165 ES79
Lakefield Rd. N22 99 DP54
Lakefields Clo., Rain. 148 FK68
Lakehall Gdns., Th.Hth. 201 DP99
Lakehall Rd., Th.Hth. 201 DP99
Lakehurst Rd., Epsom 216 CS106
Lakeland Clo., Chig. 104 EV49
Lakeland Clo., Har. 95 CD51
Lakenheath N14 81 DK44
Laker Pl. SW15 179 CZ86
Lakers Ri., Bans. 234 DE116
Lakes Clo., Guil. 259 BB140
Lakes La., Beac. 89 AM54
Lakes Rd., Kes. 222 EJ106
Lakeside N3 98 DB54
Lakeside W13 137 CJ72
Edgehill Rd.
Lakeside, Beck. 203 EB97
Lakeside, Enf. 81 DK42
Lakeside, Rain. 148 FL68
Lakeside, Red. 250 DG132
Lakeside, Wall. 201 DH104
Derek Ave.
Lakeside, Wey. 195 BS103
Lakeside, Wok. 226 AS119
Lakeside Ave. SE28 146 EU74
Lakeside Ave., Ilf. 124 EK56
Lakeside Clo. SE25 202 DU96
Lakeside Clo., Chig. 103 ET49
Lakeside Clo., Ruis. 115 BR56
Lakeside Clo., Sid. 186 EW85
Lakeside Clo., Wok. 226 AS119
Lakeside Ct. N4 121 DP61
Lakeside Ct., Borwd. 78 CN43
Cavendish Cres.
Lakeside Cres., Barn. 80 DF43
Lakeside Cres., Brwd. 108 FX48
Lakeside Cres., Wey. 195 BQ104
Churchill Dr.
Lakeside Dr., Brom. 204 EL104
Lakeside Dr., Esher 214 CC107
Lakeside Dr., Slou. 132 AS67
Lakeside Pl., St.Alb. 61 CK27
Lakeside Rd. N13 99 DM49
Lakeside Rd. W14 159 CX76
Lakeside Rd., Slou. 153 BF80
Lakeside Rd. (Cheshunt), Wal.Cr. 66 DW28
Lakeside Way, Wem. 118 CN63
Lakeswood Rd., Orp. 205 EP100
Lakeview Ct. SW19 179 CY89
Victoria Dr.
Lakeview Rd. SE27 181 DN92
Lakeview Rd., Well. 166 EV84
Lakis Clo. NW3 120 DC63
Flask Wk.
Laleham Ave. NW7 96 CR48
Laleham Ct., Wok. 226 AY116
Laleham Pk., Stai. 194 BJ99
Laleham Reach, Cher. 194 BH96
Laleham Rd. SE6 183 EC86
Laleham Rd., Shep. 194 BL98
Laleham Rd., Stai. 173 BF92
Lalor St. SW6 159 CY82
Lamb Clo., Hat. 45 CV19
Lamb Clo., Til. 171 GJ82
Coleridge Rd.
Lamb Clo., Wat. 60 BW34
Lamb La. E8 142 DV66
Lamb St. E1 275 P6
Lamb St. E1 142 DT71
Lamb Wk. SE1 279 M5
Lamb Yd., Wat. 76 BX43
Lambarde Ave. SE9 185 EN91
Lambarde Dr., Sev. 256 FG123
Lambarde Rd., Sev. 256 FG122
Lambardes Clo., Orp. 224 EW110
Lamberhurst Clo., Orp. 206 EX102
Lamberhurst Rd. SE27 181 DN91
Lamberhurst Rd., Dag. 126 EZ60
Lambert Ave., Rich. 158 CP83
Lambert Ave., Slou. 152 AY75
Lambert Clo., West. 238 EK116
Lambert Ct. (Bushey), Wat. 76 BX42
Lambert Jones Ms. EC2 142 DQ71
Beech St.
Lambert Rd. E16 144 EH72
Lambert Rd. N12 98 DD50
Lambert Rd. SW2 181 DL85
Lambert Rd., Bans. 218 DA114
Lambert St. N1 141 DN66
Lambert Wk., Wem. 117 CK62
Lambert Way N12 98 DC50
Woodhouse Rd.
Lamberts Pl., Croy. 202 DR102
Lamberts Rd., Surb. 198 CL99
Lambeth Bri. SE1 278 A8
Lambeth Bri. SE1 161 DL77
Lambeth Bri. SW1 278 A8
Lambeth Bri. SW1 161 DL77
Lambeth High St. SE1 278 B9
Lambeth High St. SE1 161 DM77
Lambeth Hill EC4 275 H10
Lambeth Hill EC4 142 DQ73
Lambeth Palace Rd. SE1 278 B7
Lambeth Palace Rd. SE1 161 DM76
Lambeth Rd. SE1 278 C7
Lambeth Rd. SE1 161 DM77
Lambeth Rd. SE11 278 C7
Lambeth Rd. SE11 161 DM77
Lambeth Rd., Croy. 201 DN101
Lambeth Wk. SE11 278 C8
Lambeth Wk. SE11 161 DM77
Lamble St. NW5 120 DG64
Lambley Rd., Dag. 146 EV65
Lambly Hill, Vir.W. 192 AY97
Lambolle Pl. NW3 140 DE65
Lambolle Rd. NW3 140 DE65
Lambourn Chase, Rad. 77 CF36
Lambourn Clo. W7 157 CF75
Lambourn Rd. SW4 161 DH83
Lambourne Ave. SW19 179 CZ91
Lambourne Clo., Chig. 104 EV47
Lambourne Rd.
Lambourne Cres., Chig. 104 EV47
Lambourne Cres., Wok. 211 BD113
Lambourne Dr., Brwd. 109 GE45
Lambourne Dr., Cob. 230 BX115
Lambourne Gdns. E4 101 EA47
Lambourne Gdns., Bark. 145 ET66
Lambourne Rd.
Lambourne Gdns., Enf. 82 DT40
Lambourne Gdns., Horn. 128 FK61
Lambourne Gro., Kings.T. 198 CP96
Kenley Rd.
Lambourne Pl. SE3 164 EH81
Shooter's Hill Rd.
Lambourne Rd. E11 123 EC59
Lambourne Rd., Bark. 145 ES66
Lambourne Rd., Chig. 103 ES49
Lambourne Rd., Ilf. 125 ES61
Lambrook Ter. SW6 159 CY81
Lamb's Bldgs. EC1 275 K5
Lambs Clo. (Cuffley), Pot.B. 65 DM29
Lambs Conduit Pas. WC1 274 B6
Lamb's Conduit St. WC1 274 B6
Lamb's Conduit St. WC1 141 DM70
Lambs La. N., Rain. 148 FJ70
Lambs La. S., Rain. 147 FH71
Lambs Meadow, Wdf.Grn. 102 EK54
Lambs Ms. N1 141 DP67
Colebrooke Row
Lamb's Pas. EC1 275 K5
Lamb's Pas. EC1 142 DR71
Lambs Ter. N9 100 DR47
Lambs Wk., Enf. 82 DQ40
Lambscroft Ave. SE9 184 EJ90
Lambscroft Way, Ger.Cr. 90 AY54
Lambton Ave., Wal.Cr. 67 DX32
Lambton Pl. W11 139 CZ72
Westbourne Gro.
Lambton Rd. N19 121 DL60
Lambton Rd. SW20 199 CW95
Lambyn Cft., Horl. 269 DJ147
Lamerock Rd., Brom. 184 EF91
Lamerton Rd., Ilf. 103 EP54
Lamerton St. SE8 163 EA79
Lamford Clo. N17 100 DR52
Lamington St. W6 159 CV77
Lamlash St. SE11 278 F8
Lammas Ave., Mitch. 200 DG96
Lammas Ct., Wind. 151 AQ82
Lammas Dr., Stai. 173 BD91
Lammas Grn. SE26 182 DV90
Lammas La., Esher 214 CA106
Lammas Mead, Brox. 49 DZ23
Lammas Pk. W5 157 CJ75
Lammas Pk. Gdns. W5 157 CJ75
Lammas Pk. Rd. W5 137 CJ74
Lammas Rd. E9 143 DX66
Lammas Rd. E10 123 DY61
Lammas Rd., Rich. 177 CJ91
Lammas Rd., Slou. 131 AK71
Lammas Rd., Wat. 76 BW43
Lammas Way, H.Wyc. 88 AC54
Lammermoor Rd. SW12 181 DH87
Lamont Rd. SW10 160 DC79
Lamont Rd. Pas. SW10 160 DD79
Lamont Rd.
Lamorbey Clo., Sid. 185 ET88
Lamorna Ave., Grav. 191 GK89
Lamorna Clo. E17 101 EC53
Lamorna Clo., Orp. 206 EU101
Lamorna Clo., Rad. 61 CH34
Lamorna Gro., Stan. 95 CK53
Lamp Office Ct. WC1 274 B5
Lampard Gro. N16 122 DT60
Lampern Sq. E2 142 DU69
Nelson Gdns.
Lampeter Clo., Wok. 226 AY118
Lampeter Sq. W6 159 CY79
Humbolt Rd.
Lampits, Hodd. 49 EB17
Lamplighter Clo. E1 142 DW70
Cleveland Way
Lamplighters Clo., Dart. 188 FM86
Lamplighters Clo., Wal.Abb. 68 EG34
Lampmead Rd. SE12 184 EE85
Lamport Clo. SE18 165 EM77
Lampton Ave., Houns. 156 CB81
Lampton Ho. Clo. SW19 179 CX91
Lampton Pk. Rd., Houns. 156 CB82
Lampton Rd., Houns. 156 CB82
Lamsey Rd., Hem.H. 40 BK22
Lamson Rd., Rain. 147 FF70
Lanacre Ave. NW9 97 CT53
Lanark Clo. W5 137 CJ71
Lanark Pl. W9 140 DC70
Lanark Rd. W9 140 DB68
Lanark Sq. E14 163 EB76
Lanata Wk., Hayes 136 BX70
Ramulis Dr.
Lanbury Rd. SE15 163 DX84
Lancashire Ct. W1 273 J10
Lancaster Ave. E18 124 EH56
Lancaster Ave. SE27 181 DP89
Lancaster Ave. SW19 179 CX92
Lancaster Ave., Bark. 145 ES66
Lancaster Ave., Barn. 80 DD38
Lancaster Ave., Mitch. 201 DL99
Lancaster Ave., Slou. 131 AQ70
Lancaster Clo. N1 142 DS66
Hertford Rd.
Lancaster Clo. N17 100 DU52
Park La.
Lancaster Clo. NW9 97 CT52
Lancaster Clo., Brwd. 108 FU43
Lancaster Clo., Brom. 204 EF98
Lancaster Clo., Egh. 172 AX92
Lancaster Clo., Kings.T. 177 CK92
Lancaster Clo., Wok. 227 BA116
Lancaster Cotts., Rich. 178 CL86
Lancaster Pk.
Lancaster Ct. SE27 181 DP89
Lancaster Ct. SW6 159 CZ80
Lancaster Ct. W2 140 DC73
Lancaster Gate
Lancaster Ct., Bans. 217 CZ114
Lancaster Ct., Walt. 195 BU101
Lancaster Dr. E14 143 EC74
Prestons Rd.
Lancaster Dr. NW3 140 DE65
Lancaster Dr., Hem.H. 57 AZ27
Lancaster Dr., Horn. 127 FH64
Lancaster Dr., Loug. 84 EL44
Lancaster Gdns. SW19 179 CY92
Lancaster Gdns. W13 157 CH75
Lancaster Gdns., Kings.T. 177 CK92
Lancaster Gate W2 140 DC73
Lancaster Gro. NW3 140 DD65
Lancaster Ms. SW18 180 DB85
East Hill
Lancaster Ms. W2 140 DC73
Lancaster Ms., Rich. 178 CL86
Richmond Hill
Lancaster Pk., Rich. 178 CL85
Lancaster Pl. SW19 179 CX92
Lancaster Rd.
Lancaster Pl. WC2 274 B10
Lancaster Pl. WC2 141 DM73
Lancaster Pl., Houns. 156 BW82
Lancaster Pl., Ilf. 125 EQ64
Staines Rd.
Lancaster Pl., Twick. 177 CG86
Lancaster Rd. E7 144 EG66
Lancaster Rd. E11 124 EE61
Lancaster Rd. E17 101 DX54
Lancaster Rd. N4 121 DN59
Lancaster Rd. N11 99 DK51
Lancaster Rd. N18 100 DT50
Lancaster Rd. NW10 119 CU64
Lancaster Rd. SE25 202 DT96
Lancaster Rd. SW19 179 CX92
Lancaster Rd. W11 139 CY72
Lancaster Rd., Barn. 80 DD43
Lancaster Rd., Enf. 82 DR39
Lancaster Rd., Epp. 70 FA26
Lancaster Rd., Grays 169 FX78
Lancaster Rd., Har. 116 CA57
Lancaster Rd., Nthlt. 136 CC65
Lancaster Rd., St.Alb. 43 CF18
Lancaster Rd., Sthl. 136 BY73
Lancaster Rd., Uxb. 134 BK65
Lancaster St. SE1 278 G5
Lancaster St. SE1 161 DP75
Lancaster Ter. W2 140 DD73
Lancaster Wk. W2 140 DC74
Lancaster Wk., Hayes 135 BQ72
Lancaster Way, Abb.L. 59 BT31
Lancaster W. W11 139 CX73
Grenfell Rd.
Lance Rd., Har. 116 CC59
Lancefield St. W10 139 CZ69
Lancell St. N16 122 DS61
Stoke Newington Ch. St.
Lancelot Ave., Wem. 117 CK63
Lancelot Clo., Slou. 151 AN75
Mitchell Clo.
Lancelot Cres., Wem. 117 CK63
Lancelot Gdns., Barn. 98 DG45
Lancelot Pl. SW7 276 D5
Lancelot Pl. SW7 160 DF75
Lancelot Rd., Ilf. 103 ES51
Lancelot Rd., Well. 166 EU84
Lancelot Rd., Wem. 117 CK64
Lancer Sq. W8 160 DB75
Old Ct. Pl.
Lancey Clo. SE7 164 EK77
Cleveley Clo.
Lanchester Rd. N6 120 DF57
Lancing Gdns. N9 100 DT46
Lancing Rd. W13 137 CH73
Drayton Grn. Rd.
Lancing Rd., Croy. 201 DM100
Lancing Rd., Felt. 175 BT89
Lancing Rd., Ilf. 125 ER58
Lancing Rd., Orp. 206 EU103
Lancing Rd., Rom. 106 FL52
Lancing St. NW1 273 M3
Lancing Way, Rick. 75 BP43
Lancresse Clo., Uxb. 134 BK65
Lancresse Ct. N1 142 DS67
Landau Way, Brox. 67 DZ26
Landau Way, Erith 168 FK78
Landcroft Rd. SE22 182 DT86
Landells Rd. SE22 182 DT86
Landen Pk., Horl. 268 DE146
Lander Rd., Grays 170 GD78
Landford Clo., Rick. 92 BL47
Landford Rd. SW15 159 CW83
Landgrove Rd. SW19 180 DA92
Landmann Way SE14 163 DX78
Landmead Rd. (Cheshunt), Wal.Cr. 67 DY29
Landon Pl. SW1 276 D6
Landon Pl. SW1 160 DF76
Landon Wk. E14 143 EB73
Cottage St.
Landon Way, Ashf. 175 BP93
Courtfield Rd.
Landons Clo. E14 143 EC74
Landor Rd. SW9 161 DL83
Landor Wk. W12 159 CU75
Landport Way SE15 162 DT80
Daniel Gdns.
Landra Gdns. N21 81 DP44
Landridge Dr., Enf. 82 DV38
Landridge Rd. SW6 159 CZ82
Landrock Rd. N8 121 DL58
Lands End, Borwd. 77 CK44
Landscape Rd., Warl. 236 DV119
Landscape Rd., Wdf.Grn. 102 EH52
Landseer Ave. E12 125 EN64
Landseer Ave., Grav. 190 GD90
Landseer Clo. SW19 200 DC95
Brangwyn Cres.
Landseer Clo., Edg. 96 CN54
Landseer Clo., Horn. 127 FH60
Landseer Rd. N19 121 DL62
Landseer Rd., Enf. 82 DU43
Landseer Rd., N.Mal. 198 CR101
Landseer Rd., Sutt. 218 DA107
Landstead Rd. SE18 165 ER80
Landway, The, Orp. 206 EW97
Lane, The NW8 140 DC68
Marlborough Pl.
Lane, The SE3 164 EG83
Lane, The, Cher. 194 BG97
Lane, The, Vir.W. 192 AY97
Lane App. NW7 97 CY50
Lane Ave., Green. 189 FW86
Lane Clo. NW2 119 CV62
Lane Clo., Add. 212 BH106
Lane End, Bexh. 167 FB83
Lane End, Epsom 216 CP114
Lane End, Harl. 52 EY15
Lane End, Hat. 45 CT21
Lane Gdns. (Bushey), Wat. 95 CE45
Lane Ms. E12 125 EM62
Colchester Ave.
Lane Wd. Clo., Amer. 72 AT39
Lanefield Wk., Welw.G.C. 29 CW09
Lanercost Clo. SW2 181 DN89
Lanercost Gdns. N14 99 DL45
Lanercost Rd. SW2 181 DN89
Lanes Ave., Grav. 191 GG91
Lanesborough Pl. SW1 276 F4
Laneside, Chis. 185 EP92
Laneside, Edg. 96 CQ50
Laneside Ave., Dag. 126 EZ59
Laneway SW15 179 CV85
Lanfranc Rd. E3 143 DY68
Lanfrey Pl. W14 159 CZ78
North End Rd.
Lang Clo., Lthd. 230 CB123
Lang St. E1 142 DW70
Langaller La., Lthd. 230 CB122
Langbourne Ave. N6 120 DG61
Langbourne Way, Esher 215 CG107
Langbrook Rd. SE3 164 EK83
Langcroft Clo., Cars. 200 DF104
Langdale Ave., Mitch. 200 DF97
Langdale Clo. SE17 162 DQ79
Langdale Clo. SW14 158 CP84
Clifford Ave.
Langdale Clo., Dag. 126 EW60
Langdale Clo., Orp. 205 EP104
Grasmere Rd.
Langdale Clo., Wok. 226 AW116
Langdale Ct., Hem.H. 40 BL17
Wharfedale
Langdale Cres., Bexh. 166 FA80
Langdale Dr., Hayes 135 BS68
Langdale Gdns., Grnf. 137 CH69
Langdale Gdns., Horn. 127 FG64
Langdale Gdns., Wal.Cr. 83 DX35
Langdale Rd. SE10 163 EC80
Langdale Rd., Th.Hth. 201 DN98
Langdale St. E1 142 DV72
Burslem St.
Langdale Wk., Grav. 190 GE90
Landseer Ave.
Langdon Ct. NW10 138 CS67
Langdon Cres. E6 145 EN68
Langdon Dr. NW9 118 CQ60
Langdon Pk. Rd. N6 121 DJ59
Langdon Pl. SW14 158 CQ83
Rosemary La.
Langdon Rd. E6 145 EN67
Langdon Rd., Brom. 204 EH97
Langdon Rd., Mord. 200 DC99
Langdon Shaw, Sid. 185 ET92
Langdon Wk., Mord. 200 DC99
Langdon Way SE1 162 DU77
Simms Rd.
Langdons Ct., Sthl. 156 CA76
Langfield Clo., Wal.Abb. 50 EE22
Langford Clo. E8 122 DU64
Langford Clo. N15 122 DS58
Langford Clo. NW8 140 DC68
Langford Pl.
Langford Ct. NW8 140 DC68
Langford Cres., Barn. 80 DF42
Langford Grn. SE5 162 DS83
Langford Grn., Brwd. 109 GC44
Langford Pl. NW8 140 DC68
Langford Pl., Sid. 186 EU90
Langford Rd. SW6 160 DB82
Langford Rd., Barn. 80 DE42
Langford Rd., Wdf.Grn. 102 EJ51
Langfords, Buck.H. 102 EK47
Langfords Way, Croy. 221 DY111
Langham Clo. N15 121 DP55
Langham Rd.
Langham Clo., St.Alb. 43 CK15
Langham Ct., Horn. 128 FK59
Langham Dene, Ken. 235 DP115
Langham Dr., Rom. 126 EV58
Langham Gdns. N21 81 DN43
Langham Gdns. W13 137 CH73
Langham Gdns., Edg. 96 CQ52
Langham Gdns., Rich. 177 CJ91
Langham Gdns., Wem. 117 CJ61
Langham Ho. Clo., Rich. 177 CK91
Langham Pl. N15 121 DP55
Langham Pl. W1 273 J7
Langham Pl. W1 141 DH71
Langham Pl. W4 158 CS79
Hogarth Roundabout
Langham Pl., Egh. 173 AZ92
Langham Rd. N15 121 DP55
Langham Rd. SW20 199 CW95
Langham Rd., Edg. 96 CQ51
Langham Rd., Tedd. 177 CH92
Langham St. W1 273 J7
Langham St. W1 141 DH71
Langhedge Clo. N18 100 DT51
Langhedge La.
Langhedge La. N18 100 DT50
Langhedge La. Ind. Est. N18 100 DT51
Langholm Clo. SW12 181 DK87
King's Ave.
Langholme (Bushey), Wat. 94 CC46
Langhorne Rd., Dag. 146 FA66
Langland Ct., Nthwd. 93 BQ52
Langland Cres., Stan. 118 CL55
Langland Dr., Pnr. 94 BY52
Langland Gdns. NW3 120 DB64
Langland Gdns., Croy. 203 DZ103
Langlands Dr., Dart. 189 FS92
Langlands Ri., Epsom 216 CQ113
Burnet Gro.

Langler Rd. NW10 139 CW68
Langley Ave., Hem.H. 40 BL23
Langley Ave., Ruis. 115 BV60
Langley Ave., Surb. 197 CK102
Langley Ave., Wor.Pk. 199 CX103
Langley Broom, Slou. 153 AZ78
Langley Business Cen., Slou. 153 BA75
Langley Clo., Epsom 232 CR119
Langley Clo., Guil. 242 AW133
Langley Clo., Rom. 106 FK52
Langley Ct. SE9 185 EN86
Langley Ct. WC2 273 P10
Langley Ct., Beck. 203 EB99
Langley Cres. E11 124 EJ59
Langley Cres., Dag. 146 EW66
Langley Cres., Edg. 96 CQ48
Langley Cres., Hayes 155 BT80
Langley Cres., Kings L. 58 BN30
Langley Cres., St.Alb. 42 CC18
Langley Dr. E11 124 EH59
Langley Dr. W3 158 CP75
Langley Dr., Brwd. 108 FU48
Langley Gdns., Brom. 204 EJ98
Langley Gdns., Dag. 146 EX66
Langley Gdns., Orp. 205 EP100
Langley Gro., N.Mal. 198 CS96
Langley Hill, Kings L. 58 BM29
Langley Hill Clo., Kings L. 58 BN29
Langley La. SW8 161 DM79
Langley La., Abb.L. 59 BT31
Langley La., Epsom 248 CQ125
Tumber St.
Langley Lo. La., Kings L. 58 BN31
Langley Meadow, Loug. 85 ER40
Langley Oaks Ave., S.Croy. 220 DU110
Langley Pk. NW7 96 CS51
Langley Pk. Rd., Iver 133 BC72
Langley Pk. Rd., Slou. 153 BA75
Langley Pk. Rd., Sutt. 218 DC106
Langley Quay, Slou. 153 BA75
Langley Rd. SW19 199 CZ95
Langley Rd., Abb.L. 59 BS31
Langley Rd., Beck. 203 DY98
Langley Rd., Islw. 157 CF82
Langley Rd., Kings L. 58 BH30
Langley Rd., Slou. 152 AW76
Langley Rd., S.Croy. 221 DX109
Langley Rd., Stai. 173 BF93
Langley Rd., Surb. 198 CL101
Langley Rd., Wat. 75 BU39
Langley Rd., Well. 166 EW79
Langley Row, Barn. 79 CZ39
Langley St. WC2 273 P9
Langley St. WC2 141 DL72
Langley Vale Rd., Epsom 232 CP120
Langley Wk., Wok. 226 AY119
Midhope Rd.
Langley Way, Wat. 75 BT39
Langley Way, W.Wick. 203 ED102
Langleybury La., Kings L. 75 BP37
Langmans La., Wok. 226 AV118
Langmans Way, Wok. 226 AS116
Langmead Dr. (Bushey), Wat. 95 CD46
Langmead St. SE27 181 DP91
Beadman St.
Langmore Ct., Bexh. 166 EX83
Regency Way
Langport Ct., Walt. 196 BW102
Langridge Ms., Hmptn. 176 BZ93
Oak Ave.
Langroyd Rd. SW17 180 DF89
Langshott, Horl. 269 DH146
Langshott Clo., Add. 211 BE111
Langshott La., Horl. 269 DH148
Langside Ave. SW15 159 CU84
Langside Cres. N14 99 DK48
Langston Hughes Clo. SE24 161 DP84
Shakespeare Rd.
Langston Rd., Loug. 85 EQ43
Langthorn Ct. EC2 275 K8
Langthorne Cres., Grays 170 GC77
Langthorne Rd. E11 123 EC62
Langthorne St. SW6 159 CX80
Langton Ave. E6 145 EN69
Langton Ave. N20 98 DC45
Langton Ave., Epsom 217 CT111
Langton Clo. WC1 274 C3
Langton Clo., Add. 194 BH104
Langton Clo., Wok. 226 AT117
Kenton Way
Langton Gro., Nthwd. 93 BQ50
Langton Pl. SW18 180 DA88
Merton Rd.
Langton Ri. SE23 182 DV87
Langton Rd. NW2 119 CW62
Langton Rd. SW9 161 DP80
Langton Rd., Har. 94 CC52
Langton Rd., Hodd. 49 DZ17
Langton Rd., W.Mol. 196 CC99
Langton St. SW10 160 DC79
Langton Way SE3 164 EF81
Langton Way, Croy. 220 DS105
Langton Way, Egh. 173 BC93
Langton Way, Grays 171 GJ77
Langton's Meadow, Slou. 131 AQ65
Langtry Rd. NW8 140 DB67
Langtry Rd., Nthlt. 136 BX68
Langtry Wk. NW8 140 DC66
Alexandra Pl.
Langwood Chase, Tedd. 177 CJ93
Langwood Gdns., Wat. 75 BU39
Langworth Clo., Dart. 188 FK90
Langworth Dr., Hayes 135 BU72
Lanhill Rd. W9 140 DA70
Lanier Rd. SE13 183 EC86
Lanigan Dr., Houns. 176 CB85
Lankaster Gdns. N2 98 DD53
Lankers Dr., Har. 116 BZ58
Lankton Clo., Beck. 203 EC95
Lannock Rd., Hayes 135 BS74
Lannoy Rd. SE9 185 EQ88
Lanrick Copse, Berk. 38 AY18
Lanrick Rd. E14 143 ED72
Lanridge Rd. SE2 166 EX76
Lansbury Ave. N18 100 DR50
Lansbury Ave., Bark. 146 EU66
Lansbury Ave., Felt. 175 BV86
Lansbury Ave., Rom. 126 EY57
Lansbury Clo. NW10 118 CQ64
Lansbury Cres., Dart. 188 FN85
Lansbury Dr., Hayes 135 BT71
Lansbury Est. E14 143 EB72
Lansbury Gdns. E14 143 ED72
Lansbury Gdns., Til. 171 GG81
Lansbury Rd., Enf. 83 DX39
Lansbury Way N18 100 DS50
Lanscombe Wk. SW8 161 DL81
Lansdell Rd., Mitch. 200 DG96
Lansdown, Guil. 243 BA134
Lansdown Clo., Walt. 196 BW102
St. Johns Dr.
Lansdown Clo., Wok. 226 AT119
Lansdown Pl., Grav. 191 GF88
Lansdown Rd. E7 144 EJ66
Lansdown Rd., Ger.Cr. 90 AX53
Lansdown Rd., Sid. 186 EV90
Lansdowne Ave., Bexh. 166 EX80
Lansdowne Ave., Orp. 205 EP102
Lansdowne Ave., Slou. 132 AS74
Lansdowne Clo. SW20 179 CX94
Lansdowne Clo., Surb. 198 CP103
Kingston Rd.
Lansdowne Clo., Twick. 177 CF88
Lion Rd.
Lansdowne Clo., Wat. 60 BX34
Lansdowne Ct., Pur. 219 DP110
Lansdowne Ct., Slou. 132 AS74
Lansdowne Ct., Wor.Pk. 199 CU103
The Ave.
Lansdowne Cres. W11 139 CY73
Lansdowne Dr. E8 142 DU65
Lansdowne Gdns. SW8 161 DL81
Lansdowne Grn. SW8 161 DL81
Hartington Rd.
Lansdowne Gro. NW10 118 CS63
Lansdowne Hill SE27 181 DP90
Lansdowne La. SE7 164 EK79
Lansdowne Ms. SE7 164 EK78
Lansdowne Ms. W11 139 CZ74
Lansdowne Rd.
Lansdowne Pl. SE1 279 L7
Lansdowne Pl. SE19 182 DT94
Lansdowne Ri. W11 139 CY73
Lansdowne Rd. E4 101 EA47
Lansdowne Rd. E11 124 EF61
Lansdowne Rd. E17 123 EA57
Lansdowne Rd. E18 124 EG55
Lansdowne Rd. N3 97 CZ52
Lansdowne Rd. N10 99 DJ54
Lansdowne Rd. N17 100 DT53
Lansdowne Rd. SW20 179 CW94
Lansdowne Rd. W11 139 CY73
Lansdowne Rd., Brom. 184 EG94
Lansdowne Rd., Chesh. 54 AQ29
Lansdowne Rd., Croy. 202 DR103
Lansdowne Rd., Epsom 216 CQ108
Lansdowne Rd., Har. 117 CE59
Lansdowne Rd., Houns. 156 CB83
Lansdowne Rd., Ilf. 125 ET60
Lansdowne Rd., Pur. 219 DN112
Lansdowne Rd., Sev. 257 FK122
Lansdowne Rd., Stai. 174 BH94
Lansdowne Rd., Stan. 95 CJ51
Lansdowne Rd., Til. 171 GF82
Lansdowne Rd., Uxb. 135 BP72
Lansdowne Row W1 277 J2
Lansdowne Sq., Grav. 191 GF86
Lansdowne Ter. WC1 274 A5
Lansdowne Ter. WC1 141 DL70
Lansdowne Wk. W11 139 CY74
Lansdowne Way SW8 161 DL81
Lansdowne Wd. Clo. SE27 181 DP90
Lansfield Ave. N18 100 DU49
Lant St. SE1 279 H4
Lant St. SE1 162 DQ75
Lantern Clo. SW15 159 CU84
Lantern Clo., Wem. 117 CK64
Lanterns Ct. E14 163 EA75
Lanvanor Rd. SE15 162 DW82
Lapford Clo. W9 139 CZ70
Lapponum Wk., Hayes 136 BX71
Lochan Clo.
Lapse Wd. Wk. SE23 182 DV88
Lapstone Gdns., Har. 117 CJ58
Lapwing Clo., Erith 167 FH80
Lapwing Clo., Hem.H. 40 BL16
Lapwing Clo., S.Croy. 221 DY110
Lapwing Ct., Surb. 198 CN104
Chaffinch Clo.
Lapwing Gro., Guil. 243 BD132
Lapwing Way, Abb.L. 59 BU31
Lapwing Way, Hayes 136 BX72
Lapwings, The, Grav. 191 GK89
Lapworth Clo., Orp. 206 EW103
Lara Clo. SE13 183 EC86
Lara Clo., Chess. 216 CL108
Larbert Rd. SW16 201 DJ95
Larby Pl., Epsom 216 CS110
Larch Ave. W3 138 CS74
Larch Ave., Guil. 242 AW132
Larch Ave., St.Alb. 60 BY30
Larch Clo. E13 144 EH70
Larch Clo. N11 98 DG52
Larch Clo. N19 121 DJ61
Bredgar Rd.
Larch Clo. SE8 163 DZ79
Clyde St.
Larch Clo. SW12 181 DH89
Larch Clo., H.Wyc. 88 AC45
Larch Clo., Red. 266 DC136
Larch Clo., Slou. 131 AP71
Larch Clo., Tad. 234 DC121
Larch Clo., Wal.Cr. 66 DS27
The Firs
Larch Clo., Warl. 237 DY119
Larch Cres., Epsom 216 CP107
Larch Cres., Hayes 136 BW70
Larch Dr. W4 158 CN78
Gunnersbury Ave.
Larch Grn. NW9 96 CS53
Clayton Fld.
Larch Gro., Sid. 185 ET88
Larch Ms. N19 121 DJ61
Bredgar Rd.
Larch Ri., Berk. 38 AU18
Larch Rd. E10 123 EA61
Walnut Rd.
Larch Rd. NW2 119 CW63
Larch Rd., Dart. 188 FK87
Larch Tree Way, Croy. 203 EA104
Larch Wk., Swan. 207 FD96
Larch Way, Brom. 205 EN101
Larchdene, Orp. 205 EN103
Larches, The N13 100 DQ48
Larches, The, Nthwd. 93 BQ51
Rickmansworth Rd.
Larches, The, St.Alb. 43 CK16
Larches, The, Uxb. 135 BP69
Larches, The, Wat. 76 BY43
Larches, The, Wok. 226 AY116
Larches Ave. SW14 158 CR84
Larches Ave., Enf. 82 DW35
Larchlands, The, H.Wyc. 88 AD46
Larchwood Ave., Rom. 105 FB51
Larchwood Clo., Bans. 233 CY115
Larchwood Clo., Rom. 105 FC51
Larchwood Dr., Egh. 172 AV93
Larchwood Gdns., Brwd. 108 FU44
Larchwood Rd. SE9 185 EP89
Larchwood Rd., Hem.H. 40 BM18
Larcom St. SE17 279 J9
Larcom St. SE17 162 DQ77
Larcombe Clo., Croy. 220 DT105
Larden Rd. W3 138 CS74
Largewood Ave., Surb. 198 CN103
Largo Wk., Erith 167 FE81
Selkirk Dr.
Larissa St. SE17 279 L10
Lark Ave., Stai. 173 BF90
Kestrel Ave.
Lark Ri., Hat. 45 CU20
Lark Ri., Lthd. 245 BS131
Lark Row E2 142 DW67
Lark Way, Cars. 200 DE101
Larkbere Rd. SE26 183 DY91
Larken Dr. (Bushey), Wat. 94 CC46
Larkfield, Cob. 213 BU113
Larkfield Ave., Har. 117 CH55
Larkfield Clo., Brom. 204 EF103
Larkfield Ct., Horl. 269 DN148
Cooper Clo.
Larkfield Rd., Rich. 158 CL84
Larkfield Rd., Sev. 256 FC123
Larkfield Rd., Sid. 185 ET90
Larkfields, Grav. 190 GE90
Larkhall Clo., Walt. 214 BW107
Larkhall Ct., Rom. 105 FC54
Larkhall La. SW4 161 DK82
Larkhall Ri. SW4 161 DJ83
Larkham Clo., Felt. 175 BS90
Larkhill Ter. SE18 165 EN80
Larkin Clo., Brwd. 109 GC45
Larkin Clo., Couls. 235 DM117
Larkin Ind. Est., Chesh. 54 AR32
Larkings La., Slou. 132 AV67
Larkins Rd., Gat. 268 DD152
Larks Gro., Bark. 145 ES66
Larks Ri., Chesh. 54 AR33
Larksfield, Egh. 172 AW94
Larksfield, Horl. 269 DH147
Larksfield Gro., Enf. 82 DV39
Larkshall Cres. E4 101 EC49
Larkshall Rd. E4 101 EC50
Larkspur Clo. E6 144 EL71
Larkspur Clo. N17 100 DR52
Fryatt Rd.
Larkspur Clo. NW9 118 CP57
Larkspur Clo., Hem.H. 39 BE19
Larkspur Clo., Orp. 206 EW103
Larkspur Clo., Ruis. 115 BQ59
Larkspur Clo., S.Ock. 149 FW69
Larkspur Gro., Edg. 96 CQ49
Larkspur Way, Dor. 263 CK139
Larkspur Way, Epsom 216 CQ106
Larkswood, Harl. 52 EW17
Larkswood Clo., Erith 167 FG81
Larkswood Ct. E4 101 ED50
Larkswood Ri., Pnr. 116 BW56
Larkswood Ri., St.Alb. 43 CJ15
Larkswood Rd. E4 101 EA49
Larkway Clo. NW9 118 CR56
Larmans Rd., Enf. 82 DW36
Larnach Rd. W6 159 CX79
Larne Rd., Ruis. 115 BT59
Larner Rd., Erith 167 FE80
Larpent Ave. SW15 179 CW85
Larsen Dr., Wal.Abb. 67 ED34
Larwood Clo., Grnf. 117 CD64
Las Palmas Est., Shep. 195 BQ101
Lascelles Ave., Har. 117 CD59
Lascelles Clo. E11 123 ED61
Lascelles Clo., Brwd. 108 FU43
Lascelles Rd., Slou. 152 AV76
Lascotts Rd. N22 99 DM51
Lassa Rd. SE9 184 EL85
Lassell St. SE10 163 ED78
Lasseter Pl. SE3 164 EF79
Vanbrugh Hill
Lasswade Rd., Cher. 193 BF101
Latchett Rd. E18 102 EH53
Latchford Pl., Chig. 104 EV49
Manford Way
Latching Clo., Rom. 106 FK49
Troopers Dr.
Latchingdon Ct. E17 123 DX56
Latchingdon Gdns., Wdf.Grn. 102 EL51
Latchmere Clo., Rich. 178 CL92
Latchmere La., Kings.T. 178 CM93
Latchmere Pas. SW11 160 DE82
Cabul Rd.
Latchmere Rd. SW11 160 DF82
Latchmere Rd., Kings.T. 178 CL94
Latchmere St. SW11 160 DF82
Latchmoor Ave., Ger.Cr. 112 AX56
Latchmoor Gro., Ger.Cr. 112 AX56
Latchmoor Way, Ger.Cr. 112 AX55
Lateward Rd., Brent. 157 CK79
Latham Clo. E6 144 EL72
Oliver Gdns.
Latham Clo., Twick. 177 CG87
Latham Clo., West. 238 EJ116
Latham Ho. E1 143 DX72
Latham Rd., Bexh. 186 FA85
Latham Rd., Twick. 177 CF87
Lathams Way, Croy. 201 DM102
Lathkill Clo., Enf. 100 DU45
Lathom Rd. E6 145 EM66
Latimer SE17 162 DS78
Beaconsfield Rd.
Latimer Ave. E6 145 EM67
Latimer Clo., Amer. 72 AW39
Latimer Clo., Hem.H. 40 BN15
Latimer Clo., Pnr. 94 BW53
Latimer Clo., Wat. 93 BS45
Latimer Clo., Wok. 227 BB116
Latimer Clo., Wor.Pk. 217 CV105
Latimer Dr., Horn. 128 FK62
Latimer Gdns., Pnr. 94 BW53
Latimer Gdns., Welw.G.C. 30 DB09
Latimer Pl. W10 139 CW72
Latimer Rd. E7 124 EH63
Latimer Rd. N15 122 DS58
Latimer Rd. SW19 180 DB93
Latimer Rd. W10 139 CW72
Latimer Rd., Barn. 80 DB41
Latimer Rd., Chesh. 54 AR34
Latimer Rd., Croy. 201 DP104
Abbey Rd.
Latimer Rd., Rick. 73 AZ38
Latimer Rd., Tedd. 177 CF92
Latimer Way, Beac. 88 AJ49
Latium Clo., St.Alb. 43 CD21
Latona Dr., Grav. 191 GM92
Latona Rd. SE15 162 DU79
Lattimer Pl. W4 158 CS79
Lattimore Rd., St.Alb. 43 CE21
Latton Clo., Esher 214 CB105
Latton Clo., Walt. 196 BY101
Latton Common Rd., Harl. 52 EU18
Latton Grn., Harl. 51 ET19
Latton Hall Clo., Harl. 36 EU14
Latton St., Harl. 36 EU14
Latymer Clo., Wey. 213 BQ105
Latymer Ct. W6 159 CX77
Latymer Rd. N9 100 DT46
Latymer Way N9 100 DR47
Laud St. SE11 278 B10
Laud St., Croy. 202 DQ104
Lauder Clo., Nthlt. 136 BX68
Lauderdale Dr., Rich. 177 CK90
Lauderdale Pl. EC2 142 DQ71
Beech St.
Lauderdale Rd. W9 140 DB69
Lauderdale Rd., Kings L. 59 BQ33
Lauderdale Twr. EC2 142 DQ71
Beech St.
Laughton Ct., Borwd. 78 CR40
Banks Rd.
Laughton Rd., Nthlt. 136 BX67
Launcelot Rd., Brom. 184 EG91
Launcelot St. SE1 278 D5
Launceston Clo., Rom. 106 FJ53
Launceston Gdns., Grnf. 137 CJ67
Launceston Pl. W8 160 DC76
Launceston Rd., Grnf. 137 CJ67
Launch St. E14 163 EC76
Launders La., Rain. 148 FM69
Laundress La. N16 122 DU62
Laundry La. N1 142 DQ67
Greenman St.
Laundry La., Wal.Abb. 68 EE25
Laundry Rd. W6 159 CY79
Laundry Rd., Guil. 258 AW135
Laura Clo. E11 124 EJ57
Laura Clo., Enf. 82 DS43
Laura Dr., Swan. 187 FG94
Laura Pl. E5 122 DW63
Lauradale Rd. N2 120 DF56
Laureate Way, Hem.H. 40 BG18
Laurel Ave., Egh. 172 AV92
Laurel Ave., Grav. 191 GJ89
Laurel Ave., Pot.B. 63 CZ32
Laurel Ave., Slou. 152 AY75
Laurel Ave., Twick. 177 CF88
Laurel Bank Gdns. SW6 159 CZ82
New Kings Rd.
Laurel Bank Rd., Enf. 82 DQ39
Laurel Bank Vil. W7 137 CE74
Lower Boston Rd.
Laurel Clo. N19 121 DJ61
Hargrave Pk.
Laurel Clo. SW17 180 DE92
Laurel Clo., Brwd. 109 GB43
Laurel Clo., Dart. 188 FJ88
Willow Rd.
Laurel Clo., Hem.H. 40 BM19
Laurel Clo., Ilf. 103 EQ51
Laurel Clo., Sid. 186 EU90
Laurel Clo., Slou. 153 BE80
Laurel Clo., Wok. 211 BD113
Laurel Cres., Croy. 203 EA104
Laurel Cres., Rom. 127 FE60
Laurel Cres., Wok. 211 BC113
Laurel Dr. N21 99 DN45
Laurel Dr., Oxt. 254 EF131
Laurel Dr., S.Ock. 149 FX70
Laurel Flds., Pot.B. 63 CZ31
Laurel Gdns. E4 101 EB45
Laurel Gdns. NW7 96 CR48
Laurel Gdns. W7 137 CE74
Laurel Gdns., Houns. 156 BY84
Laurel Gro. SE20 182 DV94
Laurel Gro. SE26 183 DX91
Laurel La., Horn. 128 FL61
Station La.
Laurel La., West Dr. 154 BL77
Laurel Lo. La., Barn. 79 CW36
Laurel Pk., Har. 95 CF52
Laurel Rd. SW13 159 CU82
Laurel Rd. SW20 199 CV95
Laurel Rd., Ger.Cr. 90 AX53
Laurel Rd., Hmptn. 177 CD92
Laurel Rd., St.Alb. 43 CF20
Laurel St. E8 142 DT65
Laurel Vw. N12 98 DB48
Laurel Way E18 124 EF56
Laurel Way N20 98 DA48
Laurels, The, Bans. 233 CZ117
Laurels, The, Berk. 39 BC17
Laurels, The, Cob. 230 BY115
Laurels, The, Dart. 188 FJ90
Laurels, The, Wal.Cr. 66 DS27
Laurels, The, Wey. 195 BR104
Laurels Rd., Iver 133 BD68
Laurelsfield, St.Alb. 42 CB23
Laurence Ms. W12 159 CU75
Askew Rd.
Laurence Pountney Hill EC4 275 K10
Laurence Pountney La. EC4 275 K10
Laurie Gro. SE14 163 DY81
Laurie Rd. W7 137 CE71
Laurie Wk., Rom. 127 FE57
Laurier Rd. NW5 121 DH62
Laurier Rd., Croy. 202 DT101
Lauries Clo., Hem.H. 39 BB22
Laurimel Clo., Stan. 95 CH51
September Way
Laurino Pl. (Bushey), Wat. 94 CC47
Lauriston Rd. E9 143 DX67
Lauriston Rd. SW19 179 CX93
Lausanne Rd. N8 121 DN56
Lausanne Rd. SE15 162 DW81
Lauser Rd., Stai. 174 BJ87
Laustan Clo., Guil. 243 BC134
Lavell St. N16 122 DR63
Lavender Ave. NW9 118 CQ60
Lavender Ave., Brwd. 108 FV43
Lavender Ave., Mitch. 200 DE95
Lavender Ave., Wor.Pk. 199 CW104
Lavender Clo. SW3 160 DD79
Danvers St.
Lavender Clo., Brom. 204 EL100
Lavender Clo., Cars. 218 DG105
Lavender Clo., Cat. 252 DQ125
Lavender Clo., Couls. 235 DJ119
Lavender Clo., Red. 267 DH139
Lavender Clo., Rom. 106 FK52
Lavender Clo. (Cheshunt), Wal.Cr. 66 DT27
Lavender Ct., W.Mol. 196 CB97
Molesham Way
Lavender Dr., Uxb. 134 BM71
Lavender Gdns. SW11 160 DF84
Lavender Gdns., Enf. 81 DP39
Lavender Gdns., Har. 95 CE51
Uxbridge Rd.
Lavender Gro. E8 142 DT66
Lavender Gro., Mitch. 200 DE95
Lavender Hill SW11 160 DE84
Lavender Hill, Enf. 81 DN39
Lavender Hill, Swan. 207 FD97
Lavender Ms., Wall. 219 DL107
Lavender Pk. Rd., W.Byf. 212 BG112
Lavender Pl., Ilf. 125 EP64
Lavender Ri., West Dr. 154 BN75
Lavender Rd. SE16 143 DY74
Lavender Rd. SW11 160 DD83
Lavender Rd., Cars. 218 DG105
Lavender Rd., Croy. 201 DM100
Lavender Rd., Enf. 82 DR39
Lavender Rd., Epsom 216 CP106
Lavender Rd., Sutt. 218 DD105
Lavender Rd., Uxb. 134 BM71
Lavender Rd., Wok. 227 BB116
Lavender Sq. E11 123 ED62
Anglian Rd.
Lavender St. E15 144 EE65
Manbey Gro.
Lavender Sweep SW11 160 DF84
Lavender Ter. SW11 160 DE83
Falcon Rd.
Lavender Vale, Wall. 219 DK107
Lavender Wk. SW11 160 DF84
Lavender Wk., Hem.H. 40 BK18
Townsend
Lavender Wk., Mitch. 200 DG97
Lavender Way, Croy. 203 DX100
Lavengro Rd. SE27 182 DQ89
Lavenham Rd. SW18 179 CZ89
Lavernock Rd., Bexh. 166 FA82
Lavers Rd. N16 122 DS62
Laverstoke Gdns. SW15 179 CU87
Laverton Ms. SW5 160 DB77
Laverton Pl.
Laverton Pl. SW5 160 DB77
Lavidge Rd. SE9 184 EL89
Lavina Gro. N1 141 DM68
Wharfdale Rd.
Lavington Rd. W13 137 CH74
Lavington Rd., Croy. 201 DM104
Lavington St. SE1 278 G3
Lavington St. SE1 141 DP74
Lavinia Ave., Wat. 60 BX34
Lavinia Rd., Dart. 188 FM86
Lavrock La., Rick. 92 BM45
Law Ho., Bark. 146 EU68
Law St. SE1 279 L6
Law St. SE1 162 DR76
Lawbrook La., Guil. 261 BQ143
Lawdons Gdns., Croy. 219 DP105
Lawford Ave., Rick. 73 BC44
Lawford Clo., Horn. 128 FJ63
Lawford Clo., Rick. 73 BC44
Lawford Clo., Wall. 219 DL109
Lawford Gdns., Dart. 188 FJ85
Lawford Gdns., Ken. 236 DQ116
Lawford Rd. N1 142 DS66
Lawford Rd. NW5 141 DJ65
Lawford Rd. W4 158 CQ80
Lawkland, Slou. 131 AQ69
Lawless St. E14 143 EB73
Lawley Rd. N14 99 DH45
Lawley St. E5 122 DW63
Lawn, The, Harl. 36 EV12
Lawn, The, Sthl. 156 CA78
Lawn Ave., West Dr. 154 BJ75
Lawn Clo. N9 100 DT45
Lawn Clo., Brom. 184 EH93
Lawn Clo., N.Mal. 198 CS96
Lawn Clo., Ruis. 115 BT62
Lawn Clo., Slou. 152 AW80
Lawn Clo., Swan. 207 FC96
Lawn Cres., Rich. 158 CN82
Lawn Fm. Gro., Rom. 126 EY56
Lawn Gdns. W7 137 CE74
Lawn Ho. Clo. E14 163 EC75
Lawn La. SW8 161 DL79
Lawn La., Hem.H. 40 BK22
Lawn Pk., Sev. 257 FH127
Lawn Pl. SE15 162 DT81
Sumner Est.
Lawn Rd. NW3 120 DF64
Lawn Rd., Beck. 183 DZ94
Lawn Rd., Grav. 190 GC86
Lawn Rd., Guil. 258 AW137
Lawn Rd., Uxb. 134 BJ66
New Windsor St.
Lawn Ter. SE3 164 EE83
Lawn Vale, Pnr. 94 BX54
Lawnfield NW2 139 CX66
Coverdale Rd.
Lawns, The E4 101 EA50
Lawns, The SE3 164 EE83
Lee Ter.
Lawns, The SE19 202 DR95
Lawns, The, Hem.H. 39 BE19
Lawns, The, Pnr. 94 CB52
Lawns, The (Shenley), Rad. 62 CL33
Lawns, The, St.Alb. 42 CC19
Lawns, The, Sid. 186 EV91
Lawns, The, Sutt. 217 CY108
Lawns, The, Welw.G.C. 29 CX06
Lawns Ct., Wem. 118 CM61
The Ave.
Lawns Cres., Grays 170 GD79
Lawns Dr., The, Brox. 49 DZ21
Lawns Way, Rom. 105 FC52
Lawnside SE3 164 EF84
Lawrance Gdns. (Cheshunt), Wal.Cr. 67 DX28
Lawrance Rd., St.Alb. 42 CC16
Lawrence Ave. E12 125 EN63
Lawrence Ave. E17 101 DX53
Lawrence Ave. N13 99 DP49
Lawrence Ave. NW7 96 CS49
Lawrence Ave., N.Mal. 198 CR100

Lawrence Ave., Ware 33 EC11
Lawrence Bldgs. N16 122 DT62
Lawrence Campe Clo. N20 98 DD48
Friern Barnet La.
Lawrence Clo. E3 143 EA68
Lawrence Clo. N15 122 DS55
Lawrence Rd.
Lawrence Clo., Guil. 243 BB129
Ladygrove Dr.
Lawrence Clo., Hert. 31 DL08
Lawrence Ct. NW7 96 CS50
Lawrence Cres., Dag. 127 FB62
Lawrence Cres., Edg. 96 CN54
Lawrence Dr., Uxb. 115 BQ63
Lawrence Gdns. NW7 97 CT48
Lawrence Gdns., Til. 171 GH80
Lawrence Hill E4 101 EA47
Lawrence Hill Gdns., Dart. 188 FJ86
Lawrence Hill Rd., Dart. 188 FJ86
Lawrence La. EC2 275 J9
Lawrence La., Bet. 249 CV132
Lawrence Moorings, Saw. 36 EZ06
Lawrence Pl. N1 141 DL67
Outram Pl.
Lawrence Rd. E6 144 EK67
Lawrence Rd. E13 144 EH67
Lawrence Rd. N15 122 DS56
Lawrence Rd. N18 100 DV49
Lawrence Rd. SE25 202 DT98
Lawrence Rd. W5 157 CK77
Lawrence Rd., Erith 167 FB80
Lawrence Rd., Hmptn. 176 BZ94
Lawrence Rd., Hayes 135 BQ68
Lawrence Rd., Houns. 156 BW84
Lawrence Rd., Pnr. 116 BX57
Lawrence Rd., Rich. 177 CJ91
Lawrence Rd., Rom. 127 FH57
Lawrence Rd., W.Wick. 222 EG105
Lawrence Sq., Grav. 191 GF90
Haynes Rd.
Lawrence St. E16 144 EF71
Lawrence St. NW7 97 CT49
Lawrence St. SW3 160 DE79
Lawrence Way NW10 118 CQ63
Lawrence Way, Slou. 131 AK71
Lawrence Weaver Clo., Mord. 200 DB100
Green La.
Lawrie Pk. Ave. SE26 182 DV92
Lawrie Pk. Cres. SE26 182 DV92
Lawrie Pk. Gdns. SE26 182 DV91
Lawrie Pk. Rd. SE26 182 DV93
Lawson Clo. E16 144 EJ71
Lawson Clo. SW19 179 CX90
Lawson Est. SE1 279 K7
Lawson Est. SE1 162 DR76
Lawson Gdns., Dart. 188 FK85
Lawson Gdns., Pnr. 115 BV55
Lawson Rd., Dart. 168 FK84
Lawson Rd., Enf. 82 DW39
Lawson Rd., Sthl. 136 BZ70
Lawton Rd. E3 143 DY69
Lawton Rd. E10 123 EC60
Lawton Rd., Barn. 80 DD41
Lawton Rd., Loug. 85 EP41
Laxcon Clo. NW10 118 CQ64
Laxey Rd., Orp. 223 ET107
Laxley Clo. SE5 161 DP80
Laxton Gdns. (Shenley), Rad. 62 CL32
Porters Pk. Dr.
Laxton Gdns., Red. 251 DK128
Laxton Pl. NW1 273 J4
Layard Rd. SE16 162 DV77
Layard Rd., Enf. 82 DT39
Layard Rd., Th.Hth. 202 DR96
Layard Sq. SE16 162 DV77
Laybrook, St.Alb. 43 CG16
Layburn Cres., Slou. 153 BB79
Laycock St. N1 141 DN65
Layer Gdns. W3 138 CN73
Layfield Clo. NW4 119 CV59
Layfield Cres. NW4 119 CV59
Layfield Rd. NW4 119 CV59
Layhams Rd., Kes. 222 EF106
Layhams Rd., W.Wick. 203 ED104
Layhill, Hem.H. 40 BK18
Laymarsh Clo., Belv. 166 EZ76
Laymead Clo., Nthlt. 136 BY65
Laystall St. EC1 274 D5
Laystall St. EC1 141 DN70
Layters Ave., Ger.Cr. 90 AW54
Layters Ave. S., Ger.Cr. 90 AW54
Layters Clo., Ger.Cr. 90 AW54
Layters End, Ger.Cr. 90 AW54
Layters Grn. La., Ger.Cr. 112 AU55
Layters Way, Ger.Cr. 112 AX56
Layton Ct., Wey. 213 BP105
Castle Vw. Rd.
Layton Cres., Croy. 219 DN106
Layton Rd. N1 141 DN68
Parkfield St.
Layton Rd., Brent. 157 CK78
Layton Rd., Houns. 156 CB84
Laytons Bldgs. SE1 279 J4
Laytons La., Sun. 195 BT96
Layzell Wk. SE9 184 EK88
Mottingham La.
Lazar Wk. N7 121 DM61
Briset Way
Le Corte Clo., Kings L. 58 BM29
Le May Ave. SE12 184 EH90
Le May Clo., Horl. 268 DG147
Le Personne Rd., Cat. 236 DR122
Lea, The, Egh. 173 BC94
Lea Bri. Rd. E5 122 DW62
Lea Bri. Rd. E10 123 DY60
Lea Bri. Rd. E17 123 ED56
Lea Bushes, Wat. 76 BY35
Lea Clo. (Bushey), Wat. 76 CB43
Lea Cres., Ruis. 115 BT63
Lea Gdns., Wem. 118 CL63
Lea Hall Rd. E10 123 EA60
Lea Mt., Wal.Cr. 66 DS28
Lea Rd., Beck. 203 EA96
Fairfield Rd.
Lea Rd., Enf. 82 DR39
Lea Rd., Grays 171 GG78
Lea Rd., Hodd. 49 EC15
Lea Rd., Sev. 257 FJ127
Lea Rd., Sthl. 156 BY77
Lea Rd., Wal.Abb. 67 EA34
Lea Vale, Dart. 167 FD84
Lea Valley Rd. E4 83 DX43
Lea Valley Rd., Enf. 83 DX43
Lea Valley Trd. Est. N18 101 DX50
Lea Valley Viaduct E4 101 DX50
Lea Valley Viaduct N18 101 DX50
Lea Vw. Hos. E5 122 DV60
Springfield
Leabank Clo., Har. 117 CE62
Leabank Sq. E9 143 EA65
Leabank Vw. N15 122 DU58
Leabourne Rd. N16 122 DU58
Leach Gro., Lthd. 231 CJ122
Leachcroft, Ger.Cr. 90 AV53
Leacroft, Stai. 174 BG92
Leacroft Ave. SW12 180 DF87
Leacroft Clo., Ken. 236 DQ116
Leacroft Clo., Stai. 174 BH91
Leacroft Clo., West Dr. 134 BL72
Leacroft Rd., Iver 133 BD72
Leadale Ave. E4 101 EA47
Leadale Rd. N15 122 DU58
Leadale Rd. N16 122 DU58
Leadbeaters Clo. N11 98 DF50
Goldsmith Rd.
Leadenhall Mkt. EC3 275 M9
Leadenhall Pl. EC3 275 M9
Leadenhall St. EC3 275 M9
Leadenhall St. EC3 142 DS72
Leader Ave. E12 125 EN64
Leadings, The, Wem. 118 CQ62
Leaf Clo., Nthwd. 93 BR52
Leaf Clo., T.Ditt. 197 CE99
Leaf Gro. SE27 181 DN92
Leafield Clo. SW16 181 DP93
Leafield Clo., Wok. 226 AV118
Winnington Way
Leafield La., Sid. 186 EZ91
Leafield Rd. SW20 199 CZ97
Leafield Rd., Sutt. 200 DA103
Leaford Cres., Wat. 75 BT37
Leaforis Rd., Wal.Cr. 66 DU28
Leafy Gro., Croy. 221 DY111
Leafy Gro., Kes. 222 EJ106
Leafy Oak Rd. SE12 184 EJ90
Leafy Way, Brwd. 109 GD46
Leafy Way, Croy. 202 DT103
Leagrave St. E5 122 DW62
Leahoe Gdns., Hert. 32 DQ10
Leaholme Gdns., Slou. 130 AJ71
Leaholme Way, Ruis. 115 BP58
Leahurst Rd. SE13 183 ED85
Leake Ct. SE1 278 C5
Leake St. SE1 278 C4
Leake St. SE1 161 DM75
Lealand Rd. N15 122 DT58
Leamington Ave. E17 123 EA57
Leamington Ave., Brom. 184 EJ92
Leamington Ave., Mord. 199 CZ98
Leamington Ave., Orp. 223 ES105
Leamington Clo. E12 124 EL64
Leamington Clo., Brom. 184 EJ92
Leamington Clo., Houns. 176 CC85
Leamington Clo., Rom. 106 FN51
Leamington Rd.
Leamington Cres., Har. 116 BY62
Leamington Gdns., Ilf. 125 ET61
Leamington Pk. W3 138 CR71
Leamington Pl., Hayes 135 BT70
Leamington Rd., Rom. 106 FN50
Leamington Rd., Sthl. 156 BX77
Leamington Rd. Vil. W11 139 CZ71
Leamore St. W6 159 CV77
Leamouth Rd. E6 144 EL72
Remington Rd.
Leamouth Rd. E14 143 ED72
Leander Ct. SE8 163 EA81
Leander Dr., Grav. 191 GM91
Leander Gdns., Wat. 76 BY37
Leander Rd. SW2 181 DM86
Leander Rd., Nthlt. 136 CA68
Leander Rd., Th.Hth. 201 DM98
Leapale La., Guil. 258 AX135
Leapale Rd., Guil. 258 AX135
Learner Dr., Har. 116 CA61
Learoyd Gdns. E6 145 EN73
Leas, The, Hem.H. 40 BN24
Leas, The, Stai. 174 BG91
Leas, The, Upmin. 129 FR59
Leas, The (Bushey), Wat. 76 BZ39
Leas Clo., Chess. 216 CM108
Leas Dale SE9 185 EN90
Leas Dr., Iver 133 BE72
Leas Grn., Chis. 185 ET93
Leas La., Warl. 237 DX118
Leas Rd., Guil. 258 AW135
Leas Rd., Warl. 237 DX118
Leaside, Hem.H. 41 BQ21
Leaside, Lthd. 230 CA123
Leaside Ave. N10 120 DG55
Leaside Ct., Uxb. 135 BP69
The Larches
Leaside Rd. E5 122 DW60
Leasowes Rd. E10 123 EA60
Leasway, Brwd. 108 FX48
Leasway, Upmin. 128 FQ62
Leathart Clo., Horn. 147 FH66
Dowding Way
Leather Bottle La., Belv. 166 EY77
Leather Clo., Mitch. 200 DG96
Leather Gdns. E15 144 EE67
Abbey Rd.
Leather La. EC1 274 E7
Leather La. EC1 141 DN71
Leather La., Horn. 128 FK60
North St.
Leatherbottle Grn., Erith 166 EZ76
Leatherdale St. E1 142 DW70
Portelet Rd.
Leatherhead Bypass Rd., Lthd. 231 CH120
Leatherhead Clo. N16 122 DT60
Leatherhead Ind. Est., Lthd. 231 CG121
Station Rd.
Leatherhead Rd., Ash. 231 CK121
Leatherhead Rd., Chess. 215 CJ111
Leatherhead Rd., Lthd. 246 CB126
Leatherhead Rd. (Great Bookham), Lthd. 231 CK121
Leatherhead Rd. (Oxshott), Lthd. 215 CD114
Leathermarket Ct. SE1 279 M5
Leathermarket Ct. SE1 162 DS75
Leathermarket St. SE1 279 M5
Leathermarket St. SE1 162 DS75
Leathersellers Clo., Barn. 79 CY42
The Ave.
Leathsail Rd., Har. 116 CB62
Leathwaite Rd. SW11 160 DF84
Leathwell Rd. SE8 163 EB82
Leaveland Clo., Beck. 203 EA98
Leaver Gdns., Grnf. 137 CD68
Leaves Grn. Cres., Kes. 222 EJ111
Leaves Grn. Rd., Kes. 222 EK111
Leavesden Rd., Stan. 95 CG51
Leavesden Rd., Wat. 75 BV38
Leavesden Rd., Wey. 213 BP106
Leaview, Wal.Abb. 67 EB33
Leaway E10 123 DX60
Leazes Ave., Cat. 235 DN124
Lebanon Ave., Felt. 176 BX92
Lebanon Clo., Wat. 75 BR36
Lebanon Ct., Twick. 177 CH87
Lebanon Dr., Cob. 214 CA113
Lebanon Gdns. SW18 180 DA86
Lebanon Gdns., West. 238 EK117
Lebanon Pk., Twick. 177 CH87
Lebanon Rd. SW18 180 DA85
Lebanon Rd., Croy. 202 DS102
Lebrun Sq. SE3 164 EH83
Lechford Rd., Horl. 268 DG149
Lechmere App., Wdf.Grn. 102 EJ54
Lechmere Ave., Chig. 103 EQ49
Lechmere Ave., Wdf.Grn. 102 EK54
Lechmere Rd. NW2 139 CV65
Leckford Rd. SW18 180 DC89
Leckwith Ave., Bexh. 166 EY79
Lecky St. SW7 160 DD78
Leconfield Ave. SW13 159 CT83
Leconfield Rd. N5 122 DR63
Leconfield Wk., Horn. 148 FJ65
Airfield Way
Lectern La., St.Alb. 43 CD24
Leda Ave., Enf. 83 DX39
Leda Rd. SE18 165 EM76
Ledborough La., Beac. 89 AK52
Ledborough Wd., Beac. 89 AL51
Ledbury Est. SE15 162 DV80
Ledbury Ms. N. W11 140 DA73
Ledbury Rd.
Ledbury Ms. W. W11 140 DA73
Ledbury Rd.
Ledbury Pl., Croy. 220 DQ105
Ledbury Rd.
Ledbury Rd. W11 139 CZ72
Ledbury Rd., Croy. 220 DQ105
Ledbury Rd., Reig. 249 CZ133
Ledbury St. SE15 162 DU80
Ledger Clo., Guil. 243 BB132
Ledger Dr., Add. 211 BF107
Ledger La., Maid. 150 AD82
Ledgers Rd., Slou. 151 AR75
Ledgers Rd., Warl. 237 EB119
Ledrington Rd. SE19 182 DU93
Anerley Hill
Ledway Dr., Wem. 118 CM59
Lee, The, Nthwd. 93 BT50
Lee Ave., Rom. 126 EY58
Lee Bri. SE13 163 EC83
Lee Ch. St. SE13 164 EE84
Lee Clo. E17 101 DX53
Lee Clo., Barn. 80 DC42
Lee Clo., Hert. 32 DQ11
Lee Clo., Ware 33 EC11
Lee Conservancy Rd. E9 123 DZ64
Lee Fm. Clo., Chesh. 56 AU30
Lee Gdns. Ave., Horn. 128 FN60
Lee Grn. SE12 184 EF85
Lee High Rd.
Lee Grn., Orp. 206 EU99
Lee Grn. La., Epsom 232 CP124
Lee Gro., Chig. 103 EN47
Lee High Rd. SE12 163 ED83
Lee High Rd. SE13 163 ED83
Lee Pk. SE3 164 EF84
Lee Pk. Way N9 101 DX49
Lee Pk. Way N18 101 DX49
Lee Rd. NW7 97 CX52
Lee Rd. SE3 164 EF83
Lee Rd. SW19 200 DB95
Lee Rd., Enf. 82 DU44
Lee Rd., Grnf. 137 CJ67
Lee St. E8 142 DT67
Lee St., Horl. 268 DE148
Lee Ter. SE3 164 EE83
Lee Ter. SE13 164 EE83
Lee Valley Technopark N17 122 DU55
Lee Vw., Enf. 81 DP39
Leech La., Epsom 248 CQ126
Leech La., Lthd. 248 CP126
Leechcroft Ave., Sid. 185 ET85
Leechcroft Ave., Swan. 207 FF97
Leechcroft Rd., Wall. 200 DG104
Leecroft Rd., Barn. 79 CY43
Leeds Clo., Orp. 206 EX103
Leeds Pl. N4 121 DM61
Tollington Pk.
Leeds Rd., Ilf. 125 ER60
Leeds Rd., Slou. 132 AS73
Leeds St. N18 100 DU50
Leefe Way, Pot.B. 65 DK28
Leefern Rd. W12 159 CU75
Leegate SE12 184 EF85
Leegate Clo., Wok. 226 AV116
Sythwood
Leeke St. WC1 274 B2
Leeke St. WC1 141 DM69
Leeland Rd. W13 137 CG74
Leeland Ter. W13 137 CG74
Leeland Way NW10 119 CT63
Leeming Rd., Borwd. 78 CM39
Leerdam Dr. E14 163 EC76
Lees, The, Croy. 203 DZ103
Lees Ave., Nthwd. 93 BT53
Lees Pl. W1 272 F10
Lees Pl. W1 140 DG73
Lees Rd., Uxb. 135 BP70
Leeside, Barn. 79 CY43
Leeside, Pot.B. 64 DD31
Wayside
Leeside Cres. NW11 119 CZ58
Leeside Rd. N17 100 DV51
Leeson Rd. SE24 161 DN84
Leesons Hill, Chis. 205 ET97
Leesons Hill, Orp. 206 EU97
Leesons Way, Orp. 205 ET96
Leeward Gdns. SW19 179 CZ93
Leeway SE8 163 DZ78
Leeway Clo., Pnr. 94 BZ52
Leewood Clo. SE12 184 EF86
Upwood Rd.
Leewood Pl., Swan. 207 FD98
Leewood Way, Lthd. 246 BW127
Lefevre Wk. E3 143 EA67
Lefroy Rd. W12 159 CT75
Legard Rd. N5 121 DP62
Legatt Rd. SE9 184 EK85
Leggatt Rd. E15 143 EC68
Leggatts Clo., Wat. 75 BT36
Leggatts Ri., Wat. 75 BU35
Leggatts Way, Wat. 75 BT36
Leggatts Wd. Ave., Wat. 75 BV36
Legge St. SE13 183 EC85
Leggfield Ter., Hem.H. 39 BF20
Leghorn Rd. NW10 139 CT68
Leghorn Rd. SE18 165 ER78
Legion Clo. N1 141 DN65
Legion Ct., Mord. 200 DA100
Legion Rd., Grnf. 136 CC67
Legion Way N12 98 DE52
Legon Ave., Rom. 127 FC60
Legrace Ave., Houns. 156 BX82
Leicester Ave., Mitch. 201 DL98
Leicester Clo., Wor.Pk. 217 CW105
Leicester Ct. WC2 273 N10
Leicester Gdns., Ilf. 125 ES59
Leicester Pl. WC2 273 N10
Leicester Rd. E11 124 EH57
Leicester Rd. N2 120 DE55
Leicester Rd. NW10 138 CR66
Leicester Rd., Barn. 80 DB43
Leicester Rd., Croy. 202 DS101
Leicester Rd., Til. 171 GF81
Leicester Sq. WC2 277 N1
Leicester Sq. WC2 141 DK73
Leicester St. WC2 273 N10
Leigh Ave., Ilf. 124 EK56
Leigh Clo., Add. 211 BF108
Leigh Clo., N.Mal. 198 CR98
Leigh Common, Welw.G.C. 29 CY11
Leigh Cor., Cob. 214 BW114
Leigh Hill Rd.
Leigh Ct., Borwd. 78 CR40
Banks Rd.
Leigh Ct., Har. 117 CE60
Leigh Ct. Clo., Cob. 214 BW114
Leigh Cres., Croy. 221 EB108
Leigh Dr., Rom. 106 FK49
Leigh Gdns. NW10 139 CW68
Leigh Hill Rd., Cob. 214 BW114
Leigh Hunt Dr. N14 99 DK46
Leigh Hunt St. SE1 279 H4
Leigh Orchard Clo. SW16 181 DM90
Leigh Pk., Slou. 152 AW80
Leigh Pl. EC1 274 D6
Leigh Pl., Cob. 214 BW114
Leigh Pl., Well. 166 EU82
Leigh Pl. La., Gdse. 253 DY132
Leigh Pl. Rd., Reig. 265 CU140
Leigh Rd. E6 145 EN65
Leigh Rd. E10 123 EC59
Leigh Rd. N5 121 DP63
Leigh Rd., Cob. 213 BV113
Leigh Rd., Grav. 191 GH89
Leigh Rd., Houns. 157 CD84
Leigh Rd., Slou. 131 AP73
Leigh Rodd, Wat. 94 BZ48
Leigh Sq., Wind. 151 AK82
Leigh St. WC1 273 P4
Leigh St. WC1 141 DL70
Leigh Ter., Orp. 206 EV97
Saxville Rd.
Leigham Ave. SW16 181 DL90
Leigham Ct., Wall. 219 DJ107
Stafford Rd.
Leigham Ct. Rd. SW16 181 DL89
Leigham Dr., Islw. 157 CE80
Leigham Vale SW2 181 DM90
Leigham Vale SW16 181 DM90
Leighton Ave. E12 125 EN64
Leighton Ave., Pnr. 116 BY55
Leighton Buzzard Rd., Hem.H. 40 BJ19
Leighton Clo., Edg. 96 CN54
Leighton Cres. NW5 121 DJ64
Leighton Gro.
Leighton Gdns. NW10 139 CV68
Leighton Gdns., S.Croy. 220 DV113
Leighton Gdns., Til. 171 GG80
Leighton Gro. NW5 121 DJ64
Leighton Pl. NW5 121 DJ64
Leighton Rd. NW5 121 DK64
Leighton Rd. W13 157 CG75
Leighton Rd., Enf. 82 DT43
Leighton Rd., Har. 95 CD54
Leighton St., Croy. 201 DP102
Leighton Way, Epsom 216 CR114
Leila Parnell Pl. SE7 164 EJ79
Leinster Ave. SW14 158 CQ83
Leinster Gdns. W2 140 DC72
Leinster Ms. W2 140 DC73
Leinster Pl. W2 140 DC72
Leinster Rd. N10 121 DH56
Leinster Rd. NW6 140 DA69
Stafford Rd.
Leinster Sq. W2 140 DA72
Leinster Ter. W2 140 DC73
Leiston Spur, Slou. 132 AS72
Leisure La., W.Byf. 212 BH112
Leisure Way N12 98 DD52
Leith Clo. NW9 118 CR60
Leith Hill, Orp. 206 EU95
Leith Hill Grn., Orp. 206 EU95
Leith Hill
Leith Hill La., Dor. 262 BY144
Leith Pk. Rd., Grav. 191 GH88
Leith Rd. N22 99 DP53
Leith Rd., Epsom 216 CS112
Leith Vw., Dor. 263 CJ140
Leith Yd. NW6 140 DA67
Quex Rd.
Leithcote Gdns. SW16 181 DM91
Leithcote Path SW16 181 DM90
Lela Ave., Houns. 156 BW82
Lelitia Clo. E8 142 DU67
Pownall Rd.
Leman St. E1 142 DT72
Lemark Clo., Stan. 95 CJ50
Lemmon Rd. SE10 164 EE79
Lemna Rd. E11 124 EE59
Lemonfield Dr., Wat. 60 BY32
Lemonwell Ct. SE9 185 EQ85
Lemonwell Dr.
Lemonwell Dr. SE9 185 EQ85
Lemsford Clo. N15 122 DU57
Lemsford Ct. N4 122 DQ61
Brownswood Rd.
Lemsford Ct., Borwd. 78 CQ42
Lemsford La., Welw.G.C. 29 CV10
Lemsford Rd., Hat. 45 CT16
Lemsford Rd., St.Alb. 43 CF20
Lemsford Rd., Welw.G.C. 29 CT11
Lemsford Village Rd., Welw.G.C. 29 CU10
Lemuel St. SW18 180 DB86
Len Freeman Pl. SW6 159 CZ80
John Smith Ave.
Lena Gdns. W6 159 CW76
Lena Kennedy Clo. E4 101 EB51
Lenanton Steps E14 163 EA75
Manilla St.
Lendal Ter. SW4 161 DK83
Lenelby Rd., Surb. 198 CN102
Lenham Rd. SE12 164 EF84
Lenham Rd., Bexh. 166 EZ79
Lenham Rd., Sutt. 218 DB105
Lenham Rd., Th.Hth. 202 DR96
Lenmore Ave., Grays 170 GC76
Lennard Ave., W.Wick. 204 EE103
Lennard Clo., W.Wick. 204 EE103
Lennard Rd. SE20 182 DW93
Lennard Rd., Beck. 183 DX93
Lennard Rd., Brom. 205 EM102
Lennard Rd., Croy. 202 DQ102
Lennard Rd., Sev. 241 FE120
Lennard Row, S.Ock. 149 FR74
Lennon Rd. NW2 119 CW64
Lennox Ave., Grav. 191 GF86
Lennox Clo., Rom. 127 FF58
Lennox Gdns. NW10 119 CT63
Lennox Gdns. SW1 276 D7
Lennox Gdns. SW1 160 DF76
Lennox Gdns., Croy. 219 DP105
Lennox Gdns., Ilf. 125 EM60
Lennox Gdns. Ms. SW1 276 D7
Lennox Gdns. Ms. SW1 160 DF76
Lennox Rd. E17 123 DZ58
Lennox Rd. N4 121 DM61
Lennox Rd., Grav. 191 GF86
Lennox Rd. E., Grav. 191 GG87
Lenor Clo., Bexh. 166 EY84
Lens Rd. E7 144 EJ66
Lensbury Clo. (Cheshunt), Wal.Cr. 67 DY28
Ashdown Cres.
Lensbury Way SE2 166 EW76
Lent Grn. La., Slou. 130 AH70
Lent Ri. Rd., Slou. 130 AH69
Lenten Clo., Guil. 261 BR142
Lenthall Ave., Grays 170 GA75
Lenthall Pl. SW7 160 DC77
Gloucester Rd.
Lenthall Rd. E8 142 DU66
Lenthall Rd., Loug. 85 ER42
Lenthorp Rd. SE10 164 EF77
Lentmead Rd., Brom. 184 EF90
Lenton Path SE18 165 ER79
Lenton Ri., Rich. 158 CL83
Evelyn Ter.
Lenton St. SE18 165 ER77
Leo St. SE15 162 DV80
Leo Yd. EC1 274 G5
Leof Cres. SE6 183 EB92
Leominster Rd., Mord. 200 DC100
Leominster Wk., Mord. 200 DC100
Leonard Ave., Mord. 200 DC99
Leonard Ave., Rom. 127 FD60
Leonard Ave., Sev. 241 FH116
Leonard Ave., Swans. 190 FY87
Leonard Rd. E4 101 EA51
Leonard Rd. E7 124 EG63
Leonard Rd. N9 100 DT48
Leonard Rd. SW16 201 DJ95
Leonard Rd., Sthl. 156 BX76
Leonard Robbins Path SE28 146 EV73
Tawney Rd.
Leonard St. E16 144 EL74
Leonard St. EC2 275 L4
Leonard St. EC2 142 DR70
Leonard Way, Brwd. 108 FS49
Leontine Clo. SE15 162 DU80
Leopards Ct. EC1 274 D6
Leopold Ave. SW19 179 CZ92
Leopold Ms. E9 142 DW67
Fremont St.
Leopold Rd. E17 123 EA57
Leopold Rd. N2 120 DD55
Leopold Rd. N18 100 DV50
Leopold Rd. NW10 138 CS66
Leopold Rd. SW19 179 CZ91
Leopold Rd. W5 138 CM74
Leopold St. E3 143 DZ71
Leopold Ter. SW19 180 DA92
Dora Rd.
Lepe Clo., Brom. 184 EE91
Winlaton Rd.
Leppoc Rd. SW4 181 DK85
Leret Way, Lthd. 231 CG121
Leroy St. SE1 279 M8
Leroy St. SE1 162 DS77
Lerwick Dr., Slou. 132 AS71
Lesbourne Rd., Reig. 266 DB135
Lescombe Clo. SE23 183 DY90
Lescombe Rd. SE23 183 DY90
Lesley Clo., Bex. 187 FB87
Lesley Clo., Grav. 191 GF94
Lesley Clo., Swan. 207 FD97
Leslie Gdns., Sutt. 218 DA108
Leslie Gro., Croy. 202 DS102
Leslie Gro. Pl., Croy. 202 DR102
Leslie Gro.
Leslie Pk. Rd., Croy. 202 DS102
Leslie Rd. E11 123 EC63
Leslie Rd. E16 144 EH72
Leslie Rd. N2 120 DD55
Leslie Rd., Dor. 247 CK134
Leslie Rd., Wok. 210 AS110
Leslie Smith Sq. SE18 165 EN79
Nightingale Vale
Lesney Fm. Est., Erith 167 FD80
Lesney Pk., Erith 167 FD79
Lesney Pk. Rd., Erith 167 FD79
Lessar Ave. SW4 181 DJ85
Lessing St. SE23 183 DY87
Lessingham Ave. SW17 180 DF91
Lessingham Ave., Ilf. 125 EN55
Lessington Ave., Rom. 127 FC58
Lessness Ave., Bexh. 166 EX80
Lessness Pk., Belv. 166 EZ78
Lessness Rd., Belv. 166 FA78
Stapley Rd.
Lessness Rd., Mord. 200 DC100
Lester Ave. E15 144 EE69
Leston Clo., Rain. 147 FG69
Leswin Pl. N16 122 DT62
Leswin Rd.
Leswin Rd. N16 122 DT62
Letchfield, Chesh. 56 AV31
Letchford Gdns. NW10 139 CU69
Letchford Ms. NW10 139 CU69
Letchford Gdns.

Letchford Ter., Har. 94 CB53
Letchmore Rd., Rad. 77 CG36
Letchworth Ave., Felt. 175 BT87
Letchworth Clo., Brom. 204 EG99
Letchworth Clo., Wat. 94 BX50
Letchworth Dr., Brom. 204 EG99
Letchworth St. SW17 180 DF91
Lethbridge Clo. SE13 163 EC81
Lett Rd. E15 143 EE66
Letter Box La., Sev. 257 FJ129
Letterstone Rd. SW6 159 CZ80
Varna Rd.
Lettice St. SW6 159 CZ81
Lettsom St. SE5 162 DS82
Lettsom Wk. E13 144 EG68
Leucha Rd. E17 123 DY57
Levana Clo. SW19 179 CY88
Levehurst Way SW4 161 DL82
Leven Clo., Wal.Cr. 67 DX33
Leven Clo., Wat. 94 BX50
Leven Dr., Wal.Cr. 67 DX33
Leven Rd. E14 143 EC71
Leven Way, Hayes 135 BS72
Leven Way, Hem.H. 40 BK16
Levendale Rd. SE23 183 DY89
Lever Sq., Grays 171 GG77
Lever St. EC1 274 G3
Lever St. EC1 141 DP69
Leveret Clo., Croy. 221 ED111
Leveret Clo., Wat. 59 BU34
Leverett St. SW3 276 C8
Leverholme Gdns. SE9 185 EN90
Leverson St. SW16 181 DJ93
Leverstock Grn. Rd., Hem.H. 41 BQ21
Leverstock Grn. Way, Hem.H. 41 BQ20
Leverton Pl. NW5 121 DJ64
Leverton St.
Leverton St. NW5 121 DJ64
Leverton Way, Wal.Abb. 67 EC33
Leveson Rd., Grays 171 GH76
Levett Gdns., Ilf. 125 ET63
Levett Rd., Bark. 145 ES65
Levett Rd., Lthd. 231 CH120
Levine Gdns., Bark. 146 EX68
Levison Way N19 121 DK61
Grovedale Rd.
Levylsdene, Guil. 243 BD134
Lewes Clo., Nthlt. 136 CA65
Lewes Rd. N12 98 DE50
Lewes Rd., Brom. 204 EK96
Lewes Rd., Rom. 106 FK49
Lewes Way, Rick. 75 BQ42
Lewesdon Clo. SW19 179 CX88
Leweston Pl. N16 122 DT59
Lewey Ho. E3 143 DZ70
Lewgars Ave. NW9 118 CQ58
Lewin Rd. SW14 158 CR83
Lewin Rd. SW16 181 DK93
Lewin Rd., Bexh. 166 EY84
Lewins Rd., Epsom 216 CP114
Lewins Rd., Ger.Cr. 112 AX55
Lewins Way, Slou. 131 AM73
Lewis Ave. E17 101 EA53
Lewis Clo. N14 99 DJ45
Orchid Rd.
Lewis Clo., Add. 212 BJ105
Lewis Clo., Brwd. 109 FZ45
Lewis Clo. (Harefield), Uxb. 92 BJ54
Lewis Cres. NW10 118 CQ64
Lewis Gdns. N2 98 DD54
Lewis Gro. SE13 163 EC83
Lewis La., Ger.Cr. 90 AY53
Lewis Rd., Horn. 128 FJ58
Lewis Rd., Mitch. 200 DD96
Lewis Rd., Rich. 177 CK85
Red Lion St.
Lewis Rd., Sid. 186 EW90
Lewis Rd., Sthl. 156 BY75
Lewis Rd., Sutt. 218 DB105
Lewis Rd., Swans. 190 FY86
Lewis Rd., Well. 166 EW83
Lewis St. NW1 141 DH66
Lewis Way, Dag. 147 FB65
Lewisham High St. SE13 163 EC83
Lewisham Hill SE13 163 EC82
Lewisham Pk. SE13 183 EB86
Lewisham Rd. SE13 163 EB81
Lewisham St. SW1 277 N5
Lewisham Way SE4 163 DZ81
Lewisham Way SE14 163 DZ81
Lexden Dr., Rom. 126 EV58
Lexden Rd. W3 138 CP73
Lexden Rd., Mitch. 201 DK98
Lexham Ct., Grnf. 137 CD67
Lexham Gdns. W8 160 DB76
Lexham Gdns., Amer. 55 AQ37
Lexham Gdns. Ms. W8 160 DB76
Lexham Ho., Bark. 145 ER67
St. Margarets
Lexham Ms. W8 160 DA77
Lexham Wk. W8 160 DB76
Lexham Gdns.
Lexington Clo., Borwd. 78 CM41
Lexington Ct., Pur. 220 DQ110
Lexington St. W1 273 L9
Lexington St. W1 141 DJ72
Lexington Way, Barn. 79 CX42
Lexington Way, Upmin. 129 FT58
Lexton Gdns. SW12 181 DK88
Ley Hill Rd., Hem.H. 56 AX30
Ley St., Ilf. 125 EP61
Ley Wk., Welw.G.C. 30 DC09
Leyborne Ave. W13 157 CH75
Leyborne Pk., Rich. 158 CN81
Leybourne Ave., W.Byf. 212 BM113
Leybourne Clo., Brom. 204 EG100
Leybourne Clo., W.Byf. 212 BM113
Leybourne Ave.
Leybourne Rd. E11 124 EF60
Leybourne Rd. NW1 141 DH66
Leybourne Rd. NW9 118 CN57
Leybourne Rd., Uxb. 135 BQ67
Leybourne St. NW1 141 DH66
Hawley St.
Leybridge Ct. SE12 184 EG85
Leyburn Clo. E17 123 EB56
Church La.
Leyburn Cres., Rom. 106 FL52
Leyburn Gdns., Croy. 202 DS103
Leyburn Gro. N18 100 DU51
Leyburn Rd. N18 100 DU51
Leyburn Rd., Rom. 106 FL52
Leycroft Clo., Loug. 85 EN43
Leycroft Gdns., Erith 167 FH81
Leyden St. E1 275 P7
Leydenhatch La., Swan. 207 FC95
Leydon Clo. SE16 143 DX74
Lagado Ms.
Leyfield, Wor.Pk. 198 CS102
Leyhill Clo., Swan. 207 FE99
Leyland Ave., Enf. 83 DY40
Leyland Ave., St.Alb. 43 CD22
Leyland Clo. (Cheshunt), Wal.Cr. 66 DW28
Leyland Gdns., Wdf.Grn. 102 EJ50
Leyland Rd. SE12 184 EG85
Leylands La., Stai. 153 BF84
Leylang Rd. SE14 163 DX80
Leys, The N2 120 DC56
Leys, The, Amer. 55 AP35
Leys, The, Har. 118 CM58
Leys, The, St.Alb. 43 CK17
Leys Ave., Dag. 147 FC66
Leys Clo., Dag. 147 FC66
Leys Clo., Har. 117 CD57
Leys Clo. (Harefield), Uxb. 92 BK53
Leys Gdns., Barn. 80 DG43
Leys Rd., Hem.H. 40 BL22
Leys Rd., Lthd. 215 CD112
Leys Rd. E., Enf. 83 DY39
Leys Rd. W., Enf. 83 DY39
Leysdown, Welw.G.C. 30 DD09
Leysdown Ave., Bexh. 167 FC84
Leysdown Rd. SE9 184 EL89
Leysfield Rd. W12 159 CU75
Leyspring Rd. E11 124 EF60
Leyswood Dr., Ilf. 125 ES57
Leythe Rd. W3 158 CQ75
Leyton Business Cen. E10 123 EA61
Leyton Cross Rd., Dart. 187 FF90
Leyton Gra. E10 123 EB60
Goldsmith Rd.
Leyton Gra. Est. E10 123 EB60
Leyton Grn. Rd. E10 123 EC58
Leyton Ind. Village E10 123 DX59
Leyton Pk. Rd. E10 123 EC62
Leyton Rd. E15 123 ED64
Leyton Rd. SW19 180 DC94
Leyton Way E11 124 EE59
Leytonstone Rd. E15 124 EE64
Leywick St. E15 144 EE68
Leywood Clo., Amer. 55 AR40
Lezayre Rd., Orp. 223 ET107
Liardet St. SE14 163 DY79
Liberia Rd. N5 141 DP65
Liberty, The, Rom. 127 FE57
Liberty Ave. SW19 200 DD95
Liberty Clo., Hert. 32 DQ12
Liberty Hall Rd., Add. 212 BG106
Liberty La., Add. 212 BG106
Liberty Ms. SW12 181 DH86
Liberty Ri., Add. 212 BG107
Liberty St. SW9 161 DM81
Libra Rd. E3 143 DZ67
Libra Rd. E13 144 EG68
Library Hill, Brwd. 108 FX47
Coptfold Rd.
Library Pl. E1 142 DV73
Cable St.
Library St. SE1 278 F5
Library St. SE1 161 DP75
Library Way, Twick. 176 CC87
Nelson Rd.
Lichfield Clo., Barn. 80 DF41
Lichfield Gdns., Rich. 158 CL84
Lichfield Gro. N3 98 DB54
Lichfield Rd. E3 143 DY69
Lichfield Rd. E6 144 EK69
Lichfield Rd. N9 100 DU47
Winchester Rd.
Lichfield Rd. NW2 119 CY63
Lichfield Rd., Dag. 126 EV63
Lichfield Rd., Houns. 156 BW83
Lichfield Rd., Nthwd. 115 BU55
Lichfield Rd., Rich. 158 CM81
Lichfield Rd., Wdf.Grn. 102 EE49
Lichfield Sq., Rich. 158 CL84
Lichfield Gdns.
Lichfield Ter., Upmin. 129 FS61
Lichfield Way, Brox. 49 DZ22
Lichfield Way, S.Croy. 221 DX110
Lichlade Clo., Orp. 223 ET105
Lidbury Rd. NW7 97 CY51
Lidcote Gdns. SW9 161 DN82
Liddall Way, West Dr. 134 BM74
Liddell Clo., Har. 117 CK55
Liddell Gdns. NW10 139 CW68
Liddell Pl., Wind. 150 AJ83
Liddell Way
Liddell Rd. NW6 140 DA65
Liddell Sq., Wind. 150 AJ83
Liddell Way
Liddell Way, Wind. 150 AJ83
Lidding Rd., Har. 117 CK57
Liddington Hall Dr., Guil. 242 AS131
Liddington New Rd., Guil. 242 AS131
Liddington Rd. E15 144 EF67
Liddon Rd. E13 144 EH69
Liddon Rd., Brom. 204 EJ97
Liden Clo. E17 123 DZ60
Hitcham Rd.
Lidfield Rd. N16 122 DR63
Lidgate Rd. SE15 162 DT80
Chandler Way
Lidiard Rd. SW18 180 DC89
Lidlington Pl. NW1 273 L1
Lidlington Pl. NW1 141 DJ68
Lido Sq. N17 100 DR54
Lidstone Clo., Wok. 226 AV117
Lidyard Rd. N19 121 DJ60
Lieutenant Ellis Way, Wal.Cr. 66 DT31
Liffler Rd. SE18 165 ES78
Lifford St. SW15 159 CX84
Liffords Pl. SW13 159 CT82
Lightcliffe Rd. N13 99 DN49
Lighter Clo. SE16 163 DY77
Lighterman Ms. E1 143 DX72
Lightermans Rd. E14 163 EA75
Lightermans Wk. SW18 160 DA84
Lightfoot Rd. N8 121 DL57
Lightley Clo., Wem. 138 CM66
Stanley Ave.
Ligonier St. E2 275 P4
Lila Pl., Swan. 207 FE98
Lilac Ave., Enf. 82 DW36
Lilac Ave., Wok. 226 AX120
Lilac Clo. E4 101 DZ51
Lilac Clo., Brwd. 108 FV43
Magnolia Way
Lilac Clo., Guil. 242 AW130
Lilac Clo. (Cheshunt), Wal.Cr. 66 DV31
Greenwood Ave.
Lilac Gdns. W5 157 CK76
Lilac Gdns., Croy. 203 EA104
Lilac Gdns., Hayes 135 BS72
Lilac Gdns., Rom. 127 FE60
Lilac Gdns., Swan. 207 FD97
Lilac Pl. SE11 278 B9
Lilac Pl. SE11 161 DM77
Lilac Pl., West Dr. 134 BM73
Cedar Ave.
Lilac Rd., Hodd. 49 EB15
Lilac St. W12 139 CU73
Lilburne Gdns. SE9 184 EL85
Lilburne Rd. SE9 184 EL85
Lilburne Wk. NW10 138 CQ65
Lile Cres. W7 137 CE71
Lilestone Est. NW8 140 DD70
Fisherton St.
Lilestone St. NW8 272 B4
Lilestone St. NW8 140 DE70
Lilford Rd. SE5 161 DP82
Lilian Barker Clo. SE12 184 EG85
Lilian Board Way, Grnf. 117 CD64
Lilian Clo. N16 122 DS62
Barbauld Rd.
Lilian Cres., Brwd. 109 GC47
Lilian Gdns., Wdf.Grn. 102 EH53
Lilian Rd. SW16 201 DJ95
Lillechurch Rd., Dag. 146 EV65
Lilleshall Rd., Mord. 200 DD100
Lilley Clo. E1 142 DU74
Hermitage Wall
Lilley Clo., Brwd. 108 FT49
Lilley Dr., Tad. 234 DB122
Lilley La. NW7 96 CR50
Lillian Ave. W3 158 CN75
Lillian Rd. SW13 159 CU79
Lilliards Clo., Hodd. 33 EB13
Lillie Rd. SW6 159 CY79
Lillie Rd., West. 238 EK118
Lillie Yd. SW6 160 DA79
Lillieshall Rd. SW4 161 DH83
Lillington Gdns. Est. SW1 277 L9
Lilliots La., Lthd. 231 CG119
Kingston Rd.
Lilliput Ave., Nthlt. 136 BZ67
Lilliput Rd., Rom. 127 FD59
Lilly La., Hem.H. 41 BR16
Lily Clo. W14 159 CY77
Lily Gdns., Wem. 137 CJ68
Lily Pl. EC1 274 E6
Lily Pl. EC1 141 DN71
Lily Rd. E17 123 EA58
Lilyville Rd. SW6 159 CZ81
Limbourne Ave., Dag. 126 EZ59
Limburg Rd. SW11 160 DF84
Lime Ave., Brwd. 109 FZ48
Lime Ave., Grav. 190 GD87
Lime Ave., Upmin. 128 FN63
Lime Ave., West Dr. 134 BM73
Lime Ave., Wind. 152 AT80
Lime Clo. E1 142 DU74
Lime Clo., Brom. 204 EL98
Lime Clo., Buck.H. 102 EK48
Lime Clo., Cars. 200 DF103
Lime Clo., Guil. 244 BH128
Lime Clo., Har. 95 CG54
Lime Clo., Pnr. 115 BT55
Lime Clo., Reig. 266 DB137
Lime Clo., Rom. 127 FC56
Lime Clo., S.Ock. 149 FW69
Lime Clo., Ware 33 DY05
Lime Clo., Wat. 94 BX45
Lime Ct., Mitch. 200 DD96
Lewis Rd.
Lime Cres., Sun. 196 BW96
Lime Gro. N20 97 CZ46
Lime Gro. W12 159 CW75
Lime Gro., Add. 212 BG105
Lime Gro., Guil. 242 AV130
Lime Gro. (West Clandon), Guil. 244 BG128
Lime Gro., Hayes 135 BR73
Lime Gro., Ilf. 103 ET51
Lime Gro., N.Mal. 198 CR97
Lime Gro., Orp. 205 EP103
Lime Gro., Ruis. 115 BV59
Lime Gro., Sid. 185 ET86
Lime Gro., Twick. 177 CF86
Lime Gro., Warl. 237 DY118
Lime Gro., Wok. 226 AY121
Lime Meadow Ave., S.Croy. 220 DU113
Lime Pit La., Sev. 241 FC117
Lime Rd., Epp. 69 ET31
Lime Rd., Rich. 158 CM84
St. Mary's Gro.
Lime Rd., Swan. 207 FD97
Lime Row, Erith 166 EZ76
Northwood Pl.
Lime St. E17 123 DY56
Lime St. EC3 275 M10
Lime St. EC3 142 DS73
Lime St. Pas. EC3 275 M9
Lime Ter. W7 137 CE73
Manor Ct. Rd.
Lime Tree Ave., Esher 197 CD102
Lime Tree Ave. (Bluewater), Green. 189 FU88
Lime Tree Ave., T.Ditt. 197 CD102
Lime Tree Clo., Lthd. 230 CA124
Lime Tree Gro., Croy. 203 DZ104
Lime Tree Pl., Mitch. 201 DH95
Lime Tree Pl., St.Alb. 43 CF21
Lime Tree Rd., Houns. 156 CB81
Lime Tree Ter. SE6 183 DZ88
Winterstoke Rd.
Lime Tree Wk., Amer. 72 AT39
Lime Tree Wk., Enf. 82 DQ38
Lime Tree Wk., Rick. 74 BH43
Lime Tree Wk., Sev. 257 FH125
Lime Tree Wk., Vir.W. 192 AY98
Lime Tree Wk. (Bushey), Wat. 95 CE46
Lime Tree Wk., W.Wick. 222 EF105
Lime Wk. E15 144 EE67
Church St. N.
Lime Wk., Guil. 260 BM139
Lime Wk., Hem.H. 40 BM22
Lime Wk. (Denham), Uxb. 114 BJ64
Lime Wks. Rd., Red. 251 DJ126
Limeburner La. EC4 274 F9
Limeburner La. EC4 141 DP72
Limebush Clo., Add. 212 BJ109
Limecroft Clo., Epsom 216 CR108
Limedene Clo., Pnr. 94 BX53
Limeharbour E14 163 EB76
Limehouse Causeway E14 143 DZ73
Limehouse Flds. Est. E14 143 DY71
Limehouse Link E14 143 DY73
Limekiln Dr. SE7 164 EH79
Limekiln Pl. SE19 182 DT94
Limerick Clo. SW12 181 DJ87
Limerick Gdns., Upmin. 129 FT59
Limerston St. SW10 160 DC79
Limes, The W2 140 DA73
Linden Gdns.
Limes, The, Amer. 55 AP35
Limes, The, Brwd. 109 FZ48
Limes, The, Brom. 204 EL103
Limes, The, Har. 95 CF54
Limes, The, Purf. 168 FN78
Tank Hill Rd.
Limes, The, St.Alb. 43 CE18
Limes, The, Welw.G.C. 30 DA11
Limes, The, Wok. 226 AX115
Limes Ave. E11 124 EH56
Limes Ave. N12 98 DC49
Limes Ave. NW7 96 CS51
Limes Ave. NW11 119 CY59
Limes Ave. SE20 182 DV94
Limes Ave. SW13 159 CT82
Limes Ave., Cars. 200 DF102
Limes Ave., Chig. 103 ER51
Limes Ave., Croy. 201 DN104
Limes Ave., Horl. 269 DH150
Limes Ave., The N11 99 DH50
Limes Clo., Ashf. 174 BN92
Limes Ct., Brwd. 108 FX46
Sawyers Hall La.
Limes Ct., Hodd. 49 EA17
Charlton Way
Limes Fld. Rd. SW14 158 CS83
White Hart La.
Limes Gdns. SW18 180 DA86
Limes Gro. SE13 163 EC84
Limes Pl., Croy. 202 DR101
Limes Rd., Beck. 203 EB96
Limes Rd., Croy. 202 DR100
Limes Rd., Egh. 173 AZ92
Limes Rd. (Cheshunt), Wal.Cr. 67 DX32
Limes Rd., Wey. 212 BN105
Limes Row, Orp. 223 EP106
Orchard Rd.
Limes Wk. SE15 162 DV84
Limes Wk. W5 157 CK75
Chestnut Gro.
Limesdale Gdns., Edg. 96 CQ54
Limesford Rd. SE15 163 DX84
Limestone Wk., Erith 166 EX76
Limetree Clo. SW2 181 DM88
Limetree Ter., Well. 166 EU83
Hook La.
Limetree Wk. SW17 180 DG92
Church La.
Limeway Ter., Dor. 247 CG134
Limewood Clo. E17 123 DZ56
Limewood Clo. W13 137 CH72
St. Stephens Rd.
Limewood Ct., Ilf. 125 EM57
Limewood Rd., Erith 167 FC80
Limpsfield Ave. SW19 179 CX89
Limpsfield Ave., Th.Hth. 201 DM99
Limpsfield Rd., S.Croy. 220 DU112
Limpsfield Rd., Warl. 236 DW116
Linacre Ct. W6 159 CX78
Linacre Rd. NW2 139 CV65
Linberry Wk. SE8 163 DZ77
Linces La., Dor. 263 CD137
Guildford Rd.
Linces Way, Welw.G.C. 30 DB11
Linchfield Rd., Slou. 152 AW81
Linchmere Rd. SE12 184 EF87
Lincoln Ave. N14 99 DJ48
Lincoln Ave. SW19 179 CX90
Lincoln Ave., Rom. 127 FD60
Lincoln Ave., Twick. 176 CB89
Lincoln Clo. SE25 202 DU100
Woodside Grn.
Lincoln Clo., Erith 167 FF82
Lincoln Clo., Grnf. 136 CC67
Lincoln Clo., Har. 116 BZ57
Lincoln Clo., Horl. 268 DG149
Lincoln Clo., Horn. 128 FN57
Lincoln Clo., Welw.G.C. 30 DC08
Lincoln Ct. N16 122 DR59
Lincoln Ct., Berk. 38 AV19
Lincoln Ct., Borwd. 78 CR43
Lincoln Cres., Enf. 82 DS43
Lincoln Dr., Rick. 75 BP42
Lincoln Dr., Wat. 94 BW48
Lincoln Dr., Wok. 227 BE115
Lincoln Gdns., Ilf. 124 EL59
Lincoln Grn. Rd., Orp. 205 ET99
Lincoln Hatch La., Slou. 130 AJ70
Lincoln Ms. NW6 139 CZ67
Willesden La.
Lincoln Ms. SE21 182 DR88
Lincoln Pk., Amer. 55 AS39
Lincoln Rd. E7 144 EK65
Lincoln Rd. E13 144 EH70
Lincoln Rd. E18 102 EG53
Grove Rd.
Lincoln Rd. N2 120 DE55
Lincoln Rd. SE25 202 DV97
Lincoln Rd., Dor. 247 CJ134
Lincoln Rd., Enf. 82 DU43
Lincoln Rd., Erith 167 FF82
Lincoln Rd., Felt. 176 BZ90
Lincoln Rd., Ger.Cr. 90 AY53
Lincoln Rd., Guil. 242 AT132
Lincoln Rd., Har. 116 BZ57
Lincoln Rd., Mitch. 201 DL99
Lincoln Rd., N.Mal. 198 CQ97
Lincoln Rd., Nthwd. 115 BT55
Lincoln Rd., Sid. 186 EV92
Lincoln Rd., Wem. 137 CK65
Lincoln Rd., Wor.Pk. 199 CV102
Lincoln St. E11 124 EE61
Lincoln St. SW3 276 D9
Lincoln St. SW3 160 DF77
Lincoln Wk., Epsom 216 CR110
Hollymoor La.
Lincoln Way, Enf. 82 DV43
Lincoln Way, Rick. 75 BP42
Lincoln Way, Slou. 131 AK73
Lincoln Way, Sun. 195 BS95
Lincolns, The NW7 97 CT48
Lincolns Clo., St.Alb. 43 CJ15
Lincolns Flds., Epp. 69 ET29
Lincoln's Inn WC2 274 C8
Lincoln's Inn WC2 141 DN72
Lincoln's Inn Flds. WC2 274 B8
Lincoln's Inn Flds. WC2 141 DM72
Lincolnshott, Grav. 190 GA92
Lincombe Rd., Brom. 184 EF90
Lind Rd., Sutt. 218 DC106
Lind St. SE8 163 EB82
Lindal Cres., Enf. 81 DL42
Lindal Rd. SE4 183 DZ85
Lindale Clo., Vir.W. 192 AT98
Lindales, The N17 100 DT51
Brantwood Rd.
Lindbergh, Welw.G.C. 30 DC09
Lindbergh Rd., Wall. 219 DL109
Linden Ave. NW10 139 CX68
Linden Ave., Couls. 235 DH116
Linden Ave., Dart. 188 FJ88
Linden Ave., Enf. 82 DU39
Linden Ave., Houns. 176 CB85
Linden Ave., Ruis. 115 BU60
Linden Ave., Th.Hth. 201 DP98
Linden Ave., Wem. 118 CM64
Linden Chase Rd., Sev. 257 FH122
Linden Clo. N14 81 DJ44
Linden Clo., Add. 212 BG111
Linden Clo., Orp. 224 EU106
Linden Clo., Purf. 168 FQ79
Linden Clo., Ruis. 115 BU60
Linden Clo., Stan. 95 CH50
Linden Clo., Tad. 233 CX120
Linden Clo., T.Ditt. 197 CF101
Linden Clo., Wal.Cr. 66 DV30
Linden Ct. W12 139 CW74
Linden Ct., Egh. 172 AV93
Linden Ct., Lthd. 231 CH121
Linden Cres., Grnf. 137 CF65
Linden Cres., Kings.T. 198 CM96
Linden Cres., St.Alb. 43 CJ20
Linden Cres., Wdf.Grn. 102 EH51
Linden Dr., Cat. 236 DQ124
Linden Dr., Ger.Cr. 90 AY54
Woodside Hill
Linden Dr., Slou. 131 AQ67
Linden Gdns. W2 140 DA73
Linden Gdns. W4 158 CR78
Linden Gdns., Enf. 82 DU39
Linden Gdns., Lthd. 231 CJ121
Linden Glade, Hem.H. 40 BG21
Linden Gro. SE15 162 DW83
Linden Gro. SE26 182 DW93
Linden Gro., N.Mal. 198 CS97
Linden Gro., Tedd. 177 CF92
Waldegrave Rd.
Linden Gro., Walt. 195 BT103
Linden Gro., Warl. 237 DY118
Linden Ho., Slou. 153 BB78
Linden Lawns, Wem. 118 CM63
Linden Lea N2 120 DC57
Linden Lea, Wat. 59 BU33
Linden Leas, W.Wick. 203 ED103
Linden Ms. N1 122 DR64
Mildmay Gro. N.
Linden Ms. W2 140 DA73
Linden Gdns.
Linden Pas. W4 158 CR78
Linden Gdns.
Linden Pit Path, Lthd. 231 CH121
Linden Pl., Epsom 216 CS112
East St.
Linden Pl., Lthd. 245 BS126
Station App.
Linden Pl., Mitch. 200 DE98
Linden Ri., Brwd. 108 FX50
Linden Rd. E17 123 DZ57
High St.
Linden Rd. N10 121 DH56
Linden Rd. N11 98 DF47
Linden Rd. N15 122 DQ56
Linden Rd., Guil. 242 AX134
Linden Rd., Hmptn. 176 CA94
Linden Rd., Lthd. 231 CH121
Linden Rd., Wey. 213 BQ109
Linden Sq., Sev. 256 FE122
London Rd.
Linden St., Rom. 127 FD56
Linden Wk. N19 121 DJ61
Hargrave Pk.
Linden Way N14 81 DJ44
Linden Way, Pur. 219 DJ110
Linden Way, Shep. 195 BQ99
Linden Way, Wok. 227 AZ121
St. Martha's Ave.
Linden Way (Send Marsh), Wok. 227 BF124
Lindenfield, Chis. 205 EP96
Lindens, The N12 98 DD50
Lindens, The W4 158 CQ81
Hartington Rd.
Lindens, The, Croy. 221 EC107
Lindens, The, Hem.H. 39 BF23
Lindens, The, Loug. 85 EM43
Lindens Clo., Lthd. 246 BY128
Mount Pleasant
Lindeth Clo., Stan. 95 CJ51
Old Ch. La.
Lindfield Gdns. NW3 120 DB64
Lindfield Gdns., Guil. 243 AZ133
Lindfield Rd. W5 137 CJ70
Lindfield Rd., Croy. 202 DT100
Lindfield Rd., Rom. 106 FL50
Lindfield St. E14 143 EA72
Lindhill Clo., Enf. 83 DX39
Lindisfarne Clo., Grav. 191 GL89
St. Benedict's Ave.
Lindisfarne Rd. SW20 179 CU94
Lindisfarne Rd., Dag. 126 EW62
Lindisfarne Way E9 123 DY63
Lindley Est. SE15 162 DU80
Bird in Bush Rd.
Lindley Rd. E10 123 EB61
Lindley Rd., Gdse. 252 DW130
Lindley Rd., Walt. 196 BX104
Lindley St. E1 142 DW71
Lindlings, Hem.H. 39 BE21
Lindo Clo., Chesh. 54 AP30
Lindo St. SE15 162 DW82
Selden Rd.
Lindore Rd. SW11 160 DF84
Lindores Rd., Cars. 200 DC101
Lindrop St. SW6 160 DC82
Lindsay Clo., Chess. 216 CL108
Lindsay Clo., Epsom 216 CQ113
Lindsay Clo., Stai. 174 BK85
Lindsay Dr., Har. 118 CL58
Lindsay Dr., Shep. 195 BR100
Lindsay Pl., Wal.Cr. 66 DV30
Lindsay Rd., Add. 212 BG110
Lindsay Rd., Hmptn. 176 CB91

Lindsay Rd., Wor.Pk. 199 CV103
Lindsay Sq. SW1 277 N10
Lindsay Sq. SW1 161 DK78
Lindsell St. SE10 163 EC81
Lindsey Clo., Brwd. 108 FU49
Lindsey Clo., Brom. 204 EK97
Lindsey Clo., Mitch. 201 DL98
Lindsey Gdns., Felt. 175 BR87
Lindsey Ms. N1 142 DQ66
Lindsey Rd., Dag. 126 EW63
Lindsey Rd. (Denham), Uxb. 114 BG62
Lindsey Smith Ho., Vir.W. 192 AY99
Lindsey St. EC1 274 G6
Lindsey St. EC1 141 DP71
Lindsey St., Epp. 69 ER28
Lindsey Way, Horn. 128 FJ57
Lindum Pl., St.Alb. 42 BZ22
Lindum Rd., Tedd. 177 CJ94
Lindvale, Wok. 226 AY115
Lindway SE27 181 DP92
Lindwood Clo. E6 144 EL71
Northumberland Rd.
Linfield Clo. NW4 119 CW55
Linfield Clo., Walt. 213 BV106
Linfields, Amer. 72 AW40
Linford Clo., Harl. 51 EP17
Linford End, Harl. 51 EP17
Linford Rd. E17 123 EC55
Linford Rd., Grays 171 GH78
Linford St. SW8 161 DJ81
Ling Rd. E16 144 EG71
Ling Rd., Erith 167 FC79
Lingards Rd. SE13 163 EC84
Lingey Clo., Sid. 185 ET89
Lingfield Ave., Dart. 188 FP87
Lingfield Ave., Kings.T. 198 CL98
Lingfield Ave., Upmin. 128 FM62
Lingfield Clo., Enf. 82 DS44
Lingfield Clo., Nthwd. 93 BS52
Lingfield Cres. SE9 165 ER84
Lingfield Gdns. N9 100 DV45
Lingfield Gdns., Couls. 235 DP119
Lingfield Rd. SW19 179 CX92
Lingfield Rd., Grav. 191 GH89
Lingfield Rd., Wor.Pk. 199 CW104
Lingfield Way, Wat. 75 BT38
Lingham St. SW9 161 DL82
Lingholm Way, Barn. 79 CX43
Lingmere Clo., Chig. 103 EQ47
Lingmoor Dr., Wat. 60 BW33
Lingrove Gdns., Buck.H. 102 EH47
Beech La.
Lings Coppice SE21 182 DR89
Lingwell Rd. SW17 180 DE90
Lingwood Gdns., Islw. 157 CE80
Lingwood Rd. E5 122 DU59
Linhope St. NW1 272 D4
Linhope St. NW1 140 DF70
Linington Ave., Chesh. 56 AU30
Link, The SE9 185 EN90
Link, The W3 138 CP72
Link, The, Enf. 83 DY39
Link, The, Nthlt. 116 BZ64
Eastcote La.
Link, The, Pnr. 116 BW59
Link, The, Slou. 132 AV72
Link, The, Wem. 117 CJ60
Nathans Rd.
Link Ave., Wok. 227 BD115
Link Clo., Hat. 45 CV18
Link Dr., Hat. 45 CV18
Link La., Wall. 219 DK107
Link Rd. N11 98 DG49
Link Rd., Add. 212 BL105
Weybridge Rd.
Link Rd., Dag. 147 FB68
Link Rd., Felt. 175 BT87
Link Rd., Slou. 152 AW80
Link Rd., Wall. 200 DG102
Link Rd. (Bushey), Wat. 76 BX40
Link St. E9 142 DW65
Link Wk., Hat. 45 CV17
Link Way, Brom. 204 EL101
Link Way, Horn. 128 FL60
Link Way, Pnr. 94 BX53
Link Way, Stai. 174 BH93
Link Way (Denham), Uxb. 114 BG58
Link Way Rd., Brwd. 108 FT48
Linkfield, Brom. 204 EG100
Linkfield, Welw.G.C. 29 CY13
Linkfield, W.Mol. 196 CB97
Linkfield Cor., Red. 250 DE133
Hatchlands Rd.
Linkfield Gdns., Red. 250 DE134
Hatchlands Rd.
Linkfield La., Red. 250 DE133
Linkfield Rd., Islw. 157 CF82
Linkfield St., Red. 250 DE134
Linklea Clo. NW9 96 CS52
Links, The E17 123 DY56
Links, The (Cheshunt), Wal.Cr. 67 DX26
Links, The, Walt. 195 BU103
Links, The, Welw.G.C. 29 CV09
Applecroft Rd.
Links Ave., Hert. 32 DV08
Links Ave., Mord. 200 DA98
Links Brow, Lthd. 231 CE124
Links Clo., Ash. 231 CJ117
Links Dr. N20 98 DA46
Links Dr., Borwd. 78 CM41
Links Dr., Rad. 61 CF33
Links Gdns. SW16 181 DN94
Links Grn. Way, Cob. 214 CA114
Links Pl., Ash. 231 CK117
Links Rd. NW2 119 CT61
Links Rd. SW17 180 DG93
Links Rd. W3 138 CN72
Links Rd., Ashf. 174 BL92
Links Rd., Ash. 231 CJ118
Links Rd., Epsom 217 CU113
Links Rd., Guil. 258 AY144
Links Rd., H.Wyc. 110 AC55
Links Rd., W.Wick. 203 EC102
Links Rd., Wdf.Grn. 102 EG50
Links Side, Enf. 81 DN41
Links Vw. N3 97 CZ52
Links Vw., Dart. 187 FH88
Links Vw., St.Alb. 42 CB18
Links Vw. Ave., Bet. 248 CN134
Links Vw. Clo., Stan. 95 CG51
Links Vw. Rd., Croy. 203 EA104
Links Vw. Rd., Hmptn. 176 CC92
Links Way, Beck. 203 EA100
Links Way, Lthd. 246 BY128
Links Way, Rick. 75 BQ41
Links Yd. E1 142 DU71
Spelman St.
Linkscroft Ave., Ashf. 175 BP93
Linkside N12 97 CZ51
Linkside, Chig. 103 EQ50
Linkside, N.Mal. 198 CS96
Linkside Clo., Enf. 81 DM41
Linkside Gdns., Enf. 81 DM41
Linksway NW4 97 CX54
Linksway, Nthwd. 93 BQ53
Linkswood Rd., Slou. 130 AJ68
Linkway N4 122 DQ59
Linkway SW20 199 CV97
Linkway, Dag. 126 EW63
Linkway, Guil. 242 AT133
Linkway, Rich. 177 CH90
Linkway, Wok. 227 BC117
Linkway, The, Barn. 80 DB44
Linkway, The, Sutt. 218 DD109
Linkwood Wk. NW1 141 DK66
Maiden La.
Linley Cres., Rom. 127 FB55
Linley Rd. N17 100 DS54
Linnell Clo. NW11 120 DB58
Linnell Dr. NW11 120 DB58
Linnell Rd. N18 100 DU50
Fairfield Rd.
Linnell Rd. SE5 162 DS82
Linnell Rd., Red. 266 DG135
Linnet Clo. N9 101 DX46
Linnet Clo. SE28 146 EW73
Linnet Clo., S.Croy. 221 DX110
Linnet Clo. (Bushey), Wat. 94 CC45
Linnet Gro., Guil. 243 BD132
Partridge Way
Linnet Ms. SW12 180 DG87
Linnet Rd., Abb.L. 59 BU31
Linnet Wk., Hat. 45 CU20
Lark Ri.
Linnet Way, Purf. 168 FP78
Linnett Clo. E4 101 EC49
Linom Rd. SW4 161 DL84
Linscott Rd. E5 122 DW63
Linsdell Rd., Bark. 145 EQ67
Linsey Clo., Hem.H. 40 BN24
Linsey St. SE16 162 DU77
Linslade Clo., Houns. 176 BY85
Frampton Rd.
Linslade Clo., Pnr. 115 BV55
Linslade Rd., Orp. 224 EU107
Linstead Ct. SE9 185 ES86
Linstead St. NW6 140 DA66
Linstead Way SW18 179 CY87
Linster Gro., Borwd. 78 CQ43
Lintaine Clo. W6 159 CY79
Moylan Rd.
Linthorpe Ave., Wem. 137 CJ65
Linthorpe Rd. N16 122 DS59
Linthorpe Rd., Barn. 80 DE41
Linton Ave., Borwd. 78 CM39
Linton Clo., Mitch. 200 DF101
Linton Clo., Well. 166 EV81
Anthony Rd.
Linton Gdns. E6 144 EL72
Linton Glade, Croy. 221 DY109
Linton Gro. SE27 181 DP92
Linton Rd., Bark. 145 EQ66
Linton St. N1 142 DQ67
Lintons, The, Bark. 145 EQ66
Lintons La., Epsom 216 CS112
Lintott Ct., Stai. 174 BK86
Linver Rd. SW6 160 DA82
Linwood, Saw. 36 EY05
Linwood Clo. SE5 162 DT82
Linwood Cres., Enf. 82 DU39
Linwood Way SE15 162 DT80
Daniel Gdns.
Linzee Rd. N8 121 DL56
Lion Ave., Twick. 177 CF88
Lion Rd.
Lion Clo. SE4 183 EA86
Lion Clo., Shep. 194 BL97
Lion Ct., Borwd. 78 CQ39
Lion Gate Gdns., Rich. 158 CM83
Lion Grn. Rd., Couls. 235 DK115
Lion La., Red. 250 DF133
Lion Pk. Ave., Chess. 216 CN105
Lion Plaza EC2 142 DR72
Threadneedle St.
Lion Rd. E6 145 EM71
Lion Rd. N9 100 DU47
Lion Rd., Bexh. 166 EZ84
Lion Rd., Croy. 202 DQ99
Lion Rd., Twick. 177 CF88
Lion Way, Brent. 157 CK80
Lion Wf. Rd., Islw. 157 CH83
Lion Yd. SW4 161 DK84
Tremadoc Rd.
Lionel Gdns. SE9 184 EK85
Lionel Ms. W10 139 CY71
Telford Rd.
Lionel Oxley Ho., Grays 170 GB79
New Rd.
Lionel Rd. SE9 184 EK85
Lionel Rd., Brent. 158 CM78
Lions Clo. SE9 184 EJ90
Liphook Clo., Horn. 127 FF63
Petworth Way
Liphook Cres. SE23 182 DW87
Liphook Rd., Wat. 94 BX49
Lippitts Hill, Loug. 84 EE39
Lipsham Clo., Bans. 218 DD113
Lipton Clo. SE28 146 EW73
Aisher Rd.
Lipton Rd. E1 143 DX72
Bower St.
Lisbon Ave., Twick. 176 CC89
Lisburne Rd. NW3 120 DF63
Lisford St. SE15 162 DT81
Lisgar Ter. W14 159 CZ77
Liskeard Clo., Chis. 185 EQ93
Liskeard Gdns. SE3 164 EG81
Liskeard Lo., Cat. 252 DU126
Lisle Clo. SW17 181 DH91
Lisle Pl., Grays 170 GA76
Lisle St. WC2 273 N10
Lisle St. WC2 141 DK73
Lismore, Hem.H. 41 BQ22
Lismore Circ. NW5 120 DG64
Lismore Clo., Islw. 157 CG82
Lismore Pk., Slou. 132 AT72
Lismore Rd. N17 122 DR55
Lismore Rd., S.Croy. 220 DS107
Lismore Wk. N1 142 DQ65
Clephane Rd.
Liss Way SE15 162 DT80
Pentridge St.
Lissenden Gdns. NW5 120 DG63
Lissoms Rd., Couls. 234 DG118
Lisson Grn. Est. NW8 272 B3
Lisson Grn. Est. NW8 140 DE69
Lisson Gro. NW1 272 B5
Lisson Gro. NW1 140 DE70
Lisson Gro. NW8 272 A3
Lisson Gro. NW8 140 DD69
Lisson St. NW1 272 B6
Lisson St. NW1 140 DE71
Lister Ave., Rom. 106 FK54
Lister Clo. W3 138 CR71
Lister Clo., Mitch. 200 DE95
Lister Gdns. N18 100 DQ50
Lister Ho. SE3 164 EE79
Lister Rd. E11 124 EE60
Lister Rd., Til. 171 GG82
Lister St. E13 144 EG69
Sewell St.
Lister Wk. SE28 146 EX73
Haldane Rd.
Liston Rd. N17 100 DU53
Liston Rd. SW4 161 DJ83
Liston Way, Wdf.Grn. 102 EJ52
Listowel Clo. SW9 161 DN80
Mandela St.
Listowel Rd., Dag. 126 FA62
Listria Pk. N16 122 DS61
Litcham Spur, Slou. 131 AR72
Litchfield Ave. E15 144 EE65
Litchfield Ave., Mord. 199 CZ101
Litchfield Gdns. NW10 139 CU65
Litchfield Rd., Sutt. 218 DC105
Litchfield St. WC2 273 N10
Litchfield St. WC2 141 DK73
Litchfield Way NW11 120 DB57
Litchfield Way, Guil. 258 AT136
Lithos Rd. NW3 140 DB65
Little Acre, Beck. 203 EA97
Little Acre, St.Alb. 43 CD17
Little Acres, Ware 33 DX07
Little Albany St. NW1 273 J4
Little Argyll St. W1 273 K9
Little Aston Rd., Rom. 106 FN52
Little Belhus Clo., S.Ock. 149 FU70
Little Benty, West Dr. 154 BK78
Little Berkhamsted La., Hat. 46 DF20
Little Berkhamsted La., Hert. 47 DJ19
Little Birch Clo., Add. 212 BK109
Little Birches, Sid. 185 ES89
Little Boltons, The SW5 160 DB78
Little Boltons, The SW10 160 DB78
Little Bookham St., Lthd. 230 BZ123
Little Bornes SE21 182 DS91
Little Borough, Bet. 264 CN135
Little Brays, Harl. 52 EU16
Little Bri. Rd., Berk. 38 AX19
Little Britain EC1 274 G7
Little Britain EC1 141 DP71
Little Brook Rd., Harl. 50 EJ15
Little Brownings SE23 182 DV89
Little Buntings, Wind. 151 AM83
Little Burrow, Welw.G.C. 29 CX11
Little Bury St. N9 100 DR46
Little Bushey La. (Bushey), Wat. 77 CD44
Little Bushey La. Footpath (Bushey), Wat. 95 CD45
Little Bushey La.
Little Catherells, Hem.H. 39 BF18
Little Cattins, Harl. 51 EM19
Little Cedars N12 98 DC49
Woodside Ave.
Little Chapels Way, Slou. 151 AN75
Little Chester St. SW1 276 G6
Little Chester St. SW1 161 DH76
Little Cloisters SW1 161 DK76
Tufton St.
Little College La. EC4 142 DR73
Garlick Hill
Little College St. SW1 277 P6
Little Collins, Red. 267 DP144
Little Common, Stan. 95 CG48
Little Common La., Red. 251 DP132
Little Ct., W.Wick. 204 EE103
Little Cranmore La., Lthd. 245 BP128
Little Dean's Yd. SW1 277 P6
Little Dell, Welw.G.C. 29 CX07
Little Dimocks SW12 181 DH89
Little Dormers, Ger.Cr. 113 AZ56
Little Dorrit Ct. SE1 279 J4
Little Dorrit Ct. SE1 162 DQ75
Little Dragons, Loug. 84 EK42
Little Ealing La. W5 157 CJ77
Little Edward St. NW1 273 J2
Little Elms, Hayes 155 BR80
Little Essex St. WC2 274 D10
Little Ferry Rd., Twick. 177 CH88
Ferry Rd.
Little Friday Rd. E4 102 EE47
Little Ganett, Welw.G.C. 30 DB11
Little Gaynes Gdns., Upmin. 128 FP63
Little Gaynes La., Upmin. 128 FM63
Little Gearies, Ilf. 125 EP56
Little George St. SW1 277 P5
Little Gerpins La., Upmin. 148 FM67
Little Gra., Grnf. 137 CG69
Perivale La.
Little Graylings, Abb.L. 59 BS33
Little Grn., Rich. 157 CK84
Little Grn. La., Cher. 193 BE104
Little Grn. La., Rick. 75 BP41
Little Grn. St. NW5 121 DH63
College La.
Little Greencroft, Chesh. 54 AN27
Little Gregories La., Epp. 85 ER35
Little Gro. (Bushey), Wat. 76 CB42
Little Gro. Fld., Harl. 51 EQ15
Little Halliards, Walt. 195 BU100
Felix Rd.
Little Hardings, Welw.G.C. 30 DC08
Little Hayes, Kings L. 58 BN29
Little Heath SE7 164 EL79
Little Heath, Rom. 126 EV56
Little Heath La., Berk. 39 BB21
Little Heath Rd., Bexh. 166 EZ81
Little Heath Rd., Wok. 210 AS109
Little Henleys, Ware 34 EK06
Little Hide, Guil. 243 BB132
Little Hill, Rick. 73 BC44
Little Hivings, Chesh. 54 AN27
Little How Cft., Abb.L. 59 BQ31
Little Ilford La. E12 125 EM63
Little Julians Hill, Sev. 256 FG128
Little Kiln, Gdmg. 258 AS143
Little Lake, Welw.G.C. 30 DB12
Little Ley, Welw.G.C. 29 CY12
Little London, Guil. 260 BL142
Little Marlborough St. W1 273 K9
Little Martins (Bushey), Wat. 76 CB43
Little Mead, Hat. 45 CV15
Little Mead, Wok. 226 AT116
Little Mimms, Hem.H. 40 BK19
Little Moreton Clo., W.Byf. 212 BH112
Little Moss La., Pnr. 94 BY54
Little Mundells, Welw.G.C. 29 CZ07
Little New St. EC4 274 E8
Little Newport St. WC2 273 N10
Little Newport St. WC2 141 DK73
Little Orchard, Add. 211 BF111
Little Orchard, Hem.H. 40 BN18
Little Orchard, Wok. 211 BA114
Little Orchard Clo., Abb.L. 59 BR32
Little Orchard Clo., Pnr. 94 BY54
Barrow Pt. La.
Little Orchard Way, Guil. 258 AY142
Little Oxhey La., Wat. 94 BX50
Little Pk., Hem.H. 57 BA28
Little Pk. Dr., Felt. 176 BX89
Little Pk. Gdns., Enf. 82 DQ41
Little Pastures, Brwd. 108 FT49
Tern Way
Little Pipers Clo. (Cheshunt), Wal.Cr. 65 DP29
Little Plucketts Way, Buck.H. 102 EJ46
Little Port Spur, Slou. 132 AS72
Little Portland St. W1 273 K8
Little Portland St. W1 141 DH72
Little Potters (Bushey), Wat. 95 CD45
Little Pynchons, Harl. 51 ET18
Little Queen St., Dart. 188 FM87
Little Queens Rd., Tedd. 177 CF93
Little Redlands, Brom. 204 EL96
Little Reeves Ave., Amer. 72 AT39
Little Ridge, Welw.G.C. 30 DA09
Little Rivers, Welw.G.C. 30 DA08
Little Rd., Croy. 202 DS102
Lower Addiscombe Rd.
Little Rd., Hayes 155 BT75
Little Rd., Hem.H. 40 BM19
Little Roke Ave., Ken. 219 DP114
Little Roke Rd., Ken. 220 DQ114
Little Russell St. WC1 273 P7
Little Russell St. WC1 141 DL71
Little Russets, Brwd. 109 GE45
Hutton Village
Little St. James's St. SW1 277 K3
Little St. James's St. SW1 141 DJ74
Little St. Leonards SW14 158 CQ83
Little Sanctuary SW1 277 N5
Little Shardeloes, Amer. 55 AN40
Little Smith St. SW1 277 N6
Little Somerset St. E1 275 P9
Little Spring, Chesh. 54 AP28
Little Strand NW9 97 CT54
Little Stream Clo., Nthwd. 93 BS50
Little St., Guil. 242 AV130
Little Sutton La., Slou. 153 BC78
Little Thistle, Welw.G.C. 30 DC11
Little Thrift, Orp. 205 EQ98
Little Titchfield St. W1 273 K7
Little Trinity La. EC4 275 J10
Little Turnstile WC1 274 B7
Little Wade, Welw.G.C. 29 CZ12
Little Wk., Harl. 51 EQ15
Little Warren Clo., Guil. 259 BB136
Little Widbury, Ware 33 DZ06
Little Widbury La., Ware 33 DZ06
Little Windmill Hill, Kings L. 57 BE32
Little Wd. Clo., Orp. 206 EU95
Little Woodcote Est., Cars. 218 DG111
Woodmansterne La.
Little Woodcote Est., Wall. 218 DG111
Woodmansterne La.
Little Woodcote La., Cars. 219 DH112
Little Woodcote La., Pur. 219 DH112
Little Woodcote La., Wall. 219 DH112
Little Woodlands, Wind. 151 AM83
Little Youngs, Welw.G.C. 29 CW09
Littlebrook Ave., Slou. 131 AL70
Littlebrook Clo., Croy. 203 DX100
Littlebrook Gdns. (Cheshunt), Wal.Cr. 66 DW30
Littlebury Rd. SW4 161 DK83
Littlecombe SE7 164 EH79
Littlecombe Clo. SW15 179 CX86
Littlecote Clo. SW19 179 CX87
Littlecote Pl., Pnr. 94 BY53
Littlecourt Rd., Sev. 256 FG124
Littlecroft SE9 165 EN83
Littlecroft, Grav. 190 GE94
Littlecroft Rd., Egh. 173 AZ92
Littledale SE2 166 EU79
Littledale, Dart. 188 FQ90
Littledown Rd., Slou. 132 AT74
Littlefield Clo. N19 121 DJ63
Tufnell Pk. Rd.
Littlefield Clo., Kings.T. 198 CL96
Fairfield W.
Littlefield Rd., Edg. 96 CQ52
Littleford La., Guil. 259 BE142
Littlegrove, Barn. 80 DE44
Littleheath La., Cob. 214 BZ114
Littleheath La., Wok. 210 AS109
Littleheath Rd., S.Croy. 220 DV108
Littlehorse La., Ware 33 DX05
Littlejohn Rd. W7 137 CF72
Littlejohn Rd., Orp. 206 EU100
Littlemead, Esher 215 CD105
Littlemede SE9 185 EM90
Littlemoor Rd., Ilf. 125 ER62
Littlemore Rd. SE2 166 EU75
Littlers Clo. SW19 200 DD95
Runnymede
Littlestone Clo., Beck. 183 EA93
Abbey La.
Littleton Ave. E4 102 EF46
Littleton Cres., Har. 117 CF61
Littleton La., Guil. 258 AU139
Littleton La., Reig. 265 CX136
Littleton La., Shep. 194 BK101
Littleton Rd., Ashf. 175 BQ94
Littleton Rd., Har. 117 CF61
Littleton St. SW18 180 DC89
Littlewick Rd., Wok. 210 AW114
Littlewood SE13 183 EC85
Littlewood, Sev. 257 FJ122
Littlewood Clo. W13 157 CH76
Littleworth Ave., Esher 215 CD106
Littleworth Common Rd., Esher 197 CD104
Littleworth La., Esher 215 CD105
Littleworth Pl., Esher 215 CD105
Littleworth Rd., Esher 215 CD106
Littleworth Rd., Slou. 110 AJ63
Litton Ct., H.Wyc. 88 AC53
Livermere Rd. E8 142 DT67
Liverpool Gro. SE17 162 DR78
Liverpool Rd. E10 123 EC58
Liverpool Rd. E16 144 EE71
Liverpool Rd. N1 141 DN68
Liverpool Rd. N7 121 DN64
Liverpool Rd. W5 157 CK75
Liverpool Rd., Kings.T. 178 CN94
Liverpool Rd., St.Alb. 43 CE20
Liverpool Rd., Slou. 131 AP72
Liverpool Rd., Th.Hth. 202 DQ97
Liverpool Rd., Wat. 75 BV43
Liverpool St. EC2 275 M7
Liverpool St. EC2 142 DS71
Livesey Clo., Kings.T. 198 CM97
Livesey Pl. SE15 162 DU79
Peckham Pk. Rd.
Livingston College Twrs. E10 123 EC58
Essex Rd.
Livingstone Gdns., Grav. 191 GK92
Livingstone Pl. E14 163 EC78
Ferry St.
Livingstone Rd. E15 143 EC67
Livingstone Rd. E17 123 EB58
Livingstone Rd. N13 99 DL51
Livingstone Rd. SW11 160 DD83
Winstanley Rd.
Livingstone Rd., Cat. 236 DR122
Livingstone Rd., Grav. 191 GK92
Livingstone Rd., Houns. 156 CC84
Livingstone Rd., Sthl. 136 BX73
Livingstone Rd., Th.Hth. 202 DQ96
Livingstone Ter., Rain. 147 FE67
Livingstone Wk. SW11 160 DD83
Livingstone Wk., Hem.H. 40 BM16
Livonia St. W1 273 L9
Lizard St. EC1 275 J3
Lizard St. EC1 142 DQ69
Lizban St. SE3 164 EH80
Llanbury Clo., Ger.Cr. 90 AY52
Llanelly Rd. NW2 119 CZ61
Llanover Rd. SE18 165 EN79
Llanover Rd., Wem. 117 CK62
Llanthony Rd., Mord. 200 DD100
Llanvanor Rd. NW2 119 CZ61
Llewellyn St. SE16 162 DU75
Chambers St.
Lloyd Ave. SW16 201 DL95
Lloyd Ave., Couls. 218 DG114
Lloyd Baker St. WC1 274 C3
Lloyd Baker St. WC1 141 DM69
Lloyd Ct., Pnr. 116 BX57
Lloyd Pk. Ave., Croy. 220 DT105
Lloyd Rd. E6 145 EM67
Lloyd Rd. E17 123 DX56
Lloyd Rd., Dag. 146 EZ65
Lloyd Rd., Wor.Pk. 199 CW104
Lloyd Sq. WC1 274 D2
Lloyd Sq. WC1 141 DN69
Lloyd St. WC1 274 D2
Lloyd St. WC1 141 DN69
Lloyd's Ave. EC3 275 N9
Lloyd's Ave. EC3 142 DS72
Lloyds Pl. SE3 164 EE82
Lloyd's Row EC1 274 E3
Lloyds Way, Beck. 203 DY99
Loampit Hill SE13 163 EA82
Loampit Vale SE13 163 EB83
Loanda Clo. E8 142 DT67
Clarissa St.
Loates La., Wat. 76 BW41
Loats Rd. SW2 181 DL86
Lobelia Clo. E6 144 EL71
Sorrel Gdns.
Local Board Rd., Wat. 76 BW43
Locarno Rd. W3 138 CQ74
High St.
Locarno Rd., Grnf. 136 CC70
Lochaber Rd. SE13 164 EE84
Lochaline St. W6 159 CW79
Lochan Clo., Hayes 136 BY70
Lochinvar Clo., Slou. 151 AP75
Haig Dr.
Lochinvar St. SW12 181 DH87
Lochmere Clo., Erith 167 FB79
Lochnagar St. E14 143 EC71
Lock Ave., Maid. 130 AC69
Lock Chase SE3 164 EF83
Lock Clo., Add. 211 BE112
Lock Clo., Sthl. 156 CC75
Navigator Dr.
Lock Island, Shep. 194 BN103
Lock La., Wok. 228 BH116
Lock Path, Wind. 151 AK79
Lock Rd., Guil. 242 AX131
Lock Rd., Rich. 177 CJ91
Locke Clo., Rain. 147 FF65
Locke Gdns., Slou. 152 AW75
Locke King Clo., Wey. 212 BN108
Locke King Rd., Wey. 212 BN108
Locke Way, Wok. 227 AZ117
The Bdy.
Lockers Pk. La., Hem.H. 40 BH20
Lockesfield Pl. E14 163 EB78
Lockesley Dr., Orp. 205 ET100
Lockesley Sq., Surb. 197 CK100
Locket Rd., Har. 117 CE55
Lockets Clo., Wind. 151 AL81
Lockfield Ave., Enf. 83 DY40
Lockfield Dr., Wok. 226 AS116
Lockgate Clo. E9 123 DZ64
Lee Conservancy Rd.
Lockhart Clo. N7 141 DM65
Lockhart Clo., Enf. 82 DV43
Derby Rd.
Lockhart Rd., Cob. 214 BW113
Lockhart St. E3 143 DZ70
Lockhurst St. E5 123 DX63
Lockie Pl. SE25 202 DU97
Lockier Wk., Wem. 117 CK62
Lockington Rd. SW8 161 DH81
Lockley Cres., Hat. 45 CV16
Lockmead Rd. N15 122 DU58
Lockmead Rd. SE13 163 EC83
Locknell Rd., Berk. 38 AT17
Lockner Holt, Guil. 259 BF141

Locks La., Mitch. 200 DF95
Locksley Dr., Wok. 226 AT118
Robin Hood Rd.
Locksley Est. E14 143 DZ72
Locksley St. E14 143 DZ71
Locksmeade Rd., Rich. 177 CJ91
Lockswood Clo., Barn. 80 DF42
Lockwood Clo. SE26 183 DX91
Lockwood Ind. Pk. N17 122 DV55
Lockwood Path, Wok. 211 BE113
Lockwood Sq. SE16 162 DV76
Lockwood Wk., Rom. 127 FE57
Lockwood Way E17 101 DX54
Lockwood Way, Chess. 216 CN106
Lockyer Est. SE1 279 L4
Lockyer Rd., Purf. 168 FQ79
Lockyer St. SE1 279 L5
Loddiges Rd. E9 142 DW66
Loddon Spur, Slou. 132 AS73
Loder Clo., Wok. 211 BD113
Loder St. SE15 162 DW81
Lodge Ave. SW14 158 CS83
Lodge Ave., Borwd. 78 CM43
Lodge Ave., Croy. 201 DN104
Lodge Ave., Dag. 146 EU67
Lodge Ave., Dart. 188 FJ86
Lodge Ave., Har. 118 CL56
Lodge Ave., Rom. 127 FG56
Lodge Clo. N18 100 DQ50
Lodge Clo., Chig. 104 EU48
Lodge Clo., Cob. 230 BZ116
Lodge Clo., Dor. 263 CJ140
Lodge Clo., Edg. 96 CM51
Lodge Clo., Egh. 172 AX92
Lodge Clo., Epsom 217 CW110
Howell Hill Gro.
Lodge Clo., Hert. 32 DQ07
Lodge Clo., Islw. 157 CH81
Lodge Clo., Lthd. 231 CD122
Lodge Clo., Orp. 206 EV102
Lodge Clo., Slou. 151 AQ75
Lodge Clo., Uxb. 134 BJ70
Lodge Clo., Wall. 200 DG102
Lodge Ct., Horn. 128 FL61
Lodge Ct., Wem. 118 CL64
Lodge Cres., Orp. 206 EV102
Lodge Cres., Wal.Cr. 67 DX34
Lodge Dr. N13 99 DN49
Lodge Dr., Hat. 45 CX15
Lodge Dr., Rick. 74 BJ42
Lodge Dr., The, Beac. 89 AL54
Lodge End, Rad. 61 CH34
Lodge End, Rick. 75 BR42
Lodge Gdns., Beck. 203 DZ99
Lodge Hall, Harl. 51 ES19
Lodge Hill SE2 166 EV80
Lodge Hill, Ilf. 124 EL56
Lodge Hill, Pur. 235 DN115
Lodge Hill, Well. 166 EV80
Lodge La. N12 98 DC50
Lodge La., Bex. 186 EX86
Lodge La., Ch.St.G. 73 AZ43
Lodge La., Croy. 221 EA107
Lodge La., Dor. 264 CL144
Lodge La., Grays 170 GA75
Lodge La., Red. 266 DE143
Lodge La., Rom. 104 FA52
Lodge La., Wal.Abb. 83 ED35
Lodge La., West. 255 EQ127
Lodge Pl., Sutt. 218 DB106
Lodge Rd. NW4 119 CW56
Lodge Rd. NW8 272 A3
Lodge Rd. NW8 140 DD69
Lodge Rd., Brom. 184 EH94
Lodge Rd., Croy. 201 DP100
Lodge Rd., Lthd. 230 CC122
Lodge Rd., Sutt. 218 DB106
Throwley Way
Lodge Rd., Wall. 219 DH106
Lodge Vil., Wdf.Grn. 102 EF52
Lodge Way, Ashf. 174 BL89
Lodge Way, Shep. 195 BQ96
Lodge Way, Wind. 151 AL83
Lodgebottom Rd., Lthd. 248 CN127
Lodgefield, Welw.G.C. 29 CY06
Lodgehill Pk. Clo., Har. 116 CB61
Lodore Gdns. NW9 118 CS57
Lodore Grn., Uxb. 114 BL62
Lodore St. E14 143 EC72
Loewen Rd., Grays 171 GG76
Lofthouse Pl., Chess. 215 CJ107
Loftie St. SE16 162 DU75
Lofting Rd. N1 141 DM66
Loftus Rd. W12 139 CV74
Logan Clo., Enf. 83 DX39
Logan Clo., Houns. 156 BZ83
Logan Ms. W8 160 DA77
Logan Pl. W8 160 DA77
Logan Rd. N9 100 DV47
Logan Rd., Wem. 118 CL61
Loggetts, The SE21 182 DS89
Logmore La., Dor. 262 CB138
Logs Hill, Brom. 184 EL94
Logs Hill, Chis. 184 EL94
Logs Hill Clo., Chis. 204 EL95
Lois Dr., Shep. 195 BP99
Lolesworth Clo. E1 142 DT71
Commercial St.
Lollard St. SE11 278 C8
Lollard St. SE11 161 DM77
Lollards Clo., Amer. 55 AQ37
Lollesworth La., Lthd. 245 BQ126
Loman Path, S.Ock. 149 FT72
Loman St. SE1 278 G4
Loman St. SE1 161 DP75
Lomas Clo., Croy. 221 EC108
Lomas Ct. E8 142 DT66
Lomas St. E1 142 DU71
Lombard Ave., Enf. 82 DW39
Lombard Ave., Ilf. 125 ES60
Lombard Business Pk. SW19 200 DC96
Lombard Ct. EC3 275 L10
Lombard Ct. W3 138 CP74
Crown St.
Lombard La. EC4 274 E9
Lombard Rd. N11 99 DH50
Lombard Rd. SW11 160 DD82
Lombard Rd. SW19 200 DB96
Lombard St. EC3 275 L9
Lombard St. EC3 142 DR72
Lombard St., Dart. 208 FQ99
Lombard Wall SE7 164 EH76
Lombards, The, Horn. 128 FM59
Lombardy Clo., Hem.H. 41 BR21
Lombardy Clo., Wok. 226 AT117
Nethercote Ave.
Lombardy Dr., Berk. 38 AX20
Lombardy Pl. W2 140 DB73
Bark Pl.
Lombardy Way, Borwd. 78 CL39
Lomond Clo. N15 122 DS56
Lomond Clo., Wem. 138 CM66
Lomond Gdns., S.Croy. 221 DY108
Lomond Gro. SE5 162 DR80
Lomond Rd., Hem.H. 40 BK16
Loncin Mead Ave., Add. 212 BJ109
Loncroft Rd. SE5 162 DS79
Londesborough Rd. N16 122 DS63
London Bri. EC4 279 L2
London Bri. EC4 142 DR74
London Bri. SE1 279 L2
London Bri. SE1 142 DR74
London Bri. St. SE1 279 K3
London Bri. St. SE1 142 DR74
London Bri. Wk. SE1 279 L2
London Bri. Wk. SE1 142 DS74
London City Airport E16 145 EM74
London Colney Bypass, St.Alb. 61 CK25
London End, Beac. 89 AM54
London Flds. E8 142 DV66
London Flds. E. Side E8 142 DV66
London Flds. W. Side E8 142 DU66
London La. E8 142 DV66
London La., Brom. 184 EF94
London La., Guil. 260 BN138
London La., Lthd. 245 BU131
London Ms. W2 272 A9
London Rd. E13 144 EG68
London Rd. SE1 278 F6
London Rd. SE1 161 DP76
London Rd. SE23 182 DU88
London Rd. SW16 201 DM95
London Rd. SW17 200 DF96
London Rd., Amer. 55 AQ40
London Rd., Ashf. 174 BJ90
London Rd., Bark. 145 EP66
London Rd., Beac. 89 AM54
London Rd., Berk. 38 AX20
London Rd., Borwd. 62 CN34
London Rd., Brent. 157 CJ80
London Rd., Brwd. 108 FT49
London Rd., Brom. 184 EF94
London Rd., Cat. 236 DR123
London Rd., Ch.St.G. 90 AW47
London Rd., Croy. 201 DP101
London Rd., Dart. 188 FP87
London Rd. (Crayford), Dart. 187 FD85
London Rd. (Farningham), Dart. 208 FL100
London Rd., Dor. 247 CH133
London Rd., Egh. 192 AW95
London Rd., Enf. 82 DR41
London Rd., Epp. 52 EV23
London Rd., Epsom 217 CT109
London Rd., Felt. 174 BH90
London Rd., Gat. 268 DF150
London Rd., Grav. 190 GD86
London Rd., Grays 169 FW79
London Rd., Green. 189 FT86
London Rd., Guil. 258 AY135
London Rd. (Old Harlow), Harl. 52 EV16
London Rd. (Potter St.), Harl. 52 EW18
London Rd. (Thornwood), Harl. 52 EV22
London Rd., Har. 117 CE61
London Rd., Hem.H. 40 BG22
London Rd., Hert. 32 DS09
London Rd., H.Wyc. 88 AD54
London Rd., Houns. 157 CD83
London Rd., Islw. 157 CF82
London Rd., Kings.T. 198 CM96
London Rd., Mitch. 200 DF96
London Rd. (Beddington Cor.), Mitch. 200 DG101
London Rd., Mord. 200 DA99
London Rd., Ong. 87 FH36
London Rd., Rad. 62 CM33
London Rd., Red. 250 DG133
London Rd., Reig. 250 DA134
London Rd., Rick. 92 BM47
London Rd., Rom. 126 FA58
London Rd. (Abridge), Rom. 85 ET42
London Rd. (Stapleford Tawney), Rom. 87 FC40
London Rd., St.Alb. 43 CD20
London Rd., Saw. 36 EY05
London Rd., Sev. 256 FF123
London Rd. (Halstead), Sev. 225 FB112
London Rd. (Longford), Sev. 241 FD119
London Rd., Slou. 152 AW76
London Rd. (Datchet), Slou. 152 AV80
London Rd., S.Ock. 148 FM74
London Rd., Stai. 173 BF91
London Rd., Stan. 95 CJ50
London Rd., Sutt. 199 CX104
London Rd., Swan. 207 FC95
London Rd., Swans. 189 FX85
London Rd., Th.Hth. 201 DN99
London Rd., Til. 171 GH82
London Rd., Twick. 177 CG87
London Rd., Vir.W. 192 AT97
London Rd., Wall. 219 DH105
London Rd., Ware 33 DX07
London Rd. (Bushey), Wat. 76 BY44
London Rd., Wem. 138 CL65
London Rd., West. 255 ER126
London Rd., Wok. 243 BD128
London Rd. E., Amer. 55 AR41
London Rd. N., Red. 251 DH126
London Rd. Purfleet, Purf. 168 FN78
London Rd. S., Red. 250 DG130
London Rd. W., Amer. 55 AQ40
London Rd. W. Thurrock, Grays 169 FS79
London Sq., Guil. 242 AY134
London Stile W4 158 CN78
Wellesley Rd.
London St. EC3 275 N10
London St. W2 272 A9
London St. W2 140 DD72
London St., Cher. 194 BG101
London Wall EC2 275 J7
London Wall EC2 142 DQ71
London Wall Bldgs. EC2 275 L7
Londons Clo., Upmin. 128 FQ64
Londrina Ter., Berk. 38 AX19
Lone Oak, Horl. 269 DP150
Lonesome La., Reig. 266 DB138
Lonesome Way SW16 201 DH95
Long Acre WC2 273 P10
Long Acre WC2 141 DL73
Long Acre, Orp. 206 EX103
Long Arrotts, Hem.H. 40 BH18
Long Banks, Harl. 51 ER19
Long Barn Clo., Wat. 59 BV32
Long Bottom La., Beac. 89 AN51
Long Chaulden, Hem.H. 39 BE20
Long Clo., Slou. 131 AP66
Long Copse Clo., Lthd. 230 CB123
Long Ct., Purf. 168 FN77
Thamley
Long Cross Rd., Wok. 192 AT104
Long Deacon Rd. E4 102 EE46
Long Dr. W3 138 CS72
Long Dr., Grnf. 136 CB67
Long Dr., Ruis. 116 BX63
Long Dr., Slou. 130 AJ69
Long Dyke, Guil. 243 BB132
Long Elmes, Har. 94 CB53
Long Elms, Abb.L. 59 BR33
Long Elms Clo., Abb.L. 59 BR33
Long Elms
Long Fallow, St.Alb. 60 CA27
Long Fld. NW9 96 CS52
Long Furlong Dr., Slou. 131 AK70
Long Gore, Gdmg. 258 AS142
Long Grn., Chig. 103 ES49
Long Gro., Beac. 89 AQ51
Long Gro., Rom. 106 FL54
Long Gro. Rd., Epsom 216 CP110
Long Hedges, Houns. 156 CA81
Long Hill, Cat. 237 DX121
Long John, Hem.H. 40 BM22
Long La. EC1 274 G6
Long La. EC1 141 DP71
Long La. N2 98 DC54
Long La. N3 98 DC54
Long La. SE1 279 K5
Long La. SE1 162 DR75
Long La., Bexh. 166 EX80
Long La., Croy. 202 DW99
Long La., Grays 170 GA75
Long La., Hem.H. 57 AZ31
Long La., Rick. 91 BF46
Long La. (Heronsgate), Rick. 73 BC44
Long La., Stai. 174 BM89
Long La., Uxb. 134 BN69
Long Ley, Harl. 51 ET15
Long Ley, Welw.G.C. 30 DC09
Long Leys E4 101 EB51
Long Lo. Dr., Walt. 196 BW104
Long Mark Rd. E16 144 EK71
Fulmer Rd.
Long Mead NW9 97 CT53
Long Meadow NW5 121 DK64
Torriano Ave.
Long Meadow, Brwd. 109 GC47
Long Meadow, Chesh. 54 AQ28
Long Meadow, Lthd. 246 BZ126
Long Meadow, Sev. 241 FD119
London Rd.
Long Meadow Clo., W.Wick. 203 EC101
Long Mimms, Hem.H. 40 BL19
Long Pk., Amer. 55 AQ36
Long Pk. Clo., Amer. 55 AQ36
Long Pk. Way, Amer. 55 AQ35
Long Pond Rd. SE3 164 EE81
Long Reach, Lthd. 245 BP125
Long Reach, Wok. 228 BN123
Long Reach Ct., Bark. 145 ER68
Long Readings La., Slou. 131 AP70
Long Ride, The, Hat. 45 CF16
Long Ridings Ave., Brwd. 109 GB43
Long Rd. SW4 161 DJ84
Long Shaw, Lthd. 231 CG120
Long Spring, St.Alb. 43 CF16
Long St. E2 275 P2
Long St. E2 142 DT69
Long St., Wal.Abb. 68 EL32
Long Vw., Berk. 38 AU17
Long Wk. SE1 279 N6
Long Wk. SE18 165 EP79
Long Wk. SW13 158 CS82
Long Wk., Ch.St.G. 72 AX41
Long Wk., Epsom 233 CW119
Long Wk., Lthd. 244 BN128
Long Wk., N.Mal. 198 CQ97
Long Wk., Wal.Abb. 67 EA30
Long Wk., W.Byf. 212 BJ114
Long Wk., The, Wind. 151 AR83
Long Wd. Dr., Beac. 90 AT51
Long Yd. WC1 274 B5
Long Yd. WC1 141 DM70
Longacre, Harl. 36 EV11
Longacre Pl., Cars. 218 DG107
Beddington Gdns.
Longacre Rd. E17 101 ED53
Longacres, St.Alb. 43 CK20
Longaford Way, Brwd. 109 GC46
Longbeach Rd. SW11 160 DF83
Longberrys NW2 119 CZ62
Longboat Row, Sthl. 136 BZ72
Longbottom La., Beac. 89 AR52
Longbourne Grn., Gdmg. 258 AS143
Barnes Rd.
Longbourne Way, Cher. 193 BF100
Longboyds, Cob. 213 BV114
Longbridge Rd., Bark. 145 EQ66
Longbridge Rd., Dag. 126 EU63
Longbridge Rd., Gat. 268 DF150
Longbridge Rd., Horl. 268 DF150
Longbridge Roundabout, Horl. 268 DE149
Longbridge Wk., Horl. 268 DF150
Longbridge Way SE13 183 EC85
Longbridge Way, Uxb. 134 BH68
Longbury Clo., Orp. 206 EV97
Longbury Dr., Orp. 206 EV97
Longchamp Clo., Horl. 269 DJ148
Carlton Tye
Longcliffe Path, Wat. 93 BU48
Gosforth La.
Longcroft SE9 185 EM90
Longcroft, Wat. 93 BV45
Longcroft Ave., Bans. 218 DC114
Longcroft Dr., Wal.Cr. 67 DZ34
Longcroft Gdns., Welw.G.C. 29 CX10
Longcroft Grn., Welw.G.C. 29 CX11
Stanborough Rd.
Longcroft La., Hem.H. 57 BC28
Longcroft La., Welw.G.C. 29 CX10
Longcroft Ri., Loug. 85 EN43
Longcroft Rd., Rick. 91 BD50
Longcrofte Rd., Edg. 95 CK52
Longcrofts, Wal.Abb. 68 EE34
Roundhills
Longcross Rd., Cher. 192 AY104
Longdean Pk., Hem.H. 40 BN24
Longdon Wd., Kes. 222 EL105
Longdown La. N., Epsom 217 CU114
Longdown Rd. SE6 183 EA91
Longdown Rd., Epsom 217 CU113
Longdown Rd., Guil. 259 BB137
Longfellow Dr., Brwd. 109 GC45
Longfellow Rd. E17 123 DZ58
Longfellow Rd., Wor.Pk. 199 CU103
Longfellow Way SE1 162 DT77
Chaucer Dr.
Longfield, Brom. 204 EF95
Longfield, Harl. 52 EU17
Longfield, Hem.H. 41 BP22
Longfield, Loug. 84 EJ43
Longfield, Slou. 111 AR62
Hedgerley Hill
Longfield Ave. E17 123 DY56
Longfield Ave. NW7 97 CU52
Longfield Ave. W5 137 CJ73
Longfield Ave., Enf. 82 DW37
Longfield Ave., Horn. 127 FF59
Longfield Ave., Wall. 200 DG102
Longfield Ave., Wem. 118 CL60
Longfield Cres. SE26 182 DW90
Longfield Cres., Tad. 233 CW120
Longfield Dr. SW14 178 CP85
Longfield Dr., Amer. 55 AP38
Longfield Dr., Mitch. 180 DE94
Longfield Est. SE1 162 DT77
Longfield La. (Cheshunt), Wal.Cr. 66 DU27
Longfield Rd. W5 137 CJ73
Longfield Rd., Chesh. 54 AM29
Longfield Rd., Dor. 263 CF137
Longfield St. SW18 180 DA87
Longfield Wk. W5 137 CJ72
Longford Ave., Felt. 175 BS86
Longford Ave., Sthl. 136 CA73
Longford Ave., Stai. 174 BL88
Longford Clo., Hmptn. 176 CA91
Longford Clo., Hayes 136 BX73
Longford Gdns.
Longford Ct. E5 123 DX63
Pedro St.
Longford Ct. NW4 119 CX56
Longford Ct., Epsom 216 CQ105
Longford Gdns., Hayes 136 BX73
Longford Gdns., Sutt. 200 DC104
Longford Rd., Twick. 176 CA88
Longford Roundabout, West Dr. 154 BH81
Longford St. NW1 273 J4
Longford St. NW1 141 DH70
Longford Wk. SW2 181 DN87
Longford Way, Stai. 174 BL88
Longhayes Ave., Rom. 126 EX56
Longhayes Ct., Rom. 126 EX56
Longhayes Ave.
Longheath Gdns., Croy. 202 DW99
Longhedge Ho. SE26 182 DT91
Longhedge St. SW11 160 DG82
Longhill Rd. SE6 183 ED89
Longhook Gdns., Nthlt. 135 BU68
Longhope Clo. SE15 162 DS79
Longhouse Rd., Grays 171 GH76
Longhurst Rd. SE13 183 ED85
Longhurst Rd., Croy. 202 DV100
Longhurst Rd., Lthd. 245 BS129
Longland Bri., B.Stort. 37 FC07
Longland Ct. SE1 162 DU78
Rolls Rd.
Longland Dr. N20 98 DB48
Longlands, Hem.H. 40 BM20
Longlands Ave., Couls. 218 DG114
Longlands Clo. (Cheshunt), Wal.Cr. 67 DX32
Longlands Ct. W11 139 CZ73
Portobello Rd.
Longlands Ct., Mitch. 200 DG95
Summerhill Way
Longlands Pk. Cres., Sid. 185 ES90
Longlands Rd., Sid. 185 ES90
Longlands Rd., Welw.G.C. 29 CZ10
Longleat Ms., Orp. 206 EW98
High St.
Longleat Rd., Enf. 82 DS43
Longleat Way, Felt. 175 BR87
Longlees, Rick. 91 BD50
Longleigh La. SE2 166 EW79
Longleigh La., Bexh. 166 EW79
Longlents Ho. NW10 138 CR67
Longley Ave., Wem. 138 CM67
Longley Rd. SW17 180 DE93
Longley Rd., Croy. 201 DP101
Longley Rd., Har. 116 CC57
Longley St. SE1 162 DU77
Longley Way NW2 119 CW62
Longmans Clo., Wat. 75 BQ44
Byewaters
Longmarsh Vw. (Sutton at Hone), Dart. 208 FP95
Longmead, Chis. 205 EN96
Longmead, Epsom 216 CR110
Longmead, Guil. 243 BC134
Longmead, Hat. 45 CV15
Longmead, Wind. 151 AL81
Longmead Business Pk., Epsom 216 CR111
Longmead Clo., Brwd. 108 FY46
Longmead Clo., Cat. 236 DS122
Longmead Dr., Sid. 186 EX89
Longmead La., Slou. 131 AK66
Longmead Rd. SW17 180 DF92
Longmead Rd., Epsom 216 CR111
Longmead Rd., Hayes 135 BT73
Longmead Rd., T.Ditt. 197 CE101
Longmeadow Rd., Sid. 185 ES88
Longmere Gdns., Tad. 233 CW119
Longmoor, Wal.Cr. 67 DY29
Longmoor Pt. SW15 179 CV88
Norley Vale
Longmoore St. SW1 277 K9
Longmoore St. SW1 161 DJ77
Longmore Ave., Barn. 80 DC44
Longmore Clo., Rick. 91 BF49
Longmore Gdns., Welw.G.C. 29 CZ09
Longmore Rd., Walt. 214 BY105
Longnor Rd. E1 143 DX69
Longport Clo., Ilf. 104 EU51
Longreach Rd., Bark. 145 ET70
Longreach Rd., Erith 167 FH80
Longridge Gro., Wok. 211 BE114
Old Woking Rd.
Longridge La., Sthl. 136 CB73
Longridge Rd. SW5 160 DA77
Longs Clo., Wok. 228 BG116
Long's Ct. WC2 273 M10
Long's Ct. WC2 141 DK73
Longs Ct., Rich. 158 CM84
Crown Ter.
Longshaw Rd. E4 101 ED48
Longshore SE8 163 DZ77
Longside Clo., Egh. 193 BC95
Longspring, Wat. 75 BV38
Longspring Wd., Sev. 256 FF130
Longstaff Cres. SW18 180 DA86
Longstaff Rd. SW18 180 DA86
Longstone Ave. NW10 139 CT66
Longstone Rd. SW17 181 DH92
Longstone Rd., Iver 133 BC68
Longthornton Rd. SW16 201 DJ96
Longton Ave. SE26 182 DU91
Longton Gro. SE26 182 DV91
Longtown Clo., Rom. 106 FJ50
Longtown Rd., Rom. 106 FJ50
Longview, Beac. 110 AF55
Longview Way, Rom. 105 FD53
Longville Rd. SE11 278 F8
Longwalk Rd., Uxb. 135 BP74
Longwood, Harl. 51 ER20
Longwood Clo., Upmin. 128 FQ64
Longwood Dr. SW15 179 CU86
Longwood Gdns., Ilf. 125 EM56
Longwood La., Amer. 55 AR39
Longwood Rd., Hert. 31 DM07
Longwood Rd., Ken. 236 DR116
Longworth Clo. SE28 146 EX72
Longworth Dr., Maid. 130 AC70
Loning, The NW9 118 CS56
Loning, The, Enf. 82 DW38
Lonsdale, Hem.H. 40 BL17
Lonsdale Ave. E6 144 EK70
Lonsdale Ave., Brwd. 109 GD44
Lonsdale Ave., Rom. 127 FC58
Lonsdale Ave., Wem. 118 CL64
Lonsdale Clo. E6 144 EL70
Lonsdale Ave.
Lonsdale Clo. SE9 184 EK90
Lonsdale Clo., Edg. 96 CM50
Orchard Dr.
Lonsdale Clo., Pnr. 94 BY52
Lonsdale Clo., Uxb. 135 BQ71
Dawley Ave.
Lonsdale Cres., Dart. 188 FQ89
Lonsdale Cres., Ilf. 125 EP58
Lonsdale Dr., Enf. 81 DL43
Lonsdale Gdns., Th.Hth. 201 DM98
Lonsdale Ms., Rich. 158 CN81
Elizabeth Cotts.
Lonsdale Pl. N1 141 DN66
Barnsbury St.
Lonsdale Rd. E11 124 EF59
Lonsdale Rd. NW6 139 CZ68
Lonsdale Rd. SE25 202 DV98
Lonsdale Rd. SW13 159 CU79
Lonsdale Rd. W4 159 CT77
Lonsdale Rd. W11 139 CZ72
Lonsdale Rd., Bexh. 166 EZ82
Lonsdale Rd., Dor. 263 CH135
Lonsdale Rd., Sthl. 156 BX76
Lonsdale Rd., Wey. 212 BN108
Lonsdale Sq. N1 141 DN66
Lonsdale Way, Maid. 150 AC78
Loobert Rd. N15 122 DS55
Looe Gdns., Ilf. 125 EP55
Loom Ct. E1 275 N5
Loom La., Rad. 77 CG37
Loom Pl., Rad. 77 CG36
Loop Rd., Chis. 185 EQ93
Loop Rd., Epsom 232 CQ116
Woodcote Side
Loop Rd., Wal.Abb. 67 EB32
Loop Rd., Wok. 227 AZ120
Lopen Rd. N18 100 DS49
Loraine Clo., Enf. 82 DW43
Loraine Gdns., Ash. 232 CL117
Loraine Rd. N7 121 DM63
Loraine Rd. W4 158 CP79
Lorane Ct., Wat. 75 BU40
Lord Amory Way E14 163 EC75
Lord Ave., Ilf. 125 EM56
Lord Chancellor Wk., Kings.T. 198 CQ95
Lord Gdns., Ilf. 124 EL56
Lord Hills Bri. W2 140 DB71
Porchester Rd.
Lord Hills Rd. W2 140 DB71
Lord Holland La. SW9 161 DN81
Myatt's Flds. S.
Lord Knyvett Clo., Stai. 174 BK86
Lord Mayors Dr., Slou. 131 AM65
Lord Napier Pl. W6 159 CU78
Upper Mall
Lord N. St. SW1 277 P7
Lord N. St. SW1 161 DL76
Lord Roberts Ms. SW6 160 DB80
Moore Pk. Rd.
Lord Roberts Ter. SE18 165 EN78
Lord St. E16 144 EL74
Lord St., Grav. 191 GH87
Lord St., Hodd. 48 DV17
Lord St., Wat. 76 BW41
Lord Warwick St. SE18 165 EM76
Lordell Pl. SW19 179 CW93
Lorden Wk. E2 142 DU69
Lord's Clo. SE21 182 DQ89
Lords Clo., Felt. 176 BY89
Lords Clo., Rad. 62 CL32
Lord's Vw. NW8 272 A3
Lords Wd., Welw.G.C. 30 DC09
Lordsbury Fld., Wall. 219 DJ110
Lordsgrove Clo., Tad. 233 CV120
Whitegate Way
Lordship Clo., Brwd. 109 GD46
Lordship Gro. N16 122 DR61
Lordship La. N17 100 DQ53
Lordship La. N22 99 DN54
Lordship La. SE22 182 DT86
Lordship La. Est. SE22 182 DU88
Lordship Pk. N16 122 DQ61
Lordship Pk. Ms. N16 122 DQ61
Allerton Rd.
Lordship Pl. SW3 160 DE79
Cheyne Row
Lordship Rd. N16 122 DR61
Lordship Rd., Nthlt. 136 BY66

Lyme Ter. NW1 141 DJ66
Royal College St.
Lymer Ave. SE19 182 DT92
Lymescote Gdns., Sutt. 200 DA103
Lyminge Clo., Sid. 185 ET91
Lyminge Gdns. SW18 180 DE88
Lymington Ave. N22 99 DN54
Lymington Clo. E6 145 EM71
Valiant Way
Lymington Clo. SW16 201 DK96
Lymington Dr., Ruis. 115 BR61
Lymington Gdns., Epsom 217 CT106
Lymington Rd. NW6 140 DB65
Lymington Rd., Dag. 126 EX60
Lympstone Gdns. SE15 162 DU80
Lyn Ms. E3 143 DZ69
Tredegar Sq.
Lynbridge Gdns. N13 99 DP49
Lynbrook Clo. SE15 162 DS80
Blakes Rd.
Lynbrook Clo., Rain. 147 FD68
Lynceley Gra., Epp. 70 EU29
Lynch, The, Hodd. 49 EB17
Lynch, The, Uxb. 134 BJ67
New Windsor St.
Lynch Clo., Uxb. 134 BJ66
New Windsor St.
Lynch Hill La., Slou. 131 AL70
Lynch Wk. SE8 163 DZ79
Prince St.
Lynchen Clo., Houns. 155 BU81
The Ave.
Lyncott Cres. SW4 161 DH84
Lyncroft Ave., Pnr. 116 BY57
Lyncroft Gdns. NW6 120 DA64
Lyncroft Gdns. W13 157 CJ75
Lyncroft Gdns., Epsom 217 CT109
Lyncroft Gdns., Houns. 156 CC84
Lyndale NW2 119 CZ63
Lyndale Ave. NW2 119 CZ62
Lyndale Clo. SE3 164 EF79
Lyndale Ct., W.Byf. 212 BG113
Parvis Rd.
Lyndale Est., Grays 169 FV79
Lyndale Rd., Red. 250 DF131
Lynden Way, Swan. 207 FC97
Lyndhurst Ave. N12 98 DF51
Lyndhurst Ave. NW7 96 CS51
Lyndhurst Ave. SW16 201 DK96
Lyndhurst Ave., Pnr. 93 BV53
Lyndhurst Ave., Sthl. 136 CB74
Lyndhurst Ave., Sun. 195 BU97
Lyndhurst Ave., Surb. 198 CP102
Lyndhurst Ave., Twick. 176 BZ88
Lyndhurst Clo. NW10 118 CR62
Lyndhurst Clo., Bexh. 167 FB83
Lyndhurst Clo., Croy. 202 DT104
Lyndhurst Clo., Orp. 223 EP105
Lyndhurst Clo., Wok. 226 AX115
Lyndhurst Dr. E10 123 EC59
Lyndhurst Dr., Horn. 128 FJ60
Lyndhurst Dr., N.Mal. 198 CS100
Lyndhurst Dr., Sev. 256 FE124
Lyndhurst Gdns. N3 97 CY53
Lyndhurst Gdns. NW3 120 DD64
Lyndhurst Gdns., Bark. 145 ES65
Lyndhurst Gdns., Enf. 82 DS42
Lyndhurst Gdns., Ilf. 125 ER58
Lyndhurst Gdns., Pnr. 93 BV53
Lyndhurst Gro. SE15 162 DS82
Lyndhurst Ri., Chig. 103 EN49
Lyndhurst Rd. E4 101 EC52
Lyndhurst Rd. N18 100 DU49
Lyndhurst Rd. N22 99 DM51
Lyndhurst Rd. NW3 120 DD64
Lyndhurst Rd., Bexh. 167 FB83
Lyndhurst Rd., Chesh. 54 AP28
Lyndhurst Rd., Couls. 234 DG116
Lyndhurst Rd., Grnf. 136 CB70
Lyndhurst Rd., Reig. 266 DA137
Lyndhurst Rd., Th.Hth. 201 DN98
Lyndhurst Sq. SE15 162 DT81
Lyndhurst Ter. NW3 120 DD64
Lyndhurst Way SE15 162 DT81
Lyndhurst Way, Brwd. 109 GC45
Lyndhurst Way, Cher. 193 BE104
Lyndhurst Way, Sutt. 218 DA108
Lyndon Ave., Pnr. 94 BY51
Lyndon Ave., Sid. 185 ET85
Lyndon Ave., Wall. 200 DG104
Lyndon Rd., Belv. 166 FA77
Lyndwood Dr., Wind. 172 AU86
Lyne Clo., Vir.W. 193 AZ100
Lyne Cres. E17 101 DZ53
Lyne Crossing Rd., Cher. 193 BA100
Lyne La., Cher. 193 BA100
Lyne La., Egh. 193 BA98
Lyne La., Vir.W. 193 BA100
Lyne Rd., Vir.W. 192 AX100
Lyne Way, Hem.H. 39 BF18
Lynegrove Ave., Ashf. 175 BQ92
Lyneham Wk. E5 123 DY64
Lyneham Wk., Pnr. 115 BT55
Lynett Rd., Dag. 126 EX61
Lynette Ave. SW4 181 DH86
Lynford Clo., Barn. 79 CT43
Rowley La.
Lynford Clo., Edg. 96 CQ52
Lynford Gdns., Edg. 96 CP48
Lynford Gdns., Ilf. 125 ET61
Lynhurst Cres., Uxb. 135 BQ66
Lynhurst Rd., Uxb. 135 BQ66
Lynmere Rd., Well. 166 EV82
Lynmouth Ave., Enf. 82 DT44
Lynmouth Ave., Mord. 199 CX101
Lynmouth Dr., Ruis. 115 BV61
Lynmouth Gdns., Grnf. 137 CH67
Lynmouth Gdns., Houns. 156 BX81
Lynmouth Ri., Orp. 206 EV98
Lynmouth Rd. E17 123 DY58
Lynmouth Rd. N2 120 DF55
Lynmouth Rd. N16 122 DT60
Lynmouth Rd., Grnf. 137 CH67
Lynmouth Rd., Welw.G.C. 29 CZ09
Lynn Clo., Ashf. 175 BR92
Goffs Rd.
Lynn Clo., Har. 95 CD54
Lynn Ms. E11 124 EE61
Lynn Rd.
Lynn Rd. E11 124 EE61
Lynn Rd. SW12 181 DH87
Lynn Rd., Ilf. 125 ER59
Lynn St., Enf. 82 DR39
Lynn Wk., Reig. 266 DB137
Lynne Clo., Orp. 223 ET107
Lynne Clo., S.Croy. 220 DW111
Lynne Wk., Esher 214 CC106
Lynne Way NW10 138 CS65
Lynne Way, Nthlt. 136 BX68
Lynross Clo., Rom. 106 FM54
Lynscott Way, S.Croy. 219 DP109
Lynsted Clo., Bexh. 187 FB85
Lynsted Clo., Brom. 204 EJ96
Lynsted Ct., Beck. 203 DY96
Churchfields Rd.
Lynsted Gdns. SE9 164 EK83
Lynton Ave. N12 98 DD49
Lynton Ave. NW9 119 CT56
Lynton Ave. W13 137 CG72
Lynton Ave., Orp. 206 EV98
Lynton Ave., Rom. 104 FA53
Lynton Ave., St.Alb. 43 CJ21
Lynton Clo. NW10 118 CS64
Lynton Clo., Chess. 216 CL105
Lynton Clo., Islw. 157 CF84
Lynton Cres., Ilf. 125 EP58
Lynton Crest, Pot.B. 64 DA32
Strafford Gate
Lynton Est. SE1 162 DU77
Lynton Rd.
Lynton Gdns. N11 99 DK51
Lynton Gdns., Enf. 100 DS45
Lynton Mead N20 98 DA48
Lynton Par., Wal.Cr. 67 DX30
Turners Hill
Lynton Rd. E4 101 EB50
Lynton Rd. N8 121 DK57
Lynton Rd. NW6 139 CZ67
Lynton Rd. SE1 162 DT77
Lynton Rd. W3 138 CN73
Lynton Rd., Chesh. 54 AP28
Lynton Rd., Croy. 201 DN100
Lynton Rd., Grav. 191 GG88
Lynton Rd., Har. 116 BY61
Lynton Rd., N.Mal. 198 CR99
Lynton Rd. S., Grav. 191 GG88
Lynton Ter. W3 138 CQ72
Lynton Rd.
Lynton Wk., Hayes 135 BS69
Lynwood, Guil. 258 AV135
Lynwood Ave., Couls. 235 DH115
Lynwood Ave., Egh. 172 AY93
Lynwood Ave., Epsom 217 CT114
Lynwood Ave., Slou. 152 AX76
Lynwood Clo. E18 102 EJ53
Lynwood Clo., Har. 116 BY62
Lynwood Clo., Rom. 105 FB51
Lynwood Clo., Wok. 211 BD113
Lynwood Dr., Nthwd. 93 BT53
Lynwood Dr., Rom. 105 FB51
Lynwood Dr., Wor.Pk. 199 CU103
Lynwood Gdns., Croy. 219 DM105
Lynwood Gdns., Sthl. 136 BZ72
Lynwood Gro. N21 99 DN46
Lynwood Gro., Orp. 205 ES101
Lynwood Hts., Rick. 74 BH43
Lynwood Rd. SW17 180 DF90
Lynwood Rd. W5 138 CL70
Lynwood Rd., Epsom 217 CT114
Lynwood Rd., Red. 250 DG132
Lynwood Rd., T.Ditt. 197 CF103
Lynx Hill, Lthd. 245 BS128
Lyon Business Pk., Bark. 145 ES68
Lyon Meade, Stan. 95 CJ53
Lyon Pk. Ave., Wem. 138 CL65
Lyon Rd. SW19 200 DC95
Lyon Rd., Har. 117 CF58
Lyon Rd., Rom. 127 FF59
Lyon Rd., Walt. 196 BY103
Lyon St. N1 141 DM66
Caledonian Rd.
Lyon Way, Grnf. 137 CE67
Lyon Way, St.Alb. 44 CN20
Lyons Ct., Dor. 263 CH136
Lyons Dr., Guil. 242 AU129
Lyons Pl. NW8 140 DD70
Lyons Wk. W14 159 CY77
Lyonsdene, Tad. 249 CZ127
Smithy La.
Lyonsdown Ave., Barn. 80 DC44
Lyonsdown Rd., Barn. 80 DC44
Lyoth Rd., Orp. 205 EQ103
Lyric Dr., Grnf. 136 CB70
Lyric Rd. SW13 159 CT81
Lys Hill Gdns., Hert. 31 DP07
Lysander Clo., Hem.H. 57 AZ27
Lysander Gdns., Surb. 198 CM100
Ewell Rd.
Lysander Gro. N19 121 DK60
Lysander Rd., Croy. 219 DM107
Lysander Rd., Ruis. 115 BR61
Lysander Way, Abb.L. 59 BU32
Lysander Way, Orp. 205 EQ104
Lysander Way, Welw.G.C. 30 DD08
Lysia St. SW6 159 CX80
Lysias Rd. SW12 180 DG86
Lysley Pl., Hat. 64 DC27
Lysons Wk. SW15 179 CU85
Swinburne Rd.
Lytchet Rd., Brom. 184 EH94
Lytchet Way, Enf. 82 DW39
Lytchgate Clo., S.Croy. 220 DS108
Lytcott Dr., W.Mol. 196 BZ97
Freeman Dr.
Lytcott Gro. SE22 182 DT85
Lyte St. E2 142 DW68
Bishops Way
Lytham Ave., Wat. 94 BX50
Lytham Gro. W5 138 CL69
Lytham St. SE17 162 DR78
Lyttelton Clo. NW3 140 DE66
Lyttelton Rd. E10 123 EB62
Lyttelton Rd. N2 120 DC57
Lyttleton Rd. N8 121 DN55
Lytton Ave. N13 99 DN47
Lytton Ave., Enf. 83 DY38
Lytton Clo. N2 120 DD57
Lytton Clo., Loug. 85 ER41
Lytton Clo., Nthlt. 136 BZ66
Lytton Gdns., Wall. 219 DK105
Lytton Gdns., Welw.G.C. 29 CX09
Lytton Gro. SW15 179 CX85
Lytton Rd. E11 124 EE59
Lytton Rd., Barn. 80 DC42
Lytton Rd., Grays 171 GG77
Lytton Rd., Pnr. 94 BY52
Lytton Rd., Rom. 127 FH57
Lytton Rd., Wok. 227 BB116
Lytton Strachey Path SE28 146 EV73
Titmuss Ave.
Lyttons Way, Hodd. 33 EA14
Lyveden Rd. SE3 164 EH80
Lyveden Rd. SW17 180 DE93
Lywood Clo., Tad. 233 CW122

M

Mabbotts, Tad. 233 CX121
Mabbutt Clo., St.Alb. 60 BY30
Mabel Rd., Swan. 187 FG93
Mabel St., Wok. 226 AX117
Maberley Cres. SE19 182 DU94
Maberley Rd. SE19 202 DT95
Maberley Rd., Beck. 203 DX97
Mabeys Wk., Saw. 36 EV06
Mabledon Pl. WC1 273 N3
Mabledon Pl. WC1 141 DK69
Mablethorpe Rd. SW6 159 CY80
Mabley St. E9 143 DY65
Macaret Clo. N20 98 DB45
MacArthur Clo. E7 144 EG65
MacArthur Ter. SE7 164 EL79
Macaulay Ave., Esher 197 CE103
Macaulay Ct. SW4 161 DH83
Macaulay Rd. E6 144 EK68
Macaulay Rd. SW4 161 DH83
Macaulay Rd., Cat. 236 DS122
Macaulay Sq. SW4 161 DH84
Macaulay Way SE28 146 EV73
Booth Clo.
Macauley Ms. SE13 163 EC82
Macbean St. SE18 165 EN76
Macbeth St. W6 159 CV78
Macclesfield Bri. NW1 140 DE68
Macclesfield Rd. EC1 275 H2
Macclesfield Rd. EC1 142 DQ69
Macclesfield Rd. SE25 202 DV99
Macclesfield St. W1 273 N10
Macclesfield St. W1 141 DK73
Macdonald Ave., Dag. 127 FB62
Macdonald Ave., Horn. 128 FL56
Macdonald Clo., Amer. 55 AR35
Macdonald Rd. E7 124 EG63
Macdonald Rd. E17 101 EC54
Macdonald Rd. N11 98 DF50
Macdonald Rd. N19 121 DJ61
Macdonald Way, Horn. 128 FL56
Macdonnell Gdns., Wat. 75 BT35
High Rd.
Macduff Rd. SW11 160 DG81
Mace Clo. E1 142 DV74
Kennet St.
Mace Ct., Grays 170 GE79
Mace La., Sev. 223 ER113
Mace St. E2 143 DX68
Macers Ct., Brox. 49 DZ24
Macers La., Brox. 49 DZ24
MacFarlane La., Islw. 157 CF79
Macfarlane Rd. W12 139 CW74
Macfarren Pl. NW1 272 G5
Macgregor Rd. E16 144 EJ71
Machell Rd. SE15 162 DW83
Macintosh Clo., Wal.Cr. 66 DR26
Mackay Rd. SW4 161 DH83
Mackennal St. NW8 272 C1
Mackennal St. NW8 140 DE68
Mackenzie Mall, Slou. 152 AT75
High St.
Mackenzie Rd. N7 141 DM65
Mackenzie Rd., Beck. 202 DW96
Mackenzie St., Slou. 132 AT74
Mackenzie Wk. E14 143 EA74
Mackenzie Way, Grav. 191 GK93
Mackeson Rd. NW3 120 DF63
Mackie Rd. SW2 181 DN87
Mackies Hill, Guil. 261 BR144
Mackintosh La. E9 123 DX64
Homerton High St.
Macklin St. WC2 274 A8
Macklin St. WC2 141 DL72
Mackrells, Red. 266 DC137
Mackrow Wk. E14 143 EC73
Robin Hood La.
Macks Rd. SE16 162 DU77
Mackworth St. NW1 273 K2
Mackworth St. NW1 141 DJ69
Maclaren Ms. SW15 159 CW84
Clarendon Dr.
Maclean Rd. SE23 183 DY86
Maclennan Ave., Rain. 148 FK69
Macleod Clo., Grays 170 GD77
Macleod Rd. N21 81 DL43
Macleod St. SE17 162 DQ78
Maclise Rd. W14 159 CY76
Macmillan Gdns., Dart. 168 FN84
Macoma Rd. SE18 165 ER79
Macoma Ter. SE18 165 ER79
Macon Way, Upmin. 129 FT59
Maconochies Rd. E14 163 EB78
Macquarie Way E14 163 EB77
Macready Pl. N7 121 DL63
Warlters Rd.
Macroom Rd. W9 139 CZ69
Mada Rd., Orp. 205 EP104
Madan Rd., West. 255 ER125
Madans Wk., Epsom 216 CR114
Maddams St. E3 143 EB70
Madden Clo., Swans. 190 FX86
Maddison Clo., Tedd. 177 CF93
Maddock Way SE17 161 DP79
Maddocks Clo., Sid. 186 EX92
Maddox La., Lthd. 230 BY123
Maddox Pk., Lthd. 230 BY123
Maddox Rd., Harl. 35 ES14
Maddox Rd., Hem.H. 41 BP20
Maddox St. W1 273 J10
Maddox St. W1 141 DH73
Madeira Ave., Brom. 184 EE94
Madeira Clo., W.Byf. 212 BG113
Brantwood Gdns.
Madeira Cres., W.Byf. 212 BG113
Brantwood Gdns.
Madeira Gro., Wdf.Grn. 102 EJ51
Madeira Rd. E11 123 ED60
Madeira Rd. N13 99 DP49
Madeira Rd. SW16 181 DL92
Madeira Rd., Mitch. 200 DF98
Madeira Rd., W.Byf. 211 BF113
Madeira Wk., Brwd. 108 FY48
Madeira Wk., Reig. 250 DD133
Madeira Wk., Wind. 151 AR81
Madeley Clo., Amer. 55 AR36
Madeley Rd. W5 138 CL72
Madeline Gro., Ilf. 125 ER64
Madeline Rd. SE20 202 DU95
Madells, Epp. 69 ET31
Madge Gill Way E6 144 EL67
Ron Leighton Way
Madgeways Clo., Ware 33 DZ10
Madgeways La., Ware 33 DZ10
Madinah Rd. E8 142 DU65
Madison Cres., Bexh. 166 EW80
Madison Gdns., Bexh. 166 EW80
Madison Gdns., Brom. 204 EF97
Madison Way, Sev. 256 FF123
Madras Pl. N7 141 DN65
Madras Rd., Ilf. 125 EP63
Madresfield Ct., Rad. 62 CL32
Russet Dr.
Madrid Rd. SW13 159 CU81
Madrid Rd., Guil. 258 AV135
Madrigal La. SE5 161 DP80
Madron St. SE17 279 N10
Madron St. SE17 162 DS78
Maesmaur Rd., West. 238 EK121
Mafeking Ave. E6 144 EK68
Mafeking Ave., Brent. 158 CL79
Mafeking Ave., Ilf. 125 ER59
Mafeking Rd. E16 144 EF70
Mafeking Rd. N17 100 DU54
Mafeking Rd., Enf. 82 DT41
Mafeking Rd., Stai. 173 BB89
Mag Ct., Beac. 111 AM55
Magazine Pl., Lthd. 231 CH122
Magazine Rd., Cat. 235 DP122
Magdala Ave. N19 121 DH61
Magdala Rd., Islw. 157 CG83
Magdala Rd., S.Croy. 220 DR108
Napier Rd.
Magdalen Clo., W.Byf. 212 BL114
Magdalen Cres., W.Byf. 212 BL114
Magdalen Gdns., Brwd. 109 GE44
Magdalen Gro., Orp. 224 EV105
Magdalen Pas. E1 142 DT73
Prescot St.
Magdalen Rd. SW18 180 DC88
Magdalen St. SE1 279 M3
Magdalen St. SE1 142 DS74
Magdalene Clo. SE15 162 DV82
Heaton Rd.
Magdalene Gdns. E6 145 EN70
Magdalene Rd., Shep. 194 BM97
Magee St. SE11 161 DN79
Magellan Pl. E14 163 EA78
Napier Ave.
Maggie Blake's Cause SE1 279 P3
Magna Carta La., Stai. 172 AX88
Magna Rd., Egh. 172 AV93
Magnaville Rd. (Bushey), Wat. 95 CE45
Magnet Est., Grays 169 FW78
Magnet Rd., Grays 169 FW79
Magnet Rd., Wem. 117 CK61
Magnin Clo. E8 142 DU67
Wilde Clo.
Magnolia Ave., Abb.L. 59 BU32
Magnolia Clo. E10 123 EA61
Magnolia Clo., Hert. 32 DU09
Magnolia Clo., Kings.T. 178 CQ93
Magnolia Clo., St.Alb. 61 CD27
Magnolia Ct., Har. 118 CM59
Magnolia Ct., Horl. 268 DG148
Magnolia Ct., Rich. 158 CP81
West Hall Rd.
Magnolia Dr., West. 238 EK116
Magnolia Gdns., Slou. 152 AW76
Magnolia Pl. SW4 181 DL85
Magnolia Pl. W5 138 CL71
Montpelier Rd.
Magnolia Rd. W4 158 CP79
Magnolia St., West Dr. 154 BK77
Magnolia Way, Brwd. 108 FV43
Magnolia Way, Dor. 263 CK139
Magnolia Way, Epsom 216 CQ106
Magnum Clo., Rain. 148 FJ70
Magpie All. EC4 274 E9
Magpie Clo. E7 124 EF64
Magpie Clo. NW9 96 CS54
Eagle Dr.
Magpie Clo., Couls. 235 DJ118
Ashbourne Clo.
Magpie Clo., Enf. 82 DU39
Magpie Hall Clo., Brom. 204 EL100
Magpie Hall La., Brom. 205 EM99
Magpie Hall Rd. (Bushey), Wat. 95 CE47
Magpie La., Amer. 89 AM45
Magpie La., Brwd. 107 FW54
Magpie Pl. SE14 163 DY79
Milton Ct. Rd.
Magpie Wk., Hat. 45 CU20
Lark Ri.
Magpie Way, Slou. 131 AL70
Pemberton Rd.
Magpies, The, Epp. 51 EP24
Magri Wk. E1 142 DW71
Ashfield St.
Maguire Dr., Rich. 177 CJ91
Maguire St. SE1 162 DT75
Mahatma Gandhi Ho., Wem. 118 CN64
Mahlon Ave., Ruis. 115 BV64
Mahogany Clo. SE16 143 DY74
Mahon Clo., Enf. 82 DT39
Maida Ave. E4 101 EB45
Maida Ave. W2 140 DC71
Maida Rd., Belv. 166 FA76
Maida Vale W9 140 DB68
Maida Vale Rd., Dart. 187 FG85
Maida Way E4 101 EB45
Maiden Erlegh Ave., Bex. 186 EY88
Maiden La. NW1 141 DK66
Maiden La. SE1 279 J2
Maiden La. WC2 278 A1
Maiden La. WC2 141 DL73
Maiden La., Dart. 167 FG83
Maiden Rd. E15 144 EE66
Maidenhead Rd., Wind. 151 AK80
Maidenhead St., Hert. 32 DR09
Maidenshaw Rd., Epsom 216 CR112
Maidenstone Hill SE10 163 EC81
Maids of Honour Row, Rich. 177 CK85
The Grn.
Maidstone Ave., Rom. 105 FC54
Maidstone Bldgs. SE1 279 J3
Maidstone Ho. E14 143 EB72
Carmen St.
Maidstone Rd. N11 99 DK51
Maidstone Rd., Grays 170 GA79
Maidstone Rd., Sev. 256 FE122
Maidstone Rd. (Seal), Sev. 257 FN121
Maidstone Rd., Sid. 186 EX93
Maidstone Rd., Swan. 207 FC95
Maidstone St. E2 142 DU68
Audrey St.
Main Ave., Enf. 82 DT43
Main Ave., Nthwd. 93 BQ48
Main Dr., Ger.Cr. 112 AW57
Main Dr., Iver 153 BE77
Main Dr., Wem. 117 CK62
Main Par., Rick. 73 BC42
Whitelands Ave.
Main Ride, Egh. 172 AS93
Main Rd. (Farningham), Dart. 208 FM100
Main Rd. (Sutton at Hone), Dart. 188 FP93
Main Rd., Eden. 255 EQ134
Main Rd., Long. 209 FX96
Main Rd., Orp. 206 EW98
Main Rd., Rom. 127 FF56
Main Rd. (Knockholt), Sev. 239 ET119
Main Rd. (Sundridge), Sev. 240 EX124
Main Rd., Sid. 185 ES90
Main Rd., Swan. 187 FF94
Main Rd. (Crockenhill), Swan. 207 FC100
Main Rd., West. 222 EJ113
Main St., Felt. 176 BX92
Mainridge Rd., Chis. 185 EN91
Maisemore St. SE15 162 DU80
Peckham Pk. Rd.
Maisie Webster Clo., Stai. 174 BK87
Lauser Rd.
Maitland Clo. SE10 163 EB80
Maitland Clo., Houns. 156 BZ83
Maitland Clo., W.Byf. 212 BG113
Maitland Pk. Est. NW3 140 DF65
Maitland Pk. Rd. NW3 140 DF65
Maitland Pk. Vil. NW3 140 DF65
Maitland Pl. E5 122 DV63
Clarence Rd.
Maitland Rd. E15 144 EF65
Maitland Rd. SE26 183 DX93
Maize Row E14 143 DZ73
Commercial Rd.
Maizecroft, Horl. 269 DJ147
Oatlands
Maizey Ct., Brwd. 108 FU43
Danes Way
Majendie Rd. SE18 165 ER78
Majestic Way, Mitch. 200 DF96
Major Rd. E15 123 ED64
Major Rd. SE16 162 DU76
Jamaica Rd.
Majors Fm. Rd., Slou. 152 AX80
Makepeace Ave. N6 120 DG61
Makepeace Rd. E11 124 EG56
Makepeace Rd., Nthlt. 136 BY68
Makins St. SW3 276 C9
Makins St. SW3 160 DE77
Malabar St. E14 163 EA75
Malacca Fm., Guil. 244 BH128
Malam Gdns. E14 143 EB73
Wades Pl.
Malan Clo., West. 238 EL117
Malan Sq., Rain. 147 FH65
Malbrook Rd. SW15 159 CV84
Malcolm Ct., Stan. 95 CJ50
Malcolm Cres. NW4 119 CU58
Malcolm Dr., Surb. 198 CL102
Malcolm Gdns., Horl. 268 DD150
Malcolm Pl. E2 142 DW70
Malcolm Rd. E1 142 DW70
Malcolm Rd. SE20 182 DW94
Malcolm Rd. SE25 202 DU100
Malcolm Rd. SW19 179 CY93
Malcolm Rd., Couls. 235 DK115
Malcolm Rd., Uxb. 114 BM63
Malcolm Way E11 124 EG57
Malcolms Way N14 81 DJ43
Malden Ave. SE25 202 DV98
Malden Ave., Grnf. 117 CE64
Malden Clo., Amer. 72 AT38
Malden Cres. NW1 140 DG65
Malden Grn. Ave., Wor.Pk. 199 CT102
Malden Hill, N.Mal. 199 CT97
Malden Hill Gdns., N.Mal. 199 CT97
Malden Pk., N.Mal. 199 CT100
Malden Pl. NW5 120 DG64
Grafton Ter.
Malden Rd. NW5 120 DG64
Malden Rd., Borwd. 78 CN41
Malden Rd., N.Mal. 198 CS99
Malden Rd., Sutt. 217 CX105
Malden Rd., Wat. 75 BV40
Malden Rd., Wor.Pk. 199 CT101
Malden Way, N.Mal. 199 CT99
Maldon Clo. E15 123 ED64
David St.
Maldon Clo. N1 142 DQ67
Maldon Clo. SE5 162 DS83
Maldon Ct., Wall. 219 DJ106
Maldon Rd.
Maldon Rd. N9 100 DT48
Maldon Rd. W3 138 CQ73
Maldon Rd., Rom. 127 FC59
Maldon Rd., Wall. 219 DH106
Maldon Wk., Wdf.Grn. 102 EJ51
Malet Clo., Egh. 173 BD93
Malet Pl. WC1 273 M5
Malet Pl. WC1 141 DK70
Malet St. WC1 273 M5
Malet St. WC1 141 DK70
Maley Ave. SE27 181 DP89
Malford Ct. E18 102 EG54
Malford Gro. E18 124 EF56
Malfort Rd. SE5 162 DS83
Malham Clo. N11 98 DG51
Catterick Clo.
Malham Rd. SE23 183 DX88
Malins Clo., Barn. 79 CV43
Malkin Dr., Beac. 88 AJ52
Mall, The E15 143 ED66
Mall, The N14 99 DL48
Mall, The SW1 277 L4
Mall, The SW1 161 DJ75
Mall, The SW14 178 CQ85
Mall, The W5 138 CL73
Mall, The, Brom. 204 EG97
High St.
Mall, The, Croy. 202 DQ103
Mall, The, Har. 118 CM58
Mall, The, Horn. 127 FH60
Mall, The, St.Alb. 60 CC27
Mall, The, Surb. 197 CK99
Mall Rd. W6 159 CV78

Mallams Ms. SW9 161 DP83
St. James's Cres.
Mallard Clo. E9 143 DZ65
Mallard Clo. NW6 140 DA68
Mallard Clo. W7 157 CE75
Mallard Clo., Barn. 80 DD44
The Hook
Mallard Clo., Dart. 188 FM85
Mallard Clo., Horl. 268 DG146
Mallard Clo., Red. 250 DG131
Mallard Clo., Twick. 176 CA87
Stephenson Rd.
Mallard Clo., Upmin. 129 FT59
Mallard Dr., Slou. 131 AM73
Mallard Path SE28 165 ER76
Mallard Pl., Twick. 177 CH90
Mallard Rd., Abb.L. 59 BU31
Mallard Rd., S.Croy. 221 DX110
Mallard Wk. SE28 165 ER76
Goosander Way
Mallard Wk., Beck. 203 DX99
Mallard Wk., Sid. 186 EW93
Cray Rd.
Mallard Way NW9 118 CQ59
Mallard Way, Brwd. 109 GB45
Mallard Way, Nthwd. 93 BQ52
Mallard Way, Wall. 219 DJ109
Mallard Way, Wat. 76 BY37
Mallards, The, Stai. 194 BH96
Thames Side
Mallards Reach, Wey. 195 BR103
Mallards Ri., Harl. 52 EX15
Mallards Rd., Wdf.Grn. 102 EH52
Mallet Dr., Nthlt. 116 BZ64
Mallet Rd. SE13 183 ED86
Malling Clo., Croy. 202 DW100
Malling Gdns., Mord. 200 DC100
Malling Way, Brom. 204 EF101
Mallinson Clo., Horn. 128 FJ64
Mallinson Rd. SW11 180 DE85
Mallinson Rd., Croy. 201 DK104
Mallion Ct., Wal.Abb. 68 EF33
Mallord St. SW3 160 DD79
Mallory Clo. SE4 163 DY84
Mallory Gdns., Barn. 98 DG45
Mallory St. NW8 272 C4
Mallory St. NW8 140 DE70
Mallow Clo., Croy. 203 DX102
Marigold Way
Mallow Clo., Grav. 190 GE91
Mallow Clo., Tad. 233 CV119
Mallow Ct., Grays 170 GD79
Mallow Cres., Guil. 243 BB131
Mallow Cft., Hat. 45 CV19
Oxlease Dr.
Mallow Mead NW7 97 CY52
Mallow St. EC1 275 K4
Mallow Wk., Wal.Cr. 66 DR28
Mallows, The, Uxb. 115 BP62
Mallows Grn., Harl. 51 EN20
Mallys Pl., Dart. 208 FQ95
Malm Clo., Rick. 92 BK47
Malmains Clo., Beck. 203 ED99
Malmains Way, Beck. 203 EC98
Malmesbury Clo., Pnr. 115 BT56
Malmesbury Rd. E3 143 DZ69
Malmesbury Rd. E16 144 EE71
Malmesbury Rd. E18 102 EF53
Malmesbury Rd., Mord. 200 DC101
Malmesbury Ter. E16 144 EF71
Malmescroft, Hem.H. 41 BQ22
Malmsdale, Welw.G.C. 29 CX05
Malmstone Ave., Red. 251 DJ128
Malpas Dr., Pnr. 116 BX57
Malpas Rd. E8 142 DV65
Malpas Rd. SE4 163 DZ82
Malpas Rd., Dag. 146 EX65
Malpas Rd., Grays 171 GJ76
Malpas Rd., Slou. 132 AV73
Malt Hill, Egh. 172 AY92
Malt Ho. Clo., Wind. 172 AV87
Malt La., Rad. 77 CG35
Malt St. SE1 162 DU79
Malta Rd. E10 123 EA60
Malta Rd., Til. 171 GF82
Malta St. EC1 274 G4
Maltby Clo., Orp. 206 EU102
Vinson Clo.
Maltby Dr., Enf. 82 DV38
Maltby Rd., Chess. 216 CN107
Maltby St. SE1 279 P5
Maltby St. SE1 162 DT75
Malthouse Dr. W4 158 CS79
Malthouse Dr., Felt. 176 BX92
Malthouse Pas. SW13 158 CS82
The Ter.
Malthouse Pl., Rad. 61 CG34
Malthouse Sq., Beac. 111 AM55
Malthus Path SE28 146 EW74
Owen Clo.
Malting Ho. E14 143 DZ73
Malting Way, Islw. 157 CF83
Maltings, The, Harl. 36 EW11
Maltings, The, Kings L. 59 BQ33
Maltings, The, Orp. 205 ET102
Maltings, The, Oxt. 254 EF131
Maltings, The, Rom. 127 FF59
Maltings, The, St.Alb. 43 CD20
Chequer St.
Maltings, The, W.Byf. 212 BM113
Maltings Clo. SW13 158 CS82
Cleveland Gdns.
Maltings Dr., Epp. 70 EU29
Palmers Hill
Maltings La., Epp. 70 EU29
Maltings Ms., Amer. 55 AP40
Maltings Ms., Sid. 186 EU90
Station Rd.
Maltings Pl. SW6 160 DC81
Maltmans La., Ger.Cr. 112 AW55
Malton Ave., Slou. 131 AP72
Malton Ms. SE18 165 ES79
Malton St.
Malton Ms. W10 139 CY72
Cambridge Gdns.
Malton Rd. W10 139 CY72
St. Marks Rd.
Malton St. SE18 165 ES79
Maltravers St. WC2 274 C10
Malus Clo., Add. 211 BF108
Malus Clo., Hem.H. 40 BN19
Malus Dr., Add. 211 BF107
Malva Clo. SW18 180 DB85
St. Ann's Hill
Malvern Ave. E4 101 ED52
Malvern Ave., Bexh. 166 EY80
Malvern Ave., Har. 116 BY62
Malvern Clo. SE20 202 DU96
Derwent Rd.
Malvern Clo. W10 139 CZ71
Malvern Clo., Cher. 211 BC107
Malvern Clo., Hat. 45 CT17
Malvern Clo., Mitch. 201 DJ97
Malvern Clo., St.Alb. 43 CJ16
Malvern Clo., Surb. 198 CL102
Malvern Clo., Uxb. 115 BP61
Malvern Ct. SE14 162 DW80
Avonley Rd.
Malvern Ct. SW7 276 A9
Malvern Ct. SW7 160 DD77
Malvern Ct., Slou. 153 BA79
Hill Ri.
Malvern Dr., Felt. 176 BX92
Malvern Dr., Ilf. 125 ET63
Malvern Dr., Wdf.Grn. 102 EJ50
Malvern Gdns. NW2 119 CY61
Malvern Gdns. NW6 139 CZ68
Carlton Vale
Malvern Gdns., Har. 118 CL55
Malvern Gdns., Loug. 85 EM44
Malvern Ms. NW6 140 DA69
Malvern Rd.
Malvern Pl. NW6 139 CZ69
Malvern Rd. E6 144 EL67
Malvern Rd. E8 142 DU66
Malvern Rd. E11 124 EE61
Malvern Rd. N8 121 DM55
Malvern Rd. N17 122 DU55
Malvern Rd. NW6 140 DA69
Malvern Rd., Enf. 83 DY37
Malvern Rd., Grays 170 GD77
Malvern Rd., Hmptn. 176 CA94
Malvern Rd., Hayes 155 BS80
Malvern Rd., Horn. 127 FG58
Malvern Rd., Orp. 224 EV105
Malvern Rd., Surb. 198 CL103
Malvern Rd., Th.Hth. 201 DN98
Malvern Ter. N1 141 DN67
Malvern Ter. N9 100 DT46
Latymer Rd.
Malvern Way W13 137 CH71
Templewood
Malvern Way, Hem.H. 40 BM18
Malvern Way, Rick. 75 BP43
Malvina Ave., Grav. 191 GH89
Malwood Rd. SW12 181 DH86
Malyons, The, Shep. 195 BR100
Gordon Rd.
Malyons Rd. SE13 183 EB85
Malyons Rd., Swan. 187 FF94
Malyons Ter. SE13 183 EB85
Managers St. E14 143 EC74
Prestons Rd.
Manan Clo., Hem.H. 41 BQ22
Manatee Pl., Wall. 201 DK104
Croydon Rd.
Manaton Clo. SE15 162 DV83
Manaton Cres., Sthl. 136 CA72
Manbey Gro. E15 144 EE65
Manbey Pk. Rd. E15 144 EE65
Manbey Rd. E15 144 EE65
Manbey St. E15 144 EE65
Manbre Rd. W6 159 CW79
Manbrough Ave. E6 145 EM69
Manchester Dr. W10 139 CY70
Manchester Gro. E14 163 EC78
Manchester Ms. W1 272 F7
Manchester Rd. E14 163 EC78
Manchester Rd. N15 122 DR58
Manchester Rd., Th.Hth. 202 DQ97
Manchester Row, Dart. 187 FE85
Manchester Sq. W1 272 F8
Manchester Sq. W1 140 DG72
Manchester St. W1 272 F7
Manchester St. W1 140 DG71
Manchester Way, Dag. 127 FB63
Manchuria Rd. SW11 180 DG86
Manciple St. SE1 279 K5
Manciple St. SE1 162 DR76
Mandalay Rd. SW4 181 DJ85
Mandarin St. E14 143 EA73
Salter St.
Mandarin Way, Hayes 136 BX71
Mandela Avenue-First Ave., Harl. 35 ES13
Mandela Clo. NW10 138 CQ66
Mandela Rd. E16 144 EG72
Mandela St. NW1 141 DJ67
Mandela St. SW9 161 DN80
Mandela Way SE1 279 P9
Mandela Way SE1 162 DS77
Mandelyns, Berk. 38 AS16
Mandeville Clo. SE3 164 EF80
Vanbrugh Pk.
Mandeville Clo. SW20 199 CY95
Mandeville Clo., Brox. 49 DZ20
Mandeville Clo., Guil. 242 AU131
Mandeville Clo., Harl. 52 EW17
Mandeville Clo., Hert. 32 DQ12
Mandeville Clo., Wat. 75 BT38
Mandeville Ct. E4 101 DY49
Mandeville Ct., Egh. 173 BA91
Mandeville Dr., St.Alb. 43 CD23
Mandeville Dr., Surb. 197 CK102
Mandeville Pl. W1 272 G8
Mandeville Pl. W1 140 DG72
Mandeville Ri., Welw.G.C. 29 CX07
Mandeville Rd. N14 99 DH47
Mandeville Rd., Enf. 83 DX36
Mandeville Rd., Hert. 32 DQ12
Mandeville Rd., Islw. 157 CG82
Mandeville Rd., Nthlt. 136 CA66
Mandeville Rd., Pot.B. 64 DC32
Mandeville Rd., Shep. 194 BN99
Mandeville St. E5 123 DY62
Mandeville Wk., Brwd. 109 GE44
Kelvedon Clo.
Mandrake Rd. SW17 180 DF90
Mandrake Way E15 144 EE66
Mandrell Rd. SW2 181 DL85
Manette St. W1 273 N9
Manette St. W1 141 DK72
Manfield Clo., Slou. 131 AN69
Manford Clo., Chig. 104 EU49
Manford Cross, Chig. 104 EU50
Manford Ind. Est., Erith 167 FG79
Manford Way, Chig. 103 ES50
Manfred Rd. SW15 179 CZ85
Manger Rd. N7 141 DL65
Mangles Rd., Guil. 242 AX132
Mangold Way, Erith 166 EY76
Mangrove Dr., Hert. 32 DS11
Mangrove La., Hert. 32 DS11
Mangrove Rd., Hert. 32 DS10
Manhattan Wf. E16 164 EG75
Manilla St. E14 163 EA75
Manister Rd. SE2 166 EU76
Manitoba Ct. SE16 162 DW75
Renforth St.
Manitoba Gdns., Orp. 223 ET107
Superior Dr.
Manley Ct. N16 122 DT62
Stoke Newington High St.
Manley Rd., Hem.H. 40 BL19
Knightsbridge Way
Manley St. NW1 140 DG67
Manly Dixon Dr., Enf. 83 DY37
Mann Clo., Croy. 202 DQ104
Salem Pl.
Mannamead, Epsom 232 CS119
Mannamead Clo., Epsom 232 CS119
Mannamead
Mannicotts, Welw.G.C. 29 CV09
Mannin Rd., Rom. 126 EV59
Manning Gdns., Har. 117 CK59
Manning Pl., Rich. 178 CM86
Grove Rd.
Manning Rd. E17 123 DY57
Southcote Rd.
Manning Rd., Dag. 146 FA65
Manning Rd., Orp. 206 EX99
Manning St., S.Ock. 148 FQ74
Manningford Clo. EC1 274 F2
Manningtree Clo. SW19 179 CY88
Manningtree Rd., Ruis. 115 BV63
Manningtree St. E1 142 DU72
White Ch. La.
Mannock Dr., Loug. 85 EQ40
Mannock Rd. N22 121 DP55
Mannock Rd., Dart. 168 FM83
Barnwell Rd.
Manns Clo., Islw. 177 CF85
Manns Rd., Edg. 96 CN51
Manoel Rd., Twick. 176 CC89
Manor Ave. SE4 163 DZ82
Manor Ave., Cat. 236 DS124
Manor Ave., Hem.H. 40 BK23
Manor Ave., Horn. 128 FJ57
Manor Ave., Houns. 156 BX83
Manor Ave., Nthlt. 136 BZ66
Manor Chase, Wey. 213 BP106
Manor Clo. E17 101 DY54
Manor Rd.
Manor Clo. NW7 96 CR50
Manor Dr.
Manor Clo. NW9 118 CP57
Manor Clo. SE28 146 EW73
Manor Clo., Barn. 79 CY42
Manor Clo., Berk. 38 AW19
Manor Clo., Dag. 147 FD65
Manor Clo. (Crayford), Dart. 167 FD84
Manor Clo. (Wilmington), Dart. 187 FG90
Manor Clo., Hat. 45 CT15
Manor Clo., Hert. 32 DR07
Manor Clo., Horl. 268 DF148
Manor Clo., Lthd. 245 BS128
Manor Clo., Rom. 127 FG57
Manor Rd.
Manor Clo., Ruis. 115 BT60
Manor Clo., S.Ock. 148 FQ74
Manor Clo., Warl. 237 DY117
Manor Clo., Wok. 227 BF116
Manor Clo., Wor.Pk. 198 CS102
Manor Clo. S., S.Ock. 148 FQ74
Manor Clo.
Manor Cotts., Nthwd. 93 BT53
Manor Cotts. App. N2 98 DC54
Manor Ct. E10 123 EB60
Grange Pk. Rd.
Manor Ct. N2 120 DF57
Manor Ct. SW6 160 DB81
Bagley's La.
Manor Ct., Enf. 82 DV36
Manor Ct., Rad. 77 CF38
Manor Ct., Slou. 131 AM74
Richards Way
Manor Ct., Twick. 176 CC89
Manor Ct., Wem. 118 CL64
Manor Ct., Wey. 213 BP105
Manor Ct. Rd. W7 137 CE73
Manor Cres., Beac. 89 AR50
Manor Cres., Epsom 216 CN112
Manor Cres., Guil. 242 AV132
Manor Cres., Horn. 128 FJ57
Manor Cres., Surb. 198 CN100
Manor Cres., W.Byf. 212 BM113
Manor Dr. N14 99 DH45
Manor Dr. N20 98 DE48
Manor Dr. NW7 96 CR50
Manor Dr., Add. 212 BG110
Manor Dr., Amer. 55 AP36
Manor Dr., Epsom 216 CS107
Manor Dr., Esher 197 CF104
Manor Dr., Felt. 176 BX92
Lebanon Ave.
Manor Dr., Horl. 268 DF148
Manor Dr., St.Alb. 60 CA27
Manor Dr., Sun. 195 BU96
Manor Dr., Surb. 198 CM100
Manor Dr., Wem. 118 CM63
Manor Dr., The, Wor.Pk. 198 CS102
Manor Dr. N., N.Mal. 198 CR101
Manor Dr. N., Wor.Pk. 198 CS102
Manor Est. SE16 162 DV77
Manor Fm. (Farningham), Dart. 208 FM101
Manor Fm. Ave., Shep. 195 BP100
Manor Fm. Clo., Wind. 151 AM83
Manor Fm. Clo., Wor.Pk. 198 CS102
Manor Fm. Dr. E4 102 EE48
Manor Fm. Est., Stai. 172 AW86
Manor Fm. La., Egh. 173 BA92
Manor Fm. Rd., Enf. 82 DV35
Manor Fm. Rd., Th.Hth. 201 DN96
Manor Fm. Rd., Wem. 137 CK68
Manor Fm. Way, Beac. 89 AR51
Orchard Rd.
Manor Flds. SW15 179 CX86
Manor Gdns. N7 121 DL62
Manor Gdns. SW20 199 CZ96
Manor Gdns. W3 158 CN77
Manor Gdns. W4 158 CS78
Devonshire Rd.
Manor Gdns., Gdmg. 258 AS144
Farncombe St.
Manor Gdns., Guil. 242 AV132
Manor Gdns., Hmptn. 176 CB94
Manor Gdns., H.Wyc. 110 AE58
Manor Gdns., Lthd. 246 BX128
Manor Gdns., Rich. 158 CM84
Manor Gdns., Ruis. 116 BW64
Manor Gdns., S.Croy. 220 DT107
Manor Gdns., Sun. 195 BU95
Manor Gate, Nthlt. 136 BY66
Manor Grn. Rd., Epsom 216 CP113
Manor Gro. SE15 162 DW79
Manor Gro., Beck. 203 EB96
Manor Gro., Maid. 150 AD80
Manor Gro., Rich. 158 CN84
Manor Hall Ave. NW4 97 CW54
Manor Hall Dr. NW4 97 CX54
Manor Hatch Clo., Harl. 52 EV16
Manor Ho. Ct., Epsom 216 CQ113
Manor Ho. Ct., Shep. 195 BP101
Manor Ho. Dr. NW6 139 CX66
Manor Ho. Dr., Nthwd. 93 BP52
Manor Ho. Est., Stan. 95 CH51
Old Ch. La.
Manor Ho. Gdns., Abb.L. 59 BR31
Manor Ho. La., Lthd. 246 BY126
Manor Ho. La., Slou. 152 AV80
Horton Rd.
Manor Ho. Way, Islw. 157 CH83
Manor La. SE12 184 EE86
Manor La. SE13 164 EE84
Manor La., Felt. 175 BU89
High St.
Manor La., Ger.Cr. 112 AX59
Manor La., Hayes 155 BR79
Manor La. (Fawkham Grn.), Long. 209 FW101
Manor La., Sev. 209 FW103
Manor La., Sun. 195 BU96
Manor La., Sutt. 218 DC106
Manor La., Tad. 250 DA129
Manor La. Ter. SE13 164 EE84
Manor Leaze, Egh. 173 BB92
Manor Lo., Guil. 242 AV132
Manor Ms. NW6 140 DA68
Cambridge Ave.
Manor Ms. SE4 163 EA82
Manor Mt. SE23 182 DW88
Manor Par. NW10 139 CT68
Station Rd.
Manor Par., Hat. 45 CT15
Green Las.
Manor Pk. SE13 163 ED84
Manor Pk., Chis. 205 ER96
Manor Pk., Rich. 158 CM84
Manor Pk. Clo., W.Wick. 203 EB102
Manor Pk. Cres., Edg. 96 CN51
Manor Pk. Dr., Har. 116 CB55
Manor Pk. Gdns., Edg. 96 CN50
Manor Pk. Par. SE13 163 ED84
Lee High Rd.
Manor Pk. Rd. E12 124 EK63
Manor Pk. Rd. N2 120 DD55
Manor Pk. Rd. NW10 139 CT67
Manor Pk. Rd., Chis. 205 EQ95
Manor Pk. Rd., Sutt. 218 DC106
Manor Pk. Rd., W.Wick. 203 EB102
Manor Pl. SE17 161 DP78
Manor Pl., Chis. 205 ER95
Manor Pl., Dart. 188 FL88
Highfield Rd. S.
Manor Pl., Felt. 175 BU88
Manor Pl., Mitch. 201 DJ97
Manor Pl., Stai. 174 BH92
Manor Pl., Sutt. 218 DB105
Manor Pl., Walt. 195 BT101
Manor Rd.
Manor Rd. E10 123 EA59
Manor Rd. E15 144 EE68
Manor Rd. E16 144 EE69
Manor Rd. E17 101 DY54
Manor Rd. N16 122 DR60
Manor Rd. N17 100 DU53
Manor Rd. N22 99 DL51
Manor Rd. SE25 202 DU98
Manor Rd. SW20 199 CZ96
Manor Rd. W13 137 CG73
Manor Rd., Ashf. 174 BM92
Manor Rd., Bark. 145 ET65
Manor Rd., Barn. 79 CY43
Manor Rd., Beac. 89 AR50
Manor Rd., Beck. 203 EB96
Manor Rd., Bex. 187 FB88
Manor Rd., Chesh. 54 AP29
Lansdowne Rd.
Manor Rd., Chig. 103 EP50
Manor Rd., Dag. 147 FC65
Manor Rd., Dart. 167 FE84
Manor Rd., E.Mol. 197 CD98
Manor Rd., Enf. 82 DR40
Manor Rd., Erith 167 FF79
Manor Rd., Grav. 191 GH86
Manor Rd., Grays 170 GC79
Manor Rd. (West Thurrock), Grays 169 FW79
Manor Rd., Guil. 242 AV131
Manor Rd., Harl. 36 EW10
Manor Rd., Har. 117 CG58
Manor Rd., Hat. 28 CR14
Manor Rd., Hayes 135 BU72
Manor Rd., Hodd. 49 EA16
Manor Rd., Loug. 84 EH44
Manor Rd. (High Beach), Loug. 84 EH38
Manor Rd., Mitch. 201 DJ98
Manor Rd., Pot.B. 63 CZ31
Manor Rd., Red. 251 DJ129
Manor Rd., Reig. 249 CZ132
Manor Rd., Rich. 158 CM83
Manor Rd., Rom. 127 FG57
Manor Rd. (Chadwell Heath), Rom. 126 EX58
Manor Rd. (Lambourne End), Rom. 104 EW47
Manor Rd., Ruis. 115 BR60
Manor Rd., St.Alb. 43 CE19
Manor Rd. (London Colney), St.Alb. 61 CJ26
Manor Rd., Sev. 240 EX124
Manor Rd., Sid. 185 ET90
Manor Rd., Sutt. 217 CZ108
Manor Rd., Swans. 189 FX86
Manor Rd., Tedd. 177 CG92
Manor Rd., Til. 171 GG82
Manor Rd., Twick. 176 CC89
Manor Rd., Wall. 219 DH105
Manor Rd., Wal.Abb. 67 ED33
Manor Rd., Walt. 195 BT101
Manor Rd., Wat. 75 BV39
Manor Rd., W.Wick. 203 EB103
Manor Rd., West. 238 EL120
Manor Rd., Wind. 151 AL82
Manor Rd., Wok. 226 AW116
Manor Rd. (Send Marsh), Wok. 227 BF123
Manor Rd., Wdf.Grn. 103 EM51
Manor Rd. N., Esher 197 CF104
Manor Rd. N., T.Ditt. 197 CG103
Manor Rd. N., Wall. 219 DH105
Manor Rd. S., Esher 215 CE105
Manor Sq., Dag. 126 EX61
Manor St., Berk. 38 AW19
Manor Vale, Brent. 157 CJ78
Manor Vw. N3 98 DB54
Manor Wk., Wey. 213 BP106
Manor Way E4 101 ED49
Manor Way NW9 118 CS55
Manor Way SE3 164 EF84
Manor Way SE28 146 EW74
Manor Way, Amer. 55 AM44
Manor Way, Bans. 234 DF116
Manor Way, Beck. 203 EA96
Manor Way, Bex. 186 FA88
Manor Way, Bexh. 167 FD83
Manor Way, Borwd. 78 CQ42
Manor Way, Brwd. 108 FU48
Manor Way, Brom. 204 EL100
Manor Way, Chesh. 54 AR30
Manor Way, Egh. 173 AZ93
Manor Way, Grays 170 GB80
Manor Way, Guil. 258 AS137
Manor Way, Har. 116 CB56
Manor Way, Lthd. 230 CC115
Manor Way, Mitch. 201 DJ97
Manor Way, Orp. 205 EQ98
Manor Way, Pot.B. 64 DA30
Manor Way, Pur. 219 DL112
Manor Way, Rain. 147 FE71
Manor Way, Rick. 74 BN42
Manor Way, Ruis. 115 BS59
Manor Way, S.Croy. 220 DS107
Manor Way, Sthl. 156 BX77
Manor Way, Swans. 169 FX84
Manor Way (Cheshunt), Wal.Cr. 67 DY31
Russells Ride
Manor Way, Wok. 227 BB121
Manor Way, Wor.Pk. 198 CS102
Manor Way, The, Wall. 219 DH105
Manor Way Ind. Est., Grays 170 GC80
Manor Waye, Uxb. 134 BK67
Manor Wd. Rd., Pur. 219 DL113
Manorbrook SE3 164 EG84
Manorcrofts Rd., Egh. 173 BA93
Manordene Clo., T.Ditt. 197 CG102
Manordene Rd. SE28 146 EW72
Manorfield Clo. N19 121 DJ63
Tufnell Pk. Rd.
Manorfields Clo., Chis. 205 ET97
Manorgate Rd., Kings.T. 198 CN95
Manorhall Gdns. E10 123 EA60
Manorside, Barn. 79 CY42
Manorside Clo. SE2 166 EW77
Manorville Rd., Hem.H. 40 BJ24
Manorway, Enf. 100 DS45
Manorway, Wdf.Grn. 102 EJ50
Manpreet Ct. E12 125 EM64
Morris Ave.
Manresa Rd. SW3 160 DE78
Mansard Beeches SW17 180 DG92
Mansard Clo., Horn. 127 FG61
Mansard Clo., Pnr. 116 BX55
Mansards, The, St.Alb. 43 CE19
Avenue Rd.
Manscroft Rd., Hem.H. 40 BH18
Manse Clo., Hayes 155 BR79
Manse Rd. N16 122 DT62
Manse Way, Swan. 207 FG98
Mansel Clo., Guil. 242 AV129
Mansel Clo., Slou. 132 AV71
Mansel Gro. E17 101 EA53
Mansel Rd. SW19 179 CY93
Mansell Clo., Wind. 151 AL82
Mansell Rd. W3 158 CR75
Mansell Rd., Grnf. 136 CB71
Mansell St. E1 142 DT72
Mansell Way, Cat. 236 DR122
Manser Rd., Rain. 147 FE69
Mansergh Clo. SE18 164 EL80
Mansfield, Saw. 36 EU06
Mansfield Ave. N15 122 DR56
Mansfield Ave., Barn. 80 DF44
Mansfield Ave., Ruis. 115 BV60
Mansfield Clo. N9 82 DU44
Mansfield Clo., Orp. 206 EX101
Mansfield Clo., Wey. 213 BP106
Mansfield Dr., Hayes 135 BS70
Mansfield Dr., Red. 251 DK128
Mansfield Gdns., Hert. 32 DQ07
Mansfield Gdns., Horn. 128 FK61
Mansfield Hill E4 101 EB46
Mansfield Ms. W1 273 H7
Mansfield Pl. NW3 120 DC63
New End
Mansfield Rd. E11 124 EH58
Mansfield Rd. E17 123 DZ56
Mansfield Rd. NW3 120 DF64
Mansfield Rd. W3 138 CP70
Mansfield Rd., Chess. 215 CJ106
Mansfield Rd., Ilf. 125 EN61
Mansfield Rd., S.Croy. 220 DR107
Mansfield Rd., Swan. 187 FE93
Mansfield St. W1 273 H7
Mansfield St. W1 141 DH71
Mansford St. E2 142 DU68
Manship Rd., Mitch. 180 DG94
Mansion Clo. SW9 161 DN81
Cowley Rd.
Mansion Gdns. NW3 120 DB62
Mansion Ho. EC4 275 K9
Mansion Ho. EC4 142 DR72
Mansion Ho. Pl. EC4 275 K9
Mansion Ho. St. EC4 275 K9
Mansion La., Iver 133 BC74
Mansion Ms. SW7 160 DC77
Manson Pl. SW7 160 DD77
Manstead Gdns., Rain. 147 FH72
Mansted Gdns., Rom. 126 EW59
Manston Ave., Sthl. 156 CA77
Manston Clo. SE20 202 DW95
Garden Rd.
Manston Clo. (Cheshunt), Wal.Cr. 66 DW30
Manston Gro., Kings.T. 177 CK92
Manston Rd., Guil. 243 BA130
Manston Rd., Harl. 51 ES15
Manston Way, Horn. 147 FH65
Manstone Rd. NW2 119 CY64

Manthorp Rd. SE18 165 EQ78
Mantilla Rd. SW17 180 DG91
Mantle Rd. SE4 163 DY83
Mantle Way E15 144 EE66
Romford Rd.
Mantlet Clo. SW16 181 DJ94
Manton Ave. W7 157 CF75
Manton Clo., Hayes 135 BS73
Manton Rd. SE2 166 EU77
Mantua St. SW11 160 DD83
Mantus Clo. E1 142 DW70
Mantus Rd.
Mantus Rd. E1 142 DW70
Manus Way N20 98 DC47
Blakeney Clo.
Manville Gdns. SW17 181 DH89
Manville Rd. SW17 180 DG89
Manwood Rd. SE4 183 DZ85
Manwood St. E16 145 EM74
Manygate La., Shep. 195 BQ101
Manygates SW12 181 DH89
Maori Rd., Guil. 243 AZ134
Mape St. E2 142 DV70
Mapesbury Rd. NW2 139 CY65
Mapeshill Pl. NW2 139 CW65
Maple Ave. E4 101 DZ50
Maple Ave. W3 138 CS74
Maple Ave., Har. 116 CB61
Maple Ave., St.Alb. 42 CC16
Maple Ave., Upmin. 128 FP62
Maple Ave., West Dr. 134 BL73
Maple Clo. N3 98 DA51
Maple Clo. N16 122 DU58
Maple Clo. SW4 181 DK86
Maple Clo., Brwd. 109 FZ48
Cherry Ave.
Maple Clo., Buck.H. 102 EK48
Maple Clo., Epp. 85 ER37
Loughton La.
Maple Clo., Hmptn. 176 BZ93
Maple Clo., Hat. 45 CU19
Elm Dr.
Maple Clo., Hayes 136 BX69
Maple Clo., Horn. 127 FH62
Maple Clo., Ilf. 103 ES50
Maple Clo., Mitch. 201 DH95
Maple Clo., Orp. 205 ER99
Maple Clo., Ruis. 115 BV58
Maple Clo., Swan. 207 FE96
Maple Clo. (Bushey), Wat. 76 BY40
Maple Clo., Whyt. 236 DT117
Maple Ct., Egh. 172 AV93
Ashwood Rd.
Maple Ct., N.Mal. 198 CS97
Maple Ct., Ware 33 ED11
Maple Cres., Sid. 186 EU86
Maple Cres., Slou. 132 AV73
Maple Cross Ind. Est., Rick. 91 BF49
Maple Dr., S.Ock. 149 FX70
Maple Gdns., Edg. 96 CS52
Maple Gdns., Stai. 174 BL89
Maple Gate, Loug. 85 EN40
Maple Grn., Hem.H. 39 BE18
Maple Gro. NW9 118 CQ59
Maple Gro. W5 157 CK76
Maple Gro., Brent. 157 CH80
Maple Gro., Guil. 242 AX132
Maple Gro., Sthl. 136 BZ71
Maple Gro., Wat. 75 BU39
Maple Gro., Welw.G.C. 29 CZ06
Maple Gro., Wok. 226 AY121
Maple Hill, Hem.H. 56 AX30
Ley Hill Rd.
Maple Ind. Est., Felt. 175 BU90
Maple Leaf Clo., Abb.L. 59 BU32
Magnolia Ave.
Maple Leaf Clo., West. 238 EK116
Main Rd.
Maple Leaf Dr., Sid. 185 ET88
Maple Leaf Sq. SE16 163 DX75
St. Elmos Rd.
Maple Lo. Clo., Rick. 91 BE49
Maple Ms. NW6 140 DB68
Kilburn Pk. Rd.
Maple Ms. SW16 181 DM92
Maple Pl. W1 273 L5
Maple Pl., Bans. 217 CX114
Maple Pl., West Dr. 134 BM73
Maple Ave.
Maple River Ind. Est., Harl. 36 EV09
Maple Rd. E11 124 EE58
Maple Rd. SE20 202 DV95
Maple Rd., Ash. 231 CK119
Maple Rd., Dart. 188 FJ88
Maple Rd., Grav. 191 GJ91
Maple Rd., Grays 170 GC79
Maple Rd., Hayes 136 BW69
Maple Rd., Red. 266 DF138
Maple Rd., Surb. 198 CL99
Maple Rd., Whyt. 236 DT117
Maple Rd., Wok. 228 BG124
Maple Springs, Wal.Abb. 68 EG33
Maple St. W1 273 K6
Maple St. W1 141 DJ71
Maple St., Rom. 127 FC56
Maple Wk. W10 139 CX70
Droop St.
Maple Wk., Sutt. 218 DB110
Maple Way, Couls. 235 DH121
Maple Way, Felt. 175 BU90
Maplecourt Wk., Wind. 151 AN77
Common Rd.
Maplecroft Clo. E6 144 EL72
Allhallows Rd.
Maplecroft La., Wal.Abb. 50 EE21
Mapledale Ave., Croy. 202 DU103
Mapledene, Chis. 185 EQ92
Kemnal Rd.
Mapledene Rd. E8 142 DT66
Maplefield, St.Alb. 60 CB29
Maplefield La., Ch.St.G. 72 AV41
Maplehurst, Lthd. 231 CD123
Maplehurst Clo., Kings.T. 198 CL98
Mapleleaf Clo., S.Croy. 221 DX111
Mapleleafe Gdns., Ilf. 125 EP55
Maples, The, Bans. 218 DB114
Maples, The, Cher. 211 BC107
Maples, The, Harl. 51 EP20
Maples, The, Wal.Cr. 66 DS28
Maples Pl. E1 142 DV71
Raven Row
Maplescombe La. (Farningham), Dart. 208 FN104
Maplestead Rd. SW2 181 DM87
Maplestead Rd., Dag. 146 EV67
Maplethorpe Rd., Th.Hth. 201 DP98
Mapleton Clo., Brom. 204 EG100
Mapleton Cres. SW18 180 DB86
Mapleton Cres., Enf. 82 DW38
Mapleton Rd. E4 101 EC48
Mapleton Rd. SW18 180 DB86
Mapleton Rd., Eden. 255 ET133
Mapleton Rd., Enf. 82 DV40
Mapleton Rd., West. 255 ES131
Maplin Clo. N21 81 DM44
Maplin Ho. SE2 166 EX75
Wolvercote Rd.
Maplin Pk., Slou. 153 BB75
Maplin Rd. E16 144 EG72
Maplin St. E3 143 DZ69
Mapperley Dr., Wdf.Grn. 102 EE52
Forest Dr.
Mar Rd., S.Ock. 149 FW70
Maran Way, Erith 166 EX75
Marban Rd. W9 139 CZ69
Marbeck Clo., Wind. 151 AK81
Marble Arch W1 272 E10
Marble Arch W1 140 DF73
Marble Clo. W3 138 CP74
Marble Dr. NW2 119 CX59
Marble Hill Clo., Twick. 177 CH87
Marble Hill Gdns., Twick. 177 CH87
Marble Ho. SE18 165 ET78
Felspar Clo.
Marble Quay E1 142 DU74
Marbles Way, Tad. 233 CX119
Marbrook Ct. SE12 184 EJ90
Marcellina Way, Orp. 205 ES104
Marcet Rd., Dart. 188 FJ85
March Rd., Twick. 177 CG87
March Rd., Wey. 212 BN106
Marchant Rd. E11 123 ED61
Marchant St. SE14 163 DY79
Sanford St.
Marchbank Rd. W14 159 CZ79
Marchmant Clo., Horn. 128 FJ62
Marchmont Gdns., Rich. 178 CM85
Marchmont Rd.
Marchmont Grn., Hem.H. 40 BK18
Paston Rd.
Marchmont Rd., Rich. 178 CM85
Marchmont Rd., Wall. 219 DJ108
Marchmont St. WC1 273 P4
Marchmont St. WC1 141 DL70
Marchside Clo., Houns. 156 BX81
Springwell Rd.
Marchwood Clo. SE5 162 DS80
Marchwood Cres. W5 137 CJ72
Marcia Ct., Slou. 131 AM74
Richards Way
Marcia Rd. SE1 279 N9
Marcia Rd. SE1 162 DS77
Marcilly Rd. SW18 180 DD85
Marco Rd. W6 159 CW76
Marcon Pl. E8 142 DV65
Marconi Rd. E10 123 EA60
Marconi Rd., Grav. 190 GD90
Marconi Way, Sthl. 136 CB72
Marcourt Lawns W5 138 CL70
Marcus Ct. E15 144 EE67
Marcus Garvey Ms. SE22 182 DV85
St. Aidan's Rd.
Marcus Garvey Way SE24 161 DN84
Marcus Rd., Dart. 187 FG87
Marcus St. E15 144 EF67
Marcus St. SW18 180 DB86
Marcus Ter. SW18 180 DB86
Marcuse Rd., Cat. 236 DQ121
Coulsdon Rd.
Mardale Dr. NW9 118 CR57
Mardell Rd., Croy. 203 DX99
Marden Ave., Brom. 204 EG100
Marden Clo., Chig. 104 EV47
Marden Cres., Bex. 187 FC85
Marden Cres., Croy. 201 DM100
Marden Pk., Cat. 253 DZ125
Marden Rd. N17 122 DS55
Marden Rd., Croy. 201 DM100
Marden Rd., Rom. 127 FE58
Kingsmead Ave.
Marden Sq. SE16 162 DV76
Marder Rd. W13 157 CG75
Mardyke Ho., Rain. 147 FD68
Lower Mardyke Ave.
Mardyke Rd., Harl. 36 EU13
Mare St. E8 142 DV67
Marechal Niel Ave., Sid. 185 ER90
Mareschal Rd., Guil. 258 AW136
Marescroft Rd., Slou. 131 AL70
Maresfield, Croy. 202 DS104
Maresfield Gdns. NW3 120 DC64
Marfleet Clo., Cars. 200 DE103
Marford Rd., St.Alb. 28 CN07
Marford Rd., Welw.G.C. 28 CR09
Margaret Ave. E4 83 EB44
Margaret Ave., Brwd. 109 FZ45
Margaret Ave., St.Alb. 43 CD18
Margaret Bondfield Ave., Bark. 146 EU66
Margaret Bldgs. N16 122 DT60
Margaret Rd.
Margaret Clo., Abb.L. 59 BT32
Margaret Clo., Epp. 70 EU29
Margaret Rd.
Margaret Clo., Pot.B. 64 DC33
Margaret Clo., Rom. 127 FH57
Margaret Rd.
Margaret Clo., Stai. 174 BK93
Charles Rd.
Margaret Clo., Wal.Abb. 67 ED33
Margaret Ct. W1 273 K8
Margaret Dr., Horn. 128 FM60
Margaret Gardner Dr. SE9 185 EM89
Margaret Ingram Clo. SW6 159 CZ79
John Smith Ave.
Margaret Lockwood Clo., Kings.T. 198 CM98
Margaret Rd. N16 122 DT60
Margaret Rd., Barn. 80 DD42
Margaret Rd., Bex. 186 EX86
Margaret Rd., Epp. 70 EU29
Margaret Rd., Guil. 258 AW135
Margaret Rd., Rom. 127 FH57
Margaret Sq., Uxb. 134 BJ67
Margaret St. W1 273 J8
Margaret St. W1 141 DH72
Margaret Way, Couls. 235 DP118
Margaret Way, Ilf. 124 EL58
Margaretta Ter. SW3 160 DE79
Margaretting Rd. E12 124 EJ60
Margate Rd. SW2 181 DL85
Margeholes, Wat. 94 BY47
Margery Gro., Tad. 249 CY129
Margery La., Tad. 249 CZ129
Margery Pk. Rd. E7 144 EG65
Margery Rd., Dag. 126 EX62
Margery St. WC1 274 D3
Margery St. WC1 141 DN69
Margery Wd., Welw.G.C. 30 DA06
Margherita Pl., Wal.Abb. 68 EF34
Margherita Rd., Wal.Abb. 68 EG34
Margin Dr. SW19 179 CX92
Margravine Gdns. W6 159 CX78
Margravine Rd. W6 159 CX79
Marham Gdns. SW18 180 DE88
Marham Gdns., Mord. 200 DC100
Maria Clo. SE1 162 DU77
Beatrice Rd.
Maria Ter. E1 143 DX70
Maria Theresa Clo., N.Mal. 198 CR99
Mariam Gdns., Horn. 128 FM61
Marian Clo., Hayes 136 BX70
Marian Ct., Sutt. 218 DB106
Marian Pl. E2 142 DV68
Marian Rd. SW16 201 DJ95
Marian Sq. E2 142 DU68
Pritchard's Rd.
Marian St. E2 142 DV68
Hackney Rd.
Marian Way NW10 139 CT66
Maricas Ave., Har. 95 CD53
Marie Lloyd Gdns. N19 121 DL59
Hornsey Ri. Gdns.
Marie Lloyd Wk. E8 142 DU65
Forest Rd.
Mariette Way, Wall. 219 DL109
Marigold All. SE1 278 F1
Marigold Clo., Sthl. 136 BY73
Lancaster Rd.
Marigold Pl., Harl. 36 EV11
Broadway Ave.
Marigold Rd. N17 100 DW52
Marigold St. SE16 162 DV75
Marigold Way E4 101 DZ51
Silver Birch Ave.
Marigold Way, Croy. 203 DX102
Marina App., Hayes 136 BY71
Marina Ave., N.Mal. 199 CV99
Marina Clo., Brom. 204 EG97
Marina Clo., Cher. 194 BH102
Marina Dr., Dart. 188 FN88
Marina Dr., Grav. 191 GF87
Marina Dr., Well. 165 ES82
Marina Gdns., Rom. 127 FC58
Marina Gdns. (Cheshunt), Wal.Cr. 66 DW30
Marina Way, Iver 133 BF73
Marina Way, Slou. 131 AK73
Marina Way, Tedd. 177 CK94
Fairways
Marine Dr. SE18 165 EM77
Marine St. SE16 162 DU76
Enid St.
Marinefield Rd. SW6 160 DB82
Mariner Gdns., Rich. 177 CJ90
Mariner Rd. E12 125 EM63
Dersingham Ave.
Mariner Way, Hem.H. 40 BN21
Mariners Ct., Green. 169 FV84
High St.
Mariners Ms. E14 163 ED77
Mariners Wk., Erith 167 FF79
Frobisher Rd.
Marion Ave., Shep. 195 BP99
Marion Clo., Ilf. 103 ER52
Marion Clo. (Bushey), Wat. 76 BZ39
Marion Cres., Orp. 206 EU99
Marion Gro., Wdf.Grn. 102 EE50
Marion Rd. NW7 97 CU50
Marion Rd., Th.Hth. 202 DQ99
Marischal Rd. SE13 163 ED83
Marisco Clo., Grays 171 GH77
Marish La., Uxb. 113 BC56
Marish Wf., Slou. 152 AY75
Maritime Clo., Green. 189 FV85
Maritime Quay E14 163 EA78
Maritime St. E3 143 DZ70
Marius Pas. SW17 180 DG89
Marius Rd.
Marius Rd. SW17 180 DG89
Marjoram Clo., Guil. 242 AU130
Marjorams Ave., Loug. 85 EM40
Marjorie Gro. SW11 160 DF84
Marjorie Ms. E1 143 DX72
Arbour Sq.
Mark Ave. E4 83 EB44
Mark Clo., Bexh. 166 EY81
Mark Clo., Sthl. 136 CB74
Longford Ave.
Mark Dr., Ger.Cr. 90 AX49
Mark Hall Moors, Harl. 36 EV12
Mark La. EC3 275 N10
Mark La. EC3 142 DS73
Mark La., Grav. 191 GL87
Mark Oak La., Lthd. 230 CA122
Mark Rd. N22 99 DP54
Mark Rd., Hem.H. 40 BN18
Mark Sq. EC2 275 M4
Mark St. E15 144 EE66
Mark St. EC2 275 M4
Mark St., Reig. 250 DB133
Mark Way, Swan. 207 FG99
Markab Rd., Nthwd. 93 BT50
Marke Clo., Kes. 222 EL105
Markedge La., Couls. 234 DE124
Markedge La., Red. 250 DF125
Markenfield Rd., Guil. 242 AX134
Markeston Grn., Wat. 94 BX49
Market Ct. W1 273 K8
Market Est. N7 141 DL65
Market Hill SE18 165 EN76
Market La., Edg. 96 CQ53
Market La., Iver 153 BC75
Market La., Slou. 153 BC76
Market Link, Rom. 127 FE56
Market Meadow, Orp. 206 EW98
Market Ms. W1 277 H3
Market Ms. W1 141 DH74
Market Oak La., Hem.H. 40 BN24
Market Par. SE15 162 DU82
Rye La.
Market Pl. N2 120 DE55
Market Pl. NW11 120 DC56
Market Pl. SE16 162 DU77
Southwark Pk. Rd.
Market Pl. W1 273 K8
Market Pl. W1 141 DJ72
Market Pl. W3 138 CQ74
Market Pl., Bexh. 166 FA84
Market Pl., Brent. 157 CJ80
Market Pl., Dart. 188 FL87
Market St.
Market Pl., Enf. 82 DR41
The Town
Market Pl., Ger.Cr. 90 AX53
Market Pl., Hat. 45 CU17
Dog Kennel La.
Market Pl., Hert. 32 DR09
Fore St.
Market Pl., Kings.T. 197 CK96
Market Pl., Rom. 127 FE57
Market Pl. (Abridge), Rom. 86 EV41
Market Pl., St.Alb. 43 CD20
Market Pl., Til. 171 GF82
Market Rd. N7 141 DL65
Market Rd., Rich. 158 CN83
Market Row SW9 161 DN84
Atlantic Rd.
Market Sq. E2 275 P2
Market Sq. E14 143 EB72
Chrisp St.
Market Sq. N9 100 DU47
New Rd.
Market Sq., Amer. 54 AP32
High St.
Market Sq., Brom. 204 EG96
Market Sq., Harl. 35 ER14
Post Office Rd.
Market Sq., Stai. 173 BE91
Clarence St.
Market Sq., Uxb. 134 BJ66
High St.
Market Sq., Wal.Abb. 67 EC33
Leverton Way
Market Sq., West. 255 EQ127
Market Sq., Wok. 226 AY117
Cawsey Way
Market St. E6 145 EM68
Market St. SE18 165 EN77
Market St., Dart. 188 FL87
Market St., Guil. 258 AX135
Market St., Harl. 36 EW11
Market St., Hert. 32 DR09
Market St., Wat. 75 BV42
Market St., Wind. 151 AR81
Castle Hill
Market Way E14 143 EB72
Kerbey St.
Market Way, Wem. 118 CL64
Turton Rd.
Market Way, West. 255 ER126
Costell's Meadow
Marketfield Rd., Red. 250 DF134
Marketfield Way, Red. 250 DF134
Markfield, Croy. 221 DZ110
Markfield Gdns. E4 101 EB45
Markfield Rd. N15 122 DU56
Markfield Rd., Cat. 252 DV126
Markham Pl. SW3 276 D10
Markham Rd. (Cheshunt), Wal.Cr. 66 DQ26
Markham Sq. SW3 276 D10
Markham Sq. SW3 160 DF78
Markham St. SW3 276 C10
Markham St. SW3 160 DE78
Markhole Clo., Hmptn. 176 BZ94
Priory Rd.
Markhouse Ave. E17 123 DY58
Markhouse Rd. E17 123 DZ57
Markmanor Ave. E17 123 DY59
Marks Rd., Rom. 127 FC57
Marks Rd., Warl. 237 DY118
Marks Sq., Grav. 191 GF91
Marksbury Ave., Rich. 158 CN83
Markville Gdns., Cat. 252 DU125
Markway, Sun. 196 BW96
Markwell Clo. SE26 182 DV91
Longton Gro.
Markwell Clo., W.Wick. 204 EE103
Deer Pk. Way
Markwell Wd., Harl. 51 EP21
Markyate Rd., Dag. 126 EV64
Marl Rd. SW18 160 DB84
Marl St. SW18 160 DC84
Marl Rd.
Marlands Rd., Ilf. 124 EL55
Marlborough Ave. E8 142 DU67
Marlborough Ave. N14 99 DJ48
Marlborough Ave., Edg. 96 CP48
Marlborough Ave., Ruis. 115 BQ58
Marlborough Bldgs. SW3 276 C8
Marlborough Bldgs. SW3 160 DE77
Marlborough Clo. N20 98 DF48
Marlborough Gdns.
Marlborough Clo. SE17 278 G9
Marlborough Clo. SW19 180 DE93
Marlborough Clo., Grays 170 GC75
Marlborough Clo., Orp. 205 ET101
Aylesham Rd.
Marlborough Clo., Upmin. 129 FS60
Marlborough Clo., Walt. 196 BX104
Arch Rd.
Marlborough Ct. W1 273 K9
Marlborough Ct. W8 160 DA77
Marlborough Ct., Dor. 263 CH136
Marlborough Rd.
Marlborough Cres. W4 158 CR76
Marlborough Cres., Sev. 256 FE124
Marlborough Dr., Ilf. 124 EL55
Marlborough Dr., Wey. 195 BQ104
Marlborough Gdns. N20 98 DF48
Marlborough Gdns., Upmin. 129 FR60
Marlborough Gate, St.Alb. 43 CE20
Marlborough Gate Ho. W2 140 DD73
Elms Ms.
Marlborough Gro. SE1 162 DU78
Marlborough Hill NW8 140 DC67
Marlborough Hill, Dor. 263 CH136
Marlborough Hill, Har. 117 CF56
Marlborough La. SE7 164 EJ79
Marlborough Pk. Ave., Sid. 186 EU88
Marlborough Pl. NW8 140 DC68
Marlborough Ri., Hem.H. 40 BL17
Marlborough Rd. E4 101 EA51
Marlborough Rd. E7 144 EJ66
Marlborough Rd. E15 124 EE63
Borthwick Rd.
Marlborough Rd. E18 124 EG55
Marlborough Rd. N9 100 DT46
Marlborough Rd. N19 121 DK61
Marlborough Rd. N22 99 DL52
Marlborough Rd. SW1 277 L3
Marlborough Rd. SW1 141 DJ74
Marlborough Rd. SW19 180 DD93
Marlborough Rd. W4 158 CQ78
Marlborough Rd. W5 157 CK75
Marlborough Rd., Ashf. 174 BK92
Marlborough Rd., Bexh. 166 EX83
Marlborough Rd., Brwd. 108 FU44
Marlborough Rd., Brom. 204 EJ98
Marlborough Rd., Dag. 126 EV63
Marlborough Rd., Dart. 188 FJ86
Marlborough Rd., Dor. 263 CH136
Marlborough Rd., Felt. 176 BX89
Marlborough Rd., Hmptn. 176 CA93
Marlborough Rd., Islw. 157 CH81
Marlborough Rd., Rich. 178 CL86
Marlborough Rd., Rom. 126 FA56
Marlborough Rd., St.Alb. 43 CE20
Marlborough Rd., Slou. 152 AX77
Marlborough Rd., S.Croy. 220 DQ108
Marlborough Rd., Sthl. 156 BW76
Marlborough Rd., Sutt. 200 DA104
Marlborough Rd., Uxb. 135 BP70
Marlborough Rd., Wat. 75 BV42
Marlborough Rd., Wok. 227 BA116
Marlborough St. SW3 276 B9
Marlborough St. SW3 160 DE77
Marlborough Yd. N19 121 DK61
Marlborough Rd.
Marld, The, Ash. 232 CM118
Marle Gdns., Wal.Abb. 67 EC32
Marler Rd. SE23 183 DY88
Marlescroft Way, Loug. 85 EP43
Marley Ave., Bexh. 166 EX79
Marley Clo. N15 121 DP56
Stanmore Rd.
Marley Clo., Add. 211 BF107
Marley Clo., Grnf. 136 CA69
Marley Ct., Brox. 49 DZ23
Marley Ri., Dor. 263 CG139
Marley Rd., Welw.G.C. 30 DA11
Marley Wk. NW2 119 CW64
Lennon Rd.
Marlin Clo., Berk. 38 AT18
Marlin Clo., Sun. 175 BS93
Marlin Copse, Berk. 38 AU20
Marlin Sq., Abb.L. 59 BT31
Marling Way, Grav. 191 GL92
Marlingdene Clo., Hmptn. 176 CA93
Marlings Clo., Chis. 205 ES98
Marlings Clo., Whyt. 236 DS117
Marlings Pk. Ave., Chis. 205 ES98
Marlins, The, Nthwd. 93 BT51
Marlins Clo., Rick. 73 BE40
Marlins Clo., Sutt. 218 DC106
Turnpike La.
Marlins Meadow, Wat. 75 BR44
Marlins Turn, Hem.H. 40 BH17
Marloes Clo., Wem. 117 CK63
Marloes Rd. W8 160 DB76
Marlow Ave., Purf. 168 FN77
Marlow Clo. SE20 202 DV97
Marlow Ct. NW6 139 CX66
Marlow Ct. NW9 119 CT55
Marlow Cres., Twick. 177 CF86
Marlow Dr., Sutt. 199 CX103
Marlow Gdns., Hayes 155 BR76
Marlow Rd. E6 145 EM69
Marlow Rd. SE20 202 DV97
Marlow Rd., Sthl. 156 BZ76
Marlow Way SE16 163 DX75
Marlowe Clo., Chis. 185 ER93
Marlowe Clo., Ilf. 103 EQ53
Marlowe Gdns. SE9 185 EN86
Marlowe Gdns., Rom. 106 FJ53
Shenstone Gdns.
Marlowe Rd. E17 123 EC56
Marlowe Sq., Mitch. 201 DJ98
Marlowe Way, Croy. 201 DL103
Marlowes, Hem.H. 40 BK21
Marlowes, The NW8 140 DD67
Marlowes, The, Dart. 167 FD84
Marlpit Ave., Couls. 235 DL117
Marlpit La., Couls. 235 DK116
Marlton St. SE10 164 EF78
Woolwich Rd.
Marlwood Clo., Sid. 185 ES89
Marlyns Clo., Guil. 243 BA130
Marlyns Dr., Guil. 243 BA130
Marlyon Rd., Ilf. 104 EV50
Marmadon Rd. SE18 165 ET77
Marmion App. E4 101 EA49
Marmion Ave. E4 101 DZ49
Marmion Clo. E4 101 DZ49
Marmion Ms. SW11 160 DG83
Taybridge Rd.
Marmion Rd. SW11 160 DG84
Marmont Rd. SE15 162 DU81
Marmora Rd. SE22 182 DW86
Marmot Rd., Houns. 156 BX83
Marne Ave. N11 99 DH49
Marne Ave., Well. 166 EU83
Marne St. W10 139 CY69
Marnell Way, Houns. 156 BX83
Marney Rd. SW11 160 DG84
Marneys Clo., Epsom 232 CN115
Marnfield Cres. SW2 181 DM87
Marnham Ave. NW2 119 CY63
Marnham Cres., Grnf. 136 CB69
Marnham Ri., Hem.H. 40 BG18
Marnock Rd. SE4 183 DY85
Maroon St. E14 143 DY71
Maroons Way SE6 183 EA92
Marquess Rd. N1 142 DR65
Marquis Clo., Wem. 138 CM66
Marquis Rd. N4 121 DM60
Marquis Rd. N22 99 DM51
Marquis Rd. NW1 141 DK65
Marrabon Clo., Sid. 186 EU88
Marram Ct., Grays 170 GE79
Medlar Rd.
Marrick Clo. SW15 159 CU84
Marrilyne Ave., Enf. 83 DZ38
Marriot Ter., Rick. 73 BF42
Marriots Clo. NW9 119 CT58
Marriott Clo., Felt. 175 BR86
Marriott Lo. Clo., Add. 212 BJ105
Marriott Rd. E15 144 EE67
Marriott Rd. N4 121 DM60
Marriott Rd. N10 98 DF53
Marriott Rd., Barn. 79 CX41
Marriott Rd., Dart. 188 FM87
Marriotts, Harl. 36 EW10
Old Rd.

Marriotts Way, Hem.H. 40 BK22
Marrods Bottom, Beac. 88 AJ47
Marrowells, Wey. 195 BS104
Marryat Pl. SW19 179 CY91
Marryat Rd. SW19 179 CX92
Marryat Rd., Enf. 82 DV35
Marryat Sq. SW6 159 CY81
Marsala Rd. SE13 163 EB84
Marsden Clo., Welw.G.C. 29 CV11
Marsden Grn., Welw.G.C. 29 CV10
Marsden Rd. N9 100 DV47
Marsden Rd. SE15 162 DT83
Marsden Rd., Welw.G.C. 29 CV10
Marsden St. NW5 140 DG65
Marsden Way, Orp. 223 ET105
Marsh Ave., Epsom 216 CS110
Marsh Ave., Mitch. 200 DG96
Marsh Clo. NW7 97 CT48
Marsh Clo., Wal.Cr. 67 DZ33
Marsh Ct. SW19 200 DC95
Marsh Dr. NW9 119 CT58
Marsh Fm. Rd., Twick. 177 CF88
Marsh Grn. Rd., Dag. 146 FA67
Marsh Hill E9 123 DY64
Marsh La. E10 123 EA61
Marsh La. N17 100 DV52
Marsh La. NW7 96 CS49
Marsh La., Add. 212 BH105
Marsh La., Harl. 36 EY10
Marsh La., Maid. 150 AF75
Marsh La., Stan. 95 CJ50
Marsh La., Ware 33 DY07
Marsh La. (Stanstead Abbotts), Ware 33 ED12
Marsh Rd., Pnr. 116 BY56
Marsh Rd., Wem. 137 CK68
Marsh St. E14 163 EB77
Harbinger Rd.
Marsh St., Dart. 168 FN82
Marsh Ter., Orp. 206 EX98
Buttermere Rd.
Marsh Wall E14 143 EA74
Marsh Way, Rain. 147 FD72
Marshall Ave., St.Alb. 43 CE17
Marshall Clo. SW18 180 DC86
Allfarthing La.
Marshall Clo., Har. 117 CD59
Bowen Rd.
Marshall Clo., Houns. 176 BZ85
Marshall Clo., S.Croy. 220 DU113
Marshall Dr., Hayes 135 BT71
Marshall Path SE28 146 EV73
Attlee Rd.
Marshall Pl., Add. 212 BJ109
Marshall Rd. E10 123 EB62
Marshall Rd. N17 100 DR53
Marshall St. W1 273 L9
Marshall St. W1 141 DJ72
Marshalls Clo. N11 99 DH49
Marshalls Clo., Epsom 216 CQ113
Marshalls Dr., Rom. 127 FE55
Marshall's Gro. SE18 164 EL77
Marshalls Pl. SE16 162 DT76
Spa Rd.
Marshalls Rd., Rom. 127 FD56
Marshall's Rd., Sutt. 218 DB105
Marshals Dr., St.Alb. 43 CF17
Marshalsea Rd. SE1 279 J4
Marshalsea Rd. SE1 162 DQ75
Marshalswick La., St.Alb. 43 CF17
Marsham Clo., Chis. 185 EP92
Marsham La., Ger.Cr. 112 AY58
Marsham Lo., Ger.Cr. 112 AY58
Marsham St. SW1 277 N7
Marsham St. SW1 161 DK76
Marsham Way, Ger.Cr. 112 AY57
Marshbrook Clo. SE3 164 EK83
Marshcroft Dr. (Cheshunt), Wal.Cr. 67 DY30
Marshe Clo., Pot.B. 64 DD32
Marshfield, Slou. 152 AW81
Marshfield St. E14 163 EC76
Marshfoot Rd., Grays 170 GE78
Marshgate, Harl. 35 ES12
School La.
Marshgate Dr., Hert. 32 DS08
Marshgate La. E15 143 EB67
Marshgate Path SE28 165 EQ77
Tom Cribb Rd.
Marshgate Sidings E15 143 EB66
Marshgate La.
Marshmoor Cres., Hat. 45 CX22
Marshmoor La.
Marshmoor La., Hat. 45 CW22
Marshside Clo. N9 100 DW46
Marsland Clo. SE17 161 DP78
Marston, Epsom 216 CQ111
Marston Ave., Chess. 216 CL107
Marston Ave., Dag. 126 FA61
Marston Clo. NW6 140 DC66
Fairfax Rd.
Marston Clo., Chesh. 54 AN27
Marston Clo., Dag. 126 FA62
Marston Clo., Hem.H. 40 BN21
Marston Ct., Walt. 196 BW102
St. Johns Dr.
Marston Dr., Warl. 237 DY118
Marston Ho., Grays 170 GA79
Marston Rd., Hodd. 49 EB16
Marston Rd., Ilf. 102 EL53
Marston Rd., Tedd. 177 CH92
Kingston Rd.
Marston Rd., Wok. 226 AV117
Marston Way SE19 181 DP94
Marsworth Ave., Pnr. 94 BX53
Marsworth Clo., Hayes 136 BY71
Marsworth Clo., Wat. 75 BS44
Mart St. WC2 274 A9
Martaban Rd. N16 122 DS61
Martel Pl. E8 142 DT65
Dalston La.
Martell Rd. SE21 182 DR90
Martello St. E8 142 DV66
Martello Ter. E8 142 DV66
Marten Gate, St.Alb. 43 CG16
Marten Rd. E17 101 EA54
Martens Ave., Bexh. 167 FC84
Martens Clo., Bexh. 167 FC84
Martha Ct. E2 142 DV68
Cambridge Heath Rd.
Martha Rd. E4 101 DZ51
Martha Rd. E15 144 EE65
Martha St. E1 142 DV72
Martham Clo. SE28 146 EX73
Marthorne Cres., Har. 95 CD54
Martian Ave., Hem.H. 40 BM17
Martin Bowes Rd. SE9 165 EM83
Martin Clo. N9 101 DX46
Martin Clo., Hat. 45 CU20
Martin Clo., S.Croy. 221 DX111
Martin Clo., Uxb. 134 BL68
Valley Rd.
Martin Clo., Warl. 236 DV116
Martin Clo., Wind. 150 AJ81
Martin Cres., Croy. 201 DN102
Martin Dene, Bexh. 186 EZ85
Martin Dr., Dart. 188 FQ86
Martin Dr., Nthlt. 116 BZ64
Martin Dr., Rain. 147 FH70
Martin Gdns., Dag. 126 EW63
Martin Gro., Mord. 200 DA97
Martin La. EC4 275 L10
Martin Ri., Bexh. 186 EZ85
Martin Rd., Dag. 126 EW63
Martin Rd., Dart. 188 FJ90
Martin Rd., Guil. 242 AU132
Martin Rd., Slou. 152 AS76
Martin Rd., S.Ock. 149 FR73
Martin Way SW20 199 CY97
Martin Way, Mord. 199 CY97
Martin Way, Wok. 226 AU118
Martinbridge Ind. Est., Enf. 82 DU43
Martindale SW14 178 CQ85
Martindale, Iver 133 BD70
Martindale Ave. E16 144 EG73
Martindale Ave., Orp. 224 EU106
Martindale Clo., Guil. 243 BD132
Gilliat Dr.
Martindale Rd. SW12 181 DH87
Martindale Rd., Hem.H. 39 BF19
Martindale Rd., Houns. 156 BY83
Martindale Rd., Wok. 226 AT118
Martineau Clo., Esher 215 CD105
Martineau Dr., Dor. 263 CH138
Martineau Ms. N5 121 DP63
Martineau Rd.
Martineau Rd. N5 121 DP63
Martineau St. E1 142 DW73
Martinfield, Welw.G.C. 29 CZ08
Martingale Clo., Sun. 195 BU98
Martingales Clo., Rich. 177 CK90
Martins Clo., Guil. 243 BC133
Martins Clo., Orp. 206 EX97
Martins Clo., Rad. 77 CE36
Martins Clo., W.Wick. 203 ED102
Martins Ct., St.Alb. 43 CH23
Cell Barnes La.
Martins Dr., Hert. 32 DV09
Martins Dr. (Cheshunt), Wal.Cr. 67 DY28
Martins Mt., Barn. 80 DA42
Martins Rd., Brom. 204 EE96
Martins Shaw, Sev. 256 FC122
Martins Wk. N10 98 DG53
Martins Wk., Borwd. 78 CN42
Siskin Clo.
Martinsfield Clo., Chig. 103 ES49
Martinstown Clo., Horn. 128 FN58
Martinsyde, Wok. 227 BC117
Martlesham, Welw.G.C. 30 DE09
Martlesham Clo., Horn. 128 FJ64
Martlet Gro., Nthlt. 136 BX69
Javelin Way
Martlett Ct. WC2 274 A9
Martley Dr., Ilf. 125 EP57
Martock Clo., Har. 117 CG56
Marton Clo. SE6 183 EA90
Marton Rd. N16 122 DS61
Martyr Clo., St.Alb. 43 CD24
Creighton Ave.
Martyr Rd., Guil. 258 AX135
Martyrs La., Wok. 211 BB112
Martys Yd. NW3 120 DD63
Hampstead High St.
Marunden Grn., Slou. 131 AM69
Marvell Ave., Hayes 135 BU71
Marvels Clo. SE12 184 EH89
Marvels La. SE12 184 EH89
Marville Rd. SW6 159 CZ80
Marvin St. E8 142 DV65
Sylvester Rd.
Marwell, West. 255 EP126
Marwell Clo., Rom. 127 FG57
Marwell Clo., W.Wick. 204 EF103
Deer Pk. Way
Marwood Clo., Kings L. 58 BN29
Marwood Clo., Well. 166 EV83
Marwood Way SE16 162 DV78
Catlin St.
Mary Adelaide Clo. SW15 178 CS91
Mary Ann Gdns. SE8 163 EA79
Mary Clo., Stan. 118 CM56
Mary Datchelor Clo. SE5 162 DR81
Mary Grn. NW8 140 DB67
Mary Kingsley Ct. N19 121 DL59
Hillrise Rd.
Mary Lawrenson Pl. SE3 164 EF80
Mary Macarthur Ho. W6 159 CY79
Field Rd.
Mary Morgan Ct., Slou. 131 AR71
Douglas Rd.
Mary Peters Dr., Grnf. 117 CD64
Mary Pl. W11 139 CY73
Mary Rd., Guil. 258 AW135
Mary Rose Clo., Hmptn. 196 CA95
Ashley Rd.
Mary Rose Mall E6 145 EN71
Frobisher Rd.
Mary Seacole Clo. E8 142 DT67
Clarissa St.
Mary St. E16 144 EF71
Barking Rd.
Mary St. N1 142 DQ67
Mary Ter. NW1 141 DH67
Maryatt Ave., Har. 116 CB61
Marybank SE18 165 EM77
Maryfield Clo., Bex. 187 FE90
Marygold Wk., Amer. 72 AV39
Maryhill Clo., Ken. 236 DQ117
Maryland, Hat. 45 CT18
Maryland Convent, St.Alb. 43 CD18
Maryland Ind. Est. E15 123 ED64
Maryland Rd.
Maryland Pk. E15 124 EE64
Maryland Pt. E15 144 EE65
Leytonstone Rd.
Maryland Rd. E15 123 ED64
Maryland Rd. N22 99 DM51
Maryland Rd., Th.Hth. 201 DP95
Maryland Sq. E15 124 EE64
Maryland St. E15 123 ED64
Maryland Wk. N1 142 DQ67
Popham St.
Maryland Way, Sun. 195 BU96
Marylands Rd. W9 140 DA70
Marylebone Flyover NW1 272 A7
Marylebone Flyover W2 272 A7
Marylebone High St. W1 272 G6
Marylebone High St. W1 140 DG71
Marylebone La. W1 273 H9
Marylebone La. W1 140 DG72
Marylebone Ms. W1 273 H7
Marylebone Ms. W1 141 DH71
Marylebone Pas. W1 273 L8
Marylebone Rd. NW1 272 C6
Marylebone Rd. NW1 140 DE71
Marylebone St. W1 272 G7
Marylebone St. W1 140 DG71
Marylee Way SE11 278 C10
Marylee Way SE11 161 DM77
Maryon Gro. SE7 164 EL77
Maryon Ms. NW3 120 DE63
South End Rd.
Maryon Rd. SE7 164 EL77
Maryon Rd. SE18 164 EL77
Maryrose Way N20 98 DD46
Mary's Clo. N17 100 DT53
Kemble Rd.
Mary's Ter., Twick. 177 CG87
Maryside, Slou. 152 AY75
Masbro Rd. W14 159 CX76
Mascalls Ct. SE7 164 EJ79
Victoria Way
Mascalls Gdns., Brwd. 108 FT49
Mascalls La., Brwd. 108 FT49
Mascalls Rd. SE7 164 EJ79
Mascotte Rd. SW15 159 CX84
Mascotts Clo. NW2 119 CV62
Masefield Ave., Borwd. 78 CP43
Masefield Ave., Sthl. 136 CA73
Masefield Ave., Stan. 95 CF50
Masefield Clo., Chesh. 54 AP28
Masefield Clo., Erith 167 FF81
Masefield Clo., Rom. 106 FJ53
Masefield Ct., Brwd. 108 FW49
Masefield Cres. N14 81 DJ44
Masefield Cres., Rom. 106 FJ53
Masefield Dr., Upmin. 128 FQ59
Masefield Gdns. E6 145 EN70
Masefield La., Hayes 135 BV70
Masefield Rd., Dart. 188 FP85
Masefield Rd., Grav. 190 GD90
Masefield Rd., Grays 170 GE75
Masefield Rd., Hmptn. 176 BZ91
Wordsworth Rd.
Masefield Vw., Orp. 205 EQ104
Masefield Way, Stai. 174 BM88
Masham Ho., Erith 166 EX75
Kale Rd.
Mashie Rd. W3 138 CS72
Mashiters Hill, Rom. 105 FD54
Mashiters Wk., Rom. 127 FE55
Maskall Clo. SW2 181 DN88
Maskani Wk. SW16 181 DJ94
Bates Cres.
Maskell Rd. SW17 180 DC90
Maskelyne Clo. SW11 160 DE81
Mason Bradbear Ct. N1 142 DR65
St. Paul's Rd.
Mason Clo. E16 144 EG73
Mason Clo. SE16 162 DU78
Stevenson Cres.
Mason Clo. SW20 199 CX95
Mason Clo., Bexh. 167 FB83
Mason Clo., Borwd. 78 CQ40
Mason Clo., Hmptn. 196 BZ95
Mason Ct., Slou. 131 AL73
Mason Dr., Rom. 106 FL54
Whitmore Ave.
Mason Rd., Sutt. 218 DB106
Manor Pl.
Mason Rd., Wdf.Grn. 102 EE49
Mason St. SE17 279 L8
Mason St. SE17 162 DR77
Mason Way, Wal.Abb. 68 EF34
Masonic Hall Rd., Cher. 193 BF100
Masons Arms Ms. W1 273 J9
Masons Ave. EC2 275 K8
Masons Ave., Croy. 202 DQ104
Masons Ave., Har. 117 CF56
Masons Bri. Rd., Red. 267 DH139
Masons Ct., Wem. 118 CN61
Mayfields
Masons Grn. La. W3 138 CN71
Masons Hill SE18 165 EP77
Masons Hill, Brom. 204 EG97
Masons Paddock, Dor. 247 CG134
Mason's Pl. EC1 274 G2
Mason's Pl. EC1 141 DP69
Masons Pl., Mitch. 200 DF95
Masons Rd., Enf. 82 DW36
Masons Rd., Hem.H. 41 BP19
Masons Rd., Slou. 131 AL73
Mason's Yd. SW1 277 L2
Mason's Yd. SW19 179 CX92
High St. Wimbledon
Massetts Rd., Horl. 268 DF149
Massey Clo. N11 99 DH50
Grove Rd.
Massie Rd. E8 142 DU65
Graham Rd.
Massingberd Way SW17 181 DH91
Massinger St. SE17 279 M9
Massingham St. E1 143 DX70
Masson Ave., Ruis. 136 BW65
Mast Ho. Ter. E14 163 EA77
Mast Leisure Pk. SE16 163 DX76
Master Clo., Oxt. 254 EE129
Church La.
Master Gunner Pl. SE18 164 EL80
Masterman Ho. SE5 162 DR80
Masterman Rd. E6 144 EL69
Masters Dr. SE16 162 DV78
Masters St. E1 143 DX71
Masthead Clo., Dart. 168 FQ84
Mastmaker Rd. E14 163 EA75
Maswell Pk. Cres., Houns. 176 CC85
Maswell Pk. Rd., Houns. 176 CB85
Matcham Rd. E11 124 EE62
Matching Rd., B.Stort. 37 FH05
Matching Rd. (Old Harlow), Harl. 37 FB11
Matching Rd., Ong. 53 FH17
Matchless Dr. SE18 165 EN80
Matfield Clo., Brom. 204 EG99
Matfield Rd., Belv. 166 FA79
Matham Gro. SE22 162 DT84
Matham Rd., E.Mol. 197 CD99
Matheson Rd. W14 159 CZ77
Mathews Ave. E6 145 EN68
Mathews Pk. Ave. E15 144 EF65
Mathias Clo., Epsom 216 CQ113
Mathisen Way, Slou. 153 BE81
Mathon Ct., Guil. 243 AZ134
Cross Las.
Matilda Clo. SE19 182 DR94
Elizabeth Way
Matilda St. N1 141 DM67
Matlock Clo. SE24 162 DQ84
Matlock Clo., Barn. 79 CX44
Matlock Ct. SE5 162 DR84
Denmark Hill Est.
Matlock Cres., Sutt. 217 CY105
Matlock Cres., Wat. 94 BW48
Matlock Gdns., Horn. 128 FL62
Matlock Gdns., Sutt. 217 CY105
Matlock Pl., Sutt. 217 CY105
Matlock Rd. E10 123 EC58
Matlock Rd., Cat. 236 DS121
Matlock St. E14 143 DY72
Matlock Way, N.Mal. 198 CR95
Matrimony Pl. SW8 161 DJ82
Matson Ct., Wdf.Grn. 102 EE52
The Bridle Path
Matthew Arnold Clo., Cob. 213 BU114
Matthew Arnold Clo., Stai. 174 BJ93
Elizabeth Ave.
Matthew Clo. W10 139 CX70
Matthew Ct., Mitch. 201 DK99
Matthew Parker St. SW1 277 N5
Matthew Parker St. SW1 161 DK75
Matthew Rd., Red. 250 DF133
Matthews Clo. (Havering-atte-Bower), Rom. 106 FM53
Oak Rd.
Matthews Gdns., Croy. 221 ED111
Matthews Rd., Grnf. 117 CD64
Matthews St. SW11 160 DF82
Matthews St., Reig. 266 DA138
Matthews Yd. WC2 273 P9
Matthias Rd. N16 122 DR64
Mattingley Way SE15 162 DT80
Daniel Gdns.
Mattison Rd. N4 121 DN58
Mattock La. W5 137 CH74
Mattock La. W13 137 CH74
Maud Cashmore Way SE18 165 EM76
Maud Gdns. E13 144 EF67
Maud Gdns., Bark. 145 ET68
Maud Rd. E10 123 EC62
Maud Rd. E13 144 EF68
Maud St. E16 144 EF71
Maude Cres., Wat. 75 BV37
Maude Rd. E17 123 DY57
Maude Rd. SE5 162 DS81
Maude Rd., Beac. 89 AN54
Maude Rd., Swan. 187 FG93
Maude Ter. E17 123 DY56
Maudesville Cotts. W7 137 CE74
The Bdy.
Maudlin's Grn. E1 142 DU74
Marble Quay
Maudslay Rd. SE9 165 EM83
Maudsley Ho., Brent. 158 CL78
Green Dragon La.
Mauleverer Rd. SW2 181 DL85
Maundeby Wk. NW10 138 CS65
Neasden La.
Maunder Rd. W7 137 CF74
Maunsel St. SW1 277 M8
Maunsel St. SW1 161 DK77
Maurice Ave. N22 99 DP54
Maurice Ave., Cat. 236 DR122
Maurice Brown Clo. NW7 97 CX50
Maurice St. W12 139 CV72
Maurice Wk. NW11 120 DC56
Maurier Clo., Nthlt. 136 BW67
Mauritius Rd. SE10 164 EE77
Maury Rd. N16 122 DU61
Mavelstone Clo., Brom. 204 EL95
Mavelstone Rd., Brom. 204 EL95
Maverton Rd. E3 143 EA67
Mavis Ave., Epsom 216 CS106
Mavis Clo., Epsom 216 CS106
Mavis Gro., Horn. 128 FL61
Mavis Wk. E6 144 EL71
Mawbey Est. SE1 162 DU78
Mawbey Pl. SE1 162 DT78
Mawbey Rd. SE1 162 DT78
Old Kent Rd.
Mawbey Rd., Cher. 211 BD107
Mawbey St. SW8 161 DL80
Mawney Clo., Rom. 105 FB54
Mawney Rd., Rom. 127 FC56
Mawson Clo. SW20 199 CY96
Mawson La. W4 159 CT79
Great W. Rd.
Maxey Gdns., Dag. 126 EY63
Maxey Rd. SE18 165 EQ77
Maxey Rd., Dag. 126 EY63
Maxfield Clo. N20 98 DC45
Maxilla Gdns. W10 139 CX72
Cambridge Gdns.
Maxilla Wk. W10 139 CX72
Kingsdown Clo.
Maxim Rd. N21 81 DN44
Maxim Rd., Dart. 187 FE85
Maxim Rd., Erith 167 FE77
Maximfeldt Rd., Erith 167 FE78
Maxted Clo., Hem.H. 41 BQ18
Maxted Pk., Har. 117 CE59
Maxted Rd. SE15 162 DT83
Maxted Rd., Hem.H. 41 BP17
Maxwell Clo., Croy. 201 DL102
Maxwell Clo., Rick. 92 BG47
Maxwell Dr., W.Byf. 212 BJ111
Maxwell Gdns., Orp. 205 ET104
Maxwell Ri., Wat. 94 BY45
Maxwell Rd. SW6 160 DB80
Maxwell Rd., Ashf. 175 BQ93
Maxwell Rd., Beac. 89 AK52
Maxwell Rd., Borwd. 78 CP41
Maxwell Rd., Nthwd. 93 BR52
Maxwell Rd., St.Alb. 43 CH21
Maxwell Rd., Well. 166 EU83
Maxwell Rd., West Dr. 154 BM77
Maxwelton Ave. NW7 96 CR50
Maxwelton Clo. NW7 96 CR50
May Ave., Grav. 191 GF88
Dover Rd. E.
May Ave., Orp. 206 EV99
May Clo., Chess. 216 CM107
May Clo., St.Alb. 43 CD18
May Cotts., Wat. 76 BW43
May Ct. SW19 200 DC95
May Ct., Grays 170 GE79
Medlar Rd.
May Gdns., Wem. 137 CJ68
May Rd. E4 101 EA51
May Rd. E13 144 EG68
May Rd., Dart. 188 FM91
May Rd., Twick. 177 CE88
May St. W14 159 CZ78
North End Rd.
May Tree La., Stan. 95 CF52
May Wk. E13 144 EH68
Maya Rd. N2 120 DC56
Mayall Rd. SE24 181 DP85
Maybank Ave. E18 102 EH54
Maybank Ave., Horn. 128 FJ64
Maybank Ave., Wem. 117 CF64
Maybank Gdns., Pnr. 115 BU57
Maybank Lo., Horn. 128 FJ64
Maybank Rd. E18 102 EH53
Maybells Commercial Est., Bark. 146 EX68
Mayberry Pl., Surb. 198 CM101
Maybourne Clo. SE26 182 DV92
Maybourne Ri., Wok. 226 AX124
Maybrick Rd., Horn. 128 FJ58
Maybrook Meadow Est., Bark. 146 EU66
Maybury Ave., Dart. 188 FQ88
Maybury Ave. (Cheshunt), Wal.Cr. 66 DV28
Maybury Clo., Enf. 82 DV38
Maybury Clo., Loug. 85 EP42
Maybury Clo., Orp. 205 EP99
Maybury Clo., Slou. 131 AK72
Maybury Clo., Tad. 233 CY119
Ballards Grn.
Maybury Gdns. NW10 139 CV65
Maybury Hill, Wok. 227 BB116
Maybury Ms. N6 121 DJ59
Maybury Rd. E13 144 EJ70
Maybury Rd., Bark. 145 ET68
Maybury Rd., Wok. 227 AZ117
Maybury St. SW17 180 DE92
Maybush Rd., Horn. 128 FL59
Maychurch Clo., Stan. 95 CK52
Maycock Gro., Nthwd. 93 BT51
Maycroft, Pnr. 93 BV54
Maycroft Ave., Grays 170 GD78
Maycroft Gdns., Grays 170 GD78
Maycroft Rd. (Cheshunt), Wal.Cr. 66 DS26
Maycross Ave., Mord. 199 CZ97
Mayday Gdns. SE3 164 EL82
Mayday Rd., Th.Hth. 201 DP100
Maydwell Lo., Borwd. 78 CM40
Mayell Clo., Lthd. 231 CJ123
Mayerne Rd. SE9 184 EK85
Mayes Clo., Swan. 207 FG98
Mayes Clo., Warl. 237 DX118
Mayes Rd. N22 99 DN54
Mayesbrook Rd., Bark. 145 ET67
Mayesbrook Rd., Dag. 126 EU62
Mayesbrook Rd., Ilf. 126 EU62
Mayesford Rd., Rom. 126 EW59
Mayeswood Rd. SE12 184 EJ90
Mayfair Ave., Bexh. 166 EX81
Mayfair Ave., Ilf. 125 EM61
Mayfair Ave., Rom. 126 EX58
Mayfair Ave., Twick. 176 CC87
Mayfair Ave., Wor.Pk. 199 CU102
Mayfair Clo., Beck. 203 EB95
Mayfair Clo., St.Alb. 43 CJ15
Mayfair Clo., Surb. 198 CL102
Mayfair Gdns. N17 100 DR51
Mayfair Gdns., Wdf.Grn. 102 EG52
Mayfair Ms. NW1 140 DF66
Regents Pk. Rd.
Mayfair Pl. W1 277 J2
Mayfair Pl. W1 141 DH74
Mayfair Rd., Dart. 188 FK85
Mayfair Ter. N14 99 DK45
Mayfare, Rick. 75 BR43
Mayfield, Bexh. 166 EZ83
Mayfield, Wal.Abb. 67 ED34
Mayfield, Welw.G.C. 29 CW05
Mayfield Ave. N12 98 DC49
Mayfield Ave. N14 99 DK47
Mayfield Ave. W4 158 CS77
Mayfield Ave. W13 157 CH76
Mayfield Ave., Add. 212 BH110
Mayfield Ave., Ger.Cr. 112 AX56
Mayfield Ave., Har. 117 CH57
Mayfield Ave., Orp. 205 ET102
Mayfield Ave., Wdf.Grn. 102 EG52
Mayfield Clo. E8 142 DT65
Forest Rd.
Mayfield Clo. SW4 181 DK85
Mayfield Clo., Add. 212 BJ110
Mayfield Clo., Ashf. 175 BP93
Mayfield Clo., Harl. 36 EZ11
Mayfield Clo., Red. 266 DG140
Brookfield Clo.
Mayfield Clo., T.Ditt. 197 CH102
Mayfield Clo., Uxb. 135 BP69
Mayfield Clo., Walt. 213 BU105
Mayfield Cres. N9 82 DV44
Mayfield Cres., Th.Hth. 201 DM98
Mayfield Dr., Pnr. 116 BZ56
Mayfield Gdns. NW4 119 CX58
Mayfield Gdns. W7 137 CD72
Mayfield Gdns., Brwd. 108 FV46
Mayfield Gdns., Stai. 173 BF93
Mayfield Gdns., Walt. 213 BU105
Mayfield Mans. SW18 179 CX87
West Hill
Mayfield Pk., West Dr. 154 BJ76
Mayfield Rd. E4 101 EC47
Mayfield Rd. E8 142 DT66
Mayfield Rd. E13 144 EF70
Mayfield Rd. E17 101 DY54
Mayfield Rd. N8 121 DM58
Mayfield Rd. SW19 199 CZ95
Mayfield Rd. W3 138 CP73
Mayfield Rd. W12 158 CS75
Mayfield Rd., Belv. 167 FC77
Mayfield Rd., Brom. 204 EL99
Mayfield Rd., Dag. 126 EW60
Mayfield Rd., Enf. 83 DX40
Mayfield Rd., Grav. 191 GF87
Mayfield Rd., H.Wyc. 110 AE57
Mayfield Rd., S.Croy. 220 DR109
Mayfield Rd., Sutt. 218 DD107
Mayfield Rd., Th.Hth. 201 DM98
Mayfield Rd., Walt. 213 BU105
Mayfield Rd., Wey. 212 BM106
Mayfields, Grays 170 GC75

Mayfields, Swans. 190 FY86
Madden Clo.
Mayfields, Wem. 118 CN61
Mayfields Clo., Wem. 118 CN61
Mayflower Ave., Hem.H. 40 BK20
Mayflower Clo. SE16 163 DX77
Greenland Quay
Mayflower Clo., Hert. 31 DL11
Mayflower Clo., Ruis. 115 BQ58
Leaholme Way
Mayflower Clo., S.Ock. 149 FW70
Mayflower Clo., Wal.Abb. 50 EE22
Mayflower Ct. SE16 162 DW75
St. Marychurch St.
Mayflower Path, Brwd. 107 FW51
Eagle Way
Mayflower Rd. SW9 161 DL83
Mayflower Rd., Grays 169 FW78
Mayflower Rd., St.Alb. 60 CB27
Mayflower St. SE16 162 DW75
Mayflower Way, Beac. 110 AG55
Mayflower Way, Slou. 111 AR63
Mayfly Clo., Pnr. 116 BW59
Mayfly Gdns., Nthlt. 136 BX69
Ruislip Rd.
Mayford Clo. SW12 180 DF87
Mayford Clo., Beck. 203 DX97
Mayford Clo., Wok. 226 AX122
Mayford Rd. SW12 180 DF87
Maygood St. N1 141 DM68
Maygoods Clo., Uxb. 134 BK71
Maygoods Grn., Uxb. 134 BK71
Worcester Rd.
Maygoods La., Uxb. 134 BK71
Maygoods Vw., Uxb. 134 BJ71
Benbow Waye
Maygreen Cres., Horn. 127 FG59
Maygrove Rd. NW6 139 CZ65
Mayhall La., Amer. 55 AP35
Mayhew Clo. E4 101 EA48
Mayhill Rd. SE7 164 EH79
Mayhill Rd., Barn. 79 CY44
Maylands Ave., Hem.H. 41 BP17
Maylands Ave., Horn. 127 FH63
Maylands Dr., Sid. 186 EX90
Maylands Dr., Uxb. 134 BK65
Maylands Rd., Wat. 94 BW49
Maylands Way, Rom. 106 FQ51
Maylins Dr., Saw. 36 EX05
Maynard Clo. N15 122 DS56
Brunswick Rd.
Maynard Clo. SW6 160 DB80
Cambria St.
Maynard Clo., Erith 167 FF80
Maynard Ct., Wal.Abb. 68 EF34
Maynard Dr., St.Alb. 43 CD23
Maynard Path E17 123 EC57
Maynard Rd.
Maynard Pl., Pot.B. 65 DL29
Maynard Rd. E17 123 EC57
Maynard Rd., Hem.H. 40 BK21
Maynards, Horn. 128 FL59
Maynards Quay E1 142 DW73
Garnet St.
Mayne Ave., St.Alb. 42 BZ22
Maynooth Gdns., Cars. 200 DF101
Middleton Rd.
Mayo Clo. (Cheshunt), Wal.Cr. 66 DW28
Mayo Rd. NW10 138 CS65
Mayo Rd., Croy. 202 DR99
Mayo Rd., Walt. 195 BT101
Mayola Rd. E5 122 DW63
Mayor's La., Dart. 188 FJ92
Mayow Rd. SE23 183 DX90
Mayow Rd. SE26 183 DX91
Mayplace Ave., Dart. 167 FG84
Mayplace Clo., Bexh. 167 FB83
Mayplace La. SE18 165 EP80
Mayplace Rd. E., Bexh. 167 FB83
Mayplace Rd. E., Dart. 167 FC83
Mayplace Rd. W., Bexh. 166 FA84
Maypole Cres., Erith 168 FK79
Maypole Cres., Ilf. 103 ER52
Maypole Dr., Chig. 104 EU48
Maypole Rd., Grav. 191 GM88
Maypole Rd., Maid. 130 AG71
Maypole Rd., Orp. 224 EZ106
Mayroyd Ave., Surb. 198 CN103
Mays Clo., Wey. 212 BM110
Mays Ct. WC2 277 P1
Mays Gro., Wok. 227 BD123
Mays Hill Rd., Brom. 204 EE96
Mays La. E4 101 ED47
Mays La., Barn. 97 CV45
Mays Rd., Tedd. 177 CD92
Maysfield Rd., Wok. 227 BD123
Maysoule Rd. SW11 160 DD84
Mayston Ms. SE10 164 EG78
Westcombe Hill
Mayswood Gdns., Dag. 147 FC65
Maythorne Clo., Wat. 75 BS42
Mayton St. N7 121 DM62
Maytree Clo., Edg. 96 CQ48
Maytree Clo., Guil. 242 AW131
Maytree Clo., Rain. 147 FE68
Maytree Cres., Wat. 75 BT35
Maytree Gdns. W5 157 CK75
South Ealing Rd.
Maytree Wk. SW2 181 DN89
Maytrees, Rad. 77 CG37
Mayville Est. N16 122 DS64
King Henry St.
Mayville Rd. E11 124 EE62
Mayville Rd., Ilf. 125 EP64
Maywater Clo., S.Croy. 220 DR111
Maywin Dr., Horn. 128 FM60
Maywood Clo., Beck. 183 EB94
Maze Hill SE3 164 EF80
Maze Hill SE10 164 EE79
Maze Rd., Rich. 158 CN80
Mazenod Ave. NW6 140 DA66
McAdam Clo., Hodd. 49 EA15
McAdam Dr., Enf. 81 DP40
Rowantree Rd.
McAuley Clo. SE1 278 D6
McAuley Clo. SE1 161 DN76
McAuley Clo. SE9 185 EP85
McAuliffe Dr., Slou. 111 AM63
McCall Clo. SW4 161 DL82
Jeffreys Rd.
McCall Cres. SE7 164 EL78
McCarthy Rd., Felt. 176 BX92
McCoid Way SE1 279 H5
McCrone Ms. NW3 140 DD65
Belsize La.
McCudden Rd., Dart. 168 FM83
Cornwall Rd.
McCullum Rd. E3 143 DZ67
McDermott Clo. SW11 160 DE83
McDermott Rd. SE15 162 DU83
McDonald Ct., Hat. 45 CU20
McDonough Clo., Chess. 216 CL105
McDowall Clo. E16 144 EF71
McDowall Rd. SE5 162 DQ81
McEntee Ave. E17 101 DY53
McEwen Way E15 143 ED67
McGrath Rd. E15 144 EF65
McGredy (Cheshunt), Wal.Cr. 66 DV29
McGregor Rd. W11 139 CZ72
McIntosh Clo., Rom. 127 FE55
McIntosh Clo., Wall. 219 DL108
McIntosh Rd., Rom. 127 FE55
McKay Rd. SW20 179 CV94
McKay Trd. Est., Slou. 153 BE82
McKellar Clo. (Bushey), Wat. 94 CC47
McKenzie Rd., Brox. 49 DZ20
McKerrell Rd. SE15 162 DU81
McLeod Rd. SE2 166 EV77
McLeod's Ms. SW7 160 DB77
McMillan Clo., Grav. 191 GJ91
McMillan St. SE8 163 EA79
McNair Rd., Sthl. 156 CB75
McNeil Rd. SE5 162 DS82
McNicol Dr. NW10 138 CQ68
McRae La., Mitch. 200 DF101
Mead, The N2 98 DC54
Mead, The W13 137 CH71
Mead, The, Ash. 232 CL119
Mead, The, Beac. 89 AL53
Mead, The, Beck. 203 EC95
Mead, The, Uxb. 114 BN61
Mead, The, Wall. 219 DK107
Mead, The (Cheshunt), Wal.Cr. 66 DW29
Mead, The, Wat. 94 BY48
Mead, The, W.Wick. 203 ED102
Mead Ave., Red. 266 DG142
Mead Ave., Slou. 153 BB75
Mead Business Pk., Hert. 32 DS08
Mead Clo., Egh. 173 BB93
Mead Clo., Grays 170 GB75
Mead Clo., Har. 95 CD53
Mead Clo., Loug. 85 EP40
Mead Clo., Red. 250 DG131
Mead Clo., Rom. 105 FG54
Mead Clo., Slou. 153 BB75
Mead Clo., Swan. 207 FG99
Mead Clo. (Denham), Uxb. 114 BG61
Mead Ct. NW9 118 CQ57
Mead Ct., Egh. 173 BC93
Holbrook Meadow
Mead Ct., Wal.Abb. 67 EB34
Mead Ct., Wok. 226 AS116
Mead Cres. E4 101 EC49
Mead Cres., Dart. 188 FK88
Beech Rd.
Mead Cres., Lthd. 246 CA125
Mead Cres., Sutt. 218 DE105
Mead End, Ash. 232 CM117
Mead Fld., Har. 116 BZ62
Kings Rd.
Mead Gro., Rom. 126 EY55
Mead Ho. La., Hayes 135 BR70
Mead La., Cher. 194 BJ102
Mead La., Hert. 32 DS08
Mead La. Caravan Pk., Cher. 194 BJ102
Mead Pk. Est., Harl. 35 ET11
Mead Path SW17 180 DC92
Mead Pl. E9 142 DW65
Mead Pl., Croy. 201 DP102
Mead Pl., Rick. 92 BH46
Mead Plat NW10 138 CQ65
Mead Rd., Cat. 236 DT123
Mead Rd., Chis. 185 EQ93
Mead Rd., Dart. 188 FK88
Mead Rd., Edg. 96 CN51
Mead Rd., Grav. 191 GH89
Mead Rd., Rad. 62 CM33
Mead Rd., Rich. 177 CJ90
Mead Rd., Uxb. 134 BK66
Mead Rd., Walt. 214 BY105
Mead Row SE1 278 D6
Mead Ter., Wem. 117 CK63
Meadow Way
Mead Wk., Slou. 153 BB75
Mead Way, Brom. 204 EF100
Mead Way, Couls. 235 DL118
Mead Way, Croy. 203 DY103
Mead Way, Slou. 131 AK71
Mead Way (Bushey), Wat. 76 BY40
Meadcroft Rd. SE11 161 DP79
Meade Clo. W4 158 CN79
Meade Ct., Tad. 233 CU124
Meades, The, Wey. 213 BR107
Meades La., Chesh. 54 AP32
Meadfield, Edg. 96 CP47
Meadfield Ave., Slou. 153 BA75
Meadfield Grn., Edg. 96 CP47
Meadfield Rd., Slou. 153 BA76
Meadfoot Rd. SW16 181 DJ94
Meadgate Ave., Wdf.Grn. 102 EL50
Meadgate Rd., Brox. 49 ED20
Meadhurst Rd., Cher. 194 BH102
Meadlands Dr., Rich. 177 CK89
Meadow, The, Chis. 185 EQ93
Meadow, The, Hert. 33 DY13
Meadow Ave., Croy. 203 DX100
Meadow Bank N21 81 DM44
Meadow Bank, Lthd. 245 BS127
Meadow Bungalows, Guil. 259 BB140
Meadow Clo. E4 101 EB46
Mount Echo Ave.
Meadow Clo. E9 123 DZ64
Meadow Clo. SE6 183 EA92
Meadow Clo. SW20 199 CW98
Meadow Clo., Barn. 79 CZ44
Meadow Clo., Bexh. 186 EZ85
Meadow Clo., Chesh. 54 AN27
Little Hivings
Meadow Clo., Chis. 185 EP92
Meadow Clo., Enf. 83 DY38
Meadow Clo., Esher 197 CF104
Meadow Clo., Gdmg. 258 AS144
Meadow Clo., Hat. 45 CX24
Meadow Clo., Hert. 32 DT08
Meadow Clo., Houns. 176 CA86
Meadow Clo., Nthlt. 136 CA68
Meadow Clo., Pur. 219 DK113
Meadow Clo., Rich. 178 CL88
Meadow Clo., Ruis. 115 BT58
Meadow Clo., St.Alb. 43 CJ17
Meadow Clo. (Bricket Wd.), St.Alb. 60 CA29
Meadow Clo. (London Colney), St.Alb. 61 CK27
Meadow Clo., Sev. 256 FG123
Meadow Clo., Sutt. 200 DB103
Aultone Way
Meadow Clo., Walt. 214 BZ105
Meadow Clo., Wind. 172 AV86
Meadow Cotts., Beac. 89 AL54
Meadow Ct., Epsom 216 CQ113
Meadow Ct., Harl. 51 ES19
Lodge Hall
Meadow Ct., Stai. 173 BE90
Moor La.
Meadow Cft., Hat. 45 CT18
Meadow Dell, Hat. 45 CT18
Meadow Dr. N10 121 DH55
Meadow Dr. NW4 97 CW54
Meadow Dr., Amer. 55 AS37
Meadow Dr., Wok. 227 BF123
Meadow Gdns., Edg. 96 CP51
Meadow Gdns., Stai. 173 BD92
Meadow Garth NW10 138 CQ65
Meadow Grn., Welw.G.C. 29 CW09
Meadow Hill, Couls. 219 DJ113
Meadow Hill, N.Mal. 198 CS100
Meadow Hill, Pur. 219 DJ113
Meadow La., Beac. 89 AM53
Meadow La., Lthd. 230 CC121
Meadow La. (Eton), Wind. 151 AQ80
Meadow Ms. SW8 161 DM79
Meadow Pl. SW8 161 DL80
Meadow Pl. W4 158 CS80
Edensor Rd.
Meadow Ri., Couls. 219 DK113
Meadow Rd. SW8 161 DM79
Meadow Rd. SW19 180 DC94
Meadow Rd., Ashf. 175 BR92
Meadow Rd., Ash. 232 CL117
Meadow Rd., Bark. 145 ET66
Meadow Rd., Berk. 38 AU17
Meadow Rd., Borwd. 78 CP40
Meadow Rd., Brom. 204 EE95
Meadow Rd., Dag. 146 EZ65
Meadow Rd., Esher 215 CE106
Meadow Rd., Felt. 176 BY89
Meadow Rd., Grav. 191 GG89
Meadow Rd., Guil. 243 BA130
Meadow Rd., Hem.H. 40 BN24
Meadow Rd., Loug. 84 EL43
Meadow Rd., Pnr. 116 BX56
Meadow Rd., Rom. 127 FC60
Meadow Rd., Slou. 152 AY76
Meadow Rd., Sthl. 136 BZ73
Meadow Rd., Sutt. 218 DE106
Meadow Rd., Vir.W. 192 AS99
Meadow Rd., Wat. 59 BU34
Meadow Rd. (Bushey), Wat. 76 CB43
Meadow Row SE1 279 H7
Meadow Row SE1 162 DQ76
Meadow Stile, Croy. 202 DQ104
High St.
Meadow Vw., Ch.St.G. 90 AU48
Meadow Vw., Har. 117 CE60
Meadow Vw., Sid. 186 EV87
Meadow Vw., Stai. 173 BF85
Meadow Vw. Rd., Hayes 135 BQ70
Meadow Vw. Rd., Th.Hth. 201 DP99
Meadow Wk. E18 124 EG56
Meadow Wk., Dag. 146 EZ65
Meadow Wk., Dart. 188 FJ91
Meadow Wk., Epsom 216 CS107
Meadow Wk., H.Wyc. 88 AC46
Meadow Wk., Tad. 233 CV124
Meadow Wk., Wall. 201 DH104
Meadow Way NW9 118 CR57
Meadow Way, Abb.L. 59 BT27
Meadow Way, Add. 212 BH105
Meadow Way, Chess. 216 CL106
Meadow Way, Chig. 103 EQ48
Meadow Way, Dart. 188 FQ87
Meadow Way, Hem.H. 39 BF23
Meadow Way, Kings L. 58 BN30
Meadow Way (Great Bookham), Lthd. 230 CB123
Meadow Way (West Horsley), Lthd. 245 BR125
Meadow Way (Dorney Reach), Maid. 150 AF75
Meadow Way (Fifield), Maid. 150 AD81
Meadow Way, Orp. 205 EN104
Meadow Way, Pot.B. 64 DA34
Meadow Way, Reig. 266 DB138
Meadow Way, Rick. 92 BJ45
Meadow Way, Ruis. 115 BV58
Meadow Way, Saw. 36 FA06
Meadow Way, Tad. 233 CY117
Meadow Way, Upmin. 128 FQ62
Meadow Way, Wem. 117 CK63
Meadow Way, Wind. 172 AV86
Meadow Way, The, Har. 95 CE53
Meadow Waye, Houns. 156 BY79
Meadowbank NW3 140 DF66
Meadowbank SE3 164 EF83
Meadowbank, Kings L. 58 BN30
Meadowbank, Surb. 198 CM100
Meadowbank, Wat. 94 BW45
Meadowbank Clo. SW6 159 CW80
Meadowbank Clo., Barn. 79 CT43
Meadowbank Gdns., Houns. 155 BU82
Meadowbank Rd. NW9 118 CR59
Meadowbanks, Barn. 79 CU43
Barnet Rd.
Meadowbrook, Oxt. 253 EC130
Meadowbrook Clo., Slou. 153 BF81
Meadowbrook Rd., Dor. 263 CG135
Meadowcot La., Amer. 55 AM44
Meadowcourt Rd. SE3 164 EF84
Meadowcroft, Brom. 205 EM97
Meadowcroft, Ger.Cr. 90 AX54
Meadowcroft, St.Alb. 43 CG23
Meadowcroft (Bushey), Wat. 76 CB44
Meadowcroft Clo., Horl. 269 DJ151
Meadowcroft Rd. N13 99 DN47
Meadowcross, Wal.Abb. 68 EE34
Meadowlands, Cob. 213 BU113
Meadowlands, Guil. 244 BH130
Meadowlands, Horn. 128 FL59
Meadowlands, Oxt. 254 EG134
Meadowlands Pk., Add. 194 BL104
Meadowlea Clo., West Dr. 154 BK79
Meadows, The, Amer. 55 AS39
Meadows, The, Guil. 258 AW137
Meadows, The, Hem.H. 39 BE19
Meadows, The, Orp. 224 EW107
Meadows, The, Saw. 36 FA05
Meadows, The, Sev. 224 EZ113
Meadows, The, Warl. 237 DX117
Meadows, The, Welw.G.C. 30 DC09
Meadows Clo. E10 123 EA61
Meadows End, Sun. 195 BU95
Meadows Leigh Clo., Wey. 195 BQ104
Meadowside SE9 164 EJ84
Meadowside, Beac. 90 AT52
Meadowside, Dart. 188 FK88
Meadowside, Horl. 269 DH147
Stockfield
Meadowside, Lthd. 230 CA123
Meadowside, Walt. 196 BW103
Meadowside Rd., Sutt. 217 CY109
Meadowside Rd., Upmin. 128 FQ64
Meadowsweet Clo. E16 144 EK71
Monarch Dr.
Meadowview, Orp. 206 EW97
Meadowview Rd. SE6 183 DZ92
Meadowview Rd., Bex. 186 EY86
Meadowview Rd., Epsom 216 CS109
Meads, The, Berk. 38 AS17
Meads, The, Edg. 96 CR51
Meads, The, St.Alb. 60 BZ29
Meads, The, Sutt. 199 CY104
Meads, The, Upmin. 129 FS61
Meads, The, Uxb. 134 BL70
Meads La., Ilf. 125 ES59
Meads Rd. N22 99 DP54
Meads Rd., Enf. 83 DY39
Meads Rd., Guil. 243 BA134
Meadsway, Brwd. 107 FV51
Meadvale Rd. W5 137 CH70
Meadvale Rd., Croy. 202 DT101
Meadview Rd., Ware 33 DX07
Meadway N14 99 DK47
Meadway NW11 120 DB58
Meadway SW20 199 CW98
Meadway, Ashf. 174 BN91
Meadway, Barn. 80 DA42
Meadway, Beck. 203 EC95
Meadway, Berk. 38 AY18
Meadway, Enf. 82 DW36
Meadway, Epsom 216 CQ112
Meadway, Esher 214 CB109
Meadway, Grays 170 GD77
Meadway, Guil. 243 BC129
Meadway, Hodd. 49 EA19
Meadway, Ilf. 125 ES63
Meadway (Effingham), Lthd. 246 BY128
Meadway (Oxshott), Lthd. 215 CD114
Meadway, Rom. 105 FG54
Meadway, Ruis. 115 BR58
Meadway, St.Alb. 44 CR23
Meadway, Sev. 224 EZ113
Meadway, Stai. 174 BG94
Meadway, Surb. 198 CQ102
Meadway, Twick. 177 CD88
Meadway, Warl. 236 DW116
Meadway, Welw.G.C. 29 CZ11
Meadway, Wdf.Grn. 102 EJ50
Meadway, The SE3 163 ED82
Heath La.
Meadway, The, Buck.H. 102 EK46
Meadway, The, Horl. 269 DJ148
Meadway, The, Loug. 85 EM44
Meadway, The, Orp. 224 EV106
Meadway, The (Cuffley), Pot.B. 65 DM28
Meadway, The, Sev. 256 FF122
Meadway Clo. NW11 120 DB58
Meadway Clo., Barn. 80 DA42
Meadway Clo., Pnr. 94 CB51
Highbanks Rd.
Meadway Clo., Stai. 173 BF94
Meadway Ct. NW11 120 DB58
Meadway Dr., Add. 212 BJ108
Meadway Dr., Wok. 226 AW116
Meadway Gdns., Ruis. 115 BR58
Meadway Gate NW11 120 DA58
Meadway Pk., Ger.Cr. 112 AX60
Meaford Way SE20 182 DV94
Meakin Est. SE1 279 M6
Meakin Est. SE1 162 DS76
Meanley Rd. E12 124 EL63
Meard St. W1 273 M9
Meard St. W1 141 DK72
Meare Clo., Tad. 233 CW123
Meare Est., H.Wyc. 110 AD55
Meath Clo., Orp. 206 EV99
Meath Grn. Ave., Horl. 268 DF146
Meath Grn. La., Horl. 266 DE143
Meath Rd. E15 144 EF68
Meath Rd., Ilf. 125 EQ62
Meath St. SW11 161 DH81
Meautys, St.Alb. 42 BZ22
Mechanics Path SE8 163 EA80
Deptford High St.
Mecklenburgh Pl. WC1 274 B4
Mecklenburgh Pl. WC1 141 DM70
Mecklenburgh Sq. WC1 274 B4
Mecklenburgh Sq. WC1 141 DM70
Mecklenburgh St. WC1 274 B4
Medburn St. NW1 141 DK68
Medbury Rd., Grav. 191 GM88
Medcalf Rd., Enf. 83 DZ37
Medcroft Gdns. SW14 158 CQ84
Mede Clo., Stai. 172 AX88
Mede Fld., Lthd. 231 CD124
Medebourne Clo. SE3 164 EG83
Medesenge Way N13 99 DP51
Medfield St. SW15 179 CV87
Medhurst Clo. E3 143 DY68
Arbery Rd.
Medhurst Clo., Wok. 210 AT109
Medhurst Cres., Grav. 191 GL90
Medhurst Gdns., Grav. 191 GM90
Medhurst Rd. E3 143 DY68
Arbery Rd.
Median Rd. E5 122 DW64
Medick Ct., Grays 170 GE79
Medina Ave., Esher 197 CE104
Medina Gro. N7 121 DN62
Medina Rd.
Medina Rd. N7 121 DN62
Medina Rd., Grays 170 GD77
Medlake Rd., Egh. 173 BC93
Medland Clo., Wall. 200 DG102
Medlar Clo., Guil. 242 AW132
Medlar Clo., Nthlt. 136 BY68
Parkfield Ave.
Medlar Ct., Slou. 132 AW74
Medlar Rd., Grays 170 GD79
Medlar St. SE5 162 DQ81
Medley Rd. NW6 140 DA65
Medman Clo., Uxb. 134 BJ68
Chiltern Vw. Rd.
Medora Rd. SW2 181 DM87
Medora Rd., Rom. 127 FD56
Medow Mead, Rad. 61 CF33
Medusa Rd. SE6 183 EB86
Medway Bldgs. E3 143 DY68
Medway Rd.
Medway Clo., Croy. 202 DW100
Medway Clo., Ilf. 125 EQ64
Medway Clo., Wat. 60 BW34
Medway Dr., Grnf. 137 CF68
Medway Gdns., Wem. 117 CG63
Medway Ms. E3 143 DY68
Medway Rd.
Medway Par., Grnf. 137 CF68
Medway Rd. E3 143 DY68
Medway Rd., Dart. 167 FG83
Medway Rd., Hem.H. 40 BM15
Medway St. SW1 277 N7
Medway St. SW1 161 DK76
Medwick Ms., Hem.H. 41 BP15
Hunters Oak
Medwin St. SW4 161 DM84
Meerbrook Rd. SE3 164 EJ83
Meeson Rd. E15 144 EF67
Meeson St. E5 123 DY63
Meesons La., Grays 170 FZ77
Meeting Flds. Path E9 142 DW65
Morning La.
Meeting Ho. La. SE15 162 DV81
Meetinghouse All. E1 142 DV74
Wapping La.
Megg La., Kings L. 58 BH29
Mehetabel Rd. E9 142 DW65
Meister Clo., Ilf. 125 ER60
Melancholy Wk., Rich. 177 CJ89
Melanda Clo., Chis. 185 EM92
Melanie Clo., Bexh. 166 EY81
Melba Gdns., Til. 171 GG80
Melba Way SE13 163 EB81
Melbourne Ave. N13 99 DM51
Melbourne Ave. W13 137 CG74
Melbourne Ave., Pnr. 116 CB55
Melbourne Ave., Slou. 131 AQ72
Melbourne Clo., Orp. 205 ES101
Melbourne Clo., St.Alb. 43 CF16
Melbourne Clo., Uxb. 114 BN63
Melbourne Clo., Wall. 219 DJ106
Melbourne Rd.
Melbourne Ct. E5 123 DY63
Daubeney Rd.
Melbourne Ct. N10 99 DH52
Sydney Rd.
Melbourne Ct. SE20 182 DU94
Melbourne Ct., Welw.G.C. 29 CV10
Melbourne Gdns., Rom. 126 EY57
Melbourne Gro. SE22 162 DS84
Melbourne Ho., Hayes 136 BW70
Melbourne Ms. SE6 183 EC87
Melbourne Ms. SW9 161 DN81
Melbourne Pl. WC2 274 C10
Melbourne Pl. WC2 141 DM72
Melbourne Rd. E6 145 EM67
Melbourne Rd. E10 123 EB59
Melbourne Rd. E17 123 DY56
Melbourne Rd. SW19 200 DA95
Melbourne Rd., Ilf. 125 EP60
Melbourne Rd., Tedd. 177 CJ93
Melbourne Rd., Til. 170 GE81
Melbourne Rd., Wall. 219 DH106
Melbourne Rd. (Bushey), Wat. 76 CB44
Melbourne Sq. SW9 161 DN81
Melbourne Ms.
Melbourne Ter. SW6 160 DB80
Waterford Rd.
Melbourne Way, Enf. 82 DT44
Melbury Ave., Sthl. 156 CB76
Melbury Clo., Cher. 194 BG101
Melbury Clo., Chis. 185 EM93
Melbury Clo., Esher 215 CH107
Melbury Clo., W.Byf. 212 BG114
Melbury Ct. W8 159 CZ76
Melbury Dr. SE5 162 DS80
Sedgmoor Pl.
Melbury Gdns. SW20 199 CV95
Melbury Rd. W14 159 CZ76
Melbury Rd., Har. 118 CM57
Melbury Ter. NW1 272 C5
Melbury Ter. NW1 140 DE70
Melcombe Gdns., Har. 118 CM58
Melcombe Pl. NW1 272 D6
Melcombe Pl. NW1 140 DF71
Melcombe St. NW1 272 E5
Melcombe St. NW1 140 DF70
Meldex Clo. NW7 97 CW51
Meldon Clo. SW6 160 DB81
Bagley's La.
Meldone Clo., Surb. 198 CP100
Meldrum Clo., Orp. 206 EW100
Killewarren Way
Meldrum Clo., Oxt. 254 EF132
Meldrum Rd., Ilf. 126 EU61
Melfield Gdns. SE6 183 EB91
Melford Ave., Bark. 145 ES65
Melford Clo., Chess. 216 CM106
Melford Rd. E6 145 EM70
Melford Rd. E11 124 EE61
Melford Rd. E17 123 DY56
Melford Rd. SE22 182 DU87
Melford Rd., Ilf. 125 ER61
Melfort Ave., Th.Hth. 201 DP97
Melfort Rd., Th.Hth. 201 DP97
Melgund Rd. N5 121 DN64
Melina Clo., Hayes 135 BR71
Middleton Rd.
Melina Pl. NW8 140 DD69
Melina Rd. W12 159 CV75
Melings, The, Hem.H. 41 BP15
Melior Pl. SE1 279 M4
Melior St. SE1 279 L4
Melior St. SE1 162 DR75
Meliot Rd. SE6 183 ED89
Melksham Clo., Rom. 106 FM52
Melksham Dr., Rom. 106 FM52
Melksham Gdns.
Melksham Gdns., Rom. 106 FL52
Melksham Grn., Rom. 106 FM52
Melksham Gdns.
Mell St. SE10 164 EE78
Trafalgar Rd.

Mel - Mil This index reads in the sequence: Street Name / Postal District or Post Town / Map Page Number / Grid Reference

Meller Clo., Croy. 201 DL104
Melling Dr., Enf. 82 DU39
Melling St. SE18 165 ES79
Mellish Clo., Bark. 145 ET67
Mellish Gdns., Wdf.Grn. 102 EG50
Mellish Ind. Est. SE18 164 EL76
Harrington Way
Mellish St. E14 163 EA76
Mellison Rd. SW17 180 DE92
Mellitus St. W12 139 CT72
Mellor Clo., Walt. 196 BZ101
Mellor Wk., Wind. 151 AR81
Bachelors Acre
Mellow Clo., Bans. 218 DB114
Mellow La. E., Hayes 135 BQ69
Mellow La. W., Uxb. 135 BQ69
Mellows Rd., Ilf. 125 EM55
Mellows Rd., Wall. 219 DK106
Mells Cres. SE9 185 EM91
Melody La. N5 121 DP64
Melody Rd. SW18 180 DC85
Melody Rd., West. 238 EJ118
Melon Pl. W8 160 DA75
Kensington Ch. St.
Melon Rd. E11 124 EE62
Melon Rd. SE15 162 DU81
Melrose Ave. N22 99 DP53
Melrose Ave. NW2 119 CW64
Melrose Ave. SW16 201 DM97
Melrose Ave. SW19 180 DA89
Melrose Ave., Borwd. 78 CP43
Melrose Ave., Grnf. 136 CB68
Melrose Ave., Mitch. 181 DH94
Melrose Ave., Pot.B. 64 DB32
Melrose Ave., Twick. 176 CB87
Melrose Clo. SE12 184 EG88
Melrose Clo., Grnf. 136 CB68
Melrose Clo., Hayes 135 BU71
Melrose Cres., Orp. 223 ER105
Melrose Dr., Sthl. 136 CA74
Melrose Gdns. W6 159 CW76
Melrose Gdns., Edg. 96 CP54
Melrose Gdns., N.Mal. 198 CR97
Melrose Gdns., Walt. 214 BW106
Melrose Pl., Wat. 75 BT38
Wentworth Clo.
Melrose Rd. SW13 159 CT82
Melrose Rd. SW18 179 CZ86
Melrose Rd. SW19 200 DA96
Melrose Rd. W3 158 CQ76
Stanley Rd.
Melrose Rd., Couls. 235 DH115
Melrose Rd., Pnr. 116 BZ56
Melrose Rd., West. 238 EJ116
Melrose Rd., Wey. 212 BN106
Melrose Ter. W6 159 CW75
Melsa Rd., Mord. 200 DC100
Melsted Rd., Hem.H. 40 BH20
Melstock Ave., Upmin. 128 FQ63
Melthorne Dr., Ruis. 116 BW62
Melthorpe Gdns. SE3 164 EL81
Melton Clo., Ruis. 116 BW60
Melton Ct. SW7 276 A9
Melton Ct. SW7 160 DD77
Melton Flds., Epsom 216 CR109
Melton Gdns., Rom. 127 FF59
Melton Pl., Epsom 216 CR109
Melton Rd., Red. 251 DJ130
Melton St. NW1 273 L3
Melton St. NW1 141 DK69
Melville Ave. SW20 179 CU94
Melville Ave., Grnf. 117 CF64
Melville Ave., S.Croy. 220 DT106
Melville Clo., Uxb. 115 BR62
Melville Gdns. N13 99 DP50
Melville Pl. N1 141 DP67
Essex Rd.
Melville Rd. E17 123 DZ55
Melville Rd. NW10 138 CR66
Melville Rd. SW13 159 CU81
Melville Rd., Rain. 147 FG70
Melville Rd., Rom. 105 FB52
Melville Rd., Sid. 186 EW89
Melville Vil. Rd. W3 138 CR74
High St.
Melvin Rd. SE20 202 DW95
Melvinshaw, Lthd. 231 CJ121
Melvyn Clo. (Cheshunt), Wal.Cr. 65 DP28
Melyn Clo. N7 121 DJ63
Anson Rd.
Memel Ct. EC1 275 H5
Memel St. EC1 275 H5
Memess Path SE18 165 EN79
Memorial Ave. E15 144 EE69
Memorial Clo., Houns. 156 BZ79
Memorial Way, Wat. 75 BU41
Mendip Clo. SE26 182 DW91
Mendip Clo. SW19 179 CY89
Queensmere Rd.
Mendip Clo., Hayes 155 BR80
Mendip Clo., St.Alb. 43 CJ15
Mendip Clo., Slou. 153 BA78
Mendip Clo., Wor.Pk. 199 CW102
Mendip Dr. NW2 119 CX61
Mendip Rd. SW11 160 DC83
Mendip Rd., Bexh. 167 FE81
Mendip Rd., Horn. 127 FG59
Mendip Rd., Ilf. 125 ES57
Mendip Rd. (Bushey), Wat. 76 CC44
Mendip Way, Hem.H. 40 BL17
Mendlesham, Welw.G.C. 30 DE09
Mendora Rd. SW6 159 CY80
Mendoza Clo., Horn. 128 FL57
Menelik Rd. NW2 119 CY63
Menlo Gdns. SE19 182 DR94
Menotti St. E2 142 DU70
Dunbridge St.
Menthone Pl., Horn. 128 FK59
Mentmore Clo., Har. 117 CJ58
Mentmore Rd., St.Alb. 43 CD22
Mentmore Ter. E8 142 DV66
Meon Clo., Tad. 233 CV122
Meon Ct., Islw. 157 CE82
Meon Rd. W3 158 CQ75
Meopham Rd., Mitch. 201 DJ95
Mepham Cres., Har. 94 CC52
Mepham Gdns., Har. 94 CC52
Mepham St. SE1 278 C3
Mepham St. SE1 141 DM74
Mera Dr., Bexh. 166 FA84
Merantun Way SW19 200 DC95
Merbury Clo. SE13 183 EC85
Merbury Rd. SE28 165 ES75
Mercator Pl. E14 163 EA78
Napier Ave.
Mercator Rd. SE13 163 ED84
Mercer Clo., T.Ditt. 197 CF101
Mercer Pl., Pnr. 94 BW54
Crossway
Mercer St. WC2 273 P9
Mercer St. WC2 141 DL72
Mercer Wk., Uxb. 134 BJ66
High St.
Merceron St. E1 142 DV70
Mercers, Harl. 51 EN17
Mercers, Hem.H. 40 BL18
Mercers Clo. SE10 164 EF77
Mercers Pl. W6 159 CW77
Mercers Rd. N19 121 DK62
Mercers Row, St.Alb. 42 CC22
Merchant Dr., Hert. 32 DT08
Merchant St. E3 143 DZ69
Merchiston Rd. SE6 183 ED89
Merchland Rd. SE9 185 EQ88
Mercia Gro. SE13 163 EC84
Mercia Wk., Wok. 227 AZ117
Church St. W.
Mercian Way, Slou. 131 AK74
Mercier Rd. SW15 179 CY85
Mercury Cen. Ind. Est., Felt. 175 BU85
Mercury Gdns., Rom. 127 FE56
Mercury Wk., Hem.H. 40 BM17
Mercury Way SE14 163 DX79
Mercy Ter. SE13 163 EB84
Mere Clo. SW15 179 CX87
Mere Clo., Orp. 205 EP103
Mere End, Croy. 203 DX101
Mere Rd., Shep. 195 BP100
Mere Rd., Slou. 152 AT76
Mere Rd., Tad. 233 CV124
Mere Rd., Wey. 195 BR104
Mere Side, Orp. 205 EN103
Merebank La., Croy. 219 DM106
Meredith Ave. NW2 119 CW64
Meredith Clo., Pnr. 94 BX52
Meredith Rd., Grays 171 GG77
Meredith St. E13 144 EG69
Meredith St. EC1 274 F3
Meredyth Rd. SW13 159 CU82
Merefield, Saw. 36 EY06
Merefield Gdns., Tad. 233 CX119
Mereside Pl., Vir.W. 192 AX100
Meretone Clo. SE4 163 DY84
Merevale Cres., Mord. 200 DC100
Mereway Rd., Twick. 177 CD88
Merewood Clo., Brom. 205 EN96
Merewood Rd., Bexh. 167 FC82
Mereworth Clo., Brom. 204 EF99
Mereworth Dr. SE18 165 EQ80
Merganser Gdns. SE28 165 ER76
Avocet Ms.
Meriden Clo., Brom. 184 EK94
Meriden Clo., Ilf. 103 EQ53
Meriden Way, Wat. 76 BY36
Meridian Gate E14 163 EC75
Meridian Gro., Horl. 269 DJ147
Wheatfield Way
Meridian Pl. E14 163 EB75
Meridian Rd. SE7 164 EK80
Meridian Trd. Est. SE7 164 EH77
Meridian Wk. N17 100 DS51
Commercial Rd.
Meridian Way N9 100 DW50
Meridian Way N18 100 DW51
Meridian Way, Enf. 83 DX44
Meridian Way, Ware 33 EB10
Merifield Rd. SE9 164 EJ84
Merino Clo. E11 124 EJ56
Merino Pl., Sid. 186 EU86
Blackfen Rd.
Merivale Rd. SW15 159 CY84
Merivale Rd., Har. 116 CC59
Merland Clo., Tad. 233 CW120
Merland Grn., Tad. 233 CW120
Merland Ri.
Merland Ri., Epsom 233 CW119
Merland Ri., Tad. 233 CW120
Merle Ave. (Harefield), Uxb. 92 BH54
Merle Clo., Cat. 236 DR120
Merlewood, Sev. 257 FH123
Merlewood Clo., Cat. 236 DR120
Merlewood Dr., Chis. 205 EM95
Merley Ct. NW9 118 CQ60
Merlin Clo., Croy. 220 DS105
Minster Dr.
Merlin Clo., Ilf. 104 EW50
Merlin Clo., Mitch. 200 DE97
Merlin Clo., Nthlt. 136 BW69
Merlin Clo., Rom. 105 FD51
Merlin Clo., Slou. 153 BB79
Merlin Clo., Wal.Abb. 68 EG34
Merlin Ct., Wok. 211 BC114
Blackmore Cres.
Merlin Cres., Edg. 96 CM53
Merlin Gdns., Brom. 184 EG90
Merlin Gdns., Rom. 105 FD51
Merlin Gro., Beck. 203 DZ98
Merlin Gro., Ilf. 103 EP52
Merlin Rd. E12 124 EK61
Merlin Rd., Rom. 105 FD51
Merlin Rd., Well. 166 EU84
Merlin Rd. N., Well. 166 EU84
Merlin St. WC1 274 D3
Merlin Way, Epp. 70 FA25
Merling Clo., Chess. 215 CK106
Coppard Gdns.
Merling Cft., Berk. 38 AS17
Merlins Ave., Har. 116 BZ62
Mermagen Dr., Rain. 147 FH66
Mermaid Ct. SE1 279 K4
Mermaid Ct. SE1 162 DR75
Mermaid Ct. SE16 143 DZ74
Mermerus Gdns., Grav. 191 GM91
Merredene St. SW2 181 DM86
Merriam Clo. E4 101 EC50
Merrick Rd., Sthl. 156 BZ75
Merrick Sq. SE1 279 J6
Merrick Sq. SE1 162 DQ76
Merridene N21 81 DP44
Merrielands Cres., Dag. 146 EZ67
Merrilands Rd., Wor.Pk. 199 CW102
Merrilees Rd., Sid. 185 ES87
Merrilyn Clo., Esher 215 CG107
Merriman Rd. SE3 164 EJ81
Merrington Rd. SW6 160 DA79
Merrion Ave., Stan. 95 CK50
Merrion Wk. SE17 162 DR78
Dawes St.
Merritt Gdns., Chess. 215 CJ107
Merritt Rd. SE4 183 DZ85
Merritt Wk., Hat. 45 CV23
Merrivale N14 81 DK44
Merrivale Ave., Ilf. 124 EK56
Merrivale Gdns., Wok. 226 AW117
Merrow Business Cen., Guil. 243 BC131
Merrow La.
Merrow Chase, Guil. 243 BC134
Merrow Common Rd., Guil. 243 BD131
Merrow Copse, Guil. 243 BB133
Merrow Ct., Guil. 243 BD134
Levylsdene
Merrow Cft., Guil. 243 BC133
Merrow Downs, Guil. 259 BD135
Merrow Dr., Hem.H. 39 BE19
Merrow La., Guil. 243 BC129
Merrow Rd., Sutt. 217 CX109
Merrow St. SE17 162 DQ79
Merrow St., Guil. 243 BD132
Merrow Wk. SE17 279 L10
Merrow Way, Croy. 221 EC107
Merrow Way, Guil. 243 BD133
Merrow Wds., Guil. 243 BB132
Merrows Clo., Nthwd. 93 BQ51
Rickmansworth Rd.
Merry Hill Mt. (Bushey), Wat. 94 CB46
Merry Hill Rd. (Bushey), Wat. 94 CB46
Merrydown Way, Chis. 204 EL95
Merryfield SE3 164 EF82
Merryfield Gdns., Stan. 95 CJ50
Merryfields, Uxb. 134 BL68
The Greenway
Merryfields Way SE6 183 EB87
Merryhill Clo. E4 101 EB45
Merryhills Clo., West. 238 EK116
Merryhills Ct. N14 81 DJ43
Merryhills Dr., Enf. 81 DK42
Merrylands, Cher. 193 BE104
Merrylands Rd., Lthd. 230 BZ123
Merrymeet, Bans. 218 DF114
Merryweather Clo., Dart. 188 FM86
Merrywood Gro., Tad. 249 CX130
Merrywood Pk., Reig. 250 DB132
Merrywood Pk., Tad. 248 CP130
Mersea Ho., Bark. 145 EP65
Mersey Ave., Upmin. 129 FR58
Mersey Pl., Hem.H. 40 BM15
Colne Way
Mersey Rd. E17 123 DZ55
Mersey Wk., Nthlt. 136 CA68
Brabazon Rd.
Mersham Dr. NW9 118 CN57
Mersham Pl. SE20 202 DV95
Mersham Rd., Th.Hth. 202 DR97
Merstham Rd., Red. 251 DM129
Merten Rd., Rom. 126 EY59
Merthyr Ter. SW13 159 CV79
Merton Ave. W4 159 CT77
Merton Ave., Nthlt. 116 CC64
Merton Ave., Uxb. 135 BP66
Merton Gdns., Orp. 205 EP99
Merton Gdns., Tad. 233 CX120
Marbles Way
Merton Hall Gdns. SW20 199 CY95
Merton Hall Rd. SW19 199 CY95
Merton High St. SW19 180 DB94
Merton Ind. Pk. SW19 200 DC95
Merton La. N6 120 DF61
Merton Mans. SW20 199 CX96
Merton Pk. Par. SW19 199 CZ95
Kingston Rd.
Merton Pl., Grays 171 GG77
Merton Ri. NW3 140 DE66
Merton Rd. E17 123 EC57
Merton Rd. SE25 202 DU99
Merton Rd. SW18 180 DA86
Merton Rd. SW19 180 DB94
Merton Rd., Bark. 145 ET66
Merton Rd., Enf. 82 DR38
Merton Rd., Har. 116 CC60
Merton Rd., Ilf. 125 ET59
Merton Rd., Slou. 152 AU76
Merton Rd., Wat. 75 BV42
Merton Wk., Lthd. 231 CG118
Merton Way
Merton Way, Lthd. 231 CG119
Merton Way, Uxb. 135 BP66
Merton Way, W.Mol. 196 CB98
Merttins Rd. SE15 183 DX85
Meru Clo. NW5 120 DG63
Mervan Rd. SW2 161 DN84
Mervyn Ave. SE9 185 EQ90
Mervyn Rd. W13 157 CG76
Mervyn Rd., Shep. 195 BQ101
Merwin Way, Wind. 151 AK83
Meryfield Clo., Borwd. 78 CM40
Mesne Way, Sev. 225 FF112
Messaline Ave. W3 138 CQ72
Messant Clo., Rom. 106 FK54
Messent Rd. SE9 184 EJ85
Messeter Pl. SE9 185 EN86
Messina Ave. NW6 140 DA66
Metcalf Rd., Ashf. 175 BP92
Metcalfe Wk., Felt. 176 BY91
Gabriel Clo.
Meteor St. SW11 160 DG84
Meteor Way, Wall. 219 DL108
Metford Cres., Enf. 83 EA38
Metheringham Way NW9 96 CS53
Methley St. SE11 161 DN78
Methuen Clo., Edg. 96 CN52
Methuen Pk. N10 99 DH54
Methuen Rd., Belv. 167 FB77
Methuen Rd., Bexh. 166 EZ84
Methuen Rd., Edg. 96 CN52
Methwold Rd. W10 139 CX71
Metro Cen., The, Islw. 157 CE82
Metropolitan Cen., The, Grnf. 136 CB67
Metropolitan Clo. E14 143 EA71
Broomfield St.
Meux Clo. (Cheshunt), Wal.Cr. 66 DU31
Mews, The N1 142 DQ67
St. Paul St.
Mews, The, Grays 170 GC77
Mews, The, Guil. 258 AW135
Walnut Tree Clo.
Mews, The, Harl. 51 ES19
Commonside Rd.
Mews, The, Ilf. 124 EK57
Mews, The, Rom. 127 FE56
Market Link
Mews, The, Sev. 256 FG123
Mews, The, Twick. 177 CH86
Bridge Rd.
Mews Deck E1 142 DV73
Mews End, West. 238 EK118
Mews Pl., Wdf.Grn. 102 EG49
Mews St. E1 142 DU74
Mexfield Rd. SW15 179 CZ85
Meyer Grn., Enf. 82 DU38
Meyer Rd., Erith 167 FC79
Meymott St. SE1 278 F3
Meymott St. SE1 141 DP74
Meynell Cres. E9 143 DX66
Meynell Gdns. E9 143 DX66
Meynell Rd. E9 143 DX66
Meynell Rd., Rom. 105 FH52
Meyrick Clo., Wok. 226 AS116
Meyrick Rd. NW10 139 CU65
Meyrick Rd. SW11 160 DD83
Mezen Clo., Nthwd. 93 BR50
Miah Ter. E1 142 DU74
Wapping High St.
Miall Wk. SE26 183 DY91
Micawber Ave., Uxb. 134 BN70
Micawber St. N1 275 J2
Micawber St. N1 142 DQ69
Michael Cres., Horl. 268 DG150
Michael Faraday Ho. SE17 162 DS78
Beaconsfield Rd.
Michael Gdns., Grav. 191 GL93
Michael Gdns., Horn. 128 FK56
Michael Gaynor Clo. W7 137 CF74
Michael Rd. E11 124 EE60
Michael Rd. SE25 202 DS97
Michael Rd. SW6 160 DB81
Michaelmas Clo. SW20 199 CW97
Michaels Clo. SE13 164 EE84
Michaels La. (Fawkham Grn.), Long. 209 FV103
Michaels La., Sev. 209 FV103
Micheldever Rd. SE12 184 EE86
Michelham Gdns., Tad. 233 CW121
Waterfield
Michelham Gdns., Twick. 177 CG90
Michels Row, Rich. 158 CL84
Kew Foot Rd.
Michigan Ave. E12 124 EL63
Michleham Down N12 97 CZ49
Micholls Ave., Ger.Cr. 90 AY49
Micklefield Rd., Hem.H. 41 BQ20
Micklefield Way, Borwd. 78 CL38
Mickleham Bypass, Dor. 247 CH128
Mickleham Clo., Orp. 205 ET96
Mickleham Downs, Dor. 247 CK127
Mickleham Dr., Lthd. 247 CJ126
Mickleham Gdns., Sutt. 217 CY107
Mickleham Rd., Orp. 205 ET95
Mickleham Way, Croy. 221 ED108
Micklem Dr., Hem.H. 39 BF19
Micklethwaite Rd. SW6 160 DA79
Mid Cross La., Ger.Cr. 91 AZ50
Mid Holmwood La., Dor. 263 CH142
Mid St., Red. 251 DM134
Midas Ind. Est., Uxb. 134 BH68
Midas Metropolitan Ind. Est., The, Mord. 199 CX102
Garth Rd.
Midcot Way, Berk. 38 AT17
Midcroft, Ruis. 115 BS60
Midcroft, Slou. 131 AP70
Middle Boy, Rom. 86 EW41
Middle Clo., Amer. 72 AT37
Middle Clo., Couls. 235 DN120
Middle Clo., Epsom 216 CS112
Middle La.
Middle Cres., Uxb. 113 BD59
Middle Dene NW7 96 CR48
Middle Dr., Beac. 89 AK50
Middle Fm. Clo., Lthd. 246 BX127
Middle Fm. Pl., Lthd. 246 BW127
Middle Fld. NW8 140 DD67
Middle Furlong (Bushey), Wat. 76 CB42
Middle Gorse, Croy. 221 DY112
Middle Grn., Bet. 264 CP136
Middle Grn., Slou. 132 AY74
Middle Grn., Stai. 174 BK94
Honnor Rd.
Middle Grn. Clo., Surb. 198 CM100
Alpha Rd.
Middle Hill, Egh. 172 AW91
Middle Hill, Hem.H. 39 BE20
Middle La. N8 121 DL57
Middle La., Epsom 216 CS112
Middle La., Hem.H. 57 BA29
Middle La., Sev. 257 FM121
Church Rd.
Middle La., Tedd. 177 CF93
Middle La. Ms. N8 121 DL57
Middle La.
Middle Meadow, Ch.St.G. 90 AW48
Middle Ope, Wat. 75 BV37
Middle Pk. Ave. SE9 184 EK86
Middle Path, Har. 117 CD60
Middle Rd.
Middle Rd. E13 144 EG68
London Rd.
Middle Rd. SW16 201 DK96
Middle Rd., Barn. 80 DE44
Middle Rd., Berk. 38 AV19
Middle Rd., Brwd. 109 GC50
Middle Rd., Har. 117 CD61
Middle Rd., Lthd. 231 CH121
Middle Rd., Uxb. 113 BC59
Middle Rd., Wal.Abb. 67 EB32
Middle Row W10 139 CY70
Middle St. EC1 275 H6
Middle St., Bet. 264 CP136
Middle St., Croy. 202 DQ104
Surrey St.
Middle St., Guil. 260 BN139
Middle St., Wal.Abb. 50 EE22
Middle Temple EC4 274 D10
Middle Temple La. EC4 274 D9
Middle Temple La. EC4 141 DN72
Middle Wk., Slou. 130 AH69
Middle Wk., Wok. 226 AY117
Commercial Way
Middle Way SW16 201 DK96
Middle Way, Erith 166 EY76
Middle Way, Hayes 136 BW70
Middle Way, Wat. 75 BV37
Middle Way, The, Har. 95 CF54
Middle Yd. SE1 279 L2
Middlefield, Hat. 45 CU17
Middlefield, Horl. 269 DJ147
Middlefield, Welw.G.C. 29 CY13
Middlefield Ave., Hodd. 49 EA15
Middlefield Clo., Hodd. 49 EA15
Middlefield Clo., St.Alb. 43 CJ17
Middlefield Gdns., Ilf. 125 EP58
Middlefield Rd., Hodd. 49 EA15
Middlefield W13 137 CH71
Middlefields, Croy. 221 DY109
Middlegreen Rd., Slou. 152 AX75
Middleham Gdns. N18 100 DU51
Middleham Rd. N18 100 DU51
Middleknights Hill, Hem.H. 40 BG17
Middlemead Clo., Lthd. 246 CA125
Middlemead Rd., Lthd. 246 BZ125
Middlesborough Rd. N18 100 DU51
Middlesex Business Cen., Sthl. 156 CA75
Middlesex Ct. W4 159 CT77
British Gro.
Middlesex Pas. EC1 274 G7
Middlesex Rd., Mitch. 201 DL99
Middlesex St. E1 275 N7
Middlesex St. E1 142 DS71
Middlesex Wf. E5 122 DW61
Middleton Ave. E4 101 DZ49
Middleton Ave., Grnf. 137 CD68
Middleton Ave., Sid. 186 EW93
Middleton Bldgs. W1 273 K7
Middleton Clo. E4 101 DZ48
Middleton Dr. SE16 163 DX75
Middleton Dr., Pnr. 115 BU55
Middleton Gdns., Ilf. 125 EP58
Middleton Gro. N7 121 DL64
Middleton Hall La., Brwd. 108 FY46
Middleton Ms. N7 121 DL64
Middleton Gro.
Middleton Rd. E8 142 DT66
Middleton Rd. NW11 120 DA59
Middleton Rd., Brwd. 108 FY46
Middleton Rd., Cars. 200 DE101
Middleton Rd., Cob. 229 BV119
Middleton Rd., Epsom 216 CR110
Middleton Rd., Hayes 135 BR71
Middleton Rd., Mord. 200 DC100
Middleton Rd., Rick. 92 BG46
Middleton St. E2 142 DV69
Middleton Way SE13 163 ED84
Middleway NW11 120 DB57
Middlings, The, Sev. 256 FF125
Middlings Ri., Sev. 256 FF126
Middlings Wd., Sev. 256 FF125
Midfield Ave., Bexh. 167 FC83
Midfield Ave., Swan. 187 FG93
Midfield Par., Bexh. 167 FC83
Midfield Way, Orp. 206 EU95
Midford Pl. W1 273 L5
Midgarth Clo., Lthd. 214 CC114
Midholm NW11 120 DB56
Midholm, Wem. 118 CN60
Midholm Clo. NW11 120 DB56
Midholm Rd., Croy. 203 DY103
Midhope Clo., Wok. 226 AY119
Midhope Gdns., Wok. 226 AY119
Midhope Rd.
Midhope Rd., Wok. 226 AY119
Midhope St. WC1 274 A3
Midhurst Ave. N10 120 DG55
Midhurst Ave., Croy. 201 DN101
Midhurst Clo., Horn. 127 FG63
Midhurst Gdns., Uxb. 135 BQ66
Midhurst Hill, Bexh. 186 FA86
Midhurst Rd. W13 157 CG75
Midland Cres. NW3 140 DC65
Finchley Rd.
Midland Pl. E14 163 EC78
Ferry St.
Midland Rd. E10 123 EC59
Midland Rd. NW1 273 N1
Midland Rd. NW1 141 DK68
Midland Rd., Hem.H. 40 BK20
Midland Ter. NW2 119 CX62
Kara Way
Midland Ter. NW10 138 CS70
Midleton Ind. Est. Rd., Guil. 242 AV133
Midleton Rd., Guil. 242 AV133
Midleton Rd., N.Mal. 198 CQ97
Midlothian Rd. E3 143 DZ71
Midmoor Rd. SW12 181 DJ88
Midmoor Rd. SW19 199 CX95
Midship Clo. SE16 143 DX74
Surrey Water Rd.
Midship Pt. E14 163 EA75
Midstrath Rd. NW10 118 CS63
Midsummer Ave., Houns. 156 BZ84
Midway, St.Alb. 42 CB23
Midway, Sutt. 199 CZ101
Midway, Walt. 195 BV103
Midway Ave., Cher. 194 BG97
Eastern Ave.
Midway Ave., Egh. 193 BB97
Midwinter Clo., Well. 166 EU83
Hook La.
Midwood Clo. NW2 119 CV62
Miena Way, Ash. 231 CK117
Miers Clo. E6 145 EN67
Mighell Ave., Ilf. 124 EK57
Mike Spring Ct., Grav. 191 GK91
Milan Rd., Sthl. 156 BZ75
Milborne Gro. SW10 160 DC78
Milborne St. E9 142 DW65
Milborough Cres. SE12 184 EE86
Milbourne La., Esher 214 CC107
Milbrook, Esher 214 CC107
Milburn Dr., West Dr. 134 BL73
Milburn Wk., Epsom 232 CS115
Milcombe Clo., Wok. 226 AV118
Inglewood
Milcote St. SE1 278 F5
Milcote St. SE1 161 DP75
Mildenhall Rd. E5 122 DW63
Mildenhall Rd., Slou. 132 AS72
Mildmay Ave. N1 142 DR65
Mildmay Gro. N. N1 122 DR64
Mildmay Gro. S. N1 122 DR64
Mildmay Pk. N1 122 DR64
Mildmay Pl. N16 122 DS64
Boleyn Rd.
Mildmay Pl., Sev. 225 FF111
Mildmay Rd. N1 122 DS64
Mildmay Rd., Ilf. 125 EP62
Winston Way
Mildmay Rd., Rom. 127 FC57
Mildmay St. N1 142 DR65
Mildred Ave., Borwd. 78 CN42
Mildred Ave., Hayes 155 BR77
Mildred Ave., Nthlt. 116 CB64
Mildred Ave., Wat. 75 BT42
Mildred Clo., Dart. 188 FN86
Mildred Rd., Erith 167 FE78
Mile Clo., Wal.Abb. 67 EC33
Mile End, The E17 101 DX53

Mile End Pl. E1 143 DX70
Mile End Rd. E1 142 DW71
Mile End Rd. E3 142 DW71
Mile Ho. Clo., St.Alb. 43 CG23
Mile Ho. La., St.Alb. 43 CG23
Mile Path, Wok. 226 AV120
Mile Rd., Wall. 201 DJ102
Miles Clo., Harl. 51 EP16
Miles La., Cob. 214 BY113
Miles Pl. NW1 272 A6
Miles Pl., Surb. 198 CM98
Villiers Ave.
Miles Rd. N8 121 DL55
Miles Rd., Epsom 216 CR112
Miles Rd., Mitch. 200 DE97
Miles St. SW8 161 DL79
Miles Way N20 98 DE47
Milespit Hill NW7 97 CV50
Milestone Clo. N9 100 DU47
Chichester Rd.
Milestone Clo., Sutt. 218 DD107
Milestone Clo., Wok. 228 BG122
Milestone Rd. SE19 182 DT93
Milestone Rd., Dart. 188 FP86
Milfoil St. W12 139 CU73
Milford Clo. SE2 166 EY79
Milford Clo., St.Alb. 43 CK16
Milford Gdns., Croy. 203 DX99
Tannery Clo.
Milford Gdns., Edg. 96 CN52
Milford Gdns., Wem. 117 CK64
Milford Gro., Sutt. 218 DC105
Milford La. WC2 274 C10
Milford La. WC2 141 DM73
Milford Ms. SW16 181 DM90
Milford Rd. W13 137 CH74
Milford Rd., Sthl. 136 CA73
Milford Way SE15 162 DT81
Sumner Est.
Milk St. E16 145 EP74
Milk St. EC2 275 J9
Milk St., Brom. 184 EH93
Milk Yd. E1 142 DW73
Milking La., Kes. 222 EK111
Milking La., Orp. 222 EL112
Milkwell Gdns., Wdf.Grn. 102 EH52
Milkwell Yd. SE5 162 DQ81
Milkwood Rd. SE24 181 DP85
Mill Ave., Uxb. 134 BJ68
Mill Bri., Hert. 32 DQ09
Mill Brook Rd., Orp. 206 EW98
Mill Clo., Cars. 200 DG103
Mill Clo., Chesh. 54 AS34
Mill Clo., Hem.H. 58 BN25
Mill Clo. (Piccotts End), Hem.H. 40 BH16
Mill Clo., Horl. 268 DE147
Mill Clo., Lthd. 230 CA124
Mill Clo., Ware 33 DX06
Mill Clo., Welw.G.C. 29 CU10
Mill Clo., West Dr. 154 BK76
Mill Cor., Barn. 79 CZ39
Mill Ct. E10 123 EC62
Mill Fm. Ave., Sun. 175 BS94
Mill Fm. Clo., Pnr. 94 BW54
Mill Fm. Cres., Houns. 176 BY88
Mill Fld., Harl. 36 EW11
Mill Gdns. SE26 182 DV91
Mill Grn., Mitch. 200 DG101
London Rd.
Mill Grn. La., Hat. 45 CY15
Mill Grn. Rd., Mitch. 200 DF101
Mill Grn. Rd., Welw.G.C. 29 CY10
Mill Hill SW13 159 CU82
Mill Hill Rd.
Mill Hill, Brwd. 108 FY45
Mill Hill Circ. NW7 97 CT50
Watford Way
Mill Hill Gro. W3 138 CP74
Mill Hill Rd.
Mill Hill La., Bet. 248 CP134
Mill Hill Rd. SW13 159 CU82
Mill Hill Rd. W3 158 CP75
Mill Ho. Clo. (Eynsford), Dart. 208 FL102
Mill La.
Mill Ho. La., Cher. 193 BD98
Mill Ho. La., Egh. 193 BB98
Mill La. E4 83 EB41
Mill La. NW6 119 CZ64
Mill La. SE18 165 EN78
Mill La., Amer. 55 AN39
Mill La., Beac. 89 AL54
Mill La., Brox. 49 DZ21
Mill La., Cars. 218 DF105
Mill La., Ch.St.G. 90 AU47
Mill La., Croy. 201 DM104
Mill La. (Eynsford), Dart. 208 FL102
Mill La., Dor. 263 CH135
Mill La., Egh. 193 BC98
Mill La., Epsom 217 CT109
Mill La., Ger.Cr. 113 AZ58
Mill La., Grays 169 FX78
Mill La., Guil. 258 AV142
Mill La. (Chilworth), Guil. 259 BF139
Dorking Rd.
Mill La., Harl. 36 EY11
Mill La., Horl. 268 DD148
Mill La., Kings L. 58 BN29
Mill La., Lthd. 231 CG122
Mill La. (Taplow), Maid. 130 AC72
Mill La. (Toot Hill), Ong. 71 FE29
Mill La. (Downe), Orp. 223 EN110
Mill La., Oxt. 254 EF132
Mill La. (The Chart), Oxt. 255 EM131
Mill La., Red. 251 DJ131
Mill La., Rick. 75 BQ44
Watford Rd.
Mill La. (Chadwell Heath), Rom. 126 EY58
Mill La. (Navestock), Rom. 87 FH38
Mill La., Sev. 257 FJ121
Mill La. (Shoreham), Sev. 225 FF110
Mill La., Slou. 153 BB83
Mill La., Wal.Cr. 67 DY28
Mill La., W.Byf. 212 BM113
Mill La., West. 255 EQ127
Mill La., Wind. 151 AN80
Mill La., Wok. 228 BK119
Mill La., Wdf.Grn. 102 EF50
Mill La. Clo., Brox. 49 DZ21
Mill La. Trd. Est., Croy. 201 DM104
Mill Mead, Stai. 173 BF91
Mill Mead Rd. N17 122 DV55
Mill Pk. Ave., Horn. 128 FL61
Mill Pl. E14 143 DZ72
East India Dock Rd.
Mill Pl., Chis. 205 EP95
Mill Pl., Dart. 167 FG84
Mill Pl., Kings.T. 198 CM97
Mill Pl., Slou. 152 AX82
Mill Pl. Caravan Pk., Slou. 152 AW82
Mill Plat, Islw. 157 CG82
Mill Plat Ave., Islw. 157 CG82
Mill Pond Clo., Sev. 257 FK121
Mill Pond Rd., Dart. 188 FL86
Mill Race, St.Alb. 42 BY15
Mill Race, Ware 33 ED11
Mill Ridge, Edg. 96 CM50
Mill Rd. E16 144 EH74
Mill Rd. SE13 163 EC83
Loampit Vale
Mill Rd. SW19 180 DC94
Mill Rd., Cob. 230 BW115
Mill Rd., Dart. 188 FM91
Mill Rd., Dor. 263 CJ144
Mill Rd., Epsom 217 CT112
Mill Rd., Erith 167 FC80
Mill Rd., Esher 196 CA103
Mill Rd., Grav. 190 GE87
Mill Rd., Hert. 32 DR09
Mill Rd., Ilf. 125 EN62
Mill Rd., Purf. 168 FP79
Mill Rd., Sev. 256 FE121
Mill Rd., S.Ock. 148 FQ73
Mill Rd., Tad. 233 CX123
Mill Rd., Twick. 176 CC89
Mill Rd., West Dr. 154 BJ76
Mill Row N1 142 DS67
Mill Shaw, Oxt. 254 EF132
Mill Shot Clo. SW6 159 CW80
Mill St. SE1 162 DT75
Mill St. W1 273 K10
Mill St. W1 141 DJ73
Mill St., Berk. 38 AW19
Mill St., Harl. 52 EY17
Mill St., Hem.H. 40 BK24
Mill St., Kings.T. 198 CL97
Mill St., Red. 266 DE135
Mill St., Slou. 132 AT74
Mill St. (Colnbrook), Slou. 153 BD80
Mill St., West. 255 ER127
Mill Vale, Brom. 204 EF96
Mill Vw., St.Alb. 61 CD27
Park St.
Mill Vw. Clo., Epsom 217 CT108
Mill Vw. Gdns., Croy. 203 DX104
Mill Way, Felt. 175 BV85
Mill Way, Lthd. 232 CM124
Mill Way, Rick. 91 BF46
Mill Way (Bushey), Wat. 76 BY40
Mill Yd. E1 142 DU73
Cable St.
Millacres, Ware 33 DX06
Station Rd.
Millais Ave. E12 125 EN64
Millais Gdns., Edg. 96 CN54
Millais Pl., Til. 171 GG80
Millais Rd. E11 123 EC63
Millais Rd., Enf. 82 DT43
Millais Rd., N.Mal. 198 CS100
Millais Way, Epsom 216 CQ105
Millan Clo., Add. 212 BH110
Milland Ct., Borwd. 78 CR39
Millard Clo. N16 122 DS64
Boleyn Rd.
Millard Ter., Dag. 146 FA65
Church Elm La.
Millbank SW1 277 P7
Millbank SW1 161 DL76
Millbank, Stai. 174 BH92
Millbank Twr. SW1 277 P9
Millbank Twr. SW1 161 DL77
Millbank Way SE12 184 EG85
Millbourne Rd., Felt. 176 BY91
Millbro, Swan. 187 FG94
Millbrook, Guil. 258 AX136
Millbrook, Wey. 213 BS105
Millbrook Ave., Well. 165 ER84
Millbrook Gdns., Rom. 105 FE54
Millbrook Gdns. (Chadwell Heath), Rom. 126 EZ58
Millbrook Pl. NW1 141 DJ68
Hampstead Rd.
Millbrook Rd. N9 100 DV46
Millbrook Rd. SW9 161 DP83
Millbrook Rd. (Bushey), Wat. 76 BZ39
Millbrook Way, Slou. 153 BE82
Millcrest Rd. (Cheshunt), Wal.Cr. 65 DP28
Millender Wk. SE16 162 DW77
Millennium Dr. E14 163 ED77
Millennium Mile SE1 278 B3
Millennium Mile SE1 141 DP73
Millennium Pl. E2 142 DV68
Millennium Sq. SE1 162 DT75
Tooley St.
Millennium Way SE10 164 EE75
Miller Clo., Mitch. 200 DF101
Miller Clo., Pnr. 94 BW54
Miller Pl., Ger.Cr. 112 AX57
Miller Rd. SW19 180 DD93
Miller Rd., Croy. 201 DM102
Miller Rd., Guil. 243 BC131
Miller St. NW1 141 DJ68
Miller Wk. SE1 278 E3
Miller Wk. SE1 141 DN74
Miller's Ave. E8 122 DT64
Millers Clo. NW7 97 CU49
Millers Clo., Chig. 104 EV46
Millers Clo., Rick. 73 BE41
Millers Clo., Stai. 174 BH92
Millers Copse, Epsom 232 CR119
Millers Copse, Red. 267 DP144
Millers Ct. W4 159 CT78
Chiswick Mall
Millers Ct., Hert. 32 DR10
Parliament Sq.
Millers Grn. Clo., Enf. 81 DP41
Miller's La., Chig. 104 EV46
Millers La., Red. 267 DP144
Millers La., Ware 33 EC11
Millers La., Wind. 172 AT86
Millers Meadow Clo. SE3 184 EF85
Meadowcourt Rd.
Millers Ri., St.Alb. 43 CE21
Miller's Ter. E8 122 DT64
Millers Way W6 159 CW75
Millersdale, Harl. 51 EP19
Millet Rd., Grnf. 136 CB69
Millfield, Berk. 38 AX18
Millfield, Sun. 195 BR95
Millfield, Welw.G.C. 30 DC08
Millfield Ave. E17 101 DY53
Millfield Dr., Grav. 190 GE89
Millfield La. N6 120 DF61
Millfield La., Tad. 249 CZ125
Millfield Pl. N6 120 DG61
Millfield Rd., Edg. 96 CQ54
Millfield Rd., Houns. 176 BY88
Millfield Wk., Hem.H. 40 BN22
Millfields, Chesh. 54 AQ33
Millfields Clo., Orp. 206 EV98
Millfields Est. E5 123 DX62
Denton Way
Millfields Rd. E5 122 DW63
Millford, Wok. 226 AV117
Millgrove St. SW11 160 DG82
Millharbour E14 163 EB76
Millhaven Clo., Rom. 126 EV58
Millhedge Clo., Cob. 230 BY116
Millhoo Ct., Wal.Abb. 68 EF34
Millhouse La., Abb.L. 59 BT27
Millhouse Pl. SE27 181 DP91
Millicent Rd. E10 123 DZ60
Milligan St. E14 143 DZ73
Milliners Ct., Loug. 85 EN40
The Cft.
Milling Rd., Edg. 96 CR52
Millington Rd., Hayes 155 BS76
Millman Ms. WC1 274 B5
Millman Ms. WC1 141 DM70
Millman Pl. WC1 141 DM70
Millman St.
Millman St. WC1 274 B5
Millman St. WC1 141 DM70
Millmark Gro. SE14 163 DY82
Millmarsh La., Enf. 83 DZ40
Millmead, Guil. 258 AW136
Millmead, W.Byf. 212 BM112
Millmead Ter., Guil. 258 AW136
Millpond Ct., Add. 212 BL106
Millpond Est. SE16 162 DV75
West La.
Mills Clo., Uxb. 134 BN68
Mills Ct. EC2 275 N3
Mills Gro. E14 143 EC71
Dewberry St.
Mills Gro. NW4 119 CX55
Mills Rd., Walt. 214 BW106
Mills Row W4 158 CR77
Mills Spur, Wind. 172 AV87
Mills Way, Brwd. 109 GC46
Millshot Dr., Amer. 55 AQ40
Millside, B.End 110 AC60
Millside, Cars. 200 DF103
Millside Ct., Iver 154 BH75
Millside Ind. Est., Dart. 168 FK84
Millside Pl., Islw. 157 CH82
Millsmead Way, Loug. 85 EM40
Millson Clo. N20 98 DD47
Millstead Clo., Tad. 233 CV122
Millstone Clo. (South Darenth), Dart. 208 FQ96
Millstone Ms., Dart. 208 FQ95
Millstream Clo. N13 99 DN50
Millstream Clo., Hert. 31 DP09
Millstream La., Slou. 131 AL74
Millstream Rd. SE1 279 P5
Millstream Rd. SE1 162 DT75
Millthorne Clo., Rick. 74 BM43
Millview Clo., Reig. 250 DD132
Millwall Dock Rd. E14 163 EA76
Millwards, Hat. 45 CV21
Millway NW7 96 CS50
Millway, Reig. 250 DD134
Millway Gdns., Nthlt. 136 BZ65
Millwell Cres., Chig. 103 ER50
Millwood Rd., Houns. 176 CC85
Millwood Rd., Orp. 206 EW97
Millwood St. W10 139 CY71
St. Charles Sq.
Milman Clo., Pnr. 116 BX55
Milman Rd. NW6 139 CY68
Milman's St. SW10 160 DD79
Milmead Ind. Cen. N17 100 DV54
Milne Feild, Pnr. 94 CA52
Milne Gdns. SE9 184 EL85
Milne Pk. E., Croy. 221 ED111
Milne Pk. W., Croy. 221 ED111
Milne Way (Harefield), Uxb. 92 BH53
Milner App., Cat. 236 DU121
Milner Clo., Cat. 236 DU121
Milner Clo., Wat. 59 BV34
Milner Ct. (Bushey), Wat. 76 CB44
Milner Dr., Cob. 214 BZ112
Milner Dr., Twick. 177 CD87
Milner Pl. N1 141 DN67
Milner Pl., Cars. 218 DG105
High St.
Milner Rd. E15 144 EE69
Milner Rd. SW19 200 DB95
Milner Rd., Cat. 236 DU122
Milner Rd., Dag. 126 EW61
Milner Rd., Kings.T. 197 CK97
Milner Rd., Mord. 200 DD99
Milner Rd., Slou. 130 AG71
Milner Rd., Th.Hth. 202 DR97
Milner Sq. N1 141 DP66
Milner St. SW3 276 D8
Milner St. SW3 160 DF77
Milner Wk. SE9 185 ER88
Milnthorpe Rd. W4 158 CR79
Milo Rd. SE22 182 DT86
Milroy Ave., Grav. 190 GE89
Milroy Wk. SE1 278 F2
Milson Rd. W14 159 CY76
Milstream Way, H.Wyc. 110 AD55
Milton Ave. E6 144 EK66
Milton Ave. N6 121 DJ59
Milton Ave. NW9 118 CQ55
Milton Ave. NW10 138 CQ67
Milton Ave., Barn. 79 CZ43
Milton Ave., Croy. 202 DR101
Milton Ave., Dor. 263 CD137
Milton Ave., Ger.Cr. 112 AX56
Milton Ave., Grav. 191 GJ88
Milton Ave., Horn. 127 FF61
Milton Ave., Sev. 225 FB110
Milton Ave., Sutt. 200 DD104
Milton Clo. N2 120 DC57
Milton Clo. SE1 279 P9
Milton Clo. SE1 162 DT77
Milton Clo., Hayes 135 BU72
Milton Clo., Slou. 153 BA83
Milton Clo., Sutt. 200 DD104
Milton Ct. EC2 275 K6
Milton Ct., Uxb. 115 BP62
Milton Ct., Wal.Abb. 67 EC34
Milton Ct. La., Dor. 263 CE136
Milton Ct. Rd. SE14 163 DY79
Milton Cres., Ilf. 125 EQ59
Milton Dene, Hem.H. 41 BP15
Milton Dr., Borwd. 78 CP43
Milton Dr., Shep. 194 BL98
Milton Flds., Ch.St.G. 90 AV48
Milton Gdn. Est. N16 122 DS63
Milton Gro.
Milton Gdns., Epsom 216 CS114
Milton Gdns., Stai. 174 BM88
Milton Gdns., Til. 171 GH81
Milton Gro. N11 99 DJ50
Milton Gro. N16 122 DR63
Milton Hall Rd., Grav. 191 GK88
Milton Hill, Ch.St.G. 90 AV48
Milton Flds.
Milton Lawns, Amer. 55 AR36
Milton Pk. N6 121 DJ59
Milton Pl. N7 121 DN64
George's Rd.
Milton Pl., Grav. 191 GJ86
Milton Rd. E17 123 EA56
Milton Rd. N6 121 DJ59
Milton Rd. N15 121 DP56
Milton Rd. NW7 97 CU50
Milton Rd. NW9 119 CU59
West Hendon Bdy.
Milton Rd. SE24 181 DP86
Milton Rd. SW14 158 CR83
Milton Rd. SW19 180 DC93
Milton Rd. W3 138 CR74
Milton Rd. W7 137 CF73
Milton Rd., Add. 212 BG107
Milton Rd., Belv. 166 FA77
Milton Rd., Brwd. 108 FW49
Milton Rd., Cat. 236 DR121
Milton Rd., Chesh. 54 AP29
Milton Rd., Croy. 202 DR102
Milton Rd., Egh. 173 AZ92
Milton Rd., Grav. 191 GH86
Milton Rd., Grays 170 GB78
Milton Rd., Hmptn. 176 CA94
Milton Rd., Har. 117 CE56
Milton Rd., Mitch. 180 DG94
Milton Rd., Rom. 127 FG58
Milton Rd., Sev. 256 FE121
Milton Rd., Slou. 131 AR70
Milton Rd., Sutt. 200 DA104
Milton Rd., Swans. 190 FY86
Milton Rd., Uxb. 115 BP63
Milton Rd., Wall. 219 DJ107
Milton Rd., Walt. 196 BX104
Milton Rd., Ware 33 DX05
Milton Rd., Well. 165 ET81
Milton St. EC2 275 K6
Milton St. EC2 142 DR71
Milton St., Dor. 263 CD137
Milton St., Swans. 189 FX86
Milton St., Wal.Abb. 67 EC34
Milton St., Wat. 75 BV38
Milton Way, Lthd. 246 CC125
Milton Way, West Dr. 154 BM77
Milverton Dr., Uxb. 115 BQ63
Milverton Gdns., Ilf. 125 ET61
Milverton Rd. NW6 139 CW66
Milverton St. SE11 161 DN78
Milverton Way SE9 185 EN91
Milward St. E1 142 DV71
Stepney Way
Milward Wk. SE18 165 EN79
Spearman St.
Milwards, Harl. 51 EP19
Mimas Rd., Hem.H. 40 BM17
Saturn Way
Mimms Hall Rd., Pot.B. 63 CX31
Mimms La., Pot.B. 62 CQ33
Mimms La., Rad. 62 CN33
Mimosa Clo., Brwd. 108 FV43
Mimosa Clo., Orp. 206 EW104
Berrylands
Mimosa Clo., Rom. 106 FJ52
Mimosa Rd., Hayes 136 BW71
Mimosa St. SW6 159 CZ81
Mimran Rd., Hert. 31 DP10
Mina Ave., Slou. 152 AX75
Mina Rd. SE17 162 DS78
Mina Rd. SW19 200 DA95
Minard Rd. SE6 184 EE87
Minchen Rd., Harl. 35 ET13
Minchenden Cres. N14 99 DJ48
Minchin Clo., Lthd. 231 CG122
Mincing La. EC3 275 M10
Mincing La. EC3 142 DS73
Mincing La., Wok. 210 AT108
Minden Rd. SE20 202 DV95
Minden Rd., Sutt. 199 CZ103
Minehead Rd. SW16 181 DM92
Minehead Rd., Har. 116 CA62
Minera Ms. SW1 276 G8
Minera Ms. SW1 160 DG77
Mineral St. SE18 165 ES77
Minerva Clo. SW9 161 DN80
Minerva Clo., Sid. 185 ES90
Minerva Dr., Wat. 75 BS36
Minerva Rd. E4 101 EB52
Minerva Rd. NW10 138 CQ69
Minerva Rd., Kings.T. 198 CM96
Minerva St. E2 142 DV68
Minerva Way, Beac. 89 AM54
Minet Ave. NW10 138 CS68
Minet Dr., Hayes 135 BU74
Minet Gdns. NW10 138 CS68
Minet Gdns., Hayes 135 BU74
Minet Rd. SW9 161 DP82
Minford Gdns. W14 159 CX75
Ming St. E14 143 EA73
Mingard Wk. N7 121 DM61
Hornsey Rd.
Minims, The, Hat. 45 CU17
Ministry Way SE9 185 EM89
Miniver Pl. EC4 142 DQ73
Garlick Hill
Mink Ct., Houns. 156 BW83
Minniecroft Rd., Slou. 130 AH69
Minniedale, Surb. 198 CM99
Minnow St. SE17 162 DS77
East St.
Minnow Wk. SE17 279 N9
Minorca Rd., Wey. 212 BN105
Minories EC3 275 P10
Minories EC3 142 DT72
Minshull Pl., Beck. 183 EA94
Minshull St. SW8 161 DK81
Wandsworth Rd.
Minson Rd. E9 143 DX67
Minstead Gdns. SW15 179 CT87
Minstead Way, N.Mal. 198 CS100
Minster Ave., Sutt. 200 DA103
Leafield Rd.
Minster Clo., Hat. 45 CU20
Minster Ct. EC3 142 DR73
Mincing La.
Minster Ct., Horn. 128 FN61
Minster Ct., St.Alb. 61 CE28
Minster Dr., Croy. 220 DS105
Minster Gdns., W.Mol. 196 BZ99
Molesey Ave.
Minster Pavement EC3 142 DR73
Mincing La.
Minster Rd. NW2 119 CY64
Minster Rd., Brom. 184 EH94
Minster Wk. N8 121 DL56
Lightfoot Rd.
Minster Way, Horn. 128 FM60
Minster Way, Slou. 153 AZ75
Minsterley Ave., Shep. 195 BS98
Minstrel Clo., Hem.H. 40 BH19
Minstrel Gdns., Surb. 198 CM98
Mint Clo., Uxb. 135 BP69
Mint Gdns., Dor. 263 CG135
Church St.
Mint Rd., Bans. 234 DC116
Mint Rd., Wall. 219 DH105
Mint St. SE1 279 H4
Mint Wk., Croy. 202 DQ104
High St.
Mint Wk., Warl. 237 DX117
Mint Wk., Wok. 226 AS117
Mintern Clo. N13 99 DP48
Mintern St. N1 142 DR68
Minterne Ave., Sthl. 156 CA77
Minterne Rd., Har. 118 CM57
Minterne Waye, Hayes 136 BW72
Minton La., Harl. 52 EW15
Minton Ms. NW6 140 DB65
Lymington Rd.
Minton Ri., Maid. 130 AH72
Mirabel Rd. SW6 159 CZ80
Mirador Cres., Slou. 132 AV73
Miramar Way, Horn. 128 FK64
Miranda Clo. E1 142 DW71
Sidney St.
Miranda Ct. W3 138 CM72
Queens Dr.
Miranda Rd. N19 121 DJ60
Mirfield St. SE7 164 EK77
Miriam Rd. SE18 165 ES78
Mirravale Trd. Est., Dag. 126 EZ59
Mirren Clo., Har. 116 BZ63
Mirrie La., Uxb. 113 BC57
Mirror Path SE9 184 EJ90
Lambscroft Ave.
Misbourne Ave., Ger.Cr. 90 AX50
Misbourne Clo., Ger.Cr. 90 AY50
Misbourne Ct., Slou. 153 BA77
High St.
Misbourne Rd., Uxb. 134 BN67
Misbourne Vale, Ger.Cr. 90 AX50
Miskin Rd., Dart. 188 FJ87
Miskin Way, Grav. 191 GK93
Missden Dr., Hem.H. 41 BQ22
Missenden Clo., Felt. 175 BT88
Missenden Gdns., Mord. 200 DC100
Missenden Gdns., Slou. 130 AH72
Missenden Rd., Chesh. 54 AL32
Mission Gro. E17 123 DY57
Mission Pl. SE15 162 DU81
Mission Sq., Brent. 158 CL79
Mistletoe Clo., Croy. 203 DX102
Marigold Way
Mistley Rd., Harl. 36 EU13
Misty's Fld., Walt. 196 BW102
Mitali Pas. E1 142 DU72
Back Ch. La.
Mitcham Gdn. Village, Mitch. 200 DG99
Mitcham Ind. Est., Mitch. 200 DG95
Mitcham La. SW16 181 DJ93
Mitcham Pk., Mitch. 200 DF98
Mitcham Rd. E6 144 EL69
Mitcham Rd. SW17 180 DF92
Mitcham Rd., Croy. 201 DL100
Mitcham Rd., Ilf. 125 ET59
Mitchell Ave., Grav. 190 GD89
Mitchell Clo. SE2 166 EW77
Mitchell Clo., Abb.L. 59 BU32
Mitchell Clo., Belv. 167 FC76
Mitchell Clo., Dart. 188 FL89
Mitchell Clo., Hem.H. 57 AZ27
Mitchell Clo., Rain. 148 FJ68
Mitchell Clo., St.Alb. 43 CD24
Mitchell Clo., Slou. 151 AN75
Mitchell Clo., Welw.G.C. 30 DC09
Mitchell Rd. N13 99 DP50
Mitchell Rd., Orp. 223 ET105
Mitchell St. EC1 275 H4
Mitchell St. EC1 142 DQ70
Mitchell Wk. E6 144 EL71
Mitchell Wk., Amer. 55 AS38
Mitchell Wk., Swans. 190 FY87
Mitchell Way NW10 138 CQ65
Mitchell Way, Brom. 204 EG95
Mitchellbrook Way NW10 138 CR65
Mitchells Clo., Guil. 258 AY140
Station Rd.
Mitchell's Pl. SE21 182 DS87
Dulwich Village
Mitchison Rd. N1 142 DR65
Mitchley Ave., Pur. 220 DQ113
Mitchley Ave., S.Croy. 220 DQ113
Mitchley Gro., S.Croy. 220 DU113
Mitchley Hill, S.Croy. 220 DT113
Mitchley Rd. N17 122 DU55
Mitchley Vw., S.Croy. 220 DU113
Mitford Clo., Chess. 215 CJ107
Merritt Gdns.
Mitford Rd. N19 121 DL61
Mitre, The E14 143 DZ73
Three Colt St.
Mitre Ave. E17 123 DZ55
Greenleaf Rd.
Mitre Clo., Brom. 204 EF96
Beckenham La.
Mitre Clo., Shep. 195 BR100
Gordon Dr.
Mitre Clo., Sutt. 218 DC108
Mitre Ct. EC2 275 J8
Mitre Ct. EC4 274 E9
Mitre Rd. E15 144 EE68
Mitre Rd. SE1 278 E4
Mitre Rd. SE1 161 DN75
Mitre Sq. EC3 275 N9
Mitre St. EC3 275 N9
Mitre St. EC3 142 DS72
Mitre Way W10 139 CV70
Mixbury Gro., Wey. 213 BR107
Mixnams La., Cher. 193 BF97

Mizen Clo., Cob. 214 BX114
Mizen Way, Cob. 230 BW115
Moat, The, N.Mal. 198 CS95
Moat, The, Ong. 71 FF29
Moat Clo., Orp. 223 ET107
Moat Clo., Sev. 256 FB123
Moat Clo. (Bushey), Wat. 76 CB43
Moat Ct., Ash. 232 CL117
Moat Cres. N3 120 DB55
Moat Cft., Well. 166 EW83
Moat Dr. E13 144 EJ68
Boundary Rd.
Moat Dr., Har. 116 CC56
Moat Dr., Ruis. 115 BS59
Moat Dr., Slou. 132 AW71
Moat Fm. Rd., Nthlt. 136 BZ65
Moat La., Erith 167 FG81
Moat Pl. SW9 161 DM83
Moat Pl. W3 138 CP72
Moat Pl. (Denham), Uxb. 114 BH63
Moatfield Rd. (Bushey), Wat. 76 CB43
Moats La., Red. 267 DN140
Moatside, Enf. 83 DX42
Moatside, Felt. 176 BW91
Moatview Ct. (Bushey), Wat. 76 CB43
Palmer Ave.
Moatwood Grn., Welw.G.C. 29 CY10
Moberley Rd. SW4 181 DK87
Modbury Gdns. NW5 140 DG65
Queens Cres.
Modder Pl. SW15 159 CX84
Model Cotts. SW14 158 CQ84
Upper Richmond Rd. W.
Model Fm. Clo. SE9 184 EL90
Modling Ho. E2 143 DX68
Moelwyn Hughes Ct. N7 121 DK64
Hilldrop Cres.
Moelyn Ms., Har. 117 CG57
Moffat Rd. N13 99 DL51
Moffat Rd. SW17 180 DE91
Moffat Rd., Th.Hth. 202 DQ96
Moffats Clo., Hat. 64 DA26
Moffats La., Hat. 63 CZ26
Mogador Cotts., Tad. 249 CX128
Mogador Rd.
Mogador Rd., Tad. 249 CY128
Mogden La., Islw. 177 CE85
Mohmmad Khan Rd. E11 124 EF60
Harvey Rd.
Moir Clo., S.Croy. 220 DU109
Moira Clo. N17 100 DS54
Moira Rd. SE9 165 EM84
Moland Mead SE16 163 DX78
Crane Mead
Molash Rd., Orp. 206 EX98
Molasses Row SW11 160 DC83
Cinnamon Row
Mole Abbey Gdns., W.Mol. 196 CA97
New Rd.
Mole Business Pk., Lthd. 231 CG121
Mole Ct., Epsom 216 CQ105
Mole Rd., Lthd. 231 CD121
Mole Rd., Walt. 214 BX106
Mole Valley Pl., Ash. 231 CK119
Molember Ct., E.Mol. 197 CE99
Molember Rd., E.Mol. 197 CD99
Moles Hill, Lthd. 215 CD111
Molescroft SE9 185 EQ90
Molesey Ave., W.Mol. 196 BZ99
Molesey Clo., Walt. 214 BX105
Molesey Dr., Sutt. 199 CY103
Molesey Pk. Ave., W.Mol. 196 CB99
Molesey Pk. Clo., E.Mol. 196 CC99
Molesey Pk. Rd., E.Mol. 196 CB99
Molesey Pk. Rd., W.Mol. 196 CB99
Molesey Rd., Walt. 196 BY101
Molesey Rd., W.Mol. 196 BY99
Molesford Rd. SW6 160 DA81
Molesham Clo., W.Mol. 196 CB97
Molesham Way, W.Mol. 196 CB97
Molesworth, Hodd. 33 EA13
Molesworth Rd., Cob. 213 BU113
Molesworth St. SE13 163 EC83
Molewood Rd., Hert. 31 DP08
Molineaux Pl., Tedd. 177 CG92
Mollands La., S.Ock. 149 FW70
Mollison Ave., Enf. 83 DY40
Mollison Dr., Wall. 219 DL107
Mollison Ri., Grav. 191 GL92
Mollison Way, Edg. 96 CN54
Molloy Ct., Wok. 227 BA116
Courtenay Rd.
Molly Huggins Clo. SW12 181 DJ87
Molteno Rd., Wat. 75 BU39
Molyneaux Ave., Hem.H. 57 AZ27
Molyneux Dr. SW17 181 DH91
Molyneux Rd., Gdmg. 258 AT144
Molyneux Rd., Wey. 212 BN106
Molyneux St. W1 272 C7
Molyneux St. W1 140 DE71
Momples Rd., Harl. 36 EV13
Mona Rd. SE15 162 DW82
Mona St. E16 144 EF71
Monahan Ave., Pur. 219 DM112
Monarch Clo., Felt. 175 BS87
Monarch Clo., Til. 171 GH82
Monarch Clo., W.Wick. 222 EF105
Monarch Dr. E16 144 EK71
Monarch Ms. E17 123 EB57
Monarch Ms. SW16 181 DN92
Monarch Pl., Buck.H. 102 EJ47
Monarch Rd., Belv. 166 FA76
Monarchs Way, Ruis. 115 BR60
Monarchs Way, Wal.Cr. 67 DY34
Monastery Gdns., Enf. 82 DR40
Monaveen Gdns., W.Mol. 196 CA97
Monck St. SW1 277 N7
Monck St. SW1 161 DK76
Monclar Rd. SE5 162 DR84
Moncorvo Clo. SW7 276 B5
Moncrieff Clo. E6 144 EL72
Linton Gdns.
Moncrieff Pl. SE15 162 DU82
Rye La.
Moncrieff St. SE15 162 DU82
Mondial Way, Hayes 155 BQ80
Monega Rd. E7 144 EJ65
Monega Rd. E12 144 EK65
Money Ave., Cat. 236 DR122
Money Hill Rd., Rick. 92 BJ46
Money Hole La., Welw.G.C. 30 DE08
Money La., West Dr. 154 BK76
Money Rd., Cat. 236 DR122
Moneyhill Par., Rick. 92 BH46
Uxbridge Rd.
Mongers La., Epsom 217 CT110
Monica Clo., Wat. 76 BW40
Monier Rd. E3 143 EA66
Monivea Rd., Beck. 183 DZ94
Monk Dr. E16 144 EG72
Monk Pas. E16 144 EG73
Monk Dr.
Monk St. SE18 165 EN77
Monkchester Clo., Loug. 85 EN39
Monkey Island La., Maid. 150 AE78
Monkfrith Ave. N14 81 DH44
Monkfrith Clo. N14 99 DH45
Monkfrith Way N14 98 DG45
Monkhams Ave., Wdf.Grn. 102 EG50
Monkhams Dr., Wdf.Grn. 102 EH49
Monkhams La., Buck.H. 102 EH48
Monkhams La., Wdf.Grn. 102 EG50
Monkleigh Rd., Mord. 199 CY97
Monks Ave., Barn. 80 DC44
Monks Ave., W.Mol. 196 BZ99
Monks Chase, Brwd. 109 GC50
Monks Clo. SE2 166 EX77
Monks Clo., Brox. 49 EA20
Monks Clo., Enf. 82 DQ40
Monks Clo., Har. 116 CB61
Monks Clo., Ruis. 116 BX63
Monks Clo., St.Alb. 43 CE22
Monks Cres., Add. 212 BH106
Monks Cres., Walt. 195 BV102
Monks Dr. W3 138 CN71
Monks Grn., Lthd. 230 CC121
Monks Horton Way, St.Alb. 43 CH19
Monks Orchard, Dart. 188 FJ89
Monks Orchard Rd., Beck. 203 EA102
Monks Pk., Wem. 138 CQ65
Monks Pk. Gdns., Wem. 138 CP65
Monks Pl., Cat. 236 DU122
Tillingdown Hill
Monks Ri., Welw.G.C. 29 CX05
Monks Rd., Bans. 234 DA116
Monks Rd., Enf. 82 DQ40
Monks Rd., Vir.W. 192 AX98
Monks Rd., Wind. 151 AK82
Monks Wk., Grav. 190 GA93
Monk's Wk., Reig. 250 DB134
Monks Way NW11 119 CZ56
Hurstwood Rd.
Monks Way, Beck. 203 EA99
Monks Way, Orp. 205 EQ102
Monks Way, Stai. 174 BK94
Monks Way, West Dr. 154 BL79
Harmondsworth La.
Monksbury, Harl. 52 EU18
Monksdene Gdns., Sutt. 200 DB104
Monksfield Way, Slou. 131 AN70
Monksgrove, Loug. 85 EN43
Monksmead, Borwd. 78 CQ42
Monkswell Ct. N10 98 DG53
Pembroke Rd.
Monkswell La., Couls. 234 DB124
Monkswick Rd., Harl. 35 ET13
Monkswood, Welw.G.C. 29 CW05
Monkswood Ave., Wal.Abb. 67 ED33
Monkswood Gdns., Borwd. 78 CR42
Monkswood Gdns., Ilf. 125 EN55
Monkton Rd., Well. 165 ET82
Monkton St. SE11 278 E8
Monkton St. SE11 161 DN77
Monkville Ave. NW11 119 CZ56
Monkwell Sq. EC2 275 J7
Monkwood Clo., Rom. 127 FG57
Monmouth Ave. E18 124 EH55
Monmouth Ave., Kings.T. 177 CJ94
Monmouth Clo. W4 158 CR76
Beaumont Rd.
Monmouth Clo., Mitch. 201 DL98
Recreation Way
Monmouth Clo., Well. 166 EU84
Monmouth Gro., Brent. 158 CL77
Sterling Pl.
Monmouth Pl. W2 140 DA72
Monmouth Rd.
Monmouth Rd. E6 145 EM69
Monmouth Rd. N9 100 DV47
Monmouth Rd. W2 140 DB72
Monmouth Rd., Dag. 126 EZ64
Monmouth Rd., Hayes 155 BS77
Monmouth Rd., Wat. 75 BV41
Monmouth St. WC2 273 P9
Monmouth St. WC2 141 DL73
Monnery Rd. N19 121 DJ62
Monnow Grn., S.Ock. 148 FQ73
Monnow Rd.
Monnow Rd. SE1 162 DU77
Monnow Rd., S.Ock. 148 FQ73
Mono La., Felt. 175 BV89
Monoux Gro. E17 101 EA53
Monro Dr., Guil. 242 AV131
Monro Gdns., Har. 95 CE52
Monroe Cres., Enf. 82 DV39
Monroe Dr. SW14 178 CP85
Mons Wk., Egh. 173 BC92
Mons Way, Brom. 204 EL100
Monsal Ct. E5 123 DX63
Redwald Rd.
Monsell Gdns., Stai. 173 BE92
Monsell Rd. N4 121 DP62
Monson Rd. NW10 139 CU68
Monson Rd. SE14 163 DX80
Monson Rd., Brox. 49 DZ20
Monson Rd., Red. 250 DF131
Montacute Rd. SE6 183 DZ87
Montacute Rd., Croy. 221 EC109
Montacute Rd., Mord. 200 DD100
Montacute Rd. (Bushey), Wat. 95 CE45
Montagu Cres. N18 100 DV49
Montagu Gdns. N18 100 DV49
Montagu Gdns., Wall. 219 DJ105
Montagu Mans. W1 272 E6
Montagu Ms. N. W1 272 E7
Montagu Ms. N. W1 140 DF71
Montagu Ms. S. W1 272 E8
Montagu Ms. W. W1 272 E8
Montagu Pl. W1 272 D7
Montagu Pl. W1 140 DF71
Montagu Rd. N9 100 DW48
Montagu Rd. N18 100 DV50
Montagu Rd. NW4 119 CU58
Montagu Rd. Ind. Est. N18 100 DW49
Montagu Row W1 272 E7
Montagu Sq. W1 272 E7
Montagu Sq. W1 140 DF71
Montagu St. W1 272 E8
Montagu St. W1 140 DF72
Montague Ave. SE4 163 DZ84
Montague Ave. W7 137 CF74
Montague Ave., S.Croy. 220 DS112
Montague Clo. SE1 279 K2
Montague Clo. SE1 142 DR74
Montague Clo., Walt. 195 BU101
Montague Dr., Cat. 236 DQ122
Drake Ave.
Montague Gdns. W3 138 CN73
Montague Hall Pl. (Bushey), Wat. 76 CA44
Montague Pl. WC1 273 N6
Montague Pl. WC1 141 DK71
Montague Rd. E8 122 DU64
Montague Rd. E11 124 EF61
Montague Rd. N8 121 DM57
Montague Rd. N15 122 DU56
Montague Rd. SW19 180 DB94
Montague Rd. W7 137 CF74
Montague Rd. W13 137 CH72
Montague Rd., Berk. 38 AV19
Montague Rd., Croy. 201 DP102
Montague Rd., Houns. 156 CB83
Montague Rd., Rich. 178 CL86
Montague Rd., Slou. 132 AT73
Montague Rd. (Datchet), Slou. 152 AV81
Montague Rd., Sthl. 156 BY77
Montague Rd., Uxb. 134 BK66
Montague Sq. SE15 162 DW80
Clifton Way
Montague St. EC1 275 H7
Montague St. EC1 142 DQ71
Montague St. WC1 273 P6
Montague St. WC1 141 DL71
Montague Waye, Sthl. 156 BY76
Montalt Rd., Wdf.Grn. 102 EF50
Montana Clo., S.Croy. 220 DR110
Montana Gdns. SE26 183 DZ91
Worsley Bri. Rd.
Montana Gdns., Sutt. 218 DC106
Lind Rd.
Montana Rd. SW17 180 DG91
Montana Rd. SW20 199 CW95
Montayne Rd. (Cheshunt), Wal.Cr. 67 DX32
Montbelle Rd. SE9 185 EP90
Montbretia Clo., Orp. 206 EW98
Montcalm Clo., Brom. 204 EG100
Montcalm Clo., Hayes 135 BV69
Ayles Rd.
Montcalm Rd. SE7 164 EK80
Montclare St. E2 275 P3
Monteagle Ave., Bark. 145 EQ65
Monteagle Way E5 122 DU62
Rendlesham Rd.
Monteagle Way SE15 162 DV83
Montefiore St. SW8 161 DH82
Montego Clo. SE24 161 DN84
Railton Rd.
Monteith Rd. E3 143 DZ67
Montem La., Slou. 131 AR74
Montem Rd. SE23 183 DZ87
Montem Rd., N.Mal. 198 CS98
Montem St. N4 121 DM60
Thorpedale Rd.
Montenotte Rd. N8 121 DJ57
Monterey Clo., Bex. 187 FC89
Montesole Ct., Pnr. 94 BW54
Montford Pl. SE11 161 DN78
Montford Rd., Sun. 195 BU98
Montfort Gdns., Ilf. 103 EQ51
Montfort Pl. SW19 179 CX88
Montfort Ri., Red. 266 DF142
Montgolfier Wk., Nthlt. 136 BY69
Jetstar Way
Montgomerie Clo., Berk. 38 AU17
Mortain Dr.
Montgomerie Dr., Guil. 242 AU129
Montgomery Ave., Esher 197 CE104
Montgomery Ave., Hem.H. 40 BN19
Montgomery Clo., Grays 170 GC75
Montgomery Clo., Mitch. 201 DL98
Montgomery Clo., Sid. 185 ET86
Montgomery Cres., Rom. 106 FJ50
Montgomery Dr. (Cheshunt), Wal.Cr. 67 DY28
Montgomery Rd. W4 158 CQ77
Montgomery Rd. (South Darenth), Dart. 209 FR95
Montgomery Rd., Edg. 96 CM51
Montgomery Rd., Wok. 226 AY118
Montholme Rd. SW11 180 DF86
Monthope Rd. E1 142 DU71
Casson St.
Montolieu Gdns. SW15 179 CV85
Montpelier Ave. W5 137 CJ71
Montpelier Ave., Bex. 186 EX87
Montpelier Clo., Uxb. 134 BN67
Montpelier Ct., Wind. 151 AQ82
St. Leonards Rd.
Montpelier Gdns. E6 144 EK69
Montpelier Gdns., Rom. 126 EW59
Montpelier Gro. NW5 121 DJ64
Montpelier Ms. SW7 276 C6
Montpelier Pl. E1 142 DW72
Montpelier Pl. SW7 276 C6
Montpelier Pl. SW7 160 DE76
Montpelier Ri. NW11 119 CY59
Montpelier Ri., Wem. 117 CK60
Montpelier Rd. N3 98 DC53
Montpelier Rd. SE15 162 DV81
Montpelier Rd. W5 137 CK71
Montpelier Rd., Pur. 219 DP110
Montpelier Rd., Sutt. 218 DC105
Montpelier Row SE3 164 EF82
Montpelier Row, Twick. 177 CH87
Montpelier Sq. SW7 276 C5
Montpelier Sq. SW7 160 DE75
Montpelier St. SW7 276 C5
Montpelier St. SW7 160 DE75
Montpelier Ter. SW7 276 C5
Montpelier Vale SE3 164 EF82
Montpelier Wk. SW7 276 C6
Montpelier Wk. SW7 160 DE76
Montpelier Way NW11 119 CY59
Montrave Rd. SE20 182 DW93
Montreal Pl. WC2 274 B10
Montreal Rd., Ilf. 125 EQ59
Montreal Rd., Sev. 256 FE123
Montreal Rd., Til. 171 GG82
Montrell Rd. SW2 181 DL88
Montrose Ave. NW6 139 CY68
Montrose Ave., Edg. 96 CQ54
Montrose Ave., Rom. 106 FJ54
Montrose Ave., Sid. 186 EU87
Montrose Ave., Slou. 131 AP72
Montrose Ave. (Datchet), Slou. 152 AW80
Montrose Ave., Twick. 176 CB87
Montrose Ave., Well. 165 ES83
Montrose Clo., Ashf. 175 BQ93
Montrose Clo., Well. 165 ET83
Montrose Clo., Wdf.Grn. 102 EG49
Montrose Ct. SW7 276 A5
Montrose Ct. SW7 160 DD75
Montrose Cres. N12 98 DC51
Montrose Cres., Wem. 138 CL65
Montrose Gdns., Lthd. 215 CD112
Montrose Gdns., Mitch. 200 DF97
Montrose Gdns., Sutt. 200 DB103
Montrose Pl. SW1 276 G5
Montrose Pl. SW1 160 DG75
Montrose Rd., Felt. 175 BR87
Montrose Rd., Har. 95 CE54
Montrose Wk., Wey. 195 BP104
Montrose Way SE23 183 DX88
Montrose Way, Slou. 152 AX81
Montrouge Cres., Epsom 233 CW116
Montserrat Ave., Wdf.Grn. 101 ED52
Montserrat Clo. SE19 182 DR92
Montserrat Rd. SW15 159 CY84
Monument Bri. Ind. Est., Wok. 227 BB115
Monument Gdns. SE13 183 EC85
Monument Grn., Wey. 213 BP105
Monument Hill, Wey. 213 BP105
Monument La., Ger.Cr. 90 AY51
Monument Rd., Wey. 213 BP105
Monument Rd., Wok. 211 BA114
Monument St. EC3 275 L10
Monument St. EC3 142 DR73
Monument Way N17 122 DT55
Monument Way E., Wok. 227 BB115
Monument Way W., Wok. 227 BA115
Monza St. E1 142 DW73
Moodkee St. SE16 162 DW76
Moody Rd. SE15 162 DT81
Moody St. E1 143 DX69
Moon La., Barn. 79 CZ41
Moon St. N1 141 DP67
Moor End, Maid. 150 AC78
Moor End Rd., Hem.H. 40 BJ21
Moor Furlong, Slou. 131 AL74
Moor Hall Rd., Harl. 36 EZ11
Moor La. EC2 275 K7
Moor La. EC2 142 DR71
Moor La., Chess. 216 CL105
Moor La., Rick. 92 BM47
Moor La. (Sarratt), Rick. 73 BE36
Moor La., Stai. 173 BD89
Moor La., Upmin. 129 FS60
Moor La., West Dr. 154 BJ79
Moor La., Wok. 226 AY122
Moor La. Crossing, Wat. 93 BQ46
Moor Mead Rd., Twick. 177 CG86
Moor Mill La., St.Alb. 61 CE29
Moor Pk. Est., Nthwd. 93 BQ49
Moor Pk. Gdns., Kings.T. 178 CS94
Moor Pk. Ind. Est., Wat. 93 BQ45
Moor Pk. Mansion, Rick. 92 BN48
Moor Pk. Rd., Nthwd. 93 BR50
Moor Pl. EC2 275 K7
Moor Rd., Chesh. 54 AQ32
Moor Rd., The, Sev. 241 FH120
Moor St. W1 273 N9
Moor Twr., Harl. 51 ET16
Moor Vw., Wat. 93 BU45
Moorcroft Gdns., Brom. 204 EL99
Southborough Rd.
Moorcroft La., Uxb. 134 BN71
Moorcroft Rd. SW16 181 DL90
Moorcroft Way, Pnr. 116 BY57
Moordown SE18 165 EN81
Moore Ave., Grays 170 FY78
Moore Ave., Til. 171 GH82
Moore Clo. SW14 158 CQ83
Little St. Leonards
Moore Clo., Add. 212 BH106
Moore Clo., Mitch. 201 DH96
Moore Clo., Slou. 151 AP75
Moore Clo., Wall. 219 DL109
Brabazon Ave.
Moore Cres., Dag. 146 EV67
Moore Gro. Cres., Egh. 172 AY94
Moore Pk. Rd. SW6 160 DB80
Moore Rd. SE19 182 DQ93
Moore Rd., Berk. 38 AT17
Moore Rd., Swans. 190 FY86
Moore St. SW3 276 D8
Moore St. SW3 160 DF77
Moore Wk. E7 124 EG63
Stracey Rd.
Moore Way SE22 182 DU88
Lordship La.
Moore Way, Sutt. 218 DA109
Moorefield Rd. N17 100 DT54
Moorehead Way SE3 164 EH83
Mooreland Rd., Brom. 184 EF94
Moorend, Welw.G.C. 30 DA12
Moores La. (Eton Wick), Wind. 151 AM77
Moores Pl., Brwd. 108 FX47
Moores Rd., Dor. 263 CH135
Moorey Clo. E15 144 EF67
Stephen's Rd.
Moorfield, Dor. 263 CK144
Moorfield, Harl. 51 EQ20
Moorfield Ave. W5 137 CK70
Moorfield Rd., Chess. 216 CL106
Moorfield Rd., Enf. 82 DW39
Moorfield Rd., Guil. 242 AX130
Moorfield Rd., Orp. 206 EU101
Moorfield Rd., Uxb. 134 BK72
Moorfield Rd. (Harefield), Uxb. 114 BG59
Moorfields EC2 275 K7
Moorfields EC2 142 DR71
Moorfields Clo., Stai. 193 BE95
Moorfields Highwalk EC2 142 DR71
Fore St.
Moorgate EC2 275 K8
Moorgate EC2 142 DR72
Moorgate Pl. EC2 275 K8
Moorhall Rd. (Harefield), Uxb. 114 BH58
Moorhayes Dr., Stai. 194 BJ97
Moorhen Clo., Erith 167 FH80
Moorholme, Wok. 226 AY119
Oak Bank
Moorhouse Rd. W2 140 DA72
Moorhouse Rd., Har. 117 CK55
Moorhouse Rd., Oxt. 255 EM131
Moorhurst Ave. (Cheshunt), Wal.Cr. 65 DN29
Moorings SE28 146 EV73
Moorland Clo., Rom. 105 FB53
Moorland Clo., Twick. 176 CA87
Telford Rd.
Moorland Rd. SW9 161 DP84
Moorland Rd., Hem.H. 40 BG22
Moorland Rd., West Dr. 154 BJ79
Moorlands, St.Alb. 61 CE28
Frogmore
Moorlands, Welw.G.C. 30 DA12
Moorlands, The, Wok. 227 AZ121
Moorlands Ave. NW7 97 CV51
Moorlands Est. SW9 161 DN84
Moorlands Reach, Saw. 36 EZ06
Moormead Dr., Epsom 216 CS106
Moormede Cres., Stai. 173 BF91
Moors, The, Welw.G.C. 30 DA08
Moors Wk., Welw.G.C. 30 DB08
Moorside, Hem.H. 40 BH23
Stratford Way
Moorside, H.Wyc. 110 AE55
Moorside, Welw.G.C. 30 DA12
Moorside Rd., Brom. 184 EE90
Moorsom Way, Couls. 235 DK117
Moortown Rd., Wat. 94 BW49
Moot Ct. NW9 118 CN57
Mora Rd. NW2 119 CW63
Mora St. EC1 275 J3
Mora St. EC1 142 DQ69
Moran Clo., St.Alb. 60 BZ31
Morant Gdns., Rom. 105 FB50
Morant Pl. N22 99 DM53
Commerce Rd.
Morant Rd., Grays 171 GH76
Morant St. E14 143 EA73
Morants Ct. Rd., Sev. 241 FC118
Morat St. SW9 161 DM81
Moravian Pl. SW10 160 DD79
Milman's St.
Moravian St. E2 142 DW69
Moray Ave., Hayes 135 BT74
Moray Clo., Edg. 96 CP47
Pentland Ave.
Moray Clo., Rom. 105 FE52
Moray Dr., Slou. 132 AU72
Moray Ms. N7 121 DM61
Durham Rd.
Moray Rd. N4 121 DM61
Moray Way, Rom. 105 FD52
Morcote Clo., Guil. 258 AY141
Mordaunt Gdns., Dag. 146 EY66
Mordaunt Ho. NW10 138 CR67
Mordaunt Rd. NW10 138 CR67
Mordaunt St. SW9 161 DM83
Morden Clo. SE13 163 EC82
Morden Clo., Tad. 233 CX120
Marbles Way
Morden Ct., Mord. 200 DB98
Morden Gdns., Grnf. 117 CF64
Morden Gdns., Mitch. 200 DD98
Morden Hall Rd., Mord. 200 DB97
Morden Hill SE13 163 EC82
Morden La. SE13 163 EC81
Morden Rd. SE3 164 EG82
Morden Rd. SW19 200 DB95
Morden Rd., Mitch. 200 DC98
Morden Rd., Rom. 126 EY59
Morden Rd. Ms. SE3 164 EG82
Morden St. SE13 163 EB81
Morden Way, Sutt. 200 DA101
Morden Wf. Rd. SE10 164 EE76
Mordon Rd., Ilf. 125 ET59
Mordred Rd. SE6 184 EE89
More Circle, Gdmg. 258 AS144
More Clo. E16 144 EF72
More Clo. W14 159 CY77
More Clo., Pur. 219 DN111
More La., Esher 196 CB103
More Rd., Gdmg. 258 AS144
Moreau Wk., Slou. 132 AY72
Alan Way
Morecambe Clo. E1 143 DX71
Morecambe Clo., Horn. 127 FH64
Morecambe Gdns., Stan. 95 CK49
Morecambe St. SE17 279 J9
Morecambe St. SE17 162 DQ77
Morecambe Ter. N18 100 DR49
Morecoombe Clo., Kings.T. 178 CP94
Moree Way N18 100 DU49
Morel Ct., Sev. 257 FH122
Moreland Ave., Grays 170 GC75
Moreland Ave., Slou. 153 BC80
Moreland Clo., Slou. 153 BC80
Moreland Ave.
Moreland Dr., Ger.Cr. 113 AZ58
Moreland St. EC1 274 G2
Moreland St. EC1 141 DP69
Moreland Way E4 101 EB48
Morell Clo., Barn. 80 DC41
Galdana Ave.
Morella Clo., Vir.W. 192 AX98
Morella Rd. SW12 180 DF87
Morello Ave., Uxb. 135 BP71
Morello Clo., Swan. 207 FD98
Morello Dr., Slou. 133 AZ74
Moremead, Wal.Abb. 67 ED33
Moremead Rd. SE6 183 DZ91
Morena St. SE6 183 EB87
Moresby Ave., Surb. 198 CP101
Moresby Rd. E5 122 DV60
Moresby Wk. SW8 161 DJ82
Moretaine Rd., Ashf. 174 BK90
Hengrove Cres.
Moreton Ave., Islw. 157 CE81
Moreton Clo. E5 122 DW61
Moreton Clo. N15 122 DR58
Moreton Clo. NW7 97 CW51
Moreton Clo., Swan. 207 FE96
Bonney Way
Moreton Clo. (Cheshunt), Wal.Cr. 66 DV27
Moreton Gdns., Wdf.Grn. 102 EL50
Moreton Ind. Est., Swan. 207 FG98
Moreton Pl. SW1 277 L10
Moreton Pl. SW1 161 DJ78
Moreton Rd. N15 122 DR58
Moreton Rd., Ong. 53 FG24
Moreton Rd., S.Croy. 220 DR106
Moreton Rd., Wor.Pk. 199 CU103
Moreton St. SW1 277 L10
Moreton St. SW1 161 DK78
Moreton Ter. SW1 277 L10

Moreton Ter. SW1 161 DJ78
Moreton Ter. Ms. N. SW1 277 L10
Moreton Ter. Ms. S. SW1 277 L10
Moreton Twr. W3 138 CP74
Moreton Way, Slou. 131 AK74
Morewood Clo., Sev. 256 FF123
Morewood Clo. Ind. Pk., Sev. 256 FF123
Morewood Clo.
Morford Clo., Ruis. 115 BV59
Morford Way, Ruis. 115 BV59
Morgan Ave. E17 123 ED56
Morgan Clo., Dag. 146 FA66
Morgan Clo., Nthwd. 93 BT51
Morgan Cres., Epp. 85 ER36
Morgan Dr., Green. 189 FS87
Morgan Gdns., Wat. 76 CB38
Morgan Rd. N7 121 DN64
Morgan Rd. W10 139 CZ71
Morgan Rd., Brom. 184 EG94
Morgan St. E3 143 DY69
Morgan St. E16 144 EF71
Morgan Way, Rain. 148 FJ69
Morgan Way, Wdf.Grn. 102 EL51
Morgans Clo., Hert. 32 DR11
Morgans La. SE1 279 M3
Morgans La. SE1 142 DS74
Morgans La., Hayes 135 BR71
Morgans Rd., Hert. 32 DR11
Moriatry Clo. N7 121 DL63
Morice Rd., Hodd. 49 DZ15
Morie St. SW18 180 DB85
Morieux Rd. E10 123 DZ60
Moring Rd. SW17 180 DG91
Morkyns Wk. SE21 182 DS90
Morland Ave., Croy. 202 DS102
Morland Ave., Dart. 187 FH85
Morland Clo. NW11 120 DB60
Morland Clo., Hmptn. 176 BZ92
Morland Clo., Mitch. 200 DE97
Morland Gdns. NW10 138 CR66
Morland Gdns., Sthl. 136 CB74
Morland Ms. N1 141 DN66
Lofting Rd.
Morland Rd. E17 123 DX57
Morland Rd. SE20 183 DX93
Morland Rd., Croy. 202 DS102
Morland Rd., Dag. 146 FA66
Morland Rd., Har. 118 CL57
Morland Rd., Ilf. 125 EP61
Morland Rd., Sutt. 218 DC106
Morland Way (Cheshunt), Wal.Cr. 67 DY28
Morley Ave. E4 101 ED52
Morley Ave. N18 100 DU49
Morley Ave. N22 99 DN54
Morley Clo., Orp. 205 EP103
Morley Clo., Slou. 153 AZ75
Morley Cres., Edg. 96 CQ47
Morley Cres., Ruis. 116 BW61
Morley Cres. E., Stan. 95 CJ54
Morley Cres. W., Stan. 95 CJ54
Morley Gro., Harl. 35 EQ13
Morley Hill, Enf. 82 DR38
Morley Rd. E10 123 EC60
Morley Rd. E15 144 EF68
Morley Rd. SE13 163 EC84
Morley Rd., Bark. 145 ER67
Morley Rd., Chis. 205 EQ95
Morley Rd., Rom. 126 EY57
Morley Rd., S.Croy. 220 DT110
Morley Rd., Sutt. 199 CZ102
Morley Rd., Twick. 177 CK86
Morley Sq., Grays 171 GG77
Morley St. SE1 278 E6
Morley St. SE1 161 DN75
Morna Rd. SE5 162 DQ82
Morning La. E9 142 DW65
Morning Ri., Rick. 74 BK41
Morningside Rd., Wor.Pk. 199 CV103
Mornington Ave. W14 159 CZ77
Mornington Ave., Brom. 204 EJ97
Mornington Ave., Ilf. 125 EN59
Mornington Clo., West. 238 EK117
Mornington Clo., Wdf.Grn. 102 EG49
Mornington Ct., Bex. 187 FC88
Mornington Cres. NW1 141 DJ68
Mornington Cres., Houns. 155 BV81
Mornington Gro. E3 143 EA69
Mornington Ms. SE5 162 DQ81
Mornington Pl. NW1 141 DH68
Mornington Ter.
Mornington Rd. E4 101 ED45
Mornington Rd. E11 124 EF60
Mornington Rd. SE8 163 DZ80
Mornington Rd., Ashf. 175 BQ92
Mornington Rd., Grnf. 136 CB71
Mornington Rd., Loug. 85 EQ41
Mornington Rd., Rad. 61 CG34
Mornington Rd., Wdf.Grn. 102 EF49
Mornington St. NW1 141 DH68
Mornington Ter. NW1 141 DH67
Mornington Wk., Rich. 177 CJ91
Morningtons, Harl. 51 EQ19
Morocco St. SE1 279 M5
Morocco St. SE1 162 DS75
Morpeth Ave., Borwd. 78 CM38
Morpeth Clo., Hem.H. 40 BL21
York Way
Morpeth Gro. E9 143 DX67
Morpeth Rd. E9 142 DW67
Morpeth St. E2 143 DX69
Morpeth Ter. SW1 277 K7
Morpeth Ter. SW1 161 DJ76
Morpeth Wk. N17 100 DV52
West Rd.
Morrab Gdns., Ilf. 125 ET62
Morrell Ct., Welw.G.C. 29 CZ08
Morrice Clo., Slou. 153 BA77
Morris Ave. E12 125 EM64
Morris Clo., Croy. 203 DY100
Morris Clo., Ger.Cr. 91 AZ53
Morris Clo., Orp. 205 ES104
Morris Ct. E4 101 EB48
Flaxen Rd.
Morris Ct., Wal.Abb. 68 EF34
Morris Gdns. SW18 180 DA87
Morris Gdns., Dart. 188 FN85
Morris Pl. N4 121 DN61
Morris Rd. E14 143 EB71
Morris Rd. E15 124 EE63
Morris Rd., Dag. 126 EZ61
Morris Rd., Islw. 157 CF83
Morris Rd., Red. 267 DL136
Morris Rd., Rom. 105 FH52
Morris St. E1 142 DV72
Morris Way, St.Alb. 62 CL26
Morrish Rd. SW2 181 DL87
Morrison Ave. N17 122 DS55
Morrison Rd., Bark. 146 EY68
Morrison Rd., Hayes 135 BV69
Morrison St. SW11 160 DG83
Morriston Clo., Wat. 94 BW50
Morse Clo. E13 144 EG69
Morse Clo. (Harefield), Uxb. 92 BJ54
Morshead Rd. W9 140 DA69
Morson Rd., Enf. 83 DY44
Morston Clo., Tad. 233 CV120
Waterfield
Morston Gdns. SE9 185 EM91
Mortain Dr., Berk. 38 AT17
Morten Clo. SW4 181 DK86
Morten Gdns. (Denham), Uxb. 114 BG59
Mortens Wd., Amer. 55 AS40
Morteyne Rd. N17 100 DR53
Mortgramit Sq. SE18 165 EN76
Powis St.
Mortham St. E15 144 EE67
Mortimer Clo. NW2 119 CZ62
Mortimer Clo. SW16 181 DK89
Mortimer Clo. (Bushey), Wat. 76 CB44
Mortimer Cres. NW6 140 DB67
Mortimer Cres., Wor.Pk. 198 CR104
Mortimer Dr., Enf. 82 DS43
Mortimer Est. NW6 140 DB67
Mortimer Gate, Wal.Cr. 67 DZ27
Mortimer Mkt. WC1 273 L5
Mortimer Pl. NW6 140 DB67
Mortimer Rd. E6 145 EM69
Mortimer Rd. N1 142 DS66
Mortimer Rd. NW10 139 CW69
Mortimer Rd. W13 137 CJ72
Mortimer Rd., Erith 167 FD79
Mortimer Rd., Mitch. 200 DF95
Mortimer Rd., Orp. 206 EU102
Mortimer Rd., Slou. 152 AX76
Mortimer Rd., West. 222 EJ112
Mortimer Sq. W11 139 CX73
St. Anns Rd.
Mortimer St. W1 273 K7
Mortimer St. W1 141 DJ72
Mortimer Ter. NW5 121 DH63
Gordon Ho. Rd.
Mortlake Clo., Croy. 201 DL104
Richmond Rd.
Mortlake Dr., Mitch. 200 DE95
Mortlake High St. SW14 158 CR83
Mortlake Rd. E16 144 EH72
Mortlake Rd., Ilf. 125 EQ63
Mortlake Rd., Rich. 158 CN80
Mortlake Ter., Rich. 158 CN80
Kew Rd.
Mortlock Clo. SE15 162 DV81
Cossall Wk.
Morton, Tad. 233 CX121
Morton Clo., Wok. 226 AX115
Morton Cres. N14 99 DK49
Morton Dr., Slou. 111 AL64
Morton Gdns., Wall. 219 DJ106
Morton Ms. SW5 160 DB77
Earls Ct. Gdns.
Morton Pl. SE1 278 D7
Morton Rd. E15 144 EF66
Morton Rd. N1 142 DQ66
Morton Rd., Mord. 200 DD99
Morton Rd., Wok. 226 AX115
Morton Way N14 99 DJ48
Morval Rd. SW2 181 DN85
Morvale Clo., Belv. 166 EZ77
Morven Clo., Pot.B. 64 DC31
Morven Rd. SW17 180 DF90
Morville St. E3 143 EA68
Morwell St. WC1 273 N7
Mosbach Gdns., Brwd. 109 GB47
Moscow Pl. W2 140 DB73
Moscow Rd.
Moscow Rd. W2 140 DA73
Moselle Ave. N22 99 DN54
Moselle Clo. N8 121 DM55
Miles Rd.
Moselle Ho. N17 100 DT52
William St.
Moselle Pl. N17 100 DT52
High Rd.
Moselle Rd., West. 238 EL118
Moselle St. N17 100 DT52
Mosford Clo., Horl. 268 DF146
Mospey Cres., Epsom 233 CT115
Moss Bank, Grays 170 FZ78
Moss Clo. E1 142 DU71
Old Montague St.
Moss Clo., Pnr. 94 BZ54
Moss Clo., Rick. 92 BK47
Moss Gdns., Felt. 175 BU89
Rose Gdns.
Moss Gdns., S.Croy. 221 DX108
Warren Ave.
Moss Grn., Welw.G.C. 29 CY11
Moss Hall Cres. N12 98 DB51
Moss Hall Gro. N12 98 DB51
Moss La., Pnr. 116 BZ55
Moss La., Rom. 127 FF58
Wheatsheaf Rd.
Moss Rd., Dag. 146 FA66
Moss Rd., S.Ock. 149 FW71
Moss Rd., Wat. 59 BV34
Moss Side, St.Alb. 60 BZ30
Moss Way, Beac. 88 AJ50
Mossborough Clo. N12 98 DB51
Mossbury Rd. SW11 160 DE83
Mossdown Clo., Belv. 166 FA77
Mossendew Clo. (Harefield), Uxb. 92 BK53
Mossfield, Cob. 213 BU113
Mossford Ct., Ilf. 125 EP55
Mossford Grn., Ilf. 125 EP55
Mossford La., Ilf. 103 EP54
Mossford St. E3 143 DZ70
Mossington Gdns. SE16 162 DW77
Abbeyfield Rd.
Mosslea Rd. SE20 182 DW93
Mosslea Rd., Brom. 204 EK99
Mosslea Rd., Orp. 205 EQ104
Mosslea Rd., Whyt. 236 DT116
Mossop St. SW3 276 C8
Mossop St. SW3 160 DE77
Mossville Gdns., Mord. 199 CZ97
Moston Clo., Hayes 155 BT78
Fuller Way
Mostyn Ave., Wem. 118 CM64
Mostyn Gdns. NW10 139 CX68
Mostyn Gro. E3 143 DZ68
Mostyn Rd. SW9 161 DN81
Mostyn Rd. SW19 199 CZ95
Mostyn Rd., Edg. 96 CR52
Mostyn Rd. (Bushey), Wat. 76 CC43
Mostyn Ter., Red. 266 DG135
Mosul Way, Brom. 204 EL100
Mosyer Dr., Orp. 206 EX103
Motcomb St. SW1 276 F6
Motcomb St. SW1 160 DG76
Mothers' Sq. E5 122 DV63
Motherwell Way, Grays 169 FU78
Motley Ave. EC2 142 DS70
Scrutton St.
Motley St. SW8 161 DJ82
St. Rule St.
Motspur Pk., N.Mal. 199 CT100
Mott St. E4 83 ED38
Mott St., Loug. 84 EF39
Mottingham Gdns. SE9 184 EK88
Mottingham La. SE9 184 EJ88
Mottingham La. SE12 184 EJ88
Mottingham Rd. N9 83 DX44
Mottingham Rd. SE9 184 EL89
Mottisfont Rd. SE2 166 EU76
Motts Hill La., Tad. 233 CU123
Mouchotte Clo., West. 222 EH112
Moulins Rd. E9 142 DW67
Moultain Hill, Swan. 207 FG98
Moulton Ave., Houns. 156 BY82
Moultrie Way, Upmin. 129 FS59
Mound, The SE9 185 EN90
Moundfield Rd. N16 122 DU58
Mount, The N20 98 DC47
Mount, The NW3 120 DC63
Heath St.
Mount, The W3 138 CQ74
High St.
Mount, The, Brwd. 108 FW48
Mount, The, Couls. 234 DG115
Mount, The (Ewell), Epsom 217 CT110
Mount, The, Esher 214 CA107
Mount, The, Guil. 258 AV137
Mount, The, Lthd. 231 CE123
Mount, The, N.Mal. 199 CT97
Mount, The, Pot.B. 64 DB30
Mount, The, Rick. 74 BJ44
Mount, The, Rom. 106 FJ48
Mount, The, Tad. 249 CZ126
Mount, The, Vir.W. 192 AX100
Mount, The (Cheshunt), Wal.Cr. 66 DR26
Mount, The, Warl. 236 DU119
Mount, The, Wem. 118 CP61
Mount, The, Wey. 195 BS103
Mount, The, Wok. 226 AX118
Mount, The (St. John's), Wok. 226 AU119
Mount, The, Wor.Pk. 217 CV105
Mount Adon Pk. SE22 182 DU87
Mount Angelus Rd. SW15 179 CT87
Mount Ararat Rd., Rich. 178 CL85
Mount Ash Rd. SE26 182 DV90
Mount Ave. E4 101 EA48
Mount Ave. W5 137 CK71
Mount Ave., Brwd. 109 GA44
Mount Ave., Cat. 236 DQ124
Mount Ave., Rom. 106 FQ51
Mount Ave., Sthl. 136 CA72
Mount Clo. W5 137 CJ71
Mount Clo., Barn. 80 DG42
Mount Clo., Brom. 204 EL95
Mount Clo., Cars. 218 DG109
Mount Clo., Hem.H. 39 BF20
Mount Clo., Ken. 236 DR116
Mount Clo., Lthd. 231 CE123
Mount Clo., Sev. 256 FF123
Mount Clo., Slou. 111 AQ63
Mount Clo., Wok. 226 AV121
Mount Clo., The, Vir.W. 192 AX100
Mount Cor., Felt. 176 BX89
Mount Ct. SW15 159 CY83
Weimar St.
Mount Ct., W.Wick. 204 EE103
Mount Cres., Brwd. 108 FX49
Mount Culver Ave., Sid. 186 EX93
Mount Dr., Bexh. 186 EY85
Mount Dr., Har. 116 BZ57
Mount Dr., St.Alb. 61 CD25
Mount Dr., Wem. 118 CQ61
Mount Dr., The, Reig. 250 DC132
Mount Echo Ave. E4 101 EB47
Mount Echo Dr. E4 101 EB46
Mount Ephraim La. SW16 181 DK90
Mount Ephraim Rd. SW16 181 DK90
Mount Est., The E5 122 DV61
Mount Pleasant La.
Mount Felix, Walt. 195 BT102
Mount Gdns. SE26 182 DV90
Mount Grace Rd., Pot.B. 64 DA31
Mount Gro., Edg. 96 CQ48
Mount Harry Rd., Sev. 256 FG123
Mount Hermon Clo., Wok. 226 AX119
Mount Hermon Rd., Wok. 226 AX119
Mount Hill La., Ger.Cr. 112 AV60
Mount La., Uxb. 113 BD61
Mount Lee, Egh. 173 AZ92
Mount Ms., Hmptn. 196 CB95
Mount Mills EC1 274 G3
Mount Nod Rd. SW16 181 DM90
Mount Nugent, Chesh. 54 AN27
Mount Pk., Cars. 218 DG109
Mount Pk. Ave., Har. 117 CD61
Mount Pk. Ave., S.Croy. 219 DP109
Mount Pk. Cres. W5 137 CK72
Mount Pk. Rd. W5 137 CK71
Mount Pk. Rd., Har. 117 CD62
Mount Pk. Rd., Pnr. 115 BU57
Mount Pl. W3 138 CP74
High St.
Mount Pl., Guil. 258 AW136
The Mt.
Mount Pleasant SE27 182 DQ91
Mount Pleasant WC1 274 C5
Mount Pleasant WC1 141 DN70
Mount Pleasant, Barn. 80 DE42
Mount Pleasant, Epsom 217 CT110
Mount Pleasant, Guil. 258 AW136
Mount Pleasant, Hert. 32 DW11
Mount Pleasant (Effingham), Lthd. 246 BY128
Mount Pleasant (West Horsley), Lthd. 245 BP129
Mount Pleasant, Ruis. 116 BW61
Mount Pleasant, St.Alb. 42 CB19
Mount Pleasant (Harefield), Uxb. 92 BG53
Mount Pleasant, Wem. 138 CL67
Mount Pleasant, West. 238 EK117
Mount Pleasant, Wey. 194 BN104
Mount Pleasant Ave., Brwd. 109 GE44
Mount Pleasant Clo., Hat. 45 CW15
Mount Pleasant Cres. N4 121 DM59
Mount Pleasant Hill E5 122 DW61
Mount Pleasant La. E5 122 DV61
Mount Pleasant La., Hat. 29 CW14
Mount Pleasant La., St.Alb. 60 BY30
Mount Pleasant Pl. SE18 165 ER77
Orchard Rd.
Mount Pleasant Rd. E17 101 DY54
Mount Pleasant Rd. N17 100 DS54
Mount Pleasant Rd. NW10 139 CW66
Mount Pleasant Rd. SE13 183 EB86
Mount Pleasant Rd. W5 137 CJ70
Mount Pleasant Rd., Cat. 236 DU123
Mount Pleasant Rd., Chig. 103 ER49
Mount Pleasant Rd., Dart. 188 FM86
Mount Pleasant Rd., N.Mal. 198 CQ97
Mount Pleasant Rd., Rom. 105 FD51
Mount Pleasant Vil. N4 121 DM59
Mount Pleasant Wk., Bex. 187 FC85
Mount Ri., Red. 266 DD136
Mount Rd. NW2 119 CV62
Mount Rd. NW4 119 CU58
Mount Rd. SE19 182 DR93
Mount Rd. SW19 180 DA89
Mount Rd., Barn. 80 DE43
Mount Rd., Bexh. 186 EX85
Mount Rd., Chess. 216 CM106
Mount Rd., Dag. 126 EZ60
Mount Rd., Dart. 187 FF86
Mount Rd., Epp. 70 EW32
Mount Rd., Felt. 176 BY90
Mount Rd., Hayes 155 BU75
Mount Rd., Hert. 31 DN10
Mount Rd., Ilf. 125 EP64
Mount Rd., Mitch. 200 DE96
Mount Rd., N.Mal. 198 CR97
Mount Rd., Wok. 226 AV121
Mount Rd. (Chobham), Wok. 210 AV112
Mount Row W1 277 H1
Mount Row W1 141 DH73
Mount Sq., The NW3 120 DC62
Heath St.
Mount Stewart Ave., Har. 117 CK58
Mount St. W1 276 G1
Mount St. W1 140 DG73
Mount St., Dor. 263 CG136
Mount Ter. E1 142 DV71
New Rd.
Mount Vernon NW3 120 DC63
Mount Vw. NW7 96 CR48
Mount Vw. W5 137 CK70
Mount Vw., Enf. 81 DM38
Mount Vw., Rick. 92 BH46
Mount Vw., St.Alb. 62 CL27
Mount Vw. Rd. E4 101 EC45
Mount Vw. Rd. N4 121 DM58
Mount Vw. Rd. NW9 118 CR56
Mount Vil. SE27 181 DP90
Mount Way, Cars. 218 DG109
Mountacre Clo. SE26 182 DT91
Mountague Pl. E14 143 EC73
Mountain Ct. (Eynsford), Dart. 208 FL103
Pollyhaugh
Mountbatten Clo. SE18 165 ES79
Mountbatten Clo. SE19 182 DS92
Mountbatten Clo., St.Alb. 43 CH23
Mountbatten Clo., Slou. 152 AU75
Mountbatten Ct. SE16 142 DW74
Rotherhithe St.
Mountbatten Ct., Buck.H. 102 EK47
Mountbatten Gdns., Beck. 203 DY98
Balmoral Ave.
Mountbatten Ms. SW18 180 DC88
Inman Rd.
Mountbatten Sq., Wind. 151 AQ81
Alma Rd.
Mountbel Rd., Stan. 95 CG53
Mountcombe Clo., Surb. 198 CL101
Mountearl Gdns. SW16 181 DM90
Mountfield Clo. SE6 183 ED87
Mountfield Rd. E6 145 EN68
Mountfield Rd. N3 120 DA55
Mountfield Rd. W5 137 CK72
Mountfield Rd., Hem.H. 40 BL20
Mountfield Way, Orp. 206 EW98
Mountford St. E1 142 DU72
Adler St.
Mountfort Cres. N1 141 DN66
Barnsbury Sq.
Mountfort Ter. N1 141 DN66
Barnsbury Sq.
Mountgrove Rd. N5 121 DP62
Mounthurst Rd., Brom. 204 EF101
Mountington Pk. Clo., Har. 117 CK58
Mountjoy Clo. SE2 166 EV75
Mountjoy Ho. EC2 142 DQ71
The Barbican
Mountnessing Bypass, Brwd. 109 GD41
Mounts Pond Rd. SE3 163 ED82
Mounts Rd., Green. 189 FV85
Mountsfield Clo., Stai. 174 BG85
Mountsfield Ct. SE13 183 ED86
Mountside, Felt. 176 BY90
Mountside, Guil. 258 AV136
Mountside, Stan. 95 CF53
Mountsorrel, Hert. 32 DT09
Mountview, Nthwd. 93 BT51
Mountview Clo., Red. 266 DE136
Mountview Ct. N8 121 DP56
Green Las.
Mountview Ct., Wat. 76 CB43
Mountview Dr., Red. 266 DE136
Mountview Rd., Esher 215 CH108
Mountview Rd., Orp. 206 EU101
Mountview Rd. (Cheshunt), Wal.Cr. 66 DS26
Mountway, Pot.B. 64 DA30
Mountway, Welw.G.C. 29 CZ12
Mountway Clo., Welw.G.C. 29 CZ12
Mountwood, W.Mol. 196 CA97
Mountwood Clo., S.Croy. 220 DV110
Movers La., Bark. 145 ES68
Mowat Ind. Est., Wat. 76 BW38
Mowatt Clo. N19 121 DK60
Mowbray Ave., W.Byf. 212 BL113
Mowbray Cres., Egh. 173 BA92
Mowbray Gdns., Dor. 247 CH134
Mowbray Rd. NW6 139 CY66
Mowbray Rd. SE19 202 DT95
Mowbray Rd., Barn. 80 DC42
Mowbray Rd., Edg. 96 CN49
Mowbray Rd., Harl. 35 ET13
Mowbray Rd., Rich. 177 CJ90
Mowbrays Clo., Rom. 105 FC53
Mowbrays Rd., Rom. 105 FC54
Mowbrey Gdns., Loug. 85 EQ40
Mowlem St. E2 142 DV68
Mowlem Trd. Est. N17 100 DW52
Mowll St. SW9 161 DN80
Moxom Ave. (Cheshunt), Wal.Cr. 67 DY30
Moxon Clo. E13 144 EF68
Whitelegg Rd.
Moxon St. W1 272 F7
Moxon St. W1 140 DG71
Moxon St., Barn. 79 CZ41
Moye Clo. E2 142 DU67
Dove Row
Moyers Rd. E10 123 EC59
Moylan Rd. W6 159 CY79
Moyne Ct., Wok. 226 AT118
Iveagh Rd.
Moyne Pl. NW10 138 CN68
Moynihan Dr. N21 81 DL43
Moys Clo., Croy. 201 DL100
Moyser Rd. SW16 181 DH92
Mozart St. W10 139 CZ69
Mozart Ter. SW1 276 G9
Mozart Ter. SW1 160 DG77
Muchelney Rd., Mord. 200 DC100
Muckhatch La., Egh. 193 BB97
Muckingford Rd., S.le H. 171 GM77
Muckingford Rd., Til. 171 GL77
Mud La. W5 137 CK71
Muddy La., Slou. 132 AS71
Mudlarks Way SE7 164 EG76
Mudlarks Way SE10 164 EG76
Muggeridge Clo., S.Croy. 220 DR106
Muggeridge Rd., Dag. 127 FB63
Muir Dr. SW18 180 DD86
Muir Rd. E5 122 DU63
Muir St. E16 145 EM74
Newland St.
Muirdown Ave. SW14 158 CR84
Muirfield W3 138 CS72
Muirfield Clo. SE16 162 DV78
Ryder Dr.
Muirfield Clo., Wat. 94 BW49
Muirfield Cres. E14 163 EB76
Millharbour
Muirfield Grn., Wat. 94 BW49
Muirfield Rd., Wat. 94 BX49
Muirfield Rd., Wok. 226 AU118
Muirkirk Rd. SE6 183 EC88
Mulberry Ave., Stai. 174 BL88
Mulberry Ave., Wind. 152 AT82
Mulberry Clo. E4 101 EA47
Mulberry Clo. N8 121 DL57
Mulberry Clo. NW3 120 DD63
Hampstead High St.
Mulberry Clo. NW4 119 CW55
Mulberry Clo. SE7 164 EK79
Mulberry Clo. SE22 182 DU85
Mulberry Clo. SW3 160 DD79
Beaufort St.
Mulberry Clo. SW16 181 DJ91
Mulberry Clo., Amer. 72 AT39
Mulberry Clo., Barn. 80 DD42
Mulberry Clo., Brox. 49 DZ24
Mulberry Clo., Nthlt. 136 BY68
Parkfield Ave.
Mulberry Clo., Rom. 127 FH56
Mulberry Clo., St.Alb. 60 CB28
Mulberry Clo., Wey. 195 BP104
Mulberry Clo., Wok. 210 AY114
Mulberry Ct., Bark. 145 ET66
Westrow Dr.
Mulberry Ct., Beac. 89 AM54
Mulberry Ct., Guil. 243 BD131
Gilliat Dr.
Mulberry Cres., Brent. 157 CH80
Mulberry Cres., West Dr. 154 BN75
Mulberry Dr., Purf. 168 FM77
Mulberry Dr., Slou. 152 AY78
Mulberry Gdns. (Shenley), Rad. 62 CL33
Mulberry Grn., Harl. 36 EX11
Mulberry Hill, Brwd. 109 FZ45
Mulberry La., Croy. 202 DT102
Mulberry Ms., Wall. 219 DJ107
Ross Rd.
Mulberry Par., West Dr. 154 BN76
Mulberry Pl. W6 159 CU78
Chiswick Mall
Mulberry Rd. E8 142 DT66
Mulberry Rd., Grav. 190 GE90
Mulberry St. E1 142 DU72
Adler St.
Mulberry Trees, Shep. 195 BR101
Mulberry Wk. SW3 160 DD79
Mulberry Way E18 102 EH54
Mulberry Way, Belv. 167 FC75
Mulberry Way, Ilf. 125 EQ56
Mulgrave Rd. NW10 119 CT63
Mulgrave Rd. SW6 159 CZ79
Mulgrave Rd. W5 137 CK69
Mulgrave Rd., Croy. 202 DR104
Mulgrave Rd., Har. 117 CG61
Mulgrave Rd., Sutt. 218 DA107
Mulgrave Way, Wok. 226 AS118
Mulholland Clo., Mitch. 201 DH96
Mulkern Rd. N19 121 DK60
Mull Wk. N1 142 DQ65
Clephane Rd.
Mullards Clo., Mitch. 200 DF102
Mullein Ct., Grays 170 GD79
Mullens Rd., Egh. 173 BB92
Muller Rd. SW4 181 DK86
Mullet Gdns. E2 142 DU68
St. Peter's Clo.
Mullins Path SW14 158 CR83
Mullion Clo., Har. 94 CB53
Mullion Wk., Wat. 94 BX49
Ormskirk Rd.
Mulready St. NW8 272 B5
Multi Way W3 158 CS75
Valetta Rd.
Multon Rd. SW18 180 DD87
Mulvaney Way SE1 279 L5
Mulvaney Way SE1 162 DR75
Mumford Ct. EC2 275 J8
Mumford Rd. SE24 181 DP85
Railton Rd.

Mumfords La., Ger.Cr. 112 AU55
Muncaster Clo., Ashf. 174 BN91
Muncaster Rd. SW11 180 DF85
Muncaster Rd., Ashf. 175 BP92
Muncies Ms. SE6 183 EC89
Mund St. W14 159 CZ78
Mundania Rd. SE22 182 DV86
Munday Rd. E16 144 EG72
Mundells, Wal.Cr. 66 DU27
Mundells, Welw.G.C. 29 CZ07
Mundells Ct., Welw.G.C. 29 CZ07
Munden Dr., Wat. 76 BY37
Munden Gro., Wat. 76 BW38
Munden St. W14 159 CY77
Munden Vw., Wat. 76 BX36
Mundesley Clo., Wat. 94 BW49
Mundesley Spur, Slou. 132 AS72
Mundford Rd. E5 122 DW61
Mundon Gdns., Ilf. 125 ER60
Mundy St. N1 275 M2
Mundy St. N1 142 DS69
Munford Dr., Swans. 190 FY87
Mungo Pk. Clo. (Bushey), Wat. 94 CC47
Mungo Pk. Rd., Grav. 191 GK92
Mungo Pk. Rd., Rain. 147 FG65
Mungo Pk. Way, Orp. 206 EW100
Munnery Way, Orp. 205 EN104
Munnings Gdns., Islw. 177 CD85
Munro Dr. N11 99 DJ51
Munro Ms. W10 139 CY71
Munro Rd. (Bushey), Wat. 76 CB43
Munro Ter. SW10 160 DD80
Munslow Gdns., Sutt. 218 DD105
Munstead Vw., Guil. 258 AV138
Munster Ave., Houns. 156 BZ84
Munster Ct., Tedd. 177 CJ93
Munster Gdns. N13 99 DP49
Munster Ms. SW6 159 CY80
Munster Rd.
Munster Rd. SW6 159 CZ81
Munster Rd., Tedd. 177 CH93
Munster Sq. NW1 273 J4
Munster Sq. NW1 141 DH69
Munton Rd. SE17 279 J8
Munton Rd. SE17 162 DQ77
Murchison Ave., Bex. 186 EX88
Murchison Rd. E10 123 EC61
Murchison Rd., Hodd. 33 EB14
Murdoch Clo., Stai. 174 BG92
Murdock Clo. E16 144 EF72
Rogers Rd.
Murdock St. SE15 162 DV79
Murfett Clo. SW19 179 CY89
Murfitt Way, Upmin. 128 FN63
Muriel Ave., Wat. 76 BW43
Muriel St. N1 141 DM68
Murillo Rd. SE13 163 ED84
Murphy St. SE1 278 D5
Murphy St. SE1 161 DN75
Murray Ave., Brom. 204 EH96
Murray Ave., Houns. 176 CB85
Murray Cres., Pnr. 94 BX53
Murray Grn., Wok. 211 BC114
Bunyard Dr.
Murray Gro. N1 275 K1
Murray Gro. N1 142 DQ68
Murray Ms. NW1 141 DK66
Murray Rd. SW19 179 CX93
Murray Rd. W5 157 CJ77
Murray Rd., Berk. 38 AV18
Murray Rd., Cher. 211 BC107
Murray Rd., Nthwd. 93 BS53
Murray Rd., Orp. 206 EV97
Murray Rd., Rich. 177 CH89
Murray Sq. E16 144 EG72
Murray St. NW1 141 DK66
Murray Ter. NW3 120 DD63
Flask Wk.
Murray Ter. W5 157 CK77
Murray Rd.
Murrays La., W.Byf. 212 BK114
Murrells Wk., Lthd. 230 CA123
Murreys, The, Ash. 231 CK118
Mursell Est. SW8 161 DM81
Murthering La., Rom. 105 FF45
Murton Ct., St.Alb. 43 CE19
Murtwell Dr., Chig. 103 EQ51
Musard Rd. W6 159 CY79
Musard Rd. W14 159 CY79
Musbury St. E1 142 DW72
Muscal W6 159 CY79
Muscatel Pl. SE5 162 DS81
Dalwood St.
Muschamp Rd. SE15 162 DT83
Muschamp Rd., Cars. 200 DE103
Muscovy Ho., Erith 166 EY75
Kale Rd.
Muscovy St. EC3 279 N1
Museum Pas. E2 142 DV69
Victoria Pk. Sq.
Museum St. WC1 273 P7
Museum St. WC1 141 DL72
Musgrave Clo., Barn. 80 DC39
Musgrave Clo., Wal.Cr. 66 DT27
Allwood Rd.
Musgrave Cres. SW6 160 DA81
Musgrave Rd., Islw. 157 CF81
Musgrove Rd. SE14 163 DX81
Musjid Rd. SW11 160 DD82
Kambala Rd.
Musk Hill, Hem.H. 39 BE21
Muskalls Clo. (Cheshunt), Wal.Cr. 66 DU27
Musket Clo., Barn. 80 DD43
East Barnet Rd.
Muskham Rd., Harl. 36 EU12
Musleigh Manor, Ware 33 DZ06
Musley Hill, Ware 33 DY05
Musley La., Ware 33 DY05
Musquash Way, Houns. 156 BW82
Mussenden La. (Horton Kirby), Dart. 208 FQ99
Mussenden La. (Fawkham Grn.), Long. 209 FT101
Mustard Mill Rd., Stai. 173 BE91
Muston Rd. E5 122 DV61
Mustow Pl. SW6 159 CZ82
Munster Rd.
Muswell Ave. N10 99 DH54
Muswell Hill N10 121 DH55
Muswell Hill Bdy. N10 121 DH55
Muswell Hill Pl. N10 121 DH56
Muswell Hill Rd. N6 120 DG58
Muswell Hill Rd. N10 120 DG56
Muswell Ms. N10 121 DH55
Muswell Rd.
Muswell Rd. N10 121 DH55
Mutchetts Clo., Wat. 60 BY33
Mutrix Rd. NW6 140 DA67
Mutton La., Pot.B. 63 CY31
Mutton Pl. NW1 141 DH65
Harmood St.
Muybridge Rd., N.Mal. 198 CQ96
Myatt Rd. SW9 161 DP81
Myatt's Flds. N. SW9 161 DN81
Eythorne Rd.
Myatt's Flds. S. SW9 161 DN82
Mycenae Rd. SE3 164 EG80
Myddelton Ave., Enf. 82 DS38
Myddelton Clo., Enf. 82 DT39
Myddelton Gdns. N21 99 DP45
Myddelton Pk. N20 98 DD48
Myddelton Pas. EC1 274 E2
Myddelton Rd. N8 121 DL56
Myddelton Sq. EC1 274 E2
Myddelton Sq. EC1 141 DN69
Myddelton St. EC1 274 E3
Myddelton St. EC1 141 DN69
Myddleton Ave. N4 122 DQ61
Myddleton Ms. N22 99 DL52
Myddleton Path (Cheshunt), Wal.Cr. 66 DV31
Myddleton Rd. N22 99 DL52
Myddleton Rd., Uxb. 134 BJ67
Myddleton Rd., Ware 33 DX07
Myers Dr., Slou. 111 AP64
Myers La. SE14 163 DX79
Mygrove Clo., Rain. 148 FK68
Mygrove Gdns., Rain. 148 FK68
Mygrove Rd., Rain. 148 FK68
Myles Ct., Wal.Cr. 66 DQ29
Mylis Clo. SE26 182 DV91
Mylius Clo. SE14 162 DW81
Kender St.
Mylne Clo., Wal.Cr. 66 DW27
Mylne St. EC1 274 D1
Mylne St. EC1 141 DN69
Mylor Clo., Wok. 210 AY114
Mymms Dr., Hat. 64 DA26
Mynchen Clo., Beac. 89 AK49
Mynchen End, Beac. 89 AK49
Mynchen Rd., Beac. 89 AK50
Mynns Clo., Epsom 216 CP114
Myra St. SE2 166 EU77
Myrdle St. E1 142 DU71
Myrke, The, Slou. 152 AT77
Myrna Clo. SW19 180 DE94
Myron Pl. SE13 163 EC83
Myrtle Ave., Felt. 155 BS84
Myrtle Ave., Ruis. 115 BU59
Myrtle Clo., Barn. 98 DF46
Myrtle Clo., Erith 167 FE80
Myrtle Clo., Slou. 153 BE81
Myrtle Clo., Uxb. 134 BM71
Violet Ave.
Myrtle Clo., West Dr. 154 BM76
Myrtle Cres., Slou. 132 AT73
Myrtle Gdns. W7 137 CE74
Myrtle Grn., Hem.H. 39 BE20
Newlands Rd.
Myrtle Gro., Enf. 82 DR38
Myrtle Gro., N.Mal. 198 CQ96
Myrtle Gro., S.Ock. 168 FQ75
Myrtle Pl., Dart. 189 FR87
Myrtle Rd. E6 144 EL67
Myrtle Rd. E17 123 DY58
Myrtle Rd. N13 100 DQ48
Myrtle Rd. W3 138 CQ74
Myrtle Rd., Brwd. 108 FW48
Myrtle Rd., Croy. 203 EA104
Myrtle Rd., Dart. 188 FK88
Myrtle Rd., Dor. 263 CG135
Myrtle Rd., Hmptn. 176 CC93
Myrtle Rd., Houns. 156 CC82
Myrtle Rd., Ilf. 125 EP61
Myrtle Rd., Rom. 106 FJ51
Myrtle Rd., Sutt. 218 DC106
Myrtle Wk. N1 275 M1
Myrtle Wk. N1 142 DS68
Myrtleberry Clo. E8 142 DT65
Beechwood Rd.
Myrtledene Rd. SE2 166 EU78
Myrtleside Clo., Nthwd. 93 BR52
Mysore Rd. SW11 160 DF83
Myton Rd. SE21 182 DR90

N

Nadine St. SE7 164 EJ78
Nafferton Ri., Loug. 84 EK43
Nagle Clo. E17 101 ED54
Nag's Head Ct. EC1 275 H5
Nags Head La., Brwd. 107 FS51
Nags Head La., Upmin. 106 FQ54
Nags Head La., Well. 166 EV83
Nags Head Rd., Enf. 82 DW42
Nailsworth Cres., Red. 251 DK129
Nailzee Clo., Ger.Cr. 112 AY59
Nairn Ct., Til. 171 GF82
Dock Rd.
Nairn Grn., Wat. 93 BU48
Nairn Rd., Ruis. 136 BW65
Nairn St. E14 143 EC71
Nairne Gro. SE24 182 DR85
Naish Ct. N1 141 DL67
Nalders Rd., Chesh. 54 AR30
Nallhead Rd., Felt. 176 BW92
Namba Roy Clo. SW16 181 DM91
Valley Rd.
Namton Dr., Th.Hth. 201 DM98
Nan Clark's La. NW7 97 CT47
Nancy Downs, Wat. 94 BW45
Nankin St. E14 143 EA72
Nansen Rd. SW11 160 DG84
Nansen Rd., Grav. 191 GK92
Nant Rd. NW2 119 CZ61
Nant St. E2 142 DV69
Cambridge Heath Rd.
Nantes Clo. SW18 160 DC84
Nantes Pas. E1 275 P6
Naoroji St. WC1 274 D3
Nap, The, Kings L. 58 BN29
Napier Ave. E14 163 EA78
Napier Ave. SW6 159 CZ83
Napier Clo. SE8 163 DZ80
Amersham Vale
Napier Clo. W14 159 CZ76
Napier Rd.
Napier Clo., Horn. 127 FH60
St. Leonards Way
Napier Clo., St.Alb. 61 CK25
Napier Clo., West Dr. 154 BM76
Napier Ct. SW6 159 CZ83
Ranelagh Gdns.
Napier Ct. (Cheshunt), Wal.Cr. 66 DV28
Flamstead End Rd.
Napier Dr. (Bushey), Wat. 76 BY42
Napier Gdns., Guil. 243 BB133
Napier Gro. N1 275 J1
Napier Gro. N1 142 DQ68
Napier Ho., Rain. 147 FF69
Napier Pl. W14 159 CZ76
Napier Rd. E6 145 EN67
Napier Rd. E11 124 EE63
Napier Rd. E15 144 EE68
Napier Rd. N17 122 DS55
Napier Rd. NW10 139 CV69
Napier Rd. SE25 202 DV98
Napier Rd. W14 159 CZ76
Napier Rd., Ashf. 175 BR94
Napier Rd., Belv. 166 EZ77
Napier Rd., Brom. 204 EH98
Napier Rd., Enf. 83 DX43
Napier Rd., Grav. 191 GF88
Napier Rd., Houns. 154 BK81
Napier Rd., Islw. 157 CG84
Napier Rd., S.Croy. 220 DR108
Napier Rd., Wem. 117 CK64
Napier Ter. N1 141 DP66
Napoleon Rd. E5 122 DV62
Napoleon Rd., Twick. 177 CH87
Napsbury Ave., St.Alb. 61 CJ26
Napsbury La., St.Alb. 43 CG23
Napton Clo., Hayes 136 BY70
Kingsash Dr.
Narbonne Ave. SW4 181 DJ85
Narboro Ct., Rom. 127 FG57
Manor Rd.
Narborough Clo., Uxb. 115 BQ61
Aylsham Dr.
Narborough St. SW6 160 DB82
Narcissus Rd. NW6 120 DA64
Narcot La., Ch.St.G. 90 AU48
Narcot La., Ger.Cr. 90 AW52
Narcot Rd., Ch.St.G. 90 AU48
Narcot Way, Ch.St.G. 90 AU49
Nare Rd., S.Ock. 148 FQ73
Naresby Fold, Stan. 95 CJ51
Bernays Clo.
Narford Rd. E5 122 DU62
Narrow La., Warl. 236 DV119
Narrow St. E14 143 DY73
Narrow Way, Brom. 204 EL100
Nascot Pl., Wat. 75 BV39
Nascot Rd., Wat. 75 BV40
Nascot St. W12 139 CW72
Nascot St., Wat. 75 BV40
Nascot Wd. Rd., Wat. 75 BT37
Naseby Clo. NW6 140 DC66
Fairfax Rd.
Naseby Clo., Islw. 157 CE81
Naseby Ct., Walt. 196 BW103
Clements Rd.
Naseby Rd. SE19 182 DR93
Naseby Rd., Dag. 126 FA62
Naseby Rd., Ilf. 103 EM53
Nash Clo., Borwd. 78 CM42
Nash Clo., Hat. 45 CX23
Nash Clo., Sutt. 200 DD104
Nash Cft., Grav. 190 GE91
Nash Dr., Red. 250 DF132
Nash Gdns., Red. 250 DF132
Nash Grn., Brom. 184 EG93
Nash Grn., Hem.H. 58 BM25
Nash La., Kes. 222 EG106
Nash Mills La., Hem.H. 58 BM26
Nash Pl. E14 143 EB74
South Colonnade
Nash Rd. N9 100 DW47
Nash Rd. SE4 163 DY84
Nash Rd., Rom. 126 EX56
Nash Rd., Slou. 153 AZ77
Nash St. NW1 273 J3
Nash Way, Har. 117 CH58
Nashdom La., Slou. 130 AF66
Nashleigh Hill, Chesh. 54 AQ29
Nash's Yd., Uxb. 134 BK66
Bakers Rd.
Nasmyth St. W6 159 CV76
Nassau Path SE28 146 EW74
Disraeli Clo.
Nassau Rd. SW13 159 CT81
Nassau St. W1 273 K7
Nassau St. W1 141 DJ71
Nassington Rd. NW3 120 DE63
Natal Rd. N11 99 DL51
Natal Rd. SW16 181 DK93
Natal Rd., Ilf. 125 EP63
Natal Rd., Th.Hth. 202 DR97
Natalie Clo., Felt. 175 BR87
Natalie Ms., Twick. 177 CD90
Sixth Cross Rd.
Nathan Clo., Upmin. 129 FS60
Nathan Way SE28 165 ES77
Nathaniel Clo. E1 142 DT71
Thrawl St.
Nathans Rd., Wem. 117 CJ60
Nation Way E4 101 EC46
Natwoke Clo., Beac. 89 AK50
Naunton Way, Horn. 128 FK62
Naval Row E14 143 EC73
Naval Wk., Brom. 204 EG97
High St.
Navarino Gro. E8 142 DU65
Navarino Rd. E8 142 DU65
Navarre Gdns., Rom. 105 FB50
Navarre Rd. E6 144 EL68
Navarre St. E2 275 P4
Navarre St. E2 142 DT70
Navenby Wk. E3 143 EA70
Rounton Rd.
Navestock Clo. E4 101 EC48
Mapleton Rd.
Navestock Cres., Wdf.Grn. 102 EJ53
Navestock Ho., Bark. 146 EV68
Navigator Dr., Sthl. 156 CC75
Navy St. SW4 161 DK83
Naylor Gro., Enf. 83 DX43
South St.
Naylor Rd. N20 98 DC47
Naylor Rd. SE15 162 DV80
Nazareth Gdns. SE15 162 DV82
Nazeing Common Rd., Wal.Abb. 50 EH24
Nazeing New Rd., Brox. 49 EA21
Nazeing Rd., Wal.Abb. 49 EC22
Nazeing Wk., Rain. 147 FE67
Ongar Way
Nazeingbury Clo., Wal.Abb. 49 ED22
Nazeingbury Par., Wal.Abb. 49 ED22
Nazeing Rd.
Nazrul St. E2 275 P2
Nazrul St. E2 142 DT69
Neagle Clo., Borwd. 78 CQ39
Balcon Way
Neal Ave., Sthl. 136 BZ70
Neal Clo., Ger.Cr. 113 BB60
Neal Clo., Nthwd. 93 BU53
Neal Ct., Hert. 32 DQ09
Neal Ct., Wal.Abb. 68 EF33
Neal St. WC2 273 P9
Neal St. WC2 141 DL72
Neal St., Wat. 76 BW43
Nealden St. SW9 161 DM83
Neale Clo. N2 120 DC55
Neal's Yd. WC2 273 P9
Near Acre NW9 97 CT53
Neasden Clo. NW10 118 CS64
Neasden La. NW10 118 CS63
Neasden La. N. NW10 118 CR62
Neasham Rd., Dag. 126 EV64
Neate St. SE5 162 DT79
Neath Gdns., Mord. 200 DC100
Neathouse Pl. SW1 277 K8
Neats Acre, Ruis. 115 BR59
Neatscourt Rd. E6 144 EK71
Neave Cres., Rom. 106 FJ53
Neb Cor. Rd., Oxt. 253 EC131
Nebraska St. SE1 279 K5
Nebraska St. SE1 162 DR75
Neckinger SE16 162 DT76
Neckinger Est. SE16 162 DT76
Neckinger St. SE1 162 DT75
Nectarine Way SE13 163 EB82
Necton Rd., St.Alb. 28 CL07
Needham Clo., Wind. 151 AL81
Needham Rd. W11 140 DA72
Westbourne Gro.
Needham Ter. NW2 119 CX62
Needleman St. SE16 163 DX75
Needles Bank, Gdse. 252 DV131
Neela Clo., Uxb. 115 BP63
Neeld Cres. NW4 119 CV57
Neeld Cres., Wem. 118 CN64
Neeld Par., Wem. 118 CN64
Harrow Rd.
Neil Clo., Ashf. 175 BQ92
Neil Wates Cres. SW2 181 DN88
Nelgarde Rd. SE6 183 EA87
Nell Gwynn Clo., Rad. 62 CL32
Nell Gwynne Ave., Shep. 195 BR100
Nell Gwynne Clo., Epsom 216 CN111
Ripley Way
Nella Rd. W6 159 CX79
Nelldale Rd. SE16 162 DW77
Nellgrove Rd., Uxb. 135 BP70
Nello James Gdns. SE27 182 DR91
Nelmes Clo., Horn. 128 FM57
Nelmes Cres., Horn. 128 FL57
Nelmes Rd., Horn. 128 FL59
Nelmes Way, Horn. 128 FL56
Nelson Ave., St.Alb. 43 CH23
Nelson Clo., Brwd. 108 FX50
Nelson Clo., Croy. 201 DP102
Nelson Clo., Felt. 175 BT88
Nelson Clo., Rom. 105 FB53
Nelson Clo., Slou. 152 AX77
Nelson Clo., Uxb. 135 BP69
Nelson Clo., Walt. 195 BV102
Nelson Clo., West. 238 EL117
Nelson Ct. SE16 142 DW74
Brunel Rd.
Nelson Gdns. E2 142 DU69
Nelson Gdns., Guil. 243 BA133
Nelson Gdns., Houns. 176 CA86
Nelson Gro. Rd. SW19 200 DB95
Nelson La., Uxb. 135 BP69
Nelson Rd.
Nelson Mandela Clo. N10 98 DG54
Nelson Mandela Rd. SE3 164 EJ83
Nelson Pas. EC1 275 J3
Nelson Pl. N1 274 G1
Nelson Pl. N1 141 DP68
Nelson Pl., Sid. 186 EU91
Nelson Rd. E4 101 EB51
Nelson Rd. E11 124 EG56
Nelson Rd. N8 121 DM57
Nelson Rd. N9 100 DV47
Nelson Rd. N15 122 DS56
Nelson Rd. SE10 163 EC79
Nelson Rd. SW19 180 DB94
Nelson Rd., Ashf. 174 BL92
Nelson Rd., Belv. 166 EZ78
Nelson Rd., Brom. 204 EJ98
Nelson Rd., Cat. 236 DR123
Nelson Rd., Dart. 188 FJ86
Nelson Rd., Enf. 83 DX44
Nelson Rd., Grav. 191 GF89
Nelson Rd., Har. 117 CD60
Nelson Rd., Houns. 176 CA86
Nelson Rd. (Heathrow Airport), Houns. 154 BM81
Nelson Rd., N.Mal. 198 CR99
Nelson Rd., Rain. 147 FF68
Nelson Rd., Sid. 186 EU91
Nelson Rd., S.Ock. 149 FW68
Nelson Rd., Stan. 95 CJ51
Nelson Rd., Twick. 176 CB87
Nelson Rd., Uxb. 135 BP69
Nelson Rd., Wind. 151 AM83
Nelson Sq. SE1 278 F4
Nelson Sq. SE1 161 DP75
Nelson St. E1 142 DV72
Nelson St. E6 145 EM68
Nelson St. E16 144 EF73
Huntingdon St.
Nelson St., Hert. 31 DP08
Nelson Ter. N1 274 G1
Nelson Ter. N1 141 DP68
Nelson Trd. Est. SW19 200 DB95
Nelson Wk. SE16 143 DY74
Rotherhithe St.
Nelson's Row SW4 161 DK84
Nelsons Yd. NW1 141 DJ68
Mornington Cres.
Nelwyn Ave., Horn. 128 FM57
Nemoure Rd. W3 138 CQ73
Nene Gdns., Felt. 176 BZ89
Nene Rd., Houns. 155 BP81
Nepaul Rd. SW11 160 DE82
Nepean St. SW15 179 CU86
Neptune Dr., Hem.H. 40 BL18
Neptune Rd., Har. 117 CD58
Neptune Rd. (Heathrow Airport), Houns. 155 BR81
Neptune St. SE16 162 DW76
Neptune Wk., Erith 167 FD77
Nesbit Rd. SE9 164 EK84
Nesbitt Clo. SE3 164 EE83
Hurren Clo.
Nesbitt Sq. SE19 182 DS94
Coxwell Rd.
Nesbitts All., Barn. 79 CZ41
Bath Pl.
Nesham St. E1 142 DU74
Ness Rd., Erith 168 FK79
Ness St. SE16 162 DU76
Spa Rd.
Nesta Rd., Wdf.Grn. 102 EE51
Nestles Ave., Hayes 155 BT76
Neston Rd., Wat. 76 BW37
Nestor Ave. N21 81 DP44
Nethan Dr., S.Ock. 148 FQ73
Nether Clo. N3 98 DA52
Nether Mt., Guil. 258 AV136
Nether St. N3 98 DA53
Nether St. N12 98 DA52
Netheravon Rd. W4 159 CT77
Netheravon Rd. W7 137 CF74
Netheravon Rd. S. W4 159 CT78
Netherbury Rd. W5 157 CK76
Netherby Gdns., Enf. 81 DL42
Netherby Pk., Wey. 213 BR106
Netherby Rd. SE23 182 DW87
Nethercote Ave., Wok. 226 AT117
Nethercourt Ave. N3 98 DA51
Netherfield Gdns., Bark. 145 ER65
Netherfield La., Ware 33 ED12
Netherfield Rd. N12 98 DB50
Netherfield Rd. SW17 180 DG90
Netherford Rd. SW4 161 DJ82
Netherhall Gdns. NW3 140 DC65
Netherhall Rd., Harl. 50 EF17
Netherhall Way NW3 120 DC64
Netherhall Gdns.
Netherlands, The, Couls. 235 DJ119
Netherlands Rd., Barn. 80 DD44
Netherleigh Clo. N6 121 DH60
Netherleigh Pk., Red. 267 DL137
Nethern Ct. Rd., Cat. 237 EA123
Netherne La., Couls. 235 DJ123
Netherne La., Red. 235 DJ123
Netherpark Dr., Rom. 105 FF54
Netherton Gro. SW10 160 DC79
Netherton Rd. N15 122 DR58
Netherton Rd., Twick. 177 CG85
Netherway, St.Alb. 42 CA23
Netherwood N2 98 DD54
Netherwood Pl. W14 159 CX76
Netherwood Rd.
Netherwood Rd. W14 159 CX76
Netherwood Rd., Beac. 89 AK50
Netherwood St. NW6 139 CZ66
Netley Clo., Croy. 221 EC108
Netley Clo., Sutt. 217 CX106
Netley Dr., Walt. 196 BZ101
Netley Gdns., Mord. 200 DC101
Netley Rd. E17 123 DZ57
Netley Rd., Brent. 158 CL79
Netley Rd. (Heathrow Airport), Houns. 155 BR81
Netley Rd., Ilf. 125 ER57
Netley Rd., Mord. 200 DC101
Netley St. NW1 273 K3
Netteswell Orchard, Harl. 35 ER14
Netteswell Rd., Harl. 35 ES13
Netteswell Twr., Harl. 35 ER14
Nettlecombe Clo., Sutt. 218 DB109
Nettlecroft, Hem.H. 40 BH21
Nettlecroft, Welw.G.C. 30 DB08
Nettleden Ave., Wem. 138 CN65
Nettleden Rd., Berk. 39 AZ17
Nettlefold Pl. SE27 181 DP90
Nettles Ter., Guil. 242 AX134
Nettlestead Clo., Beck. 183 DZ94
Copers Cope Rd.
Nettleton Rd. SE14 163 DX81
Nettleton Rd., Houns. 155 BP81
Nettleton Rd., Uxb. 114 BM63
Nettlewood Rd. SW16 181 DK94
Neuchatel Rd. SE6 183 DZ89
Nevada Clo., N.Mal. 198 CQ98
Georgia Rd.
Nevada St. SE10 163 EC79
Nevell Rd., Grays 171 GH76
Nevern Pl. SW5 160 DA77
Nevern Rd. SW5 160 DA77
Nevern Sq. SW5 160 DA78
Nevil Clo., Nthwd. 93 BQ50
Nevill Gro., Wat. 75 BV39
Nevill Rd. N16 122 DS63
Nevill Way, Loug. 102 EL45
Valley Hill
Neville Ave., N.Mal. 198 CR95
Neville Clo. E11 124 EF62
Neville Clo. NW1 273 N1
Neville Clo. NW6 139 CZ68
Neville Clo. SE15 162 DU80
Neville Clo. W3 158 CQ75
Acton La.
Neville Clo., Bans. 218 DB114
Neville Clo., Esher 214 BZ107
Neville Clo., Houns. 156 CB82
Neville Clo., Pot.B. 63 CZ31
Neville Clo., Sid. 185 ET91
Neville Clo., Slou. 132 AT65
Neville Ct., Slou. 130 AJ69
Dropmore Rd.
Neville Dr. N2 120 DC58
Neville Gdns., Dag. 126 EX62
Neville Gill Clo. SW18 180 DA86
Neville Pl. N22 99 DM53
Neville Rd. E7 144 EG66
Neville Rd. NW6 139 CZ68
Neville Rd. W5 137 CK70
Neville Rd., Croy. 202 DR101
Neville Rd., Dag. 126 EX61
Neville Rd., Ilf. 103 EQ53
Neville Rd., Kings.T. 198 CN96
Neville Rd., Rich. 177 CJ89
Neville St. SW7 160 DD78
Neville Ter. SW7 160 DD78
Neville Wk., Cars. 200 DE101
Green Wrythe La.
Nevilles Ct. NW2 119 CT62
Nevin Dr. E4 101 EB46
Nevinson Clo. SW18 180 DD86
Nevis Clo., Rom. 105 FE51
Nevis Rd. SW17 180 DG89
New Arc., Uxb. 134 BK67
High St.

New Ash Clo. N2 120 DD55
Oakridge Dr.
New Barn La., Beac. 90 AS49
New Barn La., Sev. 239 EQ116
New Barn La., West. 239 EQ118
New Barn La., Whyt. 236 DS116
New Barn Rd., Grav. 190 GC92
New Barn Rd., Swan. 207 FE95
New Barn St. E13 144 EG70
New Barnes Ave., St.Alb. 43 CG23
New Barns Ave., Mitch. 201 DK98
New Barns Way, Chig. 103 EP48
New Battlebridge La., Red. 251 DH130
New Berry La., Walt. 214 BX106
New Bond St. W1 273 J10
New Bond St. W1 141 DH73
New Brent St. NW4 119 CW57
New Bri. St. EC4 274 F9
New Bri. St. EC4 141 DP72
New Broad St. EC2 275 M7
New Broad St. EC2 142 DS71
New Bdy. W5 137 CK73
New Bdy., Hmptn. 177 CD92
Hampton Rd.
New Burlington Ms. W1 273 K10
New Burlington Pl. W1 273 K10
New Burlington St. W1 273 K10
New Burlington St. W1 141 DJ73
New Butt La. SE8 163 EA80
New Butt La. N. SE8 163 EA80
Reginald Rd.
New Causeway, Reig. 266 DB137
New Cavendish St. W1 273 J6
New Cavendish St. W1 140 DG71
New Change EC4 275 H9
New Change EC4 142 DQ72
New Chapel Sq., Felt. 175 BV88
New Charles St. EC1 274 G2
New Ch. Rd. SE5 162 DQ80
New City Rd. E13 144 EJ69
New Clo. SW19 200 DC97
New Clo., Felt. 176 BY92
New College Ct. NW3 140 DC66
College Cres.
New College Ms. N1 141 DN66
Islington Pk. St.
New College Par. NW3 140 DD65
College Cres.
New Compton St. WC2 273 N9
New Compton St. WC2 141 DK72
New Coppice, Wok. 226 AT119
New Cotts., Rain. 148 FJ72
New Ct. EC4 274 D10
New Ct., Add. 194 BJ104
New Covent Gdn. Mkt. SW8 161 DK80
New Coventry St. W1 277 N1
New Crane Pl. E1 142 DW74
Garnet St.
New Cross Rd. SE14 162 DW80
New Cross Rd., Guil. 242 AU132
New End NW3 120 DC63
New End Sq. NW3 120 DD63
New England St., St.Alb. 42 CC20
New Era Est. N1 142 DS67
Phillipp St.
New Fm. Ave., Brom. 204 EG98
New Fm. Dr., Rom. 86 EW41
New Fm. La., Nthwd. 93 BS53
New Ferry App. SE18 165 EN76
New Fetter La. EC4 274 E8
New Fetter La. EC4 141 DN72
New Ford Rd., Wal.Cr. 67 DZ34
New Forest La., Chig. 103 EN51
New Frontiers Science Pk., Harl. 51 EM16
New Gdn. Dr., West Dr. 154 BL75
Drayton Gdns.
New Globe Wk. SE1 279 H2
New Globe Wk. SE1 142 DQ74
New Goulston St. E1 275 P8
New Grn. Pl. SE19 182 DS93
Hawke Rd.
New Grns. Ave., St.Alb. 43 CD15
New Hall Clo., Hem.H. 57 BA27
New Hall Dr., Rom. 106 FL53
New Haw Rd., Add. 212 BJ106
New Heston Rd., Houns. 156 BZ80
New Horizons Ct., Brent. 157 CG79
Shield Dr.
New Ho. La., Epp. 71 FC25
New Ho. La., Grav. 191 GF90
New Ho. La., Red. 267 DK142
New Ho. Pk., St.Alb. 43 CG23
New Inn Bdy. EC2 275 N4
New Inn La., Guil. 243 BB130
New Inn Pas. WC2 274 C9
New Inn St. EC2 275 N4
New Inn Yd. EC2 275 N4
New Inn Yd. EC2 142 DS70
New James Ct. SE15 162 DV83
Nunhead La.
New Kent Rd. SE1 279 H7
New Kent Rd. SE1 162 DQ76
New Kent Rd., St.Alb. 43 CD20
New King St. SE8 163 EA79
New Kings Rd. SW6 159 CZ82
New La., Guil. 227 AZ124
New La., Wok. 226 AY122
New Lo. Dr., Oxt. 254 EF128
New London St. EC3 275 N10
New Lydenburg St. SE7 164 EJ76
New Mill Rd., Orp. 206 EW95
New Mt. St. E15 143 ED66
Bridge Rd.
New N. Pl. EC2 275 M5
New N. Rd. N1 275 L1
New N. Rd. N1 142 DR68
New N. Rd., Ilf. 103 ER52
New N. Rd., Reig. 249 CZ134
New N. St. WC1 274 B6
New N. St. WC1 141 DM71
New Oak Rd. N2 98 DC54
New Orleans Wk. N19 121 DK59
New Oxford St. WC1 273 N8
New Oxford St. WC1 141 DK72
New Par., Ashf. 174 BM91
Church Rd.
New Par., Rick. 73 BC42
Whitelands Ave.
New Pk. Ave. N13 100 DQ48
New Pk. Clo., Nthlt. 136 BY65
New Pk. Ct. SW2 181 DL87
New Pk. Dr., Hem.H. 41 BP19
New Pk. Par. SW2 181 DL86
Doverfield Rd.
New Pk. Rd. SW2 181 DK88
New Pk. Rd., Ashf. 175 BQ92
New Pk. Rd., Hert. 47 DK24
New Pk. Rd. (Harefield), Uxb. 92 BJ53
New Peachey La., Uxb. 134 BK72
New Pl. Gdns., Upmin. 129 FR61
New Pl. Sq. SE16 162 DV76
New Plaistow Rd. E15 144 EE67
New Printing Ho. Sq. WC1 141 DM70
Gray's Inn Rd.
New Priory Ct. NW6 140 DA66
Mazenod Ave.
New Quebec St. W1 272 E9
New Quebec St. W1 140 DF72
New Ride SW7 276 D4
New Ride SW7 160 DE75
New River Ave., Ware 33 EB11
New River Clo., Hodd. 49 EB16
New River Ct. (Cheshunt), Wal.Cr. 66 DV30
Pengelly Clo.
New River Cres. N13 99 DP49
New River Trd. Est. (Cheshunt), Wal.Cr. 67 DX26
New River Wk. N1 142 DQ65
New River Way N4 122 DR59
New Rd. E1 142 DV71
New Rd. E4 101 EB49
New Rd. N8 121 DL57
New Rd. N9 100 DU48
New Rd. N17 100 DT53
New Rd. N22 100 DQ53
New Rd. NW7 97 CY52
New Rd. (Barnet Gate) NW7 97 CT45
New Rd. SE2 166 EX77
New Rd., Amer. 55 AS37
New Rd. (Coleshill), Amer. 55 AM42
New Rd., Berk. 38 AX18
New Rd. (Northchurch), Berk. 38 AS17
New Rd., Borwd. 77 CK44
New Rd., Brent. 157 CK79
New Rd., Brwd. 108 FX47
New Rd., Brox. 49 DZ19
New Rd., Ch.St.G. 72 AY41
New Rd., Dag. 146 FA67
New Rd. (South Darenth), Dart. 208 FQ96
New Rd., Dor. 263 CJ137
Deepdene Ave.
New Rd., Epp. 70 FA32
New Rd., Esher 196 CC104
New Rd. (Claygate), Esher 215 CF110
New Rd., Felt. 175 BR86
New Rd. (East Bedfont), Felt. 175 BV88
New Rd. (Hanworth), Felt. 176 BY92
New Rd., Grav. 191 GH86
New Rd., Grays 170 GA79
New Rd. (Manor Way), Grays 170 GB79
New Rd., Guil. 244 BL131
New Rd. (Albury), Guil. 260 BK139
New Rd. (Chilworth), Guil. 259 BB141
New Rd. (Gomshall), Guil. 261 BQ139
New Rd. (Wonersh), Guil. 259 BB143
New Rd., Harl. 36 EX11
New Rd., Har. 117 CF63
New Rd., Hayes 155 BQ80
New Rd., Hert. 32 DQ07
New Rd., Horl. 269 DP148
New Rd., Houns. 156 CB84
Station Rd.
New Rd., Ilf. 125 ES61
New Rd., Kings L. 57 BF30
New Rd., Kings.T. 178 CN94
New Rd., Lthd. 215 CF110
New Rd., Mitch. 200 DF102
New Rd., Orp. 206 EU101
New Rd. (Limpsfield), Oxt. 254 EH130
New Rd., Pot.B. 63 CU33
New Rd., Rad. 77 CE36
New Rd. (Shenley), Rad. 62 CN34
New Rd., Rain. 147 FG69
New Rd., Rich. 177 CJ91
New Rd., Rick. 74 BN43
New Rd. (Church End), Rick. 73 BF39
New Rd., Rom. 86 EX44
New Rd., Sev. 240 EX124
New Rd., Shep. 194 BN97
New Rd. (Datchet), Slou. 152 AX81
New Rd. (Langley), Slou. 153 BA76
New Rd., Stai. 173 BC92
New Rd., Swan. 207 FF97
New Rd. (Hextable), Swan. 187 FF94
New Rd., Tad. 233 CW123
New Rd., Uxb. 135 BQ70
New Rd., Ware 33 DX06
New Rd., Wat. 76 BW42
New Rd. (Letchmore Heath), Wat. 77 CE39
New Rd., Well. 166 EV82
New Rd. (Stanborough), Welw.G.C. 29 CU12
New Rd., W.Mol. 196 CA97
New Rd., Wey. 213 BQ106
New Rd. Hill, Kes. 222 EL109
New Rd. Hill, Orp. 222 EL109
New Row WC2 273 P10
New Row WC2 141 DL73
New Spring Gdns. Wk. SE11 161 DL78
Goding St.
New Sq. WC2 274 C8
New Sq. WC2 141 DM72
New Sq., Felt. 175 BQ88
New Sq., Slou. 152 AT75
New Sq. Pas. WC2 141 DM72
New Sq.
New St. EC2 275 N7
New St. EC2 142 DS71
New St., Berk. 38 AX19
New St., Stai. 174 BG91
New St., Wat. 76 BW42
New St., West. 255 EQ127
New St. Hill, Brom. 184 EH92
New St. Sq. EC4 274 E8
New Swan Yd., Grav. 191 GH86
Bank St.
New Trinity Rd. N2 120 DD55
New Turnstile WC1 274 B7
New Union Clo. E14 163 EC76
New Union St. EC2 275 K7
New Union St. EC2 142 DR71
New Wanstead E11 124 EF58
New Way La., Harl. 53 FB16
New Way Rd. NW9 118 CS56
New Wf. Rd. N1 141 DL68
New Wickham La., Egh. 173 BA94
New Windsor St., Uxb. 134 BJ67
New Wd., Welw.G.C. 30 DC08
New Years Grn. La. (Harefield), Uxb. 114 BL58
New Years La., Orp. 239 ET115
New Years La., Sev. 239 ET115
New Zealand Ave., Walt. 195 BT102
New Zealand Way W12 139 CV73
New Zealand Way, Rain. 147 FF69
Newall Rd., Houns. 155 BQ81
Newark Clo., Guil. 243 BB129
Dairyman's Wk.
Newark Clo., Wok. 228 BG121
Newark Cotts., Wok. 228 BG121
Newark Ct., Walt. 196 BW102
St. Johns Dr.
Newark Cres. NW10 138 CR69
Newark Grn., Borwd. 78 CR41
Newark Knok E6 145 EN72
Newark La., Wok. 227 BF118
Newark Par. NW4 119 CU55
Greyhound Hill
Newark Rd., S.Croy. 220 DR107
Newark St. E1 142 DV71
Newark Way NW4 119 CU56
Newberries Ave., Rad. 77 CJ35
Newberry Cres., Wind. 151 AK82
Newbery Rd., Erith 167 FF81
Newbery Way, Slou. 151 AR75
Newbiggin Path, Wat. 94 BW49
Newbolt Ave., Sutt. 217 CW106
Newbolt Rd., Stan. 95 CF51
Newborough Grn., N.Mal. 198 CR98
Newburgh Rd. W3 138 CQ74
Newburgh Rd., Grays 170 GD78
Newburgh St. W1 273 K9
Newburgh St. W1 141 DJ72
Newburn St. SE11 278 C10
Newburn St. SE11 161 DM78
Newbury Ave., Enf. 83 DZ38
Newbury Clo., Nthlt. 136 BZ65
Newbury Clo., Rom. 106 FK51
Newbury Gdns., Epsom 217 CT105
Newbury Gdns., Rom. 106 FK51
Newbury Gdns., Upmin. 128 FM62
Newbury Ho. N22 99 DL53
Newbury Ms. NW5 140 DG65
Malden Rd.
Newbury Rd. E4 101 EC51
Newbury Rd., Brom. 204 EG97
Newbury Rd., Houns. 154 BM81
Newbury Rd., Ilf. 125 ES58
Newbury Rd., Rom. 106 FK50
Newbury St. EC1 275 H7
Newbury Wk., Rom. 106 FK50
Newbury Way, Nthlt. 136 BY65
Newby Clo., Enf. 82 DS40
Newby Pl. E14 143 EC73
Newby St. SW8 161 DH83
Newcastle Ave., Ilf. 104 EU51
Newcastle Clo. EC4 274 F8
Newcastle Pl. W2 272 A7
Newcastle Pl. W2 140 DD71
Newcastle Row EC1 274 E4
Newchurch Rd., Slou. 131 AM71
Newcombe Gdns. SW16 181 DL91
Newcombe Pk. NW7 96 CS50
Newcombe Pk., Wem. 138 CM67
Newcombe Ri., West Dr. 134 BL72
Newcombe St. W8 140 DA74
Kensington Pl.
Newcome Path, Rad. 62 CN34
Newcome Rd.
Newcome Rd., Rad. 62 CN34
Newcomen Rd. E11 124 EF62
Newcomen Rd. SW11 160 DD83
Newcomen St. SE1 279 K4
Newcomen St. SE1 162 DR75
Newcourt, Uxb. 134 BJ71
Newcourt St. NW8 272 B1
Newcourt St. NW8 140 DE68
Newcroft Clo., Uxb. 134 BM71
Newdales Clo. N9 100 DU47
Balham Rd.
Newdene Ave., Nthlt. 136 BX68
Newdigate Grn. (Harefield), Uxb. 92 BK53
Newdigate Rd. (Harefield), Uxb. 92 BJ53
Newdigate Rd. E. (Harefield), Uxb. 92 BK53
Newell Rd., Hem.H. 40 BL23
Newell St. E14 143 DZ72
Newenham Rd., Lthd. 246 CA126
Newent Clo. SE15 162 DS80
Newent Clo., Cars. 200 DF102
Newfield Clo., Hmptn. 196 CA95
Percy Rd.
Newfield La., Hem.H. 40 BL20
Newfield Ri. NW2 119 CV62
Newfield Way, St.Alb. 43 CJ22
Newfields, Welw.G.C. 29 CV10
Newford Clo., Hem.H. 41 BP19
Newgale Gdns., Edg. 96 CM53
Newgate, Croy. 202 DQ102
Newgate Clo., Felt. 176 BY89
Newgate Clo., St.Alb. 43 CK17
Newgate St. E4 102 EF48
Newgate St. EC1 274 G8
Newgate St. EC1 141 DP72
Newgate St., Hert. 47 DK21
Newgatestreet Rd. (Cheshunt), Wal.Cr. 65 DP27
Newhall Ct., Wal.Abb. 68 EF33
Newham Way E6 144 EJ71
Newham Way E16 144 EF71
Newhams Row SE1 279 N5
Newhaven Clo., Hayes 155 BT77
Newhaven Cres., Ashf. 175 BR92
Newhaven Gdns. SE9 164 EK84
Newhaven La. E16 144 EF70
Newhaven Rd. SE25 202 DR99
Newhaven Spur, Slou. 131 AP70
Newhouse Ave., Rom. 126 EX55
Newhouse Clo., N.Mal. 198 CS101
Newhouse Cres., Wat. 59 BV32
Newhouse Rd., Hem.H. 57 BA26
Newhouse Wk., Mord. 200 DC101
Newick Clo., Bex. 187 FB86
Newick Rd. E5 122 DV62
Newing Grn., Brom. 184 EK94
Newington Barrow Way N7 121 DM62
Newington Butts SE1 278 G9
Newington Butts SE1 161 DP77
Newington Butts SE11 278 G9
Newington Butts SE11 161 DP77
Newington Causeway SE1 278 G7
Newington Causeway SE1 161 DP76
Newington Grn. N1 122 DR64
Newington Grn. N16 122 DR64
Newington Grn. Rd. N1 142 DR65
Newington Way N7 121 DM61
Hornsey Rd.
Newland Clo., Pnr. 94 BY51
Newland Clo., St.Alb. 43 CG23
Newland Ct., Wem. 118 CN61
Forty Ave.
Newland Dr., Enf. 82 DV39
Newland Gdns. W13 157 CG75
Newland Rd. N8 121 DL55
Newland St. E16 144 EL74
Newlands, Abb.L. 59 BT26
Newlands, Hat. 45 CW16
Newlands, The, Wall. 219 DJ108
Newlands Ave., Rad. 61 CF34
Newlands Ave., T.Ditt. 197 CE102
Newlands Ave., Wok. 227 AZ121
Newlands Clo., Brwd. 109 GD45
Newlands Clo., Edg. 96 CL48
Newlands Clo., Horl. 268 DF146
Newlands Clo., Sthl. 156 BY78
Newlands Clo., Walt. 214 BY105
Newlands Clo., Wem. 137 CJ65
Newlands Cor., Guil. 260 BG136
Shere Rd.
Newlands Ct. SE9 185 EN86
Newlands Dr., Slou. 153 BE83
Newlands Pk. SE26 183 DX92
Newlands Pl., Barn. 79 CX43
Newlands Quay E1 142 DW73
Newlands Rd. SW16 201 DL96
Newlands Rd., Hem.H. 39 BE19
Newlands Rd., Wdf.Grn. 102 EF47
Newlands Wk., Wat. 60 BX33
Trevellance Way
Newlands Way, Chess. 215 CJ106
Newlands Way, Pot.B. 64 DB30
Newlands Wd., Croy. 221 DZ109
Newling Clo. E6 145 EM72
Porter Rd.
Newlyn Clo., St.Alb. 60 BY30
Newlyn Clo., Uxb. 134 BN71
Newlyn Gdns., Har. 116 BZ59
Newlyn Rd. N17 100 DT53
Newlyn Rd. NW2 119 CW60
Tilling Rd.
Newlyn Rd., Barn. 79 CZ42
Newlyn Rd., Well. 165 ET82
Newman Clo., Horn. 128 FL57
Newman Pas. W1 273 L7
Newman Rd. E13 144 EH69
Newman Rd. E17 123 DX57
Southcote Rd.
Newman Rd., Brom. 204 EG95
Newman Rd., Croy. 201 DM102
Newman Rd., Hayes 135 BV73
Newman St. W1 273 L7
Newman St. W1 141 DJ71
Newman Yd. W1 273 M8
Newmans Clo., Loug. 85 EP41
Newman's Ct. EC3 275 L9
Newmans Dr., Brwd. 109 GC45
Newmans La., Loug. 85 EN41
Newmans La., Surb. 197 CK100
Newmans Rd., Grav. 191 GF89
Newman's Row WC2 274 C7
Newmans Way, Barn. 80 DC39
Newmarket Ave., Nthlt. 116 CA64
Newmarket Grn. SE9 184 EK87
Middle Pk. Ave.
Newmarket Way, Horn. 128 FL63
Newminster Rd., Mord. 200 DC100
Newnes Path SW15 159 CV84
Putney Pk. La.
Newnham Ave., Ruis. 116 BW60
Newnham Clo., Loug. 84 EK44
Newnham Clo., Nthlt. 116 CC64
Newnham Clo., Slou. 132 AU74
Newnham Clo., Th.Hth. 202 DQ96
Newnham Gdns., Nthlt. 116 CC64
Newnham Ms. N22 99 DM53
Newnham Rd.
Newnham Pl., Grays 171 GG77
Newnham Rd. N22 99 DM53
Newnham Ter. SE1 278 D6
Newnham Way, Har. 118 CL57
Newnhams Clo., Brom. 205 EM97
Newnton Clo. N4 122 DR59
Newpiece, Loug. 85 EP41
Newport Ave. E13 144 EH70
Newport Ave. E14 143 ED73
Newport Clo., Enf. 83 DY37
Newport Ct. WC2 273 N10
Newport Mead, Wat. 94 BX49
Kilmarnock Rd.
Newport Pl. WC2 273 N10
Newport Pl. WC2 141 DK73
Newport Rd. E10 123 EC61
Newport Rd. E17 123 DY56
Newport Rd. SW13 159 CU81
Newport Rd., Hayes 135 BR71
Newport Rd., Houns. 154 BN81
Newport Rd., Slou. 131 AL70
Newport St. SE11 278 B9
Newport St. SE11 161 DM77
Newports, Saw. 36 EW06
Newports, Swan. 207 FD101
Newquay Cres., Har. 116 BY61
Newquay Gdns., Wat. 93 BV47
Fulford Gro.
Newquay Rd. SE6 183 EB89
Newry Rd., Twick. 157 CG84
Newsam Ave. N15 122 DR57
Newsham Rd., Wok. 226 AT117
Newsholme Dr. N21 81 DM43
Newstead, Hat. 45 CT21
Newstead Ave., Orp. 205 ER104
Newstead Ri., Cat. 252 DV126
Newstead Rd. SE12 184 EE87
Newstead Wk., Cars. 200 DC101
Newstead Way SW19 179 CX91
Newteswell Dr., Wal.Abb. 67 ED32
Newton Abbot Rd., Grav. 191 GF89
Newton Ave. N10 98 DG53
Newton Ave. W3 158 CQ75
Newton Clo. E17 123 DY58
Newton Clo., Har. 116 CA61
Newton Clo., Hodd. 33 EB13
Newton Clo., Slou. 153 AZ75
Newton Ct., Wind. 172 AU86
Newton Cres., Borwd. 78 CQ42
Newton Dr., Saw. 36 EX06
Newton Gro. W4 158 CS77
Newton La., Wind. 172 AV86
Newton Rd. E15 123 ED64
Newton Rd. N15 122 DT57
Newton Rd. NW2 119 CW62
Newton Rd. SW19 179 CY94
Newton Rd. W2 140 DA72
Newton Rd., Chig. 104 EV50
Newton Rd., Har. 95 CE54
Newton Rd., Islw. 157 CF82
Newton Rd., Pur. 219 DJ112
Newton Rd., Til. 171 GG82
Newton Rd., Well. 166 EU83
Newton Rd., Wem. 138 CM66
Newton St. WC2 274 A8
Newton St. WC2 141 DL72
Newton Wk., Edg. 96 CP53
North Rd.
Newton Way N18 100 DQ50
Newton Wd., Ash. 216 CL114
Newton Wd. Rd., Ash. 232 CM116
Newtons Clo., Rain. 147 FF66
Newtons Ct., Dart. 169 FR84
Newtons Yd. SW18 180 DB85
Wandsworth High St.
Newtonside Orchard, Wind. 172 AU86
Newtown Rd. (Denham), Uxb. 134 BH65
Newtown St. SW11 161 DH81
Strasburg Rd.
Niagara Ave. W5 157 CJ77
Niagara Clo. N1 142 DR68
Cropley St.
Niagara Clo. (Cheshunt), Wal.Cr. 67 DX29
Nibthwaite Rd., Har. 117 CE57
Nichol Clo. N14 99 DK46
Nichol La., Brom. 184 EG94
Nicholas Clo., Grnf. 136 CB68
Nicholas Clo., St.Alb. 43 CD17
Nicholas Clo., S.Ock. 149 FW69
Nicholas Clo., Wat. 75 BV37
Nicholas Ct. E13 144 EH69
Tunmarsh La.
Nicholas Dr., Sev. 257 FH126
Nicholas Gdns. W5 157 CK75
Nicholas Gdns., Wok. 227 BE116
Nicholas La. EC4 275 L10
Nicholas La., Hert. 32 DQ09
Old Cross
Nicholas Pas. EC4 275 L10
Nicholas Rd. E1 142 DW70
Nicholas Rd., Borwd. 78 CM44
Nicholas Rd., Croy. 219 DL105
Nicholas Rd., Dag. 126 EZ61
Nicholas Wk., Grays 171 GH75
Godman Rd.
Nicholas Way, Hem.H. 40 BM18
Nicholas Way, Nthwd. 93 BQ53
Nicholay Rd. N19 121 DK60
Nicholes Rd., Houns. 156 CA84
Nicholl Rd., Epp. 69 ET31
Nicholl St. E2 142 DU67
Nicholls Ave., Uxb. 134 BN70
Nicholls Fld., Harl. 52 EU16
Nicholls Wk., Wind. 150 AJ83
Nichollsfield Wk. N7 121 DM64
Hillmarton Rd.
Nichols Clo. N4 121 DN60
Osborne Rd.
Nichols Clo., Chess. 215 CJ107
Merritt Gdns.
Nichols Grn. W5 138 CL71
Montpelier Rd.
Nicholson Ms., Egh. 173 BA92
Nicholson Wk.
Nicholson Rd., Croy. 202 DT102
Nicholson St. SE1 278 F3
Nicholson St. SE1 141 DP74
Nicholson Wk., Egh. 173 BA92
Nicholson Way, Sev. 257 FK122
Nickelby Clo. SE28 146 EW72
Nickelby Clo., Uxb. 135 BP72
Dickens Ave.
Nicol Clo., Ger.Cr. 90 AX53
Nicol Clo., Twick. 177 CH86
Cassilis Rd.
Nicol End, Ger.Cr. 90 AW53
Nicol Rd., Ger.Cr. 90 AW53
Nicola Clo., Har. 95 CD54
Nicola Clo., S.Croy. 220 DQ107
Nicola Ms., Ilf. 103 EP52
Nicoll Pl. NW4 119 CV58
Nicoll Rd. NW10 138 CS67
Nicoll Way, Borwd. 78 CR43
Nicolson Dr. (Bushey), Wat. 94 CC46
Nicolson Rd., Orp. 206 EX101
Nicosia Rd. SW18 180 DE87
Nidderdale, Hem.H. 40 BM17
Wharfedale
Niederwald Rd. SE26 183 DY91
Nield Rd., Hayes 155 BT75
Nigel Clo., Nthlt. 136 BY67
Church Rd.
Nigel Ms., Ilf. 125 EP63
Nigel Playfair Ave. W6 159 CV77
King St.
Nigel Rd. E7 124 EJ64
Nigel Rd. SE15 162 DU83
Nigeria Rd. SE7 164 EJ80
Nightingale, St.Alb. 43 CJ23
Nightingale Ave. E4 102 EE50
Nightingale Ave., Lthd. 229 BR124
Nightingale Ave., Upmin. 129 FT60
Nightingale Clo. E4 102 EE49
Nightingale Clo. W4 158 CQ79
Grove Pk. Ter.
Nightingale Clo., Abb.L. 59 BU31
Nightingale Clo., Cars. 200 DG103
Nightingale Clo., Cob. 214 BX111
Nightingale Clo., Epsom 216 CN112
Nightingale Clo., Grav. 190 GE91
Nightingale Clo., Pnr. 116 BW57
Nightingale Clo., Rad. 77 CF36
Nightingale Cres., Lthd. 245 BQ125
Nightingale Dr., Epsom 216 CP107
Nightingale Est. E5 122 DU62
Nightingale Gro. SE13 183 ED85
Nightingale Gro., Dart. 168 FN84
Nightingale La. E11 124 EH57
Nightingale La. N6 120 DE60
Nightingale La. N8 121 DL56
Nightingale La. SW4 180 DF87
Nightingale La. SW12 180 DF87

Nightingale La., Brom. 204 EJ96
Nightingale La., Rich. 178 CL87
Nightingale La., St.Alb. 43 CJ24
Nightingale La., Sev. 256 FB130
Nightingale Ms. E3 143 DY68
Chisenhale Rd.
Nightingale Ms., Kings.T. 197 CK97
South La.
Nightingale Pk., Slou. 131 AM66
Nightingale Pl. SE18 165 EN79
Nightingale Pl. SW10 160 DC79
Fulham Rd.
Nightingale Pl., Rick. 92 BK45
Nightingale Rd.
Nightingale Rd. E5 122 DV62
Nightingale Rd. N9 82 DW44
Nightingale Rd. N22 99 DL53
Nightingale Rd. NW10 139 CT68
Nightingale Rd. W7 137 CF74
Nightingale Rd., Cars. 200 DF104
Nightingale Rd., Chesh. 54 AP29
Nightingale Rd., Esher 214 BZ106
Nightingale Rd., Guil. 242 AX134
Nightingale Rd., Hmptn. 176 CA92
Nightingale Rd., Lthd. 245 BT125
Nightingale Rd., Orp. 205 EQ100
Nightingale Rd., Rick. 92 BJ46
Nightingale Rd., S.Croy. 221 DX111
Nightingale Rd. (Cheshunt), Wal.Cr. 66 DQ25
Nightingale Rd., Walt. 195 BV101
Nightingale Rd. (Bushey), Wat. 76 CA43
Nightingale Rd., W.Mol. 196 CB99
Nightingale Sq. SW12 180 DG87
Nightingale Vale SE18 165 EN79
Nightingale Wk. SW4 181 DH86
Nightingale Way E6 144 EL71
Nightingale Way, Red. 252 DS134
Nightingale Way, Swan. 207 FE97
Nightingale Way, Uxb. 113 BF59
Nightingales, Wal.Abb. 68 EE34
Roundhills
Nightingales, The, Stai. 174 BM87
Nightingales La., Ch.St.G. 90 AX46
Nile Path SE18 165 EN79
Jackson St.
Nile Rd. E13 144 EJ68
Nile St. N1 275 J2
Nile St. N1 142 DR69
Nile Ter. SE15 162 DT78
Nimbus Rd., Epsom 216 CR110
Nimegen Way SE22 182 DS85
Nimmo Dr. (Bushey), Wat. 95 CD45
Nimrod Clo., Nthlt. 136 BX69
Britannia Clo.
Nimrod Pas. N1 142 DS65
Tottenham Rd.
Nimrod Rd. SW16 181 DH93
Nina Mackay Clo. E15 144 EE67
Arthingworth St.
Nine Acres, Slou. 131 AN74
Cippenham La.
Nine Acres Clo. E12 124 EL64
Nine Ashes, Ware 34 EK08
Acorn St.
Nine Elms Ave., Uxb. 134 BK71
Nine Elms Clo., Felt. 175 BT88
Nine Elms Clo., Uxb. 134 BK72
Nine Elms Gro., Grav. 191 GG87
Nine Elms La. SW8 161 DJ79
Nine Stiles Clo. (Denham), Uxb. 134 BH65
Nineacres Way, Couls. 235 DL116
Ninefields, Wal.Abb. 68 EF33
Ninehams Clo., Cat. 236 DR120
Ninehams Gdns., Cat. 236 DR120
Ninehams Rd., Cat. 236 DR121
Ninehams Rd., West. 238 EJ121
Nineteenth Rd., Mitch. 201 DL98
Ninhams Wd., Orp. 223 EN105
Ninian Rd., Hem.H. 40 BL15
Ninnings Rd., Ger.Cr. 91 AZ52
Ninnings Way, Ger.Cr. 91 AZ52
Ninth Ave., Hayes 135 BU73
Nisbet Ho. E9 123 DX64
Homerton High St.
Nita Rd., Brwd. 108 FW50
Nithdale Rd. SE18 165 EP80
Nithsdale Gro., Uxb. 115 BQ62
Tweeddale Gro.
Niton Clo., Barn. 79 CX44
Niton Rd., Rich. 158 CN83
Niton St. SW6 159 CX80
Niven Clo., Borwd. 78 CQ39
Nixey Clo., Slou. 152 AU75
Noak Hill Rd., Rom. 106 FJ49
Nobel Dr., Hayes 155 BR80
Nobel Rd. N18 100 DW50
Noble St. EC2 275 H8
Noble St. EC2 142 DQ72
Noble St., Walt. 195 BV104
Nobles Way, Egh. 172 AY93
Noel Pk. Rd. N22 99 DN54
Noel Rd. E6 144 EL70
Noel Rd. N1 141 DP68
Noel Rd. W3 138 CP72
Noel Sq., Dag. 126 EW63
Noel St. W1 273 L9
Noel St. W1 141 DJ72
Noel Ter. SE23 182 DW89
Dartmouth Rd.
Noke Dr., Red. 250 DG133
Noke La., St.Alb. 60 BY26
Noke Side, St.Alb. 60 CA27
Nokes, The, Hem.H. 40 BG18
Nolan Way E5 122 DU63
Nolton Pl., Edg. 96 CM53
Nonsuch Clo., Ilf. 103 EP51
Nonsuch Ct. Ave., Epsom 217 CV110
Nonsuch Ind. Est., Epsom 216 CS111
Nonsuch Wk., Sutt. 217 CW110
Noons Cor. Rd., Dor. 262 BZ143
Nora Gdns. NW4 119 CX56
Norbiton Ave., Kings.T. 198 CN96
Norbiton Common Rd., Kings.T. 198 CP97
Norbiton Rd. E14 143 DZ72
Norbreck Gdns. NW10 138 CM69
Lytham Gro.
Norbreck Par. NW10 138 CM69
Lytham Gro.
Norbroke St. W12 139 CT73
Norburn St. W10 139 CY71
Chesterton Rd.
Norbury Ave. SW16 201 DM95
Norbury Ave., Th.Hth. 201 DN96
Norbury Ave., Wat. 76 BW39
Norbury Clo. SW16 201 DN95
Norbury Ct. Rd. SW16 201 DL96
Norbury Cres. SW16 201 DM95
Norbury Cross SW16 201 DL97
Norbury Gdns., Rom. 126 EX57
Norbury Gro. NW7 96 CS48
Norbury Hill SW16 181 DN94
Norbury Pk., Dor. 247 CF127
Norbury Ri. SW16 201 DL97
Norbury Rd. E4 101 EA50
Norbury Rd., Reig. 249 CZ134
Norbury Rd., Th.Hth. 202 DQ96
Norbury Way, Lthd. 246 CC125
Norcombe Gdns., Har. 117 CJ58
Norcott Clo., Hayes 136 BW70
Willow Tree La.
Norcott Rd. N16 122 DU61
Norcroft Gdns. SE22 182 DU87
Norcutt Rd., Twick. 177 CE88
Nordenfeldt Rd., Erith 167 FD78
Nordmann Pl., S.Ock. 149 FX70
Norelands Dr., Slou. 130 AJ68
Norfield Rd., Dart. 187 FC91
Norfolk Ave. N13 99 DP51
Norfolk Ave. N15 122 DT58
Norfolk Ave., Slou. 131 AQ71
Norfolk Ave., S.Croy. 220 DU110
Norfolk Ave., Wat. 76 BW38
Norfolk Clo. N2 120 DE55
Park Rd.
Norfolk Clo. N13 99 DP51
Norfolk Clo., Barn. 80 DG42
Norfolk Clo., Dart. 188 FN86
Norfolk Clo., Horl. 268 DG149
Norfolk Clo., Twick. 177 CH86
Cassilis Rd.
Norfolk Cres. W2 272 C8
Norfolk Cres. W2 140 DE72
Norfolk Cres., Sid. 185 ES87
Norfolk Fm. Clo., Wok. 227 BD116
Norfolk Fm. Rd., Wok. 227 BD115
Norfolk Gdns., Bexh. 166 EZ81
Norfolk Gdns., Borwd. 78 CR42
Norfolk Ho. SE3 164 EE79
Norfolk Ho. Rd. SW16 181 DK90
Norfolk La., Dor. 263 CH142
Norfolk Ms. W10 139 CZ71
Blagrove Rd.
Norfolk Pl. W2 272 A8
Norfolk Pl. W2 140 DD72
Norfolk Pl., Well. 166 EU82
Norfolk Rd. E6 145 EM67
Norfolk Rd. E17 101 DX54
Norfolk Rd. NW8 140 DD67
Norfolk Rd. NW10 138 CS66
Norfolk Rd. SW19 180 DE94
Norfolk Rd., Bark. 145 ES66
Norfolk Rd., Barn. 80 DA41
Norfolk Rd., Dag. 127 FB64
Norfolk Rd., Dor. 263 CG136
Norfolk Rd. (South Holmwood), Dor. 263 CJ144
Norfolk Rd., Enf. 82 DV44
Norfolk Rd., Esher 215 CE106
Norfolk Rd., Felt. 176 BW88
Norfolk Rd., Grav. 191 GK86
Norfolk Rd., Har. 116 CB57
Norfolk Rd., Ilf. 125 ES60
Norfolk Rd., Rick. 92 BL46
Norfolk Rd., Rom. 127 FC58
Norfolk Rd., Th.Hth. 202 DQ97
Norfolk Rd., Upmin. 128 FN62
Norfolk Rd., Uxb. 134 BK65
Norfolk Row SE1 278 B8
Norfolk Sq. W2 272 A9
Norfolk Sq. W2 140 DD72
Norfolk Sq. Ms. W2 272 A9
Norfolk St. E7 124 EG63
Norfolk Ter. W6 159 CY78
Field Rd.
Norgrove Pk., Ger.Cr. 112 AY56
Norgrove St. SW12 180 DG87
Norheads La., Warl. 238 EG119
Norheads La., West. 238 EH117
Norhyrst Ave. SE25 202 DT97
Nork Gdns., Bans. 217 CY114
Nork Ri., Bans. 233 CX115
Norland Pl. W11 139 CY74
Norland Rd. W11 139 CX74
Norland Sq. W11 139 CY74
Norlands Cres., Chis. 205 EP95
Norlands Gate, Chis. 205 EP95
Norlands La., Egh. 193 BE97
Norley Vale SW15 179 CU88
Norlington Rd. E10 123 EC60
Norlington Rd. E11 123 EC60
Norman Ave. N22 99 DP53
Norman Ave., Epsom 217 CT112
Norman Ave., Felt. 176 BY89
Norman Ave., S.Croy. 220 DQ110
Norman Ave., Sthl. 136 BY73
Norman Ave., Twick. 177 CH87
Norman Clo., Orp. 205 EQ104
Norman Clo., Rom. 105 FB54
Norman Clo., Wal.Abb. 67 ED33
Norman Ct., Ilf. 125 ER59
Norman Ct., Pot.B. 64 DC30
Norman Cres., Brwd. 109 GA48
Norman Cres., Houns. 156 BX81
Norman Cres., Pnr. 94 BW53
Norman Gro. E3 143 DY68
Norman Rd. E6 145 EM70
Norman Rd. E11 123 ED61
Norman Rd. N15 122 DT57
Norman Rd. SE10 163 EB80
Norman Rd. SW19 180 DC94
Norman Rd., Ashf. 175 BR93
Norman Rd., Belv. 167 FB76
Norman Rd., Dart. 188 FL88
Norman Rd., Horn. 127 FG59
Norman Rd., Ilf. 125 EP64
Norman Rd., Sutt. 218 DA106
Norman Rd., Th.Hth. 201 DP99
Norman St. EC1 275 H3
Norman Way N14 99 DL47
Norman Way W3 138 CP71
Normanby Clo. SW15 179 CZ85
Manfred Rd.
Normanby Rd. NW10 119 CT63
Normand Gdns. W14 159 CY79
Greyhound Rd.
Normand Ms. W14 159 CY79
Normand Rd.
Normand Rd. W14 159 CZ79
Normandy Ave., Barn. 79 CZ43
Normandy Dr., Berk. 38 AV17
Normandy Dr., Hayes 135 BQ72
Normandy Rd. SW9 161 DN81
Normandy Rd., St.Alb. 43 CD18
Normandy Ter. E16 144 EH72
Normandy Wk., Egh. 173 BC92
Mullens Rd.
Normandy Way, Erith 167 FE81
Normanhurst, Ashf. 174 BN92
Normanhurst, Brwd. 109 GC44
Normanhurst Ave., Bexh. 166 EX81
Normanhurst Dr., Twick. 177 CH85
St. Margarets Rd.
Normanhurst Rd. SW2 181 DM89
Normanhurst Rd., Orp. 206 EV96
Normanhurst Rd., Walt. 196 BX103
Normans, The, Slou. 132 AV72
Norman's Bldgs. EC1 142 DQ69
Ironmonger Row
Normans Clo. NW10 138 CR65
Normans Clo., Grav. 191 GG87
Normans Clo., Uxb. 134 BL71
Normans Mead NW10 138 CR65
Normansfield Ave., Tedd. 177 CJ94
Normansfield Clo. (Bushey), Wat. 94 CB45
Normanshire Ave. E4 101 EC49
Normanshire Dr. E4 101 EA49
Normanton Ave. SW19 180 DA89
Normanton Pk. E4 102 EE48
Normanton Rd., S.Croy. 220 DS107
Normanton St. SE23 183 DX89
Normington Clo. SW16 181 DN92
Norrels Dr., Lthd. 245 BT126
Norrels Ride, Lthd. 245 BT125
Norrice Lea N2 120 DD57
Norris Gro., Brox. 49 DY20
Norris La., Hodd. 49 EA16
Norris Ri., Hodd. 49 DZ16
Norris Rd., Hodd. 49 EA17
Norris Rd., Stai. 173 BF91
Norris St. SW1 277 M1
Norris Way, Dart. 167 FF83
Norroy Rd. SW15 159 CX84
Norrys Clo., Barn. 80 DF43
Norrys Rd., Barn. 80 DF42
Norseman Clo., Ilf. 126 EV60
Norseman Way, Grnf. 136 CB67
Olympic Way
Norstead Pl. SW15 179 CU89
Norsted La., Orp. 224 EU112
North Access Rd. E17 123 DX58
North Acre NW9 96 CS53
North Acre, Bans. 233 CZ116
North Acton Rd. NW10 138 CR68
North App., Nthwd. 93 BQ47
North App., Wat. 75 BU35
North Audley St. W1 272 F9
North Audley St. W1 140 DG72
North Ave. N18 100 DU49
North Ave. W13 137 CH72
North Ave., Brwd. 106 FQ45
North Ave., Cars. 218 DF108
North Ave., Har. 116 CB58
North Ave., Hayes 135 BU73
North Ave., Rad. 62 CL32
North Ave., Rich. 158 CN81
Sandycombe Rd.
North Ave., Sthl. 136 BZ73
North Ave., Walt. 213 BS109
North Bank NW8 272 B3
North Bank NW8 140 DE69
North Barn, Brox. 49 EA21
North Birkbeck Rd. E11 123 ED62
North Branch Ave. W10 139 CW69
Harrow Rd.
North Burnham Clo., Slou. 130 AH68
Wyndham Cres.
North Carriage Dr. W2 272 B10
North Carriage Dr. W2 140 DD73
North Circular Rd. E4 101 DZ52
North Circular Rd. E18 102 EJ54
North Circular Rd. N3 120 DB55
North Circular Rd. N12 98 DD53
North Circular Rd. N13 99 DN50
North Circular Rd. NW2 118 CS62
North Circular Rd. NW10 138 CQ66
North Circular Rd. NW11 119 CY56
North Clo., Barn. 79 CW43
North Clo., Bexh. 166 EX84
North Clo., Chig. 104 EU50
North Clo., Dag. 146 FA67
North Clo., Dor. 263 CJ140
North Clo., Felt. 175 BR86
North Rd.
North Clo., Mord. 199 CY98
North Clo., St.Alb. 60 CB25
North Clo., Wind. 151 AM81
North Colonnade E14 143 EA74
North Common, Wey. 213 BP105
North Common Rd. W5 138 CL73
North Common Rd., Uxb. 114 BK64
North Cotts., St.Alb. 61 CG25
North Countess Rd. E17 101 DZ53
North Ct. W1 273 L6
North Ct., Rick. 92 BG46
Hall Clo.
North Cray Rd., Bex. 186 FA89
North Cray Rd., Sid. 186 EY93
North Cres. E16 143 ED70
North Cres. N3 97 CZ54
North Cres. WC1 273 M6
North Cres. WC1 141 DK71
North Cross Rd. SE22 182 DT85
North Cross Rd., Ilf. 125 EQ56
North Dene NW7 96 CR48
North Dene, Houns. 156 CB81
North Down, S.Croy. 220 DS111
North Downs Cres., Croy. 221 EB110
North Downs Rd., Croy. 221 EB110
North Downs Way, Bet. 248 CQ132
North Downs Way, Dor. 261 BU137
North Downs Way, Guil. 258 AT138
North Downs Way (Albury), Guil. 260 BJ136
North Downs Way, Oxt. 254 EE126
North Downs Way, Sev. 241 FD118
North Downs Way, Tad. 248 CQ132
North Downs Way, West. 239 ER121
North Dr. SW16 181 DJ91
North Dr., Beac. 110 AG55
North Dr., Houns. 156 CC82
North Dr., Orp. 223 ES105
North Dr., Rom. 128 FJ55
North Dr., Ruis. 115 BS59
North Dr., St.Alb. 44 CL18
North Dr., Slou. 132 AS69
North Dr., Vir.W. 192 AS100
North End NW3 120 DC61
North End, Buck.H. 102 EJ45
North End, Croy. 202 DQ103
North End Ave. NW3 120 DC61
North End Cres. W14 159 CZ77
North End Ho. W14 159 CY77
North End La., Orp. 223 EN110
North End Par. W14 159 CY77
North End Rd.
North End Rd. NW11 120 DA60
North End Rd. SW6 159 CZ79
North End Rd. W14 159 CY77
North End Rd., Wem. 118 CN62
North End Way NW3 120 DC61
North Eyot Gdns. W6 159 CT78
St. Peter's Sq.
North Flockton St. SE16 162 DU75
Chambers St.
North Gdn. E14 143 DZ74
Westferry Circ.
North Gdns. SW19 180 DD94
North Gate, Harl. 35 EQ14
North Glade, The, Bex. 186 EZ87
Camden Rd.
North Gower St. NW1 273 L3
North Gower St. NW1 141 DJ69
North Grn. NW9 96 CS52
Clayton Fld.
North Grn., Slou. 132 AS73
North Gro. N6 120 DG59
North Gro. N15 122 DR57
North Gro., Cher. 193 BF100
North Gro., Harl. 52 EU16
North Hatton Rd. (Heathrow Airport), Houns. 155 BR81
North Hill N6 120 DF58
North Hill, Rick. 73 BD40
North Hill Ave. N6 120 DG58
North Hill Dr., Rom. 106 FK48
North Hill Grn., Rom. 106 FK49
Preston Rd.
North Hyde Gdns., Hayes 155 BU77
North Hyde La., Houns. 156 BY78
North Hyde La., Sthl. 156 BY78
North Hyde Rd., Hayes 155 BT76
North Kent Ave., Grav. 190 GC86
North La., Tedd. 177 CF93
North Lo. Clo. SW15 179 CX85
Westleigh Ave.
North Mall N9 100 DV47
St. Martins Rd.
North Mead, Red. 250 DF131
North Ms. WC1 274 C5
North Ms. WC1 141 DM70
North Moors, Guil. 242 AY129
North Mymms Pk., Hat. 63 CT25
North Orbital Rd., Rick. 91 BE50
North Orbital Rd., St.Alb. 62 CL25
North Orbital Rd., Uxb. 113 BF55
North Orbital Rd., Wat. 59 BU34
North Orbital Trd. Est., St.Alb. 43 CG24
North Par., Chess. 216 CL106
North Pk. SE9 185 EM86
North Pk., Ger.Cr. 112 AY55
North Pk., Iver 153 BD76
North Pk. La., Gdse. 252 DU131
North Pas. SW18 160 DA84
North Peckham Est. SE15 162 DT80
North Perimeter Rd., Uxb. 134 BL69
Kingston La.
North Pl., Guil. 258 AX135
North Pl., Mitch. 180 DF94
North Pl., Tedd. 177 CF93
North Pl., Wal.Abb. 67 EB33
Highbridge St.
North Pl. Ind. Est., Harl. 36 EU10
North Pole La., Kes. 222 EF107
North Pole Rd. W10 139 CW71
North Ride W2 276 B1
North Ride W2 140 DE73
North Riding, St.Alb. 60 CA30
North Rd. N6 120 DG59
North Rd. N7 141 DL65
North Rd. N9 100 DV46
North Rd. SE18 165 ES77
North Rd. SW19 180 DC93
North Rd. W5 157 CK76
North Rd., Amer. 55 AQ36
North Rd., Belv. 167 FB76
North Rd., Berk. 38 AV19
North Rd., Brent. 158 CL79
North Rd., Brwd. 108 FW46
North Rd., Brom. 204 EH95
North Rd., Dart. 187 FF87
North Rd., Edg. 96 CP53
North Rd., Felt. 175 BR86
North Rd., Guil. 242 AV131
North Rd., Hayes 135 BR71
North Rd., Hert. 31 DN05
North Rd., Hodd. 49 EA16
North Rd., Ilf. 125 ES61
North Rd., Purf. 169 FR77
North Rd., Reig. 265 CZ137
North Rd., Rich. 158 CN83
North Rd., Rick. 73 BD43
North Rd., Rom. 126 EY57
North Rd. (Havering-atte-Bower), Rom. 105 FE48
North Rd., S.Ock. 149 FW68
North Rd., Sthl. 136 CA73
North Rd., Surb. 197 CK100
North Rd., Wal.Cr. 67 DY33
North Rd., Walt. 214 BW106
North Rd., West Dr. 154 BM76
North Rd., W.Wick. 203 EB102
North Rd., Wok. 227 BA116
North Rd. Ave., Brwd. 108 FW46
North Rd. Ave., Hert. 31 DN08
North Rd. Gdns., Hert. 31 DP09
North Row W1 272 E10
North Row W1 140 DF73
North Service Rd., Brwd. 108 FW47
North Several SE3 163 ED82
Orchard Dr.
North Side Wandsworth Common SW18 180 DD85
North Sq. N9 100 DV47
St. Martins Rd.
North Sq. NW11 120 DA57
North Sta. App., Red. 267 DM136
North St. E13 144 EH68
North St. NW4 119 CW57
North St. SW4 161 DJ83
North St., Bark. 145 EP65
North St., Bexh. 166 FA84
North St., Brom. 204 EG95
North St., Cars. 200 DF104
North St., Dart. 188 FK87
North St., Dor. 263 CG136
North St. (Westcott), Dor. 262 CC137
Guildford Rd.
North St., Egh. 173 AZ92
North St., Gdmg. 258 AT144
Station Rd.
North St., Grav. 191 GH87
North St., Guil. 258 AX135
North St., Horn. 128 FK59
North St., Islw. 157 CG83
North St., Lthd. 231 CG121
North St., Red. 250 DF133
North St., Rom. 127 FD55
North St., Wal.Abb. 50 EE22
North St. Pas. E13 144 EH68
North Tenter St. E1 142 DT72
North Ter. SW3 276 B7
North Ter. SW3 160 DE76
North Ter., Wind. 151 AR80
The Long Wk.
North Verbena Gdns. W6 159 CU78
St. Peter's Sq.
North Vw. SW19 179 CV92
North Vw. W5 137 CJ70
North Vw., Ilf. 104 EU52
North Vw., Pnr. 116 BW59
North Vw. Ave., Til. 171 GG81
North Vw. Cres., Epsom 233 CV117
North Vw. Dr., Wdf.Grn. 102 EK54
North Vw. Rd. N8 121 DK55
North Vw. Rd., Sev. 257 FJ121
Seal Rd.
North Vil. NW1 141 DK65
North Wk. W2 140 DC73
Bayswater Rd.
North Wk., Croy. 221 EB106
North Way N9 100 DW47
North Way N11 99 DJ51
North Way NW9 118 CP55
North Way, Pnr. 116 BW55
North Way, Uxb. 134 BL66
North Weald Ind. Est., Epp. 70 FA26
North Western Ave., Wat. 76 BW36
North Wf. Rd. W2 140 DD71
North Woolwich Rd. E16 144 EG74
North Woolwich Roundabout E16 144 EK74
North Woolwich Rd.
North Worple Way SW14 158 CR83
Northall Rd., Bexh. 167 FC82
Northallerton Way, Rom. 106 FK50
Northampton Ave., Slou. 131 AQ72
Northampton Gro. N1 122 DR64
Northampton Pk. N1 142 DQ65
Northampton Rd. EC1 274 E4
Northampton Rd. EC1 141 DN70
Northampton Rd., Croy. 202 DU103
Northampton Rd., Enf. 83 DY42
Northampton Sq. EC1 274 F3
Northampton Sq. EC1 141 DP69
Northampton St. N1 142 DQ66
Northanger Rd. SW16 181 DL93
Northaw Clo., Hem.H. 41 BP15
Northaw Pl., Pot.B. 64 DD30
Northaw Rd. E. (Cuffley), Pot.B. 65 DK31
Northaw Rd. W., Pot.B. 64 DG30
Northbank Rd. E17 101 EC54
Northborough Rd. SW16 201 DK97
Northborough Rd., Slou. 131 AN70
Northbourne, Brom. 204 EG101
Northbourne, Gdmg. 258 AT143
Northbourne Rd. SW4 161 DK84
Northbridge Rd., Berk. 38 AT17
Northbrook Dr., Nthwd. 93 BS53
Northbrook Rd. N22 99 DL52
Northbrook Rd. SE13 183 ED85
Northbrook Rd., Barn. 79 CY44
Northbrook Rd., Croy. 202 DR99
Northbrook Rd., Ilf. 125 EN61
Northbrooks, Harl. 51 EQ15
Northburgh St. EC1 274 G4
Northburgh St. EC1 141 DP70
Northchurch SE17 279 L10
Northchurch La., Berk. 38 AS21
Northchurch Rd. N1 142 DR66
Northchurch Rd., Wem. 138 CM65
Northchurch Ter. N1 142 DS66
Northcliffe Clo., Wor.Pk. 198 CS104
Northcliffe Dr. N20 97 CZ46
Northcote, Add. 212 BK105
Northcote, Pnr. 94 BW54
Northcote Ave. W5 138 CL73
Northcote Ave., Islw. 177 CG85
Northcote Ave., Sthl. 136 BY73
Northcote Ave., Surb. 198 CN101
Northcote Clo., Lthd. 245 BQ125
Northcote Cres., Lthd. 245 BQ125
Northcote Pk., Lthd. 214 CC114
Northcote Rd. E17 123 DY56
Northcote Rd. NW10 138 CS66
Northcote Rd. SW11 160 DE84
Northcote Rd., Croy. 202 DR100
Northcote Rd., Grav. 191 GF88
Northcote Rd., Lthd. 245 BQ125
Northcote Rd., N.Mal. 198 CQ97
Northcote Rd., Sid. 185 ES91
Northcote Rd., Twick. 177 CG85
Northcott Ave. N22 99 DL53
Northcotts, Abb.L. 59 BR33
Long Elms
Northcourt, Rick. 92 BG46
Springwell Ave.
Northcroft, H.Wyc. 110 AE56
Northcroft, Slou. 131 AP70
Northcroft Clo., Egh. 172 AV92
Northcroft Gdns., Egh. 172 AV92
Northcroft Rd. W13 157 CH75
Northcroft Rd., Egh. 172 AV92
Northcroft Rd., Epsom 216 CR108
Northcroft Ter. W13 157 CH75
Northcroft Rd.
Northcroft Vil., Egh. 172 AV92
Northdene, Chig. 103 ER50
Northdene Gdns. N15 122 DT58
Northdown Clo., Ruis. 115 BT62
Northdown Gdns., Ilf. 125 ES57
Northdown La., Guil. 258 AY137
Northdown Rd., Cat. 237 EA123
Northdown Rd., Ger.Cr. 90 AY51
Northdown Rd., Hat. 45 CU21
Northdown Rd., Horn. 127 FH59
Northdown Rd., Long. 209 FX96
Northdown Rd., Sutt. 218 DA110
Northdown Rd., Well. 166 EV82
Northdown St. N1 141 DM68
Northend, Brwd. 108 FW50

Northend, Hem.H. 41 BP22
Northend Clo., H.Wyc. 110 AC56
Northend Rd., Dart. 167 FF81
Northend Rd., Erith 167 FF80
Northend Trd. Est., Erith 167 FE81
Northern Av. N9 100 DT47
Northern Perimeter Rd., Houns. 155 BQ81
Northern Perimeter Rd. W., Houns. 154 BK81
Northern Relief Rd., Bark. 145 EP66
Northern Rd. E13 144 EH67
Northern Rd., Slou. 131 AR70
Northern Service Rd., Barn. 79 CY41
Northern Wds., H.Wyc. 110 AC56
Northernhay Wk., Mord. 199 CY98
Northey Ave., Sutt. 217 CZ110
Northey St. E14 143 DY73
Northfield, Guil. 258 AY142
Northfield, Hat. 45 CV15
Longmead
Northfield, Loug. 84 EK42
Northfield Ave. W5 157 CH75
Northfield Ave. W13 157 CH75
Northfield Ave., Orp. 206 EW100
Northfield Ave., Pnr. 116 BX56
Northfield Clo., Brom. 204 EL95
Northfield Clo., Hayes 155 BT76
Northfield Ct., Stai. 194 BH95
Northfield Cres., Sutt. 217 CY105
Northfield Gdns., Dag. 126 EZ63
Northfield Rd.
Northfield Gdns., Wat. 76 BW37
Northfield Pk., Hayes 155 BT76
Northfield Path, Dag. 126 EZ62
Northfield Pl., Wey. 213 BP108
Northfield Rd. E6 145 EM66
Northfield Rd. N16 122 DS59
Northfield Rd. W13 157 CH75
Northfield Rd., Barn. 80 DE41
Northfield Rd., Borwd. 78 CP39
Northfield Rd., Cob. 213 BU113
Northfield Rd., Dag. 126 EZ63
Northfield Rd., Enf. 82 DV43
Northfield Rd., Houns. 156 BX79
Northfield Rd., Stai. 194 BH95
Northfield Rd., Wal.Cr. 67 DY32
Northfield Rd. (Eton Wick), Wind. 151 AM77
Northfields SW18 160 DA84
Northfields, Ash. 232 CL119
Northfields, Grays 170 GC77
Northfields Ind. Est., Wem. 138 CN67
Northfields Rd. W3 138 CP71
Northfleet Bypass, Grav. 190 GD88
Northfleet Grn. Rd., Grav. 190 GC92
Northfleet Ind. Est., Grav. 170 FZ84
Northgate, Gat. 268 DF151
Northgate, Nthwd. 93 BQ52
Northgate Dr. NW9 118 CS58
Northgate Path, Borwd. 78 CM39
Northiam N12 98 DA48
Northiam St. E9 142 DV67
Northington St. WC1 274 C5
Northington St. WC1 141 DM70
Northlands, Pot.B. 64 DD31
Northlands Ave., Orp. 223 ES105
Northlands St. SE5 162 DQ82
Northmead Rd., Slou. 131 AM70
Northolm, Edg. 96 CR49
Northolme Clo., Grays 170 GC76
Premier Ave.
Northolme Gdns., Edg. 96 CN53
Northolme Ri., Orp. 205 ES103
Northolme Rd. N5 122 DQ63
Northolt Ave., Ruis. 115 BV64
Northolt Gdns., Grnf. 117 CF64
Northolt Rd., Har. 116 CB63
Northolt Rd., Houns. 154 BK81
Northolt Way, Horn. 148 FJ65
Northover, Brom. 184 EF90
Northport St. N1 142 DR67
Northridge Rd., Grav. 191 GJ90
Northridge Way, Hem.H. 40 BG21
Northrop Rd., Houns. 155 BS81
Northside Rd., Brom. 204 EG95
Mitchell Way
Northspur Rd., Sutt. 200 DA104
Northstead Rd. SW2 181 DN89
Northumberland All. EC3 275 N9
Northumberland All. EC3 142 DS72
Northumberland Ave. E12 124 EJ60
Northumberland Ave. WC2 277 P2
Northumberland Ave. WC2 141 DL74
Northumberland Ave., Enf. 82 DV39
Northumberland Ave., Horn. 128 FJ57
Northumberland Ave., Islw. 157 CF81
Northumberland Ave., Well. 165 ES84
Northumberland Clo., Erith 167 FC80
Northumberland Clo., Stai. 174 BL86
Northumberland Cres., Felt. 175 BS86
Northumberland Gdns. N9 100 DT48
Northumberland Gdns., Brom. 205 EN98
Northumberland Gdns., Islw. 157 CG80
Northumberland Gdns., Mitch. 201 DK99
Northumberland Gro. N17 100 DV52
Northumberland Pk. N17 100 DT52
Northumberland Pk., Erith 167 FC80
Northumberland Pl. W2 140 DA72
Northumberland Pl., Rich. 177 CK86
Northumberland Rd. E6 144 EL72
Northumberland Rd. E17 123 EA59
Northumberland Rd., Barn. 80 DC44
Northumberland Rd., Grav. 191 GF94
Northumberland Rd., Har. 116 BZ57
Northumberland Row, Twick. 177 CE88
Colne Rd.
Northumberland St. WC2 277 P2
Northumberland St. WC2 141 DL74
Northumberland Way, Erith 167 FC81
Northumbria St. E14 143 EA72
Northview, Swan. 207 FE96
Northview Cres. NW10 119 CT63
Northway NW11 120 DB57
Northway, Guil. 242 AU132
Northway, Mord. 199 CY97
Northway, Rick. 92 BK45
Northway, Wall. 219 DJ105
Northway, Welw.G.C. 29 CZ06
Nursery Hill
Northway Circ. NW7 96 CR49
Northway Cres. NW7 96 CR49
Northway Rd. SE5 162 DQ83
Northway Rd., Croy. 202 DT100
Northways Par. NW3 140 DD66
College Cres.
Northweald La., Kings.T. 177 CK92
Northwest Pl. N1 141 DN68
Chapel Mkt.
Northwick Ave., Har. 117 CG58
Northwick Circle, Har. 117 CJ58
Northwick Clo. NW8 140 DD70
Northwick Ter.
Northwick Pk. Rd., Har. 117 CF58
Northwick Rd., Wat. 94 BW49
Northwick Rd., Wem. 137 CK67
Northwick Ter. NW8 140 DD70
Northwick Wk., Har. 117 CF59
Northwold Dr., Pnr. 116 BW55
Cuckoo Hill
Northwold Est. E5 122 DU61
Northwold Rd. E5 122 DT61
Northwold Rd. N16 122 DT61
Northwood, Grays 171 GH75
Northwood, Welw.G.C. 30 DD09
Northwood Ave., Horn. 127 FG63
Northwood Ave., Pur. 219 DN113
Northwood Clo., Wal.Cr. 66 DT27
Northwood Gdns. N12 98 DD50
Northwood Gdns., Grnf. 117 CF64
Northwood Gdns., Ilf. 125 EN56
Northwood Hall N6 121 DJ59
Northwood Ho. SE27 182 DR91
Northwood Pl., Erith 166 EZ76
Northwood Rd. N6 121 DH59
Northwood Rd. SE23 183 DZ88
Northwood Rd., Cars. 218 DG107
Northwood Rd., Houns. 154 BK81
Northwood Rd., Th.Hth. 201 DP96
Northwood Rd., (Harefield) Uxb. 92 BJ53
Northwood Way SE19 182 DR93
Roman Ri.
Northwood Way, Nthwd. 93 BU52
Northwood Way (Harefield), Uxb. 92 BK53
Nortoft Rd., Ger.Cr. 91 AZ51
Norton Ave., Surb. 198 CP101
Norton Clo. E4 101 EA50
Norton Clo., Borwd. 78 CN39
Norton Clo., Enf. 82 DV40
Brick La.
Norton Folgate E1 275 N6
Norton Folgate E1 142 DS71
Norton Gdns. SW16 201 DL96
Norton La., Cob. 229 BT119
Norton Rd. E10 123 DZ60
Norton Rd., Dag. 147 FD65
Norton Rd., Uxb. 134 BK69
Norton Rd., Wem. 137 CK65
Norton Way, West. 255 ER126
Norval Rd., Wem. 117 CH61
Norway Dr., Slou. 132 AV71
Norway Gate SE16 163 DY76
Norway Pl. E14 143 DZ72
East India Dock Rd.
Norway St. SE10 163 EB79
Norway Wk., Rain. 148 FJ70
The Glen
Norwich Ho. E14 143 EB72
Cordelia St.
Norwich Ms., Ilf. 126 EU60
Ashgrove Rd.
Norwich Pl., Bexh. 166 FA84
Norwich Rd. E7 124 EG64
Norwich Rd., Dag. 146 FA68
Norwich Rd., Grnf. 136 CB67
Norwich Rd., Nthwd. 115 BT55
Norwich Rd., Th.Hth. 202 DQ97
Norwich St. EC4 274 D8
Norwich St. EC4 141 DN72
Norwich Wk., Edg. 96 CQ52
Norwich Way, Rick. 75 BP41
Norwood Ave., Rom. 127 FE59
Norwood Ave., Wem. 138 CM67
Norwood Clo., Hert. 31 DM08
Norwood Clo., Lthd. 246 BY128
Norwood Clo., Sthl. 156 CA77
Norwood Clo., Twick. 177 CD89
Fourth Cross Rd.
Norwood Ct., Amer. 55 AP40
Norwood Cres., Houns. 155 BQ81
Norwood Dr., Har. 116 BZ58
Norwood Fm. La., Cob. 213 BU111
Norwood Gdns., Hayes 136 BW70
Norwood Gdns., Sthl. 156 BZ77
Norwood Grn. Rd., Sthl. 156 CA77
Norwood High St. SE27 181 DP90
Norwood La., Iver 133 BD70
Norwood Pk. Rd. SE27 182 DQ92
Norwood Rd. SE24 181 DP88
Norwood Rd. SE27 181 DP89
Norwood Rd., Lthd. 246 BY128
Norwood Rd., Sthl. 156 BZ77
Norwood Rd. (Cheshunt), Wal.Cr. 67 DY30
Norwood Ter., Sthl. 156 CB77
Tentelow La.
Nota Ms. N3 98 DA53
Station Rd.
Notley End, Egh. 172 AW94
Notley St. SE5 162 DR80
Notre Dame Est. SW4 161 DJ84
Notson Rd. SE25 202 DV98
Notting Barn Rd. W10 139 CX70
Notting Hill Gate W11 140 DA74
Nottingdale Sq. W11 139 CY74
Wilsham St.
Nottingham Ave. E16 144 EJ71
Nottingham Clo., Wat. 59 BU33
Nottingham Clo., Wok. 226 AT118
Nottingham Ct. WC2 273 P9
Nottingham Ct., Wok. 226 AT118
Nottingham Clo.
Nottingham Pl. W1 272 F5
Nottingham Pl. W1 140 DG70
Nottingham Rd. E10 123 EC58
Nottingham Rd. SW17 180 DF88
Nottingham Rd., Islw. 157 CF82
Nottingham Rd., Rick. 91 BC45
Nottingham Rd., S.Croy. 220 DQ105
Nottingham St. W1 272 F6
Nottingham St. W1 140 DG71
Nottingham Ter. NW1 272 F5
Nova Ms., Sutt. 199 CY102
Nova Rd., Croy. 201 DP101
Novar Clo., Orp. 205 ET101
Novar Rd. SE9 185 EQ88
Novello St. SW6 160 DA81
Novello Way, Borwd. 78 CR39
Nowell Rd. SW13 159 CU79
Nower, The, Sev. 239 ET119
Nower Hill, Pnr. 116 BZ56
Nower Rd., Dor. 263 CG136
Noyna Rd. SW17 180 DF90
Nuding Clo. SE13 163 EA83
Nuffield Rd., Swan. 187 FG93
Nugent Rd. N19 121 DL60
Nugent Rd. SE25 202 DT97
Nugent Ter. NW8 140 DC68
Nugents Ct., Pnr. 94 BY53
St. Thomas' Dr.
Nugents Pk., Pnr. 94 BY53
Nun Ct. EC2 275 K8
Nunappleton Way, Oxt. 254 EG132
Nuneaton Rd., Dag. 146 EX66
Nunfield, Kings L. 58 BH31
Nunhead Cres. SE15 162 DV83
Nunhead Est. SE15 162 DV83
Nunhead Grn. SE15 162 DV83
Nunhead Grn., Uxb. 113 BF58
Nunhead Gro. SE15 162 DV83
Nunhead La. SE15 162 DV83
Nunhead Pas. SE15 162 DU83
Peckham Rye
Nunnery Clo., St.Alb. 43 CE22
Nunnery Stables, St.Alb. 43 CD22
Nunnington Clo. SE9 184 EL90
Nunns Rd., Enf. 82 DQ40
Nunns Way, Grays 170 GD77
Nuns La., St.Alb. 43 CE24
Nuns Wk., Vir.W. 192 AX99
Nunsbury Dr., Brox. 67 DY25
Nupton Dr., Barn. 79 CW44
Nurseries Rd., St.Alb. 28 CL08
Nursery, The, Erith 167 FF80
Nursery Ave. N3 98 DC54
Nursery Ave., Bexh. 166 EZ83
Nursery Ave., Croy. 203 DX103
Nursery Clo. SE4 163 DZ82
Nursery Clo. SW15 159 CX84
Nursery Clo., Add. 211 BF110
Nursery Clo., Amer. 55 AS39
Nursery Clo., Croy. 203 DX103
Nursery Clo., Dart. 188 FQ87
Nursery Clo., Enf. 83 DX39
Nursery Clo., Epsom 216 CS110
Nursery Clo., Felt. 175 BV87
Nursery Clo., H.Wyc. 88 AC47
Nursery Clo., Rom. 126 EX58
Nursery Clo., Sev. 257 FJ122
Nursery Clo., S.Ock. 149 FW70
Nursery Clo., Swan. 207 FC96
Nursery Clo., Tad. 249 CV125
Nursery Clo., Wok. 226 AW116
Nursery Clo., Wdf.Grn. 102 EH50
Nursery Ct. N17 100 DT52
Nursery St.
Nursery Dr., Maid. 130 AH72
Nursery Flds., Saw. 36 EX05
Nursery Gdns., Chis. 185 EP93
Nursery Gdns., Enf. 83 DX39
Nursery Gdns., Guil. 259 BB140
Nursery Gdns., Stai. 174 BH94
Nursery Gdns., Sun. 195 BT96
Nursery Gdns., Wal.Cr. 66 DR28
Nursery Gdns., Ware 33 DY06
Nursery Gdns., Welw.G.C. 29 CY06
Nursery Hill, Welw.G.C. 29 CY06
Nursery La. E2 142 DT67
Nursery La. E7 144 EG65
Nursery La. W10 139 CW71
Nursery La., H.Wyc. 88 AC47
Nursery La., Horl. 268 DD149
Nursery La., Slou. 132 AW74
Nursery La., Uxb. 134 BK70
Nursery Pl., Sev. 256 FD122
Nursery Rd. E9 142 DW65
Morning La.
Nursery Rd. N2 98 DD53
Nursery Rd. N14 99 DJ45
Nursery Rd. SW9 161 DM84
Nursery Rd., Brox. 67 DY25
Nursery Rd., Gdmg. 258 AT144
Nursery Rd., Hodd. 33 EB14
Nursery Rd., Loug. 84 EJ43
Nursery Rd. (High Beach), Loug. 84 EH39
Nursery Rd., Pnr. 116 BW55
Nursery Rd., Sun. 195 BS96
Nursery Rd., Sutt. 218 DC105
Nursery Rd., Tad. 249 CV125
Nursery Rd., Th.Hth. 202 DR98
Nursery Rd., Wal.Abb. 49 ED22
Nursery Rd. Merton SW19 200 DB96
Nursery Rd. Mitcham, Mitch. 200 DE97
Nursery Rd. Wimbledon SW19 179 CY94
Worple Rd.
Nursery Row SE17 279 K9
Nursery Row SE17 162 DR77
Nursery Row, Barn. 79 CY41
St. Albans Rd.
Nursery St. N17 100 DT52
Nursery Wk. NW4 119 CV55
Nursery Wk., Rom. 127 FD59
Nursery Way, Stai. 172 AX86
Nursery Waye, Uxb. 134 BK67
Nurserymans Rd. N11 98 DG47
Nurstead Rd., Erith 166 FA80
Nut Gro., Welw.G.C. 29 CX06
Nut Tree Clo., Orp. 206 EX104
Nutberry Ave., Grays 170 GA75
Nutberry Clo., Grays 170 GA75
Long La.
Nutbourne St. W10 139 CY69
Nutbrook St. SE15 162 DU83
Nutbrowne Rd., Dag. 146 EZ67
Nutcombe La., Dor. 263 CF136
Nutcroft Gro., Lthd. 231 CE121
Nutcroft Rd. SE15 162 DV80
Nutfield, Welw.G.C. 30 DA06
Nutfield Clo. N18 100 DU51
Nutfield Clo., Cars. 200 DE104
Nutfield Gdns., Ilf. 125 ET61
Nutfield Gdns., Nthlt. 136 BW68
Nutfield Marsh Rd., Red. 251 DK131
Nutfield Rd. E15 123 EC63
Nutfield Rd. NW2 119 CU61
Nutfield Rd. SE22 182 DT85
Nutfield Rd., Couls. 234 DG116
Nutfield Rd., Red. 250 DG134
Nutfield Rd. (South Merstham), Red. 251 DJ129
Nutfield Rd., Th.Hth. 201 DP98
Nutfield Way, Orp. 205 EN103
Nutford Pl. W1 272 C8
Nutford Pl. W1 140 DF72
Nuthatch Clo., Stai. 174 BM88
Nuthatch Gdns. SE28 165 ER75
Nuthatch Gdns., Reig. 266 DC138
Nuthurst Ave. SW2 181 DM89
Nutkin Wk., Uxb. 134 BL66
Park Rd.
Nutkins Way, Chesh. 54 AQ29
Nutley Clo., Swan. 207 FF95
Nutley Ct., Reig. 249 CZ134
Nutley La.
Nutley La., Reig. 249 CZ133
Nutley Ter. NW3 140 DC65
Nutmead Clo., Bex. 187 FC88
Nutmeg Clo. E16 144 EE70
Cranberry La.
Nutmeg La. E14 143 ED72
Nutt Gro., Edg. 95 CK47
Nutt St. SE15 162 DT80
Nuttall St. N1 142 DS68
Nutter La. E11 124 EJ58
Nuttfield Clo., Rick. 75 BP44
Nutty La., Shep. 195 BQ97
Nutwell St. SW17 180 DE92
Nutwood Ave., Bet. 264 CQ135
Nutwood Clo., Bet. 264 CQ135
Nuxley Rd., Belv. 166 EZ79
Nyanza St. SE18 165 ER79
Nye Bevan Est. E5 123 DX62
Nye Way, Hem.H. 57 BA28
Nyefield Pk., Tad. 249 CU126
Nylands Ave., Rich. 158 CN81
Nymans Gdns. SW20 199 CV97
Hidcote Gdns.
Nynehead St. SE14 163 DY80
Nyon Gro. SE6 183 DZ89
Nyssa Clo., Wdf.Grn. 103 EM51
Gwynne Pk. Ave.
Nyth Clo., Upmin. 129 FR58
Nyton Clo. N19 121 DL60
Courtauld Rd.

O

Oak Apple Ct. SE12 184 EG89
Oak Ave. N8 121 DL56
Oak Ave. N10 99 DH52
Oak Ave. N17 100 DR52
Oak Ave., Croy. 203 EA103
Oak Ave., Egh. 173 BC94
Oak Ave., Enf. 81 DM38
Oak Ave., Hmptn. 176 BY92
Oak Ave., Houns. 156 BX80
Oak Ave., St.Alb. 60 CA30
Oak Ave., Sev. 257 FH128
Oak Ave., Upmin. 128 FP62
Oak Ave., Uxb. 115 BP61
Oak Ave., West Dr. 154 BN76
Oak Bank, Croy. 221 EC107
Oak Bank, Wok. 226 AY119
Oak Clo. N14 99 DH45
Oak Clo., Dart. 167 FE84
Oak Clo., Gdmg. 258 AS143
Oak Clo., Hem.H. 40 BM24
Oak Clo., Sutt. 200 DC103
Oak Clo., Tad. 248 CP130
Oak Clo., Wal.Abb. 67 ED34
Oak Cottage Clo. SE6 184 EE88
Oak Cres. E16 144 EE71
Oak Dene W13 137 CH71
The Dene
Oak Dr., Berk. 38 AX20
Oak Dr., Saw. 36 EW07
Oak Dr., Tad. 248 CP130
Oak End, Harl. 51 ET17
Oak End Dr., Iver 133 BC68
Oak End Way, Add. 211 BE112
Oak End Way, Ger.Cr. 113 AZ57
Oak Fm., Borwd. 78 CQ43
Oak Gdns., Croy. 203 EA103
Oak Gdns., Edg. 96 CQ54
Oak Glade, Epp. 70 EX29
Coopersale Common
Oak Glade, Epsom 216 CN112
Christ Ch. Rd.
Oak Glade, Nthwd. 93 BP53
Oak Glen, Horn. 128 FL55
Oak Gra. Rd., Guil. 244 BG129
Oak Grn., Abb.L. 59 BS32
Oak Grn. Way, Abb.L. 59 BS32
Oak Gro. NW2 119 CY63
Oak Gro., Hat. 45 CT18
Oak Gro., Hert. 32 DS11
Oak Gro., Ruis. 115 BV60
Oak Gro., Sun. 175 BV94
Oak Gro., W.Wick. 203 EC103
Oak Gro. Rd. SE20 202 DW95
Oak Hall Rd. E11 124 EH58
Oak Hill, Epsom 232 CR116
Oak Hill, Guil. 243 BC129
Oak Hill, Surb. 198 CL101
Oak Hill, Wdf.Grn. 101 ED52
Oak Hill Clo., Wdf.Grn. 101 ED52
Oak Hill Cres., Surb. 198 CL101
Oak Hill Cres., Wdf.Grn. 101 ED52
Oak Hill Gdns., Wdf.Grn. 102 EE53
Oak Hill Gro., Surb. 198 CL100
Oak Hill Pk. NW3 120 DB63
Oak Hill Pk. Ms. NW3 120 DC63
Oak Hill Rd., Rom. 105 FD45
Oak Hill Rd., Sev. 256 FG124
Oak Hill Rd., Surb. 198 CL100
Oak Hill Way NW3 120 DC63
Oak La. E14 143 DZ73
Oak La. N2 98 DD54
Oak La. N11 99 DK51
Oak La., Egh. 172 AW90
Oak La., Islw. 157 CE84
Oak La. (Cuffley), Pot.B. 65 DM28
Oak La., Sev. 256 FF129
Oak La., Twick. 177 CG87
Oak La., Wind. 151 AN81
Oak La., Wok. 227 BC116
Beaufort Rd.
Oak La., Wdf.Grn. 102 EF49
Oak Leaf Clo., Epsom 216 CQ112
Oak Lo. Ave., Chig. 103 ER50
Oak Lo. Clo., Stan. 95 CJ50
Dennis La.
Oak Lo. Clo., Walt. 214 BW106
Oak Lo. Dr., Red. 266 DG142
Oak Lo. Dr., W.Wick. 203 EB101
Oak Lo. La., West. 255 ER125
Oak Manor Dr., Wem. 118 CM64
Oakington Manor Dr.
Oak Pk., W.Byf. 211 BE113
Oak Pk. Gdns. SW19 179 CX87
Oak Path (Bushey), Wat. 76 CB44
Ashfield Ave.
Oak Piece, Epp. 71 FC25
Oak Pl. SW18 180 DB85
East Hill
Oak Ridge, Dor. 263 CH139
Oak Ri., Buck.H. 102 EK48
Oak Rd. W5 137 CK73
The Bdy.
Oak Rd., Cat. 236 DS122
Oak Rd., Cob. 230 BX115
Oak Rd., Epp. 69 ET30
Oak Rd. (Northumberland Heath), Erith 167 FC80
Oak Rd. (Slade Grn.), Erith 167 FG81
Oak Rd., Grav. 191 GJ90
Oak Rd., Grays 170 GC79
Oak Rd., Green. 189 FS86
Oak Rd., Lthd. 231 CG119
Oak Rd., N.Mal. 198 CR96
Oak Rd., Orp. 224 EU108
Oak Rd., Reig. 250 DB133
Oak Rd., Rom. 106 FM53
Oak Rd., West. 255 ER125
Oak Row SW16 201 DJ96
Oak St., Hem.H. 40 BM24
Oak St., Rom. 127 FC57
Oak Stubbs La., Maid. 150 AF75
Oak Tree Ave. (Bluewater), Green. 189 FT87
Oak Tree Clo. W5 137 CJ72
Pinewood Gro.
Oak Tree Clo., Abb.L. 59 BR32
Oak Tree Clo. (Burpham), Guil. 243 BC129
Oak Tree Clo. (Jacobs Well), Guil. 242 AX128
Oak Tree Clo., Hat. 45 CU17
Oak Tree Clo., Hert. 32 DW12
Oak Tree Clo., Loug. 85 EQ39
Oak Tree Clo., Stan. 95 CJ52
Oak Tree Clo., Vir.W. 192 AX100
Oak Tree Ct., Borwd. 77 CK44
Barnet La.
Oak Tree Dell NW9 118 CQ57
Oak Tree Dr. N20 98 DB46
Oak Tree Dr., Egh. 172 AW92
Oak Tree Dr., Guil. 242 AW130
Oak Tree Gdns., Brom. 184 EH92
Oak Tree Rd. NW8 272 A3
Oak Tree Rd. NW8 140 DE69
Oak Village NW5 120 DG63
Oak Wk., Saw. 36 EX07
Oak Way N14 99 DH45
Oak Way W3 138 CS74
Oak Way, Ash. 232 CN116
Oak Way, Croy. 203 DX100
Oak Way, Felt. 175 BS88
Oak Way, Reig. 266 DD135
Oakapple Clo., S.Croy. 220 DV114
Oakbank, Brwd. 109 GE43
Oakbank, Lthd. 230 CC123
Oakbank Ave., Walt. 196 BZ101
Oakbank Gro. SE24 162 DQ84
Oakbrook Clo., Brom. 184 EH91
Oakbury Rd. SW6 160 DB82
Oakcombe Clo., N.Mal. 198 CS95
Traps La.
Oakcroft Clo., Pnr. 93 BV54
Oakcroft Clo., W.Byf. 211 BF114
Oakcroft Rd. SE13 163 ED82
Oakcroft Rd., Chess. 216 CM105
Oakcroft Rd., W.Byf. 211 BF114
Oakcroft Vil., Chess. 216 CM105
Oakdale N14 99 DH46
Oakdale, Welw.G.C. 29 CX05
Oakdale Ave., Har. 118 CL57
Oakdale Ave., Nthwd. 93 BU54
Oakdale Clo., Wat. 94 BW49
Oakdale Gdns. E4 101 EC50
Oakdale La., Eden. 255 EQ133
Oakdale Rd. E7 144 EH66
Oakdale Rd. E11 123 ED61
Oakdale Rd. E18 102 EH54
Oakdale Rd. N4 122 DQ58
Oakdale Rd. SE15 162 DW83
Oakdale Rd. SW16 181 DL92
Oakdale Rd., Epsom 216 CR109
Oakdale Rd., Wat. 94 BW48
Oakdale Rd., Wey. 194 BN104
Oakdale Way, Mitch. 200 DG101
Wolseley Rd.
Oakden St. SE11 278 E8
Oakden St. SE11 161 DN77
Oakdene SE15 162 DV81
Carlton Gro.
Oakdene, Beac. 89 AL52
Oakdene, Tad. 233 CY120
Oakdene (Cheshunt), Wal.Cr. 67 DY30
Oakdene, Wok. 210 AT110
Oakdene Ave., Chis. 185 EN92
Oakdene Ave., Erith 167 FC79
Oakdene Ave., T.Ditt. 197 CG102
Oakdene Clo., Bet. 264 CQ136
Oakdene Clo., Horn. 127 FH58
Oakdene Clo., Lthd. 246 CC127
Oakdene Clo., Pnr. 94 BZ52
Oakdene Dr., Surb. 198 CQ101
Oakdene Ms., Sutt. 199 CZ102
Oakdene Pk. N3 97 CZ52
Oakdene Rd., Bet. 264 CP136
Oakdene Rd., Cob. 213 BV114
Oakdene Rd., Guil. 258 AW142
Oakdene Rd., Hem.H. 40 BM24
Oakdene Rd., Lthd. 230 BZ124
Oakdene Rd., Orp. 205 ET99
Oakdene Rd., Red. 250 DE134
Oakdene Rd., Sev. 256 FG122
Oakdene Rd., Uxb. 135 BP68
Oakdene Rd., Wat. 75 BV36
Oakdene Way, St.Alb. 43 CJ20
Oake Ct. SW15 179 CY85
Oaken Coppice, Ash. 232 CN119
Oaken Dr., Esher 215 CF107
Oaken Gro., Welw.G.C. 29 CY11

Oaken La., Esher 215 CE105
Oakenholt Ho. SE2 166 EX75
Hartslock Dr.
Oakenshaw Clo., Surb. 198 CL101
Oakes Clo. E6 145 EM72
Savage Gdns.
Oakeshott Ave. N6 120 DG61
Oakey La. SE1 278 D6
Oakey La. SE1 161 DN76
Oakfield E4 101 EB50
Oakfield, Rick. 92 BG45
Oakfield, Wok. 226 AS116
Oakfield Ave., Har. 117 CH55
Oakfield Ave., Slou. 131 AP74
Oakfield Clo., N.Mal. 199 CT99
Blakes La.
Oakfield Clo., Pot.B. 63 CZ31
Oakfield Clo., Ruis. 115 BT58
Oakfield Clo., Wey. 213 BQ105
Oakfield Ct. N8 121 DL59
Oakfield Ct. NW2 119 CX59
Hendon Way
Oakfield Ct., Borwd. 78 CP41
Oakfield Dr., Reig. 250 DA132
Oakfield Gdns. N18 100 DS49
Oakfield Gdns. SE19 182 DS92
Oakfield Gdns., Beck. 203 EA99
Oakfield Gdns., Cars. 200 DE102
Oakfield Gdns., Grnf. 137 CD70
Oakfield Glade, Wey. 213 BQ105
Oakfield La., Bex. 187 FE89
Oakfield La., Dart. 187 FG89
Oakfield La., Kes. 222 EJ105
Oakfield Pk. Rd., Dart. 188 FK89
Oakfield Pl., Dart. 188 FK89
Oakfield Rd. E6 144 EL67
Oakfield Rd. E17 101 DY54
Oakfield Rd. N3 98 DB53
Oakfield Rd. N4 121 DN58
Oakfield Rd. N14 99 DL48
Oakfield Rd. SE20 182 DV94
Oakfield Rd. SW19 179 CX90
Oakfield Rd., Ashf. 175 BP91
Oakfield Rd., Ash. 231 CK117
Oakfield Rd., Cob. 213 BV113
Oakfield Rd., Croy. 202 DQ102
Oakfield Rd., Ilf. 125 EP61
Oakfield Rd., Orp. 206 EU101
Goodmead Rd.
Oakfield St. SW10 160 DC79
Oakfields, Guil. 242 AS133
Oakfields, Sev. 257 FH126
Oakfields, Walt. 195 BU102
Oakfields, W.Byf. 212 BH114
Oakfields Rd. NW11 119 CY58
Oakford Rd. NW5 121 DJ63
Oakhall Ct. E11 124 EH58
Oakhall Dr., Sun. 175 BT92
Oakham Clo. SE6 183 DZ89
Rutland Wk.
Oakham Clo., Barn. 80 DF41
Oakham Dr., Brom. 204 EF98
Oakhampton Rd. NW7 97 CX52
Oakhill, Esher 215 CG107
Oakhill Ave. NW3 120 DB63
Oakhill Ave., Pnr. 94 BY54
Oakhill Clo., Ash. 231 CJ118
Oakhill Clo., Rick. 91 BE49
Oakhill Ct. SW19 179 CX94
Oakhill Dr., Surb. 198 CL101
Oakhill Gdns., Wey. 195 BS103
Oatlands Dr.
Oakhill Path, Surb. 198 CL100
Oakhill Pl. SW15 180 DA85
Oakhill Rd.
Oakhill Rd. SW15 179 CZ85
Oakhill Rd. SW16 201 DL95
Oakhill Rd., Add. 211 BF107
Oakhill Rd., Ash. 231 CJ118
Oakhill Rd., Beck. 203 EC96
Oakhill Rd., Orp. 205 ET102
Oakhill Rd., Purf. 168 FP78
Oakhill Rd., Reig. 266 DB135
Oakhill Rd., Rick. 91 BD49
Oakhill Rd., Sutt. 200 DB104
Oakhouse Rd., Bexh. 186 FA85
Oakhurst, Wok. 210 AS109
Oakhurst Ave., Barn. 98 DE45
Oakhurst Ave., Bexh. 166 EY80
Oakhurst Clo. E17 124 EE56
Oakhurst Clo., Ilf. 103 EQ53
Oakhurst Clo., Tedd. 177 CE92
Oakhurst Gdns. E4 102 EF46
Oakhurst Gdns. E17 124 EE56
Oakhurst Gdns., Bexh. 166 EY80
Oakhurst Gro. SE22 162 DU84
Oakhurst Pl., Wat. 75 BT42
Cherrydale
Oakhurst Ri., Cars. 218 DE110
Oakhurst Rd., Enf. 83 DX36
Oakhurst Rd., Epsom 216 CQ107
Oakington, Welw.G.C. 30 DD09
Oakington Ave., Amer. 72 AX39
Oakington Ave., Har. 116 CA59
Oakington Ave., Hayes 155 BR77
Oakington Ave., Wem. 118 CM62
Oakington Dr., Sun. 196 BW96
Oakington Manor Dr., Wem. 118 CN64
Oakington Rd. W9 140 DA70
Oakington Way N8 121 DL58
Oakland Gdns., Brwd. 109 GC43
Oakland Pl., Buck.H. 102 EG47
Oakland Rd. E15 123 ED63
Oakland Way, Epsom 216 CR107
Oaklands N21 99 DM47
Oaklands, Berk. 38 AU19
Oaklands, Horl. 269 DJ147
Oaklands, Lthd. 231 CD124
Oaklands, Twick. 176 CC87
Oaklands Ave. N9 82 DV44
Oaklands Ave., Esher 197 CD102
Oaklands Ave., Hat. 63 CY27
Oaklands Ave., Islw. 157 CF79
Oaklands Ave., Rom. 127 FE55
Oaklands Ave., Sid. 185 ET87
Oaklands Ave., Th.Hth. 201 DN98
Oaklands Ave., Wat. 93 BV46
Oaklands Ave., W.Wick. 203 EB104
Oaklands Clo., Bexh. 186 EZ85
Oaklands Clo., Chess. 215 CJ105
Oaklands Clo., Guil. 258 AY142
Oaklands Clo., Orp. 205 ES100
Oaklands Ct., Add. 194 BH104
Oaklands Ct., Wat. 75 BU39
Oaklands Ct., Wem. 117 CK64
Oaklands Dr., Harl. 52 EW16
Oaklands Dr., Red. 267 DH136
Oaklands Dr., S.Ock. 149 FW71
Oaklands Est. SW4 181 DJ86
Oaklands Gdns., Ken. 220 DQ114
Oaklands Gate, Nthwd. 93 BS51
Green La.
Oaklands Gro. W12 139 CU74
Oaklands Gro., Brox. 49 DY24
Oaklands La., Barn. 79 CV42
Oaklands La., St.Alb. 44 CL18
Oaklands La., West. 222 EH113
Oaklands Pk. Ave., Ilf. 125 ER61
High Rd.
Oaklands Pl. SW4 161 DJ84
St. Alphonsus Rd.
Oaklands Rd. N20 97 CZ45
Oaklands Rd. NW2 119 CX63
Oaklands Rd. SW14 158 CR83
Oaklands Rd. W7 157 CF75
Oaklands Rd., Bexh. 166 EZ84
Oaklands Rd., Brom. 184 EE94
Oaklands Rd., Dart. 188 FP88
Oaklands Rd., Grav. 191 GF91
Oaklands Rd. (Cheshunt), Wal.Cr. 66 DS26
Oaklands Way, Tad. 233 CW122
Oaklands Way, Wall. 219 DK108
Oaklawn Rd., Lthd. 231 CE118
Oaklea Pas., Kings.T. 197 CK97
Oakleafe Gdns., Ilf. 125 EP55
Oakleigh Ave. N20 98 DD47
Oakleigh Ave., Edg. 96 CP54
Oakleigh Ave., Surb. 198 CN102
Oakleigh Clo. N20 98 DF48
Oakleigh Clo., Swan. 207 FE97
Oakleigh Ct., Barn. 80 DE44
Church Hill Rd.
Oakleigh Ct., Edg. 96 CQ54
Oakleigh Cres. N20 98 DE48
Oakleigh Dr., Rick. 75 BQ44
Oakleigh Gdns. N20 98 DC46
Oakleigh Gdns., Edg. 96 CM50
Oakleigh Gdns., Orp. 223 ES105
Oakleigh Ms. N20 98 DC47
Oakleigh Rd. N.
Oakleigh Pk. Ave., Chis. 205 EN95
Oakleigh Pk. N. N20 98 DD46
Oakleigh Pk. S. N20 98 DE47
Oakleigh Ri., Epp. 70 EU32
Bower Hill
Oakleigh Rd., Pnr. 94 BZ51
Oakleigh Rd., Uxb. 135 BQ66
Oakleigh Rd. N. N20 98 DD47
Oakleigh Rd. S. N11 98 DG48
Oakleigh Way, Mitch. 201 DH95
Oakleigh Way, Surb. 198 CN102
Oakley Ave. W5 138 CN73
Oakley Ave., Bark. 145 ET66
Oakley Ave., Croy. 219 DL105
Oakley Clo. E4 101 EC48
Mapleton Rd.
Oakley Clo. E6 144 EL72
Northumberland Rd.
Oakley Clo. W7 137 CE73
Oakley Clo., Add. 212 BK105
Oakley Clo., Grays 169 FW79
Oakley Clo., Islw. 157 CD81
Oakley Ct., Loug. 85 EN40
Hillyfields
Oakley Ct., Mitch. 200 DG102
London Rd.
Oakley Cres. EC1 274 G1
Oakley Cres., Slou. 132 AS73
Oakley Dell, Guil. 243 BC132
Oakley Dr. SE9 185 ER88
Oakley Dr. SE13 183 EC85
Hither Grn. La.
Oakley Dr., Brom. 204 EL104
Oakley Dr., Rom. 106 FN50
Oakley Gdns. N8 121 DM57
Oakley Gdns. SW3 160 DE79
Oakley Gdns., Bans. 234 DB115
Oakley Grn. Rd., Wind. 150 AG82
Oakley Pk., Bex. 186 EW87
Oakley Pl. SE1 162 DT78
Oakley Rd. N1 142 DR66
Oakley Rd. SE25 202 DV99
Oakley Rd., Brom. 204 EL104
Oakley Rd., Har. 117 CE58
Oakley Rd., Warl. 236 DU118
Oakley Sq. NW1 141 DJ68
Oakley St. SW3 160 DE79
Oakley Wk. W6 159 CX79
Oakley Yd. E2 142 DT70
Bacon St.
Oaklodge Way NW7 97 CT51
Oakmead Ave., Brom. 204 EG100
Oakmead Gdns., Edg. 96 CR49
Oakmead Grn., Epsom 232 CQ115
Oakmead Pl., Mitch. 200 DE95
Oakmead Rd. SW12 180 DG88
Oakmead Rd., Croy. 201 DK100
Oakmeade, Pnr. 94 CA51
Oakmere Ave., Pot.B. 64 DC33
Oakmere Clo., Pot.B. 64 DD31
Oakmere La., Pot.B. 64 DC32
Oakmere Rd. SE2 166 EU79
Oakmoor Way, Chig. 103 ES50
Oakmount Pl., Orp. 205 ER102
Oakridge, St.Alb. 60 BZ29
Oakridge Ave., Rad. 61 CF34
Oakridge Dr. N2 120 DD55
Oakridge La., Brom. 183 ED92
Downham Way
Oakridge La., Wat. 77 CD35
Oakridge Rd., Brom. 183 ED91
Oakroyd Ave., Pot.B. 63 CZ33
Oakroyd Clo., Pot.B. 63 CZ34
Oaks, The N12 98 DB49
Oaks, The SE18 165 EQ78
Oaks, The, Berk. 38 AU19
Oaks, The, Epsom 217 CT114
Oaks, The, Hayes 135 BQ68
Charville La.
Oaks, The, Ruis. 115 BS59
Oaks, The, Stai. 173 BF91
Moormede Cres.
Oaks, The, Swan. 207 FE96
Oaks, The, Wat. 94 BW46
Oaks, The, W.Byf. 212 BG114
Oaks, The, Wdf.Grn. 102 EE51
Oaks Ave. SE19 182 DS92
Oaks Ave., Felt. 176 BY89
Oaks Ave., Rom. 105 FC54
Oaks Ave., Wor.Pk. 199 CV104
Oaks Clo., Lthd. 231 CG121
Oaks Clo., Rad. 77 CF35
Oaks Gro. E4 102 EE47
Oaks La., Croy. 202 DW104
Oaks La., Dor. 263 CH143
Oaks La., Ilf. 125 ES57
Oaks Rd., Croy. 220 DV106
Oaks Rd., Ken. 219 DP114
Oaks Rd., Reig. 250 DD133
Oaks Rd., Stai. 174 BK86
Oaks Rd., Wok. 226 AY117
Oaks Track, Cars. 218 DF111
Oaks Track, Wall. 219 DH110
Oaks Way, Cars. 218 DF108
Oaks Way, Epsom 233 CV119
Epsom La. N.
Oaks Way, Ken. 220 DQ114
Oaks Way, Surb. 197 CK103
Oaksford Ave. SE26 182 DV90
Oakshade Rd., Brom. 183 ED91
Oakshade Rd., Lthd. 214 CC114
Oakshaw, Oxt. 253 ED127
Oakshaw Rd. SW18 180 DB87
Oakside (Denham), Uxb. 134 BH65
Oakside Ct., Horl. 269 DJ147
Oakside La.
Oakside La., Horl. 269 DJ147
Oakthorpe Rd. N13 99 DN50
Oaktree Ave. N13 99 DP48
Oaktree Clo., Brwd. 109 FZ49
Hawthorn Ave.
Oaktree Clo., Wal.Cr. 65 DP28
Oaktree Garth, Welw.G.C. 29 CY10
Oaktree Gro., Ilf. 125 ER64
Oakview Clo., Wal.Cr. 66 DV28
Oakview Gdns. N2 120 DD56
Oakview Gro., Croy. 203 DY102
Oakview Rd. SE6 183 EB92
Oakway SW20 199 CW98
Oakway, Amer. 55 AP35
Oakway, Brom. 203 ED96
Oakway, Wok. 226 AS119
Oakway Clo., Bex. 186 EY86
Oakway Pl., Rad. 61 CG34
Watling St.
Oakways SE9 185 EP86
Oakwell Dr., Pot.B. 65 DH32
Oakwood, Berk. 38 AT20
Oakwood, Guil. 242 AU129
Oakwood, Wall. 219 DH109
Oakwood, Wal.Abb. 83 ED35
Roundhills
Oakwood Ave. N14 99 DK45
Oakwood Ave., Beck. 203 EC96
Oakwood Ave., Borwd. 78 CP42
Oakwood Ave., Brwd. 109 GE44
Oakwood Ave., Brom. 204 EH97
Oakwood Ave., Mitch. 200 DD96
Oakwood Ave., Pur. 219 DP112
Oakwood Ave., Sthl. 136 CA73
Oakwood Chase, Horn. 128 FM58
Oakwood Clo. N14 81 DJ44
Oakwood Clo., Chis. 185 EM93
Oakwood Clo., Dart. 188 FP88
Oakwood Clo., Lthd. 245 BS127
Oakwood Clo., Red. 250 DG134
Oakwood Clo. (South Nutfield), Red. 267 DM136
The Ave.
Oakwood Clo., Wdf.Grn. 102 EL51
Green Wk.
Oakwood Ct. W14 159 CZ76
Oakwood Cres. N21 81 DL44
Oakwood Cres., Grnf. 137 CG65
Oakwood Dr. SE19 182 DR93
Oakwood Dr., Bexh. 167 FD84
Oakwood Dr., Edg. 96 CQ51
Oakwood Dr., Lthd. 245 BS127
Oakwood Dr., St.Alb. 43 CJ19
Oakwood Dr., Sev. 257 FH123
Oakwood Gdns., Ilf. 125 ET61
Oakwood Gdns., Orp. 205 EQ103
Oakwood Gdns., Sutt. 200 DA103
Oakwood Hill, Loug. 85 EM44
Oakwood Hill Ind. Est., Loug. 85 EQ43
Oakwood La. W14 159 CZ76
Oakwood Pk. Rd. N14 99 DK45
Oakwood Pl., Croy. 201 DN100
Oakwood Rd. NW11 120 DB57
Oakwood Rd. SW20 199 CU95
Oakwood Rd., Croy. 201 DN100
Oakwood Rd., Horl. 268 DG147
Oakwood Rd., Orp. 205 EQ103
Oakwood Rd., Pnr. 93 BV54
Oakwood Rd., Red. 251 DN129
Oakwood Rd., St.Alb. 60 BZ29
Oakwood Rd., Vir.W. 192 AW99
Oakwood Rd., Wok. 226 AS119
Oakwood Vw. N14 81 DK44
Oakworth Rd. W10 139 CW71
Oast Ho. Clo., Stai. 172 AY87
Oast Rd., Oxt. 254 EF131
Oasthouse Way, Orp. 206 EV98
Oat La. EC2 275 H8
Oat La. EC2 142 DQ72
Oates Clo., Brom. 203 ED97
Oates Rd., Rom. 105 FB50
Oatfield Rd., Orp. 205 ET102
Oatfield Rd., Tad. 233 CV121
Oatland Ri. E17 101 DY54
Oatlands, Horl. 269 DH147
Oatlands Ave., Wey. 213 BQ106
Oatlands Chase, Wey. 195 BS104
Oatlands Clo., Wey. 213 BQ105
Oatlands Dr., Slou. 131 AR72
Oatlands Dr., Wey. 195 BR104
Oatlands Grn., Wey. 195 BR104
Oatlands Dr.
Oatlands Mere, Wey. 195 BR104
Oatlands Rd., Enf. 82 DW39
Oatlands Rd., Tad. 233 CY119
Oban Clo. E13 144 EJ70
Oban Ct., Slou. 151 AR75
Montem La.
Oban Ho., Bark. 145 ER68
Wheelers Cross
Oban Rd. E13 144 EJ69
Oban Rd. SE25 202 DR98
Oban St. E14 143 ED72
Obelisk Ride, Egh. 172 AS93
Oberon Clo., Borwd. 78 CQ39
Oberon Way, Shep. 194 BL97
Oberstein Rd. SW11 160 DD84
Oborne Clo. SE24 181 DP85
Observatory Gdns. W8 160 DA75
Observatory Ms. E14 163 ED77
Storers Quay
Observatory Rd. SW14 158 CQ84
Observatory Wk., Red. 250 DF134
Lower Bri. Rd.
Occupation La. SE18 165 EP81
Occupation La. W5 157 CK77
Occupation Rd. SE17 279 H10
Occupation Rd. SE17 162 DQ78
Occupation Rd. W13 157 CH75
Occupation Rd., Wat. 75 BV43
Ocean Est. E1 143 DX70
Ocean St. E1 143 DX71
Ocean Wf. E14 163 EA75
Ockenden Clo., Wok. 227 AZ118
Ockenden Rd.
Ockenden Gdns., Wok. 227 AZ118
Ockenden Rd.
Ockenden Rd., Wok. 227 AZ118
Ockendon Rd. N1 142 DR65
Ockendon Rd., Upmin. 128 FQ64
Ockham Dr., Lthd. 229 BR124
Ockham Dr., Orp. 186 EU94
Ockham La., Cob. 229 BR120
Ockham La., Wok. 228 BN121
Ockham Rd. N., Lthd. 229 BQ123
Ockham Rd. N., Wok. 228 BL120
Ockham Rd. S., Lthd. 245 BS126
Ockley Ct., Guil. 243 BB129
Cotts Wd. Dr.
Ockley Rd. SW16 181 DL90
Ockley Rd., Croy. 201 DM101
Ockleys Mead, Gdse. 252 DW130
Octagon Arc. EC2 275 M7
Octagon Rd., Walt. 213 BS109
Octavia Clo., Mitch. 200 DE99
Octavia Rd., Islw. 157 CF82
Octavia St. SW11 160 DE81
Octavia Way SE28 146 EV73
Booth Clo.
Octavia Way, Stai. 174 BG93
Octavius St. SE8 163 EA80
Odard Rd., W.Mol. 196 CA98
Down St.
Oddesey Rd., Borwd. 78 CP39
Odencroft, Slou. 131 AN69
Odessa Rd. E7 124 EF63
Odessa Rd. NW10 139 CU68
Odessa St. SE16 163 DZ75
Odger St. SW11 160 DF82
Odhams Wk. WC2 273 P9
Odyssey Business Pk., Ruis. 115 BV64
Offa Rd., St.Alb. 42 CC20
Offa's Mead E9 123 DY63
Lindisfarne Way
Offenbach Ho. E2 143 DX68
Offenham Rd. SE9 185 EM91
Offerton Rd. SW4 161 DJ83
Offham Slope N12 97 CZ50
Offley Rd. SW9 161 DN80
Offord Clo. N17 100 DU52
Offord Rd. N1 141 DM66
Offord St. N1 141 DM66
Ogard Rd., Hodd. 49 EC15
Ogilby St. SE18 165 EM77
Oglander Rd. SE15 162 DT84
Ogle St. W1 273 K6
Ogle St. W1 141 DJ71
Oglethorpe Rd., Dag. 126 EZ62
Ohio Rd. E13 144 EF70
Oil Mill La. W6 159 CU78
Okeburn Rd. SW17 180 DG92
Okehampton Clo. N12 98 DD50
Okehampton Cres., Well. 166 EV81
Okehampton Rd. NW10 139 CW67
Okehampton Rd., Rom. 106 FJ51
Okehampton Sq., Rom. 106 FJ51
Okemore Gdns., Orp. 206 EW98
Olaf St. W11 139 CX73
Old Acre, Wok. 212 BG114
Old Amersham Rd., Ger.Cr. 113 BB60
Old Ave., W.Byf. 211 BE113
Old Ave., Wey. 213 BQ108
Old Ave. Clo., W.Byf. 211 BE113
Old Bailey EC4 274 G9
Old Bailey EC4 141 DP72
Old Bakery Ms., Guil. 260 BH139
Old Barge Ho. All. SE1 278 D2
Old Barn Clo., Sutt. 217 CY108
Old Barn La., Pur. 236 DT116
Old Barn La., Rick. 74 BM43
Old Barn Rd., Epsom 232 CQ117
Old Barn Way, Bexh. 167 FD83
Old Barrack Yd. SW1 276 F5
Old Barrowfield E15 144 EE67
New Plaistow Rd.
Old Bath Rd. (Poyle), Slou. 153 BE81
Old Bellgate Wf. E14 163 EA76
Old Bethnal Grn. Rd. E2 142 DU69
Old Bexley La., Bex. 187 FD89
Old Bexley La., Dart. 187 FF88
Old Bond St. W1 277 K1
Old Bond St. W1 141 DJ73
Old Brewers Yd. WC2 273 P9
Old Brewery Ms. NW3 120 DD63
Hampstead High St.
Old Bri. Clo., Nthlt. 136 CA68
Old Bri. St., Kings.T. 197 CK96
Old Broad St. EC2 275 L9
Old Broad St. EC2 142 DR72
Old Bromley Rd., Brom. 183 ED92
Old Brompton Rd. SW5 160 DA78
Old Brompton Rd. SW7 160 DA78
Old Bldgs. WC2 274 D8
Old Burlington St. W1 273 K10
Old Burlington St. W1 141 DJ73
Old Carriageway, The, Sev. 256 FC122
Old Castle St. E1 275 P8
Old Castle St. E1 142 DT72
Old Cavendish St. W1 273 H8
Old Cavendish St. W1 141 DH72
Old Change Ct. EC4 142 DQ72
Carter La.
Old Chapel Rd., Swan. 207 FC101
Old Charlton Rd., Shep. 195 BQ99
Old Chelsea Ms. SW3 160 DD79
Danvers St.
Old Chertsey Rd., Wok. 210 AV110
Old Chestnut Ave., Esher 214 CA107
Old Ch. La. NW9 118 CQ61
Old Ch. La., Brwd. 109 GE42
Old Ch. La., Grnf. 137 CG69
Perivale La.
Old Ch. La., Stan. 95 CJ52
Old Ch. Path, Esher 214 CB105
High St.
Old Ch. Rd. E1 143 DX72
Old Ch. Rd. E4 101 EA49
Old Ch. St. SW3 160 DD78
Old Claygate La., Esher 215 CG107
Old Clem Sq. SE18 165 EN79
Kempt St.
Old Coach Rd., Cher. 193 BD99
Old Coach Rd., The, Hert. 30 DF12
Old Common Rd., Cob. 213 BU112
Old Compton St. W1 273 M10
Old Compton St. W1 141 DK73
Old Cote Dr., Houns. 156 CA79
Old Ct., Ash. 232 CL119
Old Ct. Grn., Berk. 39 BC17
Hempstead La.
Old Ct. Pl. W8 160 DB75
Old Ct. Rd., Guil. 258 AU135
Old Crabtree La., Hem.H. 40 BL21
Old Cross, Hert. 32 DQ09
Old Dartford Rd. (Farningham), Dart. 208 FM100
Old Dean, Hem.H. 57 BA28
Old Deer Pk. Gdns., Rich. 158 CL83
Old Devonshire Rd. SW12 181 DH87
Old Dock App. Rd., Grays 170 GE77
Old Dock Clo., Rich. 158 CN79
Watcombe Cotts.
Old Dover Rd. SE3 164 EH80
Old Dr., The, Welw.G.C. 29 CV10
Old Epsom Rd., Guil. 244 BK131
Old Esher Clo., Walt. 214 BX106
Old Esher Rd.
Old Esher Rd., Walt. 214 BX106
Old Farleigh Rd., S.Croy. 220 DW110
Old Farleigh Rd., Warl. 237 DY117
Old Fm. Ave. N14 99 DJ45
Old Fm. Ave., Sid. 185 ER88
Old Fm. Clo., Beac. 88 AJ50
Old Fm. Clo., Houns. 156 BZ84
Old Fm. Gdns., Swan. 207 FF97
Old Fm. Pas., Hmptn. 196 CC95
Old Fm. Rd. N2 98 DD53
Old Fm. Rd., Guil. 242 AX131
Old Fm. Rd., Hmptn. 176 BZ93
Old Fm. Rd., West Dr. 154 BK75
Old Fm. Rd. E., Sid. 186 EU89
Old Fm. Rd. W., Sid. 185 ET89
Old Farmhouse Dr., Lthd. 231 CD115
Old Ferry Dr., Stai. 172 AW86
Old Fld. Clo., Amer. 72 AY39
Old Fish St. Hill EC4 275 H10
Old Fishery La., Hem.H. 39 BF22
Old Fives Ct., Slou. 130 AH69
Old Fleet La. EC4 274 F8
Old Fold Clo., Barn. 79 CZ39
Old Fold La.
Old Fold La., Barn. 79 CZ39
Old Fold Vw., Barn. 79 CW41
Old Ford Rd. E2 142 DW68
Old Ford Rd. E3 143 DY68
Old Forge Clo., Stan. 95 CG49
Old Forge Clo., Wat. 59 BU33
Old Forge Clo., Welw.G.C. 29 CZ05
Old Forge Cres., Shep. 195 BP100
Old Forge Ms. W12 159 CV75
Goodwin Rd.
Old Forge Rd., Enf. 82 DT38
Old Forge Rd., H.Wyc. 88 AC53
Old Forge Way, Sid. 186 EV91
Old Fox Clo., Cat. 235 DP121
Old Fox Footpath, S.Croy. 220 DS108
Essenden Rd.
Old French Horn La., Hat. 45 CW17
Old Gannon Clo., Nthwd. 93 BQ50
Old Gdn., The, Sev. 256 FD123
Old Gdn. Ct., St.Alb. 42 CC20
Old Gloucester St. WC1 274 A6
Old Gloucester St. WC1 141 DL71
Old Hall Clo., Pnr. 94 BY53
Old Hall Dr., Pnr. 94 BY53
Old Hall Ri., Harl. 52 EY15
Old Hall St., Hert. 32 DR09
Old Harpenden Rd., St.Alb. 43 CE17
Old Harrow La., West. 239 EQ119
Old Hatch Manor, Ruis. 115 BT59
Old Herns La., Welw.G.C. 30 DC07
Herns La.
Old Hertford Rd., Hat. 45 CW16
Old Highway, Hodd. 33 EB14
Old Hill, Chis. 205 EN95
Old Hill, Orp. 223 ER107
Old Hill, Wok. 226 AX120
Old Homesdale Rd., Brom. 204 EJ98
Old Hospital Clo. SW12 180 DF88
Old Ho. Clo. SW19 179 CY92
Old Ho. Clo., Epsom 217 CT110
Old Ho. Ct., Hem.H. 40 BM20
Old Ho. Rd.
Old Ho. Gdns., Twick. 177 CJ86
Old Ho. La., Harl. 50 EK18
Old Ho. La., Kings L. 74 BL35
Old Ho. La., Wal.Abb. 50 EF23
Old Ho. Rd., Hem.H. 40 BM20
Old Howlett's La., Ruis. 115 BQ58
Old Jamaica Rd. SE16 162 DU76
Old James St. SE15 162 DV83
Old Jewry EC2 275 K9
Old Jewry EC2 142 DR72
Old Kent Rd. SE1 279 M8
Old Kent Rd. SE1 162 DS77
Old Kent Rd. SE15 162 DS77
Old Kenton La. NW9 118 CP57
Old Kiln La., Bet. 264 CQ135
Old Kiln Rd. (Tylers Grn.), H.Wyc. 88 AC45
Old Kingston Rd., Wor.Pk. 198 CQ104
Old La., Cob. 229 BP117
Old La., West. 238 EK121
Old La. Gdns., Cob. 229 BT122
Old Leys, Hat. 45 CU21
Old Lo. La., Ken. 235 DN116
Old Lo. La., Pur. 219 DM114
Old Lo. Pl., Twick. 177 CH86
St. Margarets Rd.
Old Lo. Way, Stan. 95 CG50
Old London Rd., Dor. 247 CJ127
Old London Rd., Epsom 233 CU118
Old London Rd., Hert. 32 DS09
Old London Rd., Lthd. 245 BU126
Old London Rd., St.Alb. 43 CD21
Old London Rd., Sev. 224 EY109
Old London Rd. (Knockholt Pound), Sev. 240 EY115
Old Long Gro., Beac. 89 AQ51
Old Maidstone Rd., Sid. 186 EZ94
Old Malden La., Wor.Pk. 198 CR103
Old Malt Way, Wok. 226 AX117
Old Manor Dr., Grav. 191 GJ88

Street	Page	Grid
Ordnance Ms. NW8	140	DD68
St. Ann's Ter.		
Ordnance Rd. E16	144	EF71
Ordnance Rd. SE18	165	EN79
Ordnance Rd., Enf.	83	DX37
Ordnance Rd., Grav.	191	GJ86
Oregano Clo., West Dr.	134	BM72
Camomile Way		
Oregano Dr. E14	143	ED72
Oregano Way, Guil.	242	AU129
Oregon Ave. E12	125	EM63
Oregon Clo., N.Mal.	198	CQ98
Georgia Rd.		
Oregon Sq., Orp.	205	ER102
Orestan La., Lthd.	245	BV127
Orestes Ms. NW6	120	DA64
Aldred Rd.		
Oreston Rd., Rain.	148	FK69
Orewell Gdns., Reig.	266	DB136
Orford Ct. SE27	181	DP89
Orford Gdns., Twick.	177	CF89
Orford Rd. E17	123	EA57
Orford Rd. E18	124	EH55
Orford Rd. SE6	183	EB90
Organ Hall Rd., Borwd.	78	CL39
Organ La. E4	101	EC47
Oriel Clo., Mitch.	201	DK98
Oriel Ct. NW3	120	DC63
Heath St.		
Oriel Dr. SW13	159	CV79
Oriel Gdns., Ilf.	125	EM55
Oriel Pl. NW3	120	DC63
Heath St.		
Oriel Rd. E9	143	DX65
Oriel Way, Nthlt.	136	CB66
Orient Clo., St.Alb.	43	CE22
Orient Ind. Pk. E10	123	EA61
Orient St. SE11	**278**	**F8**
Orient Way E5	123	DX62
Orient Way E10	123	DY61
Oriental Clo., Wok.	227	BA117
Oriental Rd.		
Oriental Rd. E16	144	EK74
Oriental Rd., Wok.	227	AZ117
Oriental St. E14	143	EA73
Morant St.		
Oriole Clo., Abb.L.	59	BU31
Oriole Way SE28	146	EV73
Orion Rd. N11	99	DH51
Orion Way, Nthwd.	93	BT49
Orissa Rd. SE18	165	ES78
Orkney St. SW11	160	DG82
Orlando Gdns., Epsom	216	CR110
Orlando Rd. SW4	161	DJ83
Orleans Clo., Esher	197	CD103
Orleans Rd. SE19	182	DR93
Orleans Rd., Twick.	177	CH87
Orleston Ms. N7	141	DN65
Orleston Rd. N7	141	DN65
Orlestone Gdns., Orp.	224	EY106
Orley Fm. Rd., Har.	117	CE62
Orlop St. SE10	164	EE78
Ormanton Rd. SE26	182	DU91
Orme Ct. W2	140	DB73
Orme Ct. Ms. W2	140	DB73
Orme La.		
Orme La. W2	140	DB73
Orme Rd., Kings.T.	198	CP96
Orme Sq. W2	140	DB73
Bayswater Rd.		
Ormeley Rd. SW12	181	DH88
Ormerod Gdns., Mitch.	200	DG96
Ormesby Clo. SE28	146	EX73
Wroxham Rd.		
Ormesby Dr., Pot.B.	63	CX32
Ormesby Way, Har.	118	CM58
Ormiston Gro. W12	139	CV74
Ormiston Rd. SE10	164	EG78
Ormond Ave., Hmptn.	196	CB95
Ormond Ave., Rich.	177	CK85
Ormond Rd.		
Ormond Clo. WC1	**274**	**A6**
Ormond Clo., Rom.	106	FK54
Chadwick Dr.		
Ormond Cres., Hmptn.	196	CB95
Ormond Dr., Hmptn.	176	CB94
Ormond Ms. WC1	**274**	**A5**
Ormond Rd. N19	121	DL60
Ormond Rd., Rich.	177	CK85
Ormond Yd. SW1	**277**	**L2**
Ormonde Ave., Epsom	216	CR109
Ormonde Ave., Orp.	205	EQ103
Ormonde Gate SW3	160	DF78
Ormonde Pl. SW1	**276**	**F9**
Ormonde Ri., Buck.H.	102	EJ46
Ormonde Rd. SW14	158	CP83
Ormonde Rd., Nthwd.	93	BR49
Ormonde Rd., Wok.	226	AW116
Ormonde Ter. NW8	140	DF67
Ormsby Gdns., Grnf.	136	CC68
Ormsby Pl. N16	122	DT62
Victorian Gro.		
Ormsby Pt. SE18	165	EP77
Troy Ct.		
Ormsby St. E2	142	DT68
Ormside St. SE15	162	DW79
Ormside Way, Red.	251	DH130
Ormskirk Rd., Wat.	94	BX49
Ornan Rd. NW3	120	DE64
Oronsay, Hem.H.	41	BP22
Northend		
Oronsay Wk. N1	142	DQ65
Clephane Rd.		
Orpen Wk. N16	122	DS62
Orphanage Rd., Wat.	76	BW40
Orpheus St. SE5	162	DR81
Orpin Rd., Red.	251	DH130
Orpington Bypass, Orp.	224	EX106
Orpington Bypass, Sev.	224	EZ109
Orpington Gdns. N18	100	DS48
Orpington Rd. N21	99	DP46
Orpington Rd., Chis.	205	ES97
Orpwood Clo., Hmptn.	176	BZ93
Orsett Heath Cres., Grays	171	GG76
Orsett Rd., Grays	170	GA78
Orsett St. SE11	**278**	**C10**
Orsett St. SE11	161	DM78
Orsett Ter. W2	140	DC72
Orsett Ter., Wdf.Grn.	102	EJ53
Orsman Rd. N1	142	DS67
Orton Clo., St.Alb.	43	CH16
Orton St. E1	142	DU74
Hermitage Wall		
Orville Rd. SW11	160	DD82
Orwell Clo., Hayes	135	BS73
Orwell Clo., Rain.	147	FD71
Orwell Clo., Wind.	151	AR83
Orwell Ct. N5	122	DQ63
Orwell Rd. E13	144	EJ68
Osbaldeston Rd. N16	122	DU61
Osbert St. SW1	**277**	**M9**
Osberton Rd. SE12	184	EG85
Osborn Clo. E8	142	DU67
Osborn Gdns. NW7	97	CX52
Osborn La. SE23	183	DY87
Osborn St. E1	142	DT71
Osborn Ter. SE3	164	EF84
Lee Rd.		
Osborn Way, Welw.G.C.	29	CX10
Osborne Ave., Stai.	174	BL87
Osborne Clo., Barn.	80	DF41
Osborne Clo., Beck.	203	DY98
Osborne Clo., Felt.	176	BX92
Osborne Clo., Horn.	127	FH58
Osborne Clo., Pot.B.	64	DB29
Osborne Ct., Wind.	151	AQ82
Osborne Rd.		
Osborne Gdns., Pot.B.	64	DB30
Osborne Gdns., Th.Hth.	202	DQ96
Osborne Gro. E17	123	DZ56
Osborne Gro. N4	121	DN60
Osborne Ms. E17	123	DZ56
Osborne Gro.		
Osborne Ms., Wind.	151	AQ82
Osborne Pl., Sutt.	218	DD106
Osborne Rd. E7	124	EH64
Osborne Rd. E9	143	DZ65
Osborne Rd. E10	123	EB62
Osborne Rd. N4	121	DN60
Osborne Rd. N13	99	DN48
Osborne Rd. NW2	139	CV65
Osborne Rd. W3	158	CP76
Osborne Rd., Belv.	166	EZ78
Osborne Rd., Brwd.	108	FU44
Osborne Rd., Brox.	49	EA19
Osborne Rd., Buck.H.	102	EH46
Osborne Rd., Dag.	126	EZ64
Osborne Rd., Egh.	173	AZ93
Osborne Rd., Enf.	83	DY40
Osborne Rd., Horn.	127	FH58
Osborne Rd., Houns.	156	BZ83
Osborne Rd., Kings.T.	178	CL94
Osborne Rd., Pot.B.	64	DB30
Osborne Rd., Red.	250	DG131
Osborne Rd., Sthl.	136	CC72
Osborne Rd., Th.Hth.	202	DQ96
Osborne Rd., Uxb.	134	BJ66
Oxford Rd.		
Osborne Rd., Wal.Cr.	67	DY27
Osborne Rd., Walt.	195	BU102
Osborne Rd., Wat.	76	BW38
Osborne Rd., Wind.	151	AQ82
Osborne Sq., Dag.	126	EZ63
Osborne St., Slou.	152	AT75
Osborne Ter. SW17	180	DG92
Church La.		
Osbourne Ave., Kings L.	58	BM28
Osbourne Rd., Dart.	188	FP86
Oscar St. SE8	163	EA81
Oseney Cres. NW5	141	DJ65
Osgood Ave., Orp.	223	ET106
Osgood Gdns., Orp.	223	ET106
O'Shea Gro. E3	143	DZ67
Osidge La. N14	98	DG46
Osier Ms. W4	159	CT79
Osier Pl., Egh.	173	BC93
Osier St. E1	142	DW70
Osier Way E10	123	EB62
Osier Way, Bans.	217	CY114
Osier Way, Mitch.	200	DE99
Osiers Rd. SW18	160	DA84
Oslac Rd. SE6	183	EB92
Oslo Ct. NW8	**272**	**B1**
Oslo Sq. SE16	163	DY76
Norway Gate		
Osman Clo. N15	122	DR58
Tewkesbury Rd.		
Osman Rd. N9	100	DU48
Osman Rd. W6	159	CW76
Batoum Gdns.		
Osmond Clo., Har.	116	CC61
Osmond Gdns., Wall.	219	DJ106
Osmund St. W12	139	CT72
Braybrook St.		
Osnaburgh St. NW1	**273**	**J5**
Osnaburgh St. NW1	141	DH70
Osnaburgh Ter. NW1	**273**	**J4**
Osney Ho. SE2	166	EX75
Hartslock Dr.		
Osney Wk., Cars.	200	DD100
Osney Way, Grav.	191	GM89
Osprey Clo. E6	144	EL71
Dove App.		
Osprey Clo. E11	124	EG56
Osprey Clo. E17	101	DY52
Osprey Clo., Wat.	60	BY34
Falcon Way		
Osprey Clo., West Dr.	154	BL75
Osprey Ct., Wal.Abb.	68	EG34
Osprey Gdns., S.Croy.	221	DX110
Osprey Ms., Enf.	82	DV43
Osprey Rd., Wal.Abb.	68	EG34
Ospringe Clo. SE20	182	DW94
Ospringe Ct. SE9	185	ER86
Alderwood Rd.		
Ospringe Rd. NW5	121	DJ63
Osram Rd., Wem.	117	CK62
Osric Path N1	**275**	**M1**
Osric Path N1	142	DS68
Ossian Ms. N4	121	DM59
Ossian Rd. N4	121	DM59
Ossington Bldgs. W1	**272**	**F6**
Ossington Clo. W2	140	DB73
Ossington St.		
Ossington St. W2	140	DB73
Ossory Rd. SE1	162	DU78
Ossulston St. NW1	**273**	**M1**
Ossulston St. NW1	141	DK69
Ossulton Pl. N2	120	DC55
East End Rd.		
Ossulton Way N2	120	DC56
Ostade Rd. SW2	181	DM87
Osten Ms. SW7	160	DB76
McLeod's Ms.		
Oster St., St.Alb.	42	CC19
Oster Ter. E17	123	DX57
Southcote Rd.		
Osterberg Rd., Dart.	168	FM84
Osterley Ave., Islw.	157	CD80
Osterley Clo., Orp.	206	EU95
Leith Hill		
Osterley Ct., Islw.	157	CD81
Osterley Cres., Islw.	157	CE81
Osterley Gdns., Th.Hth.	202	DQ96
Osterley Ho. E14	143	EB72
Giraud St.		
Osterley La., Islw.	157	CE78
Osterley La., Sthl.	156	CA78
Osterley Pk., Islw.	157	CD78
Osterley Pk. Rd., Sthl.	156	BZ76
Osterley Pk. Vw. Rd. W7	157	CE75
Osterley Rd. N16	122	DS63
Osterley Rd., Islw.	157	CE80
Osterley Views, Sthl.	136	CC74
West Pk. Rd.		
Ostliffe Rd. N13	99	DP50
Oswald Clo., Lthd.	230	CC122
Oswald Rd., Lthd.	230	CC122
Oswald Rd., St.Alb.	43	CE21
Oswald Rd., Sthl.	136	BY74
Oswald St. E5	123	DX62
Oswald Ter. NW2	119	CW62
Temple Rd.		
Oswald's Mead E9	123	DY63
Lindisfarne Way		
Osward, Croy.	221	DZ109
Osward Pl. N9	100	DV47
Osward Rd. SW17	180	DF89
Oswell Ho. E1	142	DV74
Oswin St. SE11	**278**	**G8**
Oswin St. SE11	161	DP77
Oswyth Rd. SE5	162	DS82
Otford Clo. SE20	202	DW95
Otford Clo., Bex.	187	FB86
Southwold Rd.		
Otford Clo., Brom.	205	EN97
Otford Cres. SE4	183	DZ86
Otford La., Sev.	224	EZ112
Otford Rd., Sev.	241	FH118
Othello Clo. SE11	**278**	**F10**
Otis St. E3	143	EC69
Otley App., Ilf.	125	EP58
Otley Dr., Ilf.	125	EP57
Otley Rd. E16	144	EJ72
Otley Ter. E5	123	DX61
Otley Way, Wat.	94	BW48
Otlinge Clo., Orp.	206	EX98
Ottawa Gdns., Dag.	147	FD66
Ottawa Rd., Til.	171	GG82
Ottaway St. E5	122	DU62
Stellman Clo.		
Ottenden Clo., Orp.	223	ES105
Southfleet Rd.		
Otter Clo., Cher.	211	BB107
Otter Gdns., Hat.	45	CV19
Otter Meadow, Lthd.	231	CF119
Otter Rd., Grnf.	136	CC70
Otterbourne Rd. E4	101	ED48
Otterbourne Rd., Croy.	202	DQ103
Otterburn Gdns., Islw.	157	CG80
Otterburn Ho. SE5	162	DQ80
Otterburn St. SW17	180	DF93
Otterden St. SE6	183	EA91
Otterfield Rd., West Dr.	134	BL73
Ottermead La., Cher.	211	BC107
Otters Clo., Orp.	206	EX98
Otterspool La., Wat.	76	BY38
Otterspool Service Rd., Wat.	76	BZ39
Otterspool Way, Wat.	76	BY37
Otto Clo. SE26	182	DV90
Otto St. SE17	161	DP79
Ottoman Ter., Wat.	76	BW41
Ebury Rd.		
Ottways Ave., Ash.	231	CK119
Ottways La., Ash.	231	CK120
Otway Gdns., Wat.	95	CE45
Otways Clo., Pot.B.	64	DB32
Oulton Clo. E5	122	DW61
Mundford Rd.		
Oulton Clo. SE28	146	EW72
Rollesby Way		
Oulton Cres., Bark.	145	ET65
Oulton Cres., Pot.B.	63	CX32
Oulton Rd. N15	122	DR57
Oulton Way, Wat.	94	BY49
Oundle Ave. (Bushey), Wat.	76	CC44
Ousden Clo. (Cheshunt), Wal.Cr.	67	DY30
Ousden Dr. (Cheshunt), Wal.Cr.	67	DY30
Ouseley Rd. SW12	180	DF88
Ouseley Rd., Stai.	172	AW87
Ouseley Rd., Wind.	172	AW87
Outdowns, Lthd.	245	BV129
Outer Circle NW1	**273**	**H2**
Outer Circle NW1	141	DH68
Outfield Rd., Ger.Cr.	90	AX52
Outgate Rd. NW10	139	CT66
Outlook Dr., Ch.St.G.	90	AX48
Outram Pl. N1	141	DL67
Outram Pl., Wey.	213	BQ106
Outram Rd. E6	144	EL67
Outram Rd. N22	99	DK53
Outram Rd., Croy.	202	DT102
Outwich St. EC3	**275**	**N8**
Outwood La., Couls.	234	DE120
Outwood La., Red.	252	DR134
Outwood La., Tad.	234	DB122
Oval, The E2	142	DV68
Oval, The, Bans.	218	DA114
Oval, The, Brox.	67	DY25
Oval, The, Gdmg.	258	AT144
Oval, The, Guil.	258	AU135
Oval, The, Sid.	186	EU87
Oval Gdns., Grays	170	GC76
Oval Pl. SW8	161	DM80
Oval Rd. NW1	141	DH67
Oval Rd., Croy.	202	DS102
Oval Rd. N., Dag.	147	FB67
Oval Rd. S., Dag.	147	FB68
Oval Way SE11	161	DM78
Oval Way, Ger.Cr.	112	AY56
Ovenden Rd., Sev.	240	EX120
Over The Misbourne, Ger.Cr.	113	BA58
Over The Misbourne, Uxb.	113	BB58
Overbrae, Beck.	183	EA93
Overbrook, Lthd.	245	BP129
Overbrook Wk., Edg.	96	CN52
Overbury Ave., Beck.	203	EB97
Overbury Cres., Croy.	221	EC110
Overbury Rd. N15	122	DR58
Overbury St. E5	123	DX63
Overcliff Rd. SE13	163	EA83
Overcliff Rd., Grays	170	GD78
Overcliffe, Grav.	191	GF86
Overcourt Clo., Sid.	186	EV86
Overdale, Ash.	232	CL116
Overdale, Dor.	263	CK135
Overdale, Red.	252	DQ133
Overdale Ave., N.Mal.	198	CQ96
Overdale Rd. W5	157	CJ76
Overdale Rd., Chesh.	54	AP28
Overdown Rd. SE6	183	EA91
Overhill, Warl.	236	DW119
Overhill Rd. SE22	182	DU87
Overhill Rd., Pur.	219	DN109
Overhill Way, Beck.	203	ED99
Overlea Rd. E5	122	DU59
Overlord Clo., Brox.	49	DY20
Overmead, Sid.	185	ER87
Overmead, Swan.	207	FE99
Oversley Ho. W2	140	DA71
Overstand Clo., Beck.	203	EA99
Overstone Gdns., Croy.	203	DZ101
Overstone Rd. W6	159	CW76
Overstream, Rick.	74	BH42
Overthorpe Clo., Wok.	226	AS117
Overton Clo. NW10	138	CQ65
Overton Clo., Islw.	157	CF81
Avenue Rd.		
Overton Ct. E11	124	EG59
Overton Dr. E11	124	EH59
Overton Dr., Rom.	126	EW59
Overton Rd. E10	123	DY60
Overton Rd. N14	81	DL43
Overton Rd. SE2	166	EW76
Overton Rd. SW9	161	DN82
Overton Rd., Sutt.	218	DA107
Overton Rd. E. SE2	166	EX76
Overtons Yd., Croy.	202	DQ104
Overy St., Dart.	188	FL86
Ovesdon Ave., Har.	116	BZ60
Oveton Way, Lthd.	246	CA126
Ovett Clo. SE19	182	DS93
Ovex Clo. E14	163	EC75
Ovington Ct., Wok.	226	AT116
Roundthorn Way		
Ovington Gdns. SW3	**276**	**C7**
Ovington Gdns. SW3	160	DE76
Ovington Ms. SW3	**276**	**C7**
Ovington Ms. SW3	160	DE76
Ovington Sq. SW3	**276**	**C7**
Ovington Sq. SW3	160	DE76
Ovington St. SW3	**276**	**C7**
Ovington St. SW3	160	DE76
Owen Clo. SE28	146	EW74
Owen Clo., Croy.	202	DR100
Owen Clo., Hayes	135	BV69
Owen Gdns., Wdf.Grn.	102	EL51
Owen Pl., Lthd.	231	CH122
Church Rd.		
Owen Rd. N13	100	DQ50
Owen Rd., Hayes	135	BV69
Owen St. EC1	**274**	**F1**
Owen Wk. SE20	182	DU94
Sycamore Gro.		
Owen Waters Ho., Ilf.	103	EM53
Owen Way NW10	138	CQ65
Owenite St. SE2	166	EV77
Owen's Ct. EC1	**274**	**F2**
Owen's Row EC1	**274**	**F2**
Owens Way SE23	183	DY87
Owens Way, Rick.	74	BN43
Owgan Clo. SE5	162	DR80
Benhill Rd.		
Owl Clo., S.Croy.	221	DX110
Owl Pk., Loug.	84	EF40
Owlets Hall Clo., Horn.	128	FM55
Prospect Rd.		
Owlsears Clo., Beac.	89	AK51
Ownstead Gdns., S.Croy.	220	DT111
Ownsted Hill, Croy.	221	EC110
Ox La., Epsom	217	CU109
Church St.		
Oxberry Ave. SW6	159	CY82
Oxdowne Clo., Cob.	214	CB114
Oxenden Dr., Hodd.	49	EA18
Oxenden Wd. Rd., Orp.	224	EW108
Oxendon St. SW1	**277**	**M1**
Oxendon St. SW1	141	DK73
Oxenford St. SE15	162	DT83
Oxenholme NW1	**273**	**L1**
Oxenholme NW1	141	DJ68
Oxenpark Ave., Wem.	118	CL59
Oxestalls Rd. SE8	163	DY78
Oxfield Clo., Berk.	38	AU20
Oxford Ave. SW20	199	CY96
Oxford Ave., Grays	171	GG77
Oxford Ave., Hayes	155	BT80
Oxford Ave., Horn.	128	FN56
Oxford Ave., Houns.	156	CA78
Oxford Ave., St.Alb.	43	CJ21
Oxford Ave., Slou.	131	AM71
Oxford Ave. (Burnham), Slou.	130	AH68
Oxford Circ. Ave. W1	**273**	**K9**
Oxford Clo. N9	100	DV47
Oxford Clo., Ashf.	175	BQ94
Oxford Clo., Grav.	191	GM89
Oxford Clo., Mitch.	201	DJ97
Oxford Clo., Nthwd.	93	BQ49
Oxford Clo. (Cheshunt), Wal.Cr.	67	DX29
Oxford Ct. EC4	**275**	**K10**
Oxford Ct. W3	138	CN72
Oxford Ct., Brwd.	108	FX49
Oxford Ct., Felt.	176	BX91
Oxford Way		
Oxford Cres., N.Mal.	198	CR100
Oxford Dr., Ruis.	116	BW61
Oxford Gdns. N20	98	DD46
Oxford Gdns. N21	100	DQ45
Oxford Gdns. W4	158	CN78
Oxford Gdns. W10	139	CY72
Oxford Gate W6	159	CX77
Oxford La., Guil.	258	AX136
Sydenham Rd.		
Oxford Ms., Bex.	186	FA87
Bexley High St.		
Oxford Pl. NW10	118	CR62
Neasden La. N.		
Oxford Rd. E15	143	ED65
Oxford Rd. N4	121	DN60
Oxford Rd. N9	100	DV47
Oxford Rd. NW6	140	DA68
Oxford Rd. SE19	182	DR93
Oxford Rd. SW15	159	CY84
Oxford Rd. W5	137	CK73
Oxford Rd., Beac.	111	AP55
Oxford Rd. (Holtspur), Beac.	88	AE54
Oxford Rd., Cars.	218	DE107
Oxford Rd., Enf.	82	DV43
Oxford Rd., Ger.Cr.	112	AT56
Oxford Rd., Guil.	258	AX136
Oxford Rd., Har.	116	CC58
Oxford Rd. (Wealdstone), Har.	117	CF55
Oxford Rd., H.Wyc.	88	AE54
Oxford Rd., Ilf.	125	EQ63
Oxford Rd., Red.	250	DE133
Oxford Rd., Rom.	106	FM51
Oxford Rd., Sid.	186	EV92
Oxford Rd., Tedd.	177	CD92
Oxford Rd., Uxb.	134	BJ66
Oxford Rd., Wall.	219	DJ106
Oxford Rd., Wind.	151	AQ81
Oxford Rd., Wdf.Grn.	102	EJ50
Oxford Rd. E., Wind.	151	AQ81
Oxford Rd. N. W4	158	CP78
Oxford Rd. S. W4	158	CN78
Oxford Sq. W2	**272**	**C9**
Oxford Sq. W2	140	DE72
Oxford St. W1	**272**	**F9**
Oxford St. W1	141	DH72
Oxford St., Wat.	75	BV43
Oxford Ter., Guil.	258	AX136
Pewley Hill		
Oxford Wk., Sthl.	136	BZ74
Oxford Way, Felt.	176	BX91
Oxgate Gdns. NW2	119	CV62
Oxgate La. NW2	119	CV61
Oxhawth Cres., Brom.	205	EN99
Oxhey Ave., Wat.	94	BX45
Oxhey Dr., Nthwd.	93	BV50
Oxhey Dr., Wat.	94	BW48
Oxhey La., Har.	94	CB50
Oxhey La., Pnr.	94	CB50
Oxhey La., Wat.	94	BZ48
Oxhey Ridge Clo., Nthwd.	93	BU50
Oxhey Rd., Wat.	94	BW45
Oxleas E6	145	EP72
Oxleas Clo., Well.	165	ER82
Oxlease Dr., Hat.	45	CV19
Oxleay Ct., Har.	116	CA60
Oxleay Rd., Har.	116	CA60
Oxleigh Clo., N.Mal.	198	CS99
Oxley Clo. SE1	162	DT78
Oxley Clo., Rom.	106	FJ54
Oxleys, The, Harl.	36	EY11
Oxleys Rd. NW2	119	CV62
Oxleys Rd., Wal.Abb.	68	EG32
Oxlip Clo., Croy.	203	DX102
Marigold Way		
Oxlow La., Dag.	126	FA63
Oxonian St. SE22	162	DT84
Oxshott Ri., Cob.	214	BX113
Oxshott Rd., Lthd.	231	CE116
Oxshott Way, Cob.	230	BY115
Oxted Clo., Mitch.	200	DD97
Oxted Rd., Gdse.	252	DW130
Oxtoby Way SW16	201	DK96
Oyster Catchers Clo. E16	144	EH72
Freemasons Rd.		
Oyster La., W.Byf.	212	BK110
Oyster Row E1	142	DW72
Lukin St.		
Oysterfields, St.Alb.	42	CB19
Ozolins Way E16	144	EG72

P

Street	Page	Grid
Pablo Neruda Clo. SE24	161	DP84
Shakespeare Rd.		
Pace Pl. E1	142	DV72
Bigland St.		
Paceheath Clo., Rom.	105	FD51
Pachesham Dr., Lthd.	231	CF116
Oxshott Rd.		
Pachesham Pk., Lthd.	231	CF117
Pacific Clo., Felt.	175	BT88
Pacific Rd. E16	144	EG72
Packet Boat La., Uxb.	134	BH72
Packham Clo., Orp.	206	EW104
Berrylands		
Packham Rd., Grav.	191	GF91
Packhorse Clo., St.Alb.	43	CJ17
Packhorse La., Borwd.	78	CS37
Packhorse La., Pot.B.	62	CR31
Packhorse Rd., Ger.Cr.	112	AY55
Packhorse Rd., Sev.	256	FC123
Packington Rd. W3	158	CQ76
Packington Sq. N1	142	DQ67
Packington St. N1	141	DP67
Packmores Rd. SE9	185	ER85
Padbrook, Oxt.	254	EG129
Padbrook Clo., Oxt.	254	EG129
Padbury SE17	162	DS78
Padbury Clo., Felt.	175	BR88
Padbury Ct. E2	142	DT69
Padcroft Rd., West Dr.	134	BK74
Paddenswick Rd. W6	159	CU76
Paddick Clo., Hodd.	49	DZ16
Paddington Clo., Hayes	136	BX70
Paddington Grn. W2	**272**	**A6**
Paddington Grn. W2	140	DD71
Paddington St. W1	**272**	**F6**
Paddington St. W1	140	DG71
Paddock, The, Brox.	49	EA20
Paddock, The, Dor.	262	CB137
Paddock, The, Ger.Cr.	90	AY50
Paddock, The, Guil.	243	BD133
Paddock, The, Hat.	45	CU16
Paddock, The, Slou.	152	AV81
Paddock, The (Ickenham), Uxb.	115	BP63
Paddock, The, West.	255	EQ126
Paddock Clo. SE3	164	EG82
Paddock Clo. SE26	183	DX91
Paddock Clo. (South Darenth), Dart.	208	FQ95
Paddock Clo., Nthlt.	136	CA68
Paddock Clo., Orp.	223	EP105
State Fm. Ave.		
Paddock Clo., Oxt.	254	EF131
Paddock Clo., Ware	34	EK06
Paddock Clo., Wat.	76	BY44
Paddock Clo., Wor.Pk.	198	CS102
Paddock Gdns. SE19	182	DS93
Westow St.		
Paddock Mead, Harl.	51	EQ20
Paddock Rd. NW2	119	CU62
Paddock Rd., Bexh.	166	EY84
Paddock Rd., Ruis.	116	BX62
Paddock Wk., Warl.	236	DV119
Paddock Way, Chis.	185	ER94
Paddock Way, Hem.H.	39	BE20
Paddock Way, Oxt.	254	EF131
Paddock Way, Wok.	211	BB114
Paddocks, The, Add.	212	BH110
Paddocks, The, Barn.	80	DF41

Park Rd., Hmptn. 176 CB91
Park Rd., Hayes 135 BS71
Park Rd., Hem.H. 40 BJ22
Park Rd., Hert. 32 DS09
Park Rd., Hodd. 49 EA17
Park Rd., Houns. 156 CC84
Park Rd., Ilf. 125 ER62
Park Rd., Islw. 157 CH81
Park Rd., Ken. 235 DP115
Park Rd., Kings.T. 178 CM92
Park Rd. (Hampton Wick), Kings.T. 197 CJ95
Park Rd., N.Mal. 198 CR98
Park Rd., Orp. 206 EW99
Park Rd., Oxt. 254 EF128
Park Rd., Pot.B. 64 DG30
Park Rd., Rad. 77 CG35
Park Rd., Red. 250 DF132
Park Rd., Rich. 178 CM86
Park Rd., Rick. 92 BK45
Park Rd., Shep. 194 BN102
Park Rd., Slou. 131 AQ68
Park Rd., Stai. 174 BH86
Park Rd., Sun. 175 BV94
Park Rd., Surb. 198 CM99
Park Rd., Sutt. 217 CY107
Park Rd., Swan. 207 FF98
Park Rd., Swans. 190 FY86
Park Rd., Tedd. 177 CF94
Park Rd., Twick. 177 CJ86
Park Rd., Uxb. 134 BL66
Park Rd., Wall. 219 DH106
Park Rd. (Hackbridge), Wall. 201 DH103
Park Rd., Wal.Cr. 67 DX33
Park Rd., Ware 32 DV05
Park Rd., Warl. 222 EE114
Park Rd., Wat. 75 BU39
Park Rd. (Bushey), Wat. 76 CA44
Park Rd., Wem. 138 CL65
Park Rd., Wok. 227 AZ117
Park Rd. E. W3 158 CP75
Park Rd. E., Uxb. 134 BK68
Hillingdon Rd.
Park Rd. N. W3 158 CP75
Park Rd. N. W4 158 CR78
Park Rd. W., Kings.T. 197 CJ95
Park Row SE10 163 ED79
Park Royal Rd. NW10 138 CQ69
Park Royal Rd. W3 138 CQ69
Park Sq., Esher 214 CB105
Park Rd.
Park Sq. E. NW1 273 H4
Park Sq. E. NW1 141 DH70
Park Sq. Ms. NW1 273 H4
Park Sq. Ms. NW1 141 DH70
Park Sq. W. NW1 273 H4
Park Sq. W. NW1 141 DH70
Park St. SE1 279 H2
Park St. SE1 142 DQ74
Park St. W1 272 F10
Park St. W1 140 DG73
Park St., Berk. 38 AV18
Park St., Croy. 202 DQ103
Park St., Guil. 258 AW136
Park St., Hat. 45 CW17
Park St., St.Alb. 61 CD26
Park St., Slou. 152 AT76
Park St. (Colnbrook), Slou. 153 BD80
Park St., Tedd. 177 CE93
Park St., Wind. 151 AR81
Park St. La., St.Alb. 60 CB30
Park Ter., Green. 189 FV85
Park Ter. (Sundridge), Sev. 240 EX124
Main Rd.
Park Ter., Wor.Pk. 199 CU102
Park Vw. N21 99 DM45
Park Vw. W3 138 CQ71
Park Vw., Hat. 45 CW16
Park Vw., Hodd. 49 EA18
Park Vw., Horl. 268 DG148
Brighton Rd.
Park Vw., Lthd. 246 CA125
Park Vw., N.Mal. 199 CT97
Park Vw., Pnr. 94 BZ53
Park Vw., Pot.B. 64 DC33
Park Vw., S.Ock. 149 FR74
Park Vw., Wem. 118 CP64
Park Vw. Clo., St.Alb. 43 CG21
Park Vw. Ct., Ilf. 125 ES58
Brancaster Rd.
Park Vw. Ct., Wok. 227 AZ119
Park Vw. Cres. N11 99 DH49
Park Vw. Est. E2 143 DX68
Park Vw. Gdns. NW4 119 CW57
Park Vw. Gdns., Bark. 145 ES68
River Rd.
Park Vw. Gdns., Grays 170 GB78
Park Vw. Gdns., Ilf. 125 EM56
Park Vw. Rd. N3 98 DB53
Park Vw. Rd. N17 122 DU55
Park Vw. Rd. NW10 119 CT63
Park Vw. Rd. W5 138 CL71
Park Vw. Rd., Berk. 38 AV19
Park Vw. Rd., Cat. 237 DY122
Park Vw. Rd., Pnr. 93 BV52
Park Vw. Rd., Red. 266 DG141
Park Vw. Rd., Sthl. 136 CA74
Park Vw. Rd., Uxb. 134 BN72
Park Vw. Rd., Well. 166 EW83
Park Village E. NW1 141 DH68
Park Village W. NW1 141 DH68
Park Vil., Rom. 126 EX58
Park Vista SE10 163 ED79
Park Wk. N6 120 DG59
North Rd.
Park Wk. SE10 163 ED80
Crooms Hill
Park Wk. SW10 160 DC79
Park Wk., Ash. 232 CM119
Rectory La.
Park Way N20 98 DF49
Park Way NW11 119 CY57
Park Way, Bex. 187 FE90
Park Way, Brwd. 109 FZ46
Park Way, Edg. 96 CP53
Park Way, Enf. 81 DN40
Park Way, Felt. 175 BV87
Park Way, Horl. 268 DG148
Park Way, Lthd. 230 CA123
Park Way, Rick. 92 BJ46
Park Way, Ruis. 115 BU60
Park Way, W.Mol. 196 CB97
Park W. W2 272 C9
Park W. Pl. W2 272 C8
Park Wks. Rd., Red. 251 DM133
Parkcroft Rd. SE12 184 EF87
Parkdale Cres., Wor.Pk. 198 CR104
Parkdale Rd. SE18 165 ES78
Parke Rd. SW13 159 CU81
Parke Rd., Sun. 195 BU98
Parker Ave., Hert. 32 DR07
Parker Ave., Til. 171 GJ81
Parker Clo. E16 144 EL74
Parker Ms. WC2 274 A8
Parker Rd., Croy. 220 DQ105
Parker Rd., Grays 170 FZ78
Parker St. E16 144 EL74
Parker St. WC2 274 A8
Parker St. WC2 141 DL72
Parker St., Wat. 75 BV39
Parkers Clo., Ash. 232 CL119
Parkers Hill, Ash. 232 CL119
Parkers La., Ash. 232 CL119
Parkers Row SE1 162 DT75
Jamaica Rd.
Parkes Rd., Chig. 103 ES50
Parkfield, Rick. 73 BF42
Parkfield, Sev. 257 FM123
Parkfield Ave. SW14 158 CS84
Parkfield Ave., Amer. 55 AR37
Parkfield Ave., Felt. 175 BU90
Parkfield Ave., Har. 94 CC54
Parkfield Ave., Nthlt. 136 BX68
Parkfield Ave., Uxb. 135 BP69
Parkfield Clo., Edg. 96 CP51
Parkfield Clo., Nthlt. 136 BY68
Parkfield Cres., Felt. 175 BU90
Parkfield Cres., Har. 94 CC54
Parkfield Cres., Ruis. 116 BY62
Parkfield Dr., Nthlt. 136 BX68
Parkfield Gdns., Har. 116 CB55
Parkfield Rd. NW10 139 CU66
Parkfield Rd. SE14 163 DZ81
Parkfield Rd., Felt. 175 BU90
Parkfield Rd., Har. 116 CC62
Parkfield Rd., Nthlt. 136 BY68
Parkfield Rd. (Ickenham), Uxb. 115 BP61
Parkfield St. N1 141 DN68
Parkfield Way, Brom. 205 EM100
Parkfields SW15 159 CW84
Parkfields, Croy. 203 DZ102
Parkfields, Harl. 50 EG15
Parkfields, Lthd. 215 CD111
Parkfields, Welw.G.C. 29 CX09
Parkfields Ave. NW9 118 CR60
Parkfields Ave. SW20 199 CV95
Parkfields Clo., Cars. 218 DG105
Devonshire Rd.
Parkfields Rd., Kings.T. 178 CM92
Parkgate SE3 164 EF83
Parkgate, Slou. 130 AJ70
Parkgate Ave., Barn. 80 DC39
Parkgate Clo., Kings.T. 178 CP93
Warboys App.
Parkgate Cres., Barn. 80 DC40
Parkgate Gdns. SW14 178 CR85
Parkgate Ms. N6 121 DJ59
Stanhope Rd.
Parkgate Rd. SW11 160 DE80
Parkgate Rd., Orp. 225 FB105
Parkgate Rd., Reig. 266 DB135
Parkgate Rd., Wall. 218 DG106
Parkgate Rd., Wat. 76 BW37
Parkham Ct., Brom. 204 EE96
Parkham St. SW11 160 DE81
Parkhill Clo., Horn. 128 FJ62
Parkhill Rd. E4 101 EC46
Parkhill Rd. NW3 120 DF64
Parkhill Rd., Bex. 186 EZ87
Parkhill Rd., Hem.H. 40 BH20
Parkhill Rd., Sid. 185 ER90
Parkhill Wk. NW3 120 DF64
Parkholme Rd. E8 142 DT65
Parkhouse St. SE5 162 DR80
Parkhurst, Epsom 216 CQ110
Parkhurst Ave. E16 144 EH74
Wesley Ave.
Parkhurst Gdns., Bex. 186 FA87
Parkhurst Gro., Horl. 268 DE147
Parkhurst Rd. E12 125 EN63
Parkhurst Rd. E17 123 DY56
Parkhurst Rd. N7 121 DL63
Parkhurst Rd. N11 98 DG49
Parkhurst Rd. N17 100 DU54
Parkhurst Rd. N22 99 DM52
Parkhurst Rd., Bex. 186 FA87
Parkhurst Rd., Guil. 242 AU133
Parkhurst Rd., Hert. 31 DP08
Parkhurst Rd., Horl. 268 DE147
Parkhurst Rd., Sutt. 218 DD105
Parkland Ave., Rom. 127 FE55
Parkland Ave., Slou. 152 AX77
Parkland Ave., Upmin. 128 FP64
Parkland Clo., Chig. 103 EQ48
Parkland Clo., Hodd. 33 EB14
Parkland Clo., Sev. 257 FJ129
Parkland Dr., St.Alb. 42 CA21
Parkland Gdns. SW19 179 CX88
Parkland Gro., Ashf. 174 BN91
Parkland Rd. N22 99 DM54
Parkland Rd., Ashf. 174 BN91
Parkland Rd., Wdf.Grn. 102 EG52
Parkland Wk. N4 121 DM59
Parkland Wk. N6 121 DK59
Parkland Wk. N10 121 DH56
Parklands N6 121 DH59
Parklands, Add. 212 BJ106
Parklands, Chig. 103 EQ48
Parklands, Dor. 263 CH140
Parklands, Epp. 70 EX29
Parklands, Lthd. 230 CA123
Parklands, Oxt. 254 EE131
Parklands, Surb. 198 CM99
Parklands, Wal.Abb. 67 ED32
Parklands Clo. SW14 178 CQ85
Parklands Clo., Barn. 80 DD38
Parklands Ct., Houns. 156 BX82
Parklands Dr. N3 119 CY55
Parklands Pl., Guil. 243 BB134
Parklands Rd. SW16 181 DH92
Parklands Way, Wor.Pk. 198 CS104
Parklawn Ave., Epsom 216 CP113
Parklawn Ave., Horl. 268 DF146
Parklea Clo. NW9 96 CS53
Parkleigh Rd. SW19 200 DB96
Parkleys, Rich. 177 CK91
Parkmead SW15 179 CV86
Parkmead, Loug. 85 EN43
Parkmead Gdns. NW7 97 CT51
Parkmore Clo., Wdf.Grn. 102 EG49
Parkpale La., Bet. 264 CN139
Parkshot, Rich. 158 CL84
Parkside N3 98 DB53
Parkside NW2 119 CV62
Parkside NW7 97 CU51
Parkside SE3 164 EF80
Parkside SW19 179 CX91
Parkside, Add. 212 BH111
Parkside, Buck.H. 102 EH47
Parkside, Ger.Cr. 113 AZ56
Lower Rd.
Parkside, Grays 170 GE76
Parkside, Hmptn. 177 CD92
Parkside, Pot.B. 64 DC32
High St.
Parkside, Sev. 224 EZ113
Parkside, Sid. 186 EV89
Parkside, Sutt. 217 CY107
Parkside, Wal.Cr. 67 DY34
Parkside, Wat. 76 BW44
Parkside Ave. SW19 179 CX92
Parkside Ave., Bexh. 167 FD82
Parkside Ave., Brom. 204 EL98
Parkside Ave., Rom. 127 FD55
Parkside Ave., Til. 171 GH82
Parkside Clo. SE20 182 DW94
Parkside Clo., Lthd. 245 BT125
Parkside Ct., Wey. 212 BN105
Parkside Cres. N7 121 DN62
Parkside Cres., Surb. 198 CQ100
Parkside Cross, Bexh. 167 FE82
Parkside Dr., Edg. 96 CN48
Parkside Dr., Wat. 75 BS40
Parkside Est. E9 142 DW67
Rutland Rd.
Parkside Gdns. SW19 179 CX91
Parkside Gdns., Barn. 98 DF46
Parkside Gdns., Couls. 235 DH117
Parkside Ho., Dag. 127 FC62
Parkside Pl., Lthd. 245 BT125
Parkside Rd. SW11 160 DG81
Parkside Rd., Belv. 167 FC77
Parkside Rd., Houns. 176 CB85
Parkside Rd., Nthwd. 93 BT50
Parkside Ter. N18 100 DR49
Great Cambridge Rd.
Parkside Wk. SE10 164 EE78
Parkside Way, Har. 116 CB56
Parkstead Rd. SW15 179 CU85
Parkstone Ave. N18 100 DT50
Parkstone Ave., Horn. 128 FL58
Parkstone Rd. E17 123 EC55
Parkstone Rd. SE15 162 DU82
Rye La.
Parkthorne Clo., Har. 116 CB58
Parkthorne Dr., Har. 116 CA58
Parkthorne Rd. SW12 181 DK87
Parkview, St.Alb. 43 CG21
Parkview Chase, Slou. 131 AL72
Parkview Ct. SW18 180 DA86
Broomhill Rd.
Parkview Dr., Mitch. 200 DD96
Parkview Rd. SE9 185 EP89
Parkview Rd., Croy. 202 DU102
Parkview Vale, Guil. 243 BC132
Foxglove Gdns.
Parkville Rd. SW6 159 CZ80
Parkway N14 99 DL47
Parkway NW1 141 DH67
Parkway SW20 199 CX98
Parkway, Croy. 221 EC109
Parkway, Dor. 263 CG135
Parkway, Erith 166 EY76
Parkway, Guil. 242 AY133
Parkway, Harl. 50 EL15
Parkway, Ilf. 125 ET62
Parkway, Rain. 147 FG70
Upminster Rd. S.
Parkway, Rom. 127 FF55
Parkway, Saw. 36 EY06
Parkway, Uxb. 134 BN66
Parkway, Welw.G.C. 29 CW11
Parkway, Wey. 213 BR105
Parkway, Wdf.Grn. 102 EJ50
Parkway, The, Hayes 136 BW72
Parkway, The (Cranford), Houns. 155 BV82
Parkway, The, Iver 133 BC67
Parkway, The, Nthlt. 136 BX69
Parkway, The, Sthl. 155 BU78
Parkway Clo., Welw.G.C. 29 CW09
Parkway Ct., St.Alb. 43 CH23
Parkway Gdns., Welw.G.C. 29 CW10
Parkway Ms., Mitch. 181 DH94
Park Ave.
Parkway Trd. Est., Houns. 156 BW79
Parkwood N20 98 DF48
Parkwood, Beck. 203 EA95
Parkwood Ave., Esher 196 CC102
Parkwood Clo., Bans. 233 CX115
Parkwood Clo., Hodd. 49 DZ19
Parkwood Dr., Hem.H. 39 BF20
Parkwood Gro., Sun. 195 BU97
Parkwood Ms. N6 121 DH58
Parkwood Rd. SW19 179 CZ92
Parkwood Rd., Bans. 233 CX115
Parkwood Rd., Bex. 186 EZ87
Parkwood Rd., Islw. 157 CF81
Parkwood Rd., Red. 251 DL133
Parkwood Rd., West. 238 EL121
Parkwood Vw., Bans. 233 CW116
Parlaunt Rd., Iver 153 BC76
Parlaunt Rd., Slou. 153 BA77
Parley Dr., Wok. 226 AW117
Parliament Ct. E1 142 DS71
Sandy's Row
Parliament Hill NW3 120 DE63
Parliament La., Slou. 130 AF66
Parliament Ms. SW14 158 CQ82
Thames Bank
Parliament Sq. SW1 277 P5
Parliament Sq. SW1 161 DL75
Parliament Sq., Hert. 32 DR10
Parliament St. SW1 277 P5
Parliament St. SW1 161 DL75
Parma Cres. SW11 160 DF84
Parmiter St. E2 142 DV68
Parnall Rd., Harl. 51 ER18
Parndon Mill La., Harl. 35 EP12
Parndon Wd. Rd., Harl. 51 EQ20
Parnel Rd., Ware 33 DZ05
Parnell Clo., Abb.L. 59 BT30
Parnell Clo., Edg. 96 CP49
Parnell Rd. E3 143 DZ67
Parnham St. E14 143 DY72
Blount St.
Parolles Rd. N19 121 DJ60
Paroma Rd., Belv. 166 FA76
Parr Ave., Epsom 217 CV109
Parr Clo. N9 100 DV49
Parr Clo. N18 100 DV49
Parr Clo., Lthd. 231 CF120
Parr Ct., Felt. 176 BW91
Parr Cres., Hem.H. 41 BP15
Parr Rd. E6 144 EK67
Parr Rd., Stan. 95 CK53
Parr St. N1 142 DR68
Parris Cft., Dor. 263 CJ139
Goodwyns Rd.
Parrock, The, Grav. 191 GJ88
Parrock Ave., Grav. 191 GJ88
Parrock Rd., Grav. 191 GJ88
Parrock St., Grav. 191 GH87
Parrotts Clo., Rick. 74 BN42
Parrotts Fld., Hodd. 49 EB16
Parrs Clo., S.Croy. 220 DR109
Florence Rd.
Parrs Pl., Hmptn. 176 CA94
Parry Ave. E6 145 EM72
Parry Clo., Epsom 217 CU108
Parry Dr., Wey. 212 BN110
Parry Grn. N., Slou. 153 AZ77
Parry Grn. S., Slou. 153 AZ77
Parry Pl. SE18 165 EP77
Parry Rd. SE25 202 DS97
Parry Rd. W10 139 CY69
Parry St. SW8 161 DL79
Parsifal Rd. NW6 120 DA64
Parsley Gdns., Croy. 203 DX102
Primrose La.
Parsloe Rd., Epp. 51 EN21
Parsloe Rd., Harl. 51 EP20
Parsloes Ave., Dag. 126 EX63
Parson St. NW4 119 CW56
Parsonage Clo., Abb.L. 59 BS30
Parsonage Clo., Dor. 262 CC138
Parsonage La.
Parsonage Clo., Hayes 135 BT72
Parsonage Clo., Warl. 237 DY116
Parsonage Gdns., Enf. 82 DQ40
Parsonage La. (South Darenth), Dart. 188 FP93
Parsonage La., Dor. 262 CC137
Parsonage La., Enf. 82 DR40
Parsonage La., Hat. 45 CV23
Parsonage La., Sid. 186 EZ91
Parsonage La., Slou. 131 AQ68
Parsonage La., Wind. 151 AN81
Parsonage Leys, Harl. 51 ET15
Parsonage Manorway, Belv. 166 FA79
Parsonage Rd., Ch.St.G. 90 AV48
Parsonage Rd., Egh. 172 AX92
Parsonage Rd., Grays 169 FW79
Parsonage Rd., Hat. 45 CV23
Parsonage Rd., Rain. 148 FJ68
Parsonage Rd., Rick. 92 BK45
Parsonage Sq., Dor. 263 CG135
Parsonage St. E14 163 EC77
Parsons Clo., Horl. 268 DE147
Baden Dr.
Parsons Cres., Edg. 96 CN48
Parsons Grn. SW6 160 DA81
Parsons Grn., Guil. 242 AX132
Bellfields Rd.
Parsons Grn. Ct., Guil. 242 AX132
Bellfields Rd.
Parsons Grn. La. SW6 160 DA81
Parsons Gro., Edg. 96 CN48
Parsons Hill SE18 165 EN76
Powis St.
Parson's Ho. W2 140 DD70
Parsons La., Dart. 187 FG90
Parson's Mead, Croy. 201 DP102
Parsons Mead, E.Mol. 196 CC97
Parsons Pightle, Couls. 235 DN120
Coulsdon Rd.
Parsons Rd. E13 144 EJ68
Old St.
Parsons Wd., Slou. 131 AQ65
Parsonsfield Clo., Bans. 233 CX115
Parsonsfield Rd., Bans. 233 CX115
Parthenia Rd. SW6 160 DA81
Parthia Clo., Tad. 233 CV119
Partingdale La. NW7 97 CX50
Partington Clo. N19 121 DK60
Partridge Clo. E16 144 EK71
Fulmer Rd.
Partridge Clo., Barn. 79 CW44
Partridge Clo., Chesh. 54 AS28
Partridge Clo., Stan. 96 CL49
Partridge Clo. (Bushey), Wat. 94 CB46
Partridge Ct. EC1 141 DP70
Percival St.
Partridge Dr., Orp. 205 EQ104
Partridge Grn. SE9 185 EN90
Partridge Knoll, Pur. 219 DP112
Partridge Mead, Bans. 233 CW116
Partridge Rd., Hmptn. 176 BZ93
Partridge Rd., Harl. 51 ER17
Partridge Rd., St.Alb. 43 CD16
Partridge Rd., Sid. 185 ES90
Partridge Sq. E6 144 EL71
Nightingale Way
Partridge Way N22 99 DL53
Partridge Way, Guil. 243 BD132
Parvills, Wal.Abb. 67 ED32
Parvin St. SW8 161 DK81
Parvis Rd., W.Byf. 212 BG113
Pasadena Clo., Hayes 155 BV75
Pasadena Clo. Trd. Est., Hayes 155 BV75
Pasadena Clo.
Pascal St. SW8 161 DK80
Pascoe Rd. SE13 183 ED85
Pasfield, Wal.Abb. 67 ED33
Pasley Clo. SE17 162 DQ78
Penrose St.
Pasquier Rd. E17 123 DY55
Passey Pl. SE9 185 EM86
Passfield Dr. E14 143 EB71
Uamvar St.
Passfield Path SE28 146 EV73
Booth Clo.
Passing All. EC1 274 G5
Passmore Gdns. N11 99 DK51
Passmore St. SW1 276 F9
Passmore St. SW1 160 DG77
Pastens Rd., Oxt. 254 EJ131
Pasteur Clo. NW9 96 CS54
Pasteur Dr., Rom. 106 FK54
Pasteur Gdns. N18 99 DP50
Paston Clo. E5 123 DX62
Caldecott Way
Paston Clo., Wall. 201 DJ104
Paston Cres. SE12 184 EH87
Paston Rd., Hem.H. 40 BK18
Pastor St. SE11 278 G8
Pastor St. SE11 161 DP77
Pasture, The, St.Alb. 42 CA24
Pasture Clo. (Bushey), Wat. 94 CC45
Pasture Clo., Wem. 117 CH62
Pasture Rd. SE6 184 EF88
Pasture Rd., Dag. 126 EZ63
Pasture Rd., Wem. 117 CH61
Pastures, The N20 97 CZ46
Pastures, The, Hat. 45 CV19
Pastures, The, Hem.H. 39 BE19
Pastures, The, Wat. 94 BW45
Pastures, The, Welw.G.C. 30 DA11
Pastures Mead, Uxb. 134 BN65
Patch, The, Sev. 256 FE122
Patch Clo., Uxb. 134 BM67
Patcham Ct., Sutt. 218 DC109
Patcham Ter. SW8 161 DH81
Pater St. W8 160 DA76
Paternoster Clo., Wal.Abb. 68 EF33
Paternoster Hill, Wal.Abb. 68 EF32
Paternoster Row EC4 275 H9
Paternoster Row (Havering-atte-Bower), Rom. 106 FJ47
Paternoster Sq. EC4 274 G8
Paterson Rd., Ashf. 174 BK92
Pates Manor Dr., Felt. 175 BR87
Path, The SW19 200 DB95
Pathfield Rd. SW16 181 DK93
Pathfields, Guil. 260 BN140
Pathway, The, Rad. 77 CF36
Pathway, The, Wat. 94 BX46
Anthony Clo.
Pathway, The, Wok. 243 BF125
Patience Rd. SW11 160 DE82
Patio Clo. SW4 181 DK86
Patmore Est. SW8 161 DJ81
Patmore La., Walt. 213 BT107
Patmore Link Rd., Hem.H. 41 BQ20
Patmore Rd., Wal.Abb. 68 EE34
Patmore St. SW8 161 DJ81
Patmore Way, Rom. 105 FB50
Patmos Rd. SW9 161 DP80
Paton Clo. E3 143 EA69
Paton St. EC1 275 H3
Patricia Clo., Slou. 131 AL73
Patricia Ct., Chis. 205 ER95
Manor Pk. Rd.
Patricia Ct., Well. 166 EV80
Patricia Dr., Horn. 128 FL60
Patricia Gdns., Sutt. 218 DA111
The Cres.
Patrick Connolly Gdns. E3 143 EB69
Talwin St.
Patrick Gro., Wal.Abb. 67 EB33
Beaulieu Dr.
Patrick Pas. SW11 160 DE82
Patrick Rd. E13 144 EJ69
Patrington Clo., Uxb. 134 BJ69
Boulmer Rd.
Patriot Sq. E2 142 DV68
Patrol Pl. SE6 183 EB86
Patrons Dr., Uxb. 113 BF58
Patshull Pl. NW5 141 DJ65
Patshull Rd.
Patshull Rd. NW5 141 DJ65
Patten All., Rich. 177 CK85
The Hermitage
Patten Rd. SW18 180 DE87
Pattenden Rd. SE6 183 DZ88
Patterdale Clo., Brom. 184 EF93
Patterdale Rd. SE15 162 DW80
Patterdale Rd., Dart. 189 FR88
Patterson Ct. SE19 182 DT94
Patterson Rd. SE19 182 DT93
Patterson Rd., Chesh. 54 AP28
Pattina Wk. SE16 143 DZ74
Pattison Pt. E16 144 EG71
Fife Rd.
Pattison Rd. NW2 120 DA62
Pattison Wk. SE18 165 EQ78
Paul Clo. E15 144 EE66
Paul St.
Paul Gdns., Croy. 202 DT103
Paul Julius Clo. E14 143 ED73
Paul Robeson Clo. E6 145 EN69
Eastbourne Rd.
Paul St. E15 143 ED67
Paul St. EC2 275 L5
Paul St. EC2 142 DR70
Paulet Rd. SE5 161 DP82
Paulhan Rd., Har. 117 CK56
Paulin Dr. N21 99 DN45
Pauline Cres., Twick. 176 CC88
Paulinus Clo., Orp. 206 EW96
Pauls Grn., Wal.Cr. 67 DY33
Eleanor Rd.
Pauls Hill, H.Wyc. 88 AF48
Pauls La., Hodd. 49 EA17
Taverners Way
Paul's Pl., Ash. 232 CP119
Paul's Wk. EC4 274 G10
Paul's Wk. EC4 142 DQ73
Paultons Sq. SW3 160 DD79
Paultons St. SW3 160 DD79
Pauntley St. N19 121 DJ60
Paved Ct., Rich. 177 CK85
King St.
Paveley Dr. SW11 160 DE80
Paveley St. NW8 272 C4
Paveley St. NW8 140 DE70
Pavement, The SW4 161 DJ84
Pavement, The W5 158 CL76
Popes La.
Pavement Ms., Rom. 126 EX59
Clarissa Rd.
Pavement Sq., Croy. 202 DU102
Pavet Clo., Dag. 147 FB65
Pavilion Gdns., Stai. 174 BH94
Pavilion Ms. N3 98 DA54
Windermere Ave.
Pavilion Rd. SW1 276 E7
Pavilion Rd. SW1 160 DF75
Pavilion Rd., Ilf. 125 EM59
Pavilion St. SW1 276 E7
Pavilion Ter., E.Mol. 197 CF98
Pavilion Ter., Ilf. 125 ES57
Southdown Cres.
Pavilion Way, Amer. 72 AW39
Pavilion Way, Edg. 96 CP52
Pavilion Way, Ruis. 116 BW61
Pavilions, The, Epp. 71 FC25
Pawleyne Clo. SE20 182 DW94
Pawsey Clo. E13 144 EG67
Plashet Rd.
Pawson's Rd., Croy. 202 DQ100
Paxford Rd., Wem. 117 CH61

Paxton Ave., Slou. 151 AQ76
Paxton Clo., Rich. 158 CM82
Paxton Clo., Walt. 196 BW101
Shaw Dr.
Paxton Gdns., Wok. 211 BE112
Paxton Pl. SE27 182 DS91
Paxton Rd. N17 100 DT52
Paxton Rd. SE23 183 DY90
Paxton Rd. W4 158 CS79
Paxton Rd., Berk. 38 AX19
Paxton Rd., Brom. 184 EG94
Paxton Rd., St.Alb. 43 CE21
Paxton Ter. SW1 161 DH79
Paycock Rd., Harl. 51 EN17
Payne Rd. E3 143 EB68
Payne St. SE8 163 DZ79
Paynell Ct. SE3 164 EE83
Lawn Ter.
Paynes La., Wal.Abb. 49 EC24
Paynes Wk. W6 159 CY79
Paynesfield Ave. SW14 158 CR83
Paynesfield Rd. (Bushey), Wat. 95 CF45
Paynesfield Rd., West. 238 EJ121
Pea La., Upmin. 149 FU66
Peabody Ave. SW1 277 H10
Peabody Clo. SE10 163 EB81
Devonshire Dr.
Peabody Clo. SW1 161 DH79
Lupus St.
Peabody Clo., Croy. 202 DW102
Shirley Rd.
Peabody Dws. WC1 273 P4
Peabody Est. EC1 275 J5
Peabody Est. N17 100 DS53
Peabody Est. SE1 278 E3
Peabody Est. SE24 182 DQ87
Peabody Est. SW3 160 DE79
Margaretta Ter.
Peabody Est. W6 159 CW78
The Sq.
Peabody Est. W10 139 CW71
Peabody Hill SE21 181 DP88
Peabody Hill Est. SE21 181 DP87
Peabody Sq. N1 141 DP67
Essex Rd.
Peabody Sq. SE1 278 F5
Peabody Sq. SE1 161 DP75
Peabody Trust SE1 279 H3
Peabody Trust SE1 142 DQ74
Peabody Yd. N1 142 DQ67
Greenman St.
Peace Clo. N14 81 DH43
Peace Clo. SE25 202 DS98
Peace Clo., Wal.Cr. 66 DU29
Goffs La.
Peace Gro., Wem. 118 CP62
Peace Prospect, Wat. 75 BU41
Peace Rd., Iver 133 BB67
Peace Rd., Slou. 133 BA68
Peace St. SE18 165 EP79
Nightingale Vale
Peach Cft., Grav. 190 GE90
Peach Rd. W10 139 CX69
Peach Tree Ave., West Dr. 134 BM72
Pear Tree Ave.
Peaches Clo., Sutt. 217 CY108
Peachey Clo., Uxb. 134 BK72
Peachey La., Uxb. 134 BK71
Peachum Rd. SE3 164 EF79
Peacock Ave., Felt. 175 BR88
Peacock Clo., Horn. 128 FL56
Peacock Gdns., S.Croy. 221 DY110
Peacock St. SE17 278 G9
Peacock St., Grav. 191 GJ87
Peacock Wk. E16 144 EH72
Peacock Wk., Abb.L. 59 BU31
Peacock Wk., Dor. 263 CG137
Rose Hill
Peacock Yd. SE17 278 G9
Peacocks, Harl. 51 EM17
Peacocks Cen., Wok. 226 AY117
Victoria Way
Peacocks Clo., Berk. 38 AT17
Tortoiseshell Way
Peak, The, SE26 182 DW90
Peak Hill SE26 182 DW91
Peak Hill Ave. SE26 182 DW91
Peak Hill Gdns. SE26 182 DW91
Peak Rd., Guil. 242 AU131
Peakes La. (Cheshunt), Wal.Cr. 66 DT27
Peakes Way (Cheshunt), Wal.Cr. 66 DT27
Peaketon Ave., Ilf. 124 EK56
Peaks Hill, Pur. 219 DK110
Peaks Hill Ri., Pur. 219 DL110
Peal Gdns. W13 137 CG70
Ruislip Rd. E.
Peall Rd., Croy. 201 DM100
Pear Clo. NW9 118 CR56
Pear Clo. SE14 163 DY80
Southerngate Way
Pear Pl. SE1 278 D4
Pear Rd. E11 123 ED62
Pear Tree Ave., West Dr. 134 BM72
Pear Tree Clo. E2 142 DT67
Pear Tree Clo., Add. 212 BG106
Pear Tree Rd.
Pear Tree Clo., Beac. 89 AQ51
Pear Tree Clo., Chess. 216 CN106
Pear Tree Clo., Mitch. 200 DE96
Pear Tree Clo., Slou. 131 AM74
Pear Tree Clo., Swan. 207 FD96
Pear Tree Ct. EC1 274 E4
Pear Tree Ct. EC1 141 DN70
Pear Tree Hill, Red. 266 DG143
Pear Tree Mead, Harl. 52 EU18
Pear Tree Rd., Add. 212 BG106
Pear Tree Rd., Ashf. 175 BQ92
Pear Tree St. EC1 274 G4
Pear Tree St. EC1 141 DP70
Pear Tree Wk. (Cheshunt), Wal.Cr. 66 DR26
Pearce Clo., Mitch. 200 DG96
Pearce Rd., Chesh. 54 AP29
Pearce Rd., W.Mol. 196 CB97
Pearcefield Ave. SE23 182 DW88
Pearces Wk., St.Alb. 43 CD21
Albert St.
Pearcroft Rd. E11 123 ED61
Peardon St. SW8 161 DH82
Peareswood Gdns., Stan. 95 CK53
Peareswood Rd., Erith 167 FF81
Pearfield Rd. SE23 183 DY90
Pearl Clo. E6 145 EN72
Pearl Clo. NW2 119 CX59
Marble Dr.
Pearl Ct., Wok. 226 AS116
Langmans Way
Pearl Gdns., Slou. 131 AP74
Pearl Rd. E17 123 EA55
Pearl St. E1 142 DV74
Penang St.
Pearmain Clo., Shep. 195 BP99
Laleham Rd.
Pearman St. SE1 278 E6
Pearman St. SE1 161 DN75
Pears Rd., Houns. 156 CC83
Pearscroft Ct. SW6 160 DB81
Pearscroft Rd. SW6 160 DB81
Pearse St. SE15 162 DS79
Dragon Rd.
Pearson Ave., Hert. 32 DQ11
Pearson Clo., Hert. 32 DQ11
Pearson Ave.
Pearson Ms. SW4 161 DK83
Edgeley Rd.
Pearson St. E2 142 DT68
Pearson Way, Dart. 188 FM89
Pearsons Ave. SE14 163 EA81
Tanners Hill
Peartree Ave. SW17 180 DC90
Peartree Clo., Amer. 72 AT39
Orchard End Ave.
Peartree Clo., Erith 167 FD81
Peartree Clo., Hem.H. 40 BG19
Peartree Clo., S.Croy. 220 DV114
Peartree Clo., S.Ock. 149 FW68
Peartree Clo., Welw.G.C. 29 CY09
Peartree Ct., Welw.G.C. 29 CY10
Peartree Fm., Welw.G.C. 29 CY09
Peartree Gdns., Dag. 126 EV63
Peartree Gdns., Rom. 105 FB54
Peartree La. E1 142 DW73
Glamis Rd.
Peartree La., Welw.G.C. 29 CY10
Peartree Rd., Enf. 82 DS41
Peartree Rd., Hem.H. 40 BG19
Peartree Way SE10 164 EG77
Peary Pl. E2 142 DW69
Kirkwall Pl.
Peascod Pl., Wind. 151 AR81
Peascod St.
Peascod St., Wind. 151 AQ81
Peascroft Rd., Hem.H. 40 BN23
Pease Clo., Horn. 147 FH66
Dowding Way
Peatfield Clo., Sid. 185 ES90
Woodside Rd.
Peatmore Ave., Wok. 228 BG116
Peatmore Clo., Wok. 228 BG116
Pebble Clo., Tad. 248 CS128
Pebble Hill, Lthd. 245 BQ133
Pebble Hill Rd., Bet. 248 CS131
Pebble Hill Rd., Tad. 248 CS128
Pebble Way W3 138 CP74
Pebworth Rd., Har. 117 CG61
Peckarmans Wd. SE26 182 DU90
Peckett Sq. N5 122 DQ63
Highbury Gra.
Peckford Pl. SW9 161 DN82
Peckham Gro. SE15 162 DS80
Peckham High St. SE15 162 DU81
Peckham Hill St. SE15 162 DU80
Peckham Pk. Rd. SE15 162 DU80
Peckham Rd. SE5 162 DS81
Peckham Rd. SE15 162 DS81
Peckham Rye SE15 162 DU83
Peckham Rye SE22 162 DU84
Pecks Hill, Wal.Abb. 50 EE21
Pecks Yd. E1 275 P6
Peckwater St. NW5 121 DJ64
Pedham Pl. Est., Swan. 207 FG99
Pedlars End, Ong. 53 FH21
Pedlars Wk. N7 141 DL65
Pedley Rd., Dag. 126 EW60
Pedley St. E1 142 DT70
Pednor Rd., Chesh. 54 AM30
Pednormead End, Chesh. 54 AP32
Pedro St. E5 123 DX62
Pedworth Gdns. SE16 162 DW77
Rotherhithe New Rd.
Peek Cres. SW19 179 CX92
Peeks Brook La., Horl. 269 DL153
Peel Clo. E4 101 EB47
Peel Clo. N9 100 DU48
Plevna Rd.
Peel Clo., Wind. 151 AP83
Peel Ct., Slou. 131 AQ71
Farnburn Ave.
Peel Cres., Hert. 31 DP06
Peel Dr. NW9 119 CT55
Peel Dr., Ilf. 124 EL55
Peel Gro. E2 142 DW68
Peel Pas. W8 140 DA74
Peel St.
Peel Pl., Ilf. 102 EL54
Peel Prec. NW6 140 DA68
Peel Rd. E18 102 EF53
Peel Rd. NW6 139 CZ69
Peel Rd., Har. 117 CF55
Peel Rd., Orp. 223 EQ106
Peel Rd., Wem. 117 CK62
Peel St. W8 140 DA74
Peel Way, Rom. 106 FM54
Peel Way, Uxb. 134 BL71
Peerage Way, Horn. 128 FL59
Peerless Dr. (Harefield), Uxb. 114 BJ57
Peerless St. EC1 275 K3
Peerless St. EC1 142 DR69
Pegamoid Rd. N18 100 DW48
Pegasus Clo. N16 122 DR63
Green Las.
Pegasus Ct., Abb.L. 59 BT32
Furtherfield
Pegasus Ct., Grav. 191 GJ90
Pegasus Pl. SE11 161 DN79
Clayton St.
Pegasus Way N11 99 DH51
Pegelm Gdns., Horn. 128 FM59
Pegg Rd., Houns. 156 BX80
Peggotty Way, Uxb. 135 BP72
Dickens Ave.
Pegley Gdns. SE12 184 EG89
Pegmire La., Wat. 76 CC39
Pegrams Rd., Harl. 51 EQ18
Pegs La., Hert. 32 DR10
Pegwell St. SE18 165 ES80
Peket Clo., Stai. 193 BE95
Pekin Clo. E14 143 EA72
Pekin St.
Pekin St. E14 143 EA72
Peldon Ct., Rich. 158 CM84
Peldon Pas., Rich. 158 CM84
Worple Way
Peldon Rd., Harl. 51 EN17
Peldon Wk. N1 141 DP67
Britannia Row
Pelham Ave., Bark. 145 ET67
Pelham Clo. SE5 162 DS82
Pelham Ct., Hem.H. 41 BQ20
Pelham Ct., Welw.G.C. 30 DC10
Amwell Common
Pelham Cres. SW7 276 B9
Pelham Cres. SW7 160 DE77
Pelham Pl. SW7 276 B9
Pelham Pl. SW7 160 DE77
Pelham Rd. E18 124 EH55
Pelham Rd. N15 122 DT56
Pelham Rd. N22 99 DN54
Pelham Rd. SW19 180 DA94
Pelham Rd., Beck. 202 DW96
Pelham Rd., Bexh. 166 FA83
Pelham Rd., Grav. 191 GF88
Pelham Rd., Ilf. 125 ER61
Pelham Rd. S., Grav. 191 GF88
Pelham St. SW7 276 A8
Pelham St. SW7 160 DE77
Pelham Ter., Grav. 191 GF87
Campbell Rd.
Pelham Way, Lthd. 246 CB126
Pelhams, The, Wat. 76 BX35
Pelhams Clo., Esher 214 CA105
Pelhams Wk., Esher 196 CA104
Pelican Est. SE15 162 DT81
Pelican Pas. E1 142 DW70
Cambridge Heath Rd.
Pelican Wk. SW9 161 DP84
Loughborough Pk.
Pelier St. SE17 162 DQ79
Langdale Clo.
Pelinore Rd. SE6 184 EE89
Pellant Rd. SW6 159 CY80
Pellatt Gro. N22 99 DN53
Pellatt Rd. SE22 182 DT85
Pellatt Rd., Wem. 117 CK61
Pellerin Rd. N16 122 DS64
Pelling Hill, Wind. 172 AV87
Pelling St. E14 143 EA72
Pellipar Clo. N13 99 DN48
Pellipar Gdns. SE18 165 EM78
Pelly Ct., Epp. 69 ET31
Pelly Rd. E13 144 EG68
Pelter St. E2 275 P2
Pelter St. E2 142 DT69
Pelton Ave., Sutt. 218 DB110
Pelton Rd. SE10 164 EE78
Pembar Ave. E17 123 DY55
Pember Rd. NW10 139 CX69
Pemberley Chase (West Ewell), Epsom 216 CP106
Ruxley Clo.
Pemberley Clo. (West Ewell), Epsom 216 CP106
Ruxley Clo.
Pemberton Ave., Rom. 127 FH55
Pemberton Clo., St.Alb. 43 CD23
Pemberton Gdns. N19 121 DJ62
Pemberton Gdns., Rom. 126 EY57
Pemberton Gdns., Swan. 207 FE97
Pemberton Ho. SE26 182 DU91
High Level Dr.
Pemberton Pl. E8 142 DV66
Mare St.
Pemberton Pl., Esher 196 CC104
Carrick Gate
Pemberton Rd. N4 121 DN57
Pemberton Rd., E.Mol. 196 CC98
Pemberton Rd., Slou. 131 AL70
Pemberton Row EC4 274 E8
Pemberton Ter. N19 121 DJ62
Pembrey Way, Horn. 148 FJ65
Pembridge Ave., Twick. 176 BZ88
Pembridge Chase, Hem.H. 57 BA28
Pembridge Clo.
Pembridge Clo., Hem.H. 57 AZ28
Pembridge Cres. W11 140 DA73
Pembridge Gdns. W2 140 DA73
Pembridge La., Brox. 48 DR21
Pembridge La., Hert. 48 DQ19
Pembridge Ms. W11 140 DA73
Pembridge Pl. SW15 180 DA85
Oakhill Rd.
Pembridge Pl. W2 140 DA73
Pembridge Rd. W11 140 DA73
Pembridge Rd., Hem.H. 57 BA28
Pembridge Sq. W2 140 DA73
Pembridge Vil. W2 140 DA73
Pembridge Vil. W11 140 DA73
Pembroke Ave., Enf. 82 DV38
Pembroke Ave., Har. 117 CG55
Pembroke Ave., Pnr. 116 BX60
Pembroke Ave., Surb. 198 CP99
Pembroke Ave., Walt. 214 BX105
Pembroke Clo. SW1 276 G5
Pembroke Clo. SW1 160 DG75
Pembroke Clo., Bans. 234 DB117
Pembroke Clo., Brox. 49 DY23
Pembroke Clo., Erith 167 FD77
Pembroke Rd.
Pembroke Clo., Horn. 128 FM56
Pembroke Cotts. W8 160 DA76
Pembroke Sq.
Pembroke Dr. (Cheshunt), Wal.Cr. 65 DP29
Pembroke Gdns. W8 159 CZ77
Pembroke Gdns., Dag. 127 FB62
Pembroke Gdns., Wok. 227 BA118
Pembroke Gdns. Clo. W8 160 DA76
Pembroke Ms. E3 143 DY69
Morgan St.
Pembroke Ms. N10 98 DG53
Pembroke Rd.
Pembroke Ms. W8 160 DA76
Earls Wk.
Pembroke Ms., Sev. 257 FH125
Pembroke Rd.
Pembroke Pl. W8 160 DA76
Pembroke Pl. (Sutton at Hone), Dart. 208 FP95
Pembroke Pl., Edg. 96 CN52
Pembroke Pl., Islw. 157 CE82
Thornbury Rd.
Pembroke Rd. E6 145 EM71
Pembroke Rd. E17 123 EB57
Pembroke Rd. N8 121 DL56
Pembroke Rd. N10 98 DG53
Pembroke Rd. N13 100 DQ48
Pembroke Rd. N15 122 DT57
Pembroke Rd. SE25 202 DS98
Pembroke Rd. W8 160 DA77
Pembroke Rd., Brom. 204 EJ96
Pembroke Rd., Erith 167 FC78
Pembroke Rd., Grnf. 136 CB70
Pembroke Rd., Ilf. 125 ET60
Pembroke Rd., Mitch. 200 DG96
Pembroke Rd., Nthwd. 93 BQ48
Pembroke Rd., Ruis. 115 BT60
Pembroke Rd., Sev. 257 FH125
Pembroke Rd., Wem. 117 CK62
Pembroke Rd., Wok. 227 BA118
Pembroke Sq. W8 160 DA76
Pembroke St. N1 141 DL66
Pembroke Studios W8 159 CZ76
Pembroke Vil. W8 160 DA77
Pembroke Vil., Rich. 157 CK84
Pembroke Wk. W8 160 DA77
Pembroke Way, Hayes 155 BQ76
Pembury Ave., Wor.Pk. 199 CU101
Pembury Clo., Brom. 204 EF101
Pembury Clo., Couls. 218 DG114
Pembury Ct., Hayes 155 BR79
Pembury Cres., Sid. 186 EY90
Pembury Pl. E5 122 DV64
Pembury Rd. E5 122 DV64
Pembury Rd. N17 100 DT54
Pembury Rd. SE25 202 DU98
Pembury Rd., Bexh. 166 EY80
Pemdevon Rd., Croy. 201 DN101
Pemell Clo. E1 142 DW70
Colebert Ave.
Pemerich Clo., Hayes 155 BT78
Pempath Pl., Wem. 117 CK61
Pemsel Ct., Hem.H. 40 BK22
Crabtree La.
Penally Pl. N1 142 DR67
Shepperton Rd.
Penang St. E1 142 DV74
Penard Rd., Sthl. 156 CA76
Penarth St. SE15 162 DW79
Penates, Esher 215 CD105
Penberth Rd. SE6 183 EC88
Penbury Rd., Sthl. 156 BZ77
Pencombe Ms. W11 139 CZ73
Denbigh Rd.
Pencraig Way SE15 162 DV79
Pencroft Dr., Dart. 188 FJ87
Shepherds La.
Penda Rd., Erith 167 FB80
Pendall Clo., Barn. 80 DE42
Pendarves Rd. SW20 199 CW95
Penda's Mead E9 123 DY63
Lindisfarne Way
Pendell Ave., Hayes 155 BT80
Pendell Rd., Red. 251 DP131
Pendennis Clo., W.Byf. 212 BG114
Pendennis Rd. N17 122 DR55
Pendennis Rd. SW16 181 DL91
Pendennis Rd., Orp. 206 EW103
Pendennis Rd., Sev. 257 FH123
Penderel Rd., Houns. 176 CA85
Penderry Ri. SE6 183 ED89
Penderyn Way N7 121 DK63
Pendle Rd. SW16 181 DH93
Pendlestone Rd. E17 123 EB57
Pendleton Clo., Red. 266 DF136
Pendleton Rd., Red. 266 DC137
Pendleton Rd., Reig. 266 DC137
Pendragon Rd., Brom. 184 EF90
Pendragon Wk. NW9 118 CS58
Pendrell Rd. SE4 163 DY82
Pendrell St. SE18 165 ER80
Pendula Dr., Hayes 136 BX70
Pendulum Ms. E8 122 DT64
Birkbeck Rd.
Penerley Rd. SE6 183 EB88
Penerley Rd., Rain. 147 FH71
Penfold Clo., Croy. 201 DN104
Epsom Rd.
Penfold La., Bex. 186 EX88
Carisbrooke Ave.
Penfold Pl. NW1 272 B6
Penfold Pl. NW1 140 DE71
Penfold Rd. N9 101 DX46
Penfold St. NW1 272 A5
Penfold St. NW1 140 DD70
Penfold St. NW8 272 A5
Penfold St. NW8 140 DD70
Penford Gdns. SE9 164 EK83
Penford St. SE5 161 DP82
Pengarth Rd., Bex. 186 EX85
Penge Ho. SW11 160 DD83
Wye St.
Penge La. SE20 182 DW94
Penge Rd. E13 144 EJ66
Penge Rd. SE20 202 DU97
Penge Rd. SE25 202 DU97
Pengelly Clo. (Cheshunt), Wal.Cr. 66 DV30
Penhall Rd. SE7 164 EK77
Penhill Rd., Bex. 186 EW86
Penhurst, Wok. 211 AZ114
Penhurst Rd., Ilf. 103 EP52
Penifather La., Grnf. 137 CD69
Peninsular Clo., Felt. 175 BR86
Peninsular Pk. Rd. SE7 164 EG77
Penistone Rd. SW16 181 DL94
Penistone Wk., Rom. 106 FJ51
Okehampton Rd.
Penketh Dr., Har. 117 CD62
Penlow Rd., Harl. 51 EQ18
Penman Clo., St.Alb. 60 CA27
Penman's Grn., Kings L. 58 BG32
Penmon Rd. SE2 166 EU76
Penn Ave., Chesh. 54 AN30
Penn Bottom, H.Wyc. 88 AG45
Penn Clo., Grnf. 136 CB68
Penn Clo., Har. 117 CJ56
Penn Clo., Rick. 73 BD44
Penn Clo., Uxb. 134 BK70
Penn Dr., Uxb. 113 BF58
Penn Gdns., Chis. 205 EP96
Penn Gdns., Rom. 104 FA52
Penn Gaskell La., Ger.Cr. 91 AZ50
Penn La., Bex. 186 EX86
Penn Meadow, Slou. 132 AT67
Penn Pl., Rick. 92 BK45
Northway
Penn Rd. N7 121 DL64
Penn Rd., Beac. 88 AJ48
Penn Rd., Ger.Cr. 90 AX53
Penn Rd., Rick. 91 BF46
Penn Rd., St.Alb. 60 CC27
Penn Rd., Slou. 131 AR70
Penn Rd. (Datchet), Slou. 152 AX81
Penn Rd., Wat. 75 BV39
Penn St. N1 142 DR67
Penn Way, Rick. 73 BD44
Pennack Rd. SE15 162 DT79
Pennant Ms. W8 160 DB77
Pennant Ter. E17 101 DZ54
Pennard Rd. W12 159 CW75
Pennards, The, Sun. 196 BW96
Penne Clo., Rad. 61 CF34
Penner Clo. SW19 179 CY89
Victoria Dr.
Penners Gdns., Surb. 198 CL101
Pennethorne Clo. E9 142 DW67
Victoria Pk. Rd.
Pennethorne Rd. SE15 162 DV80
Penney Clo., Dart. 188 FK87
Pennine Dr. NW2 119 CY61
Pennine La. NW2 119 CY61
Pennine Dr.
Pennine Rd., Slou. 131 AN71
Pennine Way, Bexh. 167 FE81
Pennine Way, Grav. 190 GE90
Pennine Way, Hayes 155 BR80
Pennine Way, Hem.H. 40 BM17
Pennings Ave., Guil. 242 AT132
Pennington Clo. SE27 182 DR91
Hamilton Rd.
Pennington Clo., Rom. 104 FA51
Pennington Dr. N21 81 DL43
Pennington Dr., Wey. 195 BS104
Pennington Rd., Beac. 110 AH55
Pennington Rd., Ger.Cr. 90 AX52
Pennington St. E1 142 DU73
Pennington Way SE12 184 EH89
Penningtons, The, Amer. 55 AS37
Pennis La. (Fawkham Grn.), Long. 209 FW100
Penniston Clo. N17 100 DQ54
Penny Clo., Rain. 147 FH69
Penny La., Shep. 195 BS101
Penny Ms. SW12 181 DH87
Caistor Rd.
Penny Rd. NW10 138 CP69
Pennycroft, Croy. 221 DY109
Pennyfather La., Enf. 82 DQ41
Pennyfield, Cob. 213 BU113
Pennyfields E14 143 EA73
Pennyfields, Brwd. 108 FW49
Pennylets Grn., Slou. 132 AT66
Pennymead, Harl. 36 EU14
Pennymead Dr., Lthd. 245 BT127
Pennymead Ri., Lthd. 245 BT127
Pennymoor Wk. W9 139 CZ69
Ashmore Rd.
Pennyroyal Ave. E6 145 EN72
Pennys La., Saw. 35 ER05
Penpoll Rd. E8 142 DV65
Penpool La., Well. 166 EV83
Penrhyn Ave. E17 101 DZ53
Penrhyn Cres. E17 101 EA53
Penrhyn Cres. SW14 158 CQ84
Penrhyn Gro. E17 101 EA53
Penrhyn Rd., Kings.T. 198 CL97
Penrith Clo. SW15 179 CY85
Penrith Clo., Beck. 203 EB95
Albemarle Rd.
Penrith Clo., Reig. 250 DE133
Penrith Clo., Uxb. 134 BK66
Chippendale Waye
Penrith Cres., Rain. 127 FG64
Penrith Pl. SE27 181 DP89
Harpenden Rd.
Penrith Rd. N15 122 DR57
Penrith Rd., Ilf. 103 ET51
Penrith Rd., N.Mal. 198 CR98
Penrith Rd., Rom. 106 FN51
Penrith Rd., Th.Hth. 202 DQ96
Penrith St. SW16 181 DJ93
Penrose Ave., Wat. 94 BX47
Penrose Ct., Hem.H. 40 BL16
Penrose Dr., Epsom 216 CN111
Penrose Gro. SE17 162 DQ78
Penrose Ho. SE17 162 DQ78
Penrose Rd., Lthd. 230 CC122
Penrose St. SE17 162 DQ78
Penry St. SE1 279 N9
Penryn St. NW1 141 DK68
Pensbury Pl. SW8 161 DJ82
Pensbury St. SW8 161 DJ82
Penscroft Gdns., Borwd. 78 CR42
Pensford Ave., Rich. 158 CN82
Penshurst, Harl. 36 EV12
Penshurst Ave., Sid. 186 EU86
Penshurst Clo., Ger.Cr. 90 AX54
Penshurst Gdns., Edg. 96 CP50
Penshurst Grn., Brom. 204 EF99
Penshurst Rd. E9 143 DX66
Penshurst Rd. N17 100 DT52
Penshurst Rd., Bexh. 166 EZ81
Penshurst Rd., Pot.B. 64 DD31
Penshurst Rd., Th.Hth. 201 DP99
Penshurst Wk., Brom. 204 EF99
Hayesford Pk. Dr.
Penshurst Way, Orp. 206 EW98
Star La.
Penshurst Way, Sutt. 218 DA108
Pensilver Clo., Barn. 80 DE42
Pensons La., Ong. 71 FG28
Penstemon Clo. N3 98 DA52
Penstock Footpath N22 121 DL55
Pentavia Retail Pk. NW7 97 CT52
Bunns La.
Pentelowe Gdns., Felt. 175 BU86
Pentire Clo., Upmin. 129 FS58
Pentire Rd. E17 101 ED53
Pentland, Hem.H. 40 BM17
Mendip Way
Pentland Ave., Edg. 96 CP47
Pentland Ave., Shep. 194 BN99
Pentland Clo. NW11 119 CY61
Pentland Gdns. SW18 180 DC86
St. Ann's Hill
Pentland Pl., Nthlt. 136 BY67
Pentland Rd., Slou. 131 AN71
Pentland Rd. (Bushey), Wat. 76 CC44
Pentland St. SW18 180 DC86
Pentland Way, Uxb. 115 BQ62
Pentlands Clo., Mitch. 201 DH97
Pentley Clo., Welw.G.C. 29 CX06
Pentley Pk., Welw.G.C. 29 CX07
Pentlow St. SW15 159 CW83
Pentlow Way, Buck.H. 102 EL45
Pentney Rd. E4 101 ED46
Pentney Rd. SW12 181 DJ88
Pentney Rd. SW19 199 CY95
Midmoor Rd.
Penton Ave., Stai. 173 BF94
Penton Dr. (Cheshunt), Wal.Cr. 67 DX29
Penton Gro. N1 274 D1
Penton Hall Dr., Stai. 194 BG95

Penton Hook Rd., Stai. 174 BG94
Penton Ho. SE2 166 EX75
Hartslock Dr.
Penton Pk., Cher. 194 BH97
Penton Pl. SE17 278 G10
Penton Pl. SE17 161 DP78
Penton Ri. WC1 274 C2
Penton Ri. WC1 141 DM69
Penton Rd., Stai. 173 BF94
Penton St. N1 141 DN68
Pentonville Rd. N1 274 B1
Pentonville Rd. N1 141 DM68
Pentrich Ave., Enf. 82 DU38
Pentridge St. SE15 162 DT80
Pentyre Ave. N18 100 DR50
Penwerris Ave., Islw. 156 CC80
Penwith Rd. SW18 180 DB89
Penwith Wk., Wok. 226 AX119
Wych Hill Pk.
Penwood End, Wok. 226 AV121
Penwortham Rd. SW16 181 DH93
Penwortham Rd., S.Croy. 220 DQ110
Penylan Pl., Edg. 96 CN52
Penywern Rd. SW5 160 DA78
Penzance Clo. (Harefield), Uxb. 92 BK53
Penzance Gdns., Rom. 106 FN51
Penzance Pl. W11 139 CY74
Penzance Rd., Rom. 106 FN51
Penzance Spur, Slou. 131 AP70
Penzance St. W11 139 CY74
Peony Clo., Brwd. 108 FV44
Peony Ct., Wdf.Grn. 102 EE52
The Bridle Path
Peony Gdns. W12 139 CU73
Peplins Clo., Hat. 63 CY26
Peplins Way, Hat. 63 CY25
Peploe Rd. NW6 139 CX68
Peplow Clo., West Dr. 134 BK74
Tavistock Rd.
Pepper All., Loug. 84 EG39
Pepper Clo. E6 145 EM71
Pepper Clo., Cat. 252 DS125
Pepper Hill, Grav. 190 GC90
Pepper Hill, Ware 33 DZ10
Pepper St. E14 163 EB76
Pepper St. SE1 279 H4
Pepperhill La., Grav. 190 GC90
Peppermead Sq. SE13 183 EA85
Peppermint Clo., Croy. 201 DL101
Peppermint Pl. E11 124 EE62
Birch Gro.
Peppie Clo. N16 122 DS61
Bouverie Rd.
Pepys Clo., Ash. 232 CN117
Pepys Clo., Dart. 168 FN84
Pepys Clo., Grav. 190 GD90
Pepys Clo., Slou. 153 BB79
Pepys Clo., Til. 171 GJ81
Pepys Clo., Uxb. 115 BP63
Pepys Cres. E16 144 EG74
Britannia Gate
Pepys Cres., Barn. 79 CW43
Pepys Ri., Orp. 205 ET102
Pepys Rd. SE14 163 DX81
Pepys Rd. SW20 199 CW95
Pepys St. EC3 275 N10
Pepys St. EC3 142 DS73
Perceval Ave. NW3 120 DE64
Perch St. E8 122 DT63
Percheron Clo., Islw. 157 CG83
Percheron Rd., Borwd. 78 CR44
Percival Ct. N17 100 DT52
High Rd.
Percival Ct., Nthlt. 116 CA64
Percival Gdns., Rom. 126 EW58
Percival Rd. SW14 158 CQ84
Percival Rd., Enf. 82 DT42
Percival Rd., Felt. 175 BT89
Percival Rd., Horn. 128 FJ58
Percival Rd., Orp. 205 EP103
Percival St. EC1 274 F4
Percival St. EC1 141 DP70
Percival Way, Epsom 216 CQ105
Percy Ave., Ashf. 174 BN92
Percy Bryant Rd., Sun. 175 BS94
Percy Bush Rd., West Dr. 154 BM76
Percy Circ. WC1 274 C2
Percy Circ. WC1 141 DM69
Percy Gdns., Enf. 83 DX43
Percy Gdns., Hayes 135 BS69
Percy Gdns., Islw. 157 CG82
Percy Gdns., Wor.Pk. 198 CS102
Percy Ms. W1 273 M7
Percy Pas. W1 273 L7
Percy Pl., Slou. 152 AV81
Percy Rd. E11 124 EE59
Percy Rd. E16 144 EE71
Percy Rd. N12 98 DC50
Percy Rd. N21 100 DQ45
Percy Rd. NW6 140 DA69
Stafford Rd.
Percy Rd. SE20 203 DX95
Percy Rd. SE25 202 DU99
Percy Rd. W12 159 CU75
Percy Rd., Bexh. 166 EY82
Percy Rd., Guil. 242 AV132
Percy Rd., Hmptn. 176 CA94
Percy Rd., Ilf. 126 EU59
Percy Rd., Islw. 157 CG84
Percy Rd., Mitch. 200 DG101
Percy Rd., Rom. 127 FB55
Percy Rd., Twick. 176 CB88
Percy Rd., Wat. 75 BV42
Percy St. W1 273 M7
Percy St. W1 141 DK71
Percy St., Grays 170 GC79
Percy Ter., Ch.St.G. 90 AU48
Sycamore Rd.
Percy Way, Twick. 176 CC88
Percy Yd. WC1 274 C2
Peregrine Clo. NW10 118 CR64
Peregrine Clo., Wat. 60 BY34
Peregrine Ct. SW16 181 DM91
Leithcote Gdns.
Peregrine Ct., Well. 165 ET81
Peregrine Gdns., Croy. 203 DY103
Peregrine Ho. EC1 274 G2
Peregrine Ho. EC1 141 DP69
Peregrine Rd., Ilf. 104 EV50
Peregrine Rd., Sun. 195 BT96
Peregrine Rd., Wal.Abb. 68 EG34
Peregrine Wk., Horn. 147 FH65
Heron Flight Ave.
Peregrine Way SW19 179 CW94
Perham Rd. W14 159 CY78
Perham Way, St.Alb. 61 CK26
Peridot St. E6 144 EL71
Perifield SE21 182 DQ88
Perimeade Rd., Grnf. 137 CJ68
Perimeter Rd. E., Gat. 268 DG154
Perimeter Rd. N., Gat. 268 DD151
Perimeter Rd. S., Gat. 268 DC154
Periton Rd. SE9 164 EK84
Perivale Gdns. W13 137 CH70
Bellevue Rd.
Perivale Gdns., Wat. 59 BV34
Perivale Gra., Grnf. 137 CG69
Perivale Ind. Pk., Grnf. 137 CH68
Perivale La., Grnf. 137 CG69
Perivale New Business Cen., Grnf. 137 CH68
Perkin Clo., Wem. 117 CH64
Perkins Clo., Green. 189 FT85
Perkins Ct., Ashf. 174 BM92
Perkin's Rents SW1 277 M6
Perkin's Rents SW1 161 DK76
Perkins Rd., Ilf. 125 ER57
Perkins Sq. SE1 279 J2
Perks Clo. SE3 164 EE83
Hurren Clo.
Perleybrooke La., Wok. 226 AU117
Bampton Way
Permain Clo. (Shenley), Rad. 61 CK33
Perpins Rd. SE9 185 ES86
Perram Clo., Brox. 67 DY26
Perran Rd. SW2 181 DP89
Christchurch Rd.
Perran Wk., Brent. 158 CL78
Perren St. NW5 141 DH65
Ryland Rd.
Perrers Rd. W6 159 CV77
Perrin Clo., Ashf. 174 BM92
Fordbridge Rd.
Perrin Ct., Wok. 227 BB115
Blackmore Cres.
Perrin Rd., Wem. 117 CG63
Perrins Ct. NW3 120 DC63
Hampstead High St.
Perrins La. NW3 120 DC63
Perrin's Wk. NW3 120 DC63
Perrior Rd., Gdmg. 258 AS144
Perriors Clo. (Cheshunt), Wal.Cr. 66 DU27
Perrott St. SE18 165 EQ77
Perry Ave. W3 138 CR72
Perry Clo., Rain. 147 FD68
Lowen Rd.
Perry Clo., Uxb. 135 BQ72
Harlington Rd.
Perry Ct. E14 163 EA78
Napier Ave.
Perry Ct. N15 122 DS58
Albert Rd.
Perry Cft., Wind. 151 AL83
Perry Gdns. N9 100 DS48
Deansway
Perry Garth, Nthlt. 136 BW67
Perry Gro., Dart. 168 FN84
Perry Hall Clo., Orp. 206 EU101
Perry Hall Rd., Orp. 205 ET100
Perry Hill SE6 183 DZ90
Perry Hill, Guil. 242 AS128
Perry Hill, Wal.Abb. 50 EF23
Perry Ho., Rain. 147 FD68
Lowen Rd.
Perry How, Wor.Pk. 199 CT102
Perry Mead, Enf. 81 DP40
Perry Mead (Bushey), Wat. 94 CB45
Perry Oaks Dr. (Heathrow Airport), Houns. 154 BH82
Perry Oaks Dr., West Dr. 154 BH82
Perry Ri. SE23 183 DY90
Perry Rd., Dag. 146 EZ70
Perry Rd., Harl. 51 EQ18
Perry Spring, Harl. 52 EX17
Perry St., Chis. 185 ER93
Perry St., Dart. 167 FE84
Perry St., Grav. 190 GE88
Perry St. Gdns., Chis. 185 ES93
Old Perry St.
Perry Vale SE23 182 DW89
Perry Way, S.Ock. 148 FQ73
Perryfield Way NW9 119 CT58
Perryfield Way, Rich. 177 CH89
Perryfields Way, Slou. 130 AH70
Perrylands La., Horl. 269 DM149
Perryman Ho., Bark. 145 EQ67
The Shaftesburys
Perryman Way, Slou. 131 AM69
Perrymans Fm. Rd., Ilf. 125 ER58
Perrymead St. SW6 160 DA81
Perryn Rd. SE16 162 DV76
Drummond Rd.
Perryn Rd. W3 138 CR73
Perrys La., Sev. 224 EV113
Perrys Pl. W1 273 M8
Perrysfield Rd. (Cheshunt), Wal.Cr. 67 DY27
Perrywood Business Pk., Red. 267 DH142
Persant Rd. SE6 184 EE89
Perseverance Pl. SW9 161 DN80
Perseverance Pl., Rich. 158 CL83
Shaftesbury Rd.
Persfield Clo., Epsom 217 CU110
Pershore Clo., Ilf. 125 EP57
Pershore Gro., Cars. 200 DD100
Pert Clo. N10 99 DH52
Perth Ave. NW9 118 CR59
Perth Ave., Hayes 136 BW70
Perth Ave., Slou. 131 AP72
Perth Clo. SW20 199 CU96
Huntley Way
Perth Rd. E10 123 DY60
Perth Rd. E13 144 EH68
Perth Rd. N4 121 DN60
Perth Rd. N22 99 DP53
Perth Rd., Bark. 145 ER68
Perth Rd., Beck. 203 EC96
Perth Rd., Ilf. 125 EN58
Perth Ter., Ilf. 125 EQ59
Perwell Ave., Har. 116 BZ60
Perwell Ct., Har. 116 BZ60
Pescot Hill, Hem.H. 40 BH18
Peter Ave. NW10 139 CV66
Peter Ave., Oxt. 253 ED129
Peter James Business Cen., Hayes 155 BU75
Peter Ms., Slou. 153 BA78
Grampian Way
Peter St. W1 273 L10
Peter St. W1 141 DK73
Peter St., Grav. 191 GH87
Peterboat Clo. SE10 164 EE77
Tunnel Ave.
Peterborough Ave., Upmin. 129 FS60
Peterborough Gdns., Ilf. 124 EL59
Peterborough Ms. SW6 160 DA82
Peterborough Rd. E10 123 EC57
Peterborough Rd. SW6 160 DA82
Peterborough Rd., Cars. 200 DE100
Peterborough Rd., Guil. 242 AT132
Peterborough Rd., Har. 117 CE60
Peterborough Vil. SW6 160 DB81
Peterchurch Ho. SE15 162 DV79
Commercial Way
Petergate SW11 160 DC84
Peterhead Ms., Slou. 153 BA78
Peterhill Clo., Ger.Cr. 90 AY50
Peterlee Ct., Hem.H. 40 BM16
Peters Ave., St.Alb. 61 CJ26
Peters Clo., Dag. 126 EX60
Peters Clo., Stan. 95 CK51
Peters Clo., Well. 165 ES82
Peters Hill EC4 275 H10
Peter's La. EC1 274 G6
Peters Path SE26 182 DV91
Peters Pl., Berk. 38 AS17
Peters Wd. Hill, Ware 33 DX07
Petersfield Ave., Rom. 106 FL51
Petersfield Ave., Slou. 132 AU74
Petersfield Ave., Stai. 174 BJ92
Petersfield Clo. N18 100 DQ50
Petersfield Clo., Rom. 106 FN51
Petersfield Cres., Couls. 235 DL115
Petersfield Ri. SW15 179 CV88
Petersfield Rd. W3 158 CQ75
Petersfield Rd., Stai. 174 BJ92
Petersham Ave., W.Byf. 212 BL112
Petersham Clo., Rich. 177 CK89
Petersham Clo., Sutt. 218 DA106
Petersham Clo., W.Byf. 212 BL112
Petersham Dr., Orp. 205 ET96
Petersham Gdns., Orp. 205 ET96
Petersham La. SW7 160 DC76
Petersham Ms. SW7 160 DC76
Petersham Pl. SW7 160 DC76
Petersham Rd., Rich. 178 CL86
Petersham Ter., Croy. 201 DL104
Richmond Grn.
Peterslea, Kings L. 59 BP29
Peterstone Rd. SE2 166 EV76
Peterstow Clo. SW19 179 CY89
Peterswood, Harl. 51 ER19
Parnall Rd.
Peterwood Way, Croy. 201 DM103
Petherton Rd. N5 122 DQ64
Petley Rd. W6 159 CW79
Peto Pl. NW1 273 J4
Peto Pl. NW1 141 DH70
Peto St. N. E16 144 EF73
Victoria Dock Rd.
Petridge Rd., Red. 266 DF139
Petrie Clo. NW2 139 CY65
Pett Clo., Horn. 127 FH61
St. Leonards Way
Pett St. SE18 164 EL77
Petten Clo., Orp. 206 EX102
Petten Gro., Orp. 206 EW102
Petters Rd., Ash. 232 CM116
Petticoat La. E1 275 N7
Petticoat La. E1 142 DS71
Petticoat Sq. E1 275 P8
Petticoat Sq. E1 142 DT72
Pettits Boul., Rom. 105 FE53
Pettits Clo., Rom. 105 FE54
Pettits La., Rom. 105 FE54
Pettits La. N., Rom. 105 FD53
Pettits Pl., Dag. 126 FA64
Pettits Rd., Dag. 126 FA64
Pettiward Clo. SW15 159 CW84
Pettley Gdns., Rom. 127 FD57
Pettman Cres. SE28 165 ER76
Petts Hill, Nthlt. 116 CB64
Petts La., Shep. 194 BN98
Petts Wd. Rd., Orp. 205 EQ99
Pettsgrove Ave., Wem. 117 CJ64
Petty France SW1 277 L6
Petty France SW1 161 DJ76
Pettys Clo. (Cheshunt), Wal.Cr. 67 DX28
Petworth Clo., Couls. 235 DJ119
Petworth Clo., Nthlt. 136 BZ66
Petworth Ct., Wind. 151 AP81
Petworth Gdns. SW20 199 CV97
Hidcote Gdns.
Petworth Gdns., Uxb. 135 BQ67
Petworth Rd. N12 98 DE50
Petworth Rd., Bexh. 186 FA85
Petworth St. SW11 160 DE81
Petworth Way, Horn. 127 FF63
Petyt Pl. SW3 160 DE79
Old Ch. St.
Petyward SW3 276 C9
Petyward SW3 160 DE77
Pevel Ho., Dag. 126 FA61
Pevensey Ave. N11 99 DK50
Pevensey Ave., Enf. 82 DR40
Pevensey Clo., Islw. 156 CC80
Pevensey Rd. E7 124 EF63
Pevensey Rd. SW17 180 DD91
Pevensey Rd., Felt. 176 BY88
Pevensey Rd., Slou. 131 AN71
Peverel E6 145 EN72
Downings
Peveret Clo. N11 99 DH50
Woodland Rd.
Peveril Dr., Tedd. 177 CD92
Pewley Bank, Guil. 258 AY136
Pewley Hill, Guil. 258 AX136
Pewley Pt., Guil. 258 AY136
Pewley Way, Guil. 258 AY136
Pewsey Clo. E4 101 EA50
Peyton Pl. SE10 163 EC80
Peytons Cotts., Red. 251 DM132
Nutfield Marsh Rd.
Pharaoh Clo., Mitch. 200 DF101
Pharaoh's Island, Shep. 194 BM103
Pheasant Clo. E16 144 EG72
Maplin Rd.
Pheasant Clo., Berk. 38 AW20
Pheasant Clo., Pur. 219 DP113
Partridge Knoll
Pheasant Hill, Ch.St.G. 90 AW47
Pheasant Ri., Chesh. 54 AR33
Pheasant Wk., Ger.Cr. 90 AX49
Pheasants Way, Rick. 92 BH45
Phelips Rd., Harl. 51 EN20
Phelp St. SE17 162 DR79
Phelps Way, Hayes 155 BT77
Phene St. SW3 160 DE79
Phil Brown Pl. SW8 161 DH82
Heath Rd.
Philan Way, Rom. 105 FD51
Philanthropic Rd., Red. 266 DG135
Philbeach Gdns. SW5 160 DA78
Philchurch Pl. E1 142 DU72
Ellen St.
Philimore Clo. SE18 165 ES78
Philip Ave., Rom. 127 FD60
Philip Ave., Swan. 207 FD98
Philip Clo., Brwd. 108 FW44
Philip Clo., Rom. 127 FD60
Philip Ave.
Philip Gdns., Croy. 203 DZ103
Philip La. N15 122 DR56
Philip Rd. SE15 162 DU83
Peckham Rye
Philip Rd., Rain. 147 FE69
Philip Rd., Stai. 174 BK93
Philip St. E13 144 EG70
Philip Wk. SE15 162 DU83
Philipot Path SE9 185 EM86
Philippa Gdns. SE9 184 EK85
Philippa Way, Grays 171 GH77
Philips Clo., Cars. 200 DG102
Phillida Rd., Rom. 106 FN54
Phillimore Gdns. NW10 139 CW67
Phillimore Gdns. W8 160 DA75
Phillimore Gdns. Clo. W8 160 DA76
Phillimore Gdns.
Phillimore Pl. W8 160 DA75
Phillimore Pl., Rad. 77 CE36
Phillimore Wk. W8 160 DA76
Phillip Dr., H.Wyc. 110 AC56
Phillipers, Wat. 76 BY35
Phillipp St. N1 142 DS67
Phillips Clo., Dart. 187 FH86
Phillips Hatch, Guil. 259 BC143
Philpot La. EC3 275 M10
Philpot La., Wok. 210 AV113
Philpot Path, Ilf. 125 EQ62
Sunnyside Rd.
Philpot Sq. SW6 160 DB83
Peterborough Rd.
Philpot St. E1 142 DV72
Philpots Clo., West Dr. 134 BK73
Phineas Pett Rd. SE9 164 EL83
Phipp St. EC2 275 M4
Phipp St. EC2 142 DS70
Phipps Bri. Rd. SW19 200 DC96
Phipps Bri. Rd., Mitch. 200 DC96
Phipps Hatch La., Enf. 82 DQ38
Phipp's Ms. SW1 277 H7
Phipps Rd., Slou. 131 AL71
Phoebe Rd., Hem.H. 40 BM17
Phoebeth Rd. SE4 183 EA85
Phoenix Clo. E8 142 DT67
Stean St.
Phoenix Clo., Epsom 216 CN112
Queen Alexandra's Way
Phoenix Clo., Nthwd. 93 BT49
Phoenix Clo., W.Wick. 204 EE103
Phoenix Ct., Guil. 258 AX136
High St.
Phoenix Dr., Kes. 204 EK104
Phoenix Pk., Brent. 157 CK78
Phoenix Pl. WC1 274 C4
Phoenix Pl. WC1 141 DM70
Phoenix Pl., Dart. 188 FK87
Phoenix Rd. NW1 273 M2
Phoenix Rd. NW1 141 DK69
Phoenix Rd. SE20 182 DW93
Phoenix St. WC2 273 N9
Phoenix Way, Houns. 156 BW79
Phoenix Wf. SE10 164 EF75
Phoenix Wf. Rd. SE1 162 DT75
Druid St.
Phygtle, The, Ger.Cr. 90 AY51
Phyllis Ave., N.Mal. 199 CV99
Physic Pl. SW3 160 DF79
Royal Hospital Rd.
Piazza, The WC2 141 DL73
Covent Gdn.
Picardy Manorway, Belv. 167 FB76
Picardy Rd., Belv. 166 FA77
Picardy St., Belv. 166 FA76
Piccadilly W1 277 J3
Piccadilly W1 141 DH74
Piccadilly Arc. SW1 277 K2
Piccadilly Circ. W1 277 M1
Piccadilly Circ. W1 141 DK73
Piccadilly Pl. W1 277 L1
Piccards, The, Guil. 258 AW138
Chestnut Ave.
Piccotts End La., Hem.H. 40 BJ17
Piccotts End Rd., Hem.H. 40 BH16
Pick Hill, Wal.Abb. 68 EF32
Pickard St. EC1 274 G2
Pickering Ave. E6 145 EN68
Pickering Clo. E9 143 DX66
Cassland Rd.
Pickering Gdns., Croy. 202 DT100
Pickering Ms. W2 140 DB72
Bishops Bri. Rd.
Pickering Pl. SW1 277 L3
Pickering St. N1 141 DP67
Essex Rd.
Pickets Clo. (Bushey), Wat. 95 CD46
Pickets St. SW12 181 DH87
Pickett Cft., Stan. 95 CK53
Picketts, Welw.G.C. 29 CX06
Picketts La., Red. 267 DJ144
Picketts Lock La. N9 100 DW47
Pickford Clo., Bexh. 166 EY82
Pickford Dr., Slou. 133 AZ74
Pickford La., Bexh. 166 EY82
Pickford Rd., Bexh. 166 EY83
Pickford Rd., St.Alb. 43 CH20
Pickfords Wf. N1 275 H1
Pickfords Wf. N1 142 DQ68
Pickhurst Grn., Brom. 204 EF101
Pickhurst La., Brom. 204 EF102
Pickhurst La., W.Wick. 204 EE100
Pickhurst Mead, Brom. 204 EF101
Pickhurst Pk., Brom. 204 EE99
Pickhurst Ri., W.Wick. 203 EC101
Pickins Piece, Slou. 153 BA82
Pickle Herring St. SE1 142 DS74
Tooley St.
Pickmoss La., Sev. 241 FH116
Pickwick Clo., Houns. 176 BY85
Dorney Way
Pickwick Ct. SE9 184 EL88
West Pk.
Pickwick Gdns., Grav. 190 GD90
Pickwick Ms. N18 100 DS50
Pickwick Pl., Har. 117 CE59
Pickwick Rd. SE21 182 DR87
Pickwick St. SE1 279 H5
Pickwick Way, Chis. 185 EQ93
Pickworth Clo. SW8 161 DL80
Kenchester Clo.
Picquets Way, Bans. 233 CZ117
Picton Pl. W1 272 G9
Picton Pl., Surb. 198 CN102
Picton St. SE5 162 DR80
Piedmont Rd. SE18 165 ER78
Pield Heath Ave., Uxb. 134 BN70
Pield Heath Rd., Uxb. 134 BM71
Pier Head E1 142 DV74
Wapping High St.
Pier Par. E16 165 EN75
Pier Rd.
Pier Rd. E16 165 EM75
Pier Rd., Erith 167 FE79
Pier Rd., Felt. 175 BV85
Pier Rd., Grav. 191 GF86
Pier Rd., Green. 169 FV84
Pier St. E14 163 EC77
Pier Ter. SW18 160 DC84
Jew's Row
Pier Wk., Grays 170 GA80
Pier Way SE28 165 ER76
Piercing Hill, Epp. 85 ER35
Piermont Grn. SE22 182 DV85
Piermont Pl., Brom. 204 EL96
Piermont Rd. SE22 182 DV85
Pierrepoint Arc. N1 141 DP68
Islington High St.
Pierrepoint Rd. W3 138 CP73
Pierrepoint Row N1 141 DP68
Islington High St.
Pierson Rd., Wind. 151 AK82
Pigeon La., Hmptn. 176 CA91
Pigeonhouse La., Couls. 250 DC125
Piggotts End, Amer. 55 AP40
Piggotts Orchard, Amer. 55 AP40
Piggs Cor., Grays 170 GC76
Piggy La., Rick. 73 BB44
Bullsland La.
Pigott St. E14 143 EA72
Pike Clo., Brom. 184 EH92
Pike Clo., Uxb. 134 BM67
Pike La., Upmin. 129 FT64
Pike Rd. NW7 96 CR49
Ellesmere Ave.
Pike Way, Epp. 70 FA27
Pikes End, Pnr. 115 BV56
Pikes Hill, Epsom 216 CS113
Pikestone Clo., Hayes 136 BY70
Berrydale Rd.
Pilgrim Clo., Mord. 200 DB101
Pilgrim Clo., St.Alb. 60 CC27
Pilgrim Hill SE27 182 DQ91
Pilgrim Hill, Orp. 206 EX96
Pilgrim St. EC4 274 F9
Pilgrimage St. SE1 279 K5
Pilgrimage St. SE1 162 DR75
Pilgrims Clo. N13 99 DM49
Pilgrims Clo., Brwd. 108 FT43
Pilgrims Clo., Dor. 247 CG131
Pilgrims Clo., Guil. 260 BN139
Pilgrims Clo., Nthlt. 116 CC64
Pilgrims Clo., Wat. 60 BX33
Kytes Dr.
Pilgrims Ct. SE3 164 EG81
Pilgrim's La. NW3 120 DD63
Pilgrims La., Cat. 251 DM125
Pilgrims La., Grays 149 FW74
Pilgrims La., Oxt. 254 EH125
Pilgrims La., West. 238 EL123
Pilgrims Ms. E14 143 EC73
Blackwall Way
Pilgrims Pl. NW3 120 DD63
Hampstead High St.
Pilgrims Pl., Reig. 250 DA132
Pilgrims Ri., Barn. 80 DE43
Pilgrims Rd., Swans. 170 FY84
Pilgrims Vw., Green. 189 FW86
Pilgrims Way E6 144 EL67
High St. N.
Pilgrims Way N19 121 DK60
Pilgrims' Way, Bet. 248 CQ133
Chalkpit La.
Pilgrims Way, Dart. 188 FN88
Pilgrims' Way, Dor. 261 BT139
Pilgrims Way (Westhumble), Dor. 247 CH131
Pilgrims Way, Guil. 258 AX138
Pilgrims' Way (Albury), Guil. 259 BF138
Pilgrims Way (Shere), Guil. 260 BN139
Pilgrims' Way, Reig. 249 CZ133
Pilgrims Way (Sundridge), Sev. 240 EV121
Pilgrims Way, S.Croy. 220 DT106
Pilgrim's Way, Wem. 118 CP60
Pilgrims Way, West. 239 EM123
Pilgrims Way W., Sev. 241 FD116
Pilkington Rd. SE15 162 DV82
Pilkington Rd., Orp. 205 EQ103
Pilkingtons, Harl. 52 EX16
Kitts Riding
Pillions La., Hayes 135 BR70
Pilots Pl., Grav. 191 GJ86
Pilsdon Clo. SW19 179 CX88
Inner Pk. Rd.
Piltdown Rd., Wat. 94 BX49
Pilton Est., The, Croy. 201 DP103
Pitlake
Pilton Pl. SE17 162 DQ78
King & Queen St.
Pimento Ct. W5 157 CK76
Olive Rd.
Pimlico Rd. SW1 276 F10
Pimlico Rd. SW1 160 DG78
Pimlico Wk. N1 275 M2
Pimms Clo., Guil. 243 BA130
Pimpernel Way, Rom. 106 FK51
Pinceybrook Rd., Harl. 51 EQ19
Pinchbeck Rd., Orp. 223 ET107
Pinchfield, Rick. 91 BD50
Pinchin St. E1 142 DU73
Pincott La., Lthd. 245 BP129
Pincott Pl. SE4 163 DX83
Billingford Clo.
Pincott Rd. SW19 200 DC95
Pincott Rd., Bexh. 186 FA85
Pindar Rd., Hodd. 49 EC16
Pindar St. EC2 275 M6
Pindar St. EC2 142 DS71
Pindock Ms. W9 140 DB70
Warwick Ave.
Pine Ave. E15 123 ED64
Pine Ave., Grav. 191 GK88

Pine Ave., W.Wick. 203 EB102
Pine Clo. E10 123 EB61
Walnut Rd.
Pine Clo. N14 99 DJ45
Pine Clo. N19 121 DJ61
Hargrave Pk.
Pine Clo. SE20 202 DW95
Pine Clo., Add. 212 BH111
Pine Clo., Berk. 38 AV19
Pine Clo., Ken. 236 DR117
Pine Clo., Stan. 95 CH49
Pine Clo., Swan. 207 FF98
Pine Clo. (Cheshunt), Wal.Cr. 67 DX28
Pine Clo., Wok. 226 AW117
Pine Coombe, Croy. 221 DX105
Pine Ct., Upmin. 128 FN63
Pine Cres., Brwd. 109 GD42
Pine Cres., Cars. 218 DD111
Pine Dean, Lthd. 246 CB125
Pine Gdns., Horl. 268 DF149
Pine Gdns., Ruis. 115 BV60
Pine Gdns., Surb. 198 CN100
Pine Glade, Orp. 223 EM105
Pine Gro. N4 121 DL61
Pine Gro. N20 97 CZ46
Pine Gro. SW19 179 CZ92
Pine Gro., Hat. 64 DB25
Pine Gro., St.Alb. 60 BZ30
Pine Gro. (Bushey), Wat. 76 BZ40
Pine Gro., Wey. 213 BP106
Pine Gro. Ms., Wey. 213 BQ106
Pine Hill, Epsom 232 CR115
Pine Ms. NW10 139 CX68
Clifford Gdns.
Pine Pl., Bans. 217 CX114
Pine Pl., Hayes 135 BT70
Pine Ridge, Cars. 218 DG109
Pine Rd. N11 98 DG47
Pine Rd. NW2 119 CW63
Pine Rd., Wok. 226 AW120
Pine St. EC1 274 D4
Pine St. EC1 141 DN70
Pine Tree Clo., Hem.H. 40 BK19
Christchurch Rd.
Pine Tree Clo., Houns. 155 BV81
Pine Tree Hill, Wok. 227 BD116
Pine Trees Dr., Uxb. 114 BL63
Pine Vw. Clo., Guil. 259 BF140
Pine Vw. Manor, Epp. 70 EU30
Pine Wk., Bans. 234 DF117
Pine Wk., Brom. 204 EJ95
Pine Wk., Cars. 218 DD110
Pine Wk., Cat. 236 DS122
Pine Wk., Cob. 214 BX114
Pine Wk. (East Horsley), Lthd. 245 BT128
Pine Wk., Surb. 198 CN100
Pine Way, Egh. 172 AV93
Ashwood Rd.
Pine Wd., Sun. 195 BU95
Pineapple Ct. SW1 277 K6
Pineapple Rd., Amer. 72 AT39
Pinecrest Gdns., Orp. 223 EP105
Pinecroft, Brwd. 109 GB45
Pinecroft, Hem.H. 40 BM24
Pinecroft, Rom. 128 FJ56
Pinecroft Cres., Barn. 79 CY42
Hillside Gdns.
Pinedene SE15 162 DV81
Meeting Ho. La.
Pinefield Clo. E14 143 EA73
Pinehurst, Sev. 257 FL121
Pinehurst Clo., Abb.L. 59 BS32
Pinehurst Clo., Tad. 234 DA122
Pinehurst Wk., Orp. 205 ES102
Pinel Clo., Vir.W. 192 AY98
Pinelands Clo. SE3 164 EF80
St. John's Pk.
Pinemartin Clo. NW2 119 CW62
Pineneedle La., Sev. 257 FH123
Pines, The N14 81 DJ43
Pines, The, Borwd. 78 CM40
Anthony Rd.
Pines, The, Couls. 235 DH118
Pines, The, Dor. 263 CH137
Pines, The, Hem.H. 39 BF24
Pines, The, Pur. 219 DP113
Pines, The, Sun. 195 BU97
Pines, The, Wok. 211 AZ114
Pines, The, Wdf.Grn. 102 EG48
Pines Ave., Enf. 82 DV36
Pines Clo., Amer. 55 AP36
Pines Clo., Nthwd. 93 BS51
Pines Rd., Brom. 204 EL96
Pinetree Clo., Ger.Cr. 90 AW52
Pinewalk (Great Bookham), Lthd. 246 CB125
Pinewood, Welw.G.C. 29 CY11
Pinewood Ave., Add. 212 BJ109
Pinewood Ave., Pnr. 94 CB51
Pinewood Ave., Rain. 147 FH70
Pinewood Ave., Sev. 257 FK121
Pinewood Ave., Sid. 185 ES88
Pinewood Ave., Uxb. 134 BM72
Pinewood Clo., Borwd. 78 CR39
Pinewood Clo., Croy. 203 DY104
Pinewood Clo., Ger.Cr. 112 AY59
Dukes Wd. Ave.
Pinewood Clo., Harl. 52 EW16
Pinewood Clo., Iver 133 BC66
Pinewood Clo., Nthwd. 93 BV50
Pinewood Clo., Orp. 205 ER102
Pinewood Clo., Pnr. 94 CB51
Pinewood Clo., St.Alb. 43 CJ20
Pinewood Clo., Wat. 75 BU39
Pinewood Clo., Wok. 227 BA115
Pinewood Dr., Orp. 223 ES106
Pinewood Dr., Pot.B. 63 CZ31
Pinewood Dr., Stai. 174 BG92
Cotswold Clo.
Pinewood Gdns., Hem.H. 40 BH20
Pinewood Grn., Iver 133 BC66
Pinewood Gro. W5 137 CJ72
Pinewood Gro., Add. 212 BH110
Pinewood Pk., Add. 212 BH111
Pinewood Ride, Iver 133 BB65
Pinewood Ride, Slou. 133 BA65
Fulmer Common Rd.
Pinewood Rd. SE2 166 EX79
Pinewood Rd., Brom. 204 EG98
Pinewood Rd., Felt. 175 BV90
Pinewood Rd., Iver 133 BA65
Pinewood Rd. (Havering-atte-Bower), Rom. 105 FD49
Pinewood Rd., Vir.W. 192 AU98
Pinewood Way, Brwd. 109 GD43
Pinfold Rd. SW16 181 DL91
Pinfold Rd. (Bushey), Wat. 76 BZ40
Pinglestone Clo., West Dr. 154 BL80
Pink La., Slou. 130 AH68
Pinkcoat Clo., Felt. 175 BV90
Tanglewood Way
Pinkerton Pl. SW16 181 DK91
Riggindale Rd.
Pinkham Way N11 98 DG52
Pinkneys Ct., Maid. 130 AG72
Pinks Hill, Swan. 207 FE99
Pinkwell Ave., Hayes 155 BR77
Pinkwell La., Hayes 155 BQ77
Pinley Gdns., Dag. 146 EV67
Stamford Rd.
Pinn Clo., Uxb. 134 BK72
High Rd.
Pinn Way, Ruis. 115 BS59
Pinnacle Hill, Bexh. 167 FB84
Pinnacle Hill N., Bexh. 167 FB83
Pinnacles, Wal.Abb. 68 EE34
Pinnacles Ind. Est., Harl. 51 EM16
Pinnate Pl., Welw.G.C. 29 CY13
Pinnell Pl. SE9 164 EK84
Pinnell Rd. SE9 164 EK84
Pinner Ct., Pnr. 116 CA56
Pinner Grn., Pnr. 94 BW54
Pinner Gro., Pnr. 116 BY56
Pinner Hill, Pnr. 94 BW53
Pinner Hill Rd., Pnr. 94 BW54
Pinner Pk., Pnr. 94 CA53
Pinner Pk. Ave., Har. 116 CB55
Pinner Pk. Gdns., Har. 94 CC54
Pinner Rd., Har. 116 CB57
Pinner Rd., Nthwd. 93 BT53
Pinner Rd., Pnr. 116 BZ56
Pinner Rd., Wat. 76 BX44
Pinner Vw., Har. 116 CC58
Pinnocks Ave., Grav. 191 GH88
Pinstone Way, Ger.Cr. 113 BB61
Pintail Clo. E6 144 EL71
Swan App.
Pintail Rd., Wdf.Grn. 102 EH52
Pintail Way, Hayes 136 BX71
Pinto Clo., Borwd. 78 CR44
Percheron Rd.
Pinto Way SE3 164 EH84
Pioneer Pl., Croy. 221 EA109
Featherbed La.
Pioneer St. SE15 162 DU81
Pioneer Way W12 139 CV72
Du Cane Rd.
Pioneer Way, Swan. 207 FE97
Pioneer Way, Wat. 75 BT44
Pioneers Ind. Pk., Croy. 201 DL102
Piper Clo. N7 121 DM64
Piper Rd., Kings.T. 198 CN97
Pipers Clo., Cob. 230 BX115
Pipers Clo., Slou. 130 AJ69
Pipers End, Hert. 31 DJ13
Pipers End, Vir.W. 192 AX97
Piper's Gdns., Croy. 203 DY101
Pipers Grn. NW9 118 CQ57
Pipers Grn. La., Edg. 96 CL48
Pipewell Rd., Cars. 200 DE100
Pippbrook, Dor. 263 CH135
Pippbrook Gdns., Dor. 263 CH135
London Rd.
Pippens, Welw.G.C. 29 CY06
Pippin Clo. NW2 119 CV62
Pippin Clo., Croy. 203 DZ102
Pippin Clo. (Shenley), Rad. 61 CK33
Pippins, The, Slou. 133 AZ74
Pickford Dr.
Pippins Clo., West Dr. 154 BK76
Pippins Ct., Ashf. 175 BP93
Piquet Rd. SE20 202 DW96
Pirbright Cres., Croy. 221 EC107
Pirbright Rd. SW18 179 CZ88
Pirie Clo. SE5 162 DR83
Denmark Hill
Pirie St. E16 144 EH74
Pirrip Clo., Grav. 191 GM89
Pirton Clo., St.Alb. 43 CJ15
Pishiobury Dr., Saw. 36 EW07
Pishiobury Ms., Saw. 36 EX08
Pit Fm. Rd., Guil. 243 BA134
Pitcairn Clo., Rom. 126 FA56
Pitcairn Rd., Mitch. 180 DF94
Pitcairn's Path, Har. 116 CC62
Eastcote Rd.
Pitch Pond Clo., Beac. 88 AH50
Pitchfont La., Oxt. 238 EF124
Pitchford St. E15 143 ED66
Pitfield Cres. SE28 146 EU74
Pitfield Est. N1 275 L2
Pitfield Est. N1 142 DR69
Pitfield St. N1 275 M2
Pitfield St. N1 142 DS69
Pitfield Way NW10 138 CQ65
Pitfield Way, Enf. 82 DW39
Pitfold Clo. SE12 184 EG86
Pitfold Rd. SE12 184 EG86
Pitlake, Croy. 201 DP103
Pitman St. SE5 162 DQ80
Pitsea Pl. E1 143 DX72
Pitsea St.
Pitsea St. E1 143 DX72
Pitsfield, Welw.G.C. 29 CX06
Pitshanger La. W5 137 CH70
Pitshanger Pk. W13 137 CJ69
Pitson Clo., Add. 212 BK105
Pitstone Clo., St.Alb. 43 CJ15
Highview Gdns.
Pitt Cres. SW19 180 DB91
Pitt Pl., Epsom 216 CS114
Pitt Rd., Croy. 202 DQ99
Pitt Rd., Epsom 216 CS114
Pitt Rd., Orp. 223 EQ105
Pitt Rd., Th.Hth. 202 DQ99
Pitt St. W8 160 DA75
Pittman Clo., Brwd. 109 GC50
Pittman Gdns., Ilf. 125 EQ64
Pittmans Fld., Harl. 35 ET14
Pitt's Head Ms. W1 276 G3
Pitt's Head Ms. W1 140 DG74
Pitts Rd., Slou. 131 AQ74
Pittsmead Ave., Brom. 204 EG101
Pittville Gdns. SE25 202 DU97
Pittwood, Brwd. 109 GA46
Pitwood Grn., Tad. 233 CW120
Pix Fm. La., Hem.H. 39 BB21
Pixfield Ct., Brom. 204 EF96
Beckenham La.
Pixham La., Dor. 247 CJ133
Pixholme Gro., Dor. 247 CJ134
Pixies Hill Cres., Hem.H. 39 BF22
Pixies Hill Rd., Hem.H. 39 BF21
Pixley St. E14 143 DZ72
Pixton Way, Croy. 221 DY109
Place Fm. Ave., Orp. 205 ER102
Place Fm. Rd., Red. 252 DR130
Placehouse La., Couls. 235 DM119
Placket Way, Slou. 131 AK74
Plain, The, Epp. 70 EV29
Plaines Clo., Slou. 131 AN74
Cippenham La.
Plaistow Gro. E15 144 EF67
Plaistow Gro., Brom. 184 EH94
Plaistow La., Brom. 184 EH94
Plaistow Pk. Rd. E13 144 EH68
Plaistow Rd. E13 144 EF67
Plaistow Rd. E15 144 EF67
Plaitford Clo., Rick. 92 BL47
Plane Ave., Grav. 190 GD87
Plane St. SE26 182 DV90
Plane Tree Cres., Felt. 175 BV90
Plane Tree Wk. SE19 182 DS93
Central Hill
Planes, The, Cher. 194 BJ101
Plantaganet Pl., Wal.Abb. 67 EB33
Plantagenet Clo., Wor.Pk. 216 CR105
Plantagenet Gdns., Rom. 126 EX59
Broomfield Rd.
Plantagenet Pl., Rom. 126 EX59
Broomfield Rd.
Plantagenet Rd., Barn. 80 DC42
Plantain Gdns. E11 123 ED62
Hollydown Way
Plantain Pl. SE1 279 K4
Plantation, The SE3 164 EG82
Plantation Clo., Green. 189 FT86
Plantation Dr., Orp. 206 EX102
Plantation La., Warl. 237 DX119
Plantation Rd., Amer. 55 AS37
Plantation Rd., Erith 167 FG81
Plantation Rd., Swan. 187 FG94
Plantation Wk., Hem.H. 40 BG17
Plantation Way, Amer. 55 AS37
Plantation Wf. SW11 160 DC83
Plasel Ct. E13 144 EG67
Plashet Rd.
Plashet Gdns., Brwd. 109 GA49
Plashet Gro. E6 144 EJ67
Plashet Rd. E13 144 EG67
Plashets, B.Stort. 37 FC06
Plassy Rd. SE6 183 EB87
Platford Grn., Horn. 128 FL56
Platina St. EC2 275 L4
Plato Rd. SW2 161 DL84
Platt, The SW15 159 CX83
Platt Meadow, Guil. 243 BD131
Eustace Rd.
Platt St. NW1 141 DK68
Platts Ave., Wat. 75 BV41
Platt's Eyot, Hmptn. 196 CA96
Platt's La. NW3 120 DA63
Platts Rd., Enf. 82 DW39
Plawsfield Rd., Beck. 203 DX95
Plaxtol Clo., Brom. 204 EJ95
Plaxtol Rd., Erith 166 FA80
Playfair St. W6 159 CW78
Winslow Rd.
Playfield Ave., Rom. 105 FC53
Playfield Cres. SE22 182 DT85
Playfield Rd., Edg. 96 CQ54
Playford Rd. N4 121 DM61
Playgreen Way SE6 183 EA91
Playground Clo., Beck. 203 DX96
Churchfields Rd.
Playhouse Yd. EC4 274 F9
Plaza Par. NW6 140 DB68
Kilburn High Rd.
Plaza W., Houns. 156 CB81
Pleasance, The SW15 159 CV84
Pleasance Rd. SW15 179 CV85
Pleasance Rd., Orp. 206 EV96
Pleasant Gro., Croy. 203 DZ104
Pleasant Pl. N1 141 DP66
Pleasant Pl., Rick. 91 BE52
Pleasant Pl., Walt. 214 BW107
Pleasant Ri., Hat. 45 CV15
Pleasant Row NW1 141 DH67
Pleasant Vw., Erith 167 FE78
Pleasant Vw. Pl., Orp. 223 EP106
High St.
Pleasant Way, Wem. 137 CJ68
Pleasure Pit Rd., Ash. 232 CP118
Plender St. NW1 141 DJ67
Plender St. Est. NW1 141 DJ67
Plender St.
Pleshey Rd. N7 121 DK63
Plesman Way, Wall. 219 DL109
Plevna Cres. N15 122 DS58
Plevna Rd. N9 100 DU48
Plevna Rd., Hmptn. 196 CB95
Plevna St. E14 163 EC76
Pleydell Ave. SE19 182 DT94
Pleydell Ave. W6 159 CT77
Pleydell Ct. EC4 274 E9
Pleydell Est. EC1 142 DQ69
Radnor St.
Pleydell St. EC4 274 E9
Plimsoll Clo. E14 143 EB72
Grundy St.
Plimsoll Rd. N4 121 DN62
Plough Ct. EC3 275 L10
Plough Fm. Clo., Ruis. 115 BR58
Plough Hill (Cuffley), Pot.B. 65 DL28
Plough Ind. Est., Lthd. 231 CG120
Kingston Rd.
Plough La. SE22 182 DT86
Plough La. SW17 180 DB92
Plough La. SW19 180 DB92
Plough La., Berk. 39 BB16
Plough La., Cob. 229 BU117
Plough La., Pur. 219 DL109
Plough La., Rick. 57 BF33
Plough La., Slou. 132 AV67
Plough La., Tedd. 177 CG92
High St.
Plough La. (Harefield), Uxb. 92 BJ51
Plough La., Wall. 219 DL105
Plough La. Clo., Wall. 219 DL106
Plough Ms. SW11 160 DD84
Plough Ter.
Plough Pl. EC4 274 E8
Plough Ri., Upmin. 129 FS59
Plough Rd. SW11 160 DD83
Plough Rd., Epsom 216 CR109
Plough Rd., Horl. 269 DP148
Plough St. E1 142 DT72
Leman St.
Plough Ter. SW11 160 DD84
Plough Way SE16 163 DX77
Plough Yd. EC2 275 N5
Plough Yd. EC2 142 DS70
Ploughlees La., Slou. 132 AS73
Ploughmans Clo. NW1 141 DK67
Crofters Way
Ploughmans End, Islw. 177 CD85
Ploughmans End, Welw.G.C. 30 DC10
Plover Clo., Berk. 38 AW20
Plover Clo., Stai. 173 BF90
Waters Dr.
Plover Gdns., Upmin. 129 FT60
Plover Way SE16 163 DY76
Plover Way, Hayes 136 BX72
Plowden Bldgs. EC4 141 DN72
Middle Temple La.
Plowman Clo. N18 100 DR50
Plowman Way, Dag. 126 EW60
Ployters Rd., Harl. 51 EQ18
Plum Garth, Brent. 157 CK77
Plum La. SE18 165 EP80
Plumbers Row E1 142 DU71
Plumbridge St. SE10 163 EC81
Blackheath Hill
Plummer La., Mitch. 200 DF96
Plummer Rd. SW4 181 DK87
Plummers Cft., Sev. 256 FE121
Plumpton Ave., Horn. 128 FL63
Plumpton Clo., Nthlt. 136 CA65
Plumpton Rd., Hodd. 49 EC15
Plumpton Way, Cars. 200 DE104
Plumstead Common Rd. SE18 165 EP79
Plumstead High St. SE18 165 ES77
Plumstead Rd. SE18 165 EP77
Plumtree Clo., Dag. 147 FB65
Plumtree Clo., Wall. 219 DK108
Plumtree Ct. EC4 274 E8
Plumtree Mead, Loug. 85 EN41
Pluto Ri., Hem.H. 40 BL18
Plymouth Dr., Sev. 257 FJ124
Plymouth Ho., Rain. 147 FF69
Plymouth Pk., Sev. 257 FJ124
Plymouth Rd. E16 144 EG71
Plymouth Rd., Brom. 204 EH95
Plymouth Rd., Slou. 131 AL71
Plymouth Wf. E14 163 ED77
Plympton Ave. NW6 139 CZ66
Plympton Clo., Belv. 166 EY76
Halifield Dr.
Plympton Pl. NW8 272 B5
Plympton Rd. NW6 139 CZ66
Plympton St. NW8 272 B5
Plympton St. NW8 140 DE70
Plymstock Rd., Well. 166 EW80
Pocketsdell La., Hem.H. 56 AX28
Pocklington Clo. NW9 96 CS54
Pocock Ave., West Dr. 154 BM76
Pocock St. SE1 278 F4
Pocock St. SE1 161 DP75
Pococks La. (Eton), Wind. 152 AS78
Podmore Rd. SW18 160 DC84
Poets Chase, Hem.H. 40 BH18
Laureate Way
Poets Gate, Wal.Cr. 66 DS28
Poets Rd. N5 122 DR64
Poets Way, Har. 117 CE56
Blawith Rd.
Point, The, Ruis. 115 BU63
Bedford Rd.
Point Clo. SE10 163 EC81
Point Hill
Point Hill SE10 163 EC80
Point of Thomas Path E1 142 DW73
Glamis Rd.
Point Pl., Wem. 138 CP66
Point Pleasant SW18 160 DA84
Pointalls Clo. N3 98 DC54
Pointer Clo. SE28 146 EX72
Pointers, The, Ash. 232 CL120
Pointers Clo. E14 163 EB78
Pointers Hill, Dor. 262 CC138
Pointers Rd., Cob. 229 BQ116
Poland St. W1 273 L9
Poland St. W1 141 DJ72
Polayn Garth, Welw.G.C. 29 CW08
Pole Cat All., Brom. 204 EF103
Pole Hill Rd. E4 101 EC45
Pole Hill Rd., Hayes 135 BQ69
Pole Hill Rd., Uxb. 135 BQ69
Pole La., Ong. 53 FE17
Polebrook Rd. SE3 164 EJ83
Polecroft La. SE6 183 DZ89
Polehamptons, The, Hmptn. 176 CC94
High St.
Polehanger La., Hem.H. 39 BE18
Poles Hill, Chesh. 54 AN29
Poles Hill, Rick. 57 BE33
Polesden Gdns. SW20 199 CV96
Polesden Lacey, Dor. 246 CB130
Polesden La., Wok. 227 BF122
Polesden Rd., Lthd. 246 CB129
Polesden Vw., Lthd. 246 CB127
Polesteeple Hill, West. 238 EK117
Polesworth Ho. W2 140 DA71
Polesworth Rd., Dag. 146 EX66
Polhill, Sev. 225 FC114
Police Sta. La. (Bushey), Wat. 94 CB45
Sparrows Herne
Police Sta. Rd., Walt. 214 BW107
Pollard Ave., Uxb. 113 BF58
Pollard Clo. E16 144 EG73
Pollard Clo. N7 121 DM63
Pollard Clo., Chig. 104 EU50
Pollard Clo., Wind. 172 AV85
Pollard Hatch, Harl. 51 EP18
Pollard Rd. N20 98 DE47
Pollard Rd., Mord. 200 DD99
Pollard Rd., Wok. 227 BB116
Pollard Row E2 142 DU69
Pollard St. E2 142 DU69
Pollard Wk., Sid. 186 EW93
Evry Rd.
Pollards, Rick. 91 BD50
Pollards Clo., Loug. 84 EJ43
Pollards Clo. (Cheshunt), Wal.Cr. 66 DQ29
Pollards Cres. SW16 201 DL97
Pollards Hill E. SW16 201 DM97
Pollards Hill N. SW16 201 DL97
Pollards Hill S. SW16 201 DL97
Pollards Hill W. SW16 201 DL97
Pollards Oak Cres., Oxt. 254 EG132
Pollards Oak Rd., Oxt. 254 EG132
Pollards Wd. Hill, Oxt. 254 EH130
Pollards Wd. Rd. SW16 201 DL96
Pollards Wd. Rd., Oxt. 254 EH131
Pollen St. W1 273 J9
Pollicott Clo., St.Alb. 43 CJ15
Pollyhaugh (Eynsford), Dart. 208 FK104
Polperro Clo., Orp. 205 ET100
Cotswold Ri.
Polsted Rd. SE6 183 DZ87
Polthorne Est. SE18 165 ER77
Polthorne Gro. SE18 165 EQ77
Poltimore Rd., Guil. 258 AU136
Polworth Rd. SW16 181 DL92
Polygon, The SW4 161 DJ84
Old Town
Polygon Rd. NW1 273 M1
Polygon Rd. NW1 141 DK68
Polytechnic St. SE18 165 EN77
Pomell Way E1 142 DT72
Commercial St.
Pomeroy Clo., Amer. 55 AR39
Pomeroy Cres., Wat. 75 BV36
Pomeroy St. SE14 162 DW81
Pomfret Rd. SE5 161 DP83
Flaxman Rd.
Pomoja La. N19 121 DK61
Pompadour Clo., Brwd. 108 FW50
Queen St.
Pond Clo. N12 98 DE51
Summerfields Ave.
Pond Clo. SE3 164 EF82
Pond Clo., Ash. 232 CL117
Pond Clo. (Harefield), Uxb. 92 BJ54
Pond Clo., Walt. 213 BT107
Pond Cottage La., W.Wick. 203 EA102
Pond Cotts. SE21 182 DS88
Pond Cft., Hat. 45 CT18
Pond Cft., Welw.G.C. 29 CY10
Pond Fld., Welw.G.C. 30 DA06
Pond Fld. End, Loug. 102 EJ45
Pond Grn., Ruis. 115 BS61
Pond Hill Gdns., Sutt. 217 CY107
Pond La., Ger.Cr. 90 AV53
Pond La., Guil. 261 BQ144
Pond Mead SE21 182 DR86
Pond Meadow, Guil. 242 AS134
Pond Pk. Rd., Chesh. 54 AP29
Pond Path, Chis. 185 EP93
Heathfield La.
Pond Piece, Lthd. 214 CB113
Pond Pl. SW3 276 B9
Pond Pl. SW3 160 DE77
Pond Rd. E15 144 EE68
Pond Rd. SE3 164 EF82
Pond Rd., Egh. 173 BC93
Pond Rd., Hem.H. 58 BN25
Pond Rd., Wok. 226 AU120
Pond Sq. N6 120 DG60
South Gro.
Pond St. NW3 120 DE64
Pond Wk., Upmin. 129 FS61
Pond Way, Tedd. 177 CJ93
Holmesdale Rd.
Ponder St. N7 141 DM66
Ponders End Ind. Est., Enf. 83 DZ42
Pondfield Cres., St.Alb. 43 CH16
Pondfield La., Brwd. 109 GA49
Pondfield Rd., Brom. 204 EE102
Pondfield Rd., Dag. 127 FB64
Pondfield Rd., Gdmg. 258 AT144
Pondfield Rd., Ken. 235 DP117
Pondfield Rd., Orp. 205 EP104
Ponds, The, Wey. 213 BS107
Ellesmere Rd.
Ponds La., Guil. 260 BL142
Pondside Clo., Hayes 155 BR80
Providence La.
Pondwicks, Amer. 55 AP39
Pondwicks Clo., St.Alb. 42 CC21
Pondwood Ri., Orp. 205 ES101
Ponler St. E1 142 DV72
Ponsard Rd. NW10 139 CV69
Ponsbourne Ho., Hert. 47 DL23
Ponsford St. E9 142 DW65
Ponsonby Pl. SW1 277 N10
Ponsonby Pl. SW1 161 DK78
Ponsonby Rd. SW15 179 CV87
Ponsonby Ter. SW1 277 N10
Ponsonby Ter. SW1 161 DK78
Pont St. SW1 276 D7
Pont St. SW1 160 DF76
Pont St. Ms. SW1 276 D7
Pont St. Ms. SW1 160 DF76
Pontefract Rd., Brom. 184 EF92
Pontoise Clo., Sev. 256 FF122
Ponton Rd. SW8 161 DK79
Pontypool Pl. SE1 278 F4
Pontypool Wk., Rom. 106 FJ51
Saddleworth Rd.
Pony Chase, Cob. 214 BZ113
Pool Clo., Beck. 183 EA92
Pool Clo., W.Mol. 196 BZ99
Pool Ct. SE6 183 EA89
Pool End Clo., Shep. 194 BN99
Pool Gro., Croy. 221 DY112
Pool La., Slou. 132 AS73
Pool Rd., Har. 117 CD59
Pool Rd., W.Mol. 196 BZ99
Poole Clo., Ruis. 115 BS61
Chichester Ave.
Poole Ct. Rd., Houns. 156 BY82
Vicarage Fm. Rd.
Poole Ho., Grays 171 GJ75
Poole Rd. E9 143 DX65
Poole Rd., Epsom 216 CR107
Poole Rd., Horn. 128 FM59
Poole Rd., Wok. 226 AY117
Poole St. N1 142 DR67
Poole Way, Hayes 135 BR69
Pooles Bldgs. EC1 274 D5
Pooles La. SW10 160 DC80
Lots Rd.
Pooles La., Dag. 146 EY68
Pooles Pk. N4 121 DN61
Seven Sisters Rd.
Pooley Ave., Egh. 173 BB92
Pooley Grn. Clo., Egh. 173 BC92
Pooley Grn. Rd., Egh. 173 BB92
Pooleys La., Hat. 45 CV23
Poolmans Rd., Wind. 151 AK83
Poolmans St. SE16 163 DX75
Poolsford Rd. NW9 118 CS56
Poonah St. E1 142 DW72
Hardinge St.
Pootings Rd., Eden. 255 ER134
Pope Clo. SW19 180 DD93
Shelley Way

Pope Clo., Felt. 175 BT88
Pope Rd., Brom. 204 EK99
Pope St. SE1 279 N5
Pope St. SE1 162 DS75
Popes Ave., Twick. 177 CE89
Popes Clo., Amer. 72 AT37
Popes Clo., Slou. 153 BB80
Popes Dr. N3 98 DA53
Popes Gro., Croy. 203 DZ104
Popes Gro., Twick. 177 CE89
Pope's Head All. EC3 142 DR72
Cornhill
Popes La. W5 157 CK76
Popes La., Oxt. 254 EE134
Popes La., Wat. 75 BV37
Popes Rd. SW9 161 DN83
Popes Rd., Abb.L. 59 BS31
Popham Clo., Felt. 176 BZ90
Popham Gdns., Rich. 158 CN83
Lower Richmond Rd.
Popham Rd. N1 142 DQ67
Popham St. N1 141 DP67
Poplar Ave., Amer. 72 AT39
Poplar Ave., Grav. 191 GJ91
Poplar Ave., Lthd. 231 CH122
Poplar Ave., Mitch. 200 DF95
Poplar Ave., Orp. 205 EP103
Poplar Ave., Sthl. 156 CB76
Poplar Ave., West Dr. 134 BM73
Poplar Bath St. E14 143 EB73
Lawless St.
Poplar Business Pk. E14 143 EC73
Poplar Clo. E9 123 DZ64
Lee Conservancy Rd.
Poplar Clo., Chesh. 54 AQ28
Poplar Clo., Pnr. 94 BX53
Poplar Clo., Slou. 153 BE81
Poplar Clo., S.Ock. 149 FX70
Poplar Ct. SW19 180 DA92
Poplar Cres., Epsom 216 CQ107
Poplar Dr., Bans. 217 CX114
Poplar Dr., Brwd. 109 GC44
Poplar Fm. Clo., Epsom 216 CQ107
Poplar Gdns., N.Mal. 198 CR96
Poplar Gro. N11 98 DG51
Poplar Gro. W6 159 CW75
Poplar Gro., N.Mal. 198 CR97
Poplar Gro., Wem. 118 CQ62
Poplar Gro., Wok. 226 AY119
Poplar High St. E14 143 EA73
Poplar Mt., Belv. 167 FB77
Poplar Pl. SE28 146 EW73
Poplar Pl. W2 140 DB73
Poplar Pl., Hayes 135 BU73
Central Ave.
Poplar Rd. SE24 162 DQ84
Poplar Rd. SW19 200 DA96
Poplar Rd., Ashf. 175 BQ93
Poplar Rd., Guil. 258 AY141
Poplar Rd., Lthd. 231 CH122
Poplar Rd., Sutt. 199 CZ102
Poplar Rd. (Denham), Uxb. 114 BJ64
Poplar Rd. S. SW19 200 DA97
Poplar Row, Epp. 85 ES37
Poplar Shaw, Wal.Abb. 68 EF33
Poplar St., Rom. 127 FC56
Poplar Vw., Wem. 117 CK61
Magnet Rd.
Poplar Wk. SE24 162 DQ84
Poplar Wk., Cat. 236 DS123
Poplar Wk., Croy. 202 DQ103
Poplar Way, Felt. 175 BU90
Poplar Way, Ilf. 125 EQ56
Poplars, Welw.G.C. 30 DB08
Poplars, The N14 81 DH43
Poplars, The, Hem.H. 40 BH21
Poplars, The, Rom. 86 EV41
Hoe La.
Poplars, The, St.Alb. 43 CH24
Poplars, The, Wal.Cr. 66 DS26
Poplars Ave. NW10 139 CW65
Poplars Ave., Hat. 44 CR18
Poplars Clo., Hat. 44 CQ18
Poplars Clo., Ruis. 115 BS60
Poplars Clo., Wat. 59 BV32
Poplars Rd. E17 123 EB58
Poppins Ct. EC4 274 F9
Poppleton Rd. E11 124 EE58
Poppy Clo., Brwd. 108 FV43
Poppy Clo., Hem.H. 39 BE19
Poppy Clo., Wall. 200 DG102
Poppy La., Croy. 202 DW101
Poppy Wk., Wal.Cr. 66 DR28
Poppyfields, Welw.G.C. 30 DC09
Porch Way N20 98 DF48
Porchester Clo. SE5 162 DQ84
Porchester Clo., Horn. 128 FL58
Porchester Gdns. W2 140 DB73
Porchester Gdns. Ms. W2 140 DB72
Porchester Gdns.
Porchester Mead, Beck. 183 EB93
Porchester Ms. W2 140 DB72
Porchester Pl. W2 272 C9
Porchester Pl. W2 140 DE72
Porchester Rd. W2 140 DB72
Porchester Rd., Kings.T. 198 CP96
Porchester Sq. W2 140 DB72
Porchester Ter. W2 140 DC73
Porchester Ter. N. W2 140 DB72
Porchfield Clo., Grav. 191 GJ89
Whitehill Rd.
Porchfield Clo., Sutt. 218 DB110
Porcupine Clo. SE9 184 EL89
Porden Rd. SW2 161 DM84
Porlock Ave., Har. 116 CC60
Porlock Rd. W10 139 CX70
Ladbroke Gro.
Porlock Rd., Enf. 100 DT45
Porlock St. SE1 279 K4
Porlock St. SE1 162 DR75
Porridge Pot All., Guil. 258 AW136
Bury Flds.
Porrington Clo., Chis. 205 EM95
Port Ave., Green. 189 FV86
Port Cres. E13 144 EH70
Jenkins Rd.
Port Hill, Hert. 32 DQ09
Port Hill, Orp. 224 EV112
Port Vale, Hert. 31 DP08
Portal Clo. SE27 181 DN90
Portal Clo., Ruis. 115 BU63
Portal Clo., Uxb. 134 BL66
Portbury Clo. SE15 162 DU81
Clayton Rd.
Portcullis Lo. Rd., Enf. 82 DR41
Portelet Rd. E1 143 DX69
Porten Rd. W14 159 CY76
Porter Clo., Grays 169 FW79
Porter Rd. E6 145 EM72
Porter Sq. N19 121 DL60
Hornsey Rd.
Porter St. SE1 279 J2
Porter St. W1 272 E6
Porters Ave., Dag. 146 EV65
Porters Clo., Brwd. 108 FU46
Greenshaw
Porters Pk. Dr., Rad. 61 CK33
Porters Wk. E1 142 DV73
Pennington St.
Porters Way, West Dr. 154 BM76
Porters Wd., St.Alb. 43 CE16
Portersfield Rd., Enf. 82 DS42
Porteus Rd. W2 140 DC71
Portgate Clo. W9 139 CZ70
Porthcawe Rd. SE26 183 DY91
Porthkerry Ave., Well. 166 EU84
Portia Way E3 143 DZ70
Portinscale Rd. SW15 179 CY85
Portland Ave. N16 122 DT59
Portland Ave., Grav. 191 GH89
Portland Ave., N.Mal. 199 CT101
Portland Ave., Sid. 186 EU86
Portland Clo., Rom. 126 EY57
Portland Clo., Slou. 131 AK70
Portland Cres. SE9 184 EL89
Portland Cres., Felt. 175 BR91
Portland Cres., Grnf. 136 CB70
Portland Cres., Stan. 95 CK54
Portland Dr., Enf. 82 DS38
Portland Dr., Red. 251 DK129
Portland Dr. (Cheshunt), 66 DU31
Wal.Cr.
Portland Gdns. N4 121 DP58
Portland Gdns., Rom. 126 EX57
Portland Gro. SW8 161 DM81
Portland Hts., Nthwd. 93 BT49
Portland Ms. W1 273 L9
Portland Pl. W1 273 J7
Portland Pl. W1 141 DH71
Portland Pl., Epsom 216 CS112
Portland Pl., Hert. 32 DW11
Portland Ri. N4 121 DP60
Portland Ri. Est. N4 122 DQ60
Portland Rd. N15 122 DT56
Portland Rd. SE9 184 EL89
Portland Rd. SE25 202 DU98
Portland Rd. W11 139 CY74
Portland Rd., Ashf. 174 BL90
Portland Rd., Brom. 184 EJ91
Portland Rd., Dor. 263 CG135
Portland Rd., Grav. 191 GH88
Portland Rd., Hayes 135 BS69
Portland Rd., Kings.T. 198 CL97
Portland Rd., Mitch. 200 DE96
Portland Rd., Sthl. 156 BZ76
Portland Sq. E1 142 DV74
Watts St.
Portland St. SE17 279 K10
Portland St. SE17 162 DR78
Portland St., St.Alb. 42 CC20
Portland Ter., Rich. 157 CK84
Portland Wk. SE17 162 DR79
Portland St.
Portley La., Cat. 236 DS121
Portley Wd. Rd., Whyt. 236 DT121
Portman Ave. SW14 158 CR83
Portman Clo. W1 272 E8
Portman Clo. W1 140 DF72
Portman Clo., Bex. 187 FE88
Portman Clo., Bexh. 166 EX83
Queen Anne's Gate
Portman Clo., St.Alb. 43 CJ15
Portman Dr., Wdf.Grn. 102 EK54
Portman Gdns. NW9 96 CR54
Portman Gdns., Uxb. 134 BN66
Portman Gate NW1 272 C5
Portman Ho., St.Alb. 43 CD17
Portman Ms. S. W1 272 F9
Portman Ms. S. W1 140 DG72
Portman Pl. E2 142 DW69
Portman Rd., Kings.T. 198 CM96
Portman Sq. W1 272 F8
Portman Sq. W1 140 DF72
Portman St. W1 272 F9
Portman St. W1 140 DG72
Portmeadow Wk. SE2 166 EX75
Portmeers Clo. E17 123 DZ58
Lennox Rd.
Portmore Gdns., Rom. 104 FA50
Portmore Pk. Rd., Wey. 212 BN105
Portmore Quays, Wey. 212 BM105
Bridge Rd.
Portmore Way, Wey. 194 BN104
Portnall Dr., Vir.W. 192 AT99
Portnall Ri., Vir.W. 192 AT99
Portnall Rd. W9 139 CZ69
Portnall Rd., Vir.W. 192 AT99
Portnalls Clo., Couls. 235 DH116
Portnalls Ri., Couls. 235 DH116
Portnalls Rd., Couls. 235 DH118
Portnoi Clo., Rom. 105 FD54
Portobello Clo., Chesh. 54 AN29
Portobello Ct. W11 139 CZ73
Westbourne Gro.
Portobello Ms. W11 140 DA73
Portobello Rd.
Portobello Rd. W10 139 CZ72
Portobello Rd. W11 139 CZ72
Porton Ct., Surb. 197 CJ100
Portpool La. EC1 274 D6
Portpool La. EC1 141 DN71
Portree Clo. N22 99 DM52
Nightingale Rd.
Portree St. E14 143 ED72
Portsdown, Edg. 96 CN50
Rectory La.
Portsdown Ave. NW11 119 CZ58
Portsdown Ms. NW11 119 CZ58
Portsea Ms. W2 272 C9
Portsea Pl. W2 272 C9
Portsea Rd., Til. 171 GJ81
Portslade Rd. SW8 161 DJ82
Portsmouth Ave., T.Ditt. 197 CG101
Portsmouth Ct., Slou. 132 AS73
Portsmouth Ms. E16 144 EH74
Wesley Ave.
Portsmouth Rd. SW15 179 CV87
Portsmouth Rd., Cob. 229 BQ115
Portsmouth Rd., Esher 214 BZ108
Portsmouth Rd., Guil. 258 AV141
Portsmouth Rd., Kings.T. 197 CK98
Portsmouth Rd., Surb. 197 CJ100
Portsmouth Rd., T.Ditt. 197 CE103
Portsmouth Rd., Wok. 228 BM119
Portsmouth St. WC2 274 B9
Portsoken St. E1 275 P10
Portsoken St. E1 142 DT73
Portugal Gdns., Twick. 176 CC89
Fulwell Pk. Ave.
Portugal Rd., Wok. 227 AZ116
Portugal St. WC2 274 B9
Portugal St. WC2 141 DM72
Portway E15 144 EF67
Portway, Epsom 217 CU110
Portway Cres., Epsom 217 CU109
Portway Gdns. SE18 164 EK80
Shooter's Hill Rd.
Post Ho. La., Lthd. 246 CA125
Post La., Twick. 177 CD88
Post Meadow, Iver 133 BD69
Post Office App. E7 124 EH64
Post Office Ct. EC3 275 L9
Post Office La., Beac. 89 AK52
Post Office La., Slou. 132 AX72
Post Office Rd., Harl. 35 ER14
Post Office Row, Oxt. 254 EL131
Post Office Way SW8 161 DK80
Post Rd., Sthl. 156 CB76
Post Wd. Rd., Ware 33 DY08
Postern Grn., Enf. 81 DN40
Postfield, Welw.G.C. 30 DA06
Postmill Clo., Croy. 203 DX104
Postway Ms., Ilf. 125 EP62
Clements Rd.
Postwood Grn., Hert. 32 DW12
Potier St. SE1 279 L7
Potier St. SE1 162 DR76
Potkiln La., Beac. 111 AQ55
Pott St. E2 142 DV69
Potten End Hill, Berk. 39 BD16
Potten End Hill, Hem.H. 39 BE15
Potter Clo., Mitch. 201 DH96
Potter St., Harl. 52 EW16
Potter St., Nthwd. 93 BU53
Potter St., Pnr. 93 BV53
Potter St. Hill, Pnr. 93 BV51
Potterne Clo. SW19 179 CX87
Potters Clo., Croy. 203 DY102
Potters Clo., Loug. 84 EL40
Potters Cross, Iver 133 BE69
Potters Fld., Harl. 52 EX17
Potters Fld., St.Alb. 43 CE16
Potters Flds. SE1 142 DS74
Tooley St.
Potters Gro., N.Mal. 198 CQ98
Potters Hts. Clo., Pnr. 93 BV52
Potters La. SW16 181 DK93
Potters La., Barn. 80 DA42
Potters La., Borwd. 78 CQ39
Potters La., Wok. 227 BB123
Potters Ms., Borwd. 77 CK44
Elstree Hill N.
Potters Rd. SW6 160 DC82
Potters Rd., Barn. 80 DB42
Potters Way, Reig. 266 DC138
Pottery La. W11 139 CY73
Portland Rd.
Pottery Rd., Bex. 187 FC89
Pottery Rd., Brent. 158 CL79
Pottery St. SE16 162 DV75
Pouchen End La., 39 BD17
Hem.H.
Poulcott, Stai. 172 AY86
Poulett Gdns., Twick. 177 CF88
Poulett Rd. E6 145 EM68
Poulner Way SE15 162 DT80
Daniel Gdns.
Poulters Wd., Kes. 222 EK106
Poultney Clo., Rad. 62 CM32
Poulton Ave., Sutt. 200 DD104
Poulton Clo. E8 122 DV64
Spurstowe Ter.
Poultry EC2 275 K9
Poultry EC2 142 DR72
Pound, The, Slou. 130 AJ70
Hogfair La.
Pound Clo., Orp. 205 ER103
Pound Clo., Surb. 197 CJ102
Pound Clo., Wal.Abb. 50 EE23
Pound Ct., Ash. 232 CM118
Pound Ct. Dr., Orp. 205 ER103
Pound Cres., Lthd. 231 CD121
Pound Fld., Guil. 242 AX133
Pound La. NW10 139 CU65
Pound La., Epsom 216 CR112
Pound La., Rad. 62 CM33
Pound La., Sev. 240 EX115
Pound La. 257 FJ124
(Knockholt Pound), Sev.
Pound Pk. Rd. SE7 164 EK77
Pound Pl. SE9 185 EN86
Pound Pl., Guil. 259 AZ140
Pound Pl. Clo., Guil. 259 AZ140
Pound Rd., Bans. 233 CZ117
Pound Rd., Cher. 194 BH101
Pound St., Cars. 218 DF106
Pound Way, Chis. 185 EQ94
Royal Par.
Poundfield, Wat. 75 BT35
Ashfields
Poundfield Gdns., Wok. 227 BC120
Poundfield Rd., Loug. 85 EN43
Poundwell, Welw.G.C. 30 DA10
Pounsley Rd., Sev. 256 FE121
Pountney Rd. SW11 160 DG83
Poverest Rd., Orp. 205 ET99
Povey Cross Rd., Horl. 268 DD150
Powder Mill La., Dart. 188 FL89
Powder Mill La., Twick. 176 BZ87
Powdermill La., 67 EB33
Wal.Abb.
Powdermill Ms., 67 EB33
Wal.Abb.
Powdermill La.
Powdermill Way, 67 EB32
Wal.Abb.
Powell Clo., Chess. 215 CK106
Coppard Gdns.
Powell Clo., Edg. 96 CM51
Powell Clo., Guil. 258 AT136
Powell Clo., Horl. 268 DE147
Baden Dr.
Powell Clo., Wall. 219 DK108
Powell Gdns., Dag. 126 FA63
Powell Rd. E5 122 DV62
Powell Rd., Buck.H. 102 EJ45
Powells Clo., Dor. 263 CJ139
Goodwyns Rd.
Powell's Wk. W4 158 CS79
Power Dr., Enf. 83 DZ36
Power Ind. Est., Erith 167 FG81
Power Rd. W4 158 CN77
Powers Ct., Twick. 177 CK87
Powerscroft Rd. E5 122 DW63
Powerscroft Rd., Sid. 186 EW93
Powis Ct., Pot.B. 64 DC34
Powis Gdns. NW11 119 CZ59
Powis Gdns. W11 139 CZ72
Powis Ms. W11 139 CZ72
Westbourne Pk. Rd.
Powis Pl. WC1 274 A5
Powis Pl. WC1 141 DL70
Powis Rd. E3 143 EB69
Powis Sq. W11 139 CZ72
Powis St. SE18 165 EN76
Powis Ter. W11 139 CZ72
Powle Ter., Ilf. 125 EQ64
Oaktree Gro.
Powlett Pl. NW1 141 DH65
Harmood St.
Pownall Gdns., Houns. 156 CB84
Pownall Rd. E8 142 DT67
Pownall Rd., Houns. 156 CB84
Pownsett Ter., Ilf. 125 EQ64
Buttsbury Rd.
Powster Rd., Brom. 184 EH92
Powys Clo., Bexh. 166 EX79
Powys La. N13 99 DL50
Powys La. N14 99 DL49
Poyle Ind. Est., Slou. 153 BE82
Poyle La., Slou. 130 AH67
Poyle Rd., Guil. 258 AY136
Poyle Rd., Slou. 153 BE83
Poyle Ter., Guil. 258 AX136
Sydenham Rd.
Poynder Rd., Til. 171 GH81
Poynders Ct. SW4 181 DJ86
Poynders Rd.
Poynders Gdns. SW4 181 DJ87
Poynders Hill, Hem.H. 41 BQ21
Poynders Rd. SW4 181 DJ86
Poynes Rd., Horl. 268 DE146
Poynings, The, Iver 153 BF77
Poynings Clo., Orp. 206 EW103
Poynings Rd. N19 121 DJ62
Poynings Way N12 98 DA50
Poynings Way, Rom. 106 FL53
Arlington Gdns.
Poyntell Cres., Chis. 205 ER95
Poynter Rd., Enf. 82 DU43
Poynton Rd. N17 100 DU54
Poyntz Rd. SW11 160 DF82
Poyser St. E2 142 DV68
Prae, The, Wok. 227 BF118
Prae Clo., St.Alb. 42 CB20
Praed Ms. W2 272 A8
Praed St. W2 272 B7
Praed St. W2 140 DD72
Praetorian Ct., St.Alb. 42 CC23
Pragel St. E13 144 EH68
Pragnell Rd. SE12 184 EH89
Prague Pl. SW2 181 DL85
Prah Rd. N4 121 DN61
Prairie Clo., Add. 194 BH104
Prairie Rd., Add. 194 BH104
Prairie St. SW8 160 DG82
Pratt Ms. NW1 141 DJ67
Pratt St.
Pratt St. NW1 141 DJ67
Pratt Wk. SE11 278 C8
Pratt Wk. SE11 161 DM77
Pratts La., Walt. 214 BX105
Molesey Rd.
Pratts Pas., Kings.T. 198 CL96
Eden St.
Prayle Gro. NW2 119 CX60
Prebend Gdns. W4 159 CT76
Prebend Gdns. W6 159 CT76
Prebend St. N1 142 DQ67
Precinct, The, W.Mol. 196 CB97
Victoria Ave.
Precinct Rd., Hayes 135 BU73
Precincts, The, Mord. 200 DB100
Green La.
Precincts, The, Slou. 130 AH70
Premier Ave., Grays 170 GC75
Premier Cor. W9 139 CZ68
Kilburn La.
Premier Pk. NW10 138 CP67
Premier Pl. SW15 159 CY84
Putney High St.
Premiere Pl. E14 143 EA73
Garford St.
Prendergast Rd. SE3 164 EE83
Prentice Pl., Harl. 52 EW17
Prentis Rd. SW16 181 DK91
Prentiss Ct. SE7 164 EK77
Presburg Rd., N.Mal. 198 CS99
Presburg St. E5 123 DX62
Glyn Rd.
Prescelly Pl., Edg. 96 CM53
Prescot St. E1 142 DT73
Prescott Ave., Orp. 205 EP100
Prescott Clo. SW16 181 DL94
Prescott Clo., Horn. 127 FH60
St. Leonards Way
Prescott Grn., Loug. 85 EQ41
Prescott Ho. SE17 161 DP79
Hillingdon St.
Prescott Pl. SW4 161 DK83
Prescott Rd., Slou. 153 BE82
Prescott Rd. (Cheshunt), 67 DY27
Wal.Cr.
Presdale Dr., Ware 33 DX07
Presentation Ms. SW2 181 DM88
Palace Rd.
President Dr. E1 142 DV74
Waterman Way
President St. EC1 275 H2
Press Rd. NW10 118 CR62
Press Rd., Uxb. 134 BK65
Prestage Way E14 143 EC73
Prestbury Ct., Wok. 226 AU118
Muirfield Rd.
Prestbury Cres., Bans. 234 DF116
Prestbury Rd. E7 144 EJ66
Prestbury Sq. SE9 185 EM91
Prested Rd. SW11 160 DE84
St. John's Hill
Prestige Way NW4 119 CW57
Heriot Rd.
Preston Ave. E4 101 ED51
Preston Clo. SE1 279 M8
Preston Clo., Ash. 231 CJ116
Preston Clo., Twick. 177 CE90
Preston Ct., Walt. 196 BW102
St. Johns Dr.
Preston Dr. E11 124 EJ57
Preston Dr., Bexh. 166 EX81
Preston Dr., Epsom 216 CS107
Preston Gdns. NW10 138 CS65
Church Rd.
Preston Gdns., Enf. 83 DY37
Preston Gdns., Ilf. 124 EL58
Preston Gro., Ash. 231 CJ117
Preston Hill, Chesh. 54 AR29
Preston Hill, Har. 118 CM58
Preston La., Tad. 233 CV121
Preston Pl. NW2 139 CU65
Preston Pl., Rich. 178 CL85
Preston Rd. E11 124 EE58
Preston Rd. SE19 181 DP93
Preston Rd. SW20 179 CT94
Preston Rd., Grav. 190 GE88
Preston Rd., Har. 118 CL59
Preston Rd., Rom. 106 FK49
Preston Rd., Shep. 194 BN99
Preston Rd., Slou. 132 AW73
Preston Rd., Wem. 118 CL61
Preston Waye, Har. 118 CL60
Prestons Rd. E14 163 EC75
Prestons Rd., Brom. 204 EG104
Prestwick Clo., Sthl. 156 BY78
Ringway
Prestwick Rd., Wat. 94 BX50
Prestwood, Slou. 132 AV72
Prestwood Ave., Har. 117 CH56
Prestwood Clo. SE18 166 EU80
Prestwood Clo., Har. 117 CJ56
Prestwood Dr., Rom. 105 FC50
Prestwood Gdns., Croy. 202 DQ101
Prestwood St. N1 275 J1
Pretoria Ave. E17 123 DY56
Pretoria Clo. N17 100 DT52
Pretoria Rd.
Pretoria Cres. E4 101 EC46
Pretoria Rd. E4 101 EC46
Pretoria Rd. E11 123 ED60
Pretoria Rd. E16 144 EF69
Pretoria Rd. N17 100 DT52
Pretoria Rd. SW16 181 DH93
Pretoria Rd., Cher. 193 BF102
Pretoria Rd., Ilf. 125 EP64
Pretoria Rd., Rom. 127 FC56
Pretoria Rd., Wat. 75 BU42
Pretoria Rd. N. N18 100 DT51
Pretty La., Couls. 235 DH121
Prevost Rd. N11 98 DG47
Prey Heath, Wok. 226 AV123
Prey Heath Clo., Wok. 226 AW124
Prey Heath Rd., Wok. 226 AV124
Price Clo. NW7 97 CY51
Price Clo. SW17 180 DF90
Price Rd., Croy. 219 DP106
Price Way, Hmptn. 176 BY93
Victors Dr.
Prices La., Reig. 266 DA137
Price's Yd. N1 141 DM67
Pricklers Hill, Barn. 80 DB44
Prickley Wd., Brom. 204 EF102
Priddy's Yd., Croy. 202 DQ103
Church St.
Prideaux Pl. W3 138 CR73
Friars Pl. La.
Prideaux Pl. WC1 274 C2
Prideaux Pl. WC1 141 DM69
Prideaux Rd. SW9 161 DL83
Pridham Rd., Th.Hth. 202 DR98
Priest Ct. EC2 275 H8
Priest Hill, Egh. 172 AW90
Priest Hill, Wind. 172 AW88
Priest Pk. Ave., Har. 116 CA61
Priestfield Rd. SE23 183 DY90
Priestlands Pk. Rd., Sid. 185 ET90
Priestley Clo. N16 122 DT59
Ravensdale Rd.
Priestley Gdns., Rom. 126 EV58
Priestley Rd., Mitch. 200 DG96
Priestley Way E17 123 DX55
Priestley Way NW2 119 CU60
Priestly Gdns., Wok. 227 BA120
Priests Ave., Rom. 105 FD54
Priests Bri. SW14 158 CS83
Priests Bri. SW15 158 CS83
Priests Fld., Brwd. 109 GC50
Priests La., Brwd. 108 FY47
Prima Rd. SW9 161 DN80
Primley La., B.Stort. 37 FC06
Primrose Ave., Enf. 82 DR39
Primrose Ave., Horl. 269 DH149
Primrose Ave., Rom. 126 EV59
Primrose Clo. SE6 183 EC92
Primrose Clo., Har. 116 BZ63
Primrose Clo., Hat. 45 CV19
Primrose Clo., Hem.H. 39 BE21
Primrose Clo., Wall. 201 DH102
Primrose Dr., Hert. 32 DV09
Primrose Fld., Harl. 51 ET18
Primrose Gdns. NW3 140 DE65
Primrose Gdns., Ruis. 116 BW64
Primrose Gdns. 94 CB45
(Bushey), Wat.
Primrose Glen, Horn. 128 FL56
Primrose Hill EC4 274 E9
Primrose Hill, Brwd. 108 FW48
Primrose Hill, Kings L. 59 BP28
Primrose Hill Ct. NW3 140 DF66
Primrose Hill Rd. NW3 140 DE66
Primrose Hill Studios NW1 140 DG67
Fitzroy Rd.
Primrose La., Croy. 203 DX102
Primrose Ms. NW1 140 DF66
Sharpleshall St.
Primrose Ms. SE3 164 EH80
Primrose Ms. W5 157 CK75
St. Mary's Rd.
Primrose Path (Cheshunt), 66 DU31
Wal.Cr.
Primrose Rd. E10 123 EB60
Primrose Rd. E18 102 EH54
Primrose Rd., Walt. 214 BW106
Primrose Sq. E9 142 DW66
Primrose St. EC2 275 M6
Primrose St. EC2 142 DS71
Primrose Wk., Epsom 217 CT108
Primrose Way, Wem. 137 CK68
Primula St. W12 139 CU72
Prince Albert Rd. NW1 272 C1
Prince Albert Rd. NW1 140 DE68
Prince Albert Rd. NW8 272 C1
Prince Albert Rd. NW8 140 DE68
Prince Albert Sq., Red. 266 DF139
Prince Alberts Wk., 152 AU81
Wind.
Prince Arthur Ms. NW3 120 DC63
Perrins La.
Prince Arthur Rd. NW3 120 DC64
Prince Charles Ave. 209 FR96
(South Darenth), Dart.
Prince Charles Dr. NW4 119 CW59

Quadrangle, The W2 272 B8
Quadrangle, The, Guil. 258 AU135
The Oval
Quadrangle, The, Welw.G.C. 29 CW08
Quadrangle Ms., Stan. 95 CJ52
Quadrant, The SE24 182 DQ85
Herne Hill
Quadrant, The SW20 199 CY95
Quadrant, The, Bexh. 166 EX80
Quadrant, The, Epsom 216 CS113
Quadrant, The, Purf. 168 FQ77
Quadrant, The, Rich. 158 CL84
Quadrant, The, St.Alb. 43 CH17
Quadrant, The, Sutt. 218 DC107
Quadrant Arc. W1 277 L1
Quadrant Arc., Rom. 127 FE57
Quadrant Gro. NW5 120 DF64
Quadrant Rd., Rich. 157 CK84
Quadrant Rd., Th.Hth. 201 DP98
Quaggy Wk. SE3 164 EG84
Quail Gdns., S.Croy. 221 DY110
Quainton St. NW10 118 CR62
Quaker Clo., Sev. 257 FK123
Quaker Ct. E1 275 P5
Quaker La., Sthl. 156 CA76
Quaker La., Wal.Abb. 67 EC34
Quaker St. E1 275 P5
Quaker St. E1 142 DT70
Quakers Course NW9 97 CT53
Quakers Hall La., Sev. 257 FJ122
Quakers La., Islw. 157 CG81
Quakers La., Pot.B. 64 DB30
Quaker's Pl. E7 124 EK64
Quakers Wk. N21 82 DR44
Quality Ct. WC2 274 D8
Quality Ct. WC2 141 DN72
Quality St., Red. 251 DH128
Quantock Clo., Hayes 155 BR80
Quantock Clo., St.Alb. 43 CJ16
Quantock Clo., Slou. 153 BA78
Quantock Dr., Wor.Pk. 199 CW103
Quantock Gdns. NW2 119 CX61
Quantock Rd., Bexh. 167 FE82
Cumbrian Ave.
Quantocks, Hem.H. 40 BM17
Quarles Clo., Rom. 104 FA52
Quarley Way SE15 162 DT80
Daniel Gdns.
Quarr Rd., Cars. 200 DD100
Quarrendon Rd., Amer. 55 AR40
Quarrendon St. SW6 160 DA82
Quarry, The, Bet. 248 CS132
Station Rd.
Quarry Clo., Oxt. 254 EE130
Quarry Cotts., Sev. 256 FG123
Quarry Hill, Grays 170 GA78
Quarry Hill, Sev. 257 FK123
Quarry Hill Pk., Reig. 250 DC131
Quarry Ms., Purf. 168 FN77
Fanns Ri.
Quarry Pk. Rd., Sutt. 217 CZ107
Quarry Ri., Sutt. 217 CZ107
Quarry Rd. SW18 180 DC86
Quarry Rd., Gdse. 252 DW128
Quarry Rd., Oxt. 254 EE130
Quarry Spring, Harl. 52 EU15
Quarry St., Guil. 258 AX136
Quarryside Business Pk., Red. 251 DH131
Quarter Mile La. E10 123 EB63
Quarterdeck, The E14 163 EA75
Quartermaine Ave., Wok. 227 AZ122
Quartermass Clo., Hem.H. 40 BG19
Quartermass Rd.
Quartermass Rd., Hem.H. 40 BG19
Quaves Rd., Slou. 152 AV76
Quay La., Green. 169 FV84
Quay W., Tedd. 177 CH92
Quebec Ave., West. 255 ER126
Quebec Clo., Horl. 269 DN148
Alberta Dr.
Quebec Ms. W1 272 E9
Quebec Rd., Hayes 136 BW73
Quebec Rd., Ilf. 125 EP59
Quebec Rd., Til. 171 GG82
Quebec Sq., West. 255 ER126
Quebec Way SE16 163 DX75
Queen Adelaide Rd. SE20 182 DW93
Queen Alexandra's Ct. SW19 179 CZ92
Queen Alexandra's Way, Epsom 216 CN112
Queen Anne Ave. N15 122 DT57
Suffield Rd.
Queen Anne Ave., Brom. 204 EF97
Queen Anne Clo., Esher 215 CE108
Queen Anne Ms. W1 273 J7
Queen Anne Rd. E9 143 DX65
Queen Anne St. W1 273 H8
Queen Anne St. W1 141 DH72
Queen Anne Ter. E1 142 DV73
Sovereign Clo.
Queen Anne's Clo., Twick. 177 CD90
Queen Anne's Gdns. W4 158 CS76
Queen Annes Gdns. W5 158 CL75
Queen Annes Gdns., Enf. 82 DS44
Queen Annes Gdns., Lthd. 231 CH121
Upper Fairfield Rd.
Queen Anne's Gdns., Mitch. 200 DF97
Queen Anne's Gate SW1 277 M5
Queen Anne's Gate SW1 161 DK75
Queen Anne's Gate, Bexh. 166 EX83
Queen Anne's Gro. W4 158 CS76
Queen Annes Gro. W5 158 CL75
Queen Annes Gro., Enf. 100 DR45
Queen Annes Pl., Enf. 82 DS44
Queen Annes Rd., Wind. 151 AQ84
Queen Annes Ter., Lthd. 231 CH121
Upper Fairfield Rd.
Queen Anne's Wk. WC1 141 DL70
Guilford St.
Queen Caroline Est. W6 159 CW78
Queen Caroline St. W6 159 CW77
Queen Charlotte St., Wind. 151 AR81
High St.
Queen Eleanor's Rd., Guil. 258 AT135
Queen Elizabeth Gdns., Mord. 200 DA98
Queen Elizabeth Pl., Til. 171 GG84
Queen Elizabeth Rd. E17 123 DY55
Queen Elizabeth Rd., Kings.T. 198 CM95
Queen Elizabeth II Bri., Dart. 169 FR82
Queen Elizabeth II Bri., Grays 169 FR82
Queen Elizabeth St. SE1 279 N4
Queen Elizabeth St. SE1 162 DT75
Queen Elizabeth Wk. SW13 159 CV81
Queen Elizabeth Wk., Wind. 152 AS82
Queen Elizabeth Way, Wok. 227 AZ119
Queen Elizabeths Clo. N16 122 DR61
Queen Elizabeths Dr. N14 99 DL46
Queen Elizabeth's Dr., Croy. 221 ED110
Queen Elizabeth's Gdns., Croy. 221 ED110
Queen Elizabeth's Dr.
Queen Elizabeths Wk. N16 122 DR61
Queen Elizabeth's Wk., Wall. 219 DK105
Queen Margaret's Gro. N1 122 DS64
Queen Mary Ave., Mord. 199 CX99
Queen Mary Clo., Rom. 127 FF58
Queen Mary Clo., Surb. 198 CN104
Queen Mary Clo., Wok. 227 BC116
Queen Mary Rd. SE19 181 DP93
Queen Mary Rd., Shep. 195 BQ96
Queen Mary's Ave., Cars. 218 DF108
Queen Marys Ave., Wat. 75 BS42
Queen Marys Dr., Add. 211 BF110
Queen Mother's Dr., Uxb. 113 BF58
Queen of Denmark Ct. SE16 163 DZ76
Queen Sq. WC1 274 A5
Queen Sq. WC1 141 DL70
Queen Sq. Pl. WC1 274 A5
Queen St. EC4 275 J10
Queen St. EC4 142 DQ73
Queen St. N17 100 DS51
Queen St. W1 277 H2
Queen St. W1 141 DH74
Queen St., Bexh. 166 EZ83
Queen St., Brwd. 108 FW50
Queen St., Cher. 194 BG102
Queen St., Croy. 202 DQ104
Church Rd.
Queen St., Erith 167 FE79
Queen St., Grav. 191 GH86
Queen St., Guil. 261 BQ139
Queen St., Kings L. 58 BG32
Queen St., Rom. 127 FD58
Queen St., St.Alb. 42 CC20
Queen St. Pl. EC4 279 J1
Queen Victoria Ave., Wem. 137 CK66
Queen Victoria St. EC4 274 G10
Queen Victoria St. EC4 141 DP73
Queen Victoria Ter. E1 142 DV73
Sovereign Clo.
Queen Victoria's Wk., Wind. 152 AS80
Queenborough Gdns., Chis. 185 ER93
Queenborough Gdns., Ilf. 125 EN56
Queendale Ct., Wok. 226 AT116
Roundthorn Way
Queenhill Rd., S.Croy. 220 DV110
Queenhithe EC4 275 J10
Queenhithe EC4 142 DQ73
Queenhythe Rd., Guil. 242 AX128
Queens Acre, Sutt. 217 CX108
Queens Acre, Wind. 151 AR84
Queens All., Epp. 69 ET31
Queens Ave. N3 98 DC52
Queens Ave. N10 120 DG55
Queens Ave. N20 98 DD47
Queen's Ave. N21 99 DP46
Queens Ave., Felt. 176 BW91
Queens Ave., Grnf. 136 CB72
Queens Ave., Stan. 117 CJ55
Queens Ave., Wat. 75 BT42
Queens Ave., W.Byf. 212 BK112
Queens Ave., Wdf.Grn. 102 EH50
Queen's Circ. SW8 161 DH80
Queenstown Rd.
Queen's Circ. SW11 161 DH80
Queenstown Rd.
Queens Clo., Edg. 96 CN50
Queens Clo., Tad. 233 CU124
Queens Clo., Wall. 219 DH106
Queens Rd.
Queens Clo., Wind. 172 AU85
Queens Club Gdns. W14 159 CY79
Queens Ct. SE23 182 DW88
Queens Ct., Brox. 49 DZ24
Queens Ct., Rich. 178 CM86
Queens Ct., St.Alb. 43 CH20
Hatfield Rd.
Queens Ct., Slou. 132 AT73
Queens Ct., Wey. 213 BR106
Queens Ct. Ride, Cob. 213 BU113
Queens Cres. NW5 140 DG65
Queens Cres., Rich. 178 CM85
Queens Cres., St.Alb. 43 CH17
Queens Dr. E10 123 EA59
Queens Dr. N4 121 DP61
Queens Dr. W3 138 CM72
Queens Dr. W5 138 CM72
Queens Dr., Abb.L. 59 BT32
Queens Dr., Guil. 242 AU131
Queens Dr., Lthd. 214 CC111
Queen's Dr., Slou. 133 AZ66
Queens Dr., Surb. 198 CN101
Queens Dr., T.Ditt. 197 CG101
Queens Dr., Wal.Cr. 67 EA34
Queens Dr., The, Rick. 91 BF45
Queens Elm Par. SW3 160 DD78
Old Ch. St.
Queen's Elm Sq. SW3 160 DD78
Old Ch. St.
Queens Gdns. NW4 119 CW57
Queens Gdns. W2 140 DC73
Queens Gdns. W5 137 CJ70
Queens Gdns., Dart. 188 FP88
Queen's Gdns., Houns. 156 BY81
Queens Gdns., Rain. 147 FD68
Queens Gdns., Upmin. 129 FT58
Queen's Gate SW7 160 DC76
Queen's Gate, Gat. 268 DG152
Queen's Gate Gdns. SW7 160 DC76
Queens Gate Gdns. SW15 159 CV84
Upper Richmond Rd.
Queen's Gate Ms. SW7 160 DC75
Queen's Gate Pl. SW7 160 DC76
Queen's Gate Pl. Ms. SW7 160 DC76
Queen's Gate Ter. SW7 160 DC76
Queen's Gro. NW8 140 DD67
Queen's Gro. Ms. NW8 140 DD67
Queens Gro. Rd. E4 101 ED46
Queen's Head St. N1 141 DP67
Queens Head Wk., Brox. 49 DY23
High Rd. Wormley
Queens Head Yd. SE1 279 K3
Queens Ho., Tedd. 177 CF93
Queens La. N10 121 DH55
Queens La., Ashf. 174 BM91
Clarendon Rd.
Queens Mkt. E13 144 EJ67
Green St.
Queens Ms. W2 140 DB73
Queens Par. N11 98 DF50
Colney Hatch La.
Queens Par. W5 138 CM72
Queens Par. Clo. N11 98 DF50
Colney Hatch La.
Queens Pk. Ct. W10 139 CX69
Queens Pk. Gdns., Felt. 175 BU90
Vernon Rd.
Queens Pk. Rd., Cat. 236 DS123
Queens Pk. Rd., Rom. 106 FM53
Queens Pas., Chis. 185 EP93
High St.
Queens Pl., Mord. 200 DA98
Queens Pl., Wat. 76 BW41
Queen's Prom., Kings.T. 197 CK97
Portsmouth Rd.
Queens Reach, E.Mol. 197 CE98
Queens Ride SW13 159 CU83
Queens Ride SW15 159 CU83
Queen's Ride, Rich. 178 CP88
Queens Ri., Rich. 178 CM86
Queens Rd. E11 123 ED59
Queens Rd. E13 144 EH67
Queen's Rd. E17 123 DZ58
Queens Rd. N3 98 DC53
Queens Rd. N9 100 DV48
Queen's Rd. N11 99 DL52
Queens Rd. NW4 119 CW57
Queens Rd. SE14 162 DV81
Queens Rd. SE15 162 DV81
Queens Rd. SW14 158 CR83
Queens Rd. SW19 179 CZ93
Queens Rd. W5 138 CL72
Queens Rd., Bark. 145 EQ65
Queens Rd., Barn. 79 CX41
Queens Rd., Beck. 203 DY96
Queens Rd., Berk. 38 AU18
Queens Rd., Brwd. 108 FW48
Queens Rd., Brom. 204 EG96
Queens Rd., Buck.H. 102 EH47
Queens Rd., Chesh. 54 AQ30
Queens Rd., Chis. 185 EP93
Queen's Rd., Croy. 201 DP100
Queens Rd., Egh. 173 AZ93
Queens Rd., Enf. 82 DS42
Queens Rd., Epp. 71 FB26
Queen's Rd., Erith 167 FE79
Queens Rd., Felt. 175 BV88
Queens Rd., Grav. 191 GJ90
Queens Rd., Guil. 242 AX134
Queens Rd., Hmptn. 176 CB91
Queens Rd., Hayes 135 BS72
Queens Rd., Hert. 32 DR11
Queens Rd., Horl. 268 DG148
Queen's Rd., Houns. 156 CB83
Queens Rd., Kings.T. 178 CN94
Queens Rd., Loug. 84 EL41
Queens Rd., Mitch. 200 DD97
Queens Rd., Mord. 200 DA98
Queens Rd., N.Mal. 199 CT98
Queens Rd., Rich. 178 CL87
Queens Rd., Slou. 132 AT73
Queens Rd. (Datchet), Slou. 152 AV80
Queens Rd., Sthl. 156 BX75
Queens Rd., Sutt. 218 DA110
Queen's Rd., Tedd. 177 CE93
Queens Rd., T.Ditt. 197 CF99
Queens Rd., Twick. 177 CF87
Queen's Rd., Uxb. 134 BJ69
Queens Rd., Wall. 219 DH106
Queens Rd., Wal.Cr. 67 DY34
Queens Rd., Walt. 213 BS106
Queens Rd., Ware 33 DZ05
Queens Rd., Wat. 76 BW42
Queen's Rd., Well. 166 EV82
Queens Rd., West Dr. 154 BM75
Queens Rd., Wey. 213 BP105
Queens Rd., Wind. 151 AQ82
Queens Rd. (Eton Wick), Wind. 151 AM78
Queens Rd. W. E13 144 EG68
Queen's Row SE17 162 DR79
Queen's Sq., The, Hem.H. 40 BM20
Queens Ter. E13 144 EH67
Queen's Ter. NW8 140 DD68
Queens Ter., Islw. 157 CG84
Queens Ter. Cotts. W7 157 CE75
Boston Rd.
Queens Wk. E4 101 ED46
The Grn. Wk.
Queens Wk. NW9 118 CQ61
Queen's Wk. SW1 277 K3
Queen's Wk. SW1 141 DJ74
Queens Wk. W5 137 CJ70
Queens Wk., Ashf. 174 BK91
Queen's Wk., Har. 117 CE56
Queens Wk., Ruis. 116 BX62
Queen's Wk., The SE1 279 N2
Queen's Wk., The SE1 142 DS74
Queens Way NW4 119 CW57
Queens Way, Croy. 219 DM107
Queens Way, Felt. 176 BW91
Queens Way, Rad. 62 CL32
Queens Way, Wal.Cr. 67 DZ34
Queens Well Ave. N20 98 DE48
Queen's Wd. Rd. N10 121 DH58
Queens Yd. WC1 273 L5
Queensberry Ms. W. SW7 160 DD77
Queen's Gate
Queensberry Pl. SW7 160 DD77
Queensberry Way SW7 160 DD77
Harrington Rd.
Queensborough Ms. W2 140 DC73
Porchester Ter.
Queensborough Pas. W2 140 DC73
Porchester Ter.
Queensborough S. Bldgs. W2 140 DC73
Porchester Ter.
Queensborough Studios W2 140 DC73
Porchester Ter.
Queensborough Ter. W2 140 DB73
Queensbridge Pk., Islw. 177 CE85
Queensbridge Rd. E2 142 DT67
Queensbridge Rd. E8 142 DT66
Queensbury Circle Par., Har. 118 CL55
Streatfield Rd.
Queensbury Circle Par., Stan. 118 CL55
Streatfield Rd.
Queensbury Pl., Rich. 177 CK85
Friars La.
Queensbury Rd. NW9 118 CR59
Queensbury Rd., Wem. 138 CM68
Queensbury Sta. Par., Edg. 118 CM55
Queensbury St. N1 142 DQ66
Queenscourt, Wem. 118 CL63
Queenscroft Rd. SE9 184 EK85
Queensdale Cres. W11 139 CX74
Queensdale Pl. W11 139 CY74
Queensdale Rd. W11 139 CX74
Queensdale Wk. W11 139 CY74
Queensdown Rd. E5 122 DV63
Queensferry Wk. N17 122 DV56
Jarrow Rd.
Queensgate, Cob. 214 BX112
Queensgate, Wal.Cr. 67 DZ34
Queensgate Gdns., Chis. 205 ER95
Queensgate Pl. NW6 140 DA66
Queensland Ave. N18 100 DQ51
Queensland Ave. SW19 200 DB95
Queensland Pl. N7 121 DN63
Queensland Rd.
Queensland Rd. N7 121 DN63
Queensmead NW8 140 DD67
Queensmead, Lthd. 214 CC111
Queensmead, Slou. 152 AV81
Queensmead Ave., Epsom 217 CV110
Queensmead Rd., Brom. 204 EF96
Queensmead Rd., H.Wyc. 88 AC53
Queensmere, Slou. 152 AT75
High St.
Queensmere Clo. SW19 179 CX89
Queensmere Rd. SW19 179 CX89
Queensmere Rd., Slou. 152 AU75
Wellington St.
Queensmill Rd. SW6 159 CX80
Queensthorpe Rd. SE26 183 DX91
Queenstown Gdns., Rain. 147 FF69
Queenstown Ms. SW8 161 DH82
Queenstown Rd.
Queenstown Rd. SW8 161 DH79
Queensville Rd. SW12 181 DK87
Queensway W2 140 DB72
Queensway, Enf. 82 DV42
Queensway, Hat. 45 CU17
Queensway, Hem.H. 40 BK19
Queensway, Orp. 205 EQ99
Queensway, Red. 250 DF133
Queensway, Sun. 195 BV96
Queensway, W.Wick. 204 EE104
Queensway, The, Ger.Cr. 112 AX56
Queensway N., Walt. 214 BW105
Robinsway
Queensway S., Walt. 214 BW106
Trenchard Clo.
Queenswood Ave. E17 101 EC53
Queenswood Ave., Brwd. 109 GD42
Queenswood Ave., Hmptn. 176 CB93
Queenswood Ave., Houns. 156 BZ82
Queenswood Ave., Th.Hth. 201 DN99
Queenswood Ave., Wall. 219 DK105
Queenswood Cres., Wat. 59 BU33
Queenswood Gdns. E11 124 EH60
Queenswood Pk. N3 97 CY54
Queenswood Rd. SE23 183 DX90
Queenswood Rd., Sid. 185 ET85
Quemerford Rd. N7 121 DM64
Quendell Wk., Hem.H. 40 BL20
Quendon Dr., Wal.Abb. 67 ED33
Quennel Way, Brwd. 109 GC45
Quennell Clo., Ash. 232 CL119
Parkers La.
Quentin Pl. SE13 164 EE83
Quentin Rd. SE13 164 EE83
Quentin Way, Vir.W. 192 AV98
Quernmore Clo., Brom. 184 EG93
Quernmore Rd. N4 121 DN58
Quernmore Rd., Brom. 184 EG93
Querrin St. SW6 160 DC82
Quex Ms. NW6 140 DA67
Quex Rd.
Quex Rd. NW6 140 DA67
Quick Pl. N1 141 DP67
Quick Rd. W4 158 CS78
Quick St. N1 274 G1
Quick St. N1 141 DP68
Quick St. Ms. N1 274 F1
Quickbeams, Welw.G.C. 30 DA06
Quickberry Pl., Amer. 55 AQ39
Quickley La., Rick. 73 BB44
Quickley Ri., Rick. 73 BC44
Quickmoor La., Kings L. 58 BH33
Quicks Rd. SW19 180 DB94
Quickswood NW3 140 DE66
King Henry's Rd.
Quickwood Clo., Rick. 74 BG44
Quiet Clo., Add. 212 BG105
Quiet Nook, Brom. 204 EK104
Croydon Rd.
Quill Hall La., Amer. 55 AS37
Quill La. SW15 159 CX84
Quill St. N4 121 DN62
Quill St. W5 138 CL69
Quillot, The, Walt. 213 BT106
Quilp St. SE1 279 H4
Quilter Gdns., Orp. 206 EW102
Tintagel Rd.
Quilter Rd., Orp. 206 EW102
Quilter St. E2 142 DU69
Quilter St. SE18 165 ET78
Quinbrookes, Slou. 132 AW72
Quince Tree Clo., S.Ock. 149 FW70
Quinces Cft., Hem.H. 40 BG18
Quincy Rd., Egh. 173 BA92
Quinta Dr., Barn. 79 CV43
Quintin Ave. SW20 199 CZ95
Quintin Clo., Pnr. 115 BV57
High Rd.
Quinton Clo., Beck. 203 EC97
Quinton Clo., Houns. 155 BV80
Quinton Clo., Wall. 219 DH105
Quinton Rd., T.Ditt. 197 CG102
Quinton St. SW18 180 DC89
Quintrell Clo., Wok. 226 AV117
Quixley St. E14 143 ED73
Quorn Rd. SE22 162 DS84

R

Raans Rd., Amer. 72 AT38
Rabbit La., Walt. 213 BU108
Rabbit Row W8 140 DA74
Kensington Mall
Rabbits Rd. E12 124 EL63
Rabbits Rd. (South Darenth), Dart. 209 FR96
Rabies Heath Rd., Gdse. 252 DU134
Rabies Heath Rd., Red. 252 DS133
Rabournmead Dr., Nthlt. 116 BY64
Raby Rd., N.Mal. 198 CR98
Raby St. E14 143 DY72
Salmon La.
Raccoon Way, Houns. 156 BW82
Racecourse Way, Gat. 268 DF151
Rachel Clo., Ilf. 125 ER55
Rachel Pt. E5 122 DU63
Muir Rd.
Rachels Way, Chesh. 54 AR34
Cresswell Rd.
Rackham Clo., Well. 166 EV82
Rackham Ms. SW16 181 DJ93
Westcote Rd.
Racks Ct., Guil. 258 AX136
Racton Rd. SW6 160 DA79
Rad La., Dor. 261 BS142
Horsham Rd.
Rad La., Guil. 261 BR142
Radbourne Ave. W5 157 CJ77
Radbourne Clo. E5 123 DX63
Overbury St.
Radbourne Cres. E17 101 ED54
Radbourne Rd. SW12 181 DJ87
Radburn Clo., Harl. 52 EU19
Radcliffe Ave. NW10 139 CU68
Radcliffe Ave., Enf. 82 DQ39
Radcliffe Gdns., Cars. 218 DE108
Radcliffe Ms., Hmptn. 176 CC92
Taylor Clo.
Radcliffe Path SW8 161 DJ82
St. Rule St.
Radcliffe Rd. N21 99 DP46
Radcliffe Rd. SE1 279 N6
Radcliffe Rd., Croy. 202 DT103
Radcliffe Rd., Har. 95 CG54
Radcliffe Sq. SW15 179 CX86
Radcliffe Way, Nthlt. 136 BX69
Radcot Ave., Slou. 153 BB76
Radcot Pt. SE23 183 DX90
Radcot St. SE11 161 DN78
Raddington Rd. W10 139 CY71
Radfield Way, Sid. 185 ER87
Radford Rd. SE13 183 EC86
Radford Way, Bark. 145 ET69
Radipole Rd. SW6 159 CZ81
Radius Pk., Felt. 155 BT84
Radland Rd. E16 144 EF72
Radlet Ave. SE26 182 DV90
Radlett Clo. E7 144 EF65
Radlett La., Rad. 77 CK35
Radlett Pk. Rd., Rad. 61 CG34
Radlett Pl. NW8 140 DE67
Radlett Rd., St.Alb. 61 CE28
Radlett Rd., Wat. 76 BW41
Radlett Rd. (Aldenham), Wat. 77 CD36
Radley Ave., Ilf. 125 ET63
Radley Clo., Felt. 175 BT88
Radley Ct. SE16 163 DX75
Thame Rd.
Radley Gdns., Har. 118 CL56
Radley Ho. SE2 166 EX75
Wolvercote Rd.
Radley Ms. W8 160 DA76
Radley Rd. N17 100 DS54
Radley's La. E18 102 EG54
Radleys Mead, Dag. 147 FB65
Radlix Rd. E10 123 EA60
Radnor Ave., Har. 117 CE57
Radnor Ave., Well. 186 EV85
Radnor Clo., Chis. 185 ES93
Homewood Cres.
Radnor Clo., Mitch. 201 DL98
Radnor Cres. SE18 166 EU80
Radnor Cres., Ilf. 125 EM57
Radnor Gdns., Enf. 82 DS39
Radnor Gdns., Twick. 177 CF89
Radnor Gro., Uxb. 134 BN68
Charnwood Rd.
Radnor La., Dor. 261 BU144
Radnor Ms. W2 272 A9
Radnor Pl. W2 272 B9
Radnor Pl. W2 140 DE72
Radnor Rd. NW6 139 CY67
Radnor Rd. SE15 162 DU80
Radnor Rd., Har. 117 CD57
Radnor Rd., Twick. 177 CF88
Radnor Rd., Wey. 194 BN104
Radnor St. EC1 275 J3
Radnor St. EC1 142 DQ69
Radnor Ter. W14 159 CZ77
Radnor Wk. E14 163 EA77
Copeland Dr.
Radnor Wk. SW3 160 DE78
Radnor Wk., Croy. 203 DZ100
Radnor Way NW10 138 CP70
Radnor Way, Slou. 152 AY77
Radolphs, Tad. 233 CX122
Heathcote
Radstock Ave., Har. 117 CG55
Radstock St. SW11 160 DE80
Radstock Way, Red. 251 DK128
Radstone Ct., Wok. 227 AZ118
Radwell Path, Borwd. 78 CL39
Cromwell Rd.
Raeburn Gdns., Barn. 79 CV43
Raeburn Ave., Dart. 187 FH85
Raeburn Ave., Surb. 198 CP100
Raeburn Clo. NW11 120 DC58
Raeburn Clo., Kings.T. 177 CK94
Raeburn Rd., Edg. 96 CN53
Raeburn Rd., Hayes 135 BR68
Raeburn Rd., Sid. 185 ES86
Raeburn St. SW2 161 DL84
Raeside Clo., Beac. 89 AQ50
Rafford Way, Brom. 204 EH96

Raft Rd. SW18 160 DA84
North Pas.
Rag Hill Clo., West. 238 EL121
Rag Hill Rd., West. 238 EK121
Ragged Hall La., St.Alb. 42 BX24
Raggleswood, Chis. 205 EN95
Raglan Ave., Wal.Cr. 67 DX34
Raglan Clo., Houns. 176 BY85
Vickers Way
Raglan Clo., Reig. 250 DC132
Raglan Ct. SE12 184 EG85
Raglan Ct., S.Croy. 219 DP106
Raglan Ct., Wem. 118 CM63
Raglan Gdns., Wat. 93 BV46
Raglan Rd. E17 123 EC57
Raglan Rd. SE18 165 EQ78
Raglan Rd., Belv. 166 EZ77
Raglan Rd., Brom. 204 EJ98
Raglan Rd., Enf. 100 DS45
Raglan Rd., Reig. 250 DB131
Raglan Rd., Wok. 226 AS118
Raglan St. NW5 141 DH65
Raglan Ter., Har. 116 CB63
Raglan Way, Nthlt. 136 CC65
Ragley Clo. W3 158 CQ75
Church Rd.
Rags La. (Cheshunt), Wal.Cr. 66 DS27
Ragstone Rd., Slou. 151 AR76
Rahn Rd., Epp. 70 EU31
Raider Clo., Rom. 104 FA53
Raikes Hollow, Dor. 261 BV142
Raikes La., Dor. 261 BV143
Railey Ms. NW5 121 DJ64
Railpit La., Warl. 238 EE115
Railshead Rd., Islw. 157 CH84
Railton Rd. SE24 181 DN85
Railway App. N4 121 DN58
Wightman Rd.
Railway App. SE1 279 L2
Railway App. SE1 142 DR74
Railway App., Har. 117 CF56
Railway App., Hert. 32 DQ09
Railway App., Twick. 177 CG87
Railway App., Wall. 219 DH107
Railway Ave. SE16 162 DW75
Railway Cotts., Hat. 44 CS19
Ellenbrook La.
Railway Cotts., Wat. 75 BV39
Railway Ms. E3 143 EA69
Wellington Way
Railway Ms. W10 139 CY72
Ladbroke Gro.
Railway Pas., Tedd. 177 CG93
Victoria Rd.
Railway Pl. SW19 179 CZ93
Hartfield Rd.
Railway Pl., Belv. 166 FA76
Railway Pl., Hert. 32 DS09
Railway Ri. SE22 162 DS84
Grove Vale
Railway Rd., Tedd. 177 CF91
Railway Rd., Wal.Cr. 67 DY33
Railway Side SW13 158 CS83
Railway Sq., Brwd. 108 FW48
Fairfield Rd.
Railway St. N1 274 A1
Railway St. N1 141 DL68
Railway St., Grav. 190 GA85
Railway St., Hert. 32 DR09
Railway St., Rom. 126 EW60
Railway Ter. SE13 183 EB85
Ladywell Rd.
Railway Ter., Felt. 175 BU88
Railway Ter., Kings L. 58 BN27
Railway Ter., Slou. 132 AT74
Railway Ter., Stai. 173 BD92
Railway Ter., West. 255 ER125
Rainborough Clo. NW10 138 CQ65
Rainbow Ave. E14 163 EB78
Rainbow Ct., Wat. 76 BW44
Oxhey Rd.
Rainbow Ct., Wok. 226 AS116
Langmans Way
Rainbow Ind. Est., West Dr. 134 BK73
Rainbow Quay SE16 163 DY76
Rope St.
Rainbow Rd., Grays 169 FW77
Rainbow Rd., Harl. 37 FE12
Rainbow St. SE5 162 DS80
Raine St. E1 142 DV74
Rainer Clo. (Cheshunt), Wal.Cr. 67 DX29
Rainham Clo. SE9 185 ER86
Rainham Clo. SW11 180 DE86
Rainham Rd. NW10 139 CW69
Rainham Rd., Rain. 147 FF66
Rainham Rd. N., Dag. 127 FB61
Rainham Rd. S., Dag. 127 FB63
Rainhill Way E3 143 EA69
Rainsborough Ave. SE8 163 DY77
Rainsford Clo., Stan. 95 CJ50
Coverdale Clo.
Rainsford Rd. NW10 138 CP69
Rainsford St. W2 272 B8
Rainsford Way, Horn. 127 FG60
Rainton Rd. SE7 164 EG78
Rainville Rd. W6 159 CW79
Raisins Hill, Pnr. 116 BW55
Raith Ave. N14 99 DK48
Raleana Rd. E14 143 EC74
Raleigh Ave., Hayes 135 BV71
Raleigh Ave., Wall. 219 DK105
Raleigh Clo. NW4 119 CW57
Raleigh Clo., Erith 167 FF79
Raleigh Clo., Pnr. 116 BX59
Raleigh Clo., Ruis. 115 BT61
Raleigh Clo., Slou. 131 AN74
Raleigh Ct. SE16 143 DX74
Rotherhithe St.
Raleigh Ct., Stai. 174 BG91
Raleigh Ct., Wall. 219 DH107
Raleigh Dr. N20 98 DE48
Raleigh Dr., Esher 215 CD106
Raleigh Dr., Horl. 269 DN148
Raleigh Dr., Surb. 198 CQ102
Raleigh Gdns. SW2 181 DM86
Brixton Hill
Raleigh Gdns., Mitch. 200 DF96
Raleigh Ms. N1 141 DP67
Queen's Head St.
Raleigh Ms., Orp. 223 ET106
Osgood Ave.
Raleigh Rd. N8 121 DN56
Raleigh Rd. SE20 183 DX94
Raleigh Rd., Enf. 82 DR42
Raleigh Rd., Felt. 175 BT90
Raleigh Rd., Rich. 158 CM83
Raleigh Rd., Sthl. 156 BY78
Raleigh St. N1 141 DP67
Raleigh Way N14 99 DK46
Raleigh Way, Felt. 176 BW91
Ralliwood Rd., Ash. 232 CN119
Ralph Ct. W2 140 DB72
Queensway
Ralph Perring Ct., Beck. 203 EA98
Ralston St. SW3 160 DF78
Tedworth Sq.
Ralston Way, Wat. 94 BX47
Ram Gorse, Harl. 35 EP13
Ram Pas., Kings.T. 197 CK96
High St.
Ram Pl. E9 142 DW65
Chatham Pl.
Ram St. SW18 180 DB85
Rama Clo. SW16 181 DK94
Rama Ct., Har. 117 CE61
Ramac Way SE7 164 EH77
Rambler Clo. SW16 181 DJ91
Rambler Clo., Maid. 130 AH72
Rambler La., Slou. 152 AW76
Ramblers Way, Welw.G.C. 30 DC10
Rambling Way, Berk. 39 BC16
Rame Clo. SW17 180 DG92
Ramilles Clo. SW2 181 DL86
Ramillies Pl. W1 273 K9
Ramillies Pl. W1 141 DJ72
Ramillies Rd. NW7 96 CS47
Ramillies Rd. W4 158 CR77
Ramillies Rd., Sid. 186 EV86
Ramillies St. W1 273 K9
Ramin Ct., Guil. 242 AW131
Rowan Clo.
Ramney Dr., Enf. 83 DY37
Ramornie Clo., Walt. 214 BZ106
Rampart St. E1 142 DV72
Commercial Rd.
Ramparts, The, St.Alb. 42 CB21
Rampayne St. SW1 277 M10
Rampayne St. SW1 161 DK78
Rampton Clo. E4 101 EA48
Rams Gro., Rom. 126 EY56
Ramsay Clo., Brox. 49 DY21
Ramsay Gdns., Rom. 106 FJ53
Ramsay Ms. SW3 160 DE79
King's Rd.
Ramsay Pl., Har. 117 CE60
Ramsay Rd. E7 124 EE63
Ramsay Rd. W3 158 CQ76
Ramsbury Rd., St.Alb. 43 CE21
Ramscote La., Chesh. 54 AN25
Ramscroft Clo. N9 100 DS45
Ramsdale Rd. SW17 180 DG92
Ramsden Clo., Orp. 206 EW102
Ramsden Dr., Rom. 104 FA52
Ramsden Rd. N11 98 DF50
Ramsden Rd. SW12 180 DG87
Ramsden Rd., Erith 167 FD80
Ramsden Rd., Orp. 206 EV101
Ramsey Clo. NW9 119 CT58
West Hendon Bdy.
Ramsey Clo., Grnf. 116 CC64
Ramsey Clo., Hat. 64 DD27
Ramsey Clo., Horl. 268 DF148
Ramsey Clo., St.Alb. 43 CG22
Ramsey Ct., Slou. 131 AK70
Lower Britwell Rd.
Ramsey Ho., Wem. 138 CL65
Ramsey Lo. Ct., St.Alb. 43 CE19
Hillside Rd.
Ramsey Ms. N4 121 DP62
Monsell Rd.
Ramsey Rd., Th.Hth. 201 DM100
Ramsey St. E2 142 DU70
Ramsey Wk. N1 142 DR65
Clephane Rd.
Ramsey Way N14 99 DJ45
Ramsgate Clo. E16 144 EH74
Hanameel St.
Ramsgate St. E8 142 DT65
Dalston La.
Ramsgill App., Ilf. 125 ET56
Ramsgill Dr., Ilf. 125 ET57
Ramson Ri., Hem.H. 39 BE21
Ramulis Dr., Hayes 136 BX70
Ramus Wd. Ave., Orp. 223 ES106
Rancliffe Gdns. SE9 164 EL84
Rancliffe Rd. E6 144 EL68
Randal Cres., Reig. 266 DA136
Randall Ave. NW2 119 CT62
Randall Clo. SW11 160 DE81
Randall Clo., Erith 167 FC79
Randall Clo., Slou. 153 AZ78
Randall Dr., Horn. 128 FJ63
Randall Pl. SE10 163 EC80
Randall Rd. SE11 278 B10
Randall Rd. SE11 161 DM77
Randall Row SE11 278 B9
Randalls Cres., Lthd. 231 CG120
Randalls Dr., Brwd. 109 GE44
Randalls Pk. Ave., Lthd. 231 CG120
Randalls Pk. Dr., Lthd. 231 CG121
Randalls Rd.
Randalls Ride, Hem.H. 40 BL18
Randalls Rd., Lthd. 231 CE119
Randalls Way, Lthd. 231 CG121
Randell's Rd. N1 141 DL67
Randle Rd., Rich. 177 CJ91
Randles La., Sev. 240 EX115
Randlesdown Rd. SE6 183 EA91
Randolph App. E16 144 EK72
Randolph Ave. W9 140 DC70
Randolph Clo., Bexh. 167 FC83
Randolph Clo., Cob. 230 CA115
Randolph Clo., Kings.T. 178 CQ92
Randolph Clo., Wok. 226 AS117
Creston Ave.
Randolph Cres. W9 140 DC70
Randolph Gdns. NW6 140 DB68
Randolph Gro., Rom. 126 EW57
Donald Dr.
Randolph Ho., Croy. 202 DQ102
Randolph Ms. W9 140 DC70
Randolph Rd. E17 123 EB57
Randolph Rd. W9 140 DC70
Randolph Rd., Epsom 217 CT114
Randolph Rd., Slou. 152 AY77
Randolph Rd., Sthl. 156 BZ75
Randolph St. NW1 141 DJ66
Randolph's La., West. 255 EP126
Randon Clo., Har. 94 CB54
Ranelagh Ave. SW6 159 CZ83
Ranelagh Ave. SW13 159 CU82
Ranelagh Bri. W2 140 DB71
Gloucester Ter.
Ranelagh Clo., Edg. 96 CN49
Ranelagh Dr., Edg. 96 CN49
Ranelagh Gdns. E11 124 EJ57
Ranelagh Gdns. SW6 159 CZ83
Ranelagh Gdns. W4 158 CQ80
Grove Pk. Gdns.
Ranelagh Gdns. W6 159 CT76
Ranelagh Gdns., Grav. 191 GF87
Ranelagh Gdns., Ilf. 125 EN60
Ranelagh Gro. SW1 276 G10
Ranelagh Gro. SW1 160 DG78
Ranelagh Ms. W5 157 CK75
Ranelagh Rd.
Ranelagh Pl., N.Mal. 198 CS99
Rodney Rd.
Ranelagh Rd. E6 145 EN67
Ranelagh Rd. E11 124 EE63
Ranelagh Rd. E15 144 EE67
Ranelagh Rd. N17 122 DS55
Ranelagh Rd. N22 99 DM53
Ranelagh Rd. NW10 139 CT68
Ranelagh Rd. SW1 161 DJ78
Lupus St.
Ranelagh Rd. W5 157 CK75
Ranelagh Rd., Hem.H. 41 BP20
Ranelagh Rd., Red. 250 DE134
Ranelagh Rd., Sthl. 136 BX74
Ranelagh Rd., Wem. 117 CK64
Ranfurly Rd., Sutt. 200 DA103
Range Rd., Grav. 191 GL87
Range Way, Shep. 194 BN101
Rangefield Rd., Brom. 184 EE92
Rangemoor Rd. N15 122 DT57
Ranger Wk., Add. 212 BH106
Monks Cres.
Rangers Rd. E4 102 EE45
Rangers Rd., Loug. 102 EE45
Rangers Sq. SE10 163 ED81
Rangeworth Pl., Sid. 185 ET90
Priestlands Pk. Rd.
Rangoon St. EC3 142 DT72
Northumberland All.
Rank Ho., Harl. 51 EQ15
Rankin Clo. NW9 118 CS55
Ranleigh Gdns., Bexh. 166 EZ80
Ranmere St. SW12 181 DH88
Ormeley Rd.
Ranmoor Clo., Har. 117 CD56
Ranmoor Gdns., Har. 117 CD56
Ranmore Ave., Croy. 202 DT104
Ranmore Clo., Red. 250 DG131
Ranmore Common, Dor. 246 CA133
Ranmore Common Rd., Dor. 245 BU134
Ranmore Common Rd., Lthd. 245 BU134
Ranmore Path, Orp. 206 EU98
Ranmore Rd., Dor. 246 CC134
Ranmore Rd., Sutt. 217 CX109
Rannoch Clo., Edg. 96 CP47
Rannoch Rd. W6 159 CW79
Rannoch Wk., Hem.H. 40 BK16
Rannock Ave. NW9 118 CS59
Ranskill Rd., Borwd. 78 CN39
Ransom Clo., Wat. 94 BW45
Ransom Rd. SE7 164 EJ78
Harvey Gdns.
Ransom Wk. SE7 164 EJ78
Woolwich Rd.
Ranston Clo., Uxb. 113 BF58
Nightingale Way
Ranston St. NW1 272 B6
Rant Meadow, Hem.H. 40 BN22
Ranulf Rd. NW2 119 CZ63
Ranwell Clo. E3 143 DZ67
Beale Rd.
Ranwell St. E3 143 DZ67
Ranworth Ave., Hodd. 33 EB13
Ranworth Clo., Erith 167 FE82
Ranworth Clo., Hem.H. 40 BK22
Panxworth Rd.
Ranworth Rd. N9 100 DW47
Ranyard Clo., Chess. 198 CM104
Raphael Ave., Rom. 127 FF55
Raphael Ave., Til. 171 GG80
Raphael Clo., Rad. 62 CL32
Raphael Dr., Wat. 76 BX40
Raphael Rd., Grav. 191 GK87
Raphael St. SW7 276 D5
Raphael St. SW7 160 DF75
Rapier Clo., Purf. 168 FN77
Rasehill Clo., Rick. 74 BJ43
Rashleigh St. SW8 161 DH82
Peardon St.
Rashleigh Way (Horton Kirby), Dart. 208 FQ98
Rasper Rd. N20 98 DC47
Rastell Ave. SW2 181 DK89
Ratcliff Rd. E7 124 EJ64
Ratcliffe Clo. SE12 184 EG87
Ratcliffe Clo., Uxb. 134 BK69
Ratcliffe Cross St. E1 143 DX72
Ratcliffe La. E14 143 DY72
Ratcliffe Orchard E1 143 DX73
Rathbone Mkt. E16 144 EF71
Barking Rd.
Rathbone Pl. W1 273 M8
Rathbone Pl. W1 141 DK72
Rathbone Pt. E5 122 DU63
Nolan Way
Rathbone St. E16 144 EF71
Rathbone St. W1 273 L7
Rathbone St. W1 141 DJ71
Rathcoole Ave. N8 121 DM56
Rathcoole Gdns. N8 121 DM57
Rathfern Rd. SE6 183 DZ88
Rathgar Ave. W13 137 CH74
Rathgar Clo. N3 97 CZ54
Rathgar Clo., Red. 266 DG139
Rathgar Rd. SW9 161 DP83
Coldharbour La.
Rathlin, Hem.H. 41 BP22
Rathlin Wk. N1 142 DQ65
Clephane Rd.
Rathmell Dr. SW4 181 DK86
Rathmore Rd. SE7 164 EH78
Rathmore Rd., Grav. 191 GH87
Rathwell Path, Borwd. 78 CL39
Rats La., Loug. 84 EH38
Rattray Rd. SW2 181 DN84
Ratty's La., Hodd. 49 ED17
Raul Rd. SE15 162 DU81
Ravel Gdns., S.Ock. 148 FQ72
Ravel Rd., S.Ock. 148 FQ72
Raveley St. NW5 121 DJ63
Raven Clo. NW9 96 CS54
Eagle Dr.
Raven Clo., Rick. 92 BJ45
Raven Ct. E5 122 DU62
Stellman Clo.
Raven Ct., Hat. 45 CU19
Raven Rd. E18 102 EJ54
Raven Row E1 142 DV71
Ravencroft, Grays 171 GH75
Alexandra Clo.
Ravendale Rd., Sun. 195 BT96
Ravenet St. SW11 161 DH81
Strasburg Rd.
Ravenfield, Egh. 172 AW93
Ravenfield Rd. SW17 180 DF90
Ravenfield Rd., Welw.G.C. 29 CZ09
Ravenhill Rd. E13 144 EJ68
Ravenna Rd. SW15 179 CX85
Ravenoak Way, Chig. 103 ES50
Ravenor Pk. Rd., Grnf. 136 CB69
Ravens Clo., Brom. 204 EF96
Ravens Clo., Enf. 82 DS40
Ravens Clo., Red. 250 DF133
Ravens La., Berk. 38 AX19
Ravens Ms. SE12 184 EG85
Ravens Way
Ravens Way SE12 184 EG85
Ravens Wf., Berk. 38 AX19
Ravensbourne Ave., Beck. 183 ED94
Ravensbourne Ave., Brom. 183 ED94
Ravensbourne Ave., Stai. 174 BL88
Ravensbourne Cres., Rom. 128 FM55
Ravensbourne Gdns. W13 137 CH71
Ravensbourne Gdns., Ilf. 103 EN53
Ravensbourne Pk. SE6 183 EA87
Ravensbourne Pk. Cres. SE6 183 DZ87
Ravensbourne Pl. SE13 163 EB82
Ravensbourne Rd. SE6 183 DZ87
Ravensbourne Rd., Brom. 204 EG97
Ravensbourne Rd., Dart. 167 FG83
Ravensbourne Rd., Twick. 177 CJ86
Ravensbury Ave., Mord. 200 DC99
Ravensbury Ct., Mitch. 200 DD98
Ravensbury Gro.
Ravensbury Gro., Mitch. 200 DD98
Ravensbury La., Mitch. 200 DD98
Ravensbury Path, Mitch. 200 DD98
Ravensbury Rd. SW18 180 DA89
Ravensbury Rd., Orp. 205 ET98
Ravensbury Ter. SW18 180 DB88
Ravenscar Rd., Brom. 184 EE91
Ravenscar Rd., Surb. 198 CM103
Ravenscourt, Sun. 195 BT95
Ravenscourt Ave. W6 159 CU77
Ravenscourt Clo., Horn. 128 FL62
Ravenscourt Dr.
Ravenscourt Clo., Ruis. 115 BQ59
Ravenscourt Dr., Horn. 128 FL62
Ravenscourt Gdns. W6 159 CU77
Ravenscourt Gro., Horn. 128 FL61
Ravenscourt Pk. W6 159 CU76
Ravenscourt Pl. W6 159 CV77
Ravenscourt Rd. W6 159 CV77
Ravenscourt Rd., Orp. 206 EU97
Ravenscourt Sq. W6 159 CU76
Ravenscraig Rd. N11 99 DH49
Ravenscroft, Wat. 60 BY34
Ravenscroft Ave. NW11 119 CZ59
Ravenscroft Ave., Wem. 118 CM60
Ravenscroft Clo. E16 144 EG71
Ravenscroft Cres. SE9 185 EM90
Ravenscroft Pk., Barn. 79 CX42
Ravenscroft Rd. E16 144 EG71
Ravenscroft Rd. W4 158 CQ77
Ravenscroft Rd., Beck. 202 DW96
Ravenscroft Rd., Wey. 213 BQ111
Ravenscroft St. E2 142 DT68
Ravensdale Ave. N12 98 DC49
Ravensdale Gdns. SE19 182 DR94
Ravensdale Gdns., Houns. 156 BY83
Ravensdale Ms., Stai. 174 BH93
Ravensdale Rd. N16 122 DT59
Ravensdale Rd., Houns. 156 BY83
Ravensdell, Hem.H. 39 BF19
Ravensdon St. SE11 161 DN78
Ravensfield, Slou. 152 AX75
Ravensfield Clo., Dag. 126 EX63
Ravensfield Gdns., Epsom 216 CS106
Ravenshaw St. NW6 119 CZ64
Ravenshead Clo., S.Croy. 220 DW111
Ravenshill, Chis. 205 EP95
Ravenshurst Ave. NW4 119 CW56
Ravenside Clo. N18 101 DX51
Ravenside Retail Pk. N18 101 DX50
Ravenslea Rd. SW12 180 DF87
Ravensmead, Ger.Cr. 91 AZ50
Ravensmead Rd., Brom. 183 ED94
Ravensmede Way W4 159 CT77
Ravensmere, Epp. 70 EU31
Ravenstone SE17 162 DS78
Ravenstone Rd. N8 121 DN55
Ravenstone Rd. NW9 119 CT58
West Hendon Bdy.
Ravenstone St. SW12 180 DG88
Ravenswold, Ken. 236 DQ115
Ravenswood, Bex. 186 EY88
Ravenswood Ave., Surb. 198 CM103
Ravenswood Ave., W.Wick. 203 EC102
Ravenswood Clo., Cob. 230 BX115
Ravenswood Clo., Rom. 105 FB50
Ravenswood Ct., Kings.T. 178 CP93
Ravenswood Ct., Wok. 227 AZ118
Ravenswood Cres., Har. 116 BZ61
Ravenswood Cres., W.Wick. 203 EC102
Ravenswood Gdns., Islw. 157 CE81
Ravenswood Pk., Nthwd. 93 BU51
Ravenswood Rd. E17 123 EB56
Ravenswood Rd. SW12 181 DH87
Ravenswood Rd., Croy. 201 DP104
Ravensworth Rd. NW10 139 CV69
Ravensworth Rd. SE9 185 EM91
Ravensworth Rd., Slou. 131 AN69
Wentworth Ave.
Ravent Rd. SE11 278 C9
Ravent Rd. SE11 161 DM77
Ravey St. EC2 275 M4
Ravine Gro. SE18 165 ES79
Rawdon Dr., Hodd. 49 EA18
Rawlings La., Beac. 89 AQ48
Rawlings St. SW3 276 D8
Rawlings St. SW3 160 DF77
Rawlins Clo. N3 119 CY55
Rawlins Clo., S.Croy. 221 DY108
Rawnsley Ave., Mitch. 200 DD99
Raworth Ave., Hodd. 33 EB13
Rawreth Wk. N1 142 DQ67
Basire St.
Rawson St. SW11 160 DG81
Strasburg Rd.
Rawsthorne Clo. E16 145 EM74
Kennard St.
Rawstone Wk. E13 144 EG68
Rawstorne Pl. EC1 274 F2
Rawstorne St. EC1 274 F2
Rawstorne St. EC1 141 DP69
Ray Clo., Chess. 215 CJ107
Merritt Gdns.
Ray Fld., Welw.G.C. 29 CX06
Ray Gdns., Bark. 146 EU68
Ray Gdns., Stan. 95 CH50
Ray Lamb Way, Erith 167 FH79
Ray Lo. Rd., Wdf.Grn. 102 EJ51
Ray Massey Way E6 144 EL67
Ron Leighton Way
Ray Mead Ct., Maid. 130 AC70
Boulters La.
Ray Mead Rd., Maid. 130 AC72
Ray Rd., Rom. 105 FB50
Ray Rd., W.Mol. 196 CB99
Ray St. EC1 274 E5
Ray St. EC1 141 DN70
Ray St. Bri. EC1 274 E5
Ray Wk. N7 121 DM61
Andover Rd.
Raybarn Rd., Hem.H. 40 BG18
Rayburn Rd., Horn. 128 FN59
Raydean Rd., Barn. 80 DB43
Raydon Rd. (Cheshunt), Wal.Cr. 67 DX32
Raydon St. N19 121 DH61
Raydons Gdns., Dag. 126 EY64
Raydons Rd., Dag. 126 EY64
Rayfield, Epp. 70 EU29
Rayfield Clo., Brom. 204 EL100
Rayford Ave. SE12 184 EF87
Rayford Clo., Dart. 188 FJ85
Raylands Mead, Ger.Cr. 112 AW57
Bull La.
Rayleas Clo. SE18 165 EP81
Rayleigh Ave., Tedd. 177 CE93
Rayleigh Clo. N13 100 DR48
Rayleigh Rd.
Rayleigh Clo., Brwd. 109 GC44
Rayleigh Ct., Kings.T. 198 CM96
Rayleigh Ri., S.Croy. 220 DS107
Rayleigh Rd. E16 144 EH74
Wesley Ave.
Rayleigh Rd. N13 100 DQ48
Rayleigh Rd. SW19 199 CZ95
Rayleigh Rd., Brwd. 109 GB44
Rayleigh Rd., Wdf.Grn. 102 EJ51
Rayley La., Epp. 52 FA24
Raymead NW4 119 CW56
Tenterden Gro.
Raymead Ave., Th.Hth. 201 DN99
Raymead Clo., Lthd. 231 CE122
Raymead Way, Lthd. 231 CE122
Raymer Clo., St.Alb. 43 CE19
Raymer Wk., Horl. 269 DJ147
Raymere Gdns. SE18 165 ER80
Raymond Ave. E18 124 EF55
Raymond Ave. W13 157 CG76
Raymond Bldgs. WC1 274 C6
Raymond Clo. SE26 182 DW92
Raymond Clo., Abb.L. 59 BR32
Raymond Clo., Slou. 153 BE81
Raymond Ct. N10 98 DG52
Pembroke Rd.
Raymond Ct., Pot.B. 64 DC34
St. Francis Clo.
Raymond Cres., Guil. 258 AT135
Raymond Gdns., Chig. 104 EV48
Raymond Rd. E13 144 EJ66
Raymond Rd. SW19 179 CY93
Raymond Rd., Beck. 203 DY98
Raymond Rd., Ilf. 125 ER59
Raymond Rd., Slou. 153 BA76
Raymond Way, Esher 215 CG107
Raymonds Clo., Welw.G.C. 29 CY11
Raymonds Plain, Welw.G.C. 29 CY11
Raymouth Rd. SE16 162 DV77
Rayne Ct. E18 124 EF56
Rayner Twr. E10 123 EA59
Rayners Clo., Slou. 153 BC80
Rayners Clo., Wem. 117 CK64
Rayners Ct., Grav. 190 GB86
Rayners Ct., Har. 116 CA60
Rayners Cres., Nthlt. 135 BV69
Rayners Gdns., Nthlt. 135 BV68
Rayners La., Har. 116 CB61
Rayners La., Pnr. 116 BZ58
Rayners Rd. SW15 179 CY85
Raynes Ave. E11 124 EJ59
Raynham Ave. N18 100 DU51
Raynham Rd. N18 100 DU50
Raynham Rd. W6 159 CV77
Raynham St., Hert. 32 DS08
Raynham Ter. N18 100 DU50
Raynor Clo., Sthl. 136 BZ74
Raynor Pl. N1 142 DQ67
Elizabeth Ave.
Raynsford Rd., Ware 33 DY06
Raynton Clo., Har. 116 BY60
Raynton Clo., Hayes 135 BT70
Raynton Dr., Hayes 135 BT70
Raynton Rd., Enf. 83 DX37
Rays Ave. N18 100 DW49
Rays Ave., Wind. 151 AM80
Rays Hill, Dart. 208 FP98
Rays La., H.Wyc. 88 AC46
Rays Rd. N18 100 DW49
Rays Rd., W.Wick. 203 EC101
Raywood Clo., Hayes 155 BQ80
Raywood St. SW8 161 DH81
Gladstone Ter.
Reachview Clo. NW1 141 DJ66
Baynes St.
Read Ct., Wal.Abb. 68 EG33
Read Rd., Ash. 231 CK117
Read Way, Grav. 191 GK92
Reade Ct., Slou. 132 AV72
Victoria Rd.
Reade Wk. NW10 138 CS66
Denbigh Clo.
Readens, The, Bans. 234 DE116
Reading Arch Rd., Red. 250 DF134
Reading La. E8 142 DV65
Reading Rd., Nthlt. 116 CB64

Reading Rd., Sutt. 218 DC106
Reading Way NW7 97 CX50
Readings, The, Harl. 51 ET18
Readings, The, Rick. 73 BF41
Reads Clo., Ilf. 125 EP62
Chapel Rd.
Reads Rest La., Tad. 233 CZ119
Canons La.
Reapers Clo. NW1 141 DK67
Crofters Way
Reapers Way, Islw. 177 CD85
Hall Rd.
Reardon Ct. N21 100 DQ47
Cosgrove Clo.
Reardon Path E1 142 DV74
Reardon St. E1 142 DV74
Reaston St. SE14 163 DX80
Reckitt Rd. W4 158 CS78
Record St. SE15 162 DW79
Recovery St. SW17 180 DE92
Recreation Ave., Rom. 127 FC57
Recreation Ave. (Harold Wd.), Rom. 106 FM54
Recreation Rd. SE26 183 DX91
Recreation Rd., Brom. 204 EF96
Recreation Rd., Guil. 242 AW134
Recreation Rd., Sid. 185 ES90
Woodside Rd.
Recreation Rd., Sthl. 156 BY77
Recreation Way, Mitch. 201 DK97
Rector St. N1 142 DQ67
Rectory Chase, Brwd. 129 FX56
Rectory Clo. E4 101 EA48
Rectory Clo. N3 97 CZ53
Rectory Clo. SW20 199 CW97
Rectory Clo., Ash. 232 CM119
Rectory Clo., Dart. 167 FE84
Rectory Clo., Guil. 243 BD132
Rectory Clo., Hat. 46 DF17
Rectory Clo., Shep. 194 BN97
Rectory Clo., Sid. 186 EV91
Rectory Clo., Slou. 131 AQ69
Rectory Clo., Stan. 95 CH51
Rectory Clo., Surb. 197 CJ102
Rectory Clo., Ware 34 EK07
Rectory Clo., W.Byf. 212 BK113
Rectory Clo., Wind. 151 AN81
Rectory Cres. E11 124 EJ58
Rectory Fm. Rd., Enf. 81 DM38
Rectory Fld., Harl. 51 EP17
Rectory Fld. Cres. SE7 164 EJ80
Rectory Gdns. N8 121 DL56
Rectory Gdns. SW4 161 DJ83
Rectory Gdns., Ch.St.G. 90 AV48
Rectory Gdns., Hat. 45 CV18
Rectory Gdns., Nthlt. 136 BZ67
Rectory Gdns., Upmin. 129 FR61
Rectory Grn., Beck. 203 DZ95
Deri Ave.
Rectory Gro. SW4 161 DJ83
Rectory Gro., Croy. 201 DP103
Rectory Gro., Hmptn. 176 BZ91
Rectory Hill, Amer. 55 AP39
Rectory La. SW17 180 DG93
Rectory La., Ash. 232 CM118
Rectory La., Bans. 218 DF114
Rectory La., Berk. 38 AW19
Rectory La., Bet. 249 CT131
Rectory La., Edg. 96 CN51
Rectory La., Guil. 260 BM139
Rectory La., Harl. 51 EP17
Rectory La., Kings L. 58 BN28
Rectory La., Lthd. 246 BZ126
Rectory La., Loug. 85 EN40
Rectory La., Rad. 62 CN33
Rectory La., Rick. 92 BK46
Rectory La., Sev. 257 FJ126
Rectory La., Sid. 186 EV91
Rectory La., Stan. 95 CH50
Rectory La., Surb. 197 CH102
Rectory La., Wall. 219 DJ105
Rectory La., W.Byf. 212 BL113
Rectory La., West. 238 EL123
Rectory La. (Brasted), West. 240 EW123
Rectory Meadow, Grav. 190 GA92
Rectory Orchard SW19 179 CY91
Rectory Pk., S.Croy. 220 DS113
Rectory Pk. Ave., Nthlt. 136 BZ69
Rectory Pl. SE18 165 EN77
Rectory Rd. E12 125 EM64
Rectory Rd. E17 123 EB55
Rectory Rd. N16 122 DT62
Rectory Rd. SW13 159 CU82
Rectory Rd. W3 138 CP74
Rectory Rd., Beck. 203 EA95
Rectory Rd., Couls. 250 DB125
Rectory Rd., Dag. 146 FA66
Rectory Rd., Grays 170 GD76
Rectory Rd., Hayes 135 BU72
Rectory Rd., Houns. 155 BV81
Rectory Rd., Kes. 222 EK108
Rectory Rd., Maid. 130 AD70
Rectory Rd., Rick. 92 BK46
Rectory Rd., Sthl. 156 BZ76
Rectory Rd., Sutt. 200 DA104
Rectory Rd., Swans. 190 FY87
Rectory Rd., Til. 171 GK79
Rectory Rd., Welw.G.C. 29 CV06
Rectory Sq. E1 143 DX71
Rectory Way, Amer. 55 AP40
Rectory Way, Uxb. 115 BP62
Rectory Wd., Harl. 35 EQ14
Reculver Ms. N18 100 DU49
Lyndhurst Rd.
Reculver Rd. SE16 163 DX78
Red Anchor Clo. SW3 160 DE79
Old Ch. St.
Red Barracks Rd. SE18 165 EM77
Red Cedars Rd., Orp. 205 ES101
Red Cottage Ms., Slou. 152 AW76
Red Ct., Slou. 132 AS74
Red Hill, Chis. 185 EN92
Red Hill, Uxb. 113 BC60
Red Hills, Hodd. 48 DV19
Red Ho. Clo., Beac. 88 AH51
Red Ho. Clo., Ware 33 DY07
Red Ho. La., Bexh. 166 EX84
Red Ho. La., Walt. 195 BU103
Red Ho. Sq. N1 142 DQ65
Clephane Rd.
Red La., Dor. 264 CL141
Red La., Esher 215 CG107
Red La., Oxt. 254 EH134
Red Leaf Clo., Slou. 133 AZ74
Pickford Dr.
Red Lion Clo. SE17 162 DQ79
Red Lion Row
Red Lion Clo., Orp. 206 EW100
Red Lion Ct. EC4 274 E8
Red Lion Cres., Harl. 52 EW17
Red Lion Hill N2 98 DD54
Red Lion La. SE18 165 EN80
Red Lion La., Harl. 52 EW17
Red Lion La., Hem.H. 58 BM26
Red Lion La., Rick. 74 BG35
Red Lion La., Wok. 210 AS109
Red Lion Rd.
Red Lion Pl. SE18 165 EN81
Shooter's Hill Rd.
Red Lion Rd., Surb. 198 CM103
Red Lion Rd., Wok. 210 AS109
Red Lion Row SE17 162 DQ79
Red Lion Sq. SW18 180 DA85
Wandsworth High St.
Red Lion Sq. WC1 274 B7
Red Lion Sq. WC1 141 DM71
Red Lion St. WC1 274 B6
Red Lion St. WC1 141 DM71
Red Lion St., Chesh. 54 AP32
Red Lion St., Rich. 177 CK85
Red Lion Way, H.Wyc. 110 AE57
Red Lion Yd. W1 276 G2
Red Lion Yd., Wat. 76 BW42
High St.
Red Lo. Cres., Bex. 187 FD90
Red Lo. Gdns., Berk. 38 AU20
Red Lo. Rd., Bex. 187 FD90
Red Lo. Rd., W.Wick. 203 ED100
Red Oak Clo., Orp. 205 EP104
Red Oaks Mead, Epp. 85 ER37
Red Path E9 143 DZ65
Red Pl. W1 272 F10
Red Post Hill SE21 182 DR85
Red Post Hill SE24 162 DR84
Red Rd., Borwd. 78 CM41
Red Rd., Brwd. 108 FV49
Red St., Grav. 190 GA93
Red Willow, Harl. 51 EM18
Redan Pl. W2 140 DB72
Redan St. W14 159 CX76
Redan Ter. SE5 162 DQ82
Flaxman Rd.
Redbarn Clo., Pur. 219 DP111
Whytecliffe Rd. S.
Redberry Gro. SE26 182 DW90
Redbourn Rd., Hem.H. 40 BN16
Redbourn Rd., St.Alb. 42 CA18
Redbourne Ave. N3 98 DA53
Redbridge Enterprise Cen., Ilf. 125 EQ61
Redbridge Gdns. SE5 162 DS80
Redbridge La. E., Ilf. 124 EK58
Redbridge La. W. E11 124 EH58
Redburn St. SW3 160 DF79
Redbury Clo., Rain. 147 FH70
Redcar Clo., Nthlt. 116 CB64
Redcar Rd., Rom. 106 FM50
Redcar St. SE5 162 DQ80
Redcastle Clo. E1 142 DW73
Redchurch St. E2 275 P4
Redchurch St. E2 142 DT70
Redcliffe Clo. SW5 160 DB78
Warwick Rd.
Redcliffe Gdns. SW5 160 DB78
Redcliffe Gdns. SW10 160 DB78
Redcliffe Gdns., Ilf. 125 EN60
Redcliffe Ms. SW10 160 DB78
Redcliffe Pl. SW10 160 DC79
Redcliffe Rd. SW10 160 DC78
Redcliffe Sq. SW10 160 DB78
Redcliffe St. SW10 160 DB79
Redclose Ave., Mord. 200 DA99
Chalgrove Ave.
Redclyffe Rd. E6 144 EJ67
Redcourt, Wok. 227 BD115
Redcroft Rd., Sthl. 136 CC73
Redcross Way SE1 279 J4
Redcross Way SE1 162 DQ75
Redden Ct. Rd., Rom. 128 FL55
Redding Dr., Amer. 55 AN37
Reddings, Hem.H. 40 BN22
Reddings, Welw.G.C. 29 CW07
Reddings, The NW7 97 CT48
Reddings, The, Borwd. 78 CM41
Reddings Ave. (Bushey), Wat. 76 CB43
Reddings Clo. NW7 97 CT49
Reddington Clo., S.Croy. 220 DR109
Reddington Dr., Slou. 152 AY76
Reddins Rd. SE15 162 DU79
Redditch Ct., Hem.H. 40 BM16
Reddons Rd., Beck. 183 DY94
Reddown Rd., Couls. 235 DK118
Reddy Rd., Erith 167 FF79
Rede Ct., Wey. 195 BP104
Old Palace Rd.
Rede Pl. W2 140 DA72
Chepstow Pl.
Redehall Rd., Horl. 269 DP148
Redesdale Gdns., Islw. 157 CG80
Redesdale St. SW3 160 DF79
Redfern Ave., Houns. 176 CA87
Redfern Clo., Uxb. 134 BJ67
Redfern Gdns., Rom. 106 FK54
Redfern Rd. NW10 138 CS66
Redfern Rd. SE6 183 EC87
Redfield La. SW5 160 DA77
Redfield Ms. SW5 160 DA77
Redfield La.
Redford Ave., Couls. 219 DH114
Redford Ave., Th.Hth. 201 DM98
Redford Ave., Wall. 219 DL107
Redford Clo., Felt. 175 BT90
Redford Rd., Wind. 151 AK81
Redford Wk. N1 141 DP67
Britannia Row
Redford Way, Uxb. 134 BJ66
Redgate Dr., Brom. 204 EH103
Redgate Ter. SW15 179 CX86
Lytton Gro.
Redgrave Clo., Croy. 202 DT100
Redgrave Rd. SW15 159 CX83
Redhall Clo., Hat. 45 CT21
Redhall Ct., Cat. 236 DR123
Redhall Dr., Hat. 45 CT21
Redhall La., Rick. 74 BL39
Redheath Clo., Wat. 75 BT35
Redhill Common, Red. 266 DE135
Redhill Dr., Edg. 96 CQ54
Redhill Rd., Cob. 213 BP112
Redhill St. NW1 273 J2
Redhill St. NW1 141 DH68
Redhouse Rd., Croy. 201 DK100
Redhouse Rd., West. 238 EJ121
Redington Gdns. NW3 120 DB63
Redington Rd. NW3 120 DB63
Redland Gdns., W.Mol. 196 BZ98
Dunstable Rd.
Redlands, Couls. 235 DL116
Redlands Ct., Brom. 184 EF94
Redlands La., Dor. 263 CG142
Redlands Rd., Enf. 83 DY39
Redlands Rd., Sev. 256 FF124
Redlands Way SW2 181 DM87
Redleaf Clo., Belv. 166 FA79
Redleaves Ave., Ashf. 175 BP92
Redlees Clo., Islw. 157 CG84
Redman Clo., Nthlt. 136 BW68
Redmans La., Sev. 225 FD107
Redman's Rd. E1 142 DW71
Redmead La. E1 142 DU74
Wapping High St.
Redmead Rd., Hayes 155 BS77
Redmore Rd. W6 159 CV77
Redpoll Way, Erith 166 EX76
Redricks La., Harl. 35 ET09
Redriff Est. SE16 163 DZ76
Redriff Rd. SE16 163 DX77
Redriff Rd., Rom. 105 FB54
Redriffe Rd. E13 144 EF67
Redroofs Clo., Beck. 203 EB95
Redruth Clo. N22 99 DM52
Palmerston Rd.
Redruth Gdns., Rom. 106 FM50
Redruth Rd. E9 143 DX67
Redruth Rd., Rom. 106 FM50
Redruth Wk., Rom. 106 FM50
Redruth Rd.
Redstart Clo. E6 144 EL71
Columbine Ave.
Redstart Clo. SE14 163 DY80
Southerngate Way
Redstart Clo., Croy. 221 ED110
Redston Rd. N8 121 DK56
Redstone Hill, Red. 250 DG133
Redstone Hollow, Red. 266 DG135
Redstone Manor, Red. 250 DG134
Redstone Pk., Red. 250 DG134
Redstone Rd., Red. 266 DG135
Redvers Rd. N22 99 DN54
Redvers Rd., Warl. 237 DX118
Redvers St. N1 275 N1
Redwald Rd. E5 123 DX63
Redway Dr., Twick. 176 CC87
Redwing Clo., S.Croy. 221 DX111
Redwing Gro., Abb.L. 59 BU31
Redwing Path SE28 165 ER75
Redwing Ri., Guil. 243 BD132
Redwood, Egh. 193 BE96
Redwood, Slou. 130 AH68
Redwood Chase, S.Ock. 149 FW70
Redwood Clo. N14 99 DK45
The Vale
Redwood Clo. SE16 143 DY74
Redwood Clo., Ken. 220 DQ114
Redwood Clo., Uxb. 135 BP68
The Larches
Redwood Clo., Wat. 94 BW49
Redwood Dr., Hem.H. 40 BL22
Redwood Est., Houns. 155 BV79
Redwood Gdns. E4 83 EB44
Redwood Gdns., Chig. 104 EU50
Redwood Gdns., Slou. 131 AR73
Godolphin Rd.
Redwood Gro., Guil. 259 BC140
Redwood Ms. SW4 161 DH83
Hannington Rd.
Redwood Mt., Reig. 250 DA131
Redwood Ri., Borwd. 78 CN37
Redwood Twr. E11 123 ED62
Hollydown Way
Redwood Wk., Surb. 197 CK102
Redwood Way, Barn. 79 CX43
Redwoods SW15 179 CU88
Redwoods, Hert. 32 DQ08
Redwoods Clo., Buck.H. 102 EH47
Beech La.
Ree La. Cotts., Loug. 85 EN40
Englands La.
Reece Ms. SW7 160 DD77
Reed Ave., Orp. 205 ES104
Reed Clo. E16 144 EG71
Reed Clo. SE12 184 EG85
Reed Clo., Iver 133 BE72
Reed Clo., St.Alb. 62 CL27
Reed Pl., Shep. 194 BM102
Reed Pl., W.Byf. 211 BE113
Reed Pond Wk., Rom. 105 FF54
Reed Rd. N17 100 DT54
Reede Gdns., Dag. 127 FB64
Reede Rd., Dag. 146 FA65
Reede Way, Dag. 147 FB65
Reedham Clo. N17 122 DV56
Reedham Clo., St.Alb. 60 CA29
Reedham Dr., Pur. 219 DN113
Reedham Pk. Ave., Pur. 235 DN116
Reedham St. SE15 162 DU82
Reedholm Vil. N16 122 DR63
Winston Rd.
Reeds, The, Welw.G.C. 29 CX10
Reeds Cres., Wat. 76 BW40
Reeds Pl. NW1 141 DJ66
Royal College St.
Reeds Rest La., Tad. 233 CZ119
Reeds Wk., Wat. 76 BW40
Reedsfield Clo., Ashf. 175 BP91
The Yews
Reedsfield Rd., Ashf. 175 BP91
Reedworth St. SE11 278 E9
Reedworth St. SE11 161 DN77
Reenglass Rd., Stan. 95 CK49
Rees Dr., Stan. 96 CL49
Rees Gdns., Croy. 202 DT100
Rees St. N1 142 DQ67
Reesland Clo. E12 125 EN64
Reets Fm. Clo. NW9 118 CS58
Reeve Rd., Reig. 266 DC138
Reeves Ave. NW9 118 CR59
Reeves Cor., Croy. 201 DP103
Roman Way
Reeves Cres., Swan. 207 FD97
Reeves La., Harl. 50 EJ19
Reeves Ms. W1 276 F1
Reeves Ms. W1 140 DG73
Reeves Rd. E3 143 EB70
Reeves Rd. SE18 165 EP79
Reform Row N17 100 DT54
Reform St. SW11 160 DF82
Regal Clo. E1 142 DU71
Old Montague St.
Regal Clo. W5 137 CK71
Regal Ct. N18 100 DT50
College Clo.
Regal Cres., Wall. 201 DH104
Regal Dr. N11 99 DH50
Regal La. NW1 140 DG67
Regents Pk. Rd.
Regal Pl. E3 143 DZ69
Coborn St.
Regal Pl. SW6 160 DB80
Maxwell Rd.
Regal Row SE15 162 DW81
Queens Rd.
Regal Way, Har. 118 CL58
Regal Way, Wat. 76 BW38
Regalfield Clo., Guil. 242 AT130
Regan Clo., Guil. 242 AV129
Regan Way N1 275 M1
Regan Way N1 142 DS68
Regarder Rd., Chig. 104 EU50
Regarth Ave., Rom. 127 FE58
Regency Clo. W5 138 CL72
Regency Clo., Chig. 103 EQ50
Regency Clo., Hmptn. 176 BZ92
Regency Ct., Brwd. 108 FW47
Regency Ct., Brox. 49 DZ23
Berners Way
Regency Ct., Harl. 52 EU18
Regency Cres. NW4 97 CX54
Regency Dr., Ruis. 115 BS60
Regency Dr., W.Byf. 211 BF113
Madeira Rd.
Regency Gdns., Horn. 128 FJ59
Regency Gdns., Walt. 196 BW102
Regency Lo., Buck.H. 102 EK47
Regency Ms. NW10 139 CU65
High Rd.
Regency Ms., Beck. 203 EC95
Regency Ms., Islw. 177 CE85
Queensbridge Pk.
Regency Pl. SW1 277 N8
Regency St. SW1 277 N8
Regency St. SW1 161 DK77
Regency Ter. SW7 160 DD78
Fulham Rd.
Regency Wk., Croy. 203 DY100
Regency Wk., Rich. 178 CL86
Friars Stile Rd.
Regency Way, Bexh. 166 EX83
Regency Way, Wok. 227 BD115
Regent Ave., Uxb. 135 BP66
Regent Clo. N12 98 DC50
Nether St.
Regent Clo., Add. 212 BK109
Regent Clo., Grays 170 GC75
Regent Clo., Har. 118 CL58
Regent Clo., Houns. 155 BV81
Regent Clo., St.Alb. 43 CJ16
Regent Ct., Slou. 132 AS72
Stoke Poges La.
Regent Ct., Wind. 151 AR81
Regent Cres., Red. 250 DF132
Regent Gdns., Ilf. 126 EU58
Regent Gate, Wal.Cr. 67 DY34
Regent Pk. Ind. Est., Lthd. 231 CG118
Regent Pl. SW19 180 DB92
Haydons Rd.
Regent Pl. W1 273 L10
Regent Pl., Croy. 202 DT102
Grant Rd.
Regent Rd. SE24 181 DP86
Regent Rd., Epp. 69 ET30
Regent Rd., Surb. 198 CM99
Regent Sq. E3 143 EB69
Regent Sq. WC1 274 A3
Regent Sq. WC1 141 DL69
Regent Sq., Belv. 167 FB77
Regent St. NW10 139 CX69
Wellington Rd.
Regent St. SW1 277 M1
Regent St. SW1 141 DK73
Regent St. W1 273 J8
Regent St. W1 141 DH72
Regent St. W4 158 CN78
Regent St., Wat. 75 BV38
Regents Ave. N13 99 DM50
Regents Bri. Gdns. SW8 161 DL80
Regents Clo., Hayes 135 BS71
Park Rd.
Regents Clo., Rad. 61 CG34
Regents Clo., S.Croy. 220 DS107
Regents Clo., Whyt. 236 DS118
Regents Dr., Kes. 222 EK106
Regents Ms. NW8 140 DC68
Langford Pl.
Regent's Pk. NW1 272 E1
Regent's Pk. NW1 140 DG68
Regent's Pk. Est. NW1 273 K3
Regents Pk. Rd. N3 119 CZ55
Regents Pk. Rd. NW1 140 DF67
Regents Pk. Ter. NW1 141 DH67
Oval Rd.
Regent's Pl. NW1 273 K4
Regent's Pl. NW1 141 DJ70
Regent's Pl. SE3 164 EG82
Regents Pl., Loug. 84 EJ44
High Rd.
Regents Row E8 142 DU67
Regina Clo., Barn. 79 CX41
Regina Rd. N4 121 DM60
Regina Rd. SE25 202 DU97
Regina Rd. W13 137 CG74
Regina Rd., Sthl. 156 BY77
Regina Ter. W13 137 CH74
Reginald Rd. E7 144 EG66
Reginald Rd. SE8 163 EA80
Reginald Rd., Nthwd. 93 BT53
Reginald Rd., Rom. 106 FN53
Reginald Sq. SE8 163 EA80
Regis Pl. SW2 161 DM84
Regis Rd. NW5 121 DH64
Regnart Bldgs. NW1 273 L4
Reid Ave., Cat. 236 DR121
Reid Clo., Pnr. 115 BU56
Reidhaven Rd. SE18 165 ES77
Reigate Ave., Sutt. 200 DA102
Reigate Heath, Reig. 265 CX135
Reigate Hill, Reig. 250 DA133
Reigate Hill Clo., Reig. 250 DA131
Reigate Rd., Bet. 248 CN133
Reigate Rd., Brom. 184 EF90
Reigate Rd., Dor. 263 CJ135
Reigate Rd., Epsom 217 CT110
Reigate Rd., Horl. 268 DC146
Reigate Rd., Ilf. 125 ET61
Reigate Rd., Lthd. 231 CJ122
Reigate Rd., Red. 250 DD134
Reigate Rd., Reig. 250 DB134
Reigate Rd. (Sidlow), Reig. 266 DB141
Reigate Rd., Tad. 233 CY119
Reigate Way, Wall. 219 DL106
Reighton Rd. E5 122 DU62
Relay Rd. W12 139 CW73
Relf Rd. SE15 162 DU83
Relko Ct., Epsom 216 CR110
Relko Gdns., Sutt. 218 DD106
Relton Ms. SW7 276 C6
Rembrandt Clo. E14 163 ED76
Rembrandt Clo. SW1 276 F9
Rembrandt Ct., Epsom 217 CT107
Rembrandt Dr., Grav. 190 GD90
Rembrandt Rd. SE13 164 EE84
Rembrandt Rd., Edg. 96 CN54
Rembrandt Way, Walt. 195 BV103
Remington Rd. E6 144 EL72
Remington Rd. N15 122 DR58
Remington St. N1 274 G1
Remington St. N1 141 DP68
Remnant St. WC2 274 B8
Rempstone Ms. N1 142 DR68
Mintern St.
Remus Rd. E3 143 EA66
Monier Rd.
Rendle Clo., Croy. 202 DT99
Rendle Clo., Ware 32 DV05
Rendlesham Ave., Rad. 77 CF37
Rendlesham Rd. E5 122 DU63
Rendlesham Rd., Enf. 81 DP39
Rendlesham Way, Rick. 73 BC44
Renforth St. SE16 162 DW75
Renfree Way, Shep. 194 BM101
Renfrew Clo. E6 145 EN73
Renfrew Rd. SE11 278 F8
Renfrew Rd. SE11 161 DP77
Renfrew Rd., Houns. 156 BX82
Renfrew Rd., Kings.T. 178 CP94
Renmans, The, Ash. 232 CM116
Renmuir St. SW17 180 DF93
Rennell St. SE13 163 EC83
Rennels Way, Islw. 157 CE82
St. John's Rd.
Renness Rd. E17 123 DY55
Rennets Clo. SE9 185 ES85
Rennets Wd. Rd. SE9 185 ER85
Rennie Clo., Ashf. 174 BK90
Rennie Est. SE16 162 DV77
Rennie St. SE1 278 F2
Rennie St. SE1 141 DP74
Rennie Ter., Red. 266 DG135
Rennison Clo., Wal.Cr. 66 DT27
Allwood Rd.
Renown Clo., Croy. 201 DP102
Renown Clo., Rom. 104 FA53
Rensburg Rd. E17 123 DX57
Renshaw Clo., Belv. 166 EZ79
Grove Rd.
Renters Ave. NW4 119 CW58
Renton Dr., Orp. 206 EX101
Renwick Ind. Est., Bark. 146 EV67
Renwick Rd., Bark. 146 EV70
Repens Way, Hayes 136 BX70
Stipularis Dr.
Rephidim St. SE1 279 M7
Replingham Rd. SW18 179 CZ88
Reporton Rd. SW6 159 CY81
Repository Rd. SE18 165 EM79
Repton Ave., Hayes 155 BR77
Repton Ave., Rom. 127 FG55
Repton Ave., Wem. 117 CJ63
Repton Clo., Cars. 218 DE106
Repton Ct., Beck. 203 EB95
Repton Dr., Rom. 127 FG56
Repton Gdns., Rom. 127 FG55
Repton Grn., St.Alb. 43 CD17
Repton Gro., Ilf. 103 EM53
Repton Pl., Amer. 72 AU39
Repton Rd., Har. 118 CM56
Repton Rd., Orp. 206 EU104
Repton St. E14 143 DY72
Repton Way, Rick. 74 BN43
Repulse Clo., Rom. 105 FB53
Reservoir Clo., Th.Hth. 202 DR98
Reservoir Rd. N14 81 DJ43
Reservoir Rd. SE4 163 DY82
Reservoir Rd., Ruis. 115 BQ56
Resolution Wk. SE18 165 EM76
Reson Way, Hem.H. 40 BH21
Restell Clo. SE3 164 EE79
Restmor Way, Wall. 200 DG103
Reston Clo., Borwd. 78 CN38
Reston Path, Borwd. 78 CN38
Reston Pl. SW7 160 DC75
Hyde Pk. Gate
Restons Cres. SE9 185 ER86
Restormel Clo., Houns. 176 CA85
Retcar Clo. N19 121 DH61
Dartmouth Pk. Hill
Retcar Pl. N19 121 DH61
Retford Clo., Borwd. 78 CN38
The Campions
Retford Clo., Rom. 106 FN51
Retford Path, Rom. 106 FN51
Retford Rd., Rom. 106 FM51
Retford St. N1 275 N1
Retingham Way E4 101 EB47
Retreat, The NW9 118 CR57
Retreat, The SW14 158 CS83
South Worple Way
Retreat, The, Abb.L. 59 BQ31
Abbots Rd.
Retreat, The, Add. 212 BK106
Retreat, The, Amer. 72 AY39
Retreat, The, Brwd. 108 FV46
Costead Manor Rd.
Retreat, The (Hutton), Brwd. 109 GB44
Retreat, The, Egh. 172 AX92
Retreat, The, Grays 170 GB79
Retreat, The, Har. 116 CA59
Retreat, The, Kings L. 59 BQ31
Retreat, The, Maid. 150 AD80
Retreat, The, Orp. 224 EV107
Retreat, The, Surb. 198 CM100
Retreat, The, Th.Hth. 202 DR98
Retreat, The, Wor.Pk. 199 CV103
Retreat Clo., Har. 117 CJ57
Retreat Pl. E9 142 DW65
Retreat Rd., Rich. 177 CK85
Retreat Way, Chig. 104 EV48
Reubens Rd., Brwd. 109 GB44
Reunion Row E1 142 DV73
Pennington St.
Revel Rd., H.Wyc. 110 AD55

Reveley Sq. SE16 163 DY75
Howland Way
Revell Clo., Lthd. 230 CB122
Revell Dr., Lthd. 230 CB122
Revell Ri. SE18 165 ET79
Revell Rd., Kings.T. 198 CP95
Revell Rd., Sutt. 217 CZ107
Revelon Rd. SE4 163 DY84
Revels Clo., Hert. 32 DR07
Revels Rd., Hert. 32 DR07
Revelstoke Rd. SW18 179 CZ89
Reventlow Rd. SE9 185 EQ88
Reverdy Rd. SE1 162 DU77
Reverend Clo., Har. 116 CB62
Revesby Rd., Cars. 200 DD100
Review Rd. NW2 119 CT61
Review Rd., Dag. 147 FB67
Rewell St. SW6 160 DC80
Rewley Rd., Cars. 200 DD100
Rex Ave., Ashf. 174 BN93
Rex Clo., Rom. 105 FB52
Rex Pl. W1 276 G1
Reydon Ave. E11 124 EJ58
Reynard Clo. SE4 163 DY83
Foxwell St.
Reynard Clo., Brom. 205 EM97
Reynard Dr. SE19 182 DT94
Reynard Pl. SE14 163 DY79
Milton Ct. Rd.
Reynard Way, Hert. 32 DV09
Reynards Way, St.Alb. 60 BZ29
Reynardson Rd. N17 100 DQ52
Reynold Wk., Chesh. 54 AN27
Great Hivings
Reynolds Ave. E12 125 EN64
Reynolds Ave., Chess. 216 CL108
Reynolds Ave., Rom. 126 EW59
Reynolds Clo. NW11 120 DB59
Reynolds Clo. SW19 200 DD95
Reynolds Clo., Cars. 200 DF102
Reynolds Clo., Hem.H. 40 BG19
Reynolds Ct. E11 124 EF62
Cobbold Rd.
Reynolds Ct., Rom. 126 EX55
Reynolds Dr., Edg. 118 CM55
Reynolds Pl. SE3 164 EH80
Reynolds Pl., Rich. 178 CM86
Cambrian Rd.
Reynolds Rd. SE15 182 DW85
Reynolds Rd. W4 158 CQ76
Reynolds Rd., Beac. 88 AJ52
Reynolds Rd., Hayes 136 BW70
Reynolds Rd., N.Mal. 198 CR101
Reynolds Way, Croy. 220 DS105
Rheidol Ms. N1 142 DQ68
Rheidol Ter.
Rheidol Ter. N1 141 DP68
Rheingold Way, Wall. 219 DL109
Rheola Clo. N17 100 DT53
Rhoda St. E2 142 DT70
Brick La.
Rhodes Ave. N22 99 DJ53
Rhodes Clo., Egh. 173 BC92
Mullens Rd.
Rhodes Moorhouse Ct., Mord. 200 DA100
Rhodes St. N7 121 DM64
Mackenzie Rd.
Rhodes Way, Wat. 76 BX40
Rhodesia Rd. E11 123 ED61
Rhodesia Rd. SW9 161 DL82
Rhodeswell Rd. E14 143 DZ72
Rhododendron Ride, Egh. 172 AT93
Rhododendron Ride, Slou. 133 AZ69
Rhodrons Ave., Chess. 216 CL106
Rhondda Gro. E3 143 DY69
Rhyl Rd., Grnf. 137 CF68
Rhyl St. NW5 140 DG65
Rhys Ave. N11 99 DK52
Rialto Rd., Mitch. 200 DG96
Rib Vale, Hert. 32 DR06
Ribble Clo., Wdf.Grn. 102 EJ51
Prospect Rd.
Ribbledale, St.Alb. 62 CM27
Ribblesdale, Dor. 263 CH138
Roman Rd.
Ribblesdale, Hem.H. 40 BL17
Ribblesdale Ave. N11 98 DG51
Ribblesdale Ave., Nthlt. 136 CB65
Ribblesdale Rd. N8 121 DM56
Ribblesdale Rd. SW16 181 DH93
Ribblesdale Rd., Dart. 188 FQ88
Ribbon Dance Ms. SE5 162 DR81
Camberwell Gro.
Ribchester Ave., Grnf. 137 CF69
Ribston Clo., Brom. 205 EM102
Ribston Clo., Rad. 61 CK33
Wayside
Ricardo Path SE28 146 EW74
Byron Clo.
Ricardo Rd., Wind. 172 AV86
Meadow Way
Ricardo St. E14 143 EB72
Ricards Rd. SW19 179 CZ92
Rice Clo., Hem.H. 40 BM19
Ricebridge La., Reig. 265 CU137
Rich La. SW5 160 DB78
Warwick Rd.
Rich St. E14 143 DZ73
Richard Clo. SE18 164 EL77
Richard Foster Clo. E17 123 DZ59
Richard Ho. Dr. E16 144 EK72
Richard Stagg Clo., St.Alb. 43 CJ22
Richard St. E1 142 DV72
Commercial Rd.
Richards Ave., Rom. 127 FC57
Richards Clo., Har. 117 CG57
Richards Clo., Hayes 155 BR79
Richards Clo., Uxb. 134 BN67
Richards Clo. (Bushey), Wat. 95 CD45
Richards Fld., Epsom 216 CR109
Chessington Rd.
Richards Pl. E17 123 EA55
Richards Pl. SW3 276 C8
Richards Rd., Cob. 214 CB114
Richards Way, Slou. 131 AL74
Richardson Clo. E8 142 DT67
Clarissa St.
Richardson Clo., Green. 189 FU85
Steele Ave.
Richardson Clo., St.Alb. 62 CL27
Richardson Cres. (Cheshunt), Wal.Cr. 65 DP26
Richardson Pl., St.Alb. 44 CP22
Richardson Rd. E15 144 EE68
Richardson's Ms. W1 273 K5
Richbell Clo., Ash. 231 CK118
Richbell Pl. WC1 274 B6
Richborne Ter. SW8 161 DM80
Richborough Clo., Orp. 206 EX98
Richborough Rd. NW2 119 CX63
Richens Clo., Houns. 157 CD82
Riches Rd., Ilf. 125 EQ61
Richfield Rd. (Bushey), Wat. 94 CC45
Richford Rd. E15 144 EF67
Richford St. W6 159 CW75
Richings Way, Iver 153 BE76
Richland Ave., Couls. 218 DG114
Richlands Ave., Epsom 217 CU105
Richmer Rd., Erith 167 FG80
Richmond Ave. E4 101 ED50
Richmond Ave. N1 141 DM67
Richmond Ave. NW10 139 CW65
Richmond Ave. SW20 179 CY95
Richmond Ave., Felt. 175 BS86
Richmond Ave., Uxb. 135 BP65
Richmond Bri., Rich. 177 CK85
Richmond Bri., Twick. 177 CK86
Richmond Bldgs. W1 273 M9
Richmond Clo. E17 123 DZ58
Richmond Clo., Amer. 72 AT38
Richmond Clo., Borwd. 78 CR43
Richmond Clo., Epsom 216 CS114
Richmond Clo., Lthd. 230 CC124
Richmond Clo. (Cheshunt), Wal.Cr. 66 DW29
Richmond Clo., West. 238 EH119
Richmond Ct., Brox. 49 DZ20
Richmond Ct., Hat. 45 CV20
Cooks Way
Richmond Ct., Pot.B. 64 DC31
Richmond Cres. E4 101 ED50
Richmond Cres. N1 141 DM67
Richmond Cres. N9 100 DU46
Richmond Cres., Slou. 132 AU74
Richmond Cres., Stai. 173 BF92
Richmond Dr., Grav. 191 GL89
Richmond Dr., Shep. 195 BQ100
Richmond Dr., Wat. 75 BS39
Richmond Gdns. NW4 119 CU57
Richmond Gdns., Har. 95 CF51
Richmond Grn., Croy. 201 DL104
Richmond Gro. N1 141 DP66
Richmond Gro., Surb. 198 CM100
Richmond Hill, Rich. 178 CL86
Richmond Hill Ct., Rich. 178 CL86
Richmond Ms. W1 273 M9
Richmond Ms., Tedd. 177 CF93
Broad St.
Richmond Pk., Kings.T. 178 CQ87
Richmond Pk., Loug. 84 EJ44
High Rd.
Richmond Pk., Rich. 178 CQ87
Richmond Pk. Rd. SW14 178 CQ85
Richmond Pk. Rd., Kings.T. 178 CL94
Richmond Pl. SE18 165 EQ77
Richmond Rd. E4 101 ED46
Richmond Rd. E7 124 EH64
Richmond Rd. E8 142 DT66
Richmond Rd. E11 123 ED61
Richmond Rd. N2 98 DC54
Richmond Rd. N11 99 DL51
Richmond Rd. N15 122 DS58
Richmond Rd. SW20 199 CV95
Richmond Rd. W5 158 CL75
Richmond Rd., Barn. 80 DB43
Richmond Rd., Couls. 235 DH115
Richmond Rd., Croy. 201 DL104
Richmond Rd., Grays 170 GC79
Richmond Rd., Ilf. 125 EQ62
Richmond Rd., Islw. 157 CG83
Richmond Rd., Kings.T. 177 CK92
Richmond Rd., Pot.B. 64 DC31
Richmond Rd., Rom. 127 FF58
Richmond Rd., Stai. 173 BF92
Richmond Rd., Th.Hth. 201 DP97
Richmond Rd., Twick. 177 CG88
Richmond St. E13 144 EG68
Richmond Ter. SW1 277 P4
Richmond Ter. SW1 161 DL75
Richmond Ter. Ms. SW1 161 DL75
Parliament St.
Richmond Wk., St.Alb. 43 CK16
Richmond Way E11 124 EG61
Richmond Way W12 159 CX75
Richmond Way W14 159 CX76
Richmond Way, Lthd. 230 CB124
Richmond Way, Rick. 75 BQ42
Richmount Gdns. SE3 164 EG83
Rick Roberts Way E15 143 EC67
Rickard Clo. NW4 119 CV56
Rickard Clo. SW2 181 DM88
Rickard Clo., West Dr. 154 BK76
Rickards Clo., Surb. 198 CL102
Rickett St. SW6 160 DA79
Ricketts Hill Rd., West. 238 EK121
Rickfield Clo., Hat. 45 CU20
Rickman Cres., Add. 194 BH104
Rickman Hill, Couls. 235 DH117
Rickman Hill Rd., Couls. 235 DH118
Rickman St. E1 142 DW69
Mantus Rd.
Rickmans La., Slou. 112 AS64
Rickmansworth Bypass, Rick. 73 BF42
Rickmansworth La., Ger.Cr. 90 AY52
Rickmansworth Pk., Rick. 92 BK45
Rickmansworth Rd., Amer. 55 AQ37
Rickmansworth Rd., Nthwd. 93 BR52
Rickmansworth Rd., Pnr. 93 BV54
Rickmansworth Rd., Rick. 73 BE41
Rickmansworth Rd. (Harefield), Uxb. 92 BJ53
Rickmansworth Rd., Wat. 75 BS42
Ricksons La., Lthd. 245 BP127
Rickthorne Rd. N19 121 DL61
Landseer Rd.
Rickwood, Horl. 269 DH147
Woodhayes
Rickyard Path SE9 164 EL84
Ridding La., Grnf. 117 CF64
Riddings, The, Cat. 252 DT125
Riddings La., Harl. 51 ET19
Riddlesdown Ave., Pur. 220 DQ112
Riddlesdown Rd., Pur. 220 DQ111
Riddons Rd. SE12 184 EJ90
Ride, The, Brent. 157 CH78
Ride, The, Enf. 82 DW41
Ride La., Guil. 260 BK144
Rideout St. SE18 165 EM77
Rider Clo., Sid. 185 ES86
Riders Way, Gdse. 252 DW131
Ridgdale St. E3 143 EB68
Ridge, The, Bex. 186 EZ87
Ridge, The, Cat. 253 EB126
Ridge, The, Couls. 219 DL114
Ridge, The, Epsom 232 CQ118
Ridge, The, Lthd. 231 CD124
Ridge, The, Orp. 205 ER103
Ridge, The, Pur. 219 DJ110
Ridge, The, Surb. 198 CN99
Ridge, The, Twick. 177 CD87
Ridge, The, Wok. 227 BB117
Ridge Ave. N21 100 DQ45
Ridge Ave., Dart. 187 FF86
Ridge Clo. NW4 97 CX54
Ridge Clo. NW9 118 CR56
Ridge Clo. SE28 165 ER75
Ridge Clo., Bet. 264 CP138
Ridge Clo., Wok. 226 AV121
Ridge Crest, Enf. 81 DM39
Ridge Grn., Red. 267 DL137
Ridge Grn. Clo., Red. 267 DL137
Ridge Hill NW11 119 CY60
Ridge La., Wat. 75 BS36
Ridge Langley, S.Croy. 220 DU110
Ridge Lea, Hem.H. 39 BF20
Ridge Pk., Pur. 219 DK110
Ridge Rd. N8 121 DM58
Ridge Rd. N21 100 DQ46
Ridge Rd. NW2 119 CZ62
Ridge Rd., Mitch. 181 DH94
Ridge Rd., Sutt. 199 CY102
Ridge St., Wat. 75 BV38
Ridge Way SE19 182 DS93
Central Hill
Ridge Way, Dart. 187 FF86
Ridge Way, Felt. 176 BY90
Ridge Way, Iver 133 BE73
Ridgebank, Slou. 131 AM73
Ridgebrook Rd. SE3 164 EJ83
Ridgecroft Clo., Bex. 187 FC88
Ridgefield, Wat. 75 BS37
Ridgegate Clo., Reig. 250 DD132
Ridgehurst Ave., Wat. 59 BT34
Ridgelands, Lthd. 231 CD124
Ridgemead Rd., Egh. 172 AU90
Ridgemont Gdns., Edg. 96 CQ49
Ridgemount, Guil. 258 AV135
Ridgemount, Wey. 195 BS103
Ridgemount Ave., Couls. 235 DH117
Ridgemount Ave., Croy. 203 DX102
Ridgemount Clo. SE20 182 DV94
Anerley Pk.
Ridgemount End, Ger.Cr. 90 AY50
Ridgemount Gdns., Enf. 81 DP40
Ridgemount Way, Red. 266 DD136
Ridges, The, Guil. 258 AW139
Ridgeview Clo., Barn. 79 CX44
Ridgeview Lo., St.Alb. 62 CM28
Ridgeview Rd. N20 98 DB48
Ridgeway, Berk. 38 AT19
Ridgeway, Brwd. 109 GB46
Ridgeway, Brom. 204 EG103
Ridgeway, Dart. 189 FS92
Ridgeway, Epsom 216 CQ112
Ridgeway, Grays 170 GE77
Ridgeway, Rick. 92 BH45
Ridgeway, Welw.G.C. 30 DB09
Ridgeway, Wok. 226 AX115
Ridgeway, Wdf.Grn. 102 EJ49
Ridgeway, The E4 101 EB47
Ridgeway, The N3 98 DB52
Ridgeway, The N11 98 DF49
Ridgeway, The N14 99 DL47
Ridgeway, The NW7 97 CV49
Ridgeway, The NW9 118 CS56
Ridgeway, The NW11 119 CZ60
Ridgeway, The W3 158 CN76
Ridgeway, The, Amer. 55 AR40
Ridgeway, The, Croy. 201 DM104
Ridgeway, The, Enf. 81 DN39
Ridgeway, The, Ger.Cr. 112 AY55
Ridgeway, The, Guil. 259 BA135
Ridgeway, The, Har. 116 BZ57
Ridgeway, The (Kenton), Har. 117 CJ58
Ridgeway, The, Hert. 31 DM08
Ridgeway, The, Horl. 268 DG150
Ridgeway, The, Lthd. 214 CC114
Ridgeway, The (Oxshott), Lthd. 231 CD123
Ridgeway, The, Pot.B. 64 DD34
Ridgeway, The (Cuffley), Pot.B. 64 DE28
Ridgeway, The, Rad. 77 CF37
Ridgeway, The (Gidea Pk.), Rom. 127 FG56
Ridgeway, The (Harold Wd.), Rom. 106 FM53
Ridgeway, The, Ruis. 116 CA58
Ridgeway, The, St.Alb. 43 CG17
Ridgeway, The, S.Croy. 220 DS110
Ridgeway, The, Stan. 95 CJ51
Ridgeway, The, Wat. 75 BS37
Ridgeway Ave., Barn. 80 DF44
Ridgeway Ave., Grav. 191 GH90
Ridgeway Clo., Chesh. 54 AP28
Ridgeway Clo., Dor. 263 CG138
Ridgeway Clo., Hem.H. 58 BM26
London Rd.
Ridgeway Clo., Lthd. 214 CC114
Ridgeway Clo., Wok. 226 AX115
Ridgeway Ct., Red. 250 DF134
Ridgeway Rd.
Ridgeway Cres., Orp. 205 ES104
Ridgeway Cres. Gdns., Orp. 205 ES103
Ridgeway Dr., Brom. 184 EH91
Ridgeway Dr., Dor. 263 CG139
Ridgeway E., Sid. 185 ET85
Ridgeway Gdns. N6 121 DJ59
Ridgeway Gdns., Ilf. 124 EL57
Ridgeway Gdns., Wok. 226 AX115
Ridgeway Ind. Est., Iver 133 BF73
Ridgeway Rd. SW9 161 DP83
Ridgeway Rd., Chesh. 54 AN28
Ridgeway Rd., Dor. 263 CG138
Ridgeway Rd., Islw. 157 CE80
Ridgeway Rd., Red. 250 DE134
Ridgeway Rd. N., Islw. 157 CE79
Ridgeway Wk., Nthlt. 136 BY65
Fortunes Mead
Ridgeway W., Sid. 185 ES85
Ridgeways, Harl. 52 EY15
Ridgewell Clo. N1 142 DQ67
Basire St.
Ridgewell Clo. SE26 183 DZ91
Ridgewell Clo., Dag. 147 FB67
Ridgmont Rd., St.Alb. 43 CE21
Ridgmount Gdns. WC1 273 M5
Ridgmount Pl. WC1 273 M6
Ridgmount Rd. SW18 180 DB85
Ridgmount St. WC1 273 M6
Ridgway SW19 179 CX93
Ridgway, Wok. 228 BG115
Ridgway, The, Sutt. 218 DD108
Ridgway Gdns. SW19 179 CX94
Ridgway Pl. SW19 179 CY93
Ridgway Rd., Wok. 227 BF115
Ridgwell Rd. E16 144 EJ71
Riding, The NW11 119 CZ59
Golders Grn. Rd.
Riding, The, Wok. 211 BB114
Riding Ct. Rd., Slou. 152 AW80
Riding Hill, S.Croy. 220 DU113
Riding Ho. St. W1 273 K7
Riding Ho. St. W1 141 DH71
Riding La., Beac. 88 AF53
Ridings, The W5 138 CM70
Ridings, The, Add. 211 BE107
Ridings, The, Amer. 55 AR35
Ridings, The, Ash. 231 CK117
Ridings, The, Chesh. 72 AX36
Ridings, The, Chig. 104 EV49
Manford Way
Ridings, The, Cob. 214 CA112
Ridings, The, Epsom 232 CS115
Ridings, The (Ewell), Epsom 217 CT109
Ridings, The, Hert. 31 DN10
Ridings, The, Iver 153 BF77
Ridings, The, Lthd. 245 BS125
Ridings, The, Reig. 250 DD132
Ridings, The, Sun. 195 BU95
Ridings, The, Surb. 198 CN99
Ridings, The, Tad. 233 CZ120
Ridings, The, West. 238 EL117
Ridings, The, Wok. 228 BG123
Ridings Ave. N21 81 DP42
Ridings Clo. N6 121 DJ59
Hornsey La. Gdns.
Ridings La., Wok. 229 BP123
Ridlands Gro., Oxt. 254 EL130
Ridlands La., Oxt. 254 EK130
Ridlands Ri., Oxt. 254 EL130
Ridler Rd., Enf. 82 DS38
Ridley Ave. W13 157 CH76
Ridley Clo., Rom. 105 FH53
Ridley Rd. E7 124 EJ63
Ridley Rd. E8 122 DT64
Ridley Rd. NW10 139 CU68
Ridley Rd. SW19 180 DB94
Ridley Rd., Brom. 204 EF97
Ridley Rd., Warl. 236 DW118
Ridley Rd., Well. 166 EV81
Ridley Several SE3 164 EH82
Blackheath Pk.
Ridsdale Rd. SE20 202 DV95
Ridsdale Rd., Wok. 226 AV117
Riefield Rd. SE9 165 EQ84
Riesco Dr., Croy. 220 DW107
Riffel Rd. NW2 119 CW64
Riffhams, Brwd. 109 GB48
Rifle Pl. SE11 161 DN79
Rifle Pl. W11 139 CX74
Rifle St. E14 143 EB71
Rigault Rd. SW6 159 CY82
Rigby Clo., Croy. 201 DN104
Rigby Gdns., Grays 171 GH77
Rigby La., Hayes 155 BR75
Rigby Ms., Ilf. 125 EP61
Cranbrook Rd.
Rigden St. E14 143 EB72
Rigeley Rd. NW10 139 CU69
Rigg App. E10 123 DX60
Rigge Pl. SW4 161 DK84
Rigger Row SW11 160 DC83
Cinnamon Row
Riggindale Rd. SW16 181 DK92
Riley Rd. SE1 279 N6
Riley Rd. SE1 162 DT76
Riley Rd., Enf. 82 DW38
Riley St. SW10 160 DD79
Rinaldo Rd. SW12 181 DH87
Ring, The W2 272 B10
Ring, The W2 140 DD73
Ring Clo., Brom. 184 EH94
Garden Rd.
Ring Rd. W12 139 CW73
Ring Rd. N., Gat. 269 DH152
Ring Rd. S., Gat. 269 DH152
Ringcroft St. N7 121 DN64
Ringers Rd., Brom. 204 EG97
Ringford Rd. SW18 179 CZ85
Ringlet Clo. E16 144 EH72
Ringlewell Clo., Enf. 82 DV40
Central Ave.
Ringley Ave., Horl. 268 DG148
Ringley Pk. Ave., Reig. 266 DD135
Ringley Pk. Rd., Reig. 250 DC134
Ringmer Ave. SW6 159 CY81
Ringmer Gdns. N19 121 DL61
Sussex Way
Ringmer Pl. N21 82 DR43
Ringmer Way, Brom. 205 EM99
Ringmore Dr., Guil. 243 BC131
Ringmore Ri. SE23 182 DV87
Ringmore Rd., Walt. 196 BW104
Ringshall Rd., Orp. 206 EU97
Ringslade Rd. N22 99 DM54
Ringstead Rd. SE6 183 EB87
Ringstead Rd., Sutt. 218 DD105
Ringway N11 99 DJ51
Ringway, Sthl. 156 BY78
Ringway Rd., St.Alb. 60 CB27
Ringwold Clo., Beck. 183 DY94
Ringwood Ave. N2 98 DF54
Ringwood Ave., Croy. 201 DL101
Ringwood Ave., Horn. 128 FK61
Ringwood Ave., Orp. 224 EW110
Ringwood Ave., Red. 250 DF131
Ringwood Clo., Pnr. 116 BW55
Ringwood Gdns. E14 163 EA77
Inglewood Clo.
Ringwood Gdns. SW15 179 CU89
Ringwood Rd. E17 123 DZ58
Ringwood Way N21 99 DP46
Ringwood Way, Hmptn. 176 CA91
Ripley Ave., Egh. 172 AY93
Ripley Clo., Brom. 205 EM99
Ringmer Way
Ripley Clo., Croy. 221 EC107
Ripley Clo., Slou. 152 AY77
Ripley Gdns. SW14 158 CR83
Ripley Gdns., Sutt. 218 DC105
Ripley La., Lthd. 244 BN126
Ripley La., Wok. 228 BL123
Ripley Ms. E11 124 EE59
Wadley Rd.
Ripley Rd. E16 144 EJ72
Ripley Rd., Belv. 166 FA77
Ripley Rd., Enf. 82 DQ39
Ripley Rd., Guil. 244 BK128
Ripley Rd., Hmptn. 176 CA94
Ripley Rd., Ilf. 125 ET61
Ripley Rd., Wok. 244 BJ126
Ripley Vw., Loug. 85 EP38
Ripley Vil. W5 137 CJ72
Castlebar Rd.
Ripley Way, Epsom 216 CN111
Ripley Way, Hem.H. 39 BE19
Ripley Way (Cheshunt), Wal.Cr. 66 DV30
Riplington Ct. SW15 179 CU87
Longwood Dr.
Ripon Clo., Guil. 242 AT131
Ripon Clo., Nthlt. 116 CA64
Ripon Gdns., Chess. 215 CK106
Ripon Gdns., Ilf. 124 EL58
Ripon Rd. N9 100 DV45
Ripon Rd. N17 122 DR55
Ripon Rd. SE18 165 EP79
Ripon Way, Borwd. 78 CQ43
Ripon Way, St.Alb. 43 CK16
Rippersley Rd., Well. 166 EU81
Ripple Rd., Bark. 145 EQ66
Ripple Rd., Dag. 146 EV67
Rippleside Commercial Est., Bark. 146 EW68
Ripplevale Gro. N1 141 DM66
Rippolson Rd. SE18 165 ET78
Ripston Rd., Ashf. 175 BR92
Risborough Dr., Wor.Pk. 199 CU101
Risborough St. SE1 278 G4
Risdon St. SE16 162 DW75
Renforth St.
Rise, The E11 124 EG57
Rise, The N13 99 DN49
Rise, The NW7 97 CT51
Rise, The NW10 118 CR63
Rise, The, Amer. 55 AQ39
Rise, The, Bex. 186 EW87
Rise, The, Borwd. 78 CM43
Rise, The, Buck.H. 102 EK45
Rise, The, Dart. 167 FF84
Rise, The, Edg. 96 CP50
Rise, The, Epsom 217 CT110
Rise, The, Grav. 191 GL91
Rise, The, Grnf. 117 CG64
Rise, The, Lthd. 245 BS126
Rise, The, St.Alb. 61 CD25
Rise, The, Sev. 257 FJ129
Rise, The, Sid. 186 EW87
Rise, The, S.Croy. 220 DW109
Rise, The, Tad. 233 CW121
Rise, The, Uxb. 134 BM68
Rise Cotts., Ware 34 EK05
Widford Rd.
Rise Pk. Boul., Rom. 105 FF53
Rise Pk. Par., Rom. 105 FE54
Pettits La. N.
Risebridge Chase, Rom. 105 FF52
Risebridge Rd., Rom. 105 FF54
Risedale Clo., Hem.H. 40 BL23
Risedale Hill
Risedale Hill, Hem.H. 40 BL23
Risedale Rd., Bexh. 167 FB83
Risedale Rd., Hem.H. 40 BL23
Riseldine Rd. SE23 183 DY86
Riseway, Brwd. 108 FY48
Rising Hill Clo., Nthwd. 93 BQ51
Ducks Hill Rd.
Rising Sun Ct. EC1 274 G7
Risinghill St. N1 141 DM68
Risingholme Clo., Har. 95 CE53
Risingholme Clo. (Bushey), Wat. 94 CB45
Risingholme Rd., Har. 95 CE54
Risings, The E17 123 ED56
Risley Ave. N17 100 DQ53
Rita Rd. SW8 161 DL80
Ritches Rd. N15 122 DQ57
Ritchie Rd., Croy. 202 DV100
Ritchie St. N1 141 DN68
Ritchings Ave. E17 123 DY56
Ritcroft Clo., Hem.H. 41 BP21
Ritcroft Dr., Hem.H. 41 BP21
Ritcroft St., Hem.H. 41 BP21
Ritherdon Rd. SW17 180 DG89
Ritson Rd. E8 142 DU65
Ritter St. SE18 165 EN79
Ritz Ct., Pot.B. 64 DA31
Ritz Par. W5 138 CM70
Connell Cres.
Rivaz Pl. E9 142 DW65
Rivenhall End, Welw.G.C. 30 DC09
Rivenhall Gdns. E18 124 EF56
River Ave. N13 99 DP48
River Ave., Hodd. 49 EB16
River Ave., T.Ditt. 197 CG101
River Bank N21 100 DQ45
River Bank, E.Mol. 197 CE97
River Bank, T.Ditt. 197 CF99
River Bank, W.Mol. 196 BZ97
River Barge Clo. E14 163 EC75
Stewart St.
River Brent Business Pk. W7 157 CE76
River Clo. E11 124 EJ58
River Clo., Rain. 147 FH71
River Clo., Ruis. 115 BT58
River Clo., Sthl. 156 CC75
River Clo., Surb. 197 CK99
Catherine Rd.
River Clo., Wal.Cr. 67 EA34
River Crane Wk., Felt. 176 BX88
River Crane Wk., Twick. 177 CG86
River Dr., Upmin. 128 FQ58
River Front, Enf. 82 DR41
River Gdns., Cars. 200 DG103
River Gdns., Felt. 155 BV84
River Gdns., Maid. 150 AD75
River Gro. Pk., Beck. 203 DZ95
River Hill, Cob. 229 BV115
River Island Clo., Lthd. 231 CD121
River La., Lthd. 231 CD121
River La., Rich. 177 CK88
River Meads, Ware 33 EC11
River Pk., Berk. 38 AU18
River Pk., Hem.H. 40 BG22
River Pk. Ave., Stai. 173 BD91

River Pk. Gdns., Brom. 183 ED94
River Pk. Rd. N22 99 DM54
River Pl. N1 142 DQ66
River Reach, Tedd. 177 CJ92
River Rd., Bark. 145 ES68
River Rd., Brwd. 108 FS49
River Rd., Buck.H. 102 EL46
River Rd., Maid. 130 AC73
River Rd., Stai. 193 BF95
River Rd. Business Pk., Bark. 145 ET69
River St. EC1 274 D2
River St. EC1 141 DN69
River St., Ware 33 DY06
River St., Wind. 151 AR80
River Ter. W6 159 CW78
Crisp Rd.
River Vw., Enf. 82 DQ41
Chase Side
River Vw., Grays 171 GG77
River Vw., Welw.G.C. 29 CZ05
River Wk. (Denham), Uxb. 114 BJ64
River Wk., Walt. 195 BU100
River Way, Epsom 216 CR106
River Way, Harl. 36 EU10
River Way, Loug. 85 EN44
River Way, Twick. 176 CB89
River Wey Navigation, Guil. 242 AX132
River Wey Navigation, Wok. 227 BC122
Riverbank, Stai. 173 BF93
Riverbank Way, Brent. 157 CJ79
Rivercourt Rd. W6 159 CV77
Riverdale SE13 163 EC83
Lewisham High St.
Riverdale Dr. SW18 180 DB88
Strathville Rd.
Riverdale Dr., Wok. 227 AZ121
Riverdale Gdns., Twick. 177 CJ86
Riverdale Rd. SE18 165 ET78
Riverdale Rd., Bex. 186 EY87
Riverdale Rd., Erith 167 FB78
Riverdale Rd., Felt. 176 BZ91
Riverdale Rd., Twick. 177 CJ86
Riverdene, Edg. 96 CQ48
Riverdene Rd., Ilf. 125 EN62
Riverfield Rd., Stai. 173 BF93
Riverhead Clo. E17 101 DX54
Riverhead Dr., Sutt. 218 DA110
Riverhill, Sev. 257 FL130
Riverholme Dr., Epsom 216 CR109
Rivermead, E.Mol. 196 CC97
Rivermead, W.Byf. 212 BM113
Rivermead Clo., Add. 212 BJ108
Rivermead Clo., Tedd. 177 CH92
Rivermead Ct. SW6 159 CZ83
Rivermeads Ave., Twick. 176 CA90
Rivermill, Harl. 35 EQ13
Rivermount, Walt. 195 BT101
Rivermount Gdns., Guil. 258 AW137
Rivernook Clo., Walt. 196 BW99
Riversdale, Grav. 190 GE89
Riversdale Rd. N5 121 DP62
Riversdale Rd., Rom. 105 FB52
Riversdale Rd., T.Ditt. 197 CG99
Riversdell Clo., Cher. 193 BF101
Riversend Rd., Hem.H. 40 BJ23
Riversfield Rd., Enf. 82 DS41
Riverside NW4 119 CV59
Riverside SE7 164 EH76
Riverside, Cher. 194 BG97
Riverside (Eynsford), Dart. 208 FK103
Riverside, Dor. 247 CK134
Riverside (Runnymede), Egh. 173 BA90
Windsor Rd.
Riverside, Guil. 242 AX132
Riverside, Horl. 268 DG150
Riverside (London Colney), St.Alb. 62 CL27
Riverside, Stai. 193 BF95
Riverside (Wraysbury), Stai. 172 AW87
Riverside, Twick. 177 CH88
Riverside, The, E.Mol. 197 CD97
Riverside Ave., Brox. 49 EA22
Riverside Ave., E.Mol. 197 CD99
Riverside Business Cen. SW18 180 DB88
Riverside Clo. E5 122 DW60
Riverside Clo. W7 137 CE70
Riverside Clo., Kings L. 59 BP29
Riverside Clo., Kings.T. 197 CK98
Riverside Clo., Orp. 206 EW96
Riverside Clo., St.Alb. 43 CE21
Riverside Rd.
Riverside Clo., Stai. 193 BF95
Riverside Clo., Wall. 201 DH104
Riverside Ct. E4 83 EB44
Chelwood Clo.
Riverside Ct. SW8 161 DK79
Riverside Ct., Harl. 36 EW09
Riverside Ct., St.Alb. 43 CE22
Riverside Dr. NW11 119 CY58
Riverside Dr. W4 158 CR80
Riverside Dr., Esher 214 CA105
Riverside Dr., Guil. 259 BA144
Riverside Dr., Mitch. 200 DE99
Riverside Dr., Rich. 177 CH89
Riverside Dr., Rick. 92 BK46
Riverside Dr., Stai. 193 BF95
Riverside Dr. (Egham Hythe), Stai. 173 BE92
Riverside Gdns. N3 119 CY55
Riverside Gdns. W6 159 CV78
Riverside Gdns., Berk. 38 AU18
Riverside Gdns., Enf. 82 DQ40
Riverside Gdns., Wem. 138 CL68
Riverside Gdns., Wok. 227 BB121
Riverside Ind. Est., Bark. 146 EU69
Riverside Ind. Est., Enf. 83 DY44
Riverside Ms., Croy. 201 DL104
Wandle Rd.
Riverside Path (Cheshunt), Wal.Cr. 67 DY29
Church La.
Riverside Pl., Stai. 174 BK86
Riverside Retail Pk., Sev. 241 FH119
Riverside Rd. E15 143 EC68
Riverside Rd. N15 122 DU58
Riverside Rd. SW17 180 DB91
Riverside Rd., St.Alb. 43 CE21
Riverside Rd., Sid. 186 EY90
Riverside Rd., Stai. 173 BF94
Riverside Rd. (Stanwell), Stai. 174 BK85
Riverside Rd., Walt. 214 BX105
Riverside Rd., Wat. 75 BV44
Riverside Wk. SE1 278 B3
Riverside Wk. SE1 141 DM74
Riverside Wk., Bex. 186 EX87
Riverside Wk., Islw. 157 CE83
Riverside Wk., Kings.T. 197 CK96
High St.
Riverside Wk., Loug. 85 EP44
Riverside Way, Dart. 188 FL85
Riverside Way, St.Alb. 61 CD32
Riverside Way, Uxb. 134 BH67
Riverside W. SW18 160 DB84
Smugglers Way
Riversmead, Hodd. 49 EA18
Riversmeet, Hert. 31 DP10
Riverton Clo. W9 139 CZ69
Riverview Gdns. SW13 159 CV79
Riverview Gdns., Twick. 177 CF89
Riverview Gro. W4 158 CP79
Riverview Pk. SE6 183 EA89
Riverview Rd. W4 158 CP79
Riverview Rd., Epsom 216 CQ105
Riverview Rd., Green. 189 FU85
Riverway N13 99 DN50
Riverway, Stai. 194 BH95
Riverway Est., Guil. 258 AV142
Riverwood La., Chis. 205 ER95
Rivett Drake Rd., Guil. 242 AU130
Rivey Clo., W.Byf. 211 BF114
Rivington Ave., Wdf.Grn. 102 EK54
Rivington Ct. NW10 139 CU67
Rivington Cres. NW7 97 CT52
Rivington Pl. EC2 275 N3
Rivington St. EC2 275 M3
Rivington St. EC2 142 DS69
Rivington Wk. E8 142 DU67
Wilde Clo.
Rivulet Rd. N17 100 DQ52
Rixon Clo., Slou. 132 AY72
Rixon Ho. SE18 165 EP79
Barnfield Rd.
Rixon St. N7 121 DN62
Rixsen Rd. E12 124 EL64
Roach Rd. E3 143 EA66
Roads Pl. N19 121 DL61
Hornsey Rd.
Roakes Ave., Add. 194 BH103
Roan St. SE10 163 EC79
Roasthill La., Wind. 151 AK79
Boveney Rd.
Robarts Clo., Pnr. 115 BV57
Field End Rd.
Robb Rd., Stan. 95 CG51
Robbs Clo., Hem.H. 40 BG18
Robe End, Hem.H. 39 BF18
Robert Adam St. W1 272 F8
Robert Adam St. W1 140 DG72
Robert Ave., St.Alb. 42 CB24
Robert Clo. W9 140 DC70
Randolph Ave.
Robert Clo., Chig. 103 ET50
Robert Clo., Pot.B. 63 CY33
Robert Clo., Walt. 213 BV106
Robert Dashwood Way SE17 279 H9
Robert Dashwood Way SE17 162 DQ77
Robert Gentry Ho. W14 159 CY78
Comeragh Rd.
Robert Keen Clo. SE15 162 DU81
Cicely Rd.
Robert Lowe Clo. SE14 163 DX80
Robert Owen Ho. SW6 159 CX81
Robert Rd., Slou. 111 AR61
Robert St. E16 145 EP74
Robert St. NW1 273 J3
Robert St. NW1 141 DH69
Robert St. SE18 165 ER77
Robert St. WC2 278 A1
Robert St., Croy. 202 DQ104
High St.
Roberta St. E2 142 DU69
Roberton Dr., Brom. 204 EJ95
Roberts Clo. SE9 185 ER88
Roberts Clo., Orp. 206 EW99
Roberts Clo., Pnr. 115 BV57
Field End Rd.
Roberts Clo., Rom. 105 FH53
Roberts Clo., Stai. 174 BJ86
Roberts Clo., Sutt. 217 CX108
Roberts Clo. (Cheshunt), Wal.Cr. 67 DY30
Norwood Rd.
Roberts Clo., West Dr. 134 BL74
Roberts La., Ger.Cr. 91 BA50
Roberts Ms. SW1 276 F7
Robert's Pl. EC1 274 E4
Roberts Rd. E17 101 EB53
Roberts Rd. NW7 97 CY51
Roberts Rd., Belv. 166 FA78
Roberts Rd., Wat. 76 BW43
Tucker St.
Roberts Way, Egh. 172 AW94
Roberts Way, Hat. 45 CT19
Roberts Wd. Dr., Ger.Cr. 91 AZ50
Robertsbridge Rd., Cars. 200 DC102
Robertson Clo., Brox. 67 DY26
Robertson Ct., Wok. 226 AS118
Raglan Rd.
Robertson Rd. E15 143 EC67
Robertson St. SW8 161 DH82
Robeson St. E3 143 DZ71
Ackroyd Dr.
Robeson Way, Borwd. 78 CQ39
Robin Clo. NW7 96 CS48
Robin Clo., Add. 212 BK106
Bois Hall Rd.
Robin Clo., Hmptn. 176 BY92
Robin Clo., Rom. 105 FD52
Robin Clo., Ware 33 EC12
Robin Ct. SE16 162 DU77
Robin Cres. E6 144 EK71
Robin Gdns., Red. 250 DG132
Robin Gro. N6 120 DG61
Robin Gro., Brent. 157 CJ79
Robin Gro., Har. 118 CM58
Robin Hill, Berk. 38 AW20
Robin Hill Dr., Chis. 184 EL93
Robin Hood Clo., Slou. 131 AM74
Robin Hood Clo., Wok. 226 AT118
Robin Hood Cres., Wok. 226 AS117
Robin Hood Dr., Har. 95 CF52
Robin Hood Dr. (Bushey), Wat. 76 BZ39
Robin Hood Grn., Orp. 206 EU99
Robin Hood La. E14 143 EC73
Robin Hood La. SW15 178 CS91
Robin Hood La., Bexh. 186 EY85
Robin Hood La., Guil. 227 AZ124
Robin Hood La., Hat. 45 CU17
Robin Hood La., Sutt. 218 DA106
Robin Hood Meadow, Hem.H. 40 BM15
Robin Hood Rd. SW19 179 CV92
Robin Hood Rd., Brwd. 108 FV45
Robin Hood Rd., Wok. 226 AS117
Robin Hood Way SW15 178 CS91
Robin Hood Way SW20 178 CS91
Robin Hood Way, Grnf. 137 CF65
Robin Mead, Welw.G.C. 30 DA06
Robin Way, Guil. 242 AV130
Robin Way, Orp. 206 EV97
Robin Way (Cuffley), Pot.B. 65 DL28
Robin Way, Stai. 173 BF90
Robin Willis Way, Wind. 172 AU86
Robina Clo., Bexh. 166 EX84
Robina Clo., Nthwd. 93 BT53
Robinhood Clo., Mitch. 201 DJ97
Robinhood La., Mitch. 201 DJ97
Robinia Ave., Grav. 190 GD87
Robinia Clo., Ilf. 103 ES51
Robinia Cres. E10 123 EB61
Robins Clo., St.Alb. 62 CL27
High St.
Robins Clo., Uxb. 134 BJ71
Newcourt
Robins Ct. SE12 184 EJ90
Robins Gro., W.Wick. 204 EG104
Robins La., Epp. 85 EQ36
Robins Nest Hill, Hert. 47 DJ19
Robins Orchard, Ger.Cr. 90 AY51
Robins Rd., Hem.H. 40 BN22
Robins Way, Hat. 45 CT21
Robinscroft Ms. SE10 163 EB81
Sparta St.
Robinsfield, Hem.H. 40 BG20
Robinson Ave. (Cheshunt), Wal.Cr. 65 DP28
Robinson Clo., Horn. 147 FH66
Robinson Cres. (Bushey), Wat. 94 CC46
Robinson Rd. E2 142 DW68
Robinson Rd. SW17 180 DE93
Robinson Rd., Dag. 126 FA63
Robinson St. SW3 160 DF79
Christchurch St.
Robinsons Clo. W13 137 CG71
Robinsway, Wal.Abb. 68 EE34
Roundhills
Robinsway, Walt. 214 BW105
Robinswood Clo., Beac. 88 AJ50
Robinwood Gro., Uxb. 134 BM70
Robinwood Pl. SW15 178 CR91
Roborough Wk., Horn. 148 FJ65
Coltishall Rd.
Robsart St. SW9 161 DM82
Robson Ave. NW10 139 CU67
Robson Clo. E6 144 EL72
Linton Gdns.
Robson Clo., Enf. 81 DP40
Robson Clo., Ger.Cr. 90 AY50
Robson Rd. SE27 181 DP90
Robsons Clo., Wal.Cr. 66 DW29
Robyns Cft., Grav. 190 GE90
Robyns Way, Sev. 256 FF122
Roch Ave., Edg. 96 CM54
Rochdale Rd. E17 123 EA59
Rochdale Rd. SE2 166 EV78
Rochdale Way SE8 163 EA80
Octavius St.
Roche Rd. SW16 201 DM95
Roche Wk., Cars. 200 DD100
Rochelle Clo. SW11 160 DD84
Rochelle St. E2 275 P3
Rochemont Wk. E8 142 DT67
Pownall Rd.
Rochester Ave. E13 144 EJ67
Rochester Ave., Brom. 204 EH96
Rochester Ave., Felt. 175 BT89
Rochester Clo. SW16 181 DL94
Rochester Clo., Enf. 82 DS39
Rochester Clo., Sid. 186 EV86
Rochester Dr., Bex. 186 EZ86
Rochester Dr., Pnr. 116 BX57
Rochester Dr., Wat. 60 BW34
Rochester Gdns., Cat. 236 DS122
Rochester Gdns., Croy. 202 DS104
Rochester Gdns., Ilf. 125 EM59
Rochester Ms. NW1 141 DJ66
Rochester Pl. NW1 141 DJ65
Rochester Rd. NW1 141 DJ65
Rochester Rd., Cars. 218 DF105
Rochester Rd., Dart. 188 FN87
Rochester Rd., Grav. 191 GL87
Rochester Rd., Nthwd. 115 BT55
Rochester Rd., Stai. 173 BD92
Rochester Row SW1 277 L8
Rochester Row SW1 161 DJ77
Rochester Sq. NW1 141 DJ66
Rochester St. SW1 277 M7
Rochester St. SW1 161 DK76
Rochester Ter. NW1 141 DJ65
Rochester Wk. SE1 279 K2
Rochester Wk., Reig. 266 DB139
Castle Dr.
Rochester Way SE3 164 EH81
Rochester Way SE9 165 EM83
Rochester Way, Dart. 187 FD87
Rochester Way, Rick. 75 BP42
Rochester Way Relief Rd. SE3 164 EH81
Rochester Way Relief Rd. SE9 164 EL84
Rochford Ave., Brwd. 109 GA43
Rochford Ave., Loug. 85 EQ41
Rochford Ave., Rom. 126 EW57
Rochford Ave., Wal.Abb. 67 ED33
Rochford Clo. E6 144 EK68
Boleyn Rd.
Rochford Clo., Brox. 67 DY26
Rochford Clo., Horn. 147 FH65
Rochford Grn., Loug. 85 EQ41
Rochford St. NW5 120 DF64
Rochford Wk. E8 142 DU66
Wilman Gro.
Rochford Way, Croy. 201 DL100
Rochford Way, Maid. 130 AG72
Rochfords Gdns., Slou. 132 AW74
Rock Ave. SW14 158 CR83
South Worple Way
Rock Gdns., Dag. 127 FB64
Rock Gro. Way SE16 162 DV77
Blue Anchor La.
Rock Hill SE26 182 DT91
Rock Hill, Orp. 224 FA107
Rock St. N4 121 DN61
Rockall Ct., Slou. 153 BB76
Rockbourne Rd. SE23 183 DX88
Rockchase Gdns., Horn. 128 FL58
Rockdale Rd., Sev. 257 FH126
Rockells Pl. SE22 182 DV86
Rockfield Clo., Oxt. 254 EF131
Rockfield Rd., Oxt. 254 EF129
Rockford Ave., Grnf. 137 CG68
Rockhall Rd. NW2 119 CX63
Rockhampton Clo. SE27 181 DN91
Rockhampton Rd.
Rockhampton Rd. SE27 181 DN91
Rockhampton Rd., S.Croy. 220 DS107
Rockingham Ave., Horn. 127 FH58
Rockingham Clo. SW15 159 CT84
Rockingham Clo., Uxb. 134 BJ67
Rockingham Est. SE1 279 H7
Rockingham Est. SE1 162 DQ76
Rockingham Par., Uxb. 134 BJ66
Rockingham Rd., Uxb. 134 BH67
Rockingham St. SE1 279 H7
Rockingham St. SE1 162 DQ76
Rockland Rd. SW15 159 CY84
Rocklands Dr., Stan. 95 CH54
Rockleigh Ct., Brwd. 109 GA45
Hutton Rd.
Rockley Rd. W14 159 CX75
Rockliffe Ave., Kings L. 58 BN30
Rockmount Rd. SE18 165 ET78
Rockmount Rd. SE19 182 DR93
Rocks La. SW13 159 CU81
Rockshaw Rd., Red. 251 DJ127
Rockware Ave., Grnf. 137 CD67
Rockways, Barn. 79 CT44
Rockwell Gdns. SE19 182 DS92
Rockwell Rd., Dag. 127 FB64
Rockwood Pl. W12 159 CW75
Rocky La., Reig. 250 DF128
Rocliffe St. N1 274 G1
Rocombe Cres. SE23 182 DW87
Rocque La. SE3 164 EF83
Rodborough Rd. NW11 120 DA60
Rodborough Wk., Horn. 148 FJ65
Roden Clo., Harl. 36 EZ11
Roden Ct. N6 121 DK59
Hornsey La.
Roden Gdns., Croy. 202 DS100
Roden St. N7 121 DM62
Roden St., Ilf. 125 EN62
Rodenhurst Rd. SW4 181 DJ86
Rodeo Clo., Erith 167 FH81
Roderick Rd. NW3 120 DF63
Rodgers Clo., Borwd. 77 CK44
Roding Ave., Wdf.Grn. 102 EL51
Roding Gdns., Loug. 84 EL44
Roding La., Buck.H. 102 EL46
Roding La., Chig. 103 EN46
Roding La. N., Wdf.Grn. 102 EK54
Roding La. S., Ilf. 124 EK56
Roding La. S., Wdf.Grn. 124 EK56
Roding Ms. E1 142 DU74
Kennet St.
Roding Rd. E5 123 DX63
Roding Rd. E6 145 EP71
Roding Rd., Loug. 84 EL43
Roding Trd. Est., Bark. 145 EP66
Roding Vw., Buck.H. 102 EK46
Roding Way, Rain. 148 FK68
Rodings, The, Upmin. 129 FR58
Rodings, The, Wdf.Grn. 102 EJ51
Rodings Row, Barn. 79 CY43
Leecroft Rd.
Rodmarton St. W1 272 E7
Rodmarton St. W1 140 DF71
Rodmell Clo., Hayes 136 BY70
Rodmell Slope N12 97 CZ50
Rodmere St. SE10 164 EE78
Trafalgar Rd.
Rodmill La. SW2 181 DL87
Rodney Ave., St.Alb. 43 CG22
Rodney Clo., Croy. 201 DP102
Rodney Clo., N.Mal. 198 CS99
Rodney Clo., Pnr. 116 BY59
Rodney Clo., Walt. 196 BW102
Rodney Rd.
Rodney Ct. W9 140 DC70
Maida Vale
Rodney Cres., Hodd. 49 EA15
Rodney Gdns., Pnr. 115 BV57
Rodney Gdns., W.Wick. 222 EG105
Rodney Grn., Walt. 196 BW103
Rodney Pl. E17 101 DY54
Rodney Pl. SE17 279 J8
Rodney Pl. SE17 162 DQ77
Rodney Pl. SW19 200 DC95
Rodney Rd. E11 124 EH56
Rodney Rd. SE17 279 J8
Rodney Rd. SE17 162 DR77
Rodney Rd., Mitch. 200 DE96
Rodney Rd., N.Mal. 198 CS99
Rodney Rd., Twick. 176 CA87
Rodney Rd., Walt. 196 BW103
Rodney St. N1 141 DM68
Rodney Way, Guil. 243 BA133
Rodney Way, Rom. 104 FA53
Rodney Way, Slou. 153 BE81
Rodona Rd., Wey. 213 BR111
Rodway Rd. SW15 179 CU87
Rodway Rd., Brom. 204 EH95
Rodwell Clo., Ruis. 116 BW59
Rodwell Ct., Add. 212 BJ105
Garfield Rd.
Rodwell Pl., Edg. 96 CN51
Whitchurch La.
Rodwell Rd. SE22 182 DT86
Roe End NW9 118 CQ56
Roe Grn. NW9 118 CQ57
Roe Grn. Clo., Hat. 44 CS19
Roe Grn. La., Hat. 45 CT18
Roe Hill Clo., Hat. 45 CT19
Roe La. NW9 118 CP56
Roe Way, Wall. 219 DL108
Roebourne Way E16 165 EN75
Roebuck Clo., Ash. 232 CL120
Roebuck Clo., Felt. 175 BV91
Roebuck Clo., Reig. 250 DA134
Roebuck Grn., Slou. 131 AL74
Roebuck La. N17 100 DT51
High Rd.
Roebuck La., Buck.H. 102 EJ45
Roebuck Rd., Chess. 216 CN106
Roebuck Rd., Ilf. 104 EV50
Roedean Ave., Enf. 82 DW39
Roedean Clo., Enf. 82 DW39
Roedean Clo., Orp. 224 EV105
Roedean Cres. SW15 178 CS86
Roedean Dr., Rom. 127 FE56
Roefields Clo., Hem.H. 40 BG24
Roehampton Clo. SW15 159 CU84
Roehampton Clo., Grav. 191 GL87
Roehampton Dr., Chis. 185 EQ93
Roehampton Gate SW15 178 CS86
Roehampton High St. SW15 179 CV87
Roehampton La. SW15 159 CU84
Roehampton Vale SW15 178 CS90
Roehyde Way, Hat. 44 CS20
Roestock Gdns., St.Alb. 44 CS22
Roestock La., St.Alb. 44 CR23
Rofant Rd., Nthwd. 93 BS51
Roffes La., Cat. 236 DR124
Roffey Clo., Horl. 268 DF148
Court Lo. Rd.
Roffey Clo., Pur. 235 DP116
Roffey St. E14 163 EC75
Roffords, Wok. 226 AV117
Rogate Ho. E5 122 DU62
Muir Rd.
Roger St. WC1 274 C5
Roger St. WC1 141 DM70
Rogers Clo., Cat. 236 DV122
Tillingdown Hill
Rogers Clo., Couls. 235 DP118
Rogers Ct., Swan. 207 FG98
Rogers Gdns., Dag. 126 FA64
Rogers La., Slou. 132 AT67
Rogers La., Warl. 237 DZ118
Rogers Mead, Gdse. 252 DV132
Ivy Mill La.
Rogers Rd. E16 144 EF72
Rogers Rd. SW17 180 DD91
Rogers Rd., Dag. 126 FA64
Rogers Rd., Grays 170 GC77
Rogers Ruff, Nthwd. 93 BQ53
Rogers Wk. N12 98 DB48
Brook Meadow
Rojack Rd. SE23 183 DX88
Roke Clo., Ken. 220 DQ114
Roke Lo. Rd., Ken. 219 DP113
Roke Rd., Ken. 236 DQ115
Rokeby Ct., Wok. 226 AT117
Rokeby Gdns., Wdf.Grn. 102 EG53
Rokeby Pl. SW20 179 CV94
Rokeby Rd. SE4 163 DZ82
Rokeby St. E15 144 EE67
Roker Pk. Ave., Uxb. 114 BL63
Rokesby Clo., Well. 165 ER82
Rokesby Pl., Wem. 117 CK64
Rokesby Rd., Slou. 131 AM69
Rokesly Ave. N8 121 DL57
Rokewood Ms., Ware 33 DX05
Roland Gdns. SW7 160 DC78
Roland Gdns., Felt. 176 BZ90
Roland Ms. E1 143 DX71
Stepney Grn.
Roland Rd. E17 123 ED56
Roland St., St.Alb. 43 CG20
Roland Way SE17 162 DR78
Roland Way SW7 160 DC78
Roland Gdns.
Roland Way, Wor.Pk. 199 CT103
Roles Gro., Rom. 126 EX56
Rolfe Clo., Barn. 80 DE42
Rolfe Clo., Beac. 89 AL54
Rolinsden Way, Kes. 222 EK105
Roll Gdns., Ilf. 125 EN57
Rollesby Rd., Chess. 216 CN107
Rollesby Way SE28 146 EW73
Rolleston Ave., Orp. 205 EP100
Rolleston Clo., Orp. 205 EP101
Rolleston Rd., S.Croy. 220 DR108
Rollins St. SE15 162 DW79
Rollit Cres., Houns. 176 CA85
Rollit St. N7 121 DM64
Hornsey Rd.
Rollo Rd., Swan. 187 FF94
Rolls Bldgs. EC4 274 D8
Rolls Pk. Ave. E4 101 EA51
Rolls Pk. Rd. E4 101 EB50
Rolls Pas. EC4 274 D8
Rolls Rd. SE1 162 DT78
Rollscourt Ave. SE24 182 DQ85
Rollswood, Welw.G.C. 29 CY12
Rolt St. SE8 163 DY79
Rolvenden Gdns., Brom. 184 EK94
Rolvenden Pl. N17 100 DU53
Manor Rd.
Rom Cres., Rom. 127 FF59
Rom Valley Way, Rom. 127 FE59
Roma Read Clo. SW15 179 CV87
Bessborough Rd.
Roma Rd. E17 123 DY55
Roman Clo. W3 158 CP75
Avenue Gdns.
Roman Clo., Felt. 176 BW85
Roman Clo., Rain. 147 FD68
Roman Clo. (Harefield), Uxb. 92 BH53
Roman Gdns., Kings L. 59 BP30
Roman Ho., Rain. 147 FD68
Roman Clo.
Roman Ind. Est., Croy. 202 DS101
Roman Ms., Hodd. 49 EA16
North Rd.
Roman Ri. SE19 182 DR93
Roman Rd. E2 142 DW69
Roman Rd. E3 143 DY68
Roman Rd. E6 144 EL70
Roman Rd. N10 99 DH52
Roman Rd. NW2 119 CW62
Roman Rd. W4 159 CT77
Roman Rd., Brwd. 109 GC41
Roman Rd., Dor. 263 CG138
Roman Rd., Grav. 190 GC90
Roman Rd., Hert. 32 DV14
Roman Rd., Ilf. 145 EP65
Roman Sq. SE28 146 EU74
Roman St., Hodd. 49 EA16
Roman Vale, Harl. 36 EW10
Roman Vil. Rd. (South Darenth), Dart. 188 FQ92
Roman Way N7 141 DM65
Roman Way SE15 162 DW80
Clifton Way
Roman Way, Croy. 201 DP103
Roman Way, Dart. 187 FE85
Roman Way, Enf. 82 DT43
Roman Way, Slou. 131 AP71
Roman Way Ind. Est. N1 141 DM66
Offord St.
Romanfield Rd. SW2 181 DM87
Romanhurst Ave., Brom. 204 EE98
Romanhurst Gdns., Brom. 204 EE98

Romans End, St.Alb. 42 CC22
Romans Way, Wok. 228 BG115
Romany Gdns. E17 101 DY53
McEntee Ave.
Romany Gdns., Sutt. 200 DA101
Romany Ri., Orp. 205 EQ102
Romberg Rd. SW17 180 DG90
Romborough Gdns. SE13 183 EC85
Romborough Way SE13 183 EC85
Romeland, Borwd. 77 CK44
Romeland, Wal.Abb. 67 EC33
Romeland Hill, St.Alb. 42 CC20
Romero Clo. SW9 161 DM83
Stockwell Rd.
Romero Sq. SE3 164 EJ84
Romeyn Rd. SW16 181 DM90
Romford Rd. E7 124 EH64
Romford Rd. E12 124 EL63
Romford Rd. E15 144 EE66
Romford Rd., Chig. 104 EU48
Romford Rd., Rom. 104 EY52
Romford Rd., S.Ock. 148 FQ73
Romford St. E1 142 DU71
Romilly Dr., Wat. 94 BY48
Romilly Rd. N4 121 DP61
Romilly St. W1 273 M10
Romilly St. W1 141 DK73
Rommany Rd. SE27 182 DR91
Romney Chase, Horn. 128 FM58
Romney Clo. N17 100 DV53
Romney Clo. NW11 120 DC60
Romney Clo. SE14 162 DW80
Kender St.
Romney Clo., Ashf. 175 BQ92
Romney Clo., Chess. 216 CL105
Romney Clo., Har. 116 CA59
Romney Dr., Brom. 184 EK94
Romney Dr., Har. 116 CA59
Romney Gdns., Bexh. 166 EZ81
Romney Lock Rd., Wind. 151 AR80
Romney Ms. W1 272 F6
Romney Par., Hayes 135 BR68
Romney Rd.
Romney Rd. SE10 163 EC79
Romney Rd., Grav. 190 GE90
Romney Rd., Hayes 135 BR68
Romney Rd., N.Mal. 198 CR100
Romney Row NW2 119 CX61
Brent Ter.
Romney St. SW1 277 N7
Romney St. SW1 161 DL76
Romola Rd. SE24 181 DP88
Romsey Clo., Orp. 223 EP105
Romsey Clo., Slou. 153 AZ76
Romsey Dr., Slou. 111 AR62
Romsey Gdns., Dag. 146 EX67
Romsey Rd. W13 137 CG73
Romsey Rd., Dag. 146 EX67
Ron Leighton Way E6 144 EL67
Rona Rd. NW3 120 DG63
Rona Wk. N1 142 DR65
Clephane Rd.
Ronald Ave. E15 144 EE69
Ronald Clo., Beck. 203 DZ98
Ronald Rd., Beac. 89 AM53
Ronald Rd., Rom. 106 FN53
Ronald St. E1 142 DW72
Devonport St.
Ronalds Rd. N5 121 DN64
Ronalds Rd., Brom. 204 EG95
Ronaldsay Spur, Slou. 132 AS71
Ronaldstone Rd., Sid. 185 ES86
Ronart St., Har. 117 CF55
Stuart Rd.
Rondu Rd. NW2 119 CY64
Ronelean Rd., Surb. 198 CM104
Roneo Cor., Horn. 127 FF60
Roneo Link, Horn. 127 FF60
Ronfearn Ave., Orp. 206 EX99
Ronneby Clo., Wey. 195 BS104
Ronson Way, Lthd. 231 CG121
Randalls Rd.
Ronver Rd. SE12 184 EF87
Rood La. EC3 275 M10
Rood La. EC3 142 DS73
Rook Clo., Horn. 147 FG66
Rook La., Cat. 235 DM124
Rook Rd., H.Wyc. 110 AD59
Rook Wk. E6 144 EL72
Allhallows Rd.
Rookby Ct. N21 99 DP47
Carpenter Gdns.
Rookdean, Sev. 256 FC122
Rooke Way SE10 164 EF78
Rookeries Clo., Felt. 175 BV90
Rookery, The, Dor. 262 CA138
Rookery, The, Grays 169 FU79
Rookery Clo. NW9 119 CT57
Rookery Clo., Lthd. 231 CE124
Rookery Ct., Grays 169 FU79
Rookery Cres., Dag. 147 FB66
Rookery Dr., Chis. 205 EN95
Rookery Dr., Dor. 262 CA138
Rookery Gdns., Orp. 206 EW99
Rookery Hill, Ash. 232 CN118
Rookery Hill, Red. 269 DN145
Rookery La., Brom. 204 EK100
Rookery La., Grays 170 GD78
Rookery La., Horl. 269 DN146
Rookery Rd. SW4 161 DJ84
Rookery Rd., Orp. 223 EM110
Rookery Rd., Stai. 174 BH92
Rookery Vw., Grays 170 GD78
Rookery Way NW9 119 CT57
Rookery Way, Tad. 249 CZ127
Rookes All., Hert. 32 DR09
Gascoyne Way
Rookesley Rd., Orp. 206 EX101
Rookfield Ave. N10 121 DJ56
Rookfield Clo. N10 121 DJ56
Cranmore Way
Rookley Clo., Sutt. 218 DB110
Rooks Clo., Welw.G.C. 29 CX10
Rooks Hill, Rick. 74 BK42
Rooks Hill, Welw.G.C. 29 CW10
Rooksmead Rd., Sun. 195 BT96
Rookstone Rd. SW17 180 DF92
Rookwood Ave., Loug. 85 EQ41
Rookwood Ave., N.Mal. 199 CU98
Rookwood Ave., Wall. 219 DK105
Rookwood Clo., Grays 170 GB77
Rookwood Clo., Red. 251 DH129
Rookwood Ct., Guil. 258 AW137
Rookwood Gdns. E4 102 EF46
Whitehall Rd.
Rookwood Gdns., Loug. 85 EQ41
Rookwood Ho., Bark. 145 ER68
St. Marys
Rookwood Rd. N16 122 DT59
Roosevelt Way, Dag. 147 FD65
Rootes Dr. W10 139 CX70
Roothill La., Bet. 264 CN140
Rope St. SE16 163 DY77
Rope Wk., Sun. 196 BW97
Rope Wk. Gdns. E1 142 DU72
Commercial Rd.
Rope Yd. Rails SE18 165 EP76
Ropemaker Rd. SE16 163 DY76
Ropemaker St. EC2 275 K6
Ropemaker St. EC2 142 DR71
Ropemakers Flds. E14 143 DZ73
Narrow St.
Roper La. SE1 279 N5
Roper St. SE9 185 EM86
Roper Way, Mitch. 200 DG96
Ropers Ave. E4 101 EC50
Ropers Wk. SW2 181 DN87
Brockwell Pk. Gdns.
Ropery St. E3 143 DZ70
Ropley St. E2 142 DU68
Rosa Alba Ms. N5 122 DQ63
Kelross Rd.
Rosa Ave., Ashf. 174 BN91
Rosaline Rd. SW6 159 CY80
Rosamond St. SE26 182 DV90
Rosamun St., Sthl. 156 BY77
Rosamund Clo., S.Croy. 220 DR105
Rosary, The, Egh. 193 BE96
Rosary Clo., Houns. 156 BY82
Rosary Ct., Pot.B. 64 DB30
Rosary Gdns. SW7 160 DC77
Rosary Gdns., Ashf. 175 BP91
Rosaville Rd. SW6 159 CZ80
Roscoe St. EC1 275 J5
Roscoff Clo., Edg. 96 CQ53
Rose All. SE1 279 J2
Rose All. SE1 142 DQ74
Rose & Crown Ct. EC2 275 H8
Rose & Crown Yd. SW1 277 L2
Rose Ave. E18 102 EH54
Rose Ave., Grav. 191 GL88
Rose Ave., Mitch. 200 DF95
Rose Ave., Mord. 200 DC99
Rose Bank, Brwd. 108 FX48
Rose Bank Cotts., Wok. 226 AY122
Rose Bates Dr. NW9 118 CN56
Rose Bushes, Epsom 233 CV116
Rose Ct. E1 142 DS71
Sandy's Row
Rose Ct. SE26 182 DV89
Rose Ct., Pnr. 116 BW55
Nursery Rd.
Rose Ct., Wal.Cr. 66 DU27
Rose Dale, Orp. 205 EP103
Rose Dr., Chesh. 54 AR33
Rose End, Wor.Pk. 199 CX102
Rose Gdn. Clo., Edg. 96 CL51
Rose Gdns. W5 157 CK76
Rose Gdns., Felt. 175 BU89
Rose Gdns., Sthl. 136 CA70
Rose Gdns., Stai. 174 BK87
Diamedes Ave.
Rose Gdns., Wat. 75 BU43
Rose Glen NW9 118 CR56
Rose Glen, Rom. 127 FE60
Rose Hill, Dor. 263 CG137
Rose Hill, Slou. 130 AG67
Rose Hill, Sutt. 200 DB103
Rose La., Rom. 126 EX55
Rose La., Wok. 228 BJ121
Rose Lawn (Bushey), Wat. 94 CC46
Rose Sq. SW3 276 A10
Rose Sq. SW3 160 DD78
Rose St. WC2 273 P10
Rose St., Grav. 190 GB86
Rose Vale, Hodd. 49 EA17
Rose Valley, Brwd. 108 FW48
Rose Vil., Dart. 188 FP87
Rose Wk., Pur. 219 DK111
Rose Wk., St.Alb. 43 CJ18
Rose Wk., Slou. 131 AP71
Birch Gro.
Rose Wk., Surb. 198 CP99
Rose Wk., W.Wick. 203 ED103
Rose Wk., The, Rad. 77 CH37
Rose Way SE12 184 EG85
Rose Way, Edg. 96 CQ49
Stoneyfields La.
Roseacre, Oxt. 254 EG134
Roseacre Clo. W13 137 CH71
Middlefielde
Roseacre Clo., Horn. 128 FM60
Roseacre Clo., Shep. 194 BN99
Roseacre Gdns., Guil. 259 BF140
Roseacre Gdns., Welw.G.C. 30 DD09
Roseacre Rd., Well. 166 EV83
Roseary Clo., West Dr. 154 BK77
Rosebank SE20 182 DV94
Rosebank, Epsom 216 CQ114
Rosebank, Wal.Abb. 68 EE33
Rosebank Ave., Horn. 128 FJ64
Rosebank Ave., Wem. 117 CF63
Rosebank Clo. N12 98 DE50
Rosebank Clo., Tedd. 177 CG93
Rosebank Gdns. E3 143 DZ68
Rosebank Gro. E17 123 DZ55
Rosebank Rd. E17 123 EB58
Rosebank Rd. W7 157 CE75
Rosebank Vil. E17 123 EA56
Rosebank Wk. NW1 141 DK66
Maiden La.
Rosebank Wk. SE18 164 EL77
Woodhill
Rosebank Way W3 138 CR72
Roseberry Clo., Upmin. 129 FT58
Roseberry Ct., Wat. 75 BU39
Grandfield Ave.
Roseberry Gdns. N4 121 DP58
Roseberry Gdns., Dart. 188 FJ87
Roseberry Gdns., Orp. 205 ES104
Roseberry Gdns., Upmin. 129 FT59
Roseberry Pl. E8 142 DT65
Roseberry St. SE16 162 DV77
Rosebery Ave. E12 144 EL65
Rosebery Ave. EC1 274 D5
Rosebery Ave. EC1 141 DN70
Rosebery Ave. N17 100 DU54
Rosebery Ave., Epsom 216 CS114
Rosebery Ave., Har. 116 BZ63
Rosebery Ave., N.Mal. 199 CT96
Rosebery Ave., Sid. 185 ES87
Rosebery Ave., Th.Hth. 202 DQ96
Rosebery Clo., Mord. 199 CX100
Rosebery Ct. EC1 141 DN70
Rosebery Ave.
Rosebery Ct., Grav. 191 GF88
Rosebery Cres., Wok. 227 AZ121
Rosebery Gdns. N8 121 DL57
Rosebery Gdns. W13 137 CG72
Rosebery Gdns., Sutt. 218 DB105
Rosebery Ms. N10 99 DJ54
Rosebery Ms. SW2 181 DL86
Rosebery Rd.
Rosebery Rd. N9 100 DU48
Rosebery Rd. N10 99 DJ54
Rosebery Rd. SW2 181 DL86
Rosebery Rd., Epsom 232 CR119
Rosebery Rd., Grays 170 FY79
Rosebery Rd., Houns. 176 CC85
Rosebery Rd., Kings.T. 198 CP96
Rosebery Rd., Sutt. 217 CZ107
Rosebery Rd. (Bushey), Wat. 94 CB45
Rosebery Sq. EC1 274 D5
Rosebery Sq., Kings.T. 198 CN96
Rosebine Ave., Twick. 177 CD87
Rosebriar Clo., Wok. 228 BG116
Rosebriar Wk., Wat. 75 BT36
Rosebriars, Cat. 236 DS120
Salmons La. W.
Rosebriars, Esher 214 CC106
Rosebury Rd. SW6 160 DB82
Rosebury Vale, Ruis. 115 BT60
Rosecourt Rd., Croy. 201 DM100
Rosecroft Ave. NW3 120 DA62
Rosecroft Clo., Orp. 206 EW100
Rosecroft Clo., West. 239 EM118
Lotus Rd.
Rosecroft Dr., Wat. 75 BS36
Rosecroft Gdns. NW2 119 CU62
Rosecroft Gdns., Twick. 177 CD88
Rosecroft Rd., Sthl. 136 CA70
Rosecroft Wk., Pnr. 116 BX57
Rosecroft Wk., Wem. 117 CK64
Rosedale, Ash. 231 CJ118
Rosedale, Cat. 236 DS123
Rosedale, Welw.G.C. 29 CZ05
Rosedale Ave., Hayes 135 BR71
Rosedale Ave. (Cheshunt), Wal.Cr. 66 DT29
Rosedale Clo. SE2 166 EV76
Finchale Rd.
Rosedale Clo. W7 157 CF75
Boston Rd.
Rosedale Clo., Dart. 188 FP87
Rosedale Clo., St.Alb. 60 BY30
Rosedale Clo., Stan. 95 CH51
Rosedale Ct. N5 121 DP63
Rosedale Gdns., Dag. 146 EV66
Rosedale Rd. E7 124 EJ64
Rosedale Rd., Dag. 146 EV66
Rosedale Rd., Epsom 217 CU106
Rosedale Rd., Grays 170 GD78
Rosedale Rd., Rich. 158 CL84
Rosedale Rd., Rom. 105 FC54
Rosedale Ter. W6 159 CV76
Dalling Rd.
Rosedale Way (Cheshunt), Wal.Cr. 66 DU29
Rosedene NW6 139 CX67
Christchurch Ave.
Rosedene Ave. SW16 181 DM90
Rosedene Ave., Croy. 201 DM101
Rosedene Ave., Grnf. 136 CA69
Rosedene Ave., Mord. 200 DA99
Rosedene Ct., Dart. 188 FJ87
Shepherds La.
Rosedene Ct., Ruis. 115 BS60
Rosedene Gdns., Ilf. 125 EN56
Rosedene Ter. E10 123 EB61
Rosedew Rd. W6 159 CX79
Rosefield, Sev. 256 FG124
Rosefield Clo., Cars. 218 DE106
Alma Rd.
Rosefield Gdns. E14 143 EA73
Rosefield Gdns., Cher. 211 BD107
Rosefield Rd., Stai. 174 BG91
Roseford Ct. W12 159 CX75
Rosehart Ms. W11 140 DA72
Westbourne Gro.
Rosehatch Ave., Rom. 126 EX55
Roseheath, Hem.H. 39 BF19
Roseheath Rd., Houns. 176 BZ85
Rosehill, Esher 215 CG107
Rosehill, Hmptn. 196 CA95
Rosehill Ave., Sutt. 200 DC102
Rosehill Ave., Wok. 226 AW116
Rosehill Clo., Hodd. 49 DZ17
Rosehill Ct., Slou. 152 AU76
Yew Tree Rd.
Rosehill Fm. Meadow, Bans. 234 DB115
The Tracery
Rosehill Gdns., Abb.L. 59 BQ32
Rosehill Gdns., Grnf. 117 CF64
Rosehill Gdns., Sutt. 200 DB103
Rosehill Pk. W., Sutt. 200 DC102
Rosehill Rd. SW18 180 DC86
Rosehill Rd., West. 238 EJ117
Roseland Clo. N17 100 DR52
Cavell Rd.
Roselands Ave., Hodd. 49 DZ15
Roseleigh Ave. N5 121 DP63
Roseleigh Clo., Twick. 177 CK86
Roseley Cotts., Harl. 35 EP11
Rosemary Ave. N3 98 DB54
Rosemary Ave. N9 100 DV46
Rosemary Ave., Enf. 82 DR39
Rosemary Ave., Houns. 156 BX82
Rosemary Ave., Rom. 127 FF55
Rosemary Ave., W.Mol. 196 CA97
Rosemary Clo., Croy. 201 DL100
Rosemary Clo., Harl. 36 EW11
Rosemary Clo., Oxt. 254 EG133
Rosemary Clo., S.Ock. 149 FW69
Rosemary Clo., Uxb. 134 BN71
Rosemary Ct., Horl. 268 DE147
Rosemary Cres., Guil. 242 AT130
Rosemary Dr. E14 143 ED72
Rosemary Dr., Ilf. 124 EK57
Rosemary Gdns. SW14 158 CQ83
Rosemary La.
Rosemary Gdns., Chess. 216 CL105
Rosemary Gdns., Dag. 126 EZ60
Rosemary La. SW14 158 CQ83
Rosemary La., Egh. 193 BB97
Rosemary La., Horl. 269 DH149
Rosemary Rd. SE15 162 DT80
Rosemary Rd. SW17 180 DC90
Rosemary Rd., Well. 165 ET81
Rosemary St. N1 142 DR67
Shepperton Rd.
Rosemead NW9 119 CT59
Rosemead, Cher. 194 BH101
Rosemead, Pot.B. 64 DC30
Rosemead Ave., Felt. 175 BT89
Rosemead Ave., Mitch. 201 DJ96
Rosemead Ave., Wem. 118 CL64
Rosemead Clo., Red. 266 DD136
Rosemead Gdns., Brwd. 109 GD42
Rosemont Ave. N12 98 DC51
Rosemont Rd. NW3 140 DC65
Rosemont Rd. W3 138 CP73
Rosemont Rd., N.Mal. 198 CQ97
Rosemont Rd., Rich. 178 CL86
Rosemont Rd., Wem. 138 CL67
Rosemoor St. SW3 276 D9
Rosemoor St. SW3 160 DF77
Rosemount, Harl. 51 EP18
Rosemount Ave., W.Byf. 212 BG113
Rosemount Clo., Wdf.Grn. 103 EM51
Chapelmount Rd.
Rosemount Dr., Brom. 205 EM98
Rosemount Rd. W13 137 CG72
Rosenau Cres. SW11 160 DE81
Rosenau Rd. SW11 160 DE81
Rosendale Rd. SE21 182 DQ87
Rosendale Rd. SE24 182 DQ87
Roseneath Ave. N21 99 DP46
Roseneath Clo., Orp. 224 EW108
Roseneath Rd. SW11 180 DG86
Roseneath Wk., Enf. 82 DS42
Rosens Wk., Edg. 96 CP48
Rosenthal Rd. SE6 183 EB86
Rosenthorpe Rd. SE15 183 DX85
Roserton St. E14 163 EC75
Rosery, The, Croy. 203 DX100
Roses, The, Wdf.Grn. 102 EF52
Roses La., Wind. 151 AK82
Rosethorn Clo. SW12 181 DJ87
Rosetrees, Guil. 259 BA135
Rosetta Clo. SW8 161 DL80
Rosetti Ter., Dag. 126 EV63
Marlborough Rd.
Roseveare Rd. SE12 184 EJ91
Roseville Ave., Houns. 176 CA85
Roseville Rd., Hayes 155 BU78
Rosevine Rd. SW20 199 CW95
Rosewarne Clo., Wok. 226 AU118
Muirfield Rd.
Roseway SE21 182 DR86
Rosewell Clo. SE20 182 DV94
Rosewood, Dart. 187 FE91
Rosewood, Esher 197 CG103
Rosewood, Sutt. 218 DC110
Rosewood, Wok. 227 BA119
Rosewood Ave., Grnf. 117 CG64
Rosewood Ave., Horn. 127 FG64
Rosewood Clo., Sid. 186 EW90
Rosewood Ct., Brom. 204 EJ95
Rosewood Ct., Hem.H. 39 BE19
Rosewood Ct., Rom. 126 EW57
Rosewood Dr., Enf. 81 DN35
Rosewood Dr., Shep. 194 BM99
Rosewood Gdns. SE13 163 EC82
Lewisham Rd.
Rosewood Gro., Sutt. 200 DC103
Rosewood Sq. W12 139 CU72
Primula St.
Rosewood Ter. SE20 182 DW94
Laurel Gro.
Rosewood Way, Slou. 111 AQ64
Rosher Clo. E15 143 ED66
Rosherville Way, Grav. 190 GE87
Rosina St. E9 123 DX64
Roskell Rd. SW15 159 CX83
Rosken Gro., Slou. 131 AP68
Roslin Rd. W3 158 CP76
Roslin Way, Brom. 184 EG92
Roslyn Clo., Brox. 49 DY21
Roslyn Clo., Mitch. 200 DD96
Roslyn Ct., Wok. 226 AU118
St. John's Rd.
Roslyn Gdns., Rom. 105 FE54
Roslyn Rd. N15 122 DR57
Rosmead Rd. W11 139 CY73
Rosoman Pl. EC1 274 E4
Rosoman St. EC1 274 E3
Rosoman St. EC1 141 DN69
Ross Ave. NW7 97 CY50
Ross Ave., Dag. 126 EZ61
Ross Clo., Har. 94 CC52
Ross Clo., Hat. 45 CU15
Homestead Rd.
Ross Clo., Hayes 155 BR77
Ross Ct. SW15 179 CX87
Ross Cres., Wat. 75 BU35
Ross Par., Wall. 219 DH107
Ross Rd. SE25 202 DR97
Ross Rd., Cob. 214 BW113
Ross Rd., Dart. 187 FG86
Ross Rd., Twick. 176 CB88
Ross Rd., Wall. 219 DJ106
Ross Way SE9 164 EL83
Ross Way, Nthwd. 93 BT49
Rossall Clo., Horn. 127 FG58
Rossall Cres. NW10 138 CM69
Rossdale, Sutt. 218 DE106
Rossdale Dr. N9 82 DW44
Rossdale Dr. NW9 118 CQ60
Rossdale Rd. SW15 159 CW84
Rosse Ms. SE3 164 EH81
Rossendale St. E5 122 DV61
Rossendale Way NW1 141 DJ66
Rossetti Gdns., Couls. 235 DM118
Rossetti Rd. SE16 162 DV78
Rossgate, Hem.H. 40 BG18
Galley Hill
Rossignol Gdns., Cars. 200 DG103
Rossindel Rd., Houns. 176 CA85
Rossington Ave., Borwd. 78 CL38
Rossington Clo., Enf. 82 DV38
Rossington St. E5 122 DU61
Rossiter Clo., Slou. 152 AY77
Rossiter Flds., Barn. 79 CY44
Rossiter Rd. SW12 181 DH88
Rossland Clo., Bexh. 187 FB85
Rosslare Clo., West. 255 ER125
Rosslyn Ave. E4 102 EF47
Rosslyn Ave. SW13 158 CS83
Rosslyn Ave., Barn. 80 DE44
Rosslyn Ave., Dag. 126 EZ59
Rosslyn Ave., Felt. 175 BU86
Rosslyn Ave., Rom. 106 FM54
Rosslyn Clo., Hayes 135 BR71
Morgans La.
Rosslyn Clo., Sun. 175 BS93
Cadbury Rd.
Rosslyn Clo., W.Wick. 204 EF104
Rosslyn Cres., Har. 117 CF57
Rosslyn Cres., Wem. 118 CL63
Rosslyn Gdns., Wem. 118 CL62
Rosslyn Cres.
Rosslyn Hill NW3 120 DD63
Rosslyn Ms. NW3 120 DD63
Rosslyn Hill
Rosslyn Pk., Wey. 213 BR105
Rosslyn Pk. Ms. NW3 120 DD64
Lyndhurst Rd.
Rosslyn Rd. E17 123 EC56
Rosslyn Rd., Bark. 145 ER66
Rosslyn Rd., Twick. 177 CJ86
Rosslyn Rd., Wat. 75 BV41
Rossmore Rd. NW1 272 C5
Rossmore Rd. NW1 140 DE70
Rossway Dr. (Bushey), Wat. 76 CC43
Rosswood Gdns., Wall. 219 DJ107
Rostella Rd. SW17 180 DD91
Rostrevor Ave. N15 122 DT58
Rostrevor Gdns., Hayes 135 BS74
Rostrevor Gdns., Iver 133 BD68
Rostrevor Gdns., Sthl. 156 BY78
Rostrevor Ms. SW6 159 CZ81
Rostrevor Rd. SW6 159 CZ81
Rostrevor Rd. SW19 180 DA92
Roswell Clo. (Cheshunt), Wal.Cr. 67 DY30
Rotary St. SE1 278 F6
Roth Dr., Brwd. 109 GB47
Roth Wk. N7 121 DM62
Durham Rd.
Rothbury Ave., Rain. 147 FH71
Rothbury Gdns., Islw. 157 CG80
Rothbury Rd. E9 143 DZ66
Rothbury Wk. N17 100 DU52
Rother Clo., Wat. 60 BW34
Rotherfield Rd., Cars. 218 DG105
Rotherfield Rd., Enf. 83 DX37
Rotherfield St. N1 142 DQ66
Rotherham Wk. SE1 278 F3
Rotherhill Ave. SW16 181 DK93
Rotherhithe New Rd. SE16 162 DU78
Rotherhithe Old Rd. SE16 163 DX77
Rotherhithe St. SE16 162 DW75
Rotherhithe Tunnel E1 142 DW74
Rotherhithe Tunnel App. E14 162 DW75
Rotherhithe Tunnel App. SE16 162 DW75
Rothermere Rd., Croy. 219 DM106
Rothervale, Horl. 268 DG145
Rotherwick Hill W5 138 CM70
Rotherwick Rd. NW11 120 DA59
Rotherwood Clo. SW20 199 CY95
Rotherwood Rd. SW15 159 CX83
Rothery St. N1 141 DP67
Gaskin St.
Rothery Ter. SW9 161 DP80
Rothes Rd., Dor. 263 CH135
Rothesay Ave. SW20 199 CY96
Rothesay Ave., Grnf. 137 CD65
Rothesay Ave., Rich. 158 CP84
Rothesay Rd. SE25 202 DS98
Rothsay Rd. E7 144 EJ65
Rothsay St. SE1 279 M6
Rothsay St. SE1 162 DS76
Rothsay Wk. E14 163 EA77
Charnwood Gdns.
Rothschild Rd. W4 158 CQ77
Rothschild St. SE27 181 DP91
Rothwell Gdns., Dag. 146 EW66
Rothwell Rd., Dag. 146 EW67
Rothwell St. NW1 140 DF67
Rotten Row SW1 276 F4
Rotten Row SW1 160 DF75
Rotten Row SW7 276 B4
Rotten Row SW7 160 DE75
Rotterdam Dr. E14 163 EC76
Rouel Rd. SE16 162 DU76
Rouge La., Grav. 191 GH88
Rougemont Ave., Mord. 200 DA100
Rough Lands, Wok. 227 BE115
Rough Rew, Dor. 263 CH139
Roughdown Ave., Hem.H. 40 BG23
Roughdown Rd., Hem.H. 40 BH23
Roughdown Vil. Rd., Hem.H. 40 BG23
Roughetts La., Cat. 252 DT129
Roughetts La., Red. 252 DS129
Roughlands, Wok. 227 BE115
Roughs, The, Nthwd. 93 BT48
Roughtallys, Epp. 70 EZ27
Roughwood Clo., Wat. 75 BS38
Roughwood La., Ch.St.G. 90 AY45
Round Gro., Croy. 203 DX101
Round Hill SE26 182 DW89
Round Oak Rd., Wey. 212 BM105
Roundacre SW19 179 CX89
Inner Pk. Rd.
Roundaway Rd., Ilf. 103 EM54
Roundcroft (Cheshunt), Wal.Cr. 66 DT26
Roundel Clo. SE4 163 DZ84
Adelaide Ave.
Roundhay Clo. SE23 183 DX89
Roundheads End, Beac. 88 AH51
Roundhedge Way, Enf. 81 DM38
Roundhill, Wok. 227 BB119
Old Woking Rd.
Roundhill Dr., Enf. 81 DM42
Roundhill Dr., Wok. 227 BB118
Old Woking Rd.
Roundhill Way, Cob. 214 CB112
Roundhill Way, Guil. 242 AT134
Roundhills, Wal.Abb. 68 EE34
Roundings, The, Hert. 32 DV14
Roundmead Ave., Loug. 85 EN41
Roundmead Clo., Loug. 85 EN41
Roundmoor Dr. (Cheshunt), Wal.Cr. 67 DY29
Roundshaw Cen., Wall. 219 DL108
Meteor Way
Roundtable Rd., Brom. 184 EF90
Roundthorn Way, Wok. 226 AT116
Roundtree Rd., Wem. 117 CH64
Roundway, Egh. 173 BC92
Roundway, West. 238 EK116
Norheads La.
Roundway, The N17 100 DQ53
Roundway, The, Esher 215 CF107
Roundway, The, Wat. 75 BT44

Russell Rd., Grays 170 GA77
Russell Rd., Mitch. 200 DE97
Russell Rd., Nthlt. 116 CC64
Russell Rd., Nthwd. 93 BQ49
Russell Rd., Shep. 195 BP101
Russell Rd., Til. 170 GE81
Russell Rd., Twick. 177 CF86
Russell Rd., Walt. 195 BU100
Russell Rd., Wok. 226 AW115
Russell Sq. WC1 273 P5
Russell Sq. WC1 141 DK71
Russell Sq., Long. 209 FX97
Cavendish Sq.
Russell St. WC2 274 A10
Russell St. WC2 141 DM72
Russell St., Hert. 32 DQ09
Russell St., Wind. 151 AR81
Russell Wk., Rich. 178 CM86
Park Hill
Russell Way, Sutt. 218 DA106
Russell Way, Wat. 93 BV45
Russellcroft Rd., Welw.G.C. 29 CW08
Russells, Tad. 233 CX122
Russells Cres., Horl. 268 DG149
Russell's Footpath SW16 181 DL92
Russells Ride (Cheshunt), Wal.Cr. 67 DY31
Russet Clo., Horl. 269 DJ148
Carlton Tye
Russet Clo., Stai. 173 BF86
Russet Clo., Uxb. 135 BQ70
Uxbridge Rd.
Russet Clo., Walt. 196 BX104
Russet Cres. N7 121 DM64
Stock Orchard Cres.
Russet Dr., Croy. 203 DY102
Russet Dr., Rad. 62 CL32
Russet Dr., St.Alb. 43 CJ21
Russet Way, Dor. 263 CK140
Russets, The, Ger.Cr. 90 AX54
Austenwood Clo.
Russets Clo. E4 101 ED49
Larkshall Rd.
Russett Clo., Orp. 224 EV106
Russett Clo., Wal.Cr. 66 DS26
Russett Ct., Cat. 252 DU125
Russett Hill, Ger.Cr. 112 AY55
Russett Way SE13 163 EB82
Conington Rd.
Russett Way, Swan. 207 FD96
Russett Wd., Welw.G.C. 30 DD10
Russetts, Horn. 128 FL56
Russetts Clo., Wok. 227 AZ115
Orchard Dr.
Russia Ct. EC2 275 J8
Russia Dock Rd. SE16 143 DY74
Russia La. E2 142 DW68
Russia Row EC2 275 J9
Russia Wk. SE16 163 DY75
Russington Rd., Shep. 195 BR100
Rust Sq. SE5 162 DR80
Rusthall Ave. W4 158 CR77
Rusthall Clo., Croy. 202 DW100
Rustic Ave. SW16 181 DH94
Rustic Clo., Upmin. 129 FS60
Rustic Pl., Wem. 117 CK63
Rustic Wk. E16 144 EH72
Lambert Rd.
Rustington Wk., Mord. 199 CZ101
Ruston Ave., Surb. 198 CP101
Ruston Gdns. N14 80 DG44
Farm La.
Ruston Ms. W11 139 CY72
St. Marks Rd.
Ruston Rd. SE18 164 EL76
Ruston St. E3 143 DZ67
Rutford Rd. SW16 181 DL92
Ruth Clo., Stan. 118 CM56
Ruthen Clo., Epsom 216 CP114
Rutherford Clo., Borwd. 78 CQ40
Rutherford Clo., Sutt. 218 DD107
Rutherford Clo., Wind. 151 AM81
Rutherford St. SW1 277 M8
Rutherford St. SW1 161 DK77
Rutherford Twr., Sthl. 136 CB72
Rutherford Way (Bushey), Wat. 95 CD46
Rutherford Way, Wem. 118 CN63
Rutherglen Rd. SE2 166 EU79
Rutherwick Clo., Horl. 268 DF148
Rutherwick Ri., Couls. 235 DL117
Rutherwick Twr., Horl. 268 DF148
Rutherwyk Rd., Cher. 193 BE101
Rutherwyke Clo., Epsom 217 CU107
Ruthin Clo. NW9 118 CS58
Ruthin Rd. SE3 164 EG79
Ruthven Ave., Wal.Cr. 67 DX33
Ruthven St. E9 143 DX67
Lauriston Rd.
Rutland App., Horn. 128 FN57
Rutland Ave., Sid. 186 EU87
Rutland Ave., Slou. 131 AQ71
Rutland Clo. SW14 158 CQ83
Rutland Clo. SW19 180 DE94
Rutland Rd.
Rutland Clo., Ash. 232 CL117
Rutland Clo., Bex. 186 EX88
Rutland Clo., Chess. 216 CM107
Rutland Clo., Dart. 188 FK87
Rutland Clo., Epsom 216 CR110
Rutland Clo., Red. 250 DF133
Rutland Ct., Enf. 82 DW43
Rutland Dr., Horn. 128 FN57
Rutland Dr., Mord. 199 CZ100
Rutland Dr., Rich. 177 CK88
Rutland Gdns. N4 121 DP58
Rutland Gdns. SW7 276 C5
Rutland Gdns. SW7 160 DE75
Rutland Gdns. W13 137 CG71
Rutland Gdns., Croy. 220 DS105
Rutland Gdns., Dag. 126 EW64
Rutland Gdns., Hem.H. 40 BM19
Rutland Gdns. Ms. SW7 276 C5
Rutland Gate SW7 276 C5
Rutland Gate SW7 160 DE75
Rutland Gate, Belv. 167 FB78
Rutland Gate, Brom. 204 EF98
Rutland Gate Ms. SW7 276 B5
Rutland Gro. W6 159 CV78
Rutland Ms. NW8 140 DB67
Boundary Rd.
Rutland Ms. E. SW7 276 B6
Rutland Ms. S. SW7 276 B6
Rutland Ms. W. SW7 160 DE76
Ennismore St.
Rutland Pk. NW2 139 CW65
Rutland Pk. SE6 183 DZ89
Rutland Pk. Gdns. NW2 139 CW65
Rutland Pk.
Rutland Pk. Mans. NW2 139 CW65
Walm La.
Rutland Pl. EC1 275 H5
Rutland Pl. (Bushey), Wat. 95 CD46
The Rutts
Rutland Rd. E7 144 EK66
Rutland Rd. E9 142 DW67
Rutland Rd. E11 124 EH57
Rutland Rd. E17 123 EA58
Rutland Rd. SW19 180 DE94
Rutland Rd., Har. 116 CC58
Rutland Rd., Hayes 155 BR77
Rutland Rd., Ilf. 125 EP63
Rutland Rd., Sthl. 136 CA71
Rutland Rd., Twick. 177 CD89
Rutland St. SW7 276 C6
Rutland St. SW7 160 DE76
Rutland Wk. SE6 183 DZ89
Rutland Way, Orp. 206 EW100
Rutley Clo. SE17 161 DP79
Royal Rd.
Rutley Clo., Rom. 106 FK54
Pasteur Dr.
Rutlish Rd. SW19 200 DA95
Rutson Rd., W.Byf. 212 BM114
Rutter Gdns., Mitch. 200 DC98
Rutters Clo., West Dr. 154 BN75
Rutts, The (Bushey), Wat. 95 CD46
Rutts Ter. SE14 163 DX81
Ruvigny Gdns. SW15 159 CX83
Ruxbury Rd., Cher. 193 BC100
Ruxley Clo., Epsom 216 CP106
Ruxley Clo., Sid. 186 EY93
Ruxley Cor. Ind. Est., Sid. 186 EX93
Ruxley Cres., Esher 215 CH107
Ruxley La., Epsom 216 CR106
Ruxley Ms., Epsom 216 CP106
Ruxley Ridge, Esher 215 CG108
Ruxton Clo., Swan. 207 FE97
Ryall Clo., St.Alb. 60 BY29
Ryalls Ct. N20 98 DF48
Ryan Clo. SE3 164 EJ84
Ryan Clo., Ruis. 115 BV60
Ryan Dr., Brent. 157 CG79
Ryan Way, Wat. 76 BW39
Ryarsh Cres., Orp. 223 ES105
Rycott Path SE22 182 DU87
Lordship La.
Rycroft La., Sev. 256 FE130
Rycroft Way N17 122 DT55
Ryculff Sq. SE3 164 EF82
Rydal Clo. NW4 97 CY53
Rydal Clo., Pur. 220 DR113
Rydal Ct., Wat. 59 BV32
Grasmere Clo.
Rydal Cres., Grnf. 137 CH69
Rydal Dr., Bexh. 166 FA81
Rydal Dr., W.Wick. 204 EE103
Rydal Gdns. NW9 118 CS57
Rydal Gdns. SW15 178 CS92
Rydal Gdns., Houns. 176 CB86
Rydal Gdns., Wem. 117 CJ60
Rydal Rd. SW16 181 DK91
Rydal Way, Egh. 173 BB94
Rydal Way, Enf. 82 DW44
Rydal Way, Ruis. 116 BW63
Ryde, The, Hat. 45 CW15
Ryde, The, Stai. 194 BH95
Ryde Clo., Wok. 228 BJ121
Ryde Heron, Wok. 226 AS117
Robin Hood Rd.
Ryde Pl., Twick. 177 CJ86
Ryde Vale Rd. SW12 181 DH89
Rydens Ave., Walt. 195 BV103
Rydens Clo., Walt. 196 BW103
Rydens Gro., Walt. 214 BX105
Rydens Pk., Walt. 196 BX103
Rydens Rd.
Rydens Rd., Walt. 195 BV104
Rydens Way, Wok. 227 BA120
Ryder Ave., Hat. 44 CS20
Ryder Clo., Brom. 184 EH92
Ryder Clo., Hem.H. 57 BA28
Ryder Clo., Hert. 32 DV08
Ryder Clo. (Bushey), Wat. 76 CB44
Ryder Ct. SW1 277 L2
Ryder Dr. SE16 162 DV78
Ryder Gdns., Rain. 147 FF65
Ryder Ms. E9 122 DW64
Homerton High St.
Ryder St. SW1 277 L2
Ryder St. SW1 141 DJ74
Ryder Yd. SW1 277 L2
Ryders Ter. NW8 140 DC68
Blenheim Ter.
Rydes Ave., Guil. 242 AT131
Rydes Clo., Wok. 227 BC120
Rydes Hill Cres., Guil. 242 AT130
Rydes Hill Rd., Guil. 242 AT132
Rydings, Wind. 151 AM83
Rydon St. N1 142 DQ67
St. Paul St.
Rydons Clo. SE9 164 EL83
Rydon's La., Couls. 236 DQ120
Rydons Pk., Walt. 195 BT102
Rydon's Wd. Clo., Couls. 236 DQ120
Rydston Clo. N7 141 DM66
Sutterton St.
Rye, The N14 99 DJ45
Rye Clo., Bex. 187 FB86
Rye Clo., Guil. 242 AS132
Rye Clo., Horn. 128 FJ64
Rye Cres., Orp. 206 EW102
Rye Fld., Orp. 206 EX103
Rye Hill Pk. SE15 162 DW84
Rye Hill Rd., Epp. 52 EU22
Rye Hill Rd., Harl. 51 ER20
Rye La. SE15 162 DU81
Rye La., Sev. 241 FE120
Rye Pas. SE15 162 DU83
Rye Rd. SE15 163 DX84
Rye Rd., Hodd. 49 EB15
Rye Wk. SW15 179 CX85
Chartfield Ave.
Rye Way, Edg. 96 CM51
Canons Dr.
Ryebridge Clo., Lthd. 231 CG118
Ryebrook Rd., Lthd. 231 CG118
Ryecotes Mead SE21 182 DS88
Ryecroft, Grav. 191 GL92
Ryecroft, Harl. 51 EP15
Ryecroft, Hat. 45 CT20
Hazel Gro.
Ryecroft, Wind. 151 AM83
Ryecroft Ave., Ilf. 103 EP54
Ryecroft Ave., Twick. 176 CB87
Ryecroft Clo., Hem.H. 41 BQ21
Poynders Hill
Ryecroft Ct., St.Alb. 44 CM20
Ryecroft Cres., Barn. 79 CV43
Ryecroft Rd. SE13 183 EC85
Ryecroft Rd. SW16 181 DN93
Ryecroft Rd., Chesh. 54 AN32
Ryecroft Rd., Orp. 205 ER100
Ryecroft Rd., Sev. 241 FG116
Ryecroft St. SW6 160 DB81
Ryedale SE22 182 DV86
Ryefield Ave., Uxb. 135 BP66
Ryefield Clo., Hodd. 33 EB13
Ryefield Ct., Nthwd. 93 BU54
Ryefield Cres.
Ryefield Cres., Nthwd. 93 BU54
Ryefield Par., Nthwd. 93 BU54
Ryefield Cres.
Ryefield Path SW15 179 CU88
Ryefield Rd. SE19 182 DQ93
Ryeland Clo., West Dr. 134 BL72
Ryelands, Horl. 269 DJ147
Ryelands, Welw.G.C. 29 CZ12
Ryelands Clo., Cat. 236 DS121
Ryelands Ct., Lthd. 231 CG118
Ryelands Cres. SE12 184 EJ86
Ryelands Pl., Wey. 195 BS104
Ryfold Rd. SW19 180 DA90
Ryhope Rd. N11 99 DH49
Rykhill, Grays 171 GH76
Ryland Clo., Felt. 175 BT91
Ryland Ho., Croy. 202 DQ104
Ryland Rd. NW5 141 DH65
Rylandes Rd. NW2 119 CU62
Rylandes Rd., S.Croy. 220 DV109
Rylett Cres. W12 159 CT76
Rylett Rd. W12 159 CT75
Rylston Rd. N13 100 DR48
Rylston Rd. SW6 159 CZ79
Rymer Rd., Croy. 202 DS101
Rymer St. SE24 181 DP86
Rymill Clo., Hem.H. 57 BA28
Rymill St. E16 145 EN74
Rysbrack St. SW3 276 D6
Rysbrack St. SW3 160 DF76
Rysted La., West. 255 EQ126
Rythe Ct., T.Ditt. 197 CG101
Rythe Rd., Esher 215 CD106
Ryvers Rd., Slou. 153 AZ76

S

Sabah Ct., Ashf. 174 BN91
Sabbarton St. E16 144 EF72
Victoria Dock Rd.
Sabella Ct. E3 143 DZ68
Sabina Rd., Grays 171 GJ77
Sabine Rd. SW11 160 DF83
Sable Clo., Houns. 156 BW83
Sable St. N1 141 DP66
Canonbury Rd.
Sach Rd. E5 122 DV61
Sackville Ave., Brom. 204 EG102
Sackville Clo., Har. 117 CD62
Sackville Clo., Sev. 257 FH122
Sackville Ct., Rom. 106 FL53
Sackville Cres.
Sackville Cres., Rom. 106 FL53
Sackville Est. SW16 181 DL90
Sackville Gdns., Ilf. 125 EM60
Sackville Rd., Dart. 188 FK89
Sackville Rd., Sutt. 218 DA108
Sackville St. W1 277 L1
Sackville St. W1 141 DJ73
Sackville Way SE22 182 DU88
Dulwich Common
Sacombe Rd., Hem.H. 39 BF18
Saddington St., Grav. 191 GH87
Saddle Yd. W1 277 H2
Saddlebrook Pk., Sun. 175 BS94
Saddlers Clo., Barn. 79 CV43
Barnet Rd.
Saddlers Clo., Borwd. 78 CR44
Farriers Way
Saddlers Clo., Pnr. 94 CA51
Saddlers Mead, Harl. 52 EU16
Saddlers Ms. SW8 161 DM81
Portland Gro.
Saddlers Ms., Wem. 117 CF63
The Boltons
Saddler's Pk. (Eynsford), Dart. 208 FK104
Saddlers Path, Borwd. 78 CR43
Saddlers Way, Epsom 232 CR119
Saddlescombe Way N12 98 DA50
Saddleworth Rd., Rom. 106 FJ51
Saddleworth Sq., Rom. 106 FJ51
Sadleir Rd., St.Alb. 43 CE22
Sadler Clo., Mitch. 200 DF96
Sadler Clo. (Cheshunt), Wal.Cr. 66 DQ25
Markham Rd.
Sadlers Clo., Guil. 243 BD133
Sadlers Ride, W.Mol. 196 CB97
Sadlers Way, Hert. 31 DN09
Saffron Ave. E14 143 ED73
Saffron Clo. NW11 119 CZ57
Saffron Clo., Croy. 201 DL100
Saffron Clo., Hodd. 49 DZ16
Saffron Clo., Slou. 152 AV81
Saffron Ct., Felt. 175 BQ87
Staines Rd.
Saffron Hill EC1 274 E6
Saffron Hill EC1 141 DN70
Saffron La., Hem.H. 40 BH19
Saffron Platt, Guil. 242 AU130
Saffron Rd., Grays 169 FW77
Saffron Rd., Rom. 105 FC54
Saffron St. EC1 274 E6
Saffron Way, Surb. 197 CK102
Sage Clo. E6 145 EM71
Bradley Stone Rd.
Sage St. E1 142 DW73
Cable St.
Sage Way WC1 274 B3
Saigasso Clo. E16 144 EK72
Royal Rd.
Sail St. SE11 278 C8
Sail St. SE11 161 DM77
Sainfoin Rd. SW17 180 DG89
Sainsbury Rd. SE19 182 DS92
St. Agatha's Dr., Kings.T. 178 CM93
St. Agathas Gro., Cars. 200 DF102
St. Agnells Ct., Hem.H. 40 BN16
St. Agnells La., Hem.H. 40 BM15
St. Agnes Clo. E9 142 DW67
Gore Rd.
St. Agnes Pl. SE11 161 DN79
St. Agnes Well EC1 142 DR70
Old St.
St. Aidans Ct. W13 157 CH75
St. Aidans Rd.
St. Aidans Ct., Bark. 146 EV69
Choats Rd.
St. Aidan's Rd. SE22 182 DV86
St. Aidans Rd. W13 157 CH75
St. Aidan's Way, Grav. 191 GK90
St. Albans Ave. E6 145 EM69
St. Alban's Ave. W4 158 CR77
St. Albans Ave., Felt. 176 BX92
St. Albans Ave., Upmin. 129 FS60
St. Albans Ave., Wey. 194 BN104
St. Albans Clo. NW11 120 DA60
St. Albans Clo., Grav. 191 GK90
St. Albans Cres. N22 99 DN53
St. Alban's Cres., Wdf.Grn. 102 EG52
St. Albans Gdns., Grav. 191 GK90
St. Alban's Gdns., Tedd. 177 CG92
St. Albans Gro. W8 160 DB76
St. Alban's Gro., Cars. 200 DE101
St. Albans Hill, Hem.H. 40 BL23
St. Albans La. NW11 120 DA60
West Heath Dr.
St. Albans La., Abb.L. 59 BT26
St. Albans Ms. W2 272 A6
St. Albans Ms. W2 140 DD71
St. Alban's Pl. N1 141 DP67
St. Albans Rd. NW5 120 DG62
St. Albans Rd. NW10 138 CS67
St. Albans Rd., Barn. 79 CY39
St. Albans Rd., Dart. 188 FM87
St. Albans Rd., Epp. 70 EX29
St. Albans Rd., Hem.H. 40 BK22
St. Albans Rd., Ilf. 125 ET60
St. Alban's Rd., Kings.T. 178 CL93
St. Albans Rd. (Dancers Hill), Pot.B. 79 CV35
St. Albans Rd. (South Mimms), Pot.B. 63 CV34
St. Albans Rd., Rad. 62 CQ30
St. Albans Rd., Reig. 250 DA133
St. Albans Rd., St.Alb. 43 CF17
St. Albans Rd. (London Colney), St.Alb. 62 CN28
St. Alban's Rd., Sutt. 217 CZ105
St. Albans Rd., Wat. 75 BV40
St. Alban's Rd., Wdf.Grn. 102 EG52
St. Albans Rd. E., Hat. 45 CV17
St. Albans Rd. W., Hat. 44 CQ18
St. Albans Rd. W. (Roe Grn.), Hat. 45 CT17
St. Albans St. SW1 277 M1
St. Alban's St., Wind. 151 AR81
St. Albans Ter. W6 159 CY79
Margravine Rd.
St. Albans Twr. E4 101 DZ51
St. Alban's Vil. NW5 120 DG62
Highgate Rd.
St. Alfege Pas. SE10 163 EC79
St. Alfege Rd. SE7 164 EK79
St. Alphage Gdns. EC2 275 J7
St. Alphage Highwalk EC2 142 DR71
London Wall
St. Alphage Wk., Edg. 96 CQ54
St. Alphege Rd. N9 100 DW45
St. Alphonsus Rd. SW4 161 DJ84
St. Amunds Clo. SE6 183 EA91
St. Andrew Ms., Hert. 32 DQ09
St. Andrew St. EC4 274 E7
St. Andrew St. EC4 141 DN71
St. Andrew St., Hert. 32 DQ09
St. Andrews Ave., Horn. 127 FG64
St. Andrews Ave., Wem. 117 CG63
St. Andrews Ave., Wind. 151 AM82
St. Andrew's Clo. N12 98 DC49
Woodside Ave.
St. Andrews Clo. NW2 119 CV62
St. Andrews Clo. SE16 162 DV78
Ryder Dr.
St. Andrews Clo., Epp. 53 FD24
St. Andrew's Clo., Islw. 157 CD81
St. Andrews Clo., Reig. 266 DB135
St. Marys Rd.
St. Andrews Clo., Ruis. 116 BX61
St. Andrew's Clo., Shep. 195 BR98
St. Andrews Clo., Stai. 172 AY87
St. Andrews Clo., Stan. 95 CJ54
St. Andrews Clo., Wind. 172 AU86
St. Andrews Clo., Wok. 226 AW117
St. Mary's Rd.
St. Andrew's Ct. SW18 180 DC89
Waynflete St.
St. Andrews Ct., Wat. 75 BV39
St. Andrews Cres., Wind. 151 AM82
St. Andrews Dr., Orp. 206 EV100
St. Andrews Dr., Stan. 95 CJ53
St. Andrews Gdns., Cob. 214 BW113
St. Andrew's Gro. N16 122 DR60
St. Andrew's Hill EC4 274 G10
St. Andrew's Hill EC4 141 DP73
St. Andrew's Ms. N16 122 DS60
St. Andrews Ms. SE3 164 EG80
Mycenae Rd.
St. Andrews Pl. NW1 273 J4
St. Andrews Pl. NW1 141 DH70
St. Andrews Pl., Brwd. 109 FZ47
St. Andrews Rd. E11 124 EE58
St. Andrews Rd. E13 144 EH69
St. Andrews Rd. E17 101 DX54
St. Andrews Rd. N9 100 DW45
St. Andrews Rd. NW9 118 CR60
St. Andrews Rd. NW10 139 CV65
St. Andrews Rd. NW11 119 CZ58
St. Andrews Rd. W3 138 CS73
St. Andrews Rd. W7 157 CE75
Church Rd.
St. Andrews Rd. W14 159 CY79
St. Andrews Rd., Cars. 200 DE104
St. Andrews Rd., Couls. 235 DH116
St. Andrews Rd., Croy. 220 DQ105
Lower Coombe St.
St. Andrews Rd., Enf. 82 DR41
St. Andrew's Rd., Grav. 191 GH87
St. Andrews Rd., Hem.H. 40 BJ24
West Valley Rd.
St. Andrews Rd., Ilf. 125 EM59
St. Andrews Rd., Rom. 127 FD58
St. Andrew's Rd., Sid. 186 EX90
St. Andrew's Rd., Surb. 197 CK100
St. Andrews Rd., Til. 170 GE81
St. Andrews Rd., Uxb. 134 BM66
St. Andrews Rd., Wat. 94 BX48
St. Andrews Sq. W11 139 CY72
St. Marks Rd.
St. Andrew's Sq., Surb. 197 CK100
St. Andrews Twr., Sthl. 136 CC73
St. Andrews Wk., Cob. 229 BV115
St. Andrews Way E3 143 EB70
St. Andrews Way, Oxt. 255 EM130
St. Andrews Way, Slou. 131 AK73
St. Anna Rd., Barn. 79 CX43
Sampson Ave.
St. Anne St. E14 143 DZ72
Commercial Rd.
St. Annes Ave., Stai. 174 BK87
St. Anne's Clo. N6 120 DG62
Highgate W. Hill
St. Annes Clo., (Cheshunt) Wal.Cr. 66 DU28
St. Anne's Clo., Wat. 94 BW49
St. Anne's Ct. W1 273 M9
St. Anne's Dr., Red. 250 DG133
St. Annes Gdns. NW10 138 CM69
St. Anne's Mt., Red. 250 DG133
St. Annes Pk., Brox. 49 EA20
Friarscroft
St. Annes Pas. E14 143 DZ72
Newell St.
St. Annes Ri., Red. 250 DG133
St. Annes Rd. E11 123 ED61
St. Anne's Rd., St.Alb. 61 CK27
St. Anne's Rd. (Harefield), Uxb. 114 BJ55
St. Anne's Rd., Wem. 117 CK64
St. Anne's Row E14 143 DZ72
Commercial Rd.
St. Anne's Way, Red. 250 DG133
St. Anne's Dr.
St. Ann's, Bark. 145 EQ67
St. Anns Clo., Cher. 193 BF100
St. Ann's Cres. SW18 180 DC86
St. Ann's Gdns. NW5 140 DG65
Queens Cres.
St. Ann's Hill SW18 180 DB85
St. Anns Hill Rd., Cher. 193 BC100
St. Ann's La. SW1 277 N6
St. Ann's Pk. Rd. SW18 180 DC86
St. Ann's Pas. SW13 158 CS83
St. Anns Rd. N9 100 DT47
St. Ann's Rd. N15 121 DP57
St. Ann's Rd. SW13 159 CT82
St. Anns Rd. W11 139 CX73
St. Ann's Rd., Bark. 145 EQ67
Axe St.
St. Anns Rd., Cher. 193 BF100
St. Anns Rd., Har. 117 CE58
St. Ann's St. SW1 277 N6
St. Ann's St. SW1 161 DK76
St. Ann's Ter. NW8 140 DD68
St. Anns Vil. W11 139 CX74
St. Anns Way, S.Croy. 219 DP107
St. Anselm's Pl. W1 273 H9
St. Anselms Rd., Hayes 155 BT75
St. Anthonys Ave., Hem.H. 41 BP22
St. Anthonys Ave., Wdf.Grn. 102 EJ51
St. Anthonys Clo. E1 142 DU74
St. Anthonys Clo. SW17 180 DE89
College Gdns.
St. Anthony's Way, Felt. 155 BT84
St. Antony's Rd. E7 144 EH66
St. Arvans Clo., Croy. 202 DS104
St. Asaph Rd. SE4 163 DX83
St. Aubyn's Ave. SW19 179 CZ92
St. Aubyns Ave., Houns. 176 CA85
St. Aubyns Clo., Orp. 205 ET104
St. Aubyns Gdns., Orp. 205 ET103
St. Aubyn's Rd. SE19 182 DT93
St. Audrey Ave., Bexh. 166 FA82
St. Audreys Clo., Hat. 45 CV21
St. Audreys Grn., Welw.G.C. 29 CZ10
St. Augustine Rd., Grays 171 GH77
St. Augustine's Ave. W5 138 CL68
St. Augustines Ave., Brom. 204 EL99
St. Augustine's Ave., S.Croy. 220 DQ107
St. Augustines Ave., Wem. 118 CL62
St. Augustines Clo., Brox. 49 DZ20
St. Augustines Dr., Brox. 49 DZ19
St. Augustine's Path N5 121 DP64
St. Augustines Rd. NW1 141 DK66
St. Augustine's Rd., Belv. 166 EZ77
St. Austell Clo., Edg. 96 CM54
St. Austell Rd. SE13 163 EC82
St. Awdry's Rd., Bark. 145 ER66
St. Awdry's Wk., Bark. 145 EQ66
Station Par.
St. Barnabas Clo. SE22 182 DS85
East Dulwich Gro.
St. Barnabas Clo., Beck. 203 EC96
St. Barnabas Ct., Har. 94 CC53
St. Barnabas Rd. E17 123 EA58
St. Barnabas Rd., Mitch. 180 DG94
St. Barnabas Rd., Sutt. 218 DD106
St. Barnabas Rd., Wdf.Grn. 102 EH53
St. Barnabas St. SW1 276 G10
St. Barnabas St. SW1 160 DG78
St. Barnabas Ter. E9 123 DX64
St. Barnabas Vil. SW8 161 DL81
St. Bartholomews Clo. SE26 182 DW91
St. Bartholomews Ct., Guil. 259 AZ136
St. Bartholomew's Rd. E6 144 EL67
St. Bart's Clo., St.Alb. 43 CK21
St. Benedict's Ave., Grav. 191 GL89
St. Benedict's Clo. SW17 180 DG92
Church La.
St. Benet's Clo. SW17 180 DE89
College Gdns.
St. Benet's Gro., Cars. 200 DC101
St. Benet's Pl. EC3 275 L10
St. Benjamins Dr., Orp. 224 EW109
St. Bernards, Croy. 202 DS104
St. Bernard's Clo. SE27 182 DR91
St. Gothard Rd.

St. Luke's Ave. SW4 161 DK84
St. Lukes Ave., Enf. 82 DR38
St. Luke's Ave., Ilf. 125 EP64
St. Lukes Clo. EC1 142 DQ70
Old St.
St. Lukes Clo. SE25 202 DV100
St. Lukes Clo., Dart. 189 FS92
St. Lukes Clo., Swan. 207 FD96
St. Luke's Est. EC1 275 K3
St. Luke's Est. EC1 142 DR69
St. Lukes Ms. W11 139 CZ72
Basing St.
St. Lukes Pas., Kings.T. 198 CM95
St. Lukes Rd. W11 139 CZ71
St. Lukes Rd., Uxb. 134 BL66
St. Lukes Rd., Whyt. 236 DT118
Whyteleafe Hill
St. Lukes Rd., Wind. 172 AU86
St. Lukes Sq. E16 144 EF72
St. Lukes Sq., Guil. 259 AZ135
St. Luke's St. SW3 276 B10
St. Luke's St. SW3 160 DE78
St. Luke's Yd. W9 139 CZ68
St. Malo Ave. N9 100 DW48
St. Margaret Dr., Epsom 216 CR114
St. Margarets, Bark. 145 ER67
St. Margarets, Guil. 243 AZ133
St. Margarets Ave. N15 121 DP56
St. Margarets Ave. N20 98 DC47
St. Margarets Ave., Ashf. 175 BP92
St. Margarets Ave., Har. 116 CC62
St. Margarets Ave., Sid. 185 ER90
St. Margaret's Ave., Sutt. 199 CY104
St. Margarets Ave., Uxb. 134 BN70
St. Margarets Clo., Berk. 38 AX20
St. Margarets Clo., H.Wyc. 88 AC47
St. Margarets Clo., Iver 133 BD68
St. Margarets Gate
St. Margarets Clo., Orp. 224 EV105
St. Margaret's Ct. SE1 279 J3
St. Margarets Cres. SW15 179 CV85
St. Margaret's Cres., Grav. 191 GL90
St. Margaret's Dr., Twick. 177 CH85
St. Margarets Gate, Iver 133 BD68
St. Margaret's Gro. E11 124 EF62
St. Margaret's Gro. SE18 165 EQ79
St. Margarets Gro., Twick. 177 CG86
St. Margarets La. W8 160 DB76
St. Margarets Pas. SE13 164 EE83
Church Ter.
St. Margarets Rd. E12 124 EJ61
St. Margaret's Rd. N17 122 DS55
St. Margaret's Rd. NW10 139 CW69
St. Margarets Rd. SE4 163 DZ84
St. Margarets Rd. W7 157 CE75
St. Margarets Rd., Couls. 235 DH121
St. Margarets Rd. (South Darenth), Dart. 189 FS94
St. Margarets Rd., Edg. 96 CP50
St. Margaret's Rd., Grav. 190 GE89
St. Margarets Rd., Islw. 157 CH84
St. Margaret's Rd., Ruis. 115 BR58
St. Margarets Rd., Twick. 157 CH84
St. Margaret's Rd., Ware 33 EA13
St. Margarets Sq. SE4 163 DZ84
Adelaide Ave.
St. Margaret's St. SW1 277 P5
St. Margaret's St. SW1 161 DK77
St. Margaret's Ter. SE18 165 EQ78
St. Margarets Way, Hem.H. 41 BR20
St. Mark St. E1 142 DT72
St. Marks Ave., Grav. 190 GE87
St. Marks Clo. SE10 163 EC80
Ashburnham Gro.
St. Marks Clo. W11 139 CY72
Lancaster Rd.
St. Mark's Clo., Barn. 80 DB41
St. Marks Clo., St.Alb. 44 CP22
St. Marks Cres. NW1 140 DG67
St. Marks Gate E9 143 DZ66
Cadogan Ter.
St. Mark's Gro. SW10 160 DB79
St. Mark's Hill, Surb. 198 CL100
St. Mark's Pl. SW19 179 CZ93
Wimbledon Hill Rd.
St. Marks Pl. W11 139 CY72
St. Marks Pl., Wind. 151 AQ82
St. Marks Ri. E8 122 DT64
St. Marks Rd. SE25 202 DU98
Coventry Rd.
St. Mark's Rd. W5 138 CL74
The Common
St. Marks Rd. W7 157 CE75
St. Marks Rd. W10 139 CX72
St. Marks Rd. W11 139 CY72
St. Marks Rd., Brom. 204 EH97
St. Marks Rd., Enf. 82 DT44
St. Marks Rd., Epsom 233 CW118
St. Marks Rd., Mitch. 200 DF96
St. Mark's Rd., Tedd. 177 CH94
St. Marks Rd., Wind. 151 AQ82
St. Marks Sq. NW1 140 DG67
St. Martha's Ave., Wok. 227 AZ121
St. Martin Clo., Uxb. 134 BK72
St. Martins App., Ruis. 115 BS59
St. Martins Ave. E6 144 EK68
St. Martins Ave., Epsom 216 CS114
St. Martins Clo. NW1 141 DJ67
St. Martins Clo., Enf. 82 DV39
St. Martins Clo., Epsom 216 CS113
Church Rd.
St. Martins Clo., Erith 166 EX75
St. Helens Rd.
St. Martins Clo., Lthd. 245 BS129
St. Martin's Clo., Wat. 94 BW49
Muirfield Rd.
St. Martin's Clo., West Dr. 154 BK76
St. Martin's Rd.
St. Martin's Ct. WC2 141 DK73
St. Martin's La.
St. Martin's Ct., Ashf. 174 BJ92
St. Martins Dr., Walt. 196 BW104
St. Martins Est. SW2 181 DN88
St. Martin's La. WC2 273 P10
St. Martin's La. WC2 141 DL73
St. Martins Meadow, West. 240 EW123
St. Martin's Ms. WC2 277 P1
St. Martins Ms., Dor. 263 CG136
Church St.
St. Martin's Pl. WC2 277 P1
St. Martin's Pl. WC2 141 DL73
St. Martins Rd. N9 100 DV47
St. Martin's Rd. SW9 161 DM82
St. Martins Rd., Dart. 188 FM86
St. Martin's Rd., West Dr. 154 BJ76
St. Martin's St. WC2 277 N1
St. Martins Wk., Dor. 263 CH136
St. Martins Way SW17 180 DC90
St. Martin's-le-Grand EC1 275 H8
St. Martin's-le-Grand EC1 142 DQ72
St. Mary Abbots Pl. W8 159 CZ76
St. Mary Abbots Ter. W14 159 CZ76
St. Mary at Hill EC3 279 M1
St. Mary at Hill EC3 142 DS73
St. Mary Ave., Wall. 200 DG104
St. Mary Axe EC3 275 M9
St. Mary Axe EC3 142 DS72
St. Mary Rd. E17 123 EA56
St. Mary St. SE18 165 EM77
St. Marychurch St. SE16 162 DW75
St. Marys, Bark. 145 ER67
St. Marys App. E12 125 EM64
St. Marys Ave. E11 124 EH58
St. Mary's Ave. N3 97 CY54
St. Mary's Ave., Brwd. 109 GA43
St. Mary's Ave., Brom. 204 EE97
St. Mary's Ave., Nthwd. 93 BS50
St. Mary's Ave., Stai. 174 BK87
St. Mary's Ave., Tedd. 177 CF93
St. Mary's Ave. Cen., Sthl. 156 CB77
St. Mary's Ave. N., Sthl. 156 CB77
St. Mary's Ave. S., Sthl. 156 CB77
St. Marys Clo. N17 100 DU53
Kemble Rd.
St. Marys Clo., Chess. 216 CM108
St. Marys Clo., Epsom 217 CU108
St. Mary's Clo., Grav. 191 GJ89
St. Marys Clo., Grays 170 GD79
Dock Rd.
St. Mary's Clo., Lthd. 231 CD123
St. Marys Clo., Orp. 206 EV96
St. Mary's Clo., Oxt. 254 EE129
St. Mary's Clo., Stai. 174 BK87
St. Mary's Clo., Sun. 195 BU98
Green Way
St. Mary's Clo. (Harefield), Uxb. 114 BH55
St. Marys Clo., Wat. 75 BV42
George St.
St. Marys Ct. E6 145 EM70
St. Mary's Ct. SE7 164 EK80
St. Mary's Ct. W5 157 CK75
St. Mary's Rd.
St. Mary's Cres. NW4 119 CV55
St. Mary's Cres., Hayes 135 BT73
St. Marys Cres., Islw. 157 CD80
St. Marys Cres., Stai. 174 BK87
St. Marys Dr., Felt. 175 BQ87
St. Mary's Dr., Sev. 256 FE123
St. Mary's Gdns. SE11 278 E8
St. Mary's Gdns. SE11 161 DN77
St. Mary's Gate W8 160 DB76
St. Marys Grn. N2 120 DC55
Thomas More Way
St. Marys Grn., West. 238 EJ118
St. Mary's Gro. N1 141 DP65
St. Mary's Gro. SW13 159 CV83
St. Mary's Gro. W4 158 CP79
St. Mary's Gro., Rich. 158 CM84
St. Marys Gro., West. 238 EJ118
St. Mary's La., Hert. 31 DM11
St. Mary's La., Upmin. 128 FN61
St. Marys Mans. W2 140 DC71
St. Mary's Ms. NW6 140 DB66
Priory Rd.
St. Mary's Ms., Rich. 177 CJ90
Back La.
St. Mary's Mt., Cat. 236 DT124
St. Marys Path N1 141 DP67
St. Mary's Pl. SE9 185 EN86
Eltham High St.
St. Mary's Pl. W5 157 CK75
St. Mary's Rd.
St. Mary's Pl. W8 160 DB76
St. Marys Rd. E10 123 EC62
St. Marys Rd. E13 144 EH68
St. Marys Rd. N8 121 DL56
High St.
St. Marys Rd. N9 100 DW46
St. Mary's Rd. NW10 138 CS67
St. Mary's Rd. NW11 119 CY59
St. Mary's Rd. SE15 162 DW81
St. Mary's Rd. SE25 202 DS97
St. Mary's Rd. (Wimbledon) SW19 179 CY92
St. Mary's Rd. W5 157 CK75
St. Mary's Rd., Barn. 98 DF45
St. Marys Rd., Bex. 187 FC88
St. Marys Rd., E.Mol. 197 CD99
St. Mary's Rd., Grays 171 GH77
St. Mary's Rd., Green. 189 FS85
St. Mary's Rd., Hayes 135 BT73
St. Mary's Rd., Hem.H. 40 BK19
St. Marys Rd., Ilf. 125 EQ61
St. Marys Rd., Lthd. 231 CH122
St. Marys Rd., Reig. 266 DB135
St. Mary's Rd., Slou. 132 AY74
St. Mary's Rd., S.Croy. 220 DR110
St. Marys Rd., Surb. 197 CK100
St. Marys Rd. (Long Ditton), Surb. 197 CJ101
St. Marys Rd., Swan. 207 FD98
St. Mary's Rd. (Denham), Uxb. 113 BF58
St. Mary's Rd. (Harefield), Uxb. 114 BH56
St. Mary's Rd. (Cheshunt), Wal.Cr. 66 DW29
St. Mary's Rd., Wat. 75 BV42
St. Marys Rd., Wey. 213 BR105
St. Mary's Rd., Wok. 226 AX117
St. Mary's Rd., Wor.Pk. 198 CS103
St. Marys Sq. W2 140 DD71
St. Mary's Sq. W5 157 CK75
St. Mary's Rd.
St. Marys Ter. W2 140 DD71
St. Marys Vw., Har. 117 CJ57
St. Mary's Wk. SE11 278 E8
St. Mary's Wk. SE11 161 DN77
St. Mary's Wk., Hayes 135 BT73
St. Mary's Rd.
St. Mary's Wk., Red. 252 DR133
St. Marys Wk., St.Alb. 43 CH16
St. Mary's Way, Chesh. 54 AP31
St. Mary's Way, Chig. 103 EN50
St. Marys Way, Ger.Cr. 90 AX54
St. Matthew Clo., Uxb. 134 BK72
St. Matthew St. SW1 277 M7
St. Matthew's Ave., Surb. 198 CL102
St. Matthews Clo., Rain. 147 FG66
St. Matthews Clo., Wat. 76 BX44
St. Matthew's Dr., Brom. 205 EM97
St. Matthew's Rd. SW2 161 DM84
St. Matthews Rd. W5 138 CL74
The Common
St. Matthew's Rd., Red. 250 DF133
St. Matthew's Row E2 142 DU69
St. Matthias Clo. NW9 119 CT57
St. Maur Rd. SW6 159 CZ81
St. Merryn Clo. SE18 165 ER80
St. Michael's All. EC3 275 L9
St. Michaels Ave. N9 100 DW45
St. Michaels Ave., Hem.H. 41 BP22
St. Michael's Ave., Wem. 138 CN65
St. Michaels Clo. E16 144 EK71
Fulmer Rd.
St. Michael's Clo. N3 97 CZ54
St. Michaels Clo. N12 98 DE50
St. Michaels Clo., Brom. 204 EL97
St. Michaels Clo., Erith 166 EX75
St. Helens Rd.
St. Michaels Clo., Harl. 35 ES14
St. Michaels Clo., S.Ock. 148 FQ73
St. Michaels Clo., Walt. 196 BW103
St. Michaels Clo., Wor.Pk. 199 CT103
St. Michael's Ct., Slou. 131 AK70
St. Michaels Cres., Pnr. 116 BY58
St. Michaels Dr., Wat. 59 BV33
St. Michaels Gdns. W10 139 CY71
St. Lawrence Ter.
St. Michael's Grn., Beac. 89 AL52
St. Michaels Rd. NW2 119 CW63
St. Michael's Rd. SW9 161 DM82
St. Michael's Rd., Ashf. 174 BN92
St. Michaels Rd., Brox. 49 DZ20
St. Michaels Rd., Cat. 236 DR122
St. Michaels Rd., Croy. 202 DQ102
St. Michaels Rd., Grays 171 GH78
St. Michaels Rd., Wall. 219 DJ107
St. Michaels Rd., Well. 166 EV83
St. Michael's Rd., Wok. 211 BD114
St. Michaels St. W2 272 A8
St. Michaels St. W2 140 DE71
St. Michaels St., St.Alb. 42 CB20
St. Michaels Ter. N22 99 DL54
St. Michaels Way, Pot.B. 64 DB30
St. Mildred's Ct. EC2 142 DR72
Poultry
St. Mildreds Rd. SE12 184 EE87
St. Mildreds Rd., Guil. 243 AZ133
St. Monica's Rd., Tad. 233 CZ121
St. Nazaire Clo., Egh. 173 BC92
Mullens Rd.
St. Neots Clo., Borwd. 78 CN38
St. Neots Rd., Rom. 106 FM52
St. Nicholas Ave., Horn. 127 FG62
St. Nicholas Ave., Lthd. 246 CB125
St. Nicholas Clo., Amer. 72 AV39
St. Nicholas Clo., Borwd. 77 CK44
St. Nicholas Clo., Uxb. 134 BK72
St. Nicholas Dr., Sev. 257 FJ126
St. Nicholas Dr., Shep. 194 BN101
St. Nicholas Glebe SW17 180 DG93
St. Nicholas Hill, Lthd. 231 CH122
St. Nicholas Mt., Hem.H. 39 BF20
St. Nicholas Rd. SE18 165 ET78
St. Nicholas Rd., Sutt. 218 DB106
St. Nicholas Rd., T.Ditt. 197 CF100
St. Nicholas St. SE8 163 EA81
Lucas St.
St. Nicholas Way, Sutt. 218 DB105
St. Nicolas La., Chis. 204 EL95
St. Ninian's Ct. N20 98 DF48
St. Norbert Grn. SE4 163 DY84
St. Norbert Rd. SE4 163 DY84
St. Normans Way, Epsom 217 CU110
St. Olaf's Rd. SW6 159 CY80
St. Olaves Clo., Stai. 173 BF94
St. Olaves Ct. EC2 275 K9
St. Olave's Est. SE1 279 N4
St. Olaves Gdns. SE11 278 D8
St. Olaves Rd. E6 145 EN67
St. Olave's Wk. SW16 201 DJ96
St. Olav's Sq. SE16 162 DW76
St. Omer Ridge, Guil. 259 BA135
St. Omer Rd., Guil. 259 BA135
St. Oswald's Pl. SE11 161 DM78
St. Oswald's Rd. SW16 201 DP95
St. Oswulf St. SW1 277 N9
St. Pancras Way NW1 141 DJ66
St. Patrick's Ct., Wdf.Grn. 102 EE52
St. Patrick's Gdns., Grav. 191 GK90
St. Patricks Pl., Grays 171 GJ77
St. Paul Clo., Uxb. 134 BK71
St. Paul St. N1 142 DQ67
St. Paul's All. EC4 141 DP72
St. Paul's Chyd.
St. Pauls Ave. NW2 139 CV65
St. Paul's Ave. SE16 143 DX74
St. Pauls Ave., Har. 118 CM57
St. Paul's Ave., Slou. 132 AT73
St. Paul's Chyd. EC4 274 G9
St. Paul's Chyd. EC4 141 DP72
St. Paul's Clo. SE7 164 EK78
St. Paul's Clo. W5 158 CM74
St. Pauls Clo., Add. 212 BG106
St. Pauls Clo., Ashf. 175 BQ92
St. Paul's Clo., Cars. 200 DE102
St. Pauls Clo., Chess. 215 CK105
St. Pauls Clo., Hayes 155 BR78
St. Paul's Clo., Houns. 156 BY82
St. Pauls Clo., S.Ock. 148 FQ73
St. Pauls Clo., Swans. 190 FY87
Swanscombe St.
St. Paul's Ct. W14 159 CX77
Colet Gdns.
St. Pauls Ctyd. SE8 163 EA80
Deptford High St.
St. Pauls Cray Rd., Chis. 205 ER95
St. Paul's Cres. NW1 141 DK66
St. Pauls Dr. E15 123 ED64
St. Paul's Ms. NW1 141 DK66
St. Paul's Cres.
St. Paul's Pl. N1 142 DR65
St. Pauls Pl., St.Alb. 43 CG20
St. Pauls Pl., S.Ock. 148 FQ73
St. Pauls Ri. N13 99 DP51
St. Paul's Rd. N1 141 DP65
St. Paul's Rd. N17 100 DU52
St. Paul's Rd., Bark. 145 EQ67
St. Paul's Rd., Brent. 157 CK79
St. Paul's Rd., Erith 167 FC80
St. Pauls Rd., Hem.H. 40 BK19
St. Paul's Rd., Rich. 158 CM83
St. Pauls Rd., Stai. 173 BD92
St. Paul's Rd., Th.Hth. 202 DQ97
St. Pauls Rd., Wok. 227 BA117
St. Paul's Rd. E., Dor. 263 CH137
St. Paul's Rd. W., Dor. 263 CG137
St. Paul's Shrubbery N1 142 DR65
St. Pauls Sq., Brom. 204 EG96
St. Paul's Ter. SE17 161 DP79
Westcott Rd.
St. Pauls Twr. E10 123 EB59
St. Pauls Wk., Kings.T. 178 CN94
Alexandra Rd.
St. Paul's Way E3 143 DZ71
St. Paul's Way E14 143 DZ71
St. Paul's Way N3 98 DB52
St. Pauls Way, Wal.Abb. 67 ED33
Rochford Ave.
St. Pauls Way, Wat. 76 BW40
St. Pauls Wd. Hill, Orp. 205 ES96
St. Peter's All. EC3 275 L9
St. Peter's Ave. E2 142 DU68
St. Peter's Clo.
St. Peter's Ave. E17 124 EE56
St. Peters Ave. N18 100 DU49
St. Peter's Clo. E2 142 DU68
St. Peters Clo. SW17 180 DE89
College Gdns.
St. Peter's Clo., Barn. 79 CV43
St. Peters Clo., Chis. 185 ER94
St. Peters Clo., Ger.Cr. 90 AY53
Lewis La.
St. Peters Clo., Hat. 45 CU17
St. Peters Clo., Ilf. 125 ES56
St. Peters Clo., Rick. 92 BH46
St. Peter's Clo., Ruis. 116 BX61
St. Peters Clo., St.Alb. 43 CD19
St. Peter's Clo., Slou. 130 AH70
St. Peters Clo., Stai. 173 BF93
St. Peters Clo., Swans. 190 FZ87
Keary Rd.
St. Peters Clo. (Bushey), Wat. 95 CD46
St. Peters Clo., Wind. 172 AU85
Church Rd.
St. Peters Clo., Wok. 227 BC120
St. Peter's Ct. NW4 119 CW57
St. Peters Ct. SE3 164 EF84
Eltham Rd.
St. Peters Ct. SE4 163 DZ82
Wickham Rd.
St. Peters Ct., Ger.Cr. 90 AY53
High St.
St. Peters Ct., W.Mol. 196 CA98
St. Peter's Gdns. SE27 181 DN90
St. Peter's Gro. W6 159 CU77
St. Peters La., Orp. 206 EU96
St. Peter's Pl. W9 140 DB70
Shirland Rd.
St. Peters Rd. N9 100 DW46
St. Peter's Rd. W6 159 CU78
St. Peters Rd., Brwd. 108 FV49
Crescent Rd.
St. Peter's Rd., Croy. 220 DR105
St. Peter's Rd., Grays 171 GH77
St. Peters Rd., Kings.T. 198 CN96
St. Peters Rd., St.Alb. 43 CE20
St. Peters Rd., Sthl. 136 CA71
St. Peters Rd., Twick. 177 CH85
St. Peters Rd., Uxb. 134 BK71
St. Peter's Rd., W.Mol. 196 CA98
St. Peters Rd., Wok. 227 BB121
St. Peter's Sq. E2 142 DU68
St. Peter's Clo.
St. Peter's Sq. W6 159 CU78
St. Peters St. N1 141 DP67
St. Peters St., St.Alb. 43 CD20
St. Peter's St., S.Croy. 220 DR106
St. Peters Ter. SW6 159 CY80
St. Peter's Vil. W6 159 CU77
St. Peter's Way N1 142 DS66
St. Peters Way W5 137 CK71
St. Peters Way, Hayes 155 BR78
St. Peters Way, Rick. 73 BB42
St. Petersburgh Ms. W2 140 DB73
St. Petersburgh Pl. W2 140 DB73
St. Philip Sq. SW8 161 DH82
St. Philip St. SW8 161 DH82
St. Philip's Ave., Wor.Pk. 199 CV103
St. Philip's Rd. E8 142 DU65
St. Philips Rd., Surb. 197 CK100
St. Philip's Way N1 142 DQ67
Linton St.
St. Pinnock Ave., Stai. 194 BG95
St. Quentin Rd., Well. 165 ET83
St. Quintin Ave. W10 139 CW71
St. Quintin Gdns. W10 139 CW71
St. Quintin Rd. E13 144 EH68
St. Raphaels Ct., St.Alb. 43 CE19
Avenue Rd.
St. Raphael's Way NW10 118 CQ64
St. Regis Clo. N10 99 DH54
St. Ronan's Clo., Barn. 80 DD38
St. Ronans Cres., Wdf.Grn. 102 EG52
St. Rule St. SW8 161 DJ82
St. Saviour's Est. SE1 279 P6
St. Saviour's Est. SE1 162 DT76
St. Saviours Pl., Guil. 242 AW134
Leas Rd.
St. Saviour's Rd. SW2 181 DM85
St. Saviours Rd., Croy. 202 DQ100
St. Saviours Vw., St.Alb. 43 CF19
Avenue Rd.
St. Silas Pl. NW5 140 DG65
St. Silas St. Est. NW5 140 DG65
St. Simon's Ave. SW15 179 CW85
St. Stephens Ave. E17 123 EC57
St. Stephens Ave. W12 159 CV75
St. Stephens Ave. W13 137 CH72
St. Stephen's Ave., Ash. 232 CL116
St. Stephens Ave., St.Alb. 42 CB22
St. Stephens Clo. E17 123 EB57
St. Stephens Clo. NW8 140 DE67
St. Stephens Clo., St.Alb. 42 CB22
St. Stephens Clo., Sthl. 136 CA71
St. Stephens Cres. W2 140 DA72
St. Stephens Cres., Brwd. 109 GA49
St. Stephens Cres., Th.Hth. 201 DN97
St. Stephens Gdn. Est. W2 140 DA72
Shrewsbury Rd.
St. Stephens Gdns. SW15 179 CZ85
Manfred Rd.
St. Stephens Gdns. W2 140 DA72
St. Stephens Gdns., Twick. 177 CJ86
St. Stephens Gro. SE13 163 EC83
St. Stephens Hill, St.Alb. 42 CC22
St. Stephens Ms. W2 140 DA71
Chepstow Rd.
St. Stephen's Par. E7 144 EJ66
Green St.
St. Stephen's Pas., Twick. 177 CJ86
Richmond Rd.
St. Stephen's Rd. E3 143 DZ68
St. Stephens Rd. E6 144 EJ66
St. Stephen's Rd. E17 123 EB57
Grove Rd.
St. Stephens Rd. W13 137 CH72
St. Stephen's Rd., Barn. 79 CX43
St. Stephens Rd., Enf. 83 DX37
St. Stephens Rd., Houns. 176 CA86
St. Stephen's Rd., West Dr. 134 BK74
St. Stephens Row EC4 275 K9
St. Stephens Ter. SW8 161 DM80
St. Stephen's Wk. SW7 160 DC77
St. Swithin's La. EC4 275 K10
St. Swithin's La. EC4 142 DR73
St. Swithun's Rd. SE13 183 ED85
St. Teresa Wk., Grays 171 GH76
St. Theresa Clo., Epsom 216 CQ114
St. Theresa's Rd., Felt. 155 BT84
St. Thomas' Clo., Surb. 198 CM102
St. Thomas Clo., Wok. 226 AW117
St. Mary's Rd.
St. Thomas Ct., Bex. 186 FA87
St. Thomas Dr., Guil. 244 BL131
The St.
St. Thomas Dr., Orp. 205 EQ102
St. Thomas' Dr., Pnr. 94 BY53
St. Thomas Gdns., Ilf. 145 EQ65
St. Thomas Pl. NW1 141 DK66
St. Thomas Rd. E16 144 EG72
St. Thomas Rd. N14 99 DK45
St. Thomas' Rd. W4 158 CQ79
St. Thomas Rd., Belv. 167 FC75
St. Thomas Rd., Brwd. 108 FX47
St. Thomas Rd., Grav. 191 GF89
St. Thomas St. SE1 279 K3
St. Thomas St. SE1 142 DR74
St. Thomas Wk., Slou. 153 BD80
St. Thomas's Ave., Grav. 191 GH88
St. Thomas's Clo., Wal.Abb. 68 EH33
St. Thomas's Gdns. NW5 140 DG65
Queens Cres.
St. Thomas's Ms., Guil. 259 AZ136
St. Catherines Pk.
St. Thomas's Pl. E9 142 DW66
St. Thomas's Rd. N4 121 DN61
St. Thomas's Rd. NW10 138 CS67
St. Thomas's Sq. E9 142 DV66
St. Thomas's Way SW6 159 CZ80
St. Timothy's Ms., Brom. 204 EH95
Wharton Rd.
St. Ursula Gro., Pnr. 116 BX57
St. Ursula Rd., Sthl. 136 CA72
St. Vincent Clo. SE27 181 DP92
St. Vincent Dr., St.Alb. 43 CG23
St. Vincent Rd., Twick. 176 CC86
St. Vincent Rd., Walt. 195 BV104
St. Vincent St. W1 272 G7
St. Vincents Ave., Dart. 188 FM85
St. Vincents Rd., Dart. 188 FN86
St. Vincents Way, Pot.B. 64 DC33
St. Wilfrids Clo., Barn. 80 DE43
St. Wilfrids Rd., Barn. 80 DD43
St. Winefride's Ave. E12 125 EM64
St. Winifreds, Ken. 236 DQ115
St. Winifreds Clo., Chig. 103 EQ50
St. Winifreds Rd., Tedd. 177 CH93
St. Winifred's Rd., West. 239 EM118
St. Yon Ct., St.Alb. 44 CL20
Saints Clo. SE27 181 DP91
Wolfington Rd.
Saints Dr. E7 124 EK64
Saints Wk., Grays 171 GJ77
Sakins Cft., Harl. 51 ET18
Saladin Dr., Purf. 168 FN77
Salamanca Pl. SE1 278 B9
Salamanca St. SE1 278 A9
Salamanca St. SE1 161 DM77
Salamander Clo., Kings.T. 177 CJ92
Salamander Quay (Harefield), Uxb. 92 BG52
Coppermill La.
Salamons Way, Rain. 147 FE72
Salbrook Rd., Red. 266 DG142
Salcombe Dr., Mord. 199 CX102
Salcombe Dr., Rom. 126 EZ58
Salcombe Gdns. NW7 97 CW51
Salcombe Pk., Loug. 84 EK43
High Rd.
Salcombe Rd. E17 123 DZ59
Salcombe Rd. N16 122 DS64
Salcombe Rd., Ashf. 174 BL91
Salcombe Way, Hayes 135 BS69
Portland Rd.
Salcombe Way, Ruis. 115 BU61
Salcot Cres., Croy. 221 EC110
Salcote Rd., Grav. 191 GL92
Salcott Rd. SW11 180 DE85
Salcott Rd., Croy. 201 DL104
Sale Pl. W2 272 B7
Sale Pl. W2 140 DE71
Sale St. E2 142 DU70
Hereford St.
Salehurst Clo., Har. 118 CL57
Salehurst Rd. SE4 183 DZ86
Salem Pl., Croy. 202 DQ104
Salem Pl., Grav. 190 GD87
Shepherd St.
Salem Rd. W2 140 DB73
Salford Rd. SW2 181 DK88
Salfords Ind. Est., Red. 267 DH143
Salfords Way, Red. 266 DG142
Salhouse Clo. SE28 146 EW72
Rollesby Way
Salisbury Ave. N3 119 CZ55
Salisbury Ave., Bark. 145 ES66
Salisbury Ave., St.Alb. 43 CH19
Salisbury Ave., Slou. 131 AQ70
Salisbury Ave., Sutt. 217 CZ107
Salisbury Ave., Swan. 207 FG98
Salisbury Clo. SE17 279 K8
Salisbury Clo., Amer. 55 AS39
Salisbury Clo., Pot.B. 64 DC32
Salisbury Clo., Upmin. 129 FT61
Canterbury Ave.
Salisbury Clo., Wor.Pk. 199 CT104

Salisbury Ct. EC4 274 **F9**
Salisbury Ct. EC4 141 DP72
Salisbury Cres. (Cheshunt), Wal.Cr. 67 DX32
Salisbury Gdns. SW19 179 CY94
Salisbury Gdns., Buck.H. 102 EK47
Salisbury Gdns., Welw.G.C. 29 CZ10
Salisbury Hall Gdns. E4 101 EA51
Salisbury Ho. E14 143 EB72
Hobday St.
Salisbury Ms. SW6 159 CZ80
Dawes Rd.
Salisbury Pl. SW9 161 DP80
Salisbury Pl. W1 272 **D6**
Salisbury Pl. W1 140 DF71
Salisbury Pl., W.Byf. 212 BJ111
Salisbury Plaza, Hat. 45 CT16
Lemsford Rd.
Salisbury Rd. E4 101 EA48
Salisbury Rd. E7 144 EG65
Salisbury Rd. E10 123 EC61
Salisbury Rd. E12 124 EK64
Salisbury Rd. E17 123 EC57
Salisbury Rd. N4 121 DP57
Salisbury Rd. N9 100 DU48
Salisbury Rd. N22 99 DP53
Salisbury Rd. SE25 202 DU100
Salisbury Rd. SW19 179 CY94
Salisbury Rd. W13 157 CG75
Salisbury Rd., Bans. 218 DB114
Salisbury Rd., Barn. 79 CY41
Salisbury Rd., Bex. 186 FA88
Salisbury Rd., Brom. 204 EL99
Salisbury Rd., Cars. 218 DF107
Salisbury Rd., Dag. 147 FB65
Salisbury Rd., Dart. 188 FQ88
Salisbury Rd., Enf. 83 DZ37
Salisbury Rd., Felt. 176 BW88
Salisbury Rd., Gdse. 252 DW131
Salisbury Rd., Grav. 191 GF88
Salisbury Rd., Grays 170 GC79
Salisbury Rd., Har. 117 CD57
Salisbury Rd., Hodd. 49 EC15
Salisbury Rd., Houns. 156 BW83
Salisbury Rd. (Heathrow Airport), Houns. 175 BQ85
Salisbury Rd., Ilf. 125 ES61
Salisbury Rd., N.Mal. 198 CR97
Salisbury Rd., Pnr. 115 BU56
Salisbury Rd., Rich. 158 CL84
Salisbury Rd., Rom. 127 FH57
Salisbury Rd., Sthl. 156 BY77
Salisbury Rd., Uxb. 134 BH68
Salisbury Rd., Wat. 75 BV38
Salisbury Rd., Welw.G.C. 29 CZ10
Salisbury Rd., Wok. 226 AY119
Salisbury Rd., Wor.Pk. 199 CT104
Salisbury Sq. EC4 274 **E9**
Salisbury Sq., Hat. 45 CW17
Park St.
Salisbury St. NW8 272 **B5**
Salisbury St. NW8 140 DE70
Salisbury St. W3 158 CQ75
Salisbury Ter. SE15 162 DW83
Salisbury Wk. N19 121 DJ61
Salix Clo., Sun. 175 BV94
Oak Gro.
Salix Rd., Grays 170 GD79
Salliesfield, Twick. 177 CD86
Salmen Rd. E13 144 EF68
Salmon Clo., Welw.G.C. 30 DA06
Salmon La. E14 143 DY72
Salmon Meadow Footpath, Hem.H. 40 BK24
London Rd.
Salmon Rd., Belv. 166 FA78
Salmon Rd., Dart. 168 FM83
Salmon St. E14 143 DZ72
Salmon La.
Salmon St. NW9 118 CP60
Salmond Clo., Stan. 95 CG51
Robb Rd.
Salmons La., Cat. 236 DS120
Salmons La., Whyt. 236 DS120
Salmons La. W., Cat. 236 DS120
Salmons Rd. N9 100 DU46
Salmons Rd., Chess. 215 CK107
Salmons Rd., Lthd. 245 BV129
Salomons Rd. E13 144 EJ71
Chalk Rd.
Salop Rd. E17 123 DX58
Salt Box Hill, West. 222 EH113
Salt Box Rd., Guil. 242 AT129
Salt Hill Ave., Slou. 131 AQ74
Salt Hill Dr., Slou. 131 AQ74
Salt Hill Way, Slou. 131 AQ74
Saltash Clo., Sutt. 217 CZ105
Saltash Rd., Ilf. 103 ER52
Saltash Rd., Well. 166 EW81
Saltcoats Rd. W4 158 CS75
Saltcroft Clo., Wem. 118 CP60
Salter Clo., Har. 116 BZ62
Salter Rd. SE16 143 DX74
Salter St. E14 143 EA73
Salter St. NW10 139 CU69
Salterford Rd. SW17 180 DG93
Salters Clo., Berk. 38 AT17
Salters Clo., Rick. 92 BL46
Salters Gdns., Wat. 75 BU39
Salters Hall Ct. EC4 275 **K10**
Salters Hill SE19 182 DR92
Salters Rd. E17 123 ED56
Salters Rd. W10 139 CX70
Salterton Rd. N7 121 DL62
Saltford Clo., Erith 167 FE78
Salthill Clo., Uxb. 114 BL64
Saltley Clo. E6 144 EL72
Dunnock Rd.
Saltoun Rd. SW2 161 DN84
Saltram Clo. N15 122 DT56
Saltram Cres. W9 139 CZ69
Saltwell St. E14 143 EA73
Saltwood Clo., Orp. 224 EW105
Saltwood Gro. SE17 162 DR78
Merrow St.
Salusbury Rd. NW6 139 CY67
Salutation Rd. SE10 164 EE77
Salvia Gdns., Grnf. 137 CG68
Selborne Gdns.
Salvin Rd. SW15 159 CX83
Salway Clo., Wdf.Grn. 102 EF52
Salway Pl. E15 144 EE65
Broadway
Salway Rd. E15 143 ED65
Salwey Cres., Brox. 49 DZ20
Sam Bartram Clo. SE7 164 EJ78
Samantha Clo. E17 123 DZ59
Samantha Ms. (Havering-atte-Bower), Rom. 105 FE48
Sambruck Ms. SE6 183 EB88
Samels Ct. W6 159 CU78
South Black Lion La.
Samford St. NW8 272 **A5**
Samford St. NW8 140 DD70
Samian Gate, St.Alb. 42 BZ22
Mayne Ave.
Samos Rd. SE20 202 DV96
Samphire Ct., Grays 170 GE80
Salix Rd.
Sample Oak La., Guil. 259 BE140
Sampson Ave., Barn. 79 CX43
Sampson Clo., Belv. 166 EX76
Carrill Way
Sampson St. E1 142 DU74
Sampsons Ct., Shep. 195 BQ99
Linden Way
Samson St. E13 144 EJ68
Samuel Clo. E8 142 DT67
Pownall Rd.
Samuel Clo. SE14 163 DX79
Samuel Clo. SE18 164 EL77
Samuel Gray Gdns., Kings.T. 197 CK95
Skerne Rd.
Samuel Johnson Clo. SW16 181 DN91
Curtis Fld. Rd.
Samuel Lewis Trust Dws. E8 122 DU63
Amhurst Rd.
Samuel Lewis Trust Dws. N1 141 DN66
Liverpool Rd.
Samuel Lewis Trust Dws. SW3 276 **B9**
Samuel Lewis Trust Dws. SW6 160 DA80
Samuel St. SE15 162 DT80
Samuel St. SE18 165 EM77
Samuels Clo. W6 159 CU78
South Black Lion La.
Sancroft Clo. NW2 119 CV62
Sancroft Rd., Har. 95 CF54
Sancroft St. SE11 278 **C10**
Sancroft St. SE11 161 DM78
Sanctuary, The SW1 277 **N5**
Sanctuary, The, Bex. 186 EX86
Sanctuary, The, Mord. 200 DA100
Sanctuary Clo., Dart. 188 FJ86
Sanctuary Clo. (Harefield), Uxb. 92 BJ52
Sanctuary Rd., Houns. 174 BN86
Sanctuary St. SE1 279 **J5**
Sandal Rd. N18 100 DU50
Sandal Rd., N.Mal. 198 CR99
Sandal St. E15 144 EE67
Sandale Clo. N16 122 DR62
Stoke Newington Ch. St.
Sandall Clo. W5 138 CL70
Sandall Rd. NW5 141 DJ65
Sandall Rd. W5 138 CL70
Sandalls Spring, Hem.H. 39 BF18
Sandalwood, Guil. 258 AV135
Sandalwood Clo. E1 143 DY70
Solebay St.
Sandalwood Dr., Ruis. 115 BQ59
Sandalwood Rd., Felt. 175 BV90
Sanday Clo., Hem.H. 41 BP22
Sandbach Pl. SE18 165 EQ77
Sandbanks, Felt. 175 BS88
Sandbanks Hill, Dart. 189 FV93
Sandbourne Ave. SW19 200 DB97
Sandbourne Rd. SE4 163 DY82
Sandbrook Clo. NW7 96 CR51
Sandbrook Rd. N16 122 DS62
Sandby Grn. SE9 164 EL83
Sandcliff Rd., Erith 167 FD77
Sandcroft Clo. N13 99 DP51
Sandcross La., Reig. 265 CZ137
Sandell St. SE1 278 **D4**
Sandells Ave., Ashf. 175 BQ91
Sandels Way, Beac. 89 AK51
Sandelswood End, Beac. 89 AK50
Sanders Clo., Hmptn. 176 CC92
Sanders Clo., Hem.H. 40 BM24
Sanders Clo., St.Alb. 61 CK27
Sanders La. NW7 97 CX52
Sanders Rd., Hem.H. 40 BM23
Sanders Way N19 121 DK60
Sussex Way
Sandersfield Gdns., Bans. 234 DA115
Sandersfield Rd., Bans. 234 DB115
Sanderson Ave., Sev. 224 FA110
Sanderson Clo. NW5 121 DH63
Sanderson Rd., Uxb. 134 BJ65
Sanderstead Ave. NW2 119 CY61
Sanderstead Clo. SW12 181 DJ87
Atkins Rd.
Sanderstead Ct. Ave., S.Croy. 220 DU113
Sanderstead Hill, S.Croy. 220 DS111
Sanderstead Rd. E10 123 DY60
Sanderstead Rd., Orp. 206 EV100
Sanderstead Rd., S.Croy. 220 DR108
Sandes Pl., Lthd. 231 CG118
Sandfield, Hat. 45 CV21
Sandfield Gdns., Th.Hth. 202 DQ97
Sandfield Pas., Th.Hth. 202 DQ97
Sandfield Rd., St.Alb. 43 CG20
Sandfield Rd., Th.Hth. 201 DP97
Sandfield Ter., Guil. 258 AX135
Sandfields, Wok. 227 BD124
Sandford Ave. N22 100 DQ52
Sandford Ave., Loug. 85 EQ41
Sandford Clo. E6 145 EM70
Sandford Ct. N16 122 DS60
Sandford La. N16 122 DT61
Lawrence Bldgs.
Sandford Rd. E6 144 EL70
Sandford Rd., Bexh. 166 EY84
Sandford Rd., Brom. 204 EG98
Sandford St. SW6 160 DB80
King's Rd.
Sandgate Clo., Rom. 127 FD59
Sandgate La. SW18 180 DE88
Sandgate Rd., Well. 166 EW80
Sandgate St. SE15 162 DV79
Sandham Pt. SE18 165 EP77
Troy Ct.
Sandhills, Wall. 219 DK105
Sandhills La., Vir.W. 192 AY99
Sandhills Meadow, Shep. 195 BQ101
Sandhills Rd., Reig. 266 DA136
Sandhurst Ave., Har. 116 CB58
Sandhurst Ave., Surb. 198 CP101
Sandhurst Clo. NW9 118 CN55
Sandhurst Clo., S.Croy. 220 DS109
Sandhurst Dr., Ilf. 125 ET63
Sandhurst Rd. N9 82 DW44
Sandhurst Rd. NW9 118 CN55
Sandhurst Rd. SE6 183 ED88
Sandhurst Rd., Bex. 186 EX85
Sandhurst Rd., Orp. 206 EU104
Sandhurst Rd., Sid. 185 ET90
Sandhurst Rd., Til. 171 GJ82
Sandhurst Way, S.Croy. 220 DS108
Sandiford Rd., Sutt. 199 CZ103
Sandiland Cres., Brom. 204 EF103
Sandilands, Croy. 202 DU103
Sandilands, Sev. 256 FD122
Sandilands Rd. SW6 160 DB81
Sandison St. SE15 162 DT83
Sandland St. WC1 274 **C7**
Sandland St. WC1 141 DM71
Sandlands Gro., Tad. 233 CU123
Sandlands Rd., Tad. 233 CU123
Sandlers End, Slou. 131 AP70
Sandlewood Ave., Cher. 193 BE104
Sandling Ri. SE9 185 EN90
Sandlings, The N22 99 DN54
Sandlings Clo. SE15 162 DV82
Pilkington Rd.
Sandmere Clo., Hem.H. 40 BN21
St. Albans Rd.
Sandmere Rd. SW4 161 DL84
Sandon Clo., Esher 197 CD101
Sandon Rd. (Cheshunt), Wal.Cr. 66 DW30
Sandow Cres., Hayes 155 BT76
Sandown Ave., Dag. 147 FC65
Sandown Ave., Esher 214 CC106
Sandown Ave., Horn. 128 FK61
Sandown Clo., Houns. 155 BU81
Sandown Dr., Cars. 218 DG109
Sandown Gate, Esher 197 CD104
Sandown Ind. Pk., Esher 196 CA103
Sandown Rd. SE25 202 DV99
Sandown Rd., Couls. 234 DG116
Sandown Rd., Esher 214 CC105
Sandown Rd., Grav. 191 GJ93
Sandown Rd., Slou. 131 AM71
Sandown Rd., Wat. 76 BW38
Sandown Way, Nthlt. 136 BY65
Sandpiper Clo. E17 101 DX53
Sandpiper Clo. SE16 163 DZ75
Sandpiper Dr., Erith 167 FH80
Sandpiper Rd., S.Croy. 221 DX111
Sandpiper Way, Orp. 206 EX98
Sandpipers, The, Grav. 191 GK89
Sandpit Hall Rd., Wok. 210 AU112
Sandpit La., Brwd. 108 FT46
Sandpit La., St.Alb. 43 CE19
Sandpit Pl. SE7 164 EL78
Sandpit Rd., Brom. 184 EE92
Sandpit Rd., Dart. 168 FJ84
Sandpit Rd., Red. 266 DE135
Sandpit Rd., Welw.G.C. 29 CY11
Sandpits La., H.Wyc. 88 AC48
Sandpits Rd., Croy. 221 DX105
Sandpits Rd., Rich. 177 CK89
Sandra Clo. N22 100 DQ53
New Rd.
Sandra Clo., Houns. 176 CB85
Sandridge Clo., Har. 117 CE56
Sandridge Ct. N4 122 DQ62
Queens Dr.
Sandridge Rd., St.Alb. 43 CE18
Sandridge St. N19 121 DJ61
Sandridgebury La., St.Alb. 43 CE16
Sandringham Ave. SW20 199 CY96
Sandringham Ave., Harl. 50 EL15
Sandringham Clo. SW19 179 CX88
Sandringham Clo., Enf. 82 DS40
Sandringham Clo., Ilf. 125 EQ55
Sandringham Clo., Wok. 228 BG116
Sandringham Ct. W9 140 DC69
Maida Vale
Sandringham Ct., Slou. 131 AK72
Sandringham Cres., Har. 116 CA61
Sandringham Cres., St.Alb. 43 CG16
Sandringham Dr., Ashf. 174 BK91
Sandringham Dr., Well. 165 ES82
Sandringham Gdns. N8 121 DL58
Sandringham Gdns. N12 98 DD51
Sandringham Gdns., Houns. 155 BU81
Sandringham Gdns., Ilf. 125 EQ55
Sandringham Ms. W5 137 CK73
High St.
Sandringham Rd. E7 124 EJ64
Sandringham Rd. E8 122 DT64
Sandringham Rd. E10 123 ED58
Sandringham Rd. N22 122 DQ55
Sandringham Rd. NW2 139 CV65
Sandringham Rd. NW11 119 CY59
Sandringham Rd., Bark. 145 ET65
Sandringham Rd., Brwd. 108 FV43
Sandringham Rd., Brom. 184 EG92
Sandringham Rd., Houns. 174 BK85
Sandringham Rd., Nthlt. 136 CA66
Sandringham Rd., Pot.B. 64 DB30
Sandringham Rd., Th.Hth. 202 DQ99
Sandringham Rd., Wat. 76 BW37
Sandringham Rd., Wor.Pk. 199 CU104
Sandringham Way, Wal.Cr. 67 DX34
Sandrock Pl., Croy. 221 DX105
Sandrock Rd. SE13 163 EA83
Sandrock Rd., Dor. 262 CB138
Sandroyd Way, Cob. 214 CA113
Sand's End La. SW6 160 DB81
Sands Fm. Dr., Slou. 130 AJ70
Sands Way, Wdf.Grn. 102 EL51
Sandstone Pl. N19 121 DH61
Sandstone Rd. SE12 184 EH89
Sandtoft Rd. SE7 164 EH79
Sandway Path, Orp. 206 EW98
Okemore Gdns.
Sandway Rd., Orp. 206 EW98
Sandwell Cres. NW6 140 DA65
Sandwich St. WC1 273 **P3**
Sandwich St. WC1 141 DL69
Sandwick Clo. NW7 97 CU52
Sebergham Gro.
Sandy Bank Rd., Grav. 191 GH88
Sandy Bury, Orp. 205 ER104
Sandy Clo., Hert. 31 DP09
Sandy Clo., Wok. 227 BB117
Sandy La.
Sandy Dr., Cob. 214 CA111
Sandy Dr., Felt. 175 BS88
Sandy Hill Ave. SE18 165 EP78
Sandy Hill Rd. SE18 165 EP78
Sandy Hill Rd., Wall. 219 DJ109
Sandy La., Bet. 264 CS135
Sandy La., Cob. 214 BZ112
Sandy La., Dart. 189 FW89
Sandy La. (Chadwell St. Mary), Grays 171 GH79
Sandy La. (West Thurrock), Grays 169 FV79
London Rd.
Sandy La., Guil. 258 AU139
Sandy La. (Albury Heath), Guil. 260 BJ141
Sandy La. (Shere), Guil. 260 BN139
Sandy La., Har. 118 CM58
Sandy La., Kings.T. 197 CH95
Sandy La., Lthd. 214 CB111
Sandy La., Mitch. 200 DG95
Sandy La., Nthwd. 93 BU50
Sandy La., Orp. 206 EU101
Sandy La. (St. Paul's Cray), Orp. 206 EW96
Sandy La., Oxt. 253 EC129
Sandy La. (Limpsfield), Oxt. 254 EH127
Sandy La. (Bletchingley), Red. 251 DP132
Sandy La. (Nutfield), Red. 267 DK135
Sandy La., Reig. 265 CW135
Sandy La., Rich. 177 CJ89
Sandy La., Sev. 257 FJ123
Sandy La., Sid. 186 EX94
Sandy La., S.Ock. 148 FM73
Sandy La., Sutt. 217 CY108
Sandy La., Tad. 234 DA123
Sandy La., Tedd. 177 CG94
Sandy La., Vir.W. 193 AZ99
Sandy La., Walt. 195 BV100
Sandy La. (Bushey), Wat. 76 CC41
Sandy La., West. 255 ER125
Sandy La., Wok. 227 BC116
Sandy La. (Chobham), Wok. 228 BG116
Sandy La. (Send), Wok. 227 BC123
Sandy La. Est., Rich. 177 CK89
Sandy La. N., Wall. 219 DK106
Sandy La. S., Wall. 219 DK107
Sandy Lo. La., Nthwd. 93 BR47
Sandy Lo. Rd., Rick. 93 BP47
Sandy Lo. Way, Nthwd. 93 BS50
Sandy Mead, Maid. 150 AC78
Sandy Ridge, Chis. 185 EN93
Sandy Ri., Ger.Cr. 90 AY53
Sandy Rd. NW3 120 DB62
Sandy Rd., Add. 212 BG107
Sandy Way, Cob. 214 CA112
Sandy Way, Croy. 203 DZ104
Sandy Way, Walt. 195 BT102
Sandy Way, Wok. 227 BC117
Sandycombe Rd., Felt. 175 BU88
Sandycombe Rd., Rich. 158 CN83
Sandycombe Rd., Twick. 177 CJ86
Sandycroft SE2 166 EU79
Sandycroft, Epsom 217 CW110
Sandycroft Rd., Amer. 72 AV39
Sandyhill Rd., Ilf. 125 EP63
Sandymount Ave., Stan. 95 CJ50
Sandy's Row E1 275 **N7**
Sandy's Row E1 142 DS71
Sanfoin End, Hem.H. 40 BN18
Sanford La. N16 122 DT61
Stoke Newington High St.
Sanford St. SE14 163 DY79
Sanford Ter. N16 122 DT62
Sanford Wk. N16 122 DT61
Sanford Ter.
Sanford Wk. SE14 163 DY79
Cold Blow La.
Sanger Ave., Chess. 216 CL106
Sanger Dr., Wok. 227 BC123
Sangers Dr., Horl. 268 DF148
Sangers Wk., Horl. 268 DF148
Sangers Dr.
Sangley Rd. SE6 183 EB87
Sangley Rd. SE25 202 DS98
Sangora Rd. SW11 160 DD84
Sans Wk. EC1 274 **E4**
Sans Wk. EC1 141 DN70
Sansom Rd. E11 124 EE61
Sansom St. SE5 162 DR80
Santers La., Pot.B. 63 CY33
Santley St. SW4 161 DM84
Santos Rd. SW18 180 DA85
Santway, The, Stan. 95 CE50
Sanway Clo., W.Byf. 212 BL114
Sanway Rd., W.Byf. 212 BL114
Sapcote Trd. Cen. NW10 119 CT64
Saperton Wk. SE11 278 **C8**
Saperton Wk. SE11 161 DM77
Sapho Pk., Grav. 191 GM91
Saphora Clo., Orp. 223 ER106
Oleander Clo.
Sappers Clo., Saw. 36 EZ05
Sapphire Clo. E6 145 EN72
Sapphire Clo., Dag. 126 EW60
Sapphire Rd. SE8 163 DY77
Sappho Ct., Wok. 226 AS116
Langmans Way
Sara Ct., Beck. 203 EB95
Albemarle Rd.
Sara Cres., Green. 169 FU84
Sara Pk., Grav. 191 GL91
Saracen Clo., Croy. 202 DR100
Saracen Est., Hem.H. 41 BP18
Saracen St. E14 143 EA72
Saracens Head, Hem.H. 40 BN19
Adeyfield Rd.
Saracen's Head Yd. EC3 275 **P9**
Sarah Ho. SW15 159 CT84
Sarah St. N1 275 **N2**
Saratoga Rd. E5 122 DW63
Sardinia St. WC2 274 **B9**
Sarel Way, Horl. 269 DH146
Sargeant Clo., Uxb. 134 BK69
Ratcliffe Clo.
Sarita Clo., Har. 95 CD54
Sarjant Path SW19 179 CX89
Queensmere Rd.
Sark Clo., Houns. 156 CA80
Sark Wk. E16 144 EH72
Sarnesfield Ho. SE15 162 DV79
Pencraig Way
Sarnesfield Rd., Enf. 82 DR41
Church St.
Sarratt Ave., Hem.H. 40 BN15
Sarratt Bottom, Rick. 73 BE36
Sarratt La., Rick. 74 BH40
Sarratt Rd., Rick. 74 BM41
Sarre Ave., Horn. 148 FJ65
Sarre Rd. NW2 119 CZ64
Sarre Rd., Orp. 206 EW99
Sarsby Dr., Stai. 173 BA89
Feathers La.
Sarsen Ave., Houns. 156 BZ82
Sarsfeld Rd. SW12 180 DF88
Sarsfield Rd., Grnf. 137 CH68
Sartor Rd. SE15 163 DX84
Sarum Complex, Uxb. 134 BH68
Sarum Grn., Wey. 195 BS104
Sarum Pl., Hem.H. 40 BL16
Sarum Ter. E3 143 DZ70
Satanita Clo. E16 144 EK72
Fulmer Rd.
Satchell Mead NW9 97 CT53
Satchwell Rd. E2 142 DU69
Satinwood Ct., Hem.H. 40 BL22
Redwood Dr.
Satis Ct., Epsom 217 CT111
Windmill Ave.
Saturn Way, Hem.H. 40 BM17
Sauls Grn. E11 124 EE62
Napier Rd.
Saunder Clo., Wal.Cr. 67 DX27
Welsummer Way
Saunders Clo. E14 143 DZ73
Limehouse Causeway
Saunders Clo., Grav. 190 GE89
Saunders Copse, Wok. 226 AV122
Saunders La., Wok. 226 AS122
Saunders Ness Rd. E14 163 EC78
Saunders Rd. SE18 165 ET78
Saunders Rd., Uxb. 134 BM66
Saunders St. SE11 278 **D8**
Saunders St. SE11 161 DN77
Saunders Way SE28 146 EV73
Oriole Way
Saunders Way, Dart. 188 FM89
Saunderton Rd., Wem. 117 CH64
Saunton Ave., Hayes 155 BT80
Saunton Rd., Horn. 127 FG61
Savage Gdns. E6 145 EM72
Savage Gdns. EC3 275 **N10**
Savay Clo. (Denham), Uxb. 114 BG59
Savay La. (Denham), Uxb. 114 BG58
Savernake Rd. N9 82 DU44
Savernake Rd. NW3 120 DF63
Savile Clo., N.Mal. 198 CS99
Savile Gdns., Croy. 202 DT103
Savile Row W1 273 **K10**
Savile Row W1 141 DJ73
Savill Clo. (Cheshunt), Wal.Cr. 66 DQ25
Markham Rd.
Savill Gdns. SW20 199 CU97
Bodnant Gdns.
Savill Row, Wdf.Grn. 102 EF51
Saville Cres., Ashf. 175 BR93
Saville Rd. E16 144 EL74
Saville Rd. W4 158 CR76
Saville Rd., Rom. 126 EZ58
Saville Rd., Twick. 177 CF88
Saville Row, Brom. 204 EF102
Saville Row, Enf. 83 DX40
Savona Clo. SW19 179 CY94
Savona Est. SW8 161 DJ80
Savona St. SW8 161 DJ80
Savoy Ave., Hayes 155 BS78
Savoy Bldgs. WC2 278 **B1**
Savoy Clo. E15 144 EE67
Arthingworth St.
Savoy Clo., Edg. 96 CN50
Savoy Clo. (Harefield), Uxb. 92 BK54
Savoy Ct. WC2 278 **A1**
Savoy Hill WC2 278 **B1**
Savoy Pl. WC2 278 **A1**
Savoy Pl. WC2 141 DL73
Savoy Rd., Dart. 188 FK85
Savoy Row WC2 274 **B10**
Savoy Steps WC2 141 DM73
Savoy St.
Savoy St. WC2 274 **B10**
Savoy St. WC2 141 DM73
Savoy Way WC2 278 **B1**
Savoy Wd., Harl. 51 EP20
Sawbill Clo., Hayes 136 BX71
Sawells, Brox. 49 DZ21
Sawkins Clo. SW19 179 CY89
Sawley Rd. W12 139 CU74
Sawpit La., Guil. 244 BL131
Sawtry Clo., Cars. 200 DE101
Sawtry Way, Borwd. 78 CN38
Sawyer Clo. N9 100 DU47
Lion Rd.
Sawyer St. SE1 279 **H4**
Sawyer St. SE1 162 DQ75
Sawyers Chase, Rom. 86 EV41
Sawyers Clo., Dag. 147 FC65
Sawyers Clo., Wind. 151 AL80
Sawyers Hall La., Brwd. 108 FW45
Sawyer's Hill, Rich. 178 CP87
Sawyers La., Borwd. 77 CH40
Sawyers La., Pot.B. 63 CX34
Sawyers Lawn W13 137 CF72
Sawyers Way, Hem.H. 40 BM20
Saxby Rd. SW2 181 DL87
Saxham Rd., Bark. 145 ET67
Saxley, Horl. 269 DJ147
Ewelands
Saxlingham Rd. E4 101 ED48
Saxon Ave., Felt. 176 BY89
Saxon Clo. E17 123 EA59
Saxon Clo., Brwd. 109 GA48
Saxon Clo., Grav. 190 GC90
Saxon Clo., Rom. 106 FM54
Saxon Clo., Sev. 241 FF117
Saxon Clo., Slou. 153 AZ75
Saxon Clo., Surb. 197 CK100
Saxon Clo., Uxb. 134 BM71
Saxon Ct., Borwd. 78 CL40
Saxon Dr. W3 138 CP72
Saxon Gdns., Maid. 130 AD70
Saxon Gdns., Sthl. 136 BY73
Saxon Rd.
Saxon Pl. (Horton Kirby), Dart. 208 FQ99
Saxon Rd. E3 143 DZ68

Saxon Rd. E6 145 EM70
Saxon Rd. N22 99 DP53
Saxon Rd. SE25 202 DR99
Saxon Rd., Ashf. 175 BR93
Saxon Rd., Brom. 184 EF94
Saxon Rd., Dart. 188 FL91
Saxon Rd., Ilf. 145 EP65
Saxon Rd., Sthl. 136 BY74
Saxon Rd., Walt. 196 BX104
Saxon Rd., Wem. 118 CQ62
Saxon Shore Way, Grav. 191 GL86
Mark La.
Saxon Wk., Sid. 186 EW93
Cray Rd.
Saxon Way N14 81 DK44
Saxon Way, Reig. 249 CZ133
Saxon Way, Wal.Abb. 67 EC33
Saxon Way, West Dr. 154 BJ79
Saxon Way, Wind. 172 AV86
Saxonbury Ave., Sun. 195 BV97
Saxonbury Clo., Mitch. 200 DD97
Saxonbury Gdns., Surb. 197 CJ102
Saxonfield Clo. SW2 181 DM87
Saxons, Tad. 233 CX121
Saxony Par., Hayes 135 BQ71
Saxton Clo. SE13 163 ED83
Saxville Rd., Orp. 206 EV97
Sayer Clo., Green. 189 FU85
Sayers Clo., Lthd. 230 CC124
Sayers Gdns., Berk. 38 AU16
Sayers Wk., Rich. 178 CM87
Stafford Pl.
Sayes Ct. SE8 163 DZ78
Sayes Ct. St.
Sayes Ct., Add. 212 BJ106
Sayes Ct. Fm. Dr., Add. 212 BH106
Sayes Ct. Rd., Orp. 206 EU97
Sayes Ct. St. SE8 163 DZ79
Sayes Gdns., Saw. 36 EZ05
Sayesbury La. N18 100 DU50
Sayesbury Rd., Saw. 36 EX05
Sayward Clo., Chesh. 54 AR29
Scadbury Pk., Chis. 185 ET93
Scads Hill Clo., Orp. 205 ET100
Scafell Rd., Slou. 131 AM71
Scala St. W1 273 L6
Scala St. W1 141 DJ71
Scales Rd. N17 122 DT55
Scammel Way, Wat. 75 BT44
Scampston Ms. W10 139 CX72
Scandrett St. E1 142 DV74
Scarba Wk. N1 142 DR65
Marquess Rd.
Scarborough Clo., Sutt. 217 CZ111
Scarborough Clo., West. 238 EJ118
Scarborough Rd. E11 123 ED60
Scarborough Rd. N4 121 DN59
Scarborough Rd. N9 100 DW45
Scarborough St. E1 142 DT72
West Tenter St.
Scarborough Way, Slou. 151 AP75
Scarbrook Rd., Croy. 202 DQ104
Scarle Rd., Wem. 137 CK65
Scarlet Clo., Orp. 206 EV98
Scarlet Rd. SE6 184 EE90
Scarlett Clo., Wok. 226 AT118
Bingham Dr.
Scarlette Manor Way SW2 181 DN87
Papworth Way
Scarsbrook Rd. SE3 164 EK83
Scarsdale Pl. W8 160 DB76
Wrights La.
Scarsdale Rd., Har. 116 CC62
Scarsdale Vil. W8 160 DA76
Scarth Rd. SW13 159 CT83
Scatterdells La., Kings L. 57 BF30
Scawen Clo., Cars. 218 DG105
Scawen Rd. SE8 163 DY78
Scawfell St. E2 142 DT68
Scaynes Link N12 98 DA50
Sceaux Est. SE5 162 DS81
Sceaux Gdns. SE5 162 DT81
Sceptre Rd. E2 142 DW69
Schofield Wk. SE3 164 EH80
Dornberg Clo.
Scholars Ms., Welw.G.C. 29 CX07
Scholars Rd. E4 101 EC46
Scholars Rd. SW12 181 DJ88
Scholars Wk., Ger.Cr. 90 AY51
Scholars Wk., Hat. 45 CU21
Scholars Way, Amer. 72 AT38
Scholefield Rd. N19 121 DK60
Schonfeld Sq. N16 122 DR61
School Clo., Guil. 242 AX132
School Clo. (Essendon), Hat. 46 DF17
School La.
School Cres., Dart. 167 FF84
School Gdns., Berk. 38 AU17
School Grn. La., Epp. 71 FC25
School Hill, Red. 251 DJ128
School Ho. La., Tedd. 177 CH94
School La. SE23 182 DV89
School La., Add. 212 BG105
School La. (Amersham Old Town), Amer. 55 AM39
School La., Beac. 89 AR51
School La., Cat. 252 DT126
School La., Ch.St.G. 90 AV47
School La., Dart. 189 FW91
School La. (Horton Kirby), Dart. 208 FQ98
School La., Dor. 263 CD137
School La. (Mickleham), Dor. 247 CJ127
School La., Egh. 173 BA92
School La., Ger.Cr. 90 AX54
School La., Guil. 244 BL131
School La., Harl. 35 ES12
School La., Hat. 45 CW17
School La. (Essendon), Hat. 46 DF17
School La., Kings.T. 197 CJ95
School Rd.
School La., Lthd. 231 CD123
School La. (West Horsley), Lthd. 245 BP129
School La., Long. 209 FT102
School La., Ong. 53 FD17
School La., Pnr. 116 BY56
School La., St.Alb. 60 CA31
School La. (Seal), Sev. 257 FM121
School La., Shep. 195 BP100
High St.
School La., Slou. 132 AV66
School La., Surb. 198 CN102
School La., Swan. 207 FH95
School La., Tad. 249 CU125
Chequers La.
School La. (Bushey), Wat. 94 CB45
School La., Well. 166 EV83
School La. (Tewin), Welw. 30 DE06
School La., Wok. 229 BP122
School Mead, Abb.L. 59 BS32
School Pas., Kings.T. 198 CM96
School Pas., Sthl. 136 BZ74
School Rd. E12 125 EM63
School Rd. NW10 138 CR70
School Rd., Ashf. 175 BP93
School Rd., Chis. 205 EQ95
School Rd., Dag. 146 FA67
School Rd., E.Mol. 197 CD98
School Rd., Hmptn. 176 CC93
School Rd. (Tylers Grn.), H.Wyc. 88 AC47
School Rd. (Wooburn Grn.), H.Wyc. 110 AE57
School Rd., Houns. 156 CC83
School Rd., Kings.T. 197 CJ95
School Rd., Ong. 71 FF30
School Rd., Pot.B. 64 DC30
School Rd., West Dr. 154 BK79
School Rd. Ave., Hmptn. 176 CC93
School Row, Hem.H. 39 BF21
School Wk., Horl. 268 DE148
Thornton Clo.
School Wk., Slou. 132 AV73
Grasmere Ave.
School Wk., Sun. 195 BT98
School Way N12 98 DC49
High Rd.
School Way, Dag. 126 EW62
Schoolbell Ms. E3 143 DY68
Arbery Rd.
Schoolfield Rd., Grays 169 FU79
Schoolhouse Gdns., Loug. 85 EP42
Schoolhouse La. E1 143 DX73
Schoolway N12 98 DD51
Schooner Clo. E14 163 ED76
Schooner Clo. SE16 163 DX75
Kinburn St.
Schooner Ct., Dart. 168 FQ84
Schroder Ct., Egh. 172 AV92
Schubert Rd. SW15 179 CZ85
Schubert Rd., Borwd. 77 CK44
Scilla Ct., Grays 170 GD79
Scillonian Rd., Guil. 258 AU135
Sclater St. E1 275 P4
Sclater St. E1 142 DT70
Scoble Pl. N16 122 DT63
Amhurst Rd.
Scoles Cres. SW2 181 DN88
Scoresby St. SE1 278 F3
Scoresby St. SE1 141 DP74
Scorton Ave., Grnf. 137 CG68
Scot Gro., Pnr. 94 BX52
Scotch Common W13 137 CG71
Scoter Clo., Wdf.Grn. 102 EH52
Mallards Rd.
Scotia Rd. SW2 181 DN87
Scotland Bri. Rd., Add. 212 BG111
Scotland Grn. N17 100 DU54
Scotland Grn. Rd., Enf. 83 DX43
Scotland Grn. Rd. N., Enf. 83 DX42
Scotland Pl. SW1 277 P2
Scotland Rd., Buck.H. 102 EJ46
Scotlands Dr., Slou. 131 AP65
Scotney Wk., Horn. 128 FK64
Bonington Rd.
Scots Hill, Rick. 74 BM44
Scots Hill Clo., Rick. 74 BM44
Scots Hill
Scotscraig, Rad. 77 CF35
Scotsdale Clo., Orp. 205 ES98
Scotsdale Clo., Sutt. 217 CY108
Scotsdale Rd. SE12 184 EH85
Scotshall La., Warl. 221 EB114
Scotsmill La., Rick. 74 BM44
Scotswood Clo., Beac. 89 AK50
Scotswood St. EC1 274 E4
Scotswood Wk. N17 100 DU52
Scott Ave., Ware 33 EB11
Scott Clo. SW16 201 DM95
Scott Clo., Epsom 216 CQ106
Scott Clo., Guil. 242 AU132
Scott Clo., Slou. 111 AQ64
Scott Clo., West Dr. 154 BM77
Scott Ct. W3 158 CQ75
Petersfield Rd.
Scott Cres., Erith 167 FF81
Cloudesley Rd.
Scott Cres., Har. 116 CB60
Scott Ellis Gdns. NW8 140 DD69
Scott Fm. Clo., T.Ditt. 197 CH102
Scott Gdns., Houns. 156 BX80
Scott Ho. N18 100 DU50
Scott Lidgett Cres. SE16 162 DU75
Scott Rd., Grav. 191 GK92
Scott Rd., Grays 171 GG77
Scott Russell Pl. E14 163 EB78
Westferry Rd.
Scott St. E1 142 DV70
Scott Trimmer Way, Houns. 156 BY82
Scottes La., Dag. 126 EX60
Valence Ave.
Scotts Ave., Brom. 203 ED96
Scotts Ave., Sun. 175 BS94
Scotts Clo., Horn. 128 FJ64
Rye Clo.
Scotts Clo., Stai. 174 BK88
Scotts Clo., Ware 33 DX07
Scotts Dr., Hmptn. 176 CB94
Scotts Fm. Rd., Epsom 216 CQ107
Scotts La., Brom. 203 ED97
Scotts Rd. E10 123 EC60
Scotts Rd. W12 159 CV75
Scotts Rd., Brom. 184 EG94
Scotts Rd., Sthl. 156 BW76
Scotts Rd., Ware 33 DX07
Scotts Vw., Welw.G.C. 29 CW10
Scotts Way, Sev. 256 FE122
Scotts Way, Sun. 175 BS93
Scott's Yd. EC4 275 K10
Scottswood Clo. (Bushey), Wat. 76 BY40
Scottswood Rd.
Scottswood Rd. (Bushey) Wat. 76 BY40
Scottwell Dr. NW9 119 CT57
Crossway
Scoulding Rd. E16 144 EF72
Scouler St. E14 143 ED73
Quixley St.
Scout App. NW10 118 CS63
Scout La. SW4 161 DJ83
Old Town
Scout Way NW7 96 CR49
Scovell Cres. SE1 279 H5
Scovell Rd. SE1 279 H5
Scratchers La. (Fawkham Grn.), Long. 209 FR104
Scrattons Ter., Bark. 146 EX68
Scriven St. E8 142 DT67
Scriveners Clo., Hem.H. 40 BL20
Scrooby St. SE6 183 EB86
Scrubbitts Pk. Rd., Rad. 77 CG35
Scrubbitts Sq., Rad. 77 CG36
The Dell
Scrubs La. NW10 139 CU69
Scrubs La. W10 139 CU69
Scrutton Clo. SW12 181 DK87
Scrutton St. EC2 275 M5
Scrutton St. EC2 142 DS70
Scudamore La. NW9 118 CQ55
Scudders Hill (Fawkham Grn.), Long. 209 FV100
Scutari Rd. SE22 182 DW85
Scylla Cres., Houns. 175 BP87
Scylla Rd. SE15 162 DV83
Scylla Rd., Houns. 175 BP86
Seaborough Rd., Grays 171 GJ76
Seabright St. E2 142 DV69
Bethnal Grn. Rd.
Seabrook Dr., W.Wick. 204 EE103
Seabrook Gdns., Rom. 126 FA59
Seabrook Rd., Dag. 126 EX62
Seabrook Rd., Kings L. 59 BR27
Seabrooke Ri., Grays 170 GB79
Seaburn Clo., Rain. 147 FE68
Seacole Clo. W3 138 CR71
Seacourt Rd. SE2 166 EX75
Seacourt Rd., Slou. 153 BB77
Seacroft Gdns., Wat. 94 BX48
Seafield Rd. N11 99 DK49
Seaford Clo., Ruis. 115 BR61
Seaford Rd. E17 123 EB55
Seaford Rd. N15 122 DR57
Seaford Rd. W13 137 CH74
Seaford Rd., Enf. 82 DS42
Seaford Rd., Houns. 174 BK85
Seaford St. WC1 274 A3
Seaford St. WC1 141 DL69
Seaforth Ave., N.Mal. 199 CV99
Seaforth Clo., Rom. 105 FE52
Seaforth Cres. N5 122 DQ64
Seaforth Dr., Wal.Cr. 67 DX34
Seaforth Gdns. N21 99 DM45
Seaforth Gdns., Epsom 217 CT105
Seaforth Gdns., Wdf.Grn. 102 EJ50
Seaforth Pl. SW1 161 DJ76
Buckingham Gate
Seagrave Rd. SW6 160 DA79
Seagrave Rd., Beac. 88 AJ51
Seagry Rd. E11 124 EG58
Seal Dr., Sev. 257 FM121
Seal Hollow Rd., Sev. 257 FJ124
Seal Rd., Sev. 257 FJ121
Seal St. E8 122 DT63
Sealand Rd., Houns. 174 BN86
Sealand Wk., Nthlt. 136 BY69
Wayfarer Rd.
Seale Hill, Reig. 266 DA136
Seaman Clo., St.Alb. 61 CD25
Searches La., Abb.L. 59 BV28
Searchwood Rd., Warl. 236 DV118
Searle Pl. N4 121 DM60
Evershot Rd.
Searles Clo. SW11 160 DE80
Searles Rd. SE1 279 L8
Searles Rd. SE1 162 DR77
Sears St. SE5 162 DR80
Seasprite Clo., Nthlt. 136 BX69
Seaton Ave., Ilf. 125 ES64
Seaton Clo. E13 144 EH70
New Barn St.
Seaton Clo. SE11 278 E10
Seaton Clo. SE11 161 DN78
Seaton Clo. SW15 179 CV88
Seaton Clo., Twick. 177 CD86
Seaton Dr., Ashf. 174 BL89
Seaton Gdns., Ruis. 115 BU62
Seaton Pl. NW1 141 DJ70
Triton Sq.
Seaton Pt. E5 122 DU63
Nolan Way
Seaton Rd., Dart. 187 FG87
Seaton Rd., Hayes 155 BR77
Seaton Rd., Hem.H. 40 BK23
Seaton Rd., Mitch. 200 DE96
Seaton Rd., St.Alb. 61 CK26
Seaton Rd., Twick. 176 CC86
Seaton Rd., Well. 166 EW80
Seaton Rd., Wem. 138 CL68
Seaton St. N18 100 DU50
Sebastian Ave., Brwd. 109 GA44
Sebastian St. EC1 274 G3
Sebastian St. EC1 141 DP69
Sebastopol Rd. N9 100 DU49
Sebbon St. N1 141 DP66
Sebergham Gro. NW7 97 CU52
Sebert Rd. E7 124 EH64
Sebright Pas. E2 142 DU68
Hackney Rd.
Sebright Rd., Barn. 79 CX40
Sebright Rd., Hem.H. 40 BG21
Secker Cres., Har. 94 CC53
Secker St. SE1 278 D3
Second Ave. E12 124 EL63
Second Ave. E13 144 EG69
Second Ave. E17 123 EA57
Second Ave. N18 100 DW49
Second Ave. NW4 119 CX56
Second Ave. SW14 158 CS83
Second Ave. W3 139 CT74
Second Ave. W10 139 CY70
Second Ave., Dag. 147 FB67
Second Ave., Enf. 82 DT43
Second Ave., Grays 169 FU79
Second Ave., Harl. 51 ER15
Second Ave., Hayes 135 BT74
Second Ave., Rom. 126 EW57
Second Ave., Walt. 195 BV100
Second Ave., Wat. 76 BX35
Second Ave., Wem. 117 CK61
Second Clo., W.Mol. 196 CC98
Second Cres., Slou. 131 AQ71
Second Cross Rd., Twick. 177 CD89
Second Way, Wem. 118 CP63
Sedan Way SE17 279 M10
Sedcombe Clo., Sid. 186 EV91
Knoll Rd.
Sedcote Rd., Enf. 82 DW43
Sedding St. SW1 276 F8
Sedding St. SW1 160 DG77
Seddon Ho. EC2 142 DQ71
The Barbican
Seddon Rd., Mord. 200 DD99
Seddon St. WC1 274 C3
Sedge Ct., Grays 170 GE80
Sedge Grn., Harl. 50 EE20
Sedge Grn., Wal.Abb. 50 EE20
Sedge Rd. N17 100 DW52
Sedgebrook Rd. SE3 164 EK82
Sedgecombe Ave., Har. 117 CJ57
Sedgefield Clo., Rom. 106 FM49
Sedgefield Cres., Rom. 106 FM50
Sedgeford Rd. W12 139 CT74
Sedgehill Rd. SE6 183 EA91
Sedgemere Ave. N2 120 DC55
Sedgemere Rd. SE2 166 EW76
Sedgemoor Dr., Dag. 126 FA63
Sedgeway SE6 184 EF88
Sedgewick Ave., Uxb. 135 BP66
Sedgewood Clo., Brom. 204 EF101
Sedgmoor Pl. SE5 162 DS80
Sedgwick Rd. E10 123 EC61
Sedgwick St. E9 123 DX64
Sedleigh Rd. SW18 179 CZ86
Sedlescombe Rd. SW6 159 CZ79
Sedley, Grav. 190 GA93
Sedley Clo., Enf. 82 DV38
Sedley Gro. (Harefield), Uxb. 114 BJ56
Sedley Pl. W1 273 H9
Sedley Ri., Loug. 85 EM40
Sedum Clo. NW9 118 CP57
Seeley Dr. SE21 182 DS91
Seeleys, Harl. 36 EW12
Seeleys Clo., Beac. 88 AJ51
Seeleys La., Beac. 89 AK52
Seeleys Wk.
Seeleys Rd., Beac. 88 AJ50
Seeleys Wk., Beac. 88 AJ52
Seelig Ave. NW9 119 CU59
Seely Rd. SW17 180 DG93
Seer Grn. La., Beac. 90 AS52
Seer Mead, Beac. 89 AR51
Seething La. EC3 279 N1
Seething La. EC3 142 DS73
Seething Wells La., Surb. 197 CJ100
Sefton Ave. NW7 96 CR50
Sefton Ave., Har. 95 CD53
Sefton Clo., Orp. 205 ET98
Sefton Clo., St.Alb. 43 CF19
Blenheim Rd.
Sefton Clo., Slou. 132 AT66
Sefton Paddock, Slou. 132 AU66
Sefton Pk., Slou. 132 AU66
Sefton Rd., Croy. 202 DU102
Sefton Rd., Epsom 216 CR110
Sefton Rd., Orp. 205 ET98
Sefton St. SW15 159 CW82
Sefton Way, Uxb. 134 BJ72
Segal Clo. SE23 183 DY87
Segrave Clo., Wey. 212 BN108
Sekforde St. EC1 274 F5
Sekforde St. EC1 141 DP70
Sekhon Ter., Felt. 176 CA90
Selah Dr., Swan. 207 FC95
Selan Gdns., Hayes 135 BV71
Selbie Ave. NW10 119 CT64
Selborne Ave. E12 125 EN63
Walton Rd.
Selborne Ave., Bex. 186 EY88
Selborne Gdns. NW4 119 CU56
Selborne Gdns., Grnf. 137 CG67
Selborne Rd. E17 123 DZ57
Selborne Rd. N14 99 DL48
Selborne Rd. N22 99 DM53
Selborne Rd. SE5 162 DR82
Denmark Hill
Selborne Rd., Croy. 202 DS104
Selborne Rd., Ilf. 125 EN61
Selborne Rd., N.Mal. 198 CS96
Selborne Rd., Sid. 186 EV91
Selborne Wk. E17 123 DZ56
Selbourne Ave., Add. 212 BH110
Selbourne Ave., Surb. 198 CM103
Selbourne Clo., Add. 212 BH110
Selbourne Rd., Guil. 243 BA131
Selbourne Sq., Gdse. 252 DW130
Selby Ave., St.Alb. 43 CD20
Selby Chase, Ruis. 115 BV61
Selby Clo. E6 144 EL71
Linton Gdns.
Selby Clo., Chess. 216 CL108
Selby Clo., Chis. 185 EN93
Selby Gdns., Sthl. 136 CA70
Selby Grn., Cars. 200 DE101
Selby Rd. E11 124 EE62
Selby Rd. E13 144 EH71
Selby Rd. N17 100 DS51
Selby Rd. SE20 202 DU96
Selby Rd. W5 137 CH70
Selby Rd., Ashf. 175 BQ93
Selby Rd., Cars. 200 DE101
Selby St. E1 142 DU70
Selby Wk., Wok. 226 AV118
Wyndham Rd.
Selcroft Rd., Pur. 219 DP112
Selden Hill, Hem.H. 40 BK21
Selden Rd. SE15 162 DW82
Selden Wk. N7 121 DM61
Durham Rd.
Sele Rd., Hert. 31 DP09
Selhurst Clo. SW19 179 CX88
Selhurst Clo., Wok. 227 AZ115
Selhurst New Rd. SE25 202 DS100
Selhurst Pl. SE25 202 DS100
Selhurst Rd. N9 100 DR48
Selhurst Rd. SE25 202 DS99
Selinas La., Dag. 126 EY59
Selkirk Dr., Erith 167 FE81
Selkirk Rd. SW17 180 DE91
Selkirk Rd., Twick. 176 CC89
Sell Clo. (Cheshunt), Wal.Cr. 65 DP26
Gladding Rd.
Sellers Clo., Borwd. 78 CQ39
Sellers Hall Clo. N3 98 DA52
Sellincourt Rd. SW17 180 DE92
Sellindge Clo., Beck. 183 DZ94
Sellon Ms. SE11 278 C9
Sellons Ave. NW10 139 CT67
Sells Rd., Ware 33 DZ05
Sellwood Dr., Barn. 79 CX43
Selsdon Ave., S.Croy. 220 DR107
Selsdon Rd.
Selsdon Clo., Rom. 105 FC53
Selsdon Clo., Surb. 198 CL99
Selsdon Cres., S.Croy. 220 DW109
Selsdon Pk. Rd., S.Croy. 221 DX109
Selsdon Rd. E11 124 EG59
Selsdon Rd. E13 144 EJ67
Selsdon Rd. NW2 119 CT61
Selsdon Rd. SE27 181 DP90
Selsdon Rd., Add. 212 BG111
Selsdon Rd., S.Croy. 220 DR106
Selsdon Rd. Ind. Est., S.Croy. 220 DR107
Selsdon Rd.
Selsdon Way E14 163 EB76
Selsea Pl. N16 122 DS64
Crossway
Selsey Cres., Well. 166 EX81
Selsey St. E14 143 EA71
Selvage La. NW7 96 CR50
Selway Clo., Pnr. 115 BV56
Selwood Clo., Stai. 174 BJ86
Selwood Gdns., Stai. 174 BJ86
Selwood Pl. SW7 160 DD78
Selwood Rd., Brwd. 108 FT48
Selwood Rd., Chess. 215 CK105
Selwood Rd., Croy. 202 DV103
Selwood Rd., Sutt. 199 CZ102
Selwood Rd., Wok. 227 BB120
Selwood Ter. SW7 160 DD78
Neville Ter.
Selworthy Clo. E11 124 EG57
Selworthy Rd. SE6 183 DZ90
Selwyn Ave. E4 101 EC51
Selwyn Ave., Hat. 44 CR19
Selwyn Ave., Ilf. 125 ES58
Selwyn Ave., Rich. 158 CL83
Selwyn Clo., Houns. 156 BY84
Selwyn Ct. SE3 164 EE83
Selwyn Ct., Edg. 96 CP52
Camrose Ave.
Selwyn Cres., Hat. 44 CS18
Selwyn Cres., Well. 166 EV84
Selwyn Dr., Hat. 44 CR18
Selwyn Pl., Orp. 206 EV97
Saxville Rd.
Selwyn Rd. E3 143 DZ68
Selwyn Rd. E13 144 EH67
Selwyn Rd. NW10 138 CR66
Selwyn Rd., N.Mal. 198 CR99
Selwyn Rd., Til. 171 GF82
Dock Rd.
Semaphore Rd., Guil. 258 AY136
Semley Gate E9 143 DZ65
Eastway
Semley Pl. SW1 276 G9
Semley Pl. SW1 160 DG77
Semley Rd. SW16 201 DL96
Semper Clo., Wok. 226 AS117
Semper Rd., Grays 171 GJ75
Semphill Rd., Hem.H. 40 BL23
Senate St. SE15 162 DW82
Senator Wk. SE28 165 ER76
Broadwater Rd.
Send Barns La., Wok. 227 BD124
Send Clo., Wok. 227 BC123
Send Hill Rd., Wok. 243 BC125
Send Marsh Rd., Wok. 227 BE123
Send Par. Clo., Wok. 227 BC123
Send Rd.
Send Rd., Wok. 227 BB122
Seneca Rd., Th.Hth. 202 DQ98
Senga Rd., Wall. 200 DG102
Senhouse Rd., Sutt. 199 CX104
Senior St. W2 140 DB71
Senlac Rd. SE12 184 EH88
Sennen Rd., Enf. 100 DT45
Sennen Wk. SE9 184 EL90
Senrab St. E1 143 DX72
Sentinel Clo., Nthlt. 136 BY70
Sentinel Sq. NW4 119 CW56
Sentis Ct., Nthwd. 93 BS51
Carew Rd.
September Way, Stan. 95 CH51
Sequoia Clo. (Bushey), Wat. 95 CD46
Giant Tree Hill
Sequoia Gdns., Orp. 205 ET101
Sequoia Pk., Pnr. 94 CB51
Serbin Clo. E10 123 EC59
Sergeants Grn. La., Wal.Abb. 68 EJ33
Sergehill La., Abb.L. 59 BT27
Serjeants Inn EC4 274 E9
Serle St. WC2 274 C8
Serle St. WC2 141 DM72
Sermed Ct., Slou. 132 AW74
Sermon Dr., Swan. 207 FC97
Sermon La. EC4 275 H9
Serpentine Ct., Sev. 257 FK122
Serpentine Grn., Red. 251 DK129
Malmstone Ave.
Serpentine Rd. W2 276 D3
Serpentine Rd. W2 140 DF74
Serpentine Rd., Sev. 257 FJ123
Service Rd., The, Pot.B. 64 DA32
Serviden Dr., Brom. 204 EK95
Setchell Rd. SE1 279 P8
Setchell Way SE1 279 P8
Seth St. SE16 162 DW75
Swan Rd.
Seton Gdns., Dag. 146 EW66
Settle Pt. E13 144 EG68
London Rd.
Settle Rd. E13 144 EG68
London Rd.
Settle Rd., Rom. 106 FN49
Settles St. E1 142 DU71
Settrington Rd. SW6 160 DB82
Seven Acres, Cars. 200 DE103
Seven Acres, Nthwd. 93 BU51
Seven Acres, Swan. 207 FD100
Seven Arches Rd., Brwd. 108 FX47
Seven Hills Clo., Walt. 213 BS109
Seven Hills Rd., Cob. 213 BS110
Seven Hills Rd., Iver 133 BB65
Seven Hills Rd., Walt. 213 BS110
Seven Hills Rd. S., Cob. 213 BS113
Seven Kings Rd., Ilf. 125 ET61
Seven Sisters Rd. N4 121 DM62
Seven Sisters Rd. N7 121 DM62
Seven Sisters Rd. N15 122 DR58
Seven Stars Cor. W12 159 CU76
Goldhawk Rd.
Sevenoaks Business Cen., Sev. 257 FH121
Sevenoaks Bypass, Sev. 256 FC123
Sevenoaks Clo., Bexh. 167 FC84
Sevenoaks Clo., Rom. 106 FJ49
Sevenoaks Clo., Sutt. 218 DA110
Sevenoaks Ct., Nthwd. 93 BQ52

Sevenoaks Ho. SE25 202 DU97
Sevenoaks Rd. SE4 183 DY86
Sevenoaks Rd., Orp. 223 ET105
Sevenoaks Rd. (Green St. Grn.), Orp. 223 ET108
Sevenoaks Rd. (Otford), Sev. 241 FH116
Sevenoaks Way, Orp. 206 EW98
Sevenoaks Way, Sid. 186 EW94
Seventh Ave. E12 125 EM63
Seventh Ave., Hayes 135 BU74
Severalls Ave., Chesh. 54 AQ30
Severn Ave., Rom. 127 FH55
Severn Cres., Slou. 153 BB78
Severn Dr., Enf. 82 DU38
Severn Dr., Esher 197 CG103
Severn Dr., Upmin. 129 FR58
Severn Dr., Walt. 196 BX103
Severn Rd., S.Ock. 148 FQ72
Severn Way NW10 119 CT64
Severn Way, Wat. 60 BW34
Severnake Clo. E14 163 EA77
Severnmead, Hem.H. 40 BL17
Severns Fld., Epp. 70 EU29
Severnvale, St.Alb. 62 CM27
Thamesdale
Severus Rd. SW11 160 DE84
Seville Ms. N1 142 DS66
Seville St. SW1 276 E5
Seville St. SW1 160 DF75
Sevington Rd. NW4 119 CV58
Sevington St. W9 140 DB70
Seward Rd. W7 157 CG75
Seward Rd., Beck. 203 DX96
Seward St. EC1 274 G4
Seward St. EC1 142 DQ69
Sewardstone Gdns. E4 83 EB43
Sewardstone Rd. E2 142 DW68
Sewardstone Rd. E4 101 EB45
Sewardstone Rd., Wal.Abb. 83 EC38
Sewardstone Roundabout, Wal.Abb. 83 EC35
Sewardstone St., Wal.Abb. 67 EC34
Sewdley St. E5 123 DX62
Sewell Clo., St.Alb. 44 CL20
Sewell Harris Clo., Harl. 35 ET13
Sewell Rd. SE2 166 EU76
Sewell St. E13 144 EG69
Sewells, Welw.G.C. 29 CY05
Sextant Ave. E14 163 ED77
Sexton Clo., Rain. 147 FF67
Blake Clo.
Sexton Clo. (Cheshunt), Wal.Cr. 66 DQ25
Shambrook Rd.
Sexton Rd., Til. 171 GF81
Seymer Rd., Rom. 127 FD55
Seymour Ave. N17 100 DU54
Seymour Ave., Cat. 236 DQ122
Fairbourne La.
Seymour Ave., Epsom 217 CV109
Seymour Ave., Mord. 199 CX101
Seymour Clo., E.Mol. 196 CC99
Seymour Clo., Loug. 84 EL44
Seymour Clo., Pnr. 94 BZ53
Seymour Ct. E4 102 EF47
Seymour Cres., Hem.H. 40 BL20
Seymour Dr., Brom. 205 EM102
Seymour Gdns. SE4 163 DY83
Seymour Gdns., Felt. 176 BW91
Seymour Gdns., Ilf. 125 EM60
Seymour Gdns., Ruis. 116 BX60
Seymour Gdns., Surb. 198 CM99
Seymour Gdns., Twick. 177 CH87
Seymour Ms. W1 272 F8
Seymour Ms. W1 140 DG72
Seymour Ms., Saw. 36 EX08
Seymour Pl. SE25 202 DV98
Seymour Pl. W1 272 D7
Seymour Pl. W1 140 DE71
Seymour Rd. E4 101 EB46
Seymour Rd. E6 144 EK68
Seymour Rd. E10 123 DZ60
Seymour Rd. N3 98 DB52
Seymour Rd. N8 121 DN57
Seymour Rd. N9 100 DV47
Seymour Rd. SW18 179 CZ87
Seymour Rd. SW19 179 CX89
Seymour Rd. W4 158 CQ77
Seymour Rd., Berk. 38 AS17
Seymour Rd., Cars. 218 DG106
Seymour Rd., Ch.St.G. 90 AW49
Seymour Rd., E.Mol. 196 CC99
Seymour Rd., Grav. 191 GF88
Seymour Rd., Hmptn. 176 CC92
Seymour Rd., Kings.T. 197 CK95
Seymour Rd., Mitch. 200 DG101
Seymour Rd., St.Alb. 43 CE17
Seymour Rd., Slou. 151 AR75
Seymour Rd., Til. 171 GF81
Seymour Rd., W.Mol. 196 CC99
Seymour St. W1 272 D9
Seymour St. W1 140 DF72
Seymour St. W2 272 D9
Seymour St. W2 140 DF72
Seymour Ter. SE20 202 DV95
Seymour Vil. SE20 202 DV95
Seymour Wk. SW10 160 DC79
Seymour Wk., Swans. 190 FY87
Seymour Way, Sun. 175 BS94
Seymours, Harl. 51 EM18
Seymours, The, Loug. 85 EN39
Seyssel St. E14 163 EC77
Shaa Rd. W3 138 CR73
Shacklands Rd., Sev. 225 FB111
Shackleford Rd., Wok. 227 BA121
Shacklegate La., Tedd. 177 CE91
Shackleton Clo. SE23 182 DV89
Featherstone Ave.
Shackleton Ct. E14 163 EA78
Napier Ave.
Shackleton Rd., Slou. 132 AT73
Shackleton Rd., Sthl. 136 BZ73
Shackleton Wk., Guil. 242 AT134
Humbolt Clo.
Shackleton Way, Abb.L. 59 BU32
Lysander Way
Shackleton Way, Welw.G.C. 30 DD09
Shacklewell Grn. E8 122 DT63
Shacklewell La. E8 122 DT64
Shacklewell Rd. N16 122 DT63
Shacklewell Row E8 122 DT63
Shacklewell St. E2 142 DT70
Shad Thames SE1 279 P3
Shad Thames SE1 142 DT74
Shadbolt Ave. E4 101 DY50
Shadbolt Clo., Wor.Pk. 199 CT103
Shadwell Ct., Nthlt. 136 BZ68
Shadwell Dr.
Shadwell Dr., Nthlt. 136 BZ69
Shadwell Gdns. E1 142 DW72
Martha St.
Shadwell Pierhead E1 142 DW73
Glamis Rd.
Shadwell Pl. E1 142 DW73
Sutton St.
Shady Bush Clo. (Bushey), Wat. 94 CC45
Richfield Rd.
Shady La., Wat. 75 BV40
Shaef Way, Tedd. 177 CG94
Shafter Rd., Dag. 147 FC65
Shaftesbury, Loug. 84 EK41
Shaftesbury Ave. W1 273 M10
Shaftesbury Ave. W1 141 DK73
Shaftesbury Ave. WC2 273 M10
Shaftesbury Ave. WC2 141 DK73
Shaftesbury Ave., Barn. 80 DC42
Shaftesbury Ave., Enf. 83 DX40
Shaftesbury Ave., Felt. 175 BU86
Shaftesbury Ave., Har. 116 CB60
Shaftesbury Ave. (Kenton), Har. 117 CK58
Shaftesbury Ave., Sthl. 156 CA77
Shaftesbury Circle, Har. 116 CC60
Shaftesbury Ave.
Shaftesbury Ct. N1 142 DR68
Shaftesbury St.
Shaftesbury Cres., Stai. 174 BK94
Shaftesbury Gdns. NW10 138 CS70
Shaftesbury La., Dart. 168 FP84
Shaftesbury Ms. SW4 181 DJ85
Clapham Common S. Side
Shaftesbury Ms. W8 160 DA76
Stratford Rd.
Shaftesbury Pl. W14 159 CZ77
Warwick Rd.
Shaftesbury Pt. E13 144 EH68
High St.
Shaftesbury Rd. E4 101 ED46
Shaftesbury Rd. E7 144 EJ66
Shaftesbury Rd. E10 123 EA60
Shaftesbury Rd. E17 123 EB58
Shaftesbury Rd. N18 100 DS51
Shaftesbury Rd. N19 121 DL60
Shaftesbury Rd., Beck. 203 DZ96
Shaftesbury Rd., Cars. 200 DD101
Shaftesbury Rd., Epp. 69 ET29
Shaftesbury Rd., Rich. 158 CL83
Shaftesbury Rd., Rom. 127 FF58
Shaftesbury Rd., Wat. 76 BW41
Shaftesbury Rd., Wok. 227 BA117
Shaftesbury St. N1 275 J1
Shaftesbury St. N1 142 DQ68
Shaftesbury Way, Kings L. 59 BQ28
Shaftesbury Way, Twick. 177 CD90
Shaftesbury Waye, Hayes 135 BV71
Shaftesburys, The, Bark. 145 EN66
Shafto Ms. SW1 276 D7
Shafton Rd. E9 143 DX67
Shaggy Calf La., Slou. 132 AU73
Shakespeare Ave. N11 99 DJ50
Shakespeare Ave. NW10 138 CR67
Shakespeare Ave., Felt. 175 BU86
Shakespeare Ave., Hayes 135 BV70
Shakespeare Ave., Til. 171 GH82
Shakespeare Cres. E12 145 EM65
Shakespeare Cres. NW10 138 CR67
Shakespeare Dr., Har. 118 CN58
Shakespeare Gdns. N2 120 DF56
Shakespeare Ho. N14 99 DK47
High St.
Shakespeare Rd. E17 101 DX54
Shakespeare Rd. N3 98 DA53
Popes Dr.
Shakespeare Rd. NW7 97 CT49
Shakespeare Rd. SE24 181 DP85
Shakespeare Rd. W3 138 CQ74
Shakespeare Rd. W7 137 CF73
Shakespeare Rd., Add. 212 BK105
Shakespeare Rd., Bexh. 166 EY81
Shakespeare Rd., Dart. 168 FN84
Shakespeare Rd., Rom. 127 FF58
Shakespeare Sq., Ilf. 103 EQ51
Shakespeare St., Wat. 75 BV38
Shakespeare Twr. EC2 142 DQ71
Beech St.
Shakespeare Way, Felt. 176 BW91
Shakspeare Ms. N16 122 DS63
Shakspeare Wk.
Shakspeare Wk. N16 122 DS63
Shalcomb St. SW10 160 DC79
Shalcross Dr. (Cheshunt), Wal.Cr. 67 DZ30
Shaldon Dr., Mord. 199 CY99
Shaldon Dr., Ruis. 116 BW62
Shaldon Rd., Edg. 96 CM53
Shaldon Way, Walt. 196 BW104
Shale Grn., Red. 251 DK129
Bletchingley Rd.
Shalfleet Dr. W10 139 CX73
Shalford Clo., Orp. 223 EQ105
Shalford Rd., Guil. 258 AX138
Shalimar Gdns. W3 138 CQ73
Shalimar Rd. W3 138 CQ73
Hereford Rd.
Shallcross Cres., Hat. 45 CU21
Shallons Rd. SE9 185 EP91
Shalston Vil., Surb. 198 CM100
Shalstone Rd. SW14 158 CP83
Shambrook Rd. (Cheshunt), Wal.Cr. 65 DP25
Shamrock Clo., Lthd. 231 CD121
Shamrock Rd., Croy. 201 DM100
Shamrock Rd., Grav. 191 GL87
Shamrock St. SW4 161 DK83
Shamrock Way N14 99 DH46
Shand St. SE1 279 N4
Shand St. SE1 162 DS75
Shandon Rd. SW4 181 DJ86
Shandy St. E1 143 DX71
Shanklin Clo., Wal.Cr. 66 DT29
Hornbeam Way
Shanklin Gdns., Wat. 94 BW49
Shanklin Rd. N8 121 DK57
Shanklin Rd. N15 122 DU56
Shanklin Way SE15 162 DT80
Pentridge St.
Shannon Clo. NW2 119 CX62
Shannon Clo., Sthl. 156 BX78
Shannon Gro. SW9 161 DM84
Shannon Pl. NW8 140 DE68
Allitsen Rd.
Shannon Way, Beck. 183 EB93
Shannon Way, S.Ock. 148 FQ73
Shantock Hall La., Hem.H. 56 AY29
Shantock La., Hem.H. 56 AX30
Shap Cres., Cars. 200 DF102
Shapland Way N13 99 DM50
Shardcroft Ave. SE24 181 DP85
Shardeloes Rd. SE14 163 DZ82
Sharland Clo., Th.Hth. 201 DN100
Dunheved Rd. N.
Sharland Rd., Grav. 191 GJ89
Sharman Ct., Sid. 186 EU91
Sharnbrooke Clo., Well. 166 EW83
Sharney Ave., Slou. 153 BB76
Sharon Clo., Epsom 216 CQ113
Sharon Clo., Lthd. 230 CA124
Sharon Clo., Surb. 197 CJ102
Sharon Gdns. E9 142 DW67
Sharon Rd. W4 158 CR78
Sharon Rd., Enf. 83 DY40
Sharp Way, Dart. 168 FM83
Sharpcroft, Hem.H. 40 BK18
Sharpe Clo. W7 137 CF71
Templeman Rd.
Sharpecroft, Harl. 51 EQ15
Sharpes La., Hem.H. 39 BB22
Sharpleshall St. NW1 140 DF66
Sharpness Clo., Hayes 136 BY71
Sharps La., Ruis. 115 BR59
Sharratt St. SE15 162 DW79
Sharsted St. SE17 161 DP78
Sharvel La., Nthlt. 135 BU67
Shavers Pl. SW1 277 M1
Shaw Ave., Bark. 146 EY68
Shaw Clo. SE28 146 EV74
Shaw Clo., Cher. 211 BC107
Shaw Clo., Epsom 217 CT111
Shaw Clo., Horn. 127 FH60
Shaw Clo., S.Croy. 220 DT112
Shaw Clo. (Cheshunt), Wal.Cr. 66 DW28
Shaw Clo. (Bushey), Wat. 95 CE47
Shaw Ct., Wind. 172 AU85
Shaw Cres., Brwd. 109 GD42
Shaw Cres., S.Croy. 220 DT112
Shaw Cres., Til. 171 GH81
Shaw Dr., Walt. 196 BW101
Shaw Gdns., Bark. 146 EY68
Shaw Rd. SE22 162 DS84
Shaw Rd., Brom. 184 EF90
Shaw Rd., Enf. 83 DX39
Shaw Rd., West. 238 EJ120
Shaw Sq. E17 101 DY53
Shaw Way, Wall. 219 DL108
Shawbridge, Harl. 51 EQ18
Shawbrooke Rd. SE9 184 EJ85
Shawbury Rd. SE22 182 DT85
Shawfield Ct., West Dr. 154 BL76
Shawfield Pk., Brom. 204 EK96
Shawfield St. SW3 160 DE78
Shawford Ct. SW15 179 CU87
Shawford Rd., Epsom 216 CR107
Shawley Cres., Epsom 233 CW118
Shawley Way, Epsom 233 CV118
Shaws, The, Welw.G.C. 30 DC10
Shaws Cotts. SE23 183 DY90
Shaxton Cres., Croy. 221 EC109
Shearing Dr., Cars. 200 DC101
Stavordale Rd.
Shearling Way N7 141 DL65
Shearman Rd. SE3 164 EF84
Shearsmith Ho. E1 142 DU73
Cable St.
Shearwater Way, Hayes 136 BX72
Shearwood Cres., Dart. 167 FF83
Sheath's La., Lthd. 214 CB113
Sheaveshill Ave. NW9 118 CS56
Sheehy Way, Slou. 132 AV73
Sheen Common Dr., Rich. 158 CN84
Sheen Ct., Rich. 158 CN84
Sheen Ct. Rd., Rich. 158 CN84
Sheen Gate Gdns. SW14 158 CQ84
Sheen Gro. N1 141 DN67
Richmond Ave.
Sheen La. SW14 158 CQ83
Sheen Pk., Rich. 158 CM84
Sheen Rd., Orp. 205 ET98
Sheen Rd., Rich. 178 CL85
Sheen Way, Wall. 219 DM106
Sheen Wd. SW14 178 CQ85
Sheendale Rd., Rich. 158 CM84
Sheenewood SE26 182 DV92
Sheep La. E8 142 DV67
Sheep Wk., Epsom 232 CR122
Sheep Wk., Reig. 249 CY131
Sheep Wk., Shep. 194 BM101
Sheep Wk. Ms. SW19 179 CX93
Sheepbarn La., Warl. 222 EF112
Sheepcot Dr., Wat. 60 BW34
Sheepcot La., Wat. 59 BV34
Sheepcote, Welw.G.C. 30 DA12
Sheepcote Clo., Beac. 88 AJ51
Sheepcote Clo., Houns. 155 BU80
Sheepcote Gdns. (Denham), Uxb. 114 BG58
Sheepcote La. SW11 160 DF82
Sheepcote La., H.Wyc. 110 AG61
Sheepcote La., Orp. 206 EZ100
Sheepcote La., St.Alb. 28 CL07
Sheepcote La., Slou. 110 AF62
Sheepcote La., Swan. 206 FA98
Sheepcote Rd., Har. 117 CF58
Sheepcote Rd., Hem.H. 40 BM20
Sheepcote Rd., Wind. 151 AL82
Sheepcote Rd. (Eton Wick), Wind. 151 AN78
Sheepcotes Rd., Rom. 126 EX56
Sheepfold La., Amer. 55 AR39
Sheepfold Rd., Guil. 242 AT131
Sheephouse Grn., Dor. 262 BZ140
Sheephouse La., Dor. 262 BZ139
Sheephouse Rd., Hem.H. 40 BM22
Sheephouse Way, N.Mal. 198 CS101
Sheeplands Ave., Guil. 243 BC132
Sheepwalk La., Lthd. 245 BT134
Sheering Dr., Harl. 36 EX11
Sheering Lwr. Rd., Harl. 36 EZ09
Sheering Lwr. Rd., Saw. 36 EZ08
Sheering Mill La., Saw. 36 EZ05
Sheering Rd., B.Stort. 37 FG05
Sheering Rd., Harl. 36 EZ10
Sheerwater Ave., Add. 211 BE112
Sheerwater Business Cen., Wok. 211 BC114
Sheerwater Rd. E16 144 EK71
Sheerwater Rd., Add. 211 BE112
Sheerwater Rd., W.Byf. 211 BE113
Sheerwater Rd., Wok. 211 BE112
Sheet St., Wind. 151 AR82
Sheethanger La., Hem.H. 40 BG24
Sheffield Dr., Rom. 106 FN50
Sheffield Gdns., Rom. 106 FN50
Sheffield Rd., Slou. 131 AQ72
Sheffield Sq. E3 143 DZ69
Malmesbury Rd.
Sheffield St. WC2 274 B9
Sheffield Ter. W8 140 DA74
Shefton Ri., Nthwd. 93 BU52
Sheila Clo., Rom. 105 FB52
Sheila Rd., Rom. 105 FB52
Sheilings, The, Horn. 128 FM57
Shelbourne Clo., Pnr. 116 BZ55
Shelbourne Rd. N17 100 DV54
Shelburne Rd. N7 121 DM63
Shelbury Clo., Sid. 186 EU90
Shelbury Rd. SE22 182 DV85
Sheldon Ave. N6 120 DE59
Sheldon Ave., Ilf. 103 EP54
Sheldon Clo. SE12 184 EH85
Sheldon Clo. SE20 202 DV95
Sheldon Clo., Harl. 52 EY15
Sheldon Clo., Reig. 266 DB135
Sheldon Clo. (Cheshunt), Wal.Cr. 66 DS26
Sheldon Ct., Guil. 259 AZ135
Lower Edgeborough Rd.
Sheldon Rd. N18 100 DS49
Sheldon Rd. NW2 119 CX63
Sheldon Rd., Bexh. 166 EZ81
Sheldon Rd., Dag. 146 EY66
Sheldon St., Croy. 202 DQ104
Wandle Rd.
Sheldrake Clo. E16 145 EM74
Newland St.
Sheldrake Pl. W8 159 CZ75
Sheldrick Clo. SW19 200 DD96
Shelduck Clo. E15 124 EF64
Sheldwich Ter., Brom. 204 EL100
Shelford Pl. N16 122 DR62
Stoke Newington Ch. St.
Shelford Ri. SE19 182 DT94
Shelford Rd., Barn. 79 CW44
Shelgate Rd. SW11 180 DF85
Shell Clo., Brom. 205 EM100
Shell Rd. SE13 163 EB83
Shellbank La., Dart. 189 FU93
Shellduck Clo. NW9 96 CS54
Swan Dr.
Shelley Ave. E12 144 EL65
Shelley Ave., Grnf. 137 CD69
Shelley Ave., Horn. 127 FF61
Shelley Clo. SE15 162 DV82
Shelley Clo., Bans. 233 CX115
Shelley Clo., Couls. 235 DM117
Shelley Clo., Edg. 96 CN49
Shelley Clo., Grnf. 137 CD69
Shelley Clo., Hayes 135 BU71
Shelley Clo., H.Wyc. 110 AE55
Falcons Cft.
Shelley Clo., Nthwd. 93 BT50
Shelley Clo., Orp. 205 ES104
Shelley Clo., Slou. 153 AZ78
Shelley Cres., Houns. 156 BX82
Shelley Cres., Sthl. 136 BZ72
Shelley Dr., Well. 165 ES81
Shelley Gdns., Wem. 117 CJ61
Shelley Gro., Loug. 85 EM42
Shelley La. (Harefield), Uxb. 92 BG53
Shelley Pl., Til. 171 GH81
Kipling Ave.
Shelley Rd., Brwd. 109 GD45
Shelley Rd., Chesh. 54 AP29
Shelley Way SW19 180 DD93
Shelleys La., Sev. 239 ET116
Shellfield Clo., Stai. 174 BG85
Shellness Rd. E5 122 DV64
Shellwood Dr., Dor. 263 CJ140
Shellwood Rd. SW11 160 DF82
Shellwood Rd., Reig. 264 CQ141
Shelmerdine Clo. E3 143 EA71
Shelson Ave., Felt. 175 BT90
Shelton Ave., Warl. 236 DW117
Shelton Clo., Guil. 242 AU129
Shelton Clo., Warl. 236 DW117
Shelton Ct., Slou. 152 AW76
London Rd.
Shelton Rd. SW19 200 DA95
Shelton St. WC2 273 P9
Shelton St. WC2 141 DL72
Shelvers Grn., Tad. 233 CW121
Shelvers Hill, Tad. 233 CW121
Ashurst Rd.
Shelvers Spur, Tad. 233 CW121
Shelvers Way, Tad. 233 CW121
Shenden Clo., Sev. 257 FJ128
Shenden Way, Sev. 257 FJ128
Shendish Edge, Hem.H. 58 BM25
London Rd.
Shenfield Clo., Couls. 235 DJ119
Woodfield Clo.
Shenfield Cres., Brwd. 108 FY47
Shenfield Gdns., Brwd. 109 GB44
Shenfield Grn., Brwd. 109 GA45
Hutton Rd.
Shenfield Ho. SE18 164 EK80
Shooter's Hill Rd.
Shenfield Pl., Brwd. 108 FY45
Shenfield Rd., Brwd. 108 FX47
Shenfield Rd., Wdf.Grn. 102 EH52
Shenfield St. N1 275 N1
Shenfield St. N1 142 DS68
Shenley Ave., Ruis. 115 BT61
Shenley Hill, Rad. 77 CG35
Shenley La., St.Alb. 61 CJ27
Shenley Manor (Shenley), Rad. 61 CK33
Shenley Rd. SE5 162 DS81
Shenley Rd., Borwd. 78 CN42
Shenley Rd., Dart. 188 FN87
Shenley Rd., Hem.H. 40 BN15
Shenley Rd., Houns. 156 BY81
Shenley Rd., Rad. 61 CH34
Shenleybury, Rad. 62 CL30
Shenleybury Cotts., Rad. 62 CL31
Shenstone Clo., Dart. 167 FD84
Shenstone Dr., Slou. 131 AK70
Shenstone Gdns., Rom. 106 FJ53
Shenstone Hill, Berk. 38 AY18
Shepcot Ho. N14 81 DJ44
Shepherd Clo. W1 140 DG73
Lees Pl.
Shepherd Clo., Abb.L. 59 BT30
Shepherd Mkt. W1 277 H2
Shepherd St. W1 277 H3
Shepherd St., Grav. 190 GD87
Shepherdess Pl. N1 275 J2
Shepherdess Wk. N1 142 DQ68
Shepherds Bush Grn. W12 159 CW75
Shepherds Bush Mkt. W12 159 CW75
Shepherds Bush Pl. W12 159 CX75
Shepherds Bush Rd. W6 159 CW77
Shepherds Clo. N6 121 DH58
Shepherds Clo., Beac. 89 AM54
Shepherds Clo., Lthd. 231 CK124
Shepherds Clo., Orp. 205 ET104
Stapleton Rd.
Shepherds Clo., Rom. 126 EX57
Shepherds Clo., Shep. 195 BP100
Shepherds Clo. (Cowley), Uxb. 134 BJ70
High St.
Shepherds Ct. W12 159 CX75
Shepherds Ct., Hert. 32 DQ06
Shepherds Grn., Chis. 185 ER94
Shepherds Grn., Hem.H. 39 BE21
Shepherds Hill N6 121 DH58
Shepherds Hill, Guil. 242 AU132
Shepherds Hill, Red. 251 DJ126
Shepherds Hill, Rom. 106 FN54
Shepherds La. E9 123 DX64
Shepherds La., Beac. 89 AM54
Shepherds La., Brwd. 108 FS45
Shepherds La., Dart. 187 FG88
Shepherds La., Guil. 242 AT131
Shepherds La., Rick. 73 BD44
Shepherds Path, Nthlt. 136 BY65
Fortunes Mead
Shepherds Pl. W1 272 F10
Shepherds Pl. W1 140 DG73
Shepherds Rd., Wat. 75 BT41
Shepherds Wk. NW2 119 CU61
Shepherds Wk. NW3 120 DD64
Shepherds' Wk., Epsom 232 CP121
Shepherds Wk. (Bushey), Wat. 95 CD47
Shepherds Way, Chesh. 54 AR33
Shepherds Way, Guil. 258 AY138
Shepherds Way, Hat. 64 DC27
Shepherds Way, Rick. 92 BH45
Shepherds Way, S.Croy. 221 DX108
Shepiston La., Hayes 155 BR77
Shepiston La., West Dr. 155 BQ77
Shepley Clo., Cars. 200 DG104
Shepley Clo., Horn. 128 FK64
Chevington Way
Shepley Ms., Enf. 83 EA37
Sheppard Clo., Enf. 82 DV39
Sheppard Clo., Kings.T. 198 CL98
Beaufort Rd.
Sheppard Dr. SE16 162 DV78
Sheppard St. E16 144 EF70
Sheppards, Harl. 51 EM18
Sheppards Clo., St.Alb. 43 CE17
Shepperton Business Pk., Shep. 195 BQ99
Shepperton Clo., Borwd. 78 CR39
Shepperton Ct. Dr., Shep. 195 BP99
Shepperton Rd. N1 142 DQ67
Shepperton Rd., Orp. 205 EQ100
Shepperton Rd., Shep. 194 BL98
Shepperton Rd., Stai. 194 BJ97
Sheppey Clo., Erith 167 FH80
Sheppey Gdns., Dag. 146 EW66
Sheppey Rd.
Sheppey Rd., Dag. 146 EV66
Sheppey Wk. N1 142 DQ66
Clephane Rd.
Sheppeys La., Abb.L. 59 BS28
Sheppy Pl., Grav. 191 GH87
Sherard Ct. N7 121 DL62
Manor Gdns.
Sherard Rd. SE9 184 EL85
Sheraton Business Cen., Grnf. 137 CH68
Sheraton Clo., Borwd. 78 CM43
Sheraton Dr., Epsom 216 CQ113
Sheraton Ms., Wat. 75 BS42
Sheraton St. W1 273 M9
Sherborne Ave., Enf. 82 DW40
Sherborne Ave., Sthl. 156 CA77
Sherborne Clo., Epsom 233 CW117
Sherborne Clo., Hayes 136 BW72
Sherborne Clo., Slou. 153 BE81
Sherborne Cres., Cars. 200 DE101
Sherborne Gdns. NW9 118 CN55
Sherborne Gdns. W13 137 CH72
Sherborne Gdns., Rom. 104 FA50
Sherborne La. EC4 275 K10
Sherborne Pl., Nthwd. 93 BR51
Sherborne Rd., Chess. 216 CL106
Sherborne Rd., Felt. 175 BR87
Sherborne Rd., Orp. 205 ET98
Sherborne Rd., Sutt. 200 DA103
Sherborne St. N1 142 DR67
Sherborne Wk., Lthd. 231 CJ121
Windfield
Sherborne Way, Rick. 75 BP42
Sherboro Rd. N15 122 DT58
Ermine Rd.
Sherbourne, Guil. 260 BK139
Sherbourne Clo., Hem.H. 40 BL21
Sherbourne Cotts., Guil. 260 BL138
Shere Rd.
Sherbourne Cotts., Wat. 76 BW43
Watford Fld. Rd.
Sherbourne Dr., Wind. 151 AM84
Sherbourne Gdns., Shep. 195 BS101
Windmill Grn.
Sherbourne Wk., Slou. 111 AQ63
Sherbrook Gdns. N21 99 DP45
Sherbrooke Clo., Bexh. 166 FA84
Sherbrooke Rd. SW6 159 CZ80
Shere Ave., Sutt. 217 CW110
Shere Clo., Chess. 215 CK106
Shere Clo., Dor. 263 CJ140
Shere La., Guil. 260 BN139
Shere Rd., Guil. 260 BG136
Shere Rd., Ilf. 125 EN57
Shere Rd., Lthd. 245 BP130
Sheredan Rd. E4 101 ED50
Sheredes Dr., Hodd. 49 DZ19
Sherfield Ave., Rick. 92 BK47
Sherfield Gdns. SW15 179 CT86

Sherfield Rd., Grays 170 GB79
Sheridan Clo., Hem.H. 40 BH21
Sheridan Clo., Rom. 106 FJ52
Sheridan Clo., Swan. 207 FF97
Willow Ave.
Sheridan Clo., Uxb. 135 BQ70
Alpha Rd.
Sheridan Ct., Houns. 176 BZ85
Vickers Way
Sheridan Cres., Chis. 205 EP96
Sheridan Dr., Reig. 250 DB132
Sheridan Gdns., Har. 117 CK58
Sheridan Ms. E11 124 EG58
Woodbine Pl.
Sheridan Pl. SW13 159 CT82
Brookwood Ave.
Sheridan Pl., Hmptn. 196 CB95
Sheridan Rd. E7 124 EF62
Sheridan Rd. E12 124 EL64
Sheridan Rd. SW19 199 CZ95
Sheridan Rd., Belv. 166 FA77
Sheridan Rd., Bexh. 166 EY83
Sheridan Rd., Rich. 177 CJ90
Sheridan Rd., Wat. 94 BX45
Sheridan St. E1 142 DV72
Watney St.
Sheridan Ter., Nthlt. 116 CB64
Whitton Ave. W.
Sheridan Wk. NW11 120 DA58
Sheridan Wk., Brox. 49 DY20
Sheridan Wk., Cars. 218 DF106
Carshalton Pk. Rd.
Sheridan Way, Beck. 203 DZ95
Turners Meadow Way
Sheridans Rd., Lthd. 246 CC126
Sheriff Way, Wat. 59 BU33
Sheringham Ave. E12 125 EM63
Sheringham Ave. N14 81 DK43
Sheringham Ave., Felt. 175 BU90
Sheringham Ave., Rom. 127 FC58
Sheringham Ave., Twick. 176 BZ88
Sheringham Dr., Bark. 125 ET64
Sheringham Rd. N7 141 DM65
Sheringham Rd. SE20 202 DV97
Sheringham Twr., Sthl. 136 CB73
Sherington Ave., Pnr. 94 CA52
Sherington Rd. SE7 164 EH79
Sherland Rd., Twick. 177 CF87
Sherlies Ave., Orp. 205 ES103
Sherlock Ms. W1 272 F6
Sherman Rd., Brom. 204 EG95
Sherman Rd., Slou. 132 AS71
Shermanbury Pl., Erith 167 FF80
Betsham Rd.
Shernbroke Rd., Wal.Abb. 68 EF34
Shernhall St. E17 123 EC57
Sherrard Rd. E7 144 EJ65
Sherrard Rd. E12 124 EK64
Sherrards, Welw.G.C. 29 CV06
Sherrards Mansion, Welw.G.C. 29 CV06
Sherrards
Sherrards Ms., Welw.G.C. 29 CV06
Sherrards
Sherrards Way, Barn. 80 DA43
Sherrardspark Rd., Welw.G.C. 29 CW07
Sherrick Grn. Rd. NW10 119 CV64
Sherriff Rd. NW6 140 DA65
Sherrin Rd. E10 123 EA63
Sherringham Ave. N17 100 DU54
Sherrock Gdns. NW4 119 CU56
Sherry Ms., Bark. 145 ER66
Cecil Ave.
Sherwin Rd. SE14 163 DX81
Sherwood Ave. E18 124 EH55
Sherwood Ave. SW16 181 DK94
Sherwood Ave., Grnf. 137 CE65
Sherwood Ave., Hayes 135 BV70
Sherwood Ave., Pot.B. 63 CY32
Sherwood Ave., Ruis. 115 BS58
Sherwood Ave., St.Alb. 43 CH17
Sherwood Clo. SW13 159 CV83
Lower Common S.
Sherwood Clo. W13 137 CH74
Sherwood Clo., Bex. 186 EW86
Sherwood Clo., Lthd. 230 CC122
Sherwood Clo., Slou. 152 AY76
Sherwood Cres., Reig. 266 DB138
Sherwood Gdns. E14 163 EA77
Sherwood Gdns. SE16 162 DU78
Sherwood Gdns., Bark. 145 ER66
Sherwood Pk. Ave., Sid. 186 EU87
Sherwood Pk. Rd., Mitch. 201 DJ98
Sherwood Pk. Rd., Sutt. 218 DA106
Sherwood Pl., Hem.H. 40 BM16
Turnpike Grn.
Sherwood Rd. NW4 119 CW55
Sherwood Rd. SW19 179 CZ94
Sherwood Rd., Couls. 235 DJ116
Sherwood Rd., Croy. 202 DV101
Sherwood Rd., Hmptn. 176 CC92
Sherwood Rd., Har. 116 CC61
Sherwood Rd., Ilf. 125 ER56
Sherwood Rd., Well. 165 ES82
Sherwood Rd., Wok. 226 AS117
Sherwood St. N20 98 DD48
Sherwood St. W1 273 L10
Sherwood Ter. N20 98 DD48
Green Rd.
Sherwood Way, W.Wick. 203 EB103
Sherwoods Rd., Wat. 94 BY45
Shetland Clo., Borwd. 78 CR44
Percheron Rd.
Shetland Clo., Guil. 243 BB129
Weybrook Dr.
Shetland Rd. E3 143 DZ68
Shevon Way, Brwd. 108 FT49
Shewens Rd., Wey. 213 BR105
Shey Copse, Wok. 227 BC117
Shield Dr., Brent. 157 CG79
Shield Rd., Ashf. 175 BQ91
Shieldhall St. SE2 166 EW77
Shifford Path SE23 183 DX90
Shilburn Way, Wok. 226 AU118
Shillibeer Pl. W1 272 C6
Shillibeer Wk., Chig. 103 ET48
Shillingford St. N1 141 DP66
Cross St.
Shillitoe Ave., Pot.B. 63 CX32
Shimmings, The, Guil. 243 BA133
Shinfield St. W12 139 CW72
Shingle Ct., Wal.Abb. 68 EG33
Shinglewell Rd., Erith 166 FA80
Shinners Clo. SE25 202 DU99
Ship All. W4 158 CN79
Thames Rd.
Ship and Mermaid Row SE1 279 L4
Ship Hill, H.Wyc. 111 AL60
Ship Hill, West. 238 EJ121
Ship La. SW14 158 CQ82
Ship La. (Sutton at Hone), Dart. 208 FK95
Ship La., Purf. 169 FS76
Ship La., S.Ock. 169 FR75
Ship La., Swan. 208 FK95
Ship La. Caravan Site, S.Ock. 169 FR76
Ship St. SE8 163 EA81
Ship Tavern Pas. EC3 275 M10
Ship Yd. E14 163 EB78
Napier Ave.
Ship Yd., Wey. 213 BP105
High St.
Shipfield Clo., West. 238 EJ121
Shipka Rd. SW12 181 DH88
Shipley Bri. La., Horl. 269 DM154
Shipman Rd. E16 144 EH72
Shipman Rd. SE23 183 DX89
Shipton Clo., Dag. 126 EX62
Shipton St. E2 142 DT69
Shipwright Rd. SE16 163 DY75
Shirburn Clo. SE23 182 DW87
Tyson Rd.
Shirbutt St. E14 143 EB73
Shire Clo., Brox. 67 DZ26
Groom Rd.
Shire Ct., Epsom 217 CT108
Shire Ct., Erith 166 EX76
St. John Fisher Rd.
Shire Horse Way, Islw. 157 CF83
Shire La., Ger.Cr. 91 BB48
Shire La., Kes. 223 EM108
Shire La., Orp. 223 EM108
Shire La., Rick. 73 BB43
Shire La., Uxb. 91 BD54
Shire Pk., Welw.G.C. 29 CY07
Shire Pl. SW18 180 DC87
Whitehead Clo.
Shirebrook Rd. SE3 164 EK83
Shirehall Clo. NW4 119 CX58
Shirehall Gdns. NW4 119 CX58
Shirehall La. NW4 119 CX58
Shirehall Pk. NW4 119 CX58
Shirehall Rd., Dart. 188 FJ92
Shiremeade, Borwd. 78 CM43
Shires, The, Rich. 178 CL91
Shires Clo., Ash. 231 CK119
Shires Ho., W.Byf. 212 BL113
Eden Gro. Rd.
Shirland Ms. W9 139 CZ69
Shirland Rd. W9 140 DA70
Shirley Ave., Bex. 186 EX87
Shirley Ave., Couls. 235 DP119
Shirley Ave., Croy. 202 DW102
Shirley Ave., Red. 266 DF139
Shirley Ave., Sutt. 218 DE105
Shirley Ave. (Cheam), Sutt. 217 CZ109
Shirley Ave., Wind. 151 AM81
Shirley Ch. Rd., Croy. 203 DX104
Shirley Clo. E17 123 EB57
Addison Rd.
Shirley Clo., Brox. 49 DZ24
Shirley Clo., Dart. 168 FJ84
Shirley Clo., Houns. 176 CC85
Shirley Clo. (Cheshunt), Wal.Cr. 66 DW29
Shirley Ct., Croy. 203 DX104
Shirley Cres., Beck. 203 DY98
Shirley Dr., Houns. 176 CC85
Shirley Gdns. W7 137 CG74
Shirley Gdns., Bark. 145 ES65
Shirley Gdns., Horn. 128 FJ61
Shirley Gro. N9 100 DW45
Shirley Gro. SW11 160 DG83
Shirley Hts., Wall. 219 DJ109
Shirley Hills Rd., Croy. 221 DX106
Shirley Ho. Dr. SE7 164 EJ80
Shirley Oaks Rd., Croy. 203 DX102
Shirley Pk. Rd., Croy. 202 DV102
Shirley Rd. E15 144 EE66
Shirley Rd. W4 158 CR75
Shirley Rd., Abb.L. 59 BT32
Shirley Rd., Croy. 202 DV101
Shirley Rd., Enf. 82 DQ41
Shirley Rd., St.Alb. 43 CF21
Shirley Rd., Sid. 185 ES90
Shirley Rd., Wall. 219 DJ109
Shirley St. E16 144 EF72
Shirley Way, Croy. 203 DY104
Shirlock Rd. NW3 120 DF63
Shobden Rd. N17 100 DR53
Shobroke Clo. NW2 119 CW62
Shoe La. EC4 274 E8
Shoe La. EC4 141 DN72
Shoe La., Harl. 52 EZ16
Shoebury Rd. E6 145 EM66
Sholden Gdns., Orp. 206 EW99
Sholto Rd., Houns. 174 BM85
Shonks Mill Rd., Rom. 87 FG37
Shoot Up Hill NW2 119 CY64
Shooters Ave., Har. 117 CJ56
Shooters Dr., Wal.Abb. 50 EE22
Shooter's Hill SE18 165 EN81
Shooter's Hill, Well. 165 EN81
Shooter's Hill Rd. SE3 164 EH80
Shooter's Hill Rd. SE10 163 ED81
Shooter's Hill Rd. SE18 164 EH80
Shooters Rd., Enf. 81 DP39
Shootersway, Berk. 38 AU20
Shootersway La., Berk. 38 AT20
Shootersway Pk., Berk. 38 AT20
Shophouse La., Guil. 260 BK144
Shoplands, Welw.G.C. 29 CX05
Shord Hill, Ken. 236 DR116
Shore, The (Northfleet), Grav. 190 GC85
Shore, The (Rosherville), Grav. 191 GF86
Shore Clo., Felt. 175 BU87
Shore Clo., Hmptn. 176 BY92
Stewart Clo.
Shore Gro., Felt. 176 CA89
Shore Pl. E9 142 DW66
Shore Rd. E9 142 DW66
Shorediche Clo., Uxb. 114 BM62
Shoreditch High St. E1 275 N3
Shoreditch High St. E1 142 DS70
Shoreham Clo. SW18 180 DB85
Ram St.
Shoreham Clo., Bex. 186 EX88
Stansted Cres.
Shoreham Clo., Croy. 202 DW100
Shoreham La., Orp. 224 FA107
Shoreham La., Sev. 256 FF122
Shoreham La. (Halstead), Sev. 224 EZ112
Shoreham Pl., Sev. 225 FG112
Shoreham Ri., Slou. 131 AK70
Lower Britwell Rd.
Shoreham Rd., Orp. 206 EV95
Shoreham Rd., Sev. 225 FH112
Shoreham Rd. E., Houns. 174 BL85
Shoreham Rd. W., Houns. 174 BL85
Shoreham Way, Brom. 204 EG100
Shores Rd., Wok. 210 AY114
Shorncliffe Rd. SE1 279 P10
Shorncliffe Rd. SE1 162 DT78
Shorndean St. SE6 183 EC88
Shorne Clo., Orp. 206 EX98
Shorne Clo., Sid. 186 EV86
Shornefield Clo., Brom. 205 EN97
Shornells Way SE2 166 EW78
Willrose Cres.
Shorrolds Rd. SW6 159 CZ80
Short Hedges, Houns. 156 CB81
Short Hill, Har. 117 CE60
High St.
Short La., Oxt. 254 EH132
Short La., St.Alb. 60 BZ30
Short La., Stai. 174 BM87
Short Path SE18 165 EP79
Westdale Rd.
Short Rd. E11 124 EE61
Short Rd. E15 143 ED67
Short Rd. W4 158 CS79
Short Rd., Houns. 174 BL86
Short St. NW4 119 CW56
New Brent St.
Short St. SE1 278 E4
Short Wall E15 143 EC69
Short Way SE9 164 EL83
Short Way, Twick. 176 CC87
Shortacres, Red. 251 DM133
Shortcroft Rd., Epsom 217 CT108
Shortcrofts Rd., Dag. 146 EZ65
Shorter Ave., Brwd. 109 FZ44
Shorter St. E1 275 P10
Shorter St. E1 142 DT73
Shortern, Slou. 132 AW72
Shortgate N12 97 CZ49
Shortlands W6 159 CX77
Shortlands, Hayes 155 BR79
Shortlands Clo. N18 100 DR48
Shortlands Clo., Belv. 166 EZ76
Shortlands Gdns., Brom. 204 EE96
Shortlands Grn., Welw.G.C. 29 CZ10
Shortlands Gro., Brom. 203 ED97
Shortlands Rd. E10 123 EB59
Shortlands Rd., Brom. 203 ED97
Shortlands Rd., Kings.T. 178 CM94
Shortmead Dr. (Cheshunt), Wal.Cr. 67 DY31
Shorts Cft. NW9 118 CP56
Shorts Gdns. WC2 273 P9
Shorts Gdns. WC2 141 DL72
Shorts Rd., Cars. 218 DE105
Shortway N12 98 DE51
Shortway, Amer. 55 AR37
Shortway, Chesh. 54 AP29
Shortwood Ave., Stai. 174 BH90
Shortwood Common, Stai. 174 BH91
Shotfield, Wall. 219 DH107
Shothanger Way, Hem.H. 57 BC26
Shott Clo., Sutt. 218 DC106
Turnpike La.
Shottendane Rd. SW6 160 DA81
Shottery Clo. SE9 184 EL90
Shottfield Ave. SW14 158 CS84
Shoulder of Mutton All. E14 143 DY73
Narrow St.
Shouldham St. W1 272 C7
Shouldham St. W1 140 DE71
Showers Way, Hayes 135 BU74
Shrapnel Clo. SE18 164 EL80
Shrapnel Rd. SE9 165 EM83
Shrewsbury Ave. SW14 158 CQ84
Shrewsbury Ave., Har. 118 CL56
Shrewsbury Clo., Surb. 198 CL103
Shrewsbury Ct. EC1 142 DQ70
Whitecross St.
Shrewsbury Cres. NW10 138 CR67
Shrewsbury La. SE18 165 EP81
Shrewsbury Ms. W2 140 DA71
Chepstow Rd.
Shrewsbury Rd. E7 124 EK64
Shrewsbury Rd. N11 99 DJ51
Shrewsbury Rd. W2 140 DA72
Shrewsbury Rd., Beck. 203 DY97
Shrewsbury Rd., Cars. 200 DE100
Shrewsbury Rd., Red. 250 DE134
Shrewsbury St. W10 139 CW70
Shrewsbury Wk., Islw. 157 CG83
South St.
Shrewton Rd. SW17 180 DF94
Shrimpton Clo., Beac. 89 AK49
Shrimpton Rd., Beac. 89 AK49
Shroffold Rd., Brom. 184 EE91
Shropshire Clo., Mitch. 201 DL98
Shropshire Pl. WC1 273 L5
Shropshire Rd. N22 99 DM52
Shroton St. NW1 272 B6
Shroton St. NW1 140 DE71
Shrubberies, The E18 102 EG54
Shrubberies, The, Chig. 103 EQ50
Shrubbery, The, Hem.H. 39 BE19
Shrubbery, The, Upmin. 128 FQ62
Shrubbery Clo. N1 142 DQ67
St. Paul St.
Shrubbery Gdns. N21 99 DP45
Shrubbery Rd. N9 100 DU48
Shrubbery Rd. SW16 181 DL91
Shrubbery Rd. (South Darenth), Dart. 209 FR95
Shrubbery Rd., Grav. 191 GJ88
Shrubbery Rd., Sthl. 136 BZ74
Shrubhill Rd., Hem.H. 39 BF21
Shrubland Gro., Wor.Pk. 199 CW104
Shrubland Rd. E8 142 DU67
Shrubland Rd. E10 123 EA59
Shrubland Rd. E17 123 EA57
Shrubland Rd., Bans. 233 CZ116
Shrublands, Hat. 64 DB26
Shrublands, The, Pot.B. 63 CY33
Shrublands Ave., Berk. 38 AU19
Shrublands Ave., Croy. 221 EA105
Shrublands Clo. N20 98 DD46
Shrublands Clo. SE26 182 DW90
Shrublands Clo., Chig. 103 EQ51
Shrublands Rd., Berk. 38 AU18
Shrubs Rd., Rick. 92 BM51
Shrubsall Clo. SE9 184 EL88
Shuna Wk. N1 142 DR65
St. Paul's Rd.
Shurland Ave., Barn. 80 DD44
Shurland Gdns. SE15 162 DT80
Rosemary Rd.
Shurlock Ave., Swan. 207 FD96
Shurlock Dr., Orp. 223 EQ105
Shuters Sq. W14 159 CZ78
Sun Rd.
Shuttle Clo., Sid. 185 ET87
Shuttle Rd., Dart. 167 FG83
Shuttle St. E1 142 DU70
Buxton St.
Shuttlemead, Bex. 186 EZ87
Shuttleworth Rd. SW11 160 DE82
Sibella Rd. SW4 161 DK82
Sibley Clo., Bexh. 186 EY85
Sibley Gro. E12 144 EL66
Sibneys Grn., Harl. 51 ES19
Sibthorpe Rd. SE12 184 EH86
Sibthorpe Rd., Hat. 45 CX24
Sibton Rd., Cars. 200 DE101
Sicilian Ave. WC1 274 A7
Sicklefield Clo. (Cheshunt), Wal.Cr. 66 DT26
Sidbury St. SW6 159 CY81
Sidcup Bypass, Chis. 185 EP89
Sidcup Bypass, Orp. 186 EV93
Sidcup Bypass, Sid. 185 ES91
Sidcup High St., Sid. 186 EU91
Sidcup Hill, Sid. 186 EV91
Sidcup Hill Gdns., Sid. 186 EW92
Sidcup Hill
Sidcup Pl., Sid. 186 EU92
Sidcup Rd. SE9 184 EK87
Sidcup Rd. SE12 184 EH85
Sidcup Technology Cen., Sid. 186 EX92
Siddeley Dr., Houns. 156 BY83
Siddons La. NW1 272 E5
Siddons Rd. N17 100 DU53
Siddons Rd. SE23 183 DY89
Siddons Rd., Croy. 201 DN104
Side Rd. E17 123 DZ57
Side Rd., Uxb. 113 BD59
Sidewood Rd. SE9 185 ER88
Sidford Clo., Hem.H. 39 BF20
Sidford Pl. SE1 278 C7
Sidings, The E11 123 EC60
Sidings, The, Hat. 44 CS19
Sidings, The, Loug. 84 EL44
Sidings, The, Stai. 174 BH91
Leacroft
Sidings Ms. N7 121 DN62
Sidmouth Ave., Islw. 157 CE82
Sidmouth Clo., Wat. 93 BV47
Sidmouth Dr., Ruis. 115 BU62
Sidmouth Par. NW2 139 CW66
Sidmouth Rd.
Sidmouth Rd. E10 123 EC62
Sidmouth Rd. NW2 139 CW66
Sidmouth Rd. SE15 162 DT81
Sidmouth Rd., Orp. 206 EV99
Sidmouth Rd., Well. 166 EW80
Sidmouth St. WC1 274 A3
Sidmouth St. WC1 141 DL69
Sidney Ave. N13 99 DM50
Sidney Elson Way E6 145 EN68
Edwin Ave.
Sidney Gdns., Brent. 157 CJ79
Sidney Gro. EC1 274 F1
Sidney Rd. E7 124 EG62
Sidney Rd. N22 99 DM52
Sidney Rd. SE25 202 DU99
Sidney Rd. SW9 161 DM82
Sidney Rd., Beck. 203 DY96
Sidney Rd., Epp. 85 ER36
Sidney Rd., Har. 116 CC55
Sidney Rd., Stai. 174 BG91
Sidney Rd., Twick. 177 CG86
Sidney Rd., Walt. 195 BU101
Sidney Rd., Wind. 150 AJ83
Sidney Sq. E1 142 DW72
Sidney St. E1 142 DV71
Sidworth St. E8 142 DV66
Siebert Rd. SE3 164 EG79
Siemens Rd. SE18 164 EK76
Sigdon Rd. E8 122 DU64
Sigers, The, Pnr. 115 BV58
Signmakers Yd. NW1 141 DH67
Delancey St.
Sigrist Sq., Kings.T. 198 CL95
Silbury Ave., Mitch. 200 DE95
Silbury St. N1 275 K2
Silchester Rd. W10 139 CX72
Silecroft Rd., Bexh. 166 FA81
Silesia Bldgs. E8 142 DV66
London La.
Silex St. SE1 278 G5
Silex St. SE1 161 DP75
Silk Clo. SE12 184 EG85
Silk Mill Ct., Wat. 93 BV45
Silk Mill Rd.
Silk Mill Rd., Wat. 93 BV45
Silk Mills Clo., Sev. 257 FJ121
Silk Mills Path SE13 163 EC82
Lewisham Rd.
Silk St. EC2 275 J6
Silk St. EC2 142 DQ71
Silkfield Rd. NW9 118 CS57
Silkham Rd., Oxt. 253 ED127
Silkin Ho., Wat. 94 BW48
Silkmills Sq. E9 143 DZ65
Silkmore La., Lthd. 245 BP127
Silkstream Rd., Edg. 96 CQ53
Silo Clo., Gdmg. 258 AT143
Silo Dr., Gdmg. 258 AT143
Silo Rd., Gdmg. 258 AT143
Silsden Cres., Ch.St.G. 90 AX48
London Rd.
Silsoe Rd. N22 99 DM54
Silver Birch Ave. E4 101 DZ51
Silver Birch Ave., Epp. 70 EY27
Silver Birch Clo. N11 98 DG51
Silver Birch Clo. SE28 146 EU74
Silver Birch Clo., Add. 211 BE112
Silver Birch Clo., Dart. 187 FE91
Silver Birch Clo., Uxb. 114 BL63
Silver Birch Gdns. E6 145 EM70
Silver Birch Ms., Ilf. 103 EQ51
Fencepiece Rd.
Silver Birches, Brwd. 109 GA46
Silver Clo. SE14 163 DY80
Southerngate Way
Silver Clo., Har. 95 CD52
Silver Clo., Tad. 233 CY124
Silver Cres. W4 158 CP77
Silver Dell, Wat. 75 BT35
Silver Hill, Ch.St.G. 90 AV47
Silver Jubilee Way, Houns. 155 BV82
Silver La., Pur. 219 DK112
Silver La., W.Wick. 203 ED103
Silver Pl. W1 273 L10
Silver Rd. SE13 163 EB83
Elmira St.
Silver Rd. W12 139 CX73
Silver Rd., Grav. 191 GL89
Silver Spring Clo., Erith 167 FB79
Silver St. N18 100 DS49
Silver St., Enf. 82 DR41
Silver St., Rom. 86 EV41
Silver St., Wal.Abb. 67 EC34
Silver St. (Cheshunt), Wal.Cr. 66 DR30
Silver Tree Clo., Walt. 213 BU105
Silver Wk. SE16 143 DZ74
Silver Way, Rom. 127 FB55
Silver Way, Uxb. 135 BP68
Oakdene Rd.
Silverbirch Wk. NW3 140 DG65
Queens Cres.
Silvercliffe Gdns., Barn. 80 DE42
Silverdale SE26 182 DW91
Silverdale, Enf. 81 DL42
Silverdale Ave., Ilf. 125 ES57
Silverdale Ave., Lthd. 214 CC114
Silverdale Ave., Walt. 195 BT104
Silverdale Clo. W7 137 CE74
Silverdale Clo., Bet. 264 CP138
Silverdale Clo., Nthlt. 116 BZ64
Silverdale Clo., Sutt. 217 CZ105
Silverdale Ct., Stai. 174 BH92
Silverdale Dr. SE9 184 EL89
Silverdale Dr., Horn. 127 FH64
Silverdale Dr., Sun. 195 BV96
Silverdale Gdns., Hayes 155 BU75
Silverdale Rd. E4 101 ED51
Silverdale Rd., Bexh. 167 FB82
Silverdale Rd., Hayes 155 BU75
Silverdale Rd. (Petts Wd.), Orp. 205 EQ98
Silverdale Rd. (St. Paul's Cray), Orp. 206 EU97
Silverdale Rd. (Bushey), Wat. 76 BY43
Silverfield, Brox. 49 DZ22
Silverhall St., Islw. 157 CG83
Silverholme Clo., Har. 117 CK59
Silverland St. E16 145 EM74
Silverlea Gdns., Horl. 269 DJ149
Silverleigh Rd., Th.Hth. 201 DM98
Silverlocke Rd., Grays 170 GD79
Silvermere Ave., Rom. 105 FB51
Silvermere Rd. SE6 183 EB86
Silversmiths Way, Wok. 226 AW118
Silverstead La., West. 239 ER121
Silverston Way, Stan. 95 CJ51
Silverstone Clo., Red. 250 DF132
Goodwood Rd.
Silverthorn Dr., Hem.H. 41 BP24
Silverthorn Gdns. E4 101 EA47
Silverthorne Rd. SW8 161 DH82
Silverton Rd. W6 159 CX79
Silvertown Way E16 144 EF72
Silvertree La., Grnf. 137 CD69
Cowgate Rd.
Silvertrees, St.Alb. 60 BZ30
West Riding
Silverwood Clo., Beck. 183 EA94
Silverwood Clo., Croy. 221 DZ109
Silverwood Clo., Nthwd. 93 BQ53
Silverwood Cotts., Guil. 260 BM138
Shere Rd.
Silvester Rd. SE22 182 DT85
Silvester St. SE1 279 J5
Silvesters, Harl. 51 EM17
Silvocea Way E14 143 ED72
Silwood Est. SE16 162 DW77
Silwood St. SE16 162 DW77
Simla Clo. SE14 163 DY79
Simla Ho. SE1 279 L5
Simmil Rd., Esher 215 CE106
Simmonds Ri., Hem.H. 40 BK22
Simmons Clo. N20 98 DE46
Simmons Clo., Chess. 215 CJ107
Merritt Gdns.
Simmons Clo., Slou. 153 BA77
Common Rd.
Simmons La. E4 101 ED47
Simmons Pl., Stai. 173 BE92
Chertsey La.
Simmons Rd. SE18 165 EP78
Simmons Way N20 98 DE47
Simms Clo., Cars. 200 DE103
Simms Rd. SE1 162 DU77
Simnel Rd. SE12 184 EH87
Simon Clo. W11 139 CZ73
Portobello Rd.
Simon Dean, Hem.H. 57 BA27
Simonds Rd. E10 123 EA61
Simone Clo., Brom. 204 EK95
Simone Dr., Ken. 236 DQ116
Simons Clo., Cher. 211 BC107
Simons Wk. E15 123 ED64
Waddington St.
Simons Wk., Egh. 172 AW94
Simplemarsh Ct., Add. 212 BH105
Simplemarsh Rd.
Simplemarsh Rd., Add. 212 BG105
Simpson Clo. N21 81 DL43
Macleod Rd.
Simpson Dr. W3 138 CR72
Simpson Rd., Houns. 176 BZ86
Simpson Rd., Rain. 147 FF65
Simpson Rd., Rich. 177 CJ91
Simpson St. SW11 160 DD82
Simpsons Grn., Slou. 131 AM69
Rokesby Rd.
Simpsons Rd. E14 143 EB73
Simpsons Rd., Brom. 204 EG97
Simrose Ct. SW18 180 DA85
Wandsworth High St.
Sims Clo., Rom. 127 FF56
Sims Wk. SE3 164 EF84
Sinclair Ct., Beck. 183 EA94
Sinclair Dr., Sutt. 218 DB109
Sinclair Gdns. W14 159 CX75
Sinclair Gro. NW11 119 CX58

Sinclair Rd. E4 101 DZ50
Sinclair Rd. W14 159 CX75
Sinclair Way, Dart. 189 FR91
Sinclare Clo., Enf. 82 DT39
Sincots Rd., Red. 250 DF134
Lower Bri. Rd.
Sinderby Clo., Borwd. 78 CL39
Singapore Rd. W13 137 CG74
Singer St. EC2 275 L3
Single St., West. 239 EP115
Singles Cross La., Sev. 224 EW114
Singleton Clo. SW17 180 DF94
Singleton Clo., Croy. 202 DQ101
St. Saviours Rd.
Singleton Clo., Horn. 127 FF63
Carfax Rd.
Singleton Rd., Dag. 126 EZ64
Singleton Scarp N12 98 DA50
Singlewell Rd., Grav. 191 GH90
Singret Pl. (Cowley), Uxb. 134 BJ70
High St.
Sinnott Rd. E17 101 DX53
Sion Rd., Twick. 177 CH87
Sipson Clo., West Dr. 154 BN79
Sipson La., Hayes 154 BN79
Sipson La., West Dr. 154 BN79
Sipson Rd., West Dr. 154 BN78
Sipson Way, West Dr. 154 BN80
Sir Alexander Clo. W3 139 CT74
Sir Alexander Rd. W3 139 CT74
Sir Cyril Black Way SW19 180 DA94
Sir Francis Way, Brwd. 108 FV47
Sir Henry Peek's Dr., Slou. 131 AN65
Sir Thomas More Est. SW3 160 DD79
Beaufort St.
Sirdar Rd. N22 121 DP55
Sirdar Rd. W11 139 CX73
Sirdar Rd., Mitch. 180 DG93
Grenfell Rd.
Sirdar Strand, Grav. 191 GM92
Sirinham Pt. SW8 161 DM79
Sirius Rd., Nthwd. 93 BU50
Sise La. EC4 275 K9
Siskin Clo., Borwd. 78 CN42
Siskin Clo., Wat. 76 BY42
Sisley Rd., Bark. 145 ES67
Sispara Gdns. SW18 179 CZ86
Sissinghurst Rd., Croy. 202 DU101
Sister Mabel's Way SE15 162 DU80
Radnor Rd.
Sisters Ave. SW11 160 DF84
Sistova Rd. SW12 181 DH88
Sisulu Pl. SW9 161 DN83
Sittingbourne Ave., Enf. 82 DR44
Sitwell Gro., Stan. 95 CF50
Siverst Clo., Nthlt. 136 CB65
Sivill Ho. E2 142 DT69
Siviter Way, Dag. 147 FB66
Siward Rd. N17 100 DR53
Siward Rd. SW17 180 DC90
Siward Rd., Brom. 204 EH97
Six Acres, Hem.H. 40 BN23
Six Acres Est. N4 121 DN61
Six Bells La., Sev. 257 FJ126
Six Bridges Trd. Est. SE1 162 DU78
Sixth Ave. E12 125 EM63
Sixth Ave. W10 139 CY69
Sixth Ave., Hayes 135 BT74
Sixth Ave., Wat. 76 BX35
Sixth Cross Rd., Twick. 176 CC90
Skardu Rd. NW2 119 CY64
Skarnings Ct., Wal.Abb. 68 EG33
Skeena Hill SW18 179 CY87
Skeet Hill La., Orp. 206 EX102
Skeffington Rd. E6 145 EM67
Skelbrook St. SW18 180 DB89
Skelgill Rd. SW15 159 CZ84
Skelley Rd. E15 144 EF66
Skelton Clo. E8 142 DT65
Buttermere Wk.
Skelton Clo., Beac. 110 AG55
Skelton Rd. E7 144 EG65
Skeltons La. E10 123 EB59
Skelwith Rd. W6 159 CW79
Skenfrith Ho. SE15 162 DV79
Commercial Way
Skerne Rd., Kings.T. 197 CK95
Skerries Ct., Slou. 153 BA77
Blacksmith Row
Sketchley Gdns. SE16 163 DX78
Sketty Rd., Enf. 82 DS41
Skibbs La., Orp. 224 EY106
Skid Hill La., Warl. 222 EF113
Skidmore Way, Rick. 92 BL46
Skiers St. E15 144 EE67
Skiffington Clo. SW2 181 DN88
Skillet Hill, Wal.Abb. 84 EH35
Skimpans Clo., Hat. 45 CX24
Skinner Ct. E2 142 DV68
Parmiter St.
Skinner Pl. SW1 276 F9
Skinner St. EC1 274 E3
Skinner St. EC1 141 DN69
Skinners La. EC4 275 J10
Skinners La., Ash. 231 CK118
Skinners La., Houns. 156 CB81
Skinner's Row SE10 163 EB81
Blackheath Rd.
Skinney La., Dart. 208 FQ97
Skip La. (Harefield), Uxb. 114 BL60
Skippers Clo., Green. 189 FV85
Skipsey Ave. E6 145 EM69
Skipton Clo. N11 98 DG51
Ribblesdale Ave.
Skipton Dr., Hayes 155 BQ76
Skipton Way, Horl. 269 DH145
Skipworth Rd. E9 142 DW67
Skomer Wk. N1 142 DQ65
Clephane Rd.
Sky Peals Rd., Wdf.Grn. 101 ED53
Skydmore Path, Slou. 131 AM69
Umberville Way
Skylark Rd., Uxb. 113 BC60
Skyport Dr., West Dr. 154 BK80
Skys Wd. Rd., St.Alb. 43 CH16
Slacksbury Hatch, Harl. 51 EP15
Helions Rd.
Slade, The SE18 165 ES79
Slade Ct., Cher. 211 BD107
Slade Ct., Rad. 77 CG35
Slade End, Epp. 85 ES36
Slade Gdns., Erith 167 FF81
Slade Grn. Rd., Erith 167 FG80
Slade Ho., Houns. 176 BZ86
Slade Oak La., Ger.Cr. 113 BB55
Slade Oak La., Uxb. 113 BC57
Slade Rd., Cher. 211 BD107
Slade Twr. E10 123 EB61
Slade Wk. SE17 161 DP79
Heiron St.
Sladebrook Rd. SE3 164 EK82
Sladedale Rd. SE18 165 ES78
Slades Clo., Enf. 81 DN41
Slades Dr., Chis. 185 EQ90
Slades Gdns., Enf. 81 DN40
Slades Hill, Enf. 81 DN41
Slades Ri., Enf. 81 DN41
Slagrove Pl. SE13 183 EB85
Slaidburn St. SW10 160 DC79
Slaithwaite Rd. SE13 163 EC84
Slaney Pl. N7 121 DN64
Hornsey Rd.
Slaney Rd., Rom. 127 FE57
Slapleys, Wok. 226 AX120
Slater Clo. SE18 165 EN78
Woolwich New Rd.
Slattery Rd., Felt. 176 BW88
Sleaford Grn., Wat. 94 BX48
Sleaford St. SW8 161 DJ80
Sleapcross Gdns., St.Alb. 44 CP21
Sleapshyde La., St.Alb. 44 CP21
Sleddale, Hem.H. 40 BL17
Sledmore Ct., Felt. 175 BS88
Kilross Rd.
Sleepers Fm. Rd., Grays 171 GH75
Sleets End, Hem.H. 40 BH18
Slewins Clo., Horn. 128 FJ57
Slewins La., Horn. 128 FJ57
Slievemore Clo. SW4 161 DK83
Voltaire Rd.
Slimmons Dr., St.Alb. 43 CG16
Slines New Rd., Cat. 237 DX120
Slines Oak Rd., Cat. 237 EA123
Slines Oak Rd., Warl. 237 EA119
Slingsby Pl. WC2 273 P10
Slip, The, West. 255 EQ126
Slipe La., Brox. 49 DZ24
Slippers Hill, Hem.H. 40 BK19
Slippers Pl. SE16 162 DV76
Slipshatch Rd., Reig. 265 CX138
Slipshoe St., Reig. 249 CZ134
West St.
Sloane Ave. SW3 276 B9
Sloane Ave. SW3 160 DE77
Sloane Ct. E. SW3 276 F10
Sloane Ct. W. SW3 276 F10
Sloane Ct. W. SW3 160 DG78
Sloane Gdns. SW1 276 F9
Sloane Gdns. SW1 160 DG77
Sloane Gdns., Orp. 205 EQ104
Sloane Sq. SW1 276 F9
Sloane Sq. SW1 160 DF77
Sloane St. SW1 276 E6
Sloane St. SW1 160 DF75
Sloane Ter. SW1 276 E8
Sloane Ter. SW1 160 DF77
Sloane Wk., Croy. 203 DZ100
Sloansway, Welw.G.C. 30 DA06
Slocock Hill, Wok. 226 AW117
Slocum Clo. SE28 146 EW73
Slough La. NW9 118 CQ58
Slough La., Bet. 249 CU133
Slough La., Epp. 53 FC24
Slough La., Epsom 248 CQ125
Slough Rd., Iver 133 BC69
Slough Rd., Slou. 152 AU78
Slough Rd. (Eton), Wind. 151 AR78
Slough Trd. Est., Slou. 131 AP72
Slowmans Clo., St.Alb. 60 CC28
Sly St. E1 142 DV72
Cannon St. Rd.
Slyfield Ct., Guil. 242 AY130
Slyfield Grn.
Slyfield Grn., Guil. 242 AY130
Slyfield Ind. Est., Guil. 242 AY130
Smaldon Clo., West Dr. 154 BN76
Walnut Ave.
Small Acre, Hem.H. 39 BF20
Small Grains (Fawkham Grn.), Long. 209 FV104
Smallberry Ave., Islw. 157 CF82
Smallbrook Ms. W2 140 DD72
Craven Rd.
Smallcroft, Welw.G.C. 30 DB08
Smalley Clo. N16 122 DT62
Smalley Rd. Est. N16 122 DT62
Smalley Clo.
Smallfield Rd., Horl. 269 DH148
Smallford La., St.Alb. 44 CP21
Smallholdings Rd., Epsom 217 CW114
Smallmead, Horl. 269 DH148
Small's Hill Rd., Reig. 265 CU141
Smallwood Clo., St.Alb. 28 CL08
Smallwood Rd. SW17 180 DD91
Smardale Rd. SW18 180 DC85
Alma Rd.
Smarden Clo., Belv. 166 FA78
Essenden Rd.
Smarden Gro. SE9 185 EM91
Smart Clo., Rom. 105 FH53
Smart St. E2 143 DX69
Smarts Grn. (Cheshunt), Wal.Cr. 66 DT27
Smarts Heath La., Wok. 226 AU123
Smarts Heath Rd., Wok. 226 AT123
Smarts La., Loug. 84 EK42
Smarts Pl. N18 100 DU50
Fore St.
Smart's Pl. WC2 274 A8
Smarts Rd., Grav. 191 GH90
Smeaton Clo., Chess. 215 CK107
Merritt Gdns.
Smeaton Clo., Wal.Abb. 68 EE32
Smeaton Rd. SW18 180 DA87
Smeaton Rd., Enf. 83 EA37
Smeaton Rd., Wdf.Grn. 103 EM50
Smeaton St. E1 142 DV74
Smedley St. SW4 161 DK82
Smedley St. SW8 161 DK82
Smeed Rd. E3 143 EA66
Smiles Pl. SE13 163 EC82
Smith Clo. SE16 143 DX74
Smith Rd., Reig. 265 CZ137
Smith Sq. SW1 277 P7
Smith Sq. SW1 161 DL76
Smith St. SW3 276 D10
Smith St. SW3 160 DF78
Smith St., Surb. 198 CM100
Smith St., Wat. 76 BW42
Smith Ter. SW3 160 DF78
Smitham Bottom La., Pur. 219 DJ111
Smitham Downs Rd., Pur. 219 DK113
Smithbarn Clo., Horl. 269 DH147
Tanyard Way
Smithers, The, Bet. 264 CP136
Smithfield, Hem.H. 40 BK18
Smithfield St. EC1 274 F7
Smithies Ct. E15 123 EC64
Smithies Rd. SE2 166 EV77
Smith's Ct. W1 273 L10
Smiths Cres., St.Alb. 44 CQ21
Smiths Fm. Est., Nthlt. 136 CA68
Smiths La., Eden. 255 EQ133
Smiths La. (Cheshunt), Wal.Cr. 66 DR26
Smiths La., Wind. 151 AL82
Smiths Yd. SW18 180 DC89
Summerley St.
Smith's Yd., Croy. 202 DQ104
St. Georges Wk.
Smithson Rd. N17 100 DR53
Smithwood Clo. SW19 179 CY88
Smithy Clo., Tad. 249 CZ126
Smithy La., Tad. 249 CZ127
Smithy St. E1 142 DW71
Smock Wk., Croy. 202 DQ100
Smoke La., Reig. 266 DB136
Smokehouse Yd. EC1 274 G6
Smokehouse Yd. EC1 141 DP71
Smug Oak Grn. Business Cen., St.Alb. 60 CB30
Smug Oak La., St.Alb. 60 CB30
Smugglers Wk., Green. 189 FV85
Smugglers Way SW18 160 DB84
Smyrks Rd. SE17 162 DS78
Smyrna Rd. NW6 140 DA66
Smythe Rd. (Sutton at Hone), Dart. 208 FN95
Smythe St. E14 143 EB73
Snag La., Sev. 223 ES109
Snakeley Clo., H.Wyc. 88 AC54
Snakes La., Barn. 81 DH41
Snakes La. E., Wdf.Grn. 102 EJ51
Snakes La. W., Wdf.Grn. 102 EG51
Snape Spur, Slou. 132 AS72
Snaresbrook Dr., Stan. 95 CK49
Snaresbrook Rd. E11 124 EE56
Snarsgate St. W10 139 CW71
Snatts Hill, Oxt. 254 EF129
Sneath Ave. NW11 119 CZ59
Snelling Ave., Grav. 190 GE89
Snellings Rd., Walt. 214 BW106
Snells La., Amer. 72 AV39
Snells Pk. N18 100 DT51
Snells Wd. Ct., Amer. 72 AW40
Sneyd Rd. NW2 119 CW63
Snipe Clo., Erith 167 FH80
Snodland Clo., Orp. 223 EN110
Mill La.
Snow Hill EC1 274 F7
Snow Hill EC1 141 DP71
Snow Hill Ct. EC1 274 G8
Snowberry Clo. E15 123 ED63
Snowbury Rd. SW6 160 DB82
Snowden Ave., Uxb. 135 BP68
Snowden St. EC2 275 M5
Snowden St. EC2 142 DS70
Snowdon Clo., Wind. 151 AK83
Snowdon Cres., Hayes 155 BQ76
Snowdon Dr. NW9 118 CS58
Snowdown Clo. SE20 203 DX95
Snowdrop Clo., Hmptn. 176 CA93
Gresham Rd.
Snowdrop Path, Rom. 106 FK52
Snowerhill Rd., Bet. 264 CS136
Snowhill Cotts., Chesh. 38 AT24
Snowman Ho. NW6 140 DB67
Snowsfields SE1 279 L4
Snowsfields SE1 162 DR75
Snowshill Rd. E12 124 EL64
Snowy Fielder Waye, Islw. 157 CH82
Soames St. SE15 162 DT83
Soames Wk., N.Mal. 198 CS95
Socket La., Brom. 204 EH101
Soham Rd., Enf. 83 DZ37
Soho Cres., H.Wyc. 110 AD59
Soho Mills Ind. Est., H.Wyc. 110 AD59
Soho Sq. W1 273 M8
Soho Sq. W1 141 DK72
Soho St. W1 273 M8
Sojourner Truth Clo. E8 142 DV65
Richmond Rd.
Solander Gdns. E1 142 DV73
Dellow St.
Solar Way, Enf. 83 DZ36
Sole Fm. Ave., Lthd. 246 BZ125
Sole Fm. Clo., Lthd. 230 BZ124
Sole Fm. Rd., Lthd. 246 BZ125
Solebay St. E1 143 DY70
Solecote, Lthd. 246 CA125
Solefields Rd., Sev. 257 FH128
Solent Ri. E13 144 EG69
Solent Rd. NW6 120 DA64
Solent Rd., Houns. 174 BM86
Soleoak Dr., Sev. 257 FH127
Solesbridge Clo., Rick. 73 BF41
Solesbridge La.
Solesbridge La., Rick. 74 BG40
Soley Ms. WC1 274 D2
Solna Ave. SW15 179 CW85
Solna Rd. N21 100 DR46
Solomon Ave. N9 100 DU49
Solomons Hill, Rick. 92 BK45
Northway
Solomon's Pas. SE15 162 DV84
Solom's Ct. Rd., Bans. 234 DD117
Solon New Rd. SW4 161 DL84
Solon New Rd. Est. SW4 161 DL84
Solon New Rd.
Solon Rd. SW2 161 DL84
Solway, Hem.H. 40 BM18
Solway Clo. E8 142 DT65
Buttermere Wk.
Solway Clo., Houns. 156 BY83
Solway Rd. N22 99 DP53
Solway Rd. SE22 162 DU84
Somaford Gro., Barn. 80 DD44
Somali Rd. NW2 119 CZ63
Somerby Clo., Brox. 49 EA21
Somerby Rd., Bark. 145 ER66
Somercoates Clo., Barn. 80 DE41
Somerden Rd., Orp. 206 EX101
Somerfield Clo., Tad. 233 CY119
Somerfield Rd. N4 121 DP61
Somerford Clo., Pnr. 115 BU56
Somerford Gro. N16 122 DT63
Somerford Gro. N17 100 DU52
Somerford Gro. Est. N16 122 DT63
Somerford Gro.
Somerford St. E1 142 DV70
Somerford Way SE16 163 DY75
Somerhill Ave., Sid. 186 EV87
Somerhill Rd., Well. 166 EV82
Someries Rd., Hem.H. 39 BF18
Somerleyton Pas. SW9 161 DP84
Somerleyton Rd. SW9 161 DN84
Somers Clo. NW1 141 DK68
Platt St.
Somers Clo., Reig. 250 DA133
Somers Cres. W2 272 B9
Somers Cres. W2 140 DE72
Somers Ms. W2 272 B9
Somers Pl. SW2 181 DM87
Somers Rd. E17 123 DZ56
Somers Rd. SW2 181 DM86
Somers Rd., Hat. 45 CW24
Somers Rd., Reig. 249 CZ133
Somers Sq., Hat. 45 CW23
Somers Way (Bushey), Wat. 94 CC45
Somersby Gdns., Ilf. 125 EM57
Somerset Ave. SW20 199 CV96
Somerset Ave., Chess. 215 CK105
Somerset Ave., Well. 185 ET85
Somerset Clo. N17 100 DR54
Somerset Clo., Epsom 216 CS109
Somerset Clo., N.Mal. 198 CS100
Somerset Clo., Walt. 213 BV106
Queens Rd.
Somerset Clo., Wdf.Grn. 102 EG53
Somerset Est. SW11 160 DD81
Somerset Gdns. N6 120 DG59
Somerset Gdns. N17 100 DS52
Somerset Gdns. SE13 163 EB82
Somerset Gdns. SW16 201 DM97
Somerset Gdns., Horn. 128 FN60
Somerset Gdns., Tedd. 177 CE92
Somerset Rd. E17 123 EA57
Somerset Rd. N17 122 DT55
Somerset Rd. N18 100 DT50
Somerset Rd. NW4 119 CW56
Somerset Rd. SW19 179 CY91
Somerset Rd. W4 158 CR76
Somerset Rd. W13 137 CH74
Somerset Rd., Barn. 80 DB43
Somerset Rd., Brent. 157 CJ79
Somerset Rd., Dart. 187 FH86
Somerset Rd., Enf. 83 EA38
Somerset Rd., Har. 116 CC57
Somerset Rd., Kings.T. 198 CM96
Somerset Rd., Orp. 206 EU101
Somerset Rd., Red. 266 DD136
Somerset Rd., Sthl. 136 BZ71
Somerset Rd., Tedd. 177 CE92
Somerset Sq. W14 159 CY75
Somerset Way, Iver 153 BF75
Somerset Waye, Houns. 156 BY79
Somersham, Welw.G.C. 30 DD09
Somersham Rd., Bexh. 166 EY82
Somerswey, Guil. 258 AY142
Somerton Ave., Rich. 158 CP83
Somerton Clo., Pur. 235 DN115
Somerton Rd. NW2 119 CY62
Somerton Rd. SE15 162 DV84
Somertons Clo., Guil. 242 AU131
Somertrees Ave. SE12 184 EH89
Somervell Rd., Har. 116 BZ64
Somerville Ave. SW13 159 CV79
Somerville Rd. SE20 183 DX94
Somerville Rd., Cob. 214 CA114
Somerville Rd., Dart. 188 FM86
Somerville Rd., Rom. 126 EW58
Somerville Rd. (Eton), Wind. 151 AQ78
Sonderburg Rd. N7 121 DM61
Sondes Pl. Dr., Dor. 263 CF136
Sondes St. SE17 162 DR79
Sonia Clo., Wat. 94 BW45
Sonia Ct., Har. 117 CF58
Sonia Gdns. N12 98 DC49
Woodside Ave.
Sonia Gdns. NW10 119 CT63
Sonia Gdns., Houns. 156 CA80
Sonnet Wk., West. 238 EH118
Kings Rd.
Sonnets, The, Hem.H. 40 BH19
Sonning Gdns., Hmptn. 176 BY93
Sonning Rd. SE25 202 DU100
Soothouse Spring, St.Alb. 43 CF16
Soper Clo. E4 101 DZ50
Soper Dr., Cat. 236 DQ121
Coulsdon Rd.
Soper Ms., Enf. 83 EA38
Harston Dr.
Sopers Rd. (Cuffley), Pot.B. 65 DM29
Sophia Clo. N7 141 DM65
Mackenzie Rd.
Sophia Rd. E10 123 EB60
Sophia Rd. E16 144 EH72
Sophia Sq. SE16 143 DY73
Rotherhithe St.
Sopwell La., St.Alb. 43 CD21
Sopwith Ave., Chess. 216 CL106
Sopwith Clo., Kings.T. 178 CM92
Sopwith Clo., West. 238 EK116
Sopwith Dr., W.Byf. 212 BL112
Sopwith Dr., Wey. 212 BL111
Sopwith Rd., Houns. 156 BW80
Sopwith Way SW8 161 DH80
Sopwith Way, Kings.T. 198 CL95
Sorbie Clo., Wey. 213 BR107
Sorrel Bank, Croy. 221 DY110
Sorrel Clo. SE28 146 EU74
Sorrel Ct., Grays 170 GD79
Salix Rd.
Sorrel Gdns. E6 144 EL71
Sorrel La. E14 143 ED72
Sorrel Wk., Rom. 127 FF55
Sorrel Way, Grav. 190 GE91
Sorrell Clo. SE14 163 DY80
Southerngate Way
Sorrento Rd., Sutt. 200 DB104
Sospel Ct., Slou. 131 AQ68
Sotheby Rd. N5 121 DP62
Sotheran Clo. E8 142 DU67
Sotheron Rd. SW6 160 DB80
Sotheron Rd., Wat. 76 BW40
Soudan Rd. SW11 160 DF81
Souldern Rd. W14 159 CX76
Souldern St., Wat. 75 BU43
Sounds Lo., Swan. 207 FC100
South Access Rd. E17 123 DY59
South Acre NW9 96 CS54
South Africa Rd. W12 139 CV74
South Albert Rd., Reig. 249 CZ133
South App., Nthwd. 93 BR49
South Audley St. W1 276 G1
South Audley St. W1 140 DG73
South Ave. E4 101 EB45
South Ave., Cars. 218 DF108
South Ave., Egh. 173 BC93
South Ave., Rich. 158 CN82
Sandycombe Rd.
South Ave., Sthl. 136 BZ73
South Ave., Walt. 213 BS110
South Ave. Gdns., Sthl. 136 BZ73
South Bank, Chis. 185 EQ91
South Bank, Surb. 198 CL100
South Bank, West. 255 ER126
South Bank Rd., Berk. 38 AT17
South Bank Ter., Surb. 198 CL100
South Birkbeck Rd. E11 123 ED62
South Black Lion La. W6 159 CU78
South Bolton Gdns. SW5 160 DB78
South Border, The, Pur. 219 DK111
South Carriage Dr. SW1 276 D4
South Carriage Dr. SW1 160 DE75
South Carriage Dr. SW7 276 A5
South Carriage Dr. SW7 160 DE75
South Clo. N6 121 DH58
South Clo., Barn. 79 CZ41
South Clo., Bexh. 166 EX84
South Clo., Dag. 146 FA67
South Clo., Mord. 200 DB100
Green La.
South Clo., Pnr. 116 BZ59
South Clo., St.Alb. 60 CB25
South Clo., Slou. 131 AK73
St. George's Cres.
South Clo., Twick. 176 CA90
South Clo., West Dr. 154 BM76
South Clo., Wok. 226 AW116
South Clo. Grn., Red. 251 DH129
South Colonnade E14 143 EA74
South Common Rd., Uxb. 134 BL65
South Cottage Dr., Rick. 73 BF43
South Cottage Gdns., Rick. 73 BF43
South Countess Rd. E17 123 DZ55
South Cres. E16 143 ED70
South Cres. WC1 273 M7
South Cres. WC1 141 DK71
South Cft., Egh. 172 AV92
South Cross Rd., Ilf. 125 EQ57
South Croxted Rd. SE21 182 DR90
South Dene NW7 96 CR48
South Dr., Bans. 218 DE113
South Dr., Beac. 110 AH55
South Dr., Brwd. 108 FX49
South Dr., Couls. 235 DK115
South Dr., Dor. 263 CJ136
South Dr., Orp. 223 ES106
South Dr. (Cuffley), Pot.B. 65 DL30
South Dr., Rom. 128 FJ55
South Dr., Ruis. 115 BS60
South Dr., St.Alb. 43 CK20
South Dr., Sutt. 217 CY110
South Dr., Vir.W. 192 AU102
South Ealing Rd. W5 157 CK75
South Eastern Ave. N9 100 DT48
South Eaton Pl. SW1 276 G8
South Eaton Pl. SW1 160 DG77
South Eden Pk. Rd., Beck. 203 EB100
South Edwardes Sq. W8 159 CZ76
South End W8 160 DB76
St. Albans Gro.
South End, Croy. 220 DQ105
South End, Lthd. 246 CB126
South End Clo. NW3 120 DE63
South End Grn. NW3 120 DE63
South End Rd.
South End Rd. NW3 120 DE63
South End Rd., Horn. 147 FH65
South End Rd., Rain. 147 FG67
South End Row W8 160 DB76
South Esk Rd. E7 144 EJ65
South Gdns. SW19 180 DD94
South Gate, Harl. 51 ER15
South Gate Ave., Felt. 175 BR91
South Gipsy Rd., Well. 166 EX83
South Glade, The, Bex. 186 EZ88
Camden Rd.
South Grn. NW9 96 CS53
Clayton Fld.
South Grn., Slou. 132 AS73
South Gro. E17 123 DZ57
South Gro. N6 120 DG60
South Gro. N15 122 DR57
South Gro., Cher. 193 BF100
South Gro. Ho. N6 120 DG60
Highgate W. Hill
South Hall Clo., Dart. 208 FM101
South Hall Dr., Rain. 147 FH71
South Hill, Chis. 185 EM93
South Hill, Guil. 258 AX136
South Hill Ave., Har. 116 CC62
South Hill Gro., Har. 117 CE63
South Hill Pk. NW3 120 DE63
South Hill Pk. Gdns. NW3 120 DE63
South Hill Rd., Brom. 204 EE97
South Hill Rd., Grav. 191 GH88
South Hill Rd., Hem.H. 40 BJ20
South Huxley N18 100 DR50
South Island Pl. SW9 161 DM80
South Kensington Sta. Arc. SW7 160 DD77
Pelham St.
South Kent Ave., Grav. 190 GC87
South Lambeth Pl. SW8 161 DL79
South Lambeth Rd. SW8 161 DL80
South La., Kings.T. 197 CK97
South La., N.Mal. 198 CR98
South La. W., N.Mal. 198 CR98
South Ley, Welw.G.C. 29 CY12
South Lo. Ave., Mitch. 201 DL98
South Lo. Cres., Enf. 117 CJ61
South Lo. Dr. N14 81 DL43
South Mall N9 100 DU48
Plevna Rd.
South Mead NW9 97 CT53
South Mead, Epsom 216 CS108
South Mead, Red. 250 DF131
South Meadow La., Wind. 151 AQ79
South Meadows, Wem. 118 CM64
South Molton La. W1 273 H9
South Molton La. W1 141 DH72
South Molton Rd. E16 144 EG72
South Molton St. W1 273 H9
South Molton St. W1 141 DH72

South Mundells, Welw.G.C. 29 CZ08
South Norwood Hill SE25 202 DS96
South Oak Rd. SW16 181 DM91
South Ordnance Rd., Enf. 83 EA37
South Par. SW3 276 A10
South Par. SW3 160 DD78
South Par. W4 158 CR77
South Par., Wal.Abb. 67 EC33
Sun St.
South Pk. SW6 160 DA82
South Pk., Ger.Cr. 113 AZ57
South Pk., Sev. 257 FH125
South Pk. Ave., Rick. 73 BF43
South Pk. Cres. SE6 184 EF88
South Pk. Cres., Ger.Cr. 112 AY56
South Pk. Cres., Ilf. 125 ER62
South Pk. Dr., Bark. 125 ES63
South Pk. Dr., Ger.Cr. 112 AY56
South Pk. Dr., Ilf. 125 ES63
South Pk. Gdns., Berk. 38 AV17
South Pk. Gro., N.Mal. 198 CQ98
South Pk. Hill Rd., S.Croy. 220 DR106
South Pk. La., Red. 252 DU134
South Pk. Ms. SW6 160 DB83
South Pk. Rd. SW19 180 DA93
South Pk. Rd., Ilf. 125 ER62
South Pk. Ter., Ilf. 125 ES62
South Pk. Vw., Ger.Cr. 113 AZ56
South Pk. Way, Ruis. 136 BW65
South Path, Wind. 151 AQ81
South Penge Pk. Est. SE20 202 DV96
South Perimeter Rd., Uxb. 134 BL69
Kingston La.
South Pier Rd., Gat. 269 DH152
South Pl. EC2 275 L6
South Pl. EC2 142 DR71
South Pl., Enf. 82 DW43
South Pl., Harl. 36 EU12
South Pl., Surb. 198 CM101
South Pl. Ms. EC2 275 L7
South Ridge, Wey. 213 BP110
South Riding, St.Alb. 60 CA30
South Ri., Cars. 218 DE109
South Ri. Way SE18 165 ER78
South Rd. N9 100 DU46
South Rd. SE23 183 DX89
South Rd. SW19 180 DC93
South Rd. W5 157 CK77
South Rd., Amer. 55 AQ36
South Rd., Edg. 96 CP53
South Rd., Egh. 172 AW93
South Rd., Erith 167 FF79
South Rd., Felt. 176 BX92
South Rd., Guil. 242 AV132
South Rd., Hmptn. 176 BY93
South Rd., Harl. 36 EU12
South Rd., Reig. 266 DB135
South Rd., Rick. 73 BC43
South Rd. (Chadwell Heath), Rom. 126 EW57
South Rd. (Little Heath), Rom. 126 EY58
South Rd., S.Ock. 149 FW72
South Rd., Sthl. 156 BZ75
South Rd., Twick. 177 CD90
South Rd., West Dr. 154 BN76
South Rd., Wey. 213 BQ106
South Rd. (St. George's Hill), Wey. 212 BN110
South Rd., Wok. 210 AX114
South Row SE3 164 EF82
South Sea St. SE16 163 DZ76
South Side W6 159 CT76
South Spur, Slou. 153 BC75
South Sq. NW11 120 DB58
South Sq. WC1 274 D7
South Sta. App., Red. 267 DL136
South St. W1 276 G2
South St. W1 140 DG74
South St., Brwd. 108 FW47
South St., Brom. 204 EG96
South St., Dor. 263 CG137
South St., Enf. 83 DX43
South St., Epsom 216 CR113
South St., Grav. 191 GH87
South St., Hert. 32 DR09
South St., Islw. 157 CG83
South St., Rain. 147 FC68
South St., Rom. 127 FE57
South St., Stai. 173 BF92
South St., Ware 33 EC11
South Tenter St. E1 142 DT73
South Ter. SW7 276 B8
South Ter. SW7 160 DE77
South Ter., Dor. 263 CH137
South Ter., Surb. 198 CL100
South Vale SE19 182 DS93
South Vale, Har. 117 CE63
South Vw., Brom. 204 EH96
South Vw. Ave., Til. 171 GG81
South Vw. Ct., Wok. 226 AY118
Constitution Hill
South Vw. Dr. E18 124 EH55
South Vw. Dr., Upmin. 128 FN62
South Vw. Rd. N8 121 DK55
South Vw. Rd., Ash. 231 CK119
South Vw. Rd., Dart. 188 FK90
South Vw. Rd., Ger.Cr. 112 AX56
South Vw. Rd., Grays 169 FW79
South Vw. Rd., Loug. 85 EM44
South Vw. Rd., Pnr. 93 BV51
South Vil. NW1 141 DK65
South Wk., Hayes 135 BR71
Middleton Rd.
South Wk., Reig. 250 DB134
Church St.
South Wk., W.Wick. 204 EE104
South Way N9 100 DW47
South Way N11 99 DJ51
Ringway
South Way, Abb.L. 59 BT33
South Way, Beac. 110 AG55
South Way, Brom. 204 EG101
South Way, Croy. 203 DY104
South Way, Har. 116 CA56
South Way, Purf. 169 FS76
South Way, Wem. 118 CN64
South Weald Dr., Wal.Abb. 67 ED33
South Weald Rd., Brwd. 108 FU48
South W. India Dock Entrance E14 163 EC75
Prestons Rd.
South Western Rd., Twick. 177 CG86
South Wf. Rd. W2 140 DD72
South Woodford to Barking Relief Rd. E11 124 EJ56
South Woodford to Barking Relief Rd. E12 125 EN62
South Woodford to Barking Relief Rd. E18 124 EJ56
South Woodford to Barking Relief Rd., Bark. 125 EN62
South Woodford to Barking Relief Rd., Ilf. 125 EN62
South Worple Ave. SW14 158 CS83
South Worple Way SW14 158 CR83
Southacre Way, Pnr. 94 BW53
Southall Clo., Ware 33 DX05
Southall La., Houns. 155 BV79
Southall La., Sthl. 156 BW77
Southall Pl. SE1 279 K5
Southall Pl. SE1 162 DR75
Southall Way, Brwd. 108 FT49
Southam St. W10 139 CY70
Southampton Bldgs. WC2 274 D8
Southampton Gdns., Mitch. 201 DL99
Southampton Ms. E16 144 EH74
Wesley Ave.
Southampton Pl. WC1 274 A7
Southampton Pl. WC1 141 DL71
Southampton Rd. NW5 120 DF64
Southampton Rd., Houns. 174 BL86
Southampton Row WC1 274 A6
Southampton Row WC1 141 DL71
Southampton St. WC2 274 A10
Southampton St. WC2 141 DL73
Southampton Way SE5 162 DR80
Southbank, T.Ditt. 197 CH101
Southborough Clo., Surb. 197 CK102
Southborough La., Brom. 204 EL99
Southborough Rd. E9 142 DW67
Southborough Rd., Brom. 204 EL97
Southborough Rd., Surb. 198 CL102
Southbourne, Brom. 204 EG101
Southbourne Ave. NW9 96 CQ54
Southbourne Clo., Pnr. 116 BY59
Southbourne Cres. NW4 119 CY56
Southbourne Gdns. SE12 184 EH85
Southbourne Gdns., Ilf. 125 EQ64
Southbourne Gdns., Ruis. 115 BV60
Southbridge Pl., Croy. 220 DQ105
Southbridge Rd., Croy. 220 DQ105
Southbridge Way, Sthl. 156 BY75
Southbrook, Saw. 36 EY06
Southbrook Dr. (Cheshunt), Wal.Cr. 67 DX28
Southbrook Ms. SE12 184 EF86
Southbrook Rd. SE12 184 EF86
Southbrook Rd. SW16 201 DL95
Southbury Ave., Enf. 82 DU43
Southbury Clo., Horn. 128 FK64
Southbury Rd., Enf. 82 DR41
Southchurch Rd. E6 145 EM68
Southcliffe Dr., Ger.Cr. 90 AY50
Southcombe St. W14 159 CY77
Southcote, Wok. 226 AX115
Southcote Ave., Felt. 175 BT89
Southcote Ave., Surb. 198 CP101
Southcote Ri., Ruis. 115 BR59
Southcote Rd. E17 123 DX57
Southcote Rd. N19 121 DJ63
Southcote Rd. SE25 202 DV100
Southcote Rd., Red. 251 DJ129
Southcote Rd., S.Croy. 220 DS110
Southcroft, Slou. 131 AP70
Southcroft Ave., Well. 165 ES83
Southcroft Ave., W.Wick. 203 EC103
Southcroft Rd. SW16 180 DG93
Southcroft Rd. SW17 180 DG93
Southcroft Rd., Orp. 205 ES104
Southdale, Chig. 103 ER51
Southdean Gdns. SW19 179 CZ89
Southdene, Sev. 224 EZ113
Southdown Ave. W7 157 CG76
Southdown Ct., Hat. 45 CU21
Southdown Cres., Har. 116 CB60
Southdown Cres., Ilf. 125 ES57
Southdown Dr. SW20 179 CX94
Crescent Rd.
Southdown Rd. SW20 199 CX95
Southdown Rd., Cars. 218 DG109
Southdown Rd., Cat. 237 DZ122
Southdown Rd., Hat. 45 CU21
Southdown Rd., Horn. 127 FH59
Southdown Rd., Walt. 214 BY105
Southdowns (South Darenth), Dart. 209 FR96
Skinney La.
Southend Arterial Rd., Brwd. 129 FV57
Southend Arterial Rd., Horn. 106 FK54
Southend Arterial Rd., Rom. 106 FK54
Southend Arterial Rd., Upmin. 129 FR57
Southend Clo. SE9 185 EP86
Southend Cres. SE9 185 EN86
Southend La. SE6 183 DZ91
Southend La. SE26 183 DZ91
Southend La., Wal.Abb. 68 EH34
Southend Rd. E4 101 DY50
Southend Rd. E6 145 EM66
Southend Rd. E17 101 EB53
Southend Rd. E18 102 EG53
Southend Rd., Beck. 183 EA94
Southend Rd., Grays 170 GC77
Southend Rd., Wdf.Grn. 102 EJ54
Southerland Clo., Wey. 213 BQ105
Southern Ave. SE25 202 DT97
Southern Ave., Felt. 175 BU88
Southern Ave., Red. 266 DG142
Southern Dr., Loug. 85 EM44
Southern Gro. E3 143 DZ69
Southern Lo., Harl. 51 EQ18
Southern Perimeter Rd., Houns. 174 BJ85
Southern Pl., Swan. 207 FD98
Southern Rd. E13 144 EH68
Southern Rd. N2 120 DF56
Southern Row W10 139 CY70
Southern St. N1 141 DM68
Southern Way, Harl. 51 EN18
Southern Way, Rom. 126 FA58
Southerngate Way SE14 163 DY80
Southernhay, Loug. 84 EK43
Southerns La., Couls. 234 DD124
Southernwood Clo., Hem.H. 40 BN19
Southerton Rd. W6 159 CW76
Southerton Way (Shenley), Rad. 62 CL33
Southey Ms. E16 144 EG74
Wesley Ave.
Southey Rd. N15 122 DS57
Southey Rd. SW9 161 DN81
Southey Rd. SW19 180 DA94
Southey St. SE20 183 DX94
Southey Wk., Til. 171 GH81
Southfield, Barn. 79 CX44
Southfield, Welw.G.C. 29 CX11
Southfield Ave., Wat. 76 BW38
Southfield Clo., Uxb. 134 BN69
Southfield Clo., Wind. 150 AJ76
Southfield Cotts. W7 157 CF75
Oaklands Rd.
Southfield Gdns., Slou. 130 AH71
Southfield Gdns., Twick. 177 CF91
Southfield Pk., Har. 116 CB56
Southfield Pl., Wey. 213 BP108
Southfield Rd. N17 100 DS54
The Ave.
Southfield Rd. W4 158 CS76
Southfield Rd., Chis. 205 ET97
Southfield Rd., Enf. 82 DV44
Southfield Rd., Hodd. 49 EA16
Southfield Rd., Wal.Cr. 67 DY32
Southfield Way, St.Alb. 43 CK17
Southfields NW4 97 CU54
Southfields, E.Mol. 197 CE100
Southfields, Swan. 187 FE94
Southfields Ave., Ashf. 175 BP93
Southfields Ct. SW19 179 CY88
Southfields Pas. SW18 180 DA86
Southfields Rd. SW18 180 DA86
Southfields Rd., Cat. 237 EB124
Southfleet Rd., Dart. 189 FW91
Southfleet Rd., Grav. 191 GF89
Southfleet Rd., Orp. 205 ES104
Southfleet Rd., Swans. 190 FZ87
Southgate, Purf. 168 FQ77
Southgate Ave., Felt. 175 BR91
Southgate Circ. N14 99 DK46
The Bourne
Southgate Gro. N1 142 DR66
Southgate Rd. N1 142 DR66
Southgate Rd., Pot.B. 64 DC33
Southholme Clo. SE19 202 DS95
Southill La., Pnr. 115 BU56
Southill Rd., Chis. 184 EL94
Southill St. E14 143 EB72
Chrisp St.
Southland Rd. SE18 165 ET80
Southland Way, Houns. 177 CD85
Southlands Ave., Horl. 268 DG147
Southlands Ave., Orp. 223 ER105
Southlands Clo., Couls. 235 DM117
Southlands Dr. SW19 179 CX89
Southlands Gro., Brom. 204 EL97
Southlands La., Oxt. 253 EB134
Southlands Rd., Brom. 204 EJ98
Southlands Rd., Uxb. 113 BF62
Southlea, Wind. 152 AU84
Southlea Rd., Slou. 152 AV81
Southly Clo., Sutt. 200 DA104
Southmead Cres. (Cheshunt), Wal.Cr. 67 DY30
Southmead Rd. SW19 179 CY88
Southmont Rd., Esher 197 CE103
Southmoor Way E9 143 DZ65
Southold Ri. SE9 185 EM90
Southolm St. SW11 161 DH81
Southover N12 98 DA49
Southover, Brom. 184 EG92
Southport Rd. SE18 165 ER77
Southridge Pl. SW20 179 CX94
Southsea Ave., Wat. 75 BU42
Southsea Rd., Kings.T. 198 CL98
Southside, Ger.Cr. 112 AX55
Southside Common SW19 179 CW93
Southspring, Sid. 185 ER87
Southvale Rd. SE3 164 EE82
Southview Ave. NW10 119 CT64
Southview Clo. SW17 180 DG92
Southview Clo., Bex. 186 EZ86
Southview Clo., Swan. 207 FG98
Southview Clo. (Cheshunt), Wal.Cr. 66 DS26
Southview Cres., Ilf. 125 EP58
Southview Gdns., Wall. 219 DJ108
Southview Rd., Brom. 183 ED91
Southview Rd., Cat. 237 EB124
Southview Rd., Warl. 236 DV119
Southviews, S.Croy. 221 DX109
Southville SW8 161 DK81
Southville Clo., Epsom 216 CR109
Southville Clo., Felt. 175 BS88
Southville Cres., Felt. 175 BS88
Southville Rd., Felt. 175 BS88
Southville Rd., T.Ditt. 197 CG101
Southwark Bri. EC4 279 J2
Southwark Bri. EC4 142 DQ74
Southwark Bri. SE1 279 J2
Southwark Bri. SE1 142 DQ74
Southwark Bri. Rd. SE1 278 G6
Southwark Bri. Rd. SE1 161 DP76
Southwark Gro. SE1 279 H3
Southwark Pk. Est. SE16 162 DV77
Southwark Pk. Rd. SE16 162 DT77
Southwark Pl., Brom. 205 EM97
St. Georges Rd.
Southwark St. SE1 278 G2
Southwark St. SE1 141 DP74
Southwater Clo. E14 143 DZ72
Southwater Clo., Beck. 183 EB94
Southway N20 98 DA47
Southway NW11 120 DB58
Southway SW20 199 CW98
Southway, Cars. 218 DD110
Southway, Guil. 242 AS134
Southway, Hat. 45 CU22
Southway, Wall. 219 DJ105
Southway Ct., Guil. 242 AS134
Southwell Ave., Nthlt. 136 CA65
Southwell Gdns. SW7 160 DC77
Southwell Gro. Rd. E11 124 EE61
Southwell Rd. SE5 162 DQ83
Southwell Rd., Croy. 201 DN100
Southwell Rd., Har. 117 CK58
Southwest Rd. E11 123 ED60
Southwick Ms. W2 272 A8
Southwick Pl. W2 272 B9
Southwick Pl. W2 140 DE72
Southwick St. W2 272 B8
Southwick St. W2 140 DE72
Southwold Dr., Bark. 126 EU64
Southwold Rd. E5 122 DV61
Southwold Rd., Bex. 187 FB86
Southwold Rd., Wat. 76 BW38
Southwold Spur, Slou. 153 BC75
Southwood Ave. N6 121 DH59
Southwood Ave., Cher. 211 BC108
Southwood Ave., Couls. 235 DJ115
Southwood Ave., Kings.T. 198 CQ95
Southwood Clo., Brom. 205 EM98
Southwood Clo., Wor.Pk. 199 CX102
Southwood Dr., Surb. 198 CQ101
Southwood Gdns., Esher 197 CG104
Southwood Gdns., Ilf. 125 EP56
Southwood La. N6 120 DG59
Southwood Lawn Rd. N6 120 DG59
Southwood Rd. SE9 185 EP89
Southwood Rd. SE28 146 EV74
Southwood Smith St. N1 141 DN67
Barford St.
Soval Ct., Nthwd. 93 BR52
Maxwell Rd.
Sovereign Clo. E1 142 DV73
Sovereign Clo. W5 137 CJ71
Sovereign Clo., Pur. 219 DM110
Sovereign Clo., Ruis. 115 BS60
Sovereign Ct., Brom. 205 EM99
Sovereign Ct., W.Mol. 196 BZ98
Sovereign Cres. SE16 143 DY74
Rotherhithe St.
Sovereign Gro., Wem. 117 CK62
Sovereign Ms. E2 142 DT68
Pearson St.
Sovereign Pk. NW10 138 CP70
Sovereign Pl., Kings L. 58 BN29
Sovereign Rd., Bark. 146 EW69
Sowerby Clo. SE9 184 EL85
Sowrey Ave., Rain. 147 FF65
Soyer Ct., Wok. 226 AS118
Raglan Rd.
Spa Clo. SE25 202 DS95
Spa Dr., Epsom 216 CN114
Spa Grn. Est. EC1 274 E2
Spa Grn. Est. EC1 141 DN69
Spa Hill SE19 202 DR95
Spa Rd. SE16 279 P7
Spa Rd. SE16 162 DT76
Space Waye, Felt. 175 BU85
Spackmans Way, Slou. 151 AQ76
Spafield St. EC1 274 D4
Spalding Clo., Edg. 96 CS52
Blundell Rd.
Spalding Rd. NW4 119 CW58
Spalding Rd. SW17 181 DH92
Spalt Clo., Brwd. 109 GB47
Spanby Rd. E3 143 EA70
Spaniards Clo. NW11 120 DD60
Spaniards End NW3 120 DC60
Spaniards Rd. NW3 120 DC61
Spanish Pl. W1 272 G7
Spanish Pl. W1 140 DG72
Spanish Rd. SW18 180 DC85
Spareleaze Hill, Loug. 85 EM43
Sparepenny La. (Eynsford), Dart. 208 FK103
Sparkbridge Rd., Har. 117 CE56
Sparks Clo. W3 138 CR72
Joseph Ave.
Sparks Clo., Dag. 126 EX61
Sparks Clo., Hmptn. 176 BY93
Victors Dr.
Sparrow Clo., Hmptn. 176 BY93
Sparrow Dr., Orp. 205 EQ102
Sparrow Fm. Dr., Felt. 176 BW86
Sparrow Fm. Rd., Epsom 217 CU105
Sparrow Grn., Dag. 127 FB62
Sparrows Herne (Bushey), Wat. 94 CB45
Sparrows La. SE9 185 EQ87
Sparrows Mead, Red. 250 DG131
Sparrows Way (Bushey), Wat. 94 CC46
Sparrows Herne
Sparrowswick Ride, St.Alb. 42 CC15
Sparsholt Rd. N19 121 DM60
Sparsholt Rd., Bark. 145 ES67
Sparta St. SE10 163 EB81
Spear Ms. SW5 160 DA77
Spearman St. SE18 165 EN79
Spearpoint Gdns., Ilf. 125 ET56
Spears Rd. N19 121 DL60
Speart La., Houns. 156 BY80
Spedan Clo. NW3 120 DB62
Speed Ho. EC2 142 DR71
Silk St.
Speedbird Way, West Dr. 154 BH80
Speedgate Hill (Fawkham Grn.), Long. 209 FU103
Speedwell Clo., Guil. 243 BC131
Speedwell Clo., Hem.H. 39 BE21
Campion Rd.
Speedwell Ct., Grays 170 GE80
Speedwell St. SE8 163 EA80
Comet St.
Speedy Pl. WC1 273 P3
Speer Rd., T.Ditt. 197 CF101
Speirs Clo., N.Mal. 199 CT100
Speke Ho. SE5 162 DQ80
Speke Rd., Th.Hth. 202 DR96
Spekehill SE9 185 EM90
Speldhurst Clo., Brom. 204 EF99
Speldhurst Rd. E9 143 DX66
Speldhurst Rd. W4 158 CR76
Spellbrook Wk. N1 142 DQ67
Basire St.
Spelman St. E1 142 DU71
Spelthorne Gro., Sun. 175 BT94
Spelthorne La., Ashf. 195 BQ95
Spence Ave., W.Byf. 212 BL114
Spence Clo. SE16 163 DZ75
Vaughan St.
Spencer Ave. N13 99 DM51
Spencer Ave., Hayes 135 BU71
Spencer Ave. (Cheshunt), Wal.Cr. 66 DS26
Spencer Clo. N3 98 DA54
Spencer Clo. NW10 138 CM69
Spencer Clo., Epsom 232 CS119
Spencer Clo., Orp. 205 ES103
Spencer Clo., Uxb. 134 BJ69
Spencer Clo., Wok. 211 BC113
Spencer Clo., Wdf.Grn. 102 EJ50
Spencer Ct. NW8 140 DC68
Marlborough Pl.
Spencer Dr. N2 120 DC58
Spencer Gdns. SE9 185 EM85
Spencer Gdns. SW14 178 CQ85
Spencer Gdns., Egh. 172 AX92
Spencer Gate, St.Alb. 43 CE18
Spencer Hill SW19 179 CY93
Spencer Hill Rd. SW19 179 CY94
Spencer Ms. SW8 161 DM81
Lansdowne Way
Spencer Ms. W6 159 CY79
Greyhound Rd.
Spencer Pk. SW18 180 DD85
Spencer Pas. E2 142 DV68
Pritchard's Rd.
Spencer Pl. N1 141 DP66
Canonbury La.
Spencer Pl., Croy. 202 DR101
Gloucester Rd.
Spencer Ri. NW5 121 DH63
Spencer Rd. E6 144 EK67
Spencer Rd. E17 101 EC53
Spencer Rd. N8 121 DM57
Spencer Rd. N11 99 DH49
Spencer Rd. N17 100 DU53
Spencer Rd. SW18 160 DD84
Spencer Rd. SW20 199 CV95
Spencer Rd. W3 138 CQ74
Spencer Rd. W4 158 CQ80
Spencer Rd., Brom. 184 EE94
Spencer Rd., Cat. 236 DR121
Spencer Rd., Cob. 229 BV115
Spencer Rd., E.Mol. 197 CD98
Spencer Rd., Har. 95 CE54
Spencer Rd., Ilf. 125 ET60
Spencer Rd., Islw. 157 CD81
Spencer Rd., Mitch. 200 DG97
Spencer Rd. (Beddington Cor.), Mitch. 200 DG101
Spencer Rd., Rain. 147 FD69
Spencer Rd., Slou. 153 AZ76
Spencer Rd., S.Croy. 220 DS106
Spencer Rd., Twick. 177 CE90
Spencer Rd., Wem. 117 CJ61
Spencer St. EC1 274 F3
Spencer St. EC1 141 DP69
Spencer St., Grav. 191 GG87
Spencer St., Hert. 32 DS08
Spencer St., St.Alb. 43 CD20
Spencer St., Sthl. 156 BX75
Spencer Wk. NW3 120 DC63
Hampstead High St.
Spencer Wk. SW15 159 CX84
Spencer Wk., Rick. 74 BJ43
Spencer Wk., Til. 171 GG82
Spencer Way, Hem.H. 40 BG17
Spencer Way, Red. 266 DG139
Spencers Cft., Harl. 52 EV17
Spenser Ave., Wey. 212 BN109
Spenser Cres., Upmin. 128 FQ59
Spenser Gro. N16 122 DS63
Spenser Ms. SE21 182 DR88
Croxted Rd.
Spenser Rd. SE24 181 DN85
Spenser St. SW1 277 L6
Spenser St. SW1 161 DJ76
Spensley Wk. N16 122 DR62
Clissold Rd.
Speranza St. SE18 165 ET78
Sperling Rd. N17 100 DS54
Spert St. E14 143 DY73
Spey St. E14 143 EC71
Spey Way, Rom. 105 FE52
Speyside N14 81 DJ44
Spezia Rd. NW10 139 CU68
Sphere Ind. Est., St.Alb. 43 CG21
Spicer Clo. SW9 161 DP82
Spicer Clo., Walt. 196 BW100
Spicer St., St.Alb. 42 CC20
Spicers Fld., Lthd. 215 CD113
Spicers La., Harl. 36 EW11
Wayre St.
Spicersfield (Cheshunt), Wal.Cr. 66 DU27
Spice's Yd., Croy. 220 DQ105
Spielman Rd., Dart. 168 FM84
Spiers Way, Horl. 269 DH150
Spigurnell Rd. N17 100 DR53
Spikes Bri. Rd., Sthl. 136 BY72
Spilsby Clo. NW9 96 CS54
Kenley Ave.
Spilsby Rd., Rom. 106 FK52
Spindle Clo. SE18 164 EL76
Spindles, Til. 171 GG80
Spindlewood Gdns., Croy. 220 DS105
Spindlewoods, Tad. 233 CV122
Spindrift Ave. E14 163 EB77
Spinel Clo. SE18 165 ET78
Spingate Clo., Horn. 128 FK64
Spinnells Rd., Har. 116 BZ60
Spinners Wk., Wind. 151 AQ81
Spinney, Slou. 131 AP74
Spinney, The N21 99 DN45
Spinney, The SW16 181 DK90
Spinney, The, Barn. 80 DB40
Spinney, The, Beac. 89 AL54
Spinney, The, Berk. 38 AT20
Spinney, The, Brwd. 109 GC44
Spinney, The, Brox. 49 DZ19
Spinney, The, Chesh. 54 AR29
Spinney, The, Epsom 233 CV118
Spinney, The, Hert. 32 DT09
Spinney, The, Horl. 268 DG146
Spinney, The, Lthd. 214 CC112
Spinney, The (Great Bookham), Lthd. 230 CB124
Spinney, The, Pot.B. 64 DD31
Spinney, The, Pur. 219 DP111
Spinney, The, Sid. 186 EY91
Spinney, The, Stan. 96 CL49
Spinney, The, Sun. 195 BU95
Spinney, The, Sutt. 217 CW105
Spinney, The, Swan. 207 FE96
Spinney, The, Wat. 75 BU39
Spinney, The, Welw.G.C. 29 CY10
Spinney, The, Wem. 117 CG62
Spinney, The, Wok. 244 BJ127
Spinney Clo., Cob. 214 CA111
Spinney Clo., N.Mal. 198 CS99
Spinney Clo., Rain. 147 FE68
Spinney Clo., West Dr. 134 BL73
Yew Ave.
Spinney Clo., Wor.Pk. 199 CT103
Spinney Dr., Felt. 175 BQ87
Spinney Gdns. SE19 182 DT92
Spinney Gdns., Dag. 126 EY64
Spinney Hill, Add. 211 BE106

Spinney Oak, Brom. 204 EL96
Spinney Oak, Cher. 211 BC107
Murray Rd.
Spinney St., Hert. 32 DU09
Spinney Way, Sev. 223 ER111
Spinneycroft, Lthd. 231 CD115
Spinneys, The, Brom. 205 EM96
Spinneys Dr., St.Alb. 42 CB22
Spinning Wk., The, Guil. 260 BN139
Spinning Wheel Mead, Harl. 52 EU18
Spire Clo., Grav. 191 GH88
Spires, The, Dart. 188 FK89
Spirit Quay E1 142 DU74
Smeaton St.
Spital Heath, Dor. 263 CJ135
Spital La., Brwd. 108 FT48
Spital Sq. E1 275 N6
Spital Sq. E1 142 DS71
Spital St. E1 142 DU70
Spital St., Dart. 188 FK86
Spital Yd. E1 275 N6
Spitfire Est., Houns. 156 BW78
Spitfire Way, Houns. 156 BW78
Splendour Wk. SE16 162 DW78
Verney Rd.
Spode Wk. NW6 140 DB65
Lymington Rd.
Spondon Rd. N15 122 DU56
Spook Hill, Dor. 263 CH141
Spoonbill Way, Hayes 136 BX71
Spooner Wk., Wall. 219 DK106
Spooners Dr., St.Alb. 60 CC27
Spooners Ms. W3 138 CR74
Churchfield Rd.
Sportsbank St. SE6 183 EC87
Spottons Gro. N17 100 DQ53
Gospatrick Rd.
Spout Hill, Croy. 221 EA106
Spout La., Eden. 255 EQ133
Spout La., Stai. 174 BG85
Spout La. N., Stai. 154 BH84
Spratt Hall Rd. E11 124 EG58
Spratts All., Cher. 211 BE107
Spratts La., Cher. 211 BE107
Spray La., Twick. 177 CE86
Kneller Rd.
Spray St. SE18 165 EP77
Spreighton Rd., W.Mol. 196 CB98
Spriggs Oak, Epp. 70 EU29
Palmers Hill
Sprimont Pl. SW3 276 D10
Sprimont Pl. SW3 160 DF78
Spring Ave., Egh. 172 AY93
Spring Bottom La., Red. 251 DN127
Spring Bri. Ms. W5 137 CK73
Spring Bri. Rd.
Spring Bri. Rd. W5 137 CK73
Spring Clo., Barn. 79 CX43
Spring Clo., Borwd. 78 CN39
Spring Clo., Chesh. 72 AX36
Spring Clo., Dag. 126 EX60
Spring Clo., Gdmg. 258 AS143
Spring Clo. (Harefield), Uxb. 92 BK53
Spring Clo. La., Sutt. 217 CY107
Spring Cotts., Surb. 197 CK99
St. Leonard's Rd.
Spring Ct., Guil. 242 AV130
Day Spring
Spring Ct., Sid. 186 EU90
Station Rd.
Spring Ct. Rd., Enf. 81 DN38
Spring Cfts. (Bushey), Wat. 76 CA43
Spring Dr., Maid. 130 AD65
Yew Tree Wk.
Spring Dr., Pnr. 115 BU58
Eastcote Rd.
Spring Fm. Clo., Rain. 148 FK69
Spring Gdns. N5 122 DQ64
Grosvenor Ave.
Spring Gdns. SW1 277 N2
Spring Gdns., Dor. 263 CG136
Spring Gdns., H.Wyc. 110 AE55
Watery La.
Spring Gdns., Horn. 127 FH63
Spring Gdns., Orp. 224 EV107
Spring Gdns., Rom. 127 FC57
Spring Gdns., Wall. 219 DJ106
Spring Gdns., Wat. 76 BW35
Spring Gdns., W.Mol. 196 CC99
Spring Gdns., West. 238 EJ118
Spring Gdns., Wdf.Grn. 102 EJ52
Spring Gdns. Ind. Est., Rom. 127 FC57
Spring Glen, Hat. 45 CT19
Spring Grn., Gdmg. 258 AS143
Spring Gro. SE19 182 DT94
Alma Pl.
Spring Gro. W4 158 CN78
Spring Gro., Grav. 191 GH88
Spring Gro., Hmptn. 196 CB95
Plevna Rd.
Spring Gro., Lthd. 230 CB123
Spring Gro., Loug. 84 EK44
Spring Gro., Mitch. 200 DG95
Spring Gro. Cres., Houns. 156 CC81
Spring Gro. Rd., Houns. 156 CC81
Spring Gro. Rd., Islw. 156 CC81
Spring Gro. Rd., Rich. 178 CM85
Spring Hill E5 122 DU59
Spring Hill SE26 182 DW91
Spring Hills, Harl. 35 EN14
Spring Lake, Stan. 95 CH49
Spring La. E5 122 DV60
Spring La. N10 120 DG55
Spring La. SE25 202 DV100
Spring La., Hem.H. 39 BF18
Spring La., Oxt. 253 ED131
Spring La., Slou. 131 AM74
Spring La. (Farnham Common), Slou. 131 AP66
Spring Ms. W1 272 E6
Spring Ms., Epsom 217 CT109
Old Schools La.
Spring Pk. Ave., Croy. 203 DX103
Spring Pk. Dr. N4 122 DQ60
Spring Pk. Rd., Croy. 203 DX103
Spring Pas. SW15 159 CX83
Embankment
Spring Path NW3 120 DD64
Spring Pl. NW5 121 DH64
Spring Ri., Egh. 172 AY93
Spring Rd., Felt. 175 BT90
Spring Shaw Rd., Orp. 206 EU95
Spring St. W2 140 DD72
Spring St., Epsom 217 CT109
Spring Ter., Rich. 178 CL85
Spring Vale, Bexh. 167 FB84
Spring Vale, Green. 189 FW86
Spring Vale Clo., Swan. 187 FF94
Spring Vale N., Dart. 188 FK87
Spring Vale S., Dart. 188 FK87
Spring Vw. Rd., Ware 32 DW07
Spring Vil. Rd., Edg. 96 CN52
Spring Wk. E1 142 DU71
Old Montague St.
Spring Wk., Brox. 48 DW22
Spring Wk., Horl. 268 DF148
Court Lo. Rd.
Spring Way, Hem.H. 41 BP18
Spring Wds., Vir.W. 192 AV98
Springall St. SE15 162 DV80
Springate Fld., Slou. 152 AY75
Springbank N21 81 DM44
Springbank Ave., Horn. 128 FJ64
Springbank Rd. SE13 183 ED86
Springbank Wk. NW1 141 DK66
St. Paul's Cres.
Springbourne Ct., Beck. 203 EC95
Springcopse Rd., Reig. 266 DC135
Springcroft Ave. N2 120 DF56
Springdale Ms. N16 122 DR63
Springdale Rd.
Springdale Rd. N16 122 DR63
Springfield E5 122 DV60
Springfield, Epp. 69 ET32
Springfield, Oxt. 253 ED130
Springfield (Bushey), Wat. 95 CD46
Springfield Ave. N10 121 DJ55
Springfield Ave. SW20 199 CZ97
Springfield Ave., Brwd. 109 GE45
Springfield Ave., Hmptn. 176 CB93
Springfield Ave., Swan. 207 FF98
Springfield Clo. N12 98 DB50
Springfield Clo., Chesh. 54 AQ33
Springfield Clo., Pot.B. 64 DD31
Springfield Clo., Rick. 75 BP43
Springfield Clo., Stan. 95 CG48
Springfield Clo., Wind. 151 AP82
Springfield Clo., Wok. 226 AS118
Springfield Dr., Ilf. 125 EQ58
Springfield Dr., Lthd. 231 CE119
Springfield Gdns. E5 122 DV60
Springfield Gdns. NW9 118 CR57
Springfield Gdns., Brom. 205 EM98
Springfield Gdns., Ruis. 115 BV60
Springfield Gdns., Upmin. 128 FQ62
Springfield Gdns., W.Wick. 203 EB103
Springfield Gdns., Wdf.Grn. 102 EJ52
Springfield Gro. SE7 164 EJ79
Springfield Gro., Sun. 195 BT95
Springfield La. NW6 140 DB67
Springfield La., Wey. 213 BP105
Springfield Meadows, Wey. 213 BP105
Springfield Mt. NW9 118 CS57
Springfield Pk., Maid. 150 AC78
Springfield Pl., N.Mal. 198 CQ98
Springfield Ri. SE26 182 DV90
Springfield Rd. E4 102 EE46
Springfield Rd. E6 145 EM66
Springfield Rd. E15 144 EE69
Springfield Rd. E17 123 DZ58
Springfield Rd. N11 99 DH50
Springfield Rd. N15 122 DU56
Springfield Rd. NW8 140 DC67
Springfield Rd. SE26 182 DV92
Springfield Rd. SW19 179 CZ92
Springfield Rd. W7 137 CE74
Springfield Rd., Ashf. 174 BM92
Springfield Rd., Berk. 38 AT16
Springfield Rd., Bexh. 167 FB83
Springfield Rd., Brom. 205 EM98
Springfield Rd., Chesh. 54 AQ33
Springfield Rd., Dor. 262 CB137
Springfield Rd., Epsom 217 CW110
Springfield Rd., Grays 170 GD75
Springfield Rd., Guil. 258 AY135
Springfield Rd., Har. 117 CE58
Springfield Rd., Hayes 136 BW74
Springfield Rd., Hem.H. 40 BM19
Springfield Rd., Kings.T. 198 CL97
Springfield Rd. (Colney Heath), St.Alb. 43 CG21
Springfield Rd. (Smallford), St.Alb. 44 CP20
Springfield Rd., Slou. 153 BB80
Springfield Rd., Tedd. 177 CG92
Springfield Rd., Th.Hth. 202 DQ95
Springfield Rd., Twick. 176 CA88
Springfield Rd., Wall. 219 DH106
Springfield Rd. (Cheshunt), Wal.Cr. 67 DY32
Springfield Rd., Wat. 59 BV33
Haines Way
Springfield Rd., Well. 166 EV83
Springfield Rd., Wind. 151 AP82
Springfield Wk. NW6 140 DB67
Springfield Wk., Orp. 205 ER102
Place Fm. Ave.
Springfields, Brox. 49 DZ19
Springfields, Wal.Abb. 68 EE34
Springfields, Welw.G.C. 29 CV11
Springfields Clo., Cher. 194 BH102
Springhall La., Saw. 36 EY06
Springhall Rd., Saw. 36 EY05
Springhaven Clo., Guil. 243 BA134
Springhead Enterprise Pk., Grav. 190 GC88
Springhead Rd., Erith 167 FF79
Springhead Rd., Grav. 190 GC89
Springhill Clo. SE5 162 DR83
Springholm Clo., West. 238 EJ118
Springhurst Clo., Croy. 221 DZ105
Springle La., Hert. 33 DZ12
Springpark Dr., Beck. 203 EC97
Springpond Rd., Dag. 126 EY64
Springrice Rd. SE13 183 ED86
Springs, The, Brox. 67 DY25
Springs, The, Hert. 32 DT08
Springshaw Clo., Sev. 256 FD123
Springside Ct., Guil. 242 AW133
Springvale Ave., Brent. 157 CK78
Springvale Est. W14 159 CY76
Blythe Rd.
Springvale Ter. W14 159 CX76
Springvale Way, Orp. 206 EW97
Springwater Clo. SE18 165 EN81
Springway, Har. 117 CD59
Springwell Ave. NW10 139 CT67
Springwell Ave., Rick. 92 BG47
Springwell Clo. SW16 181 DN91
Etherstone Rd.
Springwell Ct., Houns. 156 BX82
Springwell Hill (Harefield), Uxb. 92 BH51
Springwell La., Rick. 92 BG49
Springwell La. (Harefield), Uxb. 92 BG49
Springwell Rd. SW16 181 DN91
Springwell Rd., Houns. 156 BX81
Springwood (Cheshunt), Wal.Cr. 66 DU26
Springwood Clo. (Harefield), Uxb. 92 BK53
Springwood Cres., Edg. 96 CP47
Springwood Wk., St.Alb. 43 CK17
Springwood Way, Rom. 127 FG57
Sprowston Ms. E7 144 EG65
Sprowston Rd. E7 124 EG64
Spruce Ct. W5 158 CL76
Elderberry Rd.
Spruce Hill, Harl. 51 ES20
Spruce Hills Rd. E17 101 EC54
Spruce Pk., Brom. 204 EF98
Cumberland Rd.
Spruce Rd., West. 238 EK116
Spruce Way, St.Alb. 60 CB27
Sprucedale Clo., Swan. 207 FE96
Sprucedale Gdns., Croy. 221 DX105
Sprucedale Gdns., Wall. 219 DK109
Sprules Rd. SE4 163 DY82
Spur, The, Slou. 131 AK71
Spur, The (Cheshunt), Wal.Cr. 67 DX28
Welsummer Way
Spur Clo., Abb.L. 59 BR33
Spur Clo., Rom. 86 EV41
Spur Dr., Tad. 234 DB121
Spur Rd. N15 122 DR56
Philip La.
Spur Rd. SE1 278 D4
Spur Rd. SE1 161 DN75
Spur Rd. SW1 277 K5
Spur Rd. SW1 161 DJ75
Spur Rd., Bark. 145 EQ69
Spur Rd., Edg. 96 CL49
Spur Rd., Felt. 175 BV85
Spur Rd., Islw. 157 CH80
Spur Rd., Orp. 206 EU103
Spur Rd. Est., Edg. 96 CM49
Spurfield, W.Mol. 196 CB97
Spurgate, Brwd. 109 GA47
Spurgeon Ave. SE19 202 DR95
Spurgeon Rd. SE19 202 DR95
Spurgeon St. SE1 279 K7
Spurgeon St. SE1 162 DR76
Spurling Rd. SE22 162 DT84
Spurling Rd., Dag. 146 EZ65
Spurrell Ave., Bex. 187 FD91
Spurstowe Rd. E8 142 DV65
Marcon Pl.
Spurstowe Ter. E8 122 DV64
Squadrons App., Horn. 148 FJ65
Square, The W6 159 CW78
Square, The, Berk. 39 BB16
Square, The, Brox. 49 DY23
High Rd. Wormley
Square, The, Cars. 218 DG106
Square, The, Guil. 258 AT136
Orchard Rd.
Square, The (Shere), Guil. 260 BN139
Square, The, Hayes 135 BR74
Square, The, Ilf. 125 EN59
Square, The, Rich. 177 CK85
Square, The, Saw. 36 EY05
Square, The, Sev. 256 FE122
Amherst Hill
Square, The, Swan. 207 FD97
Square, The, Wat. 75 BV37
The Harebreaks
Square, The, West Dr. 154 BH81
Square, The, West. 238 EJ120
Square, The, Wey. 213 BQ106
Square, The, Wok. 228 BL116
Square, The, Wdf.Grn. 102 EG50
Square Rigger Row SW11 160 DC83
York Pl.
Squarey St. SW17 180 DC90
Squerryes Mede, West. 255 EQ127
Squire Gdns. NW8 140 DD69
St. John's Wd. Rd.
Squires Bri. Rd., Shep. 194 BM98
Squires Ct. SW19 180 DA91
Squires Ct., Cher. 194 BH102
Springfields Clo.
Squires Fld., Swan. 207 FF95
Squires La. N3 98 DB54
Squires Mt. NW3 120 DD62
East Heath Rd.
Squires Rd., Shep. 194 BM98
Squires Wk., Ashf. 175 BR94
Napier Rd.
Squires Way, Dart. 187 FD91
Squires Wd. Dr., Chis. 184 EL94
Squirrel Chase, Hem.H. 39 BE19
Squirrel Clo., Houns. 156 BW82
Squirrel Keep, W.Byf. 212 BH112
Squirrel Ms. W13 137 CG73
Squirrel Wd., W.Byf. 212 BH112
Dartnell Ave.
Squirrels, The SE13 163 ED83
Belmont Hill
Squirrels, The, Hert. 32 DV09
Squirrels, The, Pnr. 116 BZ55
Squirrels, The (Bushey), Wat. 77 CD44
Squirrels, The, Welw.G.C. 30 DC10
Squirrels Chase, Grays 171 GG75
Hornsby La.
Squirrels Clo. N12 98 DC49
Woodside Ave.
Squirrels Clo., Uxb. 134 BN66
Squirrels Grn., Lthd. 230 CA123
Squirrels Grn., Wor.Pk. 199 CT102
Squirrels Heath Ave., Rom. 127 FH55
Squirrels Heath La., Horn. 128 FJ56
Squirrels Heath La., Rom. 128 FJ56
Squirrels Heath Rd., Rom. 128 FL55
Squirrels La., Buck.H. 102 EK48
Squirrels Trd. Est., The, Hayes 155 BU76
Squirrels Way, Epsom 232 CR115
Squirries St. E2 142 DU69
Stable Clo., Nthlt. 136 CA68
Stable La., Beac. 89 AQ51
Stable Wk. N2 98 DD53
Old Fm. Rd.
Stable Way W10 139 CW72
Latimer Rd.
Stable Yd. SW1 277 K4
Stable Yd. SW9 161 DM82
Broomgrove Rd.
Stable Yd. SW15 159 CW83
Danemere St.
Stable Yd. Rd. SW1 277 K3
Stable Yd. Rd. SW1 141 DJ74
Stables, The, Buck.H. 102 EJ45
Stables, The, Cob. 214 BZ114
Stables, The, Guil. 242 AX131
Old Fm. Rd.
Stables, The, Swan. 207 FH95
Stables End, Orp. 205 EQ104
Stables Ms. SE27 182 DQ92
Stables Way SE11 278 D10
Stables Way SE11 161 DN78
Stacey Ave. N18 100 DW49
Stacey Clo. E10 123 ED57
Halford Rd.
Stacey Clo., Grav. 191 GL92
Stacey St. N7 121 DN62
Stacey St. WC2 273 N9
Stacey St. WC2 141 DK72
Stack Rd., Dart. 209 FR97
Stackfield, Harl. 36 EU12
Stackhouse St. SW3 276 D6
Stacklands, Welw.G.C. 29 CV11
Stacy Path SE5 162 DS80
Harris St.
Stadium Rd. NW2 119 CW59
Stadium Rd. SE18 165 EM80
Stadium St. SW10 160 DC80
Stadium Way, Dart. 187 FE86
Stadium Way, Wem. 118 CM63
Staff St. EC1 275 L3
Staffa Rd. E10 123 DY60
Stafford Ave., Horn. 128 FK55
Stafford Ave., Slou. 131 AQ70
Stafford Clo. E17 123 DZ58
Stafford Clo. N14 81 DJ43
Stafford Clo. NW6 140 DA69
Stafford Clo., Cat. 236 DT123
Stafford Clo. (Chafford Hundred), Grays 169 FW77
Stafford Clo., Green. 189 FT85
Stafford Clo., Maid. 130 AH72
Stafford Clo., Sutt. 217 CY107
Stafford Clo. (Cheshunt), Wal.Cr. 66 DV29
Stafford Ct. W8 160 DA76
Stafford Cross, Croy. 219 DM106
Stafford Dr., Brox. 49 EA20
Stafford Gdns., Croy. 219 DM106
Stafford Pl. SW1 277 K6
Stafford Pl. SW1 161 DJ76
Stafford Pl., Rich. 178 CM87
Stafford Rd. E3 143 DZ68
Stafford Rd. E7 144 EJ66
Stafford Rd. NW6 140 DA69
Stafford Rd., Cat. 236 DT122
Stafford Rd., Croy. 219 DN105
Stafford Rd., Har. 94 CC52
Stafford Rd., N.Mal. 198 CQ97
Stafford Rd., Ruis. 115 BT63
Stafford Rd., Sid. 185 ES91
Stafford Rd., Wall. 219 DJ107
Stafford Sq., Wey. 213 BR105
Rosslyn Pk.
Stafford St. W1 277 K2
Stafford St. W1 141 DJ74
Stafford Ter. W8 160 DA76
Stafford Way, Sev. 257 FJ127
Staffords, Harl. 36 EY12
Staffords Pl., Horl. 269 DH149
Staffordshire St. SE15 162 DU81
Stag Clo., Edg. 96 CQ54
Stag Grn. Ave., Hat. 45 CW16
Stag Hill, Guil. 258 AU135
Stag La. NW9 96 CP54
Stag La. SW15 179 CT89
Stag La., Berk. 38 AV18
Stag La., Buck.H. 102 EH47
Stag La., Edg. 96 CP54
Stag La., Rick. 73 BC44
Stag Leys, Ash. 232 CL120
Stag Leys Clo., Bans. 234 DE115
Stag Pl. SW1 277 K6
Stag Pl. SW1 161 DJ76
Stag Ride SW19 179 CT90
Stagbury Ave., Couls. 234 DE118
Stagbury Clo., Couls. 234 DE119
Stagg Hill, Barn. 80 DD35
Stagg Hill, Pot.B. 80 DD35
Staggart Grn., Chig. 103 ET51
Stags Way, Islw. 157 CF79
Stainash Cres., Stai. 174 BH92
Stainash Par., Stai. 174 BH92
Stainbank Rd., Mitch. 201 DH97
Stainby Clo., West Dr. 154 BL76
Stainby Rd. N15 122 DT56
Stainer Rd., Borwd. 77 CK39
Stainer St. SE1 279 L3
Stainer St. SE1 142 DR74
Staines Ave., Sutt. 199 CX103
Staines Bri., Stai. 173 BE91
Staines Bypass, Ashf. 174 BK92
Staines Bypass, Stai. 173 BC89
Staines Cen. Trd. Est., Stai. 173 BE91
Staines Grn., Hert. 31 DK11
Staines La., Cher. 193 BF99
Staines La. Clo., Cher. 193 BF99
Staines Rd., Cher. 193 BF97
Staines Rd., Felt. 175 BS87
Staines Rd., Houns. 156 CB83
Staines Rd., Ilf. 125 ER63
Staines Rd., Stai. 174 BG94
Staines Rd. (Wraysbury), Stai. 172 AY87
Staines Rd., Twick. 176 CA90
Staines Rd. E., Sun. 175 BU94
Staines Rd. W., Ashf. 175 BP93
Staines Rd. W., Sun. 175 BT94
Staines Wk., Sid. 186 EW93
Evry Rd.
Stainford Clo., Ashf. 175 BR92
Stainforth Rd. E17 123 EA56
Stainforth Rd., Ilf. 125 ER59
Staining La. EC2 275 J8
Staining La. EC2 142 DQ72
Stainmore Clo., Chis. 205 ER95
Stains Clo. (Cheshunt), Wal.Cr. 67 DY28
Stainsbury St. E2 142 DW68
Royston St.
Stainsby Pl. E14 143 EA72
Stainsby Rd.
Stainsby Rd. E14 143 EA72
Stainton Rd. SE6 183 ED86
Stainton Rd., Enf. 82 DW39
Stainton Wk., Wok. 226 AW118
Inglewood
Stairfoot La., Sev. 256 FC122
Staithes Way, Tad. 233 CV120
Stakescorner Rd., Guil. 258 AU142
Stalbridge St. NW1 272 C6
Stalham St. SE16 162 DV76
Stalisfield Pl., Orp. 223 EN110
Mill La.
Stambourne Way SE19 182 DS94
Stambourne Way, W.Wick. 203 EC104
Stamford Brook Ave. W6 159 CT76
Stamford Brook Rd. W6 159 CT76
Stamford Clo. N15 122 DU56
Stamford Clo. NW3 120 DC63
Heath St.
Stamford Clo., Har. 95 CE52
Stamford Clo., Pot.B. 64 DD32
Stamford Clo., Sthl. 136 CA73
Stamford Cotts. SW10 160 DB80
Billing St.
Stamford Ct. W6 159 CT77
Goldhawk Rd.
Stamford Dr., Brom. 204 EF98
Stamford Gdns., Dag. 146 EW66
Stamford Grn. Rd., Epsom 216 CP113
Stamford Gro. E. N16 122 DU60
Oldhill St.
Stamford Gro. W. N16 122 DU60
Oldhill St.
Stamford Hill N16 122 DT61
Stamford Hill Est. N16 122 DT60
Stamford Rd. E6 144 EL67
Stamford Rd. N1 142 DS66
Stamford Rd. N15 122 DU57
Stamford Rd., Dag. 146 EV67
Stamford Rd., Walt. 196 BX104
Kenilworth Dr.
Stamford Rd., Wat. 75 BV40
Stamford St. SE1 278 D3
Stamford St. SE1 141 DN74
Stamp Pl. E2 275 P2
Stamp Pl. E2 142 DT69
Stanard Clo. N16 122 DS59
Stanborough Ave., Borwd. 78 CN37
Stanborough Clo., Borwd. 78 CN38
Stanborough Clo., Hmptn. 176 BZ93
Stanborough Clo., Welw.G.C. 29 CW10
Stanborough Grn., Welw.G.C. 29 CW11
Stanborough Pk., Wat. 75 BV35
Stanborough Pas. E8 142 DT65
Abbot St.
Stanborough Rd., Houns. 157 CD83
Stanborough Rd., Welw.G.C. 29 CV12
Stanbridge Pl. N21 99 DP47
Stanbridge Rd. SW15 159 CW83
Stanbrook Rd. SE2 166 EV75
Stanbrook Rd., Grav. 191 GF88
Stanbury Ave., Wat. 75 BS37
Stanbury Rd. SE15 162 DV81
Stancroft NW9 118 CS56
Standale Gro., Ruis. 115 BQ57
Standard Ind. Est. E16 165 EM75
Standard Pl. EC2 275 N3
Standard Rd. NW10 138 CQ70
Standard Rd., Belv. 166 FA78
Standard Rd., Bexh. 166 EY84
Standard Rd., Enf. 83 DY38
Standard Rd., Houns. 156 BY83
Standard Rd., Orp. 223 EN110
Standen Ave., Horn. 128 FK62
Standen Rd. SW18 179 CZ87
Standfield, Abb.L. 59 BS31
Standfield Gdns., Dag. 146 FA65
Standfield Rd.
Standfield Rd., Dag. 126 FA64
Standingford, Harl. 51 EP20
Phelips Rd.
Standish Rd. W6 159 CU77
Standlake Pt. SE23 183 DX90
Standring Ri., Hem.H. 40 BH23
Stane Clo. SW19 200 DB95
Hayward Clo.
Stane St., Dor. 247 CK128
Stane St., Lthd. 232 CM124
Reigate Rd.
Stane Way SE18 164 EK80
Stane Way, Epsom 217 CU110
Stanfield Rd. E3 143 DY68
Stanford Clo., Hmptn. 176 BZ93
Stanford Clo., Rom. 127 FB58
Stanford Clo., Ruis. 115 BQ58
Stanford Clo., Wdf.Grn. 102 EL50
Stanford Ct., Wal.Abb. 68 EG33
Stanford Gdns., S.Ock. 149 FR74
Stanford Ho., Bark. 146 EV68
Stanford Pl. SE17 279 M9
Stanford Rd. N11 98 DF50
Stanford Rd. SW16 201 DK96
Stanford Rd. W8 160 DB76
Stanford Rd., Grays 170 GD76
Stanford St. SW1 277 M9
Stanford Way SW16 201 DK96
Stangate Cres., Borwd. 78 CS43
Stangate Gdns., Stan. 95 CH49
Stanger Rd. SE25 202 DU98
Stanham Pl., Dart. 167 FG84
Crayford Way
Stanham Rd., Dart. 188 FJ85
Stanhope Ave. N3 119 CZ55
Stanhope Ave., Brom. 204 EF102
Stanhope Ave., Har. 95 CD53
Stanhope Clo. SE16 163 DX75
Middleton Dr.
Stanhope Gdns. N4 121 DP58
Stanhope Gdns. N6 121 DH58
Stanhope Gdns. NW7 97 CT50
Stanhope Gdns. SW7 160 DC77
Stanhope Gdns., Dag. 126 EZ62
Stanhope Gdns., Ilf. 125 EM60
Stanhope Gate W1 276 G2
Stanhope Gate W1 140 DG74
Stanhope Gro., Beck. 203 DZ99
Stanhope Heath, Stai. 174 BJ86

Station Sq. (St. Mary Cray), Orp. 206 EV98
Station Sq., Rom. 127 FH56
Station St. E15 143 EE66
Station St. E16 145 EP74
Station St., Ware 33 EA11
Station Ter. NW10 139 CX68
Station Ter. SE5 162 DQ81
Station Ter., St.Alb. 61 CD26
Park St.
Station Vw., Grnf. 137 CD67
Station Vw., Guil. 258 AW135
Station Way SE15 162 DU82
Rye La.
Station Way (Roding Valley), Buck.H. 102 EJ49
Station Way (Epsom), Epsom 216 CR113
Station Way (Claygate), Esher 215 CE107
Station Way, St.Alb. 43 CF20
Station Way (Cheam), Sutt. 217 CY107
Station Way, Welw.G.C. 29 CX08
Station Yd., Twick. 177 CG87
Stationers Hall Ct. EC4 141 DP72
Ludgate Hill
Staunton Rd., Kings.T. 178 CL93
Staunton Rd., Slou. 131 AR71
Staunton St. SE8 163 DZ79
Stave Yd. Rd. SE16 143 DY74
Staveley Clo. E9 122 DW64
Churchill Wk.
Staveley Clo. N7 121 DL63
Penn Rd.
Staveley Clo. SE15 162 DV81
Asylum Rd.
Staveley Gdns. W4 158 CR81
Staveley Rd. W4 158 CR80
Staveley Rd., Ashf. 175 BR93
Staveley Way, Wok. 226 AS117
Staverton Rd. NW2 139 CW66
Staverton Rd., Horn. 128 FK58
Stavordale Rd. N5 121 DP63
Stavordale Rd., Cars. 200 DC101
Stayne End, Vir.W. 192 AU98
Stayner's Rd. E1 143 DX70
Stayton Rd., Sutt. 200 DA104
Stead St. SE17 279 K9
Stead St. SE17 162 DR77
Steadfast Rd., Kings.T. 197 CK95
Steam Fm. La., Felt. 155 BT84
Stean St. E8 142 DT67
Stebbing Way, Bark. 146 EU68
Stebondale St. E14 163 EC78
Stedham Pl. WC1 273 P8
Stedman Clo., Bex. 187 FE90
Stedman Clo., Uxb. 114 BN62
Steed Clo., Horn. 127 FH61
St. Leonards Way
Steedman St. SE17 279 H9
Steeds Rd. N10 98 DF53
Steeds Way, Loug. 84 EL41
Steele Ave., Green. 189 FT85
Steele Rd. E11 124 EE63
Steele Rd. N17 122 DS55
Steele Rd. NW10 138 CQ68
Steele Rd. W4 158 CQ76
Steele Rd., Islw. 157 CG84
Steele Wk., Erith 167 FB79
Steeles Ms. N. NW3 140 DF65
Steeles Rd.
Steeles Ms. S. NW3 140 DF65
Steeles Rd.
Steeles Rd. NW3 140 DF65
Steel's La. E1 142 DW72
Devonport St.
Steels La., Lthd. 214 CB114
Steelyard Pas. EC4 142 DR73
Upper Thames St.
Steen Way SE22 182 DS85
East Dulwich Gro.
Steep Clo., Orp. 223 ET107
Steep Hill SW16 181 DK90
Steep Hill, Croy. 220 DS105
Steeplands (Bushey), Wat. 94 CB45
Steeple Clo. SW6 159 CY82
Steeple Clo. SW19 179 CY92
Steeple Ct. E1 142 DV70
Coventry Rd.
Steeple Gdns., Add. 212 BH106
Weatherall Clo.
Steeple Hts. Dr., West. 238 EK117
Steeple Wk. N1 142 DQ67
Basire St.
Steeplestone Clo. N18 100 DQ50
Steer Pl., Red. 266 DG143
Bonehurst Rd.
Steerforth St. SW18 180 DB89
Steers Mead, Mitch. 200 DF95
Steers Way SE16 163 DY75
Stella Rd. SW17 180 DF93
Stellar Ho. N17 100 DT51
Stelling Rd., Erith 167 FD80
Stellman Clo. E5 122 DU62
Stembridge Rd. SE20 202 DV96
Stents La., Cob. 230 BZ120
Stents La., Lthd. 230 BZ120
Cobham Rd.
Stepbridge Path, Wok. 226 AX117
Goldsworth Rd.
Stepgates, Cher. 194 BH101
Stepgates Clo., Cher. 194 BH101
Stephan Clo. E8 142 DU67
Stephen Ave., Rain. 147 FG65
Stephen Clo., Egh. 173 BC93
Stephen Clo., Orp. 205 ET104
Stephen Ms. W1 273 M7
Stephen Rd., Bexh. 167 FC83
Stephen St. W1 273 M7
Stephen St. W1 141 DK71
Stephendale Rd. SW6 160 DB82
Stephens Clo., Rom. 106 FJ50
Stephen's Rd. E15 144 EE67
Stephenson Ave., Til. 171 GG81
Stephenson Dr., Wind. 151 AP80
Stephenson Rd. E17 123 DY57
Stephenson Rd. W7 137 CF72
Stephenson Rd., Twick. 176 CA87
Stephenson St. E16 144 EE70
Stephenson St. NW10 138 CS69
Stephenson Way NW1 273 L4
Stephenson Way NW1 141 DJ70
Stephenson Way, Wat. 76 BX41
Stepney Causeway E1 143 DX72
Stepney Grn. E1 142 DW71
Stepney High St. E1 143 DX71
Stepney Way E1 142 DV71
Sterling Ave., Edg. 96 CM49
Sterling Ave., Pnr. 116 BY59
Sterling Ave., Wal.Cr. 67 DX34
Sterling Clo., Pnr. 116 BX60
Sterling Gdns. SE14 163 DY79
Sterling Ind. Est., Dag. 127 FB63
Sterling Pl. W5 158 CL77
Sterling Rd., Enf. 82 DR38
Sterling St. SW7 276 C6
Sterling Way N18 100 DR50
Stern Clo., Bark. 146 EY69
Choats Rd.
Sterndale Rd. W14 159 CX76
Sterndale Rd., Dart. 188 FM87
Sterne St. W12 159 CX75
Sternhall La. SE15 162 DU83
Sternhold Ave. SW2 181 DK89
Sterry Cres., Dag. 126 FA64
Alibon Rd.
Sterry Dr., Epsom 216 CS105
Sterry Dr., T.Ditt. 197 CE100
Sterry Gdns., Dag. 146 FA65
Sterry Rd., Bark. 145 ET67
Sterry Rd., Dag. 126 FA63
Sterry St. SE1 279 K5
Sterry St. SE1 162 DR75
Steucers La. SE23 183 DY87
Steve Biko La. SE6 183 EA91
Steve Biko Rd. N7 121 DN62
Steve Biko Way, Houns. 156 CA83
Stevedale Rd., Well. 166 EW82
Stevedore St. E1 142 DV74
Waterman Way
Stevenage Cres., Borwd. 78 CL39
Stevenage Ri., Hem.H. 40 BM16
Stevenage Rd. E6 145 EN65
Stevenage Rd. SW6 159 CX80
Stevens Ave. E9 142 DW65
Stevens Clo., Beck. 183 EA93
Stevens Clo., Bex. 187 FD91
Steven's Clo., Dart. 189 FS92
Stevens Clo., Epsom 216 CS113
Upper High St.
Stevens Clo., Hmptn. 176 BY93
Stevens Clo., Pnr. 116 BW57
Bridle Rd.
Stevens Grn. (Bushey), Wat. 94 CC46
Stevens La., Esher 215 CG108
Stevens Pl., Pur. 219 DP113
Stevens Rd., Dag. 126 EV62
Stevens St. SE1 279 N6
Steven's Wk., Croy. 221 DY111
Stevens Way, Chig. 103 ES49
Stevenson Clo., Barn. 80 DD44
Stevenson Clo., Erith 167 FH80
Stevenson Cres. SE16 162 DV78
Stevenson Rd., Slou. 111 AR61
Steventon Rd. W12 139 CT73
Stew La. EC4 275 H10
Steward Clo. (Cheshunt), Wal.Cr. 67 DY30
Steward St. E1 275 N7
Steward St. E1 142 DS71
Stewards Clo., Epp. 70 EU32
Stewards Grn. La., Epp. 70 EV32
Stewards Grn. Rd., Epp. 70 EU33
Stewards Holte Wk. N11 99 DH49
Coppies Gro.
Stewards Wk., Rom. 127 FE57
Stewart, Tad. 233 CX121
Stewart Ave., Shep. 194 BN98
Stewart Ave., Slou. 132 AT71
Stewart Ave., Upmin. 128 FP62
Stewart Clo. NW9 118 CQ58
Stewart Clo., Abb.L. 59 BT32
Stewart Clo., Chis. 185 EP92
Stewart Clo., Hmptn. 176 BY93
Stewart Clo., Maid. 150 AD81
Stewart Clo., Wok. 226 AT117
Nethercote Ave.
Stewart Rainbird Ho. E12 125 EN64
Stewart Rd. E15 123 ED63
Stewart St. E14 163 EC75
Stewart's Dr., Slou. 111 AP63
Stewart's Gro. SW3 276 A10
Stewart's Gro. SW3 160 DD77
Stewart's Rd. SW8 161 DJ80
Stewartsby Clo. N18 100 DQ50
Steyne Rd. W3 138 CQ74
Steyning Clo., Ken. 235 DP116
Steyning Gro. SE9 185 EM91
Steyning Way, Houns. 156 BW84
Steynings Way N12 98 DA50
Steynton Ave., Bex. 186 EX89
Stickland Rd., Belv. 166 FA77
Picardy Rd.
Stickleton Clo., Grnf. 136 CB69
Stifford Hill (North Stifford), Grays 149 FX74
Stifford Hill, S.Ock. 149 FW73
Stifford Rd., S.Ock. 149 FR74
Stile Hall Gdns. W4 158 CN78
Stile Hall Par. W4 158 CN78
Chiswick High Rd.
Stile Path, Sun. 195 BU97
Stile Rd., Slou. 152 AX76
Stilecroft, Harl. 52 EU17
Stilecroft Gdns., Wem. 117 CH62
Stiles Clo., Brom. 205 EM100
Stiles Clo., Erith 167 FB78
Riverdale Rd.
Stillingfleet Rd. SW13 159 CU79
Stillington St. SW1 277 L8
Stillington St. SW1 161 DJ77
Stillness Rd. SE23 183 DY86
Stilton Cres. NW10 138 CQ66
Stilton Path, Borwd. 78 CN38
Stilwell Roundabout, Uxb. 134 BN73
Stipularis Dr., Hayes 136 BX70
Stirling Clo. SW16 201 DJ95
Stirling Clo., Bans. 233 CZ117
Stirling Clo., Rain. 147 FH69
Stirling Clo., Uxb. 134 BJ69
Ferndale Cres.
Stirling Clo., Wind. 151 AK82
Stirling Cor., Barn. 78 CR44
Stirling Cor., Borwd. 78 CR44
Stirling Dr., Orp. 224 EV106
Stirling Gro., Houns. 156 CC82
Stirling Rd. E13 144 EH68
Stirling Rd. E17 123 DY55
Stirling Rd. N17 100 DU53
Stirling Rd. N22 99 DP53
Stirling Rd. SW9 161 DL82
Stirling Rd. W3 158 CP76
Stirling Rd., Har. 117 CF55
Stirling Rd., Hayes 135 BV73
Stirling Rd., Houns. 174 BM86
Stirling Rd., Slou. 131 AN71
Stirling Rd., Twick. 176 CA87
Stirling Rd. Path E17 123 DY55
Stirling Wk., N.Mal. 198 CQ99
Stirling Wk., Surb. 198 CP100
Stirling Way, Abb.L. 59 BU32
Stirling Way, Borwd. 78 CR44
Stirling Way, Croy. 201 DL101
Stirling Way, Welw.G.C. 30 DE09
Stites Hill Rd., Cat. 235 DP120
Stiven Cres., Har. 116 BZ62
Stoats Nest Rd., Couls. 219 DL114
Stoats Nest Village, Couls. 235 DL115
Stock Hill, West. 238 EK116
Stock La., Dart. 188 FJ90
Stock Orchard Cres. N7 121 DM64
Stock Orchard St. N7 121 DM64
Stock St. E13 144 EG68
Stockbreach Clo., Hat. 45 CU17
Stockbreach Rd., Hat. 45 CU17
Stockbury Rd., Croy. 202 DW100
Stockdale Rd., Dag. 126 EZ61
Stockdales Rd. (Eton Wick), Wind. 151 AM77
Stockdove Way, Grnf. 137 CF69
Stocker Gdns., Dag. 146 EW66
Ellerton Rd.
Stockers Fm. Rd., Rick. 92 BK48
Stockers La., Wok. 227 AZ120
Stockfield, Horl. 269 DH147
Stockfield Ave., Hodd. 49 EA15
Stockfield Rd. SW16 181 DM90
Stockfield Rd., Esher 215 CE106
Stockham's Clo., S.Croy. 220 DR111
Stockholm Rd. SE16 162 DW78
Stockholm Way E1 142 DU74
Stockhurst Clo. SW15 159 CW82
Stocking La. (Bayford), Hert. 47 DN18
Stockings La. (Little Berkhamsted), Hert. 47 DK18
Stockingswater La., Enf. 83 DY41
Stockland Rd., Rom. 127 FD58
Stockley Clo., West Dr. 155 BP75
Stockley Fm. Rd., West Dr. 155 BP76
Stockley Rd.
Stockley Pk., Uxb. 135 BP74
Stockley Pk. Roundabout, Uxb. 135 BP74
Stockley Rd., Uxb. 135 BP73
Stockley Rd., West Dr. 155 BP77
Stockport Rd. SW16 201 DK95
Stockport Rd., Rick. 91 BC45
Stocks Clo., Horl. 269 DH149
Stocks Pl. E14 143 DZ73
Grenade St.
Stocksfield Rd. E17 123 EC55
Stockton Gdns. N17 100 DQ52
Stockton Rd.
Stockton Gdns. NW7 96 CS48
Stockton Rd. N17 100 DQ52
Stockton Rd. N18 100 DU51
Stockton Rd., Reig. 266 DA137
Stockwell Ave. SW9 161 DM83
Stockwell Clo., Brom. 204 EH96
Stockwell Clo. (Cheshunt), Wal.Cr. 66 DU28
Stockwell Gdns. SW9 161 DM82
Stockwell Gdns. Est. SW9 161 DL82
Stockwell Grn. SW9 161 DM82
Stockwell La. SW9 161 DM82
Stockwell La. (Cheshunt), Wal.Cr. 66 DU28
Stockwell Ms. SW9 161 DM82
Stockwell Rd.
Stockwell Pk. Cres. SW9 161 DM82
Stockwell Pk. Est. SW9 161 DN82
Stockwell Pk. Rd. SW9 161 DM81
Stockwell Pk. Wk. SW9 161 DM83
Stockwell Rd. SW9 161 DM82
Stockwell St. SE10 163 EC79
Stockwell Ter. SW9 161 DM81
Stockwells, Maid. 130 AD70
Stocton Clo., Guil. 242 AW133
Stocton Rd., Guil. 242 AW133
Stodart Rd. SE20 202 DW95
Stofield Gdns. SE9 184 EK90
Aldersgrove Ave.
Stoford Clo. SW19 179 CY87
Stoke Ave., Ilf. 104 EU51
Stoke Clo., Cob. 230 BZ116
Stoke Common Rd., Slou. 112 AU63
Stoke Ct. Dr., Slou. 132 AS67
Stoke Flds., Guil. 258 AX135
York Rd.
Stoke Gdns., Slou. 132 AS74
Stoke Grn., Slou. 132 AU70
Stoke Gro., Guil. 242 AX134
York Rd.
Stoke Ms., Guil. 258 AX135
Stoke Rd.
Stoke Newington Ch. St. N16 122 DR62
Stoke Newington Common N16 122 DT62
Stoke Newington High St. N16 122 DT62
Stoke Newington Rd. N16 122 DT64
Stoke Pk. Ave., Slou. 131 AQ69
Stoke Pl. NW10 139 CT69
Stoke Pl. Conference Cen., Slou. 132 AU70
Stoke Poges La., Slou. 132 AS74
Stoke Rd., Cob. 230 BW115
Stoke Rd., Guil. 242 AX133
Stoke Rd., Kings.T. 178 CQ94
Stoke Rd., Rain. 148 FK68
Stoke Rd., Slou. 132 AT74
Stoke Rd., Walt. 196 BW104
Stoke Wd., Slou. 112 AT63
Stokenchurch St. SW6 160 DB81
Stokers Clo., Horl. 268 DE151
Stokes Ridings, Tad. 233 CX123
Stokes Rd. E6 144 EL70
Stokes Rd., Croy. 203 DX100
Stokesay, Slou. 132 AT73
Stokesby Rd., Chess. 216 CM107
Stokesheath Rd., Lthd. 214 CC111
Stokesley Ri., H.Wyc. 110 AE55
Wootton Dr.
Stokesley St. W12 139 CT72
Stoll Clo. NW2 119 CW62
Stomp Rd., Slou. 130 AH71
Stompond La., Walt. 195 BU103
Stoms Path SE6 183 EA92
Stonard Rd. N13 99 DN48
Stonard Rd., Dag. 126 EV64
Stonards Hill, Epp. 70 EU29
Stonards Hill, Loug. 85 EM44
Stondon Pk. SE23 183 DY87
Stondon Wk. E6 144 EK68
Stone Bldgs. WC2 274 C7
Stone Bldgs. WC2 141 DM71
Stone Clo. SW4 161 DJ82
Larkhall Ri.
Stone Clo., Dag. 126 EZ61
Stone Clo., West Dr. 134 BM74
Stone Cres., Felt. 175 BT87
Stone Cross, Harl. 35 ER14
Post Office Rd.
Stone Hall Gdns. W8 160 DB76
St. Mary's Gate
Stone Hall Pl. W8 160 DB76
St. Mary's Gate
Stone Hall Rd. N21 99 DM45
Stone Ho. Ct. EC3 275 M8
Stone Ness Rd., Grays 169 FV79
Stone Pk. Ave., Beck. 203 EA98
Stone Pl., Wor.Pk. 199 CU103
Stone Pl. Rd., Green. 189 FS85
Stone Rd., Brom. 204 EF99
Stone St., Croy. 219 DN106
Stone St., Grav. 191 GH86
Stonebanks, Walt. 195 BU101
Stonebridge Common E8 142 DT66
Mayfield Rd.
Stonebridge Fld., Wind. 151 AP78
Stonebridge Flds., Guil. 258 AX141
Stonebridge Pk. NW10 138 CR66
Stonebridge Rd. N15 122 DS57
Stonebridge Rd., Grav. 190 GA85
Stonebridge Way, Wem. 138 CP65
Stonebridge Wf., Guil. 258 AX141
Stonechat Sq. E6 144 EL71
Peridot St.
Stonecot Clo., Sutt. 199 CY102
Stonecot Hill, Sutt. 199 CY102
Stonecourt Clo., Horl. 269 DJ148
Stonecroft Ave., Iver 133 BE72
Stonecroft Clo., Barn. 79 CV42
Stonecroft Rd., Erith 167 FC80
Stonecroft Way, Croy. 201 DL101
Stonecrop Clo. NW9 118 CR55
Colindale Ave.
Stonecrop Rd., Guil. 243 BC132
Kingfisher Dr.
Stonecross, St.Alb. 43 CE19
Stonecross Clo., St.Alb. 43 CE19
Stonecross
Stonecross Rd., Hat. 45 CV16
Stonecutter Ct. EC4 141 DP72
Stonecutter St.
Stonecutter St. EC4 274 F8
Stonecutter St. EC4 141 DP72
Stonefield Clo., Bexh. 166 FA83
Stonefield Clo., Ruis. 116 BY64
Stonefield St. N1 141 DN67
Stonefield Way SE7 164 EK80
Greenbay Rd.
Stonefield Way, Ruis. 116 BY63
Stonegate Clo., Orp. 206 EW97
Main Rd.
Stonegrove, Edg. 96 CL49
Stonegrove Est., Edg. 96 CM49
Stonegrove Gdns., Edg. 96 CM50
Stonehall Ave., Ilf. 124 EL58
Stoneham Rd. N11 99 DJ51
Stonehill Clo. SW14 178 CR85
Stonehill Clo., Lthd. 246 CA125
Stonehill Grn. Rd., Dart. 187 FC94
Birchwood Rd.
Stonehill Rd. SW14 178 CQ85
Stonehill Rd. W4 158 CN78
Wellesley Rd.
Stonehill Rd., Cher. 210 AY107
Stonehill Rd., Wok. 210 AW108
Stonehill Woods Caravan Pk., Sid. 187 FB93
Stonehills, Welw.G.C. 29 CX08
Stonehills Ct. SE21 182 DS90
Stonehorse Rd., Enf. 82 DW43
Stonehouse Gdns., Cat. 252 DS125
Stonehouse La., Purf. 169 FS79
Stonehouse La., Sev. 224 EX109
Stonehouse Rd., Sev. 224 EW110
Stoneings La., Sev. 239 ET118
Stonelea Rd., Hem.H. 40 BM23
Stoneleigh Ave., Enf. 82 DV39
Stoneleigh Ave., Wor.Pk. 217 CU105
Stoneleigh Bdy., Epsom 217 CU106
Stoneleigh Clo., Wal.Cr. 67 DX33
Stoneleigh Cres., Epsom 217 CT106
Stoneleigh Dr., Hodd. 33 EB14
Stoneleigh Pk., Wey. 213 BQ106
Stoneleigh Pk. Ave., Croy. 203 DX100
Stoneleigh Pk. Rd., Epsom 217 CT107
Stoneleigh Pl. W11 139 CX73
Stoneleigh Rd. N17 122 DT55
Stoneleigh Rd., Cars. 200 DE101
Stoneleigh Rd., Ilf. 124 EL55
Stoneleigh Rd., Oxt. 254 EL130
Stoneleigh St. W11 139 CX73
Stoneleigh Ter. N19 121 DH61
Stonells Rd. SW11 180 DF85
Chatham Rd.
Stonemasons Clo. N15 122 DR56
Stonenest St. N4 121 DM60
Stones All., Wat. 75 BV42
Stones Cross Rd., Swan. 207 FC99
Stones End St. SE1 279 H5
Stones End St. SE1 162 DQ75
Stones La., Dor. 262 CC137
Stones Rd., Epsom 216 CS112
Stoneswood Rd., Oxt. 254 EH130
Stonewall E6 145 EN71
Stonewood, Dart. 189 FW90
Stonewood Rd., Erith 167 FE78
Stoney All. SE18 165 EN82
Stoney Brook, Guil. 242 AS133
Stoney Cft., Hem.H. 40 BG20
Stoney Cft., Welw.G.C. 30 DA08
Stoney Gro., Chesh. 54 AR30
Stoney La. E1 275 N8
Stoney La. SE19 182 DT93
Church Rd.
Stoney La., Hem.H. 57 BB27
Stoney La., Kings L. 57 BE30
Stoney La., Slou. 131 AN67
Stoney Meade, Slou. 131 AP74
Weekes Dr.
Stoney St. SE1 279 K2
Stoney St. SE1 142 DR74
Stoneyard La. E14 143 EB73
Poplar High St.
Stoneycroft, Hem.H. 40 BG20
Long Chaulden
Stoneycroft Clo. SE12 184 EF87
Stoneycroft Rd., Wdf.Grn. 102 EL51
Stoneydeep, Tedd. 177 CG91
Twickenham Rd.
Stoneydown E17 123 DY56
Stoneydown Ave. E17 123 DY56
Stoneyfield Rd., Couls. 235 DM117
Stoneyfields Gdns., Edg. 96 CQ49
Stoneyfields La., Edg. 96 CQ50
Stoneylands Ct., Egh. 173 AZ92
Stoneylands Rd., Egh. 173 AZ92
Stonhouse St. SW4 161 DK83
Stonny Cft., Ash. 232 CM117
Stonor Rd. W14 159 CZ77
Stony La., Amer. 72 AY38
Stony Path, Loug. 85 EM40
Stony Wd., Harl. 51 ES16
Stonycroft Clo., Enf. 83 DY40
Brimsdown Ave.
Stonyrock La., Dor. 246 BY134
Stonyshotts, Wal.Abb. 68 EE34
Stoop Ct., W.Byf. 212 BH112
Stopes St. SE15 162 DT80
Stopford Rd. E13 144 EG67
Stopford Rd. SE17 161 DP78
Store Gdns., Brwd. 109 GD43
Store Rd. E16 165 EN75
Store St. E15 123 ED64
Store St. WC1 273 M7
Store St. WC1 141 DK71
Storers Quay E14 163 ED77
Storey Rd. E17 123 DZ56
Storey Rd. N6 120 DF58
Storey St. E16 145 EN74
Storey St., Hem.H. 40 BK24
Storey's Gate SW1 277 N5
Storey's Gate SW1 161 DK75
Stories Ms. SE5 162 DS82
Stories Rd. SE5 162 DS83
Stork Rd. E7 144 EF65
Storks Rd. SE16 162 DU76
Storksmead Rd., Edg. 96 CS52
Stormont Rd. N6 120 DF59
Stormont Rd. SW11 160 DG83
Stormont Way, Chess. 215 CJ106
Stormount Dr., Hayes 155 BQ75
Stornaway Strand, Grav. 191 GM91
Stornoway, Hem.H. 41 BP22
Storr Gdns., Brwd. 109 GD43
Storrington Rd., Croy. 202 DT102
Stort Mill, Harl. 36 EV09
Stort Twr., Harl. 35 ET13
Stortford Rd., Hodd. 49 EB16
Story St. N1 141 DM66
Carnoustie Dr.
Stothard Pl. EC2 142 DS71
Bishopsgate
Stothard St. E1 142 DW70
Colebert Ave.
Stott Clo. SW18 180 DD86
Stoughton Ave., Sutt. 217 CX106
Stoughton Clo. SE11 278 C9
Stoughton Clo. SW15 179 CU88
Bessborough Rd.
Stoughton Rd., Guil. 242 AU131
Stour Ave., Sthl. 156 CA76
Stour Clo., Kes. 222 EJ105
Stour Clo., Slou. 151 AP76
Stour Rd. E3 143 EA66
Stour Rd., Dag. 126 FA61
Stour Rd., Dart. 167 FG83
Stour Rd., Grays 171 GG78
Stour Way, Upmin. 129 FS58
Stourcliffe St. W1 272 D9
Stourcliffe St. W1 140 DF72
Stourhead Clo. SW19 179 CX87
Castlecombe Dr.
Stourhead Gdns. SW20 199 CU97
Stourton Ave., Felt. 176 BZ91
Stovell Rd., Wind. 151 AP80
Stow, The, Harl. 35 ET13
Stow Cres. E17 101 DY52
Stowage SE8 163 EA79
Stowe Ct., Dart. 188 FQ87
Stowe Cres., Ruis. 115 BP58
Stowe Gdns. N9 100 DT46
Latymer Rd.
Stowe Pl. N15 122 DS55
Stowe Rd. W12 159 CV75
Stowe Rd., Orp. 224 EV105
Stowe Rd., Slou. 131 AL73
Stowell Ave., Croy. 221 ED110
Stowting Rd., Orp. 223 ES105
Stox Mead, Har. 95 CD53
Stracey Rd. E7 124 EG63
Stracey Rd. NW10 138 CR67
Strachan Pl. SW19 179 CW93
Woodhayes Rd.
Stradbroke Dr., Chig. 103 EN51
Stradbroke Gro., Buck.H. 102 EK46
Stradbroke Gro., Ilf. 124 EL55
Stradbroke Pk., Chig. 103 EP51
Stradbroke Rd. N5 122 DQ63
Stradbrook Clo., Har. 116 BZ62
Stiven Cres.
Stradella Rd. SE24 182 DQ86
Strafford Ave., Ilf. 103 EN54
Strafford Clo., Pot.B. 64 DA32
Strafford Gate
Strafford Gate, Pot.B. 64 DA32
Strafford Rd. W3 158 CQ75
Strafford Rd., Barn. 79 CY41
Strafford Rd., Houns. 156 BZ83
Strafford Rd., Twick. 177 CG87
Strafford St. E14 163 EA75
Strahan Rd. E3 143 DY69
Straight, The, Sthl. 156 BX75
Straight Bit, H.Wyc. 110 AC55
Straight Rd., Rom. 105 FH50
Straight Rd., Wind. 172 AU85
Straightsmouth SE10 163 EC80
Strait Rd. E6 144 EL73
Straker's Rd. SE15 162 DV84
Strand WC2 277 P1
Strand WC2 141 DL73
Strand Clo., Epsom 232 CR119
Strand La. WC2 274 C10
Strand on the Grn. W4 158 CN79
Strand Pl. N18 100 DR49
Strand Sch. App. W4 158 CN79
Thames Rd.
Strandfield Clo. SE18 165 ES78
Strangeways, Wat. 75 BS36

Sunnycroft Rd. SE25 202 DU97
Sunnycroft Rd., Houns. 156 CB82
Sunnycroft Rd., Sthl. 136 CA71
Sunnydale, Orp. 205 EN103
Sunnydale Gdns. NW7 96 CR51
Sunnydale Rd. SE12 184 EH85
Sunnydell, St.Alb. 60 CB26
Sunnydene Ave. E4 101 ED50
Sunnydene Ave., Ruis. 115 BU61
Sunnydene Clo., Rom. 106 FM52
Sunnydene Gdns., Wem. 137 CJ65
Sunnydene Rd., Pur. 219 DP113
Sunnydene St. SE26 183 DY91
Sunnyfield NW7 97 CT49
Sunnyfield, Hat. 45 CX15
Sunnyfield Rd., Chis. 206 EU97
Sunnyhill Clo. E5 123 DY63
Sunnyhill Rd. SW16 181 DL91
Sunnyhill Rd., Hem.H. 40 BH20
Sunnyhill Rd., Rick. 91 BD51
Sunnyhurst Clo., Sutt. 200 DA104
Sunnymead Ave., Mitch. 201 DJ97
Sunnymead Rd. NW9 118 CR59
Sunnymead Rd. SW15 179 CV85
Sunnymede, Chig. 104 EV47
Sunnymede Ave., Cars. 218 DD111
Sunnymede Ave., Chesh. 54 AS28
Sunnymede Ave., Epsom 216 CS109
Sunnymede Dr., Ilf. 125 EP56
Sunnyside NW2 119 CZ62
Sunnyside SW19 179 CY93
Sunnyside, Wal.Abb. 50 EF22
Sunnyside, Walt. 196 BW99
Sunnyside Cotts., Chesh. 38 AT24
Two Dells La.
Sunnyside Dr. E4 101 EC45
Sunnyside Gdns., Upmin. 128 FQ61
Sunnyside Pas. SW19 179 CY93
Sunnyside Pl. SW19 179 CY93
Sunnyside
Sunnyside Rd. E10 123 EA60
Sunnyside Rd. N19 121 DK59
Sunnyside Rd. W5 137 CK74
Sunnyside Rd., Chesh. 54 AP30
Sunnyside Rd., Epp. 69 ET32
Sunnyside Rd., Ilf. 125 EQ62
Sunnyside Rd., Tedd. 177 CD91
Sunnyside Rd. E. N9 100 DU48
Sunnyside Rd. N. N9 100 DT48
Sunnyside Rd. S. N9 100 DT48
Sunnyside Ter. NW9 118 CR55
Edgware Rd.
Sunray Ave. SE24 162 DR84
Sunray Ave., Brwd. 109 GE44
Sunray Ave., Brom. 204 EL100
Sunray Ave., Surb. 198 CP103
Sunray Ave., West Dr. 154 BK75
Sunrise Ave., Horn. 128 FJ62
Sunrise Clo., Felt. 176 BZ90
Exeter Rd.
Sunrise Cres., Hem.H. 40 BM23
Sunset Ave. E4 101 EB46
Sunset Ave., Wdf.Grn. 102 EF49
Sunset Clo., Erith 167 FH81
Sunset Dr. 105 FH50
(Havering-atte-Bower), Rom.
Sunset Gdns. SE25 202 DT96
Sunset Rd. SE5 162 DQ84
Sunset Rd. SE28 166 EU75
Sunset Vw., Barn. 79 CY40
Sunshine Way, Mitch. 200 DF96
Sunstone Gro., Red. 251 DL129
Sunwell Clo. SE15 162 DV81
Cossall Wk.
Superior Dr., Orp. 223 ET107
Surbiton Ct., Surb. 197 CJ100
Surbiton Cres., Kings.T. 198 CL98
Surbiton Hall Clo., Kings.T. 198 CL98
Surbiton Hill Pk., Surb. 198 CN99
Surbiton Hill Rd., Surb. 198 CL98
Surbiton Par., Surb. 198 CL100
St. Mark's Hill
Surbiton Rd., Kings.T. 198 CL98
Surlingham Clo. SE28 146 EX73
Surly Hall Wk., Wind. 151 AM81
Surma Clo. E1 142 DV70
Surman Cres., Brwd. 109 GC45
Surr St. N7 121 DL64
Surrendale Pl. W9 140 DA70
Surrey Ave., Slou. 131 AQ71
Surrey Canal Rd. SE14 162 DW79
Surrey Canal Rd. SE15 162 DW79
Surrey Cres. W4 158 CN78
Surrey Dr., Horn. 128 FN56
Surrey Gdns. N4 122 DQ58
Finsbury Pk. Ave.
Surrey Gdns., Lthd. 229 BU122
Surrey Gro. SE17 162 DS78
Surrey Sq.
Surrey Gro., Sutt. 200 DD104
Surrey Hills, Tad. 248 CP130
Surrey Hills Ave., Tad. 248 CQ130
Surrey La. SW11 160 DE81
Surrey La. Est. SW11 160 DE81
Surrey Lo. SE1 278 D7
Surrey Ms. SE27 182 DS91
Hamilton Rd.
Surrey Mt. SE23 182 DV88
Surrey Quays Rd. SE16 163 DX75
Surrey Rd. SE15 183 DX85
Surrey Rd., Bark. 145 ES67
Surrey Rd., Dag. 127 FB64
Surrey Rd., Har. 116 CC57
Surrey Rd., W.Wick. 203 EB102
Surrey Row SE1 278 F4
Surrey Row SE1 161 DP75
Surrey Sq. SE17 279 M10
Surrey Sq. SE17 162 DS78
Surrey St. E13 144 EH69
Surrey St. WC2 274 C10
Surrey St. WC2 141 DM73
Surrey St., Croy. 202 DQ104
Surrey Ter. SE17 279 N10
Surrey Ter. SE17 162 DS78
Surrey Twr. SE20 182 DW94
Surrey Water Rd. SE16 163 DX74
Surridge Clo., Rain. 148 FJ69
Surridge Gdns. SE19 182 DR93
Hancock Rd.
Susan Clo., Rom. 127 FC55
Susan Rd. SE3 164 EH82
Susan Wd., Chis. 205 EN95
Susannah St. E14 143 EB72
Sussex Ave., Islw. 157 CE83
Sussex Ave., Rom. 106 FM52
Sussex Border Path, Horl. 268 DA152
Sussex Clo. N19 121 DL61
Cornwallis Rd.
Sussex Clo., Ch.St.G. 90 AV47
Sussex Clo., Hodd. 49 EA16
Roman St.
Sussex Clo., Ilf. 125 EM57
Sussex Clo., N.Mal. 198 CS98
Sussex Clo., Reig. 266 DD135
Sussex Clo., Slou. 152 AV75
Sussex Clo., Twick. 177 CH86
Westmorland Clo.
Sussex Cres., Nthlt. 136 CA65
Sussex Gdns. N4 122 DQ57
Sussex Gdns. N6 120 DF57
Great N. Rd.
Sussex Gdns. W2 140 DD72
Sussex Gdns., Chess. 215 CK107
Sussex Keep, Slou. 152 AV75
Sussex Clo.
Sussex Ms. E. W2 272 A9
Sussex Ms. W. W2 272 A10
Sussex Pl. NW1 272 D4
Sussex Pl. NW1 140 DF70
Sussex Pl. W2 272 A9
Sussex Pl. W2 140 DD72
Sussex Pl. W6 159 CW78
Sussex Pl., Erith 167 FB80
Sussex Pl., N.Mal. 198 CS98
Sussex Pl., Slou. 152 AV75
Sussex Ring N12 98 DA50
Sussex Rd. E6 145 EN67
Sussex Rd., Brwd. 108 FV49
Sussex Rd., Cars. 218 DF107
Sussex Rd., Dart. 188 FN87
Sussex Rd., Erith 167 FB80
Sussex Rd., Har. 116 CC57
Sussex Rd., Mitch. 201 DL99
Lincoln Rd.
Sussex Rd., N.Mal. 198 CS98
Sussex Rd., Orp. 206 EW100
Sussex Rd., Sid. 186 EV92
Sussex Rd., S.Croy. 220 DR107
Sussex Rd., Sthl. 156 BX76
Sussex Rd., Uxb. 115 BQ63
Sussex Rd., Wat. 75 BU38
Sussex Rd., W.Wick. 203 EB102
Sussex Sq. W2 272 A10
Sussex Sq. W2 140 DD73
Sussex St. E13 144 EH69
Sussex St. SW1 161 DH78
Sussex Wk. SW9 161 DP84
Sussex Way N7 121 DL61
Sussex Way N19 121 DL60
Sussex Way, Barn. 80 DG43
Sussex Way, Uxb. 113 BF57
Sutcliffe Clo. NW11 120 DB57
Sutcliffe Clo. 76 CC42
(Bushey), Wat.
Sutcliffe Ho., Hayes 135 BU72
Sutcliffe Rd. SE18 165 ES79
Sutcliffe Rd., Well. 166 EW82
Sutherland Ave. W9 140 DC69
Sutherland Ave. W13 137 CH72
Sutherland Ave., Guil. 242 AX128
Sutherland Ave., Hayes 155 BU77
Sutherland Ave., Orp. 205 ET100
Sutherland Ave. 65 DK28
(Cuffley), Pot.B.
Sutherland Ave., Sun. 195 BT96
Sutherland Ave., Well. 165 ES84
Sutherland Ave., West. 238 EK117
Sutherland Clo., Barn. 79 CY42
Sutherland Clo., Green. 189 FT85
Sutherland Ct. NW9 118 CP57
Sutherland Ct., Welw.G.C. 29 CZ08
Sutherland Dr. SW19 200 DD95
Willow Vw.
Sutherland Dr., Guil. 243 AZ131
Sutherland Gdns. SW14 158 CS83
Sutherland Gdns., Sun. 195 BT96
Sutherland Ave.
Sutherland Gdns., Wor.Pk. 199 CV102
Sutherland Gro. SW18 179 CY86
Sutherland Gro., Tedd. 177 CE92
Sutherland Pl. W2 140 DA72
Sutherland Pt. E5 122 DV63
Tiger Way
Sutherland Rd. E17 101 DX54
Sutherland Rd. N9 100 DU46
Sutherland Rd. N17 100 DU52
Sutherland Rd. W4 158 CS79
Sutherland Rd. W13 137 CG72
Sutherland Rd., Belv. 166 FA76
Sutherland Rd., Croy. 201 DN101
Sutherland Rd., Enf. 83 DX43
Sutherland Rd., Sthl. 136 BZ72
Sutherland Rd. Path E17 123 DX55
Sutherland Row SW1 277 J10
Sutherland Row SW1 161 DH78
Sutherland Sq. SE17 162 DQ78
Sutherland St. SW1 277 H10
Sutherland St. SW1 161 DH78
Sutherland Wk. SE17 162 DQ78
Sutherland Way 65 DK28
(Cuffley), Pot.B.
Sutlej Rd. SE7 164 EJ80
Sutterton St. N7 141 DM65
Sutton Ave., Slou. 152 AW75
Sutton Ave., Wok. 226 AS119
Sutton Clo., Beck. 203 EB95
Albemarle Rd.
Sutton Clo., Brox. 49 DY20
Sutton Clo., Loug. 102 EL45
Sutton Clo., Pnr. 115 BU57
Sutton Common Rd., Sutt. 199 CZ101
Sutton Ct. W4 158 CQ79
Sutton Ct. Rd. E13 144 EJ69
Sutton Ct. Rd. W4 158 CQ80
Sutton Ct. Rd., Sutt. 218 DC107
Sutton Ct. Rd., Uxb. 135 BP67
Sutton Cres., Barn. 79 CX43
Sutton Dene, Houns. 156 CB81
Sutton Est. SW3 276 C10
Sutton Est. SW3 160 DE78
Sutton Est. W10 139 CW71
Sutton Est., The N1 141 DP66
Sutton Gdns., Bark. 145 ES67
Sutton Rd.
Sutton Gdns., Croy. 202 DT99
Sutton Gdns., Red. 251 DK129
Sutton Grn., Bark. 145 ES67
Sutton Rd.
Sutton Grn. Rd., Guil. 242 AY126
Sutton Gro., Sutt. 218 DD105
Sutton Hall Rd., Houns. 156 CA80
Sutton Ho., Hem.H. 40 BL16
Sutton La., Bans. 234 DB115
Sutton La., Dor. 261 BV143
Sutton La., Houns. 156 BZ83
Sutton La., Slou. 153 BB79
Sutton La., Sutt. 218 DB111
Sutton La. N. W4 158 CQ78
Sutton La. S. W4 158 CQ79
Sutton Par. NW4 119 CW56
Church Rd.
Sutton Pk., Guil. 243 AZ127
Sutton Pk. Rd., Sutt. 218 DB107
Sutton Path, Borwd. 78 CN40
Stratfield Rd.
Sutton Pl. E9 122 DW64
Sutton Pl., Dor. 261 BT143
Sutton Pl., Slou. 153 BB79
Sutton Rd. E13 144 EF70
Sutton Rd. E17 101 DX53
Sutton Rd. N10 98 DG54
Sutton Rd., Bark. 145 ES68
Sutton Rd., Houns. 156 CA81
Sutton Rd., St.Alb. 43 CH21
Sutton Rd., Wat. 76 BW41
Sutton Row W1 273 N8
Sutton Row W1 141 DK72
Sutton Sq. E9 122 DW64
Urswick Rd.
Sutton Sq., Houns. 156 BZ81
Sutton St. E1 142 DW72
Sutton Way W10 139 CW71
Sutton Way, Houns. 156 BZ81
Suttons Ave., Horn. 128 FJ62
Suttons Gdns., Horn. 128 FK62
Suttons La., Horn. 128 FK64
Sutton's Way EC1 275 J5
Swabey Rd., Slou. 153 BA77
Swaby Rd. SW18 180 DC88
Swaffham Way N22 99 DP52
White Hart La.
Swaffield Rd. SW18 180 DB87
Swaffield Rd., Sev. 257 FJ122
Swain Clo. SW16 181 DH93
Swain Rd., Th.Hth. 202 DQ99
Swains Clo., West Dr. 154 BL75
Swains La. N6 120 DG62
Swains Rd. SW17 180 DF94
Swainson Rd. W3 159 CT75
Swaisland Dr., Dart. 187 FF85
Swaisland Rd., Dart. 187 FH85
Swakeleys Dr., Uxb. 114 BN63
Swakeleys Rd. 114 BM62
(Ickenham), Uxb.
Swale Clo., S.Ock. 148 FQ72
Swale Rd., Dart. 167 FG83
Swaledale Clo. N11 98 DG51
Ribblesdale Ave.
Swaledale Rd., Dart. 188 FQ88
Swallands Rd. SE6 183 EA90
Swallow Clo. SE14 162 DW81
Swallow Clo., Erith 167 FE81
Swallow Clo. (Chafford 169 FW77
Hundred), Grays
Swallow Clo., Green. 189 FT85
Swallow Clo., Rick. 92 BJ45
Swallow Clo., Stai. 173 BF91
Swallow Clo. 94 CC46
(Bushey), Wat.
Swallow Ct., Hert. 32 DQ09
Swallow Dr. NW10 138 CR65
Kingfisher Way
Swallow Dr., Nthlt. 136 CA68
Swallow End, Welw.G.C. 29 CZ09
Swallow Gdns. SW16 181 DK92
Swallow Gdns., Hat. 45 CU20
Swallow La., Dor. 263 CH142
Swallow La., St.Alb. 43 CH23
Swallow Pas. W1 273 J9
Swallow Pl. W1 273 J9
Swallow St. E6 144 EL71
Swallow St. W1 277 L1
Swallow St., Iver 133 BD69
Swallow Wk., Horn. 147 FH65
Heron Flight Ave.
Swallowdale, Iver 133 BD69
Swallowdale, S.Croy. 221 DX109
Swallowdale La., Hem.H. 40 BN17
Swallowfield, Egh. 172 AV93
Heronfield
Swallowfield Rd. SE7 164 EH78
Swallowfield Way, Hayes 155 BR75
Swallowfields, Grav. 190 GE90
Hillary Ave.
Swallowfields, Welw.G.C. 29 CZ09
Swallows, Harl. 36 EW11
Station Rd.
Swallows, The, Welw.G.C. 29 CZ05
Swallows Oak, Abb.L. 59 BT31
Swan & Pike Rd., Enf. 83 EA38
Swan App. E6 144 EL71
Swan Ave., Upmin. 129 FT60
Swan Clo. E17 101 DY53
Swan Clo., Chesh. 54 AP27
Swan Clo., Croy. 202 DS101
Swan Clo., Felt. 176 BY91
Swan Clo., Orp. 206 EU97
Swan Clo., Rick. 92 BK45
Parsonage Rd.
Swan Ct. SW3 160 DE78
Flood St.
Swan Ct., Guil. 242 AX132
Swan Dr. NW9 96 CS54
Swan La. EC4 279 K1
Swan La. N20 98 DC48
Swan La., Dart. 187 FF87
Swan La., Guil. 258 AX135
Swan La., Loug. 102 EJ45
Swan Mead SE1 279 M7
Swan Mead SE1 162 DS76
Swan Mill Gdns., Dor. 247 CJ134
Swan Pas. E1 142 DT73
Cartwright St.
Swan Path E10 123 EC60
Jesse Rd.
Swan Pl. SW13 159 CT82
Swan Rd. SE16 162 DW75
Swan Rd. SE18 164 EK76
Swan Rd., Felt. 176 BY92
Swan Rd., Iver 133 BF72
Swan Rd., Sthl. 136 CB72
Swan Rd., West Dr. 154 BK75
Swan St. SE1 279 J6
Swan St. SE1 162 DQ76
Swan St., Islw. 157 CH83
Swan Ter., Wind. 151 AP80
Mill La.
Swan Wk. SW3 160 DF79
Swan Wk., Rom. 127 FE57
Swan Wk., Shep. 195 BS101
Swan Way, Enf. 83 DX40
Swan Yd. N1 141 DP65
Highbury Sta. Rd.
Swanage Rd. E4 101 EC52
Swanage Rd. SW18 180 DC86
Swanage Waye, Hayes 136 BW72
Swanbourne Dr., Horn. 128 FJ64
Swanbridge Rd., Bexh. 166 FA81
Swandon Way SW18 160 DB84
Swanfield Rd., Wal.Cr. 67 DY33
Swanfield St. E2 275 P3
Swanfield St. E2 142 DT69
Swanhill, Welw.G.C. 30 DA06
Swanland Rd., Hat. 63 CV31
Swanland Rd., Pot.B. 63 CV33
Swanley Bar La., Pot.B. 64 DB28
Swanley Bypass, Sid. 207 FC96
Swanley Bypass, Swan. 207 FC96
Swanley Cres., Pot.B. 64 DB29
Swanley La., Swan. 207 FF97
Swanley Rd., Well. 166 EW81
Swanley Village Rd., Swan. 207 FH95
Swanns Meadow, Lthd. 246 CA126
Swans Clo., St.Alb. 44 CL21
Swanscombe Rd. W4 158 CS78
Swanscombe Rd. W11 139 CX74
Swanscombe St., Swans. 190 FY87
Swansea Rd., Enf. 82 DW42
Swanshope, Loug. 85 EP40
Swansland Gdns. E17 101 DY53
McEntee Ave.
Swanston Path, Wat. 94 BW48
Swanton Gdns. SW19 179 CX88
Swanton Rd., Erith 167 FB80
Swanwick Clo. SW15 179 CT87
Swanworth La., Dor. 247 CH128
Sward Rd., Orp. 206 EU100
Swaton Rd. E3 143 EA70
Swaylands Rd., Belv. 166 FA79
Swaynes La., Guil. 243 BE134
Swaynesland Rd., Eden. 255 EM134
Swaythling Clo. N18 100 DV49
Sweden Gate SE16 163 DY76
Swedenborg Gdns. E1 142 DU73
Sweeney Cres. SE1 162 DT75
Sweeps Ditch Clo., Stai. 174 BG94
Sweeps La., Egh. 173 AZ92
Sweeps La., Orp. 206 EX99
Sweet Briar, Welw.G.C. 30 DA11
Sweet Briar Grn. N9 100 DT48
Sweet Briar Gro. N9 100 DT48
Sweet Briar La., Epsom 216 CR114
Sweet Briar Wk. N18 100 DT49
Sweet La., Guil. 261 BR143
Sweetbriar Clo., Hem.H. 40 BG17
Sweetcroft La., Uxb. 134 BN66
Sweetmans Ave., Pnr. 116 BX55
Sweets Way N20 98 DD47
Swete St. E13 144 EG68
Swetenham Wk. SE18 165 EQ78
Sandbach Pl.
Sweyn Pl. SE3 164 EG82
Sweyne Rd., Swans. 190 FY86
Sweyns, Harl. 52 EX17
Swievelands Rd., West. 238 EH119
Swift Clo. E17 101 DY52
Swift Clo., Har. 116 CB61
Swift Clo., Hayes 135 BT72
Church Rd.
Swift Clo., Upmin. 129 FS60
Swift Clo., Ware 33 EC12
Swift Rd., Felt. 176 BX91
Swift Rd., Sthl. 156 BZ76
Swift St. SW6 159 CZ81
Swiftfields, Welw.G.C. 29 CZ08
Swiftsden Way, Brom. 184 EE93
Swiftsure Rd. (Chafford 169 FW77
Hundred), Grays
Swinbrook Rd. W10 139 CY71
Swinburne Ct. SE5 162 DR84
Basingdon Way
Swinburne Cres., Croy. 202 DW100
Swinburne Gdns., Til. 171 GH82
Swinburne Rd. SW15 159 CU84
Swinderby Rd., Wem. 138 CL65
Swindon Clo., Ilf. 125 ES61
Salisbury Rd.
Swindon Clo., Rom. 106 FM50
Swindon Gdns., Rom. 106 FM50
Swindon La., Rom. 106 FM50
Swindon Rd., Houns. 175 BQ86
Southern Perimeter Rd.
Swindon St. W12 139 CV74
Swinfield Clo., Felt. 176 BY91
Swinford Gdns. SW9 161 DP83
Swing Gate La., Berk. 38 AX21
Swingate La. SE18 165 ES79
Swinnerton St. E9 123 DY64
Swinton Clo., Wem. 118 CP60
Swinton Pl. WC1 274 B2
Swinton Pl. WC1 141 DM69
Swinton St. WC1 274 B2
Swinton St. WC1 141 DM69
Swires Shaw, Kes. 222 EK105
Swiss Ave., Wat. 75 BS42
Swiss Clo., Wat. 75 BS41
Swiss Ter. NW6 140 DD66
Swithland Gdns. SE9 185 EN91
Sword Clo., Brox. 49 DX20
Swyncombe Ave. W5 157 CH77
Swynford Gdns. NW4 119 CU56
Handowe Clo.
Sybil Ms. N4 121 DP58
Lothair Rd. N.
Sybil Phoenix Clo. SE8 163 DX78
Sybil Thorndike Ho. N1 142 DQ65
Clephane Rd.
Sybourn St. E17 123 DZ59
Sycamore App., Rick. 75 BQ43
Sycamore Ave. W5 157 CK76
Sycamore Ave., Hat. 45 CU19
Sycamore Ave., Hayes 135 BS73
Sycamore Ave., Sid. 185 ET86
Sycamore Ave., Upmin. 128 FN62
Sycamore Clo. E16 144 EE70
Clarence Rd.
Sycamore Clo. N9 100 DU49
Pycroft Way
Sycamore Clo. SE9 184 EL89
Sycamore Clo. W3 138 CS74
Bromyard Ave.
Sycamore Clo., Amer. 55 AR37
Sycamore Clo., Barn. 80 DD44
Sycamore Clo., Cars. 218 DF105
Sycamore Clo., Ch.St.G. 90 AU48
Sycamore Clo., Felt. 175 BU90
Sycamore Clo., Grav. 191 GK87
Sycamore Clo., Lthd. 231 CE123
Sycamore Clo., Loug. 85 EP40
Cedar Dr.
Sycamore Clo., Nthlt. 136 BY67
Sycamore Clo., Wal.Cr. 66 DT27
Sycamore Clo., Wat. 75 BV35
Sycamore Clo. 76 BY40
(Bushey), Wat.
Sycamore Clo., West Dr. 134 BM73
Whitethorn Ave.
Sycamore Ct., Surb. 198 CL101
Penners Gdns.
Sycamore Dene, Chesh. 54 AR28
Sycamore Dr., Brwd. 108 FW46
Copperfield Gdns.
Sycamore Dr., St.Alb. 61 CD27
Sycamore Dr., Swan. 207 FE97
Sycamore Fld., Harl. 51 EN19
Broadley Rd.
Sycamore Gdns. W6 159 CV75
Sycamore Gdns., Mitch. 200 DD96
Sycamore Gro. NW9 118 CQ59
Sycamore Gro. SE6 183 EC86
Sycamore Gro. SE20 182 DU94
Sycamore Gro., N.Mal. 198 CR97
Sycamore Hill N11 98 DG51
Sycamore Ms. SW4 161 DJ83
Sycamore Ri., Bans. 217 CX114
Sycamore Ri., Berk. 38 AX20
Sycamore Ri., Ch.St.G. 90 AU48
Sycamore Rd. SW19 179 CW93
Sycamore Rd., Amer. 55 AQ37
Sycamore Rd., Ch.St.G. 90 AU48
Sycamore Rd., Dart. 188 FK87
Sycamore Rd., Guil. 242 AX134
Sycamore Rd., Rick. 75 BQ43
Sycamore St. EC1 275 H5
Sycamore Wk. W10 139 CY70
Fifth Ave.
Sycamore Wk., Egh. 172 AV93
Sycamore Wk., Ilf. 125 EQ56
Civic Way
Sycamore Wk., Reig. 266 DC136
Sycamore Wk., Slou. 132 AY72
Sycamore Way, S.Ock. 149 FX70
Sycamore Way, Tedd. 177 CJ93
Sycamore Way, Th.Hth. 201 DN99
Sycamores, The, Hem.H. 39 BF23
Sycamores, The, Rad. 61 CH34
The Ave.
Sycamores, The, S.Ock. 149 FR74
Dacre Ave.
Sydenham Ave. N21 81 DM43
Sydenham Ave. SE26 182 DV92
Sydenham Clo., Rom. 127 FF56
Sydenham Cotts. SE12 184 EJ89
Sydenham Hill SE23 182 DV88
Sydenham Hill SE26 182 DU90
Sydenham Hill Est. SE26 182 DU90
Sydenham Pk. SE26 182 DW90
Sydenham Pk. Rd. SE26 182 DW90
Sydenham Ri. SE23 182 DV89
Sydenham Rd. SE26 182 DW92
Sydenham Rd., Croy. 202 DR101
Sydenham Rd., Guil. 258 AX136
Sydmons Ct. SE23 182 DW87
Sydner Ms. N16 122 DT63
Sydner Rd.
Sydner Rd. N16 122 DT63
Sydney Ave., Pur. 219 DM112
Sydney Clo. SW3 276 A9
Sydney Clo. SW3 160 DD77
Sydney Cres., Ashf. 175 BP93
Sydney Gro. NW4 119 CW57
Sydney Gro., Slou. 131 AQ72
Sydney Ms. SW3 276 A9
Sydney Ms. SW3 160 DD77
Sydney Pl. SW7 276 A9
Sydney Pl. SW7 160 DD77
Sydney Pl., Guil. 259 AZ135
Sydney Rd. E11 124 EH58
Mansfield Rd.
Sydney Rd. N8 121 DN56
Sydney Rd. N10 98 DG53
Sydney Rd. SE2 166 EW76
Sydney Rd. SW20 199 CX96
Sydney Rd. W13 137 CG74
Sydney Rd., Bexh. 166 EX84
Sydney Rd., Enf. 82 DR42
Sydney Rd., Felt. 175 BU88
Sydney Rd., Guil. 259 AZ135
Sydney Rd., Ilf. 103 EQ54
Sydney Rd., Rich. 158 CL84
Sydney Rd., Sid. 185 ES91
Sydney Rd., Sutt. 218 DA105
Sydney Rd., Tedd. 177 CF92
Sydney Rd., Til. 171 GG82
Sydney Rd., Wat. 75 BS43
Sydney Rd., Wdf.Grn. 102 EG49
Sydney St. SW3 276 B10
Sydney St. SW3 160 DE77
Syke Cluan, Iver 153 BE75
Syke Ings, Iver 153 BE76
Sykes Dr., Stai. 174 BH92
Sykes Rd., Slou. 131 AP72
Sylvan Ave. N3 98 DA54
Sylvan Ave. N22 99 DM52
Sylvan Ave. NW7 97 CT51
Sylvan Ave., Horn. 128 FL58
Sylvan Ave., Rom. 126 EZ58
Sylvan Clo., Grays 170 FY77
Warren La.
Sylvan Clo., Hem.H. 40 BN21
Sylvan Clo., Oxt. 254 EH129
Sylvan Clo., S.Croy. 220 DV110
Sylvan Clo., Wok. 227 BB117
Sylvan Est. SE19 202 DT95
Sylvan Gdns., Surb. 197 CK101
Sylvan Gro. NW2 119 CX63
Sylvan Gro. SE15 162 DV79
Sylvan Hill SE19 202 DS95
Sylvan Rd. E7 144 EG65
Sylvan Rd. E11 124 EG57
Sylvan Rd. E17 123 EA57
Sylvan Rd. SE19 202 DT95
Sylvan Rd., Ilf. 125 EQ61
Hainault St.
Sylvan Wk., Brom. 205 EM97
Sylvan Way, Chig. 104 EV48
Sylvan Way, Dag. 126 EV62
Sylvan Way, Red. 266 DG135
Sylvan Way, W.Wick. 222 EE105
Sylvana Clo., Uxb. 134 BM67
Sylvandale, Welw.G.C. 30 DC10
Sylverdale Rd., Croy. 201 DP104
Sylverdale Rd., Pur. 219 DP113
Sylvester Ave., Chis. 185 EM93
Sylvester Gdns., Ilf. 104 EV50

Sylvester Path E8 142 DV65
Sylvester Rd.
Sylvester Rd. E8 142 DV65
Sylvester Rd. E17 123 DZ59
Sylvester Rd. N2 98 DC54
Sylvester Rd., Wem. 117 CJ64
Sylvestres, Sev. 241 FD119
London Rd.
Sylvestrus Clo., Kings.T. 198 CN95
Sylvia Ave., Brwd. 109 GC47
Sylvia Ave., Pnr. 94 BZ51
Sylvia Ct., Wem. 138 CP66
Harrow Rd.
Sylvia Gdns., Wem. 138 CP66
Symes Ms. NW1 141 DJ68
Camden High St.
Symonds Ct. (Cheshunt), Wal.Cr. 67 DX28
High St.
Symons St. SW3 276 E9
Symons St. SW3 160 DF77
Syon Gate Way, Brent. 157 CG80
Syon La., Islw. 157 CH80
Syon Pk. Gdns., Islw. 157 CF80
Syon Vista, Rich. 157 CK81
Syracuse Ave., Rain. 148 FL69
Syringa Ct., Grays 170 GD80
Sythwood, Wok. 226 AV117

T

Tabard Gdn. Est. SE1 279 L5
Tabard Gdn. Est. SE1 162 DR75
Tabard St. SE1 279 K5
Tabard St. SE1 162 DR75
Tabarin Way, Epsom 233 CW116
Tabernacle Ave. E13 144 EG70
Barking Rd.
Tabernacle St. EC2 275 L5
Tabernacle St. EC2 142 DR70
Tableer Ave. SW4 181 DK85
Tabley Rd. N7 121 DL63
Tabor Gdns., Sutt. 217 CZ107
Tabor Gro. SW19 179 CY94
Tabor Rd. W6 159 CV76
Tabrums Way, Upmin. 129 FS59
Tachbrook Est. SW1 161 DK78
Tachbrook Ms. SW1 277 K8
Tachbrook Rd., Felt. 175 BT87
Tachbrook Rd., Sthl. 156 BX77
Tachbrook Rd., Uxb. 134 BJ68
Tachbrook St. SW1 277 L9
Tachbrook St. SW1 161 DJ77
Tack Ms. SE4 163 EA83
Tadema Rd. SW10 160 DC80
Tadlows Clo., Upmin. 128 FP64
Tadmor Clo., Sun. 195 BT98
Tadmor St. W12 139 CX74
Tadorne Rd., Tad. 233 CW121
Tadworth Ave., N.Mal. 199 CT99
Tadworth Clo., Tad. 233 CX122
Tadworth Par., Horn. 127 FH63
Maylands Ave.
Tadworth Rd. NW2 119 CU61
Tadworth St., Tad. 233 CW123
Taeping St. E14 163 EB77
Taffy's How, Mitch. 200 DE97
Taft Way E3 143 EB69
St. Leonards St.
Tagalie Pl. (Shenley), Rad. 62 CL32
Porters Pk. Dr.
Tagg's Island, Hmptn. 197 CD96
Tailworth St. E1 142 DU71
Chicksand St.
Tait Rd., Croy. 202 DS101
Takeley Clo., Rom. 105 FD54
Takeley Clo., Wal.Abb. 67 ED33
Takhar Ms. SW11 160 DE82
Cabul Rd.
Talacre Rd. NW5 140 DG65
Talbot Ave. N2 120 DD55
Talbot Ave., Slou. 153 AZ76
Talbot Ave., Wat. 94 BY45
Talbot Clo. N15 122 DT56
Talbot Clo., Reig. 266 DB135
Talbot Ct. EC3 275 L10
Talbot Ct., Hem.H. 40 BK22
Crabtree La.
Talbot Cres. NW4 119 CU57
Talbot Gdns., Ilf. 126 EU61
Talbot Ho. E14 143 EB72
Giraud St.
Talbot Pl. SE3 164 EE82
Talbot Pl., Slou. 152 AW81
Talbot Rd. E6 145 EN68
Talbot Rd. E7 124 EG63
Talbot Rd. N6 120 DG58
Talbot Rd. N15 122 DT56
Talbot Rd. N22 99 DJ54
Talbot Rd. SE22 162 DS84
Talbot Rd. W2 139 CZ72
Talbot Rd. W11 139 CZ72
Talbot Rd. W13 137 CG73
Talbot Rd., Ashf. 174 BK92
Talbot Rd., Brom. 204 EH98
Masons Hill
Talbot Rd., Cars. 218 DG106
Talbot Rd., Dag. 146 EZ65
Talbot Rd., Har. 95 CF54
Talbot Rd., Hat. 45 CU15
Talbot Rd., Islw. 157 CG84
Talbot Rd., Rick. 92 BL46
Talbot Rd., Sthl. 156 BY77
Talbot Rd., Th.Hth. 202 DR98
Talbot Rd., Twick. 177 CE88
Talbot Rd., Wem. 117 CK64
Talbot Sq. W2 272 A9
Talbot Sq. W2 140 DD72
Talbot St., Hert. 32 DS09
Talbot Wk. NW10 138 CS65
Garnet Rd.
Talbot Wk. W11 139 CY72
Talbot Yd. SE1 279 K3
Talbrook, Brwd. 108 FT48
Taleworth Clo., Ash. 231 CK120
Taleworth Pk., Ash. 231 CK120
Taleworth Rd., Ash. 231 CK119
Talfourd Pl. SE15 162 DT81
Talfourd Rd. SE15 162 DT81
Talgarth Rd. W6 159 CY78
Talgarth Rd. W14 159 CY78
Talgarth Wk. NW9 118 CS57
Talisman Clo., Ilf. 126 EV60
Talisman Sq. SE26 182 DU91
Talisman Way, Epsom 233 CW116
Talisman Way, Wem. 118 CM62
Tall Elms Clo., Brom. 204 EF99
Tall Oaks, Amer. 55 AR37
Tall Trees SW16 201 DM97
Tall Trees, Slou. 153 BE81
Tall Trees Clo., Horn. 128 FK58
Tallack Clo., Har. 95 CE52
College Hill Rd.
Tallack Rd. E10 123 DZ60
Tallents Clo. (Sutton at Hone), Dart. 188 FP94
Tallis Clo. E16 144 EH72
Tallis Gro. SE7 164 EH79
Tallis St. EC4 274 E10
Tallis St. EC4 141 DN73
Tallis Vw. NW10 138 CR65
Tallis Way, Borwd. 77 CK39
Tallon Rd., Brwd. 109 GE43
Tally Ho Cor. N12 98 DC50
Tally Rd., Oxt. 254 EL131
Talma Gdns., Twick. 177 CE86
Talma Rd. SW2 161 DN84
Talmage Clo. SE23 182 DW87
Tyson Rd.
Talman Gro., Stan. 95 CK51
Talus Clo., Purf. 169 FR77
Brimfield Rd.
Talwin St. E3 143 EB69
Tamar Clo. E3 143 DZ67
Lefevre Wk.
Tamar Clo., Upmin. 129 FS58
Tamar Dr., S.Ock. 148 FQ72
Tamar Grn., Hem.H. 40 BM15
Tamar Sq., Wdf.Grn. 102 EH51
Tamar St. SE7 164 EL76
Woolwich Rd.
Tamar Way N17 122 DU55
Tamar Way, Slou. 153 BB78
Tamarind Clo., Guil. 242 AU129
Tamarind Yd. E1 142 DU74
Asher Way
Tamarisk Clo., St.Alb. 43 CD16
New Grns. Ave.
Tamarisk Clo., S.Ock. 149 FW70
Tamarisk Rd., S.Ock. 149 FW69
Tamarisk Sq. W12 139 CT73
Tamarisk Way, Slou. 151 AN75
Tamerton Sq., Wok. 226 AY118
Tamesis Gdns., Wor.Pk. 198 CS102
Tamesis Strand, Grav. 191 GL92
Tamian Way, Houns. 156 BW84
Tamworth Ave., Wdf.Grn. 102 EE51
Tamworth La., Mitch. 201 DH96
Tamworth Pk., Mitch. 201 DH98
Tamworth Pl., Croy. 202 DQ103
Tamworth Rd., Croy. 201 DP103
Tamworth Rd., Hert. 32 DT08
Tamworth St. SW6 160 DA79
Tancred Rd. N4 121 DP58
Tandridge Ct., Cat. 236 DU122
Tandridge Dr., Orp. 205 ER102
Tandridge Gdns., S.Croy. 220 DT113
Tandridge Hill La., Gdse. 253 DZ128
Tandridge La., Oxt. 253 EA131
Tandridge Pl., Orp. 205 ER101
Tandridge Dr.
Tandridge Rd., Warl. 237 DX119
Tanfield Ave. NW2 119 CT63
Tanfield Clo., Wal.Cr. 66 DU27
Tanfield Rd., Croy. 220 DQ105
Tangent Rd., Rom. 106 FK53
Ashton Rd.
Tangier La. (Eton), Wind. 151 AR79
Tangier Rd., Guil. 259 BA135
Tangier Rd., Rich. 158 CP83
Tangier Way, Tad. 233 CY117
Tangier Wd., Tad. 233 CY118
Tangle Tree Clo. N3 98 DB54
Tanglebury Clo., Brom. 205 EM98
Tanglewood Clo., Cher. 192 AV104
Tanglewood Clo., Croy. 202 DW104
Tanglewood Clo., Stan. 95 CE47
Tanglewood Clo., Uxb. 134 BN69
Tanglewood Clo., Wok. 227 BD116
Tanglewood Way, Felt. 175 BV90
Tangley Gro. SW15 179 CT86
Tangley La., Guil. 242 AT130
Tangley Pk. Rd., Hmptn. 176 BZ92
Tanglyn Ave., Shep. 194 BN99
Tangmere Cres., Horn. 147 FH65
Tangmere Gdns., Nthlt. 136 BW68
Tangmere Gro., Kings.T. 177 CK92
Tangmere Way NW9 96 CS54
Tanhouse Rd., Oxt. 253 ED132
Tanhurst Wk. SE2 166 EX76
Alsike Rd.
Tank Hill Rd., Purf. 168 FN78
Tank La., Purf. 168 FN77
Tankerton Rd., Surb. 198 CM103
Tankerton St. WC1 274 A3
Tankerville Rd. SW16 181 DK93
Tankridge Rd. NW2 119 CV61
Tanner St. SE1 279 N5
Tanner St. SE1 162 DS75
Tanner St., Bark. 145 EQ65
Tanners Clo., St.Alb. 42 CC19
Tanners Clo., Walt. 195 BV100
Tanners Cres., Hert. 32 DQ11
Tanners Dean, Lthd. 231 CJ122
Tanners End La. N18 100 DS49
Tanners Hill SE8 163 DZ81
Tanners Hill, Abb.L. 59 BT31
Tanners La., Ilf. 125 EQ55
Tanners Meadow, Bet. 264 CP138
Tanners Way, Ware 34 EJ06
Tanners Wd. Clo., Abb.L. 59 BS32
Tanners Wd. La.
Tanners Wd. La., Abb.L. 59 BS32
Tannersfield, Guil. 258 AY142
Tannery, The, Red. 250 DE134
Oakdene Rd.
Tannery Clo., Beck. 203 DX99
Tannery Clo., Dag. 127 FB62
Tannery La., Guil. 258 AY144
Tannery La., Wok. 227 BD123
Tannington Ter. N5 121 DN62
Tannsfeld Rd. SE26 183 DX92
Tannsfield Dr., Hem.H. 40 BM18
Tannsmore Clo., Hem.H. 40 BM18
Tansley Clo. N7 121 DK64
Hilldrop Rd.
Tanswell Est. SE1 278 E5
Tanswell St. SE1 278 D5
Tansy Clo. E6 145 EN72
Tansy Clo., Guil. 243 BC132
Tansy Clo., Rom. 106 FL51
Tansycroft, Welw.G.C. 30 DB08
Tant Ave. E16 144 EF72
Tantallon Rd. SW12 180 DG88
Tantony Gro., Rom. 126 EX55
Tanworth Clo., Nthwd. 93 BQ51
Tanworth Gdns., Pnr. 93 BV54
Tanyard La., Bex. 186 FA87
Bexley High St.
Tanyard Way, Horl. 269 DH146
Tanys Dell, Harl. 36 EU12
Tanza Rd. NW3 120 DF63
Tapestry Clo., Sutt. 218 DB108
Taplow NW3 140 DD66
Taplow SE17 162 DS78
Thurlow St.
Taplow Common Rd., Slou. 130 AF65
Taplow Rd. N13 100 DQ49
Taplow Rd., Maid. 130 AG71
Taplow St. N1 275 J1
Taplow St. N1 142 DQ68
Tapners Rd., Reig. 265 CT139
Tapp St. E1 142 DV70
Tappesfield Rd. SE15 162 DW83
Tapster St., Barn. 79 CZ42
Taransay, Hem.H. 41 BP22
Taransay Wk. N1 142 DR65
Marquess Rd.
Tarbay La., Wind. 150 AH82
Tarbert Rd. SE22 182 DS85
Tarbert Wk. E1 142 DW73
Juniper St.
Target Clo., Felt. 175 BS86
Tarham Clo., Horl. 268 DE146
Tariff Cres. SE8 163 DZ77
Tariff Rd. N17 100 DU51
Tarleton Gdns. SE23 182 DV88
Tarling Clo., Sid. 186 EV90
Tarling Rd. E16 144 EF72
Tarling Rd. N2 98 DC54
Tarling St. E1 142 DV72
Tarling St. Est. E1 142 DW72
Tarmac Way, West Dr. 154 BH80
Tarn St. SE1 279 H7
Tarnbank, Enf. 81 DL43
Tarnwood Pk. SE9 185 EM88
Tarnworth Rd., Rom. 106 FN50
Tarpan Way, Brox. 67 DZ26
Tarquin Ho. SE26 182 DU91
Tarragon Clo. SE14 163 DY80
Tarragon Dr., Guil. 242 AU129
Tarragon Gro. SE26 183 DX93
Tarrant Pl. W1 272 D7
Tarrington Clo. SW16 181 DK90
Tarry La. SE8 163 DY77
Tartar Rd., Cob. 214 BW113
Tarver Rd. SE17 161 DP78
Tarves Way SE10 163 EB80
Tash Pl. N11 99 DH50
Woodland Rd.
Tasker Clo., Hayes 155 BQ80
Tasker Ho., Bark. 145 ER68
Dovehouse Mead
Tasker Rd. NW3 120 DF64
Tasker Rd., Grays 171 GH76
Tasman Rd. SW9 161 DL83
Tasman Wk. E16 144 EK72
Royal Rd.
Tasmania Ho., Til. 171 GG81
Hobart Rd.
Tasmania Ter. N18 100 DQ51
Tasso Rd. W6 159 CY79
Tatam Rd. NW10 138 CQ66
Tate & Lyle Jetty E16 164 EL75
Tate Clo., Lthd. 231 CJ123
Windmill Dr.
Tate Rd. E16 145 EM74
Newland St.
Tate Rd., Ger.Cr. 91 AZ50
Tate Rd., Sutt. 218 DA106
Tatnell Rd. SE23 183 DY86
Tatsfield App. Rd., West. 238 EH123
Tatsfield Ave., Wal.Abb. 49 ED23
Tatsfield La., West. 238 EL121
Tattenham Cor. Rd., Epsom 232 CS117
Tattenham Cres., Epsom 233 CU118
Tattenham Gro., Epsom 233 CV118
Tattenham Way, Tad. 233 CX118
Tattersall Clo. SE9 184 EL85
Tattle Hill, Hert. 31 DL05
Tatton Cres. N16 122 DT59
Clapton Common
Tatum St. SE17 279 L9
Tatum St. SE17 162 DR77
Tauber Clo., Borwd. 78 CM42
Tauheed Clo. N4 122 DQ61
Taunton Ave. SW20 199 CV96
Taunton Ave., Cat. 236 DT123
Taunton Ave., Houns. 156 CC82
Taunton Clo., Bexh. 167 FD82
Taunton Clo., Ilf. 103 ET51
Taunton Clo., Sutt. 200 DA102
Taunton Dr. N2 98 DC54
Taunton Dr., Enf. 81 DN41
Taunton La., Couls. 235 DN119
Taunton Ms. NW1 272 D5
Taunton Pl. NW1 272 D4
Taunton Pl. NW1 140 DF70
Taunton Rd. SE12 184 EE85
Taunton Rd., Grav. 190 GA85
Taunton Rd., Grnf. 136 CB67
Taunton Rd., Rom. 106 FJ49
Taunton Vale, Grav. 191 GK89
Taunton Way, Stan. 118 CL55
Tavern Clo., Cars. 200 DE101
Tavern La. SW9 161 DN82
Taverner Sq. N5 122 DQ63
Highbury Gra.
Taverners, Hem.H. 40 BL18
Taverners Clo. W11 139 CY74
Addison Ave.
Taverners Way E4 102 EE46
Douglas Rd.
Taverners Way, Hodd. 49 EA17
Tavistock Ave. E17 123 DY55
Tavistock Ave., Grnf. 137 CG68
Tavistock Ave., St.Alb. 43 CD23
Tavistock Clo. N16 122 DS64
Crossway
Tavistock Clo., Pot.B. 64 DD31
Tavistock Clo., Rom. 106 FK53
Tavistock Clo., St.Alb. 43 CD23
Tavistock Clo., Stai. 174 BK94
Tavistock Cres. W11 139 CZ71
Tavistock Cres., Mitch. 201 DL98
Tavistock Gdns., Ilf. 125 ES63
Tavistock Gate, Croy. 202 DR102
Tavistock Gro., Croy. 202 DR101
Tavistock Ms. E18 124 EG56
Avon Way
Tavistock Ms. W11 139 CZ72
Lancaster Rd.
Tavistock Pl. E18 124 EG55
Avon Way
Tavistock Pl. N14 99 DH45
Chase Side
Tavistock Pl. WC1 273 N4
Tavistock Pl. WC1 141 DL70
Tavistock Rd. E7 124 EF63
Tavistock Rd. E15 144 EF65
Tavistock Rd. E18 124 EG55
Tavistock Rd. N4 122 DR58
Tavistock Rd. NW10 139 CT68
Tavistock Rd. W11 139 CZ71
Tavistock Rd., Brom. 204 EF98
Tavistock Rd., Cars. 200 DD102
Tavistock Rd., Croy. 202 DR102
Tavistock Rd., Edg. 96 CN53
Tavistock Rd., Uxb. 115 BQ64
Tavistock Rd., Wat. 76 BX39
Tavistock Rd., Well. 166 EW81
Tavistock Rd., West Dr. 134 BK74
Tavistock Sq. WC1 273 N4
Tavistock Sq. WC1 141 DK70
Tavistock St. WC2 274 A10
Tavistock St. WC2 141 DL73
Tavistock Ter. N19 121 DK62
Tavistock Wk., Cars. 200 DD102
Tavistock Rd.
Taviton St. WC1 273 M4
Taviton St. WC1 141 DK70
Tavy Clo. SE11 278 E10
Tavy Clo. SE11 161 DN78
Tawney Common, Epp. 70 FA32
Tawney Rd. SE28 146 EV73
Tawneys Rd., Harl. 51 ES16
Tawny Ave., Upmin. 128 FP64
Tawny Clo. W13 137 CH74
Tawny Clo., Felt. 175 BU90
Chervil Clo.
Tawny Way SE16 163 DX77
Tay Way, Rom. 105 FF53
Tayben Ave., Twick. 177 CE86
Taybridge Rd. SW11 160 DG83
Tayburn Clo. E14 143 EC72
Tayfield Clo., Uxb. 115 BQ62
Tayler Cotts., Pot.B. 63 CT34
Crossoaks La.
Tayles Hill, Epsom 217 CT110
Tayles Hill Dr.
Tayles Hill Dr., Epsom 217 CT110
Taylifers, Harl. 51 EN20
Taylor Ave., Rich. 158 CP82
Taylor Clo. N17 100 DU52
Taylor Clo., Epsom 216 CN111
Williams Evans Rd.
Taylor Clo., Hmptn. 176 CC92
Taylor Clo., Houns. 156 CC81
Taylor Clo., Orp. 223 ET105
Taylor Clo., Rom. 104 FA52
Taylor Clo., St.Alb. 43 CG15
Taylor Clo., Uxb. 92 BJ53
High St.
Taylor Ct. E15 123 EC64
Clays La.
Taylor Rd., Ash. 231 CK117
Taylor Rd., Mitch. 180 DE94
Taylor Rd., Wall. 219 DH106
Taylors Ave., Hodd. 49 EA18
Taylors Bldgs. SE18 165 EP77
Spray St.
Taylors Clo., Sid. 185 ET91
Taylors Grn. W3 138 CS72
Long Dr.
Taylors La. NW10 138 CS66
Taylors La. SE26 182 DV91
Taylors La., Barn. 79 CZ39
Taylors Rd., Chesh. 54 AR29
Taymount Ri. SE23 182 DW89
Taynton Dr., Red. 251 DK129
Tayport Clo. N1 141 DL66
Tayside Dr., Edg. 96 CP48
Taywood Rd., Nthlt. 136 BZ69
Teak Clo. SE16 143 DY74
Teal Ave., Orp. 206 EX98
Teal Clo. E16 144 EK71
Fulmer Rd.
Teal Clo., S.Croy. 221 DX111
Teal Dr., Nthwd. 93 BQ52
Teale St. E2 142 DU68
Tealing Dr., Epsom 216 CR105
Teardrop Ind. Est., Swan. 207 FH99
Teasel Clo., Croy. 203 DX102
Teasel Way E15 144 EE69
Teazle Wd. Hill, Lthd. 231 CE117
Oaklawn Rd.
Teazlewood Pk., Lthd. 231 CG117
Tebworth Rd. N17 100 DT52
Teck Clo., Islw. 157 CG82
Tedder Clo., Chess. 215 CJ107
Tedder Clo., Ruis. 115 BV64
West End Rd.
Tedder Clo., Uxb. 134 BM66
Tedder Rd., Hem.H. 40 BN19
Tedder Rd., S.Croy. 220 DW108
Teddington Clo., Epsom 216 CR110
Teddington Lock, Tedd. 177 CG91
Teddington Pk., Tedd. 177 CF92
Teddington Pk. Rd., Tedd. 177 CF91
Tedworth Gdns. SW3 160 DF78
Tedworth Sq.
Tedworth Sq. SW3 160 DF78
Tee, The W3 138 CS72
Tee Side, Hert. 32 DV08
Tees Ave., Grnf. 137 CE68
Tees Clo., Upmin. 129 FR59
Tees Dr., Rom. 106 FK48
Teesdale, Hem.H. 40 BL17
Teesdale Ave., Islw. 157 CG81
Teesdale Clo. E2 142 DV68
Teesdale Gdns. SE25 202 DS96
Teesdale Gdns., Islw. 157 CG81
Teesdale Rd. E11 124 EF58
Teesdale Rd., Dart. 188 FQ88
Teesdale Rd., Slou. 131 AM70
Teesdale St. E2 142 DV68
Teesdale Yd. E2 142 DV68
Teesdale St.
Teeswater Ct., Erith 166 EX76
Middle Way
Teevan Clo., Croy. 202 DU101
Teevan Rd., Croy. 202 DU101
Teggs La., Wok. 227 BF116
Teignmouth Clo. SW4 161 DK84
Teignmouth Clo., Edg. 96 CM54
Teignmouth Gdns., Grnf. 137 CG68
Teignmouth Rd. NW2 119 CX64
Teignmouth Rd., Well. 166 EW82
Telcote Way, Ruis. 116 BW59
Woodlands Ave.
Telegraph Hill NW3 120 DB62
Telegraph La., Esher 215 CF107
Telegraph Ms., Ilf. 126 EU60
Telegraph Pl. E14 163 EB77
Telegraph Rd. SW15 179 CV87
Telegraph St. EC2 275 K8
Telegraph Track, Cars. 218 DG110
Telemann Sq. SE3 164 EH83
Telephone Pl. SW6 159 CZ79
Lillie Rd.
Telfer Clo. W3 158 CQ75
Church Rd.
Telferscot Rd. SW12 181 DK88
Telford Ave. SW2 181 DL88
Telford Clo. E17 123 DY59
Telford Clo. SE19 182 DT93
St. Aubyn's Rd.
Telford Clo. W3 158 CQ75
Church Rd.
Telford Clo., Wat. 76 BX35
Telford Ct., Guil. 258 AY135
Clandon Rd.
Telford Ct., St.Alb. 43 CE21
Telford Dr., Slou. 151 AN75
Telford Dr., Walt. 196 BW101
Telford Rd. N11 99 DJ51
Telford Rd. NW9 119 CU58
West Hendon Bdy.
Telford Rd. SE9 185 ER89
Telford Rd. W10 139 CY71
Telford Rd., St.Alb. 61 CJ27
Telford Rd., Sthl. 136 CB73
Telford Rd., Twick. 176 CA87
Telford Ter. SW1 161 DJ79
Telford Way W3 138 CS71
Telford Way, Hayes 136 BY71
Telfords Yd. E1 142 DU73
The Highway
Telham Rd. E6 145 EN68
Tell Gro. SE22 162 DT84
Tellisford, Esher 214 CB105
Tellson Ave. SE18 164 EK81
Telscombe Clo., Orp. 205 ES103
Telston La., Sev. 241 FF117
Temeraire St. SE16 162 DW75
Albion St.
Temperance St., St.Alb. 42 CC20
Temperley Rd. SW12 180 DG87
Tempest Ave., Pot.B. 64 DC32
Tempest Rd., Egh. 173 BC93
Tempest Way, Rain. 147 FG65
Templar Dr. SE28 146 EX72
Templar Dr., Grav. 191 GG92
Templar Ho. NW2 139 CZ65
Shoot Up Hill
Templar Ho., Rain. 147 FD68
Chantry Way
Templar Pl., Hmptn. 176 CA94
Templar St. SE5 161 DP82
Templars Ave. NW11 119 CZ58
Templars Cres. N3 98 DA54
Templars Dr., Har. 95 CD51
Temple EC4 274 D9
Temple EC4 141 DN73
Temple Ave. EC4 274 E10
Temple Ave. EC4 141 DN73
Temple Ave. N20 98 DD45
Temple Ave., Croy. 203 DZ103
Temple Ave., Dag. 126 FA60
Temple Bank, Harl. 36 EV09
Temple Bar Rd., Wok. 226 AT119
Temple Clo. E11 124 EE59
Wadley Rd.
Temple Clo. N3 97 CZ54
Cyprus Rd.
Temple Clo. SE28 165 EQ76
Temple Clo., Epsom 216 CR112
Hazon Way
Temple Clo. (Cheshunt), Wal.Cr. 66 DU31
Temple Clo., Wat. 75 BT40
Temple Ct., Hert. 32 DR06
Temple Ct., Pot.B. 63 CY31
Temple Flds., Hert. 32 DR06
Temple Flds. Ind. Area, Harl. 36 EU11
Temple Fortune Hill NW11 120 DA57
Temple Fortune La. NW11 120 DA58
Temple Fortune Par. NW11 119 CZ57
Finchley Rd.
Temple Gdns. N21 99 DP47
Barrowell Grn.
Temple Gdns. NW11 119 CZ58
Temple Gdns., Dag. 126 EX62
Temple Gdns., Rick. 93 BP49
Temple Gdns., Stai. 193 BF95
Temple Gro. NW11 120 DA58
Temple Gro., Enf. 81 DP41
Temple Hill, Dart. 188 FM86
Temple Hill Sq., Dart. 188 FM85
Temple La. EC4 274 E9
Temple Mead, Harl. 50 EH15
Temple Mead, Hem.H. 40 BK18
Temple Mead Clo., Stan. 95 CH51
Temple Mill La. E15 123 EB63
Temple Pk., Uxb. 134 BN69
Temple Pl. WC2 274 C10
Temple Pl. WC2 141 DM73
Temple Rd. E6 144 EL67
Temple Rd. N8 121 DM56
Temple Rd. NW2 119 CW63
Temple Rd. W4 158 CQ76
Temple Rd. W5 157 CK76
Temple Rd., Croy. 220 DR105
Temple Rd., Epsom 216 CR112
Temple Rd., Houns. 156 CB84
Temple Rd., Rich. 158 CM83
Temple Rd., West. 238 EK117
Temple Rd., Wind. 151 AQ82
Temple Sheen SW14 178 CQ85
Temple Sheen Rd. SW14 158 CP84
Temple St. E2 142 DV68
Temple Vw., St.Alb. 42 CC18
Temple Way, Slou. 111 AQ64
Temple Way, Sutt. 200 DD104
Temple W. Ms. SE11 278 F7
Temple W. Ms. SE11 161 DP76
Temple Wd. Dr., Red. 250 DF131
Templecombe Ms., Wok. 227 BA116
Dorchester Ct.
Templecombe Rd. E9 142 DW67
Templecombe Way, Mord. 199 CY99
Templecroft, Ashf. 175 BR93
Templedene Ave., Stai. 174 BH94
Templefield Clo., Add. 212 BH107

Templehof Ave. NW2 119 CW59
Templeman Clo., Pur. 235 DP116
Croftleigh Ave.
Templeman Rd. W7 137 CF71
Templemead Clo. W3 138 CS72
Templemere, Wey. 195 BR104
Templepan La., Rick. 74 BL37
Templer Ave., Grays 171 GG77
Templeton Ave. E4 101 EA49
Templeton Clo. N16 122 DS64
Truman's Rd.
Templeton Clo. SE19 202 DR95
Templeton Pl. SW5 160 DA77
Templeton Rd. N15 122 DR58
Templewood W13 137 CH71
Templewood, Welw.G.C. 29 CX06
Templewood Ave. NW3 120 DB62
Templewood Gdns. NW3 120 DB62
Templewood La., Slou. 111 AQ64
Templewood Pk., Slou. 112 AT63
Tempsford, Welw.G.C. 30 DD09
Tempsford Ave., Borwd. 78 CR42
Tempsford Clo., Enf. 82 DQ41
Gladbeck Way
Temsford Clo., Har. 94 CC54
Ten Acre, Wok. 226 AU118
Abercorn Way
Ten Acre La., Egh. 193 BC96
Ten Acres, Lthd. 231 CD124
Ten Acres Clo., Lthd. 231 CD124
Tenbury Clo. E7 124 EK64
Romford Rd.
Tenbury Ct. SW2 181 DK88
Tenby Ave., Har. 95 CH54
Tenby Clo. N15 122 DT56
Hanover Rd.
Tenby Clo., Rom. 126 EY58
Tenby Gdns., Nthlt. 136 CA65
Tenby Rd. E17 123 DY57
Tenby Rd., Edg. 96 CM53
Tenby Rd., Enf. 82 DW41
Tenby Rd., Rom. 126 EY58
Tenby Rd., Well. 166 EX81
Tench St. E1 142 DV74
Tenchleys La., Oxt. 254 EK131
Tenda Rd. SE16 162 DV77
Roseberry St.
Tendring Rd., Harl. 51 EQ17
Tendring Way, Rom. 126 EW57
Tenham Ave. SW2 181 DK88
Tenison Ct. W1 273 K10
Tenison Way SE1 278 D3
Tenison Way SE1 141 DM74
Tennand Clo. (Cheshunt), Wal.Cr. 66 DT26
Tenniel Clo. W2 140 DC72
Porchester Gdns.
Tennis Ct. La., E.Mol. 197 CF97
Hampton Ct. Way
Tennis St. SE1 279 K4
Tennis St. SE1 162 DR75
Tennison Ave., Borwd. 78 CP43
Tennison Clo., Couls. 235 DP120
Tennison Rd. SE25 202 DT98
Tenniswood Rd., Enf. 82 DT39
Tennyson Ave. E11 124 EG59
Tennyson Ave. E12 144 EL66
Tennyson Ave. NW9 118 CQ55
Tennyson Ave., Grays 170 GB76
Tennyson Ave., N.Mal. 199 CV99
Tennyson Ave., Twick. 177 CF88
Tennyson Ave., Wal.Abb. 68 EE34
Tennyson Clo., Enf. 83 DX43
Tennyson Clo., Felt. 175 BT86
Tennyson Clo., Well. 165 ET81
Tennyson Rd. E10 123 EB61
Tennyson Rd. E15 144 EE66
Tennyson Rd. E17 123 DZ58
Tennyson Rd. NW6 139 CZ67
Tennyson Rd. NW7 97 CU50
Tennyson Rd. SE20 183 DX94
Tennyson Rd. SW19 180 DC93
Tennyson Rd. W7 137 CF73
Tennyson Rd., Add. 212 BL105
Tennyson Rd., Ashf. 174 BL92
Tennyson Rd., Brwd. 109 GC45
Tennyson Rd., Dart. 188 FN85
Tennyson Rd., Houns. 156 CC82
Tennyson Rd., Rom. 106 FJ52
Tennyson Rd., St.Alb. 60 CA26
Tennyson St. SW8 161 DH82
Tennyson Wk., Grav. 190 GD90
Tennyson Wk., Til. 171 GH82
Tennyson Way, Horn. 127 FF61
Tennyson Way, Slou. 131 AL70
Wordsworth Rd.
Tensing Ave., Grav. 190 GE90
Tensing Rd., Sthl. 156 CA76
Tent Peg La., Orp. 205 EQ99
Tent St. E1 142 DV70
Tentelow La., Sthl. 156 CA78
Tenter Grd. E1 275 P7
Tenter Pas. E1 142 DT72
Mansell St.
Tenterden Clo. NW4 119 CX55
Tenterden Clo. SE9 185 EM91
Tenterden Dr. NW4 119 CX55
Tenterden Gdns. NW4 119 CX55
Tenterden Gdns., Croy. 202 DU101
Tenterden Gro. NW4 119 CX56
Tenterden Rd. N17 100 DT52
Tenterden Rd., Croy. 202 DU101
Tenterden Rd., Dag. 126 EZ61
Tenterden St. W1 273 J9
Tenterden St. W1 141 DH72
Tenzing Rd., Hem.H. 40 BN20
Terborch Way SE22 182 DS85
East Dulwich Gro.
Tercel Path, Chig. 104 EV49
Teredo St. SE16 163 DX76
Terence Clo., Grav. 191 GM89
Terence Ct., Belv. 166 EZ79
Nuxley Rd.
Teresa Gdns., Wal.Cr. 66 DW34
Teresa Ms. E17 123 EA56
Teresa Wk. N10 121 DH57
Connaught Gdns.
Terling Clo. E11 124 EF62
Terling Rd., Dag. 126 FA61
Terling Wk. N1 142 DQ67
Britannia Row
Terlings, The, Brwd. 108 FU48
Terminus Ho., Harl. 35 ER14
Terminus Pl. SW1 277 J7
Terminus Pl. SW1 161 DH76
Terminus St., Harl. 35 ER14
Tern Gdns., Upmin. 129 FS60
Tern Way, Brwd. 108 FS49
Terrace, The E4 102 EE48
Chingdale Rd.
Terrace, The N3 97 CZ54
Hendon La.
Terrace, The NW6 140 DA67
Terrace, The SW13 158 CS82
Terrace, The, Add. 212 BL106
Terrace, The, Dor. 263 CJ137
Deepdene Wd.
Terrace, The, Grav. 191 GH86
Terrace, The, Har. 117 CH60
Terrace, The, Maid. 150 AC76
Terrace, The, Sev. 256 FD122
Terrace, The, Wdf.Grn. 102 EG51
Broadmead Rd.
Terrace Gdns. SW13 159 CT82
Terrace Gdns., Wat. 75 BV40
Terrace La., Rich. 178 CL86
Terrace Rd. E9 142 DW66
Terrace Rd. E13 144 EG67
Terrace Rd., Walt. 195 BU101
Terrace St., Grav. 191 GH86
Terrace Wk., Dag. 126 EY64
Terraces, The, Dart. 188 FQ87
Terrapin Rd. SW17 181 DH90
Terretts Pl. N1 141 DP66
Upper St.
Terrick Rd. N22 99 DL53
Terrick St. W12 139 CV72
Terrilands, Pnr. 116 BZ55
Terront Rd. N15 122 DQ57
Tessa Sanderson Pl. SW8 161 DH83
Tessa Sanderson Way, Grnf. 117 CD64
Lilian Board Way
Testard Rd., Guil. 258 AW136
Testers Clo., Oxt. 254 EH132
Testerton Wk. W11 139 CX73
Testwood Rd., Wind. 151 AK81
Tetbury Pl. N1 141 DP67
Upper St.
Tetcott Rd. SW10 160 DC80
Tetherdown N10 120 DG55
Tethys Rd., Hem.H. 40 BM17
Tetty Way, Brom. 204 EG96
Teversham La. SW8 161 DL81
Teviot Ave., S.Ock. 148 FQ72
Teviot Clo., Guil. 242 AU131
Teviot Clo., Well. 166 EV81
Teviot St. E14 143 EC71
Tewin Clo., St.Alb. 43 CJ16
Tewin Ct., Welw.G.C. 29 CZ09
Tewin Rd., Hem.H. 41 BQ20
Tewin Rd., Welw.G.C. 29 CZ09
Tewkesbury Ave. SE23 182 DV88
Tewkesbury Ave., Pnr. 116 BY57
Tewkesbury Clo. N15 122 DR58
Tewkesbury Rd.
Tewkesbury Clo., Loug. 84 EL44
Tewkesbury Clo., W.Byf. 212 BK111
Tewkesbury Gdns. NW9 118 CP55
Tewkesbury Rd. N15 122 DR58
Tewkesbury Rd. W13 137 CG73
Tewkesbury Rd., Cars. 200 DD102
Tewkesbury Ter. N11 99 DJ51
Tewson Rd. SE18 165 ES78
Teynham Ave., Enf. 82 DR44
Teynham Grn., Brom. 204 EG99
Teynton Ter. N17 100 DQ53
Thackeray Ave. N17 100 DU54
Thackeray Ave., Til. 171 GH81
Thackeray Clo. SW19 179 CX94
Thackeray Clo., Har. 116 CA60
Thackeray Clo., Islw. 157 CG82
Thackeray Clo., Uxb. 135 BP72
Dickens Ave.
Thackeray Dr., Rom. 126 EU59
Thackeray Rd. E6 144 EK68
Thackeray Rd. SW8 161 DH82
Thackeray St. W8 160 DB75
Thackrah Clo. N2 98 DC54
Thakeham Clo. SE26 182 DV92
Thalia Clo. SE10 163 ED79
Thalmassing Clo., Brwd. 109 GB47
Thame Rd. SE16 163 DX75
Thames Ave. SW10 160 DC81
Thames Ave., Cher. 194 BG97
Thames Ave., Dag. 147 FB70
Thames Ave., Grnf. 137 CF68
Thames Ave., Hem.H. 40 BM15
Thames Ave., Wind. 151 AR80
Thames Bank SW14 158 CQ82
Thames Circle E14 163 EA77
Westferry Rd.
Thames Clo., Cher. 194 BH101
Thames Clo., Hmptn. 196 CB96
Thames Clo., Rain. 147 FH72
Thames Ct., W.Mol. 196 CB96
Thames Dr., Grays 171 GG78
Thames Dr., Ruis. 115 BQ58
Thames Gate, Dart. 168 FN84
St. Edmunds Rd.
Thames Gateway, Dag. 146 EZ68
Thames Gateway, Rain. 147 FG72
Thames Gateway, S.Ock. 168 FP75
Thames Mead, Walt. 195 BU101
Thames Mead, Wind. 151 AL81
Thames Meadow, Shep. 195 BR102
Thames Meadow, W.Mol. 196 CA96
Thames Path SE1 278 E1
Thames Path SE1 141 DN73
Thames Path SE7 164 EJ76
Thames Pl. SW15 159 CX83
Thames Rd. E16 144 EK74
Thames Rd. W4 158 CN79
Thames Rd., Bark. 145 ET69
Thames Rd., Dart. 167 FF82
Thames Rd., Grays 170 GB80
Thames Rd., Slou. 153 BA77
Thames Side, Cher. 194 BJ99
Thames Side, Kings.T. 197 CK95
Thames Side, Stai. 194 BH96
Thames Side, Tedd. 177 CK94
Thames Side, Wind. 151 AR80
Thames St. SE10 163 EB79
Thames St., Hmptn. 196 CB95
Thames St., Kings.T. 197 CK96
Thames St., Stai. 173 BE91
Thames St., Sun. 195 BU98
Thames St., Walt. 195 BT101
Thames St., Wey. 195 BP103
Thames St., Wind. 151 AR81
Thames Vw., Grays 171 GG78
Thames Village W4 158 CQ81
Thames Way, Grav. 190 GC88
Thames Wf. E16 144 EF74
Thamesbank Pl. SE28 146 EW72
Thamesdale, St.Alb. 62 CM27
Thamesfield Ct., Shep. 195 BQ101
Thamesgate Clo., Rich. 177 CH91
Locksmeade Rd.
Thameshill Ave., Rom. 105 FC54
Thameside, Tedd. 177 CJ94
Thameside Ind. Est. E16 164 EL75
Thameside Wk. SE28 145 ET72
Thamesmead, Walt. 195 BU101
Thamesmead Spine Rd., Belv. 167 FC75
Thamesmere Dr. SE28 146 EU73
Thamesvale Clo., Houns. 156 CA83
Thamley, Purf. 168 FN77
Thane Vil. N7 121 DM62
Thane Wks. N7 121 DM62
Thane Vil.
Thanescroft Gdns., Croy. 202 DS104
Thanet Dr., Kes. 204 EK104
Phoenix Dr.
Thanet Pl., Croy. 220 DQ105
Thanet Rd., Bex. 186 FA87
Thanet Rd., Erith 167 FE80
Thanet St. WC1 273 P3
Thanet St. WC1 141 DL69
Thanington Ct. SE9 185 ES86
Thant Clo. E10 123 EB62
Tharp Rd., Wall. 219 DK106
Thatcham Gdns. N20 98 DC45
Thatcher Clo., West Dr. 154 BL75
Classon Clo.
Thatchers Clo., Horl. 269 DH146
Wheatfield Way
Thatchers Clo., Loug. 85 EQ40
Thatchers Cft., Hem.H. 40 BL16
Marlborough Ri.
Thatchers Way, Islw. 177 CD85
Thatches Gro., Rom. 126 EY56
Thavies Inn EC1 274 E8
Thaxted Grn., Brwd. 109 GC43
Thaxted Ho., Dag. 147 FB66
Thaxted Pl. SW20 179 CX94
Thaxted Rd. SE9 185 EQ89
Thaxted Rd., Buck.H. 102 EL45
Thaxted Wk., Rain. 147 FF67
Ongar Way
Thaxted Way, Wal.Abb. 67 ED33
Thaxton Rd. W14 159 CZ79
Thayer St. W1 272 G7
Thayer St. W1 140 DG71
Thayers Fm. Rd., Beck. 203 DY95
Thaynesfield, Pot.B. 64 DD31
The Floats, Sev. 241 FD119
London Rd.
Theatre Sq. E15 143 ED65
Salway Rd.
Theatre St. SW11 160 DF83
Theberton St. N1 141 DN67
Theed St. SE1 278 D3
Theed St. SE1 141 DN74
Thele Ave., Ware 33 ED11
Thellusson Way, Rick. 91 BF45
Thelma Clo., Grav. 191 GM92
Thelma Gdns. SE3 164 EK81
Thelma Gdns., Felt. 176 BY90
Thelma Gro., Tedd. 177 CG93
Theobald Cres., Har. 94 CB53
Theobald Rd. E17 123 DZ59
Theobald Rd., Croy. 201 DP103
Theobald St. SE1 279 K7
Theobald St., Borwd. 78 CM40
Theobald St., Rad. 77 CH36
Theobalds Ave. N12 98 DC49
Theobalds Ave., Grays 170 GC78
Theobalds Clo. (Cuffley), Pot.B. 65 DM30
Theobalds Ct. N4 122 DQ61
Queens Dr.
Theobalds La. (Cheshunt), Wal.Cr. 66 DV32
Theobalds Pk. Rd., Enf. 81 DP35
Theobald's Rd. WC1 274 B6
Theobald's Rd. WC1 141 DM71
Theobalds Rd. (Cuffley), Pot.B. 65 DL30
Theodora Way, Pnr. 115 BT55
Theodore Rd. SE13 183 EC86
Thepps Clo., Red. 267 DM137
Therapia La., Croy. 201 DL100
Therapia Rd. SE22 182 DW86
Theresa Rd. W6 159 CU77
Theresas Wk., S.Croy. 220 DR110
Sanderstead Rd.
Therfield Ct. N4 122 DQ61
Brownswood Rd.
Therfield Rd., St.Alb. 43 CD16
Thermopylae Gate E14 163 EB77
Theseus Wk. N1 274 G1
Thesiger Rd. SE20 183 DX94
Thessaly Rd. SW8 161 DJ80
Thetford Clo. N13 99 DP51
Thetford Gdns., Dag. 146 EX66
Thetford Rd., Ashf. 174 BL91
Thetford Rd., Dag. 146 EX67
Thetford Rd., N.Mal. 198 CR100
Thetis Ter., Rich. 158 CN79
Kew Grn.
Theydon Bower, Epp. 70 EU31
Theydon Ct., Wal.Abb. 68 EG33
Theydon Gdns., Rain. 147 FE66
Theydon Gate, Epp. 85 ES37
Coppice Row
Theydon Gro., Epp. 70 EU30
Theydon Gro., Wdf.Grn. 102 EJ51
Theydon Pk. Rd., Epp. 85 ES39
Theydon Pl., Epp. 69 ET31
Theydon Rd. E5 122 DW61
Theydon Rd., Epp. 69 ER34
Theydon St. E17 123 DZ59
Thicket, The, West Dr. 134 BL72
Thicket Cres., Sutt. 218 DC105
Thicket Gro. SE20 182 DU94
Anerley Rd.
Thicket Gro., Dag. 146 EW65
Thicket Rd. SE20 182 DU94
Thicket Rd., Sutt. 218 DC105
Thicketts, Sev. 257 FJ123
Thickthorne La., Stai. 174 BJ94
Berryscroft Rd.
Thieves La., Hert. 31 DM10
Thieves La., Ware 32 DW08
Third Ave. E12 124 EL63
Third Ave. E13 144 EG69
Third Ave. E17 123 EA57
Third Ave. W3 139 CT74
Third Ave. W10 139 CY69
Third Ave., Dag. 147 FB67
Third Ave., Enf. 82 DT43
Third Ave., Grays 169 FU79
Third Ave., Harl. 51 EM16
Third Ave., Hayes 135 BT74
Third Ave., Rom. 126 EW58
Third Ave., Wat. 76 BX35
Third Ave., Wem. 117 CK61
Third Clo., W.Mol. 196 CB98
Third Cres., Slou. 131 AQ71
Third Cross Rd., Twick. 177 CD89
Third Way, Wem. 118 CP63
Thirkleby Clo., Slou. 131 AQ74
Thirleby Rd. SW1 277 L7
Thirleby Rd. SW1 161 DJ76
Thirleby Rd., Edg. 96 CR53
Thirlmere Ave., Grnf. 137 CJ69
Thirlmere Ave., Slou. 130 AJ71
Thirlmere Clo., Egh. 173 BB94
Keswick Rd.
Thirlmere Dr., St.Alb. 43 CH22
Thirlmere Gdns., Nthwd. 93 BQ51
Thirlmere Gdns., Wem. 117 CJ60
Thirlmere Ho., Islw. 177 CF85
Thirlmere Ri., Brom. 184 EF93
Thirlmere Rd. N10 99 DH53
Thirlmere Rd. SW16 181 DK91
Thirlmere Rd., Bexh. 167 FC82
Thirlstane, St.Alb. 43 CF19
Thirsk Clo., Nthlt. 136 CA65
Thirsk Rd. SE25 202 DR98
Thirsk Rd. SW11 160 DG83
Thirsk Rd., Borwd. 78 CN37
Thirsk Rd., Mitch. 180 DG94
Thirston Path, Borwd. 78 CN40
Thirza Rd., Dart. 188 FM86
Thistle Clo., Hem.H. 39 BE21
Thistle Gro. SW10 160 DC78
Thistle Gro., Welw.G.C. 30 DC11
Thistle Mead, Loug. 85 EN41
Thistle Rd., Grav. 191 GL87
Thistlebrook SE2 166 EW76
Thistlebrook Ind. Est. SE2 166 EW75
Thistlecroft, Hem.H. 40 BH21
Thistlecroft Gdns., Stan. 95 CK53
Thistlecroft Rd., Walt. 214 BW105
Thistledene, T.Ditt. 197 CE100
Thistledene, W.Byf. 211 BF113
Thistledene Ave., Har. 116 BY62
Thistledene Ave., Rom. 105 FB50
Thistledown, Grav. 191 GK93
Thistlemead, Chis. 205 EP96
Thistles, The, Hem.H. 40 BH19
Thistlewaite Rd. E5 122 DV62
Thistlewood Clo. N7 121 DM61
Thistlewood Cres., Croy. 221 ED112
Thistleworth Clo., Islw. 157 CD80
Thistley Clo. N12 98 DE51
Summerfields Ave.
Thomas a'Beckett Clo., Wem. 117 CF63
Thomas Ave., Cat. 236 DQ121
Thomas Baines Rd. SW11 160 DD83
Thomas Clo., Brwd. 108 FY48
Thomas Darby Ct. W11 139 CY72
Thomas Dean Rd. SE26 183 DZ91
Kangley Bri. Rd.
Thomas Dinwiddy Rd. SE12 184 EH89
Thomas Doyle St. SE1 278 F6
Thomas Doyle St. SE1 161 DP76
Thomas Dr., Grav. 191 GK89
Thomas Hardy Ho. N22 99 DM52
Thomas La. SE6 183 EA87
Thomas More Ho. EC2 142 DQ71
The Barbican
Thomas More St. E1 142 DU73
Thomas More Way N2 120 DC55
Thomas Pl. W8 160 DB76
St. Mary's Pl.
Thomas Rd. E14 143 DZ72
Thomas Rd., H.Wyc. 110 AD59
Thomas Rochford Way, Wal.Cr. 67 DZ27
Thomas Sims Ct., Horn. 127 FH64
Thomas St. SE18 165 EP77
Thomas Wall Clo., Sutt. 218 DB106
Clarence Rd.
Thompkins La., Slou. 131 AM66
Thompson Ave., Rich. 158 CN83
Thompson Clo., Ilf. 125 EQ61
High Rd.
Thompson Clo., Slou. 153 BA77
Thompson Rd. SE22 182 DT86
Thompson Rd., Dag. 126 EZ62
Thompson Rd., Uxb. 134 BL66
Thompson's Ave. SE5 162 DQ80
Thompsons Clo., Wal.Cr. 66 DT29
Thompson's La., Loug. 84 EF39
Thomson Cres., Croy. 201 DN102
Thomson Rd., Har. 117 CE55
Thong La., Grav. 191 GM91
Thorburn Sq. SE1 162 DU77
Thorburn Way SW19 200 DD95
Willow Vw.
Thoresby St. N1 275 J2
Thoresby St. N1 142 DQ69
Thorkhill Gdns., T.Ditt. 197 CG102
Thorkhill Rd., T.Ditt. 197 CG102
Thorley Clo., W.Byf. 212 BG114
Thorley Gdns., Wok. 212 BG114
Thorn Ave. (Bushey), Wat. 94 CC46
Thorn Bank, Guil. 258 AU136
Thorn Clo., Brom. 205 EN100
Thorn Clo., Nthlt. 136 BZ69
Thorn Dr., Slou. 132 AY72
Thorn Hill Clo., Amer. 55 AP40
Thorn Ho., Beck. 203 DY95
Thorn La., Rain. 148 FK68
Thorn Ter. SE15 162 DW83
Nunhead Gro.
Thornaby Gdns. N18 100 DU51
Thornaby Pl., H.Wyc. 110 AE55
Wootton Dr.
Thornash Clo., Wok. 226 AW115
Thornash Rd., Wok. 226 AW115
Thornash Way, Wok. 226 AW115
Thornbank Clo., Stai. 174 BG85
Thornbridge Rd., Iver 133 BC67
Thornbury Ave., Islw. 157 CD80
Thornbury Clo. N16 122 DS64
Truman's Rd.
Thornbury Clo., Hodd. 33 EB13
Thornbury Gdns., Borwd. 78 CQ42
Thornbury Rd. SW2 181 DL86
Thornbury Rd., Islw. 157 CD81
Thornbury Sq. N6 121 DJ60
Thornby Rd. E5 122 DW62
Thorncliffe Rd. SW2 181 DL86
Thorncliffe Rd., Sthl. 156 BZ78
Thorncombe Rd. SE22 182 DS85
Thorncroft, Egh. 172 AW94
Thorncroft, Hem.H. 41 BP22
Thorncroft, Horn. 127 FH58
Thorncroft Clo., Couls. 235 DN120
Waddington Ave.
Thorncroft Dr., Lthd. 231 CH123
Thorncroft Rd., Sutt. 218 DB105
Thorncroft St. SW8 161 DL80
Thorndales, Brwd. 108 FX49
Thorndean St. SW18 180 DC89
Thorndene Ave. N11 98 DG46
Thorndike, Slou. 131 AN71
Thorndike Ave., Nthlt. 136 BX67
Thorndike Clo. SW10 160 DC80
Thorndike St. SW1 277 M10
Thorndike St. SW1 161 DJ77
Thorndon Clo., Orp. 205 ET96
Thorndon Gdns., Epsom 216 CS105
Thorndon Gate, Brwd. 109 GC50
Thorndon Rd., Orp. 205 ET96
Thorndyke Ct., Pnr. 94 BZ52
Westfield Pk.
Thorne Clo. E11 124 EE63
Thorne Clo. E16 144 EG72
Thorne Clo., Ashf. 175 BQ94
Thorne Clo., Erith 167 FC79
Thorne Pas. SW13 158 CS82
Thorne Rd. SW8 161 DL80
Thorne St. E16 144 EF72
Thorne St. SW13 158 CS83
Thorneloe Gdns., Croy. 219 DN106
Thornes Clo., Beck. 203 EC97
Thornet Wd. Rd., Brom. 205 EN97
Thorney Cres. SW11 160 DD80
Thorney Hedge Rd. W4 158 CP77
Thorney La. N., Iver 133 BF72
Thorney La. S., Iver 153 BF75
Thorney Mill Rd., Iver 154 BG76
Thorney Mill Rd., West Dr. 154 BG76
Thorney St. SW1 277 P8
Thorney St. SW1 161 DL77
Thorneycroft Clo., Walt. 196 BW100
Thornfield Ave. NW7 97 CY53
Thornfield Rd. W12 159 CV75
Thornfield Rd., Bans. 234 DA117
Thornford Rd. SE13 183 EC85
Thorngate Rd. W9 140 DA70
Thorngrove Rd. E13 144 EH67
Thornham Gro. E15 123 ED64
Thornham St. SE10 163 EB79
Thornhaugh Ms. WC1 273 N5
Thornhaugh St. WC1 273 N6
Thornhaugh St. WC1 141 DK70
Thornhill, Epp. 71 FC26
Thornhill Ave. SE18 165 ES80
Thornhill Ave., Surb. 198 CL103
Thornhill Bri. Wf. N1 141 DM67
Caledonian Rd.
Thornhill Cres. N1 141 DM66
Thornhill Gdns. E10 123 EB61
Thornhill Gdns., Bark. 145 ES66
Thornhill Gro. N1 141 DM66
Lofting Rd.
Thornhill Ho. N1 141 DN66
Thornhill Rd.
Thornhill Rd. E10 123 EB61
Thornhill Rd. N1 141 DN66
Thornhill Rd., Croy. 202 DQ101
Thornhill Rd., Nthwd. 93 BQ49
Thornhill Rd., Surb. 198 CL103
Thornhill Rd., Uxb. 114 BM63
Thornhill Sq. N1 141 DM66
Thornhill Way, Shep. 194 BN99
Thornlaw Rd. SE27 181 DN91
Thornleas Pl., Lthd. 245 BS126
Station App.
Thornley Clo. N17 100 DU52
Thornley Dr., Har. 116 CB61
Thornley Pl. SE10 164 EE78
Caradoc St.
Thornridge, Brwd. 108 FV45
Thorns, The, Reig. 250 DC131
Thorns Meadow, West. 240 EW123
Thornsbeach Rd. SE6 183 EC88
Thornsett Pl. SE20 202 DV96
Thornsett Rd. SE20 202 DV96
Thornsett Rd. SW18 180 DB89
Thornside, Edg. 96 CN51
High St.
Thornton Ave. SW2 181 DK88
Thornton Ave. W4 158 CS77
Thornton Ave., Croy. 201 DM100
Thornton Ave., West Dr. 154 BM76
Thornton Clo., Guil. 242 AU130
Thornton Clo., Horl. 268 DE148
Thornton Clo., West Dr. 154 BM76
Thornton Ct. SW20 199 CX99
Thornton Cres., Couls. 235 DN119
Thornton Dene, Beck. 203 EA96
Thornton Gdns. SW12 181 DK88
Thornton Gro., Pnr. 94 CA51
Thornton Hill SW19 179 CY94
Thornton Pl. W1 272 E6
Thornton Pl. W1 140 DF71
Thornton Pl., Horl. 268 DE147
Thornton Rd. E11 123 ED61
Thornton Rd. N18 100 DW48
Thornton Rd. SW12 181 DK87
Thornton Rd. SW14 158 CR83
Thornton Rd. SW19 179 CX93
Thornton Rd., Barn. 79 CY41
Thornton Rd., Belv. 167 FB77
Thornton Rd., Brom. 184 EG92
Thornton Rd., Cars. 200 DD102
Thornton Rd., Croy. 201 DM101
Thornton Rd., Ilf. 125 EP63
Thornton Rd., Pot.B. 64 DC30
Thornton Rd., Th.Hth. 201 DM101
Thornton Rd. E. SW19 179 CX93
Thornton Rd.
Thornton Rd. Retail Pk., Croy. 201 DM100
Thornton Row, Th.Hth. 201 DN99
London Rd.
Thornton St. SW9 161 DN82
Thornton St., Hert. 32 DR09
Thornton St., St.Alb. 42 CC19
Thornton Wk., Horl. 268 DE148
Thornton Pl.
Thornton Way NW11 120 DB57
Thorntons Fm. Ave., Rom. 127 FD60
Thorntree Rd. SE7 164 EK78

Thornville Gro., Mitch. 200 DC96
Thornville St. SE8 163 EA81
Thornwood Clo. E18 102 EH54
Thornwood Rd. SE13 184 EE85
Thornwood Rd., Epp. 70 EV29
Thorogood Gdns. E15 124 EE64
Thorogood Way, Rain. 147 FE67
Thorold Clo., S.Croy. 221 DX110
Thorold Rd. N22 99 DL52
Thorold Rd., Ilf. 125 EP61
Thoroughfare, The, Tad. 249 CU125
Chequers La.
Thorparch Rd. SW8 161 DK81
Thorpe Bypass, Egh. 193 BB96
Thorpe Clo. W10 139 CY72
Cambridge Gdns.
Thorpe Clo., Croy. 221 EC111
Thorpe Clo., Orp. 205 ES103
Thorpe Cres. E17 101 DZ54
Thorpe Cres., Wat. 94 BW45
Thorpe Hall Rd. E17 101 EC53
Thorpe Ind. Pk., Egh. 193 BC95
Thorpe Lea Rd., Egh. 173 BB93
Thorpe Lo., Horn. 128 FL59
Thorpe Rd. E6 145 EM67
Thorpe Rd. E7 124 EF63
Thorpe Rd. E17 101 EC54
Thorpe Rd. N15 122 DS58
Thorpe Rd., Bark. 145 ER66
Thorpe Rd., Cher. 193 BD99
Thorpe Rd., Kings.T. 178 CL94
Thorpe Rd., St.Alb. 43 CD21
Thorpe Rd., Stai. 173 BD93
Thorpebank Rd. W12 139 CU74
Thorpedale Gdns., Ilf. 125 EN56
Thorpedale Rd. N4 121 DL60
Thorpefield Clo., St.Alb. 43 CK17
Thorpes Clo., Guil. 242 AU131
Thorpeside Clo., Stai. 193 BE95
Thorpewood Ave. SE26 182 DV89
Thorpland Ave., Uxb. 115 BQ62
Thorsden Clo., Wok. 226 AY119
Thorsden Ct., Wok. 226 AY118
Guildford Rd.
Thorsden Way SE19 182 DS91
Oaks Ave.
Thorverton Rd. NW2 119 CY62
Thoydon Rd. E3 143 DY68
Thrale Rd. SW16 181 DJ92
Thrale St. SE1 279 J3
Thrale St. SE1 142 DQ74
Thrasher Clo. E8 142 DT67
Stean St.
Thrawl St. E1 142 DT71
Threadneedle St. EC2 275 L9
Threadneedle St. EC2 142 DR72
Three Arch Rd., Red. 266 DF138
Three Barrels Wk. EC4 275 J10
Three Cherry Trees La., Hem.H. 41 BP16
Three Clo. La., Berk. 38 AW20
Three Colt St. E14 143 DZ73
Three Colts Cor. E2 142 DU70
Weaver St.
Three Colts La. E2 142 DV70
Three Cors., Bexh. 167 FB82
Three Cors., Hem.H. 40 BN22
Three Cups Yd. WC1 274 C7
Three Forest Way, Epp. 51 EM22
Three Forest Way, Harl. 34 EG14
Three Forest Way (Mark Hall N.), Harl. 36 EU10
Three Forest Way, Wal.Abb. 51 EM21
Three Forest Way, Ware 35 EM12
Three Forests Way, Chig. 104 EW48
Three Forests Way, Loug. 84 EK38
The Clay Rd.
Three Forests Way, Wal.Abb. 84 EL36
Woodridden Hill
Three Gates, Guil. 243 BC132
Three Gates Rd. (Fawkham Grn.), Long. 209 FT104
Three Horseshoes Rd., Harl. 51 EP17
Three Households, Ch.St.G. 90 AT49
Three Kings Rd., Mitch. 200 DG97
Three Kings Yd. W1 273 H10
Three Kings Yd. W1 141 DH73
Three Mill La. E3 143 EC69
Three Oak La. SE1 279 P4
Three Oaks Clo., Uxb. 114 BM62
Three Pears Rd., Guil. 243 BE134
Threshers Bush, Harl. 36 FA14
Threshers Pl. W11 139 CY73
Thriffwood SE26 182 DW90
Thrift, The, Dart. 189 FW90
Thrift Fm. La., Borwd. 78 CP40
Thrift Grn., Brwd. 109 GA48
Knight's Way
Thrift La., Sev. 239 ER116
Cudham La. S.
Thrift Vale, Guil. 243 BD131
Thriftfield, Hem.H. 40 BK18
Thrifts Mead, Epp. 85 ES37
Thrigby Rd., Chess. 216 CM107
Throckmorten Rd. E16 144 EH72
Throgmorton Ave. EC2 275 L8
Throgmorton Ave. EC2 142 DR72
Throgmorton St. EC2 275 L8
Throgmorton St. EC2 142 DR72
Throwley Clo. SE2 166 EW76
Throwley Rd., Sutt. 218 DB106
Throwley Way, Sutt. 218 DB105
Thrums, The, Wat. 75 BV37
Thrupp Clo., Mitch. 201 DH96
Thrupps Ave., Walt. 214 BX106
Thrupps La., Walt. 214 BX106
Thrush Ave., Hat. 45 CU20
Thrush Grn., Har. 116 CA56
Thrush Grn., Rick. 92 BJ45
Thrush La. (Cuffley), Pot.B. 65 DL28
Thrush St. SE17 279 H10
Thruxton Way SE15 162 DT80
Daniel Gdns.
Thumbswood, Welw.G.C. 30 DA12
Thumpers, Hem.H. 40 BL18
Thundercourt, Ware 33 DX05
Thunderer Rd., Dag. 146 EY70
Thundridge Clo., Welw.G.C. 30 DB10
Amwell Common
Thurbarn Rd. SE6 183 EB92
Thurgood Rd., Hodd. 49 EA15
Thurland Rd. SE16 162 DU76
Thurlby Clo., Har. 117 CG58
Gayton Rd.
Thurlby Clo., Wdf.Grn. 103 EM50
Thurlby Rd. SE27 181 DN91
Thurlby Rd., Wem. 137 CK65
Thurleigh Ave. SW12 180 DG86
Thurleigh Rd. SW12 180 DG86
Thurleston Ave., Mord. 199 CY99
Thurlestone Ave. N12 98 DF51
Thurlestone Ave., Ilf. 125 ET63
Thurlestone Clo., Shep. 195 BQ100
Thurlestone Rd. SE27 181 DN90
Thurloe Clo. SW7 276 B8
Thurloe Clo. SW7 160 DE76
Thurloe Gdns., Rom. 127 FF58
Thurloe Pl. SW7 276 A8
Thurloe Pl. SW7 160 DD77
Thurloe Pl. Ms. SW7 276 A8
Thurloe Sq. SW7 276 B8
Thurloe Sq. SW7 160 DE77
Thurloe St. SW7 276 A8
Thurloe St. SW7 160 DD77
Thurloe Wk., Grays 170 GA76
Thurlow Clo. E4 101 EB51
Higham Sta. Ave.
Thurlow Gdns., Ilf. 103 ER51
Thurlow Gdns., Wem. 117 CK64
Thurlow Hill SE21 182 DQ88
Thurlow Pk. Rd. SE21 181 DP88
Thurlow Rd. NW3 120 DD64
Thurlow Rd. W7 157 CG75
Thurlow St. SE17 279 L10
Thurlow St. SE17 162 DR78
Thurlow Ter. NW5 120 DG64
Thurlstone Rd., Ruis. 115 BU62
Thurlton Ct., Wok. 226 AY116
Chobham Rd.
Thurnby Ct., Twick. 177 CE90
Thurnham Way, Tad. 233 CW120
Thurrock Lakeside, Grays 169 FV77
Thurrock Pk. Ind. Est., Til. 170 GD80
Thurrock Pk. Way, Til. 170 GD80
Thursby Rd., Wok. 226 AU118
Thursland Rd., Sid. 186 EY92
Thursley Cres., Croy. 221 ED108
Thursley Gdns. SW19 179 CX89
Thursley Rd. SE9 185 EM90
Thurso Clo., Rom. 106 FP51
Thurso St. SW17 180 DD91
Thurstan Rd. SW20 179 CV94
Thurstans, Harl. 51 EQ20
Thurston Rd. SE13 163 EB82
Thurston Rd., Slou. 132 AS72
Thurston Rd., Sthl. 136 BZ72
Thurtle Rd. E2 142 DT67
Thwaite Clo., Erith 167 FC79
Thyer Clo., Orp. 223 EQ105
Isabella Dr.
Thyme Ct., Guil. 243 BB131
Mallow Cres.
Thyra Gro. N12 98 DB51
Tibbatts Rd. E3 143 EB70
Tibbenham Wk. E13 144 EF68
Tibberton Sq. N1 142 DQ66
Popham Rd.
Tibbets Clo. SW19 179 CX88
Tibbet's Cor. SW15 179 CX87
Tibbet's Cor. Underpass SW15 179 CX87
West Hill
Tibbet's Ride SW15 179 CX87
Tibbles Clo., Wat. 76 BY35
Tibbs Hill Rd., Abb.L. 59 BT30
Tiber Gdns. N1 141 DM67
Treaty St.
Ticehurst Clo., Orp. 186 EU94
Grovelands Rd.
Ticehurst Rd. SE23 183 DY89
Tichborne Wd., Rick. 91 BD50
Tichmarsh, Epsom 216 CQ110
Tickenhall Dr., Harl. 52 EX15
Tickford Clo. SE2 166 EW75
Ampleforth Rd.
Tidal Basin Rd. E16 144 EF73
Tidenham Gdns., Croy. 202 DS104
Tideswell Rd. SW15 179 CW85
Tideswell Rd., Croy. 203 EA104
Tideway Clo., Rich. 177 CH91
Locksmeade Rd.
Tidey St. E3 143 EA71
Tidford Rd., Well. 165 ET82
Tidworth Rd. E3 143 EA70
Tidy's La., Epp. 70 EV29
Tiepigs La., Brom. 204 EE103
Tiepigs La., W.Wick. 204 EE103
Tierney Rd. SW2 181 DL88
Tiger La., Brom. 204 EH98
Tiger Way E5 122 DV63
Tilbrook Rd. SE3 164 EJ83
Tilburstow Hill Rd., Gdse. 252 DW132
Tilbury Clo. SE15 162 DT80
Willowbrook Rd.
Tilbury Clo., Orp. 206 EV96
Tilbury Docks, Til. 170 GE84
Tilbury Gdns., Til. 171 GG84
Tilbury Hotel Rd., Til. 171 GG84
Tilbury Mead, Harl. 52 EU17
Tilbury Rd. E6 145 EM68
Tilbury Rd. E10 123 EC59
Tildesley Rd. SW15 179 CW86
Tile Fm. Rd., Orp. 205 ER104
Tile Kiln Clo., Hem.H. 41 BP21
Tile Kiln Cres., Hem.H. 41 BP21
Tile Kiln La. N6 121 DH60
Winchester Rd.
Tile Kiln La. N13 100 DQ50
Tile Kiln La., Bex. 187 FC89
Tile Kiln La., Hem.H. 41 BP21
Tile Kiln La. (Harefield), Uxb. 115 BP59
Tile Yd. E14 143 DZ72
Commercial Rd.
Tilecroft, Welw.G.C. 29 CX05
Tilegate Rd., Harl. 51 ET17
Tilegate Rd., Ong. 53 FC19
Tilehost, Guil. 242 AU130
Tilehouse Clo., Borwd. 78 CM41
Tilehouse La., Ger.Cr. 91 BE53
Tilehouse La., Rick. 91 BE53
Tilehouse La., Uxb. 113 BE55
Tilehouse Rd., Guil. 258 AY138
Tilehouse Way, Uxb. 113 BF59
Tilehurst La., Dor. 263 CK137
Tilehurst Pt. SE2 166 EW75
Yarnton Way
Tilehurst Rd. SW18 180 DD88
Tilehurst Rd., Sutt. 217 CY106
Tilekiln Clo., Wal.Cr. 66 DT29
Tiler's Wk., Reig. 266 DC138
Tiler's Way, Reig. 266 DC138
Tileyard Rd. N7 141 DL66
Tilford Ave., Croy. 221 EC109
Tilford Gdns. SW19 179 CX89
Tilia Clo., Sutt. 217 CZ106
Tilia Rd. E5 122 DV63
Clarence Rd.
Tilia Wk. SW9 161 DP84
Moorland Rd.
Till Ave. (Farningham), Dart. 208 FM102
Tiller Rd. E14 163 EA76
Tillett Clo. NW10 138 CQ65
Tillett Sq. SE16 163 DY75
Howland Way
Tillett Way E2 142 DU69
Gosset St.
Tilley La., Epsom 232 CQ123
Tillgate Common, Red. 252 DQ133
Tilling Rd. NW2 119 CW60
Tilling Way, Wem. 117 CK61
Tillingbourne Gdns. N3 119 CZ55
Tillingbourne Rd., Guil. 258 AY140
Tillingbourne Way N3 119 CZ55
Tillingbourne Gdns.
Tillingdown Hill, Cat. 236 DU122
Tillingdown La., Cat. 252 DV125
Tillingham Ct., Wal.Abb. 68 EG33
Tillingham Way N12 98 DA49
Tillman St. E1 142 DV72
Bigland St.
Tilloch St. N1 141 DM66
Carnoustie Dr.
Tillotson Rd. N9 100 DT47
Tillotson Rd., Har. 94 CB52
Tillotson Rd., Ilf. 125 EN59
Tillwicks Rd., Harl. 51 ET16
Tilly's La., Stai. 173 BF91
Tilmans Mead (Farningham), Dart. 208 FM101
Tilney Ct. EC1 275 J4
Tilney Dr., Buck.H. 102 EG47
Tilney Gdns. N1 142 DR65
Tilney Rd., Dag. 146 EZ65
Tilney Rd., Sthl. 156 BW77
Tilney St. W1 276 G2
Tilney St. W1 140 DG74
Tilson Gdns. SW2 181 DL87
Tilson Ho. SW2 181 DL87
Tilson Gdns.
Tilson Rd. N17 100 DU53
Tilstone Ave. (Eton Wick), Wind. 151 AL78
Tilstone Clo. (Eton Wick), Wind. 151 AL78
Tilsworth Rd., Beac. 88 AJ54
Tilsworth Wk., St.Alb. 43 CJ15
Sandringham Cres.
Tilt Clo., Cob. 230 BY116
Tilt Meadow, Cob. 230 BY116
Tilt Rd., Cob. 230 BW115
Tilt Yd. App. SE9 185 EM86
Tilthams Cor. Rd., Gdmg. 258 AV143
Tilthams Grn., Gdmg. 258 AV143
Tilton St. SW6 159 CY79
Tiltwood, The W3 138 CQ73
Acacia Rd.
Timber Clo., Chis. 205 EN96
Timber Clo., Lthd. 246 CC126
Timber Clo., Wok. 211 BF114
Hacketts La.
Timber Hill Rd., Cat. 236 DU124
Timber La., Cat. 236 DU124
Timber Hill Rd.
Timber Mill Way SW4 161 DK83
Timber Orchard, Hert. 31 DN05
Timber Pond Rd. SE16 163 DX75
Timber Ridge, Rick. 74 BK42
Timber St. EC1 275 H4
Timbercroft, Epsom 216 CS105
Timbercroft, Welw.G.C. 29 CZ06
Timbercroft La. SE18 165 ES79
Timberdene NW4 97 CX54
Timberdene Ave., Ilf. 103 EP53
Timberham Fm. Rd., Gat. 268 DD151
Timberham Way, Horl. 268 DE151
Timberhill, Ash. 232 CL119
Ottways La.
Timberland Rd. E1 142 DV72
Timberling Gdns., S.Croy. 220 DR109
Sanderstead Rd.
Timberslip Dr., Wall. 219 DK109
Timbertop Rd., West. 238 EJ118
Timberwharf Rd. N16 122 DU58
Timberwood, Slou. 111 AR62
Timbrell Pl. SE16 143 DZ74
Silver Wk.
Time Sq. E8 122 DT64
Times Sq., Sutt. 218 DB106
Timothy Clo. SW4 181 DJ85
Elms Rd.
Timothy Clo., Bexh. 186 EY85
Timothy Ho., Erith 166 EY75
Kale Rd.
Timothy Rd. E3 143 DZ71
Timperley Gdns., Red. 250 DE132
Timplings Row, Hem.H. 40 BH18
Timsbury Wk. SW15 179 CU88
Timsway, Stai. 173 BF92
Tindal St. SW9 161 DP81
Tindale Clo., S.Croy. 220 DR111
Tindall Clo., Rom. 106 FM54
Tinderbox All. SW14 158 CR83
Tine Rd., Chig. 103 ES50
Tingeys Top La., Enf. 81 DN36
Tinkers La., Wind. 151 AK82
Tinniswood Clo. N5 121 DN64
Drayton Pk.
Tinsey Clo., Egh. 173 BB92
Tinsley Rd. E1 142 DW71
Tintagel Clo., Epsom 217 CT114
Tintagel Clo., Hem.H. 40 BK15
Tintagel Cres. SE22 162 DT84
Tintagel Dr., Stan. 95 CK49
Tintagel Gdns. SE22 162 DT84
Oxonian St.
Tintagel Rd., Orp. 206 EW103
Tintagel Way, Wok. 227 BA116
Tintells La., Lthd. 245 BP128
Tintern Ave. NW9 118 CP55
Tintern Clo. SW15 179 CY85
Tintern Clo. SW19 180 DC94
Tintern Clo., Slou. 151 AQ76
Tintern Gdns. N14 99 DL45
Tintern Path NW9 118 CS58
Ruthin Clo.
Tintern Rd. N22 100 DQ53
Tintern Rd., Cars. 200 DD102
Tintern St. SW4 161 DL84
Tintern Way, Har. 116 CB60
Tinto Rd. E16 144 EG70
Tinwell Ms., Borwd. 78 CQ43
Cranes Way
Tinworth St. SE11 278 A10
Tinworth St. SE11 161 DM78
Tippendell La., St.Alb. 60 CB26
Tippetts Clo., Enf. 82 DQ39
Tipthorpe Rd. SW11 160 DG83
Tipton Cotts., Add. 212 BG105
Oliver Clo.
Tipton Dr., Croy. 220 DS105
Tiptree Clo. E4 101 EC48
Mapleton Rd.
Tiptree Clo., Horn. 128 FN60
Tiptree Cres., Ilf. 125 EN55
Tiptree Dr., Enf. 82 DR42
Tiptree Est., Ilf. 125 EN55
Tiptree Rd., Ruis. 115 BV63
Tiree Clo., Hem.H. 41 BP22
Tirlemont Rd., S.Croy. 220 DQ108
Tirrell Rd., Croy. 202 DQ100
Tisbury Ct. W1 141 DK73
Rupert St.
Tisbury Rd. SW16 201 DL96
Tisdall Pl. SE17 279 L9
Tisdall Pl. SE17 162 DR77
Titan Rd., Grays 170 GA78
Titan Rd., Hem.H. 40 BM17
Titchborne Row W2 272 C9
Titchfield Rd. NW8 140 DF67
Titchfield Rd., Cars. 200 DD102
Titchfield Rd., Enf. 83 DY37
Titchfield Wk., Cars. 200 DD101
Titchfield Rd.
Titchwell Rd. SW18 180 DD87
Tite Hill, Egh. 172 AX92
Tite St. SW3 160 DF78
Tithe Barn Clo., Kings.T. 198 CM95
Tithe Barn Clo., St.Alb. 42 CC23
Tithe Barn Ct., Abb.L. 59 BT29
Tithe Barn Dr., Maid. 150 AD78
Tithe Barn Est., St.Alb. 42 CC24
Tithe Barn Way, Nthlt. 135 BV69
Tithe Clo. NW7 97 CU53
Tithe Clo., Hayes 135 BT71
Gledwood Dr.
Tithe Clo., Maid. 150 AC78
Tithe Ct., Slou. 153 BA77
Tithe Fm. Ave., Har. 116 CA62
Tithe Fm. Clo., Har. 116 CA62
Tithe La., Stai. 173 BA86
Tithe Meadow, Vir.W. 192 AX100
Tithe Meadow, Wat. 75 BR44
Tithe Wk. NW7 97 CU53
Tithebarns La., Wok. 244 BG126
Tithelands, Harl. 51 EN18
Tithepit Shaw La., Warl. 236 DV117
Titian Ave. (Bushey), Wat. 95 CE45
Titley Clo. E4 101 EA50
Titmus Clo., Uxb. 135 BQ72
Titmuss Ave. SE28 146 EV73
Titmuss St. W12 159 CV75
Titsey Hill, Oxt. 238 EF123
Titsey Rd., Oxt. 254 EG128
Tiverton Ave., Ilf. 125 EN55
Tiverton Dr. SE9 185 EQ88
Tiverton Gro., Rom. 106 FN50
Tiverton Rd. N15 122 DR58
Tiverton Rd. N18 100 DS50
Tiverton Rd. NW10 139 CX67
Tiverton Rd., Edg. 96 CM54
Tiverton Rd., Houns. 156 CC82
Tiverton Rd., Pot.B. 64 DD31
Tiverton Rd., Ruis. 115 BU62
Tiverton Rd., Th.Hth. 201 DN99
Willett Rd.
Tiverton Rd., Wem. 138 CL68
Tiverton St. SE1 279 H7
Tiverton St. SE1 162 DQ76
Tiverton Way, Chess. 215 CJ106
Tivoli Ct. SE16 163 DZ75
Tivoli Gdns. SE18 164 EL77
Tivoli Rd. N8 121 DK57
Tivoli Rd. SE27 182 DQ92
Tivoli Rd., Houns. 156 BY84
Toad La., Houns. 156 BZ84
Tobacco Quay E1 142 DV73
Wapping La.
Tobago St. E14 163 EA75
Manilla St.
Tobin Clo. NW3 140 DE66
Toby La. E1 143 DY70
Toby Way, Surb. 198 CP103
Tockley Rd., Slou. 130 AH69
Todd Clo., Rain. 148 FK70
Toddbrook, Harl. 51 EP16
Harberts Rd.
Todds Clo., Horl. 268 DE146
Todds Wk. N7 121 DM61
Andover Rd.
Toft Ave., Grays 170 GD77
Token Yd. SW15 159 CY84
Montserrat Rd.
Tokenhouse Yd. EC2 275 K8
Tokyngton Ave., Wem. 138 CN65
Toland Sq. SW15 179 CU85
Tolcarne Dr., Pnr. 115 BV55
Toley Ave., Wem. 118 CL59
Tollbridge Clo. W10 139 CY70
Kensal Rd.
Tolldene Clo., Wok. 226 AS117
Robin Hood Rd.
Tollers La., Couls. 235 DM119
Tollesbury Gdns., Ilf. 125 ER55
Tollet St. E1 143 DX70
Tollgate, Guil. 243 BD133
Tollgate Ave., Red. 266 DF139
Tollgate Clo., Rick. 73 BF41
Tollgate Dr. SE21 182 DS89
Tollgate Gdns. NW6 140 DB68
Tollgate Rd. E6 144 EK71
Tollgate Rd. E16 144 EJ71
Tollgate Rd., Dart. 189 FR87
Tollgate Rd., Dor. 263 CH139
Tollgate Rd., St.Alb. 44 CR23
Tollgate Rd., Wal.Cr. 83 DX35
Tollhouse La., Wall. 219 DJ109
Tollhouse Way N19 121 DJ61
Tollington Pk. N4 121 DM61
Tollington Pl. N4 121 DM61
Tollington Rd. N7 121 DM63
Tollington Way N7 121 DL62
Tollpit End, Hem.H. 40 BG17
Tolmers Ave. (Cuffley), Pot.B. 65 DL28
Tolmers Gdns. (Cuffley), Pot.B. 65 DL29
Tolmers Ms., Hert. 65 DL25
Tolmers Pk., Hert. 65 DL25
Tolmers Rd. (Cuffley), Pot.B. 65 DL27
Tolmers Sq. NW1 273 L4
Tolpits Clo., Wat. 75 BT43
Tolpits La., Wat. 75 BT44
Tolpuddle Ave. E13 144 EJ67
Rochester Ave.
Tolpuddle St. N1 141 DN68
Tolsford Rd. E5 122 DV64
Tolson Rd., Islw. 157 CG83
Tolvaddon, Wok. 226 AU117
Cardingham
Tolverne Rd. SW20 199 CW95
Tolworth Clo., Surb. 198 CP102
Tolworth Gdns., Rom. 126 EX57
Tolworth Pk. Rd., Surb. 198 CM103
Tolworth Ri. N., Surb. 198 CQ101
Elmbridge Ave.
Tolworth Ri. S., Surb. 198 CQ102
Warren Dr. S.
Tolworth Rd., Surb. 198 CL103
Tolworth Twr., Surb. 198 CP103
Tom Coombs Clo. SE9 164 EL84
Well Hall Rd.
Tom Cribb Rd. SE28 165 EQ76
Tom Gros. Clo. E15 123 ED64
Maryland St.
Tom Hood Clo. E15 123 ED64
Maryland St.
Tom Jenkinson Rd. E16 144 EG74
Tom Mann Clo., Bark. 145 ES67
Tom Nolan Clo. E15 144 EE68
Tom Smith Clo. SE10 164 EE79
Maze Hill
Tom Thumbs Arch E3 143 EA68
Malmesbury Rd.
Tomahawk Gdns., Nthlt. 136 BX69
Javelin Way
Tomkins Clo., Borwd. 78 CL39
Tallis Way
Tomkyns La., Upmin. 129 FR56
Tomlin Clo., Epsom 216 CR111
Tomlin Rd., Slou. 131 AL70
Tomlins Gro. E3 143 EA69
Tomlins Orchard, Bark. 145 EQ67
Tomlins Ter. E14 143 DZ71
Rhodeswell Rd.
Tomlins Wk. N7 121 DM61
Briset Way
Tomlinson Clo. E2 142 DT69
Tomlinson Clo. W4 158 CP78
Oxford Rd. N.
Tomlyns Clo., Brwd. 109 GE44
Tomo Ind. Est., Uxb. 134 BJ72
Tompion St. EC1 274 F3
Toms Cft., Hem.H. 40 BL21
Toms Hill, Rick. 74 BL36
Toms La., Abb.L. 59 BR28
Toms La., Kings L. 59 BP29
Tomsfield, Hat. 44 CS19
Tomswood Ct., Ilf. 103 EQ53
Tomswood Hill, Ilf. 103 EP52
Tomswood Rd., Chig. 103 EN51
Tonbridge Clo., Bans. 218 DF114
Tonbridge Cres., Har. 118 CL56
Tonbridge Ho. SE25 202 DU97
Tonbridge Rd., Rom. 106 FK52
Tonbridge Rd., Sev. 257 FJ126
Tonbridge Rd., W.Mol. 196 BY98
Tonbridge St. WC1 273 P2
Tonbridge St. WC1 141 DL69
Tonbridge Wk. WC1 141 DL69
Tonbridge St.
Tonfield Rd., Sutt. 199 CZ102
Tonge Clo., Beck. 203 EA99
Tonsley Hill SW18 180 DB85
Tonsley Pl. SW18 180 DB85
Tonsley Rd. SW18 180 DB85
Tonsley St. SW18 180 DB85
Tonstall Rd., Epsom 216 CR110
Tonstall Rd., Mitch. 200 DG96
Tony Cannell Ms. E3 143 DZ69
Maplin St.
Tooke Clo., Pnr. 94 BY53
Took's Ct. EC4 274 D8
Tooley St. SE1 279 L2
Tooley St. SE1 142 DR74
Tooley St., Grav. 190 GD87
Toorack Rd., Har. 95 CD54
Toot Hill Rd., Ong. 71 FF30
Tooting Bec Gdns. SW16 181 DK91
Tooting Bec Rd. SW16 180 DG90
Tooting Bec Rd. SW17 180 DG90
Tooting Gro. SW17 180 DE92
Tooting High St. SW17 180 DE93
Tootswood Rd., Brom. 204 EE99
Tooveys Mill Clo., Kings L. 58 BN28
Top Dartford Rd., Swan. 187 FF94
Top Ho. Ri. E4 101 EC45
Parkhill Rd.
Top Pk., Beck. 204 EE99
Top Pk., Ger.Cr. 112 AW58
Topaz Clo., Slou. 131 AP74
Pearl Gdns.
Topaz Wk. NW2 119 CX59
Marble Dr.
Topcliffe Dr., Orp. 223 ER105
Topham Sq. N17 100 DQ53
Topham St. EC1 274 D4
Topiary, The, Ash. 232 CL121
Topiary Sq., Rich. 158 CM83
Topland Rd., Ger.Cr. 90 AX52
Toplands Ave., S.Ock. 148 FP74
Topley St. SE9 164 EK84
Topmast Pt. E14 163 EA75
Topp Wk. NW2 119 CW61
Topping La., Uxb. 134 BK69
Topsfield Clo. N8 121 DK57
Wolseley Rd.
Topsfield Par. N8 121 DL57
Tottenham La.
Topsfield Rd. N8 121 DL57
Topsham Rd. SW17 180 DF90
Tor Gdns. W8 160 DA75
Tor La., Wey. 213 BQ111
Tor Rd., Well. 166 EW81
Torbay Rd. NW6 139 CZ66
Torbay Rd., Har. 116 BY61
Torbay St. NW1 141 DH66
Hawley Rd.
Torbitt Way, Ilf. 125 ET57

Torbridge Clo., Edg. 96 CL52
Torbrook Clo., Bex. 186 EY86
Torcross Dr. SE23 182 DW89
Torcross Rd., Ruis. 115 BV62
Torin Ct., Egh. 172 AW92
Torland Dr., Lthd. 215 CD114
Tormead Clo., Sutt. 218 DA107
Tormead Rd., Guil. 243 AZ134
Tormount Rd. SE18 165 ES79
Toronto Ave. E12 125 EM63
Toronto Dr., Horl. 269 DN148
Toronto Rd. E11 123 ED63
Toronto Rd., Ilf. 125 EP60
Toronto Rd., Til. 171 GG82
Torquay Gdns., Ilf. 124 EK56
Torquay Spur, Slou. 131 AP69
Torquay St. W2 140 DB71
Harrow Rd.
Torr Rd. SE20 183 DX94
Torrance Clo., Horn. 127 FH60
Torre Wk., Cars. 200 DE102
Torrens Clo., Guil. 242 AU131
Torrens Rd. E15 144 EF65
Torrens Rd. SW2 181 DM85
Torrens Sq. E15 144 EE65
Torrens St. EC1 274 E1
Torrens St. EC1 141 DN68
Torrens Wk., Grav. 191 GL92
Torres Sq. E14 163 EA78
Napier Ave.
Torriano Ave. NW5 121 DK64
Torriano Cotts. NW5 121 DJ64
Torriano Ave.
Torriano Ms. NW5 121 DK64
Torriano Ave.
Torridge Gdns. SE15 162 DW84
Torridge Rd., Slou. 153 BB79
Torridge Rd., Th.Hth. 201 DP99
Torridge Wk., Hem.H. 40 BM15
The Dee
Torridon Clo., Wok. 226 AV117
Torridon Rd. SE6 183 ED88
Torridon Rd. SE13 183 ED87
Torrington Ave. N12 98 DD50
Torrington Clo. N12 98 DD49
Torrington Clo., Esher 215 CE107
Torrington Dr., Har. 116 CB63
Torrington Dr., Loug. 85 EQ42
Torrington Dr., Pot.B. 64 DD32
Torrington Gdns. N11 99 DJ51
Torrington Gdns., Grnf. 137 CJ66
Torrington Gdns., Loug. 85 EQ42
Torrington Gro. N12 98 DE50
Torrington Pk. N12 98 DD50
Torrington Pl. E1 142 DU74
Torrington Pl. WC1 273 M6
Torrington Pl. WC1 141 DK71
Torrington Rd. E18 124 EG55
Torrington Rd., Berk. 38 AV19
Torrington Rd., Dag. 126 EZ60
Torrington Rd., Esher 215 CE107
Torrington Rd., Grnf. 137 CJ67
Torrington Rd., Ruis. 115 BT62
Torrington Sq. WC1 273 N5
Torrington Sq. WC1 141 DK70
Torrington Sq., Croy. 202 DR101
Tavistock Gro.
Torrington Way, Mord. 200 DA100
Tortoiseshell Way, Berk. 38 AT17
Torver Rd., Har. 117 CE56
Torver Way, Orp. 205 ER104
Torwood Clo., Berk. 38 AT19
Torwood La., Whyt. 236 DT120
Torwood Rd. SW15 179 CU85
Torworth Rd., Borwd. 78 CM39
Tothill St. SW1 277 M5
Tothill St. SW1 161 DK75
Totnes Rd., Well. 166 EV80
Totnes Wk. N2 120 DD56
Tottan Ter. E1 143 DX72
Tottenhall Rd. N13 99 DN51
Tottenham Ct. Rd. W1 273 L5
Tottenham Ct. Rd. W1 141 DJ70
Tottenham Grn. E. N15 122 DT56
Tottenham La. N8 121 DL57
Tottenham Ms. W1 273 L6
Tottenham Rd. N1 142 DS65
Tottenham St. W1 273 L7
Tottenham St. W1 141 DJ71
Totterdown St. SW17 180 DF91
Totteridge Common N20 97 CU47
Totteridge Grn. N20 98 DA47
Totteridge La. N20 98 DA47
Totteridge Rd., Enf. 83 DX37
Totteridge Village N20 97 CY46
Totternhoe Clo., Har. 117 CJ57
Totton Rd., Th.Hth. 201 DN97
Toulmin Dr., St.Alb. 42 CC16
Toulmin St. SE1 279 H5
Toulmin St. SE1 162 DQ75
Toulon St. SE5 162 DQ80
Tournay Rd. SW6 159 CZ80
Toussaint Wk. SE16 162 DU76
John Roll Way
Tovey Ave., Hodd. 49 EA15
Tovey Clo., St.Alb. 61 CK26
Tovey Clo., Wal.Abb. 50 EE23
Tovil Clo. SE20 202 DU96
Towcester Rd. E3 143 EB70
Tower Bri. E1 279 P3
Tower Bri. E1 142 DT74
Tower Bri. SE1 279 P3
Tower Bri. SE1 142 DT74
Tower Bri. App. E1 279 P2
Tower Bri. App. E1 142 DT74
Tower Bri. Piazza SE1 142 DT74
Horselydown La.
Tower Bri. Rd. SE1 279 M7
Tower Bri. Rd. SE1 162 DS76
Tower Clo. NW3 120 DD64
Lyndhurst Rd.
Tower Clo. SE20 182 DV94
Tower Clo., Berk. 38 AU20
Tower Clo., Epp. 53 FD24
Tower Clo., Grav. 191 GL92
Tower Clo., H.Wyc. 110 AC56
Tower Clo., Horl. 268 DF148
Tower Clo., Ilf. 103 EP51
Tower Clo., Orp. 205 ET103
Tower Clo., Wok. 226 AX117
Tower Ct. WC2 273 P9
Tower Ct., Brwd. 108 FV47
Tower Cft. (Eynsford), Dart. 208 FL103
High St.
Tower Gdns. Rd. N17 100 DQ53
Tower Gro., Wey. 195 BS103
Tower Hamlets Rd. E7 124 EF63
Tower Hamlets Rd. E17 123 EA55
Tower Hill EC3 279 N1
Tower Hill EC3 142 DS73
Tower Hill, Brwd. 108 FW47
Tower Hill, Dor. 263 CH138
Tower Hill, Guil. 261 BQ140
Tower Hill, Kings L. 57 BE29
Tower Hill La., Guil. 261 BQ140
Tower Hill
Tower Hill La., St.Alb. 28 CM10
Tower Hill Ri., Guil. 261 BQ140
Tower Hill Rd., Dor. 263 CH138
Tower Hill Ter. EC3 142 DS73
Byward St.
Tower La., Guil. 261 BQ140
Tower La., Wem. 117 CK62
Main Dr.
Tower Ms. E17 123 EA56
Tower Mill Rd. SE15 162 DS79
Wells Way
Tower Pier EC3 279 N2
Tower Pier EC3 142 DT74
Tower Pl. EC3 279 N1
Tower Pt., Enf. 82 DR42
Tower Ri., Rich. 158 CL83
Jocelyn Rd.
Tower Rd. NW10 139 CU66
Tower Rd., Amer. 55 AN43
Tower Rd., Belv. 167 FC77
Tower Rd., Bexh. 167 FB84
Tower Rd., Dart. 188 FJ87
Tower Rd., Epp. 69 ES30
Tower Rd., Orp. 205 ET103
Tower Rd., Tad. 233 CW123
Tower Rd., Twick. 177 CF90
Tower Rd., Ware 33 DY05
Tower Royal EC4 275 J10
Tower St. WC2 273 N9
Tower St. WC2 141 DK72
Tower St., Hert. 32 DQ07
Tower Ter. N22 99 DM54
Mayes Rd.
Tower Vw., Croy. 203 DX101
Towers, The, Ken. 236 DQ115
Towers Ave., Uxb. 135 BQ69
Towers Pl., Rich. 178 CL85
Eton St.
Towers Rd., Grays 170 GC78
Towers Rd., Hem.H. 40 BL19
Towers Rd., Pnr. 94 BY53
Towers Rd., Sthl. 136 CA70
Towers Wk., Wey. 213 BP107
Towers Wd., Dart. 209 FR95
Towfield Rd., Felt. 176 BZ89
Towing Path, Guil. 242 AW132
Towing Path Wk. N1 141 DK67
York Way
Town, The, Enf. 82 DR41
Town Bri. Ct., Chesh. 54 AP32
Water Meadow
Town Cen., Hat. 45 CU17
Town Ct. Path N4 122 DQ60
Town End, Cat. 236 DS122
Town End Clo., Cat. 236 DS122
Town Fld. La., Ch.St.G. 90 AW48
Town Fld. Way, Islw. 157 CG82
Town Hall App. N16 122 DS63
Milton Gro.
Town Hall App. Rd. N15 122 DT56
Town Hall Ave. W4 158 CR78
Town Hall Rd. SW11 160 DF83
Town La., H.Wyc. 110 AD59
Town La., Stai. 174 BK86
Town Meadow, Brent. 157 CK80
Town Path, Egh. 173 BA92
Town Quay, Bark. 145 EP67
Town Rd. N9 100 DV47
Town Sq., Erith 167 FE79
Pier Rd.
Town Sq. Cres. (Bluewater), Green. 189 FT87
Town Tree Rd., Ashf. 174 BN92
Towncourt Cres., Orp. 205 EQ99
Towncourt La., Orp. 205 ER100
Towney Mead, Nthlt. 136 BZ68
Towney Mead Ct., Nthlt. 136 BZ68
Towney Mead
Townfield, Chesh. 54 AP32
Townfield, Rick. 92 BJ45
Townfield Cor., Grav. 191 GJ88
Townfield Rd., Dor. 263 CG137
Townfield Rd., Hayes 135 BT74
Townfield Sq., Hayes 135 BT73
Townfields, Hat. 45 CU17
Towngate, Cob. 230 BY115
Townholm Cres. W7 157 CF76
Townley Ct. E15 144 EF65
Townley Rd. SE22 182 DS85
Townley Rd., Bexh. 186 EZ86
Townley St. SE17 279 K10
Townmead, Red. 252 DR133
Townmead Rd. SW6 160 DC82
Townmead Rd., Rich. 158 CP82
Townmead Rd., Wal.Abb. 67 EC34
Townsend, Hem.H. 40 BK18
Townsend Ave. N14 99 DK49
Townsend Ave., St.Alb. 43 CE19
Townsend Dr., St.Alb. 43 CD17
Townsend Ind. Est. NW10 138 CR68
Townsend La. NW9 118 CR59
Townsend La., Wok. 227 BB121
St. Peters Rd.
Townsend Rd. N15 122 DT57
Townsend Rd., Ashf. 174 BL92
Townsend Rd., Chesh. 54 AP30
Townsend Rd., Sthl. 136 BY74
Townsend St. SE17 279 L9
Townsend St. SE17 162 DR77
Townsend Way, Nthwd. 93 BT52
Townsend Yd. N6 121 DH60
Townshend Clo., Sid. 186 EV93
Townshend Est. NW8 140 DE68
Townshend Rd. NW8 140 DE67
Townshend Rd., Chis. 185 EP92
Townshend Rd., Rich. 158 CM84
Townshend St., Hert. 32 DS09
Townshend Ter., Rich. 158 CM84
Townshott Clo., Lthd. 246 CA125
Townslow La., Wok. 228 BK116
Townson Ave., Nthlt. 135 BU69
Townson Way, Nthlt. 135 BU68
Townson Ave.
Towpath, Shep. 194 BM102
Dockett Eddy La.
Towpath Wk. E9 123 DZ64
Towpath Way, Croy. 202 DT100
Towton Rd. SE27 182 DQ89
Toynbec Clo., Chis. 185 EP91
Beechwood Ri.
Toynbee Rd. SW20 199 CY95
Toynbee St. E1 275 P7
Toynbee St. E1 142 DT71
Toyne Way N6 120 DF58
Gaskell Rd.
Tozer Wk., Wind. 151 AK83
Tinkers La.
Tracery, The, Bans. 234 DB115
Tracey Ave. NW2 119 CW64
Tracious Clo., Wok. 226 AV116
Sythwood
Tracious La., Wok. 226 AV116
Tracy Ct., Stan. 95 CJ52
Tracyes Rd., Harl. 52 EV17
Trade Clo. N13 99 DN49
Trader Rd. E6 145 EP72
Tradescant Rd. SW8 161 DL80
Trading Est. Rd. NW10 138 CQ70
Trafalgar Ave. N17 100 DS51
Trafalgar Ave. SE15 162 DT78
Trafalgar Ave., Brox. 49 DZ21
Trafalgar Ave., Wor.Pk. 199 CX102
Trafalgar Business Cen., Bark. 145 ET70
Trafalgar Clo. SE16 163 DY77
Greenland Quay
Trafalgar Ct., Cob. 213 BU113
Trafalgar Dr., Walt. 195 BU104
Trafalgar Gdns. E1 143 DX71
Trafalgar Gdns. W8 160 DB76
South End Row
Trafalgar Gro. SE10 163 ED79
Trafalgar Pl. E11 124 EG56
Trafalgar Pl. N18 100 DU50
Trafalgar Rd. SE10 163 ED79
Trafalgar Rd. SW19 180 DB94
Trafalgar Rd., Dart. 188 FL89
Trafalgar Rd., Grav. 191 GG87
Trafalgar Rd., Rain. 147 FF68
Trafalgar Rd., Twick. 177 CD89
Trafalgar Sq. SW1 277 N2
Trafalgar Sq. SW1 141 DK74
Trafalgar Sq. WC2 277 N2
Trafalgar Sq. WC2 141 DK74
Trafalgar St. SE17 279 K10
Trafalgar St. SE17 162 DR78
Trafalgar Ter., Har. 117 CE60
Nelson Rd.
Trafalgar Way E14 143 EC74
Trafalgar Way, Croy. 201 DM103
Trafford Clo. E15 123 EB64
Trafford Clo., Ilf. 103 ET51
Trafford Clo., Rad. 62 CL32
Trafford Rd., Th.Hth. 201 DM99
Tralee Ct. SE16 162 DV78
Masters Dr.
Tramway Ave. E15 144 EE66
Tramway Ave. N9 100 DV45
Tramway Path, Mitch. 200 DF99
Tranby Pl. E9 123 DX64
Homerton High St.
Tranley Ms. NW3 120 DE63
Fleet Rd.
Tranmere Rd. N9 100 DT45
Tranmere Rd. SW18 180 DC89
Tranmere Rd., Twick. 176 CB87
Tranquil Dale, Bet. 249 CT132
Tranquil Pas. SE3 164 EF82
Tranquil Vale
Tranquil Ri., Erith 167 FE78
West St.
Tranquil Vale SE3 164 EE82
Transay Wk. N1 142 DR65
Marquess Rd.
Transept St. NW1 272 B7
Transept St. NW1 140 DE71
Transmere Clo., Orp. 205 EQ100
Transmere Rd., Orp. 205 EQ100
Transom Clo. SE16 163 DY77
Plough Way
Transom Sq. E14 163 EB78
Transport Ave., Brent. 157 CH78
Tranton Rd. SE16 162 DU76
Trapps La., Chesh. 54 AR32
Traps Hill, Loug. 85 EM41
Traps La., N.Mal. 198 CS95
Trapstyle Rd., Ware 32 DU05
Trasher Mead, Dor. 263 CJ139
Travellers Clo., Hat. 45 CW23
Travellers La., Hat. 45 CU19
Travellers La. (Welham Grn.), Hat. 45 CV21
Travellers Way, Houns. 156 BW82
Travers Clo. E17 101 DX53
Travers Rd. N7 121 DN62
Travic Rd., Slou. 131 AM69
Travis Ct., Slou. 131 AP69
Treachers Clo., Chesh. 54 AP31
Treacy Clo. (Bushey), Wat. 94 CC47
Treadgold St. W11 139 CX73
Treadway St. E2 142 DV68
Treadwell Rd., Epsom 232 CS116
Treaty Rd., Houns. 156 CB83
Hanworth Rd.
Treaty St. N1 141 DM67
Trebble Rd., Swans. 190 FY86
Trebeck St. W1 277 H2
Trebellan Dr., Hem.H. 40 BM19
Trebovir Rd. SW5 160 DA78
Treby St. E3 143 DZ70
Trecastle Way N7 121 DK63
Carleton Rd.
Tredegar Ms. E3 143 DZ69
Tredegar Ter.
Tredegar Rd. E3 143 DZ68
Tredegar Rd. N11 99 DK52
Tredegar Rd., Dart. 187 FG89
Tredegar Sq. E3 143 DZ69
Tredegar Ter. E3 143 DZ69
Trederwen Rd. E8 142 DU67
Tredown Rd. SE26 182 DW92
Tredwell Clo. SW2 181 DM89
Hillside Rd.
Tredwell Clo., Brom. 204 EL98
Tredwell Rd. SE27 181 DP91
Tree Clo., Rich. 177 CK88
Tree Rd. E16 144 EJ72
Tree Tops, Brwd. 108 FW46
Tree Way, Reig. 250 DB131
Treebourne Rd., West. 238 EJ117
Treebys Ave., Guil. 242 AX128
Treelands, Dor. 263 CJ139
Treen Ave. SW13 159 CT83
Treeside Clo., West Dr. 154 BK77
Treetops, Grav. 191 GH92
Treetops, Whyt. 236 DU118
Treetops Clo. SE2 166 EY78
Treetops Clo., Nthwd. 93 BR50
Treetops Vw., Loug. 84 EJ44
High Rd.
Treeview Clo. SE19 202 DS95
Treewall Gdns., Brom. 184 EH91
Trefgarne Rd., Dag. 126 FA61
Trefil Wk. N7 121 DL63
Trefoil Ho., Erith 166 EY75
Kale Rd.
Trefoil Rd. SW18 180 DC85
Trefusis Wk., Wat. 75 BS39
Tregaron Ave. N8 121 DL58
Tregaron Gdns., N.Mal. 198 CS98
Avenue Rd.
Tregarth Pl., Wok. 226 AT117
Tregarthen Pl., Lthd. 231 CJ121
Tregarvon Rd. SW11 160 DG84
Tregelles Rd., Hodd. 33 EA14
Tregenna Ave., Har. 116 BZ63
Tregenna Clo. N14 81 DJ43
Tregenna Ct., Har. 116 CA63
Trego Rd. E9 143 EA66
Tregothnan Rd. SW9 161 DL83
Tregunter Rd. SW10 160 DC79
Trehearn Rd., Ilf. 103 ER52
Trehern Rd. SW14 158 CR83
Treherne Ct. SW9 161 DN81
Eythorne Rd.
Treherne Ct. SW17 180 DG91
Trehurst St. E5 123 DY64
Trelawn Clo., Cher. 211 BC108
Trelawn Rd. E10 123 EC62
Trelawn Rd. SW2 181 DN85
Trelawney Ave., Slou. 152 AX76
Trelawney Clo. E17 123 EB56
Orford Rd.
Trelawney Est. E9 142 DW65
Trelawney Gro., Wey. 212 BN107
Trelawney Rd., Ilf. 103 ER52
Trellick Twr. W10 139 CZ70
Trellis Sq. E3 143 DZ69
Malmesbury Rd.
Treloar Gdns. SE19 182 DR93
Hancock Rd.
Tremadoc Rd. SW4 161 DK84
Tremaine Clo. SE4 163 EA82
Tremaine Gro., Hem.H. 40 BL16
Tremaine Rd. SE20 202 DV96
Trematon Pl., Tedd. 177 CJ94
Tremlett Gro. N19 121 DJ62
Tremlett Ms. N19 121 DJ62
Trenance, Wok. 226 AU117
Cardingham
Trenance Gdns., Ilf. 126 EU62
Trench Yd. Ct., Mord. 200 DB100
Green La.
Trenchard Ave., Ruis. 115 BV63
Trenchard Clo. NW9 96 CS53
Fulbeck Dr.
Trenchard Clo., Stan. 95 CG51
Trenchard Clo., Walt. 214 BW106
Trenchard Ct., Mord. 200 DB100
Green La.
Trenchard St. SE10 163 ED78
Trenches La., Slou. 133 BA73
Trenchold St. SW8 161 DL79
Trenham Dr., Warl. 236 DW116
Trenholme Clo. SE20 182 DV94
Trenholme Ct., Cat. 236 DU122
Trenholme Rd. SE20 182 DV94
Trenholme Ter. SE20 182 DV94
Trenmar Gdns. NW10 139 CV69
Trent Ave. W5 157 CJ76
Trent Ave., Upmin. 129 FR58
Trent Clo., Rad. 62 CL32
Edgbaston Dr.
Trent Gdns. N14 81 DH44
Trent Rd. SW2 181 DM85
Trent Rd., Buck.H. 102 EH46
Trent Rd., Slou. 153 BB79
Trent Way, Hayes 135 BS68
Trent Way, Wor.Pk. 199 CW104
Trentbridge Clo., Ilf. 103 ET51
Trentham Cres., Wok. 227 BA121
Trentham Dr., Orp. 206 EU98
Trentham Rd., Red. 266 DG136
Trentham St. SW18 180 DA88
Trentwood Side, Enf. 81 DM41
Treport St. SW18 180 DB87
Tresco Clo., Brom. 184 EE93
Tresco Gdns., Ilf. 126 EU61
Tresco Rd. SE15 162 DV84
Tresco Rd., Berk. 38 AT18
Trescoe Gdns., Har. 116 BY59
Trescoe Gdns., Rom. 105 FC50
Tresham Cres. NW8 272 B4
Tresham Cres. NW8 140 DE70
Tresham Rd., Bark. 145 ET66
Tresham Wk. E9 122 DW64
Churchill Wk.
Tresilian Ave. N21 81 DM43
Tresilian Sq., Hem.H. 40 BM15
The Dee
Tresillian Way, Wok. 226 AU116
Tressell Clo. N1 141 DP66
Sebbon St.
Tressillian Cres. SE4 163 EA83
Tressillian Rd. SE4 163 DZ84
Tresta Wk., Wok. 226 AU115
Trestis Clo., Hayes 136 BY71
Jollys La.
Treston Ct., Stai. 173 BF92
Treswell Rd., Dag. 146 EY67
Tretawn Gdns. NW7 96 CS49
Tretawn Pk. NW7 96 CS49
Trevalga Way, Hem.H. 40 BL16
Trevanion Rd. W14 159 CY78
Treve Ave., Har. 116 CC59
Trevellance Way, Wat. 60 BW33
Trevelyan Ave. E12 125 EM63
Trevelyan Clo., Dart. 168 FM84
Trevelyan Cres., Har. 117 CK59
Trevelyan Gdns. NW10 139 CW67
Trevelyan Rd. E15 124 EF63
Trevelyan Rd. SW17 180 DE92
Trevelyan Way, Berk. 38 AV17
Trevereux Hill, Oxt. 255 EM131
Treveris St. SE1 278 F3
Treverton St. W10 139 CX70
Treves Clo. N21 81 DM43
Treville St. SW15 179 CV87
Treviso Rd. SE23 183 DX89
Farren Rd.
Trevithick Clo., Felt. 175 BT88
Trevithick Dr., Dart. 168 FM84
Trevithick St. SE8 163 EA78
Trevone Gdns., Pnr. 116 BY58
Trevor Clo., Barn. 80 DD43
Trevor Clo., Brom. 204 EF101
Trevor Clo., Har. 95 CF52
Kenton La.
Trevor Clo., Islw. 177 CF85
Trevor Clo., Nthlt. 136 BW68
Trevor Cres., Ruis. 115 BT63
Trevor Gdns., Edg. 96 CR53
Trevor Gdns., Nthlt. 136 BW68
Trevor Gdns., Ruis. 115 BU63
Clyfford Rd.
Trevor Pl. SW7 276 C5
Trevor Pl. SW7 160 DE75
Trevor Rd. SW19 179 CY94
Trevor Rd., Edg. 96 CR53
Trevor Rd., Hayes 155 BS75
Trevor Rd., Wdf.Grn. 102 EG52
Trevor Sq. SW7 276 D5
Trevor Sq. SW7 160 DF75
Trevor St. SW7 276 C5
Trevor St. SW7 160 DE75
Trevor Wk. SW7 160 DF75
Trevor Sq.
Trevose Ave., W.Byf. 211 BF114
Trevose Rd. E17 101 ED53
Trevose Way, Wat. 94 BW48
Trewarden Ave., Iver 133 BD68
Trewenna Dr., Chess. 215 CK106
Trewenna Dr., Pot.B. 64 DD32
Trewince Rd. SW20 199 CW95
Trewint St. SW18 180 DC89
Trewsbury Ho. SE2 166 EX75
Hartslock Dr.
Trewsbury Rd. SE26 183 DX92
Triandra Way, Hayes 136 BX71
Triangle, The EC1 141 DP70
Goswell Rd.
Triangle, The N13 99 DN49
Lodge Dr.
Triangle, The, Bark. 145 EQ65
Tanner St.
Triangle, The, Hmptn. 196 CC95
High St.
Triangle, The, Kings.T. 198 CQ96
Kenley Rd.
Triangle, The, Wok. 226 AW118
St. John's Rd.
Triangle Ct. E16 144 EK71
Tollgate Rd.
Triangle Pas., Barn. 80 DC42
Triangle Pl. SW4 161 DK84
Triangle Rd. E8 142 DV67
Trident Gdns., Nthlt. 136 BX69
Jetstar Way
Trident Ind. Est., Hodd. 49 EB17
Trident Ind. Est., Slou. 153 BE83
Trident Rd., Wat. 59 BT34
Trident St. SE16 163 DX77
Trident Way, Sthl. 155 BV76
Trig La. EC4 275 H10
Trigg's Clo., Wok. 226 AX119
Trigg's La., Wok. 226 AX118
Trigo Ct., Epsom 216 CR111
Blakeney Clo.
Trigon Rd. SW8 161 DM80
Trilby Rd. SE23 183 DX89
Trim St. SE14 163 DZ79
Trimmer Wk., Brent. 158 CL79
Trinder Gdns. N19 121 DL60
Trinder Rd.
Trinder Rd. N19 121 DL60
Trinder Rd., Barn. 79 CW43
Trindles Rd., Red. 267 DM136
Tring Ave. W5 138 CM74
Tring Ave., Sthl. 136 BZ72
Tring Ave., Wem. 138 CN65
Tring Clo., Ilf. 125 EQ57
Tring Clo., Rom. 106 FM49
Tring Gdns., Rom. 106 FL49
Tring Grn., Rom. 106 FL49
Tring Gdns.
Tring Wk., Rom. 106 FL49
Tring Gdns.
Tringham Clo., Cher. 211 BC106
Trinidad Gdns., Dag. 147 FD66
Trinidad St. E14 143 DZ73
Trinity Ave. N2 120 DD55
Trinity Ave., Enf. 82 DT44
Trinity Buoy Wf. E14 144 EF73
Trinity Ch. Pas. SW13 159 CV79
Trinity Ch. Rd. SW13 159 CV79
Trinity Ch. Sq. SE1 279 J6
Trinity Ch. Sq. SE1 162 DQ76
Trinity Chyd., Guil. 258 AX136
High St.
Trinity Clo. E8 142 DT65
Trinity Clo. E11 124 EE61
Trinity Clo. NW3 120 DD63
Hampstead High St.
Trinity Clo. SE13 163 ED84
Wisteria Rd.
Trinity Clo., Brom. 204 EL102
Trinity Clo., Houns. 156 BY84
Trinity Clo., Nthwd. 93 BS51
Trinity Clo., S.Croy. 220 DS109
Trinity Clo., Stai. 174 BJ86
Trinity Cotts., Rich. 158 CM83
Trinity Rd.
Trinity Ct. N1 142 DS66
Downham Rd.
Trinity Ct. SE7 164 EK77
Charlton La.
Trinity Cres. SW17 180 DF89
Trinity Gdns. E16 144 EF70
Cliff Wk.
Trinity Gdns. SW9 161 DM84
Trinity Gro. SE10 163 EC81
Trinity Gro., Hert. 32 DQ07
Trinity Hall Clo., Wat. 76 BW41
Trinity La., Wal.Cr. 67 DY32
Trinity Ms. SE20 202 DV95
Trinity Ms. W10 139 CX72
Cambridge Gdns.
Trinity Ms., Hem.H. 41 BR21
Pancake La.
Trinity Path SE26 182 DW90
Trinity Pl., Bexh. 166 EZ84
Trinity Pl., Wind. 151 AQ82
Trinity Ri. SW2 181 DN88
Trinity Rd. N2 120 DD55
Trinity Rd. N22 99 DL53
Trinity Rd. SW17 180 DF89
Trinity Rd. SW18 180 DD85
Trinity Rd. SW19 180 DA93
Trinity Rd., Grav. 191 GJ87
Trinity Rd., Hert. 32 DW12

Ullswater Clo., Slou. 130 AJ71
Buttermere Ave.
Ullswater Ct., Har. 116 CA59
Oakington Ave.
Ullswater Cres. SW15 178 CR91
Ullswater Cres., Couls. 235 DL116
Ullswater Rd. SE27 181 DP89
Ullswater Rd. SW13 159 CU80
Ullswater Rd., Hem.H. 41 BQ22
Ullswater Way, Horn. 127 FG64
Ulstan Clo., Cat. 237 EA123
Ulster Gdns. N13 100 DQ49
Ulster Pl. NW1 273 H5
Ulster Ter. NW1 273 H4
Ulundi Rd. SE3 164 EE79
Ulva Rd. SW15 179 CX85
Ravenna Rd.
Ulverscroft Rd. SE22 182 DT85
Ulverston Rd. E17 101 ED54
Ulverstone Rd. SE27 181 DP89
Ulwin Ave., W.Byf. 212 BL113
Ulysses Rd. NW6 119 CZ64
Umberston St. E1 142 DV72
Hessel St.
Umberville Way, Slou. 131 AM69
Umbria St. SW15 179 CU86
Umfreville Rd. N4 121 DP58
Underacres Clo., Hem.H. 40 BN19
Undercliff Rd. SE13 163 EA83
Underhill, Barn. 80 DA43
Underhill Pk. Rd., Reig. 250 DA131
Underhill Pas. NW1 141 DH67
Camden High St.
Underhill Rd. SE22 182 DV86
Underhill St. NW1 141 DH67
Camden High St.
Underne Ave. N14 99 DH47
Underriver Ho. Rd., Sev. 257 FP130
Undershaft EC3 275 M9
Undershaft EC3 142 DS72
Undershaw Rd., Brom. 184 EE90
Underwood, Croy. 221 EC106
Underwood, The SE9 185 EM89
Underwood Rd. E1 142 DU70
Underwood Rd. E4 101 EB50
Underwood Rd., Cat. 252 DS126
Underwood Rd., Wdf.Grn. 102 EK52
Underwood Row N1 275 J2
Underwood Row N1 142 DQ69
Underwood St. N1 275 J2
Underwood St. N1 142 DQ69
Undine Rd. E14 163 EB77
Undine St. SW17 180 DF92
Uneeda Dr., Grnf. 137 CD67
Unicorn Wk., Green. 189 FT85
Union Clo. E11 123 ED63
Union Cotts. E15 144 EE66
Welfare Rd.
Union Ct. EC2 275 M8
Union Ct., Rich. 178 CL85
Eton St.
Union Dr. E1 143 DY70
Canal Clo.
Union Grn., Hem.H. 40 BK19
Union Gro. SW8 161 DK82
Union Rd. N11 99 DK51
Union Rd. SW4 161 DK82
Union Rd. SW8 161 DK82
Union Rd., Brom. 204 EK99
Union Rd., Croy. 202 DQ101
Union Rd., Nthlt. 136 CA68
Union Rd., Wem. 138 CL65
Union Sq. N1 142 DQ67
Union St. E15 143 EC67
Union St. SE1 278 G3
Union St. SE1 141 DP74
Union St., Barn. 79 CY42
Union St., Kings.T. 197 CK96
Union Wk. E2 275 N2
Unity Clo. NW10 139 CU65
Unity Clo. SE19 182 DQ92
Crown Dale
Unity Clo., Croy. 221 EB109
Castle Hill Ave.
Unity Rd., Enf. 82 DW37
Unity Way SE18 164 EK76
Unity Wf. SE1 162 DT75
Mill St.
University Clo. NW7 97 CT52
University Clo., Wat. 76 CA42
University Gdns., Bex. 186 EZ87
University Pl., Erith 167 FB80
Belmont Rd.
University Rd. SW19 180 DD93
University St. WC1 273 L5
University St. WC1 141 DJ70
University Way E16 145 EN73
University Way, Dart. 168 FJ84
Unstead La., Guil. 258 AW144
Unstead Wd., Guil. 258 AW142
Unwin Ave., Felt. 175 BR85
Unwin Clo. SE15 162 DU79
Unwin Rd. SW7 276 A6
Unwin Rd., Islw. 157 CE83
Up Cor., Ch.St.G. 90 AW47
Up Cor. Clo., Ch.St.G. 90 AV47
Upbrook Ms. W2 140 DC72
Chilworth St.
Upcerne Rd. SW10 160 DC80
Upchurch Clo. SE20 182 DV94
Upcroft, Wind. 151 AP83
Upcroft Ave., Edg. 96 CQ50
Updale Clo., Pot.B. 63 CY33
Updale Rd., Sid. 185 ET91
Upfield, Croy. 202 DV103
Upfield, Horl. 268 DG149
Upfield Clo., Horl. 268 DG150
Upfield Rd. W7 137 CF70
Upfolds Grn., Guil. 243 BC130
Upgrove Manor Way SW2 181 DN87
Trinity Ri.
Uphall Rd., Ilf. 125 EP64
Upham Pk. Rd. W4 158 CS77
Uphill Dr. NW7 96 CS50
Uphill Dr. NW9 118 CQ57
Uphill Gro. NW7 96 CS49
Uphill Rd. NW7 96 CS49
Upland Ave., Chesh. 54 AP28
Upland Ct. Rd., Rom. 106 FM54
Upland Dr., Hat. 64 DB25
Upland Ms. SE22 182 DU85
Upland Rd.
Upland Rd. E13 144 EF70
Sutton Rd.
Upland Rd. SE22 182 DU85
Upland Rd., Bexh. 166 EZ83
Upland Rd., Cat. 237 EA120
Upland Rd., Epp. 69 ET25
Upland Rd., S.Croy. 220 DR106
Upland Rd., Sutt. 218 DD108
Upland Way, Epsom 233 CW118
Uplands, Ash. 231 CK120
Uplands, Beck. 203 EA96
Uplands, Rick. 74 BM44
Uplands, Ware 33 DZ05
Uplands, Welw.G.C. 29 CW05
Uplands, The, Ger.Cr. 112 AY60
Uplands, The, Loug. 85 EM41
Uplands, The, Ruis. 115 BU60
Uplands, The, St.Alb. 60 BY30
Uplands Ave. E17 101 DX54
Blackhorse La.
Uplands Business Pk. E17 101 DX54
Uplands Clo. SW14 178 CP85
Monroe Dr.
Uplands Clo., Ger.Cr. 112 AY60
Uplands Clo., Sev. 256 FF123
Uplands Dr., Lthd. 215 CD113
Uplands End, Wdf.Grn. 102 EL52
Uplands Pk. Rd., Enf. 81 DN41
Uplands Rd. N8 121 DM57
Uplands Rd., Barn. 98 DG46
Uplands Rd., Brwd. 108 FY50
Uplands Rd., Ken. 236 DQ116
Uplands Rd., Orp. 206 EV102
Uplands Rd., Rom. 126 EX55
Uplands Rd., Wdf.Grn. 102 EL52
Uplands Way N21 81 DN43
Uplands Way, Sev. 256 FF123
Upminster Rd., Horn. 128 FM61
Upminster Rd., Upmin. 128 FM61
Upminster Rd. N., Rain. 148 FJ69
Upminster Rd. S., Rain. 147 FG70
Upminster Trd. Pk., Upmin. 129 FX59
Upney Clo., Horn. 128 FJ64
Tylers Cres.
Upney La., Bark. 145 ES65
Upnor Way SE17 279 N10
Uppark Dr., Ilf. 125 EQ58
Upper Abbey Rd., Belv. 166 EZ77
Upper Addison Gdns. W14 159 CY75
Upper Ashlyns Rd., Berk. 38 AV20
Upper Bardsey Wk. N1 142 DQ65
Clephane Rd.
Upper Barn, Hem.H. 40 BM23
Upper Belgrave St. SW1 276 G6
Upper Belgrave St. SW1 160 DG76
Upper Belmont Rd., Chesh. 54 AP28
Upper Berkeley St. W1 272 D9
Upper Berkeley St. W1 140 DF72
Upper Beulah Hill SE19 202 DS95
Upper Bourne End La., Hem.H. 57 BA25
Upper Bray Rd., Maid. 150 AC77
Upper Brentwood Rd., Rom. 128 FJ56
Upper Bri. Rd., Red. 250 DE134
Upper Brighton Rd., Surb. 197 CK100
Upper Brockley Rd. SE4 163 DZ82
Upper Brook St. W1 276 F1
Upper Brook St. W1 140 DG73
Upper Butts, Brent. 157 CJ79
Upper Caldy Wk. N1 142 DQ65
Clephane Rd.
Upper Camelford Wk. W11 139 CY72
Lancaster Rd.
Upper Cavendish Ave. N3 120 DA55
Upper Cheyne Row SW3 160 DE79
Upper Ch. Hill, Green. 189 FS85
Upper Clabdens, Ware 33 DZ06
Upper Clapton Rd. E5 122 DV60
Upper Clarendon Wk. W11 139 CY72
Lancaster Rd.
Upper Cornsland, Brwd. 108 FX48
Upper Ct. Rd., Cat. 237 EA123
Upper Ct. Rd., Epsom 216 CQ111
Upper Culver Rd., St.Alb. 43 CE18
Upper Dagnall St., St.Alb. 43 CD20
Upper Dengie Wk. N1 142 DQ67
Popham Rd.
Upper Dr., Beac. 89 AK50
Upper Dr., West. 238 EJ118
Upper Dunnymans, Bans. 217 CZ114
Basing Rd.
Upper Edgeborough Rd., Guil. 259 AZ135
Upper Elmers End Rd., Beck. 203 DY98
Upper Fairfield Rd., Lthd. 231 CH121
Upper Fm. Rd., W.Mol. 196 BZ98
Upper Forecourt, Gat. 269 DH152
Upper Fosters NW4 119 CW57
New Brent St.
Upper George St., Chesh. 54 AQ30
Frances St.
Upper Gladstone Rd., Chesh. 54 AQ30
Upper Grn. E., Mitch. 200 DF97
Upper Grn. W., Mitch. 200 DF97
London Rd.
Upper Grenfell Wk. W11 139 CX73
Whitchurch Rd.
Upper Grosvenor St. W1 276 F1
Upper Grosvenor St. W1 140 DG73
Upper Grotto Rd., Twick. 177 CF89
Upper Grd. SE1 278 D2
Upper Grd. SE1 141 DP74
Upper Gro. SE25 202 DS98
Upper Gro. Rd., Belv. 166 EZ79
Upper Guild Hall (Bluewater), Green. 189 FU88
Bluewater Parkway
Upper Guildown Rd., Guil. 258 AV137
Upper Gulland Wk. N1 142 DQ65
Clephane Rd.
Upper Hall Pk., Berk. 38 AX20
Upper Halliford Bypass, Shep. 195 BS99
Upper Halliford Grn., Shep. 195 BS98
Holmbank Dr.
Upper Halliford Rd., Shep. 195 BS98
Upper Ham Rd., Rich. 177 CK91
Upper Handa Wk. N1 142 DR65
Clephane Rd.
Upper Harley St. NW1 272 G4
Upper Harley St. NW1 140 DG70
Upper Hawkwell Wk. N1 142 DQ67
Popham Rd.
Upper Heath Rd., St.Alb. 43 CF18
Upper High St., Epsom 216 CS113
Upper Highway, Abb.L. 59 BR33
Upper Highway, Kings L. 59 BQ32
Upper Hill Ri., Rick. 74 BH44
Upper Hitch, Wat. 94 BY46
Upper Holly Hill Rd., Belv. 167 FB78
Upper Hook, Harl. 51 ES17
Upper James St. W1 273 L10
Upper John St. W1 273 L10
Upper Lattimore Rd., St.Alb. 43 CE20
Upper Lees Rd., Slou. 131 AP69
Upper Lismore Wk. N1 142 DQ65
Clephane Rd.
Upper Mall W6 159 CU78
Upper Manor Rd., Gdmg. 258 AS144
Upper Marlborough Rd., St.Alb. 43 CE20
Upper Marsh SE1 278 C6
Upper Marsh SE1 161 DM76
Upper Marsh La., Hodd. 49 EA18
Upper Mealines, Harl. 52 EU18
Upper Montagu St. W1 272 D6
Upper Montagu St. W1 140 DF71
Upper Mulgrave Rd., Sutt. 217 CZ108
Upper N. St. E14 143 EA71
Upper Paddock Rd., Wat. 76 BY44
Upper Palace Rd., E.Mol. 196 CC97
Upper Pk., Harl. 35 EP14
Upper Pk., Loug. 84 EK42
Upper Pk. Rd. N11 99 DH50
Upper Pk. Rd. NW3 120 DF64
Upper Pk. Rd., Belv. 167 FB77
Upper Pk. Rd., Brom. 204 EH95
Upper Pk. Rd., Kings.T. 178 CN93
Upper Phillimore Gdns. W8 160 DA75
Upper Pillory Down, Cars. 218 DG113
Upper Pines, Bans. 234 DF117
Upper Rainham Rd., Horn. 127 FF63
Upper Ramsey Wk. N1 142 DR65
Clephane Rd.
Upper Rawreth Wk. N1 142 DQ67
Popham Rd.
Upper Richmond Rd. SW15 159 CY84
Upper Richmond Rd. W. SW14 158 CP84
Upper Richmond Rd. W., Rich. 158 CN84
Upper Riding, Beac. 88 AG54
Upper Rd. E13 144 EG69
Upper Rd., Uxb. 113 BD59
Upper Rd., Wall. 219 DK106
Upper Rose Gallery (Bluewater), Green. 189 FU88
Bluewater Parkway
Upper Rose Hill, Dor. 263 CH137
Upper Ryle, Brwd. 108 FW45
Upper St. Martin's La. WC2 273 P10
Upper Sales, Hem.H. 39 BF21
Upper Sawley Wd., Bans. 217 CZ114
Upper Selsdon Rd., S.Croy. 220 DT108
Upper Sheppey Wk. N1 142 DQ66
Clephane Rd.
Upper Sheridan Rd., Belv. 166 FA77
Coleman Rd.
Upper Shirley Rd., Croy. 202 DW103
Upper Shot, Welw.G.C. 30 DA08
Upper Shott (Cheshunt), Wal.Cr. 66 DT26
Upper Sq., Islw. 157 CG83
North St.
Upper Sta. Rd., Rad. 77 CG35
Upper Stonyfield, Harl. 51 EP15
Upper St. N1 141 DN68
Upper St., Guil. 260 BM139
Upper Sunbury Rd., Hmptn. 196 BY95
Upper Sutton La., Houns. 156 CA80
Upper Swaines, Epp. 69 ET30
Upper Tachbrook St. SW1 277 K8
Upper Tachbrook St. SW1 161 DJ77
Upper Tail, Wat. 94 BY48
Upper Talbot Wk. W11 139 CY72
Lancaster Rd.
Upper Teddington Rd., Kings.T. 177 CJ94
Upper Ter. NW3 120 DC62
Upper Thames St. EC4 274 G10
Upper Thames St. EC4 142 DQ73
Upper Thames Wk. (Bluewater), Green. 189 FU88
Bluewater Parkway
Upper Tollington Pk. N4 121 DN60
Upper Tooting Pk. SW17 180 DF89
Upper Tooting Rd. SW17 180 DF91
Upper Town Rd., Grnf. 136 CB70
Upper Tulse Hill SW2 181 DM87
Upper Vernon Rd., Sutt. 218 DD106
Upper Wk., Vir.W. 192 AY98
Upper Walthamstow Rd. E17 123 ED56
Upper W. St., Reig. 249 CZ134
Upper Wickham La., Well. 166 EV80
Upper Wimpole St. W1 273 H6
Upper Wimpole St. W1 140 DG71
Upper Woburn Pl. WC1 273 N3
Upper Woburn Pl. WC1 141 DK69
Upper Woodcote Village, Pur. 219 DK112
Upperfield Rd., Welw.G.C. 29 CZ10
Upperton Rd., Guil. 258 AW135
Upperton Rd., Sid. 185 ET92
Upperton Rd. E. E13 144 EJ69
Inniskilling Rd.
Upperton Rd. W. E13 144 EJ69
Uppingham Ave., Stan. 95 CH53
Upsdell Ave. N13 99 DN51
Upshire Rd., Wal.Abb. 68 EF32
Upshott La., Wok. 227 BF117
Upstall St. SE5 161 DP81
Upton, Wok. 226 AV117
Upton Ave. E7 144 EG66
Upton Ave., St.Alb. 43 CD19
Upton Clo., Bex. 186 EZ86
Upton Clo., St.Alb. 61 CD25
Upton Clo., Slou. 152 AT76
Upton Ct. SE20 182 DW94
Blean Gro.
Upton Ct. Rd., Slou. 152 AU76
Upton Dene, Sutt. 218 DB108
Upton Gdns., Har. 117 CH57
Upton La. E7 144 EG66
Upton Lo. Clo. (Bushey), Wat. 94 CC45
Upton Pk., Slou. 152 AS76
Upton Pk. Rd. E7 144 EH66
Upton Rd. N18 100 DU50
Upton Rd. SE18 165 EQ79
Upton Rd., Bex. 186 EZ86
Upton Rd., Bexh. 166 EY84
Upton Rd., Houns. 156 CA83
Upton Rd., Slou. 152 AU76
Upton Rd., Th.Hth. 202 DR96
Upton Rd., Wat. 75 BV42
Upton Rd. S., Bex. 186 EZ86
Upway N12 98 DE52
Upway, Ger.Cr. 91 AZ52
Upwood Rd. SE12 184 EG86
Upwood Rd. SW16 201 DL95
Uranus Rd., Hem.H. 40 BM18
Urban Ave., Horn. 128 FJ62
Urlwin St. SE5 162 DQ79
Urlwin Wk. SW9 161 DN82
Urmston Dr. SW19 179 CY88
Ursula Ms. N4 122 DQ60
Portland Ri.
Ursula St. SW11 160 DE81
Urswick Gdns., Dag. 146 EY66
Urswick Rd.
Urswick Rd. E9 122 DW64
Urswick Rd., Dag. 146 EX66
Usborne Ms. SW8 161 DM80
Usher Rd. E3 143 DZ68
Usherwood Clo., Tad. 248 CP131
Usk Rd. SW11 160 DC84
Usk Rd., S.Ock. 148 FQ72
Usk St. E2 143 DX69
Utopia Village NW1 140 DG67
Chalcot Rd.
Uvedale Clo., Croy. 221 ED111
Uvedale Cres.
Uvedale Cres., Croy. 221 ED111
Uvedale Rd., Dag. 126 FA62
Uvedale Rd., Enf. 82 DR43
Uvedale Rd., Oxt. 254 EF129
Uverdale Rd. SW10 160 DC80
Uxbridge Gdns., Felt. 176 BX89
Marlborough Rd.
Uxbridge Rd. W3 138 CL73
Uxbridge Rd. W5 138 CL73
Uxbridge Rd. W7 137 CF74
Uxbridge Rd. W12 139 CU74
Uxbridge Rd. W13 137 CF74
Uxbridge Rd., Felt. 176 BW88
Uxbridge Rd., Hmptn. 176 CA91
Uxbridge Rd., Har. 94 CC52
Uxbridge Rd., Hayes 136 BW73
Uxbridge Rd., Iver 132 AY71
Uxbridge Rd., Kings.T. 197 CK98
Uxbridge Rd., Pnr. 94 CB52
Uxbridge Rd., Rick. 91 BF47
Uxbridge Rd., Slou. 152 AU75
Uxbridge Rd., Sthl. 136 CA74
Uxbridge Rd., Stan. 95 CF51
Uxbridge Rd., Uxb. 135 BV72
Uxbridge St. W8 140 DA74
Uxendon Cres., Wem. 118 CL60
Uxendon Hill, Wem. 118 CM60

V

Vache La., Ch.St.G. 90 AW47
Vaillant Rd., Wey. 213 BQ105
Valan Leas, Brom. 204 EE97
Valance Ave. E4 102 EF46
Vale, The N10 98 DG53
Vale, The N14 99 DK45
Vale, The NW11 119 CX62
Vale, The SW3 160 DD79
Vale, The W3 138 CR74
Vale, The, Brwd. 108 FW46
Vale, The, Chesh. 54 AQ26
Vale, The, Couls. 219 DK114
Vale, The, Croy. 203 DX103
Vale, The, Felt. 175 BV86
Vale, The, Ger.Cr. 90 AX53
Vale, The, Houns. 156 BY79
Vale, The, Ruis. 116 BW63
Vale, The, Sun. 175 BU93
Ashridge Way
Vale, The, Wdf.Grn. 102 EG52
Vale Ave., Borwd. 78 CP43
Vale Border, Croy. 221 DX111
Vale Clo. N2 120 DF55
Church Vale
Vale Clo. W9 140 DC69
Maida Vale
Vale Clo., Brwd. 108 FT43
Vale Clo., Ger.Cr. 90 AX53
Vale Clo., Orp. 223 EN105
Vale Clo., Wey. 195 BR104
Vale Clo., Wok. 226 AY116
The Larches
Vale Cotts. SW15 178 CR91
Kingston Vale
Vale Ct. W9 140 DC69
Maida Vale
Vale Ct., Wey. 195 BR104
Vale Cres. SW15 178 CS90
Vale Cft., Esher 215 CE109
Vale Cft., Pnr. 116 BY57
Vale Dr., Barn. 79 CZ42
Vale End SE22 162 DS84
Grove Vale
Vale Fm. Rd., Wok. 226 AX117
Vale Gro. N4 122 DQ59
Vale Gro. W3 138 CR74
The Vale
Vale Gro., Slou. 152 AS76
Vale Ind. Est., Wat. 93 BQ46
Vale La. W3 138 CN71
Vale of Health NW3 120 DD62
East Heath Rd.
Vale Par. SW15 178 CR91
Kingston Vale
Vale Ri. NW11 119 CZ60
Vale Ri., Chesh. 54 AQ28
Vale Rd. E7 144 EH65
Vale Rd. N4 122 DQ59
Vale Rd., Brom. 205 EN96
Vale Rd., Chesh. 54 AQ28
Vale Rd., Dart. 187 FH88
Vale Rd., Epsom 217 CT105
Vale Rd., Esher 215 CE109
Vale Rd., Grav. 190 GD87
Vale Rd., Mitch. 201 DK97
Vale Rd., Sutt. 218 DB105
Vale Rd. (Bushey), Wat. 76 BY43
Vale Rd., Wey. 195 BR104
Vale Rd., Wind. 151 AM80
Vale Rd., Wor.Pk. 217 CT105
Vale Rd. N., Surb. 198 CL103
Vale Rd. S., Surb. 198 CL103
Vale Row N5 121 DP62
Gillespie Rd.
Vale Royal N7 141 DL66
Vale St. SE27 182 DR90
Vale Ter. N4 122 DQ58
Valence Ave., Dag. 126 EX62
Valence Circ., Dag. 126 EX62
Valence Dr. (Cheshunt), Wal.Cr. 66 DU28
Valence Rd., Erith 167 FD80
Valence Wd. Rd., Dag. 126 EX62
Valencia Rd., Stan. 95 CJ49
Valency Clo., Nthwd. 93 BT49
Valentia Pl. SW9 161 DN84
Brixton Sta. Rd.
Valentine Ave., Bex. 186 EY89
Valentine Ct. SE23 183 DX89
Valentine Pl. SE1 278 F4
Valentine Pl. SE1 161 DP75
Valentine Rd. E9 143 DX65
Valentine Rd., Har. 116 CC62
Valentine Row SE1 278 F5
Valentine Row SE1 161 DP75
Valentine Way, Ch.St.G. 90 AX48
Valentines Rd., Ilf. 125 EP60
Valentines Way, Rom. 127 FE61
Valentyne Clo., Croy. 222 EE111
Warbank Cres.
Valerian Way E15 144 EE69
Valerie Clo., St.Alb. 43 CH20
Valerie Ct. (Bushey), Wat. 94 CC45
Valeside, Hert. 31 DN10
Valeswood Rd., Brom. 184 EF92
Valetta Gro. E13 144 EG68
Valetta Rd. W3 158 CS75
Valette St. E9 142 DV65
Valiant Clo., Nthlt. 136 BX69
Ruislip Rd.
Valiant Clo., Rom. 104 FA54
Valiant Ho. SE7 164 EJ78
Valiant Path NW9 96 CS52
Blundell Rd.
Valiant Way E6 145 EM71
Vallance Rd. E1 142 DU70
Vallance Rd. E2 142 DU69
Vallance Rd. N22 99 DJ54
Vallentin Rd. E17 123 EC56
Valley, The, Guil. 258 AW138
Portsmouth Rd.
Valley Ave. N12 98 DD49
Valley Clo., Dart. 187 FF86
Valley Clo., Hert. 32 DR09
Valley Clo., Loug. 85 EM44
Valley Clo., Pnr. 93 BV54
Alandale Dr.
Valley Clo., Wal.Abb. 67 EC32
Valley Clo., Ware 32 DV05
Valley Ct., Ken. 220 DQ114
Hayes La.
Valley Dr. NW9 118 CN58
Valley Dr., Grav. 191 GK89
Valley Dr., Sev. 257 FH125
Valley Flds. Cres., Enf. 81 DN40
Valley Gdns. SW19 180 DD94
Valley Gdns., Wem. 138 CM66
Valley Grn., The, Welw.G.C. 29 CW08
Valley Gro. SE7 164 EJ78
Valley Hill, Loug. 102 EL45
Valley Link Ind. Est., Enf. 83 DY44
Valley Ms., Twick. 177 CG89
Cross Deep
Valley Ri., Wat. 59 BV33
Valley Rd. SW16 181 DM91
Valley Rd., Belv. 167 FB77
Valley Rd., Berk. 38 AT17
Valley Rd., Brom. 204 EE96
Valley Rd., Dart. 187 FF86
Valley Rd., Erith 167 FD77
Valley Rd., Ken. 236 DR115
Valley Rd. (Fawkham Grn.), Long. 209 FV103
Valley Rd., Orp. 206 EV95
Valley Rd., Rick. 74 BG43
Valley Rd., St.Alb. 43 CE16
Valley Rd., Uxb. 134 BL68
Valley Rd., Welw.G.C. 29 CV10
Valley Side E4 101 EA47
Valley Side Par. E4 101 EA47
Valley Side
Valley Vw., Barn. 79 CY44
Valley Vw., Chesh. 54 AN32
Valley Vw., Green. 189 FV86
Valley Vw. (Cheshunt), Wal.Cr. 66 DQ28
Valley Vw., West. 238 EJ118
Valley Vw. Gdns., Ken. 236 DS115
Godstone Rd.
Valley Wk., Croy. 202 DW103
Valley Wk., Rick. 75 BQ43
Valley Way, Ger.Cr. 112 AW58
Valleyfield Rd. SW16 181 DM92
Valleyside, Hem.H. 39 BF20
Valliere Rd. NW10 139 CV69
Valliers Wd. Rd., Sid. 185 ER88
Vallis Way W13 137 CG71
Vallis Way, Chess. 215 CK105
Valmar Rd. SE5 162 DQ81
Valnay St. SW17 180 DF92
Valognes Ave. E17 101 DY53
Valonia Gdns. SW18 179 CZ86
Vambery Rd. SE18 165 EQ79
Van Dyck Ave., N.Mal. 198 CR101
Vanbrough Cres., Nthlt. 136 BW67
Vanbrugh Clo. E16 144 EK71
Fulmer Rd.
Vanbrugh Dr., Walt. 196 BW101
Vanbrugh Flds. SE3 164 EF80
Vanbrugh Hill SE3 164 EF78
Vanbrugh Hill SE10 164 EF78
Vanbrugh Pk. SE3 164 EF80
Vanbrugh Pk. Rd. SE3 164 EF80
Vanbrugh Pk. Rd. W. SE3 164 EF80
Vanbrugh Rd. W4 158 CR76
Vanbrugh Ter. SE3 164 EF81
Vanburgh Clo., Orp. 205 ES102
Vancouver Clo., Epsom 216 CQ111
Vancouver Ct., Horl. 269 DN148
Vancouver Rd. SE23 183 DY89
Vancouver Rd., Edg. 96 CP53
Vancouver Rd., Hayes 135 BV70
Vancouver Rd., Rich. 177 CJ91
Vanda Cres., St.Alb. 43 CF21

Villiers Rd., Islw. 157 CE82
Villiers Rd., Kings.T. 198 CM97
Villiers Rd., Slou. 131 AR71
Villiers Rd., Sthl. 136 BZ74
Villiers Rd., Wat. 76 BY44
Villiers St. WC2 277 P1
Villiers St. WC2 141 DL73
Villiers St., Hert. 32 DS09
Vincam Clo., Twick. 176 CA87
Vince St. EC1 275 L3
Vince St. EC1 142 DR69
Vincent Ave., Cars. 218 DD111
Vincent Ave., Croy. 221 DY111
Vincent Ave., Surb. 198 CP102
Vincent Clo. SE16 163 DY75
Vincent Clo., Barn. 80 DA41
Vincent Clo., Brom. 204 EH98
Vincent Clo., Cher. 193 BE101
Vincent Clo., Couls. 234 DF120
Vincent Clo., Esher 196 CB104
Vincent Clo., Ilf. 103 EQ51
Vincent Clo., Lthd. 230 CB123
Vincent Clo., Sid. 185 ES88
Vincent Clo. (Cheshunt), Wal.Cr. 67 DY28
Vincent Clo., West Dr. 154 BN79
Vincent Dr., Dor. 263 CG137
Vincent Dr., Shep. 195 BS97
Vincent Dr., Uxb. 134 BM67
Birch Cres.
Vincent Gdns. NW2 119 CT62
Vincent Grn., Couls. 234 DF120
High Rd.
Vincent La., Dor. 263 CG136
Vincent Ms. E3 143 EA68
Vincent Rd. E4 101 ED51
Vincent Rd. N15 122 DQ56
Vincent Rd. N22 99 DN54
Vincent Rd. SE18 165 EP77
Vincent Rd. W3 158 CQ76
Vincent Rd., Cher. 193 BE101
Vincent Rd., Cob. 230 BY116
Vincent Rd., Couls. 235 DJ116
Vincent Rd., Croy. 202 DS101
Vincent Rd., Dag. 146 EY66
Vincent Rd., Dor. 263 CG136
Vincent Rd., Houns. 156 BX82
Vincent Rd., Islw. 157 CD81
Vincent Rd., Kings.T. 198 CN97
Vincent Rd., Rain. 148 FJ70
Vincent Rd., Wem. 138 CM66
Vincent Row, Hmptn. 176 CC93
Vincent Sq. SW1 277 L8
Vincent Sq. SW1 161 DJ77
Vincent Sq., West. 222 EJ113
Vincent St. E16 144 EF71
Vincent St. SW1 277 M8
Vincent St. SW1 161 DK77
Vincent Ter. N1 141 DP68
Vincents Dr., Dor. 263 CG137
Nower Rd.
Vincents Path, Nthlt. 136 BY65
Arnold Rd.
Vincents Wk., Dor. 263 CG136
Arundel Rd.
Vincenzo Clo., Hat. 45 CW23
Vine, The, Sev. 257 FJ124
Vine Ave., Sev. 257 FH124
Vine Clo., Stai. 174 BG85
Vine Clo., Surb. 198 CM100
Vine Clo., Sutt. 200 DC104
Vine Clo., Welw.G.C. 29 CY07
Vine Clo., West Dr. 154 BN77
Vine Ct. E1 142 DU71
Whitechapel Rd.
Vine Ct., Har. 118 CL58
Vine Ct. Rd., Sev. 257 FJ124
Vine Gdns., Ilf. 125 EQ64
Vine Gate, Slou. 131 AQ65
Vine Gro., Harl. 35 ER10
Eastwick Rd.
Vine Gro., Uxb. 134 BN66
Vine Hill EC1 274 D5
Vine La. SE1 279 N3
Vine La., Uxb. 134 BM67
Vine Pl. W5 138 CL74
The Common
Vine Pl., Houns. 156 CB84
Vine Rd. E15 144 EF66
Vine Rd. SW13 159 CT83
Vine Rd., E.Mol. 196 CC98
Vine Rd., Orp. 223 ET107
Vine Rd., Slou. 132 AT65
Vine Sq. W14 159 CZ78
Vine St. EC3 275 P10
Vine St. W1 277 L1
Vine St., Rom. 127 FC57
Vine St., Uxb. 134 BK67
Vine St. Bri. EC1 274 E5
Vine St. Bri. EC1 141 DN70
Vine Way, Brwd. 108 FW46
Vine Yd. SE1 279 J4
Vinegar All. E17 123 EB56
Vinegar St. E1 142 DV74
Reardon St.
Vinegar Yd. SE1 279 M4
Viner Clo., Walt. 196 BW100
Vineries, The N14 81 DJ44
Vineries, The, Enf. 82 DS41
Vineries Bank NW7 97 CV50
Vineries Clo., Dag. 146 FA65
Heathway
Vineries Clo., West Dr. 154 BN79
Vines Ave. N3 98 DB53
Viney Bank, Croy. 221 DZ109
Viney Rd. SE13 163 EB83
Vineyard, The, Rich. 178 CL85
Vineyard, The, Ware 33 EA05
Vineyard, The, Welw.G.C. 29 CX07
Vineyard Ave. NW7 97 CY52
Vineyard Clo. SE6 183 EA88
Vineyard Clo., Kings.T. 198 CM97
Vineyard Gro. N3 98 DB53
Vineyard Hill, Pot.B. 64 DG29
Vineyard Hill Rd. SW19 180 DA91
Vineyard Pas., Rich. 178 CL85
Paradise Rd.
Vineyard Path SW14 158 CR83
Vineyard Rd., Felt. 175 BU90
Vineyard Row, Kings.T. 197 CJ95
Vineyard Wk. EC1 274 D4
Vineyard Wk. EC1 141 DN70
Vineyards Rd., Pot.B. 64 DG30
Vining St. SW9 161 DN84
Vinlake Ave., Uxb. 114 BM62
Vinson Clo., Orp. 206 EU102
Vintry Ms. E17 123 EA56
Cleveland Pk. Cres.
Viola Ave. SE2 166 EV77
Viola Ave., Felt. 176 BW86
Viola Ave., Stai. 174 BL88
Viola Clo., S.Ock. 149 FW69
Viola Sq. W12 139 CT73
Violet Ave., Enf. 82 DR38
Violet Ave., Uxb. 134 BM71
Violet Clo. E16 144 EE70
Violet Clo., Wall. 201 DH102
Violet Gdns., Croy. 219 DP106
Violet Hill NW8 140 DC68
Violet La., Croy. 219 DP106
Violet Rd. E3 143 EB70
Violet Rd. E17 123 EA58
Violet Rd. E18 102 EH54
Violet St. E2 142 DV70
Three Colts La.
Violet Way, Rick. 74 BJ42
Virgil Dr., Brox. 49 DZ23
Virgil Pl. W1 272 D7
Virgil St. SE1 278 C6
Virgil St. SE1 161 DM76
Virginia Ave., Vir.W. 192 AW99
Virginia Beeches, Vir.W. 192 AW97
Virginia Clo., Ash. 231 CK118
Skinners La.
Virginia Clo., N.Mal. 198 CQ98
Willow Rd.
Virginia Clo., Wey. 213 BQ107
Virginia Dr., Vir.W. 192 AW99
Virginia Gdns., Ilf. 103 EQ54
Virginia Rd. E2 275 P3
Virginia Rd. E2 142 DT69
Virginia Rd., Th.Hth. 201 DP95
Virginia St. E1 142 DU73
Virginia Wk. SW2 181 DM86
Virginia Wk., Grav. 191 GK93
Viscount Clo. N11 99 DH50
Viscount Dr. E6 145 EM71
Viscount Gdns., W.Byf. 212 BL112
Viscount Gro., Nthlt. 136 BX69
Wayfarer Rd.
Viscount Rd., Stai. 174 BL88
Viscount St. EC1 275 H5
Viscount Way, Houns. 155 BS84
Vista, The SE9 184 EK86
Vista, The, Sid. 185 ET92
Langdon Shaw
Vista Ave., Enf. 83 DX40
Vista Dr., Ilf. 124 EK57
Vista Way, Har. 118 CL58
Viveash Clo., Hayes 155 BT76
Vivian Ave. NW4 119 CV57
Vivian Ave., Wem. 118 CN64
Vivian Clo., Wat. 93 BU46
Vivian Ct., Wat. 93 BU46
Vivian Gdns., Wem. 118 CN64
Vivian Rd. E3 143 DY68
Vivian Sq. SE15 162 DV83
Scylla Rd.
Vivian Way N2 120 DD57
Vivien Clo., Chess. 216 CL108
Vivienne Clo., Twick. 177 CK86
Vixen Dr., Hert. 32 DU09
Voce Rd. SE18 165 ER80
Voewood Clo., N.Mal. 199 CT100
Vogan Clo., Reig. 266 DB137
Volta Way, Croy. 201 DM102
Voltaire Rd. SW4 161 DK83
Voltaire Way, Hayes 135 BS73
Judge Heath La.
Voluntary Pl. E11 124 EG58
Vorley Rd. N19 121 DJ61
Voss Ct. SW16 181 DL93
Voss St. E2 142 DU69
Voyagers Clo. SE28 146 EW72
Vulcan Clo., Wall. 219 DM108
Vulcan Gate, Enf. 81 DN40
Vulcan Rd. SE4 163 DZ82
Vulcan Sq. E14 163 EA77
Britannia Rd.
Vulcan Ter. SE4 163 DZ82
Vulcan Way N7 141 DM65
Vulcan Way, Croy. 222 EE110
Vyne, The, Bexh. 167 FB83
Vyner Rd. W3 138 CR73
Vyner St. E2 142 DV67
Vyners Way, Uxb. 114 BN64
Vyse Clo., Barn. 79 CW42

W

Wacketts (Cheshunt), Wal.Cr. 66 DU27
Spicersfield
Wadding St. SE17 279 K9
Wadding St. SE17 162 DR77
Waddington Ave., Couls. 235 DN120
Waddington Clo., Couls. 235 DP119
Waddington Clo., Enf. 82 DS42
Waddington Rd. E15 123 ED64
Waddington Rd., St.Alb. 43 CD20
Waddington St. E15 143 ED65
Waddington Way SE19 182 DQ94
Waddon Clo., Croy. 201 DN104
Waddon Ct. Rd., Croy. 219 DN105
Waddon Marsh Way, Croy. 201 DM102
Waddon New Rd., Croy. 201 DP104
Waddon Pk. Ave., Croy. 201 DN104
Waddon Rd., Croy. 201 DN104
Waddon Way, Croy. 219 DN107
Wade, The, Welw.G.C. 29 CZ12
Wade Ave., Orp. 206 EX101
Wade Dr., Slou. 131 AN74
Wades, The, Hat. 45 CU21
Wades Gro. N21 99 DN45
Wades Hill N21 81 DN44
Wades La., Tedd. 177 CG92
High St.
Wades Ms. N21 99 DN45
Wades Hill
Wades Pl. E14 143 EB73
Wadesmill Rd., Hert. 32 DQ06
Wadeson St. E2 142 DV68
Wadeville Ave., Rom. 126 EZ59
Wadeville Clo., Belv. 166 FA79
Wadham Ave. E17 101 EB52
Wadham Clo., Shep. 195 BQ101
Wadham Gdns. NW3 140 DE67
Wadham Gdns., Grnf. 137 CD65
Wadham Rd. E17 101 EB53
Wadham Rd. SW15 159 CY84
Wadham Rd., Abb.L. 59 BT31
Wadhurst Clo. SE20 202 DV96
Wadhurst Rd. SW8 161 DJ81
Wadhurst Rd. W4 158 CR76
Wadley Clo., Hem.H. 40 BM21
White Hart Dr.
Wadley Rd. E11 124 EE59
Wadsworth Business Cen., Grnf. 137 CJ68
Wadsworth Clo., Enf. 83 DX43
Wadsworth Clo., Grnf. 137 CJ68
Wadsworth Rd., Grnf. 137 CH68
Wager St. E3 143 DZ70
Waggon Clo., Guil. 242 AS133
Waggon Ms. N14 99 DJ46
Chase Side
Waggon Rd., Barn. 80 DC37
Waghorn Rd. E13 144 EJ67
Waghorn Rd., Har. 117 CK55
Waghorn St. SE15 162 DU83
Wagner St. SE15 162 DW80
Wagon Rd., Barn. 80 DB36
Wagon Way, Rick. 74 BJ41
Wagstaff Gdns., Dag. 146 EW66
Ellerton Rd.
Wagtail Clo. NW9 96 CS54
Swan Dr.
Wagtail Gdns., S.Croy. 221 DY110
Wagtail Way, Orp. 206 EX98
Waid Clo., Dart. 188 FM86
Waights Ct., Kings.T. 198 CL95
Wain Clo., Pot.B. 64 DB29
Wainfleet Ave., Rom. 105 FC54
Wainford Clo. SW19 179 CX88
Windlesham Gro.
Wainwright Ave., Brwd. 109 GD44
Wainwright Gro., Islw. 157 CD84
Waite Davies Rd. SE12 184 EF87
Waite St. SE15 162 DT79
Waithman St. EC4 274 F9
Wake Rd., Loug. 84 EJ38
Wakefield Clo., W.Byf. 212 BL112
Wakefield Cres., Slou. 132 AT65
Wakefield Gdns. SE19 182 DS94
Wakefield Gdns., Ilf. 124 EL58
Wakefield Ms. WC1 274 A3
Wakefield Rd. N11 99 DK50
Wakefield Rd. N15 122 DT57
Wakefield Rd., Green. 189 FW85
Wakefield Rd., Rich. 177 CK85
Wakefield St. E6 144 EK67
Wakefield St. N18 100 DU50
Wakefield St. WC1 274 A4
Wakefield St. WC1 141 DL69
Wakefield Wk., Wal.Cr. 67 DY31
Wakeham St. N1 142 DR65
Wakehams Hill, Pnr. 116 BZ55
Wakehurst Path, Wok. 211 BC114
Bunyard Dr.
Wakehurst Rd. SW11 180 DE85
Wakelin Rd. E15 144 EE68
Wakeling Rd. W7 137 CF71
Wakeling St. E14 143 DY72
Wakely Clo., West. 238 EJ118
Wakeman Rd. NW10 139 CW69
Wakemans Hill Ave. NW9 118 CR57
Wakerfield Clo., Horn. 128 FM57
Wakering Rd., Bark. 145 EQ65
Wakerley Clo. E6 145 EM72
Truesdale Rd.
Wakley St. EC1 274 F2
Wakley St. EC1 141 DP68
Walberswick St. SW8 161 DL80
Walbrook EC4 275 K10
Walbrook EC4 142 DR73
Walbrook Ho. N9 100 DW46
Walbrook Wf. EC4 142 DQ73
Upper Thames St.
Walburgh St. E1 142 DV72
Bigland St.
Walburton Rd., Pur. 219 DJ113
Walcorde Ave. SE17 279 J9
Walcot Rd., Enf. 83 DZ40
Walcot Sq. SE11 278 E8
Walcot Sq. SE11 161 DN77
Walcott St. SW1 277 L8
Waldair Ct. E16 165 EP75
Barge Ho. Rd.
Waldair Wf. E16 165 EP75
Waldeck Gro. SE27 181 DP90
Waldeck Rd. N15 121 DP56
Waldeck Rd. SW14 158 CQ83
Lower Richmond Rd.
Waldeck Rd. W4 158 CN79
Waldeck Rd. W13 137 CH72
Waldeck Rd., Dart. 188 FM86
Waldeck Ter. SW14 158 CQ83
Lower Richmond Rd.
Waldegrave Ave., Tedd. 177 CF92
Waldegrave Rd.
Waldegrave Ct., Upmin. 128 FP60
Waldegrave Gdns., Twick. 177 CF89
Waldegrave Gdns., Upmin. 128 FP60
Waldegrave Pk., Twick. 177 CF91
Waldegrave Rd. N8 121 DN55
Waldegrave Rd. SE19 182 DT94
Waldegrave Rd. W5 138 CM72
Waldegrave Rd., Brom. 204 EL98
Waldegrave Rd., Dag. 126 EW61
Waldegrave Rd., Tedd. 177 CF91
Waldegrave Rd., Twick. 177 CF91
Waldegrove, Croy. 202 DT104
Waldemar Ave. SW6 159 CY81
Waldemar Ave. W13 137 CJ74
Waldemar Rd. SW19 180 DA92
Walden Ave. N13 100 DQ49
Walden Ave., Chis. 185 EM91
Walden Ave., Rain. 147 FD68
Walden Clo., Belv. 166 EZ78
Walden Gdns., Th.Hth. 201 DM97
Walden Pl., Welw.G.C. 29 CX07
Walden Rd. N17 100 DR53
Walden Rd., Chis. 185 EM93
Walden Rd., Horn. 128 FK58
Walden Rd., Welw.G.C. 29 CX07
Walden St. E1 142 DV72
Walden Way NW7 97 CX51
Walden Way, Horn. 128 FK58
Walden Way, Ilf. 103 ES52
Waldenhurst Rd., Orp. 206 EX101
Waldens Clo., Orp. 206 EX101
Waldens Pk. Rd., Wok. 226 AW116
Waldens Rd., Orp. 206 EY101
Waldens Rd., Wok. 226 AX117
Waldenshaw Rd. SE23 182 DW88
Waldo Clo. SW4 181 DJ85
Waldo Pl., Mitch. 180 DE94
Waldo Rd. NW10 139 CU69
Waldo Rd., Brom. 204 EK97
Waldorf Clo., S.Croy. 219 DP109
Waldram Cres. SE23 182 DW88
Waldram Pk. Rd. SE23 183 DX88
Waldram Pl. SE23 182 DW88
Waldram Cres.
Waldrist Way, Erith 166 EZ75
Waldron Gdns., Brom. 203 ED97
Waldron Ms. SW3 160 DD79
Old Ch. St.
Waldron Rd. SW18 180 DC90
Waldron Rd., Har. 117 CE60
Waldronhyrst, S.Croy. 219 DP105
Waldrons, The, Croy. 219 DP105
Waldrons, The, Oxt. 254 EF131
Waldrons Path, S.Croy. 220 DQ105
Waldstock Rd. SE28 146 EU73
Waleran Clo., Stan. 95 CF51
Chenduit Way
Waleran Flats SE1 162 DS77
Old Kent Rd.
Walerand Rd. SE13 163 EC82
Wales Ave., Cars. 218 DF106
Wales Clo. SE15 162 DV80
Wales Fm. Rd. W3 138 CR71
Waley St. E1 143 DX71
Walfield Ave. N20 98 DB45
Walford Clo., Harl. 36 EW12
Walford Rd. N16 122 DS63
Walford Rd., Dor. 263 CH140
Walford Rd., Uxb. 134 BJ68
Walfrey Gdns., Dag. 146 EY66
Walham Grn. Ct. SW6 160 DB80
Waterford Rd.
Walham Gro. SW6 160 DA80
Walham Ri. SW19 179 CY93
Walham Yd. SW6 160 DA80
Walham Gro.
Walk, The, Horn. 128 FM61
Walk, The, Oxt. 253 EA133
Walk, The, Pot.B. 64 DA32
Walk, The, Sun. 175 BT94
Walk, The (Eton Wick), Wind. 151 AN78
Walkden Rd., Chis. 185 EN92
Walker Clo. N11 99 DJ49
Walker Clo. SE18 165 EQ77
Walker Clo. W7 137 CE74
Walker Clo., Dart. 167 FF83
Walker Clo., Hmptn. 176 BZ93
Fearnley Cres.
Walkers Ct. E8 142 DU65
Wilton Way
Walkers Ct. W1 273 M10
Walkers Pl. SW15 159 CY83
Felsham Rd.
Walkerscroft Mead SE21 182 DQ88
Walkfield Dr., Epsom 233 CV117
Walkford Way SE15 162 DT80
Daniel Gdns.
Walkley Rd., Dart. 187 FH85
Walks, The N2 120 DD55
Walkwood End, Beac. 88 AJ54
Walkwood Ri., Beac. 110 AJ55
Wall End Rd. E6 145 EN66
Wall St. N1 142 DR65
Wallace Clo. SE28 146 EX73
Haldane Rd.
Wallace Clo., Shep. 195 BR98
Wallace Clo., Uxb. 134 BL68
Grays Rd.
Wallace Cres., Cars. 218 DF106
Wallace Flds., Epsom 217 CT112
Wallace Gdns., Swans. 190 FY86
Milton St.
Wallace Rd. N1 142 DQ65
Wallace Rd., Grays 170 GA76
Wallace Wk., Add. 212 BJ105
Wallace Way N19 121 DK61
Giesbach Rd.
Wallasey Cres., Uxb. 114 BN61
Wallbutton Rd. SE4 163 DY82
Wallcote Ave. NW2 119 CX60
Walled Gdn., The, Bet. 264 CR135
Walled Gdn., The, Tad. 233 CX122
Heathcote
Wallenger Ave., Rom. 127 FH55
Waller Dr., Nthwd. 93 BU54
Waller La., Cat. 236 DT123
Waller Rd. SE14 163 DX81
Waller Rd., Beac. 89 AM53
Wallers Clo., Dag. 146 EY67
Wallers Clo., Wdf.Grn. 103 EM51
Wallers Hoppit, Loug. 84 EL40
Wallers Way, Hodd. 33 EB14
Wallfield All., Hert. 32 DQ10
Wallflower St. W12 139 CT73
Wallgrave Rd. SW5 160 DB77
Wallhouse Rd., Erith 167 FH80
Wallingford Ave. W10 139 CX71
Wallingford Rd., Uxb. 134 BH68
Wallingford Wk., St.Alb. 43 CD23
Wallington Clo., Ruis. 115 BQ58
Wallington Cor., Wall. 219 DH105
Manor Rd. N.
Wallington Rd., Chesh. 54 AP30
Wallington Rd., Ilf. 125 ET59
Wallington Sq., Wall. 219 DH107
Woodcote Rd.
Wallis All. SE1 279 J5
Wallis Clo. SW11 160 DD83
Wallis Clo., Dart. 187 FG90
Wallis Clo., Horn. 127 FH60
Wallis Ct., Slou. 152 AU76
Nixey Clo.
Wallis Ms. N22 121 DN55
Brampton Pk. Rd.
Wallis Ms., Lthd. 231 CG122
Wallis Pk., Grav. 190 GB85
Wallis Rd. E9 143 DZ65
Wallis Rd., Sthl. 136 CB72
Wallis's Cotts. SW2 181 DL87
Wallman Pl. N22 99 DM53
Bounds Grn. Rd.
Wallorton Gdns. SW14 158 CR84
Wallside EC2 142 DQ71
Wood St.
Wallwood Rd. E11 123 ED59
Wallwood St. E14 143 DZ71
Walm La. NW2 119 CX64
Walmar Clo., Barn. 80 DD39
Walmer Clo. E4 101 EB47
Walmer Clo., Orp. 223 ER105
Tubbenden La. S.
Walmer Clo., Rom. 105 FB54
Walmer Gdns. W13 157 CG75
Walmer Ho. N9 100 DT45
Walmer Pl. W1 272 D6
Walmer Rd. W10 139 CW72
Latimer Rd.
Walmer Rd. W11 139 CY73
Walmer St. W1 272 D6
Walmer Ter. SE18 165 EQ77
Walmgate Rd., Grnf. 137 CH67
Walmington Fold N12 98 DA51
Walney Wk. N1 142 DQ65
St. Paul's Rd.
Walnut Ave., West Dr. 154 BN76
Walnut Clo. SE8 163 DZ79
Clyde St.
Walnut Clo., Cars. 218 DF106
Walnut Clo. (Eynsford), Dart. 208 FK104
Walnut Clo., Epsom 233 CT115
Walnut Clo., Hayes 135 BS73
Walnut Clo., Ilf. 125 EQ56
Civic Way
Walnut Clo., St.Alb. 60 CB27
Walnut Ct. W5 158 CL75
Rowan Clo.
Walnut Ct., Welw.G.C. 29 CY12
Walnut Dr., Tad. 233 CY124
Warren Lo. Dr.
Walnut Flds., Epsom 217 CT109
Walnut Gdns. E15 124 EE63
Burgess Rd.
Walnut Grn. (Bushey), Wat. 76 BZ40
Walnut Gro., Bans. 217 CX114
Walnut Gro., Enf. 82 DR43
Walnut Gro., Hem.H. 40 BK20
Walnut Gro., Welw.G.C. 29 CY12
Walnut Ms., Sutt. 218 DC108
Walnut Rd. E10 123 EA61
Walnut Tree Ave., Dart. 188 FL89
Walnut Tree Ave., Mitch. 200 DE97
De'Arn Gdns.
Walnut Tree Clo. SW13 159 CT81
Walnut Tree Clo., Bans. 217 CY112
Walnut Tree Clo., Chis. 205 EQ95
Walnut Tree Clo., Guil. 242 AW134
Walnut Tree Clo., Hodd. 49 EA17
Walnut Tree Clo. (Cheshunt), Wal.Cr. 67 DX31
Walnut Tree Cotts. SW19 179 CY91
Church Rd.
Walnut Tree La., W.Byf. 212 BK112
Walnut Tree Pk., Guil. 242 AW134
Walnut Tree Rd. SE10 164 EE78
Walnut Tree Rd., Brent. 158 CL79
Walnut Tree Rd., Dag. 126 EX61
Walnut Tree Rd., Erith 167 FE78
Walnut Tree Rd., Houns. 156 BZ79
Walnut Tree Rd., Shep. 195 BQ96
Walnut Tree Wk. SE11 278 D8
Walnut Tree Wk. SE11 161 DN77
Walnut Tree Wk., Ware 33 DX08
Walnut Way, Buck.H. 102 EK48
Walnut Way, Ruis. 136 BW65
Walnut Way, Swan. 207 FD96
Walnuts, The, Orp. 206 EU102
High St.
Walnuts Rd., Orp. 206 EU102
Walpole Ave., Couls. 234 DF119
Walpole Ave., Rich. 158 CM82
Walpole Clo. W13 157 CJ75
Walpole Clo., Grays 170 GC77
Palmers Dr.
Walpole Clo., Pnr. 94 CA51
Walpole Cres., Tedd. 177 CF92
Walpole Gdns. W4 158 CQ78
Walpole Gdns., Twick. 177 CE89
Walpole Ms. NW8 140 DD67
Queen's Gro.
Walpole Ms. SW19 180 DD93
Walpole Rd.
Walpole Pk. W5 137 CJ74
Walpole Pk., Wey. 212 BN108
Walpole Pl. SE18 165 EP77
Anglesea Rd.
Walpole Pl., Tedd. 177 CF92
Walpole Rd. E6 144 EJ66
Walpole Rd. E17 123 DY56
Walpole Rd. E18 102 EF53
Walpole Rd. (Downhills Way) N17 122 DQ55
Walpole Rd. (Lordship La.) N17 100 DQ54
Walpole Rd. SW19 180 DD93
Walpole Rd., Brom. 204 EK99
Walpole Rd., Croy. 202 DR103
Walpole Rd., Slou. 131 AK72
Walpole Rd., Surb. 198 CL100
Walpole Rd., Tedd. 177 CF92
Walpole Rd., Twick. 177 CE89
Walpole Rd., Wind. 172 AV87
Walpole St. SW3 276 D10
Walpole St. SW3 160 DF78
Walrond Ave., Wem. 118 CL64
Walsh Cres., Croy. 222 EE112
Walsham Clo. N16 122 DU59
Braydon Rd.
Walsham Clo. SE28 146 EX73
Walsham Rd. SE14 163 DX82
Walsham Rd., Felt. 175 BV87
Walshford Way, Borwd. 78 CN38
Walsingham Clo., Hat. 45 CT17
Walsingham Gdns., Epsom 216 CS105
Walsingham Pk., Chis. 205 ER96
Walsingham Pl. SW4 160 DF84
Clapham Common W. Side
Walsingham Pl. SW11 180 DG86
Walsingham Rd. E5 122 DU62
Walsingham Rd. W13 137 CG74
Walsingham Rd., Croy. 221 EC110
Walsingham Rd., Enf. 82 DR42
Walsingham Rd., Mitch. 200 DF99
Walsingham Rd., Orp. 206 EV95
Walsingham Wk., Belv. 166 FA79
Walsingham Way, St.Alb. 61 CJ27
Walt Whitman Clo. SE24 161 DP84
Shakespeare Rd.
Walter Rodney Clo. E6 145 EM65
Stevenage Rd.
Walter St. E2 143 DX69
Walter St., Kings.T. 198 CL95
Sopwith Way
Walter Ter. E1 143 DX72
Walter Wk., Edg. 96 CQ51
Walters Clo. (Cheshunt), Wal.Cr. 65 DP25
Walters Ho. SE17 161 DP79
Otto St.
Walters Mead, Ash. 232 CL117
Walters Rd. SE25 202 DS98

Walters Rd., Enf. 82 DW43
Walters Way SE23 183 DX86
Walters Yd., Brom. 204 EG96
Walterton Rd. W9 139 CZ70
Waltham Ave. NW9 118 CN58
Waltham Ave., Guil. 242 AV131
Waltham Ave., Hayes 155 BQ76
Waltham Clo., Brwd. 109 GC44
Bannister Dr.
Waltham Clo., Dart. 187 FG86
Waltham Clo., Orp. 206 EX102
Waltham Dr., Edg. 96 CN54
Waltham Gdns., Enf. 82 DW36
Waltham Gate, Wal.Cr. 67 DZ26
Waltham Pk. Way E17 101 EA53
Waltham Rd., Cars. 200 DD101
Waltham Rd., Cat. 236 DV122
Waltham Rd., Sthl. 156 BY76
Waltham Rd., Wal.Abb. 68 EF26
Waltham Rd., Wdf.Grn. 102 EL51
Waltham Way E4 101 DZ48
Walthamstow Ave. E4 101 EA52
Walthamstow Business Cen. E17 101 EC54
Waltheof Ave. N17 100 DR53
Waltheof Gdns. N17 100 DR53
Walton Ave., Har. 116 BZ64
Walton Ave., N.Mal. 199 CT98
Walton Ave., Sutt. 199 CZ104
Walton Bri., Shep. 195 BS101
Walton Bri. Rd., Shep. 195 BR100
Walton Clo. E5 123 DX62
Orient Way
Walton Clo. NW2 119 CV61
Walton Clo. SW8 161 DL80
Walton Clo., Har. 117 CD56
Walton Ct., Wok. 227 BA116
Walton Cres., Har. 116 BZ63
Walton Dr. NW10 138 CR65
Mitchellbrook Way
Walton Dr., Har. 117 CD56
Walton Gdns. W3 138 CP71
Walton Gdns., Brwd. 109 GC43
Walton Gdns., Felt. 175 BT91
Walton Gdns., Wal.Abb. 67 EB33
Walton Gdns., Wem. 118 CL61
Walton Grn., Croy. 221 EC108
Walton La., Shep. 195 BR101
Walton La., Slou. 131 AL69
Walton La., Wey. 195 BP103
Walton Pk., Walt. 196 BX103
Walton Pk. La., Walt. 196 BX103
Walton Pl. SW3 276 D6
Walton Pl. SW3 160 DF76
Walton Rd. E12 125 EN63
Walton Rd. E13 144 EJ68
Walton Rd. N15 122 DT57
Walton Rd., E.Mol. 196 BY98
Walton Rd. (Epsom Downs), Epsom 233 CT117
Walton Rd. (Headley), Epsom 232 CQ121
Walton Rd., Har. 117 CD56
Walton Rd., Hodd. 49 EB15
Walton Rd., Rom. 104 EZ52
Walton Rd., Sid. 186 EW89
Walton Rd., Walt. 196 BW99
Walton Rd., Ware 33 DX07
Walton Rd. (Bushey), Wat. 76 BX42
Walton Rd., W.Mol. 196 BY98
Walton Rd., Wok. 227 AZ116
Walton St. SW3 276 C8
Walton St. SW3 160 DE77
Walton St., Enf. 82 DR39
Walton St., St.Alb. 43 CF19
Walton St., Tad. 233 CU124
Walton Ter., Wok. 227 BB115
Walton Way W3 138 CP71
Walton Way, Mitch. 201 DJ98
Walverns Clo., Wat. 76 BW44
Walworth Pl. SE17 162 DQ78
Walworth Rd. SE1 279 H8
Walworth Rd. SE1 162 DQ77
Walworth Rd. SE17 279 H8
Walworth Rd. SE17 162 DQ77
Walwyn Ave., Brom. 204 EK97
Wambrook Clo., Brwd. 109 GC46
Wanborough Dr. SW15 179 CV88
Wanderer Dr., Bark. 146 EV69
Wandle Bank SW19 180 DD93
Wandle Bank, Croy. 201 DL104
Wandle Ct., Epsom 216 CQ105
Wandle Ct. Gdns., Croy. 219 DL105
Wandle Rd. SW17 180 DE89
Wandle Rd., Croy. 202 DQ104
Wandle Rd. (Waddon), Croy. 201 DL104
Wandle Rd., Mord. 200 DC98
Wandle Rd., Wall. 201 DH103
Wandle Side, Croy. 201 DM104
Wandle Side, Wall. 201 DH104
Wandle Way SW18 180 DB88
Wandle Way, Mitch. 200 DF99
Wandon Rd. SW6 160 DB80
Wandsworth Bri. SW6 160 DB83
Wandsworth Bri. SW18 160 DB83
Wandsworth Bri. Rd. SW6 160 DB81
Wandsworth Common SW12 180 DE86
Wandsworth Common W. Side SW18 180 DC85
Wandsworth High St. SW18 180 DA85
Wandsworth Plain SW18 180 DB85
Wandsworth Rd. SW8 161 DK80
Wangey Rd., Rom. 126 EX59
Wanless Rd. SE24 162 DQ83
Wanley Rd. SE5 162 DR84
Wanlip Rd. E13 144 EH70
Wanmer Ct., Reig. 250 DA133
Birkheads Rd.
Wannions Clo., Chesh. 56 AU30
Wannock Gdns., Ilf. 103 EP52
Wansbeck Rd. E9 143 DZ66
Wansbury Way, Swan. 207 FG99
Wansdown Pl. SW6 160 DB80
Fulham Rd.
Wansey St. SE17 279 H9
Wansey St. SE17 162 DQ77
Wansford Clo., Brwd. 108 FT48
Wansford Grn., Wok. 226 AT117
Kenton Way
Wansford Pk., Borwd. 78 CS42
Wansford Rd., Wdf.Grn. 102 EJ53
Wanstead Clo., Brom. 204 EJ96
Wanstead La., Ilf. 124 EK58
Wanstead Pk. E11 124 EK59
Wanstead Pk. Ave. E12 124 EK61
Wanstead Pk. Rd., Ilf. 125 EM60
Wanstead Pl. E11 124 EG58
Wanstead Rd., Brom. 204 EJ96
Wansunt Rd., Bex. 187 FC88
Wantage Rd. SE12 184 EF85
Wantz La., Rain. 147 FH70
Wantz Rd., Dag. 127 FB63
Waplings, The, Tad. 233 CV124
Deans La.
Wapping Dock St. E1 142 DV74
Cinnamon St.
Wapping High St. E1 142 DU74
Wapping La. E1 142 DV73
Wapping Wall E1 142 DW74
Wapseys La., Slou. 112 AS58
Wapshott Rd., Stai. 173 BE93
War Coppice Rd., Cat. 252 DR127
Warbank Clo., Croy. 222 EE111
Warbank Cres., Croy. 222 EE110
Warbank La., Kings.T. 179 CT94
Warbeck Rd. W12 139 CV74
Warberry Rd. N22 99 DM54
Warblers Grn., Cob. 214 BZ114
Warboys App., Kings.T. 178 CP93
Warboys Cres. E4 101 EC50
Warboys Rd., Kings.T. 178 CP93
Warburton Clo. N1 142 DS65
Culford Rd.
Warburton Clo., Har. 95 CD51
Warburton Rd. E8 142 DV66
Warburton Rd., Twick. 176 CB88
Warburton St. E8 142 DV67
Warburton Rd.
Warburton Ter. E17 101 EB54
Ward Ave., Grays 170 GA77
Ward Clo., Erith 167 FD79
Ward Clo., Iver 133 BF72
Ward Clo., S.Croy. 220 DS106
Ward Clo. (Cheshunt), Wal.Cr. 66 DU27
Spicersfield
Ward Clo., Ware 32 DW05
Ward Gdns., Rom. 106 FK54
Whitmore Ave.
Ward Gdns., Slou. 131 AL73
Ward Hatch, Harl. 36 EU12
Mowbray Rd.
Ward La., Warl. 236 DW116
Ward Pl., Amer. 55 AP40
Ward Rd. E15 143 ED67
Ward Rd. N19 121 DJ62
Ward Royal, Wind. 151 AQ81
Alma Rd.
Ward St., Guil. 258 AX135
Martyr Rd.
Wardalls Gro. SE14 162 DW80
Wardell Clo. NW7 96 CS52
Wardell Fld. NW9 96 CS53
Warden Ave., Har. 116 BZ60
Warden Ave., Rom. 105 FC50
Warden Rd. NW5 140 DG65
Wardens Fld. Clo., Orp. 223 ES107
Wardens Gro. SE1 279 H3
Wardle St. E9 123 DX64
Wardley St. SW18 180 DB87
Garratt La.
Wardo Ave. SW6 159 CY81
Wardour Ms. W1 273 L9
Wardour St. W1 273 M10
Wardour St. W1 141 DK73
Wardrobe Pl. EC4 274 G10
Wardrobe Ter. EC4 274 G10
Wards La., Borwd. 77 CG40
Ward's Pl., Egh. 173 BC93
Wards Rd., Ilf. 125 ER59
Ware Pk. Rd., Hert. 32 DR07
Ware Pt. Dr. SE28 165 ER75
Ware Rd., Hert. 32 DS09
Ware Rd. (Hertford Heath), Hert. 33 EA12
Ware Rd., Hodd. 49 EA15
Ware Rd., Ware 33 EC05
Ware Rd. (Chadwell Springs), Ware 32 DS09
Wareham Clo., Houns. 156 CB84
Warehams La., Hert. 32 DQ10
Waremead Rd., Ilf. 125 EP57
Warenford Way, Borwd. 78 CN39
Warenne Hts., Red. 266 DD136
Warenne Rd., Lthd. 230 CC122
Warescot Clo., Brwd. 108 FV45
Warescot Rd., Brwd. 108 FV45
Wareside Clo., Welw.G.C. 30 DB10
Warfield Rd. NW10 139 CX69
Warfield Rd., Felt. 175 BS87
Warfield Rd., Hmptn. 196 CB95
Warfield Yd. NW10 139 CX69
Warfield Rd.
Wargrave Ave. N15 122 DT58
Wargrave Rd., Har. 116 CC62
Warham Rd. N4 121 DN57
Warham Rd., Har. 95 CF54
Warham Rd., Sev. 241 FH116
Warham Rd., S.Croy. 220 DQ106
Warham St. SE5 161 DP80
Waring Clo., Orp. 223 ET107
Waring Dr., Orp. 223 ET107
Waring Rd., Sid. 186 EW93
Waring St. SE27 182 DQ91
Warkworth Gdns., Islw. 157 CG80
Warkworth Rd. N17 100 DR52
Warland Rd. SE18 165 ER80
Warley Ave., Dag. 126 EZ59
Warley Ave., Hayes 135 BU71
Warley Clo. E10 123 DZ60
Millicent Rd.
Warley Gap, Brwd. 107 FV52
Warley Hill, Brwd. 107 FV51
Warley Mt., Brwd. 108 FW49
Warley Rd. N9 100 DW47
Warley Rd., Brwd. 107 FU53
Warley Rd., Hayes 135 BU72
Warley Rd., Ilf. 103 EN53
Warley Rd., Upmin. 106 FQ54
Warley Rd., Wdf.Grn. 102 EH52
Warley St., E2 143 DX69
Warley St., Brwd. 129 FW58
Warley St., Upmin. 129 FW58
Warlingham Rd., Th.Hth. 201 DP98
Warlock Rd. W9 140 DA70
Warlters Clo. N7 121 DL63
Warlters Rd.
Warlters Rd. N7 121 DL63
Warltersville Rd. N19 121 DL59
Warltersville Way, Horl. 269 DJ150
Warmark Rd., Hem.H. 39 BE18
Warmington Clo. E5 123 DX62
Orient Way
Warmington Rd. SE24 182 DQ86
Warmington St. E13 144 EG70
Barking Rd.
Warminster Gdns. SE25 202 DU96
Warminster Rd. SE25 202 DT96
Warminster Sq. SE25 202 DU96
Warminster Rd.
Warminster Way, Mitch. 201 DH95
Warndon St. SE16 163 DX77
Warne Pl., Sid. 186 EV86
Westerham Dr.
Warneford Pl., Wat. 76 BY44
Warneford Rd., Har. 117 CK55
Warneford St. E9 142 DV67
Warner Ave., Sutt. 199 CY103
Warner Clo. E15 124 EE64
Warner Clo. NW9 119 CT59
Warner Clo., Hmptn. 176 BZ92
Tangley Pk. Rd.
Warner Clo., Hayes 155 BR80
Warner Clo., Slou. 131 AL74
Warner Par., Hayes 155 BR80
Warner Pl. E2 142 DU68
Warner Rd. E17 123 DY56
Warner Rd. N8 121 DK56
Warner Rd. SE5 162 DQ81
Warner Rd., Brom. 184 EF94
Warner Rd., Ware 33 DX07
Warner St. EC1 274 D5
Warner St. EC1 141 DN70
Warner Ter. E14 143 EA71
Broomfield St.
Warner Yd. EC1 274 D5
Warners Ave., Hodd. 49 DZ19
Warners Clo., Wdf.Grn. 102 EG50
Warners End Rd., Hem.H. 40 BG20
Warners La., Guil. 260 BL141
Warners La., Kings.T. 177 CK92
Warners Path, Wdf.Grn. 102 EG50
Warnford Ind. Est., Hayes 155 BS75
Warnford Rd., Orp. 223 ET106
Warnham Ct. Rd., Cars. 218 DF108
Warnham Rd. N12 98 DE50
Warple Ms. W3 158 CS75
Warple Way
Warple Way W3 158 CS75
Warren, The E12 124 EL63
Warren, The, Ash. 232 CL119
Warren, The, Cars. 218 DD109
Warren, The, Chesh. 54 AL28
Warren, The, Ger.Cr. 91 AZ52
Warren, The, Grav. 191 GK91
Warren, The, Hayes 135 BU72
Warren, The, Houns. 156 BZ80
Warren, The, Lthd. 214 CC112
Warren, The (East Horsley), Lthd. 245 BT130
Warren, The, Rad. 61 CG33
Warren, The, Tad. 233 CY123
Warren, The, Wor.Pk. 216 CR105
Warren Ave. E10 123 EC62
Warren Ave., Brom. 184 EE94
Warren Ave., Orp. 223 ET106
Warren Ave., Rich. 158 CP84
Warren Ave., S.Croy. 221 DX108
Warren Ave., Sutt. 217 CZ110
Warren Clo. N9 101 DX45
Warren Clo. SE21 182 DQ87
Lairdale Clo.
Warren Clo., Bexh. 186 FA85
Pincott Rd.
Warren Clo., Esher 214 CB105
Warren Clo., Hat. 45 CV15
Warren Clo., Hayes 136 BW71
Warren Clo., Slou. 152 AY76
Warren Clo., Wem. 117 CK61
Warren Ct., Chig. 103 ER49
Warren Ct., Sev. 257 FJ125
Warren Ct., Wey. 212 BN106
Warren Cres. N9 100 DT45
Warren Cutting, Kings.T. 178 CR94
Warren Dale, Welw.G.C. 29 CX06
Warren Dr., Grnf. 136 CB70
Warren Dr., Horn. 127 FG62
Warren Dr., Orp. 224 EV106
Warren Dr., Ruis. 116 BX59
Warren Dr., Tad. 233 CZ122
Warren Dr., The E11 124 EJ59
Warren Dr. N., Surb. 198 CP102
Warren Dr. S., Surb. 198 CQ102
Warren Fld., Epp. 70 EU32
Warren Fld., Iver 133 BC68
Warren Flds., Stan. 95 CJ49
Valencia Rd.
Warren Footpath, Twick. 177 CJ88
Warren Gdns. E15 123 ED64
Ashton Rd.
Warren Gdns., Orp. 224 EU106
Warren Grn., Hat. 45 CV15
Warren Gro., Borwd. 78 CR42
Warren Hastings Ct., Grav. 191 GF86
Pier Rd.
Warren Hts., Grays 170 FY77
Warren Hill, Epsom 232 CR116
Warren Hill, Loug. 84 EJ44
Warren Ho. E3 143 EB69
Bromley High St.
Warren La. SE18 165 EP76
Warren La., Grays 169 FW77
Warren La., Guil. 260 BJ139
Warren La., Lthd. 214 CC111
Warren La., Oxt. 254 EG134
Warren La., Stan. 95 CG47
Warren La., Wok. 228 BG118
Warren Lo. Dr., Tad. 233 CY124
Warren Mead, Bans. 233 CW115
Warren Ms. W1 273 K5
Warren Pk., Kings.T. 178 CQ93
Warren Pk., Warl. 237 DX118
Warren Pk. Rd., Hert. 32 DQ08
Warren Pk. Rd., Sutt. 218 DD107
Warren Pl. E1 143 DX72
Pitsea St.
Warren Pond Rd. E4 102 EF46
Warren Ri., N.Mal. 198 CR95
Warren Rd. E4 101 EC47
Warren Rd. E10 123 EC62
Warren Rd. E11 124 EJ60
Warren Rd. NW2 119 CT61
Warren Rd. SW19 180 DE93
Warren Rd., Add. 212 BG110
Warren Rd., Ashf. 175 BS94
Warren Rd., Bans. 217 CW114
Warren Rd., Bexh. 186 FA85
Warren Rd., Brom. 204 EG103
Warren Rd., Croy. 202 DS102
Warren Rd., Dart. 188 FL90
Warren Rd., Gdmg. 258 AS144
Warren Rd., Grav. 190 GB92
Warren Rd., Guil. 259 AZ135
Warren Rd., Ilf. 125 ER57
Warren Rd., Kings.T. 178 CQ93
Warren Rd., Orp. 223 ET106
Warren Rd., Pur. 219 DP112
Warren Rd., Reig. 250 DB133
Warren Rd., St.Alb. 42 CC24
Warren Rd., Sid. 186 EW90
Warren Rd., Twick. 176 CC86
Warren Rd., Uxb. 114 BL63
Warren Rd. (Bushey), Wat. 94 CC46
Warren St. W1 273 K5
Warren St. W1 141 DJ70
Warren Ter., Grays 169 FX75
Arterial Rd.
W. Thurrock
Warren Ter., Hert. 32 DR07
Warren Ter., Rom. 126 EX56
Warren Wk. SE7 164 EJ79
Warren Way NW7 97 CY51
Warren Way, Wey. 213 BQ106
Warren Wd. Clo., Brom. 204 EF103
Warrender Rd. N19 121 DJ62
Warrender Rd., Chesh. 54 AS29
Warrender Way, Ruis. 115 BU59
Warreners La., Wey. 213 BR109
Warrenfield Clo. (Cheshunt), Wal.Cr. 66 DU31
Portland Dr.
Warrengate La., Pot.B. 63 CW31
Warrengate Rd., Hat. 63 CW28
Warrenhyrst, Guil. 259 BA135
Warren Rd.
Warrenne Rd., Bet. 264 CQ136
Warrenne Way, Reig. 250 DA134
Warrens Shawe La., Edg. 96 CP46
Warriner Ave., Horn. 128 FK61
Warriner Dr. N9 100 DU48
Warriner Gdns. SW11 160 DF81
Warrington Ave., Slou. 131 AQ72
Warrington Cres. W9 140 DC70
Warrington Gdns. W9 140 DC70
Warwick Ave.
Warrington Gdns., Horn. 128 FJ58
Warrington Pl. E14 143 EC74
Yabsley St.
Warrington Rd., Croy. 201 DP104
Warrington Rd., Dag. 126 EX61
Warrington Rd., Har. 117 CE57
Warrington Rd., Rich. 177 CK85
Warrington Spur, Wind. 172 AV87
Warrington Sq., Dag. 126 EX61
Warrington St. E13 144 EG70
Doherty Rd.
Warrior Ave., Grav. 191 GJ91
Warrior Sq. E12 125 EN63
Warsaw Clo., Ruis. 135 BV65
Glebe Ave.
Warsdale Dr. NW9 118 CR57
Mardale Dr.
Warspite Rd. SE18 164 EL76
Warton Rd. E15 143 EC66
Warwall E6 145 EP72
Warwick Ave. W2 140 DC70
Warwick Ave. W9 140 DB70
Warwick Ave., Edg. 96 CP48
Warwick Ave., Egh. 193 BC95
Warwick Ave., Har. 116 BZ63
Warwick Ave. (Cuffley), Pot.B. 65 DK27
Warwick Ave., Slou. 131 AQ70
Warwick Ave., Stai. 174 BJ93
Warwick Clo., Barn. 80 DD43
Warwick Clo., Bex. 186 EZ87
Warwick Clo., Dor. 263 CH144
Warwick Clo., Hmptn. 176 CC94
Warwick Clo., Hert. 32 DQ11
Warwick Clo., Orp. 206 EU104
Warwick Clo. (Cuffley), Pot.B. 65 DK27
Warwick Clo. (Bushey), Wat. 95 CE45
Magnaville Rd.
Warwick Ct. SE15 162 DU82
Warwick Ct. WC1 274 C7
Warwick Ct., Surb. 198 CL103
Hook Rd.
Warwick Cres. W2 140 DC71
Warwick Cres., Hayes 135 BT70
Warwick Deeping Pl., Cher. 211 BC106
Warwick Dene W5 138 CL74
Warwick Dr. SW15 159 CV83
Warwick Dr. (Cheshunt), Wal.Cr. 67 DX28
Warwick Est. W2 140 DB71
Warwick Gdns. N4 122 DQ57
Warwick Gdns. W14 159 CZ76
Warwick Gdns., Ash. 231 CJ117
Warwick Gdns., Barn. 79 CZ38
Great N. Rd.
Warwick Gdns., Ilf. 125 EP60
Warwick Gdns., Rom. 128 FJ55
Warwick Gdns., T.Ditt. 197 CF99
Warwick Gro. E5 122 DV60
Warwick Gro., Surb. 198 CM101
Warwick Ho. St. SW1 277 N2
Warwick Ho. St. SW1 141 DK74
Warwick La. EC4 274 G9
Warwick La. EC4 141 DP72
Warwick La., Rain. 148 FM68
Warwick La., Upmin. 148 FP68
Warwick La., Wok. 226 AU119
Warwick Pas. EC4 274 G8
Warwick Pl. W5 157 CK75
Warwick Rd.
Warwick Pl. W9 140 DC71
Warwick Pl., Grav. 190 GB85
Warwick Pl., Uxb. 134 BJ66
Warwick Pl. N. SW1 277 K9
Warwick Pl. N. SW1 161 DJ77
Warwick Rd. E4 101 EA50
Warwick Rd. E11 124 EH57
Warwick Rd. E12 124 EL64
Warwick Rd. E15 144 EF65
Warwick Rd. E17 101 DZ53
Warwick Rd. N11 99 DK51
Warwick Rd. N18 100 DS49
Warwick Rd. SE20 202 DV97
Warwick Rd. SW5 159 CZ77
Warwick Rd. W5 157 CK75
Warwick Rd. W14 159 CZ77
Warwick Rd., Ashf. 174 BL92
Warwick Rd., Barn. 80 DB42
Warwick Rd., Beac. 89 AK52
Warwick Rd., Borwd. 78 CR41
Warwick Rd., Couls. 219 DJ114
Warwick Rd., Dor. 263 CJ144
Warwick Rd., Enf. 83 DZ37
Warwick Rd., Houns. 155 BV83
Warwick Rd., Kings.T. 197 CJ95
Warwick Rd., N.Mal. 198 CQ97
Warwick Rd., Rain. 148 FJ70
Warwick Rd., Red. 250 DF133
Warwick Rd., St.Alb. 43 CF18
Warwick Rd., Sid. 186 EV92
Warwick Rd., Sthl. 156 BZ76
Warwick Rd., Sutt. 218 DC105
Warwick Rd., T.Ditt. 197 CF99
Warwick Rd., Th.Hth. 201 DN97
Warwick Rd., Twick. 177 CE88
Warwick Rd., Well. 166 EW83
Warwick Rd., West Dr. 134 BL74
Warwick Row SW1 277 J6
Warwick Row SW1 161 DH76
Warwick Sq. EC4 274 G8
Warwick Sq. SW1 277 K9
Warwick Sq. SW1 161 DJ78
Warwick Sq. Ms. SW1 277 K9
Warwick Sq. Ms. SW1 161 DJ77
Warwick St. W1 273 L10
Warwick St. W1 141 DJ73
Warwick Ter. SE18 165 ER79
Warwick Way SW1 277 K9
Warwick Way SW1 161 DJ77
Warwick Way, Rick. 75 BQ42
Warwick Wold Rd., Red. 251 DN129
Warwick Yd. EC1 275 J5
Warwicks Bench, Guil. 258 AX136
Warwicks Bench La., Guil. 259 AZ137
Warwicks Bench Rd., Guil. 258 AY137
Warwickshire Path SE8 163 DZ80
Wash, The, Hert. 32 DR09
Wash Hill, H.Wyc. 110 AE59
Wash Hill Lea, H.Wyc. 110 AD59
Wash La., Pot.B. 63 CV33
Wash Rd., Brwd. 109 GD44
Washington Ave. E12 124 EL63
Washington Ave., Hem.H. 40 BL15
Washington Clo. E3 143 EC72
Washington Clo., Reig. 250 DA131
Washington Dr., Slou. 131 AK73
Washington Dr., Wind. 151 AL83
Washington Rd. E6 144 EJ66
St. Stephens Rd.
Washington Rd. E18 102 EF54
Washington Rd. SW13 159 CU80
Washington Rd., Kings.T. 198 CN96
Washington Rd., Wor.Pk. 199 CV103
Washington Row, Amer. 55 AQ40
London Rd. W.
Washneys La., Orp. 224 EU114
Washneys Rd., Orp. 224 EV113
Washpond La., Warl. 237 EC118
Wastdale Rd. SE23 183 DX88
Wat Tyler Rd. SE3 163 EC82
Wat Tyler Rd. SE10 163 EC82
Watchfield Ct. W4 158 CQ78
Watchgate, Dart. 189 FR91
Watchlytes, Welw.G.C. 30 DC09
Watchmead, Welw.G.C. 30 DA09
Watcombe Cotts., Rich. 158 CN79
Watcombe Pl. SE25 202 DV99
Albert Rd.
Watcombe Rd. SE25 202 DV99
Water Circ. (Bluewater), Green. 189 FT88
Water End Rd., Berk. 39 BB17
Water Gdns., Stan. 95 CH51
Water Gdns., The W2 140 DE72
Burwood Pl.
Water La. E15 144 EE65
Water La. N9 100 DV46
Water La. NW1 141 DH66
Kentish Town Rd.
Water La. SE14 162 DW80
Water La., Berk. 38 AW19
Water La., Chesh. 54 AP32
Water La., Cob. 230 BY115
Water La., Dor. 261 BV143
Water La., Guil. 260 BH138
Water La., Harl. 50 EL19
Water La., Hem.H. 57 BA29
Water La., Ilf. 125 ES62
Water La., Kings L. 59 BP29
Water La., Kings.T. 197 CK95
Water La., Lthd. 246 BY126
Water La., Oxt. 254 EG127
Water La., Purf. 168 FN77
Water La., Rich. 177 CK85
Water La., Sev. 225 FF112
Water La., Sid. 186 EZ90
Water La., Twick. 177 CG88
The Embk.
Water La., Wat. 76 BW42
Water La., West. 255 ER127
Water Lily Clo., Sthl. 156 CC75
Navigator Dr.
Water Meadow, Chesh. 54 AP32
Water Ms. SE15 162 DW84
Water Mill Way (South Darenth), Dart. 208 FP96
Water Rd., Wem. 138 CM67
Water Row, Ware 33 DX06
Water Side, Kings L. 58 BN29
Water St. WC2 274 C10
Water Twr. Clo., Uxb. 114 BL64
Water Twr. Hill, Croy. 220 DR105
Water Twr. Pl. N1 141 DN67
Liverpool Rd.
Water Vw., Horl. 269 DJ148
Carlton Tye
Waterbank Rd. SE6 183 EB90
Waterbeach, Welw.G.C. 30 DD09
Waterbeach Rd., Dag. 146 EW65
Waterbeach Rd., Slou. 131 AR72
Waterbrook La. NW4 119 CW57
Watercress Pl. N1 142 DS66
Hertford Rd.
Watercress Way, Wok. 226 AV116
Watercroft Rd., Sev. 224 EZ110
Waterdale, Hert. 32 DQ11
Waterdale Rd. SE2 166 EU79
Waterdales, Grav. 190 GC89
Waterdell Pl., Rick. 92 BG47
Uxbridge Rd.
Waterden Clo., Guil. 259 AZ135
Waterden Rd. E15 123 EA64
Waterden Rd., Guil. 258 AY135
Waterend La., St.Alb. 28 CQ07
Waterend La., Welw. 28 CS06
Waterer Gdns., Tad. 233 CX118

Waterer Ri., Wall. 219 DK107
Waterfall Clo. N14 99 DJ48
Waterfall Clo., Vir.W. 192 AU97
Waterfall Cotts. SW19 180 DD93
Waterfall Rd. N11 99 DH49
Waterfall Rd. N14 99 DJ48
Waterfall Rd. SW19 180 DD93
Waterfall Ter. SW17 180 DE93
Waterfield, Rick. 91 BC45
Waterfield, Tad. 233 CV119
Waterfield, Welw.G.C. 30 DB08
Waterfield Clo. SE28 146 EV74
Waterfield Clo., Belv. 166 FA76
Waterfield Dr., Warl. 236 DW119
Waterfield Gdns. SE25 202 DS99
Waterfield Grn., Tad. 233 CV120
Waterfields, Lthd. 231 CH119
Waterfields Way, Wat. 76 BX42
Waterford Common, Hert. 31 DP05
Waterford Grn., Welw.G.C. 30 DB09
Waterford Rd. SW6 160 DB81
Watergardens, The, Kings.T. 178 CQ93
Watergate EC4 274 F10
Watergate, The, Wat. 94 BX47
Watergate St. SE8 163 EA79
Watergate Wk. WC2 278 A2
Waterglade Ind. Pk., Grays 169 FT78
Waterhall Ave. E4 102 EE49
Waterhall Clo. E17 101 DX53
Waterhead Clo., Erith 167 FE80
Waterhouse Clo. E16 144 EK71
Waterhouse Clo. NW3 120 DD64
Lyndhurst Rd.
Waterhouse Clo. W6 159 CX77
Great Ch. La.
Waterhouse La., Ken. 236 DQ119
Hayes La.
Waterhouse La., Red. 252 DT132
Waterhouse La., Tad. 233 CZ121
Waterhouse Moor, Harl. 51 ET16
Waterhouse Sq. EC1 274 D7
Waterhouse Sq. EC1 141 DN71
Waterhouse St., Hem.H. 40 BJ20
Wateridge Clo. E14 163 EA76
Westferry Rd.
Wateringbury Clo., Orp. 206 EV97
Waterloo Bri. SE1 278 B1
Waterloo Bri. SE1 141 DM73
Waterloo Bri. WC2 278 B1
Waterloo Bri. WC2 141 DM73
Waterloo Clo. E9 122 DW64
Churchill Wk.
Waterloo Clo., Felt. 175 BT88
Waterloo Est. E2 142 DW68
Waterloo Gdns. E2 142 DW68
Waterloo Gdns. N1 141 DP66
Barnsbury St.
Waterloo Gdns., Rom. 127 FD58
Waterloo Pas. NW6 140 DA66
Waterloo Pl. SW1 277 M2
Waterloo Pl. SW1 141 DK74
Waterloo Pl., Rich. 178 CL85
Sheen Rd.
Waterloo Pl. (Kew), Rich. 158 CN79
Waterloo Rd. E6 144 EJ66
Waterloo Rd. E7 124 EF64
Wellington Rd.
Waterloo Rd. E10 123 EA59
Waterloo Rd. NW2 119 CU60
Waterloo Rd. SE1 278 D4
Waterloo Rd. SE1 161 DN75
Waterloo Rd., Brwd. 108 FW46
Waterloo Rd., Epsom 216 CR112
Waterloo Rd., Ilf. 103 EQ54
Waterloo Rd., Rom. 127 FE57
Waterloo Rd., Sutt. 218 DD106
Waterloo Rd., Uxb. 134 BJ67
Waterloo St., Grav. 191 GJ87
Waterloo Ter. N1 141 DP66
Waterlow Ct. NW11 120 DB59
Heath Clo.
Waterlow Rd. N19 121 DJ60
Waterlow Rd., Reig. 266 DC135
Waterman Clo., Wat. 75 BV44
Waterman Ct., Slou. 131 AL74
Waterman St. SW15 159 CX83
Waterman Way E1 142 DV74
Waterman's Clo., Kings.T. 178 CL94
Woodside Rd.
Watermans Wk. SE16 163 DY76
Watermans Way, Epp. 70 FA27
Watermark Way, Hert. 32 DT09
Watermead, Felt. 175 BS88
Watermead, Tad. 233 CV121
Watermead, Wok. 226 AT116
Watermead La., Cars. 200 DF101
Watermead Rd. SE6 183 EC91
Watermead Way N17 122 DV55
Watermeadow Clo., Erith 167 FH81
Watermeadow La. SW6 160 DC82
Watermen's Sq. SE20 182 DW94
Watermill Clo., Rich. 177 CJ90
Watermill La. N18 100 DS50
Watermill La., Hert. 32 DR06
Watermill La. N., Hert. 32 DQ06
Watermill Way SW19 200 DC95
Watermill Way, Felt. 176 BZ89
Watermint Clo., Orp. 206 EX98
Wagtail Way
Watermint Quay N16 122 DU59
Waterperry La., Wok. 210 AT110
Waters Dr., Rick. 92 BL46
Waters Dr., Stai. 173 BF90
Waters Gdns., Dag. 126 FA64
Waters Pl. SW15 159 CW82
Danemere St.
Waters Rd. SE6 184 EE90
Waters Rd., Kings.T. 198 CP96
Waters Sq., Kings.T. 198 CP97
Watersedge, Epsom 216 CQ105
Watersfield Way, Edg. 95 CK52
Waterside, Beck. 203 EA95
Rectory Rd.
Waterside, Berk. 38 AX19
Holliday St.
Waterside, Chesh. 54 AQ32
Waterside, Dart. 187 FE85
Waterside, H.Wyc. 110 AE56
Waterside, Horl. 268 DG146
Waterside, Rad. 61 CH34
Waterside, St.Alb. 62 CL27
Waterside, Uxb. 134 BJ71
Waterside, Welw.G.C. 30 DA07
Waterside Clo. E3 143 DZ67
Waterside Clo. SE16 162 DU75
Bevington St.
Waterside Clo., Bark. 126 EU63
Waterside Clo., Nthlt. 136 BZ69
Waterside Clo., Rom. 106 FN52
Waterside Clo., Surb. 198 CL103
Culsac Rd.
Waterside Ct., Kings L. 59 BP29
Water Side
Waterside Dr., Slou. 153 AZ75
Waterside Dr., Walt. 195 BU99
Waterside Ms., Guil. 242 AW132
Waterside Pl. NW1 140 DG67
Princess Rd.
Waterside Pl., Saw. 36 FA05
Waterside Pt. SW11 160 DE80
Waterside Rd., Guil. 242 AX131
Waterside Rd., Sthl. 156 CA76
Waterside Trd. Cen. W7 157 CE76
Waterside Way SW17 180 DC91
Waterside Way, Wok. 226 AV118
Winnington Way
Watersmeet, Harl. 51 EP19
Watersmeet Clo., Guil. 243 BA129
Cotts Wd. Dr.
Watersmeet Way SE28 146 EW72
Waterson Rd., Grays 171 GH77
Waterson St. E2 275 N2
Waterson St. E2 142 DS69
Watersplash Clo., Kings.T. 198 CL97
Watersplash La., Hayes 155 BU77
Watersplash La., Houns. 155 BV78
Watersplash Rd., Shep. 194 BN99
Waterton Ave., Grav. 191 GL87
Waterview Ho. E14 143 DY71
Waterway Rd., Lthd. 231 CG122
Waterworks Cotts., Brox. 49 DY22
Waterworks La. E5 123 DX61
Waterworks Rd. SW2 181 DM86
Waterworks Yd., Croy. 202 DQ104
Surrey St.
Watery La. SW20 199 CZ96
Watery La., Cher. 193 BD101
Watery La., Hat. 44 CS19
Watery La., H.Wyc. 110 AE55
Watery La., Nthlt. 136 BW68
Watery La., St.Alb. 61 CK28
Watery La., Sid. 186 EV93
Wates Way, Brwd. 108 FX46
Wates Way, Mitch. 200 DF100
Wateville Rd. N17 100 DQ53
Watford Bypass, Borwd. 95 CG45
Watford Clo. SW11 160 DE81
Petworth St.
Watford Clo., Guil. 243 AZ134
Watford Fld. Rd., Wat. 76 BW43
Watford Heath, Wat. 94 BX45
Watford Rd. E16 144 EG71
Watford Rd., Borwd. 77 CJ44
Watford Rd., Har. 117 CG61
Watford Rd., Kings L. 59 BP32
Watford Rd., Nthwd. 93 BT51
Watford Rd., Rad. 77 CE36
Watford Rd., Rick. 75 BQ43
Watford Rd., St.Alb. 60 CA27
Watford Rd., Wem. 117 CG61
Watford Way NW4 119 CU56
Watford Way NW7 119 CU56
Wathen Rd., Dor. 263 CH135
Watkin Rd., Wem. 118 CP62
Watkinson Rd. N7 141 DM65
Watling Ave., Edg. 96 CR52
Watling Clo., Hem.H. 40 BL17
Watling Ct. EC4 275 J9
Watling Ct., Borwd. 77 CK44
Watling Fm. Clo., Stan. 95 CJ46
Watling Gdns. NW2 139 CY65
Watling Knoll, Rad. 61 CF33
Watling St. EC4 275 H9
Watling St. EC4 142 DQ72
Watling St. SE15 162 DS79
Dragon Rd.
Watling St., Bexh. 167 FB84
Watling St., Borwd. 77 CJ40
Watling St., Dart. 189 FR88
Watling St., Grav. 191 GG92
Watling St., Rad. 61 CF32
Watling St., St.Alb. 61 CD25
Watling St. Caravan Site (Travellers), St.Alb. 60 CC25
Watling Vw., St.Alb. 42 CC23
Watlings Clo., Croy. 203 DY100
Watlington Gro. SE26 183 DY92
Watlington Rd., Harl. 36 EX11
Watney Mkt. E1 142 DV72
Commercial Rd.
Watney Rd. SW14 158 CQ83
Watney St. E1 142 DV72
Watneys Rd., Mitch. 201 DK99
Watson Ave. E6 145 EN66
Watson Ave., St.Alb. 43 CF17
Watson Ave., Sutt. 199 CY103
Watson Clo. N16 122 DR64
Matthias Rd.
Watson Clo. SW19 180 DE93
Watson Clo., Grays 169 FU81
Watson Gdns., Rom. 106 FK54
Watson Rd., Dor. 262 CC137
Watson St. E13 144 EH68
Watson's Ms. W1 272 C7
Watsons Rd. N22 99 DM53
Watson's St. SE8 163 EA80
Watsons Wk., St.Alb. 43 CE21
Watsons Yd. NW2 119 CT61
North Circular Rd.
Wattendon Rd., Ken. 235 DP116
Wattisfield Rd. E5 122 DW62
Wattleton Rd., Beac. 110 AJ55
Watts Bri. Rd., Erith 167 FF79
Reddy Rd.
Watts Clo. N15 122 DS57
Seaford Rd.
Watts Clo., Tad. 233 CX122
Watts Cres., Purf. 168 FQ77
Watts Fm. Par., Wok. 210 AT110
Barnmead
Watts Gro. E3 143 EB71
Watts La., Chis. 205 EP95
Watts La., Tad. 233 CX122
Watts La., Tedd. 177 CG92
Watts Mead, Tad. 233 CX122
Watts Rd., T.Ditt. 197 CG101
Watts St. E1 142 DV74
Watts St. SE15 162 DT81
Watts Way SW7 276 A6
Wauthier Clo. N13 99 DP50
Wavel Ms. N8 121 DK56
Wavel Ms. NW6 140 DB66
Acol Rd.
Wavel Pl. SE26 182 DT91
Sydenham Hill
Wavell Clo. (Cheshunt), Wal.Cr. 67 DY27
Wavell Dr., Sid. 185 ES86
Wavell Gdns., Slou. 131 AM69
Wavell Rd., Beac. 89 AP54
Wavendene Ave., Egh. 173 BB94
Wavendon Ave. W4 158 CR78
Waveney, Hem.H. 40 BM15
Waveney Ave. SE15 162 DV84
Waveney Clo. E1 142 DU74
Kennet St.
Waverley Ave. E4 101 DZ49
Waverley Ave. E17 123 ED55
Waverley Ave., Ken. 236 DS116
Waverley Ave., Surb. 198 CP100
Waverley Ave., Sutt. 200 DB103
Waverley Ave., Twick. 176 BZ88
Waverley Ave., Wem. 118 CM64
Waverley Clo. E18 102 EJ53
Waverley Clo., Brom. 204 EK99
Waverley Clo., Hayes 155 BR77
Waverley Ct., Wok. 226 AY117
Waverley Cres. SE18 165 ER78
Waverley Cres., Rom. 106 FJ52
Waverley Dr., Cher. 193 BD104
Waverley Dr., Vir.W. 192 AU97
Waverley Gdns. E6 144 EL71
Oliver Gdns.
Waverley Gdns. NW10 138 CM69
Waverley Gdns., Bark. 145 ES68
Waverley Gdns., Grays 170 GA75
Waverley Gdns., Ilf. 103 EQ54
Waverley Gdns., Nthwd. 93 BU53
Waverley Gro. N3 119 CY55
Waverley Ind. Est., Har. 117 CD55
Waverley Pl. N4 121 DP61
Adolphus Rd.
Waverley Pl. NW8 140 DD68
Waverley Pl., Lthd. 231 CH122
Church Rd.
Waverley Rd. E17 123 EC55
Waverley Rd. E18 102 EJ53
Waverley Rd. N8 121 DK58
Waverley Rd. N17 100 DV52
Waverley Rd. SE18 165 ER78
Waverley Rd. SE25 202 DV98
Waverley Rd., Cob. 214 CB114
Waverley Rd., Enf. 81 DP42
Waverley Rd., Epsom 217 CV106
Waverley Rd., Har. 116 BZ60
Waverley Rd., Lthd. 214 CB114
Waverley Rd., Rain. 147 FH69
Waverley Rd., St.Alb. 42 CC18
Waverley Rd., Slou. 131 AQ71
Waverley Rd., Sthl. 136 CA73
Waverley Rd., Wey. 212 BN106
Waverley Vil. N17 100 DT54
Waverley Wk. W2 140 DA71
Waverley Way, Cars. 218 DE107
Waverton Ho. E3 143 DZ67
Waverton Rd. SW18 180 DC87
Waverton St. W1 276 G2
Waverton St. W1 140 DG74
Wavertree Ct. SW2 181 DM88
Streatham Hill
Wavertree Rd. E18 102 EG54
Wavertree Rd. SW2 181 DL88
Waxlow Cres., Sthl. 136 CA72
Waxlow Rd. NW10 138 CQ68
Waxwell Clo., Pnr. 94 BX54
Waxwell La., Pnr. 94 BX54
Waxwell Ter. SE1 278 C5
Way, The, Reig. 250 DD133
Way Volante, Grav. 191 GL91
Wayborne Gro., Ruis. 115 BQ58
Waycross Rd., Upmin. 129 FS58
Waye Ave., Houns. 155 BU81
Wayfarer Rd., Nthlt. 136 BX70
Wayfarers Pk., Berk. 38 AT19
Wayfaring Grn., Grays 170 FZ78
Curling La.
Wayfield Link SE9 185 ER86
Wayford St. SW11 160 DE82
Wayland Ave. E8 122 DU64
Waylands, Hayes 135 BR71
Waylands, Swan. 207 FF98
Waylands Clo., Sev. 240 EY115
Waylands Mead, Beck. 203 EB95
Wayleave, The SE28 146 EV73
Waylett Pl. SE27 181 DP90
Waylett Pl., Wem. 117 CK63
Wayman Ct. E8 142 DV65
Wayne Clo., Orp. 205 ET104
Wayneflete Twr. Ave., Esher 196 CA104
Waynflete Ave., Croy. 201 DP104
Waynflete Sq. W10 139 CX73
Waynflete St. SW18 180 DC89
Wayre, The, Harl. 36 EW11
Wayre St., Harl. 36 EW11
Wayside NW11 119 CY60
Wayside SW14 178 CQ85
Wayside, Croy. 221 EB107
Field Way
Wayside, Kings L. 58 BH30
Wayside, Pot.B. 64 DD33
Wayside, Rad. 61 CK33
Wayside, The, Hem.H. 41 BQ21
Wayside Ave., Horn. 128 FK61
Wayside Ave. (Bushey), Wat. 77 CD44
Wayside Clo. N14 81 DJ44
Wayside Clo., Rom. 127 FF55
Wayside Commercial Est., Bark. 146 EU67
Wayside Ct., Twick. 177 CJ86
Wayside Ct., Wem. 118 CN62
Oakington Ave.
Wayside Ct., Wok. 226 AS116
Langmans Way
Wayside Gdns. SE9 185 EM91
Wayside Gro.
Wayside Gdns., Dag. 126 FA64
Wayside Gdns., Ger.Cr. 112 AX59
Wayside Gro. SE9 185 EM91
Wayside Ms., Ilf. 125 EN57
Gaysham Ave.
Wayville Rd., Dart. 188 FP87
Weald, The, Chis. 185 EM93
Weald Bri. Rd., Epp. 53 FD24
Weald Clo. SE16 162 DV78
Stevenson Cres.
Weald Clo., Brwd. 108 FU48
Weald Clo., Brom. 204 EL103
Weald Clo., Grav. 190 GE94
Weald Clo., Guil. 258 AY140
Station Rd.
Weald Hall La., Epp. 70 EW25
Weald La., Har. 95 CD54
Weald Pk. Way, Brwd. 108 FS47
Weald Ri., Har. 95 CF52
Weald Rd., Brwd. 106 FM46
Weald Rd., Sev. 257 FH129
Weald Rd., Uxb. 134 BN68
Weald Sq. E5 122 DV61
Rossington St.
Weald Way, Cat. 252 DS128
Weald Way, Hayes 135 BS69
Weald Way, Reig. 266 DC138
Weald Way, Rom. 127 FB58
Wealdon Ct., Guil. 242 AT134
Humbolt Clo.
Wealdstone Rd., Sutt. 199 CZ103
Wealdway, Grav. 191 GH93
Wealdwood Gdns., Pnr. 94 CB51
Highbanks Rd.
Weale Rd. E4 101 ED48
Weall Grn., Wat. 59 BV32
Wear Pl. E2 142 DV69
Weardale Ave., Dart. 188 FQ89
Weardale Gdns., Enf. 82 DR39
Weardale Rd. SE13 163 ED84
Wearside Rd. SE13 163 EB84
Weasdale Ct., Wok. 226 AT116
Roundthorn Way
Weatherall Clo., Add. 212 BH106
Weatherhill Clo., Horl. 269 DM148
Weatherhill Common, Horl. 269 DM147
Weatherhill Rd., Horl. 269 DM148
Weatherley Clo. E3 143 DZ71
Weaver Clo. E6 145 EP73
Trader Rd.
Weaver St. E1 142 DU70
Weaver Wk. SE27 181 DP91
Weavers Clo., Grav. 191 GG88
Weavers Clo., Islw. 157 CE84
Weavers La., Sev. 257 FJ121
Weavers Orchard, Grav. 190 GA93
Weavers Ter. SW6 160 DA79
Weavers Way NW1 141 DK67
Webb Clo. W10 139 CW70
Webb Clo., Chesh. 54 AP30
Webb Clo., Slou. 152 AX77
Webb Est. E5 122 DU59
Webb Gdns. E13 144 EG70
Kelland Rd.
Webb Pl. NW10 139 CT69
Old Oak La.
Webb Rd. SE3 164 EF79
Webb St. SE1 279 M7
Webb St. SE1 162 DS76
Webber Clo., Borwd. 77 CK44
Rodgers Clo.
Webber Clo., Erith 167 FH80
Webber Row SE1 278 E5
Webber Row SE1 161 DP75
Webber St. SE1 278 E4
Webber St. SE1 161 DP75
Webb's All., Sev. 257 FJ125
Webbs Rd. SW11 180 DF85
Webbs Rd., Hayes 135 BV69
Webbscroft Rd., Dag. 127 FB63
Webster Clo., Horn. 128 FK62
Latimer Dr.
Webster Clo., Lthd. 214 CB114
Webster Clo., Wal.Abb. 68 EG33
Webster Gdns. W5 137 CK74
Webster Rd. E11 123 EC62
Webster Rd. SE16 162 DU76
Websters Clo., Wok. 226 AV120
Wedderburn Rd. NW3 120 DD64
Wedderburn Rd., Bark. 145 ES67
Wedgewood Clo., Epp. 70 EU30
Wedgewood Clo., Nthwd. 93 BQ51
Wedgewood Dr., Harl. 52 EX16
Wedgewood Wk. NW6 120 DB64
Lymington Rd.
Wedgewoods, West. 238 EJ121
Westmore Rd.
Wedgwood Ms. W1 273 N9
Wedgwood Way SE19 182 DQ94
Wedhey, Harl. 51 EQ15
Wedlake Clo., Horn. 128 FL60
Wedlake St. W10 139 CY70
Kensal Rd.
Wedmore Ave., Ilf. 103 EN53
Wedmore Gdns. N19 121 DK61
Wedmore Ms. N19 121 DK62
Wedmore St.
Wedmore Rd., Grnf. 137 CD69
Wedmore St. N19 121 DK62
Wednesbury Gdns., Rom. 106 FM52
Wednesbury Grn., Rom. 106 FM52
Wednesbury Gdns.
Wednesbury Rd., Rom. 106 FM52
Weech Rd. NW6 120 DA63
Weedington Rd. NW5 120 DG64
Weedon Clo., Ger.Cr. 90 AV53
Weedon La., Amer. 55 AN36
Weekes Dr., Slou. 131 AP74
Weekley Sq. SW11 160 DD83
Thomas Baines Rd.
Weigall Rd. SE12 164 EG84
Weighhouse St. W1 272 G9
Weighhouse St. W1 140 DG72
Weighton Rd. SE20 202 DV96
Weighton Rd., Har. 95 CD53
Weihurst Gdns., Sutt. 218 DD106
Weimar St. SW15 159 CY83
Weind, The, Epp. 85 ES36
Weir Est. SW12 181 DJ87
Weir Hall Ave. N18 100 DR51
Weir Hall Gdns. N18 100 DR50
Weir Hall Rd. N17 100 DR50
Weir Hall Rd. N18 100 DR50
Weir Pl., Stai. 193 BE95
Weir Rd. SW12 181 DJ87
Weir Rd. SW19 180 DB90
Weir Rd., Bex. 187 FB87
Weir Rd., Cher. 194 BH101
Weir Rd., Walt. 195 BU100
Weirdale Ave. N20 98 DF47
Weir's Pas. NW1 273 N2
Weir's Pas. NW1 141 DK69
Weirside Gdns., West Dr. 134 BK74
Weiss Rd. SW15 159 CX83
Welbeck Ave., Brom. 184 EG91
Welbeck Ave., Hayes 135 BV70
Welbeck Ave., Sid. 186 EU88
Welbeck Clo. N12 98 DD50
Torrington Pk.
Welbeck Clo., Borwd. 78 CN41
Welbeck Clo., Epsom 217 CU108
Welbeck Clo., N.Mal. 199 CT99
Welbeck Rd. E6 144 EK69
Welbeck Rd., Barn. 80 DD44
Welbeck Rd., Cars. 200 DE102
Welbeck Rd., Har. 116 CB60
Welbeck Rd., Sutt. 200 DD103
Welbeck St. W1 273 H8
Welbeck St. W1 140 DG71
Welbeck Wk., Cars. 200 DE102
Welbeck Rd.
Welbeck Way W1 273 H8
Welbeck Way W1 141 DH72
Welby St. SE5 161 DP81
Welch Pl., Pnr. 94 BW53
Welclose St., St.Alb. 42 CC20
Welcomes Rd., Ken. 236 DQ116
Welcote Dr., Nthwd. 93 BR51
Weld Pl. N11 99 DH50
Welden, Slou. 132 AW72
Welders La., Beac. 90 AT52
Welders La., Ger.Cr. 90 AV52
Weldon Clo., Ruis. 135 BV65
Weldon Dr., W.Mol. 196 BZ98
Weldon Way, Red. 251 DK129
Welfare Rd. E15 144 EE66
Welford Clo. E5 123 DX62
Denton Way
Welford Pl. SW19 179 CY91
Welham Clo., Hat. 45 CW24
Welham Ct., Hat. 45 CW24
Dixons Hill Rd.
Welham Manor, Hat. 45 CW24
Welham Rd. SW16 180 DG92
Welham Rd. SW17 180 DG92
Welhouse Rd., Cars. 200 DE102
Well App., Barn. 79 CW43
Well Clo. SW16 181 DM91
Well Clo., Ruis. 116 BY62
Parkfield Cres.
Well Clo., Wok. 226 AW117
Well Cottage Clo. E11 124 EJ59
Well Ct. EC4 275 J9
Well Ct. SW16 181 DM91
Well Cft., Hem.H. 40 BH19
Gadebridge Rd.
Well End Rd., Borwd. 78 CQ37
Well Fm. Rd., Whyt. 236 DU119
Well Garth, Welw.G.C. 29 CY10
Well Gro. N20 98 DC45
Well Hall Par. SE9 165 EM84
Well Hall Rd.
Well Hall Rd. SE9 165 EM83
Well Hill, Orp. 225 FB107
Well Hill La., Orp. 225 FB108
Well Hill Rd., Sev. 225 FC107
Well La. SW14 178 CQ85
Well La., Brwd. 108 FT41
Well La., Harl. 35 EN14
Well La., Wok. 226 AW117
Well Pas. NW3 120 DD62
Well Path, Wok. 226 AW117
Well La.
Well Rd. NW3 120 DD62
Well Rd., Barn. 79 CW43
Well Rd., Pot.B. 64 DE28
Well Row, Hert. 47 DM17
Well St. E9 142 DW66
Well St. E15 144 EE65
Well Wk. NW3 120 DD63
Well Way, Epsom 232 CN115
Wellacre Rd., Har. 117 CH58
Wellan Clo., Sid. 186 EV85
Welland Clo., Slou. 153 BB79
Welland Gdns., Grnf. 137 CF68
Welland Ms. E1 142 DU74
Kennet St.
Welland St. SE10 163 EC79
Wellands, Hat. 45 CU16
Wellands Clo., Brom. 205 EM96
Wellbank, Maid. 130 AE70
Rectory Rd.
Wellbrook Rd., Orp. 223 EN105
Wellbury Ter., Hem.H. 41 BQ20
Wellclose Sq. E1 142 DU73
Wellclose St. E1 142 DU73
The Highway
Wellcome Ave., Dart. 168 FM84
Wellcome Chemical Wks., Dart. 188 FM85
Wellcroft Clo., Welw.G.C. 30 DA11
Wellcroft Rd., Slou. 131 AP74
Wellcroft Rd., Welw.G.C. 30 DA10
Welldon Cres., Har. 117 CE58
Wellen Ri., Hem.H. 40 BL23
Weller Clo., Amer. 55 AS37
Weller Rd., Amer. 55 AS37
Weller St. SE1 279 H4
Wellers Clo., West. 255 EQ127
Weller's Ct. N1 273 P1
Wellers Ct., Guil. 260 BN139
Wellers Gro. (Cheshunt), Wal.Cr. 66 DU28
Wellesford Clo., Bans. 233 CZ117
Wellesley, Harl. 51 EN20
Wellesley Ave. W6 159 CV76
Wellesley Ave., Iver 153 BF76
Wellesley Ave., Nthwd. 93 BT50
Wellesley Ct. W9 140 DC69
Maida Vale
Wellesley Ct. Rd., Croy. 202 DR103
Wellesley Cres., Pot.B. 63 CY33
Wellesley Cres., Twick. 177 CE89
Wellesley Gro., Croy. 202 DR103
Wellesley Pk. Ms., Enf. 81 DP40
Wellesley Path, Slou. 152 AU75
Wellesley Rd.
Wellesley Pl. NW1 273 M3
Wellesley Rd. E11 124 EG57
Wellesley Rd. E17 123 EA58
Wellesley Rd. N22 99 DN54
Wellesley Rd. NW5 120 DG64
Wellesley Rd. W4 158 CN78
Wellesley Rd., Brwd. 108 FW46
Wellesley Rd., Croy. 202 DQ102
Wellesley Rd., Har. 117 CE57
Wellesley Rd., Ilf. 125 EP61
Wellesley Rd., Slou. 152 AU75
Wellesley Rd., Sutt. 218 DC107
Wellesley Rd., Twick. 177 CD90
Wellesley St. E1 143 DX71
Wellesley Ter. N1 275 J2
Wellesley Ter. N1 142 DQ69
Welley Ave., Stai. 152 AY84
Welley Rd., Stai. 172 AX85

Wellfield Ave. N10 121 DH55
Wellfield Clo., Hat. 45 CU17
Wellfield Gdns., Cars. 218 DE109
Wellfield Rd. SW16 181 DL91
Wellfield Rd., Hat. 45 CU16
Wellfield Wk. SW16 181 DM92
Wellfields, Loug. 85 EN41
Wellfit St. SE24 161 DP83
Hinton Rd.
Wellgarth, Grnf. 137 CH65
Wellgarth Rd. NW11 120 DB60
Wellhouse La., Barn. 79 CW42
Wellhouse La., Bet. 264 CQ138
Wellhouse Rd., Beck. 203 DZ98
Welling High St., Well. 166 EV83
Welling Way SE9 165 ER83
Welling Way, Well. 165 ER83
Wellings Ho., Hayes 135 BV74
Wellington Ave. E4 101 EA47
Wellington Ave. N9 100 DV48
Wellington Ave. N15 122 DT58
Wellington Ave., Houns. 176 CA85
Wellington Ave., Pnr. 94 BZ53
Wellington Ave., Sid. 186 EU86
Wellington Ave., Vir.W. 192 AV99
Wellington Ave., Wor.Pk. 217 CW105
Wellington Bldgs. SW1 161 DH78
Ebury Bri. Rd.
Wellington Clo. SE14 163 DX81
Rutts Ter.
Wellington Clo. W11 140 DA72
Ledbury Rd.
Wellington Clo., Dag. 147 FC66
Wellington Clo., Walt. 195 BT102
Hepworth Way
Wellington Clo., Wat. 94 BY46
Highfield
Wellington Cotts, Lthd. 245 BS129
Wellington Ct. NW8 140 DD68
Wellington Rd.
Wellington Ct., Stai. 174 BL87
Wellington Cres., N.Mal. 198 CQ97
Wellington Dr., Dag. 147 FC66
Wellington Dr., Pur. 219 DM110
Wellington Dr., Welw.G.C. 30 DC09
Wellington Gdns. SE7 164 EJ79
Wellington Gdns., Twick. 177 CD91
Wellington Gro. SE10 163 ED80
Crooms Hill
Wellington Hill, Loug. 84 EH37
Wellington Ms. SE7 164 EJ79
Wellington Ms. SE22 162 DU84
Peckham Rye
Wellington Pk. Est. NW2 119 CU61
Wellington Pas. E11 124 EG57
Wellington Rd.
Wellington Pl. N2 120 DE57
Great N. Rd.
Wellington Pl. NW8 272 B1
Wellington Pl. NW8 140 DE68
Wellington Pl., Brwd. 108 FW50
Wellington Pl., Brox. 48 DW23
Wellington Rd. E6 145 EM68
Wellington Rd. E7 124 EF63
Wellington Rd. E10 123 DY60
Wellington Rd. E11 124 EG57
Wellington Rd. E17 123 DY56
Wellington Rd. NW8 140 DD68
Wellington Rd. NW10 139 CX69
Wellington Rd. SW19 180 DA89
Wellington Rd. W5 157 CJ76
Wellington Rd., Ashf. 174 BL92
Wellington Rd., Belv. 166 EZ78
Wellington Rd., Bex. 186 EX85
Wellington Rd., Brom. 204 EJ98
Wellington Rd., Cat. 236 DQ122
Wellington Rd., Croy. 201 DP101
Wellington Rd., Dart. 188 FJ86
Wellington Rd., Enf. 82 DS43
Wellington Rd., Epp. 70 FA27
Wellington Rd., Felt. 175 BS85
Wellington Rd., Hmptn. 177 CD92
Wellington Rd., Har. 117 CE55
Wellington Rd., Orp. 206 EV100
Wellington Rd., Pnr. 94 BZ53
Wellington Rd., St.Alb. 43 CH21
Wellington Rd. (London Colney), St.Alb. 61 CK26
Wellington Rd., Til. 171 GG83
Wellington Rd., Twick. 177 CD91
Wellington Rd., Uxb. 134 BJ67
Wellington Rd., Wat. 75 BV40
Wellington Rd. N., Houns. 156 BZ83
Wellington Rd. S., Houns. 156 BZ84
Wellington Row E2 142 DT69
Wellington Sq. SW3 276 D10
Wellington Sq. SW3 160 DF78
Wellington St. SE18 165 EN77
Wellington St. WC2 274 A10
Wellington St. WC2 141 DL73
Wellington St., Bark. 145 EQ67
Axe St.
Wellington St., Grav. 191 GJ87
Wellington St., Hert. 31 DP08
Wellington St., Slou. 152 AT75
Wellington Ter. E1 142 DV74
Wellington Ter. N8 121 DN55
Turnpike La.
Wellington Ter. W2 140 DB73
Notting Hill Gate
Wellington Ter., Har. 117 CD60
West St.
Wellington Way E3 143 EA69
Wellington Way, Horl. 268 DF146
Wellington Way, Wey. 212 BM110
Wellingtonia Ave. (Havering-atte-Bower), Rom. 105 FE48
Wellmeade Dr., Sev. 257 FH127
Wellmeadow Rd. SE6 184 EE87
Wellmeadow Rd. SE13 184 EE86
Wellmeadow Rd. W7 157 CG77
Wellow Wk., Cars. 200 DD102
Wells, The N14 99 DK45
Wells Clo., Lthd. 230 CB124
Wells Clo., Nthlt. 136 BW69
Yeading La.
Wells Clo., St.Alb. 42 CC19
Artisan Cres.
Wells Clo. (Cheshunt), Wal.Cr. 66 DQ25
Bloomfield Rd.
Wells Clo., Wind. 151 AN81
Wells Dr. NW9 118 CR60
Wells Gdns., Dag. 127 FB64
Wells Gdns., Ilf. 124 EL59
Wells Gdns., Rain. 147 FF65
Wells Ho. Rd. NW10 138 CS71
Wells Ms. W1 273 L8
Wells Pk. Rd. SE26 182 DU90
Wells Path, Hayes 135 BS69
Wells Pl., Red. 251 DH130
Wells Ri. NW8 140 DF67
Wells Rd. W12 159 CW75
Wells Rd., Brom. 205 EM96
Wells Rd., Epsom 216 CN114
Wells Rd., Guil. 243 BC131
Wells Sq. WC1 274 B3
Wells St. W1 273 K7
Wells St. W1 141 DJ72
Wells Ter. N4 121 DN61
Wells Way SE5 162 DS79
Wells Way SW7 160 DD76
Wells Yd. N7 121 DN64
Holloway Rd.
Wellside Clo., Barn. 79 CW42
Wellside Gdns. SW14 178 CQ85
Well La.
Wellsmoor Gdns., Brom. 205 EN97
Wellsprings Cres., Wem. 118 CP62
Wellstead Ave. N9 101 DX45
Wellstead Rd. E6 145 EN68
Wellstones, Wat. 75 BV41
Wellstones Yd., Wat. 75 BV41
Wellstones
Wellswood Clo., Hem.H. 41 BP19
Wellwood Clo., Couls. 219 DL114
The Vale
Wellwood Rd., Ilf. 126 EU60
Welsford St. SE1 162 DU78
Welsh Clo. E13 144 EG69
Welshpool Ho. E8 142 DU67
Benjamin Clo.
Welshpool St. E8 142 DV67
Broadway Mkt.
Welshside Wk. NW9 118 CS58
Fryent Gro.
Welstead Way W4 158 CS78
Bath Rd.
Welsummer Way, Wal.Cr. 67 DX27
Weltje Rd. W6 159 CU77
Welton Rd. SE18 165 ES80
Welwyn Ave., Felt. 175 BT86
Welwyn Ct., Hem.H. 40 BM16
Welwyn Rd., Hert. 30 DG08
Welwyn St. E2 142 DW69
Globe Rd.
Welwyn Way, Hayes 135 BS70
Wembley Commercial Cen., Wem. 117 CK61
Wembley Hill Rd., Wem. 118 CM64
Wembley Pk. Business Cen., Wem. 118 CP62
Wembley Pk. Dr., Wem. 118 CM62
Wembley Pt., Wem. 138 CP66
Wembley Rd., Hmptn. 176 CA94
Wembley Way, Wem. 138 CP65
Wemborough Rd., Stan. 95 CJ52
Wembury Rd. N6 121 DH59
Wemyss Rd. SE3 164 EF82
Wend, The, Couls. 219 DK114
Wend, The, Croy. 221 DZ111
Wendela Clo., Wok. 227 AZ118
Wendela Ct., Har. 117 CE62
Wendell Rd. W12 159 CT75
Wendle Ct. SW8 161 DL79
Wendley Dr., Add. 211 BF110
Wendling Rd., Sutt. 200 DD102
Wendon St. E3 143 DZ67
Wendover SE17 162 DS78
Wendover Clo., Hayes 136 BY70
Kingsash Dr.
Wendover Clo., St.Alb. 43 CJ15
Highview Gdns.
Wendover Dr., N.Mal. 199 CT100
Wendover Gdns., Brwd. 109 GB47
Wendover Pl., Stai. 173 BD92
Wendover Rd. NW10 139 CT68
Wendover Rd. SE9 164 EK83
Wendover Rd., Brom. 204 EH97
Wendover Rd., Slou. 130 AH71
Wendover Rd., Stai. 173 BC92
Wendover Way, Horn. 128 FJ64
Wendover Way, Orp. 206 EU100
Glendower Cres.
Wendover Way (Bushey), Wat. 76 CC44
Wendover Way, Well. 186 EU85
Wendron Clo., Wok. 226 AU118
Shilburn Way
Wendy Clo., Enf. 82 DT44
Wendy Cres., Guil. 242 AU132
Wendy Way, Wem. 138 CL67
Wengeo La., Ware 32 DV05
Wenham Gdns., Brwd. 109 GC44
Bannister Dr.
Wenlack Clo. (Denham), Uxb. 114 BG62
Lindsey Rd.
Wenlock Ct. N1 275 L1
Wenlock Gdns. NW4 119 CU56
Rickard Clo.
Wenlock Rd. N1 275 H1
Wenlock Rd. N1 142 DQ68
Wenlock Rd., Edg. 96 CP52
Wenlock St. N1 275 J1
Wenlock St. N1 142 DQ68
Wennington Rd. E3 143 DX68
Wennington Rd., Rain. 147 FG70
Wensley Ave., Wdf.Grn. 102 EF52
Wensley Clo. SE9 185 EM86
Wensley Clo., Rom. 104 FA50
Wensley Rd. N18 100 DV51
Wensleydale, Hem.H. 40 BM17
Wensleydale Ave., Ilf. 102 EL54
Wensleydale Gdns., Hmptn. 176 CB94
Wensleydale Pas., Hmptn. 196 CA95
Wensleydale Rd., Hmptn. 176 CA93
Wensum Way, Rick. 92 BK46
Wentbridge Path, Borwd. 78 CN38
Wentland Clo. SE6 183 ED89
Wentland Rd. SE6 183 ED89
Wentworth Ave. N3 98 DA52
Wentworth Ave., Borwd. 78 CM43
Wentworth Ave., Slou. 131 AN68
Wentworth Clo. N3 98 DB52
Wentworth Clo. SE28 146 EX72
Wentworth Clo., Ashf. 175 BP91
Reedsfield Rd.
Wentworth Clo., Brom. 204 EG103
Hillside La.
Wentworth Clo., Grav. 191 GG92
Wentworth Clo., Mord. 200 DA101
Wentworth Clo., Orp. 223 ES106
Wentworth Clo., Pot.B. 64 DA31
Strafford Gate
Wentworth Clo., Surb. 197 CK103
Wentworth Clo., Wat. 75 BT38
Wentworth Clo., Wok. 228 BH121
Wentworth Cotts., Brox. 49 DY22
Wentworth Cres. SE15 162 DU80
Wentworth Cres., Hayes 155 BR76
Wentworth Dr., Dart. 187 FG86
Wentworth Dr., Pnr. 115 BU57
Wentworth Dr., Vir.W. 192 AT98
Wentworth Gdns. N13 99 DP49
Wentworth Hill, Wem. 118 CM60
Wentworth Ms. E3 143 DZ70
Eric St.
Wentworth Pk. N3 98 DA52
Wentworth Pl., Grays 170 GD76
Wentworth Pl., Stan. 95 CH51
Greenacres Dr.
Wentworth Rd. E12 124 EK63
Wentworth Rd. NW11 119 CZ58
Wentworth Rd., Barn. 79 CX41
Wentworth Rd., Croy. 201 DN101
Wentworth Rd., Hert. 32 DQ12
Wentworth Rd., Sthl. 156 BW77
Wentworth St. E1 275 P8
Wentworth St. E1 142 DT72
Wentworth Way, Pnr. 116 BY56
Wentworth Way, Rain. 147 FH69
Wentworth Way, S.Croy. 220 DU114
Wenvoe Ave., Bexh. 167 FB82
Wernbrook St. SE18 165 EQ79
Werndee Rd. SE25 202 DU98
Werneth Hall Rd., Ilf. 125 EM55
Werrington St. NW1 273 L1
Werrington St. NW1 141 DJ68
Werter Rd. SW15 159 CY84
Wescott Way, Uxb. 134 BJ68
Wesley Ave. E16 144 EG74
Wesley Ave. NW10 138 CR69
Wesley Ave., Hert. 32 DR10
Hale Rd.
Wesley Ave., Houns. 156 BY82
Wesley Clo. N7 121 DM61
Wesley Clo. SE17 278 G9
Wesley Clo. SE17 161 DP77
Wesley Clo., Har. 116 CC61
Wesley Clo., Horl. 268 DG146
Wesley Clo., Orp. 206 EW97
Wesley Clo., Reig. 265 CZ135
Wesley Clo. (Cheshunt), Wal.Cr. 66 DQ28
Wesley Dr., Egh. 173 BA93
Wesley Hill, Chesh. 54 AP30
Wesley Rd. E10 123 EC59
Wesley Rd. NW10 138 CQ67
Wesley Rd., Hayes 135 BU73
Wesley Sq. W11 139 CY72
Bartle Rd.
Wesley St. W1 272 G7
Wesleyan Pl. NW5 121 DH63
Gordon Ho. Rd.
Wessels, Tad. 233 CX121
Wessex Ave. SW19 200 DA96
Wessex Clo., Ilf. 125 ES58
Wessex Clo., Kings.T. 198 CP95
Gloucester Rd.
Wessex Dr., Erith 167 FE81
Wessex Dr., Pnr. 94 BY52
Wessex Gdns. NW11 119 CY60
Wessex La., Grnf. 137 CD68
Wessex Rd., Houns. 154 BK82
Wessex St. E2 142 DW69
Wessex Way NW11 119 CY60
West Acres, Amer. 55 AR40
West App., Orp. 205 EQ99
West Arbour St. E1 143 DX72
West Ave. E17 123 EB56
West Ave. N3 98 DA51
West Ave. NW4 119 CX57
West Ave., Hayes 135 BT73
West Ave., H.Wyc. 88 AC46
West Ave., Pnr. 116 BZ58
West Ave., Red. 266 DG140
West Ave., St.Alb. 60 CB25
West Ave., Sthl. 136 BZ73
West Ave., Wall. 219 DL106
West Ave., Walt. 213 BS109
West Ave. Rd. E17 123 EA56
West Bank N16 122 DS59
West Bank, Bark. 145 EP67
Highbridge Rd.
West Bank, Dor. 263 CF137
West Bank, Enf. 82 DQ40
West Barnes La. SW20 199 CV96
West Barnes La., N.Mal. 199 CV97
West Burrow Fld., Welw.G.C. 29 CX11
West Carriage Dr. W2 276 A3
West Carriage Dr. W2 140 DD73
West Cen. St. WC1 273 P8
West Cen. Ave. W10 139 CV69
Harrow Rd.
West Chantry, Har. 94 CB53
Chantry Rd.
West Clo. N9 100 DT48
West Clo., Ashf. 174 BL91
West Clo., Barn. 79 CV43
West Clo. (Cockfosters), Barn. 80 DG42
West Clo., Grnf. 136 CC68
West Clo., Hmptn. 176 BY93
Oak Ave.
West Clo., Hodd. 49 EA16
West Clo., Rain. 147 FH70
West Clo., Wem. 118 CM60
West Common, Ger.Cr. 112 AX57
West Common Clo., Ger.Cr. 112 AY57
West Common Rd., Brom. 204 EG103
West Common Rd., Kes. 222 EH105
West Common Rd., Uxb. 114 BK64
West Cotts. NW6 120 DA64
West Ct. SE18 165 EM81
Prince Imperial Rd.
West Ct., Wem. 117 CJ61
West Cres., Wind. 151 AM81
West Cres. Rd., Grav. 170 FZ81
West Cromwell Rd. SW5 159 CZ77
West Cromwell Rd. W14 159 CZ77
West Cross Cen., Brent. 157 CG79
West Cross Route W10 139 CX73
West Cross Route W11 139 CX73
West Cross Way, Brent. 157 CH79
West Dene, Sutt. 217 CY107
Park La.
West Dene Dr., Rom. 106 FK50
West Down, Lthd. 246 CB127
West Drayton Pk. Ave., West Dr. 154 BL76
West Drayton Rd., Uxb. 135 BQ71
West Dr. SW16 181 DJ91
West Dr., Cars. 218 DD110
West Dr., Har. 95 CD51
West Dr. (Cheam), Sutt. 217 CX109
West Dr., Tad. 233 CX118
West Dr., Vir.W. 192 AS101
West Dr., Wat. 75 BV36
West Dr. Gdns., Har. 95 CD51
West Eaton Pl. SW1 276 F8
West Eaton Pl. SW1 160 DG77
West Eaton Pl. Ms. SW1 276 F8
West Ella Rd. NW10 138 CS66
West End Ave. E10 123 EC57
West End Ave., Pnr. 116 BX56
West End Ct., Pnr. 116 BX56
West End Ct., Slou. 132 AT67
West End Gdns., Esher 214 BZ106
West End Gdns., Nthlt. 136 BW68
Edward Clo.
West End La. NW6 140 DA67
West End La., Barn. 79 CX42
West End La., Esher 214 BZ108
West End La., Hat. 46 DC18
West End La., Hayes 155 BQ80
West End La., Pnr. 116 BX55
West End La., Slou. 132 AS68
West End Rd., Brox. 48 DS23
West End Rd., Nthlt. 136 BW66
West End Rd., Ruis. 115 BV64
West End Rd., Sthl. 136 BY74
West Fm. Ave., Ash. 231 CJ118
West Fm. Clo., Ash. 231 CJ119
West Fm. Dr., Ash. 231 CK119
West Gdn. Pl. W2 272 C9
West Gdns. E1 142 DV73
West Gdns. SW17 180 DE93
West Gdns., Epsom 216 CS110
West Gate W5 138 CL69
West Gate, Harl. 51 EQ15
West Gorse, Croy. 221 DY112
West Grn. Pl., Grnf. 137 CD67
Uneeda Dr.
West Grn. Rd. N15 122 DR56
West Gro. SE10 163 EC81
West Gro., Walt. 213 BV106
West Gro., Wdf.Grn. 102 EJ51
West Halkin St. SW1 276 F6
West Halkin St. SW1 160 DG76
West Hall Rd., Rich. 158 CP81
West Hallowes SE9 184 EK88
West Ham La. E15 144 EE66
West Ham Pk. E7 144 EG66
West Hampstead Ms. NW6 140 DB65
West Harding St. EC4 274 E8
West Harold, Swan. 207 FD97
West Hatch Manor, Ruis. 115 BT60
West Heath Ave. NW11 120 DA60
West Heath Clo. NW3 120 DA62
West Heath Clo., Dart. 187 FF86
West Heath Rd.
West Heath Dr. NW11 120 DA60
West Heath Gdns. NW3 120 DA62
West Heath La., Sev. 257 FH128
West Heath Rd. NW3 120 DA61
West Heath Rd. SE2 166 EX79
West Heath Rd., Dart. 187 FF86
West Hendon Bdy. NW9 119 CT58
West Hill SW15 179 CX87
West Hill SW18 180 DA85
West Hill, Dart. 188 FJ86
West Hill, Epsom 216 CQ113
West Hill, Har. 117 CE61
West Hill, Orp. 223 EM112
West Hill, Oxt. 253 ED130
West Hill, S.Croy. 220 DS110
West Hill, Wem. 118 CM60
West Hill Ave., Epsom 216 CQ112
West Hill Bank, Oxt. 253 ED130
West Hill Ct. N6 120 DG62
West Hill Dr., Dart. 188 FJ86
West Hill Pk. N6 120 DF61
Merton La.
West Hill Ri., Dart. 188 FK86
West Hill Rd. SW18 180 DA86
West Hill Rd., Wok. 226 AX119
West Hill Way N20 98 DB46
West Holme, Erith 167 FC81
West Ho. Clo. SW19 179 CY88
West Hyde La., Ger.Cr. 91 AZ52
West India Ave. E14 143 EA74
West India Dock Rd. E14 143 DZ72
West Kent Ave., Grav. 190 GC86
West Kentish Town Est. NW5 120 DG64
West La. SE16 162 DV75
West La., Dor. 262 BX139
West Lo. Ave. W3 138 CN74
West Mall W8 140 DA74
Palace Gdns. Ter.
West Malling Way, Horn. 128 FJ64
West Mead, Epsom 216 CS107
West Mead, Ruis. 116 BW63
West Mead, Welw.G.C. 30 DB12
West Meads, Guil. 258 AT136
West Mersea Clo. E16 144 EH74
Hanameel St.
West Ms. N17 100 DV51
West Ms. SW1 277 K9
West Mill, Grav. 191 GF86
West Mt., Guil. 258 AW136
The Mt.
West Oak, Beck. 203 ED95
West Palace Gdns., Wey. 195 BP104
West Pk. SE9 184 EL89
West Pk. Ave., Rich. 158 CN81
West Pk. Clo., Houns. 156 BZ79
Heston Gra. La.
West Pk. Clo., Rom. 126 EX57
West Pk. Hill, Brwd. 108 FU48
West Pk. Rd., Epsom 216 CM112
West Pk. Rd., Rich. 158 CN81
West Pk. Rd., Sthl. 136 CC74
West Parkside SE10 164 EE75
West Pier E1 142 DV74
Wapping High St.
West Pl. SW19 179 CW92
West Pt., Slou. 131 AK74
West Poultry Ave. EC1 274 F7
West Quarters W12 139 CU72
West Quay Dr., Hayes 136 BY71
West Ramp, Houns. 154 BN81
West Ridge Gdns., Grnf. 136 CC68
West Riding, St.Alb. 60 BZ30
West Rd. E15 144 EF67
West Rd. N17 100 DV51
West Rd. SW3 160 DF79
West Rd. SW4 181 DK85
West Rd. W5 138 CL71
West Rd., Barn. 98 DG46
West Rd., Berk. 38 AU18
West Rd., Chess. 215 CJ111
West Rd., Felt. 175 BR86
West Rd., Guil. 258 AY135
West Rd., Harl. 36 EU11
West Rd., Kings.T. 198 CQ95
West Rd., Reig. 266 DB135
West Rd. (Chadwell Heath), Rom. 126 EX58
West Rd. (Rush Grn.), Rom. 127 FD59
West Rd., S.Ock. 149 FV69
West Rd., West Dr. 154 BM76
West Rd., Wey. 213 BP109
West Row W10 139 CY70
West Shaw, Long. 209 FX96
West Sheen Vale, Rich. 158 CM84
West Side, Brox. 67 DY25
High Rd. Turnford
West Side Common SW19 179 CW92
West Smithfield EC1 274 F7
West Smithfield EC1 141 DP71
West Spur Rd., Uxb. 134 BK69
West Sq. SE11 278 F7
West Sq. SE11 161 DP76
West Sq., Iver 133 BF72
High St.
West St. E2 142 DV68
West St. E11 124 EE62
West St. E17 123 EB57
Grove Rd.
West St. WC2 273 N9
West St., Bexh. 166 EZ84
West St., Brent. 157 CJ79
West St., Brom. 204 EG95
West St., Cars. 200 DF104
West St., Croy. 220 DQ105
West St., Dor. 263 CG136
West St., Epsom 216 CR113
West St. (Ewell), Epsom 216 CS110
West St., Erith 167 FD77
West St., Grav. 191 GH86
West St., Grays 170 GA79
West St., Har. 117 CD60
West St., Hert. 32 DQ10
West St., Reig. 249 CY134
West St., Sutt. 218 DB106
West St., Ware 33 DX06
West St., Wat. 75 BV40
West St., Wok. 227 AZ117
Church St. E.
West St. La., Cars. 218 DF105
West Temple Sheen SW14 158 CP84
West Tenter St. E1 142 DT72
West Thurrock Way, Grays 169 FT77
West Twrs., Pnr. 116 BX58
West Valley Rd., Hem.H. 58 BJ25
West Vw. NW4 119 CW56
West Vw., Chesh. 54 AR29
West Vw., Felt. 175 BQ87
West Vw., Loug. 85 EM41
West Vw. Ave., Whyt. 236 DU118
Station Rd.
West Vw. Ct., Borwd. 77 CK44
High St.
West Vw. Gdns., Borwd. 77 CK44
High St.
West Vw. Rd., Dart. 188 FM86
West Vw. Rd., St.Alb. 43 CD19
West Vw. Rd., Swan. 207 FG98
West Vw. Rd. (Crockenhill), Swan. 207 FD100
West Wk. W5 138 CL71
West Wk., Barn. 98 DG45
West Wk., Harl. 35 EQ14
West Wk., Hayes 135 BU74
West Walkway, The, Sutt. 218 DB111
Cheam Rd.
West Warwick Pl. SW1 277 J9
West Warwick Pl. SW1 161 DH77
West Way N18 100 DR49
West Way NW10 118 CR62
West Way, Beac. 88 AF54
West Way, Brwd. 108 FU48
West Way, Cars. 218 DD110
West Way, Croy. 203 DY103
West Way, Edg. 96 CP51
West Way, Houns. 156 BZ81
West Way, Pnr. 116 BX56
West Way, Rick. 92 BH46
West Way, Ruis. 115 BT60
West Way, Shep. 195 BR100
West Way, W.Wick. 203 ED100
West Way Gdns., Croy. 203 DX103
West Woodside, Bex. 186 EY87
West World W5 138 CL69
West Yoke, Sev. 209 FW103
Westacott, Hayes 135 BS71
Westacott Clo. N19 121 DK60
Westacres, Esher 214 BZ108
Westall Clo., Hert. 32 DQ10
Westall Rd., Loug. 85 EP41
Westanley Ave., Amer. 55 AR39
Westbank Rd., Hmptn. 176 CC93
Westbeech Rd. N22 121 DN55
Westbere Dr., Stan. 95 CK49
Westbere Rd. NW2 119 CY64
Westbourne Ave. W3 138 CR72
Westbourne Ave., Sutt. 199 CY103
Westbourne Bri. W2 140 DC71
Westbourne Clo., Hayes 135 BV70
Westbourne Cres. W2 140 DD73
Westbourne Cres. Ms. W2 140 DD73
Westbourne Cres.
Westbourne Dr. SE23 183 DX89
Westbourne Dr., Brwd. 108 FT49
Westbourne Gdns. W2 140 DB72
Westbourne Gro. W2 140 DA72
Westbourne Gro. W11 139 CZ73
Westbourne Gro. Ms. W11 140 DA72
Westbourne Gro.
Westbourne Gro. Ter. W2 140 DB72
Westbourne Pk. Ms. W2 140 DB72
Westbourne Gdns.
Westbourne Pk. Pas. W2 140 DA71
Westbourne Pk. Vil.
Westbourne Pk. Rd. W2 140 DA71
Westbourne Pk. Rd. W11 139 CY72
Westbourne Pk. Vil. W2 140 DA71
Westbourne Pl. N9 100 DV48
Eastbournia Ave.
Westbourne Rd. N7 141 DN65

Westbourne Rd. SE26 183 DX93
Westbourne Rd., Bexh. 166 EY80
Westbourne Rd., Croy. 202 DT100
Westbourne Rd., Felt. 175 BT90
Westbourne Rd., Stai. 174 BH94
Westbourne Rd., Uxb. 135 BP70
Westbourne St. W2 140 DD73
Westbourne Ter. SE23 183 DX89
Westbourne Dr.
Westbourne Ter. W2 140 DD72
Westbourne Ter. Ms. W2 140 DC72
Westbourne Ter. Rd. W2 140 DC71
Westbridge Rd. SW11 160 DD81
Westbrook, Maid. 150 AE78
Westbrook Ave., Hmptn. 176 BZ94
Westbrook Clo., Barn. 80 DD41
Westbrook Cres., Barn. 80 DD41
Westbrook Dr., Orp. 206 EW102
Westbrook Rd. SE3 164 EH81
Westbrook Rd., Houns. 156 BZ80
Westbrook Rd., Stai. 173 BF92
South St.
Westbrook Rd., Th.Hth. 202 DR95
Westbrook Sq., Barn. 80 DD41
Westbrook Cres.
Westbrooke Cres., Well. 166 EW83
Westbrooke Rd., Sid. 185 ER89
Westbrooke Rd., Well. 166 EV83
Westbury Ave. N22 121 DP55
Westbury Ave., Esher 215 CF107
Westbury Ave., Sthl. 136 CA70
Westbury Ave., Wem. 138 CL66
Westbury Clo., Ruis. 115 BU59
Westbury Clo., Shep. 195 BP100
Burchetts Way
Westbury Clo., Whyt. 236 DS116
Beverley Rd.
Westbury Dr., Brwd. 108 FV48
Westbury Gro. N12 98 DA51
Westbury La., Buck.H. 102 EJ47
Westbury Lo. Clo., Pnr. 116 BX55
Westbury Par. SW12 181 DH86
Balham Hill
Westbury Pl., Brent. 157 CK79
Westbury Ri., Harl. 52 EX16
Westbury Rd. E7 124 EH64
Westbury Rd. E17 123 EA56
Westbury Rd. N11 99 DL51
Westbury Rd. N12 98 DA51
Westbury Rd. SE20 203 DX95
Westbury Rd. W5 138 CL72
Westbury Rd., Bark. 145 ER67
Westbury Rd., Beck. 203 DY97
Westbury Rd., Brwd. 108 FW47
Westbury Rd., Brom. 204 EK95
Westbury Rd., Buck.H. 102 EJ47
Westbury Rd., Croy. 202 DR100
Westbury Rd., Felt. 176 BX88
Westbury Rd., Ilf. 125 EN61
Westbury Rd., N.Mal. 198 CR98
Westbury Rd., Nthwd. 93 BS49
Westbury Rd. (Cheshunt), Wal.Cr. 67 DX30
Turners Hill
Westbury Rd., Wat. 75 BV43
Westbury Rd., Wem. 138 CL66
Westbury St. SW8 161 DJ82
Westbury Ter. E7 144 EH65
Westbury Ter., Upmin. 129 FS61
Westbury Ter., West. 255 EQ127
Westbush Clo., Hodd. 33 DZ14
Westcar La., Walt. 213 BV107
Westchester Dr. NW4 119 CX55
Westcombe Ave., Croy. 201 DL100
Westcombe Ct. SE3 164 EF80
Westcombe Pk. Rd.
Westcombe Dr., Barn. 80 DA43
Westcombe Hill SE3 164 EG79
Westcombe Hill SE10 164 EG78
Westcombe Lo. Dr., Hayes 135 BR71
Westcombe Pk. Rd. SE3 164 EE79
Westcoombe Ave. SW20 199 CT95
Westcote Ri., Ruis. 115 BQ59
Westcote Rd. SW16 181 DJ92
Westcott, Welw.G.C. 30 DD08
Westcott Ave., Grav. 191 GG90
Westcott Clo. N15 122 DT58
Ermine Rd.
Westcott Clo., Brom. 204 EL99
Ringmer Way
Westcott Clo., Croy. 221 EB109
Castle Hill Ave.
Westcott Cres. W7 137 CE72
Westcott Rd. SE17 161 DP79
Westcott Rd., Dor. 263 CE137
Westcott St., Dor. 262 CB137
Westcott Way, Sutt. 217 CW110
Westcourt, Sun. 195 BV96
Westcroft, Slou. 131 AP70
Westcroft Clo. NW2 119 CY63
Westcroft Clo., Enf. 82 DW38
Westcroft Ct., Brox. 49 EA19
Westcroft Gdns., Mord. 199 CZ97
Westcroft Rd., Cars. 218 DG105
Westcroft Rd., Wall. 218 DG105
Westcroft Sq. W6 159 CU77
Westcroft Way NW2 119 CY63
Westdale Pas. SE18 165 EP79
Westdale Rd. SE18 165 EP79
Westdean Ave. SE12 184 EH88
Westdean Clo. SW18 180 DB86
Westdene Way, Wey. 195 BS104
Westdown Rd. E15 123 EC63
Westdown Rd. SE6 183 EA87
Wested La., Swan. 207 FG101
Westerdale, Hem.H. 40 BL17
Westerdale Rd. SE10 164 EG78
Westerfield Rd. N15 122 DT57
Westerfolds Clo., Wok. 227 BC116
Westergate Rd. SE2 166 EY78
Westerham Ave. N9 100 DR48
Westerham Clo., Add. 212 BJ107
Westerham Clo., Sutt. 218 DA110
Westerham Dr., Sid. 186 EV86
Westerham Hill, West. 239 EN120
Westerham Rd. E10 123 EB59
Westerham Rd., Kes. 222 EK107
Westerham Rd., Oxt. 254 EF129
Westerham Rd., Sev. 256 FC123
Westerham Rd., West. 255 EM128
Westerley Cres. SE26 183 DZ92
Westerley Ware, Rich. 158 CN79
Kew Grn.
Western Ave. NW11 119 CX58
Western Ave. W3 138 CR71
Western Ave. W5 138 CM70
Western Ave., Brwd. 108 FW46
Western Ave., Cher. 194 BG97
Western Ave., Dag. 147 FC65
Western Ave., Egh. 193 BB97
Western Ave., Epp. 69 ET32
Western Ave., Grays 169 FT78
Western Ave., Grnf. 137 CK69
Western Ave., Nthlt. 136 BZ67
Western Ave., Rom. 106 FJ54
Western Ave., Ruis. 135 BP65
Western Ave. (Denham), Uxb. 114 BJ63
Western Ave. (Ickenham), Uxb. 135 BP65
Western Ave. Underpass W5 138 CM69
Western Ave.
Western Clo., Cher. 194 BG97
Western Ave.
Western Ct. N3 98 DA51
Huntley Dr.
Western Cross Clo., Green. 189 FW86
Johnsons Way
Western Dr., H.Wyc. 110 AE58
Western Dr., Shep. 195 BR100
Western Gdns. W5 138 CN73
Western Gdns., Brwd. 108 FW47
Western Gateway E16 144 EG73
Western La. SW12 180 DG87
Western Ms. W9 139 CZ70
Great Western Rd.
Western Par., Reig. 266 DA137
Prices La.
Western Pathway, Horn. 148 FJ65
Western Perimeter Rd., Houns. 154 BH83
Western Perimeter Rd., West Dr. 154 BH82
Western Pl. SE16 162 DW75
Canon Beck Rd.
Western Rd. E13 144 EJ67
Western Rd. E17 123 EC57
Western Rd. N2 120 DF56
Western Rd. N22 99 DM54
Western Rd. NW10 138 CQ70
Western Rd. SW9 161 DN83
Western Rd. SW19 200 DD95
Western Rd. W5 137 CK73
Western Rd., Brwd. 108 FW47
Western Rd., Epp. 69 ET32
Western Rd., Mitch. 200 DD95
Western Rd., Rom. 127 FE57
Western Rd., Sthl. 156 BX76
Western Rd., Sutt. 218 DA106
Western Rd., Wal.Abb. 50 EE22
Western Ter. W6 159 CU78
Chiswick Mall
Western Trd. Est. NW10 138 CQ70
Western Vw., Hayes 155 BT75
Station Rd.
Western Way SE28 165 ER76
Western Way, Barn. 80 DA44
Westernville Gdns., Ilf. 125 EQ59
Westferry Circ. E14 143 DZ74
Westferry Rd. E14 143 EA74
Westfield, Ash. 232 CM118
Westfield, Dor. 261 BT143
Westfield, Harl. 51 ES16
Westfield, Hat. 46 DA23
Westfield, Loug. 84 EJ43
Westfield, Reig. 250 DB131
Westfield, Sev. 257 FJ122
Westfield, Welw.G.C. 30 DA08
Westfield Ave., S.Croy. 220 DR113
Westfield Ave., Wat. 76 BX37
Westfield Ave., Wok. 226 AY121
Westfield Clo. NW9 118 CQ55
Westfield Clo. SW10 160 DC80
Westfield Clo., Enf. 83 DY41
Westfield Clo., Grav. 191 GJ93
Westfield Clo., Sutt. 217 CZ105
Westfield Clo., Wal.Cr. 67 DZ31
Westfield Common, Wok. 226 AY122
Westfield Ct., St.Alb. 43 CK17
Westfield Dr., Har. 117 CK56
Westfield Dr., Lthd. 230 CA122
Westfield Gdns., Har. 117 CK56
Westfield Gro., Wok. 226 AY120
Westfield La., Har. 117 CK56
Westfield La., Slou. 132 AX72
Westfield Par., Add. 212 BK110
Westfield Pk., Pnr. 94 BZ52
Westfield Pk. Dr., Wdf.Grn. 102 EL51
Westfield Rd. NW7 96 CR48
Westfield Rd. W13 137 CG74
Westfield Rd., Beac. 88 AJ54
Westfield Rd., Beck. 203 DZ96
Westfield Rd., Berk. 38 AS17
Westfield Rd., Bexh. 167 FC82
Westfield Rd., Croy. 201 DP103
Westfield Rd., Dag. 126 EY63
Westfield Rd., Guil. 242 AY130
Westfield Rd., Hert. 32 DQ07
Westfield Rd., Hodd. 49 DZ16
Westfield Rd., Mitch. 200 DF96
Westfield Rd., Slou. 131 AP70
Westfield Rd., Surb. 197 CK99
Westfield Rd., Sutt. 217 CZ105
Westfield Rd., Walt. 196 BY101
Westfield Rd., Wok. 226 AX122
Westfield St. SE18 164 EK76
Westfield Wk., Wal.Cr. 67 DZ31
Westfield Clo.
Westfield Way E1 143 DY69
Westfield Way, Ruis. 115 BS62
Westfield Way, Wok. 226 AY122
Westfields SW13 159 CT83
Westfields, St.Alb. 42 CA22
Westfields Ave. SW13 158 CS83
Westfields Rd. W3 138 CP71
Westgate Clo., Epsom 232 CR115
Chalk La.
Westgate Ct., Wal.Cr. 83 DX35
Holmesdale
Westgate Cres., Slou. 131 AM73
Westgate Rd. SE25 202 DV98
Westgate Rd., Beck. 203 EB95
Westgate Rd., Dart. 188 FK86
Westgate St. E8 142 DV67
Westgate Ter. SW10 160 DB78
Westglade Ct., Har. 117 CK57
Westgrove La. SE10 163 EC81
Westhall Pk., Warl. 236 DW119
Westhall Rd., Warl. 236 DU118
Westhay Gdns. SW14 178 CP85
Westhill Clo., Grav. 191 GH88
Leith Pk. Rd.
Westhill Rd., Hodd. 49 DZ16
Westholm NW11 120 DB56
Westholme, Orp. 205 ES101
Westholme Gdns., Ruis. 115 BU60
Westhorne Ave. SE9 184 EJ86
Westhorne Ave. SE12 184 EG87
Westhorpe Gdns. NW4 119 CW55
Westhorpe Rd. SW15 159 CW83
Westhumble St., Dor. 247 CH131
Westhurst Dr., Chis. 185 EP92
Westlake Clo. N13 99 DN48
Westlake Clo., Hayes 136 BY70
Lochan Clo.
Westlake Rd., Wem. 117 CK61
Westland Ave., Horn. 128 FL60
Westland Clo., Stai. 174 BL86
Westland Dr., Brom. 204 EF103
Westland Dr., Hat. 63 CY27
Westland Pl. N1 275 K2
Westland Rd., Wat. 75 BV40
Westlands Ave., Slou. 130 AJ72
Westlands Clo., Hayes 155 BU77
Granville Rd.
Westlands Clo., Slou. 130 AJ72
Westlands Ave.
Westlands Ct., Epsom 232 CQ115
Westlands Ter. SW12 181 DJ86
Gaskarth Rd.
Westlands Way, Oxt. 253 ED127
Westlea Ave., Wat. 76 BY37
Westlea Clo., Brox. 49 DZ24
Westlea Rd. W7 157 CG76
Westlea Rd., Brox. 49 DZ23
Westleas, Horl. 268 DE146
Westlees Clo., Dor. 263 CK139
Wildcroft Dr.
Westleigh Ave. SW15 179 CV85
Westleigh Ave., Couls. 234 DG116
Westleigh Dr., Brom. 204 EL95
Westleigh Gdns., Edg. 96 CN53
Westlinks, Wem. 137 CK69
Alperton La.
Westlinton Clo. NW7 97 CY51
Frith La.
Westly Wd., Welw.G.C. 30 DA08
Westlyn Clo., Rain. 148 FJ69
Westmacott Dr., Felt. 175 BT87
Westmead SW15 179 CV86
Westmead, Wind. 151 AP83
Westmead, Wok. 226 AV117
Westmead Cor., Cars. 218 DE105
Colston Ave.
Westmead Dr., Red. 266 DG142
Westmead Rd., Sutt. 218 DD105
Westmeade Clo. (Cheshunt), Wal.Cr. 66 DV29
Westmede, Chig. 103 EQ51
Westmere Dr. NW7 96 CR48
Westmill Ct. N4 122 DQ61
Brownswood Rd.
Westminster Ave., Th.Hth. 201 DP96
Westminster Bri. SE1 278 A5
Westminster Bri. SE1 161 DL75
Westminster Bri. SW1 278 A5
Westminster Bri. SW1 161 DL75
Westminster Bri. Rd. SE1 278 C5
Westminster Bri. Rd. SE1 161 DN76
Westminster Clo., Felt. 175 BU88
Westminster Clo., Ilf. 103 ER54
Westminster Clo., Tedd. 177 CG92
Westminster Ct., St.Alb. 42 CC22
Westminster Dr. N13 99 DL50
Westminster Gdns. E4 102 EE46
Westminster Gdns., Bark. 145 ES68
Westminster Gdns., Ilf. 103 EQ54
Westminster Rd. N9 100 DV46
Westminster Rd. W7 137 CE74
Westminster Rd., Sutt. 200 DD103
Westmoat Clo., Beck. 183 EC94
Westmont Rd., Esher 197 CE103
Westmoor Gdns., Enf. 83 DX40
Westmoor Rd., Enf. 83 DX40
Westmoor St. SE7 164 EK76
Westmore Grn., West. 238 EJ121
Westmore Rd., West. 238 EJ121
Westmoreland Ave., Horn. 128 FJ57
Westmoreland Ave., Well. 165 ES83
Westmoreland Bldgs. EC1 142 DQ71
Bartholomew Clo.
Westmoreland Dr., Sutt. 218 DB109
Westmoreland Pl. SW1 161 DH78
Westmoreland Pl. W5 137 CK71
Mount Ave.
Westmoreland Pl., Brom. 204 EG97
Westmoreland Rd. NW9 118 CN56
Westmoreland Rd. SE17 162 DR79
Westmoreland Rd. SW13 159 CT81
Westmoreland Rd., Brom. 204 EE99
Westmoreland St. W1 272 G7
Westmoreland St. W1 140 DG71
Westmoreland Ter. SW1 161 DH78
Westmoreland Wk. SE17 162 DR79
Westmoreland Rd.
Westmorland Clo. E12 124 EK61
Westmorland Clo., Epsom 216 CS110
Westmorland Clo., Twick. 177 CH86
Westmorland Rd. E17 123 EA58
Westmorland Rd., Har. 116 CB57
Westmorland Sq., Mitch. 201 DL99
Westmorland Way
Westmorland Ter. SE20 182 DV94
Westmorland Way, Mitch. 201 DL99
Westmount Ave., Amer. 55 AQ39
Westmount Rd. SE9 165 EM82
Westoe Rd. N9 100 DV47
Weston Ave., Add. 212 BG105
Weston Ave., Grays 169 FT77
Weston Ave., T.Ditt. 197 CE101
Weston Ave., W.Mol. 196 BY97
Weston Clo., Brwd. 109 GC45
Weston Clo., Couls. 235 DM120
Weston Clo., Pot.B. 63 CZ32
Weston Ct. N4 122 DQ62
Queens Dr.
Weston Dr., Stan. 95 CH53
Weston Gdns., Islw. 157 CE81
Weston Gdns., Wok. 227 BE116
Weston Grn., Dag. 126 EZ63
Weston Grn., T.Ditt. 197 CE102
Weston Grn. Rd., Esher 197 CD102
Weston Grn. Rd., T.Ditt. 197 CE102
Weston Gro., Brom. 204 EF95
Weston Lea, Lthd. 245 BR125
Weston Pk. N8 121 DL58
Weston Pk., Kings.T. 198 CL96
Fairfield W.
Weston Pk., T.Ditt. 197 CE102
Weston Pk. Clo., T.Ditt. 197 CE102
Weston Pk.
Weston Ri. WC1 274 C1
Weston Ri. WC1 141 DM68
Weston Rd. W4 158 CQ76
Weston Rd., Brom. 184 EF94
Weston Rd., Dag. 126 EY63
Weston Rd., Enf. 82 DR39
Weston Rd., Epsom 216 CS111
Weston Rd., Guil. 242 AU133
Weston Rd., Slou. 131 AM71
Weston Rd., T.Ditt. 197 CE102
Weston St. SE1 279 L6
Weston St. SE1 162 DR76
Weston Wk. E8 142 DV66
Mare St.
Weston Way, Wok. 227 BE116
Weston Yd., Guil. 260 BJ139
Westonfields, Guil. 260 BJ139
Westover Clo., Sutt. 218 DB109
Westover Hill NW3 120 DA61
Westover Rd. SW18 180 DC86
Westow Hill SE19 182 DS93
Westow St. SE19 182 DS93
Westpoint Trd. Est. W3 138 CP70
Westpole Ave., Barn. 80 DG42
Westport Rd. E13 144 EH70
Westport St. E1 143 DX72
Westray, Hem.H. 41 BQ22
Westridge Clo., Hem.H. 39 BF20
Westrow SW15 179 CW85
Westrow Dr., Bark. 145 ET65
Westrow Gdns., Ilf. 125 ET61
Westside NW4 97 CV54
Westvale Ms. W3 138 CS74
Westview, Hat. 45 CU16
Westview Clo. NW10 119 CT64
Westview Clo. W7 137 CE72
Westview Clo. W10 139 CW72
Westview Clo., Rain. 148 FJ69
Westview Clo., Red. 266 DE136
Westview Cres. N9 100 DS45
Westview Dr., Wdf.Grn. 102 EK54
Westview Ri., Hem.H. 40 BK19
Westview Rd., Warl. 236 DV119
Westville Rd. W12 159 CU75
Westville Rd., T.Ditt. 197 CG102
Westward Ho, Guil. 243 AZ132
Westward Rd. E4 101 DZ50
Westward Way, Har. 118 CL58
Westway SW20 199 CV97
Westway W2 140 DA71
Westway W9 140 DA71
Westway W10 139 CY72
Westway W12 139 CU73
Westway, Cat. 236 DR122
Westway, Gat. 269 DH152
Westway, Guil. 242 AT132
Westway, Orp. 205 ER99
Westway Clo. SW20 199 CV97
Westway Gdns., Red. 251 DH131
Westways, Epsom 217 CT105
Westways, West. 255 EQ126
Westwell Clo., Orp. 206 EX102
Westwell Rd. SW16 181 DL93
Westwell Rd. App. SW16 181 DL93
Westwell Rd.
Westwick Clo., Hem.H. 41 BR21
Westwick Gdns. W14 159 CX75
Westwick Gdns., Houns. 155 BV82
Westwick Pl., Wat. 60 BW34
Westwick Row, Hem.H. 41 BR20
Westwood Ave. SE19 202 DQ95
Westwood Ave., Add. 211 BF112
Westwood Ave., Brwd. 108 FU49
Westwood Ave., Har. 116 CB63
Westwood Clo., Amer. 72 AX39
Westwood Clo., Brom. 204 EK97
Westwood Clo., Esher 196 CC104
Westwood Clo., Pot.B. 64 DA30
Westwood Clo., Ruis. 115 BP58
Westwood Ct., Guil. 242 AT133
Hillcrest Rd.
Westwood Dr., Amer. 72 AX39
Westwood Gdns. SW13 159 CT83
Westwood Hill SE26 182 DU92
Westwood La., Sid. 186 EU85
Westwood La., Well. 165 ET83
Westwood Pk. SE23 182 DV87
Westwood Rd. E16 144 EH74
Westwood Rd. SW13 159 CT83
Westwood Rd., Couls. 235 DK118
Westwood Rd., Grav. 189 FX94
Westwood Rd., Ilf. 125 ET60
Westwood Way, Sev. 256 FF122
Wetheral Dr., Stan. 95 CH53
Wetherby Clo., Nthlt. 136 CB65
Wetherby Gdns. SW5 160 DC77
Wetherby Ms. SW5 160 DB78
Bolton Gdns.
Wetherby Pl. SW7 160 DC77
Wetherby Rd., Borwd. 78 CL39
Wetherby Rd., Enf. 82 DQ39
Wetherby Way, Chess. 216 CL108
Wetherden St. E17 123 DZ59
Wethered Dr., Slou. 130 AH71
Wetherell Rd. E9 143 DX67
Wetherill Rd. N10 98 DG53
Wetherly Clo., Harl. 36 EZ11
Moor Hall Rd.
Wettern Clo., S.Croy. 220 DS110
Purley Oaks Rd.
Wetton Pl., Egh. 173 BA92
High St.
Wexfenne Gdns., Wok. 228 BH116
Wexford Rd. SW12 180 DF87
Wexham Pk. La., Slou. 132 AW70
Wexham Rd., Slou. 152 AU75
Wexham St., Slou. 132 AV70
Wexham Wds., Slou. 132 AW71
Wey Ave., Cher. 194 BG97
Wey Barton, W.Byf. 212 BM113
Wey Clo., W.Byf. 212 BH113
Broadoaks Cres.
Wey Ct., Add. 212 BK109
Wey Ct., Epsom 216 CQ105
Wey La., Chesh. 54 AP32
Wey Manor Rd., Add. 212 BK109
Wey Meadows, Wey. 212 BL106
Wey Rd., Wey. 194 BM104
Wey Vw. Ct., Guil. 258 AW135
Walnut Tree Clo.
Weybank, Wok. 228 BL116
Weybourne Pl., S.Croy. 220 DR110
Weybourne St. SW18 180 DC89
Weybridge Business Pk., Add. 212 BL105
Weybridge Ct. SE16 162 DU78
Argyle Way
Weybridge Pk., Wey. 212 BN106
Weybridge Pt. SW11 160 DG82
Weybridge Rd., Add. 194 BK104
Weybridge Rd., Th.Hth. 201 DN98
Weybridge Rd., Wey. 194 BK104
Weybrook Dr., Guil. 243 BB129
Weydown Clo. SW19 179 CY88
Weydown Clo., Guil. 242 AU129
Weydown La., Guil. 242 AU129
Cumberland Ave.
Weyhill Rd. E1 142 DU72
Commercial Rd.
Weylands Clo., Walt. 196 BZ102
Weylands Pk., Wey. 213 BS107
Ellesmere Rd.
Weylea Ave., Guil. 243 BA131
Weylond Rd., Dag. 126 EZ62
Weyman Rd. SE3 164 EJ81
Weymead Clo., Cher. 194 BJ102
Weymede, W.Byf. 212 BM112
Weymouth Ave. NW7 96 CS50
Weymouth Ave. W5 157 CJ76
Weymouth Clo. E6 145 EP72
Covelees Wall
Weymouth Ct., Sutt. 218 DA108
Weymouth Ms. W1 273 H6
Weymouth Ms. W1 141 DH71
Weymouth Rd., Hayes 135 BS69
Weymouth St. W1 272 G7
Weymouth St. W1 141 DH71
Weymouth St., Hem.H. 40 BK24
Weymouth Ter. E2 142 DT68
Weymouth Wk., Stan. 95 CG51
Weyside Clo., W.Byf. 212 BM112
Weyside Gdns., Guil. 242 AW132
Weyside Rd., Guil. 242 AV133
Weystone Rd., Add. 212 BM105
Weybridge Rd.
Whadcote St. N4 121 DN61
Seven Sisters Rd.
Whalebone Ave., Rom. 126 EZ58
Whalebone Ct. EC2 275 L8
Whalebone Gro., Rom. 126 EZ58
Whalebone La. E15 144 EE66
West Ham La.
Whalebone La. N., Rom. 126 EY57
Whalebone La. S., Dag. 126 EZ59
Whalebone La. S., Rom. 126 EZ59
Whaley Rd., Pot.B. 64 DC33
Wharf La., Rick. 92 BL46
Wharf La., Twick. 177 CG88
Wharf La. (Ripley), Wok. 228 BK119
Mill La.
Wharf La. (Send), Wok. 227 BC123
Wharf Pl. E2 142 DU67
Wharf Rd. E15 143 ED67
Wharf Rd. N1 275 H1
Wharf Rd. N1 142 DQ68
Wharf Rd., Brwd. 108 FW48
Wharf Rd., Brox. 49 DZ23
Wharf Rd., Enf. 83 DY44
Wharf Rd., Grav. 191 GL86
Wharf Rd., Grays 170 FZ79
Wharf Rd., Guil. 242 AW134
Wharf Rd., Hem.H. 40 BH22
Wharf Rd., Stai. 172 AW87
Wharf Rd. S., Grays 170 FZ79
Wharf St. E16 144 EE71
Wharfdale Ct. E5 123 DX63
Rushmore Rd.
Wharfdale Rd. N1 141 DL68
Wharfedale, Hem.H. 40 BL17
Wharfedale Gdns., Th.Hth. 201 DM98
Wharfedale Rd., Dart. 188 FQ88
Wharfedale St. SW10 160 DB78
Wharfside Rd. E16 144 EE71
Wharley Hook, Harl. 51 ET18
Wharncliffe Dr., Sthl. 137 CD74
Wharncliffe Gdns. SE25 202 DS96
Wharncliffe Rd. SE25 202 DS96
Wharton Clo. NW10 138 CS65
Wharton Rd., Brom. 204 EH95
Wharton St. WC1 274 C3
Wharton St. WC1 141 DM69
Whateley Rd. SE20 183 DX94
Whateley Rd. SE22 182 DT85
Whateley Rd., Guil. 242 AV130
Whatley Ave. SW20 199 CY97
Whatman Rd. SE23 183 DX87
Whatmore Clo., Stai. 174 BG86
Wheat Clo., St.Alb. 43 CG16
Wheat Knoll, Ken. 236 DQ116
Wheat Leys, St.Alb. 43 CJ18
Wheat Sheaf Clo. E14 163 EB77
Wheatash Rd., Add. 194 BH103
Wheatbarn, Welw.G.C. 30 DB08
Wheatbutts, The (Eton Wick), Wind. 151 AM77
Wheatcroft (Cheshunt), Wal.Cr. 66 DV28
Wheatfield, Hat. 45 CV17
Crop Common
Wheatfield, Hem.H. 40 BK18
Wheatfield Way, Horl. 269 DH147
Wheatfield Way, Kings.T. 198 CL96
Wheatfields E6 145 EP72
Oxleas
Wheatfields, Enf. 83 DY40
Wheatfields, Harl. 36 EX09
Wheathill Rd. SE20 202 DV97
Wheatlands, Houns. 156 CA79
Wheatlands Rd. SW17 180 DG90
Stapleton Rd.
Wheatlands Rd., Slou. 152 AW76
Wheatley Clo. NW4 97 CU54
Wheatley Clo., Green. 189 FU85
Steele Ave.
Wheatley Clo., Horn. 128 FK57
Wheatley Clo., Saw. 36 EW06
Wheatley Clo., Welw.G.C. 30 DA11
Wheatley Cres., Hayes 135 BU73
Wheatley Gdns. N9 100 DS47
Wheatley Rd., Islw. 157 CF83
Wheatley Rd., Welw.G.C. 30 DA10
Wheatley St. W1 272 G7
Wheatley Ter. Rd., Erith 167 FF79
Wheatley Way, Ger.Cr. 90 AY51
Wheatsheaf Clo., Cher. 211 BD107

Wheatsheaf Clo., Nthlt. 116 BY64
Wheatsheaf Clo., Wok. 226 AY116
Wheatsheaf Hill (Halstead), Sev. 224 EZ109
Wheatsheaf La. SW6 159 CW80
Wheatsheaf La. SW8 161 DL80
Wheatsheaf La., Stai. 173 BF94
Wheatsheaf Rd., Rom. 127 FF58
Wheatsheaf Rd., Ware 34 EK05
Wheatsheaf Ter. SW6 159 CZ80
Wheatstone Clo., Mitch. 200 DE95
Wheatstone Rd. W10 139 CY71
Wheel Fm. Dr., Dag. 127 FC62
Wheeler Ave., H.Wyc. 88 AC47
Wheeler Ave., Oxt. 253 ED129
Wheeler Clo., Wdf.Grn. 103 EM50
Chigwell Rd.
Wheeler Gdns. N1 141 DL67
Outram Pl.
Wheelers, Epp. 69 ET29
Wheelers Clo., Wal.Abb. 50 EE22
Wheelers Cross, Bark. 145 ER68
Wheelers Dr., Ruis. 115 BQ58
Wallington Clo.
Wheelers Fm. Gdns., Epp. 71 FB26
Wheelers La., Bet. 264 CP136
Wheelers La., Epsom 216 CP113
Wheelers La., Hem.H. 40 BL22
Wheelers La., Horl. 269 DN149
Wheelers Orchard, Ger.Cr. 90 AY51
Wheelock Clo., Erith 167 FB80
Wheelwright Clo. (Bushey), Wat. 76 CB44
Ashfield Ave.
Wheelwright St. N7 141 DM66
Whelan Way, Wall. 201 DK104
Wheler St. E1 275 P5
Wheler St. E1 142 DT70
Whellock Rd. W4 158 CS76
Whenman Ave., Bex. 187 FC89
Whernside Clo. SE28 146 EW73
Wherwell Rd., Guil. 258 AW136
Whetstone Clo. N20 98 DD47
Oakleigh Rd. N.
Whetstone Pk. WC2 274 B8
Whetstone Rd. SE3 164 EJ82
Whewell Rd. N19 121 DL61
Whichcote Gdns., Chesh. 54 AR33
Pheasant Ri.
Whichcote St. SE1 278 D3
Whichert Clo., Beac. 88 AJ49
Whidborne Clo. SE8 163 EA82
Cliff Ter.
Whidborne St. WC1 274 A3
Whidborne St. WC1 141 DL69
Whielden Gate, Amer. 55 AL43
Whielden Grn., Amer. 55 AP40
Whielden La., Amer. 55 AL43
Whielden St., Amer. 55 AN41
Whiffins Orchard, Epp. 70 EX29
Whimbrel Clo. SE28 146 EW73
Whimbrel Clo., S.Croy. 220 DR111
Whimbrel Way, Hayes 136 BX72
Whinchat Rd. SE28 165 ER76
Whinfell Clo. SW16 181 DK92
Whinfell Way, Grav. 191 GM91
Whinneys Rd., H.Wyc. 88 AC52
Whinyates Rd. SE9 164 EL83
Whipley Clo., Guil. 243 BB129
Weybrook Dr.
Whippendell Clo., Orp. 206 EV95
Whippendell Hill, Kings L. 58 BJ30
Whippendell Rd., Wat. 75 BU43
Whippendell Way, Orp. 206 EV95
Whipps Cross Rd. E11 123 ED57
Whiskin St. EC1 274 F3
Whiskin St. EC1 141 DP69
Whisperwood, Rick. 74 BH41
Whisperwood Clo., Har. 95 CE52
Whistler Gdns., Edg. 96 CM54
Whistler Ms. SE15 162 DT80
Commercial Way
Whistler Ms., Dag. 126 EV64
Fitzstephen Rd.
Whistler St. N5 121 DP63
Whistler Wk. SW10 160 DD80
World's End Est.
Whistlers Ave. SW11 160 DD80
Whiston Rd. E2 142 DT68
Whit Hern Ct., Wal.Cr. 66 DW30
College Rd.
Whitakers Way, Loug. 85 EM39
Whitbread Clo. N17 100 DU53
Whitbread Rd. SE4 163 DY84
Whitburn Rd. SE13 163 EB84
Whitby Ave. NW10 138 CP69
Whitby Clo., Green. 189 FU85
Whitby Clo., West. 238 EH119
Whitby Gdns. NW9 118 CN55
Whitby Gdns., Sutt. 200 DD103
Whitby Rd. SE18 165 EM77
Whitby Rd., Har. 116 CC62
Whitby Rd., Ruis. 115 BV62
Whitby Rd., Slou. 131 AQ73
Whitby Rd., Sutt. 200 DD103
Whitby St. E1 275 P4
Whitcher Clo. SE14 163 DY79
Whitcher Pl. NW1 141 DJ66
Rochester Rd.
Whitchurch Ave., Edg. 96 CM52
Whitchurch Clo., Edg. 96 CM51
Whitchurch Gdns., Edg. 96 CM51
Whitchurch La., Edg. 95 CK52
Whitchurch Rd. W11 139 CX73
Whitchurch Rd., Rom. 106 FK49
Whitcomb Ct. WC2 141 DK73
Whitcomb St.
Whitcomb St. WC2 277 N1
Whitcomb St. WC2 141 DK73
White Acre NW9 96 CS54
White Ave., Grav. 191 GF90
White Beam Way, Tad. 233 CU121
White Beams, St.Alb. 60 CC28
White Bear Pl. NW3 120 DD63
New End Sq.
White Bri. Ave., Mitch. 200 DD98
Belgrave Wk.
White Butts Rd., Ruis. 116 BX62
White Ch. La. E1 142 DU72
White Ch. Pas. E1 142 DU72
White Ch. La.
White City Clo. W12 139 CW73
White City Est. W12 139 CV73
White City Rd. W12 139 CV73
White Clo., Slou. 131 AR74
White Conduit St. N1 141 DN68
Chapel Mkt.
White Craig Clo., Pnr. 94 CA50
White Down Rd., Dor. 261 BV139
White Friars, Sev. 256 FG127
White Gdns., Dag. 146 FA65
White Gates, Horn. 128 FJ61
White Hall, Rom. 86 EV41
Market Pl.
White Hart Clo., Ch.St.G. 90 AU48
White Hart Clo., Sev. 257 FJ128
White Hart Ct. EC2 142 DS72
Bishopsgate
White Hart Ct., Wok. 228 BJ121
White Hart Dr., Hem.H. 40 BM21
White Hart La. N17 100 DR52
White Hart La. N22 99 DN53
White Hart La. NW10 139 CT65
Church Rd.
White Hart La. SW13 158 CS83
White Hart La., Rom. 104 FA53
White Hart Meadow, Beac. 89 AL54
White Hart Meadows, Wok. 228 BJ121
White Hart Rd. SE18 165 ES77
White Hart Rd., Hem.H. 40 BN21
White Hart Rd., Slou. 151 AR76
White Hart Row, Cher. 194 BG101
Heriot Rd.
White Hart Slip, Brom. 204 EG96
Market Sq.
White Hart St. SE11 278 E10
White Hart St. SE11 161 DN78
White Hart Wd., Sev. 257 FJ129
White Hart Yd. SE1 279 K3
White Hedge Dr., St.Alb. 42 CC19
White Heron Ms., Tedd. 177 CF93
White Hill, Chesh. 54 AQ31
White Hill, Couls. 234 DC124
White Hill, Hem.H. 39 BF21
White Hill, Nthwd. 92 BN51
White Hill, Rick. 92 BN51
White Hill, S.Croy. 220 DR109
St. Mary's Rd.
White Hill, Welw. 29 CU05
White Hill Clo., Chesh. 54 AQ30
White Hill Ct., Berk. 38 AX18
Whitehill
White Hill Rd., Berk. 38 AV21
White Hill Rd., Chesh. 56 AX26
White Hill Rd., Hem.H. 56 AY27
White Horse Dr., Epsom 216 CQ114
White Horse Hill, Chis. 185 EN91
White Horse La. E1 143 DX70
White Horse La., St.Alb. 62 CL25
White Horse La., Wok. 228 BJ121
White Horse Ms. SE1 278 E6
White Horse Rd. E1 143 DY72
White Horse Rd. E6 145 EM69
White Horse Rd., Wind. 151 AK83
White Horse St. W1 277 H3
White Horse St. W1 141 DH74
White Horse Yd. EC2 275 K8
White Ho. Clo., Ger.Cr. 90 AY52
White Ho. Dr., Guil. 243 BB134
White Ho. Dr., Stan. 95 CJ49
White Ho. La., Guil. 242 AX129
White Ho. Rd., Sev. 256 FF130
White Kennett St. E1 275 N8
White Knights Rd., Wey. 213 BQ108
White Knobs Way, Cat. 252 DU125
White La., Guil. 259 BC136
White La., Oxt. 238 EH124
White La., Warl. 238 EH123
White Lion Clo., Amer. 72 AU39
White Lion Ct. EC3 275 M9
White Lion Hill EC4 274 G10
White Lion Hill EC4 141 DP73
White Lion Hos., Hat. 45 CU17
Robin Hood La.
White Lion Rd., Amer. 72 AT38
White Lion Sq., Hat. 45 CU17
Robin Hood La.
White Lion St. N1 274 D1
White Lion St. N1 141 DN68
White Lion St., Hem.H. 40 BK24
White Lion Wk., Guil. 258 AX136
High St.
White Lo. SE19 181 DP94
White Lo. Clo. N2 120 DE58
White Lo. Clo., Sev. 257 FH123
White Lo. Clo., Sutt. 218 DC108
White Lo. Gdns., Red. 266 DG142
White Lyon Ct. EC2 142 DQ70
Fann St.
White Lyons Rd., Brwd. 108 FW47
White Oak Business Pk., Swan. 207 FE97
London Rd.
White Oak Dr., Beck. 203 EC96
White Oak Gdns., Sid. 185 ET87
White Orchards N20 97 CZ45
White Orchards, Stan. 95 CG50
White Post Fld., Saw. 36 EX05
White Post Hill (Farningham), Dart. 208 FN101
White Post La. E9 143 DZ66
White Post La. SE13 163 EA83
White Post St. SE15 162 DW80
White Rd. E15 144 EE66
White Rd., Bet. 248 CN133
White Rd., Tad. 248 CN133
White Rose La., Wok. 227 AZ118
White Shack La., Rick. 74 BM37
White St., Sthl. 156 BX75
White Stubbs La., Brox. 48 DS22
White Stubbs La., Hert. 47 DK21
White Swan Ms. W4 158 CS79
Bennett St.
White Way, Lthd. 246 CB126
Whiteadder Way E14 163 EB77
Whitear Wk. E15 143 ED65
Whitebarn La., Dag. 146 FA67
Whitebeam Ave., Brom. 205 EN100
Whitebeam Clo. SW9 161 DM80
Clapham Rd.
Whitebeam Clo. (Shenley), Rad. 62 CM33
Mulberry Gdns.
Whitebeam Clo., Wal.Cr. 66 DS26
The Laurels
Whitebeam Dr., Reig. 266 DB137
Whitebeam Dr., S.Ock. 149 FW69
Whitebeam Twr. E17 123 DY55
Hillyfield
Whitebeams, Hat. 45 CU21
Whiteberry Rd., Dor. 262 CB143
Whitebridge Clo., Felt. 175 BT86
Whitebroom Rd., Hem.H. 39 BE18
Whitechapel High St. E1 142 DT72
Whitechapel Rd. E1 142 DU71
Whitecote Rd., Sthl. 136 CB72
Whitecroft, Horl. 269 DH147
Woodhayes
Whitecroft, St.Alb. 43 CH23
Whitecroft, Swan. 207 FE96
Whitecroft Clo., Beck. 203 ED98
Whitecroft Way, Beck. 203 EC99
Whitecross Pl. EC2 275 L6
Whitecross St. EC1 275 J4
Whitecross St. EC1 142 DQ70
Whitefield Ave. NW2 119 CW59
Whitefield Ave., Pur. 235 DN116
Whitefield Clo. SW15 179 CY86
Whitefield Clo., Orp. 206 EW97
Whitefields Rd. (Cheshunt), Wal.Cr. 66 DW28
Whitefoot La., Brom. 183 EC91
Whitefoot Ter., Brom. 184 EE90
Whiteford Rd., Slou. 132 AS71
Whitefriars Ave., Har. 95 CE54
Whitefriars Dr., Har. 95 CD54
Whitefriars St. EC4 274 E9
Whitefriars St. EC4 141 DN72
Whitegate Gdns., Har. 95 CF52
Whitegate Way, Tad. 233 CV120
Whitegates, Whyt. 236 DU119
Court Bushes Rd.
Whitegates, Wok. 227 AZ120
Loop Rd.
Whitegates Clo., Rick. 74 BN42
Whitehall SW1 277 P2
Whitehall SW1 141 DL74
Whitehall Clo., Chig. 104 EU47
Whitehall Clo., Uxb. 134 BJ67
Whitehall Clo., Wal.Abb. 50 EE22
Whitehall Ct. SW1 277 P3
Whitehall Ct. SW1 141 DL74
Whitehall Cres., Chess. 215 CK106
Whitehall Est., Har. 50 EL16
Whitehall Fm. La., Vir.W. 192 AY97
Whitehall Gdns. E4 101 ED46
Whitehall Gdns. SW1 277 P3
Whitehall Gdns. W3 138 CN74
Whitehall Gdns. W4 158 CP79
Whitehall La., Buck.H. 102 EG47
Whitehall La., Egh. 173 AZ94
Whitehall La., Erith 167 FF82
Whitehall La., Grays 170 GC78
Whitehall La., Reig. 265 CZ138
Whitehall La., Stai. 173 BA86
Whitehall Pk. N19 121 DJ60
Whitehall Pk. Rd. W4 158 CP79
Whitehall Pl. E7 124 EG64
Station Rd.
Whitehall Pl. SW1 277 P3
Whitehall Pl. SW1 141 DL74
Whitehall Pl., Wall. 219 DH105
Bernard Rd.
Whitehall Rd. E4 102 EE47
Whitehall Rd. W7 157 CG75
Whitehall Rd., Brom. 204 EK99
Whitehall Rd., Grays 170 GC77
Whitehall Rd., Har. 117 CE59
Whitehall Rd., Th.Hth. 201 DN99
Whitehall Rd., Uxb. 134 BK67
Whitehall Rd., Wdf.Grn. 102 EE47
Whitehall St. N17 100 DT52
Whitehands Clo., Hodd. 49 DZ17
Whitehart Rd., Orp. 206 EU101
Whitehaven, Slou. 132 AT73
Whitehaven Clo., Brom. 204 EG98
Whitehaven St. NW8 272 B5
Whitehead Clo. N18 100 DR50
Whitehead Clo. SW18 180 DC87
Whitehead Clo., Dart. 188 FJ90
Whitehead's Gro. SW3 276 C10
Whitehead's Gro. SW3 160 DE78
Whiteheart Ave., Uxb. 135 BQ71
Whiteheath Ave., Ruis. 115 BQ59
Whitehill, Berk. 38 AW18
Whitehill Clo., Berk. 38 AX18
Whitehill
Whitehill La., Grav. 191 GJ89
Whitehill La., Red. 252 DR127
Whitehill La., Wok. 229 BQ123
Whitehill Par., Grav. 191 GJ90
Whitehill Pl., Vir.W. 192 AY99
Whitehill Rd., Dart. 187 FG85
Whitehill Rd., Grav. 191 GJ89
Whitehill Rd. (Hook Grn.), Grav. 209 FX96
Whitehill Rd., Long. 209 FX96
Whitehills Rd., Loug. 85 EN41
Whitehorse La. SE25 202 DR98
Whitehorse Rd., Croy. 202 DQ101
Whitehorse Rd., Th.Hth. 202 DR100
Whitehouse Ave., Borwd. 78 CP41
Whitehouse Clo., H.Wyc. 88 AE54
Whitehouse La., Abb.L. 59 BV26
Whitehouse La., Enf. 82 DQ39
Brigadier Hill
Whitehouse La., H.Wyc. 88 AE54
Whitehouse Way N14 99 DH47
Whitehouse Way, Iver 133 BD69
Whitelands Ave., Rick. 73 BB41
Whitelands Way, Rom. 106 FK53
Whiteleaf Rd., Hem.H. 40 BJ23
Whiteledges W13 137 CJ72
Whitelegg Rd. E13 144 EF68
Whiteley, Wind. 151 AL80
Whiteley Rd. SE19 182 DR92
Whiteleys Cotts. W14 159 CZ77
Whiteleys Way, Felt. 176 CA90
Whitemore Rd., Guil. 242 AX130
Whiteoaks, Bans. 218 DB113
Whiteoaks La., Grnf. 137 CD68
Whitepit La., H.Wyc. 110 AC56
Whitepost Hill, Red. 250 DE134
Whites Ave., Ilf. 125 ES58
Whites Clo., Green. 189 FW86
Whites Grds. SE1 279 N5
Whites Grds. SE1 162 DS75
Whites Grds. Est. SE1 279 N4
Whites La., Slou. 152 AV79
White's Row E1 275 P7
White's Row E1 142 DT71
White's Sq. SW4 161 DK84
Nelson's Row
Whitestile Rd., Brent. 157 CJ78
Whitestone La. NW3 120 DC62
Heath St.
Whitestone Wk. NW3 120 DC62
North End Way
Whitestone Wk., Hem.H. 40 BG17
Fennycroft Rd.
Whitethorn, Welw.G.C. 30 DB10
Whitethorn Ave., Couls. 234 DG115
Whitethorn Ave., West Dr. 134 BL73
Whitethorn Gdns., Croy. 202 DV103
Whitethorn Gdns., Enf. 82 DR43
Whitethorn Gdns., Horn. 128 FJ58
Whitethorn Pl., West Dr. 134 BM74
Whitethorn Ave.
Whitethorn St. E3 143 EA70
Whitewaits, Harl. 35 ES14
Whiteways Ct., Stai. 174 BH94
Pavilion Gdns.
Whitewebbs La., Enf. 82 DS35
Whitewebbs Pk., Enf. 82 DQ35
Whitewebbs Rd., Enf. 81 DP35
Whitewebbs Way, Orp. 205 ET95
Whitewood Cotts., West. 238 EJ120
Whitewood Rd., Berk. 38 AU19
Whitfield Clo., Guil. 242 AU131
Whitfield Pl. W1 273 K5
Whitfield Rd. E6 144 EJ66
Whitfield Rd. SE3 163 ED81
Whitfield Rd., Bexh. 166 EZ80
Whitfield St. W1 273 M7
Whitfield St. W1 141 DK71
Whitfield Way, Rick. 91 BF46
Whitford Gdns., Mitch. 200 DF97
Whitgift Ave., S.Croy. 220 DQ106
Whitgift Cen., Croy. 202 DQ103
Whitgift St. SE11 278 B8
Whitgift St. SE11 161 DM77
Whitgift St., Croy. 202 DQ104
Whiting Ave., Bark. 145 EP66
Whitings, Ilf. 125 ER57
Whitings Rd., Barn. 79 CW43
Whitings Way E6 145 EN71
Whitland Rd., Cars. 200 DD102
Whitlars Dr., Kings L. 58 BM28
Whitley Clo., Abb.L. 59 BU32
Whitley Clo., Stai. 174 BL86
Whitley Rd. N17 100 DS54
Whitley Rd., Hodd. 49 EB15
Whitlock Dr. SW19 179 CY87
Whitman Rd. E3 143 DY70
Whitmead Clo., S.Croy. 220 DS107
Whitmoor Common, Guil. 242 AV127
Whitmoor La., Guil. 242 AX126
Whitmore Ave., Rom. 106 FL54
Whitmore Clo. N11 99 DH50
Whitmore Est. N1 142 DS67
Whitmore Gdns. NW10 139 CW68
Whitmore Rd. N1 142 DS67
Whitmore Rd., Beck. 203 DZ97
Whitmore Rd., Har. 116 CC59
Whitmore Way, Horl. 268 DE147
Whitmores Clo., Epsom 232 CQ115
Whitnell Way SW15 179 CX85
Whitney Ave., Ilf. 124 EK56
Whitney Rd. E10 123 EB59
Whitney Wk., Sid. 186 EY93
Whitstable Clo., Beck. 203 DZ95
Whitstable Clo., Ruis. 115 BS61
Chichester Ave.
Whitstable Ho. W10 139 CX72
Whitstable Pl., Croy. 220 DQ105
Whitta Rd. E12 124 EK63
Whittaker Ave., Rich. 177 CK85
Hill St.
Whittaker Rd. E6 144 EJ66
Whittaker Rd., Slou. 131 AK70
Whittaker Rd., Sutt. 199 CZ104
Whittaker St. SW1 276 F9
Whittaker St. SW1 160 DG77
Whittaker Way SE1 162 DU77
Lynton Rd.
Whittell Gdns. SE26 182 DW90
Whittenham Clo., Slou. 132 AU74
Whittingstall Rd. SW6 159 CZ81
Whittingstall Rd., Hodd. 49 EB15
Whittington Ave. EC3 275 M9
Whittington Ave., Hayes 135 BT71
Whittington Ct. N2 120 DF57
Whittington Ms. N12 98 DC49
Fredericks Pl.
Whittington Rd. N22 99 DL52
Whittington Rd., Brwd. 109 GC44
Whittington Way, Pnr. 116 BY57
Whittle Clo. E17 123 DY58
Whittle Clo., Sthl. 136 CB72
Whittle Parkway, Slou. 131 AK72
Whittle Rd., Houns. 156 BW80
Whittle Rd., Sthl. 156 CB75
Post Rd.
Whittlebury Clo., Cars. 218 DF108
Whittlesea Clo., Har. 94 CC52
Whittlesea Path, Har. 94 CC53
Whittlesea Rd., Har. 94 CC53
Whittlesey St. SE1 278 D3
Whitton Ave. E., Grnf. 117 CE64
Whitton Ave. W., Grnf. 116 CC64
Whitton Ave. W., Nthlt. 116 CC64
Whitton Clo., Grnf. 137 CH65
Whitton Dene, Houns. 176 CB85
Whitton Dene, Islw. 177 CD85
Whitton Dr., Grnf. 137 CG65
Whitton Manor Rd., Islw. 176 CC85
Whitton Rd., Houns. 156 CB84
Whitton Rd., Twick. 177 CE86
Whitton Wk. E3 143 EA68
Whitton Waye, Houns. 176 CA86
Whitwell Rd. E13 144 EG69
Whitwell Rd., Wat. 76 BX35
Whitworth Pl. SE18 165 EP77
Whitworth Rd. SE18 165 EN80
Whitworth Rd. SE25 202 DS97
Whitworth St. SE10 164 EE78
Whopshott Ave., Wok. 226 AW116
Whopshott Clo., Wok. 226 AW116
Whopshott Dr., Wok. 226 AW116
Whorlton Rd. SE15 162 DV83
Whybridge Clo., Rain. 147 FE67
Whymark Ave. N22 121 DN55
Whytebeam Vw., Whyt. 236 DT118
Whytecliffe Rd. N., Pur. 219 DP111
Whytecliffe Rd. S., Pur. 219 DN111
Whytecroft, Houns. 156 BX80
Whyteleafe Hill, Whyt. 236 DS120
Whyteleafe Rd., Cat. 236 DS122
Whyteville Rd. E7 144 EH65
Wichling Clo., Orp. 206 EX102
Wick, The, Hert. 31 DP06
Wick La. E3 143 EA68
Wick La., Egh. 172 AT92
Wick Rd. E9 143 DX65
Wick Rd., Egh. 192 AU95
Wick Rd., Tedd. 177 CH94
Wick Sq. E9 143 DZ65
Eastway
Wick Way, St.Alb. 43 CH17
Marshalswick La.
Wickenden Rd., Sev. 257 FJ122
Wicker St. E1 142 DV72
Burslem St.
Wickers Oake SE19 182 DT91
Wickersley Rd. SW11 160 DG82
Wicket, The, Croy. 221 EA106
Wicket Rd., Grnf. 137 CG69
Wickets, The, Ashf. 174 BL91
Wickets End (Shenley), Rad. 62 CL33
Wickets Way, Ilf. 103 ET51
Wickford Clo., Rom. 106 FM50
Wickford Dr.
Wickford Dr., Rom. 106 FM50
Wickford St. E1 142 DW70
Wickford Way E17 123 DX56
Wickham Ave., Croy. 203 DY103
Wickham Ave., Sutt. 217 CW106
Wickham Chase, W.Wick. 203 ED101
Wickham Clo., Enf. 82 DV41
Wickham Clo., Horl. 268 DF147
Wickham Clo., N.Mal. 199 CT99
Wickham Clo. (Harefield), Uxb. 92 BK53
Wickham Ct., St.Alb. 43 CH18
Wickham Ct. Rd., W.Wick. 203 EC103
Wickham Cres., W.Wick. 203 EC103
Wickham Fld., Sev. 241 FF116
Wickham Gdns. SE4 163 DZ83
Wickham Ho. E1 143 DX71
Wickham La. SE2 166 EU78
Wickham La., Egh. 173 BA94
Wickham La., Well. 166 EU78
Wickham Ms. SE4 163 DZ82
Wickham Rd. E4 101 EC52
Wickham Rd. SE4 163 DZ83
Wickham Rd., Beck. 203 EB96
Wickham Rd., Croy. 203 DX103
Wickham Rd., Grays 171 GJ75
Wickham Rd., Har. 95 CD54
Wickham St. SE11 278 B10
Wickham St. SE11 161 DM78
Wickham St., Well. 165 ES82
Wickham Way, Beck. 203 EC98
Wicklands Rd. (Hunsdon), Ware 34 EK07
Wickliffe Ave. N3 97 CY54
Wickliffe Gdns., Wem. 118 CP61
Wicklow St. WC1 274 B2
Wicklow St. WC1 141 DM69
Wicks Clo. SE9 184 EK91
Wicksteed Clo., Bex. 187 FD90
Wicksteed Ho., Brent. 158 CM78
Green Dragon La.
Wickwood St. SE5 161 DP82
Wid Clo., Brwd. 109 GD43
Widbury Gdns., Ware 33 DZ06
Widbury Hill, Ware 33 DZ06
Widdecombe Ave., Har. 116 BY61
Widdenham Rd. N7 121 DM63
Widdin St. E15 143 ED66
Wide Way, Mitch. 201 DK97
Widecombe Clo., Rom. 106 FK53
Widecombe Gdns., Ilf. 124 EL56
Widecombe Rd. SE9 184 EL90
Widecombe Way N2 120 DD57
Widecroft Rd., Iver 133 BE72
Widegate St. E1 275 N7
Widenham Clo., Pnr. 116 BW57
Bridle Rd.
Widford Rd. (Hunsdon), Ware 34 EK05
Widford Rd., Welw.G.C. 30 DB09
Widgeon Clo. E16 144 EH72
Maplin Rd.
Widgeon Rd., Erith 167 FH80
Widgeon Way, Wat. 76 BY36
Widley Rd. W9 140 DA69
Widmoor, H.Wyc. 110 AE60
Widmore Dr., Hem.H. 40 BN18
Widmore Lo. Rd., Brom. 204 EK96
Widmore Rd., Brom. 204 EG96
Widmore Rd., Uxb. 135 BP70
Widworthy Hayes, Brwd. 109 GB46
Wieland Rd., Nthwd. 93 BU52
Wigan Ho. E5 122 DV60
Warwick Gro.
Wigeon Path SE28 165 ER76
Wigeon Way, Hayes 136 BX72
Wiggenhall Rd., Wat. 75 BV43
Wiggie La., Red. 250 DG132
Wiggins Mead NW9 97 CT52
Wigginton Ave., Wem. 138 CP65
Wigham Ho., Bark. 145 EQ66
Wightman Rd. N4 121 DN57
Wightman Rd. N8 121 DN56
Wigley Bush La., Brwd. 108 FS47
Wigley Rd., Felt. 176 BX89
Wigmore Pl. W1 273 H8
Wigmore Pl. W1 141 DH72
Wigmore Rd., Cars. 200 DD103
Wigmore St. W1 272 F9
Wigmore St. W1 140 DG72
Wigmore Wk., Cars. 200 DD103
Wigmores N., Welw.G.C. 29 CX08
Wigmores S., Welw.G.C. 29 CX09
Wigram Rd. E11 124 EJ58
Wigram Sq. E17 123 EC55
Wigston Clo. N18 100 DS50
Wigston Rd. E13 144 EH70
Wigton Gdns., Stan. 96 CL53
Wigton Pl. SE11 161 DN78
Milverton St.
Wigton Rd. E17 101 DZ53
Wigton Rd., Rom. 106 FL49
Wigton Way, Rom. 106 FL49
Wilberforce Rd. N4 121 DP62
Wilberforce Rd. NW9 119 CU58
Wilberforce Way SW19 179 CX93
Wilberforce Way, Grav. 191 GK92
Wilbraham Pl. SW1 276 E8
Wilbraham Pl. SW1 160 DF77
Wilbury Ave., Sutt. 217 CZ110
Wilbury Rd., Wok. 226 AX117
Wilbury Way N18 100 DR50
Wilby Ms. W11 139 CZ74
Wilcot Ave., Wat. 94 BY45
Wilcot Clo., Wat. 94 BY45
Wilcot Ave.
Wilcox Clo. SW8 161 DL80
Wilcox Clo., Borwd. 78 CQ39
Wilcox Gdns., Shep. 194 BM97
Wilcox Pl. SW1 277 L7
Wilcox Rd. SW8 161 DL80
Wilcox Rd., Sutt. 218 DB105
Wilcox Rd., Tedd. 177 CD91

Wild Ct. WC2 274 B8
Wild Ct. WC2 141 DM72
Wild Goose Dr. SE14 162 DW81
Wild Grn. N., Slou. 153 BA77
Verney Rd.
Wild Grn. S., Slou. 153 BA77
Swabey Rd.
Wild Hatch NW11 120 DA58
Wild Oaks Clo., Nthwd. 93 BT51
Wild St. WC2 274 A9
Wild St. WC2 141 DL72
Wildacres, W.Byf. 212 BJ111
Wildbank Ct., Wok. 227 AZ118
White Rose La.
Wildcroft Dr., Dor. 263 CK139
Wildcroft Gdns., Edg. 95 CK51
Wildcroft Rd. SW15 179 CW87
Wilde Clo. E8 142 DU67
Wilde Clo., Til. 171 GJ82
Coleridge Rd.
Wilde Pl. N13 99 DP51
Medesenge Way
Wilde Pl. SW18 180 DD87
Heathfield Rd.
Wilde Rd., Erith 167 FB80
Wilder Clo., Ruis. 115 BV60
Wilderness, The, Berk. 38 AW19
Wilderness, The, Hmptn. 176 CB91
Park Rd.
Wilderness Rd., Chis. 185 EP94
Wilderness Rd., Guil. 258 AT135
Wilderness Rd., Oxt. 254 EE130
Wildernesse Ave., Sev. 257 FL122
Wildernesse Mt., Sev. 257 FK122
Wilders Clo., Wok. 226 AW118
Wilderton Rd. N16 122 DS59
Wildfell Rd. SE6 183 EB87
Wildhill Rd., Hat. 45 CY23
Wild's Rents SE1 279 M6
Wild's Rents SE1 162 DS76
Wildwood, Nthwd. 93 BR51
Wildwood Ave., St.Alb. 60 BZ30
Wildwood Clo. SE12 184 EF87
Wildwood Clo., Lthd. 245 BT125
Wildwood Clo., Wok. 227 BF115
Wildwood Ct., Ken. 236 DR115
Wildwood Gro. NW3 120 DC60
North End Way
Wildwood Ri. NW11 120 DC60
Wildwood Rd. NW11 120 DC59
Wildwood Ter. NW3 120 DC60
Wilford Clo., Enf. 82 DR41
Wilford Clo., Nthwd. 93 BR52
Wilford Rd., Slou. 152 AY77
Wilfred Ave., Rain. 147 FG71
Wilfred Owen Clo. SW19 180 DC93
Tennyson Rd.
Wilfred St. SW1 277 K6
Wilfred St. SW1 161 DJ76
Wilfred St., Grav. 191 GH86
Wilfred St., Wok. 226 AX118
Wilfrid Gdns. W3 138 CQ71
Wilhelmina Ave., Couls. 235 DJ119
Wilkes Rd., Brent. 158 CL79
Wilkes Rd., Brwd. 109 GD43
Wilkes St. E1 142 DT71
Wilkie Way SE22 182 DU88
Lordship La.
Wilkin St. NW5 141 DH65
Wilkin St. Ms. NW5 141 DH65
Wilkin St.
Wilkins Clo., Hayes 155 BT78
Wilkins Clo., Mitch. 200 DE95
Wilkins Grn. La., Hat. 44 CR19
Wilkins Grn. La., St.Alb. 44 CP20
Wilkins Gro., Welw.G.C. 29 CX10
Wilkins Way, West. 240 EV124
Wilkinson Clo., Dart. 168 FM84
Wilkinson Clo., Uxb. 135 BP67
Wilkinson Clo. 66 DQ26
(Cheshunt), Wal.Cr.
Wilkinson Rd. E16 144 EJ72
Wilkinson St. SW8 161 DM80
Wilkinson Way W4 158 CR75
Wilks Ave., Dart. 188 FM89
Wilks Gdns., Croy. 203 DY102
Wilks Pl. N1 275 N1
Will Crooks Gdns. SE9 164 EJ84
Willan Rd. N17 100 DR54
Willan Wall E16 144 EF73
Victoria Dock Rd.
Willard St. SW8 161 DH83
Willcocks Clo., Chess. 198 CL104
Willcott Rd. W3 138 CP74
Willen Fld. Rd. NW10 138 CQ68
Willenhall Ave., Barn. 80 DC44
Willenhall Dr., Hayes 135 BS73
Willenhall Rd. SE18 165 EP78
Willersley Ave., Orp. 205 ER104
Willersley Ave., Sid. 185 ET88
Willersley Clo., Sid. 185 ET88
Willes Rd. NW5 141 DH65
Willesden La. NW2 139 CX65
Willesden La. NW6 139 CX65
Willett Clo., Nthlt. 136 BW69
Broomcroft Ave.
Willett Clo., Orp. 205 ES100
Willett Pl., Th.Hth. 201 DN99
Willett Rd.
Willett Rd., Th.Hth. 201 DN99
Willett Way, Orp. 205 ER99
Willetts La., Uxb. 113 BF63
Willey Broom La., Cat. 251 DN125
Willey Fm. La., Cat. 252 DQ126
Willey La., Cat. 252 DR125
William Barefoot Dr. SE9 185 EN91
William Bonney Est. SW4 161 DK84
William Booth Rd. SE20 202 DU95
William Carey Way, Har. 117 CE59
William Clo. N2 120 DD55
King St.
William Clo., Rom. 105 FC53
William Clo., Sthl. 156 CC75
Windmill Ave.
William Cory Prom., Erith 167 FE78
William Ct., Hem.H. 40 BK24
King Edward St.
William Covell Clo., Enf. 81 DM38
William Dunbar Ho. NW6 139 CZ68
William Dyce Ms. SW16 181 DK91
Babington Rd.
William Ellis Clo., Wind. 172 AU85
William Ellis Way SE16 162 DU76
St. James's Rd.
William Evelyn Ct., Dor. 262 BZ139
William IV St. WC2 277 P1
William IV St. WC2 141 DL73
William Gdns. SW15 179 CV85
William Guy Gdns. E3 143 EB69
Talwin St.
William Margrie Clo. SE15 162 DU82
Moncrieff St.
William Ms. SW1 276 E5
William Morley Clo. E6 144 EK67
William Morris Clo. E17 123 DZ55
William Morris Way SW6 160 DC83
William Moulder Ct., Chesh. 54 AP28
William Nash Ct., Orp. 206 EW97
Brantwood Way
William Pl. E3 143 DZ68
Roman Rd.
William Rd. NW1 273 J3
William Rd. NW1 141 DH69
William Rd. SW19 179 CY94
William Rd., Cat. 236 DR122
William Rd., Guil. 242 AW134
William Rd., Sutt. 218 DC106
William Russell Ct., Wok. 226 AS118
Raglan Rd.
William Saville Ho. NW6 139 CZ68
William Sq. SE16 143 DY73
Rotherhithe St.
William St. E10 123 EB58
William St. N17 100 DT52
William St. SW1 276 E5
William St. SW1 160 DF75
William St., Bark. 145 EQ66
William St., Berk. 38 AX19
William St., Cars. 200 DE104
William St., Grav. 191 GH87
William St., Grays 170 GB79
William St., Slou. 132 AT74
William St. (Bushey), Wat. 76 BX41
William St., Wind. 151 AR81
William Swayne Pl., Guil. 258 AY135
Station App.
Williams Ave. E17 101 DZ53
Williams Bldgs. E2 142 DW70
Williams Clo. N8 121 DK58
Coolhurst Rd.
Williams Clo., Add. 212 BH106
Monks Cres.
Williams Evans Rd., Epsom 216 CN111
Williams Gro. N22 99 DN53
William's La. SW14 158 CQ82
Williams La., Mord. 200 DC99
Williams Rd. W13 137 CG73
Williams Rd., Sthl. 156 BY77
Williams Ter., Croy. 219 DN107
Williams Wk., Guil. 242 AV130
Grange Rd.
Williams Way, Rad. 77 CJ35
Williamson Clo. SE10 164 EF77
Lenthorp Rd.
Williamson Rd. N4 121 DP58
Williamson St. N7 121 DL63
Williamson Way NW7 97 CY51
Williamson Way, Rick. 92 BG46
Willifield Way NW11 119 CZ57
Willingale Clo., Brwd. 109 GE44
Fairview Ave.
Willingale Clo., Loug. 85 EQ40
Willingale Rd.
Willingale Clo., Wdf.Grn. 102 EK51
Willingale Rd., Loug. 85 EQ41
Willingdon Rd. N22 99 DP54
Willinghall Clo., Wal.Abb. 67 ED32
Willingham Clo. NW5 121 DJ64
Leighton Rd.
Willingham Ter. NW5 121 DJ64
Leighton Rd.
Willingham Way, Kings.T. 198 CN97
Willington Ct. E5 123 DY62
Mandeville St.
Willington Rd. SW9 161 DL83
Willis Ave., Sutt. 218 DE107
Willis Clo., Epsom 216 CP114
Willis Rd. E15 144 EF67
Willis Rd., Croy. 202 DQ101
Willis Rd., Erith 167 FC77
Willis St. E14 143 EB72
Willmore End SW19 200 DB95
Willoughby Ave., Croy. 219 DM105
Willoughby Clo., Brox. 49 DY21
Willoughby Ct., St.Alb. 61 CK26
Willoughby Dr., Rain. 147 FE66
Willoughby Gro. N17 100 DV52
Willoughby Ho. EC2 142 DR71
Moor La.
Willoughby La. N17 100 DV52
Willoughby Ms. SW4 161 DH84
Wixs La.
Willoughby Pk. Rd. N17 100 DV52
Willoughby Pas. E14 143 EA74
Willoughby Rd. N8 121 DN55
Willoughby Rd. NW3 120 DD63
Willoughby Rd., Kings.T. 198 CM95
Willoughby Rd., Slou. 153 BA76
Willoughby Rd., Twick. 177 CK86
Willoughby St. WC1 273 P7
Willoughby Way SE7 164 EH77
Willoughbys, The SW14 158 CS84
Upper Richmond Rd. W.
Willow Ave. SW13 159 CT82
Willow Ave., Sid. 186 EU86
Willow Ave., Swan. 207 FF97
Willow Ave. (Denham), Uxb. 114 BJ64
Willow Ave., West Dr. 134 BM73
Willow Bank SW6 159 CY83
Willow Bank, Rich. 177 CH90
Willow Bank, Wok. 226 AY122
Willow Brean, Horl. 268 DE146
Willow Bri. Rd. N1 142 DQ65
Willow Business Cen., Mitch. 200 DF99
Willow Clo., Add. 211 BF111
Willow Clo., Bex. 186 EZ86
Willow Clo., Brent. 157 CJ79
Willow Clo., Brwd. 109 GB44
Willow Clo., Brom. 205 EM99
Willow Clo., Buck.H. 102 EK48
Willow Clo., Erith 167 FG81
Willow Rd.
Willow Clo., H.Wyc. 110 AC57
Willow Clo., Horn. 127 FH62
Willow Clo., Orp. 206 EV101
Willow Clo., Slou. 153 BC80
Willow Clo., Th.Hth. 201 DP100
Willow Clo. (Cheshunt), Wal.Cr. 66 DS26
Willow Cotts., Mitch. 201 DJ97
Willow Cotts., Rich. 158 CN79
Kew Grn.
Willow Ct. EC2 275 M4
Willow Ct., Edg. 96 CL49
Willow Ct., Horl. 269 DH145
Willow Cres., St.Alb. 43 CJ20
Willow Cres. E. (Denham), Uxb. 114 BJ64
Willow Cres. W. (Denham), Uxb. 114 BJ64
Willow Dene, Pnr. 94 BX54
Willow Dene (Bushey), Wat. 95 CE45
Willow Dr., Barn. 79 CY42
Willow Dr., Wok. 228 BG124
Willow Edge, Kings L. 58 BN29
Willow End N20 98 DA47
Willow End, Nthwd. 93 BU51
Willow End, Surb. 198 CL102
Willow Fm. La. SW15 159 CV83
Queens Ride
Willow Gdns., Houns. 156 CA81
Willow Gdns., Ruis. 115 BT61
Willow Grn. NW9 96 CS53
Clayton Fld.
Willow Grn., Borwd. 78 CR43
Willow Grn., Dor. 263 CH140
Holmesdale Rd.
Willow Gro. E13 144 EG68
Libra Rd.
Willow Gro., Chis. 185 EN93
Willow Gro., Ruis. 115 BT61
Willow La., Amer. 72 AT41
Willow La., Guil. 243 BA133
Boxgrove Rd.
Willow La., Mitch. 200 DF99
Willow La., Wat. 75 BU43
Willow Mead, Chig. 104 EU48
Willow Mead, Dor. 263 CG135
Portland Rd.
Willow Mead, Saw. 36 EY06
Willow Mt., Croy. 202 DS104
Langton Way
Willow Pk., Sev. 241 FF117
Willow Pk., Slou. 132 AU66
Willow Path, Wal.Abb. 68 EE34
Willow Pl. SW1 277 L8
Willow Pl. SW1 161 DJ77
Willow Pl., Wind. 151 AQ79
Willow Rd. NW3 120 DD63
Willow Rd. W5 158 CL75
Willow Rd., Dart. 188 FJ88
Willow Rd., Enf. 82 DS41
Willow Rd., Erith 167 FG81
Willow Rd., Gdmg. 258 AT143
Willow Rd., N.Mal. 198 CQ98
Willow Rd., Red. 266 DC137
Willow Rd., Rom. 126 EY58
Willow Rd., Slou. 153 BE82
Willow Rd., Wall. 219 DH108
Willow St. E4 101 ED45
Willow St. EC2 275 M4
Willow St. EC2 142 DS70
Willow St., Rom. 127 FC56
Willow Tree Clo. E3 143 DZ67
Birdsfield La.
Willow Tree Clo. SW18 180 DB88
Cargill Rd.
Willow Tree Clo., Hayes 136 BW70
Willow Tree Clo., Uxb. 115 BQ62
Willow Tree La., Hayes 136 BW70
Willow Tree Wk., Brom. 204 EH95
Willow Vale W12 139 CU74
Willow Vale, Chis. 185 EP93
Willow Vale, Lthd. 230 CB123
Willow Vw. SW19 200 DD95
Willow Wk. E17 123 DZ57
Willow Wk. N2 98 DD54
Willow Wk. N15 121 DP56
Willow Wk. N21 81 DM44
Willow Wk. SE1 279 N8
Willow Wk. SE1 162 DS77
Willow Wk., Cher. 194 BG101
Willow Wk., Dart. 188 FK85
Francis Rd.
Willow Wk., Egh. 172 AW92
Willow Wk., Guil. 260 BN139
Willow Wk., Orp. 205 EP104
Willow Wk., Red. 267 DH136
Ash Dr.
Willow Wk., Sutt. 199 CZ104
Willow Wk., Tad. 248 CQ130
Oak Dr.
Willow Wk., Upmin. 129 FS60
Willow Way N3 98 DB52
Willow Way SE26 182 DV90
Willow Way W11 139 CX74
Freston Rd.
Willow Way, Epsom 216 CR107
Willow Way, Gdse. 252 DU132
Willow Way, Guil. 242 AV130
Willow Way, Hat. 45 CT21
Willow Way, Hem.H. 40 BH18
Willow Way, Pot.B. 64 DB33
Willow Way, Rad. 77 CE36
Willow Way, Rom. 106 FP51
Willow Way, St.Alb. 60 CA27
Willow Way, Sun. 195 BU98
Willow Way, Tad. 248 CP130
Oak Dr.
Willow Way, Twick. 176 CB89
Willow Way, Wem. 117 CG62
Willow Way, W.Byf. 212 BJ111
Willow Way, Wok. 226 AX121
Willow Wd. Cres. SE25 202 DS100
Willowbank Gdns., Tad. 233 CV122
Willowbrook (Eton), Wind. 151 AR77
Willowbrook Rd. SE15 162 DT79
Willowbrook Rd., Sthl. 156 CA76
Willowbrook Rd., Stai. 174 BL89
Willowcourt Ave., Har. 117 CH57
Willowdene N6 120 DF59
Denewood Rd.
Willowdene, Brwd. 108 FT43
Willowdene, Wal.Cr. 67 DY27
Willowdene Clo., Twick. 176 CC87
Willowdene Ct., Brwd. 108 FW49
Willowfield, Harl. 51 ER17
Willowhayne Dr., Walt. 195 BV101
Willowhayne Gdns., Wor.Pk. 199 CW104
Willowherb Wk., Rom. 106 FJ52
Clematis Clo.
Willowmead, Hert. 31 DP10
Willowmead, Stai. 194 BH95
Northfield Rd.
Willowmead Clo. W5 137 CK71
Willowmead Clo., Wok. 226 AU116
Willowmere, Esher 214 CC105
Willows, The, Amer. 55 AP35
Willows, The, Buck.H. 102 EK48
Willows, The, Esher 215 CE107
Albany Cres.
Willows, The, Grays 170 GE79
Willows, The, Rick. 92 BG47
Uxbridge Rd.
Willows, The, St.Alb. 43 CH24
Willows, The, Wat. 93 BV45
Brookside Rd.
Willows, The, W.Byf. 212 BL113
Willows, The, Wey. 194 BN104
Willows Ave., Mord. 200 DB99
Willows Clo., Pnr. 94 BW54
Willows Path, Epsom 216 CP114
Willows Path, Wind. 150 AJ81
Willowside, St.Alb. 62 CL27
Willowtree Way, Th.Hth. 201 DN95
Kensington Ave.
Willrose Cres. SE2 166 EW78
Wills Cres., Houns. 176 CB86
Wills Gro. NW7 97 CU50
Willson Rd., Egh. 172 AV92
Wilman Gro. E8 142 DU66
Wilmar Clo., Hayes 135 BR70
Wilmar Clo., Uxb. 134 BK66
Wilmar Gdns., W.Wick. 203 EB102
Wilmcote Ho. W2 140 DB71
Wilmer Clo., Kings.T. 178 CM92
Wilmer Cres., Kings.T. 178 CM92
Wilmer Gdns. N1 142 DS67
Wilmer Lea Clo. E15 143 ED66
Wilmer Pl. N16 122 DT61
Stoke Newington Ch. St.
Wilmer Way N14 99 DK50
Wilmerhatch La., Epsom 232 CP118
Wilmington Ave. W4 158 CR80
Wilmington Ave., Orp. 206 EW103
Wilmington Ct. Rd., Dart. 187 FG90
Wilmington Gdns., Bark. 145 ER65
Wilmington Sq. WC1 274 D3
Wilmington Sq. WC1 141 DN69
Wilmington St. WC1 274 D3
Wilmington St. WC1 141 DN69
Wilmot Clo. N2 98 DC54
Wilmot Clo. SE15 162 DU80
Wilmot Grn., Brwd. 107 FW51
Wilmot Pl. NW1 141 DJ66
Wilmot Pl. W7 137 CE74
Boston Rd.
Wilmot Rd. E10 123 EB61
Wilmot Rd. N17 122 DR55
Wilmot Rd., Cars. 218 DF106
Wilmot Rd., Dart. 187 FG85
Wilmot Rd., Pur. 219 DN112
Wilmot Rd., Slou. 130 AH69
Wilmot St. E2 142 DV70
Wilmot Way, Bans. 218 DA114
Wilmots Clo., Reig. 250 DC133
Wilmount St. SE18 165 EP77
Wilna Rd. SW18 180 DC87
Wilsham St. W11 139 CX74
Wilshaw St. SE14 163 EA81
Wilshere Ave., St.Alb. 42 CC23
Wilsman Rd., S.Ock. 149 FW68
Wilsmere Dr., Har. 95 CF52
Wilsmere Dr., Nthlt. 136 BY65
Wilson Ave., Mitch. 180 DE94
Wilson Clo., S.Croy. 220 DR106
Bartlett St.
Wilson Clo., Wem. 118 CM59
Wilson Clo., West Dr. 154 BK79
Hatch La.
Wilson Dr., Cher. 211 BB106
Wilson Dr., Wem. 118 CM59
Wilson Gdns., Har. 116 CC59
Wilson Gro. SE16 162 DV75
Wilson La., Dart. 209 FT96
Wilson Rd. E6 144 EK69
Wilson Rd. SE5 162 DS81
Wilson Rd., Chess. 216 CM107
Wilson Rd., Ilf. 125 EM59
Wilson St. E17 123 EC57
Wilson St. EC2 275 L6
Wilson St. EC2 142 DR71
Wilson St. N21 99 DN45
Wilson Way, Wok. 226 AX116
Wilsons, Tad. 233 CX121
Heathcote
Wilsons Pl. E14 143 DZ72
Salmon La.
Wilsons Rd. W6 159 CX78
Wilstone Clo., Hayes 136 BY70
Kingsash Dr.
Wilstone Dr., St.Alb. 43 CJ15
Wilthorne Gdns., Dag. 147 FB66
Acre Rd.
Wilton Ave. W4 158 CS78
Wilton Clo., West Dr. 154 BK79
Hatch La.
Wilton Cres. SW1 276 F5
Wilton Cres. SW1 160 DG75
Wilton Cres. SW19 199 CZ95
Wilton Cres., Beac. 89 AL52
Wilton Cres., Hert. 32 DQ12
Wilton Cres., Wind. 151 AK84
Wilton Dr., Rom. 105 FC52
Wilton Gdns., Walt. 196 BX102
Wilton Gdns., W.Mol. 196 CA97
Wilton Gro. SW19 199 CZ95
Wilton Gro., N.Mal. 199 CT100
Wilton La., Beac. 89 AR52
Wilton Ms. SW1 276 G6
Wilton Ms. SW1 160 DG76
Wilton Par., Felt. 175 BU89
Highfield Rd.
Wilton Pk. Ct. SE18 165 EN81
Prince Imperial Rd.
Wilton Pl. SW1 276 F5
Wilton Pl. SW1 160 DG75
Wilton Pl., Add. 212 BK108
Wilton Rd. N10 98 DG54
Wilton Rd. SE2 166 EW76
Wilton Rd. SW1 277 J7
Wilton Rd. SW1 161 DJ76
Wilton Rd. SW19 180 DE94
Wilton Rd., Barn. 80 DF42
Wilton Rd., Beac. 89 AL51
Wilton Rd., Houns. 156 BX83
Wilton Rd., Ilf. 125 EP62
Ilford La.
Wilton Rd., Red. 266 DF135
Wilton Row SW1 276 F5
Wilton Row SW1 160 DG75
Wilton Sq. N1 142 DR67
Wilton St. SW1 277 H6
Wilton St. SW1 161 DH76
Wilton Ter. SW1 276 F6
Wilton Ter. SW1 160 DG76
Wilton Vil. N1 142 DR67
Wilton Way E8 142 DU65
Wilton Way, Hert. 32 DQ11
Wiltshire Ave., Horn. 128 FM56
Wiltshire Ave., Slou. 131 AQ70
Wiltshire Clo. NW7 97 CT50
Wiltshire Clo. SW3 276 D8
Wiltshire Clo., Dart. 189 FR87
Wiltshire Gdns. N4 122 DQ58
Wiltshire Gdns., Twick. 176 CC88
Wiltshire La., Pnr. 115 BT55
Wiltshire Rd. SW9 161 DN83
Wiltshire Rd., Orp. 206 EU101
Wiltshire Rd., Th.Hth. 201 DN97
Wiltshire Row N1 142 DR67
Wilverley Cres., N.Mal. 198 CS100
Wimbart Rd. SW2 181 DM87
Wimbledon Bri. SW19 179 CZ93
Wimbledon Common SW19 179 CU91
Wimbledon Hill Rd. SW19 179 CY93
Wimbledon Pk. SW19 179 CZ89
Wimbledon Pk. Est. SW19 179 CY88
Wimbledon Pk. Rd. SW18 179 CZ87
Wimbledon Pk. Rd. SW19 179 CZ88
Wimbledon Pk. Side SW19 179 CX89
Wimbledon Rd. SW17 180 DC91
Wimbledon Sta. SW19 179 CZ93
The Bdy.
Wimbolt St. E2 142 DU69
Wimborne Ave., Hayes 135 BV72
Wimborne Ave., Sthl. 156 CA77
Wimborne Clo. SE12 184 EF85
Wimborne Clo., Buck.H. 102 EH47
Wimborne Clo., Epsom 216 CS113
Wimborne Clo., Saw. 36 EX05
Wimborne Clo., Wor.Pk. 199 CW102
Wimborne Dr. NW9 118 CN55
Wimborne Dr., Pnr. 116 BX59
Wimborne Gdns. W13 137 CH72
Wimborne Gro., Wat. 75 BS37
Wimborne Rd. N9 100 DU47
Wimborne Rd. N17 100 DS54
Wimborne Way, Beck. 203 DX97
Wimbourne Ave., Orp. 205 ET98
Wimbourne Ave., Red. 266 DF139
Wimbourne Ct. N1 142 DR68
Wimbourne St.
Wimbourne St. N1 142 DR68
Wimpole Clo., Brom. 204 EJ98
Stanley Rd.
Wimpole Clo., Kings.T. 198 CM96
Wimpole Ms. W1 273 H6
Wimpole Ms. W1 141 DH71
Wimpole Rd., West Dr. 134 BK74
Wimpole St. W1 273 H8
Wimpole St. W1 141 DH72
Wimshurst Clo., Croy. 201 DL102
Winans Wk. SW9 161 DN82
Wincanton Cres., Nthlt. 116 CA64
Wincanton Gdns., Ilf. 103 EP54
Wincanton Rd. SW18 179 CZ87
Wincanton Rd., Rom. 106 FK48
Winchcomb Gdns. SE9 164 EK83
Winchdells, Hem.H. 40 BN23
Winchelsea Ave., Bexh. 166 EZ80
Winchelsea Clo. SW15 179 CX85
Winchelsea Rd. E7 124 EG63
Winchelsea Rd. N17 122 DS55
Winchelsea Rd. NW10 138 CR67
Winchelsey Ri., S.Croy. 220 DT107
Winchendon Rd. SW6 159 CZ80
Winchendon Rd., Tedd. 177 CD91
Winchester Ave. NW6 139 CY67
Winchester Ave. NW9 118 CN55
Winchester Ave., Houns. 156 BZ79
Winchester Ave., Upmin. 129 FT60
Winchester Clo. E6 144 EL72
Boultwood Rd.
Winchester Clo. SE17 278 G9
Winchester Clo. SE17 161 DP77
Winchester Clo., Amer. 55 AS39
Lincoln Pk.
Winchester Clo., Brom. 204 EF97
Winchester Clo., Enf. 82 DS43
Winchester Clo., Esher 214 CA105
Winchester Clo., Kings.T. 178 CP94
Winchester Clo., Slou. 153 BE81
Winchester Cres., Grav. 191 GK90
Winchester Cres., H.Wyc. 88 AC53
Winchester Dr., Pnr. 116 BX57
Winchester Gro., Sev. 257 FH123
Winchester Ho. SE18 164 EK80
Shooter's Hill Rd.
Winchester Ms. NW3 140 DD66
Winchester Rd.
Winchester Pk., Brom. 204 EF97
Winchester Pl. E8 122 DT64
Kingsland High St.
Winchester Pl. N6 121 DH60
Winchester Pl. W3 158 CQ75
Avenue Rd.
Winchester Rd. E4 101 EC52
Winchester Rd. N6 121 DH59
Winchester Rd. N9 100 DU46
Winchester Rd. NW3 140 DD66
Winchester Rd., Bexh. 166 EX82
Winchester Rd., Brom. 204 EF97
Winchester Rd., Felt. 176 BZ90
Winchester Rd., Har. 118 CL56
Winchester Rd., Hayes 155 BS80
Winchester Rd., Ilf. 125 ER62
Winchester Rd., Nthwd. 115 BT55
Winchester Rd., Orp. 224 EW105
Winchester Rd., Twick. 177 CH87
Winchester Rd., Walt. 195 BU102
Winchester Sq. SE1 279 K2
Winchester Sq. SE1 142 DR74
Winchester St. SW1 277 J10
Winchester St. SW1 161 DH78
Winchester St. W3 138 CQ74
Winchester Wk. SE1 279 K2
Winchester Wk. SE1 142 DR74
Winchester Way, Rick. 75 BP43
Winchet Wk., Croy. 202 DW100
Medway Clo.
Winchfield Clo., Har. 117 CJ58
Winchfield Rd. SE26 183 DY92
Winchfield Way, Rick. 92 BJ45
Winchilsea Cres., W.Mol. 196 CC96

Winchmore Hill Rd. N14 99 DK46
Winchmore Hill Rd. N21 99 DK46
Winchstone Clo., Shep. 194 BM98
Winckley Clo., Har. 118 CM57
Wincott St. SE11 278 E8
Wincott St. SE11 161 DN77
Wincrofts Dr. SE9 165 ER84
Wind Hill, Ong. 53 FF20
Windall Clo. SE19 202 DU95
Windborough Rd., Cars. 218 DG108
Windermere Ave. N3 120 DA55
Windermere Ave. NW6 139 CY67
Windermere Ave. SW19 200 DB97
Windermere Ave., Har. 117 CJ59
Windermere Ave., Horn. 127 FG64
Windermere Ave., Ruis. 116 BW59
Windermere Ave., St.Alb. 43 CH22
Windermere Ave., Wem. 117 CJ59
Windermere Clo., Dart. 187 FH88
Windermere Clo., Egh. 173 BB94
Derwent Rd.
Windermere Clo., Felt. 175 BT88
Windermere Clo., Hem.H. 41 BQ21
Windermere Clo., Orp. 205 EP104
Windermere Clo., Rick. 73 BD44
Windermere Clo., Stai. 174 BL88
Viola Ave.
Windermere Ct. SW13 159 CT79
Windermere Ct., Ken. 235 DP115
Windermere Ct., Wem. 117 CJ59
Windermere Ave.
Windermere Gdns., Ilf. 124 EL57
Windermere Gro., Wem. 117 CJ60
Windermere Ave.
Windermere Ho., Islw. 177 CF85
Windermere Rd. N10 99 DH53
Windermere Rd. N19 121 DJ61
Holloway Rd.
Windermere Rd. SW15 178 CS91
Windermere Rd. SW16 201 DJ95
Windermere Rd. W5 157 CJ76
Windermere Rd., Bexh. 167 FC82
Windermere Rd., Couls. 235 DL115
Windermere Rd., Croy. 202 DT102
Windermere Rd., Sthl. 136 BZ71
Windermere Rd., W.Wick. 204 EE103
Windermere Way, Reig. 250 DE133
Windermere Way, West Dr. 134 BM74
Providence Rd.
Winders Rd. SW11 160 DE82
Windfield, Lthd. 231 CH121
Windfield Clo. SE26 183 DX91
Windgates, Guil. 243 BC131
Tychbourne Dr.
Windham Ave., Croy. 221 ED110
Windham Rd., Rich. 158 CM83
Windhill, Welw.G.C. 30 DA08
Windhover Way, Grav. 191 GL91
Winding Shot, Hem.H. 40 BG19
Winding Way, Dag. 126 EW62
Winding Way, Har. 117 CE63
Windings, The, S.Croy. 220 DT111
Windlass Pl. SE8 163 DY77
Windlesham Gro. SW19 179 CX88
Windley Clo. SE23 182 DW89
Windmere Way, Slou. 130 AJ71
Windmill All. W4 158 CS77
Windmill Rd.
Windmill Ave., Epsom 217 CT111
Windmill Ave., St.Alb. 43 CJ16
Windmill Ave., Sthl. 156 CC75
Windmill Bri. Ho., Croy. 202 DS102
Windmill Clo. SE1 162 DU77
Beatrice Rd.
Windmill Clo. SE13 163 EC82
Windmill Clo., Cat. 236 DQ121
Windmill Clo., Epsom 217 CT112
Windmill Clo., Horl. 269 DH148
Windmill Clo., Sun. 175 BS94
Windmill Clo., Surb. 197 CJ102
Windmill Clo., Upmin. 128 FN61
Windmill Clo., Wal.Abb. 68 EE34
Windmill Clo., Wind. 151 AP82
Windmill Ct. NW2 139 CY65
Windmill Dr. SW4 181 DJ85
Windmill Dr., Kes. 222 EJ105
Windmill Dr., Lthd. 231 CJ123
Windmill Dr., Reig. 250 DD132
Windmill Dr., Rick. 74 BM44
Windmill End, Epsom 217 CT112
Windmill Fld., Ware 33 DX07
Windmill Flds., Harl. 36 EZ11
Windmill Gdns., Enf. 81 DN41
Windmill Grn., Shep. 195 BS101
Windmill Gro., Croy. 202 DQ101
Windmill Hill NW3 120 DC62
Windmill Hill, Amer. 89 AM45
Windmill Hill, Enf. 81 DP41
Windmill Hill, Kings L. 57 BF32
Windmill Hill, Ruis. 115 BT59
Windmill La. E15 143 ED65
Windmill La., Barn. 79 CT44
Windmill La., Epsom 217 CT112
Windmill La., Grnf. 136 CC71
Windmill La., Islw. 157 CE77
Windmill La., Sthl. 156 CC76
Windmill La., Surb. 197 CH100
Windmill La. (Cheshunt), Wal.Cr. 67 DY30
Windmill La. (Bushey), Wat. 95 CE46
Windmill Ms. W4 158 CS77
Windmill Rd.
Windmill Pas. W4 158 CS77
Windmill Ri., Kings.T. 178 CP94
Windmill Rd. N18 100 DR49
Windmill Rd. SW18 180 DD86
Windmill Rd. SW19 179 CV88
Windmill Rd. W4 158 CS77
Windmill Rd. W5 157 CJ77
Windmill Rd., Brent. 157 CK78
Windmill Rd., Croy. 202 DQ101
Windmill Rd., Ger.Cr. 90 AX52
Windmill Rd., Hmptn. 176 CB92
Windmill Rd., Hem.H. 40 BL20
Windmill Rd., Mitch. 201 DJ99
Windmill Rd., Sev. 257 FH130
Windmill Rd., Slou. 131 AR74
Windmill Rd. (Fulmer), Slou. 112 AX64
Windmill Rd., Sun. 195 BS95
Windmill Rd. W., Sun. 195 BS96
Windmill Row SE11 161 DN78
Windmill St. W1 273 M7
Windmill St. W1 141 DK71
Windmill St., Grav. 191 GH87
Windmill St. (Bushey), Wat. 95 CE46
Windmill Wk. SE1 278 E3
Windmill Wk. SE1 141 DN74
Windmill Way, Reig. 250 DD132
Windmill Way, Ruis. 115 BT60
Windmill Wd., Amer. 55 AN37
Windmore Ave., Pot.B. 63 CW31
Windover Ave. NW9 118 CR56
Windridge Clo., St.Alb. 42 CA22
Windridge Rd., St.Alb. 42 BX24
Windrose Clo. SE16 163 DX75
Windrush Ave., Slou. 153 BB76
Windrush Clo. SW11 160 DD84
Maysoule Rd.
Windrush Clo. W4 158 CQ81
Windrush Clo., Uxb. 114 BM63
Windrush La. SE23 183 DX90
Windrush Sq. SW2 161 DN84
Rushcroft Rd.
Winds End Clo., Hem.H. 40 BN18
Winds Ridge, Wok. 243 BC125
Windsock Clo. SE16 163 DZ77
Windsor & Eton Relief Rd., Wind. 151 AP81
Windsor Ave. E17 101 DY54
Windsor Ave. SW19 200 DC95
Windsor Ave., Edg. 96 CP49
Windsor Ave., Grays 170 GB75
Windsor Ave., N.Mal. 198 CQ99
Windsor Ave., Sutt. 199 CY104
Windsor Ave., Uxb. 135 BP67
Windsor Ave., W.Mol. 196 CA97
Windsor Castle, Wind. 152 AS80
Windsor Cen., The SE27 182 DQ91
Advance Rd.
Windsor Clo. N3 97 CY54
Windsor Clo. SE27 182 DQ91
Windsor Clo., Borwd. 78 CN39
Windsor Clo., Brent. 157 CH79
Windsor Clo., Chis. 185 EP92
Windsor Clo., Guil. 258 AT136
Windsor Clo., Har. 116 CA62
Windsor Clo., Hem.H. 40 BL22
Windsor Clo. (Bovingdon), Hem.H. 57 BA28
Windsor Clo., Nthwd. 93 BU54
Windsor Clo. (Cheshunt), Wal.Cr. 66 DU30
Windsor Ct. N14 99 DJ45
Windsor Ct., Sun. 175 BU93
Windsor Rd.
Windsor Ct. Rd., Wok. 210 AS109
Windsor Cres., Har. 116 CA63
Windsor Cres., Wem. 118 CP62
Windsor Dr., Ashf. 174 BK91
Windsor Dr., Barn. 80 DF44
Windsor Dr., Dart. 187 FG86
Windsor Dr., Hert. 31 DM09
Windsor Dr., Orp. 224 EU107
Windsor End, Beac. 111 AM55
Windsor Gdns. W9 140 DA71
Windsor Gdns., Croy. 201 DL104
Richmond Rd.
Windsor Gdns., Hayes 155 BR76
Windsor Gro. SE27 182 DQ91
Windsor Hill, H.Wyc. 110 AF58
Windsor La., H.Wyc. 110 AE58
Windsor La., Slou. 130 AJ70
Windsor Pk. Rd., Hayes 155 BT80
Windsor Pl. SW1 277 L7
Windsor Pl., Cher. 194 BG100
Windsor St.
Windsor Rd. E4 101 EB49
Chivers Rd.
Windsor Rd. E7 124 EH64
Windsor Rd. E10 123 EB61
Windsor Rd. E11 124 EG60
Windsor Rd. N3 97 CY54
Windsor Rd. N7 121 DL62
Windsor Rd. N13 99 DN48
Windsor Rd. N17 100 DU54
Windsor Rd. NW2 139 CV65
Windsor Rd. W5 138 CL73
Windsor Rd., Barn. 79 CX44
Windsor Rd., Beac. 111 AN57
Windsor Rd., Bexh. 166 EY84
Windsor Rd., Brwd. 108 FV44
Windsor Rd., Chesh. 54 AP28
Windsor Rd., Dag. 126 EY62
Windsor Rd., Egh. 172 AW88
Windsor Rd., Enf. 83 DX36
Windsor Rd., Ger.Cr. 112 AW60
Windsor Rd., Grav. 191 GH90
Windsor Rd., Har. 95 CD53
Windsor Rd., Horn. 128 FJ59
Windsor Rd., Houns. 155 BV82
Windsor Rd., Ilf. 125 EP63
Windsor Rd., Kings.T. 178 CL94
Windsor Rd., Maid. 150 AE79
Windsor Rd., Rich. 158 CM82
Windsor Rd., Slou. 152 AS76
Windsor Rd. (Datchet), Slou. 152 AU80
Windsor Rd. (Fulmer), Slou. 112 AU62
Windsor Rd., Sthl. 156 BZ76
Windsor Rd., Stai. 172 AY86
Windsor Rd., Sun. 175 BU93
Windsor Rd., Tedd. 177 CD92
Windsor Rd., Th.Hth. 201 DP96
Windsor Rd., Wat. 76 BW38
Windsor Rd., Wind. 150 AE79
Windsor Rd. (Eton), Wind. 151 AR79
Windsor Rd., Wok. 210 AS109
Windsor Rd., Wor.Pk. 199 CU103
Windsor St. N1 141 DP67
Windsor St., Cher. 194 BG100
Windsor St., Uxb. 134 BJ66
Windsor Ter. N1 275 J2
Windsor Ter. N1 142 DQ69
Windsor Wk. SE5 162 DR82
Windsor Wk., Walt. 196 BX102
King George Ave.
Windsor Wk., Wey. 213 BP106
Windsor Way W14 159 CY77
Windsor Way, Rick. 92 BG46
Windsor Way, Wok. 227 BC116
Windsor Wf. E9 123 DZ64
Windsor Wd., Wal.Abb. 68 EE33
Monkswood Ave.
Windsors, The, Buck.H. 102 EL47
Windspoint Dr. SE15 162 DV79
Ethnard Rd.
Windus Rd. N16 122 DT60
Windus Wk. N16 122 DT60
Windward Clo., Enf. 83 DX35
Bullsmoor La.
Windy Hill, Brwd. 109 GC46
Windy Ridge, Brom. 204 EL95
Windycroft Clo., Pur. 219 DK113
Windyridge Clo. SW19 179 CX92
Wine Clo. E1 142 DW73
Wine Office Ct. EC4 274 E8
Winern Glebe, W.Byf. 212 BK113
Winery La., Kings.T. 198 CM97
Winfield Mobile Home Pk., Wat. 76 CB39
Winford Dr., Brox. 49 DZ22
Winford Ho. E3 143 DZ66
Winford Par., Sthl. 136 CB72
Telford Rd.
Winforton St. SE10 163 EC81
Winfrith Rd. SW18 180 DC87
Wing Way, Brwd. 108 FW46
Geary Dr.
Wingate Cres., Croy. 201 DK100
Wingate Rd. W6 159 CV76
Wingate Rd., Ilf. 125 EP64
Wingate Rd., Sid. 186 EW93
Wingate Trd. Est. N17 100 DU52
Wingate Way, St.Alb. 43 CG21
Wingfield, Grays 170 FZ78
Wingfield Bank, Grav. 190 GC89
Wingfield Clo., Add. 212 BH110
Wingfield Clo., Brwd. 109 GA48
Pondfield La.
Wingfield Gdns., Upmin. 129 FT58
Wingfield Ms. SE15 162 DU83
Wingfield St.
Wingfield Rd. E15 124 EE63
Wingfield Rd. E17 123 EB57
Wingfield Rd., Grav. 191 GH87
Wingfield Rd., Kings.T. 178 CN93
Wingfield St. SE15 162 DU83
Wingfield Way, Ruis. 135 BV65
Wingford Rd. SW2 181 DL86
Wingletye La., Horn. 128 FM60
Wingmore Rd. SE24 162 DQ83
Wingrave Cres., Brwd. 108 FS49
Wingrave Rd. W6 159 CW79
Wingrove Rd. SE6 184 EE89
Wings Clo., Sutt. 218 DA105
Winifred Ave., Horn. 128 FK63
Winifred Gro. SW11 160 DF84
Winifred Pl. N12 98 DC50
High Rd.
Winifred Rd. SW19 200 DA95
Winifred Rd., Couls. 234 DG116
Winifred Rd., Dag. 126 EY61
Winifred Rd., Dart. 187 FH85
Winifred Rd., Erith 167 FE78
Winifred Rd., Hmptn. 176 CA91
Winifred Rd., Hem.H. 40 BK24
Winifred St. E16 145 EM74
Winifred Ter. E13 144 EG68
Victoria Rd.
Winifred Ter., Enf. 100 DT45
Great Cambridge Rd.
Winkers Clo., Ger.Cr. 91 AZ53
Winkers La., Ger.Cr. 91 AZ53
Winkfield Rd. E13 144 EH68
Winkfield Rd. N22 99 DN53
Winkley St. E2 142 DV68
Winkwell, Hem.H. 39 BD22
Winkworth Pl., Bans. 217 CZ114
Bolters La.
Winkworth Rd., Bans. 218 DA114
Winlaton Rd., Brom. 183 ED91
Winmill Rd., Dag. 126 EZ62
Winn Common Rd. SE18 165 ES79
Winn Rd. SE12 184 EG88
Winnards, Wok. 226 AV118
Abercorn Way
Winnett St. W1 273 M10
Winnings Wk., Nthlt. 136 BY65
Arnold Rd.
Winnington Clo. N2 120 DD58
Winnington Rd. N2 120 DD59
Winnington Rd., Enf. 82 DW38
Winnington Way, Wok. 226 AV118
Winnipeg Dr., Orp. 223 ET107
Winnock Rd., West Dr. 134 BK74
Winns Ave. E17 123 DZ55
Winns Ms. N15 122 DS56
Grove Pk. Rd.
Winns Ter. E17 101 EA54
Winsbeach E17 123 ED55
Winscombe Cres. W5 137 CK70
Winscombe St. N19 121 DH61
Winscombe Way, Stan. 95 CG50
Winsford Rd. SE6 183 DZ90
Winsford Ter. N18 100 DR50
Winsham Gro. SW11 180 DG85
Winslade Rd. SW2 181 DL85
Winslade Way SE6 183 EB87
Rushey Grn.
Winsland Ms. W2 140 DD72
London St.
Winsland St. W2 140 DD72
Winsley St. W1 273 L8
Winsley St. W1 141 DJ72
Winslow SE17 162 DS78
Winslow Clo. NW10 118 CS62
Neasden La. N.
Winslow Clo., Pnr. 115 BV58
Winslow Gro. E4 102 EE47
Winslow Rd. W6 159 CW79
Winslow Way, Felt. 176 BX90
Winslow Way, Walt. 196 BW104
Winsor Ter. E6 145 EN71
Winsor Ter. Roundabout E6 145 EP71
Royal Docks Rd.
Winstanley Clo., Cob. 213 BV114
Winstanley Est. SW11 160 DD83
Winstanley Rd. SW11 160 DD83
Winstead Gdns., Dag. 127 FC64
Winston Ave. NW9 118 CS59
Winston Clo., Green. 189 FT85
Winston Clo., Har. 95 CF51
Winston Clo., Rom. 127 FB56
Winston Ct., Har. 94 CB52
Winston Dr., Cob. 230 BY116
Winston Gdns., Berk. 38 AT19
Winston Rd. N16 122 DR63
Winston Wk. W4 158 CR77
Acton La.
Winston Way, Ilf. 125 EP62
Winston Way, Pot.B. 64 DA34
Winston Way, Wok. 227 BB120
Winstone Clo., Amer. 54 AP34
Winstre Rd., Borwd. 78 CN39
Winter Ave. E6 144 EL67
Winter Box Wk., Rich. 158 CM84
Winter Gdn. Cres. (Bluewater), Green. 189 FU88
Winterborne Ave., Orp. 205 ER104
Winterbourne Gro., Wey. 213 BQ107
Winterbourne Rd. SE6 183 DZ88
Winterbourne Rd., Dag. 126 EW61
Winterbourne Rd., Th.Hth. 201 DN97
Winterbrook Rd. SE24 182 DQ86
Winterburn Clo. N11 98 DG51
Winterdown Gdns., Esher 214 BZ107
Winterdown Rd., Esher 214 BZ107
Winterfold Clo. SW19 179 CY89
Wintergarden (Bluewater), Green. 189 FU88
Bluewater Parkway
Wintergreen Clo. E6 144 EL71
Yarrow Cres.
Winterhill Way, Guil. 243 BB130
Winters Cft., Grav. 191 GK93
Winters Rd., T.Ditt. 197 CH101
Winters Way, Wal.Abb. 68 EG33
Winterscroft Rd., Hodd. 49 DZ16
Wintersells Rd., W.Byf. 212 BK110
Winterstoke Gdns. NW7 97 CU50
Winterstoke Rd. SE6 183 DZ88
Winterton Ho. E1 142 DV72
Winterton Pl. SW10 160 DC79
Park Wk.
Winterwell Rd. SW2 181 DL85
Winthorpe Rd. SW15 159 CY84
Winthrop St. E1 142 DV71
Winthrop Wk., Wem. 118 CL62
Everard Way
Winton App., Rick. 75 BQ43
Winton Ave. N11 99 DJ52
Winton Clo. N9 101 DX45
Winton Cres., Rick. 75 BP43
Winton Dr., Rick. 75 BP43
Winton Dr. (Cheshunt), Wal.Cr. 67 DY29
Winton Gdns., Edg. 96 CM52
Winton Rd., Orp. 223 EP105
Winton Rd., Ware 33 DZ06
Winton Way SW16 181 DN92
Wintoun Path, Slou. 131 AL70
Winvale, Slou. 152 AS76
Winwood, Slou. 132 AW72
Wireless Rd., West. 238 EK115
Wisbeach Rd., Croy. 202 DR99
Wisborough Rd., S.Croy. 220 DT109
Wisdons Clo., Dag. 127 FB60
Wise La. NW7 97 CV51
Wise La., West Dr. 154 BK77
Wise Rd. E15 143 ED67
Wiseman Ct. SE19 182 DS92
Wiseman Rd. E10 123 EA61
Wisemans Gdns., Saw. 36 EW06
High Wych Rd.
Wise's La., Hat. 63 CW27
Wiseton Rd. SW17 180 DE88
Wishart Rd. SE3 164 EK81
Wishbone Way, Wok. 226 AT116
Wishford Ct., Ash. 232 CM118
The Marld
Wisley Common, Wok. 228 BM117
Wisley Ct., S.Croy. 220 DS110
Sanderstead Rd.
Wisley La., Wok. 228 BJ116
Wisley Rd. SW11 180 DG85
Wisley Rd., Orp. 186 EU94
Wissants, Harl. 51 EP19
Wisteria Clo. NW7 97 CT51
Wisteria Clo., Brwd. 108 FV43
Wisteria Clo., Ilf. 125 EP64
Wisteria Clo., Orp. 205 EP103
Wisteria Gdns., Swan. 207 FD96
Wisteria Rd. SE13 163 ED84
Wistlea Cres., St.Alb. 44 CP22
Witan St. E2 142 DV69
Witches La., Sev. 256 FD123
Witchford, Welw.G.C. 30 DD09
Witham Clo., Loug. 84 EL44
Witham Rd. SE20 202 DW97
Witham Rd. W13 137 CG74
Witham Rd., Dag. 126 FA64
Witham Rd., Islw. 157 CD81
Witham Rd., Rom. 127 FH57
Withens Clo., Orp. 206 EW98
Wither Dale, Horl. 268 DE147
Witherby Clo., Croy. 220 DS106
Witheridge La., H.Wyc. 88 AF48
Witherings, The, Horn. 128 FL57
Witherington Rd. N5 121 DN64
Withers Clo., Chess. 215 CJ107
Coppard Gdns.
Withers Mead NW9 97 CT53
Witherston Way SE9 185 EN89
Withey Clo., Wind. 151 AL81
Withey Meadows, Horl. 268 DD150
Witheygate Ave., Stai. 174 BH93
Withies, The, Lthd. 231 CH121
Withies, The, Wok. 226 AS117
Withy La., Ruis. 115 BQ57
Withy Mead E4 101 ED48
Withy Pl., St.Alb. 60 CC28
Withybed Cor., Tad. 233 CV123
Withycombe Rd. SW19 179 CX87
Withycroft, Slou. 132 AY72
Witley Cres., Croy. 221 EC107
Witley Gdns., Sthl. 156 BZ77
Witley Rd. N19 121 DJ61
Holloway Rd.
Witney Clo., Pnr. 94 BZ51
Witney Clo., Uxb. 114 BM63
Witney Path SE23 183 DX90
Wittenham Way E4 101 ED48
Wittering Clo., Kings.T. 177 CK92
Wittering Wk., Horn. 148 FJ65
Wittersham Rd., Brom. 184 EF92
Wivenhoe Clo. SE15 162 DV83
Wivenhoe Ct., Houns. 156 BZ84
Wivenhoe Rd., Bark. 146 EU68
Wiverton Rd. SE26 182 DW93
Wix Hill, Lthd. 245 BP130
Wix Hill Clo., Lthd. 245 BP131
Wix Rd., Dag. 146 EX67
Wixs La. SW4 161 DH84
Woburn Ave., Epp. 85 ES37
Woburn Ave., Horn. 127 FG63
Woburn Ave., Pur. 219 DN111
High St.
Woburn Clo. SE28 146 EX72
Summerton Way
Woburn Clo. SW19 180 DC93
Tintern Clo.
Woburn Clo. (Bushey), Wat. 76 CC43
Woburn Ct. SE16 162 DV78
Masters Dr.
Woburn Hill, Add. 194 BJ103
Woburn Pl. WC1 273 N4
Woburn Pl. WC1 141 DL70
Woburn Rd., Cars. 200 DE102
Woburn Rd., Croy. 202 DQ102
Woburn Sq. WC1 273 N5
Woburn Sq. WC1 141 DK70
Woburn Wk. WC1 273 N3
Woburn Wk. WC1 141 DK69
Wodehouse Ave. SE5 162 DT81
Wodehouse Rd., Dart. 168 FN84
Wodeland Ave., Guil. 258 AV136
Woffington Clo., Kings.T. 197 CJ95
Wokindon Rd., Grays 171 GH76
Woking Business Pk., Wok. 227 BB115
Woking Clo. SW15 159 CT84
Woking Rd., Guil. 242 AW128
Wold, The, Cat. 237 EA122
Woldham Pl., Brom. 204 EJ98
Woldham Rd., Brom. 204 EJ98
Woldingham Rd., Cat. 236 DV120
Wolds Dr., Orp. 223 EN105
Wolf La., Wind. 151 AK83
Wolfe Clo., Brom. 204 EG100
Wolfe Clo., Hayes 135 BV69
Ayles Rd.
Wolfe Cres. SE7 164 EK78
Wolfe Cres. SE16 163 DX75
Wolferton Rd. E12 125 EM63
Wolffe Gdns. E15 144 EF65
Wolffram Clo. SE13 184 EE85
Wolfington Rd. SE27 181 DP91
Wolfs Hill, Oxt. 254 EG131
Wolf's Row, Oxt. 254 EH130
Wolfs Wd., Oxt. 254 EG132
Wolftencroft Clo. SW11 160 DD83
Wollaston Clo. SE1 279 H8
Wolmer Clo., Edg. 96 CP49
Wolmer Gdns., Edg. 96 CN48
Wolseley Ave. SW19 180 DA89
Wolseley Gdns. W4 158 CP79
Wolseley Rd. E7 144 EH66
Wolseley Rd. N8 121 DK58
Wolseley Rd. N22 99 DM53
Wolseley Rd. W4 158 CQ77
Wolseley Rd., Har. 117 CE55
Wolseley Rd., Mitch. 200 DG101
Wolseley Rd., Rom. 127 FD59
Wolseley St. SE1 162 DT75
Wolsey Ave. E6 145 EN69
Wolsey Ave. E17 123 DZ55
Wolsey Ave., T.Ditt. 197 CF99
Aragon Ave.
Wolsey Ave. (Cheshunt), Wal.Cr. 66 DT29
Wolsey Business Pk., Wat. 93 BR45
Wolsey Clo. SW20 179 CV94
Wolsey Clo., Houns. 156 CC84
Wolsey Clo., Kings.T. 198 CP95
Wolsey Clo., Sthl. 156 CC76
Wolsey Clo., Wor.Pk. 217 CU105
Wolsey Cres., Croy. 221 EC109
Wolsey Cres., Mord. 199 CY101
Wolsey Dr., Kings.T. 178 CL92
Wolsey Dr., Walt. 196 BX102
Wolsey Gdns., Ilf. 103 EQ51
Wolsey Gro., Edg. 96 CR52
Wolsey Gro., Esher 214 CB105
Wolsey Ms. NW5 141 DJ65
Wolsey Ms., Orp. 223 ET106
Osgood Ave.
Wolsey Rd. N1 122 DR64
Wolsey Rd., Ashf. 174 BL91
Wolsey Rd., E.Mol. 197 CD98
Wolsey Rd., Enf. 82 DV40
Wolsey Rd., Esher 214 CB105
Wolsey Rd., Hmptn. 176 CB93
Wolsey Rd., Hem.H. 40 BK21
Wolsey Rd., Nthwd. 93 BQ47
Wolsey Rd., Sun. 175 BT94
Wolsey St. E1 142 DW71
Sidney St.
Wolsey Wk., Wok. 226 AY117
Church St. W.
Wolsey Way, Chess. 216 CN106
Wolsley Clo., Dart. 187 FE85
Wolstan Clo. (Denham), Uxb. 114 BG62
Lindsey Rd.
Wolstonbury N12 98 DA50
Wolvens La., Dor. 262 CA140
Wolvercote Rd. SE2 166 EX75
Wolverley St. E2 142 DV69
Bethnal Grn. Rd.
Wolverton SE17 279 M10
Wolverton Ave., Kings.T. 198 CN95
Wolverton Clo., Horl. 268 DF150
Wolverton Gdns. W5 138 CM73
Wolverton Gdns. W6 159 CX77
Wolverton Gdns., Horl. 268 DF149
Wolverton Rd., Stan. 95 CH51
Wolverton Way N14 81 DJ43
Wolves La. N13 99 DN52
Wolves La. N22 99 DN52
Wombwell Gdns., Grav. 190 GE89
Womersley Rd. N8 121 DM58
Wonersh Common, Guil. 259 BB141
Wonersh Common Rd., Guil. 259 BB142
Wonersh Way, Sutt. 217 CX109
Wonford Clo., Kings.T. 198 CS95
Wonford Clo., Tad. 249 CU126
Wonham La., Bet. 264 CS135
Wonham Way, Guil. 261 BR139
Wontford Rd., Pur. 235 DN115
Wontner Clo. N1 142 DQ66
Greenman St.
Wontner Rd. SW17 180 DF89
Wooburn Clo., Uxb. 135 BP70
Aldenham Dr.
Wooburn Common, H.Wyc. 110 AF59
Wooburn Common Rd., H.Wyc. 110 AG59
Wooburn Gra., H.Wyc. 110 AD60
Wooburn Grn. La., Beac. 110 AG56
Wooburn Manor Pk., H.Wyc. 110 AE58
Wooburn Ms., H.Wyc. 110 AE58
Wooburn Town, H.Wyc. 110 AD59
Wood Ave., Purf. 168 FQ77
Wood Clo. E2 142 DU70
Wood Clo. NW9 118 CR59
Wood Clo., Bex. 187 FE90
Wood Clo., Har. 117 CD59

Wood Clo., Hat. 45 CV18
Wood Clo., Red. 266 DG143
Wood Clo., Wind. 151 AQ84
Wood Common, Hat. 45 CV15
Wood Cres., Hem.H. 40 BK21
Wood Dr., Chis. 184 EL93
Wood Dr., Sev. 256 FF126
Wood End, Hayes 135 BS72
Wood End, St.Alb. 60 CC28
Wood End Ave., Har. 116 CB63
Wood End Clo., Hem.H. 41 BQ19
Wood End Clo., Nthlt. 117 CD64
Wood End Clo., Slou. 111 AR62
Wood End Gdns., Nthlt. 116 CC64
Wood End Grn. Rd., Hayes 135 BR71
Wood End La., Nthlt. 136 CB65
Wood End Rd., Har. 117 CD63
Wood End Way, Nthlt. 116 CC64
Wood Fm. Rd., Hem.H. 40 BL20
Wood Grn. Way (Cheshunt), Wal.Cr. 67 DY31
Wood Ho. La., Brox. 48 DT21
Wood La. N6 121 DH58
Wood La. NW9 118 CS59
Wood La. W12 139 CW72
Wood La., Cat. 236 DR124
Wood La., Dag. 126 EW63
Wood La., Dart. 189 FR91
Wood La., Horn. 127 FG64
Wood La., Islw. 157 CF80
Wood La., Iver 133 BC69
Wood La., Ruis. 115 BR60
Wood La., Slou. 151 AM76
Wood La., Stan. 95 CG48
Wood La., Tad. 233 CZ117
Brighton Rd.
Wood La., Ware 33 EA05
Wood La., Wey. 213 BQ109
Wood La., Wdf.Grn. 102 EF50
Wood La. Clo., Iver 133 BB69
Wood La. End, Hem.H. 40 BN19
Wood Lo. Gdns., Brom. 184 EL94
Wood Lo. La., W.Wick. 203 EC104
Wood Meads, Epp. 70 EU29
Wood Pt. E16 144 EG71
Fife Rd.
Wood Pond Clo., Beac. 89 AQ51
Wood Retreat SE18 165 ER80
Wood Ride, Barn. 80 DD39
Wood Ride, Orp. 205 ER98
Wood Riding, Wok. 227 BF115
Pyrford Wds. Rd.
Wood Ri., Guil. 242 AS132
Wood Ri., Pnr. 115 BU57
Wood Rd., Gdmg. 258 AT144
Wood Rd., Shep. 194 BN98
Wood Rd., West. 238 EJ118
Wood St. E16 144 EH73
Ethel Rd.
Wood St. E17 123 EC55
Wood St. EC2 275 J9
Wood St. EC2 142 DQ72
Wood St. W4 158 CS78
Wood St., Barn. 79 CX42
Wood St., Grays 170 GC79
Wood St., Kings.T. 197 CK95
Wood St., Mitch. 200 DG101
Wood St., Red. 251 DJ129
Wood St., Swan. 208 FJ95
Wood Vale N10 121 DJ57
Wood Vale SE23 182 DV88
Wood Vale, Hat. 45 CV18
Wood Vale Est. SE23 182 DW86
Wood Vw., Hem.H. 40 BH18
Wood Vw. (Cuffley), Pot.B. 65 DL27
Wood Wk., Rick. 73 BE40
Wood Way, Beac. 88 AF54
Wood Way, Orp. 205 EN103
Wood Wf. SE10 163 EB79
Woodall Clo. E14 143 EB73
Lawless St.
Woodall Rd., Enf. 83 DX44
Woodbank, Rick. 74 BJ44
Woodbank Ave., Ger.Cr. 112 AX58
Woodbank Dr., Ch.St.G. 90 AX48
Woodbank Rd., Brom. 184 EF90
Woodbastwick Rd. SE26 183 DX92
Woodberry Ave. N21 99 DN47
Woodberry Ave., Har. 116 CB56
Woodberry Clo., Sun. 175 BU93
Ashridge Way
Woodberry Cres. N10 121 DH55
Woodberry Down N4 122 DQ59
Woodberry Down, Epp. 70 EU29
Woodberry Down Est. N4 122 DQ59
Woodberry Gdns. N12 98 DC51
Woodberry Gro. N4 122 DQ59
Woodberry Gro. N12 98 DC51
Woodberry Gro., Bex. 187 FD90
Woodberry Way E4 101 EC46
Woodberry Way N12 98 DC51
Woodbine Clo., Harl. 51 EQ17
Linford End
Woodbine Clo., Twick. 177 CD89
Woodbine Clo., Wal.Abb. 84 EJ35
Woodbine Gro. SE20 182 DV94
Woodbine Gro., Enf. 82 DR38
Woodbine La., Wor.Pk. 199 CW104
Woodbine Pl. E11 124 EG58
Woodbine Rd., Sid. 185 ES88
Woodbine Ter. E9 142 DW65
Morning La.
Woodbines Ave., Kings.T. 197 CK97
Woodborough Rd. SW15 159 CV84
Woodbourne Ave. SW16 181 DK90
Woodbourne Clo. SW16 181 DL90
Woodbourne Ave.
Woodbourne Dr., Esher 215 CF107
Woodbourne Gdns., Wall. 219 DH108
Woodbridge Ave., Lthd. 231 CG118
Woodbridge Clo. N7 121 DM61
Woodbridge Clo. NW2 119 CU62
Woodbridge Clo., Rom. 106 FK49
Woodbridge Ct., Wdf.Grn. 102 EL52
Woodbridge Gro., Lthd. 231 CG118
Woodbridge Hill, Guil. 242 AV133
Woodbridge Hill Gdns., Guil. 242 AU133
Woodbridge La., Rom. 106 FK48
Woodbridge Meadows, Guil. 242 AW133
Woodbridge Rd., Bark. 125 ET64
Woodbridge Rd., Guil. 242 AV133
Woodbridge St. EC1 274 F4
Woodbridge St. EC1 141 DP70
Woodbrook Gdns., Wal.Abb. 68 EE33
Woodbrook Rd. SE2 166 EU79
Woodburn Clo. NW4 119 CX57
Woodbury, B.End 110 AC59
Woodbury Clo. E11 124 EH56
Woodbury Clo., Croy. 202 DT103
Woodbury Clo., West. 239 EM118
Woodbury Dr., Sutt. 218 DC110
Woodbury Hill, Loug. 84 EL41
Woodbury Hollow, Loug. 84 EL40
Woodbury Pk. Rd. W13 137 CH70
Woodbury Rd. E17 123 EB56
Woodbury Rd., West. 239 EM118
Woodbury St. SW17 180 DE92
Woodchester Pk., Beac. 88 AJ49
Woodchester Sq. W2 140 DB71
Woodchurch Clo., Sid. 185 ER90
Woodchurch Dr., Brom. 184 EK94
Woodchurch Rd. NW6 140 DA66
Woodclyffe Dr., Chis. 205 EN96
Woodcock Ct., Har. 118 CL59
Woodcock Dell Ave., Har. 117 CK59
Woodcock Hill, Har. 117 CK59
Woodcock Hill, Rick. 92 BL50
Woodcock Hill, St.Alb. 28 CN14
Woodcocks E16 144 EJ71
Woodcombe Cres. SE23 182 DW88
Woodcote, Guil. 258 AV138
Woodcote, Horl. 269 DJ147
The Fieldings
Woodcote Ave. NW7 97 CW51
Woodcote Ave., Horn. 127 FG63
Woodcote Ave., Th.Hth. 201 DP98
Woodcote Ave., Wall. 219 DH108
Woodcote Clo., Enf. 82 DW44
Woodcote Clo., Epsom 216 CR114
Woodcote Clo., Kings.T. 178 CM92
Woodcote Clo. (Cheshunt), Wal.Cr. 66 DW30
Woodcote Dr., Orp. 205 ER102
Woodcote Dr., Pur. 219 DK110
Woodcote End, Epsom 232 CR115
Woodcote Grn., Wall. 219 DJ109
Woodcote Grn. Rd., Epsom 232 CQ116
Woodcote Gro., Couls. 219 DH112
Woodcote Gro. Rd., Couls. 235 DK115
Woodcote Hurst, Epsom 232 CQ116
Woodcote La., Pur. 219 DK111
Woodcote Ms., Wall. 219 DH107
Woodcote Pk. Ave., Pur. 219 DJ112
Woodcote Pk. Rd., Epsom 232 CQ116
Woodcote Pl. SE27 181 DP92
Woodcote Rd. E11 124 EG59
Woodcote Rd., Epsom 216 CR114
Woodcote Rd., Pur. 219 DJ109
Woodcote Rd., Wall. 219 DH107
Woodcote Side, Epsom 232 CP115
Woodcote Valley Rd., Pur. 219 DK113
Woodcrest Rd., Pur. 219 DL113
Woodcrest Wk., Reig. 250 DE132
Woodcroft N21 99 DM46
Woodcroft SE9 185 EM90
Woodcroft, Grnf. 137 CG65
Woodcroft, Harl. 51 EQ17
Woodcroft Ave. NW7 96 CS52
Woodcroft Ave., Stan. 95 CF53
Woodcroft Ave., Ware 33 ED11
Woodcroft Cres., Uxb. 135 BP67
Woodcroft Ms. SE8 163 DY77
Croft St.
Woodcroft Rd., Chesh. 54 AR28
Woodcroft Rd., Th.Hth. 201 DP99
Woodcutters Ave., Grays 170 GC75
Woodedge Clo. E4 102 EF46
Woodend SE19 182 DQ93
Woodend, Esher 196 CC103
Woodend, Lthd. 247 CJ125
Woodend, Sutt. 200 DC103
Woodend, The, Wall. 219 DH109
Woodend Clo., Wok. 226 AU119
Woodend Gdns., Enf. 81 DL42
Woodend Pk., Cob. 230 BX115
Woodend Rd. E17 101 EC54
Wooder Gdns. E7 124 EF63
Wooderson Clo. SE25 202 DS98
Woodfall Ave., Barn. 79 CZ43
Woodfall Dr., Dart. 167 FE84
Woodfall Rd. N4 121 DN60
Woodfall St. SW3 160 DF78
Woodfarrs SE5 162 DR84
Woodfield, Ash. 231 CK117
Woodfield Ave. NW9 118 CS56
Woodfield Ave. SW16 181 DK90
Woodfield Ave. W5 137 CJ70
Woodfield Ave., Cars. 218 DG107
Woodfield Ave., Grav. 191 GH88
Woodfield Ave., Nthwd. 93 BS49
Woodfield Ave., Wem. 117 CJ62
Woodfield Clo. SE19 182 DQ94
Woodfield Clo., Ash. 231 CK117
Woodfield Clo., Couls. 235 DJ119
Woodfield Clo., Enf. 82 DS42
Woodfield Clo., Red. 250 DE133
Woodfield Cres. W5 137 CJ70
Woodfield Dr., Barn. 98 DG46
Woodfield Dr., Hem.H. 41 BR22
Woodfield Dr., Rom. 127 FG56
Woodfield Gdns. W9 139 CZ71
Woodfield Rd.
Woodfield Gdns., Hem.H. 41 BR22
Woodfield Gdns., N.Mal. 199 CT99
Woodfield Gro. SW16 181 DK90
Woodfield Hill, Couls. 235 DH119
Woodfield La. SW16 181 DK90
Woodfield La., Ash. 232 CL117
Woodfield La., Hat. 46 DD23
Woodfield La., Hert. 46 DD23
Woodfield Pk., Amer. 55 AN37
Woodfield Pl. W9 139 CZ70
Woodfield Ri. (Bushey), Wat. 95 CD45
Woodfield Rd. W5 137 CJ70
Woodfield Rd. W9 139 CZ71
Woodfield Rd., Ash. 231 CK117
Woodfield Rd., Houns. 155 BV82
Woodfield Rd., Rad. 77 CG36
Woodfield Rd., T.Ditt. 197 CF103
Woodfield Rd., Welw.G.C. 29 CZ09
Woodfield Ter., Epp. 70 EW25
High Rd.
Woodfield Ter. (Harefield), Uxb. 92 BH54
Woodfield Way N11 99 DK52
Woodfield Way, Horn. 128 FK60
Woodfield Way, Red. 250 DE132
Woodfield Way, St.Alb. 43 CJ17
Woodfields, Sev. 256 FD122
Woodfields, The, S.Croy. 220 DT111
Woodfines, The, Horn. 128 FK58
Woodford Ave., Ilf. 125 EM57
Woodford Ave., Wdf.Grn. 124 EL55
Woodford Bri. Rd., Ilf. 124 EK55
Woodford Ct. W12 159 CX75
Shepherds Bush Grn.
Woodford Ct., Wal.Abb. 68 EG33
Woodford Cres., Pnr. 93 BV54
Woodford New Rd. E17 124 EE56
Woodford New Rd. E18 102 EE53
Woodford New Rd., Wdf.Grn. 102 EE53
Woodford Pl., Wem. 118 CL60
Woodford Rd. E7 124 EH63
Woodford Rd. E18 124 EG56
Woodford Rd., Wat. 75 BV40
Woodford Trd. Est., Wdf.Grn. 124 EK55
Woodford Way, Slou. 131 AN69
Woodgate, Wat. 59 BV33
Woodgate Ave., Chess. 215 CK106
Woodgate Ave., Pot.B. 65 DH33
Woodgate Cres., Nthwd. 93 BU51
Woodgate Dr. SW16 181 DK94
Woodgavil, Bans. 233 CZ116
Woodger Clo., Guil. 243 BC132
Kingfisher Dr.
Woodger Rd. W12 159 CW75
Goldhawk Rd.
Woodgers Gro., Swan. 207 FF96
Woodget Clo. E6 144 EL72
Remington Rd.
Woodgrange Ave. N12 98 DD51
Woodgrange Ave. W5 138 CN74
Woodgrange Ave., Enf. 82 DU44
Woodgrange Ave., Har. 117 CJ57
Woodgrange Clo., Har. 117 CK57
Woodgrange Gdns., Enf. 82 DU44
Woodgrange Rd. E7 124 EH63
Woodgrange Ter., Enf. 82 DU44
Great Cambridge Rd.
Woodgreen Rd., Wal.Abb. 84 EJ35
Woodhall Ave. SE21 182 DT90
Woodhall Ave., Pnr. 94 BY54
Woodhall Clo., Hert. 32 DQ07
Woodhall Clo., Uxb. 114 BK64
Woodhall Ct., Welw.G.C. 29 CY10
Woodhall Cres., Horn. 128 FM59
Woodhall Dr. SE21 182 DT90
Woodhall Dr., Pnr. 94 BX53
Woodhall Gate, Pnr. 94 BX52
Woodhall La., Hem.H. 40 BL19
Woodhall La., Rad. 78 CL35
Woodhall La., Wat. 94 BX49
Woodhall La., Welw.G.C. 29 CY10
Woodhall Par., Welw.G.C. 29 CZ11
Woodhall Rd., Pnr. 94 BX52
Woodham Ct. E18 124 EF56
Woodham La., Add. 212 BG110
Woodham La., Wok. 211 BB114
Woodham Pk. Rd., Add. 211 BF109
Woodham Pk. Way, Add. 211 BF111
Woodham Ri., Wok. 211 AZ114
Woodham Rd. SE6 183 EC90
Woodham Rd., Wok. 211 AZ114
Woodham Waye, Wok. 211 BB114
Woodhatch Clo. E6 144 EL72
Remington Rd.
Woodhatch Rd., Red. 266 DC137
Woodhatch Rd., Reig. 266 DB137
Woodhatch Spinney, Couls. 235 DL116
Woodhaven Gdns., Ilf. 125 EQ55
Brandville Gdns.
Woodhaw, Egh. 173 BB91
Woodhayes, Horl. 269 DH147
Woodhayes Rd. SW19 179 CW94
Woodhead Dr., Orp. 205 ES103
Sherlies Ave.
Woodheyes Rd. NW10 118 CR64
Woodhill SE18 164 EL77
Woodhill, Harl. 51 ES19
Woodhill, Wok. 243 BD126
Woodhill Ave., Ger.Cr. 113 AZ58
Woodhill Cres., Har. 117 CK58
Woodhouse Ave., Grnf. 137 CF68
Woodhouse Clo., Grnf. 137 CF68
Woodhouse Clo., Hayes 155 BS76
Woodhouse Eaves, Nthwd. 93 BU50
Woodhouse Gro. E12 144 EL65
Woodhouse La., Dor. 261 BU143
Woodhouse Rd. E11 124 EF62
Woodhouse Rd. N12 98 DD51
Woodhurst Ave., Orp. 205 EQ100
Woodhurst Ave., Wat. 76 BX35
Woodhurst Dr., Uxb. 113 BF57
Woodhurst La., Oxt. 254 EE131
Woodhurst Pk., Oxt. 254 EE130
Woodhurst Rd. SE2 166 EU78
Woodhurst Rd. W3 138 CQ73
Woodhyrst Gdns., Ken. 235 DP115
Firs Rd.
Wooding Gro., Harl. 51 EP15
Woodington Clo. SE9 185 EN86
Woodison St. E3 143 DY70
Woodknoll Dr., Chis. 205 EM95
Woodland App., Grnf. 137 CG65
Woodland Ave., Brwd. 109 GC43
Woodland Ave., Hem.H. 40 BH21
Woodland Ave., Slou. 131 AR73
Woodland Ave., Wind. 151 AM84
Woodland Clo. NW9 118 CQ58
Woodland Clo. SE19 182 DS93
Woodland Hill
Woodland Clo., Brwd. 109 GC43
Woodland Clo., Epsom 216 CS107
Woodland Clo., Hem.H. 40 BH21
Woodland Clo., Lthd. 245 BT127
Woodland Clo. (Ickenham), Uxb. 115 BP61
Woodland Clo., Wey. 213 BR105
Woodland Gro.
Woodland Clo., Wdf.Grn. 102 EH48
Woodland Ct., Oxt. 253 ED128
Woodland Cres. SE10 164 EE79
Woodland Cres. SE16 163 DX75
Woodland Dr., Lthd. 245 BT127
Woodland Dr., St.Alb. 43 CJ19
Woodland Dr., Wat. 75 BT39
Woodland Gdns. N10 121 DH57
Woodland Gdns., Islw. 157 CE82
Woodland Gdns., S.Croy. 220 DW111
Woodland Gro. SE10 164 EE78
Woodland Gro., Epp. 70 EU31
Woodland Gro., Wey. 213 BR105
Woodland Hill SE19 182 DS93
Woodland La., Rick. 73 BD41
Woodland Mt., Hert. 32 DT09
Woodland Pl., Hem.H. 40 BH21
Woodland Pl., Rick. 73 BF42
Woodland Ri. N10 121 DH56
Woodland Ri., Grnf. 137 CG65
Woodland Ri., Oxt. 254 EE130
Woodland Ri., Sev. 257 FL123
Woodland Ri., Welw.G.C. 29 CW07
Woodland Rd. E4 101 EC46
Woodland Rd. N11 99 DH50
Woodland Rd. SE19 182 DS92
Woodland Rd., Hert. 32 DW12
Woodland Rd., Loug. 84 EL41
Woodland Rd., Rick. 91 BD50
Woodland Rd., Th.Hth. 201 DN98
Woodland St. E8 142 DT65
Dalston La.
Woodland Ter. SE7 164 EL77
Woodland Vw., Chesh. 54 AR33
Woodland Vw., Gdmg. 258 AS142
Woodland Wk. NW3 120 DE64
Woodland Wk. SE10 164 EE78
Woodland Gro.
Woodland Wk., Brom. 184 EE91
Woodland Way N21 99 DN47
Woodland Way NW7 96 CS51
Woodland Way SE2 166 EX77
Woodland Way, Abb.L. 59 BT27
Woodland Way, Cat. 252 DS128
Woodland Way, Croy. 203 DY102
Woodland Way, Epp. 85 ER35
Woodland Way, Green. 169 FU84
Woodland Way, Mitch. 180 DG94
Woodland Way, Mord. 199 CZ98
Woodland Way, Orp. 205 EQ98
Woodland Way, Pur. 219 DN113
Woodland Way, Surb. 198 CP103
Woodland Way, Tad. 233 CY122
Woodland Way (Cheshunt), Wal.Cr. 65 DP28
Woodland Way, W.Wick. 221 EB105
Woodland Way, Wey. 213 BR106
Woodland Way, Wdf.Grn. 102 EH48
Woodlands NW11 119 CY58
Woodlands SW20 199 CW98
Woodlands, Ger.Cr. 113 AZ57
Woodlands, Har. 116 CA56
Woodlands, Hat. 64 DB26
Woodlands, Horl. 269 DJ147
Woodlands, Rad. 61 CG34
Woodlands, St.Alb. 60 CC27
Woodlands, Wok. 226 AY118
Constitution Hill
Woodlands, The N14 99 DH46
Woodlands, The SE13 183 ED87
Woodlands, The SE19 182 DQ94
Woodlands, The, Amer. 55 AQ35
Woodlands, The, Esher 196 CC103
Woodlands, The, Hem.H. 41 BP19
Woodlands, The, Horl. 269 DP148
Woodlands, The, Islw. 157 CF82
Woodlands, The, Orp. 224 EV107
Woodlands, The, Wall. 219 DH109
Woodlands Ave. E11 124 EH60
Woodlands Ave. N3 98 DC52
Woodlands Ave. W3 138 CP74
Woodlands Ave., Berk. 38 AW20
Woodlands Ave., Horn. 128 FK57
Woodlands Ave., N.Mal. 198 CQ95
Woodlands Ave., Red. 266 DF135
Woodlands Ave., Rom. 126 EY58
Woodlands Ave., Ruis. 116 BX60
Woodlands Ave., Sid. 185 ES88
Woodlands Ave., W.Byf. 211 BF113
Woodlands Ave., Wor.Pk. 199 CT103
Woodlands Clo. NW11 119 CY57
Woodlands Clo., Borwd. 78 CP42
Woodlands Clo., Brom. 205 EM96
Woodlands Clo., Cher. 211 BB110
Woodlands Clo., Esher 215 CF108
Woodlands Clo., Ger.Cr. 113 BA58
Woodlands Clo., Grays 170 GE76
Woodlands Clo., Hodd. 49 EA18
Woodlands Clo., Swan. 207 FF97
Woodlands Ct., Wok. 226 AY119
Constitution Hill
Woodlands Dr., Beac. 88 AJ51
Woodlands Dr., Hodd. 49 EA19
Woodlands Dr., Kings L. 59 BQ28
Woodlands Dr., Stan. 95 CF51
Woodlands Dr., Sun. 196 BW96
Woodlands Glade, Beac. 88 AJ51
Woodlands Glade, Slou. 111 AR62
Woodlands Gro., Couls. 234 DG117
Woodlands Gro., Islw. 157 CE82
Woodlands Hill, Beac. 111 AL58
Woodlands La., Cob. 230 BY117
Woodlands Par., Ashf. 175 BQ93
Woodlands Pk., Add. 211 BF106
Woodlands Pk., Bex. 187 FC91
Woodlands Pk., Guil. 243 BB133
Woodlands Pk., Tad. 248 CP131
Woodlands Pk., Wok. 211 BC114
Blackmore Cres.
Woodlands Pk. Rd. N15 121 DP57
Woodlands Pk. Rd. SE10 164 EE79
Woodlands Ri., Swan. 207 FF96
Woodlands Rd. E11 124 EE61
Woodlands Rd. E17 123 EC55
Woodlands Rd. N9 100 DW46
Woodlands Rd. SW13 159 CT83
Woodlands Rd., Bexh. 166 EY83
Woodlands Rd., Brom. 204 EL96
Woodlands Rd., Enf. 82 DR39
Woodlands Rd., Epsom 232 CN115
Woodlands Rd., Guil. 242 AX130
Woodlands Rd., Har. 117 CF57
Woodlands Rd., Hem.H. 58 BN27
Woodlands Rd., Hert. 32 DT09
Woodlands Rd., Ilf. 125 EQ62
Woodlands Rd., Islw. 157 CE82
Woodlands Rd., Lthd. 231 CD117
Woodlands Rd. (Effingham), Lthd. 246 BY128
Woodlands Rd., Orp. 224 EU107
Woodlands Rd., Red. 266 DF136
Woodlands Rd., Rom. 127 FF55
Woodlands Rd. (Harold Wd.), Rom. 106 FN53
Fitzilian Ave.
Woodlands Rd., Sthl. 136 BX74
Woodlands Rd., Surb. 197 CK101
Woodlands Rd., Vir.W. 192 AW98
Woodlands Rd. (Bushey), Wat. 76 BY43
Woodlands Rd., W.Byf. 211 BF114
Woodlands Rd. E., Vir.W. 192 AW98
Woodlands Rd. W., Vir.W. 192 AW98
Woodlands St. SE13 183 ED87
Woodlands Vw., Dor. 263 CH142
Woodlands Vw., Sev. 224 FA110
Woodlands Way SW15 179 CZ85
Oakhill Rd.
Woodlands Way, Ash. 232 CN116
Woodlands Way, Tad. 248 CQ130
Woodlawn Clo. SW15 179 CZ85
Woodlawn Cres., Twick. 176 CB89
Woodlawn Dr., Felt. 176 BX89
Woodlawn Gro., Wok. 227 AZ115
Woodlawn Rd. SW6 159 CX80
Woodlea Dr., Brom. 204 EE99
Woodlea Gro., Nthwd. 93 BQ51
Woodlea Rd. N16 122 DS62
Woodleigh Ave. N12 98 DE51
Woodleigh Gdns. SW16 181 DL90
Woodley Clo. SW17 180 DF94
Arnold Rd.
Woodley Hill, Chesh. 54 AR34
Woodley La., Cars. 200 DD104
Woodley Rd., Orp. 206 EW103
Woodley Rd., Ware 33 DZ05
Woodman La. E4 84 EE43
Woodman Path, Ilf. 103 ES51
Woodman Rd., Brwd. 108 FW50
Woodman Rd., Couls. 235 DJ115
Woodman Rd., Hem.H. 40 BL22
Woodman St. E16 145 EN74
Woodmancote Gdns., W.Byf. 212 BG113
Woodmans Gro. NW10 119 CT64
Woodmans Ms. W12 139 CV71
Woodman's Yd., Wat. 76 BX42
Woodmansterne La., Bans. 234 DB115
Woodmansterne La., Cars. 218 DF112
Woodmansterne La., Wall. 219 DH111
Woodmansterne Rd. SW16 181 DK94
Woodmansterne Rd., Cars. 218 DE109
Woodmansterne Rd., Couls. 235 DJ115
Woodmansterne St., Bans. 234 DE115
Woodmere SE9 185 EM88
Woodmere Ave., Croy. 203 DX101
Woodmere Ave., Wat. 76 BX38
Woodmere Clo. SW11 160 DG83
Lavender Hill
Woodmere Clo., Croy. 203 DX101
Woodmere Gdns., Croy. 203 DX101
Woodmere Way, Beck. 203 ED99
Woodmill Ms., Hodd. 49 EB15
Whittingstall Rd.
Woodmount, Swan. 207 FC101
Woodnook Rd. SW16 181 DH92
Woodpecker Clo. N9 82 DV44
Woodpecker Clo., Cob. 214 BY112
Woodpecker Clo., Har. 95 CF53
Woodpecker Clo., Hat. 45 CT21
Woodpecker Clo. (Bushey), Wat. 94 CC46
Woodpecker Mt., Croy. 221 DY109
Woodpecker Rd. SE14 163 DY79
Woodpecker Rd. SE28 146 EW73
Woodpecker Way, Wok. 226 AX123
Woodplace Clo., Couls. 235 DJ119
Woodplace La., Couls. 235 DJ118
Woodquest Ave. SE24 182 DQ85
Woodredon Clo., Harl. 50 EH16
Epping Rd.
Woodredon Fm. La., Wal.Abb. 84 EK35
Woodridden Hill, Wal.Abb. 84 EK35
Woodridge Clo., Enf. 81 DN39
Woodridge Way, Nthwd. 93 BS51
Woodridings Ave., Pnr. 94 BZ53
Woodridings Clo., Pnr. 94 BY52
Woodriffe Rd. E11 123 ED59
Woodrow SE18 165 EM77
Woodrow Ave., Hayes 135 BT71
Woodrow Clo., Grnf. 137 CH66
Woodrow Ct. N17 100 DV52
Heybourne Rd.
Woodroyd Ave., Horl. 268 DF149
Woodroyd Gdns., Horl. 268 DF150
Woodruff Ave., Guil. 243 BA131
Woodrush Clo. SE14 163 DY80
Southerngate Way
Woodrush Way, Rom. 126 EX56
Woods, The, Nthwd. 93 BU50
Woods, The, Rad. 61 CH34
Woods, The, Uxb. 115 BP63
Woods Ave., Hat. 45 CU20
Woods Clo. SE19 182 DS93
Woodland Hill
Woods Dr., Slou. 111 AM64
Woods Ms. W1 272 E10
Woods Ms. W1 140 DG73
Woods Pl. SE1 279 N7
Woods Rd. SE15 162 DV81
Woodseer St. E1 142 DT71
Woodsford SE17 162 DR78
Portland St.
Woodsford Sq. W14 159 CY75
Woodshire Rd., Dag. 127 FB62
Woodshore Clo., Vir.W. 192 AV100
Woodshots Meadow, Wat. 75 BR43
Woodside NW11 120 DA57
Woodside SW19 179 CZ93
Woodside, Borwd. 78 CM42
Woodside, Buck.H. 102 EJ47
Woodside, Epp. 70 EW26
Woodside, Hert. 32 DW12
Woodside, Lthd. 230 CB122
Woodside (West Horsley), Lthd. 245 BQ126
Woodside, Orp. 224 EU106
Woodside, Tad. 249 CZ128
Woodside (Cheshunt), Wal.Cr. 66 DU31
Woodside, Walt. 195 BU102
Ashley Rd.
Woodside, Wat. 75 BU36
Woodside Ave. N6 120 DF57
Woodside Ave. N10 120 DF57
Woodside Ave. N12 98 DC49
Woodside Ave. SE25 202 DV100
Woodside Ave., Amer. 55 AR36
Woodside Ave., Beac. 88 AJ52
Woodside Ave., Chis. 185 EQ92

Wyvern Rd., Pur. 219 DP110
Wyvern Way, Uxb. 134 BH66
Wyvil Est. SW8 161 DL80
Luscombe Way
Wyvil Rd. SW8 161 DL79
Wyvis St. E14 143 EB71

Y

Yabsley St. E14 143 EC74
Yaffle Rd., Wey. 213 BQ110
Yalding Clo., Orp. 206 EX98
Yalding Rd. SE16 162 DU76
Yale Clo., Houns. 176 BZ85
Bramley Way
Yale Way, Horn. 127 FG63
Yarborough Rd. SW19 200 DD95
Runnymede
Yarbridge Clo., Sutt. 218 DB110
Yard Mead, Egh. 173 BA90
Yardley Clo. E4 83 EB43
Yardley Clo., Reig. 250 DB132
Yardley La. E4 83 EB43
Yardley St. WC1 274 D3
Yardley St. WC1 141 DN69
Yarm Clo., Lthd. 231 CJ123
Yarm Ct. Rd., Lthd. 231 CJ123
Yarm Way, Lthd. 231 CJ123
Yarmouth Cres. N17 122 DV57
Yarmouth Pl. W1 277 H3
Yarmouth Rd., Slou. 131 AQ73
Yarmouth Rd., Wat. 76 BW38
Yarnfield Sq. SE15 162 DU81
Clayton Rd.
Yarnton Way SE2 166 EX75
Yarnton Way, Erith 166 EZ76
Yarrow Cres. E6 144 EL71
Yarrowfield, Wok. 226 AX123
Yarrowside, Amer. 72 AV40
Yateley St. SE18 164 EK76
Yates Ct. NW2 139 CX65
Yattendon Rd., Horl. 269 DH148
Ye Cor., Wat. 76 BY44
Yeading Ave., Har. 116 BY61
Yeading Fork, Hayes 136 BW71
Yeading Gdns., Hayes 135 BV71
Yeading La., Hayes 135 BV72
Yeading La., Nthlt. 136 BW69
Yeames Clo. W13 137 CG72
Yeate St. N1 142 DR66
Yeatman Rd. N6 120 DF58
Yeats Clo. NW10 138 CS65
Yeats Clo. SE13 163 ED82
Eliot Pk.
Yeats Clo., Red. 266 DC137
Yeldham Rd. W6 159 CX78
Yellow Hammer Ct. NW9 96 CS54
Eagle Dr.
Yellowpine Way, Chig. 104 EV49
Yelverton Clo., Rom. 106 FK53
Yelverton Rd. SW11 160 DD82
Yenston Clo., Mord. 200 DA100
Yeo St. E3 143 EB71
Yeoman Clo. E6 145 EP73
Ferndale St.
Yeoman Clo. SE27 181 DP90
Yeoman Rd., Nthlt. 136 BY66
Yeoman St. SE8 163 DY77
Yeoman Way, Red. 267 DH139
Yeomanry Clo., Epsom 217 CT112
Dirdene Gdns.
Yeomans Acre, Ruis. 115 BU58
Yeomans Keep, Rick. 73 BF41
Rickmansworth Rd.
Yeomans Meadow, Sev. 256 FG126
Yeoman's Ms., Islw. 177 CE85
Queensbridge Pk.
Yeoman's Row SW3 276 C7
Yeoman's Row SW3 160 DE76
Yeomans Way, Enf. 82 DW40
Yeomans Yd. E1 142 DT73
Chamber St.
Yeomen Way, Ilf. 103 EQ51
Yeoveney Clo., Stai. 173 BD89
Yeovil Clo., Orp. 205 ES103
Yeovil Rd., Slou. 131 AL71
Yeovilton Pl., Kings.T. 177 CK92
Yerbury Rd. N19 121 DK62
Yester Dr., Chis. 184 EL94
Yester Pk., Chis. 185 EM94
Yester Rd., Chis. 185 EM94
Yevele Way, Horn. 128 FL59
Yew Ave., West Dr. 134 BL73
Yew Clo., Buck.H. 102 EK47
Yew Clo., Wal.Cr. 66 DS27
Yew Gro. NW2 119 CX63
Yew Gro., Welw.G.C. 30 DC10
Yew Pl., Wey. 195 BT104
Yew Tree Bottom Rd., Epsom 233 CV116
Yew Tree Clo. N21 99 DN45
Yew Tree Clo., Beac. 89 AM54
Yew Tree Clo., Brwd. 109 GB44
Yew Tree Clo., Chesh. 56 AU30
Botley Rd.
Yew Tree Clo., Couls. 234 DF119
Yew Tree Clo., Hem.H. 40 BG22
Fishery Rd.
Yew Tree Clo., Horl. 268 DG146
Yew Tree Clo., Sev. 256 FD123
Yew Tree Clo., Well. 166 EU81
Yew Tree Clo., Wor.Pk. 198 CS102
Yew Tree Ct., Borwd. 77 CK44
Barnet La.
Yew Tree Dr., Cat. 252 DT125
Yew Tree Dr., Guil. 242 AV130
Yew Tree Dr., Hem.H. 57 BB28
Yew Tree Gdns., Rom. 127 FD57
Yew Tree Gdns. (Chadwell Heath), Rom. 126 EY57
Yew Tree La., Reig. 250 DB131
Yew Tree Rd. W12 139 CT73
Yew Tree Rd., Dor. 247 CG134
Yew Tree Rd., Slou. 152 AU76
Yew Tree Rd., Uxb. 134 BM67
Yew Tree Wk., Houns. 176 BZ85
Yew Tree Wk., Lthd. 246 BX127
Yew Tree Wk., Maid. 110 AC64
Yew Tree Wk., Pur. 220 DQ110
Yew Tree Way, Croy. 221 DY110
Yew Trees, Egh. 193 BC97
Yew Trees, Shep. 194 BM98
Laleham Rd.
Yew Wk., Har. 117 CE60
Yew Wk., Hodd. 49 EA18
Yewbank Clo., Ken. 236 DR115
Yewdale Clo., Brom. 184 EE93
Yewdells Clo., Bet. 249 CU133
Yewfield Rd. NW10 139 CT66
Yewlands, Hodd. 49 EA18
Yewlands, Saw. 36 EY06
Yewlands Clo., Bans. 234 DB115
Yewlands Dr., Hodd. 49 EA18
Yews, The, Ashf. 175 BP91
Yews, The, Grav. 191 GK89
Yews Ave., Enf. 82 DV36
Yewtree Clo. N22 99 DJ53
Yewtree Clo., Har. 116 CB56
Yewtree End, St.Alb. 60 CB27
Yewtree Gdns., Epsom 232 CP115
Yewtree Rd., Beck. 203 DZ96
Yoakley Rd. N16 122 DS61
Yoke Clo. N7 141 DL65
Ewe Clo.
Yolande Gdns. SE9 184 EL85
Yonge Pk. N4 121 DN62
York Ave. SW14 178 CQ85
York Ave. W7 137 CE74
York Ave., Hayes 135 BQ71
York Ave., Sid. 185 ES89
York Ave., Slou. 131 AQ72
York Ave., Stan. 95 CH53
York Ave., Wind. 151 AP82
York Bri. NW1 272 F4
York Bri. NW1 140 DG70
York Bldgs. WC2 278 A1
York Clo. E6 145 EM72
Boultwood Rd.
York Clo. W7 137 CE74
York Ave.
York Clo., Amer. 72 AT39
York Clo., Brwd. 109 FZ45
York Clo., Kings L. 58 BN29
York Clo., Mord. 200 DB98
York Clo., W.Byf. 212 BL112
York Cres., Borwd. 78 CR40
York Cres., Loug. 84 EL41
York Gdns., Walt. 196 BX103
York Gate N14 99 DL45
York Gate NW1 272 F5
York Gate NW1 140 DG70
York Gro. SE15 162 DW81
York Hill SE27 181 DP90
York Hill, Loug. 84 EL41
York Hill Est. SE27 181 DP90
York Ho., Wem. 118 CM63
York Ho. Pl. W8 160 DB75
York Ms. NW5 121 DH64
Kentish Town Rd.
York Ms., Ilf. 125 EN62
York Rd.
York Par., Brent. 157 CK78
York Pl. SW11 160 DD83
York Pl. WC2 278 A1
York Pl., Dag. 147 FC65
York Pl., Grays 170 GA79
York Pl., Ilf. 125 EN61
York Rd.
York Ri. NW5 121 DH62
York Ri., Orp. 205 ES102
York Rd. E4 101 EA50
York Rd. E7 144 EG65
York Rd. E10 123 EC62
York Rd. E17 123 DX57
York Rd. N11 99 DK51
York Rd. N18 100 DV51
York Rd. N21 100 DR45
York Rd. SE1 278 C5
York Rd. SE1 161 DM75
York Rd. SW11 160 DC83
York Rd. SW18 160 DC83
York Rd. SW19 180 DC93
York Rd. W3 138 CQ72
York Rd. W5 157 CJ76
York Rd., Barn. 80 DC43
York Rd., Brent. 157 CK78
York Rd., Brwd. 109 FZ45
York Rd., Croy. 201 DN101
York Rd., Dart. 188 FM87
York Rd., Epp. 70 FA27
York Rd., Grav. 191 GJ90
York Rd. (Northfleet), . Grav 190 GD87
York Rd., Guil. 258 AX135
York Rd., Houns. 156 CB83
York Rd., Ilf. 125 EN62
York Rd., Kings.T. 178 CM94
York Rd., Nthwd. 93 BU54
York Rd., Rain. 147 FD66
York Rd., Rich. 178 CM85
Albert Rd.
York Rd., St.Alb. 43 CF19
York Rd., S.Croy. 221 DX110
York Rd., Sutt. 218 DA107
York Rd., Tedd. 177 CE91
York Rd., Uxb. 134 BK66
York Rd., Wal.Cr. 67 DY34
York Rd., Wat. 76 BW43
York Rd., W.Byf. 212 BK112
York Rd., West. 238 EH119
York Rd., Wey. 213 BQ105
York Rd., Wind. 151 AP82
York Rd., Wok. 226 AX119
York Sq. E14 143 DY72
York St. W1 272 E6
York St. W1 140 DF71
York St., Bark. 145 EQ67
Abbey Rd.
York St., Mitch. 200 DG101
York St., Twick. 177 CG88
York Ter., Enf. 82 DQ38
York Ter., Erith 167 FC81
York Ter. E. NW1 272 G5
York Ter. E. NW1 140 DG70
York Ter. W. NW1 272 F5
York Ter. W. NW1 140 DG70
York Way N1 141 DL67
York Way N7 141 DK65
York Way N20 98 DF48
York Way, Borwd. 78 CR40
York Way, Chess. 216 CL108
York Way, Felt. 176 BZ90
York Way, Hem.H. 40 BL21
York Way, Wat. 76 BY36
York Way Ct. N1 141 DL67
York Way Est. N7 141 DL65
York Way
Yorke Gdns., Reig. 250 DA133
Yorke Gate Rd., Cat. 236 DR122
Yorke Rd., Reig. 249 CZ133
Yorke Rd., Rick. 74 BN44
Yorkes, Harl. 51 ET17
Yorkland Ave., Well. 165 ET83
Yorkshire Clo. N16 122 DS62
Yorkshire Gdns. N18 100 DV50
Yorkshire Grey Pl. NW3 120 DC63
Heath St.
Yorkshire Grey Yd. WC1 274 B7
Yorkshire Rd. E14 143 DY72
Yorkshire Rd., Mitch. 201 DL99
Yorkton St. E2 142 DU68
Young Rd. E16 144 EJ72
Young St. W8 160 DB75
Young St., Lthd. 247 CE125
Youngfield Rd., Hem.H. 39 BF19
Youngmans Clo., Enf. 82 DQ39
Young's Bldgs. EC1 275 J4
Youngs Ri., Welw.G.C. 29 CV09
Youngs Rd., Ilf. 125 ER57
Youngstroat La., Wok. 210 AY110
Yoxley App., Ilf. 125 EQ58
Yoxley Dr., Ilf. 125 EQ58
Yukon Rd. SW12 181 DH87
Yule Clo., St.Alb. 60 BZ30
Yuletide Clo. NW10 138 CS66
Yunus Khan Clo. E17 123 EA57

Z

Zampa Rd. SE16 162 DW78
Zander Ct. E2 142 DU68
St. Peter's Clo.
Zangwill Rd. SE3 164 EK81
Zealand Ave., West Dr. 154 BK80
Zealand Rd. E3 143 DY68
Zelah Rd., Orp. 206 EV101
Zennor Rd. SW12 181 DJ88
Zenoria St. SE22 162 DT84
Zermatt Rd., Th.Hth. 202 DQ98
Zetland St. E14 143 EB71
Zig Zag Rd., Dor. 247 CJ130
Zig Zag Rd., Tad. 247 CK132
Zig-Zag Rd., Ken. 236 DQ116
Zion Pl., Grav. 191 GH87
Zion Pl., Th.Hth. 202 DR98
Zion Rd., Th.Hth. 202 DR98
Zion St., Sev. 257 FM121
Church Rd.
Zoar St. SE1 279 H2
Zoffany St. N19 121 DK61

The following is a comprehensive listing of all the railway stations which appear in this atlas. Bold references can be found within the Central London enlarged scale section (pages 272-279).

INDEX TO LONDON REGIONAL TRANSPORT STATIONS

The following is a comprehensive listing of all London Regional Transport Stations which appear in this atlas. Bold references can be found within the Central London enlarged scale section (pages 272-279). A London Underground map can be found on page 431. Restricted line services are indicated by brackets.

London Undergound Line Abbreviations

Bak.	Bakerloo	*Dist.*	District	*Met.*	Metropolitan
Cen.	Central	*E.L.*	East London	*North.*	Northern
Circ.	Circle	*H. & C.*	Hammersmith & City	*Picc.*	Piccadilly
C.T.	Croydon Tramlink	*Jub.*	Jubilee	*Vic.*	Victoria
D.L.R.	Docklands Light Railway				

Station	Lines	Page	Grid
Acton Town	Dist.; Picc.	158	CN75
Addington Village	C.T.	221	EA107
Aldgate	**Circ.; Met.**	**275**	**P8**
Aldgate East	Dist.; H. & C.	142	DT72
All Saints	D.L.R.	143	EB73
Alperton	Picc.	138	CL67
Amersham	Met.	55	AQ38
Angel	North.	141	DN68
Archway	North.	121	DJ61
Arena	C.T.	202	DW99
Arnos Grove	Picc.	99	DJ49
Arsenal	Picc.	121	DN62
Avenue Road	C.T.	203	DX96
Baker Street	**Bak.; Circ.; H. & C.; Jub.; Met.**	**272**	**E5**
Balham	North.	181	DH88
Bank	**Cen.; D.L.R.; North.**	**275**	**K9**
Barbican	**Circ.; H. & C.; Met.**	**274**	**G6**
Barking	Dist.; (H. & C.)	145	EQ66
Barkingside	Cen.	125	ER56
Barons Court	Dist.; Picc.	159	CY78
Bayswater	Circ.; Dist.	140	DB73
Beckenham Junction	C.T.	203	EA95
Beckenham Road	C.T.	203	DY95
Beckton	D.L.R.	145	EN71
Beckton Park	D.L.R.	145	EM73
Becontree	Dist.	146	EW66
Beddington Lane	C.T.	201	DJ100
Belgrave Walk	C.T.	200	DD97
Belsize Park	North.	120	DE64
Bermondsey	Jub.	162	DU76
Bethnal Green	Cen.	142	DW69
Bingham Road	C.T.	202	DU102
Birkbeck	C.T.	202	DW97
Blackfriars	**Circ.; Dist.**	**274**	**G10**
Blackhorse Lane	C.T.	202	DU101
Blackhorse Road	Vic.	123	DX56
Blackwall	D.L.R.	143	EC73
Bond Street	**Cen.; Jub.**	**272**	**G9**
Borough	**North.**	**279**	**J5**
Boston Manor	Picc.	157	CG77
Bounds Green	Picc.	99	DK51
Bow Church	D.L.R.	143	EA69
Bow Road	Dist.; (H. & C.)	143	DZ69
Brent Cross	North.	119	CX59
Brixton	Vic.	161	DN84
Bromley-by-Bow	Dist.; (H. & C.)	143	EC69
Buckhurst Hill	Cen.	102	EK47
Burnt Oak	North.	96	CQ53
Caledonian Road	Picc.	141	DM65
Camden Town	North.	141	DH67
Canada Water	Jub.	162	DW75
Canary Wharf	D.L.R.; Jub.	143	EA74
Canning Town	D.L.R.; Jub.	144	EE72
Cannon Street	**Circ.; Dist.**	**279**	**K1**
Canons Park	Jub.	96	CL52
Chalfont & Latimer	Met.	72	AW39
Chalk Farm	North.	140	DG66
Chancery Lane	**Cen.**	**274**	**D7**
Charing Cross	**Bak.; Jub.; North.**	**277**	**P2**
Chesham	Met.	54	AQ31
Chigwell	(Cen.)	103	EP49
Chiswick Park	Dist.	158	CQ77
Chorleywood	Met.	73	BD42
Church Street	C.T.	202	DQ103
Clapham Common	North.	161	DJ84
Clapham North	North.	161	DL83
Clapham South	North.	181	DH86
Cockfosters	Picc.	80	DG42
Colindale	North.	118	CS55
Colliers Wood	North.	180	DD94
Coombe Lane	C.T.	220	DW106
Covent Garden	**Picc.**	**273**	**P10**
Crossharbour & London Arena	D.L.R.	163	EB76
Croxley	Met.	75	BP44
Croydon Central	C.T.	202	DQ103
Custom House	D.L.R.	144	EH73
Cutty Sark	D.L.R.	163	EC79
Cyprus	D.L.R.	145	EN73
Dagenham East	Dist.	127	FC64
Dagenham Heathway	Dist.	146	EZ65
Debden	Cen.	85	EQ42
Deptford Bridge	D.L.R.	163	EA81
Devons Road	D.L.R.	143	EB70
Dollis Hill	Jub.	119	CU64
Dundonald Road	C.T.	179	CZ94
Ealing Broadway	Cen.; Dist.	137	CK73
Ealing Common	Dist.; Picc.	138	CM74
Earls Court	Dist.; Picc.	160	DA78
East Acton	Cen.	139	CT72
East Croydon	C.T.	202	DR103
East Finchley	North.	120	DE56
East Ham	Dist.; (H. & C.)	144	EL66
East India	D.L.R.	143	ED73
East Putney	Dist.	179	CY85
Eastcote	Met.; Picc.	116	BW59
Edgware	North.	96	CP51
Edgware Road	**Bak.; Circ.; Dist.; H. & C.**	**272**	**B7**
Elephant & Castle	**Bak.; North.**	**278**	**G8**
Elm Park	Dist.	127	FH63
Elverson Road	D.L.R.	163	EB82
Embankment	**Bak.; Circ.; Dist.; North.**	**278**	**A2**
Epping	Cen.	70	EU31
Euston	**North.; Vic.**	**273**	**L2**
Euston Square	**Circ.; H. & C.; Met.**	**273**	**L4**
Fairlop	Cen.	103	ER53
Farringdon	**Circ.; H. & C.; Met.**	**274**	**E6**
Fieldway	C.T.	221	EB108
Finchley Central	North.	98	DA53
Finchley Road	Jub.; Met.	140	DC65
Finsbury Park	Picc.; Vic.	121	DN61
Fulham Broadway	Dist.	160	DA80

Station	Lines	Page	Grid
Gallions Reach	D.L.R.	145	EP72
Gants Hill	Cen.	125	EN58
Gloucester Road	Circ.; Dist.; Picc.	160	DC77
Golders Green	North.	120	DA59
Goldhawk Road	H. & C.	159	CW75
Goodge Street	**North.**	**273**	**L6**
Grange Hill	(Cen.)	103	ER49
Gravel Hill	C.T.	221	DY107
Great Portland Street	**Circ.; H. & C.; Met.**	**273**	**J5**
Green Park	**Jub.; Picc.; Vic.**	**277**	**K3**
Greenford	Cen.	137	CD67
Greenwich	D.L.R.	163	EB80
Gunnersbury	Dist.	158	CP78
Hainault	(Cen.)	103	ES52
Hammersmith	Dist.; H. & C.; Picc.	159	CW77
Hampstead	North.	120	DC63
Hanger Lane	Cen.	138	CM69
Harlesden	Bak.	138	CR68
Harrington Road	C.T.	202	DW97
Harrow & Wealdstone	Bak.	117	CE56
Harrow on the Hill	Met.	117	CE58
Hatton Cross	Picc.	155	BS84
Heathrow Terminal 4	Picc.	175	BP85
Heathrow Terminals 1,2,3	Picc.	155	BP83
Hendon Central	North.	119	CW57
Heron Quays	D.L.R.	143	EA74
High Barnet	North.	80	DA42
High Street Kensington	Circ.; Dist.	160	DB75
Highbury & Islington	Vic.	141	DP65
Highgate	North.	121	DH58
Hillingdon	Met.; (Picc.)	114	BN64
Holborn	**Cen.; Picc.**	**274**	**A7**
Holland Park	Cen.	139	CZ74
Holloway Road	Picc.	121	DM64
Hornchurch	Dist.	128	FK62
Hounslow Central	Picc.	156	CA83
Hounslow East	Picc.	156	CC82
Hounslow West	Picc.	156	BY82
Hyde Park Corner	**Picc.**	**276**	**F4**
Ickenham	Met.; (Picc.)	115	BQ63
Island Gardens	D.L.R.	163	EC77
Kennington	**North.**	**278**	**F10**
Kensal Green	Bak.	139	CW69
Kensington (Olympia)	(Dist.)	159	CY76
Kentish Town	North.	121	DJ64
Kenton	Bak.	117	CH58
Kew Gardens	Dist.	158	CN81
Kilburn	Jub.	139	CZ65
Kilburn Park	Bak.	140	DA68
King Henry's Drive	C.T.	221	EB109
King's Cross St. Pancras	**Circ.; H. & C.; Met.; North.; Picc.; Vic.**	**274**	**A1**
Kingsbury	Jub.	118	CN57
Knightsbridge	**Picc.**	**276**	**D5**
Ladbroke Grove	H. & C.	139	CY72
Lambeth North	**Bak.**	**278**	**D5**
Lancaster Gate	Cen.	140	DD73
Latimer Road	H. & C.	139	CX73
Lebanon Road	C.T.	202	DS103
Leicester Square	**North.; Picc.**	**273**	**N10**
Lewisham	D.L.R.	163	EC83
Leyton	Cen.	123	EC62
Leytonstone	Cen.	124	EE60
Limehouse	D.L.R.	143	DY72
Liverpool Street	**Cen.; Circ.; H. & C.; Met.**	**275**	**M7**
Lloyd Park	C.T.	220	DT105
London Bridge	**Jub.; North.**	**279**	**M3**
Loughton	Cen.	84	EL43
Maida Vale	Bak.	140	DB69
Manor House	Picc.	121	DP59
Mansion House	**Circ.; Dist.**	**275**	**J10**
Marble Arch	**Cen.**	**272**	**E10**
Marylebone	**Bak.**	**272**	**D5**
Merton Park	C.T.	200	DA95
Mile End	Cen.; Dist.; (H. & C.)	143	DY69
Mill Hill East	North.	97	CX52
Mitcham	C.T.	200	DE98
Mitcham Junction	C.T.	200	DG99
Monument	**Circ.; Dist.; D.L.R.**	**275**	**L10**
Moor Park	Met.	93	BR48
Moorgate	**Circ.; H. & C.; Met.; North.**	**275**	**K7**
Morden	North.	200	DB97
Morden Road	C.T.	200	DB96
Mornington Crescent	North.	141	DJ68
Mudchute	D.L.R.	163	EB77
Neasden	Jub.	118	CS64
New Addington	C.T.	221	EC110
New Cross	E.L.	163	DZ80
New Cross Gate	E.L.	163	DY80
Newbury Park	Cen.	125	ER58
North Acton	Cen.	138	CR71
North Ealing	Picc.	138	CM72
North Greenwich	Jub.	164	EE75
North Harrow	Met.	116	CA57
North Wembley	Bak.	117	CK62
Northfields	Picc.	157	CH76
Northolt	Cen.	136	CA66
Northwick Park	Met.	117	CG59
Northwood	Met.	93	BS52
Northwood Hills	Met.	93	BU54
Notting Hill Gate	Cen.; Circ.; Dist.	140	DA73
Oakwood	Picc.	81	DJ43
Old Street	**North.**	**275**	**K3**
Osterley	Picc.	157	CD80
Oval	North.	161	DN79
Oxford Circus	**Bak.; Cen.; Vic.**	**273**	**K8**
Paddington	Bak.; Circ.; Dist.; H. & C.	140	DC72
Park Royal	Picc.	138	CN70
Parsons Green	Dist.	160	DA81
Perivale	Cen.	137	CG68
Phipps Bridge	C.T.	200	DC97

Station	Lines	Page	Grid
Piccadilly Circus	**Bak.; Picc.**	**277**	**L1**
Pimlico	**Vic.**	**277**	**M10**
Pinner	Met.	116	BY56
Plaistow	Dist.; (H. & C.)	144	EF68
Poplar	D.L.R.	143	EB73
Preston Road	Met.	118	CL60
Prince Regent	D.L.R.	144	EJ73
Pudding Mill Lane	D.L.R.	143	EB67
Putney Bridge	Dist.	159	CY83
Queen's Park	Bak.	139	CY68
Queensbury	Jub.	118	CM55
Queensway	Cen.	140	DB73
Ravenscourt Park	Dist.	159	CU77
Rayners Lane	Met.; Picc.	116	BZ59
Redbridge	Cen.	124	EK58
Regent's Park	**Bak.**	**273**	**H5**
Richmond	Dist.	158	CL84
Rickmansworth	Met.	92	BK45
Roding Valley	(Cen.)	102	EK49
Rotherhithe	E.L.	162	DW75
Royal Albert	D.L.R.	144	EL73
Royal Oak	H. & C.	140	DB71
Royal Victoria	D.L.R.	144	EG73
Ruislip	Met.; (Picc.)	115	BS60
Ruislip Gardens	Cen.	115	BU63
Ruislip Manor	Met.; (Picc.)	115	BU60
Russell Square	**Picc.**	**273**	**P5**
St. James's Park	**Circ.; Dist.**	**277**	**M5**
St. John's Wood	Jub.	140	DD68
St. Paul's	**Cen.**	**275**	**H8**
Sandilands	C.T.	202	DT103
Seven Sisters	Vic.	122	DS57
Shadwell	D.L.R.; E.L.	142	DW73
Shepherd's Bush	Cen.; H. & C.	139	CW74
Shoreditch	(E.L.)	142	DT70
Sloane Square	**Circ.; Dist.**	**276**	**F9**
Snaresbrook	Cen.	124	EG57
South Ealing	Picc.	157	CK76
South Harrow	Picc.	116	CC62
South Kensington	**Circ.; Dist.; Picc.**	**276**	**A8**
South Kenton	Bak.	117	CJ60
South Quay	D.L.R.	163	EB75
South Ruislip	Cen.	116	BW63
South Wimbledon	North.	180	DB94
South Woodford	Cen.	102	EG54
Southfields	Dist.	179	CZ88
Southgate	Picc.	99	DK46
Southwark	**Jub.**	**278**	**F3**
Stamford Brook	Dist.	159	CT77
Stanmore	Jub.	95	CK50
Stepney Green	Dist.; (H. & C.)	143	DX70
Stockwell	North.; Vic.	161	DL81
Stonebridge Park	Bak.	138	CP66
Stratford	Cen.; D.L.R.; Jub.	143	EC66
Sudbury Hill	Picc.	117	CE63
Sudbury Town	Picc.	137	CH65
Surrey Quays	E.L.	163	DX76
Swiss Cottage	Jub.	140	DD66
Temple	**Circ.; Dist.**	**274**	**C10**
Therapia Lane	C.T.	201	DL101
Theydon Bois	Cen.	85	ET36
Tooting Bec	North.	180	DG90
Tooting Broadway	North.	180	DE92
Tottenham Court Road	**Cen.; North.**	**273**	**M8**
Tottenham Hale	Vic.	122	DV55
Totteridge & Whetstone	North.	98	DB47
Tower Gateway	D.L.R.	142	DT73
Tower Hill	**Circ.; Dist.**	**275**	**P10**
Tufnell Park	North.	121	DJ63
Turnham Green	Dist.; Picc.	158	CS77
Turnpike Lane	Picc.	121	DN55
Upminster	Dist.	128	FQ61
Upminster Bridge	Dist.	128	FN61
Upney	Dist.	145	ET66
Upton Park	Dist.; (H. & C.)	144	EH67
Uxbridge	Met.; (Picc.)	134	BK66
Vauxhall	Vic.	161	DL78
Victoria	**Circ.; Dist.; Vic.**	**277**	**J7**
Waddon Marsh	C.T.	201	DM102
Walthamstow Central	Vic.	123	EA56
Wandle Park	C.T.	201	DN103
Wanstead	Cen.	124	EH58
Wapping	E.L.	142	DW74
Warren Street	**North.; Vic.**	**273**	**L4**
Warwick Avenue	Bak.	140	DC70
Waterloo	**Bak.; Jub.; North.**	**278**	**D4**
Watford	Met.	75	BT41
Wellesley Road	C.T.	202	DQ103
Wembley Central	Bak.	118	CL64
Wembley Park	Jub.; Met.	118	CN62
West Acton	Cen.	138	CN72
West Brompton	Dist.	160	DA78
West Croydon	C.T.	202	DQ102
West Finchley	North.	98	DB51
West Ham	Dist.; (H. & C.); Jub.	144	EE69
West Hampstead	Jub.	140	DA65
West Harrow	Met.	116	CC58
West India Quay	D.L.R.	143	EA73
West Kensington	Dist.	159	CZ78
West Ruislip	Cen.	115	BQ61
Westbourne Park	H. & C.	139	CZ71
Westferry	D.L.R.	143	EA73
Westminster	**Circ.; Dist.**	**278**	**A5**
White City	Cen.	139	CW73
Whitechapel	Dist.; E.L.; H. & C.	142	DV71
Willesden Green	Jub.	139	CW65
Willesden Junction	Bak.	139	CT69
Wimbledon	C.T.; Dist.	179	CZ93
Wimbledon Park	Dist.	180	DA90
Wood Green	Picc.	99	DM54
Woodford	Cen.	102	EH51
Woodside	C.T.	202	DV100
Woodside Park	North.	98	DB49

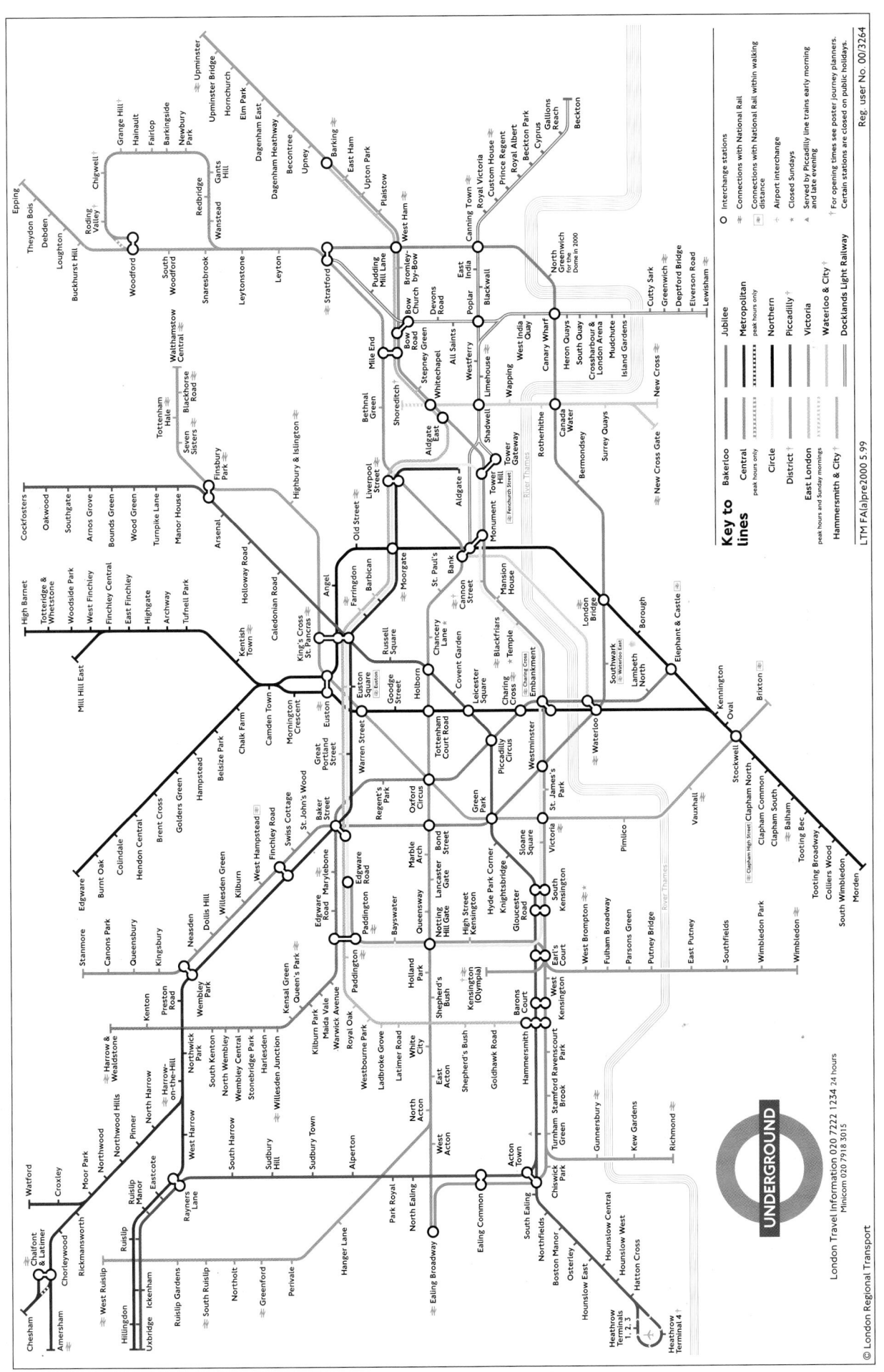

UNDERGROUND

London Travel Information 020 7222 1234 24 hours
Minicom 020 7918 3015

© London Regional Transport

Key to lines

Bakerloo	Jubilee
Central	Metropolitan
peak hours only	peak hours only
Circle	Northern
District	Piccadilly †
East London	Victoria
peak hours and Sunday mornings	Waterloo & City †
Hammersmith & City	Docklands Light Railway

○ Interchange stations
⊖ Connections with National Rail
◉ Connections with National Rail within walking distance
✈ Airport interchange
✻ Closed Sundays
▲ Closed Sundays
† Served by Piccadilly line trains early morning and late evening
For opening times see poster journey planners.
Certain stations are closed on public holidays.

LTM FA(a)pre2000 5.99   Reg. user No. 00/3264

AYLESBURY VALE

D A C O R U M

ST.
ALBANS

WELWYN

28   29   30

HATFIELD

38   39   40   41   42   43   44   45   46

CHILTERN

54   56   57   58   59   60   61   62   63   64

WYCOMBE

THREE
RIVERS

WATFORD

HERTSMERE

55   72   73   74   75   76   77   78   79   80

88   89   90   91   92   93   94   95   96   97   98

BARNET

HARROW

110   111   112   113   114   115   116   117   118   119   120

SOUTH BUCKS

HILLINGDON

BRENT

CAMDEN

130   131   132   133   134   135   136   137   138   139   140

SLOUGH

EALING

WESTMINS

HAMMERSMITH &
FULHAM

KENSINGTON &
CHELSEA

150   151   152   153   154   155   156   157   158   159   160

WINDSOR & MAIDENHEAD

HOUNSLOW

WANDSWORTH

RICHMOND
UPON THAMES

172   173   174   175   176   177   178   179   180

SPELTHORNE

WOKINGHAM

BRACKNELL
FOREST

MERTON

KINGSTON
UPON THAMES

192   193   194   195   196   197   198   199   200

RUNNYMEDE

SUTTON

ELMBRIDGE

210   211   212   213   214   215   216   217   218

SURREY HEATH

EPSOM
& EWELL

WOKING

226   227   228   229   230   231   232   233   234

HART

242   243   244   245   246   247   248   249   250

RUSHMOOR

REIGATE &
BANSTEAD

GUILDFORD

258   259   260   261   262   263   264   265   266

EAST
HANTS

MOLE VALLEY

268

W A V E R L E Y

CRAWL

E

H